JOURNAL OF RESEARCH

OF THE U.S. GEOLOGICAL SURVEY

JANUARY-FEBRUARY 1973
VOLUME 1, NUMBER 1

Scientific notes and summaries of investigations in geology, hydrology, and related fields

U.S. DEPARTMENT OF THE INTERIOR

UNITED STATES DEPARTMENT OF THE INTERIOR
ROGERS C. B. MORTON, Secretary
GEOLOGICAL SURVEY
V. E. McKelvey, Director

For sale by the Superintendent of Documents, U.S. Government Printing Office, Washington, D.C., 20402. Order by SD Catalog No. JRGS. Annual subscription rate $8.50 (plus $2.25 for foreign mailing). Single copy $1.50. Make checks or money orders payable to the Superintendent of Documents.

Send all subscription inquiries and address changes to the Superintendent of Documents at the above address.

Purchase orders should not be sent to the U.S. Geological Survey library.

Library of Congress Card No. 72-600241

The Journal of Research consists of six issues a year (January-February, March-April, May-June, July-August, September-October, November-December) published in Washington, D.C., by the U.S. Geological Survey. It contains papers by members of the Geological Survey on geologic, hydrologic, topographic, and other scientific and technical subjects.

The Journal supersedes the short-papers chapters (B, C, and D) of the former Geological Survey Research ("Annual Review") series of professional papers. The synopsis chapter (A) of the former Geological Survey Research series will be published as a separate professional paper each year.

Correspondence and inquiries concerning the Journal (other than subscription inquiries and address changes) should be directed to the Managing Editor, Journal of Research, Publications Division, U.S. Geological Survey, Washington, D.C., 20242.

Papers for the Journal should be submitted through regular Division publication channels.

The Secretary of the Interior has determined that the publication of this periodical is necessary in the transaction of the public business required by law of this Department. Use of funds for printing this periodical has been approved by the Director of the Office of Management and Budget through February 11, 1975.

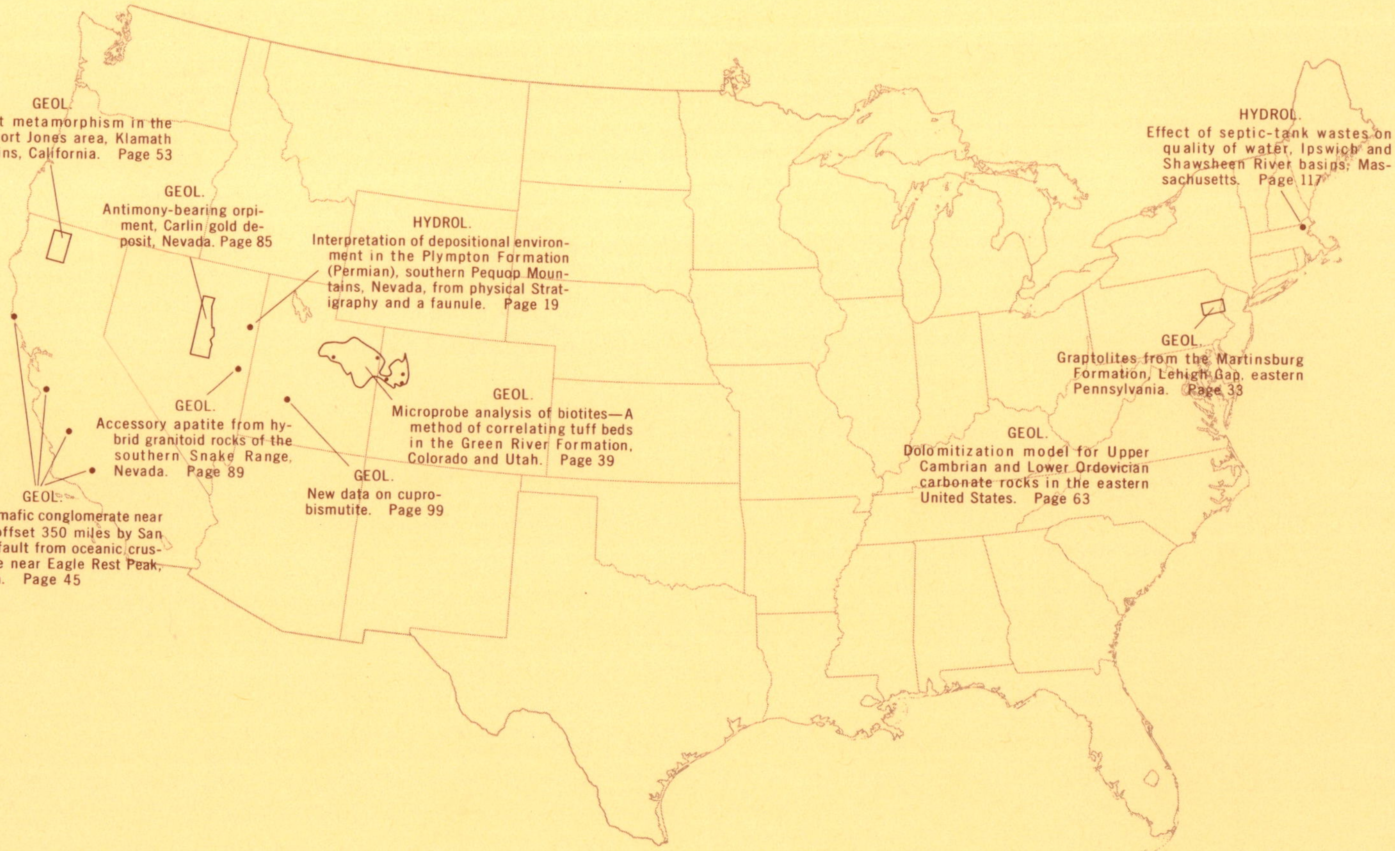

GEOGRAPHIC INDEX TO ARTICLES

[See Contents for articles concerning areas outside the United States and articles without geographic orientation]

JOURNAL OF RESEARCH

of the

U.S. Geological Survey

Vol. 1 No. 1 Jan.—Feb. 1973

CONTENTS

Foreword, by V. E. McKelvey, Director, U.S. Geological Survey III
Abbreviations IV

GEOLOGIC STUDIES

Geologic implications of the Apollo 14 Fra Mauro breccias and comparison with ejecta from the Ries Crater, Germany .... *E. C. T. Chao* 1
Interpretation of depositional environment in the Plympton Formation (Permian), southern Pequop Mountains, Nev., from physical stratigraphy and a faunule .... *E. L. Yochelson and G. D. Fraser* 19
Graptolites from the Martinsburg Formation, Lehigh Gap, eastern Pennsylvania .... *J. B. Epstein and W. B. N. Berry* 33
Microprobe analysis of biotites—A method of correlating tuff beds in the Green River Formation, Colorado and Utah .... *G. A. Desborough, J. K. Pitman, and J. R. Donnell* 39
Cretaceous mafic conglomerate near Gualala offset 350 miles by San Andreas fault from oceanic crustal source near Eagle Rest Peak, Calif. .... *D. C. Ross, C. M. Wentworth, and E. H. McKee* 45
Blueschist metamorphism in the Yreka-Fort Jones area, Klamath Mountains, Calif. .... *P. E. Hotz* 53
Dolomitization model for Upper Cambrian and Lower Ordovician carbonate rocks in the eastern United States .... *L. D. Harris* 63
Determination of gold in phosphates by activation analysis using epithermal neutrons .... *J. J. Rowe* 79
Rapid determination of sulfur in rocks .... *Leonard Shapiro* 81
Antimony-bearing orpiment, Carlin gold deposit, Nevada ... *A. S. Radtke, C. M. Taylor, and Chris Heropoulos* 85
Accessory apatite from hybrid granitoid rocks of the southern Snake Range, Nev. .... *D. E. Lee, R. E. Van Loenen, and R. E. Mays* 89
New data on cuprobismutite .... *C. M. Taylor, A. S. Radtke, and C. L. Christ* 99

HYDROLOGIC STUDIES

Chemical composition of a saline lake on Enderbury Island, Phoenix Island Group, Pacific Ocean .... *D. W. Brown and R. A. Gulbrandsen* 105
A rapid method for the determination of radioactive cesium isotopes in water .... *V. J. Janzer* 113
Effect of septic-tank wastes on quality of water, Ipswich and Shawsheen River basins, Massachusetts .... *G. B. Morrill III and L. G. Toler* 117
The great Tunisian flood .... *F. E. Clarke* 121

Recent publications of the U.S. Geological Survey .... Inside of back cover

FOREWORD

Publication of the "Journal of Research of the U.S. Geological Survey" is an evolutionary advance in the publications program of the Geological Survey. The Journal is an outgrowth of the 13-year series of Geological Survey professional papers entitled "Geological Survey Research," also known informally as the "Annual Review" series.

The Geological Survey Research series was begun in 1960 as a means of more rapid publication of the results of Geological Survey research. Over a span of several years it evolved into a series of annual volumes containing four chapters each, one of which (chapter A) was an annual summary of results of Survey activities during the year, and the other three of which (chapters B, C, and D) were collections of short scientific papers. The short papers were primarily of two types—some were announcements of new discoveries or observations on problems of limited scope, whereas others were summaries of the conclusions of larger investigations that were to be published in greater detail later. An annual summary will continue to be published as a separate professional paper each year; short papers of the type that formerly appeared in chapters B, C, and D will now be published in the Journal of Research. The Journal will also contain listings of recently released Survey publications.

The Journal, which will be published six times a year, will enable the Survey to make the results of its research more readily available to readers. It will be easier to acquire because of its availability by subscription as well as on an individual-copy basis. Moreover, use of annual printing contracts will permit closer control of publication schedules.

The Journal shows more completely than any other Survey publication the wide range of research done by the Geological Survey. Papers will be drawn from all Divisions and all disciplines of the Survey, and thus will present a wide spectrum of subject matter in the earth sciences and related fields. This is in harmony with the interdisciplinary approach that is followed more and more in the study of problems in the natural sciences.

Just as the Journal has evolved from an earlier publication series, it is anticipated that it will continue to develop in style, format, and content in order better to meet future publications needs.

V. E. McKelvey

V. E. McKelvey
Director

ABBREVIATIONS

[Singular and plural forms for abbreviations of units of measure are the same]

A	angstrom units
A^3	cubic angstroms
a-c	alternating current
b.y.	billion years
cm	centimeters
cm^2	square centimeters
cm^3	cubic centimeters
cpm	counts per minute
cu ft	cubic feet
cu mi	cubic miles
eV	electron volts
emu	electromagnetic units
ft	feet
g	grams
gal	gallons
gpd	gallons per day
hr	hours
in.	inches
kb	kilobars
kg	kilograms
km	kilometers
km^2	square kilometers
km^3	cubic kilometers
kV	kilovolts
l	liters
lb	pounds
m	meters
m	molal (concentration)
m^2	square meters
m^3	cubic meters
MeV	million electron volts
mg	milligrams
ml	milliliters
mm	millimeters
mol	moles
mr	milliroentgens
mV	millivolts
m.y.	million years
μ	microns
μm	micrometers
μmhos	micromhos
n	neutrons
N	normal (concentration)
ng	nanograms
nm	nanometers
Oe	oersteds
pCi	picocuries
pH	pH (measure of hydrogen ion activity)
ppb	parts per billion
ppm	parts per million
rad	radiometric
rpm	revolutions per minute
sec	seconds
sq ft	square feet
sq mi	square miles
yr	years

Jour. Research U.S. Geol. Survey
Vol. 1, No. 1, Jan.—Feb. 1973, p. 1—18

GEOLOGIC IMPLICATIONS OF THE APOLLO 14 FRA MAURO BRECCIAS AND COMPARISON WITH EJECTA FROM THE RIES CRATER, GERMANY

By E. C. T. CHAO, Washington, D.C.

Work done in cooperation with the National Aeronautics and Space Administration under NASA contracts T-75412 and W13,130

Abstract.—On the basis of petrographic and laboratory and active seismic data for the Fra Mauro breccias, and by comparison with the nature and distribution of the ejecta from the Ries crater, Germany, some tentative conclusions regarding the geologic significance of the Fra Mauro Formation on the moon can be drawn. The Fra Mauro Formation, as a whole, consists of unwelded, porous ejecta, slightly less porous than the regolith. It contains hand-specimen and larger size clasts of strongly annealed complex breccias, partly to slightly annealed breccias, basalts, and perhaps spherule-rich breccias. These clasts are embedded in a matrix of porous aggregate dominated by mineral and breccia fragments and probably largely free of undevitrified glass. All strongly annealed hand-specimen-size breccias are clasts in the Fra Mauro Formation. To account for the porous, unwelded state of the Fra Mauro Formation, the ejecta must have been deposited at a temperature below that required for welding and annealing. Large boulders probably compacted by the Cone crater event occur near the rim of the crater. They probably consist of a similar suite of fragments, but are probably less porous than the formation. The geochronologic clocks of fragments in the Fra Mauro Formation, with textures ranging from unannealed to strongly annealed, were not reset or strongly modified by the Imbrian event. Strongly annealed breccia clasts and basalt clasts are pre-Imbrian, and probably existed as ejecta mixed with basalt flows in the Imbrium Basin prior to the Imbrian event. The Imbrian event probably occurred between 3.90 or 3.88 and 3.65 b.y. ago.

Prior studies of Apollo 14 breccias (Warner, 1972; Jackson and Wilshire, 1972; Wilshire and Jackson, 1972; Chao and others, 1972) show that thermally metamorphosed, strongly annealed breccias are dominant among the hand specimens returned from the Fra Mauro site on the moon. Associated with these are porous, friable feldspathic breccias. A prevalent view (LSPET, 1971; Wilshire and Jackson, 1972; Warner, 1972; McKay and others, 1972) is that the strongly annealed breccias are representative of the Fra Mauro Formation. The Fra Mauro Formation is postulated to represent a hot ejecta blanket from the Imbrium Basin, deposited at a high temperature. Citing the thermal blanketing effect after deposition, proponents of this theory infer that materials of the ejecta were annealed, some more than others. The high temperature would have reset the geochronological clock of most if not all of the Fra Mauro materials. Hence the annealing or the age of thermal metamorphism would date the Imbrian event. Other investigators (Dence and others, 1972; Chao and others, 1972) seriously question this view.

In order to interpret the Fra Mauro Formation correctly, three important questions must be answered: (1) Are the well-annealed hand-specimen-size breccias representative of the entire Fra Mauro Formation, or are they only clasts in the Fra Mauro Formation? (2) Were the breccias of the Fra Mauro Formation annealed and welded together after deposition of the Imbrian ejecta at the Fra Mauro site? (3) How should the ages determined on various lithic fragments in the Fra Mauro breccias be interpreted, and what is the age of the Imbrian event?

In order to answer these questions, this paper presents (1) a schematic geologic cross section of the Fra Mauro site based on photogeologic and active seismic onsite data, (2) a summary of the petrology of the breccias of the Fra Mauro Formation, (3) a summary of the nature and distribution of the ejecta of the Ries crater, illustrated by a geologic cross section and map, and a reconstruction of the development of this crater for comparison with the Imbrium Basin structure, and (4) an interpretation of age data and the age of the Imbrian event.

GEOLOGIC SETTING OF THE FRA MAURO SITE

The Fra Mauro Formation has been interpreted as an ejecta blanket excavated and ejected from the Imbrium Basin by the Imbrian impact event which produced the Imbrium multi-ring structure (Eggleton, 1970). This generally accepted interpretation is based principally on the ejecta topography; hummocky ejecta deposits can be traced more or less continuously from the rim of the Imbrium Basin to the Fra Mauro site. The

Apollo 14 landing site is within the type locality of the Fra Mauro Formation (Wilhelms, 1970).

The geology of the Fra Mauro site can be best illustrated by a schematic geologic cross section from the Neighbor crater just north of the LM (lunar module) landing site in the west to beyond Cone crater in the east (fig. 1). The profile of the cross section is from T. W. Offield (unpub. data). Areas of impact ejecta, mostly from Cone crater, are determined by field geologic data (Swann and others, 1971). The thickness of the regolith layer and the estimated thickness of the Fra Mauro Formation are based on the active seismic experiment data of Watkins and Kovach (1972). Neighbor crater is interpreted photogeologically as of Eratosthenian age (Eggleton, 1970) on the basis of its subdued and degraded morphology. Cone crater is much more recent, about 25 m.y. old (Ar^{38} cosmic ray exposure age, Burnett and others, 1972); thus a thin layer of regolith is shown over the ejecta of Neighbor crater and none over the Cone crater ejecta because of its young age.

Cone crater, which is about 320 m in diameter and about 70 m deep, has penetrated the regolith layer into the Fra Mauro Formation. Hence the boulders and coarse ejecta around Cone crater should essentially be from the Fra Mauro Formation.

According to Watkins and Kovach (1972), the regolith layer at the Fra Mauro site is 8.5 m thick and has a compressional wave velocity of 104 m/sec. It probably consists of a mixture of fines, fragments, and chunks of porous regolith microbreccias, which are compacted from fines by small impact events with an effective pressure of only a few kilobars (Chao and others, 1971; Warren and others, 1971). Ray materials, some from the Copernicus crater and others from more distant sources, are probably also present in the regolith.

The compressional wave velocity of the material that underlies the regolith is 299 m/sec. It is easily distinguishable from that of the regolith. The thickness of this layer is calculated to be between 16 and 76 m. Watkins and Kovach (1972) interpreted this layer as the Fra Mauro Formation. They contend that in order to account for such velocity the material must have a porosity of between 35 and 55 percent. Hence the Fra Mauro Formation must be highly porous.

The pre-Fra Mauro Formation material is probably also porous ejecta, with a compressive wave velocity of greater than 370 m/sec (Watkins and Kovach, 1972). The upper limit of compressive wave velocity and the depth of this layer are not given. Cone crater probably did not penetrate beyond the Fra Mauro Formation. Otherwise, some of the clasts from the Cone crater ejecta might belong to the pre-Fra Mauro materials.

Samples from both the regolith and the Cone crater ejecta were collected. Among the hand specimens returned from the Fra Mauro site, two are basalts, 14310 and 14053; the rest are breccias. The location from which 14310 was collected is uncertain. It may have been collected near station G near the Triplet craters (Swann and others, 1971). Specimen 14053 was collected near the rim of the Cone crater; hence it came from the Fra Mauro Formation.

Many of the hand specimens of gray, coherent breccias were collected from boulder fields. Some are from small to car-size boulders from the Cone crater ejecta. For example, samples 14312, 14314, 14315, 14318, and 14319 were collected at station H, in a boulder field of the Cone crater ejecta nearest to the LM site (Swann and others, 1971). Hand-specimen-size samples of white friable breccias (14063 and 14082) and the largest moderately coherent gray breccia (14312) were collected near the rim of Cone crater; 14082 was chipped off a car-size boulder at the Cone crater rim. Brownish-gray friable to coherent breccias such as 14042, 14047, 14049, 14055, and

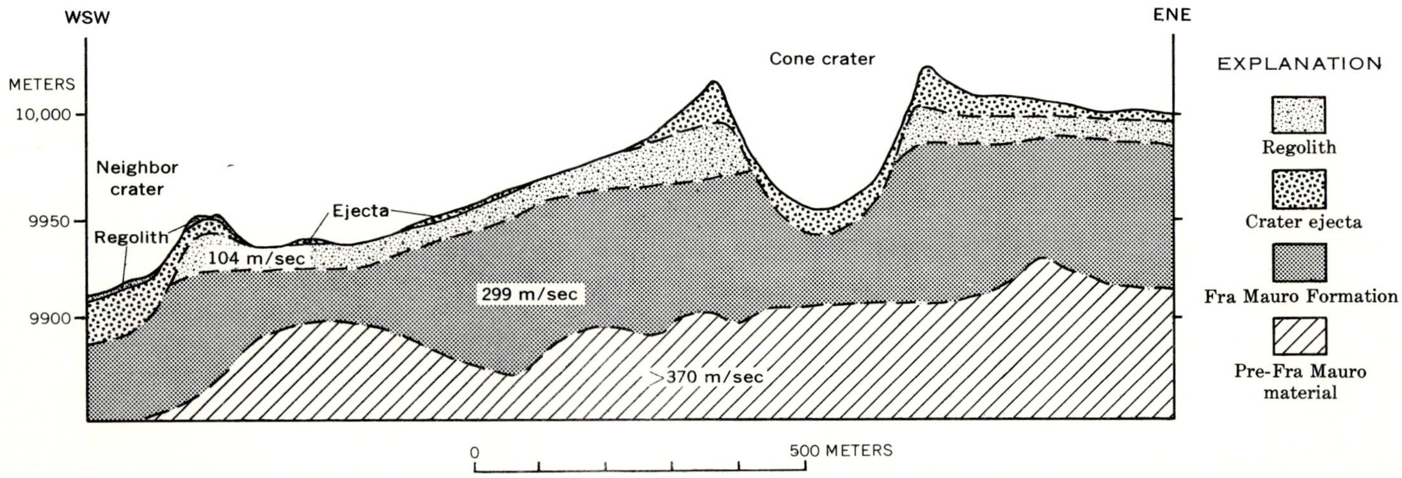

Figure 1.—Schematic geologic cross section of the Fra Mauro site. The section is drawn just north of the Apollo 14 lunar module landing site across Neighbor crater in the west to Cone crater in the east. Thickness of geologic units is principally based on active seismic data. Compressional wave velocities of some units are indicated on the cross section. The elevations shown in the vertical scale of the cross section are based on a reference elevation chosen to correspond to the mean radius of the moon of 1,738 km.

14301 were collected from areas mapped as regolith (Swann and others, 1971) east of the LM site.

DESCRIPTION OF FRA MAURO BRECCIAS

According to the genetic classification of Chao, Minkin, and Best (1972), the breccias from the Fra Mauro site can be divided into regolith microbreccias, Fra Mauro breccias, and spherule-rich microbreccias. Twenty-six hand-specimen-size breccias were so classified (table 1). The name Fra Mauro breccias was used because these samples were collected from the boulder field near the rim of Cone crater or from well-defined ejecta of the crater and hence they are derived from the Fra Mauro Formation. They also can be distinguished as different rock types from the regolith microbreccias. Among the hand specimens, the Fra Mauro breccias predominate over regolith microbreccias. Only two samples (14315 and 14318) are classified as spherule-rich microbreccias. Comparison of classification of the Apollo 14 breccias with that by Jackson and Wilshire (1972) has been given in a previous paper (Chao and others, 1972).

Table 1.—*Classification of Apollo 14 breccias based on the study of polished thin sections*

[Asterisk (*) indicates samples with fragment populations differing from others in same subgroup. From Chao, Minkin, and Best (1972)]

Classification	*Samples*
1. Regolith microbreccias:	
a. Unshocked, porous	14042, 14047, 14049, 14055, 14301*
b. Compact, nonporous	14313
c. Shocked	14307
2. Fra Mauro breccias:	
a. Unannealed or slightly annealed feldspatic breccias.	14063, 14082
b. Partly annealed breccias	14312
c. Strongly annealed (thermally metamorphosed) breccias:	
Unshocked	14006, 14270, 14311
Shocked	14066, 14171, 14303, 14304, 14305, 14306*, 14308, 14312*, 14314, 14319*, 14320
3. Spherule-rich microbreccias	14315*, 14318

Porous regolith microbreccias are poorly compacted and weakly lithified lunar fines. They generally consist chiefly of fine-grained mineral and lithic fragments and a large amount (about 50 volume percent) of glass particles. Their bulk chemical composition is generally very similar to or identical with that of the regolith. Except for a small but significant amount of exotic lithic and glass particles, and except for ray materials, most of the lithic fragments in the regolith are derived from underlying formation. In this paper, we are mainly concerned with the interpretation of the Fra Mauro breccias, rocks representative of the Fra Mauro Formation.

The Fra Mauro breccias are very complex and are characterized by a wide range of clast types and textures. The two principal types of Fra Mauro breccias are (1) a light-gray to grayish-white, generally friable, porous, unannealed to slightly annealed, highly feldspathic microbreccia, and (2) a gray, slightly or partly annealed (found principally among the coarse fines) to strongly annealed, highly coherent microbreccia. These two types are believed to be representative of the white and gray materials in the boulders near the rim of Cone crater. Most hand specimens of Fra Mauro breccias contain more than six types of lithic fragments, some as many as ten or more. Not only does the fragment population of a single Fra Mauro breccia vary, but the texture of the matrix which surrounds various clasts also varies in porosity and extent of annealing.

Principal lithic fragments

The principal categories of lithic fragments in the Fra Mauro breccias are (1) very fine grained hornfelsed noritic microbreccias and annealed fragment-laden glasses, (2) somewhat coarser grained micronorite hornfelses, (3) dark devitrified glasses, and (4) basalts. Other types of lithic fragments generally form less than a few percent of any single hand-specimen-size breccia. Most abundant among these less common types are vitrophyres, fine-grained anorthositic rocks, troctolitic rocks, and olivine-rich microbreccias. Some of the less common lithic types often occur as small inclusions in either the very fine grained hornfelsed noritic microbreccias or in annealed fragment-laden glasses or devitrified glasses. Some of the small breccia chips contain several types of breccia fragments of an earlier generation.

The very fine grained hornfelsed noritic microbreccias and annealed fragment-laden glasses may be roughly divided into three subtypes (1a, 1b, and lc) on the basis of grain size of matrix (Chao and others, 1972). The extremely fine grained type (lc) is an annealed vuggy to vesicular impactite glass charged with fine xenocrysts and a few plagioclase-rich xenoliths. The two slightly coarser grained types (1a and 1b) probably have similar origin but are better annealed than those of type lc. Their appearance is that of a vuggy hornfelsed noritic microbreccia with xenocrysts set in a granular crystalline matrix. The xenocrysts consist dominantly of plagioclase, clinopyroxenes, orthopyroxenes, and olivine, and subordinately of ilmenite, pink spinel, and nickel-iron. They are embedded in an annealed matrix consisting of lath-shaped to irregular grains of plagioclase, stubby and irregular grains of orthopyroxenes, and platy to granular ilmenite. The color of a noritic microbreccia fragment is directly related to the grain size and proportions of minerals in its annealed matrix, particularly ilmenite.

Micronorite hornfels fragments (type 2, Chao and others, 1972) are also hornfelsed fragmental rocks, but they are coarser and better recrystallized than the hornfelsed noritic microbreccias, and distinctions between fragments and matrix are more obscure. These fragments consist mainly of calcic plagioclase and inclusion-laden orthopyroxenes. They contain accessory olivine, ilmenite, a phosphate mineral, zircon, and a distinct silica and potassium-rich mesostasis. This fine-grained mesostasis gives the rock a microporphyritic texture despite the fact that the amount of the mesostasis is small. Limited or large amounts of xenocrysts of plagioclase, pyroxene, and olivine, and a few xenoliths are also present. Some of the fragments are distinctly vesicular; most are vuggy.

A distinctive type of dark, devitrified glass with xenocrysts (type 3, Chao and others, 1972) is abundant in a few of the breccias. It contains abundant skeletal plagioclase crystals and crystallites, sparse ilmenite, and is more feldspathic than noritic in composition.

Basalt fragments (type 4, Chao and others, 1972) are rare in all Fra Mauro breccias except 14321. There are several types which differ in amounts of plagioclase, pyroxene, and ilmenite, and in textures. The most abundant type is a subophitic to ophitic basalt with pyroxene dominating over calcic plagioclase. These are commonly olivine bearing, and contain 1–5 percent ilmenite.

Fragment population and textures

Light-gray to grayish-white, friable, porous, largely unannealed, highly feldspathic microbreccias.—Samples 14063 and 14082 are representative of this type. Sample 14063 contains two main types of lithic fragments, brownish-gray devitrified glass (lithic type 3) and grayish-white micronorite hornfels (lithic type 2). The fragment populations measured from two thin sections are shown in table 2. Most large crystal or lithic fragments are free of evidence of mineral reactions. The rock is porous (38–51 percent porosity, table 2, see also figures 2 and 3). Because one of these samples, 14082, was chipped off from a car-size boulder near the Cone crater rim, this type of porous, largely unannealed feldspathic breccia is closely associated with the gray Fra Mauro breccias described below.

Figure 2.—A chip of slightly annealed grayish-white, friable, porous, feldspathic Fra Mauro breccia 14063. It contains fragments of well-recrystallized micronorite hornfels (right center) and dark-purplish-brown devitrified glass (center and lower center).

Gray, partly annealed, moderately coherent breccia.—In hand specimen size the only example of this type is 14321, the largest rock returned from the Fra Mauro site. It contains abundant black fragments of annealed extremely fine grained fragment-laden glass (lithic type 1c), and several types of basalt fragments (with subophitic olivine basalt similar to 14053 dominant) in a matrix of broken basaltic fragments (fig.

Table 2.—*Fragment population of some Apollo 14 Fra Mauro and spherule-rich breccias, in volume percent*

[From Chao, Minkin, and Best (1972)]

	Slightly annealed feldspathic		Partly annealed	Annealed	Spherule rich
	14063,13	14063,46	14321,241	14303,2	14315,8
Fine-grained hornfelsed noritic microbreccia (1a).	....	....	....	44.4	0.2
Very fine grained hornfelsed noritic microbreccia (1b).	0.8	3.1	....	11.1	16.8
Extremely fine grained annealed fragment-laden glass (1c).	....	....	59.3	....	2.6
Micronorite hornfels (2)	21.4	33.0	.3	....	.8
Feldspathic devitrified glass (3).	16.0	19.0	3.3	....	....
Basalt (4)	.6	.3	27.5	8.2	.4
Other lithic fragments	11.0	1.8	1.0	3.6	3.6
Devitrified glass spheroids	....	....	....	....	38.9
Undevitrified glass spheroids	....	....	....	....	1.9
Mineral fragments and matrix (<25μ).	50.3	42.9	8.2	32.6	34.8
Pores	(51)[1]	(38)[1]	(18)[1]	....	....

[1] The percentage of pores is excluded in mineral mode.

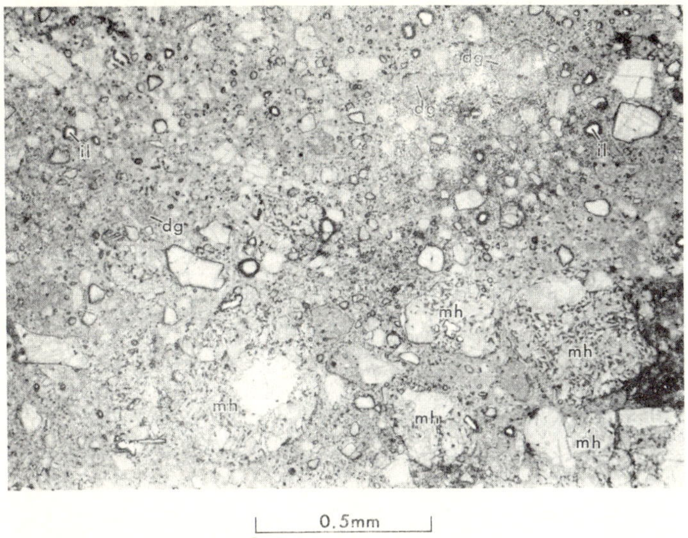

Figure 3.—Photomicrograph of part of polished thin section 14063,13, slightly annealed feldspathic Fra Mauro breccia, showing fragments of micronorite hornfels (mh, mottled light-gray fragments) and devitrified glass (dg, gray areas with high relief surrounded by thin black borders). Pores and open space are medium gray in low relief. Light areas in high relief are ilmenite (il). Reflected light.

4). A tentative estimate of the fragment population based on a large thin section is given in table 2.

Strongly annealed, coherent, gray breccias.—This is the most abundant group of hand specimens returned from the Fra Mauro site (table 1). They are generally light gray to gray. Except for vugs in annealed lithic or devitrified glass fragments within them, they are nonporous (fig. 5). In polished thin sections viewed in reflected light, fragment boundaries are distinguished only by changes in texture (fig. 6). Reaction rims around olivine and spinel are common (Wilshire and Jackson, 1972). Under high magnification, xenocrysts and surrounding matrix grains show interlocking textures.

The complexity of the strongly annealed breccias is evident from the wide range of fragment populations that they contain. Each sample contains a collection of annealed breccia fragments of multiple generations or sources. Hornfelsed noritic microbreccia fragments with strongly contrasting grain size of recrystallized matrix occur side by side (fig. 6). Preliminary study of thin sections shows that 14303, 14305, and 14311 are similar in fragment population, with fine-grained and very fine grained hornfelsed noritic microbreccia fragments (types 1a and 1b) dominant (see 14303 in table 2) and basalt fragments present in small but significant amounts.

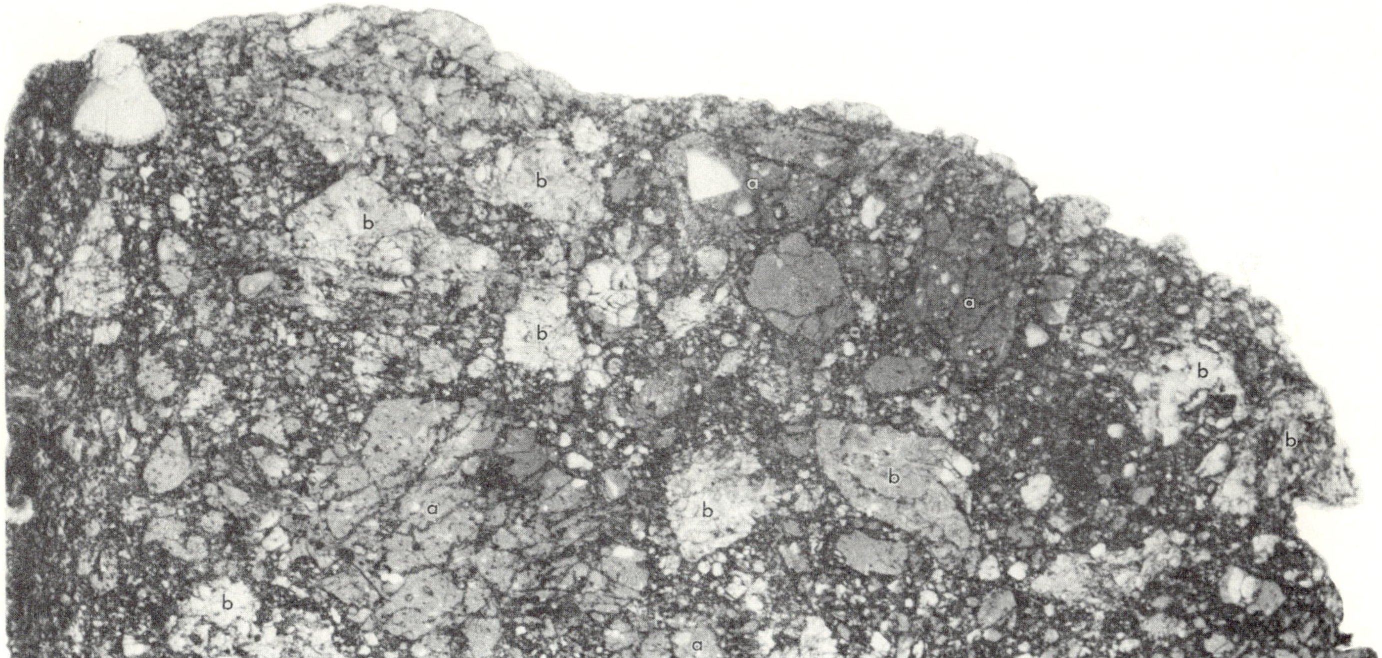

Figure 4.—Photomicrograph of polished thin section 14321,241-4, a partly annealed Fra Mauro breccia, showing the dominant fragments of basalt (b) and annealed extremely fine grained fragment-laden glass (a) in a granular matrix of moderate porosity. Reflected light.

Figure 5.–Hand specimen of strongly annealed Fra Mauro breccia 14319, showing fragments of annealed very fine grained noritic microbreccias (gray) in a well-annealed lighter colored matrix. Dark fragment in upper left is an annealed extremely fine grained fragment-laden glass.

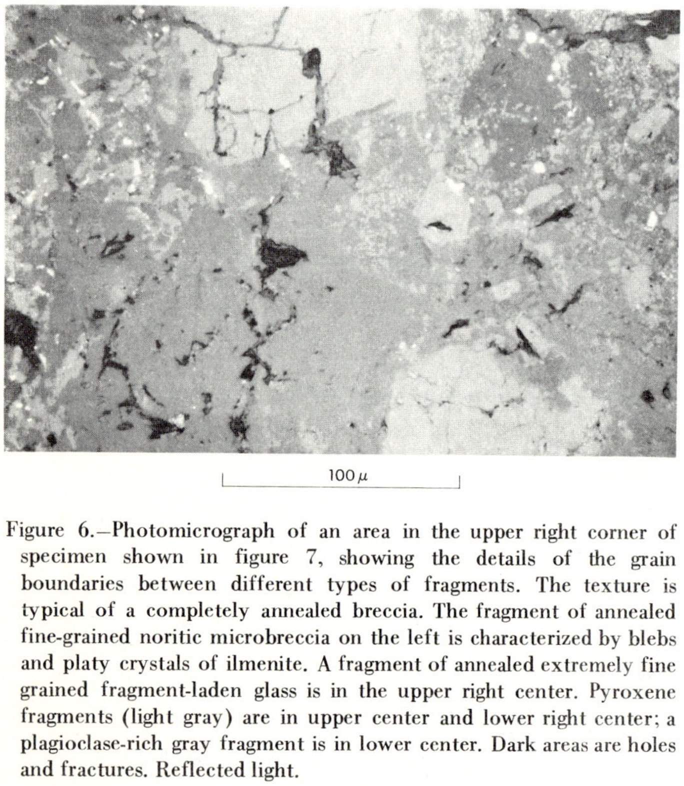

Figure 6.–Photomicrograph of an area in the upper right corner of specimen shown in figure 7, showing the details of the grain boundaries between different types of fragments. The texture is typical of a completely annealed breccia. The fragment of annealed fine-grained noritic microbreccia on the left is characterized by blebs and platy crystals of ilmenite. A fragment of annealed extremely fine grained fragment-laden glass is in the upper right center. Pyroxene fragments (light gray) are in upper center and lower right center; a plagioclase-rich gray fragment is in lower center. Dark areas are holes and fractures. Reflected light.

14312 and 14319 are similar to each other and distinct from the previous samples in fragment population. In these samples, fine-grained hornfelsed microbreccias (type 1a) are dominant, as in the first group, but basalts are very rare, and dark, devitrified pyroxene-dominant vitrophyric fragments generally free of xenocrysts are common. The fragment population of 14306 is unique. This sample contains fragments of fine-grained to very fine grained hornfelsed noritic microbreccias, similar to those in the other samples, but in addition dark extremely fine grained annealed fragment-laden glass is abundant, appreciable numbers of fragments of felsite (microgranite) are present, and basalt fragments are virtually absent (fig. 7).

Despite this complexity of textures of fragments, however, there appear to be only a few dominant types if bulk composition alone is considered. The predominant fragments in all the Fra Mauro breccias are noritic, troctolitic, or highly feldspathic (anorthositic gabbro). Basaltic rocks in which mafic minerals predominate over plagioclase are sparse, and ilmenite-rich rocks are extremely rare.

All the glass or glassy fragments in the well-annealed breccias are completely devitrified or annealed. Some are very well recrystallized. Undevitrified glass is very rare or absent. The amount of devitrified or annealed glass is generally less than 50 percent, less than the amount of mineral and crystalline rock fragments present.

Among the xenocrysts and crystalline rock fragments present in the well-annealed breccias, fragments with evidence of moderate to strong shock (such as vitrification and vesiculation) are generally lacking. Nearly all the well-annealed Fra Maura breccias are clasts made up of aggregates of crushed impact ejecta that have undergone only low shock. Effects of shock compression can be observed in many of the well-annealed hand-specimen-size breccias. They were probably produced by the Cone crater event.

Spherule-rich microbreccias.–Two microbreccias (14315 and 14318) are of this type and are characterized by abundant devitrified spherules and spheroids of varied composition, and by subrounded to rounded lithic fragments whose long dimensions are alined in a subparallel manner (particularly in 14315). The fragment population for 14315,8 is given in table 2. 14315 is nonporous and thoroughly indurated. 14318 contains fewer devitrified glass spheroids and more lithic fragments. How 14315 and 14318 are related to the Fra Mauro breccias is not clear.

Porosity and seismic velocity

Porosity of breccias reflects the degree of shock compaction (Chao and others, 1971) and annealing, and is reflected in the compressive seismic wave velocities. The compressive seismic wave velocity in Apollo 11 regolith microbreccia 10046 (26 percent porosity) measured by Anderson and others (1970) is 1.20 km/sec. The velocity in a similar microbreccia, 10065 (bulk density of 2.34 g/cm^3 and estimated porosity of about 22 percent), measured by Kanamori and others (1970) is 1.50 km/sec. The compressive seismic wave velocity in Apollo 14 regolith microbreccia 14313 (estimated porosity of 21 per-

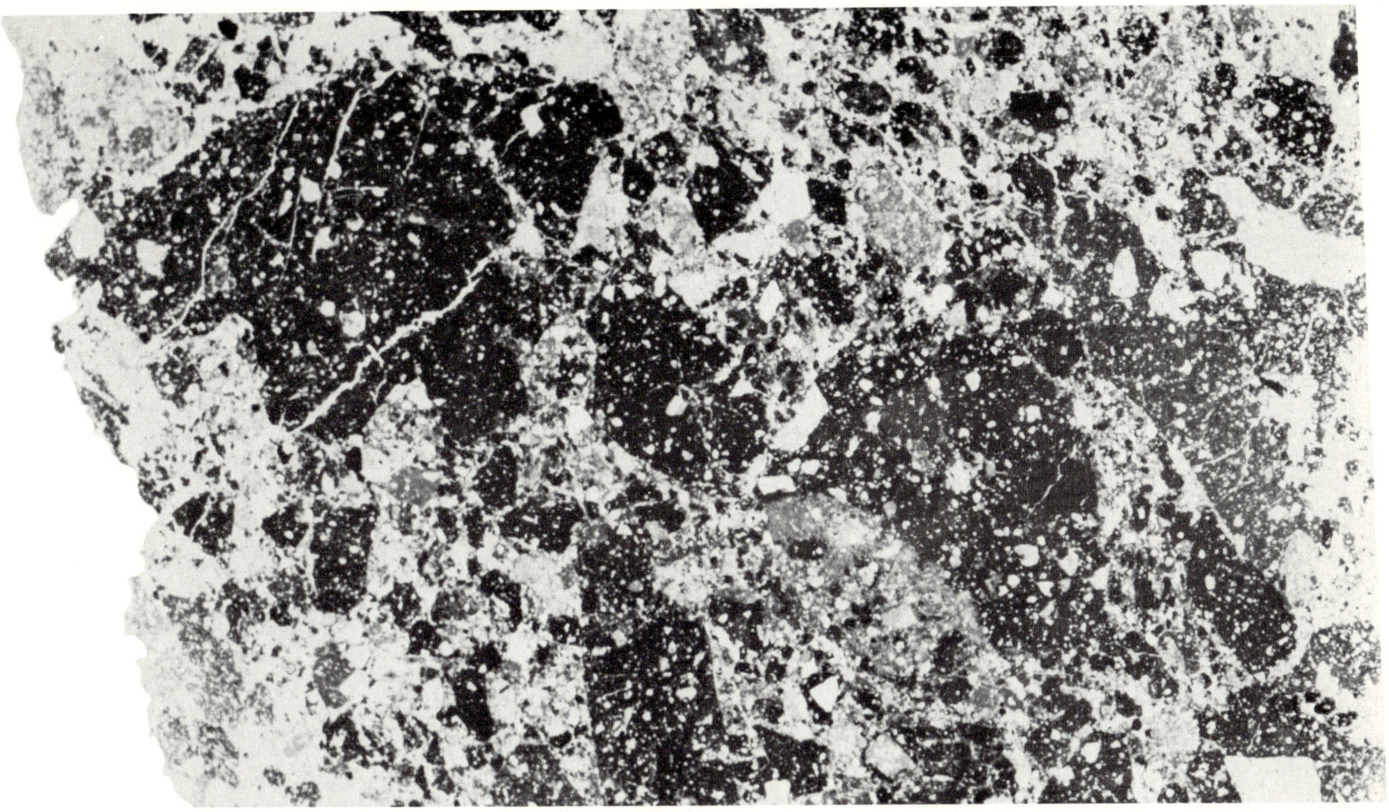

Figure 7.—Photomicrograph of polished thin section 14306,58, a strongly annealed Fra Mauro breccia. The black fragments are annealed very fine grained noritic microbreccias. The gray fragments are annealed fine-grained noritic microbreccias. The gradation in gray reflects the contrast in grain size. The sample is nonporous and strongly annealed. Transmitted plane-polarized light.

cent) is 2.25 km/sec (Mizutani and others, 1972). In contrast, Apollo 14 well-annealed Fra Mauro breccia 14311 has a much higher seismic velocity measured by the same authors, 5.65 km/sec. This seismic velocity is even higher than many of the Apollo 12 basalts measured (4.30 km/sec for 12052, 3.27 km/sec for 12065, Kanamori and others, 1971; 2.51–3.32 km/sec for 12063, 1.79–2.04 km/sec for 12018, Warren and others, 1971).

THE NATURE AND DISTRIBUTION OF THE EJECTA AND THE RECONSTRUCTED DEVELOPMENT OF THE RIES CRATER

Probably the best preserved terrestrial meteorite crater larger than 20 km in diameter is the Ries crater (Rieskessel) in southern Bavaria, Germany. The general structure and the stratigraphic section and basement crystalline rocks underlying the Ries are now fairly well known (Schmidt-Kaler, 1969; Dressler and others, 1969). Although partly eroded, the ejecta of the Ries are well preserved. A condensed summary of the reconstructed development of the Ries crater is given below. This summary includes the nature and distribution of the ejecta, their sequence of production and ejection trajectories. This summary is based on selected published literature and limited personal observations of the Ries ejecta material in the laboratory and during three short field trips in 1961, 1964, and 1971.

The geologic literature of the Ries crater is voluminous. A review of this literature up to 1969 citing earlier reviews by Löffle, Kranz, Preuss, and Barthel was made by Preuss (1969). A collection of many of the recent investigations in geology, stratigraphy, geophysics, and petrology concerning the Ries, including a geologic map (1:100,000), was published in a single volume of Geologica Bavarica (no. 61, 1969). A separate brief review has been published by Dennis (1971).

Geologic setting

The Ries crater is on the Schwabian-Frankian Alb, a low cuesta or plateau that extends east-northeasterly across Bavaria. The Alb is underlain by gently southeastwardly dipping Mesozoic sedimentary rocks (fig. 8) which in turn unconformably overlie basement crystalline rocks of Hercynian and pre-Hercynian age. The basement

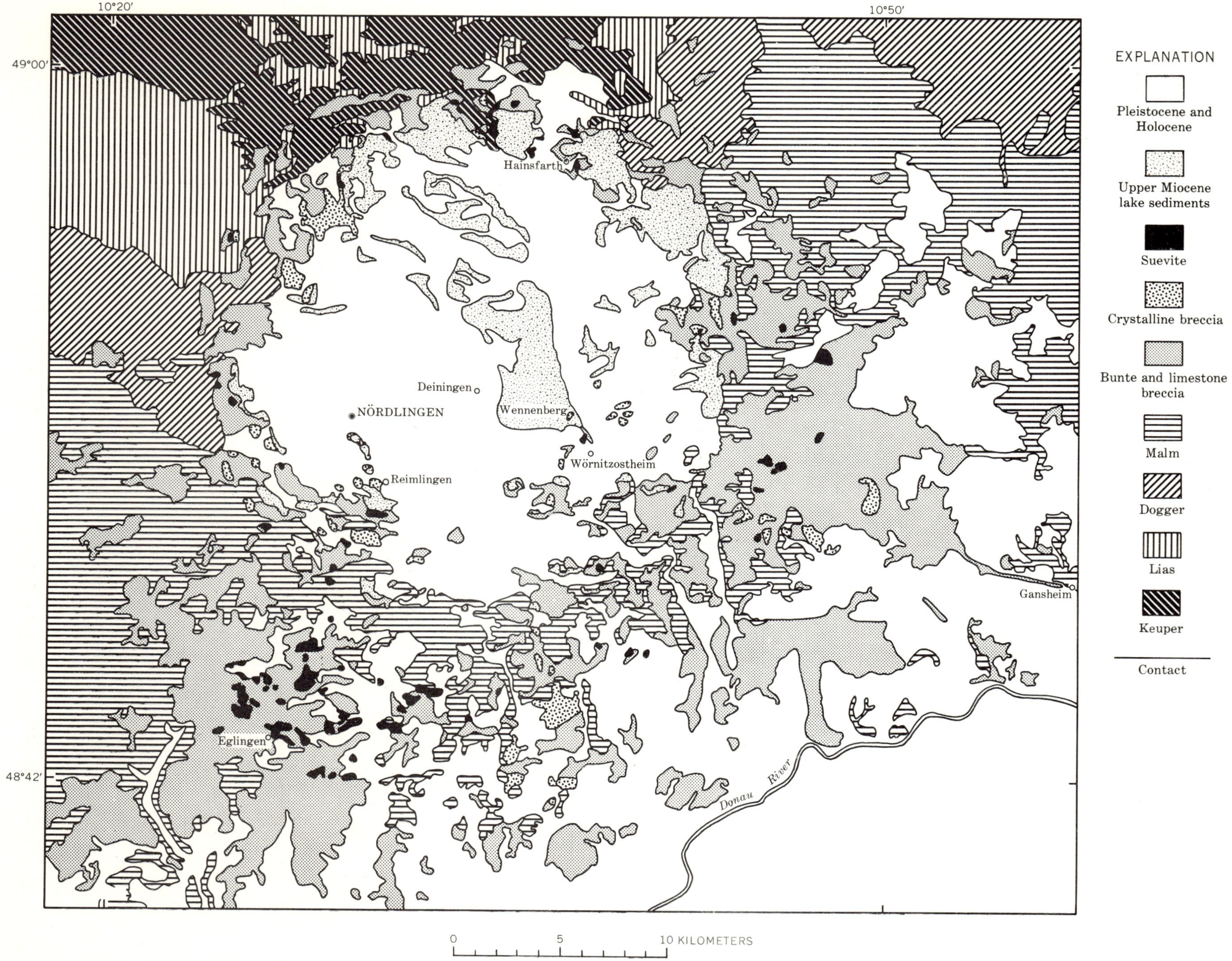

Figure 8.—Geologic map of the Ries crater. Compiled from large-scale geologic maps and the 1:100,000 geologic map by Hüttner, Schmidt-Kaler, and Treibs (1969).

crystalline rocks consist of fine-grained to medium-coarse-grained granodiorite, dioritic and granitic rocks, granitic gneisses, amphibolites, and dark lamprophyres and other dike rocks. They have been described by Dressler and others (1969). According to Schmidt-Kaler (1969), Wirth (1969), and Preuss (1969), the reconstructed Ries sedimentary section consists of 700 to nearly 1,000 m of chiefly Mesozoic sedimentary rocks. In ascending order, these rocks consist of (1) Rotliegendes sandstones and shales (Permian?, 30 to 200 m) and some limestones in the upper part (Muschelkalk about 50 m), (2) Triassic Keuper sandstones and shales (about 250 m), (3) Lias (Black Jura) bluish-gray shales (about 30 m), (4) Dogger (Brown Jura) shale and oolitic and pisolitic ferrugenous sandstone (about 140 m), and (5) Malm (White Jura) limestones consisting of thin-bedded limestone followed by massive limestone (about 300 m). Both geologic and geophysical data show that the bottom of the Ries crater lies within the basement crystalline rocks. Hence the crater has penetrated a minimum of several hundred meters of Mesozoic sedimentary rocks. After the crater was formed, the crater depression was filled with upper Miocene fossiliferous lacustrine deposits of shales and limestones having a maximum estimated thickness of about 350 m (Angenheister and Pöhl, 1969). Hence, based on the geology and the potassium-argon ages determined on Ries glass (Gentner and Wagner, 1969), the Ries crater was formed in late Miocene time about 14.5 m.y. ago. Since that time the crater and its ejecta have been partly eroded. Pleistocene loess and other periglacial deposits cover parts of the structure.

Nature of ejecta

Because of the distinctive lithologies of the various Mesozoic formations and the basement crystalline rocks, four types of ejecta can be recognized on the basis of the dominant lithic types in the ejecta: (1) suevite, a breccia rich in fragmental glass and containing lithic fragments predominantly of crystalline rock, (2) crystalline rock breccia, consisting of fractured and brecciated blocks of granitic rocks, amphibolites, and other metamorphic basement crystalline rocks, (3) "Bunte breccia," a mixed breccia of predominantly variegated shale and sandstone, limestone, and some crystalline rocks, and (4) "Gries," an intensely shattered and finely brecciated limestone. The nature of these four types of ejecta is summarized below.

Suevite, a term traced to Sauer (1901), is a poorly sorted, unstratified, brownish-gray, moderately indurated breccia deposit. The rock is soft, somewhat compacted, and moderately coherent because of cementation in many instances by secondary minerals. It resembles tuff-breccia but contains abundant strongly shocked granitic rock fragments and abundant glass particles and "bombs" (fig. 9). This unique rock type is found only in the vicinity of the Ries and nowhere else in Germany. Petrographic descriptions of suevite have been

Figure 9.—Suevite, west side of quarry wall in Otting, Ries, Germany. Dark fragments are glass. White fragments are granitic rocks, and many are strongly shocked. The lack of bedding is characteristic. The area selected for fragment count is outlined by strings.

given by Sauer (1901), Oberdorfer (1905), and Ackermann (1959) from the volcanic point of view. Suevite was reinterpreted by Shoemaker and Chao (1961) and Chao and Littler (1963) as impact ejecta on the basis of the shock effects in fragments and the occurrence of coesite and stishovite in strongly shocked fragments of granitic rocks. Additional evidence of shock or meteorite impact origin of suevite was reported later by Chao (1967, 1968), Engelhardt and Stöffler (1968), and Engelhardt and others (1968, 1969). Hence the impact origin of the Ries crater has been firmly established.

In suevite the fragment size varies from less than a millimeter to a little more than 25 cm (Chao, unpub. data). Glass bombs are as much as 25 cm. Most bombs appear to have cooled quickly and show no sign of recrystallization or annealing, although small clusters of trichites of pyroxene are present in some samples. A small number show more extensive devitrification. There is no mineral reaction of any kind between adjacent fragments. Except for a thin veneer of small particles, most fragments adjacent to the glass bombs do not stick to the glass.

Other than glass, most of the fragments in suevite are mineral fragments and fragments of granitic crystalline rocks. Some of the lithic fragments are coated by glass whose composition may be similar to or different from the rock fragment; thus the glasses coating such fragments are not products of in-place melting of the enclosed fragment. The predominant crystalline rock types in suevite appear to vary with respect to their geographic location in the ejecta deposits, perhaps reflecting the proximity to the sources of the basement crystalline rocks. Suevite also contains small amounts of shale, sandstone, and limestone fragments; a few of these show evidence of fusion and thermal metamorphism.

Fragment population data on suevite are sparse. Some estimates of the proportions of glass "bombs" in suevite were reported by Ackermann (in Engelhardt and others, 1969), and a fragment count of sedimentary fragments in suevite was done by Barani (in Engelhardt and others, 1969). Fragment counts, by a method similar to the Rosiwal method, of those fragments in suevite larger than 1 cm were made on outcrops of suevite in several quarries in the Ries by the author in 1971. The lithology of each rock fragment and the degree of shock of granitic fragments were determined with a 20X hand lens. These fragment counts were obtained from outcrop areas of about 1 m^2. Hand samples of breccias containing only fragments finer than 1 cm from the same outcrops were collected. Fragment population study of these samples in thin sections has yet to be completed.

A preliminary fragment count (table 3) indicates that the Ries suevite contains a very high percentage (50–75) of glass fragments. Where the glass fragment content is high, fragments of strongly shocked crystalline rock predominate over moderately shocked fragments. Fragment count of a sample of suevite from St. George's Church in Nördlingen shows that as the percentage of glass fragments decreases, the quantities of

Table 3.—*Fragment population, in percent of fragments larger than 1 cm, determined for suevite from the Ries crater area, Germany*

	Locality				
	Otting	Hainsfarth	Bollstadt	Aufhausen	St. George's Church
Vesicular glass.	74.7	70.0	67.9	62.4	51.5
Granodiorite, moderately shocked.	4.2	1.0	. . . .	.9	4.8
Granodiorite, strongly shocked.	9.0	4.0	5.7	7.3	2.4
Granite gneiss, moderately shocked.	.6	9.0	3.8	3.7	5.4
Granite gneiss, strongly shocked.	4.2	9.0	13.2	18.3	. . . .
Glass-coated fragments.	4.8	2.0	1.9	2.8	6.1
Shales, sandstones.	1.8	5.0	5.7	3.7	19.4
Limestones . . .	. . . .	. . . .	1.9	.9	7.9
Metamorphic rocks.	.6	. . . .	Trace	. . . .	2.4

the moderately shocked granitic fragments and sedimentary rock fragments from the overlying Mesozoic section increase notably.

Crystalline rock breccias consist of intensely shattered and highly fractured house-size or larger blocks of basement crystalline rocks (monomict) and breccias of mixed varieties of crystalline rocks (polymict; see Stöffler in Engelhardt and others, 1969). The monomict breccias are generally deeply weathered and highly friable. The intense shattering is the only shock effect observed; evidence of shock strong enough to produce plastic deformation is generally absent (see also Stöffler in Engelhardt and others, 1969). The polymict crystalline rock breccias, such as those from Meyer's Keller (about 2 km south of Nördlingen), contain many lithic fragments that show a somewhat greater degree of shock (see also Stöffler in Engelhardt and others, 1969). Some of these breccias also contain mixed bunte breccias, but the degree of mixing between crystalline rock breccias and bunte breccias appears to be very limited. Most of the polymict breccias are slightly to moderately coherent. Because of weathering, they are highly friable and crumbly. Fragment size is seriate rather than bimodal. The maximum degree of shock effects observed so far in fragments in crystalline rock breccias is low to moderate (classification presented in Chao, 1968). The presence of vesiculated rocks or glasses has not been reported from any crystalline rock breccias so far. There is no evidence of annealing or welding of fragments.

Bunte breccia is weakly to moderately coherent, variegated, mixed breccia, consisting predominantly of variegated shales and sandstones of Keuper, Lias, and Dogger, and limestones of Malm. Descriptions of bunte breccias have been summarized by Hüttner (1969) and by W. Schneider (in Engelhardt and others, 1969). Although the proportions of kinds of sedimentary rocks vary, and a small number of basement crystalline rock fragments are commonly present, bunte breccias consist of fragments derived principally from the lower part of the Mesozoic section (fig. 10). According to Schneider (in Engelhardt and others, 1969) fragments from the lower part of the Mesozoic section tend to be more abundant in the upper part of the bunte breccias and those from the upper part of the Mesozoic section tend to be abundant in the lower part, similar to an inverted section. He also noted that blocks of older Mesozoic sedimentary rocks are more abundant near the crater rim and that fragments from the upper Mesozoic section are more abundant in bunte breccias farther away from the rim. Bunte breccias in general are free of fragments that have undergone any optically detectable shock effects.

The Gries consists chiefly of light-gray to yellowish-white intensely shattered, highly fractured and brecciated limestone derived largely from Malm. A description of the nature and occurrences of Gries was given by Hüttner (1969). Figure 11 shows some detail of a quarry wall in this type of material. Besides intense shattering, calcite in thin sections of such limestones shows abundant shock-induced lamellar twinning. Because of the lack of experimental shock data on calcite, the shock undergone by most of the brecciated limestones can only be estimated, but the shock effects are clearly all of low degree.

Relative abundance and distribution of the Ries ejecta materials

The best exposures showing the relationships of the different types of Ries ejecta are in quarries and roadcuts. The ejecta deposits were also exposed in a 2-m deep trench for an oil pipeline extending from north of Nördlingen to Gansheim (Treibs, 1965). The areal distribution of the ejecta is shown on the geologic map (fig. 8). The vertical distribution is illustrated in the geologic cross section from Hainsfarth in the northeast to beyond Eglingen in the southwest (fig. 12).

Figure 10.—North wall of Harburg-N quarry, showing large blocks of Jurassic limestone (light) in loosely cemented bunte breccia overlying flat-lying to gently dipping Jurassic limestone of the crater wall. The contact is marked by a striated surface (Schliff-Fläche). Bulldozer in lower right provides scale.

Figure 11.—Fractured, brecciated, and shattered limestone of the Gries (limestone breccia) exposed in a quarry wall near Wörnitzstein. Bedding structures in the limestone have been obliterated. Hammer in lower right provides scale.

The total amount and the relative abundance of the different types of Ries ejecta can be roughly estimated because (1) the reconstructed thickness of the sedimentary section is available, (2) the position of the undisturbed crystalline rocks corresponding to the bottom of the crater cavity has been estimated to be 1 to 1.4 km below the normal unconformity contact (Angenheister and Pöhl, 1969), and (3) the diameter of the crater is known (average 23 km). Thus, the calculated total amount of Ries ejecta is about 400 km^3, of which 155 km^3 are crystalline rock breccias and suevite and 245 km^3 are sedimentary rock breccias (bunte breccias and Gries). It is evident from the geologic map (fig. 8) that the bulk of the fallback and fallout breccias are the crystalline breccias and suevite, whereas the throwout breccias are dominated by the sedimentary rock breccias. The crystalline rock breccias and suevite occur within a distance about equal to one crater radius of the rim of the crater. The sedimentary rock breccias are distributed about a crater diameter or more beyond the crater rim.

Within the crater, suevite, as fallback breccia, occurs below the upper Miocene lacustrine sediments and above fractured or brecciated basement crystalline rocks. This is demonstrated by rocks from drill holes at Deiningen and Wörnitzostheim (Förstner, 1967) and by geophysical data (Angenheister and Pöhl, 1969). Although the thicknesses of suevite penetrated by the two drill holes are about 40 m and 85 m, respectively, the maximum thickness of suevite underlying the Ries lake deposits is estimated to range from 300 to 400 m (Angenheister and Pöhl, 1969). This estimate has not been verified by drilling.

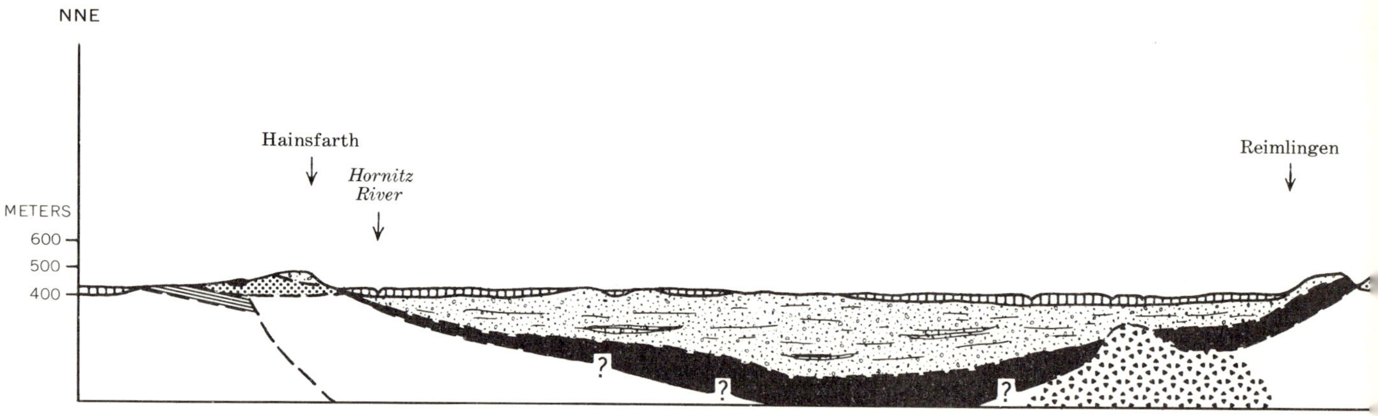

Figure 12.–Geologic cross section of the Ries from near Hainsfarth in the northeast to beyond Eglingen in the southwest. The profile is based c 1:100,000 topographic maps (AMS M642). The surface geology is from figure 8. Most of the subsurface geology is from geophysical da (Angenheister and Pöhl, 1969; Reich and Horrix, 1955) and extrapolation from the drill holes at Deiningen and Wörnitzostheim (Förstne 1967). Small suevite bodies near Eglingen have been slightly exaggerated in size. Bunte and limestone breccias extend nearly twice as far o from the crater rim as the scattered overlying suevite fallout breccias. Some of the former overlie Paleocene-Eocene(?) sand, which is tc thin to show in the cross section. The general limit of the crater cavity is marked by the dashed line.

The thickness of suevite deposits that occur outside of the crater rim ranges from a few meters to about 20 m. Suevite in many cases occurs in steep contact with bunte breccias or limestone breccias. As observed along the trench of the pipeline (Treibs, 1965) and in the Otting and Hainsfarth quarries (fig. 13) suevite overlies bunte breccia. This relationship has also been observed in other localities by other investigators (Hüttner, 1969; Engelhardt and others, 1969). The fact that suevite overlies the bunte breccias indicates that it was the last to settle or deposit and that it must have been produced in the late stage of cratering and have had a high-angle trajectory.

Shattered and fractured crystalline blocks and mixed crystalline rock breccias occur in isolated outcrops both within and outside the rim of the crater. Those that occur within the crater, such as that of Wennenberg, may be a part of a horseshoe-shaped crystalline rock wall that is buried beneath the surface sediments (Reich and Horrix, 1955). The other outcrops of crystalline rock breccias within the crater are located largely outside of this horseshoe ridge. This raised crystalline rockwall may be part of the brecciated and fractured basement rock which in most places underlies a blanket of suevite inside the crater. If so, instead of a central hill, the Ries structure has a horseshoe-shaped raised central ridge (now buried). Dislodged blocks and breccias of crystalline rocks also occur outside the crater rim but not far away from the rim. Areas of scattered crystalline rocks that extend farthest away from the rim are located near Stillnau and Hochstein southward from the rim and near Mündling, Sulzdorf, and Itzing in the southeastern part of Vorries.

Bunte breccias are best exposed high above the crater wall from quarries such as at Harburg-N, where large blocks of inverted and rotated Malm limestone were enclosed in the bunte breccia (fig. 10).

Although some outcrops of bunte breccias occur within the crater, most are outside the crater and far beyond outcrops of suevite and the crystalline rock breccias (fig. 12). In many localities bunte breccias were deposited on the flat-lying limestones of the crater wall, above a distinctly striated surface known as Schliff-Fläche similar to surfaces produced by glaciation (Wagner, 1964; Hüttner, 1969). The striated or grooved surfaces are generally flat, and the direction of striae or grooves is basically radial with respect to the crater (Wagner, 1964). Such surfaces were probably produced by gouging and scraping of fragments at the base of the bunte breccia as the large volume of brecciated rock moved laterally and radially away out of the crater. If so, the angles of trajectory of the bunte breccias were flat to low, and the bunte breccias were deposited before the suevite which was ejected at high angles. Such lateral movement of breccias is also strong evidence against a simple overturning of the stratigraphic section.

Deposits of brecciated and shattered limestone are most extensive to the southwest and southeast of the crater, outside the rim. They overlie the eroded surface of white Jurassic limestones, and in places occur on Paleocene and Eocene(?) sand (fig. 12). They are among the farthest throwout ejecta from the Ries (shown as an undifferentiated unit from bunte breccia, in fig. 8).

Rare veins of fine-grained clayey to sandy bunte breccia materials occur in shattered and brecciated limestone such as at Holheim (east quarry) and at the Schwalbenberg quarry near Fünfstetten. These veins were probably produced by injection of crushed rock along fractures when the crater was formed.

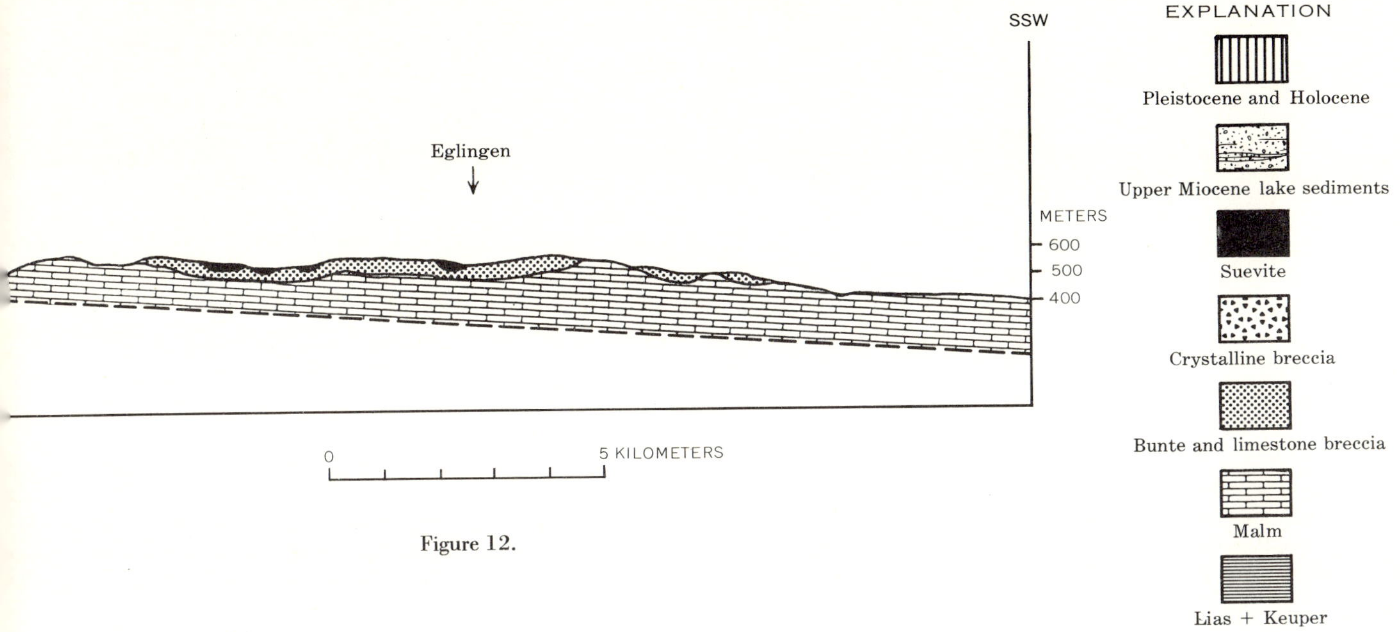

Figure 12.

Reconstructed development of the Ries crater

On the basis of the nature and the lateral and vertical distribution of the four types of Ries ejecta, the cratering event that produced the Ries structure may be reconstructed as outlined below. The entire sequence described occurred within a few seconds or perhaps even a fraction of a second.

1. The impacting body (probably a tough meteoritic body) penetrated at least 700 m of the Mesozoic section of the Schwabian-Frankian Alb; the crater bottom lies within the basement crystalline rocks.

2. Before the impacting body reached the basement crystalline rocks, the Mesozoic sedimentary rocks in the upper part of the section were compressed, crushed, dislodged, and ejected at low angles radially outward from the center of the crater. Movement of this material produced the slickensided surfaces above the crater wall. The deposits of this material are the bunte breccias and Gries and they occur farther out from the crater center than the other types of Ries ejecta deposits. The fragments are only weakly shocked, and the shock-induced temperatures must have been very low.

3. As the impacting body continued to penetrate, the compression of the target materials and the impacting body increased, and the shock-induced temperature in the immediate region appears to have exceeded the melting temperatures at just about the time that the impacting body penetrated the basement crystalline rocks. This is the moment when the peak transient pressure and shock-induced temperature were reached and when the particles of molten crystalline rocks and fragments of strongly shocked crystalline rocks were formed. Deposits of these materials are the suevites, and their distribution indicates that the fragments were ejected at high angles. Crystalline rock farther from the immediate area of penetration of the impacting body was moderately to weakly shocked and compressed; then it was fractured, brecciated, and dislodged and pushed up and, in part, beyond the crater rim to form deposits of throwout breccias.

Two modes of ejecta transport that have been proposed for impact cratering apparently were not important in the Ries event. These are: (1) jetting upon first contact between the impacting body and the target materials (suggested by small-scale hypervelocity impact experiments by Gault and others, 1968) and (2) base surge (suggested by underwater nuclear explosion, Young, 1965).

In laboratory hypervelocity experiments using principally lexan projectiles impacting in sand, Gault and others (1968) presented evidence of the occurrence of the highest temperature ejected phase by jetting upon contact. In the Ries event, however, producing a large amount of melt or glass by jetting upon contact is not consistent with the time sequence of development of suevite, the Ries ejecta deposit that contains the hottest ejecta. Suevite could not have been produced until the impacting body had penetrated, or the impact momentum had been transferred into, the basement crystalline rocks where the apparent origin of shock is located. The Ries impact event is probably similar to that proposed by Shoemaker (1960) in his analysis of the penetration mechanics of Meteor Crater in Arizona, where the meteorite-impact penetration by hydrodynamic flow was accomplished by lateral deflection of material at the leading end of the still fast-moving system of compressed rock and meteorite. The depth of penetration of the impacting body is directly proportional to the square root of the ratio of the density of the impacting body and the target material (cited by Shoemaker, 1960). Hence the impacting body producing the Ries structure should have been dense; probably an iron meteorite.

Figure 13—Weathered lighter colored suevite overlying slightly darker bunte breccia. Coin (2 cm in diameter) marks the contact. Glass (dark spots) is only found in suevite. Dark spots in bunte breccia below are gray and purple shale of Lias and Keuper, respectively. Hainsfarth quarry, north of Hainsfarth, Ries, Germany.

The phenomenon of base surge was first observed in the Baker underwater nuclear test at Bikini in 1947. According to Young (1965) the primary base surge of this test occurred 11 seconds after the detonation of the nuclear device. The primary base surge was produced by spillout, caused principally by gaseous (steam) expansion (G. A. Young, oral commun., 1972). The secondary base surge of this same test was the result of lateral displacement produced by the fallback of the ejected water column. Once produced, a base surge behaves more or less as a density current. Base surge has also been observed in cratering events of high-energy chemical explosives and underground detonation of nuclear devices (Young, 1965; R. B. Colton, written commun., 1963). The base-surge deposit of the Sedan nuclear event consists of dust a few millimeters thick, and the dust was so fine that its distribution was controlled by a southerly wind (R. B. Colton, written commun., 1963). The phenomenon of base surge has also been observed in recent volcanic eruptions (Moore, 1967). All these observed instances of base-surge transport have one thing in common—gaseous expansion—and all involve fluid- or gas-entrained materials that are only a small fraction of the total ejecta. None of the four major types of ejecta of the Ries can be identified as base-surge deposits. Although a small fraction of the rocks may be vaporized in a meteorite-impact event, meteorite impact (particularly on the outgassed moon) is not an effective process for the production of a lot of gases by vaporization of rocks. Because the occurrence of a base surge depends principally on gaseous expansion, it should not be surprising to find that base-surge deposits are not a part of impact-originated ejecta. Base surge produced by fallback also would be hardly significant.

INTERPRETATION OF THE FRA MAURO FORMATION

The data presented here suggest that the Fra Mauro Formation, as a whole, consists of unwelded, porous ejecta, slightly less porous than the regolith. It contains hand-specimen and larger size clasts of strongly annealed breccias, partly to slightly annealed breccias, basalts, and perhaps spherule-rich breccias. These clasts are embedded in a matrix of porous aggregate dominated by mineral and breccia fragments and probably largely free of undevitrified glass. Large boulders occurring near the rim of Cone crater are probably blocks of indurated materials of the Fra Mauro Formation. They are probably less porous than the underlying formation and could have been compacted into large blocks by the Cone crater event.

To account for the porous, unwelded state of the Fra Mauro Formation, the ejecta must have been deposited at a temperature below that required for welding and annealing. All strongly annealed hand-specimen-size breccias are clasts in this ejecta deposit. The strongly annealed breccia clasts and the basalt clasts are pre-Imbrian. They probably existed in an ejecta deposit, mixed perhaps with basalt flows, at the site of the Imbrian Basin prior to the Imbrian event.

Major lines of evidence for these interpretations are as follows:

1. Onsite active seismic data indicate that the Fra Mauro Formation has a compressive wave velocity much lower than that of porous regolith microbreccias, and almost as low as that of regolith material. This means that the material of the Fra Mauro Formation is more porous than porous regolith microbreccia and only slightly less porous than regolith. The seismic velocity of strongly annealed, nonporous Fra Mauro breccias such as 14311 is 5.65 km/sec, much greater than that of the formation as a whole and greater even than that of most of the basalts measured. If 14311 were representative of the whole Fra Mauro Formation, the seismic velocity of the formation as a whole would be more than an order of magnitude greater than it is. The low porosity of the formation

cannot be accounted for by fracturing of the annealed breccias. The returned clasts of strongly annealed Fra Mauro breccias are not intensely fractured. They are subrounded and coherent, neither bounded by angular fracture surfaces nor intensely shattered. Thus, the seismic data are not consistent with the view that the Fra Mauro Formation was deposited hot by the Imbrian event and that the annealing of the breccias occurred at the Fra Mauro site in this hot debris blanket. (Warner, 1972; Wilshire and Jackson, 1972; McKay and others, 1972).

2. Largely unannealed, very friable and porous feldspathic microbreccias, such as 14063, evidently coexist with strongly annealed breccias, resembling 14303 and 14311, in car-size boulders on the rim of the Cone crater. The difference in porosity and in degree of annealing between these two types of breccias is striking. If the strongly annealed breccias were annealed after deposition at the Fra Mauro site, it would be difficult to explain why the coexisting unannealed feldspathic breccias were not also strongly annealed.

3. The hand-specimen-size Fra Mauro breccias have a wide range of distinctive fragment populations and probably are products of different impact events in different source areas. Many contain fragments showing a wide range of annealed textures and fragments of breccias of still earlier generations. It is unlikely that a single impact event would produce an ejecta deposit that differed so radically in fragment population over very short distances, as would be required if the annealed breccias had been annealed at the Fra Mauro site.

4. The hottest ejecta deposit from the Ries crater, the suevite, shows little or no annealing after deposition. Suevite is characterized by a large amount of glass particles and significant amounts of strongly shocked fragments. Thus it had appreciable sources of internal heat. In contrast, the annealed breccias of the Fra Mauro Formation contain only small amounts of strongly shocked fragments and small amounts of material that was demonstrably hot glass when the breccia was formed. Without glasses and strongly shocked fragments as an internal source of heat, it is unlikely that these latter represent hot ejecta deposits.

5. By extrapolation, the distribution of the different types of ejecta deposits produced by the Ries event may be compared to the probable distribution of ejecta deposits produced by the Imbrian event. Such a comparison is informative in spite of the hazard that some drastic modification may be necessary because of the difference in size (Ries, 23 km in diameter; Imbrium, about 900 km in diameter) and the low gravity and the lack of atmospheric aerodynamic drag on the moon. The ejecta at the Fra Mauro site is about 450 km from the Carpathian Mountains, the southern rim of the Imbrium Basin, about one crater radius away. By analogy with the Ries crater, the ejecta at the Fra Mauro site should be equivalent to the bunte breccias and limestone breccias of the Ries, not to the suevite. If so, the Fra Mauro Formation at the Apollo 14 site was derived from the upper part of the stratigraphic section of the site of the Imbrian event and was probably transported at low-angle trajectories. The corresponding deposits from the Ries do not contain abundant strongly shocked material and were deposited at low temperatures, far below the temperatures necessary for annealing of the fragments within the ejecta. They were not products of jetting, nor were they transported laterally by base surge.

AGE OF FRAGMENTS IN FRA MAURO BRECCIAS AND AGE OF THE IMBRIAN EVENT

Several basalt samples (among them 14310, 14073, and 14053) have been dated both by the Rb-Sr and the ^{40}Ar-^{39}Ar methods. In addition, fragments from several breccias have been investigated by the ^{40}Ar-^{39}Ar method. The Rb-Sr or the ^{40}Ar-^{39}Ar age of an unmodified basalt is the age of crystallization or solidification of the basalt, but both shock and thermal metamorphism can modify isotopic ratios and cause the age dating methods to give younger ages than the age of crystallization. The age of thoroughly thermally annealed breccia or basalt should date the age of the thermal metamorphism. An example of one such thoroughly annealed and reequilibrated breccia is 12013 (Turner, 1970). The ^{40}Ar-^{39}Ar release pattern in this sample has a well-defined plateau; hence it is readily interpreted as the age of thermal metamorphism. Complex ^{40}Ar-^{39}Ar release patterns have been obtained for many fragments from Apollo 14 breccias, however, and these are not understood and the ages they yield cannot be interpreted at this time.

Age of basalt fragments

The age of 14310, a fine-grained feldspathic basalt, has been determined by Rb-Sr and ^{40}Ar-^{39}Ar methods to be 3.88 b.y. (Papanastassiou and Wasserburg, 1971; Wasserburg and others, 1972). Unfortunately, sample 14310 is not well documented and its location is uncertain. It has tentatively been located at station G (Swann and others, 1971). The Rb-Sr and ^{40}Ar-^{39}Ar age of another fragment of very similar basalt, 14073, is also 3.88 b.y. (Papanastassiou and Wasserburg, 1971; Wasserburg and others, 1972), and this sample was definitely collected at station G (Swann and others, 1971). These basalt fragments could have been excavated from the Fra Mauro Formation by either the center or the south crater of Triplet. However, it is also possible that both samples could be from ray ejecta from an unknown source and be unrelated to the Fra Mauro Formation.

A pyroxene-dominant basalt, 14053, was collected from station C2 from the Cone crater ejecta. Its Rb-Sr and ^{40}Ar-^{39}Ar age is 3.92–3.95 b.y. (Papanastassiou and Wasserburg 1971; Turner and others, 1971; Wasserburg and others, 1972; Schaeffer and others, 1972).

Two chips from an olivine-bearing pyroxene-dominant basalt (14072,6) collected from station C at the Cone crater rim were also dated by the ^{40}Ar-^{39}Ar method (York and others, 1972). Both have well-defined plateaus in their gas-release patterns indicating ages of 4.0 b.y.

Several fragments of basalt from the partly annealed Fra Mauro breccia 14321 have been investigated by the ^{40}Ar-^{39}Ar method by several laboratories. A basalt clast from 14321,191 gave an age of 3.95 b.y. (Papanastassiou and Wasserburg, 1971). Three basalt clasts from 14321,184 gave ^{40}Ar-^{39}Ar plateau ages of 3.90, 3.95, and 3.99 b.y. (York and others, 1972). A 72-mg sample consisting of multiple fragments of basalt clasts from 14321,144 gave an age of 3.92 b.y. (Turner and others, 1971). However, this multiple sample of basalt has a complex ^{40}Ar-^{39}Ar release pattern that is not easily interpreted, suggesting that the basalt clasts from 14321 may not all be of the same type or have the same thermal history.

Evidently we have two main groups of basalts, one group represented by the feldspathic basalts 14310 and 14073 yielding ages of 3.88 b.y., the other group represented by pyroxene-dominant basalts 14053, 14072, and clasts from 14321 yielding plateau ^{40}Ar-^{39}Ar ages of 3.90 to 4.0 b.y. Basalts of the latter group were all collected from the Cone crater rim and should have come from the Fra Mauro Formation. Basalts of the former group may or may not be derived from the Fra Mauro Formation.

Age of fragments in well-annealed breccias

Two clasts, one of basalt and one of annealed microbreccia, from sample 14303,13, a well-annealed Fra Mauro breccia, have been investigated by the ^{40}Ar-^{39}Ar method (Kirsten and others, 1972). The basalt clast shows a complex gas-release pattern but gives a high-temperature plateau age (800°–1,000°C) of 3.91±0.04 b.y. (Schaeffer and others, 1972). The gas-release pattern of the annealed microbreccia fragment shows a narrow plateau followed by a strong drop at temperatures above 800°C; the plateau age is reported to be 3.78±0.14 b.y. Perhaps these complex gas-release patterns and age differences between fragments indicate that annealing in sample 14303 has not proceeded to the same degree as in sample 12013, so that an age for the thermal metamorphism of the hand specimen cannot easily be determined. A breccia clast (No. 17) from 14066,21, another hand sample of well-annealed Fra Mauro breccia, was dated at 4.0 b.y. by the Rb-Sr method (Cliff and others, 1972). Again, the meaning of this age depends on the degree of reequilibration caused by the thermal metamorphism.

Age of fragments in slightly to partly annealed breccias

The ages of clasts in unannealed nonregolith breccias should reflect the last dominant event that these clasts underwent prior to incorporation in the unannealed breccias. The least annealed Fra Mauro breccia is probably 14063. Two separate clasts from 14063,37 have been studied by the ^{40}Ar-^{39}Ar method by Derek York (oral commun., 1972). The petrology of these clasts has not been described, but both gave well-defined plateau ages of 3.95 b.y. This suggests that some of the source materials of 14063 are 3.95 b.y. old. Since they have been largely unaffected by the Imbrian impact, their ages are useful as indicators of the maximum age of the Imbrian event.

Various chips of breccias from coarse fines 14167,6 and 14257,12 (Sutter and others, 1971) and from 14321 (Turner and others, 1971) have been investigated by the ^{40}Ar-^{39}Ar method. The gas-release patterns were complex; their origins are not understood and their age significance cannot be determined at present.

Age of the Imbrian event

The age of the youngest basalt clast from the Fra Mauro Formation should set an upper limit on the date of the Imbrian event. The youngest dated basalt clast clearly derived from the Fra Mauro material is from 14321, and its age is 3.90 b.y. Whether 14310 or 14073 are also from the Fra Mauro Formation is unknown. If they are, then the maximum age of the Imbrian event is 3.88 b.y.

The minimum age of the Imbrian event can be determined by geological reasoning. The Imbrian event must have occurred before 3.65 b.y., the age of the ilmenite basalt which filled Mare Tranquillitatis, for the Imbrian sculpture affected the basin wall of Mare Tranquillitatis but not the ilmenite basalts that filled it. Hence, the best estimate of the age of the Imbrian event that can be made with the data available at present is between 3.90 or 3.88 and 3.65 b.y.

ACKNOWLEDGMENTS

I thank my colleagues, Odette B. James, and Newell Trask for their helpful review of this paper. I am particularly indebted to Odette B. James for discussion of many aspects of this paper. I appreciate the assistance of Judith B. Best in the preparation of the map and geologic cross sections and some of the photomicrographs.

REFERENCES CITED

Ackermann, Wilhelm, 1959, Geologisch-petrographische Untersuchungen im Ries: Germany, Geol. Landesanst., Geol. Jahrb., v. 75 (1958), p. 135–182.

Anderson, O. L., Scholz, Christopher, Soga, Naohiro, Warner, Nicholas, and Schreiber, Edward, 1970, Elastic properties of a micro-breccia, igneous rock and lunar fines from Apollo 11 mission, *in* Apollo 11 Lunar Sci. Conf., Houston, Tex., 1970, Proc., V. 3, Physical properties: New York, Pergamon Press (Geochim. et Cosmochim. Acta Supp. 1), p. 1959–1973.

Angenheister, Gustav, and Pöhl, Jean, 1969, Die seismischen Messungen im Ries von 1948–1969: Geologica Bavarica, no. 61, p. 304–326.

Burnett, D. S., Huneke, J. C., Podosek, F. A., Russ, G. P., III, Turner, G., and Wasserburg, G. J., 1972, The irradiation history of lunar samples [abs.], *in* Lunar Sci. Conf., 3d, Houston, Tex., 1972, Revised abs.: Houston, Tex., Lunar Science Institute, p. 105–107.

Chao, E. C. T., 1967, Shock effects in certain rock-forming minerals: Science, v. 156, no. 3772, p. 192–202.

—— 1968, Pressure and temperature histories of impact metamorphosed rocks—Based on petrographic observations, *in* French, B. M., and Short, N. M., eds., Shock metamorphism of natural materials—1st Conf., Greenbelt, Md., 1966, Proc.: Baltimore, Md., Mono Book Corp., p. 135–158.

Chao, E. C. T., Boreman, J. A., and Desborough, G. A., 1971, The petrology of unshocked and shocked Apollo 11 and Apollo 12 microbreccias, *in* Lunar Sci. Conf., 2d, Houston, Tex., 1971, Proc., V. 1, Mineralogy and petrology: Cambridge, Mass., MIT Press (Geochim. et Cosmochim. Acta Supp. 2), p. 797–816.

Chao, E. C. T., and Littler, Janet, 1963, Additional evidence for the impact origin of the Ries basin, Bavaria, Germany [abs.]: Geol. Soc. America Spec. Paper 73, p. 127.

Chao, E. C. T., Minkin, J. A., and Best, J. B., 1972, Apollo 14 breccias—General characteristics and classification, *in* Lunar Sci. Conf., 3d, Houston, Tex., 1972, Proc., v. 1, Mineralogy and petrology: Cambridge, Mass., MIT Press (Geochim. et Cosmochim. Acta Supp. 3), p. 645–659.

Cliff, R. A., Lee-Hu, C., and Wetherill, G. W., 1972, K, Rb, and Sr measurements in Apollo 14 and 15 material [abs.], *in* Lunar Sci. Conf., 3d, Houston, Tex., 1972, Revised abs.: Houston, Tex., Lunar Science Institute, p. 146–147.

Dence, M. R., Plant, A. G., and Traill, R. J., 1972, Impact-generated shock and thermal metamorphism in Fra Mauro lunar samples [abs.], *in* Lunar Sci. Conf., 3d, Houston, Tex., 1972, Revised abs.: Houston, Tex., Lunar Science Institute, p. 174–176.

Dennis, J. G., 1971, Ries structure, southern Germany, a review: Jour. Geophys. Research, v. 76, no. 23, p. 5394–5406.

Dressler, Burkhard, Graup, Günther, and Matzke, Klaus, 1969, Die Gesteine des kristallinen Grundgebirges im Nördlingen Ries: Geologica Bavarica, no. 61, p. 201–228.

Eggleton, R. E., 1970, Geologic map of the Fra Mauro region of the Moon, *in* Offield, T. W., and Eggleton, R. E., Geologic maps of the Fra Mauro region of the Moon: U.S. Geol. Survey Misc. Geol. Inv. Map I-708, sheet 2, scale 1:250,000.

Engelhardt, Wolf von., Hörz, F., Stöffler, D., and Bertsch, W., 1968, Observations on quartz deformation in the breccias of West Clearwater Lake, Canada, and the Ries basin, Germany, *in* French, B. M., and Short, N. M., eds., Shock metamorphism of natural materials—1st Conf., Greenbelt, Md., 1966, Proc.: Baltimore, Md., Mono Book Corp., p. 475–482.

Engelhardt, Wolf von, and Stöffler, D., 1968, Stages of shock metamorphism in the crystalline rocks of the Ries basin, Germany, *in* French B. M., and Short, N. M., eds., Shock metamorphism of natural materials—1st Conf., Greenbelt, Md., 1966, Proc.: Baltimore, Md., Mono Book Corp., p. 159–168.

Engelhardt, Wolf von, Stöffler, Dieter, and Schneider, Werner, 1969, Petrologische Untersuchungen im Ries: Geologica Bavarica, no. 61, p. 229–295.

Förstner, U., 1967, Petrographische Untersuchungen des Suevits aus den Bohrungen Deiningen und Wörnitzostheim im Ries von Nördlingen: Contr. Mineralogy and Petrology, v. 15, p. 281–308.

Gault, D. E., Quaide, W. L., and Oberbeck, V. R., 1968, Impact cratering mechanics and structures, *in* French, B. M., and Short, N. M., eds., Shock metamorphism of natural materials—1st Conf., Greenbelt, Md., 1966, Proc.: Baltimore, Md., Mono Book Corp., p. 87–99.

Gentner, Wolfgang, and Wagner, G. A., 1969, Altersbestimmungen an Riesgläsern und Moldaviten: Geologica Bavarica, no. 61, p. 296–303.

Hüttner, Rudolf, 1969, Bunte Trümmermassen und Suevit: Geologica Bavarica, no. 61, p. 142–200.

Hüttner, Rudolf, Schmidt-Kaler, Hermann, and Treibs, Walter, 1969, Anmerkungen zur geologischen Übersichtskarte (Beilage 1): Geologica Bavarica, no. 61, p. 451–454.

Jackson, E. D., and Wilshire, H. G., 1972, Classification of the samples returned from the Apollo 14 landing site [abs.], *in* Lunar Sci. Conf., 3d, Houston, Tex., 1972, Revised abs.: Houston, Tex., Lunar Science Institute, p. 418–420.

Kanamori, Hiroo, Mizutani, H., and Hamano, Y., 1971, Elastic wave velocities of Apollo 12 rocks at high pressures, *in* Lunar Sci. Conf., 2d, Houston, Tex., 1971, Proc., V. 3, Physical properties: Cambridge, Mass., MIT Press (Geochim. et Cosmochim. Acta Supp. 2), p. 2323–2326.

Kanamori, Hiroo, Nur, Amos, Chung, D. H., and Simmons, Gene, 1970, Elastic wave velocities of lunar samples at high pressures and their geophysical implications, *in* Apollo 11 Lunar Sci. Conf., Houston, Tex., 1970, Proc., V. 3, Physical properties: New York, Pergamon Press (Geochim. et Cosmochim. Acta Supp. 1), p. 2289–2293.

Kirsten, T., Deubner, J., Horn, P., Kaneoka, I., Kiko, J., Schaeffer, O. A., Thio, S. K., 1972, The rare gas record of Apollo 14 and 15 samples, *in* Lunar Sci. Conf., 3d, Houston, Tex., 1972, Proc. V. 2: Cambridge, Mass., MIT Press (Geochim. et Cosmochim. Acta Supp. 3). [In press]

LSPET (Lunar Sample Preliminary Examination Team), 1971, Preliminary examination of lunar samples from Apollo 14: Science, v. 173, no. 3998, p. 681–693.

McKay, D. S., Clanton, U. S., Heiken, G. H., Morrison, D. A., and Taylor, R. M., 1972, Vapor phase crystallization in Apollo 14 breccias and size analysis of Apollo 14 soils [abs.], *in* Lunar Sci. Conf., 3d, Houston, Tex., 1972, Revised abs.: Houston, Tex., Lunar Science Institute, p. 529–531.

Mizutani, H., Fujii, N., Hamano, Y., Osako, M., and Kanamori, H., 1972, Elastic wave velocities and thermal diffusivities of Apollo 14 rocks [abs.], *in* Lunar Sci. Conf., 3d, Houston, Tex., 1972, Revised abs.: Houston, Tex., Lunar Science Institute, p. 547–549.

Moore, J. G., 1967, Base surge in recent volcanic eruptions: Bull. Volcanol., v. 30, p. 337–363.

Oberdorfer, R., 1905, Die vulkanischen Tuffe des Ries bei Nördlingen: Ver. vaterl. Naturkunde Württemberg, Jahresh., v. 61, p. 1–40.

Papanastassiou, D. A., and Wasserburg, G. J., 1971, Rb-Sr ages of igneous rocks from the Apollo 14 mission and the age of the Fra Mauro Formation: Earth and Planetary Sci. Letters, v. 12, no. 1, p. 36–48.

Preuss, Ekkehard, 1969, Einführung in die Ries-Forschung: Geologica Bavarica, no. 61, p. 12–24.

Reich, Hermann, and Horrix, W., 1955, Geophysikalische Untersuchungen im Ries und Vorries und deren geologische Deutung: Germany, Geol. Landesanst., Geol. Jahrb. Beihefte, Heft 19, 119 p.

Sauer, Adolf, 1901, Petrographische Studien an den Lavabomben aus dem Ries: Ver. vaterl. Naturkunde Württemberg, Jahresh., v. 57, p. lxxxviii.

Schaeffer, O. A., Husain, L., Sutter, J., and Funkhouser, J., 1972, The ages of lunar material from Fra Mauro and the Hadley Rille–Appenine Front area [abs.], *in* Lunar Sci. Conf. 3d, Houston, Tex., 1972, Revised abs.: Houston, Tex., Lunar Science Institute, p. 675–677.

Schmidt-Kaler, Hermann, 1969, Versuch einer Profildarstellung für das Rieszentrum vor der Kraterbildung (Beilage 5): Geologica Bavarica, no. 61, p. 38–40.

Shoemaker, E. M., 1960, Penetration mechanics of high velocity meteorites, illustrated by Meteor crater, Arizona: Internat. Geol. Cong., 21st, Copenhagen, 1960, Rept., pt. 18, p. 418–434.

Shoemaker, E. M., and Chao, E. C. T., 1961, New evidence for the impact origin of the Ries basin, Bavaria, Germany: Jour. Geophys. Research, v. 66, p. 3371–3378.

Sutter, J. F., Husain, L., and Schaeffer, O. A., 1971, ^{40}Ar-^{39}Ar ages from Fra Mauro: Earth and Planetary Sci. Letters, v. 11, no. 4, p. 249–253.

Swann, G. A., Trask, N. J., Hait, M. H., and Sutton, R. L., 1971, Geologic setting of the Apollo 14 samples: Science, v. 173, no. 3998, p. 716–719.

Treibs, W., 1965, Beitrag zur Kenntnis der Geologie des Rieses und östlichen Vorries nach Beobachtungen in Rohrgraben der Rhein-Donau-Ölleitung: Geologica Bavarica, no. 55, p. 310–316.

Turner, G., 1970, ^{40}Ar-^{39}Ar age determination of lunar rock 12013: Earth and Planetary Sci. Letters, v. 9, no. 2, p. 177–180.

Turner, G., Huneke, J. C., Podosek, F. A., and Wasserburg, G. J., 1971, ^{40}Ar-^{39}Ar ages and cosmic ray exposure ages of Apollo 14 samples: Earth and Planetary Sci. Letters, v. 12, no. 1, p. 19–35.

Wagner, G. H., 1964, Kleintektonische Untersuchungen im Gebiet des Nördlinger Ries: Geol. Jahrb., v. 81, p. 519–600.

Warner, J. L., 1972, Apollo 14 breccias–Metamorphic origin and classification [abs.], *in* Lunar Sci. Conf., 3d, Houston, Tex., 1972, Revised abs.: Houston, Tex., Lunar Science Institute, p. 782–784.

Warren, N., Schreiber, E., Scholz, C., Morrison, J. A., Norton, P. R., Kumazawa, M., and Anderson, O. L., 1971, Elastic and thermal properties of Apollo 11 and Apollo 12 rocks, *in* Lunar Sci. Conf., 2d, Houston, Tex., 1971, Proc., V. 3, Physical properties: Cambridge, Mass., MIT Press (Geochim. et Cosmochim. Acta Supp. 2), p. 2345–2360.

Wasserburg, G. J., Turner, G., Tera, F., Podosek, F. A., Papanastassiou, D. A., and Huneke, J. C., 1972, Comparison of Rb-Sr, K-Ar, and U-Th-Pb ages; lunar chronology and evolution [abs.], *in* Lunar Sci. Conf., 3d, Houston, Tex., 1972, Revised abs.: Houston, Tex., Lunar Science Institute, p. 788–790.

Watkins, J. S., and Kovach, R. L., 1972, Apollo 14 active seismic experiment: Science, v. 175, no. 4027, p. 1244–1245.

Wilhelms, D. E., 1970, Summary of lunar stratigraphy–Telescopic observations: U.S. Geol. Survey Prof. Paper 599-F, 47 p.

Wilshire, H. G., and Jackson, E. D., 1972, Petrology and stratigraphy of the Fra Mauro Formation at the Apollo 14 site: U.S. Geol. Survey Prof. Paper 785, 26 p.

Wirth, E., 1969, Ein Profil vom Malm bis ins Rotliegendes südöstlich des Rieses–Kurzprofit der Erdölaufschlussbohrung Daiting 1: Geologica Bavarica, no. 61, p. 41–42.

York, D., Kenyon, W. J., and Doyle, R. J., 1972, ^{40}Ar-^{39}Ar ages of Apollo XIV and XV samples [abs.], *in* Lunar Sci. Conf., 3d, Houston, Tex., 1972, Revised abs.: Houston, Tex., Lunar Science Institute, p. 822–824.

Young, G. A., 1965, The physics of the base surge: White Oak, Md., U.S. Naval Ordnance Laboratory Rept. NOLTR 64–103, 284 p.

Jour. Research U.S. Geol. Survey
Vol. 1, No. 1, Jan.—Feb. 1973, p. 19—32

INTERPRETATION OF DEPOSITIONAL ENVIRONMENT IN THE PLYMPTON FORMATION (PERMIAN), SOUTHERN PEQUOP MOUNTAINS, NEVADA, FROM PHYSICAL STRATIGRAPHY AND A FAUNULE

By ELLIS L. YOCHELSON and GEORGE D. FRASER,
Washington, D.C., Denver, Colo.

Abstract.—Field mapping in the southern part of the Pequop Mountains has shown the presence of a major structural high which has profoundly affected the stratigraphy of Pennsylvanian and Lower Permian beds; lesser effects of this high persisted into the later Permian. Within the Park City Group (Permian), the Plympton Formation, overlying the Kaibab Limestone, is divided informally into five parts. The uppermost Plympton has yielded silicified fossils. The faunule studied is characterized by the scaphopod *Plagioglypta* and by bellerophontacean and neritacean gastropods, suggestive of a middle Permian age. Specimens are worn, and several lines of evidence suggest that this is a high-energy beach deposit associated with a residual high. The interpretation supplements the field evidence of a hiatus between the Plympton and the overlying Gerster Formation. Other occurrences of elements of the faunule in the equivalent Phosphoria rock complex are noted, but only a few were probably deposited in a high-energy beach environment. A new species of *Naticopsis* that has the color pattern preserved is named and described.

This paper is a combination of specific paleontological information regarding a silicified scaphopod faunule found locally at the top of the Plympton Formation and general stratigraphic information about a larger part of the thick Permian section in the southern Pequop Mountains, northeast Nevada (fig. 1). The paper compares environmental interpretations based on the independent laboratory study of the fossils with environmental interpretations based on field study of the physical stratigraphy. The two studies complement and reinforce each other; both indicate high-energy beach or shallow-water conditions and a local disconformity at the top of the Plympton where the fossils were found. The stratigraphic study suggests further that an ancient positive area, which was transverse to the present mountains and which had its south flank in the area of this report, controlled Late Pennsylvanian-Early Permian stratigraphic patterns and exerted a lesser modifying effect on subsequent depositional patterns throughout latest Paleozoic and earliest Mesozoic time.

The outcrop of silicified mollusks discussed (USGS locality 23819-PC) is at the top of the Plympton Formation on the northwest side of the hill 700 feet north of the water tank in sec. 3, T. 31 N., R. 65 E., Spruce Mountain 4 quadrangle, Nevada (fig. 2). That 15-minute quadrangle includes nearly all the southern Pequop Mountains. The railroad tunnel through a pass in the northern part of the quadrangle, 28 miles west of Wendover, Nev., is a convenient dividing line between the southern and northern Pequop Mountains, as those terms are used in this report.

The parts of this report relating primarily to identification and interpretation of the silicified mollusks are by Yochelson; the new species is named by him. The parts relating to physical stratigraphy and its interpretation are by Fraser. Fraser was aided in his fieldwork (1965–71) by H. A. Waldrop (1966), M. T. Naney (1968), and G. P. Eager (1970–71). Fieldwork included geologic mapping of the quadrangle, section measuring, and special phosphate studies in the basal part of the Plympton Formation; these activities are part of a continuing program of Federal land classification by the U.S. Geological Survey.

RECURRENT STRUCTURAL CONTROL OF STRATIGRAPHIC CHANGES

In the southern Pequop Mountains, obvious stratigraphic changes occur in the upper part of the Pennsylvanian and lower part of the Permian section, thousands of feet below the Plympton Formation and seemingly unrelated to it. Nevertheless, these older changes are so great and the structures which caused them so large that one suspects that subtle changes higher in the section and in nearly the same geographic area are related in some way to the older events.

Early stratigraphic studies in the area by Steele (1960), Robinson (1961), and Bissell (1964) indicated a great difference between the Lower Permian sections in the southern and northern Pequop Mountains. Mapping in the southern area shows additional changes and suggests that most or all of them were caused by an east- or southeast-trending Pennsylvanian-Permian positive area that began a conspicuous rise in Late Pennsylvanian (Virgilian) time. Limestone and chert boulders, cobbles, and pebbles derived from Ely Limestone of Pennsyl-

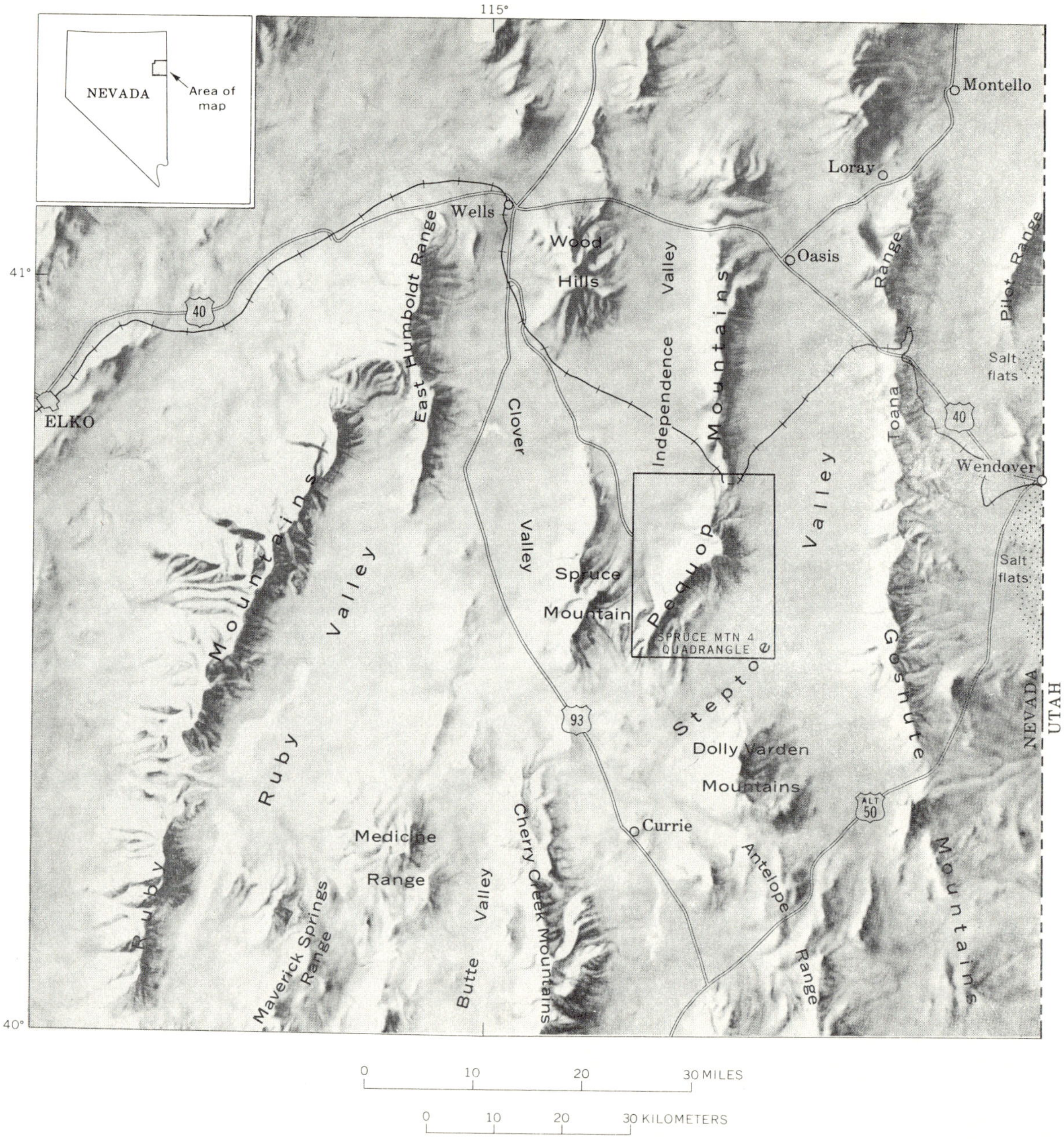

Figure 1.—Index map showing location of Spruce Mountain 4 quadrangle in southern Pequop Mountains, northeast Nevada.

vanian age were shed southward into a local basin where an unusually thick and complete deposit of Pennsylvanian and Permian limestone is preserved. No unconformity has been found in the basin, and the one on the positive area does not coincide with the systemic boundary.

By a combination of erosion and transgressive overlap on the south flank of the positive area (fig. 2), the total thickness of Pennsylvanian-Permian rock was reduced northward by about 5,000 feet in 6 miles. About 2,200 feet of nonconglomeratic Upper and Middle Pennsylvanian rock was eroded in this small area. In the same area, the conglomeratic overlap unit, mostly Permian limestone, thins northward from 1,390 feet to 250 feet and changes to a thin tongue of nearly pure conglomerate. The overlying Rib Hill(?) Sandstone thins abruptly northward and loses most of its diagnostic sandstone to become the basal (upper Wolfcampian) part of the type Pequop Formation of Steele (1960; Robinson, 1961). These major stratigraphic changes, which introduce many nomenclature problems, require a more detailed explanation (G. D. Fraser and R. C. Douglass, unpub. data).

The indicated positive area extended at least 23 miles north of the quadrangle boundary, where a thin basal conglomerate

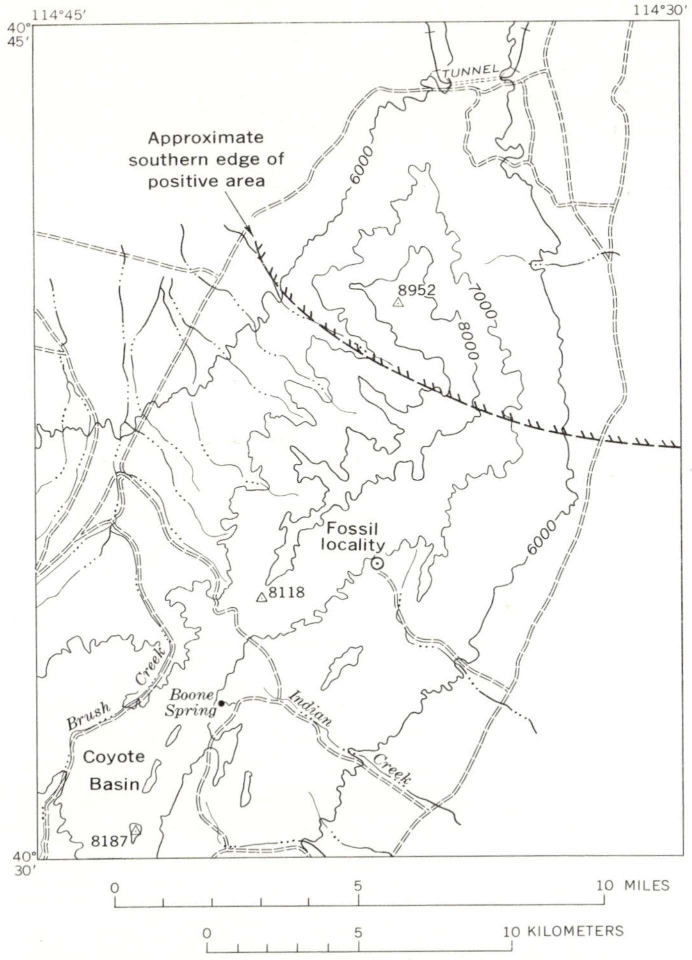

Figure 2.—Map of Spruce Mountain 4 quadrangle in southern Pequop Mountains, showing principal access roads and molluscan fossil locality. Southern edge of positive area refers only to Late Pennsylvanian-Early Permian structure. Contour interval 1,000 feet.

of the Pequop Formation rests unconformably on Mississippian rocks near the highway on the east side of the northern Pequop Mountains (fig. 1; Thorman, 1970, fig. 4). In that area, about 7,000 feet of the section exposed in the southern Pequop Mountains is missing. Fraser's investigations show further that the south flank of the positive area was not eroded evenly, but it is not known what fraction of the unusually thick Pennsylvanian section in the southern basin may never have been deposited on the crest of the positive area. After prolonged erosion, the positive area was inundated by the Early Permian (Leonardian) sea and deeply covered by limestone and the limited amount of sandstone composing the Pequop Formation.

Diffuse and ill-defined versions of the ancient structures were recurrently active, and their subdued late-stage effects can be found in many units younger than the Pequop Formation. The Loray(?) Formation of Steele (1960) and formations in the Park City Group thin northward erratically, apparently onto the same positive area. Conglomerates have been found locally at the base of the Kaibab Limestone, within and at the top of the Plympton Formation, at the base of the Gerster Formation, and at the base of the Thaynes Formation (Lower Triassic). Doubtless, the Permian-Triassic hiatus (Hose and Repenning, 1959, p. 2189; Collinson, 1968, p. 33) and perhaps some older disconformities were regional events, which however, were locally exaggerated on positive areas and damped out in basins, on structures similar to those described here.

The recurrent southerly margin of the uplift, where successive formations thinned and patches of conglomerate accumulated, seems to have shifted progressively southward in response either to a structural shift or to the broadening effect of thousands of feet of sediment on the uplift. The late-stage uplift probably was marked only by scattered ephemeral shoals or low islands, because late-stage conglomerates, unlike the earlier ones, are thin and discontinuous and contain no boulders and few cobbles. Several thick Pennsylvanian and Lower Permian units, but none of the younger formations within or above the Park City Group, pinch out or change to different formations within the Spruce Mountain 4 quadrangle.

Brief examination of the stratigraphic section in the mountains west of Montello, Nev. (fig. 1), suggests approximate geographic limits on the width of the positive area and indicates a deeper basin on the north side of the positive area, at least in Late Permian and Early Triassic time. In the basin, at least the lowest and highest formations within the Park City Group are much thicker and contain far more chert than they do to the south, so that a different stratigraphic nomenclature, more like that of the western phosphate field, may be required. The tectonic breccia everywhere present in the Plympton Formation of the southern Pequop Mountains was not found near Montello; only the lowest conglomerate of that formation extends northward from the southern Pequops to the vicinity of Montello. A very thick Lower Triassic section is present in both areas, but no conglomerate was found at its base near Montello. A pre-Thaynes (pre-*Meekoceras* zone) "flat-clam" and shale unit, not present in the southern Pequops, confirms a deeper basin on the north and a shorter hiatus between Permian and Triassic deposition.

PARK CITY GROUP

The Park City Group (Hose and Repenning, 1959) can be extrapolated into the southern Pequop Mountains and homotaxis maintained if it can be shown that the underlying Arcturus Group of Bissell (1964) is equivalent to the Arcturus Formation. Field studies indicate that the Arcturus Group of Bissell is characterized in the southern Pequop Mountains by intertonguing facies relationships (lithosomes) similar to those described in other areas by Stevens (1965). Everywhere in the quadrangle the Pequop lithosome is dominant; on the south flank of the positive area, the Pequop Formation commonly is the only mappable unit below the Park City Group and above the conglomeratic tongue of pre-Rib Hill rock noted above. These observations confirm generally the regional correlations by previously cited authors; although different stratigraphers may use different boundaries and names for the local facies, there can be little doubt about homotaxis.

As used here, the Park City Group contains only the original three formations of Hose and Repenning (1959): Kaibab Limestone (oldest), Plympton Formation, and Gerster Limestone. The Indian Canyon Formation of Hodgkinson (1961) is included here as approximately the upper half of the Plympton (see below, parts 4 and 5 of the Plympton Formation) because in the field one could not map the base of the Indian Canyon consistently and because its lithology is chiefly a Plympton lithology. As noted by Hose and Repenning (1959, p. 2182), the upper part of the Plympton Formation is more variable than the lower part. Mudstone, siltstone, or sandstone is common in the upper half. In the Pequop Mountains, abundant dolomite and chert, algal structures, conglomeratic lenses, phosphorite or phosphatic black chert, and a molluscan rather than a brachiopod fauna tie the lower to the upper Plympton and clearly separate both from limestone formations above and below. For structural mapping and phosphate studies, Fraser found it convenient to split the Plympton only at the base of the tectonic breccia (see below, part 2 of the Plympton Formation), which is about 200 feet above the base.

In the Medicine Range (fig. 1), Collinson (1968, p. 32) included the probable Indian Canyon equivalent in a more inclusive Gerster Formation, even though he too considered the Indian Canyon equivalent to be part of the type Plympton. The brachiopod fauna used by Collinson to make this reasonable assignment cannot be used in the Pequop Mountains, where a molluscan fauna and other Plympton attributes persist to the base of the Gerster Formation, where there is an abrupt change.

Kaibab Limestone

In the southern Pequop Mountains, the Kaibab is mostly light-gray, resistant, and thick-bedded coarsely bioclastic crinoidal limestone or dolomitic limestone. The basal part, generally darker, thinner bedded, and finer grained, grades downward into the less resistant Pequop Formation or Loray(?) Formation of Steele (1960), whichever lithosome is present locally. A thin basal chert-pebble conglomerate was found in only one small area near the railroad tunnel. Light- to dark-gray bedded and nodular chert is common in middle and upper parts of the formation, particularly in northern areas, but chert is less abundant than in the Plympton. Large silicified productoid brachiopods are locally present near the base, and poorly preserved *Composita* occur where darker and thinner beds are present at the top. The formation thins irregularly northward from 300 to 150 feet or less locally.

Plympton Formation

The Plympton is mainly dolomite, bedded chert, and dolomitic mudstone or siltstone. Generally it is more iron stained, more fractured, less resistant, finer grained, and supports less vegetation than the limestone formations. The Plympton can be divided informally into five parts:

1. A basal zone about 200 feet thick, mostly brown to black chert interbedded with subordinate gray, yellow, or reddish-brown mudstone and capped in most areas by about 35 feet of light-gray sugary limestone or dolomite. The chert contains thin beds of impure and commonly pelletal phosphorite, especially near base and top, and rare low-spired gastropods, spicules, and fossil hash. Thin algal mats are present very locally at the top of the carbonate caprock where the flat faults of part 2 have not cut too deeply into the section.

2. A brown-weathering tectonic breccia[1] 2 to 200 feet thick with an average thickness of about 75 feet. The breccia is composed of coarse dark chert fragments as much as 2 feet in diameter and subordinate carbonate-rock fragments, all cemented by calcite.

3. Interbedded light-gray thin- to thick-bedded medium-crystalline to finely crystalline dolomite, dolomitic limestone, bedded gray to brown chert, and yellowish-gray dolomitic mudstone, totaling about 300 feet stratigraphically. This part has a thin lenticular but widespread chert-pebble conglomerate at its base in areas north of Indian Creek. The bed may mark an intraformational disconformity that helped to localize the tectonic breccia zone. The conglomerate is locally coarse and about 10 feet thick in some northern areas. One or more thin beds of phosphorite or black phosphatic chert are also present in areas both north and south of Indian Creek. Local beds of shell fragments and ghost structures of large pelecypods(?) are

[1] The breccia indicates a stratigraphically localized and fold-generated zone of bedding-plane slip present wherever the Plympton is exposed in the quadrangle. The movement zone never cuts up-section through part 3 of the Plympton but does cut down-section on the stretched limbs of some folds. In these areas, flat normal faults are indicated, and 1,500 feet or more of the stratigraphic section may be missing; part 1 of the Plympton, all of the Kaibab, all of the Loray(?) Formation of Steele where that lithosome was deposited, and part of the Pequop Formation are cut out; part 3 of the Plympton rests on structurally truncated Pequop Formation with only a screen of the tectonic breccia between. A parallel deeper slip zone, localized by weak beds directly below the Kaibab, is also involved in these unusual structures but generally is covered and rarely can be mapped.

The brittle and conspicuous Kaibab acts as a marker bed to reveal large tectonic lenses similar to boudins on the crests and troughs of folds and broad tectonic gaps on the stretched flanks of the folds. Needless to say, the stratigraphic anomalies created by this incipient diapirism are many. In Fraser's opinion, some of the so-called younger-over-older thrusts, common in the eastern Great Basin but rare elsewhere, are not explicable by gravitational gliding tectonics; they are explicable in terms of bedding faults and flat normal faults controlled by folding in a thick and differentially plastic carbonate section.

present north of Indian Creek. Numerous geodelike chert rosettes (Hodgkinson, 1961, p. 181), ¼- to 3-inch ovoids, characterize this and most other parts of the Plympton in all areas. Many rosettes are partly filled with secondary quartz and calcite. Although the scattered rosettes are variable in size, in some beds where they are abundant the size is consistent, and originally they might have been organic in origin.

4. Interbedded yellowish- to reddish-brown-weathering gray platy dolomitic siltstone, thin-bedded gray dolomite, and bedded chert, about 300 feet thick and mostly covered. The base of part 4 is probably the base of the Indian Canyon Formation of Hodgkinson (1961), which is a locally mappable member of the Plympton but not, in Fraser's opinion, a separate formation.

5. A highly variable and partly covered zone, generally about 200 feet thick, of interbedded thin- to thick-bedded dolomite, dolomitic limestone, chert, dolomitic mudstone, thin local beds of phosphatic black chert, siltstone, yellowish-brown quartzitic sandstone, and lenticular or disseminated chert-pebble conglomerate or gritstone locally scattered through at least the upper 100 feet of section. North of Indian Creek, near the fossil locality discussed below, the extreme top of the formation has the following stratigraphic sequence, in ascending order: light-gray thin- to medium-bedded dolomite or dolomitic limestone; 10 feet or more of yellowish-brown quartzitic sandstone; a thin 1- to 5-foot zone or zones of silicified molluscan coquina or pelecypod fragments, and as much as 10 feet of fine to coarse well-rounded chert-pebble conglomerate. Because of erosional truncation or extremely local deposition patterns, any of the rock types may form the uppermost beds in the formation. A thick silicified algal mat was found directly below the pelecypod fragments in one area. No evaporites were found in the quadrangle (compare Hose and Repenning, 1959, p. 2182).

Much of the Plympton is covered, but parts 2 and 3 commonly form ridges, and platy brown scree slopes derived from part 4 are locally conspicuous. Apparent thickness is variable because the formation localizes flat faults 200 feet above the base and, less commonly, at the top. Stratigraphic thickness probably ranges from about 1,000 to 1,200 feet. The upper part is differentially bevelled by pre-Gerster erosion north of Indian Creek, where the disconformity at the top of the formation is most conspicuous.

Gerster Formation

The Gerster is a light-gray resistant limestone, which is thin to thick bedded and which contains variable gray to brown nodular and bedded chert in less abundant quantities than in the Plympton. Much of the formation is a brachiopod coquina, but near the base of the formation, this may be reduced locally to a fossil hash containing thin lenticles of fine-grained conglomerate or gritstone. Thickness ranges from at least 376 feet to less than 140 feet. Rapid northward thinning was observed south of Indian Creek on the east side of the range. The formation is generally but variably thin north of Indian Creek. Erosional unconformities at the base, and particularly at the top, may explain reddish and purplish tints in those parts of the formation. A prolonged Permian-Triassic hiatus in this area may also explain the rapid thickness changes and the general thinness of the formation as compared with most other parts of the eastern Great Basin.

THAYNES FORMATION

The thick Lower Triassic section is assigned here entirely to the Thaynes Formation. The well-known *Meekoceras* zone, generally marking the base of the Thaynes in other areas, is present here in all areas where the base of the formation is exposed; other Early Triassic fossils have been found at the extreme top of the formation. Details of the formation are not discussed here. The Thaynes is about 3,300 feet thick in the southern part of the area, but generally most of it is covered. A rarely exposed thin lenticular chert-pebble conglomerate is widespread at the base. The coarsest known conglomerate is found in areas north of Indian Creek.

The Thaynes is the youngest marine formation in the area and the only known Mesozoic unit. Jurassic rocks have been reported from the Currie area, some distance south of the Pequop Mountains (fig. 1).

INTERPRETATION OF ENVIRONMENT AT THE TOP OF THE PLYMPTON FORMATION

In many areas north of Indian Creek, the top of the Plympton can be interpreted on the field evidence as indicative of a very shallow water environment peripheral to low islands and including some beach or tidal-flat deposits. Limy muds, silts, sands, and gravels mixed with molluscan shells were commonly reworked, and the youngest beds were locally truncated by erosion.

The silicified scaphopod-bellerophontid faunule discussed in detail below is a rare and extremely limited development in a much more extensive deposit of silicified pelecypod fragments, a thin coquina which is part of a still more extensive chert-pebble conglomerate. All this material is much more abundant north of Indian Creek than it is to the south, and the associated brown quartzite was found only north of Indian Creek. Exposures of this upper facies of the Plympton are best on the east side of the range.

During Gerster time the water was deeper, no coarse conglomerates were deposited, and productid brachiopods were the characteristic fossils. Locally, at the base of the Gerster the brachiopods were ground to a fossil hash and mixed with silicified molluscan debris derived from the underlying Plympton. Grits and fine-grained local lenticular conglomerates in the base of the Gerster appear to be largely reworked shells.

ONE PLYMPTON FOSSIL OCCURRENCE

A large collection (USGS locality 23819-PC, fig. 2) of silicified molluscan material was obtained from a limestone in part 5 of the Plympton Formation just below the conglomerate that marks the top of the formation. In the rocks collected from locality 23819-PC, the fossils have been completely replaced by silica, but there is no additional silica in the form of nodules. The original collection was not weighed, but it is estimated that about 50 pounds of limestone was treated with hydrochloric acid. The residue consisted exclusively of replaced organic remains. Excess silica is not present to cement the individual fossils together, as at several other Permian localities that contain a similar fossil assemblage. Part of the residue, after acid solution of the matrix, is shown in figure 3. The assemblage was washed in running water to remove any mud and to dissolve calcium chloride but was little disturbed by that process. It is apparent that several sedimentary grade sizes are present.

The following fossils have been recovered from the insoluble residue of rock collected at locality 23819-PC:

Scaphopoda:
- *Plagioglypta canna* (White) (abundant)

Gastropoda:
- *Euphemites imperator* Yochelson (abundant)
- *Euphemites* or *Euphemitopsis* fragment (one specimen)
- *Knightites* (*Retispira*) *modesta* (Girty) (one complete specimen and four fragments)
- *Naticopsis* (?*Naticopsis*) *rosewateri* n. sp. (abundant)
- Neritacean gastropod, new genus (three specimens)

Pelecypoda:
- ?*Permophorus* sp. indet. (one specimen)
- Crassitellid pelecypod indet. (two specimens)

As noted above, except for quantitatively insignificant minor additions, the fauna is limited to more than 100 examples each of three forms: a scaphopod, *Plagioglypta* (fig. 4); a large bellerophontacean gastropod, *Euphemites* (fig. 5); and a neritacean gastropod, *Naticopsis* (?*Naticopsis*) *rosewateri* n. sp. (fig. 7). In the shell debris, almost all pieces large enough to identify are assigned to the first two taxa.

Plagioglypta canna (White) is a well-known form, though the type specimens have never been redescribed or reillustrated. *Knightites* (*Retispira*) *modesta* (Girty) was reillustrated by Yochelson (1960, p. 275, pl. 56, figs. 15–19) in the same publication in which *Euphemites imperator* was described (Yochelson, 1960, p. 247). The new species of *Naticopsis* is described in the systematics part of this paper; the remaining material, including the new genus, is inadequate for description or meaningful illustration.

Sedimentary character of the fossil remains

The scaphopod shells show one remarkable feature which apparently has not been reported previously. Some examples have a smaller specimen lodged within a larger. Occasional specimens have two smaller shells nested or telescoped. The rare Middle Ordovician genus *Polylopia* often has multiple nestings of shells (Yochelson, 1968a). Hyolithids at some localities may be found nested; the resulting nonbiologic assemblage is often misinterpreted, and the name *Biconulites* is based on such a misinterpretation. However, both *Polylopia* and "*Biconulites*" are tubes with a closed apex. Even the telescoped orthoconic cephalopods, perhaps best known from the Maquoketa Shale (Upper Ordovician) of Iowa (Tasch, 1955), are septate. Geometrically, all these fossils are quite unlike the scaphopod tube which is open at both anterior and posterior. Flume or wave-tank studies of the currents required to cause the nestings of these various forms of fossils might provide useful data for paleoecologic interpretations.

A few of the scaphopod tubes are at an oblique angle to the bedding plane (fig. 6); at first glance, the tubes might be interpreted as being in life position. However, several of these show a smaller specimen jammed within a larger, and accordingly they cannot have lived in the bottom as they are now presently seen. Most specimens are parallel to bedding, and some scaphopods appear to be current oriented, but without preference for the larger or smaller ends; observations on orientation are based on insoluble residues from each block, and there might have been some slight movement of the material during the etching and subsequent washing.

Most of the bellerophontacean gastropods are 3.5–4.0 cm wide, very few being smaller than 3.0 cm. Thus, they do not resemble a sample of a life population in which small specimens are far more common than large individuals (compare with Yochelson, 1960, p. 221, fig. 2). The specimens show no orientation, but as their shape is somewhat spherical, the lack of orientation is not surprising. Most *Plagioglypta* are short segments of the long tube, generally 2–5 cm long. Few juvenile specimens are present. Specimens as long as 10 cm are present, though rare. Comparison with material from other localities suggests that some of these individuals may have attained a length of about 20 cm during life.

Many of the specimens are not well preserved. Although in part this is the result of fracture of the thick silicified shells, damage of this sort is the exception rather than the rule. Rather, almost all the bellerophontaceans and scaphopods show evidence of erosion by mechanical wear. In most *Euphemites* and *Plagioglypta*, the shell is 2 to 3 mm thick, so that wear of the thin marginal edge is obvious.

In addition to wear, about 5 percent of bellerophontacean shells also show a large number of elongate holes, such as have been ascribed to the action of boring barnacles (Tomlinson, 1969). The percentage of long-dead shells which accumulated on the bottom may be underrepresented in the sample because the bored shells are weaker and therefore more easily destroyed than those unbored. None of the scaphopod shells show indication of borings.

About half the rock volume is composed of *Plagioglypta* and *Euphemites*. The interstices are filled mainly with worn shell

Figure 3.—Part of the insoluble residue from collection 23819-PC in which a large number of *Euphemites* are present in varying states of preservation. Scaphopods are obvious on the right side of the photograph but are scattered in both horizontal and vertical position within the residue. Natural size.

fragments which range in size from about 1 cm in maximum diameter down to the smallest fragments that can still be identified as organic. The individual particles of the shell coquina thus are held together with a minor amount of calcium carbonate cement.

Scattered randomly through the shell fragments are neritacean gastropods. Most of these range from 0.5 to 1 cm in width, but a few are wider than 1 cm. Individuals less than 0.5 cm are virtually unknown; were this a life population they should be the most common size. Several hundred specimens

Figure 4.–*Plagioglypta canna* (White) in several orientations. Most specimens are worn, are nested, or show both features. The specimen near the center has two tubes telescoped within the outermost specimen. Natural size.

have been recovered, or about as many as the *Euphemites* and *Plagioglypta* combined. Some of these neritaceans are also worn, but collectively they are better preserved than the larger fossils. Many specimens retain a conspicuous color pattern which would likely have been removed had any significant part of the shell thickness been worn away, for the color is confined to the outer layer of the shell.

Interpretation of the faunule

Every obvious feature of the fossils supports their interpretation as a death assemblage gathered together under conditions of relatively strong water movement. The wear of most large fossils, the high percentage and large size of shell debris, and the telescoping of the *Plagioglypta* tubes all indicate a high-energy environment. From this one-spot locality, it is impossible to determine the geometry of the deposit, but similar assemblages elsewhere in the Permian of the west are variable and laterally discontinuous over distances of a few feet. Accumulation of the fossils at or near the strandline is a reasonable conclusion.

Specimens have probably been moved a few feet to a maximum of a few tens of feet vertically. On modern beaches after heavy storms, unworn shells are found of mollusks that lived at shallow depths. Most wear was probably accomplished by movement back and forth, with only limited transport. The amount of lateral transport can only be guessed, but the large volume of fossils still identifiable, even though worn, would seem to imply a short time of such transport. If transported for extended distances, it might be expected that the bellerophontacean shell would be breached and specimens worn so that only the columella remained, whereas, in fact, most are complete shells. A short violent stage of transport is in keeping with interpretation of storm-driven waves moving up a relatively steep outer beach slope; it is somewhat less in keeping with their moving up a long, very gently sloping mudflat.

Figure 5.—*Euphemites imperator* Yochelson in several orientations. Although a few specimens preserve spiral ornament, most are worn on the outer surface and the aperture. The specimen in the lower left is bored, and the fragment above it is that of a worn columella; other shell fragments are shown in the lower right. Natural size.

Living neritacean gastropods occupy a variety of habitats, but they are particularly characteristic of shores, many forms living between the tide lines and some in the spray zone above high-tide level. It may be that the *Euphemites* and *Plagioglypta* shells were swept shoreward, there to be mixed with the neritaceans. Some transport of the neritaceans must certainly have taken place, as indicated by shell wear, but it was far less than that affecting the other specimens.

Speculations on feeding habits of the fossils support the general picture built up from the physical evidence. By comparison with living Neritacea, one may confidently assume that the fossil forms were microherbivores. Within this broad niche, the most likely method of feeding was scraping algae from hard surfaces, rather than clinging to algal fronds or digesting of algal mats. The bellerophontaceans probably were also herbivores. The large size of specimens precluded life on algal fronds. It seems more likely that they lived on algal mats rather than on the shoreline, but no evidence directly supports this assertion. Thus, one can speculate that the bellerophontaceans in the faunule were large specimens from a very shallow water sand-algal mat environment, which were transported to a nearshore bottom area and then perhaps were moved along a beach.

Limited data are available on the habits of living scaphopods. Morton (1959, p. 225, fig. 1) described a species in some detail, noting that it burrowed in "fairly clean sand of medium grade," at an oblique angle to the substrate. Dinamani (1964b) described another species which lives with the shell at an even more acute angle to the upper surface of the substrate. Trueman (1968, p. 27), in a detailed discussion of the burrowing process, concluded that in contrast to the pelecypods, the scaphopods are only able to burrow shallowly and obliquely. Both Morton (1959) and Dinamani (1964a) discussed the role of captacula, highly specialized tentacles, in feeding. Although there are some differences in the accounts, they agree on the importance of these structures in trapping benthonic foraminifers; the radula of living North Atlantic species seems to be well suited for crushing foram shells (John Kraeuter, oral commun., 1971). Dinamani (1964a) suggested that organic detritus also forms an important part of the diet and noted that stirring of the sediment by the probing foot is reflected on the surface, another indication of the extreme shallowness of burrowing. From these data, one would be inclined to guess that large specimens such as are found at the Pequop Mountains locality lived in a sand bottom rather than in mud. If water movement were sufficiently strong to move sand grains, the tubes would be readily dislodged.

Ever since the work of Nicol (1944), which compared a *Plagioglypta*-bearing faunule with two others in the Kaibab Limestone of Arizona, it has been traditional to assume that an abundance of scaphopods is suggestive of restricted water circulation and hypersaline conditions. Lateral and vertical facies changes do support such an assumption at the locality studied by Nicol and in places within the slightly older Arcturus Formation (Permian) of the Ely, Nev., district. In other areas, evidence is equivocal, and the assumption of

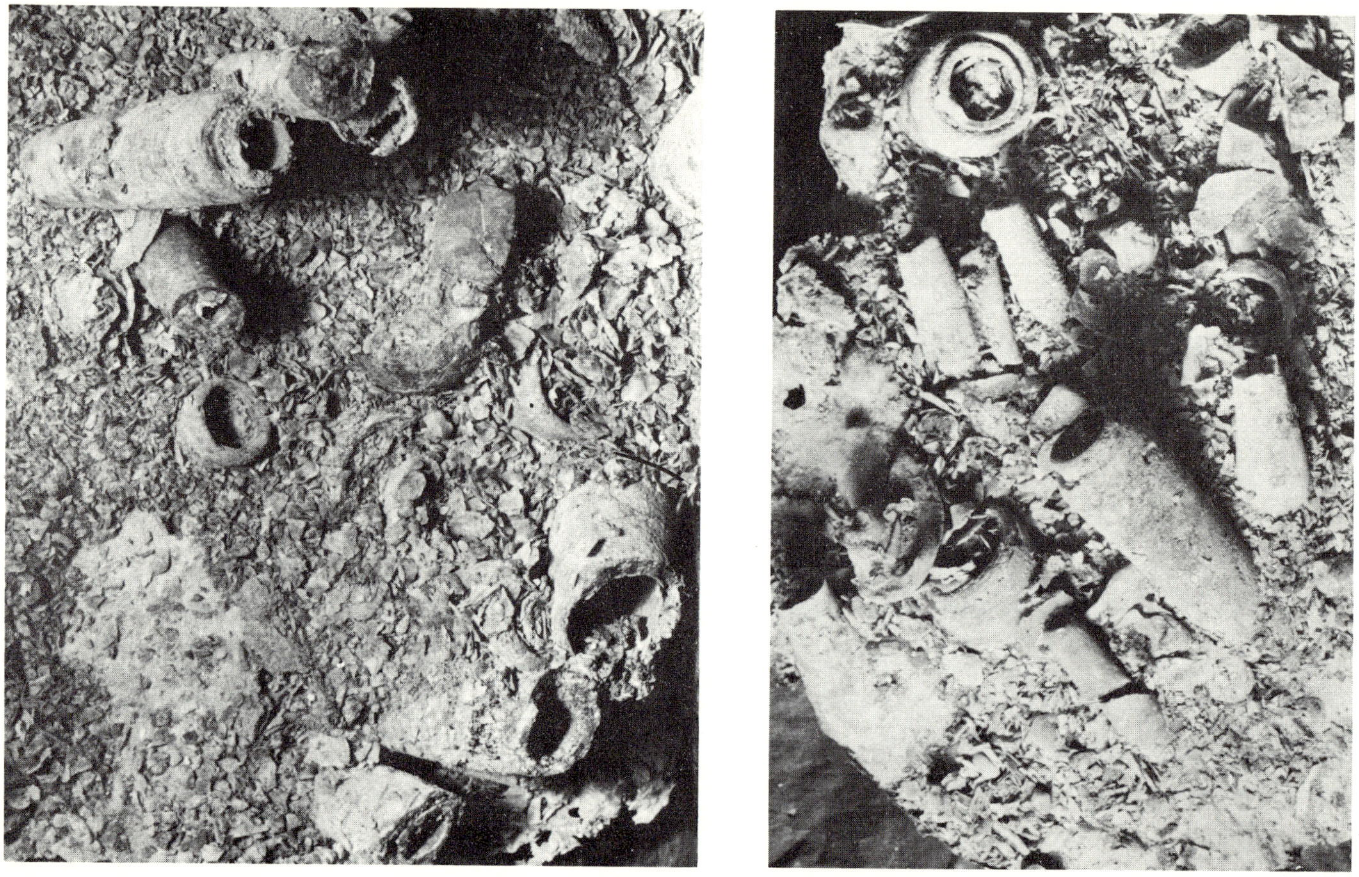

Figure 6.—View from above of two limestone blocks, partly etched, showing nested scaphopod tubes standing at various angles to the horizontal bedding plane. Natural size.

hypersalinity may be in error. At the Pequop locality, the interpretation of the fossils as an exceedingly shallow water deposit laid down by strong currents is difficult to reconcile with a restricted basin, though such a hydrographic situation is certainly possible. No evaporites have been found in the Plympton Formation in the Pequop Mountains, but evaporites have been found in the upper part of the formation 100 miles to the southeast (Hose and Repenning, 1959, p. 2182).

The evidence of a storm bed—the wear of fossils and the mixing of forms from slightly different environments—seems clear. The changes observed in the regional pattern of stratigraphy indicate moderately pronounced relief and a hiatus at the top of the Plympton Formation. The two fundamentally different approaches thus complement each other.

Age of the faunule

In spite of its limited variety, this faunule is readily dated as late Leonardian-early Wordian in age, in terms of the western Texas Permian section. An important fossil for dating is *Euphemites imperator;* this is the first known occurrence of the species since its description from localities in western Texas (Yochelson, 1960).

Knightites (*Retispira*) *modesta* is known from western Texas as well as from the Kaibab Limestone in Arizona. It also occurs in Montana in the Franson Member of the Park City Formation at Big Sheep Canyon (USGS locality 18581-PC) and at Cedar Creek (loc. 10829-PC), probably in the upper member of the Shedhorn Sandstone. The very abundant *Naticopsis* does not appear to be represented in collections from the Permian of western Texas, and the other rare gastropods and pelecypods add no information on the age of the deposit.

Mr. S. D. Olmore, University of Utah, has recently contributed a collection from the "*Bellerophon* limestone horizon" within the Harrisburg Gypsiferous Member of the Kaibab Limestone in the East Mormon Mountains; except for several small *Bellerophon*, only *Plagioglypta canna* (White) has been collected. The locality (22282-PC) is in the NW¼SW¼, sec. 13, T. 10 S., R. 69 E., Nevada, approximately 200 miles almost due south of the Pequop Mountains locality. This new occurrence of exceptionally well preserved material provides an intermediate point between the Pequop Mountains and

Relief Spring, Ariz. White (1874, p. 23) described *Dentalium canna* originally from both that locality and Salt Lake, N. Mex. *Plagioglypta canna* is conventionally used in the sense of specimens known from the Kaibab Plateau region; a type locality has never been designated.

Paleozoic scaphopods have received little study in the United States from the standpoint of either their biology or stratigraphic occurrence; in part, this is because their relatively simple shell shows only a limited number of characters. Accordingly, it is impossible to document conclusively the range of even such a well-known species as *Plagioglypta canna* (White). Nevertheless, the common occurrence of this taxon in certain facies of the Kaibab Limestone and Franson Member of the Park City suggests that it is an excellent guide to rocks of upper Leonardian-lower Wordian equivalents. This supposition can be tested when the scaphopods of the American standard Permian section are studied in detail.

DISTRIBUTION OF THE PERMIAN PLAGIOGLYPTA FACIES IN THE NORTHWESTERN UNITED STATES

The *Plagioglypta* faunule from the southern Pequop Mountains is similar to category 6 of Yochelson (1968b, p. 592), who summarized the fossil collections within the Phosphoria rock complex by their principal faunal components. Some useful data might be gathered by comparing these occurrences. As any attempt to generalize inevitably leads to loss of precision, one must immediately note that of the several dozen occurrences of *Plagioglypta* included in category 6, only about half a dozen are closely comparable to the Pequop occurrence. Locality details and other pertinent matters concerned with the Phosphoria fossils are given in Yochelson (1968b; see also Yochelson, 1968c) and need not be repeated here. Bretsky and Bermingham (1970) summarized the paleoecologic setting of reported Paleozoic scaphopods, but they did not review the occurrences in the Phosphoria rock complex in any detail.

Although a great deal of effort has gone into interpretation and reconstruction of the Phosphoria sea (McKelvey and others, 1959; Sheldon, 1963; Cressman and Swanson, 1964; Sheldon and others, 1967), many details still remain to be worked out. If the Permian phosphate deposits of the Western United States are the result of deposition from upwelling waters, studies of position of shoreline may be important. Further, the general nature of the shoreline slope could be critical, for a steep gradient is more likely to promote local upwelling than a shallow shelf area some miles wide. As indicated, a steep gradient is more likely to produce a storm-tossed beach deposit.

Viewed in this aspect, only two areas where *Plagioglypta* occur are particularly comparable. The first area is on the south side of the Uinta Mountains in Utah at Coulter Ranger Station (USGS loc. 10019-PC, 19406-PC) and at Split Mountain (19407-PC). The second is in the disturbed belt of southwestern Wyoming at Deadline Ridge (13350-PC; 18633-PC). At these localities, observation of fossil assemblages is inhibited because secondary silicification has changed the matrix to a mass composed of solid chert.

Several attempts to collect silicified faunules in both areas met with quite limited success and make the Pequop Mountains material all the more meaningful, for none of this Phosphoria matrix can be disaggregated. No information is available on what factors might govern silicification of fossils and oversilicification of the matrix. As a consequence of this strong secondary silicification, the Phosphoria localities are now chert. There appears little merit in equating these local deposits with the Rex Chert Member of the Phosphoria Formation, rather than the Franson Member of the Park City. Whatever the conditions of Rex deposition may have been, they do not appear to have been nearshore. The point is raised here simply to caution the unwary as to the potential effects of secondary silicification.

Orientation of fossils, degree of sorting from a life population, amount of wear, and the general character of preservation are features which fall between the interests of the stratigraphic paleontologist and the sedimentologist.

With those qualifications clearly understood, one would judge that, at the localities in southwestern Wyoming, fossils show deposition near the strandline in the most striking manner; therefore, presumably quite strong currents were involved. In the Uinta Mountains area, the evidence of high-energy deposition is not quite so obvious. The Pequop Mountains locality seems intermediate in character, but much closer to the environment of deposition of the southwestern Wyoming fossils. A locality near Big Timber in eastern Montana (USGS loc. 18843-PC) may be similar in depositional environment to that of the Uinta Mountains, but the fossils are not silicified, and observations on wear and orientation cannot be made so readily.

At the presumed beach localities in the Phosphoria rock complex that have been noted above, pelecypods are abundant and bellerophontacean gastropods are rare. The only previously known locality that approaches the faunal composition of the Pequop Mountains faunule is at Cedar Creek, Mont. (10528-PC); we have not investigated this locality and do not know if it represents a beach. In that collection, *Plagioglypta* and the bellerophontaceans *Bellerophon* and *Knightites* are present in about equal numbers, along with a few pelecypods (*Permophorus*).

At a few other localities, such as Hidden Pastures (18581-PC) and Sappington Canyon (18588-PC) in south-central Montana and Blind Stream (19408-PC) and Dry Bread Hollow (19415-PC) in the Uinta Mountains and northern Utah, respectively, the faunules consist predominantly of *Plagioglypta* and pelecypods. None of the material at these four localities shows obvious evidence of transport. The available material does not show a large amount of wear, though some specimens may have been discarded before being examined by Yochelson (1968b). Although these assemblages may be similar to *Plagioglypta*-bellerophontacean faunules, so little is known of the ecological requirements of the organisms that it may be premature to assume that they lived under the same general conditions.

For the sake of completeness, it is appropriate to mention a slab from La Marche Gulch (12629-PC) in central Montana, which contains only large *Plagioglypta*, and collections from Cinnabar Mountain (12695-PC; 18844-PC) in extreme southeastern Montana, which has yielded *Bellerophon* and *Euphemites* but no *Plagioglypta. Plagioglypta* have been collected at other localities reported by Yochelson (1968c), but they appear to have a somewhat different aspect than those outlined above.

SYSTEMATIC PALEONTOLOGY

Class GASTROPODA
Order NERITOPSIDA Cox and Knight
Superfamily NERITACEA Rafinesque
Family NERITOPSIDAE Gray
Subfamily NATICOPSINAE Miller
Genus NATICOPSIS M'Coy
Subgenus NATICOPSIS M'Coy
Naticopsis (?Naticopsis) rosewateri Yochelson n. sp.

Figure 7, *a–t*

Description.—Elongate neritiform gastropods with a thickened but quite restricted inductura. Nucleus unknown. Shell exceedingly low spired, the upper part of the early growth stages seemingly relatively lower than that of the penultimate whorl. Suture obscure. Whorl profile that of a flattened ovoid, the short upper segment being only gently inclined and almost ramplike before curving abruptly downward to the outer face; periphery at or just above midwhorl, the whorl segment above it being more flattened than the part below; lower part of whorl profile a smooth curve following the arc of a circle and continuing this curvature to the base of the columella. Outer lip unknown; basal lip simple and smoothly curved. Shell surface smooth; growth lines unknown. Shell presumably has a thin outer layer and a thick inner layer. Inductura distinct and clearly set off from underlying shell, limited to a narrow zone parallel to the aperture and extending through less than one-eighth the circumference of the body whorl; inductura thin at the upper part of the aperture and at its farthest lateral extension, raised and nearly bosslike adjacent to the middle part of the aperture; not quite so thick near the lower part of the aperture and in early growth stages, but in later growth stages thicker and bounded by a distinct ridge. Inductura appears to be partially filling a shallow columellar depression. Ornamented by light and dark color bands, the dark bands being crescentic in early stages and elongating at later stages to form a variable zigzag pattern.

Discussion.—Conventionally, the Neritacea are placed within the Archaeogastropoda. Morton and Yonge (1964, p. 2) have formally raised this superfamily to the rank of order, basing this change on anatomical distinctions between present-day Neritacea and all other forms assigned to the Archaeogastropoda. There is no reason to challenge this new classification, and the rather mysterious appearance of the neritacean stock in the Devonian, without any obvious ancestral forms, provides slight additional support for this view. Although no rules of priority apply at the ordinal level, it should be noted that Cox and Knight (1960, p. 263) earlier had differentiated as a suborder a group termed by them Neritopsina.

The common late Paleozoic genus *Naticopsis* has never been subjected to monographic treatment. Because it has a relatively simple shell form and lacks many of the features, such as elaborate ornament, which are of use in distinguishing members of other gastropod groups, *Naticopsis* has been divided into subgenera on the basis of features of shell shape (Yochelson, 1953), the limits of which are more or less subjective. This new species differs in shape from typical *Naticopsis* in being somewhat narrower. However, it is more similar to that form than it is to any of the other subgenera currently recognized; questioned placement on the subgeneric level is better practice at this time than any ill-founded attempt to characterize yet another subgenus.

Naticopsis (?*Naticopsis*) *rosewateri* is distinguished by its somewhat peculiar whorl profile, being elongate but flattened above. In apertural view, as in figure 7, *f* or *k*, the shell appears compressed, whereas in the adapertural view it appears more inflated. This is clearly an optical illusion, heightened possibly because the outer lip is broken back, but it is the best expression of the low spire and the elongate whorl profile.

North American late Paleozoic species of *Naticopsis* have been listed by Yochelson and Saunders (1967, p. 139–144), who supplied the pertinent references to literature. Among the named Permian taxa, *N. remex* is based on indeterminate material, and *N. diminuta* is incorrectly assigned to genus, for it has a denticulate aperture. *N. transversa* has prominent colabral ornament and may not belong to this genus. *N. deformis*, *N. gracilis*, and *N. oblatus* are all relatively wider than this new form. *N. apachensis* and *N. oblatus* are more similar than other named forms, but each has a teardrop-shaped profile with virtually no development of an inclined upper surface. The difficulty in distinguishing species emphasizes the need for some scheme to describe more quantitatively the overall shape of the whorl profile. Though *N.* (?*N.*) *rosewateri* appears to be distinctive, several of the forms distinguished from it may be synonymous with others listed above.

Preservation of the *Naticopsis* is better than that of the other fossils in the faunule, but it leaves something to be desired. Many specimens have the early whorls worn, as in figure 7, *r*, so that the species appears even lower spired than it actually is. A few specimens are crushed, as on the side of the specimen in figure 7, *j*, or near the base of the aperture (fig. 7, *k*). All specimens have the outer lip broken back so that the aperture is not known in detail. Undoubted growth lines are not preserved, even though striations shown in figure 7, *n*,

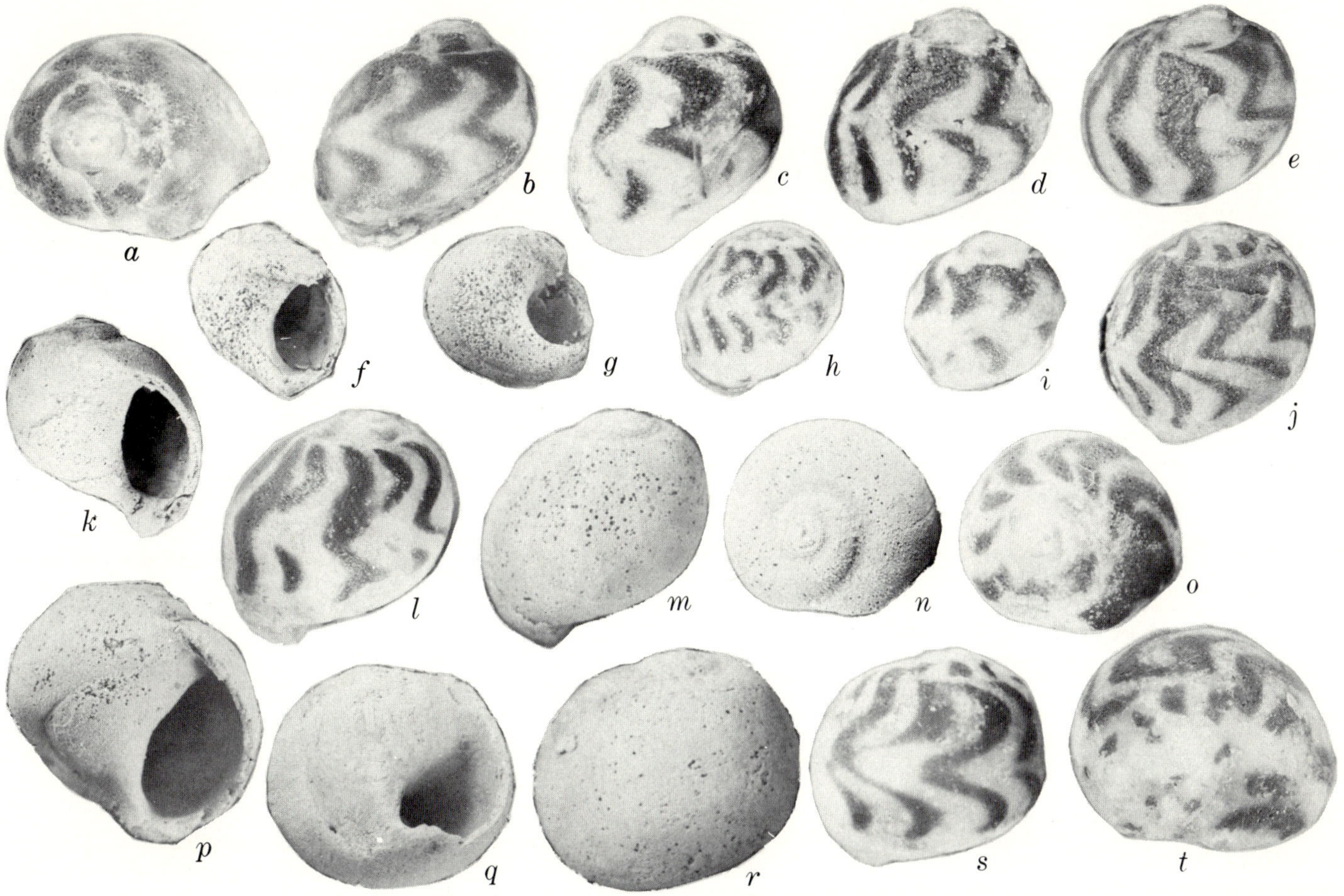

Figure 7.—*Naticopsis* (?*Naticopsis*) *rosewateri* n. sp. All illustrations × 3. *f, g, k, m, n,* and *p–r* coated with ammonium chloride; for other illustrations the specimens were moistened to accentuate the dark color bands. *a, b,* top and side views of paratype, USNM 183540; *c,* side view of paratype, USNM 183541; *d,* side view of paratype, USNM 183542; *e,* slightly oblique side view of paratype, USNM 183543; *f–h,* apertural view, oblique basal view to emphasize inductura, and side view of paratype, USNM 183544; *i,* side view of paratype, USNM 183545; *j,* side view of paratype, USNM 183546, *k–o,* apertural view, side views, and top views of paratype, USNM 183547; *p–t,* apertural view, oblique basal view, side views, and top view of holotype, USNM 183548.

might suggest that the apertural lip was nearly orthocline. The lack of growth lines does not seem to be a factor of poor preservation but rather a reflection of an originally highly polished shell surface.

The color pattern preserved on so many individuals is certainly the most eye-catching feature of this species. What the original colors may have been is not known and cannot be surmised. Color patterns preserved in silicified Permian specimens are not common, but they do occur at some localities. Any consideration of the mechanism of silicification must take into account the retention of this pattern during the replacement process. It does not persist through the shell but is limited to the thinner outer shell layer.

As demonstrated by the specimens illustrated in figure 7, there is a high degree of individual variation in the precise details of light and dark stripes that follow a general zigzag pattern. As it is likely that the zigzag stripes were used for camouflage by complicating predator recognition of the shell shape, evolutionary theory supports the notion that there would not be rigorous natural selection toward a precise unvarying form. Variation in this pattern, as shown for example in figure 7, *c, e,* and *s,* is not uncommon. Even the early stages (fig. 7, *h* and *i*) do not have a definite pattern.

During the early days of conchology, many varieties were named among elaborately patterned modern forms. Further study has shown that some populations are highly variable in many details of coloration and that this feature is of limited taxonomic significance, even if only the general pattern is considered. In fossils, the preservation of color pattern is such a special event—even at this locality more than half the specimens lack the pattern—that such patterns should not be used as a feature for distinguishing species.

The specific name acknowledges a debt of long standing to Dr. Joseph Rosewater, of the National Museum of Natural History, for his assistance, in ways too numerous to detail, in my attempts to draw comparisons between features of Paleozoic gastropods and those of the modern fauna.

Types.—Holotype, USNM 183548; figured paratypes, USNM 183540–183547.

REFERENCES CITED

Bissell, H. J., 1964, Ely, Arcturus, and Park City Groups (Pennsylvanian-Permian) in eastern Nevada and western Utah: Am. Assoc. Petroleum Geologists Bull., v. 48, no. 5, p. 565–636.

Bretsky, P. W., and Bermingham, J. J., 1970, Ecology of the Paleozoic scaphopod genus *Plagioglypta* with special reference to the Ordovician of eastern Iowa: Jour. Paleontology, v. 44, no. 5, p. 908–924.

Collinson, J. W., 1968, Permian and Triassic biostratigraphy of the Medicine Range, northeastern Nevada: Earth Sci. Bull., v. 1, no. 4, p. 25–44.

Cox, L. R., and Knight, J. B., 1960, Suborders of Archaeogastropoda: Malacological Soc. London Proc., v. 33, p. 262–264.

Cressman, E. R., and Swanson, R. W., 1964, Stratigraphy and petrology of the Permian rocks of southwestern Montana: U.S. Geol. Survey Prof. Paper 313-C, p. 275–569, pls. 14–25.

Dinamani, P., 1964a, Feeding in *Dentalium conspicuum:* Malacological Soc. London Proc., v. 36, p. 1–5.

—— 1964b, Burrowing behavior of *Dentalium:* Biol. Bull., v. 126, p. 28–32.

Hodgkinson, K. A., 1961, Permian stratigraphy of northeastern Nevada and northwestern Utah: Brigham Young Univ. Geology Studies, v. 8, p. 167–196.

Hose, R. K., and Repenning, C. A., 1959, Stratigraphy of Pennsylvanian, Permian, and Lower Triassic rocks of Confusion Range, west-central Utah. Am. Assoc. Petroleum Geologists Bull., v. 43, no. 9, p. 2167–2196.

McKelvey, V. E., and others 1959, The Phosphoria, Park City, and Shedhorn formations in the western phosphate field: U.S. Geol. Survey Prof. Paper 313–A, p. 1–47, pls. 1–3.

Morton, J. E., 1959, The habits and feeding organs of *Dentalium entalis:* Marine Biol. Assoc. United Kingdom Jour., v. 38, p. 225–238.

Morton, J. E., and Yonge, C. M., 1964, Classification and structure of the Mollusca, *in* Wilber, K. W., and Yonge, C. M., Physiology of the Mollusca: New York, Academic Press, v. 1, p. 1–58.

Nicol, David, 1944, Paleoecology of three faunules in the Permian Kaibab Formation at Flagstaff, Arizona: Jour. Paleontology, v. 18, no. 6, p. 553–557.

Robinson, G. B., Jr., 1961, Stratigraphy and Leonardian fusulinid paleontology in central Pequop Mountains, Elko County, Nevada: Brigham Young Univ. Geology Studies, v. 8, p. 93–145.

Sheldon, R. P., 1963, Physical stratigraphy and mineral resources of Permian rocks in western Wyoming: U.S. Geol. Survey Prof. Paper 313-B, p. 49–273, pls. 4–13.

Sheldon, R. P., Cressman, E. R., Cheney, T. M., and McKelvey, V. E., 1967, Paleotectonic investigations of the Permian System in the United States—Middle Rocky Mountains and northeastern Great Basin: U.S. Geol. Survey Prof. Paper 515–H, p. 159–170.

Steele, Grant, 1960, Pennsylvanian-Permian stratigraphy of east-central Nevada and adjacent Utah, *in* Intermtn. Assoc. Petroleum Geologists, Guidebook to the geology of east-central Nevada, 11th annual field conference, 1960: Salt Lake City, Utah Geol. and Mineralog. Survey, p. 91–113.

Stevens, C. H., 1965, Pre-Kaibab Permian stratigraphy and history of Butte basin, Nevada and Utah: Am. Assoc. Petroleum Geologists Bull., v. 49, no. 2, p. 139–156.

Tasch, Paul, 1955, Paleoecologic observations on the orthoceratid coquina beds of the Maquoketa at Graf, Iowa: Jour. Paleontology, v. 29, no. 3, p. 510–518.

Thorman, C. H., 1970, Metamorphosed and nonmetamorphosed Paleozoic rocks in the Wood Hills and Pequop Mountains, northeast Nevada. Geol. Soc. America Bull., v. 81, no. 8, p. 2417–2448.

Tomlinson, J. T., 1969, The burrowing barnacles (Cirripedia: Order Acrothoracica): U.S. Natl. Mus. Bull. 296, 162 p.

Trueman, E. R., 1968, The burrowing process of *Dentalium* (Scaphopoda): Zool. Soc. London Jour., v. 154, p. 19–27.

White, C. A., 1874, Preliminary report upon invertebrate fossils collected by expeditions of 1871, 1872, and 1873, with descriptions of new species: U.S. Geog. Explor. W. 100th meridian (Wheeler), 27 p.

Yochelson, E. L., 1953, *Jedria*, a new subgenus of *Naticopsis:* Washington Acad. Sci. Jour., v. 43, no. 3, p. 65.

—— 1960, Permian Gastropoda of the southwestern United States* * *–3. Bellerophontacea and Patellacea: Am. Mus. Nat. History Bull., v. 119, art. 4, p. 207–294, pls. 46–57.

—— 1968a, On the nature of *Polylopia:* U.S. Geol. Survey Prof. Paper 593-F, p. F1-F7, pl. 1.

—— 1968b, Biostratigraphy of the Phosphoria, Park City, and Shedhorn Formations: U.S. Geol. Survey Prof. Paper 313-D, p. 571–660.

—— 1968c, Charts showing distribution and abundance of fossils in the Phosphoria, Park City, and Shedhorn Formations in Wyoming, Idaho, Utah, and Montana: U.S. Geol. Survey open-file report, 8 sheets.

Yochelson, E. L., and Saunders, B. W., 1967, A bibliographic index of North American late Paleozoic Hyolitha, Amphineura, Scaphopoda, and Gastropoda: U.S. Geol. Survey Bull. 1210, 271 p.

Jour. Research U.S. Geol. Survey
Vol. 1, No. 1, Jan.—Feb. 1973, p. 33—37

GRAPTOLITES FROM THE MARTINSBURG FORMATION, LEHIGH GAP, EASTERN PENNSYLVANIA

By JACK B. EPSTEIN and WILLIAM B. N. BERRY[1]
Beltsville, Md., Berkeley, Calif.

Work done in cooperation with the Pennsylvania Department of Environmental Resources, Bureau of Topographic and Geologic Survey

Abstract.—Graptolites collected from the uppermost part of the Martinsburg Formation (Pen Argyl Member) at and near the contact with the overlying Shawangunk Formation at Lehigh Gap, Pa., indicate that the uppermost Martinsburg is as young as Edenian to early Maysvillian (upper subzone [*Climacograptus spiniferus* subzone] of zone 13 [*Orthograptus truncatus intermedius* zone]). The Martinsburg gradationally overlies the Jacksonburg Limestone of late Middle Ordovician age, suggesting a lower age limit for the Martinsburg.

The Martinsburg Formation in easternmost Pennsylvania and northwestern New Jersey consists predominantly of 9,800 to 12,800 feet of slate, graywacke, and graywacke siltstone. Three members were defined by Drake and Epstein (1967), namely a middle graywacke-bearing member (Ramseyburg) separating lower (Bushkill) and upper (Pen Argyl) slate-dominated members. The distribution of these is shown in figure 1.

The upper age of the Martinsburg in eastern Pennsylvania has generally been given as early Maysvillian (for example, Twenhofel and others, 1954) based on shelly fossils identified by Ulrich (in Stose, 1930, p. 648–649) from the Shochary Ridge area west of Lehigh River. The Shochary Sandstone and what is here called the Ramseyburg Member were originally thought to be contiguous units by Behre (1933). Reconnaissance by A. A. Drake, Jr., and J. B. Epstein (see Epstein and others, 1972) suggests that the rocks in Shochary Ridge may be separated from the Martinsburg of the slate belt to the east by a fault of large displacement. The abundant shelly fauna in the sandstone in Shochary Ridge (named the Shochary Sandstone by Willard and Cleaves, 1939) has not been found in sandstone of the Ramseyburg Member of the slate-belt Martinsburg. Only very sparse brachiopod and crinoid debris have been found in the Ramseyburg during the past decade of mapping in eastern Pennsylvania by members of the U.S. Geological Survey.

[1] Department of Paleontology, University of California.

Previously, few fossils have been found in the slate-belt Martinsburg that yielded a precise age determination. Beerbower (1956) found the trilobite *Triarthrus beckii* just below the contact of the Martinsburg and Shawangunk Formations at Delaware Water Gap in New Jersey. *Triarthrus* ranges from Barnveldian through Edenian (Twenhofel and others, 1954; see fig. 2 for stage names used in this report). The fossil was collected from the upper part of the Ramseyburg Member, whose contact with the overlying Pen Argyl Member is truncated by the Shawangunk 0.75 mile southwest of the gap (fig. 1). Willard and Cleaves (1939, p. 1184) found poorly preserved fossils at Lehigh Gap—identification was not possible. Schuchert (1916, p. 548), however, reported *Diplograptus foliaceus* var. *vespertinus* Ruedemann (=*Glyptograptus vespertinus* (Ruedemann), suggestive of zone 13) from the Martinsburg (Pen Argyl Member) from within 75 feet of the overlying Shawangunk. Unspecified fossils in the Ramseyburg Member north of Klecknersville, Pa., were believed to be of probable Trenton age (late Middle Ordovician?) by Ulrich (in Stose, 1930, p. 638), but Behre (1933, p. 142) maintained that their poor state of preservation shed doubt on the age determination.

More recently, Aldrich (1967) discovered *Glyptograptus* cf. *G. teretiusculus* (Hisinger) and a variety of *Orthograptus calcaratus* Lapworth in the Bushkill Member of the Martinsburg Formation near Seemsville, Pa. These graptolites also occur in the Normanskill Shale and the Canajoharie Shale in New York (Ruedemann, 1947; Berry, 1962; Riva, 1969) and are, therefore, indicative of the zone 12-lower subzone of zone 13 interval.

NEW GRAPTOLITE COLLECTIONS FROM LEHIGH GAP—UPPER AGE LIMIT OF THE MARTINSBURG FORMATION

Graptolites have been found at four localities in the Pen Argyl Member of the Martinsburg Formation in the Palmerton quadrangle immediately south of Lehigh Gap (fig. 3). The Pen Argyl is nearly 6,000 feet thick in the Lehigh Valley.

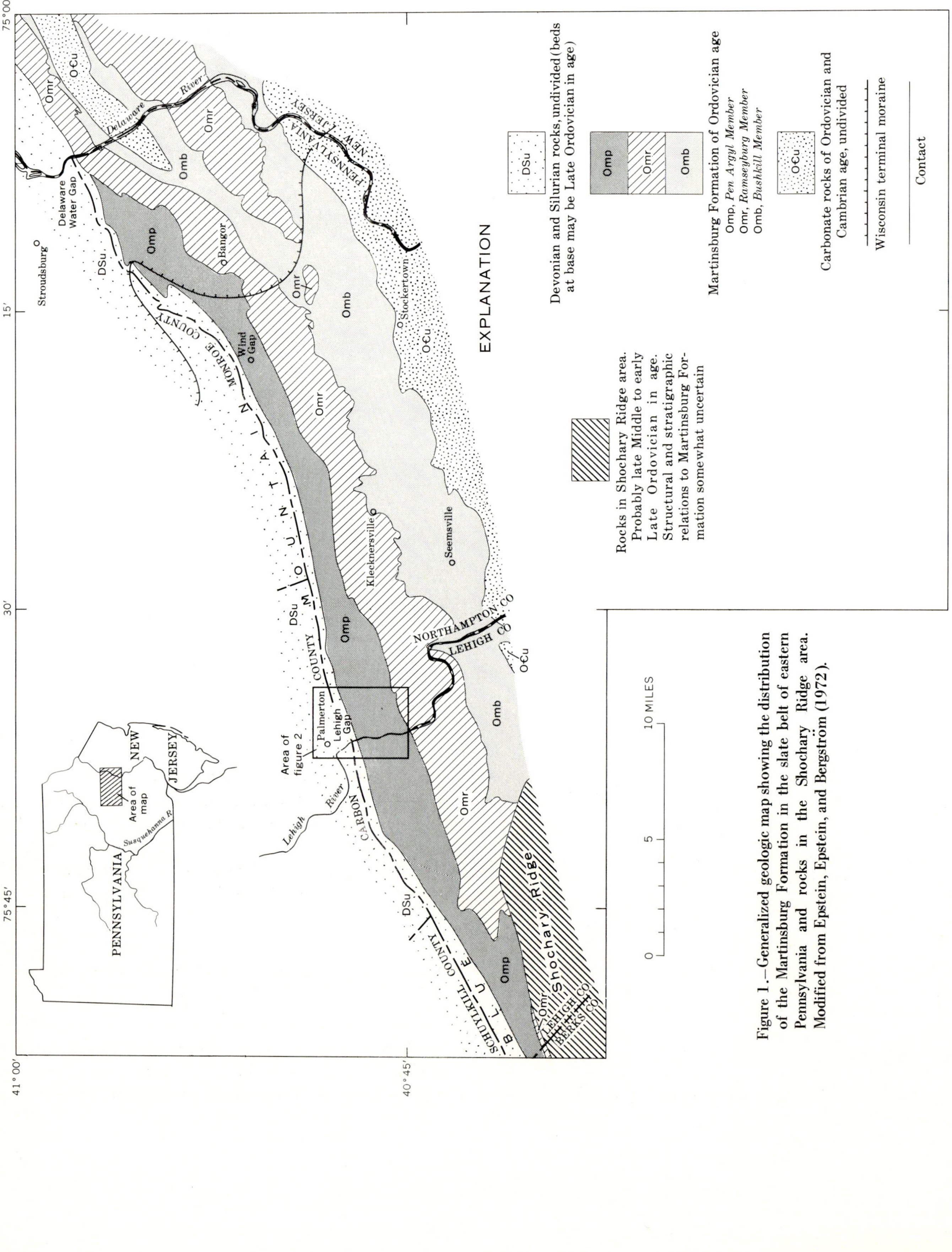

Figure 1.—Generalized geologic map showing the distribution of the Martinsburg Formation in the slate belt of eastern Pennsylvania and rocks in the Shochary Ridge area. Modified from Epstein, Epstein, and Bergström (1972).

Series	North American stages	Graptolite zones	Formations in slate-belt area, eastern Pennsylvania	
Upper Ordovician (Cincinnatian)	Richmondian	15	Shawangunk Formation (part) ?	
	Maysvillian	14		
	Edenian	13 Upper subzone	Martinsburg Formation	Pen Argyl Member
				Ramseyburg Member
Middle Ordovician (Champlainian)	Barnveldian	13 Lower subzone		Bushkill Member ?
	Wildernessian	12	Jacksonburg Limestone	

Figure 2.—Age of the Martinsburg Formation in the slate belt of eastern Pennsylvania and upper Middle and Upper Ordovician stages and graptolite zones used in this report. Many of the reports cited in this paper present age determinations in reference to either the Trenton Group or "Trentonian" stage. Conodont faunas in the type areas of the "Trentonian" and Edenian (Bergström and Sweet, 1966; Schopf, 1966; Sweet and Bergström, 1970) indicate that the upper part of the Trenton Group is Edenian, so that "Trenton" is Wildernessian through early Edenian in age.

The graptolites collected at each locality and the structural setting are listed in table 1. The stratigraphic and structural positions of the graptolite localities are shown in the cross section in figure 3. Stratigraphic and structural details are given in Epstein and Epstein (1969).

The association of *Climacograptus spiniferus*, *C. typicalis*, and *Dicranograptus nicholsoni* var. *minor* with orthograptids of the *O. quadrimucronatus* and *O. truncatus* groups in collections from the Pen Argyl Member is indicative of the upper subzone of zone 13 of Berry (1970). The upper subzone of zone 13 (the *Climacograptus spiniferus* subzone of the *Orthograptus truncatus intermedius* zone) is equivalent to the *Climacograptus spiniferus* zone of Riva (1969). Riva (1969) indicated that the *Climacograptus spiniferus* zone is in the lower part of the Utica Shale in the Mohawk Valley, N.Y. He (Riva, 1969) correlated the lower part of the Utica Shale in the Mohawk Valley with the Cobourg Limestone in the Trenton Group. Sweet and Bergström (1971) correlated the Cobourg Limestone with the entire Edenian and the lower part of the Maysvillian in the Cincinnati area on the basis of their conodont studies. The upper part of the Martinsburg Formation in eastern Pennsylvania (the Pen Argyl Member) may thus be correlated with at least a part of the Edenian-Maysvillian interval. If the youngest rocks in Shochary Ridge west of the Lehigh River are Maysvillian in age as suggested by Stose (1930), then the upper part of the Martinsburg in the slate belt could be about the same age. However, modern paleontologic studies of Shochary Ridge rocks have not been undertaken as yet to prove the Maysvillian correlation.

LOWER AGE LIMIT OF THE MARTINSBURG FORMATION

The Martinsburg Formation grades down into the Jacksonburg Limestone in easternmost Pennsylvania. Miller (1937) indicated that the uppermost part of the Jacksonburg Limestone is correlative with the Sherman Fall Formation (Barnveldian in age) in New York and Ontario. Twenhofel and others (1954) correlated the uppermost part of the Jacksonburg with the lower part of the Sherman Fall. Barnett (1965), on the basis of conodont studies, concluded that the Jacksonburg probably correlates with the Rockland, Kirkfield, and lower Shoreham Formations. Barnett's (1965) conclusions are supported by conodont collections made by J. B. Epstein near Stockertown, Pa. (fig. 1). J. W. Huddle, of the U.S. Geological Survey, identified the conodonts (written commun., 1970; USGS loc. 6974-CO and 6975-CO) and cited the presence of *Phragmodus undatus* Branson and Mehl which suggests that the beds bearing it in the Jacksonburg Limestone are no older than the Rockland Formation. The Rockland is in the upper part of the Wildernessian Stage (Cooper, 1954). Thus, precise dating of the top of the Jacksonburg and the transitional beds in the basal Martinsburg remains to be established, but it seems likely that the basal Martinsburg is late Wildernessian to early Barnveldian (or late zone 12 to lower subzone of zone 13) in age.

SUGGESTIONS FOR FUTURE COLLECTING IN THE SLATE BELT

The graptolite-bearing rocks of the Pen Argyl Member have several characteristics in common that may aid in future discovery of other fossil localities in the eastern Pennsylvania slate belt. In general, bedding and cleavage are nearly parallel at the localities from which the graptolites were obtained. In areas where cleavage is at an appreciable angle to the bedding, the slate will not split parallel to bedding. Thus, bedding surfaces are not exposed as in the case where bedding and cleavage are subparallel. Cleavage is poorly developed at locality 1 which is regarded as a pressure-shadow area (Epstein and Epstein, 1969, p. 166–167). Other pressure-shadow areas near the contact with the Shawangunk Formation may be good sites for inspection. They include exposures in the Delaware Water Gap and at the Yards Creek hydroelectric project near Blairstown, N.J. (Epstein and Epstein, 1969, p. 135, fig. 3).

The graptolites from most of the localities are dark brown and stand out against the lighter colored, weathered slate that bears them. Weathered outcrops that fulfill the near-parallel bedding-cleavage requirement are excellent sites for examination for future collecting. As the weathering took place primarily prior to Wisconsin glaciation (Epstein and Hosterman, 1969), outcrops south and west of the Wisconsin terminal moraine (fig. 1) are generally more favorable for finding graptolites.

CONCLUSIONS

The faunal evidence suggests that the Martinsburg Formation in the eastern Pennsylvania slate belt ranges in age from late Middle Ordovician at its base to an age in the span of Edenian-Maysvillian (the upper subzone of zone 13 of Berry, 1970) at the top. This dates the youngest beds exposed beneath the Taconic unconformity in this part of eastern Pennsylvania. Berry (1970) has previously discussed the significance of the graptolite collections from the Pen Argyl Member near Lehigh Gap, Pa., in his reevaluation and refinement of graptolite zone 13 in New York and Pennsylvania.

ACKNOWLEDGMENTS

We wish to acknowledge P. B. Myers, Jr., Lehigh University, who first discovered graptolites in the Lehigh Gap area (loc. 3, fig. 3), and J. W. Huddle for identifying the conodonts from the Jacksonburg Limestone. We give our sincere thanks to A. A. Drake, Jr., U.S. Geological Survey, for his exchange of ideas on the stratigraphy on the Martinsburg Formation.

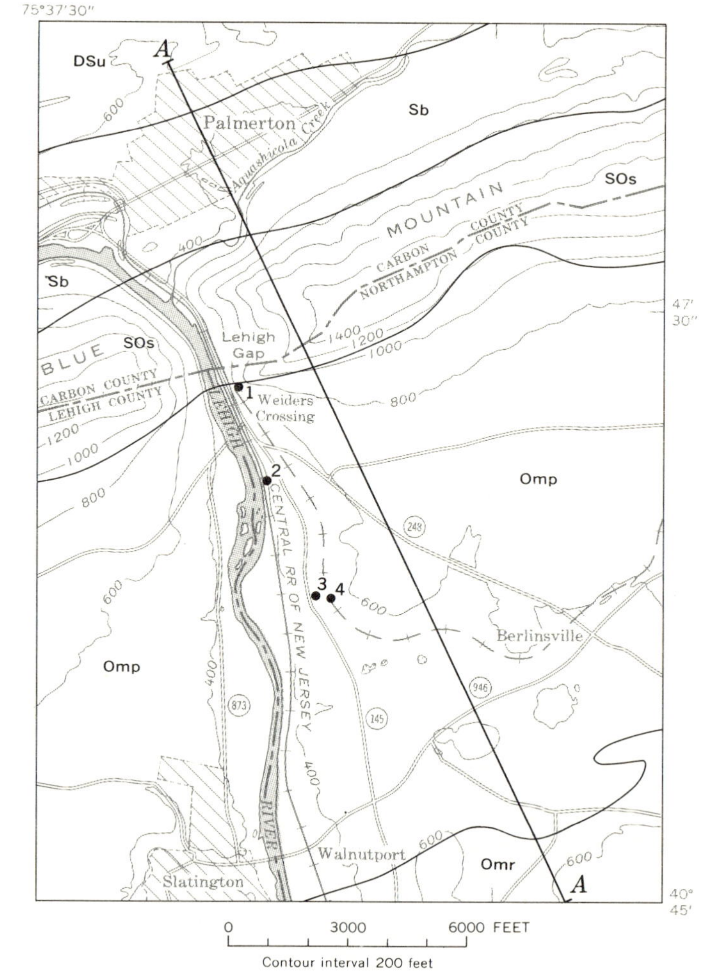

Figure 3.

Table 1.—*Ordovician graptolites in the Pen Argyl Member of the Martinsburg Formation near Lehigh Gap, Pa.*

Locality	Description	Graptolites
1.	Abandoned railroad cut. Slightly weathered argillite, cleavage poorly developed. Samples 80 to 100 feet below contact with overlying Shawangunk Formation. Locality described by Epstein and Epstein (1969, p. 180–181).	*Climacograptus spiniferus* Ruedemann
2.	Railroad cut. Weathered slate in cleavage arch, cleavage and bedding nearly parallel. Sample about 2,400 feet below contact with overlying Shawangunk Formation.	*Climacograptus* cf. *C. bicornis* var. *longispina* T. S. Hall *C. spiniferus* Ruedemann *C. typicalis* J. Hall *Diplograptus* sp. *Orthograptus truncatus* cf. var. *pertenuis* (Ruedemann)
3.	Shale pit. Weathered slate in vertical beds, cleavage and bedding nearly parallel. Samples collected from 300-foot interval about 3,000 feet below the Shawangunk Formation.	*C. spiniferus* Ruedemann *C. typicalis* J. Hall *Dicranograptus nicholsoni* var. *minor* Bulman *Diplograptus mohawkensis* Ruedemann *Leptograptus* sp. *Orthograptus quadrimucronatus* cf. var. *approximatus* (Ruedemann) *O. truncatus* var. *intermedius* (Elles and Wood)
4.	Same as at locality 3 but from abandoned railroad cut above locality 3.	*Climacograptus spiniferus* Ruedemann *C. typicalis* J. Hall *Diplograptus mohawkensis* Ruedemann? *Diplograptus* sp. *Orthograptus quadrimucronatus* cf. var. *approximatus* (Ruedemann) *Orthograptus* sp. (of the *O. truncatus* group)

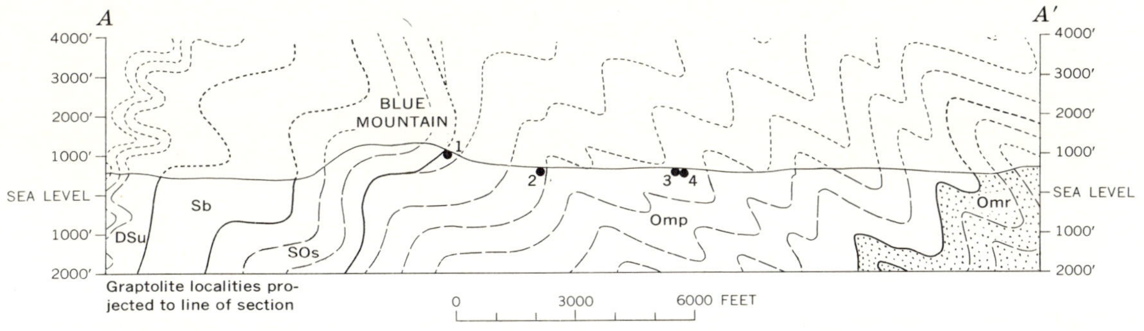

Figure 3.—Generalized geologic map and section showing graptolite localities in the Lehigh Gap area, Pennsylvania. DSu, Devonian and Upper Silurian rocks, undivided; Sb, Bloomsburg Red Beds; SOs, Shawangunk Formation; Omp, Pen Argyl Member of Martinsburg Formation; Omr, Ramseyburg Member of Martinsburg Formation. Base from U.S. Geological Survey, Palmerton, Pa., 7½-minute quadrangle, 1960.

REFERENCES CITED

Aldrich, M. J., Jr., 1967, Cambrian dolomite in the Martinsburg Formation, eastern Pennsylvania: Pennsylvania Acad. Sci. Proc., v. 41, p. 133–140.

Barnett, S. G., III, 1965, Conodonts of the Jacksonburg Limestone (Middle Ordovician) of northwestern New Jersey and eastern Pennsylvania: Micropaleontology, v. 11, no. 1, p. 59–80.

Beerbower, J. R., 1956, The Ordovician-Silurian contact, Delaware Water Gap, New Jersey: Pennsylvania Acad. Sci. Proc., v. 30, p. 146–149.

Behre, C. H., Jr., 1933, Slate in Pennsylvania: Pennsylvania Geol. Survey, 4th ser., Bull. M16, 400 p.

Bergström, S. M., and Sweet, W. C., 1966, Conodonts from the Lexington Limestone (Middle Ordovician) of Kentucky, and its lateral equivalents in Ohio and Indiana: Bulls. Am. Paleontology, v. 50, no. 229 p. 271–441.

Berry, W. B. N., 1962, Stratigraphy, zonation, and age of Schaghticoke, Deepkill, and Normanskill shales, eastern New York: Geol. Soc. America Bull., v. 73, p. 695–718.

——1970, Review of late Middle Ordovician graptolites in eastern New York and Pennsylvania: Am. Jour. Sci., v. 269, p. 304–313.

Cooper, G. A., 1954, Chazyan and related brachiopods: Smithsonian Misc. Colln., v. 127, pts. 1 and 2, 1245 p.

Drake, A. A., Jr., and Epstein, J. B., 1967, The Martinsburg Formation (Middle and Upper Ordovician) in the Delaware Valley, Pennsylvania-New Jersey: U.S. Geol. Survey Bull. 1244-H, p. H1–H16.

Epstein, J. B., and Epstein, A. G., 1969, Geology of the Valley and Ridge province between Delaware Water Gap and Lehigh Gap, Pennsylvania, *in* Subitzky, Seymour, ed., Geology of selected areas in New Jersey and eastern Pennsylvania and guidebook of excursions: New Brunswick, N.J., Rutgers Univ. Press, p. 132–205.

Epstein, J. B., Epstein, A. G., and Bergström, S. M., 1972, Significance of Lower Ordovician exotic blocks in the Hamburg klippe, eastern Pennsylvania, *in* Geological Survey Research 1972: U.S. Geol. Survey Prof. Paper 800-D, p. D29–D36.

Epstein, J. B., and Hosterman, J. W., 1969, Residual clay deposits in rocks of Early and Middle Devonian age near Kunkletown, Pennsylvania, *in* Geological Survey Research 1969: U.S. Geol. Survey Prof. Paper 650-D, p. D94–D105.

Miller, R. L., 1937, Stratigraphy of the Jacksonburg Limestone: Geol. Soc. America Bull., v. 48, p. 1687–1717.

Riva, John, 1969, Utica and Canajoharie Shales in the Mohawk Valley, *in* Bird, J. M., ed., New England Intercollegiate Geological Conf., 61st Ann. Mtg., Oct. 10–12, 1969, Guidebook for field trips in New York, Massachusetts, and Vermont, 7 p. (paged separately).

Ruedemann, Rudolf, 1947, Graptolites of North America: Geol. Soc. America Mem. 19, 652 p.

Schopf, T. J. M., 1966, Conodonts of the Trenton Group (Ordovician) in New York, southern Ontario, and Quebec: New York State Mus. and Sci. Ser. Bull. 405, 105 p.

Schuchert, Charles, 1916, Silurian formations of southeastern New York, New Jersey, and Pennsylvania: Geol. Soc. America Bull., v. 27, p. 531–554.

Stose, G. W., 1930, Unconformity at the base of the Silurian in southeastern Pennsylvania: Geol. Soc. America Bull., v. 41, p. 629–658.

Sweet, W. C., and Bergström, S. M., 1970, Stratigraphic significance of conodonts from the Lexington Limestone and Kope Formation in the Cincinnati region [abs.]: Geol. Soc. America Abs. with Programs, v. 2, no. 3, p. 242–243.

—— 1971, The American Upper Ordovician standard XIII–A revised time-stratigraphic classification of North American upper Middle and Upper Ordovician rocks: Geol. Soc. America Bull., v. 82, p. 613–628.

Twenhofel, W. H., and others, 1954, Correlation of the Ordovician formations of North America: Geol. Soc. America Bull., v. 65, p. 247–298.

Willard, Bradford, and Cleaves, A. B., 1939, Ordovician-Silurian relations in Pennsylvania: Geol. Soc. America Bull., v. 50, p. 1165–1198.

Jour. Research U.S. Geol. Survey
Vol. 1, No. 1, Jan.—Feb. 1973, p. 39—44

MICROPROBE ANALYSIS OF BIOTITES—A METHOD OF CORRELATING TUFF BEDS IN THE GREEN RIVER FORMATION, COLORADO AND UTAH

By GEORGE A. DESBOROUGH, JANET K. PITMAN, and JOHN R. DONNELL, Denver, Colo.

Abstract.—Quantitative electron microprobe analyses of biotite grains for iron, magnesium, and titanium from tuff beds in the lacustrine Green River Formation (Eocene) of Colorado and Utah provide a tentative method of identification and a permissive stratigraphic correlation of tuffs. Tuff beds that have been identified and correlated by stratigraphic means were sampled at five localities in Colorado and Utah to determine if microprobe analyses of biotite could be used as a method of correlation. Although most of the original phenocrysts and glass shards of these pyroclastic beds have undergone extensive postdepositional alteration, biotite seems to have been unaffected. The iron, magnesium, and titanium contents of the biotite do not uniquely characterize individual tuff beds, but when the proportions of these elements are compared in a continuous stratigraphic sequence of beds, correlation of individual tuffs or groups of tuffs is possible over areas exceeding several hundred square miles. The method may be used for detailed correlation of pyroclastic beds where stratigraphic, faunal, and radiometric methods have been unsatisfactory.

Biotites from certain thin, persistent tuff beds in the lacustrine Green River Formation (Eocene) of Colorado and Utah have been studied by electron microprobe analysis in an effort to provide a method of characterizing these beds. This information might facilitate the correlation of stratigraphic sequences from one depositional basin to another, particularly in those areas where lacustrine and fluviatile facies of the Green River Formation interfinger and coalesce.

This report gives results of analyses for iron, magnesium, and titanium in biotites from tuff beds of the Green River Formation in Colorado and Utah. The study consisted of two parts: (1) Well-known tuff beds in the Mahogany ledge, Parachute Creek Member, were used as a model to test the consistency in chemical composition of the biotites from tuff beds at one locality with biotites of the same beds at other localities; and (2) biotites from two stratigraphic sequences of unknown tuffs were analyzed to determine if correlation between the sequences might be made from the chemical composition of biotite in each bed.

Upper-Tertiary tuffs that are widely distributed in western North America have been successfully correlated by means of quantitative electron microprobe analysis of "fresh" glass (Smith and Westgate, 1969; Izett and others, 1970). However, the Eocene ash beds of the Green River Formation were subjected to such intensive postdepositional alteration that the original glass shards were converted to zeolites (primarily analcime), quartz, and carbonates (Bradley, 1964). Therefore, we studied only biotites in the tuffs, because they apparently have undergone only minimal alteration. Unaltered hornblende occurs in a few tuffs, but only in trace amounts.

For the sequence of tuffs studied, the radiometric age difference between the oldest and youngest bed is approximately 5 m.y. (R. L. Mauger, written commun, 1971). The precision of K/Ar dating is about ±0.9 m.y. for beds 45 m.y. old; this amount prevents correlation of individual tuffs by absolute age in sequences such as those shown in figures 1 and 2.

Microprobe analysis of biotites, which was used as a method of correlation, was found to be valuable in distinguishing individual beds in a sequence of beds for which stratigraphic, faunal, and radiometric dating methods of identification have not been particularly successful.

ANALYTICAL METHODS

Tuff samples were prepared for analysis by one of three methods. Biotites from selected tuff beds were concentrated in bromoform (method 1), or were separated by electromagnetic techniques (method 2). These grains were mounted in epoxy and polished with diamond pastes. Rock slabs of the tuffs showing biotite were polished in a similar manner (method 3). For one tuff bed, the arithmetic means of iron, magnesium, and titanium in biotite separated by each of the three methods are the same within one standard deviation; therefore, because of the considerable time saving involved, most of the biotite grains analyzed were prepared by polishing rock slabs.

Three chemically homogeneous biotite concentrates, whose iron, magnesium, and titanium content had previously been determined by wet chemical analysis, were used as quantitative standards. Each standard contains the following weight percentage of iron, magnesium, and titanium calculated as an oxide:

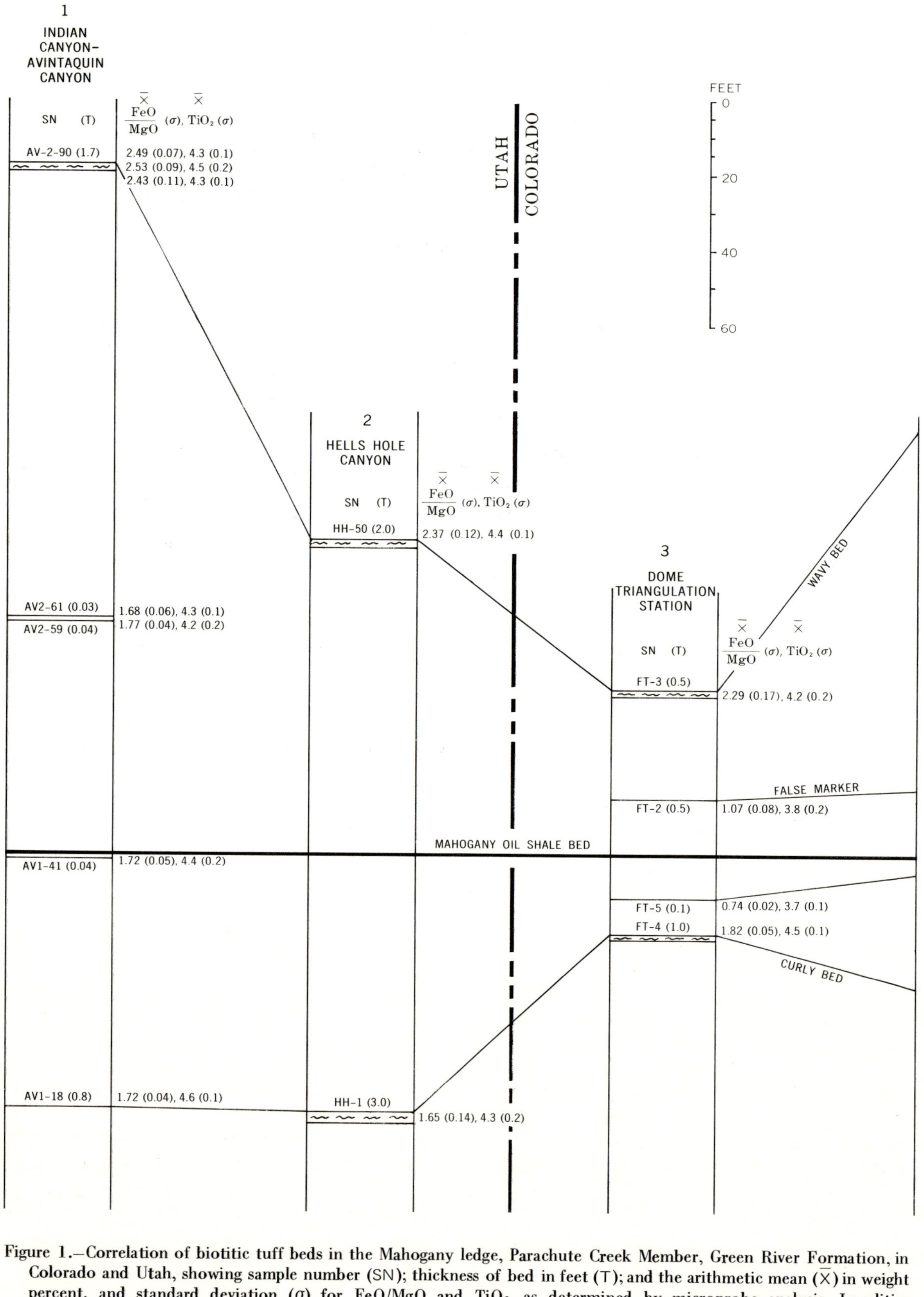

Figure 1.—Correlation of biotitic tuff beds in the Mahogany ledge, Parachute Creek Member, Green River Formation, in Colorado and Utah, showing sample number (SN); thickness of bed in feet (T); and the arithmetic mean ($\overline{X}$) in weight percent, and standard deviation (σ) for FeO/MgO and TiO_2 as determined by microprobe analysis. Localities correspond to those in table 1.

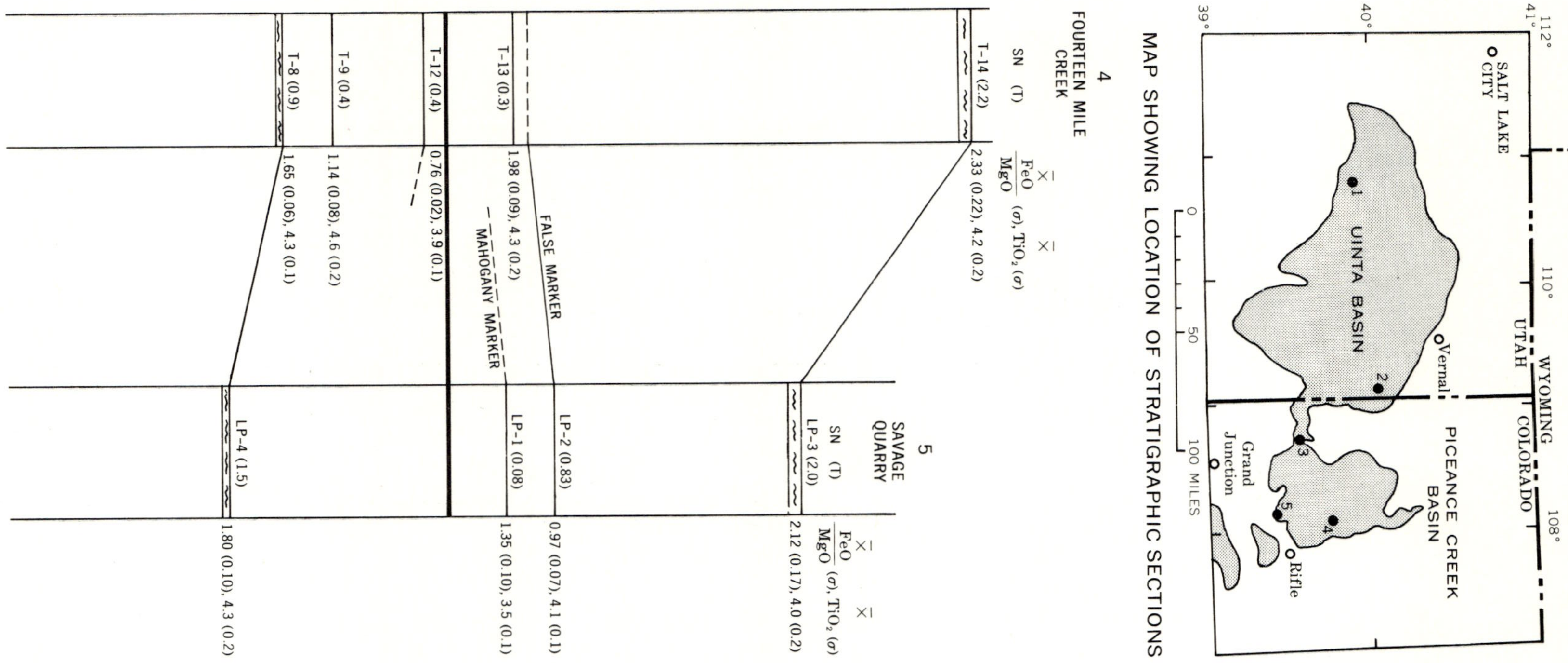

Figure 1.

Table 1.—*Mean weight percentage* ($\bar{X}$) *and standard deviation* (σ) *for* FeO, MgO, *and* TiO_2 *in biotite of selected tuff beds in the Mahogany ledge, Parachute Creek Member, Green River Formation, in Colorado and Utah*

[Locality numbers correspond to those on figure 1]

Bed name	1 Indian Canyon–Avintaquin Canyon, Utah Sec. 14, T. 5 S., R. 4 W.			2 Hells Hole Canyon, Utah Sec. 17, T. 10 S., R. 25 E.			3 Dome triangulation station, Colo. Sec. 7, T. 5 S., R. 10 W.			4 Fourteen Mile Creek, Colo. Sec. 12, T. 3 S., R. 97 W.			5 Savage quarry, Logan Peak, Colo. Sec. 36, T. 7 S., R. 97 W.		
	FeO $\bar{X}$ (σ)	MgO $\bar{X}$ (σ)	TiO_2 $\bar{X}$ (σ)	FeO $\bar{X}$ (σ)	MgO $\bar{X}$ (σ)	TiO_2 $\bar{X}$ (σ)	FeO $\bar{X}$ (σ)	MgO $\bar{X}$ (σ)	TiO_2 $\bar{X}$ (σ)	FeO $\bar{X}$ (σ)	MgO $\bar{X}$ (σ)	TiO_2 $\bar{X}$ (σ)	FeO $\bar{X}$ (σ)	MgO $\bar{X}$ (σ)	TiO_2 $\bar{X}$ (σ)
Wavy	[1]22.9(0.4)	9.2(0.2)	4.3(0.1)	22.0(0.5)	9.3(0.3)	4.4(0.1)	22.1(0.7)	9.7(0.5)	4.2(0.2)	21.3(1.4)	9.2(0.3)	4.2(0.2)	21.7(0.7)	10.2(0.6)	[1]4.0(0.2)
	[2]22.7(0.4)	9.0(0.2)	4.5(0.2)	....	....	....	....	....	....	....	....	....	....	....	....
	22.5(0.4)	9.3(0.5)	4.3(0.1)	....	....	....	....	....	....	....	....	....	....	....	....
Unnamed	21.0(0.4)	12.5(0.5)	4.3(0.1)	....	....	....	....	....	....	....	....	....	....	....	....
Do.	19.5(0.4)	11.0(0.3)	4.2(0.2)	....	....	....	....	....	....	....	....	....	....	....	....
False marker	....	....	....	....	....	....	15.3(0.5)	14.3(0.3)	3.8(0.2)	....	....	....	14.3(0.8)	14.7(0.6)	4.1(0.1)
Mahogany marker	....	....	....	....	....	....	....	....	....	....	....	....	16.8(0.8)	12.4(0.5)	3.5(0.1)
Unnamed	....	....	....	....	....	....	....	....	....	20.8(0.9)	10.5(0.4)	4.3(0.2)	....	....	....
Do.	19.6(0.4)	11.4(0.3)	4.4(0.2)	....	....	....	....	....	....	....	....	....	....	....	....
Do.	....	....	....	....	....	....	12.6(0.2)	17.0(0.4)	3.7(0.1)	13.1(0.2)	17.2(0.2)	3.9(0.1)	....	....	....
Do.	....	....	....	....	....	....	....	....	....	15.5(0.8)	13.6(0.5)	4.6(0.2)	....	....	....
Curly	19.1(0.4)	11.1(0.2)	4.6(0.1)	19.0(0.67)	11.6(0.8)	4.3(0.2)	20.2(0.3)	11.1(0.2)	4.5(0.1)	19.4(0.4)	11.2(0.3)	4.3(0.1)	19.5(0.7)	10.8(0.5)	4.3(0.2)

[1] Magnetic concentrate.

[2] Bromoform concentrate.

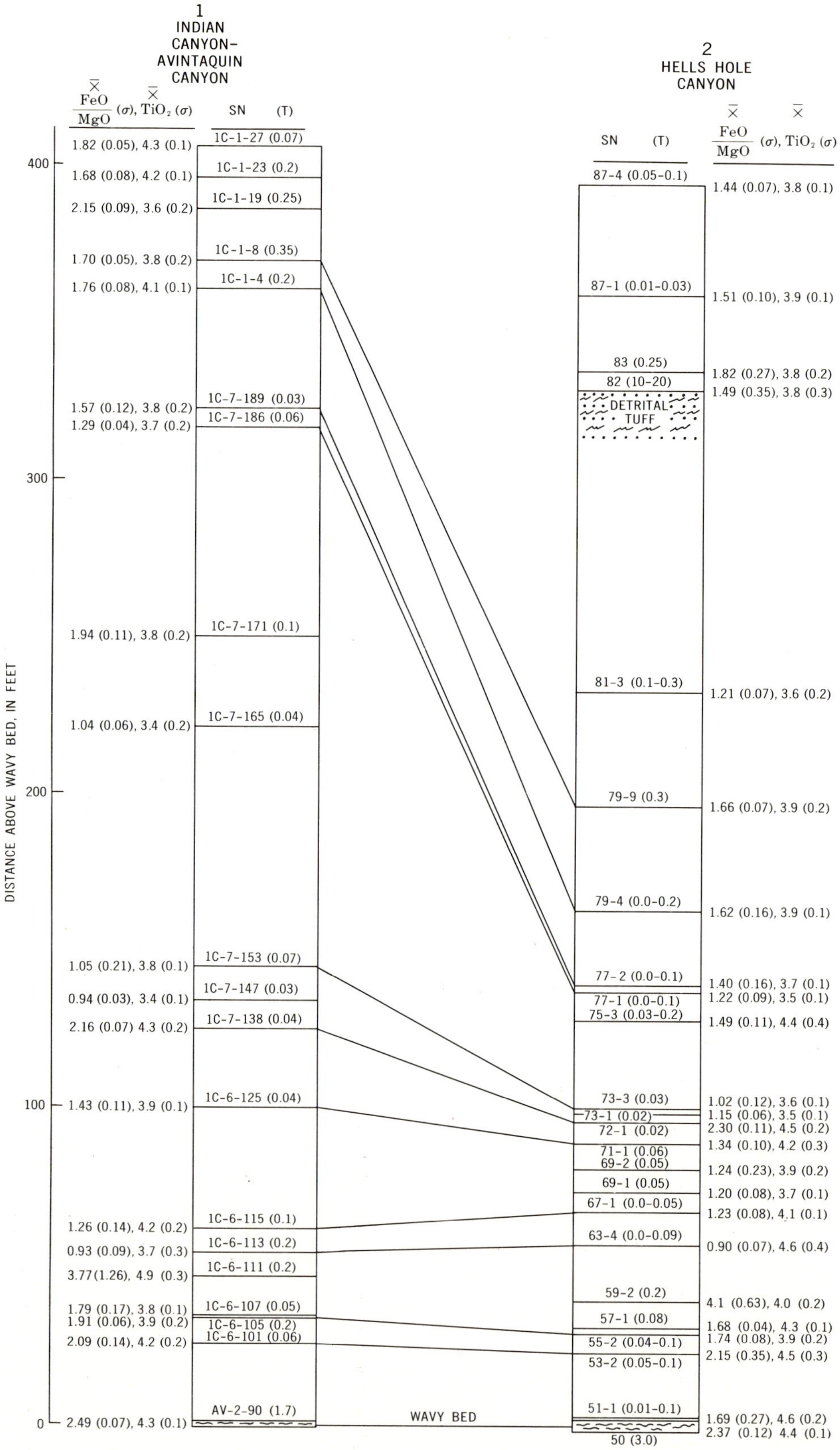

Figure 2.—Correlation based on microprobe analysis of biotitic tuffs above the wavy bed, Parachute Creek Member, Green River Formation, in the Uinta Basin, showing sample number (SN); thickness of bed in feet (T); and the arithmetic mean ($\bar{X}$) in weight percent, and standard deviation (σ) for FeO/MgO and TiO_2. Localities are shown on figure 1.

	FeO	MgO	TiO_2
1	31.39	2.93	1.45
2	34.71	1.24	3.85
3	11.00	19.90	1.58

Because iron in the divalent and trivalent state cannot be distinguished by microprobe analysis, all iron is reported as FeO. Measurements of X-ray intensities (counts) of the $K\alpha$ lines for the elements were recorded before and after analysis of the samples. Calibration curves were constructed by plotting elemental weight percentage against accumulated counts. These procedures corrected for background and instrument drift. All analyses were performed at 10 kV with 2×10^{-4} amperes emission current, 2×10^{-8} amperes sample current, an integrated beam current, and electron beam size of 5–10 μm.

Twenty-five biotite grains per sample were analyzed for iron, magnesium, and titanium with two to four measurements obtained for each grain. A mean weight percentage and a standard deviation for FeO, MgO, TiO_2 and FeO/MgO were calculated for each grain. For each sample, a mean weight percentage and a standard deviation were computed for each element and for the FeO/MgO ratio from results calculated for each of the individual grains. This method permitted an FeO/MgO ratio to be computed for a sample as well as allowing equal emphasis to the ratio of each grain. High compositional homogeneity among individual biotite grains in each sample was indicated by the small variation in counts.

STRATIGRAPHY

The Parachute Creek Member of the Green River Formation underlies large areas of the Piceance Creek basin in Colorado and the Uinta Basin in Utah. This interval is well known because of detailed studies of the rich oil shale. The lower part of the member is composed of oil shale, interbedded with thin, persistent tuff beds ranging in thickness from 0.5 inches to 3 feet. Certain rich oil shale units within the Parachute Creek Member are used as key stratigraphic markers. The Mahogany ledge is one of the thickest and richest of these units. Within the Mahogany ledge is a thin, persistent, exceedingly rich bed known as the Mahogany bed; it serves as an excellent stratigraphic marker and is laterally persistent for several hundred miles along the outcrop (Donnell, 1961).

The upper part of the Parachute Creek Member consists of marlstone, siltstone, and some tuffaceous sandstone. In this rock sequence, the volume of clastic material varies considerably, and as a result the thickness of the stratigraphic intervals between individual beds may vary significantly over short distances. Donnell (1961) has described and mapped beds of the Green River Formation in the Piceance Creek basin, and Cashion (1967) has studied time-equivalent beds in the Uinta Basin. These investigations as well as other subsequent studies provide the stratigraphic information upon which this report is based.

Numerous tuff beds are in the Parachute Creek Member, but only a few have been widely correlated (Donnell, 1961; Cashion, 1967; Cashion and Donnell, 1972). Many of the tuffs do not have sufficient thickness, lateral extent, or unique lithologic characteristics to permit field identification over large areas. Several of the tuffs contain biotite suitable for our study; however, many tuff beds throughout the sequence studied are nonbiotitic and have not been discussed in this report. Among the key tuff beds that have been widely recognized and that have been studied for this report is the wavy bed. This tuff marks the base of the "tuff zone," Parachute Creek Member (Dane, 1955), and is equivalent to the "wavy bedded analcitized tuff" (Cashion, 1967, pl. 3; Donnell, 1961, pl. 53). The wavy bed is an excellent time-stratigraphic marker and is present throughout the southern part of the Piceance Creek basin and the Uinta Basin.

RESULTS OF ANALYSES

In the first part of the present study, well-known tuff beds below the wavy bed were sampled from five localities in Colorado and Utah. Figure 1 shows the stratigraphic positions of these beds at each of the localities. Microprobe analyses of biotites from corresponding beds are listed in table 1. The chemical data indicate that the biotite from any specific tuff bed has almost the same chemical composition as the biotite from the same bed at a different locality. The biotite composition among tuff beds is sufficiently different to permit some tuffs to be distinguished from others. The arithmetic means for the weight percentages of FeO, MgO, and TiO_2 for a particular bed may be distinctly different from those of other beds within a sequence. However, samples of an individual tuff bed but from various localities have the same mean within 1½ standard deviations.

The lateral consistency in composition shown by the analyses indicates that postdepositional alteration had little or no effect on biotites in any of the tuff beds, regardless of the geographic locality, and that detrital biotite has not been added to any of the tuffs studied. Because the contents of FeO, MgO, and TiO_2 in the biotite grains of a single tuff sample follow a normal distribution about a mean, it is assumed that little if any mixing of ash from more than one source occurred.

In the second part of the study, biotites from stratigraphic sequences of tuff beds above the wavy bed at two localities were analyzed. Correlations of these tuffs between localities by use of other methods have been unsuccessful. Stratigraphic positions and the mean FeO/MgO ratio and TiO_2 content for biotites in these tuffs are reported in figure 2. The mean FeO/MgO ratio and mean TiO_2 contents of individual tuffs may not be distinctive taken alone; however, they can be used with confidence in correlating a sequence of tuff beds. For example, the mean FeO/MgO ratio of samples IC-6-113 and 63-4 (fig. 2) is about 0.9, in a sequence of beds having ratios from 1.2 to 4.1. Samples IC-7-138 and 72-1 have a mean

FeO/MgO of 2.2 in a sequence with ratios ranging from 1.0 to 1.4. Correlations might be made on one bed with such distinctive FeO/MgO ratios, but the chemical composition of adjacent beds in a stratigraphic sequence establishes a pattern which remains relatively constant at localities 1 and 2. This pattern may allow one to determine if some beds are absent or if they are unrecognizable.

CONCLUSIONS

Microprobe analysis may provide a quantitative method of identifying tuff beds within a sequence of biotite-bearing beds in the absence of other stratigraphic controls, and it is useful in extending correlations over relatively long distances without detailed stratigraphic measurements between localities.

ACKNOWLEDGMENTS

The authors acknowledge the following individuals for their cooperation in providing measured stratigraphic sections and field consultation: J. R. Dyni and W. B. Cashion for Indian Canyon–Avintaquin Canyon, Utah; W. B. Cashion for Hells Hole Canyon, Utah; and R. B. O'Sullivan for Fourteen Mile Creek, Colo. R. L. Mauger provided unpublished K/Ar radiometric dates. We thank Jacquie Tripp for aid in sample preparation and data reduction. We appreciate helpful suggestions provided by Charles Maxwell, W. B. Cashion, J. R. Dyni, and W. J. Mapel on the manuscript.

REFERENCES CITED

Bradley, W. H., 1964, Geology of the Green River Formation and associated Eocene rocks in southwestern Wyoming and adjacent parts of Colorado and Utah: U.S. Geol. Survey Prof. Paper 496-A, 86 p.

Cashion, W. B., 1967, Geology and fuel resources of the Green River Formation, southeastern Uinta Basin, Utah and Colorado: U.S. Geol. Survey Prof. Paper 548, 48 p.

Cashion, W. B., and Donnell, J. R., 1972, Chart showing correlation of selected key units in the organic-rich sequence of the Green River Formation, Piceance Creek Basin, Colorado, and Uinta Basin, Utah: U.S. Geol. Survey Oil and Gas Inv. Chart OC-65.

Dane, C. H., 1955, Stratigraphic and facies relationships of the upper part of the Green River formation and the lower part of the Uinta formation in Duchesne, Uintah, and Wasatch Counties, Utah: U.S. Geol. Survey Oil and Gas Inv. Chart OC-52.

Donnell, J. R., 1961, Tertiary geology and oil-shale resources of the Piceance Creek basin between the Colorado and White Rivers, northwestern Colorado: U.S. Geol. Survey Bull. 1082-L, p. 835–891.

Izett, G. A., Wilcox, R. E., Powers, H. A., and Desborough, G. A., 1970, The Bishop Ash bed, a Pleistocene marker bed in the Western United States: Quaternary Research, v. 1, no. 1, p. 121–132.

Smith, D. G. W., and Westgate, J. A., 1969, Electron probe technique for characterising pyroclastic deposits: Earth and Planetary Sci. Letters, v. 5, p. 313–319.

Jour. Research U.S. Geol. Survey
Vol. 1, No. 1, Jan.—Feb. 1973, p. 45—52

CRETACEOUS MAFIC CONGLOMERATE NEAR GUALALA OFFSET 350 MILES BY SAN ANDREAS FAULT FROM OCEANIC CRUSTAL SOURCE NEAR EAGLE REST PEAK, CALIFORNIA

By DONALD C. ROSS, CARL M. WENTWORTH, and EDWIN H. McKEE,
Menlo Park, Calif.

Abstract.—Upper Cretaceous mafic conglomerate and quartz-plagioclase arkose that crop out on the southwest side of the San Andreas fault near Gualala, Calif., may have been eroded from a gabbroic terrane that now lies about 350 miles to the southeast, on the opposite side of the San Andreas fault. The plagioclase arkose near Gualala contains little or no K-feldspar, and the conglomerate is characterized by quartz-bearing mafic rocks that lack K-feldspar—volcanic rocks, diabase, and diorite to gabbro. Hornblendes from these clasts yield K/Ar ages of 141±4, 175±7, and 186±7 m.y. The arkose and conglomerate appear to have been eroded from a chert-poor ophiolite (oceanic crust) sequence that, according to paleocurrent evidence, lay east of the present San Andreas fault. Near Eagle Rest Peak, 350 miles southeast of Gualala, similar mafic quartz-bearing volcanic rocks, diabase, and gabbro are exposed in a small structurally isolated area that abuts the San Andreas fault on the southwest. These rocks yield hornblende K/Ar ages of 134±4, 165±4, and 207±10 m.y. They may also be the source of two small fault slivers of similar mafic rocks, which yield hornblende K/Ar ages between 144 and 172 m.y. These slivers now lie 100 and 200 miles to the northwest along the San Andreas fault at Gold Hill and Logan.

Upper Cretaceous sedimentary rocks near Gualala, Calif., offer a possible key to a Late Cretaceous tie across the San Andreas fault because of their unusual mafic composition and present separation from their source by that fault. Studies of basement rocks along the San Andreas fault by Ross (1970, 1972) and of the Cretaceous and Tertiary sedimentary rocks near Gualala by Wentworth (1966, 1968) have led to proposals that these unusual sedimentary rocks were eroded from a terrane of oceanic crust, a remnant of which is preserved as the gabbroic rocks in the western San Emigdio Mountains, now offset about 350 miles from Gualala by the San Andreas fault. In contrast, Cretaceous and lower Tertiary arkose and granitic conglomerate associated with the mafic sedimentary rocks were probably derived from Salinian granitic basement.

This report provides additional petrographic data on the mafic and granitic clasts in the two types of Gualala conglomerates, records seven K/Ar mineral dates from those clasts and the possible mafic source terrane, and discusses the limitations that these data place on the characteristics of the basement source areas of the two conglomerates.

THE SEDIMENTARY SEQUENCE NEAR GUALALA

The conglomerates occur scattered throughout a tripartite stratigraphic sequence of marine sandstone, mudstone, and conglomerate. The sequence consists of two intertonguing Upper Cretaceous facies, one of K-feldspar arkose and granitic conglomerate and one of plagioclase arkose and mafic conglomerate, which together are overlain by K-feldspar arkose and granitic conglomerate of Paleocene and Eocene age (fig. 1). The entire sequence, including the conglomerate, was deposited at bathyal depths by turbidity currents, as indicated by sedimentary structures and by interbedding of sandstone and conglomerate beds, some of which contain abundant shallow-water megafossils, with mudstone beds containing deepwater foraminifers. The foraminifers indicate that both the K-feldspar and the plagioclase arkoses were deposited contemporaneously during late Campanian and (or) early Maestrichtian time.

The orientation of the more regular cross-laminations and of some linear structures in the plagioclase arkose and in the younger (Tertiary) K-feldspar arkose suggests that the two lithologies were supplied from opposite sides of a northwest-trending basin (fig. 1). The source of the Cretaceous K-feldspar arkose, which lacks mesoscopic paleocurrent indicators, is assumed to be the same as that of the Tertiary arkose because the two rocks are similar in composition and contain the same kinds of granitic conglomerate clasts. The currents that deposited both the plagioclase and K-feldspar parts flowed northwestward for the most part, suggesting deposition in a northwest-trending basin. However, some northward and northeastward directional components in the K-feldspar arkose and contrasting westward and southwestward components in the plagioclase arkose suggest that the two lithologies were supplied from opposite sides of the northwest-trending basin.

Conglomerate occurs scattered throughout the two units and, like the sandstone, has distinctly contrasting compositions in the two lithologies. The conglomerate associated with the plagioclase arkose is characterized by a gabbroic suite, which is the sole component of conglomerate in the Anchor

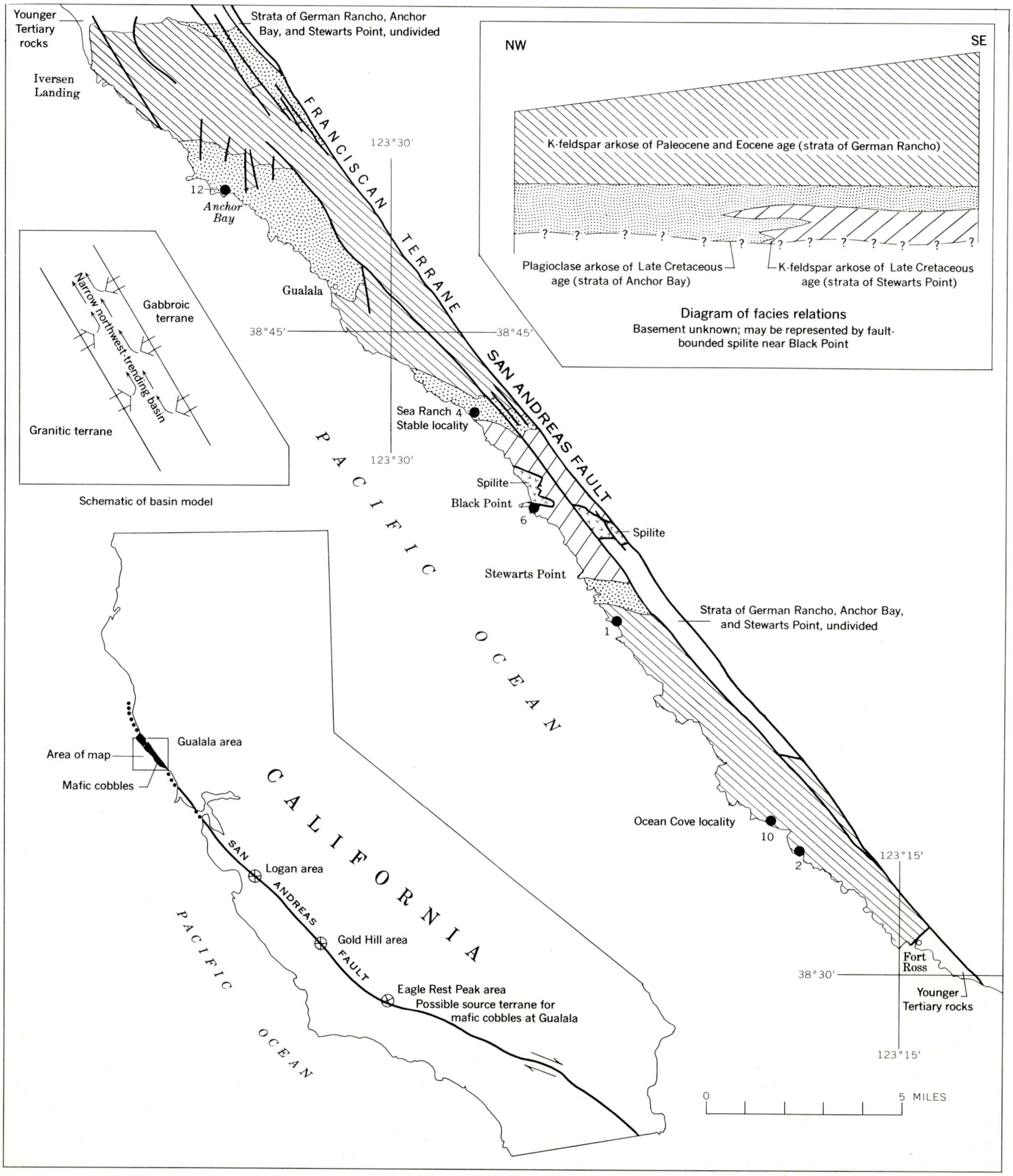

Figure 1.—Index map, generalized geologic map, basin model, and diagram of facies relations in the Gualala area, California. Dots indicate sample localities of modally analyzed conglomerate clasts; number of modes shown for each locality.

Bay area, and is diluted in the Sea Ranch Stable locality by resistant siliceous volcanic clasts at least superficially similar to those present throughout the sedimentary section in the Coast Ranges. Conglomerate in the K-feldspar arkose lacks gabbroic clasts entirely and is characterized by granitic clasts, which are accompanied by abundant siliceous volcanic clasts in the Cretaceous part and by various metamorphic clasts in the Tertiary part. The conglomerate beds consist of coarse pebbles, cobbles, and sparse boulders and occur both scattered in the sequence and to a greater extent concentrated in sequences a few feet to hundreds of feet thick. The samples discussed in this report were collected from most of the major occurrences of conglomerate in the section exposed along the sea cliffs.

CONGLOMERATE CLASTS FROM THE K-FELDSPAR ARKOSE

Four localities where conglomeratic layers in the K-feldspar arkose are particularly well exposed are shown on figure 1. These localities are dominated by granitic clasts ranging in size from small pebbles to boulders more than 1 foot in diameter. Clasts of marble, felsic gneiss, mica schist, amphibolite, quartzite, and volcanic rocks are also present in the conglomerates, but this report will concentrate on the granitic debris. The granitic clasts range from white alaskite to quartz diorite with 15 to 20 percent dark minerals and from fine- to coarse-grained varieties. Quartz is generally abundant, plagioclase is oligoclase to andesine, biotite is yellow and brown, and green hornblende commonly is intensely altered. These clasts form a rather prosaic suite of granitic rocks ranging from quartz monzonite to quartz diorite.

The northernmost locality, near Black Point (fig. 1), is part of Wentworth's (1968) strata of Stewarts Point of Cretaceous age, whereas the other three localities to the south are part of his strata of German Rancho of Paleocene and Eocene age. Although only a limited number of samples were studied, the same range of rock types and compositions is found in both age groups. The limited modal data plotted on figure 2, however, suggest that the Cretaceous strata may have a higher percentage of felsic rock types.

Clasts from both the Cretaceous and the Paleocene and Eocene strata define a somewhat linear, nearly horizontal modal field (fig. 2), showing that the quartz content is relatively constant throughout the compositional range. Another diagnostic feature of these clasts is the rarity or complete absence of metallic opaque minerals even in rocks containing as much as 15 percent biotite and hornblende. Several percent of garnet was found in some clasts.

CONGLOMERATE CLASTS FROM THE PLAGIOCLASE ARKOSE

Two of the best exposures of the conglomeratic layers in the plagioclase arkose, the Anchor Bay and Sea Ranch Stable localities (fig. 1), were extensively sampled. The clasts are dominantly fine- to medium-grained gabbro and diorite, fine-grained diabase, and quartz-bearing mafic volcanic rock. The absence of K-feldspar in most specimens, even some that are relatively light colored and rich in quartz, is characteristic. Olivine-bearing ultramafic clasts are present but extremely rare. Some of the gabbroic rocks are gneissic, but metamorphic clasts appear to be lacking. The modal plot (fig. 2) is mostly of quartz diorite and gabbro specimens, with minor representation of diabase. Additional diabase and mafic volcanic specimens would not markedly alter the modal field but would add points on the plagioclase-quartz tieline in the range of 0 to 20 percent quartz.

The most abundant clast type, and consequently the most extensively sampled, at both the Anchor Bay and Sea Ranch Stable localities is quartz diorite-quartz gabbro, which ranges from fine to medium grained; coarse-grained types are also present but rare. Dark-mineral content, and hence color, varies considerably, but more of these rocks look like average diorite and gabbro, even though many contain abundant quartz. The complete absence of K-feldspar is particularly surprising in the lighter colored clasts, some of which have rather large masses of quartz. Plagioclase is in the andesine-labradorite range and is in part intensely altered. The dark minerals, which range from 10 to 40 percent, consist dominantly of hornblende, with lesser biotite, and minor clinopyroxene as cores of some hornblende. Fresh biotite is rare in these rocks, but a few traces of unchloritized reddish-brown biotite remain. Hornblende is also intensely altered, but most rocks preserve a little relatively fresh hornblende that is pleochroic from moderate greenish yellow to light olive and grayish green.

Clasts of medium- to coarse-grained gabbro rich in amphibole and clinopyroxene that have well-developed bladed plagioclase crystals are abundant at the Sea Ranch Stable locality but are virtually absent in the Anchor Bay area. These rocks are in part diabasic and grade to coarser anorthositic gabbro. Plagioclase is as calcic as bytownite in some of these specimens.

Finer grained rocks with typical diabasic texture are also present. These rocks are in part quartz bearing, seem to have about the same composition as the gabbros, and may be gradational in grain size with the gabbros. Some contain both clinopyroxene and amphibole, others only amphibole. The most distinctive feature of these rather prosaic dark diabases is that some contain 10 percent of quartz or more.

Another locally abundant rock type is a dense, dark-gray rock with a pilotaxitic mat of plagioclase laths as much as 1 mm long set in a groundmass of amphibole, chlorite, epidote, and some interstitial quartz. Varieties of these volcanic rocks also have small quartz phenocrysts as large as 1 mm across as well as plagioclase and amphibole phenocrysts of about the same size. The variety of gabbroic rocks suggests that there are all gradations from these dense pilotaxitic volcanic types, through diabasic types, to medium- to coarse-grained anorthositic gabbro of possible cumulate origin.

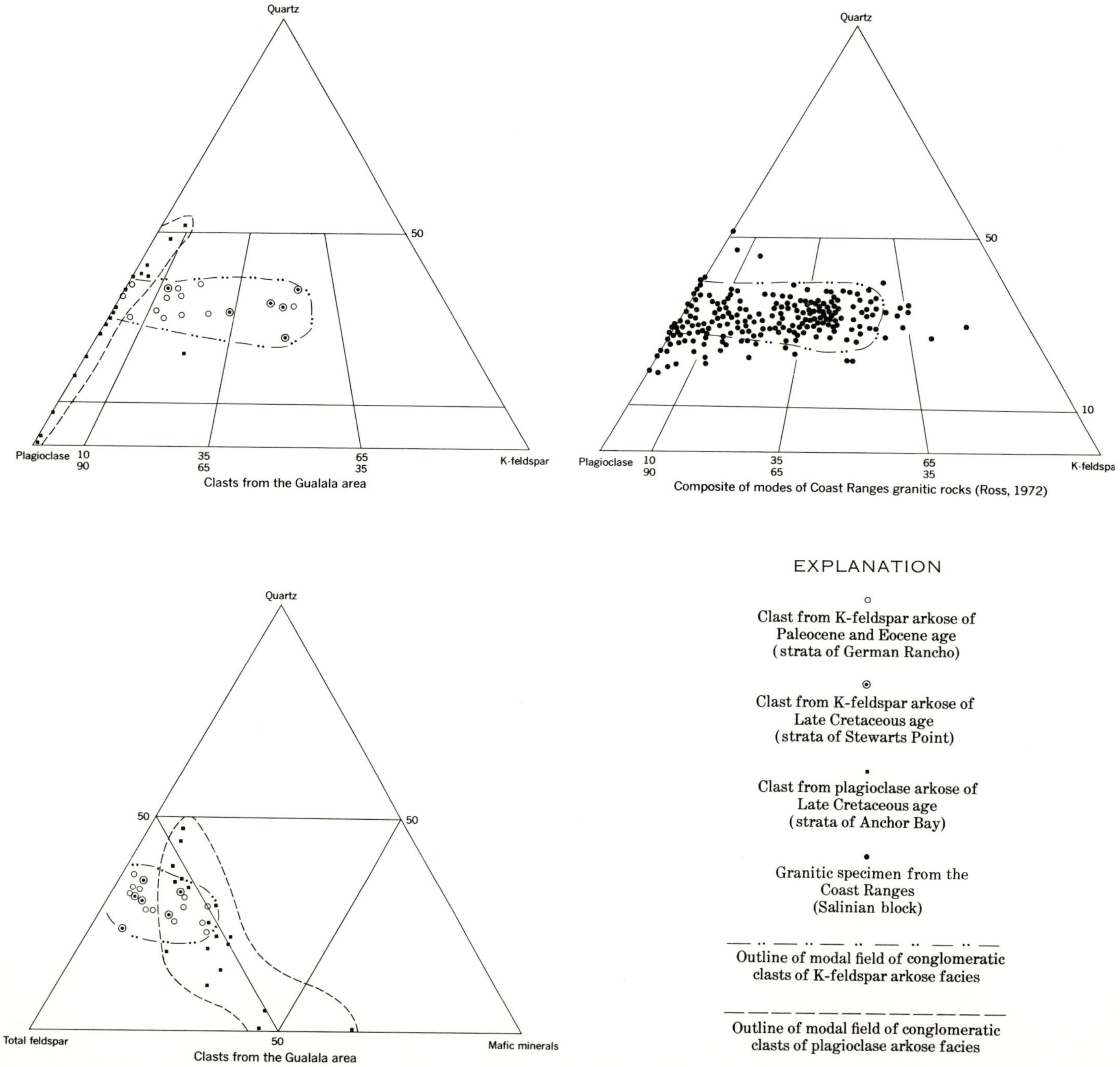

Figure 2.—Modal plots of conglomerate clasts from the Gualala area and of granitic rocks in the California Coast Ranges.

SOURCE OF THE CONGLOMERATE CLASTS IN THE K-FELDSPAR ARKOSE

The basement terrane that supplied the K-feldspar arkose and associated conglomerate must have had an abundance of relatively quartz-rich granitic rocks ranging from quartz monzonite to quartz diorite. In addition, significant amounts of calcareous, micaceous, and siliceous metamorphic rocks were present, and mafic plutonic rocks were rare. Such conditions are easily satisfied throughout much of the Cordilleran batholithic belt, but the nearest and most obvious source area is the Salinian block of the California Coast Ranges. The general basement rock types in the Salinian block (Ross, 1972) are similar to those in the clasts of the K-feldspar arkose facies. More specifically, as shown by figure 2, the modal field of the conglomerate clasts bears a close correspondence to the composite plot of modes for specimens from the granitic rocks of the Salinian block. The Salinian modal trend is unusual because it is more horizontal than the modal trend of most other granitic suites in the Cordilleran batholithic belt (Ross, 1972), which strengthens the case for correlation.

The physical and petrographic qualifications of the Salinian block as a source for the conglomerate clasts of the K-feldspar arkose facies are convincing. Coupled with this is the paleocurrent evidence that the K-feldspar arkose material was derived from southwest of the Gualala basin. In addition, a K/Ar age of 82±3 m.y. (table 1) was obtained from hornblende separated from a clast at the Ocean Cove locality (fig. 1). This age lies within the 70- to 90-m.y. determinations that have been made on numerous biotites and hornblendes from the Salinian block of the California Coast Ranges (Curtis and others, 1958; Evernden and Kistler, 1970; Huffman, 1970). Together, these factors strongly indicate that the Salinian block granitic terrane is the source for the K-feldspar arkose and associated granitic conglomerate.

SOURCE OF THE CONGLOMERATE CLASTS IN THE PLAGIOCLASE ARKOSE

The basement source that supplied the sediment for the plagioclase arkose and mafic conglomerate was rich in gabbro, diorite, diabase, and dark volcanic rocks, all characterized by the common presence of quartz, and was virtually devoid of K-feldspar-bearing rocks. The sediment must have been derived from a terrane virtually free of granitic rocks, for any granitic rock present would have been concentrated to some degree in the weathering cycle at the expense of the less stable gabbroic rocks (Goldich, 1938). Such a quartz-bearing mafic terrane is not easy to locate in the region—in fact, no such basement terrane large enough to supply cubic miles of gabbroic sedimentary debris now exists anywhere in the western Cordilleran batholithic belt. The difficulty is further compounded by paleocurrents that indicate that the sediments were derived from northeast of the Gualala basin, where the presently exposed basement is the Franciscan Formation, an unsuitable source terrane for the clasts of the plagioclase arkose. As Wentworth pointed out in 1968, the search for a suitable source area should probably focus on the area of the San Emigdio Mountains far to the southeast across the San Andreas fault. Ross later (1970) noted that the bulk of the San Emigdio basement was relatively rich in K-feldspar-bearing granitic rocks, which were not suitable as a source terrane for the gabbroic suite of the plagioclase arkose facies. However, the Eagle Rest Peak area (fig. 1; Ross, 1970, fig. 1), which may be structurally separate from the rest of the San Emigdio basement, contains a suite of gabbro, diabase and hornfels (in part quartz bearing), quartz diorite-quartz gabbro, anorthositic gabbro, minor pyroxenite and serpentine, and virtually no K-feldspar-bearing rock. Though the few square miles of present gabbroic exposures are not large enough to have supplied the cubic miles of plagioclase arkose at Gualala, this may be all that is left of what was originally a much larger

Table 1.—*Hornblende mineral ages*

[Potassium measurements were made on an I. L. flame photometer with a lithium internal standard. Argon measurements were made using standard techniques of isotope dilution. Ages were calculated using these constants: K^{40} decay constants: λ_ϵ = 0.585×10^{-10} year^{-1}; λ_β = 4.72×10^{-10} year^{-1}. Abundance ratio: K^{40}/K = 1.19×10^{-4} atom percent. Analysts: Potassium measurements, Lois Schlocker; argon measurements and age calculation, E. H. McKee, except ABc-4 and DR-1169A by J. C. Von Essen]

Sample	K_2O (percent)	Ar^{40}rad (moles/g$\times10^{-11}$)	Ar^{40}rad / Ar^{40}total	Calculated age (m.y.)
Gualala area:				
Anchor Bay:				
ABc-1	0.207	5.608	0.09	175±8
ABc-4	.098	2.135	.52	141±4
ABi-1	.250	7.20	.54	186±7
Ocean Cove:				
OC-3	.198	1.99	.22	82±3
Eagle Rest Peak area:				
DR-1169A ...	.204	4.202	.55	134±4
DR-1182C ...	.190	4.82	.26	165±6
DR-1189C ...	.107	3.46	.41	207±10

Location and description of samples:

Gualala area:

Anchor Bay: Gualala 7½-minute quadrangle, Mendocino County, Calif., lat 38°48′ N., long 123°35′ W. Clasts from plagioclase arkose facies.

ABc-1, Hornblende quartz diorite-quartz gabbro (andesine-labradorite 49 percent, hornblende 25, quartz 22, biotite 2, opaque minerals 2).

ABc-4, Hornblende quartz gabbro (labradorite 50 percent, hornblende 40, quartz 10, minor biotite, clinopyroxene, and opaque minerals).

ABi-1, Hornblende quartz diabase (andesine 59 percent, hornblende 26, quartz 11, opaque minerals 4).

Ocean Cove: Plantation 7½-minute quadrangle, Sonoma County, Calif., lat 38°33′ N., long 123°19′ W. Clast from K-feldspar arkose facies.

OC-3, Biotite granodiorite (oligoclase(?) 43 percent, K-feldspar 12, quartz 34, biotite 8, pale-green hornblende 3).

Eagle Rest Peak area:

DR-1169A: Eagle Rest Peak 7½-minute quadrangle, Kern County, Calif., lat 34°56′ N., long 119°13′ W. Hornblende-quartz gabbro (labradorite, grayish-green hornblende, quartz, abundant opaque minerals, minor clinopyroxene).

DR-1182C: Santiago Creek 7½-minute quadrangle, Kern County, Calif., lat 34°56′, long 119°15′ W. Hornblende-quartz gabbro (labradorite, grayish-green hornblende, quartz, minor biotite, and opaque minerals).

DR-1189C: Eagle Rest Peak 7½-minute quadrangle, Kern County, Calif., lat 34°56′ N., long 119°14′ W. Hornblende-rich pegmatite composed of andesine, euhedral green hornblende in crystals as long as 20 mm (n_α = 1.636±, n_γ = 1.651±), and quartz. Occurs as dikes or "sweated out" patches in gabbro-pyroxenite suite that is comparable to the anorthositic gabbro at Gold Hill and Logan (Ross, 1970).

gabbroic terrane, because the Eagle Rest Peak area abuts against the San Andreas fault. Added to this tantalizing possible correlation are similar gabbroic blocks at Gold Hill and Logan (fig. 1) that seem to be slivers of this basement terrane strewn out along the San Andreas fault.

In appearance and petrography, the anorthositic gabbro at Eagle Rest Peak is strikingly similar to the bladed coarse anorthositic gabbro of the Sea Ranch Stable locality. Also, the presence in both areas of similar quartz diorite-quartz gabbro is noteworthy. In addition, fine-grained dark diabasic rocks and finer grained volcanic varieties are common to both the Gualala and Eagle Rest Peak areas.

Ross (1970, p. 3656), postulated, largely on the basis of earlier work by Hammond (1958), that the Eagle Rest Peak area was a remnant of a pile of volcanic and diabasic rocks intruded by a gabbro-pyroxenite sequence, which in turn was intruded by a quartz diorite-quartz gabbro mass. Such an assemblage would furnish a suitable source terrane for the clasts of the plagioclase arkose and mafic conglomerate of Gualala. Though the percentage of conglomerate clasts of the various rock types has not been determined in the plagioclase arkose facies of Gualala, the dominant rock types are probably gabbro, quartz diorite-quartz gabbro, diabase, and volcanic rocks; one ultramafic clast was found.

To test further the compatibility of the Eagle Rest Peak and Gualala terranes, K/Ar determinations were made on several hornblendes from both terranes (table 1). Figure 3 summarizes these data from the clasts of the plagioclase arkose facies of the Gualala area and the possible parent area of Eagle Rest Peak, and from previously published hornblende ages on similar rocks that may be fault slivers caught between Gualala and Eagle Rest Peak (Ross, 1970). The age range is wide but grossly similar in both terranes. Although these sparse data by no means prove that the Eagle Rest Peak area is the source area for the Gualala clasts, they at least permit that possibility. Hornblende ages from the hornblende quartz gabbro of both areas seem to group at about 135 to 140 m.y. and about 165 to 175 m.y. The diabase clast from Gualala and the gabbro pegmatite from Eagle Rest Peak give expectably older, somewhat comparable hornblende ages. Virtually the same range of ages was found in both areas.

It is interesting to speculate on the meaning of the rather wide range of hornblende ages from these terranes (fig. 3), which we would have expected to have a much more restricted age range. Two distinct ages of hornblende quartz gabbro are at least suggested by the radiometric data, and the Eagle Rest Peak basement would permit two such ages; the two dated localities are separated by a fault but are only 2 miles apart and are petrographically similar. Furthermore, the possible intermediate slivers (Ross, 1970) at Gold Hill and Logan bridge the time gap between the two Eagle Rest Peak specimens. However, in such a spread of ages in what looks like a related suite of similar rocks, the younger ages may reflect argon loss. The intrusive age of the hornblende quartz gabbro is more likely somewhere in the range of 165 to 175 m.y., or even older.

The hornblende determinations from a diabase clast and gabbro pegmatite in the range of 180 to 220 m.y. push the possible age of these gabbroic terranes down into the very earliest Jurrassic or even into the Triassic. Whatever the true age and range of ages of these gabbroic terranes, we can at least say that a similar range of ages at both Eagle Rest Peak and Gualala supports the view that these two terranes could be related. Furthermore, this range of ages is distinctly different from anything in the Salinian block or in the "Sierran basement" of the Transverse Ranges. The only other somewhat comparable ages from plutonic rocks in this region are from gabbros in the California Coast Ranges that Lanphere (1971, p. 3211) has dated as about 155 m.y. (fig. 3).

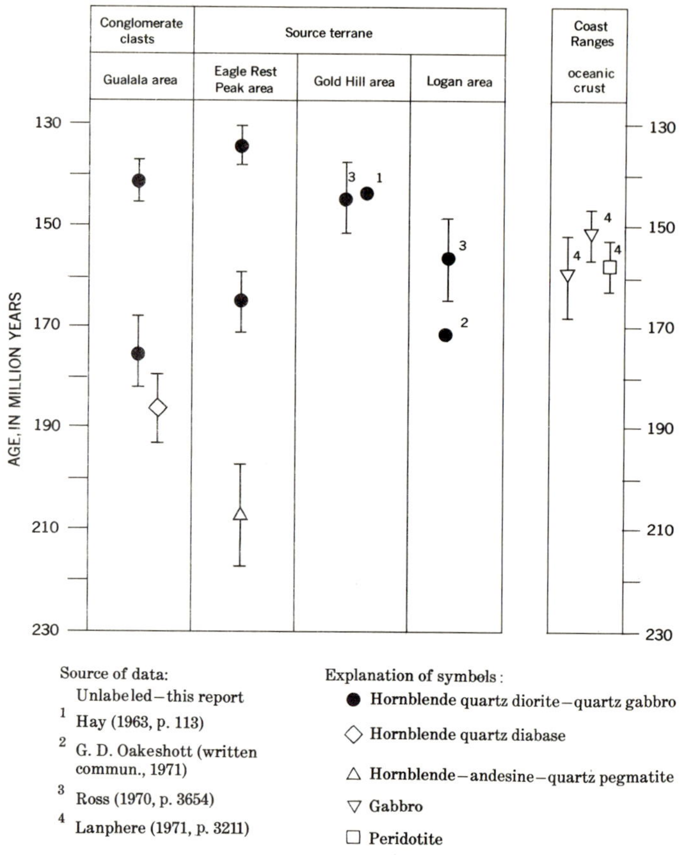

Figure 3.–Comparison of K/Ar ages of hornblendes from conglomerate clasts of the Gualala area, granitic rocks of the Eagle Rest Peak, Gold Hill, and Logan areas, and oceanic crust in the California Coast Ranges.

OCEANIC CRUSTAL ORIGIN OF THE GABBROIC ROCKS AND CLASTS

The gabbroic and related clasts in the conglomerates of the plagioclase arkose in the Gualala area require a very special and unusual source terrane. The rarity of granitic and metamorphic debris in these conglomerates rules out virtually any present-day basement exposures as a source of the more than 20 cu mi of plagioclase arkose and conglomerate (Wentworth, 1968, p. 136). The gabbroic and related rocks at Eagle Rest Peak are a petrographically suitable source, but what we see now is only a small remnant of a terrane large enough to father the observed sedimentary product. Wentworth (1968, p. 36) suggested that the source terrane could have been several hundred square miles in area, as the minimum volume of the Gualala plagioclase arkose and conglomerate would cover an area of 100,000 sq mi to a depth of 1 foot.

The type of terrane that best qualifies as a source for the Gualala mafic debris is ophiolitic oceanic crust. Ross (1970, p. 3660) has already speculated that the Eagle Rest Peak locality might be a remnant of ophiolitic oceanic crust. The quartz-bearing gabbro-diabase-volcanic assemblage with minor ultramafic rocks, both at Gualala and Eagle Rest Peak, is compatible with the rock types in ophiolitic oceanic crust as described from various localities in California by Bailey, Blake, and Jones (1970). The K/Ar ages on hornblendes from the gabbroic rocks of Gualala and Eagle Rest Peak are also grossly compatible with K/Ar ages determined by Lanphere (1971, p. 3211) from gabbros from suspected oceanic crust in the California Coast Ranges (fig. 3). The major obstacles to such an identity are the paucity of ultramafic rocks or serpentine and the absence of chert in both the Gualala and Eagle Rest Peak areas. The absence or rarity of some of the members of the common ophiolitic suite at Eagle Rest Peak can be accounted for by assuming that a somewhat nonrepresentative sample of oceanic crust is preserved in the rather limited area now exposed. But this argument is not sufficient to account for the absence of these rocks at Gualala, where many cubic miles of sedimentary debris attest to a large mafic source area.

The lack of chert in the Gualala beds may not pose a serious problem. Though chert is considered one of the "trinity" in the ophiolite suite along with serpentinite and pillow lava, Maxwell (1969, p. 489) noted that it is not everywhere present. Bailey, Blake, and Jones (1970, p. C73) in ten columnar sections of ophiolitic successions in the California Coast Ranges showed no chert in five of the sections. Thus it seems reasonable that chert could be missing from rather wide terranes of oceanic crust, and therefore its absence at Gualala does not preclude derivation of the plagioclase arkose from an oceanic crustal source.

The general absence of ultramafic rock or serpentine clasts in the conglomerates could have resulted from weathering and disaggregation of such rocks in the source area, rather than from their absence there, although the disposition of any resultant finer serpentine sediment is unknown at present. Maxwell (1969, p. 490), in a review of ophiolitic sequences, noted that ultramafic rocks make up 65 to 85 percent of the Tethyan ophiolitic sequences. If this percentage is representative of ophiolitic oceanic crustal sequences, then one might expect considerable ultramafic debris in the Gualala beds if they were derived from an ophiolitic sequence. However, in the suspected ophiolite sequences in the California Coast Ranges that might be expected to represent the kind of terrane that furnished the Gualala debris, Bailey, Blake, and Jones (1970) noted that much of the ultramafic part of the sequence is serpentinized. Such rocks might not survive to become well-rounded clasts in the relatively mature Gualala conglomerates.

The rarity of ultramafic clasts may also be due to their selective alteration and dissaggregation in the weathering and transportation processes attendant to the production of the Gualala conglomerates. The stability series of Goldich (1938) shows that the susceptibility to weathering of the dark-minerals series olivine-pyroxene-amphibole-biotite parallels their order of crystallization in the well-known Bowen reaction series. Thus olivine and pyroxene are highly susceptible to weathering and are less stable than amphibole or biotite. As the biotite and hornblende are almost universally highly altered in the Gualala clasts—at least in part owing to weathering—we consider clasts rich in olivine and pyroxene less likely to survive, even though they may have been abundant in the source area.

It seems reasonable that from a chert-poor ophiolitic sequence, gabbro, quartz gabbro-quartz diorite, diabase, and dense crystallized volcanic rocks (those with little or no glass) could be concentrated in a relatively mature conglomerate. Even though the fit is far from perfect, and regardless of the presence or absence of ultramafic rocks or serpentine in the source area, oceanic crust seems to be the most plausible source for these gabbroic terranes. It is virtually impossible to find a gabbroic continental basement area lacking granitic rocks along the western margin of North America that is large enough to supply the mafic debris of the Gualala area.

SUMMARY AND CONCLUSIONS

Mafic conglomerate and quartz-plagioclase arkose of Late Cretaceous age near Gualala, Calif., may well have been eroded from a gabbroic oceanic crustal terrane that is now offset about 350 miles southeastward from Gualala by the intervening San Andreas fault. This tentative conclusion has resulted from study of basement rocks along the San Andreas fault by Ross (1970, 1972) and study of the Cretaceous and Tertiary sedimentary rocks near Gualala by Wentworth (1966, 1968), in the context of abundant evidence of large right-lateral slip on the San Andreas fault. The character of the Gualala conglomerates is thus a possible key to a Late Cretaceous tie across the San Andreas fault.

Two distinct clastic lithologies near Gualala, one consisting of quartz-plagioclase arkose with mafic conglomerate and one of quartz–K-feldspar–plagioclase arkose with granitic conglomerate, are inferred from paleocurrent indicators to have been derived from opposite sides of a northwest-trending depositional basin. The Salinian granitic terrane southwest of the Gualala rocks seems an adequate source for the K-feldspar arkose facies. But the apparent lack of an adequate source for the plagioclase arkose facies in the Franciscan terrane northeast of and across the San Andreas fault from the Gualala rocks led Wentworth (1968) to suggest right-lateral offset of the source to at least southeast of the Diablo Range (270 miles). Possible spilitic basement with Franciscan affinities beneath granitic sediment derived from the south and west further led him to suggest offset of the Gualala block from an original position near the presumed intersection of the San Andreas fault and the Sierran-Franciscan basement contact 350 miles to the southeast along the fault. This evidence in turn suggests a source for the mafic conglomerate near the west end of the San Emigdio Mountains.

Ross (1970) concluded that two very similar bodies of quartz gabbro and anorthositic gabbro located about 100 miles apart along the San Andreas fault at Gold Hill and Logan probably were once part of a single gabbroic terrane. Similar rocks in a small gabbroic terrane 100 miles farther to the southeast at the west end of the San Emigdio Mountains near Eagle Rest Peak suggest that the Gold Hill and Logan bodies have been sliced by the San Andreas fault from a once larger gabbroic terrane there.

The mafic Gualala conglomerates contain clasts of the distinctive anorthositic gabbro common to the three localities mentioned above, as well as quartz diorite-quartz gabbro and dark, dense, fine-grained volcanic and diabasic rocks similar to rocks in the Eagle Rest Peak terrane. We conclude that a large area of oceanic crustal material exposed near Eagle Rest Peak in Late Cretaceous time may have yielded the gabbroic sediment rich in quartz and lacking K-feldspar that formed the plagioclase arkose of the Gualala section. Subsequent right-lateral slip on the San Andreas fault then carried the sediment about 350 miles away from the source and also carried two slices of the gabbroic basement terrane to their present intermediate positions at Gold Hill and Logan.

REFERENCES CITED

Bailey, E. H., Blake, M. C., Jr., and Jones, D. L., 1970, On-land Mesozoic oceanic crust in California Coast Ranges, *in* Geological Survey Research 1970: U.S. Geol. Survey Prof. Paper 700-C, p. C70–C81.

Curtis, G. H., Evernden, J. F., and Lipson, J., 1958, Age determinations of some granitic rocks in California by the potassium-argon method: California Div. Mines Spec. Rept. 54, 16 p.

Evernden, J. F., and Kistler, R. W., 1970, Chronology of emplacement of Mesozoic batholithic complexes in California and western Nevada: U.S. Geol. Survey Prof. Paper 623, 42 p.

Goldich, S. S., 1938, A study in rock-weathering: Jour. Geology, v. 46, p. 17–58.

Hammond, P. E., 1958, Geology of the lower Santiago Creek area, San Emigdio Mountains, Kern County, California: California Univ., Los Angeles, unpub. M.S. thesis, 108 p.

Hay, E. A., 1963, Age and relationships of the Gold Hill pluton, Cholame Valley, California, *in* Geology of Salinas Valley and the San Andreas fault: Am. Assoc. Petroleum Geologists, Pacific Sec. Guidebook, p. 113–115.

Huffman, O. F., 1970, Miocene and post-Miocene offset on the San Andreas fault in central California: Geol. Soc. America Abs. with Programs, v. 2, no. 2, p. 104–105.

Lanphere, Marvin, 1971, Age of Mesozoic oceanic crust in the California Coast Ranges: Geol. Soc. America Bull., v. 82, no. 11, p. 3209–3212.

Maxwell, J. C., 1969, "Alpine" mafic and ultramafic rocks—The ophiolite suite: A contribution to the discussion of the paper, "The origin of ultramafic and ultrabasic rocks" by P. J. Wylie: Tectonophysics, p. 489–494.

Ross, D. C., 1970, Quartz gabbro and anorthositic gabbro-markers of offset along the San Andreas fault in the California Coast Ranges: Geol. Soc. America Bull., v. 81, p. 3647–3662.

—— 1972, Petrographic and chemical reconnaissance of some granitic and gneissic rocks near the San Andreas fault from Bodega Head to Cajon Pass, California: U.S. Geol. Survey Prof. Paper 698, 93 p.

Wentworth, C. M., Jr., 1966, The Upper Cretaceous and lower Tertiary rocks of the Gualala area, northern Coast Ranges, California: Stanford Univ., unpub. Ph. D. thesis, 197 p.

—— 1968, Upper Cretaceous and lower Tertiary strata near Gualala, California, and inferred large right lateral slip on the San Andreas fault: Stanford Univ. Pubs. Geol. Sci., v. 11, p. 130–143.

Jour. Research U.S. Geol. Survey
Vol. 1, No. 1, Jan.—Feb. 1973, p. 53—61

BLUESCHIST METAMORPHISM IN THE YREKA—FORT JONES AREA, KLAMATH MOUNTAINS, CALIFORNIA

By PRESTON E. HOTZ, Menlo Park, Calif.

Abstract.—Blueschist is plentiful in the Yreka—Fort Jones area, eastern Klamath Mountains, adjacent to a belt of serpentinite that marks the boundary between two fundamental lithologic units, an eastern belt of early Paleozoic sedimentary and metamorphic rocks, and a western greenstone-chert assemblage of late Paleozoic and Triassic(?) age. The blueschists, which contain lawsonite and glaucophane or crossite, occur with phyllitic quartzite and siliceous phyllite of the Stuart Fork Formation, which is overthrust northwestward on the greenstone-chert terrane. The blueschist facies metamorphism probably was synchronous with Middle and Late Jurassic metamorphism of the Stuart Fork Formation. The blueschist-serpentinite terrane possibly marks the site of collision between the eastern Klamath plate and an oceanic western Paleozoic and Triassic plate.

Although blueschist facies metamorphic rocks occur at many places adjacent to the Klamath Mountains in the Coast Ranges of northern California and southwestern Oregon (Blake and others, 1967; Blake, 1969; Coleman and Lanphere, 1971), they are unusual within the Klamath Mountains province. They were first reported in this province by Masson (1949), who discovered an outcrop of glaucophane-lawsonite rock north of Fort Jones in Siskiyou County, Calif. Recent mapping by the writer in the Hornbrook, Yreka, and Fort Jones 15-minute quadrangles has shown that blueschist is plentiful in this region. Blueschist and ultramafic rock occur near the boundary between two distinctive lithologic belts: the western Paleozoic and Triassic belt and the eastern Klamath belt, as defined by Irwin (1960, 1966). The former, lying to the northwest, comprises a greenstone-chert assemblage; the latter, to the southeast, Paleozoic sedimentary and metamorphic rocks. (See fig. 1.)

The only other occurrences of blueschist that have been found in the Klamath Mountains are south of Cecilville, Calif. (Davis, 1968) (fig. 2), and an isolated occurrence in the southern part of the Helena quadrangle (Cox, 1956).

GEOLOGIC SETTING

In the Yreka—Fort Jones area a belt of ultramafic rocks as much as 2½ miles wide trends northeast-southwest and separates the western Paleozoic and Triassic belt from the eastern Klamath belt. At its northeast end it narrows to a few feet and is overlapped by Upper Cretaceous sedimentary rocks. It extends southward beyond the area of figure 1 and apparently is continuous with a large ultramafic body in the southeastern Klamath Mountains (fig. 2). The ultramafic rocks have not been studied in detail, but at most places they are highly sheared serpentinites. In some places where they are less sheared, harzburgite and dunite can be recognized. Minor amounts of fine-grained gabbro are associated with the serpentinite.

The serpentinite is bordered on its east side by a narrow belt of fine-grained epidote amphibolite. Southward the serpentinite interfingers with amphibolite and schistose micaceous marble. The ages of the amphibolite and marble are unknown, but these rocks are lithologically similar to the Salmon Hornblende Schist and Abrams Mica Schist of the southern Klamath Mountains, whose metamorphic age is Devonian (Lanphere and others, 1968). A thrust fault separates the amphibolite from sedimentary rocks of the Duzel and Gazell Formations which include phyllitic calcareous siltstone, calcareous quartz wacke, quartzite (quartz arenite), recrystallized chert, and lenticular bodies of marble. These sedimentary rocks are part of a northeast-trending oblong belt more than 30 miles long and 12 miles wide that contains the only known Ordovician and Silurian strata in the Klamath Mountains (Churkin and Langenheim, 1960; Churkin, 1965; Potter and Boucot, 1971; Wells and others, 1959; Zdanowicz, 1971).

West of the serpentinite are rocks of the western Paleozoic and Triassic belt, including a belt of highly deformed phyllitic quartzite and siliceous phyllite and closely associated blueschist facies rocks thrust over a greenstone-chert assemblage. The siliceous rocks lithologically resemble the Stuart Fork Formation of the southern Klamath Mountains (Davis and Lipman, 1962), which Davis (1968) regards as a metamorphic equivalent of the western Paleozoic and Triassic belt. Meager paleontologic data indicate that rocks in this subprovince range from late Paleozoic to Late Triassic. Northeast of Yreka a limestone lens in the greenstone-chert assemblage has yielded Late Permian (Ochoan) fossils (Elliott, 1971, p. 13).

Stuart Fork Formation

The Stuart Fork Formation was named by Davis and Lipman (1962, p. 1548) for excellent exposures along the

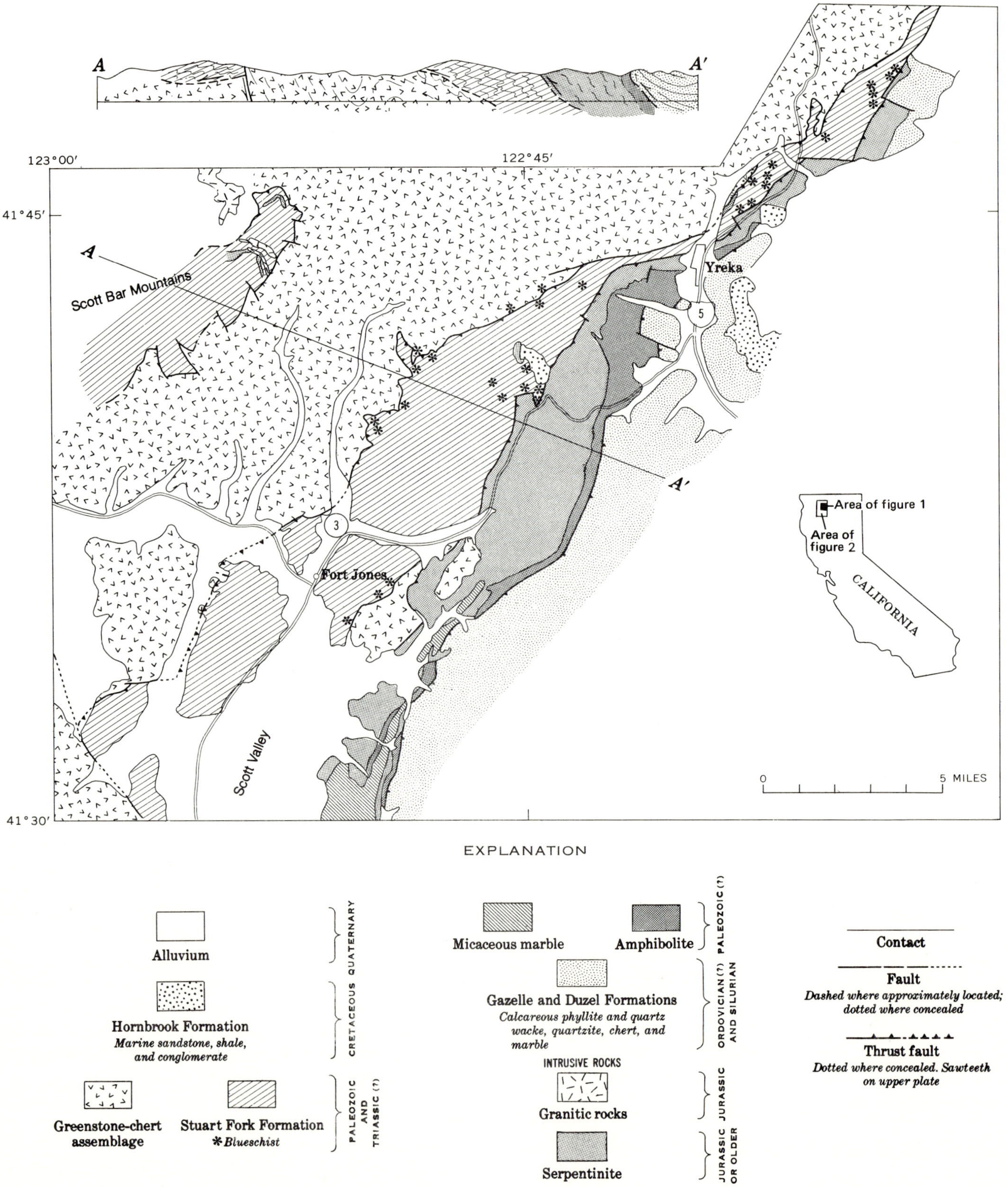

Figure 1.—Geologic map of the Yreka–Fort Jones area, California, and cross section along line *A–A′*.

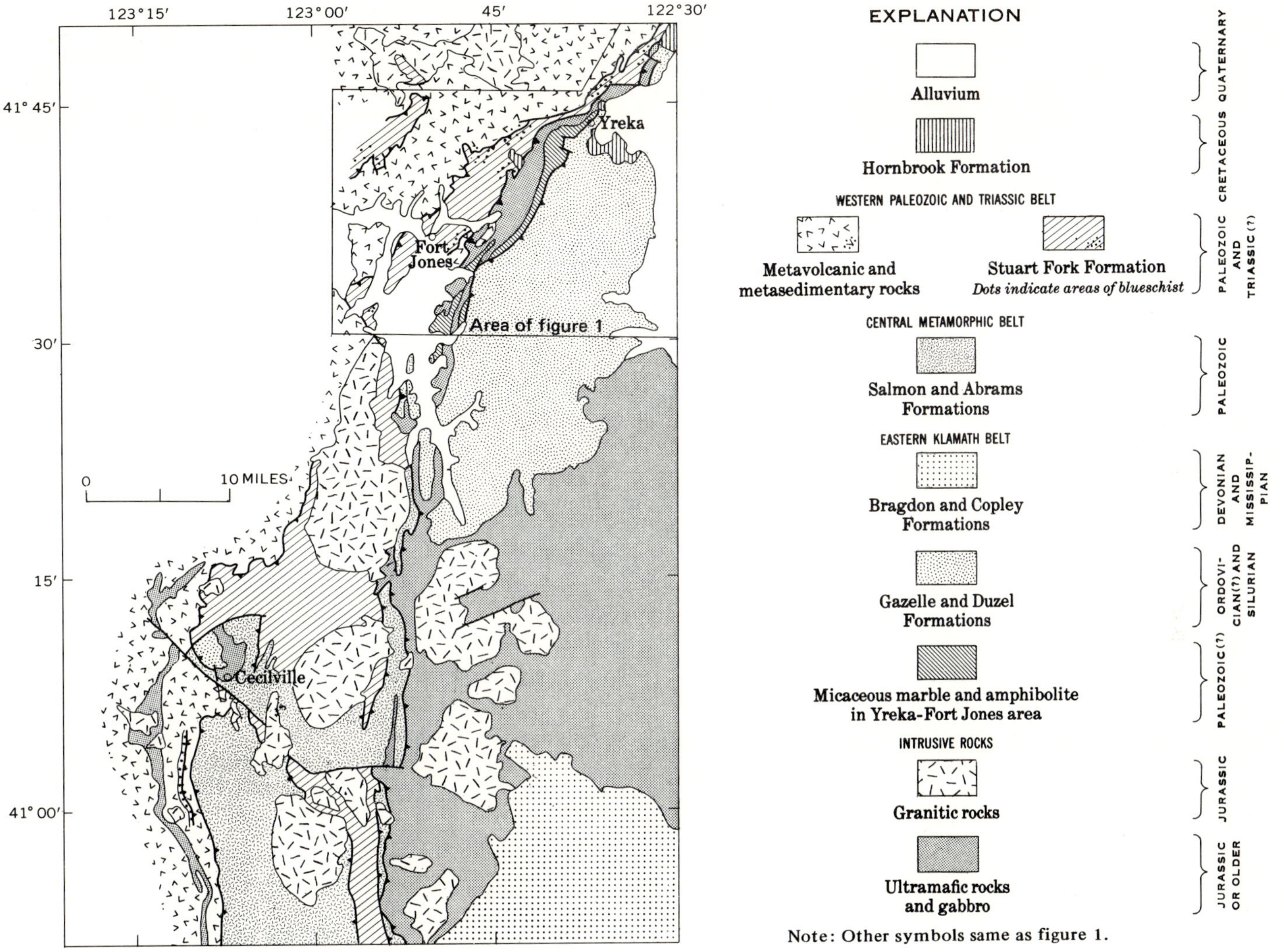

Figure 2.—Geologic map of the east-central Klamath Mountains, Calif.

Stuart Fork of the Trinity River between Deep and Van Matre Creek tributaries. In the Yreka–Fort Jones area the Stuart Fork Formation is composed predominantly of phyllitic quartzite. This rock is mainly light colored, thinly layered, and complexly deformed, even on a microscopic scale. The layering is conspicuous but is commonly discontinuous and extensively disrupted by close folding and transposition. Layers of fine-grained crystalloblastic quartz 1 to 5 mm thick alternate with micaceous lamellae composed of white mica and pale-green chlorite. A distinctive variety of phyllitic quartzite that is plentiful in the vicinity of Fort Jones has a pale-reddish coloration on cleavage surfaces owing to an abundance of microscopic hematite in the micaceous laminae.

Coarsely crystalline marble in small lenticular bodies constitutes an uncommon rock type in the Stuart Fork of this area.

Greenstone-chert assemblage

Metavolcanic rocks of basaltic composition predominate in the greenstone-chert assemblage. They are mainly massive, fine-grained flow rocks, but locally they show pillow structure. Breccias and agglomerates as well as vesicular and amygdaloidal metavolcanic rocks are less common varieties. Calcium carbonate commonly occurs in interstices as cavity fillings and as matrix material. Dike- and sill-like bodies of fine-grained diabase are recognizable in some places.

Original structures and textures of the metavolcanic rocks generally are well preserved. Common mineral phases are albite to sodic oligoclase + chlorite + actinolite + sphene ± calcite ± clinozoisite ± magnetite ± quartz, an assemblage characteristic of the greenschist metamorphic facies. Some specimens contain the assemblage albite + chlorite + unaltered clinopyroxene (augite), plus accessory epidote, sphene, calcite, and opaque minerals. The association of fresh clinopyroxene with albite and chlorite is typical of spilite.

Sedimentary rocks interbedded with the metavolcanic rocks range from thin beds a few feet thick to units several hundred feet thick that contain minor amounts of intercalated volcanic rock. Most of the sedimentary rock is very fine grained black argillite, slaty argillite, and phyllite. Chert is very common and includes both the rhythmically bedded variety and the massive, poorly bedded type. The cherts are recrystallized to fine-grained quartzite. Other sedimentary rocks include minor amounts of fine-grained graywacke and occasional discontinuous, commonly lenticular bodies of marble.

DISTRIBUTION AND MODE OF OCCURRENCE OF THE BLUESCHIST

Blueschist of the Yreka–Fort Jones area is restricted to the Stuart Fork Formation, except for a few occurrences in rocks of the greenstone-chert assemblage very close to the contact with the Stuart Fork (fig. 1). All exposures found thus far have been close to either the contact with the serpentinite body or the contact of the Stuart Fork with the underlying greenstone-chert assemblage; however, this distribution may be more apparent than real, because most field traverses were near these contacts. The correlation between occurrences of blueschist and distribution of the Stuart Fork Formation is emphasized by the presence of blueschist minerals in a faulted outlier of the Stuart Fork in the Scott Bar Mountains, and their absence in the area between the outlier and the main Yreka–Fort Jones belt.

The blueschist occurs as isolated bodies that range in size from as much as 10 feet in many exposures to a few which may be 1,000 feet or more in length and several hundred feet in width. In some exposures, foliated blueschist is interlayered with fine-grained crossite-bearing quartzite and siliceous mica schist. Many schist bodies are ellipsoidal masses surrounded by siliceous schist, and one is enclosed by marble.

PETROGRAPHY OF THE BLUESCHIST

Blueschist in the Yreka–Fort Jones area contains the diagnostic metamorphic mineral assemblage lawsonite plus blue sodic amphibole. Common accessory minerals are white mica and sphene. Other accessory minerals, present in some rocks but not in others, are stilpnomelane, jadeite, aegerine, quartz, albite, pumpellyite, garnet, calcium carbonate, and chlorite. The blueschist formed from both basaltic and sedimentary rocks (table 1), with metabasalts apparently more common than metasedimentary varieties.

Metabasaltic rocks

The metabasalts commonly are very fine grained, hard, and massive, although some are phyllitic or schistose. Commonly, original structures and textures are obliterated by recrystallization, but in some thin sections faint relics of an ophitic or diabasic texture are visible. The specific gravity of these rocks ranges from 2.91 to 3.14; the average of 19 measurements is 3.08.

Glaucophane is plentiful in the metabasalts and is predominant in some. It is commonly very finely fibrous and may form a "mat" in which the other minerals occur, although in many specimens the fibers have a distinct parallelism.

Lawsonite commonly occurs as subhedral to strongly euhedral stubby prisms which may be scattered through a mat of glaucophane, or as crystals in glaucophane-lawsonite laminae with the glaucophane fibers wrapping around the lawsonite crystals (fig. 3*A*). In some specimens monomineralic folia and lenses of lawsonite alternate with layers in which glaucophane predominates (fig. 3*B*). Uncommonly, in some unsheared nonfoliated specimens, lawsonite is pseudomorphic after original plagioclase laths.

Sphene is a ubiquitous accessory mineral. It occurs as scattered anhedral grains and clusters and trains of granules. Commonly it is partly altered to a gray, opaque substance, presumably leucoxene.

Minor amounts of white mica are usually present in these rocks, as well as a little quartz. Small amounts of chlorite and stilpnomelane are also present. X-ray patterns of whole-rock powders indicate that some samples contain small quantities of albite, although none was positively identified under the microscope.

Jadeitic pyroxene was recognized in a few thin sections, but it is not a common constituent of blueschists in the Yreka–Fort Jones area. Where present it is a plentiful accessory, occurring as colorless to pale-brown anhedral, commonly radiating, masses. Some metabasalts contain a green pyroxene identified as aegerine from its optical properties and X-ray pattern (fig. 3*C*).

Pumpellyite was found in only a few thin sections.

Calcium carbonate is not abundant, but small amounts occur in some specimens. X-ray data indicate that it is calcite, not the aragonite which is commonly reported from blueschist terranes.

Pyrite is a common minor constituent, although there seldom is more than a percent or so. Magnetite, ilmenite, and hematite appear to be absent, a fact noted by Coleman and Lee at Cazadero, Calif. (1963, p. 275), and attributed to a relatively high sulfur fugacity for the metamorphic environment.

In figure 4 the analyzed metabasaltic rocks of table 1 are plotted in an Alk-F-M diagram and compared with analyzed metavolcanic rocks from the greenstone-chert assemblage of the Condrey Mountain and Hornbrook quadrangles. The similarity in composition is apparent.

Metasedimentary rocks

Siliceous metasedimentary rocks containing lawsonite and a sodic amphibole are less plentiful than the metabasaltic blueschist facies rocks. Probably they originally were impure quartzites or graywackes (table 1), for composition of relatively pure quartzite and chert is not suitable for formation of lawsonite. The specific gravity of eight samples was measured; it averaged 2.71.

Table 1.—*Chemical, semiquantitative spectrographic, and modal analyses of blueschist facies rocks*

[Tr., trace]

	Metabasalt						Metasedimentary rocks		
	FJ-4-66	FJ-3C-67	H-1-69	H-7-71	Y-3-65	Y-37-71	FJ-3B-67	H-6-71	Y-2-65
Chemical analyses[1] (weight percent)									
SiO_2	48.7	48.7	49.1	47.4	47.5	51.4	89.7	83.7	85.9
Al_2O_3	17.0	14.2	15.6	17.4	13.9	16.5	2.2	6.6	4.0
Fe_2O_3	1.6	3.8	3.6	4.8	5.8	2.3	2.1	1.2	1.6
FeO	6.8	7.3	8.0	5.9	6.5	6.9	.92	1.3	2.1
MgO	7.7	6.5	4.7	4.6	6.2	6.1	.89	1.3	1.4
CaO	5.6	9.0	7.5	8.3	9.3	6.5	.99	1.6	1.6
Na_2O	2.8	2.3	4.0	3.3	2.3	4.2	.78	.46	1.1
K_2O	.54	.18	.29	.15	.51	.11	.22	1.3	.23
H_2O+	5.9	5.6	4.4	6.0	5.7	4.1	.85	1.9	1.3
H_2O-	.32	.14	.08	.20	.32	.07	.02	.05	.03
TiO_2	2.0	1.5	1.6	1.5	.51	.94	.11	.27	.26
P_2O_5	.29	.11	.33	.20	.24	.02	.16	.00	.06
MnO	.14	.19	.13	.11	.26	.16	.14	.07	.07
CO_2	<.05	<.05	<.05	<.05	<.05	<.05	<.05	<.05	<.05
Total	99.39	99.52	99.33	99.86	99.04	99.03	99.08	99.75	99.65
Specific gravity	2.91	3.08	3.09	3.08	3.11	3.11	2.69	2.73	2.74
Semiquantitative spectrographic analyses[2] (parts per million)									
B	......	......	......	......	......	......	......	......	100
Ba	150	70	300	20	200	20	300	300	500
Co	30	50	30	50	30	30	5	7	3
Cr	500	300	......	500	200	500	10	30	10
Cu	70	100	15	50	70	70	70	50	7
Ga	20	20	20	15	20	20	3	10	7
Nb	15	......	......	......	......	......	......	......	7
Ni	150	100	10	100	70	70	50	20	15
Sc	20	70	30	30	50	70	50	5	10	7
Sr	500	70	200	150	100	300	15	50	50
V	150	300	150	300	300	300	70	50	30
Y	50	50	50	50	50	30	15	15	15
Yb	3	5	5	5	5	3	2	2	2
Zr	100	50	100	70	70	20	30	50	100
Modal analyses (volumetric percent)									
Crossite	......	......	......	......	......	......	10	8	17
Glaucophane	6	42	53	57	61	57	......	......	......
Lawsonite	26	49	27	34	31	40	6	11	11
Sphene	10	4	6	7	6	3	......	2	1
Aegerine	......	3	10	1.5	......	......	......	......	......
Jadeite	13	Tr.	......	......	......	......	......	......	......
Muscovite	......	.5	4	.3	Tr.	......	Tr.	13	3
Quartz	8	1	......	......	1	......	83	66	68
Chlorite	37	......	Tr.	......	1	......	......	......	......
Stilpnomelane	......	......	......	......	......	......	Tr.	......	Tr.
Garnet	......	......	......	......	......	......	Tr.	......	......

[1] Methods used are those described by Shapiro and Brannock (1962), supplemented by atomic absorption. Analysts: P. L. D. Elmore, James Kelsey, H. Smith, J. L. Glenn.

[2] Analyst: Chris Heropoulos.

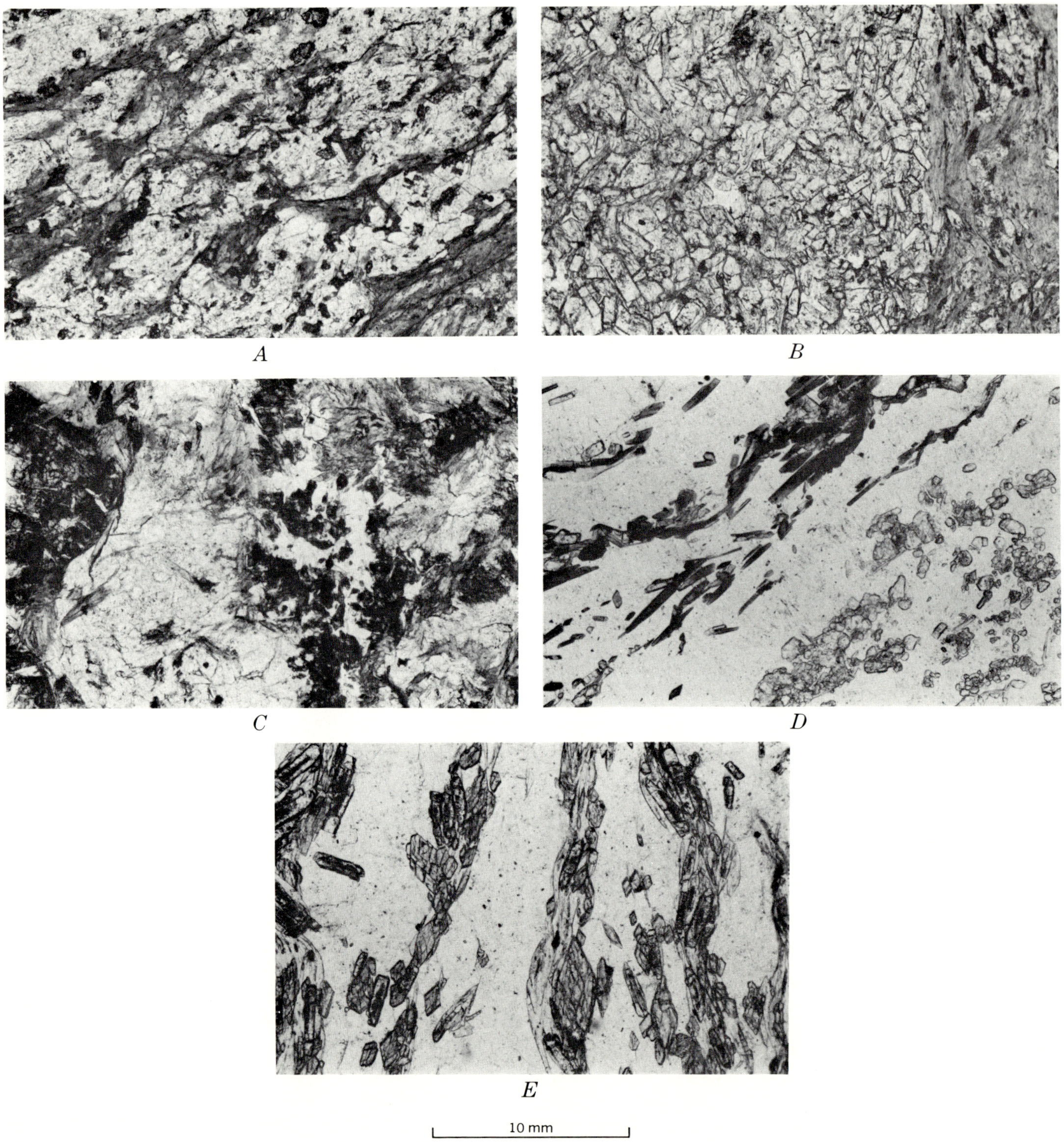

Figure 3.—Photomicrographs of blueschist facies rocks from Yreka—Fort Jones area.

A. Glaucophane-lawsonite schist. Gray is fibrous glaucophane; light gray, prismatic lawsonite; small dark grains, sphene.

B. Glaucophane-lawsonite phyllite. Gray is wispy glaucophane; light gray, lawsonite; dark scattered granules, sphene.

C. Glaucophane-lawsonite rock with aegerine. Light-gray masses are lawsonite; gray, fibrous glaucophane; white, irregular patches of muscovite; dark areas in left and right central parts of figure, aegerine.

D. Crossite-lawsonite quartzite. Low-relief light matrix is quartz; dark-gray blades, crossite, accompanied by stubby, prismatic lawsonite; light-gray high-relief grains in lower right part of figure are mostly colorless garnet (grossular) accompanied by a few prismatic lawsonite crystals.

E. Lawsonite-crossite-quartz-muscovite schist. Light-gray matrix is quartz; gray mineral with amphibole cross section (cleavage), crossite; lighter gray, moderate relief, muscovite; darker gray prisms, lawsonite. Crossite, muscovite, and lawsonite intergrown in close-spaced micaceous folia. Central parts of lawsonite crystals commonly cloudy with dustlike inclusions.

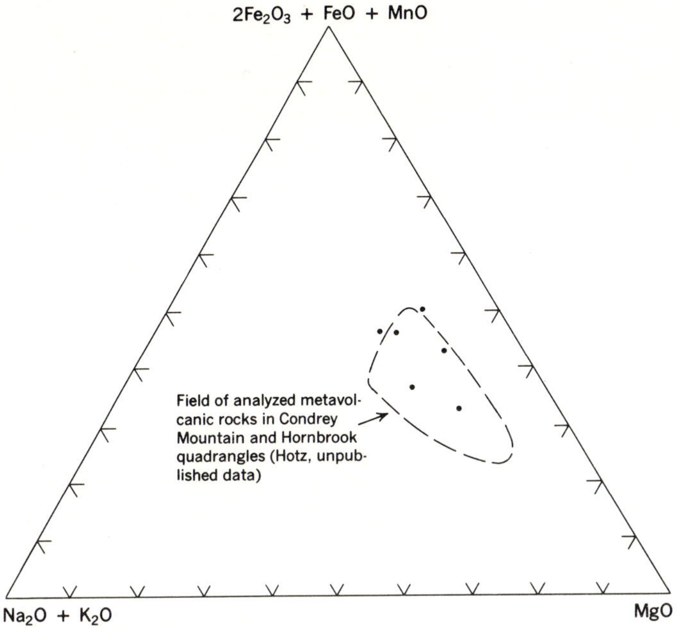

Figure 4.—Alk-F-M plot comparing blueschists of basaltic composition with metavolcanic rocks of the greenstone-chert assemblage.

Recrystallization destroyed the original fabric, and in hand specimens the rocks are fine grained and foliated with thin, alternating dark and light laminae parallel to the cleavage. Under the microscope the crystalloblastic texture of these rocks is clear. Anhedral interlocking quartz with irregular to sutured boundaries predominates. In some, the quartz grains are equidimensional, but in others they are somewhat elongate with nearly parallel orientation.

Dark-blue acicular crossite crystals in parallel arrangement and accompanied by strongly idioblastic prismatic lawsonite are concentrated in thin laminae (fig. 3*D*). In some specimens the laminae are fairly continuous; in others they are discontinuous wispy streaks and lenses. Amphibole needles commonly wrap around and enclose the lawsonite crystals. In some rocks, the laminae are highly contorted by microfolds. Crossite is the common soda amphibole in the metasedimentary rocks, but in some, presumably of lower original iron content, pale-blue glaucophane was formed instead.

White mica, although common, is a minor constituent (fig. 3*E*), but in some specimens it is more plentiful than the soda amphibole. Traces of chlorite and stilpnomelane are not uncommon. Minor quantities of colorless garnet occur as small grains in a few specimens (fig. 3*D*).

STRUCTURE

The contact of the Stuart Fork Formation with the underlying metavolcanic rocks, chert, and argillite is not exposed, but it can be placed within narrow limits because of the contrasting lithologies and structural styles. The metavolcanic and sedimentary rocks dip moderately to steeply southeast and northwest. They are deformed, but not as intensely as the overlying highly contorted and crumpled rocks of the Stuart Fork Formation. At several places near the contact, however, the underlying rocks are intensely deformed: chert beds are closely folded, siliceous argillites strongly sheared and crumpled, and greenstone sheared and brecciated. The sinuous trace of the contact at many places in areas of moderate to steep topography indicates a gentle dip. At other places the trace is straight and steep. This contact is interpreted as an east-dipping, undulatory, low-angle fault, modified by steeply dipping faults, on which a plate of Stuart Fork Formation has overridden the greenstone-chert assemblage (fig. 1). The partly mapped patch of Stuart Fork in the Scott Bar Mountains may be an outlier of this thrust plate. The moderate to steep eastward-dipping contact of the serpentinite with the Stuart Fork is interpreted to be a thrust fault on which the serpentinite and overlying metamorphic and lower Paleozoic sedimentary rocks overrode rocks of the western Paleozoic and Triassic belt.

CONCLUSIONS

In mineralogy, texture, and density the blueschists of the Yreka–Fort Jones area are comparable to the low-grade, Cazadero type III blueschists of Coleman and Lee (1963). The occurrences of blueschist in the Yreka–Fort Jones area are restricted to the Stuart Fork Formation and to greenstone of the underlying greenstone-chert assemblage immediately beneath the thrust plate of Stuart Fork Formation. Although many of the occurrences of blueschist of basaltic composition quite obviously are discontinuous bodies within the metasedimentary rocks, some of the metasedimentary blueschists are interlayered with siliceous phyllites that contain no critical blueschist facies minerals. Greenstones interfinger with the siliceous Stuart Fork Formation in its type area (Davis and others, 1965; Davis and Lipman, 1962) and may have had a similar relationship in the Yreka–Fort Jones area but became isolated by tectonic disruption. The similarity between the chemical composition of the metavolcanic rocks in the greenstone-chert assemblage and that of the basaltic blueschist supports the concept that some of the blueschist now within the plate of Stuart Fork rocks is metamorphosed greenstone from the greenstone-chert assemblage of the underlying plate.

The high-pressure and low-temperature conditions under which blueschist facies metamorphism takes place are reasonably well established (Coleman and Lee, 1962; Coleman, 1967; Ernst and others, 1970). Pressures on the order of 5–8 kb and temperatures of 200°–300°C are appropriate for the formation of low-grade blueschists of the kind that occur in the Yreka–Fort Jones area. The tectonic environment under which such temperature-pressure conditions are attained, however, is somewhat obscure and under dispute. Rapid, deep burial followed by rapid uplift (Bailey and others, 1964; Ernst and others, 1970), and development of tectonic overpressures at the sole of overthrusts (Blake and others, 1967; Coleman, 1967) are two radically different models which have been proposed to satisfy the peculiar conditions of blueschist metamorphism. Regardless of the tectonic circumstances under which blueschists form, the terranes in which they occur throughout the world have many features in common. These include narrow, elongate belts that have developed along continental margins. Characteristically they are closely associated with elongate, parallel belts of alpine-type ultramafic rocks. In terms of plate tectonic theory, these tectonic environments can be regarded as suture zones marking the collision site between plates, the blueschists having been formed in the subduction zone between a descending oceanic plate and a continental plate (Blake and others, 1969; Ernst, 1970; Coleman, 1971).

Blueschist metamorphism in the Yreka–Fort Jones area may have been synchronous with metamorphism of the Stuart Fork Formation at its type area. A Middle or Late Jurassic age has been postulated for this event, on the basis of limited isotopic age determinations ranging from 133 to 158 m.y. (Lanphere and others, 1968). In the Scott Barr Mountains (fig. 1) and their northern extension in the Condrey Mountain quadrangle (Hotz, 1967), klippen composed of the Stuart Fork are intruded by Middle or Late Jurassic (145 to 155 m.y.) granitic plutons, while to the south in the Trinity Alps and Salmon Mountains granitic plutons 127 to 140 m.y. old intrude the Stuart Fork (Lanphere and others, 1968). Metamorphism probably occurred during the Nevadan orogeny, before the multiple Cretaceous deformations (Irwin, 1964) that produced the regional blueschist metamorphism in the Coast Ranges of California and southwestern Oregon (Suppe, 1969; Suppe and Armstrong, 1972).

The Yreka–Fort Jones blueschist belt probably developed along thrust faults that separate two tectonic plates. The phyllitic quartzite and siliceous phyllite of the Stuart Fork Formation may represent fine siliceous sediments deposited in a trench on late Paleozoic and Triassic(?) oceanic crust. These rocks collided with a continental plate composed of early Paleozoic metamorphic and sedimentary rocks. Underthrusting of the oceanic plate could account for the extreme deformation of the Stuart Fork Formation and for its blueschist metamorphism that developed as the sedimentary and volcanic rocks were scraped off against the landward plate and rapidly buried in the subduction zone. The serpentinite belt that now separates the two plates may be the basement (oceanic crust and upper mantle) of the eastern plate against which the younger oceanic plate collided.

REFERENCES CITED

Bailey, E. H., Irwin, W. P., and Jones, D. L., 1964, Franciscan and related rocks and their significance in the geology of western California: California Dept. Nat. Resources Div. Mines Bull. 183, 171 p.

Blake, M. C., Jr., 1969, Blueschist facies metamorphism related to regional thrust faulting: Tectonophysics, v. 8, p. 237–246.

Blake, M. C., Jr., Irwin, W. P., and Coleman, R. G., 1967, Upside-down metamorphic zonation, blueschist facies, along a regional thrust in California and Oregon, *in* Geological Survey Research 1967: U.S. Geol. Survey Prof. Paper 575-C, p. C1–C9.

Churkin, Michael, Jr., 1965, First occurrence of graptolites in the Klamath Mountains, California, *in* Geological Survey Research 1965: U.S. Geol. Survey Prof. Paper 525-C, p. C72–C73.

Churkin, Michael, Jr., and Langenheim, R. L., Jr., 1960, Silurian strata of the Klamath Mountains, California: Am. Jour. Sci., v. 258, no. 4, p. 258–273.

Coleman, R. G., 1967, Glaucophane schists from California and New Caledonia: Tectonophysics, v. 4, p. 479–498.

—— 1971, Plate tectonic emplacement of upper mantle peridotites along continental edges: Jour. Geophys. Research, v. 76, p. 1212–1222.

Coleman, R. G., and Lanphere, M. A., 1971, Distribution and age of high-grade blueschists, associated eclogites, and amphibolites from Oregon and California: Geol. Soc. America Bull., v. 82, p. 2397–2412.

Coleman, R. G., and Lee, D. E., 1962, Metamorphic aragonite in the glaucophane schists of Cazadero, California: Am. Jour. Sci., v. 260, no. 8, p. 577–595.

—— 1963, Glaucophane-bearing metamorphic rock types of the Cazadero area, California: Jour. Petrology, v. 4, no. 2, p. 260–301.

Cox, D. P., 1956, Geology of the Helena quadrangle, Trinity County, California: Stanford, Calif., Stanford Univ., unpub. Ph. D. thesis, 123 p.

Davis, G. A., 1968, Westward thrust faulting in the south-central Klamath Mountains, California: Geol. Soc. America Bull., v. 79, p. 911–934.

Davis, G. A., Holdaway, J. J., Lipman, P. W., and Romey, W. D., 1965, Structure, metamorphism, and plutonism in the south-central Klamath Mountains, California: Geol. Soc. America Bull., v. 76, no. 8, p. 933–966.

Davis, G. A., and Lipman, P. W., 1962, Revised structural sequence of pre-Cretaceous metamorphic rocks in the southern Klamath Mountains, California: Geol. Soc. America Bull., v. 73, p. 1547–1552.

Elliott, M. A., 1971, Stratigraphy and petrology of the Late Cretaceous rocks near Hilt and Hornbrook, Siskiyou County, California, and Jackson County, Oregon: Corvallis, Oreg., Oregon State Univ., unpub. Ph.D. thesis, 171 p.

Ernst, W. G., 1970, Tectonic contact between the Franciscan mélange and the Great Valley sequence–Crustal expression of a late Mesozoic Benioff zone: Jour. Geophys. Research, v. 75, p. 886–901.

Ernst, W. G., Seki, Y., Onuki, H., and Gilbert, M. C., 1970, Comparative study of low-grade metamorphism in the California Coast Ranges and the outer metamorphic belt of Japan: Geol. Soc. America Mem. 124, 276 p.

Hotz, P. E., 1967, Geologic map of the Condrey Mountain quadrangle and parts of the Seiad Valley and Hornbrook quadrangles, California: U.S. Geol. Survey Geol. Quad. Map GQ-618, scale 1:62,500.

Irwin, W. P., 1960, Geological reconnaissance of the northern Coast Ranges and Klamath Mountains, California, with a summary of the mineral resources: California Div. Mines Bull. 179, 80 p.

—— 1964, Late Mesozoic orogenies in the ultramafic belts of northwestern California and southwestern Oregon, *in* Geological Survey Research 1964: U.S. Geol. Survey Prof. Paper 501-C, p. C1–C9.

—— 1966, Geology of the Klamath Mountains province, *in* Bailey, E. H., ed., Geology of northern California: California Div. Mines and Geology Bull. 190, p. 19–38.

Lanphere, M. A., Irwin, W. P., and Hotz, P. E., 1968, Isotopic age of the Nevadan orogeny and older plutonic and metamorphic events in the Klamath Mountains, California: Geol. Soc. America Bull., v. 79, p. 1027–1052.

Masson, P. H., 1949, Geology of the Gunsight Peak district, Siskiyou County, California: Berkeley, Calif., California Univ., unpub. M.A. thesis, 74 p.

Potter, A. W., and Boucot, A. J., 1971, Ashgillian, Late Ordovician brachiopods from the eastern Klamath Mountains of northern California: Geol. Soc. America Abs. with Programs, v. 3, no. 2, p. 180.

Shapiro, Leonard, and Brannock, W. W., 1962, Rapid analysis of silicate, carbonate, and phosphate rocks: U.S. Geol. Survey Bull. 1144-A, 56 p.

Suppe, John, 1969, Times of metamorphism in the Franciscan terrain of the northern Coast Ranges, California: Geol. Soc. America Bull., v. 80, no. 1, p. 135–142.

Suppe, John, and Armstrong, R. L., 1972, Potassium-argon dating of Franciscan metamorphic rocks: Am. Jour. Sci., v. 272, no. 3, p. 217–233.

Wells, F. G., Walker, G. W., and Merriam, C. W., 1959, Upper Ordovician (?) and Upper Silurian formations of the northern Klamath Mountains, California: Geol. Soc. America Bull., v. 70, no. 5, p. 645–649.

Zdanowicz, Ted, 1971, The folded mallethead thrust, eastern Klamath Mountains, California: Geol. Soc. America Abs. with Programs, v. 3, no. 2, p. 223.

Jour. Research U.S. Geol. Survey
Vol. 1, No. 1, Jan.—Feb. 1973, p. 63—78

DOLOMITIZATION MODEL FOR UPPER CAMBRIAN AND LOWER ORDOVICIAN CARBONATE ROCKS IN THE EASTERN UNITED STATES

By LEONARD D. HARRIS, Knoxville, Tenn.

Abstract.—Existing models for dolomitization emphasize that penecontemporaneous dolomitization can occur in both subtidal and supratidal environments if the necessary chemical and physical factors favorable for the development of magnesium-rich hypersaline waters exist. Holocene shallow-water hypersaline environments that have the potential to produce dolomite without deposition of more soluble evaporite minerals are found in Shark Bay, Australia, and on the Great Bahama Bank. These hypersalinity systems are characterized by near-vertical isosalinity layers of increasing concentration landward from the open ocean and show little or no relationship to bottom topography. I suggest that a similar but larger scale epicontinental salinity system covering the Late Cambrian and Early Ordovician carbonate continental shelf produced a broad wedge of subtidally deposited dolomite in the eastern half of the United States from Mexico to Canada. The distribution of limestone and dolomite in this region is closely keyed to the salinity gradient and accounts for the natural progression from a normal marine limestone facies through a transition zone to a highly saline dolomite facies phase. Algal stromatolite mats and domes occupied low-energy niches in both the limestone and dolomite facies, whereas stratiform algal stromatolites were confined to the areas of moderate energy within the dolomite facies.

In the past, construction of environmental models that account for the large-scale deposition of dolomite in ancient widespread carbonate environments has defied resolution because the feasibility of the suggested processes could not be confirmed experimentally nor compared to natural modern sedimentary conditions. Recently some progress concerning the origin of dolomite has been gained through the discovery of dolomite in Holocene carbonate rocks and the subsequent study of its environmental parameters. The major contribution from these studies is the general acceptance of the idea that penecontemporaneous dolomitization is common where sediments in high intertidal or supratidal areas contain pore fluids consisting of concentrated magnesium-rich brines, as for example along wide salt flats, termed "sabkhas" in the Persian Gulf (Illing and others, 1965) and carbonate mudflats in the Bahamas (Shinn and others, 1965). The model of supratidal penecontemporaneous dolomitization has been widely used in interpreting ancient carbonate environments; however, it seems to be most applicable to relatively restricted geographic areas (commonly less than 10,000 sq mi) where thin carbonate units can be demonstrated to change from subtidal and intertidal limestone to supratidal dolomite. It is less applicable as a principal site of dolomitization in regionally extensive megacarbonate environments (approximately 1 million square miles) such as the Late Cambrian and Early Ordovician, where nearly 90 percent of the carbonate is dolomite. Some widespread uniform process, other than the supratidal model, must have been operating to have dolomitized thousands of square miles of carbonate as much as 3,000 feet thick. This report questions the currently popular usage of the intertidal and supratidal environments as exclusive sites for large-scale regional dolomitization, and offers an alternate hypothesis involving a magnesium-rich subtidal environment.

UPPER CAMBRIAN AND LOWER ORDOVICIAN CARBONATE ROCKS

A paleogeographic and lithofacies map of the Late Cambrian and Early Ordovician shows that during this time a vast continental shelf, about 2,000 miles long and from 100 to 1,000 miles wide, occupied much of the eastern half of the United States (fig. 1). Maximum development of the shelf and its attendant epicontinental sea occurred late in Cambrian time and persisted with apparent continuous sedimentation until late in Early Ordovician time. Facies of Late Cambrian and Early Ordovician age show an almost classic relationship to near-shore clastic sediments containing subordinate dolomite interfingering with offshore carbonate rocks. A multitude of stratigraphic names has been used to subdivide this ancient sequence of strata into stratigraphic units of differing ranks. Because the nomenclatural complexities are not critical to this study the reader is referred to the latest summary report (Holland, 1971). One major subdivision, the Knox Group, has been widely recognized in the southern and central Appalachians within the predominantly carbonate sequence, and I suggest that many of the general features of the Knox can be applied on a shelf-wide basis.

The Knox Group, as much as 3,000 feet thick, occupies most of the middle segment of the offshore carbonate sequence, crops out in Georgia, Alabama, eastern Tennessee, and southwestern Virginia, and lies in the subsurface of middle

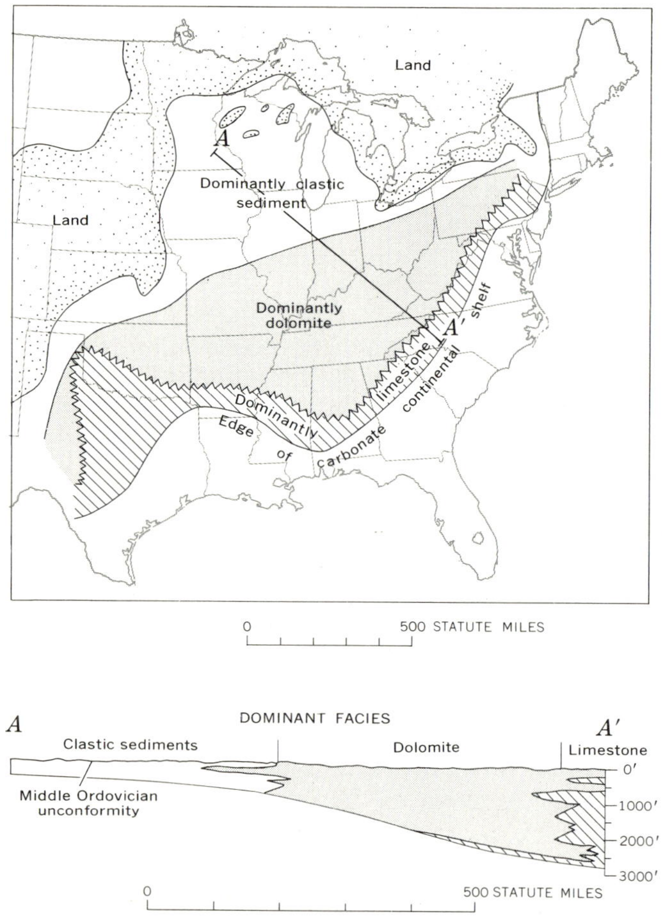

Figure 1.—Generalized paleogeographic map of Late Cambrian and Early Ordovician time, showing regional distribution of facies of the Knox Group and equivalent rocks on the ancient continental shelf. Based on Chenoweth (1968), Donaldson and Page (1964), Folk (1959), Lochman-Balk (1971), Perry (1964), Rodgers (1968), Swartz (1948), and Williams (1969).

and western Tennessee, Kentucky, West Virginia, Ohio, and parts of Indiana and Illinois. Throughout most of this area the Knox is dolomite, but in easternmost Tennessee and southwestern Virginia it is divided into a western dolomite facies and an eastern limestone facies. Recently Laporte (1971) summarized the view of sedimentologists concerned with the change of limestone to dolomite in Upper Cambrian and Lower Ordovician carbonate strata in the eastern United States. They suggest that the change is a response to the environment of deposition and indicate that the limestone has a subtidal origin, whereas the dolomite had an intertidal and supratidal origin. In their view each facies characteristically contains recognizable stratigraphic criteria imposed by environmental controls: subtidal limestone units, although exhibiting regional change and variation, tend to be uniform and may commonly show great lateral persistence. In contrast, variable conditions of sedimentation in the intertidal and supratidal dolomite regime produce abrupt and frequent changes in lithologic units, so that correlation of dolomite beds even between adjacent outcrops is nearly impossible. These apparent clear-cut differences between limestone and dolomite facies of Cambrian and Ordovician age as summarized by Laporte have not been corroborated by the studies of economic geologists in eastern Tennessee, who concentrated on details of stratigraphy without preconceived ideas of environmental constraints.

More than 40 years ago, when geologists realized that commercial quantities of zinc were confined regionally to a 200-foot zone in the upper part of the dolomite phase of the Knox Group of eastern Tennessee, zinc mining companies initiated intensive foot-by-foot stratigraphic studies in search of key beds to aid in exploration and in mine development. Detailed studies of mine workings demonstrated that, rather than a series of laterally discontinuous lithologic units, almost any distinctive stratum, such as a 1-inch sandstone or shale bed, a chert nodule zone, minor bedding or color variation, and so on, could be correlated from mine to mine in the Mascot-Jefferson City zinc district. Continuing surface and subsurface studies of approximately the upper 900 feet of the Knox in Tennessee have resulted in the careful documentation of an average of one key bed per approximately 11 feet of vertical section, many of which have regional significance (Oder and Miller, 1945; Crawford, 1945; Oder and Ricketts, 1961; Harris, 1969; Stagg and Fischer, 1970). In the past 20 years thousands of core holes have penetrated parts of the predominantly dolomite facies of the Knox in search for economic zinc deposits throughout much of Tennessee and in parts of Kentucky, Alabama, and Virginia. In every area, where enough closely spaced drilling has been done to develop a stratigraphic sequence, laterally extensive key beds can be recognized and can be correlated for considerable distances. In central and northern Virginia, far removed from the Tennessee zinc district, Young and Wedow (1962) and Herbert and Young (1956) experienced no difficulty in recognizing and using thin key units in rocks of the Beekmantown Dolomite, the lateral equivalent of the upper part of the Knox. The widespread uniformity of multiple key units in the dolomite facies of the Knox Group and equivalent rocks, rather than being characteristic of discontinuous intertidal-supratidal sedimentation, is more characteristic of the uniform subtidal sedimentation of Laporte (1971). Consequently many of the criteria summarized by Laporte and used to distinguish between subtidal, intertidal, and supratidal environments need to be critically analyzed.

PRIMARY FEATURES AS ENVIRONMENTAL INDICATORS

Identification of ancient intertidal and supratidal sediments is based on the recognition of features similar to those found on modern carbonate tidal flats. Unfortunately, there is a tendency to ignore the possibility that many of the primary features found on Holocene tidal flats may not necessarily be limited to that environment. In fact, few primary features are infallible. Both shrinkage cracks and algal stromatolites are excellent examples of "infallible guides" used to identify positively the intertidal and supratidal environments. Shrinkage cracks are common features of modern intertidal and supratidal areas; however, Burst (1965) has experimentally confirmed that shrinkage cracks can form subaqueously, in response to an increase in salinity, in mud that contains a small quantity of swelling clay. In the Knox Group, shrinkage cracks are found in about equal abundance in both the limestone and dolomite facies. Detailed facies studies and insoluble residue contents suggest that cracked beds show a close affinity for niches within a subtidal environment where clay-mineral abundance, usually greater than 5 percent, is sufficient to react to major fluctuations in salinity. Major changes in salinity are undoubtedly common along the transition zone between masses of normal marine and penesaline water. Consequently, shrinkage cracks, although useful in many places as indicators of subaerial exposure, may just as commonly indicate fluctuations in salinity within subtidal environments.

Holocene algal stromatolites

Algal stromatolites are laminated structures formed by the trapping and binding of sediment by an algal film. They are organosedimentary features in which only the gross structure of the algal films is preserved; cellular and other detailed structure are not preserved. Logan, Rezak, and Ginsburg (1964) suggested that the form of a Holocene stromatolite is related to environmental conditions, and does not lend itself to the limited definition of form genera or form species. They proposed to abandon all generic and specific names, substituting a descriptive nomenclature based on the arrangement of certain geometric forms. Their classification contains two basic forms—the hemispheroid and the spheroid in three major arrangements: (1) laterally linked hemispheroids (LLH), (2) discrete, vertically stacked hemispheroids (SH), and (3) discrete spheroids (SS). Usefulness of algal stromatolites as environmental indicators was stressed by their suggesting that LLH and SH forms were restricted to intertidal areas and SS forms restricted to subtidal areas of shallow agitated water. Other studies of Holocene algal stromatolites (Ginsburg, 1960; Monty, 1965; Kendall and Skipwith, 1968; Gebelein, 1969; and G. R. Davis, 1970) have not fully confirmed either the form distribution or environmental parameters proposed by Logan, Rezak, and Ginsburg (1964), but generally all agree that there are three dominant geometric forms—mats, hemispheroids, and spheroids. Investigations of intertidal algal stromatolites by Kendall and Skipwith (1968) in the Persian Gulf and by G. R. Davis (1970) in Shark Bay, Western Australia, indicate that the dominant geometric growth form is a subparallel mat rather than a hemispheroid or a spheroid. The mat may be altered mechanically to many subforms depending upon its position within the intertidal and supratidal area. A summary of Holocene stromatolite reports suggests that the intertidal and supratidal areas can be subdivided into as many as five distinct zones (fig. 2).

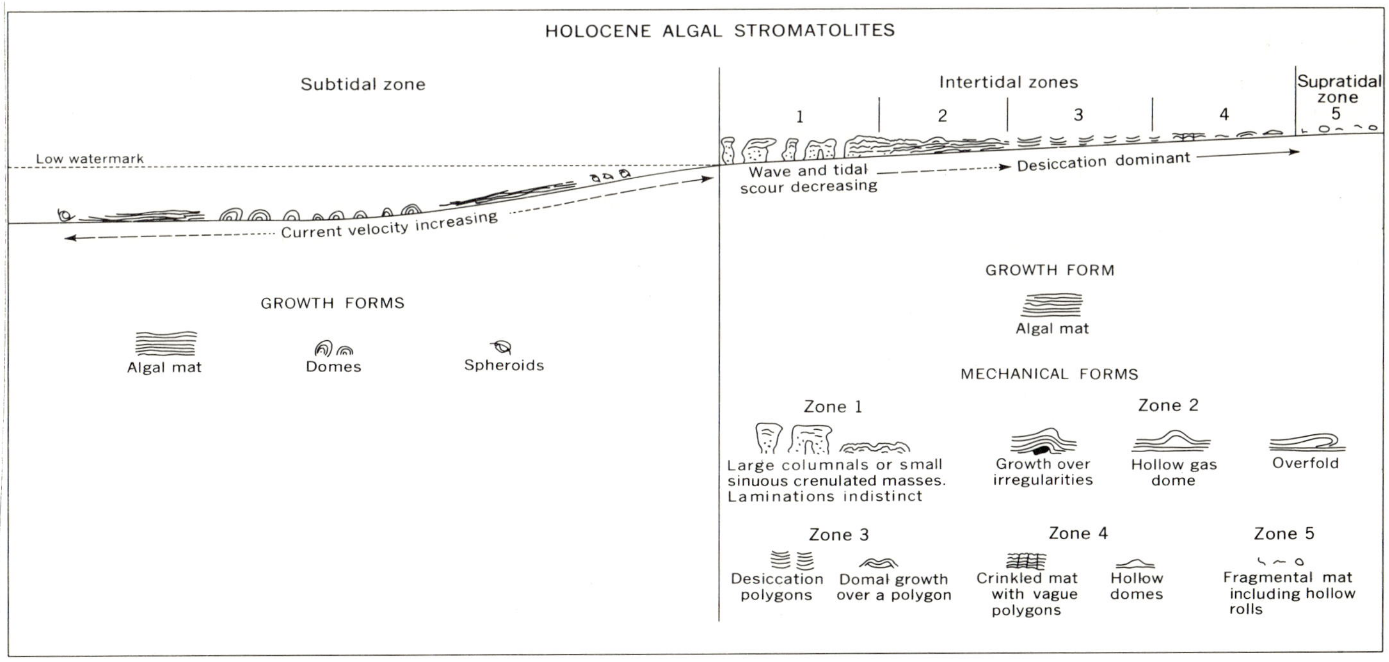

Figure 2.—Form distribution of Holocene algal stromatolites. Based on Black (1933); Ginsburg (1960); Logan, Rezak, and Ginsburg (1964); Kendall and Skipwith (1968); Gebelein (1969); and G. R. Davis (1970).

Zone 1.—A continuous algal mat may develop almost to the low watermark in a protected intertidal mudflat environment, but varieties of forms ranging from sinuous domes or ridges to columnar structures result where waves and tides have increased erosive force. Logan (1961) attributed the development of columnar forms to upward growth of algal stromatolites by progressive stacking of hemispheroidal laminae (SH-V). However, their development seems much more complex, and, as suggested by Logan (1961, figs. 2 and 3) and G. R. Davis (1970, p. 199), they appear to result from scour and beach-rock formation in conjunction with algal growth. Active algal mats are not mechanically resistant to moderate erosive forces (Gebelein, 1969, p. 56) and a slight increase in erosive energy scours the mat irregularly. Once the mat is breached, beach rock, which results from cementation caused by alternate wetting and drying in the intertidal zone, may begin to line the walls of channels. The protection on the walls afforded by the beach-rock formation causes erosion to proceed in a dominantly vertical direction, thereby inducing the development of characteristic SH-V columnar forms of Logan, Rezak and Ginsburg (1964). Along the low watermark, beach rock is sculptured by erosion into columnar structures that grade toward the high watermark into sinuous mounds or ridges, which may or may not be indurated, and finally into unbroken algal mat. Within the beach-rock environment the growth of algal mat is restricted to the top of structures where erosive forces are less. Continued growth of the mat adds to the development of sculptured forms, but its effect is minimal as suggested by the restriction of crudely defined laminations to the upper part of the structures.

Zone 2.—Smooth, nearly flat algal mats characteristically occupy diurnally flooded intertidal areas of low energy. Irregular domelike structures result from growth over irregularities, obstructions, or from erosion and slight desiccation. Superficially these domelike structures resemble the laterally linked hemispheroidal (LLH) structures of Logan, Rezak, and Ginsburg (1964), but they lack symmetry, and their mechanical origin is clearly discernible.

Zone 3.—Desiccation of the algal mat produces a typical polygonal pattern in which individual polygons are saucer shaped and exhibit a wide range in size depending upon the grain size of local sediment and the moisture distribution.

Zone 4.—The algal mat in this zone has a poorly defined polygonal pattern but exhibits abundant hollow domes and a crinkled surface produced by trapped gases. Locally this zone may change to a relatively flat mat similar to that of zone 2.

Zone 5.—Above the high watermark, in the supratidal zone, algal growth is inhibited, as shown by detrital fragments and spheroidally coiled pieces of algal mat.

Subtidal Holocene algal stromatolites have not received the same amount of study as the intertidal forms because they are more difficult to observe and classify. Although these forms were noted by Ginsburg (1960) and Monty (1965) in Florida and the Bahamas, a thorough study of their distribution and environmental parameters did not emerge until Gebelein (1969) published a paper on subtidal algal stromatolites of Bermuda. Gebelein found that algal development is favored in the lee of islands and on wide, shallow shelf areas where reduced wave and current scour takes place. Form distribution is closely keyed to current velocity and sediment supply (fig. 2). Areas of moderate current velocity and ample sediment supply develop algal mats, similar to those described in zone 2 of the intertidal zone, in water as much as 35 feet deep. In areas of reduced velocity where sediment supply is small, algal mats differentiate into discrete small domes; where sediment supply is large, they differentiate into large domes. Both domes tend to elongate in the direction of current movement. Lamination within small domes is distinct, convex, regular, and symmetrical; in contrast, lamination within domes is convex, indistinct, and irregular in thickness.

To summarize, Logan, Rezak, and Ginsburg (1964) based their classification of algal stromatolites on the assumption that hemispheroids or spheroids were the basic growth forms of algal stromatolites. Other studies (Kendall and Skipwith, 1968; Gebelein, 1969; G. R. Davis, 1970) indicated that there are three growth forms—mats, hemispheroids, and spheroids. The basic structural element of each form is a simple lamina. Logan, Rezak, and Ginsburg (1964) showed that development of laminae and form differentiation are controlled by physical, chemical, and biological constraints of the environment. Thus, wide variation in type and intensity of environmental constraints between subtidal and intertidal settings results in the development of distinctive algal stromatolite forms keyed to the particular environment (fig. 2). Natural growth of hemispheroidal forms is favored in subtidal areas where sediment supply is ample and current velocity is low. Spheroidal forms are more likely to develop in subtidal areas where current velocity alternates between low and moderate. Algal mats grow in both subtidal and intertidal environments because the controlling physical constraints of moderate current velocity and sediment supply are similar. The distinguishing characteristic between subtidal and intertidal algal mats is the greater diversity of forms mechanically produced in the intertidal zone in conjunction with erosion, beach rock formation, gas generation, and desiccation. Because Logan, Rezak, and Ginsburg (1964) did not recognize the algal mat as a distinct form and did not distinguish between intertidally mechanically produced forms and subtidal growth forms, they unintentionally limited the usefulness of algal stromatolites as environmental indicators of ancient carbonate depositional environments.

Algal stromatolites of the Knox Group

Preservation of algal stromatolites in the Knox Group of Tennessee and southwestern Virginia ranges from vague outlines in dolomite to minute detailed structures in chert. Because of intense weathering, the residuum from the Knox contains vast quantities of chertified algal stromatolites. On the basis of detailed study of bedrock and residual products, ancient algal structures in the Knox are limited to algal mats, stratiform layers, and growth domes, with only a rare spheroidal structure (fig. 3). By analogy with Holocene algal stromatolite zonation (fig. 2) the absence of mechanically produced structures, such as polygonal forms and mechanical domes, suggests that intertidal and supratidal environments were absent or poorly developed during deposition of the Knox.

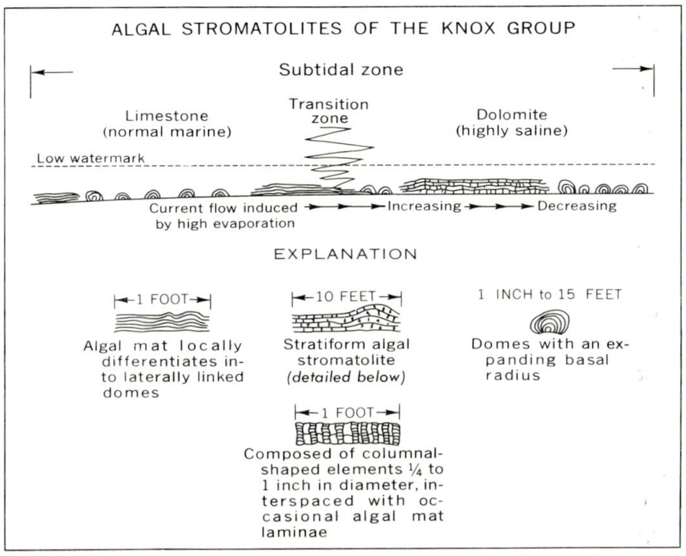

Figure 3.—Forms and distribution of Late Cambrian and Early Ordovician algal stromatolites in the Knox Group. Comparison of the small-scale algal mat structure with the large-scale stratiform algal structures suggests many similarities; the main difference is size.

Beds consisting of near-parallel paper-thin laminae, similar to those described (Black, 1933, p. 170–171) as the result of rhythmic alternation of Holocene carbonate sediments and dark algal films, are common in the Knox Group. Unfortunately, rhythmic alternation in organic content does not in itself identify laminated algal structures. Periodic changes in salinity, which are not unlikely in the highly saline environment suggested for the Knox, could cause mass mortality in phytoplankton (Emery and Stevenson, 1957, p. 687), which in turn would result in the deposition of a lamina high in organic matter, resembling a primary algal lamina. The lack of suitable criteria to differentiate between laminated algal sediments and organic lamination from other processes limits the number of such beds that can be assigned to an algal origin.

Paper-thin laminated beds in the Knox Group without exception have been found to have a clay content ranging from 10 to more than 25 percent, strongly suggesting that the lamination primarily resulted from rhythmic changes in clay content. That rhythmic changes in amounts of clay alternate with algal mat development is implied by the fact that locally some paper-thin laminated beds are found to differentiate into LLH structures.

The most abundant algal stromatolite in the Knox Group is in regionally persistent stratiform units in which the basic structural element is a crude column exhibiting paper-thin and vertically stacked hemispheroidal laminae. Thousands of the individual basic columnar elements, from ¼ inch to 1 inch in diameter, are in laterally continuous layers from 1 inch to 3 feet thick. Silicified specimens in which many primary structures are preserved in detail, suggest that the layering results from periodic interruption in upward growth of individual columnal elements. These interruptions are recorded as laminae which form natural partings that present-day weathering tends to accentuate. In all respects the growth layers imitate algal mat development—they form laterally continuous subparallel stratiform layers that locally differentiate into a series of hemispheroids several feet in height and more than 10 feet in diameter. The major difference between the laminae of an algal mat and the layers in the columnar structures is a matter of scale, plus the fact that each growth layer is composed of thousands of individual units (fig. 3).

Stratiform algal stromatolites in massive units from 3 to 140 feet thick are confined to the dolomite facies of the Knox Group of eastern Tennessee and southwestern Virginia. Detailed studies indicate that many of these thick stratiform zones persist laterally for more than 50 miles. Intercalated within these zones are thin beds of oolite, intraformational round-pebble conglomerate, and dololutite. Lateral facies changes from algal to nonalgal material involving individual beds within the zone can be transitional or abrupt. Where transitional, the stratiform algal beds change laterally to algal debris, then to oolite and dololutite, and finally to dololutite containing abundant growth domes; where abrupt, they change directly to dololutite with thin beds of oolite, intraformational round-pebble conglomerate, and growth domes. Distribution of insoluble residues across the facies boundaries shows a direct relationship between the amount of clay residue and rock type. Clay content of stratiform algal stromatolites, oolite, and some debris beds is less than 1 percent; in contrast, the clay content of all dololutite beds exceeds 5 percent. The low clay content of the algal beds, oolites, and algal debris suggests that these rocks were deposited in an environment where the energy level was sufficiently great to prevent the mechanical accumulation of clay, whereas dololutite with higher clay content accumulated in areas of lower energy.

The laterally continuous nature of stratiform algal stromatolite deposits suggests that uniformly widespread subtidal environmental conditions must be responsible for their development. Low clay content and presence of oolite and round-pebble intraformational conglomerate implies that stratiform algal deposits developed in areas of moderate current activity where scouring action of the current prevented growth between columnals. Periodic reduction in current velocities encouraged limited growth of laterally continuous algal laminae. Exceptional conditions exist in present-day hypersaline environments where water lost to high evaporation is continuously replaced by oceanic water (Emery and Stevenson, 1957, p. 686). The continuous inflow of marine water to replace water lost to evaporation in hypersaline environments may be the mechanism which accounts for the widespread development of laterally persistent stratiform algal zones and their restriction to the dolomite facies of the Knox Group.

Unlike the SH-C domes of Logan, Rezak, and Ginsburg (1964), which are defined as discrete structures in which succeeding hemispheroidal laminae develop without an increase in the basal radius, algal growth domes in the Knox Group develop with an increasing basal radius. Growth domes are distinct and nearly symmetrical structures markedly different from the randomly disposed and asymmetrical mechanical domes developed in Holocene intertidal settings. Normally, growth domes in the Knox are arranged in laterally continuous layers composed of hundreds or thousands of individual domes. The size of individual domes within a layer ranges from a few inches up to 15 feet in diameter. The initial spacing of individual domes within a layer is critical and determines the ultimate size and configuration of the mature structures. If growth is initiated at widely spaced intervals, individual elements develop without interference into large, wide-spaced domes; but if development starts at more closely spaced intervals, the growing domes soon impinge on one another and compound forms with complex growth patterns develop.

That both limestone and dolomite facies contain domes demonstrates that their growth was not dependent on variations in salinity. However, their growth does appear to be keyed to subtidal zones with low current velocities, where they are associated with low-energy lithologies such as calcilutite and dololutite containing more than 5 percent insoluble clay.

MODELS OF DOLOMITIZATION

Studies of Holocene massive carbonate deposits have emphasized that dolomite is formed as a penecontemporaneous replacement of calcium carbonate and that the process of dolomitization is operative in supratidal areas in which magnesium-rich hypersaline solutions are developed (Illing and others, 1965; Shinn and others, 1965). Similarly, studies of ancient evaporite deposits have emphasized that subtidal dolomite can be an early primary deposit (Irwin, 1965) or can form late in the evaporite cycle as a consequence of refluxion of magnesium-rich brines (Adams and Rhodes, 1960). The unifying theme emerging from these studies is that dolomitization can occur in both supratidal and subtidal environments, where high evaporation rate and low fresh-water dilution produce magnesium-rich brines. Salinity systems with the potential to develop and maintain the necessary chemical and physical factors favoring widespread subtidal dolomitization through a considerable time span have been described for the deepwater barred basin and the shallow epicontinental sea model (fig. 4).

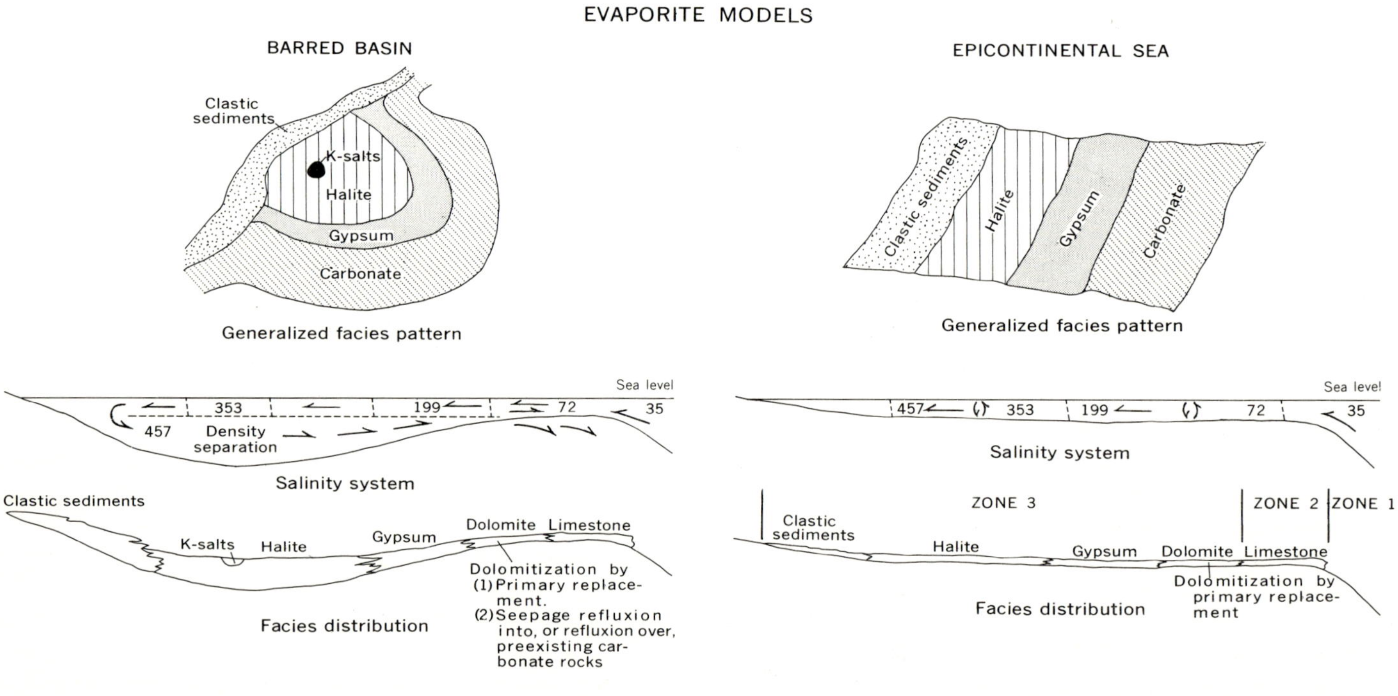

Figure 4.—The salinity systems, facies distributions, and generalized facies patterns of the barred-basin and epicontinental sea evaporite models. Based on data from King (1947), Scruton (1953), Adams and Rhodes (1960), Shaw (1964), Irwin (1965), and Hite (1968, 1970). The values given in the salinity systems are parts per thousand.

Barred basin

The barred-basin evaporite model (Ochsenius, 1877; King, 1947), which is operative in warm arid areas where evaporation exceeds dilution by fresh and oceanic water, is generally a relatively deep topographic depression separated from the open ocean by a shallower physical barrier. Commonly the barrier has been a shelf covering thousands of square miles (Hite, 1970, p. 50) that nearly or completely surrounds the basin. As sea water moves across the shallow shelf toward the basin, a strong horizontally increasing salinity gradient is produced in response to high evaporation rates (Lang, 1937). Continued evaporation establishes a circulatory system in the basin because of density stratification and density flow. Dense brine in the farthest reaches of the basin sinks and flows back beneath the less dense influxing current toward the bottom of the basin; some of this brine is refluxed back over the barrier to the sea (King, 1947, p. 474). The combination of chemical and physical factors controlling the circulation in a barred basin produces a distinctive and somewhat circular facies pattern in which chemical and biochemical carbonates occur on the fringing shelf and the more soluble salts occur near the center (fig. 4). A large part of the shelf carbonate is thought to have been dolomitized by seepage refluxion through permeable beds (Adams and Rhodes, 1960) or by refluxion of the brines over the carbonate shelf (Hite, 1970, p. 53).

Continental shelf

Although several shallow-water sedimentation models have been proposed to explain sedimentary patterns in a variety of carbonate and evaporite sequences, only relatively recently has it been recognized that certain elements were common to all shallow-water models, enabling Shaw (1964) and Irwin (1965) to describe a generalized model for epicontinental sedimentation. Shaw and Irwin emphasize that an epicontinental sea environment is characterized by the great width of the shelf (hundreds of miles) where bottom depositional slopes are on the order of less than 1 foot per mile, and where circulation, except near the edge, is restricted by the shallow depth of the sea. According to Shaw and Irwin, lateral variation in biochemical, chemical, and physical factors from shore to deeper water results in the development of three major zones of sedimentation. These sedimentary zones, in contrast to the nearly circular sedimentary pattern of a barred basin, tend to form a series of broad bands roughly parallel to the shore (fig. 4). Their three zones include:

1. An open ocean zone of low energy, hundreds of miles wide, where the depth of water restricts the hydraulic energy. Sediments are largely derived from zone 2 (see below) and consist of fine-grained organic debris. Bottom conditions tend to be reducing, thus preserving introduced organic matter and producing dark sediments.
2. A zone of high energy, tens of miles wide extending from the point where waves first strike the bottom to the limit of tidal action. Physical, chemical, and organic activity within this zone causes an orderly shoreward progression of facies ranging from biogenetic sediments to oolites and coated grains to pellets to mud.
3. A zone of low energy, free from the effects of oceanic waves and tides, extending from zone 2 to shore. In areas of high evaporation and low fresh-water runoff, salinities should increase progressively shoreward, initiating chemical precipitation keyed to that gradient. Precipitation begins with calcium carbonate and progresses consecutively through dolomite to gypsum, halite, and other more soluble salts.

Wind-generated currents within a shallow epicontinental sea tend to homogenize the water mass to a depth of at least 65 feet, thereby preventing the development of vertical density stratification. Instead, a horizontal gradient is established with increasing salinity and density toward the shore (fig. 4). The higher density water mass is prevented from free refluxion to the open ocean by the lack of sufficient hydrologic head to overcome the frictional resistance of the gently sloping sea bottom (Scruton, 1953). This frictional entrapment of highly saline water is in contrast to the hydrologic system of the deeper barred basin, where circulation is dependent upon a density differential between influxing surface currents and refluxing bottom currents. The existence at the present time of hydrologic condition similar to the epicontinental sea model but on a smaller scale seems well established (Emery and Stevenson, 1957), particularly by the long-term measurements (13 years) in Shark Bay, Western Australia (Logan and Cebulski, 1970), and the consistencies in data obtained through a 29-year time span for the Great Bahama Bank (Black, 1933; Smith, 1940; Newell and others, 1959; Cloud, 1962).

Shark Bay, Western Australia, with a semiarid subtropical climate is a shallow-water embayment open to the ocean, whereas the Great Bahama Bank with a humid subtropical climate is a shallow-water carbonate shelf surrounded by the open ocean. Despite these environmental differences, the hydrologic systems of both areas are similar in that high salinities are formed in response to high evaporation, small tidal influx, and low fresh-water dilution. Surface and bottom salinity in Shark Bay shows a gradient from normal marine salinity at the bay mouth to hypersalinity in the bay head (Logan and Cebulski, 1970, fig. 6). Cross sections drawn through the long axis of the bay show no horizontal density stratification, nor do isohalines show any relationship to bottom topography (fig. 5). Instead, the structure of the high-salinity water mass is nearly vertical, with increasing salinity and density toward the bay head. The vertical isosalinity zones, which are uniformly oxygenated from top to bottom, result from continuous homogenization by currents and wave action (Logan and Cebulski, 1970, p. 14). Surface

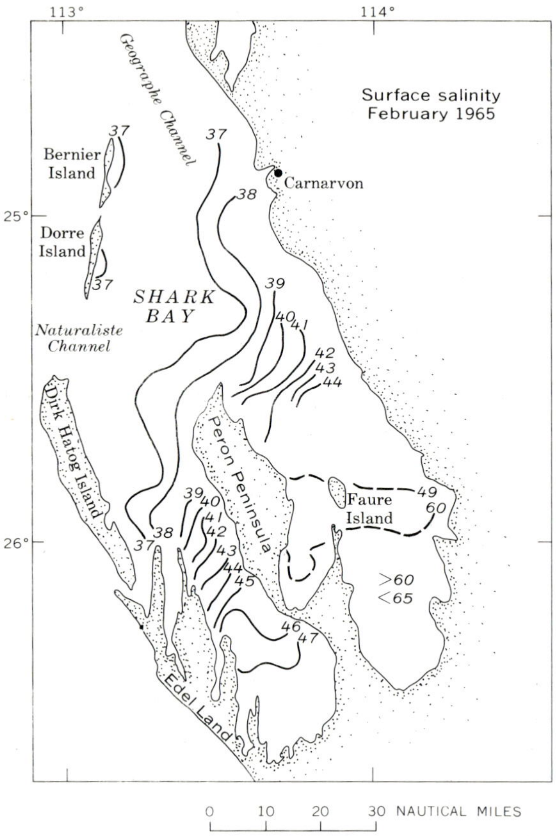

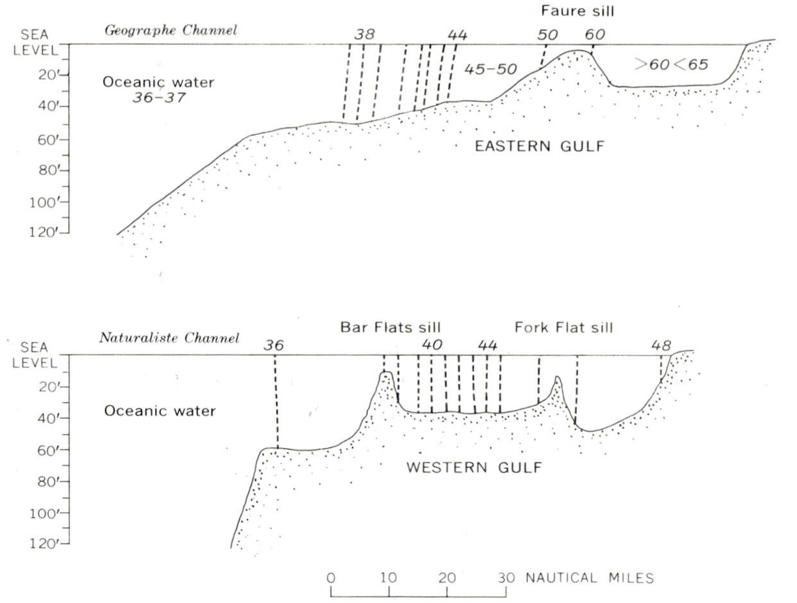

Figure 5.—Distribution of salinity (in parts per thousand) in Shark Bay, Western Australia, and cross sections showing the nearly vertical isohalines and the horizontal increase of the salinity gradients toward the heads of the two gulfs. From Logan and Cebulski (1970).

and bottom salinity gradients (Cloud, 1962, table 25) for part of the Great Bahama Bank show that the structure of the Bahama high-salinity mass is defined by steeply inclined isohalines, similar to the configuration at Shark Bay (fig. 6).

Circulation in Shark Bay and on the Great Bahama Bank is sluggish, having an estimated residual time for a particular water mass to complete a circuit from open ocean and back to be on the order of 5 months in Shark Bay (Logan and Cebulski, 1970, p. 21) and 3 months in the Bahamas (Smith, 1940, p. 156). An equilibrium condition between evaporation rate and oceanic exchange has been accomplished in Shark Bay by the constant slow movement of tidal currents bringing oceanic water in on east-facing shores and a reflux of higher salinity water out along west-facing shores (Logan and Cebulski, 1970, p. 21). Tidal currents play a minor role as a controlling factor in the circulation on the Great Bahama Bank. The direction of tidal flooding is such that its effect is largely canceled out; thus, residual current directions are determined by seasonal changes in prevailing winds (Smith, 1940, p. 15). During the summer months when prevailing winds are from the east, continuing evaporation results in the development of a high-salinity water mass with its apex off the northwest shore of Andros Island (fig. 6). Water with salinities greater than 39 parts per thousand is carried westward by persistent residual currents to cover much of the bank. Apparently, 40 to 60 inches of rain, mainly during the summer months, tends to prevent the salinity of the Bahama water mass from attaining concentrations greater than 45 parts per thousand. During the winter months the wind shifts to the northwest and oceanic water of lower salinity is carried shoreward to dilute the high-salinity mass. Thus, the salinity system developed on the bank is dynamic and tends to move and deteriorate seasonally.

DOLOMITIZATION

Studies of Holocene dolomitization, especially that of Illing, Wells, and Taylor (1965), emphasize that magnesium-ion concentrations are sufficiently great early in the evaporite cycle to initiate dolomitization before large concentrations of gypsum or anhydrite are deposited. The relationship is well illustrated by a plot of Illing, Wells, and Taylor's data from the Persian Gulf (fig. 7). Incipient dolomitization begins subtidally as suggested by the combination of minor dolomite and abundant magnesian calcite. Supratidally, where dolomitization is more complete, dolomite is abundant and magnesian calcite is sparse. The mole Mg-Ca ratio of pore water increases to about 19 at the seaward edge of the supratidal area, where gypsum first appears in the sediments; thereafter it decreases as magnesium is subtracted by the process of dolomitization. The relatively slight increase in chlorinity across the supratidal sabkha suggests that the system is near equilibrium and that

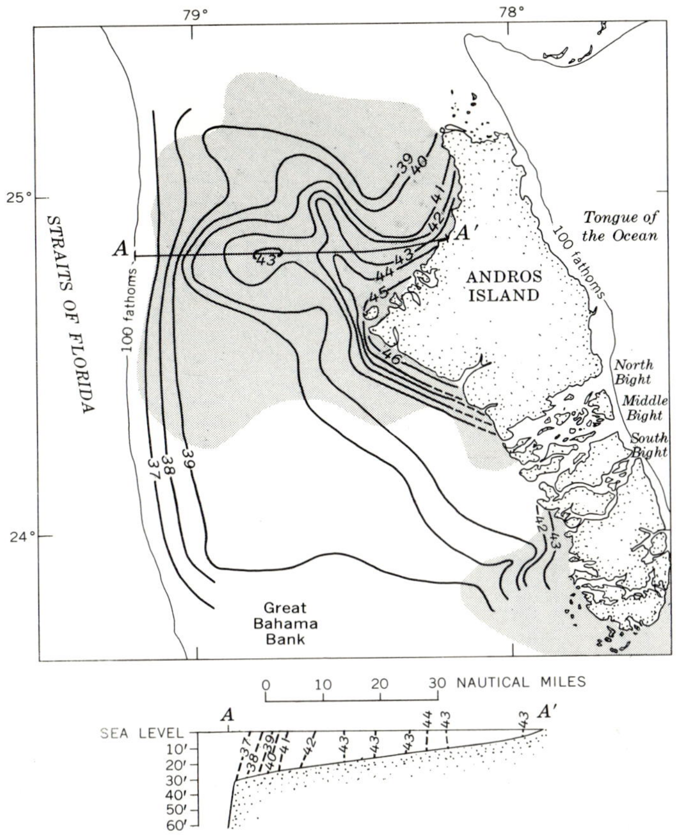

Figure 6.—Distribution of salinity (in parts per thousand) on the Great Bahama Bank, and cross section showing the nearly vertical isohalines and the horizontal increase of the salinity gradient shoreward. Shaded areas contain more than 3 percent magnesium carbonate. Data from Newell and Rigby (1957) and Cloud (1962).

dolomitization is proceeding rapidly, accompanied by deposition of small amounts of gypsum. Accordingly, dolomitization occurs early in the evaporite cycle during the transition from deposition of calcium carbonate to gypsum. Significantly, many ancient evaporite deposits have a marked deficiency of magnesium relative to its abundance in sea water (Stewart, 1963, p. 40), lending support to the concept that magnesium in ancient evaporite basins was extracted early in the process of dolomitization, thereby depleting residual brines so that only small quantities of magnesium salts were available for precipitation and refluxion. The natural progression of facies from limestone to dolomite to gypsum to halite to potassium salt is simply a reflection of the varying concentration of salts within a salinity system.

The process of magnesium concentration in sediments appears to be operative subtidally within a present-day shallow carbonate environment. This is suggested by the comparison of the distribution of salinity on the Great Bahama Bank (Cloud, 1962, table 25) to distribution of magnesium (Newell and Rigby, 1957, fig. 13). Areas of greatest magnesium in the bottom sediment appear to be closely allied to the configuration of the Bahama salinity system; in contrast, sediments with low magnesium content are deposited where oceanic water with lower salinities circulates more freely, such as north of and southwest of Andros Island and in the area of the bights near the center of Andros (figs. 6, 8). Cloud (1962, p. 94) suggests that most high-magnesium calcite in the bottom sediment of the bank is probably related to the skeletal content of the sediment. However, the amount of magnesium in skeletal material is thought to be dependent upon temperatures and salinity of the environment as well as the genetic effect of the organism (Chave, 1954; Lowenstam, 1954; Chilingar, 1962). Magnesium in the Bahamas may well be all concentrated in skeletal material, but this simply reflects the high-salinity environment within which the material formed. Magnesium distribution superimposed on a facies map of the Great Bank (Imbrie and Purdy, 1962, fig. 10) demonstrates that no clear-cut relation exists between facies and magnesium content (fig. 8). The lack of control by facies lends credence to the inference that the distribution of magnesium in the bottom sediments is related to the configuration of the salinity system on the Great Bahama Bank.

The epicontinental-sea salinity system of Shaw (1964) and Irwin (1965) and its shoreward horizontally increasing salinity gradient has the potential to develop the necessary chemical and physical factors to promote widespread subtidal dolomitization. I believe that such a system is responsible for the regional development of subtidal dolomite during Late Cambrian and Early Ordovician time.

LATE CAMBRIAN AND EARLY ORDOVICIAN SEDIMENTATION MODEL

Massive evaporite deposits attributed to deepwater deposition have not been described in the Knox Group. Minor amounts of anhydrite in vugs, small veins, and thin laminae have been observed in Tennessee and also in Lower Ordovician carbonate rocks in Texas (Barnes, 1959, p. 57) and Illinois (Saxby and Lamar, 1957, p. 14). The limited amounts of anhydrite and the broad-band facies distributions (figs. 1 and 4) tend to rule out the barred-basin model as a means of explaining deposition of dolomite in the Knox. Instead, the epicontinental-sea salinity system of Shaw (1964) and Irwin (1965) and its shoreward increasing salinity gradient is postulated as a more likely environment for the deposition of this facies. Characteristically, the deposition of limestone and dolomite in the Knox was related to the epicontinental salinity gradient, so that a shoreward succession exists from normal marine limestone on the east through a transitional zone to a highly saline dolomite phase on the west (fig. 9). Subsurface information (summarized by Lochman-Balk, 1971) shows that the Knox gradually thins northwestward toward Illinois and is replaced by a dominantly clastic sequence (fig. 1). Primary characteristics of outcropping Upper Cambrian and Lower Ordovician rocks of Wisconsin (Ostrom, 1970; R. A. Davis, 1970) compared to the primary characteristics of equivalent

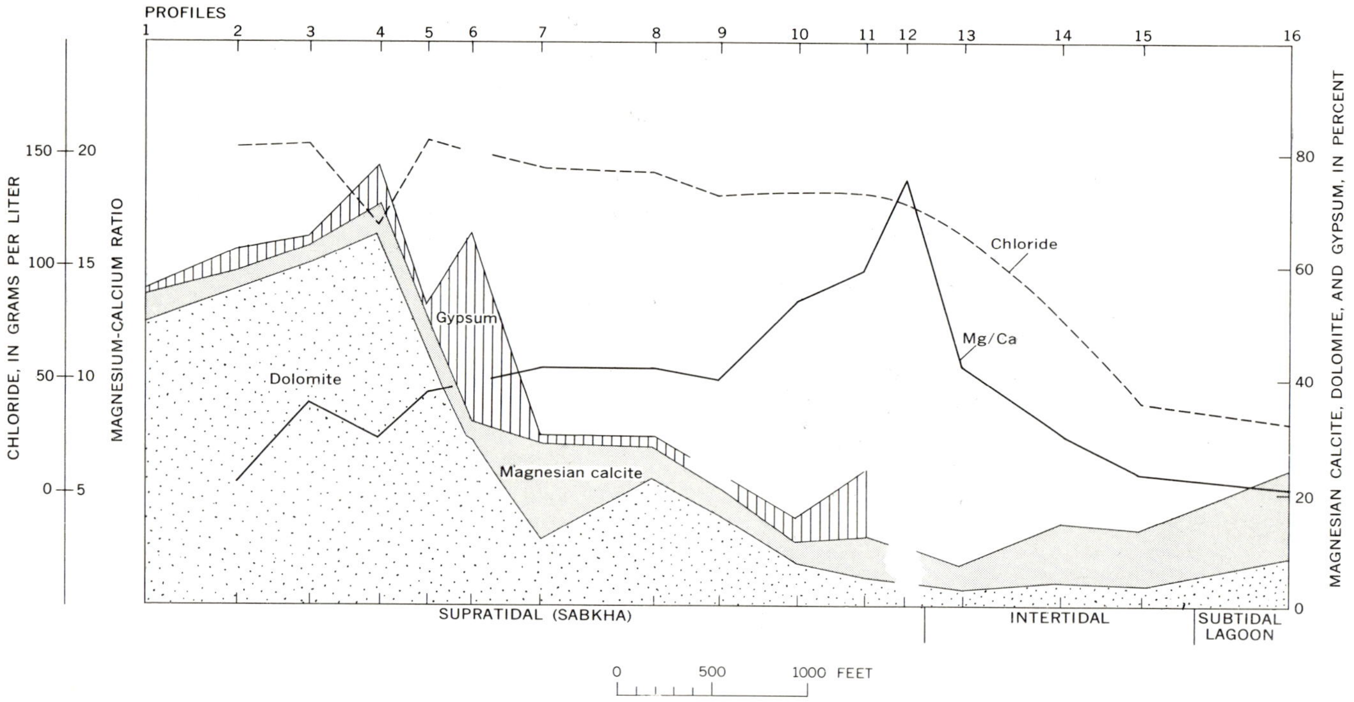

Figure 7.—Profiles to a depth of 58 cm across the Sabkha Faishakh on the Persian Gulf, showing changes in chlorinity, Mg-Ca ratio, and percentage of magnesian calcite, dolomite, and gypsum. The process of dolomitization appears to intensify progressively from incipient dolomitization subtidally to massive dolomitization in the high supratidal area. Adapted from Illing, Wells, and Taylor (1965).

age rocks of the Knox Group suggest that in near-shore areas the ancient salinity system did not continue to increase (fig. 10). Apparently fresh-water dilution from the bordering land lowered salinities to the point that a more diverse fauna developed, as well as contributed toward the preservation of minor amounts of limestone.

Reconstruction of the configuration of the original carbonate shelf of the Knox Group is hampered by numerous thrust faults of regional extent in eastern Tennessee (fig. 11). These faults with displacements on the order of miles obscure regional facies trends by burying large segments of the original depositional shelf and bringing into juxtaposition the facies which accumulated on separate parts of the shelf. This is especially true in regard to the limestone facies. Before faulting, the original width of the area of limestone deposition was on the order of 100 miles (fig. 1). Mass transport by faults has buried the easternmost edge of the original shelf where sediments reflecting high energy were deposited. Consequently, only that part of the limestone sequence deposited under a low-energy condition is preserved in eastern Tennessee. Despite the fact that parts of the record are obscure, generalized facies trends can be ascertained in a series of stratigraphic sections extending from the easternmost outcrop belt in eastern Tennessee to deep wells in eastern Kentucky (fig. 9). A summary of selected primary features of the limestone facies, the transition zone, and the dolomite facies clearly indicates that many of the same primary elements are found throughout all facies of the Knox Group (fig. 12), emphasizing the regional impress of the overall subtidal environment. However, physical and chemical differences within the subtidal environment tended to restrict the abundance and even the presence of few elements to particular facies.

Where the limestone facies is present, it is characterized by dark-gray calcilutite containing thin zones of paper-thin laminated beds, angular intraclasts, oolite, arenite, and domal algal stromatolites. This combination of lithologies and algal domes suggests that the eastern limestone facies was deposited in water of normal salinity near wave base but not below the zone of photosynthesis. The energy level as suggested by the abundance of dark-gray calcilutite was normally low, although intraclasts and arenite beds record an occasional short-term increase in energy from strong storm currents. That a low-energy level was maintained throughout deposition of the limestone sequence is probably related to the fact that much of the ocean's energy from tides and wave action was largely dissipated before reaching that part of the facies now preserved in eastern Tennessee.

The transition zone between the dominantly limestone facies on the east and the dolomite facies on the west is confined to a relatively narrow geographic belt (fig. 9). Prouty (1947; 1948, p. 1618) thought that this abrupt facies change was related to a structural barrier, but my stratigraphic work shows no unusual thickening or thinning across the so-called

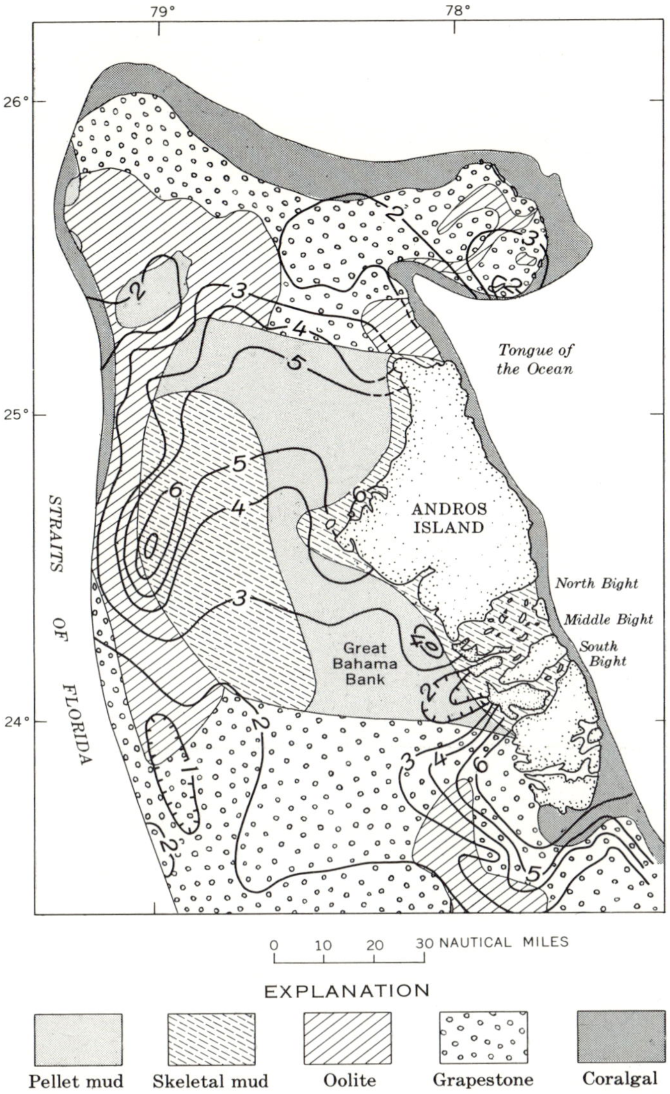

Figure 8.—Map of part of the Great Bahama Bank, showing the distribution of facies and magnesian carbonate content of sediments, in percent. From Newell and Rigby (1957) and Imbrie and Purdy (1962).

barrier. I believe that the transition zone, which has been partly telescoped by Appalachian thrusting, marks the location of a relatively constant geographic zone of change from normal marine water to penesaline water within an epicontinental sea. Surface and subsurface studies (Swartz, 1948; Donaldson and Page, 1964; Perry, 1964; Barnes, 1959; Chenoweth, 1968; Williams, 1969) suggest that this same transition zone within carbonate rocks equivalent to the Knox Group persists from New York to Texas (fig. 1), thus implying that the change from normal marine water to penesaline water existed completely around the edge of the ancient continental shelf.

The transition zone characteristically contains about equal proportions of dolomite and limestone, apparently reflecting the gradual lateral shift of the eastern part of the high-salinity water mass where magnesium concentration was large enough to promote dolomitization. The facies within the transition zone contains a higher proportion of oolite in relation to intraclasts and records the first stratiform algal stromatolites in dolomite. The transition facies apparently accumulated near the limit of oceanic wave and tidal effect, but under the influence of induced currents produced by water loss to evaporation.

The dolomite facies of the Knox Group contains a diversity of rock types ranging from dololutite to oolite, produced by widely different levels of depositional energy within a high-salinity environment. Forcefully emphasizing that although dolomitization may be controlled by the concentration of magnesium ions within an epicontinental sea, it does not follow that concentration of magnesium can only occur in low-energy environments. Despite the fact that a dolomite facies was deposited largely beyond the reach of oceanic waves and tidal currents, circulation within the high-salinity water mass was not static. Instead, high evaporation induced a constant shoreward current flow, which had a profound effect upon the kind and lateral distribution of facies. These induced currents were uniform and widespread, and caused the deposition of laterally persistent lithologic units as little as 1 inch thick. Where these currents were moderate, oolite and massive-bedded stratiform algal stromatolite as much as 140 feet thick accumulated; where current velocities were low, dololutite with domal algal stromatolites accumulated. Because of the similarity in energy levels, the distribution of dololutite, oolite, and stratiform algal stromatolite of the highly saline environment closely resembles the distribution pattern of like lithologic elements in the normal marine limestone phase of Shaw (1964) and Irwin (1965), where oolite and reefs accumulated in the higher energy zones at the shelf edge and calcilutite accumulated in areas of lower energy.

SUMMARY

Approximately 90 percent of the Upper Cambrian and Lower Ordovician carbonate strata is dolomite. This is in sharp contrast to Holocene carbonate deposition sites where most of the carbonate strata are limestone and only a small percentage of the total sediment is dolomite, mainly confined to the supratidal area. The epicontinental-sea sedimentation model and its shoreward increasing salinity gradient is postulated to be the likely mechanism responsible for widespread subtidal dolomitization during Late Cambrian and Early Ordovician time. Comparison of the epicontinental sedimentation model to present-day carbonate depositional sites suggests that Holocene sites represent only the normal marine limestone phase of the epicontinental model.

Present-day examples of the epicontinental salinity system, although measured only by tens of miles, illustrate that appreciable salinity increase can occur without physical

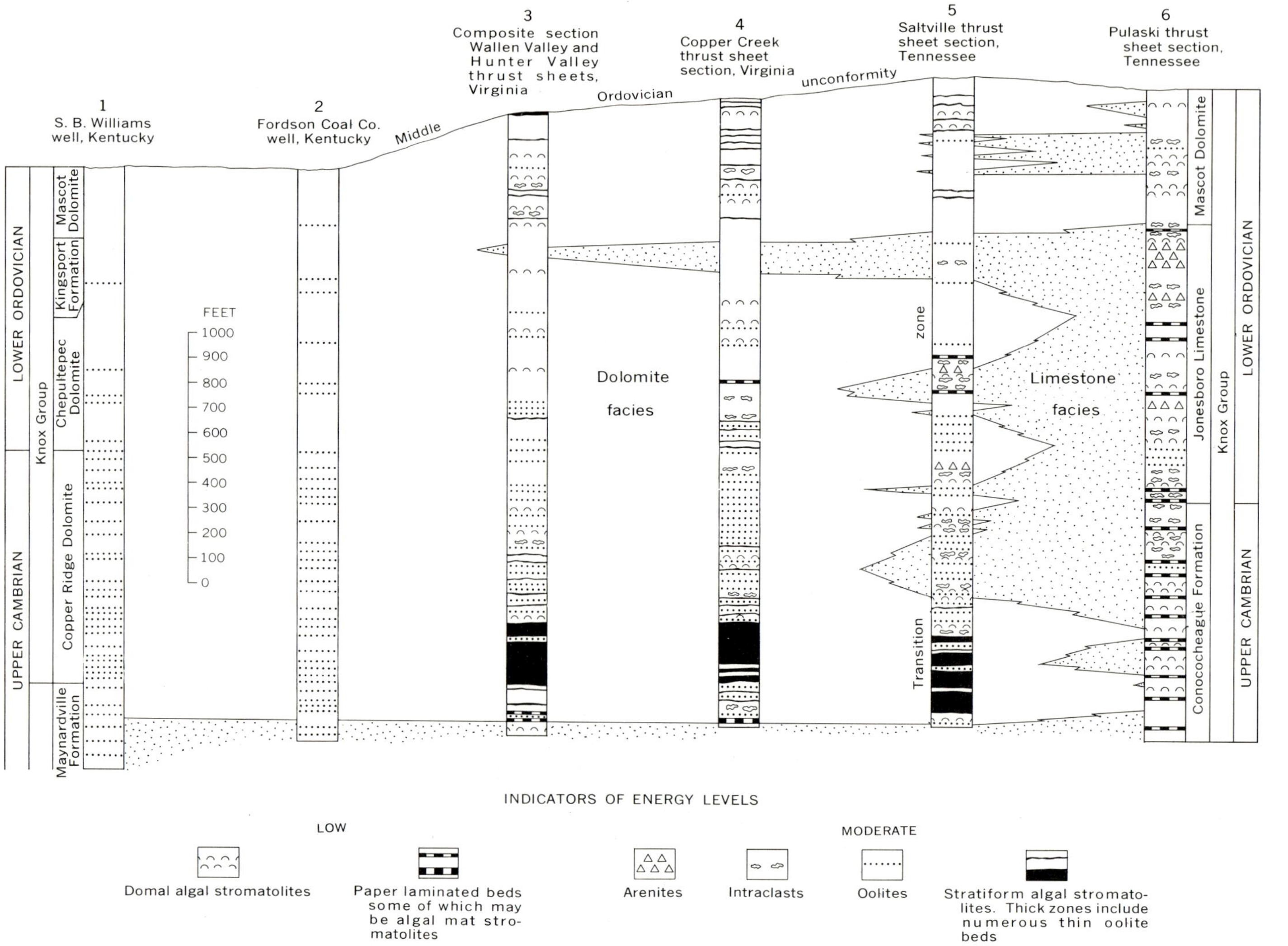

Figure 9.—Sections showing the distribution of energy-indicative beds in the Upper Cambrian and Lower Ordovician carbonate strata in wells in Kentucky and surface sections in Virginia and Tennessee. Algal stromatolites could not be identified in well cuttings from Kentucky. (See fig. 11 for line of section.)

barriers. Such a system developed on an ancient, shallow continental shelf, hundreds of miles wide, could easily concentrate sea water to the point of gypsum saturation. This would result in the development of subtidal dolomite on a regional scale. Increased fresh-water runoff from land or seasonal shifts in wind direction, as in the Bahamas, would contribute to a seasonal deterioration of the ancient salinity system. Resolution of calcium sulfate during the period of lower salinity would account for only trace amounts of gypsum now found in the rocks of Late Cambrian and Early Ordovician age.

Sedimentation within an epicontinental sea, as typified by the Knox Group of Late Cambrian and Early Ordovician age in the southern Appalachians, is closely related to a westward-increasing salinity gradient, so that a lateral transition from normal marine limestone facies to a transition zone to a dolomite facies exists. Domal algal stromatolites are abundant throughout both the limestone and dolomite facies of the Knox, indicating that variation in salinity has little effect on their growth, but that water depth during deposition of either facies was not below the zone of photosynthesis. Limestone deposition was restricted to a rather narrow band at the oceanic bordering edge of the epicontinental sea, where continual flushing by wave and tidal currents prevented extensive buildup in salinity. The transition zone developed near the limit of tidal exchange, thus it occupies a relatively fixed geographic position throughout deposition of the Knox. Although the dolomite facies was deposited in high-salinity water beyond the reach of oceanic and tidal currents, energy levels within that environment were not uniformly low. Instead, the diversity in rock type, from dololutite to oolite, suggests that energy levels ranged from low to moderate. The

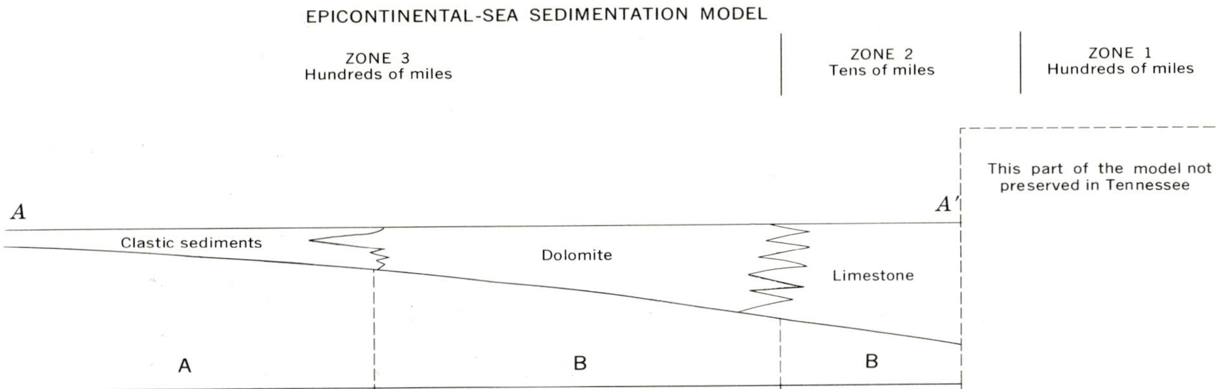

	A	B	B
Lithology	Sandstone with some siltstone and shale. Carbonate rocks increasing upward and to the southeast. Glauconite	Dolomite with minor beds of sandstone and shale	Limestone with minor beds of sandstone and shale
Crossbedding and ripple marks	Abundant	Rare	
Oolite content	Locally abundant in carbonate rocks	Low to abundant	Low
Shrinkage cracks	Generally rare in sequence, but can be locally abundant		
Intraclast content	Abundant	Low to moderate	Moderate
Laminations	Few	Locally abundant	Abundant
Burrows	Common	Locally common	
Algal stromatolites	Abundant in carbonate rocks	Abundant	
Other fossils	Diverse to restricted	Restricted to a few forms	Diverse
Salinity	Fluctuating from normal to high because of fresh water dilution from land	High	Normal ← Increasing
Dominant energy level	High → Low to moderate	Low to moderate	Low
Source of energy	← Wind; Longshore currents due to density differential produced by fresh water runoff; Induced currents →	→ Induced current flow from high rate of evaporation ←	Oceanic wave and tidal
Environment	Intertidal to subtidal	Subtidal	

Figure 10.—Summary of primary characteristics and interpretive environments of the rocks of the Knox Group of Tennessee (B) compared with similar parameters of equivalent age rocks in Wisconsin (A). Cross section is line *A–A′* of figure 1. (Wisconsin data from Ostrom, 1970, and R. A. Davis, 1970).

distribution of the different rock types was related to circulatory patterns induced where a constant shoreward current flow developed from replacement of water by evaporation loss. Where velocities of the induced current were moderate, oolite and stratiform algal stromatolite development is favored; where velocities were low, dololutite with domal algal stromatolites accumulated.

REFERENCES CITED

Adams, J. E., and Rhodes, M. L., 1960, Dolomitization by seepage refluxion: Am. Assoc. Petroleum Geologists Bull., v. 44, no. 12, p. 1912–1920.

Barnes, V. E., 1959, Stratigraphy of the pre-Simpson Paleozoic subsurface rocks of Texas and southeast New Mexico, V. 1–2: Texas Univ. Pub. no. 5924, 836 p.

Black, Maurice, 1933, The algal sedimentation of Andros Island, Bahamas: Royal Soc. London Philos. Trans. ser. B, vol. 222, p. 165–192.

Burst, J. F., 1965, Subaqueously formed shrinkage cracks in clay: Jour. Sed. Petrology, v. 35, no. 2, p. 348–353.

Chave, K. E., 1954, Aspects of the biochemistry of magnesium–[Pt.] 1, Calcareous marine organisms: Jour. Geology v. 62, no. 3, p. 266–283.

Chenoweth, P. A., 1968, Early Paleozoic (Arbuckle) overlap, southern Mid-continent, United States: Am. Assoc. Petroleum Geologists Bull. v. 52, no. 9, p. 1670–1688.

Chilingar, G. V., 1962, Dependence on temperature of Ca/Mg ratio of skeletal structure of organisms and direct chemical precipitation out of sea water: Southern California Acad. Sci. Bull., v. 61, p. 45–60.

Cloud, P. E., Jr., 1962, Environment of calcium carbonate deposition west of Andros Island, Bahamas: U.S. Geol. Survey Prof. Paper 350, 138 p.

Crawford, Johnson, 1945, Structural and stratigraphic control of zinc deposits in East Tennessee: Econ. Geology, v. 40, p. 408–415.

Davis, G. R., 1970, Algal-laminated sediments, Gladstone embayment, Shark Bay, Western Australia, *in* Carbonate sedimentation and environments, Shark Bay, Western Australia: Am. Assoc. Petroleum Geologists Mem. 13, p. 169–205.

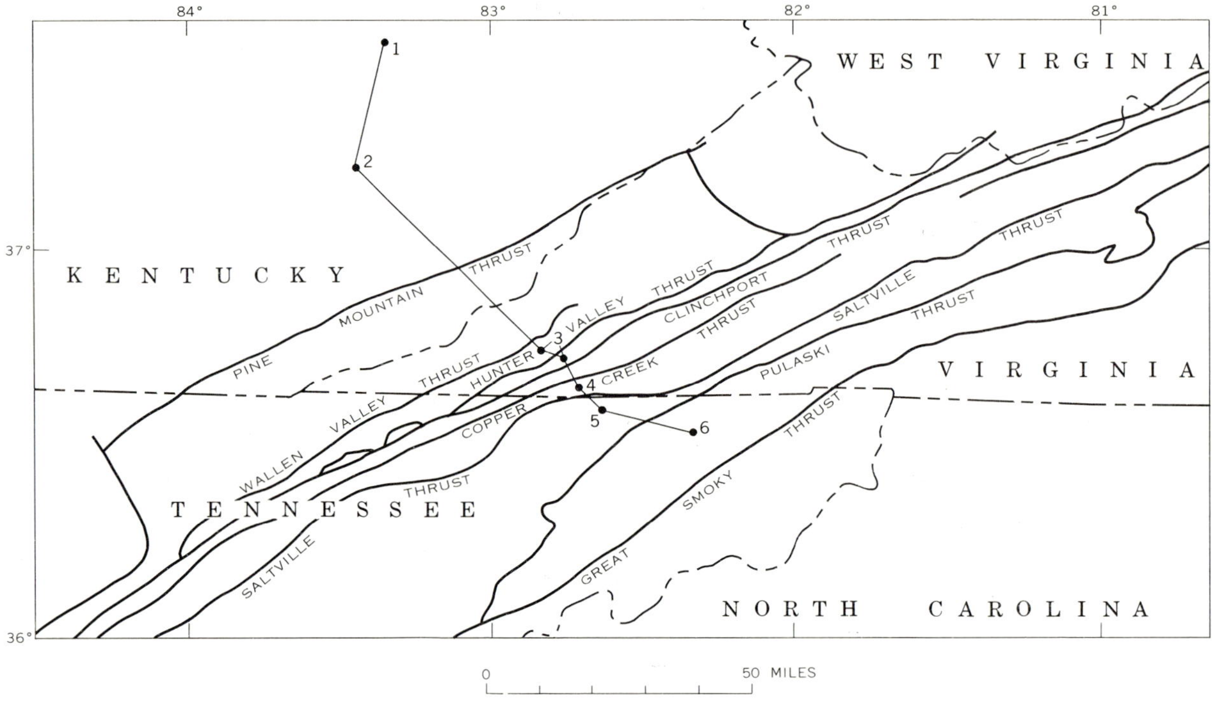

Figure 11.—Map showing the location of wells and measured sections in figure 9 and the trace of major thrust faults in the area.

Davis, R. A., Jr., 1970, Prairie Du Chien Group in the Upper Mississippi Valley, *in* Field trip guidebook for Cambrian-Ordovician geology of western Wisconsin—Geol. Soc. America, Ann. Mtg., Milwaukee, Wis., 1970: Wisconsin Geol. and Nat. History Survey Inf. Circ. 11, p. 35–44.

Donaldson, Alan, and Page, Ronald, 1964, Stratigraphic reference sections of Elbrook and Conococheague Formations (Middle and Upper Cambrian) and Beekmantown Group (Lower Ordovician) in Berkeley and Jefferson Counties, West Virginia: West Virginia Acad. Sci. Proc., v. 35, p. 149–171.

Emery, K. O., and Stevenson, R. E., 1957, Estuaries and lagoons—[Pt.] 1, Physical and chemical characteristics, *in* Chap. 23 *of* Hedgpeth, J. W., ed., Ecology: Geol. Soc. America Mem. 67, p. 673–693.

Folk, R. L., 1959, Thin-section examination of pre-Simpson Paleozoic rocks, *in* V. 1 *of* Barnes, V. E., Stratigraphy of the pre-Simpson Paleozoic subsurface rocks of Texas and southeast New Mexico: Texas Univ. Pub., no. 5924, p. 95–130.

Gebelein, C. D., 1969, Distribution, morphology, and accretion rate of Recent subtidal algal stromatolites, Bermuda: Jour. Sed. Petrology, v. 39, no. 1, p. 49–69.

Ginsburg, R. N., 1960, Ancient analogues of Recent stromatolites: Internat. Geol. Cong., 21st, Copenhagen, 1960, Rept., pt. 22, p. 26–35.

Harris, L. D., 1969, Kingsport Formation and Mascot Dolomite (Lower Ordovician) of East Tennessee, *in* Papers on the stratigraphy and mine geology of the Kingsport and Mascot Formations (Lower Ordovician) of East Tennessee: Tennessee Div. Geology Rept. Inv. 23, p. 1–39.

Herbert, Paul, Jr., and Young, R. S., 1956, Sulfide mineralization in the Shenandoah Valley of Virginia: Virginia Div. Geology Bull. 70, 58 p.

Hite, R. J., 1968, Distribution and geologic habitat of marine halite and associated potash deposits, *in* Seminar on sources of mineral raw materials for the fertilizer industry in Asia and the Far East: U.N. ECAFE Mineral Resources Devel. Ser. 32, p. 307–326.

——1970, Shelf carbonate sedimentation controlled by salinity in the Paradox basin, southeast Utah, *in* Rau, J. L., and Dellwig, L. F., eds., Third symposium on salt, V. 1: Cleveland, Ohio, Northern Ohio Geol. Soc., p. 48–66.

Holland, C. H., ed., 1971, Cambrian of the New World, V. 1: New York and London, Interscience Publishers, 456 p.

Illing, L. V., Wells, A. J., and Taylor, J. C. M., 1965, Penecontemporary dolomite in the Persian Gulf, *in* Dolomitization and limestone diagenesis—A symposium: Soc. Econ. Paleontologists and Mineralogists Spec. Pub. 13, p. 89–111.

Imbrie, John, and Purdy, E. C., 1962, Classification of modern Bahamian carbonate sediments, *in* Classification of carbonate rocks—A symposium: Am. Assoc. Petroleum Geologists Mem. 1, p. 253–272.

Irwin, M. L., 1965, General theory of epeiric clear water sedimentation: Am. Assoc. Petroleum Geologists Bull., v. 49, no. 4, p. 445–459.

Kendall, C. G., and Skipwith, P. A., 1968, Recent algal mats of a Persian Gulf lagoon: Jour. Sed. Petrology, v. 38, no. 4, p. 1040–1058.

King, R. H., 1947, Sedimentation in Permian Castile Sea: Am. Assoc. Petroleum Geologists Bull. v. 31, no. 3, p. 470–477.

Lang, W. T. B., 1937, The Permian formation of the Pecos Valley of New Mexico and Texas: Am. Assoc. Petroleum Geologists Bull., v. 21, p. 833–898.

Laporte, L. F., 1971, Paleozoic carbonate facies of the central Appalachian shelf: Jour. Sed. Petrology, v. 41, no. 3, p. 724–740.

Lochman-Balk, Christina, 1971, The Cambrian of the craton of the United States, *in* Cambrian of the New World, V. 1: New York and London, Interscience Publishers, p. 79–167.

Logan, B. W., 1961, Cryptozoon and associate stromatolites from the Recent Shark Bay, Western Australia: Jour. Geology, v. 69, no. 5, p. 517–533.

Logan, B. W., and Cebulski, D. E., 1970, Sedimentary environments of Shark Bay, Western Australia, *in* Carbonate sedimentation and environments, Shark Bay, Western Australia: Am. Assoc. Petroleum Geologists Mem. 13, p. 1–37.

Logan, B. W., Rezak, Richard, and Ginsburg, R. N., 1964, Classification and environmental significance of algal stromatolites: Jour. Geology, v. 72, no. 3, p. 68–83.

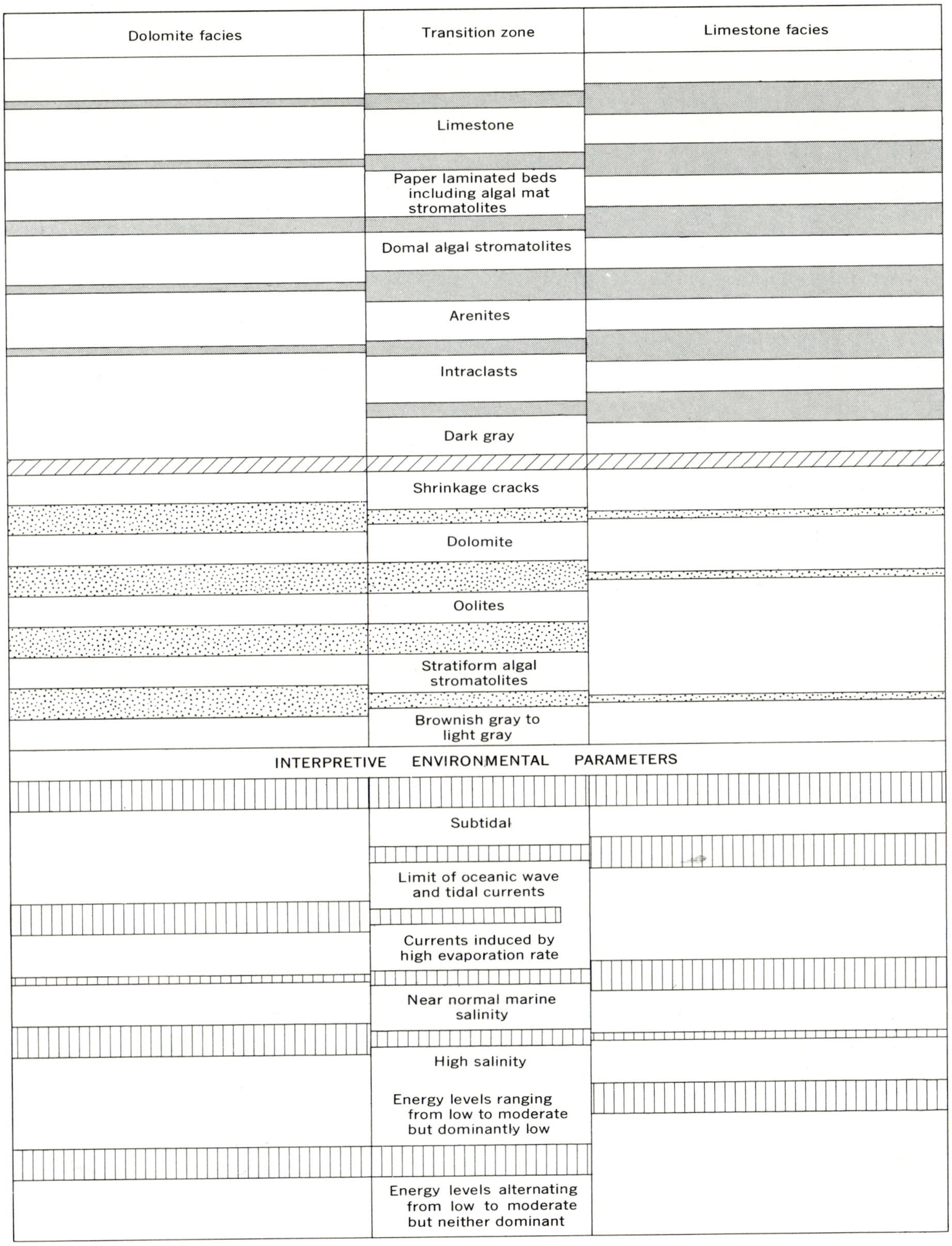

Figure 12.—The distribution of common elements of the dolomite, transition, and limestone facies of the Knox Group, and interpretive environmental parameters. Thickness of the bar emphasizes the relative importance of each element within each facies.

Lowenstam, H. A., 1954, Factors affecting the aragonite-calcite ratios in carbonate-secreting marine organisms: Jour. Geology v. 62, p. 284–322.

Monty, Claude, 1965, Recent algal stromatolites in the Windward Lagoon, Andros Island, Bahamas: Soc. Géol. Belgique Annales, v. 88, p. 269–276.

Newell, N. D., Imbrie, John, Purdy, E. G., and Thurber, D. L., 1959, Organism communities and bottom facies, Great Bahama Bank: Am. Mus. Nat. History Bull. v. 117, p. 177–228.

Newell, N. D., and Rigby, J. K., 1957, Geological studies on the Great Bahama Bank, *in* Regional aspects of carbonate deposition–A symposium: Soc. Econ. Paleontologists and Mineralogists Spec. Pub. 5, p. 15–72.

Ochsenius, Karl, 1877, Die Bildung der Steinsalzlager und ihrer Mutterlaugensalze: Halle, C. E. M. Pfeffer, 172 p.

Oder, C. R. L., and Miller, H. W., 1945, Stratigraphy of the Mascot-Jefferson City zinc district [Tenn.]: Am. Inst. Mining Metall. Engineers Tech. Pub. 1818, 9 p.; A.I.M.E. Trans., v. 178, p. 223–231 (1948).

Oder, C. R. L., and Ricketts, J. E., 1961, Geology of the Mascot-Jefferson City zinc district, Tennessee: Tennessee Div. Geology Rept. Inv. 12, 29 p.

Ostrom, M. E., 1970, Sedimentation cycles in the Lower Paleozoic rocks of western Wisconsin, *in* Field trip guidebook for Cambrian-Ordovician geology of western Wisconsin–Geol. Soc. America, Ann. Mtg., Milwaukee, Wis. 1970: Wisconsin Geol. and Nat. History Survey Inf. Circ. 11, p. 10–34.

Perry, W. J., Jr., 1964, Geology of Ray Sponaugle well, Pendleton County, West Virginia: Am. Assoc. Petroleum Geologists Bull., v. 48, no. 5, p. 659–669.

Prouty, C. E., 1947, Relationship of Cambro-Ordovician dolomites to facies barriers in Tennessee and Virginia [abs.]: Geol. Soc. America Bull., v. 58, no. 12, pt. 2, p. 1218–1219.

——1948, Trenton and sub-Trenton stratigraphy of northwest belts of Virginia and Tennessee, *in* Appalachian Basin Ordovician symposium: Am. Assoc. Petroleum Geologists Bull., v. 32, no. 8, p. 1596–1626.

Rodgers, John, 1968, The eastern edge of the North American Continent during the Cambrian and Early Ordovician, Chap. 10 *in* Zen, E-an, and others, eds., Studies of Appalachian geology, northern and maritime: New York and London, Interscience Publishers, p. 141–149.

Saxby, D. B., and Lamar, J. E., 1957, Gypsum and anhydrite in Illinois: Illinois State Geol. Survey Circ. 226, 26 p.

Scruton, P. C., 1953, Deposition of evaporites: Am. Assoc. Petroleum Geologists Bull., v. 37, no. 11, p. 2498–2512.

Shaw, A. B., 1964, Time in stratigraphy: New York, McGraw-Hill Book Co., 365 p.

Shinn, E. A., Ginsburg, R. N., and Lloyd, R. M., 1965, Recent supratidal dolomite from Andros Island, Bahamas, *in* Dolomitization and limestone diagenesis–A symposium: Soc. Econ. Paleontologists and Mineralogists Spec. Pub. 13, p. 112–123.

Smith, C. L., 1940, The Great Bahama Bank–[Pt.] 1, General hydrographical and chemical features: Jour. Marine Research, v. 3, no. 2, p. 147–170.

Stagg, A. K., and Fischer, F. T., 1970, Upper Knox stratigraphy of Middle Tennessee [abs.]: Geol. Soc. America Abstracts with Programs, v. 2, no. 7, p. 693.

Stewart, F. H., 1963, Marine evaporites, Chap. Y *of* Data of Geochemistry, 6th ed.: U.S. Geol. Survey Prof. Paper 440-Y, 52 p.

Swartz, F. M., 1948, Trenton and sub-Trenton of outcrop areas in New York, Pennsylvania, and Maryland, *in* Appalachian Basin Ordovician symposium: Am. Assoc. Petroleum Geologist Bull., v. 32, no. 8, p. 1493–1595.

Williams, C. H., Jr., 1969, Cross section from Mississippi-Tennessee State line to Horn Island in Gulf of Mexico: Jackson, Miss., Mississippi Geol. Survey, map.

Young, R. S., and Wedow, Helmuth, Jr., 1962, Geologic setting of the Myers zinc prospect, Smyth County, Virginia [abs.]: Geol. Soc. America Spec. Paper 68, p. 82.

Jour. Research U.S. Geol. Survey
Vol. 1, No. 1, Jan.—Feb. 1973, p. 79—80

DETERMINATION OF GOLD IN PHOSPHATES BY ACTIVATION ANALYSIS USING EPITHERMAL NEUTRONS

By JACK J. ROWE, Washington, D.C.

Abstract.—A simple method is described for determining gold in phosphates and phosphatic materials. Samples in a cadmium container are irradiated with epithermal neutrons to minimize the formation of ^{32}P, while permitting the formation of adequate amounts of ^{198}Au. Fire assay-radiochemical methods are used to separate the ^{198}Au. Concentrations as low as 0.1 ppb can be determined readily while maintaining low radiation levels.

The routine determination of gold in geologic materials using the method of Rowe and Simon (1968) provides for a 10-hour irradiation at a flux of 5×10^{12} n per cm^2 per sec and 10 days of cooling to permit the decay of 15-hour ^{24}Na, the principal source of matrix radioactivity in rocks and minerals. When this procedure is applied to phosphatic materials, high levels of 16-day ^{32}P are formed. Because of its biological effect, it is undesirable to expose personnel to the hazards of radioactive phosphorus. It is not practical to wait for the decay of ^{32}P because the 2.7-day ^{198}Au decays much more rapidly than the 16-day ^{32}P. The use of epithermal neutron irradiation permits the determination of gold while reducing the amount of ^{32}P formed.

The "advantage factor" obtained by using epithermal neutrons for irradiations rather than the entire reactor spectrum (thermal plus epithermal) can be defined by the ratio R_{Cd}^{m}/R_{Cd}^{a} where R_{Cd} is the cadmium ratio, m is the matrix, and a is the element being studied. The cadmium ratio can be determined experimentally or by calculation. If the cadmium ratio of a standard isotope, usually ^{198}Au, has been determined, the corresponding R_{Cd} for another nuclide can be calculated from the following formula given by Brunfelt and Steinnes (1969):

$$R_{Cd} = 1 + \frac{\sigma_o}{\sigma_o{}^{Au}} \cdot \frac{0.44\,\sigma_o{}^{Au} + I^{Au}}{0.44\,\sigma_o + I} \quad (R_{Cd}^{Au} - 1),$$

where σ_o = the thermal neutron cross section and I = the resonance activation integral excluding the $1/v$ contribution for the nuclide.

Experimentally, the cadmium ratio (R_{Cd}) can be defined as:

$$R_{Cd} = \frac{A_{th} + A_r}{A_r},$$

where A_{th} and A_r are the activities produced from thermal and epithermal neutrons, respectively. Hence the cadmium ratio is a measure of the decrease in activity of an isotope irradiated by epithermal neutrons compared to irradiation with the total neutron flux.

Brunfelt and Steinnes (1969) have shown that the calculated values for the cadmium ratio agree with experimentally determined values for many elements. Table 1 shows the cadmium ratio and the gold advantage factor for some of the nuclides observed in studies of rocks and phosphatic materials. The advantage factors are favorable not only for the determination of gold in a phosphorus matrix, but also for matrices containing Na, Fe, Co, Cr, and Ca. Hence epithermal neutron irradiations can be applied to many materials.

IRRADIATION PROCEDURE

Approximately 1 g of each sample was weighed into 2/5-dram polyethylene vials. Monitors containing 50 ng of gold were prepared by accurately pipetting 0.2 ml of a solution containing 250 ng of gold per ml onto 0.2 g of spectrographic grade silica in a 2/5-dram vial. Usually 10 samples plus four monitors were irradiated together. Vials were heat sealed and placed in a cadmium cylinder (1 mm thick) fitted with cadmium caps at top and bottom and formed to fit inside the usual irradiation polybucket. The cadmium absorbed neutrons below 0.4 eV, hence the induced activity in the samples was due to epithermal neutrons.

Samples and monitors were irradiated for 30 minutes in the U.S. Naval Research Laboratory reactor (thermal flux = 5×10^{12} n per cm^2 per sec; R_{Cd}^{Au} = 3.2). After cooling overnight, the overall radioactivity of the samples was generally less than 2 mr per hour at 6 inches, unshielded. This low amount reduced the hazards involved in handling the irradiated samples.

Table 1.—*Cadmium ratio and gold advantage factor for various nuclides*

Nuclide	Half-life[1]	R_{Cd}	Advantage factor R^{m}_{Cd}/R^{Au}_{Cd}
^{198}Au	2.7 d	3.2	....
^{86}Rb	18.6 d	3.1	0.97
^{122}Sb	2.8 d	2.5	.8
^{124}Sb	60 d	1.6	.5
^{134}Cs	2.3 y	3.3	1.03
^{131}Ba	12 d	2.5	.8
^{153}Sm	47 h	3.3	1.03
^{160}Tb	73 d	2.7	.8
^{181}Hf	46 d	21	6.6
^{182}Ta	111 d	2.3	.7
^{233}Pa(Th)	27 d	4.0	1.25
^{24}Na	15 h	60	18.7
^{47}Ca	150 d	27	8.4
^{46}Sc	85 d	74	23
^{59}Fe	45 d	32	10
^{60}Co	5.3 y	18	5.6
^{140}La	40 h	26	8
^{152}Eu	12 y	45	14
^{152m}Eu	9.5 h	34	10.6
^{32}P	16 d	39	12.1
^{51}Cr	27 d	26	8.4

[1] Abbreviations: h, hour; d, day; y, year.

RADIOCHEMISTRY

Because of the low concentrations of gold in the samples being analyzed, it was necessary to perform a radiochemical separation of the gold. The procedure used was the fire assay-radiochemical method of Rowe and Simon (1968). Samples were processed through fire assay with gold carrier. The final gold bead was weighed for yield determination. Samples were counted in a 3- by 3-inch well-type NaI(Tl) detector coupled to a multichannel analyzer. The 0.413-MeV peak of ^{198}Au was used for the calculations.

DISCUSSION

Epithermal neutron irradiations have been applied by de Lange and others (1968) and Lobanov and others (1966) to reduce the interferences from ^{24}Na and ^{59}Fe in the instrumental determination of gold in ores. Brunfelt and Steinnes (1969) showed an improvement in the instrumental neutron activation determination of many elements through the use of epithermal irradiations. It can be seen from table 1 that the technique is applicable to the determination of Ta, Ba, Sb, Rb, Cs, Sm, Tb, and Th to overcome interferences from Na, Fe, Co, Eu, Sc, Ca and P.

Gamma-ray spectra obtained after fire assay radiochemistry of phosphates were virtually free of other nuclides. The only isotope observed was ^{144}Ce (31-hour). It has a peak at 0.296 MeV, which does not interfere with the 0.413-MeV peak for ^{198}Au. The ^{198}Au activity was sufficient to provide 150 counts per min per ng of gold in the photopeak using Covell's (1959) method for calculating peak area. Samples of phosphates were irradiated one afternoon, processed the next morning, and counted by the close of the day, providing for rapid analyses with only negligible exposure of analysts to radioactivity.

This method was applied to the determination of gold in Florida phosphates where the gold content ranged from 0.4 to 5 ppb. It was also used for the determination of gold in deer antlers in connection with a study by Jones (1970, p. 12) of the gold content of animals. Gold in the ash of deer antlers ranged from 0.3 to 28.3 ppb. Each irradiation included at least one 0.1-g sample of gold quartz standard GQS-1 (Millard and others, 1969). Results for this standard agree with the published values.

ACKNOWLEDGMENTS

The author wishes to acknowledge the assistance and cooperation of L. P. Harris, of the U.S. Naval Research Laboratory, and the helpful suggestions of L. P. Greenland.

REFERENCES CITED

Brunfelt, A. O., and Steinnes, E., 1969, Instrumental activation analysis of silicate rocks with epithermal neutrons: Anal. Chim. Acta, v. 48, no. 1, p. 13–24.

Covell, D. F., 1959, Determination of gamma-ray abundance directly from total absorption peak: Anal. Chemistry, v. 31, p. 1785–1790.

deLange, P. W., deWet, W. J., Turkstra, J., and Venter, J. H., 1968, Nondestructive neutron activation analysis of small samples of Witwatersrand ore for gold: Anal. Chemistry, v. 40, no. 2, p. 451–454.

Jones, R. S., 1970, Gold content of water, plants, and animals: U.S. Geol. Survey Circ. 625, 15 p.

Lobanov, E. M., Miranskii, I. A., Pozychanyuk, V. F., Saifutdinova, D. G., and Khaidarov, A. A., 1966, A more effective determination of gold in ores by activation analysis, *in* Lobanov, E. M., ed., Activation analysis; Proceedings of First All-Union Coordinating Conference, Tashkent, Oct. 24–28, 1962: Jerusalem, Israel Program for Sci. Translation, p. 60–63, available from Natl. Tech. Inf. Service, U.S. Dept. Commerce, Springfield, Va.

Millard, H. T., Jr., Marinenko, John, and McLane, J. E., 1969, Establishment of gold-quartz standard GQS-1: U.S. Geol. Survey Circ. 598, 6 p.

Rowe, J. J., and Simon, F. O., 1968, The determination of gold in geologic materials by neutron-activation analysis using fire assay for the radiochemical separations: U.S. Geol. Survey Circ. 599, 4 p.

Jour. Research U.S. Geol. Survey
Vol. 1, No. 1, Jan.—Feb. 1973, p. 81—84

RAPID DETERMINATION OF SULFUR IN ROCKS

By LEONARD SHAPIRO, Washington, D.C.

Abstract.—Sulfur is determined turbidimetrically as barium sulfate after an aqua regia attack. The turbidity is formed in an ammoniacal solution from which R_2O_3 has been centrifuged. Reproducibility of turbidity is obtained by adding barium chloride as a solid rather than as a solution. Sulfur is determined in the range 0.01–4 percent within ±0.02 absolute, or approximately 5 percent of the amount present, whichever is larger. A 100-mg sample is used for sulfur concentrations of up to 0.50 percent S, a 20-mg sample for higher levels. A determination requires about 5 minutes.

Conventional chemical procedures for the determination of sulfur in rocks are generally based on an oxidizing sodium carbonate fusion to decompose the sample, followed by a separation of the sulfur from possible interferences and the subsequent precipitation and weighing of barium sulphate. An excellent summary of currently used procedures for sulfur determinations is given by Maxwell (1968). All the procedures described can give excellent results, but they are lengthy. An excellent summary of methods for sulfur in materials other than rocks is given by Patterson (1958), who also gives a general review of turbidimetric methods for sulfur.

The precipitation of sulfur with barium is probably the most widely used turbidimetric determination (Fisher, 1966, p. 277–282). The precision of this determination is dependent on the reproducibility of the turbidity which is itself dependent on the conditions at the time of initiation of precipitation. Fisher refers to the complexity and irreproducibility of nucleation and crystal growth. Solid barium chloride has been used in water and soil analysis (American Public Health Association, 1965, p. 291–292; Bardsley and Lancaster, 1965) to obtain reproducible turbidity, and in our laboratory it was found that when barium chloride is introduced as a solid and the precipitation made in ammoniacal solution, reproducibility is remarkably better than when it is added as a solution.

The method described in this paper is a chemical technique which is more rapid and simple than previous chemical techniques and requires no complex instrumentation. To a solution made by attacking a 100-mg sample with aqua regia in a test tube, calcium chloride is added. The solution is boiled, made ammoniacal, and the precipitate centrifuged off. About 5 ml of the clear supernatant liquid is transferred by pipet to a dry test tube to which a small spike of sulfate has been added. The sulfate is precipitated by adding powdered barium chloride, and the absorbance of the resultant turbidity is measured in a spectrophotometer after a few minutes. A solution prepared from pure sodium sulfate is used as a reference standard. The result obtained represents all the sulfide which has been converted to sulfate plus all the acid-soluble sulfate.

The procedure may be repeated using hydrochloric acid in place of aqua regia to obtain a value for the acid-soluble sulfate. Samples containing as much as 4 percent S can be analyzed.

REAGENTS AND APPARATUS

Reagents

Barium chloride: Crush the crystals with a mortar and pestle.
HNO_3, concentrated.
HCl, concentrated.
Dilute HNO_3, 1+3 dilution with water.
NH_4OH, 1+1 dilution with water.
Standard sulfate solution: Dissolve 177.5 mg Na_2SO_4 in 250 ml H_2O. One ml contains 0.4 mg SO_3 or 0.16 mg S.
Calcium chloride solution: Dissolve 5 g $CaCl_2 \cdot 2H_2O$ in 100 ml H_2O.

Apparatus

Spectrophotometer, fitted for test tubes.
Centrifuge.
Test tubes, 18 by 150 mm.
Bunsen burner.
Pipets, squeeze type, 2-ml and 5-ml capacities.
Dipper, about 2 mm deep and 5 mm in diameter capable of measuring 30±10 mg of the powdered barium chloride.

PROCEDURE

Transfer 100-mg samples (100 mesh or finer) through a funnel to each of a series of test tubes. To an additional test tube add 2 ml of standard sulfate solution. Another test tube serves as a blank. Add 0.2 ml of concentrated HNO_3 to all test tubes with a squeeze-type pipet. Pass each test tube containing a sample over a flame for several seconds to bring the solution to a boil. Allow each test tube to cool for at least a minute, then repeat the heating after adding 0.4 ml of concentrated HCl. Add 1 ml of $CaCl_2$ solution to all test tubes. Add 5 ml of water to the first sample with the squeeze-type pipet, bring to a boil over a burner and maintain at or near boiling for 30 seconds, and then add 2 ml of (1+1) NH_4OH by squeeze pipet and agitate briefly. Add 5 ml of water and agitate briefly. Repeat this treatment with each of the samples. Add 2 ml (1+1) NH_4OH to the blank and standard. Add 10 ml of water to the blank and 8 ml to the standard test tube and agitate the blank and standard. Centrifuge all the samples at about 1,200 rpm for 1½ minutes.

To each of a second set of dry test tubes add 0.1 ml of the standard sulfate solution to serve as a spike, and then transfer 5 ml of the supernatant liquids previously prepared, using a squeeze pipet, to this second set of test tubes.

Set the spectrophotometer to read 0 absorbance at 650 nm using a test tube containing water. Record the absorbance of each test tube of the second set. These readings provide a means of correcting for any color, cloudiness, or tube variations. By use of the dipper transfer approximately 30 mg of powdered $BaCl_2$ to each tube, without agitation. Note the time and then agitate each tube for a few seconds. It is not necessary to dissolve all the barium chloride. Two minutes after the first tube has been agitated start reading absorbance. The addition and agitation steps should be done with not more than 10 tubes at a time.

Calculate sulfur concentrations by subtracting the absorbance readings prior to precipitation from those after precipitation for each tube and then subtracting the value for the blank from those of the samples and the standard. The standard corresponds to 0.32 percent S, and its absorbance should be about 0.400.

If the sulfur is higher than 0.5 percent, the procedure should be repeated with a 20-mg sample, and a standard curve should be made using 0, 1, 2, 3, 4, and 5 ml of the standard sulfate solution. The curve is linear to 3 ml of standard sulfate solution, but is usable to 5 ml which corresponds to 4 percent S in a sample.

DISCUSSION AND RESULTS

The results shown in table 1 illustrate the greater reproducibility obtained when $BaCl_2$ is added by dipper as powder than that obtained when 0.2 ml of 30-percent $BaCl_2$ is added by pipet.

The variation in weight of 10 dipperfuls was found to be about 20 percent when a spatula was used to level the powder in the dipper. The turbidity was then measured using a 1-ml aliquot of the sulfate standard solution (equivalent to 0.16 percent S) in the described procedure and 20, 40, and 80 mg of powdered $BaCl_2$. The turbidity produced by 20 mg and 40 mg was the same, whereas that produced by 80 mg was about

Table 1.—*Comparison of absorbances produced by* $BaCl_2$ *added as a solid and as a solution*

30 mg of solid	*0.2 ml of 30-percent solution*
0.170	0.205
.170	.170
.170	.155
.160	.130
.165	.115
.165	.105

10 percent less. The tests were done in triplicate. In the procedure described, a 30-mg dipper is used which allows considerable variation in the amount dispensed without noticeable effect on the resultant turbidity.

The stability and the time required for the turbidity to reach a maximum vary with the sulfate level. When 0.5 mg S is used, the maximum for which linearity is obtained, maximum absorbance occurs in several seconds and is stable for about 5 minutes; after this it begins to decline. At low levels of sulfate the maximum absorbance is reached in 2–3 minutes and is stable for a much longer time than that obtained from the high levels of sulfate. Adding some known stabilizers tends to have an adverse effect on the rate of turbidity formation.

At very low levels of sulfur, equivalent to a few hundredths of a milligram, the initiation of turbidity is variable and sometimes fails to occur. This problem is eliminated by the addition of a spike of 0.016 mg S to all solutions. This ensures that enough sulfur is always present to initiate turbidity. If the standards and samples are measured 2–4 minutes after dissolving the powdered barium chloride, the standards show a near linearity, beginning to fall off slightly above 0.5 mg S.

The slope of the absorbance-concentration curve is steeper (about 15 percent) when aqua regia instead of hydrochloric acid is used in decomposing the sample. This is of concern if one were to determine soluble sulfate where hydrochloric acid alone would be used. The difference can be eliminated if a small amount of nitric acid is added to the hydrochloric acid solution along with the sulfate spike prior to the addition of barium chloride. When 0.2, 0.4, and 0.6 ml (1+3) HNO_3 is used the turbidity obtained is nearly the same. For determining acid-soluble sulfate, 0.4 ml was chosen. Three times this amount perceptibly reduces the turbidity.

When the procedure was applied to several hundred rocks, some of them, particularly those with organic matter, inhibited the formation of turbidity, even that which would normally occur from the spike. Inhibition was sufficient at times to prevent precipitation in the presence of three times the concentration of the spike. This effect is completely eliminated by the addition of calcium prior to ammonium hydroxide addition. The mechanism for this is not understood by the author but probably involves a chelating effect between barium and organic matter which is displaced by calcium.

After the R_2O_3 has been precipitated by ammonium hydroxide, the solution, which is strongly alkaline, is used for the sulfate precipitation. When attempts are made to acidify the solution prior to precipitation, the pH becomes a critical factor because the turbidity characteristics vary with acidity. In addition, at low pH readings the slope is about half of that found when precipitation is made from alkaline solutions. The only drawback to working on the alkaline side is that the determination must be completed within three hours after ammonium hydroxide has been added or sufficient carbon dioxide will be absorbed to initiate precipitation of barium carbonate.

To evaluate the procedure a series of samples was run by the described method. Table 2 shows that results of the new procedure compare favorably with those of existing methods. Data are not shown here on the discrimination between sulfide and sulfate by the use of an aqua regia attack and a hydrochloric acid attack. It may sometimes be useful to determine whether the sulfur in a sample is predominantly sulfide or sulfate for the purpose of reporting a value in one form or the other, but the accuracy of this discrimination has not been ascertained.

The method of attack is based on the assumption that a rock consists of an assemblage of minerals from which the aqua regia will effectively dissolve all but a few rare sulfur minerals. Aqua regia does not attack, to a significant degree, most silicate minerals present. The procedure therefore fails with obsidian and other glasses where the sulfur may be enclosed within a protective siliceous shield. It also fails if barium is present in excess of about half a percent When iron is present up to about 15 percent calculated as Fe_2O_3 no noticeable loss of sulfur is observed with the R_2O_3. Above this and especially at iron ore levels, some percentage of the sulfur goes with the R_2O_3 precipitate. In iron ores a fairly good result can still be obtained if a similar material is used as a reference standard so that approximately the same proportion of sulfur is absorbed with both the standard and sample. A similar situation prevails with phosphate rocks. Sulfur, which is frequently high in phosphate rocks, tends to be absorbed to some extent on the calcium phosphate precipitated so that the results are about 10 percent too low. This is easily corrected if a standard phosphate rock is carried through the procedure and used as the comparison standard when analyzing phosphate rocks.

Organic matter, which may contain sulfur, is not decomposed by the attack described. Organic matter found in such materials as shale, carbonates, and phosphates generally contains about 1 percent S, and the rocks rarely contain more than 5 percent organic matter so that a potential error as great as 0.05 percent S could occur. If a substantially greater amount of organic matter is present, one of the conventional oxidizing fusion procedures should be used. The yellow coloration produced where 5 percent or less of organic matter is present has such little absorbance at 650 nm that it does not interfere with the determination. Elemental sulfur present in small amounts will go into solution; it rarely occurs in amounts in excess of that which can go into solution by the decomposition procedure.

Table 2.—*Sulfur content of silicate rocks determined by turbidimetry and other methods*

Sample	Sulfur (percent)	Other methods	
		Sulfur (percent)	Source of data
Granite, G-2	0.01	0.01, 0.08, 0.01, 0.02	Flanagan (1969, p. 84–89).
Granodiorite, GSP-1	.03	.03, .02, .21	Do.
Andesite, AGV-1	.00	.01, .01, .02	Do.
Peridotite, PCC-1	.01	.02	Do.
Dunite, DTS-1	.00	.00, .00, .00	Do.
Basalt, BCR-1	.05	.04, .02, .04, .05	Do.
Bauxite, NBS-69A	.03	.02	National Bureau of Standards certificate value.
Dolomite, NBS-88	.03	.02	Do.
Fleet clay, NBS-97	.02	.02	Do.
Plastic clay, NBS-98	.03	.03	Do.
Limestone, NBS-1A	.30	.28	Do.
Phosphate rock, NBS-56	2.5	2.7	Do.
Portland cement, NBS-117	.62	.64	Do.
Portland cement, NBS-1013	.72	.72	Do.
Granite, G-1	.02	.01, .01, .02, .01	Stevens (1960, table 1).
Diabase, W-1	.01	.02, .02, .03	Stevens (1960, table 2).
Lab sample 1	1.8	1.7	Shapiro, gravimetric analysis.
2	1.5	1.4	Do.
3	.60	.55	Do.
4	.33	.28	Do.

REFERENCES CITED

American Public Health Association, 1965, Standard method for the examination of water and waste water: New York, Am. Public Health Assoc., 769 p.

Bardsley, C. E. and Lancaster, J. D., 1965, Sulfur, *in* Black, C. A., ed. Methods of soil analysis: Madison, Wis., Am. Soc. Agronomy, p. 1102–1116.

Fisher, R. B., 1966, Turbidimetry and nephelometry, *in* Welcher, F. J., ed., Standard methods of chemical analysis, v. 3: Princeton, N.J., D. Van Nostrand Co., 974 p.

Flanagan, F. J., 1969, U.S. Geological Survey Standards–[Pt.] 2, First compilation of data for new U.S.G.S. rocks: Geochim. et Cosmochim. Acta, v. 33, no. 1, p. 81–120.

Maxwell, J. A., 1968, Rock and mineral analysis: New York, Interscience Publishers, 584 p.

Patterson, G. D., Jr., 1958, Sulphur *in* Boltz D. F., ed., Colorimetric determination of nonmetals: New York, Interscience Publishers, p. 261–308.

Stevens, R. E., and others. 1960, Second report on a cooperative investigation of the composition of two silicate rocks: U.S. Geol. Survey Bull. 1113, 126 p.

Jour. Research U.S. Geol. Survey
Vol. 1, No. 1, Jan.—Feb. 1973, p. 85—87

ANTIMONY-BEARING ORPIMENT, CARLIN GOLD DEPOSIT, NEVADA

By ARTHUR S. RADTKE, CHARLES M. TAYLOR[1], and CHRIS HEROPOULOS,
Menlo Park, Calif., Stanford, Calif., Menlo Park, Calif.

Abstract.—Orpiment, As_2S_3, containing up to 1.5 percent antimony has been recognized in carbonaceous arsenic-rich gold ores in the unoxidized East ore body of the Carlin gold deposit. Associated hydrothermal minerals include realgar (AsS) and quartz. Stibnite, commonly associated with realgar in the ores, has not been observed associated with this type of orpiment.

Orpiment, As_2S_3, has been recognized in several disseminated replacement-type gold deposits in the Western United States. These include the Getchell deposit in Nevada (Joralemon, 1951; Weissberg, 1965), the White Caps deposit at Manhattan, Nev. (Ferguson, 1924), the Carlin deposit in Nevada (Radtke and Scheiner, 1970), and the Mercur deposit in Utah (Gilluly, 1932). Deposits of this general type are usually in limestones from which significant amounts of carbonate have been removed and silica added. The characteristic hydrothermal mineral assemblage includes fine-grained metallic gold, quartz, pyrite, pyrrhotite, arsenopyrite, cinnabar, stibnite, realgar, orpiment, sphalerite, galena, and several other sulfide and sulfosalt minerals. Barite is also an important hydrothermal mineral in the Carlin ores.

Although no data are available on the content of antimony in orpiment from the other deposits, samples of the mineral from the Carlin deposit were found to contain significant amounts of the element. To the best of the writers' knowledge, there have been no reports of antimony substituting for arsenic in the mineral orpiment.

Acknowledgments.—We wish to thank Richard C. Erd, U.S. Geological Survey, for his assistance in X-ray diffraction studies and Mel Essington, mine geologist, Carlin Gold Mining Co., for his help in sampling within the mine. Permission to publish information on the Carlin deposit was kindly given by Newmont Mining Corp.

OCCURRENCE AND ASSOCIATIONS

The Carlin gold deposit is in northern Eureka County, Nev., about 33 miles northwest of the town of Elko (fig. 1). Host rocks for the gold ore bodies are dark- to medium-gray, thin-bedded, siliceous, argillaceous, dolomitic limestone of the Silurian Roberts Mountains Formation. The gold ores probably were formed from a low-temperature, acid, hydrothermal solution which transported silica, iron, barium, sulfur, gold, mercury, and other elements. After ore deposition the upper parts of the ore bodies were altered by oxygen-bearing meteoric waters. Important chemical and mineralogical changes that took place during ore deposition and subsequent oxidation are summarized in Radtke and others (1972).

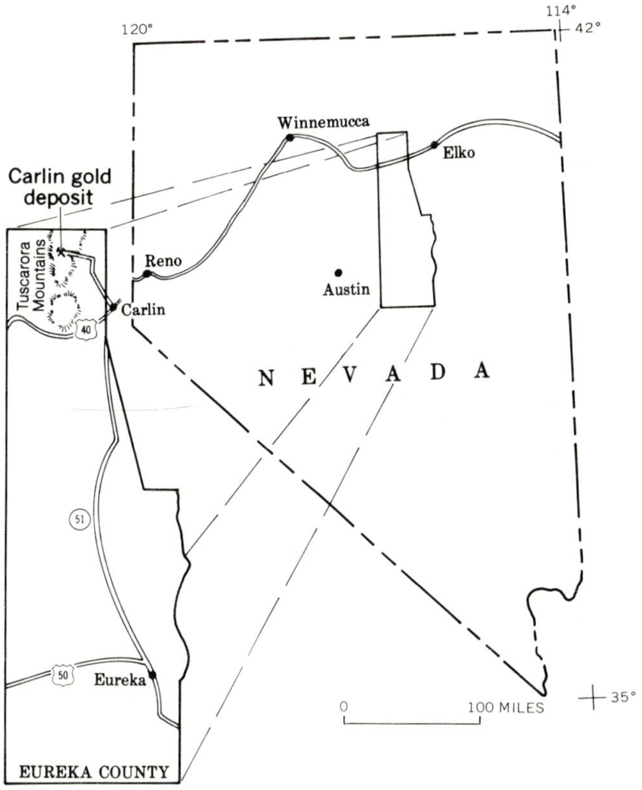

Figure 1.—Index map showing the location of the Carlin gold deposit in north-central Nevada.

The primary unoxidized gold ores of the Carlin deposit may be classified into several types according to (1) the amount of silica and organic carbon, (2) the form and associations of

[1] Stanford University.

gold, and (3) the ratios and abundance of the various hydrothermal minerals.

Although all the primary ores contain significant amounts of arsenic, one variety contains a very large concentration of the element, most of which is present as realgar (AsS) (fig. 2). The arsenic content may exceed 10,000 ppm, and more than 1 percent of the rock commonly is made up of arsenic sulfide. Most of the realgar occurs with barite in narrow veinlets that fill small fractures and cut the gold-bearing limestones. The realgar-barite veinlets may contain fine-grained metallic gold, pyrite, and other sulfide minerals, including stibnite, interlocked with quartz. Physical relations and textural features indicate that the realgar may have been deposited from the hydrothermal solution after the gold and most of the quartz and pyrite had been precipitated.

Figure 2.—Specimen of carbonaceous gold ore, showing small veinlets (outlined) of realgar and barite cutting host rock (limestone). Realgar appears dark gray, similar to the limestone, and barite is light gray.

Locally, the veinlets contain large amounts of orpiment and small amounts of realgar. Foliated and columnar crystals of orpiment as much as 8 mm long are interlocked with fragments of the dark-gray silicified limestone host rock (fig. 3). Only small amounts of fine-grained quartz and realgar are scattered through and intergrown with the orpiment, and no other hydrothermal minerals, including those usually associated with realgar, have been recognized.

CHEMICAL COMPOSITION

Orpiment in this particular type of occurrence in arsenic-rich gold ores at the Carlin deposit usually contains significant amounts of antimony. A semiquantitative spectrographic analysis of hand-picked fragments of orpiment is given in table 1. High values for silica and calcium shown in table 1 reflect the presence of minor amounts of hydrothermal quartz inclusions in orpiment as well as quartz and calcite from small limestone fragments.

Figure 3.—Specimens of antimony-bearing orpiment. Light-gray shiny areas are orpiment crystals. Dark areas are limestone fragments.

Table 1.—*Semiquantitative spectrographic analysis of antimony-bearing orpiment*

[Sought but not found: Ag, Au, B, Be, Bi, Cd, Ce, Co, Eu, Ga, Ge, Hf, In, K, La, Li, Mn, Mo, Na, Nb, Ni, P, Pb, Pd, Pt, Re, Sc, Sn, Sr, Ta, Te, Th, Ti, Tl, U, V, W, Y, Yb, Zr. Values are in weight percent. Analyst: Chris Heropoulos]

Si.......	1.5	Ca......	0.5	Cu......	0.0002
Al.......	.007	As.......	>20	Sb.......	1
Fe.......	.005	Ba.......	.002	Zn.......	.03
Mg......	.0015	Cr.......	.0002		

Eight small grains of orpiment were mounted and polished for electron microprobe analysis. Qualitative spectral scans and quantitative analyses were made using the Applied Research Laboratory EMX-SM model electron microprobe in the Department of Geology, Stanford University, California.

Arsenic, sulfur, and antimony were the only elements detected from spectral scans. Five grains were selected for quantitative analysis, and 10 to 15 points on each grain were analyzed for these three elements. Analytical conditions used were: (1) arsenic, $K\alpha$ characteristic line, LiF crystal, 25 kV, and realgar (AsS) standard; (2) sulfur, $K\alpha$ characteristic line, ADP crystal, 15 kV, and realgar standard; and (3) antimony, $L\alpha_1$ characteristic line, LiF crystal, 15 kV, and stibnite (Sb_2S_3) standard.

Although the content of antimony varied from grain to grain (0.10 to 1.50 percent Sb), the amount present within individual grains was generally uniform. The composition of five grains is shown in table 2.

Table 2.—*Chemical analyses of antimony-bearing orpiment*

Grain No.	As	Sb	S	Total
1	59.6	1.1	39.2	99.9
2	59.4	1.5	39.1	100.0
3	60.1	.5	39.3	99.9
4	59.2	1.2	39.4	99.8
5	59.7	1.0	39.2	99.9

It is apparent that under certain conditions antimony may substitute for arsenic in orpiment. Some experimental study to determine the solubility of antimony in As_2S_3 is justified.

REFERENCES CITED

Ferguson, H. G., 1924, Geology and ore deposits of the Manhattan district, Nevada: U.S. Geol. Survey Bull. 723, 163 p.

Gilluly, James, 1932, Geology and ore deposits of the Stockton and Fairfield quadrangles, Utah: U.S. Geol. Survey Prof. Paper 173, 171 p.

Joralemon, Peter, 1951, The occurrence of gold at the Getchell mine, Nevada: Econ. Geology, v. 46, no. 3, p. 267–310.

Radtke, A. S., Heropoulos, Chris, Fabbi, B. P., Scheiner, B. J., and Essington, Mel, 1972, Data on major and minor elements in host rocks and ores, Carlin gold deposit, Nevada: Econ. Geology. [In press]

Radtke, A. S., and Scheiner, B. J., 1970, Studies of hydrothermal gold deposition (I). Carlin gold deposit, Nevada—The role of carbonaceous materials in gold deposition: Econ. Geology, v. 65, no. 2, p. 87–102.

Weissberg, B. G., 1965, Getchellite, $AsSbS_3$, a new mineral from Humboldt County, Nevada: Am. Mineralogist, v. 50, nos. 11–12, p. 1817–1826.

Jour. Research U.S. Geol. Survey
Vol. 1, No. 1, Jan.—Feb. 1973, p. 89—98

ACCESSORY APATITE FROM HYBRID GRANITOID ROCKS OF THE SOUTHERN SNAKE RANGE, NEVADA

By DONALD E. LEE, RICHARD E. VAN LOENEN; and
ROBERT E. MAYS, Denver, Colo.; Menlo Park, Calif.

Abstract.—Analytical data, optical properties, and unit-cell parameters are presented for 24 samples of accessory apatites recovered from hybrid granitoid rocks of the southern Snake Range, Nev. A complete chemical analysis is given for one. In the Snake Creek—Williams Canyon outcrop area, where the hybrid rocks grade from granodiorite with 63 percent SiO_2 to a quartz monzonite with 76 percent SiO_2 within a horizontal distance of about 3 miles, abundance and crystal habit of the apatite change with rock chemistry. The apatite probably is slightly more than 90 mole percent fluorapatite in the most felsic rocks, slightly less in the most mafic. The range of $F \rightleftharpoons OH$ substitution in apatite from this outcrop area is much smaller than in the coexisting biotites. Except for manganese, strontium, sodium, and the rare earths, there is very limited substitution for calcium in the crystal structure of these apatites. Apatites from the more mafic rocks tend to contain a lighter, more basic assemblage of rare earths, in agreement with results obtained for coexisting allanites, monazites, and zircons.

Granitoid rocks of Jurassic age crop out a few miles north of the Mount Wheeler mine in the southern part of the Snake Range, about 50 miles southeast of Ely, Nev. (Lee and Van Loenen, 1970, fig. 1; 1971). The many well-defined differences in the chemistry and mineralogy of these granitoid rocks within an outcrop area of about 20 square miles are believed by Lee and Van Loenen (1971) to have resulted mainly from assimilation of chemically distinct host rocks. The 1971 report is a comprehensive field and laboratory study and includes a geologic map and sample locality data. The present paper describes the chemical and physical properties of 24 samples of accessory apatite recovered from these granitoid rocks and associated aplites.

Petrologically and structurally, the hybrid granitoid rocks from which these apatites were recovered fall into three separate study units: the Snake Creek—Williams Canyon area, the Pole Canyon—Can Young Canyon area, and the Young Canyon—Kious Basin area. The 18 samples of apatite from the Snake Creek—Williams Canyon area are discussed first, and then the six apatites from the other areas, including two apatites from aplitic phases.

Special care was taken to recover apatite fractions having a high degree of purity. After the preliminary concentration described by Lee and Dodge (1964), the apatite was centrifuged in a mixture of methylene iodide and bromoform, the specific gravity of the liquid being controlled by means of a Christian Becker specific gravity balance before each operation. Specific gravity of the apatite was determined by the suspension method during centrifuging. Each fraction analyzed was centrifuged on either side of a very narrow specific gravity range. This method, often with repeated processing of a given fraction, enabled us to reject (heavier) apatite grains having relatively abundant inclusions of zircon, or (lighter) apatite grains having relatively abundant inclusions of quartz. After exposure to heavy liquids, each fraction was cleaned by ultrasonic vibration in 25 ml of distilled water for about an hour; the effectiveness of the cleaning action was evident from the fact that the water surrounding the mineral became milky. Finally, apatite grains with tiny inclusions of biotite were drawn away from the main fraction by means of the Frantz isodynamic separator.

Indices of refraction were determined by the immersion method, by use of a spindle stage (Wilcox, 1959) and focal masking technique (Wilcox, 1962). Cell parameters were obtained by least-squares refinement of powder diffractometer data, with an internal standard of CaF_2 and a self-indexing computer program developed by Evans, Appleman, and Handwerker (1963).

Quantitative spectrographic analyses have an overall accuracy of ±15 percent except near limits of detection, where only one digit is reported. Semiquantitative spectrographic results are based on their identity with geometric brackets whose boundaries are 1.2, 0.83, 0.56, 0.38, 0.26, 0.18, 0.12 percent, and so forth; and the results are reported arbitrarily as midpoints of these brackets, 1.0, 0.7, 0.5, 0.3, 0.2, 0.15, and 0.1 percent, respectively. The precision of a reported value is approximately one bracket at 68-percent or two brackets at 95-percent confidence.

APATITE OCCURRENCE AND ANALYSES

Apatites from Snake Creek—Williams Canyon area

The influence of host rock on chemistry and mineralogy of intrusive rocks of the southern Snake Range is most clearly shown in the Snake Creek–Williams Canyon area. There the intrusive is undeformed, probably has not been eroded to a depth of much more than 1,000 feet, and is well exposed in contact with limestone, shale, and quartzite. Within a horizontal distance of 3 miles the intrusive grades from a granodiorite (63 percent SiO_2, 4.5 percent CaO) where the host rock is limestone to quartz monzonite (76 percent SiO_2, 0.5 percent CaO) where the host rock is quartzite. The amount of apatite present in the intrusive increases rather systematically from less than 0.02 weight percent in the most felsic rocks to about 0.3 weight percent in the most mafic rocks. The apatite tends to be associated with biotite, although in the more mafic rocks (CaO>2.5 percent) euhedra of apatite are readily found in all the essential minerals.

Crystal habit of the apatite changes with rock chemistry (fig. 1). The sparse apatite in the most felsic rocks is present as relatively large grains with a stubby habit; length-to-width ratio seldom exceeds 2:1. Apatite recovered from the more mafic rocks tends to be more acicular, and where the CaO content of the rock is 2.5 percent or more, the apatite crystals commonly have a length-to-width ratio that exceeds 4:1. In the more mafic rocks tiny euhedral apatite needles about 25μ long were found to be intimately intergrown with biotite crystals (Lee and Van Loenen, 1970, p. D199).

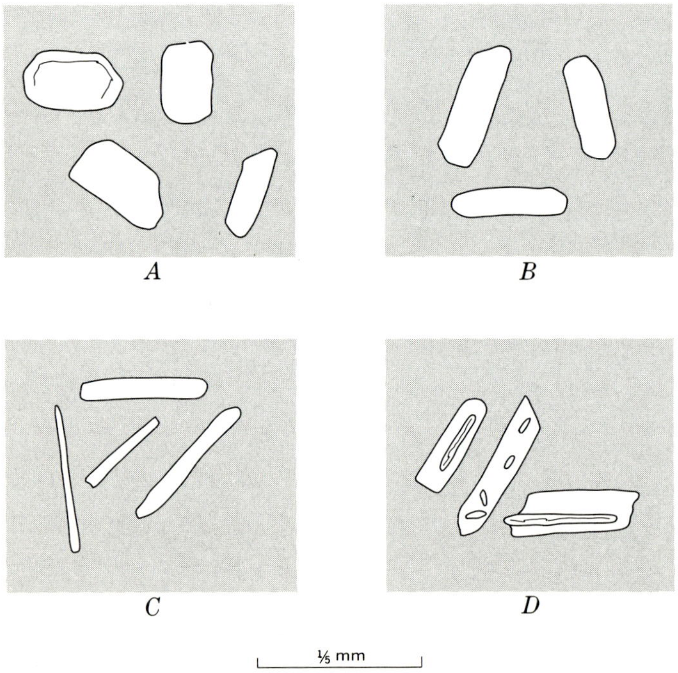

Figure 1.–Representative apatite crystals recovered from the Snake Creek–Williams Canyon area. Broken fragments of larger grains, especially abundant in *A* and *B*, not sketched.

A. Sample 238-MW-61, 0.78 percent CaO in rock. The apatite in this rock is so sparse that we were unable to recover enough for analytical work.
B. Sample 174-MW-61, 1.5 percent CaO in rock.
C. Sample 40B-MW-60, 3.5 percent CaO in rock.
D. Types of inclusions found in some apatite crystals. The middle grain contains some colorless inclusions with index of refraction (n)> apatite (probably zircon), and some with n < apatite (probably quartz). The other two grains contain biotite inclusions and could easily be separated from biotite-free apatite by means of the Frantz isodynamic separator.

Many observers, the earliest being Harker (1895), have recorded the relative abundance and acicular form of apatite crystals in the more contaminated parts of hybrid rocks. Nockolds (1933, p. 563) wrote:

> This conclusion was based partly on the relative abundance of apatite found in the xenoliths and more contaminated portions of the magma when compared with the amount present in the invaded or invading rock. This apatite is characteristically present as thin needles penetrating the other minerals and often of exceedingly small dimensions.

Moreover, Nockolds cited 14 reports describing the relative abundance of apatite in hybrid rocks. Many of these authors mentioned "apatite needles" or otherwise referred to the acicular habit of the apatite.

Results of experimental work bear on these relations. Wyllie, Cox, and Biggar (1962) found that apatite crystals coexisting with liquid or with vapor are equant, whereas crystals precipitated from a liquid during a quench are greatly elongated parallel to the *c* axis. If the material added to a magma is nearer the high-temperature end of the solid solution series than the crystals with which the magma is saturated (as happened in the more mafic parts of the Snake Creek–Williams Canyon area), the reaction is exothermic and decreases the amount of liquid (Bowen, 1922, p. 531). This in effect is a quenching action, and according to the findings by Wyllie, Cox, and Biggar would be expected to lead to the development of elongated apatite crystals. Bowen showed that if the material added to a magma is nearer the lower end of the solid solution series than the crystals with which the liquid is saturated (as happened in the most felsic parts of the Snake Creek–Williams Canyon rocks), the reaction is endothermic and increases slightly the amount of liquid. This would allow the apatite crystals to coexist longer with the liquid or vapor and might be expected to result in larger apatite crystals with a more equant habit.

We note that the occurrence of zircon (also a tetragonal mineral) in some hybrid rocks is similar to that just described for apatite. After studying the Monadhliath granite in Scotland, Wyatt concluded (1954, p. 988) that "the evidence indicated that very elongated zircon is produced only in granite which has been contaminated * * *." Taubeneck (1957) and Huang (1958) emphasized the greater elongation ratio of zircon from hybrid rocks. In the Snake Creek–Williams Canyon area, zircon is both more acicular and more abundant in the more mafic parts of the exposure (Lee and others, 1968).

A wet chemical analysis of apatite 40A-MW-60 (table 1) is calculated on the basis of 26 (O, OH, Cl, F) to the apatite formula $Ca_5(PO_4)_3(F,Cl,OH)$, by use of the computer

Table 1.—*Chemical analysis and physical properties of apatite 40A-MW-60*

[Chemical analysis by Elaine L. Munson]

Chemical analysis (weight percent)	
SiO_2	0.18
Al_2O_3	.08
Fe_2O_3	.06
FeO	.04
CaO	54.87
Na_2O	.06
K_2O	.01
P_2O_5	41.97
MnO	.13
Cl	.02
F	3.36
R_2O_3	[1] .45
Insoluble	[2] .23
Subtotal	101.46
Less O≡Cl,F	1.41
Total	100.05

Number of ions, on basis of 26 (O,OH,F,Cl)		
P	6.001	6.031
Si	.030	
Al	.016	10.025
Fe^{+3}	.008	
Fe^{+2}	.006	
Mn	.019	
Ca	9.928	
Na	.020	
K	.002	
Ce^{+3}*	.026	
F	1.795	1.801
Cl	.006	

Optical and other properties	
Specific gravity observed	3.215±0.005
Density calculated	3.210 g/cm³
Cell volume measured	523.6±0.1 A³
Cell volume calculated	522.8 A³
ϵ	1.631±0.001
ω	1.633±0.001
$\omega-\epsilon$	.002
a	9.373±0.001 A
c	6.881±0.001 A
c/a	.7342

[1] Rare-earth oxide precipitate. See table 2 for analysis.

[2] Insoluble in 1:1 HCl at 100°C. From X-ray diffraction study this material is estimated to be 40 percent quartz, 40 percent zircon, and 20 percent zoisite.

*For simplicity, entire rare-earth oxide precipitate calculated as Ce_2O_3.

program described by Jackson, Stevens, and Bowen (1967). The analysis shows 0.23 weight percent material insoluble in 1:1 HCl at 100°C, and thus the material analyzed was 99.77 percent pure. The 0.23-percent impurity is estimated to be 40 percent quartz, 40 percent zircon, and 20 percent zoisite; probably all of it was present as inclusions in the apatite grains. The analysis also shows 0.45 weight percent rare-earth oxide precipitate. An X-ray spectrographic analysis of this precipitate was calculated to atomic percent of total rare earths in the apatite (table 2); the low rare-earth oxide total probably results from the presence of filter-paper ash in the precipitate.

Table 2.—*Analysis of rare-earth precipitate and calculation of* Σ(La+Ce+Pr) *for apatite 40A-MW-60*

[X-ray spectrographic analysis by Frank Cuttitta, Ralph Christian, and Harry J. Rose, Jr. Sc_2O_3 not detected. Low total probably due to presence of filter-paper ash in precipitate]

X-ray spectrographic analysis (weight percent)			
Y_2O_3	22.9	Tb_2O_3	1.01
La_2O_3	7.04	Dy_2O_3	3.32
CeO_2	22.1	Ho_2O_3	1.21
Pr_2O_3	3.52	Er_2O_3	1.76
Nd_2O_3	15.6	Tm_2O_3	.55
Sm_2O_3	5.03	Yb_2O_3	1.71
Eu_2O_3	2.01	Lu_2O_3	.65
Gd_2O_3	3.27	Total	91.68

Atomic percent of total rare earths in apatite			
Y	33.77	Dy	2.96
La	7.19	Ho	1.07
Ce	21.38	Er	1.53
Pr	3.56	Tm	.47
Nd	15.44	Yb	1.44
Sm	4.81	Lu	.54
Eu	1.91	Total	100.00
Gd	3.01	Σ(La+Ce+Pr)	32.5
Tb	.92		

The fluorine content of 40A-MW-60 shows it to be about 90 mole percent fluorapatite. Virtually all of the remaining 10 mole percent must be hydroxylapatite, for the chlorine content of the mineral is negligible, and no effervescence occurred when the mineral was immersed in 1:1 HCl, indicating absence of CO_2 in the structure. The amount of material was not sufficient for direct determination of H_2O.

Analytical and physical data for 18 apatites (including 40A-MW-60) from the Snake Creek–Williams Canyon area are shown in table 3. The major-element data and physical properties (tables 1, 3) indicate that all 18 minerals are hydroxyl-fluorapatites, and despite certain variations in physical properties (discussed below) they indicate a narrow range of major-element composition. The large and complex variations in composition within the apatite group make accurate correlation of physical properties difficult. Generally, however, cell parameters and indices of refraction of hydroxyl-fluorapatites depend mostly on the extent of substitution of

Table 3.—*Analytical data and physical properties for accessory apatites from*

[Samples arranged in order of increasing CaO content of whole rock. Sample localities are shown on plate 1 of Lee and Van Loenen (1971). elements by Robena Brown and H. J. Rose, Jr. Spectrographic analyses by R. E. Mays. Results for Si, Na, and Pb are semiquantitative; all

	Sample No.	147-MW-61	151-MW-61	190-DL-62	14-MW-60	36-DL-62	8-DL-62	31-DL-62	40A-MW-60	
	CaO in rock (weight percent)	1.5	1.8	2.0	2.2	2.2	2.3	2.4	2.4	
	Specific gravity (±0.005)	3.221	3.220	3.220	3.211	3.210	3.212	3.215	3.215	
	Indices of refraction									
1	$\epsilon(\pm0.001)$	1.629	1.630	1.629	1.630	1.630	1.630	1.630	1.631	1
2	$\omega(\pm0.001)$	1.631	1.632	1.631	1.632	1.632	1.632	1.632	1.633	2
3	$\omega-\epsilon$	.002	.002	.002	.002	.002	.002	.002	.002	3
	Cell parameters									
4	a(±0.001 A)	9.369	9.370	9.370	9.374	9.374	9.368	9.376	9.373	4
5	c(±0.001 A)	6.881	6.880	6.881	6.881	6.882	6.879	6.883	6.881	5
6	c/a	.7344	.7343	.7343	.7341	.7342	.7344	.7341	.7342	6
7	Volume (±0.1 A^3)	523.2	523.1	523.2	523.7	523.7	523.2	523.9	523.6	7
	Major elements (weight percent)[2]									
8	CaO	....	54.0	....	54.4	....	53.9	53.8	[3]54.87	8
9	P_2O_5	....	41.6	....	41.7	....	41.8	41.3	[3]41.97	9
10	F	....	....	....	....	....	....	....	[3]3.36	10
11	Cl	....	<.02	[4].02	<.02	[4].02	<.02	<.02	[3].02	11
	Spectrographic analyses (weight percent)									
12	Al	0.130	0.042	0.038	0.020	0.016	0.023	0.014	....	12
13	Ba	.0006	<.0005	<.0005	<.0005	<.0005	<.0005	<.0005	<.0005	13
14	Cu	.0004	.0005	.0006	.0002	.0003	.0005	.0005	.0003	14
15	Fe	.044	.042	.036	.028	.022	.030	.034	....	15
16	Mg	.0060	.0050	.0050	.0030	.0020	.0050	.0060	.0050	16
17	Mn	.25	.25	.29	.11	.13	.14	.13	....	17
18	Na	.15	.1	.1	.07	.05	.05	.07	....	18
19	Pb	.0015	.002	.002	.001	0	.001	.001	.001	19
20	Si	.3	.15	.15	.07	.2	.1	.1	....	20
21	Sr	.050	.042	.038	.050	.040	.060	.050	.036	21
22	Ti	.014	.014	.026	.0055	.0060	.013	.010	.014	22
23	V	.002	.002	.004	.002	.0022	.002	.002	.002	23
24	Zr	.020	.040	.026	.012	.021	.020	.016	.014	24

[1] Apatite from xenolith. [2] X-ray fluorescence analyses performed on 25-mg samples.

OH for F. Cell parameters indicate slightly increased substitution of OH for F in apatites from the more mafic rocks. Thus the *a* dimension tends to increase with CaO content of the whole rock (Deer and others, 1962, p. 324). The rising indices of refraction (table 3) with increased CaO content of the whole rock also indicate slightly increased substitution of OH for F (Deer and others, 1962, p. 331) in apatites from the more mafic rocks. (Admittedly, the 3.53 percent F in apatite 16-MW-60 does not conform.)

In terms of fluorapatite-hydroxylapatite end members, the total range of composition deduced from the physical properties just discussed is on the order of 10–15 mole percent. Chemical analyses of biotites coexisting with most of the apatites listed in table 3 show a similar but much sharper change in the F:OH ratio, with fluorine ranging from 0.33 percent in biotite from mafic rocks to 1.13 percent in biotite from felsic rocks (Lee and Van Loenen, 1970). Stormer and Carmichael (1971) calculated the distribution of F and OH between apatite and biotite for various temperatures of crystallization by using free-energy data for the simple fluorides and hydroxides; but our data do not fit their hypothetical distribution diagram. That is, plotting F/(F+OH) in biotite against F/(F+OH) in apatite gives points that fall near or below the 127°C temperature curve.

Analytical results for apatite 40A-MW-60 (table 1) provide a good indication of the amount (0.23 percent) and type (quartz, zircon, and zoisite) of impurity to be expected in the other samples included in table 3. We conclude that all the zirconium values listed therein are due to tiny inclusions of zircon in the analyzed apatites. Also, the titanium found might result from inclusions of sphene, closely associated with apatite in these rocks; however, we were unable to detect any sphene peaks during X-ray diffraction work on the insoluble residue of apatite 40A-MW-60. The copper values probably come from heavy liquids used, despite the subsequent ultrasonic cleaning of each apatite fraction, for these liquids are *the Snake Creek–Williams Canyon area, southern Snake Range, Nev.*

Determination of specific gravity, indices of refraction, and cell parameters explained in text. X-ray fluorescence analysis for major other results are quantitative. General limitations of the two methods given in text]

	38-MW-60	25-DL-61	152-MW-60	21A-MW-60	40B-MW-60[1]	126-MW-60[1]	43-DL-61	27-DL-61[1]	16-MW-60	98-DL-62[1]	
	2.5	3.1	3.2	3.4	3.5	3.5	3.9	4.1	4.3	4.5	
	3.215	3.210	3.206	3.205	3.205	3.221	3.210	3.211	3.202	3.215	
					Indices of refraction						
1	1.630	1.630	1.630	1.630	1.631	1.629	1.631	1.630	1.630	....	1
2	1.632	1.632	1.633	1.632	1.633	1.632	1.634	1.633	1.632	....	2
3	.002	.002	.003	.002	.002	.003	.003	.003	.002	....	3
					Cell parameters						
4	9.375	9.375	9.376	9.371	9.373	9.369	9.377	9.376	9.370	9.367	4
5	6.882	6.882	6.882	6.883	6.882	6.882	6.882	6.880	6.881	6.879	5
6	.7340	.7341	.7341	.7345	.7342	.7346	.7340	.7338	.7344	.7345	6
7	523.8	523.9	523.9	523.5	523.6	523.2	524.1	523.8	523.2	522.7	7
					Major elements (weight percent)[2]						
8	53.3	54.3	....	54.0	54.9	54.0	54.3	....	53.9	54.4	8
9	41.3	41.4	....	42.0	42.1	42.0	42.1	....	41.3	41.6	9
10	....	....	....	....	....	....	....	....	[4]3.53	....	10
11	<.02	<.02	....	<.02	<.02	<.02	<.02	....	[4].00	[4].01	11
					Spectrographic analyses (weight percent)						
12	0.042	0.02	0.026	0.060	0.024	0.046	0.020	0.022	0.024	0.014	12
13	<.0005	<.0005	<.0005	.0006	<.0005	<.0005	.0026	<.0005	.0006	<.0005	13
14	.0003	.0004	.0005	.0006	.0004	.0012	.0005	.0005	.0006	.0007	14
15	.034	.036	.044	.055	.050	.014	.036	.028	.030	.028	15
16	.0060	.0070	.0090	.013	.0010	.0070	.010	.0060	.0070	.0050	16
17	.15	.10	.11	.055	.10	.18	.075	.075	.050	.060	17
18	.1	.1	.07	.1	.07	.1	.05	.1	.07	.07	18
19	.001	.001	.001	.0015	0	.001	0	.001	.001	.001	19
20	.15	.15	.15	.15	.1	.15	.15	.2	.15	.15	20
21	.075	.070	.050	.060	.036	.026	.085	.050	.050	.036	21
22	.014	.014	.014	.0090	.0070	.015	.013	.013	.0048	.012	22
23	.001	.003	.002	.002	<.001	.002	.002	.002	.002	.007	23
24	.022	.022	.016	.030	.024	.030	.018	.016	.014	.003	24

[3] See table 1. [4] Wet chemical determination by E. L. Munson.

kept standing over copper foil to prevent their breakdown. Although silicon-bearing apatites have been recognized (for example, Cruft, 1966, p. 379), and the analysis of 40A-MW-60 (table 1) does show 0.18 percent SiO_2, we conclude that the silicon values in table 3 result mainly from inclusions of quartz and silicates. We attribute the aluminum values mostly to the presence of zoisite and possibly other aluminosilicates.

The tiny amounts of barium, lead, and vanadium listed are probably present in the crystal structure of the apatites. The values for sodium are equivalent to the range (of Na_2O) for apatites from plutonic rocks of the Odenwald Mountains, Germany, reported by Taborszky (1962), who found Na_2O content of apatite to be unrelated to rock type. Scatter diagrams based on table 3 show a slight tendency for sodium to decrease with whole-rock CaO. A similar trend for biotites from these rocks was found to relate to activity of albite in the system (Lee and Van Loenen, 1970, p. D199). The amounts of iron and magnesium listed are so small that they might have been trapped in the crystal structure of apatite (Cruft, 1962, p. 391), or they might be in inclusions.

Cruft noted that the strontium content is highest in apatite from the ultrabasic rocks, decreasing with increasing acidity of the rocks. The same trend is apparent in our data but is not pronounced, probably because strontium in these rocks is concentrated in epidote, a mineral that is well developed in the more mafic parts of the Snake Creek–Williams Canyon exposure (Lee and others, 1971).

Several observers, including Otto (1935), have noted that larger amounts of manganese are likely to be found in apatites from more felsic rocks. This is well illustrated by the data in table 3—those apatites that are richer in manganese tend to have higher specific gravities. In general, however, these same apatites contain a heavier assemblage of rare-earth elements, as described later in this paper.

Apatites from other areas, and from aplites

Most of the Young Canyon–Kious Basin area intrusive was sheared and deformed by Miocene movement on a regional thrust fault (Lee and others, 1971, fig. 2). The undeformed part of this intrusive outcrop is a quartz monzonite that is petrologically similar to, though not identical with, some of the more felsic parts of the Snake Creek–Williams Canyon exposure.

The Pole Canyon–Can Young Canyon area intrusive is an unusual hybrid rock that has developed through assimilation of argillite. It is distinguished in part by the presence of large muscovite phenocrysts, many of which contain euhedral crystals of biotite. The apatite in this rock is present in large (+150 mesh), poorly formed grains, and almost all the zircon in the rock is present as acicular inclusions within the apatite grains (fig. 2).

Analytical data and physical properties are presented (table 4) for four apatites from granitoid rocks (two from the Young Canyon–Kious Basin area and two from the Pole Canyon–Can Young Canyon area) and for two apatites from aplites. We

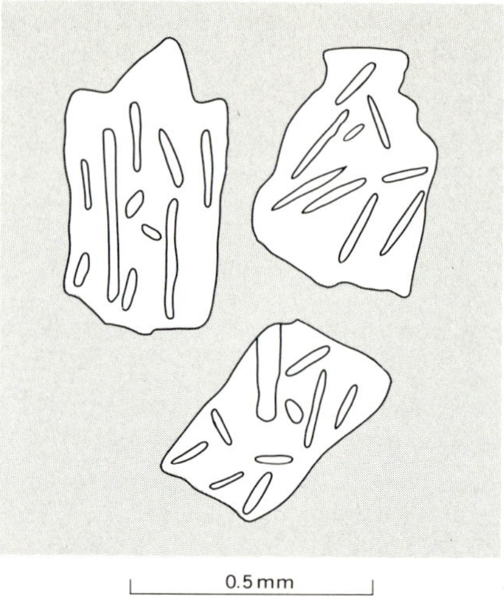

Figure 2.–Representative apatite from the Pole Canyon–Can Young Canyon area. Sample 135-DL-62, fragments of apatite crystals containing many inclusions of zircon. Almost all the zircon in the rock is present as inclusions in the apatite.

Table 4.–*Analytical data and physical properties for accessory apatites from the Young Canyon–Kious Basin area, the Pole Canyon–Can Young Canyon area, and from aplites, southern Snake Range, Nev.*

[Sample localities are shown on plate 1 of Lee and Van Loenen (1971). Determination of specific gravity, indices of refraction, and cell parameters explained in text. Spectrographic analyses by R. E. Mays. Results for Si, Na, and Pb are semiquantitative; all other results are quantitative. General limitations of the two methods given in text]

	Young Canyon–Kious Basin area		Pole Canyon–Can Young Canyon area		Aplites	
Sample No.	190-MW-61	234-MW-61	135-DL-62	120-MW-60	119-MW-60	121-MW-60
CaO in rock, (weight percent)	1.2	1.6	0.98	1.3	0.63	0.70
Specific gravity (±0.005)	3.225	3.225	3.210	3.220	3.215	3.230
Indices of refraction						
$\epsilon(\pm 0.001)$	1.629	1.629	1.629	1.630	1.629	1.629
$\omega(\pm 0.001)$	1.631	1.631	1.631	1.632	1.631	1.631
$\omega-\epsilon$	.002	.002	.002	.002	.002	.002
Cell parameters						
$a(\pm 0.001$ A)	9.366	9.367	9.369	9.367	9.365	9.366
$c(\pm 0.001$ A)	6.878	6.878	6.881	6.879	6.878	6.878
c/a	.7343	.7344	.7345	.7343	.7345	.7343
Volume (±0.1 A^3)	522.5	522.6	523.0	522.7	522.5	522.5
Spectrographic analyses (weight percent)						
Al	0.034	0.050	0.026	0.070	0.26	0.022
Ba	<.0005	<.0005	<.0005	<.0005	.0008	<.0005
Cr	<.0002	<.0002	<.0002	<.0002	.0008	<.0002
Cu	.0004	.0004	.0005	.0004	.0011	.0003
Fe	.055	.048	.044	.055	.055	.060
Mg	.0030	.0040	.0030	.0035	.0070	.0030
Mn	.50	.38	.19	.34	.50	.80
Na	.15	.15	.1	.1	.07	.07
Ni	<.0004	<.0004	.0024	<.0004	<.0004	<.0004
Si	.15	.1	.15	.15	.5	.02
Sr	.024	.036	.042	.042	.019	.006
Ti	.025	.017	.012	.010	.028	.0090
V	.002	.002	<.0010	<.0010	.001	.001
Zr	.015	.022	.17	.013	.018	.010

were unable to obtain major-element data for these six samples, but values for indices of refraction and cell parameters suggest that all are hydroxyl-fluorapatites. The minor-element data in table 4 require no comment beyond the previous discussion of similar data for apatites from the Snake Creek–Williams Canyon area (table 3).

DISTRIBUTION OF RARE-EARTH ELEMENTS

Distribution of rare earths in the hybrid granitoid rocks of the southern Snake Range has proved to be one of the most interesting features of the geochemistry of these rocks. In the Snake Creek–Williams Canyon area, where the equivalent of a large part (63–76 percent SiO_2) of the classic differentiation sequence is exposed, analyses of 87 rocks show an increase in total rare-earth content from the more felsic toward the more mafic parts of the exposure. Moreover, the rare-earth assemblage is increasingly enriched in the lighter, more basic lanthanides in the more mafic parts of the exposure (Lee and Van Loenen, 1971, table 5, fig. 6).

In treating rare-earth analyses of minerals recovered from these hybrid rocks, we have followed the procedure devised by Murata, Rose, and Carron (1953), who sought to denote the composition of each sample by means of a single number. They proposed the quantity $\Sigma(La + Ce + Pr)$ in atomic percent of total rare-earth elements as a numerical index of the composition and the stage of fractionation attained by the rare-earth elements. Thus, higher values of $\Sigma(La + Ce + Pr)$ represent greater enrichment of the lighter, more basic rare-earth elements. In the following discussion, this quantity $\Sigma(La + Ce + Pr)$ is referred to simply as sigma.

The quantitative data for 40A-MW-60 (table 2) and the semiquantitative data for other apatites from the Snake Creek–Williams Canyon area (table 5) are calculated to atomic percent of rare-earth elements, and the sigma value is given for each apatite. Values of sigma range from 17 to 48 atomic percent, representing an appreciable range of composition in terms of the rare-earth elements; obviously, apatites from the more mafic rocks tend to have the higher sigma values.

Results for apatites from the Young Canyon–Kious Basin area and the Pole Canyon–Can Young Canyon area (table 6) fit this trend; they were recovered from felsic rocks, and they contain a relatively heavy assemblage of rare-earth elements. Results for two apatites recovered from aplites (table 6) also fit this trend.

Fleischer and Altschuler (1969) have summarized available data on the rare-earth contents of apatites from different geological environments. Our data (tables 5, 6) would plot within the field that Fleischer and Altschuler (1969, p. 729, fig. 3) have outlined for apatites from "granitic" rocks.

Quantitative data for 20 allanites and 13 monazites, many of which coexist with the apatites listed in tables 2, 5, and 6, show sigma values ranging from 61 to 81 atomic percent (Lee and Bastron, 1967), with higher values found in those minerals from the more mafic rocks. Semiquantitative data for 25 zircons from these rocks show the same trend (Lee and others, 1968). However, although sphenes from these rocks contain significant amounts of rare-earth elements, their sigma values are not very obviously related to whole-rock chemistry (Lee and others, 1969). Under the conditions of formation of these hybrid rocks, crystallochemical selection was perhaps more important than the chemistry of the rock-forming medium in determining fractionation of rare earths in sphene. Only minor amounts of rare-earth elements were found in the epidotes analyzed.

Therefore, apatites recovered from the more mafic rocks tend to contain a lighter, more basic assemblage of rare earths, in agreement with results obtained for coexisting allanites, monazites, and zircons. The distribution of rare earths in these hybrid rocks and in their constituent allanites, apatites, monazites, and zircons has been cited (Lee and Bastron, 1967; Lee and Van Loenen, 1971, p. 20, 21) as evidence that the chemical processes once operative in these rocks might be similar to processes which contribute to the formation of alkalic rocks and carbonatites.

SUMMARY

In the Snake Creek–Williams Canyon area, where the hybrid rocks grade from granodiorite with 63 percent SiO_2 to quartz monzonite with 76 percent SiO_2 within a horizontal distance of 3 miles, the following relations have been found:

1. Abundance of apatite increases from less than 0.02 weight percent in the most felsic rocks to about 0.3 weight percent in the most mafic.
2. Crystal habit of the apatite relates to rock chemistry. In the most felsic rocks the apatite has a stubby habit, whereas in the most mafic rocks the mineral has an acicular habit and a length-to-width ratio that commonly exceeds 4:1.
3. In terms of the fluorapatite-hydroxylapatite end members, the span of composition deduced from analytical data and physical properties is 10–15 mole percent. The mineral probably is slightly more than 90 mole percent fluorapatite in the most felsic rocks, slightly less in the most mafic. The range of $F \leftrightharpoons OH$ substitution in apatite from this outcrop area is much smaller than in the coexisting biotites.
4. Except for manganese, strontium, sodium, and the rare earths, there is very limited substitution for calcium in the crystal structure of these apatites.
5. Apatites recovered from the more mafic rocks tend to contain a lighter, more basic assemblage of rare earths, corresponding to results obtained previously for coexisting allanites, monazites, and zircons.
6. In the Pole Canyon–Can Young Canyon area, where a distinctive muscovite-rich granitoid rock has resulted from assimilation of argillite, almost all the zircon in the rock is present as acicular inclusions in large, equant apatite crystals.

Table 5.—*Rare-earth contents of accessory apatites from the Snake*

[Samples arranged in order of increasing CaO content of whole rock. Sample localities are shown on plate 1 of Lee and Van Loenen (1971). General limitations of the two methods given in text. Looked for but

	Sample No.	147-MW-61	151-MW-61	190-DL-62	14-MW-60	36-DL-62	8-DL-62	31-DL-62	
	CaO in rock (weight percent)	1.5	1.8	2.0	2.2	2.2	2.3	2.4	
	Rare earths in apatite (weight percent)								
1	Y	0.21	0.25	0.23	0.06	0.1	0.08	0.065	1
2	La	.036	.034	.026	.03	.044	.032	.036	2
3	Ce	.15	.1	.1	.1	.15	.1	.1	3
4	Pr	.015	.02	.02	.015	.03	.02	.02	4
5	Nd	.15	.15	.15	.1	.15	.1	.07	5
6	Sm	.05	.07	.03	.05	0	.05	.015	6
7	Eu	.005	.003	0	.003	0	.003	0	7
8	Gd	.05	.07	0	.02	.02	.02	.015	8
9	Dy	.05	.05	.05	.003	.015	.007	.015	9
10	Ho	.01	.01	.007	.003	.005	.003	.005	10
11	Er	.03	.015	.015	0	0	0	0	11
12	Tm	0	.003	0	.001	0	.0015	0	12
13	Yb	.017	.021	.017	.0055	.007	.008	.0046	13
14	Lu	0	.005	0	0	0	0	0	14
15	Total	.773	.801	.645	.3905	.521	.4195	.3456	15
	Total rare-earth elements in apatite (atomic percent)[2]								
16	Y	38.2	43.1	47.9	22.9	27.6	26.1	27.2	16
17	La	4.2	3.8	3.5	7.4	7.9	7.2	9.7	17
18	Ce	17.3	10.9	13.2	23.9	26.4	22.1	26.5	18
19	Pr	1.8	2.2	2.6	3.7	5.4	4.4	5.3	19
20	Nd	16.9	15.9	19.2	23.2	25.5	21.5	18.3	20
21	Sm	5.4	7.2	3.7	11.1	0	10.3	3.7	21
22	Eu	.5	.3	0	.7	0	.6	0	22
23	Gd	5.2	6.9	0	4.4	3.2	4.1	3.7	23
24	Dy	5.0	4.8	5.7	.7	2.2	1.2	3.4	24
25	Ho	1.0	.9	.7	.7	.8	.6	1.1	25
26	Er	2.9	1.4	1.7	0	0	0	0	26
27	Tm	0	.3	0	.3	0	.3	0	27
28	Yb	1.6	1.8	1.8	1.0	1.0	1.6	1.1	28
29	Lu	0	.5	0	0	0	0	0	29
30	Total	100.0	100.0	100.0	100.0	100.0	100.0	100.0	30
31	Σ(La+Ce+Pr)	23.3	16.9	26.2	35.0	39.7	33.7	41.5	31

[1] Apatite from xenolith.

[2] Results of conversion to atomic percent are given in more significant figures than justified by

REFERENCES CITED

Bowen, N. L., 1922, The behavior of inclusions in igneous magmas: Jour. Geology, v. 30, supp. to no. 6, p. 513–570.

Cruft, E. F., 1966, Minor elements in igneous and metamorphic apatite: Geochim. et Cosmochim. Acta, v. 30, no. 4, p. 375–398.

Deer, W. A., Howie, R. A., and Zussman, J., 1962, Rock-forming minerals—v. 5, Non-silicates: New York, John Wiley and Sons, Inc., 371 p.

Evans, H. T., Jr., Appleman, D. E., and Handwerker, D. S., 1963, The least squares refinement of crystal unit cells with powder diffraction data by an automatic computer indexing method [abs.]: Am. Crystallog. Assoc. Program and Abs. 1963 Ann. Mtg., p. 42–43.

Fleischer, Michael, and Altschuler, Z. S., 1969, The relationship of the rare-earth composition of minerals to geological environment: Geochim. et Cosmochim. Acta, v. 33, no. 6, p. 725–732.

Harker, Alfred, 1895, Carrock Fell—A study in the variation of igneous rock masses; Pt. 2, The Carrock Fell Granophyre: Geol. Soc. London Quart. Jour., v. 51, p. 125–139.

Huang, W. W. T., 1958, Zircons in the Precambrian igneous rocks, Wichita Mountains, Oklahoma [abs.]: Geol. Soc. America Bull., v. 69, no. 12, pt. 2, p. 1589.

Jackson, E. D., Stevens, R. E., and Bowen, R. W., 1967, A computer-based procedure for deriving mineral formulas from mineral analyses, *in* Geological Survey Research 1967: U.S. Geol. Survey Prof. Paper 575-C, p. C23–C31.

Lee, D. E., and Bastron, Harry, 1967, Fractionation of rare-earth elements in allanite and monazite as related to geology of the Mt. Wheeler mine area, Nevada: Geochim. et Cosmochim. Acta, v. 31, no. 3, p. 339–356.

Lee, D. E., and Dodge, F. C. W., 1964, Accessory minerals in some granitic rocks in California and Nevada as a function of calcium content: Am. Mineralogist, v. 49, nos. 11–12, p. 1660–1669.

Lee, D. E., Mays, R. E., Van Loenen, R. E., and Rose, H. J., Jr., 1969, Accessory sphene from hybrid rocks of the Mount Wheeler mine area, Nevada, *in* Geological Survey Research 1969: U.S. Geol. Survey Prof. Paper 650-B, p. B41–B46.

—— 1971, Accessory epidote from hybrid granitoid rocks of the Mount Wheeler mine area, Nevada, *in* Geological Survey Research

Creek–Williams Canyon area, southern Snake Range, Nev.

Spectrographic analyses by R. E. Mays. Results for Y, La, and Yb are quantitative; results for all other elements are semiquantitative. not found: Tb (limit of detection 0.005 percent). Σ discussed in text]

	38-MW-60 2.5	25-DL-61 3.1	152-MW-60 3.2	21A-MW-60 3.4	40B-MW-60[1] 3.5	126-MW-60[1] 3.5	43-DL-61 3.9	27-DL-6[1] 4.1	16-MW-60 4.3	98-DL-62[1] 4.5	
	Rare earths in apatite (weight percent)										
1	0.12	0.11	0.07	0.03	0.085	0.13	0.06	0.09	0.034	0.055	1
2	.032	.03	.032	.03	.019	.038	.03	.044	.019	.036	2
3	.1	.1	.15	.1	.07	.15	.15	.15	.1	.15	3
4	.015	.02	.015	.015	.015	.02	.015	.02	.015	.015	4
5	.1	.07	.15	.1	.05	.15	.1	.1	.1	.1	5
6	.015	.07	.015	.01	.07	.05	0	.02	0	.015	6
7	0	.003	.003	.003	.003	.003	.003	.005	0	.003	7
8	.015	.05	.03	.01	.02	.05	.02	.03	0	.01	8
9	.015	.05	.015	.005	.007	.015	.005	.015	.0015	.007	9
10	.005	.005	.003	.0015	.003	.007	.0015	.005	0	.0015	10
11	0	.01	0	0	.015	0	0	0	0	0	11
12	0	.0015	0	0	.001	0	0	0	0	0	12
13	.012	.009	.007	.0025	.009	.01	.004	.006	.0025	.004	13
14	0	0	0	0	0	0	0	0	0	0	14
15	.429	.5285	.490	.307	.367	.623	.3885	.485	.272	.3965	15
	Total rare-earth elements in apatite (atomic percent)[2]										
16	38.8	30.5	21.4	15.0	33.4	30.2	22.8	27.1	18.6	20.6	16
17	6.6	5.4	6.2	9.7	4.9	5.6	7.4	8.6	6.8	8.7	17
18	20.4	17.5	29.0	31.3	17.4	22.1	35.9	28.7	34.6	35.7	18
19	3.2	3.5	3.0	4.9	3.9	2.9	3.7	3.8	5.4	3.7	19
20	19.8	12.0	28.1	30.4	12.2	21.5	23.1	18.4	33.6	23.0	20
21	2.9	11.5	2.7	3.1	16.4	6.8	0	3.5	0	3.3	21
22	0	.5	.5	.9	0	.4	.7	.8	0	.7	22
23	2.8	7.9	5.1	2.6	4.5	6.6	4.4	5.1	0	2.0	23
24	2.6	7.6	2.4	1.3	1.4	1.9	1.0	2.4	.5	1.3	24
25	.9	.7	.5	.4	.7	.8	.3	.8	0	.3	25
26	0	1.5	0	0	3.1	0	0	0	0	0	26
27	0	.2	0	0	.4	0	0	0	0	0	27
28	2.0	1.2	1.1	.4	1.7	1.2	.7	.8	.5	.7	28
29	0	0	0	0	0	0	0	0	0	0	29
30	100.0	100.0	100.0	100.0	100.0	100.0	100.0	100.0	100.0	100.0	30
31	30.2	26.4	38.2	45.9	26.2	30.6	47.0	41.1	46.8	48.1	31

precision of original data.

1971: U.S. Geol. Survey Prof. Paper 750-C, p. C112–C116.

Lee, D. E., Stern, T. W., Mays, R. E., and Van Loenen, R. E., 1968, Accessory zircon from granitoid rocks of the Mount Wheeler mine area, Nevada, *in* Geological Survey Research 1968: U.S. Geol. Survey Prof. Paper 600-D, p. D197–D203.

Lee, D. E., and Van Loenen, R. E., 1970, Biotites from hybrid granitoid rocks of the southern Snake Range, Nevada, *in* Geological Survey Research 1970: U.S. Geol. Survey Prof. Paper 700-D, p. D196–D206.

—— 1971, Hybrid granitoid rocks of the southern Snake Range, Nevada: U.S. Geol. Survey Prof. Paper 668, 48 p.

Murata, K. J., Rose, H. J., Jr., and Carron, M. K., 1953, Systematic variation of rare earths in monazite: Geochim. et Cosmochim. Acta, v. 4, no. 6, p. 292–300.

Nockolds, S. R., 1933, Some theoretical aspects of contamination in acid magmas: Jour. Geology, v. 41, no. 6, p. 561–589.

Otto, Helmut, 1935, Die Rolle des Mangans in den Mineralien: Tschermaks Mineralog. u. Petrog. Mitt., v. 47, p. 89–140.

Stormer, J. C., and Carmichael, I. S. E., 1971, Fluorine-hydroxyl exchange in apatite and biotite—A potential igneous geothermometer: Contr. Mineralogy and Petrology, v. 31, no. 2, p. 121–131.

Taborszky, F. K., 1962, Geochemie des Apatits in Tiefengesteinen am Beispiel des Odenwaldes: Beitr. Mineralogie u. Petrographie, v. 8, no. 5, p. 354–392.

Taubeneck, W. H., 1957, Zircons in the metamorphic aureole of the Bald Mountain batholith, Elkhorn Mountains, northwestern Oregon [abs.]: Geol. Soc. America Bull., v. 68, no. 12, pt. 2, p. 1803–1804.

Wilcox, R. E., 1959, Use of the spindle stage for determination of principal indices of refraction of crystal fragments: Am. Mineralogist, v. 44, nos. 11–12, p. 1272–1293.

—— 1962, Cherkasov's "focal screening" for determination of refractive index by the immersion method, *in* McCrone, W. C., ed., Internat. Microscopy Symposium, Chicago, 1960 [1962], Proc.: p. 160–165.

Wyatt, Michael, 1954, Zircons as provenance indicators: Am. Mineralogist, v. 39, nos. 11–12, p. 983–990.

Wyllie, P. J., Cox, K. G., and Biggar, G. M., 1962, The habit of apatite in synthetic systems and igneous rocks: Jour. Petrology, v. 3, pt. 2, p. 238–243.

Table 6.—*Rare-earth contents of accessory apatites from the Young Canyon—Kious Basin area, the Pole Canyon—Can Young Canyon area, and from aplites, southern Snake Range, Nev.*

[Sample localities are shown on plate 1 of Lee and Van Loenen (1971). Spectrographic analyses by R. E. Mays. Results for Y, La, and Yb are quantitative; results for all other elements are semiquantitative. General limitations of two methods given in text. Looked for but not found: Tb (limit of detection 0.005 percent). Σ discussed in text]

	Young Canyon—Kious Basin area		Pole Canyon—Can Young Canyon area		Aplites	
Sample No.	190-MW-61	234-MW-61	135-DL-62	120-MW-60	119-MW-60	121-MW-60
CaO in rock (weight percent)	1.2	1.6	0.98	1.3	0.63	0.70
			Rare earths in apatite (weight percent)			
Y	0.20	0.30	0.15	0.16	0.2	0.1
La	.046	.050	.026	.026	.032	.034
Ce	.2	.15	.15	.07	.1	.15
Pr	.03	.02	.015	.015	.02	.03
Nd	.2	.15	.1	.1	.15	.15
Sm	.07	.05	.15	.015	.05	.07
Eu	.005	.005	.003	.005	.005	.005
Gd	.07	.07	.07	.03	.05	.1
Dy	.07	.05	.07	.02	.03	.03
Ho	.015	.007	.01	.01	.005	.005
Er	.05	.03	.015	0	0	0
Tm	0	0	.002	0	0	0
Yb	.021	.023	.007	.0095	.005	.002
Lu	.005	.015	0	0	0	0
Total	.982	.920	.768	.4605	.647	.676
			Total rare-earth elements in apatite (atomic percent)[1]			
Y	29.9	44.7	29.4	46.8	42.5	22.3
La	4.4	4.8	3.3	5.0	4.3	4.9
Ce	19.0	14.2	18.7	13.0	13.4	21.1
Pr	2.8	1.9	1.9	2.9	2.6	4.1
Nd	18.4	13.8	12.0	18.0	19.6	20.5
Sm	6.2	4.4	17.4	2.6	6.2	9.3
Eu	.4	.4	.4	.8	.6	.6
Gd	6.0	5.9	7.9	4.9	6.0	12.6
Dy	5.7	4.1	5.4	3.1	3.6	3.8
Ho	1.2	.5	1.1	1.6	.6	.6
Er	4.0	2.4	1.6	0	0	0
Tm	0	0	.2	0	0	0
Yb	1.6	1.7	.7	1.3	.6	.2
Lu	.4	1.2	0	0	0	0
Total	100.0	100.0	100.0	100.0	100.0	100.0
Σ(La+Ce+Pr)	26.2	20.9	23.9	20.9	20.3	30.1

[1] Results of conversion to atomic percent are given in more significant figures than justified by precision of original data.

Jour. Research U.S. Geol. Survey
Vol. 1, No. 1, Jan.—Feb. 1973, p. 99—103

NEW DATA ON CUPROBISMUTITE

By CHARLES M. TAYLOR[1]; ARTHUR S. RADTKE, and
C. L. CHRIST, Stanford, Calif.; Menlo Park, Calif.

Abstract.—Cuprobismutite from Tunnel Extension Number Two mine, Ohio mining district, Utah, was chemically analyzed using the electron microprobe. Its empirical formula was determined to be $Cu_{20.8}Ag_{0.97}Pb_{0.35}Mn_{0.22}Bi_{26.7}Sb_{0.06}Te_{0.05}Se_{0.55}S_{50.4}$. The tentative conclusion is that unsubstituted cuprobismutite has the chemical formula $5Cu_2S{\cdot}6Bi_2S_3$ rather than the previously ascribed formula $6Cu_2S{\cdot}6Bi_2S_3$ and that cuprobismutite is therefore not dimorphous with emplectite.

Microscopic examination of polished sections of gold- and silver-bearing sulfide ore from the Tunnel Extension Number Two mine, Ohio mining district, Utah, showed that the ore contains a variety of bismuth-bearing minerals, including cuprobismutite, bismuthinite, emplectite, and tetradymite. Electron microprobe studies also indicate the presence of a secondary hydrated bismuth sulfate mineral, the data for which will be given separately. This paper presents data on the micromineralogy of the ore minerals and defines the chemical composition of cuprobismutite.

The Ohio mining district is located along the east flank of the Tushar Range, about 6 miles southwest of Marysvale (fig. 1) in Piute County, Utah. Most of the sulfide ore bodies in the Tunnel Extension Number Two mine are tabular and occur within steeply dipping shear or fault zones. Locally, small amounts of ore replace the wallrocks which are latite and agglomerate units of the Bullion Canyon Volcanics of Oligocene age.

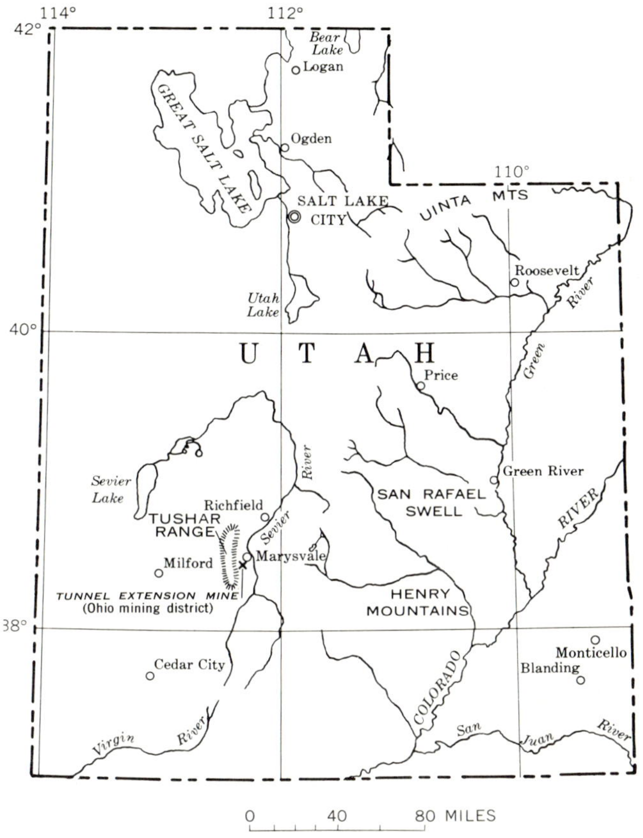

Figure 1.—Index map of Utah, showing location of the Tunnel Extension mine (Ohio mining district) (Radtke and others, 1967).

The ore bodies in the Tunnel Extension Number Two mine, as well as other deposits in the Ohio district described by Butler, Loughlin, Heikes, and others (1920), were mined principally for their high content of gold and silver. Although the other deposits in the district may contain the same suite of bismuth-bearing minerals, the only specimens used in this study came from the 400-foot level of the Tunnel Extension Number Two mine.

Acknowledgments.—All electron microprobe analyses were done on the Model 400 electron microprobe analyzer at Materials Analysis Co., Palo Alto, Calif., which is now a division of ETEC Corp. We wish to thank Richard Wolf of Microspec Corp., Palo Alto, Calif., for the use of his computer program for electron microprobe quantitative data reduction, and the following members of the U.S. Geological Survey: Richard C. Erd and Joan R. Clark for critical review of the manuscript; Richard C. Erd for assistance in X-ray diffraction analysis; Chris Heropoulos for spectrographic analyses; Brent P. Fabbi for X-ray fluorescence analyses; and W. W. Brannock for specific gravity determinations. The ore specimens were generously provided by John E. Frost, Mineral Department Manager, Esso Eastern, Inc., Houston, Texas.

[1] School of Earth Sciences, Stanford University.

ORE CHEMISTRY AND MINERALOGY

The chemical and mineralogical associations in this ore were described previously by Radtke, Taylor, and Frost (1967). Results of this earlier work and more recent study of these ores as they apply to the detailed study of the bismuth-bearing minerals are summarized below.

The fine-grained siliceous sulfide ores are composed mainly of cuprobismutite, quartz, and bismuthinite. The approximate percentage by volume of these and other minerals is shown in table 1. Primary ore minerals are cuprobismutite, bismuthinite,

Table 1.—*Mineralogy of massive sulfide ores*

[Abundance, in percentage by volume of total sample, was estimated visually. (From Radtke and others, 1967.)]

Mineral	Abundance	Mineral	Abundance
Cuprobismutite	40	Tetrahedrite	1
Bismuthinite	30	Cassiterite	1
Quartz	20	Tetradymite	<1
Hydrated bismuth sulfate	5	Chalcopyrite	<1
Covellite	1	Gold	<1
Chalcocite	1	Calcite	<1

tetrahedrite, tetradymite, chalcopyrite, and native gold. Secondary or alteration minerals are chalcocite, covellite, and a hydrated bismuth sulfate. Quartz makes up most of the gangue. Other gangue minerals include significant amounts of cassiterite (Radtke and others, 1967) and small amounts of calcite. The three most abundant minerals, cuprobismutite, bismuthinite, and quartz, are intergrown and interlocked in the ore (fig. 2).

A semiquantitative spectrographic analysis of a typical specimen of ore is given in table 2. This analysis, plus several other spectrographic analyses performed by Taylor and Radtke on other ore samples indicate that the principal elements in the ore are bismuth (>20 percent), silicon (7–10 percent), copper (5–7 percent), tin (1–1.5 percent), and silver (0.3–1 percent). Although the ore contains small amounts of selenium and tellurium, data on these elements are not given in table 2. Owing to poor sensitivity and spectral interference, selenium is not sought in the standard method used. However,

Table 2.—*Semiquantitative spectrographic analysis of massive sulfide ore*

[Sought but not found: As, B, Be, Cd, Ce, Co, Eu, Ga, Ge, Hf, Hg, In, K, La, Li, Na, Nb, P, Pd, Pt, Re, Sc, Sr, Ta, Te, Th, Tl, U, Y, Yb, Zn, and Zr. Values are in weight percent. Analyst: Chris Heropoulos. (From Radtke and others, 1967.)]

Element	Amount	Element	Amount	Element	Amount
Si	10	Ag	1	Ni	0.001
Al	.02	Au	.003	Pb	.3
Fe	.015	Ba	.001	Sb	.1
Mg	.0003	Bi	>10	Sn	1.5
Ca	.001	Cr	.0002	V	.005
Ti	.007	Cu	7	W	.01
Mn	.07	Mo	.001		

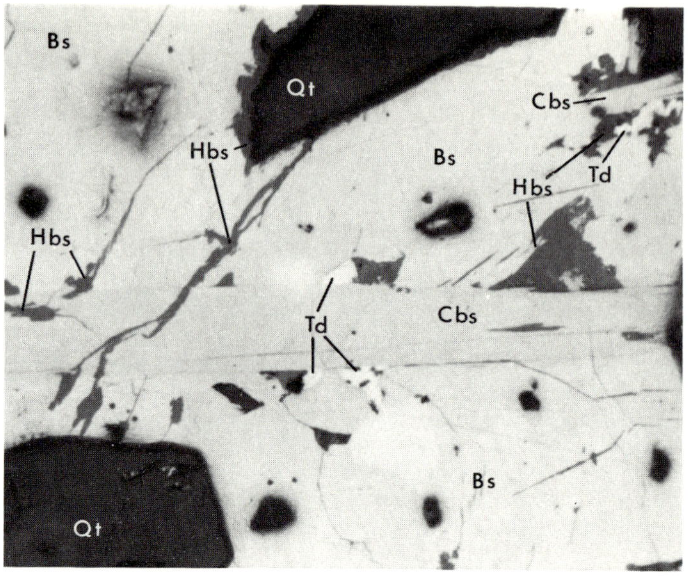

Figure 2.—Photomicrograph showing intergrowths of medium-gray bladed cuprobismutite (Cbs) and small white grains of tetradymite (Td) in pale-gray bismuthinite (Bs). Darkest areas are euhedral quartz (Qt) grains. Note alteration of primary bismuth minerals to a hydrous bismuth sulfate (Hbs) along fractures and grain boundaries. X 340. (From Radtke and others, 1967.)

X-ray fluorescence analysis shows the content of selenium to be approximately 0.2–0.3 weight percent; the content of tellurium is <0.1 percent.

CUPROBISMUTITE

Because one of the purposes of this paper is to establish the composition of cuprobismutite and because the validity of this mineral as a distinct species has been questioned in the past, a brief review of the literature is necessary. Hillebrand (1884) reported the presence of "a sulpho-bismuthite of copper and silver in ore specimens" from the Missouri mine, Halls Valley, Park County, Colo. He recognized this as "a probably new mineral" and proposed the formula $3(Cu,Ag)_2S \cdot 4Bi_2S_3$. Dana (1892) listed the data collected by Hillebrand and named the mineral cuprobismutite. Schneiderhöhn and Ramdohr (1931) presented some data on the physical and optical properties of cuprobismutite and indicated that the mineral also occurred at Arnsberg, Westphalia.

On the basis of study of polished sections of specimens from the type locality, Halls Valley, Colo., Short (1931) reported that cuprobismutite was identical with emplectite ($Cu_2S \cdot Bi_2S_3$) and listed cuprobismutite as a discredited or doubtful mineral. Palache (1940) examined the type specimen, USNM 92902, from Halls Valley, identified bismuthinite (Bi_2S_3) and emplectite, and concluded (p. 611) "since a mixture of these two phases would give the composition revealed by Hillebrand's analysis, the species has no validity." Palache, Berman, and Frondel (1944) also classified cuprobismutite as a discredited species.

Nuffield (1952) examined the type specimen and showed that cuprobismutite was a valid species and not a mixture of bismuthinite and emplectite. Because of the presence of several intergrown phases, Nuffield was not able to determine the exact chemical formula. However, he argued that since the Bi-Cu ratio was close to 1:1, it was reasonable to suggest that its chemical formula was $Cu_2S \cdot Bi_2S_3$ and that cuprobismutite was dimorphous with emplectite. Ramdohr (1969, p. 707) stated that the composition was "presumably $3Cu_2S \cdot 4Bi_2S_3$, but in the classic occurrence according to the structure probably $CuBiS_2$, i.e., dimorphous with emplectite."

Electron microprobe analysis

Polished sections of the ore were prepared for microscopic examination and electron microprobe analysis following the method outlined by Taylor and Radtke (1965). The polished section containing the standards for electron microprobe analysis and the section for analysis were simultaneously carbon coated to uniform thicknesses. Numerous grains of cuprobismutite were analyzed by spectral scans, and all elements detected were subsequently analyzed quantitatively.

Corrections in electron microprobe intensity data were made taking into account: (1) drift of the incident electron beam, (2) background from the continuous spectrum, (3) characteristic fluorescence by other radiations, (4) absorption effects, and (5) atomic number effects. $K\alpha$ characteristic lines were used for S, Se, Cu, and Mn; $L\alpha$ characteristic lines were used for Te, Sb, and Ag; and $M\alpha$ characteristic lines were used for Bi and Pb. Operating voltages were 20 kV for S, Ag, Te, and Bi; 25 kV for Sb and Pb; and 30 kV for Mn, Cu, and Se. Standards used for the quantitative analyses include Mn, Cu, Se, Ag, Sb, Te, PbS, and Bi_2S_3. The quantitative data were reduced at the Stanford University Computing Center according to a program developed by Richard Wolf, of Microspec Corp. Results of the analysis of numerous grains of cuprobismutite showed the composition to be remarkably uniform. The chemical analysis of a typical grain is given in table 3.

These analytical results yield the complex empirical formula $Cu_{20.8}Ag_{0.97}Pb_{0.35}Mn_{0.22}Bi_{26.7}Sb_{0.06}Te_{0.05}Se_{0.55}S_{50.4}$

Table 3.—*Electron microprobe analysis of cuprobismutite*

Element	Weight percent	Precision[1]	Atomic percent
S	18.5	±0.20	50.38
Se	.50	±.04	.55
Te	.07	±.02	.05
Bi	63.8	±.30	26.66
Sb	.08	±.02	.06
Cu	15.1	±.20	20.75
Ag	1.19	±.03	.97
Pb	.84	±.03	.35
Mn	.14	±.02	.22
Total	100.2		99.99

[1] Precision is calculated from the standard counting error from an average of 18 points in two separate but near-together grains. The values of precision listed indicate that the elements are distributed uniformly within and between the two grains. The values listed in the weight percentage column are considered to be accurate to ±2 percent.

for cuprobismutite. For this formula, the total charge for the anions is −102.0, taking S, Se, and Te as −2, and that for the cations is +103.2, taking Cu and Ag to be +1, Pb and Mn to be +2, and Bi and Sb to be +3. This agreement, which is within 1.2 percent, is entirely satisfactory, considering the errors of analysis and the complex chemistry of the mineral. The charge-balance calculation is, of course, based on the assumption that the valence rule is valid and that cuprobismutite is a "sulfosalt" and not a "complex sulfide" (such as binnite, $Cu_{12}As_4S_{13}$), as defined by Nowacki (1971).

X-ray data

From single-crystal X-ray diffraction studies of type specimen cuprobismutite, Nuffield (1952) found that the mineral is monoclinic with cell constants a=17.65, b=3.93, c=15.24 A, and β=100.5°. He observed that the phase gave systematic X-ray extinctions for the general class of hkl reflections for which $h+k \neq 2n$, and he correctly stated that this result is consistent with the space group $C2/m$. Actually, these extinction conditions are also consistent with the space groups $C2$ and Cm.

In the present study, X-ray powder data were obtained from four different grains of the Tunnel Extension Number Two cuprobismutite, each of which had the same chemical composition, within limits of error. The measured d spacings and intensities did not differ significantly from pattern to pattern. The measured data from a typical pattern are listed in table 4 for the specimen designated as MU-1. Starting with the cell constants of Nuffield (1952), the d_{hkl} values for MU-1 were treated by the computer program of Evans, Appleman, and Handwerker (1963) to index the pattern and to obtain a least-squares refinement of the cell constants. The cell constants obtained for MU-1 are a=17.628±0.01, b=3.911±0.002, c=15.190±0.01 A, and β=101°16′; the volume of the unit cell is 1,027.0±0.8 A^3, and the errors given represent 1 standard error. The calculated d spacings and indices are listed in table 4, as are the data for cuprobismutite from the type specimen (USNM 92902) reported by Berry and Thompson (1962).

Mineral chemistry

As shown by the quantitative electron microprobe analysis (table 3), the cuprobismutite studied here has as major constituents copper, bismuth, and sulfur and also contains a significant amount of silver and minor amounts of selenium, tellurium, antimony, lead, and manganese. Starting with the empirical formula, $Cu_{20.8}Ag_{0.97}Pb_{0.35}Mn_{0.22}Bi_{26.7}Sb_{0.06}Te_{0.05}Se_{0.55}S_{50.4}$, and summing the atomic percentages of the elements as (Cu+Ag+Pb+Mn)=22.3, (Bi+Sb)=26.8, and (S+Se+Te)=51.0, the ratio of (Bi+Sb) to (Cu+Ag+Pb+Mn) is 12 to 10. This result suggests that the correct chemical formula for unsubstituted cuprobismutite is $5Cu_2S \cdot 6Bi_2S_3$, or

Table 4.—*X-ray powder diffraction data for cuprobismutite from the Ohio mining d*

Calculated[1]		Cuprobism Tunnel Ext Number Tw Ohio mining district, Utah		Cuprobismutite[3] Missouri mine, Halls Valley, Park County, Colo.	
		Observed		Observed	
hkl	d_{hkl} (A)	d_{hkl} (A)	I/I_0	d_{hkl} (A)	I/I_0
001	14.898	.....	....	.....	....
200	8.644	.....	....	.....	....
$\bar{2}01$	8.204	.....	....	.....	....
002	7.449	.....	....	.....	....
201	6.914	6.94	12	.....	....
$\bar{2}02$	6.282	6.28	35	6.24	20
202	5.166	.....	....	.....	....
003	4.966	4.96	15	.....	....
$\bar{2}03$	4.723	.....	....	.....	....
$\bar{4}01$	4.386	.....	....	.....	....
400	4.322	4.32	40	4.31	30
$\bar{4}02$	4.102	.....	....	.....	....
203	3.983	.....	....	.....	....
401	3.950	3.941	10	.....	....
110	3.814	.....	....	.....	....
$\bar{1}11$	3.734	.....	....	.....	....
004	3.724	.....	....	.....	....
$\bar{2}04$	3.693	.....	....	.....	....
111	3.658	.....	....	} 3.65	40B
$\bar{4}03$	3.630	3.632	70		
402	3.457	.....	....	} 3.47	10
$\bar{1}12$	3.456	3.452	45		
112	3.338	.....	....	.....	....
$\bar{3}11$	3.237	.....	....		
310	3.236	3.220	70	} 3.23	40
204	3.201	.....	....		
$\bar{4}04$	3.141	.....	....	.....	....
$\bar{3}12$	3.095	.....	....		
311	3.093	.....	....	} 3.10	100
$\bar{1}13$	3.090	3.090	100		
$\bar{2}05$	3.003	.....	....	.....	....
403	2.984	.....	....	.....	....
005	2.980	.....	....		
113	2.964	2.971	12	} 2.96	5B
$\bar{6}01$	2.938	.....	....		
$\bar{6}02$	2.883	.....	....		
600	2.881	.....	....		
$\bar{3}13$	2.858	2.860	30	} 2.86	10B
312	2.856	.....	....		
$\bar{6}03$	2.735	.....	....		
601	2.731	.....	....		
$\bar{1}14$	2.724	2.721	80	} 2.73	60
$\bar{4}05$	2.713	.....	....		
		2.580	40	2.58	10
		2.501	10	2.49	5
		2.291	12	2.30	5
		2.160	35	2.17	20
		2.091	30	2.09	20
		1.995	25	2.00	5
		1.955	40	.....	....
		1.862	12	.....	....
		1.825	15	.....	....

Table 4.—*X-ray powder diffraction data for cuprobismutite from the Ohio mining district, Utah.*—Continued

Calculated[1]		Cuprobismutite[2] Tunnel Extension Number Two mine, Ohio mining district, Utah		Cuprobismutite[3] Missouri mine, Halls Valley, Park County, Colo.	
		Observed		Observed	
hkl	d_{hkl} (A)	d_{hkl} (A)	I/I_0	d_{hkl} (A)	I/I_0
		1.722	30	.....	....
		1.669	15	.....	....
		1.610	5B	.....	....
		1.485	7	.....	....
		1.454	10	.....	....
		1.435	10	.....	....

[1] Calculated from least-squares refinement of the observed X-ray powder data from specimen MU-1 (see footnote 2) by use of the computer program of Appleman, Evans, and Handwerker (1972).

[2] Specimen MU-1, private collection of C. M. Taylor, School of Earth Sciences, Stanford University; film ASR-1, 1968; Cu/Ni; radiation $CuK\alpha = 1.5418$ A; camera diameter 114.6 mm.

[3] Specimen 92902, U.S. National Museum, type specimen of cuprobismutite; Cu/Ni; radiation $CuK\alpha = 1.5418$ A; data from Berry and Thompson (1962, p. 143).

$Cu_{10}Bi_{12}S_{23}$. For this formula, and adjusting for the abundances of the other elements present, the formula weight of the cuprobismutite is 3,933. Using a unit-cell weight of 3,933 and the calculated unit-cell volume of 1,027 A^3, the calculated density is 6.36 g cm^{-3}. Unfortunately, no single crystals of the specimen studied were available, so that no direct measurement could be made to check this calculated density. However, it was possible to arrive at a specific gravity value in the following way: The specific gravity of a sample containing about 50 percent cuprobismutite was measured. A small sample of ore was crushed to −225 mesh and treated with hydrochloric acid to remove any carbonates. The heavy minerals were separated from the quartz using methylene iodide, and the concentrate was cleaned and dried. The specific gravity of the heavy-media concentrate was determined to be 6.35.

The contents of copper, bismuth, silica, and tin in the heavy-media concentrate were determined using standard X-ray fluorescence methods. By solving two simultaneous equations set up on the basis of the weight balance and the copper balance in the sample, it was determined that the heavy-mineral concentrate contained 53.2 percent cuprobismutite and 44.2 percent bismuthinite. Chemical analysis showed that the concentrate contained 2.4 percent quartz and 0.1 percent cassiterite. Covellite, the only other mineral identified, was estimated at 0.1 percent. The specific gravity of cuprobismutite was then calculated by setting up an equation in which the weight percent of each mineral divided by its specific gravity was added and the summation made equal to 100 divided by the specific gravity of the bulk concentrate. The specific gravity of cuprobismutite was determined to be 6.36.

Obviously, the excellent agreement between the calculated density and measured specific gravity of cuprobismutite is somewhat fortuitous, considering the assumptions made, but it does tend to confirm the cell contents of the unsubstituted mineral to be $5Cu_2S \cdot 6Bi_2S_3$ (or some integral multiple of this formula) and indicates that cuprobismutite is not dimorphous with emplectite, $6Cu_2S \cdot 6Bi_2S_3$.

A unit-cell content of $Cu_{10}B_{12}S_{23}$ is not consistent with the *C*-centered cell found by Nuffield (1952) if all crystallographically equivalent sites are occupied. A *C*-centered cell must, of necessity, contain equivalent atoms in at least multiples of 2 (in special positions). For *Cm* or *C*2, general positions are fourfold, and for *C*2/*m*, general positions are eightfold. A unit-cell content of 23 atoms of sulfur is not in agreement with these requirements. Thus, the possibility exists that some of the equivalent sites are vacant and that cuprobismutite forms a defect structure if the data of Nuffield (1952) are correct. On the other hand, it is quite possible that the unit cell determined by Nuffield (1952) is actually a submultiple of the true unit cell, or that the symmetry assigned to the structure is incorrect, or that a combination of all of these possibilities exists. Obviously, further work is necessary to resolve this problem. Ideally, this would involve a complete crystal structure determination on chemically well-characterized single crystals. Short of a structure determination, it would be considerably helpful to redetermine the symmetry and unit-cell constants by modern single-crystal X-ray techniques, such as the precession camera method. As pointed out in the foregoing, single crystals suitable for X-ray study are not available in the specimens studied.

BISMUTHINITE

Large amounts of bismuthinite are also present in the sulfide ores of the Tunnel Extension Number Two mine. Microscopic examination of polished sections shows that the bulk ore contains approximately 30 percent bismuthinite by volume and may in some samples contain as much as 45 percent.

Although the composition of bismuthinite is, in essence, Bi_2S_3, analyses summarized in Palache, Berman, and Frondel (1944) indicate that small amounts of lead, copper, iron, and tellurium, and larger amounts of antimony and selenium may be present in the structure. Quantitative electron-microprobe analyses of numerous grains of bismuthinite show that in these ores, this mineral contains 0.43–0.47 weight percent Cu, 0.93–0.98 weight percent Pb, 0.12–0.15 weight percent Sb, 0.68–0.73 weight percent Se, and 0.05–0.07 weight percent Te.

REFERENCES CITED

Appleman, D. E., Evans, H. T., Jr., and Handwerker, D. S., 1972, Job 9214; Indexing and least-squares refinement of powder diffraction data, U.S. Geol. Survey Computer Contr. 20: Springfield, Va., Natl. Tech. Inf. Service.

Berry, L. G., and Thompson, R. M., 1962, X-ray powder data for ore minerals—the Peacock atlas: Geol. Soc. America Mem. 85, 281 p.

Butler, B. S., Loughlin, G. F., Heikes, V. C., and others, 1920, The ore deposits of Utah: U.S. Geol. Survey Prof. Paper 111, 672 p.

Dana, E. S., 1892, The system of mineralogy of James Dwight Dana, 1837–1868, 6th ed.: New York, John Wiley and Sons, Inc., 1,134 p.

Hillebrand, W. F., 1884, On an interesting variety of löllingite and other minerals: Am. Jour. Sci., v. 27, p. 349–358.

Nowacki, W., 1971, Introductory talk: Japan Mining Geol. Soc., Spec. Issue 2, p. 3–9.

Nuffield, E. W., 1952, Studies of mineral sulpho-salts—[Pt.] 16, Cuprobismuthite: Am. Mineralogist, v. 37, nos. 5–6, p. 447–452.

Palache, Charles, 1940, Cuprobismutite—a mixture: Am. Mineralogist, v. 25, no. 9, p. 611–613.

Palache, Charles, Berman, Harry, and Frondel, Clifford, 1944, The system of mineralogy of James Dwight Dana and Edward Salisbury Dana, v. 1, Elements, sulfides, sulfosalts, oxides, 7th ed., rev.: New York, John Wiley and Sons, Inc., 834 p.

Radtke, A. S., Taylor, C. M., and Frost, J. E., 1967, Bismuth and tin minerals in gold- and silver-bearing sulfide ores, Ohio mining district, Marysvale, Utah, *in* Geological Survey Research 1967: U.S. Geol. Survey Prof. Paper 575-D, p. D127–D130.

Ramdohr, Paul, 1969, The ore minerals and their intergrowths, 3d ed.: London, Pergamon Press, 1,174 p.

Schneiderhöhn, Hans, and Ramdohr, Paul, 1931, Lehrbuch der Erzmikroskopie, 2d ed.: Berlin, Germany, Verlag von Gebrüder, 714 p.

Short, M. N., 1931, Microscopic determination of the ore minerals: U.S. Geol. Survey Bull. 825, 204 p.

Taylor, C. M., and Radtke, A. S., 1965, Preparation and polishing of ores and mill products for microscopic examination and electron microprobe analysis: Econ. Geology, v. 60, no. 6, p. 1306–1319.

Jour. Research U.S. Geol. Survey
Vol. 1, No. 1, Jan.—Feb. 1973, p. 105—111

CHEMICAL COMPOSITION OF A SALINE LAKE ON ENDERBURY ISLAND, PHOENIX ISLAND GROUP, PACIFIC OCEAN

By DAVID W. BROWN and ROBERT A. GULBRANDSEN,
Menlo Park, Calif.

Abstract.—Ion activity products for the dissolution of calcite, aragonite, gypsum, monetite, brushite, dolomite, magnesite, hydroxyapatite, and fluorapatite were calculated for a South Pacific guano island brine with an ionic strength of 6.4. Environmental conditions for the brine at the time of analysis and of sampling indicated saturation with respect to calcite, aragonite, gypsum, hydroxyapatite and fluorapatite; a comparison of the ion activity products and equilibrium constants indicated saturation or supersaturation with respect to most minerals found in lake sediments or elsewhere on the island. The results suggest that chemical thermodynamic calculations for brines may have some usefulness despite the many assumptions and estimations that must be made.

Enderbury Island is one of the atolls of the Phoenix Island Group in the central equatorial Pacific Ocean (fig. 1). It is a small island about 3 miles in length and about a mile in greatest breadth. The highest point is 33 feet, the top of an old phosphate stockpile. The surface of the island in cross section is concave, and most drainage is to the interior. Because of the great porosity of the surface material, all drainage is underground. The climate is arid, even though the mean annual rainfall is around 25 inches (Hutchinson, 1950, p. 166), and vegetation is sparse.

The bulk of the island is coral, but many kinds of shells and other skeletal material are incorporated in the coral reefs and mixed with coral fragments in the sands of the beaches and of much of the interior of the island. Phosphate, as guano and guano-derived phosphate rock and sediment, is widespread on the island but not now abundant. Hutchinson (1950, p. 180) estimated that about 100,000 tons of phosphate ore was shipped from Enderbury in the latter half of the nineteenth century.

A shallow saline lake is located in the southern half of the island (fig. 1) and occupies the site of a former lagoon that became filled with sediment. The depth of the lake probably never exceeds a few feet. The small islands within the lake are old reefs, now above sea level. The water of the lake is derived directly from rain on its surface, from rainwater drained from the island, from sea-water spray, and possibly from beach-ridge overwash during large storms. Ground water under the lake may be sea water. Because the drainage terrain is of restricted composition, composed almost entirely of calcium and magnesium carbonates and phosphates, and because of the existence of an evaporitic environment, a sample was collected from the lake to determine the composition of the water. One of the purposes of this study is to relate the existence of any remaining phosphate deposits to the water composition. Mineral equilibria calculations were attempted in order to assess the extent of saturation in the water of phosphate and other minerals found on the island and in the lake sediment. These calculations also serve to illustrate the applicability of chemical thermodynamic calculations to brines of very high dissolved solids content.

Acknowledgments.—The water sample was collected in the course of an investigation of the economic potential of phosphate deposits on the island. This work was a joint effort of the United Kingdom and the United States, and it was performed by Brian D. Hackman, on behalf of the United Kingdom, and by Joshua I. Tracey, Jr., and the junior author of this paper on behalf of the United States. We are grateful to the U.S. Air Force for the opportunity to make this study.

WATER ANALYSIS

The water sample was collected on the eastern edge of the lake (fig. 1). Temperature of the water at the time of collection was 40°C.

All chemical species were measured according to accepted procedures (Brown and others, 1970). In these procedures, all cation concentrations were determined by atomic absorption spectrophotometry. Alkalinity was measured by acid titration. Total halides (excluding fluoride) were determined by the Mohr method. Bromide and iodide were measured iodometrically after appropriate oxidation to bromate and iodate. Sulfate was determined by the thorin barium titration method by use of a spectrophotometrically determined end point. Silica and phosphate concentrations were determined colorimetrically by use of their respective molybdate complexing methods. Boron and fluoride concentrations were also determined colorimetrically, with the dianthrimide and Zirconium-Eriochrome Cyanide R methods, respectively.

The composition of the water is presented in table 1. The lake is highly saline, about 10 times more concentrated with

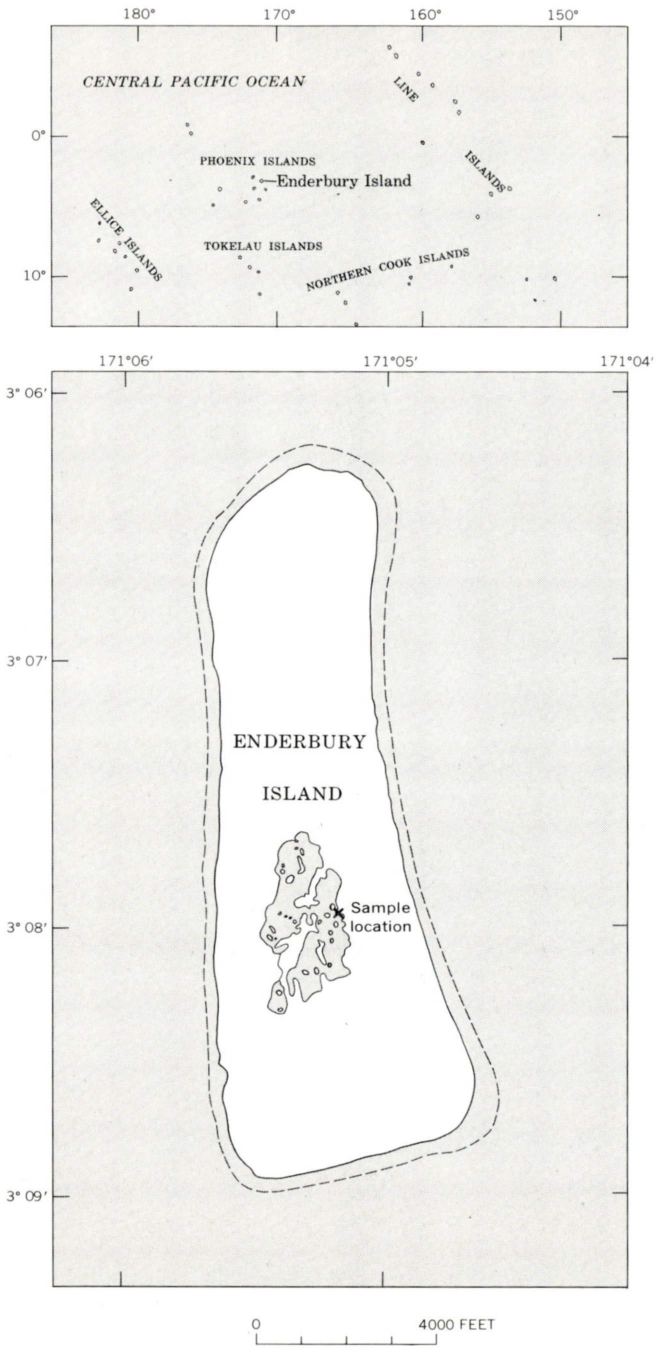

Figure 1.—Map showing outline of Enderbury Island and saline lake in southern part of island. Dashed line around island marks the approximate position of low tide.

Table 1.—*Analysis of Enderbury lake water*

Species	Method	Concentration Mg/l	Molarity (Major ions only)	Normality (Major ions only)
Neutral:				
SiO_2 ..	Colorimetric (molybdate).	0.5	......	......
Cations:				
Cu....	Atomic absorption.	3.6	......	......
Ca....	........do.........	885	0.022	0.044
Mg....	........do.........	7,800	.32	.64
Sr....	........do.........	42	......	......
Na....	........do.........	104,000	4.52	4.52
K....	........do.........	2,000	.051	.051
Li....	........do.........	1.0	......	......
Anions:				
HCO_3 .	Acid titration.	442	.0072	.0072
CO_3 ..	........do.........	0	......	......
OH ...	........do.........	0	......	......
SO_4...	Ba^{+2} titration (thorin).	14,100	.147	.294
Cl....	Ag^{+} titration (Mohr).	176,000	4.96	4.96
F.....	Colorimetric (cyanine).	10	......	......
Br....	Hypochlorite oxidation, titration with thiosulfate.	104	.001	.001
I.....	Bromine oxidation, titration with thiosulfate.	[1]19±7	......	......
PO_4...	Colorimetric (molybdate).	1.6	......	......
B.....	Colorimetric (1, 1-dianthrimide).	30	......	......

Normality total cations: 5.26 *N*
Normality total anions: 5.27 *N*
Total dissolved solids: 305,000 mg/l
pH: 7.70
Density: 1.202 g/ml
Appearance: Light pink with some suspended solids.
Mg/Ca molar ratio: 14.5

[1] Inadequate sample for accurate determination.

respect to sodium chloride than sea water. The sodium and chloride contents show well the contribution of sea water to the present composition of the lake. Magnesium is more concentrated relative to calcium in the lake water than in sea water; the Mg/Ca molar ratios are 14.5 and 5.4 (Goldberg, 1965, p. 164), respectively. A ratio of 35.7 was found for a brine pool on Jarvis Island, east of Enderbury in the southern Line Islands, by Schlanger and Tracey (1970, p. 676). They also found calcium-rich dolomite in the nearby evaporitic sediments. Bottom sediment of the Enderbury lake has not been sampled, but two sediment cores, collected by Joshua Tracey, Jr., and Brian Hackman, one on the east edge and one on the west edge of the lake, both contain high-magnesium calcite (about 35–40 mol percent $MgCO_3$) 2 to 3 feet below the surface. A study of these cores that is in progress shows that gypsum and bassanite layers are also present and that aragonite, low-magnesium calcite, and gypsum are the principal minerals in the upper few inches of the cores. Apatite, probably a carbonate hydroxyfluorapatite, is present in all of the sediment in small amounts.

The copper content of the water, 3.6 mg/l, is of special interest. It is more than 1,000 times greater than the amount reported in sea water, 0.003 mg/l (Goldberg, 1965, p. 164), and much more than can be accounted for by the contribution of sea water to the lake's composition. A source for the copper, however, is not difficult to explain. A sample of guano spectrographically analyzed by R. E. Mays contains 20 ppm Cu, and skeletal parts of a number of organisms, including corals, contain from 11 to 25 ppm Cu (Bowen, 1966, p. 72). The island's drainage of rainwater into the lake, therefore, should provide an adequate supply of copper. The fact that copper can occur in such a high amount in saline water may help to explain the copper deposits in evaporitic sequences such as in the Permian Flowerpot Shale in Oklahoma (Ham and Johnson, 1964).

THEORETICAL CONSIDERATIONS

The fact that a closed-basin lake on a phosphate-rich island contains only 1.6 mg total phosphate (as PO_4) per liter may possibly be explained by assuming the phosphate to be in equilibrium with the large concentrations of calcium and (or) magnesium. Since there are primarily three types of phosphate ions present in any orthophosphate solution, there are several possible combinations of equilibrium species.

In a solution of known ionic strength, hydrogen ion activity, and extent of complex ion formation, the relative activities of the three phosphate ions $H_2PO_4^{-1}$, HPO_4^{-2}, and PO_4^{-3} may be calculated. If the activities of the ions which are suspected of being in equilibrium with phosphate are also calculated, one may determine whether the appropriate cation–phosphate ion activity products are characteristic of a system in chemical equilibrium with respect to these ions.

With regard to complex ion formation we first estimated the complexing effect of sulfate on the major cations to determine the cation activities, then we calculated the complexing effect of those cations on bicarbonate, fluoride, and finally phosphate. It was assumed that only sulfate significantly affects the cation activities because it is the only strongly complexing anion present in quantities comparable to the cation concentrations.

From the four cation-sulfate complex dissociation relations,

$$K_{CaSO_4} = \frac{[Ca^{+2}][SO_4^{-2}]}{[CaSO_4^{0}]},\ K_{MgSO_4} = \frac{[Mg^{+2}][SO_4^{-2}]}{[MgSO_4^{0}]},$$

$$K_{NaSO_4} = \frac{[Na^{+}][SO_4^{-2}]}{[NaSO_4^{-}]},\ \text{and}\ K_{KSO_4} = \frac{[K^{+}][SO_4^{-2}]}{[KSO_4^{-}]}.$$

For the $CaSO_4^{0}$, $MgSO_4^{0}$, $NaSO_4^{-}$, and KSO_4^{-} complex ions and the concentration relations

$$C_{Ca} = \frac{[Ca^{+2}]}{\gamma_{Ca}} + \frac{[CaSO_4^{0}]}{\gamma_{CaSO_4}},\ C_{Mg} = \frac{[Mg^{+2}]}{\gamma_{Mg}} + \frac{[MgSO_4^{0}]}{\gamma_{MgSO_4}},$$

$$C_{Na} = \frac{[Na^{+}]}{\gamma_{Na}} + \frac{[NaSO_4^{-}]}{\gamma_{NaSO_4}},\ C_{K} = \frac{[K^{+}]}{\gamma_{K}} + \frac{[KSO_4^{-}]}{\gamma_{KSO_4}},\ \text{and}$$

$$C_{SO_4} = \frac{[SO_4^{-2}]}{\gamma_{SO_4}} + \frac{[CaSO_4^{0}]}{\gamma_{CaSO_4}} + \frac{[MgSO_4^{0}]}{\gamma_{MgSO_4}} + \frac{[NaSO_4^{-}]}{\gamma_{NaSO_4}} + \frac{[KSO_4^{-}]}{\gamma_{KSO_4}},$$

it can be shown that

$$[Ca^{+2}] = \frac{C_{Ca}}{\dfrac{1}{\gamma_{Ca}} + \dfrac{[SO_4^{-2}]}{K_{CaSO_4}\gamma_{CaSO_4}}},\ \text{with similar relations for}$$

$[Mg^{+2}]$, $[Na^{+}]$, and $[K^{+}]$, or more generally,

$$[i^{+z}] = \frac{C_i}{\dfrac{1}{\gamma_i} + \dfrac{[SO_4^{-2}]}{K_{iSO_4}\gamma_{iSO_4}}},\ \text{where } i \text{ represents Ca, Mg, Na, or}$$

K, and z is the ionic charge. It can also be shown that

$$[SO_4^{-2}] = \frac{C_{SO_4}}{\left\{\dfrac{1}{\gamma_{SO_4}} + \sum_{i = \text{Ca, Mg, Na, K}} \left(\dfrac{C_i}{\dfrac{K_{iSO_4}\gamma_{iSO_4}}{\gamma_i} + [SO_4^{-2}]}\right)\right\}}$$

This equation can be solved by several successive iterations, with $[SO_4^{-2}] = C_{SO_4}\gamma_{SO_4}$ (no complexing) as the first approximation. Bracketed terms are the molal thermodynamic activities of the particular ions in brackets. K_{CaSO_4}, K_{MgSO_4}, K_{NaSO_4}, and K_{KSO_4} are the ion complex dissociation constants. The total molal cation and sulfate concentrations are represented by C_{Ca}, C_{Mg}, C_{Na}, C_K, and C_{SO_4}, respectively. The terms γ_{Ca}, γ_{Mg}, γ_{Na}, γ_K, γ_{CaSO_4}, γ_{MgSO_4}, γ_{NaSO_4}, γ_{KSO_4}, and γ_{SO_4} are the activity coefficients of Ca^{+2}, Mg^{+2}, Na^{+}, K^{+}, $CaSO_4^{0}$, $MgSO_4^{0}$, $NaSO_4^{-}$, KSO_4^{-}, and SO_4^{-2}, respectively, and are a function of the solution's ionic strength. The ionic strength, a measure of the total dissolved electrolytes, can be calculated from the molal concentrations of the major ionic species in solution by the relation

$$\mu = \frac{\Sigma m_i z_i^2}{2},$$

where μ is the molal ionic strength, m_i is the molality of the *i*th ion, and *z* is the unit charge on that ion. In dilute solutions, molarity can be substituted for molality, introducing only negligible error, but in solutions such as ours having very high total dissolved solids concentrations, the difference between molality and molarity is no longer negligible. Molality can be expressed by the relation

$$m = \frac{M}{\rho - S},$$

where M is molarity, ρ is the density of the solution in grams per milliliter, and S is the total grams dissolved solids per milliliter solution. In our specific case the relation is

$$m = \frac{M}{\rho - S} = \frac{M}{(1.202 - 0.305)\mathrm{g/ml}} = 1.115\,M.$$

The major ionic species present in our sample are listed in table 2 with their molarities, molalities, and contributions to total ionic strength.

At this very high ionic strength, the original assumptions used in deriving the Debye-Hükel and Davies equations (Butler, 1964, p. 437) are no longer valid. These equations cannot be used to calculate ion activity coefficients in this solution. Such coefficients must be estimated from experimentally determined mean activity coefficients. Polzer and Roberson (1967, p. C117) have calculated such activity coefficients for various species at an ionic strength of 6.3. For most uncharged species ($CaSO_4^0$, $MgSO_4^0$), the activity coefficient is 3.0. For most monovalent cations and anions (K^+, $NaSO_4^-$, KSO_4^-), it is taken as 0.8 (1.3 for Na^+), for divalent anions (SO_4^{-2}) as 0.03, and for Ca^{+2} and Mg^{+2} ions as 0.9 and 2.2, respectively. Given this data and the following dissociation constants (Garrels and Thompson, 1962, p. 58), summarized below, we can solve for the cation and sulfate activities:

$$C_{SO_4} = 0.164\ m;\ \gamma_{SO_4} = 0.03$$

i	C_i (molal)	K_{iSO_4} at 25°C	γ_i	γ_{iSO_4}
Ca	0.024	$10^{-2.31}$	0.9	3.0
Mg	.36	$10^{-2.36}$	2.2	3.0
Na	5.04	$10^{-0.72}$	1.3	.8
K	.057	$10^{-0.96}$	.8	.8

Substituting into the appropriate aforementioned relations, we obtain activities and p values as follows:

Species	Activity (molal)	p[ ]
SO_4^{-2}	0.0013	2.89
Ca^{+2}	.020	1.70
Mg^{+2}	.65	.19
Na^+	6.45	-.81
K^+	.045	1.35

Table 2.—*Molarities, molalities, and ionic strength contributions of major ions*

Ion	Molarity (M)	Molality (m)	$\frac{m_i z_i^2}{2}$
Ca^{+2}	0.022	0.024	0.048
Mg^{+2}	.32	.36	.72
Na^+	4.52	5.04	2.52
K^+	.051	.057	.028
HCO_3^-	.007	.008	.004
SO_4^{-2}	.147	.164	.328
Cl^-	4.96	5.53	2.76

Total ionic strength $= \frac{\Sigma m_i z_i^2}{2} = 6.4$

In examining the bicarbonate complex ion system, we note that no potassium-bicarbonate complex ion is thought to exist. We need only consider the complexes $CaHCO_3^+$, $MgHCO_3^+$, and $NaHCO_3^0$. We write the concentration and equilibrium dissociation relations:

$$K_{CaHCO_3} = \frac{[Ca^{+2}][HCO_3^-]}{[CaHCO_3^+]},\ K_{MgHCO_3} = \frac{[Mg^{+2}][HCO_3^-]}{[MgHCO_3^+]},$$

$$K_{NaHCO_3} = \frac{[Na^+][HCO_3^-]}{[NaHCO_3^0]},$$

$$\text{and } C_{HCO_3} = \frac{[HCO_3^-]}{\gamma_{HCO_3}} + \frac{[CaHCO_3^+]}{\gamma_{CaHCO_3}} + \frac{[MgHCO_3^+]}{\gamma_{MgHCO_3}} + \frac{[NaHCO_3^0]}{\gamma_{NaHCO_3}},$$

from which can be derived the relation

$$[HCO_3^-] = \frac{C_{HCO_3}}{\left\{\frac{1}{\gamma_{HCO_3}} + \sum_{i=\mathrm{Ca,Mg,Na}} \left(\frac{[i^{+z}]}{K_{iHCO_3}\ \gamma_{iHCO_3}}\right)\right\}}$$

Substituting C_{HCO_3}, the previously calculated cation activities, and the appropriate activity coefficients (Polzer and Roberson, 1967, p. C117) and dissociation constants (Garrels and Thompson, 1962, p. 58),

$$C_{HCO_3} = 0.0077\ m;\ \gamma_{HCO_3} = 0.8$$

i	$[i]$ (molal)	K_{iHCO_3} at 25°C	γ_{iHCO_3}
Ca	0.020	$10^{-1.26}$	0.8
Mg	.65	$10^{-1.16}$	.8
Na	6.45	$10^{+0.25}$	3.0

we obtain $[HCO_3^-] = 0.00052\ m$, or $pHCO_3 = 3.28$. Carbonate-bicarbonate equilibrium dictates that

$$\frac{[CO_3^{-2}][H^+]}{[HCO_3^-]} = 10^{-10.33}$$ at 25°C (Sillén and Martell, 1964, p. 135).

Therefore $pCO_3 + pH - pHCO_3 = 10.33$, or $pCO_3 = 10.33 + pHCO_3 - pH = 5.91$, for our pH of 7.70 at 25°C.

We may calculate the fluoride activity in the same manner, taking into consideration the ion complexes CaF^+ and MgF^+, for which the activity coefficients are assumed to be 0.8. The activity coefficient for F^- is estimated at 1.2 from mean activity coefficients for KF (Harned and Owen, 1967, p. 732). Sillén and Martell (1964, p. 257–258) report dissociation constants at 25°C for CaF^+ and MgF^+ as $>10^{-1.04}$ and $10^{-1.82}$, respectively. Substituting this data, and also $C_F = 0.00059$, $[Ca^{+2}] = 0.020\ m$, and $[Mg^{+2}] = 0.65\ m$ into the relation

$$[F^-] = \frac{C_F}{\left\{\frac{1}{\gamma_F} + \sum_{i=Ca, Mg}\left(\frac{[i]}{K_{iF}\gamma_{iF}}\right)\right\}},$$

we obtain $[F^-] = 0.000011\ m$, or $pF = 4.96$.

In calculating the activities of the three orthophosphate ions $H_2PO_4^-$, HPO_4^{-2}, and PO_4^{-3}, we shall consider the known complex ions $CaH_2PO_4^+$, $CaHPO_4^0$, $CaPO_4^-$, $MgHPO_4^0$, $MgPO_4^-$, $NaHPO_4^-$, and $KHPO_4^-$. Our equilibrium and concentration relations are

$$K_2 = \frac{[HPO_4^{-2}][H^+]}{[H_2PO_4^-]} \text{ and } K_3 = \frac{[PO_4^{-3}][H^+]}{[HPO_4^{-2}]}$$ (second and third dissociation constants of phosphoric acid).

$$K_{CaH_2PO_4} = \frac{[Ca^{+2}][H_2PO_4^-]}{[CaH_2PO_4^+]},\ K_{CaHPO_4} = \frac{[Ca^{+2}][HPO_4^{-2}]}{[CaHPO_4^0]},$$

$$K_{CaPO_4} = \frac{[Ca^{+2}][PO_4^{-3}]}{[CaPO_4^-]},\ K_{MgHPO_4} = \frac{[Mg^{+2}][HPO_4^{+2}]}{[MgHPO_4^0]},$$

$$K_{MgPO_4} = \frac{[Mg^{+2}][PO_4^{-3}]}{[MgPO_4^-]},\ K_{NaHPO_4} = \frac{[Na^+][HPO_4^{-2}]}{[NaHPO_4^-]},$$

$$K_{KHPO_4} = \frac{[K^+][HPO_4^{-2}]}{[KHPO_4^-]},$$ and

$$C_{PO_4} = \frac{[H_2PO_4^-]}{\gamma_{H_2PO_4}} + \frac{[HPO_4^{-2}]}{\gamma_{HPO_4}} + \frac{[PO_4^{-3}]}{\gamma_{PO_4}} + \frac{[CaH_2PO_4^+]}{\gamma_{CaH_2PO_4}} + \frac{[CaHPO_4^0]}{\gamma_{CaHPO_4}} + \frac{[CaPO_4^-]}{\gamma_{CaPO_4}} + \frac{[MgHPO_4^0]}{\gamma_{MgHPO_4}} + \frac{[MgPO_4^-]}{\gamma_{MgPO_4}} + \frac{[NaHPO_4^-]}{\gamma_{NaHPO_4}} + \frac{[KHPO_4^-]}{\gamma_{KHPO_4}}.$$

From these relations it may be shown that

$$\frac{C_{PO_4}}{[PO_4^{-3}]} = \frac{1}{\gamma_{PO_4}} + \frac{[H^+]}{K_3\gamma_{HPO_4}} + \frac{[H^+]^2}{K_2K_3\gamma_{H_2PO_4}} + \frac{[Ca^{+2}][H^+]^2}{K_2K_3\gamma_{CaH_2PO_4}K_{CaH_2PO_4}} + \frac{[Ca^{+2}][H^+]}{K_3\gamma_{CaHPO_4}K_{CaHPO_4}} + \frac{[Ca^{+2}]}{\gamma_{CaPO_4}K_{CaPO_4}} + \frac{[Mg^{+2}][H^+]}{K_3\gamma_{MgHPO_4}K_{MgHPO_4}} + \frac{[Mg^{+2}]}{\gamma_{MgPO_4}K_{MgPO_4}} + \frac{[Na^+][H^+]}{K_3\gamma_{NaHPO_4}K_{NaHPO_4}} + \frac{[K^+][H^+]}{K_3\gamma_{KHPO_4}K_{KHPO_4}}.$$

Activity coefficients are estimated as earlier:

Uncharged species: ($CaHPO_4^0$, $MgHPO_4^0$) $\gamma = 3.0$.

Monovalent cations, anions: ($H_2PO_4^-$, $CaH_2PO_4^+$, $MgH_2PO_4^+$, $NaHPO_4^-$, $KHPO_4^-$) $\gamma = 0.8$.

Divalent anions: (HPO_4^{-2}) $\gamma = 0.03$.

Using the assumption (from the Debye-Hückel equation) that the negative logarithm of the activity coefficients for divalent and trivalent ions is proportional to the square of the unit ionic charge (z) by the same constant, we may arrive at a fairly reasonable value for γ_{PO_4}. If

$$\frac{-\log \gamma_{HPO_4}}{-\log \gamma_{PO_4}} = \frac{\log 0.03}{\log \gamma_{PO_4}} = \frac{(-2)^2}{(-3)^2} = \frac{4}{9},$$

then

$$\log \gamma_{PO_4} = -3.43, \text{ and } \gamma_{PO_4} = 10^{-3.43} = 0.0004.$$

However, the accuracy of this term is not critical, for the term $\frac{1}{\gamma_{PO_4}}$ will be negligible as compared to other terms in the denominator of our phosphate concentration relation.

We have the following dissociation constants: $K_2 = 10^{-7.2}$; $K_3 = 10^{-12.2}$ (Roberson, 1966, p. D181), $K_{CaH_2PO_4} = 10^{-1.41}$, $K_{CaHPO_4} = 10^{-2.74}$, $K_{CaPO_4} = 10^{-6.46}$, $K_{MgHPO_4} = 10^{-2.5}$, $K_{MgPO_4} = 10^{-6.46}$ (estimated), $K_{NaHPO_4} = 10^{-1.15}$, and $K_{KHPO_4} = 10^{-1.04}$ (R. A. Gulbrandsen and C. E. Roberson, written commun., 1972).

Most thermodynamic data is referenced at 25°C, but the temperature of our sample at the time of collection was 40°C. However, it can be thermodynamically shown that for most reactions between ions that concern us, the change in the pK value is small over a 15°C temperature range. Where the heat of reaction, $\Delta H_R{}^\circ$, valid within the 25°–40°C temperature range, is expressed in kilocalories, the change in pK is equal to $-0.035\ \Delta H_R{}^\circ$. For the reactions of the dissociation of phosphoric acid these changes are seen as quite small, for at 25°C pK_2 and pK_3 are 7.2 and 12.2, and at 40°C they are 7.2 and 12.1. Owing to the many approximations we are forced to make in our treatment, our margins of error will often exceed small differences such as these; therefore we may still use data valid at 25°C. Substituting this data, our cation activities, and a total phosphate concentration (C_{PO_4}) of $10^{-4.72}$ m (1.6 mg/l), we obtain $[PO_4^{-3}] = 10^{-11.69}$, or $pPO_4 = 11.69$.

Since phosphate-hydrogen ion equilibrium dictates that

$$\frac{[PO_4^{-3}][H^+]}{[HPO_4^{-2}]} = 10^{-12.2} \text{ and } \frac{[HPO_4^{-2}][H^+]}{[H_2PO_4^-]} = 10^{-7.2},$$

then

$$pPO_4 + pH - pHPO_4 = 12.2 \text{ and } pHPO_4 + pH - pH_2PO_4 = 7.2,$$

which yield

$$pHPO_4 = 7.19 \text{ and } pH_2PO_4 = 7.69.$$

The activity of water was estimated as 0.75 ($pH_2O = 0.12$) by Polzer and Roberson (1967, p. C118) from data for the NaCl-H_2O system listed by Robinson and Stokes (1959). (All ion activities calculated in this paper are summarized in table 3.)

Table 3.—*Ion activities*

Ion	Activity (molal)	p[ ]
Ca^{+2}	0.020	1.70
Mg^{+2}	.65	.19
Na^+	6.45	−.81
K^+	.045	1.35
H^+	$10^{-7.70}$	7.70
HCO_3^-	.00052	3.28
CO_3^{-2}	($pCO_3 = 10.33 + pHCO_3 - pH$ at 25°C)	5.91
OH^-	($pOH = 14.00 - pH$ at 25°C)	6.30
SO_4^{-2}	.0013	2.89
F^-	.000011	4.96
PO_4^{-3}	$10^{-11.69}$	11.69
HPO_4^{-2}	($pHPO_4 = pPO_4 - 12.2 + pH$ at 25°C)	7.19
$H_2PO_4^-$	($pH_2PO_4 = pHPO_4 - 7.2 + pH$ at 25°C)	7.69

The appropriate ion activities may be multiplied to determine whether our sample is saturated with respect to various species. Our calculated ion activity products are compared in table 4 with values calculated for 25° and 40°C from heats of formation and entropy values (Garrels and Christ, 1965; Robie and Waldbaum, 1968; and Sillén and Martell, 1964). This comparison points to the conclusion that our sample is near equilibrium with respect to gypsum, aragonite, and calcite, and supersaturated with respect to dolomite, magnesite, and apatite. Such calculations are only suggestive for solutions of this nature, because the calculations involve the following assumptions: (1) the activity and ion complex dissociation constants for all ions are reasonably accurate, and (2) the sample's pH as measured by a pH electrode is accurate (such accuracy decreases with increasing ionic strength). The electrode method for determining ion activities depends on the assumed constancy of the reference electrode's liquid-junction potential for the unknown and for the calibrating standard. If there is a large difference in ionic strength between the unknown and the standard, the liquid-junction potential (caused by differences in mobility between cations and anions of the same absolute charge as they migrate across a membrane from one solution to the other) is probably not constant, and

Table 4.—*Comparison of solubility products and experimental ion activity products*

Species	pK_{s0} at 25°C	pK_{s0} at 40°C	ΔH_f°, S_f° source	p (ion activity product)	Comments
Aragonite ($CaCO_3$)	8.16	8.26	1	$pCa + pCO_3 = 7.61$	Present in lake sediments.
Calcite ($CaCO_3$)	8.35	8.45	1	$pCa + pCO_3 = 7.61$	Do.
Gypsum ($CaSO_4 \cdot 2H_2O$)	4.63	4.64	1	$pCa + pSO_4 + 2pH_2O = 4.83$	Do.
Monetite ($CaHPO_4$)	5.71	5.88	1	$pCa + pHPO_4 = 8.89$	Present on island, not in lake.
Brushite ($CaHPO_4 \cdot 2H_2O$)	5.62	5.64	1	$pCa + pHPO_4 + 2pH_2O = 9.13$	Do.
Dolomite ($CaMg(CO_3)_2$)	18.43	18.63	2	$pCa + pMg + 2pCO_3 = 13.71$	High-magnesium calcite present in lake sediments.
Magnesite ($MgCO_3$)	8.00	8.21	1	$pMg + pCO_3 = 6.10$	
Hydroxyapatite ($Ca_{10}(PO_4)_6(OH)_2$)	113.99	115.3	5	$10pCa + 6pPO_4 + 2pOH = 99.74$	Hydroxyfluorapatite present in lake sediments (no thermodynamic data available for this mineral).
Fluorapatite ($Ca_{10}(PO_4)_6F_2$)	120.86	121.82	3, 4	$10pCa + 6pPO_4 + 2pF = 97.06$	

Sources: 1. Garrels and Christ (1965, p. 408, 416).
2. Robie and Waldbaum (1968, p. 20, 22).
3. Roberson (1966, p. D180).
4. Sillén and Martell (1964, p. 183).
5. Kramer (1964, p. 637). (pK_{s0} at 40°C obtained by extrapolation of values at 0, 5, 15, 25, and 30°C)

the measured activity could be in error. The use of a saturated KCl solution as a salt bridge between the reference electrode and the test solution minimizes this problem unless the test solution's ionic strength is very high, as ours is.

With the admission that all of the above assumptions are suspect, the calculations, along with geological evidence (the physical presence of various minerals in lake sediment samples and elsewhere on the island), indicate that crude calculations for equilibrium in highly saline systems may have some merit.

REFERENCES CITED

Bowen, H. J. M., 1966, Trace elements in biochemistry: New York, Academic Press, 241 p.

Brown, Eugene, Skougstad, M. W., and Fishman, M. J., 1970, Methods for collection and analysis of water samples for dissolved minerals and gases: U.S. Geol. Survey Techniques Water Resources Inv., book 3, chap. A1, 160 p.

Butler, J. N., 1964, Ionic equilibrium–a mathematical approach: Reading, Mass., Addison-Wesley, 547 p.

Garrels, R. M., and Christ, C. L., 1965, Solutions, minerals, and equilibria: New York, Harper and Row, 450 p.

Garrels, R. M., and Thompson, M. E., 1962, A chemical model for sea water at 25°C and one atmosphere total pressure: Am. Jour. Sci., v. 260, no. 1, p. 57–65.

Goldberg, E. D., 1965, Minor elements in sea water, *in* Riley, J. P., and Skirrow, G., eds., Chemical oceanography, v. 1: New York, Academic Press, p. 163–196.

Ham, W. E., and Johnson, K. S., 1964, Copper in the Flowerpot Shale (Permian) of the Creta area, Jackson County, Oklahoma: Oklahoma Geol. Survey Circ. 64, 32 p.

Harned, H. S., and Owen, B. B., 1967, The physical chemistry of electrolytic solutions: New York, Reinhold, 803 p.

Hutchinson, G. E., 1950, The biogeochemistry of vertebrate excretion: Am. Museum Nat. History Bull., v. 96, 594 p.

Kramer, J. R., 1964, Sea water: Saturation with apatites and carbonates: Science, v. 146, no. 3644, p. 637–638.

Polzer, W. L., and Roberson, C. E., 1967, Calculation of ion activity products for a brine from the Bonneville Salt Flats, Utah, *in* Geological Survey Research 1967: U.S. Geol. Survey Prof. Paper 575-C, p. C116–C119.

Roberson, C. E., 1966, Solubility implications of apatite in sea water, *in* Geological Survey Research 1966: U.S. Geol. Survey Prof. Paper 550-D, p. D178–D185.

Robie, R. A., and Waldbaum, D. R., 1968, Thermodynamic properties of minerals and related substances at 298.15°K (25.0°C) and one atmosphere (1.013 bars) pressure and at high temperatures: U.S. Geol. Survey Bull. 1259, 256 p.

Robinson, R. A., and Stokes, R. H., 1959, Electrolyte solutions: London, Butterworths, 559 p.

Schlanger, S. O., and Tracey, J. I., Jr., 1970, Dolomitization related to recent emergence of Jarvis Island, Southern Line Islands (Pacific Ocean): Geol. Soc. America Abs. with Programs, v. 2, no. 7, p. 676.

Sillén, L. G., and Martell, A. E., 1964, Stability constants of metal-ion complexes: London, The Chemical Society, 754 p.

Jour. Research U.S. Geol. Survey
Vol. 1, No. 1, Jan.—Feb. 1973, p. 113—115

A RAPID METHOD FOR THE DETERMINATION OF RADIOACTIVE CESIUM ISOTOPES IN WATER

By V. J. JANZER, Lakewood, Colo.

Abstract.—Radioactive cesium in water is concentrated by ion-exchange on finely divided ammonium hexacyanocobalt ferrate (NCFC), and then determined by beta counting. No carrier is added, and the method can be used to determine beta-emitting cesium isotopes at the 10-pCi/l level using a 100-ml sample. Five samples can be prepared for counting in approximately 3 hours, and the method is applicable to fresh and saline waters.

Eleven radioactive cesium isotopes, and stable cesium-133, which yields radioactive cesium-134 by a neutron-gamma reaction, are produced by the slow neutron fission of uranium-235. Most of the radiocesium isotopes have such short half lives that they are of little importance in natural waters. The longer lived isotopes, cesium-134 and cesium-137, have been deposited over most of the earth's surface primarily as the result of nuclear weapons use and testing.

Cesium-137 is produced in excess of 6-percent yield by thermal neutron fission of uranium-233, uranium-238, plutonium-239, and thorium-232 (Finston and Kinsley, 1961). Owing to a 30-year half life, cesium-137 and daughter barium-137m account for approximately 8 percent of the total activity of 2-year-old fission products (U.S. Public Health Service, 1960).

Detectable quantities of cesium-137 may consequently be found in most surface water, in surficial soil, and in most land plants and animals. The relatively high fission yield of cesium-137 combined with a half life of 30 years and a physiological similarity to potassium account for its importance as a potential water pollutant and a biological hazard. Measurements of the cesium-137 concentrations which occur in natural waters are necessary to evaluate its movement and fate in the hydrologic environment.

Many techniques for the separation and determination of radiocesium are given by Finston and Kinsley (1961). Most of these techniques, however, are time consuming or are not satisfactory for the determination of cesium at the picocurie per liter levels in relatively small-volume samples.

Prout, Russell, and Groh (1965) reported the determination of cesium-137 by gamma counting methods, using the inorganic salt, potassium hexacyanocobalt(II) ferrate(II) (KCFC), as a highly specific ion exchanger.

Boni (1966) described the use of KCFC for the rapid determination of radiocesium in milk, urine, sea water, and environmental samples by various gamma counting techniques. He reported a detection limit of 3 pCi/l, using a 1-gallon water sample and a 9- by 9-inch sodium iodide crystal with 3- by 6-inch well in a gamma spectrometer system. Direct concentration of radiocesium from water samples was hindered by absorption of ruthenium, zirconium, niobium, cobalt, and zinc.

With the exception of cobalt, these interferences were eliminated by preparing the sample in 1 *N* HCl and 0.5 *N* HF. Elimination of all radionuclide interferences including cobalt was reported when the hydrochloric acid concentration was increased to 10 *N*. No cobalt or zinc radioactivity was detected by gamma spectrum analyses of the samples which Boni analyzed by this technique.

Ellenburg and McCown (1968) described a batch technique in which KCFC was used to separate cesium-137 from a mixture of fission products in normal reactor fuel solutions. They reported that 50 mg of 60-mesh KCFC in contact with 50 ml of solution for more than 5 minutes was sufficient to enable complete recovery of all cesium-137 present. Samples ranging in activity from approximately 2×10^4 to 2×10^6 cpm were analyzed by use of a 3- by 3-inch NaI (Tl) crystal and a multichannel analyzer.

Petrow and Levine (1967) reported the use of ammonium hexacyanocobalt ferrate (NCFC) as an improved inorganic exchange material for the determination of cesium-137. The use of the ammonium-ion-exchange salt rather than the potassium salt resulted in much purer gamma spectra and enabled the measurement of exchanged cesium at lower detection levels.

Batch exchange of cesium-137 from dilute solutions by means of NCFC, and subsequent beta counting by the use of low background proportional counting systems has been used by this laboratory to rapidly determine cesium-137 at levels as low as 1—5 pCi/l.

APPARATUS AND REAGENTS

Beta counter, low-background. Sharp Widebeta automatic proportional counter, thin-window, flowing-gas.

Filtration apparatus:
Ring and disk assemblies to accommodate 47-mm filters.
Millipore Sterifil plastic 47-mm filter holder.
Nitrocellulose membrane filters, 0.45 μm, 47-mm diameter.
Plastic film, kitchen-wrap type.
Teflon beakers, 100- to 800-ml capacity.
Ammonium hexacyanocobalt ferrate (NCFC). Prepared as described by Petrow and Levine (1967) and sieved to pass 100-mesh screen.
Cesium-137 standardized solution. Obtained commercially. Contains about 100 pCi/ml of cesium-137.

PROCEDURE

1. Transfer a measured volume of sample to a Teflon beaker of suitable size. A sample of 100 to 500 ml is usually adequate.
2. Filter the sample through a 0.45-μm nitrocellulose membrane filter if turbid.
3. Add concentrated hydrochloric and hydrofluoric acids to adjust the acidity to 1.0 *N* in HCl and 0.5 *N* in HF, respectively. Handle samples in hood, and use plastic gloves and appropriate precautions required with hydrofluoric acid. For a 500-ml sample, add 45 ml of concentrated HCl and 10 ml of concentrated HF; this results in a final volume of approximately 550 ml. For smaller samples, use proportionately smaller volumes of acid.
4. Stir to mix.
5. Add 100 mg (±1 mg) of NCFC fines, and stir for 5 to 10 minutes on a stir plate.
6. Remove from stir plate, allow fines to settle, and filter through a 0.45-μm, 47-mm diameter nitrocellulose filter by using suction. By means of liquid still remaining in the beaker in the last stages of filtration, transfer the major part of the NCFC fines to the filter to produce a uniform deposit, then release suction and transfer the clear filtrate to the Teflon beaker.
7. Filter the solution through the NCFC pad a second time, and quantitatively transfer all the NCFC remaining in the beaker to the filter.
8. Rinse the beaker with several small volumes of distilled water; rinse down the funnel sides, and wash the filter and retained NCFC several times. To maintain a uniform deposit do not disturb the filter pad.
9. Apply suction until the pad is free of wash water, and then mount on a ring and disk assembly and dry under a heat lamp.
10. Cover with a single layer of plastic film, and count in the beta counter. Three 50-minute counts are generally adequate.
11. Prepare blank NCFC planchets by slurrying 100 mg of NCFC fines in a volume of 0.5 *N* HF—1.0 *N* HCl equal to the volume of the samples to be analyzed and prepared in the same manner as the samples.
12. Prepare cesium-137 standards in triplicate, each with 100 mg of NCFC in the same volume of mixed hydrochloric-hydrofluoric acids as the samples plus 5-ml parts of approximately 100 pCi/ml of cesium-137 standard solution. The ring-and-disk standards can be used repeatedly if the plastic covers are not torn and NCFC is not lost.

CALCULATIONS

Cesium-137 concentrations in the samples analyzed are determined by the following calculations:

1. Determine the standard deviation of the net counting rate, as described by Barker and Robinson (1963), from the equation:

$$\sigma_N = \left(\frac{B}{t_b} + \frac{R}{t_s}\right)^{1/2},$$

where

σ_N = standard deviation of the net counting rate,
B = blank counting rate, in counts per minute,
t_b = time, in minutes, that blank was counted,
R = gross sample counting rate, in counts per minute, and
t_s = time, in minutes, that sample was counted.

2. If the net counting rate is equal to or in excess of two standard deviations of the net counting rate, that is, $R - B \geqslant 2\sigma_N$, calculate the cesium-137 concentration in the sample from the equation:

Cesium concentration, in picocuries per liter

$$= \frac{1{,}000}{V}\left[\frac{(R-B)\pm 2\sigma_N}{E}\right],$$

where

E = counting efficiency of system, in counts per minute per picocurie, and
V = volume of sample analyzed, in milliliters.

Counting efficiency (E) of the system is determined by:

$$E = \frac{(R_s - B)}{V_s C_s},$$

where

R_s = gross counting rate of standard, in counts per minute,
V_s = volume of standard solution used, in milliliters, and
C_s = concentration of cesium-137 standard, in picocuries per milliliter.

3. If the net counting rate does not exceed two standard deviations of the net counting rate, report the result as less than the minimum detection level (MDL). The MDL is calculated from the equation

$$\text{Cs-137 MDL} = \frac{2\sigma_N\,(1{,}000)}{EV}.$$

Precision data for this method based on replicate analysis of duplicate samples are not available. However, based only on counting statistics, the 95-percent confidence limit, that is, two standard deviations of the net counting rate for 1 pCi of cesium-137 determined in 100 ml of sample and yielding a net count of 0.6 cpm, could be calculated as follows:

$$2\sigma_N = 2\left(\frac{2.2}{100}+\frac{2.8}{100}\right)^{1/2}$$

$$= 2(0.224)$$

$$= 0.448 \text{ cpm.}$$

The net counting rate 0.6 cpm exceeds 0.448 cpm ($2\sigma_N$), and a value and error is calculated and reported as follows:

$$\text{Cs-137 pCi/l} = \frac{1{,}000}{V}\,\frac{(2.8-2.2)\pm 2\sigma_N}{E}$$

$$= 10\,\frac{0.6\pm 0.45}{0.6}$$

$$= 10\pm 7.5 \text{ pCi/l.}$$

DISCUSSION

Strontium-90 present in some of the samples was found to interfere in the determination of cesium by the NCFC method. The short-lived daughter of strontium-90, yttrium-90, as well as cesium was absorbed by the NCFC exchanger. Boni (1966) reported the elimination of zirconium-95, niobium-95, ruthenium-103, and ruthenium-106 fission product interference when using gamma counting to determine cesium absorbed on KCFC by preparing the sample in 1 *N* HCl and 0.5 *N* HF prior to ion exchange. Similar acidification of the samples analyzed in this study using NCFC, eliminated the yttrium-90 interference. No other interfering fission product activity detectable by gamma spectroscopy was present in the samples tested.

If cesium-134 as well as cesium-137 is present in the sample, and the ratio of the concentrations of these two nuclides is desired, other techniques such as those described by Yamamoto (1966) must be used.

A plastic filtration apparatus is necessary for filtering the mixed hydrochloric-hydrofluoric acidified samples. The fritted glass filter support in the usual vacuum filter apparatus disintegrates rapidly when used with hydrofluoric acid solutions.

A lower recovery and counting efficiency was obtained for 500-ml than for 100-ml standards. Counting efficiency for standards prepared in volumes of 100 and 500 ml using 100 mg of NCFC mounted and counted in the matter described has ranged from 0.56 to 0.69 cpm/pCi of cesium-137. The results shown in table 1 were calculated by using an average counting efficiency of 0.64 and 0.60 cpm/pCi of cesium-137 for sample volumes of 100 and 500 ml, respectively.

All standards listed in table 1 were counted for 100 minutes. Blank planchets prepared in the same manner but without added cesium-137 counted an average of 2.21 cpm.

To minimize variations in the cesium-absorption efficiency of NCFC with variations in solution volumes, all samples are adjusted to the same volume or a set of standards is prepared that spans the volume range of the samples to be analyzed. The samples are stirred with the NCFC and filtered, and the filtered solution is refiltered through the exchanger bed to further increase the degree of contact and improve the precision of the method.

Table 1.—*Recovery of cesium-137 from standard solutions*

Sample No.	Standard volume (ml)	Cesium-137	
		Added (pCi)	Found (pCi)
1	100	11	10.5
2	100	11	11.5
3	100	23	21.9
4	100	23	22.6
5	100	56	58.6
6	100	56	57.8
7	100	113	108
8	100	113	115
9	500	11	12.6
10	500	11	11.0
11	500	56	56.9
12	500	56	54.1
13	500	113	107.4
14	500	113	105.5

REFERENCES CITED

Barker, F. B., and Robinson, B. P., 1963, Determination of beta activity in water: U.S. Geol. Survey Water-Supply Paper 1696-A, 32 p.

Boni, A. L., 1966, Rapid ion exchange analysis of radiocesium in milk, urine, sea water and environmental samples: Anal. Chemistry, v. 38, no. 1, p. 89–92.

Ellenburg, E. J., and McCown, J. J., 1968, Rapid carrier-free method for the radiochemical determination of cesium-137: Anal. Letters, v. 1, no. 11, p. 697–706.

Finston, H. L., and Kinsley, M. T., 1961, The radiochemistry of cesium: U.S. Dept. Commerce Nuclear Sci. Ser. NAS-NS, no. 3035, 68 p.

Petrow, H. G., and Levine, H., 1967, Ammonium hexacyanocobalt ferrate as an improved inorganic exchange material for determination of cesium-137: Anal. Chemistry, v. 39, no. 3, p. 360–362.

Prout, W. E., Russell, E. R., and Groh, H. J., 1965, Ion exchange absorption of cesium by potassium hexacyanocobalt (II) ferrate (II): Jour. Inorganic and Nuclear Chemistry, v. 27, p. 473–479.

U.S. Public Health Service, 1960, Radiological health handbook: U.S. Dept. Health, Education and Welfare, 468 p.

Yamamoto, S., 1966, Analysis of cesium-134–cesium-137 mixtures by gamma ray spectrometric methods: Anal. Chemistry, v. 38, no. 9, p. 1261–1264.

Jour. Research U.S. Geol. Survey
Vol. 1, No. 1, Jan.—Feb. 1973, p. 117—120

EFFECT OF SEPTIC-TANK WASTES ON QUALITY OF WATER, IPSWICH AND SHAWSHEEN RIVER BASINS, MASSACHUSETTS

By GEORGE B. MORRILL III and LARRY G. TOLER,
Boston, Mass.

Abstract.—Many housing projects in the metropolitan area of Boston are beyond the reach of municipal sewer systems. Waste water disposed of through septic-tank or cesspool systems percolates to ground-water reservoirs and eventually reaches the streams. The dissolved-solids load in the streams receiving septic-tank effluent is increased by an amount that can be predicted from the housing density. In the study area, highway deicing salts are the only materials other than septic-tank discharge that contribute to water-quality degradation. The effect of these salts on the relationship with housing density is eliminated by subtracting the specific conductance due to sodium chloride from the measured specific conductance of a water sample. The difference is called residual conductance and is proportional to the dissolved-solids content minus the concentration of sodium chloride.

Development of housing beyond the reach of municipal sewer systems of metropolitan areas has lowered the quality of the environment in many of the developments and has created health hazards in others. Waste-water disposal through septic tanks and cesspools is common practice in many developments in the Boston area. The purpose of this study is to determine if there is a relationship between the number of septic-tank disposal systems in a drainage basin and some parameter describing quality of water in streams draining the basin.

LOCATION AND DESCRIPTION

Seventeen small drainage basins, all but one less than 1 square mile in area, were selected for study. All are in the Ipswich and Shawsheen River basins (fig. 1), in the communities of Andover, Burlington, North Reading, Tewksbury, Wilmington, and Peabody, Mass. All the basins are served by public water supplies, but none have municipal sewer systems, and individual houses are served by on-site disposal systems. The basins differ considerably in size, stream gradient, topography, amount of drainage through culverts, and age of houses; housing density ranges from 0 to 900 units per sq mi.

Typically, the drainage basins are characterized by low rounded hills surrounded by swamp-dotted lowlands where drainage is generally poor. The low hills are underlain by bedrock or glacial till—a relatively impermeable mixture of unsorted silt, sand, rounded to angular gravel, and boulders. The till forms a thin mantle overlying bedrock. In the lowlands the till is covered by permeable sand and gravel. Many of the housing developments are located in the lowlands because the level terrain is easy to develop and the good soil permeability permits installation of on-site disposal systems. The water table is only a few feet below land surface, and about one-fifth of the area is subject to seasonal flooding (Sammel and others, 1966, p. 6). The high water table and flooding make operations of on-site disposal systems inefficient at least part of the year.

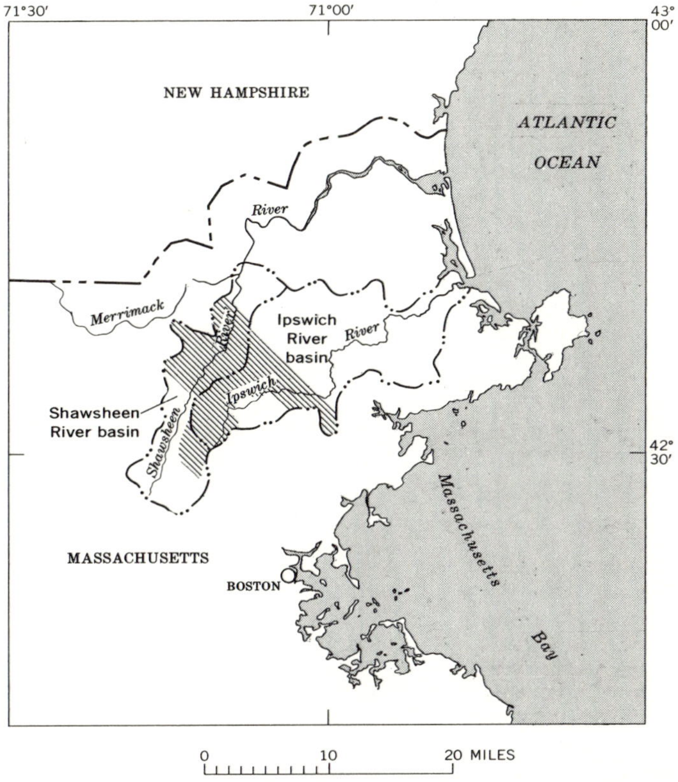

Figure 1.—Index map showing location of study area (patterned) in northeastern Massachusetts.

Streams draining developed areas are frequently malodorous and support a luxuriant growth of weeds and brush. Residents with whom the problems have been discussed have expressed their concern about the sanitary and esthetic qualities of the streams, and some have prevailed upon public health officials to take action. The action, for the most part, has been to install culverts to convey the streams underground through the developments to swamps. Many of the swamps into which these streams flow contain foul-smelling stagnant water. The absence of other obvious sources of the foul smell suggests that it comes from domestic waste-water disposal systems by way of ground-water seepage into the streams.

The 17 small basins were chosen to meet two requirements: (1) that they were drained by a stream or ditch from which representative base-flow samples could be taken, and (2) that they had no apparent source of extraneous material other than septic-tank and cesspool wastes and highway deicing chemicals.

METHOD OF STUDY

Base runoff from ground-water discharge in the Ipswich River basin averages approximately 13 inches per year, or 6.2×10^5 gpd per sq mi (Sammel and others, 1966, p. 52). Although ground-water discharge can be expected to vary considerably in small basins having a wide range of terrain and ground cover, 13 inches per year is used as an average.

Average water consumption in east coast suburbs with metered water and septic tanks was determined by Linaweaver, Geyer, and Wolff (1967) to be 245 gpd per dwelling, of which 42 gpd was used for irrigation of lawns and gardens. Unmetered areas were found to use more water for lawns but about the same for household purposes. Septic-tank flow per house is estimated to be 200 gpd.

The 42 gpd or more used for watering gardens, lawns, and shrubs is applied during the growing season, a time when evapotranspiration normally exceeds precipitation. Most of this water is evaporated and transpired, so little reaches the water table and does not contribute significantly to base flow of streams. The water applied for irrigation, therefore, is not included in this analysis.

Samples of water from the streams were collected periodically during periods of base flow from March through August 1968. The samples were analyzed in the field for chloride concentration and specific conductance and the results averaged for each site.

The specific electrical conductance of water is a good indicator of its dissolved-solids content. Because the measurement is easy to make, specific conductance is widely used in geochemical studies of water. For natural water, the dissolved solids, in milligrams per liter, usually range from 0.55 to 0.75 times the specific conductance, in micromhos per centimeter at 25°C (Hem, 1959, p. 40).

Highway salting in most of the basins affects both chloride concentration and conductivity. To correct for this effect, a residual conductivity, the difference between the measured specific conductance and that calculated to be caused by sodium chloride, the principal highway deicing agent, was used for defining the quality of the water. The residual conductivity is proportional to the dissolved-solids content minus the sodium chloride concentration. The specific conductance of sodium chloride is approximately 3.5 times the chloride concentration, in milligrams per liter.

Average values of specific conductance and chloride concentration for natural water were obtained by sampling several small unpolluted streams in the basins during base flow. The average specific conductance was 48 μmhos, and the average concentration of chloride was 5 mg/l. The average residual conductance is 30 μmhos.

Almost no data are available defining septic-tank effluent in terms of the concentrations of its dissolved constituents. Published data on untreated sewage do not include specific conductance. An average residual conductivity of 785 μmhos was determined from analysis of two samples of septic-tank liquor from the project area. The concentration of chloride was about 50 mg/l higher than that of the tapwater entering the septic tank.

Tapwater contributes significant concentrations of some minerals to the ground water. Chloride concentrations of tapwater samples taken in the towns in the study area ranged from 17 to 54 mg/l and averaged about 35 mg/l. Residual conductance ranged from 87 to 150 μmhos and averaged 120 μmhos.

Base flow in the basins is derived from precipitation and imported municipal water. Some precipitation percolates to the water table, forming "natural" ground water, whereas the municipal water is used in homes and discharged to ground-water reservoirs by way of septic tanks and cesspools. If the storage of both water and dissolved solids in the aquifer is assumed to be constant, the dissolved-solids load, in excess of that of natural ground water, leaving the ground-water reservoir by way of base flow is the sum of the loads carried in by precipitation and septic-tank effluent.

Description of terms

A = Drainage basin area (sq mi).
n = Number of houses in the basin (houses).
d = Housing density = n/A (houses per sq mi).
q_b = Average annual base flow per unit area (gpd per sq mi).
q_n = Natural base flow per unit area derived from average annual infiltration of precipitation (gpd per sq mi).
q_s = Average combined septic-tank and cesspool flow per house (gpd per house).
C = Quality parameter, concentration in base flow.
C_n = Quality parameter, concentration in natural ground water.
C_s = Quality parameter, concentration in domestic septic-tank effluent.

Calculations

The average annual base flow of a specific drainage basin is equal to the sum of two components, one derived from precipitation and one derived from septic tank effluent, according to the equation

$$q_b A = q_n A + q_s n, \quad (1)$$

which may be made more general by eliminating the terms for area and restating equation 1 in terms of housing density as

$$q_b = q_n + q_s d. \quad (2)$$

This equation multiplied by the appropriate concentrations of the quality parameter yields

$$q_b C = q_n C_n + q_s d C_s. \quad (3)$$

When one combines equations 2 and 3 to express base-flow concentration, C, as a function of housing density, one obtains the working equation

$$C = \frac{C_n}{1+\dfrac{q_s d}{q_n}} + \frac{C_s}{1+\dfrac{q_n}{q_s d}}. \quad (4)$$

This equation for C gives the average annual base-flow concentration of any contaminant for which C_n and C_s can be determined.

The residual conductance in base flow (C_{RC}) in the study area in terms of housing density may be estimated by substituting the following in equation 4:

C_n = residual conductance in natural water (average 30 μmhos),
C_s = residual conductance in septic-tank effluent (average 785 μmhos),
q_s = 200 gpd per house, and
q_n = 6.2×10^5 gpd per sq mi,
which results in

$$C_{RC} = \frac{93{,}000 + 785d}{3{,}100 + d}. \quad (5)$$

Figure 2 was developed to evaluate sampling sites and to identify those with probable sources of extraneous material other than domestic waste water. The graph in figure 2 was developed for chloride but should be adaptable to other parameters. To use the graph, the specific conductance and concentration of chloride of a sample of water from a study site and the average concentration of chloride in public water serving the study site must be known.

A line from a point (X) representing the specific conductance and chloride concentration of a sample, drawn parallel to the housing-density lines, intercepts the horizontal specific-conductance scale at the value for residual conductance. The concentration of chloride contributed by domestic waste water is read on the vertical chloride scale at the intercept of a horizontal line from the point (O), where the line, previously drawn parallel to the housing-density lines, intersects a line representing average concentration of chloride in tapwater. The difference between the concentration of chloride in the sample and the concentration of chloride from domestic waste water represents chloride from other sources. The initial plot of specific conductance and chloride concentration should lie on or near the housing-density line, approximating the housing density in the basin. If this plot does not approximate the actual housing density, extraneous material other than domestic waste and sodium chloride is indicated.

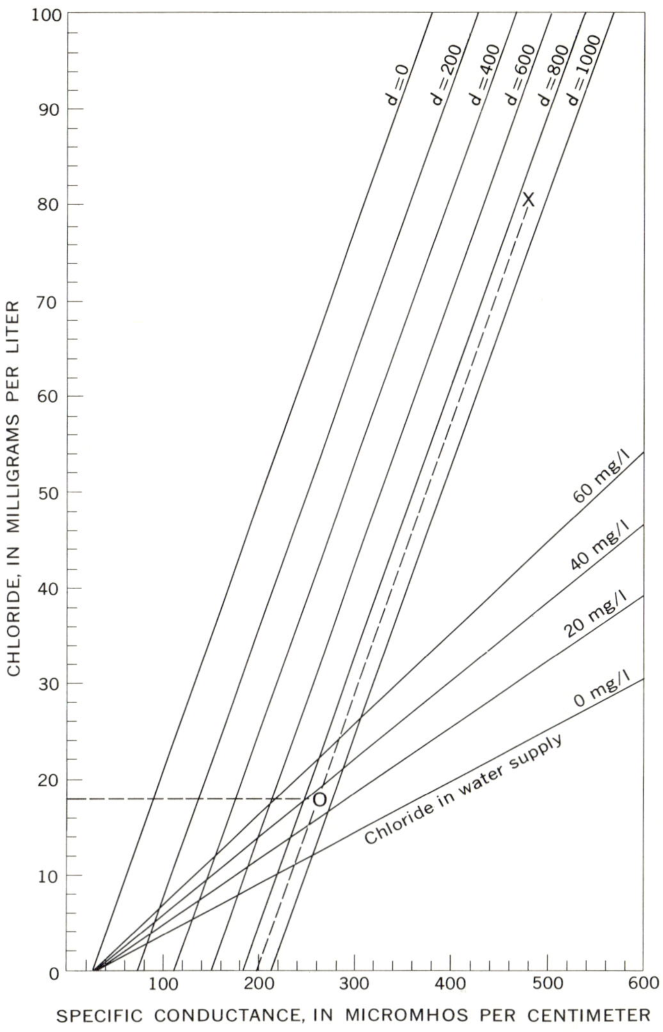

Figure 2.—Graph to evaluate sampling sites for sources of extraneous material in terms of residual conductance and chloride. See text for explanation of use.

RESULTS

The residual conductivity data from the 17 sites in table 1 generally agree with the relationship predicted by equation 5 (fig. 3) and indicate that most dissolved solids from septic-tank systems reach the streams. The dissolved-solids-accretion scale

Table 1.—*Sampling site data*

Site No.	Housing density in drainage basin (houses per sq mi)	Drainage basin area (sq mi)	Average specific conductance (μmhos at 25° C)	Average base-flow residual conductivity (μmhos)	Average chloride (mg/l)	Number of samples
	d	*A*	*C*	C_{RC}		
1......	0	0.031	46	29	5	1
2......	75	.120	94	59	10	3
3......	105	.210	53	35	5	2
4......	150	.040	52	34	5	3
5......	170	.110	144	102	12	3
6......	275	.215	187	124	18	2
7......	325	.037	174	108	19	3
8......	350	.210	170	128	15	6
9......	360	.165	176	89	25	3
10......	370	.165	127	78	14	5
11......	440	.032	140	98	12	1
12......	510	1.85	474	173	86	5
13......	585	.075	292	128	47	4
14......	590	.027	225	180	13	2
15......	730	.115	225	155	20	8
16......	830	.420	440	177	75	5
17......	900	.525	434	210	64	4

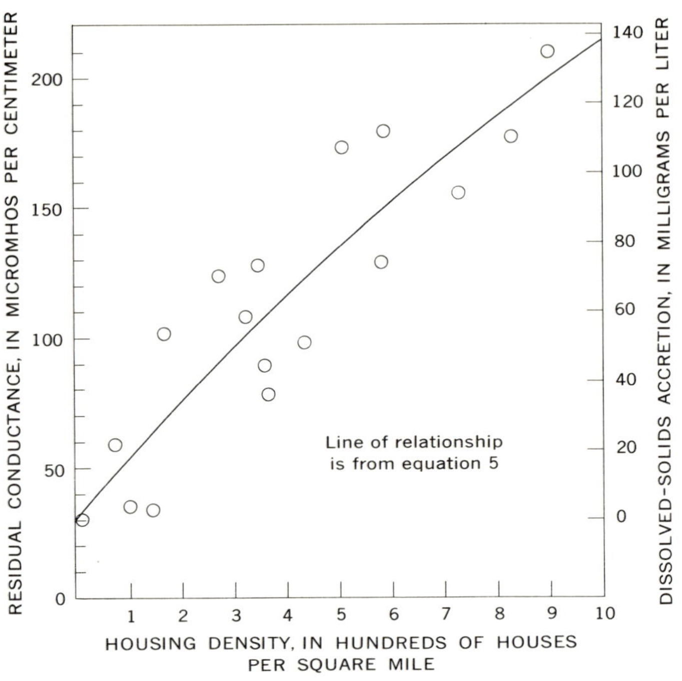

Figure 3.—Relationship of housing density to residual conductance and accretion of dissolved solids in base flow of streams.

on the right of figure 3 shows the estimated increase of dissolved solids in base runoff caused by various housing densities. Dissolved-solids accretion was calculated by multiplying the increase in residual conductance in base flow of a polluted stream over that of natural ground water by 0.65 (Hem, 1959, p. 40) and adding the increase in dissolved solids caused by domestic waste-water chloride (50 mg/l concentration of chloride in 200 gpd per house), which was excluded from residual conductance.

The scatter of the data points in figure 3 may be in large part due to deviations from the average values used for (1) volume of infiltration and subsequent ground-water discharge, (2) concentration of chloride in public water supplies, and (3) volume of septic-tank effluent. Undetected sources of extraneous material may also cause deviation from the line of relationship predicted from equation 5.

The graph indicates that the amount of dissolved solids in base flow of streams is dependent on housing density. In the range of housing densities observed, dissolved solids in stream base flow can be expected to increase 10 to 15 mg/l per 100 houses per sq mi.

REFERENCES CITED

Hem, J. D., 1959, Study and interpretation of the chemical characteristics of natural water: U.S. Geol. Survey Water-Supply Paper 1473, 269 p. [4th printing, 1967]

Linaweaver, F. P., Jr., Geyer, J. E., and Wolff, J. B., 1967, Summary report on the residential water use research project: Am. Water Works Assoc. Jour., no. 3, v. 59, p. 267–270.

Sammel, E. A., Baker, J. A., and Brackley, R. A., 1966, Water resources of the Ipswich River basin, Massachusetts: U.S. Geol. Survey Water-Supply Paper 1826, 83 p. [1967].

Jour. Research U.S. Geol. Survey
Vol. 1, No. 1, Jan.—Feb. 1973, p. 121—124

THE GREAT TUNISIAN FLOOD

By FRANK E. CLARKE, Washington, D.C.

Abstract.—In the autumn of 1969, unusual meteorological conditions over Europe and northern Africa caused an enormous persistent desert storm in Tunisia and eastern Algeria. Poorly developed drainage patterns and gypsum-encrusted surfaces of these desert regions intensified effects of the storm and contributed to the heavy loss of life and property. Destruction of Roman bridges suggests that such storms may have recurrence probabilities of several thousands of years. The event also suggests that, although desert storms are less frequent than those of temperate regions, they can be similar in magnitude.

Collection of field data for a U.S. Geological Survey report (Clarke and Jones, 1972) was brought to a close prematurely on September 25, 1969, by a desert storm and resulting flood of enormous proportions—an event with a presumed recurrence interval of thousands of years. This summary is provided to document the relatively few facts available on a rare type of meteorological phenomenon which undoubtedly has affected desert hydrology significantly through geologic time.

Meteorologists attribute the unusual storm to a shift in the Azores high-pressure pattern from lat 35° N., the normal center, to 45° N. This change reduced rainfall and resulted in unusually warm and sunny weather in most of Europe during the summer of 1969. Apparently, it also triggered movement of cool air from Europe toward the Mediterranean Sea, and meteorological conditions over North Africa directed the moisture-laden northern airmass across Tunisia to the Atlas Mountains, where it stalled on September 25, 1969, and created the persistent cyclonic pattern shown in figure 1.

FACTORS AFFECTING SEVERITY OF DAMAGE

Geologic and hydrologic factors.—The area of Tunisia and adjoining Algeria immediately south of the Atlas Mountains receives little rainfall, about 7.5 cm (3 inches) per year. Its surface drainage pattern is poorly developed, with a limited river (oued) network and many internal sinks (chotts).

The relatively high temperature and corresponding high evaporation rate, together with the abundance of calcium sulfate in both earth strata and ground waters, produce a gypsum-encrusted surface or subsurface which is highly impermeable to water. Windblown silt and sand which veneer the gypsum surface to shallow depths are relatively unstable and offer little resistance to wind and water.

Cultural factors.—Because of the dearth of precipitation, inhabitants of these semiarid and desert regions take little account of the possibility of occasional floods. Oueds and chotts, which are dry for the most part and gentle in grade, are systematically used for roads and other transportation routes. Villages encroach on ancient flood plains; buildings lack the substantial construction that predominates in more stormy climates, and they often occupy sites which can easily be isolated by high water. Pastures and related facilities involve the same hazards for livestock. Desert societies generally lack facilities for rapid response to natural disasters.

Precipitation.—Intense steady rainfall started late on the afternoon of September 25, after several hours of severe duststorms and intermittent thundershowers. Flooding in the relatively impermeable desert terrain was almost instantaneous over a wide area. In the study area near El Hamma, Tunisia, arroyos were raging torrents, and highways resembled oueds in less than 20 minutes. Forty centimeters (15 inches) of rain fell in the environs of Gabès, Tunisia, during the first 24-hour period—about 5 times the annual rainfall for the area. Figures 2, 3, 4, and 5 show the extent of early flooding. Intermittent heavy precipitation continued for 38 days. The author has been unable to obtain a figure for total rainfall or for variations in pattern over the 162,750 sq km (63,000 sq mi) affected.

FLOODING AND EFFECTS

Tunisia.—Nine of Tunisia's 13 provinces were seriously affected by overland runoff, filling of chotts, and flooding of oueds. Stages as much as 11 m (36 feet) above normal were recorded. The Zeroud and Marguelil oueds combined to form a single torrent 13 km (8 miles) wide. Innumerable flooded chotts, some as much as 13 km in diameter, existed at the end of the storm. The exceptional magnitude of flooding is indicated by the destruction of several massive Roman bridges which have stood the test of the elements for thousands of years.

The unique combination of meteorological, geologic, and cultural factors in the desert storm wreaked unbelievable

Figure 1.—Storm pattern of record-breaking North Sahara flood. Photograph taken from Nimbus meteorological satellite.

Figure 2.—Highway to Gafsa, 20 km (12.5 miles) west of Gabès, Tunisia, 18 hours after rain began.

Figure 3.—Flooded olive grove, 20 km (12.5 miles) west of Gabès.

Figure 4.—Gabès-Sfax highway, 40 km (25 miles) north of Gabès, 42 hours after rain began.

havoc on Tunisia. The relatively small population of 4.5 million suffered 600 dead and 300,000 homeless. Other losses included an estimated 1 million livestock, 10,000 olive trees, 35 bridges, and virtually the entire network of highways and railroads in 80 percent of the country, including transportation links which serviced the vitally important phosphate industry at Gafsa. This disruption alone represented a loss to the country of $4.8 million weekly in mineral revenue during the time of outage.

The specific losses were accompanied by profound surface changes which literally revised the map of Tunisia. In the Kairouan Plain, 130 km (81 miles) south of Tunis, removal of 1 m (3 feet) of accumulated soil exposed a sizable Roman village. At the same time, the great flood deposited sediment

Figure 5.—Flood-damaged Gabès-Sfax highway, about 40 km (25 miles) north of Gabès. The highway followed an ancient broad, shallow drainage channel.

from 0.4 to 1.8 m (1 to 6 feet) in depth on a 14-km- (9-mile-) wide coastal plain between Gabès and Sfax, Tunisia, thereby converting the barren gypsum-encrusted area to fertile green pasture. Such alterations must have been widespread and highly significant. Similar changes undoubtedly have occurred at widely scattered intervals throughout time.

Algeria.—The somewhat smaller losses in neighboring Algeria are explained by the limited area affected. They included 60 dead (250 injured), 18,800 homes (13,000 damaged), 10,000 livestock, 2,000 hectares (5,000 acres) of crops, hundreds of trees, 50 km (31 miles) of rail line, and 2,600 wells. In final count, 91,000 people of Algeria were homeless, and total dollar value of damage in that country was approximately $96 million.

Response.—The Tunisian-Algerian flood was recognized from the beginning as an unusual natural disaster of international importance. At least 24 countries, including the United States, and a number of international organizations, sent prompt and substantial aid.

The U.S. Geological Survey worked with the United Nations Educational, Scientific, and Cultural Organization in an effort to document effects of the flood by aerial mapping and other remote-sensing techniques. Unfortunately, the plan could not be implemented.

Hydrologic significance.—Destruction of Roman bridges suggests a recurrence probability of thousands of years for desert storms of this kind. The long duration and great intensity of precipitation also suggest that, despite their infrequency, the magnitude of desert storms may equal that of temperate-zone storms.

REFERENCE CITED

Clarke, F. E., and Jones, B. F., 1972, Significance of ground-water chemistry in performance of North Sahara tube wells in Algeria and Tunisia: U.S. Geol. Survey Water-Supply Paper 1757-M. [In press]

RECENT PUBLICATIONS OF THE U.S. GEOLOGICAL SURVEY

(Books may be ordered from the Superintendent of Documents, Government Printing Office, Washington, D.C., 20402, to whom remittances should be sent by check or money order. Give title, series No., stock No. (shown in parentheses in this list), and catalog No. [shown in brackets])

Professional Papers

562-J. Summary of alluvial-channel data from Rio Grande conveyance channel, New Mexico, 1965–69, by J. K. Culbertson, C. H. Scott, and J. P. Bennett. 1972. p. J1–J49. 70¢. (2401-2184) [I 19:16:562-J]

599-J. The contributions of Ranger photographs to understanding the geology of the Moon, by N. J. Trask. 1972. p. J1–J16. 40¢. (2401-2111) [I 19:16:599-J]

689. Sedimentary processes and distribution of particulate gold in the northern Bering Sea, by C. H. Nelson and D. M. Hopkins. 1972. 27 p. 75¢. (2401-2107) [I 19:16:689]

698. Petrographic and chemical reconnaissance study of some granitic and gneissic rocks near the San Andreas fault from Bodega Head to Cajon Pass, Calif., by D. C. Ross. 1972. 92 p. $2.25. (2401-2090) [I 19:16:698]

707. Interpretation of an aeromagnetic survey of the Amchitka Island area, Alaska, by G. D. Bath, W. J. Carr, L. M. Gard, Jr., and W. D. Quinlivan. 1972. 25 p. $1.75. (2401-2087) [I 19:16:707]

714. Mineral resource evaluation of the U.S. Forest Service Sierra Demonstration Project area, Sierra National Forest, Calif., by J. P. Lockwood, P. C. Bateman, and J. S. Sullivan. 1972. 59 p. $1. (2401-2103) [I 19:16:714]

716-A. Geology and copper mineralization of the Saindak quadrangle, Chagai District, West Pakistan, by Waheeduddin Ahmed, S. N. Khan, and R. G. Schmidt. 1972. p. A1–A21. $1. (2401-2108) [I 19:16:716-A]

726-A. Aeromagnetic, Bouguer gravity, and generalized geologic studies of the Great Falls-Mission Range area, northwestern Montana, by M. D. Kleinkopf and M. R. Mudge. 1972. p. A1–A19. $1.75. (2401-2075) [I 19:16:726-A]

738. Silurian rugose corals of the Klamath Mountains region, California, by C. W. Merriam. 1972. 50 p.; 8 plates. $1. (2401-2077) [I 19:16:738]

739. Geology of Isla Desecheo, Puerto Rico, with notes on the great southern Puerto Rico fault zone and Quaternary stillstands of the sea, by V. M. Seiders, R. P. Briggs, and Lynn Glover III. 1972. 22 p. 45¢. (2401-2106) [I 19:16:739]

741. The quinary reciprocal salt system Na,K,Mg,Ca/Cl,SO_4—A review of the literature with new data, by J. J. Rowe, G. W. Morey, and C. S. Zen. 1972. 37 p. 50¢. (2401-2140) [I 19:16:741]

742. Characteristics of estuarine sediments of the United States, by D. W. Folger. 1972. 94 p. $1.25. (2401-2112) [I 19:16:742]

745. Geology and uranium deposits, Shirley Basin area, Wyoming, by E. N. Harshman. 1972. 82 p. $1.50. (2401-2138) [I 19:16:745]

749. Distribution of the Middle Ordovician Copenhagen Formation and its trilobites in Nevada, by R. J. Ross, Jr., and F. C. Shaw. 1972. 33 p.; 8 plates. 70¢. (2401-2109) [I 19:16:749]

751-A. Preliminary results of injecting highly treated sewage-plant effluent into a deep sand aquifer at Bay Park, N.Y., by John Vecchioli and H. F. H. Ku. 1972. p. A1–A14. 30¢. (2401-2181) [I 19:16:751-A]

753. Geophysical, geohydrological, and geochemical reconnaissance of the Luke salt body, central Arizona, by G. P. Eaton, D. L. Peterson, and H. H. Schumann. 1972. 28 p. 40¢. (2401-2161) [I 19:16:753]

755. Calorimeters for heat of solution and low-temperature heat capacity measurements, by R. A. Robie and B. S. Hemingway. 1972. 32 p. 40¢. (2401-2182) [I 19:16:755]

760. Paleomagnetism of some Lake Superior Keweenawan rocks, by K. G. Books. 1972. 42 p. 50¢. (2401-2180) [I 19:16:760]

Bulletins

1314-F. Trace-element contents of some plutonic rocks of the Sierra Nevada batholith, by F. C. W. Dodge. 1972. p. F1–F13. 55¢. (2401-2137) [I 19:3:1314-F]

1342. Massive sulfide deposits near Shellabarger Pass, southern Alaska Range, Alaska, by B. L. Reed and G. D. Eberlein. 1972. 45 p. $1. (2401-2088) [I 19:3:1342]

1372-B. Stratigraphic nomenclature of Cambrian and Lower Ordovician rocks of easternmost southern Arizona and adjacent westernmost New Mexico, by P. T. Hayes. 1972. p. B1–B21. 25¢. (2401-2183) [I 19:3:1372-B]

1377. Bibliography and index of U.S. Geological Survey publications relating to coal, 1882–1970, by Paul Averitt and Lorreda Lopez. 1972. 173 p. 75¢. (2401-2175) [I 19:3:1377]

Water-Supply Papers

1663-H. Origin of mineralized water in Precambrian rocks of the upper Paraíba basin, Paraíba, Brazil, by S. L. Schoff. 1972. p. H1–H38. 60¢. (2401-2143) [I 19:13:1663-H]

1798-K. Fluvial sediment in Salem Fork watershed, West Virginia, by R. F. Flint. 1972. p. K1–K29. 30¢. (2401-2165) [I 19:13:1798-K]

1938. Water supply for the Nuclear Rocket Development Station at the U.S. Atomic Energy Commission's Nevada Test Site, by R. A. Young. 1972. 19 p. $1.25. (2401-2069) [I 19:13:1938]

1939-D. Chemical quality of the water in the Tucson basin, Arizona, by R. L. Laney. 1972. p. D1–D46; plates in separate case. $4.25. (2401-2076) [I 19:13:1939-D]

2008. Sediment transport in a Mississippi River distributary—Bayou Lafourche, La., by W. H. Doyle, Jr. 1972. 48 p. 40¢. (2401-2197) [I 19:13:2008]

2016. Quality of surface waters of the United States, 1967—Parts 12–16, North Pacific slope basins, Alaska, and Hawaii and other Pacific areas. 1972. 431 p. $2. (2401-2174) [I 19:13:2016]

2021. Evaluation of yields of wells in consolidated rocks, Virginia to Maine, by D. J. Cederstrom. 1972. 38 p. 65¢. (2401-2159) [I 19:13:2021]

U.S. GOVERNMENT
PRINTING OFFICE
PUBLIC DOCUMENTS DEPARTMENT
WASHINGTON, D.C. 20402

OFFICIAL BUSINESS
PENALTY FOR PRIVATE USE $300

POSTAGE AND FEES PAID
U.S. GOVERNMENT
PRINTING OFFICE
375

U.S.MAIL

JOURNAL OF RESEARCH

OF THE U.S. GEOLOGICAL SURVEY

MARCH–APRIL 1973
VOLUME 1, NUMBER 2

Scientific notes and summaries of investigations in geology, hydrology, and related fields

U.S. DEPARTMENT OF THE INTERIOR

UNITED STATES DEPARTMENT OF THE INTERIOR
ROGERS C. B. MORTON, Secretary
GEOLOGICAL SURVEY
V. E. McKelvey, Director

For sale by the Superintendent of Documents, U.S. Government Printing Office, Washington, D.C., 20402. Order by SD Catalog No. JRGS. Annual subscription rate $8.50 (plus $2.25 for foreign mailing). Single copy $1.50. Prices valid until July 1, 1973, at which time a price increase is scheduled. Make checks or money orders payable to the Superintendent of Documents.

Send all subscription inquiries and address changes to the Superintendent of Documents at the above address.

Purchase orders should not be sent to the U.S. Geological Survey library.

Library of Congress Card No. 72-600241

The Journal of Research consists of six issues a year (January-February, March-April, May-June, July-August, September-October, November-December) published in Washington, D.C., by the U.S. Geological Survey. It contains papers by members of the Geological Survey on geologic, hydrologic, topographic, and other scientific and technical subjects.

The Journal supersedes the short-papers chapters (B, C, and D) of the former Geological Survey Research ("Annual Review") series of professional papers. The synopsis chapter (A) of the former Geological Survey Research series will be published as a separate professional paper each year.

Correspondence and inquiries concerning the Journal (other than subscription inquiries and address changes) should be directed to the Managing Editor, Journal of Research, Publications Division, U.S. Geological Survey, Washington, D.C., 20242.

Papers for the Journal should be submitted through regular Division publication channels.

The Secretary of the Interior has determined that the publication of this periodical is necessary in the transaction of the public business required by law of this Department. Use of funds for printing this periodical has been approved by the Director of the Office of Management and Budget through February 11, 1975.

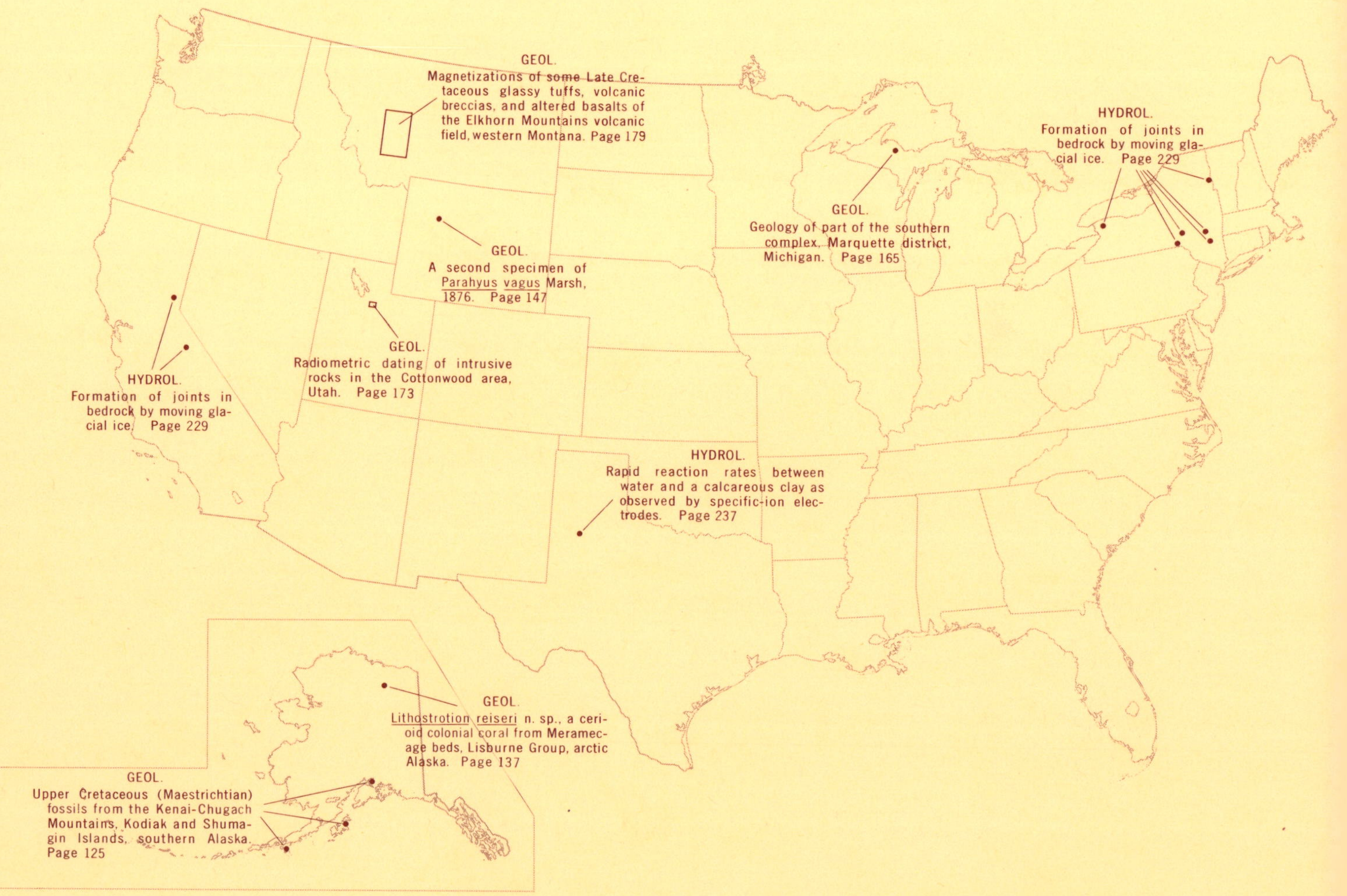

GEOGRAPHIC INDEX TO ARTICLES

[See Contents for articles concerning areas outside the United States and articles without geographic orientation]

JOURNAL OF RESEARCH

of the

U.S. Geological Survey

Vol. 1 No. 2 Mar.-Apr. 1973

CONTENTS

Abbreviations II

GEOLOGIC STUDIES

Upper Cretaceous (Maestrichtian) fossils from the Kenai-Chugach Mountains, Kodiak and Shumagin Islands, southern Alaska .... *D. L. Jones and S. H. B. Clark* 125

Lithostrotion reiseri n. sp., a cerioid colonial coral from Meramec-age beds, Lisburne Group, arctic Alaska .... *A. K. Armstrong* 137

A second specimen of *Parahyus vagus* Marsh, 1876 .... *G. E. Lewis* 147

The concept of growth and maturity of ore-stage pyrite in roll-type uranium deposits .... *C. G. Warren and H. C. Granger* 151

Age and tectonic implications of some low-grade metamorphic rocks from the Yucatan Channel .... *J. G. Vedder, N. S. MacLeod, M. A. Lanphere, and W. P. Dillon* 157

Geology of part of the southern complex, Marquette district, Michigan .... *W. F. Cannon and G. C. Simmons* 165

Radiometric dating of intrusive rocks in the Cottonwood area, Utah .... *M. D. Crittenden, Jr., J. S. Stuckless, R. W. Kistler, and T. W. Stern* 173

Magnetizations of some Late Cretaceous glassy tuffs, volcanic breccias, and altered basalts of the Elkhorn Mountains volcanic field, western Montana .... *W. F. Hanna* 179

Geologic bench marks by terrestrial photography .... *H. E. Malde* 193

The microgravimetric determination of acid-insoluble impurities in the complete analysis of small samples of acid-soluble minerals .... *Robert Meyrowitz* 207

Effects of laboratory treatments on silver and other elements in native gold .... *W. L. Campbell, E. L. Mosier, and J. C. Antweiler* 211

A precautionary note on the use of mixed solvents in soxhlet extraction procedures .... *A. A. Roberts and J. G. Palacas* 221

TOPOGRAPHIC STUDIES

Photomechanical experiments in automated cartography .... *C. R. Gilman* 223

HYDROLOGIC STUDIES

Formation of joints in bedrock by moving glacial ice .... *F. W. Trainer* 229

Rapid reaction rates between water and a calcareous clay as observed by specific-ion electrodes .... *W. W. Wood* 237

Hydraulic sand-model studies of miscible-fluid flow .... *J. M. Cahill* 243

Recent publications of the U.S. Geological Survey .... Inside of back cover

ABBREVIATIONS

[Singular and plural forms for abbreviations of units of measure are the same]

A	angstrom units
A^3	cubic angstroms
a-c	alternating current
B.P.	Before Present
b.y.	billion years
cal	calories
cm	centimeters
cm^2	square centimeters
cm^3	cubic centimeters
cpm	counts per minute
cu ft	cubic feet
cu mi	cubic miles
emu	electromagnetic units
eV	electron volts
ft	feet
g	grams
gal	gallons
gpd	gallons per day
gpm	gallons per minute
hr	hours
in.	inches
kb	kilobars
kg	kilograms
km	kilometers
km^2	square kilometers
km^3	cubic kilometers
kV	kilovolts
l	liters
lb	pounds
m	meters
m	molal (concentration)
m^2	square meters
m^3	cubic meters
me	milliequivalents
MeV	million electron volts
mg	milligrams
min	minutes
ml	milliliters
mm	millimeters
mol	moles
mr	milliroentgens
mV	millivolts
m.y.	million years
μ	microns
μm	micrometers
μmhos	micromhos
n	neutrons
N	normal (concentration)
ng	nanograms
nm	nanometers
Oe	oersteds
pCi	picocuries
pH	pH (measure of hydrogen ion activity)
ppb	parts per billion
ppm	parts per million
rad	radiometric
rpm	revolutions per minute
sec	seconds
sq ft	square feet
sq mi	square miles
yr	years

Jour. Research U.S. Geol. Survey
Vol. 1, No. 2, Mar.—Apr. 1973, p. 125—136

UPPER CRETACEOUS (MAESTRICHTIAN) FOSSILS FROM THE KENAI-CHUGACH MOUNTAINS, KODIAK AND SHUMAGIN ISLANDS, SOUTHERN ALASKA

By DAVID L. JONES and SANDRA H. B. CLARK,
Menlo Park, Calif.

Abstract.—A thick sequence of highly deformed flyschlike metasandstone, slate, and argillite crops out in southern Alaska in the Kenai-Chugach Mountains and on Kodiak and the Shumagin Islands to the southwest. These poorly fossiliferous rocks have long been considered Cretaceous in age because of scattered occurrences of fragmentary shells of *Inoceramus.* Mainly on the basis of new fossil collections, the age of some of these rocks can now be firmly established as Late Cretaceous (Maestrichtian); the critical fossil is *Inoceramus kusiroensis* Nagao and Matsumoto. *Inoceramus kusiroensis* also occurs in the much more fossiliferous and only slightly deformed Matanuska Formation that forms a parallel belt north of the Chugach Mountains. On the basis of faunal, lithologic, and bedding characteristics, the Matanuska Formation is the shelf equivalent of the deepwater, trench, or continental-rise deposits of the Kenai-Chugach Mountains and islands to the southwest. "*Inoceramya concentrica*" Ulrich occurs with *Inoceramus kusiroensis* and is Maestrichtian in age, not Early Jurassic as E. O. Ulrich suggested in 1910. The syntypes of *I. concentrica* are refigured and a lectotype is designated.

A thick sequence of Mesozoic metasandstone, slate, and argillite is exposed in an arcuate belt near the Pacific Coast in southern Alaska (fig. 1). These rocks, which are many thousands of feet thick, complexly deformed, and poorly fossiliferous, have long been considered to be Cretaceous, but firm evidence for their age has hiterto not been published. The purpose of this report is to describe and illustrate Upper Cretaceous fossils, mainly collected within the past 2 or 3 years, that permit close dating of some of these rocks. Descriptions of fossil localities are given in table 1 on page 135.

REGIONAL GEOLOGY

Sedimentary rocks of the Chugach and Kenai Mountains in southern Alaska and islands along the strike to the southwest include the Valdez Group, named for exposures near Valdez in Prince William Sound (Schrader, 1900; Moffit, 1954), similar rocks (Valdez? Group) widely and well exposed near Anchorage (Clark, 1972a, b), the Kodiak Formation of Kodiak Island (Moore, 1969), and the Shumagin Formation of Burk (1965) of the Shumagin Islands and Sanak Island (Moore, 1972). These formations are grossly similar in lithology, bedding characteristics, age, and depositional environment. They differ markedly from nearby highly fossiliferous and only slightly deformed Cretaceous rocks that occur to the north in the Wrangell Mountains, Talkeetna Mountains, Matanuska Valley, and Alaska Peninsula.

Despite the general similarity of rocks and structures in the Kenai-Chugach Mountains and on islands to the southwest, there is no name in general use that embraces the rocks in all these localities. This lack, together with the recent proliferation of local formational names and uncertainties in correlation, makes discussion of the entire belt cumbersome. Payne (1955) included the rocks of the Kenai and Chugach Mountains and Kodiak Island in the Chugach Mountains geosyncline. Similar rocks from the Shumagin Islands were placed in the Shumagin Shelf unit. Moore (1972) referred to these rocks as "Cretaceous trench sediments," which they may be, but general use of a genetic term such as "trench" seems unwarranted. Berg and others (1972) have referred to these rocks as the "Chugach terrane," here accepted as the most useful informal name applicable to the entire belt of highly deformed upper Mesozoic rocks of coastal southern Alaska.

On the basis of detailed mapping in the Chugach Mountains near Anchorage, Clark (1972b) subdivided the upper Mesozoic rocks into a heterogeneous assemblage of metavolcanic and metaclastic rocks of presumed Late Jurassic and (or) Cretaceous age named the McHugh Complex and a structurally lower sparsely fossiliferous flysch deposit termed the Valdez(?) Group (fig. 2).

Rocks of the Valdez(?) Group comprise very thick sequences of rhythmically interbedded metasandstone (mostly metagraywacke) and argillite that alternate with thick, massive beds of metasandstone and rare beds of conglomeratic argillite. Small-scale sedimentary structures in these rocks include graded bedding, small-scale crossbedding, flame structures, convolute laminations, and disturbed bedding. Sole markings are difficult to observe because of shearing along the base of the beds, although on the Shumagin Islands where deformation is less intense, sole markings are abundant and well preserved (Moore, 1972).

Figure 1.—Map of southern Alaska showing distribution of major geologic elements (modified from King, 1969), fossil localities discussed in text, and locations of figures 2, 6, and 8.

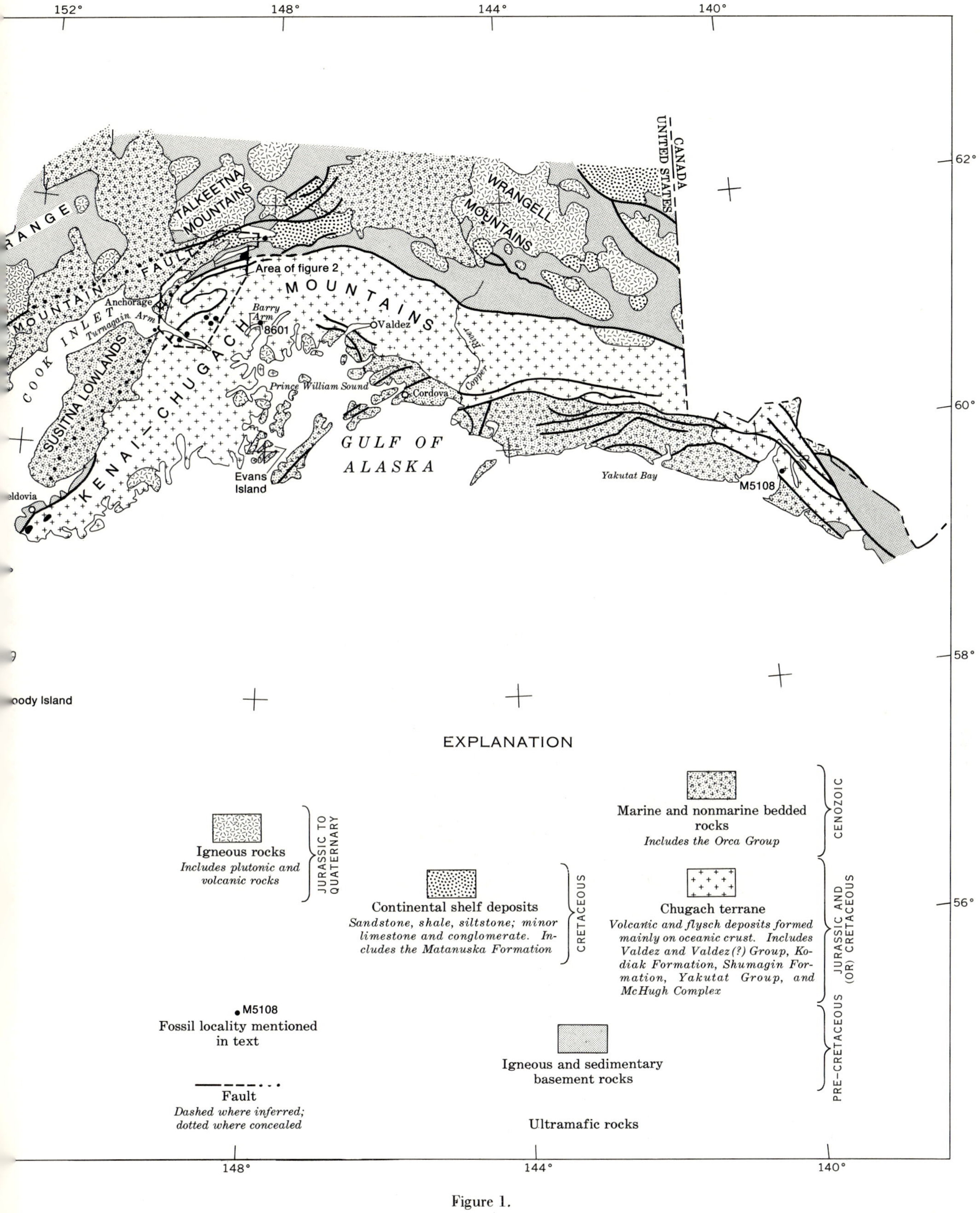
152°
148°
144°
140°
62°
60°
58°
56°
CANADA
UNITED STATES
TALKEETNA MOUNTAINS
WRANGELL MOUNTAINS
RANGE
MOUNTAIN FAULT
Area of figure 2
CHUGACH MOUNTAINS
Anchorage
Turnagain Arm
COOK INLET
Barry Arm
8601
Valdez
Copper River
SUSITNA LOWLANDS
KENAI
Prince William Sound
Cordova
GULF OF ALASKA
Evans Island
Yakutat Bay
M5108
ldovia
ody Island
EXPLANATION
Marine and nonmarine bedded rocks
Includes the Orca Group
CENOZOIC
Igneous rocks
Includes plutonic and volcanic rocks
JURASSIC TO QUATERNARY
Continental shelf deposits
Sandstone, shale, siltstone; minor limestone and conglomerate. Includes the Matanuska Formation
CRETACEOUS
Chugach terrane
Volcanic and flysch deposits formed mainly on oceanic crust. Includes Valdez and Valdez(?) Group, Kodiak Formation, Shumagin Formation, Yakutat Group, and McHugh Complex
JURASSIC AND (OR) CRETACEOUS
M5108
Fossil locality mentioned in text
Igneous and sedimentary basement rocks
PRE-CRETACEOUS
Fault
Dashed where inferred; dotted where concealed
Ultramafic rocks
148°
144°
140°

Figure 1.

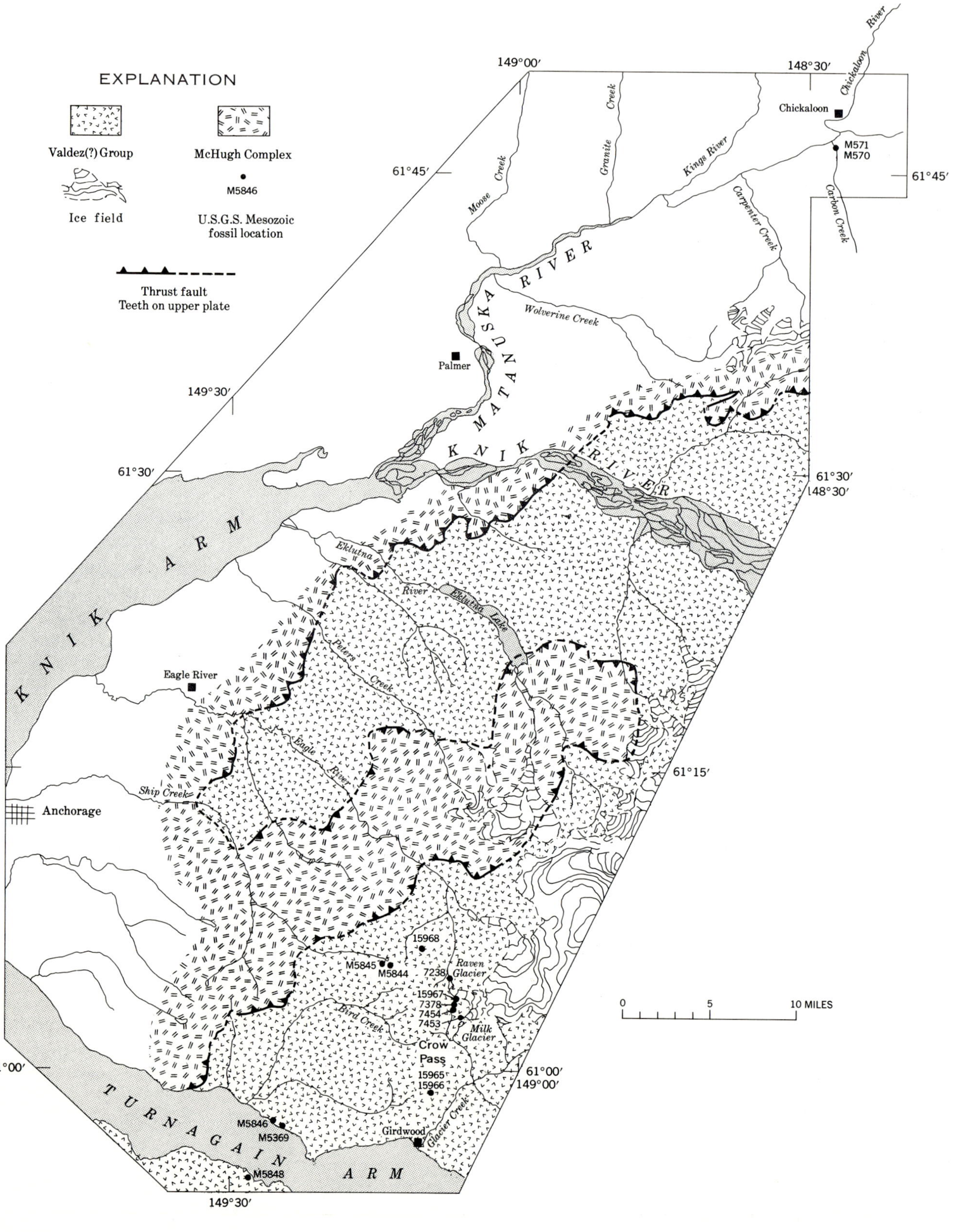

Figure 2.–Map of Anchorage-Turnagain Arm area, showing distribution of the Valdez(?) Group, McHugh Complex, and location of fossil localities described in text.

Fossils are very scarce in the Valdez(?) Group and related rocks, and many stratigraphic sequences thousands of feet thick fail to show even traces of organisms. In a few places bedding surfaces are covered with fossil "hash" composed of broken fragments and rare but nearly complete specimens of *Inoceramus*. Although these fossils have been known for many years (Martin, 1926; Park, 1933; Imlay and Reeside, 1954), it has only been within the past few years that specimens well-enough preserved to permit reliable identification have been found. The Valdez(?) Group near Anchorage is highly deformed, and the rocks have been metamorphosed to lower greenschist facies. Tight similar folds predominate with well-developed axial-plane slaty cleavage. The folds generally trend north-northeast and axial surfaces dip steeply northwest or southeast. In some areas the rocks are phyllitic and have undergone two periods of folding, for previously formed cleavage or schistosity is itself folded around steeply plunging axes.

Such highly deformed rocks offer poor opportunity for finding fossils as they tend to part along planes of cleavage or schistosity and not along bedding planes where the fossils are concentrated.

FOSSILS FROM THE CHUGACH TERRANE OF SOUTHERN ALASKA

The first molluscan fossils discovered in rocks of the Chugach Mountains in southern Alaska and correlative strata to the southwest were found by W. H. Dall in 1895 and described by E. O. Ulrich in 1910 (1910, p. 51, 134, 135; pls. 12, 13) as *Inoceramya concentrica* Ulrich, genus and species new. Specimens obtained from Woody Island near Kodiak were believed by Ulrich (1910, p. 432) to be a link between late Paleozoic *Posidonomya* (= *Posidonia*) and Cretaceous *Inoceramus*. Because of this presumed evolutionary relation, he suggested an Early Jurassic age.

Since Dall's original discovery of fossils on Woody Island, specimens of *Inoceramus* have been found near Girdwood on the north side of Turnagain Arm (fig. 2) and on Barry Arm (fig. 1) in the Port Wells district north of Prince William Sound. Concerning the fossils from these three localities, Imlay and Reeside (1954, p. 228) stated, "Curiously, these three areas contain identical species of *Inoceramus* characterized by bearing radial markings." They also pointed out that on the same slab as the type of *Inoceramya concentrica*, but not figured by Ulrich, is the radially ribbed species that occurs at Turnagain Arm. Imlay and Reeside (1954, p. 228) believed that both *I. concentrica* and the radially ribbed forms could be matched with Upper Cretaceous species that occur in Utah and Wyoming in the zone of *Scaphites binneyi*, suggesting a stratigraphic position corresponding to the upper Coniacian or lower Santonian. Following a review of Cretaceous fossils from southern Alaska, Jones (1967, p. 15) questioned this age assignment that was based on comparison with species in another faunal province because similar species were not known to occur in nearby fossiliferous Coniacian strata of the Matanuska Formation, nor had they been recognized in any of the more fossiliferous Cretaceous deposits in Alaska or elsewhere along the Pacific Coast of North America.

Since that time, much better preserved fossils have been found in the Chugach Mountains, identical fossils have been found in the Matanuska Formation, and a Late Cretaceous (Maestrichtian) age can be assigned with considerable confidence. The critical species is *Inoceramus kusiroensis* Nagao and Matsumoto, previously described from Upper Cretaceous strata of Japan and northeastern U.S.S.R.

Another fossil cited by Imlay and Reeside (1954, p. 228) in support of a Late Cretaceous age for rocks of the Chugach Mountains is a comatulid crinoid found on the west side of Evans Island in the western part of Prince William Sound. According to Plafker (oral commun., 1971), strata on Evans Island belong to the Orca Group, of early Tertiary age. Imlay and Reeside pointed out that this fossil has a long range (Jurassic to Holocene) thus it obviously contributes nothing to solution of the problem of the age of the Mesozoic rocks.

Inoceramus kusiroensis was first described by Nagao and Matsumoto (1940, p. 56, pl. 22, fig. 4) from Upper Cretaceous deposits of Hokkaido, Japan. The characteristic ornamentation of this species is concentric rings and narrow, sharp radial ribs. The concentric rings are widely spaced in early growth stages, closely spaced during midgrowth stages, and widely spaced again in mature stages (1940, p. 56). Radial ribs appear only at midgrowth stage, at about the time of change from widely to narrowly spaced concentric ribs.

The Alaskan specimens show close similarities to the holotype of *I. kusiroensis*, although on some the early concentric ribs are much more widely spaced (fig. 3, *h*). In this regard, the Alaskan forms are nearly identical to a specimen of *I. kusiroensis* from the Koryak Range of northeast U.S.S.R. figured by Vereshchagin and others (1965, pl. 63, fig. 2; see fig. 4, *e* of this report for a copy of their photograph). Because Alaskan specimens also show quite a wide range in variation in strength of early concentric ribbing, this minor difference from the holotype is not considered to be significant.

Radial ribs are well developed on the Alaskan specimens, and the reticulate pattern produced by the intersection of the concentric and radial ornamentation is sufficiently distinctive to permit identification of fragments. Some specimens have radial ribs that are relatively broad folds (fig. 4, *g*) rather than sharp, narrow ribs. Some of these broader structures may be secondary features formed by deformation of the shell.

A remarkable specimen from Woody Island (USGS Mesozoic loc. M5963) shows that at a mature growth stage, peculiar fingerlike projections develop along the ventral margin. Four fingers are clearly shown on fig. 5, but the total number cannot be observed because of the fragmentary nature of this specimen. The purpose of this unusual feature is unknown, but possibly the fingers supported mantle flaps or folds that aided in maintaining buoyancy. Another kind of inoceramid is

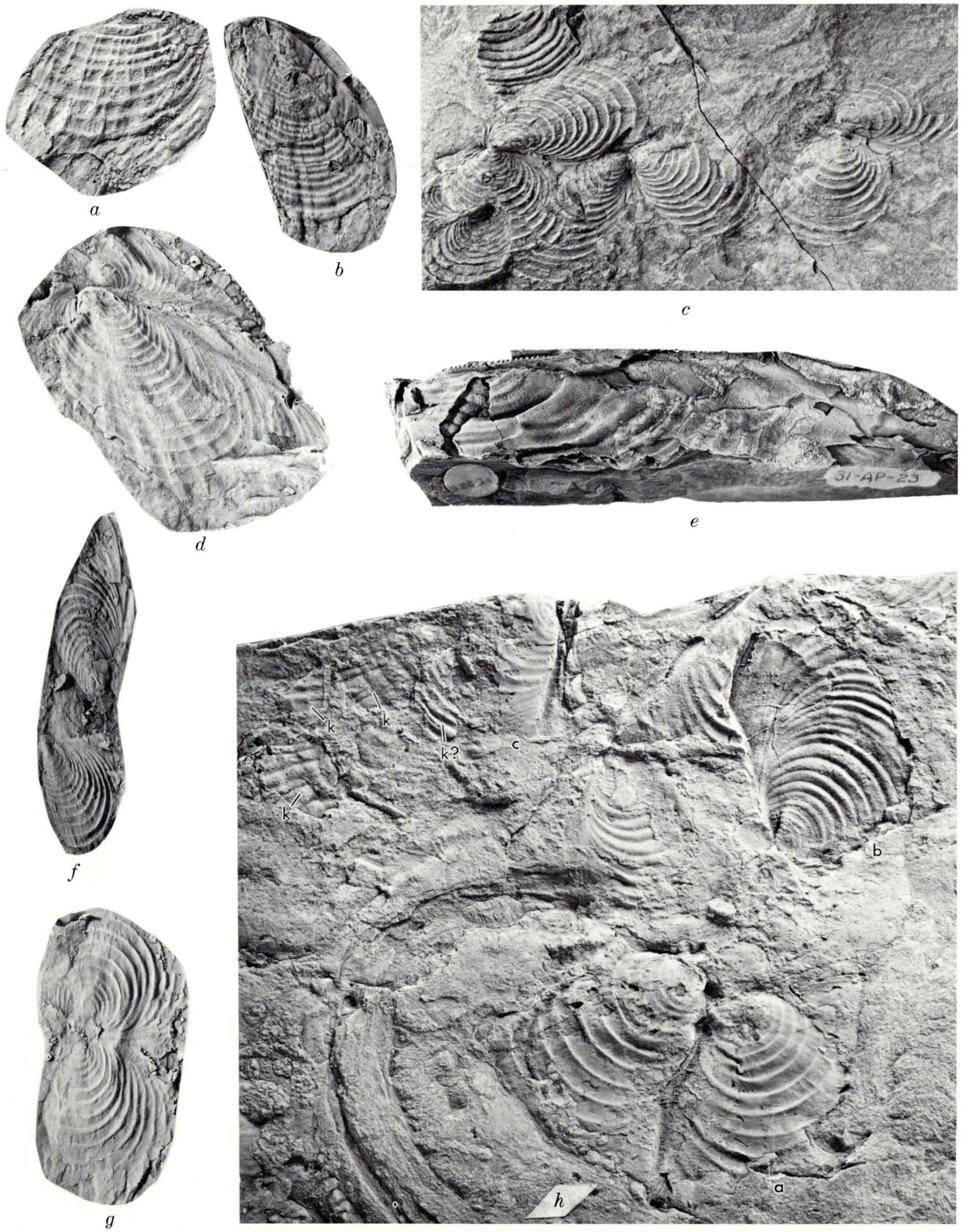

Figure 3.

associated with *I. kusiroensis* in a few localities in the Chugach Mountains and on Woody Island. This is *Inoceramya concentrica* Ulrich (1910, p. 134), the syntypes of which are refigured on figure 3, *h*. At least six fragmentary specimens are exposed on the type slab; Ulrich figured three of them (these are labeled on figure 3, *h* as a, b, c). Because a holotype was not specified by Ulrich, we designated as lectotype of *Inoceramya concentrica* the bivalved fragment labeled a.

This specimen shows well-developed concentric ribs that are separated by nearly flat, broad, interrib areas. Spacing between ribs increases with growth, attaining a maximum of about 4 mm. Faint radial striae are visible between ribs on the preserved anterior parts of the valves. Concentric ribs become faint on the flattened posterodorsal part of the valves. Anterior and ventral margins and hinge plate are not preserved.

The other syntypes differ somewhat from the lectotype. Specimen b shows well-preserved concentric rings that are more closely spaced than on the lectotype and become more closely spaced with growth. Specimen c is a well-preserved umbonal fragment that shows the ligament pits. Several other fragments found near specimen c, that may or may not belong with this specimen, show the reticulate rib pattern of *I. kusiroensis*; these are labeled k on figure 3, *h*. The umbonal part may also be of this species, but a positive determination is not possible. In any case, it is not clear that these syntypes belong to the same species as the lectotype.

The status of the genus *Inoceramya* is questionable, and its differentiation from *Inoceramus* sensu lato is in doubt.

Figure 3.—Photographs of *Inoceramus kusiroensis* Nagao and Matsumoto and of *I. concentrica* Ulrich. Natural size.

a–g. *Inoceramus kusiroensis* Nagao and Matsumoto.

- *a*. Fragment of right valve, USNM 183441b from USGS Mesozoic loc. M5369, showing reticulate pattern of ornamentation. This specimen is on the same large slab as that of figure 4, *f*. Rubber cast.
- *b*. Left valve, USNM 183645 from USGS Mesozoic loc. M571 (Matanuska Formation), showing well-developed radial ribs.
- *c*. Slab, USNM 183646 from USGS Mesozoic loc. M570 (Matanuska Formation). Juvenile specimens that lack well-developed radial ribs.
- *d*. Left valve and umbo of right valve, USNM 183647 from USGS Mesozoic loc. 7378. Rubber cast.
- *e*. Crushed left valve, USNM 183648a from USGS Mesozoic loc. 15966, showing ligament pits on hinge.
- *f*. Left and right valves, USNM 183648b from USGS Mesozoic loc. 15966. Note similarity to specimens from Matanuska Formation shown in this figure, *c*. Rubber cast.
- *g*. Left and right valves, USNM 183649 from USGS Mesozoic loc. M5369. Note close similarity to *Inoceramya concentrica*, *h* of this figure, which has more widely spaced concentric ribs. Rubber cast.

h. *Inoceramya concentrica* Ulrich.

Type slab, USNM 30210, from Woody Island. Syntypes figured by Ulrich are labeled a, b, and c. Specimen a is herein designated as the lectotype of *I. concentrica*. Fragments of *Inoceramus kusiroensis* are indicated by k.

According to Ulrich (1910) and Cox (1969, p. N317) the main characters that separate *Inoceramya* from *Inoceramus* are: lack of prismatic shell, ligament pits that are small and numerous and decrease in size toward the ends of the hinge margin, presence of an internal riblike swelling that extends obliquely backward from the umbo, regular concentric ribs that are absent from the posterodorsal region, and nonprotruding umbones located near the middle of the hinge margin. Of these features, the lack of prismatic shell is due to nonpreservation, and only the regular concentric ornamentation can be accredited assuredly to *Inoceramya concentrica*. The other features are not displayed by the lectotype and may indeed be characteristics of another species.

The type locality of *Inoceramya concentrica* was not precisely located in the original report, although on the basis of a drawing of the islands in Kodiak harbor (Emerson, 1910, p. 52, fig. 12) and a brief description of the locality (p. 51), it is apparent that the fossils were obtained from the northwest shore of Woody Island. A detailed search of the entire island by the writers resulted in discovery of three *Inoceramus*-bearing fossil localities, all on the northwest shore. This is the only place on the island where the metamorphic grade is relatively low and where the top surfaces of beds are well exposed. The position of our new localities is shown on figure 6. In addition to the *Inoceramus* shells, tubes of *Terebellina palachei* Ulrich and trace fossils are fairly common in these exposures, and most of the forms described by Ulrich can be found. The strike of the beds is approximately parallel to the shoreline, and only a small stratigraphic interval is exposed there. Hence, our localities must lie nearly at the same stratigraphic horizon as Ulrich's original specimens.

Unfortunately, no well-preserved specimens of *Inoceramya concentrica* were found that shed more light on the nature of this poorly known form. Several specimens were found with well-developed concentric ribs, but these could be either *I. concentrica* or *Inoceramus kusiroensis*. A large specimen of the latter from USGS Mesozoic loc. M5963 is illustrated in figure 5.

AGE, CORRELATION, AND DEPOSITIONAL ENVIRONMENT

Inoceramus kusiroensis occurs in Hokkaido, Japan, in association with *I. shikotanensis* Nagao and Matsumoto, a guide fossil to the Japanese upper Hetonaian (K6β) substage (Matsumoto, 1954, p. 37; 1959, pl. 8), which is correlated by Japanese paleontologists with the lower part of the Maestrichtian Stage of Europe. A comparable age seems warranted for the Chugach specimens.

Inoceramus kusiroensis is locally abundant in the Matanuska Formation in the lower Matanuska Valley (see identifications by Jones *in* Grantz, 1964, p. 124). The best fossils are from USGS Mesozoic localities 6692, M570, M571, M584, M585, and M589 (see Grantz, 1964, p. 125 and fig. 2 for location of these collections) in the upper part of the Matanuska

Figure 4.

Formation, as determined by Grantz; some occur with ammonites of the *Pachydiscus kamishakensis* zone of late Campanian and Maestrichtian age.

The Matanuska Formation is relatively fossiliferous, and locally contains abundant specimens of ammonites and *Inoceramus* (Jones, 1963, 1967). It thus contrasts markedly with the poorly fossiliferous flysch deposits of the Chugach terrane, which have yielded no molluscan fossils except for the *Inoceramus* described in this report. The Matanuska Formation probably accumulated on a narrow, unstable continental shelf where depths of water were mainly in the neritic to upper bathyal zones (Grantz, 1964, p. 122; Jones and others, 1971; Berg and others, 1972). The rocks of the Chugach terrane lying to the south apparently formed in much deeper water, perhaps on a continental rise or in a trench at the margin of the continent (Payne, 1955; Moore, 1972; Berg and others, 1972). This postulated environment is supported not only by the lack of shallow-water fossils but also by the character of bedding and sedimentary structures, which are typical of deepwater deposits (Burk, 1965; Plafker and MacNeil, 1966; Moore, 1972; Clark, 1972a, b).

The presence of *Inoceramus kusiroensis* in both the shallow-water deposits of the Matanuska Formation and the deepwater deposits of the Chugach Mountains raises a question as to the environmental conditions under which this organism lived. It seems doubtful that this species, alone among the Late Cretaceous marine mollusks of southern Alaska, actually could inhabit such a wide ecological niche. It seems more likely that

Figure 4.—Photographs of *Inoceramus kusiroensis* Nagao and Matsumoto and of *Inoceramus* cf. *I. kusiroensis*. Natural size.

a, c–h; Inoceramus kusiroensis Nagao and Matsumoto.

a. Left valve, USNM 183639 from USGS Mesozoic loc. M5369. Concentric ribs are evenly spaced throughout in constrast to most specimens that have narrowly spaced ribs in midgrowth stages. Rubber cast.

c. Holotype, Hk. 7271a. Reproduced from Nagao and Matsumoto, 1940, pl. 22, fig. 4.

d. Fragment of left(?) valve, USNM 183640 from USGS Mesozoic loc. M571 (Matanuska Formation), showing reticulate ornamentation. Rubber cast.

e. Left valve and part of right valve, from Koryak Range, northeastern U.S.S.R. Reproduced from Vereshchagin and others, 1965, pl. 63, fig. 2.

f. Fragment of large specimen, USNM 183641a from USGS Mesozoic loc. M5369, showing well-developed reticulate ornamentation. Rubber cast.

g. Right and left valves, USNM 183642 from USGS Mesozoic loc. M5846. Note very coarse radial ribs. Rubber cast.

h. Slab, USNM 183643 from USGS Mesozoic loc. M5846. Note very coarse concentric rings on the two specimens on the right-hand part of slab. Rubber cast.

b. Inoceramus cf. *I. kusiroensis.*

USNM 183644 from USGS Mesozoic loc. M5868, Shumagin Islands. Radial ribs are not as strongly developed on Shumagin Islands specimens as on most forms from the Chugach Mountains and Woody Island.

Figure 5.—*Inoceramus kusiroensis*, USNM 185747 from USGS Mesozoic loc. M5963, Woody Island. Note strong radial ribs and development of fingerlike projections on ventral margin.

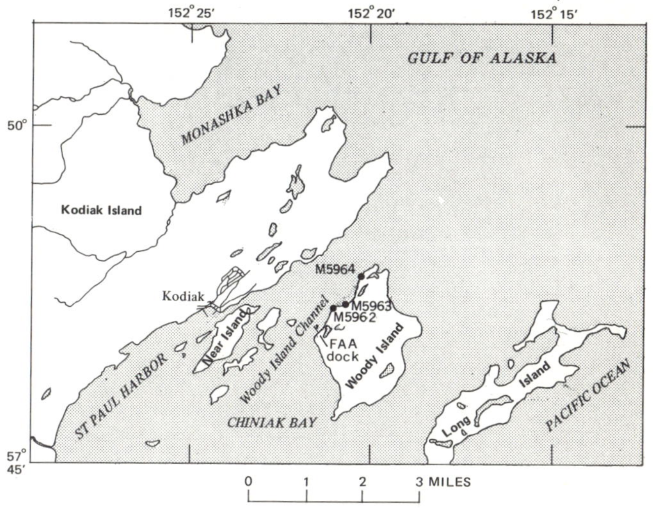

Figure 6.—Map showing fossil localities on Woody Island.

the *Inoceramus* shells were transported from shallow water where they lived, to deep water, where they became entombed in the sediment. But if this is so, why were only the *Inoceramus* transported, and not shells of ammonites and other forms that are so common in the Matanuska Formation but totally unknown from the Chugach rocks? And what was the mode of transportation that carried these thin-shelled, fragile mollusks without breaking them into small fragments?

A possible explanation for the distribution of *Inoceramus kusiroensis* in both shallow-water and deepwater deposits is that it had a pseudoplanktonic habit (Hayami, 1969) and lived suspended in the near-surface waters, perhaps attached to drifting seaweed. Upon death the shells would settle to the bottom and accumulate on bedding planes. A number of specimens show both valves still together, but spread open and lying flat along the bedding plane (fig. 7; fig. 4, *g*). These specimens have not been carried far by bottom currents; otherwise the two valves, which lack hinge teeth, would have been separated.

If this interpretation of a pseudoplanktonic habit is correct, the presence of *I. kusiroensis* provides no direct information about the environment of deposition of the enclosing sediments. As this species does appear to be more abundant in the deeper water deposits than in the shelf deposits, it may have flourished well offshore.

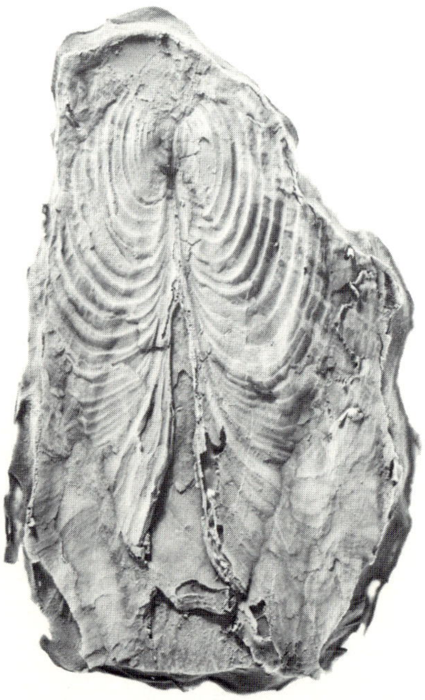

Figure 7.—*Inoceramus kusiroensis*, USNM 183650, from USGS Mesozoic locality 15965 (fig. 2). Rubber cast. Left and right valves of nearly complete specimen spread open along bedding plane in black argillite. The two valves, which lack hinge teeth, could not have been carried to the burial site by strong bottom currents without disarticulation.

Specimens of *Inoceramus* are locally abundant on the Shumagin Islands to the southwest, particularly on Nagai Island (fig. 8). Some of these closely resemble *I. kusiroensis*, except that radial ribs are not as strongly developed (see fig. 4, *b*). The significance of this difference is not known; it may be

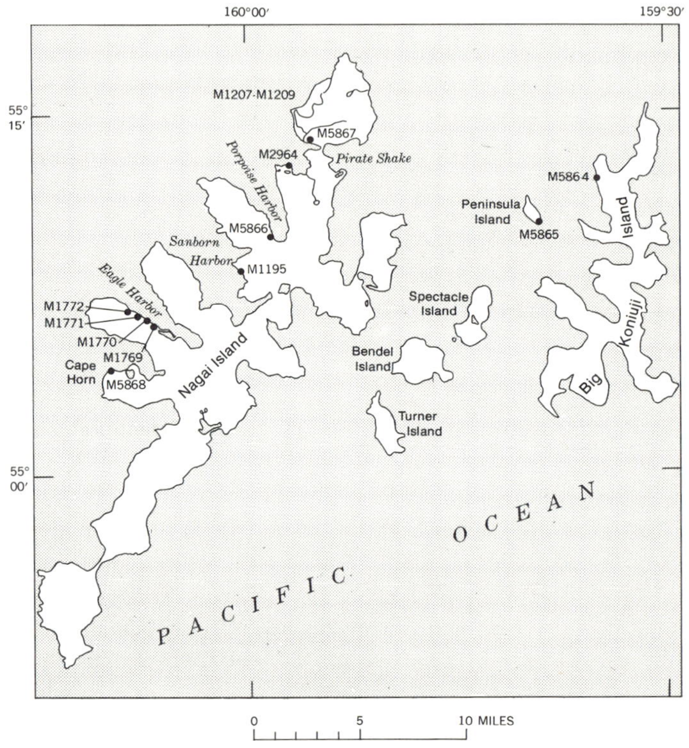

Figure 8.—Map of Shumagin Islands, showing fossil locations.

normal variation in a slightly younger or older subspecies, or it might be related to somewhat different ecological conditions. In any case, the Shumagin Islands rocks appear to be grossly similar in age to those of the Valdez Group and related rocks near Anchorage.

The Valdez Group and related rocks of the Chugach terrane in southern Alaska are similar in lithological character to rocks exposed in the Chugach Mountains east of the Copper River (Yakutat Group) as pointed out by Plafker and MacNeil (1966, p. B63–B64). They are also grossly similar to rocks in southeastern Alaska on Baranof and Chichagof Islands (Sitka Graywacke of Loney and others, 1963, 1964). As both the Yakutat Group and the Sitka Graywacke contain *Buchia* of earliest Cretaceous (Berriasian) age, they are in part much older than any of the *Inoceramus kusiroensis*-bearing rocks identified in southern Alaska. Some of the rocks of the Yakutat Group, however, are nearly contemporaneous with these Maestrichtian rocks, as Plafker and Perkins have found *Inoceramus schmidti* of Campanian age in Yakutat Bay (USGS Mesozoic loc. M5108). This fossil is well known from the

Matanuska Formation (Jones, 1963), where it occurs in a faunal zone directly below that containing *Inoceramus kusiroensis*. Because of this close proximity in age, and judged by the great thickness of rocks involved in both the Yakutat and the Valdez Group and related rocks, it seems reasonable to suppose that they are, in part, coeval, even though an exact equivalency cannot be demonstrated on a faunal basis.

The absence of older fossils from the Chugach terrane of southern Alaska is surprising in view of the fairly large number and wide distribution of the known fossil localities. The same Maestrichtian fossils occur near the northwestern boundary of the belt (Turnagain Arm), near the southeastern boundary (Woody Island), and also near the center of the belt (Barry Arm). Such a wide distribution suggests that if older rocks are present at all, they may be very limited in extent.

Table 1.—*Description of Upper Cretaceous fossil localities referred to in text*

U.S. Geol Survey Mesozoic loc. No.	Field No.	Collector, year of collection, description of locality, and fossil identifications
	Chugach Mountains	
7238	....	G. C. Martin, 1911. Turnagain Arm area, head of Raven Creek. *Inoceramus kusiroensis.*
7378	....	E. J. Barnes, 1911. Slide near foot of East Fork Crow Creek Glacier. *Inoceramus kusiroensis.*
7453	....	B. L. Johnson, 1911. Moraine on west side of Milk Creek Glacier, tributary to Crow Creek. *Inoceramus kusiroensis.*
7454	....	B. L. Johnson, 1911. Near head of Crow Creek. *Inoceramus kusiroensis.*
8601	13-AJ-128	B. L. Johnson, 1913. East side of Point Doran, Barry Arm of Port Wells. *Inoceramus ulrichi, Inoceramus kusiroensis*(?).
9495	15-AJ-19	B. L. Johnson, 1915. Float on Valdez Glacier near Wilson cabin. *Inoceramus* sp. indet.
15965	31-AP-22	C. F. Park, Jr., 1931. 1.2 miles N. 10° W. from Girdwood station, on ridge between California and Crow Creeks. *Inoceramus kusiroensis.*
15966	31-AP-23	C. F. Park, Jr. Same as 15965. *Inoceramus kusiroensis.*
15967	31-AP-63	C. F. Park, Jr., 1931. Just northeast of trail across summit between Crow and Raven Creeks. *Inoceramus kusiroensis.*
15968	31-AP-120	C. F. Park, Jr., 1931. 3.6 miles S. 22° W. from Eagle River Road house, in moraine. *Inoceramus kusiroensis.*
M5369	69-ACs-68, 69-ACs-388	S. Clark, 1969. Turnagain Arm, Seward D-7 quadrangle, sec. 14, T. 10 N., R. 1 W., lat 60°57.1′ N.; long 149°24.2′ W. *Inoceramus kusiroensis.*
M5844	71-ACs-171D	S. Clark and D. L. Jones, 1971. Anchorage A-6 quadrangle. Ridge south of lake at head of North Fork Ship Creek, 1,500 ft S., 2,000 ft E. of NW. cor. sec. 35, T. 12 N., R. 1 E. *Inoceramus kusiroensis.*
M5845	71-ACs-175	S. Clark and D. L. Jones, 1971. Anchorage A-6 quadrangle. Ridge south of lake at head of North Fork Ship Creek, 2,000 ft S., 250 ft E. of NW. cor. sec. 35, T. 12 N., R. 1 E. *Inoceramus* cf. *I. kusiroensis.*
M5846	71-ACs-328	S. Clark and G. R. Winkler, 1971. North shore of Turnagain Arm, Anchorage Highway, 2,000 ft S., 400 ft W. of NE. cor. sec. 15, T. 10 N., R. 1 W. *Inoceramus kusiroensis.*
M5848	71-ACs-2033	S. Clark, M. E. Yount, and P. S. Morse, 1971. Seward D-7 quadrangle. South shore of Turnagain Arm, Hope Highway east of Sunset Creek, 1,500 ft N., 2,800 ft E. of SW. cor. sec. 33, T. 10 N., R. 1 W. *Inoceramus kusiroensis.*
	Kodiak and Shumagin Islands	
USNM 30210	....	W. H. Dall, 1895. Woody Island near Kodiak, on shore facing Chiniak Bay. "*Inoceramya concentrica*" (= *Inoceramus ulrichi* Jones and Clark) and *Inoceramus kusiroensis.*
M1195	134-A1-3	C. A. Burk, 1961. Shumagin Islands, Sanborn Harbor, lat 55°8.5′ N.; long 160°0.5′ W. *Inoceramus* cf. *I. kusiroensis.*
M1207 ..... M1209	135-A4-5 135-A4-15	C. A. Burk, 1958–61. West of Pirate Shake, Nagai Island. *Inoceramus* cf. *I. kusiroensis.*
M1770	62-AGz-9	Arthur Grantz, 1962. Shumagin Islands, Nagai Island, Eagle Harbor, lat 55°6.4′ N.; long 160°7.3′ W. *Inoceramus* cf. *I. kusiroensis.*
M1771	62-AGz-10	Arthur Grantz, 1962. Shumagin Islands, Nagai Island, Eagle Harbor, lat 55°6.6′ N.; long 160°7.7′ W. *Inoceramus* cf. *I. kusiroensis.*
M1772	62-AGz-11	Arthur Grantz, 1962. Shumagin Islands, Nagai Island, Eagle Harbor, lat 55°6.6′ N.; long 160°7.9′ W. *Inoceramus* cf. *I. kusiroensis.*
M2964	16098-19	Standard Oil Company of California, year unknown. Nagai Island, lat 55°12.8′ N.; long 159°56.7′ W., Northeast shore of eastern point at Porpoise Harbor. *Inoceramus* cf. *I. kusiroensis.*
M5864	N-140F	J. C. Moore, 1969–1970. Big Koniuji Island, northeastern peninsula, 2.1 miles N. 38°30′ W. of triangulation station Koniuji. *Inoceramus* cf. *I. kusiroensis* and *Inoceramus* sp.
M5867	N-115E	J. C. Moore, 1969–1970. Nagai Island, south side of stream east of Porpoise Rocks, 2.5 miles N. 50°30′ W. of triangulation station Wreck. *Inoceramus* cf. *I. kusiroensis.*

Table 1.—*Description of Upper Cretaceous fossil localities referred to in text*—Continued

U.S. Geol. Survey Mesozoic loc. No.	Field No.	Collector, year of collection, description of locality, and fossil identifications
Kodiak and Shumagin Islands—Continued		
M5868	N-8A	J. C. Moore, 1969–1970. Nagai Island, Cape Horn. *Inoceramus* cf *I. kusiroensis.*
M5962	72Acs 489	S. Clark and D. L. Jones, 1972. Woody Island, Kodiak (D-1) quadrangle, 600 ft E., 700 ft N. of SW. cor. sec. 34, T. 27 S., R. 19 W., at triangulation station Eider. *Inoceramya concentrica*(?).
M5963	72Acs 490	S. Clark and D. L. Jones, 1972. Woody Island, Kodiak (D-1) quadrangle, 1,700 ft E., 1,000 ft N. of SW. cor. sec. 34, T. 27 S., R. 19 W. *Inoceramya concentrica*(?), *Inoceramus kusiroensis.*
M5964	72Acs 492	S. Clark and D. L. Jones, Woody Island, Kodiak (D-1) quadrangle, 3,200 ft E., 3,650 ft N. of SW. cor. sec. 34, T. 27 S., R. 19 W. *I. kusiroensis*(?).
Location of *Inoceramus schmidti* from Yakutat Group		
M5108	68-APs-72E	G. Plafker and M. Perkins, 1968 and 1969. Yakutat 1:250,000 quadrangle, SE¼ sec. 23, T. 25 S., R. 35 E., above Rasmussen Glacier. Yakutat Group.
Location of figured specimens from Matanuska Valley		
M570	59-AGz-M35	D. L. Jones and Arthur Grantz, 1959. Carbon Creek, lat 61°46′20″ N.; long 148°27′35″ W. Matanuska Formation, *Inoceramus kusiroensis.*
M571	59-AGz-M36A	D. L. Jones and Arthur Grantz, 1959. Carbon Creek, lat 61°46′15″ N.; long 148°27′30″ W. Matanuska Formation, *Inoceramus kusiroensis.*

REFERENCES CITED

Berg, H. C., Jones, D. L., and Richter, D. H., 1972, Gravina-Nutzotin belt—Tectonic significance of an upper Mesozoic sedimentary and volcanic sequence in southern and southeastern Alaska, *in* Geological Survey Research 1972: U.S. Geol. Survey Prof. Paper 800-D, p. D1–D24.

Burk, C. A., 1965, Geology of the Alaska Peninsula—Island arc and continental margin: Geol. Soc. America Mem. 99, pt. 1, 250 p.

Clark, S. H. B., 1972a, Reconnaissance bedrock geologic map of the Chugach Mountains near Anchorage, Alaska: U.S. Geol. Survey Misc. Inv. Field Studies Map MF-350. [In press]

—— 1972b, The McHugh Complex of south-central Alaska: U.S. Geol. Survey Bull. 1372-D.

Cox, L. R., 1969, Family Inoceramidae, *in* Moore, R. C., ed., Treatise on Invertebrate Paleontology, pt. N. v. 1, Mollusca 6: Boulder, Colo., and Lawrence, Kans., Geol. Soc. America (and Kansas Univ. Press), p. N314–N321.

Emerson, B. K., 1910, Notes on the stratigraphy and igneous rocks, *in* Harriman Alaska series, v. 4, Geology and Paleontology, p. 11–56.

Grantz, Arthur, 1964, Stratigraphic reconnaissance of the Matanuska Formation in the Matanuska Valley, Alaska: U.S. Geol. Survey Bull. 1181-I, p. I1–I33.

Hayami, Itaru, 1969, Notes on Mesozoic "planktonic" bivalves: Jour. Geology [Japan], v. 75, no. 7, p. 375–385 [English abs. p. 385].

Imlay, R. W., and Reeside, J. B., Jr., 1954, Correlation of the Cretaceous Formations of Greenland and Alaska: Geol. Soc. America Bull., v. 65, p. 223–246.

Jones, D. L., 1963, Upper Cretaceous (Campanian and Maestrichtian) ammonites from southern Alaska: U.S. Geol. Survey Prof. Paper 432, 53 p. [1964]

—— 1967, Cretaceous ammonites from the lower part of the Matanuska Formation, southern Alaska: U.S. Geol. Survey Prof. Paper 547, 49 p.

Jones, D. L., MacKevett, E. M., Jr., and Plafker, George, 1971, Speculations on late Mesozoic tectonic history of part of southern Alaska: Am. Assoc. Petroleum Geologists, Second Internat. Symposium on Arctic Geology, Program Abs., p. 30.

King, P. B., compiler, 1969, Tectonic map of North America: U.S. Geol. Survey, scale 1:5,000,000.

Loney, R. A., Berg, H. C., Pomeroy, J. S., and Brew, D. A., 1963, Reconnaissance geologic map of Chichagof Island and northwestern Baranof Island, Alaska: U.S. Geol. Survey Misc. Geol. Inv. Map I-388, scale 1:250,000.

Loney, R. A., Pomeroy, J. S., Brew, D. A., and Muffler, L. J. P., 1964, Reconnaissance geologic map of Baranof and Kruzof Islands, Alaska: U.S. Geol. Survey Misc. Geol. Inv. Map I-411, scale 1:250,000.

Martin, G. C., 1926, The Mesozoic stratigraphy of Alaska: U.S. Geol. Survey Bull. 776, 493 p.

Matsumoto, Tatsuro, 1954, The Cretaceous system in the Japanese Islands: Tokyo, Japan, Japanese Soc. Promotion Sci. Research, 324 p.

—— 1959, Zonation of Upper Cretaceous in Japan: Kyushu Univ. Fac. Sci. Mem., ser. D, Geology, v. 9, no. 2, p.55–93.

Moffit, F. H., 1954, Geology of the Prince William Sound region, Alaska: U.S. Geol. Survey Bull. 989-E, p. 225–310.

Moore, C. W., 1969, New formations on Kodiak and adjacent islands, Alaska, *in* Changes in stratigraphic nomenclature by the U.S. Geological Survey, 1967: U.S. Geol. Survey Bull. 1274-A p. A27-A35.

Moore, J. C., 1972, Uplifted trench sediments—southwest Alaska-Bering Shelf edge: Science, v. 175, no. 4026, p. 1103–1105.

Nagao, Tukumi, and Matsumoto, Tatsuro, 1940, A monograph of the Cretaceous *Inoceramus* of Japan, pt. 2: Hokkaido Univ., Fac. Sci., Jour., ser. 4, v. 6, no. 1, p. 1–64.

Park, C. F., Jr., 1933, The Girdwood district, Alaska: U.S. Geol. Survey Bull. 849-G, p. 381–424.

Payne, T. G., (compiler), 1955, Mesozoic and Cenozoic tectonic elements of Alaska: U.S. Geol. Survey Misc. Geol. Inv. Map I-84, scale 1:5,000,000.

Plafker, George, and MacNeil, F. S., 1966, Stratigraphic significance of Tertiary fossils from the Orca Group in the Prince William Sound region, Alaska, *in* Geological Survey Research 1966: U.S. Geol. Survey Prof. Paper 550-B, p. B62–B68.

Schrader, F. C., 1900, A reconnaissance of a part of Prince William Sound and the Copper River district, Alaska, in 1898: U.S. Geol. Survey 20th Ann. Rept., pt. 7, p. 408–410, 413.

Ulrich, E. O., 1910, Fossils and age of the Yakutat Formation, *in* Harriman Alaska Series, v. 4, Geology and Paleontology, p. 125–146.

Vereshchagin, V. N., Kinasov, V. P., Paraketsov, K. V., and Terekhova, G. P., 1965, Polevoi Atlas, Melovoi fauni Severo-Vostoka S.S.S.R.: Magadan, Gosudarst. Proizvodst. Geol. Dom. RSFSR, Servero-Vostoch. Geol. Upravlenie, 66 p. [In Russian]

Jour. Research U.S. Geol. Survey
Vol. 1, No. 2, Mar.—Apr. 1973, p. 137—145

LITHOSTROTION REISERI N. SP., A CERIOID COLONIAL CORAL FROM MERAMEC-AGE BEDS, LISBURNE GROUP, ARCTIC ALASKA

By AUGUSTUS K. ARMSTRONG, Menlo Park, Calif.

Abstract.—*Lithostrotion reiseri* n. sp. is a cerioid, colonial coral, index fossil for microfossil zones 12-13 (Meramec) in the Lisburne Group in the central and eastern Brooks Range, arctic Alaska.

The studies of the Carboniferous biostratigraphy and the rugose colonial corals of arctic Alaska (fig. 1) (Armstrong, 1970b, 1972a, 1972b; Armstrong and others, 1971; Mamet and Armstrong, 1972) have resulted in the description and delineation of the stratigraphic ranges of a number of species of cerioid lithostrotionoids (fig. 2). The genera are *Lithostrotionella*, *Thysanophyllum*, and *Sciophyllum*, each of which is characterized by major and minor septa that are discontinuous in the dissepimentarium. The genus *Lithostrotion* Fleming, whose major and minor septa are continuous through the dissepimentarium, is represented by five species of fasiculate *Lithostrotion*, subgenus *Siphonodendron*, and only one known species of cerioid *Lithostrotion* Fleming. *Lithostrotion reiseri* n. sp. is of interest not only because it is cerioid, but also because it can be readily recognized in the field by its continuous major and minor septa. In the area of its known occurrence in the central and eastern Brooks Range, it is an index fossil to zones 12-13 (Meramec) of the Lisburne Group (fig. 3).

The stratigraphic distribution of *Lithostrotion reiseri* n. sp. together with other known species of colonial rugose corals and B. L. Mamet's microfossil zonation in the Lisburne Group are shown in figure 2.

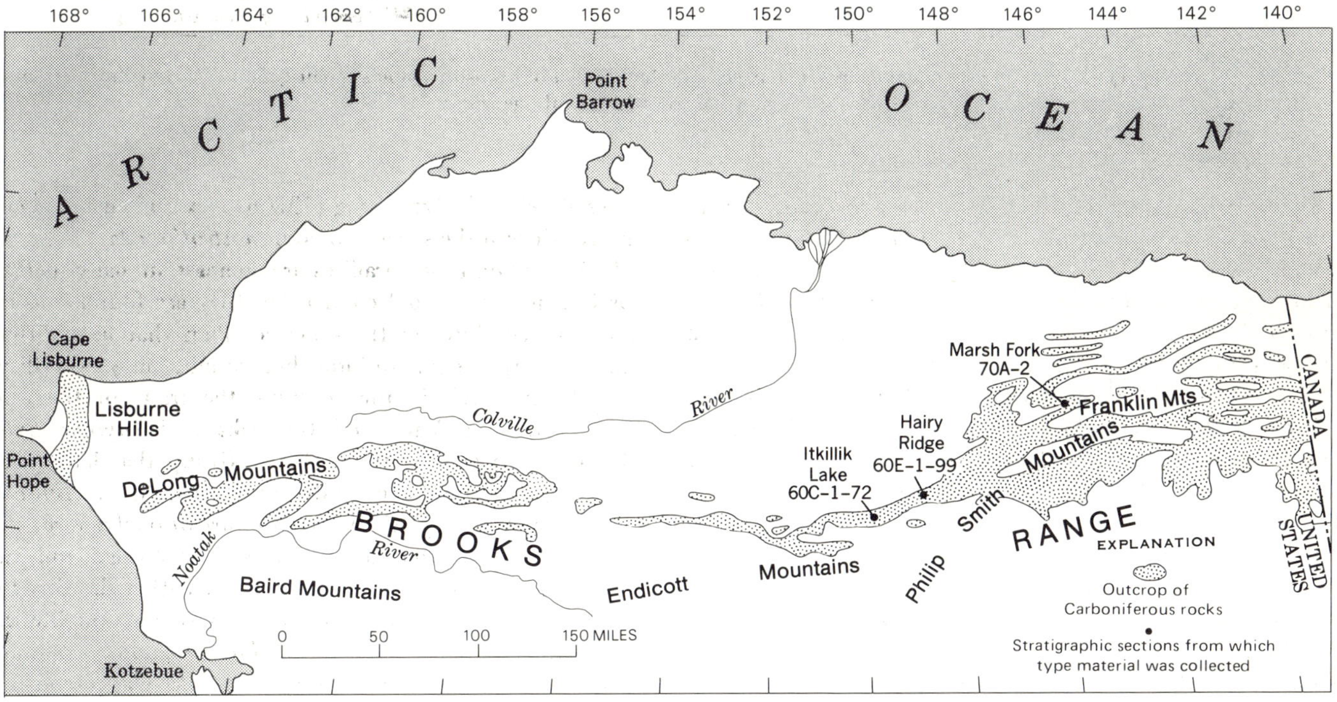

Figure 1.—Map of arctic Alaska, showing generalized locations of Carboniferous rock outcrops and of the type material for *Lithostrotion reiseri* n. sp.

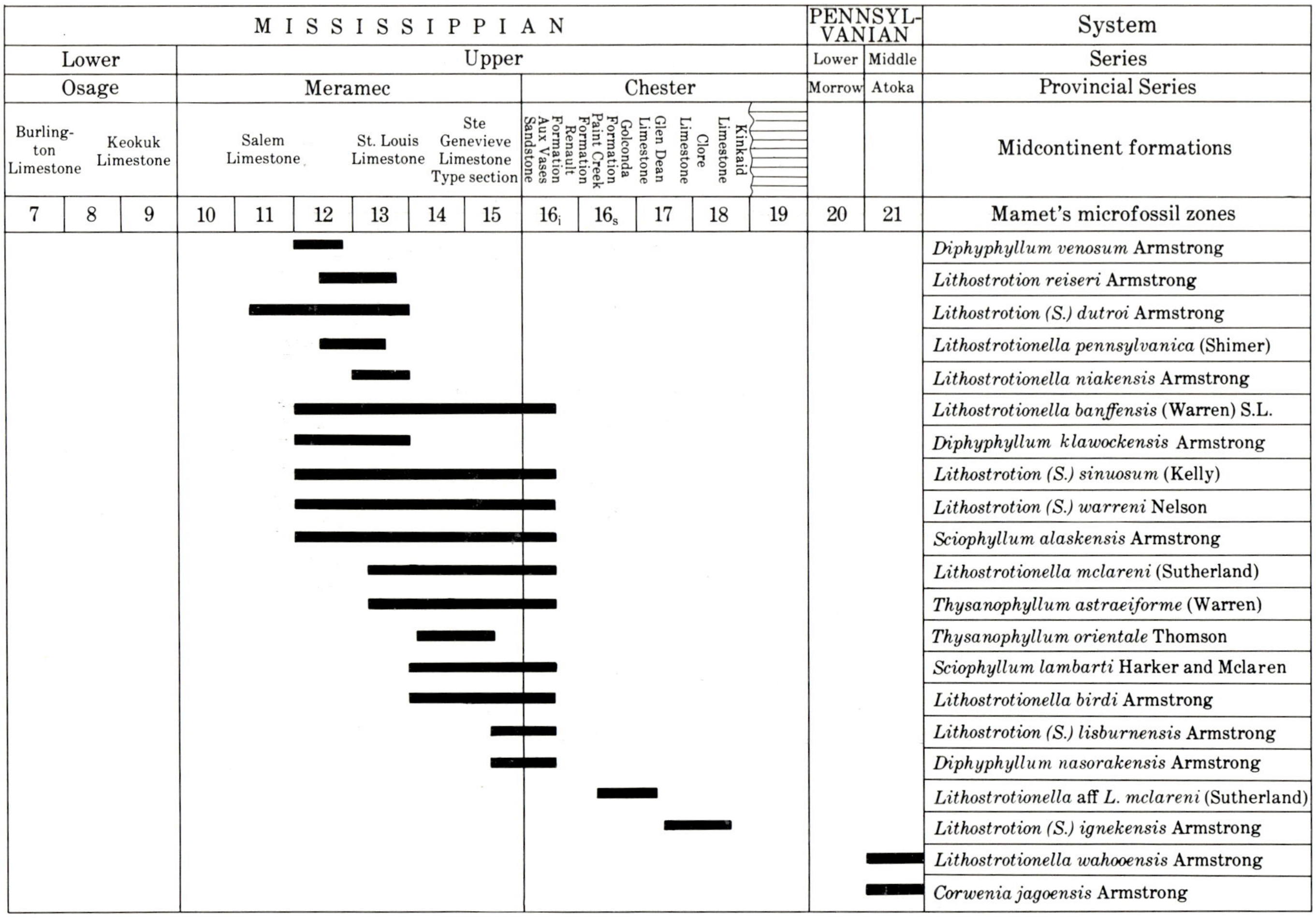

Figure 2.—Stratigraphic distribution of *Lithostrotion reiseri* n. sp. and other species of lithostrotionoids in The Lisburne Group. Zones are based on B. L. Mamet's microfossil-assemblage zones.

Kelly (1942) recognized that all the cerioid corals studied to that date which were considered to be *Lithostrotion* Fleming from the western United States and Canada, had discontinuous major septa in the dissepimentarium and were, in fact, *Lithostrotionella* Yabe and Hayasaka. Subsequent studies by Armstrong (1962, 1970a, 1970b, 1972a, 1972b), Sutherland (1958), Nelson (1960), Bamber (1966), Macqueen and Bamber (1967, 1968), Sando, Mamet, and Dutro (1969), Stensaas and Langenheim (1960), Langenheim and Tischler (1960), Sando (1960, 1963, 1969), Easton, Sanders, Knight, and Miller (1958), Bowsher (1961), Easton and Gutschick (1953), and Parks (1951) have failed to reveal cerioid corals from the North American Mississippian that can be placed without equivocation in the genus *Lithostrotion*. Lambe (1901) described a form, *Lithostrotion macouni*, which has small corallites about 2 to 3 mm in diameter, in which the majority of septa are continuous. Sutherland (1958, p. 94) believed the species to be a true *Lithostrotion*, but Nelson (1960, p. 122) stated, "The species is questionably referred to *Lithostrotion* because of the sublonsdaleoid dissepimentarium which sometimes develops." Armstrong (1970b) reexamined the syntype and considered the species to be *Lithostrotionella*.

Lithostrotion-type corallites are common in many species of corals that have cerioid coralla, but they are found in association with corallites in the same corallum that have differing generic morphology. An individual corallite may even display at different levels in the corallum the traits of the genera *Lithostrotionella* Yabe and Hayasaka and *Thysanophyllum* Thomson. Species of the Lisburne Group that have generic polymorphism in the corallites of the coralla are *Lithostrotionella mclareni* (Sutherland), *Lithostrotionella birdi* Armstrong, *Lithostrotionella niakensis* Armstrong, and *Sciophyllum lambarti* Harker and McLaren. Within the first three of these species, generally, the majority of the corallites have the characteristics of the genus *Lithostrotion*. These three species also display some corallites that have continuous major and minor septa through the dissepimentarium. Other corallites have the morphology of *Thysanophyllum*.

Lithostrotion reiseri n. sp., in contrast to all other known species of cerioid Mississippian corals in western North Amer-

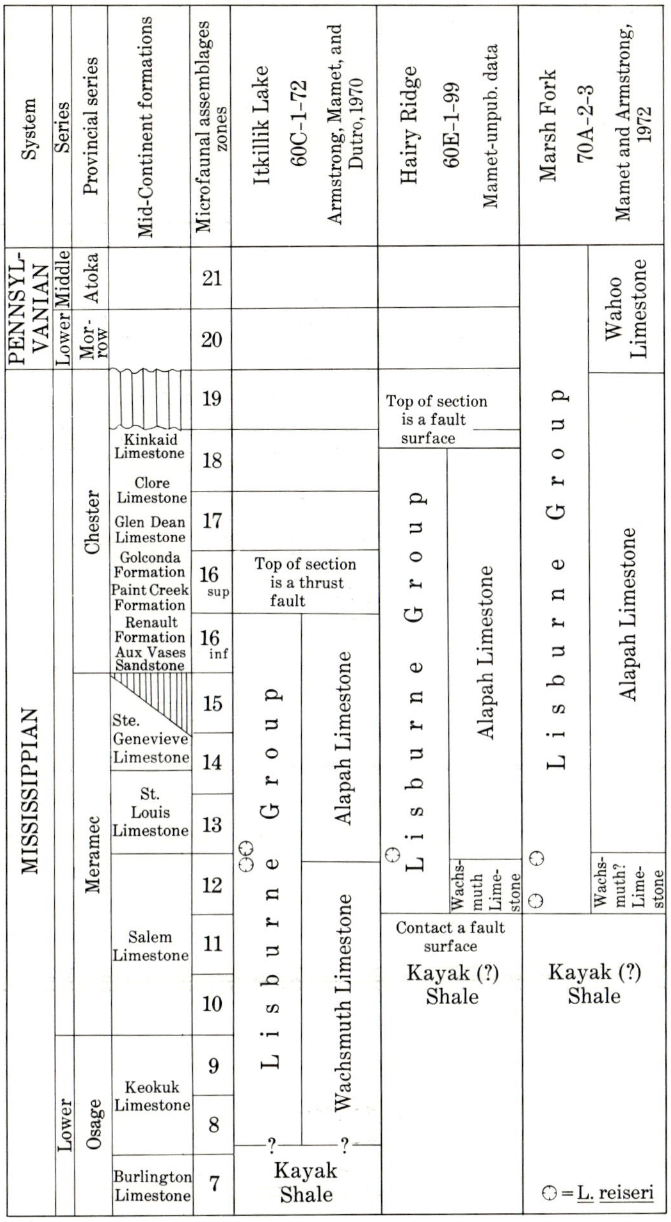

Figure 3.—Correlation chart for sections 60C–1–72, Itkillik Lake; 60E-1-99, Hairy Ridge; and 70A-2, Marsh Fork.

ica, has corallites with continuous septa in the dissepimentarium in all the corallites of the corallum. The corallites average about 7 mm in diameter and are relatively uniform in their internal structures. The corallite diameters and the number of major septa in *Lithostrotion reiseri* n. sp. are shown on figure 4.

Acknowledgments.—I wish to express my appreciation to Hillard Reiser, the party chief during the summers of 1969, 1970, and 1971, for his generosity in supporting my coral collecting and stratigraphic studies of the Lisburne Group. I wish to thank the Naval Arctic Research Laboratory (Barrow), Office of Naval Research, for their logistical support of field work in the summers of 1969–1971. Large collections of corals, Foraminifera, and thin sections used in this study were collected by Shell Oil Co. geologists in 1959–1964. The collections I made in 1964 while employed by the company were given to the U.S. Geological Survey. Appreciation is extended to R. C. McAdams and G. E. Burton, vice presidents of Shell Oil Co. Dr. Bernard L. Mamet, of the Université de Montreal, kindly examined all the petrographic thin sections and made the microfossil and zone determinations used in this study. The photographs were made by Kenji Sakamoto, and the thin sections were made by Robert Shely and R. W. Hershiser, all of the U.S. Geological Survey.

SYSTEMATIC PALEONTOLOGY

Phylum COELENTERATA

Class ANTHOZOA

Order RUGOSA Milne-Edwards and Haime, 1850

Family LITHOSTROTIONIDAE d'Orbigny, 1851

Genus LITHOSTROTION Fleming, 1828

Lithostrotion reiseri n. sp.

Figures 5–7

Material.—The material and specimens available for study are shown in Table 1.

Description.—The holotype USNM 161095 (fig. 5*a*, *b*, *d*, *e*; 6*b*, *c*) is a cerioid corallum. In transverse section, corallites are

Table 1.—*Description of materials and specimens available for study*

Stratigraphic section No.	USNM No.	Size of corallite fragment collected (cm)	Quantity and type of thin sections and number of corallites			
			Transverse	Corallites	Longitudinal	Corallites
60C-25+22B	161095......	9 by 9 by 12	6	190	6	45
60C-28	161091......	7 by 7 by 10	4	140	2	25
60C-29A	161092......	7 by 7 by 10	1	35	3	27
60C-29B	161093......	7 by 7 by 10	1	18	2	20
60E-67+2	161094......	5 by 8 by 9	2	55	3	25
70A-2+1220D	161096......	8 by 9 by 10	1	95	1	15
70A-2+1220F	161097......	8 by 10 by 10	1	77	1	14

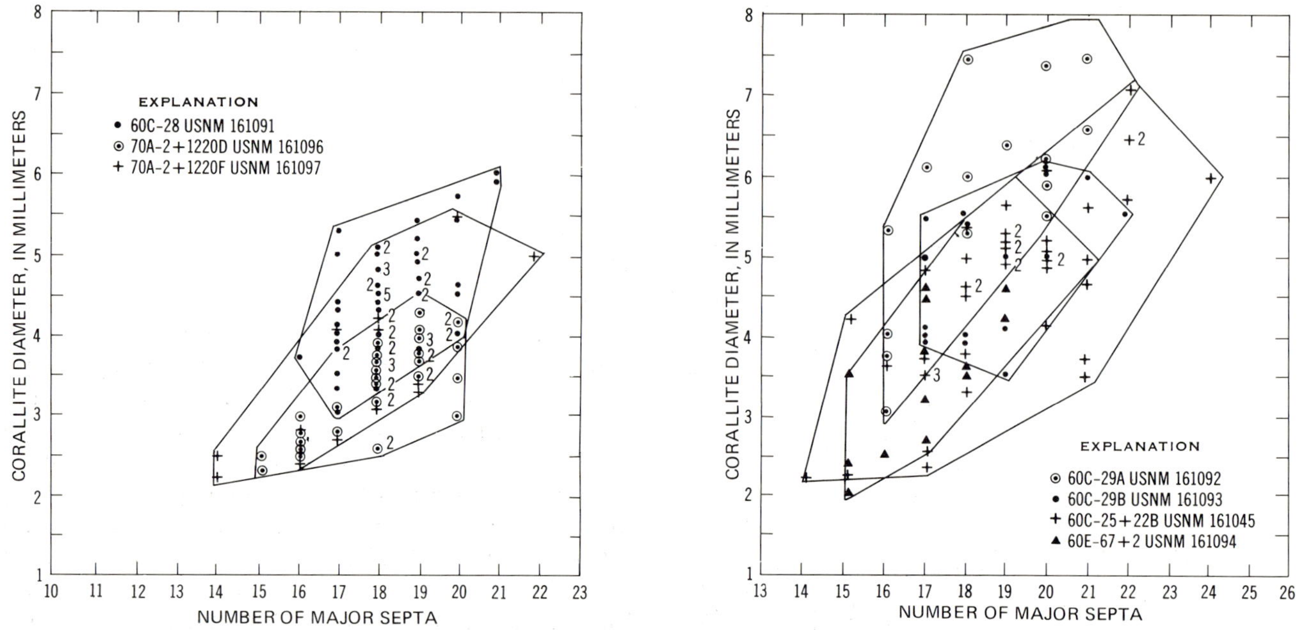

Figure 4.—Graphs showing corallite diameter and number of major septa in *Lithostrotion reiseri* n. sp. Each unnumbered symbol represents a single corallite; if more than one corallite shows the same diameter and number of septa, the number of similar corallites is shown.

2.2 to 7.2 mm in diameter and have 14 to 24 long major septa that are continuous through the dissepimentarium. The dissepiments are 0.03 to 0.05 mm wide in the dissepimentarium. Within the tabularium, the major septa are dilated, 0.25 to 0.35 mm thick at the tabularium wall, and taper gradually to their distal ends. Minor septa are well developed, long, and continuous through the dissepimentarium and extend 0.2 to 0.35 mm into the tabularium. The counter septa and, in some specimens, the cardinal septa are continuous with the columella, which is formed by the dilation of the axial end of the counter septum. Other major septa are generally withdrawn from the axial region, except as ridges on the upper surfaces of the tabulae, where the major septa fuse with the columella. The columella is oval in shape and may be from 0.6 mm long and 0.3 mm wide to 1.4 mm long and 0.8 mm wide.

The dissepiments are arranged in a herringbone pattern. Microstructure is well preserved. The common corallite wall is about 0.2 mm thick, has a dark central band about 0.02 to 0.03 mm thick, is formed of calcite deposited at right angles to the wall (fig. 5*e*), and can be described as fibrous. The major and minor septa have a very different microstructure from the walls, and the junction of the septa with the wall is distinct. The septal microstructure has been altered by the growth of calcite grains but appears to have been trabecular. Longitudinal thin sections (figs. 5*d*, 6*c*) show that the tabulae and dissepiments are thin, only about 0.02 to 0.03 mm thick, and formed by interlocking calcite crystals less than 5μ in size.

In transverse section, the dissepimentarium is formed by three to six rows of globose dissepiments typically 0.5 by 0.5 mm as seen in longitudinal sections. The tabulae are generally incomplete and can be divided into an inner and outer series of tabellae. The series next to the dissepiments may be flat or have a slope of 35°, and the inner series has a slope of 15° to 25° (figs. 5*d*; 6*b*, *c*). The columella is well developed and persistent. The inner tabellae generally are not strongly arched upwards near the columella.

Paratype USNM 161091 (fig. 6*d*, *e*, *f*) differs from the holotype by having corallites that show less variation in size, 3 to 6 mm in diameter with 16 to 21 major septa. Again, all the major and minor septa are continuous through the dissepimentarium. Paratypes USNM 161092 and 161093 are very similar to the holotype (fig. 5*c*; fig. 6*a*; fig. 7*c*, *d*). Paratype USNM 161094 (fig. 7*b*) is also similar to the holotype except that the major septa are not so strongly dilated in the tabularium.

The specimens USNM 161096 and 161097 (fig. 7*c*, *d*, and *a*, *g*, respectively) from the Franklin Mountains are characterized by weakly dilated septa and corallites of smaller diameter than those of the holotype.

Remarks.—*Lithostrotion reiseri* n. sp. shows close affinities to a group of Eurasian cerioid *Lithostrotion*. The Scottish species *L. clavaticum* Thomson as described by Hill (1939, p. 178) is very similar to the arctic species. *L. clavaticum* in

Figure 5.—*Lithostrotion reiseri* n. sp., all from Itkillik Lake section, 60C-1-72.

a transverse section; *b*, longitudinal section, × 3, holotype, USNM 161095.

c, transverse section, × 3, paratype, USNM 161093.

d, longitudinal section; *e*, transverse section, × 9, holotype, USNM 161095.

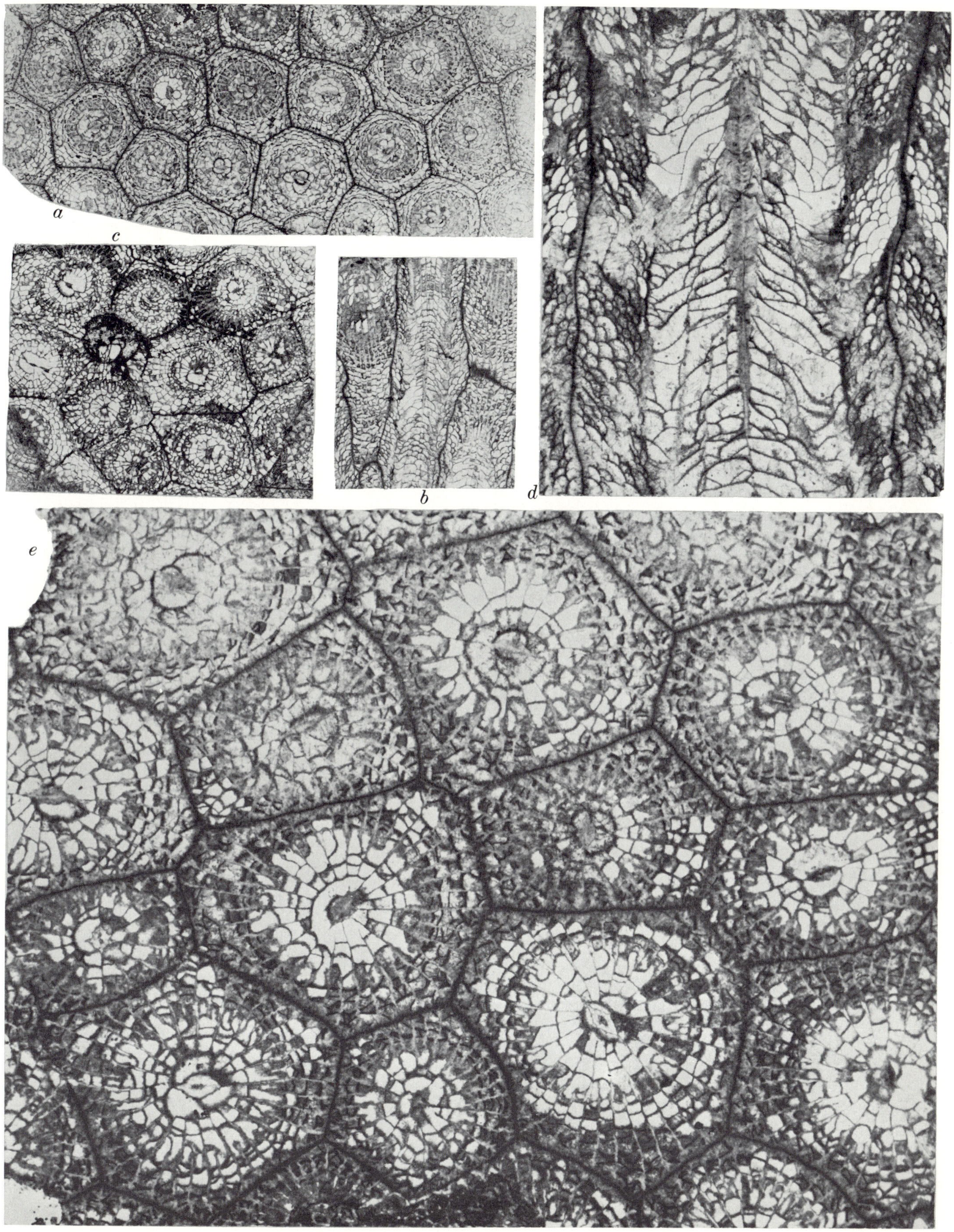

Figure 5.

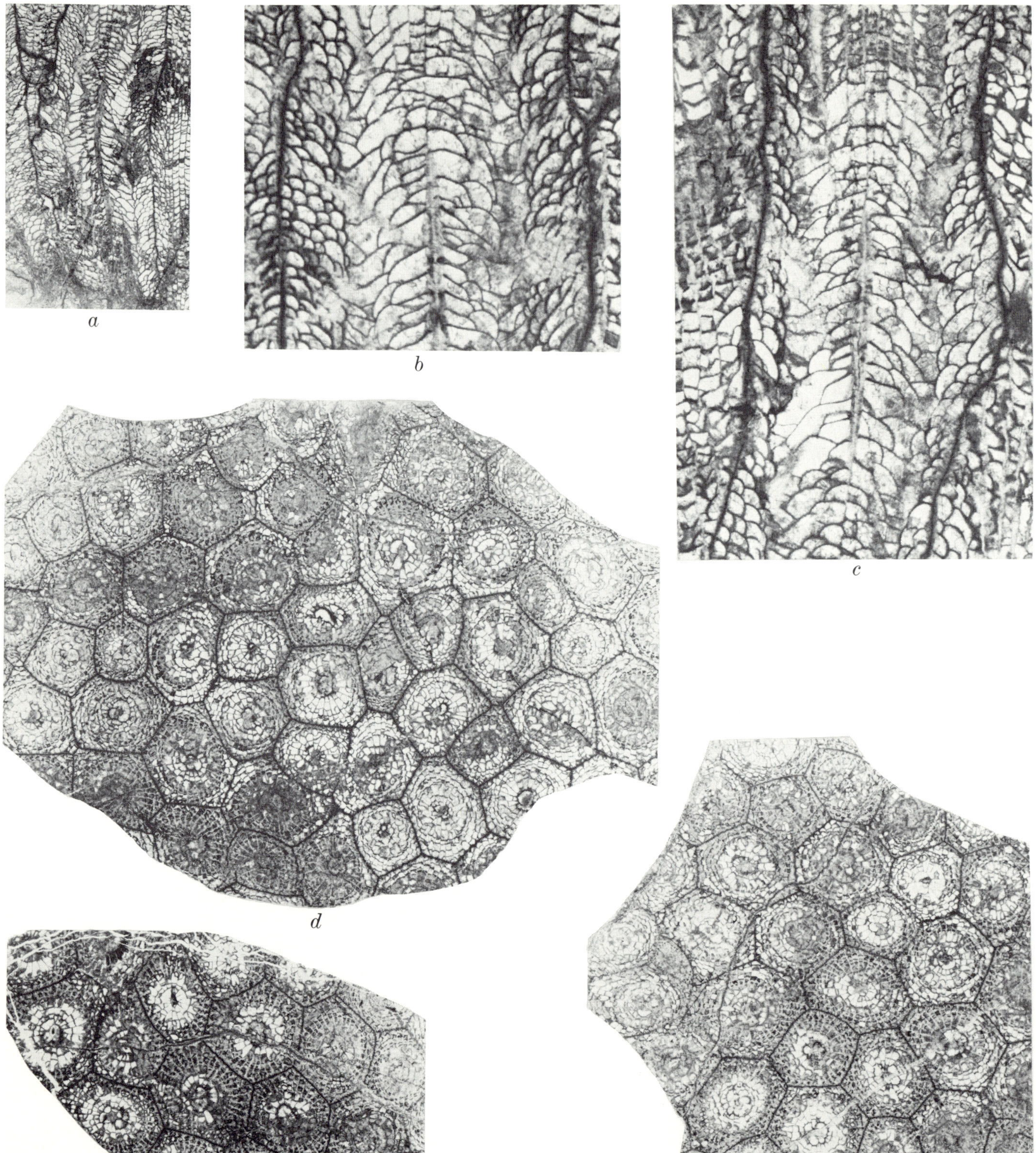

Figure 6.

Figure 6.—*Lithostrotion reiseri* n. sp., all from Itkillik Lake section, 60C-1-72.
a, longitudinal section, X 3, paratype, USNM 161093.
b, c, longitudinal sections, X 9, holotype, USNM 161095.
d, e, f, transverse sections, X 3, paratype, USNM 161091.

contrast to *L. reiseri* has longer major septa and generally complete tabulae. Yü (1933, p. 89–93) described two species of lower Carboniferous corals from China that are also close to *L. reiseri*. They have similar corallite diameters, but *Lithostrotion portlocki* Edwards and Haime, var. *depasophylloides* Yü has only 14 to 15 long major septa and a wider dissepimentarium. *Lithostrotion planocystatum* Yü also has only 13 to 15 major septa, a much wider dissepimentarium, and longer septa. *Lithostrotion basaltiforme* (Phillips) from the Russian Platform as described by Dobroljubova (1958, pl. 28, figs. 2a-2b) shows only a few traits similar to *L. reiseri*. The immature and smaller corallites in the Russian form are somewhat similar in form to the mature corallites in *L. reiseri*. The Russian specimen typically has larger corallites that are 11 to 16 mm in diameter with 22 to 26 major septa.

Occurrence.—The holotype USNM 161095 was collected 970 feet below the top of the Itkillik Lake section 60C-1-72 (fig. 8). Paratype USNM 161091 was collected at 1,190 feet, and specimens USNM 161092 and 161093 were collected at 1,220 feet below the top of the same section. All four of the specimens occur in carbonates that contain a large Foraminifera fauna of Meramec (zone 12-13) age (Armstrong and others, 1970). Shell Oil Co.'s stratigraphic section of the Lisburne Group, "Hairy Ridge, 60E-1-99," measured by Richard Emmons, is about 30 miles northeast of the Itkillik Lake section, near the Sagavanirktok River (fig. 9), and has yielded paratype USNM 161094. This specimen was collected about 2,070 feet below the top of the Lisburne Group in limestones that have a rich microfauna of Meramec (zone 12-13) age. Paratypes USNM 161096 and 161097 were collected 1,220 feet above the base of section 70A-2 (Mamet and Armstrong, 1972) in zone 12-13 of the Wachsmuth(?) Limestone. This section is near the junction of Marsh Fork and the Canning River in the Franklin Mountains (fig. 10).

The specimens available for study have been found only in beds associated with a microfauna of Meramec age (zone 12-13). The species has not been found west of the Itkillik River. Extensive coral collections that J. Thomas Dutro and I made from the Lisburne Group of the DeLong Mountains and the Lisburne Hills do not contain *Lithostrotion reiseri* n. sp.

REFERENCES CITED

Armstrong, A. K., 1962, Stratigraphy and paleontology of the Mississippian system in southwestern New Mexico and adjacent southeastern Arizona: New Mexico Bur. Mines and Mineral Resources Mem. 8, 99 p., 12 pls.

——1970a, Mississippian rugose corals, Peratrovich Formation, west coast of Prince of Wales Island, southeastern Alaska: U.S. Geol. Survey Prof. Paper 534, 43 p., 13 pls., 30 figs.

——1970b, Carbonate facies and the lithostrotionid corals of the Mississippian Kogruk Formation, DeLong Mountains, northwestern Alaska: U.S. Geol. Survey Prof. Paper 664, 38 p., 14 pls., 37 figs.

——1972a, Biostratigraphy of Mississippian lithostrotionoid corals, Lisburne Group, Arctic Alaska: U.S. Geol. Survey Prof. Paper 743-A, 28 p.

——1972b, Pennsylvania carbonates, paleoecology and colonial corals, north flank, eastern Brooks Range, Arctic Alaska: U.S. Geol. Survey Prof. Paper 747. [In press]

Armstrong, A. K., Mamet, B. L., and Dutro, J. T., Jr., 1970, Foraminiferal zonation and carbonate facies of the Mississippian and Pennsylvanian Lisburne Group, central and eastern Brooks Range, Alaska: Am. Assoc. Petroleum Geologists Bull., v. 54, no. 5, p. 687–698, 4 figs.

——1971, Lisburne Group, Cape Lewis-Niak Creek, northwestern Alaska, *in* Geological Survey Research 1971: U.S. Geol. Survey Prof. Paper 750-B, p. B23–B34, 9 figs.

Bamber, E. W., 1966, Type lithostrotionid corals from the Mississippian of western Canada: Canada Geol. Survey Bull. 135, 28 p., 6 pls.

Bowsher, A. L., 1961, The stratigraphic occurrence of some Lower Mississippian corals from New Mexico and Missouri: Jour. Paleontology, v. 35, no. 5, p. 955–962.

Dobroljubova, T. A., 1958, Nizhnekamennogol'nye kolonial'nye chetyrokhluchevye korally Russkoi platformy [Lower Carboniferous colonial tetracorals of the Russian Platform]: Akad. Nauk SSSR Paleont. Inst. Trudy, v. 70, 216 p., 38 pls., 34 figs.

Easton, W. H., and Gutschick, R. C., 1953, Corals from the Redwall limestone (Mississippian) of Arizona: Southern California Acad. Sci. Bull., v. 52, pt. 1, p. 1–27.

Easton, W. H., Sanders, J. E., Knight, J. B., and Miller, A. K., 1958, Mississippian fauna in northwestern Sonora, Mexico: Smithsonian Misc. Colln., v. 119, no. 3, 87 p.

Hill, Dorothy, 1939, A monograph on the Carboniferous rugose corals of Scotland, pt. 2: Palaeontographical Soc. London, 213 p., 11 pls.

Kelly, W. A., 1942, Lithostrotiontidae in the Rocky Mountains: Jour. Paleontology, v. 16, no. 3, p. 351–361, pls. 50, 51, 1 text fig.

Lambe, L. M., 1901, A revision of the genera and species of Canadian Paleozoic corals; the Madreporaria Aporosa and the Madreporaria Rugosa: Canada Geol. Survey, Contr. Canadian Palaeontology, v. 4, pt. 2, p. 97–197.

Langenheim, R. L., Jr., and Tischler, Herbert, 1960, Mississippian and Devonian paleontology and stratigraphy, Quartz Spring area, Inyo County, California: California Univ. Pubs. Geol. Sci., v. 38, no. 2, p. 89–150.

Macqueen, R. W., and Bamber, E. W., 1967, Stratigraphy of Banff Formation and lower Rundle Group (Mississippian), southwestern Alberta: Canada Geol. Survey Paper 67–47, 37 p., 3 pls., 9 figs.

——1968, Stratigraphy and facies relationships of the Upper Mississippian Mount Head Formation, Rocky Mountains and foothills, southwestern Alberta: Canadian Petroleum Geology Bull., v. 16, no. 3, p. 225–287, 11 figs.

Mamet, B. L., and Armstrong, A. K., 1972, Lisburne Group, Franklin and Romanzof Mountains, northeastern Alaska, *in* Geological Survey Research 1972: U.S. Geol. Survey Prof. Paper 800–C, p. C127–C144.

Nelson, S. J., 1960, Mississippian lithostrotionid zones of the southern Canadian Rocky Mountains: Jour. Paleontology, v. 34, no. 1, p. 107–125, pls. 21–25, 3 text figs.

Parks, J. M., 1951, Corals from the Brazer Formation (Mississippian) of northern Utah: Jour. Paleontology, v. 25, no. 2, p. 171–186, pls. 29–33, 3 text figs.

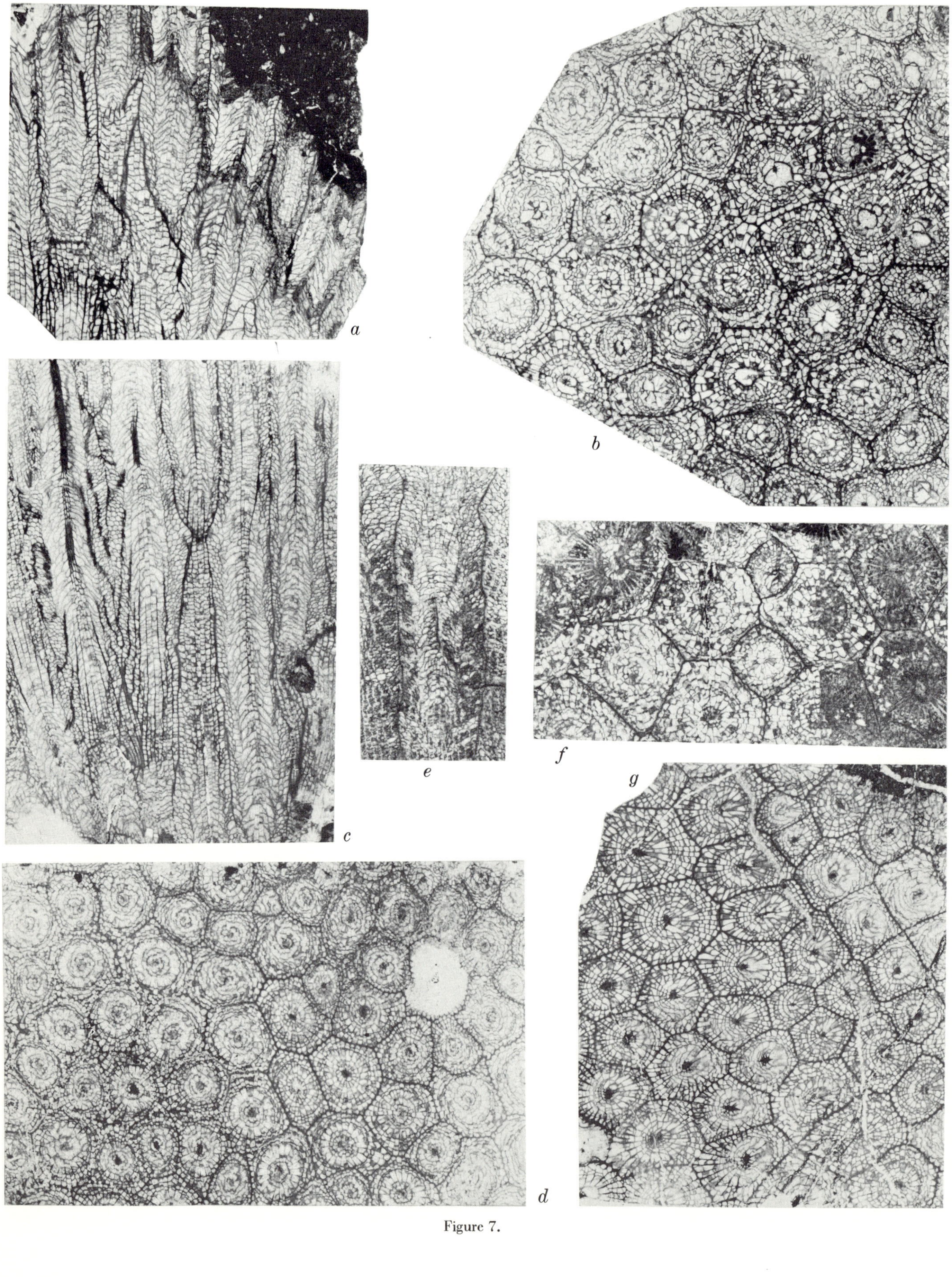

Figure 7.

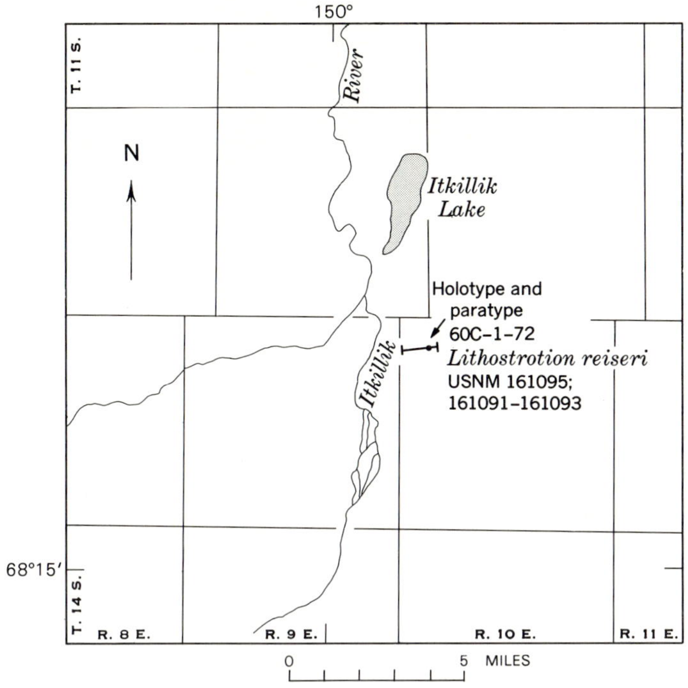

Figure 8.—Map of Itkillik Lake section 60C-1-72, showing collection localities of the holotype and paratypes of *Lithostrotion reiseri* n. sp.

Sando, W. J., 1960, Corals from well cores of Madison group, Williston basin [Montana]: U.S. Geol. Survey Bull. 1071-F, p. 157–190 [1961].

—— 1963, New species of colonial rugose corals from the Mississippian of northern Arizona: Jour. Paleontology, v. 37, no. 5, p. 1074–1079, pls. 145, 146.

—— 1969, Corals, *in* McKee, E. D., and Gutschick, R. C., eds., History of Redwall Limestone in northern Arizona: Geol. Soc. America Mem. 114, p. 257–342, pls. 29–40.

Sando, W. J., Mamet, B. L., and Dutro, J. T., Jr., 1969, Carboniferous megafaunal and microfaunal zonation in the northern Cordillera of the United States: U.S. Geol. Survey Prof. Paper 613–E, 29 p., 7 figs.

Stensaas, L. J., and Langenheim, R. L., Jr., 1960, Rugose corals from the Lower Mississippian Joana Limestone of Nevada: Jour. Paleontology, v. 34, no. 1, p. 179–188, 10 figs.

Sutherland, P. K., 1958, Carboniferous stratigraphy and rugose coral faunas of northeastern British Columbia: Canada Geol. Survey Mem. 295, 177 p., 33 pls., 4 figs.

Yü, C. C., 1933, Lower Carboniferous corals of China: China Geol. Survey, Palaeontologica Sinica, ser. B, v. 12, pt. 3, 211 p., 24 pls.

Figure 7.—*Lithostrotion reiseri* n. sp. *a, c, d, g*, from Marsh Fork section 70A-2; *b*, from Hairy Ridge section 60E-1-99; and *e, f*, from Itkillik Lake section 60C-1-72.

a, g, longitudinal and transverse sections, × 3, paratypes, USNM 161097.

b, transverse section, × 3, paratype, USNM 161094.

c, d, longitudinal and transverse thin sections, × 3, paratype, USNM 161096.

e, f, longitudinal and transverse thin sections, × 3, paratype, USNM 161092.

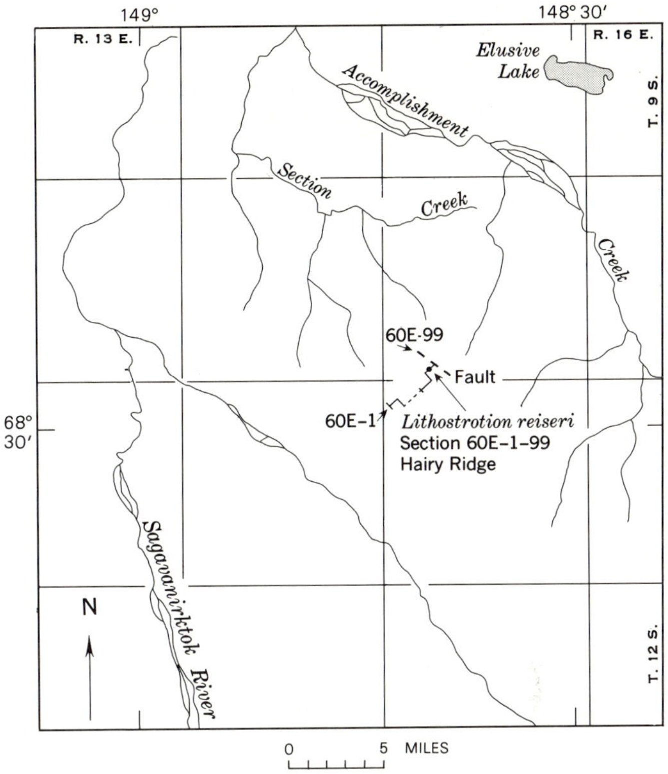

Figure 9.—Map of Hairy Ridge section 60E-1-99, showing collection localities of the paratypes of *Lithostrotion reiseri* n. sp.

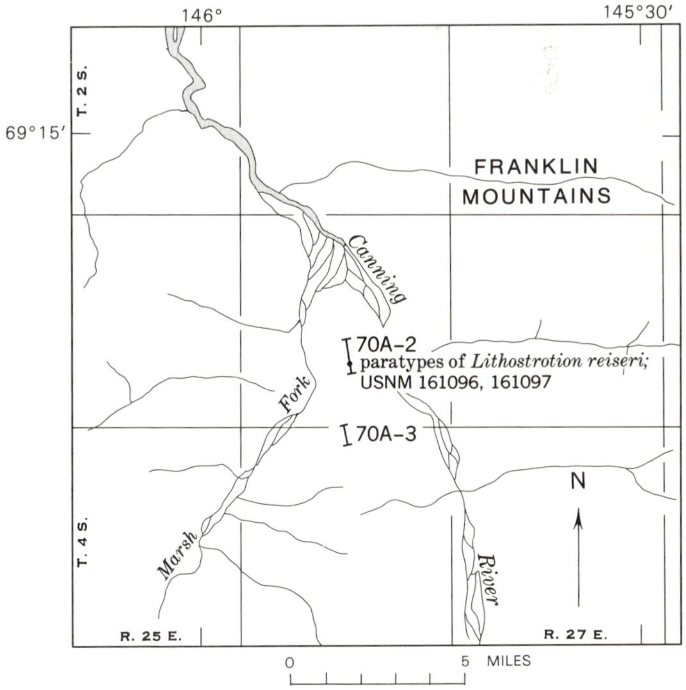

Figure 10.—Map of Marsh Fork section 70A-2, showing collection localities of paratypes of *Lithostrotion reiseri* n. sp.

Jour. Research U.S. Geol. Survey
Vol. 1, No. 2, Mar.—Apr. 1973, p. 147—149

A SECOND SPECIMEN OF PARAHYUS VAGUS MARSH, 1876

By G. EDWARD LEWIS, Denver, Colo.

Abstract.—The occurrence of the second known specimen of *Parahyus vagus*, from the Tepee Trail Formation, Wyoming, is recorded. As the first specimen was reported from the lower Eocene, this second occurrence casts doubt on the supposed age ranges of both *Parahyus* and the Tepee Trail.

PALEONTOLOGY

In 1876 (p. 402), Marsh named and described *Parahyus vagus*, a palaeodont artiodactyl hoofed animal very remotely related to the swine, on the basis of a right mandibular ramal fragment with alveolus of P_2, root-stump of /C, P_{3-4}, and M_{1-3} (Yale Peabody Museum No. 10972) "from the lower Eocene of Wyoming." The purpose of the present report is to record the discovery of the second known specimen of *Parahyus*. It adds nothing to our knowledge of the morphology of the genus because the entire specimen consists of a left mandibular ramal fragment with $P_{3-4}M_{1-3}$ (fig. 1) but no skull or other parts of the skeleton. It is a mirror image of all but the anteriormost, toothless portion of the type of *P. vagus*. The specimen was found by J. D. Love in 1936, collected by me at his request in 1938, and, with pertinent field records, added to the collections of the Yale Peabody Museum where it has since been mislaid or lost and so the specimen is not available to me for comparisons and measurements at this time. Fortunately, I had duplicate photographic prints that have been used for the illustrations in figure 1 of this report.

STRATIGRAPHY AND AGE

I am indebted to J. D. Love for the opportunity to record the discovery of this rare specimen, and for the following information about the locality (oral commun., June 8, 1972): the specimen was found in 1936 in the type section of the Tepee Trail Formation (Love, 1939, p. 74), T. 44 N., R. 104 W., Fremont County, Wyo., on the top of the high river cliffs on the east side of East Fork of the Wind River, 10 feet 8 inches above the base of unit 30 as described in the published type section.

The holotype was collected by J. Heisey for Marsh in 1876, and the tray label reads "Lower Eocene Washakie?, Coryphodon zone, Wyoming, Bitter Creek Station." This usage of the stratigraphic name "Washakie" is the correct, original usage of Hayden (1869, p. 90, with the spelling "Washakee"), who later (1877, p. 181–183) stated that he "named the Washakie * * * which is probably the same as * * * the Wasatch." The usage of Wood and others (1941, p. 36, pl. 1) is a misuse of Hayden's name. No other specimen positively referable to this genus has ever been described.

Love (1939, p. 78) "provisionally correlated * * * the Tepee Trail formation * * * with at least part of the Uinta formation of Upper Eocene age" but stated that "on the basis of the few fragmentary fossils, specific age determinations and long-range correlations are not justified". Wood and others (1941, p. 33, pl. 1) and most writers since 1941 have listed the Tepee Trail as upper Eocene equivalent to the Uinta without the careful reservation of Love's original description. In the field, while the Tepee Trail specimen was still largely in the enclosing rock with the dentition only partly visible, and with the provisional upper Eocene stratigraphic position in mind, I had guessed that the specimen might be referable to the characteristic late Eocene genus *Achaenodon*. When, after Love's report (1939) had gone to press, the Tepee Trail specimen was prepared for study and identification, it cast doubt on the provisional upper Eocene correlation of the Tepee Trail, and also on the supposed lower Eocene stratigraphic position of the type of *Parahyus vagus*, because it was clear that the Tepee Trail specimen could only be a *Parahyus*, very close morphologically to the genotype.

Gazin, in his review of the Eocene Artiodactyla (1955, p. 38, 42–43) argued that (1) he "cannot believe * * * the type * * * described by Marsh as coming from the Lower Eocene of Wyoming" really came from lower Eocene rocks because "*Parahyus vagus* is clearly and in every respect at a stage of development intermediate between Bridger *Helohyus lentus* and * * * Uinta B *Achaenodon insolens*. (2) Moreover, during an intensive field program * * * no further evidence has been discovered of such a form in the" lower Eocene, but (3) he added that "*Parahyus vagus* is apparently, though not necessarily, too advanced for Bridger D * * * ." His first observation is good professional opinion and fully correct, but not a conclusive argument for relative stratigraphic position; all faunas, including today's living animals, show contem-

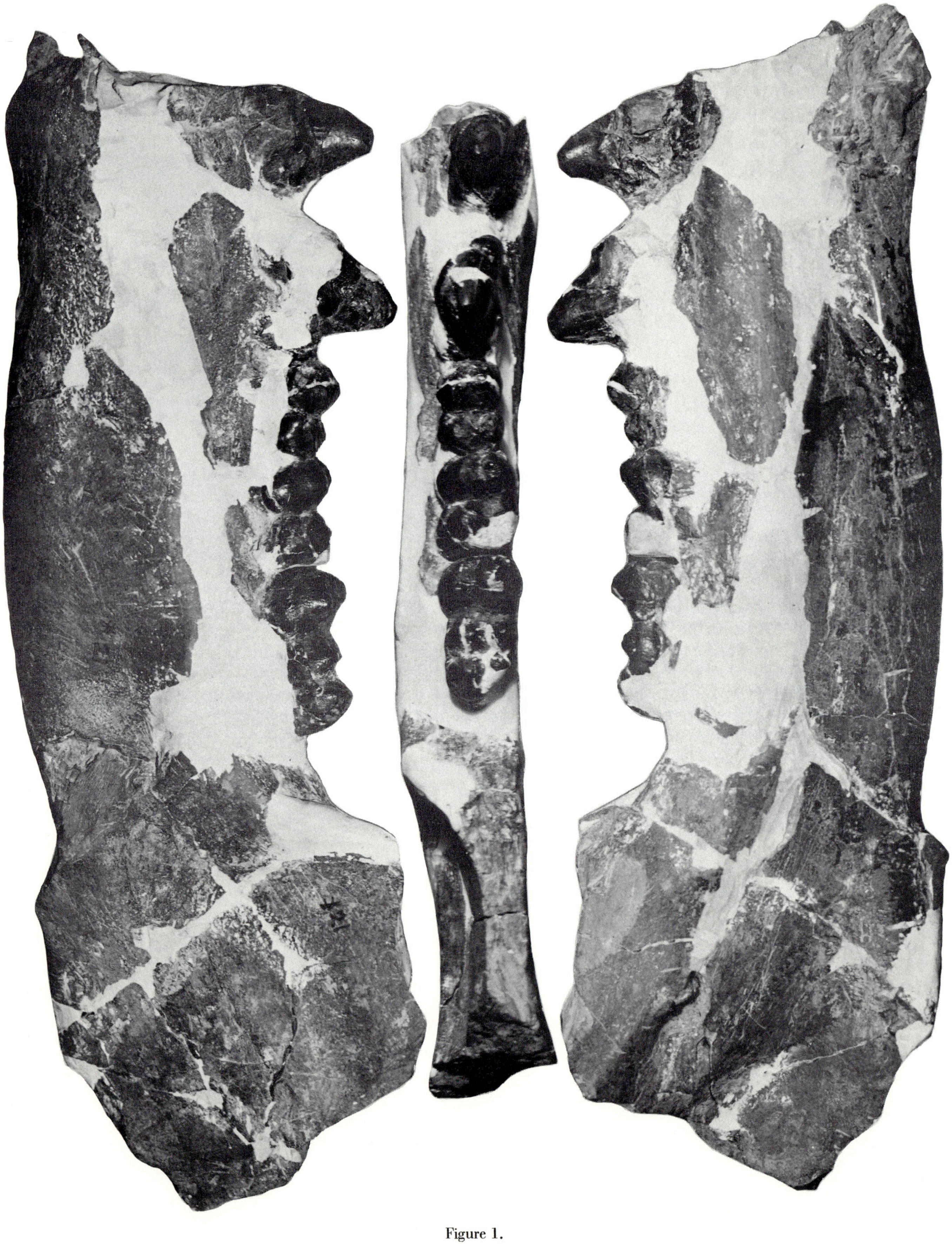

Figure 1.

Figure 1.—Fragment of left mandibular ramus of *Parahyus vagus*, about natural size. Left, labial-buccal view; center, occlusal view; right, lingual view.

porary morphologically primitive and advanced genera. His second observation is correct negative evidence but even more inconclusive because for the 97 years preceding the present report, more intensive field programs in richly fossiliferous middle and upper Eocene rocks have failed to report the positive evidence of upper or middle Eocene specimens of *Parahyus*. His third observation speculates that *Parahyus* might occur in rocks of middle Eocene stratigraphic position; I would concur in this speculation. But Marsh's information is all the direct evidence we have had to the present time.

It seems impossible that the Tepee Trail Formation could be lower Eocene, whether or not the type of *Parahyus vagus* did in fact come from lower Eocene rocks: underlying the Tepee Trail is the Aycross Formation, which has yielded vertebrate fossils of middle Eocene (Bridger fauna) age according to Love (1939, p. 70, 73). Possibly the Tepee Trail and its *Parahyus vagus* are either of post-Aycross middle Eocene age or of late Eocene age as suggested by Love.

The stratigraphic and age ranges of *Parahyus* are still moot, but Love's specimen of *Parahyus vagus* establishes an upper stratigraphic limit for this genus above the lower Eocene. The radiometric age range may not be great: J. D. Obradovich has stated (oral commun., June 15, 1972) that the Tepee Trail cannot be younger than 46 m.y. B.P., so only 3 m.y. separates it from the Wasatch Formation.

REFERENCES CITED

Gazin, C. L., 1955, A review of the upper Eocene Artiodactyla of North America: Smithsonian Misc. Colln., v. 128, no. 8, 96 p.

Hayden, F. V., 1869, Preliminary field report [third annual] of the United States Geological Survey of Colorado and New Mexico: Washington, U.S. Govt. Printing Office, 155 p.

—— 1877, Notes on some artesian borings along the line of the Union Pacific Railroad in Wyoming Territory: U.S. Geol. and Geog. Survey Terr. Bull. 3, p. 181–185.

Love, J. D., 1939, Geology along the southern margin of the Absaroka Range, Wyoming: Geol. Soc. America Spec. Paper 20, 134 p.

Marsh, O. C., 1876, Notice of new Tertiary mammals, V: Am. Jour. Sci., ser. 3, v. 12, p. 401–404.

Wood, H. E., 2d, Chaney, R. W., Clark, John, Colbert, E. H., Jepsen, G. L., Reeside, J. B., Jr., and Stock, Chester, 1941, Nomenclature and correlation of the North American continental Tertiary: Geo' Soc. America Bull., v. 52, no. 1, p. 1–48.

Jour. Research U.S. Geol. Survey
Vol. 1, No. 2, Mar.—Apr. 1973, p. 151—155

THE CONCEPT OF GROWTH AND MATURITY OF ORE-STAGE PYRITE IN ROLL-TYPE URANIUM DEPOSITS

By C. G. WARREN[1] and H. C. GRANGER,
Fort Collins, Colo., Denver, Colo.

Abstract.—Roll-type uranium deposits contain both ore-stage pyrite and preore or diagenetic pyrite that was present in the host rock before the deposits began to form. Ore-stage pyrite forms as the result of redistribution and accretion from the preore pyrite. Accretion of the ore-stage pyrite seems to be governed by natural laws that limit its concentration to only a few times the concentration of the preore pyrite. Accumulations of ore-stage pyrite build up along the leading edge of a supergene oxidation zone which spreads through the host rocks, literally pushing the ore deposits ahead of it. The ore-stage pyrite probably progresses much as a wave that first grows to a nearly fixed amplitude and thereafter is steadily maintained as the mature deposit continues to advance.

Roll-type uranium deposits have now been recognized and studied for more than a decade but, although much is known about their size, shape, geologic setting, element distribution, and mineralogy, some aspects of their genesis remain unknown or clouded in controversy. Pyrite and sparse marcasite are always associated with the uranium minerals in these deposits, and it is the chemical and (or) isotopic behavior of iron and sulfur that have yielded the most definitive information about the depositional geochemistry and genesis of roll-type deposits. In this paper we examine some additional implications that are provided by the distribution pattern of the sulfide minerals, which will hereafter be referred to collectively as pyrite.

A concept of maturity followed by a steady-state process in the genesis of roll-type uranium deposits has been developed through a series of earlier papers (Granger and Warren, 1969; Warren, 1971, 1972) but may have been inadequately explained and justified. One purpose of this paper, therefore, is to show how the pyrite accumulations associated with roll-type deposits might have evolved. The exact chemical or biogenic reactions involved do not have to be specified, because this concept deals largely with the quantitative efficiency of the process and not with details of the process itself.

Roll-type uranium deposits now constitute one of the world's principal resources of uranium ore and are known to occur in Wyoming (Harshman, 1962, 1966, 1970; Armstrong, 1970; Melin, 1964, 1969; King and Austin, 1966; Davis, 1969; Bailey, 1969), Texas (Eargle and Weeks, 1968; Harshman, 1970), New Mexico (Shawe and Granger, 1965), and at several places in the Soviet Union (Germanov, 1960; Lisitsyn and Kuznetsova, 1967; Kholodov and others, 1961; Kashirtseva, 1964). Although rather thorough descriptions and speculation regarding the genesis of the deposits are included in the cited reports, it may be well to review, briefly, the salient features common to most of the deposits.

[1] Colorado State University.

GENERAL DESCRIPTION OF DEPOSITS

With very few exceptions (Kholodov and others, 1961) the host rocks are gently dipping, permeable, fluvial sandstone strata underlain and overlain by less permeable strata (fig. 1). Where unaltered, they typically contain small quantities of organic matter that may range from finely disseminated kerogenlike material to coaly tree limbs, trunks, and other fragmental plant fossils. At least some of the deposits of the U.S.S.R. are said to be in strata that contain petroleum or petroleum residues.

Before the deposits began to develop, the host rocks invariably contained from a few tenths percent to 2 percent disseminated pyrite. This pyrite is presumed to have formed during diagenesis by biogenic bacterial reduction of sulfate to sulfide species. Indeed, only a biogenic process seems adequate

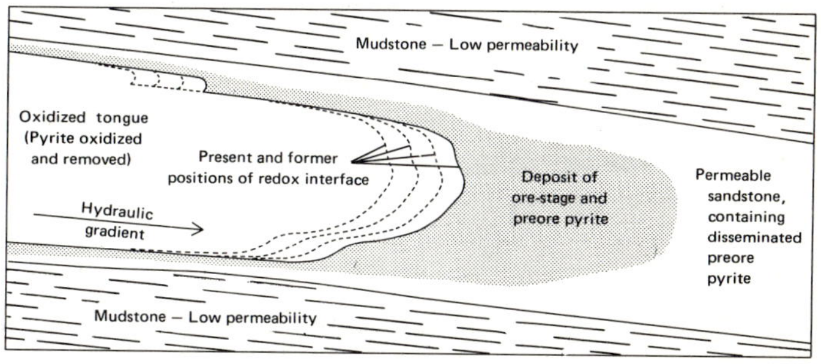

Figure 1.—Some characteristics of a roll-type deposit.

to explain thoroughly disseminated sulfide minerals produced solely at low temperature during diagenesis of a sedimentary rock. Although this pyrite may make up only a small part of the unaltered host rock, its importance to the processes that form roll-type uranium deposits should not be underestimated.

The uranium deposits are all closely associated with an altered zone within the host rocks. This is typically a large, irregular tongue-shaped mass in which most of the original pyrite has been destroyed by oxidation. The "base" or updip part of the tongue is now exposed at the surface or can be inferred to have once cropped out—a characteristic that establishes an inferential relation between the oxidized rock and oxygen-rich meteoric waters.

An envelope of anomalously pyritic rock virtually encloses each oxidized tongue like a huge sack (fig. 1). This envelope can range in thickness from a few inches along the upper and lower surfaces of the tongue to 200 feet along the bordering edges of the tongue. Much of the pyritic envelope is also uraniferous, and uranium ore bodies are distributed within the thicker parts of the envelope along the margins or "front" of each tongue, where the surface of the tongue—the redox interface—rolls sharply across the layers of stratification.

Oxidation of the host rock within the tongue (in terms of the oxidation of pyrite) was presumably caused by an extension of the weathering process to considerable depth through downward percolation of oxygen-bearing meteoric water. Ore-stage minerals in the envelope surrounding the tongue are believed to have migrated in these waters by means of a continuous cyclic process of dissolving and then reforming a short distance down the hydraulic gradient. The prevailing opinion is that the ore body accumulated and migrated along the leading edges of the tongue as it expanded into the host rocks.

Most tongues are only a few feet to a few tens of feet thick, but they can have an areal extent measurable in square miles. If we assume that the oxidized rock within the tongue once contained pyrite commensurate with the unoxidized, nonuraniferous host rock which contains even the smallest amounts of pyrite, it is obvious that vast amounts of pyrite have been removed from the oxidized tongue. In most places, even near and in uranium ore bodies, the richest representative samples from the pyritic envelope contain only a few times more pyrite than the pristine unoxidized host rock well away from the tongue, and in many places the added secondary pyrite is nearly imperceptible. Definitive data, admittedly, are scanty for rock at some distance from uranium deposits, and there is little reliable information to indicate whether all parts of the roll front (the rounded margins of the tongue) are anomalously pyritic. For this reason we shall direct our appraisal principally to the pyrite associated with the uranium deposits, although presumably pyrite elsewhere along the oxidized envelope follows the same geochemical pattern of genesis and distribution.

The altered tongue once contained more than enough pyrite to account for all the ore-stage pyrite now present; however, the same relation may not hold for other ore-stage components such as uranium and selenium. An intrinsic source within the host rocks seems to be a reasonable assumption for pyrite, but an extrinsic source may provide a better explanation for some of the other ore-stage minerals. The genesis of ore components other than pyrite and related sulfide minerals, however, is not within the scope of this paper.

If the pyrite redistribution process was heterogeneous, varying widely in type or efficiency of reactions from place to place, we might expect to see enormous concentrations of pyrite at some places, contrasted with virtually no anomalous concentration elsewhere. Some controlling mechanism must have operated during redistribution of the pyrite to permit a severalfold concentration but prevent the accumulations from building up until the pore spaces were blocked. The occurrence of generally low-grade accumulations of pyrite along the roll front indicates that only a part of the pyrite removed from the oxidized tongue has been redeposited.

MATURITY AND THE STEADY-STATE CONCEPT

The assumption is, then, that the ore-stage pyrite in the envelope was derived either solely or largely by a redistribution process, while the grade remained fairly constant and seemingly showed no correlation to the size of the oxidized zone; it seems probable that the deposits of ore-stage pyrite first built up to a somewhat uniform size and grade and then continued to move in advance of the oxidized tongue without undergoing significant changes. This implies that throughout most of its active history the advance of the oxidized tongue continually destroyed and lost an amount of pyrite equal to the diagenetic pyrite but figuratively pushed a "bow wave" of redistributed pyrite ahead of it. The distance over which pyrite is anomalously concentrated can be thought of as a cycle. Accordingly, a fundamental concept of roll-type ore formation was proposed by Warren (1971): when the pyrite being oxidized and lost to redeposition in each cycle is equal to the pyrite already present in the rock, the amount of sulfide sulfur in the deposit neither increases nor decreases, but remains constant, cycle after cycle and over extended distances and periods of time. When a deposit first begins to accumulate, the pyrite lost in each cycle must be less than the pyrite originally present in the rock. Although the proportion of pyrite destroyed and lost in each cycle may not change, larger and larger actual quantities of pyrite are lost as the deposit grows in size. When the lost pyrite equals the original pyrite, the deposit may be said to be mature and will maintain this steady state no matter how far it moves. If the efficiency of transfer and redeposition of pyrite remains constant, maturity is inevitable. It is this principle that we will examine further. Speculation on the mechanism(s) of pyrite redistribution must then be compatible with these findings.

We continue to discuss the deposits as if pyrite being oxidized at the roll front were the only source of components for the reconstituted pyrite. The steady-state concept can apply, however, even if the oxidizing solutions should introduce components which can recombine as pyrite. When maturity is reached, in this situation, the total loss of components from oxidized rock must include an amount equal to both the preore pyrite and the introduced material.

Figure 2 illustrates what happens when pyrite is oxidized at the redox interface and some fraction of it is repeatedly

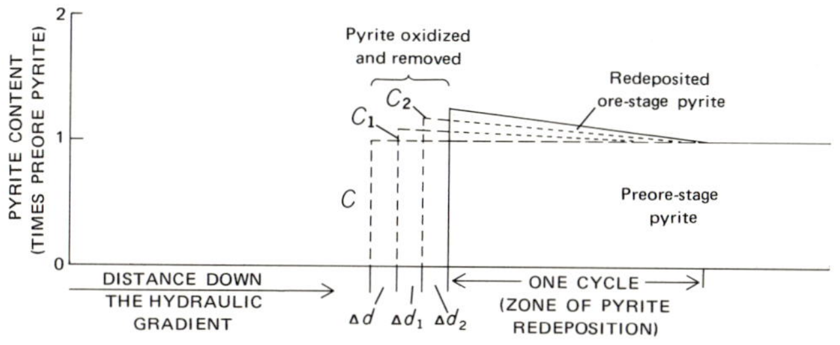

Figure 2.—Graph depicting initial growth stages of ore-stage pyrite in a roll-type deposit. Refer to text for explanation.

transported and redeposited in the ore zone. It depicts the early stages of a process that is 50-percent efficient; that is, as the pyrite is oxidized over a distance Δd, half of it is redeposited and half is lost. Losses can occur either if some components of pyrite become oxidized and lag behind in the oxidized zone or if they become soluble and are swept out of the system. Presumably, the rate at which pyrite is redeposited is a function of the concentrations, in solution, of the active components of pyrite. These concentrations should be greatest just beyond the redox interface and continually diminish as deposition proceeds. Hence, at the inception of a roll, the first pyrite oxidized can be represented graphically (fig. 2) by the rectangle whose area is $C\Delta d$; almost simultaneously, the first pyrite redeposited becomes the flat-lying triangle with vertical leg, C_1. The next tiny advance of the redox interface causes the oxidation of the preore pyrite in $C\Delta d_1$, and also a little of the ore-stage pyrite deposited during the previous step. The pyrite redeposited as a result of the d_1 advance of the redox interface can be represented by the quadrilateral with one side equal to C_2, and which directly overlies the triangular area representing pyrite deposited in the previous step.

At each step the amount of ore-stage pyrite oxidized increases slightly, and the amount of pyrite redeposited increases correspondingly. Concurrently, the pyrite lost during each step increases, and eventually (fig. 3*A*) the amount of pyrite lost is virtually equal to the preore pyrite being oxidized. The deposit can then be said to have attained maturity. Subsequently, as the redox interface continues further, the amount of ore-stage pyrite oxidized equals the amount of ore-stage pyrite being redeposited. The mature deposit can be said to move according to a steady-state process. As ore-stage pyrite is removed from one part of the deposit, it is continually replenished by deposition in other parts of the deposit. We are, of course, speaking of equivalent

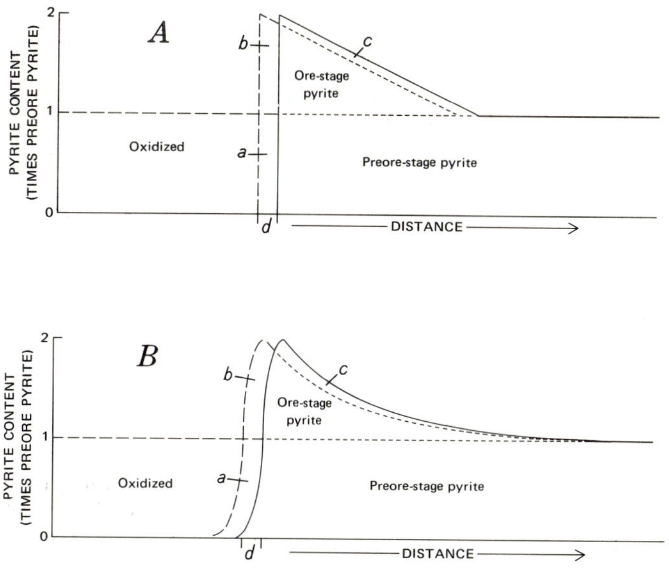

Figure 3.—Graphs depicting ore-stage pyrite cycle in a mature roll-type deposit. Arbitrary efficiency of redeposition is 50 percent. Area *a*, preore pyrite oxidized but not redeposited; area *b*, ore-stage pyrite oxidized; area *c*, redeposited pyrite; area *b* = area *c*. *A*, Representation that must follow from growth pattern depicted schematically by figure 2. *B*, More probable idealized pattern at maturity where pyrite redeposited is related to concentration of components remaining in solution. Efficiency of the process is the ratio between total pyrite redeposited and total pyrite oxidized.

$$\text{Efficiency} = \frac{c}{a+b}, \text{ Substituting } b \text{ for } c,$$

$$= \frac{b}{a+b}, \text{ or}$$

$$= \frac{\text{Maximum ore-stage pyrite}}{\text{Maximum total pyrite}}$$

amounts of oxidized pyrite and transported pyrite, it being immaterial to the process whether a molecule deposited as ore-stage pyrite was previously derived from ore-stage pyrite or preore pyrite.

Efficiency—the ratio of pyrite continually being redeposited to the pyrite dissolved—is a function of the processes involved. If the process is 50-percent efficient, as shown in figures 2 and 3, the maximum (preore plus ore-stage) pyrite content at maturity is double the preore pyrite concentration. If two-thirds of the oxidized pyrite is reprecipitated, a maximum pyrite content three times the preore pyrite content is maintained. If the efficiency is 75 percent, the pyrite buildup is fourfold, and so on. This can be represented by the formula:

$$P_t = P_p/(1-f),$$

where

P_p is the preore pyrite content,

f, or efficiency, is the fraction of pyrite redeposited relative to that dissolved in each cycle, and

P_t is the total pyrite concentration at the redox interface.

The formula merely says that, after maturity is achieved and as the pyrite is continuously dissolved at the redox interface, some fraction of that pyrite will be continuously and commensurately redeposited in advance of the interface. That fraction is f and the amount redeposited is fP_t. The pattern of redistribution of the ore-stage pyrite is immaterial. Derivation of the same formula from a variety of hypothetical patterns of pyrite distribution can be proved mathematically; the principle is shown graphically in figure 2. If the efficiency of the process of dissolution and redeposition remains constant and if the amount of pyrite being dissolved minus the pyrite being redeposited is equal to the preore pyrite, the requirements for a steady-state system are satisfied.

A simplified graphic presentation like figure 2 does not accurately represent the natural situation. For example, figure 2 suggests that the rate of redeposition decreases with distance from the oxidation front. Figure 2 is probably a reasonably valid representation, because the amount of pyrite redeposited is expected to be proportional to the concentration of components remaining in solution. Continued increments as shown in figure 2 ultimately result in a state of maturity that can be represented as in figure 3*A*. This straight-line graphic approach necessitates that the rate of redeposition at maturity (fig. 3*A*), however, remain constant from the redox interface nearly to the tail of the deposit. Such constant rate throughout the deposit, though chemically possible, is obviously improbable, because it implies some significant change in the type, or order, of geochemical reaction between inception (fig. 2) and maturity (fig. 3*A*). Neither does the distribution indicated in figure 3*A* faithfully mimic the pattern of pyrite concentrations actually observed in the deposits. In natural occurrences, the graphed shape of the pyrite concentrations plotted across roll-type deposits is invariably uneven, but such a curve, when smoothed, tends to look much like figure 3*B*. This configuration suggests an exponential or inversely proportional decrease in deposition across the deposits. Nearly all chemical precipitations occur by either first-order or second-order processes and would be expected to produce just such a distribution from a dynamic system as proposed for roll-type ore genesis.

If we imagine each ore-stage sulfur increment as having a curved upper surface in figure 2, the generation of figure 3*B* at maturity is easily visualized. We chose, as first approximations, the representations shown in figures 2 and 3*A* because they can be more readily manipulated geometrically.

The approach to maturity is asymptotic, but for all practical purposes maturity is reached when the redox interface has traveled a relatively short distance. If the process involved has an efficiency of 50 percent, virtual (say, 95 percent) maturity is reached in a distance of three cycles; if it has an 80-percent efficiency, maturity is approximately completed only after the front travels nearly eight cycles. This is illustrated in figure 4, which shows curves generated by the maximum ore-stage pyrite contents during growth to maturity; each curve represents a different efficiency. The greater the efficiency, the longer the time required for the process to attain maturity.

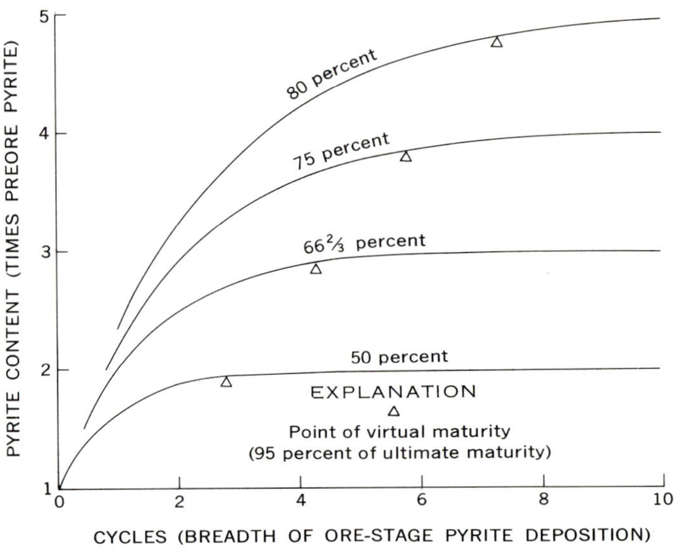

Figure 4.—Growth curves for maximum pyrite content at various efficiencies of redeposition of ore-stage pyrite.

The natural distribution of preore pyrite is never perfectly uniform (fig. 5). Redistribution during the roll-forming process tends to compensate for these variations, however. Any given concentration of pyrite in a deposit must be maintained by a complementary amount of preore pyrite; the effects of local, unusually high or unusually low concentrations of preore pyrite are lost within a few cycles as the redox interface advances, and the amount of ore-stage pyrite is governed by the average preore pyrite content. Highly efficient processes take longer than less efficient processes do to adjust completely to a local fluctuation in the preore pyrite content (fig. 4). On the other hand, the highly efficient process results in the more regular distribution of ore-stage pyrite because it averages the effects of fluctuations in the preore pyrite content over a longer distance. Broad-scale fluctuations in the preore pyrite content, of course, result in correspondingly broad-scale fluctuations in the amount and distributions of ore-stage pyrite.

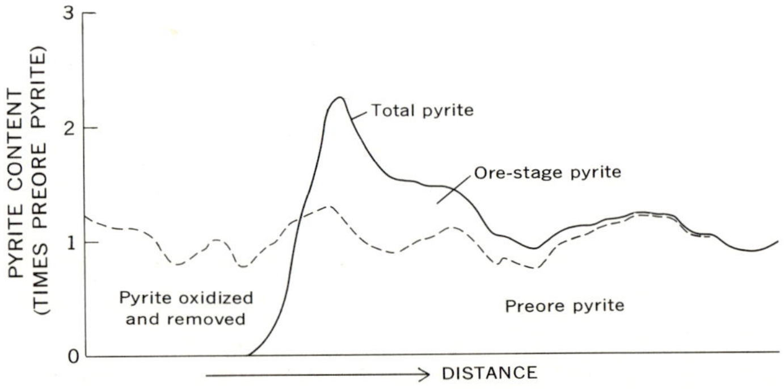

Figure 5.—Typical pyrite distribution in a roll-type deposit showing irregularities that can result from uneven distribution of preore pyrite.

The maximum concentrations of pyrite in the rolls are generally, but not always, just in advance of the redox interface. Presumably, the pyrite content that might be expectable at a given place in a deposit can vary owing to previously existing, greater-than-normal accumulations of preore pyrite or to some unspecified factor which enhanced ore-stage pyrite deposition at that point. Such expectable irregularities do not constitute a valid objection to the steady-state concept.

Ideally, the efficiency of the redepositional process is a parameter of the particular system involved. If, for example, the system entails oxidation of pyrite sulfur to an active sulfur species which then disproportionates (Granger and Warren, 1969) in such a way that exactly half the sulfur is reconverted to a sulfide, the total pyrite at the redox interface in a mature deposit should, ideally, be twice the preore pyrite content. Other chemical processes of disproportionation could produce equally distinctive earmarks of the exact process involved. Whether or not such definite limitations can be placed on natural systems by use of less precise field and analytical data is not yet known.

If the concept of maturity and steady state is valid with regard to the amount and distribution of total ore-stage sulfide sulfur, then the concept should also be applicable to each isotope of sulfur. The results of applying the concept should be no more susceptible to local variations in isotopic composition of the preore pyrite than to the quantity of pyrite. Patterns of isotope distribution should grow, mature, and then continue as part of a steady-state process much as the total sulfide content changes, but perhaps at a different initial rate of growth. This idea, more thoroughly explored by Warren (1972), is mentioned here because regularities of sulfur isotope distribution known to occur in some roll-type deposits (King and Austin, 1966; Austin, 1970) are compatible with a steady-state process.

SUMMARY

In summary, the accumulation of ore-stage pyrite in a roll-type deposit is largely, or entirely, a process of continuous redistribution. The process starts by dissolution of pyrite that is already present in the rock and reprecipitation of a part of it in advance of the point of dissolution, or at redox interface. The ratio of the amount reprecipitated to the amount dissolved can be called the efficiency of the reaction and is a positive function of the maximum pyrite accumulations. The reprecipitated pyrite steadily accumulates until the amount lost in each cycle is equal to the amount initially present in the rock. At this time the deposit has reached maturity and the accumulated pyrite moves along in advance of the redox interface as a continuous wave, neither significantly increasing nor decreasing in size so long as the other parameters remain unchanged. The principal reason that large, rich accumulations of ore-stage pyrite are rarely, if ever, seen in these deposits seems to be that only an extremely efficient process would permit more than a few-fold compounding of the original preore pyrite content.

REFERENCES CITED

Armstrong, F. C., 1970, Geologic factors controlling uranium resources in the Gas Hills district, Wyoming: Wyoming Geol. Assoc. Guidebook, 22d Ann. Field Conf., p. 31–44.

Austin, S. R., 1970, Some patterns of sulfur isotope distribution in uranium deposits: Wyoming Geol. Assoc. Earth Sci. Bull., p. 5–22.

Bailey, R. V., 1969, Uranium deposits in the Great Divide Basin–Crooks Gap Area, Fremont and Sweetwater Counties, Wyoming, *in* Wyoming Uranium Issue, Contribution to Geology, Univ. of Wyoming, v. 8, no. 2, pt. 1, p. 105–120.

Davis, J. F., 1969, Uranium deposits of the Powder River Basin, *in* Wyoming Uranium Issue, Contributions to Geology, Univ. of Wyoming, v. 8, no. 2, pt. 1, p. 131–141.

Eargle, D. H., and Weeks, A. M. D., 1968, Factors in the formation of uranium deposits, Coastal Plain of Texas: South Texas Geol. Soc. Bull., v. 9, no. 3, p. 1–11.

Germanov, A. N., 1960, Main genetic features of some infiltration-type hydrothermal uranium deposits: Akad. Nauk SSSR Izv. Ser. Geol., no. 8, p. 60–71. [English translation]

Granger, H. C., and Warren C. G., 1969, Unstable sulfur compounds and the origin of roll-type uranium deposits: Econ. Geology, v. 64, no. 2, p. 160–171.

Harshman, E. N., 1962, Alteration as a guide to uranium ore, Shirley Basin, Wyoming: Art. 122 *in* U.S. Geol. Survey Prof. Paper 450-D, p. D8–D10.

—— 1966, Genetic implications of some elements associated with uranium deposits, Shirley Basin, Wyoming, *in* Geological Survey Research 1966: U.S. Geol. Survey Prof. Paper 550–C, p. C167–C173.

—— 1970, Uranium ore rolls in the United States: Uranium Exploration Geology, Internat. Atomic Energy Agency, Vienna, Austria, p. 219–232.

Kashirtseva, M. F., 1964, Mineral and geochemical zonation of infiltration uranium ores: Soviet Geology, no. 10, p. 51–65. [English translation]

Kholodov, V. N., Lisitsyn, A. K., Komarova, G. V., and Kondrat'yeva, I. A., 1961, Epigene zoning of uranium mineralization in petroliferous carbonate rocks: Akad. Nauk SSSR Izv., Ser. Geol., no. 11, p. 43–56.

King, J. W., and Austin, S. R., 1966, Some characteristics of roll-type uranium deposits at Gas Hills, Wyoming: Mining Eng., v. 18, no. 5, p. 73–80.

Lisitsyn, A. K., and Kuznetsova, E. C., 1967, Role of microorganisms in development of geochemical reduction barriers where limonitization bedded zones wedge-out: Akad. Nauk SSSR Izv. Ser. Geol., no. 1, p. 31–44. [English translation, Internat. Geology Rev., v. 9, no. 9, p. 1180–1191, 1967]

Melin, R. E., 1964, Description and origin of uranium deposits in Shirley Basin, Wyoming: Econ. Geology, v. 59, no. 5, p. 835–849.

—— 1969, Uranium deposits in Shirley Basin, Wyoming, *in* Wyoming Uranium Issue: Wyoming Univ. Contr. Geology, v. 8, no. 2, pt. 1, p. 143–149.

Shawe, D. R., and Granger, H. C., 1965, Uranium ore rolls—An analysis: Econ. Geology, v. 60, no. 2, p. 240–250.

Warren, C. G., 1971, A method for discriminating between biogenic and chemical origins of the ore-stage pyrite in a roll-type uranium deposit: Econ. Geology, v. 66, no. 6, p. 919–928.

—— 1972, The use of sulfur isotopes as a clue to the genetic geochemistry of a roll-type uranium deposit: Econ. Geology, v. 67, no. 6, p. 759–767.

Jour. Research U.S. Geol. Survey
Vol. 1, No. 2, Mar.—Apr. 1973, p. 157—164

AGE AND TECTONIC IMPLICATIONS OF SOME LOW-GRADE METAMORPHIC ROCKS FROM THE YUCATAN CHANNEL

By J. G. VEDDER, N. S. MacLEOD, M. A. LANPHERE; and
W. P. DILLON, Menlo Park, Calif.; Woods Hole, Mass.

Abstract.—Phyllite and marble dredged from the lower part of the continental slope between Cuba and the Yucatan Peninsula seem to support the contention that a pre-early Tertiary metamorphic belt extends from the western Greater Antilles into northern Central America. The minimum K-Ar ages derived from the samples suggest that the metamorphic event was pre-Late Cretaceous, and evaluation of the K-Ar data implies that this metamorphic event is not older than Late Jurassic. Greater antiquity, however, is inferred from structural and stratigraphic relations in British Honduras, where the latest regional metamorphic event was post-Early Permian and pre-Middle Jurassic. Rifting and extension related to plate motions along the British Honduras—Quintana Roo margin through Mesozoic and earliest Cenozoic time presumably would preclude extensive regional metamorphism, permitting only limited development of schistose rocks there during that interval. The timing of metamorphic events in western Cuba is uncertain, but a pre-Middle Jurassic episode possibly is reflected in the phyllite and marble terranes of Isla de Piños and Sierra de Trinidad. Local incipient metamorphism of Early and Middle Jurassic strata in the Sierra de los Órganos may have resulted from severe tectonism that began in Late Cretaceous time and diminished in the Eocene.

During the U.S. Geological Survey—International Decade of Ocean Exploration (USGS-IDOE) Leg 2 study of the east continental margin of the Yucatan Peninsula in June and July 1971, dredge samples were taken to determine the age and composition of sea floor outcrops in the region where geophysical data were being acquired (Vedder and others, 1971). Two dredge hauls (fig. 1), one 94 km southwest of Cabo San Antonio, Cuba, the other 85 km southeast of Punta Molas, Isla de Cozumel, Mexico, yielded abundant low-grade metamorphic rocks from near the base of the continental slope. These rocks are critical to the interpretation of the structural evolution of the Yucatan Channel and the continental margin southwest of it. Unfortunately, precise stratigraphic correlation and radiometric age of the dredged samples cannot be resolved at present, and the relationship of these rocks to similar metamorphic terranes in northern Central America and Cuba is conjectural.

GEOLOGIC SETTING

Yucatan region

The Yucatan Peninsula is underlain by crystalline basement rocks that are Paleozoic in age in central Guatemala and southern British Honduras (Kesler, 1971), perhaps older in adjacent areas. This basement is overlain by late Paleozoic clastic sedimentary rocks that are partly metamorphosed and by unmetamorphosed Mesozoic and Cenozoic rocks composed mainly of carbonates. Several episodes of igneous intrusion and tectonism have deformed these strata, and two folding events, one Paleozoic and the other Mesozoic, have been recognized throughout northern Central America (Dengo, 1969). In the northern part of the peninsula, pre-Middle-Jurassic felsic metaporphyry was penetrated in Yucatan 1 well beneath more than 3,000 m of Cretaceous and Tertiary anhydrite and limestone and about 400 m of Jurassic red beds (Bass and Zartman, 1969; Viniegra, 1971). Similar rocks were drilled in Yucatan 2 well beneath a slightly thinner sedimentary sequence. Andesite of probable pre-Cretaceous age underlies Turonian(?) and younger carbonates and evaporites in wells near Mérida (Mina, 1966; Bryant and others, 1969).

In the Maya Mountains of British Honduras, the oldest exposed sedimentary rocks are marine shale, sandstone, and limestone of late Paleozoic age that are locally metamorphosed (Dixon, 1956). These deformed clastic rocks are locally interlayered with felsic volcanic porphyry and are cut by granitic intrusive bodies that are assigned an age range of Pennsylvanian to Triassic (Bateson and Hall, 1971; Hall and Bateson, 1972; Bateson, 1972). The absence of latest Paleozoic and early Mesozoic strata suggests that the region was positive during that time interval.

Another cycle of sedimentation began throughout northern Central America during Late Jurassic to Early Cretaceous time with limited deposition of thin, discontinuous successions of Jurassic red beds followed by thicker sequences of Cretaceous shallow-water marine sediments. Widespread deposition of shallow-water carbonates, evaporites, and clastic strata continued in broader, deeper basins in Late Cretaceous and early

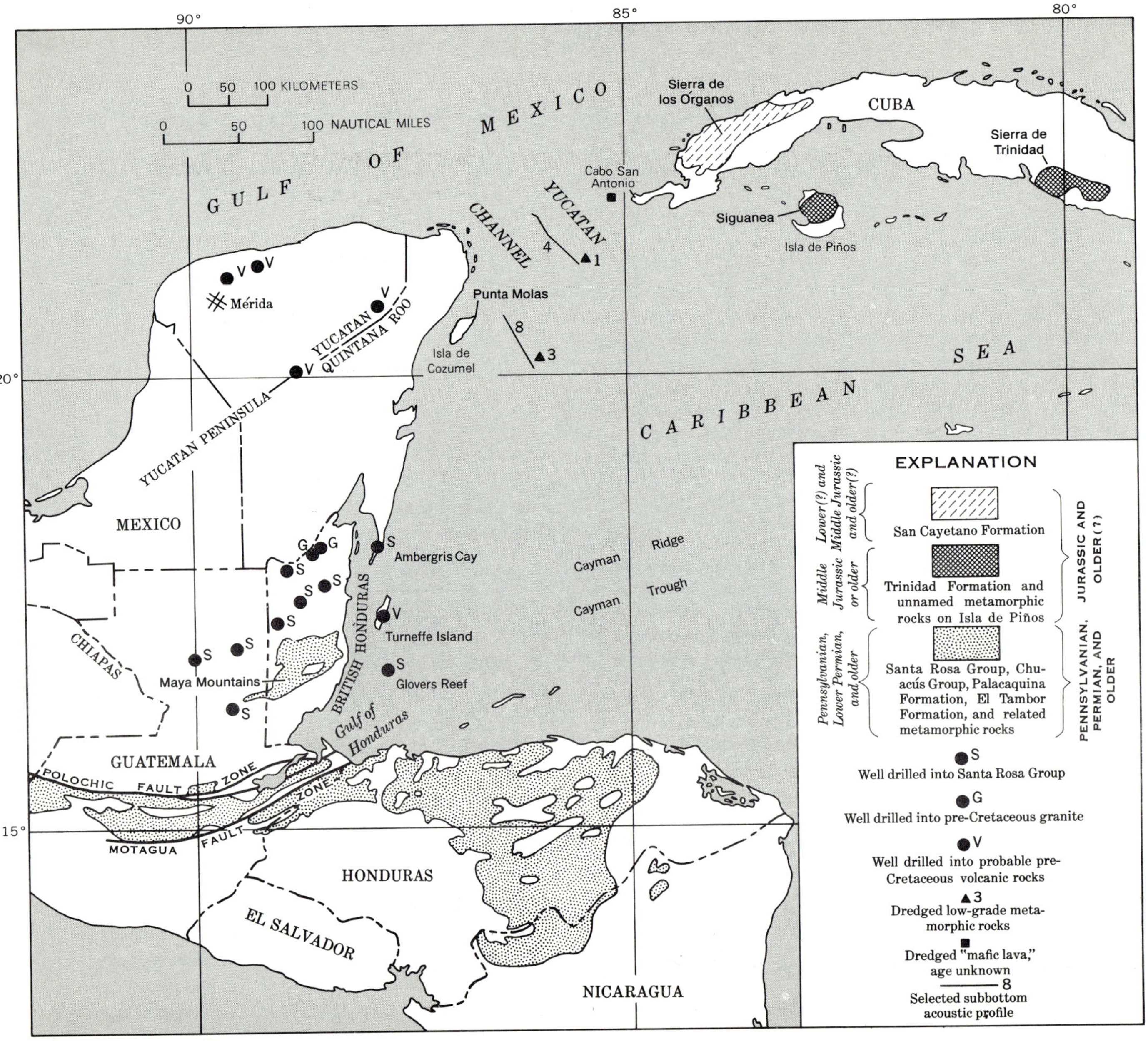

Figure 1.–Generalized map showing the distribution of low-grade metamorphic rocks, related sedimentary rocks, and drilled igneous rocks in northern Central America and western Cuba. Modified from Dengo (1969) and Khudoley and Meyerhoff (1971).

Tertiary time, during which plutonic intrusions locally were emplaced in the southeastern part of Guatemala (Williams and McBirney, 1969; Clemons and Long, 1971). Relatively thin, slightly deformed carbonate platform deposits constitute the bulk of the Tertiary strata on the northeastern part of the Yucatan Peninsula, where all the series except Oligocene are represented in the stratigraphic succession (Flores, 1952).

Northeast-trending normal faults cut the Tertiary section in northwestern British Honduras and Quintana Roo (Alvarez, 1954), and a similar set of faults along the continental margin is postulated by Dengo and Bohnenberger (1969) and Dillon and Vedder (1972). A possibly older set of faults, on which there may have been recurrent movement, displaces the Paleozoic and Mesozoic sequences of the Maya Mountains. These faults trend eastward in the western part of the mountains, but some curve northeast as they approach the coast (Dixon, 1956). A major east-trending zone of faults (Motagua-Polochic system) in central Guatemala apparently extends eastward into the Cayman Ridge and Trough. This fault zone seems to separate widespread phyllite and schist of the greenschist facies on the south from mildly metamorphosed and unmetamorphosed strata in the Maya Mountains (Dengo, 1969). The belt of rocks between the bounding faults of the zone consists in large part of pre-Pennsylvanian schist and gneiss (Kesler, 1971) and contains elongate bodies of serpentinite that probably were intruded in Late Cretaceous time.

Western Cuba

The age of the so-called basement complex of western Cuba is unknown. Metamorphosed sedimentary rocks exposed on Isla de Piños are unconformably overlain by marine pyroclastics of Albian to Cenomanian age (Kuman and Gavilán, 1965); somewhat similar pre-Upper Cretaceous metamorphic rocks underlie much of the Sierra de Trinidad (Hill, 1959). Hatten (1967) believes that both sequences are Paleozoic, but Khudoley (1967) and Kuman and Gavilán (1965) correlate them with the Jurassic San Cayetano Formation and Viñales Limestone of the Sierra de los Órganos. The San Cayetano is composed of a thick, repetitious succession of beds of marine and nonmarine quartzose sandstone, siltstone, and shale that are locally mildly metamorphosed and that contain a Bathonian and Callovian marine fauna in the upper part (Hatten, 1967; Meyerhoff and others, 1969; Hatten and Meyerhoff, 1970). Volcanic detritus is absent. The formation is intruded by serpentinite, primarily along faults; and it may be partly equivalent in age to the evaporite deposits in the Punta Alegre Formation on the Cuban north coast (Meyerhoff and Hatten, 1968). The San Cayetano is overlain by a Late Jurassic clastic and carbonate sequence, which in turn is overlain by a succession of pelagic carbonate units of Cretaceous age (Khudoley and Meyerhoff, 1971).

From Albian through Turonian time, gentle folding interrupted normal deposition, volcanic activity ceased in the west-central part of the island, and dioritic rocks probably began to be emplaced in central and eastern Cuba near the end of this time interval. At the end of Cretaceous time, orogenic activity intensified and during the earliest Tertiary culminated with the formation of nappe structures and the intrusion of granitic plutons (Meyerhoff and others, 1969; Meyerhoff *in* Khudoley and Meyerhoff, 1971). By the end of Eocene time, large-scale faulting and folding had diminished in western Cuba; younger Tertiary rocks are only slightly deformed.

Continental margin east of Yucatan Peninsula

Little is known about the geology of the sea floor in the segment of continental margin that extends southwestward from Cabo San Antonio, Cuba, into the Gulf of Honduras. Subbottom reflection profiles show that narrow, sediment-damming ridges extend southward from the Yucatan Channel to British Honduras to form a pattern of linear structures that are alined approximately parallel to the edge of the continent (Baie, 1970; Vedder and others, 1971; Dillon and Vedder, 1972). Parts of two subbottom acoustic profiles (fig. 2) illustrate one of these well-defined ridges of acoustic basement. Large northeast-trending faults are assumed to bound individual blocks but are not discernible on the original profiles. The slightly deformed reflectors in the basins that lie shoreward of the ridge are inferred to be in a carbonate-dominated sedimentary sequence that includes strata of both Cretaceous and Tertiary age similar to that in basins offshore from British Honduras (Dillon and Vedder, 1972). The age range of the thin wedges of sediment that flank the seaward side of the ridge in both profiles is not certain, but foraminifers dredged from this slope indicate that some of it is mid-Tertiary. Quaternary deposits, chiefly pelagic, presumably mantle most of the older rocks.

DREDGED METAMORPHIC ROCKS

Station 1

Numerous angular pieces of rock, primarily phyllite and marble, were dredged at station 1 (lat 21°13.2′ N.; long 83°31.0′ W.). They average about 5 cm in maximum dimension; the largest fragment is about 25 cm long. Many have fresh surfaces as though broken from outcrops, although some are weathered and partly manganese coated. The haul was made up the steep part of the slope (fig. 2, profile 4) in a depth range of 2,715–2,490 m. A large amount of Pleistocene(?) and Holocene pteropod-globigerine ooze in the dredged sample may be from the thin wedge of bedded sediment over the acoustic basement on the slope about 2–3 km south of the dredge site shown on profile 4 (fig. 2). The steep slopes and peaks of acoustic basement are assumed to be underlain chiefly by metamorphic rocks similar to those recovered in the haul, although intrusive igneous rocks and serpentinite bodies probably are present in adjacent areas.

The largest pieces of rock from station 1 are angular fragments of marble that typically are streaked with irregular dark and light bands. The dark bands consist of laminated dark-gray fine-grained impure limestone that are as much as 1 cm thick; the laminae are parallel in some fragments but are tightly folded in others. The light bands are veins of white coarsely crystalline limestone that disrupt both the dark layers and the folds. Thin lenses and laminae of phyllite, 1–8 mm thick, are interlayered with the dark-gray limestone.

Three typical phyllite fragments from station 1 were studied in thin section. These rocks represent the greenschist facies (quartz-albite-muscovite-chlorite or quartz-albite-biotite-muscovite assemblage) and presumably were derived from mudstone or siltstone and silty limestone. The first consists of quartz, albite, chlorite, muscovite, and biotite, with accessory calcite, sphene, zircon, hydrous iron oxides, and opaque minerals. It has well-developed bands of quartzo-feldspathic and micaceous layers that are shear folded into tight, almost isoclinal, microfolds with sheared limbs. The amplitude of the larger folds averages about 1 cm, but fold limbs and crests are highly crenulated. Most quartz and albite grains are less than 0.05 mm in diameter. They recrystallized after deformation, as

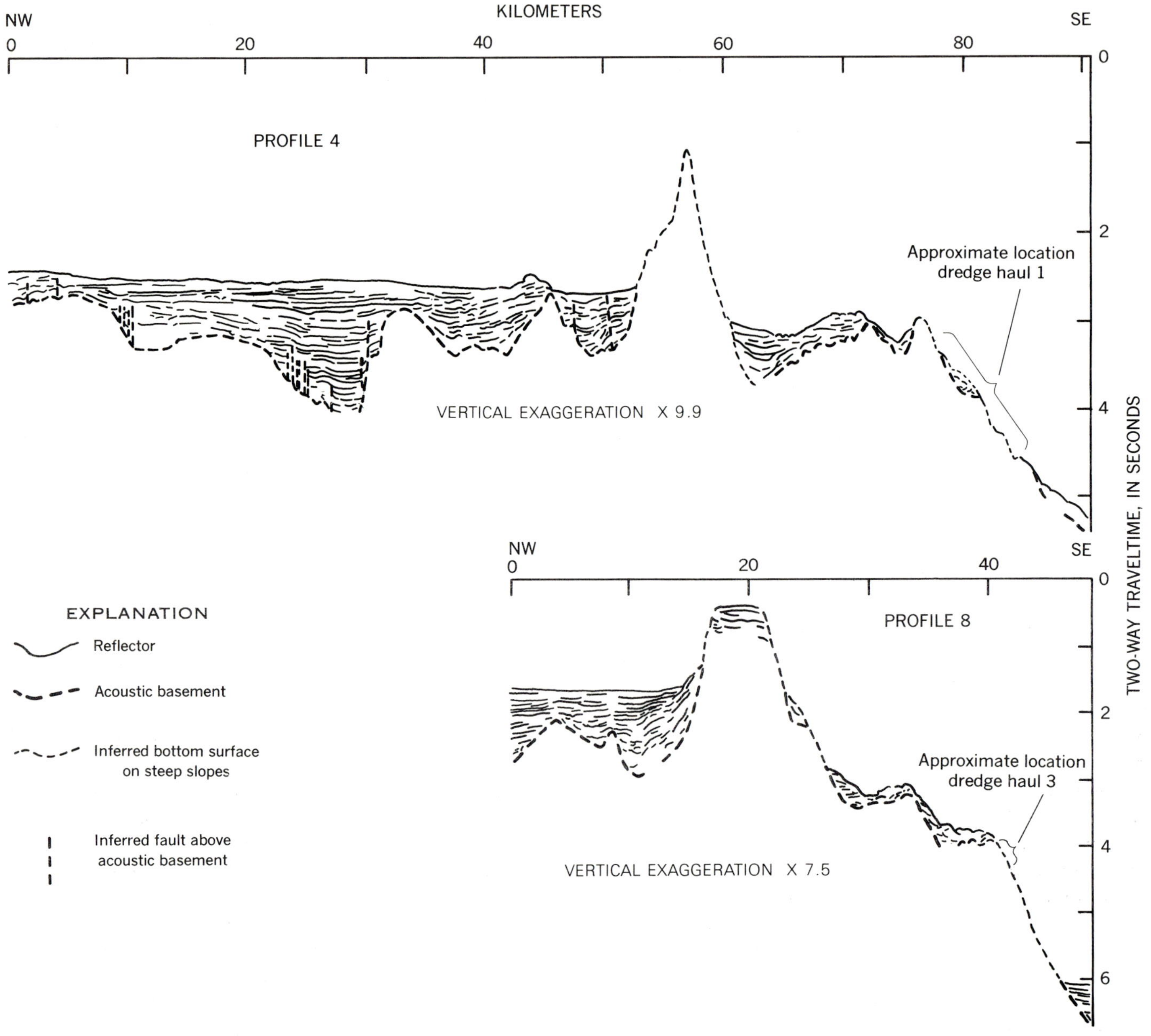

Figure 2.—Interpreted subbottom acoustic profiles showing the relation of dredge hauls to exposures of acoustic basement and to position on the continental slope. The profiles and dredge stations are numbered to agree with those of the original survey (Vedder and others, 1972).

shown by their mosaic texture and lack of strain or preferred orientation. A few larger quartz ovoids as much as 0.3 mm long are highly strained but are recrystallized at their margins to a granoblastic mosaic of unstrained quartz. Rhombs of calcite and plates of muscovite, chlorite, and biotite are scattered through the quartzo-feldspathic layers. The micaceous layers interleaved between the quartzo-feldspathic layers are typically 0.1 mm thick and are composed of chlorite, muscovite, and biotite, with lesser quartz and albite.

The second sample of phyllitic rock consists of muscovite, quartz, albite, and chlorite with accessory calcite, sphene, rutile, and apatite. It has a very well developed foliation and poorly developed crenulation lineation. The surfaces of fragments have a pronounced sheen produced by minute mica flakes. Small (1 by 5 mm) to microscopic (0.1 mm) ovoid porphyroblasts of albite and quartz and discontinuous quartzo-feldspathic layers constitute a small proportion of the rock.

The third sample is a phyllitic marble that consists of calcite, quartz, muscovite, and chlorite, with accessory sphene and epidote. Unlike the other phyllite samples, it contains no detectable albite. Calcite makes up 80–90 percent of the sample and occurs as lenses of minute grains that have a mosaic texture and layers of interleaved elongate grains

0.1–0.3 mm wide and as much as 0.5 mm long. Slightly strained quartz grains are generally scattered throughout the calcite but show greater concentrations along some foliation planes, where they occur with muscovite and chlorite in addition to calcite.

A single small piece of highly sheared serpentinite was collected from dredge station 1 and was identified by petrographic and X-ray methods. Its occurrence is supporting evidence for a southwestward continuation of the Cuban ultramafic belt, which in turn may be related to similar intrusive zones that were most active during latest Cretaceous and earliest Tertiary time in the circum-Caribbean region (Dengo, 1969; MacGillavry, 1970). Small, perhaps older, serpentinite bodies occur in a northwest-trending zone through the north-central part of Isla de Piños (Kuman and Gavilán, 1965; Khudoley and Meyerhoff, 1971), where they intrude phyllite and schist that may correlate with the metamorphic rocks from both dredge stations. Mafic lava(?) of unknown age reported from a Russian dredge haul about 20 km west of Cabo San Antonio (Khudoley and Meyerhoff, 1971) possibly is related to Cretaceous diabasic rocks that are exposed in western Cuba (unit vCr_2, Khudoley and others, 1963).

Station 3

The haul from station 3 (lat 20°10.5′ N.; long 86°03.6 W.) consists of numerous angular fragments of phyllite and a few small pieces of schist pebble conglomerate that were dredged in the depth range of 3,090–2,920 m. The phyllite fragments range in length from a few millimeters to 21 cm. Most have weathered surfaces coated with manganese oxide and seem to be from submarine scree derived from the top of the steep lower slope (fig. 2, profile 8); a few large fragments with freshly broken surfaces may have been torn from outcrops during dredging. Pleistocene and Holocene pteropod-globigerine ooze constitutes the remainder of the haul and is assumed to represent a thin cover of sediment on the metamorphic rocks. The pebble-conglomerate fragments may be slumped material from thicker sediment accumulations that lie between the steep lower slope and the high basement ridge, but the precise relations are uncertain, as the dredge site is 1–2 km north of the profile. The matrix of the conglomerate contains *Lepidocyclina* sp. and other smaller foraminifers that suggest deposition during late Eocene to early Miocene time, possibly Oligocene, and a water depth much shallower than that at the site today if the fossils are not displaced. Reflectors atop the high-standing basement ridge may indicate the presence of ancient coral reefs that were drowned by subsidence of the continental margin (Vedder and others, 1971).

The quartz-albite-muscovite-chlorite assemblage in the phyllite samples from station 3 indicates that the rocks represent the greenschist facies. The phyllite probably was derived from siltstone or silty sandstone, and the abundant calcite in one sample suggests that some of the original sediment may have been rich in carbonate.

All phyllite samples examined from station 3 have a well-developed foliation, and a few also have a weakly developed lineation produced by intersection of the principal foliation with a later shear foliation that is oriented 30°–60° oblique to the principal foliation. The foliation surfaces have a silky sheen imparted by parallel muscovite plates that are barely visible to the unaided eye. Most samples show segregation layering with quartzo-feldspathic layers 1–5 mm thick between the micaceous layers.

Two samples studied in thin section consist of quartz, albite, muscovite, and chlorite; a third contains the same minerals plus abundant calcite. Accessory and secondary minerals include apatite, biotite, sphene, rutile, zircon, opaque minerals, and hydrous iron oxide. Quartzo-feldspathic bands make up about half of each sample, although in the calcite-bearing phyllite the segregation into quartzo-feldspathic and micaceous bands is poorly defined. Some quartzo-feldspathic layers are devoid of muscovite and chlorite; others contain abundant chlorite. Quartz and albite in these layers are highly strained, and the quartz shows a preferred orientation. Grain size is mostly less than 0.2 mm, but some irregular albite crystals and strained quartz ovoids are as large as 1 by 2 mm. Larger quartz grains contain small fluid inclusions. The chlorite occurs as parallel crystals scattered with quartz and albite through the micaceous layers, whereas the muscovite is principally confined to 0.1–0.2-mm-thick bands consisting almost entirely of interleaved muscovite crystals. Some muscovite and chlorite is alined along secondary shear surfaces. Biotite occurs in minute amounts interleaved with chlorite. Disrupted albite grains and strongly undulatory quartz ovoids with irregular boundaries indicate additional shearing during or after crystallization.

POTASSIUM-ARGON AGE MEASUREMENTS

It was not possible to separate pure muscovite or biotite from the dredged samples, for these minerals are too fine grained and intricately intergrown with chlorite. The concentrate of sheet-structure minerals from station 1 was split into three fractions by use of magnetic techniques; the least magnetic fraction, "muscovite," and most magnetic fraction, "chlorite," were analyzed. Inasmuch as the quantity of material in the sheet-structure mineral concentrate from station 3 was too small to split into separate fractions, the total chlorite-muscovite-biotite mixture, "biotite," was analyzed. X-ray diffraction patterns and the relatively low K_2O content indicate that chlorite is equal to or more abundant than mica in all three analyzed samples.

Argon measurements by isotope-dilution methods were made using equipment and techniques previously described (Dalrymple and Lanphere, 1969). Potassium content was measured by flame photometry using a lithium internal standard. The plus-or-minus value assigned to each age measurement (table 1) is an estimate of the standard deviation of analytical precision, using the method of Cox and Dalrymple (1967), together with an estimate of accuracy

Table 1.—*Analytical data and potassium-argon ages for samples dredged from stations 1 and 2*

[Constants used: $K^{40}\lambda_\epsilon=0.585\times10^{-10}yr^{-1}$; $K^{40}\lambda_\beta=4.72\times10^{-10}yr^{-1}$. Abundance: $K^{40}=1.19\times10^{-4}$ atom percent. Analysts: L. B. Schlocker, potassium measurements; J. C. Von Essen, argon measurements and age calculations]

Sample No.	Mineral	K_2O content[1] (percent)	Radiogenic argon (10^{-10} moles/g)	Ar^{40} radiogenic / Ar^{40} total	Calculated age (m.y.)
1.	"Muscovite"	4.73, 4.75 (4.74)	6.638	0.81	92.5±2.8
2.	"Chlorite"	2.77, 2.78 (2.78)	3.074	.63	73.5±2.3
3.	"Biotite"	1.373, 1.377 (1.375)	1.223	.54	59.3±2.0

[1] Percentage values in parentheses are averages.

based on evaluation of the uncertainties in the isotope composition and concentration of the Ar^{38} tracer and concentrations of the flame photometer standards.

The three potassium-argon ages (table 1) are not in agreement, and the two fractions from station 1 differ by much more than the uncertainty of the individual measurements. The age of 92.5 m.y. for the "muscovite" fraction from station 1 is interpreted as a minimum age for the development of the mineral assemblage.

A maximum age for the time of metamorphic recrystallization can be inferred from a plot of the results for station 1 on an age-versus-K_2O diagram in which it is assumed that the two fractions define a mixing line that can be extrapolated to a "pure" muscovite end member and that all the chlorite is derived from muscovite. This construction results in inferred ages of 134 m.y. and 154 m.y. for K_2O contents of 9 and 11 percent, respectively. As it is unlikely that the "pure" muscovite contains more than 11 percent K_2O, an inferred maximum age of metamorphism is about 155 m.y. This age is Late Jurassic on most compilations of the geologic time scale, but the inferred maximum age of metamorphism could be as young as Early Cretaceous, depending on the K_2O content of the "pure" muscovite. The age of 59.3 m.y. for the sample from station 3 is a minimum value for the metamorphic event in which the mineral assemblage was produced.

In summary, the potassium-argon results indicate minimum ages of 92.5 and 59.3 m.y. for the metamorphism of the phyllites at stations 1 and 3, respectively. Evidence for possible systematic loss of Ar^{40} suggests that these phyllites were more likely produced by older metamorphism, perhaps during mid-Mesozoic time.

REGIONAL DISTRIBUTION OF LOW-GRADE METAMORPHIC ROCKS

Low-grade metamorphic rocks, chiefly phyllite and schist, are common in pre-Cretaceous terranes throughout the western Greater Antilles and northern Central America (fig. 1) (Dengo, 1969; Meyerhoff and others, 1969; Khudoley, 1967; Williams and McBirney, 1969; McBirney and Bass, 1969; Khudoley and Meyerhoff, 1971). In the Maya Mountains of southern British Honduras, a thick sequence of locally metamorphosed sedimentary rocks has been assigned a Pennsylvanian to Late Permian age. Dixon (1956) called the metamorphosed part of the sequence the Maya Series and separated it from shales and sandstones that he assigned to the Macal Series. Dengo (1969) provisionally accepted this interpretation and correlated the metamorphic rocks with the Chuacús Group (McBirney, 1963) in Guatemala and Chiapas, Mexico. Later detailed work by Kesler and others (1971), Bateson and Hall (1971), and Bateson (1972) has demonstrated that the Maya and Macal Series are coeval in part and that they correlate with the Santa Rosa Group of Pennsylvanian and Permian age in Guatemala (Bohnenberger, 1966). Precise correlation with the metamorphic rocks of the Palacaguina Formation in southern Guatemala and Honduras, south of the Motagua-Polochic fault system, is uncertain (Dengo, 1969).

Muscovite phyllite that presumably is equivalent to that exposed in the Maya Mountains was penetrated below about 2,218 m in the Gulf-Shell Basil Jones 1 well on Ambergris Cay about 111 km northeast of the northeasternmost outcrops in British Honduras (fig. 1). The Shell Oil Co. Glover well at the south end of Glovers Reef also penetrated rocks that may correlate with the Santa Rosa Group. Here 182 m of shale and phyllite was drilled below Eocene and Upper Cretaceous strata in the depth interval 777–959 m. On Turneffe Island, the Shell Oil Co. Turneffe well did not recover phyllite but drilled into pre-Upper Cretaceous extrusive andesitic(?) volcanic rocks at 1,692 m that may be related to the rhyolitic Bladen Volcanic Member of the Santa Rosa Group (Bateson and Hall, 1971; Hall and Bateson, 1972) but are more likely to represent younger intermediate to mafic rocks in the Antillean geosynclinal belt.

Muscovite phyllite and schist with intercalated limestone and marble from Isla de Piños, Cuba, have been described by Rutten (1934), Page and McAllister (1944), Kuman and Gavilán (1965), and Tijomirov (1967). J. E. McAllister (oral commun., 1971) briefly examined a few hand specimens from the dredge hauls and remarked that they closely resemble rocks from the Siguanea district. Kuman and Gavilán correlate the unfossiliferous succession on the island with the San Cayetano Formation and Vinales Limestone of Jurassic age in western Cuba; Hatten (1967) disagrees with this comparison and assigns it to the Paleozoic. Similar low-grade metamorphic rocks are exposed in the Sierra de Trinidad in central Cuba and perhaps in eastern Oriente Province in the Sierra Maestra in southeastern Cuba (Palmer, 1945; Hill, 1959; Khudoley, 1967; Skvor, 1969; Khudoley and Meyerhoff, 1971).

The abundance of phyllite and marble fragments dredged from near the base of the slope suggests that the basement ridges are composed primarily of low-grade metamorphic rocks, although intrusive igneous rocks and serpentinite bodies are presumed to be present. The wide distribution of similar metamorphic rocks both in western Cuba and northern Central America indicates that a broad, fragmented belt of low-grade metamorphic rocks may underlie the margin of the northwestern Caribbean. It is unlikely that these mildly metamorphosed sedimentary terranes developed from rocks of the same age, and the evidence for suggesting that the metamorphic event was everywhere the same age is lacking.

SUMMARY AND CONCLUSIONS

In northern Central America, two major episodes of tectonism that could have produced regional metamorphism followed the deposition of the late Paleozoic Santa Rosa Group. The first event included wide-ranging deformation by north-south compression, intrusion by granitic plutons, and uplift of large segments of "nuclear Central America" sometime during the interval between Early Permian and Middle or Late Triassic time. This event was followed by extensional tectonics that formed the ancestral Gulf of Honduras in Late Jurassic through Early Cretaceous time. A second significant orogenic event developed through Late Cretaceous and earliest Tertiary time and seems to have affected the entire western Caribbean. Concurrently, the rocks of the Sierras of northern Central America were intensely folded and thrust northward, strike-slip movement may have begun along the Motagua-Polochic fault system, and granitic intrusions were again emplaced. At the same time, mobilization of serpentinite occurred around the Caribbean margins, and a new set of plate movements was initiated that resulted in continued extensional faulting and subsidence at the eastern continental margin of the Yucatan Peninsula.

In Cuba, the sequence of pre-Cretaceous events is more obscure. The depositional age of the phyllites and marbles of the Sierra de Trinidad and Isla de Piños is uncertain, and the latest metamorphic episode there can be established only as pre-mid-Cretaceous on stratigraphic evidence. The age and provenance of the San Cayetano Formation are critical in the interpretation of the tectonic history of western Cuba, yet the unfossiliferous lower part of the succession can be designated only Middle Jurassic or older, and the source terrane is unknown. The correlation of the metamorphic rocks on Isla de Piños with the sedimentary rocks of the San Cayetano Formation and Viñales Limestone is tenuous at best; the alternative age assignment of the island rocks to the Paleozoic may be correct. Perhaps the phyllites of Sierra de Trinidad and Isla de Piños are equivalent to those of the Santa Rosa Group, as Murray (1961) implies in his discussion of a Paleozoic fold belt between northern Central America and western Cuba. The presence of serpentinite at station 1 suggests a southwestward continuation of the Antillean ultramafic belt and further supports the inferred link.

Although the potassium-argon measurements are inadequate for precise age determination, the dredged phyllite samples indicate a pre-Tertiary metamorphic event, and evaluation of the data suggests that this event is not as old as the Late Permian to Late Triassic orogeny in northern Central America. Isotope ages on muscovite schist from Isla de Piños reported by Meyerhoff, Khudoley, and Hatten (1969), 73±4, 76±2, and 78±4 m.y., indicate a metamorphic event that occurred before the end of Cretaceous time. These workers imply that the dates may be rejuvenescent as a result of degassing during an Eocene(?) thermal event and that, on the basis of stratigraphic evidence, the metamorphism was pre-Campanian.

Structural and stratigraphic interpretations seem to favor the Late Permian to Late Triassic orogenic episode as the cause of metamorphism in the Yucatan Channel. If the phyllite samples from the dredge stations and Isla de Piños correlate with the Pennsylvanian and Early Permian Santa Rosa Group, then their metamorphism predates continental rifting, and a broad distribution of similar rocks through the submerged continental remnants in the western Caribbean is to be expected. Alternatively, the San Cayetano Formation and the metamorphic rocks of Isla de Piños and Sierra de Trinidad may be equivalent and entirely of Early and Middle Jurassic age. If they are, the corresponding dredged phyllites would not correlate with the subsurface and outcrop occurrences of strikingly similar older rocks in British Honduras but would reflect a post-Middle Jurassic metamorphic event. The central Yucatan Basin apparently opened progressively southwestward by sphenochasmic rifting that began in Late Triassic or Early Jurassic time and continued through the Cretaceous (Dillon and Vedder, 1972). Extensional tectonics along the eastern continental margin of the Yucatan Peninsula during Late Jurassic through Late Cretaceous time seem to preclude regional metamorphism of preexisting continental terranes in the Yucatan Channel within the same time interval.

ACKNOWLEDGMENTS

Identification of Foraminifera and their age assignment were provided expeditiously by Ruth Todd and K. N. Sachs. L. B. Schlocker made the potassium measurements, and J. C. Von Essen did the argon measurements and calculations. H. C. MacGillavry, of the University of Amsterdam, and G. W. Moore and R. A. Loney read the manuscript and offered pertinent suggestions for its improvement. We are grateful for the assistance of the scientific party and the crew of the *Unitedgeo I* during the cruise.

REFERENCES CITED

Alvarez, Manuel, Jr., 1954, Exploración geológica preliminar del Rio Hondo, Quintana Roo: Asoc. Mexicana Geólogos Petroleros Bol., v. 6, p. 207–213.

Baie, L. F., 1970, Possible structural link between Yucatan and Cuba: Am. Assoc. Petroleum Geologists Bull., v. 54, p. 2204–2207.

Bass, M. N., and Zartman, R. E., 1969, The basement of Yucatan Peninsula: EOS (Am. Geophys. Union Trans.), v. 50, no. 4, p. 313.

Bateson, J. H., 1972, New interpretation of geology of Maya Mountains, British Honduras: Am. Assoc. Petroleum Geologists Bull., v. 56, p. 956–963.

Bateson, J. H., and Hall, I. H. S., 1971, Revised geologic nomenclature for pre-Cretaceous rocks of British Honduras: Am. Assoc. Petroleum Geologists Bull., v. 55, p. 529–530.

Bohnenberger, O. H., 1966, Nomenclatura de las capas Santa Rosa en Guatemala: Inst. Centroamericano Inv. y Technología Indus. Pub. Geol., no. 1, p. 47–51.

Bryant, W. R., Meyerhoff, A. A., Brown, N. K., Jr., Furrer, M. A., Pyle, T. A., and Antoine, J. W., 1969, Escarpments, reef trends, and diapiric structures, eastern Gulf of Mexico: Am. Assoc. Petroleum Geologists, v. 53, p. 2506–2542.

Clemons, R. E., and Long, L. E., 1971, Petrologic and isotopic study of the Chiquimula pluton, southeastern Guatemala: Geol. Soc. America Bull., v. 82, no. 10, p. 2729–2740.

Cox, Allan, and Dalrymple, G. B., 1967, Statistical analysis of geomagnetic reversal data and the precision of potassium-argon dating: Jour. Geophys. Research, v. 72, no. 10, p. 2603–2614.

Dalrymple, G. B., and Lanphere, M. A., 1969, Potassium-argon dating–Principles, techniques and applications to geochronology: San Francisco, Calif., W. H. Freeman and Co., 258 p.

Dengo, G., 1969, Problems of tectonic relations between Central America and the Caribbean: Gulf Coast Assoc. Geol. Soc. Trans., v. 19, p. 311–320.

Dengo, G., and Bohnenberger, O. H., 1969, Structural development of northern Central America: Am. Assoc. Petroleum Geologists Mem. 11, p. 203–220.

Dillon, W. P., and Vedder, J. G., 1972, Structure and development of the continental margin of British Honduras: Geol. Soc. America Abs. with Programs, v. 4, no. 7, p. 488.

Dixon, C. G., 1956, Geology of southern British Honduras, with notes on adjacent areas: Belize Govt. Printer, 85 p.

Evernden, J. F., and Kistler, R. W., 1970, Chronology of emplacement of Mesozoic complexes in California and western Nevada: U.S. Geol. Survey Prof. Paper 623, 42 p.

Flores, G., 1952, Geology of northern British Honduras: Am. Assoc. Petroleum Geologists Bull., v. 36, p. 404–409.

Hall, I. H. S., and Bateson, J. H., 1972, Late Paleozoic lavas in Maya Mountains, British Honduras, and their possible regional significance: Am. Assoc. Petroleum Geologists Bull., v. 56, p. 950–953.

Hatten, C. W., 1967, Principal features of Cuban geology: Am. Assoc. Petroleum Geologists Bull., v. 51, p. 780–789.

Hatten, C. W., and Meyerhoff, A. A., 1970, The Caribbean area: a case of destruction and regeneration of a continent: Geol. Soc. America Bull., v. 81, p. 1855–1862.

Hill, P. A., 1959, Geology and structure of the northwest Trinidad Mountains, Las Villas Province, Cuba: Geol. Soc. America Bull., v. 70, p. 1459–1478.

Kesler, S. E., 1971, Nature of ancestral orogenic zone in nuclear Central America: Am. Assoc. Petroleum Geologists Bull., v. 55, p. 2116–2129.

Kesler, S. E., Bateson, J. H., Josey, W. L., Cramer, G. H., and Simmons, W. A., 1971, Mesoscopic structural homogeneity of Maya Series and Macal Series, Mountain Pine Ridge, British Honduras: Am. Assoc. Petroleum Geologists Bull., v. 55, no. 1, p. 97–103.

Khudoley, K. M., 1967, Principal features of Cuban geology: Am. Assoc. Petroleum Geologists Bull., v. 51, p. 668–677.

Khudoley, K. M., and Meyerhoff, A. A., 1971, Paleogeography and geologic history of Greater Antilles: Geol. Soc. America Mem. 129, 199 p.

Khudoley [Judoley], K. M., Krasnor, V. I., Novojasky, I. P., and Skriabina, E., eds., 1963, Mapa de Yacimientos minerales de Cuba: Cuba Inst. Recursos Minerales, 4 sheets, 1:500,000. [1965]

Kuman, V. E., and Gavilán, R. R., 1965, Geología de Isla de Piños: Nuestra Industria–Rev. Tecnológica, v. 3, no. 4, p. 20–38.

McBirney, A. R., 1963, Geology of a part of the central Guatemala Cordillera: California Univ. Pubs. Geol. Sci., v. 38, no. 4, p. 177–242.

McBirney, A. R., and Bass, M. N., 1969, Structural relations of pre-Mesozoic rocks of northern Central America: Am. Assoc. Petroleum Geologists Mem. 11, p. 269–280.

MacGillavry, H. J., 1970, Geological history of the Caribbean: Koninkl Nederlandse Akad. Wetensch. Proc., ser. B, v. 73, no. 1, p. 64–96.

Meyerhoff, A. A., and Hatten, C. W., 1968, Diapiric structures in central Cuba: Am. Assoc. Petroleum Geologists Mem. 8, p. 315–357.

Meyerhoff, A. A., Khudoley, K. M., and Hatten, C. W., 1969, Geologic significance of radiometric dates from Cuba: Am. Assoc. Petroleum Geologists Bull., v. 53, p. 2494–2500.

Mina V., Federico, 1966, Petroleum developments in Mexico in 1965: Am. Assoc. Petroleum Geologists Bull., v. 50, p. 1553–1563.

Murray, G. E., 1961, Geology of the Atlantic and Gulf coastal province of North America: New York, Harper and Bros., 692 p.

Page, L. R., and McAllister, J. F., 1944, Tungsten deposits, Isla de Piños, Cuba: U.S. Geol. Survey Bull. 935-D, p. 177–246.

Palmer, R. H., 1945, Outline of the geology of Cuba: Jour. Geology, v. 53, no. 1, p. 1–34.

Rutten, L. M. R., 1934, Geology of Isla de Piños, Cuba: Koninkl. Akad. Wetensch. Amsterdam, Sec. Sci. Proc., v. 37, no. 7, p. 401–406.

Skvor, Vladimir, 1969, The Caribbean area: a case of destruction and regeneration of a continent: Geol. Soc. America Bull., v. 80, p. 961–968.

Tijomirov, I. N., 1967, Formaciones magmaticas de Cuba y algunas particularidades de su metalogenia: Nuestra Industria–Rev. Technológica, v. 5, no. 4, p. 13–22 [1968]

Vedder, J. G., and others, 1971, USGS–IDOE Leg 2: Geotimes, v. 16, p. 10–12.

Vedder, J. G., and others, 1972, Acoustic reflection profiles–East margin, Yucatan Peninsula: U.S. Geol Survey Rept. USGS-GD-70-003, 33 p.; available only from U.S. Dept. Commerce Natl. Tech. Inf. Service, Springfield, Va. 22151, as Rept. PB2-0795.

Viniegra, O. F., 1971, Age and evolution of salt basins of southeastern Mexico: Am. Assoc. Petroleum Geologists Bull., v. 55, p. 478–494.

Williams, H., and McBirney, A. R., 1969, Volcanic history of Honduras: California Univ. Pubs. Geol. Sci., v. 85, 101 p.

Jour. Research U.S. Geol. Survey
Vol. 1, No. 2, Mar.—Apr. 1973, p. 165—172

GEOLOGY OF PART OF THE SOUTHERN COMPLEX, MARQUETTE DISTRICT, MICHIGAN

By W. F. CANNON and GEORGE C. SIMMONS,
Washington, D.C., Denver, Colo.

Work done in cooperation with the Geological Survey Division, Michigan Department of Natural Resources

Abstract.—The southern complex, south of the Marquette synclinorium in the Marquette district of Michigan, is dominantly granitic. The granitic parts of the complex have Rb-Sr ages of about 2.5 b.y. and are classed as of Precambrian W age. The rocks are divided into two major units: (1) Bell Creek Gneiss consisting mostly of coarse megacrystic granitic rocks and lesser amounts of mafic gneiss and metasedimentary rocks in layers concordant to the foliation of the granitic gneiss, and (2) Compeau Creek Gneiss, previously described to the east, which is mostly medium-grained granitic gneiss and lesser amounts of massive granitic rocks and locally abundant xenoliths of mafic and metasedimentary rocks. Compeau Creek Gneiss intrudes Bell Creek Gneiss throughout the area. Mafic and metasedimentary rocks in the Bell Creek Gneiss are interpreted as remnants of a greenstone belt. The granitic parts of the Bell Creek Gneiss are of problematic origin. Their composition suggests a magmatic origin, but they do not intrude any rocks with which they are in contact; they form concordant layers in all observed places. Granitic parts of the Compeau Creek Gneiss are suspected to be highly altered and partly melted sedimentary rocks. The mafic parts are probably xenoliths of mafic rocks from the Bell Creek Gneiss.

The Marquette district is in the Northern Peninsula of Michigan (fig. 1), and has been famous as a producer of iron ore during the past 120 years. Because of its economic importance, the district has been extensively studied, and the literature describing the iron-bearing formation and the rocks folded with it in the Marquette synclinorium is voluminous. Rocks south of the synclinorium, in what has become known as the southern complex, have received less attention, and the extant literature presents a confusing and contradictory account of the geology. Recent detailed mapping by the U.S. Geological Survey provides significant data for the geologic interpretation of this area.

This paper describes the lithology, distribution, and age of rocks of part of the southern complex underlying about 110 sq mi within the Ishpeming, Greenwood, and Republic 7½-minute quadrangles, and introduces a new stratigraphic name for a major gneiss unit. The origin of many of the rock types is problematical, is still under study, and is mentioned only briefly.

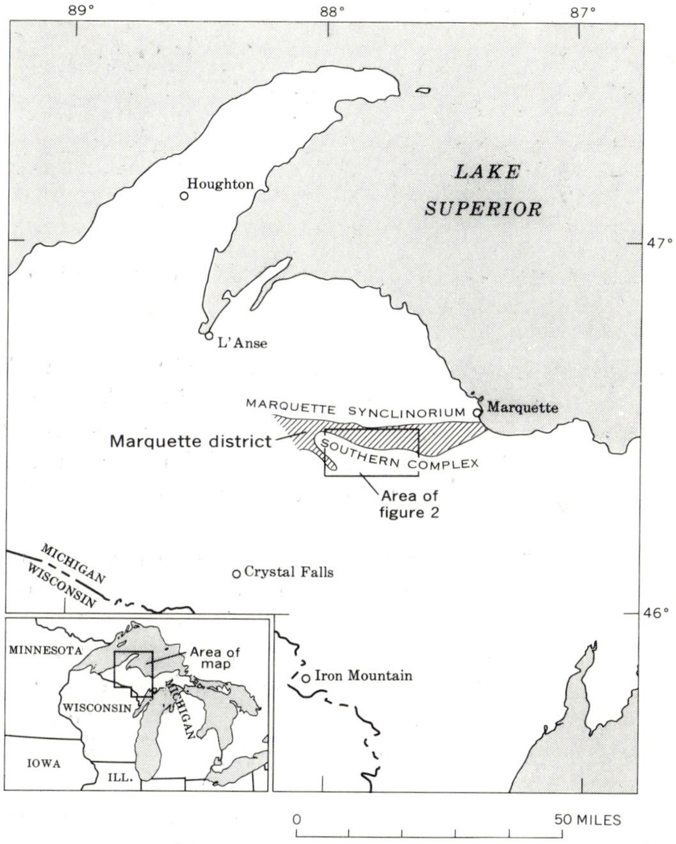

Figure 1.—Map showing the location of the Marquette district, Marquette synclinorium (diagonal pattern), and the southern complex.

PREVIOUS WORK

A variety of stratigraphic names has been used for rocks in

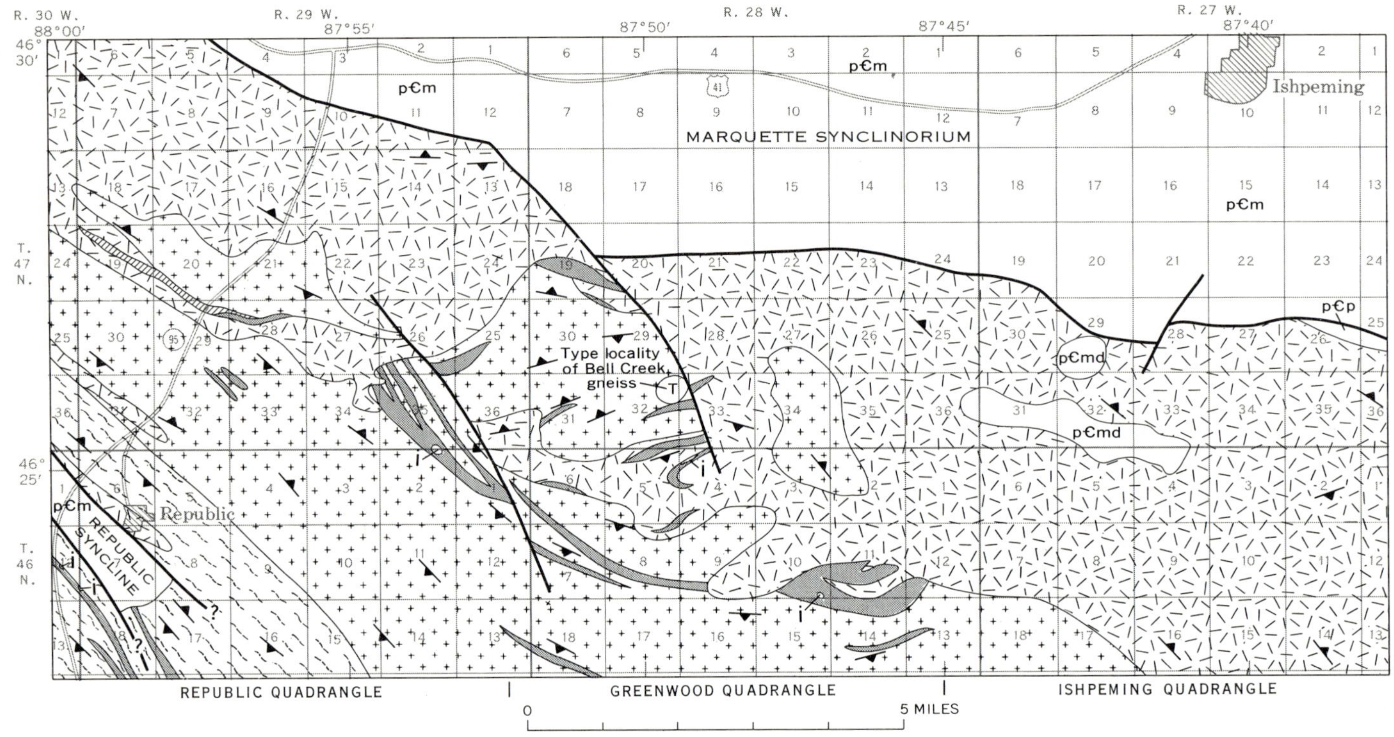

Figure 2.—Generalized geologic map of the southern complex in the Republic, Greenwood, and Ishpeming 7½-minute quadrangles, Michigan.

the Marquette district. Rocks presently called Precambrian W have also been called "Archean" and lower Precambrian. The Marquette Range Supergroup (Precambrian X) has been called middle Precambrian, Animikie Series, and Huronian. In this report, the terms in quotation marks are those used by the author to which reference is made.

The name "southern complex" was introduced by Van Hise and Bayley (1897) for the crystalline rocks south of the Marquette synclinorium; although they did not map the area, they published the first detailed petrographic descriptions of the rocks, which they considered "Archean." Lamey (1931, 1933, 1934, 1935) disagreed with Van Hise and Bayley and presented evidence for a "post-Huronian" age (post-Marquette Range Supergroup of present usage) for the granitic rocks. In response to Lamey's work, Dickey (1936) reasserted an "Archean" age for these rocks and described relations indicating two ages of "Archean" granite. Later, Dickey (1938) changed his opinion and adopted a "post-lower Huronian—pre-middle Huronian" age for the southern complex (post-Chocolay Group—pre-Menominee Group of present usage), on the basis of intrusive relations with supposed "lower Huronian" rocks in northern Dickinson County. Snelgrove, Seaman, and Ayres (1944) described intrusive relations near Republic and concluded that the granitic rocks of the southern complex were entirely "post-Huronian." James (1955, 1958) reasserted a "lower Precambrian" age for the granitic rocks because they are intruded by diabase dikes that are older than the Precambrian X Penokean orogeny. Dickey's earlier interpretation (1936) was invalidated because his "lower Huronian" rocks were reassigned a "lower Precambrian" age (Dickinson Group). Taylor (1967) studied structures in the western part of the area discussed in this paper, proposed a sequence of multiple intrusion and deformation, and suggested that a major part of the southern complex is of "post-Animikie" age. Gair and Thaden (1968) described in detail part of the southern complex near the east end of the Marquette Range and presented evidence indicating a "lower Precambrian" age. Zainuddin (1971) described the petrology of granitic rocks near Republic and devised a tripartite division based on lithology. Although his division is similar to ours, the relative ages that he suggested are the reverse of those which we propose later in this paper. He suggested that a major part of the southern complex is "post-Animikie," but this is refuted by radiometric dates by Woolsey (1971), which show that all major granitic units in our map area are of Precambrian W age.

GENERAL GEOLOGY

The rocks of the southern complex are chiefly granitic gneisses and lesser amounts of mafic gneiss, massive granitic rocks, migmatite, and highly metamorphosed rocks of probable metasedimentary origin. Our mapping has defined two major units whose distribution is shown in figure 2: (1) an older unit, here named the Bell Creek Gneiss, and (2) the Compeau Creek Gneiss, a unit first described by Gair and Thaden (1968) near the east end of the Marquette Range.

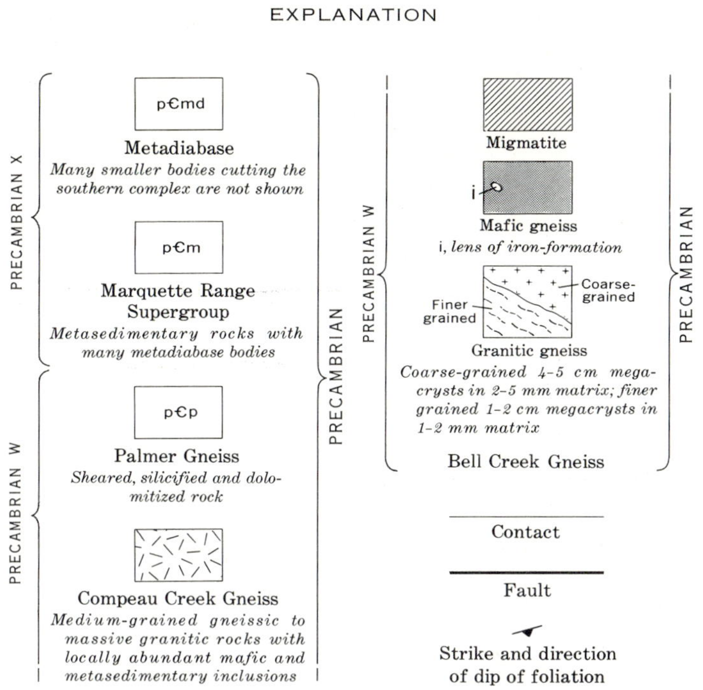

Figure 2.

Figure 3.—Dike of Compeau Creek Gneiss (finer grained) cutting foliation of Bell Creek Gneiss (coarser grained rock in lower left). Outcrop at type locality of Bell Creek Gneiss, NW¼, sec. 32, T. 47 N., R. 28 W. Hammer about 10 inches long.

The Bell Creek Gneiss consists largely of very coarse grained megacrystic[1] granitic rocks, mostly of adamellite composition, and lesser amounts of mafic gneiss containing lenses of iron-formation. Migmatite forms a small part of the Bell Creek Gneiss in the Republic quadrangle.

The Compeau Creek Gneiss consists mostly of foliated granodiorite and tonalite containing locally abundant inclusions of amphibolitic gneiss; gneisses of adamellite and monzonitic composition, and granite, are less common. The Compeau Creek Gneiss truncates units of the Bell Creek Gneiss in many places. Figure 3, for example, shows crosscutting relationships near the type locality of the Bell Creek Gneiss where megacryst foliation in the Bell Creek granitic gneiss is truncated by a dike of Compeau Creek granitic gneiss. The granitic rocks of the southern complex lack crosscutting relations with the rocks of the Marquette Range Supergroup, which are folded in the Marquette synclinorium, but like the Marquette Range Supergroup, they are cut by dikes of metadiabase which are older than the late Precambrian X Penokean orogeny. Thus, the formation of the southern complex must likewise predate the Penokean orogeny. Because there are no other thermal events in Precambrian X time to which the rocks of the southern complex can be related, they must have formed during one or more Precambrian W orogenies.

The southern complex was deeply eroded and probably peneplaned before the deposition of the Marquette Range Supergroup. Before being folded in the Marquette synclinorium and Republic syncline, the Marquette Range Supergroup unconformably overlay the southern complex but is now in fault contact with it in most of the area.

The southern complex is cut by mafic dike rocks of probably two Precambrian X ages (both sets of rocks having been metamorphosed by the late Precambrian X Penokean orogeny) and by nonmetamorphosed diabase dikes of Keweenawan age.

Pegmatite dikes, which are most abundant in the southern complex near Republic, are similar both texturally and mineralogically to pegmatites that cut Precambrian X rocks in the Republic syncline and are believed to be the only Precambrian X granitic rocks in the complex. They are rare and form only a small part of the southern complex.

Although the southern complex predates the Penokean orogeny, it was little affected by that orogeny; all folds in the complex, and most of the mineralogic features, are the result of one or more Precambrian W orogenies. Folds in the gneissic rocks are cut by metadiabase dikes which are older than the Penokean orogeny but are not folded, indicating that no Penokean folding of the gneissic rocks occurred. Some sheared zones and locally penetrative shear foliation, most conspicuous near Republic, may have formed during the Penokean orogeny. Mineral assemblages in the Precambrian W rocks are unrelated to the isograds of Penokean regional metamorphism defined from Precambrian X rocks by James (1955). Assemblages in Precambrian W rocks generally indicate meta-

[1] Because the origin of these rocks is undetermined, the term "megacryst" is used for those grains in an inequigranular rock that are distinctly larger than grains of the groundmass. Terms such as "phenocryst" and "porphyroblast," that imply an origin, are avoided.

morphism more intense than the Penokean metamorphism. Retrograde metamorphism of the high-grade Precambrian W assemblages was minimal during the Penokean metamorphism, probably because of a scarcity of water, which prevented rehydration of the largely dehydrated Precambrian W assemblages.

BELL CREEK GNEISS

The rocks here named Bell Creek Gneiss are a layered sequence of coarse-grained megacrystic granitic gneiss and concordant layers, some 1,000 feet or more thick, of mostly moderately to weakly foliated mafic gneiss. At several localities, lenses of highly metamorphosed iron-formation are within the mafic gneiss. Near Republic is a belt 3–4 miles wide of finer grained megacrystic granite. Thin layers, most only a few feet thick, are rare but widely distributed and consist of fine- to medium-grained granite and rarely of biotitic or hornblendic quartzite. The Bell Creek also includes one conspicuous unit of migmatite. The Bell Creek Gneiss is named for Bell Creek in the Greenwood quadrangle, and the type locality is in secs. 32 and 33, T. 47, N., R. 28 W., where most phases of the gneiss are well exposed along the valley of Bell Creek and in artificial exposures along a recently constructed pipeline.

Granitic gneiss.—The most abundant rock type in the Bell Creek Gneiss is coarse-grained granitic gneiss, a very distinctive rock consisting of large pink megacrysts of microcline microperthite, typically 4–5 cm long, set in a coarse matrix of quartz, feldspar, and biotite with an average grain size of 2–5 mm (fig. 4). Pink, white, and gray are common colors for both weathered and fresh surfaces. The megacrysts are commonly carlsbad twins and are generally moderately to strongly alined, which imparts a distinctly gneissic appearance. Layers 1 to 5 feet thick are apparent in some outcrops because of variations in the abundance of megacrysts. The composition of the groundmass is uniform, regardless of the concentration of the megacrysts, and the layers are parallel to the gneissic structure (alinement of the megacrysts).

The mineralogic and chemical compositions are relatively homogeneous, as indicated by the proportions of quartz, plagioclase, and potassium feldspar plotted in figure 5*A* and the chemical analyses in table 1. The rock is predominantly adamellite with lesser amounts of granodiorite and granite; tonalite is rare.

A finer grained phase of this rock occurs in a belt 3 to 4 miles wide in the southwest corner of the mapped area (fig. 2); the belt trends parallel to the northwest strike of the regional foliation and appears to be a concordant body in the coarser grained gneiss. The northeast contact of this unit is gradational; the grain size gradually increases across a zone roughly a few hundred feet wide in which the finer grained rocks pass into typical coarse-grained granitic gneiss. The southwest contact of this unit is southwest of the map area; here, also, reconnaissance indicates that the finer grained rocks pass into typical coarse-grained granitic gneiss. In hand specimen, the rock is mineralogically identical to the coarser grained variety and is texturally similar, except for the diminished size of all components. Microcline megacrysts are 1–2 cm long, and groundmass grains are about 1–2 mm.

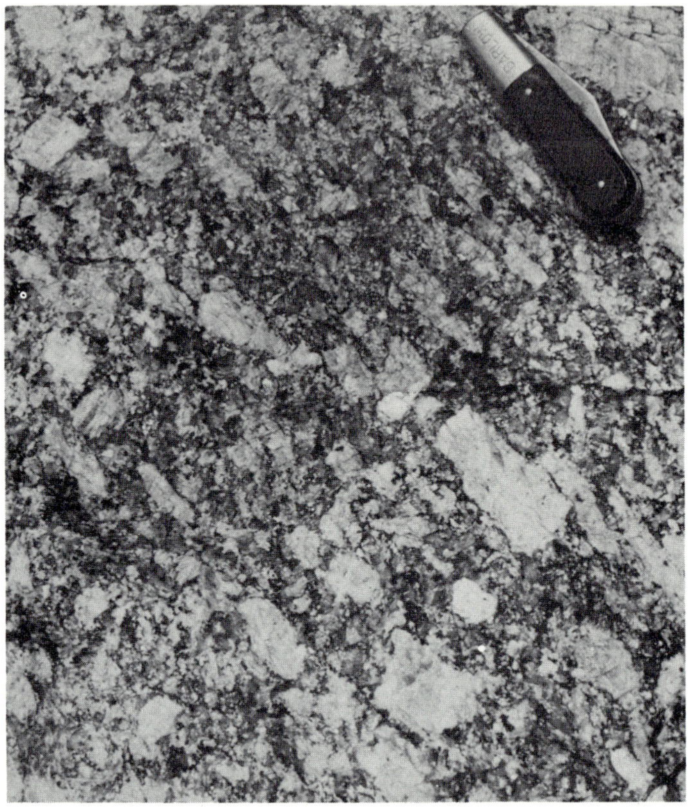

Figure 4.—Granitic phase of Bell Creek Gneiss at type locality in pipeline cut 100 feet west of Marquette County Road 478; 500 ft S., 2,000 ft W., NE cor. sec. 32, T. 47 N., R. 28 W.

Mafic gneiss.—Layers of mafic gneiss of mappable extent are common and widely distributed throughout the granitic gneiss. They occur parallel to the foliation of the granitic gneiss, and intrusion of one rock by the other has not been found. The most common mafic gneiss is black to dark green and chiefly consists of plagioclase and hornblende, and, locally, clinopyroxene. In outcrop, the clinopyroxene is generally distinguishable from hornblende by its somewhat golden-weathering surface which is distinct from the black hornblende. The texture is characteristically granoblastic, with little preferred orientation of grains, and is distinct from the relict diabasic texture of younger mafic rocks. Equant grains 1 mm across are typical. In hand specimen, the rock is either massive or compositionally layered, but at outcrop scale some compositional layering can always be found, even where the rock is largely massive. In a few places, the rock contains elongated ellipsoidal structures suggestive of stretched pillows.

Mafic rocks, in masses too small to show on figure 2, are widely distributed throughout the Bell Creek Gneiss. The relative age of these rocks is commonly difficult to determine, but it is clear that these rocks are of several different ages and

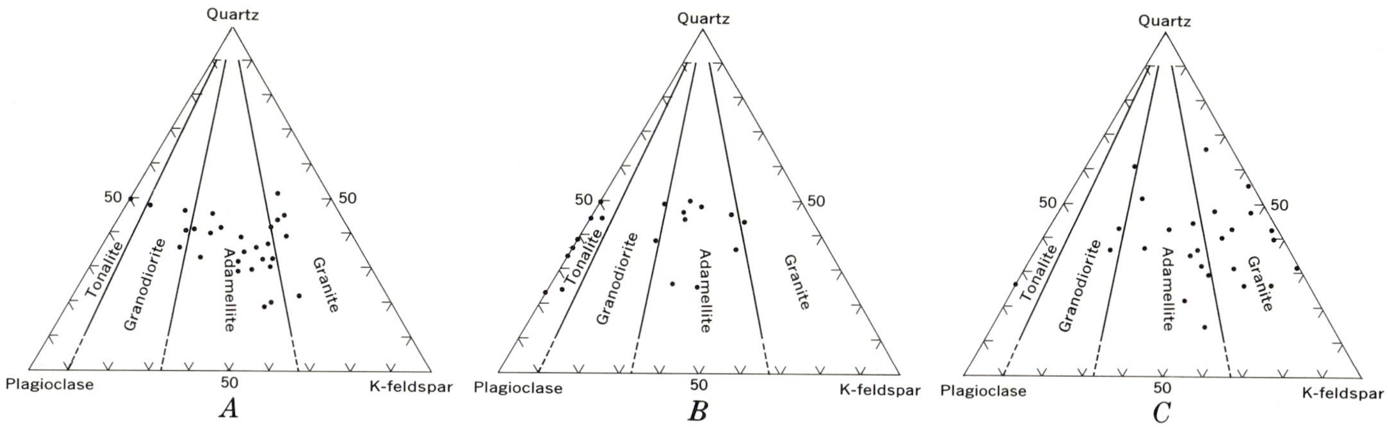

Figure 5.—Ternary diagrams showing the relative modal proportions of quartz, plagioclase (mostly oligoclase), and potassium feldspar in granitic gneiss of the Bell Creek Gneiss (*A*), granitic gneiss of the Compeau Creek Gneiss (*B*), and massive granitic rocks of the Compeau Creek Gneiss (*C*).

Table 1.—*Chemical analyses of rocks from the southern complex, Marquette district, Michigan*
[Method used was a single-solution procedure described by Shapiro (1967)]

Field No	GS-1-71	GS-2-71	GS-3-71	GS-35-71	GS-36-71	GS-38-71	GS-40-71	GS-41-71	GS-43-71	GS-44-71	GS-45-71
SiO_2	74.2	73.4	74.0	74.9	75.1	74.5	49.3	47.1	71.2	51.0	75.7
Al_2O_3	13.7	13.7	13.5	12.4	12.9	13.7	15.8	13.7	14.0	15.7	13.3
Fe_2O_3	.50	.50	.50	.40	.18	.30	1.2	2.0	.30	1.2	.40
FeO	1.4	1.6	1.8	1.4	.32	.84	10.2	11.4	2.4	10.9	.68
MgO	.42	.51	.39	.60	.24	.60	6.4	8.9	1.2	8.5	.21
CaO	1.1	1.5	1.1	1.7	.12	1.8	12.1	11.9	3.9	1.6	.16
Na_2O	2.6	2.9	2.6	2.4	2.0	3.5	2.4	1.3	4.1	.70	2.2
K_2O	5.4	4.7	4.8	5.0	7.0	4.5	.53	.50	1.2	4.1	6.1
H_2O+	.84	.83	.40	.78	.47	.71	1.6	1.4	.86	4.0	.71
H_2O-	.09	.09	.65	.04	.01	.09	.03	.03	.02	.12	.05
TiO_2	.24	.28	.29	.15	.03	.09	.89	.93	.38	2.2	.07
P_2O_5	.06	.06	.10	.17	.00	.00	.08	.06	.24	.12	.01
MnO	.05	.05	.05	.07	.06	.05	.18	.22	.41	.04	.19
CO_2	.06	.02	.26	.22	.15	.10	.10	.09	.14	.06	.08
Sum	101	100	100	100	99	101	101	100	100	100	100

Locations of samples:

GS-1-71. Bell Creek Gneiss, bridge abutment on north side of Middle Branch, Escanaba River, 2,200 ft S., 1,550 ft W., NE cor. sec. 13, T. 46 N., R. 28 W.

GS-2-71. Bell Creek Gneiss, 560 ft S., 0 ft W., NE cor. sec. 18, T. 46 N., R. 27 W. (on section line of secs. 17 and 18).

GS-3-71. Bell Creek Gneiss, type locality on pipeline 100 ft W. of Marquette County Road 478, 500 ft S., 2,000 ft W., NE cor. sec. 32, T. 47 N., R. 28 W.

GS-35-71. Compeau Creek Gneiss, granitic phase, 2,000 ft S., 2,080 ft E., NW cor. sec. 1, T. 46 N., R. 27 W.

GS-36-71. Compeau Creek Gneiss, Granitic phase, 400 ft S., 2,060 ft W., NE cor. sec. 3, T. 46 N., R. 27 W.

GS-38-71. Compeau Creek Gneiss (weakly foliated gneiss), 1,760 ft S., 2,540 ft E., NW cor. sec. 14, T. 46 N., R. 27 W.

GS-40-71. Compeau Creek Gneiss, amphibole gneiss, 1,640 ft N., 2,000 ft E., SW cor. sec. 15, T. 46 N., R. 27 W.

GS-41-71. Compeau Creek Gneiss, amphibole gneiss, 1,500 ft N., 1,550 ft W., SE cor. sec. 15, T. 46 N., R. 27 W.

GS-43-71. Compeau Creek Gneiss, 2,300 ft S., 2,200 ft E., SW cor. sec. 10, T. 46 N., R. 27 W.

GS-44-71. Compeau Creek Gneiss, amphibole gneiss, 1,300 ft N., 2,550 ft W., SE cor. sec. 30, T. 47 N., R. 27 W.

GS-45-71. Compeau Creek Gneiss, garnetiferous granodiorite, 2,550 ft N., 650 ft E., SW cor. sec. 29, T. 47 N., R. 27 W.

are in part younger than the large mafic gneiss masses shown on figure 2.

Iron-formation.—At several localities are lenses of highly metamorphosed iron-formation (see fig. 2) in mafic gneiss. The iron-formation consists of grunerite, iron-rich orthopyroxene and clinopyroxene, garnet, magnetite, and quartz in various combinations. The average grain size is 1 mm. Most iron-formation is layered; the layers are 1/2–1 inch thick. The iron-formation is pale brown or green on fresh surfaces and weathers buff. Layers of nearly pure quartz are common, and although coarse grained now, they were probably originally chert. Magnetite content is generally less than 10 percent, but may be as much as 30 percent. Although the iron-formation units are generally small, being at most about 100 feet thick and probably no more than a few thousand feet long, some are reflected as northwest-trending positive magnetic anomalies on aeromagnetic maps (Case and Gair, 1965). Other northwest-trending anomalies over the southern complex may be caused by unexposed units of iron-formation.

Migmatite.—In the Republic quadrangle, a layer of migmatite lies between the Bell Creek granitic gneiss on the north and the Compeau Creek Gneiss on the south. The migmatite layer is nearly 1,000 feet in maximum thickness and has been mapped for about 3 miles along the strike. It terminates to the northwest in a poorly exposed area where it strikes directly into the Compeau Creek Gneiss; to the southeast it pinches out between Bell Creek granitic and mafic gneiss (fig. 2). The unit consists of conspicuously layered rocks, the layers typically 1–2 feet thick and composed of light- to dark-gray quartzo-feldspathic gneiss with variable amounts of mafic minerals, mostly biotite. These layers are interlayered with pink to white, gneissic to massive granitic gneiss of the Compeau Creek Gneiss. The migmatite is believed to have originally been a unit of metasedimentary rocks within the Bell Creek Gneiss which was later migmatized during emplacement of the Compeau Creek Gneiss.

Other lithologies.—A very small volume of the Bell Creek Gneiss consists of layers of biotitic and hornblendic quartzite and fine- to medium-grained granitic rocks. These occur as layers as much as a few feet thick which are parallel to the foliation of granitic or mafic gneiss.

COMPEAU CREEK GNEISS

The Compeau Creek Gneiss was named and described by Gair and Thaden (1968) from its type locality in the northern complex, north of the Marquette synclinorium. Although there is no surface continuity between gneisses on opposite sides of the synclinorium, the gneisses were correlated on the basis of lithologic and structural similarities, and Gair and Thaden mapped the Compeau Creek Gneiss in both the northern and southern complexes near the east end of the Marquette Range. Later, Gair (1968) mapped the Compeau Creek Gneiss westward in the southern complex to the east boundary of the area discussed in this paper, and the same rocks crop out in a large part of our map area. In addition to the large areas shown in figure 2, Compeau Creek Gneiss occurs as bodies too small to be shown, which intrude the Bell Creek Gneiss at many other localities.

Massive and gneissic granitic rocks.—Most of the Compeau Creek Gneiss consists of granitic rocks which vary from gneissic to massive. They are distinct from the granitic gneiss of the Bell Creek Gneiss in their finer grain size, tendency toward more sodic composition, and common intermingling of rock types on outcrop scale. The rocks in the Compeau Creek are mostly equigranular and medium grained. Crystals larger than a few millimeters in diameter occur mostly with pegmatitic clots and veins, or more rarely as individual roughly euhedral microcline megacrysts as much as 2 inches long. Modal compositions are shown in figures 5*B* and *C*, and chemical analyses appear in table 1. Gneissic rocks are more abundant than massive rocks and are mostly tonalite and adamellite in composition, with lesser amounts of granodiorite and granite (fig. 5*B*). The massive rocks are chiefly granite and adamellite (fig. 5*C*). Layering is best shown by biotitic layers and schlieren, or in some cases by alinement of biotite, chlorite, and biotite-garnet and chlorite-garnet clots. These clots are generally about 0.5 cm in diameter and consist of randomly oriented biotite flakes; some clots contain cores of one or more fragments of anhedral garnet. In many areas, the massive granitic rocks contain abundant layers and xenoliths of older gneissic rocks of probable metasedimentary origin.

Amphibolite.—Small bodies of amphibolite are common within the Compeau Creek granitic gneiss. Most are represented by a single outcrop or parts of an outcrop, and many are clearly xenoliths. All are too small to be represented on figure 2.

The rocks are typically light to dark green and, at most places, are conspicuously gneissic (fig. 6*A*). They consist mostly of hornblende and plagioclase with minor amounts, usually less than 5 percent, of quartz. They commonly show a strong preferred orientation of *c*-axes of hornblende, and some are compositionally layered on a scale of a few inches. In places they are feldspathized by reaction with Compeau Creek granitic rocks (fig. 6*B*).

STRUCTURE

The most conspicuous structural feature of the Bell Creek Gneiss is the west to northwest trend of lithologic units and foliation. Emplacement of Compeau Creek granitic rocks obscured earlier structures of the Bell Creek Gneiss in much of the area, but the distribution of foliation-plane attitudes of the Bell Creek and trends of units suggests a northwest-plunging antiform. Immediately west of our map area, reconnaissance mapping by Taylor (1967), involving the tracing of migmatitic and granitic units, indicates closure on this northwest-plunging structure. The emplacement of the Compeau Creek Gneiss occurred, at least in part, independently of the structures in the Bell Creek Gneiss, but offshoots and satellitic bodies from the main mass of Compeau Creek Gneiss are commonly elongated parallel to the regional trend of the Bell Creek Gneiss. Foliation in the Compeau Creek Gneiss is also mostly west and northwest, but much of the unit is largely structureless, and no large-scale structures are evident.

AGE

The age of the southern complex has been debated for many years. Although many authors have favored a post-Marquette Range Supergroup age for at least part of the complex, their evidence is equivocal. Our observations agree with relations

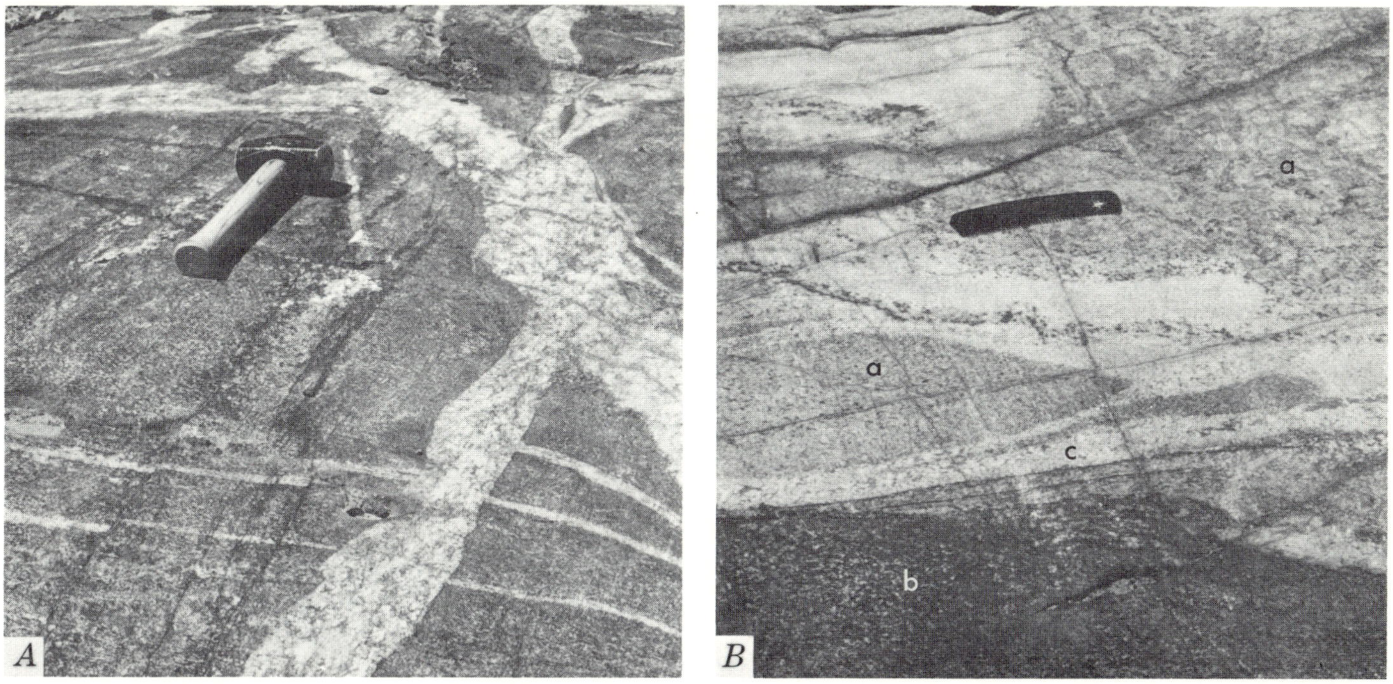

Figure 6.—Compeau Creek Gneiss.
A. Amphibolite cut by dikes of granitic pegmatite; 2,400 ft N., 500 ft W., SE cor. sec. 9, T. 46 N., R. 27 W.
B. Chloritic, biotitic, and hornblendic gneiss (a), presumably derived from amphibolite (b), at the time of emplacement of granitic pegmatite (c); 2,400 ft N., 500 ft W., SE cor. sec. 9, T. 46 N., R. 27 W.

presented by James (1955, 1958) and Gair and Thaden (1968). In our opinion, the general lack of crosscutting relationships of the granitic rocks of the southern complex to rocks of the Marquette Range Supergroup (a few pegmatites cut the Marquette Range Supergroup as well as the southern complex) and the presence of pre-Penokean diabase dikes cutting all major units of the southern complex are persuasive arguments for a Precambrian W age for the complex. This view is supported by radiometric ages from Woolsey (1971) who reported a whole-rock Rb-Sr age of 2,494±179 m.y. for 10 samples of granitic rocks from in or near our map area. Although this age is very slightly younger than the 2.5-b.y. dividing line between Precambrian W and X time, we feel that a Precambrian W age for the rocks is justified. On an isochron plot, Woolsey's data show excessive scatter, beyond experimental error, and the initial Sr^{87}/Sr^{86} ratio of 0.7097 is unusually high for granitic rocks of this age. Minerals from these rocks give much younger ages of 1,620 to 1,760 m.y., indicating a strong thermal event at this time. Some open-system behavior of the total rock systems during this younger event could well have lowered the primary isochron age, as suggested by the scatter and initial ratio, and it is very likely that the granitic rocks are 2,500 m.y. old or older (Precambrian W).

In areas about 30 miles to the south, Aldrich, Davis, and James (1965) dated similar, and probably in part correlative, rocks at 2,700 m.y. We consider that the Precambrian W age for all major units in the southern complex in our map area is now established beyond reasonable doubt.

The absolute time difference between the Bell Creek and Compeau Creek Gneiss is unknown. The 2,494-m.y. isochron (Woolsey, 1971) was derived using samples from both Bell Creek and Compeau Creek Gneisses. The Bell Creek Gneiss appears to have been isotopically homogeneous at the time of Compeau Creek emplacement, but this does not preclude the possibility that it is an older rock whose age was reset by thermal activity related to the Compeau Creek Gneiss.

ORIGIN

Bell Creek Gneiss.—The origin of the Bell Creek Gneiss is obscured by later metamorphism and deformation. Precambrian W metamorphism attained at least upper amphibolite facies, and Penokean metamorphism ranged from biotite to sillimanite grade in this area. At some places the parent material for the present rock units seems well established. The metamorphosed iron-formations are almost certainly reconstituted iron-rich precipitates of subaqueous origin. The mafic gneiss units with which they are invariably associated are, by implication, also of subaqueous origin. These units together are believed to be remnants of a Precambrian W greenstone terrane.

The origin of Bell Creek granitic gneiss presents a major problem. The clustering of modal compositions near a likely cotectic minimum, as shown in figure 5, suggests an igneous origin. These rocks are not easily interpreted as intrusive rocks, however, because they do not appear to intrude any of the units with which they are in contact. In spite of being complexly interlayered with mafic gneiss and other rock types in some areas, the granitic gneiss nowhere clearly truncates or breaches other units and contains no rock bodies which can be clearly assigned a xenolithic origin. The origin is largely an open question, but structural relationships indicate that an origin other than an intrusive igneous rock must be given serious consideration.

Compeau Creek Gneiss.—Gair and Thaden (1968) expressed little doubt that the granitic parts of the Compeau Creek Gneiss are of magmatic origin. Our work supports their findings. The complex and widespread intrusion of the granitic rocks into older rocks of the Bell Creek Gneiss, local feldspathization of older rocks near contacts with Compeau Creek granitic gneiss, and widespread pegmatitic phases in the granitic rocks all suggest a magmatic origin.

Figure 5 shows an interesting variation in modal compositions between massive and gneissic granitic rocks. Although a distinction based on the presence or lack of gneissic structure is not necessarily significant in terms of magmatic evolution, the differences shown in figure 5 suggest that the two are at least in part related in the Compeau Creek Gneiss. We suggest that the gneissic rocks, which tend to be sodic, may be the residue of partially melted sedimentary rocks whose initial composition was more sodic than the composition of the cotectic minimum in the quartz-albite-orthoclase system. The partial melting of such rocks would produce a magma more potassic than the original bulk composition, and a crystalline residue, now preserved as the gneissic rocks, which would become progressively more sodic as melting progressed. The massive rocks, which tend to be potassic, may be the crystallization products of the anatectic magma. This mechanism alone does not explain the highly potassic compositions of some of the massive rocks, but these compositions may be the result of fractional crystallization.

The origin of the schlieren and amphibolitic septa is open to question. Some amphibolite units seem to be clearly xenoliths of Bell Creek mafic gneiss. Others, that bear less resemblance to Bell Creek mafic gneiss, may be more highly altered Bell Creek Gneiss or remnants of some other unknown mafic rock. Many xenoliths are well banded, and their composition suggests a sedimentary origin. At one place in the Ishpeming quadrangle, a conglomerate layer a little more than an inch thick occurs in granitic gneiss; the layer contains abundant quartz clasts and a few pebbles, as much as 1 inch in diameter, of quartzite and ferruginous quartzite.

REFERENCES CITED

Aldrich, L. T., Davis, G. L., and James, H. L., 1965, Ages of minerals from metamorphic and igneous rocks near Iron Mountain, Michigan: Jour. Petrology, v. 6, pt. 3, p. 445–472.

Case, J. E., and Gair, J. E., 1965, Aeromagnetic map of parts of Marquette, Dickinson, Baraga, Alger, and Schoolcraft Counties, Michigan, and its geologic interpretation: U.S. Geol. Survey Geophys. Inv. Map GP-467, 3 sheets.

Dickey, R. M., 1936, The granitic sequence in the southern complex of upper Michigan: Jour. Geology, v. 44, no. 3, p. 317–340.

—— 1938, The Ford River granite of the southern complex of upper Michigan: Jour. Geology, v. 46, no. 3, pt. 1, p. 321–335.

Gair, J. E., 1968, Preliminary geologic map of the Palmer 7½-minute quadrangle, Marquette County, Michigan: U.S. Geol. Survey open-file map, scale 1:12,000.

Gair, J. E., and Thaden, R. E., 1968, Geology of the Marquette and Sands quadrangles, Marquette County, Michigan: U.S. Geol. Survey Prof. Paper 397, 77 p.

James, H. L., 1955, Zones of regional metamorphism in the Precambrian of northern Michigan: Geol. Soc. America Bull., v. 66, no. 12, pt. 1, p. 1455–1488.

—— 1958, Stratigraphy of pre-Keweenawan rocks in parts of northern Michigan: U.S. Geol. Survey Prof. Paper 314-C, p. 27–44.

Lamey, C. A., 1931, Granite intrusions in the Huronian formations of northern Michigan: Jour. Geology, v. 39, no. 3, p. 288–295.

—— 1933, The intrusive relations of the Republic granite: Jour. Geology, v. 41, no. 5, p. 487–500.

—— 1934, Some metamorphic effects of the Republic granite: Jour. Geology, v. 42, no. 3, p. 248–263.

—— 1935, The Palmer gneiss: Geol. Soc. America Bull., v. 46, no. 7, p. 1137–1162.

Shapiro, Leonard, 1967, Rapid analysis of rocks and minerals by a single-solution method, *in* Geological Survey Research 1967: U.S. Geol. Survey Prof. Paper 575-B, p. B187–B191.

Snelgrove, A. K. Seaman, W. A., and Ayres, V. L., 1944, Strategic minerals investigations, Marquette and Baraga Counties [Mich.], 1943: Michigan Geol. Survey Prog. Rept. 10, 69 p.

Taylor, W. E. G., 1967, The geology of the lower Precambrian rocks of the Champion area of upper Michigan: Northwestern Univ. Rept. 13 (Natl. Aeronautics and Space Admin. Research Grant NGR 14-007-27), 34 p.

Van Hise, C. R., and Bayley, W. S., 1897, The Marquette iron-bearing district of Michigan: U.S. Geol. Survey Mon. 28, 608 p.

Woolsey, L. L., 1971, A Rb-Sr geochronological study of the Republic metamorphic node, Republic, Michigan: Lawrence, Univ. Kansas, M.S. thesis.

Zainuddin, S. M., 1971, Petrology of the granitic rocks in the vicinity of Republic Trough in the Upper Peninsula of Michigan: East Lansing, Michigan State Univ. Ph. D. dissert., 76 p.

Jour. Research U.S. Geol. Survey
Vol. 1, No. 2, Mar.—Apr. 1973, p. 173—178

RADIOMETRIC DATING OF INTRUSIVE ROCKS IN THE COTTONWOOD AREA, UTAH

By M. D. CRITTENDEN, JR., J. S. STUCKLESS[1], R. W. KISTLER;
and T. W. STERN, Menlo Park, Calif.; Washington, D.C.

Abstract.—Recently completed fission-track and K-Ar dating of zircon, sphene, apatite, muscovite, biotite, and hornblende indicate that the Clayton Peak stock was intruded 37–41 m.y. ago, the Alta stock about 32–33 m.y. ago, and the Little Cottonwood stock between 24 and 31 m.y. ago. Pb-α ages on zircon, though showing the same sequence, are about twice as great and are inferred to represent a partial mixing of inherited Precambrian zircons. Acceptance of a middle Tertiary age for the Little Cottonwood stock requires revision of earlier interpretations that it could be as old as Late Cretaceous. K-Ar dates also indicate that the Keetley Volcanics are 32 to 35 m.y. old, and a single date of 37.3 m.y. was obtained on the Traverse Volcanics, suggesting that they are more closely related to volcanic activity in the adjoining Oquirrh Mountains.

The Cottonwood area is in north-central Utah, about 20 miles airline southeast of Salt Lake City (fig. 1). The area is bounded on the west by the Wasatch fault, a normal fault, which separates it from the Salt Lake Valley. On the east it adjoins the Park City mining district, and the series of igneous rocks considered here extend from one area to the other.

The Cottonwood area lies at the intersection of two of the major tectonic elements of northern Utah (fig. 1), the west-trending Uinta arch (Crittenden, 1964) and the north-trending belt of folds and thrusts of the Sevier orogenic belt (Armstrong, 1968). The interaction of these two elements has long been regarded as significant in localizing the intrusive rocks and the associated ore deposits (Butler and others, 1911; Calkins and Butler, 1943; Tooker, 1971).

The major intrusive bodies of the Cottonwood area comprise three stocks alined in an east-west direction roughly along the Uinta arch; they are, from east to west, the Clayton Peak, Alta, and Little Cottonwood stocks (fig. 1) (Boutwell, 1912; Calkins and Butler, 1943). These bodies form a coherent sequence in both age and composition, being oldest on the east and youngest on the west, and ranging from moderately mafic quartz diorite (Clayton Peak) to quartz monzonite (Little Cottonwood). The central Alta stock intrudes the Clayton Peak, but the Little Cottonwood stock is not in contact with either of the others. All are coarse-grained holocrystalline plutonic rocks. In this respect, they differ markedly from the porphyries of the adjoining Park City district, most of which have an aphanitic or fine- to medium-grained groundmass like those that characterize many other mining districts of western Utah. Recent mapping in the Cottonwood area (Crittenden, 1965; Baker and others, 1966; Bromfield and others, 1970) has shown that each of the western stocks (Alta and Little Cottonwood) contains a younger, porphyritic, and generally more silicic phase (fig. 1). Though each appears to intrude the enclosing nonporphyritic phase, radiometric dating does not reveal a significant difference in age.

[1] Present address: Northern Illinois University, DeKalb, Ill. 60115

RADIOMETRIC DATING

Attempts to date the intrusive rocks of the Cottonwood area were begun by E. S. Larsen, Jr., of the U.S. Geological Survey, soon after the lead-alpha method was devised, and preliminary results were reported by Crittenden, Sharp, and Calkins (1952) and by Jaffe and others (1959, p. 75). Improvements in the technique for lead analysis (Rose and Stern, 1960, p. 1243) resulted in new determinations on the original samples, and these later measurements (reported here) supersede those by Jaffe. Table 1 summarizes these Pb-α ages, together with K-Ar ages on biotite, muscovite, and hornblende, and recently completed fission-track ages on zircon, sphene, and apatite. Analytical and sample localities are included in tables 2, 3, and 4.

Argon analyses were made using standard isotope dilution techniques (Dalrymple and Lanphere, 1969) and a Nier-type 6-inch radius, 60°-sector mass spectrometer. The errors shown as plus-or-minus (±) values range from 2 to 4 percent of the calculated ages and are assigned on the basis of experience with duplicate analyses and uncertainties in individual analyses.

The techniques of fission-track analysis are described by Naeser and McKee (1970) for zircon and apatite and by Stuckless and Sheridan (1971) for sphene. The decay constant used in these calculations was $6.85 \times 10^{-17} yr^{-1}$. The "±" after a determination on a single grain or a population of apatites represents one standard deviation based on the number of

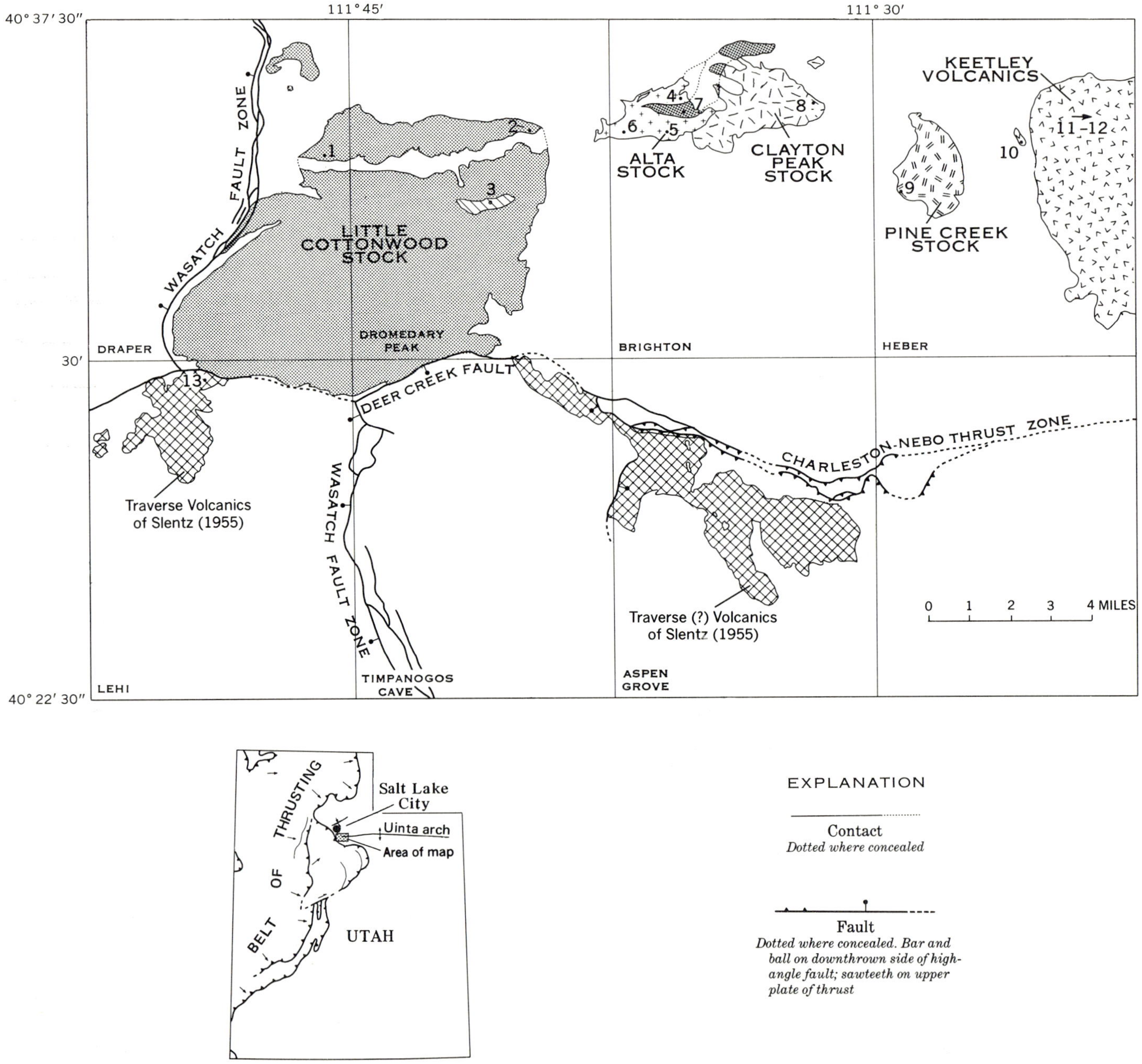

Figure 1.—Map showing regional setting of Cottonwood area, Utah. Numbers refer to sample localities listed in table 1.

fossil, induced, and standard tracks counted. The "±" assigned to an average mineral age is twice the standard error of the mean.

INTERPRETATION AND DISCUSSION

The Pb-α ages (tables 1 and 2) are consistent with the relative age relations determined from field mapping but (except for thorite from the Clayton Peak stock) are nearly twice as high as the ages obtained by other methods. The close agreement of ages for each intrusive body by the K-Ar dates on muscovite, biotite, and hornblende and by fission-track dates on zircon, sphene, and apatite suggests that the Pb-α ages do not represent the time of crystallization. This inference is supported also by the Pb-α ages of 200 to 270 m.y. obtained for the Pine Creek stock (LSH-4 and 4a), whose relations to other porphyritic rocks of the Park City district strongly suggest a Tertiary age.

The zircons in samples LSH-1, 2, and 3 appear almost identical optically, but each sample contains zircons of two

Table 1.—*Summary of radiometric dates, in millions of years*

Locality (fig. 1)	Sample No.	Apatite[1]		Zircon		Sphene[1]		Biotite	Hornblende	Muscovite	Assigned age
Little Cottonwood stock											
1...	LSH-1	8.5±1.0		[1]25.1±3.5	[2]24.5±0.6	24.0±3.9	[2]24.1±0.6	[3]24.8±0.8			
				[1]24.5±7.1		24.0±3.7		[3]25.4±0.8			
				[1]23.8±2.9		23.4±4.0					
				[4]50±10		25.1±3.2					
						25.0±4.9		[5]24±6			Early
						23.1±3.0					Miocene.
1...	63-mc-64								[6]31.1±0.9		
2...	146							[7]26.2±0.5			
2...	63-mc-63							[6]28.4±1.4			
3...	64-mc-20									[3]25.5±0.8	
Alta stock											
4...	LSH-2	35.6±3.6		[1]33.4±4.6	[2]33.7±0.9	34.2±5.3	[2]32.7±0.9				
				[1]34.7±4.6		31.4±5.1					
				[1]32.9±6.9		32.4±5.7					
				[4]60±10		31.4±4.9					
						31.9±5.1					Early
						35.4±6.3					Oligocene.
4...	64-mc-5							[3]32.1±1.0	[3]33.5±1.0		
5...	58-FC-53							[6]32.6±1.0	[6]30.9±1.5		
6...	145							[7]32.8±0.7			
7...	64-mc-4							[3]32.4±1.0	[3]35.1±1.1		
Clayton Peak stock											
8...	LSH-3	36.2±12.3		[1]40.1±5.7	[2]40.9±2.2			[8]36.7±1.5			
		50.5±15.7		[1]39.1±5.0							
		42.4±13.0		[1]43.5±5.7							
		38.8±13.9	[2]41.2±3.0	[4]70±10							Late
		41.9±13.2		[9]40±4 (thorite)							Eocene.
		36.3±11.8									
		43.6±12.2									
		39.9±14.3									
Pine Creek stock											
9...	LSH-4a			[4]270±30				[6]36.8±1.1			Early
				[4]200±25							Oligocene.
Keetley Volcanics											
10...	63-mc-47							[6]35.1±1.1			Early
11...	62-mc-12							[6]32.7±1.0			Oligocene.
12...	62-mc-15							[6]34.0±1.0			
Traverse Volcanics of Slentz (1955)											
13...	63-mc-66							[6]37.3±1.1			Eocene-Oligocene boundary.

[1] Fission track (J. S. Stuckless, this report).
[2] Average.
[3] K-Ar (J. C. Engels, this report).
[4] Pb-α (T. W. Stern, this report).
[5] Rb-Sr (Aldrich, 1961).
[6] K-Ar (R. W. Kistler, this report).
[7] K-Ar (Armstrong, 1963).
[8] K-Ar (J. D. Obradovich, this report).
[9] Pb-α (Jaffe and others, 1959).

distinct shapes. Both kinds are generally euhedral, but in one the *c* direction is greater than *a* and *b*, whereas the other form is roughly equidimensional. The proportions of the two forms are different from sample to sample. In LSH-3 the equidimensional form is most abundant; in LSH-2 the elongate form makes up slightly more than half the zircon; in LSH-1 the elongate form strongly predominates. Stern, Phair, and Newell (1971) noted a similar bimodal distribution of zircons

Table 2.—*Lead-alpha analytical data*

Sample No.	Mineral	α/mg-hr	Lead (ppm)	Calculated age[1] (m.y.)
LSH-1	Zircon	517	[2]10.2	50±10
LSH-2	. . do. .	308	[2]6.9	60±10
LSH-3	. . do. .	218	[2]6.0	70±10
LSH-3	Thorite[3]	5,795	115	40
LSH-4	Zircon	120	[2]13.3	270±30
LSH-4a . . .	. . do. .	126	[2]10.0	200±25

[1] The lead-alpha age was calculated from the following equations:

$$t = \mathrm{C\ Pb}/\alpha,$$

where t is the calculated age in millions of years, C is a constant based upon the U/Th ratio, Pb is the lead content in parts per million, and α is the alpha counts per milligram per hour.

$$T = t - \tfrac{1}{2}\mathrm{k}t^2,$$

where T is the age in millions of years corrected for decay of uranium and thorium, and k is a decay constant based upon the U/Th ratio. These constants were used for zircon:

Assumed Th/U ratio	C	k
1.0	2,483	1.56×10^{-6}

Age is rounded off to nearest 10 m.y. The error quoted here is that resulting only from uncertainties in analytical techniques.

[2] Lead determinations by Charles Annell and Harold Westley. All values are average of duplicate determinations.

[3] Jaffe and others (1959).

Table 3.—*Potassium-argon analytical data*

[K determinations by H. C. Whitehead and L. B. Schlocker, using flame photometry and a lithium internal standard. Constants used for K^{40} are $\lambda_\epsilon = 0.585\times10^{-10}\mathrm{yr}^{-1}$, $\lambda_\beta = 4.72\times10^{-10}\mathrm{yr}^{-1}$, and atomic abundance of $K^{40} = 1.19\times10^{-4}$ moles/mole]

Sample No.	Mineral	K_2O (percent)	Ar^{40}_{rad} (moles/g)	$Ar^{40}_{rad}/Ar^{40}_{total}$	Age (m.y.)
LSH-1 . . .	Biotite	6.96	2.570×10^{-10}	0.73	24.8±0.8
	. . .do. . .	. . . .	2.629×10^{-10}	.87	25.4±0.8
63-mc-64	Hornblende	.961	4.448×10^{-11}	.62	31.1±0.9
63-mc-63	. . .do. . .	9.01	3.807×10^{-10}	.54	28.4±1.4
64-mc-20	Muscovite	10.24	3.880×10^{-10}	.78	25.5±0.8
64-mc-5	Biotite	9.15	4.376×10^{-10}	.47	32.1±1.0
	Hornblende	.531	2.650×10^{-11}	.53	33.5±1.0
58-FC-53	Biotite	8.54	4.149×10^{-10}	.70	32.6±1.0
	Hornblende	.55	2.550×10^{-11}	.27	30.9±1.5
64-mc-4	Biotite	8.59	4.149×10^{-10}	.88	32.4±1.0
	Hornblende	.487	2.551×10^{-11}	.47	35.1±1.1
LSH-3 . . .	Biotite	8.13	4.435×10^{-10}	.90	36.7±1.5
LSH-4a . . .	. .do. . .	5.01	2.745×10^{-10}	.73	36.8±1.1
63-mc-47	. . .do. . .	7.81	4.079×10^{-10}	.85	35.1±1.1
62-mc-12	. . .do. . .	7.92	3.847×10^{-10}	.86	32.7±1.0
62-mc-15	. . .do. . .	7.48	3.791×10^{-10}	.77	34.0±1.0
63-mc-66	. . .do. . .	5.85	3.262×10^{-10}	.89	37.3±1.1

Table 4.—*Sample locality data*

Locality No. (fig. 1)	Sample No.	Location: Lat (N.) Long (W.)	Location: Specific
1	LSH-1 and 63-mc-64.	40°34′22.8″ 111°45′15.6″	Temple quarry, near mouth of Little Cottonwood Canyon.
2	146 and 63-mc-63.	40°35′0″ 111°39′30″	1½ miles WSW of Alta, Little Cottonwood Canyon.
3	64-mc-20. . .	40°33′20.4″ 111°40′52.2″	White Pine Canyon.
4	LSH-2	40°35′55″ 111°35′00″	Brighton area, Big Cottonwood Canyon. Freshly blasted glacial erratic, nonporphyritic phase.
4	64-mc-5 . . .	40°35′57.6″ 111°35′10.8″	Outcrops just north of line of Mount Millicent ski lift, nonporphyritic phase.
5	58-FC-53. . .	40°34′55″ 111°35′41.5″	Outcrops west of Lake Catherine, nonporphyritic phase.
6	145	40°34′50″ 111°36′55″	1 mile SE of Alta, Little Cottonwood Canyon, nonporphyritic phase.
7	64-mc-4 . . .	40°35′21.6″ 111°35′13.8″	Small quarry immediately south of Lake Mary dam, porphyritic phase.
8	LSH-3	40°36′03″ 111°32′24″	Southwest edge of Lake Brimhall, head of Pine Creek, Brighton quadrangle.
9	LSH-4a	40°33′47″ 111°29′30″	Quarry beside road in Pine Creek Canyon, Heber quadrangle.
10	63-mc-47 . .	40°34′43″ 111°25′52″	Quarry west of Provo River at mouth of Cottonwood Canyon.
11	62-mc-12. . .	40°36′17″ 111°17′45″	Quarry on point of ridge 0.9 mile WSW of Francis.
12	62-mc-15. . .	40°28′0″ 111°3′30″	Cliffs overlooking Leonards Lake.
13	63-mc-66. . .	40°29′38″ 111°49′30″	Roadcuts on north slope of Traverse Range.

in the Boulder Creek batholith, Colorado, and concluded that the anhedral zircons with lower length to width ratios were inherited by assimilation from older rocks. Although the equidimensional zircons in the Cottonwood area are not anhedral, it is possible that some of them may be inherited.

That a large proportion of zircons is inherited is the most reasonable way to account for the anomalously high Pb-α ages of samples LSH-4 and 4a and is inferred to contribute to the other dates also. It seems probable that the inherited zircons were heated sufficiently by the magma to anneal their inherited fission tracks and to remove any radiation damage which might be used to distinguish them optically but not sufficiently to bring their lead-uranium content into equilibrium. Hence the fission-track age gives the age of crystallization, whereas the Pb-α ages still bear the partial imprint of the previous history of these rocks.

Two other explanations for the older Pb-α ages that cannot be excluded are the presence of nonradiogenic lead in the concentrates and systematically high lead values. The majority of the zircon concentrates contain less than 10 ppm Pb, and it is possible that the errors exceed the 5 percent commonly assumed for isotope dilution and chemical values determined for zircon of higher lead content. If so, however, one would not expect to find ages so systematically related to those determined by two other age techniques.

The Clayton Peak stock is regarded as having been emplaced between 37 and 41 m.y. ago (late Eocene). The relatively large statistical uncertainties in dates for the apatite grains result from the small number of fossil fission tracks counted. Nevertheless, the agreement between the average of these results and those from zircon suggests relatively rapid cooling and absence of later thermal events (Naeser and others, 1971).

The Alta stock yields a strikingly concordant array of ages, indicating that it was intruded between 32 and 33 m.y. ago (early Oligocene). Ages on different minerals by different methods on both the nonporphyritic and younger porphyritic phases agree within the limits of analytical error. The concordance of the apatite fission-track age with those for zircon and sphene suggests relatively rapid cooling and the absence of later thermal events.

The Little Cottonwood stock yields ages with the largest spread and involves structural complications that have led to speculation that it could be as old as Cretaceous (Baker and Crittenden, 1961). This interpretation depends on field relations which show that the stock is bounded on the south and west by rocks of the upper plate of the Charleston-Nebo thrust. To the southeast the thrust is overlapped by latest Cretaceous and Paleocene rocks, which places a minimum age of Cretaceous on the thrust. The rocks of the upper plate are separated from the Little Cottonwood stock and its contact metamorphic aureole by many tens of feet of dense mylonite. The mylonite was believed to have been developed by the Charleston-Nebo thrust, thereby requiring the stock to be older than the thrust.

If the Cretaceous age were accepted, the numerous radiometric dates around 25 m.y. would have to be explained by a thermal resetting of the mineral ages. Regional heating, centered west of the area shown in figure 1, could accomplish this resetting and still leave the proper relative ages for the various intrusives since the ages increase eastward, but there is no independent evidence for such a heat source. Furthermore, the temperature required to completely reset zircon during a period of 1 m.y. is 450° to 600°C (Naeser and others, 1971). In order for apatite in the nearby Alta stock to retain all its fission tracks and therefore to yield an age concordant with zircon, it could not have been heated above 75°C for more than 1 m.y. (Naeser and Faul, 1969). Such a steep thermal gradient on a regional scale seems unreasonable. Thus the concordant sphene and zircon fission-track and the nearly concordant K-Ar dates coupled with the possible explanation for the older Pb-α dates suggest that the earlier Cretaceous age assignment for the Little Cottonwood stock is not correct.

The above argument supports an alternate age assignment for the mylonite. Crittenden, Sharp, and Calkins (1952, p. 30) and Armstrong (1963, p. 168) proposed that the mylonite might be the product of movement along the Deer Creek fault, a normal fault with unknown but large middle Tertiary displacement. In addition to the stock, this fault cuts volcanic and clastic sediments of the Tibble Formation (Baker and Crittenden, 1961). These sediments are assigned to the Tertiary and are believed to be closely related in origin to the volcanic rocks of the Traverse Range, which have yielded a K-Ar date of 37 m.y.

The present data suggest that the Little Cottonwood stock was intruded between 24 and 31 m.y. ago. The two biotite ages from the eastern margin of the stock are significantly older than most of the ages from Temple quarry (loc. 1, fig. 1) near the western edge. That these older ages may more nearly represent the time of intrusion than do the more abundant 24- to 25-m.y. ages is suggested by the discordance of both the one hornblende age and the younger apatite ages. The 8.5-m.y. date for the apatite clearly indicates a thermal resetting. Higher temperatures are required to reset hornblende (650°C) than are required for biotite (325°C) (Evernden and Kistler, 1970), and it seems possible that near the Temple quarry, temperatures were reached that affected all the mineral ages, except that of the K-Ar in hornblende.

The coincidence of the 24- to 25-m.y. ages with that obtained for the muscovite from the greisen in White Pine Canyon (loc. 3) suggests that this hydrothermal mineralization may have accompanied local heating in the western part of the stock. Alternatively, the proposed regional heating may not have been great enough to affect any minerals except apatite. If so, the older hornblende age may be the result of incorporated material that was not completely outgassed or of extraneous argon which would affect the age of the low-potassium phase (hornblende) more than the higher potassium mineral (biotite).

The 8.5-m.y. age on the apatite from LSH-1 cannot be interpreted directly because the rate of annealing is dependent on both time and temperature. Thus the age may represent either the end of complete annealing at 8.5 m.y. or an averaging by partial annealing of an earlier and a later episode. It is most reasonable to infer that the 8.5-m.y. date represents the approximate time of cooling through the 100°C isotherm. Assuming typical geothermal gradients, this cooling might be accounted for by an uplift of about 3 km (10,000 feet) and subsequent denudation on the order of 6 to 10 m.y. ago, implying an episode of rapid uplift on the Wasatch fault in the early Pliocene.

REGIONAL RELATIONS

The chronology of igneous activity in the Cottonwood and Park City district, reported here, and in the Bingham district of the Oquirrh Mountains to the west (Moore and Lanphere, 1971) is summarized in figure 2. Although the data from Park City are limited, it appears that intrusive activity began in all three areas at about the same time in the late Eocene to early Oligocene (37–41 m.y. ago). Volcanism in and east of the Park City district continued until 32–34 m.y. ago, according to dates on the Keetley Volcanics. Geologic relations near Keetley show that the volcanic rocks are intruded by shallow stocks and locally are mineralized (Bromfield and others, 1970; Bromfield and Crittenden, 1971), suggesting that ore deposition also took place during this interval. At Bingham, mineralization ended before 35 m.y. ago. In the Cottonwood area, plutonism and associated greisen mineralization apparently continued about 10 m.y. longer, until very late in Oligocene time. If volcanic activity accompanied the Cottonwood intrusions, any record of it has been erased by uplift and erosion. Hypabyssal dikes ranging from lamprophyres to rhyolites are widespread in the Cottonwood area (Calkins and Butler, 1943) but do not seem abundant enough to represent the roots of a volcano.

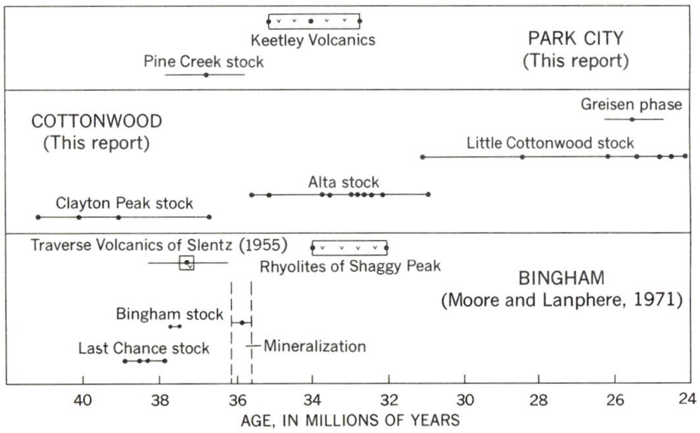

Figure 2.–Radiometric dates from Park City, Cottonwood, and Bingham areas, Utah.

REFERENCES CITED

Aldrich, L. T., 1961, Discussion *in* Kulp, J. L., ed., Geochronology of rock systems: New York Acad. Sci. Annals, v. 91, p. 463.

Armstrong, R. L., 1963, Geochronology and geology of the eastern Great Basin in Nevada and Utah: New Haven, Conn., Yale Univ., unpub. Ph. D. thesis, 202 p.

——1968, Sevier orogenic belt in Nevada and Utah: Geol. Soc. America Bull., v. 79, p. 429–458.

——1970, K-Ar dating using neutron activation for Ar analysis: Comparison with isotope dilution Ar analyses: Geochim. et Cosmochim. Acta, v. 34, p. 233–236.

Baker, A. A., Calkins, F. C., Crittenden, M. D., Jr., and Bromfield, C. S., 1966, Geologic map of the Brighton quadrangle, Utah: U.S. Geol. Survey Geol. Quad. Map GQ-534, scale 1:24,000.

Baker, A. A., and Crittenden, M. D., Jr., 1961, Geology of the Timpanogos Cave quadrangle, Utah: U.S. Geol. Survey Geol. Quad. Map GQ-132, scale 1:24,000.

Boutwell, J. M., 1912, Geology and ore deposits of the Park City district, Utah: U.S. Geol. Survey Prof. Paper 77, 231 p.

Bromfield, C. S., Baker, A. A., and Crittenden, M. D., Jr., 1970, Geologic map of the Heber quadrangle: U.S. Geol. Survey Geol. Quad. Map GQ-864, scale 1:24,000.

Bromfield, C. S., and Crittenden, M. D., Jr., 1971, Geologic map of the Park City East quadrangle: U.S. Geol. Survey Geol. Quad. Map GQ-852, scale 1:24,000.

Butler, B. S., Loughlin, G. F., Heikes, V. C., and others, 1911, Ore deposits of Utah: U.S. Geol. Survey Prof. Paper 111, 672 p.

Calkins, F. C., and Butler, B. S., 1943, Geology and ore deposits of the Cottonwood-American Fork area, Utah: U.S. Geol. Survey Prof. Paper 201, 152 p.

Crittenden, M. D., Jr., 1964, General geology of Salt Lake County, Sec. 1 *in* Geology of Salt Lake County: Utah Geol. and Mineralog. Survey Bull. 69, p. 11–48.

——1965, Geology of the Draper, Dromedary Peak, Mount Aire, and Sugar House quadrangles, Utah: U.S. Geol. Survey Geol. Quad. Maps GQ-377, GQ-378, GQ-389, and GQ-380, scale 1:24,000.

Crittenden, M. D., Jr., Sharp, B. J., and Calkins, F. C., 1952, Geology of the Wasatch Mountains east of Salt Lake City, Parleys Canyon, and Traverse Range: Utah Geol. Soc., Guidebook to the geology of Utah, no. 8, p. 1–37.

Dalrymple, G. B., and Lanphere, M. A., 1969, Potassium-argon dating; principles, techniques, and applications to geochronology: San Francisco, W. H. Freeman and Co., 258 p.

Evernden, J. F., and Kistler, R. W., 1970, Chronology of emplacement of Mesozoic batholithic complexes in California and western Nevada: U.S. Geol. Survey Prof. Paper 623, 42 p.

Jaffe, H. W., Gottfried, David, Waring, C. L., and Worthing, H. W., 1959, Lead-alpha age determinations of accessory minerals of igneous rocks (1953–1957): U.S. Geol. Survey Bull. 1097-B, p. 65–148.

Moore, W. J., and Lanphere, M. A., 1971, The age of porphyry-type copper mineralization in the Bingham district, Utah–A refined estimate: Econ. Geology, v. 66, p. 331–334.

Naeser, C. W., and Faul, H. O., 1969, Fission track annealing in apatite and sphene: Jour. Geophys. Research, v. 74, p. 705–710.

Naeser, C. W., Kistler, R. W., and Dodge, F. C. W., 1971, Ages of coexisting minerals from heat-flow borehole sites, central Sierra Nevada batholith: Jour. Geophys. Research, v. 76, p. 6462–6463.

Naeser, C. W., and McKee, E. H., 1970, Fission-track and K-Ar ages of Tertiary ash-flow tuffs, north-central Nevada: Geol. Soc. America Bull., v. 81, p. 3375–3384.

Rose, H. J., Jr., and Stern, T. W., 1960, Spectrochemical determination of lead in zircon for lead-alpha age measurements: Am. Mineralogist, v. 45, p. 1243–1256.

Slentz, L. W., 1955, Salt Lake group in lower Jordan Valley, Utah: Utah Geol. Soc., Guidebook to the geology of Utah, no. 10, p. 23–36.

Stern, T. W., Phair, George, and Newell, M. F., 1971, Boulder Creek batholith–Part II, Isotopic age of emplacement and morphology of zircon: Geol. Soc. America Bull., v. 82, p. 1615–1634.

Stuckless, J. S., and Sheridan, M. F., 1971, Tertiary volcanic stratigraphy in the Goldfield and Superstition Mountains, Arizona: Geol. Soc. America Bull., v. 82, p. 3235–3240.

Tooker, E. W., 1971, Regional structural controls of the deposits, Bingham mining district, Utah, U.S.A.: Japan Geol. Soc., Spec. Issue 3, p. 76–81 [Internat. Mineralog. Assoc.–Internat. Assoc. Genesis of Ore Deposits Mtgs. Proc.]

Jour. Research U.S. Geol. Survey
Vol. 1, No. 2, Mar.—Apr. 1973, p. 179—192

MAGNETIZATIONS OF SOME LATE CRETACEOUS GLASSY TUFFS, VOLCANIC BRECCIAS, AND ALTERED BASALTS OF THE ELKHORN MOUNTAINS VOLCANIC FIELD, WESTERN MONTANA

By W. F. HANNA, Menlo Park, Calif.

Abstract.—New magnetization data for Late Cretaceous glassy welded tuffs, volcanic breccias, and altered basalts from the Elkhorn Mountains volcanic field, together with geologic, mineralogic, and K-Ar data, indicate that (1) the glassy tuffs have unusually strong, uniform remanent magnetizations which are reversely polarized, much of the remanence perhaps residing in submicroscopic single-domain iron oxide particles within the glass itself, (2) breccias emplaced at minimum temperatures of about 400°C have moderately dispersed remanent magnetization directions which are normally polarized, and (3) basalts that occur within a broad area of hydrothermal alteration have remanent magnetization directions which are normally, horizontally, and reversely polarized. Present and previous studies indicate the occurrence of from two to eight complete field reversal cycles during emplacement of the volcanic field about 78 m.y. ago. Among the rocks studied, only basalt from the Zosell mining district is important as a major aeromagnetic anomaly source.

After original paleomagnetic studies on the Elkhorn Mountains Volcanics (Colville, 1961; Hanna, 1965, 1967) were completed, two pieces of new information about the volcanic field that offered an opportunity to further the paleomagnetic understanding of the rocks were published. First, radiometric dates obtained for welded tuffs and breccias not previously sampled (Robinson and Marvin, 1967; Robinson and others, 1968) provided a firm time base for previous inferences about paleomagnetic field directions and polarities. Second, an aeromagnetic map covering parts of the Elkhorn Mountains volcanic field (Johnson and others, 1965) showed an anomalous zone of field values over basalts that occur within or near an extensive mining district, suggesting that the basalts have anomalous magnetizations. In order to update and supplement the previous magnetic work, the dated tuffs and breccias as well as the basalts suspected of having anomalous magnetizations were sampled. Results are treated together here for the purpose of presenting a complete summary of new magnetic data from the Elkhorn Mountains volcanic field.

All three groups of sampled rocks (tuffs, breccias, and basalts) have features that are distinctive from those of rocks previously sampled in the volcanic field. For example, two of the welded tuffs have high glass content and are among the oldest glassy rocks reported in the United States. These glassy tuffs were the first rocks radiometrically dated from the volcanic field. Although the radiometric data are not in perfect harmony with relative ages inferred from observed structural relations and limited paleontological data, they firmly establish the Late Cretaceous age of the rocks. The volcanic breccias, which are lithologically similar to previously sampled breccias in the volcanic field (although it is not possible to infer their temperature of formation from outcrop inspection), were the second rocks radiometrically dated. The dates obtained agree well with relative ages inferred from observed field relations. The basalts are unlike previously sampled rocks from the volcanic field in that they occur within an area subjected to regional hydrothermal alteration which accompanied extensive mineralization. One basalt sample was highly altered, and two others were slightly altered.

MEASUREMENT PROCEDURES

Magnetic measurements were made with spinner magnetometers of the types described by Doell and Cox (1965a) and Phillips and Kuckes (1967) and a magnetic susceptibility apparatus slightly modified from that described by Hanna (1968a). Oriented samples were collected by portable drill (Doell and Cox, 1965a) or, in areas of rugged terrain, by hand. Remanent magnetization measurements were made by W. E. Huff and Arthur Conradi in U.S. Geological Survey laboratories in Silver Spring, Md., and Menlo Park, Calif.

Selected specimens were partly demagnetized in peak fields of 400 Oe, by use of equipment described by Doell and Cox (1967a). Thermomagnetic data for 12 specimens, measured in air, were provided by E. A. Mankinen, who used a recording magnetic balance (Doell and Cox, 1967b). Curie temperatures were estimated from plots of magnetization versus temperature in fields of 1,500 to 5,000 Oe, with a linear sampling rate of 10°C per minute within the temperature interval 30° to 700°C.

The spinner magnetometers provided remanent magnetization directions accurate to within about 2° and magnetization intensities accurate to approximately 5 percent. Susceptibility values are estimated to be accurate to within about 1 or 2 percent. The accuracy of the temperature calibration for the magnetic balance is approximately 2°C (Grommé and others, 1969).

GLASSY WELDED TUFFS

Occurrence and description

Two outcrops of Late Cretaceous glassy welded tuff were sampled near Wolf Creek and Three Forks, about 125 km apart (fig. 1). At each site, stony welded tuffs in stratigraphic contact above and below the glassy rocks were also sampled for comparison.

The welded tuffs near Wolf Creek are exposed in a quarry next to the Great Northern Railway approximately 1.5 km south of Wolf Creek (lat 46°59.66′ N., long 112°04.40′ W.). They were identified by Adolf Knopf in 1947, were described by Barksdale (1951), and were stratigraphically reassigned from the Adel Mountain Volcanics of Lyons (1944, p. 449 and 459) to the western facies of the Two Medicine Formation (R. G. Schmidt, 1963; written commun., 1968), which is the northern equivalent of the Elkhorn Mountains Volcanics

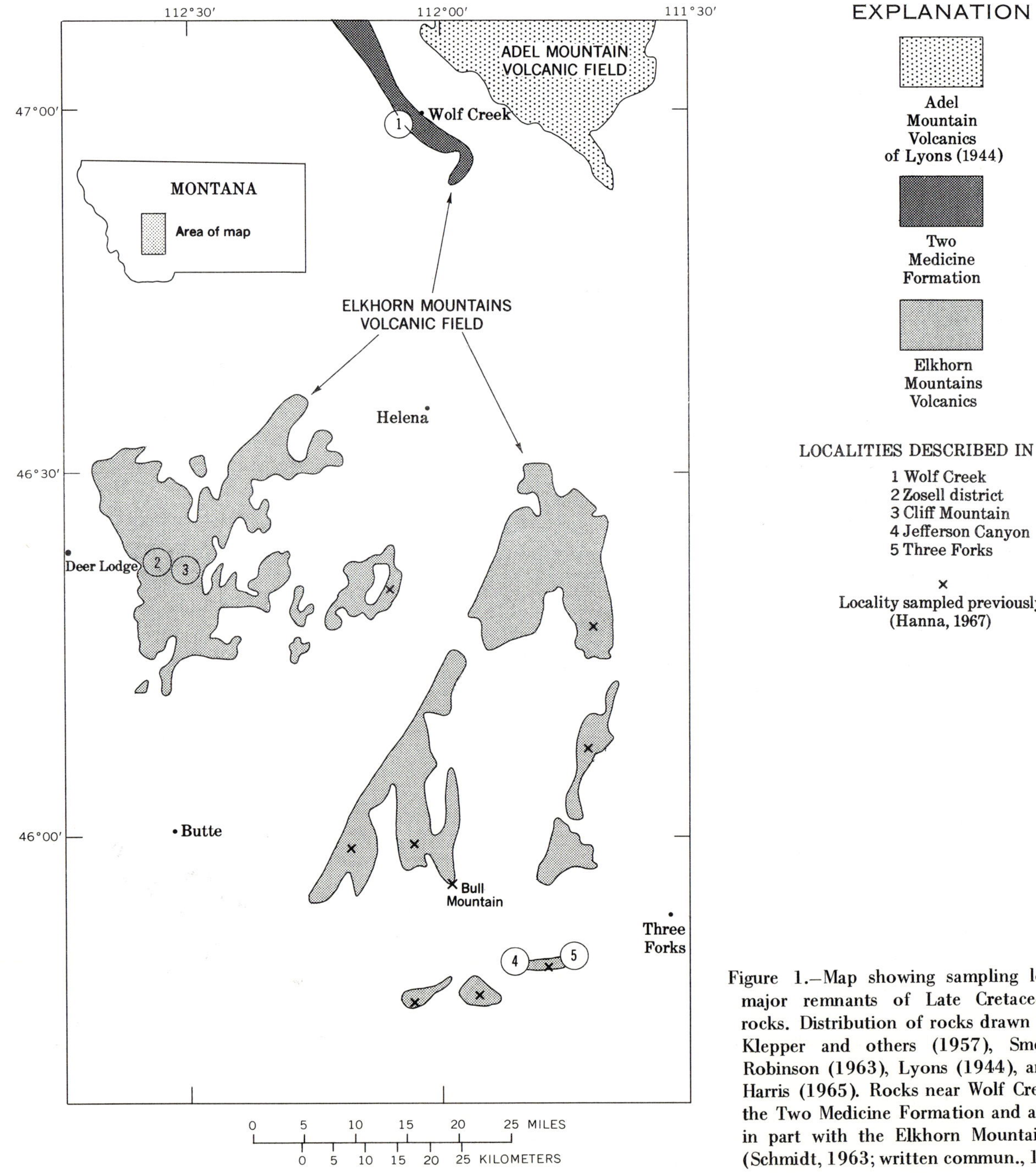

Figure 1.—Map showing sampling localities and major remnants of Late Cretaceous volcanic rocks. Distribution of rocks drawn from data of Klepper and others (1957), Smedes (1966), Robinson (1963), Lyons (1944), and Viele and Harris (1965). Rocks near Wolf Creek belong to the Two Medicine Formation and are correlative in part with the Elkhorn Mountains Volcanics (Schmidt, 1963; written commun., 1968).

(Klepper and Smedes, 1959; Viele and Harris, 1965). Magnetic data here will be compared with other results previously obtained (Hanna 1965, 1967, 1969) within the Elkhorn Mountains volcanic field to the south.

The welded tuffs near Three Forks are exposed in an isolated outcrop 15 km southwest of Three Forks and 5 km northeast of Sappington (lat 45°49.85′ N., long 111°43.32′ W.) They were described by G. D. Robinson and H. F. Barnett and were assigned to the Elkhorn Mountains Volcanics (Robinson, 1963, p. 88–89; p. 92–93).

The sampled rocks near Wolf Creek have an average strike of N. 37° W. and a dip of 26½° SW., whereas those near Three Forks have an average strike of east-west and a dip of 70° N. Field relations indicate that the Wolf Creek section is right-side-up. However, field evidence at the Three Forks site is insufficient to dismiss the possibility that the section is overturned.

The geologic settings of the Wolf Creek and Three Forks sites are similar insofar as both rock sequences consist largely of devitrified welded tuffs and lava flows at the margin of the Elkhorn Mountains volcanic field, and both are on soles of major thrusts involving Precambrian rocks (Robinson and Marvin, 1967, p. 606). However, detailed petrologic and chemical characteristics of the glassy rocks from the two areas are sharply contrasting.

Petrologically, the glassy rocks near Wolf Creek contain more highly mafic phenocrysts and have a more distinct welded fabric than those near Three Forks. Volume percentages of black iron oxide grains (exceeding 10 μm) also differ somewhat on the basis of thin-section inspection. The upper stony tuff, glassy tuff, and lower stony tuff sequence at Wolf Creek has modal iron oxide contents of 1.0, 1.3, and 0.9 percent, respectively, whereas the analogous sequence at Three Forks contains 0.9, 1.1, and 0.7 percent, respectively. Glassy rocks at each site contain a few iron oxide phenocrysts as much as 0.3–0.6 mm in diameter.

Chemically, the glassy rocks near Wolf Creek contain less Fe_2O_3 and FeO than those near Three Forks (Knopf, 1957, p. 84; Robinson, 1963, p. 91; Robinson and Marvin, 1967, p. 604). It is of interest that the iron oxide content for the glass alone at the Three Forks site is a high percentage (about 65 to 80 percent) of that for the whole glassy rock at that site. This relation suggests that, if this iron oxide is largely in the form of magnetic particles, much of the magnetization is contained in the glass itself. It is not known whether the same relation between glass and whole rock also obtains at Wolf Creek.[1]

Thermomagnetic curves for the glasses at Wolf Creek and Three Forks (fig. 2), shown with a curve obtained for resampled tuffs of the Elkhorn Mountains Volcanics at Conrow Creek (X near Bull Mountain, fig. 1), provide further information about iron oxide content. The estimated Curie temperatures of 560°C and 575°C for the glasses at Wolf Creek and Three Forks are consistent with those for titanium-poor titanomagnetite (Akimoto and Katsura, 1959, p. 81; Nagata, 1967, p. 502). The curve for the tuff, in contrast, indicates that two kinds of magnetic mineral are present, one having a Curie temperature of 360°C and the other, 580°C. The observed irreversibility of the heating and cooling curves, accompanied by slight decreases in Curie temperatures, may be an expression of a change in the magnetic mineral to a more stable state (Nagata, 1961, p. 96) or to oxidation (Ade-Hall and others, 1965; Wilson and others, 1968; Wasilewski, 1968; Creer and Peterson, 1969; Sanver and O'Reilly, 1969).

Stony tuffs at the sites of glassy rocks have thermomagnetic curves (not shown) similar to those of the glasses, suggesting that nearly pure magnetite is the predominant magnetic constituent throughout the cooling units. There is some possibility that small amounts of minerals of the ilmenite-hematite group would go undetected in high-field thermo-

[1] It is of further interest that the rocks near Three Forks are unusually high in potassium (Robinson and Marvin, 1967, p. 604). The author's discovery in 1962 of leucite-rich flows (Hanna, 1965, p. 129) in the eastward continuation of the volcanic section from the glassy rock site suggested that this sequence of Elkhorn Mountains Volcanics might be more alkalic than the normally calc-alkalic rocks elsewhere in the volcanic field. The author suggested that these alkalic rocks might be in some way related to similar rocks in the Big Belt, Little Belt, and Highwood Mountains to the northeast.

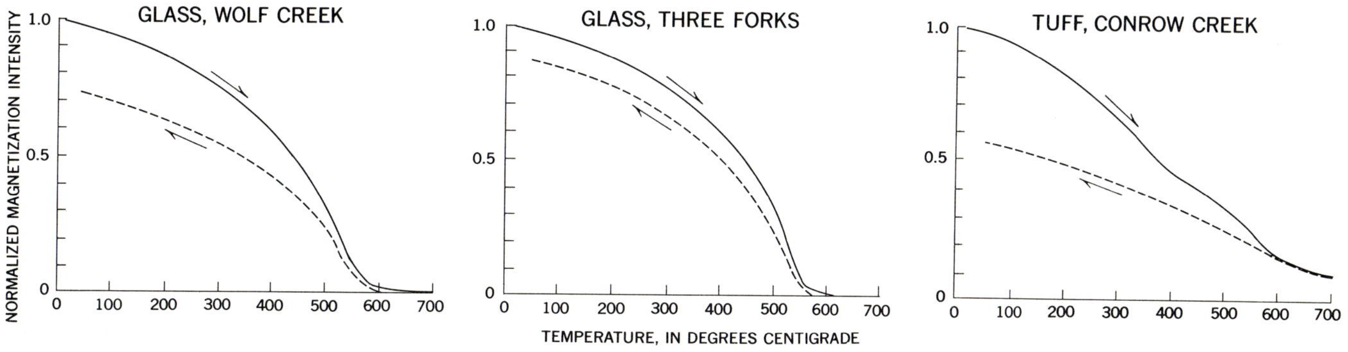

Figure 2.—Thermomagnetic curves for glasses at Wolf Creek and Three Forks and for previously sampled tuff at Conrow Creek. Plots of normalized magnetization intensity versus temperature are for external fields of 2,000 Oe for the glasses and 5,000 Oe for the tuff. Measurements made in air. Solid line represents heating cycle; dashed line, cooling cycle.

magnetic measurements made in air, as experienced by Uyeda (1958, p. 30). However, no ilmenohematite lamellas were observed in spinel-type iron oxide grains, even at highest power settings, under the reflecting microscope.

Age

A Late Cretaceous age for both sites of glassy rocks is supported by radiometric age data. Robinson and Marvin (1967, p. 605) reported K-Ar dates of 73±2 and 72±7 m.y. for biotite and plagioclase from glassy rocks 2.2 km northwest of the sampled quarry near Wolf Creek, and dates of 74±4 m.y. for both biotite and plagioclase at the Three Forks site. Robinson and Marvin (1967, p. 607) and Robinson, Klepper, and Obradovich (1968, p. 567–568) further suggested that the glassy tuffs are several million years older than the biotite and plagioclase data indicate, mainly on the basis of more recent radiometric data on hornblende from the Elkhorn Mountains Volcanics (discussed in the section on volcanic breccias in this paper) and on the basis of recent stratigraphic and paleontologic work.

Magnetization

The most striking magnetic feature of the welded tuff sites is the strong remanent magnetization intensities of the glassy rocks relative to those of their stony equivalents (table 1; fig. 3). The glassy rocks, as expected, weigh less than their stratigraphic neighbors, and thus an inverse correlation exists between magnetization intensity and rock density. This inverse correlation is rare for geologic materials; it is usually restricted to large-scale counterparts such as contrasts between fresh and serpentinized ultramafic rocks and contrasts between granitic rocks and metamorphic rocks into which they intrude. Where found on a large enough scale, the inverse density-magnetization contrast can cause a direct association of positive magnetic anomalies (depending upon the magnetization direction) and negative gravity anomalies.

The glassy rocks at Wolf Creek and Three Forks are also characterized by highly uniform or homogeneous remanent magnetizations relative to other rocks of the Elkhorn Mountains Volcanics. This uniformity may reflect a homogeneous assemblage of submicroscopic magnetic oxides within the glass itself. The only rock unit of the Elkhorn Mountains Volcanics having a substantially more uniform remanent magnetization is tuff M of Conrow Creek, discovered by Colville (1961) and extensively resampled and studied by Hanna (1965, 1967; new data in table 1 of this report), which provided the first reliable Late Cretaceous pole position and evidence for field reversals within the volcanic field.

The Koenigsberger ratios, or Q values (ratios of remanent to induced magnetization intensity), of the glassy tuffs at Wolf Creek and Three Forks are about 15 times and 3 times, respectively, greater than their stony counterparts. The much higher Q value of Wolf Creek glassy tuff (about 64) relative to Three Forks glassy tuff (about 3) suggests that the average size of magnetic constituents in Wolf Creek tuff may be smaller than that in Three Forks tuff, a conclusion based on work of others (Nagata, 1961; Parry, 1965) but not obvious from petrographic work.

Remanent magnetizations of the glassy and stony tuffs at each site are reversed (opposite in sense to the present north-seeking pole in Montana). If the in-place pole positions at each site are corrected for structural deformation by rotation about the present strike direction equal to the amount of present dip, the corrected poles fall within the upper southeastern octant (fig. 3) of the projection. This octant contains the reversed pole position previously obtained for the Elkhorn Mountains Volcanics (Hanna, 1967, p. 607).

If we assume that the previously obtained reversed pole position is rigorously precise, then we may infer that the tuffs at Wolf Creek underwent an azimuthal rotation (Hanna, 1968b) of about 35° in addition to their downward tilting, or that the rocks are now on the flank of a broad anticline plunging 10° to 15° north-northwest. By the same argument, we may infer that the rocks at Three Forks underwent little, if any, azimuthal rotation, that any existing fold axis is horizontal, and that the rocks may have assumed initial dips of as much as 5° to 15° northward at the time of deposition, although geologic field relations do not suggest large initial dips. Although there is reason to believe that the mean reversed pole position is valid on the basis of comparison with other North American data (Hanna, 1967, p. 607), it is not to be expected that individual volcanic units were all magnetized exactly parallel to this mean direction. Magnetizations of individual units may reflect short-term variations in the ancient magnetic field, or they may consist of some recently acquired magnetization components not randomized in the partial demagnetization process. We may conclude broadly that (1) the Late Cretaceous magnetic field was reversed during emplacement of the tuffs at each site, although it is not known whether emplacements at each site occurred during the same reversed epoch, and locally that (2) if the field was reversed, the tuff sequence at Three Forks is also right-side-up, not an unexpected fact.

An outstanding problem regarding the glassy tuffs at each site, in addition to their unexplained resistance to devitrification over a period exceeding 70 m.y., is the source of their strong remanent magnetization intensity relative to adjacent stony tuffs. It is suggested on the basis of the previously described petrological and chemical data and on the basis of previously established relations of increasing magnetic coercivities with decreasing grain size and increasing internal stress (Nagata, 1961) that much of the remanent magnetization of the vitreous tuffs is contained in single-domain submicroscopic iron oxide constituents within the glass itself. Rigorous documentation of this suggestion awaits future work.

Table 1.—*Magnetic data of selected Late Cretaceous volcanic rocks, western Montana*

Site	Rock unit	N	H_d	REM D	REM I	REM J	k	a_{95}	δ	K	TOT D	TOT I	TOT J	Q	Tc	ρ
Wolf Creek	C	12	0	215.4 (127.6)	−64.5 (−82.2)	0.72±.74	292	2.5	4.7	0.30±.15	219.0	−62.2	0.55	4.2	575	2.55±.03
	B	29	0	214.6 (110.6)	−67.0 (−81.6)	175±79.1	76.5	3.1	9.3	4.78±1.53	214.8	−66.9	172	64	560	2.36±.03
	A	13	0	201.3 (97.2)	−71.1 (−75.8)	1.33±.94	230	2.7	5.3	.82±.28	202.8	−71.1	.86	2.8	580	2.57±.01
Three Forks	C	11	400	3.1 (178.9)	−73.2 (−36.8)	1.27±.92	17.8	11.1	19.4	2.42±1.13	11.6	7.0	.82	.91	580	2.51±.05
	B	25	400	20.5 (163.3)	−57.8 (−49.4)	19.3±7.9	43.0	4.5	12.6	16.3±2.8	20.0	−29.3	15.3	2.1	575	2.44±.02
	A	14	400	19.6 (167.3)	−62.5 (−45.4)	9.65±9.59	23.7	8.3	16.8	20.4±12.2	19.1	17.0	8.65	.82	575	2.55±.02
Cliff Mountain		25	0	303.8	39.0	1.63±.77	3.8	17.4	43.5	6.46±1.87	[18.5]	[71.0]	[3.71]	.44	575	2.54±.04
Jefferson Canyon		27	0	335.9	53.0	14.0±11.9	1.3	45.5	91.4	31.0±10.3	[18.5]	[71.0]	[17.8]	.78	575	2.51±.07
			200	200.8	−14.8	8.56±9.88	1.1	71.2	89.5							
Zosell district	I	15	0	35.0	4.9	304±281	35.0	6.6	13.7	14.2±1.8	34.9	5.7	306	37	580	2.73±.04
			200	41.8	15.0	8.45±5.11	37.9	6.3	13.2		38.2	34.6	11.6	1.8		
	II	11	0	170.4	−53.5	2.14±1.42	31.2	8.3	14.6	4.36±2.26	135.6	44.0	.94	.85	595	2.54±.14
	III	13	0	69.4	73.8	1.80±1.05	44.1	6.3	12.2	.63±.60	60.3	74.2	2.15	5.0	225	2.79±.04
Conrow Creek	M	20	0	66.5 (136.8)	−31.7 (−63.0)	1.09±.01	348	1.8	4.3	.57±.16	62.0	−14.8	1.03	3.3	580	2.63±.02

Explanation of terms:

N—Number of samples consisting of one or two specimens.

H_d—Peak field used in partial demagnetization, in oersteds.

REM D—Declination of remanent magnetization, in degrees east of north. Numbers in parentheses are structurally corrected values.

REM I—Inclination of remanent magnetization, in degrees below horizontal. Numbers in parentheses are structurally corrected values.

REM J—Intensity of remanent magnetization, $\times 10^{-4}$ emu/cm^3. Standard deviation follows mean value.

k—Between-sample precision parameter estimate (Fisher, 1953).

a_{95}—95-percent confidence angle about the estimated mean direction, in degrees.

δ—Angular standard deviation (Wilson, 1959).

K—Apparent volume magnetic susceptibility, $\times 10^{-4}$ emu/cm^3. Standard deviation follows mean value.

TOT D—Declination of total magnetization, in degrees east of north.

TOT I—Inclination of total magnetization, in degrees below horizontal.

TOT J—Intensity of total magnetization, $\times 10^{-4}$ emu/cm^3.

Q—Koenigsberger ratio of remanent magnetization intensity to induced magnetization intensity.

Tc—Curie point, in degrees centigrade.

ρ—Dry bulk density, in grams per cubic centimeter.

Bracketed numbers indicate present magnetic field direction and maximum total magnetization intensities.

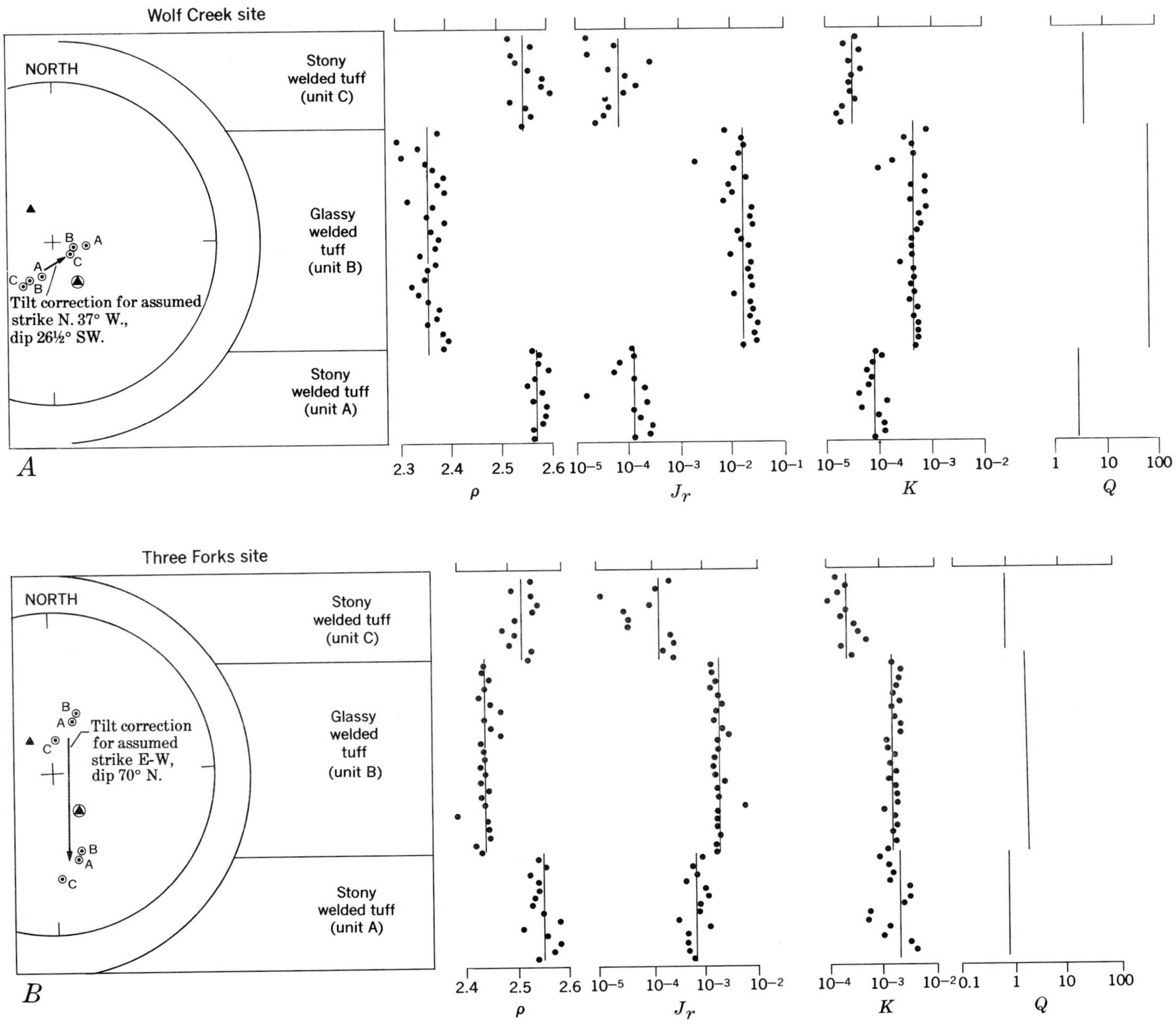

EXPLANATION

▲ Normal Late Cretaceous Elkhorn Mountains Volcanics. Pole position based on previous work

Ⓐ Reversed Late Cretaceous Elkhorn Mountains Volcanics. Pole position based on previous work

⊙ Upper hemisphere projection (reversed polarity)

ρ = dry bulk density in grams per cubic centimeter

J_r = remanent intensity of magnetization in emu per cubic centimeter

K = apparent volume magnetic susceptibility in emu per cubic centimeter

Q = Koenigsberger ratio of remanent magnetization intensity to induced magnetization intensity

| = mean value

Figure 3.—Inverse relation between rock density and magnetization for glassy and stony welded tuffs from the Wolf Creek and Three Forks sites. Equal-area projections at left show mean remanent magnetization directions before and after structural correction. *A*, Wolf Creek site. The glassy welded tuff unit is approximately 2 m thick. *B*, Three Forks site. The glassy welded tuff unit is approximately 5 m thick.

VOLCANIC BRECCIAS

Occurrence and description

Two units of breccia about 75 km apart are considered to have the most precise K-Ar dates among rocks of the Elkhorn Mountains volcanic field. The northern occurrence (locality 3; lat 46°22.09′ N., long 112°30.18′ W.) is part of a sequence of flow breccias (Ruppel, 1961; 1963) that crop out near the crest of Cliff Mountain, about 18 km east-southeast of Deer Lodge (fig. 1). At the collecting site, the rocks have an average strike of N. 25° W. and an average dip of 10° SW. The southern occurrence (loc. 4; lat 45°49.63′ N., long 111°51.07′ W.) is a unit of autoclastic flow breccia (Robinson and others, 1968, p. 567) that crops out in Jefferson Canyon, 7 km northwest of Sappington and only 10 km west of the Three Forks glassy tuff site previously discussed. Breccias at both localities are in the lower member of the Elkhorn Mountains Volcanics (Robinson and others, 1968, p. 567). They have an average strike of east-west and an average dip of 80° N., although part of this may be initial dip of the volcaniclastic material.

Age

K-Ar dating of hornblende from rocks at the Cliff Mountain site gives an age of 77.6±2.4 m.y. Hornblende K-Ar dates of two samples from the Jefferson Canyon site are 78.8±2.4 m.y. and 77.6±2.4 m.y. (Robinson and others, 1968, p. 567). These ages not only are internally consistent but also conform well to the inferred history of volcanism and plutonism in the area (Robinson and others, 1968; Tilling and others, 1968).

Magnetization

The chief magnetic characteristic of the breccias at each site is the relatively large dispersion of remanent magnetization directions (figs. 4 and 5). This dispersion is reflected in the large angular standard deviation values, δ, and small precision parameter estimates, k, corresponding to the data of each site (table 1), the δ values having greater significance in view of the non-Fisherian geometry (Fisher, 1953) of the distributions.

At Cliff Mountain, the remanent magnetization directions of 24 out of 25 samples from a 75-sq-mi outcrop area are generally confined to the lower northwest octant of the projection (fig. 4). This octant contains the mean normal pole position previously obtained for the Elkhorn Mountains Volcanics (Hanna, 1967). Hardness of remanence was confirmed in a-c demagnetization work. If a fossil magnetization of, say, some combination of thermoremanent, chemical, or detrital origin is assumed, the data indicate that the earth's field was normal at the time of cooling or deposition of the unit. The structural correction required to obtain the predeformation magnetization direction is not sufficiently large at this site to affect this interpretation.

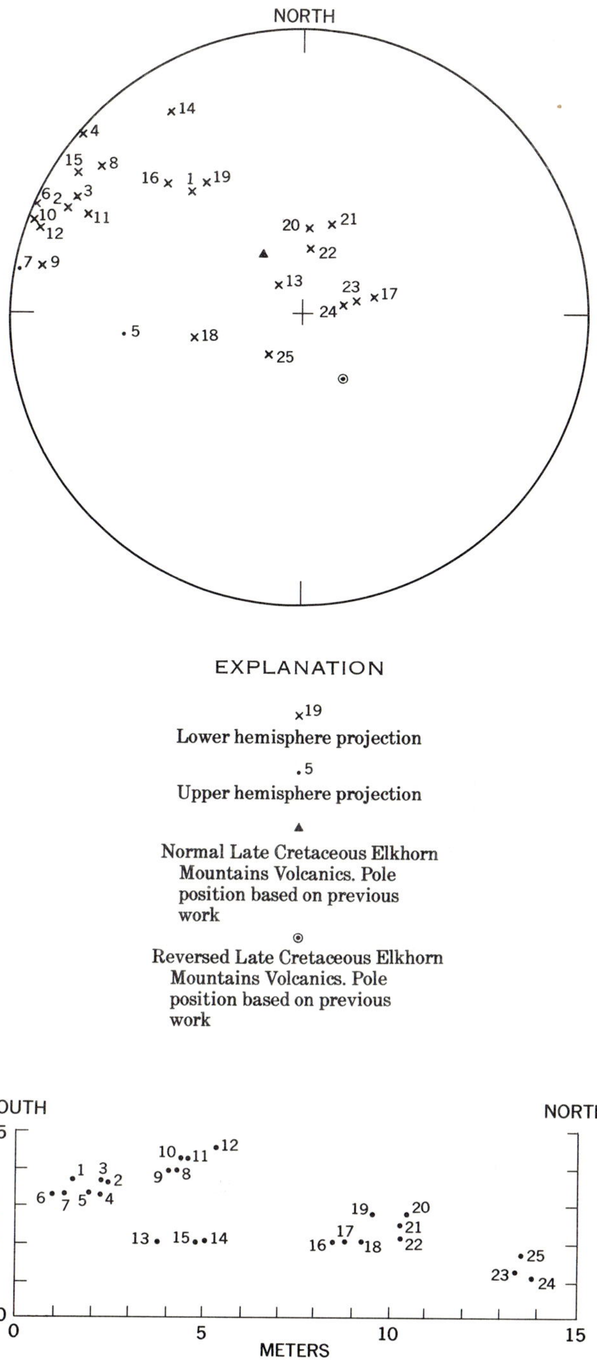

Figure 4.—Equal-area projection of remanent magnetization directions of volcanic breccia from the Cliff Mountain site. Relative locations of samples within the outcrop are shown in lower diagram.

At Jefferson Canyon, where a total of 16 samples are used to illustrate results in figure 5, samples 1 through 8 were collected from a fresh unoxidized outcrop face solidly in place, and samples 9 through 16 were collected from the outcrop face of a nearby oxidized, slightly disoriented block. Initial remanent magnetization directions of samples from the fresh outcrop are normal but somewhat dispersed, whereas those from the oxidized outcrop are reversed and tightly clustered (fig. 5*A*). Partial demagnetization in peak fields of 200 to 400 Oe indicates that the fresh rock has a soft magnetization component and that the oxidized rock is magnetically hard (fig. 5*B*). This difference in response to partial demagnetization is an expression of the low-coercivity spinel-type magnetic oxide content of the fresh rock as opposed to the high-coercivity rhombohedral-type oxide content of the oxidized rock.

Structural correction at the Jefferson Canyon site produces remanent magnetization directions corresponding to the fresh outcrop within the lower northwest octant of the projection (fig. 5*C*) and directions corresponding to the oxidized block to a southerly, nearly horizontal position (not shown in figure). Data corresponding to the fresh rock are considered to indicate reliably that the ancient field was normal at the time of cooling. Data corresponding to the oxidized rock suggest that a hard magnetization, possibly chemical in origin, was acquired after cooling by magnetic mineral constituents of the ilmenite-hematite series. Although a self-reversal mechanism may have operated within the oxidized rock to produce the resulting reversed magnetization, it is also possible and consistent with other data that a chemical remanent magnetization was acquired after folding in a reversed Late Cretaceous magnetic field. If true, the paleomagnetic field direction is inferred from the original remanent magnetizations, uncorrected for tilt. This latter possibility is strengthened by the Three Forks welded tuff data, which imply the presence of a prefolding reversed magnetic field, and by data from elsewhere in the Elkhorn Mountains volcanic field (Hanna, 1965; 1967), which suggest the occurrence of multiple field reversals during volcanic emplacement.

The amount of scatter of remanent magnetization directions in breccias and conglomerates can be used to help distinguish between a relatively hot and cold environment of final deposition (Graham, 1949; Aramaki and Akimoto, 1957; Hanna, 1967; Starkey and Palmer, 1971; Chadwick, 1971). Stated simply, if such rocks have highly dispersed remanent magnetization directions and if the magnetization is thermoremanent in origin, we may infer that clasts have moved somewhat randomly after passing through their Curie temperature range, as they would in cold depositional environments of some mudflows, tuffs, conglomerates, and breccias. If magnetization directions are tightly grouped, we may infer that clasts have not moved after acquiring thermoremanent magnetization, as in warm depositional environments of some breccias and tuffs.

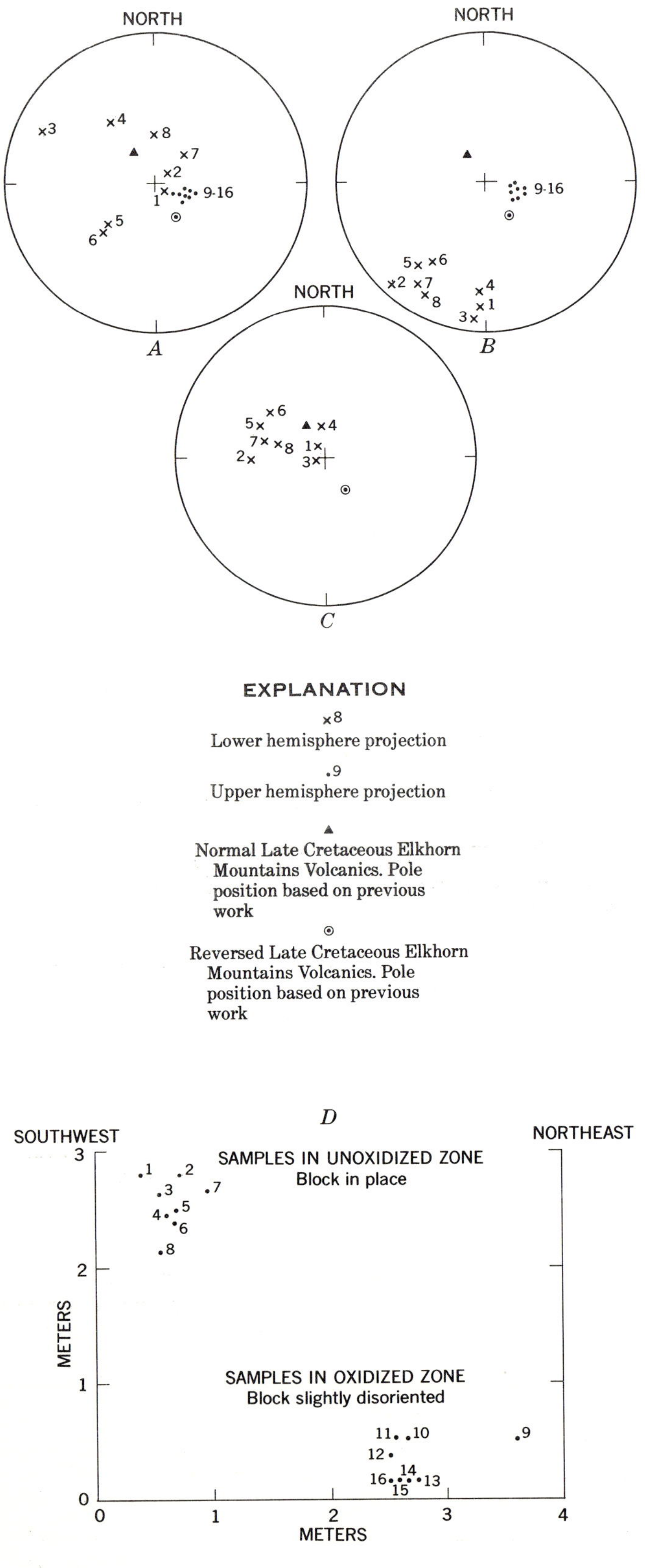

Figure 5.—Equal-area projections of remanent magnetization directions of 16 samples of volcanic breccia from the Jefferson Canyon site. *A*, Original magnetization directions for samples. *B*, Directions for samples after a-c partial demagnetization in peak fields of 200 to 400 Oe. *C*, Directions for partly demagnetized samples (1–8) from unoxidized zone after correction for structural tilt of strike east-west and dip 80° N. *D*, Relative locations of samples.

The amount of dispersion in the data from Cliff Mountain and Jefferson Canyon is not considered great enough to imply a cold environment of deposition but is sufficiently great to suggest a warm one in which limited motion of clasts occurred after passing through blocking temperatures of about 575°C, on the basis of Curie temperature data from representative rock specimens (table 1). If the partial thermoremanent magnetization spectrums of the sampled breccias are similar to those obtained elsewhere for basalt and magnetite powder (Nagata, 1961, p. 159, 163), as we might expect them to be on the basis of the magnetite Curie temperatures measured, we may infer that almost all of the magnetization of the breccias was acquired at temperatures above 400°C. This temperature may be used as a best estimate of the minimum temperature of breccia deposition.

ALTERED BASALTS

Three localities of basaltic rocks within the Zosell (Emery) mining district, 13 km east of Deer Lodge (loc. 2, fig. 1), were sampled. Because they occur in an area characterized by a major negative aeromagnetic anomaly (Hanna, 1969, p. D162), these rocks were suspected of having either reversed, anomalously directed, or very weak magnetizations compared to basalts and andesites in other parts of the Elkhorn Mountains volcanic field. In fact, this outcrop area is the only occurrence of the Elkhorn Mountains Volcanics associated with a major aeromagnetic low within the Boulder batholith area, even though many units of the volcanic field have reversed magnetization polarities (Hanna, 1967). Ordinarily, negative aeromagnetic features in the Boulder batholith area are associated with plutonic rocks of the batholith itself or with relatively felsic Lowland Creek Volcanics in broad zones of mineralization.

Rocks within the Zosell district were sampled at three separate locations within a 1-km radius but for purposes of discussion are treated as a single collecting site. Designated I, II, and III in table 1, these outcrop locations have specific geographical coordinates, respectively, of lat 46°22.52′ N., long 112°34.37′ W.; 46°22.38′, 112°34.53′; and 46°23.16′, 112°34.28′.

Under the petrologic nomenclature of Robertson (1953, p. 7), outcrops I and II consist of feldspar-pyroxene basalt, and outcrop III consists of pyroxene basalt. Although all three outcrops occur in mineralized zones, only rocks from outcrop II show appreciable megascopic alteration. Black iron oxide is relatively abundant as an accessory mineral in all of the basalts sampled. A modal analysis of pyroxene basalt similar to that of outcrop III shows a magnetite abundance of 4.5 percent (Robertson, 1953, p. 8). Comparison of chemical analyses of pyroxene basalt with those of feldspar-pyroxene basalt similar to rocks sampled suggests that the feldspar-pyroxene unit has a modal magnetite abundance of about 3.5 to 4.0 percent.

The present structural attitudes of rocks at the three outcrops are very difficult, if not impossible, to establish precisely. In areas immediately north and south of the mining district, flows generally strike N. 30° W. to north-south and dip 10° to 20° W. (Robertson, 1953, p. 8). Within the mining district a small, tight, west-plunging syncline has been produced in which low-angle reverse fractures and high-angle normal faults occur. The low-angle reverse fractures are considered to be nearly parallel to bedding, whereas the normal faults probably represent tension fractures (Robertson, 1953, p. 8–9).

Attempts were made to determine bedding orientation by use of the alinement of subplanar feldspar laths and amygdules; however, abrupt changes in these orientations suggest occurrences of locally turbulent flow. The ambiguity of structural orientation of the flows where sampled gives rise to corresponding ambiguity of predeformation remanent magnetization directions, as will be seen in a following section.

Thermomagnetic curves for basalts at each locality (fig. 6) are highly contrasting and indicate that the rocks have somewhat different magnetic constituents. The curve for the sample from outcrop I is similar to those of the glasses previously discussed (fig. 2) and is typical for that of nearly

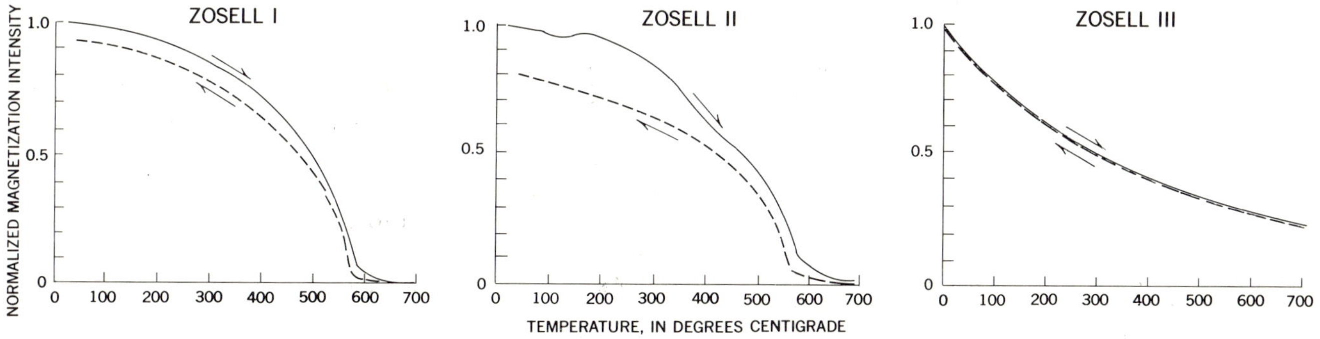

Figure 6.—Thermomagnetic curves for basalts at locations I, II, and III of the Zosell district. Plots of normalized magnetization intensity versus temperature are for external fields of 1,500, 2,000, and 4,000 Oe, respectively. Measurements made in air. Solid line represents heating cycle; dashed line, cooling cycle.

pure magnetite. The curve for the sample from outcrop II possesses a conspicuous hump not previously observed in other units of the Elkhorn Mountains Volcanics. The curve for the sample from outcrop III is concave upward throughout the sampled temperature interval and is also unique among curves previously obtained.

Because the flows occur within a mining district rich in hydrothermal deposits and because some specimens of outcrop II show megascopic alteration, it is instructive to compare the thermomagnetic curves with curves obtained elsewhere (Ade-Hall, 1971, p. 8078) for certain hydrothermally and deuterically altered basalt containing class I magnetites (Wilson and others, 1968). If one assumes a general absence of deuteric alteration, on the basis of inspection of thin sections, the curve of outcrop I is similar to that of Ade-Hall's (1971, p. 8078) Mull specimen C120-1, which is characterized by a high regional hydrothermal alteration, inferred by Ade-Hall to have involved maximum reheating temperatures of over 200°C. The humped curve of outcrop II is similar to that of Ade-Hall's (1971, p. 8078) Mull specimen C190-1, which is characterized by high regional hydrothermal alteration and moderate deuteric oxidation. The rise in magnetization within the temperature interval 150°–375°C may be attributable to a relatively rapid change of the magnetic mineral to material having a higher Curie temperature during the heating process, as suggested by Ade-Hall (1971, p. 8078) for other rocks. The smooth, reversible, concave-upward curve for outcrop III, which was exactly reproduced in duplicate thermomagnetic experiments, has no sharply defined Curie temperature. A temperature of 225°C was estimated, which would suggest a spinel-phase ferromagnetic mineral intermediate in composition between pure magnetite and ulvospinel (Nagata, 1967, p. 502). Curves of this type for samples heated in air are unknown to the author in the literature, and they indicate a resistance of the magnetic mineral against further oxidation as well as an anomalously high retentivity of magnetic moment at temperatures exceeding 700°C. The curve might indicate the presence of a spectrum of titanomagnetites of varying composition within the rock such as Doell and Cox (1965b, p. 3383) inferred for Hawaiian basaltic flows having thermomagnetic curves with no well-defined knees. The presence of abundant hemoilmenite within the rock having a Curie temperature of 225°C has been ruled out on the basis of its absence in petrographic analysis and the response of the rock to demagnetizing fields.

Age

Although none of the basalts sampled have been radiometrically dated, all belong to the Elkhorn Mountains Volcanics (Klepper and others, 1957; Smedes, 1966) of Late Cretaceous age (Robinson and others, 1968). The basalts were provisionally included in the uppermost unit of the Elkhorn Mountains Volcanics by E. T. Ruppel in 1957 (Ruppel, 1961), although the outcrops are only about 5 km from the 78-m.y.-old volcanic breccia of Cliff Mountain, assigned to the upper part of the lower unit of the Elkhorn Mountains Volcanics (Robinson and others, 1968, p. 567). For purposes of the present investigation, the rocks are adequately time bracketed by the assigned Late Cretaceous age.

Magnetization

Mean remanent magnetization directions of the flows at outcrops I, II, and III are highly contrasting, having inclinations that are horizontal, reversed, and normal, respectively. These directions, together with possible predeformation directions inferred from various structural corrections, are shown in figure 7. The ambiguity of the various possible predeformation directions is reduced by recognizing that the most reliable structural corrections are based on regional structure, the local synclinal structure, and the low-angle reverse fractures (designated 1, 2, and 3 for each outcrop in figure 7). Any one or combination of inferred structurally corrected directions 1, 2, or 3 of each outcrop locality indicates that (a) the predeformation direction of outcrop I was anomalous, being nearly horizontal, (b) that of outcrop II was reversed with moderate inclination, and (c) that of outcrop III was normal and steeply inclined.

The possibility of self-reversed magnetization or anomalous chemical remanent magnetization must be admitted for each of the localities sampled within the mining district in view of the thermomagnetic data and field evidence of regional hydrothermal activity. However, there is a lack of definite petrographic evidence for oxidized or exsolved rhombohedral-phase magnetic mineral often suggestive of self-reversal, and a-c demagnetization indicates no evidence of anomalously high coercitivities characteristic of the rhombohedral phase. Thus, with caution, we may allow for the possibility that any one or all of the localities express the polarity of the ancient field at the time of cooling. If the magnetization is fossil, a relatively rapid reversal of the ancient field was presumably required because of the inferred short time interval required for extrusion.

The most significant magnetic intensity characteristic of the sampled basalts is the strong total magnetization intensity of about 3×10^{-2} emu/cm^3 for outcrop I. Rocks from outcrops II and III have total magnetizations about one and two orders of magnitude weaker and are less important as active sources of aeromagnetic anomalies.

SIGNIFICANCE OF RESULTS

Paleomagnetic interpretation

The most important conclusion of the present study is the confirmation of previous inferences about multiple field reversals accompanying extrusion of the Elkhorn Mountains Volcanics, now fixed at about 78 m.y. ago. The exact polarity

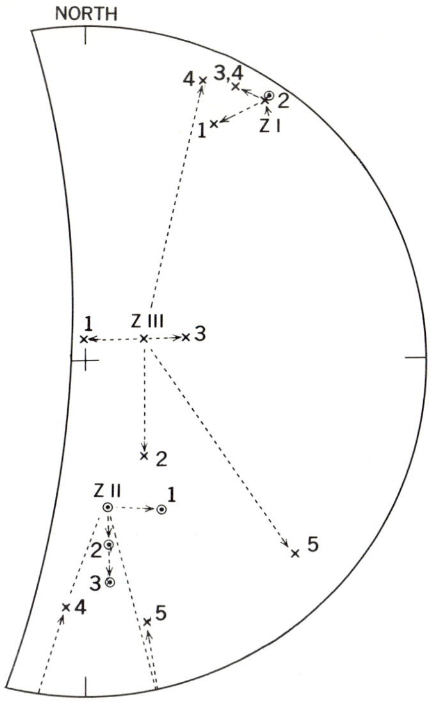

EXPLANATION

× Lower hemisphere projection

⊙ Upper hemisphere projection

ORIGINAL REMANENT MAGNETIZATIONS

Z I: Zosell location I
Z II: Zosell location II
Z III: Zosell location III

POSSIBLE STRUCTURAL CORRECTIONS

1 Regional structure
2 Local synclinal structure
3 Low-angle reverse fractures
4 Steep-dipping veined fractures
5 Local alinement of vesicles and feldspar laths

Figure 7.—Equal-area projection of mean remanent magnetization directions of basalt from three locations in the Zosell district. Numbers refer to various structural corrections that might be made to establish predeformation mean pole positions.

sequence still cannot be precisely established, but it is evident from present and previous work that a minimum of two complete field reversal cycles occurred and that as many as eight complete cycles may have occurred during volcanic rock emplacement.

The firm establishment of multiple field reversals approximately 78 m.y. ago is important for two reasons. First, the data serve to revise the chronology of field polarities inferred by Heirtzler and others (1968, p. 2123) on the basis of marine magnetic anomalies near the maximum point of extrapolation at about 79 m.y. Second, the data indicate that a 30-m.y. interval of normal field polarity preceding 78 m.y., cited by Helsley and Steiner (1969, p. 328) on the basis of compilations of paleomagnetic data, was interrupted not by a simple reversed epoch but rather by a series of field reversal cycles. It is anticipated that paleomagnetic work on the Late Cretaceous Boulder batholith, which was intruded into the Elkhorn Mountains volcanic field between 78 and 68 m.y. ago, will help determine whether or not this succession of polarity reversals continued to the close of the Cretaceous Period.

The northeasterly, nearly horizontal remanent magnetization of basalt I at the Zosell district, if primary, may represent another example of rapid paleomagnetic field migration previously suggested by Grommé and Gluskoter (1965) and Saad (1969) on the basis of results from the Jurassic and Cretaceous Franciscan Formation of California and by Spall (1968) on the basis of results from late Mesozoic dolerites of Norway. Somewhat similar anomalous magnetization directions have been found in the Late Cretaceous Boulder batholith of Montana (Hanna, unpub. data, 1966–68), the Eocene Siletz River Volcanics of Oregon (Cox, 1957), and the Eocene Lowland Creek Volcanics of Montana (Hanna, unpub. data).

Aeromagnetic interpretation

Among the three groups of rocks discussed (tuffs, breccias, and basalts), three individual rock units have sufficiently strong remanent magnetizations and one rock unit has a sufficiently strong induced magnetization to be important as possible sources of aeromagnetic anomalies. The rock units with strong remanent magnetizations are the glasses of Wolf Creek and Three Forks and the basalt of locality I in the Zosell mining district, all having total magnetization intensities of greater than 10^{-3} emu/cm^3. These units are designated 1, 2, and 5 on the aeromagnetic maps and equal-area projection of figure 8. The rock unit with strong induced magnetization is the breccia at Jefferson Canyon, which also has a total magnetization of greater than 10^{-3} emu/cm^3, whether or not the somewhat dispersed, normally polarized remanent magnetization is considered to contribute to the total magnetization. This breccia unit is designated 4 in figure 8 and is shown with the breccia from Cliff Mountain (3, fig. 8) because of the latter's proximity to the Zosell site.

In view of the criteria necessary for a rock to constitute the source of an aeromagnetic anomaly, namely, that its magnetization must be strong relative to surrounding rocks and that its volume in the subsurface must be large relative to the distance between source and magnetometer, only the basalt from the Zosell district and the breccia from Jefferson Canyon meet both requirements. Thus, the major negative anomaly centered near the basalt exposure and the weaker positive anomaly nose at the breccia site may be inferred to be caused, at least in part, by the sampled rocks extending into the subsurface (fig. 8). The glasses at Wolf Creek and Three Forks, which are very

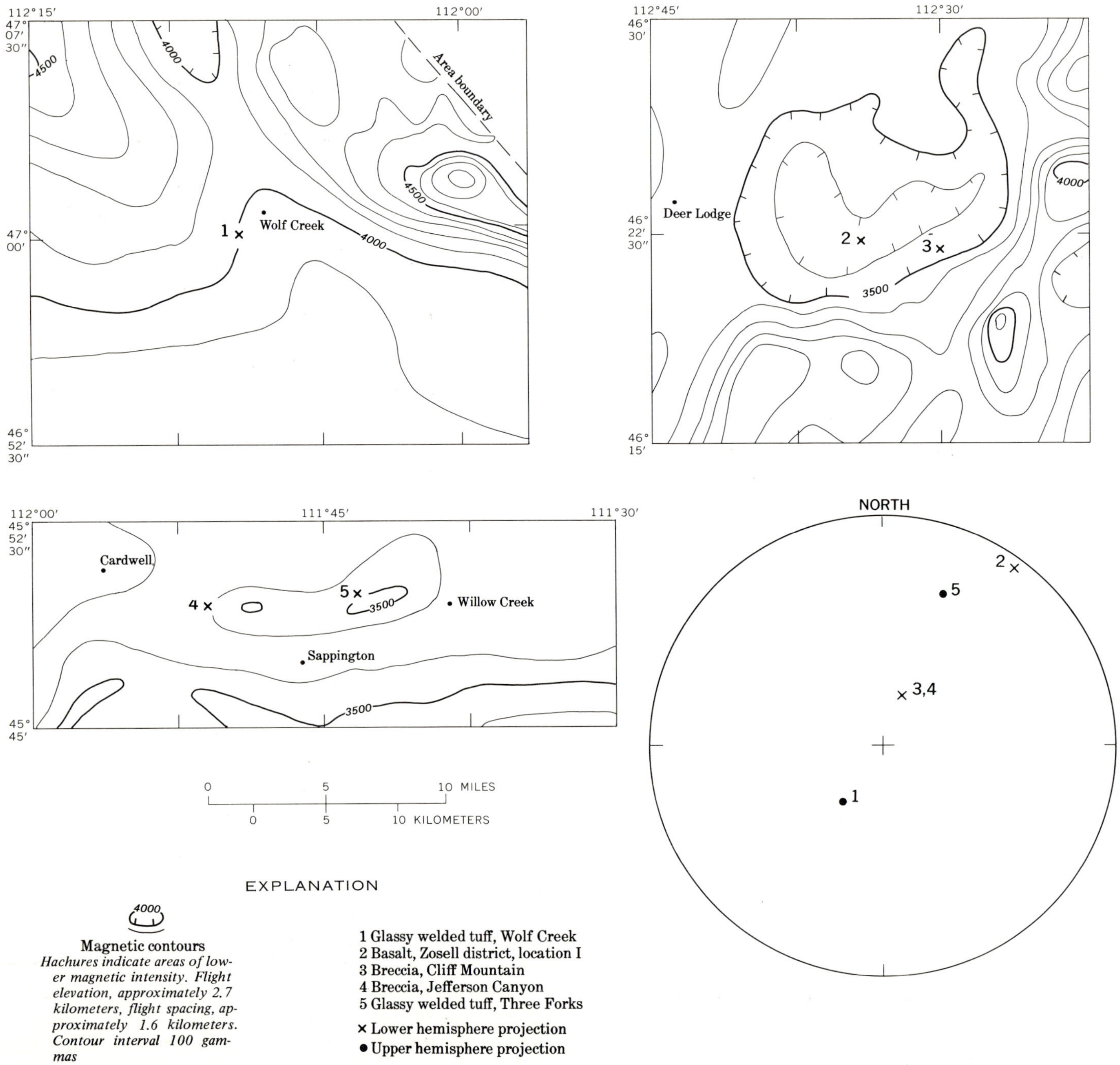

Figure 8.—Generalized aeromagnetic maps of sampling localities, and equal-area projections of mean total magnetizations of rocks sufficiently magnetic to be considered in aeromagnetic interpretation. Magnetic intensities are listed in table 1. Sources of aeromagnetic data: upper left, Kleinkopf and Mudge (1972); upper right, Johnson, Henderson, and Tyson (1965); and lower left, Davis, Kinoshita, and Robinson (1965).

limited in outcrop extent and which were relatively distant from the surveying magnetometer, do not have the volume needed to contribute appreciably to the aeromagnetic patterns, despite their strong magnetizations. The absence of negative anomalies associated with the reversed magnetizations of these glassy tuffs indicates that the glasses are minor elements within the volcanic piles.

Of primary interest in aeromagnetic interpretation are the basalts that occur within the Zosell mining district. On the basis of measured magnetizations and previous magnetic model calculations (Hanna, 1969), the broad negative aeromagnetic anomaly centered near the district is generated not so much by rocks with strong reversed magnetizations but rather by rocks with strong horizontal magnetizations in association with other rocks having variously polarized weak magnetizations. If the correlation between negative aeromagnetic anomalies and zones of hydrothermal alteration continues to be valid for subsurface rocks extending northward from the Zosell district, the aeromagnetic data to the north may define undiscovered zones of subsurface mineralization and therefore have economic value.

REFERENCES CITED

Ade-Hall, J. M., 1971, Discussion of paper by Minoru Ozima and Mituko Ozima, "Characteristic thermomagnetic curve in submarine basalts": Jour. Geophys. Research, v. 76, no. 32, p. 8077–8079.

Ade-Hall, J. M., Wilson, R. L., and Smith, P. J., 1965, The petrology, Curie points, and natural magnetizations of basic lavas: Royal Astron. Soc. Geophys. Jour., v. 9, no. 4, p. 323–326.

Akimoto, Syun-iti, and Katsura, Takashi, 1959, Magneto-chemical study of the generalized titanomagnetite in volcanic rocks: Jour. Geomagnetism and Geoelectricity [Kyoto], v. 10, no. 3, p. 69–90.

Aramaki, Shigeo, and Akimoto, Syun-iti, 1957, Temperature estimation of pyroclastic deposits by natural remanent magnetism: Am. Jour. Sci., v. 255, no. 9, p. 619–627.

Barksdale, J. D., 1951, Cretaceous glassy welded tuffs–Lewis and Clark County, Montana: Am. Jour. Sci., v. 249, no. 6, p. 439–443.

Chadwick, R. A., 1971, Paleomagnetic criteria for volcanic breccia emplacement: Geol. Soc. America Bull., v. 82, no. 8, p. 2285–2294.

Colville, A. A., 1961, Paleomagnetic investigation in the vicinity of the northern Tobacco Root Mountains, Madison County, Montana: Indiana Univ., Bloomington, Ind., Ph. D. thesis, 148 p.

Cox, Allan, 1957, Remanent magnetism of lower to middle Eocene basalt flows from Oregon: Nature, v. 179, no. 4561, p. 685–686.

Creer, K. M., and Petersen, N., 1969, Thermochemical magnetization in basalts: Zeitschr. Geophysik, v. 35, no. 5, p. 501–516.

Davis, W. E., Kinoshita, W. T., and Robinson, G. D., 1965, Bouguer gravity, aeromagnetic, and generalized geologic map of the western part of the Three Forks Basin, Jefferson, Broadwater, Madison, and Gallatin Counties, Montana: U.S. Geol. Survey Geophys. Inv. Map GP-497, scale 1:62,500.

Doell, R. R., and Cox, Allan, 1965a, Measurement of the remanent magnetization of igneous rocks: U.S. Geol. Survey Bull. 1203-A, p. A1–A32.

———1965b, Paleomagnetism of Hawaiian lava flows: Jour. Geophys. Research, v. 70, no. 14, p. 3377–3405.

———1967a, Analysis of alternating field demagnetization equipment, *in* Collinson, D. W., Creer, K. M., and Runcorn, S. K., eds., Methods in paleomagnetism: Amsterdam, Elsevier Co., p. 241–253.

———1967b, Recording magnetic balance, *in* Collinson, D. W., Creer, K. M., and Runcorn, S. K., eds., Methods in paleomagnetism: Amsterdam, Elsevier Co., p. 440–444.

Fisher, R. A., 1953, Dispersion on a sphere: Royal Soc. London Proc., ser. A, v. 217, no. A1130, p. 295–305.

Graham, J. W., 1949, The stability and significance of magnetism in sedimentary rocks: Jour. Geophys. Research, v. 54, no. 2, p. 131–167.

Grommé, C. S., and Gluskoter, H. J., 1965, Remanent magnetization of spilite and diabase in the Franciscan Formation, western Marin County: Jour. Geology, v. 73, no. 1, p. 74–94.

Grommé, C. S., Wright, T. L., and Peck, D. L., 1969, Magnetic properties and oxidation of iron-titanium oxide minerals in Alae and Makaopuhi lava lakes, Hawaii: Jour. Geophys. Research, v. 74, no. 22, p. 5277–5293.

Hanna, W. F., 1965, Magnetic properties of selected volcanic rocks of southwestern Montana: Indiana Univ., Bloomington, Ind., Ph. D. thesis, 207 p.

Hanna, W. F., 1967, Paleomagnetism of upper Cretaceous volcanic rocks of southwestern Montana: Jour. Geophys. Research, v. 72, no. 2, p. 595–610.

———1968a, Preliminary analysis of an induction-type apparatus for measuring magnetic susceptibility [abs.]: Am. Geophys. Union Trans., v. 49, no. 4, p. 673.

———1968b, Remanent magnetization of two late Cretaceous glassy volcanic rocks from Montana [abs.]: Am. Geophys. Union Trans., v. 49, no. 4, p. 671.

———1969, Negative aeromagnetic anomalies over mineralized areas of the Boulder batholith, Montana, *in* Geological Survey Research 1969: U.S. Geol. Survey Prof. Paper 650-D, p. D159–D167.

Heirtzler, J. R., Dickson, G. O., Herron, E. M., Pitman, W. C., and LePichon, Xavier, 1968, Marine magnetic anomalies, geomagnetic field reversals, and motions of the ocean floor and continents: Jour. Geophys. Research, v. 73, no. 6, p. 2119–2136.

Helsley, C. E., and Steiner, M. B., 1969, Evidence for long intervals of normal polarity during the Cretaceous period: Earth and Planetary Sci. Letters, v. 5, no. 5, p. 325–332.

Johnson, R. W., Jr., Henderson, J. R., and Tyson, N. S., 1965, Aeromagnetic map of the Boulder batholith area, southwestern Montana: U.S. Geol. Survey Geophys. Inv. Map GP-538, scale 1:250,000.

Kleinkopf, M. D., and Mudge, M. R., 1972, Aeromagnetic, Bouguer gravity, and generalized geology of the Great Falls-Mission Range area, northwestern Montana: U.S. Geol. Survey Prof. Paper 726-A. [In press]

Klepper, M. R., and Smedes, H. W., 1959, Elkhorn Mountains volcanic field, western Montana [abs.]: Geol. Soc. America Bull., v. 70, no. 12, pt. 2, p. 1631.

Klepper, M. R., Weeks, R. A., and Ruppel, E. T., 1957, Geology of the southern Elkhorn Mountains, Jefferson and Broadwater Counties, Montana: U.S. Geol. Survey Prof. Paper 292, 82 p.

Knopf, Adolph, 1957, The Boulder bathylith of Montana: Am. Jour. Sci., v. 255, no. 2, p. 81–103.

Lyons, J. B., 1944, Igneous rocks of the northern Big Belt Range, Montana: Geol. Soc. America Bull., v. 55, no. 4, p. 445–472.

Nagata, Takesi, 1961, Rock magnetism: Tokyo, Japan, Maruzen Co. Ltd., 350 p.

———1967, Identification of magnetic minerals in rocks using methods based on their magnetic properties, *in* Collinson, D. W., Creer, K. M., and Runcorn, S. K., eds., Methods in paleomagnetism: Amsterdam, Elsevier Co., p. 501–513.

Parry, L. G., 1965, Magnetic properties of dispersed magnetite powders: Philos. Mag., v. 11, no. 110, p. 303–312.

Phillips, J. D., and Kuckes, A. F., 1967, A spinner magnetometer: Jour. Geophys. Research, v. 72, no. 8, p. 2209–2212.

Robertson, F. S., 1953, Geology and mineral deposits of the Zosell (Emery) mining district, Powell County, Montana: Montana Bur. Mines and Geology Mem. 34, 29 p.

Robinson, G. D., 1963, Geology of the Three Forks quadrangle, Montana, with section on the petrography of igneous rocks, by H. F. Barnett: U.S. Geol. Survey Prof. Paper 370, 143 p.

Robinson, G. D., and Marvin, R. F., 1967, Upper Cretaceous volcanic glass from western Montana: Geol. Soc. America Bull., v. 78, no. 5, p. 601–608.

Robinson, G. D., Klepper, M. R., and Obradovich, J. D., 1968, Overlapping plutonism, volcanism, and tectonism in the Boulder batholith region, western Montana, *in* Coats, R. R., Hay, R. L., and Anderson, C. A., eds., Studies in volcanology: Geol. Soc. America Mem. 116, p. 557–576.

Ruppel, E. T., 1961, Reconnaissance geologic map of the Deer Lodge quadrangle, Powell, Deer Lodge, and Jefferson Counties, Montana: U.S. Geol. Survey Mineral Inv. Field Studies Map MF-174, scale 1:48,000.

——1963, Geology of the Basin quadrangle, Jefferson, Lewis and Clark, and Powell Counties, Montana: U.S. Geol. Survey Bull. 1151, 121 p.

Saad, A. H., 1969, Paleomagnetism of Franciscan ultramafic rocks from Red Mountain, California: Jour. Geophys. Research, v. 74, no. 27, p. 6567–6578.

Sanver, M., and O'Reilly, W., 1969, Identification of naturally occurring non-stoichiometric titanomagnetites: Physics Earth and Planetary Interiors, v. 2, no. 3, p. 166–174.

Schmidt, R. G., 1963, Preliminary geologic map and sections of the Hogan 4 Southeast quadrangle, Lewis and Clark County, Montana: U.S. Geol. Survey Misc. Geol. Inv. Map I-379, scale 1:24,000.

Smedes, H. W., 1966, Geology and igneous petrology of the northern Elkhorn Mountains, Jefferson and Broadwater Counties, Montana: U.S. Geol. Survey Prof. Paper 510, 116 p.

Spall, Henry, 1968, Anomalous paleomagnetic poles from late Mesozoic dolerites from Spitsbergen: Earth and Planetary Sci. Letters, v. 4, no. 1, p. 73–78.

Starkey, J., and Palmer, H. C., 1971, The sensitivity of the conglomerate test in paleomagnetism: Royal Astron. Soc. Geophys. Jour., v. 22, no. 3, p. 235–240.

Tilling, R. I., Klepper, M. R., and Obradovich, J. D., 1968, K-Ar ages and time span of emplacement of the Boulder batholith, Montana: Am. Jour. Sci., v. 266, no. 8, p. 671–689.

Uyeda, Seiya, 1958, Thermo-remanent magnetism as a medium of paleomagnetism, with special reference to reverse thermo-remanent magnetism: Japanese Jour. Geophysics, v. 2, no. 1, p. 1–123.

Viele, G. W., and Harris, F. G., III, 1965, Montana Group stratigraphy, Lewis and Clark County, Montana: Am. Assoc. Petroleum Geologists Bull., v. 49, no. 4, p. 379–417.

Wasilewski, P. J., 1968, Magnetization of ocean basalts: Jour. Geomagnetism and Geoelectricity [Kyoto], v. 20, no. 3, p. 129–154.

Wilson, R. L., 1959, Remanent magnetism of Late Secondary and Early Tertiary British rocks: Philos. Mag., v. 4, no. 42, p. 750–755.

Wilson, R. L., Haggerty, S. E., and Watkins, N. D., 1968, Variation of paleomagnetic stability and other parameters in a vertical traverse of a single Icelandic lava: Royal Astron. Soc. Geophys. Jour., v. 16, no. 1, p. 79–96.

Jour. Research U.S. Geol. Survey
Vol. 1, No. 2, Mar.—Apr. 1973, p. 193—206

GEOLOGIC BENCH MARKS BY TERRESTRIAL PHOTOGRAPHY

By HAROLD E. MALDE, Denver, Colo.

Abstract.—A photograph made with a level camera, if taken at a known height above a permanent mark on the ground, can be later repeated with exactness for measurement of changes in terrain. Such a photograph is one of several means for establishing a geologic bench mark and is especially useful for monitoring the subtle qualities of a landscape that are otherwise hard to map and describe, including the effects of man's use. Moreover, the geometry of such a photograph provides the same angular measurements between objects as can be made with a transit. A measurement of distance on a single photograph, however, requires control points. These can be surveyed at any convenient time, not necessarily when the initial photograph is made. Distances can also be determined by simple stereophotography from a base line of suitable length.

This paper deals with the use of repeated photographs in field geology as records of a changing land. I began to think about this subject years ago when I heard Ansel Adams, the famous photographer and teacher, tell about his troubles in finding the exact site from which an old photograph had been taken in Canyon de Chelly, Ariz.—a search that fortunately resulted in his celebrated picture of White House Ruin. Mr. Adams, of course, did not precisely duplicate the older photograph; he improved on it. His creative impulse was nonetheless stimulated by a photographic document of the past. Like others before him, Mr. Adams had benefited from the added value of a photograph after a lapse of time.

My thesis is that the value of terrestrial photographs for the future measurement of change can be enhanced by some simple techniques: mainly the marking of the camera position and, where practical, the making of photographs as stereopairs. These techniques make an ordinary field photograph an exceedingly detailed document of the existing landscape, and photographs made by these methods can be routinely repeated with exactness at some future time with whatever camera is then available. In short, the camera becomes a tool for establishing a geologic bench mark.

Terrestrial photographs have many obvious advantages over other methods of recording changes in landscapes, although standard methods of surveying (including vertical aerial photographs) can never be replaced. Observations for the Vigil Network, for example, although derived mainly by standard surveys, depend also on photographs (Emmett and Hadley, 1968). The camera sees all the intricate qualities of terrain that may otherwise escape notice: the staining of outcrops, the cracking of soil, small rills made by runoff on bare ground, the growth of plants, the impact of man's use, and countless other features that are virtually impossible to map and describe by other means. These aspects, moreover, are recorded by the camera impartially and completely, without the bias of observing only selected features that are expected to change. In an article on stream pollution, Wolman (1971, p. 916) remarked that the quality of the rivers themselves should be monitored, not just the quality of the water. The camera is an ideal tool for this purpose. From a stance on the ground, the camera accurately documents the landscape as the eye then sees it, even though the mind may later forget. Moreover, the qualities that can be pictured by photography can be determined at small expense in the ordinary course of fieldwork.

I recently became directly involved with the documentary qualities of photographs when I retraced the steps of several pioneer geologists in New Mexico by finding the places that they had photographed. With their photographs in hand, I was able to determine the actual sites where their tripods had stood and also, in some instances, the hour-by-hour routine of their daily rounds. My motive in this search, besides a desire to know their life on the trail, was to compare new photographs with the old and thereby to document changes in the land. In this pleasant work I was following the example of Hastings and Turner (1965), who had measured the changing plant cover of southern Arizona and adjacent Mexico by repeated photography. In a similar way, my duplicates of early photographs showed me that the landscape of New Mexico had also changed perceptibly in a relatively short time. I further learned that the early photographs would have been easier to repeat if the pioneer geologists had marked their localities. The degree of my success, at least for some of the early photographs, can be judged from figures 1—4.

The idea of using photography for field documentation is, of course, as old as the camera itself. Frederick Catherwood, the architect who traveled with John Lloyd Stephens in 1838—42 in Central America and Yucatán, besides making extraordinarily accurate drawings of the Maya ruins with a camera lucida, also tried to use a daguerreotype apparatus for the same purpose shortly after Daguerre's invention was introduced in Europe (von Hagen, 1947, p. 209, 232). Later,

Figure 1.–The White Bluffs in the Ojo Hedionda and Wildhorse Mesa 7½-minute quadrangles, Santa Fe County, N. Mex., as seen from the grassy alluvial bottomland along Arroyo de la Jara, 0.4 mile southeast of the Pueblo Chey ruins. The center of view is N. 7° E., but the photograph has been cropped on the right. Arroyo de la Jara lies beyond the field of view at the left and is probably incised, as shown by the bank of a tributary arroyo in the middle distance. The photograph is enlarged from a 5- by 7-inch glass-plate negative made with a lens of 200-mm focal length by N.H. Darton in September 1915. (Darton photograph 1478 in field records of U.S. Geological Survey, Denver, Colo.)

as photographic methods were perfected, terrestrial photogrammetry got its start in repeated surveys by Prof. Sabastian Finsterwald of the changing aspect of glaciers in the eastern Alps in 1888 and 1889 (Hattersley-Smith, 1966). This surveying technique has been actively practiced in rugged terrain ever since, building on the pioneer work of Finsterwald and his son, Richard (Case, 1961; Konecny, 1966). The more elementary technique of making repeated photographs from marked locations for geologic observation was probably first conceived in the United States in 1896 by Israel Russell who, as a member of a U.S. Geological Survey group on a reconnaissance of Mount Rainier, recommended systematic photography and measurement of the terminus of Nisqually Glacier (Russell, 1898, p. 399–400).

Despite Russell's early endorsement, repeated photography has seldom been practiced as a method of geologic research, although many geologists have been avid photographers of landscapes. Russell's recommendation for photography of Nisqually Glacier was eventually adopted nearly half a century later with establishment in 1942 of a network of regularly scheduled photographs (Veatch, 1969). Hastings and Turner (1965) gave credit to a botanist, Homer L. Shantz of the University of Arizona, as a dedicated photographer of representative landscapes. At the time of his death in 1958, Shantz was repeating his early photographs in the northern Great Plains that date back to 1908—a project since completed by his associate of the time, Walter S. Phillips (1963). The examples from geology, other than the photographs of Nisqually Glacier, have been published sparingly at wide intervals—perhaps the most remarkable of these being the recent duplicates by Hal G. Stephens of photographs taken by E.O. Beaman during the 1871 Powell Expedition, of which only a few have been published thus far as matched pairs (Baars and Molenaar, 1971, p. 89–99). Some other examples

Figure 2.–Duplicate of Darton photograph 1478 (fig. 1), taken August 10, 1970, at 1525 hours mountain daylight time. The photograph has been cropped on the right to match the cropping of the photograph by Darton. Gully erosion since Darton's time is conspicuous in the alluvium of the foreground, but very little change is visible in the grassland beyond. The juniper-pinyon woodland of the middle distance is also substantially the same. Blocks that lie as talus below the White Bluffs appear to be unchanged. The photograph is enlarged from a 4- by 5-inch stable-film negative made with a lens of 162-mm focal length. (Malde photograph 546 in field records of U.S. Geological Survey, Denver, Colo.)

of the use of photographs to interpret geologic change are in reports by Shepard and Grant (1947), Leopold (1951), Harrison (1960), and Bryant (1971). In this paper, I hope to encourage more geologists to adopt the idea of Russell by making reproducible photographs of all types of geologic landscapes as a means for future measurement of change. The purpose is not to use the photographs for measurement when they are first made, but is rather to accumulate archives of photographs that can be later repeated from marked localities.

MAKING PHOTOGRAPHIC RECORDS

Most geologists take photographs, but their usual photographs are impossible to duplicate exactly. The accurate matching of photographs for the measurement of change requires records that specify the position of the camera that was used for the original photograph. Foreground details, which are often the features easiest to measure because they have the largest apparent size in a field photograph, are especially hard to locate precisely without a record of the initial camera position. Thus, records of current photographs must be kept if the photographs are to be accurately duplicated later. Such records make a photograph a geologic bench mark.

The primary record of the camera position is a permanent mark on the ground. If possible, this mark should be placed by hanging a plumb bob from the center of the lens, with the camera mounted on a tripod. A steel rod half an inch in diameter makes a good mark when driven into the ground. The rod then becomes a datum for surveys of control points in the photograph, when needed later to determine the amount of change. The height of such a rod above the ground can also be noted for subsequent measurement of erosion or the buildup of sediment.

Figure 3.–The White Bluffs in the Ojo Hedionda 7½-minute quadrangle, Santa Fe County, N. Mex., as seen from the nearby edge of Arroyo de la Jara, 0.6 mile west-northwest of the Pueblo Chey ruins. The center of view is N. 22° E., but the photograph has been cropped on both the left and right, and a leftward tilt of 8° in the attitude of the camera has been corrected. The photograph is enlarged from a 5- by 7-inch glass-plate negative made with a lens of 200-mm focal length by N.H. Darton in September 1915. (Darton photograph 1477 in field records of U.S. Geological Survey, Denver, Colo.)

Other records about the initial camera position enable later photographers to place a camera above a mark with a high degree of exactness. These records are the height of the camera lens above the mark, the inclination of the camera if not level, and the azimuth of the camera axis. Quite obviously, these variables can be determined accurately only by placing the camera on a tripod.

The inclination can be read with a Brunton compass, but a better method is to place the camera level; the gain in additional foreground or height from an inclined perspective is not usually worth the trouble of duplicating the camera angle at a later time. An inclined camera also makes the geometry of a photograph needlessly complicated for subsequent measurement of geologic change (Williams, 1969, p. 139–147; Janke, 1972).

Finding the azimuth of the camera amounts to measuring the direction of the central aiming point. Clearly, the photograph can be repeated more easily if the aiming point is a conspicuous object at a distance, and such an aiming point can be described in the notes for later reference. Of course, to aim a level camera, the aiming point can be anywhere along a vertical line through the center of the field of view. Some cameras, however, lack a focusing screen with marks to determine the aiming point. In this circumstance, the center of the photograph is itself a rather accurate indicator of the aim of the camera, and the azimuth can be noted approximately.

A note about the date and hour of a photograph, although not absolutely essential for repeated photography, enhances the value of a field photograph as a geologic document.

Geologists who anticipate that active geologic processes might influence the vegetation of a landscape, or that changes in the vegetation might modify the geologic processes, may wish to collect voucher specimens of the plants and soils when a photograph is made.

Figure 4.–Duplicate of Darton photograph 1477 (fig. 3), taken August 11, 1970, at 1425 hours mountain daylight time. The trees of Darton's day in the middle distance, although now larger, mark the headward growth of the foreground gullies. Large blocks have fallen from three places along the cliff, as marked by circles, thus adding to the talus below. The photograph is enlarged from a 4- by 5-inch stable-film negative made with a lens of 162-mm focal length. (Malde photograph 551 in field records of U.S. Geological Survey, Denver, Colo.)

Records giving the positions of control points in a photograph, although helpful, are not needed for the initial photograph. These points can be identified and surveyed at the time of subsequent photography. An object of known size in a photograph is nonetheless useful in providing a reference for comparison with other objects nearby. A measured object can also be of help in detecting small changes in its vicinity.

A scheme for systematically recording the variables of a level camera at a station, including useful information about the type of film and filter as well as other technical data about the actual photograph, is shown in figure 5. Space is provided for notes on the lateral and vertical movements of the lens on a view camera, relative to the center of the film plane, and for information about the lens and focus. The format is intended for printing on either a 4- by 5-inch card or an envelope for 4- by 5-inch negatives; either way, the record stays with the negative, and a permanent document is provided for storage in an archive. Of course, a working file of these records of photographs should also be kept, partly for convenience, but mainly as a precaution against loss or damage. The notes about a photograph used for a geologic bench mark might include a supplemental photograph that shows the environs of the camera at its marked location. This photograph can be invaluable if the marker is lost.

DUPLICATING PHOTOGRAPHS WITHOUT RECORDS

If the record of a photograph is missing, the photograph can still be duplicated rather closely, although great care is needed to match details of the foreground. The record that is kept for the new photograph then makes both the old and the new photographs a geologic bench mark for later use. Finding the former placement of a camera depends on the familiar principle of parallax. With the photograph in hand, a position

Station________ Date________ Time________
Location________
Subject________

Film number				
Film type				
Filter (X)				
Exposure				
f-Stop				
Development				
Axis right				
Axis left				
Lens up				
Lens down				

Lens____ Focus________ Azimuth________ Height____

Photographer________ Camera________ REMARKS OVERLEAF

Figure 5.—A format for recording the data of photographs used for geologic bench marks.

is found such that near and distant objects in the center of the field of view are brought into approximate alinement. Then, by moving along the centerline, objects at the periphery are alined so that their apparent parallax is also correct. This procedure identifies the aiming point and fixes the camera at the proper distance from the subject. The height of the camera at this distance can generally be determined only by observing the parallax of identifiable objects in the foreground. If the nearby objects are well defined, a few inches of error in the camera position is quite noticeable in the photographic image, and a close match between the old and new photographs thus gives confidence that the original camera placement has been found.

A common fallacy about making duplicate photographs is that the focal length of the new camera should be proportional to that of the old (Curry, 1967b). All that is actually required is that the two cameras occupy the same position (meaning the position of the lens on each camera) and that they be aimed at the same point. These circumstances determine the perspective and all the geometrical properties of the two photographs (assuming that the focal plane of each camera is perpendicular to the lens axis). The broad view of a wide-angle lens obviously cannot be covered by a lens with a narrow angle of view, but a photograph made with a lens of narrow coverage will match the central part of a wide-angle photograph (suitably enlarged) if both photographs are taken from the same place. A similar comment applies to photographs made with different sizes of negatives. For example, Darton used a 5- by 7-inch camera and a 200-mm lens in New Mexico. His photographs thus covered a lateral angle of view of 47°. The camera I used covered a view of 41°, but the photographs made from his negatives and mine could be matched by enlarging them to the same size.

MEASUREMENT OF THE FOCAL LENGTH

A knowledge of the focal length of a camera is fundamental for photographic measurements, even on photographs for which the positions of control points have been measured on the ground. The focal length marked on a typical lens is only approximate and is not intended for accurate work, but the true focal length can be measured quickly with ordinary tools that are available to any geologist. The method of measurement that is outlined below is based on a procedure described by G. A. Fischer, formerly of the U.S. Geological Survey (unpub. data). (See fig. 6.)

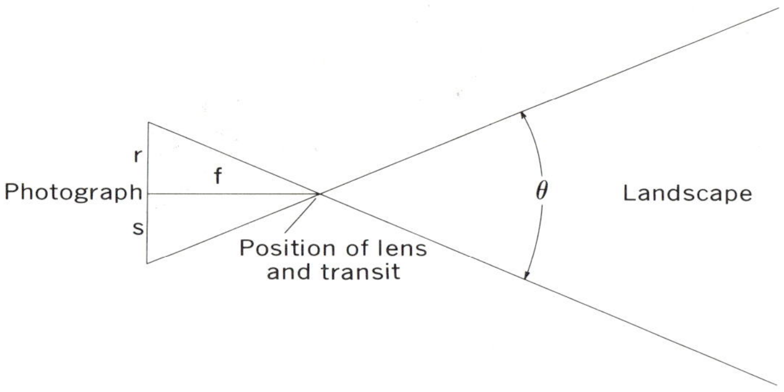

Figure 6.—Diagram of method for measurement of focal length. The symbols are explained in the text.

1. The camera is placed level, a plumb bob is used to mark a point on the ground below the center of the lens, and a photograph is made of a distant landscape that contains sharply defined objects such as church steeples and telephone poles for targets.
2. A transit is placed above the point marked on the ground, and the horizontal angle between targets near the left and right margins of the photograph is measured. Call this angle θ.
3. The distances from the center of the photograph to the images of the two target points are measured, preferably on the negative, calling one distance r and the other distance s. The measurements are made at right angles to a vertical line through the center. They can be made with an instrument as precise as a comparator or as simple as a glass scale.
4. The focal length, f, is computed from the quadratic equation,

$$f^2 - \left(\frac{r+s}{\tan\theta} \right) f - rs = 0,$$

which can be solved by standard algebraic methods.

The accuracy of the final result depends on the precision of measurement of the quantities r, s, and θ, but Fischer pointed out that a small error in locating the true center of the photograph (which introduces small complementary errors in r and s, although not an actual error in their sum) is immaterial. Still, the sum of r and s (meaning the distance between the target points on the negative) must be determined as accurately as possible. For an accuracy of one part in 4,000, which is the practical standard for photogrammetric work, the r and s distance must be measured to a tolerance of 0.04 mm if the negative is made with a lens having a nominal focal length of 150 mm. For the same accuracy, the angle θ must be measured to the nearest half minute. The computed focal length would then have a maximum error of 0.05 mm.

In practice, because the focus of a camera may be set for various distances, the focal length should be determined when the camera is focused on nearby objects (for instance, an object at a standard hyperfocal distance marked on the focusing scale), as well as when the camera is focused at infinity. When a field photograph is made, the correction factor for the actual position of focus is recorded.

GEOMETRY OF A HORIZONTAL PHOTOGRAPH

A photograph made with a level camera of known focal length provides the same general information that can be obtained by surveys with a transit, namely the horizontal and vertical angles between objects in the field of view. The information on the photograph, however, is entirely in terms of distances between these objects as they are pictured in the focal plane. Although the angular relations can be accurately determined with a special instrument—that is, a photogoniometer—the angles are easily calculated from direct measurements of distances on the photograph. These distances can be conveniently measured with either a comparator, a stereometer, or an ordinary glass scale. In practice, the measurements should be made directly on the negative.

The angular relations of a point, Q, with respect to the center of a photograph, as determined from measurements of two distances and the focal length, are evident in figure 7. For any two points in a photograph, their angular relations are calculated merely by relating their respective horizontal and vertical angles to each other.

The horizontal angle between two points on a photograph can also be calculated directly, as follows. Let r and s be the horizontal distances from the center. Then,

$$\tan\theta = f\left(\frac{r+s}{f^2 - rs}\right),$$

where f is the focal length and θ is the horizontal angle. This formula is simply a transposition of the formula used for the experimental measurement of the focal length. As before, the r and s distance should be measured as accurately as possible, but small complementary errors in r and s that result from a small error in locating the true center are insignificant.

The vertical angles that can be determined from a photograph depend on distances that are measured from the center

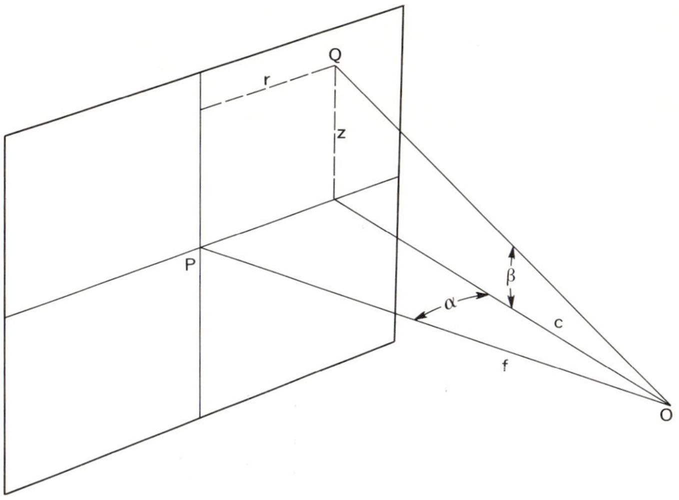

$$\tan\alpha = \frac{r}{f}$$

$$\tan\beta = \frac{z}{c} = \frac{z}{\sqrt{f^2+r^2}},$$

Figure 7.—Perspective diagram of the geometry of a horizontal photograph, where O is the position of the lens, f is the focal length, P is the center of the photograph (also called the principal point), and Q is the image of an object in the focal plane. The horizontal and vertical angles, α and β, are determined by the focal length and by measurements of r and z, using the indicated formulas. (Slightly modified from Strain and Case, 1966, fig. 19-11.)

of the photograph. The center point should be located rather precisely, but even the approximate position of the center point, which can be closely estimated by measurement from the edges or the corners of a photograph, might give a value for the vertical angle that is within the desired tolerance.

A camera can be modified to locate the center point by directly imprinting marks along the edges of the negative at the time of exposure. These should resemble the fiducial marks made by cameras used for aerial mapping. Several methods for adding such marks to negatives are technically feasible, including the direct approach of making notches at suitable places along the frame of the focal plane (Curry, 1967a). The notches should be made to close tolerances in an instrument shop by use of machine tools. The specifications for a metal slide for making fiducial marks on 4- by 5-inch film are given on figure 8. Whatever method is used for making the fiducial marks, their accuracy is uncertain unless they have been calibrated with the actual center of the photographic image. This is an optical procedure beyond the scope of this paper and is best done in an instrument shop equipped for this work.

The task of making measurements on negatives is facilitated by using cameras of large format, even though the burden in the field is greater. In reality, the accuracy of the measurements does not depend on the film size but on the focal length, and lenses of long focal length are typically used mainly on large cameras. Another advantage of larger film sizes

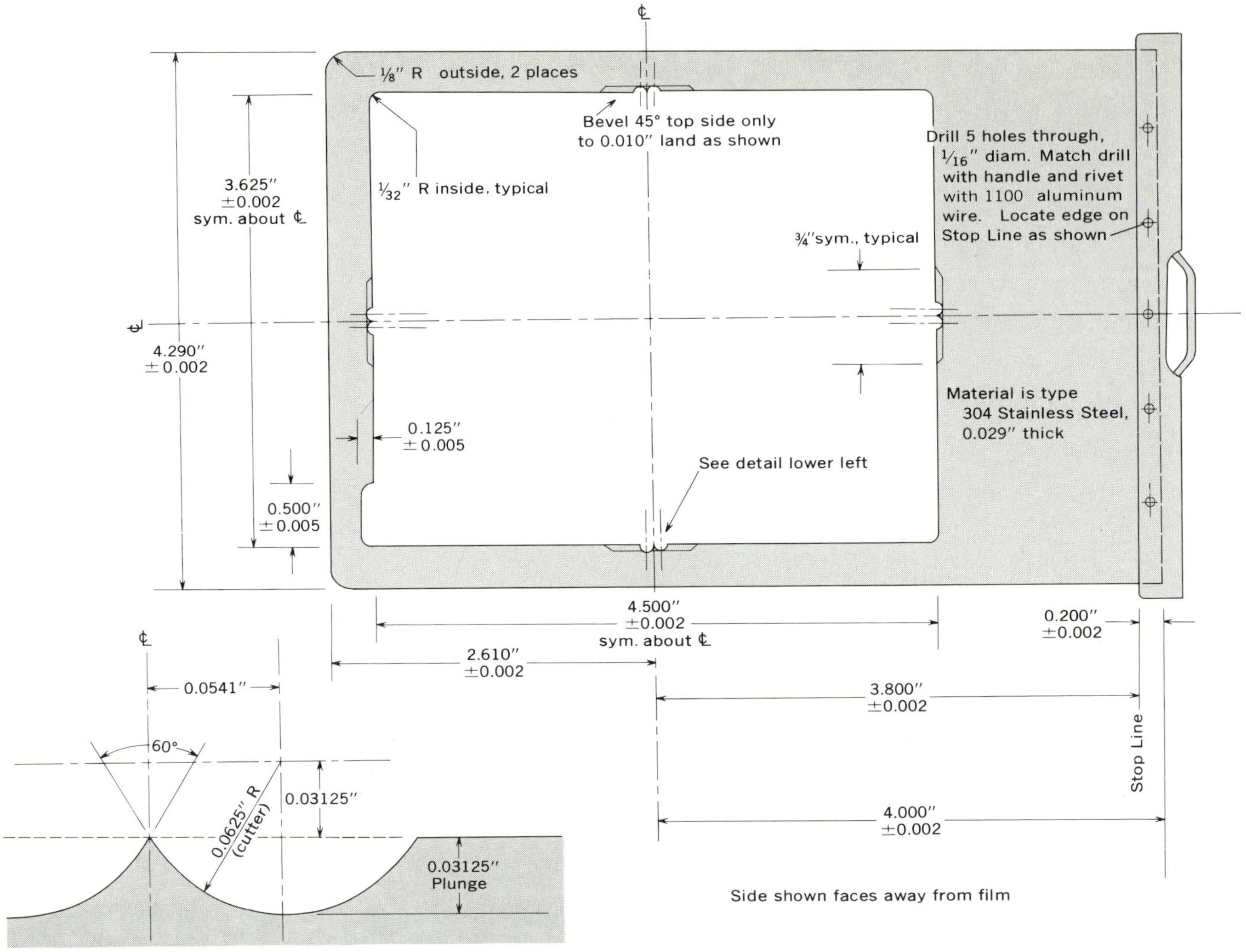

Figure 8.—Engineering drawing of a metal slide for imprinting fiducial marks at the time of exposure on 4- by 5-inch film in a standard film holder. The dark slide of the film holder is removed, and this metal slide is inserted when the photograph is made. After the film is exposed, the metal slide is pulled past the fabric of the light trap with the aid of a sheet of stainless steel, 0.003 inch thick, which is cut to the same size as the metal slide. The sheet of stainless steel is slipped in behind the metal slide, on the side toward the film, and the sheet and metal slide are removed together from the film holder. The marks that are imprinted with this device are not as accurate as those that can be made with rigid markers in other cameras, because of inaccuracies caused by a movable marker in a movable film holder, but the device is a simple means of making fiducial marks that are accurate enough for general work. The design is by Leon B. Lacey, National Center for Atmospheric Research, Boulder, Colo.

(70 mm and 4 by 5 inches) is that they are currently available in stable polyester material, which is almost as permanent as glass negatives. If work must be done with miniature negatives that are made with lenses of short focal length (35-mm cameras, for instance), the measurements should be made with a precise comparator, not with an instrument of lesser accuracy. Enlargements made from miniature negatives have been suggested as a means of achieving a photograph of convenient size (Williams, 1969; Janke, 1972), but the scale of these enlargements is hard to control, and the enlargements should preferably be made on print film to avoid the differential shrinkage of prints on paper.

The angles that can be measured with a level camera, particularly the horizontal angles, are obviously a direct means of making a map when the distances between a few control points are known. The map can be made either by analytical methods, when the greatest possible accuracy is needed in measuring the position of objects, or by graphical methods, when a lesser accuracy is sufficient. Procedures for mapping from photographs are beyond the scope of this paper, but Williams (1969) gives many practical examples that emphasize graphical techniques. Procedures that depend on plotting instruments are explained by Strain and Case (1966).

SIMPLE STEREOPHOTOGRAPHY

Geologists have become familiar with stereophotography from their regular use of aerial photographs in geologic mapping; but, as Professor Finsterwald showed in the early days of photogrammetry, the principles of stereophotography also apply to pairs of photographs made from the ground. Such stereopairs can be used either to enhance the perception of depth in a photograph of a landscape (Moseley, 1972) or to make actual measurements of terrain, depending on the distance between the pairs and the distance of the subject. Although stereophotographs are widely appreciated, geologists have rarely used them to document the geologic features of landscapes. Fortunately, stereopairs can be made simply and routinely for this purpose. In the discussion that follows, which is based on the use of a level camera, the general principles of terrestrial stereophotographs are outlined, and the methods of making them are explained.

Stereopairs can be made with a single camera either by placing the camera alternately at the ends of a short bar designed for this purpose (See, for example, Curry, 1967a) or by setting the camera successively over the ends of a base line of suitable length. Photographs from a bar would ordinarily be used with a stereoscope for visual study of landscapes, and those from a base line would be used primarily for analytical measurements of distances to nearby objects. The marked ends of the base line provide bench marks for the measurement of distances to control points. These distances, as will be seen, can also be measured directly from the stereophotographs.

Whatever means are used to make stereophotographs, they are all similar in geometry. The essential variables for measurement of a horizontal distance from the base line, using a stereopair, are shown on the diagram of figure 9. In applying this diagram, the distances r and s can be measured without knowing the true centers of the respective photographs. These measurements can be made from the image of a distant object near the center of the field of view, which is identifiable on both photographs. In this way, an increment that is added to r, for example, is subtracted from s, and the sum of r and s (or their difference) remains constant.

The range of distance that can be mapped with stereophotographs varies directly with the base line, and a common rule of thumb is that the distance to objects that are to be mapped should be from four to 15 times the length of the base line. This rule stems from a standard formula in photogrammetry, which expresses the error in the measurement of distance as follows:

$$d = \frac{h^2}{bf} e,$$

where d is the error in the distance, h is the distance from the camera to the object, b is the length of the base line, f is the focal length of the camera, and e is the error of measurement on the photograph. For example, if the measurement error is 0.1 mm, a stereopair made with a 150-mm lens from a base line 10 m long would have a resultant distance error of 1.5 m for an object 150 m away (an error of 1 percent)—the distance

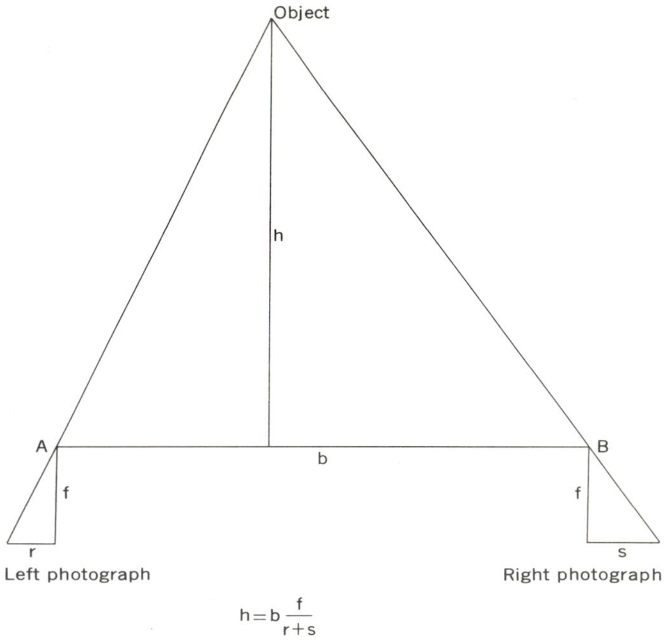

Figure 9.–Diagram of the geometry of a pair of photographs made with a level camera pointed straight ahead from the ends of a base line, AB, where b is the length of the base line, h is the distance from the base line to an object in the field of view, f is the focal length, r is the distance from the center of the left photograph to the image of the object, and s is the related distance in the right photograph. The distance to the object is calculated from the indicated formula. The geometry for an object to the left or right of the base line is similar, but the difference between r and s (not their sum) is used in the formula; that is, attention is paid to the sign of r and s.

to the object thus being 15 times the length of the base line. The recommended distance to near objects by this rule of thumb is derived from the amount of overlap of typical photographs (Strain and Case, 1966, fig. 19-17).

The preceding formula can be used to determine a suitable length for the base line, once the accuracy of measurement on the photograph is known and a tolerance has been adopted for the measurement of objects within the selected range of distance. If objects closer than this range must be mapped, an intermediate camera station can be located along the base line.

After the distance to an object has been determined from a stereopair, the vertical difference in elevation of the object with respect to the camera, if desired, can be calculated from the angular measurements previously described.

The procedure for making stereophotographs of landscapes with a short bar requires only that the bar be designed such that a camera can be placed level on the bar and aimed at the same subject from two adjacent positions—for instance, two places at a known distance along the bar. With the bar mounted on a tripod, a mark is made on the ground below the camera lens when the camera is located at a middle position on the bar, thus marking the site of the stereophotograph. Various devices that can be modified for stereophotography

Figure 10.

are sold by the makers of photographic equipment, but a bar specifically designed for a particular camera must generally be made in an instrument shop. The horizontal movements of a view camera, which permit the camera axis to be shifted from side to side, can also be used for stereophotography.

Those who see a stereophotograph of a landscape for the first time are impressed by its startling realism, and they usually misjudge the separation of the paired photographs that create the enhanced perception of depth. Even experienced users of stereophotographs of other kinds often mistakenly think that the separation between a typical stereopair of a landscape is at least 1 foot. On the contrary, a separation of 1 foot would produce an image of a landscape that cannot be viewed stereoscopically in its entirety from front to back, although the near and far areas can be viewed individually. In theory, the separation should be the distance between the eyes, which amounts to about 6.4 cm for most people. However, in actual practice, a separation of 8 cm between the paired photographs of a landscape, taken from the ground, forms a slightly exaggerated image that can still be viewed comfortably. Such stereophotographs can be studied as enlargements with the aid of a mirror stereoscope, or they can be printed side by side at a separation of 6.4 cm for viewing with either a pocket stereoscope or the unaided eyes. An example of repeated landscape photography by stereopairs is illustrated by figure 10.

Figure 10.—Stereophotographs of an area before and after a flood in New Mexico.

A. A former road breached by the arroyo of Pueblo Cañon, 12 miles south-southwest of Santa Fe, N. Mex. Since the road was last used, which was surely within the present century, the arroyo has cut headward 573 feet. This stereopair was made on July 3, 1971, at 1338 hours mountain daylight time. The arroyo was then 50 feet wide and 6.7 feet deep along the opposite bank. The two photographs of this pair were made at a separation of 8 cm and a height of 2 m, using a lens of 213-mm focal length and 4- by 5-inch stable film. The camera was level, but the lens was lowered 35 mm with respect to the center of the focal plane to increase the foreground area. The center of view bears S. 57° W. (Malde photograph 627 in field records of U.S. Geological Survey, Denver, Colo.)

B. Duplicate of Malde photograph 627 (fig. 10*A*), taken August 1, 1971, at 1336 hours mountain daylight time. A few days earlier, on July 26, the arroyo overflowed as a result of heavy rain. This flood had a calculated discharge of 5,000 cubic feet per second for a period of less than half an hour. The arroyo cut headward an additional 34 feet, and the channel was deepened as much as 2 feet. Although bank erosion as a consequence of this flood was typically unmeasurable along the length of the arroyo, the near bank at this place was cut back several feet. (Malde photograph 685 in field records of U.S. Geological Survey, Denver, Colo.)

Stereophotographs of landscapes can also be used to measure the approximate distances to nearby objects, even though their main use is for improved visual realism. The distances are calculated from measurements on the paired photographs, as previously described. Because the base line is short, the measurements on the photographs are best done with a precise comparator. For example, if a stereopair is made with a 150-mm lens from a base line 8 cm long, assuming a measurement error of 0.1 mm on the photographs, the distance to an object 12 m away can be determined with an error of 10 percent.

When greater accuracy is required in the measurement of distances by stereophotography, a procedure must be devised to make an accurate stereopair from the ends of a longer base line. Such a procedure might be needed, for instance, to measure the intricate changes in a landscape vulnerable to erosion, or to monitor the changing quality of a landscape under the impact of new forms of land use. Fortunately, the procedure for making stereophotographs from a base line requires only that the camera be placed level at the two ends and be aimed in a direction perpendicular to the base line. I will describe the simple steps that can be used with short and long base lines and then discuss the consequences of an error in the aiming point.

The simplest procedure for making an accurate stereopair from a base line makes use of a well-defined object at a considerable distance, preferably a distance several hundred times the selected length of the base line. The procedure requires some means for aiming the camera so that the distant object lies along a vertical line through the center of the field of view. If the camera lacks a focusing screen with a central mark, some other method of aiming it usually can be improvised, such as an open-sight alidade held against one side. The direction to the aiming point is first read with a compass, and the base line is laid out at right angles. Alternatively, the line of sight to the aiming point can be marked on the ground, and the perpendicular direction of the base line can then be located by ground measurements of the familiar 3-4-5 right triangle. With the direction of the base line established, photographs are made from two places along it, with the camera placed level and aimed at the distant object. Marks made with a plumb bob at the two positions give the length of the base line. The camera at these positions should be approximately at the same height, but small differences in height have no effect on the measurements that can be made from the photographs. Also, as I explain below, the slight amount of convergence that results from this procedure can be ignored. With a little practice, these steps can be completed in 30 minutes. An example of a stereopair made by this method is given in figure 11.

If a distant aiming point perpendicular to the desired base line cannot be found, or if the base line is very long, a second procedure for orienting the camera can be used. In this procedure, the base line itself is oriented toward a distant object—a circumstance that can be an advantage if stereophotographs are to be made in opposite directions from the base line. The procedure requires a device for alining the focal plane of the camera along the direction of the base line, aimed at the distant object. With the aid of this aiming device, the camera is thereby pointed at right angles to the base line. Photographs are made from two places, with the camera thus alined and placed level. As before, marks made with a plumb bob at these places define the length of the base line. The practical matters of alining the aiming device with the focal plane naturally differ among various types of cameras, and a satisfactory technique must be worked out individually for each one. This procedure for making stereophotographs from a base line is not quite as easy as the direct method of aiming the camera at a distant object, but the results are geometrically nearly the same. The choice between these alternate procedures for simple stereophotography depends only on the character of the terrain that is being photographed.

Small errors in the aim of the camera have little practical effect on measurements that can be made with stereopairs. In figure 12, for example, if the camera is averted 2° from the aiming point, the image distance of an object at a field angle of 15° would be shortened by one part in 100. Fortunately, the error decreases with the field angle. Furthermore, a camera usually can be aimed much closer than 2°. If the error in the aiming point is half a degree, which amounts to pointing the camera with the accuracy of a Brunton compass, the error of measurement is only two parts in 1,000. Because of these small errors, stereopairs made by convergent photography, whereby the camera is aimed slightly inward from the two ends of a base line, are quite usable if optimum accuracy is not required.

Figure 11.—A stereopair taken from a base line 14.91 m long oriented perpendicular to a line of sight to Bear Peak, a sharply pointed mountain in the foothills of the Front Range near Boulder, Colo. Bear Peak lies S. 21° W. in the center of each photograph at a distance of 14 km. This stereopair was made from a camera height of 1.6 m on February 29, 1972, at about 0815 hours mountain standard time, using a lens of 150.6-mm focal length and 4- by 5-inch stable film. The fiducial marks at the edges were made with the metal slide described in the text. The measured distance from the base line to the ranging pole, which is marked in intervals of half a meter, is 23.34 m. From measurements on the negatives, the distances from a central point to the image of the ranging pole are 47.94 mm and 48.14 mm on the right and left photographs, respectively. By the formula explained elsewhere in the text, the calculated distance on the ground to the ranging pole is 23.37 m, which amounts to an error of 0.13 percent at this distance. (Malde photographs 694 and 695 in field records of U.S. Geological Survey, Denver, Colo.) The stereoimage formed by this pair of photographs can be viewed with a mirror stereoscope.

CONCLUSION

Geologists of the past left behind innumerable photographs of their travels, which increase in value with each passing day. Meanwhile, photographic techniques have steadily improved over those used by early geologists, and further improvements surely lie ahead. Even so, the existing methods of photography have hardly yet been tapped by geologists for documenting the changing qualities of landscapes. With present techniques and equipment, the routine practice of marking the positions of photographs taken in the field, at times making them as stereopairs, would provide growing archives of geologic bench marks that would greatly benefit the future knowledge of geologic change.

REFERENCES CITED

Baars, D. L., and Molenaar, C. M., 1971, Geology of Canyonlands and Cataract Canyon: Four Corners Geol. Soc., 6th Field Conf., Cataract Canyon River Expedition, 1971, 99 p.

Bryant, Bruce, 1971, Movement measurements on two rock glaciers in the eastern Elk Mountains, Colorado, *in* Geological Survey Research 1971: U.S. Geol. Survey Prof. Paper 750-B, p. B108–B116.

Case, J. B., 1961, Glacier-mapping activities in the United States: Internat. Assoc. Sci. Hydrology Pub. 54, p. 359–365.

Curry, R. R., 1967a, Photography and stereophotography, *in* Field methods for the study of slope and fluvial processes—A contribution to the International Hydrological Decade: Rev. Géomorphologie Dynam., v. 17, no. 4, p. 174–175.

——1967b, On repeated photographs, *in* Field methods for the study of slope and fluvial processes—A contribution to the International Hydrological Decade: Rev. Géomorphologie Dynam., v. 17, no. 4, p. 175–176.

Emmett, W. W., and Hadley, R. F., 1968, The Vigil Network—Pt. C, preservation and access of data: U.S. Geol. Survey Circ. 460-C, 21 p.

Harrison, A. E., 1960, Exploring glaciers with a camera: San Francisco, Calif., Sierra Club, 71 p.

Hastings, J. R., and Turner, R. M., 1965, The changing mile, an ecological study of vegetation change with time in the lower mile of an arid and semiarid region: Tucson, Ariz., Univ. Arizona Press, 317 p.

Figure 11.

Hattersley-Smith, G., 1966, The symposium on glacier mapping: Canadian Jour. Earth Sci., v. 3, no. 6, p. 737–743.

Janke, N. C., 1972, Field measurements with common equipment: Photogramm. Eng., v. 38, no. 1., p. 37–47.

Konecny, Gottfried, 1966, Applications of photogrammetry to surveys of glaciers in Canada and Alaska, *in* Symposium on glacier mapping, Ottawa, 1965: Canadian Jour. Earth Sci., v. 3, no. 6, p. 783–798.

Leopold, L. B., 1951, Vegetation of southwestern watersheds in the nineteenth century: Geog. Rev., v. 41, no. 2, p. 295–316.

Moseley, F., 1972, Stereoscopic ground photographs in field geology: Mercian Geologist, v. 4, no. 2, p. 97–99.

Phillips, W. S., 1963, Photographic documentation, vegetational changes in northern Great Plains: Arizona Univ., Agr. Experiment Sta. Rept. 214, 185 p.

Russell, I. C., 1898, Glaciers of Mount Rainier: U.S. Geol. Survey 18th Ann. Rept. 1896–97, pt. 2, p. 349–415.

Shepard, F. P., and Grant, U. S., 4th, 1947, Wave erosion along the southern California coast: Geol. Soc. America Bull., v. 58, no. 10, p. 919–926.

Strain, M. B., and Case, J. B., 1966, Terrestrial photogrammetry, *in* Thompson, M. M., and others, eds., Manual of photogrammetry, 3d ed., v. 2: Am. Soc. Photogrammetry, p. 919–959.

Veatch, F. M., 1969, Analysis of a 24-year photographic record of Nisqually Glacier, Mount Rainier National Park, Washington: U.S. Geol. Survey Prof. Paper 631, 52 p.

von Hagen, V. W., 1947, Maya explorer, John Lloyd Stephens and the lost cities of Central America and Yucatán: Norman, Okla., Univ. Oklahoma Press, 324 p.

Williams, J. C. C., 1969, Simple photogrammetry: London and New York, Academic Press, 211 p.

Wolman, M. G., 1971, The nation's rivers: Science, v. 174, no. 4012, p. 905–918.

Note: Figure 12 is on the following page.

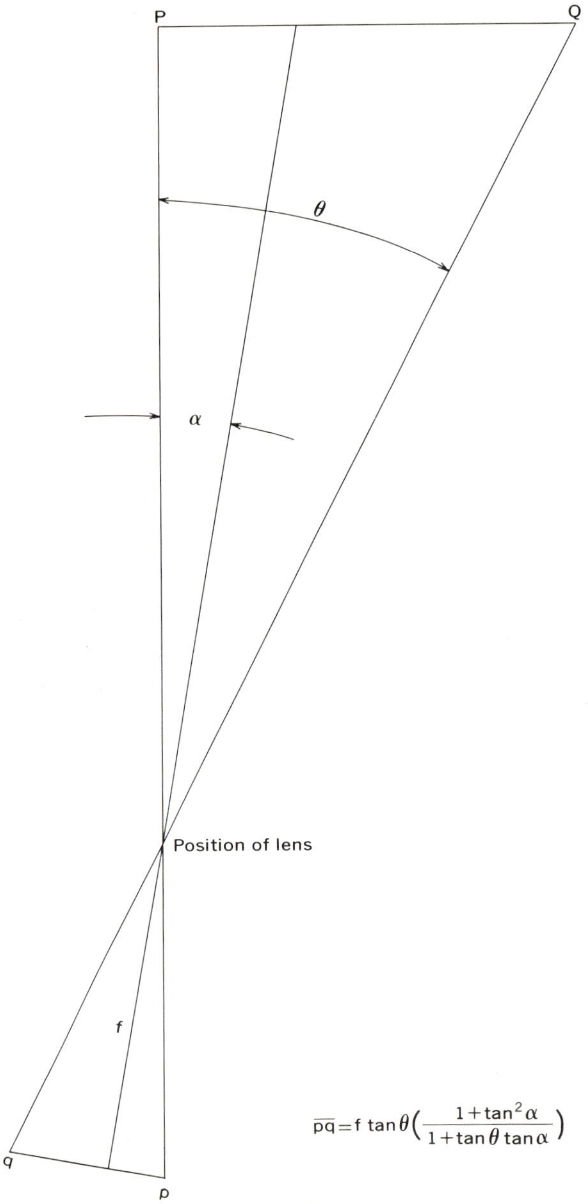

Figure 12.—Diagram of the geometry of a horizontal photograph made with a camera averted by a small angle, α, from the nominal aiming point, *P*. The aiming point is pictured in the focal plane at *p*, and an object at *Q* is pictured at *q*. If *f* is the focal length, and if θ is the field angle between *P* and *Q*, the distance in the focal plane between *p* and *q* is given by the indicated formula. This distance is slightly less than it would be if the camera were aimed directly at *P*, but the formula shows that small errors in the aiming point cause errors in the image that are too small for practical measurement. Even these errors are reduced when the field angle is small.

Jour. Research U.S. Geol. Survey
Vol. 1, No. 2, Mar.—Apr. 1973, p. 207—209

THE MICROGRAVIMETRIC DETERMINATION OF ACID-INSOLUBLE IMPURITIES IN THE COMPLETE ANALYSIS OF SMALL SAMPLES OF ACID-SOLUBLE MINERALS

By ROBERT MEYROWITZ, Washington, D.C.

Abstract.—The acid-insoluble impurities of small samples of minerals are determined by a microgravimetric procedure. A Schwarz von Bergkampf glass filter stick with paper filter medium is used to separate the insoluble material. The filtration apparatus and procedural details are described.

Frequently, minerals contain impurities which cannot be separated mechanically. Data resulting from complete decomposition and chemical analysis of both the mineral and its contaminants cannot be used to calculate the correct molecular formula of the mineral, especially if the mineral is new and the mineral and its contaminants contain elements common to both. The following procedure is recommended for the separation and microgravimetric determination of acid-insoluble impurities in small samples of acid-soluble minerals.

The application of the Schwarz von Bergkampf (1930) filter stick in the analysis of small samples of minerals has been neglected in recent years. It provides an efficient technique for the collection of very small amounts of precipitate which require treatment with hydrofluoric acid or subsequent fusion.

REAGENTS AND APPARATUS

Sulfuric acid, 9 *N*.
Sulfuric acid, 0.5 *N*.
Filtration apparatus. Letters A–I identify apparatus shown in figure 1.
(A) Crucible and cover (not shown), platinum, 15-ml capacity.
(B) Filter paper, low-ash; rolled into cylinder.
(C) Schwarz von Bergkampf (1930) filter stick; borosilicate-glass tubing with standard 0.8-mm wall, 4-mm outside diameter, and 80- to 90-mm overall length. The center of the constriction is 10 to 13 mm from the end, and a 5- to 6-mm section of tubing of undiminished bore below the constriction provides for the placement of the paper cylinder.
(D) Tubing, microchemical, thin-wall rubber, 13 mm long.
(E) Siphon; borosilicate-glass capillary tubing with 5- to 6-mm outside diameter and 0.25- to 0.75-mm bore. The outside diameter of the curved end is 2 to 4 mm and that of other end is the same as that of the filter stick, namely 4 mm.
(F) Stopper, rubber, one-hole.
(G) Bell jar, micro. Available from Corning Glass Works, Corning, N.Y., catalog No. 6880 (with ground glass plate) or from Kimble Products by Owens-Illinois, Toledo, Ohio, catalog No. 32450 (without ground glass plate).
(H) Beaker, borosilicate-glass, 50-ml capacity.
(I) Plate, ground glass.
Plate, quartz; for bottom of furnace.
Tweezers, platinum-tipped.
Thermometer, surface-temperature, 0°–540°C.
Air bath, micro. This consists of a thermostatically controlled hotplate and a vented glass dome provided with an additional hole on top for insertion of a glass thermometer. (See Rulfs, 1951, p. 48, fig. 2.)
Cooling block, brass, chromium-plated.
Jack, positioner, laboratory.
Filter paper, low-ash, rectangular, 9 by 35 mm and 9 by 12 mm.

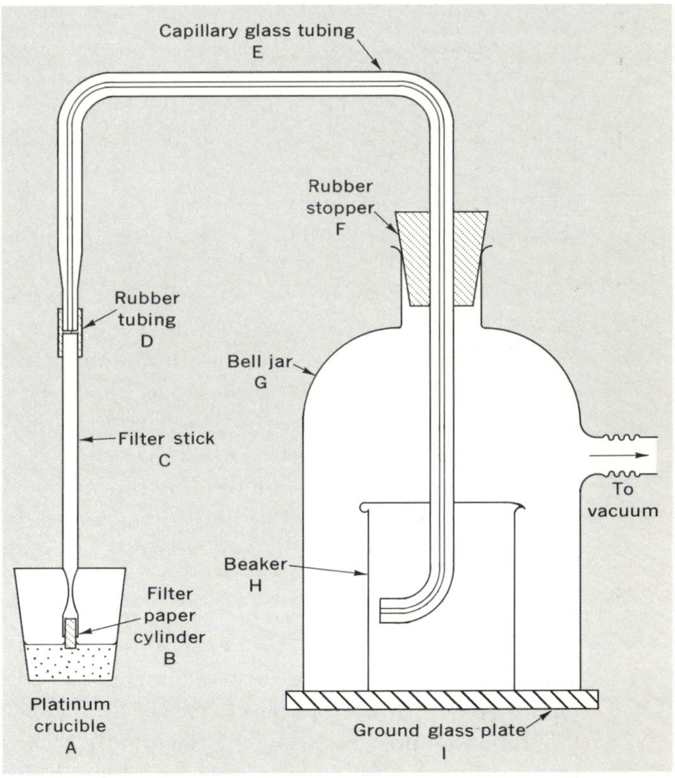

Figure 1.—Filtration apparatus. Description is given in text.

PROCEDURE

1. Weigh a 20- to 50-mg (±0.01 mg) sample in a 15-ml platinum crucible (with cover) which has been ignited to constant weight (±0.02 mg) at 850°C in an electric furnace.
2. Place crucible (uncovered) and crucible cover in the air bath at 110°±5°C for 2 hours. Cover the crucible with cover, and cool in desiccator for 20 minutes. Weigh. Calculate the percentage of H_2O lost.
3. Place crucible cover in desiccator or other clean and safe place until needed.
4. Add from a few drops to 1 ml of water down the side of the crucible to moisten the sample of mineral. Add 4 ml of 9 *N* H_2SO_4 slowly down the side of the crucible. Mix by gentle swirling.
5. Place in hot air bath (approximately 100°C) for as long as it is necessary to decompose the mineral. Add water at necessary intervals to replace evaporated water.
6. Evaporate to first appearance of sulfuric acid fumes. Cool. Add 5.0 ml of water and again evaporate to first appearance of sulfuric acid fumes. Cool.
7. Add 5.0 ml of water and warm in hot air bath (approximately 100°C) to dissolve soluble salts.
8. Prepare the filter stick by rolling a 9- by 35-mm piece of low-ash filter paper between the fingers into a tight cylinder and until the hole in the center disappears. If the cylinder does not fit into the end of the filter stick, cut a small part off the loose end. Roll cylinder again until it is compact and then insert it into the filter stick when the proper thickness has been obtained. The paper cylinder projects approximately 3 mm beyond the end of the filter stick, the other end of which is attached to the siphon tube by means of a glass-to-glass butt connection.

   Test the filter stick for the proper rate of filtration by moistening the paper cylinder with a few drops of water, connecting it to the siphon tube, and filtering distilled water. The paper cylinder swells when wetted. The water should come over dropwise at a steady rate. If no filtrate comes through, remove the cylinder, cut off a very small part of it, reinsert it in the filter stick, and test again. Replace the beaker containing the distilled water filtrate with an empty beaker before the sample is filtered.
9. Position the crucible on a laboratory jack so that the paper cylinder of the filter stick just dips into the solution. Apply suction slowly and increase suction until there is a slow dropwise but steady filtration. As the filtration proceeds, raise the laboratory jack to keep pace with the lowering surface of the solution, taking care to see that the paper cylinder just dips into the solution.
10. Raise the crucible at the last stages of filtration so that the filter stick touches the bottom of the crucible to draw off the liquid as completely as possible. While the head of the filter stick is still touching the bottom of the crucible and the suction is still on, rinse down the lower part of the filter stick with 1.0 ml of 0.5 *N* H_2SO_4.
11. Lower the crucible from the filter stick after the wash solution has been drawn off and suction is still on, and rotate the crucible in an inclined position while 2.0 ml of 0.5 *N* H_2SO_4 is added dropwise down its side. Rerinse the entire inside of the crucible at least once while rotating the crucible in an inclined position. Warm in the hot air bath for 2 minutes. Filter off the liquid as described in step 9.
12. Repeat step 11 three times.
13. Hold the filter stick over the crucible and, using the platinum-tipped tweezers, remove the paper cylinder from the filter stick and drop it into the crucible.
14. Pick up a small rectangular piece of filter paper and moisten it slightly with water. Use it to wipe the opening and outside bottom of the filter stick to remove any silicic acid present and drop it into the crucible.
15. Use a second piece of moistened filter paper to wipe the platinum tips of the tweezers and drop it into the crucible.
16. Place the crucible in a hot air bath (approximately 100°C) to remove water and then place it on a clean surface on a hotplate (surface temperature approximately 100°C). Raise the temperature of the hotplate slowly to 270°C to remove all the H_2SO_4.
17. Cover the crucible with a cover and place in an electric furnace at room temperature. Set the controller at 550°C. When this temperature has been reached, remove crucible from furnace, place on the cooling block, and allow to cool to room temperature. If all the carbon has not burned off, again place crucible in the furnace and heat until all the carbon has been removed. Set controller at 850°C. When the temperature has reached 850°C, place crucible in the furnace for 10 minutes, remove from furnace, place in a desiccator for 30 minutes, and weigh. Weigh to constant weight (±0.02 mg).
18. Calculate the percentage of acid-insoluble material.

DISCUSSION

Silica present either as an impurity of soluble silica or as silica in an acid-soluble silicate will dissolve in the acid. The decomposition mixture is brought to fumes of sulfuric acid to render the silica insoluble for filtration with the other insoluble material. The procedure describes the use of sulfuric acid because it is the acid most likely to be used. However, other acids can be used if they are suitable. Sulfuric acid is relatively inert except primarily in the presence of barium, strontium, or lead, which precludes its use. The presence of silver precludes the use of hydrochloric acid, and the presence of chloride precludes the use of nitric acid if a platinum crucible is to be used. The presence of oxidizing agents such as manganese dioxide, ferric iron, nitrate, and vanadate also obviates the use of hydrochloric acid if a platinum crucible is to be used. The filtrate collected in the 50-ml beaker is used for the analysis of the remainder of the sample. The procedures used for these analyses often require that a particular anion be absent. All of these considerations must be dovetailed in the selection of the dissolving acid.

Sometimes it is necessary to boil the sample (step 5) in order to dissolve the mineral. The correction for the ash content of the filter paper is negligible. It is assumed that there is no loss in weight on ignition of the insoluble material other than nonessential water and that an insignificant amount of water will remain with any solubilized and subsequently precipitated silica. The nature of the insoluble material may be determined by microscopic examination, qualitative microspectrographic analysis, and X-ray diffraction.

This type of filter stick was first described by Schwarz von Bergkampf (1930) and used by others, especially Benedetti-Pichler (1942, p. 198–221). Both ends are cut on the square and are carefully fire-polished so that the ends remain flat and the bore at the ends is not reduced. If the bore at the lower end of the filterstick becomes reduced, there will be a vacant space between the paper cylinder and the inside wall of the filter stick. The ends of the siphon tube are also cut on the square. The diameter of the end which is attached to the filter stick by the small piece of rubber tubing is reduced to match that of the filter stick in order to minimize the amount of filtrate that might be caught in the space between the two tubes.

The end of the siphon tube is drawn out to make the drops of falling filtrate small, and it is curved to direct the filtrate against the side of the beaker rather than the surface of the filtrate to prevent loss by spattering.

REFERENCES CITED

Benedetti-Pichler, A. A., 1942, Introduction to the microtechnique of inorganic analysis: New York, John Wiley and Sons, 302 p.

Rulfs, C. L., 1951, Quantitative semimicro inorganic procedures: Anal. Chim. Acta, v. 5, p. 46–54.

Schwarz von Bergkampf, Erich, 1930, Eine neue anwendung der filterstäbchen: Mikrochemie, Friedrich Emich Festschrift, p. 269–274.

Jour. Research U.S. Geol. Survey
Vol. 1, No. 2, Mar.—Apr. 1973, p. 211—220

EFFECTS OF LABORATORY TREATMENTS ON SILVER AND OTHER ELEMENTS IN NATIVE GOLD

By W. L. CAMPBELL, E. L. MOSIER,
and J. C. ANTWEILER, Denver, Colo.

Abstract.—Interpretation of the element content of gold and of alloy proportions of gold and silver may have useful applications in prospecting and ore genesis studies. The commonly used methods of concentration and recovery of gold for analysis (acid leach, roasting, or amalgamation), however, alter the content of silver and other elements in the gold. The treatment of gold with four mineral acids (HF, HCL, H_2SO_4, and HNO_3) and combinations of these acids, amalgamation of the gold, and roasting the gold in a muffle furnace at 650°C for 8 hours caused losses of 0–100 percent of the elements studied. In some of the samples studied these treatments also caused losses totaling as much as 50 percent, by weight, of the silver content (which made up 20 percent of the total sample weight). The other elements studied show similar behavior to a lesser extent. The results of these studies show that before one interprets compositional analyses for prospecting or other applications he must know to what extent a recovery treatment changes the composition of the elements.

Gold from various types of ore deposits has diagnostic compositional features consisting of variations in the content of elements present in trace amounts in the gold and alloy proportions of gold and silver (Antweiler and Sutton, 1970, p. 11–15). Interpretation of gold compositional data may, therefore, have useful application in prospecting and ore genesis studies. Gold occurs not only in placer deposits, but also in a great variety of lode deposits, in some as the most economically important metal, but in most as a minor constituent. The potential prospecting application of gold compositional data may therefore be extensive. The methods commonly used to concentrate and recover gold (treatment by HF, HCl, H_2SO_4, and HNO_3; amalgamation; and roasting) may alter the elemental content of the gold to the extent that the original compositional characteristics of the gold cannot be determined. The purpose of this paper is to show the amount of change in the content of silver and other elements in gold recovered by the different laboratory procedures.

COMMON METHODS OF GOLD CONCENTRATION AND RECOVERY

Gravity concentration methods including careful panning followed by handpicking under a microscope are satisfactory for recovering gold for analysis from placer deposits or free-milling or oxidized ores. Gold particles as small as 75μ in diameter can be recovered in this way, but repeated panning and patience are necessary to recover the small particles. Alternatively, gold particles can be separated from other heavy minerals by adding a small quantity of mercury to amalgamate the gold. Contact of clean mercury with clean gold particles effectively segregates gold from all the other heavy minerals. Gold can be recovered from the mercury amalgam either by solution of mercury with nitric acid, by driving off mercury with heat, by filtration, or by freezing. An obvious disadvantage of amalgamation is that the natural mercury content of the samples cannot be determined.

Procedures for obtaining gold from sulfides or tellurides are necessarily more complex than those used for obtaining free gold. Several acid-leaching and roasting procedures can be used, either alone or in combination with one another. Preconcentration by panning is usually done to remove lighter minerals. In general, if pyrite or arsenopyrite are dominant minerals, the sample is roasted at 650°C. If galena or chalcopyrite are dominant minerals, a nitric acid leach effectively removes them. If gold is intimately associated with quartz, and is not released by coarse grinding of the sample, a hydrofluoric acid leach usually removes the quartz. Iron-rich minerals such as limonite can be removed by hydrochloric acid. If tellurides are dominant minerals, one must decide whether to recover and analyze the tellurides, or destroy them by roasting or with acids to recover and analyze only the gold. After any acid-leaching or roasting procedure, final cleanup of gold particles must be done by amalgamation or by handpicking the gold.

LABORATORY STUDIES

This study was prompted in part by our observations that tiny gold grains, when recovered by acid leaching of ore material, showed a marked decrease in silver near the edges, as determined by electron-beam microprobe analyses. In contrast, silver-depleted edges were not detected in grains obtained simply by panning oxidized ore. Further tests suggested that for these tiny gold grains even mild acid cleaning prior to spectrographic analysis created a bias in the analytical results through loss of silver and other elements. Obviously, loss of silver and other elements would be easier to observe on small-particle gold than on nuggets because the percentage of gold exposed to surface contact increases with decreasing particle size. To minimize that variation for this study, samples of uniform size were used for nugget gold and random splits were used for lode gold.

To study the effects of the concentration and recovery treatments on gold composition, replicate analyses were made on treated and untreated native gold from two localities: lode gold from the Seafoam mine, Custer County, Idaho (Ross, 1930, p. 3), and placer nugget gold from the Apache Oro mine, Lost Basin, Mohave County, Ariz. Both the lode and nugget gold samples were split into fractions, and the fractions were subjected to various acid-leaching procedures. The lode samples were also subjected to amalgamation and roasting procedures. The laboratory treatments and changes in element content in the gold samples are discussed in detail in the following section.

LABORATORY TREATMENTS USED

Sericitized and oxidized vein material from the Seafoam mine was ground to pass a 35-mesh screen and panned to remove gangue minerals and sulfides. Finely divided free gold particles left in the pan (75μ–100μ in diameter) were then recovered by handpicking under a binocular microscope. The gold was then randomly split into 11 fractions of approximately 25 mg each.

A nugget (approximately 10 mm in diameter) from the Apache Oro mine was cut into 45 fractions weighing approximately 5 mg each.

1. The following acids and acid combinations were used for leaching the gold for testing:

   On lode and placer samples (five splits used for each leach):

   - 1:1 hydrofluoric acid:distilled water
   - 1:1 hydrochloric acid:distilled water
   - 1:1 sulfuric acid:distilled water
   - 1:1 nitric acid:distilled water
   - 1:1:1 hydrofluoric acid:hydrochloric acid:distilled water
   - 1:1:1 hydrofluoric acid:nitric acid:distilled water

   On lode samples only (five splits used for each leach):

   - 1:1:1 hydrofluoric acid:sulfuric acid:distilled water
   - 1:1:1 hydrochloric acid:sulfuric acid:distilled water

All samples were leached at about 85°C for 24 hours on a steam bath. Because of the limited amount of nugget gold available, only the first six acid solutions were used. After leaching, the samples were washed four times with distilled water and dried prior to analysis.

2. Roasting (five splits of the lode and placer sample were roasted):

The splits were roasted in a muffle furnace for 8 hours at 650°C to simulate the temperature effect that would be produced by roasting a gold-rich pyrite sample long enough to oxidize the pyrite.

3. Amalgamation (five splits of the lode sample were amalgamated):

The splits were amalgamated with triple-mercury, and gold was recovered by digesting the amalgam with 1:1 nitric acid-distilled water. The splits were then rinsed with distilled water, and dried prior to analysis.

ANALYSIS

A direct-arc six-step semiquantitative spectrographic method, designed for 5 mg or less (E. L. Mosier, unpub. data, 1972), was used to analyze the samples for silver and other elements. Five replicate analyses were made on raw gold from the Seafoam mine and on each treated fraction except that only two were made on the fraction treated with hydrochloric-sulfuric acid. Fifteen replicate analyses were made on raw gold from the nugget, and five replicate analyses on each treated fraction. Approximately 5 mg was used for most of the analyses, but the actual weight, which was governed by the size of the particles and the amount available, ranged from 2.5 to 6 mg.

A small amount of the lode gold was analyzed for silver variations by electron-beam microprobe by use of the method and standards described by Desborough (1970). Because the concentration of all other elements was less than the lower limit of detection, no other elements could be determined by this method.

RESULTS OF SPECTROGRAPHIC ANALYSES

The results of spectrographic analyses are shown in tables 1 and 2. The analyses of untreated gold serve as a point of reference to determine the effects of the various procedures on the content of silver and the other elements in the treated gold. The results indicate that the element content of gold is altered by recovery procedures.

The detection of Ba, B, Cr, Mn, Mo, Ni, Pt, W, and Zr in some analyses but not in others suggests that these elements probably occur in discrete mineral impurities rather than as alloy lattice components. This characteristic dramatically illustrates the heterogeneity not only among lode gold grains deposited close to one another in a vein, but also within a single gold nugget. The irregular occurrences of these elements in the gold make interpretations of the analytical data difficult and suggest that a single analysis may have little value in determining the elemental composition of gold.

A somewhat different trace element assemblage occurs in gold from the two localities. The Lost Basin placer gold contains traces of chromium, tungsten, vanadium, and zirconium—none of which were detected in the Seafoam lode gold—and contains slightly more magnesium, manganese,

Table 1.—*Direct-arc six-step spectrographic analyses of placer nugget gold from Lost Basin, Mohave County, Ariz.*

[Values for silver are in percent and are quantitative; other elements are in parts per million and are semiquantitative. Number in parentheses indicates sensitivity of method for 5-mg sample. Symbols: L, element was detected but in an amount below the sensitivity limits; N, element was looked for but not found. Also looked for but not found: As(50), Te(50), Mn(5), La(20), Ta(500), Be(1), Sb(10), Pt(10), Pd(5), Zn(50), V(5), Zr(10), Ni(10), Cd(10), B(2), Y(2), Mo(10), Sn(5), Co(5), W(50), Nb(10), Sc(2), Cr(5), Ba(10), Sr(50), In(5), Ga(5), Ge(5). "Other elements" column, occasionally detected elements—not frequent enough for statistical study]

Treatment		Ag (0.0001)	Cu(1)	Hg(50)	Pb(1)	Bi(1)	Mn(5)	Fe(10)	Ca(10)	Mg(5)	Ti(5)	Si(10)	Other elements
1. Untreated	1.	10.0	200	2,000	700	N	10	500	15	50	N	2,000	B
	2.	15.0	200	2,000	500	N	15	1,000	30	200	N	2,000	B
	3.	10.0	150	1,500	200	N	10	700	15	200	N	2,000	B
	4.	10.0	200	1,000	500	N	7	300	20	200	100	1,500	B
	5.	15.0	150	1,500	500	N	10	700	15	150	10	5,000	B
	6.	15.0	500	2,000	100	15	10	500	30	200	50	7,000	B
	7.	10.0	200	100	1,000	10	5	500	15	200	70	500	
	8.	10.0	200	2,000	150	2	5	200	70	50	100	1,000	
	9.	10.0	150	1,500	30	10	7	500	200	100	50	1,500	B
	10.	10.0	200	1,000	100	10	5	150	50	150	100	1,500	
	11.	4.2	150	200	20	3	1.5	30	50	100	70	1,500	B
	12.	10.0	100	300	2	3	7	700	100	30	5	3,000	
	13.	2.5	300	500	5	2	10	70	50	100	20	N	
	14.	9.9	150	300	50	1.5	2	N	50	30	70	2,000	V
	15.	9.5	10	300	30	2	N	50	20	150	20	300	B
Mean (M)		10.0	191	1,080	259	3.9	7	393	49	127	44	2,050	
Standard deviation (d)		3.4	106	748	307	4.8	4	305	49	66	39	1,800	
2. HF+H_2O	1.	10.0	150	1,000	N	N	N	5	7	3	N	10	
	2.	16.7	300	700	15	N	1.5	30	50	20	N	30	
	3.	6.3	70	300	5	N	N	10	10	5	N	300	
	4.	9.5	200	5,000	2	N	3	200	100	50	N	500	
	5.	.7	3	150	3	N	N	N	30	15	50	30	
	M	8.6	145	1,430	5	...	.9	49	39	19	10	174	
	d.	5.8	115	2,023	6	...	1.3	85	38	19	22	218	
3. HCl+H_2O	1.	3.8	10	200	2	N	N	N	L(20)	10	N	1,000	
	2.	6.0	70	300	3	N	N	N	20	10	N	200	
	3.	4.2	70	1,000	1	N	N	9	10	7	N	300	
	4.	4.8	50	150	1.5	N	N	15	15	7	N	300	Mo, W
	5.	5.1	70	300	1.5	N	N	15	15	7	N	500	Mo, Ni
	M	4.8	54	390	1.8	...	...	7.8	L(16)	8.2	...	460	
	d.	.8	26	347	.8	...	...	7.5	4	1.6	...	320	
4. H_2SO_4+H_2O	1.	6.0	70	300	N	N	L	15	10	50	N	700	
	2.	5.8	70	500	N	N	N	15	10	5	N	200	
	3.	7.0	100	200	2	N	L	50	15	20	N	3,000	Mo, Zr
	4.	15.0	150	500	1.5	N	1.5	15	15	20	100	1,500	
	5.	7.0	100	200	1	N	N	N	10	10	5	500	
	M	8.2	98	340	.9	...	.3	19	12	21	21	1,180	
	d.	3.9	33	150	.9	...	.7	18.5	2.7	11	44	1,125	
5. HNO_3+H_2O	1.	7.0	100	500	1	N	1	30	10	10	N	500	
	2.	12.0	150	300	1	N	1	30	10	15	N	1,500	Cr, Ni
	3.	8.1	100	500	N	N	N	5	10	5	N	20	
	4.	4.5	30	500	1.5	N	N	15	15	10	N	300	
	5.	3.6	20	200	3	N	N	N	30	20	100	2,000	
	M	7.0	80	400	1.3	...	.4	16	15	12	20	860	
	d.	3.3	54	140	1.1	...	.5	14	8.7	6	45	845	
6. HF+HCl+H_2O	1.	.6	1.5	150	1.5	N	N	N	15	7	N	15	
	2.	2.0	10	300	N	N	N	7	15	7	N	15	Mo
	3.	8.0	70	300	1.5	N	N	N	15	5	N	30	
	4.	2.4	N	200	N	N	N	N	20	10	N	30	
	5.	1.3	30	200	2	N	N	N	20	10	N	20	
	M	2.9	22	230	1	...	...	1.4	17	7.8	...	22	
	d.	3.0	29	67	.9	...	...	3.1	3	2.2	...	7.6	

Table 1.—*Direct-arc six-step spectrographic analyses of placer nugget gold from Lost Basin, Mohave County, Ariz.*—Continued

[Values for silver are in percent and are quantitative; other elements are in parts per million and are semiquantitative. Number in parentheses indicates sensitivity of method for 5-mg sample. Symbols: L, element was detected but in an amount below the sensitivity limits; N, element was looked for but not found. Also looked for but not found: As(50), Te(50), Mn(5), La(20), Ta(500), Be(1), Sb(10), Pt(10), Pd(5), Zn(50), V(5), Zr(10), Ni(10), Cd(10), B(2), Y(2), Mo(10), Sn(5), Co(5), W(50), Nb(10), Sc(2), Cr(5), Ba(10), Sr(50), In(5), Ga(5), Ge(5). "Other elements" column, occasionally detected elements—not frequent enough for statistical study]

Treatment	Ag (0.0001)	Cu(1)	Hg(50)	Pb(1)	Bi(1)	Mn(5)	Fe(10)	Ca(10)	Mg(5)	Ti(5)	Si(10)	Other elements
7. $HF+HNO_3+H_2O$ .. 1....	5.5	50	1,000	N	N	N	10	10	5	N	10	
2....	5.8	50	1,000	N	N	N	5	10	5	N	10	Mo
3....	4.5	70	300	N	N	N	7	15	10	N	15	
4....	10.5	150	1,000	3	N	N	N	15	7	N	15	
5....	5.0	50	300	2	N	N	N	20	10	N	20	
M...	6.3	74	720	1	...	...	4.4	.4	7.4	...	14	
d....	2.4	43	380	1.4	...	...	4.4	4.2	2.5	...	4.2	

Table 2.—*Direct-arc six-step spectrographic analyses of lode gold from Seafoam mine, Custer County, Idaho*

[Values for silver are in percent and are quantitative; other elements are in parts per million and are semiquantitative. Number in parentheses indicates sensitivity of method for 5-mg sample. Symbols: L, element was detected but in an amount below the sensitivity limit; N, element was looked for but not found; NA, not analyzed. Also looked for but not found: As(50), Te(50), Mn(5), La(20), Ta(500), Be(1), Pt(10), Pd(5), Zn(50), V(5), Zr(10), Ni(10), Cd(10), B(2), Y(2), Mo(10), Sn(5), Co(5), N(50), Nb(10), Sc(2), Cr(5), Ba(10), Sr(50), In(5), Ga(5), and Ge(5). "Other elements" column, occasionally detected elements—not frequent enough for statistical study]

Treatment	Ag (0.0001)	Cu(1)	Hg(50)	Pb(1)	Bi(1)	Sb(1)	Fe(10)	Ca(10)	Mg(5)	Ti(5)	Si(10)	Other elements
1. Untreated .... 1....	12.5	50	50	175	12.5	25	250	N	25	40	700	Mo
2....	25.0	70	50	125	12.5	25	325	N	20	12.5	700	Mo
3....	12.5	25	50	50	5	25	325	50	12	12.5	500	
4....	25.0	50	50	125	12.5	25	500	25	25	50	500	
5....	25.0	50	70	250	15	25	125	25	25	25	700	Y
Mean (M)	20.0	49	54	145	11.5	25	305	20	21	28	620	
Standard deviation (d)	7	16	9	74	3.8	0	136	21	6	17	110	
2. $HG+H_2O$ .... 1....	20.0	40	30	10	3	20	4	N	L	N	40	
2....	20.0	40	N	4	3	20	2	N	L	N	30	
3....	20.0	40	N	6	4	20	10	N	L	N	30	
4....	14.0	40	N	6	3	20	4	N	L	N	150	
5....	28.0	70	20	14	3	20	7	N	15	7	70	
M...	20.4	46	10	8	3.2	20	5	...	L(7)	1.4	64	
d....	5	13	14	4	.5	0	3	...	4.5	3.1	50	
3. $HCl+H_2O$ .... 1....	5.0	5	N	10	N	N	5	25	25	N	250	Mn
2....	5.0	10	N	10	N	N	10	50	25	N	150	
3....	7.0	5	N	15	N	N	L	N	35	N	350	
4....	15.0	7	N	20	N	N	10	N	L	N	350	
5....	17.0	9	N	25	N	N	50	50	17	17	500	Y
M...	9.9	7	N	16	...	...	L(10)	25	L(20)	3.4	320	
d....	5.7	2.3	...	6.5	...	...	19	25	11	7.6	130	
4. $H_2SO_4+H_2O$ ..... 1....	17.0	50	25	17	3	30	30	30	17	30	850	
2....	12.0	25	25	8	2	17	30	50	8	7	500	
3....	17.0	30	25	25	3	17	17	7	8	17	500	Y
4....	13.0	25	20	3	2	15	20	7	10	13	600	
5....	20.0	50	20	50	7	20	30	20	10	70	1,000	Pt
M...	15.8	36	23	21	3.4	20	25	23	10.6	27	690	
d....	33	13	2.7	18.5	2	6	6.4	18	3.7	2.5	224	

Table 2.—*Direct-arc six-step spectrographic analyses of lode gold from Seafoam mine, Custer County, Idaho*—Continued

Treatment		Ag (0.0001)	Cu(1)	Hg(50)	Pb(1)	Bi(1)	Sb(1)	Fe(10)	Ca(10)	Mg(5)	Ti(5)	Si(10)	Other elements
5. HNO_3+H_2O	1	20.0	40	N	60	2	20	30	10	14	10	600	Mn
	2	14.0	30	N	6	N	20	20	10	10	40	600	
	3	20.0	60	N	10	4	30	60	10	20	15	1,000	Mn
	4	14.0	40	N	6	2	20	10	10	10	N	600	
	5	15.0	30	N	8	2	25	30	20	15	N	800	Mn
	M	16.6	40	...	18	2	23	30	12	14	13	720	
	d	3.1	12	...	24	1.5	4.5	19	4.5	4	16	180	
6. $HF+HCl+H_2O$	1	12.5	25	N	5	N	N	L	L	15	N	175	
	2	17.5	25	N	7	N	N	2.5	L	10	N	L	Mo
	3	5.0	12.5	N	5	N	N	L	L	L	N	L	
	4	25.0	50	N	12	N	N	5	L	15	N	12	Mo
	5	10.0	20	N	4	2	25	10	L	10	200	L	Mo
	M	14.0	27	...	7	.4	5	L(4.3)	...	L(11)	40	L(43)	
	d	7.6	14	...	3	.9	11	3.4	...	4.2	89	74	
7. $HF+HNO_3+H_2O$	1	12.0	30	L	2	4	N	5	L	8	N	17	
	2	8.5	17	L	2	1.5	N	12	L	8	N	8	
	3	10.0	30	L	2	N	N	4	L	15	N	10	
	4	14.0	40	L	2	N	N	6	L	10	N	30	
	5	6.0	20	25	3	N	17	2	L	7	N	12	Mo
	M	10.1	27	5	2.2	1.1	3.4	5.8	...	9.6	...	15	
	d	3.0	9	11.2	.5	1.7	7.6	3.8	...	3.2	...	8.8	
8. $HF+H_2SO_4+H_2O$	1	12.5	40	N	5	5	25	2	L	10	N	15	
	2	17.5	50	N	5	2	25	3	L	10	N	15	
	3	17.5	50	N	15	10	25	10	L	10	N	50	
	4	25.0	70	N	10	5	N	10	L	15	N	25	
	5	20.0	40	N	5	5	N	5	L	20	20	20	Mo
	M	18.5	50	...	8	5.4	15	6	...	13	4	25	
	d	4.5	12	...	4.5	2.9	14	3.8	...	4.5	9	15	
9. $HCl+H_2SO_4+H_2O$	1	5.0	15	N	5	N	N	5	L	25	N	L	Mo
	2	30.0	50	N	30	3	30	70	L	20	15	100	Mo
	M	17.5	32.5	...	17.5	1.5	15	37.5	...	22.5	7.5	L(62.3)	
	d	17.7	24.7	...	17.7	2.1	21	46	...	46	11	53	
10. Hg+HNO	1	10.0	20	NA	20	7	10	50	30	50	N	500	Mn, B, Ba
	2	15.0	30	NA	15	2	10	30	30	30	5	500	Mn
	3	11.0	20	NA	8	1.5	10	15	20	15	10	200	Mn, Mo, Ni
	4	11.0	30	NA	8	1	10	20	30	20	5	300	Mn
	5	19.0	30	NA	15	2	10	190	60	190	100	600	Mn
	M	13.2	26	....	13	2.7	10	61	34	61	24	420	
	d	3.8	5.5	....	5	2.4	0	73	15	73	43	164	
11. Muffle at 650°C	1	8.0	15	N	80	5	15	115	15	115	N	300	Mn
	2	8.0	25	N	80	5	15	80	8	80	N	500	Mn
	3	25.0	50	N	330	15	30	80	8	80	N	1,000	Mn, B
	4	8.0	25	N	110	8	15	115	8	115	N	500	Mn
	5	13.0	40	N	130	13	25	260	13	260	90	250	Mn, B, Y
	M	12.4	31	...	246	9.2	20	130	10.4	130	18	960	
	d	7.3	14	...	105	4.6	7	75	3.4	75	41	900	

boron, and nickel than the Seafoam lode gold. On the other hand, the Seafoam gold contains antimony, barium, platinum, and yttrium—none of which were detected in the Lost Basin gold—and also contains appreciably more bismuth, calcium, titanium, lead, and silicon than the Lost Basin placer gold.

All the samples, whether treated or untreated, contain silver, copper and magnesium; silver and copper are alloy lattice constituents, but presumably may also occur in mineral impurities. Elements of high crustal abundance such as iron, calcium, magnesium, and silicon which occur in all or nearly all the samples analyzed probably represent either mineral impurities or grain boundary inclusions; for the nugget sample, at least, these elements cannot be regarded as surface coatings because most of the samples analyzed came from the interior of the nugget.

Mercury, an element of relatively low crustal abundance, is a major constituent of the Lost Basin placer nugget, but is scarcely identifiable in most of the Seafoam lode samples.

Reasons for this difference are not obvious, but one might speculate that the nugget accumulated mercury in its detrital environment or that much more mercury was present when mineralization occurred.

Lead was found in all the Seafoam splits, whether treated or not, and in most of the Lost Basin splits. Bismuth was detected more frequently in the Seafoam samples, but was also found in some Lost Basin samples. Antimony was found in some Seafoam samples, but in none of the Lost Basin samples. These chalcophilic elements probably occur as sulfide inclusions, and may be related to ore-forming processes, not only in the lode samples but in the nugget as well.

Iron was present in most of the splits. It is usually present in or on gold (Gay, 1963, p. 28) as sulfide or oxide inclusions rather than as an alloy constituent.

Platinum was detected in only one of the 97 splits. In general platinum occurs only rarely in gold (Antweiler and Sutton, 1970). Platinum in this sample may have been present either as a grain of the native metal or as an alloy constituent in a gold grain; in any event presence of platinum was confirmed by analyses of other samples from the Seafoam mine that were not a part of this test (Antweiler and Campbell, unpub. data).

Molybdenum was occasionally detected in the analysis of splits from both localities, but not consistently enough to justify conclusions about its behavior. The fact that it was detected in samples treated by several of the methods indicates that, if present, it may be able to withstand several of the procedures more effectively than the other elements do.

STATISTICAL ANALYSIS

Figures 1 and 2 show the mean value ± one standard deviation of each element for each sample run with each treatment. Iron, lead, antimony, and bismuth show very significant variations caused by the leaching and also show a decrease in the amount of deviation around the mean. The value for lead in the roasted lode gold sample is virtually unaltered, but all other lead values decrease. The other elements (magnesium, silver, copper, mercury, and silicon) show an overall decrease in amounts present as compared to the untreated reference sample values. The elements least affected are silver (normally present in percentile values) and copper, but they still indicate an overall drop in content in the treated samples.

The results of a one-sided normal test (table 3) also show a difference for most elements and treatments in the average of the untreated reference samples compared to the average of the treated samples. If the difference in the means M′ is greater than the computed values of μ, it is concluded that there is

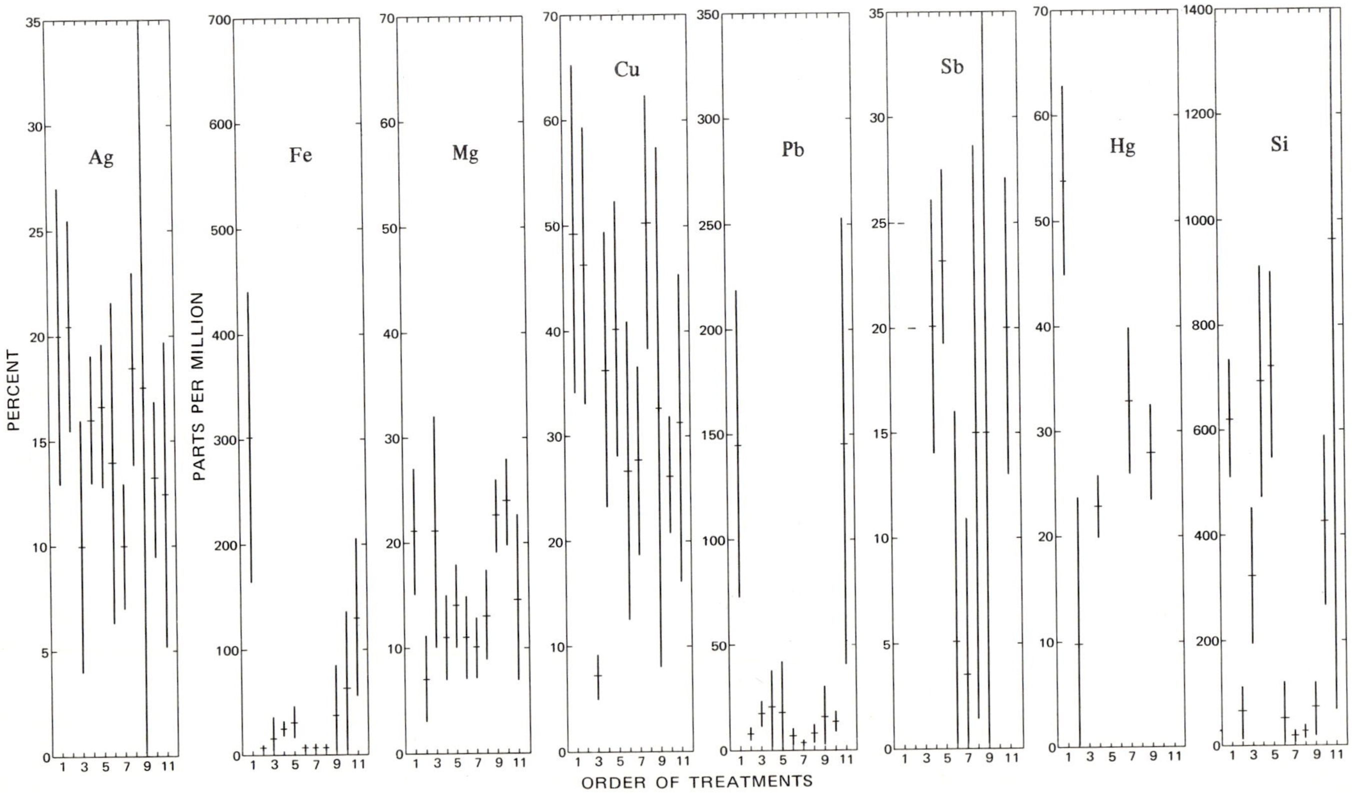

Figure 1.—Mean value ± one standard deviation for elements in lode gold caused by various treatments. Numbers indicate order of treatments: (1) untreated, (2) HF, (3) HCl, (4) H_2SO_4, (5) HNO_3, (6) HF+HCl, (7) HF+HNO_3, (8) HF+H_2SO_4, (9) HCl+H_2SO_4, (10) amalgam, (11) muffle. Dash, mean value; vertical line, ± one standard deviation.

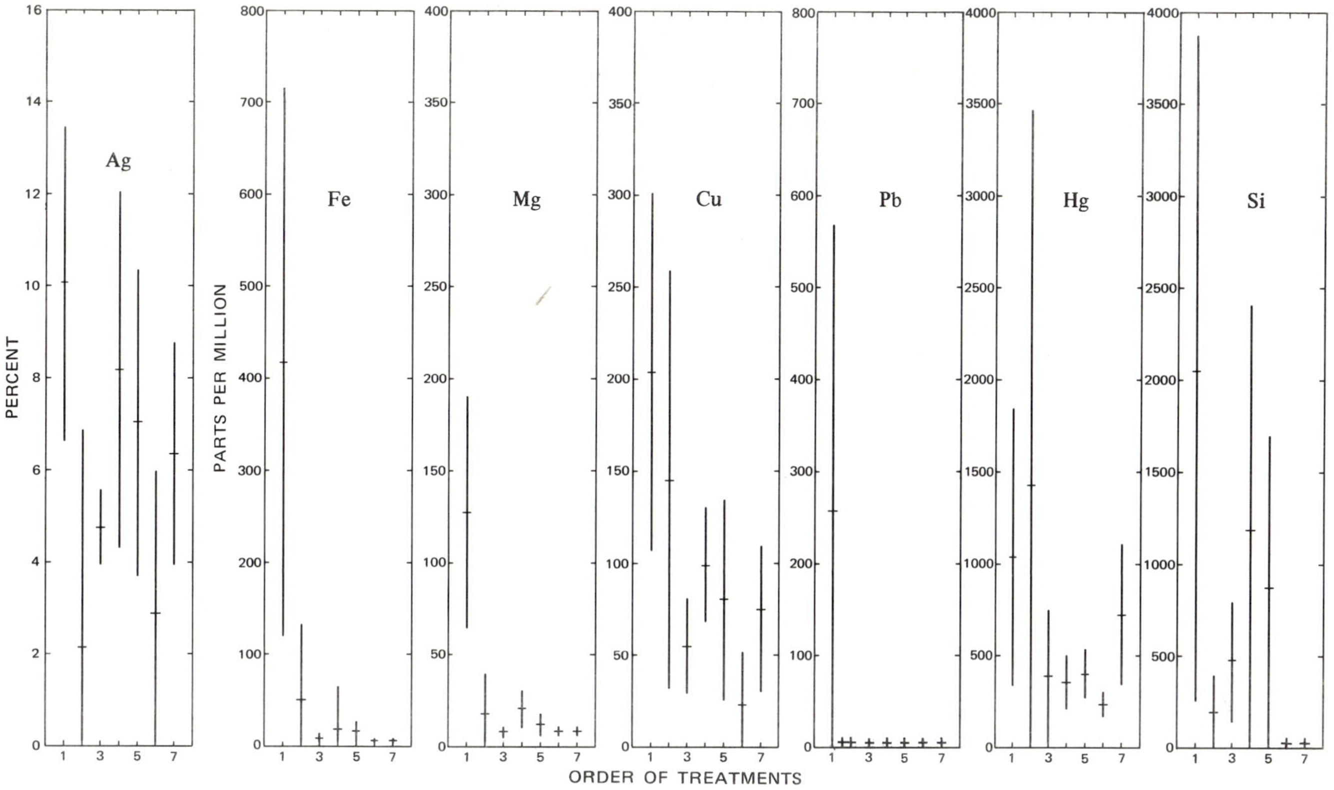

Figure 2.—Mean value ± one standard deviation for elements in placer gold caused by various treatments. Numbers indicate order of treatments: (1) untreated, (2) HF, (3) HCl, (4) H_2SO_4, (5) HNO_3, (6) HF+HCl, (7) HF+HNO_3. Dash, mean value; vertical line, ± one standard deviation.

reason to believe that the average of the reference sample exceeds that of the treated samples (Natrella, 1962, p. 3–20). Inasmuch as the treated samples and the reference sample were splits of one original sample, it must be surmised that the lower values in the treated samples are caused by the laboratory treatments.

To ascertain which of the treatments caused the smallest loss of elements from the gold, the determined amounts of all the elements, except silver, were combined and totaled. The total percentage loss was calculated by adding the totals of the element losses (in parts per million) for each fraction treated and dividing by the element totals (parts per million) in the untreated samples. These percentage losses are graphed on figure 3.

For the Seafoam gold, the most corrosive treatment was 1:1:1 HF:HNO_3:H_2O solution, which leached 91 percent of the elements from the gold. The least corrosive was the roasting procedure, which caused a loss of 28 percent of the elements from the gold. These treatments, respectively, caused losses of 50 and 34 percent of the silver content.

The most corrosive leach on the Lost Basin gold was 1:1:1 HF:HCl:H_2O solution (the treatment used by Crook (1939) to remove the gangue from the surface of gold prior to spectrographic analysis), which leached 86 percent of the elements from the gold. The least corrosive was 1:1

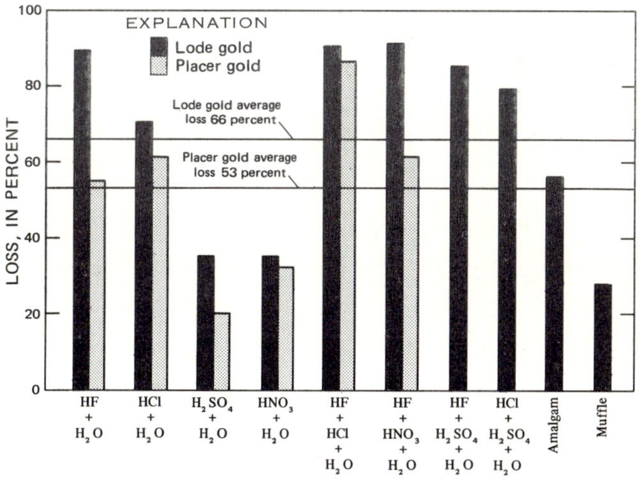

Figure 3.—Percentage losses of combined elements (except silver) based on total combined element content (except silver) of untreated gold samples.

H_2SO_4:H_2O solution, which leached 21 percent of the elements from the gold.

Amalgamation of the Seafoam mine lode gold sample followed by 1:1 HNO_3:H_2O solution leaching to remove mercury caused a loss of 34 percent of the silver in the gold,

Table 3.—*One-sided normal test on placer nugget gold and on lode gold at 90-percent confidence level*

[M′ = Mean of untreated reference sample minus mean of treated sample. $\mu = T_{1-\alpha}\frac{S}{\sqrt{n}}$, where $1-\alpha = 0.9$, S = standard deviation, and n = number of samples ($T_{0.9}$ = table values for cumulative normal distribution (Natrella, 1962, sec. 5, table A-4)). Italicized values show a significant difference]

Treatment	Ag M′	Ag μ	Cu M′	Cu μ	Hg M′	Hg μ	Pb M′	Pb μ	Bi M′	Bi μ	Fe M′	Fe μ
Placer nugget gold												
$HF+H_2O$	*8.0*	3.3	47	79	−350	1,400	*254*	4	.....	.....	*344*	59
$HCl+H_2O$	*5.3*	.56	*138*	17.7	*690*	242	*257*	1	.....	.....	*385*	6
$H_2SO_4+H_2O$	1.9	2.6	*94*	22.4	*740*	104	*258*	1	.....	.....	*374*	13
HNO_3+H_2O	*3.0*	2.2	*111*	37.3	*680*	93	*258*	1	.....	.....	*377*	93
$HF+HCl+H_2O$	*7.2*	2.1	*169*	20.5	*850*	47	*258*	1	.....	.....	*392*	2
$HF+HNO_3+H_2O$	*3.8*	1.7	*118*	29.8	*360*	260	*258*	1	.....	.....	*389*	3
Lode gold												
$HF+H_2O$	−0.4	3.4	0.3	9.2	*44*	9.3	*137*	2.7	*8.3*	0.3	*300*	2.1
$HCl+H_2O$	*10.1*	3.9	*42*	1.6	*54*	0	*130*	4.5	*11.5*	0	*289*	13
$H_2SO_4+H_2O$	*4.2*	2.2	*13*	8.9	*31*	1.9	*124*	12.7	*8.1*	2	*280*	4.4
HNO_3+H_2O	*3.4*	2.1	*9*	8.4	*54*	0	*127*	16.1	*10*	1	*275*	13
$HF+HCl+H_2O$	*6.0*	5.2	*23*	9.3	*54*	0	*138*	2.2	*11*	.7	*301*	2.3
$HF+HNO_3+H_2O$	*9.9*	2.1	*22*	6.2	*21*	4.6	*143*	.3	*10*	.9	*299*	2.6
$HF+H_2SO_4+H_2O$	1.5	3.1	−1	8.4	*4*	0	*137*	3.1	*6*	2	*299*	2.6
$HCl+H_2SO_4+H_2O$	2.5	12.1	*17*	16.8	*54*	0	*128*	12.1	*10*	2	*267*	31.7
Hg amalgam	*6.8*	2.6	*23*	3.7	.....	.....	*132*	3.5	*9*	2	*244*	50.3
Muffle at 650°C	7.6	5.0	*18*	9.3	*26*	3.0	−1	21.8	2.3	3.2	*175*	51.3

Treatment	Ca M′	Ca μ	Mg M′	Mg μ	Ti M′	Ti μ	Si M′	Si μ	Al M′	Al μ	Sb M′	Sb μ
Placer nugget gold												
$HF+H_2O$	10	26	*109*	13	*34*	15	*1,900*	149	*26*	13	.....	.....
$HCl+H_2O$	*33*	3	*120*	1	*44*	0	*1,600*	224	*36*	2	.....	.....
$H_2SO_4+H_2O$	*37*	2	*106*	8	23	30	*810*	773	*29*	13	.....	.....
HNO_3+H_2O	*34*	6	*115*	4	24	30	*1,200*	578	*32*	8	.....	.....
$HF+HCl+H_2O$	*32*	2	*119*	2	*44*	0	*2,000*	6	*38*	3	.....	.....
$HF+HNO_3+H_2O$	*35*	3	*120*	2	*44*	0	*2,000*	3	*39*	3	.....	.....
Lode gold												
$HF+H_2O$	*20*	0	*14.4*	3.1	*27*	11.2	*560*	37	*104*	0	*5*	0
$HCl+H_2O$	−5	17	0	7.6	*27*	1.9	*300*	93	*86*	8	*25*	0
$H_2SO_4+H_2O$	−2	12	*9.8*	2.5	*25*	5.6	−70	158	*70*	10	*5.2*	4
HNO_3+H_2O	*8*	3	*7.6*	2.9	1	16	−100	121	*72*	11	2	3
$HF+HCl+H_2O$	−4	2	*10.4*	2.9	*15*	11.2	*580*	503	*94*	0	*20*	8
$HF+HNO_3+H_2O$	*2.8*	2	*11.8*	2.2	−12	61	*605*	6.5	*97*	2	*22*	5
$HF+H_2SO_4+H_2O$	−8	4.7	*8.4*	3.1	*24*	6.5	*600*	10	*104*	0	*10*	9
$HCl+H_2SO_4+H_2O$	−20	9.3	−1.1	2.4	*20*	7.5	*560*	37	*97*	8	10	15
Hg amalgam	−14	10	−2.6	2.9	4	29	*200*	112	*68*	12	*15*	0
Muffle at 650°C	*9.6*	2.3	*7.0*	5.3	10	27	−340	7	*67*	11	5	5

but 1:1 $HNO_3:H_2O$ leach without prior amalgamation caused only a 17-percent loss. The difference in the two values can probably be attributed to differential removal of silver caused by solution of gold with mercury.

The percentage loss of total minor trace elements for Seafoam lode gold was higher than the loss for the Lost Basin nugget sample. The 13-percent difference (fig. 3) could be a function of the particle size because the vein gold was approximately 200 mesh in size, whereas the nugget gold samples were about 40 mesh. But it may also reflect, in part, natural refining in the detrital environment.

RESULTS OF MICROPROBE ANALYSIS

Seafoam lode gold treated with mercury and nitric acid develops rims which are comparable to the leached rims on placer gold samples reported by Desborough (1970, p. 310).

These rims are visible on carbon-coated gold prepared for the electron-beam microprobe analyses, are very distinct under high magnification, and are verified by analysis.

The effects of amalgamation, 1:1:1 HF:HCl:H_2O leaching, and roasting in the muffle furnace on the profile cross section as determined by spot analysis with the electron-beam microprobe across the individual grains (fig. 4) show that the surface rims are greatly reduced in silver content with most all the silver being removed from the outer 4μ of the grains. The profile of untreated samples, on the other hand, shows some variation in silver content, but no indication of silver-deficient edges.

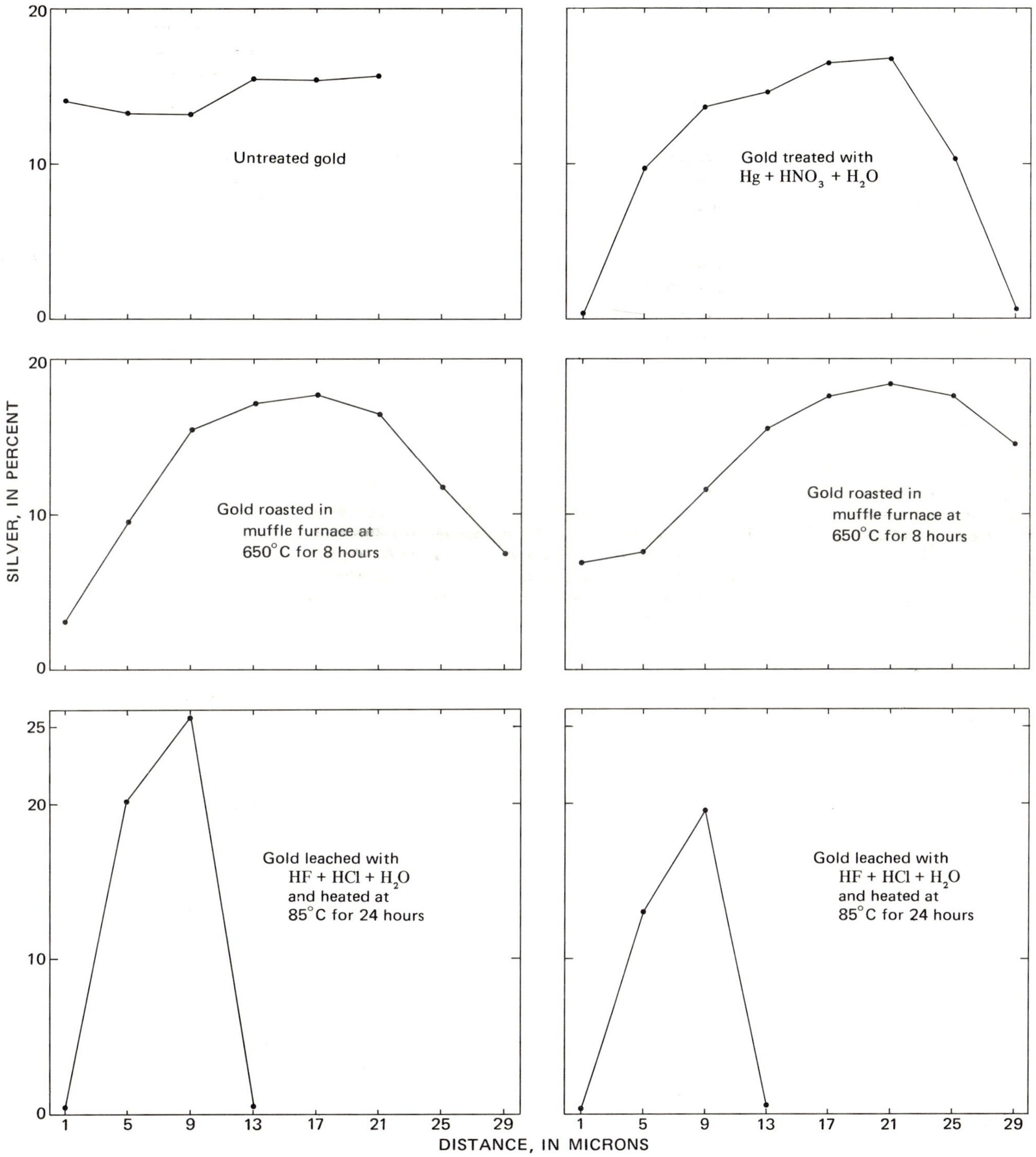

Figure 4.—The effects of laboratory treatment on silver profiles of lode gold as determined by electron-beam microprobe step scan of single grains.

CONCLUSIONS

Trace-element assemblages and concentrations in native gold are the means by which the characteristic signature of gold deposits can be determined. Although some samples must be roasted, amalgamated, or leached to recover gold, the data of the study show that these recovery procedures cause losses of most elements associated with or contained in the gold. Thus, unless specific knowledge of the effects produced by recovery procedures on a particular sample of gold are understood, interpretation of compositional data may not be valid.

REFERENCES CITED

Antweiler, J. C., and Sutton, A. L., Jr., 1970, Spectrochemical analyses of native gold samples: U.S. Geol. Survey Rept. USGS-GD-70-003, 28 p.; available only from U.S. Dept. Commerce Natl. Tech. Inf. Service, Springfield, Va. 22151, as Rept. PB1-94809.

Crook, W. S., 1939, Preliminary spectrographic and metallographic study of native gold: Am. Inst. Mining Metall. Engineers, Tech. Pub. 998.

Desborough, G. A., 1970, Silver depletion indicated by microanalysis of gold from placer occurrences, Western United States: Econ. Geology, v. 65, p. 304–311.

Gay, N. C., 1963, A review of the geochemical characteristics of gold in ore deposits: Witwatersrand Univ. Econ. Geology Research Unit Inf. Circ. 12, 70 p.

Natrella, M. G., 1962, Comparing materials or products with respect to average performance, chap. 3, p. 3–1 to 3–42, *in* Experimental statistics—Sec. 1, Basic statistical concepts and standard techniques for analysis and interpretation of measurement data: U.S. Natl. Bur. Standards Ordnance Eng. Design Handb., Ordnance Corps Pamph. ORDP 20-110, 178 p.; *also* Sec. 5, Tables, Ordnance Corps Pamph. ORDP 20-114, 89 p. [Reprinted 1963]

Ross, C. P., 1930, Geology and ore deposits of the Seafoam, Alder Creek, Little Smoky, and Willow Creek mining districts, Custer and Camas Counties, Idaho: Idaho Bur. Mines and Geology Pamph. 33, 26 p.

Jour. Research U.S. Geol. Survey
Vol. 1, No. 2, Mar.—Apr. 1973, p. 221—222

A PRECAUTIONARY NOTE ON THE USE OF MIXED SOLVENTS IN SOXHLET EXTRACTION PROCEDURES

By ALAN A. ROBERTS and JAMES G. PALACAS, Denver, Colo.

Abstract.—The variation in solvent composition of a mixed solvent used in Soxhlet extraction of sediments has apparently often been overlooked. Owing to azeotropic distillation of the solvent introduced into the apparatus, care must be taken to determine the composition of the solvent actually doing the extracting.

During our studies on hydrocarbons in recent sediments, several methods were tested to extract organic matter from samples. One of these methods, extraction of sediment samples in a Soxhlet apparatus using a variety of mixed solvents, has been used by many research workers. One of the most common solvent mixtures used in such Soxhlet extractions is a benzene-methanol mixture with ratios of benzene to methanol ranging from 9:1 to 1:2. In a cursory examination of the geochemical literature of the past 5 years we have noted in at least 15 papers in some eight different periodicals what appears to be a common oversight involved in such extractions—that the sample is assumed to be extracted by mixed solvent of the same composition as that introduced into the Soxhlet apparatus.

A Soxhlet apparatus allows repeated extraction of the sample with freshly distilled solvent. Because of the formation of an azeotrope, the composition of the mixed solvent that is distilled in such an extraction apparatus, however, is generally somewhat different from that which was introduced into the flask. For example, boiling-point (phase) diagrams for benzene-methanol mixtures (fig. 1) indicate a constant vapor concentration of about 58 volume percent benzene for distillation of liquid mixtures between about 45 and 90 volume percent benzene (Williams and others, 1948; Timmermans, 1959, p. 51–52). Outside this range the vapor will be enriched in one or the other solvent.

We have experimentally determined that the distillation within a Soxhlet apparatus of benzene-methanol mixtures that contain between 50 and 90 volume percent benzene does indeed yield a distillate composed of 58.5±0.5 volume percent benzene. Therefore, even if one were to use a starting solution of 90 volume percent benzene and 10 volume percent methanol, the distillate, which does the extracting, would initially be only about 60 percent benzene. As this distillate is removed, the liquid, and hence the vapor, will gradually become more enriched in benzene until all the methanol has distilled off or the solvent in the Soxhlet thimble has siphoned over, restarting the cycle. Thus, the extraction solvent would not be the 9:1 benzene-methanol mixture introduced into the apparatus.

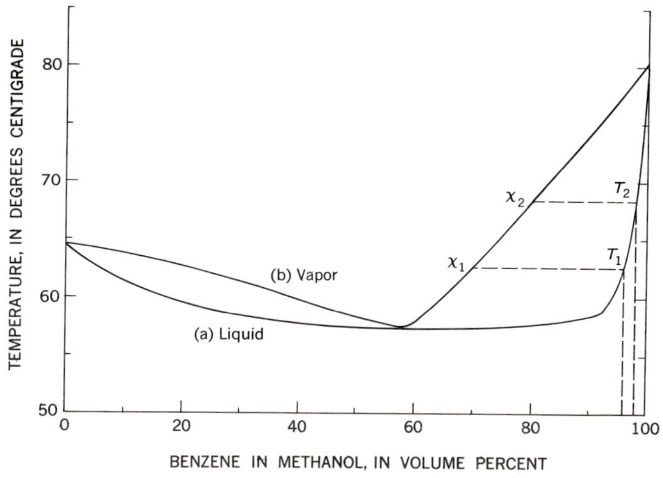

Figure 1.—Boiling point—composition diagram for benzene-methanol mixtures (data from Timmermans, 1959). The 63° boiling-point value at T_1 of a 96 volume percent benzene in methanol mixture projected to χ_1 indicates that the vapor-phase composition is 70 volume percent benzene. Inasmuch as the vapor has a higher concentration of methanol than the liquid, the liquid becomes enriched in benzene as the distillation proceeds. When the liquid reaches a composition of 98 volume percent benzene and 2 volume percent methanol, it boils at 68°C (T_2) and the vapor has an 80 volume percent composition (χ_2). With further distillation the liquid is enriched in benzene until only pure benzene results. The relative flatness of curve a between 45 and 90 volume percent benzene indicates that within this range of liquid composition the vapors are very close to the minimum-boiling azeotropic composition of 58 volume percent benzene.

One further noteworthy example in which the composition of the Soxhlet extract could be significantly altered by the effect of azeotrope formation is found in the toluene-methanol system. In this case the azeotropic mixture that would be distilled and do the extracting is mostly methanol (toluene:methanol = 2:5 by volume) in contrast to the usually desired and apparently expected ratio of toluene to methanol of 3 or 4 to 1. Other solvent systems forming azeotropes should behave in a similar manner.

We, therefore, emphasize that whenever mixed solvents are used in Soxhlet extraction the composition of the liquid mixture should be identical with that of the constant-boiling azeotropic mixture, where applicable, in order to ensure that the extraction is being done by solvent of known and constant composition. For the benzene-methanol system this composition is 58 volume percent benzene and 42 volume percent methanol.

Acknowledgments.—We wish to thank Dr. William S. Ferguson, Colorado State University, Fort Collins, Colo., for his helpful discussions and critical review of this note.

REFERENCES CITED

Timmermans, Jean, ed., 1959, The physico-chemical constants of binary systems in concentrated solutions: New York, Interscience Publishers, v. 2, 1284 p.

Williams, G. C., Rosenberg, S., and Rothenberg, H. A., 1948, Physical properties of benzene-methanol mixtures: Indus. Eng. Chemistry, v. 40, p. 1273–1275.

Jour. Research U.S. Geol. Survey
Vol. 1, No. 2, Mar.—Apr. 1973, p. 223—227

PHOTOMECHANICAL EXPERIMENTS IN AUTOMATED CARTOGRAPHY

By C. R. GILMAN, McLean, Va.

Abstract.—The U.S. Geological Survey recently undertook the investigation of two seemingly unrelated cartographic tasks: (1) the preparation of map copy for digitizing and (2) the production of experimental slope maps. Both tasks, however, require techniques and equipment for changing or manipulating the line weights of existing map symbols and producing suitable reproduction copy. After a study of existing equipment, a prototype revolving illuminator was designed and fabricated for experiments in line-weight manipulation. Sufficient exposures have been made with the device to indicate that positive control of line-weight increases and decreases up to 0.2 inch is attainable. The device has been used for photomechanical experiments in slope mapping, hill shading, and preparation of map copy for digitizing.

PHOTOMECHANICAL MANIPULATION OF MAP SYMBOLS

A major effort in U.S. Geological Survey research is devoted to developing automated techniques for increasing speed and efficiency in the cartographic phases of map revision. The goal is to produce a digitally generated map with input derived from color-separation materials of an existing map and graphic revision data.

Concurrently, a project was undertaken to develop techniques and associated equipment for slope-map production. A fast, reliable, economical way was needed to replace the tedious hand method of delineating slope zones. A computer-assisted type of compilation was first investigated, but this approach was abandoned because of the overwhelming tasks of digitizing all the contours and preparing programs to extract and plot the slope zones. The approach now under investigation is a photomechanical technique that widens contours by predetermined amounts so that contours touching each other indicate specific slope zones.

If the line weights could be controlled in reducing as well as in widening, it was reasoned, then the approach used in slope mapping experiments could also be used in separating other types of map symbols into groups convenient for digitizing.

Methods of line-weight manipulation

Methods of line-weight manipulation can be divided into three general categories:

1. Spreading and compression. In this process, the recording film is separated from the line copy by a transparent spacer and overexposed so that the recorded lines are spread if exposed through negative copy or compressed if exposed through positive copy. The amount and predictability of line-weight change is limited with this method.

2. Orbiting of images. There are methods of moving images projected from the original copy in a circular motion over the surface of the recording film so that the dimensions of the original symbols can be increased or decreased by a controlled amount. This action produces the same effect as if the original copy were being moved. In these methods, negative copy is used to generate added dimension, and positive copy is used to reduce dimensions. The amount added or subtracted is equal to the diameter of the circular movement of the image.

3. Shaking. This term could be applied to methods of moving the original copy by controlled amounts in relation to the recording film, or conversely, moving the recording film in relation to the original copy. The task would be difficult to achieve because the film and original copy would have to remain in close contact during exposure. We are not aware of any devices for accomplishing this task.

Revolving illuminator

Of these methods, the ones that appear easiest to control are those of the orbiting type. Accordingly, a revolving illuminator was developed and tested by the U.S. Geological Survey as an aid to photomechanical map-symbol manipulation. It offers a means of changing line weights without affecting the shapes of map symbols, and with no appreciable change in map scale. As the term implies, it is the illuminating lamps which revolve and thereby generate the image motion on the recording film. Map copy in the form of a film positive or negative is contained in a vacuum frame and separated from the recording film by a transparent spacer. Light rays from the revolving lamps pass through the film copy at preset angles and through the spacer to expose the recording film. The angles at which the rays pass to the recording film can be controlled by the distance between the lamps and the distance between the illuminator and the vacuum frame (fig. 1). Exposures can be controlled by the illumination level and exposure time.

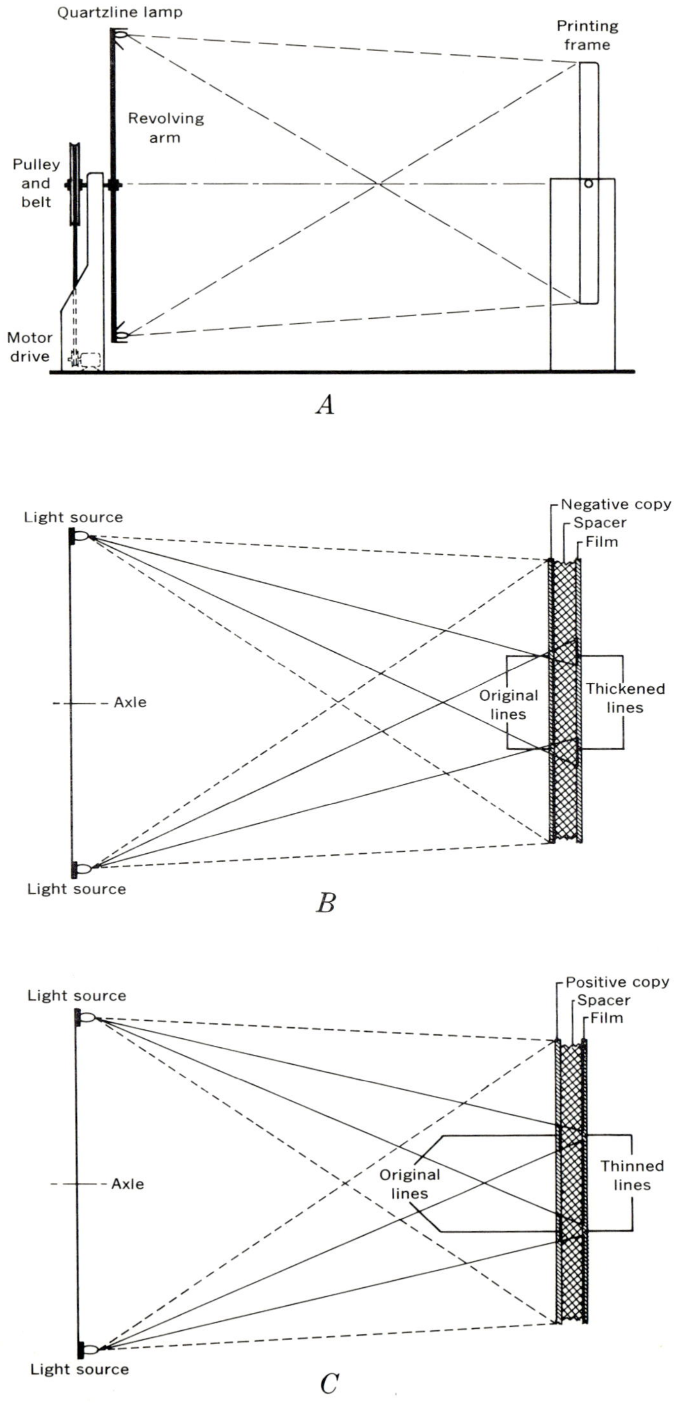

Figure 1.—Diagrams of the revolving illuminator. *A*. Relationship of revolving illuminator to printing frame. *B*. Arrangement for increasing line weight or symbol size. *C*. Arrangement for reducing line weight or symbol size.

The revolving illuminator consists principally of a stand, which houses the electrical-mechanical parts and supports the revolving arm; the controls for illumination and the driving motor; and the revolving arm, which holds the lamps. The lamps are of the quartz-halogen type, 19 volts, 80 watts. The control box contains independent on-off switches for illumination and the drive motor. An autotransformer is used for varying the illumination and the revolving speed. The lamps can be moved to any desired position along the arm, and the hoods on the lamps prevent stray light from causing spurious exposures.

In manipulating line weights, the period of exposure and the intensity of illumination are relatively important for obtaining the desired photographic product. If simple contact exposures were being made, relatively short exposures would be sufficient to equally expose lines of various weights. However, with image movement involved, each part of the negative copy acts as an individual aperture; and the wider lines, of course, provide larger apertures. Thus narrow lines must get more exposure than wider lines, either by more time or increased illumination. Tradeoffs can be made in exposure time and illumination intensity to provide both quality of product and efficiency in processing. Most experimental exposures were made at a distance of 6 feet, with the lights separated 60 inches. Transparent spacers used thus far have been 0.005-inch Mylar, 0.010- and 0.020-inch acetate, and 1/32-, 1/16-, 1/10-, 1/8-, and 1/4-inch Plexiglas. It is entirely practical to sandwich two or three spacers to arrive at a desired thickness. Line-weight increases and decreases ranging from 0.003 to 0.190 inch have been recorded repeatedly.

Advantages of the revolving illuminator are:

1. A copy camera is not needed.
2. Large or small adjustments can be made in distance between lamps, distance to vacuum frame, and intensity of illumination.
3. Orientation of the illuminator relative to the plane of the vacuum frame can be changed, depending on the task at hand.
4. Working models can be economically constructed in sizes tailored to fit laboratory spaces or the size of map copy.
5. Line-weight additions or reductions are consistent throughout the format.
6. The range of line-weight change is considerable.

The principal disadvantage appears to be the slight outward radial displacement of the recorded images. For some purposes this displacement might be of no concern; for others of exacting requirements, it might be excessive. Radial displacement can be minimized by maintaining a maximum separation between the illuminating lamps. When successive exposures are made, radial displacement is always cumulative, whether the line weights are increased or reduced. It therefore behooves the cartographer to plan the processing in as few steps as possible. If the end product exceeds the allowable limits of scale, it must be processed through a copy camera to recover the desired scale.

PREPARATION OF MAP COPY FOR DIGITIZING

The U.S. Geological Survey is developing automated techniques for producing a digitally generated map from color-separation materials of an existing map, new aerial photographs, and ground information. The culture (black) plate contains the widest variety of map symbols (fig. 2A). To reduce manual editing of digitized information, culture symbols must be separated into categories before being scanned. Other color-separation drawings—contours, woodland, drainage—can be scanned with little or no modification. A functional automatic scanning system records symbols by groups in digital format. Such digital cartographic information would be a principal input to an automated system for map revision.

All culture symbols in current use for topographic mapping were classified by dimension and analyzed to determine the possibility of photomechanically separating them for scanning. It was found that many symbols fall in two categories, and a few fall in three categories. It therefore seems impossible to separate symbols completely on the basis of equal-dimension categories. The analysis did indicate, however, that many symbols, or parts of them, could be separated into groups having the dimensions, in inches, of 0.002 and 0.003; 0.005–0.008; 0.010 and 0.012; 0.016 and 0.017; and 0.020 and larger.

In experiments with black-plate symbols, a photomechanical method was developed for deleting or retaining selected groups of symbols by line-width discrimination. This method involves the revolving illuminator to selectively and predictably control the spreading and reducing of line widths on lithographic films. Combinations of these films and the original plate are used in intermediate masking steps to produce plates with different categories of symbols. The series of resultant abridged plates can serve as input for digitizing. Since the experiments began, the process has been refined so that now fewer intermediate steps are needed to arrive at the desired product. Figures 2B and 2C illustrate some of the categories of symbols that can be isolated.

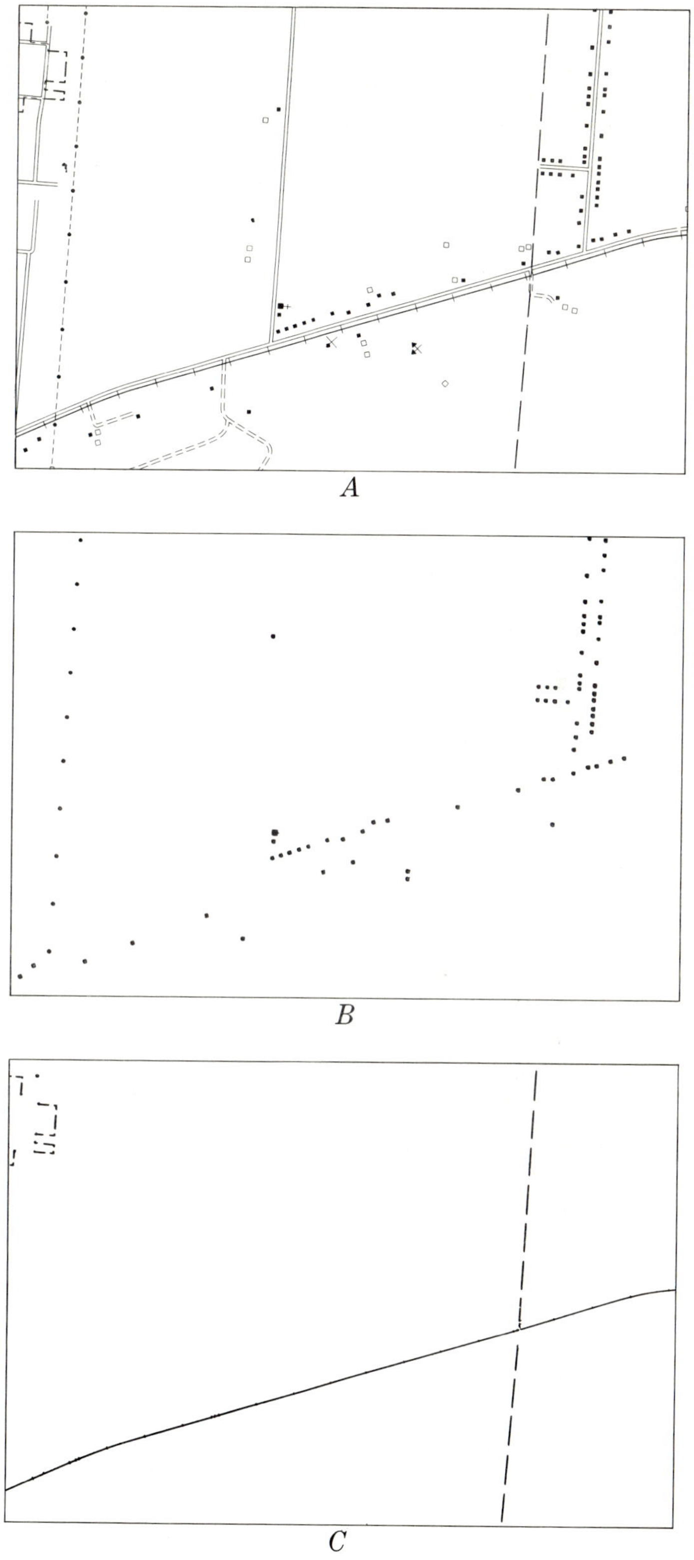

Figure 2.—Categories of map symbols with similar line weights that can be isolated from the original plate by photomechanical methods. *A*. Original culture (black) plate with variety of map symbols. *B*. Isolated symbols 0.02-inch and larger line dimension. *C*. Isolated symbols 0.005- to 0.008-inch line dimension.

SLOPE MAPPING

A slope map is a special-purpose map on which areas of similar slope are represented by a distinguishable pattern or color. Slope maps can be designed with a wide range in the number of slope categories. A simple map may include three slope categories, whereas a detailed large-scale map might contain 15 to 20 categories, usually with greater detail in the lower gradients. By looking at a good topographic map we can tell at a glance which areas are steep, flat, or in between; but without actually converting a topographic map to a slope map in some way, it is difficult to go beyond these simple slope categories with any degree of accuracy.

In a series of experiments in Menlo Park, Calif., and McLean, Va., modified 10-foot-interval contour negatives at 1:24,000 scale were used as source data for generating slope maps by photomechanical methods. To eliminate sources of spurious slope zones, contour labels, spot elevations, and other disruptive symbols had to be removed from the contour copy. The revolving illuminator was used in a process to bring the index contours to the same line weight as the intermediate contours. Limited amounts of the normal cartographic techniques of opaquing, masking, etching, and scribing were also used to modify the contour copy. Figure 3*A* illustrates a part of the modified contour plate used for generating slope zones.

In producing the color-separation copy for the various slope zones, the revolving illuminator was used, with the modified contour copy as original input, in a series of controlled manipulations of line weight and masking steps. The slope map illustrated in figure 3*B* contains five slope zones which were photomechanically generated in a series of 15 steps. Each of the zones is separated so that it can be printed in any distinctive color. The map contains some spurious slope zones which have been generated by proximity of parts of the same contour line at drain reentrants and tops of hills or ridges.

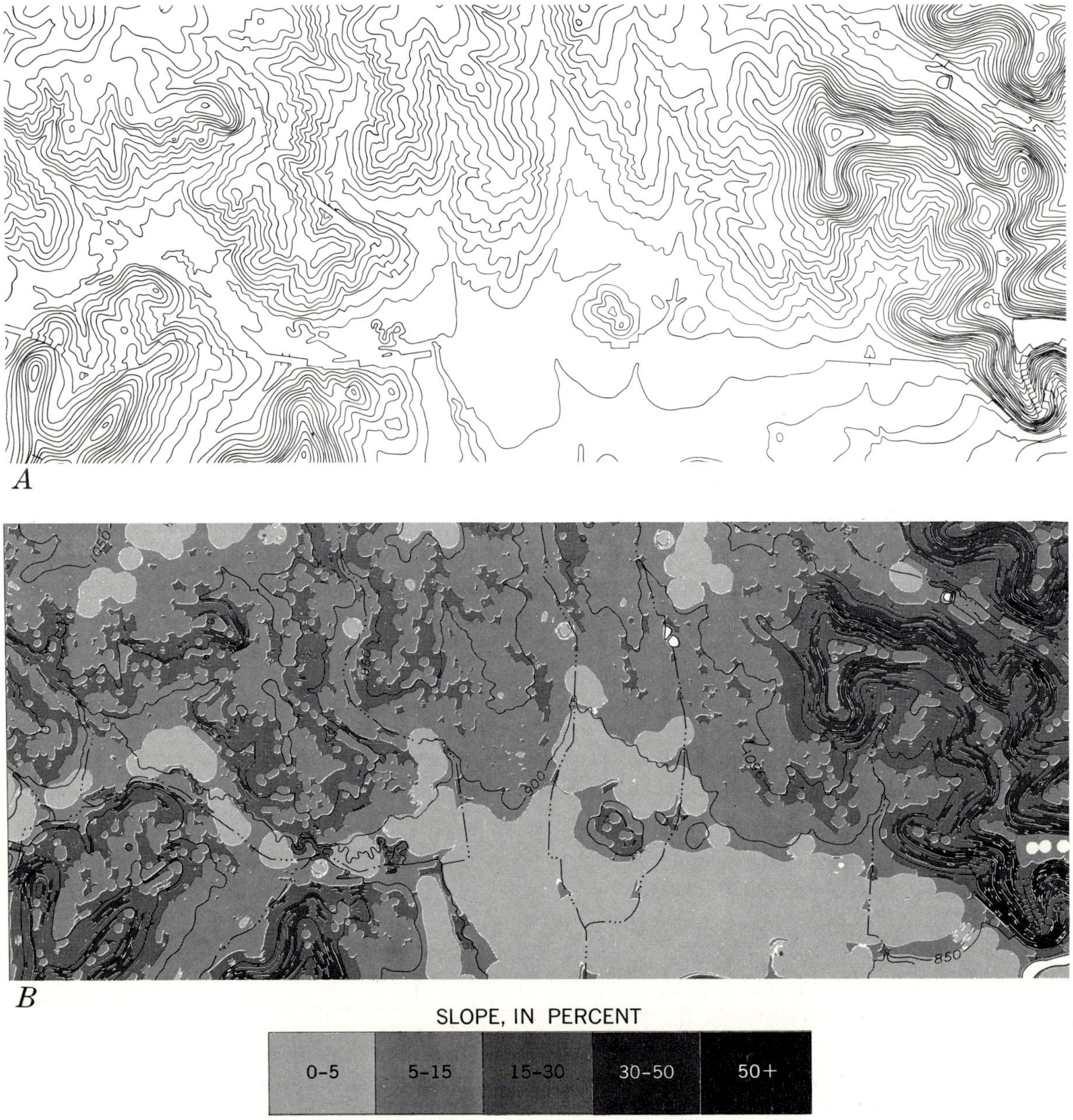

Figure 3.—Input and product of photomechanical slope mapping. *A*. Modified contour copy used for generating slope map. Width of index contours was reduced by photomechanical techniques, and contour numbers were removed manually. *B*. Part of a slope map produced by photomechanical methods.

SEMIAUTOMATIC RELIEF SHADING

The Geological Survey publishes shaded-relief editions of selected topographic maps that show physiographic features of special interest. On these editions, the shading accentuates the physical features by simulating the appearance of sunlight and shadows on the terrain and conveys an illusion of a three-dimensional land surface. Until now, the shading for these maps has been rendered by airbrush.

The photomechanical method of relief shading now being developed shows promise of replacing the tedious manual method. The cartographer chooses the direction of illumination and constructs a mask to separate illuminated slopes from shaded slopes. A negative image of the contour lines is then subjected to a line-enhancing process in which contours are thickened in the direction of illumination. In this process the revolving illuminator is turned edgewise to the copy and thus widens the contour lines in a direction controlled by the orientation of the copy. Then in a series of photographic steps, the mask, the enhanced contours, and a 40-percent screen are combined on a film which conveys a three-dimensional illusion (fig. 4*A*).

The composite is then used as copy for further processing into a more conventional shaded-relief form that resembles a hand rendering by airbrush (fig. 4*B*). In this procedure, continuous-tone film is exposed through a sandwich of the composite copy, a translucent diffuser, and a 0.1-inch transparent spacer. Thus, the varying tones on the illuminated and shaded slopes are effectively blended with the background tint. The resultant shadings can be reproduced in halftone and overprinted on the topographic map (fig. 4*C*).

Further relief-shading experiments with maps of other scales and formats are in progress. Hopefully, the technique will assist us in producing more economical, but satisfactory, relief shading. In particular, we are anxious to determine if these semiautomatically generated products are practical for use on orthophotomaps and on 1:500,000-scale State maps.

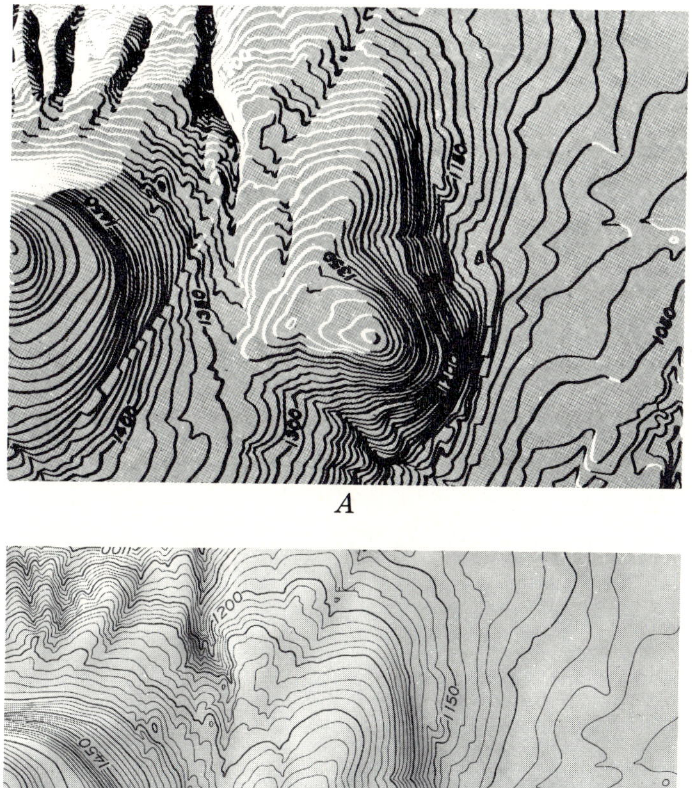

A

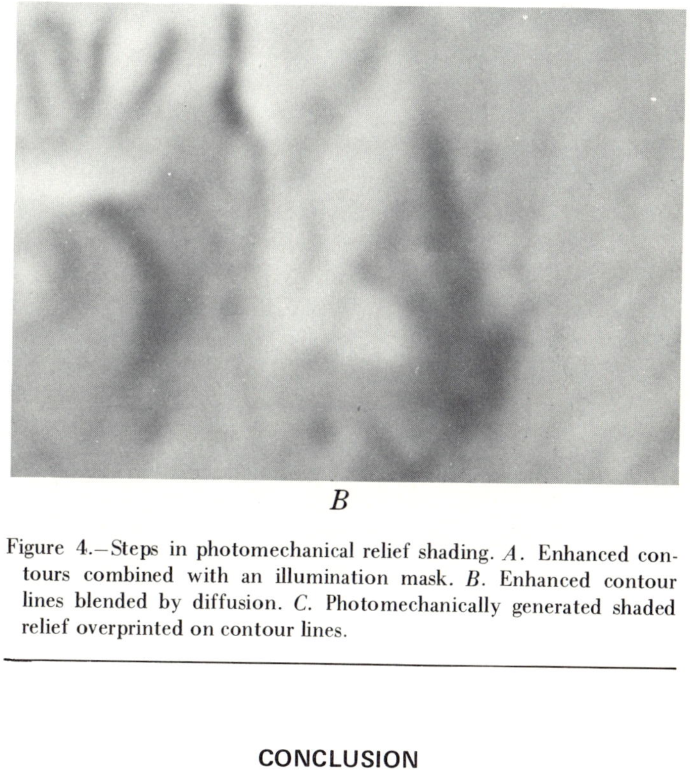

B

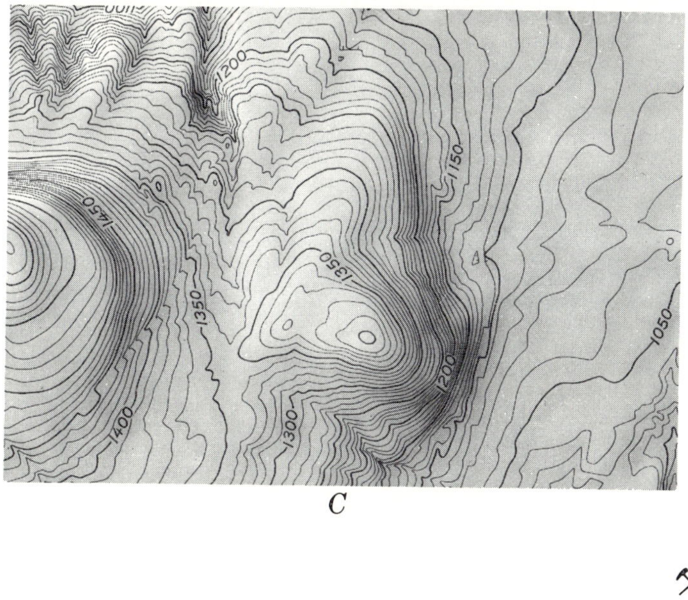

C

Figure 4.—Steps in photomechanical relief shading. *A*. Enhanced contours combined with an illumination mask. *B*. Enhanced contour lines blended by diffusion. *C*. Photomechanically generated shaded relief overprinted on contour lines.

CONCLUSION

In view of the present state of the art in cartographic equipment and techniques and the trend toward new cartographic products, additional research, experimentation, design, and testing of photomechanical devices and their products are both desirable and necessary. Photomechanical automation has been proved to be feasible, and the potential of this field should not be overlooked because of the rapid advances being made in automation by digital techniques.

Jour. Research U.S. Geol. Survey
Vol. 1, No. 2, Mar.—Apr. 1973, p. 229—235

FORMATION OF JOINTS IN BEDROCK BY MOVING GLACIAL ICE

By FRANK W. TRAINER, Albuquerque, N.M.

Abstract.—The orientation of joints in igneous and sedimentary rocks was measured at 21 localities in California, Maine, and New York to investigate the hypothesis that glaciation may open joints in bedrock. A summary of strikes of all joint sets shows the following pattern relative to the direction of glacial advance: two sets, thought to be extension joints, flank the direction of advance and are separated from it by about 10°; two sets, thought to be shear joints, flank the direction of advance by about 40°; and two sets, thought to be release joints, are about 70° to 80° from the direction of advance, or nearly perpendicular to the extension joints. An average of five joint sets, including three or four in this pattern, was found at each locality. The joints are believed to have been opened, in response to stress applied by the moving ice, along preexisting zones of weakness (potential regional joints) in the rock. Some new joints may have formed where no such zone was present near the position required for fracture under the applied stress. Additional investigation of the hypothesis is desirable because of its possible bearing on glacial erosion by quarrying, on interpretation of joint patterns in glaciated regions, and on the nature of aquifers in glaciated bedrock.

Several observers have interpreted jointing in glaciated rock as an effect of the glaciation. Lewis (1954, p. 418–419), Battey (1960, p. 8–9), and Linton (1963, p. 17–18) suggested that sheeting, formed as a result of dilatation after glacial erosion, has contributed significantly to deep glacial erosion in mountain valleys in Norway. Johnston (1964, p. 27) suggested that bedding joints in horizontal sedimentary rocks in western New York were opened or expanded as a result of pressure release during deglaciation.

Nonsheeting joints, vertical or steeply dipping, are common in many glaciated terrains. One can infer that they are regional joints, inherited from the preglacial history of the rock, which are present as either potential or incipient fractures to considerable depth. Kupsch (1955, 1965) described jointing in boulders in a deposit of glacial drift—jointing which he attributed to stress applied by glacial ice that had moved across the deposit. At least two other references have been made to the possible role of glacial stress in opening bedrock joints. Chapman (1958, p. 557) concluded that glacial ice shove had opened some joints in granite on Mount Desert Island, Maine. Yatsu (1966, p. 45) listed compression failure due to glacial action in a table of geomorphic agents and types of destruction but did not elaborate this interpretation.

This report presents the hypothesis that stress applied by a moving glacier opens joints in the underlying bedrock. Most of these joints are believed to have formed along preexisting zones of weakness whose positions are near those required for fracturing under the applied stress, but it is suggested that new joints may be formed in sound rock where older zones of weakness do not occur near the required positions.

Acknowledgments.—The assistance of John T. Collier, David M. Hopkins, and Robert A. Loney, through their discussion and review of this study and report, is gratefully acknowledged.

SOURCES OF DATA

The orientations of joints were measured at 21 localities: eight in granite or rhyolite in the Sierra Nevada in east-central California; three in granite on Mount Desert Island, Maine; and 10 in sandstone or carbonate rock in New York. Table 1 summarizes the observations, and figure 1 shows the locations of the areas in which data were obtained.

The eastern part of the Sierra Nevada is characterized by a regional system of steeply dipping conjugate joints (Bateman and Wahrhaftig, 1966, p. 121–122). At most places two principal joint sets can be identified; they are nearly at right angles, one striking northeast and one northwest. In this investigation joints were studied in two parts of the range: in Yosemite National Park (No. 1 in table 1), and near Interstate Highway 80, which crosses the crest of the range near Donner Pass in the region between Sacramento, Calif., and Reno, Nev. (Nos. 2–8, table 1).

On Mount Desert Island, Maine, two or three sets of well-developed joints and one to three sets of poorly developed joints are commonly present at a given locality; the sets which are best developed are believed to be those whose orientation relative to the local topography or to sheeting surfaces is favorable for dilatation (Chapman, 1958, p. 556–557). As part of the present study the orientations of joints were measured at three places at or near the summit of Cadillac Mountain (Nos. 9–11).

Joints were studied in horizontally bedded sedimentary rocks in western New York (Nos. 12–16), in southeastern New York (17–20), and near the south end of Lake Cham-

Table 1.—*Joint sets identified on contoured equal-area plots, and other data, for 21 localities in California, New York, and Maine*

Locality No. (fig. 1)	Brief name	Location[1] (long W., lat N.)	Number of joints	Rock[2]	Average strike of scratches	Average strike and dip of joint sets[3] (degrees)
					California	
1	Tuolumne Meadows	119°20′43″, 37°52′24″	210	G	N. 76 W.	N. 84 W., 88 NE. (5); N. 60 W., 80 SW. (5); N. 44 W., 90 (5); N. 8 E., 87 SE (4); N. 25 E., 90 (8) R; N. 42 E., 35 NW. (2).
2	Long Lake	120°25′52″, 39°17′37″	99	G	N. 15 E.	N. 66 W., 80 NE. (9) R; N. 40 W., 65 SW. (4); N. 15 E., 77 SE. (8); N. 45 E., 90 (6) R; N. 52 E., 47 NW. (2); N. 70 E., 90 (6).
3	Hill near Long Lake	120°25′18″, 39°18′00″	100	G	N. 8 W.	N. 75 W., 80 NE. (14) R; N. 62 W., 78 SW. (10) R; N. 64 E., 72 NW. (11).
4	Near Palisade Lake	120°24′38″, 39°18′24″	112	R	N. 1 E.	N. 88 W., 88 NE. (5); N. 41 W., 90 (8) R?; N. 0 E., 90 (6); N. 13 E., 82 NW. (4); N. 30 E., 90 (5); N. 58 E., 90 (9) R?.
5	Cold Springs	120°27′56″, 39°19′01″	100	G	N. 66 E.	N. 35 W., 90 (12) R; N. 18 W., 90 (12); N. 22 E., 75 NW. (5); N. 50 E., 72 SE. (7) R; N. 75 E., 80 SE. (4).
6	Lower Lola Montez Lake.	120°25′23″, 39°21′00″	102	G	N. 2 E.	N. 82 W., 85 SW. (3); N. 58 W., 90 (5) R; N. 20 W., 72 SW. (8); N. 35 E., 63 NW. (3); N. 55 E., 65 SE. (5) R?; N. 75 E., 90 (3).
7	Euer Saddle	120°20′28″, 39°20′45″	100	G	N. 48 W.	N. 47 W., 60 NE. (9) R?; N. 27 W., 78 SW. (8); N. 20 E., 90 (9); N. 57 E., 83 NW. (11) R?; N. 85 E., 90 (2).
8	Donner Pass	120°19′37″, 39°19′06″	100	G	N. 73 E.	N. 66 W., 90 (7) R; N. 45 W., 83 SW. (7); N. 30 W.,90 (7); N. 15 W., 90 (10); N. 5 W., 90 (8); N. 20 E., 90 (4) R?; N. 55 E., 70 NW. (3); N. 75 E., 78 NW. (5).
					Maine	
9	Mt. Desert Island	Summit, Cadillac Mtn.	108	G	N. 27 W.	N. 85 W., 88 NE. (5); N. 60 W., 90 (8); N. 20 W., 89 NE. (6); N. 0 E., 88 E. (6); N. 42 E., 88 NW. (8).
10	do	Ridge NE. of summit.	125	G	N. 27 W.	N. 89 W., 90 (11); N. 38 W., 80 SW. (5); N. 10 W., 90 (8); N. 15 E., 85 SE. (8).
11	do	W. face mountain, near summit.	100	G	N. 18 W.	N. 75 W., 85 SW. (6); N. 28 W., 90 (8); N. 20 E., 90 (7); N. 80 E., 88 NW. (13).
					New York	
12	Pekin	Quarry 2.0 miles NW. of Pekin.	146	S	N. 75 E.	N. 38 W., 88 SW. (18) R; N. 23 W., 82 SW. (5); N. 12 E., 90 (4); N. 84 E., 87 SE. (10) R.
13	Lockport	Outwater Park	91	L	N. 41 E.	N. 76 W., 78 SW. (2); N. 58 W., 87 NE. (24) R; N. 32 W., 90 (6) R?; N. 3 E., 87 SE. (4); N. 23 E., 83 SE. (3); N. 81 E., 86 NW. (16) R.
14	do	Gooding Street	143	L	N. 11 E.	N. 58 W., 88 NE. (12) R; N. 9 E., 87 NW. (4); N. 22 E., 90 (2); N. 53 E., 75 NW. (3); N. 87 E., 88 SE. (20) R.
15	do	Quarry, Frontier Stone Products.	317	L	N. 35 E.	N. 45 W. R; N. 5 W; N. 20 E; N. 80 E. R[4].
16	Gasport	Bolton Road	115	L	N. 23 E.	N. 78 W., 88 NE. (25); N. 35 W., 88 NE. (5) R?; N. 15 W., 90 (4); N. 32 E., 88 NW. (8); N. 87 E., 88 NW. (8) R.
17	McClure	Highway 17, 4.7 miles W.	127	S	N. 21 E.	N. 85 W., 83 SW. (12); N. 60 W., 88 SW. (2); N. 50 W., 78 NE. (2); N. 8 E., 88 NW. (16); N. 35 E., 80 SE. (2); N. 48 E., 75 SE. (3); N. 70 E., 50 SE. (2).
18	Otego	Highway 7, 2.3 miles SW.	93	S	N. 57 E.	N. 65 W., 73 SW. (4); N. 30 W., 78 SW. (4); N. 5 W., 75 NE. (4); N. 15 E., 90 (2); N. 66 E., 78 SE. (7); N. 81 E., 67 SE. (9).
19	Windham	Highway 23, 1.6 miles E.	80	S	N. 50 E.	N. 66 W., 80 NE. (10); N. 16 E., 55 NW. (2); N. 38 E., 80 SE. (22).
20	Kingston	Highway 209 at S. edge of village.	94	L	N. 29 E.	N. 82 W., 88 SW. (5); N. 30 W., 87 SW. (2); N. 3 E., 88 NW. (20).
21	Crown Point	Shore, Lake Champlain, near bridge, Highway 8.	84	L	N. 19 E.	N. 88 W., 88 NE. (15); N. 60 W., 85 NE. (6); N. 45 W., 88 SW. (4); N. 22 W., 88 NE. (2); N. 13 E., 80 SE. (6).

[1] Where adequate, a brief verbal description is given instead of longitude and latitude.

[2] G, granite; R, rhyolite; L, carbonate rock; S, sandstone.

[3] Concentration (in percent) in parentheses; R, regional joint set.

[4] Joints observed on horizontal rock surface, plotted as vertical joints.

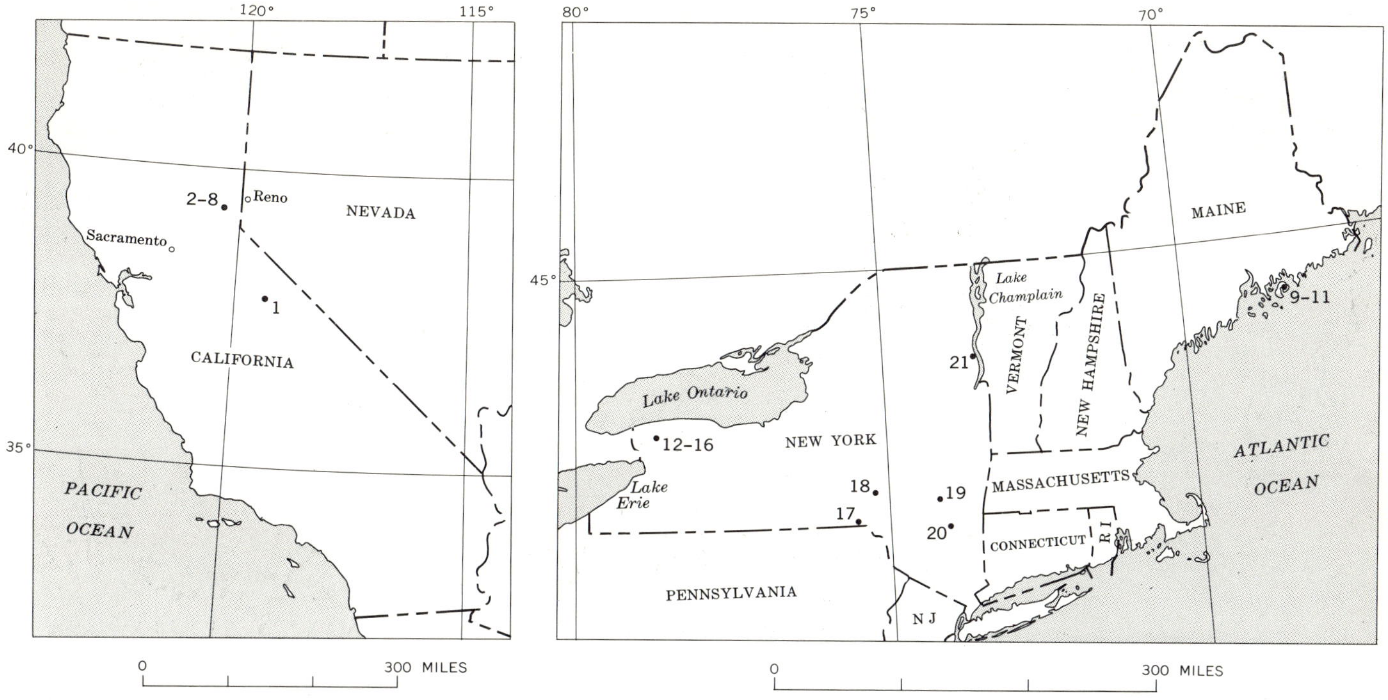

Figure 1.—Locations of areas in California, Maine, and New York where orientations of joints were measured.

plain (21). In western New York the joints are in the Lockport Dolomite (Silurian) and in sandstone in the Albion Group (Silurian). Two sets of regional joints are present; they strike about N. 81 E. and N. 47 W. In southeastern New York three regional joint sets have been recognized (Parker, 1942); two, approximately perpendicular, whose strikes shift progressively in a clockwise direction as the observer moves eastward across northern Pennsylvania and southern New York, and a third set which strikes northeast throughout the region. Joints measured in this region as part of this study are in sandstones of the Katsberg Formation of Chadwick (1933) and of the Genesee Formation, and in Onondaga Limestone, all of Devonian age. Near Lake Champlain the joints are in limestone of the Chazy Group.

METHODS OF STUDY

The strike and dip of joints were measured at each of the 21 localities. Samples represent from 80 to 317 joints; at most localities a sample of about 100 joints was measured. In the granites only steeply dipping joints that are at a high angle to the sheeting were measured; near-horizontal sheeting is present at most of these places. In the sedimentary rocks both near-horizontal bedding joints and near-vertical joints were measured, but the bedding joints constitute only a small proportion of the total. At each locality, observations were made in the smallest practicable area. At most localities a hundred joints were found within a tract of land surface of 2,000 to 5,000 sq ft (about 200 to 500 m^2) or in a roadcut 200 to 300 feet (about 65 to 100 m) long.

The strikes of glacial scratches and grooves on the bedrock surface were measured in order to determine the last direction of glacier movement.

Regional joints were identified through such criteria as length, depth, and continuity (most clearly seen in the Sierra Nevada and on Mount Desert Island); relative frequency at a locality; and similarity of strikes with those of joints at nearby localities. Joints were also measured at several localities which are not listed in table 1 because glacial scratches were not found; some of these data were used in identification of the sets of regional joints.

Observations were plotted and joint sets identified on a Schmidt or equal-area net using the lower hemisphere.

PATTERN OF JOINT SETS

The distribution of strikes of joints is broadly similar at many localities. Thus, it is common to find joints which strike along or at a small angle to the direction of glacial advance, joints which are at a large angle to the direction of advance, and joints which are near an angle of 45° with respect to the direction of advance. Figure 2*A*, which represents the orientation of joints in granite at one locality in the Sierra Nevada, illustrates this pattern. Five sets of joints are identified in the diagram; their average strikes are N. 35° W., N. 18° W., N. 22° E., N. 50° E., and N. 75° E. Two sets (N. 35° W. and N. 50° E.) are believed to be regional joints. At this locality the direction of ice movement was along the line N. 66° E. If the diagram is rotated so that the line of glacial advance becomes N. 0° E., the strikes of the five joint sets become N. 79° E., N.

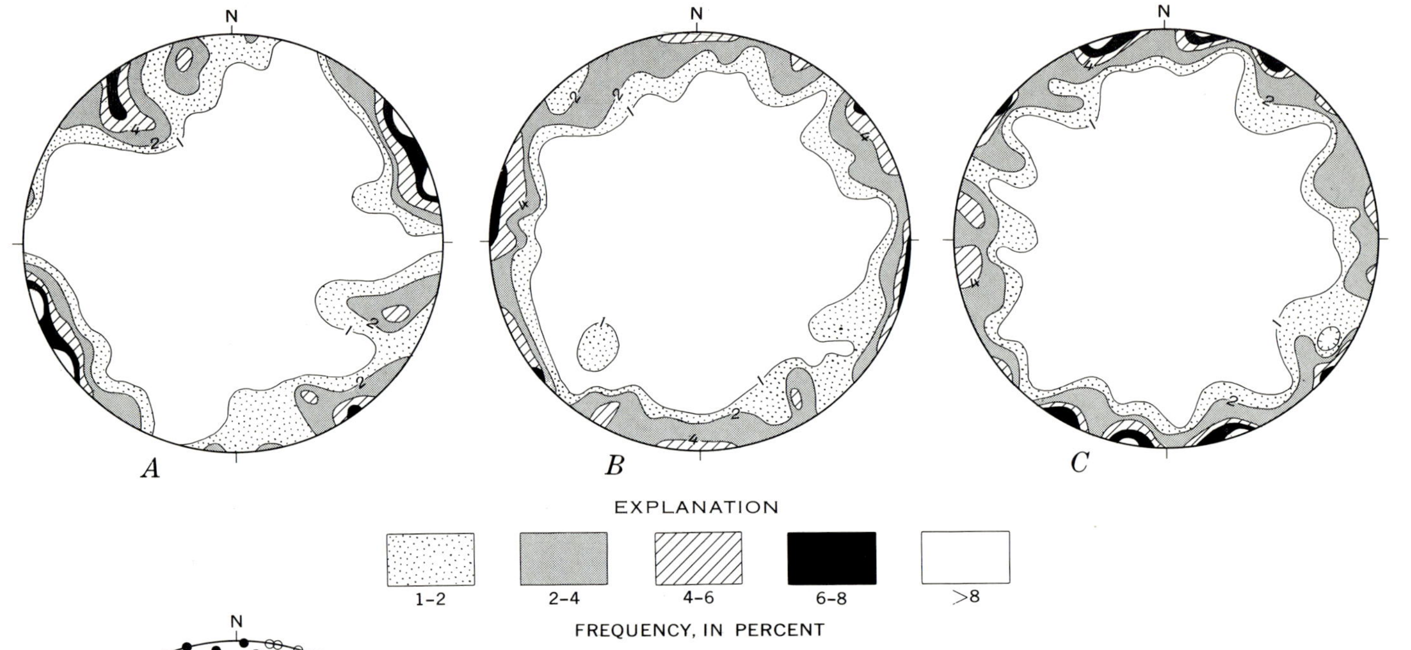

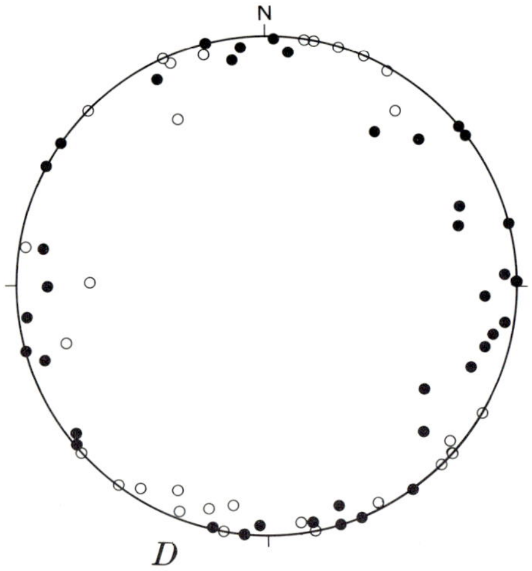

Figure 2.—Equal-area diagrams (lower hemisphere plots).
A. Contours drawn on poles of joints in granite at locality 5, table 1; 100 joints. Average strike of glacial scratches on bedrock surface is N. 66° E.
B. Contours based on 94 points, each of which is the average position of a joint set with a concentration greater than 2 percent. All 21 localities in table 1 are represented.
C. Contours based on the same 94 points, after adjustment of the strike of each set to its position relative to the direction of glacial advance (arbitrarily taken as N. 0° E.).
D. Joint sets at localities where regional joints were identified. Strikes have been adjusted as in diagram *C*. Open circles represent sets identified as regional joint sets; solid circles represent sets not so identified.

84° W., N. 44° W., N. 16° W., and N. 9° E., respectively.

A total of 107 joint sets was identified in the equal-area diagrams for the 21 localities. From three to eight sets were found at individual localities. In order to see the distribution of joint sets more clearly, summary diagrams (fig. 2*B*, *C*) were prepared by an extension of a method used by Spencer (1959, p. 480–481). The mean position of each joint set having a concentration greater than 2 percent (94 of the 107 sets) was plotted as a pole on each of the two equal-area diagrams. Figure 2*B* is a summary diagram for the 94 points, plotted in their observed positions with respect to geographic north. Figure 2*C* is a summary diagram for these 94 points in which their strikes have been rotated to positions relative to the direction of glacial advance (taken arbitrarily as N. 0° E.).

The summary diagram of adjusted poles (fig. 2*C*) reveals seven well-defined concentrations whose average strikes relative to the direction of glacial advance (N. 0° E.) are N. 9° W., N. 8° E., N. 40° E., N. 40° W., N. 58° W., N. 72° E., and N. 80° W. A diagram (not shown) similar to figure 2*C* was prepared by plotting the percentage-concentration value of each of the 94 sets, rather than a single point having weight equal to that of every other point. Contouring this plot eliminated the concentration at N. 58° W.; the remaining six concentrations of figure 2*C* were duplicated almost precisely. Each of these concentrations exhibits a range of about 15° to 20°, with most of the points falling within a span of 10° or less.

The summary diagram of unadjusted poles (fig. 2*B*) was prepared as a semiquantitative test of the significance of the apparent orderly arrangement of concentrations in figure 2*C*. It seems possible that if two or more diagrams, each of which had several well-defined joint sets, were rotated through random angles and then combined, the resulting summary diagram might show clearly defined concentrations. The pattern of concentrations in the adjusted plot is much more orderly than that in the unadjusted plot. This common pattern in the adjusted diagram for the 21 samples, which represent unlike rock types and structural histories, suggests a similar response of these rocks to the stress applied by moving ice.

How many of the six joint sets are likely to be found at a single locality? Three arbitrary ranges of average strike, based on examination of figure 2*C*, were used to estimate the frequency of occurrence of these joint sets. (1) At 16 of the 21 localities studied there is one joint set whose average strike is within 15° of the direction of glacier movement. At one locality there are two such sets, and at four localities there are none. (2) At nine of the 21 localities there is one set whose average strike is 35°–45° from the direction of advance; at two localities there are two such sets, one to each side, and at 10 localities there are no sets in this range. (3) At 11 of the 21 localities there is one set whose average strike is 65°–85° to one side of the direction of advance, and at eight localities there are two sets, one to each side. There is thus a high degree of similarity in the patterns of joints at the localities studied.

INTERPRETATION OF JOINT PATTERN

Kupsch (1955, p. 332–336) found three sets of joints in the boulder deposit that he studied. Two near-vertical sets, each of which strikes about 45° to one side of the direction of glacial advance, were interpreted as shear joints. The third near-vertical set, approximately parallel to the direction of advance, was interpreted as a set of extension joints. In the present study the writer concludes tentatively that joints in these glaciated areas include two sets of shear joints which flank the direction of ice advance and strike at about 40° to it, two sets of extension joints which flank the direction of advance and strike within about 10° of it, and two sets of release joints which are nearly perpendicular to the sets of extension joints. There commonly is considerable departure from this idealized average pattern. As was noted in the preceding section, at many localities some of these sets are missing or are poorly represented. Nonetheless, if one considers the nonhomogeneity of the rocks, the range in direction of application of the glacial stress (at least 10° to 15° at many localities), and the unknown effect of topography on the glacial stress, the agreement of the strikes of observed joint sets with those expected on the basis of theory is considered satisfactory.

Observations by Kupsch (1955, p. 330; 1965, p. 114), which show that individual joints in boulders in a drumlin may extend through adjacent boulders, leave no doubt that those joints are related to stress applied by the moving glacier; they are not preglacial. Kupsch (1955, p. 336) concluded that the jointing occurred when the glacier advanced across a frozen mass of sediment and interstitial ice. Where joints cut bedrock rather than boulders, it is possible that the glaciation opened joints along preexisting zones of weakness, and identification of the regional joints is therefore necessary. The data obtained in the present study are not adequate to show whether all the joints were opened along old zones of weakness in the rock. From two to several sets of regional joints are probably present at each of the localities studied, and it seems likely that joints of any of these sets, if near the positions required for fracture, could be opened as a result of glacial stress. However, the regional joints could not be identified at all 21 localities. Figure 2*D* is a plot of the poles of all joint sets for the localities at which regional joints were recognized. (Strikes of the joint sets have been adjusted to the direction of glacial movement.) It is clear that each concentration of joint sets in figure 2*C* is a regional set in at least some of the localities studied, and that the possible role of glacial stress in forming new joints in sound rock cannot be evaluated with the available evidence. The abundance of joint sets at most localities studied, however, favors the interpretation that some were formed in sound rock and do not lie along preexisting zones of weakness.

It is desirable that further tests of the hypothesis of the glacial opening of joints, and of the possible role of new (nonregional) joints in this process, should include comparison of joint patterns and abundance in similar rocks in adjacent glaciated and unglaciated regions, and an attempt to relate characteristics of the jointing to such factors as slope of the bedrock surface and thickness of the glacier. One such study could well be made in the Appalachian Plateaus region, which is discussed briefly in the next section.

SOME IMPLICATIONS OF GLACIAL JOINTING

The writer believes that the foregoing hypothesis warrants further examination and testing because the formation of fractures in this way would be a significant consideration in several types of studies. Three of these are noted briefly below.

Geomorphology

At many places sheeting is an incomplete answer to the problem of why bedrock is susceptible to glacial quarrying in mountainous regions. Other joints, at high angles to the sheeting, are required to break the rock into blocks which can be removed by plucking. Joints opened by moving glacial ice would serve this function and thus would facilitate glacial erosion.

Locality 1 in table 1 is on a small ice-rounded hill. Visible joints are sparse on the adjacent ice-scoured rock surface of low relief. On the hill, however, joints are abundant. Six sets of nonsheeting joints, all near the vertical, were found on the gently rounded upstream end of the hill. Three of these sets (those with strikes N. 84° W., N. 25° E., and N. 42° E.) were also found on the cliffy downstream end of the hill. There, with sheeting joints and an additional near-vertical set, they facilitated partial destruction of the hill by glacial quarrying.

Structural geology

If joints were opened as a result of glacial stress their presence in the bedrock of a glaciated region would complicate tectonic interpretation of the joint pattern, particularly if the joints included some unrelated to preglacial stresses.

The Appalachian Plateaus province in western New York and Pennsylvania is a region where reexamination of the joints would be of interest in light of the hypothesis of glacial jointing. In addition to the report by Parker (1942) already cited, many other reports treat the joints in this region. (See, for example, Badgley, 1965, p. 101–103; de Sitter, 1956, p. 125–126; Muehlberger, 1961; Nickelsen and Hough, 1967; and Wood and others, 1969.) A striking feature of Parker's report is his observation that the north-trending set of joints in this region is double, consisting of two subsets whose average strikes are separated by about 19°. Several of the writers cited above have discussed and reinterpreted this observation. Nickelsen and Hough (1967, p. 622) noted that few of the exposures they studied in Pennsylvania, and few they observed during reconnaissance in New York, show these acutely intersecting joints; they believe that the few acutely intersecting sets found represent "overprinting" of sets from adjacent areas, in each of which one set dominates. This interpretation is reasonable in light of the fact that Parker's diagrams do not represent single localities but are summaries for 15-minute quadrangles based on a few observations at each of many localities. But it seems less reasonable in light of the large region of southern New York covered by Parker's observations. Under an alternative explanation, one member of Parker's paired joints may have been opened by moving ice at places where the direction of glacial advance was at a large acute angle to the strike of a single north-trending set of regional joints.

Ground water

Substantial changes in the occurrence of shallow ground water have occurred in many glaciated regions as a result of the glaciation. One of the most significant of these changes has been the removal of much or all of the layer of broken and weathered rock which formerly covered the bedrock, and the deposition of drift in its place. Quantitative change in the hydrologic character of the bedrock has probably been greatest in limestone and dolomite, where the solution-riddled upper part of the rock has been partly or completely removed, leaving an eroded surface of fresh and relatively impermeable rock.

Field studies of ground water in some glaciated regions of carbonate rock have shown, however, that the uppermost part of the glacially eroded rock has appreciable secondary permeability. In some of these regions sufficient evidence is available from drillers' logs to show that there are few cavernous openings or other solution-widened joints in the rock; evidently the permeability is due to relatively unmodified fractures. Well records from glaciated carbonate-rock terrains in Michigan, Ohio, and New York (Norris, 1959; Sinclair, 1960; Trainer and Salvas, 1962; Vanlier, 1963) were examined to determine the depth of penetration of glaciated carbonate rock which is adequate to insure a domestic or farm water supply—probably one to a few gallons per minute, on the average. In the sample of 982 wells the median depth of penetration is about 24 feet; 44 percent of the wells penetrate 20 feet of rock, or less, and 25 percent penetrate 10 feet or less. These data, in light of the hypothesis of glacial jointing, suggest that a fracture zone of low to moderate permeability is typical of the upper part of the glaciated bedrock in these regions. The effect of deep glacial erosion of the carbonate rock is thought to have been the removal of the upper part of the rock, a karst aquifer of low to high permeability, and the substitution for it of a fractured-rock aquifer of low permeability.

This conclusion is of potential significance for its bearing on both water supply and waste disposal. Thus, we may conclude that a thin aquifer is likely to occur generally in the upper part of glaciated bedrock. Where covered by till it commonly is hydraulically confined, or artesian; where covered by washed drift it is more likely to be unconfined. It may generally be a source of small water supplies. But where the drift cover is both relatively permeable and thin, or where it is absent, this bedrock aquifer also provides a potential medium for the migration of substances derived from septic tanks and other sites for the disposal of wastes to the ground at shallow depth. For this reason protection of surface and near-surface material from disposal and from accidental spills of noxious substances is particularly important where glaciated bedrock is not covered by a thick layer of till which would serve to protect the aquifer from contamination.

REFERENCES CITED

Badgley, P. C., 1965, Structural and tectonic principles: New York, Harper and Row, 521 p.

Bateman, P. C., and Wahrhaftig, Clyde, 1966, Geology of the Sierra Nevada, p. 107–172 *in* Bailey, E. H., ed., Geology of northern California: California Div. Mines and Geology Bull. 190.

Battey, M. H., 1960, Geological factors in the development of Veslgjuv-botn and Vesl-Skaubotn, p. 5–10 *in* Lewis, W. V., ed., Investigations on Norwegian cirque glaciers: Royal Geog. Soc., Research Ser., no. 4, 104 p.

Chadwick, G. H., 1933, Catskill as a geologic name: Am. Jour. Sci., 5th ser., v. 26, no. 155, p. 479–484.

Chapman, C. A., 1958, Control of jointing by topography: Jour. Geology, v. 66, no. 5, p. 552–558.

de Sitter, L. U., 1956, Structural geology: New York, McGraw-Hill Book Company, Inc., 552 p.

Johnston, R. H., 1964, Ground water in the Niagara Falls area, New York, with emphasis on the water-bearing characteristics of the bedrock: New York Water Resources Comm. Bull. GW-53, 93 p.

Kupsch, W. O., 1955, Drumlins with jointed boulders near Dollard, Saskatchewan: Geol. Soc. America Bull., v. 66, no. 3, p. 327–338.

—— 1965, Jointing of boulders caused by flowing ice: Alberta Soc. Petroleum Geologists, 15th Ann. Field Conf. Guidebook, Pt. 1, Cypress Hills Plateau, p. 112–115.

Lewis, W. V., 1954, Pressure release and glacial erosion: Jour. Glaciology, v. 2, no. 11, p. 417–422.

Linton, D. L., 1963, The forms of glacial erosion: Inst. British Geographers Trans., Pub. 33, p. 1–28.

Muehlberger, W. R., 1961, Conjugate joint sets of small dihedral angle: Jour. Geology, v. 69, p. 211–219.

Nickelsen, R. P., and Hough, V. D., 1967, Jointing in the Appalachian Plateau of Pennsylvania: Geol. Soc. America Bull., v. 78, no. 5, p. 609–630.

Norris, S. E., 1959, The water resources of Madison County, Ohio: Ohio Dept. Nat. Res., Div. Water, Bull. 33, 63 p.

Parker, J. M., III, 1942, Regional systematic jointing in slightly deformed sedimentary rocks: Geol. Soc. America Bull., v. 53, p. 381–408.

Sinclair, W. C., 1960, Reconnaissance of the ground-water resources of Delta County, Michigan: Michigan Geol. Survey Prog. Rept. no. 24, 93 p.

Spencer, E. W., 1959, Geologic evolution of the Beartooth Mountains, Montana and Wyoming. Part 2. Fracture patterns: Geol. Soc. America Bull., v. 70, no. 4, p. 467–508.

Trainer, F. W., and Salvas, E. H., 1962, Ground-water resources of the Massena-Waddington area, St. Lawrence County, New York, with emphasis on the effect of Lake St. Lawrence on ground water: New York Water Resources Comm. Bull. GW-47, 227 p.

Vanlier, K. E., 1963, Ground water in Menominee County: Michigan Geol. Survey Water Inv. 2, 42 p.

Wood, G. H., Jr., Arndt, H. H., and Carter, M. D., 1969, Systematic jointing in the western part of the Anthracite Region of eastern Pennsylvania: U.S. Geol. Survey Bull. 1271-D, 17 p.

Yatsu, Eiju, 1966, Rock control in geomorphology: Tokyo, Sozosha, 135 p.

Jour. Research U.S. Geol. Survey
Vol. 1, No. 2, Mar.—Apr. 1973, p. 237—241

RAPID REACTION RATES BETWEEN WATER AND A CALCAREOUS CLAY AS OBSERVED BY SPECIFIC-ION ELECTRODES

By WARREN W. WOOD, Lubbock, Tex.

Abstract.—Specific-ion electrodes were used to simultaneously determine the activity changes of calcium, hydrogen, sodium, fluoride, and divalent ions when 50 g of a natural, untreated material containing calcium-rich mixed-layer illite-montmorillonite clay, quartz sand, and calcium carbonate was added to 250 ml of natural Canadian River water containing 220 mg/l Na. Calcium and magnesium were displaced from the clay by the sodium; the exchanged and dissolved noncarbonate calcium precipitated as calcium carbonate, and the magnesium remained in solution. Fluoride entered into both a rapid reaction and a long-term reaction, indicating solution from the material. The pH decreased rapidly. The reactions for all observed ions, other than fluoride, were faster than the response time of their respective electrodes and were complete in less than one minute. Rapid solution of material containing calcium, magnesium, sodium, and fluoride was also observed when a duplicate sample of the earth material was added to distilled water; pH also changed rapidly in this mixture. These results suggest that many important water-rock reactions can be considered nearly instantaneous for purposes of digital modeling of the geochemical changes during artificial recharge.

This report presents data on the rate of ion exchange and mineral solution when distilled and high-sodium waters were mixed with a natural, untreated, clay-sized material. The laboratory experiment simulates a field condition that will be developed by artificial recharge through surface spreading on the southern High Plains of Texas.

Research for this paper was done as part of a study of chemical reactions occurring during artificial recharge when water is rapidly introduced into a chemically different environment. Predicting the quality of recharge water with time and space is a major goal of this recharge project. One phase of the study is an investigation of the rate at which these reactions occur. If they are slow—taking months or years—then the recharge water could be withdrawn before reactions proceed very far, and chemical changes would not be a problem. If the reactions are rapid, their effects must be considered; if the reactions are faster than flow velocity, they can be considered as instantaneous, which greatly simplifies digital modeling of the chemical system.

Field and laboratory experiments have been designed to test the rate of reaction of several important ions. One site where experiments will examine the chemical effects of recharge has been established north of Lubbock, Tex. The site has 27 m of saturated material overlain by 37 m of unsaturated material; it consists of a series of unconsolidated sands, silts, calcium-rich clays, and zones rich in calcium carbonate.

Untreated water from the Lubbock municipal supply will be the source of recharge water. This water, imported from the Canadian River north of Amarillo, Tex., is a sodium chloride, sodium sulfate water which contains approximately 1,000 mg/l dissolved solids. Native ground water is a calcium magnesium bicarbonate water with less than 400 mg/l dissolved solids.

Malcolm and Kennedy (1969) used a monovalent-ion electrode to measure the rate of cation exchange on clay minerals that had been treated and prepared by grinding, blending, saturating with potassium chloride solution, and adjusting pH. These authors observed exchange rates of K^+ for Ba^{+2} that were faster than the 3-second response time of the electrode. The technique of using specific-ion electrodes to measure rapid chemical reactions was expanded for the present study to include several electrodes operating simultaneously. Untreated earth materials from the field-test site were used to duplicate natural conditions as nearly as possible.

A laboratory experiment using Canadian River water and earth materials taken from the field site was designed to measure the rate of ion exchange and mineral solution of five constituents. Na^+, H^+, Ca^{+2}, and Mg^{+2} were selected because of the potential loss of hydraulic conductivity caused either by clay swelling upon the addition of sodium or by precipitation of calcium carbonate. F^- was measured because the native water contains up to 10 mg/l, and it is important to know if recharge water would acquire this concentration.

EXPERIMENTAL METHODS

The material used in this study was obtained from a clay layer approximately 1 m thick and 30 m below land surface in the Ogallala Formation. The clay was removed from a core taken near the Lubbock Regional Airport. The sample containing the clay was air dried at room temperature, mechanically disaggregated to pass through a 149-micron screen, and split into eight 50-g samples. X-ray analysis indicated that 65 percent of the sample was a mixed-layer illite-montmorillonite clay with 15 percent quartz, 15 percent calcium carbonate, and traces of potash and plagioclase feldspars. Magnetite is a dominant accessory mineral. The clay, which is deep red, has a cation-exchange capacity of approximately 49 meq/100 g.

Canadian River water used in this experiment has the composition given in table 1.

Table 1.—*Average chemical analyses, in milligrams per liter, of water before and after batch tests*

Constituent	Canadian River water (30 minutes contact time)		Distilled water (20 minutes contact time)	
	Initial	Final	Initial	Final
Ca	57	58	0.0	24
Mg	23	46	.0	12
Na	220	165	.0	8.4
HCO_3	191	160	2.4	53
SO_4	230	235	.0	15
Cl	231	240	.0	40
F	1.0	4.2	.0	2.0
pH	7.85	7.70	5.62	8.28

Orion[1] specific electrode model 92-20 was used to determine calcium activity, Orion model 92-32 was used to determine divalent cation activity, Orion 94-09 was used to determine fluoride activity, Orion 94-11 was used to determine sodium activity, and a Corning[1] triple purpose glass electrode was used to determine pH. Orion model 90-01 single junction reference electrodes filled with the manufacturer's recommended reference solution (Orion 90-00-01) were used with all the electrodes except sodium. Orion model 90-02 double junction reference electrode was used with the sodium electrode. Three Orion models 401 and one model 407 specific-ion meters were used with outputs connected to a modified potentiometric strip-chart recorder.

The response of a specific-ion electrode to changes in ionic activity is controlled by the time lag inherent in the electrode. Response lag was determined by adding known amounts of the specific ion to the water used in the study and recording the rate of change of the electrode potential.

For example, sodium chloride was added to the tap water at the same temperature and stirring rate used in the experiment, and the Na^+ electrode output was recorded on the potentiometric strip-chart recorder. Different activities of Na^+ were added nearly instantaneously, and no significant difference in response time of the electrode was observed in the range of interest (250–500 mg/l). This empirical method of testing electrode lag integrates effects of stirring rates and temperature on the response time of the electrodes.

Calcium chloride was used in the same manner to check the response of divalent- and calcium-ion electrodes; the pH electrode was checked by adding hydrochloric acid; and the flouride electrode was checked by adding sodium fluoride. These electrode response times were also virtually unaffected by an activity increase in the range of interest of this study. Response time of all electrodes was similar to that observed by Malcolm and Kennedy (1969)—90 percent of full-scale reading was observed in approximately 40 seconds. Orion literature[2] supplied with the electrodes states that their electrodes respond more rapidly to an increase in activity than to a decrease. In this study, declining activity of sodium nevertheless gave a Na^+ electrode response that was very rapid (fig. 1).

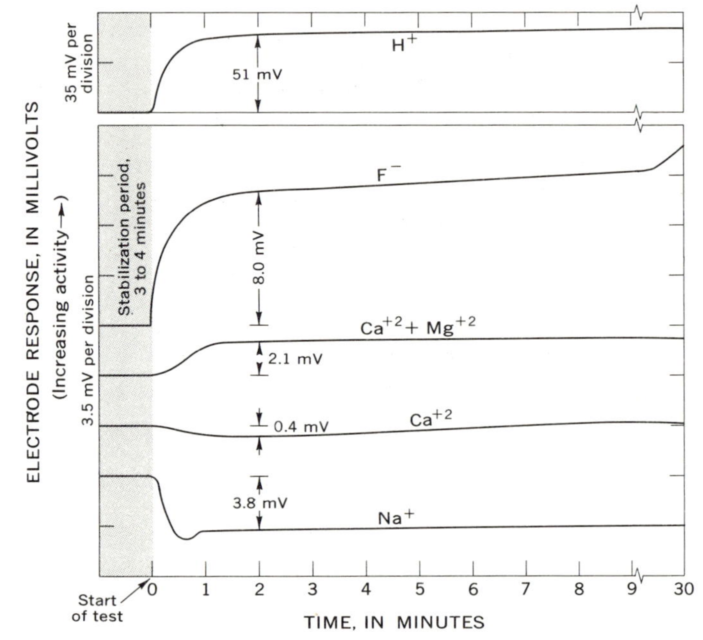

COMPARISON OF ION ACTIVITIES

	Ion activity (mg/l) Initial (0 min)	Ion activity (mg/l) Final (30 min)
Ca^{+2}	7.5×10^{-4}	7.5×10^{-4}
$Ca^{+2}+ Mg^{+2}$	1.2×10^{-3}	1.8×10^{-3}
Na^+	8.3×10^{-3}	6.7×10^{-3}
F^-	5.2×10^{-5}	2.2×10^{-4}
H^+	1.41×10^{-8}	1.95×10^{-8}

Figure 1.—Specific-ion electrode traces from 250 ml of Canadian River water and 50 g of clay-sized material from the Ogallala Formation, Lubbock, Tex.

The divalent electrode was used in this study to follow changes in the activity of magnesium. This was accomplished by simultaneously monitoring changes in calcium activity with the calcium specific-ion electrode. The difference in output between these electrodes represents changes in magnesium activity. Although the divalent electrode responds to the activity of any divalent ion, only the activities of calcium and magnesium were sufficiently large to be significant in this study.

[1] The mention of brand names is for a complete description of the methods used and does not constitute an endorsement of the product by the U.S. Geological Survey.

[2] Instruction manual, sodium ion electrode, model 94—11, 1969, 17 p. Available from Orion Research, Inc., Cambridge, Mass.

The electrodes were calibrated within the activity ranges that bracketed the expected range of the sample. The electrodes were then suspended in a polyethylene beaker, and 250 ml of Canadian River water was added and allowed to equilibrate with the electrodes. The recorder was activated and the electrode output was recorded to check for drift.

When the system stabilized, the 50-g sample was introduced into the water directly on and above a magnetic stirring bar that was rotating at medium speed. The sample was rapidly and thoroughly mixed by the stirring bar. The slurry was monitored until no further potentiometric changes were observed on the recorder. The slurry was then removed, and the electrodes were rinsed in the same type of water used in the experiment and then allowed to reequilibrate in a duplicate water sample. The recorder was reactivated, and the difference between the original and the final reading was considered as electronic drift and applied linearly to the particular electrode trace affected by the drift.

The system was stable, and it was only necessary to make one drift correction on one electrode in the six tests that were conducted. The slurry was filtered under pressure of nitrogen gas immediately after it was removed from the electrodes. Filtering took about 20 minutes. Alkalinity was determined on the first 25 ml of filtrate by use of 0.02 N H_2SO_4 and a pH electrode and meter. The remainder of the filtrate was acidified and saved for conventional chemical analysis.

Before the tests were conducted, the response of the calcium electrode was checked for sensitivity to the Mg^{+2} ion. El-Swaify and Gazdar (1969) reported that the Orion calcium electrode responded to changes in Mg^{+2} activities in contradiction to the information supplied by the manufacturer. Virtually the same experiment as conducted by these authors was rerun. The results indicated that the calcium electrode used in this experiment was selective and did not respond to the Mg^{+2} activity.

EXPERIMENTAL RESULTS

Because of an interest in five constituents and the availability of only four meters, four similar tests were conducted with different combinations of four electrodes in each test. Figure 1 was drawn from the averages of these four tests, whereas figure 2 was drawn from an average of two tests.

Most of the reactions shown in figure 1 occurred before the electrode could respond; that is, the initial traces of the electrode outputs are determined by the response lag of the electrode. The rapidity of the reactions is a result of ion exchange between the minerals and water, according to the work of Malcolm and Kennedy (1969).

Ion-exchange hypothesis for this rapid reaction is supported by examination of figure 1, which illustrates a decrease in sodium while a similar but smaller increase in the divalent ions takes place. The response of these two electrodes is not equivalent because of calcium precipitation and solution of minerals in the sample.

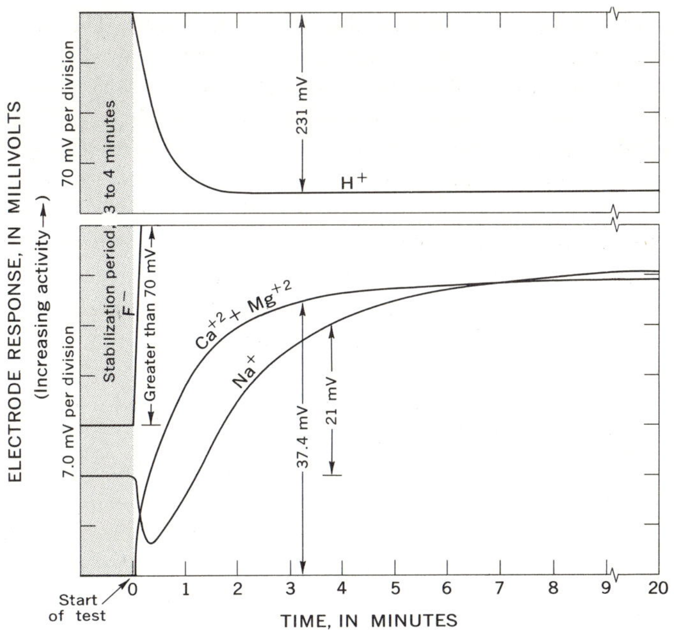

COMPARISON OF ION ACTIVITIES

	Ion activity (mg/l) Initial (0 min)	Final (30 min)
F^-	5.9×10^{-7}	1.1×10^{-4}
$Ca^{+2} + Mg^{+2}$	4.3×10^{-5}	8.0×10^{-4}
Na^+	3.1×10^{-5}	3.4×10^{-4}
H^+	2.40×10^{-6}	5.25×10^{-9}

Figure 2.—Specific-ion electrode traces from 250 ml of distilled, deionized water and 50 g of clay-sized material from the Ogallala Formation, Lubbock, Tex.

Examination of figures 1 and 2 shows that the Na^+ trace exhibits a small decrease near the start of the experiment. This decrease is unique to the electrode in that it exhibits a brief transient response to changes in hydrogen-ion activity, according to the manufacturer's literature, and is not a function of the solution being examined. The initial response of this particular electrode indicates a lower sodium activity regardless of the increase or decrease in hydrogen-ion activity.

Calcium precipitation is indicated by the lack of potentiometric change of the calcium specific-ion electrode and the loss of 31 mg/l HCO_3^- from the water. The Canadian River water was in thermodynamic equilibrium with calcite at the time of the test. It is, therefore, not surprising that the combination of stirring and availability of calcium carbonate nucleation sites resulted in precipitation of calcium as it exchanged and dissolved from the sample.

The calcium electrode indicates an initial decline in calcium activity that returns to the original activity within a few minutes. This slight drop probably is the result of the water being initially slightly supersaturated with respect to calcite and therefore seeking equilibrium as more calcium is introduced. The decline may also be in response to some transient inorganic complex, or perhaps it is the electrode-ion exchanger equilibrating to a rapidly changing environment. This slight drop, regardless of its origin, is not significant in this study.

Fluoride apparently enters the water by an exchange reaction as well as from mineral solution. By analogy with the divalent and sodium electrodes, the early part of the fluoride curve indicates ion exchange, probably for the hydroxyl (OH^-) ion, while a longer term (30 minutes) increase is interpreted as the solution of some fluoride-rich mineral. However, fluoride dissolved very rapidly from the sample when it was mixed with distilled water. It is possible that the rapid as well as the longer term responses result from mineral solution. X-ray analyses did not indicate detectable quantities of any fluoride mineral. However, volcanic ash in the Ogallala (Sidwell and Bronaugh, 1946) could have furnished small quantities of fluoride-rich minerals which escaped detection.

The hydrogen-ion activity increased very rapidly. This increase in activity is probably a function of the precipitation of calcium carbonate. The pH remains constant after the first 2 minutes of the test and does not appear to respond to the adjustment of the calcium ion.

To examine the rate of solubility of the clay-sized material, distilled water was used in place of Canadian River water for the test shown in figure 2. This substitution assured that the dominant chemical control would be solution and not ion exchange in this environment, although ion exchange would undoubtedly occur as ions were made available through solution.

The general shape of electrode traces in figure 2 is one of a gradual attainment of a steady-state condition and does not appear to be that of electrode response as was exhibited in figure 1. The difference is more apparent when it is recognized that the millivolt scale in figure 2 is double that of figure 1.

Figure 2 illustrates the speed of the fluoride reaction; the trace of this electrode goes off scale in less than 1 minute. This rapid reaction appears to indicate an ion-exchange reaction or the presence of an extremely soluble mineral. In the initial acidic environment in which this test was run, it is improbable that there should be ion exchange of OH^-, although there may be some small amount of exchange with SO_4^{-2} or Cl^- if some of the F^- is held on nonspecific positive sites. Therefore, it would appear that there is a very soluble fluoride mineral present. Because of the large range in millivolt output and the manner in which signals were recorded, it was not possible to follow the fluoride through to a steady-state condition while monitoring the other electrodes.

The calcium electrode was not used in the test with distilled water because of the lack of sample on which to run more than two tests. However, the analyses indicate that there were soluble calcium minerals present and that the divalent electrode response was from both calcium and magnesium. The pH changed rapidly and attained a steady state in approximately 2 minutes. Sodium required nearly 9 minutes, while the divalent electrode required about 4 minutes to attain a steady-state condition.

The electrodes in distilled water are near their limit of detection, which is approximately 10^{-6} mole for fluoride, 10^{-6} mole for sodium, and 10^{-8} mole for the divalent electrode. Consequently, the large change in potential exhibited by the electrodes in figure 2 represents significant changes in activity; however, because the electrodes are logarithmic devices, the absolute values of the changes in concentration are relatively small (table 1). The presence of 15 mg/l SO_4^{-2} and 40 mg/l Cl^- in the water and the 62 mg/l noncarbonate hardness as $CaCO_3$ indicate that sulfate and chloride minerals, not detected by X-ray analyses, furnish part of the calcium and magnesium to the water.

The filtered effluent from the distilled water test is not in thermodynamic equilibrium with common minerals. The effluent is undersaturated with respect to calcite, aragonite, anhydrite, gypsum, dolomite, and magnesite. Undersaturation with respect to these calcium minerals is not surprising because of the limited amount of material present for solution and the total contact time of less than 1 hour.

In the natural geologic environment, mineral solution and ion exchange would not continue indefinitely. Reaction rims of altered material would probably form around mineral grains, and the rate of reaction would then be controlled by slow diffusion through the rims (Malcolm and Kennedy, 1970; Helgeson, 1971). Ion exchange, though initially rapid, would eventually cease to operate as exchange sites are occupied and an equilibrium condition is formed. Thus, when water is initially introduced into a natural environment it will approach equilibrium with that environment in a short period of time.

During artificial recharge, water moves through the natural environment forming an advancing front. Water near the point of recharge will quickly approach equilibrium. Mineral solution and ion exchange will take place rapidly only as long as there is fresh material available. As this fresh material is exhausted, a chemical reaction front will advance in the direction of hydraulic flow.

CONCLUSIONS

Experiments with distilled and Canadian River water indicate that ion exchange and solution of certain common minerals are relatively rapid. The speed of solution of sulfate, chloride, fluoride, and carbonate minerals in the sample permit the assumption of instantaneous mineral solution for the purposes of modeling the coupled chemical and hydrologic environment. It is anticipated that reactions such as these will take place at an advancing front of recharged water. The problem associated with mineral precipitation is not so readily solved. In the experiment, the stirring and availability of nucleation sites most certainly prevents supersaturation of the water with respect to many of the mineral phases, but the problem of predicting the rate of mineral precipitation in the natural environment is as yet unanswered.

REFERENCES CITED

El-Swaify, S. A., and Gazdar, M. N., 1969, Evaluating the use of Na^{+}, Ca^{++}, and divalent cation electrodes in some soil extracting solutions: Soil Sci. Soc. America Proc., v. 33, p. 665–667.

Helgeson, H. C., 1971, Kinetics of mass transfer among silicates and aqueous solutions: Geochim. et Cosmochim. Acta, v. 35, no. 5, p. 421–469.

Malcolm, R. L., and Kennedy, V. C., 1969, Rate of cation exchange on clay minerals as determined by specific-ion electrode techniques: Soil Sci. Soc. America Proc., v. 33, no. 2, p. 247–253.

—— 1970, Variation of cation exchange capacity and rate with particle size in stream sediment: Jour. Water Pollution Control Federation, v. 42, no. 5, pt. 2, p. R153–R160.

Sidwell, R. L., and Bronaugh, R. L., 1946, Volcanic sediments in northern Texas: Jour. Sed. Petrology, v. 16, p. 15–18.

Jour. Research U.S. Geol. Survey
Vol. 1, No. 2, Mar.—Apr. 1973, p. 243—250

HYDRAULIC SAND-MODEL STUDIES OF MISCIBLE-FLUID FLOW

By J. M. CAHILL, Lakewood, Colo.

Abstract.—Hydraulic sand models are useful physical tools in the investigation of the transition zone that occurs between salt and fresh ground water in coastal aquifers. Such models are used to demonstrate the effects of transport mechanisms that influence the dynamic behavior and the shape of the transition zone. The techniques employed in obtaining in-place measurements of solute concentrations are generally the stumbling block in generating data for two-dimensional dispersion systems. Two in-place measurement techniques were used in the studies described: (1) conductivity probes when salt was used as a tracer; and (2) photoelectric cells when organic dye was used as a tracer. Results indicate that conductivity methods are more reliable; however, care must be exercised inasmuch as the probes tend to disturb the fluid flow.

In investigations of fluid-flow behavior, mathematical and physical models may be used. Limitations in using such models result from the complexity of the mathematical language or the inability to properly construct an accurate physical counterpart. The mathematical model is used when the governing equations are known, and the solution of these equations can be used for data analysis. Physical models, such as electrical analogs and hydraulic models, are most useful for studying systems having complex boundary conditions. However, scaling requirements for the model impose some restrictions on model construction as do available methods for measuring response in the model. Further, obtaining reliable data from physical models is related to the experience of the individual experimenter.

The theory of models is based on the concept of similarity of the three fundamental dimensions—length, time, and mass. In detailing the transport process in hydraulic sand models, the internal geometry of the medium presents some difficulty if strict adherence to this similitude is maintained. This is especially true when ordinary fluids such as clear water or water-based fluids are used. This difficulty occurs because grain diameter is a characteristic geometric length. Maintaining the scaling of grain diameters would require the reduction of the pore size, which also influences the dispersion process. Thus, scaling the grain size in a small laboratory model will reduce the pore size in the model to molecular dimensions, and physical activity in the model would be similar to the process of diffusion through solid material.

The models used in these studies were not for the purpose of detailing the transport process for any particular ground-water system. Rather, the primary purpose of the models was to view dispersion of two miscible fluids. Miscible-fluid systems are those in which fluids mix in any ratio without separation. Because the transport process is controlled largely by pore geometry and fluid velocity, it can be assumed that fluid behavior in the models will have a similar response in nature under the same boundary conditions.

Problems in modeling the dynamics of miscible-fluid flow involve controls established by both external and internal geometry. Systems such as salt-water encroachment are difficult to describe mathematically because of the dynamic boundary between fluids of different densities. These systems can be physically modeled with less effort, and various methods have been discussed in the literature for many years. For example, Bear and Todd (1960) extended the study of salt-water encroachment to include both miscible and immiscible systems. Mathematical models give the approximate shape of the fresh water—salt water interface. The derived expression as indicated by Henry (1964, p. C35–C59, *in* Cooper and others) gives a good approximation for the position of the interface at some distance from the ocean. Cooper and others (1964), using an area in Florida, also described the diffused zone in terms of a "cyclic-flow" phenomenon. Cyclic flow takes place as the salt water flows inland from the sea floor into the zone of diffusion and back to the sea through an upper flow region. The body of water flowing towards the sea is within the upper flow region.

Although small sand models are valuable tools for studying the dynamics of miscible-fluid flow, they also have limitations. One of the primary difficulties in modeling this type of system is the lack of a reliable means of measuring the mixing ratios of the miscible fluids with minimum disturbance to the flow regime. This report describes the construction and operation of one- and two-dimensional sand models and techniques used to measure the tracer concentrations. In addition, some preliminary data are presented.

METHODS OF STUDY

Hydraulic sand models were used to study the dynamics and transport process of a coastal aquifer in two dimensions. Orientation of the models was perpendicular to the coastline or parallel to the direction of fluid flow. A photograph of a typical hydraulic model is shown on figure 1. The models were designed so that both visual observations and internal measurements of tracer concentrations could be made. Loose sand or glass beads, the principal aquifer material, were encased in transparent acrylic plastic. The clear-plastic wall facilitated measurement because it allowed visual detection of the tracer fluid.

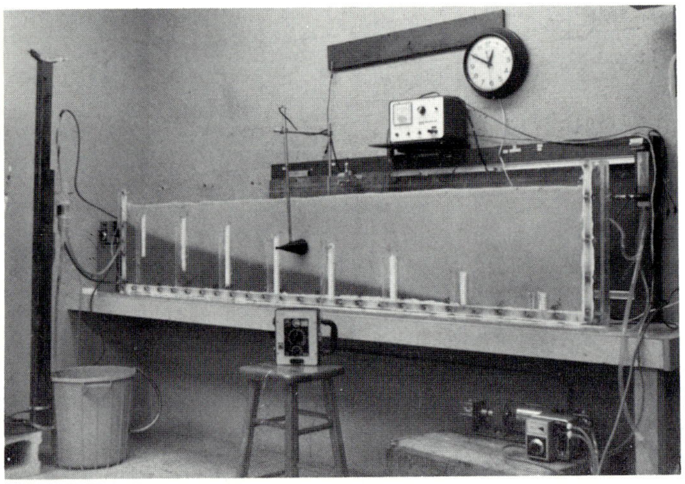

Figure 1.—Hydraulic sand model used in salt-water encroachment studies. Fluid movement is "landward" to the right and "seaward" to the left.

Model fluids

Tap water (sp gr = 1.000) was used as the original fluid or the less dense fluid in the models. The second or heavier fluid (sp gr = 1.025) was a mixture of one part commercial grade glycerine and nine parts of tap water. Organic dye and sodium chloride were added to the heavier fluid as tracer indicators. The organic dyes were different commercial brands of recorder inks.

Rumer and Harleman (1963), in addition to other investigators, have used sugar to make up the heavier fluid. Glycerine was the preferred additive in this study because of ease and accuracy in duplicating mixtures when additional amounts were needed. In addition, the glycerine remained in solution with the tap water for many months. Data obtained in this study indicated that glycerine and sodium chloride solutions traveled at almost the same rate. In tests involving pore velocities of 0.2 to 2.0 cm/min, the differences in the distribution of the concentrations of glycerine and salt were less than the precision with which their concentrations could be measured. The determinations of concentration were made with an electrical-conductivity probe for chloride and a hand refractometer for glycerine.

The results shown on figure 2 are for a flow rate of 0.3 cm/min. These curves are the breakthrough concentrations of the heavy fluid composed of glycerine and sodium chloride. The results show good correlation between salt and glycerine.

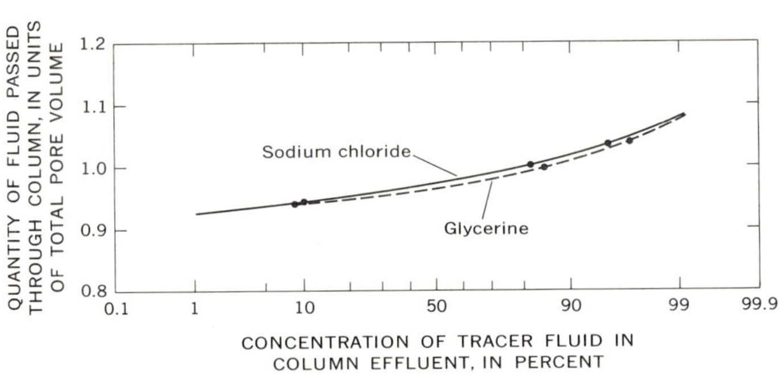

Figure 2.—Changes in concentration of tracer in effluent from column of spherical beads with passage of tagged fluids through column.

Tracer-concentration measurement

Bear (1961), in his investigation of fluid dispersion, described a method of measurement involving transmission of light through a Christiansen model. Cahill (1966) also showed that this method of measurement was effective with the use of organic dye tracers. The concentration profile of the dye tracer in the models is determined by correlating the measured light intensity with that of known dye-tracer concentrations. The system, as shown in figure 3*A*, is not a Christiansen model in that the index of refraction of the glass beads was not matched against that of the fluid. However, the system of measurement was similar to Bear's in that a cadmium sulfide photocell was used as the measuring device. The measurement apparatus included a light source and photocell mounted on a parallel arm extending downward from the top of the model on a continuous screw. This arrangement allowed positioning the source and the cell simultaneously. The cadmium sulfide cell was located in a tapered housing with a slit opening to obtain near-point measurement (figure 3*B*).

The cadmium sulfide cell was well suited for measuring the intensity of illumination in this test apparatus because of its size and operating characteristics. The available range allowed use of standard supporting instrumentation. Photocells of the type used are known as photoresistors or light-dependent resistors (Radio Corp. of America, 1964), and their resistance to the flow of electricity depends on the intensity of light impinging on the cell. The response of the cell, which is proportional to the illumination, can be measured with an ohmmeter. In these experiments, the light beam from the constant-intensity source is randomly scattered and adsorbed by the dye molecules and the matrix material. Where the porous material is chemically stable, the measured resistance is dependent only on the dye concentration.

Various studies, such as by Kaufman and Orlob (1956), show that chloride ions in low concentrations are the simplest tracers to use. Chloride is readily available, economical, and easy to detect. Chloride, in a salt solution, is electrolytic and can be detected by measuring the electrical conductivity of the fluid between two electrodes. With an increase in concentra-

A

B

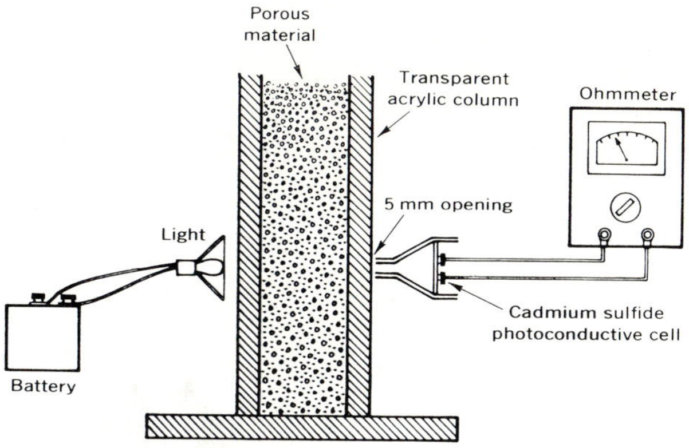

Figure 3.—Apparatus used to detect movement and to measure the concentration of dye tracers in the model.
A. Photograph shows the light source at the left and the photocell at the right of the column. The ohmmeter measures the photocell's response to the light transmitted throughout the length of the column. It is raised and lowered by lead screw and hand crank.
B. Schematic diagram shows the components of the model.

tion of the electrolyte, there is an increase in the ability of the fluid to transmit electricity. The change in conductivity can be measured by means of a conductivity bridge meter and probe consisting of a pair of electrodes.

Generally, rating curves are developed for each probe in the model. This procedure is necessary because nonuniform packing of the material and slight physical differences in each probe will contribute to differences in probe response. Rating curves are obtained by introducing fluids of known concentrations into the column and correlating the tracer concentrations with the meter readings. In the column studies, it was observed that changes in conditions near the probes or in the characteristic of the probes were sufficient to give errant readings with time. Therefore, tracer concentration plotted against percentage of meter deflection was used to obtain consistent results with a representative single-calibration curve.

The construction of the conductivity probes affects the dispersion process because insertion of the probes disturbs the fluid. Initially, probes made of 1-mm-diameter platinum wire were embedded in the plastic wall of the model, but later these were replaced by probes made of stainless-steel 26-gage (0.48-mm) hypodermic needles. The needles were inserted through small holes filled with silicone-rubber sealer. The sealer did not leak when punctured by the needle or when the needle was pulled out.

The fixed-probe system was used initially in both the vertical column and two-dimensional model. It was found that disturbance created by the fixed probes was not severe for low flow rates, but these probes exhibited changes in characteristics and frequent recalibration was needed. The hypodermic needle probes proved reliable when the single-calibration curve was used. The flexibility of the needles was the only difficulty encountered, and at times they required more than one insertion into the model.

HYDRAULIC SAND MODELS

Column model

A vertical-hydraulic or column model (fig. 4) was used for analysis of the dispersive characteristics of both steady and unsteady flow in one dimension. The column was investigated first to provide information for the two-dimensional flow model. In the two-dimensional system, fresh water flows over the heavier salt water (fig. 1); therefore, prior determination of dispersion in one direction is necessary to define the transport process.

In constructing the sand model, glass beads were slowly poured into the container filled with tap water. This minimized entrapment of air in the voids. During and after pouring, the sides of the containers were tapped lightly to obtain compaction. Because this procedure separates the particles, variations in fall velocity caused some layering. However, because the glass beads were nearly uniform, layering should not have affected the results.

The glass beads, which were spherical and translucent, had an average diameter of 0.58 mm. Porosity was calculated from data on the weight of beads in a given volume of container. Although variations in porosity were small, variations in permeabilities were large, ranging from 30 to 40 cm/min. These values of permeabilities and porosity were determined prior to and, on some occasions, after the test runs were completed.

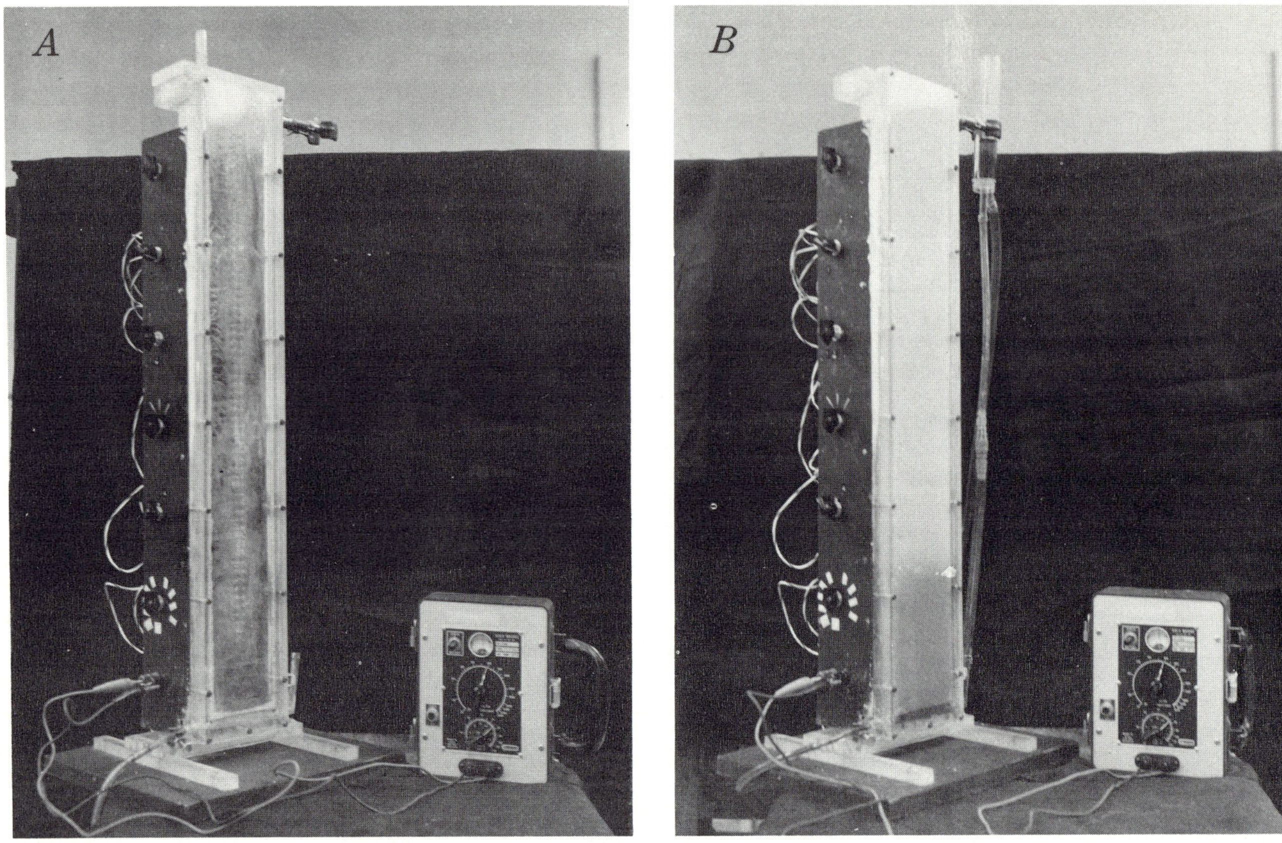

Figure 4.—Vertical column used to measure the one-dimensional dispersion characteristics of the porous medium. *A*. Column without porous medium. The buttonlike probe electrodes are faintly visible in the column. The rotary switches at the left choose the appropriate set of probes, and response is measured with the conductivity meter. *B*. Movement of invading fluid (dark) is from the bottom upward.

Salt concentration in the one-dimension column model was measured by paired electrodes. The initial test model had 61 pairs of probes spaced 1 cm apart in the direction of flow. The readings of each pair were obtained by manual selection using a series of rotary switches attached to the vertical column (figure 4*A*).

Flow to the models was controlled by a constant-rate piston pump, which fed a reservoir or constant-head tank which in turn fed directly into the models. Although this method introduced a pulsing at the reservoir tank because of the characteristics of the piston pumps, this effect was relatively minor when flow rate was averaged over time. Smaller pulses were noted when peristaltic pumps, such as "sigmoid worm" pumps, were used. However, tubing fatigue caused a change in the input rate after 2 or 3 days of operation.

Two-dimensional model

The two-dimensional model (fig. 1) required that the heavier fluid be introduced at a lower level. The salt-water input rate was controlled by a constant-head tank in response to the amount of salt flowing out of the system. To induce unsteady flow that simulated tidal fluctuations in both the one- and two-dimensional models, the salt-water input tank was oscillated vertically by a pulley system shown at the left on figure 1.

For the two-dimensional model, the control needed to maintain a given front or contact region of salt and fresh water at the desired location was the determining factor in sizing of the model. Models less than 200 cm long were unsatisfactory because a small change in head caused salt water to enter the fresh-water source area. The dimensions of the model shown in figure 1 were 240 cm long, 30 cm high, and 2 cm thick (inside dimensions). These dimensions were chosen because it was possible to establish at least three steady positions of the salt water—fresh water contact in the model without too much difficulty.

The discharge of the model was collected in a separate compartment to prevent the progressive change in density of the salt water input. The tagged-fluid effluent was removed from the model at the upper left as shown in figure 1. This enabled monitoring of the discharge by means of an electrical probe. All measurements of the position and the concentration along the contact zone were taken after steady-state condition was realized or at midtide in the models when the salt-water level was oscillated.

DISCUSSION OF RESULTS

The one-dimensional model was used to generate data under two different boundary conditions—constant and sinusoidal input. In all test runs, the model initially contained clear tap water. After stable conditions were reached, the test fluid was introduced into the column. The flow in the column was upward to minimize fingering which is generally caused by a gravitational effect. In the test series, the sinusoidal input-boundary condition was imposed by oscillating the head tank about the mean elevation. Maintaining a frequency of one cycle every 20 minutes, three different amplitudes of oscillation, 1, 2, and 4 cm were used to determine the effects of the nonsteady fluid motion on the dispersion of tagged particles. The average pore velocities of various tests ranged from 0.02 to 2 cm/min. The concentrations of tracer material at selected points in the column were determined with the electrical probes.

Computation of the preliminary values of longitudinal dispersion coefficients for unsteady flow in the one-dimensional model was based on the expression described by Harleman and Rumer (1963, p. 388):

$$C/C_o = \tfrac{1}{2}\text{erfc}\left[\frac{x-ut}{\sqrt{4Dt}}\right] = \left[\tfrac{1}{2}\left(1\text{-erf}\,\frac{x-ut}{\sqrt{2Dt}}\right)\right] \quad (1)$$

where

C_o = concentration of the injected tracer fluid before mixing occurs,

C = concentration of tracer of the mixed fluid at the point of observation,

x = distance from the injection face to the point of observation,

t = time for the tracer concentration to travel the distance x,

u = mean pore velocity of the fluid,

D = dispersion coefficient,

erf = error function, and

erfc = complementary error function.

Values of the erfc can be found in Abramowitz and Stegum (1964, p. 310–315).

An easy means of solving for D is by the analytical method. Thus, to compute D we define $\xi = ut/x$ and $\zeta = D/ux$. Equation 1 is now expressed as:

$$C/C_o = \tfrac{1}{2}\text{erfc}\left[\frac{1-\xi}{2\sqrt{\xi\zeta}}\right] = \tfrac{1}{2}\text{erfc}\,\Phi. \quad (2)$$

In this expression, D is the only unknown. Because C/C_o is known, Φ can be determined from tables of error functions. D can be eliminated temporarily from the equation by expressing ξ as a function Φ, thus $\Phi(\xi) = \frac{1-\xi}{2\sqrt{\xi}}$. Because u, t, and x are known, $\Phi(\xi)$ can be computed for corresponding values of C/C_o; that is, values of Φ can be obtained and related to values of $\Phi(\xi)$ for specific C/C_o values.

The values of Φ and corresponding values of $\Phi(\xi)$ are plotted graphically on coordinate paper. The values of Φ are plotted on the abscissa and values of $\Phi(\xi)$ on the ordinate in the Cartesian coordinate system. A best-fit straight line is drawn through the experimentally determined values, and the slope of this line is determined. The dispersion coefficient D can now be computed by reasoning that

$$\text{slope} = \frac{\Phi(\xi)}{\Phi} = \sqrt{\zeta} = \sqrt{\frac{D}{ux}}\,. \quad (3)$$

The computed values of dispersion in square centimeters per minute for two boundary conditions are given in table 1. These boundary conditions account for oscillatory and nonoscillatory effects on the fluid body as it moved through the column.

Preliminary comparison of the effects of two boundary conditions (nonoscillatory and oscillatory) showed that there was only a slight difference in the width of the frontal diffused zone for both conditions. In other words, concentration distribution determined at each station remained about the same in the steady and unsteady systems. Computations as shown in table 1 indicate that for low flow, the calculated dispersion coefficient varied by a factor of 3 with changing tidal amplitude. With the higher flow rates, the values became erratic.

These results indicate that the fixed probes influence the flow pattern and, therefore, the dispersion mechanism. The geometry of the probes attached to the wall of the vertical column may have been such that only the fluid channeled near the wall was measured. Because the dispersion coefficient is a function of fluid velocity, some changes in dispersion were detected with an increase in fluid velocity. However, failure to detect additional changes in the dispersion coefficient with tidal-amplitude changes indicates that the fixed probes were most likely the cause. Further testing will be required before the cause can be definitely established.

It should be noted that these column tests, although repetitious, were carried out for two reasons. The first was to establish the effectiveness of using chlorides or color as a standard measuring technique. The second was to establish the dispersion coefficient in one dimension for extension into the two-dimensional horizontal model. Initially, verification of published data was desired to establish the reliability of the testing procedure. When measurement of light transmission was used, it was noted that the organic dye tracer tended to fade with time (fig. 5).

Correcting for the fading was impractical because the dye completely faded with time at the low flow rates. It was found that the dye lagged as much as 2 cm behind the chloride when the fluid traveled 16 cm in 13 hours. Thus it was apparent that only for fast fluid velocities could the dye be used as a reliable

Table 1.—*Preliminary calculations of the longitudinal dispersion coefficient for nonoscillatory and oscillatory flow in a rectangular vertical sand column*

Test No.	Fluid pore velocity (cm/min)	Oscillation amplitude (cm)	Computed dispersion (cm^2/min): Travel distance of tracer fluid from injection face to station (cm)				
			17	18	19	20	21
1	0.021	0	0.0013	0.0010	0.0010	......	......
	.023	1	.0012	.0011	.0011	0.0010	0.0008
	.022	2	.0014	.0016	.0023	.0020	.0021
	.022	4	.0018	.0023	.0028	.0028	.0018
			10	19	20	31	32
2	0.105	0	0.0019	0.0021	0.0020	0.0019	0.0017
	.105	1	.0034	.0035	.0030	.0032	.0038
	.106	2	.0049	.0034	.0035	.0042	.0021
	.108	4	.0056	.0039	.0038	.0037	.0037
			10	11	12	13	14
3	0.208	0	0.0140	0.0140	0.0140	0.0150	0.0110
	.190	1	.0052	.0065	.0065	.0089	.0080
	.202	2	.0110	.0096	.0110	.0070	.0060
	.190	4	.0068	.0070	.0050	.0073	.0051
			18	27	35		
4	0.42	0	0.023	0.014	0.013		
	.43	1	.018	.015	.015		
	.42	2	.021	.014	.016		
	.43	4	.022	.021	.032		
			17	27	37		
5	1.17	0	0.083	0.079	0.048		
	.86	1	.057	.028	.083		
	.86	2	.058	.040	.039		
	.90	4	.044	.039	.062		

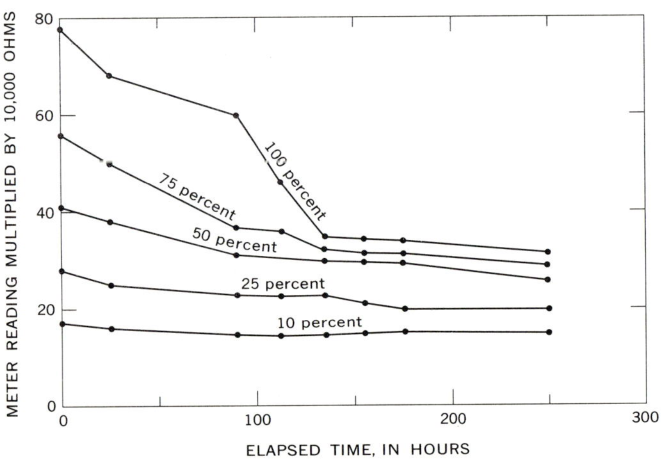

Figure 5.—Changes in resistance registered by the photo-electric cell as color concentration of dye tracer fades with time.

indicator of the concentration profile in studying the transport mechanism in porous material. Because of its simplicity and the ability to measure the required property outside of the region of flow, this method of measurement is desirable if a reliable dye tracer is available.

The two-dimensional models were used initially without oscillating the salt-water body to verify published data. For each experiment, a quantity of fresh-water input or average flow was established, and the denser fluid containing the tracer substance was allowed to reach equilibrium with this fresh-water flow. When dynamic equilibrium was attained, the position of the wedge was recorded by measuring the concentration profile of the mixed zone with either fixed or removable conductivity probes. For unsteady flow systems, the salt-water head tank was oscillated while a given amount of fresh water flowed through the model. After some experience it was possible to determine the number of oscillations required before the concentration profile in the mixed zone was stable. Various tests were conducted for different fresh-water flow rates and amplitudes in tidal fluctuations.

A typical concentration profile of the dispersed zone as mapped by traversing vertically at each station is shown on figure 6. Entrances to use the removable electrical probe to measure the chloride-tracer concentration in the mixed zone were spaced at vertical intervals of 1 cm. These concentration profiles, which are not normal to the interface, need to be corrected before analysis. Because a narrow dispersed zone was obtained in the model and because entrances for concentration detection were spaced 1 cm apart, only seven points were established for any one station (fig. 6). The curve does represent a characteristic dispersion-concentration profile, but is wider than expected because measurements were not taken normal to the interface.

A typical distribution of salt water at the interface of the

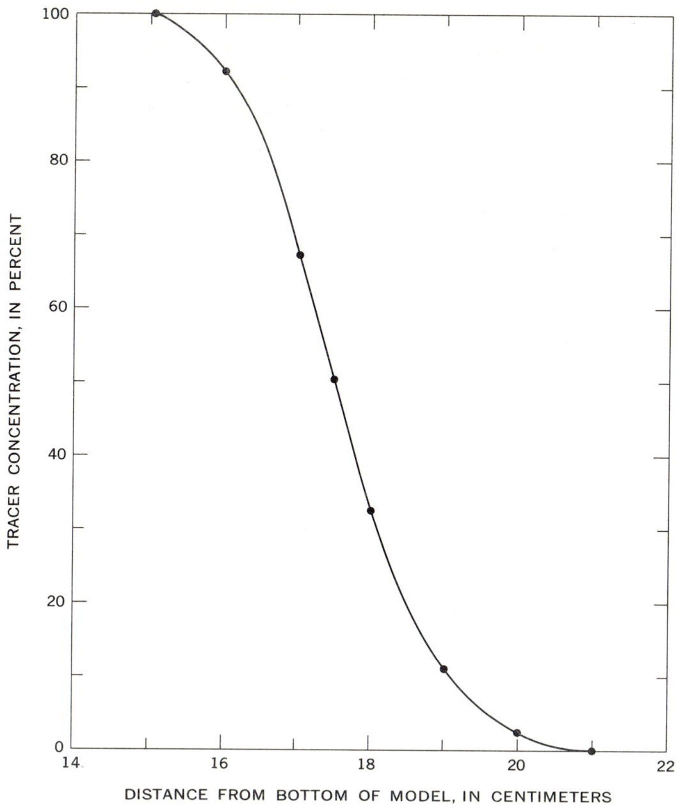

Figure 6.—Typical tracer-concentration profile in the "zone of diffusion" of a two-dimensional hydraulic sand model.

fluids is shown on figure 7. For this test, the quantity of fresh-water flow in the model was 4.5 ml/min. Each station was measured to determine the line of equal concentration. The concentrations of 10, 50, and 90 percent, shown by solid lines, were determined for the steady-flow system. The effluent for this condition contained 12 percent salt water.

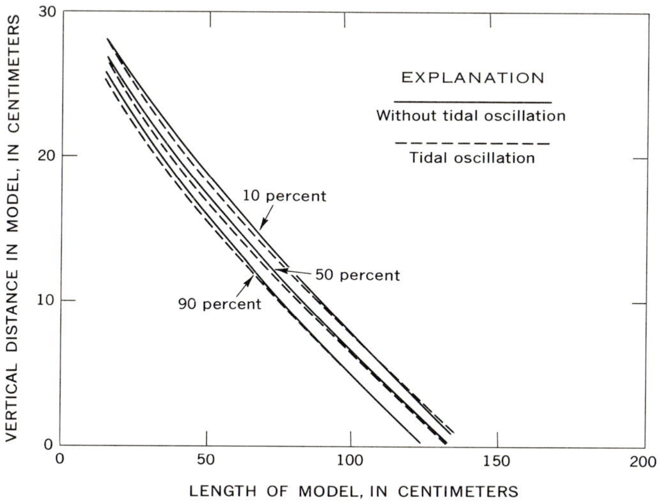

Figure 7.—Salt-water concentration profile at fresh water–salt water interface for steady and unsteady flow.

The dashed lines on figure 7 show the concentration distribution for the oscillating system with full fluctuation amplitude of 1 cm. These readings were taken at the midpoint of an oscillation cycle after a given time of oscillation so that a good average was attained. The oscillation was about the mean head established in the steady-flow model. For the oscillating condition, a 14-percent salt concentration was detected in the effluent. Thus the effect of tidal fluctuations increases the salt-water flow back to the ocean, but does not change significantly the equilibrium profile of the dispersed zone.

The interface location for an intrusive salt-water wedge in equilibrium has been presented by Rumer and Harleman (1963, p. 200) as:

$$y_i = \left[2\left(\frac{q_f}{K\frac{\Delta\rho}{\rho}}\right)x + 0.55\left(\frac{q_f}{K\frac{\Delta\rho}{\rho}}\right)^2\right]^{1/2} \qquad (4)$$

where

y_i = distance from top of aquifer to salt water–fresh water interface,
q_f = fresh-water flow per unit width of ocean front,
K = permeability of the porous medium,
x = distance from ocean to wedge toe,
$\Delta\rho$ = difference in density between salt and fresh water, and
ρ = density of fresh water.

Computations based on the use of this dynamic mathematical expression were compared to data obtained from model results and shown as a solid line on figure 8. The graph shows that, except for the region near the shoreline, the mathematical expression gives a good approximation of the dynamic-equilibrium position of the 50-percent concentration line in two-fluid flow. The 50-percent concentration position was chosen because this concentration could be more accurately defined in the model.

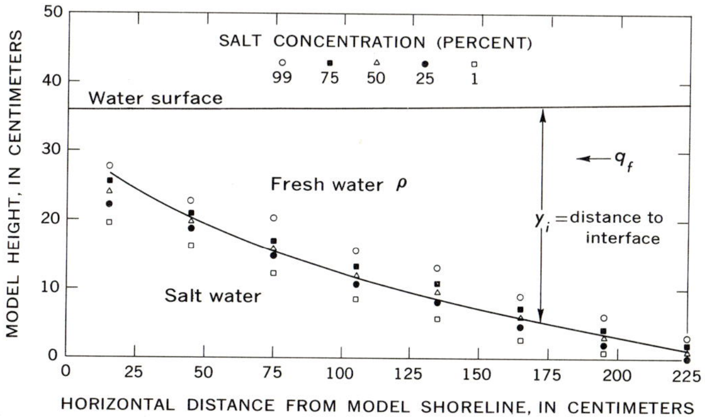

Figure 8.—Comparison of theoretical calculated values (solid line) and data obtained from model at the 50-percent concentration line in two-fluid flow.

CONCLUSIONS

Laboratory studies of the two-fluid system reported here are preliminary. The in-place measurement required for study of any two-dimensional flow requires careful modeling techniques. The initial endeavor was towards development of satisfactory measurement techniques. Because a fixed probe left in the saline solution tends to change in characteristics, either a removable-probe technique or a method of remote measurement is desirable. The method of inserting probe electrodes into the model proved satisfactory. The biggest disadvantage of the electrical probe is its effect on the microscopic flow system even for a short time because the probes are generally larger than the sand grains. Further investigation in the use of measurements of light transmission through the medium is also needed.

The use of a dye tracer in the model has a physical disadvantage in that most organic dye lags behind the carrier fluid because of adsorption. This becomes especially noticeable when typical ground-water flow velocities are used. However, in tests requiring only 2 or 3 hours for completion, the results obtained are generally satisfactory (Cahill, 1966). Because of the ease with which transmission of light through the models filled with glass beads can be measured and because of the possibility of obtaining measurements without disturbing the flow, this method is promising if suitable tracers can be found. Further tests are needed to evaluate this method, using various dyes, especially in recording the long-term characteristics and the possible use of adsorption-rate correction.

Because of the physical modeling difficulties, the investigation of miscible flow is still in its initial stage. Additional data for this system are needed for further studies, which should consider other mechanisms, such as pumpage and aquifer heterogeneity, that control the shape and position of the salt water-fresh water interface. More detailed investigations will be needed to include the boundary effects of pumpage and interior controls of aquifer heterogeneity and their effect on the transport mechanism. How these factors influence the dispersion process, which in turn governs the dynamic positioning of the two-fluid boundaries, must be assessed before mathematical formulation is possible.

Data obtained from these preliminary model experiments can be used to evaluate methodology and reproducibility. Agreement with published studies will determine to a large extent whether a valid method for the study of salt-water encroachment is available or if new methods need to be developed.

REFERENCES CITED

Abramowitz, M., and Stegum, A. S., 1964, Handbook of mathematical functions: U.S. Natl. Bur. Standards, Appl. Math. Ser. 55, 1046 p.

Bear, Jacob, 1961, Some experiments in dispersion: Jour. Geophys. Research, v. 66, no. 8, p. 2455–2467.

Bear, Jacob, and Todd, D. K., 1960, The transition zone between fresh and salt waters in coastal aquifers: California Univ. Water Resources Center Contr. 29, 156 p.

Cahill, J. M., 1966, Preliminary evaluation of three tracers used in hydraulic experiments on sand models, *in* Geological Survey Research 1966: U.S. Geol. Survey Prof. Paper 550-B, p. B213–B217.

Cooper, H. H., Jr., Kohout, F. A., Henry, H. R., and Glover, R. E., 1964, Sea water in coastal aquifers: U.S. Geol. Survey Water-Supply Paper 1613-C, p. C1–C84.

Harlemann, D. R. F., and Rumer, R. R., Jr., 1963, Longitudinal and lateral dispersion in an isotropic porous medium: Jour. Fluid Mechanics, v. 16, pt. 3, p. 385–394.

Kaufman, W. J., and Orlob, G. T., 1956, An evaluation of ground-water tracers: Am. Geophys. Union Trans., v. 37, no. 3, p. 297–306.

Radio Corp. of America, 1964, Photocells, solid-state photosensitive devices: Radio Corp. of America, Electronic Components and Devices, Harrison, N.J., 35 p.

Rumer, R. R., Jr., and Harleman, D. R. F., 1963, Intruded salt-water wedge in porous media: Am. Soc. Civil Engineers Proc., Jour. Hydraulics Div., v. 89, no. HY-6, p. 193–220.

RECENT PUBLICATIONS OF THE U.S. GEOLOGICAL SURVEY

(Books may be ordered from the Superintendent of Documents, Government Printing Office, Washington, D.C., 20402, to whom remittances should be sent by check or money order. Give title, series No., stock No. (shown in parentheses in this list), and catalog No. [shown in brackets])

Professional Papers

440-N-1. Data of geochemistry, sixth edition, Michael Fleischer, technical editor, Chapter N. Chemistry of igneous rocks—Part 1, The chemistry of the peralkaline oversaturated obsidians, by Ray MacDonald and D. K. Bailey. 1973 (1972). p. N1–N37. 75¢. (2401-00253) [I 19:16:440-N-1]

529-K. Atlantic Continental Shelf and Slope of the United States—Sand-size fraction of bottom sediments, New Jersey to Nova Scotia, by J. V. A. Trumbull. 1972. p. K1-K45. 55¢. (2401-2185) [I 19:16:529-K]

532. Cenozoic fossil mollusks from western Pacific Islands; gastropods (Turritellidae through Strombidae), by H. S. Ladd. 1972. 79 p.; 20 plates. $1.50. (2401-2133) [I 19:16:532]

582-C. Transverse diffusion of solutes in natural streams, by Nobuhiro Yotsukura and E. D. Cobb. 1972. p. C1–C19. 55¢. (2401-2147) [I 19:16:582-C]

585-A. Hydrologic investigations of prairie potholes in North Dakota, 1959-68, by W. S. Eisenlohr, Jr., and others. 1972 p. A1–A102; plates in pocket. $3. (2401-2156) [I 19:16:585-A]

655-E. Soil-moisture and energy relationships associated with riparian vegetation near San Carlos, Ariz., by I. S. McQueen and R. F. Miller. 1972. p. E1–E51. 60¢. (2401-2055) [I 19:16:655-E]

685. Fossils from the Ordovician Bioherm at Meikelejohn Peak, Nev., by R. J. Ross, Jr. 1972. 47 p.; 18 plates showing fossils. $1.25. (2401-2048) [I 19:16:685]

690. Stratigraphy and origin of the Chinle Formation and related Upper Triassic strata in the Colorado Plateau region, by J. H. Stewart, F. G. Poole, and R. F. Wilson, *with a section on* Sedimentary petrology, by R. A. Cadigan, *and a section on* Conglomerate studies, by William Thordarson, H. F. Albee, and J. H. Stewart. 1972. 336 p. $8.25. (2401-2186) [I 19:16:690]

702. Stratigraphy and structure of Middle and Upper Ordovician rocks in the Sedgwick basin and adjacent areas, south-central Kansas, by W. L. Adkison. 1972. 33 p.; plates in pocket. $1.50. (2401-2148) [I 19:16:702]

710. Jasperoid in the United States—Its characteristics, origin, and economic significance, by T. G. Lovering. 1972. 164 p. $1.75. (2401-1218) [I 19:16:710]

724-A. Huntington Lake quadrangle, central Sierra Nevada, Calif.—Analytic data, by P. C. Bateman and D. R. Wones. 1972. p. A1–A18. 55¢. (2401-00226) [I 19:16:724-A]

729-C. Stratigraphic framework of the Absaroka Volcanic Supergroup in the Yellowstone National Park region, by H. W. Smedes and H. J. Prostka. 1972. p. C1–C33. 50¢. (2401-2151) [I 19:16:729-C]

746. Cenozoic rocks of the Santa Rita Mountains, southeast of Tucson, Ariz., by Harald Drewes. 1972. 66 p. $1.50. (2401-2187) [I 19:16:746]

761. Geochemical anomalies and alteration in the Moenkopi Formation, Skull Creek, Moffat County, Colo., by R. A. Cadigan. 1972. 21 p. 70¢. (2401-00221) [I 19:16:761]

762. Instrumentation studies of earth tremors related to geology and to mining at the Somerset coal mine, Colorado, by F. W. Osterwald, C. R. Dunrud, J. B. Bennetti, Jr., and J. O. Maberry. 1972. 27 p. 70¢. (2401-00227) [I 19:16:762]

795. Lower Cretaceous, Jurassic(?), and Triassic Ostracoda from the Atlantic Coastal region, by F. M. Swain and P. M. Brown. 1972. 55 p.; 9 plates. $2.00. (2401-00250) [I 19:16:795]

796. Structural and stratigraphic framework, and spatial distribution of permeability of the Atlantic Coastal Plain, North Carolina to New York, by P. M. Brown, J. A. Miller, and F. M. Swain. 1972. 79 p.; text and plates in case. $50. (2401-00243) [I 19:16:796]

800-D. Geological Survey Research 1972, Chapter D. 1972. p.

Bulletins

1331-A. Mississippian stratigraphy of northwestern Pennsylvania, by G. R. Schiner and G. E. Kimmel. 1972. p. A1–A27. $1.25. (2401-2169) [I 19:3:1331-A]

1336. Precambrian geology of the northern Bradshaw Mountains, Yavapai County, Ariz., by C. A. Anderson and P. M. Blacet. 1972. 82 p. $2.75. (2401-2101) [I 19:3:1336]

1340. Geology of the Moxie pluton in the Moosehead Lake–Jo-Mary Mountain area, Piscataquis County, Maine, by G. H. Espenshade. 1972. 40 p. $3. (2401-2113) [I 19:3:1340]

1355. Placer gold deposits of Arizona, by M. G. Johnson. 1972. 103 p. $1. (2401-2155) [I 19:3:1355]

1360. Geochemistry and diagenesis of tidal-marsh sediment, northeastern Gulf of Mexico, by V. E. Swanson, A. H. Love, and I. C. Frost. 1972. 83 p. 55¢. (2401-2093) [I 19:3:1360]

1363. Underclay deposits of Somerset and eastern Fayette Counties, Pa., by J. W. Hosterman. 1972. 17 p.; plates in pocket. 65¢. (2401-2155) [I 19:3:1363]

1364. Arsenic as an indicator element for mineralized volcanic pipes in the Red Mountains area, western San Juan Mountains, Colo., by W. S. Burbank, R. G. Luedke, and F. N. Ward. 1972. 31 p. 25¢. (2401-2195) [I 19:3:1364]

1371-B. Mineral resources of the Salmon-Trinity Alps Primitive Area, Calif., by P. E. Hotz, H. K. Thurber, L. Y. Marks, and R. K. Evans, *with a section on* An aeromagnetic survey and interpretation, by Andrew Griscom. 1972. p. B1–B267. $3.75. (2401-2199) [I 19:3:1371-B]

1371-C. Mineral resources of the Cloud Peak Primitive Area, Wyo., by T. H. Kiilsgaard, G. E. Ericksen, L. L. Patten, and C. L. Bieniewski. 1972. p. C1–C60; plates in pocket. $1.75. (2401-00219) [I 19:3:1371-C]

Water-Supply Papers

1532-G. Hydrology and effects of conservation structures, Willow Creek basin, Valley County, Mont., 1954-68, by D. G. Frickel. 1972. p. G1–G34. 30¢. (2401-02210) [I 19:13:1532-G]

1542-B. Accuracy of low-flow characteristics estimated by correlation of base-flow measurements, by C. H. Hardison and M. E. Moss, *with a section on* Outline of derivations by E. J. Gilroy. 1972. p. B1–B55. 40¢. (2401-2168) [I 19:13:1542-B]

1586-J. Tracer simulation study of potential solute movement in Port Royal Sound, S.C., by F. A. Kilpatrick and T. R. Cummings. 1972. p. J1–J27. 55¢. (2401-2196) [I 19:13:1586-J]

1798-J. Sediment transport in the western tributaries of the Sacramento River, Calif., by B. L. Jones, N. L. Hawley, and J. R. Crippen. 1972. p. J1–J27. 25¢. (2401-2163) [I 19:13:1798-J]

1873-D. Measurement of salt-wedge excursion distance in the Duwamish River estuary, Seattle, Wash., by means of the dissolved-oxygen gradient, by W. A. Dawson and L. J. Tilley. 1972. p. D1–D27. 25¢. (2401-2166) [I 19:13:1873-D]

1873-F. Determination of mass balance and entrainment in the stratified Duwamish River estuary, King County, Wash., by J. D. Stoner. 1972. p. F1–F17. 30¢. (2401-00252) [I 19:13:1873-F]

1999-N. Quality of the ground water in basalt of the Columbia River Group, Wash., Oreg., and Idaho, by R. C. Newcomb. 1972. p. N1–N71. 75¢. (2401-2149) [I 19:13:1999-N]

2009-A. Runoff characteristics of California streams, by S. E. Rantz. 1972. p. A1–A38. 70¢. (2401-00216) [I 19:13:2009-A]

2025. Glossary of selected terms useful in studies of the mechanics of aquifer systems and land subsidence due to fluid withdrawal, by J. F. Poland, B. E. Lofgren, and F. S. Riley. 1972. 9 p. 15¢.

U.S. GOVERNMENT
PRINTING OFFICE
PUBLIC DOCUMENTS DEPARTMENT
WASHINGTON, D.C. 20402

OFFICIAL BUSINESS
PENALTY FOR PRIVATE USE $300

POSTAGE AND FEES PAID
U.S. GOVERNMENT
PRINTING OFFICE
375

U.S.MAIL

JOURNAL OF RESEARCH OF THE U.S. GEOLOGICAL SURVEY

MAY–JUNE 1973
VOLUME 1, NUMBER 3

Scientific notes and summaries of investigations in geology, hydrology, and related fields

U.S. DEPARTMENT OF THE INTERIOR

UNITED STATES DEPARTMENT OF THE INTERIOR

ROGERS C. B. MORTON, Secretary

GEOLOGICAL SURVEY

V. E. McKelvey, Director

For sale by the Superintendent of Documents, U.S. Government Printing Office, Washington, D.C., 20402. Order by SD Catalog No. JRGS. Annual subscription rate $8.50 (plus $2.25 for foreign mailing). Single copy $1.50. Prices valid until July 1, 1973, at which time a price increase is scheduled. Make checks or money orders payable to the Superintendent of Documents.

Send all subscription inquiries and address changes to the Superintendent of Documents at the above address.

Purchase orders should not be sent to the U.S. Geological Survey library.

Library of Congress Card No. 72-600241

The Journal of Research consists of six issues a year (January-February, March-April, May-June, July-August, September-October, November-December) published in Washington, D.C., by the U.S. Geological Survey. It contains papers by members of the Geological Survey on geologic, hydrologic, topographic, and other scientific and technical subjects.

The Journal supersedes the short-papers chapters (B, C, and D) of the former Geological Survey Research ("Annual Review") series of professional papers. The synopsis chapter (A) of the former Geological Survey Research series will be published as a separate professional paper each year.

Correspondence and inquiries concerning the Journal (other than subscription inquiries and address changes) should be directed to the Managing Editor, Journal of Research, Publications Division, U.S. Geological Survey, Washington, D.C., 20244.

Papers for the Journal should be submitted through regular Division publication channels.

The Secretary of the Interior has determined that the publication of this periodical is necessary in the transaction of the public business required by law of this Department. Use of funds for printing this periodical has been approved by the Director of the Office of Management and Budget through February 11, 1975.

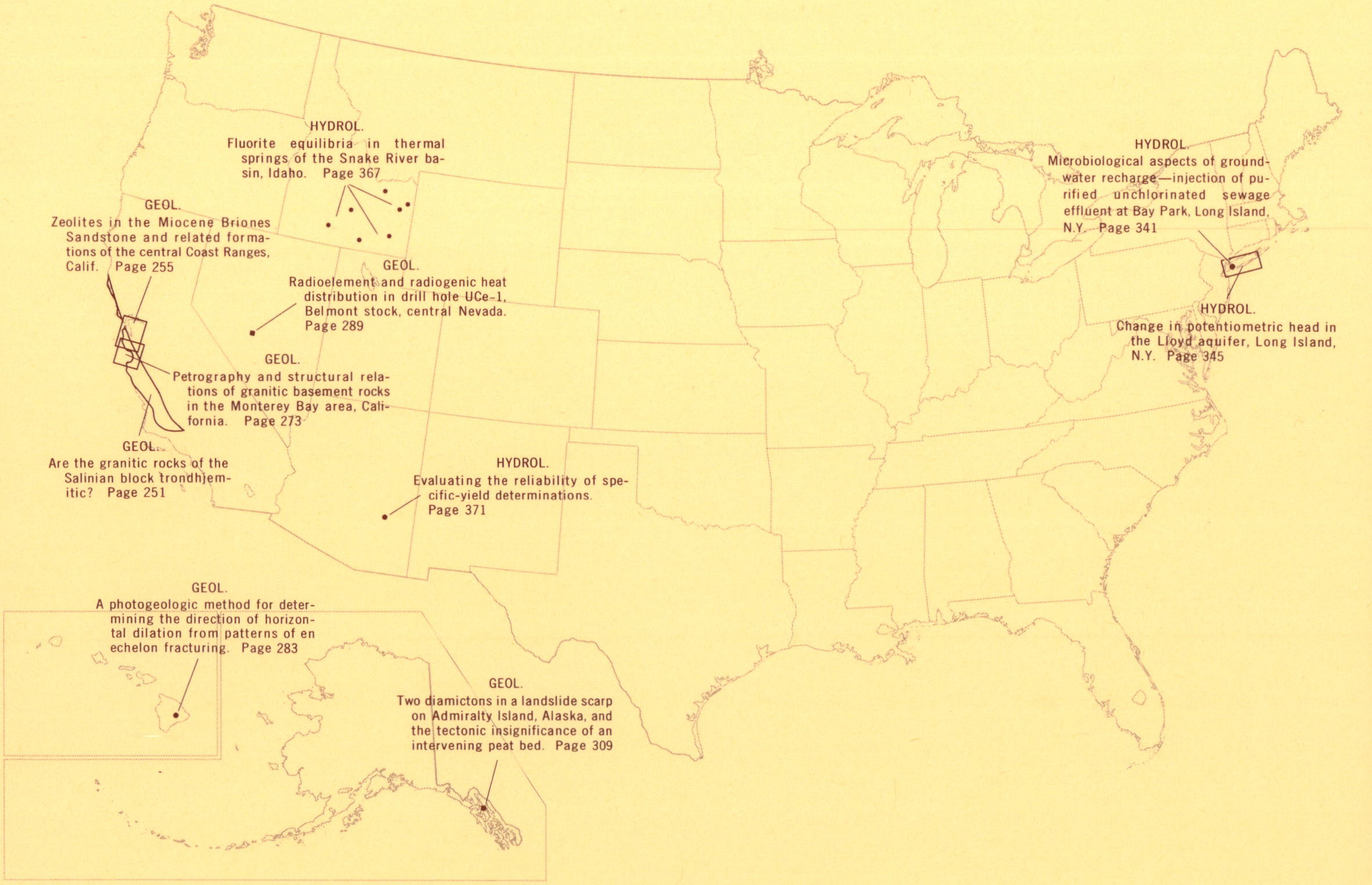

GEOGRAPHIC INDEX TO ARTICLES

[See Contents for articles concerning areas outside the United States and articles without geographic orientation]

JOURNAL OF RESEARCH

of the

U.S. Geological Survey

Vol. 1 No. 3 May-June 1973

CONTENTS

Abbreviations II

GEOLOGIC STUDIES

Are the granitic rocks of the Salinian block trondhjemitic? . . . . *D. C. Ross* 251

Zeolites in the Miocene Briones Sandstone and related formations of the central Coast Ranges, Calif. . . . . *K. J. Murata and K. R. Whiteley* 255

The chemistry of five accessory rock-forming apatites . . . . *D. E. Lee, E. L. M. Brandt, R. E. Van Loenen, and H. J. Rose, Jr.* 267

Petrography and structural relations of granitic basement rocks in the Monterey Bay area, California . . . . *D. C. Ross and E. E. Brabb* 273

A photogeologic method for determining the direction of horizontal dilation from patterns of en echelon fracturing . . . . *W. A. Duffield and Kazuaki Nakamura* 283

Radioelement and radiogenic heat distribution in drill hole UCe-1, Belmont stock, central Nevada . . . . *C. M. Bunker and C. A. Bush* 289

Geology of a system of submarine canyons south of Puerto Rico . . . . *J. V. A. Trumbull and L. E. Garrison* 293

A spectrochemical method for determining the composition of native gold . . . . *A. L. Sutton, R. G. Havens, and C. L. Sainsbury* 301

Two diamictons in a landslide scarp on Admiralty Island, Alaska, and the tectonic insignificance of an intervening peat bed . . . . *R. D. Miller* 309

TOPOGRAPHIC STUDIES

Can satellite photography contribute to topographic mapping? . . . . *F. J. Doyle* 315

Photoimages for map bases . . . . *Morris L. McKenzie* 327

HYDROLOGIC STUDIES

Microbiological aspects of ground-water recharge—Injection of purified unchlorinated sewage effluent at Bay Park, Long Island, N.Y. . . . . *G. G. Ehrlich, T. A. Ehlke, and John Vecchioli* 341

Change in potentiometric head in the Lloyd aquifer, Long Island, N.Y. . . . . *G. E. Kimmel* 345

Concepts of karst development in relation to interpretation of surface runoff. . *H. E. LeGrand and V. T. Stringfield* 351

The fractionation of humic acids from natural water systems . . . . *R. L. Wershaw and D. J. Pinckney* 361

Fluorite equilibria in thermal springs of the Snake River basin, Idaho. . . . . *C. E. Roberson and Robert Schoen* 367

Evaluating the reliability of specific-yield determinations . . . . *R. L. Hanson* 371

Recent publications of the U.S. Geological Survey . . . . Inside of back cover

ABBREVIATIONS AND SYMBOLS

[Singular and plural forms for abbreviations of units of measure are the same]

A	angstrom units
A^3	cubic angstroms
a-c	alternating current
amp	amperes
atm	atmospheres
B.P.	Before Present
b.y.	billion years
c	crystalline state
C_x	molal concentration (of substance x)
cal	calories
cfs	cubic feet per second
Ci	Curies
cm	centimeters
cm^2	square centimeters
cm^3	cubic centimeters
cpm	counts per minute
cu ft.	cubic feet
cu mi	cubic miles
d-c	direct current
eV	electron volts
emu	electromagnetic units
ft	feet
g	grams
gal	gallons
gpd	gallons per day
gpm	gallons per minute
hr	hours
in.	inches
kb	kilobars
kg	kilograms
km	kilometers
km^2	square kilometers
km^3	cubic kilometers
kV	kilovolts
l	liters
lb	pounds
m	meters
m	molal (concentration)
m^2	square meters
m^3	cubic meters
M	molar (concentration)
me	milliequivalents
MeV	million electron volts
mg	milligrams
mgd	million gallons per day
min	minutes
ml	milliliters
mm	millimeters
mol	moles
mr	milliroentgens
mV	millivolts
m.y.	million years
μ	microns
μm	micrometers
μmho	micromhos
n	neutrons
N	normal
ng	nanograms
nm	nanometers
Oe	oersteds
pCi	picocuries
pH	pH (measure of hydrogen ion activity)
ppb	parts per billion
ppm	parts per million
rad	radiometric
rpm	revolutions per minute
sec	seconds
sq ft	square feet
sq mi	square miles
yr	years

Jour. Research U.S. Geol. Survey
Vol. 1, No. 3, May-June 1973, p. 251–254

ARE THE GRANITIC ROCKS OF THE SALINIAN BLOCK TRONDHJEMITIC?

By DONALD C. ROSS, Menlo Park, Calif.

Abstract.—Trondhjemitic rocks are relatively abundant in the granitic terranes of the western Sierra Nevada and the Klamath Mountains but have not been found in the granitic plutons of the Salinian block, which lies westward, across the San Andreas fault. A ternary plot of modal quartz : K-feldspar : plagioclase from more than 200 granitic samples from the Salinian block has an elongate, nearly horizontal, quartz-rich trend that appears trondhjemitic to some observers. However, petrographic and chemical comparison of these rocks with trondhjemite from the type area in Norway and with rocks called trondhjemite in the Western United States shows that the granitic rocks of the Salinian block are not trondhjemitic. The absence of trondhjemite in the Salinian block further supports the contention that this terrane is not merely a westward continuation of Sierran basement but is a displaced basement block.

Trondhjemite has been identified from various localities in the nearest granitic terranes east and north of the Salinian block of the California Coast Ranges (fig. 1)—the western Sierra Nevada (Turner, 1894; Hietanen, 1951; Larsen and Poldervaart, 1961; Olmsted, 1971; and L. D. Clark, written commun., 1972) and the Klamath Mountains (Davis, 1963; Lipman, 1963; and Hotz, 1971). Trondhjemite has also been described to the west of the Salinian block where it is associated with gabbroic intrusions in an oceanic crust sequence (Page, 1972). Recently, a reference has been made to a "hornblende-biotite trondhjemite" in the Salinian block near Point Reyes (Mattinson and others, 1971). In a rather widespread study of granitic outcrops in the Salinian block I have identified no trondhjemites. Nevertheless, a ternary plot of modal quartz : K-feldspar : plagioclase of more than 200 samples from this study (fig. 2) has an elongate, nearly horizontal, quartz-rich trend which some colleagues suggest is trondhjemitic.

In view of the possibly erroneous conclusion that can be drawn from the trend on the modal plot of the granitic rocks of the Salinian block, it seems worthwhile at this time to compare these Salinian rocks with trondhjemite as originally defined and currently used.

The term "trondhjemite" was first applied by Goldschmidt (1916) to quartz-rich tonalites from the Trondhjem (Trondheim) area of Norway. Johannsen (1932) translated Goldschmidt's definition of trondhjemite as:

> leucocratic acid plutonic rocks, whose essential constituents are soda-rich plagioclase (oligoclase or andesine) and quartz. Potash-feldspar is entirely wanting or is present only in subordinate amounts. Biotite is the most important of the mafic constituents, although it is present in small quantity. Muscovite is often present * * *.

Current usage of the term "trondhjemite" seems to correspond fairly well to the original definition. For example, Williams, Turner, and Gilbert (1955) stated that trondhjemite is "essentially an oligoclase-biotite-quartz diorite." Five representative trondhjemite modes of Goldschmidt (1916, 1921) are shown in figure 3; plagioclase is oligoclase in four specimens and andesine in the fifth. These rocks have about the same quartz content as many rocks that are now called trondhjemites. In contrast, rocks called trondhjemites from the Western United States (Klamath Mountains, western Sierra Nevada, Idaho) contain considerably more K-feldspar than those of the type area, and some have several percent of hornblende (fig. 3). Davis (1963, p. 343) has described some trondhjemites whose average plagioclase is more calcic than An_{30}, for which he suggested the name "calcic trondhjemite." These variations notwithstanding, oligoclase-biotite quartz diorite appears to describe trondhjemite generally, as commonly used in the Western United States.

The modes of numerous granitic rocks of the Salinian block determined by Ross (1972a) are plotted on figure 2. Modes of rocks chemically analyzed are identified separately, and their distribution on the diagram shows them to be representative of the entire compositional range. Geographically, the samples range from Bodega Head on the north to the La Panza Range on the south.

Feldspar-quartz ternary modal plots, such as figures 2 and 3, which indicate neither the anorthite content of the plagioclase nor the kind and amount of dark minerals, will not by themselves distinguish trondhjemites from quartz-rich tonalites. More diagnostic are chemical characteristics, such as the ratio K_2O:Na_2O:CaO, or the somewhat comparable ratio of normative Or:Ab:An shown in figures 4 and 5, respectively. On these figures, it is evident that the granitic rocks of the Salinian block are markedly different from trondhjemites. The

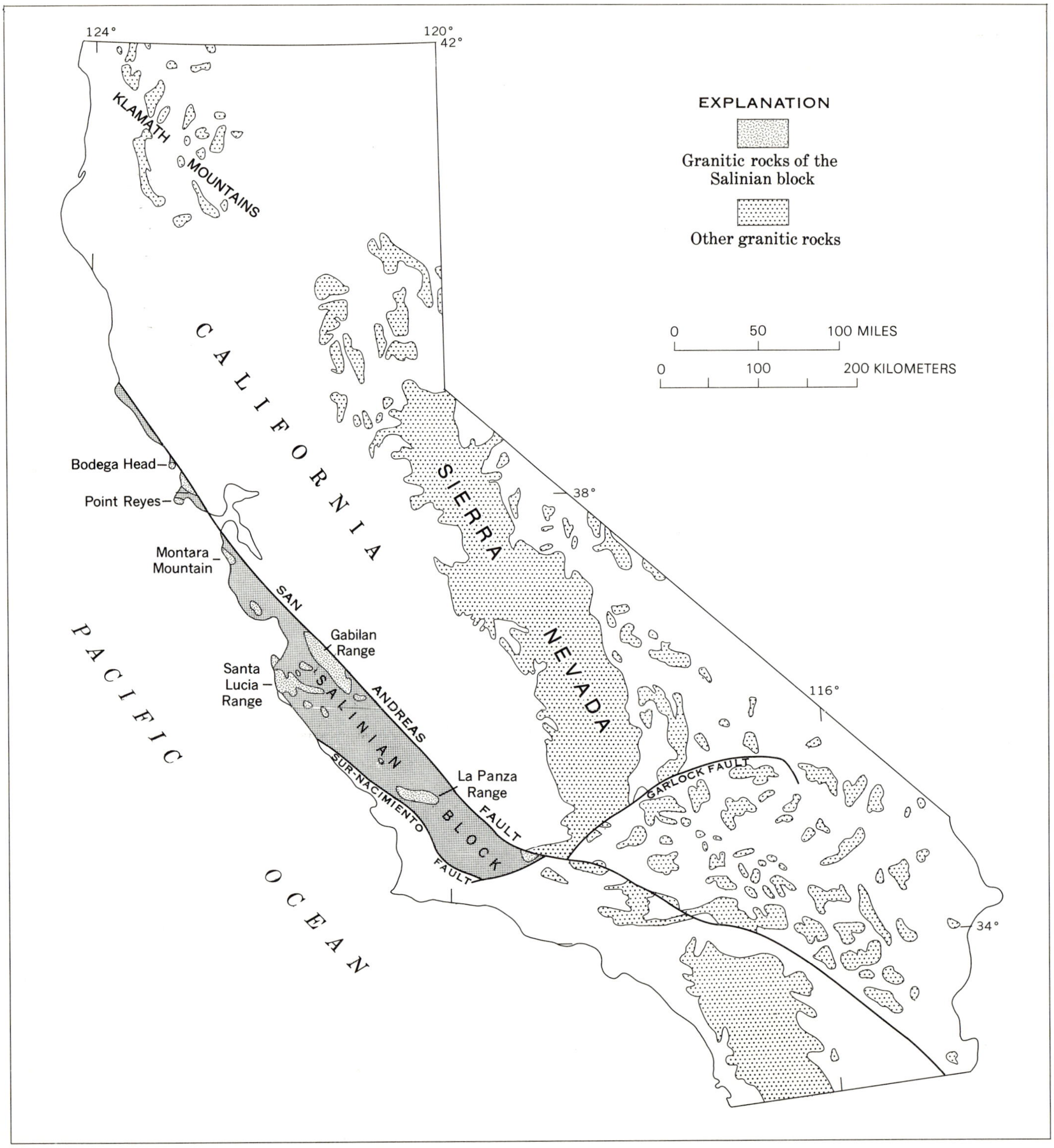

Figure 1.—Index map of Salinian block localities, California.

trondhjemite fields lie significantly closer to the Na_2O and Ab corners than the specimens from the Salinian block do.

Only one mass from the Salinian block, a gneissic quartz diorite from the southern part of the Gabilan Range (gneissic quartz diorite of Stonewall Canyon, Ross, 1972b), plots near the trondhjemite field. No chemical analyses were available from this mass, but chemical analyses were calculated from seven modes and estimated compositions of constituent minerals. These rocks contain 35 to 60 percent plagioclase (intermediate andesine), 25 to 45 percent quartz, 10 to 20 percent

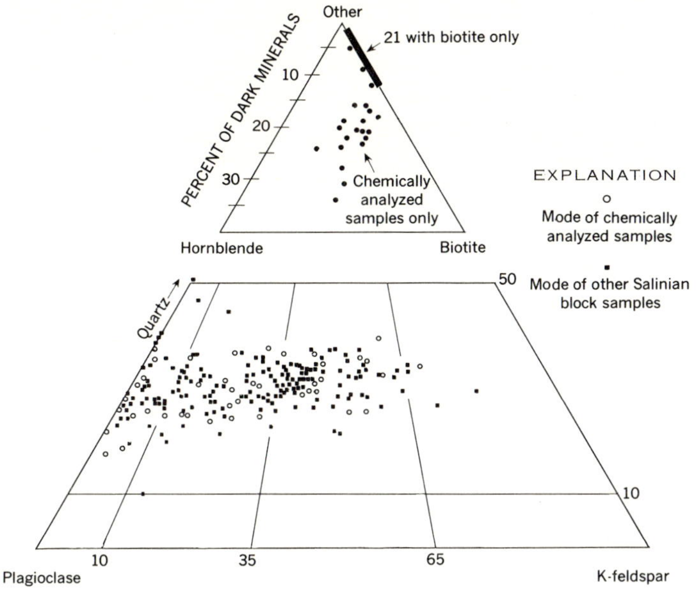

Figure 2.—Modes of granitic samples, Salinian block, California.

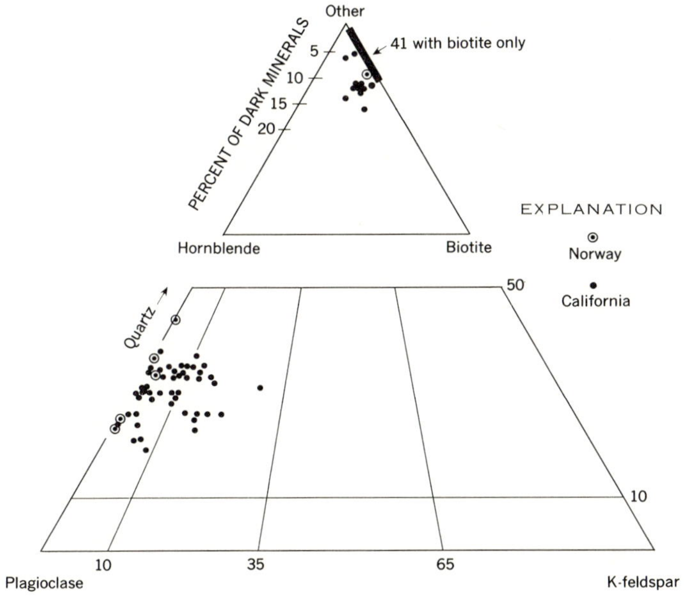

Figure 3.—Modal data on trondhjemites from California and Norway.

biotite, 0 to 11 percent K-feldspar (3 percent or less in all but one specimen), and traces of hornblende and accessory minerals. Though these rocks have some of the modal character of a trondhjemite, the plagioclase, about An_{40}, seems too calcic. Also, this mass may possibly be an ultrametamorphosed metasedimentary rock that looks similar to a normal intrusive rock. Abundant gneiss, schist, and calc-hornfels are associated and mixed with the more homogeneous granitoid samples. The percentage of quartz (three samples have 40, 41, and 44 percent, respectively) is also somewhat high for a "normal" granitic rock.

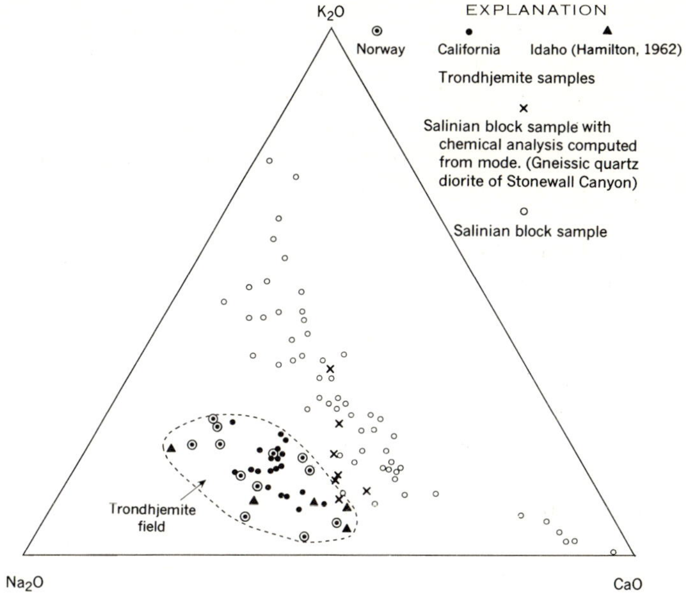

Figure 4.—Ternary K_2O – Na_2O – CaO diagram comparing trondhjemites with chemically analyzed samples from the Salinian block.

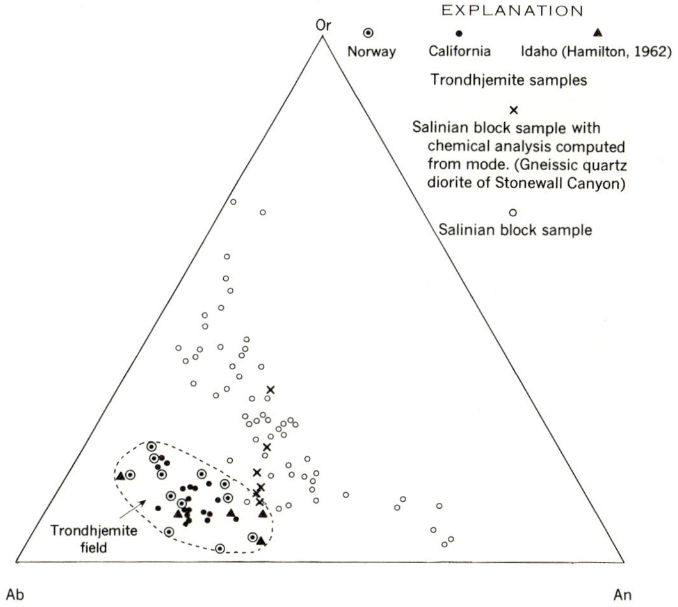

Figure 5.—Ternary diagram of normative Or–Ab–An comparing trondhjemites with chemically analyzed samples from the Salinian block.

One specimen from the granitic mass of Montara Mountain also plots on the edge of the trondhjemite field. This rock is strongly sheared and extensively saussuritized, which could explain why it differs from the general trend of the Salinian granitic rocks. With these exceptions, the Salinian block granitic rocks that have been analyzed are chemically distinct from analyzed trondhjemites.

The average of 37 trondhjemite analyses used in figures 4 and 5 is 3.2 percent CaO, 5.0 percent Na_2O, and 1.5 percent

K_2O. The comparable average for the normative feldspar constituents is "or," 7.5; "ab," 43.5; and "an," 15.6. The SiO_2 ranges from 66 to 76 percent and averages 70.7 percent, so that as a class, these are rather silicic rocks. In contrast, the five specimens from the gneissic body in the southern Gabilan Range that are closest to the trondhjemite field average 4.2 percent CaO, 3.8 percent Na_2O, and 1.3 percent K_2O and have normative "or" = 13, "ab" = 53, and "an" = 34; they are considerably different from trondhjemites. The saussuritized sample from Montara Mountain has almost the same K_2O, Na_2O, and CaO contents as the average for the gneissic mass from the Gabilan Range.

In conclusion, both petrographically and chemically, the granitic rocks of the Salinian block that I have studied are not trondhjemitic. It is possible that some individual specimens might qualify as "calcic trondhjemite" because they are intermediate andesine-bearing quartz diorite with biotite as their only dark mineral. However, these are all local variations from "normal" hornblende-bearing quartz diorites; in other words, none of the granitic masses in the Salinian block that have been studied are trondhjemites. Although not all the granitic masses in the Santa Lucia Range have been studied, where granitic rocks have been mapped by Compton (1966), Pearson, Hayes, and Fillo (1967), and Wiebe (1970), no trondhjemite has been noted.

The granitic terranes that are the closest to the Salinian block on the north and east, the Klamath Mountains and the western Sierra Nevada, contain significant amounts of trondhjemite. The contrasting absence of trondhjemite in the Salinian block seems to suggest that this block is not a westward continuation of the Sierran basement that has merely been differentially uplifted to expose the granitic terrane. Ross (1972a) has already suggested that the chemical character of the granitic rocks of the Salinian block does not seem to be a logical projection of the east-west chemical trends across the central Sierra Nevada, as reported by Bateman and Dodge (1970). The absence of trondhjemite in the Salinian block reinforces this chemical contrast and supports the suggestion that the Salinian block has been laterally transported to its present position.

REFERENCES CITED

Bateman, P. C., and Dodge, F. C. W., 1970, Variations of major chemical constituents across the central Sierra Nevada batholith: Geol. Soc. America Bull., v. 81, p. 409–420.

Compton, R. R., 1966, Granitic and metamorphic rocks of the Salinian block, California Coast Ranges: California Div. Mines and Geology Bull. 190, p. 277–287.

Davis, G. A., 1963, Structure and mode of emplacement of Caribou Mountain pluton, Klamath Mountains, California: Geol. Soc. America Bull., v. 74, p. 331–348.

Goldschmidt, V. M., 1916, Geologisch–petrographische studien im Hochgebirges des Südlichen Norwegens; IV, übersicht der Eruptivegesteine in Kaledonischen Gebirge zwischen Stavanger und Trondhjem: Vidensk. Selsk. Skr., Kristiana, no. 2, 140 p.

—— 1921, Geologisch–petrographische Studien im Hochgebirge des Südlichen Norwegens, V, die Injectionsmetamorphose im Stavanger–Gebiete: Vidensk. Selsk. Skr., Kristiana No. 10, p. 142.

Hamilton, Warren, 1962, Trondhjemite in the Riggins quadrangle, western Idaho: Art. 205 *in* U.S. Geol. Survey Prof. Paper 450-E, p. E98–E101.

Hietanen, Anna, 1951, Metamorphic and igneous rocks of the Merrimac area, Plumas National Forest, California: Geol. Soc. America Bull., v. 62, p. 565–608.

Hotz, P. E., 1971, Plutonic rocks of the Klamath Mountains, California and Oregon: U.S. Geol. Survey Prof. Paper 684-B, p. B1–B20.

Johannsen, Albert, 1932, A descriptive petrography of the igneous rocks, Volume II, the quartz-bearing rocks: Chicago, Chicago Univ. Press, 428 p.

Larsen, L. H., and Poldervaart, Arie, 1961, Petrologic study of Bald Rock batholith, near Bidwell Bar, California: Geol. Soc. America Bull., v. 72, p. 69–92.

Lipman, P. W., 1963, Gibson Peak pluton: A discordant composite intrusion in the southeastern Trinity Alps, northern California: Geol. Soc. America Bull., v. 74, p. 1259–1280.

Mattinson, J. M., Davis, T. E., and Hopson, C. A., 1971, U-Pb studies in the Salinian block of California: Annual Rept. of the Director, Geophys. Lab, *in* Carnegie Inst. Washington Year Book 70, p. 248–251.

Olmsted, F. H., 1971, Pre-Cenozoic geology of the south half of the Auburn 15-minute quadrangle, California: U.S. Geol. Survey Bull. 1341, 30 p.

Page, B. M., 1972, Oceanic crust and mantle fragment in subduction complex near San Luis Obispo, California: Geol. Soc. America Bull., v. 83, p. 957–972.

Pearson, R. C., Hayes, P. T., Fillo, P. V., 1967, Mineral resources of the Ventana primitive area, Monterey County, California: U.S. Geol. Survey Bull. 1261-B, 42 p.

Ross, D. C., 1972a, Petrographic and chemical reconnaissance of some granitic and gneissic rocks near the San Andreas fault from Bodega Head to Cajon Pass, California: U.S. Geol. Survey Prof. Paper 698, 92 p.

—— 1972b, Geologic map of the pre-Cenozoic basement rocks, Gabilan Range, Monterey and San Benito Counties, California: U.S. Geol. Survey Misc. Field Inv. Map MF-357, scale 1:125,000.

Turner, H. W., 1894, Rocks of the Sierra Nevada: U.S. Geol. Survey Ann. Rept. 14, pt. 2, p. 435–495.

Wiebe, R. A., 1970, Relations of granitic and gabbroic rocks, northern Santa Lucia Range, California: Geol. Soc. America Bull., v. 81, p. 105–116.

Williams, Howel, Turner, F. J., and Gilbert, C. M., 1955, Petrography, an introduction to the study of rocks in thin sections: San Francisco, W. H. Freeman and Co., 406 p.

Jour. Research U.S. Geol. Survey
Vol. 1, No. 3, May-June 1973, p. 255–265

ZEOLITES IN THE MIOCENE BRIONES SANDSTONE AND RELATED FORMATIONS OF THE CENTRAL COAST RANGES, CALIFORNIA

By K. J. MURATA and KAREN R. WHITELEY,
Menlo Park, Calif.

Abstract.—Authigenic zeolites present in the generally tuffaceous Miocene Briones Sandstone and related formations of the central Coast Ranges of California indicate three stages of diagenetic history: (1) Initial alteration of pyroclastic materials to clinoptilolite (and montmorillonite) that is widely distributed in small amounts throughout the region. (2) Subsequent crystallization of heulandite followed by stilbite in fractures at a few places. (3) Widespread development of laumontite in only the southern part of the region, where the sandstone appears to have been downfolded and faulted to greater depths than elsewhere. Laumontite occurs both as pervasive cement of sandstone and as filling of fractures, and was produced through the reaction of interstitial solutions with other zeolites and with such major constituents of the sandstone as plagioclase, montmorillonite, and calcite at temperatures of 100°C or higher. Mordenite was found at only one locality, closely associated with clinoptilolite and opal. Analcite occurs in diverse settings, and its relation to the other zeolites is obscure. Sparry calcite and coexisting stilbite, laumontite, or analcite in veins seem to make up nonequilibrium assemblages.

The widely scattered occurrences of diagenetic laumontite in Tertiary marine sandstones of California Coast Ranges were described recently by Madsen and Murata (1970). A subsequent study restricted to Miocene sandstones of the central Coast Ranges east of San Francisco Bay has clarified some of the factors that control the distribution of laumontite and has led to the discovery of several other zeolites (clinoptilolite, mordenite, heulandite, stilbite, and analcite) in these sandstones. Although most of them occur in small amounts, these zeolites merit careful study because they can provide new insights into the diagenetic history of the host sandstone.

Acknowledgments.—Paleontologic and geologic data on the several formations that we sampled were provided by W. O. Addicott, E. H. Bailey, M. D. Crittenden, T. W. Dibblee, Jr., J. W. Miller, and Julius Schlocker. Ranchers of the region and administrators of the San Francisco Water Department and the Sunol Valley Regional Park kindly granted access to lands under their control. Authenticated samples of different zeolites were made available by R. C. Erd, Robert Fournier, R. A. Gulbrandsen, W. H. Lee, and M. B. Norman II. We are also indebted to J. D. Gleason and J. R. O'Neil for isotopic analyses of calcites, to N. F. Prime for the photomicrographs of tiny zeolite crystals shown in figure 4, and to Elizabeth Murata for help with the fieldwork.

OCCURRENCE OF ZEOLITES

The stratigraphy of middle and upper Miocene rocks of the central Coast Ranges and environs was originally defined by Lawson (1914), and subsequently refined and extended by Trask (1922), Taliaferro (1943), Weaver (1949), Crittenden (1951), Page (1966), and many others. The sedimentary units that have been mapped in different parts of the region are listed below, in order of increasing geologic age.

Upper Miocene	San Pablo Group	Neroly Sandstone
		Cierbo Sandstone
		Briones Sandstone
Middle Miocene	Monterey Group	Rodeo Shale
		Hambre Sandstone
		Tice Shale
		Oursan Sandstone
		Claremont Shale
		Sobrante Sandstone

All these formations except the Rodeo Shale were sampled by us; by far the largest number of samples were collected from the widely distributed upper Miocene Briones Sandstone.

The combined outcrop areas of the middle and upper Miocene marine formations (fig. 1, table 1) delineate the broadly folded structure of the central Coast Ranges. Pyroclastic material in the form of andesitic to rhyolitic debris is a common constituent in these formations (Taliaferro, 1933; Lerbekmo, 1957) along with occasional beds of ash or bentonite. Clinoptilolite and laumontite are the most common zeolites; clinoptilolite is widely distributed, whereas laumontite is restricted to the southern area (south of lat 37°40′ and west of the Calaveras fault zone). The extensive development of laumontite in the southern area in the Briones but not in the northern area suggests that the diagenetic history of the

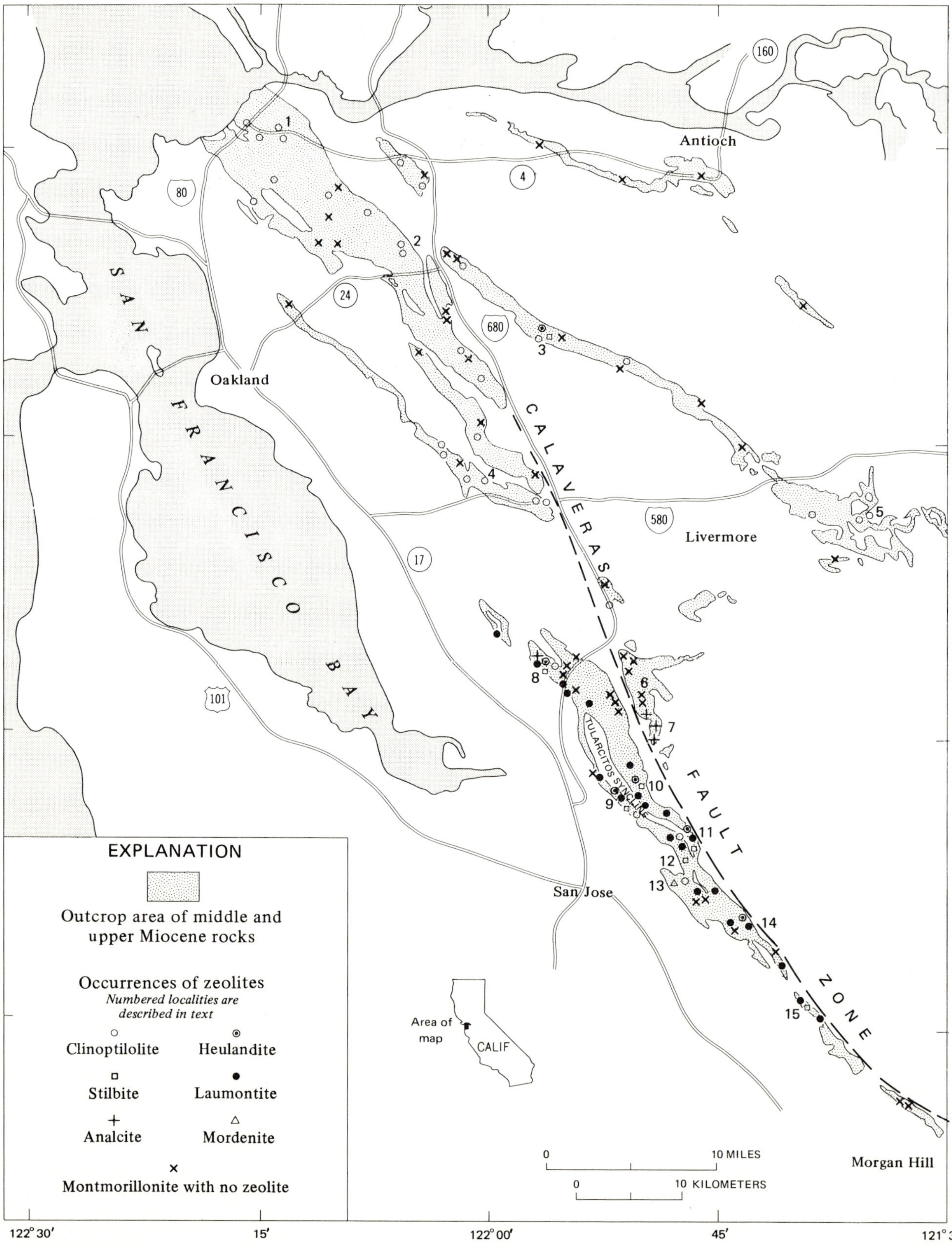

Figure 1.—Map showing outcrop areas of middle and upper Miocene formations in the central Coast Ranges east of San Francisco Bay (based on compilations by Jennings and Burnett, 1961; Koenig, 1963; Strand and Koenig, 1965; Rogers, 1966; and Brabb and others, 1971) and localities of studied samples. Zeolites from the numbered localities are discussed in the text, and the details of these localities are given in table 1. Montmorillonite is ubiquitous, and the zeolite-bearing samples also contain this common alteration product of volcanic ash.

Table 1.—*Data on numbered localities shown on figure 1*

Locality	Lat. N., long. W.	Sedimentary unit
	Contra Costa County	
1. Santa Fe RR., right-of-way.	38°01′, 122°14′	Bentonite bed in Hercules Shale Member of Briones Sandstone.
2. Briones Hills	37°57′, 122°07′	Briones Sandstone.
3. Mount Diablo	37°50′, 121°56′	Do.
	Alameda County	
4. Eden Canyon	37°43′, 122°00′	Briones Sandstone.
5. Patterson Pass	37°41′, 121°35′	Cierbo Sandstone.
6. Welch Creek	37°33′, 121°50′	Lower part of Briones Sandstone.
7. Alameda Creek	37°30′, 121°49′	Oursan Sandstone.
8. Morrison Canyon ...	37°34′, 121°57′	Hambre Sandstone.
	Santa Clara County	
9. Calaveras Road	37°27′, 121°51′	Briones Sandstone.
10. Weller Road	37°27′, 121°50′	Do.
11. Sierra Road	37°25′, 121°47′	Do.
12. Penitencia Creek....	37°24′, 121°47′	Do.
13. Mount Hamilton Road.	37°21′, 121°46′	Do.
14. Quimby Road	37°21′, 121°43′	Do.
15. San Felipe Valley ...	37°16′, 121°40′	Do.

two areas differs considerably. The hardness of noncalcareous Briones Sandstone differs concomitantly in the two areas; the sandstone is dense and hard to the south and porous and friable to the north.

ZEOLITE ASSEMBLAGES AND DIAGENETIC STAGES

Field studies of zonation by depth of zeolites in sedimentary sections (for example, Coombs, 1954; Hay, 1966; Castano and Sparks, 1970; Iijima and Utada, 1971) and laboratory investigations of phase relations (for example, Coombs and others, 1959; Fyfe and Mackenzie, 1969; Thompson, 1970; Liou, 1971) suggest that different assemblages of zeolites indicate different pressure-temperature conditions of diagenesis. Pressures and temperatures involved in the zeolitic stage of diagenesis are exemplified below by data obtained from deep drill holes by Iijima and Utada (1971). The tabulated values pertain to conditions prevailing at the tops of several zeolite zones in Neogene sedimentary deposits of Niigata oil field of Japan.

Zone	*Temperature (°C)*	*Pressure (kb)*	*Depth (km)*
Clinoptilolite	41–49	....	0.8–1.9
Mordenite	55–59	0.4–0.7	1.4–2.4
Analcite	84–91	.9–1.1	2.9–3.5
Laumontite	≈100	≈1.0	≈3.0

Similar zeolite relations are found at much shallower depths in the hydrothermal hot-spring environment, according to Steiner (1953) and Honda and Muffler (1970).

In contrast to such a zonation that is controlled mainly by physical parameters of temperature and pressure, other similar but generally shallower zonations seem to depend more on systematic variations in the chemistry of migrating solutions. Some chemical reactions or factors that are likely to affect the composition of interstitial solutions are:

1. Changing chemistry of solutions involved in hydrolysis of glassy shards (Hay, 1963, 1964; Hoover, 1968; Sheppard and Gude, 1969; and Moiola, 1970; among others).
2. Reduction in the activity of dissolved silica induced by sequential changes in the nature of deposited silica, namely, opal-cristobalite-quartz (Coombs and others, 1959; Campbell and Fyfe, 1960).
3. The dependence of the nature of the zeolite formed on the concentrations of the large cations, Na, K, Ca, and Mg; for example, the localization of laumontite in the middle part of the Briones Sandstone, where numerous shell beds constitute a rich source of calcium (Madsen and Murata, 1970).

Three main zeolite assemblages, characteristic of three successive stages of diagenesis, are apparent in the Briones and related sandstones of the Central Coast Ranges:

1. Clinoptilolite (with montmorillonite) that is pseudomorphous after glassy shards and widely distributed in small amounts throughout the studied region.
2. Heulandite together with stilbite as rare fillings of fractures in sandstone.
3. Laumontite, abundantly developed as pervasive cement or as filling of joints and other fractures, and restricted to sandstone in the southern part of the studied region. These zeolites will be described in the following sections.

Clinoptilolite

In their pioneering study of zeolitic alteration of pyroclastics, Bramlette and Posnjak (1933) identified clinoptilolite as a widespread diagenetic mineral in marine Miocene formations of California. Sheppard (1971) compiled all known American localities of this mineral and concluded that "Clinoptilolite is probably the most abundant authigenic zeolite that occurs in sedimentary rocks." The mineral is also common in Tertiary sedimentary formations of central Russia (Senderov and Khitarov, 1970) and of Japan (Utada, 1970).

Clinoptilolite is widespread among the Miocene formations of the central Coast Ranges (fig. 1), in which it is one of the earliest products of alteration of volcanic glass. Unaltered glass (fig. 2*A*) is rare in these formations.

Clinoptilolite is a common minor constituent in cores of tuffaceous Miocene deep-sea oozes drilled off the west coast of Mexico (Murata and Erd, 1964) and has been found in sediments dredged or drilled from the bottom of the Atlantic

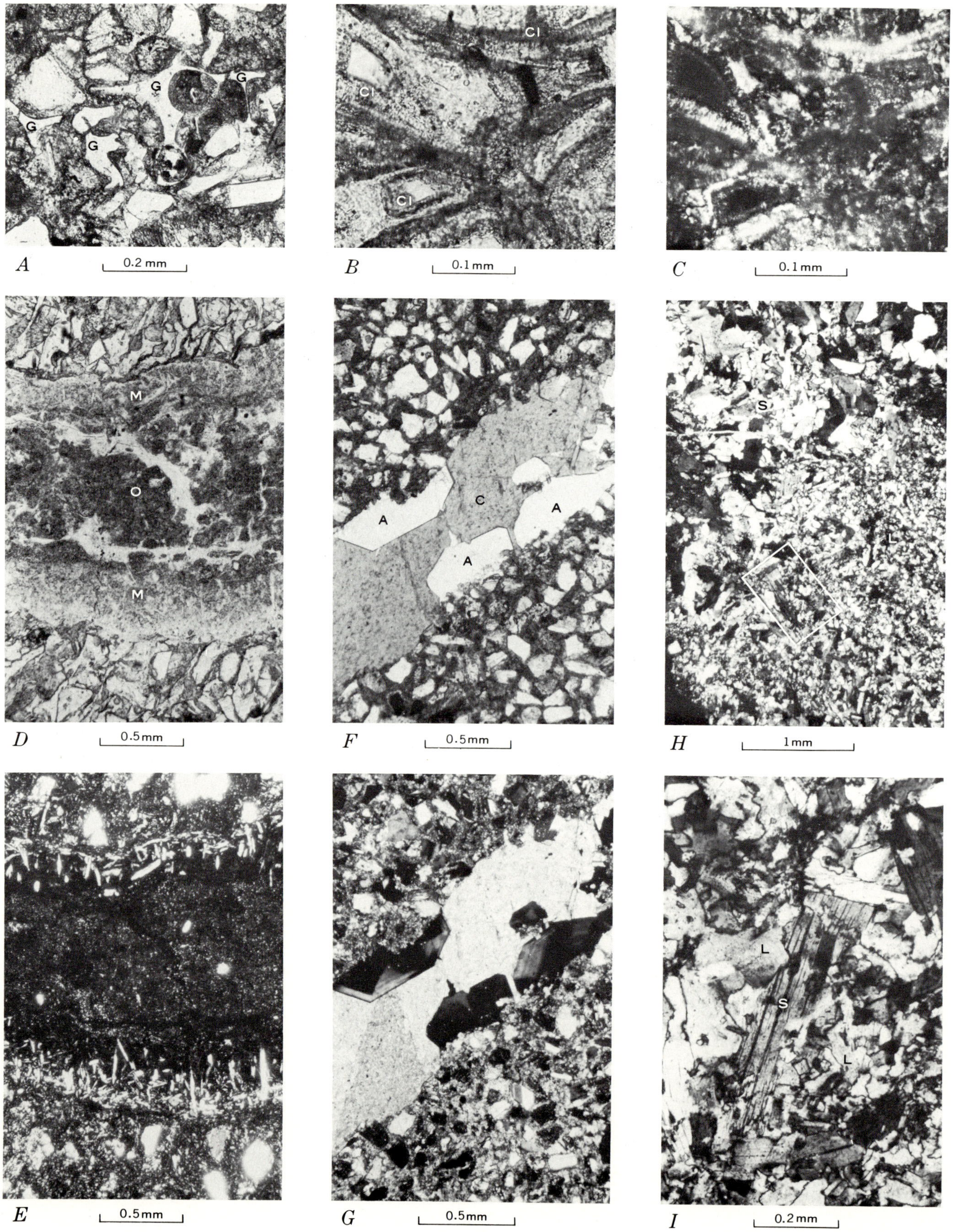
G
G
G
G
Cl
Cl
Cl
A
0.2 mm
B
0.1 mm
C
0.1 mm
M
O
M
D
0.5 mm
C
A
A
A
F
0.5 mm
S
L
H
1 mm
E
0.5 mm
G
0.5 mm
L
S
L
I
0.2 mm

Figure 2.

(Hathaway and Sachs, 1965; Peterson and others, 1970, p. 423). These occurrences suggest that clinoptilolite can be produced diagenetically at an appreciable rate even at low temperatures of the order of 10°C. The mineral is one of the more siliceous of the zeolites, and its Si/Al atomic ratio generally falls between 4 and 6 (Sheppard, 1971).

A bed of volcanic ash, which occurs in the lower part of the Briones at locality 13, was the only rock sufficiently rich in clinoptilolite to be studied directly. The mineral occurs as minutely fibrous replacement of glassy shards (figs. 2*B*,*C*). Clinoptilolite, concentrated out of sandstone from other localities (Nos. 1, 2, 4, 8, 9, 12) by means of heavy liquids, has the same fibrous replacement texture.

A heating test (400°C for 3 hours) was used to distinguish clinoptilolite from heulandite (Mumpton, 1960) on the basis of the absence of an X-ray reflection at 8.3 A in the heated sample for clinoptilolite. Upon heating, clinoptilolite from localities 1 and 4 showed very little weakening or displacement of the principal X-ray reflection at 9.0 A (exemplified by fig. 3*B*), whereas that from localities 2, 8, 9, 12, and 13 manifested an appreciable weakening of the principal reflection and a displacement to 8.7 A (fig. 3*C*). The thermal behavior of the latter type of clinoptilolite is somewhat like that of the calcium clinoptilolite described by Shepard and Starkey (1964, fig. 138.2) and by Utada (1970, fig. 10). When treated overnight with 1*M* Na_2SO_4, the sample from locality 12 released a substantial amount of calcium to solution and became appreciably more resistant to heating, though not completely so. Although differing in thermal behavior, none of the above-mentioned clinoptilolites developed a strong reflection at 8.3 A (fig. 3*A*) that is characteristic of heulandite. Also, the gamma refractive index of these clinoptilolites was determined to be less than 1.488 (Mason and Sand, 1960).

Samples separated from the vein-free sandstone of locality 3 and from the bulk sandstone of locality 5 also had the minutely fibrous habit of clinoptilolite, but many of the grains showed a gamma refractive index between 1.488 and 1.508. When heated, these two samples yielded X-ray patterns indicative of both clinoptilolite and heulandite (fig. 3*D*). This mixed type resembles the material from Nevada described by Shepard (1961), and a detailed study of it may throw light on factors that control the formation of heulandite and clinoptilolite.

Clinoptilolite, pseudomorphous after volcanic shards, formed early in the sandstones at low temperatures and shallow depths of burial. It is the characteristic zeolite in rocks of the northern half of the studied region and indicates what we shall call stage 1 of diagenesis.

Mordenite

In California, mordenite, a relatively minor zeolite most commonly associated with clinoptilolite, has been previously found with clinoptilolite in Miocene tuffs of the marine Obispo Formation of Surdam and Hall (1968) and in continental tuffaceous beds of Tertiary age in the Mojave Desert (Sheppard and Gude, 1964, 1969).

In the central Coast Ranges, small amounts of mordenite have been found only within the previously mentioned clinoptilolite-rich ash bed of locality 13, where it is localized as small stubby crystals along the borders of some opal (cristobalite) veins (figs. 2*D* and 2*E*). The close association with opal suggests that mordenite, whose Si/Al ratio is similar to that of clinoptilolite, formed from solutions with high silica activity (Coombs and others, 1959).

Heulandite

Heulandite typically grows on walls of fractures in sandstone, either as druses of minute tabular crystals (fig. 4*C*) or as sheaves of thin plates, like the sheaves of stilbite shown in figure 4*E*. The two minerals look much alike, although heulandite is generally much finer grained. Their X-ray patterns (Deer and others, 1963) are sufficiently different to distinguish one mineral from the other.

Fracture-filling heulandite has been found at localities 3, 8, 9, 10, 11, and 14, among which only locality 3 lies in the northern area characterized by the lowest stage of diagenesis. At most localities, the mineral is covered by coarse crystals of stilbite, which has a very similar crystal structure and chemical composition (Deer and others, 1963). With an average Si/Al ratio of around 3.0, heulandite and stilbite are distinctly less siliceous than clinoptilolite or mordenite (Si/Al = 5).

Figure 2.—Photomicrographs of thin sections illustrating modes of occurrence of zeolites and associated minerals.

A. Unaltered shards of rhyolitic glass (G) in lower part of Briones Sandstone of locality 6. Plane light. Such fresh glass is rare in the studied formations.

B. Zeolitized shards of a tuff bed in Briones Sandstone of locality 13. The shards may have hollow interiors (white) or centers of unaltered or altered glass. The rim of the shards has been converted to fibrous clinoptilolite (Cl). Plane light.

C. Section *B* under crossed nicols. The constant-exposure method used to obtain the photomicrographs exaggerates the apparent birefringence of the clinoptilolite fibers.

D. A vein of opal (O) in the tuff bed of preceding section *B-C*. The vein has a border zone rich in mordenite (M). Plane light.

E. Section *D* under crossed nicols. The opal consists mostly of specks of cristobalite, and tiny needles of mordenite are concentrated along the borders of the opal vein.

F. Cross section of the analcite-calcite vein shown in figure 4*A*. Analcite (A) grows on both walls of the fracture, and sparry calcite (C) fills the remaining space. Plane light.

G. Section *F* under crossed nicols. The analcite is birefringent and zoned.

H. The upper left half of this view of a vein from locality 9 is occupied by stilbite (S) crystals which are partly replaced by laumontite (L), the finer grained material occupying the lower right half. The marked rectangular area is shown enlarged below in photograph *I*. Crossed nicols.

I. An elongate section of a crystal of stilbite (S) that is partly replaced on all sides by laumontite (L). Crossed nicols.

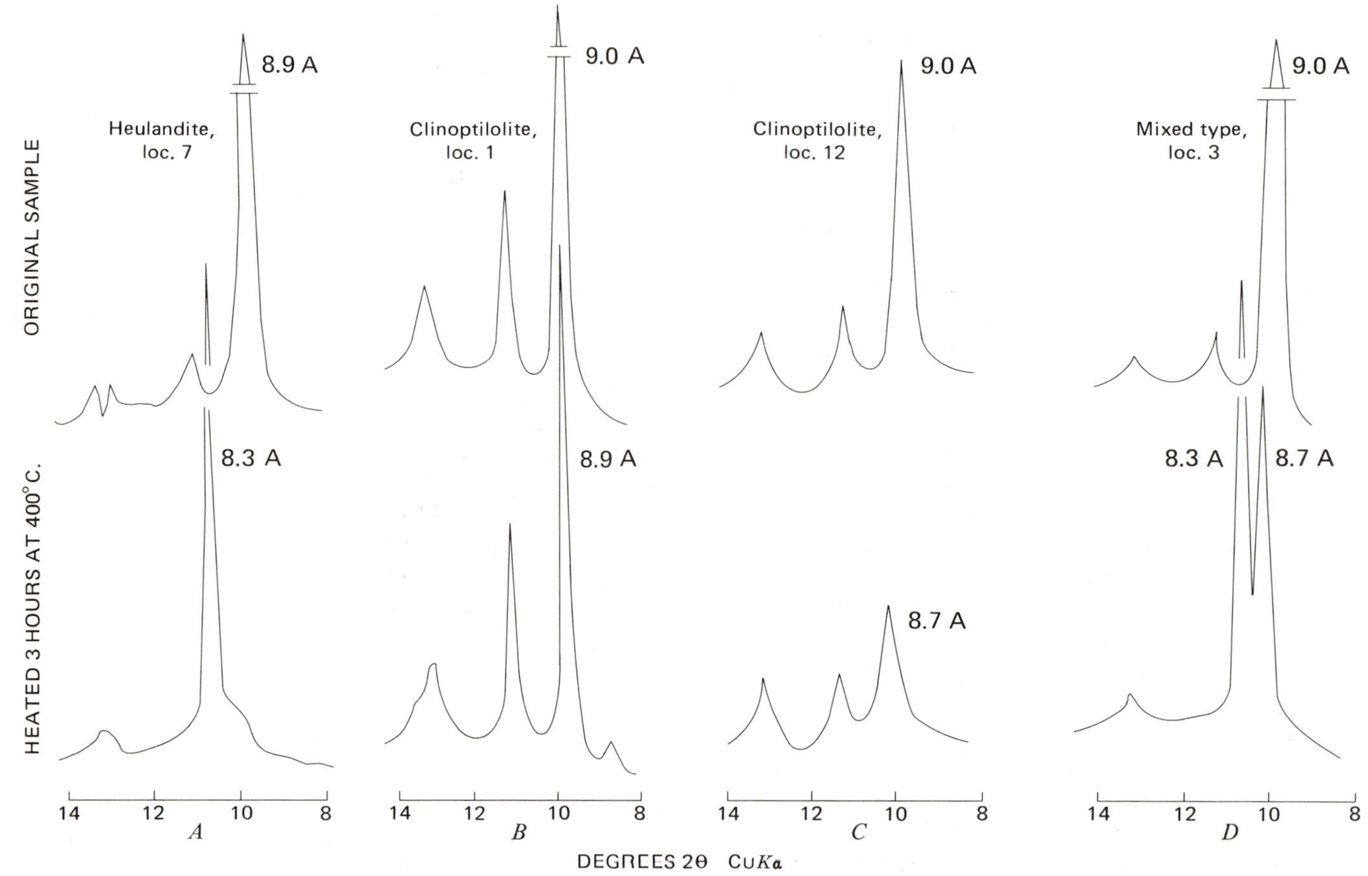

Figure 3.—X-ray diffractometer patterns of original and heated samples of heulandite-group minerals.

Stilbite

Stilbite is preeminent among fracture-filling zeolites, occurring exclusively in fractures as large and well-formed crystals. The mineral has been found at localities 3, 8, 9, 10, 11, 12, and 15, either as sheaves of glistening plates (fig. 4*E*) or as coarse druses (fig. 4*F*), commonly grown over finely crystallized heulandite. The frequent association of chemically and structurally similar stilbite and heulandite suggests that this pair of minerals represents a second stage of diagenesis, which is more advanced than the stage 1 of clinoptilolite. By the time of stage 2, the sediment probably would have been buried deeper into a hotter zone and hardened sufficiently to fracture under stress.

Locality 3 (fig. 1) is interpreted as an unusual spot where diagenetic stage 2 became developed locally in a region generally at rest in stage 1. The more numerous occurrences of stilbite-heulandite in the southern area were apparently formed while the rocks of the area were undergoing progressively more intense alteration toward diagenetic stage 3 characterized by laumontite. In the most intensely laumontized parts of the area, the stilbite-heulandite fracture fillings are replaced by laumontite.

Laumontite

Figure 5 illustrates the way in which laumontite fills joints and pervades the host sandstone throughout the southern part of the studied region. Where well developed, laumontite amounts to 5–10 percent by weight of the rock, as determined by an X-ray diffraction method that was calibrated with known mixtures of the mineral and a sandstone blank. Such percentages far exceed the percentage of clinoptilolite or other zeolites in the average Briones, so they could not have been attained solely through conversion of preexisting zeolites into laumontite. Much of the laumontite was produced through reaction of interstitial solutions with major constituents of sandstone like plagioclase, montmorillonite, and calcite (Madsen and Murata, 1970).

Stilbite, crystallized in joints at localities 9 and 12, is partially replaced by laumontite (figs. 2*H*, *I*), showing that temperature and pressure in the host rock had gone beyond those of stage 2 to those of stage 3. The temperature and pressure attained were probably similar to those observed in laumontite-bearing Miocene sandstones in the Tejon oil field of California, about 100°C and 320 bars hydrostatic pressure (Castano and Sparks, 1970). That the pressure-temperature

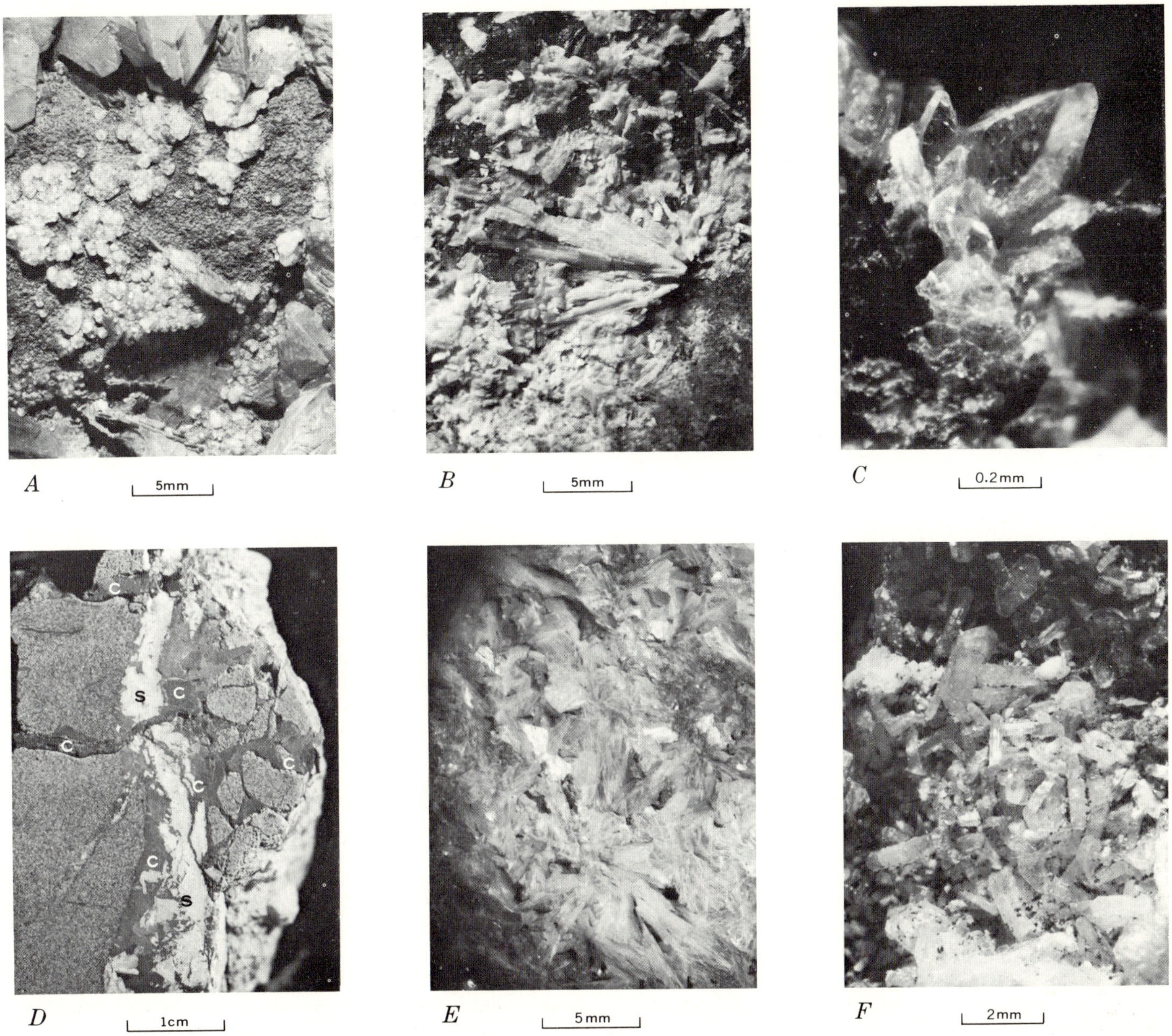

Figure 4.—Photomicrographs of zeolites and associated minerals of veins in Miocene sandstones. The direction of view, except for photographs *C* and *D*, is normal to the wall of the opened vein. Photograph *C* is an edgewise view of a heulandite druse; *D* is an edgewise view of a vein of stilbite.

A. Clusters of analcite trapezohedra (white) surrounded and overgrown by sparry calcite (gray). Oursan Sandstone of locality 7. A thin-section cut across this vein is shown in figure 2*F*.

B. A radiating group of unusually coarse prismatic crystals of laumontite in Briones Sandstone of locality 9.

C. Drusy heulandite in Briones Sandstone of locality 11. The minute crystals are tabular on (010) and elongate along the *c* axis. Commonly, they are overgrown by coarse stilbite like that of *E* below.

D. Sawed section of a fractured vein of stilbite (S) with the fractures filled by late sparry calcite (C); locality 10. Calcite is dark because it was stained with Alizarin Red S.

E. Stilbite consisting of radiating or irregularly stacked platy twin crystals in Briones Sandstone of locality 12.

F. Twin crystals of stilbite of more regular habit than those of *E*. Briones Sandstone of locality 8.

conditions did not exceed those appropriate for stage-3 laumontite is suggested by the apparent absence of higher grade minerals, such as wairakite, epidote, and lawsonite (Thompson, 1971; Liou, 1971).

The Si/Al ratio of the zeolites that characterize the three diagenetic stages decreases progressively as follows: clinoptilolite-mordenite, about 5; heulandite-stilbite, about 3; and laumontite, about 2. As noted by Kostov (1969), such a compositional progression must generally be explained in terms of an increase in temperature or a decrease in activity of

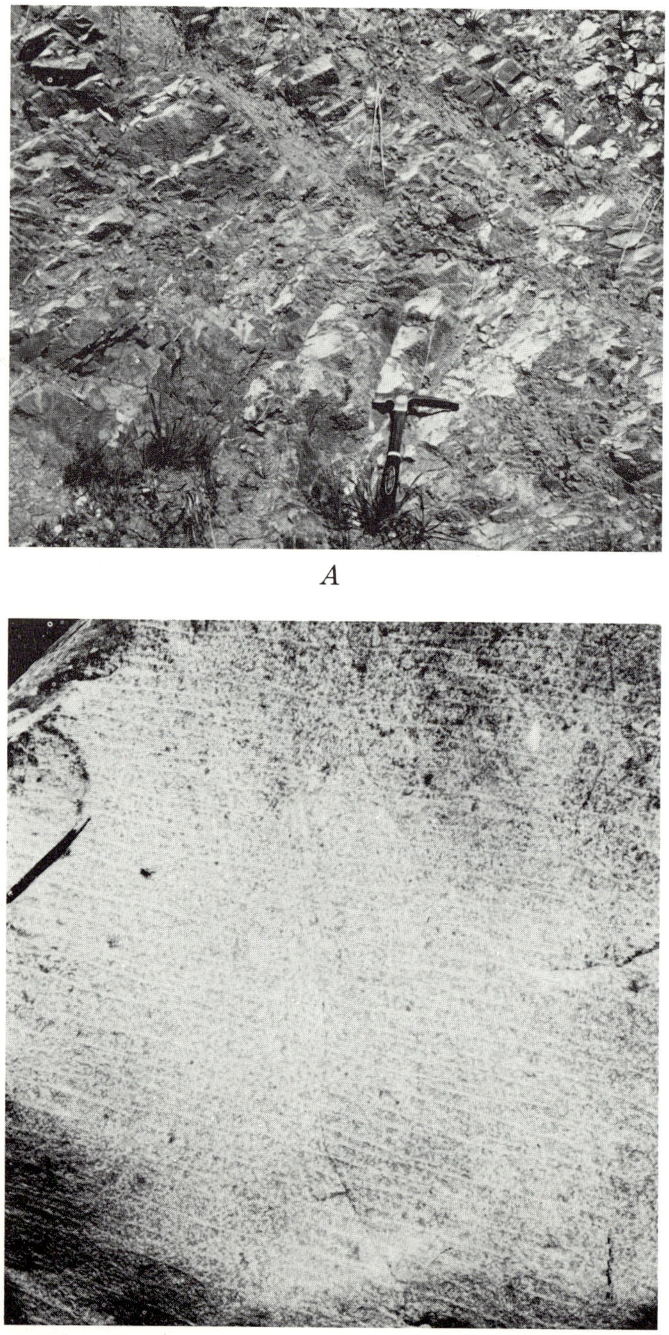

A

B

Figure 5.—Modes of occurrence of laumontite in the Briones Sandstone. *A*, white laumontite coating the walls of subparallel joints and reflecting the sunlight. The joints are nearly perpendicular to the bedding, which dips about 45° to the right. Laumontite is also dispersed throughout the sandstone. Locality 9. *B*, Laumontite dispersed through sandstone and also concentrated along bedding planes. Pencil is 14 cm long. Locality 12.

dissolved silica. The data on the geology and geography of zeolite occurrences in the central Coast Ranges favor the explanation based on increasing temperature.

Significance of laumontite occurrence

The Briones Sandstone is the principal host rock for laumontite, but only in the 30-mile stretch south of lat 37°40′ and west of Calaveras fault zone (fig. 1). Elsewhere, the sandstone and related formations generally have clinoptilolite as a characteristic diagenetic mineral. The strikingly restricted distribution of laumontite suggests that the Briones either differs compositionally or has undergone different pressure-temperature conditions of diagenesis in its northern and southern parts. Materials such as plagioclase, volcanic debris, montmorillonite, and calcite previously noted to be involved in the formation of laumontite (Madsen and Murata, 1970) are all present in the Briones Sandstone throughout the entire region. The widespread shell beds in the generally clean sands of the middle Briones point to shallow waters of open bays as the probable depositional environment. There are no indications of heterogeneities in the depositional environment which might have led to regional differences in salinity or composition of interstitial waters or in porosity of the sands. The localization of laumontite (fig. 1) thus cannot be explained in terms of the intrinsic properties of the Briones.

From the standpoint of depth metamorphism, the localization of laumontite could be understood if the Briones Sandstone of the southern area had been buried under a greater thickness of younger sedimentary deposits than elsewhere. But according to Crittenden (1951), the cover there (excluding localized Pleistocene deposits) is at most only about 2,000 feet thick stratigraphically, and to the north, others (Ham, 1952; Robinson, 1956; Hall, 1958) have found maximum thickness of cover 3,000–12,000 feet, just the opposite of what would be expected. Although these data are somewhat uncertain because the amount of post-Briones sediments that might have been eroded away is unknown, they suggest that laumontite of the southern area did not result from burial of the Briones under a thicker cover of sediments.

T. W. Dibblee, Jr., who recently remapped a large part of the region shown in figure 1, has stressed to us (oral commun., 1972) that the Briones and related formations are more strongly deformed in the southern than in the northern area. The tightly folded, overturned, and faulted Tularcitos syncline (fig. 1) is a dominant structural feature of the southern area (Crittenden, 1951), and it stands in sharp contrast to the generally more open folds to the north. It seems highly probable that the Briones of only the southern area was downfolded and faulted to depths where temperature and pressure were appropriate for laumontite generation. This interesting relation between intensity of tectonism and metamorphic grade has been noted elsewhere (Haller, 1962; Rast, 1962).

Analcite

The few places where we found analcite have not yielded enough information to put the mineral definitely within the three-stage scheme of diagenesis. Analcite occurs with clinoptilolite as minor cement of clasts in middle Miocene Hambre Sandstone at locality 8, and as well-formed trapezohedra (figs. *2F*, *2G*, and *4A*) in fractures in the middle Miocene Oursan Sandstone of locality 7, where it is associated with no other zeolite. A third locality is in the continental Pliocene Mulholland Formation of Ham (1952) of Cull Canyon in the region of locality 4, where analcite forms tiny spherical aggregates in a thin bed of bentonite. This occurrence in bentonite seems comparable to those in the lacustrine tuffs of the Green River Formation of Wyoming (Bradley, 1928).

The refractive index of analcite from locality 7 and from Cull Canyon falls in the range 1.484–1.486, which indicates a rather siliceous composition (Saha, 1959). X-ray determinations by the method of Saha (1961) on crystals from two different places in locality 7 uniformly gave a Si/Al ratio of 2.36, compared with the 2.00 of the conventional formula $NaAlSi_2O_6 \cdot H_2O$.

Chemical, more so than physical, factors seem to have been important in the genesis of analcite. Very likely, high-sodium alkaline and saline solutions (VanHouten, 1962; Hay, 1966; Baldar and Whittig, 1968; Boles, 1971), generated by processes unrelated to the main chemistry of regional diagenesis, were involved in forming analcite in diverse settings.

ISOTOPIC COMPOSITION OF CALCITE ASSOCIATED WITH ZEOLITES IN FRACTURES

Sparry calcite commonly occurs with zeolites in both sedimentary and altered igneous rocks, and Thompson (1971) has recently discussed the significance of this association. Among our samples, an obviously late calcite fills and transects a vein of stilbite (fig. *4D*), and calcite also fills voids in analcite-lined fractures (figs. *2F*, *2G*, *4A*). Similar laumontite-calcite veins have also been collected. The possibility that calcite can coexist with zeolite, on the basis of an equilibrium reaction of the type calcite + kaolinite + 2 quartz + $2H_2O$ = laumontite + CO_2, was considered by Thompson, who concluded that most associations of calcite with zeolite are nonequilibrium assemblages.

With the hope of shedding light on the origin of calcite that coexists with zeolite, samples from four veins were submitted for isotopic analysis; the results are given in table 2.

As the last three lines of table 2 show, the ranges of carbon and oxygen isotopic compositions in calcite formed in the hydrothermal environment (exemplified by lead-zinc deposits) and those in calcite deposited from cool fresh water coincide, except that carbon can be much lighter in some fresh-water calcites. The isotopic compositions of samples 1, 2, and 4 fall in the coincident ranges, so whether these associates of zeolites were formed at low or high temperatures is unknown. The excessively light carbon (−23.9 per mil) of sample 3, however, strongly suggests very late deposition from ground water containing more than usual amounts of bicarbonate derived from soil humus.

Table 2.—*Isotopic analyses of sparry calcite associated with zeolite in the central Coast Ranges and of comparative calcites from other localities*

Locality	Sample No.	Associated mineral	δO^{18} (per mil SMOW)[1]	δC^{13} (per mil PDB)[2]	Analyst or reference
11.	1	Stilbite	+15.5	−7.5	J. D. Gleason.
9.	2	Laumontite	+12.0	−6.6	Do.
12.	3	do	+23.5	−23.9	J. R. O'Neil.
7.	4	Analcite	+22.5	+.6	J. D. Gleason.
Mexico		Pb-Zn ores	+11 to +20	−8 to −1	Rye (1966).
Kansas		do	+15 to +23	−7 to −1	Hall and Friedman (1969).
Worldwide		Fresh-water calcite	+9 to +24	−18 to −3	Clayton and Degens (1959); Graf (1960); O'Neil and Barnes (1971).

[1] SMOW, standard mean ocean water.
[2] PDB, Pee Dee Belemnite standard.

A similar late origin for the other samples of calcite is not excluded by the isotopic data. Elementary considerations, such as the median position of calcite in the veins (fig. *2F*), the cutting of some zeolite veins by calcite (fig. *4D*), and the occurrence of zeolites in some veins devoid of calcite, also suggest that zeolite and calcite formed successively, not simultaneously, and were not in equilibrium with each other.

REFERENCES CITED

Baldar, N. A., and Whittig, L. D., 1968, Occurrence and synthesis of soil zeolites: Soil Sci. Soc. Am. Proc., v. 32, p. 235–240.

Boles, J. R., 1971, Synthesis of analcime from natural heulandite and clinoptilolite: Am. Mineralogist, v. 56, nos. 9–10, p. 1724–1734.

Brabb, E. E., Sonneman, H. S., and Switzer, J. R., Jr., compilers, 1971, Geologic map of the Mount Diablo-Byron area, Contra Costa, Alameda, and San Joaquin Counties, California: U.S. Geol. Survey open-file rept., scale 1:62,500.

Bradley, W. H., 1928, Zeolite beds in the Green River Formation: Science, v. 67, p. 73–74.

Bramlette, M. N., and Posnjak, Eugen, 1933, Zeolitic alteration of pyroclastics: Am. Mineralogist, v. 18, no. 4, p. 167–171.

Campbell, A. S., and Fyfe, W. S., 1960, Hydroxyl-ion catalysis of the hydrothermal crystallization of amorphous silica; a possible high-temperature indicator: Am. Mineralogist, v. 45, nos. 3–4, p. 464–468.

Castano, J. R., and Sparks, D. M., 1970, Interpretation of vitrinite reflectance measurements in sedimentary rocks and determination of burial history using vitrinite reflectance and authigenic minerals: Geol. Soc. America Abs. with Programs, v. 2, no. 7, p. 516–517.

Clayton, R. N., and Degens, E. T., 1959, Use of carbon isotope analysis of carbonates for differentiating fresh-water and marine sediments: Am. Assoc. Petroleum Geologists Bull., v. 43, no. 4, p. 890–897.

Coombs, D. S., 1954, The nature and alteration of some Triassic sediments from Southland, New Zealand: Royal Soc. New Zealand Trans., v. 82, pt. 1, p. 65–109.

Coombs, D. S., Ellis, J. A., Fyfe, W. S., and Taylor, A. M., 1959, The zeolite facies, with comments on the interpretation of hydrothermal synthesis: Geochim. et Cosmochim. Acta, v. 17, nos. 1–2, p. 53–107.

Crittenden, M. D., 1951, Geology of the San Jose-Mount Hamilton Area, California: California Div. Mines and Geology Bull. 157, 74 p.

Deer, W. A., Howie, R. A., and Zussman, J., 1963, Rock-forming minerals, v. 4, Framework silicates: London, Longmans, Green, and Co., 435 p.

Fyfe, W. S., and Mackenzie, W. S., 1969, Aspects of experimental petrology: Earth-Sci. Rev., v. 5, no. 3, p. 185–215.

Graf, D. L., 1960, Geochemistry of carbonate sediments and sedimentary carbonate rocks—Pt. 4A, Isotopic composition, chemical analysis: Illinois Geol. Survey Circ. 308, 42 p.

Hall, C. A., Jr., 1958, Geology and paleontology of the Pleasanton Area, Alameda and Contra Costa Counties, California: California Univ. Pubs. Geol. Sci., v. 34, no. 1, p. 1–90.

Hall, W. E., and Friedman, Irving, 1969, Oxygen and carbon isotopic composition of ore and host rock of selected Mississippi Valley deposits, *in* Geological Survey Research 1969: U.S. Geol. Survey Prof. Paper 650-C, p. C140–C148.

Haller, J., 1962, Structural control of regional metamorphism in East Greenland Caledonides: Geol. Soc. London Proc., no. 1594, p. 21–25.

Ham, C. K., 1952, Geology of Las Trampas Ridge, Berkeley Hills, California: California Div. Mines and Geology Spec. Rept. 22, 26 p.

Hathaway, J. C., and Sachs, P. L., 1965, Sepiolite and clinoptilolite from the Mid-Atlantic Ridge: Am. Mineralogist, v. 50, nos. 7–8, p. 852–867.

Hay, R. L., 1963, Stratigraphy and zeolitic diagenesis of the John Day Formation of Oregon: California Univ. Pubs. Geol. Sci., v. 42, p. 199–262.

—— 1964, Phillipsite of saline lakes and soils: Am. Mineralogist, v. 49, nos. 9–10, p. 1366–1387.

—— 1966, Zeolites and zeolitic reactions in sedimentary rocks: Geol. Soc. America Spec. Paper 85, 130 p.

Honda, Sakuro, and Muffler, L. J. P., 1970, Hydrothermal alteration in core from research drill hole Y-1, Upper Geyser Basin, Yellowstone National Park, Wyoming: Am. Mineralogist, v. 55, nos. 9–10, p. 1714–1737.

Hoover, D. L., 1968, Genesis of zeolites, Nevada Test Site, *in* Eckel, E. B., ed., Nevada Test Site: Geol. Soc. America Mem. 110, p. 275–284.

Iijima, Azuma, and Utada, Minoru, 1971, Present-day zeolitic diagenesis of the Neogene geosynclinal deposits in the Niigata oilfield, Japan, *in* Molecular sieve zeolites [Pt.] 1: Am. Chem. Soc. Advances in Chemistry Ser., no. 101, p. 342–349.

Jennings, C. W., and Burnett, J. L., 1961, Geologic map of California, San Francisco sheet: California Div. Mines and Geology Map Sheet, scale 1:250,000.

Koenig, J. B., 1963, Geologic map of California, Santa Rosa sheet: California Div. Mines and Geology Map Sheet, scale 1:250,000.

Kostov, Ivan, 1969, Zoning in the development of the volcanogenic zeolites: Neues Jahrb. Mineralogie Abh., v. 3, p. 264–278.

Lawson A. C., 1914, Description of the San Francisco district; Tamalpais, San Francisco, Concord, San Mateo, and Hayward quadrangles: U.S. Geol. Survey Geol. Atlas, Folio 193, 24 p.

Lerbekmo, J. F., 1957, Authigenic montmorillonoid cement in andesitic sandstones of central California: Jour. Sed. Petrology, v. 27, no. 3, p. 298–305.

Liou, J. G., 1971, Stilbite-laumontite equilibrium: Contr. Mineralogy and Petrology, v. 31, p. 171–177.

Madsen, B. M., and Murata, K. J., 1970, Occurrence of laumontite in Tertiary sandstones of the central Coast Ranges, California, *in* Geological Survey Research 1970: U.S. Geol. Survey Prof. Paper 700-D, p. D188–D195.

Mason, B. H., and Sand, L. B., 1960, Clinoptilolite from Patagonia—The relationship between clinoptilolite and heulandite: Am. Mineralogist, v. 45, nos. 3–4, p. 341–350.

Moiola, R. J., 1970, Authigenic zeolites and K-feldspar in the Esmeralda Formation, Nevada: Am. Mineralogist, v. 55, nos. 9–10, p. 1681–1691.

Mumpton, F. A., 1960, Clinoptilolite redefined: Am. Mineralogist, v. 45, nos. 3–4, p. 351–369.

Murata, K. J., and Erd, R. C., 1964, Composition of sediments from the experimental Mohole project (Guadalupe site): Jour. Sed. Petrology, v. 34, no. 3, p. 633–655.

O'Neil, J. R., and Barnes, Ivan, 1971, C^{13} and O^{18} compositions in some fresh-water carbonates associated with ultramafic rocks and serpentinites: Geochim. et Cosmochim. Acta, v. 35, no. 7, p. 687–697.

Page, B. M., 1966, Geology of the Coast Ranges of California, *in* Bailey, E. H., ed., Geology of northern California: California Div. Mines and Geology Bull. 190, p. 255–276.

Peterson, N. M. A., and others, 1970, Deep Sea Drilling Project—Initial Rept., v. 2: Washington, U.S. Govt. Printing Office, 501 p.

Rast, Nicholas, 1962, The relationship between tectonic deformation and regional metamorphism. Geol. Soc. London Proc., no. 1594, p. 25–26.

Robinson, G. D., 1956, Geology of the Hayward quadrangle, California: U.S. Geol. Survey Geol. Quad. Map GQ-88.

Rogers, T. H., 1966, Geologic map of California, San Jose sheet: California Div. Mines and Geology Map Sheet, scale 1:250,000.

Rye, R. O., 1966, The carbon, hydrogen, and oxygen isotopic composition of the hydrothermal fluids responsible for the lead-zinc deposits at Providencia, Zacatecas, Mexico: Econ. Geology, v. 61, no. 8, p. 1399–1427.

Saha, Prasenjit, 1959, Geochemical and X-ray investigation of natural and synthetic analcites: Am. Mineralogist, v. 44, nos. 3–4, p. 300–313.

—— 1961, The system $NaAlSiO_4$ (nepheline)–$NaAlSi_3O_8$ (albite)–H_2O: Am. Mineralogist, v. 46, nos. 7–8, p. 859–884.

Senderov, E. E., and Khitarov, N. I., 1970, Zeolites, their synthesis and conditions of formation in nature: Moscow, Nauka Publishing House, 283 p. [In Russian].

Shepard, A. O., 1961, A heulandite-like mineral associated with clinoptilolite in tuffs of Oak Springs Formation, Nevada Test Site, Nye County, Nevada: Art. 264 *in* U.S. Geol. Survey Prof. Paper 424-C, p. C320–C322.

Shepard, A. O., and Starkey, H. C., 1964, Effect of cation exchange on the thermal behavior of heulandite and clinoptilolite: Art. 138 *in* U.S. Geol. Survey Prof. Paper 475-D, p. D89–D92.

Sheppard, R. A., 1971, Clinoptilolite of possible economic value in sedimentary deposits of the conterminous United States: U.S. Geol. Survey Bull. 1332-B, p. B1–B15.

Sheppard, R. A., and Gude, A. J., 1964, Reconnaissance of zeolite deposits in tuffaceous rocks of the western Mojave Desert and vicinity, California, *in* Geological Survey Research 1964: U.S. Geol. Survey Prof. Paper 501-C, p. C114–C116.

—— 1969, Diagenesis of tuffs in the Barstow Formation, Mud Hills, San Bernardino County, California: U.S. Geol. Survey Prof. Paper 634, 35 p.

Steiner, Alfred, 1953, Hydrothermal rock alteration at Wairakei, New Zealand: Econ. Geology, v. 48, no. 1, p. 1–13.

Strand, R. G., and Koenig, J. B., 1965, Geologic map of California, Sacramento sheet: California Div. Mines and Geology Map Sheet, scale 1:250,000.

Surdam, R. C., and Hall, C. A., 1968, Zeolitization of the Obispo Formation, Coast Ranges of California [abs.]: Geol. Soc. America Spec. Paper 101, p. 338.

Taliaferro, N. L., 1933, The relation of volcanism to diatomaceous and associated siliceous sediments: California Univ. Pubs. Geol. Sci., v. 23, no. 1, p. 1–56.

—— 1943, Geologic history and structure of the central Coast Ranges of California: California Div. Mines and Geology Bull. 118, p. 119–163.

Thompson, A. B., 1970, Laumontite equilibria and the zeolite facies: Am. Jour. Sci., v. 269, p. 267–275.

—— 1971, PCO_2 in low-grade metamorphism; zeolite, carbonate, clay mineral, prehnite relations in the system $CaO-Al_2O_3-SiO_2-CO_2-H_2O$: Contr. Mineralogy and Petrology, v. 33, p. 145–161.

Trask, P. D., 1922, The Briones formation of Middle California: California Univ. Pubs. Geol. Sci., v. 13, p. 133–174.

Utada, Minoru, 1970, Occurrence and distribution of authigenic zeolites in the Neogene pyroclastic rocks in Japan: Tokyo Univ., Coll. Gen. Educ., Sci. Paper, v. 20, no. 2, p. 191–262.

VanHouten, F. B., 1962, Cyclic sedimentation and the origin of analcime-rich Upper Triassic Lockatong Formation, west-central New Jersey and adjacent Pennsylvania: Am. Jour. Sci., v. 260, p. 561–576.

Weaver, C. E., 1949, Geology of the Coast Ranges immediately north of the San Francisco Bay region, California: Geol. Soc. America Mem. 35, 242 p.

Jour. Research U.S. Geol. Survey
Vol. 1, No. 3, May-June 1973, p. 267—272

THE CHEMISTRY OF FIVE ACCESSORY ROCK-FORMING APATITES

By DONALD E. LEE, ELAINE L. MUNSON BRANDT,
RICHARD E. VAN LOENEN; and HARRY J. ROSE, JR.,
Denver, Colo.; Washington, D.C.

Abstract.—Chemical and physical data are given for five samples of rock-forming apatite from diverse geologic environments in Nevada and Colorado. Four of these apatites contain rare-earth assemblages in which the cerium group is well represented but the yttrium group predominates. The fifth apatite contains a highly fractionated assemblage of the lighter (cerium group) rare earths similar to the assemblage typical of alkalic rocks.

Before the advent of modern techniques of mineral purification many minerals being considered for analysis were selected on the basis of their easy availablity, and thus many of the early analyses were performed on minerals from pegmatites, tactites, or drusy cavities, from which large crystals could be handpicked with minimal effort. Fewer analyses were performed on minerals from some of the more common igneous and metamorphic rocks, especially rather fine-grained rocks. During the past 20 years or so, many analyses of the more common rock-forming minerals have been published. However, for some of the accessory (as opposed to essential) minerals—including apatite—there still is a dearth of chemical data on samples recovered from some of the more common rock types. This paper presents chemical data for four samples of accessory apatite and one sample of placer apatite.

The apatites described here were purified by the same methods used on accessory apatites from the southern Snake Range, Nev. (Lee and others, 1973). Indices of refraction were determined by the immersion method, using a spindle stage (Wilcox, 1959) and focal masking technique (Wilcox, 1962). Cell parameters were obtained by least-squares refinement of powder diffractometer data, using an internal standard of CaF_2 and a self-indexing computer program developed by Evans, Appleman, and Handwerker (1963).

Semiquantitative spectrographic results are based on their identity with geometric brackets whose boundaries are 1.2, 0.83, 0.56, 0.38, 0.26, 0.18, 0.12, and so forth, and are reported arbitrarily as midpoints of these brackets, 1., 0.7, 0.5, 0.3, 0.2, 0.15, and 0.1, respectively. The precision of a reported value is approximately one bracket at 68-percent confidence, or two brackets at 95-percent confidence.

FIELD SETTING OF APATITES

Apatite 244-MW-60 was recovered from a muscovite-rich granitoid rock collected at lat 39°35′55″ N.; long 114°7′55″ W., in the Kern Mountains of White Pine County, Nev. This granitoid rock is almost identical with the (southern Snake Range) Pole Canyon—Can Young Canyon intrusive type described in detail by Lee and Van Loenen (1971, p. 5, 38, 39), who ascribed its distinctive nature to assimilation of argillite. According to R. K. Hose and M. C. Blake, Jr. (oral commun., 1971), who prepared the geologic map of White Pine County, the distinctive nature of the granitoid rock from which apatite 244-MW-60 was recovered might also result from assimilation of argillite. Whatever the origin, the great similarity of these two granitoid rocks extends to the peculiar apatite-zircon relation described by Lee and Van Loenen (1971, p. 5, 39) and illustrated by Lee and others (1973, fig. 2). In each rock almost all the zircon is present as tiny, acicular inclusions in large, equant, rather poorly formed, and sparsely distributed apatite crystals.

Apatite 300-DL-64 was recovered from a placer concentrate collected at the mouth of Hampton Creek at lat 39°14′45″ N.; long 114°3′50″ W., in White Pine County, Nev. Except for some Middle Cambrian limestones resting above a thrust surface, all the Hampton Creek drainage is underlain by Lower Cambrian metaquartzites and metashales, as shown on the geologic map of White Pine County, Nev. (Hose and Blake, 1970). The ultimate environment(s) in which the crystals of apatite 300-DL-64 may have formed is problematical. However, the sample analyzed appeared to be homogeneous, for it gave an X-ray diffraction pattern with sharp peaks which in turn gave a good refinement of the unit cell parameters (table 1). Moreover, the Lower Cambrian metasedimentary rocks were the source of most or perhaps almost all of this placer apatite. In connection with potassium-argon age studies in the area (Lee and others, 1970; and unpub. data), we have done mineral separation work on several samples of these metasedimentary rocks. Minor amounts of apatite were commonly recovered, and petrographic study shows the apatite to be present as well-formed crystals that appear to be part of the metamorphic assemblage.

Table 1.—*Analytical data for five apatites*

[Descriptions of sample localities, methods of determination of physical properties, and general limitations of the semiquantitative method are given in text. Chemical analyses by E. L. Munson Brandt; semiquantitative analyses by L. D. Forshey]

Area of collection	White Pine County, Nev.			Elko County Nev.	Gilpin County, Colo.
Sample No.	244-MW-60	300-DL-64	301-DL-65	363-DL-66	1-CC
Physical properties					
Indices of refraction:					
ϵ (±0.001)	1.630	.....	1.630	1.634	1.630
ω (±0.001)	1.632	.....	1.632	1.640	1.632
$\omega-\epsilon$	.002	.....	.002	.006	.002
Specific gravity:					
Observed	3.20±.01	3.20±.01	3.20±.01	[1] 3.226±.005	3.20±.01
Calculated	3.21	3.22	3.22	3.227	.....
Unit cell parameters:					
a (±0.001 A)	9.367	9.373	9.366	9.407	9.376
c (±0.001 A)	6.880	6.875	6.880	6.876	6.877
c/a	.734	.733	.734	.731	.733
Cell volume:					
Measured (±0.2 A^3)	522.9	523.1	522.6	527.0	523.6
Calculated	523.7	525.6	525.6	527.2	....
Chemical analyses (weight percent)					
SiO_2	0.06	0.04	0.24	0.55	0.11
Al_2O_3	.07	.06	.09	.04	.....
Fe_2O_3	.06	.02	.05	.14	.05
FeO	.03	.12	.04	.24	.04
MgO	.....	.05	......	.....	.....
CaO	54.54	54.97	54.21	53.91	55.09
Na_2O	.07	.05	......	.10	.....
K_2O	.01	.01	......	.01	.....
H_2O+	.....	.00	......	.....	.....
H_2O-	.....	.00	.....	.....	.....
P_2O_5	42.22	42.21	41.78	41.13	.....
MnO	.11	.08	.15	.08	.....
Cl	.....	.02	.....	.71	.....
F	3.64	2.98	3.49	2.93	2.92
[2] R_2O_3	.41	.29	.88	1.69	.39
Insoluble residues[3]	.59	.22	.36	.13	.07
Subtotal	101.81	101.06	101.29	101.66	.....
Less O≡Cl,F	1.53	1.25	1.47	1.23	.....
Total	100.28	99.81	99.82	100.43	.....

Ions on basis of 26(O,OH,F,Cl)

	244-MW-60		300-DL-64		301-DL-65		363-DL-66		1-CC
P	6.024	6.034	6.048	6.055	5.996	6.037	5.930	6.024	.....
Si	.010		.007		.041		.094		.....
Al	.014		.012		.018		.008		.....
Fe^{3+}	.008		.003		.006		.018		.....
Fe^{2+}	.004		.017		.006		.034		.....
Mg	.....		.013		.....		.....		.....
Mn	.016	9.940	.012	10.061	.022	9.954	.012	10.048	.....
Ca	9.848		9.968		9.847		9.836		.....
Na	.023		.016		.....		.033		.....
K	.002		.002		.....		.002		.....
[4] Ce^{3+}	.025		.018		.055		.105		.....
F	1.940	1.940	1.595	1.601	1.871	1.871	1.578	1.783	.....
Cl	.....		.006		....		.205		.....

Table 1.—*Analytical data for five apatites*—Continued

[Descriptions of sample localities, methods of determination of physical properties, and general limitations of the semiquantitative method are given in text. Chemical analyses by E. L. Munson Brandt; semiquantitative analyses by L. D. Forshey]

Area of collection	White Pine County, Nev.			Elko County Nev.	Gilpin County, Colo.
Sample No.	244-MW-60	300-DL-64	301-DL-65	363-DL-66	1-CC
Semiquantitative spectrographic analyses (weight percent)					
Ba	0.0002	0.0002	0.0003	0.0005	0.0002
Cu	.0005	.0003	.0005	.005	.0007
Pb	.001	.0015	.0015	.0015	.001
Sr	.05	.05	.03	.15	.03
Ti	.005	.007	.01	.0002	.002
V	0	0	.0015	.007	.0007
Zr	.15	.01	.005	0	.003

[1] Specific gravity of sample 363-DL-66 was determined with greater precision than others.
[2] Rare-earth oxide precipitates. See table 2 for analyses.
[3] Insoluble in 1:1 HCl at 100°C. Results of X-ray diffraction work on these insoluble residues are given in text.
[4] Each rare-earth oxide precipitate calculated as Ce_2O_3 for sake of simplicity.

Apatite 301-DL-65 was recovered from a xenolith (of shaly quartzite?) collected at lat 38°56′49″ N.; long 114°16′26″ W., within the area of a detailed field and laboratory study by Lee and Van Loenen (1971).

Apatite 363-DL-66 was recovered from a granitoid rock collected at lat 40°20′55″ N.; long 114°34′ W., in the upper drainage of Cougar Canyon of the Dolly Varden Mountains, Elko County, Nev. This rock is the "augite monzonite" of Snow (1964, p. 69, 78), who described the various igneous rock types exposed in the area. On the basis of our mineral separation work we estimate that this apatite makes up more than 1 percent of the rock from which it was recovered.

Apatite 1-CC was recovered from a Precambrian metamorphic rock collected at lat 39°47′49″ N.; long 105°30′25″ W., about 1 mile south-southeast of Central City in Gilpin County, Colo. The rock is a fine-grained biotite-rich schist that occurs as a layer about 3 inches thick within a migmatitic biotite gneiss.

APATITE ANALYSES

Chemical analyses of the apatites (table 1) are calculated on the basis of 26(O,OH,F,Cl) to the apatite formula $Ca_5(PO_4)_3$ (F,Cl,OH), using the computer program described by Jackson, Stevens, and Bowen (1967).

Each analysis includes the weight percent of material insoluble in 1:1 HCl at 100°C., giving a good indication of the degree of purity of the apatites analyzed. Amount of impurity (insoluble material) ranges from 0.07 weight percent of apatite 1-CC to 0.54 weight percent in apatite 244-MW-60, and in each apatite probably all the insoluble material was present as inclusions in the apatite grains.

Each analysis also includes weight percent of the rare-earth oxide precipitate recovered. X-ray spectrographic analyses of these precipitates are calculated to atomic percent of total rare earths in each of the apatites (table 2) and discussed in some detail later in this paper.

The compositions (table 1) range from about 79 to 92 mole percent end-member fluorapatite. Sample 363-DL-66 is about 10 mole percent chlorapatite; the other four minerals are for the most part hydroxyfluorapatites, as indicated by the indices of refraction and unit cell parameters listed in table 1 (See Deer, Howie, and Zussman, 1962, p. 324, 331). There was enough material for determination of $H_2O(+)$ in only sample 300-DL-64. Each apatite in table 1 completely lacked effervescence when immersed in 1:1 HCl at 100°C., indicating absence of the carbonate ion.

Aside from rare earths, only minor amounts of other cations proxy for Ca^{2+} in the structural formulas (table 1). There is very nearly a straight-line relation between amounts of Si and rare earths present in the structural formulas, owing probably to the coupled $Si^{4+}RE^{3+,4+} \leftrightharpoons P^{5+}Ca^{2+}$ substitution.

The insoluble residues (table 1) were identified by means of X-ray diffraction study as follows: 244-MW-60, predominantly zircon; 300-DL-64, subequal amounts of quartz and zircon; and the other three, predominantly quartz. We attribute the zirconium values (table 1) to zircon inclusions in the apatite (0.02 weight percent zircon about equivalent to 100 ppm zirconium). The tiny amounts of the other minor elements listed most probably are present in the crystal structures of the apatites.

There are several methods of assessing the degree of fractionation of rare earths included in the structures of minerals from various geologic environments, a subject of considerable interest. Murata, Rose, and Carron (1953) pro-

Table 2.—*Analyses of rare-earth precipitates and calculation of* $\Sigma(La+Ce+Pr)$ *for apatites in table 1*

Sample No.	244-MW-60	300-DL-64	301-DL-65	363-DL-66	1-CC
Weight percent of rare-earth precipitate[1]					
Y_2O_3	36.7	28.9	40.5	2.95	34.7
La_2O_3	3.11	1.85	2.53	21.3	1.76
CeO_2	11.0	6.71	9.16	41.6	7.06
Pr_2O_3	1.98	1.34	1.93	5.11	1.71
Nd_2O_3	10.5	7.73	10.4	14.3	9.47
Sm_2O_3	5.65	4.40	5.54	3.80	5.00
Eu_2O_3	1.13	1.85	1.20	1.69	1.47
Gd_2O_3	5.31	4.86	5.04	1.52	4.53
Tb_2O_3	1.69	1.62	1.45	.42	1.47
Dy_2O_3	6.79	7.27	6.39	.51	7.47
Ho_2O_3	2.26	2.18	2.17	.0	1.88
Er_2O_3	2.88	2.31	2.84	.21	3.00
Tm_2O_3	.62	.60	.77	.08	.71
Yb_2O_3	1.75	1.53	2.34	.0	2.76
Lu_2O_3	.90	.83	1.01	.0	.94
Total	92.27	73.98	93.27	93.40	83.88
Atomic percent of total rare earths in apatite					
Y	50.81	50.25	54.43	4.65	52.63
La	2.98	2.23	2.36	23.31	1.85
Ce	10.00	7.65	8.40	43.11	7.03
Pr	1.88	1.60	1.77	5.53	1.78
Nd	9.75	9.02	9.38	15.16	9.64
Sm	5.06	4.95	4.85	3.89	4.91
Eu	1.01	2.06	1.04	1.71	1.43
Gd	4.57	5.27	4.22	1.50	4.28
Tb	1.44	1.74	1.20	.40	1.38
Dy	5.68	7.64	5.20	.48	6.86
Ho	1.87	2.27	1.73	.0	1.70
Er	2.36	2.37	2.25	.19	2.68
Tm	.50	.61	.60	.07	.63
Yb	1.39	1.52	1.80	.0	2.39
Lu	.70	.82	.77	.0	.81
Total	100.00	100.00	100.00	100.00	100.00
$\Sigma(La+Ce+Pr)$	14.86	11.48	12.53	69.95	10.66

[1] X-ray spectrographic analysis by Frank Cuttitta, Ralph Christian, and Harry J. Rose, Jr. Sc_2O_3 not detected. Low totals probably due to presence of filter-paper ash in precipitate.

posed the quantity $\Sigma(La+Ce+Pr)$ in atomic percent of total rare-earth elements as a numerical index of the composition and stage of fractionation attained by the rare-earth elements. Thus higher values of $\Sigma(La+Ce+Pr)$ represent greater enrichment of the lighter, more basic rare-earth elements. Apatite 363-DL-66 has a sigma value of about 70, representing a much lighter assemblage of rare earths than any of the other four (with sigmas of 10.7–14.9, table 2).

Fleischer and Altschuler (1969, p. 729) based their discussion of the fractionation of lanthanides (excluding yttrium) on a triangular diagram with corners featuring (in atomic percent) the groups La–Nd, Sm–Ho, and Er–Lu. If the results in table

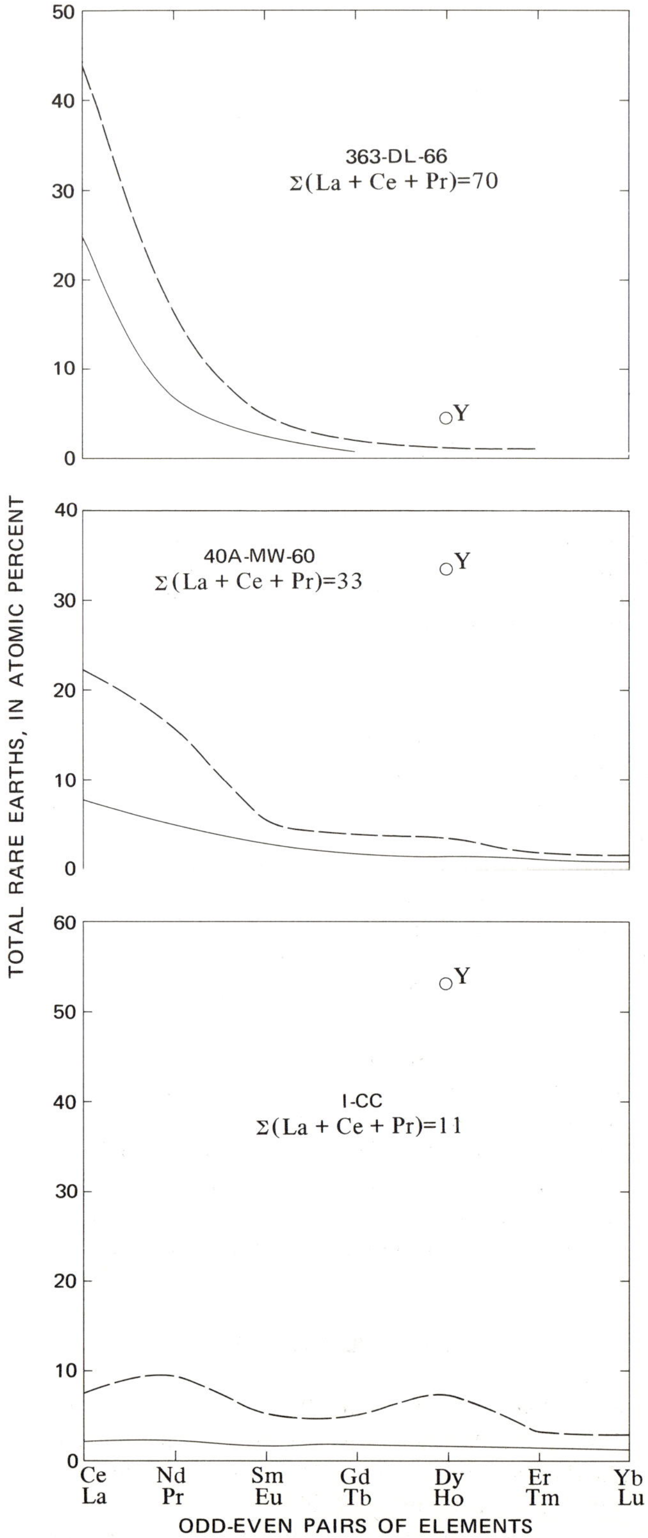

Figure 1.—Range of distribution of rare earths shown by three apatites, with $\Sigma(La+Ce+Pr)$ value for each. Data for apatite 40A-MW-60 from Lee, Van Loenen, and Mays (1973); data for other two from table 2, this report. The relationship of yttritum (Y) to the other rare earths is indicated. Odd-even pairs of elements are arranged, left to right, in order of increasing atomic number.

2 are plotted on such a diagram, they include nearly the whole range of lanthanide compositions published for apatites from various environments, excluding a few apatites from pegmatites that show an extreme concentration of the heavier rare earths.

Adams (1969) summarized the several mechanisms (ionic radii differences, basicity, and accommodation in crystal lattices) that may contribute to fractionation of the lanthanide group of elements in rare-earth-bearing minerals. He illustrated lanthanide assemblages found in various minerals by means of graphs plotted in the form suggested by Semenov and Barinskii (1958), in which odd-even pairs of elements are arranged in order of increasing atomic number along the abscissa, and abundance in atomic percent along the ordinate.

The rare-earth assemblages of apatites 363-DL-66 and 1-CC are plotted in this way (fig. 1). Graphs for the other three apatites (table 2) are very similar to the one for 1-CC. A plot of the rare-earth assemblage present in apatite 40A-MW-60, from a hybrid granitoid rock (Lee and others, 1973), is included in figure 1. Fractionation of lanthanides in apatite 363-DL-66 is similar to that found in allanite, or even in bastnaesite (Adams, 1969, figs. 4*C* and 1*C*, respectively), while the assemblage in apatite 1-CC is similar to that found in gadolinite (Adams, 1969, fig. 1*E*). The plot for 40A-MW-60 does not resemble very closely any of the plots for various minerals featured by Adams (1969). As Fleischer and Altschuler (1969, p. 729) stated, "* * * the lanthanides in apatite * * * vary greatly in composition." Adams (1969, p. C43) also mentioned apatite as a mineral with a tolerance for all the rare earths, and a mineral which may therefore be a valuable guide "to changes in rare-earth composition that have taken place during the development of the rocks in which they are found."

The changes in rare-earth composition that took place during the development of the rock from which apatite 363-DL-66 was recovered may be similar to processes that lead to the formation of alkalic rocks and carbonatites. Goldschmidt, Hauptmann, and Peters (1933) and Goldschmidt (1937) first recognized the unusual abundance of rare-earth elements and the predominance of the most basic (lightest) of these elements in alkalic rocks, and Murata, Ross, Carron, and Glass (1957) emphasized the fact that cerium-earth minerals from alkalic rocks and carbonatites are rich in the most basic rare earths. Moreover, apatite is commonly well developed in alkalic rocks and carbonatites (see for example Deer, Howie, and Zussman, 1962, p. 333), and apatite 363-DL-66 makes up more than 1 percent of the host rock, as well as being unusually rich in total rare earths (table 1). Finally, the highest barium and strontium values were found in apatite 363-DL-66 (table 1), and these two elements are commonly enriched in alkalic rocks and carbonatites (Pecora, 1956).

Although it would be unwise to overinterpret data for a single mineral, we note finally that the granitoid rock containing apatite 363-DL-66 is exposed in contact with thinly interbedded limestones and sandstones (the Permian Pequop Formation of Steele, 1959; Snow, 1964, pl. 1). In a study of hybrid granitoid rocks from the southern Snake Range, Nev., Lee and Bastron (1967) found accessory allanite to contain a more basic assemblage of rare earths where the granitoid rock is in contact with limestone; and the rare-earth assemblages in accessory apatites from the same rocks show the same trend (Lee and others, 1973).

REFERENCES CITED

Adams, J. W., 1969, Distribution of lanthanides in minerals, *in* Geological Survey Research 1969: U.S. Geol. Survey Prof. Paper 650-C, p.C38–C44.

Deer, W. A., Howie, R. A., and Zussman, J., 1962, Non-silicates, v. 5 *of* Rock-forming minerals: New York, John Wiley and Sons, Inc., 371 p.

Evans, H. T., Jr., Appleman, D. E., and Handwerker, D. S., 1963, The least squares refinement of crystal unit cells with powder diffraction data by an automatic computer indexing method [abs.]: Am. Cryst. Assoc. Program and Abs., Ann. Mtg., 1963, no. E-10, p. 42–43.

Fleischer, Michael, and Altschuler, Z. S., 1969, The relationship of the rare-earth composition of minerals to geologic environment: Geochim. et Cosmochim. Acta, v. 33, p. 725–732.

Goldschmidt, V. M., 1937, The principles of distribution of chemical elements in minerals and rocks: Jour. Chem. Soc. London, 1937, p. 655.

Goldschmidt, V. M., Hauptmann, H., and Peters, C., 1933, Über die Berücksichtigung "seltener" Elemente bei Gesteins-Analysen: Naturwissenschaften, v. 21, p. 362–365.

Hose, R. K., and Blake, M. C., Jr., 1970, Geologic map of White Pine County, Nevada: U.S. Geol. Survey open-file map, scale 1:150,000.

Jackson, E. D., Stevens, R. E., and Bowen, R. W., 1967, A computer-based procedure for deriving mineral formulas from mineral analyses, *in* Geological Survey Research 1967: U.S. Geol. Survey Prof. Paper 575-C, p. C23–C31.

Lee, D. E., and Bastron, Harry, 1967, Fractionation of rare-earth elements in allanite and monazite as related to geology of the Mount Wheeler mine area, Nevada: Geochim. et Cosmochim. Acta, v. 31, p. 339–356.

Lee, D. E., Marvin, R. F., Stern, T. W., and Peterman, Z. E., 1970, Modification of potassium-argon ages by Tertiary thrusting in the Snake Range, White Pine County, Nevada, *in* Geological Survey Research 1970: U.S. Geol. Survey Prof. Paper 700-D, p. D92–D102.

Lee, D. E., and Van Loenen, R. E., 1971, Hybrid granitoid rocks of the southern Snake Range, Nevada: U.S. Geol. Survey Prof. Paper 668, 48 p.

Lee, D. E., Van Loenen, R. E., and Mays, R. E., 1973, Accessory apatite from hybrid granitoid rocks of the southern Snake Range, Nevada: U.S. Geol. Survey Jour. Research, v. 1, no. 1, p. 89–98.

Murata, K. J., Rose, H. J., Jr., and Carron, M. K., 1953, Systematic variation of rare-earths in monazite: Geochim. et Cosmochim. Acta, v. 4, p. 292–300.

Murata, K. J., Rose, H. J., Jr., Carron, M. K., and Glass, J. J., 1957, Systematic variation of rare-earth elements in cerium-earth minerals: Geochim. et Cosmochim. Acta, v. 11, p. 141–161.

Pecora, W. T., 1956, Carbonatites—A review: Geol. Soc. America Bull., v. 67, p. 1537–1555.

Semenov, E. J., and Barinskii, R. L., 1958, The composition characteristics of the rare earths in minerals: Geokhimiya, 1958, no. 4, p. 314–333 [In Russian]; translation in Geochemistry 1958, no. 4, p. 398–419.

Snow, G. G., 1964, Mineralogy and geology of the Dolly Varden Mountains, Elko County, Nevada: Utah Univ. Ph. D. thesis, 153 p., University Microfilms, Inc., Ann Arbor, Mich.

Steele, Grant, 1959, Basin and Range structure reflects Paleozoic tectonics and sedimentation [abs]: Am. Assoc. Petroleum Geologists Bull., v. 43, no. 5, p. 1105.

Wilcox, R. E., 1959, Use of the spindle stage for determination of principal indices of refraction of crystal fragments: Am. Mineralogist, v. 44, p. 1272–1293.

—— 1962, Cherkasov's "focal screening" for determination of refractive index by the immersion method, *in* McCrone, W. C., ed., Proceedings of the International Microscopy Symposium, Chicago, 1960–1962: Chicago, McCrone Associates, p. 160–165.

Jour. Research U.S. Geol. Survey
Vol. 1, No. 3, May-June 1973, p. 273–282

PETROGRAPHY AND STRUCTURAL RELATIONS OF GRANITIC BASEMENT ROCKS IN THE MONTEREY BAY AREA, CALIFORNIA

By DONALD C. ROSS and EARL E. BRABB, Menlo Park, Calif.

Abstract.—In the past, the granitic basement of the Coast Ranges has been thought to be dominantly quartz diorite and low in K-feldspar. However, a study of outcrops around Monterey Bay, basement well samples, and dredge samples from Monterey Bay shows that the granitic basement averages about 15 to 20 percent K-feldspar. Therefore, as a sedimentary provenance, the basement around Monterey Bay could have contributed abundant K-feldspar to the Cenozoic sedimentary deposits of the region; that is, in the Monterey Bay area the local basement is an adequate source for the abundant K-feldspar in the sedimentary units. The distribution of basement rocks and mapped faults, coupled with gravity-geophysical data, suggests that the area between the San Andreas and Sur-Nacimiento fault zones (the Salinian block) near Monterey Bay is broken into several discrete structural blocks. Some of these blocks juxtapose not only different basement rocks, but also different contour patterns on the buried basement surface. These features suggest large strike-slip movements along some faults within the Salinian block in the Monterey Bay area.

The Monterey Bay area (fig. 1) appears to be underlain by a dominantly granitic basement of Mesozoic age containing inclusions and roof pendants of older marble, schist, quartzite, and other metamorphic types (fig. 2). The granitic rocks range in composition from very felsic alaskites to dark gabbros, but the bulk of the outcrops is intermediate between these end types. Outcrops are mainly in the Ben Lomond area on the north, the Gabilan Range on the east, and the Monterey Peninsula and adjacent Monterey Bay on the south; farther south, the Santa Lucia Range is underlain by a mixture of metamorphic and granitic types.

This summary report provides a general picture of the composition and areal distribution of the granitic basement rocks in the Monterey Bay area. From this it may be possible to determine the provenance of Late Cretaceous and Tertiary sedimentary rocks in this area. Although in the past the granitic rocks of the Coast Ranges have been considered to be dominantly quartz diorite and low in K-feldspar, some of the Tertiary sedimentary units in this area contain abundant K-feldspar, which raises the question of whether or not there are suitable K-feldspar-rich rocks in this area to supply this Tertiary debris. Also, discontinuities in the present distribution and structural trends of the various basement types may reveal the presence of possible large faults.

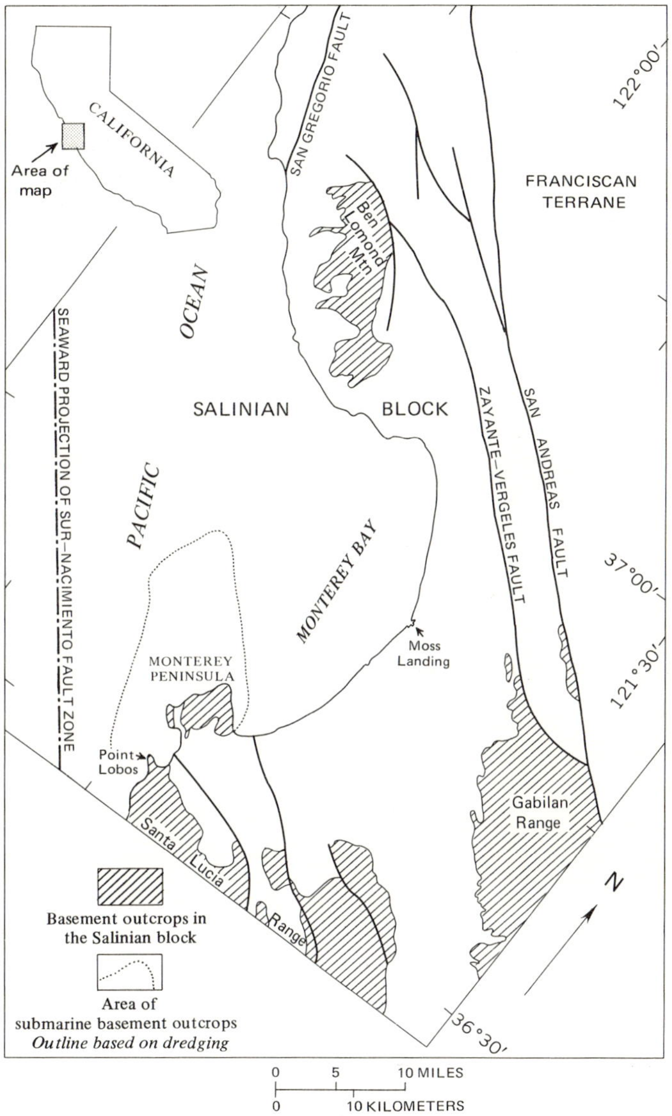

Figure 1.—Map of the Monterey Bay area, California.

Acknowledgments.—Texaco, Inc., and Union Oil Co. of California kindly provided cores of basement rocks in the Monterey Bay area. H. G. Greene, of the U.S. Geological

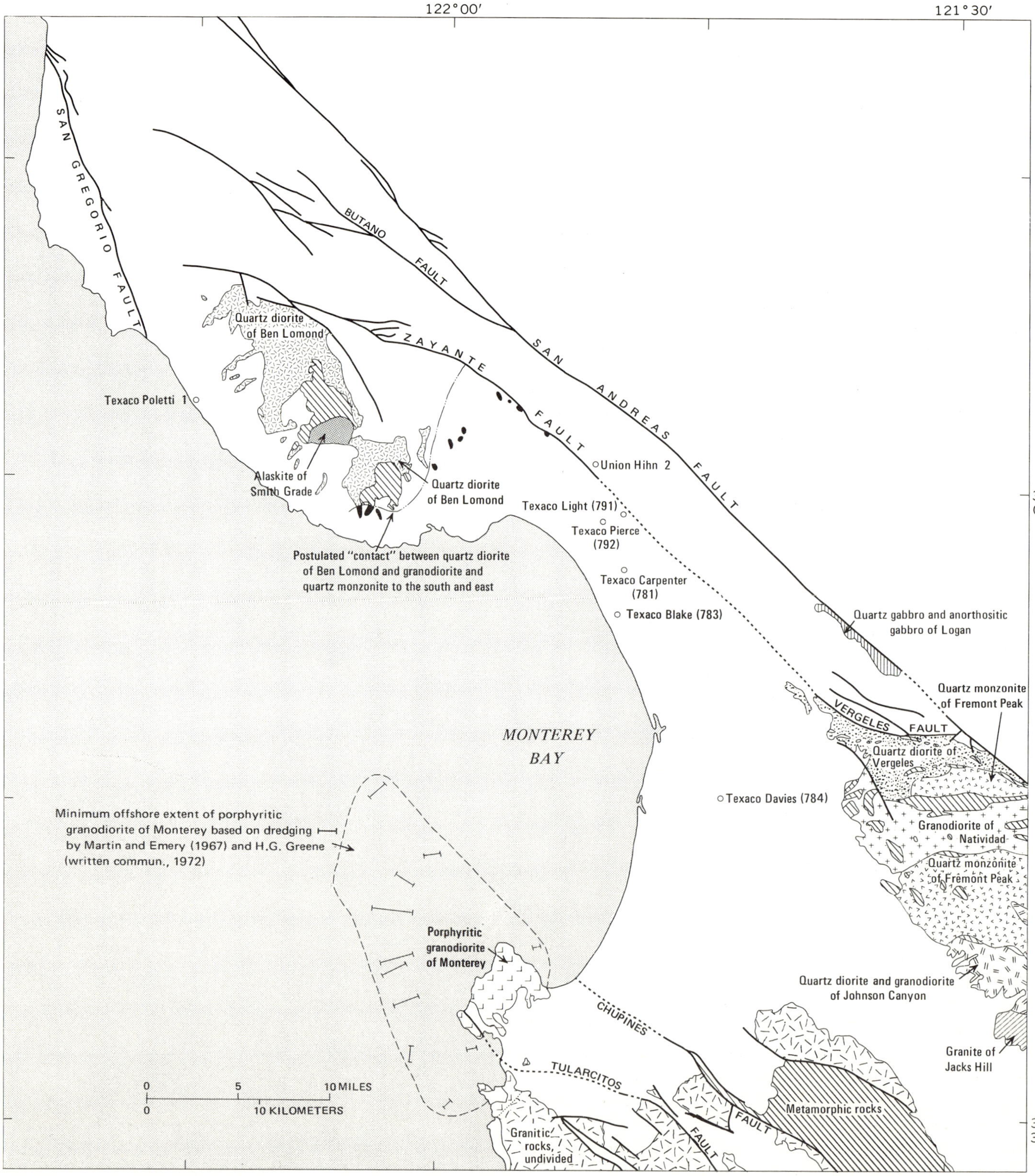

Figure 2.—Basement rock exposures in and around Monterey Bay, Calif. Open circles, locations of wells from which basement rock samples were studied.

Survey, furnished dredge samples from Monterey Bay. We also wish to thank D. L. Durham and T. W. Dibblee for their helpful reviews.

BEN LOMOND MOUNTAIN AREA

About 40 sq mi (104 km^2) of basement rocks is exposed in the Ben Lomond Mountain area. The dominant rock type, the hornblende-biotite quartz diorite of Ben Lomond Mountain, engulfs and intrudes a pendant composed of mica schist, marble, and quartzite several square miles in area. The alaskite of Smith Grade and several smaller alaskitic masses also cover a few square miles (fig. 2). The modal and petrographic data on the Ben Lomond rocks are taken in part from Leo (1967) and are supplemented by additional data from Ross (1972a).

Figure 3 shows the general modal distribution of the two main granitic masses. The alaskite of Smith Grade is a medium- to coarse-grained rock composed of nearly equal amounts of sodic plagioclase, K-feldspar, and quartz, together with a couple percent of biotite and trace amounts of garnet. There is some controversy about the relative age of this unit. Compton (1966, p. 285) thinks that it predates the main Ben Lomond mass, and Ross (1972) thinks it is a late plug related to garnet-bearing dikes that cut the Ben Lomond mass. Nonetheless, the largest body of alaskite is almost completely surrounded by the quartz diorite of Ben Lomond (fig. 2) and probably extends for no more than twice its exposed size under the overlying sediments to the south. Judging from the exposed basement sample of the Ben Lomond area, which contains only a few small alaskite plugs and dikes, we do not think that there are any very large alaskite masses in the buried basement nearby.

The more important basement unit, and the one that is more likely to have substantial subsurface extent, is the quartz diorite of Ben Lomond. This rock consists of about one-half andesine, one-quarter quartz, and one-quarter biotite and hornblende. K-feldspar normally is only a few percent, but Leo (1967) reported as much as 12 percent locally. The ternary plot of feldspar and quartz (fig. 3) shows that most specimens from the main mass fall in the quartz diorite field, but that isolated masses to the east stretch the composition well over into the quartz monzonite field. East of the main mass, the K-feldspar content of the granitic rocks is considerably higher over a rather large area. Leo (1967, p. 37) described the granodiorite of Wilder Creek at the south end of the main mass and suggested that this rather felsic biotite-bearing rock may be a gradational phase of the Ben Lomond mass. It is interesting to note that the modes of the Wilder Creek rocks recorded by Leo (fig. 3) are in the same general range as those of the isolated masses east of the main Ben Lomond body. J. C. Clarke, who was able to study several well cores, in addition to outcrops, in the area of Wilder Creek, reported gradations of rock types from quartz diorite to quartz monzonite (oral commun., 1970). It appears that both to the south and east the Ben Lomond basement becomes considerably richer in K-feldspar. A "contact" on figure 2 emphasizes this relation; however, limited examination of some of the small, isolated bodies east of Ben Lomond suggests that these are variations of the quartz diorite, rather than a separate intrusive mass.

GABILAN RANGE

The Gabilan Range is a dominantly granitic massif covering more than 300 sq mi. At the northern end of the range, which is of most interest in this report, the main rock types are the quartz diorite of Vergeles, the granodiorite of Natividad, and the quartz monzonite of Fremont Peak (fig. 2). The metamorphic rocks in the northern part of the range are dominantly marble and mica schist, with lesser calc-hornfels and tactite, and rare quartzite. Additional petrographic and modal data on these rocks are given by Ross (1972a).

The quartz diorite of Vergeles ranges to granodiorite (fig. 3), and the modal average is probably close to the boundary between these two types. The Vergeles mass is a normal granitic-looking rock composed of about 50 percent plagioclase, 20 to 30 percent quartz, about 20 percent biotite and hornblende, and as much as 15 percent K-feldspar. The Vergeles mass seems to be abruptly cut off to the northeast by the Vergeles fault. Ross (1972a, p. 33) has suggested that this mass may be correlative with the quartz diorite of Ben Lomond.

The granodiorite of Natividad is finer grained and physically distinguishable from the Vergeles unit, but the two rocks have somewhat similar modal compositions. Some question exists as to whether these are two separate intrusives or two facies of one mass, but nevertheless both units could contribute about the same sort of debris to sedimentary deposits.

The quartz monzonite of Fremont Peak is coarse-grained felsic granitic rock composed of about equal amounts of sodic plagioclase, K-feldspar, and quartz, and a few percent of biotite. This mass, which intrudes the Vergeles and Natividad units, underlies two large areas in the northern part of the range.

North of the Gabilan Range (fig. 2) is a thin sliver of basement rocks along the San Andreas fault. These rocks, quartz gabbro and anorthositic gabbro, are quite distinct from any of the granitic basement units in this region (Ross, 1970). They are composed of calcic plagioclase, hornblende, pyroxene, and less quartz and are virtually devoid of K-feldspar, except for some minor pegmatitic dikes.

MONTEREY PENINSULA AND BAY

The Monterey Peninsula and the Point Lobos areas to the south are both underlain by coarse-grained porphyritic granodiorite. Present outcrops span some 20 sq mi, and these rocks almost certainly extend some as yet unkown distance to the south and east. For example, nearly 20 miles to the southeast in the Santa Lucia Mountains, similar granitic rocks are

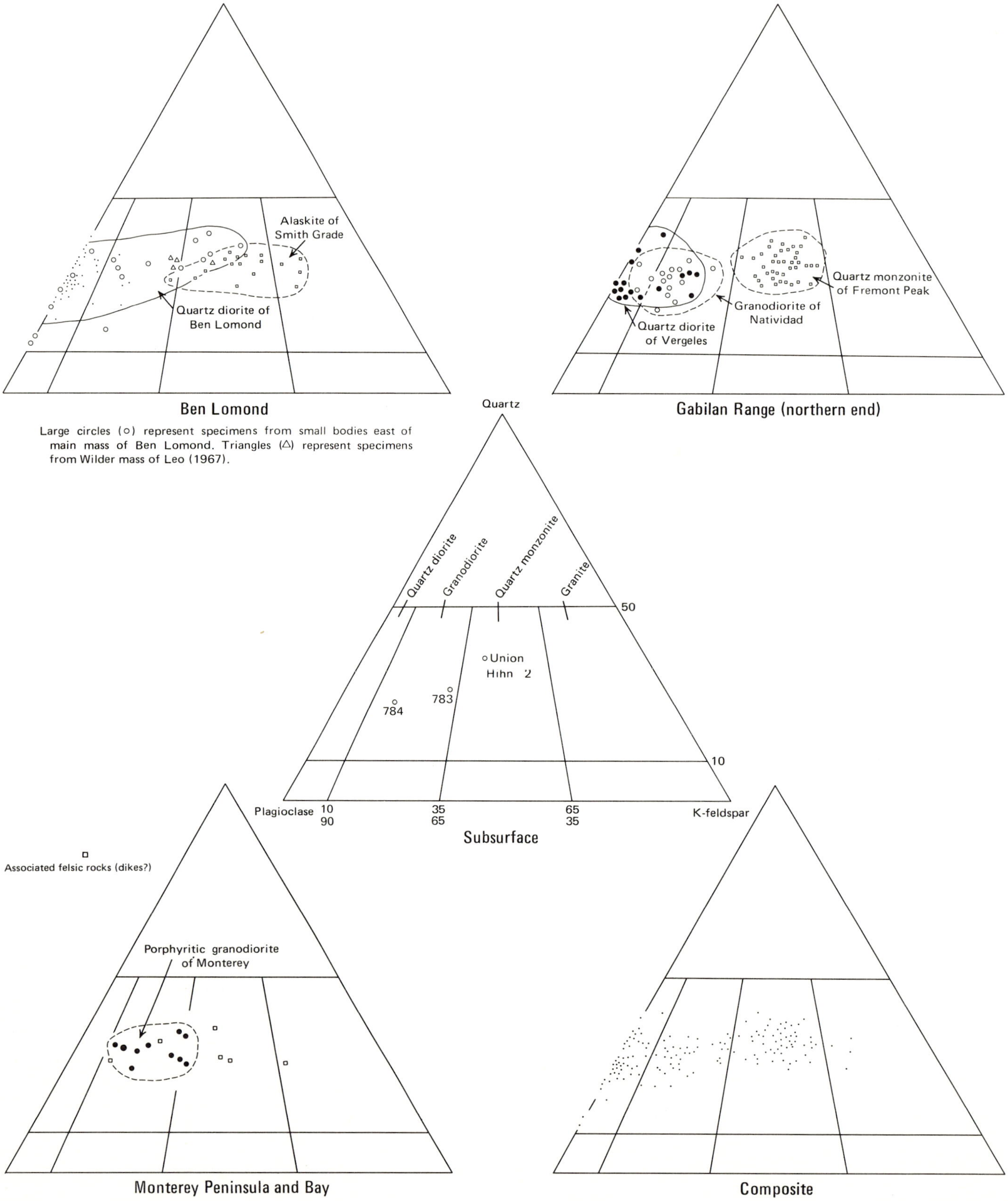

Figure 3.—Ternary diagrams showing modal data for the Monterey Bay area, California.

exposed (Alf Piwinskii, oral commun., 1969). The detailed granitic geology has not yet been worked out for the area of figure 2 labeled "granitic rocks, undivided." However, from the work of Compton (1966) and Wiebe (1970), we know that the granitic basement of the Santa Lucia Range encompasses a wide range of compositions and includes abundant quartz monzonite and granodiorite.

According to the few samples analyzed, the Monterey mass is a granodiorite having a modal composition of about 50 percent sodic plagioclase, 30 percent quartz, 15 to 20 percent K-feldspar, and 5 to 10 percent biotite. Primary muscovite is also present in this body. K-feldspar phenocrysts as large as 30 mm in longest dimension are distinctive in this rock. Rocks as coarsely porphyritic as the Monterey mass do not lend themselves to accurate modal analysis, but the overall abundance of K-feldspar in this mass is nevertheless indisputable, judging from the abundance of K-feldspar phenocrysts in many outcrops.

The extension of this mass offshore from the Monterey Peninsula has been confirmed by dredging. Martin and Emery (1969, p. 2288) briefly described dredged specimens in which they noted that, though mineral percentages varied, a typical sample was 35 percent quartz, 30 percent K-feldspar, 20 percent oligoclase, 10 percent biotite, and 5 percent chlorite. Further dredging in 1971 and 1972 by H. G. Greene extended the area of known granitic outcrop in the bay both north and south of the area of Martin's and Emery's work. The present known extent of offshore granitic outcrops is shown by the dashed line on figure 2. Greene kindly furnished us with specimens from these dredge hauls; the dominant material was found to be porphyritic granodiorite that was similar to the exposures on Monterey Peninsula. Associated with the porphyritic rocks were finer grained rocks, rich in K-feldspar, that may be from satellitic bodies or dikes. Thus it seems highly likely that an offshore area of more than 100 sq mi is underlain by rocks rich in K-feldspar and generally similar to the rocks on the Monterey Peninsula. These rocks almost surely also extend some distance farther north under the sediments of the bay. They do not appear to extend very far south, however, at least along the coast. One of the samples from the southernmost dredge line is a quartz diorite containing pseudomorphs of hornblende as well as abundant biotite; quartz diorite containing abundant hornblende and biotite is also found along State Highway 1 about 4 miles south of Point Lobos.

DATA ON SUBSURFACE GRANITIC BASEMENT ROCKS

The outcrop data have been supplemented by the acquisition of basement samples from cores of six wells drilled for oil between Ben Lomond Mountain and Gabilan Range and another sample core west of Ben Lomond. The locations of these wells are plotted on figure 2. These widely isolated core samples are particularly valuable to help determine the types of basement rock between the exposures of Ben Lomond and the Gabilan Range and therefore deserve individual description. The limitation on drawing conclusions from these scattered cores is, we trust, readily obvious to readers.

Union Hihn Well 2.—From this well we have four samples from 3,436 feet, where basement was first found, to 3,507 feet, and a fifth sample from the interval 3,565 to 3,569 feet, the total depth of the well. An additional sample of arkosic sand, rich in K-feldspar, from the interval 3,413 to 3,436 feet appears to overlie the basement immediately. All the quartz-rich, felsic granitic samples are very similar. They are quartz monzonite with an average mode of 35 percent andesine, 26 percent K-feldspar, 36 percent quartz, and 3 percent medium-brown biotite. Zircon is present in all samples; metallic opaque grains are extremely rare, and at least some of them are pyrite. Modally, these rocks resemble some of those exposed east of the main Ben Lomond basement outcrops. Texturally, they are somewhat finer grained, aplitic in part, and contain lacy, irregular growths of K-feldspar, but they bear textural resemblance to some of the finer grained and less felsic rocks east of Ben Lomond. These rocks are very tenuously considered to be a continuation of the quartz diorite of Ben Lomond; but even if the correlation is erroneous, they still provide another sample point of granitic basement relatively rich in K-feldspar.

The plotted position of Union Hihn well 2 is about 1,000 feet east of the mapped trace of the Zayante fault; yet the granitic material at the bottom of the hole seems to be related to the basement rocks west of the fault in the Ben Lomond-Gabilan block, which crop out only 3 miles to the northwest. A short distance northeast of the Hihn well 2, Union Hihn 1 went down 7,747 feet and was still in Miocene rocks, which suggests that there is a basement break (the Zayante fault) between the bottoms of Hihn wells 1 and 2. A dip of 70° or less to the east on the Zayante fault would permit the Union Hihn 2 to bottom on the west side of the fault; a southwestward deflection of the well would also produce the same effect. With the present limited data, it seems most logical to speculate that the Hihn 2 basement rocks belong to the Ben Lomond-Gabilan block.

Texaco Light (791).—Two samples are available from this well. One from 3,240 feet is a "granitic breccia" that could represent either fragmental material near the contact with the basement rocks or tectonic breccia; it is probably the former. The other sample from 3,620 feet is extensively weathered but appears to be quartz diorite containing abundant black biotite. Both specimens contain little K-feldspar. It is impossible to relate these samples adequately to any granitic basement of the region. General composition and appearance make correlation with the Ben Lomond rocks permissible; little more can be said.

Texaco Pierce (792).—Three samples from intervals 2,633 to 2,637, 2,637 to 2,642, and 2,642 to 2,655 feet are light-gray aplitic rocks that are liberally sprinkled with small flakes of yellowish-orange biotite, grains of sphene, and as much as 2 percent small pyrite crystals. Thin-section appearance definitely suggests that these rocks are aplite, but it is possible that they are fine-grained hornfelses.

Texaco Carpenter (781).—Samples from 3,050 and 3,096 feet are both dark-gray medium- to fine-grained quartz-bearing diorite containing small plagioclase phenocrysts as long as 3 mm. In general appearance the specimens resemble inclusion material that is common in granitic rocks, but the fact that the hole passed through at least 46 feet of this material and that no other basement rock type was recovered suggests that a diorite body was penetrated. The mode of this rock is 41 percent intermediate andesine, 5 percent quartz, 43 percent pale-greenish-yellow to pale-olive hornblende, and 11 percent yellowish-orange to moderate-reddish-brown biotite. Accessory apatite, zircon, and magnetite are also present.

Texaco Blake (783).—Samples were obtained from the basement rocks at 2,426, 2,458, and 2,462 feet. The upper and lower samples are light-gray aplites that are somewhat banded by variation in grain size and K-feldspar content and somewhat streaked with yellowish-orange to brown biotite. These samples look much like those from the Texaco Pierce (792) hole. The sample from 2,458 feet, however, is a medium- to coarse-grained, weakly porphyritic granitic rock. It is composed of 40 percent zoned sodic to intermediate andesine, 20 percent K-feldspar, 24 percent moderately strained quartz, and 16 percent brown biotite. Trace amounts of grayish-green hornblende are present, as are sphene, allanite, epidote, apatite, and zircon. No metallic opaque grains were seen in the specimen studied. This biotite granodiorite bears a striking resemblance to much of the rock in the isolated outcrops east of the main Ben Lomond mass and is considered here to be correlative of those rocks. The aplites are presumably dikes or small masses, which are also present in the Ben Lomond area.

Texaco Davies (784).—One basement sample from 2,194 feet is a relatively fresh, medium-light-gray granitic rock containing abundant dark minerals in fairly large crystals. This rock is a granodiorite that is hypautomorphic granular and is composed of 51 percent sodic andesine, 10 percent K-feldspar, 21 percent quartz, 11 percent dark-yellowish-brown biotite, and 7 percent grayish- to medium-green hornblende. Some of the dark mineral plates are as much as 5 mm across. Sphene crystals as large as 3 mm across are most abundant as an accessory mineral; minor apatite, zircon, allanite, and the merest traces of metallic opaque minerals are also seen. The K-feldspar tends to occur in large, lacy, interstitial masses rather than in discrete crystals.

The general appearance of this rock as well as its modal composition suggest that it is a correlative of the Vergeles mass of the Gabilan Range. Rocks with abundant, large, discrete dark-mineral plates like those in this specimen are not only characteristic of the Vergeles mass but also are present in the Ben Lomond mass, as well as in other Coast Ranges granitic outcrops farther north. This recurring, rather distinctive texture has led Ross (1972a) to suggest that the Vergeles mass and the rest of the granitic basement north to Bodega Head are a comagmatic, closely related granodiorite-quartz diorite terrane, or possibly even one large pluton, into which numerous, younger, more felsic masses have been intruded.

Texaco Poletti 1.—In this well near the coast west of Ben Lomond, basement was hit at about 9,000 feet, and three samples were examined from 9,163, 9,191, and 9,193 feet. Another basement sample is available from an unknown depth below 9,000 feet, and still another sample was examined briefly and subsequently lost. The sample from an unknown depth is a massive medium-grained biotite quartz monzonite to granodiorite with schistose to gneissose layers. Some concentrations of pinkish K-feldspar are present but not quite discrete enought to be phenocrysts; K-feldspar crystals about 55 mm long were observed in the core that was lost. The schistose-gneissose layers are composed of quartz, sodic plagioclase, and olive-brown biotite, as well as abundant secondary calcite. The layered part of the specimen appears to lack K-feldspar, in sharp contrast to its abundance in the adjoining granitic rock. This rock somewhat resembles the porphyritic granodiorite of Monterey and, probably more importantly, does not seem to resemble the nearby surface outcrops of the Ben Lomond mass.

The three basement samples from near the top of the basement in this well are all brecciated to some extent with anastomosing shear zones rich in chloritic material. There is no mylonite, but crushing and shearing are suggested from the specimens. The original rock in all three samples was a relatively quartz-rich biotite granodiorite. None of these samples resemble the nearby Ben Lomond basement rocks.

REGIONAL CONSIDERATIONS

The new well-core data allow us to extend the Ben Lomond granitic basement tentatively some 12 miles farther southeast. But more significantly they allow us to enlarge the area of granitic rocks relatively rich in K-feldspar east and south of the Ben Lomond mass. Well 784 permits us to extend the Vergeles mass of the Gabilan Range some 7 miles farther west. Even with these new data, however, there is still a 10-mile gap between the Gabilan outcrops and the nearest well with granitic rock like that in the Ben Lomond area.

Figure 4 is a highly speculative interpretation of the configuration of granitic basement rocks beneath the cover of Mesozoic and Cenozoic sedimentary and volcanic rocks and sediments. It was constructed partly from oil test-well data, partly from gravity data or profiles by Clark (1970), H. C. Sieck (unpub. data), and J. W. Fairborn (unpub. data), and partly from an analysis of geologic maps by Clark (1970), Bowen (1965), and Brabb (1970). Even though the data points are few and scattered, the abrupt change in depth to granitic basement rocks across inferred faults is well established. Some of the irregularities in the surface of these granitic basement rocks, such as the reentrant in the Moss Landing area, could be due to erosion by fluvial process prior to submergence, as suggested by Starke and Howard (1968), but other irregularities seem related to folding or warping of the basement rocks.

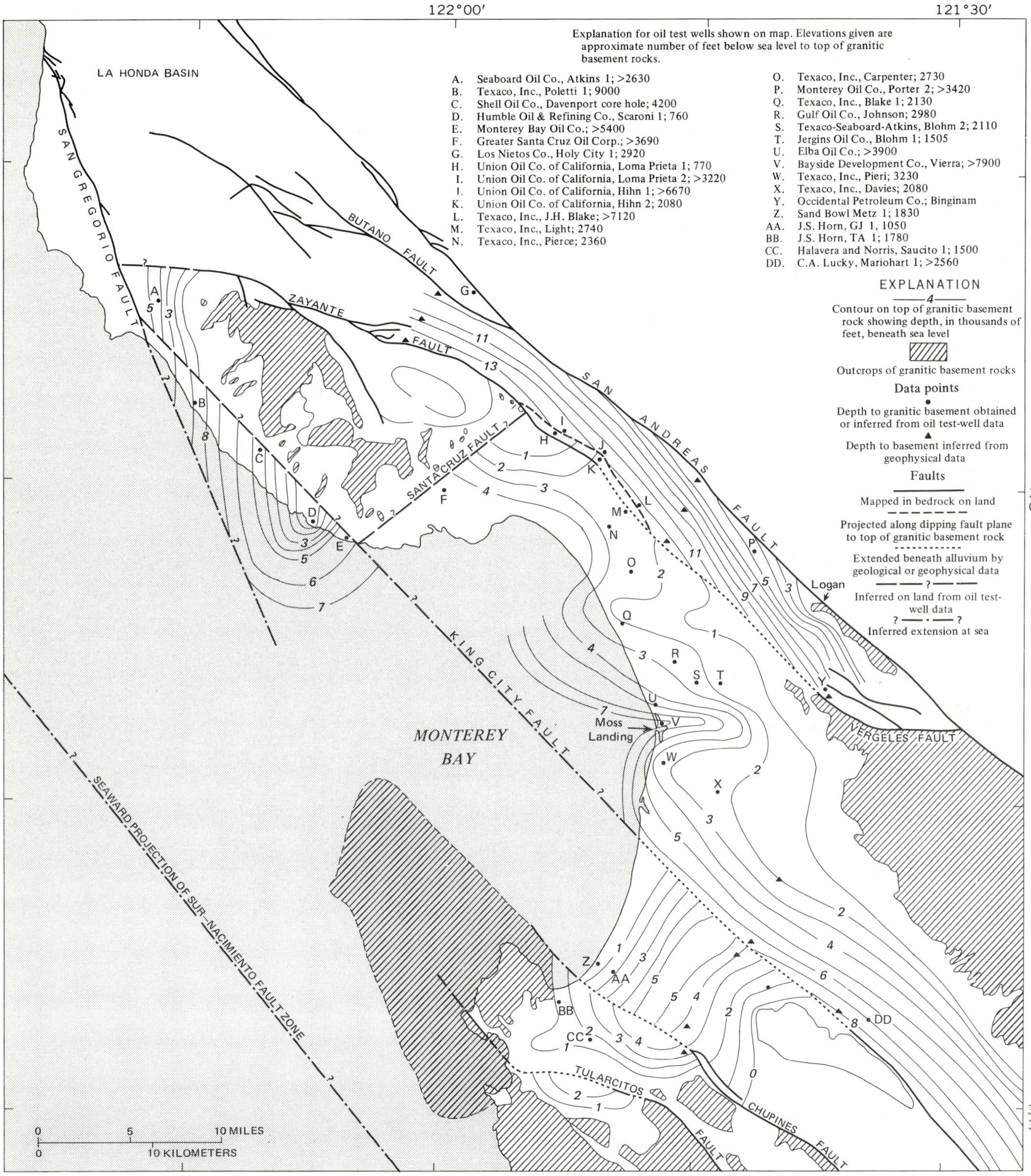

Figure 4.—Map showing depth to granitic basement rocks and major fault systems in the Monterey Bay area, California. The map is highly speculative and is based on relatively few data points.

Such deformation was postulated many years ago, mainly on geomorphic evidence, by Rode (1930), and more recently by Cummings, Touring, and Brabb (1962, p. 214) and Gribi (1957, fig. 6). Termination of the folded surfaces at faults and the abrupt change in strike of these surfaces across faults suggest that the deformation was not related to simple up-and-down movement of the faults or simple compression of the blocks, but rather that it was complex and associated with extensive strike-slip movement. In support of this argument, Bowen (1965, p. 66) has postulated at least some right-lateral movement on the Tularcitos and Chupines faults, largely on the basis of offset of a middle Miocene formation. If so, then the granitic rocks in the Monterey area may be juxtaposed from terranes that were once widely separated.

Two new faults are proposed to explain abrupt changes in depth to basement rocks reached by oil test wells. Neither fault has any known surface expression, and both seem to be older than late Miocene. The Santa Cruz fault seems to extend northeastward from Santa Cruz at least to the Zayante fault. A slight deflection in the San Andreas fault along the extension of the Santa Cruz fault may or may not be coincidental. The King City fault, as mapped originally by Clark (1929) and later by Bowen (1965) in the Salinas River area, is extended across Monterey Bay and northwestward from Santa Cruz at least to the San Gregorio fault. The extension of the King City fault was also recognized but not mapped or named by Starke and Howard (1968, p. 822–823) on the basis of the same oil test-well data. Directly on strike to the south of the King City fault is the Reliz-Espinosa-San Marcos-Rinconada fault zone, a regionally significant feature that is probably continuous with the King City fault in the Monterey Bay area. Dibblee (1972, p. 145–146) has noted that drag folding associated with this fault zone indicates right-lateral movement. He postulates that strata of Late Cretaceous to early Tertiary age have been offset in a right-lateral sense nearly 40 miles along this zone.

On the basis of the distribution of basement rock types, we can speculate that the striking contrasts in basement rocks across both the Zayante-Vergeles and King City faults (fig. 4) require some lateral movement, whereas the distribution of basement across the Santa Cruz fault requires only moderate dip-slip movement. At both the north and south ends of the Zayante-Vergeles fault zone, petrographically similar granitic rocks abut the west side of the fault. In between those larger outcrop areas, isolated granitic outcrops and well and gravity data suggest a relatively shallow movement along the west side of the fault. East of the fault there are no exposures of Salinian block-type granitic rocks. The only basement exposed is the unusual gabbro of Logan, which Ross (1970) has suggested may be exotic and unrelated to the granitic rocks of the Salinian block to the west. The contrast in basement contours across the fault (fig. 4) could possibly result solely from vertical fault movement, but the markedly different basements across the fault suggest that lateral movement has juxtaposed these different rocks. From the present data, we must also entertain the possibility that the Zayante-Vergeles block is underlain by Franciscan basement, rather than Salinian granitic basement.

The Santa Cruz fault, in contrast, has similar, possibly correlative granitic basement rocks on both sides. Basement evidence suggests that this may be a dip-slip fault of moderate displacement that has had little effect on distribution of the basement rocks.

The King City fault, however, appears to have had significant effect on the distribution of the basement rocks. The core material from the Texaco Poletti well 1 has some resemblance to the basement of Monterey Peninsula, but none to the nearby exposures of granitic rocks of the Ben Lomond area. Also, Ross (1972a) has suggested that the basement of the Gabilan Range is different from the basement of the Santa Lucia Range of the Monterey block west of the King City fault. Preliminary study suggests that the dominantly granitic Gabilan basement has little in common with the largely metamorphic Santa Lucia basement, although many areas in the Santa Lucia Range have not yet been examined in detail. The contrast in basement rocks across the proposed King City fault seems to require more than dip-slip fault movement. It seems more probable that strike-slip movement on the King City fault has juxtaposed these contrasting basement terranes.

From the surface and subsurface data around and under Monterey Bay, we can make some generalizations about the overall composition of the basement rocks. More specifically, for the purposes of this report, we can generalize about the K-feldspar content of the basement rocks in this area. From the preceding discussion of modal composition and structural blocks in this region, a generalized basement map can be constructed (fig. 5). Within the outlined semicircular area, an average K-feldspar content can be estimated for each postulated basement block. Weighting each area according to size, an average K-feldspar content of 15 percent is obtained for the approximately 1,000-sq-mi area. It is also possible to estimate an average granitic composition for this area by assuming that the Monterey Bay area is representative of the granitic basement of the entire Coast Ranges. For the 450 sq mi of granitic rocks exposed in the Coast Ranges (excluding the Santa Lucia Range), Ross (1972a) has estimated that they consist of 40 percent quartz monzonite, 36 percent granodiorite, 23 percent quartz diorite, and 1 percent diorite and gabbro. It should be remembered, however, that the Monterey Bay area is between the central Coast Ranges with a generally higher proportion of quartz diorite and the southern Coast Ranges (Gabilan Range and to the south) where granodiorite and quartz monzonite greatly predominate. Nevertheless, if we use these average amounts, we could postulate about 20 to 25 percent K-feldspar as a general amount for the Monterey Bay area. However, considering all the uncertainties that result from both these methods based on limited data, 15 to 20 percent of K-feldspar is probably a fair estimate of overall content in the granitic rocks of the Monterey Bay area. The composite plot of all the modal data from the Monterey Bay area (fig. 3) shows that there is a wide range of composition

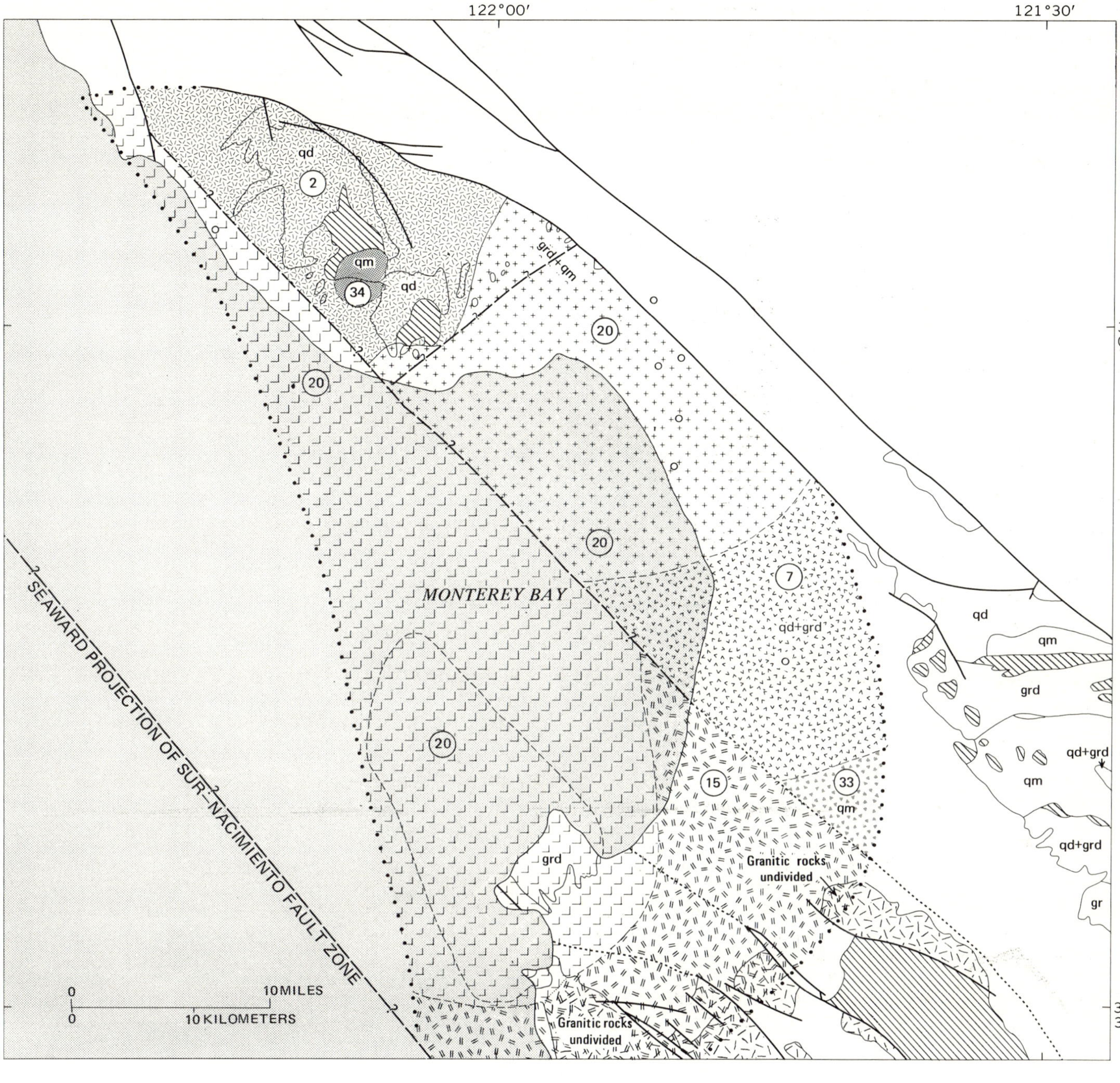

Figure 5.—Estimated percentage of K-feldspar (circled numbers in patterned areas) in granitic basement in and around Monterey Bay, Calif., within area enclosed by heavy dotted line. Generalized granitic type shown for each basement segment by letter symbols: qd, quartz diorite; grd, granodiorite; qm, quartz monzonite; gr, granite. Metamorphic rocks (diagonal line pattern) are presumed to occupy only a small part of the area outlined by the heavy dotted line. Open circles, locations of wells (see fig. 2).

and relatively abundant source material for significant amounts of K-feldspar in the sedimentary section derived from this basement, even though the plot is somewhat weighted in favor of the K-feldspar-rich rocks, which were more densely sampled in the Ben Lomond area.

Generally, the Monterey Bay area rocks have 20 to 30 percent quartz and from 10 to 25 percent dark minerals, so we can predict an overall range of plagioclase from 25 to 50 percent. Thus sedimentary units that received granitic debris might be expected to receive about twice as much plagioclase as K-feldspar. However, a relative enrichment of K-feldspar over plagioclase may take place during the weathering process because much of the plagioclase in the granitic rocks is to some extent altered, whereas K-feldspar is generally much fresher. The plagioclase of these granitic rocks is much more likely to break down during mechanical weathering than is the K-feldspar because much of it is already partly saturated with micaceous and clayey alteration material. Also these somewhat altered plagioclase crystals should be much more receptive to additional chemical alteration during the weathering process.

Some of the Tertiary sedimentary rocks that could have been derived from granitic basement rocks surrounding Monterey Bay have been described by Cummings, Touring, and Brabb (1962). These sedimentary rocks occur in the La Honda basin, north of Ben Lomond Mountain (fig. 2). Cummings and his colleagues found that sandstones of Eocene and Oligocene age have about 30 percent K-feldspar and 10 percent plagioclase, whereas sandstones of Miocene age, according to Brabb (1960, p. 72), contain as much as 92 percent plagioclase and only 5 percent K-feldspar. The change in ratio of feldspar is attributed to a significant change in source areas during early or Middle Miocene time. The source for the Eocene and Oligocene sediments was thought by these authors to be south and west of the present outcrops of predominantly quartz diorite on Ben Lomond Mountain, in what is now the Pacific Ocean, whereas the Miocene sediments were thought to come directly from the Ben Lomond Mountain area. Corroboration for at least the southern source during the Eocene has been provided by Nilsen (1971).

These data provide additional clues to understanding the structural framework of granitic basement rocks in the Monterey Bay area. If major strike-slip dislocations have occurred, then movement of the Monterey block away from the La Honda basin probably occurred in early or middle Miocene time.

REFERENCES CITED

Bowen, O. E., 1965, Stratigraphy, structure and oil possibilities in Monterey and Salinas quadrangles, California: Am Assoc. Petroleum Geologists, 40th Ann. Mtg., Pacific Sec., Bakersfield, Calif., 1965, p. 48–67.

Brabb, E. E., 1960, Geology of the Big Basin area, Santa Cruz Mountains, California: Stanford Univ., Stanford, Calif., Ph. D. thesis, 197 p.

—— compiler, 1970, Preliminary geologic map of the central Santa Cruz Mountains, California: U.S. Geol. Survey open-file rept.

Clark, B. L., 1929, Tectonics of the Valle Grande of California: Am. Assoc. Petroleum Geologists Bull., v. 13, no. 3, p. 199–238.

Clark, J. C., compiler, 1970, Preliminary geologic and gravity maps of the Santa Cruz–San Juan Bautista area, Santa Cruz, Santa Clara, Monterey, and San Benito Counties, California: U.S. Geol. Survey open-file rept.

Compton, R. R., 1966, Granitic and metamorphic rocks of the Salinian block, California Coast Ranges: California Div. Mines and Geology Bull. 190, p. 277–287.

Cummings, J. C., Touring, R. M., and Brabb, E. E., 1962, Geology of the northern Santa Cruz Mountains, California: California Div. Mines and Geology Bull. 181, p. 179–220.

Dibblee, T. W., Jr., 1972, Rinconada fault in the southern Coast Ranges, California, and its significance: Geol. Soc. America Abs. with Programs, v. 4, no. 3, p. 145–146.

Gribi, E. A., Jr., 1957, Santa Cruz basin holds important promise: Oil and Gas Jour., v. 55, no. 13, p. 113–116.

Leo, G. W., 1967, The plutonic and metamorphic rocks of the Ben Lomond Mountain area, Santa Cruz County, California: California Div. Mines and Geology Spec. Rept. 91, p. 27–43.

Martin, B. D., and Emery, K. O., 1967, Geology of Monterey Canyon, California: Am. Assoc. Petroleum Geologists Bull., v. 51, p. 2281–2304.

Nilsen, T. H., 1971, Sedimentology of the Eocene Butano Sandstone, a continental borderland submarine fan deposit, central Coast Ranges of California [abs.]: Geol. Soc. America Abs. with Program, v. 3, no. 7, p. 659–660.

Rode, Karl, 1930, Geomorphogenie des Ben Lomond, Kalifornien: Zeitschr. P. Geomorph., v. 5, p. 16–78, Trans. by John E. Kesseli, Dept. of Geography, California Univ. (manuscript).

Ross, D. C., 1970, Quartz gabbro and anorthositic gabbro—Markers of offset along the San Andreas fault in the California Coast Ranges: Geol. Soc. America Bull., v. 81, no. 12, p. 3647–3662.

—— 1972a, Petrographic and chemical reconnaissance of some granitic and gneissic rocks near the San Andreas fault from Bodega Head to Cajon Pass, California: U.S. Geol. Survey Prof. Paper 698, 92 p.

—— 1972b, Geologic map of the pre-Cenozoic basement rocks, Gabilan Range, Monterey and San Benito Counties, California: U.S. Geol. Survey Misc. Field Studies Map MF-357, scale 1:125,000.

Starke, G. W., and Howard, A. D., 1968, Polygenetic origin of Monterey Submarine Canyon: Geol. Soc. America Bull., v. 79, no. 7, p. 813–826.

Wiebe, R. A., 1970, Relations of granitic and gabbroic rocks, northern Santa Lucia Range, California: Geol. Soc. America Bull., v. 81, no. 1, p. 105–116.

Jour. Research U.S. Geol. Survey
Vol. 1, No. 3, May-June 1973, p. 283–287

A PHOTOGEOLOGIC METHOD FOR DETERMINING THE DIRECTION OF HORIZONTAL DILATION FROM PATTERNS OF EN ECHELON FRACTURING

By WENDELL A. DUFFIELD and KAZUAKI NAKAMURA[1],
Menlo Park, Calif., Tokyo, Japan

Abstract.—The direction of horizontal dilation in areas characterized by tensional tectonics can be determined from a statistical study of en echelon patterns of fracturing observed on aerial photographs. Relative to a north-south dilation, nearly all directions of zones of dextral (right-lateral) en echelon fractures lie in the northeast quadrant, while those of sinistral (left-lateral) en echelon fractures concentrate in the northwest quadrant. Statistically, directions of the two types of zones define unimodal frequency curves that intersect at about 90 degrees to, and thus define the direction of, applied dilation. The method has been field tested twice and is believed to be suitable for any area characterized by (1) generally unidirectional horizontal strain and (2) an adequate population of geologically contemporaneous fissures, including roughly equal development of sinistral and dextral en echelon arrays. Where exposures and aerial photograph coverage are adequate, the direction can be determined quickly to within about 10 degrees accuracy without fieldwork. The method should be useful for preliminary structural studies, especially in inaccessible areas.

A recently developed photogeologic method for determining the azimuth of horizontal extension for areas characterized by tensional tectonics has been tested in the median zone of southwest Iceland (Nakamura, 1970) and in the Koae fault system of Kilauea Volcano, Hawaii. The method predicts the direction of horizontal extension from the interrelations of the azimuthal frequencies of zones of en echelon fractures and non-en-echelon or neutral fractures.

For both the Icelandic and Hawaiian examples, this predicted direction was initially determined by a quantitative study of the azimuthal frequency of zones of fissures on vertical aerial photographs. Subsequently, a brief field check in Iceland substantiated the predicted results there, and abundant measurements made directly on open cracks and normal faults proved those of the Hawaiian study to be nearly correct within the errors of the field measurements. Thus the photogeologic procedure may have general applicability in all areas that are characterized by (1) generally unidirectional extensional horizontal strain and (2) an adequate population of geologically contemporaneous fissures—neutral and about equally developed sinistral and dextral en echelon arrays. Accordingly, the method should be useful for preliminary structural studies of areas that lie astride loci of spreading in the upper mantle, zones such as the Koae fault system in Hawaii that are being forcibly torn apart by localized volcanic processes, areas where gravity sliding is common, and similar areas where generally unidirectional extensional tectonics prevail.

Acknowledgments.—We thank R. S. Fiske, M. D. Crittenden, and D. A. Swanson for helpful discussions of our study and useful suggestions for improving the manuscript. This paper is an outgrowth of related independent studies by both of us. Nakamura completed the analysis of aerial photographs of the Koae fault system while visiting Kilauea in the fall of 1970, and Duffield later contributed the field measurements. Nakamura thanks R. S. Fiske, D. L. Peck, H. A. Powers, and D. W. Peterson, of the U.S. Geological Survey, for the opportunity to visit the Hawaiian Volcano Observatory at Kilauea.

EXPERIMENTAL BASIS OF METHOD

The primary experimental basis for the new method of study is that a homogeneous brittle material tends to fail by fracturing perpendicular to the direction of pull under an applied tension (for example, see Billings, 1954, p. 94). There are, of course, many combinations of physical-chemical environments and materials under which simple right-angle brittle fractures would not form from such an applied tension, but in general, rocks at and near the surface of the earth will fail in this manner; it is to this environment that the proposed method is applied.

The reasons that tensional fractures often form en echelon patterns are not well understood, but apparently such an arrangement can result from several markedly different states of stress. Nakamura (1970) reported that en echelon arrangement of fractures is common when the trend of the zone of such fractures is oblique to the direction of dilation; Riedel shears are the extreme example in which the zone of fractures parallels dilation. Patterns of en echelon fractures may result from mechanical inhomogenieties in the failing material and

[1] Earthquake Research Institute.

also may result in surface rocks from a nonperpendicular arrangement between tension and a master fracture at some relatively shallow depth. The effectiveness of such master faults in producing en echelon patterns of fractures in overlying material has been demonstrated by Fiske and Cloos (see Fiske and Kinoshita, 1969) and by Fiske and Duffield (unpub. data) in experiments involving the fracturing of clay cakes.

En echelon fracturing resulting from underlying or related strike-slip movement on a master fault is either sinistral or dextral, depending upon the sense of strike-slip offset. However, in general, for areas under active unidirectional horizontal tension, both contemporaneous dextral and sinistral arrays can be expected, and such arrays are evidence of non-strike-slip origin. This criterion together with other types of evidence (for example, the presence of graben-horst topography and the absence of strike-slip offset and structures caused by compression) indicates areas to which the new method may be applied.

CLASSIFICATION OF ZONES OF FRACTURES

Although the arrangement of individual fractures into en echelon arrays may be simple (fig. 1*B*), natural examples are rarely, if ever, so clearly indicated, and their recognition normally requires judgment by the observer. If three or more parallel or semiparallel, generally partly overlapping fractures define a zone that is oblique to the trend of the fractures, we classify them as en echelon. If the zone and the individual fractures parallel one another, we classify the fractures as neutral.

These are simple and standard definitions, but natural sets of fractures may be confusing when studied at different scales. In general, fractures of both en echelon and neutral arrangement form zones of some finite width, and within each type of zone, the length of all fractures is not the same. Thus at one scale a group of fractures may be classified as a single zone of neutral type, but more detailed examination might well indicate the presence of many zones of both neutral and en echelon types.

In practice, the degree of detail of analysis is limited by the scale of available aerial photographs, and we have found that the classification of zones of fractures from photographs agrees very well with classification based on direct field observations, although a greater number of all types of zones is recognized from field study. Presumably, the results should be roughly the same at any scale of examination, but we suggest using a single scale which is most convenient for a given photogeologic study.

IDEAL MODEL AND PROCEDURE

Suppose that an area is characterized by fissures that formed in response to horizontal north-south tension. Experimental studies predict that such breaks will dip steeply and trend east-west. If zones of en echelon fractures are present, those zones which trend between north and east will show a right-lateral or dextral arrangement of fractures, and those between north and west a left-lateral or sinistral arrangement of fractures. Figure 1 is a sketch of a clay cake experiment by R. S. Fiske and Duffield which demonstrates this pattern.

The direction of horizontal extension for such a pattern of fracturing may be determined from the azimuthal frequencies of zones of en echelon fractures (fig. 2). Two smooth unimodal frequency curves, dextral arrays in the northeast quadrant and sinistral arrays in the northwest quadrant, intersect at an azimuth that is approximately perpendicular to the direction of tension. The frequency curve for zones of neutral fractures is centered in this same direction. The relative abundance of any single type of zone is a function of the shape of the underlying template and its relation to the actual direction of pull.

In practice the azimuth and length of the three types of fracture zones are measured and plotted separately, using

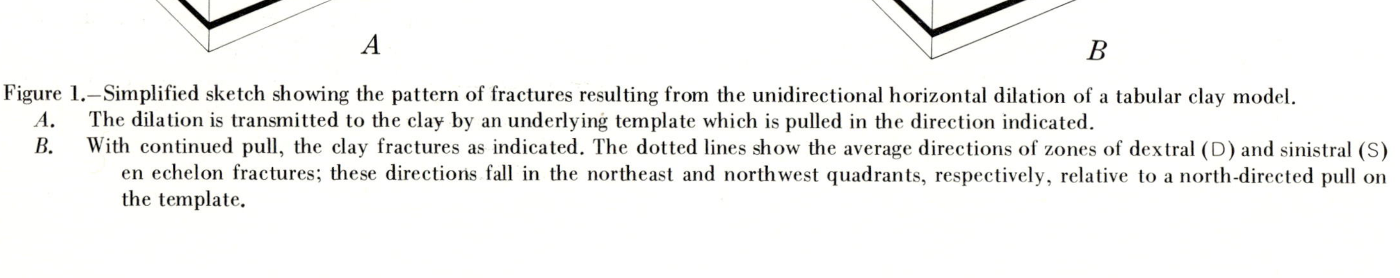

Figure 1.—Simplified sketch showing the pattern of fractures resulting from the unidirectional horizontal dilation of a tabular clay model.
A. The dilation is transmitted to the clay by an underlying template which is pulled in the direction indicated.
B. With continued pull, the clay fractures as indicated. The dotted lines show the average directions of zones of dextral (D) and sinistral (S) en echelon fractures; these directions fall in the northeast and northwest quadrants, respectively, relative to a north-directed pull on the template.

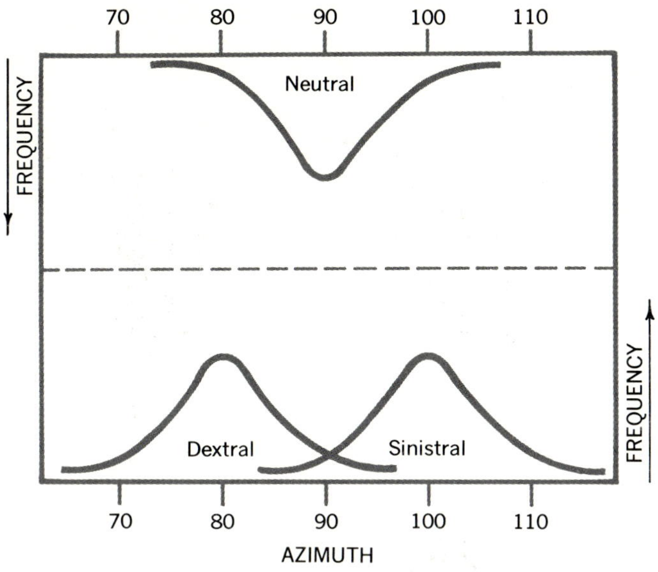

Figure 2.—Summary diagram showing the ideal arrangement of azimuthal frequency of zones of fractures resulting from a unidirectional horizontal tension along a north-south direction. Note that the maximum of the neutral curve and the intersection of curves for the en echelon zones lie on the east-west line.

Table 1.—*Lengths and azimuths for zones of fissures in the Koae fault system*

Sinistral			Neutral			Dextral		
Photograph length (cm)	True length (km)	Azimuth	Photograph length (cm)	True length (km)	Azimuth	Photograph length (cm)	True length (km)	Azimuth
15	0.72	112	12.5	0.60	99	5	0.24	46
30	1.44	75	11	.53	89	14	.67	54
40	1.92	94	27.5	1.32	59	2.5	.12	59
15	.72	77	4.5	.22	70	4	.19	61
25.5	1.22	74	8	.38	58	5	.24	41
7	.34	89	10	.48	69	3	.14	60
19	.91	68	16	.77	64	7	.34	48
15	.72	62	12	.58	79	14	.67	54
6	.29	90	9.5	.46	66	8	.38	65
7	.34	63	5	.24	90	15	.72	54
26.5	1.27	69	13	.62	55	9.5	.46	36
11.5	.55	61	11	.53	60	9.5	.46	35
7	.34	79	9.5	.46	68	7	.34	77
7	.34	88	4	.19	68	7.5	.36	67
14	.67	60	7	.34	53	27	1.30	48
11	.53	81	4	.19	80	5.5	.26	69
8	.38	78	11	.53	68	15	.72	60
24.5	1.18	84	7	.34	70	14	.67	41
23	1.10	73	15.5	.74	78	3	.14	56
11	.53	77	8.5	.41	77	2	.10	61
9	.43	69	19.5	.94	68	14	.67	58
27	1.30	90	17	.82	66	9.5	.46	69
10	.48	80	19	.91	70	6	.29	73
4.5	.22	70						
5	.24	90						

length as a measure of frequency. Measurement can be made most accurately from constant-scale aerial photographs (orthophotographs) but can also be made adequately by less direct methods.

HAWAIIAN STUDY

The Hawaiian example provided a rigorous test of the new method because a detailed field study was completed subsequent to the preliminary determination of horizontal extension. This procedure permitted a check not only on the validity of the method, but also on the judgment of the photoinvestigator in deciding which fractures are indeed arranged en echelon.

The studied area is the Koae fault system, on the south flank of Kilauea Volcano, Hawaii. This system is about 2 km wide and 12 km long and is characterized by steeply dipping open cracks and normal faults. The fractures occur on a well-exposed part of the volcano and are well preserved since they are relatively young; the fault system itself is still active.

For the preliminary study, both uncorrected and constant-scale vertical aerial photographs were available. Most measurements of azimuth and length were made on zones of normal faulting since they were easiest to interpret; patterns of fracturing for small open cracks were often ambiguous at the scale of available photographs. The measurements were tabulated (table 1) and subsequently compiled as histograms (fig. 3). The histograms compare favorably with the ideal case illustrated in figure 2 and suggest that the direction of horizontal extension across the Koae fault system is about N. 30° W., S. 30° E. Neutral fissures favor a N. 65°–70° E. strike,

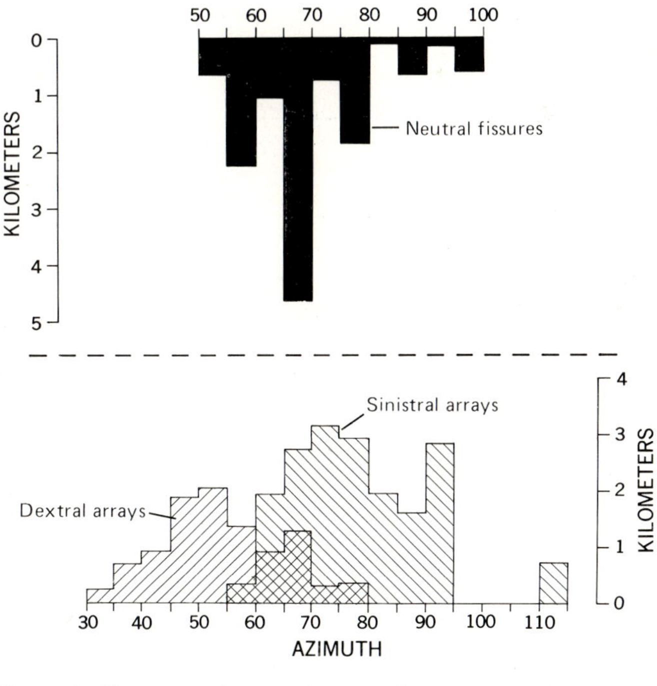

Figure 3.—Histograms showing the azimuthal frequency of zones of fractures for the Koae fault system as determined from aerial photographs. The data from which the histograms were constructed are listed in table 1. Note the similarity between this diagram and figure 2.

approximately at right angles to this indicated opening and parallel to the trend of the entire Koae fault system itself.

Field data used for comparison with these results are part of a detailed (1:4,800 scale) structural mapping project in the Koae fault system. During mapping, individual fissures were routinely measured for trend, and where possible, the azimuth of horizontal opening was also determined. Since most fissures have serrate edges that can mentally be fitted together like pieces of a jigsaw puzzle, nearly all measurements are paired, that is, the trend of fissure and azimuth of opening. Measurements generally are distributed evenly throughout the fault system with regard to approximate total surface length of fracturing per unit area, and fractures of both neutral and en echelon zones are included.

Most measurements were made on open cracks showing little or no vertical offset. Almost invariably, these could be mentally reconstructed easily and unambiguously to yield paired measurements. Normal faults with more than about 1 m of vertical offset were often impossible to reconstruct because of slumping along the plane of the fissure. Thus, the population sampled for the photostudy differed from that of the field study in terms of vertical offset, but the two are believed to be completely comparable in terms of horizontal offset.

All field measurements are subject to some error, mostly caused by slight nonlinearity of individual fissures and by minor difficulties in establishing the precise sense of opening on gaping cracks. The estimated average error for these uncertainties is ±5 degrees. This quantity permits the limits of error to be applied to derived results and also makes it possible to smooth out histograms by redistributing data points within any 10-degree interval. Such smoothing has not been done in this study, but the reader should bear its potential effect in mind.

One hundred and fifty-three paired measurements (trend of fracture and trend of horizontal opening) are summarized in figure 4. Histograms of the trend of individual fissures and the trend of horizontal dilation, which are shown on the same figure, define maxima at azimuths of about 75 degrees (N. 75° E.) and 345 degrees (N. 15° W.), respectively. Thus, within the errors of the method, this azimuth of horizontal dilation as determined from the field measurements differs from that determined from aerial photographs by about 10 degrees. Unrecognized sources of field error may account for this discrepancy. The favored trend of all fractures is essentially the same as that of the neutral fissures of figure 3, indicating that the individual fissures that form en echelon patterns are parallel to each other, to the neutral fissures, and to the entire fault system itself. The slightly elongated pattern of data points in figure 4 reflects a tendency for any individual fissure to open at about right angles to its trend, even though statistically, the two directions favor the above-mentioned orientations.

A comparison of zones of fractures categorized from aerial photographs (table 1) with actual mapped patterns indicates

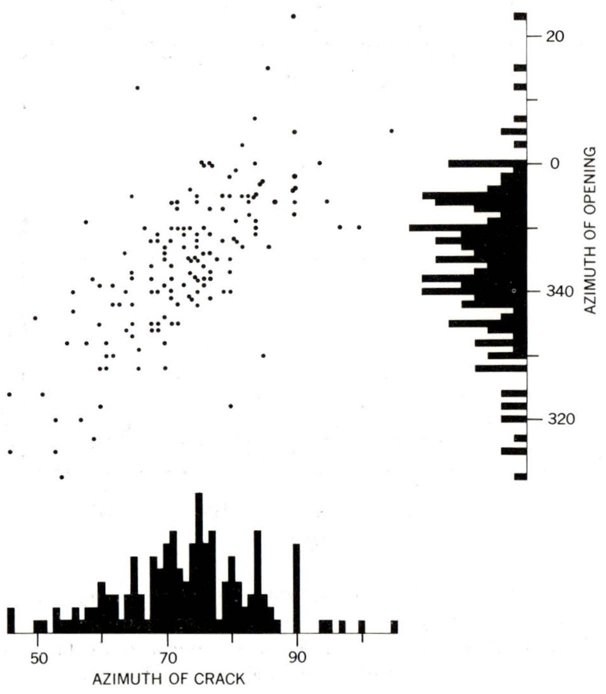

Figure 4.—Graph of paired measurements, trend of crack and trend of horizontal opening, for 153 open cracks of the Koae fault system. Histograms show maxima at about 345-degree azimuth for trend of opening and 75-degree azimuth for trend of crack.

that these predicted classifications are about 90 percent correct. Such "reading error" depends primarily on the degree of preservation and exposure of fissures, the quality of available aerial photographs, and the ability of the photo-investigator to analyze materials correctly. In the Hawaiian study, these sources of error were so small that essentially correct results were obtained; under other similar conditions, sound results can also be expected.

The general validity of the method is confirmed also by the formation of contemporaneous arrays of sinistral and dextral en echelon fractures at Kilauea Volcano in recent years. During the 1955 eruption on the east rift zone of Kilauea, for example, eruptive fissures formed an en echelon array of each sense (Macdonald and Eaton, 1964); direct examination of the fissures and comparison of preeruption and posteruption triangulation surveys indicate that all individual fractures are roughly parallel to one another and that the horizontal opening on them was at right angles to this direction. The azimuth and sense of en echelon arrays relative to this direction were the same as shown in figure 2, the ideal case. Even more recently (September 24–29, 1971), ground cracking associated with an eruption on the southwest rift zone of Kilauea formed similar patterns of fractures with the same interrelations of the various elements (W. A. Duffield, unpub. data).

CONCLUDING REMARKS

Perhaps the most useful aspect of the new method is that sound results can be obtained after only a brief photostudy rather than after lengthy fieldwork. Whenever possible, we recommend that the results of any photostudy be briefly field checked. However, there are circumstances where fieldwork is impractical or impossible, and to these situations the new method has especially valuable applications. Furthermore, for many areas, direct field measurements of horizontal dilation on individual fissures may be impossible; slumping, erosion, and similar destructive processes may quickly destroy the evidence for reconstructing open fissures. Under such conditions, the most detailed of field studies can test only how accurately the arrangement of fissures into en echelon zones was initially determined from aerial photographs.

The type of tectonics (formed by unidirectional tension) to which the method may be applied is restricted, but as more attempts are made to relate structural data to the extensional motions of global plate tectonics, especially on continental regions, this method may become widely applied. The Icelandic study (Nakamura, 1970) provides one example of such an application, and analogous areas, such as the Ethiopian rift system of East Africa, might benefit from a similar analysis. The new method can provide a test for any area which is thought to owe its pattern of fracturing to the transmitted tensional stress of an underlying zone of spreading.

REFERENCES CITED

Billings, M. P., 1954, Structural geology: Englewood Cliffs, N.J., Prentice-Hall, 514 p.

Fiske, R. S., and Kinoshita, W. T., 1969, Rift dilation and seaward displacement of the south flank of Kilauea Volcano, Hawaii [abs.]: Internat. Assoc. Volcanology and Chemistry of the Earth's Interior, Symposium on Volcanoes and their Roots, Oxford, England, p. 53–54.

Macdonald, G. A., and Eaton, J. P., 1964, Hawaiian volcanoes during 1955: U.S. Geol. Survey Bull. 1171, 170 p.

Nakamura, Kazuaki, 1970, En echelon features of Icelandic ground fissures: Acta Naturalia Islandica, v. 2, no. 8, p. 1–15.

Jour. Research U.S. Geol. Survey
Vol. 1, No. 3, May-June 1973, p. 289—292

RADIOELEMENT AND RADIOGENIC HEAT DISTRIBUTION IN DRILL HOLE UCe-1, BELMONT STOCK, CENTRAL NEVADA

By C. M. BUNKER and C. A. BUSH, Denver, Colo.

Abstract.—Uranium, thorium, and potassium concentrations were measured in 60 samples collected from an exploratory hole drilled in the Belmont stock about 40 miles north-northeast of Tonopah, Nev. The results indicate that, at least within 2,000 feet of the surface, the granitic pluton contains radioelement concentrations similar to those in average granodiorites and that local variations in concentrations may reflect the effects of argillic alteration.

An exploratory drill hole, UCe-1, was drilled to provide geologic and geophysical data for evaluating a supplementary nuclear test site. The hole was drilled 2,000 feet into the Belmont stock, a granitic pluton, at approximate Nevada State coordinates N. 1,395,000; E. 429,400 (lat 38°36′ N.; long 116°55′ W.) at an elevation of 7,050±50 feet above mean sea level, about 40 miles north-northeast of Tonopah, Nev. (fig. 1).

In the 340- to 2,000-foot-depth interval the hole penetrated very light gray, medium-grained hypidiomorphic granular granite of Mesozoic age. The granite is well jointed and contains many zones of argillic alteration which are generally joint controlled. The argillized zones are not mineralized and are probably caused by percolating water rather than by hydrothermal solutions (D.C. Hedlund and G.S. Corchary, written commun., 1967). Zones that are moderately or strongly argillized are at the following depths, in feet: 460–468; 1,404–1,407; 1,438–1,444; 1,648–1,650; 1,694–1,694.7; 1,895–1,915; 1,959–1,961; and 1,963–1,966 (D. L. Hoover, written commun., 1967).

Radioelement concentrations were measured in 60 samples selected at intervals of 20 to 50 feet from depths between 365 and 1,997 feet (table 1). These data were obtained initially to determine the radiogenic heat contribution to inhole temperature and heat flow being investigated by A. H. Lachenbruch and John Sass, U.S. Geological Survey. The average values of the data reported here have been compared with averages from other drill holes in a report by Lachenbruch and Bunker (1971). The present report describes the vertical distribution of the radioelements and radiogenic heat in the granite stock.

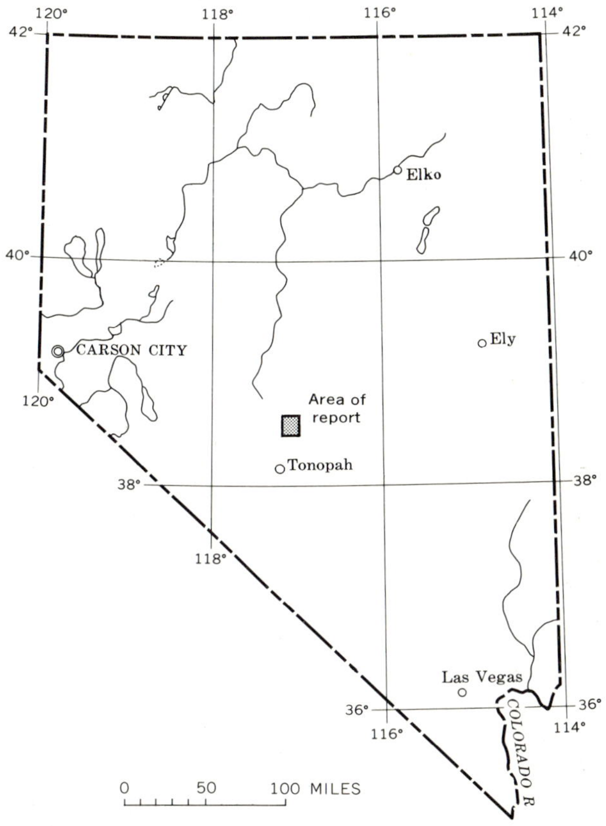

Figure 1.—Index map of Nevada showing area of report.

ANALYTICAL METHOD

The concentrations of the radioelements in the samples were measured by gamma-ray spectrometry. The basic operational procedures and calibration techniques have been described previously (Bunker and Bush, 1966, 1967). The spectra were interpreted with the aid of a linear least-squares computer method which matches the spectrum from a sample to a library of radioelement standards and calculates the concentrations of the radioelements in the sample. The computer method is a modification of a program written by Schonfeld (1966).

Uranium concentrations are determined indirectly by measuring the radium daughters to obtain radium equivalent uranium (RaeU) values. Radium equivalent uranium is the

Table 1.—*Summary of radioelement and radiogenic heat analyses, drill hole UCe-1*
[RaeU, radium equivalent uranium]

Sample depth (feet)	RaeU (ppm)	Th (ppm)	K (percent)	Heat (μcal/g-yr)	Th/RaeU	RaeU/K×10⁻⁴	Th/K×10⁻⁴
365 . . .	2.91	12.83	3.83	5.72	4.41	0.76	3.35
391 . . .	2.96	15.00	3.67	6.15	5.07	.81	4.09
426 . . .	2.70	11.29	3.58	5.20	4.18	.75	3.15
465 . . .	10.71	12.23	3.72	11.27	1.14	2.88	3.29
501 . . .	2.85	11.01	3.65	5.27	3.86	.78	3.02
550 . . .	2.95	11.75	3.76	5.52	3.98	.78	3.12
573 . . .	3.15	11.45	3.79	5.61	3.63	.83	3.02
644 . . .	2.56	10.93	3.66	5.04	4.27	.70	2.99
672 . . .	2.44	11.85	3.67	5.14	4.86	.66	3.23
713 . . .	2.86	11.60	3.78	5.43	4.06	.76	3.07
738 . . .	3.40	11.63	3.82	5.84	3.42	.89	3.04
763 . . .	4.83	10.72	4.68	6.93	2.22	1.03	2.29
795.5 . .	2.50	11.90	3.81	5.23	4.76	.66	3.12
824 . . .	2.83	11.41	3.78	5.37	4.03	.75	3.02
851 . . .	2.70	11.52	3.65	5.26	4.27	.74	3.16
883 . . .	2.96	12.05	3.76	5.59	4.07	.79	3.20
906 . . .	2.86	11.82	3.62	5.43	4.13	.79	3.27
933 . . .	3.62	11.93	3.63	6.01	3.30	1.00	3.29
956 . . .	2.91	11.96	3.64	5.50	4.11	.80	3.29
984 . . .	3.63	11.35	3.76	5.94	3.13	.97	3.02
1,013 . . .	1.77	10.86	3.79	4.49	6.14	.47	2.87
1,027 . . .	2.78	11.52	3.22	5.20	4.14	.86	3.58
1,055 . . .	2.87	12.22	3.59	5.51	4.26	.80	3.40
1,080 . . .	2.35	10.99	3.76	4.93	4.68	.62	2.92
1,107 . . .	6.65	14.47	3.65	8.73	2.18	1.82	3.96
1,129 . . .	3.05	11.00	3.64	5.41	3.61	.84	3.02
1,159 . . .	2.64	11.81	3.53	5.24	4.47	.75	3.35
1,183 . . .	2.33	10.31	3.55	4.72	4.42	.66	2.90
1,206 . . .	2.60	11.34	3.55	5.12	4.36	.73	3.19
1,232 . . .	2.49	12.74	3.59	5.33	5.12	.69	3.55
1,252 . . .	2.33	10.24	3.47	4.69	4.39	.67	2.95
1,280 . . .	2.80	9.60	3.47	4.90	3.43	.81	2.77
1,308 . . .	1.92	12.79	3.67	4.95	6.66	.52	3.49
1,339 . . .	1.81	8.91	3.64	4.09	4.92	.50	2.45
1,374 . . .	1.99	9.90	3.50	4.38	4.97	.57	2.83
1,399 . . .	1.90	8.78	3.52	4.09	4.62	.54	2.49
1,427 . . .	2.18	10.88	3.50	4.71	4.99	.62	3.11
1,454 . . .	2.37	11.07	3.69	4.94	4.67	.64	3.00
1,481 . . .	2.95	10.47	3.53	5.20	3.55	.84	2.97
1,501 . . .	2.22	10.70	3.75	4.77	4.82	.59	2.85
1,526 . . .	3.61	10.85	3.46	5.74	3.01	1.04	3.14
1,552 . . .	3.31	9.91	4.08	5.50	2.99	.81	2.43
1,587 . . .	2.29	10.23	3.62	4.70	4.47	.63	2.83
1,604 . . .	2.35	9.86	3.58	4.65	4.20	.66	2.75
1,633 . . .	2.54	9.77	3.75	4.82	3.85	.68	2.61
1,657 . . .	2.43	11.24	3.39	4.94	4.63	.72	3.32
1,681 . . .	2.22	9.76	3.38	4.49	4.40	.66	2.89
1,706 . . .	3.42	8.56	3.40	5.13	2.50	1.01	2.52
1,731 . . .	2.16	8.46	3.47	4.21	3.92	.62	2.44
1,762 . . .	2.46	11.80	3.57	5.12	4.80	.69	3.31
1,778 . . .	2.19	14.82	3.52	5.51	6.77	.62	4.21
1,809 . . .	2.55	12.65	3.78	5.41	4.96	.67	3.35
1,833 . . .	2.94	11.26	3.39	5.31	3.83	.87	3.32
1,859 . . .	3.84	11.77	3.58	6.12	3.07	1.07	3.29
1,884 . . .	4.50	11.11	3.52	6.46	2.47	1.28	3.16
1,912 . . .	3.95	12.31	4.37	6.53	3.12	.90	2.82
1,931 . . .	2.87	10.17	3.51	5.08	3.54	.82	2.90
1,950 . . .	2.43	9.84	3.57	4.71	4.05	.68	2.76
1,979 . . .	3.41	13.66	3.33	6.12	4.01	1.02	4.10
1,997 . . .	3.03	9.76	3.26	5.04	3.22	.93	2.99

amount of uranium, under the assumption of radioactive equilibrium, required to support the amount of daughter products that emit the radioactivity measured in a sample. Throughout the report where "U" and "uranium" are used "radium equivalent uranium" is implicit. Although thorium is also measured from daughter products, disequilibrium is improbable because of short half-lives; therefore, the concentrations are considered to be a direct measurement of parent thorium. Potassium is determined from its K^{40} constituent which is proportional to the total potassium. The coefficients of variation for the accuracy of the data included in this report (table 1) are about 5 percent for uranium and thorium and 1 percent for potassium when compared to standards analyzed by isotope dilution methods.

RESULTS

The vertical distributions of the radioelements (fig. 2) indicate a fairly homogeneous rock intersected by zones containing greater concentrations of the radioelements. The character of the distribution is compatible with the available geologic data: variations in concentrations can be expected in well-jointed and altered rock. The data appear to indicate a change in the rock at a depth of about 1,150 feet, below which the radioelement concentrations decrease, although the lower part of the section contains some zones of relatively high concentrations. The apparent differences in the rock above and below 1,150 feet which are observable on the vertical distribution plots are also indicated in histograms of the data (fig. 3). The apparent differences are confirmed by the averages and standard deviations for both potassium and radiogenic heat. However, statistically, uranium and thorium in the upper and lower levels are not significantly different at the 95-percent confidence level. Thus, the apparent differences in uranium and thorium shown on the vertical distribution plots and histograms are really a reflection of the greater variability in concentrations below that depth. The generally higher concentrations in the upper part of the section might be caused by either deep alteration resulting from water moving through the numerous joints or differentiation during intrusion; the available lithologic data do not suggest an explanation. The upper and lower zones are too thin to determine whether systematic changes in concentrations exist that are related to depth (Lachenbruch and Bunker, 1971).

The averages and standard deviations of the radioelements, their ratios, and radiogenic heat are shown in table 2 for the samples above and below 1,150 feet. Values which differed from the mean by more than 3 standard deviations were

Table 2.—*Comparison of radioelement data in drill hole UCe-1 and average concentrations in similar rocks*

	Concentrations in drill hole UCe-1[1] (average ± standard deviation)		Average concentrations (Clark and others, 1966)		
	Above 1,150 ft	Below 1,150 ft	Diorite, quartz diorite	Grano-diorite	Silicic igneous rocks
U (ppm)	2.85±0.41	2.60±0.64	2	2.6	4.7
Th (ppm).	11.58± .51	11.24±1.5	8.5	9.3	20.0
K (percent)	3.71± .08	3.53± .12	1.10	2.55	3.9
Th/U	4.06± .45	4.21± .98	4.3	3.6	4.0
U/K×10⁻⁴	.77± .11	.74± .18	1.8	1	1.3
Th/K×10⁻⁴	3.13± .14	3.06± .42	7.7	3.6	5.0
Heat[2] (μcal/g-yr) . . .	5.40± .35	5.02± .55	3.5	4.4	8.5

[1] Average concentrations calculated after excluding values which differ from mean by more than 3 standard deviations.
[2] Heat = 0.73 U + 0.20 Th + 0.27 K.

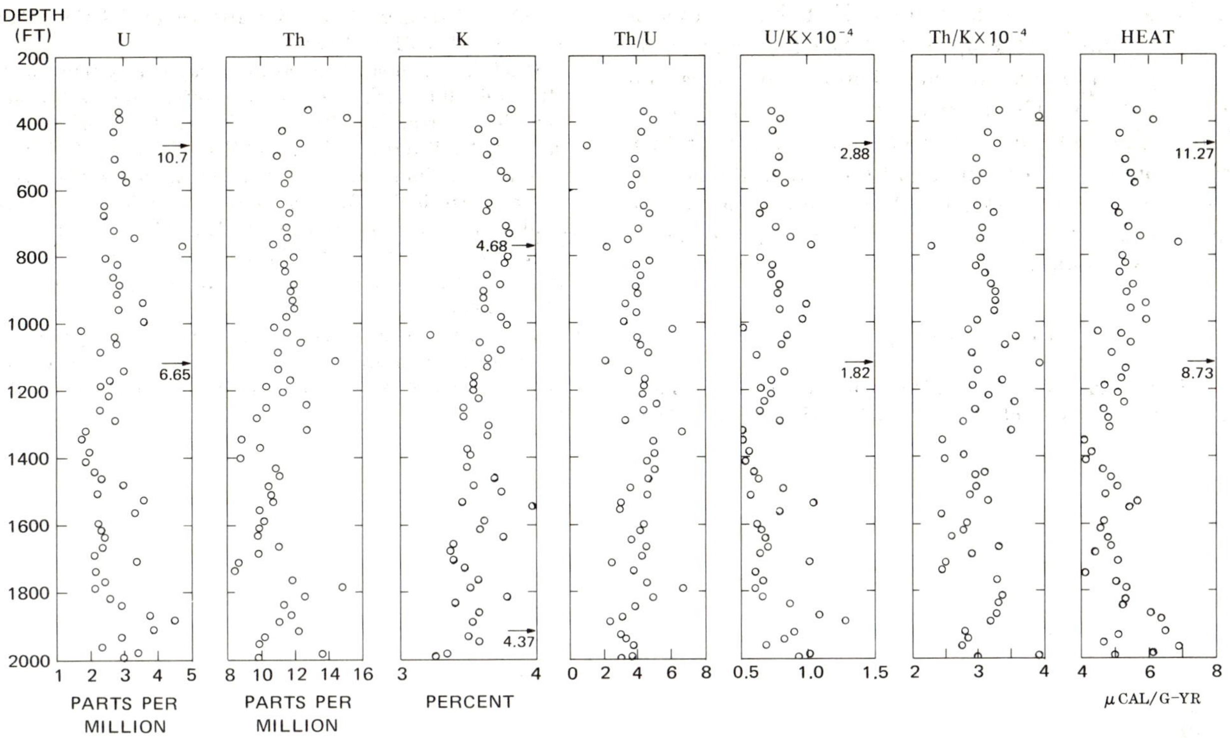

Figure 2.—Radioelement concentrations and ratios, and radiogenic heat in drill hole UCe-1. Arrows indicate points beyond scale limit.

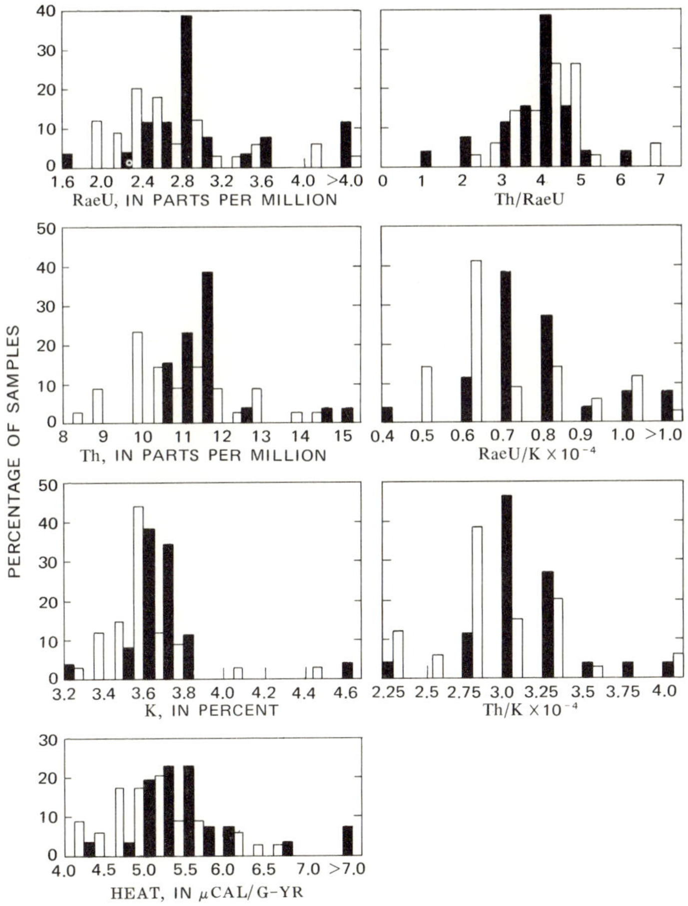

Figure 3.—Frequency distribution of radioelement concentrations and ratios and radiogenic heat. Shaded bars are from interval 365–1,129 feet (26 samples); others are from 1,159–1,997 feet (34 samples).

excluded from the calculations. For comparison, data are included for average abundances in similar rocks as summarized by Clark, Peterman, and Heier (1966).

Uranium concentration ranges from 1.8 to 10.7 ppm, but in most samples it ranges from 1.9 to 3.4 ppm, which is similar to the average concentrations in diorite, quartz diorite, and granodiorite. Thorium concentration ranges from 8.4 to 15 ppm, but in most samples it ranges from 9.6 to 12.2 ppm, slightly more than the average for granodiorite. The potassium concentration is remarkably constant throughout the depth of the hole, and with few exceptions it ranges from 3.4 to 3.8 percent; this range lies between the averages for granodiorite and monzonite. The constancy of the potassium concentrations supports the conclusion of D. C. Hedlund and G. S. Corchary (written commun., 1967) that the argillized alteration is caused by percolating water; hydrothermal alteration often causes changes in potassium concentrations. Most of the Th/U ratios range from 3 to 5, which is normal for granitic rocks. The $U/K\times10^{-4}$ ratios in most of the samples range from 0.5 to 0.9, which is lower than normal for silicic rocks containing the concentrations measured here, and indicates that the rock either contains excess potassium or is deficient in uranium. $Th/K\times10^{-4}$ ratios, which range from 2.8 to 3.3, are slightly lower than the average for granodiorite. The radiogenic heat, calculated from the radioelement concentrations, ranges mostly from 4.4 to 5.8 μcal/g-yr, which is slightly higher than that calculated for the average granodiorite.

The radioelement data indicate that the Belmont stock is not a typical granite in the upper 2,000 feet penetrated by drill hole UCe-1. The uranium and thorium concentrations indicate a rock in the intermediate class, similar to a granodiorite. The potassium concentrations are greater than the average for granodiorite and slightly less than the average for more silicic igneous rocks. Local variations from average concentrations may be caused by the effects of the numerous zones of argillic alteration.

REFERENCES CITED

Bunker, C. M., and Bush, C. A., 1966, Uranium, thorium, and radium analyses by gamma-ray spectrometry (0.184–0.352 million electron volts), *in* Geological Survey Research 1966: U.S. Geol. Survey Prof. Paper 550-B, p. B176–B181.

—— 1967, A comparison of potassium analyses by gamma-ray spectrometry and other techniques, *in* Geological Survey Research 1967: U.S. Geol. Survey Prof. Paper 575-B, p. B164–B169.

Clark, S. P., Jr., Peterman, Z. E., and Heier, K. S., 1966, Abundances of uranium, thorium, and potassium, Sec. 24 *in* Handbook of physical constants (revised ed.): Geol. Soc. America Mem. 97, p. 521–541.

Lachenbruch, A. H., and Bunker, C. M., 1971, Vertical gradients of heat production in the continental crust, 2. Some estimates from borehole data: Jour. Geophys. Research, v. 76, no. 17, p. 3852–3860.

Schonfeld, Ernest, 1966, Alpha M—An improved computer program for determining radioisotopes by least-squares resolution of the gamma-ray spectra: U.S. Natl. Lab., Oak Ridge, Tenn. [Pub.] ORNL-3975, 42 p.

Jour. Research U.S. Geol. Survey
Vol. 1, No. 3, May-June 1973, p. 293—299

GEOLOGY OF A SYSTEM OF SUBMARINE CANYONS SOUTH OF PUERTO RICO

By JAMES V. A. TRUMBULL and LOUIS E. GARRISON,
Corpus Christi, Tex.

Work done in cooperation with the Puerto Rico Economic Development Administration

Abstract.—A strongly dendritic submarine canyon system with four major canyons occupies a 30-km indentation in the insular shelf off the south coast of Puerto Rico between Guánica and Ponce. Each canyon has several headward branches at depths of 100 to 1,100 m. Each of the five major rivers that reach the coast between Guánica and Ponce is opposite a canyon head, and off each of the rivers a channel 20 to 30 m deep is incised into the insular shelf. The entire canyon system is 40 km long and terminates at a depth of about 3.3 km; no fan or other constructional feature appears to have been formed. A 410-km continuous seismic profiling survey shows that three unconformable stratigraphic units underlie the canyon area. One sample of indurated clay of probable Miocene age was dredged from a canyon-wall outcrop of the middle stratigraphic unit. The three stratigraphic units may be roughly correlative with (in ascending order) the Juana Díaz Formation, the Ponce Limestone, and an unnamed upper section found in a nearby drill hole ashore. Canyon-axis sediment at depths of 700 to 2,200 m is entirely of pelagic origin, indicating that sediment is not now being transported down the canyons.

During the conduct of marine geophysical work by the U.S. Geological Survey off the south coast of Puerto Rico in January 1968, bathymetric records indicated the presence of a small submarine canyon trending south-southwest off Punta Cuchara. Through the cooperation of the National Ocean Survey (then the U.S. Coast and Geodetic Survey), detailed soundings were made in the area of the suspected canyon in 1969, and the preliminary data were released to the Geological Survey. From those uncorrected soundings, a bathymetric map (fig. 1) was made that revealed the presence of a major submarine canyon system on the insular slope between Guánica and Ponce. This canyon system is here referred to as the Guayanilla Canyon system; its four feeder canyons are here called, from west to east, Guánica Canyon, Guayanilla Canyon, Cuchara Canyon, and Muertos Canyon. The existence of all four canyons was pointed out by Athearn (1971), but his bathymetric map did not extend far enough seaward to show that the four canyons form one dendritic system.

During a cruise to the area in 1970, the bathymetric map was field checked, more than 410 km of continuous seismic reflection profiles were made, and samples were gathered from the wallrock and from the unconsolidated sediment along the canyon axes. Preliminary results of that work are presented here.

The continuous seismic reflection profiler used in this study discharged 9,000 joules of stored electrical energy at intervals of 4 seconds. For simplicity, reflection traveltimes have been converted to depth, with an assumed sound velocity in sediment of 2 km/sec. Selection of this figure is based on the presumed carbonate lithology inferred from onshore mapping (Briggs and Akers, 1965) and on results of seismic refraction work on the south coastal plain of Puerto Rico (Denning, 1955).

Acknowledgments.—We thank our U.S. Geological Survey colleagues Jacky W. Lee and Stephen C. Wolf for their skilled operation of seismic equipment and other assistance at sea; Ruth Todd for identification of Foraminifera; Ray Martin for contouring the canyon bathymetry; and John Aaron for information added during review. We also thank the National Ocean Survey for the sounding data from which the bathymetric chart was derived. Arnie Junger gave valuable advice in the technique of determining the effect of rough topography on seismic records.

TOPOGRAPHY

The bathymetry of the Guayanilla Canyon system and adjacent insular shelf is shown in figure 1, and the salient characteristics of the canyons are listed and compared with the characteristics of other known submarine canyons of the world in table 1.

The four canyons form a well-developed tributary system. Each of them has at least three headward branches. Muertos Canyon joins Cuchara Canyon at a depth of about 1,550 m, and Cuchara Canyon joins Guayanilla Canyon at about 1,900 m. Guánica Canyon loses its V-shaped cross section at a closed topographic depression at a depth of about 1,700 m, and it loses its identification as a canyon a few kilometers further downslope. It too is clearly confluent with Guayanilla Canyon

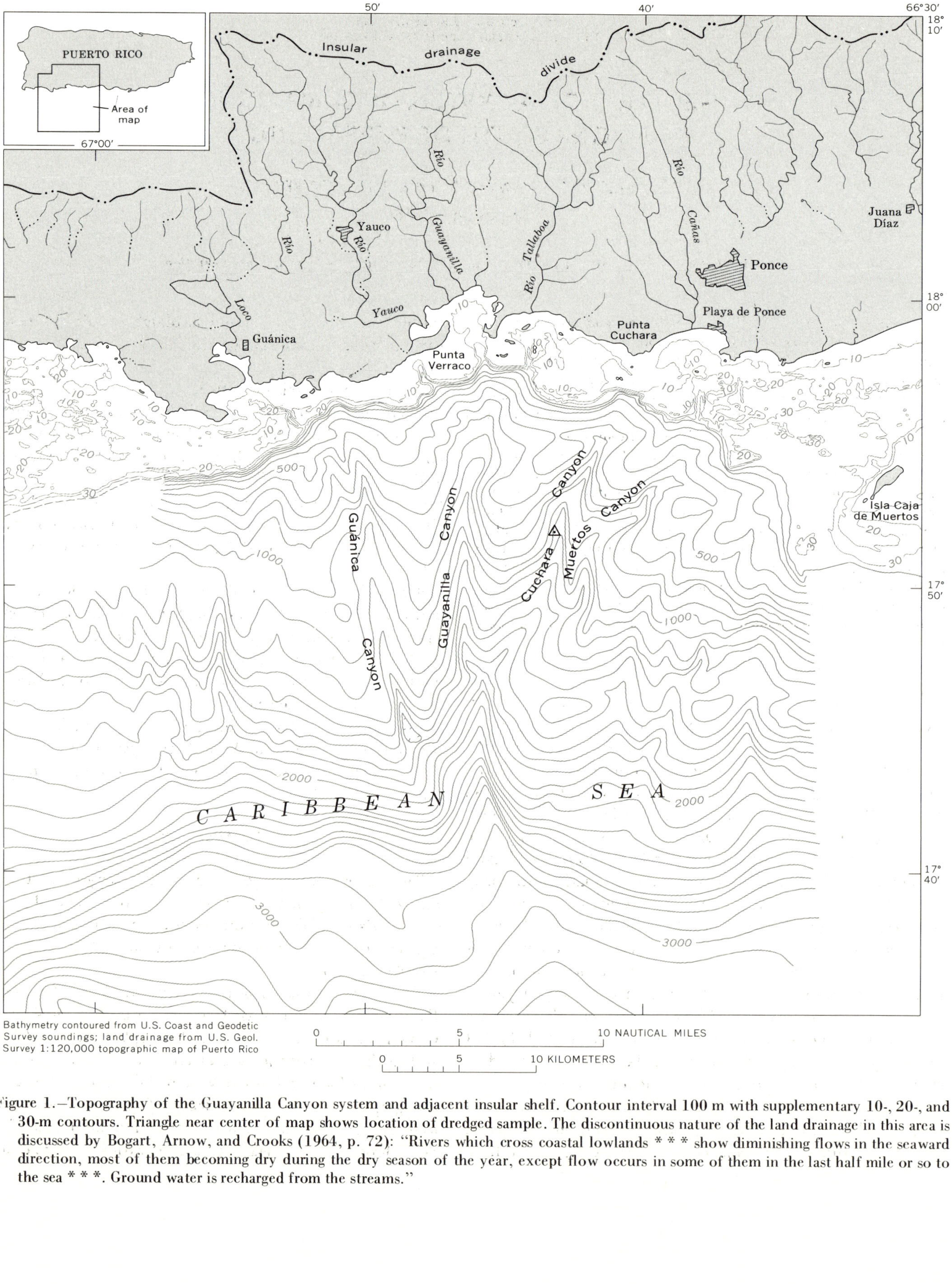

Figure 1.—Topography of the Guayanilla Canyon system and adjacent insular shelf. Contour interval 100 m with supplementary 10-, 20-, and 30-m contours. Triangle near center of map shows location of dredged sample. The discontinuous nature of the land drainage in this area is discussed by Bogart, Arnow, and Crooks (1964, p. 72): "Rivers which cross coastal lowlands * * * show diminishing flows in the seaward direction, most of them becoming dry during the dry season of the year, except flow occurs in some of them in the last half mile or so to the sea * * *. Ground water is recharged from the streams."

Table 1.—*Comparison of four Puerto Rico submarine canyons with other known submarine canyons of the world*

[Data on averages for other canyons are from Shepard and Dill (1966)]

Canyon characteristic		Four Puerto Rico canyons	Average of all other canyons
Length	km	40	55
Depth at head	m	100–400	107
Depth at outer termination.	km	3	2.1
Coast embayed or straight.		Embayed.	Equal numbers of each type.
Distance of head from land.	km	2–5	Majority are close.
Relation to land valleys.		Strongly related.	80 percent related.
Shelf channels		Small, well developed.	Rare.
Land sediment now entering.		No	57 percent no.
Gradient	m/km	63	58
Profile		Relatively even below steeper head.	Most concave upward.
Maximum wall height	m	500–1,000	915
Axial trend		Gently curving.	Sinuous to gently curving.
Tributaries below heads.		All have tributaries.	87 percent have tributaries.
Transverse profile		Mostly V-shaped.	80 percent V-shaped.
Wall material		Sedimentary rock.	Virtually all rock, 55 percent sedimentary.

as a hanging valley. Thus Guayanilla Canyon is the master canyon of the system.

On the evidence of available soundings, Guayanilla Canyon loses its valley characteristics at about lat 17°35′ N., the lower border of figure 1. Farther south is Muertos Trough, whose east-trending axis, with greatest depths near 5,050 m, is at about lat 17°20′ N. Small inflections in bathymetric contours as deep as 4,300 m indicate that Guayanilla Canyon may continue in some form to that depth. No depositional fan or other constructional feature formed of material excavated from or carried through the canyon appears to be present.

Five samples of unconsolidated sediment from the axes of Guayanilla and Cuchara Canyons at depths ranging from 700 to 2,200 m are composed entirely of the remains of pelagic organisms, indicating that little or no land-derived sediment is now being transported down those canyons.

The most striking characteristic of the four submarine canyons is their close relationship to the width of the insular shelf, to the nearby river systems, and to channels in the insular shelf.

The upper reaches of the four canyons occupy an indentation in the insular shelf that extends about 35 km from Guánica to Playa de Ponce (fig. 1). The shelf is only 1 to 5 km wide in the area occupied by the canyons, but it is 9 to 10 km wide west of the canyon system, and 15 to 18 km wide to the east. Figure 1 also shows that in this part of Puerto Rico, the larger rivers are opposite the canyon area and that the rivers east and west of the canyon area are discontinuous.

The geology of the land area opposite the canyon system and the narrow part of the shelf is also distinctive. As pointed out by our colleague John Aaron, that area is the only part of the south coastal plain where middle Tertiary rocks are extensive. East of Juana Díaz and west of Guánica they occur only as very isolated and very small patches. All else is alluvium or volcanic complex. This might mean that canyon formation could have been promoted by, among other factors, the relatively incompetent nature of these rocks.

The heads of the submarine canyons are directly opposite the mouths of major rivers, excepting only the head of Cuchara Canyon, discussed in the next paragraph. As figure 1 shows, the head of Guánica Canyon is opposite the Bahia de Guánica, into which the Río Loco flows. The three major headward branches of Guayanilla Canyon are directly in line with Ríos Guayanilla and Tallaboa and the previous trend of the Río Yauco (see below). The head of Muertos Canyon is opposite the Bahia de Ponce, into which the Río Cañas flows. Furthermore, each of the canyons except Cuchara is linked to its river by a channel cut into the shelf. The shelf channels are well developed, although not of impressive dimensions: the 20- and 30-m depth contours extend 2 to 3½ km across the insular shelf (fig. 1).

Cuchara Canyon alone is not associated with a shelf channel. Clearly Muertos Canyon connects with the Río Cañas system through the shelf channel southwest of Playa de Ponce. Because Cuchara Canyon and Muertos Canyon both are east of the divide separating the Río Tallaboa system from the Río Cañas system, and because this divide continues seaward to the confluence of those two canyons with the main Guayanilla Canyon, it seems likely that both canyons are related to the Río Cañas. Cuchara Canyon may therefore be an older extension of the Río Cañas system that was closed off, perhaps by uplift or upbuilding of the present shelf, Muertos Canyon being formed later.

The relation between the Río Yauco and the shelf channel south of Punta Verraco is not immediately clear from the map (fig. 1), for the Río Yauco does not now discharge near the shelf channel. It previously did, however, as is shown in a report on the Guánica-Guayanilla Bay area by Grossman (1963, p. B116), who stated:

> That the Río Yauco formerly followed a more direct course to the Caribbean is indicated by the broad valley that extends from the present valley of the river southeastward * * * to the Caribbean Sea * * * [west of Punta Verraco] * * *. This "abandoned" valley is drained by an undersized ephemeral stream that flows southeastward to the blocked exit to the sea and then doubles back [northeastward] and empties into Guayanilla Bay.

STRATIGRAPHY

Interpretation of the seismic profiler records (fig. 2) shows that three bedded rock units are present throughout most of the upper canyon area.

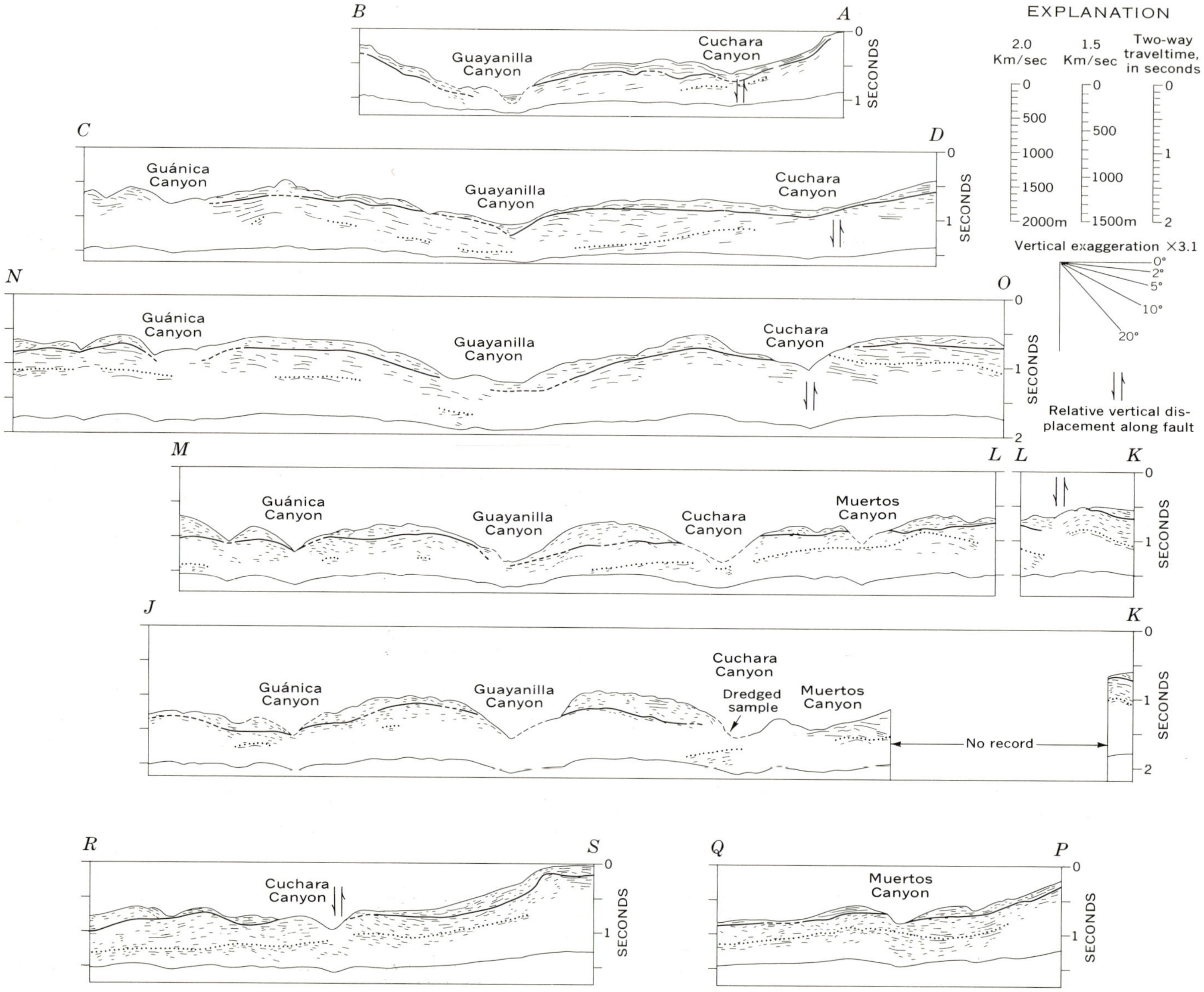

Figure 2.—Simplified tracings of selected seismic profiles. See figure 3 for locations. Heavy line designates contact between upper and middle stratigraphic units; dotted line designates contact between middle and lower units. Continuous line profile below each seismic profile shows the calculated distorting effect of topography on a theoretical horizontal reflecting bed at depth. Horizontal scale is not the same in all profiles because strong current in survey area caused variation in ship speed over the ground.

The upper unit averages about 150 m in thickness on the topographically high areas between canyons, becomes progressively thinner down the canyon flanks, and is absent below depths ranging from 700 m in the upper reaches of Cuchara and Muertos Canyons to 1,000 m in the middle reaches of Guayanilla Canyon (fig. 3). The upper unit is characterized by strong, closely spaced internal reflectors, especially on the profiles near land. These internal reflecting horizons are generally parallel both to the present topographic surface and to the eroded surface of the underlying middle unit. The progressive thinning and pinchout of the upper unit on the canyon flanks is therefore predominantly a result of nondeposition rather than of erosion, though some erosion on the canyon flanks is evident. The surface on which the upper unit was deposited had the general topographic form of the present surface, so that sediment deposited on the intercanyon areas and not in the canyons acted to preserve and accentuate the preexisting topography. Age of the upper unit is not directly known, but it lies unconformably on beds of probable Miocene age.

The middle stratigraphic unit lacks prominent continuous reflecting horizons. Bedding is generally even, though slight internal unconformities are not uncommon. The middle unit was deposited throughout the area covered by seismic profiles. In general, it is 400 to 500 m thick in the area of upper Guayanilla Canyon in the north-central part of the area, and

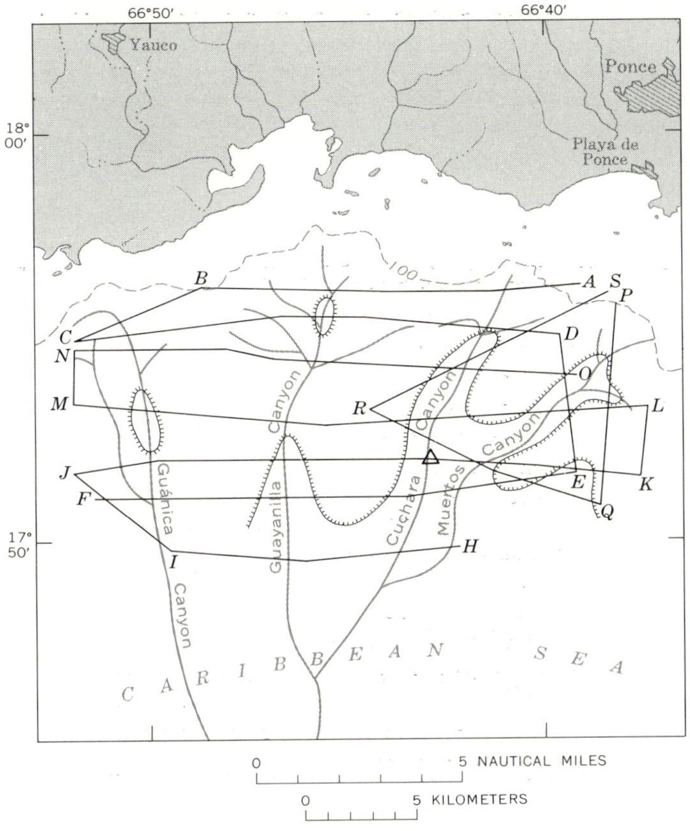

Figure 3.—Location of seismic profiles (fig. 2) and extent of upper stratigraphic unit. Ticks indicate the side of the boundary line on which the upper stratigraphic unit is present. Dashed 100-m bathymetric contour indicates approximate edge of insular shelf. Heavy gray lines are canyon axes.

250 to 300-m thick in the upper reaches of Cuchara and Muertos Canyons. Thickness variations of the middle unit are not correlative with the location of canyon axes or the intercanyon topographic highs.

It appears that at least the tributary canyons Cuchara and Muertos were cut into the middle unit, as shown by the truncation of middle unit reflectors in profiles *R–S* and *Q–P* (fig. 2). In Guayanilla Canyon, downcutting into the middle unit is indicated by an apparent truncation of reflectors in profiles *B–A* and *C–D*; thinning of this unit beneath the canyon is apparent in many of the profiles.

In most places the middle unit lies conformably on the lower unit, but unconformity exists, indicating at least a slight erosional cycle between deposition of the lower and middle units.

The top of the lower unit is characterized by a prominent reflector, but the reflector and hence the unit could be identified on less than half the total length of profiles. The character of seismic returns from within the lower unit shows that, like the middle unit, it is rather even bedded and contains minor internal unconformities. Maximum seismic penetration into the lower unit was 450 m. No base could be defined, and no change in character with depth was noted. Erosion of the top of the lower unit is evident in only a few places. Within the area surveyed, the lower unit crops out only in the east bank of Cuchara Canyon on line *N–O*, in the upthrown block of a fault.

On most profiles where it could be identified, the top of the lower unit is subparallel to the topography of the sea floor. Much of this is caused by the effect of topography on the attitude of subbottom reflectors as shown in the profiles. As illustrated by the continuous line profiles below each seismic profile in figure 2, the effect of topography in other than level areas is to rotate all reflectors toward parallelism with the bottom. Thus a truly horizontal reflector would appear to dip toward a canyon axis.

Only one sample of what appears to be canyon wallrock has been obtained to date. Dredging at a depth of 1,030–1,170 m on the west side of Cuchara Canyon (fig. 1) produced pieces of moderately well indurated, light-olive-gray clay from what is thought to be the middle unit (fig. 2, profile *J–K*). Four species of Foraminifera from this sample indicate a probable Miocene age (Ruth Todd, written commun., 1970). Rounded limestone fragments found in the same dredge haul are tentatively dated as no younger than Oligocene on the basis of one species of Foraminifera. Presumably they were eroded from farther up the canyon, where they may have been derived from the lower unit.

According to Ruth Todd (written commun., 1970), the units sampled and the Holocene ooze with which the samples are mixed were probably deposited at generally similar depths.

The stratigraphic relations and terminology of the Tertiary rocks of the land bordering the canyon area are complex (Zapp and others, 1948; Seiglie and Bermúdez, 1969; Moussa and Seiglie, 1970), but as a simplification we can say that the Juana Díaz Formation is of Oligocene and early Miocene age and is composed of shale, sandy limestone, and conglomerate. It is as much as 655 m thick. The Ponce Limestone is of Miocene age and is principally limestone with lenses of clay. It is as much as 1,300 m thick.

In an exploratory well drilled near the coast southeast of Ponce, about 9 km from the nearest seismic profile of this study, the Juana Díaz Formation was found to be about 335 m thick, and the Ponce Limestone to be about 366 m thick (Glover, 1971, fig. 30). Overlying the Ponce Limestone is an unnamed sequence of sand, gravel, and limestone beds about 150 m thick.

On the basis of geologic age and thickness, the lower stratigraphic unit in the seismic profiles may correlate with the Juana Díaz Formation, the middle stratigraphic unit with the Ponce Limestone, and the upper stratigraphic unit with the unnamed upper section of the exploratory well.

STRUCTURE

The well-developed dendritic pattern of the Guayanilla Canyon system would seem to preclude any extensive structural control of canyon location. Furthermore the primarily north-south orientation of the canyons is not in accord with the main nearby structural trends. In the exposed coastal plain to the north, the principal alinement of faulting and folding is east and northwest, in accordance with the older structural trends of that part of the island (Zapp and others, 1948; Briggs and Akers, 1965). To the east on the submerged Muertos shelf, faulting of the rocks along northeasterly trends has been described (Garrison, 1969).

Some faulting in the eastern part of the canyon system is seen in the seismic profiles, however, and the upper part of Cuchara Canyon may be fault controlled. The fault shown near the east end of profile *N–O* (fig. 2) has an estimated vertical displacement of slightly less than 500 m on the basis of the offset of the middle stratigraphic unit. The upthrown block of the fault forms the east wall of Cuchara Canyon. This fault can also be tentatively identified beneath Cuchara Canyon in profiles *R–S*, *C–D*, and *B–A*, but it is not evident on profiles crossing Cuchara Canyon south of profile *N–O*.

A second fault is seen on profile *L–K*, where the estimated vertical displacement is 250–400 m. This fault is not discernible on any of the adjacent profiles; whether this is because it dies out or because of poor records is not known.

DISCUSSION

The close correspondence between river-cut land valleys and the heads of submarine canyons surely shows a genetic relationship. The canyons have cut into the middle stratigraphic unit, which is of probable Miocene age, and the youngest rocks eroded by the rivers are in the Ponce Limestone, also of Miocene age (Briggs and Akers, 1965). Thus the land and the submarine valleys may have started forming at the same time.

The excellent correspondence of land and sea valleys across the insular shelf could be taken as an indication of subaerial canyon origin, as could the dendritic tributary pattern of the canyons on the insular slope. These characteristics are shared by most of the submarine canyons throughout the world, however (table 1), and the hypothesis of worldwide subaerial canyon erosion requires an episode of worldwide sea-level lowering on the order of several kilometers. The absence of evidence for this makes it difficult to invoke a subaerial origin for other than perhaps the shallow part of the Guayanilla Canyon system.

The insular shelf forms a prominent nickpoint in the overall longitudinal profile of the Guayanilla river-canyon system shown in figure 4. In a detailed study of a land valley–sea valley system of similar longitudinal profile, Woodford (1951) concluded that a prominent nickpoint eliminated submergence of a river valley as a possible mode of canyon origin. In observing that Woodford's conclusion was justified, Shepard and Dill (1966, p. 319) went on to say that:

> It seems apparent that the typical concave profile of submarine canyons, with its steepest element in shallow water near the canyon head, is an indication that the profile is adjusted to the present sea level, or at least a sea level close to that of the present day. This does not disprove an original subaerial cutting of the submarine canyons, but it does show that some form of submarine erosion must have greatly reshaped these valleys.

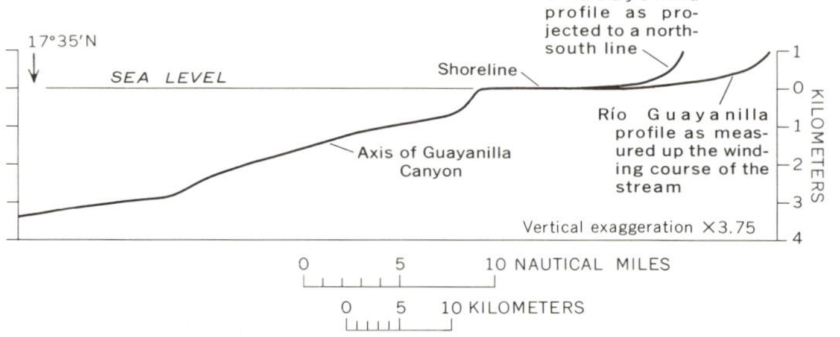

Figure 4.—Longitudinal profile of Río Guayanilla and Guayanilla Canyon.

The prism of sediments beneath the insular shelf forms the nickpoint in figure 4. If that prism was cut through early in the erosion cycle and later filled, or if it was formed after the main erosion cycle, the river-canyon system could well have had a continuous gradient. This would accord with the hypothesis of subaerial canyon erosion. We have as yet no information whether such extensive cutting and filling took place in the heads of the Guayanilla Canyon system. As to the possibility of upbuilding of the insular shelf as a whole since canyon formation, profiles *B–A* and *R–S* of figure 2 show that the middle stratigraphic unit forms a significant part of the prism of shelf sediments. The canyon has eroded the middle unit and therefore postdates it. Presumably then the insular shelf was present in some form when the canyon was eroded.

The extensive headward branching of all four canyons shown in figure 3 appears to be a response to the steep gradient of the outer edge of the prism of sediment that forms the insular shelf. Thus at least some canyon erosion at depths generally between 100 and 1,100 m has occurred since formation of the shelf.

The small channels cut into the surface of the outer shelf between river mouths and canyon heads are at the most only slightly more than 30 m deep. They were probably formed subaerially during Pleistocene glacial-stage withdrawals of sea level.

REFERENCES CITED

Athearn, W. D., 1971, Upper slope bathymetry off Guayanilla and Ponce, Puerto Rico, *in* Caribbean Geol. Conf., 5th, St. Thomas, Virgin Islands, 1968, Trans.: Flushing, N.Y., Queens College Press (New York City Univ. Queens Coll., Dept. Geology Geol. Bull. 5), p. 41–43.

Bogart, D. B., Arnow, Ted, and Crooks, J. W., 1964, Water resources of Puerto Rico—A progress report: Puerto Rico Water Resources Authority Water-Resources Bull. 4, [120 p].

Briggs, R. P., and Akers, J. P., 1965, Hydrogeologic map of Puerto Rico and adjacent islands: U.S. Geol. Survey Hydrol. Inv. Atlas HA-197.

Denning, W. H., 1955, Preliminary results of geophysical exploration for gas and oil on the south coast of Puerto Rico: Puerto Rico, Dept. Indus. Research, Div. Mineralogy and Geology Bull. 2, 17 p. (mimeo).

Garrison, L. E., 1969, Structural geology of the Muertos insular shelf, Puerto Rico: U.S. Geol. Survey open-file report, 9 p.

Glover, Lynn, III, 1971, Geology of the Coamo area, Puerto Rico, and its relation to the volcanic arc-trench phenomena: U.S. Geol. Survey Prof. Paper 636, 102 p.

Grossman, I. G., 1963, Geology of the Guánica-Guayanilla Bay area, southwestern Puerto Rico: Art. 29 *in* U.S. Geol. Survey Prof. Paper 475-B, p. B114–B116.

Moussa, M. T., and Seiglie, G. A., 1970, Revision of mid-Tertiary stratigraphy of southwestern Puerto Rico: Am. Assoc. Petroleum Geologists Bull., v. 54, no. 10, p. 1887–1898.

Seiglie, G. A., and Bermúdez, P. J., 1969, Informe preliminar sobre los foraminíferos del terciario del sur de Puerto Rico, Pt. 1: Caribbean Jour. Sci., v. 9, nos. 1–2, p. 67–80.

Shepard, F. P., and Dill, R. F., 1966, Submarine canyons and other sea valleys: Chicago, Rand McNally and Co., 381 p.

Woodford, A. O., 1951, Stream gradients and Monterey sea valley: Geol. Soc. America Bull., v. 62, no. 7, p. 799–852.

Zapp, A. D., Bergquist, H. R., and Thomas, C. R., 1948, Tertiary geology of the coastal plains of Puerto Rico: U.S. Geol. Survey Oil and Gas Inv. Prelim. Map OM-85, 2 sheets.

Jour. Research U.S. Geol. Survey
Vol. 1, No. 3, May-June 1973, p. 301—307

A SPECTROCHEMICAL METHOD FOR DETERMINING THE COMPOSITION OF NATIVE GOLD

By A. L. SUTTON, R. G. HAVENS, and
C. L. SAINSBURY, Denver, Colo.

Abstract.—The spectrochemical method described herein for determining trace, minor, and major element distribution in native gold is applicable over a wide range of particle sizes and over a very large concentration range. The matrices of samples and standards are very closely matched. The method was tested on 100 nuggets from a gold sample collected in Alaska. The data show that the method is adequate for 30 of the 31 elements checked; only the mercury values are not acceptable. The data also show that more than one sample is necessary for a complete evaluation of all elements in one geologic location.

The following spectrochemical method was developed to satisfy requests by U.S. Geological Survey geologists for the determination of trace and minor elemental composition of native gold. A d-c arc technique was used because low detection limits were of interest. Warren and Thompson (1944) used a d-c arc excitation to determine minor element composition of gold. They reported the elements as either faint (<0.1 percent), medium (0.1–0.5 percent), or strong (>0.5 percent). For this study we believed that a six-step semiquantitative method was adequate. The procedure had to apply to samples with large variations in both weight and particle size.

Later, requests for more quantitative results for copper and silver were received. The small size of most of the samples eliminated the possibility of an additional method for these two elements. The heterogeneity of the samples also made the use of two separate methods for each element undesirable if relationships between elements were to be determined. The basic method was changed slightly at this time in an attempt to improve the copper and silver results. Owing to the limited number of analytical lines available for both elements, only silver showed any improvement.

Also included in this report is the analysis of 100 randomly selected nuggets from a small locality in Alaska to illustrate the variation in their composition. Additional information on variation is included in a paper by Antweiler and Sutton (1970). Desborough (1970), Desborough, Raymond, and Iagmin (1970), and Desborough, Raymond, and Soule (1970) have investigated major and minor element distributions within grains using the electron microprobe. The spectrochemical method described in this paper cannot show distribution within a single grain, but it does furnish data on many trace elements as well as major and minor elements for a whole grain.

Prior to the analysis of the 100 nuggets, the question of sample preparation arose. Most samples have a coating of oxides that contain trace elements. This was also noted by Crook (1939). Samples were analyzed both with and without cleaning, and the results are given in the present paper.

REAGENTS AND EQUIPMENT

Hydrofluoric acid: Reagent grade.
Hydrochloric acid: Triple distilled, constant boiling.
Nitric acid: Triple distilled.
$HAuCl_4 \cdot 3H_2O$: B&A purified grade.
Gold solution: Dissolve 10 g $HAuCl_4 \cdot 3H_2O$ in 20 ml of constant-boiling hydrochloric acid and dilute to 25 ml.
Gold control sample 1: To approximate the composition of the samples, melt quantities of Johnson and Matthey gold, silver, and copper in a graphite electrode using an acetylene flame.
Gold control sample 2: Weigh 10 mg of any good silicate reference sample (such as W-1, G-1, Glass reference standards) into a plastic test tube. (See below.) Add 50 μl of gold solution, 1 ml of concentrated hydrofluoric acid, and evaporate to dryness on a steam bath.
Sealing solution: Dissolve 100 ml of Fletch-lac glue in 100 ml of acetone. Fletch-lac is available from R. A. Bohning Adhesives Co.
Standard stock solutions: Three stock solutions for silver are made to contain 10, 4.64, and 2.15 mg in 100 μl of 2 *N* nitric acid. Each solution is diluted by factors of 10 to give a complete range of 10 to 0.00001 mg of silver per 100 μl of solution.
Silicate standards: Silicate standards are prepared as described by Myers, Havens, and Dunton (1961).
Test tubes: 12 by 75 mm polypropylene.
Pipets: 5¾ inches by 7.0 mm OD disposable capillary pipet (heavy wall glass).
Ultrasonic cleaner: Any small ultrasonic cleaner with an output of at least 25 watts.
Hotplate: A block of aluminum with holes to accommodate 12 electrodes is placed on a hotplate and the temperature controlled with a Variac. The holes are 1 inch deep. In one corner of the block a thermometer is suspended in a well filled with mineral oil.
Spectrograph: A Wadsworth-mounted grating spectrograph, equipped with a 600-grooves-per-mm grating and having a reciprocal linear dispersion of 5.24 A per mm in the first order.

Electrodes: Lower electrode, 0.242-inch diameter, with a thin wall cavity. Ultra Carbon Corp. type, performed electrode No. 3170. Upper electrode, 0.125-inch diameter by 1.5 inches long, cut from graphite rods obtained from Union Carbide Corp.
Graphite powder: Ultra Carbon Corp., type UCP-2 nonpelletizing graphite powder.
Photographic plates: Eastman Kodak type III-O X-thin plates, developed at 20°C in D-19 developer for 4 minutes with intermittent nitrogen agitation.
Microdensitometer: Direct reading projection microdensitometer fitted with a line-width measuring device described by Barnett (1967).

SAMPLE PREPARATION PROCEDURE

[Note.—This sample preparation procedure is not used when a submitter requests that the sample be analyzed "as received."]

1. Weigh half of the sample (not to exceed 500 mg) into a plastic tube. Add 1 ml of concentrated hydrofluoric acid and leach for 16 hours on a steam bath.
2. Transfer the test tube to the ultrasonic cleaner for 10 minutes.
3. Decant off the hydrofluoric acid solution and reserve it for analysis.
4. Add 1 ml of distilled water to the test tube and place it in the ultrasonic cleaner for 10 minutes. Discard this wash.
5. Examine each sample under a binocular microscope for any remaining coatings, foreign material, and inclusions.
6. Flatten the larger nuggets, using the base of an agate mortar as an anvil and the pestle as a hammer. Place a foam pad under the mortar to absorb part of the shock. Light taps are sufficient to flatten the gold.
7. With a pair of small scissors, cut the sample into small squares weighing 5–10 mg and containing no visible inclusions.

ANALYTICAL PROCEDURE

A. *Preparation of standard plates (quantitative method).*— Add 100 μl of each stock silver solution and 100 μl of distilled water as a blank to plastic tubes. Treat each solution as follows:

1. Add 50 μl of gold solution.
2. Heat on a steam bath until about two drops of solution remain in each test tube.
3. While the samples are on the steam bath, seal a quantity of electrodes by adding six drops of sealing solution to each electrode. Allow the solvent to evaporate at room temperature and repeat this step.
4. Transfer the contents with a disposable pipet to a sealed electrode, preheated to 75°–85°C.
5. Add 15 mg of graphite powder.
6. Add two drops of acetone to settle graphite powder, and dry at room temperature.

Each standard plate should contain 16 concentrations of the silver standard, one blank solution, three pegmatite bases containing 1 percent Fe_2O_3 for emulsion calibration, and three No. 1 gold control samples.

B. *Preparation of standard plates (semiquantitative method).*— Weigh 10 mg of each silicate standard into plastic test tubes. The elements in each standard are grouped according to table 1. Treat each standard as follows:

1. Add 50 μl of gold solution.
2. Add 0.5 ml of hydrofluoric acid to remove silica.
3. Heat to dryness on a steam bath.
4. Add three drops of nitric acid and six drops of hydrochloric acid and evaporate to about two drops.
5. Transfer the contents to a sealed, preheated electrode and evaporate to dryness.
6. Add 15 mg of graphite powder.
7. Add two drops of acetone and dry at room temperature.

Table 1.—*Standards for part B of procedure*

Standard	Elements	Concentration range (percent)
1	Ag	0.0001–100
	Cu	.0001–1
2	Fe	.001–1
3	Ti, Mn, Co, Ni, Zr	.0001–1
4	Ba, La, Ga	.0001–1
5	Be, V, Cr, Mo, Sn	.0001–1
6	Zn, Cd, Bi, Te	.001–1
7	Pb, Sc, B	.0001–1
8	Nb	.0001–1
9	Pd, Pt, Rh	.0001–.1
10	Ir, Os, Ru	.0001–.1

C. *Preparation of sample plates.*—

1. Weigh a sample of as much as 10 mg into a plastic test tube.
2. Add six drops of hydrochloric acid and two drops of nitric acid to each test tube.
3. Heat on a steam bath until the reaction of aqua regia on the gold stops. Samples with a silver content between about 20 and 70 percent will not completely go into solution. Place the test tubes in the ultrasonic cleaner to assist digestion.
4. When about two drops of sample remain in the test tubes, transfer both solid and liquid to a sealed, preheated electrode. Wash the test tubes twice with two-drop portions of concentrated hydrochloric acid. Repeat steps 6 and 7 of the previous section.

Each plate of samples should also contain wash solutions from the sample preparation procedure, three No. 2 gold control samples, and three pegmatite bases containing approximately 1 percent Fe_2O_3 for emulsion calibration.

D. *Spectrographic procedure.*—

1. Arc the samples and standards in a 5-amp d-c arc for 20 seconds and then 13 amps for an additional 80 seconds.
2. Measure the silver lines on a microdensitometer. Line width measurements are used when the transmission falls below 10 percent.

Table 2.—*Analytical lines and their analytical ranges*

Element	Wavelength (angstroms)	Analytical range (micrograms)
Ag	3280.68	100–0.01
	3382.89	100–.01
	2721.77	10,000–100
B	2496.78	100–.7
	2497.73	100–.5
Ba	4554.03	100–.1
Be	2348.61	100–.05
Bi	3067.72	100–.5
Cd	3261.06	100–1
Co	3453.50	100–.1
Cr	4254.35	100–.1
Cu	3273.96	[1]10–.05
	3247.54	[1]10–.05
	2824.37	100–.5
Fe	3020.64	10–.5
	3021.07	10–.5
	3222.07	100–.5
	3225.79	100–.5
	3217.38	100–10
Ga	2943.64	100–0.1
Ir	3220.78	10–.5
La	4333.73	100–.5
Mn	2933.06	100–.5
	2939.30	100–.5
	2801.06	.5–.1
Mo	3170.35	100–.05
	3193.97	100–.05
Nb	3163.40	100–.2
Ni	3414.76	100–.1
Os	3301.56	10–.5
Pb	2833.07	20–.5
	2663.17	100–20
Pd	3404.58	10–.05
Pt	2659.45	10–.2
Rh	3396.85	10–.05
Ru	3436.74	10–0.5
Sc	4246.83	100–.1
Sn	2839.99	100–.3
	3175.05	100–.3
Te	2385.76	100–20
	2383.25	100–20
Ti	3088.02	10–.1
	3152.25	100–10
V	4379.24	10–.1
	3183.98	100–.1
Y	3242.28	100–.1
Yb	3289.37	100–.1
Zn	3345.02	100–5
	3345.57	100–5
	3302.59	100–2
Zr	3273.05	100–2
	3279.26	100–.1

[1] Lower limit due to a reagent blank.

3. Prepare analytical curves and report silver as a quantitative value.
4. All other elements are compared visually and reported as six-step semiquantitative values.
5. Wash solutions from the sample preparation procedure are compared visually and reported qualitatively.

The lines and analytical ranges for the elements are reported in table 2. The methods of emulsion calibration and determination of exposure conditions are described by Bastron, Barnett, and Murata (1960).

VARIABILITY STUDIES

The analyses of 100 nuggets split from a sample collected at a single placer on the Seward Peninsula, Alaska, are reported in this paper. The sample came from a placer being mined by Mr. Bon Davis and Mr. W. Dickman on the south headwater of Gold Run (lat 65°4′25″ N.; long 166°25′30″ W.). Because of the limited area, it was assumed that this sample was derived from a single mineralized source, and that the 100 nuggets would provide a statistically reliable answer on the variation in trace elements in placer gold from a single source.

Many of the nuggets in this sample were coated with iron oxides; others had distinct inclusions of silicates and (or) sulfides. Two grams of this sample was split into four parts and cleaned in hydrofluoric acid for 16 hours. Two splits were recombined and 100 random nuggets from these splits were selected for emission spectrographic analysis, and 10 random nuggets from a third split were submitted for atomic absorption analysis. The fourth split was heated to its melting point and homogenized for 5 minutes. The melted bead was flattened and cut into pieces weighing 5–10 mg. Of these pieces, 10 were submitted for emission spectrographic analysis and 10 for atomic absorption analysis. The difference between the distribution of copper and silver in the melted and unmelted samples was used to estimate the precision and accuracy for the analytical methods used. For comparison with the analyzed nuggets, an additional 188 nuggets from the original sample were mounted in cold-setting plastic, polished, and examined with the reflecting microscope for inclusions and zoning.

RESULTS AND DISCUSSION

Sample preparation

Table 3 shows the analytical data for four nuggets of gold, selected at random from the original 100 nuggets, of which two were cleaned and two were not cleaned. This is just one of several such sets of data—all showing a similar pattern.

The concentration of the various elements in the wash solution was calculated on the basis of parts per million from the original 2-g sample. These values plus the values determined from the cleaned nuggets should equal the values from the uncleaned nuggets. The checks are well within the error of the procedure for Al, Co, Cr, Mg, Mn, Ni, Ti, and V. The iron values are disappointing because iron determinations are usually better than this. No explanation other than a random sampling error is available. The poor checks on the results of the elements calcium, boron, and sodium are due to contamination by the hydrofluoric acid. Because of a lack of interest in these three elements, no attempt was made to purify the hydrofluoric acid.

We believe that these results explain why some reports show a larger number of trace elements in gold than we are finding. Nevertheless, we realize that this cleaning process will not remove all of the sulfides nor all of the heavy minerals.

On the basis of the very small amount of silver, gold, and copper detected in the wash solution—less than 1 percent of the total if they all came from the gold—we believe that we are

Table 3.—*Comparison of values (in parts per million) in two cleaned nuggets and two uncleaned nuggets of gold*

Element	Cleaned nuggets: Values in cleaned nuggets	Values in wash solution[1]	Total	Uncleaned nuggets
Ag	>100,000	0.2	>100,000	>100,000
Au	>100,000	10	>100,000	>100,000
B	<50; <50	.3	<50	10; 200
Ba	10; 10	20	30	50; 300
Be	<5; <5	.02	<5	<5; <5
Bi	<50; <50	<.1	<50	<50; <50
Cd	<100; <100	<.5	<100	<100; <100
Co	<10; <10	2	2	<10; <10
Cr	3; 3	3	6	5; 5
Cu	700; 1,000	7	700; 1,000	1,000; 1,000
Fe	10; 10	150	160	2,000; 2,000
Ga	<10; <10	.3	<10	<10; <10
Mn	<5; <5	5	5	5; 7
Mo	<5; <5	<.03	<5	<5; <5
Nb	<20; <20	.5	<20	<20; <20
Ni	<10; <20	10	<20	10; 10
Pb	<50; <50	10	<60	<50; <50
Pd	<2; <2	<.02	<2	<2; <2
Pt	<20; <20	<.5	<20	<20; <20
Sc	<10; <10	.7	<10	<10; <10
Sn	<30; <50	<.1	<30	<30; <30
Ti	10; 10	100	110	500; 500
V	<10; <10	7	7	7; 7
Y	<10; <10	.3	<10	<10; <10
Yb	<10; <10	.....	<10	<10; <10
Zn	<200; <200	<2	<200	<200; <200
Zr	<10 <10	2	2	10; 10
Al	<10; <10	200	200	100; 100
Ca	<50 <50	100	100	<50; 1,500
Na	<500; <500	300	<800	<500; 1,500
Hg[2]	1,500; 10,000	.....	....	2,000; 2,000

[1] Calculated for a 10-mg sample. Detection limits are lower because the starting sample weight was 2 g.
[2] Not normally looked for.

not significantly changing the original composition of the gold by our washing technique. Extremely small particles of gold and the presence of mercury could present a problem, however. One sample containing gold tellurides did show significant amounts of tellurium in the wash solution and only minor concentrations of tellurium in the washed gold.

The washing time of 16 hours seems long, but several shorter washes did not completely remove the coatings. After the original washing and splitting of the 2-g sample there was an insufficient number of nuggets for the emission spectrographic analysis, so a few additional nuggets were taken and washed for only 8 hours. The effects of this shorter washing time are demonstrated by the fact that most of the samples (table 5) that contained titanium (18 of 22 samples) and most of those that contained iron (seven of 12 samples) were washed only 8 hours.

Analytical procedure

Table 4 gives the trace element content of the control samples used to evaluate this method. Over a period of 3 years 93 control samples were analyzed; the results should give a realistic measure of accuracy and precision for one operator and one laboratory.

Table 4.—*Control sample data*

Element	Best known value	Geometric mean	Geometric deviation[1]	Results
Gold alloys (values in percent)				
Ag	9.41	8.17	1.14	6.43–9.43
	33.10	30.3	1.19	24.8–34
	36.00	34.9	1.13	32.0–38
Cu	.056	.0644	1.30	.05–.1
	[2].20±.03	.1931	1.44	.15–.3
	[2].53±.10	.5107	1.44	.3–.7
	[3]<.001	....	....	.0002
Gold control samples prepared from silicate reference samples (values in ppm in the rock)				
Fe	48,000	....	....	>10,000
Ag	36	50	1.55	20–70
B	55	45	3.12	20–100
Ba[4]	85	116	1.23	100–147
Be	50	17	1.62	7–20
Bi	40	55	1.22	50–70
Cd	30	....	....	<30
Co	30	74	1.29	50–100
Cr	50	44	1.35	30–50
Cu	55	88	1.21	70–100
Ga	5	[5]4.1	[5]2.00	<5–7
Ir	30	....	....	<50
La	55	68	1.59	30–100
Mn	250	171	1.51	100–300
Mo	45	26	1.52	15–50
Nb	42	20	1.00	20–20
Ni	55	88	1.21	70–100
Os	....	....	....	<50
Pb	70	31	1.25	20–50
Pd	45	39	1.22	30–50
Pt	<50	....	....	<50
Rh	18	16	1.35	10–20
Ru	<10	....	....	<50
Sc	<5	....	....	<10
Sn	45	....	....	<30–70
Ti	45	82	1.23	30–100
V	45	51	1.51	30–100
Y	50	62	1.38	50–100
Yb	<1	....	....	<1
Zn	50	....	....	<200
Zr	40	44	1.34	30–70

[1] Geometric deviation or antilog of the log standard deviation.
[2] Electron microprobe analysis by George Desborough.
[3] Sigmund Cohn Corp. 5-9/s gold wire (10 determinations).
[4] Several obvious contaminations not included in this calculation.
[5] A value one order of magnitude below the "less-than value" is used for the calculation of the geometric mean and deviation.

Quantitative silver values are biased low, but the precision is good. Copper values are well within the six-step semiquantitative precision and accuracy limits. Low-level copper values, although more precise than the higher level copper values, tend to be biased about one step high. Niobium is very precise, but is low compared to the known values. Molybdenum and lead are low, probably owing to the presence of volatile chlorides and fluorides. Beryllium is also low, but the reason for the low value is not known.

The extremely volatile $SnCl_4$ is lost completely in some samples in which tin is near the detection limit; in samples of high tin concentrations some tin remains but results are low.

Table 5.—*Atomic absorption (AA) and emission spectrographic (ES) data for the 100-nugget study*

Element	Method	Geometric mean (ppm, except as noted)	Geometric deviation	Range of values (ppm except as noted)	Number of samples in which detected
Ag....	AA[1]	[2]8.02	1.26	[2]6.10–12.8	[3]10
Ag....	ES	[2]7.04	1.30	[2]3.7–18	100
Cu....	ES	660	2.52	70–5,000	100
Pb[4] ...	ES	2.92	4.10	<15–150	20
Co[4] ...	ES	1.11	1.75	<7–70	4
Cr....	ES	......	....	<3–5	2
Ni....	ES	......	....	<2–7	2
Ti....	ES	......	....	<10–200	22
Fe....	ES	......	....	<7–70	12

[1] Atomic absorption analyses by Claude Huffman, Jr.
[2] Values in percent.
[3] Only 10 samples were run by atomic absorption.
[4] A value one order of magnitude below the lowest value reported is substituted for N (not detected).

(Somewhere in the procedure there is an erratic source of barium contamination which we have tried several times to locate but without success.) The remaining elements exhibit reasonable accuracy and precision for a semiquantitative method. Platinum, palladium, and rhodium give good analytical curves and could be done quantitatively.

The principal advantage of the procedure described in this paper is the ability to make standards that very closely approximate the samples. It is extremely difficult and impractical to make alloys that contain 1–100 ppm of many elements, but in solution these elements can be added easily. Failure to use standards closely approximating the sample can cause errors of orders of magnitude for some elements.

Contamination from solutions and the necessity of handling the samples several times are the primary disadvantages of this procedure. Fortunately the elements that contaminate most often (Ba, Cu, Mg) either are high enough that a small blank does not cause an appreciable error or they are of little interest. Owing to the gold matrix, detection limits are two to three steps higher on some elements than they are in a silicate matrix.

Additional information on the accuracy and precision of copper and silver determinations follows.

Variability studies

For the 100 nuggets used in the present study the element concentrations were determined by the emission spectrographic method, and for 10 additional nuggets the concentrations were also determined by the atomic absorption method (table 5). The two methods show good agreement for silver, as shown by the geometric mean values of 8.02 and 7.04, respectively. The geometric deviation of both methods is about the same—1.26 and 1.30. Geometric means and deviations were not calculated for iron and titanium because these elements are present primarily in the coatings.

Table 6.—*Data on homogenized nugget for variability studies*

Element	Method	Geometric mean (percent)	Geometric deviation	Range of results (percent)	Number of determinations
Ag	AA[1]	7.89	1.07	7.22–8.87	10
Ag	ES[2]	7.70	1.09	7.14–8.93	10
Cu	ES[2]	.0584	1.22	.0500–.0700	10

[1] Atomic absorption analyses, by J. A. Thomas, Claude Huffman, Jr., and A. L. Sutton, Jr.
[2] Emission spectrographic analyses, by A. L. Sutton, Jr.

Table 6 gives the results of the sample split after it was melted into one nugget, flattened, and cut into individual samples. The geometric deviations of the original sample and the homogenized sample show that the portion of the total deviation due to the analytical procedures is small by comparison. This is especially true of the copper results.

Figures 1, 2, and 3 are histograms of the silver, copper, and lead in one split of the sample and in the homogenized split. Lead values in the homogenized split are all below the detection limit, thus no "after" histogram was drawn for this element. For the purpose of these diagrams, quantitative silver values were converted to 12-step brackets.

Silver shows a fairly normal distribution curve, but copper is far from normal. The distributions for the homogenized samples show that the copper distribution cannot be attributed to analytical error. There is some hint of a bimodal distribution of copper, and thus the possibility of separate small veins as sources for the gold cannot be ruled out.

Only gold, silver, and copper were detected in all 100 nuggets from the sample used for this study. Lead was detected in 20 percent of the samples, cobalt in 4 percent, and nickel and chromium in 2 percent. Only two nuggets out of 188 mounted nuggets examined with the microscope were found to have visible sulfide inclusions, so it is doubtful that all the lead was in this form. In addition, figure 3 indicates the possibility of a distribution of lead with a mean below the detection limit. Titanium and iron have not been discussed here because the major contribution to these elements appears to be from the coatings. This points out the need for more than a single sample to obtain an overall estimate of the trace elements to be found in one area. Additional unpublished work on trace and minor elements in gold has shown that this sample was relatively pure in comparison with samples representing geologic sources larger than the one picked for this study.

In addition to the elements reported here, mercury was detected in most of the samples. Because of the volatility of mercury, we were not able to determine its concentrations to our satisfaction, and thus it was not reported. We believe, however, that future studies must take mercury into consideration.

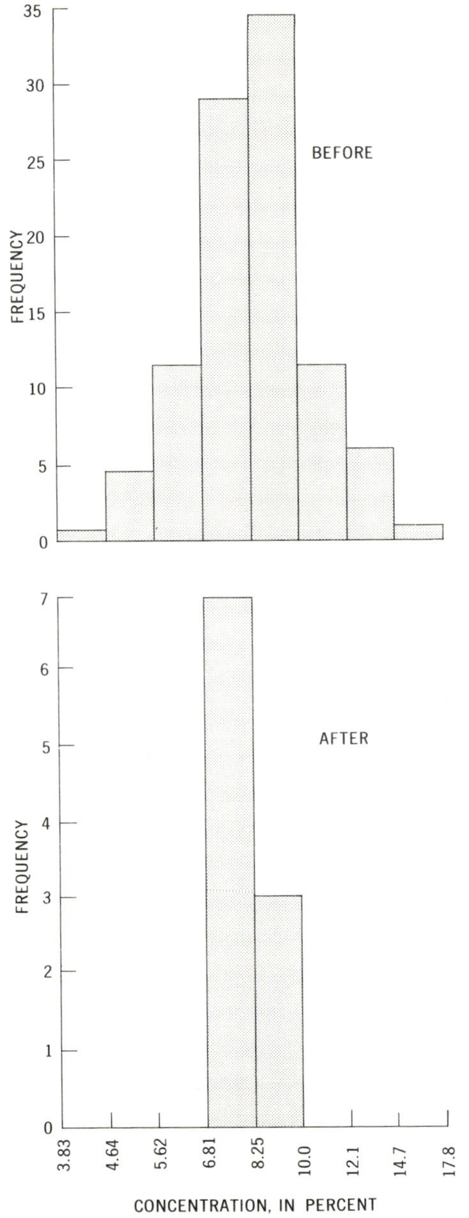

Figure 1.—Histograms of the silver content in gold nuggets before and after the nuggets were homogenized at 1,300° C.

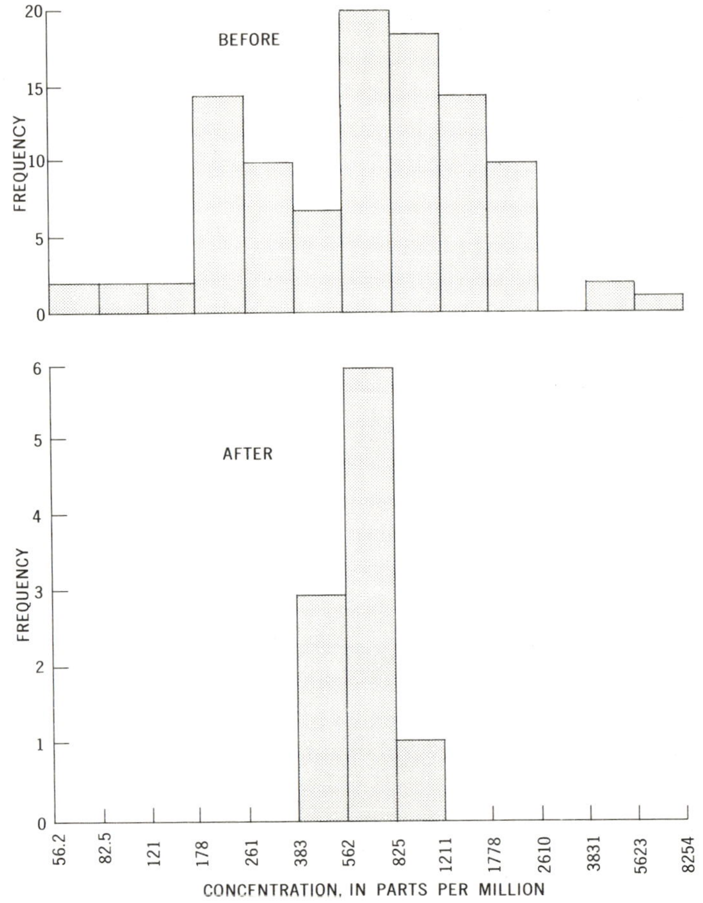

Figure 2.—Histograms of the copper content in gold nuggets before and after the nuggets were homogenized at 1,300° C.

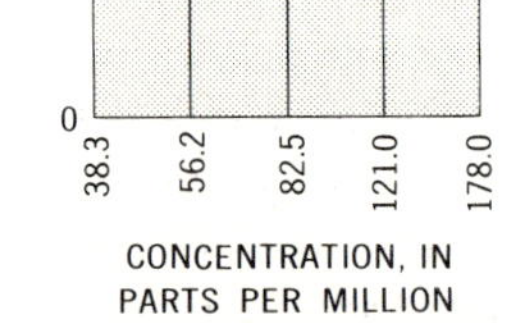

Figure 3.—Histogram of the lead content in gold nuggets before the nuggets were heated to 1,300° C.

REFERENCES CITED

Antweiler, J. C., and Sutton, A. L., Jr., 1970, Spectrochemical analyses of native gold samples: U.S. Geol. Survey Rept. USGS GD-70-003, 28 p.; available only from U.S. Dept. Commerce, Natl. Tech. Inf. Service, Springfield, Va. 22151, as Rept. PB1-94809.

Barnett, P. R., 1967, Device for measuring spectral linewidths: Appl. Spectroscopy, v. 21, no. 2, p. 128–130.

Bastron, Harry, Barnett, P. R., and Murata, K. J., 1960, Method for the quantitative spectrochemical analysis of rocks, minerals, ores, and other materials by a powder d-c arc technique: U.S. Geol. Survey Bull. 1084-G, p. 165–182.

Crook, W. J., 1939, Preliminary spectrographic and metallographic study of native gold: Metals Technology, v. 6, no. 2, Tech. Pub. 998, p. 1–14.

Desborough, G. A., 1970, Silver depletion indicated by microanalysis of gold from placer occurrences, Western United States: Econ. Geology, v. 65, no. 3, p. 304–311.

Desborough, G. A., Raymond, W. H., and Iagmin, P. J., 1970, Distribution of silver and copper in placer gold derived from the northeastern part of the Colorado mineral belt: Econ. Geology, v. 65, no. 8, p. 937–944.

Desborough, G. A., Raymond, W. H., and Soule, Courtney, 1970, Placer gold of unique fineness in Douglas and Elbert Counties, Colorado, *in* Geological Survey Research 1970: U.S. Geol. Survey Prof. Paper 700-D, p. D134–D139.

Myers, A. T., Havens, R. G., and Dunton, P. J., 1961, A spectrochemical method for the semiquantitative analysis of rocks, minerals, and ores: U.S. Geol. Survey Bull. 1084-I, p. 207–229.

Warren, H. V., and Thompson, R. M., 1944, Minor elements in gold: Econ. Geology, v. 39, no. 7, p. 457–471.

Jour. Research U.S. Geol. Survey
Vol. 1, No. 3, May-June 1973, p. 309—314

TWO DIAMICTONS IN A LANDSLIDE SCARP ON ADMIRALTY ISLAND, ALASKA, AND THE TECTONIC INSIGNIFICANCE OF AN INTERVENING PEAT BED

By ROBERT D. MILLER, Denver, Colo.

Abstract.—Two till-like diamictons, 700 feet above present sea level on Admiralty Island, Alaska, are separated by peat near the top of a landslide scarp. The lower diamicton is glaciomarine; the upper diamicton is probably a mudflow. The lower diamicton contains the foraminifer *Elphidium clavatum* Cushman, a species typical of fiords. Similar diamicton crops out along Gastineau Channel near Juneau, 15 miles eastward. Diamicton in both areas reflects deposition in glacier-free fiords during land depression and sea transgression. Consequently, till-like deposits less than 700 feet above sea level elsewhere in southeastern Alaska should be considered as possibly glaciomarine. Sliding occurred after late 1962, but before July 1964; the March 27, 1964, Alaska earthquake might have caused sliding of diamicton saturated by melting snow and spring rains. The peat in the landslide scarp has a published radiocarbon date of 3,400±250 years B.P. (W-1955). The peat was expected to be older, and to relate to Holocene tectonic movement of Admiralty Island. The unexpectedly young date led to additional field study that showed the material over the peat to be a probable mudflow derived from glaciomarine diamicton upvalley; the date has no tectonic significance.

Two till-like diamictons, which are separated by a woody peaty layer, are exposed in the scarp of a large landslide about 15 miles westward from Juneau, Alaska, on Mansfield Peninsula, Admiralty Island, Alaska (fig. 1). A radiocarbon date places the age of the peaty layer, which lies about 5 feet below the top of the scarp, at 3,400±250 years B.P. (Marsters and others, 1969, p. 224). The lower diamicton is glaciomarine in origin and is composed of heterogeneous till-like mixtures of clay-sized particles, silt, sand, and pebbles, and scattered cobbles and boulders; broken barnacle and mollusk shells and unbroken Foraminifera are scattered throughout the deposit. The diamicton overlying the peaty layer has similar textural characteristics, but it is believed to be a mudflow derived from glaciomarine diamicton exposed upvalley.

This report describes the glaciomarine deposit on Admiralty Island, relates this deposit to the glaciomarine deposits on Douglas Island and the mainland near Juneau, emphasizes that these shell-rich diamictons are glaciomarine in orgin—not "marine till"—and presents data to prevent misinterpretation of the tectonic meaning of the woody peaty layer. In addition, the landslide is deemed worthy of description because of its location, type of material involved, the multiple types of movement related to the landslide, and the relationship of the landslide to the geologic environment.

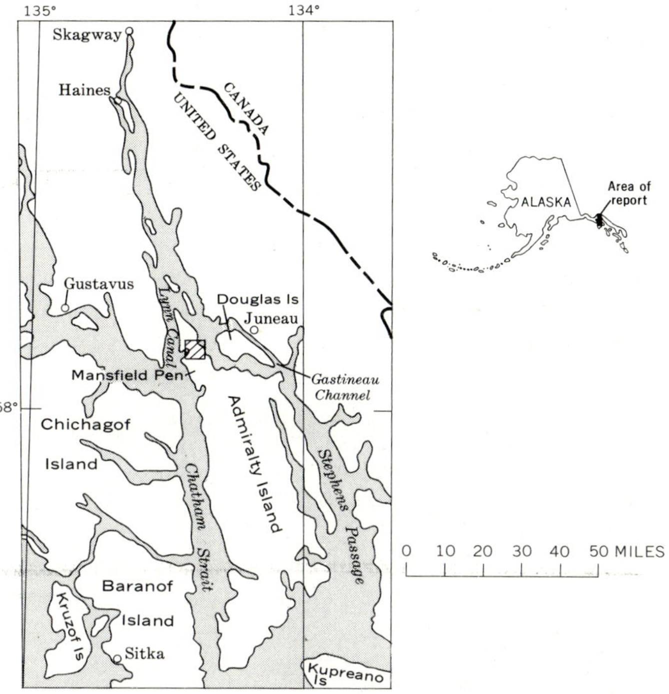

Figure 1.—Sketch map showing the portion of Mansfield Peninsula, Admiralty Island, that is enlarged in figure 2.

DESCRIPTION OF THE LANDSLIDE

The landslide that provided the exposure of diamicton occurred sometime before the last week of July 1964, but to my knowledge was not visited by anyone until the fall of 1965. This massive landslide is in an area of Admiralty Island that is somewhat off the path of most hikers and of most aircraft flying westward from Juneau. Keith Hart, Auke Bay, Alaska, kindly provided me with a resumé of the events that led to his visit to the landslide (written commun., 1967).

The possibility of a landslide on Admiralty Island apparently was inferred first by Keith Hart and A. J. Carr while they were hiking along Bear Creek (fig. 2) in the last week of July 1964. They noticed an intense coloration of the water in the lower part of Bear Creek and high-water marks conspicuously indicated by layers of silt covering the vegetation high on the stream bank. The turbidity was as pronounced during subsequent visits to the Bear Creek area in 1964, and later in July 1965, as it was during the first visit. In September 1965, Hart and Alfred Gordon, Juneau, followed the turbid water upstream along the southern branch of Bear Creek that flows from the northeastern slope of Robert Barron Peak. About 1½ miles from the junction with Bear Creek, they stood at the base of the main scarp of the landslide (fig. 3).

Keith Hart collected a sample of the diamicton from the northernmost part of the main scarp at an altitude of about 695 feet above sea level. In the summer of 1966, Hart gave the sample to me for analysis (fig. 4, sample 2). The sample contained numerous individuals of the foraminifer *Elphidium clavatum* Cushman (Ruth Todd and Doris Low, written commun., 1967), one of the most widely distributed species in the glaciomarine deposits on the mainland near Juneau (Miller, 1972, tables 5 and 7).

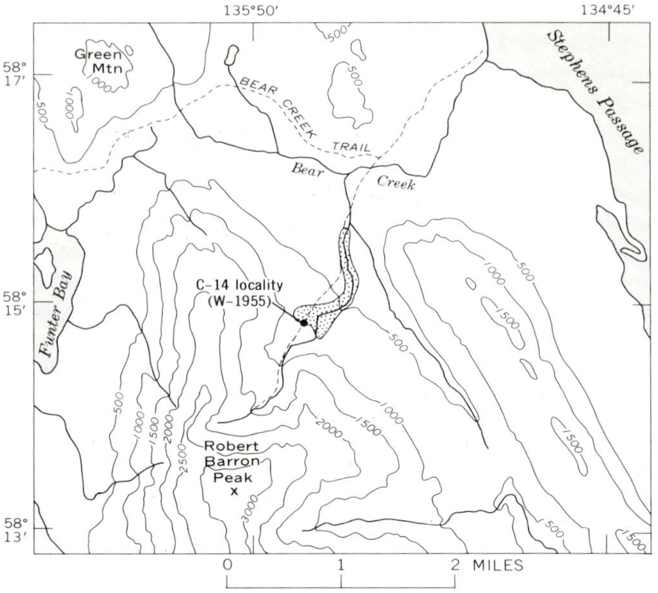

Figure 2.—Sketch map showing the areal extent of the landslide, emphasized by stipple pattern, on the northeastern slope of Robert Barron Peak, Mansfield Peninsula, Admiralty Island, Alaska. Base from U.S. Geological Survey topographic quadrangles: Juneau A-3, 1950, and Juneau B-3, 1962. Contour interval 500 feet.

Figure 3.—Aerial oblique view of the landslide, September 1966. Locations of C^{14} sample W-1955 and materials samples 1, 2, and 3 are indicated. H is the position of the helicopter in figure 5*A*; S marks the area of slump blocks with slight reverse dips shown by the trees; cb marks the area of coherent blocks of slump and slide material.

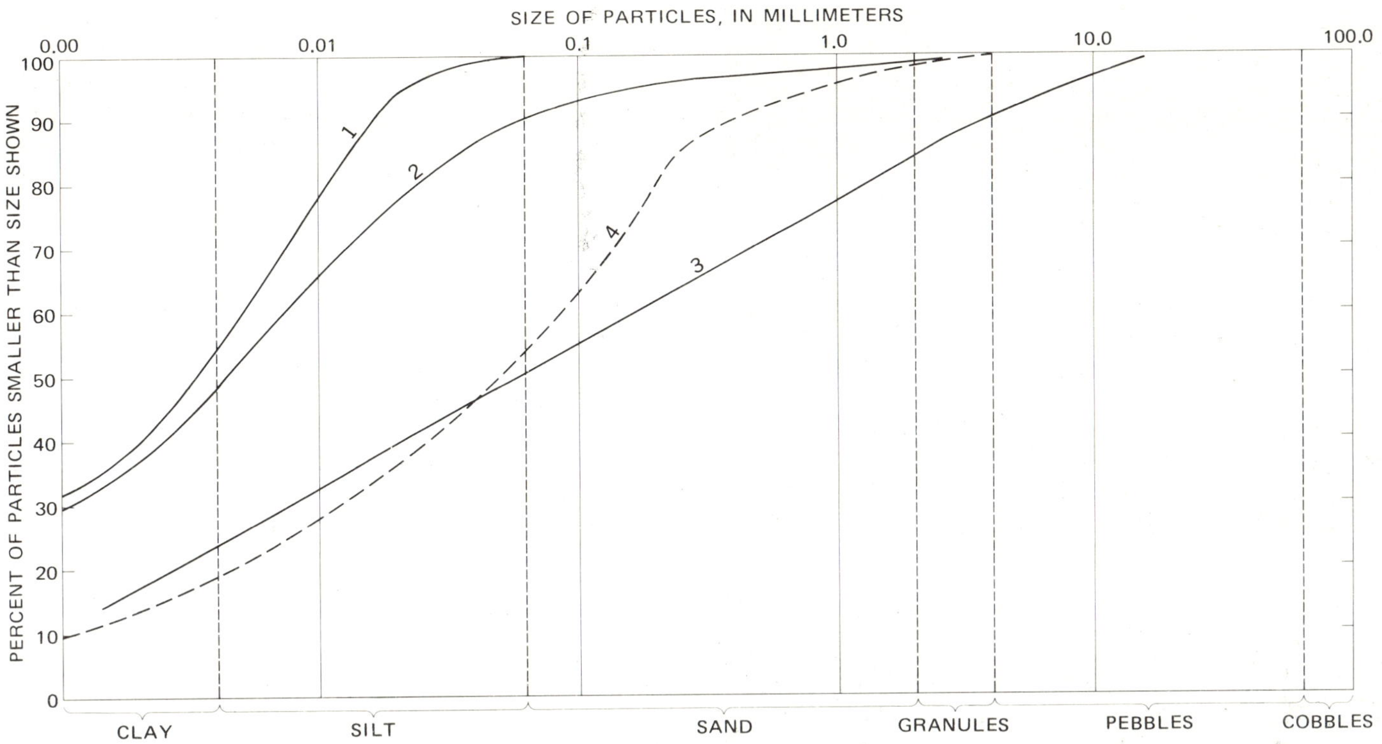

Figure 4.—Particle-size distribution curves comparing samples 1 and 2, collected below the peat zone in glaciomarine deposit in the main scarp of the landslide, and sample 3, collected above the peat zone, with a composite curve (4) of the average of 12 samples of glaciomarine material collected on the mainland near Juneau and on Douglas Island.

I subsequently made two visits to the landslide area by helicopter: one in 1966, with V. K. Berwick, and one in 1968, with J. A. McConaghy, both with the U.S. Geological Survey in Juneau. The landslide was clearly visible from the air in 1966 (fig. 3) as a mass of jumbled tree-covered blocks on a bluish scar in the dark-green forest. In 1968, the landslide was less conspicuous when viewed from the air although still visible; grass and brush mottled the bluish scar and obscured landforms previously identifiable from the air and from the ground (fig. 5*A* and *B*).

The main scarp of the landslide is slightly more than one-quarter mile long. The northern end of the scarp is 95 feet high and has an altitude at the top of 735 feet above sea level, as determined from the altimeter in the helicopter. The woody peaty zone 1½ feet thick crops out 5 feet below the surface and is found only near the northern end of the scarp. A low sag separates the northern end from the southern end of the scarp, which is only 50 to 60 feet high.

The landslide apparently moved from a slope that had failed in the past. Preslide aerial photographs (taken July 1962) of this part of Mansfield Peninsula reveal a steep tree-covered slope where the landslide scarp now exists. This steep slope is interpreted to be an old landslide scarp. Similar tree-covered slopes are found in nearly identical topographic situations along the streams south of this particular branch of Bear Creek. The terrain above the steep slope on the southern branch of Bear Creek is covered by trees and muskeg. The stream valley at this point of the steep slope is incised into the general surface that bounds the stream on either side.

The volume involved in the landslide is not known. From the appearance of the landslide scarp, and by locating the area on the prelandslide photography, I estimate that a relatively small thickness of the prelandslide slope was involved in the landslide.

Water necessary to cause the slide by lubrication and possible saturation of the slope material probably came from several sources: the southern branch of Bear Creek, which flows over the landslide scarp at the southern edge of the main scarp; several smaller streams whose boulder-laden channels hang at the edge of the scarp; and melting snow and spring rains.

Surface expression of the landslide material reflects at least three types of movement: flowage, horizontal translation, and rotation. Natural levees are well developed along the northern edge of the slide and range in height from 1 to 10 feet. The presence of these levees suggests at least local flowage. Excessive lubrication elsewhere along the landslide scarp permitted some of the tree-covered terrain to glide relatively short distances downvalley as discrete units. The more saturated material flowed downvalley to form a narrow lobe that now marks the maximum extent of this particular landslide. Older landslides may have extended farther downstream, but the area near the confluence of the southern branch with Bear Creek was not examined on the ground.

Landslide blocks of all sizes cover the path of the landslide. Large blocks of material that slid on a gently inclined surface

Figure 5.–Landslide scarp, Admiralty Island, Alaska. *A*, photograph taken September 1966; *B*, photograph taken July 1968. Selected identical features in the two photographs are marked by matching numbers. H in photograph *B* is the position occupied by the helicopter in photograph *A*. The trees at 4 moved downslope during the 2-year interval between photographs.

have almost upright trees and are generally confined to the wide upper part of the valley below the main scarp. Smaller blocks that have nearly vertically standing trees form islands separated by the glaciomarine diamicton floor, which retains striations that extend beneath the transported blocks. Small rotated blocks almost line the base of the landslide scarp (fig. 5, points 5 and 3) and contain trees with more than 10° of backward tilt. One of the largest rotated blocks is several hundred feet long; it moved from the southern margin of the landslide toward the center of the valley (fig. 3, point S). A small scarp separates this block from the undisturbed hillside. Trees on this block have backward tilts of about 10°.

Erosion subsequent to the 1964 sliding provided the silt that discolored Bear Creek for several years. Erosion channels, which are floored with boulders 1–3 feet in diameter, separate mounds of tree-covered glaciomarine diamicton 30–40 feet high. Whether these eroded mounds represent glide blocks or material that did not slide is not known. Such erosion apparently continued intermittently for at least several years. Figure 5*A* shows one group of trees (point 4) standing high on the main landslide scarp in 1966; figure 5*B* shows the same trees at the base of the scarp in 1968. Thus, it is also probable that the scarp as exposed in 1966 was modified from the original configuration of the scarp that existed immediately after the original slide took place.

The isolation of the landslide area resulted in an apparent delay between the occurrence and recognition of the landslide. Consequently, absolute determination of the triggering action is not possible. Photographs taken July 1962 show that the terrain had no fresh landslide scars. One event that occurred regionally during the interval between late 1962 and mid-1964 was the March 27, 1964, Alaska earthquake. The Juneau area, only 15 miles away, was affected to differing degrees. The heaviest rolling shocks apparently were concentrated in the valley of the Mendenhall River, about 8 miles northwest of Juneau, and the control tower at the airport located at the lower end of the valley was temporarily abandoned (von Hake and Cloud, 1966, p. 54). It seems plausible to assume that parts of Admiralty Island were equally affected by the shocks; if so, one might speculate and tentatively attribute the triggering action of the Admiralty Island landslide to the shock waves and shaking caused by the earthquake.

DEPOSITS IN THE LANDSLIDE SCARP

The material in the landslide scarp is considered here to correlate with the diamicton of the glaciomarine deposits exposed along the mountain slopes bounding the fiords in the Juneau area, and in the bluffs along Gastineau Channel. All these deposits—whether accumulated on Admiralty or Douglas Islands, or on the mainland—contain numerous scattered boulders 3 feet or more in diameter dispersed throughout a relatively fine grained matrix. Fragments larger than cobbles were not collected in samples of the diamicton, and all remaining pieces larger than 64 mm were removed before the samples were subjected to mechanical analysis. The fine-grained matrix in the landslide scarp is predominantly silt and clay. Two samples collected from the diamicton below the peat layer (fig. 4, curves 1 and 2) reflect the same general textural distribution as the samples of the more sandy matrix reflected in curve 4, which is the average of 12 samples of glaciomarine deposits collected on the mainland and Douglas Island. In addition, the species of Foraminifera from the diamicton in the landslide scarp is part of the fauna that is typical of accumulation in fiords where the water was probably less than 50 fathoms deep (Ruth Todd and Doris Low, written commun., 1967). The finer grained character of the Admiralty Island samples probably is due to the more quiet water associated with the former fiord that extended as an elongate valley into which this part of the glaciomarine sequence was deposited. The fiords nearer Juneau are closer to the mainland source areas that provided much of the materials that were deposited as glaciomarine diamicton.

Judged from available field and laboratory data, the glaciomarine diamicton accumulated on Admiralty Island in the same manner as the diamicton accumulated on the mainland. Much of the diamicton on the mainland near Juneau has been called "marine till" in the past, but as determined from geologic field evidence in the Juneau area, a glacier-free environment existed along the fiords during deposition of the diamicton. Radiocarbon dates determined for shells within the older delta deposits that lie about 200–250 feet above sea level along the mountain slopes bounding the fiords and the dates determined for shells in diamicton beneath the delta deposits and elsewhere along the fiord walls are similar. The presence of deltas rather than kames along the fiords requires that the glaciers retreated from the area before the deltas formed in open water. The similar ages for the diamicton and the delta deposits indicate a similar glacier-free environment for the diamicton as well. According to the interpretation of the depositional story in the Juneau area (Miller, 1972), the first phase of deposition was the accumulation of the stony fossiliferous diamicton during a maximum submergence of the land in latest Pleistocene time and earliest Holocene time and during the first part of land emergence in early Holocene time. Marine waters occupied the formerly ice-filled but still depressed fiords around Juneau, and by inference, Admiralty Island. As the land rebounded and the galciomarine diamicton emerged above water, waves reworked the upper few feet of the material and helped stratify the deposits in an environment of nearshore shallow water. The numerous coarse fragments typical of the diamicton are believed to represent transport by bergs and sea ice. Nearly midway through the emergence cycle, a slowing or halting of unknown duration apparently occurred, as shown by the older deltas perched along the mountain slopes. These deposits probably were graded to sea level at the time of deposition. During this interval, the rise in sea level apparently exceeded land uplift and relatively quiet water existed along the shores. A fossiliferous stony clayey silty sandy layer of glaciomarine diamicton then buried the delta deposits. Land emergence subsequently accelerated and exceeded the rise in sea level. Glaciomarine deposits accumulated in the water until the total emergence was completed, thereby exposing fossiliferous deposits high on the slopes of the mountains and far up fiords and tributary valleys.

Apparently most of the fossiliferous diamicton, in at least this part of southeastern alaska, that lies below a minimum altitude of about 700 feet above sea level is a glaciomarine deposit rather than marine till. The main landslide scarp is one of two high exposures of Foraminifera-bearing diamicton currently known to me in this region. The second exposure is slightly higher, cropping out at 750 feet above sea level, and is on the mainland northwest of Juneau, along Montana Creek (Miller, 1972, p. 94). The closeness in altitude of these two deposits lends support to the interpretation that the Juneau-Admiralty Island area was more or less uniformly depressed as a result of the weight from glacial ice of Pleistocene age. The ice-free fiords in this area filled with marine waters and slowly emerged above water level at about the same time in response to the absence of the load from the glaciers.

INTERPRETATION OF THE WOODY PEATY LAYER AND THE RADIOCARBON DATE

The woody peaty layer in the main scarp of the landslide (fig. 6) was interpreted in 1966 as lying in normal depositional and stratigraphic position and as reflecting an interruption of glaciomarine deposition. It was anticipated that similar ages would be found for materials from the peat layer and from shell materials collected from older delta deposits near Juneau. Accordingly, the potential importance of a date from the peaty horizon is emphasized in my transmittal comment regarding the anticipated radiocarbon date, as reported in Marsters, Spiker, and Rubin (1969, p. 224) "*** peat in

Figure 6.—Part of the main scarp of the landslide; September 1966. Locality of radiocarbon sample W-1955 is indicated. Bedding in the washed area of the scarp is shown by the arrow. Note numerous cobbles and boulders in diamicton away from drainage channels; these fragments are in place.

highest known marine deposit in area; age critical for determination of rate of uplift and detection of possible tectonic movement between Admiralty Island and Douglas and the mainland."

The radiocarbon age of 3,400±250 years B.P. (W-1955, Marsters and others, 1969, p. 224) determined for the Admiralty Island sample, however, is younger than the 10,000–12,000-year ages obtained from shells in the older delta deposits on the mainland (Miller, 1972, p. 70). Glaciomarine deposits above the sand and gravel deposits in the older deltas are slightly younger; one such deposit on Douglas Island contains molluscan shells dated at 9,150±800 years B.P. (W-2395, Meyer Rubin, written commun., Jan. 15, 1970). Glaciomarine deposits beneath the older delta at this locality are dated at 10,760±500 years B.P. (W-2394, Meyer Rubin, written commun., Jan. 15, 1970). Earlier determinations of dates from diamicton led me to expect a date within the 10,000-year range for the peat sample from Admiralty Island. The resulting younger date could be misinterpreted from the comment in Marsters, Spiker, and Rubin (1969, p. 224) to mean that Admiralty Island had an enormous amount of rebound after an abnormally prolonged period of submergence.

In 1968, I reexamined the peat bed in the light of the 3,400-year-old radiocarbon date and found that the depositional relationship between the peat bed and the fossiliferous diamicton was not as clearly exposed in 1966 as I had believed; consequently, the importance of the peat bed is overstated in Marsters, Spiker, and Rubin (1969). By 1968, erosion of the main scarp had created gullies 4–6 feet deep which exposed the relationship of the peat bed to the overlying materials.

The deposit on top of the peaty layer apparently is composed of material that moved down the valley and buried a land surface composed of peat and wood fragments. The particle-size curves in figure 4 provide contrasts that seem to indicate different depositional conditions. The nearly straight line curve (3) derived for the material above the peat layer indicates a deposit that has a wide distribution of grain sizes; this curve is in contrast with those curves of the better sorted materials that show a dominance of one particular grain size. Such curves are 1 and 2 from the diamicton in the main scarp below the peat layer, and curve 4 from the deposits of diamicton on the mainland. Curves similar to 4 were obtained for glaciomarine deposits on the mainland of British Columbia and Vancouver Island, British Columbia, Canada (Armstrong, 1957, p. 4; Fyles, 1963, p. 21). I interpret the straight-line curve to be indicative of depositional conditions that are completely different from those of a glaciomarine environment.

Straight-line curves are typical of deposits related to mass movement and glacial deposition. Straight-line curves have been obtained from lahars and mudflows on Mount St. Helens, Oreg. (Mullineaux and Crandell, 1962, p. 860, 863), and on Mount Rainier, Wash. (Crandell, 1971, p. 28, 41, 55, 66), and from glacial till in the Puget Sound area (Mullineaux, 1970, p. 35).

The brief examination of the exposures in and near the landslide scarp did not resolve the mode of origin of the material above the peat bed. However, the young age of the peat requires that any overlying till be Neoglacial in age; the Neoglaciation apparently started in the Juneau area about 3,500 years ago (Heusser, 1960, p. 186). Deposits of this glaciation characteristically retain recognizable topographic forms where seen in the Juneau area (Miller, 1972, p. 53). There are no such recognizable glacial features in the valley directly above the landslide on Admiralty Island.

Mass movement, probably a mudflow, is a likely origin for the material above the peat. The texture, color, and consistency of this material and of the material beneath the peat are similar. In addition, laboratory tests of mainland diamicton, to which I relate the Admiralty Island deposits, show that many of the deposits of diamicton have a high affinity for water, but a correspondingly critical range between stability and flowage as the percentage of moisture increases (Miller, 1972, p. 99). It seems reasonable to me to consider the deposit that buried the ground surface about 3,400 years ago as a mudflow that was derived from saturated glaciomarine diamicton exposed upvalley from the present landslide scarp. Such an interpretation does not require recent tectonic activity to account for the young age of the peat.

REFERENCES CITED

Armstrong, J. E, 1957, Surficial geology of New Westminster map-area, British Columbia: Canada Geol. Survey Paper 57-5, rept. and map 16-1957, 25 p.

Crandell, D. R., 1971, Postglacial lahars from Mount Rainier volcano, Washington: U.S. Geol. Survey Prof. Paper 677, 75 p.

Fyles, J. G., 1963, Surficial geology of Horne Lake and Parksville map-areas, Vancouver Island, British Columbia: Canada Geol. Survey Mem. 318, 142 p.

Heusser, C. J., 1960, Late-Pleistocene environments of North Pacific North America; an elaboration of late-glacial and postglacial climatic, physiographic, and biotic changes: Am. Geog. Soc. Spec. Pub. 35, 308 p.

Marsters, Beverly, Spiker, Elliott, and Rubin, Meyer, 1969, U.S. Geological Survey radiocarbon dates X: Radiocarbon, v. 11, no. 1, p. 210–227.

Miller, R. D., 1972, Surficial geology of the Juneau urban area and vicinity, Alaska, with emphasis on earthquake and other geologic hazards: U.S. Geol. Survey open-file report, 107 p.

Mullineaux, D. R., 1970, Geology of the Renton, Auburn, and Black Diamond quadrangles, King County, Washington: U.S. Geol. Survey Prof. Paper 672, 92 p.

Mullineaux, D. R., and Crandell, D. R., 1962, Recent lahars from Mount St. Helens, Washington: Geol. Soc. America Bull., v. 73, no. 7, p. 855–870.

von Hake, C. A., and Cloud, W. K., 1966, United States earthquakes, 1964: U.S. Coast and Geod. Survey [Pub.], 91 p.

Jour. Research U.S. Geol. Survey
Vol. 1, No. 3, May-June 1973, p. 315–325

CAN SATELLITE PHOTOGRAPHY CONTRIBUTE TO TOPOGRAPHIC MAPPING?

By FREDERICK J. DOYLE, McLean, Va.

Abstract.—Photographs taken on early space missions, in the Gemini-Apollo series, demonstrated the usefulness of the long view for cartography despite acknowledged shortcomings. Later developments, such as ERTS and Skylab, will provide far more data about Earth, but mostly in planimetric form. The third dimension, height, which makes the map representation topographic, is not easy to measure at orbital altitudes. The capability of current and near-future systems is not likely to do much for topographic mapping at scales larger than 1:250,000, but the benefits in planimetric mapping may be better than even the optimists hoped for.

As one reviews the accomplishments of the last decade, there can be little doubt that the routine achievement of successful missions in space is the most technologically significant. Photogrammetrists and cartographers naturally look upon orbiting spacecraft as a logical step in the progression from planetable to aircraft to satellite. They can foresee the same kind of quantum jump in production, geometric accuracy, and content of topographic maps which occurred when aerial photogrammetry replaced ground surveys. At the same time they are frustrated because as of this date there has been only one space camera system in which photogrammetric principles were considered in the design and operation of the camera.

HASSELBLAD PHOTOGRAPHY

Throughout the manned space program, Hasselblad and Maurer cameras were used for still photography. These are both 70-mm film cameras with interchangeable lenses of various focal lengths. In the Mercury and Gemini programs, over 2,400 color photographs were obtained. Many of them are exceptionally beautiful and certainly historical. Scientifically they demonstrated the utility of the synoptic view for geologic, hydrologic, and geographic interpretation of the Earth's surface. They also demonstrated that, apart from cloud cover, photographing through the Earth's atmosphere did not impose as great a problem as had been anticipated.

Though cartography was not an objective for the Gemini missions, and photographs were not acquired in typical mapping sequences, some attempts were made to demonstrate the potential usefulness of space photographs for map compilation. A single frame exposed from Gemini 7 over the Cape Kennedy, Fla., area was compared with the existing 1:250,000-scale map, and new cultural features were located. Mosaics of Peru and the Southwestern United States were assembled from rectified prints of the Gemini photographs. Geologic and land-use maps were compiled to demonstrate the utility for small-scale thematic mapping.

In April 1968, the unmanned Apollo 6 Earth-orbiting mission carried an intervalometer-controlled Maurer 70-mm film camera with 76-mm focal length. A sequence of near-vertical stereophotographs over the Southwestern United States was obtained. One photograph at original scale 1:2,730,000 of the Dallas-Fort Worth, Tex., area was compared with the existing 1:250,000 topographic map. By measuring the coordinates of identified points on an enlarged and rectified print and comparing them with coordinates scaled from large-scale (1:24,000) maps, it was found that the space photograph could be used to check the planimetric accuracy of the small-scale map. Furthermore it was clearly demonstrated that linear cultural features such as roads and railroads, whose actual dimensions were far less than the ground resolution of the photograph, could be detected and indeed recognized on the photograph. In addition the limits of urbanized areas were easily visible on the photograph. The report on the study concluded that the space photograph was useful for map revision in terms of both planimetric position and content.

The Apollo 9 manned Earth-orbiting mission in March 1969 carried an experiment known as SO-65. The principal objective of the experiment was to simulate the multispectral photographs of the Earth Resources Technology Satellite (ERTS). Four 70-mm Hasselblad cameras with 80-mm lenses were mounted in a fixture which held their optical axes parallel and provided simultaneous exposures by all four shutters. The camera array was mounted in the hatch window of the Apollo Command Module. The spacecraft was oriented so that the camera axes were vertical, and five strips of pictures across the Southern United States were obtained under exceptionally favorable weather conditions. Three black-and-white films were exposed through appropriate filters to give the red, green, and near-infrared spectral bands proposed for the ERTS television cameras. The fourth camera obtained color infrared photographs which simulate the effects of superimposing the three black-and-white pictures. These pictures have been used extensively to determine the procedures for automatic thematic mapping of Earth resources.

Two frames of the red band covered approximately the area of the 1:250,000 Phoenix, Ariz., map sheet. These were rectified and enlarged nearly 10 times by fitting to detail points identified on the map and the photographs. The mosaic was then printed as an image base for the standard line map. A number of different color schemes were tried, and versions were produced both with and without contours (fig. 1). The maps have been widely circulated in the cartographic community, and the reaction has been overwhelmingly, though not unanimously, favorable. The black and white reproductions in this paper do not show the added advantages of color enhancement of the image base.

On the standard line map, wherever white paper appears there is no information. The terrain morphology, the field patterns, and other characteristics of the area are more clearly shown by the photographic image. At the same time, all the information from the conventional line map is also available.

Though the Phoenix line map had been recently checked for accuracy and revised for content, the photoimage base disclosed corrections to both accuracy and content. In several areas there was an obvious mismatch between the photographic and the line data. Checking against large-scale maps disclosed that the error was in the line map and not in the image. In other areas, the photoimage showed new cultural features constructed since the line map was revised.

Though the Phoenix 1:250,000 space photomap may be considered a qualified success, it should be evaluated more as a forerunner of things to come rather than as an example of the limits of utility of space photographs for cartography.

LUNAR CAMERA SYSTEMS

Photogrammetrists will readily recognize that the Hasselblad cameras are not to be compared with the sophisticated mapping cameras used in aircraft. When focal lengths of 150 and 600 mm and formats of 230 mm are used at altitudes up to 10,000 m in aircraft, it is patently absurd to expect comparable information with focal lengths of 80 mm and formats of 70 mm from spacecraft at nearly 20 times the altitude.

For reasons difficult to rationalize, the lunar exploration program has been able to obtain better cameras than have been used in the Earth program. Through lunar Apollo mission 12, the Hasselblad camera was again used with interchangeable lenses of focal lengths 60, 80, 250, and 500 mm. The 60-mm lens was used primarily for documentary photographs within the spacecraft and for operations on the lunar surface. The 80-mm lens was used with the camera mounted on a bracket in the Command Module hatch window to obtain near-vertical stereo strips from lunar orbit much like the Apollo Earth photography. The 250-mm lens was used handheld to take oblique photographs of sites of particular geologic interest. On Apollo 12 an attempt was made to photograph potential landing sites for future missions by using the 500-mm lens. To provide both forward-motion compensation and adequate stereo base, the camera was bracket mounted in the hatch window. The entire spacecraft was pitched in synchronism with its forward motion to keep the same scene in the field of view. This complicated operation restricted the number of targets that could be photographed, because of the necessity of completely reorienting the spacecraft as a unit between scenes, and it was only marginally successful in providing the hoped-for high resolution.

In October 1969 the Apollo Orbital Science Photographic Team was formed to recommend the photographic equipment and operations which would get the maximum scientific return from the remaining missions. However, the team was not completely free in selecting the camera systems to be employed. It was necessary to choose cameras that were either available or developed to the extent that they could meet the rigid timetable of qualification for the Apollo missions, which were at that time scheduled at approximately 4-month intervals. Furthermore, severe space and operating requirements had to be met. Consequently the cameras selected were compromises adapted from existing equipment.

Lunar Topographic Camera

The first new photographic system was a modified Hycon (now Actron Industries, Inc.) KA-74 reconnaissance camera of 460-mm focal length, exposing 430 frames in each magazine of 130-mm roll film. The camera was mounted on a special fixture in the Command Module hatch window. Forward-motion compensation was provided by rocking the entire camera in its mount during the exposure. Adequate stereo base was obtained by taking pictures with the camera axis vertical on one revolution and directed 20° aft on the succeeding revolution.

The camera was carried aboard Apollo 13 and was actually mounted in position ready for lunar approach photography when the oxygen tanks exploded and the mission was aborted. It was carried again on Apollo 14, but a transistor failure resulted in only about 80 good frames being obtained. A further modified version of the KA-74 will be carried on Skylab as the S-190B Earth Terrain Camera.

Lunar Panoramic Camera

With Apollo 15, 16, and 17, lunar photography took on new dimensions. In a section of the Service Module known as the SIM (Scientific Instrumentation Module) various orbital science experiments were mounted. A major component of the SIM was a panoramic camera to provide high-resolution photographs of large areas of the lunar surface. The camera

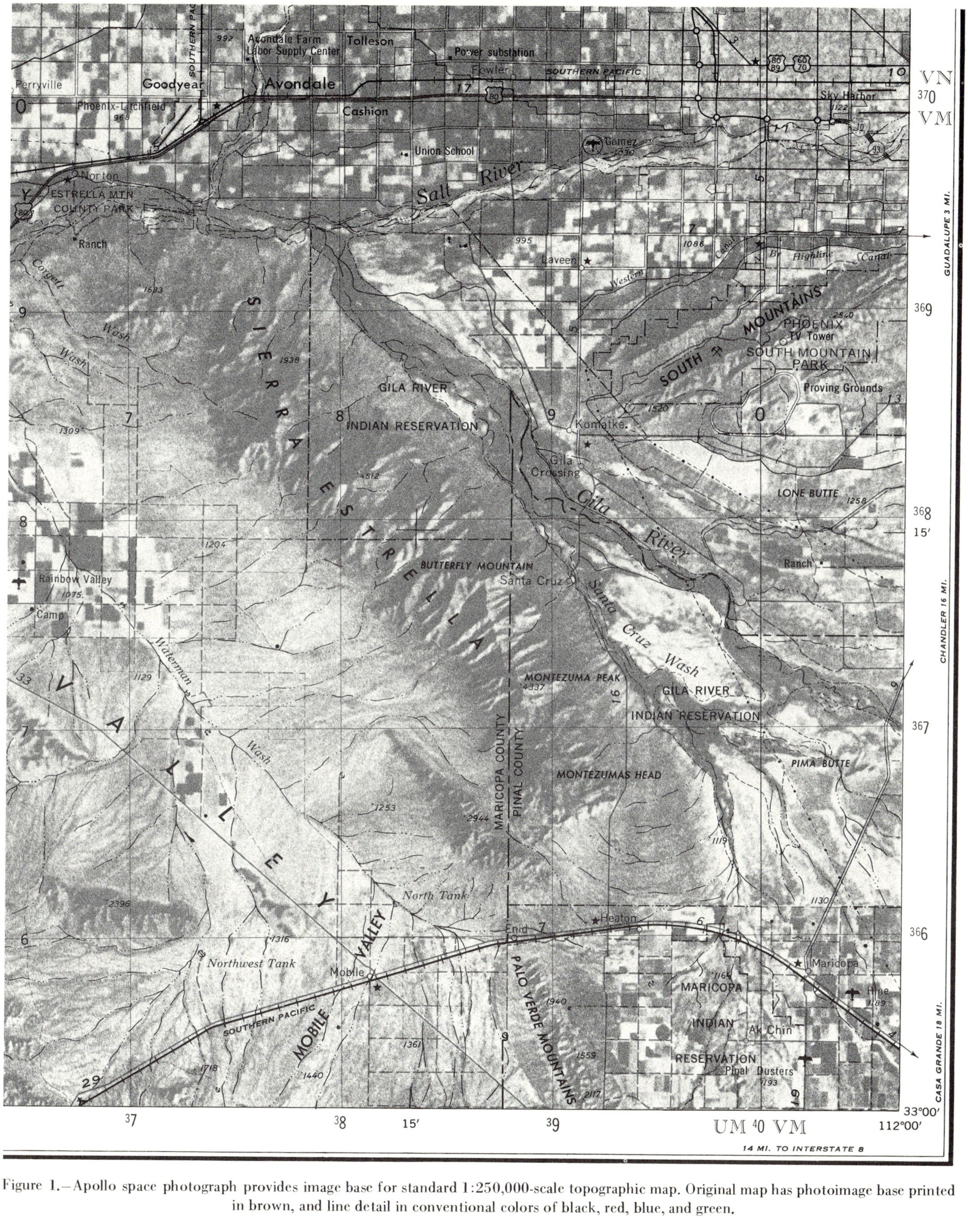

Figure 1.—Apollo space photograph provides image base for standard 1:250,000-scale topographic map. Original map has photoimage base printed in brown, and line detail in conventional colors of black, red, blue, and green.

had a 610-mm focal length and an aperture of f/3.5. The 108° sweep angle exposed a frame 115 by 1,270 mm on 130-mm roll film. A total of 1,900 m of thin-base film provided 1,650 exposures.

The camera, constructed by Itek Corp., is a modification of an existing rotating-optical-bar camera. Its principal elements (fig. 2) are the main frame, which mounts rigidly to the spacecraft and carries the supply and takeup film rolls; the stereo gimbal assembly, which can rotate about a transverse axis to provide stereo convergence and forward-motion compensation; and the roll-frame assembly, which carries the rotating lens and moving-film rollers.

Stereo coverage can be obtained by rocking the camera 12.5° forward or aft between succeeding exposures. A V/H (velocity/height) sensor provides the signal for controlling the forward-motion compensation, which is also obtained by rocking the camera. A light sensor mounted on the stereo gimbal adjusts the exposure time by modifying the width of the slit. From the nominal operating altitude of 111 km, the camera provides about 2-m surface resolution at the spacecraft

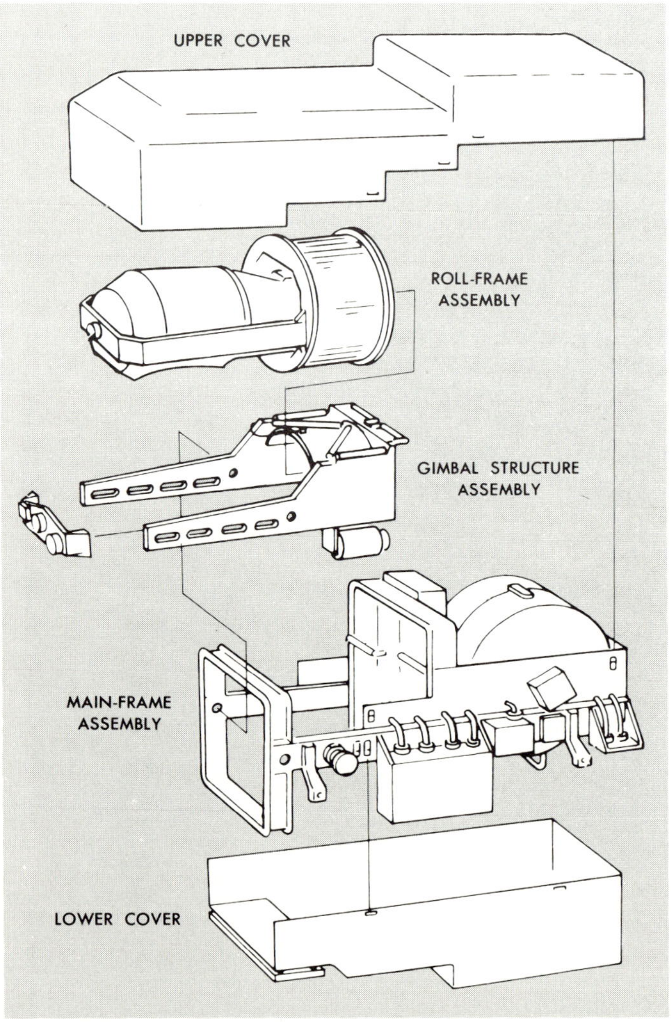

Figure 2.—Principal elements of Lunar Panoramic Camera.

nadir. In the monoscopic mode each frame covers 300 km across track by 20 km along track, and each vertical photograph overlaps the preceding one by 10 percent at the nadir. In the stereo mode, the camera rocks through the 25° convergence angle between each pair of exposures. The forward exposure from station 1 and the aft exposure from station 6 overlap by 100 percent to form a stereomodel, and each succeeding stereomodel overlaps the preceding one by 10 percent.

For many applications it is desirable to transform the panoramic photographs into equivalent vertical photographs, and a special transforming printer was constructed to do so. The rectifier (fig. 3) is an analog of the camera system. The film is carried on a cylindrical platen whose radius is equal to the 610-m equivalent focal length of the camera. Longitudinal

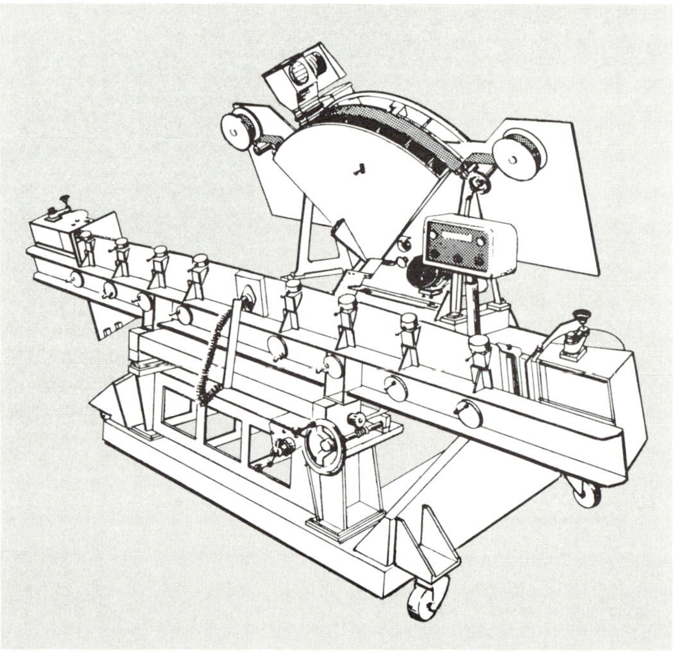

Figure 3.—Rectifier for lunar panoramic photographs.

displacement of the film with respect to the center of the arc compensates for roll of the spacecraft. A moving light source traverses the length of the film to make the exposure. The projection lens rotates at a variable rate to assure sharp focus at all positions. The projected image is then reflected to the easel. The tilt of the easel can be adjusted to compensate for the 12.5° stereo convergence as well as for spacecraft pitch. The longitudinal curvature of the easel can be adjusted to simulate the curvature of the lunar surface for orbital altitudes up to 150 km.

The rectified pictures have a nadir enlargement of approximately 1.8 times but are restricted to a scan angle of 35° on either side of the nadir. The resolution, measured at the input scale, varies from 90 line pairs per millimeter on axis to 50 line pairs per millimeter at 35° maximum scan. The displacement of images from all causes is specified as 1 mm circular probable error. Thus the rectified pictures are not designed for photogrammetric use but have adequate geometry for photo-interpretation.

Mapping Camera System

Mounted on the front shelf of the SIM on Apollo missions 15 through 17 was a Mapping Camera System (fig. 4) composed of a terrain camera, a stellar camera, a laser altimeter, and a precise timing mechanism.

The terrain camera had a 75-mm focal length, f/4.5 lens and exposed a 115- by 115-mm format on 130-mm roll film. The glass-plate focal plane was engraved with a 10-mm reseau. Two sets of artificially illuminated fiducials and one set of naturally illuminated fiducials were provided. A data block on each frame of the terrain camera recorded the midpoint of each exposure to ±1 msec. The flight height measured by the laser altimeter and the shutter open time to ±0.1 msec were also recorded. A manually adjusted V/H mechanism provided forward-motion compensation with an accuracy of 3 percent by moving the focal plane during the camera exposure. Automatic exposure control set the between-the-lens shutter in five steps between 1/15 and 1/240 second.

The resolution on the lunar surface depends upon solar altitude and the accuracy of forward-motion compensation. For the nominal altitude of 111 km and exposure on Kodak 3400 film, the high-contrast resolution at low solar altitude was about 20 m per line pair, decreasing to about 50 m for low-contrast resolution at high solar altitude.

The forward overlap of successive frames was adjusted preflight. The available 3,600 exposures permitted the total overflown area to be photographed with 78 percent forward overlap and 55 percent side overlap, meaning that every point on the ground was seen on four consecutive photographs with a maximum base-height ratio of 1.0. In addition to providing geometric strength for triangulation, the four views permit study of the Moon's peculiar photometric characteristics.

The stellar camera was directed to the side of the orbital plane and 4° above the horizon so that no part of the lunar surface was included in the field of view. The lens is 75-mm focal length, f/2.8, and exposes a 25- by 32-mm format on 35-mm film. Four fiducials and a 5-mm reseau on the glass focal plane were edge illuminated to record on the film. Prefogging has the additional advantage of hypersensitizing the film for stellar exposure. A fixed exposure time of 1.5 seconds provided an average of 25 star images per frame, depending on the location of the field of view in the celestial sphere. The laser altimeter was mounted with its transmission and receiving optical axes parallel to those of the terrain camera, and its accuracy was about ±2 m.

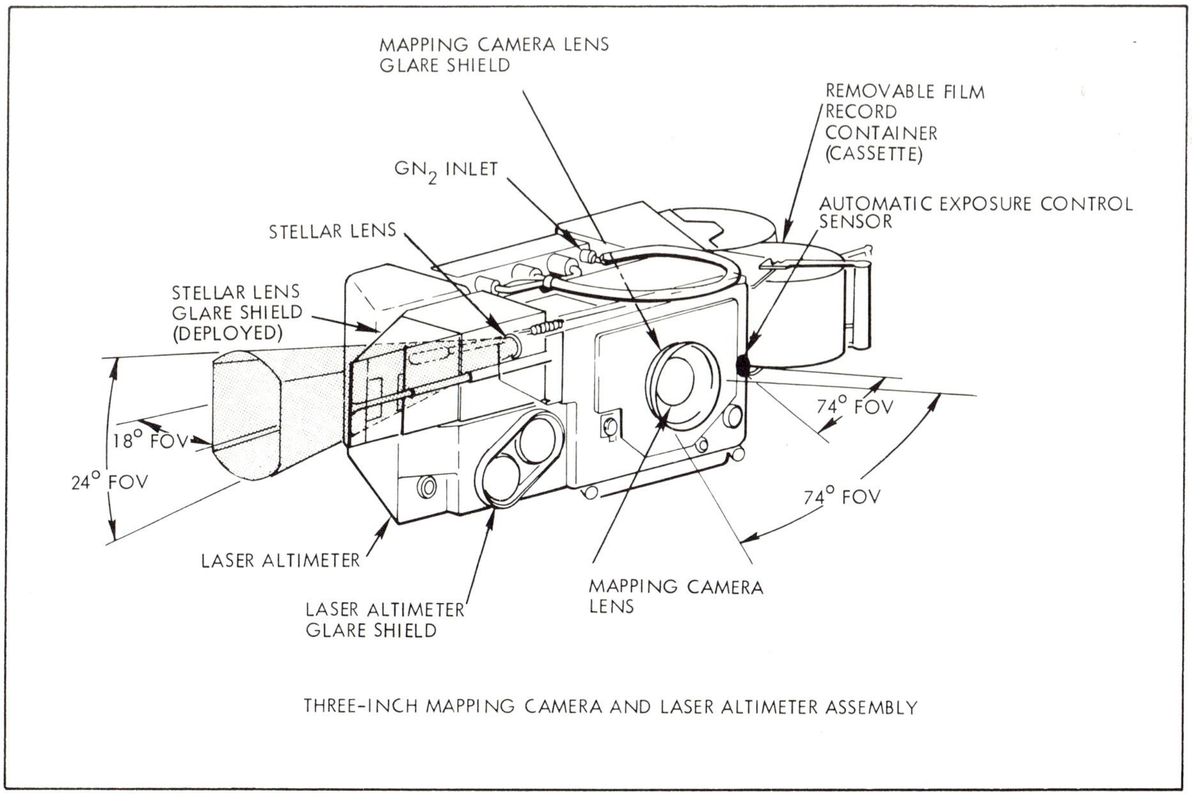

Figure 4.–Mapping Camera System for Apollo 15–17.

The terrain and stellar cameras were built by Fairchild Space and Defense Systems. The laser altimeter was built by RCA Aerospace Systems, but Fairchild was responsible for integrating it into the mapping camera package. The installation of all systems in the SIM was the responsibility of North American Rockwell.

Film recovery

The photographic films from both the panoramic and the mapping camera systems were accumulated in special quick-release magazines. The astronaut left the Command Module, activated a single handle which cut the film, closed the light-tight compartment, and released the film-return magazine. The magazines were stowed in the Command Module for the journey back to Earth.

The design and construction of these complicated camera systems, their qualification for operation in a manned spacecraft, and extensive planning for the data analysis of the lunar photographs inspire confidence that an adequate system could be devised for topographic mapping of the Earth at scales compatible with existing cartographic standards.

RATIONALE FOR AN EARTH MAPPING SYSTEM

Before attempting to define a useful system of topographic mapping from space data, we must examine some of the factors involved. A topographic map contains three kinds of information:

Content—the details represented on the map.

Position—the reference graticule.

Elevation—spot heights and contour lines.

Any mapping system must be able to provide all of these.

Map content is obtained from photographic resolution and scale, or more directly from ground resolution. It is difficult to establish a linear relation between map scale and required ground resolution because some features, like roads and railroads, must be shown on a map regardless of its scale. However, by considering the photograph as an image base (photomosaic or orthophotograph) for the map, a useful criterion can be produced.

Under normal conditions the unaided human eye resolves about 5 line pairs per millimeter. To retain that resolution in the final map, the photograph should have better resolution, say at least 10 line pairs per millimeter, to allow for inevitable losses in processing. Therefore the ground resolution of the image base map would be 1/10 mm times the map scale number:

$$R_g = 10^{-4} S_m \,, \qquad (1)$$

where

R_g = ground resolution, in meters, and

S_m = map scale number.

Obviously not all map content is obtainable directly from photographs, regardless of scale or ground resolution, whether taken from aircraft or space. Data such as political boundaries, place names, and detail obscured by vegetation must be compiled on the ground or from other sources. The fact that linear features whose lateral dimension is well below the resolution limit can nevertheless be identified works in favor of small-scale photographs.

In aircraft photography, external factors such as attitude rates, vibration, and atmospheric anomalies generally restrict photographic resolution to 25 to 30 line pairs per millimeter regardless of the laboratory-determined lens-film performance. In the space environment all the degrading factors are considerably reduced so that the actual photographs may have nearly the same resolution as measured in the laboratory.

Large-scale maps (S_m<25,000) are usually compiled with up to 5 times enlargement between airphotograph and map scale. Medium-scale maps (25,000<S_m<100,000) are compiled at 1 to 2 times enlargement between photograph and map. Small-scale maps (S_m>100,000) are usually assembled from existing larger scale source materials rather than compiled directly from photographs. The restrictions, however, generally result from the operational limits of aircraft, cameras, and photogrammetric instruments, rather than from the information inherent in the photographs. According to the criterion established, high-resolution space photographs can be enlarged until their equivalent resolution is 10 line pairs per millimeter.

$$M_a = r_p/10, \qquad (2)$$

where

M_a = allowable enlargement from photo to map scale, and

r_p = original photo resolution, in line pairs per millimeter.

The second kind of map information is planimetric position. Absolute position is generally provided by reference to ground control points. For a space system, however, orbital tracking data can provide spacecraft position to a high order of accuracy. When the tracking data are coupled with precise camera attitude data and time of exposure, an independent means of determining absolute position is available.

Within a stereomodel or a photogrammetric triangulation, the internal positional accuracy is equal to the product of the photograph scale and the error in measuring or identifying a point on the picture:

$$\sigma_p = S_p \sigma_r \,, \qquad (3)$$

where

σ_p = standard error in position of a ground point,

σ_r = residual measuring error, and

S_p = photograph scale number.

U.S. National Map Accuracy Standards (NMAS) require that the standard error of point positions should not exceed 0.3

mm at the published map scale:

$$\sigma_p = 3\times10^{-4}\ S_m \ . \qquad (4)$$

The third kind of information on a topographic map is terrain relief depicted by contour lines, spot elevations, and sometimes shaded relief. In conventional aerial mapping, vertical control points are established with an accuracy of 0.1 to 0.2 of the contour interval. A statistical interpretation of NMAS requires that

$$\sigma_h = 0.3 \text{ c.i.} \ , \qquad (5)$$

where

σ_h = standard error of elevation, and
c.i. = contour interval.

It may be noted in passing, however, that recent tests by the U.S. Geological Survey have demonstrated that if a stereomodel is properly adjusted to redundant vertical control points, contours at an interval equal to the standard error can be compiled and still meet NMAS.

Elevation data are obtained from aerial photographs by means of image parallax, which depends on the camera configuration, the image scale, and the measuring accuracy:

$$\sigma_h = S_p(H/B)\sigma_r \ , \qquad (6)$$

where H/B is the reciprocal of the base-height ratio.

The critical requirements for maps at various scales can be derived by applying formulas 1, 4, and 5, with the results given in table 1. A fixed contour interval does not necessarily go with a given map scale. An interval fine enough to depict the character of the terrain will be chosen. The values listed in table 1 represent the performance objectives against which a space cartographic system should be evaluated.

Table 1.—*Map accuracy requirements, in meters*

Map scale number S_m	Ground resolution R_g	Std. error position σ_p	Contour interval c.i.	Std. error elevation σ_h
1,000,000	100	300	100	30
250,000	25	75	50	15
100,000	10	30	25	8
50,000	5	15	10	3
25,000	2.5	7.5	5	1.5

SPACE CAMERA SYSTEM FOR EARTH MAPPING

In the summer of 1967, NASA (National Aeronautics and Space Administration) asked the National Academy of Sciences to study "Useful Applications of Earth Oriented Satellites." Thirteen panel reports were presented, discussing a variety of interests. Although differing in details, the Forestry, Agriculture, Geography, Geology, and Hydrology Panels confirmed their requirements for a television system providing repetitive cover at relatively coarse resolution.

The Geodesy-Cartography Panel attacked the problems of providing data for geodetic control and topographic mapping on a worldwide basis. The Geodetic Satellite Program is now producing a worldwide network of some 40 stations in a unified geocentric coordinate system. Continental intensification networks, if carried to completion as recommended by the panel, will locate points with better than 3-m accuracy at about 800-km spacing. These points, together with existing geodetic control, can form the foundation for map compilation at scales as large as 1:25,000.

The panel recommended two camera systems: a metric camera system for complete small-scale mapping and establishing control for large-scale mapping, and a long-focal-length convergent camera system for providing the detail necessary for large-scale map compilation. The recommended metric camera system would comprise:

A vertical frame camera with 305-mm focal length, 230- by 365-mm format, and 70-percent forward overlap between frames.

A stellar-altitude camera with 150-mm focal length and 70-mm format, synchronized with the terrain camera.

A laser altimeter measuring the distance from camera to terrain in synchronism with each camera exposure.

A timing device to record the midpoint of each exposure.

Though the panel did not define the large-scale camera in detail, the panoramic camera from the lunar program would be an obvious candidate. The major parameters of the camera systems are summarized in table 2.

To retain the geometric integrity of the photographs, the panel recommended physical recovery of the film rather than transmission of the images by some form of television system. The general procedure would be to mount the cameras in the spacecraft and feed the exposed film to the attached reentry capsule (fig. 5). When the photographic mission has been

Table 2.—*Parameters of space camera systems*

	Control camera (frame)	Stellar camera (frame)	Compilation camera (panoramic)
Focal length . . . mm	305	150	610
Film width . . . mm	240	70	125
Sweep angle . . . degrees	....	....	70
Format . . . mm	230 by 365	60 by 60	115 by 1270
Convergent angle . . . degrees	....	....	30
Overlap between frames . . . percent	70	....	100
Base-height ratio	.72	....	.54
Resolution (AWAR[1], in line pairs per mm)	50	....	135

[1] AWAR, area weighted average resolutions.

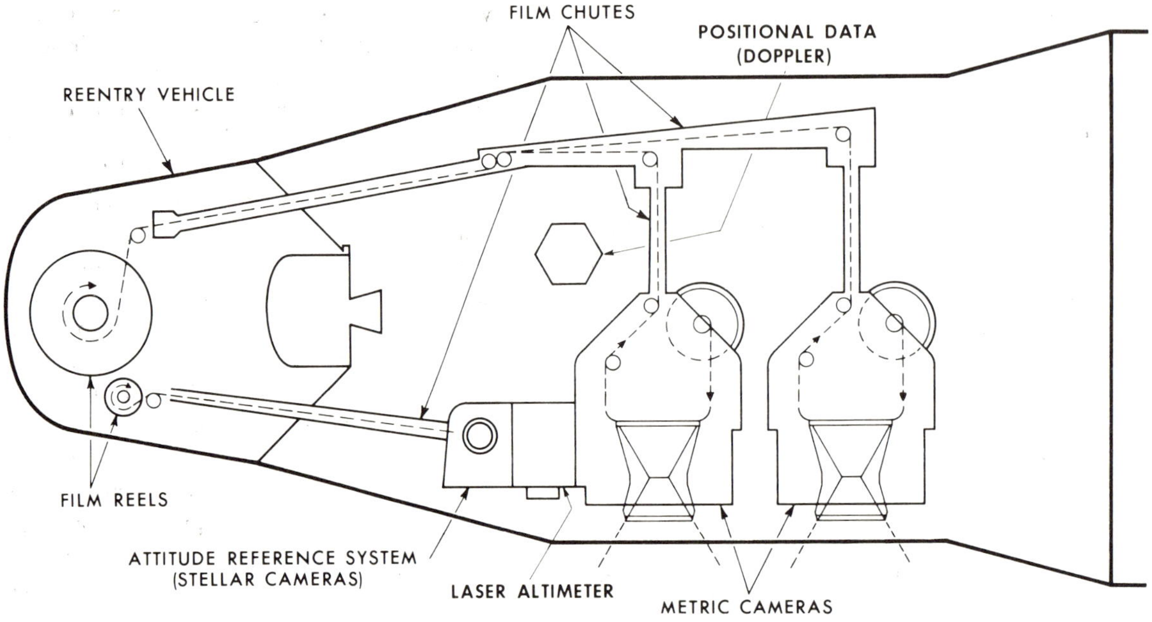

Figure 5.—Design of film-return system.

completed, the recovery vehicle would be separated from the spacecraft and reenter the atmosphere. A parachute would be deployed, and the film package would be picked up by aircraft. An operating altitude of about 200 km was recommended in order to obtain an adequate lifetime for the satellite.

In evaluating the expected performance of the system, a critical factor is the residual image coordinate error, σ_r. In analytical triangulation with conventional aerial photographs, σ_r = 7 μm is regularly obtained in a single stereomodel, and σ_r = 15 μm in a strip of 6 to 10 photographs between control points. With space photography there is good reason to believe that these values can be appreciably reduced. Contributing factors include:

Better photograph resolution.
Reseau to indicate film deformations.
Attitude constraints for each stereopair, obtained from the stellar photographs.
Exposure-station positions, obtained from orbital tracking data.
Scale restraint in each stereopair, obtained from the laser altimetry.

It is expected that σ_r = 5 μm can be obtained in a single stereomodel and σ_r = 10 μm in a triangulated block.

When the appropriate values are substituted in formulas 2, 3, and 6, the expected performance of the two camera systems is as listed in table 3. It should be noted that no absolute values are listed for the panoramic photographs because the panoramic camera has very poor inherent geometry. The concept, therefore, is to establish the control for large-scale mapping with photographs taken by the frame camera, and then use the high-resolution panoramic photographs to compile the planimetry and contours.

Table 3.—*Expected performance of space cameras*

		Control camera	Compilation camera
Photograph scale S_p		655,000	328,000
Ground resolution R_g	m	13	2.4
Allowable enlargement M_a		5	13.5
Maximum map scale S_m		130,000	24,000
Coverage per frame	km	150 by 240	38 by 280
Relative accuracy (σ_r=5μm):			
Position σ_p	m	3.3	1.6
Elevation σ_h	m	4.6	3.0
Contour interval	m	13.7	9.0
Absolute accuracy (σ_r=10μm):			
Position σ_p	m	6.5	....
Elevation σ_h	m	9.2	....
Contour interval	m	27.5	....

By comparing the performance values in table 3 with the map requirement values in table 1, it is apparent that the systems can satisfy mapping needs as shown in table 4.

If the photographs from the control camera were enlarged 2.6 times to form a photoimage base for a map at 1:250,000 scale, a single frame would more than cover a standard map sheet. Within the limits of a stereomodel—the central third of each frame—terrain relief of nearly 400 m could be accommodated without exceeding the allowable planimetric displacement. One can imagine the improvement in the Phoenix 1:250,000 space photomap if the resolution of the photoimagery were increased fourfold.

Table 4.—*Maximum mapping capacity of recommended camera systems*

	Control camera	Compilation camera
Relative mapping		
Content for map scale	130,000	25,000
Position accuracy for map scale	25,000	25,000
Elevation accuracy for contour interval (meters)	15	10
Absolute mapping		
Content for map scale	130,000	25,000
Position accuracy for map scale	25,000	25,000
Elevation accuracy for contour interval (meters)	25	....

Similarly if a 1:25,000-scale map sheet is located near the center of a panoramic photograph, nearly 300 m of relief can be accommodated without exceeding planimetric accuracy requirements.

Contours at the indicated intervals of 10 to 25 m will not be easily obtained. Conventional photogrammetric instruments operate at a C-factor (C = altitude/c.i.) of 1,000 to 2,500. It would require C = 8,000 to 20,000 to reach the values inherent in the photography. Analytical plotting instruments or computer derivation of contours from digitized elevations are possible solutions to the problem. One should not be surprised that new data handling techniques may be needed to exploit the capability of space photography. After all, the optical-mechanical plotting instrument required for aerial photogrammetry represented quite a development beyond the planetable and alidade used in ground surveys.

Obviously, one could argue that any of the assumed values should be a factor of 2 larger or smaller. What is needed is an experiment to determine how well actual performance will conform to that predicted. The U.S. Geological Survey has proposed to NASA that a system with the characteristics of the control camera be flown. It is not yet a funded project, but topographic mappers look forward to it as the best approach to the application of space photography to their requirements.

WHAT ABOUT ECONOMICS?

Several contractors have submitted proposals to NASA to build a photogrammetric satellite as described at a cost between $15 and $20 million per mission. The exact capability cannot be determined until the system is designed, but the National Academy of Sciences estimated that 90 kg of film could be carried—enough to photograph 20 million km^2, or enough to cover the entire United States twice. The cost per square kilometer is directly competitive with the most economical aircraft photography. The obvious problem, however, is that 1,000 km^2 would cost the same amount as 20 million km^2. Thus space photography is economical only for extremely large areas.

The economic analysis must include the photogrammetric and cartographic reduction as well as the cost of photography. To cover the United States with the proposed space frame photographs would require less than 1,000 stereomodels as opposed to over 100,000 with high-altitude aircraft photographs. A large part of the advantage might be lost if conventional line drafting methods are employed for map production. But as has been pointed out, the central part of each frame is orthographic within the limits of the National Map Accuracy Standards. Therefore, one can conclude that annotated orthophotomaps might be the most practical way of producing useful maps of extensive areas on a timely basis.

The formats and focal lengths of space photographs are, to a large extent, incompatible with current photogrammetric instrumentation. Clearly, if satellite photography is to be useful for production, detailed consideration and planning is required throughout the whole course of the mapping cycle, extending as far as a reeducation of map users who may find it necessary to revise their notions of what an acceptable map is.

WHAT ABOUT CLOUDS?

Extensive studies of weather-satellite pictures to predict the probability of obtaining cloud-free photographs from space indicate that a space system with a lifetime adequate for four passes over each area will achieve about 97 percent successful photography. The system will require ground control of the satellite cameras in accordance with weather predictions.

WHAT ARE THE IMMEDIATE PROSPECTS?

Apart from weather satellites, only two NASA projects for photographing the Earth from space are currently funded. The first of these is the Earth Resources Technology Satellite (ERTS), which carries three television cameras and a four-channel multispectral scanner. It is designed fundamentally to provide repetitive coverage for monitoring time-variant phenomena. Thematic mapping is an important part of the utilization of the records, and the resolution of the pictures is adequate as an image base for maps at scale 1:1,000,000 and possibly larger. But the system does not provide stereoscopic coverage, and topographic mapping is not an objective.

The other project is Skylab, designed primarily to investigate the problems of man operating for extended periods in space. An empty S-IVB rocket will be converted into a laboratory capable of supporting three men for periods of up to 56 days. The Apollo Command and Service Module will be used as a ferry to change crews in Skylab, which will be occupied three different times during its lifetime of one year. It is planned to launch Skylab in the spring of 1973. Its operating altitude will be 435 km, and the orbit inclination will be 50°. It will carry two photographic systems.

The first is a multispectral photographic experiment designated S-190A. Itek Corporation developed an array of six cameras (fig. 6), of 150-mm focal length and f/2.8 aperture, recording on 70-mm film. The optical axes of all cameras are accurately alined, and the focal length and lens distortions are matched so that all pictures can be accurately registered. Forward-motion compensation will be provided by rocking the frame that carries the six cameras. Four black-and-white spectral bands of 0.1-μm bandwidth between 0.5 and 0.9 μm are planned. The other two cameras will carry color and color-infrared film.

The second photographic experiment carried on Skylab A will be the 460-mm Actron camera from the lunar program. It has been modified for operation in Earth orbit and is designated S-190B, the Earth Terrain Camera (ETC)(fig. 7). A fixed mount is contemplated, with convergent stereo provided by pitching the entire spacecraft as it passes over an experimental area.

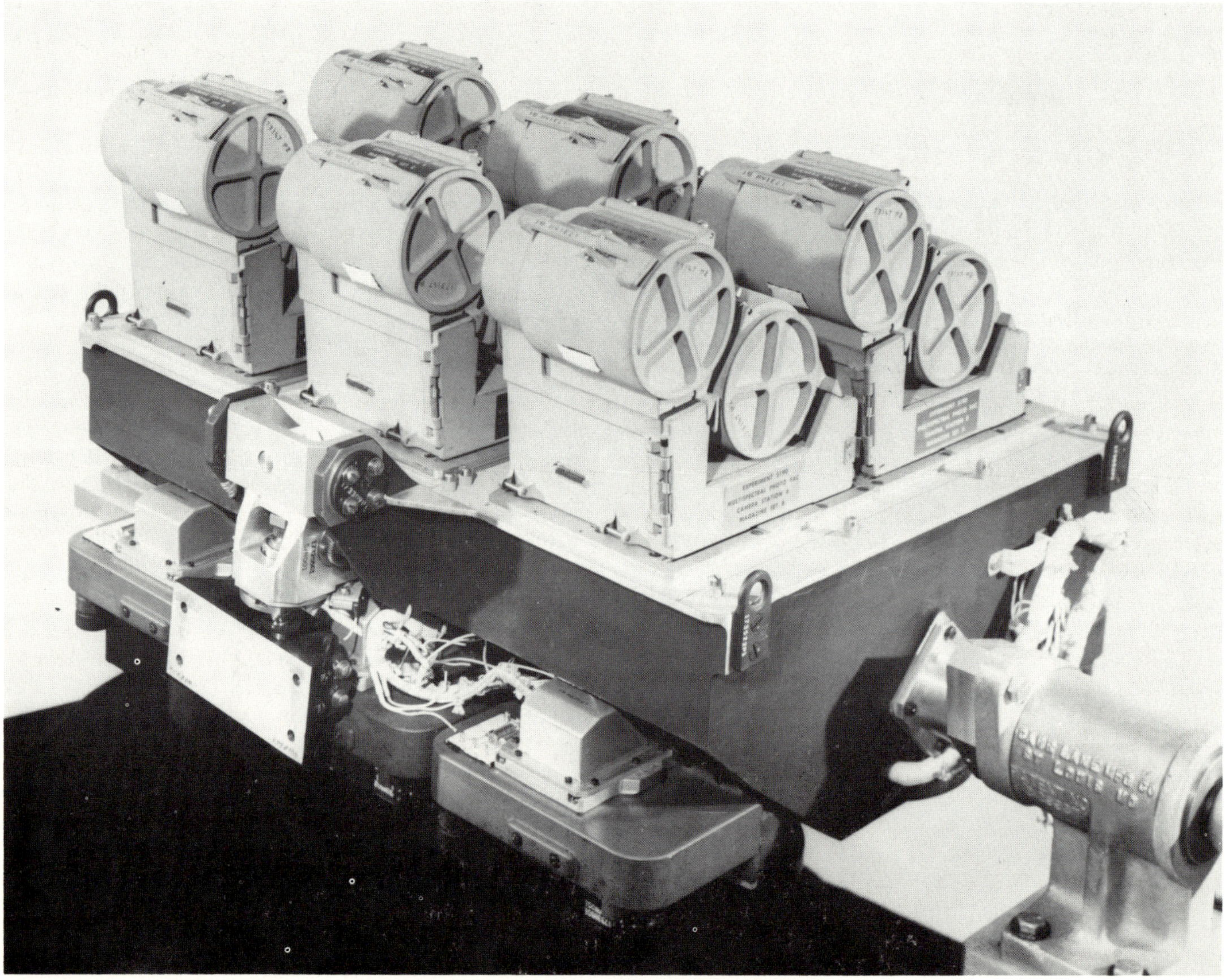

Figure 6.—Skylab S-190A Multispectral Camera.

Both systems will resolve about 80 line pairs per millimeter for usual ground-object contrasts. Neither system will have precise timing, attitude, or altimetry support data. Primary application will be for interpretation of Earth resources information. Mapping potential, evaluated by formulas 2, 3, 5, and 6, is given in table 5.

The tabulated values obviously do not approach those expected from the proposed 305-mm frame camera system, supplemented by the 610-mm panoramic camera. Nevertheless the photographs will be an appreciable improvement over those obtained from Gemini and Apollo.

CONCLUSION

The space program to date has produced some astonishing photographs. Many of them have been of compelling interest from the historical, pictorial, and interpretative points of view. So far as photogrammetrists are concerned, however, the pictures have presented far more problems than they have solved. It is easy to question why things have been done and are being done in the ways described. Most of the reasons have nothing to do with science, but with finances and politics. However, there can be no doubt that, as the difficulties of operation for men and machines in space are overcome, the advantages of space will be applied to the routine production of both thematic and topographic maps for the benefit of all mankind.

Table 5.—*Cartographic potential of S-190A and S-190B cameras in Skylab*

	S-190A	S-190B
Photo scale S_p	2,900,000	945,000
Ground resolution R_g . . . m . .	36	12
Allowable enlargement M_a	8	8
Maximum map scale S_m	360,000	118,000
Coverage per frame . . . km . .	174 by 174	109 by 109
Base-height ratio	.16	0.45 (25° conv.)
Accuracy (σ_r=10μm):		
Position σ_p . . . m . .	30	10
Elevation σ_h . . . m . .	180	20
Contour interval . . . m . .	550	60

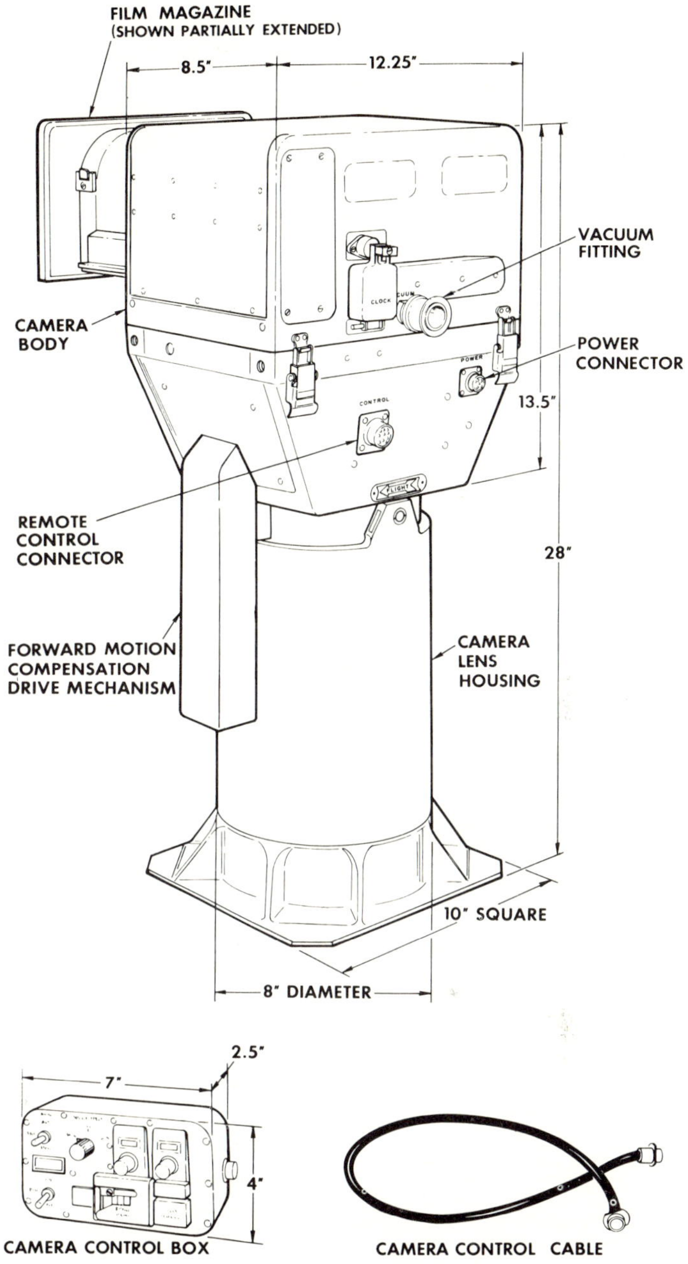

Figure 7.—Diagram of S-190B Earth Terrain Camera.

Jour. Research U.S. Geol. Survey
Vol. 1, No. 3, May-June 1973, p. 327—339

PHOTOIMAGES FOR MAP BASES

By MORRIS L. McKENZIE, McLean, Va.

Abstract.—Maps with aerial photograph image bases have gained wide popularity. The orthophotomap presents an abundance of ground detail and information that cannot be shown on a line map with standard cartographic symbols. In preparing a map base covering areas of little relief, the imagery is fitted to map control with a conventional rectifier, but for areas of significant relief, the photographs are reproduced in an orthophotoscope to remove the effects of both camera tilt and terrain relief.

The photoimage map has attained high status with both the map user and mapmaker. Geologists, geographers, hydrologists, engineers, surveyors, and city planners are finding photomaps useful as working bases. Photoimage map bases can be produced quickly and thus provide current map information either as a separate product or in combination with line symbols. The production of a photoimage base lends itself to automation with the use of equipment already developed. The automatic production of a true line map has not yet been attained.

TYPES OF PHOTOIMAGE MAPS

Terminology and definitions for various photoimage products and processes have not been universally established. Consequently, some agencies, including the U.S. Geological Survey, have their own terminology. The descriptions below are based on Geological Survey usage.

A photomap is a map on a base containing photoimagery which is retained as a part of the representation. It may incorporate special cartographic treatment, image enhancement, color separation, or a combination of these.

An orthophotomap (fig. 1) is a photomap prepared from an orthophotograph or a precisely controlled assembly of orthophotographs. It is generally published in standard map format with a geographic graticule and plane coordinate grid ticks. Color-enhanced imagery and cartographic symbols—including contours and (or) elevations, boundaries, and labels—are added as required to suit the area and intended use of the map. The prefix "ortho" implies that the horizontal position of the image base is within limits specified by the National Map Accuracy Standards.

An orthophotoquad (fig. 2) is a map of standard accuracy prepared from an orthophotograph or a mosaic of orthophotographs in quadrangle format, with little or no cartographic enhancement. It contains a geographic graticule, a reference grid or grid ticks, and appropriate map collar information, but no cartographic symbols or contours. Orthophotoquads are reproduced in final form either photographically, lithographically, or by the diazo process.

PHOTOMAPPING INSTRUMENTS

The relative positions of images in an aerial photograph are seriously influenced by camera tilt and terrain relief. If the terrain is relatively flat, then image displacements due to camera tilt are removed with a conventional rectifier. The photograph to be rectified is tilted and positioned relative to the film plane so that image points projected from the photographs are fitted to the plotted positions of these points on the film plane.

If the amount of distortion in the photograph due to relief is too great for correction by simple rectification, then the photograph is scanned in an orthophotoscope (fig. 3). In this instrument, images are projected onto a platen having a slot about 5 mm in length, which exposes the film beneath. The platen is automatically driven in the *y* direction (perpendicular to the flight line) with automatic stepover in the *x* direction (along the flight line) at the end of each *y* scan. The operator controls the *z* motion (up and down) of the platen so as to keep the exposing slot in contact with the apparent surface of the three-dimensional terrain model. Thus the photoimagery is reproduced at a common scale in a series of narrow contiguous strips (Scher, 1964).

PROCESSING

Positive photographic prints are made, all at a common scale, of the various orthophotonegatives covering the area to be mapped. They are then mosaicked to form a single photoimage base. Some orthophotos are made from a single high-altitude photograph that covers the entire area to be mapped, and mosaicking is not needed.

If the map is to be produced lithographically, the continuous-tone imagery of the mosaic is converted to minute, random-dot patterns for making pressplates (Clark, 1971).

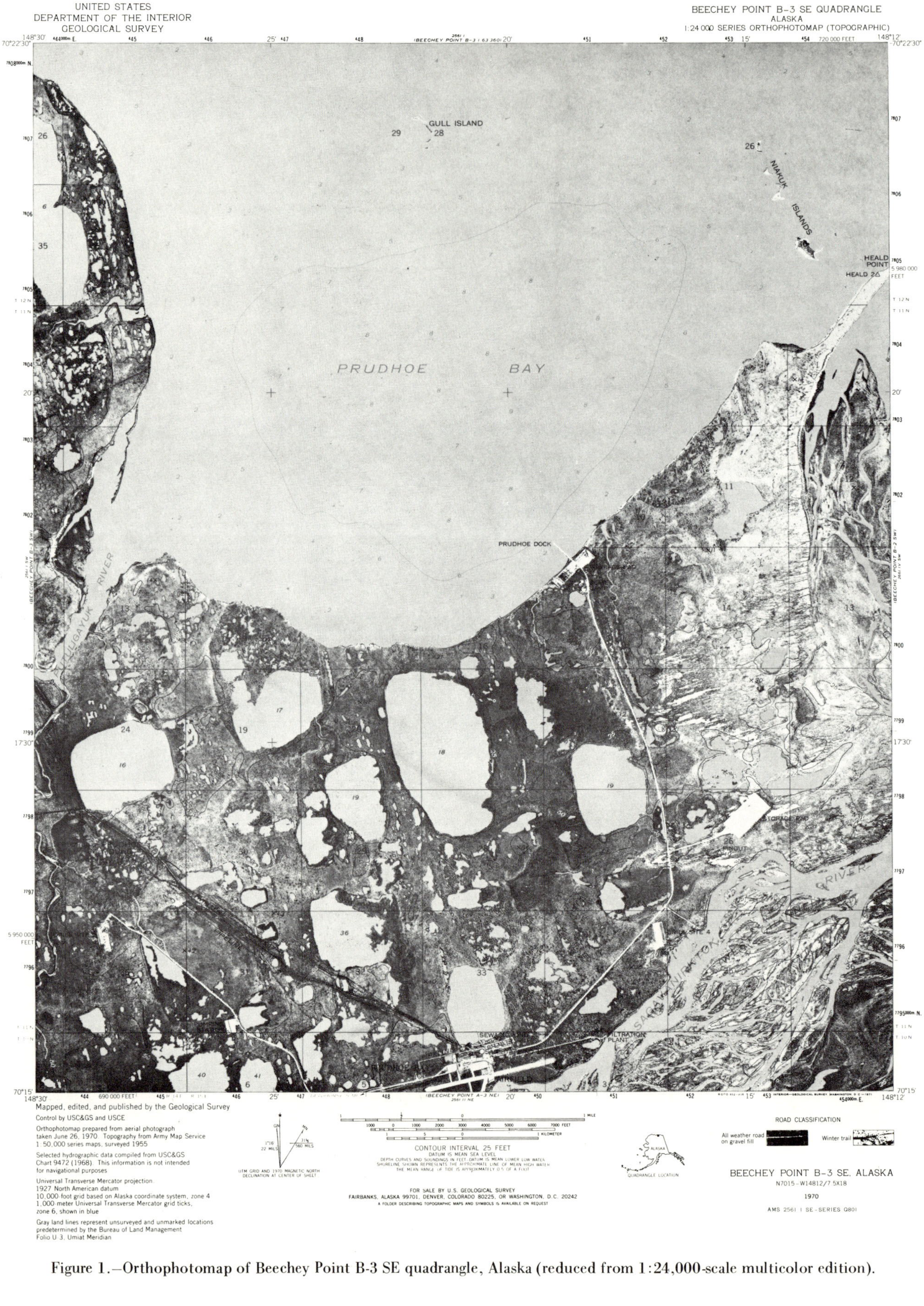

Figure 1.—Orthophotomap of Beechey Point B-3 SE quadrangle, Alaska (reduced from 1:24,000-scale multicolor edition).

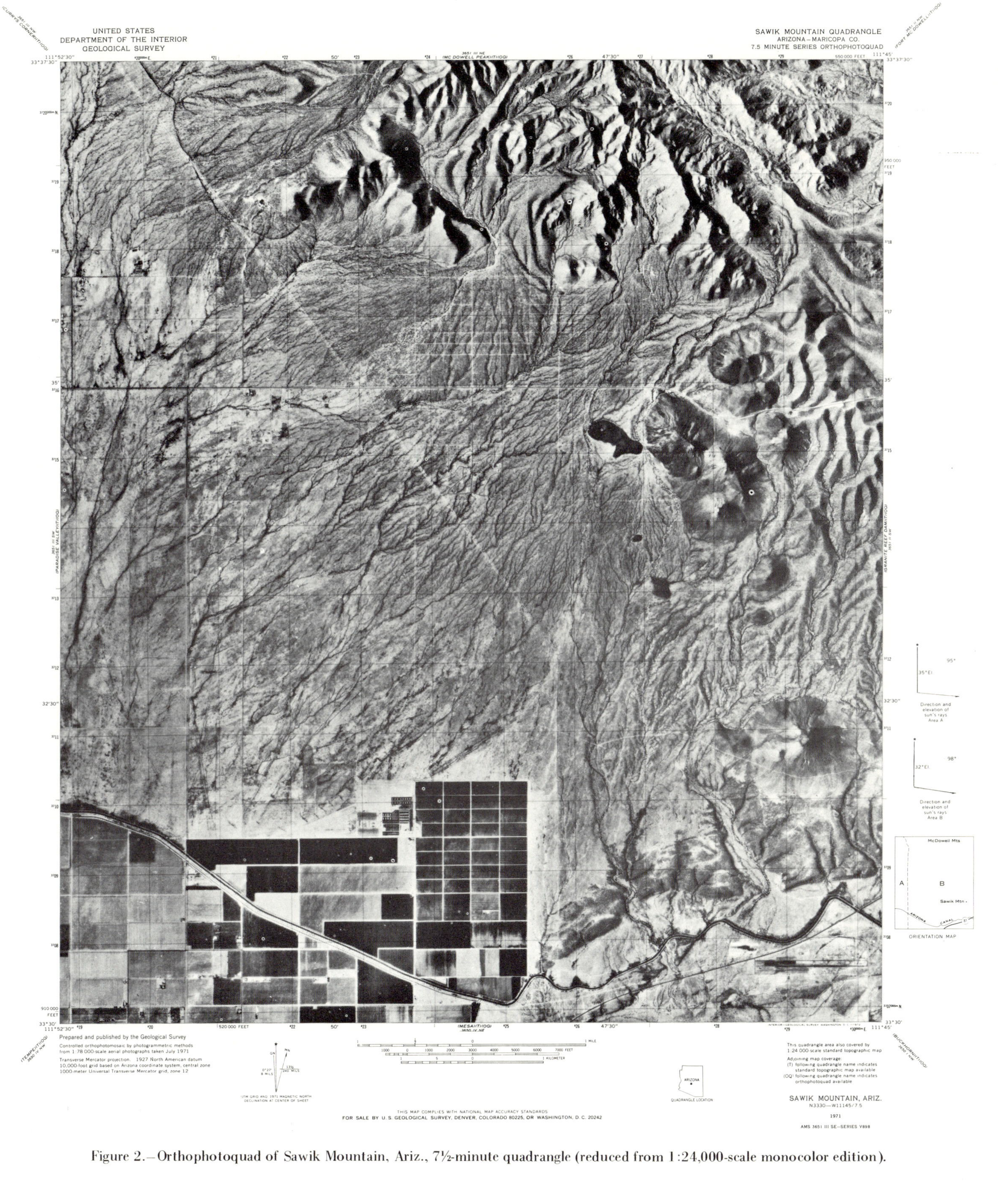

Figure 2.—Orthophotoquad of Sawik Mountain, Ariz., 7½-minute quadrangle (reduced from 1:24,000-scale monocolor edition).

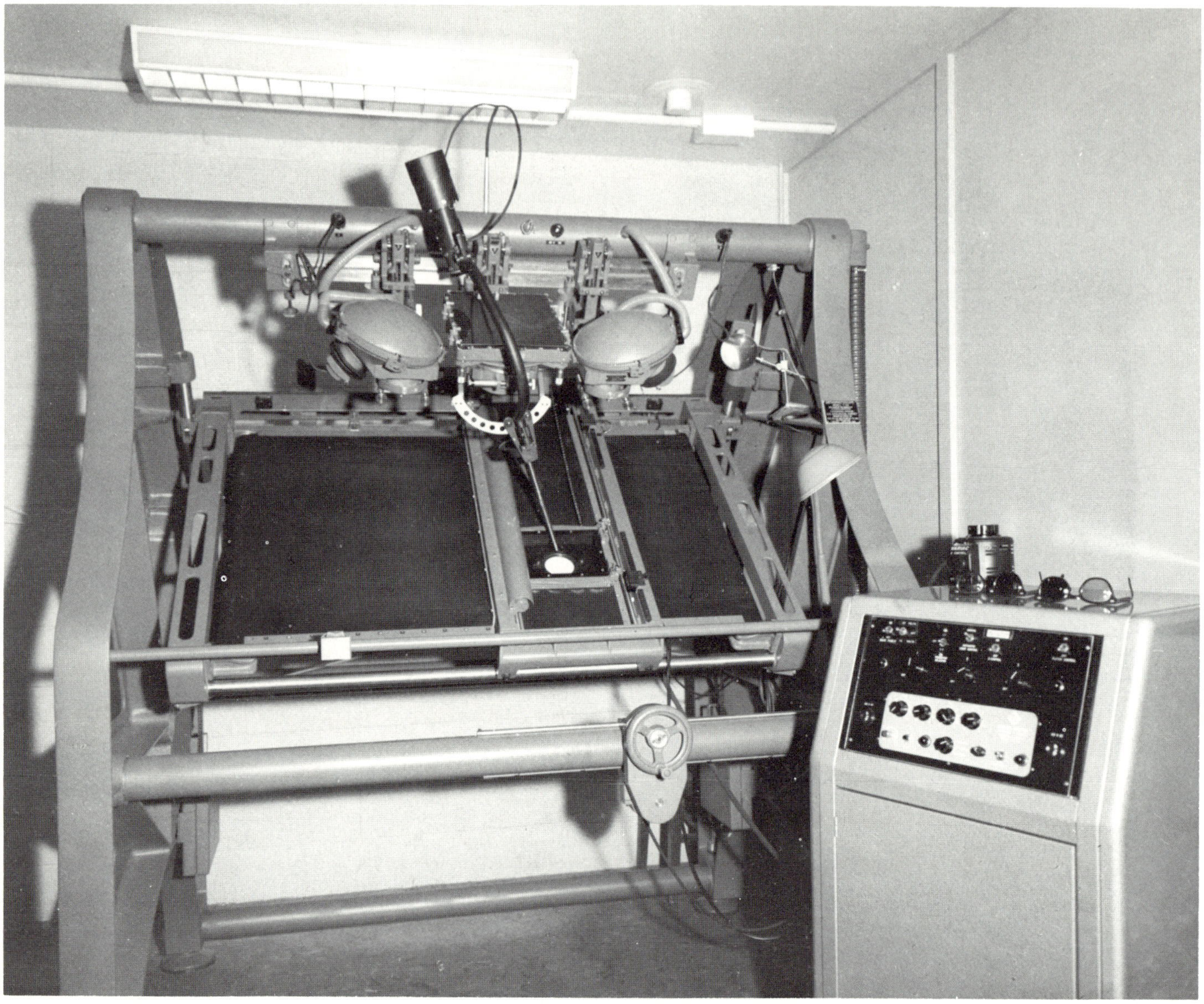

Figure 3.—Orthophotoscope, used to print orthophotographs corrected for distortion due to high relief.

Best results have been obtained with a method known as photolysis, in which a continuous-tone negative is contact printed to a matte-surface film by prolonged exposure to high-intensity ultraviolet light. The matte-surface film thus produces an extremely low contrast positive. Contact printing from the positive produces a random-dot negative on high-contrast lithographic film. Imagery from the random-dot negative can be transferred to the pressplate without the use of a halftone screen.

Orthophotomaps are usually made from black-and-white photographs, and therefore color imagery on the printed map must be artificially produced by appropriate ink colors. By masking techniques, pressplates are made for printing selected parts of the photoimagery in basic colors or a combination of colors. Thus a variety of tones and colors are available for depicting ground imagery in more recognizable colors than nature provides; that is, woodland can be accentuated with green, water features with blue, barren lands with tan or brown, and so on.

UTILITY OF PHOTOIMAGERY

Geology.—Geologists deserve much credit for fostering the development of the first Geological Survey orthophotoscope in the early 1950's. They recognized the usefulness of a true-scale photograph for geologic studies. Figure 4, top, is a part of a topographic line map of North Emblem Reservoir, Wyo., containing prominent geologic features. Figure 4, bottom, is an orthophotomap of the same area. One needs

Figure 4.—Part of the North Emblem Reservoir, Wyo., 7½-minute quadrangle. Top, topographic map; bottom, orthophotomap. (Reproduced from multicolor editions.)

only to compare these two products to appreciate the value of the photoimage base to the geologist.[1]

Hydrology.—On the orthophotomap of Antelope Island, Utah (fig. 5), the extent of water recession of the Great Salt Lake is clearly discernible, and bottom features can be seen in shallow-water areas. This type of detail is not depicted on the line map covering the same area.

Urban planning.—Figure 6 is a part of an orthophotomap of the Dallas, Tex., area. The amount of urban detail vital to city planners that is shown automatically on an orthophotomap is not practical or even possible to show on a conventional line map.

Natural resources survey.—Figure 7, bottom, is a part of an orthophotomap of Royal Palm Ranger Station, Fla., and figure 7, top, is a part of the line map of the same area. The line map appears grossly inadequate when compared with the wealth of information and detail imaged in the orthophotomap. Even such detail as salt-water encroachment and marshland limits can be discerned on the photographs and portrayed in distinctive colors in the printed map. The orthophotomap provides many images for orienting the map to ground features, a valuable aid to the explorer.

Line map complement.—Figure 8, top, is a part of a line map of the Asbury Park, N.J., area which has undergone extensive development. Figure 8, bottom, a part of an orthophotoquad of the same area, shows the extent of development since the line map was published. The monocolor orthophotoquad provides a convenient method of providing the map user with up-to-date map information. The time required to produce an orthophotoquad is a fraction of that required to publish a standard orthophotomap or line map.

ORTHOPHOTOMAPPING RESEARCH

The two prime goals of orthophotomapping research are improved image quality and automation of the process. Instruments are being designed with the intent of reaching both of these objectives. The newly designed Orthophotomat (fig. 9) is equipped with a single projector rather than two or three projectors that require anaglyphic filtering (Hughes and others, 1971). The single plate is leveled and positioned to predetermined locations of pass points on a base sheet. The x, y, and z motions of the film platen and exposing slot of the Orthophotomat are automatically driven by the Autoline (fig. 10), which locks onto and follows the profiles previously extracted from a stereomodel.

The only link in this approach that has not been fully developed is the process of automatically extracting profiles from stereomodels. Profiles are now being extracted manually with a modified projection-type stereoplotter. The tracing table of the plotter is equipped with a special coordinatograph, which records vertical profiles in a horizontal plane as the operator scans the stereomodel in strips. The operator must keep the floating mark in contact with the ground surface in the stereomodel by manually manipulating the floating mark.

An automatic approach for extracting profiles is under development (Lewis and Hughes, 1970). The trace of intersecting, corresponding rays at ground level is recorded on film (fig. 11) by moving the stereoplotter projectors upwards as film is pulled across a slot extending the full length of the stereomodel. A profile is formed along a line of intersecting ray traces. For the next profile, the slot is moved over one increment and the process cycle repeated (fig. 12); or multiple slots are used to extract multiple profiles in one cycle. The research effort is now aimed at automatically isolating the profiles from the extraneous images formed in the process.

FUTURE PROSPECTS

During the first few years of development, the orthophotomap was not widely accepted, but the demand for this type of map is increasing rapidly. At present, most orthophotomaps supplement or complement the corresponding line map. However, the orthophotomap, in some terrain types, is coming into demand as a product preferred over the line map. It is conceivable that in the not-too-distant future the Geological Survey will provide a photoimage base as a standard product, either as content of an orthophotomap or as a separate orthophotoquad to complement the standard line map.

REFERENCES CITED

Clark, Clyde, 1971, Reproduction of orthophotographics: Am. Soc. Photogrammetry Orthophoto Workshop, Washington, D.C., Jan. 18–21, 1971, Proc.

Hughes, T. A., Shope, A. R., and Baxter, F. S., 1971, USGS Automatic Orthophoto System: Photogramm. Eng., v. 37, no. 10, p. 1055–1062.

Lewis, J. G., and Hughes, T. A., 1970, Stereoscopic profiling by intersection of ray traces: Am. Soc. Photogrammetry and Am. Cong. on Surveying and Mapping Fall Tech. Conf., Denver, Colo., Oct. 7–11, 1970, Proc.

Scher, M. B., 1964, Research in orthophotography: Photogramm. Eng., v. 30, no. 5, p. 756–762.

[1] The black-and-white reproductions in this paper do not show the added advantages of color enhancement of the imagery on orthophotomaps.

[Figures 5–12 follow this page]

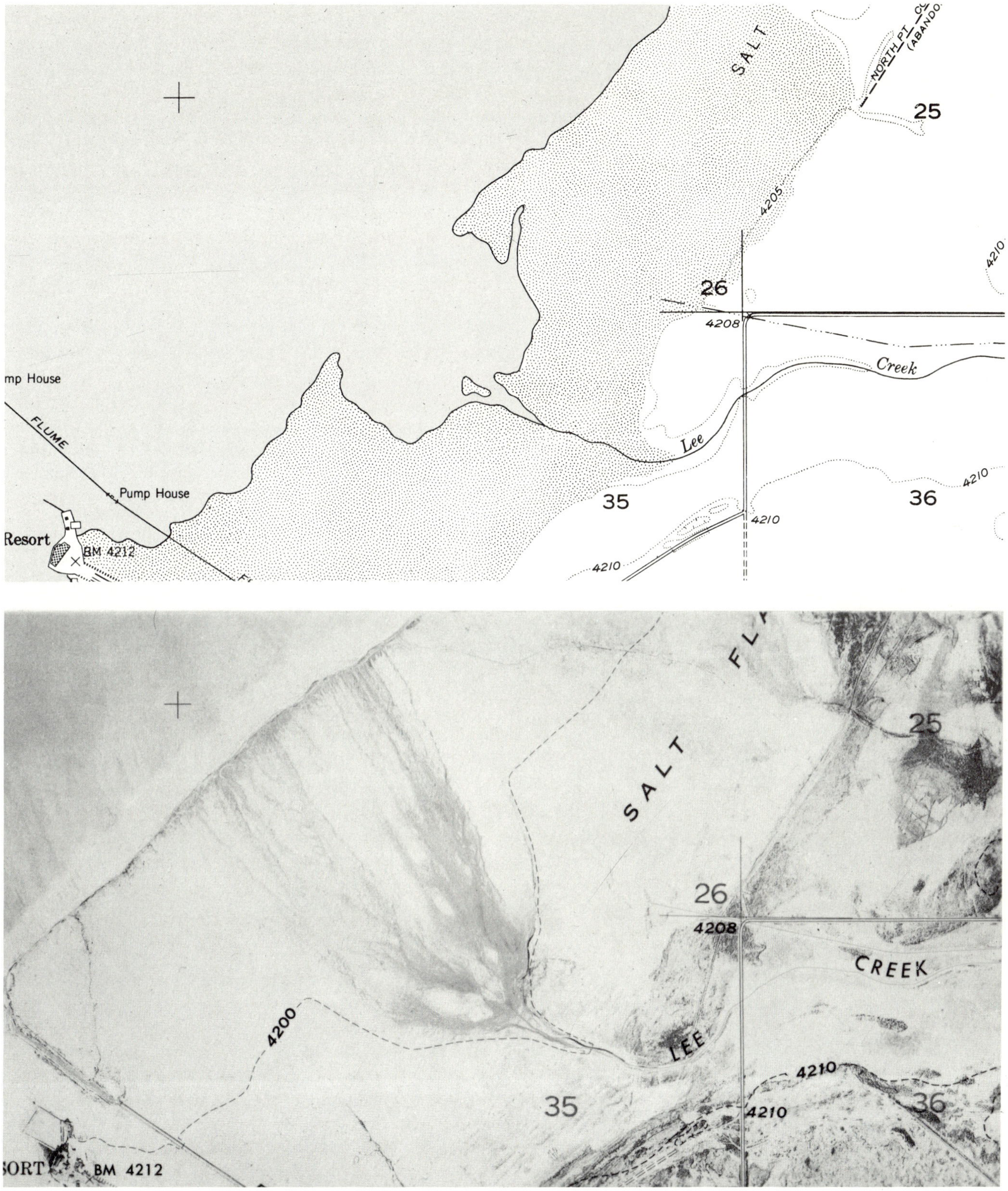

Figure 5.—Part of the Antelope Island, Utah, 7½-minute quadrangle. Top, topographic map; bottom, orthophotomap. (Reproduced from multicolor editions.)

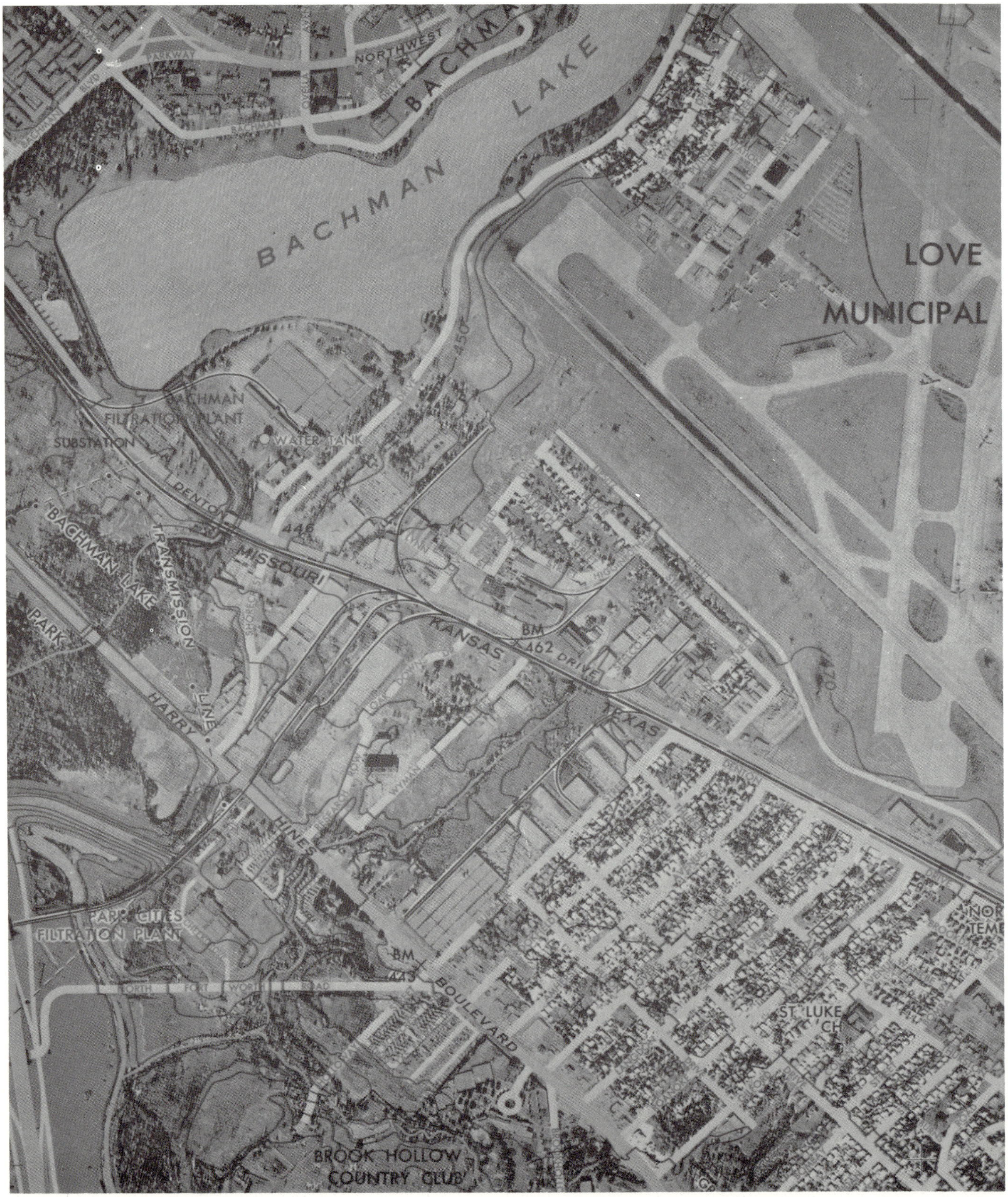

Figure 6.–Part of Dallas, Tex., experimental orthophotomap. (Reproduced from multicolor edition.)

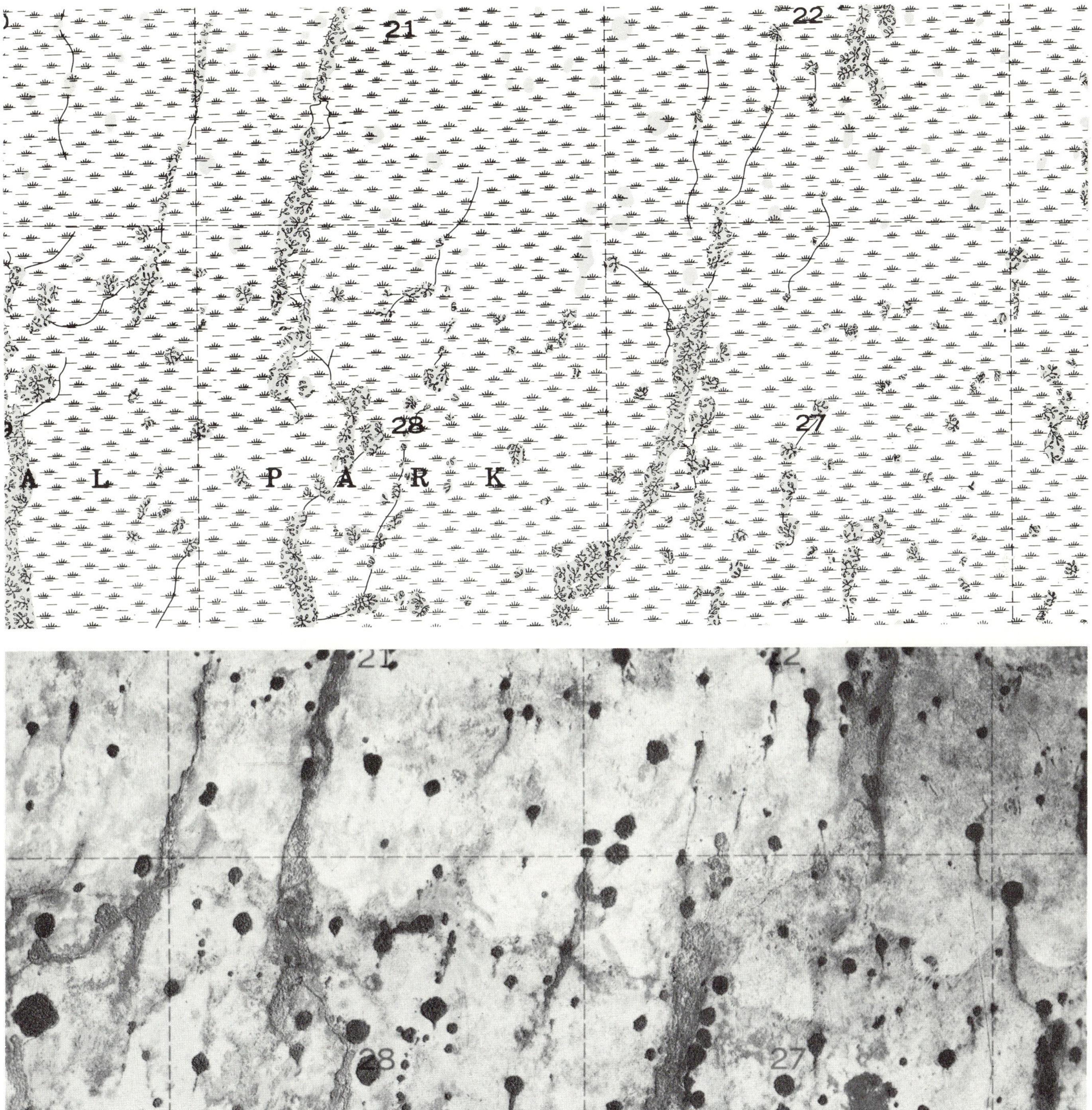

Figure 7.—Part of the Royal Palm Ranger Station, Fla., 7½-minute quadrangle. Top, topographic map; bottom, orthophotomap. (Reproduced from multicolor editions.)

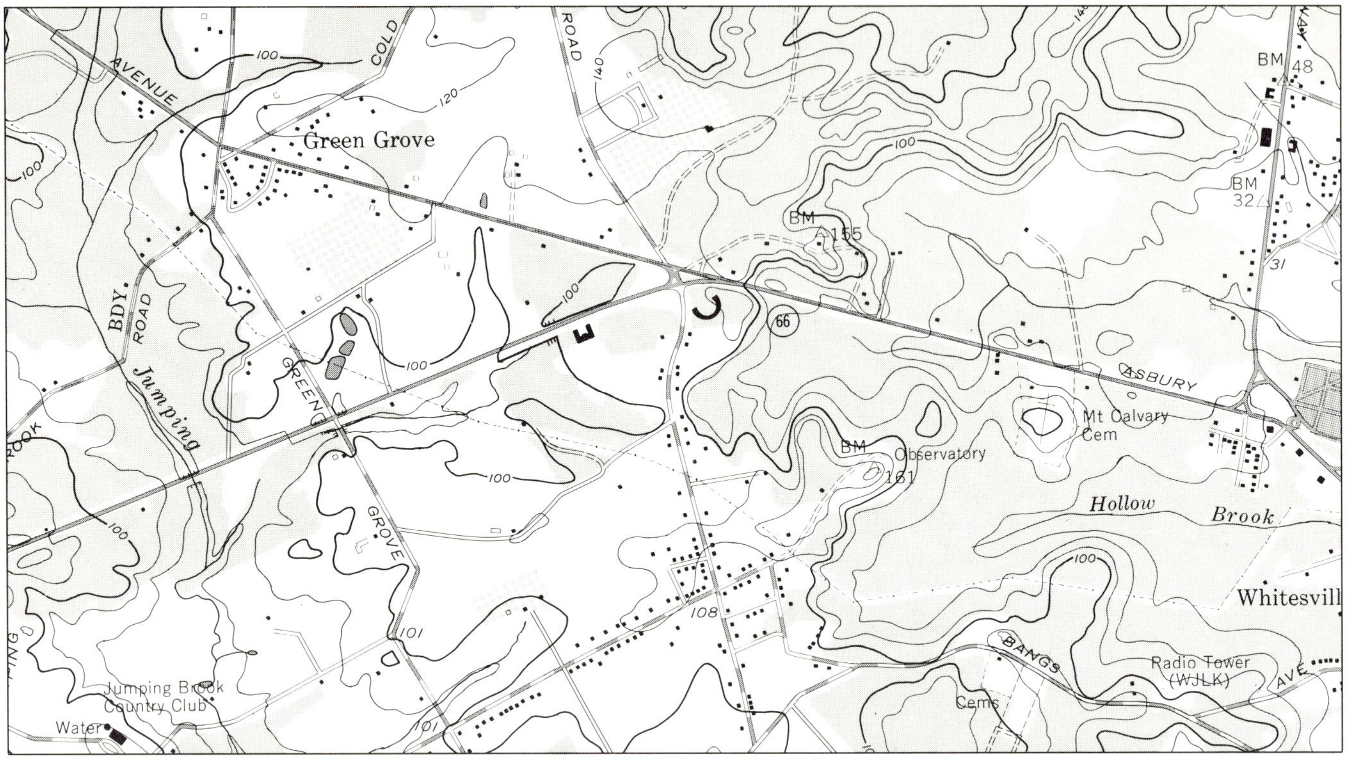

Figure 8.—Part of the Asbury Park, N.J., 7½-minute quadrangle. Top, topographic map; bottom, orthophotoquad. (Reproduced from multicolor and monocolor editions.)

Figure 9.—Orthophotomat, used with Autoline (fig. 10) to print orthophotographs.

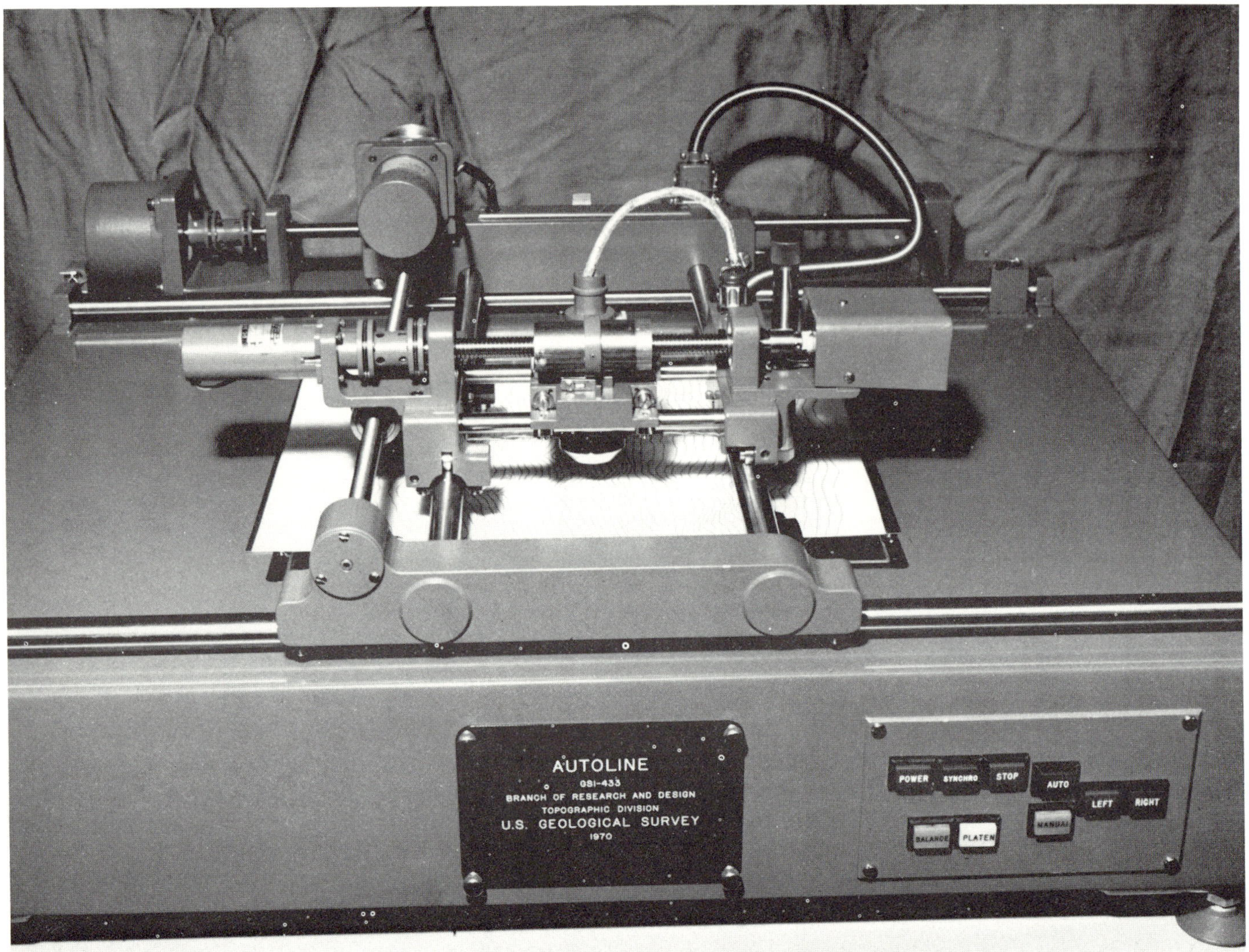

Figure 10.—Autoline, used with terrain profiles to drive the scanning motions of the Orthophotomat (fig. 9).

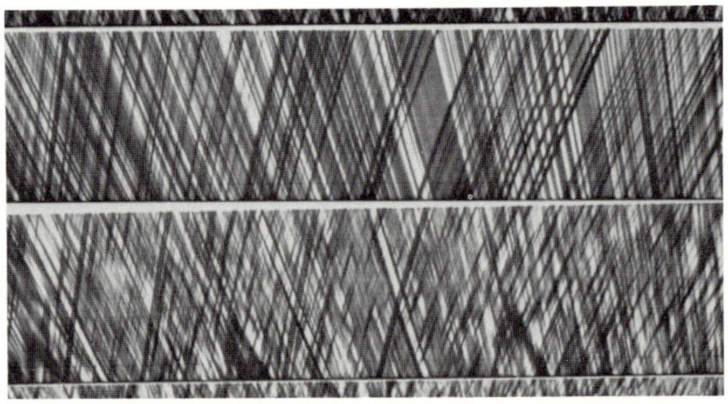

Figure 11.—Profiles formed by the intersection of corresponding image rays.

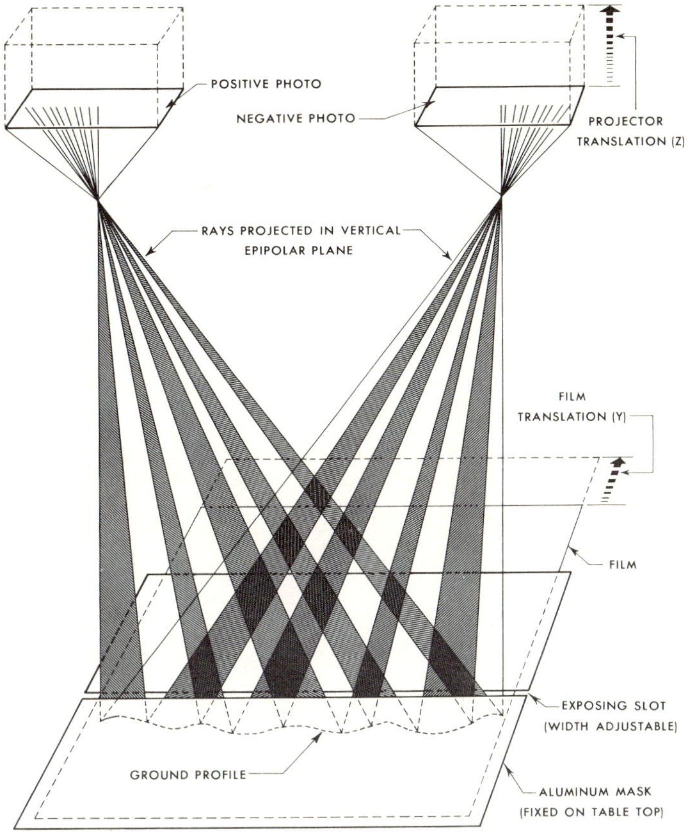

Figure 12.—Schematic of profile scanning operation.

Jour. Research U.S. Geol. Survey
Vol. 1, No. 3, May-June 1973, p. 341—344

MICROBIOLOGICAL ASPECTS OF GROUND-WATER RECHARGE—INJECTION OF PURIFIED UNCHLORINATED SEWAGE EFFLUENT AT BAY PARK, LONG ISLAND, NEW YORK

By GARRY G. EHRLICH, THEODORE A. EHLKE, and JOHN VECCHIOLI,
Menlo Park, Calif., Albany, N.Y., Mineola, N.Y.

Prepared in cooperation with the Nassau County Department of Public Works

Abstract.—Unchlorinated, tertiary-treated sewage effluent was injected through a well at Bay Park, Long Island, N.Y., into a sand aquifer at a rate of 340 gpm for 10 days. Massive, biologically produced slime deposits formed in the filter pack immediately adjacent to the well screen. Observed head buildup in the recharge well was correlated with the formation of these deposits. Comparison of results from this test with results of earlier tests suggests that formation of these deposits may be avoided by addition of chlorine to the injectant.

The performance of a recharge well is adversely affected by factors that decrease the permeability of the receiving formation in the vicinity of the well. Clogging caused by the accumulation of organic and inorganic particulate matter in a mat at the aquifer face is one such factor. Evidence for particulate clogging of injection wells was presented by the California State Water Pollution Control Board (1954) and Rebhun and Schwarz (1968). The California group (1954, p. 165) found that the rate of clogging was directly proportional to the amount of solids injected in any period of time. They further concluded that biological activity in the particulate mat decreased the rate of accumulation of organic solids and thereby reduced the rate of clogging. Rebhun and Schwarz suggested that bacterial growth and its associated decomposition products enhanced the rate of solids buildup and therefore increased the rate of well clogging. These apparently contradictory conclusions may have resulted from different circumstances in the two studies, and each might be correct for the conditions that prevailed during the tests.

Using reclaimed water (tertiary-treated sewage effluent) as the injectant, Ehrlich, Ehlke, and Vecchioli (1972) found that microbial growth near a recharge well at Bay Park, Long Island, N.Y., was effectively suppressed if the residual chlorine level of the injectant was maintained at about 2 mg/l. In a further evaluation of the specific effect of microbial growth on clogging of the Bay Park well, the authors injected unchlorinated reclaimed water into the well. They found that in the absence of the high residual chlorine level vigorous microbial growth occurred in the vicinity of the well.

METHODS

The experimental recharge facility and the water-treatment process at Bay Park have been described previously (Cohen and Durfor, 1967; Peters and Rose, 1968). Reclaimed water from the tertiary treatment process was injected into the Bay Park well under positive head at a rate of 340 gpm for 10 days. The total quantity of reclaimed water injected was about 5 million gallons. Chemical quality of the water used in this test (table 1) was virtually the same as that used in earlier tests (Vecchioli, 1970; Ehrlich and others, 1972) except that the water was not chlorinated before injection.

Total-coliform, fecal-coliform, and fecal-streptococci counts were made by membrane-filter methods described by the American Public Health Association and others (1971, p. 678–688; p. 690–691). Total bacteria counts were made by filtering measured volumes of water through membrane filters (mean pore size, 0.45 μm). The exposed filters were placed on plates of plate-count agar, bacterial-laden side up, and incubated at 30°C (Celsius). Plates were counted after 24 hours of incubation. Bacterial quality of the injectant is listed in table 2.

The bacterial population of the aquifer near the well screen was determined by evaluating the contents of a special probe. This probe was built from a piece of stainless-steel well screen 2 inches in diameter and 19 inches in length. After the probe had been filled with sand from the aquifer, it was autoclaved until the contents were sterile. Before the start of injection, the sterile sand-filled probe was lowered into an observation well in the filter pack surrounding the recharge well and was suspended at about the midlength of the filter pack (at a depth of about 450 feet). The precise distance between the observation well and the main screen of the injection well is unknown, but it is probably less than 9 inches. The probe was removed

Table 1.—*Chemical and physical quality of the recharge water in the test of November 30 to December 10, 1970*

[Observed values are based on 10 daily composite samples. Each composite sample consists of four samples collected throughout the day. Values for aluminum, iron, and manganese are in micrograms per liter; all other parameters except pH, specific conductance, and water temperature are in milligrams per liter]

Parameter	Observed values		Median
	Maximum	Minimum	
Silica (SiO_2)	14	13	14
Aluminum (Al), total	400	0	100
Iron (Fe), total	580	200	310
Manganese (Mn), dissolved	100	6	70
Calcium (Ca)	18	14	16
Magnesium (Mg)	7.2	6.2	6.3
Sodium (Na)	84	79	81
Potassium (K)	12	11	11
Bicarbonate (HCO_3)	64	0	6
Sulfate (SO_4)	161	119	136
Chloride (Cl)	92	83	86
Fluoride (F)	.1	0	.1
Organic nitrogen (N)	5.0	.82	1.4
Nitrite nitrogen (N)	.01	.00	.00
Ammonia nitrogen (N)	28	25	26
Nitrate nitrogen (N)	.0	.0	.0
Phosphate as PO_4, total	.49	.20	.34
Dissolved solids, residue at 180°C	396	365	376
Dissolved solids, calculated from determined constituents.	464	333	373
Total solids, residue, volatile	51	17	34
Hardness as $CaCO_3$ (Ca, Mg)	74	61	67
Noncarbonate hardness	67	22	59
Specific conductance (μmhos/cm at 25°C).	840	778	815
pH	6.3	6.0	6.1
Water temperature (°C)	19	18	18
Dissolved oxygen (DO)	5.2	3.8	4.3
Chemical oxygen demand (COD), 0.025*N* $K_2Cr_2O_7$.	17	7	14
Detergents (MBAS)	.18	.04	.14

Table 2.—*Bacterial quality of the recharge water in the test of November 30 to December 10, 1970*

[All results in colonies per 100 ml]

Elapsed time (days)	Total bacteria	Total coliforms	Fecal coliforms	Fecal streptococci
1	2.2×10^5	1.0×10^4	200	[1] 1
2	29×10^5	2.7×10^4	1,200	80
3	1.4×10^5	1.0×10^4	.....	[1] 11
4	3.7×10^5	4.7×10^4	2,000	39
5	3.3×10^5	6.0×10^4	1,500	31
6	2.9×10^5	6.1×10^4	[1] 750	30
7	1.2×10^5	6.0×10^4	1,100	[1] 10
8	1.2×10^5	5.4×10^4	2,200	[1] 15
9	1.9×10^5	5.5×10^4	960	22

[1] Estimated count based on nonideal colony count.

Table 3.—*Bacterial counts made by membrane-filter methods of material recovered from sand probe*

[All counts given as colonies per 100 ml of pore volume. Pore volume, calculated on the basis of weight of sand sampled, was assumed to be 30 percent of the total volume; bulk density was assumed to be 2 g/cm³]

Type of bacteria	Bacterial count
Total	1.0×10^8
Coliform	1.0×10^6
Fecal coliform	3.5×10^3
Fecal streptococci	Not detected.

Table 4.—*Bacterial counts made by membrane-filter methods of water recovered from injection well at Bay Park, Long Island, N.Y., after injection test of November 30 to December 10, 1970*

[All counts given as colonies per 100 ml of pore volume]

Type of bacteria	Bacterial count
Total	2.0×10^5
Coliform	8.3×10^4
Fecal coliform	2.8×10^3
Fecal streptococci	57

immediately after injection ended. A known weight of material from the center of the probe was suspended in sterile, buffered dilution water. Samples of the suspension and dilutions were planted in plate-count agar as described by the American Public Health Association and others (1971, p. 660–662). Bacterial counts of probe material were calculated on the basis of estimated pore volume of the sample based on sample weight, bulk density, and an assumed void volume of 30 percent (table 3).

Redevelopment of the injection well was started immediately after the end of the injection test. Samples for microbiological study were taken immediately after the water in the well casing had been removed. (table 4).

RESULTS AND DISCUSSION

Specific capacity of the injection well decreased from 26.5 gpm per foot of head buildup at the start of the test to 11 gpm per foot of head buildup after 10 days. Curves showing rate of head buildup in the present test (test 8) and three other tests in which the injectant was chlorinated are given in figure 1. Earlier testing at comparable injection rates showed that the rate of clogging depended mainly on the turbidity of the injectant (Vecchioli and Ku, 1970; Ehrlich and others, 1972). Turbidity of the injectant in this test was consistently low, and averaged less than the turbidities in the other tests (table 5). Turbidity is a measure of the suspended-solids content of the

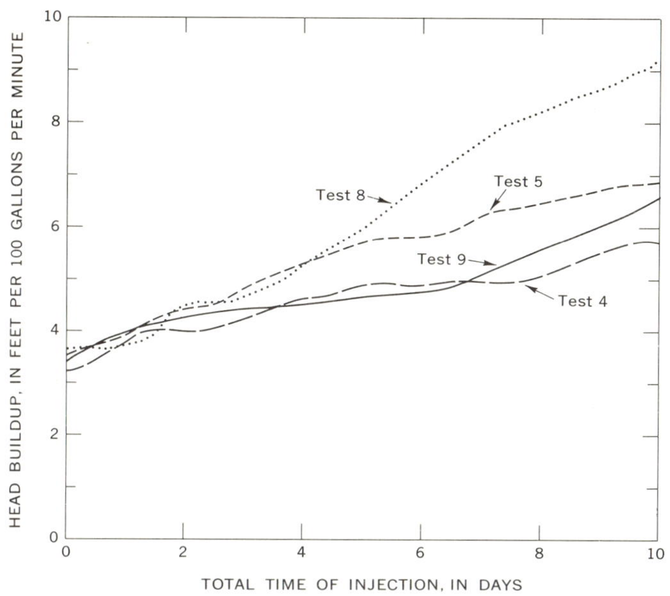

Figure 1.—Head buildup at the injection well as a function of time for present test (test 8) and three other tests. Chlorinated effluent was used in tests 4, 5, and 9.

Table 5.—*Turbidity of injectant*

Injection test	Turbidity (mg/l as SiO_2)	
	Range	Average
4	0.2–1.8	0.9
5	.1–1.6	.6
8	0–.3	.1
9	0–1.5	.3

injectant. Thus, the increased rate of head buildup observed in test 8 (fig. 1) could not be ascribed to physical clogging by inert particulate matter.

In all injection tests but test 8, the head buildup in an observation well within the filter pack of the recharge well was virtually the same as that in the injection well. In this test, however, after the second day of injection, the head in the injection well rose at a more rapid rate than that in the filter pack (fig. 2). Near the end of the test the head in the injection well (well N7884) was about 12 feet higher than that in the observation well (well 7885). The observed head difference suggests that much of the clogging in this test occurred in the filter pack immediately adjacent to the recharge-well screen or on the recharge-well screen. A lesser amount of clogging probably occurred beyond the filter pack at the aquifer face where most of the clogging had occurred in other tests.

The filter pack of the injection well consists almost entirely of subrounded, moderately spherical particles of quartz, chert, and quartzite (Cohen and Durfor, 1966, p. D257). At least 95 percent of this material is in the size range from 1 to 3 mm. Hence, because of the large size of the filter-pack pores, it is unlikely that the observed clogging of the filter pack resulted

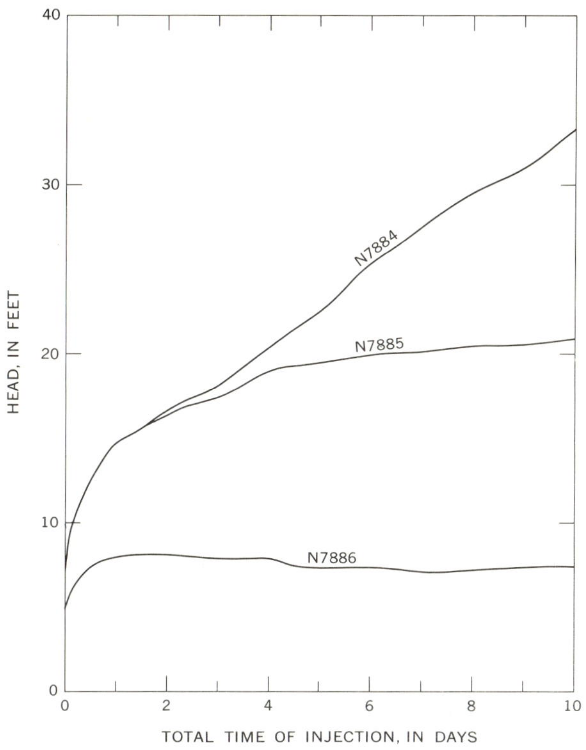

Figure 2.—Head as a function of time for the recharge well (N7884), the observation well in the filter pack (N7885), and an observation well 20 feet from the recharge well (N7886), for recharge test 8.

directly from filtration of particulate matter or bacterial cells in the injectant.

The first water recovered from the formation after the end of test 8 was moderately turbid and showed little tendency for settlement of suspended material on standing. Approximately 75 percent of the suspended material was volatile at 550°C. This property suggests that the material was composed largely of organic matter. In an earlier test in which chlorinated reclaimed water was used as the injectant the volatility of the suspended matter was only about 25 percent (Ehrlich and others, 1972, p. B242). Because the injectant had received virtually the same treatment before injection in both tests (except for chlorination) the threefold increase in volatile matter noticed in the particulate material recovered after test 8 cannot be ascribed solely to differences in preinjection treatment.

Bacterial counts of the first water to be recovered from the filter pack were much higher after test 8 than in comparable samples recovered after injection of chlorinated reclaimed water (2.0×10^5 colonies per milliliter in this sample versus 5×10^3 colonies per milliliter; Ehrlich and others, 1972, p. B243). Total-bacteria, total-coliform, and fecal-coliform counts of the repumped water were approximately the same as in the injectant.

The sand-filled probe, suspended in the filter-pack observation well during the test, was observed to be coated with a slimy gelatinous material when recovered after test 8. Sand grains inside the probe were cemented into larger aggregates by this slimy material. Such slime formation had not been observed when chlorinated injectant was recharged. Bacterial densities of 1.0×10^8 colonies per 100 cm^3 of pore volume were recorded for material from the center of the probe (table 3). The bacterial density of the interstices of the sand probe was about 500 times the bacterial densities of the injectant or the repumped water. The coliform-bacteria count of the probe was about 10 times that of the injectant and the first repumped water. Fecal-coliform and fecal-streptococcal counts were about the same in the probe, the injectant, and the first repumped water.

Coliform bacteria, which accounted for about half the total bacterial count of the injectant during much of the test, constituted only about 1 percent of the probe bacterial population. If one assumes that the ratio of coliform bacteria to total bacteria captured in the probe by filtration was the same as the ratio in the injectant, then the observed reduced ratio results either from more rapid die-off of coliform organisms relative to other bacterial species or slower multiplication of coliform bacteria relative to other species. In any event, these results indicate that coliform bacteria are less significant in the injection regime than other species of bacteria. This suggests that increased attention to other bacterial types would be desirable in future studies rather than the restricted attention to coliform and other pollution-indicating organisms that has characterized earlier work on the microbiology of artificial recharge.

The results of test 8 suggest that microbial growths and associated slimes generated by new growth caused much of the observed loss in specific capacity of the recharge well. There was no evidence for the establishment of a biological equilibrium as suggested by the California workers (1954, p. 165). Growth of bacteria in the filter pack and at the formation face and attendant clogging may be avoided by addition of chlorine to the injectant as shown in previous tests (Ehrlich and others, 1972).

REFERENCES CITED

American Public Health Association, American Waterworks Association, and Water Pollution Control Federation, 1971 (13th ed.), Standard methods for the examination of water and wastewater: New York, Am. Public Health Assoc., 874 p.

California State Water Pollution Control Board, 1954, Report on the investigation of travel of pollution: Sacramento, Calif., California State Water Pollution Control Board Pub. 11, 218 p.

Cohen, Philip, and Durfor, C. N., 1966, Design and construction of a unique injection well on Long Island, N.Y., *in* Geological Survey Research 1966: U.S. Geol. Survey Prof. Paper 550-D, p. D253–D257.

——1967, Artificial recharge experiments utilizing renovated sewage-plant effluent—A feasibility study at Bay Park, New York, U.S.A., *in* Artificial recharge and management of aquifers—Symposium of Haifa, 1967: Internat. Assoc. Sci. Hydrology Pub. 72, p. 193–199.

Ehrlich, G. G., Ehlke, T. A., and Vecchioli, John, 1972, Microbiological aspects of ground-water recharge—Injection of purified chlorinated sewage effluent, *in* Geological Survey Research 1972: U.S. Geol. Survey Prof. Paper 800-B, p. B241–B245.

Peters, J. H., and Rose, J. L., 1968, Water conservation by reclamation and recharge: Am. Soc. Civil Engineers Proc., Jour. Sanitary Eng. Div., v. 94, no. SA4, p. 625–639.

Rebhun, M., and Schwarz, J., 1968, Clogging and contamination processes in recharge wells: Water Resources Research, v. 4, no. 6, p. 1207–1217.

Vecchioli, John, 1970, A note on bacterial growth around a recharge well at Bay Park, Long Island, N.Y.: Water Resources Research, v. 6, no. 5, p. 1415–1419.

Vecchioli, John, and Ku, H. F. H., 1970, Preliminary results of injecting highly treated sewage-plant effluent into a deep sand aquifer at Bay Park, New York: U.S. Geol. Survey open-file rept., 53 p., 6 figs.

Jour. Research U.S. Geol. Survey
Vol. 1, No. 3, May-June 1973, p. 345–350

CHANGE IN POTENTIOMETRIC HEAD IN THE LLOYD AQUIFER, LONG ISLAND, NEW YORK

By G. E. KIMMEL, Mineola, N.Y.

Work done in cooperation with the Nassau County Department of Public Works, the New York State Department of Environmental Conservation, Division of Water Resources, the Suffolk County Department of Health, and the Suffolk County Water Authority

Abstract.—The potentiometric surface of the Lloyd aquifer in 1970 locally was as much as 40 feet lower than in 1900. During this period, withdrawal of water from wells was estimated to exceed 300 billion gallons, and the amount of water released from aquifer storage by compressive forces was estimated to be 1.6 billion gallons (about 0.5 percent of the withdrawal). The remainder of the withdrawal was derived from downward leakage through overlying aquifers and confining layers and by the displacement of fresh water in the aquifer by landward movement of salty ground water.

The ground-water reservoir of Long Island is the source of water supply for about 4 million people. The Lloyd aquifer, the lowest unit of this reservoir, is a major source of water for public supply and industrial use in places where overlying units contain salty water or where such units are heavily pumped.

Much of the historical information for this report was collected by the U.S. Geological Survey as part of various State and county cooperative programs from 1930 to 1970. The data collected by N. J. Lusczynski were especially helpful. The cooperation of water companies, water districts, and industries on Long Island in the water-level-measurement program is greatly appreciated.

This report documents the regional changes in potentiometric head in the Lloyd aquifer from 1900 to 1970 and considers the sources of the water withdrawn from the aquifer.

GEOHYDROLOGY

Long Island is underlain by a wedge of unconsolidated deposits, which overlies a southeastward-dipping bedrock floor (fig. 1). The bedrock is overlain by three major units of Cretaceous age—the Lloyd and Magothy aquifers and the intervening Raritan clay. The Cretaceous units are overlain by deposits of Pleistocene age whose thickness varies widely. In the northern part of the island, deep channels cut in the deposits of Cretaceous age have been filled with as much as several hundred feet of undifferentiated deposits of clay and gravel of Pleistocene age. Along the south shore, the Gardiners Clay of Pleistocene age overlies the Magothy aquifer.

Moraine and outwash deposits overlie the Magothy aquifer, the undifferentiated deposits of Pleistocene age, and the Gardiners Clay. The saturated parts of the moraine and the outwash deposits are termed "the upper glacial aquifer" (Cohen and others, 1968, p. 18), and that aquifer ranges in thickness from 0 to 100 feet. Generally, in the central part of the island, the flow of water from the upper glacial aquifer to the Magothy aquifer is unrestricted by intervening clay layers. However, along the south shore, and also in other places along the margins of the island, the Gardiners Clay or other clay layers of Pleistocene age confine water in the underlying deposits.

The ground-water reservoir extends vertically from the bedrock floor to the water table, which is at an altitude of 60 to 80 feet in the central part of the island, and laterally to the interfaces between fresh and salty water. The interfaces lie mainly at the shore or seaward from it. Locally, however, salty water underlies parts of the ground-water reservoir in the western part of the island (Lusczynski, 1952; Lusczynski and Swarzenski, 1966; Perlmutter and others, 1959; and Soren, 1971). Salty water also underlies fresh-water lenses on the north and south forks at the east end of the island (Crandell, 1963; Perlmutter and Crandell, 1959; and Perlmutter and DeLuca, 1963). Data considered later in this report suggest that, with the exception of the north and south forks and part of northern Queens County, the Lloyd aquifer contains fresh water everywhere beneath Long Island. In other words, except as noted, the interfaces between fresh and salty water in the Lloyd aquifer are seaward of the shores of Long Island.

LLOYD AQUIFER

The Lloyd aquifer overlies bedrock and is the basal unit of the ground-water reservoir on Long Island. In a study of the regional aspects of the ground-water reservoir on Long Island,

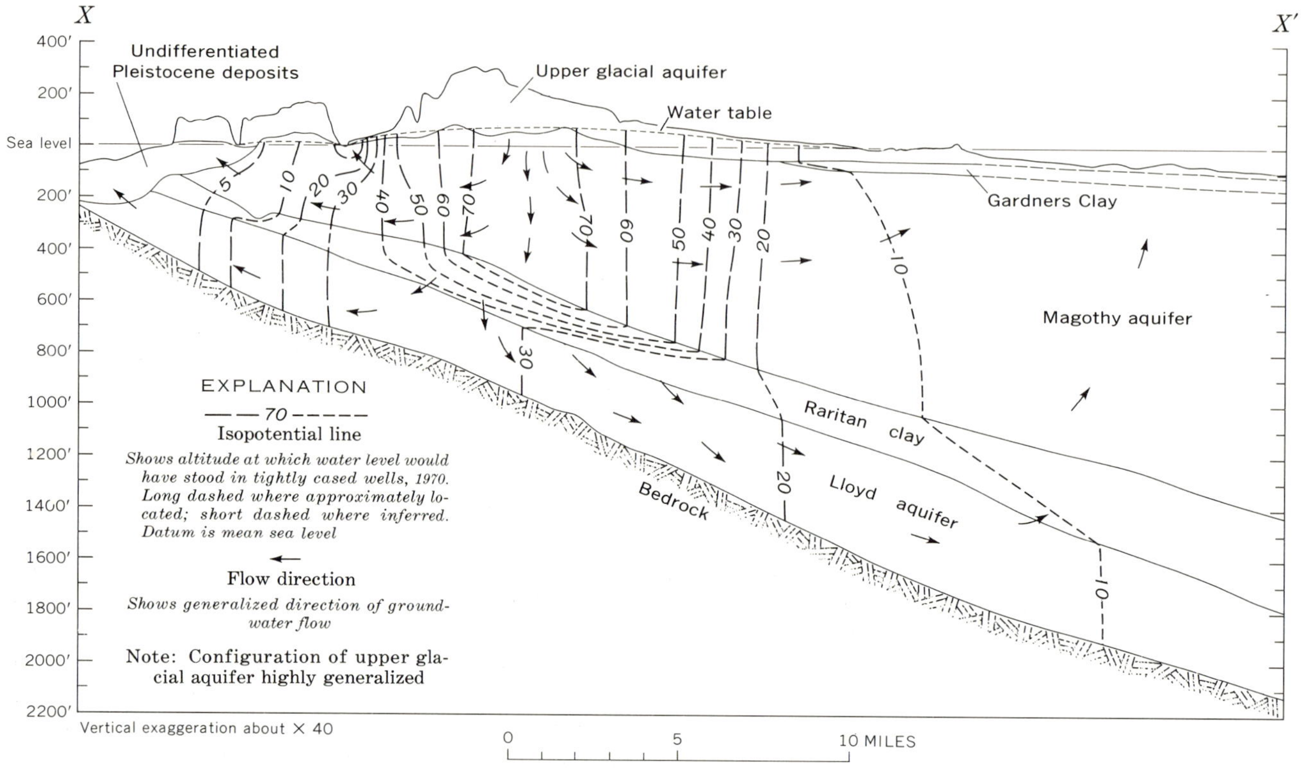

Figure 1.—Generalized hydrogeologic section showing isopotential lines in 1970 in the ground-water reservoir near the Nassau-Suffolk County line on Long Island, N.Y. Location of section is shown in figure 4. Hydrogeologic units from Cohen, Franke, and Foxworthy (1968).

McClymonds and Franke (1972) found that the thickness of the Lloyd increases irregularly in a southeasterly direction in western Long Island and in a southerly direction in central and eastern Long Island. The Lloyd pinches out between the bedrock and the overlying Raritan clay in the northwestern part of the island (fig. 4) and increases in thickness to a maximum of 450 feet in the southern part of the island. McClymonds and Franke estimated that the transmissivity of the Lloyd ranges from less than 20,000 gal day^{-1} ft^{-1} (2,700 ft^2 day^{-1}) along the north shore to 140,000 gal day^{-1} ft^{-1} (19,000 ft^2 day^{-1}) in southern Nassau County. The transmissivity ranges from 60,000 to 100,000 gal day^{-1} ft^{-1} (8,000–13,000 ft^2 day^{-1}) in Suffolk County, mainly owing to the lower hydraulic conductivity there. The top of the Lloyd aquifer slopes southeastward about 60 ft/mi (Suter and others, 1949).

Near the north shore of Long Island, east of central Queens County, the Lloyd aquifer is truncated and abuts undifferentiated deposits of Pleistocene age. (See figure 4.) The geologic and the hydrologic relations between the Lloyd aquifer and the abutting undifferentiated deposits of Pleistocene age suggest that these deposits are in close lateral hydraulic continuity. (For example, see Swarzenski, 1963, pl. 4.) Thus, some wells tapping the contiguous deposits of Pleistocene age north of the Lloyd aquifer were used to construct the potentiometric maps and the net-change map in this report.

The Lloyd is recharged from precipitation along a narrow band in the middle of the island. From there, ground water moves downward through the overlying aquifers and confining layers into the Lloyd (fig. 1). In several places near the northern part of the island, channels have been cut into the Lloyd and have been backfilled with highly permeable sand and gravel of Pleistocene age (Soren, 1971, pl. 1). These channels facilitate movement of water into and out of the Lloyd aquifer.

As of 1971, most of the discharge from the Lloyd in western Long Island was through wells; but, under the more nearly natural conditions that prevail in eastern Long Island, most of the discharge from the aquifer occurs by movement of the water laterally outward toward the shore and then upward into the bays and the ocean.

Withdrawals

From 1910 to 1970, cumulative withdrawal from wells from the Lloyd aquifer was estimated to be 300 billion gallons (fig. 2). Although major development of the aquifer began in Kings and western Queens Counties, centers of major withdrawals have shifted eastward to central Queens and Nassau Counties. By 1970 the cumulative withdrawal from wells from the Lloyd in Nassau County was 160 billion gallons and in Queens County was 120 billion gallons. By 1950, cumulative with-

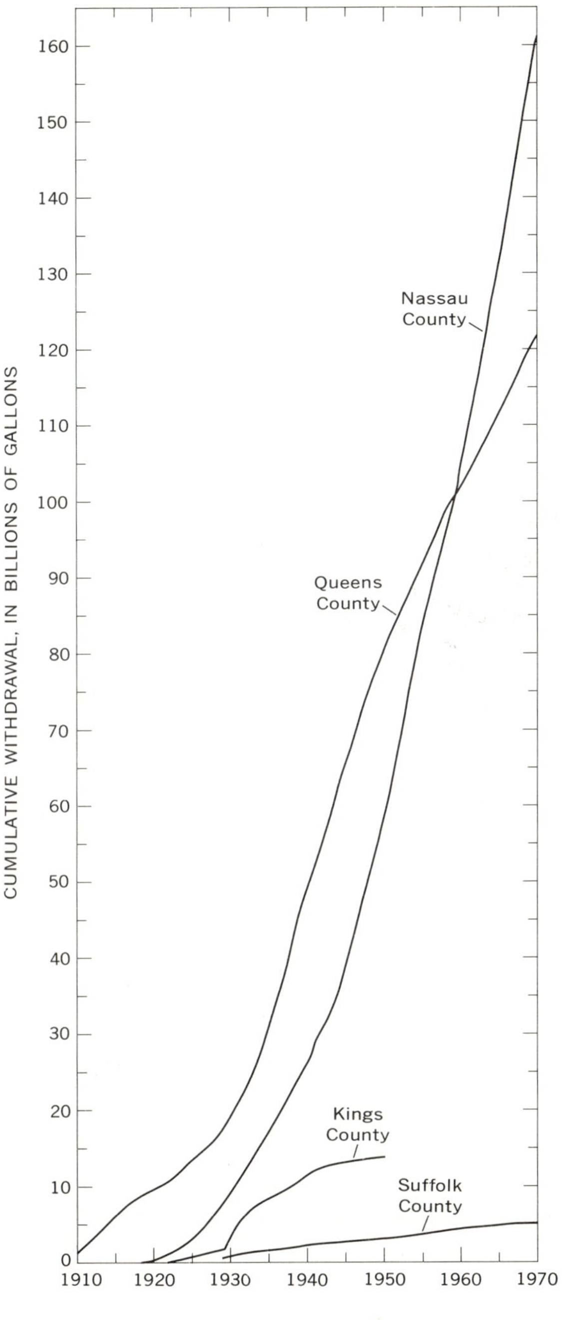

Figure 2.—Cumulative withdrawals of water from wells from the Lloyd aquifer on Long Island, N.Y., 1910 to 1970. Data for 1910 to 1950 are from Lusczynski and Roberts (1952), and data for 1950 to 1970 are from New York State Department of Environmental Conservation (written commun., 1971).

drawal in Kings County was 14 billion gallons. Withdrawals in Kings County have been insignificant since then. The cumulative withdrawal in Suffolk County was 6 billion gallons by 1970.

Major centers of withdrawal from the Lloyd in 1970 (fig. 3) were the peninsula areas along the north shore of Nassau County, central Queens County, and Long Beach. In this part

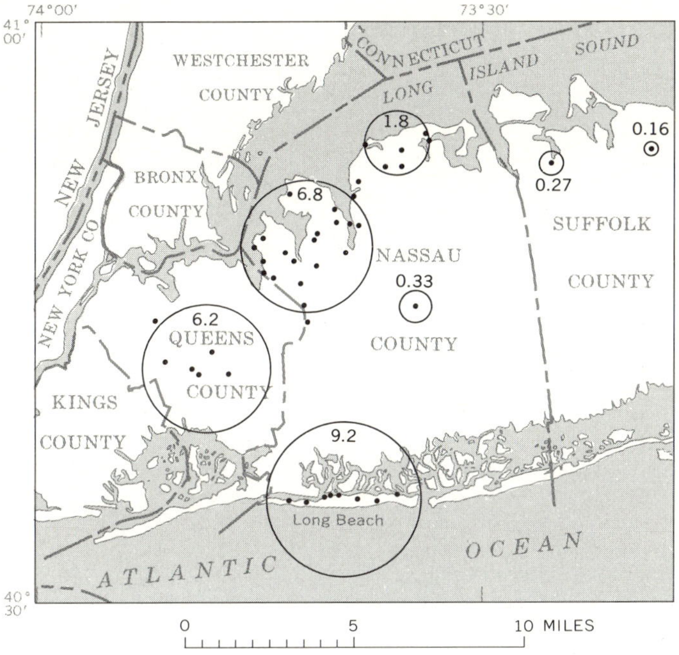

Figure 3.—Withdrawal from the Lloyd aquifer in western Long Island, N.Y., 1970. Dot indicates location of pumping well; figure is withdrawal in millions of gallons per day from wells in and near circle; diameter of circle is proportional to withdrawal.

of western Long Island, withdrawal from the Lloyd aquifer averaged 24 million gal day^{-1} in 1970. In central Nassau County and in northwestern Suffolk County, respectively, withdrawal averaged 0.3 and 0.4 million gal day^{-1} in 1970.

Potentiometric surfaces

Potentiometric maps of the Lloyd aquifer are shown for various times and parts of Long Island in reports by Isbister (1966, fig. 12), Lusczynski and Swarzenski (1966, fig. 9), Swarzenski (1963, pl. 11), Soren (1971, pl. 2), and Warren, de Laguna, and Lusczynski (1968, fig. 34). A report of the U.S. Geological Survey (1952) contains a potentiometric map of the Lloyd for western Long Island.

The most recent potentiometric map (fig. 4) was constructed from measurements in observation and public-supply wells in December 1970 and in January 1971. In areas where water levels are known to be significantly affected by nearby pumping, most of the pumping wells were shut off before measurements were made in either the pumping well or in nearby observation wells; however, one well in Long Beach and two wells in central Queens County could not be shut off. Because most of the measured wells are in heavily pumped areas, potentiometric heads at the time of measurements (December 1970–January 1971) were higher than during most of the year. Wells affected by tidal fluctuations were measured at high tide, or the water-level measurements were converted to equivalent high-tide readings.

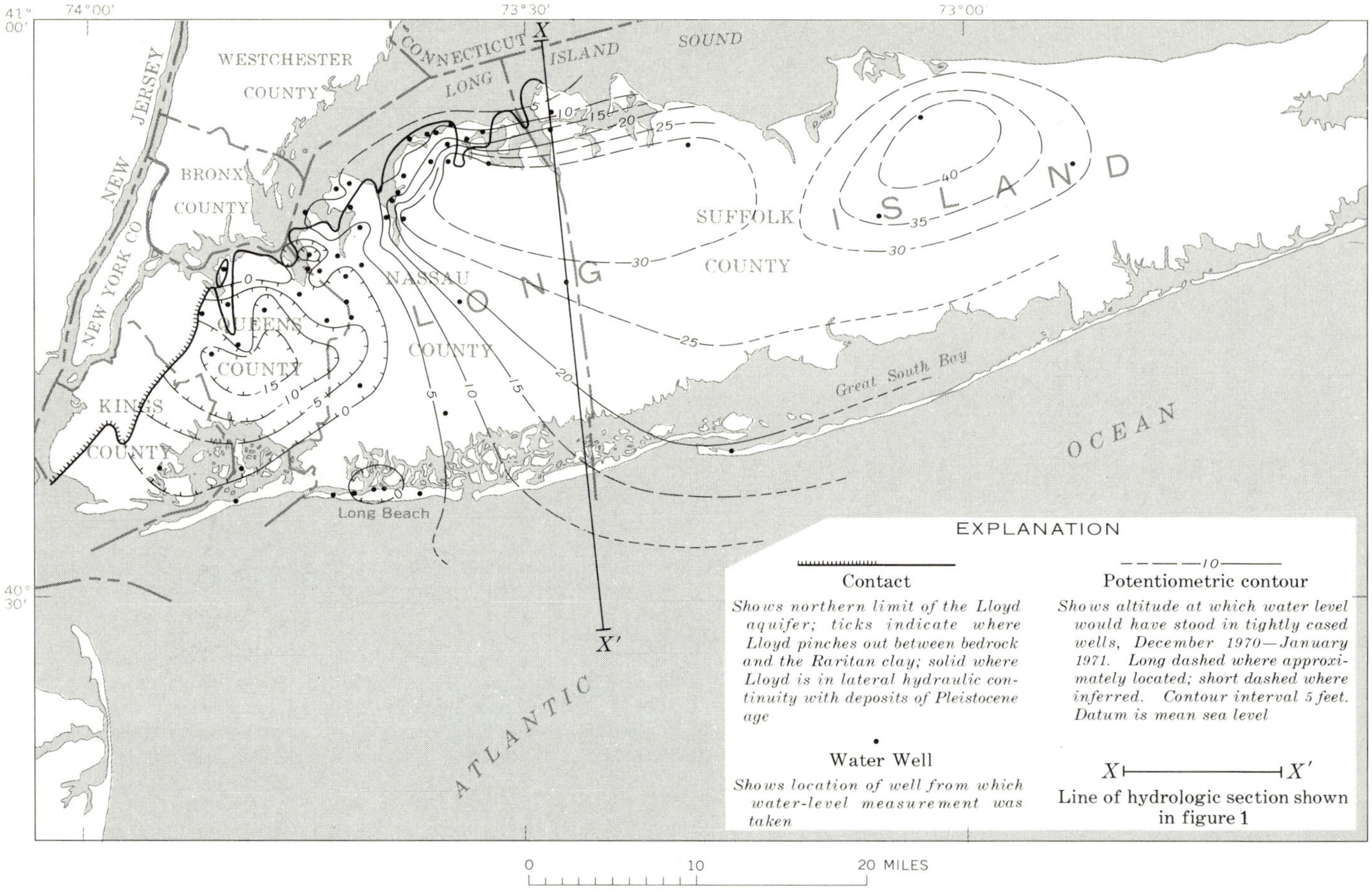

Figure 4.—Potentiometric surface of water in the Lloyd aquifer and contiguous hydraulically equivalent aquifers on Long Island, N.Y., December 1970–January 1971.

In central Queens County the potentiometric surface in 1970 (fig. 4) showed a major depression, which, locally, was more than 15 feet below sea level. Although the maximum depth of this depression could not be determined accurately, it may have been as much as 30 feet below sea level under nonpumping conditions. The effect of pumping is also evident from the contorted contours in northwestern Nassau and the depression on southern Nassau County.

Under natural predevelopment conditions and over a long period of time, average annual recharge to and discharge from the Lloyd aquifer were equal, and the potentiometric head remained virtually unchanged except for minor short-term fluctuations. Withdrawals of water from wells since the early 1900's have upset the balance between recharge and discharge and have caused significant widespread declines in potentiometric head. To assess the declines, the inferred potentiometric surface in about 1900, before significant withdrawals affected heads in the Lloyd (fig. 5), was reconstructed. This potentiometric surface is based on the earliest available data and in places is adjusted empirically to compensate for the effects of local pumpage at the time or before the time that the earliest water levels were measured.

Net change in head

The inferred net change in head in the Lloyd aquifer in western Long Island from 1900 to 1970 is shown on figure 6. Some features on the map deserve special note. First, the lines of equal change terminate in the west, where the aquifer overlaps bedrock and thins to a featheredge. Second, the areas of greatest declines in head do not coincide with the areas of greatest withdrawal in 1970 (fig. 3) because of numerous factors, including the history of withdrawal, areal differences in the hydraulic properties of the aquifer (transmissivity and storage coefficient), and marked differences in the geometry and the boundaries of the aquifer.

Source of water withdrawn

The estimated decrease in the amount of water in storage in the Lloyd aquifer from 1900 to 1970 can be computed by mutiplying the volume of net decline (based on the net-change map shown in fig. 6) by the estimated average storage coefficeint of the deposits in which the head declined. The storage coefficient is defined as the volume of water an aquifer

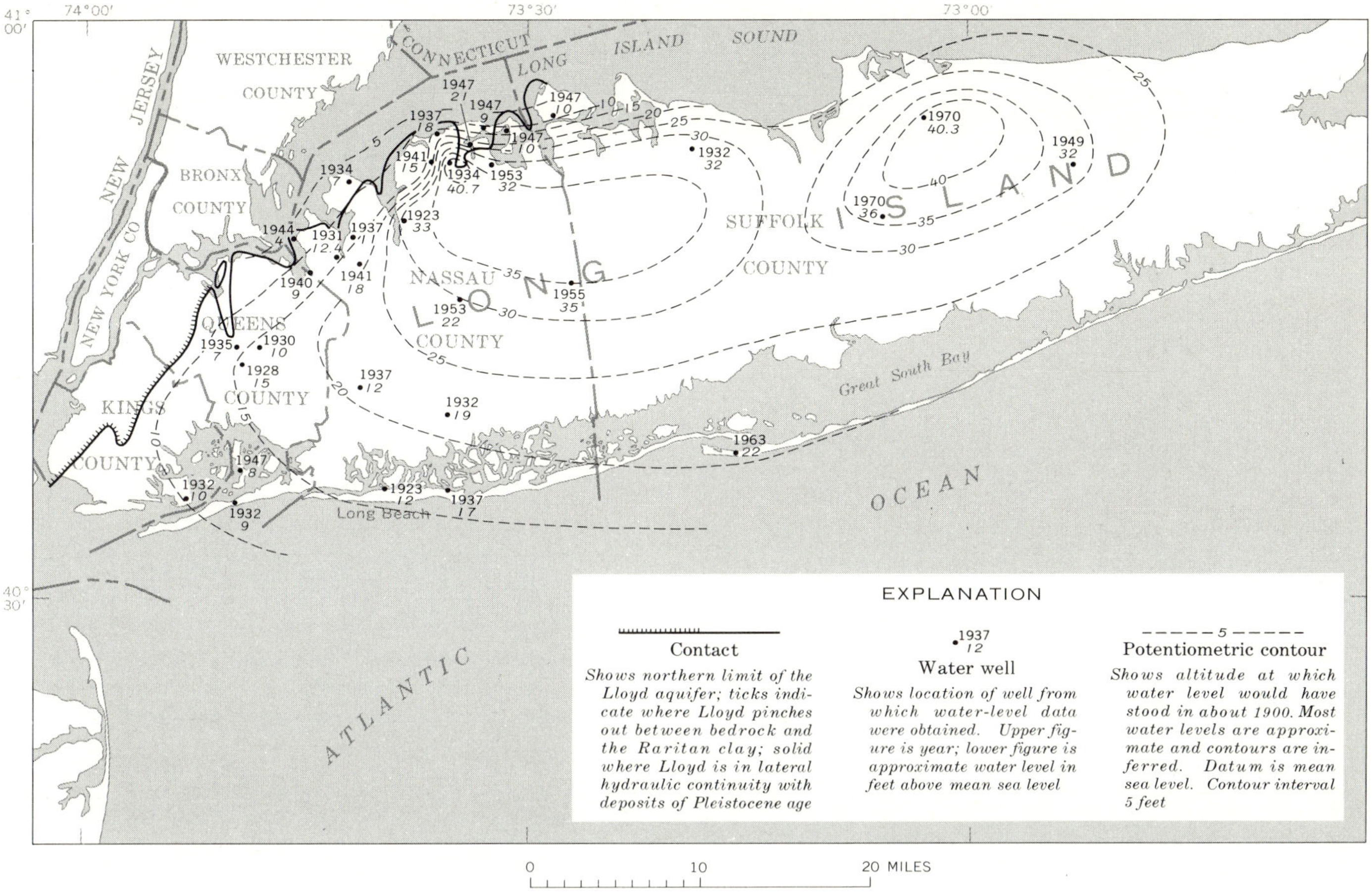

Figure 5.—Inferred potentiometric surface of water in the Lloyd aquifer and contiguous hydraulically equivalent aquifers on Long Island, N.Y., in about 1900.

releases from or takes into storage per unit of surface area of the aquifer per unit change in head. The storage coefficient S for confined aquifers, such as the Lloyd, reportedly ranges from 10^{-3} to 10^{-5} (Ferris and others, 1962). Jacob (1941) found that the storage coefficient in the Lloyd in southern Queens County was about 3×10^{-4}. When one uses the largest probable value for the storage coefficient of the Lloyd, 10^{-3}, the computed maximum decrease in the amount of water in storage in the Lloyd aquifer from 1900 to 1970 is 1.6 billion gallons. This figure represents only about 0.5 percent of the gross withdrawals from the aquifer during that period (estimated to exceed 300 billion gallons). The source of most of the withdrawal from the Lloyd aquifer was probably a combination of downward leakage from and through the confining layers and downward leakage through highly permeable channel-fill deposits.

A significant but unknown quantity of fresh water also was displaced in the Lloyd aquifer by the landward movement of salty ground water. The chloride content of water from some wells tapping the Lloyd aquifer and the Pleistocene deposits hydraulically connected to the Lloyd along the north shore of Long Island has increased from time to time because of local salt-water intrusion (Soren, 1971, p. A32–A34; Swarzenski, 1963, p. 52–53). In 1971, the chloride content of two public-supply wells screened in Pleistocene deposits adjacent to the Lloyd in northeastern Nassau County was more than 100 mg/l (Nassau County Department of Health, written commun., 1972).

The interface between fresh and salty water in the Lloyd is still (1971) seaward of Long Beach and the other barrier beaches along the south shore of Long Island (Lusczynski and Swarzenski, 1966; Cohen and Kimmel, 1970). However, withdrawal from the Lloyd and the net declines in head shown in figure 6 almost certainly have caused and (or) have accelerated the landward movement of salty water in the Lloyd aquifer along the south shore. The rate and the extent of that movement are unknown.

REFERENCES CITED

Cohen, Philip, Franke, O. L., and Foxworthy, B. L., 1968, An atlas of Long Island's water resources: New York State Water Resources Comm. Bull. 62, 117 p.

Cohen, Philip, and Kimmel, G. E., 1970, Status of salt-water encroachment in 1969 in southern Nassau and southeastern Queens Counties,

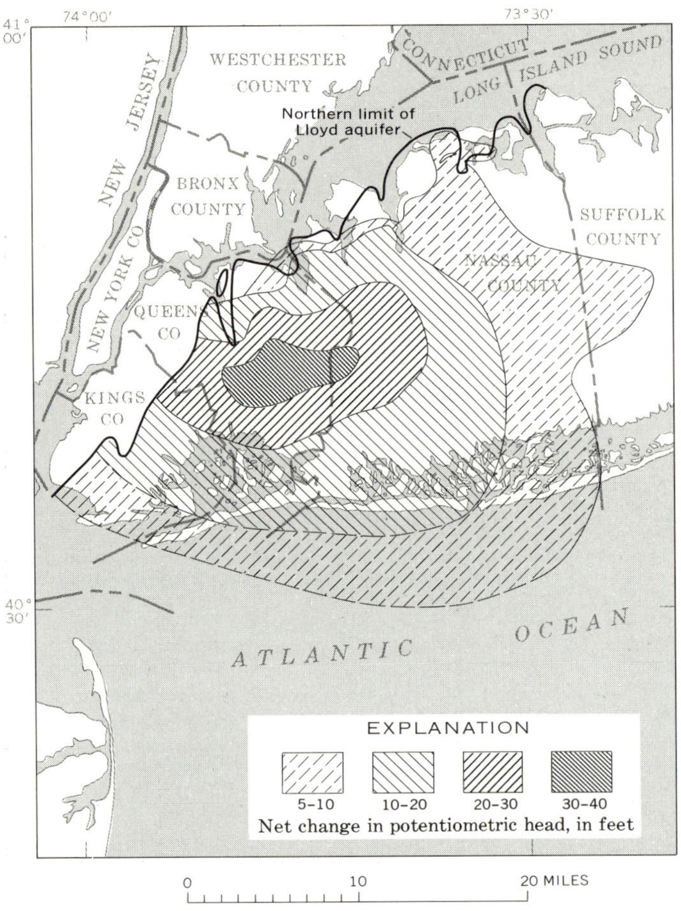

Figure 6.—Inferred net change in potentiometric head in the Lloyd aquifer and contiguous hydraulically equivalent aquifers from about 1900 to 1970 in western Long Island, N.Y. Lines of equal net change are dashed where uncertain.

Long Island, New York, *in* Geological Survey Research 1970: U.S. Geol. Survey Prof. Paper 700–D, p. D281–D286.

Crandell, H. C., 1963, Geology and ground-water resources of the town of Southold, Suffolk County, New York: U.S. Geol. Survey Water-Supply Paper 1619–GG, 36 p.

Ferris, J. G., Knowles, D. B., Brown, R. H., and Stallman, R. W., 1962, Theory of aquifer tests: U.S. Geol. Survey Water-Supply Paper 1536–E, p. 69–174.

Isbister, John, 1966, Geology and hydrology of northeastern Nassau County, Long Island, New York: U.S. Geol. Survey Water-Supply Paper 1825, 89 p. [1967]

Jacob, C. E., 1941, Notes on the elasticity of the Lloyd sand on Long Island, New York: Am. Geophys. Union Trans., v. 22, pt. 3, p. 783–787.

Lusczynski, N. J., 1952, The recovery of ground-water levels in Brooklyn, New York, from 1947 to 1950: U.S. Geol. Survey Circ. 167, 29 p.

Lusczynski, N. J., and Roberts, C. M., 1952, Withdrawal of ground water from the Lloyd sand member on Long Island, N.Y., from 1904 to 1950: U.S. Geol. Survey open-file rept., 7 figs, 6 tables, 4 pls.

Lusczynski, N. J., and Swarzenski, W. V., 1966, Salt-water encroachment in southern Nassau and southeastern Queens Counties, Long Island, New York: U.S. Geol. Survey Water-Supply Paper 1613–F, 76 p.

McClymonds, N. E., and Franke, O. L., 1972, Water-transmitting properties of aquifers on Long Island, New York: U.S. Geol. Survey Prof. Paper 627–E, 24 p.

Perlmutter, N. M., and Crandell, H. C., 1959, Geology and ground-water supplies of the south-shore beaches of Long Island, New York *in* Lowe, K. E., ed., Modern aspects of the geology of New York City and environs: New York Acad. Sci. Annals, v. 80, art. 4, p. 1060–1076.

Perlmutter, N. M., Geraghty, J. J., and Upson, J. E., 1959, The relation between fresh and salty ground water in southern Nassau and southeastern Queens Counties, Long Island, New York: Econ. Geology, v. 54, p. 416–435.

Perlmutter, N. M., and DeLuca, F. A., 1963, Availability of fresh ground water, Montauk Point area, Suffolk County, Long Island, New York: U.S. Geol. Survey Water-Supply Paper 1613–B, 39 p.

Soren, Julian, 1971, Ground-water and geohydrologic conditions in Queens County, Long Island, New York: U.S. Geol. Survey Water-Supply Paper 2001–A, 39 p.

Suter, Russell, de Laguna, Wallace, and Perlmutter, N. M., 1949, Mapping of geologic formations and aquifers of Long Island, New York: New York State Water Power and Control Comm. Bull. GW–18, 212 p.

Swarzenski, W. V., 1963, Hydrogeology of northwestern Nassau and northeastern Queens Counties, Long Island, New York: U.S. Geol. Survey Water-Supply Paper 1657, 90 p.

U.S. Geological Survey, 1952, The piezometric surface of the Lloyd sand, Long Island, New York in 1947: U.S. Geol. Survey open-file rept. 1 table, 1 map, 3 pls.

Warren, M. A., de Laguna, Wallace, and Lusczynski, N. J., 1968, Hydrology of Brookhaven National Laboratory and vicinity, Suffolk County, New York: U.S. Geol. Survey Bulletin 1156-C, 127 p.

Jour. Research U.S. Geol. Survey
Vol. 1, No. 3, May-June 1973, p. 351—360

CONCEPTS OF KARST DEVELOPMENT IN RELATION TO INTERPRETATION OF SURFACE RUNOFF

By H. E. LeGRAND and V. T. STRINGFIELD,
Raleigh, N.C., Washington, D.C.

Abstract.—Some unusual characteristics of streamflow occur in regions underlain by carbonate rocks. The streamflow characteristics are related to processes of karstification, these processes being dependent on circulation of subsurface water and solution of the rock to form characteristic topography and underground cavern systems. Very highly cavernous and permeable unsaturated zones tend to keep the water table depressed below land surface in many karst regions, a condition that leads to a low density of perennial streams. The uneven distribution of permeability beneath surface karst streams causes them to lose or gain water, depending on the position of the water table with reference to stream level. The conventional techniques of interpolation and extrapolation that have been reasonably successful in approximating streamflow of ungaged sites in nonkarstic regions have only limited use in karst regions. An understanding of principles of karstification and an understanding of the hydrogeologic framework of a carbonate terrane provide a useful basis for evaluating the streamflow characteristics.

The science of surface-water hydrology has developed greatly during the past two decades, and sophisticated techniques have been devised to predict critical high-flow and low-flow characteristics of streams. Although recognition has been made of the importance of geology to streamflow, distinctive relationships between rock terranes and streamflow have not been fully explored. Streams in some carbonate-rock terranes have unusual characteristics, and even the spectacular phenomena of disappearing and reappearing streams are fairly common; the disappearing stream flows into a sinkhole or swallow hole, where the stream has an underground flow for some distance before emerging as a large spring, from where its surface course continues. The unusual streamflow characteristics are related to the general processes of karstification, these processes being dependent on circulation of subsurface water and solution of the carbonate rock to form characteristic topography, as well as cavern systems. The purpose of this paper is to give concepts on the development of stream networks and on stream characteristics in regions underlain by carbonate rocks that have undergone karstification. Through a better understanding of the processes involved in karstification, more accurate interpretation of runoff from such regions will result.

KARST FEATURES AND THEIR DEVELOPMENT

Where carbonate rocks are widespread there are generally surface and subsurface features that differ from those of less soluble rocks. Depressions sometimes develop that reflect areas where the underlying rock has been carried away in solution. These depressions, called sinkholes, usually form where the surface collapses into a large cavity beneath. The depressions are commonly somewhat round, and where they coalesce there is a tendency for elongated solution valleys to form. Surface water drains into the sinks, dissolving the rock as it moves into the ground-water system. A wide range of topographic conditions occurs on carbonate terranes. The term "karst topography" has been applied to carbonate-rock areas where sinkholes abound and streamless valleys are common. Even karst forms differ from place to place, some of these differences having led to the concept of a karst cycle (Grund, 1914, p. 621—640) in which a distinct sequence of topographic forms has been recognized. As will be indicated later, certain discernible karst features that are related in a sense to stages of karst development are also related to surface water and to other hydrologic conditions.

In the early youthful stage, surface streams cut valleys into the carbonate rocks and drain off the circulating ground water that has percolated downward through fractures in the rock to the water table and then moved somewhat laterally toward the surface streams. The fractures become enlarged by solutional erosion while water readily infiltrates the terrane and readily discharges from it. The enlarged fractures represent an increase in permeability. As a result of the increasing permeability, the water table becomes progressively lower in the terrane, and some local subsidence of the surface occurs as sinks. Some of the fractures continue to be enlarged into caverns and other large openings as interstream drainage is diverted underground. During the late youthful stage almost all of the original surface streams have been diverted to underground courses. Topographic relief may be appreciable; deep sinks, and in some places cone-shaped hills, are common on the landscape.

The youthful stage passes into maturity as sinks enlarge and coalesce into dry valleys. Very little of the original plateau surface remains. Sinkholes and undulating topography are common, and almost all precipitation goes underground immediately; this diffused infiltrating water tends to move to a low level and tends to become concentrated in a large opening, emerging as a large spring. During the mature stage the air-filled cavern systems are at their ultimate size, especially beneath the higher topographic features. Also during the mature stage the underlying aquifer is fully developed from the viewpoint of having its arterial solution openings fully enlarged.

In the old-age stage the valleys have become wide and somewhat flat, and most of the ridges between the valleys have been reduced except for isolated hills and knobs. Caverns that were once air-filled have been destroyed by collapse of the land surface. The land surface in general has been lowered to the extent that the water table is near land surface, and surface streams no longer go underground.

The concept of the karst cycle would have little merit if it were regarded as a cycle involving only time. The karst cycle considered here represents a sequence of topographic features to which a sequence of time should be applied only when referring to a restricted part of the carbonate-rock terrane. Youthful, mature, and old-age topographic features are considered as migratory in space with geologic time. Mature karst topography is generally widespread and is the setting for much of the discussion in this paper. An understanding of the evolution of karst topography leads to advanced understanding of the development and distribution of permeability in carbonate-rock aquifers and to the character of surface water.

The chief karst regions of the United States are shown in general on figure 1; some of them are briefly described by Stringfield and LeGrand (1969, p. 361–371). There are many informative publications on karst as indicated in an annotated bibliography (LaMoreaux and others, 1970); a recent book (Herak and Stringfield, eds., 1971) summarizes the karst of the Northern Hemisphere. Yet some aspects of karst, such as the relation of surface-water hydrology to ground-water hydrology, have not been fully studied.

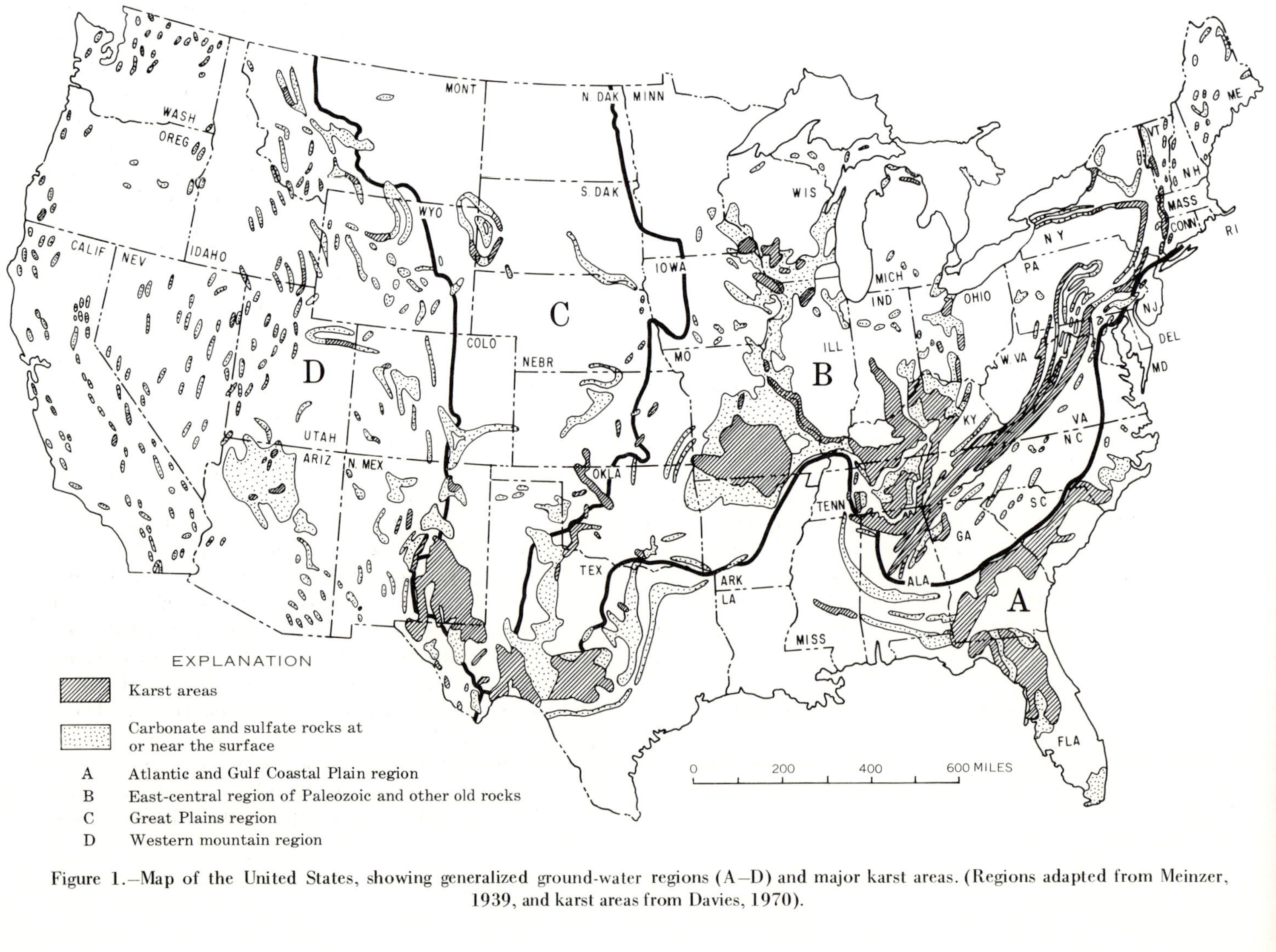

Figure 1.—Map of the United States, showing generalized ground-water regions (A–D) and major karst areas. (Regions adapted from Meinzer, 1939, and karst areas from Davies, 1970).

SURFACE DRAINAGE NETWORK IN KARST REGIONS

Fully developed karst regions are characterized by the scarcity of surface streams, even under humid conditions. In fact, the combination of thin soils and absence of surface streams causes some humid karst regions to appear more arid than they are. Many coastal karst regions, such as parts of the Mediterranean coast, the Yucatan Peninsula, and some islands of the Caribbean, have no streams; in these places water from precipitation moves downward into the limestone quickly, and then it travels laterally to coastal discharge points at or below sea level. The discharge points are less obscure in interior karst regions because at least one spring or surface stream must drain water to a low place at the land surface. If not within the karst region, the discharge may be along the contact with surrounding less soluble rocks.

Major trunk streams are the general rule, these streams representing the base level toward which much of the ground water moves laterally. The trunk streams do not necessarily have a dendritic or treelike pattern, so common in nearby structureless terranes of clastic rocks. Trellis drainage is not common except where structural control is strong; an example of trellis karst drainage is the folded Appalachian region where long parallel karst valleys alternate with sandstone ridges. A characteristic feature of the trunk stream is the scarcity of tributary surface streams. Suggestions of former tributary streams are elongated dry valleys with hummocky topography leading from the trunk stream outward into coves and reentrants in upland areas. An example can be seen on the Sparta, Tenn., 7½-minute quadrangle, where Bear Cove extends eastward from Calfkiller River through the town of Sparta into the higher Cumberland Plateau.

Most trunk streams are cut into karst plateaus. Strongly meandering courses in deep channels are common, Calfkiller River in Tennessee and the White and Gasconade Rivers on the Salem Plateau in Missouri being examples. Among the most spectacular entrenched meanders in a karst region is the Ardeche River in southern France, which flows in a canyon 31 km long (Avias, 1972, p. 141). Flood plains along karst streams are not especially common, although broad solution plains in which trunk streams flow represent lowland plateaus that may be bordered by an escarpment and a higher plateau (fig. 2).

The scarcity of streams in karst regions is related to the distribution of permeability; the caverns and enlarged solution openings are a result of the permeability that has developed by the karstification processes. Although not specifically considering karst terranes, both Jacob (1944, p. 566) and Carlston (1963, p. 5) demonstrated that as permeability, or transmissivity, increases, drainage density should decrease, and as transmissivity decreases, drainage density should increase. A relation of low stream density and high permeability in karst regions is readily observable, but LeGrand (1970, p. 1247) showed that high density of streams does not necessarily prevail in poorly karstified impermeable carbonate rocks.

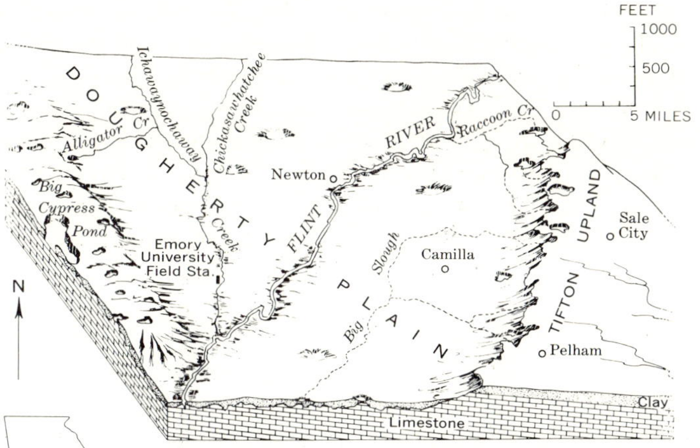

Figure 2.—Diagrammatic sketch of Flint River valley, Baker and Mitchell Counties, Ga. Clay beneath the Tifton Upland belongs to the Hawthorn Formation and that beneath the Dougherty Plain represents downslumped masses of the Hawthorn as well as insoluble residue of former limestone beds (after Hendricks and Goodwin, 1952; Herrick and LeGrand, 1964).

CHARACTER OF DRAINAGE BASINS IN KARST REGIONS

Hydrologists in the United States have conventionally used "flow per square mile" as the comparative unit of surface flow measurement. The size of the contributing drainage basin in nonkarstic regions has generally been easy to derive because topographic and ground-water divides almost coincide. In karst regions, however, there is little or no relation between topographic and ground-water divides in many places.

A study by White and Schmidt (1966) in a maturely karsted limestone system in Pocahontas County, W. Va., by use of dye tracing and underground mapping techniques, shows that the Swago Creek underground drainage is unrelated to surface drainage. They indicate that underground drainage lines cross major surface divides, and that the water table is almost flat but has a gentle slope toward Swago Creek.

In artesian systems of both carbonate and noncarbonate aquifers far from major recharge and discharge areas, the surface and subsurface flows of water are not closely related. However, where carbonate aquifers extend from a water-table recharge area to an artesian system a variety of surface and subsurface flow relations exists (Stringfield, 1964, p. C168). Surface stream characteristics generally should change considerably where a stream cuts through the noncarbonate and less soluble cover into underlying soluble carbonate rocks. Solution by circulating water then initiates karstification and increases the permeability of the rocks in the stream valley. This phenomenon may be noted in some regions, such as in north-central Florida. Here the Santa Fe River rises east of the Suwannee River and flows westward on an upland region where the noncarbonate beds of the Hawthorn Formation overlie the principal artesian carbonate aquifer (Stringfield, 1966, p. 14). In its lower course, the Santa Fe River flows on and in the cavernous limestone aquifer. As described by Clark and others (1962, p. 39–48) the flow characteristics of the upper part and the lower part of the Santa Fe basin differ considerably. The flow characteristics change abruptly in the vicinity of O'leno State Park, about 6 miles north of High Springs, where the river disappears underground, then reappears about 3 miles away. Below that point, streamflow increases rapidly as the river flows through the channel cut in the limestone. Almost all of the increase in flow in the lower basin is from the artesian aquifer. Few tributary streams feed the lower river except those that flow from springs such as Ichatucknee Springs near Hildreth. In the lower part of the basin the section of the river between High Springs and Fort White has an average annual runoff of 84.7 inches, more than 1½ times the annual rainfall on the 130-sq-mi area. This runoff is the highest of any area of like size in Florida.

The polje type of karst, typically displayed in the Dalmatian area of Yugoslavia and shown in figure 3, offers a good example of underground drainage beneath topographic divides. The Ljubljanica River, in the polje area, has several alternate surface and subsurface stretches as it burrows through at least three carbonate-rock ridges (Lewicki, 1967, p. 261). A similar situation of water traversing an area beneath carbonate ridges in Nevada has been described (Winograd, 1962; Maxey, 1968).

The complexities of subsurface drainage divides are greatest in broad karst regions having several perennial streams. The problem is less complex where the karst is confined between nonkarstic rocks and where one major karst stream is present. Such a stream is the Sequatchie River in east Tennessee, which is entrenched in a karst valley a few miles wide and about 75 miles long.

The indefinite boundaries of the subsurface karst drainage areas as discussed above are spatial because there are many examples to show that the topographic divides are not the same as the ground-water divides. In addition to this lack of concordance of topographic and ground-water divides in karst regions, there can be a change in the size of a ground-water drainage area with time, especially with changes of precipitation during seasons of the year. The drying up of some streams is common in karst areas, a fact that may be evidence of the gaining ability of an adjacent karst stream. The migration of subsurface drainage divides between wet and dry seasons is a significant aspect of karst hydrology that has not been fully recognized. A study of the cyclic regime of karst streams between wet and dry seasons, coupled with subsurface water tracing experiments, gives evidence that creeping of divides does occur (fig. 3).

FLOODS AND HIGH FLOW

An understanding of karstification leads to the suggestion that floods in carbonate-rock terranes may be less severe than those in other terranes. It may be reasoned that precipitation in karst regions does not run off rapidly on the surface but is largely diverted to temporary storage in caverns. This water in temporary storage is soon depleted because water moves readily from the large openings through circuitous channels to springs and surface streams, but the rate of subsurface movement is slower than that of surface water which might otherwise move overland to a stream. There is evidence that temporary storage of precipitation in karst regions results in subdued high-water stages of streams during floods.

The behavior of annual floods in limestone basins in Pennsylvania has been described by White and Reich (1970). They show the mean annual floods per square mile of basin area for parts of several physiographic provinces which include noncarbonate rocks and limestones. The flood data in figure 4 were compiled by White and Reich from data taken from U.S. Geological Survey Water-Supply Papers containing records of streamflow. The limestone basins which are located in the thick carbonate part of the geologic section are shown as solid triangles in figure 4. The mean annual floods per unit area for these basins are low and are independent of drainage area. Those basins lying mainly on noncarbonate rocks have mean annual floods three to nine times greater than those underlain by carbonate rock. According to White and Reich (1970, p.

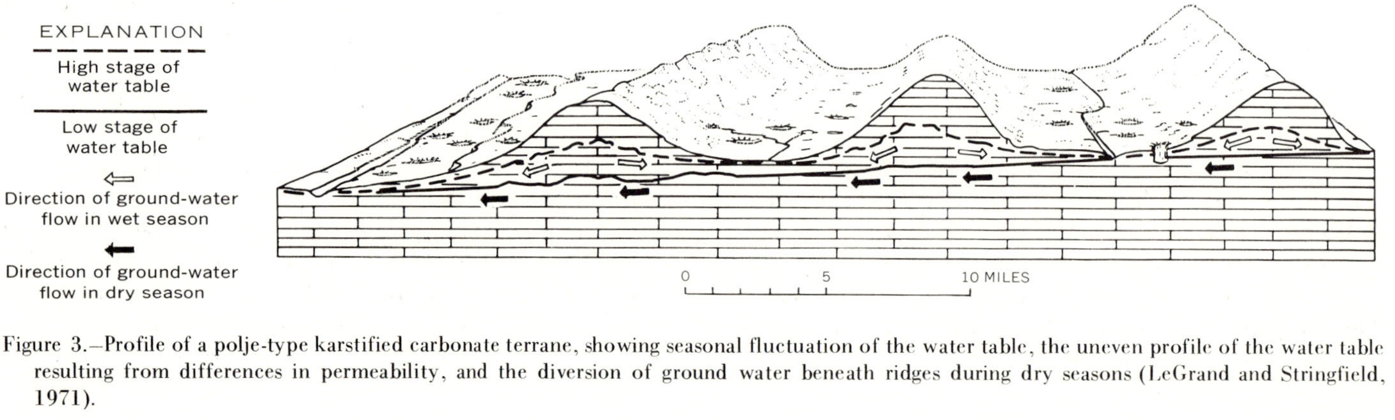

Figure 3.—Profile of a polje-type karstified carbonate terrane, showing seasonal fluctuation of the water table, the uneven profile of the water table resulting from differences in permeability, and the diversion of ground water beneath ridges during dry seasons (LeGrand and Stringfield, 1971).

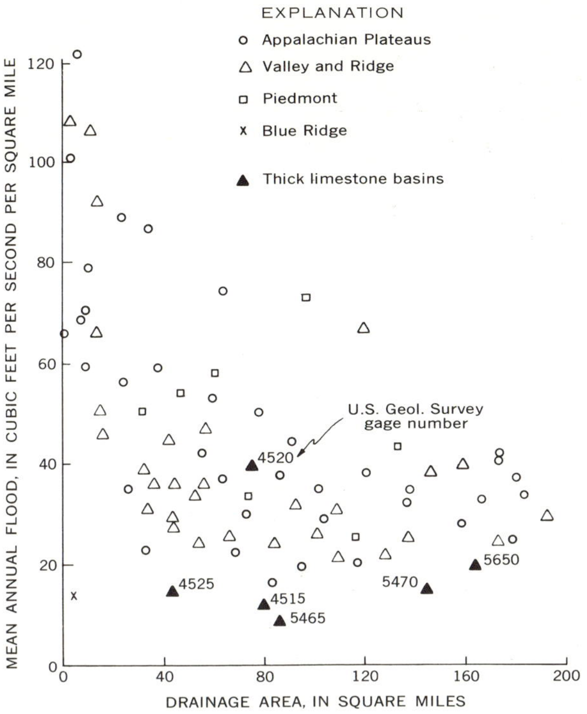

Figure 4.—Mean annual floods for carbonate and noncarbonate drainage basins, Pennsylvania. Comparatively low mean annual floods occur in the valleys underlain by thick carbonate rocks in the Valley and Ridge province (after White and Reich, 1970).

193), the mean annual floods were calculated for 114 basins which ranged from 2 to 200 sq mi in area. The average period of record used was 25 years. High values were obtained from watersheds on shales and sandstones. Extremely low mean annual floods occurred where there was extensive thick and cavernous limestone above the water table within the basin.

Another hydrologic parameter that can be used to show the effect of lithology is the shape of the flood hydrograph as indicated by the peak discharge and the high-flow duration. White and Reich (1970, p. 194) concluded:

> An important effect of the presence of limestone is the smoothing action on the flood peak. The open sinkholes can accept storm excess and thus add temporarily to the ground water storage. Water is then released, via the springs, over the next few days. The temporary storage lasts a short duration with respect to ground-water discharge but a long duration with respect to passage of a flood crest.

Hydrographs of a carbonate basin, Spring Creek, and a typical Pennsylvania noncarbonate basin, Little Fishing Creek, are shown in figure 5 to illustrate this smoothing action. The reduced peaks illustrated are the result of spreading the volume of water over long periods in the limestone basin.

The influence of karst on the hydrological characteristics of rivers in Russia has been studied by Gavrilov (1967, p. 544). He reports that the influence of karst on maximum discharge is indicated by the smoothing of the flood hydrograph and by the lower peak discharge.

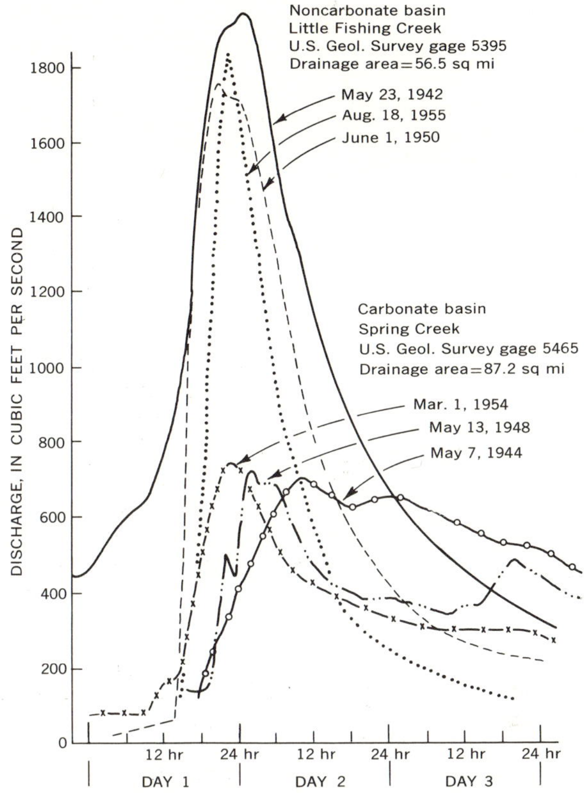

Figure 5.—Distinction between a limestone and noncarbonate basin in Pennsylvania, on the basis of the variation of peak discharge and high-flow duration during floods (after White and Reich, 1970).

LOW-FLOW CHARACTERISTICS OF KARST STREAMS

The tendency toward a smooth effect or moderation of flood flow in karst regions might be expected to lead to a smoothing effect of low flow also to the extent that a karst stream might have an annual lowest 7-day flow somewhat higher than that of a stream on noncarbonate rocks. Major trunk streams do have higher than normal base flows, but erratic patterns of base flow characterize many tributary or smaller karst streams.

The erratic pattern of base flow is demonstrated in Swatara Creek basin, Pennsylvania, where streams in the limestone area have a greater range in low-flow yields than those in adjacent noncarbonate rocks; the low flows in the limestone range from 0.60 to 0 mgd per sq mi (Stuart and others, 1967, p. 3). Almost all karst regions have streams that go dry during dry seasons, but less obvious are the many streams that lose part of their flow in certain places. Skelton (1966, p. 17) made a series of discharge measurements (fig. 6) during base flow periods in 1953 which indicated that large water losses occurred in a reach of the Gasconade River in Missouri that is underlain by solution channels. Burchett and Moore (1971, p. 37) pointed out that during dry weather periods a stretch of East Fork Stones River in central Tennessee loses considerable

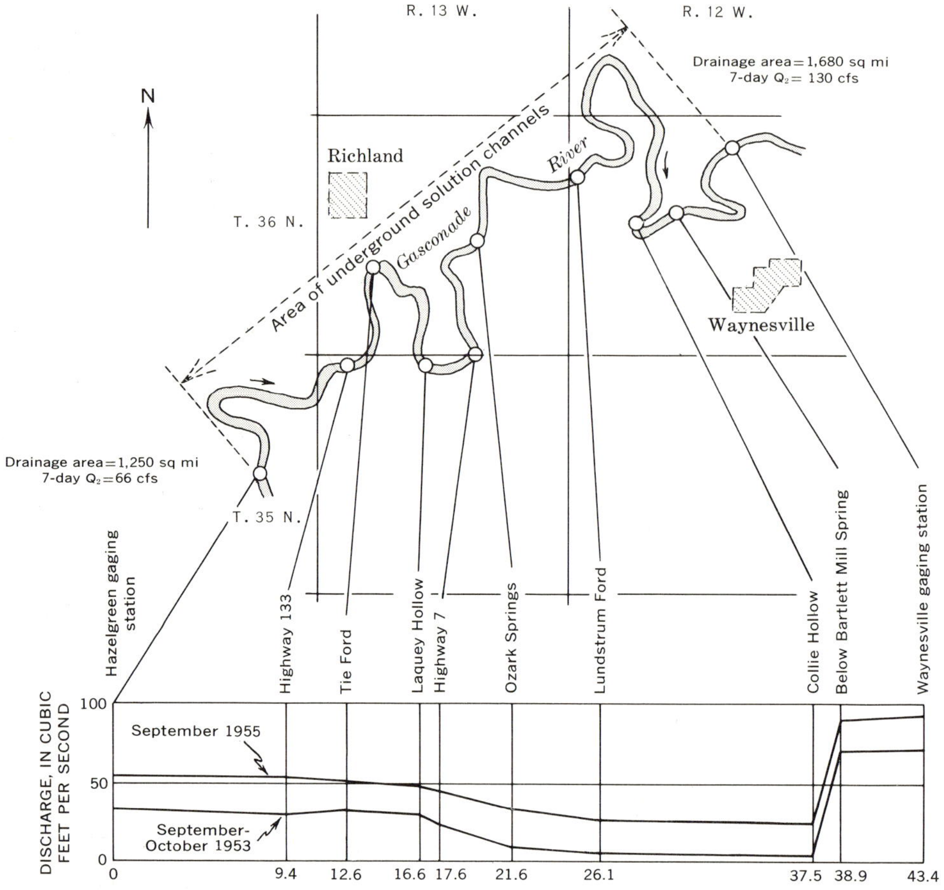

Figure 6.—How streamflow is decreased by infiltration to underground solution channels as evidenced by decreasing base flow in a reach of Gasconade River, Mo. (Skelton, 1966).

water by underflow to subsurface solution cavities, although no points of large water losses are visible.

DISCONTINUITIES OF SURFACE STREAMS DRAINING KARST

Almost all humid karst regions have surface streams that are discontinuous in certain stretches. Most such streams lose water in a specific place, commonly referred to as a swallow hole, from which place the water flows in subsurface conduits to a place of emergence, called a resurgence. For instance, Malott (1952) noted the Lost River in southern Indiana as an excellent example of a disappearing and reappearing stream (fig. 7). Thornbury (1965, p. 194) described this river:

> The Lost River drainage basin encompasses some 350 square miles and can be divided into three rather distinct parts: a lower part in which the stream is a deeply entrenched surface stream, a middle abandoned dry-bed stretch that is used only after heavy rains, and an upper part in which Lost River is an unentrenched surface stream. The middle part of its route crosses the portion of the karst plain upon the St. Louis and Ste. Genevieve limestones. This limestone plain is dotted with thousands of sinkholes and is practically devoid of surface streams. The meandering abandoned dry-bed route of Lost River across this plain *** is 22 miles long, whereas its underground route is only 8 miles long and is directly down the regional dip. Lost River sinks in a series of swallow holes ranging in altitude from 620 to 560 feet. After extremely heavy rains all its water may not be accommodated by these swallow holes, and the excess goes around the dry-bed channel. Lost River reappears at the end of its underground route as a karst spring at an altitude of 490 feet.

The northern part of Puerto Rico is another karst area having numerous discontinuous surface streams. These streams head in the volcanic region to the south before cutting rather narrow but deep gorges in rugged karst, after which they have underground courses for a distance of a mile or more. The underground courses of such streams as the Río Camuy and Río Tanama are suggested at the land surface beneath long irregular dry valleys. Both streams reappear as large springs emerging from coves.

In the central United States where noncarbonate rocks lie above low-lying karst regions small surface streams emerge from coves in noncarbonate rocks and have perennial flows until they go underground in the bordering karst areas; their underground courses can be approximated by the long dry

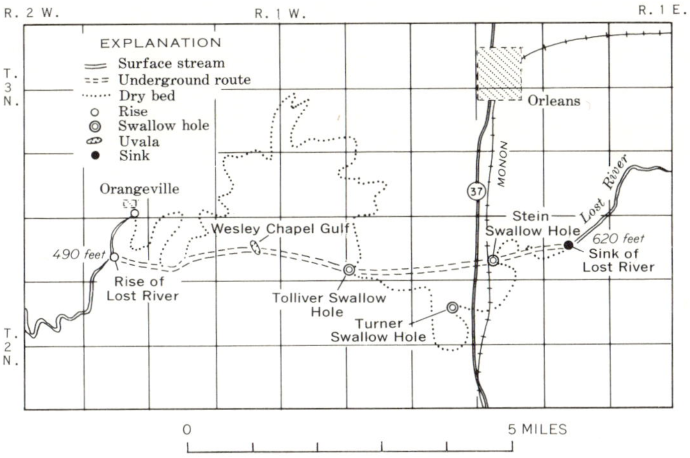

Figure 7.—Map of middle part of Lost River, Orange County, Ind., showing discontinuous flow (after Malott, 1952).

Figure 8.—Typical master trunk conduit. A view of the 3-mile-long stream passage in Overholt Blowing Cave, W. Va. (photograph by W. B. White).

valleys leading to trunk streams. Several examples of these short disappearing streams can be seen on the Sparta, Tenn., 7½-minute quadrangle.

It is reasonable to assume that beneath the discontinuous stretches of karst streams the waters are not diffused but flow as subsurface cave streams. This is evidenced by speleologists, who have noted cave streams in many karst lands (see fig. 8). Cave streams are very abundant and form a sort of arterial flow pattern in the upper part of the saturated zone in many karst areas.

White and Schmidt (1966) gave an elaborate discussion of cave streams in east-central West Virginia and showed (p. 553) that

> some of the drainage more or less follows the surface drainage lines, and thus merely has the effect of underdraining the valleys. These drainage lines are termed "well behaved". In other parts of the area, subsurface drainage conduits do not parallel surface drainage lines but cross surface divides and carry water out of the small drainage basins by unobvious routes. These drainage lines are termed "misbehaved".

Some carbonate-rock streams lose water gradually instead of suddenly through a swallow hole. Excellent examples are the Nueces, Frio, and Sabinal Rivers which flow on the Edwards limestone aquifer in the Balcones Fault Zone of south-central Texas. These streams head in and drain the Edwards Plateau upstream from the fault zone. In the Balcones Fault Zone, the Edwards is downfaulted along numerous faults and as a consequence the streams lose water by seepage into solution openings along fractures where the streams flow on the limestone (Sayre and Bennett, 1942). Infiltration of river water into the underlying limestone contributes most of the recharge to the aquifer that supplies water for the city of San Antonio. The capability of water in the streams to infiltrate the limestone is exemplified by the Nueces River within the recharge area to the Edwards aquifer as shown by the following data at Laguna weather gage. On October 20, 1962, the average daily flow at the Laguna gage was 901 cfs, the peak discharge for that day being 3,210 cfs; the difference between the average flow and the peak flow for that day represents some of the water lost by seepage into the underlying Edwards aquifer (U.S. Army Corps Engineers, 1970). The Martha Brae River, of northern Jamaica, West Indies, is another example of a stream that loses part, but not all, of its water in a stretch through a karst region.

Streams flowing eastward from the structural dome of the Black Hills in South Dakota cross a belt of cavernous limestone several miles wide. Here many small streams lose their entire flow to sinkholes, and even the larger streams show perceptibly decreased flow at the eastern border of the outcrop belt (Gries and others, 1968, p. 57–58). The streams tend to regain their lost water from large springs located slightly east of and downgradient from the limestone belt (Rahn and Gries, 1971).

In many karst regions the loss of water from a stream is local, and the water is generally regained at some resurgence less than several miles from the point of loss; however, in the Edwards aquifer in Texas and others in broad karst plateaus, the regain of water may be tens of miles away, even in different drainage basins. Where streams in coastal karst areas lose water by seepage into streambeds and sinkholes, there may be no regain of water as it moves in subsurface channels to the sea.

The uneven distribution of permeability and of topographic conditions is responsible for the intriguing karst phenomena of disappearing and reappearing surface streams. These seemingly mysterious phenomena can best be understood by considering the underground and missing segment of the stream as being in a relatively permeable zone and a segment upgradient from the swallow hole as being in a relatively impermeable zone.

There are current and potential problems relating to streams that have discontinuous surface courses. Harvey and Skelton

(1968) have described the movement of effluent from a sewage treatment plant at Springfield, Mo., into Wilson Creek; near the outfall of the treatment plant both water and effluent are lost underground before reappearing at a resurgence 1.4 miles away, where the surface course of the creek continues. The effluent at Springfield received secondary treatment—a condition that might not be objectionable along surface stretches of some streams where aeration is effective—but the limited aeration in the subsurface stretch made the effluent objectionable. In addition to the problem of poor aeration in the ground, any polluted water in the subsurface stretch of a karst river might be easily drawn toward pumping wells. Also there is no assurance that it will be contained in a single subsurface channel of flow; instead it might spread in two or more branching directions of flow.

Stretches of some surface streams in karst areas may have channels in relatively impermeable carbonate rocks or in an intervening shale bed, the level of the stream being higher than the underlying karst water table. If a natural or manmade opening develops between the streambed and underlying karst water a partial or complete loss of surface water could result. The lower course of the Río Cobre, draining the karstland of south-central Jamaica, is such a stream as it flows on clays of an alluvial plain. Near the border of the karst and alluvial plain the underlying karst water level is lower than river level, a condition that represents a potential loss of river water in this zone. The streamflow records show no water loss during low flows, and the stream level is above the water level in the limestone (Richard Davis, Hydrogeologist, United Nations Food and Agricultural Organization, Kingston, Jamaica, West Indies, oral commun., May 1971). Probably there is loss of water to the limestone during flood stages when the water level in the river rises above the silted part of the channel. The water level of stretches of stream channels with respect to a karst water table is an important hydrological consideration, and on karst hydrological maps a distinction between the terms "karst water-table stretches" and "nonkarstic stretches" would be helpful.

SURFACE RESERVOIRS IN KARST REGIONS

The problem of leaky reservoirs in karst areas centers on the distribution of permeability in karstified rocks. The permeability is unevenly distributed, and, unlike in insoluble rocks, the permeability is developed as water high in dissolved carbon dioxide content moves through joints and other openings to places of discharge. The following well-established generalizations indicate that the permeability of carbonate aquifers is commonly different from that of other aquifers:

1. Circulation of water and solution activity tend to be greatest in the upper part of the zone of saturation and tend to lessen with increased depth.
2. The moderately large openings in the path of bulk flow of ground water tend to enlarge by solution action, in contrast to small openings not in the path of bulk flow which enlarge only slightly.

Almost all surface reservoirs are hydrologically connected with the saturated zone of the ground-water system. A dam designed to raise the water level of the reservoir must also raise the adjacent and subjacent water table. A rise in the water table around a reservoir in nonkarstic rocks, especially of poor to moderate permeability, is nearly always certain; in karst rocks, on the other hand, a rise in the water table is less certain. Karst topography is characteristically underlain by carbonate rocks in which large solution channels are separated by large volumes of poorly permeable carbonates. The large solution channels in the zone of saturation resemble in some ways the surface drainage network on some noncarbonate rocks of humid regions. The volume of solution channels, representing the gross permeability, tends to decline almost exponentially with increasing distance below the water table. The zone of saturation of the aquifer is commonly thin, lenticular, and elongate, and its base is indefinite or arbitrary. The unsaturated zone tends to be very permeable and cavernous. The reservoir problems must focus on the very permeable material around the reservoirs that allows water to flow away freely and that thwarts a rise in the water table. The general nature of solution openings can be approximated by hydrogeological observations and inferences, but techniques of outlining specific solution openings before drilling are not available.

CONCLUSIONS

The great ranges of natural conditions that influence streamflow in carbonate-rock terranes and the scarcity of a synthesis of data prevent a useful statistical analysis of the characteristics of streamflow in these terranes. The conventional techniques of interpolation and extrapolation that have been reasonably successful in approximating streamflow of ungaged sites in nonkarstic regions have only limited use in karst regions. An understanding of principles of karstification and an understanding of the hydrogeologic framework of a carbonate terrane provide a useful basis for evaluating the streamflow characteristics.

A karst terrane has its own characteristic distribution of permeability, both in the unsaturated and saturated zones, which is a major factor in controlling the streamflow. The very highly cavernous and permeable unsaturated zone tends to keep the water table depressed below land surface in much of karst regions and in turn leads to a low density of perennial streams. The major trunk stream tends to have a high base flow because ground water continues to drain toward it after the water table falls below the level of some tributary streams, at which time the tributary streams go dry. A shifting of ground-water divides away from the major trunk stream during dry seasons causes a temporary enlargement of some drainage basins and the movement of ground water as underflow beneath some upland areas. The high permeability in the unsaturated zone tends to cause flood stages to be smoothed out to the extent that the floods are lower in height and longer in time than those in noncarbonate regions. The smoothing out of flood stages occurs because (1) precipitation is quickly drained underground where it has a somewhat slower movement through solution channels to a surface stream than would overland flow, and (2) water in a rising stream tends to spread laterally during a flood into adjacent air-filled cavities and thereby to subdue a potential flood.

Big springs, rather than small springs and diffuse seepage, are the general rule in mature karst regions. The big springs emerge from underground streams or cave rivers. Some of the underground streams are the subsurface links in discontinuous surface streams that disappear underground and reappear as springs elsewhere. Most of the underground streams, however, are large solution openings at the top of the saturated zone which carry much of the ground water to springs. The underground streams tend to branch upgradient in arterial fashion and represent the more permeable parts of the saturated zone; the water table is depressed along the arterial system so that the underground stream meets the surface stream almost at grade.

The uneven distribution of permeability beneath surface karst streams causes them to lose or gain water, depending on the position of the water table with reference to stream level. A surface stream may disappear or lose water where the losing stretch is very permeable, and it may gain water where the rock is less permeable to the extent that the water table is above stream level.

The uneven distribution of both permeability and topography between karst and adjacent nonkarst terranes causes many surface streams to gain or lose much water near the rock boundaries. Many surface streams flowing from clastic rocks onto lower lying karst rocks disappear into swallow holes before reappearing elsewhere as karst springs. Many underground karst streams emerge as springs at the boundary of nonkarst rocks where they then follow a surface course.

REFERENCES CITED

Avias, J., 1972, Karst of France, *in* Important karst regions of the Northern Hemisphere, chap. 5: Amsterdam, Elsevier Publishing Co., p. 124–184.

Burchett, C. R., and Moore, G. K., 1971, Water resources in the upper Stones River basin, central Tennessee: Tennessee Div. Water Resources, Water Resources Ser. No. 8, 62 p.

Carlston, C. W., 1963, Drainage density and streamflow: U.S. Geol. Survey Prof. Paper 422-C, 8 p.

Clark, W. E., Musgrove, R. H., Menke, C. G., and Cagle, J. W., Jr., 1962, Interim report on the water resources of Alachua, Bradford, Clay, and Union Counties, Florida: Florida Geol. Survey Inf. Circ. 36, 92 p.

Davies, W. E., 1970, Map of karst areas, *in* National atlas of the United States of America: U.S. Geol. Survey, p. 77.

Gavrilov, A. M., 1967, On the problem of the influence of karst on the hydrological regime of rivers, *in* Hydrology of fractured rocks: Dubrovnik Symposium, October 1965, Proc. Internat. Assoc. Sci. Hydrology Pub. 74, v. 2, p. 544–562.

Gries, J. P., Niven, D. W., and Crooks, T. J., 1968, Recharge of the Pahasapa Limestone aquifer from stream losses, Black Hills, South Dakota: South Dakota Acad. Sci. Proc., v. 47, p. 56–61.

Grund, Alfred, 1914, Der Geographische Zyklus im karst: Zeitschr. der Gesellschaft fur Erdkunde zu Berlin, p. 621–640.

Harvey, E. J., and Skelton, John, 1968, Hydrologic study of a waste-disposal problem in a karst area at Springfield, Missouri, *in* Geological Survey Research 1968: U.S. Geol. Survey Prof. Paper 600-C, p. C217–C220.

Hendricks, E. L., and Goodwin, M. H., Jr., 1952, Water-level fluctuations in limestone sinks in southwestern Georgia: U.S. Geol. Survey Water-Supply Paper 1110-E, p. 157–246.

Herak, Milan, and Stringfield, V. T., eds., 1971, Important karst regions of the Northern Hemisphere: Amsterdam, Elsevier Publishing Co., 488 p.

Herrick, S. M., and LeGrand, H. E., 1964, Solution subsidence of a limestone terrane in southwest Georgia: Internat. Assoc. Sci. Hydrology Bull., v. 9, no. 2, p. 25–36.

Jacob, C. E., 1944, Correlation of ground-water levels and precipitation on Long Island, New York, Pt. 1, Theory: Am. Geophys. Union Trans., 24th Ann. Mtg., p. 564–573.

LaMoreaux, P. E., Raymond, Dorothy, and Joiner, T. J., 1970, Hydrology of limestone terranes, annotated bibliography of carbonate rocks: Alabama Geol. Survey Bull. 94, pt. A, 242 p.

LeGrand, H. E., 1970, Comparative hydrogeology: An example of its use: Geol. Soc. America Bull., v. 81, p. 1243–1248.

LeGrand, H. E., and Stringfield, V. T., 1971, Water levels in carbonate rock terranes: Ground Water, v. 9, no. 3, p. 4–10.

Lewicki, Friderik, 1967, The basic hydrologic characteristics of the karst river Ljubljanica, *in* Hydrology of fractured rocks: Dubrovnik Symposium, October 1965, Proc., Internat. Assoc. Sci. Hydrology Pub. 73, v. 1, p. 255–262.

Malott, C. A., 1952, The swallow-holes of Lost River, Orange County, Indiana: Indiana Acad. Sci. Proc., v. 61, p. 187–231.

Maxey, G. B., 1968, Hydrogeology of desert basins: Ground Water, v. 6, no. 5, p. 10–22.

Meinzer, O. E., 1939, Ground water in the United States, a summary of ground-water conditions and resources, utilization of water from wells and springs, methods of scientific investigation, and literature relating to the subject: U.S. Geol. Survey Water-Supply Paper 836-D, p. 157–232.

Rahn, P. H., and Gries, J. P., 1971, Estimating recharge to limestone aquifers based on spring discharge: Geol. Soc. America, Abs. with Programs, v. 3, no. 7, p. 677.

Sayre, A. N., and Bennett, R. R., 1942, Recharge, movement, and discharge in the Edwards limestone reservoir, Texas: Am. Geophys. Union Trans., v. 23, p. 19–27.

Skelton, John, 1966, Low flow characteristics of Missouri streams: Missouri Geol. Survey and Water Resources, Water Resources Rept. 20, 95 p.

Stringfield, V. T., 1964, Relation of surface-water hydrology to the principal artesian aquifer in Florida and southeastern Georgia, *in* Geological Survey Research 1964: U.S. Geol. Survey Prof. Paper 501-C, p. C164–C169.

—— 1966, Artesian water in Tertiary limestone in the southeastern States: U.S. Geol. Survey Prof. Paper 517, 226 p. [1967]

Stringfield, V. T., and LeGrand, H. E., 1969, Hydrology of carbonate-rock terranes—A review, with special reference to the United States: Jour. Hydrology, v. 8, nos. 3 and 4, p. 349–417.

Stuart, W. T., Schneider, W. J., and Crooks, J. W., 1967, Swatara Creek basin of southeastern Pennsylvania—An evaluation of its hydrologic system: U.S. Geol. Survey Water-Supply Paper 1829, 79 p.

Thornbury, W. D., 1965, Regional geomorphology of the United States: New York, John Wiley & Sons, 609 p.

U.S. Army Corps Engineers, 1970, Survey report on Edwards underground reservoir, Guadalupe, San Antonio, and Nueces River and tributaries: U.S. Army Corps Engineers, Fort Worth District, v. 2, app. 2, p. II–67.

White, E. L., and Reich, B. M., 1970, Behavior of annual floods in limestone basins in Pennsylvania: Jour. Hydrology, v. 10, p. 193–198.

White, W. B., and Schmidt, V. A., 1966, Hydrology of a karst area in east-central West Virginia: Water Resources Research, v. 2, no. 3, p. 549–560.

Winograd, I. J., 1962, Interbasin movement of ground water at the Nevada Test Site, Nevada: Art. 104 *in* U.S. Geol. Survey Prof. Paper 450-C, p. C108–C111.

Jour. Research U.S. Geol. Survey
Vol. 1, No. 3, May-June 1973, p. 361–366

THE FRACTIONATION OF HUMIC ACIDS FROM NATURAL WATER SYSTEMS

By R. L. WERSHAW and D. J. PINCKNEY, Lakewood, Colo.

Abstract.—Humic acids, the most abundant organic components of natural water systems, are complex mixtures of molecular aggregates of different chemical and physical properties. The first step in the study of such a mixture is the fractionation of the mixture. The most common approach with humic acids is to attempt to obtain a molecular weight fractionation by gel-permeation chromatography. However, since the preponderance of evidence indicates that the components of humic acid do not fulfill the basic criteria of uniform shape and chemical structure necessary for obtaining a molecular fractionation on gel-permeation media, molecular weight distributions in humic acids cannot be evaluated by this method. A fractionation dependent upon chemical structure can be obtained by the manipulation of elution conditions on a gel-permeation column. This procedure provides a beginning in the isolation and identification of discrete components of humic acids.

Progress in the elucidation of molecular structure of humic acid and also of fulvic acid has been extremely slow. As a consequence, a detailed understanding of their interactions in soil and water systems is lacking. It has been realized for a long time that the humic and fulvic acid extracts from soils, sediments, and waters are complex mixtures of chemically different molecular species. Any study of the chemistry of humic or fulvic acids must therefore begin with the isolation of these various molecular species.

Sephadex[1] gel-permeation chromatography, which has been particularly valuable in the molecular weight fractionation of mixtures of closely related molecules such as globular proteins or polysaccharides, has been used extensively in attempts to fractionate humic and fulvic acids according to molecular weight (see review by Swift and Posner, 1971). Most of the workers have tacitly assumed in interpreting their data that all the particles in a given humic or fulvic acid sample were of the same shape and chemical structure, for if these two conditions did not obtain then one could not evaluate relative molecular weights from elution volumes (Determann, 1969).

The effect of differences in shape on apparent molecular weights calculated from Sephadex elution volumes has been graphically demonstrated by the work of Chao and Einstein (1969) on globular and flexible, disordered proteins. They have shown that the molecular weights of flexible, disordered proteins calculated by comparing the elution volumes of the proteins with those of globular proteins are considerably higher than the molecular weights obtained by equilibrium ultracentrifugation. Schnitzer and Skinner (1968), working with fulvic acids, which are apparently similar to humic acids, found that the molecular weights of the fulvic acid fractions calculated from gel-permeation chromatography data were 3 to 10 times higher than those determined for the same fractions by vapor pressure osmometry, freezing point depression, and ultracentrifugation. Therefore, since it has not been established that humic acid molecules are uniform in shape or in chemical structure, molecular weight distributions determined by gel-permeation chromatography are, at best, of doubtful value.

In the absence of evidence to the contrary, one can only assume that a given humic acid sample is a heterogeneous mixture of particles of different shapes and different chemical structures. In a heterogeneous mixture of different chemical species, it is more fruitful to attempt to increase the chemical homogeneity of the fractions than to try to obtain a molecular weight fractionation. This is especially true for humic and fulvic acids which form molecular aggregates in solution (Wershaw and Pinckney, 1971, 1973).

The work of Wershaw and Burcar (1967), Wildenhain and Henseke (1967), and Bailly and Margulis (1968) suggests that it should be possible to increase the chemical homogeneity of humic acid fractions by adsorption chromatography on Sephadex gels. In order to obtain chemical fractionation the functional groups of various humic acid fractions must interact with the functional groups of the gel-permeation medium. The amount of interaction between a given humic acid molecule and the gel will be dependent on the functional-group composition of the molecule; therefore, different types of molecules will move through the gel column at different speeds. In order to obtain maximum fractionation, we have attempted to enhance this differential interaction. This is exactly the opposite of the practice in normal gel-permeation chromatography, where it is desired that the interactions between gel molecules and the sample molecules be minimized.

[1] Sephadex is a registered trademark of Pharmacia Fine Chemicals, Inc. Use of the term in this paper is for descriptive purposes only and does not constitute an endorsement of the product by the U.S. Geological Survey.

There is very little detailed information on the chemical structure of humic acids. However, that information which is available suggests that humic acids are principally aromatic in nature, containing phenol, quinone, and acid groups. In addition to the aromatic functional groups, amine and alcohol groups and ether linkages are apparently also present in most humic acids (see Flaig, 1970, and Kononova, 1966).

Phenols, quinones, and aromatic acids in general strongly interact with Sephadex dextran gels. Gelotte (1960) was the first to make a detailed study of sorption of compounds by Sephadex. He found that compounds containing aromatic and heterocyclic groups, and basic compounds were adsorbed to Sephadex. The adsorptions were most pronounced when the Sephadex column was equilibrated with distilled water, and when distilled water was used an an eluant. Demetriou and others (1968) have demonstrated that by manipulation of the ion strength of eluant, it is possible to obtain fractionation of substituted phenolic and heterocyclic compounds. Adsorptive effects were found to be operative in both distilled water and electrolyte solutions. Janson (1967) has shown in his review of the literature on adsorption on Sephadex that there are two types of departure from ideal molecular sieving behavior on Sephadex gels. Some solutes may be retarded in their movement through the gel by adsorption or attractive electrostatic interactions, whereas others will be excluded from the gel by repressive forces and will move through the column more rapidly than normal. Janson has pointed out that dextran gels, such as Sephadex, have a particular affinity for aromatic compounds and other compounds with large numbers of π electrons. Brook and Munday (1970) have shown that the hydroxyl, amino, or carboxyl groups of monosubstituted derivatives of phenols, anilines, and benzoic acids interact with the ether linkage and the hydroxyl groups on the dextran chains. Their work also indicates that the degree of interaction between these monosubstituted derivatives and dextran gels can be correlated by the Hammett equation.

Sephadex adsorption chromatography has been used for separation of closely related aromatic and heterocyclic compounds (Miranda and others, 1962, Demetriou and others, 1968, and Woof and Pierce, 1967). Reeves, Kaiser, and Finley (1970) have devised a method for the separation of azo and azomethine dyes by gel-permeation chromatography on Sephadex G-25 and G-50. Using 0.01 *N* KOH as an eluant they were able to separate dye isomers.

The fact that sodium humates form aggregates will also affect their fractionation on Sephadex. As Andrews (1970) has pointed out, compounds which form molecular aggregates in solution will behave in at least three different ways on gel-permeation columns. Those compounds which form stable aggregates that do not dissociate under the physical and chemical conditions of the procedure will move through the column as though the aggregates were simply large molecules. If, however, the aggregates are in equilibrium with their dissociated constituent units, then the elution volume of the aggregated system will be concentration dependent. In addition, there will be some spreading of the solute on the column. If the aggregates are complexes of different molecular species, then in some instances gel-permeation chromatography will bring about dissociation of the otherwise stable aggregates.

EXPERIMENTAL PROCEDURE

The humic acids used in this study were extracted from both soils and natural waters. The soil extraction procedure with 0.1 *N* NaOH was the same as that outlined in Wershaw and others (1967) except that the extractions were carried out in closed Teflon bottles that were completely filled with soil and extraction solution. The water samples were concentrated to about 20 percent of the original volume by freeze concentration (Shapiro, 1961). The humic acid in both the soil and water samples was precipitated by lowering the pH of the solution to 1 with hydrochloric acid. The humic acid was separated from the solution by centrifugation and washed three times with water. After washing, the sodium salt of the humic acid was prepared by dissolving the humic acid in excess sodium hydroxide. In our early work, we dialyzed the solutions to remove excess sodium hydroxide; however, we found that we were losing some material. Therefore, we now add only enough sodium hydroxide to dissolve the humic acid; the pH of the solutions after the addition of sodium hydroxide is between 7 and 9. This product is then lyophilized.

Column chromatography of the sodium humate samples from various environments was carried out on Sephadex G-50, G-25, and G-100 columns prepared in the usual manner prescribed by the manufacturer. All of the Sephadex was allowed to swell in distilled water, and the columns were packed with Sephadex suspended in distilled water.

A variety of column sizes was used; however, most of the work was done on columns 4.2 cm in diameter and 30.5 cm in length. One-percent solutions of the various sodium humate samples to be fractionated were prepared, and the pH of each solution was adjusted to values between 11.2 and 11.6 with sodium hydroxide. A 10-ml aliquot of the solution was applied to the Sephadex column, and the column was eluted with distilled water. The first fractionation of each sample was carried out on a Sephadex Superfine G-50 column, and the fractions were collected and lyophilized. The first fraction to come off the G-50 column was refractionated on Sephadex Superfine G-100 columns, and the rest of the fractions were refractionated on Sephadex Superfine G-25 columns. From 10 to 12 subfractions were obtained. In the refractionation procedure, the lyophilized fractions were dissolved in water and eluted from the columns with water; these subfractions were then lyophilized.

Results similar to those of Sephadex column chromatography may be obtained by Sephadex thin-layer chromatography. The thin-layer technique permits the comparison of a number of small samples on the same thin-layer plate under the same elution conditions.

The procedure for the low-angle X-ray scattering studies to determine particle size distribution of fractions in solution is described in Wershaw and Pinckney (1973).

Description of soils extracted for humic acids

North Carolina sandy soil.—This soil was taken from the Bh horizon of the Leon-Lakewood soil association, of the coastal plain, Brunswick County, N.C. It is a dark medium sand with a very low clay content and about 2 percent organic carbon. (For a complete description, see Malcolm, 1964).

Florida sandy soil.—This sample of Rutledge mucky fine sand was collected from the poorly drained area along Cypress Creek, Vineland, Orange County, Fla. This soil is a sandy surface soil which is normally 4 to 12 inches thick. It has been classified as a humic clay soil by Leighty and others (1960).

Lagunita soil.—This soil was taken from an alpine bog in the Sangre de Cristo Mountains, Mora County, N. Mex. (sec. 25, T. 23 N., R. 14 E., New Mexico Principal Meridian) at an elevation of about 11,040 feet. The upper 3 to 4 inches of vegetation was removed, and the next 12 inches of soil was sampled. It is high in decaying organic matter consisting mainly of dead roots. Before extraction, as much of the root material as possible was removed. (For a more complete description of the soils in the area, see Carleton, 1971.)

Washington organic soil.—A composite sample made up of Spalding peat, Rifle peat, and undifferentiated alluvial soil was taken from eight sampling sites along Grovers Creek, Kitsap County, Wash. The peats consist mainly of organic material with little or no mineral material. The undifferentiated alluvial soil occurs in strips 100 to 200 feet wide along the stream. In addition to peat, it contains decaying organic matter, sand, and clay (Wildermuth and others, 1939).

Description of water sample extracted for humic acid

Alamosa water.—The water comes from a zone 200 to 400 feet beneath the land surface; it normally has a color of about 520 APHA (American Public Health Association) units, and the pH is about 8. This water is in contact with peat beds of the Alamosa Formation, and apparently the humic acids in the water come from these beds. The well from which this water was taken is in sec. 13, T. 39 N., R. 10 E., Alamosa County, Colo.

Discussion of the results

The characterization of the elution behavior of a particular fraction from a gel-permeation chromatography column requires the use of a parameter which is independent of the column dimensions. The parameter most frequently used for this is K_d, which is defined by the equation

$$K_d = \frac{V_e - V_o}{V_t - V_o},$$

where V_e is the elution volume of the fraction, V_o is the void volume of the column, and V_t is the total volume of the column. It is generally assumed that K_d values less than one indicate that normal molecular sieving is taking place and that values greater than one indicate that the fraction is being sorbed by the column medium. However, the work of Baetz and Diehl (1968) suggests that adsorption may even play a role in the fractionation of compounds with K_d values less than one. They were able to separate mixtures of 0,0'-dihydroxyazobenzene dyes on Sephadex G-10 using 0.001 *N* NaOH as an eluant. All of the dyes had K_d values less than one; however, they found that the normal elution order of higher molecular weight compounds coming off the column before lower molecular weight compounds was not followed. A compound of molecular weight 504 was eluted from the column after a dye with a molecular weight of 359. Baetz and Diehl (1968) have attributed this reversal in elution order to differential adsorption of the two species.

Elution curves for several different sodium humates from Sephadex G-50 columns are given in figure 1. In general it will be noted that the chromatograms are very similar for the fractionation of the various sodium humate samples on G-50. The first fraction is eluted at the void volume of the column in every instance (K_d = 0). Another fraction is eluted at approximately the total column volume (K_d = 1); this fraction is in general the most abundant fraction. Between this fraction, which is designated fraction 4, and the first fraction, normally two other fractions are eluted. The relative positions and abundances of these fractions are different in different humic acids. In addition to these fractions, in several of the humic acids that were studied, two other fractions have been detected. One of these comes off the column much later than fraction 4 and has been designated fraction 5; between this fraction and fraction 4 a green band is sometimes seen on the column. This band is generally so weak that it does not show up as an absorption peak on the spectrophotometer trace.

The North Carolina humic acid green band has been tentatively identified as being the same as the so-called green humic acid isolated by Kumada and Hurst (1967). Sato and Kumada (1967) have identified this substance as a derivative of 4,9-dihydroxyperylene-3,10-quinone. Kumada and Hurst (1967) isolated the green humic acid fraction by chromatography of a humic acid sample on a Sephadex G-25 column. Lowe and Tsang (1970), using the same procedure, have been able to isolate green humic acids from different forest soils in British Columbia. The isolation of what appears to be a single chemical compound or at least a group of closely related compounds lends support to the proposition that the separation of chemically distinct species can be accomplished by Sephadex chromatography.

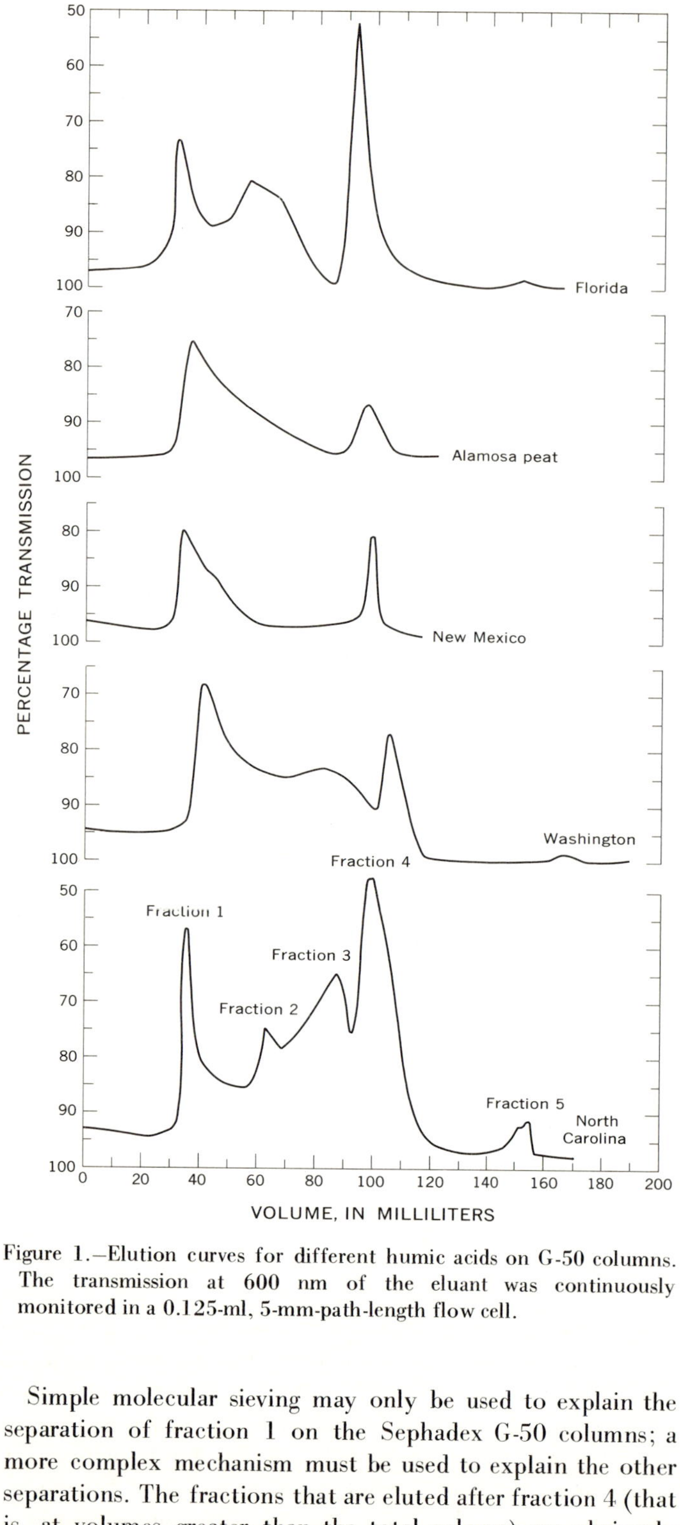

Figure 1.—Elution curves for different humic acids on G-50 columns. The transmission at 600 nm of the eluant was continuously monitored in a 0.125-ml, 5-mm-path-length flow cell.

Simple molecular sieving may only be used to explain the separation of fraction 1 on the Sephadex G-50 columns; a more complex mechanism must be used to explain the other separations. The fractions that are eluted after fraction 4 (that is, at volumes greater than the total column) are obviously being separated by a mechanism other than molecular sieving. Generally this type of behavior has been attributed to adsorption of the fraction by gel. The separation of fractions 2, 3, and 4 cannot be explained by molecular sieving alone, for low-angle X-ray scattering showed that each of these fractions is polydisperse under conditions found in the column (Wershaw and Pinckney, 1971). The smallest particles in most of these polydisperse systems are small enough to enter the Sephadex G-50 gel. Therefore, the fractionation that is taking place is most likely due to both adsorption of the sodium humate molecules by the gel and molecular sieving. The sorption of the fractions probably takes place both on the outer surfaces of gel spheres and in their interiors. However, the adsorption properties of the interiors of the Sephadex beads are apparently different from those of the outside surfaces of the beads (Dr. Monty Lee, oral commun., 1971).

Generalized diagrams of the appearance of the G-25 and G-100 columns on which the G-50 fractions were refractionated are shown in figure 2. The diagrams depict the column appearance at the time that the first fraction reached the bottom of the column. These diagrams show that the G-50 fractions will refractionate into discrete bands on G-25 and G-100 columns.

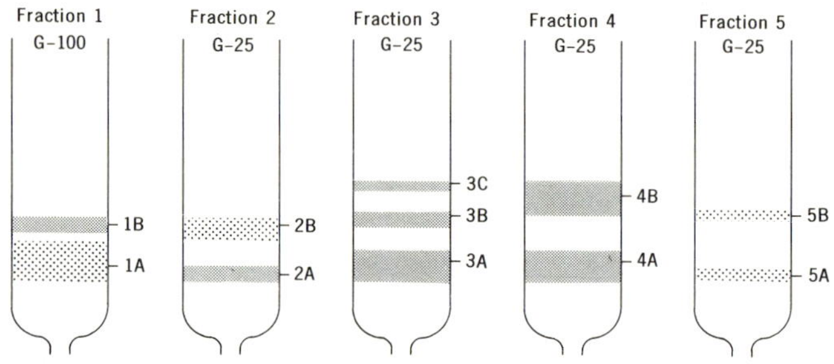

Figure 2.—The refractionation of G-50 fractions on G-100 and G-25 columns.

The additional fractionation that is obtained on one grade of Sephadex after initial fractionation on another grade probably results from differences in both pore size and functional-group distribution between the various grades. Sephadex is a cross-linked dextran polysaccharide in which the dextran strands are cross-linked by hydroxyether groups. The degree of cross-linking is greater the lower the Sephadex number, thus Sephadex G-50 has fewer cross-links and larger voids than G-25. The differences in cross-link distribution between the various grades of Sephadex affect not only the molecular sieving properties of the Sephadex but also its adsorption properties. The cross-linked dextran chains contain a few terminal carboxylic acid groups which will act as ion exchange sites. In Sephadex grades with more cross-links, more ion exchange sites are present; therefore, in distilled water these grades will act as weak ion exchangers.

A detailed study by Wershaw and Pinckney (1973) of the particle size distributions in solutions of these subfractions at different pH values provides us with an insight into the complexity of the separation mechanism on the Sephadex columns. The subfractions that we have isolated form molecular aggregates in solution; the degree of aggregation is a function of pH. All of the subfractions are highly aggregated at pH 3.5; however at higher pH values three different types of behavior have been detected:

1. Little change in degree of aggregation above pH 3.5;
2. Continual decrease in amount of aggregation with increasing pH; and
3. Decrease in aggregation with increasing pH up to about pH 7 at which point the particles are completely disaggregated, and then reaggregation above pH 7 (Wershaw and Pinckney, 1971).

The subfractions 1A from most of the samples exhibit type 1 behavior. However, the subfractions 1A from some of the sodium humates after collection and freeze drying could not be completely redissolved in some or all of the buffers that were used. Examination of these samples by X-ray diffraction revealed that they contained appreciable amounts of montmorillonite which was probably bound to the sodium humate.

The third category of behavior is sometimes detected in some of the subfractions of fraction 2. However, since fraction 2 is indistinct in many samples, it is not always possible to compare its subfractions from one sample to another.

Most of the subfractions exhibit behavior of the second category. Even in highly alkaline solutions the molecules of these fractions are aggregated to some extent in a continuous distribution of particle sizes from those that are larger than pores of G-50 or even G-100 to those that are smaller than the pores.

As Janson (1967) has pointed out, since much more surface is exposed on the inside of the gel beads than on the outside, the molecules that are being fractionated must enter the gel medium before an appreciable amount of material can interact with the gel. Therefore, in attempting to understand the mechanism of interaction of sodium humate particles with Sephadex gels it is necessary to know the sizes of pores in the gel beads. These sizes may be evaluated from data on the exclusion limits for globular proteins. Since the Sephadex gels have been widely used for fractionation of globular proteins, the minimum molecular weights of globular proteins that are excluded from the gels have been well established.[2] Therefore by plotting radii of gyration versus molecular weights of globular proteins, one can determine the minimum sizes of the molecules that are excluded from the gels. These data indicate that molecules having a radii of gyration greater than about 12 A will be excluded from G-25, greater than 21 A from G-50, and greater than 35 A from G-100. Thus the larger sodium humate aggregates will be completely excluded from the gel along with the associated clay–humic acid particles.

The elution behavior of the aggregate will be altered if the component particles of the aggregate enter and interact with the particles of the gel. Since, in general, sodium humates are more disaggregated at high pH values, the introduction of the samples onto the G-50 columns at pH values of about 11 will enhance the penetration of the sodium humate into gel pores. The molecules of the various fractions will migrate through the column at different rates that are dependent on both the chemical and physical properties of the fractions. This process will tend to disaggregate a mixed aggregate into its component fractions. This mechanism for the fractionation of mixed aggregates probably accounts for the initial fractionation of sodium humate on Sephadex G-50 columns.

[2] See "Sephadex gel filtration in theory and practice," 1970, available from Pharmacia Fine Chemicals, Inc., Piscataway, N.J.

Werhsaw and others (1967) have detected particles with radii of gyration in excess of 100 A in an unfractionated sodium humate sample. Further work has revealed, however, that particles small enough to penetrate the pores of Sephadex G-50 are also present. The distribution of particle sizes changes with pH, and therefore there is apparently a dynamic equilibrium between the mixed aggregates and their component particles. The entrance of smaller particles into the pores of the Sephadex will create osmotic pressure differences between the inside and outside of gel beads and further complicate the fractionation mechanism (Well, 1972).

Monahan, DeLuca, and Wershaw (1972) have demonstrated by ultraviolet-visible absorption spectrophotometry and fluorescence spectrophotometry that the degree of aggregation of the sodium humate molecules is also a function of concentration. Their results also show that the different subfractions of the North Carolina sodium humate are chemically different. At very low concentrations, each of the fractions has a distinctive spectrum which is due to an unassociated monomer. At higher concentrations aggregation of the monomers markedly alters the spectra and obscures the spectral differences.

CONCLUSIONS

The fractionation of humic acid salts on Sephadex is probably due to the interaction of at least three different processes; molecular sieving, adsorption, and ion exchange. Since the different grades of Sephadex have different molecular sieving, adsorption, and ion exchange properties, it is not surprising that one grade of Sephadex will fractionate a material that was not fractionated on another grade. Chromatography on Sephadex gels, therefore, provides a convenient means for chemically fractionating and comparing sodium humates from different environments.

The fractionation procedures described here provide a first step in the continuing effort to unravel the complex chemical and physical structure of humic acids. In order to obtain detailed structural information about the components of a complex mixture such as natural humic acid, one must first isolate the components and then subject each one of them to analysis. It is hopeless to attempt to work with the unfractionated mixture.

Additional fractionation procedures must now be devised for the refinement of the separations that have already been obtained. In this way an eventual capability to isolate homogeneous, identifiable components will be reached. Assay procedures will then be necessary to identify and assess the purity of these components.

REFERENCES CITED

Andrews, P., 1970, Estimation of molecular size and molecular weights of biological compounds by gel filtration, *in* David Glick, ed., Methods of biological analysis, v. 18: New York, Interscience, p. 1–53.

Baetz, A. L., and Diehl, Harvey, 1968, Separation on a Sephadex column of a complex mixture of azo dyes used as fluorometric chelating agents: Jour. Chromatography, v. 34, p. 534–536.

Bailly, Jean-Rene, and Margulis, Henri, 1968, Etude de quelques acides humiques sur gel de dextrane: Plant and Soil, v. 29, p. 343–361.

Brook, A. J. W., and Munday, K. C., 1970, The interaction of phenols, anilines and benzoic acids with Sephadex gels: Jour. Chromatography, v. 47, p. 1–8.

Carleton, J. O., 1971, Soil resource inventory for the east half Carson National Forest: U.S. Forest Service in-service report, 220 p. (Available in Santa Fe, N. Mex., office.)

Chao, Li-Pen, and Einstein, E. R., 1969, Estimation of the molecular weight of flexible disordered proteins by exclusion chromatography: Jour. Chromatography, v. 42, p. 485–492.

Demetriou, J. A., Macias R., F. M., McArthur, M. J., and Beattie, J. M., 1968, Gel filtration chromatography of fluorescent phenolic and heterocyclic compounds: Jour. Chromatography, v. 34, p. 342–350.

Determann, Helmut, 1969, Principles of gel chromatography, *in* Giddings, J. C., and Keller, R. A., Advances in chromatography, v. 8: New York, Marcel Dekker, p. 3–45.

Flaig, Wolfgang, 1970, Contribution à la connaissance de la constitution et de la synthèse des acides humiques: Extrait de Science du Sol, no. 2, Supplément au Bulletin de L'Association Francaise pour l'Etude du Sol, p. 39–72.

Gelotte, Bertil, 1960, Studies on gel filtration sorption properties of the bed material Sephadex: Jour. Chromatography, v. 3, p. 330–342.

Janson, Jan-Christer, 1967, Adsorption phenomena on Sephadex: Jour. Chromatography, v. 28, p. 12–20.

Kononova, M. M., 1966, Soil organic matter, its nature, its role in soil formation and in soil fertility: London, Pergamon Press, 544 p.

Kumada, Kyoichi, and Hurst, H. M., 1967, Green humic acid and its possible origin as a fungal metabolite: Nature, v. 214, p. 631–633.

Leighty, R. G., Brewer, D. T., Smith, W. R., Cruz, O. E., Evenson, E. H., Matanzo, F., Taylor, D. S., Craig, R. M., Diamond, W. G., Mathews, E. D., Morgan, M. S., White, H. O., and Hasty, A. H., 1960, Soil survey, Orange County, Florida: U.S. Dept. Agriculture Soil Conservation Service Series 1957, no. 5, 63 p.

Lowe, L. E., and Tsang, W-C., 1970, Distribution of a green humic acid component in forest humus layers of British Columbia: Canadian Jour. Soil Sci., v. 50, p. 456–457.

Malcolm, R. L., 1964, Mobile soil organic matter and its interactions with clay minerals and sesquioxides: North Carolina State Univ. Ph. D. thesis, 148 p.; available on microfilm, Univ. Micro Films, Ann Arbor, Mich.

Miranda, Francois, Rochat, Hervé, and Lissitzky, Serge, 1962, Propriétés échangeuses d'ions du gel de dextrane (Sephadex) application á la mise au point d'une technique de rétention réversible des protéines basiques de faible poids moléculaire: Jour. Chromatography, v. 7, p. 142–154.

Monahan, A. R., DeLuca, A. F., and Wershaw, R. L., 1972, Spectroscopic characterization of humic acid fractions in aqueous media: Am. Chem. Soc. mtg., New York, Aug. 27–Sept. 1, 1972, Proc. (In press)

Reeves, R. L., Kaiser, R. S., and Finley, K. T., 1970, The separation and purification of ionic azo and azomethine dyes by gel permeation chromatography: Jour. Chromatography, v. 47, p. 217–223.

Sato, Osamu, and Kumada, Kyoichi, 1967, The chemical nature of the green fraction of p type humic acid: Soil Sci. and Plant Nutrition, v. 13, p. 121–122.

Schnitzer, M., and Skinner, S. I. M., 1968, Gel filtration of fulvic acid, a soil humic compound, *in* Isotopes and radiation in soil organic-matter studies: Vienna, Internat. Atomic Energy Agency, p. 41–55.

Shapiro, Joseph, 1961, Freezing-out, a safe technique for concentration of dilute solutions: Science, v. 133, p. 2063–2064.

Swift, R. S., and Posner, A. M., 1971, Gel chromatography of humic acid: Jour. Soil Sci., v. 22, p. 237–249.

Well, J. D., 1972, Possible source of error in osmometry with salt-free polyelectrolyte solutions: Nature Physical Science, v. 237, p. 59–60.

Wershaw, R. L., and Burcar, P. J., 1967, Physical-chemical properties of naturally occurring polyelectrolytes—I. Sodium humate: Am. Water Resources Conf., 3d, San Francisco, Calif., Nov. 8–10, 1967, Proc., p. 351–364.

Wershaw, R. L., Burcar, P. J., Sutula, C. L., and Wiginton, B. J., 1967, Sodium humate solution studied with small-angle X-ray scattering: Science, v. 157, no. 3795, p. 1429–1431.

Wershaw, R. L., and Pinckney, D. J., 1971, Association and dissociation of a humic acid fraction as a function of pH, *in* Geological Survey Research 1971: U.S. Geol. Survey Prof. Paper 750-D, p. D216–D218.

—— 1973, Determination of the association and dissociation of humic acid fractions by small angle X-ray scattering: U.S. Geol. Survey Jour. Research (In press).

Wildenhain, Wolfgang, and Henseke, Günter, 1967, Fraktionierung von fulvosäuren an Sephadex und charakterisierung durch farbreaktionen: Zeitschr. Anal. Chemie, v. 229, p. 271–281.

Wildermuth, Robert, Perkins, S. O., Pasco, R. E., and Hubbard, E. H., 1939, Soil survey, Kitsap County, Washington: U.S. Dept. Agriculture, Bureau of Chemistry and Soils Series 1934, no. 12, 41 p.

Woof, J. B., and Pierce, J. S., 1967, Separation of complex mixtures of polyhydroxy phenols on columns of Sephadex: Jour. Chromatography, v. 28, p. 94–103.

Jour. Research U.S. Geol. Survey
Vol. 1, No. 3, May-June 1973, p. 367–370

FLUORITE EQUILIBRIA IN THERMAL SPRINGS OF THE SNAKE RIVER BASIN, IDAHO

By C. E. ROBERSON and ROBERT SCHOEN, Menlo Park, Calif.

Abstract.—Some thermal water sources of the Snake River basin, Idaho, are near saturation with respect to fluorite. That mineral was identified by X-ray diffraction in precipitates induced in three water samples by adding sodium fluoride. The derived solubility product (K_{S0}) for zero ionic strength was close to that calculated from Latimer's thermodynamic data ($10^{-9.77}$). The relative ease of precipitation of fluorite from these water samples indicates that equilibrium with respect to fluorite may occur in some ground-water systems.

A recent study by one of us (Schoen, 1972) of the hydrochemistry at the National Reactor Testing Station (NRTS) included some discussion of thermal waters which have relatively high fluoride-ion (F^-) concentrations (up to 15 mg F^-/l). Calculation of activity products suggested that some of the sources were near equilibrium with respect to fluorite ($CaF_{2\ c}$). Implications relating to geochemistry as well as to possible sampling difficulties led us to examine more closely fluoride equilibria in the water sources in question. To demonstrate experimentally that the solutions were near equilibrium with respect to fluorite, small amounts of sodium fluoride were added to each. This caused calcium fluoride (CaF_2) to precipitate from filtered portions of the source samples. Activity products, before and after precipitation, were compared with data in the literature for the solubility product for fluorite.

Acknowledgments.—We thank our colleagues of the U.S. Geological Survey—J. D. Hem for his very helpful comments and D. W. Brown for doing computer calculations in connection with his review.

EXPERIMENTAL METHODS

Samples 2095–2101 were first analyzed for major and other constituents (table 1) by methods described by Brown,

Table 1.—*Chemical analyses of water samples from thermal sources, Idaho*

[Values are in milligrams per liter, except for values in parentheses]

Sample No.	2095	2096	2097	2098	2099	2100	2101
SiO_2	34	24	33	44	80	97	27
Al	<0.2	<0.2	<0.2	<0.2	<0.2	<0.2	<0.2
Fe	.08	.04	.10	.05	.00	.00	.27
Mn	.05	.01	.22	.02	.02	.00	.00
Ca	90	133	430	150	51	1.0	55
Mg	16	31	81	30	.2	.01	11
Na	28	3.9	1,530	311	541	106	63
K	15	4.4	192	71	20	1.5	22
Li	.05	.02	2.3	.47	1.4	.04	.08
NH_4	.26	.32	5.2	.00	.24	.13	.80
Alkalinity (as HCO_3^-)	171	165	1,080	736	48	159	367
SO_4	184	314	756	144	56	28	25
Cl	7.7	1.0	2,360	361	869	25	13
F	5.6	1.6	4.8	1.1	7.7	15	1.6
NO_3	.0	.4	2.6	1.4	1.5	.0	.2
PO_4	.02	.03	.06	.06	.01	.07	.02
B	.09	.00	4.6	.95	.20	.20	.26
Specific conductance (mhos×10^{-6}, 25°C)	(687)	(839)	(9,190)	(2,410)	(3,020)	(479)	(652)
pH	(7.84)	(7.52)	(6.67)	(7.56)	(7.94)	(9.14)	(7.68)
Dissolved solids (calculated)	470	595	5,950	1,480	1,650	358	401
Temperature (°C)	(48.2)	(42.2)	(47.8)	(48.9)	(95.6)	(59.4)	(50.0)

Sample localities in Idaho

2095, Lidy Hot Springs, Clark County.
2096, Green Canyon Hot Springs, Madison County.
2097, Heise Hot Springs, Jefferson County.
2098, Lava Hot Springs, Bannock County.
2099, Frazier boiling well, Cassia County.
2100, Banbury Hot Springs, Twin Falls County.
2101, Condie Hot Springs, Blaine County.

Skougstad, and Fishman (1970). Fluoride concentrations in table 1 were determined by both a colorimetric method and a specific-ion electrode method. The latter method employed a pH 8 buffer rather than that described by Brown, Skougstad, and Fishman (1970). Results by both methods were in close agreement. Then portions of samples 2095, 2097, 2099, and 2100 were filtered through membranes having 0.1-μm porosity. To 100.0-ml portions of the filtrate, 1.00 ml 0.100 *M* NaF was added, increasing the total fluoride content in each by 1.9 mg F^- (or by 19 mg/l).

The solutions were stored at room temperature. Fluoride activities were measured at 10 days and again at 30 days; at the latter time visible precipitates were noted. Also at 30 days analytical concentrations for Ca^{2+} and F^- were determined. Calcium activities were measured by an Orion 92-20 electrode, and fluoride activities by an Orion 94-09 electrode.[1] Measurements were made at 25°±0.1°C.

The precipitates were identified as fluorite by X-ray diffraction.

RESULTS AND DISCUSSION

To test the sample sources for saturation with respect to fluorite, the data of table 1 were used to calculate activity products (table 2) for the reaction $CaF_{2\,c} = Ca^{2+} + 2F^-$. The values for ionic strength, log $[Ca^{2+}]$, log $[F^-]$, and log $[Ca^{2+}][F^-]^2$ expressed in table 2 were calculated from total analytical (complexed and uncomplexed) concentrations, using a computer program (Kharaka and others, written commun., 1973) which calculates thermodynamic activities of individual aqueous ions and their complexes. These calculations are performed by first calculating approximate ionic strength from total analytical concentrations. Then approximate activities for all aqueous species are obtained from the resultant temperature-corrected Debye-Hückel activity coefficients, complex-ion dissociation constants, and total analytical concentrations. The ionic strength is then recalculated and the calculations are repeated until no significant changes (±0.5 percent) in ion activities occur with successive iteration cycles.

[1] The use of brand names in this report does not imply endorsement by the U.S. Geological Survey. Equivalent equipment can be used for the processes.

The principal ligands which involved from 10 to 27 percent of the calcium in the different samples were $SO_4{}^{2-}$ and $HCO_3{}^-$, whereas the predominant fluoride complex involving only 0.1 to 6 percent of the fluoride was MgF^+.

Equilibrium constants representing in-place temperatures were estimated from the relation,

$$\int_{T_1}^{T_2} d\ln K = \int_{T_1}^{T_2} \frac{\Delta H^\circ{}_R\, dT}{RT_2} \text{(Klotz, 1964, p. 159)}.$$

Integration and rearrangement provides

$$\log K_{T_2} = \frac{\Delta H^\circ{}_R/RT_1 - \Delta H^\circ{}_R/RT_2}{2.303} + \log K_{T_1}$$

where T_1 is taken as 25°C (298°K). The equilibrium constant K_{T_1} (later called K_{S0}) is taken as $10^{-9.77}$ (discussed in next section). The heat of reaction $\Delta H^\circ{}_R$ is calculated from heats of formation values (Latimer, 1952) for the species in the fluorite solubility reaction.

The effect of pressure on the equilibrium constant or the activity product was not considered.

Comparison of activity products $[Ca^{2+}][F^-]^2$ with K_{S0} (table 2) suggests that three water samples (2095, 2097, and 2099) are only slightly undersaturated with respect to fluorite at temperatures measured when the samples were collected. Upon cooling, the samples would be even closer to saturation ($-\log K_{S0}$ at 25°C = 9.77).

To four of the samples (2095, 2097, 2099 and 2100), sodium fluoride was added (1.9 mg F^-/100-ml sample) to supersaturate the solutions with respect to fluorite and to observe whether precipitation would be readily induced in this way. Actually, for sample 2100, the amount of fluoride added was not sufficient to cause precipitation that could be observed visually or analytically ($-\log [Ca^{2+}][F^-]^2 = 10.3$). The other samples, after adding sodium fluoride, were supersaturated with respect to fluorite by nearly an order of magnitude. Precipitates were visible in these samples (2095, 2097, and 2099) within 30 days. Activities of fluoride $[F^-]$ were measured before, 10 days after, and 30 days after adding sodium fluoride (table 3).

Table 2.–*Calculations to test equilibrium with respect to fluorite*

Sample No.	Temperature (°C)	Ionic strength	Calcium mg/l	Calcium Log $[Ca^{2+}]$	Fluoride mg/l	Fluoride Log $[F^-]$	Log K_{S0} at sample temperature	Log $[Ca^{2+}][F^-]^2$
2095	48.2	0.0100	90	-2.921	5.6	-3.593	-9.60	-10.11
2096	42.2	.0135	133	-2.783	1.6	-4.153	-9.64	-11.09
2097	47.8	.1090	430	-2.521	4.8	-3.772	-9.60	-10.07
2098	48.9	.0283	150	-2.824	1.1	-4.335	-9.59	-11.49
2099	95.6	.0279	51	-3.230	7.7	-3.472	-9.32	-10.18
2100	59.4	.0053	1.0	-4.892	15	-3.139	-9.53	-11.17
2101	50.0	.0083	55	-3.114	1.6	-4.130	-9.59	-11.37

Table 3.—*Data from measurements made on solutions to which 1.9 mg F^- (as sodium fluoride) was added to 100-ml sample (25°C, 1 atm)*

Sample No.	–Log $[F^-]$[a]		–Log $[Ca^{2+}]$[b]	–Log $[Ca^{2+}][F^-]^2$ [c] (–log K_{SO}=9.77)
	10 days	30 days	30 days	
2095	3.23	3.26	3.24	9.76
2097	3.25	3.30	3.01	9.61
2099	3.25	3.28	3.33	9.89
2100	2.80	2.78	4.89[d]	10.21

[a]Measured by Orion 94-09 electrode.
[b]Measured by Orion 92-20 electrode.
[c]Calculated from –log $[Ca^{2+}]$ and –log $[F^-]$, both after 30-day aging.
[d]Electrode measurement, not shown, was in error. This value (same as in table 2) is used because analytical measurement showed that the calcium concentration had not changed.

The fact that $[F^-]$ measured at 10 days after adding sodium fluoride was nearly the same as that observed after 30 days suggests that a precipitate may have been present at 10 days, but it could not be detected visually; therefore, no attempt was made to examine it. After 30 days the precipitates were removed by filtration through 1-inch-diameter filter membranes having a porosity of 0.1 μm. The membranes were cemented to glass slides with rubber cement and examined by X-ray diffraction. Diffraction patterns indicated well-crystallized material having the three strongest lines for $CaF_{2\ c}$ (3.16 A, 1.93 A, and 1.65 A). The lines were present in the diffractograms for samples 2095, 2097, and 2099. Sample 2100 was not examined, because of the lack of evidence that precipitation had taken place (no visible precipitate, and no change in Ca^{2+} concentration or in F^- activity).

SOLUBILITY OF FLUORITE

The activity products, log $[Ca^{2+}][F^-]^2$, for the three solutions from which synthetic fluorite precipitated were -9.76, -9.61, and -9.89 (table 3). These are close to the thermodynamic activity product constant log K_{SO} = -9.77 calculated from Latimer's (1952) free energy data. More negative values, generally around $10^{-10.4}$, for this constant are quoted by Sillén and Martell (1964, p. 258), and data in the more recent literature seem to indicate that the solubility product for fluorite is not well known. It is possible a somewhat more negative value would have been reached in our solutions after longer aging. The results do show, however, that precipitation of fluorite can occur readily at 25°C from moderately supersaturated solutions.

IMPLICATIONS

That certain thermal water sources in the Snake River basin are near saturation with respect to fluorite appears reasonably assured. This despite the fact that pressure and temperature effects and thermodynamic data are not known well enough to place rigorous boundaries for fluorite precipitation in the ground-water environment.

As a good first approximation, for a water source having a calcium activity of 400 mg/l, a fluoride activity of 2.5 mg/l is permitted before saturation with respect to $CaF_{2\ c}$ is attained (log K_{SO} = -9.77, 25°C). The degree of supersaturation required to cause the onset of precipitation of $CaF_{2\ c}$ is not known to us, but it would probably be influenced by nucleating surfaces in the ground-water environment. That is, mineral surfaces would probably lower the activation energy for the precipitation reaction. Therefore, because precipitation of $CaF_{2\ c}$ did occur in filtered solutions whose fluoride concentrations were increased by factors of only 4, 5, and 3 in samples 2095, 2097, and 2099, respectively, it appears quite likely that fluorite could precipitate at least as readily under conditions in the ground-water aquifer. In that ground-water environment, plenty of nucleating sites are obviously available, and lower degrees of supersaturation are probably required; lower perhaps than those of the spiked solutions (table 3) before precipitation. It would be of interest to look for fluorite in the mineral assemblages related to certain thermal water samples.

The probable source of fluoride in thermal waters of the Snake River basin is the dissolution of volcanic glass in extensive siliceous volcanic rocks as well as hydrolysis of fluorapatite from the Phosphoria Formation (Schoen, 1972). Mixing of water from different lithologic assemblages could occur as water moves toward a thermal spring orifice and possibly supersaturation with respect to $CaF_{2\ c}$ could result in the mixture. If other conditions were favorable, precipitation could occur at the mixing point or beyond it in the flow path, especially if the temperature of the water decreased significantly. For example, at 1 atmosphere pressure and neglecting ionic strength effects, a solution which is saturated at 100°C (K_{SO} = $10^{-9.29}$) would be supersaturated by a factor of 3 if the solution were cooled to 25°C. This is a somewhat lower degree of supersaturation than that of our solutions, in which sodium fluoride addition had induced precipitation of fluorite. However, a factor of 3 may be sufficient to induce precipitation, particularly in the natural environment.

The calcium and fluoride specific-ion electrodes provide a means of studying chemical equilibrium under field conditions and can be substantial aids toward improving our understanding of natural systems.

REFERENCES CITED

Brown, Eugene, Skougstad, M. W., and Fishman, M. J., 1970, Methods for collection and analysis of water samples for dissolved minerals and gases: U.S. Geol. Survey Techniques Water-Resources Inv., Book 5, Chap. A-1, 160 p.

Klotz, I. M., 1964, Chemical thermodynamics: New York, W. A. Benjamin, Inc., 468 p.

Latimer, W. M., 1952, Oxidation potentials: Englewood Cliffs, N.J., Prentice-Hall, 392 p.

Schoen, Robert, 1972, Hydrochemical study of the National Reactor Testing Station, Idaho: Internat. Geol. Cong., 24th, Montreal 1972, Hydrogeology, sec. 11, p. 306–314.

Sillén, L. G., and Martell, A. E., 1964, Stability constants of metal-ion complexes: Chemical Soc. [London] Spec. Pub. 17, 754 p.

Jour. Research U.S. Geol. Survey
Vol. 1, No. 3, May-June 1973, p. 371–376

EVALUATING THE RELIABILITY OF SPECIFIC-YIELD DETERMINATIONS

By RONALD L. HANSON, Tucson, Ariz.

Abstract.—The specific yield of the alluvial aquifer in the Gila River flood plain in southeastern Arizona has been determined using two methods of analysis—the time-drawdown method and the soil-moisture-content method. Time-drawdown data measured at 17 observation wells during a 3.5-day aquifer test define an average apparent specific yield of 0.13. Soil-moisture-content data measured at nine access holes during the aquifer test indicate that complete gravity drainage had not been attained in the cone of depression by the end of the drawdown period. The moisture-content data were therefore extrapolated with time to define an average specific yield in the range 0.13 to 0.15. The results obtained by the two methods are in close agreement. However, the significantly lower standard deviation of the results from the moisture-content analysis indicates that extrapolation of the apparent values derived by this method may provide a more reliable estimate of the true specific yield than the apparent values derived by the time-drawdown method. Reliable estimates of specific yield in the zone of seasonal water-level fluctuations are also possible from an evaluation of the soil-moisture change in the spring and summer recession period.

Specific yield (S_y) is the ratio of the volume of water a saturated material will yield by gravity to the volume of the material (Meinzer, 1923, p. 28). This definition generally is restricted to unconfined aquifers and implies complete gravity drainage from the zone of water-level decline (Lohman and others, 1972). Specific yield may be used to evaluate the amount of water stored in an unconfined aquifer or to predict water-level changes in the aquifer owing to recharge or discharge.

The most common method used to determine the specific yield of an unconfined aquifer is the analysis of the time-drawdown data collected while pumping water from the aquifer. In recent years a method has been developed for evaluating S_y by measuring the change in soil-moisture content with a neutron moisture probe during times of pumping or seasonal water-level change. Both of these methods define the storage capacity of the aquifer as a result of gravity drainage from the zone of water-level change. Incomplete gravity drainage from the zone will define an apparent specific yield, which is smaller than the true specific yield; therefore, the magnitude of apparent specific yield is time dependent and approaches the true value asymptotically depending on the duration of pumping or water-level change.

This paper compares the specific-yield values determined by the time-drawdown and soil-moisture-content methods, evaluates their variability, and illustrates the effect that duration of drainage has on the values. The paper includes an evaluation of specific yield derived from the depletion of the soil-moisture content that occurs in the spring and summer water-level recession period.

Meyer (1962) found close agreement between the S_y derived from time-drawdown data and S_y derived from moisture-content data for an unconfined aquifer having a water level about 20 feet below the land surface. Meyer derived his S_y values from time-drawdown data collected at five observation wells during a 6.3-day aquifer test and from moisture-content data collected at one access hole during the first 1.03 days of the test. Jones and Schneider (1969) studied an unconfined aquifer having a water level 150 feet below the land surface and found that the S_y values derived from moisture-content data were 50 percent more than the S_y values obtained from time-drawdown data. Jones and Schneider based their S_y values on time-drawdown data collected at 13 observation wells and on moisture-content data collected at one access hole during an 11-day aquifer test.

The time-drawdown and soil-moisture-content data used for this study were obtained at a test site in the flood-plain alluvium in the Gila River valley in south-central Arizona. The test site is near the upstream end of a 15-mile reach of the Gila River flood plain in the Gila River Phreatophyte Project area (Culler and others, 1970). The alluvium at the test site is composed of a 55-foot layer of lenticular gravel, sand, and silt, which overlies the much less permeable basin-fill deposits (Weist, 1971). The depth to water in the alluvium ranges from 10 to 15 feet below the land surface.

Instrumentation at the test site is on the right bank of the Gila River about 800 feet from the channel. Well C1 (fig. 1), the pumped well, is 6 inches in diameter, screened, and penetrates the entire thickness of the aquifer. The 17 observation wells are unscreened and open ended, partly penetrate the aquifer, and are within 400 feet of the pumped well. The 10 soil-moisture access holes are cased with 2-inch-diameter aluminum tubing, extend several feet below the water level, and are adjacent to observation wells (fig. 1).

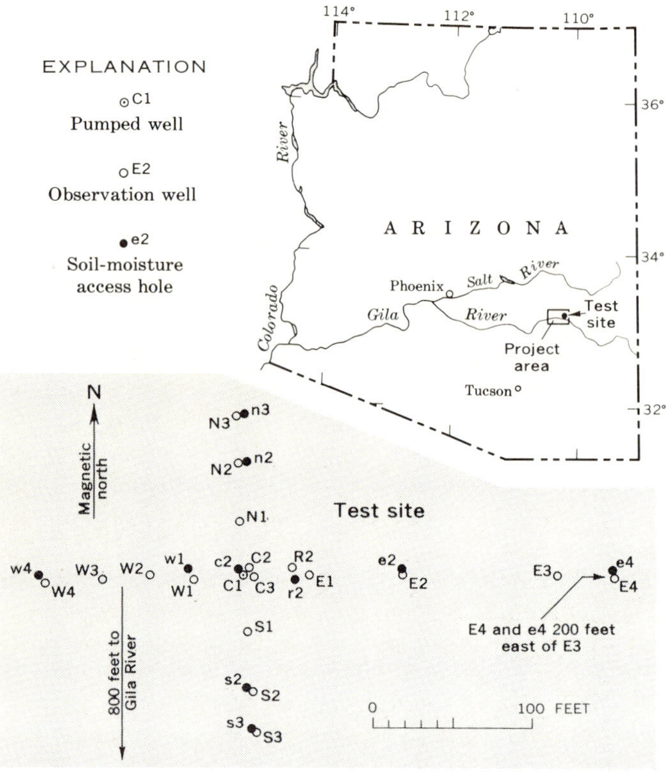

Figure 1.—Map showing the location and type of wells in the test site. The index map of Arizona shows the general location of the test site in the Gila River Phreatophyte Project area.

DETERMINATION OF SPECIFIC YIELD FROM TIME-DRAWDOWN DATA

Estimates of the transmissivity and specific yield of the alluvium were made using data obtained during the aquifer test conducted from April 16 to 20, 1964. Well C1 was pumped at a constant rate of 0.34 $ft^3 sec^{-1}$ or 152 gal min^{-1} for 3.5 days; a longer aquifer test was scheduled, but a leak in the gasline ended the test prematurely. Water levels were measured in the 17 observation wells at regular intervals during the 3.5-day aquifer test and the subsequent 3.6-day recovery period.

A correction for dewatering was applied to the water-level data by subtracting $s^2/2b$ from all measured drawdowns, where s is the drawdown and b is the saturated thickness of the alluvium (Jacob, 1963). The corrected data were then used to prepare time-drawdown plots for each observation well on logarithmic paper. Estimates of transmissivity (T), the instantaneous specific yield (S), and the delayed specific yield (S') were obtained for each observation well by matching the time-drawdown plots to type curves developed by Boulton (1963, fig. 1, p. 472). The early time-drawdown data define S, which represents that water released instantaneously from storage as a result of elastic compaction of the aquifer and expansion of water in response to a reduction in hydrostatic pressure. The later-drawdown data define S', which represents delayed gravity drainage from the interstices above the cone of depression. Table 1 lists the values of T, S, and S' for each well. The average transmissivity for the 17 observation wells is 86,900 gal $day^{-1} ft^{-1}$ with a standard deviation of 18 percent. The average combined specific yield ($S + S'$) for the total period of pumping is 0.13 with a standard deviation of ±0.12 (±92 percent).

Table 1.—*Distance from pumped well to observation wells,* r; *transmissivity,* T; *time from start of pumping to negligible delayed gravity drainage,* t_0; *instantaneous specific yield,* S; *and delayed specific yield,* S'

Well No.	r (feet)	T (gal $day^{-1} ft^{-1}$)	t_0 (hours)	S	S'
C2	6	51,200	21.5	0.002	0.285
C3	7	102,500	3.7	.005	.326
E1	41	91,700	5.0	0	.020
E2	100	87,100	7.2	.016	.078
E3	200	79,200	15.8	.034	.112
E4	400	87,100	23.9	.025	.081
N1	34	96,800	8.5	.002	.053
N2	70	116,000	3.8	.001	.025
N3	100	82,900	12.1	.010	.089
R2	31	79,200	5.2	.018	.186
S1	37	87,100	7.4	.002	.076
S2	74	79,200	.4	.016	.134
S3	99	87,100	4.3	.010	.082
W1	30	67,100	9.1	.033	.387
W2	60	116,100	.7	.005	.048
W3	90	87,100	1.5	0	.004
W4	125	79,200	16.3	.018	.073
Average		86,900	8.6	0.012	0.121
Standard deviation.		±15,800	±7.0	±.011	±.111

Included in table 1 is the time after the start of pumping, t_0, when the effect of delayed gravity drainage ceases to influence drawdown. The values of t_0 were determined from a graph defined by Boulton (1963, fig. 3, p. 477) which relates a given type curve to αt_0 where α is the reciprocal of a delay index. The t_0 values in table 1 suggest that delayed gravity drainage became negligible at all wells within 24 hours after pumping started.

The equations which describe the type curves used in this analysis assume that the aquifer is unconfined, homogeneous, isotropic, and of infinite areal extent with the same saturated thickness throughout. These equations also assume that flow to the pumped well is precisely radial. Because these assumptions are only partly satisfied at the test site, the results of this analysis are questionable.

Part of the large variation in the specific-yield values given in table 1 may be attributed to the uncertainty in the graphical interpretation required for the time-drawdown analysis. The specific-yield values obtained from data for wells near the pumped well may be in error owing to the increase in curvature of the equipotential lines near the pumped well. Some of the variation in specific yield probably is real, however, and reflects the lithologic differences within the aquifer.

Weist (1971, table 2, p. D10) and S. G. Brown (in Hanson, 1972, table 3, p. F10) each made independent determinations of T and S_y by applying a modification of the nonequilibrium equation (Ferris and others, 1962, p. 100) to the drawdown data measured late in the test. The average T values obtained by Weist and Brown are 79,400 and 73,600 gal day^{-1} ft^{-1}, respectively; and the average S_y values are 0.12 and 0.16, respectively. These values do not differ appreciably from the average transmissivity and combined specific-yield values in table 1; however, the analyses of Weist and Brown indicate that delayed gravity drainage was not complete at all observation wells when pumping ceased.

DETERMINATION OF SPECIFIC YIELD FROM SOIL-MOISTURE-CONTENT DATA

Estimates of specific yield may be obtained from measurements of the change in soil-moisture content as the result of water-level rises or declines. The estimates are computed from the ratio $\Delta c/\Delta h$, where Δc is the change in soil-moisture content, in feet, resulting from a water-level change, and Δh is the water-level change, in feet (Stallman, 1967, p. 183).

Two typical soil-moisture profiles and the corresponding water levels are shown in figure 2; the soil-moisture content and water levels in the profiles were measured in access hole r2 in April and September 1964.

The profiles show the change in soil-moisture content (Δc) in the water-level zone, which extends from about 2 feet above the top of the upper water level to about 1 foot below the lower water level. The part of the zone that is above the water level is considered to be representative of the capillary fringe. The soil-moisture content above the water-level zone is assumed to be unaffected by changes in water level and is not included in the computation of S_y. The difference in the profiles below the lower water level is due to measurement error. In order to obtain reliable estimates of specific yield from the $\Delta c/\Delta h$ ratio, gravity drainage from the capillary fringe must be virtually complete before and after the water-level change.

Soil-moisture measurements were made in 10 access holes at regular intervals during the pumping and recovery periods of the aquifer test; the measurements were made using one of four neutron probes at ¼-foot intervals. Readings were taken at each ¼-foot interval for a duration of 1 minute to minimize the randomness of the count of slow neutrons returning to the probe. Two of the probes have radium-beryllium sources of 5 mCi, one has a radium-beryllium source of 4 mCi, and one has an actinium-beryllium source of 20 mCi. Prior to the aquifer test, each probe was calibrated in barrels containing sand, gravel, and flood-plain alluvium of known moisture content, which was determined from volumetric samples.

Graphs showing the relation between soil-moisture content in the water-level zone and the depth to water in the adjacent observation well were made for each access hole. An example of this relation is shown in figure 3 for access hole r2. The solid line shows the average water level and soil-moisture

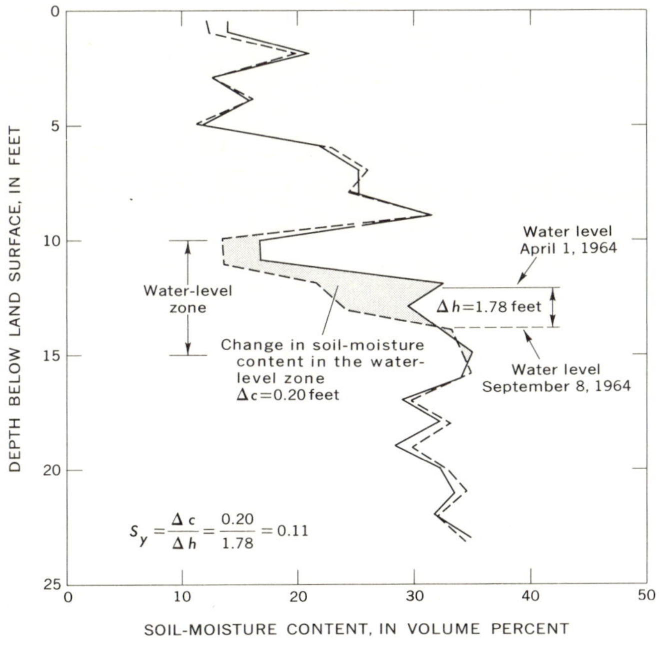

Figure 2.—Profiles showing water-level declines and depletion of soil-moisture content in the water-level zone in access hole r2.

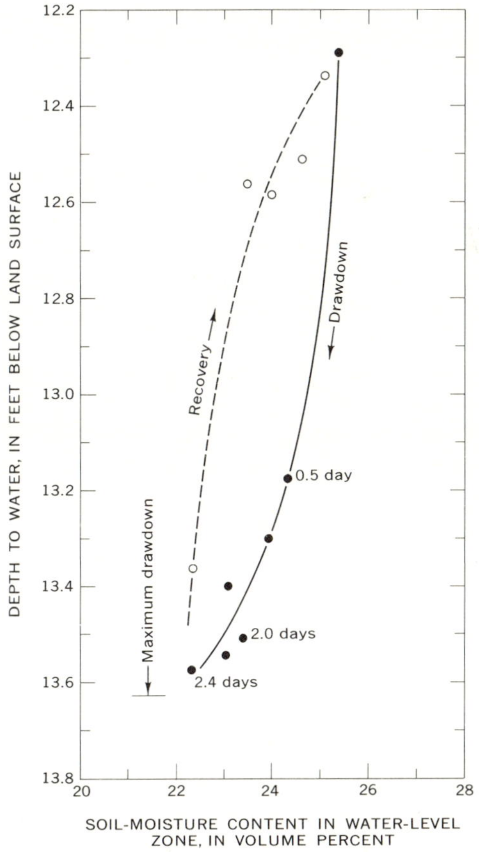

Figure 3.—Graph showing the relation between water-level change and soil-moisture content at access hole r2 during the pumping and recovery periods.

content measured during the 3.5-day pumping period, and the dashed line shows the average water level and soil-moisture content measured during the 3.6-day recovery period. The number of days since pumping started is shown at selected points on the drawdown curve. The hysteresis of soil moisture shows that there is less moisture in the water-level zone during the recovery period than during the drawdown period. The scatter of points along the drawdown and recovery curves is about ±0.5 percent by volume, which indicates an average error of measurement of ±2 percent in the soil-moisture content. This error is attributed to inconsistent depth settings of the probe, misreading of the scaler, water-level changes during the measurement, inaccurate water-level readings, and instrument variability. Although the probes were calibrated prior to the test, calibration inaccuracies also may have contributed to the error because different probes were used in the same access hole.

The extent to which gravity drainage from the water-level zone was complete at the end of the pumping period is unknown, but the data points indicate that about 90 percent of the drawdown and about 75 percent of the soil-moisture depletion occurred during the first 2 days of the pumping test (fig. 3). Similar trends were noted during the recovery period; however, the water level and the soil-moisture content had not reached full recovery 3.6 days after pumping was stopped.

The apparent specific yield at different times after pumping began was computed for each access hole using the ratio of the change in soil-moisture content to the change in water level. Figure 4 shows the relation between apparent specific yield and duration of pumping at the 10 access holes with a line of best fit drawn through the data points in each plot. Little weight was given to those points occurring within the first 12 hours of pumping because of the relatively rapid rate of change in water level during this period. Although the data points for some of the holes suggest a curvilinear rather than a linear relation (for example, hole n2), scatter of the data points does not justify this refinement. The lines through the data points for access holes s2 and c2 indicate virtually no change in apparent S_y during the last 3 days and 2 days of the test, respectively. The estimates of apparent S_y for access hole e4, which is the most distant hole from the pumped well, are not considered reliable because of the very small changes in water level and soil-moisture content measured during the test, and, therefore, the data for this hole are not included in the analysis. The data for the other seven access holes indicate an increase in apparent specific yield with the duration of pumping. Table 2 gives the drawdown and corresponding apparent specific-yield values for the access holes at the end of the 3.5-day aquifer test.

The data from most of the access holes indicate that delayed gravity drainage from the zone of water-level change was not complete at the end of the aquifer test (fig. 4). These results are contrary to the results shown by the t_0 values in table 1 which indicate no significant delayed yield after the first 24 hours of pumping. The reliability of the t_0 values is

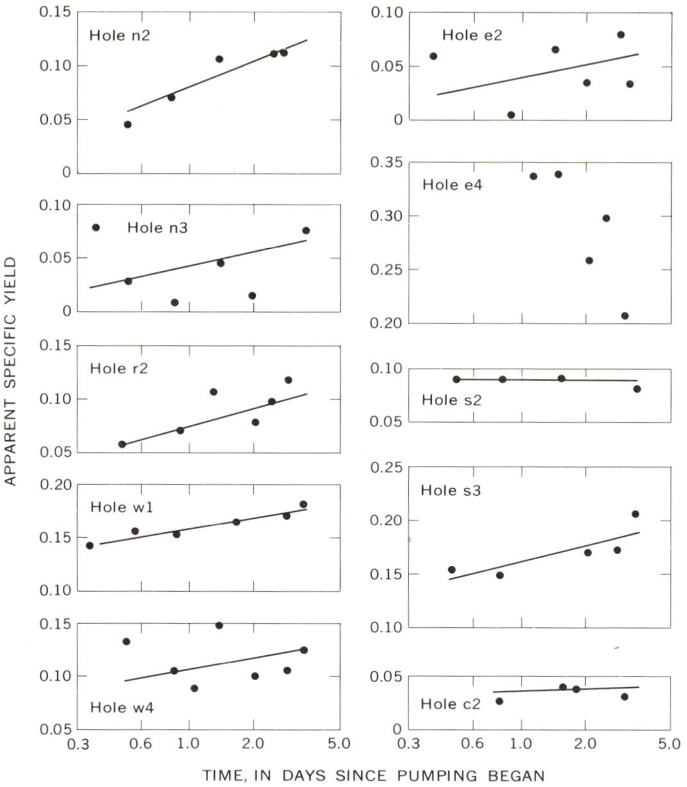

Figure 4.—Graphs showing the relation between apparent specific yield and duration of pumping at 10 soil-moisture access holes.

questionable, however, because of their large deviation (±81 percent) and the many constraints associated with their determination. The average apparent specific yield of 0.11 in table 2 is therefore assumed to represent only partial drainage and is considered to be a minimum value. Distance from the pumped well and the amount of drawdown that occurred in the access holes during the aquifer test do not appear to have significant effects on the apparent specific yield. The standard deviation of ±0.05 (±45 percent) probably reflects soil-moisture content and water-level measurement errors but may

Table 2.—*Drawdown and corresponding apparent specific-yield values computed from the change in soil-moisture content measured at the access holes during the aquifer test*

Access hole No.	Depth of water-level zone (feet)	Distance from pumped well (feet)	Drawdown (feet)	Apparent specific yield
n2	6.75–11.75	71	1.13	0.12
n3	7.25–12.25	101	.92	.07
c2	11.00–17.00	5	2.93	.04
r2	10.00–15.00	32	1.33	.11
e2	10.00–14.00	100	.99	.06
e4	9.50–12.50	400	.39	....
s2	9.75–14.75	72	1.03	.09
s3	9.50–14.50	98	.98	.19
w1	11.75–15.75	34	1.34	.18
w4	10.75–15.75	127	.92	.13
Average				.11
Standard deviation				±.05

include real variations in the extent of delayed gravity drainage at the end of the aquifer test owing to lithologic differences in the aquifer.

In an analysis of the rate of drainage from a column of saturated medium-grained Fresno sand, Prill and others (1965) showed that 90 percent of the moisture in the column was removed after 25 hours of drainage and that sufficient depletion for practical estimates of S_y was attained after 4 days of drainage; they concluded, however, that complete gravity drainage would require several months. Jones and Schneider (1969) showed that 90 percent of the specific yield in the fine sand, caliche, and clay of the Ogallala Formation occurred in the first 6 days of an 11-day aquifer test. The flood-plain alluvium in the Gila River valley is stratified and poorly sorted, and its permeability is probably less than that for the Fresno sand but may be similar to that for the Ogallala Formation. The drainage time for the flood-plain alluvium may, therefore, approximate that for the Ogallala Formation.

The degree to which gravity drainage from the zone of water-level change was complete at the end of the aquifer test is not apparent in figure 4. However, if gravity drainage is assumed to be 90 percent complete after 6 days of pumping, a straight-line extrapolation of the data gives an average apparent specific yield of 0.12 at the end of the 6 days; extrapolation to 10 days increases this value to 0.13, and extrapolation of the data to 30 days increases this value to 0.15. The true specific yield representing complete gravity drainage is highly conjectural, but the small rate of change in the extrapolated values indicates that a specific yield within the range of 0.13 to 0.15 may be more representative than the apparent value of 0.11. Any value within this range also compares favorably with the average S_y of 0.13 derived from the time-drawdown analysis. The significantly lower standard deviation of the average S_y obtained from the moisture-content analysis suggests that the extrapolated apparent values derived by this method define a more reliable estimate of the true S_y than the apparent values derived by the time-drawdown method.

Figure 5 shows the apparent specific-yield values for data from access hole r2 computed from the change in soil-moisture content during the seasonal 160-day water-level recession period from April 1, 1964, to September 8, 1964. The soil-moisture content in the capillary fringe was assumed to be stable at the beginning and end of the recession period because the water level was nearly static for 24 days before April 1 and for 15 days before September 8. These data define an apparent specific yield of 0.13 at the end of the seasonal recession period. Because the data points in figure 5 indicate little change in apparent specific yield during the last 40 days of the recession period, the data were not extrapolated, and the value of 0.13 is considered to represent complete gravity drainage from the water-level zone. Good agreement exists between this value and the apparent S_y of 0.11 for access hole r2 (table 2) derived from the moisture-content data obtained during the aquifer test; even closer agreement could be obtained if the

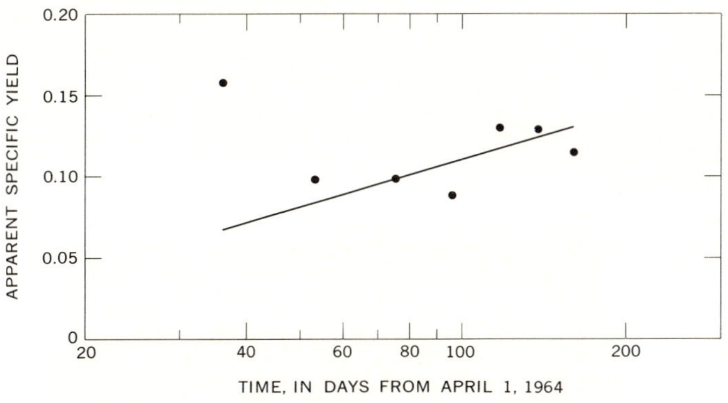

Figure 5.—Graph showing the relation between apparent specific yield and duration of the seasonal recession period at access hole r2.

apparent values for hole r2 in figure 4 are extrapolated to account for delayed gravity drainage. The water-level declines for both the 3.5-day aquifer test and the seasonal 160-day recession period were of about the same magnitude (1.3 and 1.8 feet, respectively) and both declines occurred between 12 and 14 feet below the land surface.

Determinations of S_y from a seasonal change in soil-moisture content may give erroneous results if plant activity or subsurface temperature fluctuations cause a redistribution of moisture in the unsaturated zone during the season. The effects of plant activity are not a factor in this analysis as no vegetation exists within several hundred feet of the test site. The effects of subsurface temperature fluctuations on the seasonal determination of S_y at hole r2 are unknown, but are probably negligible as indicated in figure 2 by the agreement in the April and September moisture profiles above the water-level zone.

CONCLUSIONS

Estimates of specific yield obtained from a typical short-term aquifer test are generally low because complete gravity drainage in the zone of water-level change is seldom achieved during the test. A more reliable estimate of the true specific yield may be obtained by graphical extrapolation of the relation of apparent specific yield versus time. Extrapolation of apparent specific-yield values determined from changes in soil-moisture content at nine access holes during a 3.5-day aquifer test suggests that the average apparent specific yield of 0.11 should be increased to a value between 0.13 and 0.15.

The specific-yield values determined from the time-drawdown analysis are not considered reliable because of the large standard deviation of the values and the subjectivity associated with the method of analysis. The substantially smaller deviation of the apparent specific-yield values obtained from the moisture-content analysis suggests that this method may provide a more reliable estimate of the true specific yield when the apparent values are extrapolated to account for delayed gravity drainage.

A specific yield in the range 0.13 to 0.15 is considered representative of the storage capacity at depths ranging from about 10 to 15 feet below the land surface and may be applied when estimating water-level changes caused by pumping from this depth zone.

Estimates of specific yield in the zone of natural seasonal water-level fluctuations are possible from an evaluation of the soil-moisture change in the spring and summer recession period. In order to obtain reliable estimates, however, the moisture content in the water-level zone must be stable at the beginning and at the end of the recession period, and the redistribution of moisture in the zone due to subsurface temperature fluctuations and plant activity must be minimal during the period.

REFERENCES CITED

Boulton, N. S., 1963, Analysis of data from non-equilibrium pumping tests allowing for delayed yield from storage: Inst. Civil Engineers Proc. v. 26, p. 469–482.

Culler, R. C., and others, 1970, Objectives, methods, and environment—Gila River Phreatophyte Project, Graham County, Arizona: U.S. Geol. Survey Prof. Paper 655-A, 25 p.

Ferris, J. G., Knowles, D. B., Brown, R. H., and Stallman, R. W., 1962, Theory of aquifer tests: U.S. Geol. Survey Water-Supply Paper 1536-E, p. 69–174.

Hanson, R. L., 1972, Subsurface hydraulics in the area of the Gila River Phreatophyte Project, Graham County, Arizona: U.S. Geol. Survey Prof. Paper 655-F, 27 p.

Jacob, C. E., 1963, Determining the permeability of water-table aquifers, *in* Bentall, Ray, compiler, Methods of determining permeability, transmissibility, and drawdown: U.S. Geol. Survey Water-Supply Paper 1536-I, p. 243–341.

Jones, O. R., and Schneider, A. D., 1969, Determining specific yield of the Ogallala aquifer by the neutron method: Water Resources Research, v. 5, no. 6, p. 1267–1272.

Lohman, S. W., and others, 1972, Definitions of selected ground-water terms—Revisions and conceptual refinements: U.S. Geol. Survey Water-Supply Paper 1988, 21 p.

Meinzer, O. E., 1923, Outline of ground-water hydrology, with definitions: U.S. Geol. Survey Water-Supply Paper 494, 71 p.

Meyer, W. R., 1962, Use of a neutron moisture probe to determine the storage coefficient of an unconfined aquifer: Art. 235 *in* U.S. Geol. Survey Prof. Paper 450-E, p. E174–E176.

Prill, R. C., Johnson, A. I., and Morris, D. A., 1965, Specific yield—Laboratory experiments showing the effect of time on column drainage: U.S. Geol. Survey Water-Supply Paper 1662-B, 55 p.

Stallman, R. W., 1967, Flow in the zone of aeration, *in* Chow, Van Te, ed., Advances in hydroscience: New York, Academic Press, v. 4, 428 p.

Weist, W. G., Jr., 1971, Geology and the ground-water system in the Gila River Phreatophyte Project area, Graham County, Arizona: U.S. Geol. Survey Prof. Paper 655-D, 22 p.

RECENT PUBLICATIONS OF THE U.S. GEOLOGICAL SURVEY

(Books may be ordered from the Superintendent of Documents, Government Printing Office, Washington, D.C., 20402, to whom remittances should be sent by check or money order. Give title, series No., stock No. (shown in parentheses in this list), and catalog No. [shown in brackets])

Professional Papers

420-C. Geology and oil resources of the western Puente Hills area, southern California, by R. F. Yerkes. 1972 (1973). p. C1–C63; plates in pocket. $3.10. (2401-2100) [I 19:16:420-C]

585-C. Ground-water hydrology of prairie potholes in North Dakota, by C. E. Sloan. 1972 (1973). p. C1–C28; plate in pocket. 70c. (2401-2157) [I 19:16:585-C]

645. Stratigraphy and ammonite fauna of the Graneros Shale and Greenhorn Limestone near Pueblo, Colo., by W. A. Cobban and G. R. Scott. 1972 (1973). 108 p.; 39 plates showing fossils; plates in pocket. $4.25. (2401-00257) [I 19:16:645]

655-G. Channel changes of the Gila River in Safford Valley, Ariz., 1846–1970, by D. E. Burkham. 1972 (1973). p. G1–G24; plates in pocket. $2. (2401-2065) [I 19:16:655-G]

726-C. Gravity and magnetic features as related to geology in the Leadville 30-minute quadrangle, Colorado, by Ogden Tweto and J. E. Case. 1972 (1973). p. C1–C31; plates in pocket. $1.75. (2401-2145) [I 19:16:726-C]

734-B. Sedimentary petrology and paleocurrents of the Harebell Formation, Pinyon Conglomerate, and associated coarse clastic deposits, northwestern Wyoming, by D. A. Lindsey. 1972 (1973). p. B1–B68. $1.50. (2401-00249) [I 19:16:734-B]

747. Pennsylvanian carbonates, paleoecology, and rugose colonial corals, north flank, eastern Brooks Range, arctic Alaska, by A. K. Armstrong. 1972 (1973). 21 p.; 8 plates showing fossils. $1. (2401-2150) [I 19:16:747]

771. Chemical composition of sedimentary rocks in Alaska, Idaho, Oregon, and Washington, compiled by T. P. Hill and M. A. Werner. 1972 (1973). 319 p. $4.50. (2401-00254) [I 19:16:771]

787. The Borrego Mountain earthquake of April 9, 1968. 1972 (1973). 207 p.; plates in pocket. $6.25. (2401-00218) [I 19:16:787]

790. Stratigraphy, morphology, and paleoecology of a fossil peccary herd from western Kentucky, by W. I. Finch, F. C. Whitmore, Jr., and J. D. Sims. 1972 (1973). 25 p. 70c. (2401-00248) [I 19:16:790]

800-A. Geological Survey Research 1972, Chapter A. 1972 (1973). p. A1–A320. $3.45. (2401-00278) [I 19:16:800-A]

817. Summary petroleum and selected mineral statistics for 120 countries, including offshore areas, by J. P. Albers, M. D. Carter, A. L. Clark, A. B. Coury, and S. P. Schweinfurth. 1973. 149 p. $2.10. (2401-00279) [I 19:16:817]

Bulletins

1314-G. Cadmium in plants, by H. T. Shacklette. 1972 (1973). p. G1–G28. 40c. (2401-00251) [I 19:3:1314-G]

1331-D. Stratigraphy of the Glenns Ferry Formation from Hammett to Hagerman, Idaho, by H. E. Malde. 1972 (1973). p. D1–D19; plates in pocket. $1.25. (2401-02206) [I 19:3:1331-D]

1348. Placer gold deposits of New Mexico, by M. G. Johnson. 1972 (1973). 46 p.; plate in pocket. $1.25. (2401-2162) [I 19:3:1348]

1356. Placer gold deposits of Nevada, by M. G. Johnson. 1973. 118 p.; plate in pocket. $2. (2401-02211) [I 19:3:1356]

1359. Geology and mineral resources of the northern part of the North Cascades National Park, Wash., by M. H. Staatz, R. W. Tabor, P. L. Weis, J. F. Robertson, R. M. Van Noy, and E. C. Pattee. 1972 (1973). 132 p.; plates in pocket. $2. (2401-2135) [I 19:3:1359]

1362. Neogene marine mollusks of the Pacific coast of North America: An annotated bibliography, 1797–1969, by W. O. Addicott. 1973. 201 p. $1.50. (2401-2164) [I 19:3:1362]

1372-C. Strodes Creek Member (Upper Ordovician)—A new map unit in the Lexington Limestone of north-central Kentucky, by D. F. B. Black and N. P. Cuppels. 1973. p. C1–C16. 30c. (2401-00290) [I 19:3:1372-C]

1372-F. The upper Paleozoic Madera Group in the Manzano Mountains, N. Mex., by D. A. Myers. 1973. p. F1–F13. 25c. (2401-00287) [I 19:3:1372-F]

Water-Supply Papers

1757-M. Significance of ground-water chemistry in performance of North Sahara tube wells in Algeria and Tunisia, by F. E. Clarke and B. F. Jones. 1972 (1973). p. M1–M39. 55c. (2401-00256) [I 19:13:1757-M]

1940. Effects of coal mining on the water resources of the Tradewater River basin, Kentucky, by H. F. Grubb and P. D. Ryder. 1972 (1973). 83 p.; plates in pocket. $2.10. (2401-2158) [I 19:13:1940]

1970-B. Summary of floods in the United States during 1968, by J. O. Rostvedt and others. 1972 (1973). p. B1–B73. 60c. (Includes title page and contents for volume, Floods of 1968 in the United States.) (2401-2171) [I 19:13:1970-B]

2099. Quality of surface waters of the United States, 1968—Part 11, Pacific slope basins in California. 1972 (1973). 359 p. $2.75. (2401-00268) [I 19:13:2099]

2119. Surface water supply of the United States, 1966-70—Part 6, Missouri River basin—Volume 4, Missouri River basin below Nebraska City, Nebr. 1972 (1973). 901 p. $5.75. (2401-00267) [I 19:13:2119]

U.S. GOVERNMENT
PRINTING OFFICE
PUBLIC DOCUMENTS DEPARTMENT
WASHINGTON, D.C. 20402

OFFICIAL BUSINESS
PENALTY FOR PRIVATE USE $300

POSTAGE AND FEES PAID
U.S. GOVERNMENT
PRINTING OFFICE
375

U.S.MAIL

JRGS HARTWOOOH R 1
HARTWICK CLG LIB
ONEONTA NY 13820

JOURNAL OF RESEARCH OF THE U.S. GEOLOGICAL SURVEY

JULY–AUGUST 1973
VOLUME 1, NUMBER 4

Scientific notes and summaries of investigations in geology, hydrology, and related fields

U.S. DEPARTMENT OF THE INTERIOR

UNITED STATES DEPARTMENT OF THE INTERIOR

ROGERS C. B. MORTON, Secretary

GEOLOGICAL SURVEY

V. E. McKelvey, Director

For sale by the Superintendent of Documents, U.S. Government Printing Office, Washington, D.C., 20402. Order by SD Catalog No. JRGS. Annual subscription rate, effective July 1, 1973, $15.50 (plus $3.75 for foreign mailing). Single copy $2.75. Make checks or money orders payable to the Superintendent of Documents.

Send all subscription inquiries and address changes to the Superintendent of Documents at the above address.

Purchase orders should not be sent to the U.S. Geological Survey library.

Library of Congress Card No. 72-600241

The Journal of Research consists of six issues a year (January-February, March-April, May-June, July-August, September-October, November-December) published in Washington, D.C., by the U.S. Geological Survey. It contains papers by members of the Geological Survey on geologic, hydrologic, topographic, and other scientific and technical subjects.

The Journal supersedes the short-papers chapters (B, C, and D) of the former Geological Survey Research ("Annual Review") series of professional papers. The synopsis chapter (A) of the former Geological Survey Research series will be published as a separate professional paper each year.

Correspondence and inquiries concerning the Journal (other than subscription inquiries and address changes) should be directed to the Managing Editor, Journal of Research, Publications Division, U.S. Geological Survey, Washington, D.C. 20244.

Papers for the Journal should be submitted through regular Division publication channels.

The Secretary of the Interior has determined that the publication of this periodical is necessary in the transaction of the public business required by law of this Department. Use of funds for printing this periodical has been approved by the Director of the Office of Management and Budget through February 11, 1975.

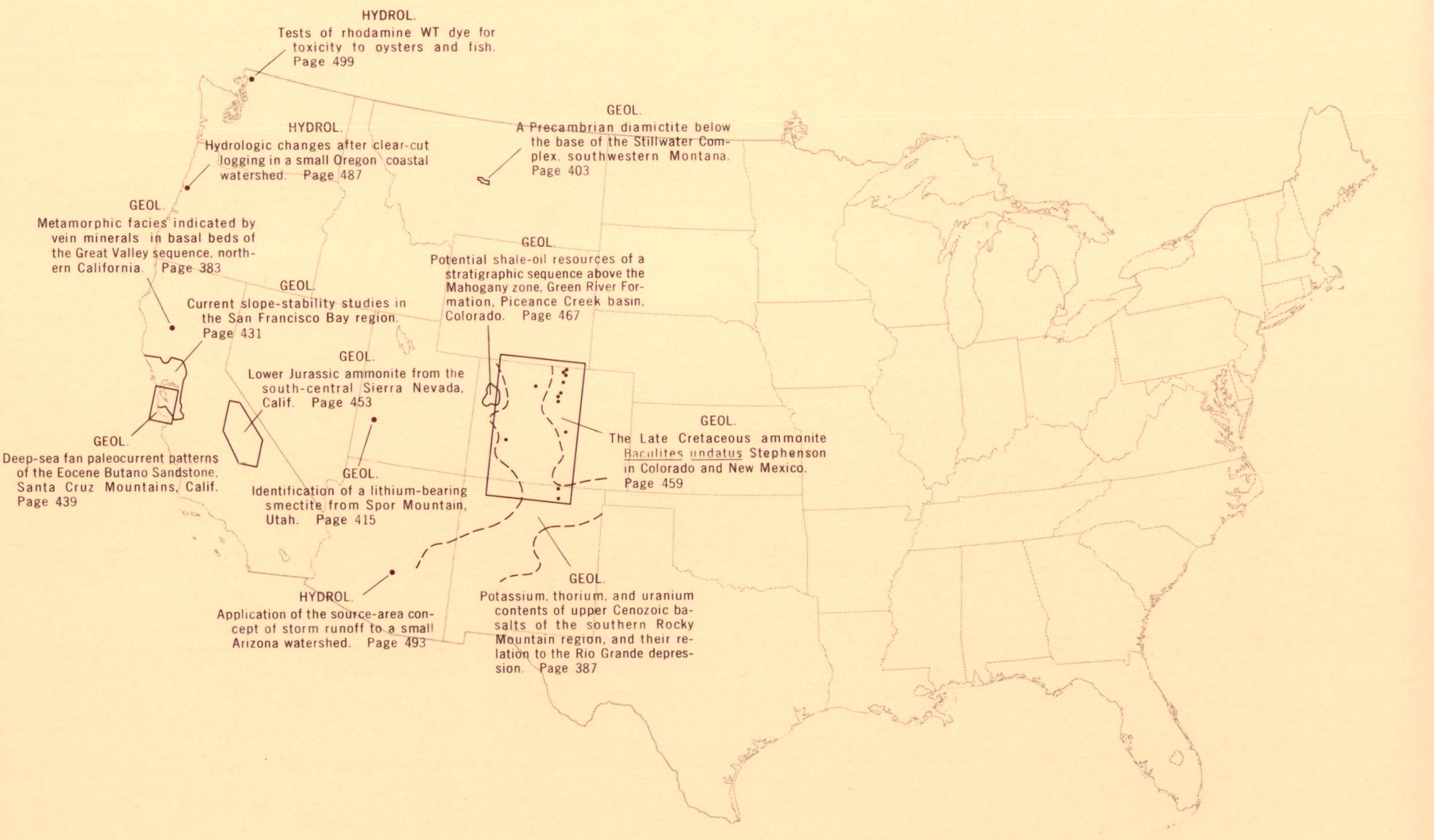

GEOGRAPHIC INDEX TO ARTICLES

[See Contents for articles concerning areas outside the United States and articles without geographic orientation]

JOURNAL OF RESEARCH

of the

U.S. Geological Survey

Vol. 1 No. 4 July-Aug. 1973

CONTENTS

Abbreviations and symbols II

GEOLOGIC STUDIES

Boron-bearing potassium feldspar of authigenic origin in closed-basin deposits.. *R. A. Sheppard and A. J. Gude 3d* 377

Metamorphic facies indicated by vein minerals in basal beds of the Great Valley sequence, northern California .... *E. H. Bailey and D. L. Jones* 383

Potassium, thorium, and uranium contents of upper Cenozoic basalts of the southern Rocky Mountain region, and their relation to the Rio Grande depression .... *P. W. Lipman, C. M. Bunker, and C. A. Bush* 387

A Precambrian diamictite below the base of the Stillwater Complex, southwestern Montana .... *N. J Page and R. A. Koski* 403

Identification of a lithium-bearing smectite from Spor Mountain, Utah ...... *H. C. Starkey and Wayne Mountjoy* 415

Stream-profile analysis and stream-gradient index .... *J. T. Hack* 421

Current slope-stability studies in the San Francisco Bay region .... *T. H. Nilsen and E. E. Brabb* 431

Deep-sea fan paleocurrent patterns of the Eocene Butano Sandstone, Santa Cruz Mountains, California .... *T. H. Nilsen and T. R. Simoni, Jr.* 439

Lower Jurassic ammonite from the south-central Sierra Nevada, California.......... *D. L. Jones and J. G. Moore* 453

The Late Cretaceous ammonite ***Baculites undatus*** Stephenson in Colorado and New Mexico .... *W. A. Cobban* 459

Potential shale-oil resources of a stratigraphic sequence above the Mahogany zone, Green River Formation, Piceance Creek basin, Colorado .... *J. K. Pitman and J. R. Donnell* 467

Spectrochemical computer analysis—Instrumentation.......... *A. W. Helz* 475

Solubility of cryolite at 25°C and 1 atmosphere pressure .... *C. E. Roberson and J. D. Hem* 483

HYDROLOGIC STUDIES

Hydrologic changes after clear-cut logging in a small Oregon coastal watershed .... *D. D. Harris* 487

Application of the source-area concept of storm runoff to a small Arizona watershed .... *F. E. Arteaga and S. E. Rantz* 493

Tests of rhodamine WT dye for toxicity to oysters and fish .... *G. G. Parker, Jr.* 499

Recent publications of the U.S. Geological Survey .... Inside of back cover

ABBREVIATIONS

[Singular and plural forms for abbreviations of units of measure are the same]

A .... angstrom units
A^3 .... cubic angstroms
a-c .... alternating current
amp .... amperes
atm .... atmospheres
bbl .... barrels
B.C. .... Before Christ
B.P. .... Before Present
b.y. .... billion years
c .... crystalline state
C_x .... molal concentration (of substance x)
cal .... calories
cfs .... cubic feet per second
Ci .... Curies
cm .... centimeters
cm^2 .... square centimeters
cm^3 .... cubic centimeters
cpm .... counts per minute
cu ft .... cubic feet
cu mi .... cubic miles
d-c .... direct current
emu .... electromagnetic units
eV .... electron volts
ft .... feet
ft^3 .... cubic feet
g .... grams
gal .... gallons
gpd .... gallons per day
gpm .... gallons per minute
hr .... hours
in. .... inches
kb .... kilobars
kg .... kilograms
km .... kilometers
km^2 .... square kilometers
km^3 .... cubic kilometers
kV .... kilovolts
l .... liters
lb .... pounds
m .... meters
m .... molal (concentration)
m^2 .... square meters
m^3 .... cubic meters
M .... molar (concentration)
me .... milliequivalents
MeV .... million electron volts
mg .... milligrams
mgd .... million gallons per day
mi^2 .... square miles
min .... minutes
ml .... milliliters
mm .... millimeters
mol .... moles
mr .... milliroentgens
mV .... millivolts
m.y. .... million years
μ .... microns
μm .... micrometers
μmho .... micromhos
n .... neutrons
N .... normal
ng .... nanograms
nm .... nanometers
Oe .... oersteds
pCi .... picocuries
pH .... pH (measure of hydrogen ion activity)
ppb .... parts per billion
ppm .... parts per million
rad .... radiometric
rpm .... revolutions per minute
sec .... seconds
sq ft .... square feet
sq mi .... square miles
yr .... years
v .... volts
wt .... weight

Jour. Research U.S. Geol. Survey
Vol. 1, No. 4, July—Aug. 1973, p. 377—382

BORON-BEARING POTASSIUM FELDSPAR OF AUTHIGENIC ORIGIN IN CLOSED-BASIN DEPOSITS

By RICHARD A. SHEPPARD and ARTHUR J. GUDE 3d,
Denver, Colo.

Abstract.—Silicic vitric tuffs in saline, alkaline lacustrine deposits are commonly altered to a variety of zeolites and potassium feldspar. The tuffs generally show a lateral gradation, in a basinward direction, of fresh glass to zeolites and then to potassium feldspar. Zeolites were formed early in diagenesis by reaction of the glass with the interstitial water. The feldspar, however, was formed later by reaction of the zeolites with interstitial water, and its formation can be correlated with water of relatively high salinity and alkalinity. Semiquantitative spectrographic analyses for boron in the zeolites and potassium feldspar show that most of the boron resides in the relatively late feldspar. The boron content of the zeolites is commonly less than 100 ppm, whereas the boron content of the potassium feldspar is commonly greater than 1,000 ppm. Boron apparently substitutes for aluminum in the feldspar structure and causes distortion of the monoclinic unit cell such that the *b* and *c* dimensions are shortened. These boron-bearing potassium feldspars having anomalous cell parameters seem unique to saline, alkaline lacustrine deposits and could serve as a prospecting aid for locating buried saline minerals.

Authigenic silicate minerals in silicic vitric tuffs of closed-basin deposits show a consistent distribution pattern (Hay, 1966). In a general way, there is a lateral gradation, basinward, of fresh glass to zeolites and then to potassium feldspar. The authigenic silicate minerals in the tuffs of Pleistocene Lake Tecopa, Inyo County, Calif. (Sheppard and Gude, 1968), are characteristic of this distribution pattern. Fresh glass occurs along the margin and at the inlets of the ancient lake. The glass is succeeded inwardly first by a zone of zeolites and then, in the central part of the lake basin, by potassium feldspar. Zeolites in the Lake Tecopa deposits are chiefly phillipsite, erionite, and clinoptilolite. At Lake Tecopa, the tuffs containing authigenic potassium feldspar also commonly contain searlesite ($NaBSi_2O_6 \cdot H_2O$).

A variation in the distribution pattern of authigenic silicate minerals in tuffs of closed-basin deposits is illustrated by the Pliocene Big Sandy Formation (Sheppard and Gude, 1972). The Big Sandy Formation consists of lacustrine strata that were deposited in the valley of the Big Sandy River near Wikieup, Mohave County, Ariz. A nonanalcimic zeolite facies occurs along the margin of the ancient lacustrine deposit and is succeeded basinward first by the analcime facies and then by the potassium feldspar facies. Zeolites in the nonanalcimic zeolite facies are chiefly chabazite, clinoptilolite, erionite, and phillipsite. A similar distribution pattern of authigenic silicate minerals was recognized in the Miocene Barstow Formation of California (Sheppard and Gude, 1969a) and in the Eocene Green River Formation of Wyoming (Surdam and Parker, 1972).

GENESIS OF THE SILICATE MINERALS

The zeolites and potassium feldspar in the originally silicic vitric tuffs formed during diagenesis; the probable paragenetic sequence is shown schematically in figure 1. The silicic glass

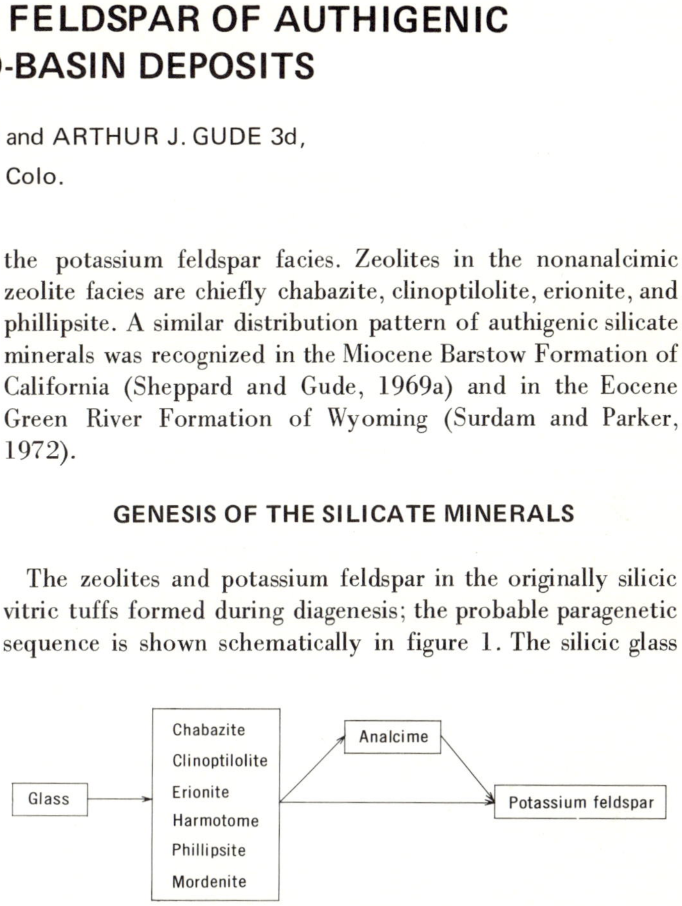

Figure 1.—Schematic representation of the paragenetic sequence that leads to the crystallization of potassium feldspar in tuffs of closed-basin deposits.

reacted with the alkaline and saline interstitial water to form all of the zeolites except analcime. Mariner and Surdam (1970) recently suggested that aluminosilicate gels may be an intermediate stage between the glass and the zeolites. Analcime formed later by the reaction of these relatively early zeolites with the interstitial fluids. The potassium feldspar is the end product of the series of reactions and formed from analcime as well as directly from the other zeolites. The formation of potassium feldspar can be correlated with interstitial water of the highest salinity and pH (Sheppard and Gude, 1969a).

BORON CONTENT OF THE SILICATE MINERALS

While studying the authigenic silicate minerals in tuffs of the Miocene Barstow Formation, Mud Hills, Calif., in 1964, we

Table 1.—*Boron, in parts per million, in authigenic zeolites and potassium feldspars from closed-basin deposits*

[Number of specimens analyzed is given in parentheses]

Deposit	Boron					
	Zeolites			Potassium feldspar		
	Range	Average		Range	Average	
Pleistocene Lake Tecopa, near Shoshone, Inyo County, Calif.	50–200	130	(6)	1,000–2,000	1,700	(3)
Unnamed deposit of Pliocene age, near Rome, Malheur County, Oreg.	0–150	90	(6)	700–1,500	1,050	(4)
Pliocene Big Sandy Formation, near Wikieup, Mohave County, Ariz.	0–150	40	(26)	500–1,500	950	(6)
Miocene Barstow Formation, Mud Hills, San Bernardino County, Calif.	0–150	30	(11)	1,000–5,000	3,400	(9)

discovered that the potassium feldspar contains substantial amounts of boron and is deficient in aluminum (Sheppard and Gude, 1965). The boron substitutes for aluminum in the feldspar structure. Inasmuch as there were insufficient data on the boron contents of zeolites and feldspars, we obtained semiquantitative spectrographic analyses of these minerals from the Barstow Formation and several other closed-basin deposits.

The boron contents of the authigenic zeolites and potassium feldspars from these deposits are shown in table 1. The analyses were performed either on pure separates or on bulk samples of tuff that were monomineralic as determined by X-ray powder diffraction. The average and the range of boron contents are shown for the zeolites and potassium feldspar from each of these closed-basin deposits, which range in age from Pleistocene to Miocene. The boron content of the zeolites is much lower than that of the feldspars. The boron content is commonly less than 100 ppm in the zeolites, whereas it is commonly greater than 1,000 ppm in the feldspar. Although analcime, chabazite, clinoptilolite, erionite, harmotome, mordenite, and phillipsite were analyzed, no consistent difference in the boron content of the different zeolites was found.

DESCRIPTION OF THE POTASSIUM FELDSPAR-RICH TUFFS

The potassium feldspar-rich tuffs are difficult to identify as such in the field because of their fine crystallinity. Commonly, vitroclastic texture in the feldspathic tuffs is poorly preserved in contrast with that of most of the zeolitic tuffs. If the feldspar-rich tuffs are free of opal, quartz, or searlesite, they are generally friable—much more so than their zeolitic counterparts. Tuffs altered chiefly to potassium feldspar are generally white to light gray or locally pastel shades of green or yellow. Nearly monomineralic feldspathic tuffs range in thickness from less than an inch to several feet.

Thin sections of the potassium feldspar-rich tuffs do not reveal much about the character of the feldspar except that it is finely crystalline; most crystals are less than 10 μm in size. We examined feldspathic tuffs from closed-basin deposits that range in age from Quaternary to Eocene and found that all samples have about the same range in crystal size. Optically, the feldspar seems to occur as aggregates of minute anhedral crystals, somewhat resembling chert. Electron microscopy, however, has shown that the feldspar occurs as subhedral to euhedral crystals. The well-developed crystal forms of this authigenic potassium feldspar from three different deposits are shown in figure 2.

Potassium feldspar in the tuffs is most easily identified by X-ray powder diffraction techniques. A typical X-ray diffractometer trace of a bulk sample of monomineralic feldspathic tuff from the Miocene Barstow Formation is shown in figure 3.

CELL DIMENSIONS OF THE FELDSPAR

The boron-bearing authigenic potassium feldspar, first recognized in the Barstow Formation, has a distorted monoclinic unit cell (Sheppard and Gude, 1965). Cell parameters were obtained by a least-squares refinement of X-ray powder diffractometer data of 14 specimens from four deposits by use of the U.S. Geological Survey's FORTRAN IV computer program W9214. The cell parameters and the boron contents of these authigenic potassium feldspars are given in table 2. The cell parameters show the following ranges: a=8.570–8.611 A, b=12.957–12.998 A, c=7.156–7.179 A, β=115°54.7′–116°8.9′, and V=715.0–721.1 A^3.

The b and c dimensions for feldspars from the four closed-basin deposits are plotted in figure 4, the potassic portion of Wright and Stewart's (1968) b-c quadrilateral for alkali feldspars. All these authigenic potassium feldspars plot near the high sanidine corner but well within the quadrilateral. On the basis of the potassic composition of the feldspars as determined by chemical analyses and inferred from the indices of refraction, the feldspars would be expected to plot along the maximum microcline—high sanidine sideline. Inasmuch as the authigenic feldspars are monoclinic, they would be expected to plot at the high sanidine corner. Thus, the feldspars have an anomalous unit cell, and b is shortened by as much as about 0.07 A and c is shortened by as much as about 0.02 A. The a dimension is not plotted in figure 4; however, a is consistent with the potassic composition of the feldspar. Another measure of the distortion of the monoclinic unit cell is shown by the a dimension inferred from the b-c plot. The measured *a* dimension is about 8.57–8.61 A, but the inferred *a* dimension is about 8.32–8.40 A.

Two possible explanations for the distortion are: (1) Inasmuch as the feldspar formed from zeolites, some relict structure may have been inherited from the zeolites, or (2) the substitution of boron for aluminum in the framework may have distorted the feldspar structure. Martin (1971) confirmed the second possibility. On the basis of cation exchange and heating experiments on natural specimens from Lake Tecopa and the Barstow Formation, as well as the synthesis of a series of boron-bearing potassium feldspars, Martin concluded that substitution of relatively small amounts of boron for aluminum in the authigenic feldspar causes appreciable distortion of the unit cell. Eugster and McIver (1959) had previously synthesized a potassium feldspar having boron completely replacing aluminum.

POTENTIAL PROSPECTING GUIDE TO SALINE DEPOSITS

Localities where similar authigenic potassium feldspars have been found in tuffs of lacustrine deposits of the Western United States are shown in figure 5. The deposits range in age from Pleistocene to Eocene, and many contain bedded saline minerals of economic interest such as borax, colemanite, halite, nahcolite, and trona, or molds of saline minerals. A careful search at those deposits where saline minerals have not been reported may also reveal saline minerals or their molds.

With respect to authigenic zeolites and potassium feldspar, boron resides chiefly in the relatively late feldspar. The boron apparently remains in the interstitial fluid in the tuff and eventually enters the feldspar structure, causing distortion of the unit cell. This boron-bearing potassium feldspar seems unique to saline lacustrine deposits. Thus, the recognition of this distinctive authigenic feldspar in lacustrine deposits may be useful as a prospecting guide for the location of buried saline minerals.

Figure 2.—Electron micrographs of authigenic potassium feldspar in tuffs. *A*, Pleistocene Lake Tecopa deposit, California. *B*, Pliocene Big Sandy Formation, Arizona. *C*, Miocene Barstow Formation, California. Electron micrographs by Paul D. Blackmon.

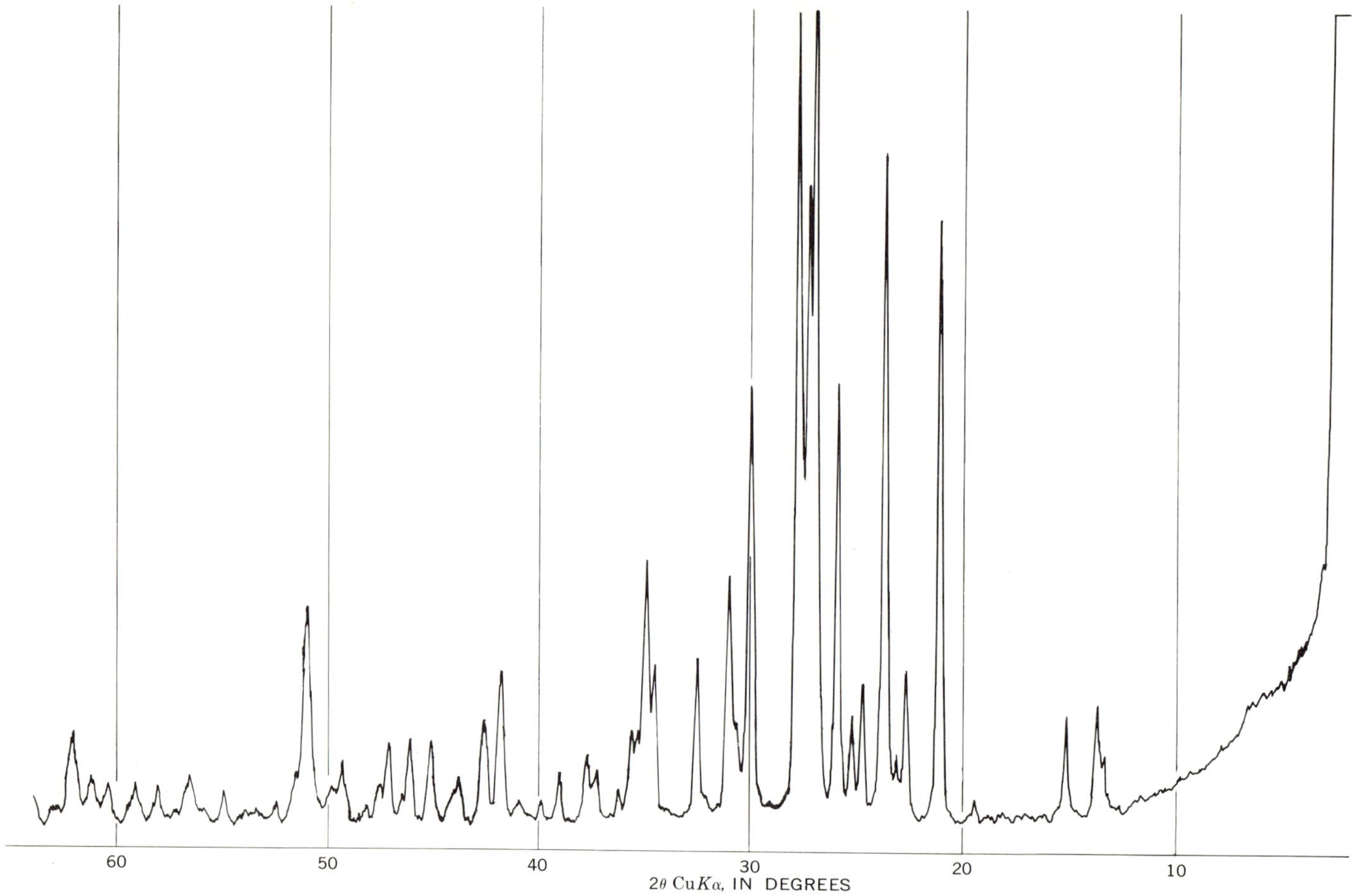

Figure 3.—X-ray diffractometer trace of authigenic potassium feldspar from a tuff in the Barstow Formation of California.

Table 2.—*Unit cell parameters and boron contents of authigenic potassium feldspars from closed-basin deposits*

[Cell parameters were obtained by a least-squares refinement of X-ray diffractometer data, by use of the U.S. Geological Survey's FORTRAN IV computer program W9214. The boron content was determined by semiquantitative spectrographic analysis by L. A. Bradley, W. B. Crandel, J. C. Hamilton, B. W. Lanthorn, Harriet Neiman, and Barbara Tobin]

Deposit	Sample	*a* (A)	*b* (A)	*c* (A)	*β*	*V* (A³)	Boron content (ppm)
Pleistocene Lake Tecopa, near Shoshone, Inyo County, Calif.	1	8.583±0.003	12.969±0.003	7.169±0.002	115°59.9′±2.0′	718.2±0.3	2,000
	2	8.576±0.004	12.990±0.006	7.169±0.002	116°5.3′±2.6′	717.3±0.5	1,000
Unnamed deposit of Pliocene age, near Rome, Malheur County, Oreg.	3	8.604±0.005	12.983±0.004	7.175±0.002	116°6.7′±2.2′	719.8±0.4	1,000
	4	8.601±0.010	12.988±0.010	7.174±0.005	116°2.0′±5.6′	720.1±1.0	1,000
Pliocene Big Sandy Formation, near Wikieup, Mohave County, Ariz.	5	8.589±0.003	12.976±0.003	7.164±0.001	115°59.2′±1.2′	717.7±0.2	1,000
	6	8.583±0.004	12.974±0.003	7.167±0.002	116°0.6′±1.8′	717.2±0.3	1,000
	7	8.578±0.004	12.986±0.004	7.170±0.003	116°3.2′±1.4′	717.6±0.3	500
	8	8.589±0.002	12.984±0.002	7.169±0.002	115°59.3′±1.4′	718.6±0.2	1,500
	9	8.589±0.002	12.982±0.002	7.168±0.002	115°55.7′±1.0′	718.8±0.2	700
	10	8.573±0.003	12.966±0.006	7.167±0.002	116°1.4′±1.1′	715.9±0.3′	1,000
Miocene Barstow Formation, Mud Hills, San Bernardino County, Calif.	11	8.593±0.002	12.967±0.003	7.165±0.001	116°3.3′±1.0′	717.2±0.2	1,500
	12	8.582±0.004	12.962±0.005	7.158±0.002	116°2.3′±2.5′	715.4±0.4	2,000
	13	8.592±0.003	12.976±0.005	7.164±0.003	116°0.4′±1.6′	717.8±0.3	5,000
	14	8.590±0.003	12.986±0.004	7.171±0.003	116°0.9′±1.7′	718.9±0.3	2,000

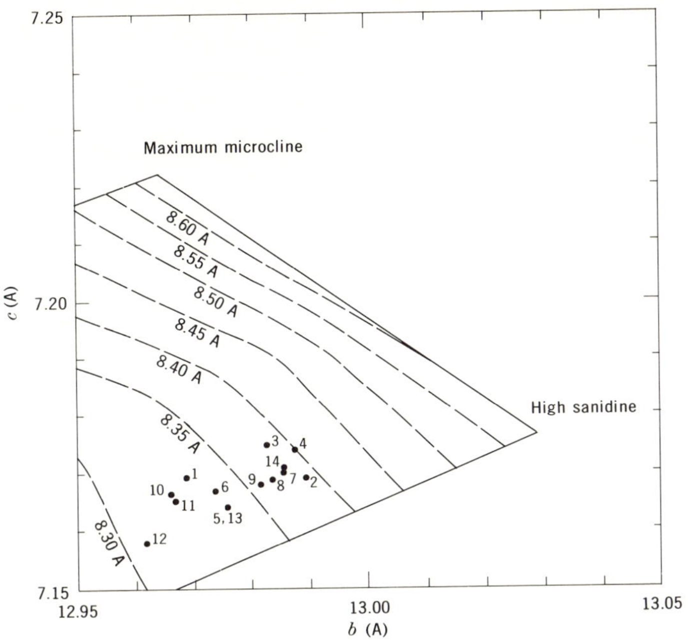

Figure 4.—Potassium-rich portion of Wright and Stewart's (1968) *b-c* quadrilateral for alkali feldspars which has been contoured for *a* (dashed). The *b-c* dimensions are plotted for the 14 specimens given in table 2.

Figure 5.—Map showing occurrences of authigenic potassium feldspar in tuffs of lacustrine deposits. Closed circle, potassium feldspar associated with saline minerals or their molds; open circle, potassium feldspar not associated with saline minerals or their molds. Data for numbered localities are as follows:

1. Unnamed deposit of Pliocene age, near Durkee, Baker County, Oreg. (Sheppard and Gude, unpub. data).

Figure 5—Continued

2. Danforth Formation of Pliocene age, Harney Lake, Harney County, Oreg. (Walker and Swanson, 1968).
3. Unnamed deposit of Pliocene age, near Rome, Malheur County, Oreg. (Sheppard and Gude, 1969b).
4. Unnamed deposit of Pliocene age, Jersey Valley, Pershing County, Nev. (Sheppard and Gude, unpub. data).
5. Horse Camp Formation of Miocene to Pliocene age, near Currant, Nye County, Nev. (Moores, 1968).
6. Unnamed deposit of Pliocene age, Silver Peak Range, Esmeralda County, Nev. (Robinson, 1966).
7. Unnamed deposit of Pleistocene Lake Tecopa, near Shoshone, Inyo County, Calif. (Sheppard and Gude, 1968).
8. Mixed layer of Pleistocene Searles Lake, San Bernardino County, Calif. (Hay and Moiola, 1963; Smith and Haines, 1964).
9. Unnamed deposit of Miocene age, near Kramer, San Bernardino County, Calif. (Hay, 1966).
10. Barstow Formation of Miocene age, Mud Hills, San Bernardino County, Calif. (Sheppard and Gude, 1969a).
11. Big Sandy Formation of Pliocene age, near Wikieup, Mohave County, Ariz. (Sheppard and Gude, 1972).
12. Unnamed deposit of Eocene age, Lysite Mountain, Hot Springs County, Wyo. (Bay, 1969).
13. Wagon Bed Formation of Eocene age, Beaver Rim, Fremont County, Wyo. (Boles, 1968).
14. Green River Formation of Eocene age, near Green River, Sweetwater County, Wyo. (Iijima and Hay, 1968; Surdam and Parker, 1972).
15. Green River Formation of Eocene age, Piceance Creek basin, Rio Blanco County, Colo. (Hite and Dyni, 1967; Brobst and Tucker, 1973).

REFERENCES CITED

Bay, K. W., 1969, Stratigraphy of Eocene sedimentary rocks in the Lysite Mountain area, Hot Springs, Fremont, and Washakie Counties, Wyoming: Wyoming Univ., unpub. Ph. D. thesis, 181 p.

Boles, J. R., 1968, Zeolites and authigenic feldspar along a part of the Beaver Rim, Fremont County, Wyoming: Wyoming Univ., unpub. M.S. thesis, 64 p.

Brobst, D. A., and Tucker, J. D., 1973, X-ray mineralogy of the Parachute Creek Member, Green River Formation, in the northern Piceance Creek basin, Colorado: U.S. Geol. Survey Prof. Paper 803 (In press).

Eugster, H. P., and McIver, N. L., 1959, Boron analogues of alkali feldspars and related silicates [abs.]: Geol. Soc. America Bull., v. 70, no. 12, pt. 2, p. 1598–1599.

Hay, R. L., 1966, Zeolites and zeolitic reactions in sedimentary rocks: Geol. Soc. America Spec. Paper 85, 130 p.

Hay, R. L., and Moiola, R. J., 1963, Authigenic silicate minerals in Searles Lake, California: Sedimentology, v. 2, no. 4, p. 312–332.

Hite, R. J., and Dyni, J. R., 1967, Potential resources of dawsonite and nahcolite in the Piceance Creek basin, northwest Colorado: Colorado School Mines Quart., v. 62, no. 3, p. 25–38.

Iijima, Azuma, and Hay, R. L., 1968, Analcime composition in tuffs of the Green River Formation of Wyoming: Am. Mineralogist, v. 53, nos. 1–2, p. 184–200.

Mariner, R. H., and Surdam, R. C., 1970, Alkalinity and formation of zeolites in saline alkaline lakes: Science, v. 170, no. 3961, p. 977–980.

Martin, R. F., 1971, Disordered authigenic feldspars of the series $KAlSi_3O_8$-$KBSi_3O_8$ from southern California: Am. Mineralogist, v. 56, nos. 1–2, p. 281–291.

Moores, E. M., 1968, Mio-Pliocene sediments, gravity slides, and their tectonic significance, east-central Nevada: Jour. Geology, v. 76, no. 1, p. 88–98.

Robinson, P. T., 1966, Zeolitic diagenesis of Mio-Pliocene rocks of the Silver Peak Range, Esmeralda County, Nevada: Jour. Sed. Petrology, v. 36, no. 4, p. 1007–1015.

Sheppard, R. A., and Gude, A. J., 3d, 1965, Potash feldspar of possible economic value in the Barstow Formation, San Bernardino County, California: U.S. Geol. Survey Circ. 500, 7 p.

—— 1968, Distribution and genesis of authigenic silicate minerals in tuffs of Pleistocene Lake Tecopa, Inyo County, California: U.S. Geol. Survey Prof. Paper 597, 38 p.

—— 1969a, Diagenesis of tuffs in the Barstow Formation, Mud Hills, San Bernardino County, California: U.S. Geol. Survey Prof. Paper 634, 35 p.

—— 1969b, Authigenic fluorite in Pliocene lacustrine rocks near Rome, Malheur County, Oregon, *in* Geological Survey Research 1969: U.S. Geol. Survey Prof. Paper 650-D, p. D69–D74.

—— 1972, Big Sandy Formation near Wikieup, Mohave County, Arizona: U.S. Geol. Survey Bull. 1354-C, 10 p.

Smith, G. I., and Haines, D. V., 1964, Character and distribution of nonclastic minerals in the Searles Lake evaporite deposit, California: U.S. Geol. Survey Bull. 1181-P, 58 p.

Surdam, R. C., and Parker, R. D., 1972, Authigenic aluminosilicate minerals in the tuffaceous rocks of the Green River Formation, Wyoming: Geol. Soc. America Bull., v. 83, no. 3, p. 689–700.

Walker, G. W., and Swanson, D. A., 1968, Summary report on the geology and mineral resources of the Harney Lake and Malheur Lake areas of the Malheur National Wildlife Refuge, north-central Harney County, Oregon: U.S. Geol. Survey Bull. 1260-L, 17 p.

Wright, T. L., and Stewart, D. B., 1968, X-ray and optical study of alkali feldspar—[Pt.] I. Determination of composition and structural state from refined unit-cell parameters and $2V$: Am. Mineralogist, v. 53, nos. 1–2, p. 38–87.

Jour. Research U.S. Geol. Survey
Vol. 1, No. 4, July—Aug. 1973, p. 383—385

METAMORPHIC FACIES INDICATED BY VEIN MINERALS IN BASAL BEDS OF THE GREAT VALLEY SEQUENCE, NORTHERN CALIFORNIA

By EDGAR H. BAILEY and DAVID L. JONES, Menlo Park, Calif.

Abstract.—A reexamination of reported blueschist mineral localities in the basal strata of the Great Valley sequence revealed only prehnite-pumpellyite facies minerals. Franciscan graywacke thrust below the Great Valley rocks contains lawsonite-quartz blueschist assemblages. At a common pressure of about 4 kb, the Franciscan blueschists formed at lower temperatures than the overlying Great Valley prehnite-bearing rocks, lending support to tectonic models that involve rapid subduction of the Franciscan rocks.

The Great Valley sequence in California consists of a conformable section of about 50,000 feet (15,000 m) of marine sedimentary rock of Late Jurassic and Cretaceous age deposited on an ophiolite sequence having basalt, or locally keratophyre, in its upper part, gabbro below, and serpentinized ultramafic rocks at the base (Bailey and others, 1970). Beneath the serpentinite lies the Coast Range thrust, a late Mesozoic subduction zone along which eugeosynclinal Franciscan rocks have been thrust under the Great Valley rocks. The Franciscan rocks beneath the Coast Range thrust are converted to blueschist metamorphic assemblages in which lawsonite, jadeite, glaucophane, and aragonite are key minerals (Blake and others, 1967). In contrast, the Great Valley rocks above the Coast Range thrust typically are altered only to zeolite, or locally prehnite-pumpellyite facies (Bailey and Blake, 1969; Dickinson and others, 1969). The Franciscan blueschists are believed to require temperatures of 150°–300°C and pressure of about 5 kb or more for their formation (Taylor and Coleman, 1968; Ernst and others, 1970), whereas the formation of zeolite (laumontite) or prehnite-pumpellyite facies of the Great Valley rocks are generally believed to be indicative of slightly lower temperatures and significantly less pressure (Crawford and Fyfe, 1965; Fyfe, 1970; Coombs and others, 1970). Thus, the difference in metamorphic facies across the Coast Range thrust, particularly as it has been interpreted to indicate major pressure difference, is striking (Bailey and Blake, 1969; Ernst, 1971a).

In one area, veins containing the key blueschist minerals lawsonite and aragonite have been reported from the basal sedimentary rocks of the Great Valley sequence above the Coast Range thrust (McKee, 1965). As the pressure-temperature significance of the metamorphic mineral assemblages became better known, their occurrence in an environment that had not been subjected to shearing or metamorphic pressures other than those resulting from the load of 50,000 feet (15,000 m) of overlying sediments seemed anomalous. To reevaluate this apparently unique find, we obtained through the generous cooperation of Bates McKee, University of Washington, one of his original thin sections and locality data that permitted us to reexamine these blueschist mineral occurrences.

The chief localities are near the north end of the Sacramento Valley about 5 miles northwest of Paskenta in two canyons at the west edges of secs. 23 and 26, T. 24 N., R. 7 W., Mount Diablo base line (fig. 1). In both canyons graywacke and shale of the Great Valley sequence lie on basaltic breccia and contain mafic and ultramafic clasts. Small discontinuous veins and veinlets are conspicuous in the sedimentary rocks within tens of meters of the contact. Most veins are chiefly quartz, although carbonate veins also are common. Rarer albite and albite-quartz veins traverse the sedimentary strata. Prehnite forms crystals several millimeters long in some quartz-calcite veins, and larger barite crystals occur in coarsely crystalline

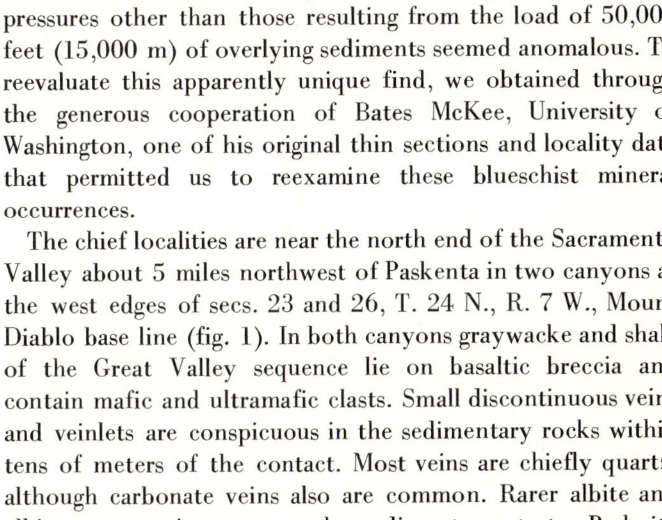

Figure 1.—Sketch map showing location of prehnite-quartz veins.

calcite veins. Both prehnite and barite were confirmed by X-ray, spectroscopic, and optical examination. No lawsonite was found, but as seen in both specimens and thin sections, the blades of prehnite might be easily mistaken for tablets of lawsonite (fig. 2). Some of the carbonate mineral shows a little separation of isogyres in optic axial interference figures, but all specimens we checked by X-ray proved to be calcite, not aragonite. Three miles farther south along Thomes Creek, indurated mudstone near the same contact contains abundant veins of laumontite.

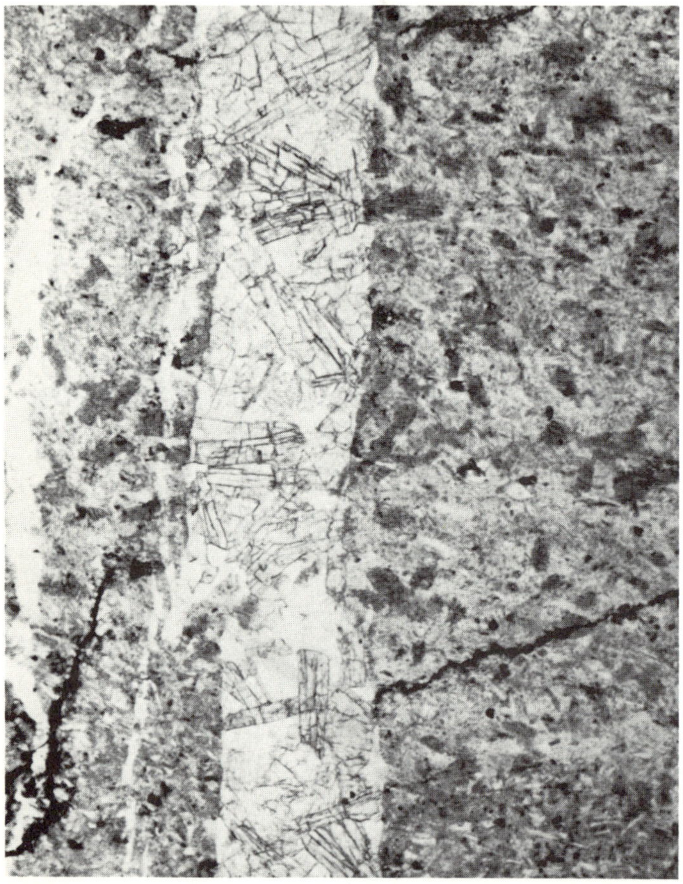

Figure 2.–Prehnite-quartz vein in metagraywacke of the Great Valley sequence. Width of vein is ½ mm.

The mineral assemblages of the veinlets in these sedimentary rocks clearly are representative of conditions under which the Great Valley strata have been altered. Where we found quartz-prehnite veins, the host graywackes also contained prehnite, and where albite veins occur, the feldspar clasts are albitized. We know of no other alleged occurrences of blueschist minerals above the Coast Range thrust in the basal sedimentary rocks of the Great Valley sequence. Until such an occurrence can be documented, the metamorphic facies above the thrust should be regarded as of no higher grade than prehnite-pumpellyite. Veins in the basalts of the ophiolite immediately below the sedimentary rocks of the Great Valley sequence also locally contain quartz, prehnite, pumpellyite, thomsonite, and epidote, but one cannot be certain that they did not form prior to the deposition of the sedimentary strata under different pressure-temperature conditions. Certainly some epidote formed earlier, as it occurs as detrital grains in the lowest beds of the Great Valley sequence.

The Franciscan metagraywackes below these Great Valley sequence localities contain a lawsonite-plus-quartz mineral assemblage (Blake and others, 1967). The experimental work of Liou (1971) on the stability field of prehnite indicates that at 4 kb fluid pressure, prehnite and quartz are stable between 300° and 400°C, and at the same pressure lawsonite plus quartz is stable at temperatures below 300°C. The presence of the lower temperature assemblage in the Franciscan plate below the Coast Range thrust doubtless is the result of rapid subduction of colder Franciscan rocks beneath the warmer Great Valley sequence (fig. 3), and lends support to the tectonic models of Bailey and Blake (1969), Hamilton (1969), and Ernst (1970). However, where jadeite plus quartz occurs directly beneath rock of the prehnite-pumpellyite-bearing Great Valley sequence rocks, a metamorphic pressure discontinuity seems to exist (Ernst, 1971b).

REFERENCES CITED

Bailey, E. H., and Blake, M. C., 1969, Tectonic development of western California during the late Mesozoic: Geotektonika, pt. 3, p. 17–30; pt. 4, p. 24–34.

Bailey, E. H., Blake, M. C., Jr., and Jones, D. L., 1970, On-land Mesozoic oceanic crust in California Coast Ranges, *in* Geological Survey Research 1970: U.S. Geol. Survey Prof. Paper 700-C, p. C70–C81.

Blake, M. C., Jr., Irwin, W. P., and Coleman, R. G., 1967, Upside-down metamorphic zonation, blueschist facies, along a regional thrust in California and Oregon, *in* Geological Survey Research 1967: U.S. Geol. Survey Prof. Paper 575-C, p. C1–C9.

Coombs, D. S., Horodyski, R. J., and Naylor, R. S., 1970, Occurrence of prehnite-pumpellyite facies metamorphism in northern Maine: Am. Jour. Sci., v. 268, p. 142–156.

Crawford, W. A., and Fyfe, W. S., 1965, Lawsonite equilibria: Am. Jour. Sci. v. 263, p. 262–270.

Dickinson, W. R., Ojakangas, R. W., and Stewart, R. J., 1969, Burial metamorphism of the late Mesozoic Great Valley sequence, Cache Creek, California: Geol. Soc. America Bull., v. 80, p. 519–526.

Ernst, W. G., 1970, Tectonic contact between the Franciscan mélange and the Great Valley sequence–crustal expression of late Mesozoic Benioff zone: Jour. Geophys. Research, v. 75, no. 5, p. 886–901.

—— 1971a, Metamorphic zonations on presumably subducted lithospheric plates from Japan, California, and the Alps: Contr. Mineralogy and Petrology, v. 34, p. 43–59.

—— 1971b, Do mineral parageneses reflect unusually high-pressure conditions of Franciscan metamorphism?: Am. Jour. Sci., v. 270, p. 81–108.

Ernst, W. G., Seki, Y., Onuki, H., and Gilbert, M. C., 1970, Comparative study of low-grade metamorphism in the California Coast Ranges and the outer metamorphic belt of Japan: Geol. Soc. America Mem. 124, 276 p.

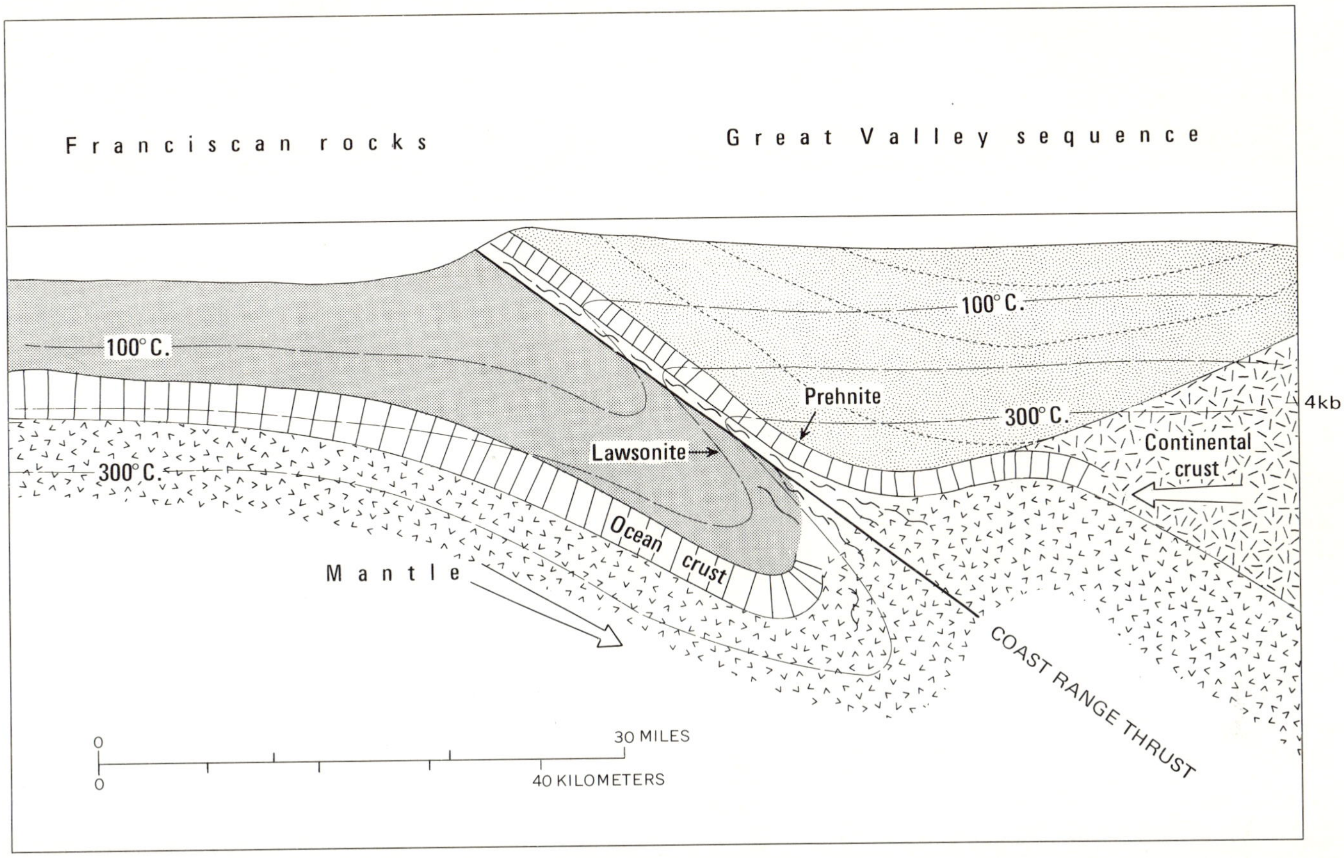

Figure 3.—Schematic section showing the Coast Range thrust subduction zone and Franciscan rocks plunging beneath rocks of the Great Valley sequence. Complex internal deformation of Franciscan rocks is not shown. Rapid underthrusting results in depression of isotherms beneath the subduction zone. At the 4-kb pressure level, prehnite developed in the rocks of the upper plate while lawsonite developed in the colder Franciscan rocks beneath the Coast Range thrust.

Fyfe, W. S., 1970, Phase changes in the earth's crust—the record of crustal geophysics: Sci. Progress, v. 58, p. 47–70.

Hamilton, Warren, 1969, Mesozoic California and the underflow of Pacific Mantle: Geol. Soc. America Bull., v. 80, p. 2409–2430.

Liou, J. G., 1971, Synthesis and stability relations of prehnite, $Ca_2Al_2Si_3O_{10}(OH)_2$: Am. Mineralogist, v. 56, p. 507–531.

McKee, Bates, 1965, Knoxville-Franciscan contact near Paskenta, western Sacramento Valley, California: Geol. Soc. America Spec. Paper 87, p. 215–216.

Taylor, H. P., and Coleman, R. G., 1968, O^{18}/O^{16} ratios of coexisting minerals in glaucophane-bearing metamorphic rocks: Geol. Soc. America Bull., v. 79, p. 1727–1756.

Jour. Research U.S. Geol. Survey
Vol. 1, No. 4, July—Aug. 1973, p. 387—401

POTASSIUM, THORIUM, AND URANIUM CONTENTS OF UPPER CENOZOIC BASALTS OF THE SOUTHERN ROCKY MOUNTAIN REGION, AND THEIR RELATION TO THE RIO GRANDE DEPRESSION

By PETER W. LIPMAN, CARL M. BUNKER,
and CHARLES A. BUSH, Denver, Colo.

Abstract.—Late Cenozoic basaltic volcanism in southern Colorado and northern New Mexico was most intense near the Rio Grande rift depression but extended onto stable platforms to the west (Colorado Plateau) and to the east (High Plains). Tholeiitic rocks are largely confined to the Rio Grande depression, and the basalts become increasingly alkalic with distance from the depression. The K, Th, and U contents and the Th/K and U/K ratios consistently increase away from the depression, and Th/U ratios also tend to increase slightly. Geographically distinct suites of petrographically related basalts that are very similar in major-oxide compositions are readily distinguishable by K, Th, and U contents. Sialic crustal contamination did not contribute significantly to development of these compositional variations, and the lateral change from tholeiitic to alkalic basaltic volcanism may be related to different depths of or degrees of partial melting in the mantle. The compositions and compositional ranges of basalts in the southern Rocky Mountain region are similar to those of many Pacific islands, despite the contrasting geologic settings.

Basaltic volcanism and extensional block faulting have been the dominant volcano-tectonic association in the Western United States over much of late Cenozoic time (Christiansen and Lipman, 1972). In much of this region, extensional faulting occurred across a broad zone, as in the Basin and Range province, but in the southern Rocky Mountains the Rio Grande depression (Bryan, 1938; Kelley, 1952, 1956; Chapin, 1971) forms a well-defined rift valley that separates the stable platforms of the Colorado Plateau and the High Plains in its central part and extends northward at least as far as central Colorado (fig. 1).

In Colorado and northern New Mexico, the San Luis Valley segment of the Rio Grande depression is a complexly faulted graben containing as much as 8 km of sedimentary fill, as indicated by gravity data (Gaca and Karig, 1966). The major bounding fault system is on the east side of the graben against the Sangre de Cristo Mountains, and the west boundary is a dip slope of eastward-tilted volcanic rocks of the San Juan Mountains. From Sante Fe to Socorro, N. Mex., the Albuquerque basin is a similar asymmetrical graben with its axis shifted en echelon to the west. South of Socorro, the Rio Grande depression merges with the Basin and Range province and is a less pronounced structure than to the north.

Previous reconnaissance studies have suggested that upper Cenozoic basaltic rocks in the southern Rocky Mountain region vary in petrology with distance from the Rio Grande depression (Lipman, 1969; Kudo and others, 1971). In general, basalt and basaltic andesite of alkalic affinities are thought to have erupted east and west of the depression concurrently with its formation, whereas tholeiitic basalt flooded parts of the depression late in its history. We here report additional chemical data on 170 samples (see table 2 at end of article), mainly K, Th, and U concentrations determined by gamma-ray spectrometry, that demonstrate more precisely some aspects of these petrologic variations.

ANALYTICAL TECHNIQUES

Samples weighing at least 4—5 kg were collected by sledge hammer, trimmed of all weathered surfaces, and crushed to −30 mesh. So far as possible, porous vesicular parts of flows were avoided in sampling. Samples were sealed in an aluminum container consisting of a double-walled cylinder closed on one end. A 2.5-cm-thick layer of sample is contained between the annuli and within the closed end; this amount of material weighs 3,000—5,000 g, depending on the bulk density of the powdered rock. The sample container is placed on and around a 12.5-cm-diameter by 10-cm-thick sodium iodide crystal. The radiation penetrating the crystal is sorted by the spectrometer system and stored in a 100-channel memory. The spectra were interpreted with the aid of a linear least-squares computer method which matches the spectrum from a sample to a library of radioelement standards and calculates the concentrations of the radioelement in the sample; the computer method is a modification of a program written by Schonfeld (1966). The spectrometer data are calibrated to U and Th

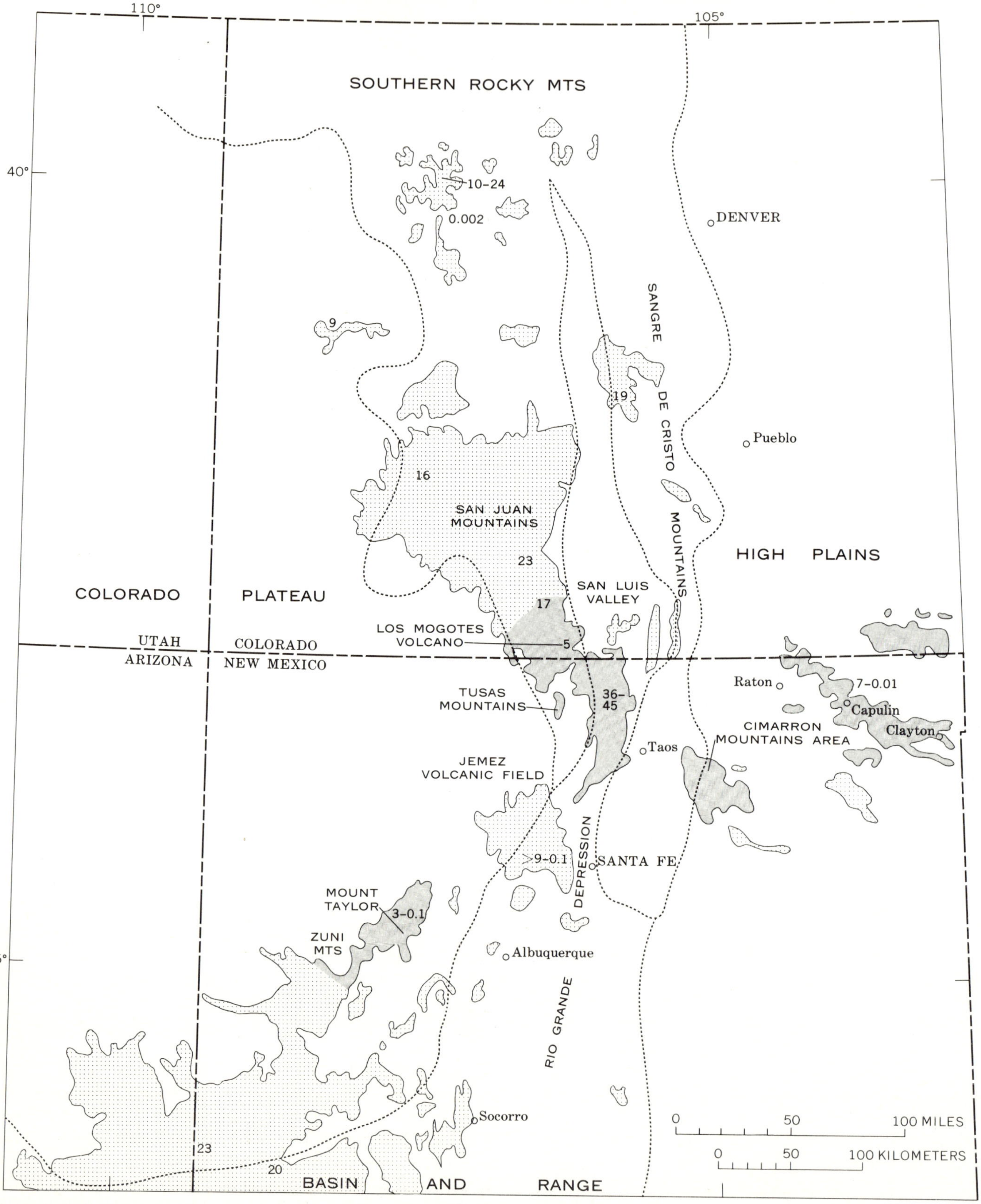

Figure 1.—Index map of the southern Rocky Mountain region, showing general distribution of upper Cenozoic volcanic rocks (coarse pattern; modified from Cohee, 1961), major structural provinces (Kelley, 1952), and areas discussed in this report (fine pattern). Numbers indicate K-Ar ages, in millions of years, of upper Cenozoic basaltic rocks; these are taken from references cited in text.

standards measured by isotope dilution and mass or alpha spectrometry in a group of rocks.

Uranium concentrations are determined indirectly by measuring the radium daughters to obtain radium-equivalent uranium (RaeU) values. Radium-equivalent uranium is the amount of uranium, under the assumption of radioactive equilibrium, required to support the amount of daughter products that emit the radioactivity measured in a sample; disequilibrium in unaltered mafic igneous rocks is unlikely to exceed 5–10 percent. Throughout the report where "U" and "uranium" are used, "radium-equivalent uranium" is implicit. Although thorium is also measured from daughter products, disequilibrium is improbable because of short half-lives, and the concentrations are considered to be a direct measurement of parent thorium. Potassium is determined from its K^{40} constituent which is proportional to total potassium. The coefficients of variation for the accuracy of the data included in this report, when compared to samples analyzed by isotope-dilution techniques, are about 5 percent for U and Th and about 3 percent for K. At low concentrations these percentages are in addition to minimum standard deviations of about 0.01 ppm U, 0.02 ppm Th, and 0.01 percent K.

Acknowledgments.—We thank Robert J. Kirkpatrick for assistance in collecting the basalt samples and Gerald T. Cebula for help in sample preparation.

BASALTS

Basalts in the southern Rocky Mountain region range in age from Miocene to Holocene (Lipman and others, 1970; Strangway and others, 1969; Christiansen and Lipman, 1972), approximately contemporaneous with the period of extensional block faulting. These basalts represent the latest phase of widespread Cenozoic volcanism in the southern Rocky Mountains. The earlier volcanism was more silicic, ranging from andesite to rhyolite, and was mainly Oligocene in age (Steven and Epis, 1968).

For convenience, the basalt data are discussed in six geographic groups (fig. 1): (1) tholeiitic basalts, alkalic basalts, and xenocrystic basaltic andesites of the Rio Grande depression, (2) alkalic basalts of Los Mogotes volcano in the southeastern San Juan Mountains, (3) the alkalic Brazos Basalt (of Doney, 1968) in the Tusas Mountains, (4) several basalt groups from the Mount Taylor area, (5) alkalic basalt of the Cimarron Mountains, and (6) the alkalic Raton, Clayton, and Capulin Basalts (of Collins, 1949) on the High Plains of northeastern New Mexico.

Rio Grande depression

Mafic flows that flood the southern San Luis Valley are divisible into three distinct types: olivine tholeiite, silicic alkalic basalt, and xenocrystic alkalic basaltic andesite.

The flows of olivine tholeiite are volumetrically the most abundant (Aoki, 1967a; Lipman, 1969). They form an impressive volcanic plateau north of Taos, N. Mex., and constitute the dominant basalt type in sections as much as 200 m thick in the Rio Grande gorge, where they have been dated as 3.6 to 4.5 m.y. old (Ozima and others, 1967). These basalts are coarse grained, porous, and characterized by diktytaxitic textures. They are also distinctive chemically in comparison with all the alkalic rocks of the region, being characterized by higher Fe, Al, Mg, and lower Ti, P, Sr, Ba, Rb, K, U, and Th (Lipman, 1969). Total alkalis are sufficiently low that these rocks plot within the field of tholeiitic basalts of Hawaii (fig. 2*A*). The contents of K, U, and Th are the lowest in the region and are only slightly variable (fig. 3*A*).

Interlayered in the Rio Grande gorge with the typical diktytaxitic olivine tholeiites are subordinate flows of fine-grained dense silicic alkali-olivine basalt (Aoki, 1967a, table 1, Nos. 11, 14, 15). Cinder-cone vents for similar flows are exposed along the west margin of the southern San Luis Valley in northernmost New Mexico, but it is not clear whether the alkalic basalts exposed along the Rio Grande gorge were erupted from vents within the main part of the rift or whether they flowed in from the sides. All these flows petrologically resemble the nearby alkalic basalts in the Tusas Mountains and southeastern San Juan Mountains: in addition to higher total alkalis than the tholeiites (fig. 2*A*), they contain higher contents of K, Th, and U (table 1; fig. 3*A*).

Also exposed along the west margin of the San Luis Valley, near the Colorado-New Mexico line, are several distinctive flows of alkalic basaltic andesite that are characterized by abundant xenocrysts of quartz and plagioclase. These flows are similar to upper Cenozoic xenocrystic basalts that occur farther northwest in the San Juan volcanic field (Larsen and others, 1938; Doe and others, 1969; Lipman, 1969, pls. 1, 2). Some of these xenocrystic flows are clearly older than the olivine tholeiite flows, for example the Dorado Basalt of Butler (1971) that is exposed along the east edge of the Tusas Mountains. Other xenocrystic flows farther east within the Rio Grande depression may be younger than some of the tholeiitic basalts or, alternatively, these flows may represent older hills partly buried by the tholeiitic basalts. The xenocrystic flows of basaltic andesite are only slightly higher in K than the nonxenocrystic alkalic basalts of the same general area, but they are distinctly higher in Th and U (fig. 3*A*).

Southeastern San Juan Mountains

Basaltic lavas of the Miocene-Pliocene Hinsdale Formation are the dominant type of late Cenozoic volcanism throughout the San Juan Mountains, but interpretation of these rocks is hampered by uncertain location of the vents for many flows. All analyses reported here are of samples from Los Mogotes volcano, a small 5-m.y.-old shield (Lipman and others, 1970) near the west edge of the San Luis Valley in the southeastern

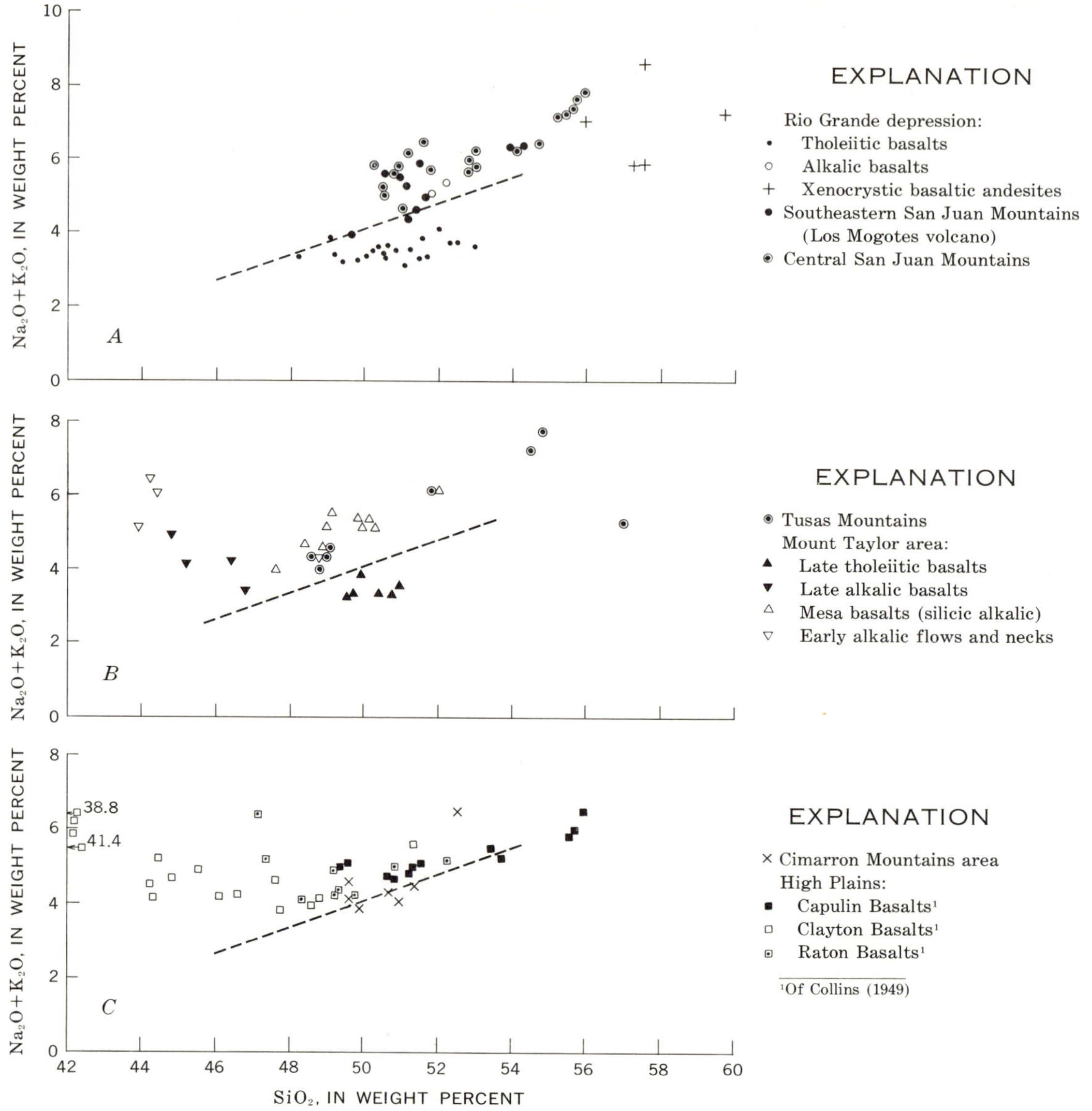

Figure 2.—Plots of total alkalis and SiO_2 for basalts of the southern Rocky Mountain region. Data from Aoki (1967a, b), Renault (1970), Laughlin and others (1971), Baldwin and Muehlberger (1959), Larsen and Cross (1956), Stormer (1972), Lipman and Moench (1972), and Lipman (1969 and unpub. data). All analyses plotted have been recalculated to 100 percent without H_2O or CO_2. Dashed line separates fields of Hawaiian tholeiitic and alkalic basalts (Macdonald and Katsura, 1964). Although arbitrary, this field boundary is used because it emphasizes seemingly significant petrographic and geographic distinctions; alternative boundaries (Kudo and others, 1971) result in slightly different nomenclature for the basalts of the region.
A. Basalts of the Rio Grande depression and the southeastern and central San Juan Mountains.
B. Basalts west of the Rio Grande depression (Tusas Mountains and Mount Taylor areas).
C. Basalts east of the Rio Grande depression (Cimarron Mountains and High Plains areas).

San Juan Mountains (fig. 1). Basaltic lava flows originally extended outward 15–20 km in all directions from a central cinder cone, but the shield has been tilted about 5° toward the San Luis Valley and asymmetrically dissected. Where the flank of the volcano has been cut across by the canyon of the Conajos River, at least 10 individual basalt flows are exposed. In the field these flows appear to be monotonously uniform dense basalt with sparse olivine phenocrysts, but chemical analyses indicate that they decrease systematically upward in silica, alkalis, and other elements—from about 54 percent silica at the base of the sequence to less than 50 percent silica for the latest erupted flows (P. W. Lipman, unpub. data). The Los Mogotes flows are relatively silicic alkali-olivine basalts, generally similar in petrography and chemistry to the other basalts

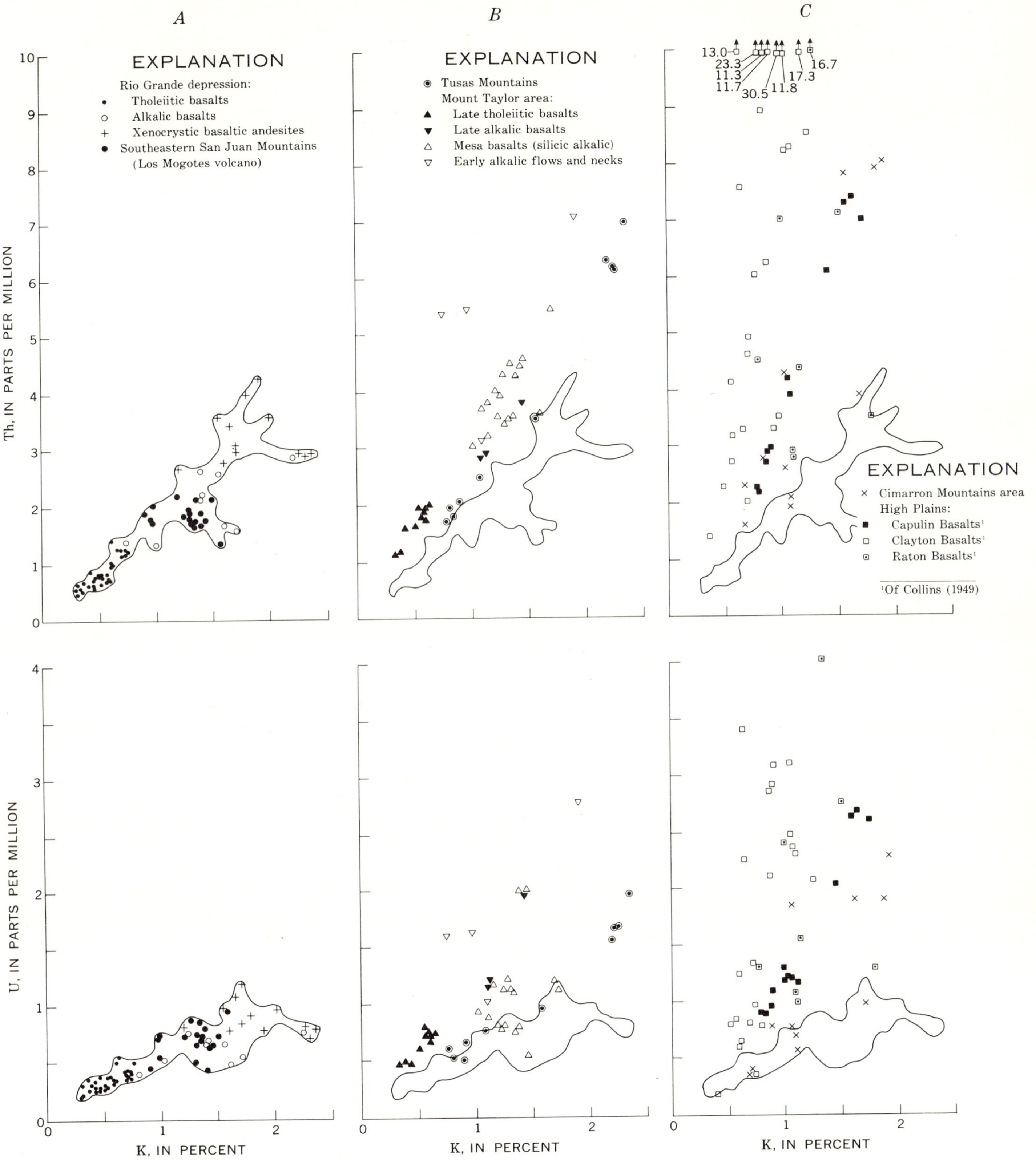

Figure 3.—Plots of K, Th, and U contents of basalts of the southern Rocky Mountain region. Data from table 2.

A. Basalts of the Rio Grande depression and the southeastern San Juan Mountains. Empirically estimated field boundary of Rio Grande depression basalts is repeated in *B* and *C*.

B. Basalts west of the Rio Grande depression (Tusas Mountains and Mount Taylor areas).

C. Basalts east of the Rio Grande depression (Cimarron Mountains and High Plains areas).

of the Hinsdale Formation. Their contents of K, Th, and U are generally similar to those of nearby alkalic basalts within the Rio Grande depression (fig. 2*A*).

Tusas Mountains

A north-trending zone of at least five little-eroded cinder cones and related lava flows of probable Pleistocene age along the west flank of the Tusas Mountains in northern New Mexico, which have been termed the Brazos Basalt by Doney (1968), forms a partial link between the San Juan volcanic field and the Jemez field to the south. Although younger than any known basalt of the Hinsdale Formation of the San Juan Mountains, the Brazos Basalt is a generally similar type of silicic alkali-olivine basalt (fig. 2*B*). The most silicic flows of Brazos Basalt contain sparse xenocrysts of quartz and plagioclase. The Brazos Basalt, which is well west of the Rio Grande depression, is slightly higher in U and Th contents than otherwise petrographically similar alkalic basalts along the west edge of the San Luis Valley and in the Rio Grande gorge (fig. 3*B*).

Mount Taylor area

Petrologically diverse Pliocene and younger basalts occur in the vicinity of Mount Taylor (Lipman and Moench, 1972), near the south margin of the Colorado Plateau, about 50 km west of the Rio Grande depression (fig. 1).

The oldest basalts in this area are flows and necks, mainly low-silica nepheline-normative alkali-olivine basalt (fig. 2*B*), that were emplaced prior to the formation of the Mount Taylor stratovolcano. Flows of intermediate age (mesa basalts), which now cap erosional mesas around Mount Taylor, consist of silicic alkalic basalt that is generally similar in mineralogy, texture, and major-oxide composition to basalts of the San Juan Mountains and Tusas Mountains (fig. 2). Pleistocene and Holocene basalts of the Mount Taylor area, which occur near modern drainage levels, include both alkalic and tholeiitic types. Diktytaxitic olivine tholeiites that are similar to the tholeiitic basalts of the Rio Grande depression in mineralogy, texture, and major-oxide composition occur around the southwest, south, and southeast margins of the Mount Taylor area (Lipman and Moench, 1972; Renault, 1970). Late alkalic basalts, some sufficiently low in silica to be nepheline normative, are closely associated with olivine tholeiites in the Zuni Mountains, about 30 km southwest of Mount Taylor (Renault, 1970; Kudo and others, 1971; Laughlin and others, 1971).

These diverse basalts in the Mount Taylor area are predictably variable in K, Th, and U contents (fig. 3*B*; table 1), but at any K content, both Th and U are distinctly higher than for basalts near or within the Rio Grande depression (fig. 3*A*). Especially striking are the distinctly separate fields for the olivine tholeiites from the two areas, and also the virtually complete separation of the two groups of silicic alkalic basalts (fig. 3*B*). The low-silica alkalic basalts from the Mount Taylor area are especially rich in Th and U; no petrologically comparable basalts occur within or near the Rio Grande depression to the east.

Cimarron Mountains area

On the east side of the Rio Grande depression, a large basalt field that extends from near Wagon Mound, N. Mex., across the Cimarron Mountains, to the flank of the southern Sangre de Cristo Mountains (fig. 1), is virtually unstudied except for reconnaissance geochemical sampling (Kudo and others, 1971; this report). Most of the flows are late Cenozoic, as indicated by limited erosional dissection, but no radiometric ages are available. These basalts are mostly silicic alkalic types (fig. 2*C*), similar in texture and mineralogy to those of Los Mogotes volcano, the Tusas Mountains, and the mesas of the Mount Taylor area. Although a few of the samples analyzed for this study have diktytaxitic textures, megascopically resemble the tholeiites of the Rio Grande depression, and plot marginally within the field of Hawaiian tholeiitic basalts (fig. 2*C*), none are as low in alkalis and other dispersed elements as the tholeiites of the depression. In contents of K, Th, and U, basalts of the Cimarron Mountains are rather like the silicic alkalic basalts of the Mount Taylor area: they are distinctly enriched in U and Th at any given K content, in comparison with otherwise similar rocks within or near the Rio Grande depression (fig. 3*A*). Xenocrystic basaltic andesites, which are common in the western Cimarron Mountains, contain exceptionally high K, Th, and U contents.

High Plains of northeastern New Mexico

The large area of Pliocene to Holocene basaltic lavas in northeastern New Mexico (fig. 1) has been described by Lee (1922), Collins (1949), Stobbe (1949), Baldwin and Muehlberger (1959), Aoki (1967b), and Stormer (1972). The older basalts cap high mesas and have been extensively eroded, but the younger basalts follow present drainages and are only slightly eroded. Several of the older flows have yielded K-Ar ages of 7–8 m.y. (Stormer, 1972). One of the youngest basaltic centers of this area, Capulin cone, was active between 8,000 and 2,500 B.C. (Baldwin and Muehlberger, 1959).

These basalts can be divided into several groups on the basis of petrology and age. The oldest, the Raton Basalts of Collins (1949), are mostly silicic alkalic basalts similar in chemistry and petrography to the basalts of the San Juan Mountains and the mesa basalts of the Mount Taylor area (fig. 2). The intermediate-age Clayton Basalts of Collins (1949) consist in part of silicic alkalic basalt similar to the Raton Basalts, but they also include distinctive highly alkalic basalts low in silica and containing feldspathoids in the groundmass. These feldspathoidal basalts are generally like the nepheline-normative early basalts of the Mount Taylor area (fig. 2*B*), but some are even more mafic and alkalic, with silica contents of 40 percent or less. The youngest lavas, the Capulin Basalts of Collins (1949), are silicic alkalic basalts chemically and petrographically similar to the Raton Basalts. These flows contain olivine phenocrysts, and some flows from Capulin cone contain abundant xenocrysts of quartz and plagioclase.

All these High Plains basalts are rich in Th and U, in comparison with otherwise petrologically similar basalts nearer the Rio Grande depression (fig. 3). The feldspathoidal Clayton Basalts are the most enriched, containing as much as 30.0 ppm Th and 7.2 ppm U, but even the more ordinary silicic alkalic flows of Clayton Basalts are much higher in these elements than any of the basalts near the Rio Grande depression. The Raton and Capulin Basalts, which are restricted to western parts of the High Plains basalt field, have contents of Th and U that are intermediate between those of the Clayton Basalts and basalt fields nearer the Rio Grande depression (fig. 3). The Clayton Basalts that are lowest in K, Th, and U have fine-grained diktytaxitic textures, generally resembling some tholeiites of the Rio Grande depression, but the Th/K and most of the U/K ratios of these Clayton Basalts are much higher (fig. 3*C*; table 1).

DISCUSSION

The most interesting general feature of the distribution of K, Th, and U in basalts of the southern Rocky Mountain region is the increase in Th and U with respect to K with distance from the Rio Grande depression. The volumetrically predominant olivine tholeiites of the depression have the lowest K, Th, and U contents of any basalts in the region. The less abundant alkalic basalts and xenocrystic basaltic andesites of the western Rio Grande depression have higher contents of these elements but the Th/K and U/K ratios remain very low, averaging about 1.7×10^{-4} and 0.5×10^{-4}, respectively (table 1).

Away from the Rio Grande depression, tholeiitic rocks low in K, Th, and U are rare in the southern Rocky Mountain region. The only major exception would seem to be the olivine tholeiites south of Mount Taylor, which are similar to tholeiites of the depression in texture, mineralogy, and major-oxide chemistry (fig. 2*B*), but which have distinctly higher average Th/K and U/K ratios, about 3.1×10^{-4} and 1.1×10^{-4} (table 1, fig. 3). The presence of tholeiitic basalts near Mount Taylor has been interpreted as related to the structural discontinuity between the Colorado Plateau and Basin and Range provinces (Lipman, 1969; Lipman and Moench, 1972). Compositionally transitional basalts with diktytaxitic textures, that are low-potassium components of the basalt suites in the Cimarron Mountains and in the Clayton Basalts on the High Plains, are also distinctly enriched in Th and U relative to K, in comparison with similar-textured tholeiites of the Rio Grande depression (fig. 3).

These large variations in K, Th, and U contents and ratios between suites of olivine tholeiites from different geographic regions, and similar variations between suites of silicic alkalic basalts from different regions, permit distinctions among basalt suites that are very similar in texture, mineralogy, and major-oxide chemistry.

The silicic alkalic basalts that are the dominant type in the southern Rocky Mountain region all have higher K, Th, and U contents than the tholeiitic basalts. In addition, the Th/K and U/K ratios of these basalts increase with distance from the Rio Grande depression (table 1). The lowest ratios of these elements occur in the basalts of Los Mogotes volcano on the west margin of the Rio Grande depression and in the sparse similar silicic alkalic basalts interlayered with the tholeiitic basalts farther south within the depression (fig. 3*A*). Concentrations and ratios of these elements increase westward across the San Juan volcanic field: preliminary results of our minor-element studies, currently in progress on western San Juan basalts, indicate average U/K and Th/K ratios of 0.86 and

Table 1.—*Averages and ranges of* Th/U, U/K, *and* Th/K *in basalts of the southern Rocky Mountain region*

[Data from table 2; U/K and Th/K ratios $\times10^{-4}$]

Area and rock type	No. of samples	Th/U	U/K	Th/K
Rio Grande depression:				
Tholeiitic basalts	31	2.7 (1.9–3.8)	0.64 (0.51–1.1)	1.7 (1.3–2.3)
Alkalic basalts	9	3.4 (2.7–3.8)	.45 (.28–.67)	1.6 (1.0–2.3)
Xenocrystic basaltic andesites	12	4.0 (2.9–4.6)	.46 (.27–.63)	1.8 (1.2–2.3)
Southeastern San Juan Mountains	18	2.9 (1.5–4.6)	.51 (.30–.67)	1.5 (.87–2.1)
Tusas Mountains	10	3.7 (3.0–4.3)	.67 (.56–.83)	2.5 (2.2–2.9)
Mount Taylor area:				
Early alkalic flows and necks	4	3.3 (2.9–3.6)	1.4 (.87–2.0)	4.8 (2.8–7.0)
Mesa basalts	17	4.2 (2.3–9.2)	.75 (.33–1.3)	2.9 (2.1–3.3)
Late tholeiitic basalts	10	2.8 (2.5–3.6)	1.1 (.87–1.3)	3.1 (2.4–3.6)
Late alkalic basalts	3	2.3 (2.2–2.5)	1.1 (.92–1.2)	2.4 (2.1–2.7)
Cimarron Mountains	11	4.0 (2.5–6.4)	.79 (.48–1.6)	3.1 (1.7–4.8)
High Plains:				
Raton Basalts	8	3.1 (2.3–4.1)	1.6 (.69–2.9)	5.0 (1.8–12.2)
Clayton Basalts	23	4.5 (3.2–9.4)	2.3 (.35–7.6)	9.4 (2.5–26.4)
Capulin Basalts	14	2.9 (2.5–4.4)	1.2 (.86–1.6)	3.6 (2.8–4.5)

2.8, respectively, for these rocks (compare with table 1). These ratios also are higher in the silicic alkalic basalts of the Cimarron and Tusas Mountains, east and west of the Rio Grande depression, respectively; they are even higher in the otherwise petrologically similar mesa basalts of the Mount Taylor area and Capulin Basalts of the High Plains at greater distances from the Rio Grande depression. Extremely high Th and U contents—as much as 30 and 7 ppm, respectively—and high Th/K and U/K ratios occur only at large distances from the Rio Grande depression; on the High Plains to the east and at Mount Taylor on the southeastern Colorado Plateau. High Th/K and U/K ratios characterize basalts of the western Colorado Plateau region (fig. 4A), as noted by Best, Hamblin, and Brimhall (1966, 1969) and Best and Brimhall (1970); the

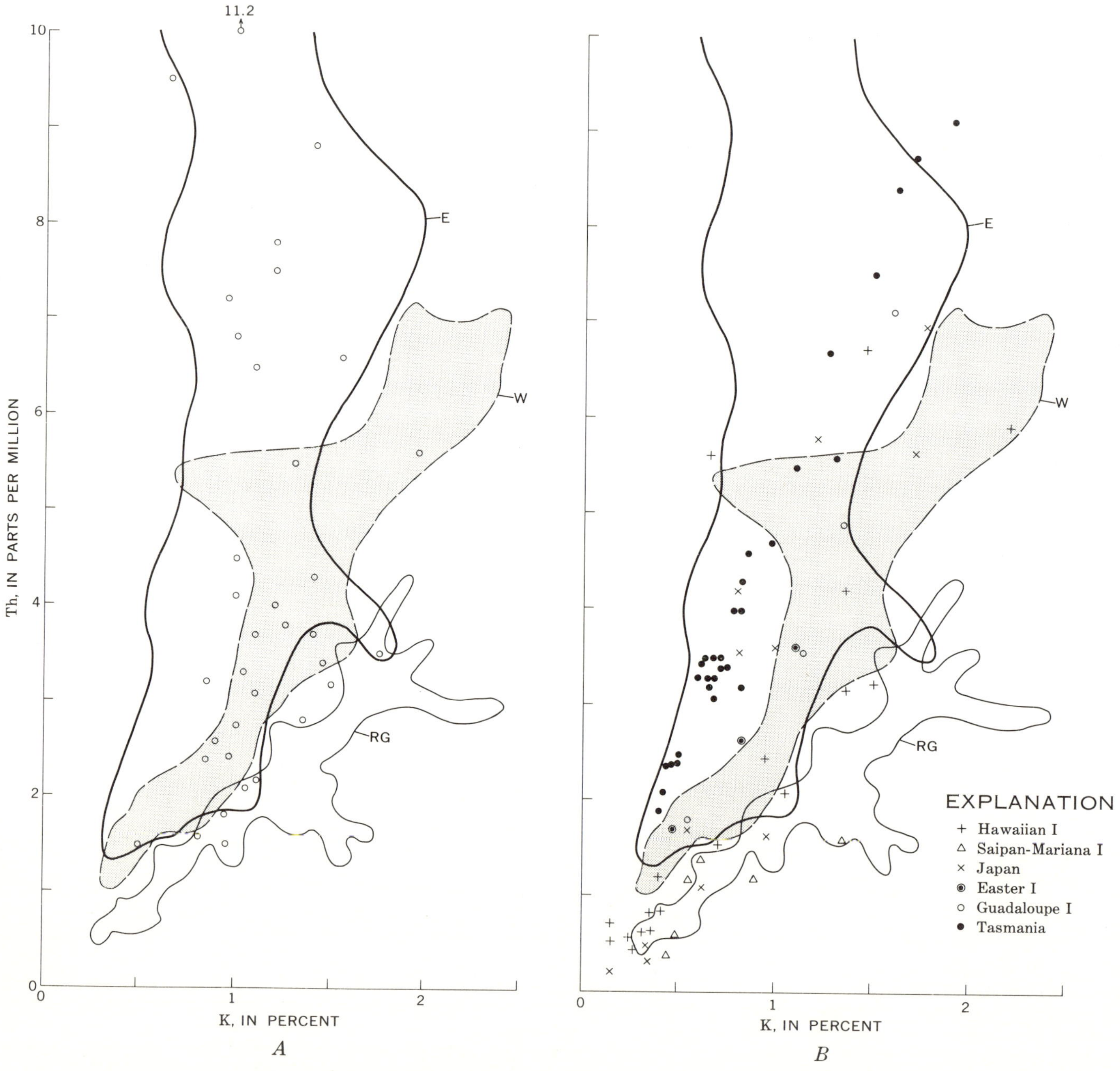

Figure 4.—Comparisons of K and Th contents of basalts of the southern Rocky Mountain region with mafic volcanic rocks from other regions. Plots of K and U also show similar patterns for these regions. Empirically estimated field boundaries for basalts of the Rio Grande depression (RG), basalts west of the depression (W), and basalts east of the depression (E) are taken from figure 3.

A. Western Grand Canyon region. Data are from Best, Hamblin, and Brimhall (1966) and Embree (1970).

B. Oceanic-island and island-arc basalts. Data are from Heier and Rogers (1963), Heier, McDougall, and Adams (1964), Heier, Compston, and McDougall (1965), Tatsumoto (1966a, b), Gottfried, Moore, and Campbell (1963), and Hedge and Knight (1969).

western Colorado Plateau basalts seem generally petrologically similar to basalts of the Mount Taylor and High Plains areas discussed in this report.

Large variations in U and Th contents and ratios within some individual lava flows have been interpreted as related to oxidation and leaching processes (Watkins and Haggerty, 1967; Watkins and others, 1967; Heier and Rogers, 1963), but processes of this type seem unlikely to have affected significantly the basalts studied here. Paired samples of black cinders (reduced) and red cinders (oxidized) from four individual cinder cones differ only slightly in Th, K, and U contents or ratios (table 2, Nos. 45–47, 160–161, 164–165, and 165–166). A detailed study by Embree (1970) also found only insignificant lateral variation and only slight vertical variation within a single large basalt flow in the western Grand Canyon region.

The Th/K and U/K ratios of basalts of the southern Rocky Mountain region vary by more than an order of magnitude (table 1), a larger range than has previously been reported for basaltic rocks in general (Heier and Rogers, 1963). The geochemical coherence of these elements seems less ideal than previously thought, and the present data show a closer coherence between Th (and U) and Sr (fig. 5) than between Th (and U) and K (fig. 3). The highest Th/K and U/K ratios of the basalts approach those of lunar basalts (Fanale and Nash, 1971) and terrestrial ultramafic rocks (Fisher, 1970), although the concentrations of these elements are much greater in the basalts of the southern Rocky Mountain region.

The Th/U ratios are also quite variable, although less so than the Th/K or U/K ratios (table 1). In general, the most alkalic basalts have the highest Th/U ratios, and the tholeiitic rocks have low ratios. Significant exceptions are the late alkalic basalts of the Mount Taylor area, which have atypically low Th/U ratios, apparently because of anomalously high U contents. These variations in Th/U ratios in basalts of the southern Rocky Mountain region are interesting, as most of the values are below the estimated mantle ratio (3.9–4.1) required to generate observed ranges of Pb-isotopic compositions through time (Russell and Farquhar, 1960; Patterson and Tatsumoto, 1964). In the ocean basins, the ridge tholeiites also have lower Th/U ratios than the more alkalic island basalts, and the Th/U ratios of the ridge tholeiites are too low to have generated their observed Pb-isotopic ratios (Tatsumoto, 1966a). Sparse available Pb-isotopic data (Doe and others, 1969) suggest the possibility of a similar relation for the low Th/U basalts of the southern Rocky Mountain region. Either the mantle underlying the southern Rocky Mountain region has been variably depleted in Th relative to U by pre-late Cenozoic events, or varying conditions of melting during generation of the upper Cenozoic basalts were capable of significantly fractionating the Th/U ratios.

The variations in K, Th, and U are parallel to the major-oxide chemical variations of the southern Rocky Mountain basalts, which become generally more alkalic away from the Rio Grande depression (Lipman, 1969; Kudo and others, 1971): basalts and basaltic andesites of alkalic affinities were

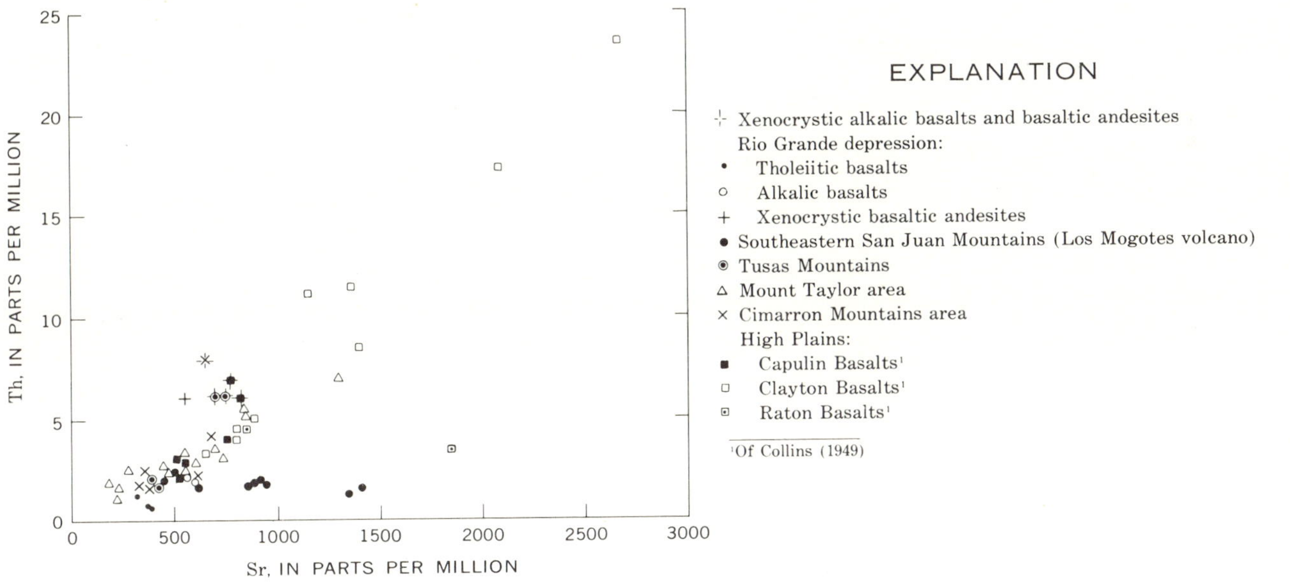

Figure 5.—Plot of Th and Sr for basalts of the southern Rocky Mountain region, showing general coherence of these two elements. The major exceptions are samples from Los Mogotes volcano, which define a divergent trend in which Sr increases as Th remains nearly constant; the Los Mogotes rocks are also atypical in several other elemental trends (P. W. Lipman and C. E. Hedge, unpub. data). Also, xenocrystic alkalic basalts and basaltic andesites tend to contain higher Th contents than nonxenocrystic basalts of similar Sr content from the same area. Sr concentrations are by X-ray fluorescence (C. E. Hedge, written commun., 1971) except for Mount Taylor (Lipman and Moench, 1972) and Cimarron Mountains (Lipman, unpub. data), which are by emission-spectrographic methods.

erupted east and west of the depression concurrently with its formation, and tholeiitic basalts filled parts of the depression late in its history. Nepheline-normative alkalic basalts occur only at distances of about 100 km or more from the depression. Extremely alkalic rocks are present in the interior of the Colorado Plateau (Williams, 1936) and on the High Plains (Clayton Basalts). Thus, the increasing Th/K and U/K ratios of the basalts of the southern Rocky Mountain region correlate well with alkalinity of the basalt suites. This correlation is probably valid for basalts in general. A similar increase in Th and U in basalts across Japan, as the basalts change from tholeiitic to alkalic (Kuno, 1959; Sugimura, 1960), was noted by Heier and Rogers (1963), and systematic correlation between Th and U contents and alkali-lime indices has been demonstrated for igneous suites in general by Tilling and Gottfried (1969, fig. 6).

The overall range in compositions, both major oxides and minor elements, in basalts of the southern Rocky Mountain region is large and encompasses virtually the entire known range of oceanic-island or other continental basalts (Hedge and Lipman, 1972). This similarity seems especially evident for the K, Th, and U data (fig. 4), although adequate analyses are sparse for many regions. The only conspicuous exceptions are the oceanic ridge tholeiites, which are extremely low in elements such as K, Th, U, Sr, Rb, and Ba (Engel and others, 1965; Tatsumoto, 1966a; Kay and others, 1970), and even here the tholeiitic basalts of the Rio Grande depression are transitional toward the ridge tholeiites (Cohen and others, 1967; Lipman, 1969), containing contents of these minor elements as low as or lower than most Hawaiian or Japanese tholeiites (fig. *4B*; Hedge and Lipman, 1972). The low-silica alkalic basalts of the High Plains and the Mount Taylor areas are generally similar to the nepheline-normative alkalic basalts of oceanic islands. The silicic alkalic basalts, although generally similar in elemental composition to hawaiites and mugearites of oceanic islands, form a significantly greater proportion of the total basalt accumulation in the southern Rocky Mountains, and for that matter throughout the Western United States (Lipman, 1969; Leeman and Rogers, 1970).

The diversity of basalt types in the southern Rocky Mountain region seems most plausibly interpreted as related to depth of magma generation (Lipman, 1969; Lipman and Moench, 1972; Stormer, 1972). The general trends of chemical variations from tholeiitic to nepheline-normative alkalic basalts, involving increase of alkalis as silica decreases, cannot be produced by crystal-liquid fractionation at low pressures (Powers, 1935; Yoder and Tilley, 1962). Furthermore, compositional variations within basalt sequences related to some individual centers, such as Los Mogotes volcano, cannot be accounted for by addition or subtraction of the low-pressure phenocryst phases present in the basalts, and seemingly must also be due to high-pressure fractionation (P. W. Lipman and C. E. Hedge, unpub. data). It therefore appears likely that much of the chemical variation among basalts of the southern Rocky Mountain region reflects fundamental differences in the conditions of magma generation at depth in the source area, presumably in the mantle. Either the source area differs in composition roughly symmetrically across the area of the Rio Grande depression or, more likely, the pressure-temperature conditions of magma generation vary symmetrically across the region.

Crystallization experiments on basalts at high pressures (Green and Ringwood, 1967; Green, 1968; Kushiro, 1968) have shown that basaltic magmas can be generated by partial melting of probable mantle constituents and that the composition of the basaltic melt is determined by the depth of melting and the depth at which the melt last equilibrates with the refractory residium (O'Hara and Yoder, 1967). Experimental fraction trends at different pressures suggest that tholeiitic basalt should be generated at lesser depths than alkalic basalt, and these relations have been cited to interpret the origin of compositionally varied basalt associations in the Western United States like those of the southern Rocky Mountain region (Wise, 1969; Leeman and Rogers, 1970; Condie and Barsky, 1972) and also to account for basalt variations in oceanic areas (Kuno, 1959, 1968; Jackson and Wright, 1970).

Effects of sialic crustal contamination on basalts of the southern Rocky Mountain region, although locally significant in affecting concentrations and isotopic compositions of some elements (Doe and others, 1969; Laughlin and others, 1972), seem generally to have played an insignificant role in generation of the diversity of basalt types. In the present study the rocks with the highest Th and U contents are the low-silica alkalic basalts; these high Th and U values cannot be due to contamination by sialic crust, which would have concurrently increased the silica contents of these basalts. Interpretation of Sr data leads to similar conclusions: the rocks richest in U and Th also have the highest Sr contents—as much as 2,500 ppm Sr, in contrast with 250–300 ppm Sr in the Th- and U-poor olivine tholeiites (C. E. Hedge, written commun., 1971)—but contamination by any plausible crustal material would lower the Sr concentration in these basalts, not increase it. The Sr-poor rocks should also be much more sensitive to effects of contamination than the Sr-rich rocks, yet the Sr^{87}/Sr^{86} ratios of the most Sr-rich Clayton Basalts of the High Plains (0.7041–0.7049; four samples) bracket the radiogenic Sr of the Sr-poor tholeiitic basalts of the Rio Grande depression (0.7042–0.7048; four samples); data from Hedge and Lipman (1972 and unpub. data).

Perhaps the slightly high Th/K and U/K ratios of the xenocrystic basaltic andesites of the Rio Grande depression, in comparison with silicic alkalic basalts from the same area (fig. *2A*), are due to effects of sialic crustal contamination, as Pb-isotopic comparisons of similar rocks show significant differences (Doe and others, 1969). However, the origin of such xenocrystic rocks is in doubt. In addition to possible derivation from Precambrian sialic crust, they may represent disequilibrium remnants from high-pressure crystallization in the upper mantle (Nicholls and others, 1971) or result from mixing with phenocryst-bearing rhyolitic magma, as can be demonstrated for a few small basalt rhyolite mix-lava complexes in the southeastern San Juan Mountains (Lipman, unpub data).

Table 2.—*Analyses of* K, Th, *and* U *in basalts of the southern Rocky Mountain region*

No.	Field sample No.	U (ppm)	Th (ppm)	K (percent)	Th/U	$\frac{U}{K\times10^{-4}}$	$\frac{Th}{K\times10^{-4}}$
	Rio Grande depression—tholeiitic basalt						
1.	68L-10.....	0.51	1.02	0.62	1.99	0.82	1.65
2.	14A....	.36	.81	.60	2.25	.60	1.35
3.	14B....	.36	.83	.53	2.31	.68	1.57
4.	14C ...	.36	.86	.55	2.39	.65	1.56
5.	14D ...	.38	1.17	.71	3.08	.54	1.65
6.	14E ...	.50	1.21	.77	2.42	.65	1.57
7.	14F ...	.38	1.27	.69	3.34	.55	1.84
8.	14G ...	.39	1.30	.68	3.33	.57	1.91
9.	14H ...	.38	1.29	.75	3.39	.51	1.72
10.	18B4 ..	.29	.81	.53	2.79	.55	1.53
11.	19.....	.52	1.42	.62	2.73	.84	2.29
12.	111....	.23	.52	.32	2.26	.72	1.62
13.	112....	.32	.63	.38	1.97	.84	1.66
14.	113....	.37	.79	.62	2.14	.60	1.27
15.	114....	.29	.88	.51	3.03	.57	1.73
16.	119C ..	.26	.80	.47	3.08	.55	1.70
17.	119D ..	.42	1.20	.75	2.86	.56	1.60
18.	119E ..	.36	1.03	.63	2.86	.57	1.63
19.	119F ..	.18	.69	.31	3.83	.58	2.23
20.	119G ..	.28	.70	.54	2.50	.52	1.30
21.	120....	.24	.73	.37	3.04	.65	1.97
22.	121....	.27	.63	.34	2.33	.79	1.85
23.	125....	.30	.71	.42	2.37	.71	1.69
24.	126....	.32	.76	.58	2.38	.55	1.31
25.	127....	.24	.64	.46	2.67	.52	1.39
26.	128....	.32	.94	.42	2.94	.76	2.24
27.	129....	.34	1.14	.62	3.35	.55	1.84
28.	140....	.32	.62	.30	1.94	1.07	2.07
29.	145A ..	.31	.89	.59	2.87	.53	1.51
30.	145B ..	.35	1.00	.61	2.86	.57	1.64
31.	147....	.38	.79	.45	2.14	.82	1.76
	Rio Grande depression—alkalic basalt						
32.	68L-116....	0.76	2.62	1.24	3.45	0.61	2.11
33.	119A ..	.65	2.17	1.43	3.34	.45	1.52
34.	119B ..	.64	2.17	1.40	3.39	.46	1.55
35.	137....	.57	1.59	1.70	2.79	.34	.94
36.	138....	.81	3.10	1.57	3.83	.52	1.97
37.	139....	.79	2.95	2.27	3.73	.35	1.30
38.	141....	.50	1.71	.75	3.42	.67	2.28
39.	142....	.42	1.41	1.04	3.36	.40	1.36
40.	146....	.45	1.64	1.63	3.64	.28	1.01
	Rio Grande depression—xenocrystic basaltic andesite						
41.	67L-102....	0.77	4.29	1.94	5.56	0.40	2.21
42.	68L-115....	.74	2.83	1.64	3.82	.45	1.73
43.	117....	.69	2.68	1.21	3.88	.57	2.21
44.	118....	.91	3.55	1.58	3.90	.58	2.25
45.	122A ..	.86	2.83	2.28	3.29	.38	1.24
46.	122B1 .	.63	2.93	2.36	4.65	.27	1.24
47.	122B2 .	.74	2.98	2.39	4.03	.31	1.25
48.	123....	.92	3.63	2.05	3.95	.45	1.77
49.	131....	1.09	3.17	1.72	2.91	.63	1.84
50.	143A ..	.88	4.05	1.80	4.60	.49	2.25
51.	143B ..	1.03	3.49	1.65	3.39	.62	2.12
52.	144....	.80	2.99	1.73	3.74	.46	1.73
	Southeastern San Juan Mountains						
53.	67L-12.....	0.71	2.08	1.53	2.93	0.46	1.36
54.	13.....	.59	1.73	1.48	2.93	.40	1.17
55.	16.....	.54	2.04	1.01	3.78	.53	2.02
56.	103....	.42	1.91	1.40	4.55	.30	1.36

Table 2.—*Analyses of* K, Th, *and* U *in basalts of the southern Rocky Mountain region—Continued*

No.	Field sample No.	U (ppm)	Th (ppm)	K (percent)	Th/U	$\frac{U}{K\times10^{-4}}$	$\frac{Th}{K\times10^{-4}}$
	Southeastern San Juan Mountains—*Continued*						
57.	68L-16A ...	0.69	2.17	1.20	3.14	0.58	1.81
58.	16B ...	.72	2.19	1.21	3.04	.60	1.81
59.	17B2 ..	.48	1.76	1.30	3.67	.37	1.35
60.	134A ..	.68	1.78	1.01	2.62	.67	1.76
61.	134B ..	.68	1.77	1.01	2.60	.67	1.75
62.	134C ..	.85	1.91	1.27	2.25	.67	1.50
63.	134D ..	.73	1.97	1.32	2.70	.55	1.49
64.	134E ..	.90	1.38	1.59	1.53	.57	.87
65.	134F ..	.65	1.67	1.36	2.57	.48	1.23
66.	134G ..	.70	1.79	1.38	2.56	.51	1.30
67.	134H ..	.78	2.17	1.40	2.78	.56	1.55
68.	134I...	.83	1.78	1.35	2.14	.61	1.32
69.	135....	.58	1.69	1.44	2.91	.40	1.17
70.	136....	.44	1.89	.90	4.30	.49	2.10
	Tusas Mountains						
71.	68L-92.....	0.51	2.09	0.91	4.10	0.56	2.30
72.	93.....	1.43	6.20	2.23	4.34	.64	2.78
73.	94.....	1.58	6.25	2.28	3.96	.69	2.74
74.	95.....	.50	1.81	.83	3.62	.60	2.18
75.	96.....	.71	2.52	1.10	3.55	.65	2.29
76.	97.....	1.62	6.55	2.25	4.04	.72	2.91
77.	98.....	1.96	6.86	2.35	3.50	.83	2.92
78.	99.....	.57	1.75	.79	3.07	.72	2.22
79.	100....	.89	3.51	1.61	3.94	.55	2.18
80.	101....	.63	2.04	.83	3.24	.76	2.46
	Mount Taylor area—early alkalic flows and necks						
81.	68L-202A ..	0.99	3.14	1.14	3.17	0.87	2.75
82.	202B ..	1.53	5.35	.77	3.50	1.99	6.95
83.	215....	2.47	7.10	1.96	2.87	1.26	3.62
84.	217....	1.51	5.48	.98	3.63	1.54	5.59
	Mount Taylor area—mesa basalts						
85.	68L-7A	1.07	5.42	1.75	5.07	0.61	3.10
86.	7B(2) ..	.83	3.69	1.12	4.45	.74	3.29
87.	7C.....	.79	3.14	1.22	3.97	.65	2.57
88.	7D	.76	3.56	1.40	4.68	.54	2.54
89.	200A ..	.73	3.54	1.27	4.85	.57	2.79
90.	200B ..	.73	4.06	1.24	5.56	.59	3.27
91.	200C ..	.73	4.42	1.36	6.05	.54	3.25
92.	200D ..	1.14	3.58	1.70	3.14	.67	2.11
93.	201A ..	1.84	4.33	1.42	2.35	1.30	3.05
94.	201B ..	1.87	4.52	1.47	2.42	1.27	3.07
95.	201C ..	1.03	3.97	1.27	3.85	.81	3.13
96.	202C ..	.49	4.52	1.49	9.22	.33	3.03
97.	202D ..	1.17	4.25	1.31	3.63	.89	3.24
98.	203....	1.09	3.78	1.18	3.47	.92	3.20
99.	205....	.89	3.05	1.06	3.43	.84	2.88
100.	216A ..	1.05	3.54	1.36	3.37	.77	2.60
101.	216B ..	1.06	3.44	1.34	3.25	.79	2.57
	Mount Taylor area—late tholeiitic basalts						
102.	68L-8......	0.44	1.60	0.45	3.64	0.98	3.56
103.	206....	.43	1.13	.35	2.63	1.23	3.23
104.	207....	.47	1.24	.40	2.64	1.17	3.10
105.	208....	.67	1.95	.61	2.91	1.10	3.20
106.	209....	.67	1.89	.60	2.82	1.12	3.15
107.	213....	.71	2.03	.65	2.86	1.09	3.12
108.	214....	.76	1.92	.57	2.53	1.33	3.37
109.	218....	.57	1.66	.51	2.91	1.12	3.25
110.	219....	.62	1.72	.62	2.77	1.00	2.77
111.	220....	.66	1.83	.76	2.77	.87	2.41
	Mount Taylor area—late alkalic basalts						
112.	68L-210....	1.16	2.93	1.16	2.53	1.00	2.53
113.	211....	1.82	3.92	1.46	2.15	1.25	2.68
114.	212....	1.05	2.43	1.14	2.31	.92	2.13
	Cimarron Mountains						
115.	68L-187....	0.38	1.58	0.71	4.16	0.54	2.23
116.	188.....	1.70	4.24	1.07	2.49	1.59	3.96

Table 2.—*Analyses of* K, Th, *and* U *in basalts of the southern Rocky Mountain region*—Continued

No.	Field sample No.	U (ppm)	Th (ppm)	K (percent)	Th/U	$\frac{U}{K\times10^{-4}}$	$\frac{Th}{K\times10^{-4}}$
Cimarron Mountains—*Continued*							
117.	68L-189....	0.76	2.76	0.90	3.63	0.84	3.07
118.	190....	.64	2.62	1.07	4.09	.60	2.45
119.	191....	.92	3.91	1.73	4.25	.53	2.26
120.	192....	.37	2.38	.70	6.43	.53	3.40
121.	193....	.62	1.93	1.12	3.11	.55	1.72
122.	194....	2.12	7.97	1.96	3.76	1.08	4.07
123.	195....	1.71	7.86	1.91	4.60	.90	4.12
124.	196....	1.85	7.86	1.64	4.25	1.13	4.79
125.	228....	.54	2.10	1.13	3.89	.48	1.86
High Plains—Raton Basalts							
126.	68L-1A.....	1.04	2.93	1.12	2.82	0.93	2.62
127.	1B.....	.92	2.82	1.13	3.07	.81	2.50
128.	148....	4.08	16.92	1.39	4.15	2.94	12.17
129.	149....	1.50	4.36	1.16	2.91	1.29	3.76
130.	156A ..	2.99	6.94	1.51	2.32	1.98	4.60
131.	156B ..	2.28	7.14	1.02	3.13	2.24	7.00
132.	164....	1.25	3.25	1.80	2.60	.69	1.81
133.	197....	1.27	4.41	.79	3.47	1.61	5.58
High Plains—Clayton Basalts							
134.	68L-151....	4.54	17.29	1.25	3.81	3.63	13.83
135.	157....	6.74	23.46	.89	3.48	7.57	26.36
136.	160....	1.88	8.47	1.33	4.51	1.41	6.37
137.	165....	2.73	11.55	.96	4.23	2.84	12.03
138.	167....	7.22	30.02	1.23	4.16	5.87	24.41
139.	168....	2.99	12.81	.68	4.28	4.40	18.84
140.	169....	2.55	11.21	.91	4.40	2.80	12.32
141.	170....	2.59	11.40	1.09	4.40	2.38	10.46
142.	171....	.88	4.93	.80	5.60	1.10	6.16
143.	172....	.73	3.27	.73	4.48	1.00	4.48
144.	174....	1.19	4.49	.76	3.77	1.57	5.91
145.	175....	.31	2.00	.79	6.45	.39	2.53
146.	176....	.15	1.41	.43	9.40	.35	3.28
147.	177....	2.57	8.70	.88	3.39	2.92	9.89
148.	178....	1.11	4.07	.64	3.67	1.73	6.36
149.	179....	.63	3.20	.63	5.08	1.00	5.08
150.	180....	.82	6.04	.78	7.37	1.05	7.74
151.	181....	2.16	8.16	1.13	3.78	1.91	7.22
152.	182....	2.19	8.09	1.18	3.69	1.86	6.86
153.	183....	.76	2.70	.61	3.55	1.25	4.43
154.	184....	.71	2.28	.55	3.21	1.29	4.15
155.	185....	1.97	7.52	.69	3.82	2.86	10.90
156.	186....	1.83	6.19	.91	3.38	2.01	6.80
High Plains—Capulin Basalts							
157.	68L-2......	0.96	4.18	1.11	4.35	0.86	3.77
158.	152....	2.72	6.82	1.76	2.51	1.55	3.88
159.	153....	1.07	3.85	1.12	3.60	.96	3.44
160.	154A ..	2.66	7.15	1.60	2.69	1.66	4.47
161.	154B ..	2.47	7.42	1.68	3.00	1.47	4.42
162.	155....	2.03	5.96	1.48	2.94	1.37	4.03
163.	158....	1.08	2.90	.92	2.69	1.17	3.15
164.	159A ..	1.19	3.74	1.03	3.14	1.16	3.63
165.	159B ..	1.15	3.49	1.08	3.03	1.06	3.23
166.	161A ..	1.18	3.34	.98	2.83	1.20	3.41
167.	161B ..	1.11	3.24	1.00	2.92	1.11	3.24
168.	162....	.86	2.65	.89	3.08	.97	2.98
169.	163....	1.18	2.91	.90	2.47	1.31	3.23
170.	166....	.79	2.27	.82	2.87	.96	2.77

Basalt sample localities and comments:

1. Low cliff, east side of north-trending arroyo, 0.5 km southeast of San Antonio, Colo.

2–9. Sequence of flow units or separate rapidly erupted lava flows, from top of section down; nose of ridge between Rio de los Pinos and Rio San Antonio, 0.4 km southeast of Ortiz, N. Mex.

10. La Jara Canyon road, 4 km southwest of Capulin, Colo., at bend in road around low cliff of basalt.

11. South of road intersection, 1.5 km south of Capulin, Colo.

12. 1.6 km east of U.S. Route 285 on gravel road; lat 36°58′ N., long 105°59′ W.; at spot elevation 8,073 ft. Especially coarse grained.

13. Same road 5 km east of U.S. 285; 36°57′ N., 105°56′ W.; at spot elevation 7,953 ft. Zeolite vesicle coatings.

14. Same road, about 9 km east of U.S. 285; 36°57′ N., 105°54′ W.; west side of small hill with spot elevation 7,967 ft.

15. Road through saddle about 2 km west of No. 13; at 8,050 ft on west side of 8,113-ft hill. Relatively dense and fine grained.

16–20. Rio Grande gorge at Dunn Bridge; sequence of five flows, from base up. Lowest flow (Nos. 33–34) is alkalic basalt.

21. Road to Dunn Bridge, at first main arroyo, about 4.5 km southeast of intersection with N. Mex. 111.

22. Along N. Mex. 111, about 0.5 km southeast of intersection with Dunn Bridge road; first roadcut.

23. Roadcut, U.S. 285, west of La Segita Peaks, 0.2 km south of spot elevation 8,460 ft.

24. N. Mex. 111, 1.3 km east of Tres Piedras intersection, at Arroyo Aguaje de la Petaca.

25. Roadcut, U.S. 285, at arroyo 4.5 km northeast of Cerro Mojimo.

26. South slope of Cerro Mojimo, at about 7,750-ft elevation. Cerro Mojimo is a small tholeiitic shield volcano.

27. Roadcut, U.S. 285, 2 km south of Stong, N. Mex.

28. Lower flow, Arroyo Aguaje de la Petaca, along gravel road 1.5 km northeast of Red Hill.

29–30. Lower and upper flows in roadcut, U.S. 285, 0.2 km north of Arroyo Aguaje de la Petaca, 0.9 km north of No Agua mill road.

31. Rio Grande gorge bridge, N. Mex. 111, west abutment.

32. Southeast Pinabetoso Peak; thin lava flow interlayered with cinders in dissected remnant of old cone.

33–34. Rio Grande gorge at Dunn Bridge; base and top of lowest flow, overlain by tholeiitic flows (Nos. 16–20).

35. Red Hill, flow on north ridge at 8,560 ft.

36. Red Hill, red cinders from most northwesterly prospect on east side, at about 8,560 ft.

37. Same locality as No. 28, upper flow; zeolitic vesicle linings.

38. Los Cerritos de la Cruz, northwest cone; cinders from pit on southeast side at about 9,020 ft.

39. Los Cerritos de la Cruz; flow in arroyo 0.9 km southeast of northwest cone, at 8,850-ft elevation.

40. Roadcut, U.S. 285, west of No Agua Peaks, 0.2 km north of Bareta Canyon. Fine-grained dense texture.

41. Mouth, Ra Jadero Canyon, west of La Jara, Colo.; same locality as analyzed sample (Lipman, 1969, table 1, No. 7).

42. Same locality as No. 15; from top of hill. Uncertain whether older or younger than flanking tholeiitic flows.

43. Crest of north La Segita Peak.

44. North La Segita Peak, south slope at 8,540 ft. Flattened vesicles partly filled by zeolite.

45–47. Cinder cone at northeast base of San Antonio Mountain. No. 45, black cinders; Nos. 46–47, two different horizons of red cinders.

48. Northeast side of San Antonio Mountain; flow along road to cinder quarry, at about 8,340-ft elevation.

49. Flow on Petaca Mesa; talus block along road about 1.0 km north of Petaca, N. Mex.

50–51. Los Cerritos de la Cruz, east slope of south cone at about 8,900 ft. No. 50, upper flow, is rather oxidized; No. 51, lower flow, appears less oxidized but has zeolite-coated vesicles.

52. Flow, 1.5 km northeast of south cone, Los Cerritos de la Cruz, knob south of road; probably erupted from this cone.

53. Southeast flank of Los Mogotes volcano, top flow on mesa rim, along road, 2.5 km northwest of Mecitas, Colo.

54. Flow at base of dissected main cone, along road, about 1 km east of central peak.

55. North rim of crater; fairly coarse interior of dense flow.

56. Ridge south of Ra Jadero Canyon, west of La Jara, Colo.; knob east of logging road, at about 8,850 ft.

57–58. Lower La Jara Canyon, lower and upper parts of lowest flow, mouth of Vicente Canyon. May not have been erupted from Los Mogotes volcano.

59. Lower La Jara Canyon, middle flow; along road about 3.5 km northeast of locality 57–58.

60–68. Sequence of nine flows, from top down, on south mesa rim about 5 km west of Mecitas, south flank of Los Mogotes volcano.

69. Flow along road, east flank of main cone; about same locality as 54.

70. Flow on north crater rim; about same locality as 55.

71. Tierra Amarilla flow; roadcut, U.S. 84, at 7,400-ft elevation, just south of Park View, N. Mex.
72. Cebolla flow; along logging road at 8,750 ft, about 6 km east of Cebolla, N. Mex.
73. Cebolla flow; along logging road at about 8,500 ft, about 5 km east of Cebolla, N. Mex.
74. Tierra Amarilla flow; north of road (N. Mex. 112), 1.0 km northeast of La Puente, N. Mex.
75. Tierra Amarilla flow; along N. Mex. 112, 2.2 km southwest of La Puente.
76. Agua Fria flow; south of road, about 1 km west of junction of Rito de Tierra Amarilla and Rito de Agua Fria. Rather vesicular.
77. Agua Fria flow; about 1 km above mouth of Rito de Agua Fria.
78–80. Cluster of cinder cones, about 4 km southeast of Brazos Box. No. 78 is agglutinate spatter from near the crest of the west cone; No. 79 is a flow on the southwest side of the north cone; and No. 80 is a flow on the west side of the east cone.
81. Flow 1; see Lipman and Moench (1972, table 1, No. 1).
82. Flow 2; see Lipman and Moench (1972, table 1, No. 2).
83. Picacho Peak plug; see Lipman and Moench (1972, table 1, No. 4).
84. Flow 2; see Lipman and Moench (1972, table 1, No. 3).
85. Flow 4; same locality as Lipman and Moench (1972, table 1, No. 7).
86. Flow 6; see Lipman and Moench (1972, table 1, No. 7).
87. Flow 8; see Lipman and Moench (1972, table 1, No. 8).
88. Flow 13; same locality as Lipman and Moench (1972, table 1, No. 7).
89. Flow 3? Rio Paguate, about 1 km northeast of Evans Ranch.
90. Flow 5? Same locality as 89.
91. Flow 6; same locality as 89.
92. Flow 8? Same locality as 89.
93. Flow 9; see Lipman and Moench (1972, table 1, No. 9).
94. Flow 11; see Lipman and Moench (1972, table 1, No. 10).
95. Flow 4? See Lipman and Moench (1972, table 1, No. 6).
96. Flow 4; see Lipman and Moench (1972, table 1, No. 5).
97. Flow 5; same locality as 96.
98. High basalt of La Jara Mesa: Lobo Canyon road, San Mateo quadrangle.
99. Basalt of Horace Mesa; see Lipman and Moench (1972, table 1, No. 11).
100. Flow 12; see Lipman and Moench (1972, table 1, No. 12).
101. Flow 13; see Lipman and Moench (1972, table 1, No. 13).
102. Laguna flow at Laguna, N. Mex., just east of bridge across Rio San Jose.
103. Bluewater flow; roadcut, U.S. 66, about 1.5 km west of Anaconda mill.
104. Bluewater flow; see Lipman and Moench (1972, table 1, No. 16).
105. Fine-grained vesicular flow, southeast end of Zuni uplift; N. Mex. 53, at about 6,800-ft elevation.
106. Olivine-rich flow, N. Mex. 53, at about 7,250 ft just east of Continental Divide.
107. McCarty flow; see Lipman and Moench (1972, table 1, No. 15).
108. McCarty flow; roadcut, U.S. 66, 11 km southeast of Grants, north end of Las Ventanas Ridge.
109. Laguna flow; see Lipman and Moench (1972, table 1, No. 14).
110. Diktytaxitic flow; N. Mex. 6, 8 km southeast of intersection with U.S. 66.
111. Fine-grained porous flow with large olivine phenocrysts; N. Mex. 6, about 10 km east of Rio Puerco.
112. Roadcut, N. Mex. 53, just west of Continental Divide.
113. Junction of Zuni and La Jara Canyons; flow came down La Jara Canyon.
114. Zuni Canyon flow; see Lipman and Moench (1972, table 1, No. 17).
115. High flow, U.S. 85, 1.5 km north of Wagon Mound, N. Mex.
116. High flow, in quarry 2 km east of Wagon Mound.
117. Maxson flow, roadcut, U.S. 85, at hillcrest southeast of Maxson crater.
118. Dense basalt, probably welded spatter; eroded cinder cone 0.5 km north of N. Mex. 120, 13 km northwest of Wagon Mound.
119. Xenocrystic basalt on low mesa; just north of N. Mex. 120, 1.5 km east of Naranjos, N. Mex.
120. Diktytaxitic flow; N. Mex. 21, 1 km south of Ocate.
121. Dense fine-grained flow; N. Mex. 21, about 2 km south of Ojo Felix.
122. Xenocrystic flow; N. Mex. 38, about 3.5 km north of Guadalupita.
123. Basaltic andesite; N. Mex. 38, at pass south of Black Lakes.
124. Basaltic andesite(?); outlet of Black Lake.
125. Low flow; west of U.S. 85, about 9 km north of Wagon Mound, N. Mex.
126–127. Northwest end of Mesa de Maya, 5 km south of Tobe, Colo., upper and lower flows.
128. Johnson Mesa, upper flow; roadcut, N. Mex. 72, about 3 km northwest of Windrow Peak at about 8,000-ft elevation.
129. Johnson Mesa, pressure ridge, top of flow; roadcut, just south of intersection with N. Mex. 72, 1.5 km west of Windrow Peak.
130–131. Mesa rim, 2.5 km northwest of Capulin cone. No. 130 is top blocky ledge; 131 is lower ledge of denser and finer grained basalt. Probably same locality as that of sample analyzed by Baldwin and Muehlberger (1959, table 4, RBC).
132. East rim of Johnson Mesa; first major roadcut, N. Mex. 72, at about 7,400 ft. Probably same locality as that of sample analyzed by Aoki (1967b, table 1, No. 1).
133. Bartlett Mesa; talus block on slope at Raton Pass, rest area on I-25.
134. Flow from Yankee volcano; south of N. Mex. 72 at Yankee, N. Mex. Approximately same locality as that of samples analyzed by Lee (1922).
135. Mud Hill cinder cone; small fine-grained dense flow on west side.
136. Purvine Mesa flow; from vent No. 4 (south of main line of cones) in Purvine Hills.
137. Bellisle Mountain flow; N. Mex. 72, at west boundary of Union County.
138. East Big Hill; N. Mex. 325, about 5 km northeast of Folsom, N. Mex. May be a dike within the cinder cone.
139. Emory Peak flow; underlies sample 138 at same locality.
140. Emory Peak flow; west end of flow at falls over Baby Capulin flow. Locality of sample analyzed by Baldwin and Muehlberger (1959, table 4, EP).
141. Bellisle Mountain flow; N. Mex. 325, about 3 km northeast of Folsom, N. Mex.
142. Robinson Mountain flow; about 4 km west of Folsom, N. Mex., at about 6,400-ft elevation, in tributary of Dry Cimarron Creek; fine diktytaxitic texture.
143. Jose Butte flow, as mapped by Baldwin and Muehlberger (1959), but appears continuous with Robinson Mountain flow locality 142; collected 0.5 km upstream from locality 142.
144. Van Cleve flow, at Weatherly Lake; about same locality as that of sample analyzed by Baldwin and Muehlberger (1959, table 4, VC).
145. Gaps flow; 5 km south of Weatherly Lake, from scarp west of road; fine-grained diktytaxitic texture.
146. At road intersection, 1.5 km northeast of Greenville, N. Mex.; fairly coarse diktytaxitic texture.
147. Flow from Cienquilla del Barro Mountain; at railway cut, 1.5 km east of Mount Dora. A few large quartz xenocrysts; some zeolites in vesicles.
148. Flow at Royce; along gravel road, about 0.1 km north of railway. Some calcite-filled vesicles. Near locality of sample analyzed by Aoki (1967b, table 1, No. 7).
149. Roadcut, N. Mex. 370, about 3 km northwest of Clayton, N. Mex.
150. Mesa rim flow, south of Clayton Reservoir, on access road.
151. Middle-level flow; N. Mex. 370, about 4 km northwest of Rabbit Ear Mountain, at 4,900-ft elevation; erupted from Rabbit Ear vent.
152. High flow; N. Mex. 370, about 1.5 km west of Rabbit Ear Mountain, at 4,500 ft; erupted from Rabbit Ear vent.
153. Carrizo flow; N. Mex. 56, about 20 km southwest of Clayton, N. Mex.
154. Flow at southeast edge of San Carlos Hills; N. Mex. 56, just west of Passamonte Ranch.
155. Similar flow; N. Mex. 56, about 4 km east of Gladstone, N. Mex.
156. Higher level flow; N. Mex. 56, about 10 km east of Gladstone, N. Mex.
157. Capulin cone; dense flow, at campground on south side of cone.
158. Xenocrystic flow from Capulin cone; roadcut, N. Mex. 64. Probably locality of sample analyzed by Aoki (1967b, table 1, No. 8).
159. Capulin cone; flow or large block within scoria fall on south side of cone.
160–161. Capulin cone; scoria fall along road 0.1 km north of crater parking lot. No. 160 is red cinders; 161, black cinders.
162. Capulin cone; xenocrystic flow on west side; roadcut, N. Mex. 325.
163. Baby Capulin; flow on west side of cone, about 0.1 km east of N. Mex. 325.

164–165. Baby Capulin; scoria fall, east quarry pit. No. 164 is red cinders; 165, black cinders.
166–167. Twin Mountain; scoria fall, east quarry pit. No. 166 is red cinders; 167, black cinders.
168. Flow probably from west Purvine Hill vent; 0.5 km east of Twin Mountain, on cinder quarry road.
169. Twin Mountain flow; tumulus south of paved road, just north of Twin Mountain.
170. Baby Capulin flow near toe; along Cimarron River south of Devoys Peak. Probably near locality of sample analyzed by Baldwin and Muehlberger (1959, table 4, BC).

REFERENCES CITED

Aoki, Ken-ichiro, 1967a, Petrography and petrochemistry of latest Pliocene olivine-tholeiites of Taos area, northern New Mexico, U.S.A.: Contr. Mineralogy and Petrology, v. 14, no. 3, p. 190–203.

——1967b, Alkaline and calc-alkaline basalts from Capulin Mountain, northeastern New Mexico, U.S.A.: Japanese Assoc. Mineralogists, Petrologists and Econ. Geologists Jour., v. 58, no. 4, p. 143–151.

Baldwin, Brewster, and Muehlberger, W. R., 1959, Geologic studies of Union County, New Mexico: New Mexico Bur. Mines and Mineral Resources Bull. 63, 171 p.

Best, M. G., and Brimhall, W. H., 1970, Late Cenozoic basalt types in the western Grand Canyon region, *in* Hamblin, W. K., and Best, M. G., eds., The western Grand Canyon district: Utah Geol. Soc. Guidebook 23, p. 57–74.

Best, M. G., Hamblin, W. K., and Brimhall, W. H., 1966, Preliminary petrology and chemistry of Late Cenozoic basalts in the western Grand Canyon region: Brigham Young Univ. Geology Studies, v. 13, p. 109–123.

——1969, Late Cenozoic basalts on the western margin of the Colorado Plateaus, Utah and Arizona: Brigham Young Univ. Research Rept. 69-1, 39 p.

Bryan, Kirk, 1938, Geology and ground water conditions of the Rio Grande depression in Colorado and New Mexico, *in* Regional planning, Pt. 6, Rio Grande joint investigation in the upper Rio Grande Basin: Washington, Natl. Resources Comm., v. 1, pt. 2, sec. 1, p. 197–225.

Butler, A. P., Jr., 1971, Tertiary volcanic stratigraphy of the eastern Tusas Mountains, southwest of the San Luis Valley, Colorado-New Mexico, *in* New Mexico Geol. Soc. Guidebook 22d Field Conf.: p. 289–300.

Chapin, C. E., 1971, The Rio Grande Rift, Pt. I—Modifications and additions, *in* New Mexico Geol. Soc. Guidebook 22d Field Conf.: p. 191–202.

Christiansen, R. L., and Lipman, P. W., 1972, Cenozoic volcanism and plate tectonic evolution of the Western United States—II. Late Cenozoic: Royal Soc. London Philos. Trans., v. 271, no. 1213, p. 249–284.

Cohee, G. V., chm., and others, 1961, Tectonic map of the United States, exclusive of Alaska and Hawaii: U.S. Geol. Survey and Am. Assoc. Petroleum Geologists, scale 1:2,500,000 [1962].

Cohen, L. H., Ito, Keisuke, and Kennedy, G. C., 1967, Melting and phase relations in an anhydrous basalt to 40 kilobars: Am. Jour. Sci., v. 265, no. 6, p. 475–518.

Collins, R. F., 1949, Volcanic rocks of northeastern New Mexico: Geol. Soc. America Bull., v. 60, no. 6, p. 1017–1040.

Condie, K. C., and Barsky, C. K., 1972, Origin of Quaternary basalts from the Black Rock Desert region, Utah: Geol. Soc. America Bull., v. 83, no. 2, p. 333–352.

Doe, B. R., Lipman, P. W., Hedge, C. E., and Kurasawa, Hajime, 1969, Primitive and contaminated basalts from the southern Rocky Mountains, U.S.A.: Contr. Mineralogy and Petrology, v. 21, no. 2, p. 142–156.

Doney, H. H., 1968, Geology of the Cebolla quadrangle, Rio Arriba County, New Mexico: New Mexico State Bur. Mines and Mineral Resources Bull. 92, 114 p.

Embree, G. F., 1970, Lateral and vertical variations in a Quaternary basalt flow—Petrography and chemistry of the Gunlock flow, southwestern Utah: Brigham Young Univ. Geology Studies, v. 17, pt. 1, p. 67–115.

Engel, A. E. J., Engel, C. G., and Havens, R. G., 1965, Chemical characteristics of oceanic basalts and the upper mantle: Geol. Soc. America Bull., v. 76, no. 7, p. 719–734.

Fanale, F. P., and Nash, D. B., 1971, Potassium-uranium systematics of Apollo 11 and Apollo 12 samples—Implications for lunar material history: Science, v. 171, no. 3968, p. 282–284.

Fisher, D. E., 1970, Homogenized fission track analysis of uranium in some ultramafic rocks of known potassium content: Geochim. et Cosmochim. Acta, v. 34, no. 5, p. 630–634.

Gaca, J. R., and Karig, D. E., 1966, Gravity survey in the San Luis Valley area, Colorado: U.S. Geol. Survey open-file report, 43 p.

Gottfried, David, Moore, Roosevelt, and Campbell, Esma, 1963, Thorium and uranium in some volcanic rocks from the circum-Pacific province: Art. 202 *in* U.S. Geol. Survey Prof. Paper 450-E, p. E85–E89.

Green, D. H., 1968, Origin of basaltic magmas, *in* Hess, H. H., and Poldervaart, Arie, eds., Basalts—The Poldervaart treatise on rocks of basaltic composition, V. 2: New York and London, Intersci. Publishers, p. 835–862.

Green, D. H., and Ringwood, A. E., 1967, The genesis of basaltic magmas: Contr. Mineralogy and Petrology, v. 15, no. 2, p. 103–190.

Hedge, C. E., and Knight, R. J., 1969, Lead and strontium isotopes in volcanic rocks from northern Honshu, Japan: Geochem. Jour., v. 3, no. 1, p. 15–24.

Hedge, C. E., and Lipman, P. W., 1972, Upper Cenozoic basalts of the southern Rocky Mountain region—Pt. 2, Strontium isotopes and the geochemistry of Sr, Rb, and Ba: Geol. Soc. America, Cordilleran Sec., Abs. with Programs, v. 4, no. 3, p. 169.

Heier, K. S., Compston, W., and McDougall, I., 1965, Thorium and uranium concentrations, and the isotopic composition of strontium in the differentiated Tasmanian dolerites: Geochim. et Cosmochim. Acta, v. 29, no. 6, p. 643–659.

Heier, K. S., McDougall, Ian, and Adams, J. A. S., 1964, Thorium, uranium and potassium concentrations in Hawaiian lavas: Nature, v. 201, no. 4916, p. 254–256.

Heier, K. S., and Rogers, J. J. W., 1963, Radiometric determination of thorium, uranium and potassium in basalts and in two magmatic differentiation series: Geochim. et Cosmochim. Acta, v. 27, no. 2, p. 137–154.

Jackson, E. D., and Wright, T. L., 1970, Xenoliths in the Honolulu volcanic series, Hawaii: Jour. Petrology, v. 11, pt. 2, p. 405–430.

Kay, R., Hubbard, N. J., and Gast, P. W., 1970, Chemical characteristics and origin of oceanic ridge volcanic rocks: Jour. Geophys. Research, v. 75, no. 8, p. 1585–1614.

Kelley, V. C., 1952, Tectonics of the Rio Grande depression of central New Mexico, *in* New Mexico Geol. Soc. Guidebook 3d Field Conf., Rio Grande Country, central New Mexico, 1952: p. 93–105.

——1956, The Rio Grande depression from Taos to Santa Fe, *in* New Mexico Geol. Soc. Guidebook 7th Field Conf., southeastern Sangre de Cristo Mountains, New Mexico, 1956: p. 109–114.

Kudo, A. M., Aoki, Ken-ichiro, and Brookins, D. G., 1971, The origin of Pliocene-Holocene basalts of New Mexico in the light of strontium-isotope and major-element abundances: Earth and Planetary Sci. Letters, v. 13, no. 1, p. 200–240.

Kuno, Hisashi, 1959, Origin of Cenozoic petrographic provinces of Japan and surrounding areas: Bull. Volcanol., ser. 2, v. 20, p. 37–76.

——1968, Differentiation of basalt magmas, *in* Hess, H. H., and Poldervaart, Arie, eds., Basalts—The Poldervaart treatise on rocks of basaltic composition, V. 2: New York and London, Intersci. Publishers, p. 623–688.

Kushiro, Ikuo, 1968, Compositions of magmas formed by partial zone melting of the earth's upper mantle: Jour. Geophys. Research, v. 73, no. 2, p. 619–634.

Larsen, E. S., Jr., and Cross, Whitman, 1956, Geology and petrology of the San Juan region, southwestern Colorado: U.S. Geol. Survey Prof. Paper 258, 303 p.

Larsen, E. S., Irving, John, Gonyer, F. A., and Larsen, E. S., 3d, 1938, Petrologic results of a study of the minerals from the Tertiary volcanic rocks of the San Juan region, Colorado: Am. Mineralogist, v. 23, no. 7, p. 417–429.

Laughlin, A. W., Brookins, D. G., and Carden, J. R., 1972, Variations in the initial strontium ratios of a single basalt flow: Earth and Planetary Sci. Letters, v. 14, p. 79–82.

Laughlin, A. W., Brookins, D. G., Kudo, A. M., and Causey, J. D., 1971, Chemical and strontium isotopic investigations of ultramafic inclusions and basalt, Bandera Crater, New Mexico: Geochim. et Cosmochim. Acta, v. 35, no. 1, p. 107–113.

Lee, W. T., 1922, Description of the Raton, Brilliant, and Koehler quadrangles [New Mexico]: U.S. Geol. Survey Geol. Atlas Folio 214.

Leeman, W. P., and Rogers, J. W. J., 1970, Late Cenozoic alkali-olivine basalts of the basin-range province, USA: Contr. Mineralogy and Petrology, v. 25, p. 1–24.

Lipman, P. W., 1969, Alkalic and tholeiitic basaltic volcanism related to the Rio Grande depression, southern Colorado and northern New Mexico: Geol. Soc. America Bull., v. 80, no. 7, p. 1343–1353.

Lipman, P. W., and Moench, R. H., 1972, Basalts of the Mount Taylor volcanic field, New Mexico: Geol. Soc. America Bull., v. 83, no. 5, p. 1335–1344.

Lipman, P. W., Steven, T. A., and Mehnert, H. H., 1970, Volcanic history of the San Juan Mountains, Colorado, as indicated by potassium-argon dating: Geol. Soc. America Bull., v. 81, no. 8, p. 2329–2352.

Macdonald, G. A., and Katsura, T., 1964, Chemical composition of Hawaiian lavas: Jour. Petrology, v. 5, pt. 1, p. 82–133.

Nicholls, J., Carmichael, I. S. E., and Stormer, J. C., Jr., 1971, Silica activity and P_{total} in igneous rocks: Contr. Mineralogy and Petrology, v. 33, no. 1, p. 1–20.

O'Hara, M. J., and Yoder, H. S., Jr., 1967, Formation and fractionation of basic magmas at high pressures: Scottish Jour. Geology, v. 3, pt. 1, p. 67–117.

Ozima, M., Kono, M., Kaneoka, I., Kinoshita, H., Kobayashi, Kazuo, Nagata, T., Larson, E. E., and Strangway, D. W., 1967, Paleomagnetism and potassium-argon ages of some volcanic rocks from the Rio Grande gorge, New Mexico: Jour. Geophys. Research, v. 72, no. 10, p. 2615–2622.

Patterson, Claire, and Tatsumoto, M., 1964, The significance of lead isotopes in detrital feldspar with respect to chemical differentiation within the earth's mantle: Geochim. et Cosmochim. Acta, v. 28, no. 1, p. 1–22.

Powers, H. A., 1935, Differentiation of Hawaiian lavas: Am. Jour. Sci., 5th ser., v. 30, no. 175, p. 57–71.

Renault, Jacques, 1970, Major-element variations in the Potrillo, Carrizozo, and McCartys basalt fields, New Mexico: New Mexico Bur. Mines and Mineral Resources Circ. 113, 22 p.

Russell, R. D., and Farquhar, R. M., 1960, Dating galenas by means of their isotopic constitutions—II: Geochim. et Cosmochim. Acta, v. 19, no. 1, p. 41–52.

Schonfeld, Ernest, 1966, Alpha M—An improved computer program for determining radioisotopes by least-squares resolution of the gamma-ray spectra: U.S. Natl. Lab. Oak Ridge ORNL-3975, 42 p.

Steven, T. A., and Epis, R. C., 1968, Oligocene volcanism in south-central Colorado, *in* Cenozoic volcanism in the southern Rocky Mountains: Colorado School Mines Quart., v. 63, no. 3, p. 241–258.

Stobbe, H. R., 1949, Petrology of volcanic rocks of northeastern New Mexico: Geol. Soc. America Bull., v. 60, no. 6, p. 1041–1095.

Stormer, J. C., Jr., 1972, Ages and nature of volcanic activity on the southern High Plains, New Mexico and Colorado: Geol. Soc. America Bull., v. 83, no. 8, p. 2443–2448.

Strangway, D. W., Larson, E. E., and York D., 1969, A middle Tertiary magnetic transition in northwestern Colorado [abs.]: EOS (Am. Geophys. Union Trans.), v. 50, no. 4, p. 131.

Sugimura, Arata, 1960, Zonal arrangement of some geophysical and petrological features in Japan and its environs: Tokyo Univ. Fac. Sci. Jour., sec. 2, v. 12, pt. 2 p. 133–153.

Tatsumoto, M., 1966a, Genetic relations of oceanic basalts as indicated by lead isotopes: Science, v. 153, no. 3740, p. 1094–1101.

——1966b, Isotopic composition of lead in volcanic rocks from Hawaii, Iwo-Jima and Japan: Jour. Geophys. Research, v. 71, no. 6, p. 1721–1733.

Tilling, R. I., and Gottfried, David, 1969, Distribution of thorium, uranium, and potassium in igneous rocks of the Boulder batholith region, Montana, and its bearing on radiogenic heat production and heat flow: U.S. Geol. Survey Prof. Paper 614-E, 29 p.

Watkins, N. D., and Haggerty, S. E., 1967, Primary oxidation variation and petrogenesis in a single lava: Contr. Mineralogy and Petrology, v. 15, p. 251–271.

Watkins, N. D., Holmes, C. W., and Haggerty, S. E., 1967, Primary oxidation variation and distribution of uranium and thorium in a lava flow: Science, v. 155, no. 3762, p. 579–581.

Williams, Howel, 1936, Pliocene volcanoes of the Navajo-Hopi country: Geol. Soc. America Bull., v. 47, no. 1, p. 111–172.

Wise, W. S., 1969, Origin of basaltic magmas in the Mojave desert area, California: Contr. Mineralogy and Petrology, v. 23, p. 53–64.

Yoder, H. S., Jr., and Tilley, C. E., 1962, Origin of basalt magmas—An experimental study of natural and synthetic rock systems: Jour. Petrology, v. 3, pt. 3, p. 342–532.

Jour. Research U.S. Geol. Survey
Vol. 1, No. 4, July—Aug. 1973, p. 403—414

A PRECAMBRIAN DIAMICTITE BELOW THE BASE OF THE STILLWATER COMPLEX, SOUTHWESTERN MONTANA

By NORMAN J PAGE and RANDOLPH A. KOSKI, Menlo Park, Calif.

Abstract.—The metasedimentary rocks of Precambrian age below the base of the Stillwater Complex, southwestern Montana, contain a metamorphosed diamictite similar to diamictite in strata of late Precambrian and Early Cambrian age in Canada and the Western United States. The diamictite consists of a quartz-cordierite matrix containing an average 10–15 percent of rock fragments diverse in shape, size, angularity, lithologic types, and textures. The diamictite unit is poorly sorted, crops out discontinuously for 14 miles, and locally has a crude layering containing dropstones. Its origin is debatable, but the rock is suggestive of glacial marine deposition. The minimum age of the diamictite of the complex is 2,750 m.y. from U-Pb determination on zircon of intrusive quartz monzonite, the maximum 3,140 m.y. as determined on zircon from metasedimentary rocks interbedded with the diamictite.

Recently Gabrielse in Canada (1967, 1972) and Crittenden and others in the Western United States (1971) have called attention to a widespread but discontinuous diamictite in strata of late Precambrian and Early Cambrian age. This diamictite is commonly interpreted as glacial in origin (Aalto, 1971; Crittenden and others, 1971; Troxel, 1967) and is used as a synchronous unit for correlation in Western North America (Stewart, 1972). Similar diamictites occur in the hornfelsed metasedimentary rocks that form the basement below the Stillwater Complex of Precambrian age in southwestern Montana. As the age of the diamictite-bearing metasediments by U-Pb determinations of Nunes and Tilton (1971) on zircon is between 2,750 and 3,140 m.y., these pre-Stillwater diamictites are not correlative with those in the upper Precambrian, although they may be similar in aspect and origin. Because the aspect of the diamictites below the Stillwater Complex is distinctive, this report presents a detailed description of the rocks for comparison with other diamictites. Such rocks might furnish a lithologic basis for correlation in the older Precambrian strata.

The fragmental rocks, though now hornfelsed, will be referred to in this paper as diamictite, a term used to describe a nonsorted rock of sedimentary origin consisting of sand-size and (or) larger particles in a mud matrix (modified from Flint and others, 1960). Diamictites crop out discontinuously along a northwest trend for 14 or 15 miles, some immediately adjacent to the Basal zone of the Stillwater, others almost a mile from the Basal zone (fig. 1). Owing to the complexity of the geology and the sparsity of outcrops (Page and Nokleberg, 1970), continuity of the diamictite over the extent of the trend cannot be proved, but within areas of continuous outcrop and simple structure, diamictite units 100–200 feet thick can be traced in the hornfelsed metasedimentary rocks.

Although the stratigraphic sequence within the hornfelsed metasedimentary rocks is not well established because of the structural complexity, the rocks contain a magnetite-silicate mineral iron-formation; a blue-gray metaquartzite; a sequence of layered rocks that contain relict small-scale crossbedding, graded bedding, and cut-and-fill structures; and sequences of finely banded rocks. But most of the exposed hornfelses are massive, structureless rocks. The position of the diamictites in the sequence is difficult to establish except on a local scale, but their known occurrences appear to be at the same stratigraphic horizon.

The metasedimentary rocks have had a long, complicated geologic history that includes the following sequence of events: (1) at least two generations of folding (Page and Nokleberg, 1972), (2) intrusion and hornfelsing by the basaltic magma that formed the Stillwater Complex (Jones and others, (1960), (3) local intrusion by quartz-monzonites and aplites (Page and Nokleberg, 1970), (4) possible low-grade regional metamorphism, deformation, faulting, and intrusion of diabase dikes (Page and Nokleberg, 1972), and (5) normal and thrust faulting (Jones and others, 1960). Events 1 to 4 occurred in the Precambrian, event 5 during Laramide time (Jones and others, 1960). The geologic complexity introduced by these events must be borne in mind throughout the discussion of the diamictite rocks.

GEOLOGIC OCCURRENCE AND METHODOLOGY

Two of the better exposed and more accessible areas of diamictite were chosen for study, one near the Mountain View area, the other at the head of Bobcat Creek (fig. 1). The Mountain View area was studied by mapping the fragmental rocks exposed in five roadcuts across a cliff face in Verdigris Creek on a geologic base map at a scale of 1 inch to 100 feet

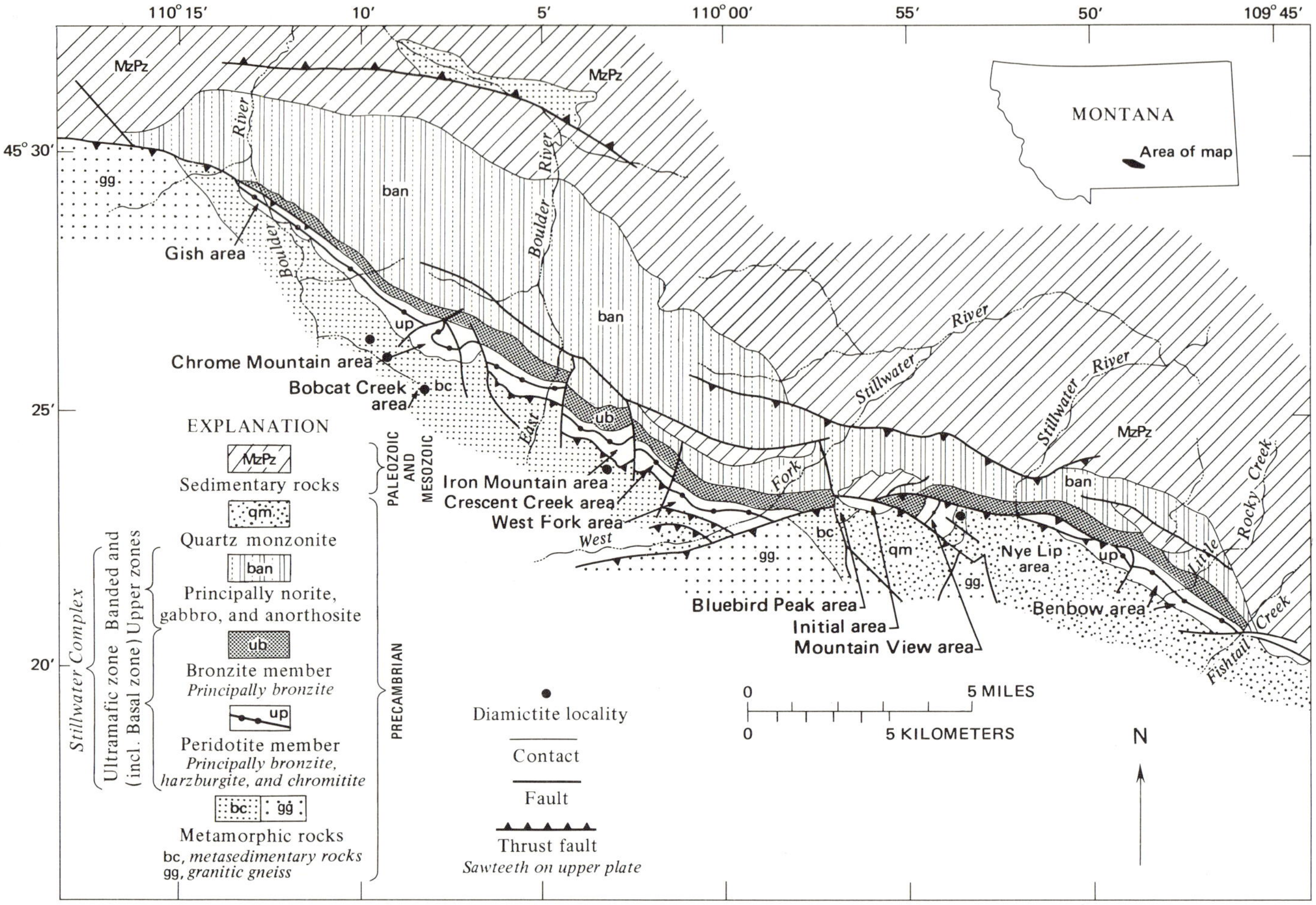

Figure 1.—Geologic sketch map of the Stillwater Complex, Montana, showing occurrences of diamictite. After Page and Nokleberg (1970).

(Peoples and others, 1954) and in greater detail at a scale of 1 inch to 20 feet. This area (fig. 2) was selected for study partly because it is intruded by noritic rocks of the Basal zone of the Stillwater Complex. The diamictite forms a layer 100–150 feet wide between finely layered hornfelses and massive structureless hornfelses that probably form a limb of a complex fold. No interfingering between the different rock types was observed.

Exposures at the Bobcat Creek locality (fig. 1) are in cliffs at the head of the creek about three-fifths of a mile south of the Basal zone of the Stillwater Complex. The locality is between two faults and apparently is part of a continuous unfaulted section from the Basal zone to the diamictite. A reconstructed geologic column based on Page and Nokleberg's map (1970) indicates that the diamictite is separated from the Stillwater Complex (fig. 3) by about 2,860 feet of diabase massive cordierite-orthopyroxene-biotite-quartz-plagioclase hornfels, blue metaquartzite, and iron-formation. At this locality the diamictite, matrix and megaclasts, was examined in nine subareas totalling more than 1,200 sq ft; all visible fragments were cataloged.

Other localities shown on the geologic sketch map (fig. 1) were not studied in detail but were briefly examined during mapping.

At both localities all visible megaclasts, about an eighth of an inch to tens of feet in diameter, were described and cataloged according to texture, size (maximum and minimum dimensions), shape, angularity, and probable original rock type before metamorphism. Examination of the megaclasts in three dimensions in the field was hindered because the outcrops were in cliffs and roadcuts, where most exposures were two-dimensional, and because there is little differential weathering between the matrix and the megaclasts. Where possible, megaclast attitudes were estimated in order to determine structural orientation (long dimension or planar feature) within the diamictite. Samples were collected for thin-section and analytical studies.

DESCRIPTION OF THE DIAMICTITE

The general aspect presented by outcrops of the diamictite is one of a minor proportion of megaclasts with diverse shapes,

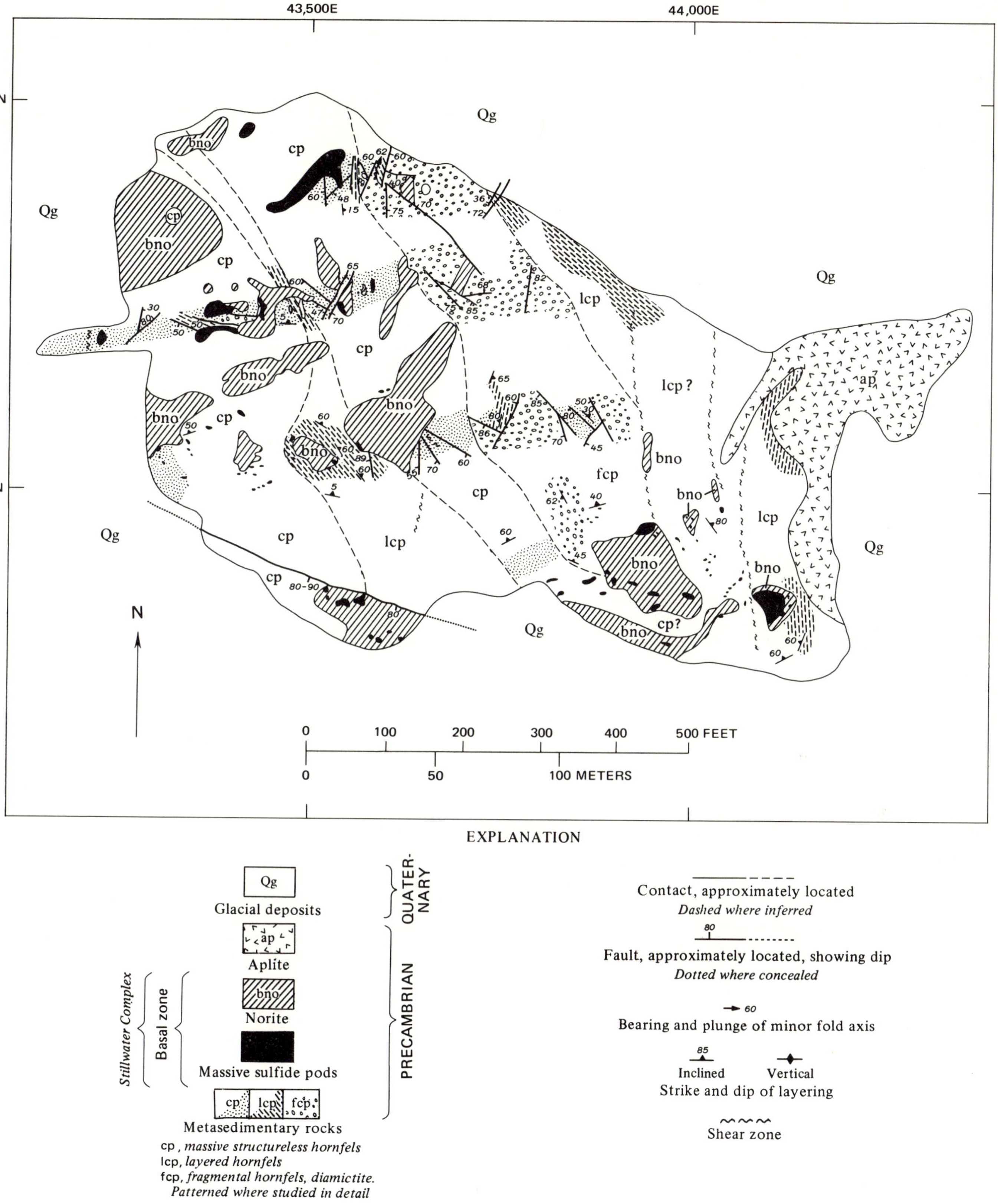

Figure 2.–Geologic map of the Mountain View area, showing outcrop north of Verdigris Creek (modified from Peoples and others, 1954; coordinates refer to coordinates on their map).

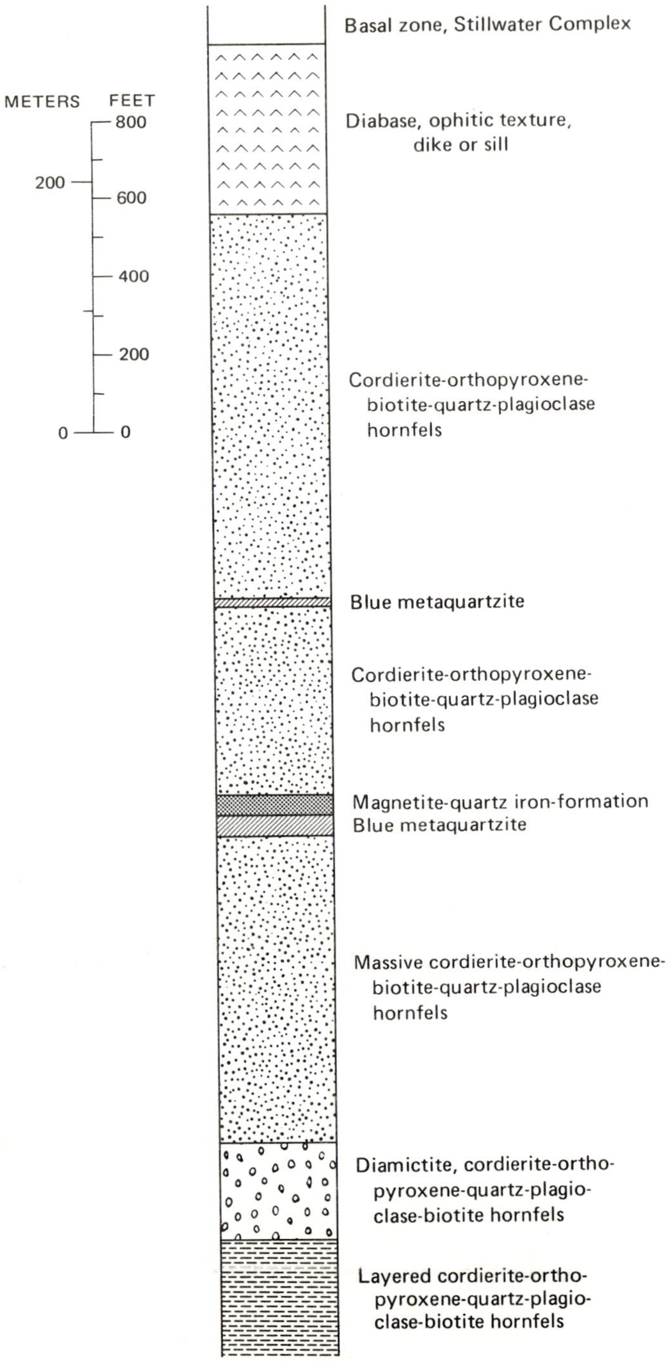

Figure 3.—Reconstructed geologic column for the Bobcat Creek locality, based on an approximate north-south section drawn from Page and Nokleberg (1970).

sizes, and angularity floating in a dark, fine-grained matrix (fig. 4). Some zones contain more megaclasts than others, suggesting weak stratification. Estimates of the volume of megaclasts in the matrix from subareas at the two localities range from less than 1 percent to 65 percent (table 1) but average 10 to 15 percent. Two methods were used to make these estimates: one was to measure the surface area of rock, sum the area covered by megaclasts, and derive a volume percentage; the other was to estimate the megaclasts visually.

Figure 4.—Diamictite outcrop in the Mountain View area. Maximum length of visible megaclasts 30 cm.

Table 1.—*Estimated volume percentages of megaclasts in matrix at the Mountain View and Bobcat Creek localities*

Subarea	Volume of megaclasts	
	Measured by areas	Visual estimate
Mountain View locality		
Traverse 1	1.4	......
2	55.4	......
3	6.4	......
4	2.3	......
Area 2	....	30.0
3	....	<1–65
4a	....	<5
4c	....	25
5	....	50
Bobcat Creek locality		
Area 1	3.8	......
2	8.1	......
3	13.5	......
4	.3	......
5	.3	......
6	14.1	......
7	11	......
8	12.8	......

Properties of Megaclasts

Textural varieties

The abundance of visible megaclasts in the diamictite, cataloged by texture recognized in the field, is given in table 2 for the Mountain View and Bobcat Creek localities. All of the textures are relict, and all megaclasts except the metaquartzites are composed of varying proportions of cordierite, orthopyroxene, plagioclase, biotite, and quartz. It should be emphasized that classification based on texture is by necessity rather crude. One of our main objectives, however, is to point

Table 2.—*Abundance of rock megaclasts classified by textural categories at the Mountain View and Bobcat Creek localities*

[Based on megaclast counts in the outcrops]

Textural category	Mountain View			Bobcat Creek		
	Number	Percentage	Group	Number	Percentage	Group
Layered, banded, or foliated.	101	35.2	56.1	40	36.4	80.0
Massive, homogeneous.	60	20.9		48	43.6	
Blue or gray metaquartzite.	50	17.4	35.9	11	10	11.8
Gneissic	45	15.7		2	1.8	
Schistose	8	2.8		0	0	
Granitoid, equigranular.	13	4.5	4.5	4	3.6	8.1
Volcanic	0	0		5	4.5	
Not classified	10	3.5		0	0	
Total	287	100		110	99.9	

out the heterogeneity of megaclasts found in the diamictite, a diversity that has survived several periods of intense deformation and metamorphism. The textures and mineralogy cannot be used directly to imply the source of the megaclasts as in sedimentary rocks.

Banded, layered, or foliated megaclasts are most easily recognized and one of the more abundant types. The layering consists of two types: (1) alternating dark and light laminations reflecting varying percentages of plagioclase, cordierite, and orthopyroxene; and (2) layering formed by abrupt changes in grain size. The layers are typically undeformed and display no sedimentary structures; a few banded megaclasts appear to contain folds or slump structures. Figure 5 shows several examples. Layered megaclasts showing effects of deformation are uncommon, but a number of clasts at Bobcat Creek (fig. 5*E*) display a peculiar convolute (disharmonic?) folding of alternating light and dark layers with attenuated fold limbs. Some of these distorted layers are finely laminated or massive and somewhat coarser than intervening thicker massive layers of very fine grained material. Septa of light massive material often terminate or penetrate darker seams. Whether this irregular deformation occurred before, during, or after emplacement of the diamictite is not known.

Layers within megaclasts range in thickness from less than 1 mm to greater than 15 cm, a single megaclast containing two layers or more. Some of the more finely layered megaclasts are suggestive of varves formed in lacustrine environments; other, coarsely layered megaclasts resemble interlayered sandstones and siltstones.

Of the samples examined, the rock exhibiting the most spectacular layering in a megaclast at the Mountain View locality is the block shown as figure 5*F*, which contains a near-linear contact between two contrasting fabrics, one fine-grained, massive, and cordierite-rich, the other medium-grained and granitoid, with prismatic, euhedral pyroxenes interlocked with plagioclase. The coarse segment of the megaclast appears to be devoid of cordierite. Closer examination of the contact reveals several tonguelike protuberances of coarser grained material penetrating approximately 0.5 cm into the massive portion of the fragment. Neither segment of this clast resembles the matrix texturally, and the megaclast boundaries are clearly marked. Other binary fragments were observed in the outcrop.

Massive megaclasts, the other most abundant category, are fine grained, dense, rich in cordierite and plagioclase or combinations of these minerals, and have a texture closely resembling that of the granofels matrix. These blocks are commonly somewhat bleached, especially near their perimeters, owing to surface weathering of cordierite and plagioclase and to a decrease of quartz in the megaclast. Some staining of megaclasts results from oxidation of sulfides and iron-bearing silicates. Microscopic examination of massive megaclasts reveals a relict texture with plagioclase and rounded or subrounded grains of quartz surrounded by orthopyroxene and cordierite. Locally the orthopyroxene exhibits sieve texture (fig. 5*H*). Where pyroxene is less common, quartz and cordierite have a distinct arrangement of isolated, round to subround grains of quartz being surrounded by clots or patches in which individual cordierite grains form a mosaic. The massive nature of these megaclasts at the outcrop is less apparent in thin section.

Megaclasts with a metamorphic fabric distinct from the granofels matrix are the third most abundant group at both localities. Most conspicuous are the blue and gray metaquartzite clasts that are easily spotted in the field and occur in slightly greater abundance at the Mountain View locality. Although common throughout the localities, generally they are so thoroughly dispersed that rarely do several metaquartzite megaclasts occur in 4 or 5 sq ft of outcrop. Textures are typically coarse grained with intergrown crystals of granular quartz and a few accessory minerals.

Megaclasts with a gneissic texture have a unique color banding resulting from differing proportions of quartz, cordierite, and orthopyroxene. The bands usually parallel the longest particle axes. In some megaclasts the variation in thickness of individual bands is slight, in others the bands are discontinuous and form lenses and "eyes" suggestive of augen gneisses. Light bands tend to have greater thickness, producing a pronounced color contrast between clast and matrix.

More difficult to distinguish at the outcrop are schistose megaclasts, so termed because planar orientation of fine-grained biotite results in the development of a pronounced cleavage or fracture.

The fourth group of megaclasts have textures that resemble those in igneous rocks. The majority of igneouslike megaclasts are granitoid or coarse-grained equigranular; the equant grains are easily observed without a hand lens and show interlocking and penetrating relations. No foliation or banding was seen in those megaclasts roughly classed as igneous. Megaclasts unique to Bobcat Creek have a blastoporphyritic texture consisting of sparse fine- to medium-grained phenocrysts of plagioclase set in a fine-grained massive matrix of plagioclase, cordierite,

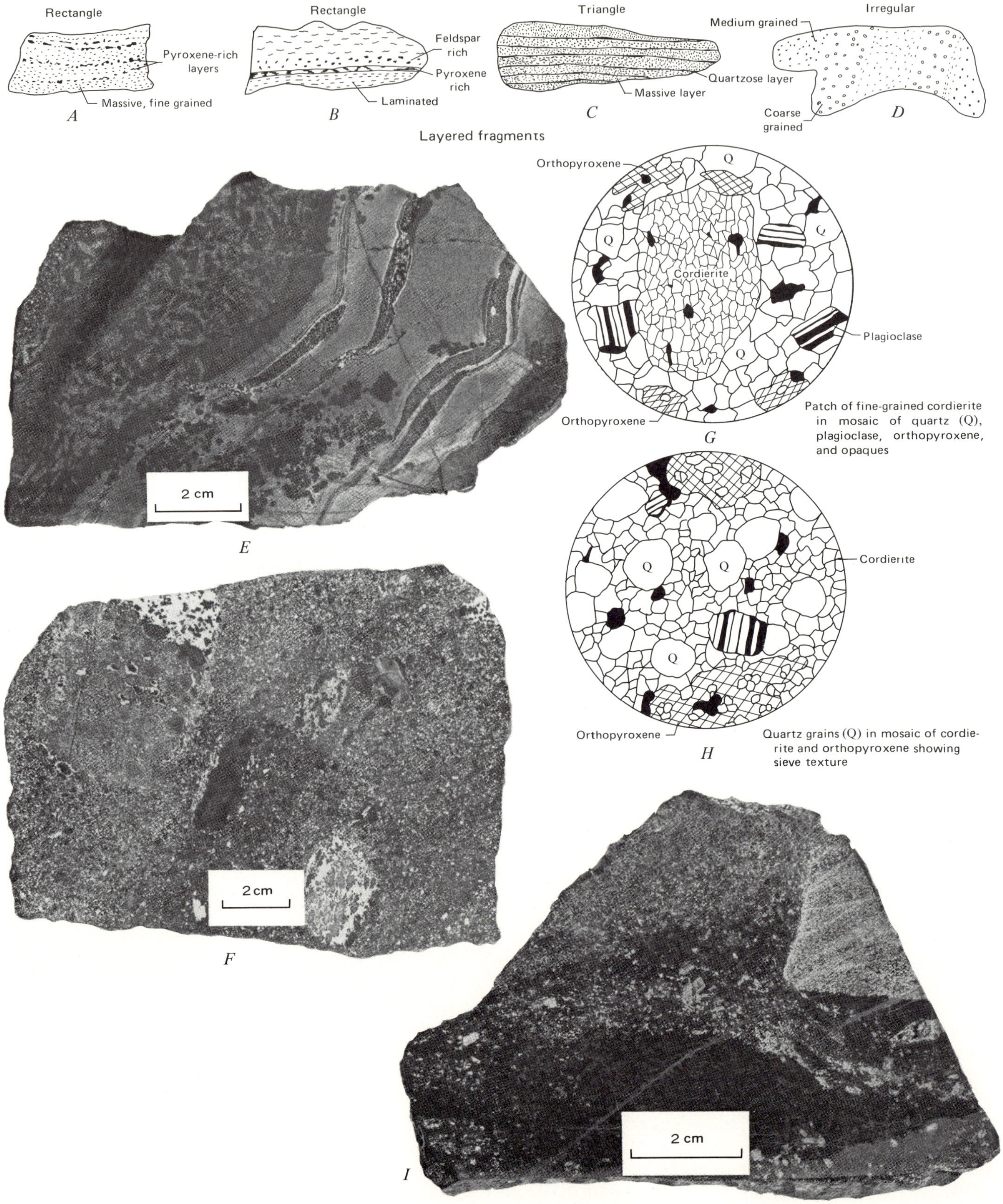
Rectangle
Pyroxene-rich layers
Massive, fine grained
A
Rectangle
Feldspar rich
Pyroxene rich
Laminated
B
Triangle
Quartzose layer
Massive layer
C
Irregular
Medium grained
Coarse grained
D
Layered fragments
Orthopyroxene
Q
Cordierite
Plagioclase
Orthopyroxene
Patch of fine-grained cordierite in mosaic of quartz (Q), plagioclase, orthopyroxene, and opaques
G
2 cm
E
Cordierite
Orthopyroxene
Quartz grains (Q) in mosaic of cordierite and orthopyroxene showing sieve texture
H
2 cm
F
2 cm
I

Figure 5.

pyroxene, and quartz; such clasts are considered to represent relict textures of volcanic rocks.

The layered and massive megaclasts that predominate at both the Mountain View and Bobcat Creek localities may be fragments of sedimentary rocks. The blue or gray metaquartzites could have been sedimentary rocks before they were hornfelsed but may also represent a contribution from an older metamorphic terrane, as do the gneissic and schistose megaclasts. Layered, massive, and metaquartzite megaclasts all have lithologic counterparts within a few miles of the exposed diamictite and within the same extensive metasedimentary unit. The blue-gray metaquartzite megaclasts, in particular, are suggestive of blue metaquartzite units in the hornfels unit adjacent to the base of the complex. Layered megaclasts closely resemble finely laminated metasediments that crop out elsewhere in the Mountain View area. Local provenances for the megaclasts of suspected metamorphic and igneous origins are not known.

Size characteristics

The diamictite at the Mountain View locality is marked by an extremely large range in particle size, from microscopic single grains of quartz to room-sized heterogeneous boulders. This millionfold size range is found along the entire strike of the diamictite horizon. At Bobcat Creek, a wide distribution of particle sizes exists, but unlike the Mountain View area, no megaclasts with an average diameter greater than 1 m were observed. The cumulative size-frequency curves based on the average of the apparent maximum and minimum diameters of megaclasts observed in only two dimensions at the Mountain View and Bobcat Creek localities are compared in figure 6, along with their statistical parameters. Since these curves represent field data, which omit microscopic particles, they do not represent a true size distribution for the diamictite. If microscopic fragments less than 8 mm in size were included, the dispersion, or coefficient of sorting, would be increased by several units and probably would make the size distribution curves bimodal. The size distributions of megaclasts at Mountain View and Bobcat Creek differ slightly. The median size is between 15 and 18 cm; distribution for both localities shows moderate to poor sorting characteristics and some skewness.

An accumulation of points relating apparent long and short dimensions of megaclasts at the Mountain View and Bobcat Creek localities (fig. 7) shows that the average of length-to-width ratios can be roughly represented by a straight line having a positive slope of about one-half. Megaclasts tend to be elongate rather than equant in two dimensions. Three-dimensional data from the few megaclasts so observed yield a range of ratios of 1:1.13:1.13 to 1:9.6:1.6.

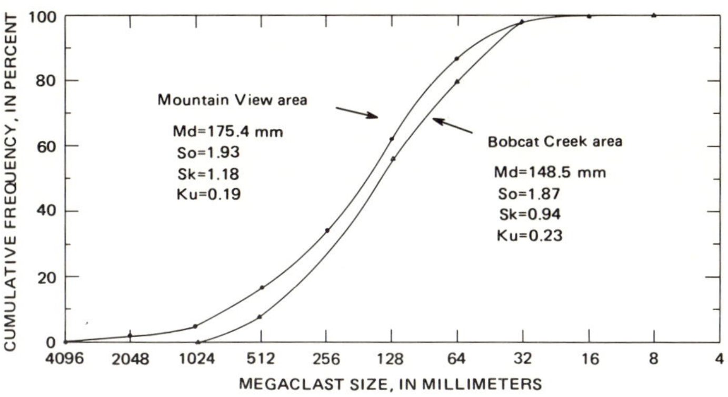

Figure 6.—Diagram showing cumulative frequency curves of megaclasts observed on outcrops. Md, median; So, sorting coefficient; Sk, skewness coefficient; Ku, kurtosis coefficient.

The extremely large size variation common to all megaclasts regardless of texture is readily seen from the median and range by category (table 3). Massive, gneissic, and layered megaclasts tend to have the largest median diameters, greater than that of metaquartzites; granitoid and volcanic megaclasts, the smallest. Megaclasts of diameter less than 8 mm certainly exist but were not readily observed in the field. Several boulder-sized chunks of diamictite were brought back to the laboratory for more detailed examination. By etching slabbed sections of diamictite in hydrofluoric acid, several suspicions held in the field were confirmed: (1) all particle sizes are present down to a few tenths of a millimeter in diameter; (2) fragment density is much greater than suggested by weathered surfaces; and (3) no textural type can be placed within a restricted class size.

Shape characteristics

The shape of megaclasts at Bobcat Creek and Mountain View can be determined in only two dimensions on the face formed by the intersection of the clast and the weathered surface. Rarely can the three-dimensional form be ascertained at the outcrop, but where observed, megaclasts tend to be prismatic. The heterogeneous shape characteristics of megaclasts of various textures at Bobcat Creek and Mountain View are apparent in the diagram of shape abundance (fig. 8) and the samples shown in figure 5. Nonetheless, a numerical preference for rectangular or elliptical shapes consistent with the length-width plots (given in fig. 7) prevails at the Mountain View and Bobcat Creek localities. Elongate megaclasts displaying one or both ends tapering to a blunt or broad tip (ellipses, triangles, pears, cigars) are more than twice as abundant at Bobcat Creek than at Mountain View.

Figure 5.—Sketches and photographs of megaclasts. *A*, layered rectangular megaclast, length 25 cm; *B*, layered rectangular megaclast, length 23 cm; *C*, layered triangular megaclast, length 61 cm; *D*, layered irregular megaclast, length 15 cm; *E*, etched slab of layered megaclast containing folds (?); *F*, etched slab of megaclasts in matrix; fragment in upper left consists of two rock types in contact; *G* and *H*, microscopic texture of megaclast, diameter of circles about 2 cm; *I*, megaclast in matrix—possible dropstone.

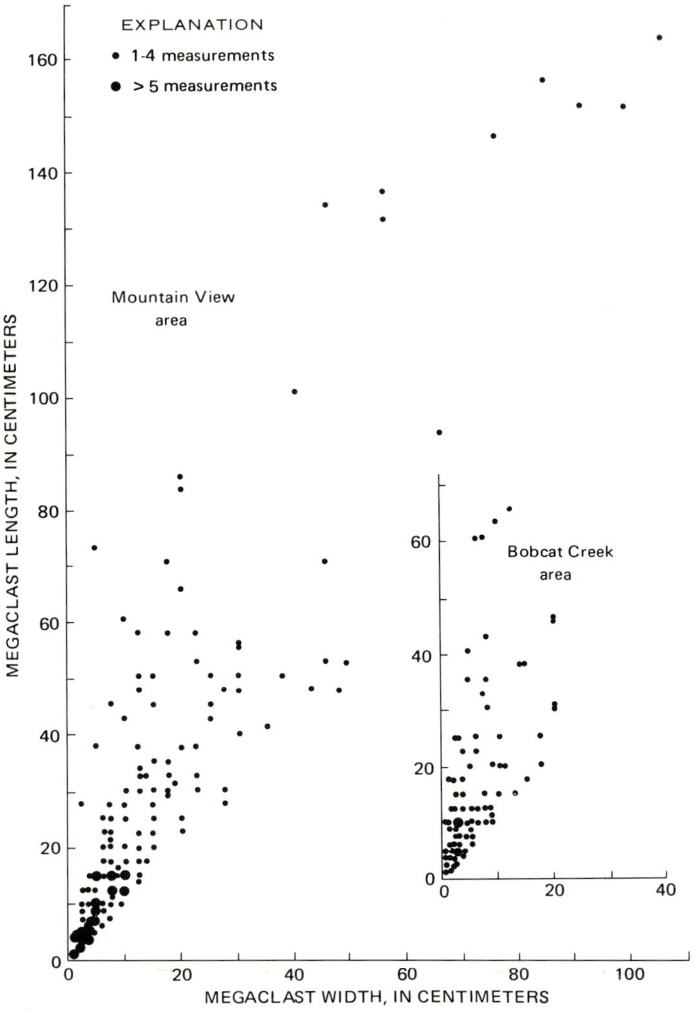

Figure 7.–Diagram showing length-to-width ratios of megaclasts at the Mountain View and Bobcat Creek localities.

Table 3.–*Median diameters and ranges of the megaclasts of the different textural categories at the Mountain View and Bobcat Creek localities*

[In millimeters]

Textural category	Mountain View		Bobcat Creek	
	Median	Range	Median	Range
Layered, banded, or foliated.	179.2	>2,048–16	243.20	512–16
Massive, homogeneous	208	>2,048–16	88	512–32
Blue or gray metaquartzite	136.3	>2,048–16	198.40	256–8
Gneissic	221.4	>2,048–16	......	128–32
Schistose	.....	....	......	....
Granitoid, equigranular	.....	....	......	128–32
Volcanic	.....	....	198.40	512–64

When particle shape is compared with texture (fig. 8), several affinities become apparent. Rectangular megaclasts are most commonly layered or banded, whereas elliptical megaclasts tend to be massive or metaquartzite. These associations probably reflect not only the agent of transportation but also the mechanism by which the megaclasts were formed.

Comparison of particle shape to particle size shows that at both the Mountain View and Bobcat Creek localities rectangular and elliptical shapes make up 55 to 80 percent of the megaclasts with average diameters between 1,024 and 16 mm. There are few differences in shape-size correlations between the two areas except for the apparent greater abundance of elongate megaclasts at Bobcat Creek.

Roundness characteristics

Each megaclast observed in the diamictite at the Mountain View and Bobcat Creek localities was placed in a roundness classification consisting of four categories: angular, subangular, subrounded, and rounded. Assignment to a particular category is based mainly on primary corners and edges as seen in outcrop; secondary corners are obscured by metamorphic effects and fuzzy boundaries on smaller clasts; thin sections show that recrystallization has greatly changed original clast edges. At Mountain View, about 19.5 percent are round, 27.1 percent subround, 30.1 percent subangular, and 23.3 percent angular, whereas at Bobcat Creek, 14.6 percent are round, 29.1 percent subround, 20 percent subangular, and 36.3 percent angular. As a group the megaclasts are predominantly subround to subangular.

Degree of rounding varies according to megaclast texture, size, and shape. In general, layered megaclasts tend to be subround to angular, quartzite megaclasts rounded, massive megaclasts round to subangular, gneissic megaclasts subround to angular, granitic megaclasts round, and schistose round to angular. In general, coarse clasts tend to be more angular, finer clasts more rounded, with some convergence in the intermediate size range of 256–128 mm.

Orientation

Wherever possible, megaclast attitudes were measured according to fabric or structural elements within each megaclast. Features used for megaclast orientation include foliation or schistosity, coarse banding, and fine lamination. In many places, a rough parallelism exists between planar elements in elongate megaclasts and their long dimensional surfaces. This direction of elongation of the megaclast and a rough estimation of plunge were recorded as a lineation.

Contoured fabric diagrams representing poles to megaclast foliations and lineations (plunge) are shown in figure 9. Foliation within megaclasts (fig. 9*A*) is represented by a weakly developed girdle that trends approximately east-west and dips 40° S. This pattern probably indicates deformation by folding after formation of the diamictite and is similar to the pattern obtained from layering in folded hornfelses within the same fault block (fig. 9*B*). An expanded discussion of the complexities of folding is given in Page and Nokleberg (1970, 1972) and other work of Page (unpub. data, 1972). Megaclast

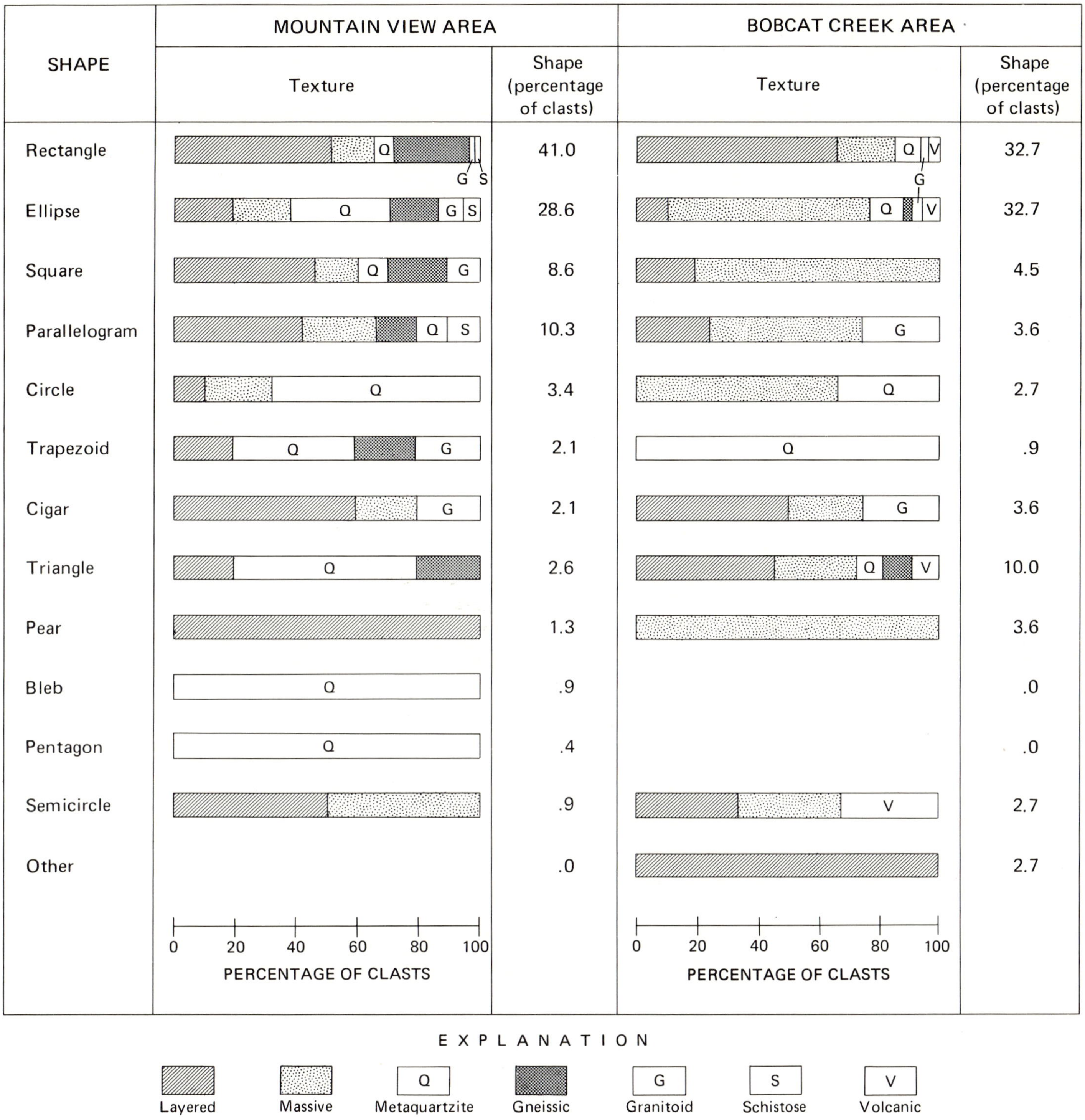

Figure 8.—Diagram showing shape abundance correlated with textural categories at Mountain View and Bobcat Creek.

elongations (maximum diameter) (fig. 9C) form a maximum plunging N. 226° E. at 47° SW., nearly in the plane of the megaclast foliation girdle. Some caution is necessary in interpreting lineation data, because bias may have been introduced in securing these "lineations" from nearly vertical cliff faces striking east-west to N. 70° E. If the elongation represented an original prefolding lineation, one would expect it to be distributed as a small circle around the fold axis or as a great circle with respect to the fold axes. Therefore, it would appear that the orientation of the maximum diameter of the megaclasts is a function of the nature of tectonism, as is the present orientation of foliation in the megaclast.

A fabric diagram of 51 recorded megaclast foliations at Bobcat Creek, figure 9*D*, shows a single maximum with minor girdling indicating a preferred orientation of planar elements striking northwest-southeast and dipping to the northeast. This orientation is roughly similar to the general attitude of layering in the adjacent hornfels and is probably a result of tectonism.

From examining foliations within megaclasts and comparing these with layering and its tectonic history in adjacent rocks, it appears that the megaclasts with preexisting structures and the layering in adjacent rocks behaved in a similar fashion. The correspondence between elongate, flattened megaclast shape and foliation suggests that these blocks were deposited in an equilibrium position, that is, with the largest surface parallel with sedimentary layering. From the study of the orientation of maximum diameters, it is probable that the long axes were oriented randomly in the bedding plane.

Matrix Material

The dark matrix containing the megaclasts consists by volume of 20–40 percent quartz, 30–40 percent cordierite, 15–20 percent orthopyroxene, 5–10 percent plagioclase, 0.5–3 percent biotite, less than 3 percent sulfide and oxide minerals, and minor amounts of zircon, garnet, chlorite, and sericite. The subrounded to subangular quartz grains (fig. 5*H*), averaging less than a millimeter in diameter (0.2–3.5 mm) and locally composed of more than one quartz crystal, appear to represent remnants of a clastic texture. The quartz grains are enclosed by sieve-textured orthopyroxene and anhedral masses of twinned and untwinned cordierite that could be metamorphic equivalents of various combinations of chlorite and clay minerals.

Comparison of chemical analyses of the matrix material with analyses of sedimentary rocks (Pettijohn, 1963) suggests that the matrix material has a composition similar to subgraywackes and graywackes but with higher MgO, FeO, Ni, and Cr contents than an average graywacke.

Although most field observations indicate a complete absence of bedding in the matrix material, laboratory studies suggest that some may be present. Crude layering can be recognized in the matrix upon etched surfaces and at places in megaclast-layering relations. At one locality we found what is interpreted to be bedding containing a dropstone (fig. 5*I*), a

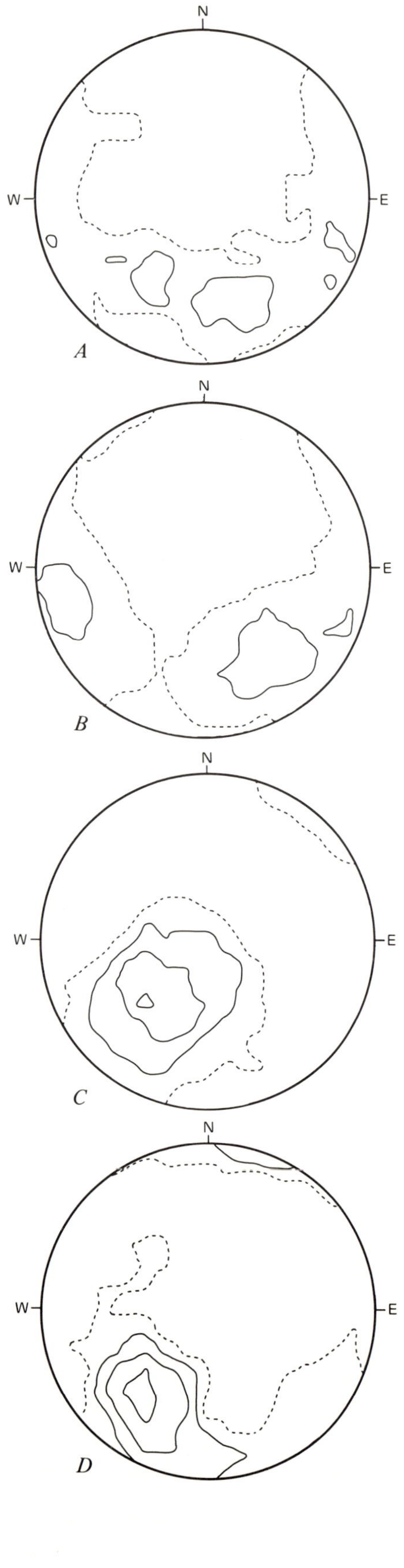

Figure 9.—Contoured fabric diagrams showing orientation of fragments. Contoured at 1E intervals where E is the expected number of points within the counting area for a random pattern using a method developed by Kamb (1959) and computerized by C. E. Corbato (written commun., 1970). Dashed contour is the 1E contour, solid contours are contours greater than 1E. *A*, poles to foliation in fragments, Mountain View area, 55 points, E = 3.73. *B*, poles to layering in hornfels from the Mountain View area, 22 points, E = 3.38. *C*, elongate orientation of fragment axes, Mountain View area, 21 points, E = 3.36. *D*, poles to foliation in fragments, Bobcat Creek area, 51 points, E = 3.71.

megaclast that has disturbed the underlying bedding and has been buried by later deposits.

AGE

Some of the recent age dating by Nunes and Tilton (1971) using U-Pb zircon methods on various rocks from the Stillwater Complex area can be used to establish limits on the age of the diamictite. The metasedimentary rocks intruded by the Stillwater Complex contain detrital zircons approximately 3,140 m.y. old, which establishes that these rocks are at least that old. Quartz monzonites intrude both the Stillwater Complex and the metasedimentary rocks (Page and Nokleberg, 1970, 1972). These siliceous igneous rocks yield an age of about 2,750 m.y. (Nunes and Tilton, 1971), which represents a minimum age for the metasedimentary rocks. The diamictite forms a layer or lenses within the metasedimentary rocks and has been involved in the same complex folding and faulting as the metasedimentary rocks. The age of the diamictite must be between the above two dates.

POSSIBLE ORIGINS

The composition, shape, and provenance of the megaclasts and the thickness, areal extent, and stratigraphic relations of the diamictite suggest that it is not a volcanic, fault, intrusive, or collapse breccia. The volume, abundant matrix, and bimodal texture of the diamictite imply that the megaclasts and matrix were transported by a viscous medium, either subaerially or subaqueously, which did little sorting, or that the megaclasts and matrix were separately transported to the areas of deposition. Flint (1961, p. 148–149) lists several depositional mechanisms that fit these qualifications, and Harland, Herod, and Krinsley (1966) review and reassess the criteria for the recognition of the products of these processes. Another possible origin of the diamictite is by meteoritic impact, as has been suggested for similar breccias associated with the Sudbury irruptive (French, 1968). Characteristics not supporting this origin are the appearance of megaclasts with no local provenance and the folded nature of the diamictite. In addition, the matrix fabric shows no evidence of flowage but does retain crude layering which at places contains dropstones. The most likely processes remain transport by a viscous medium or separate deposition of megaclasts and matrix.

The lack of evidence for channels, weathered zones, lag gravels, and alluvial sand and gravel deposits with channeling and current structures (Blackwelder, 1928) suggests that the diamictite did not originate as a subaerial mudflow, landslide, alluvial fan, or slumped debris. It is difficult to envision five or six drainage channels perpendicular to the general strike of the diamictite that would contribute megaclasts and matrix of a very similar nature, including clasts for which no local provenance is known.

Triangular and pentagonal clasts and dropstones could be taken as evidence of rafting, possibly by ice. All of the other described features of the diamictite are consistent with such an origin in a glacial marine environment, including deposits of drift and ice-rafted material, possibly reworked by slumping and sliding. Crowell (1964) and others have emphasized the difficulty of distinguishing such glacial marine deposits without a study of paleotectonics, paleogeography, and sediment sources, all of which are difficult, if not impossible, to evaluate in this diamictite. Although a glacial marine origin seems possible, the origin of the diamictite cannot be resolved with the available data and may be similar to the origin of the nonglacial pebbly mudstones in California described by Crowell (1957).

REFERENCES CITED

Aalto, K. R., 1971, Glacial marine sedimentation and stratigraphy of the Toby Conglomerate (upper Proterozoic), southeastern British Columbia, northwestern Idaho and northeastern Washington: Canadian Jour. Earth Sci., v. 8, no. 7, p. 753–787.

Blackwelder, Eliot, 1928, Mudflow as a geologic agent in semiarid mountains: Geol. Soc. America Bull., v. 39, p. 465–483.

Crittenden, M. D., Jr., Schaeffer, F. E., Trimble, D. E., and Woodward, L. A., 1971, Nomenclature and correlation of some upper Precambrian and basal Cambrian sequences in western Utah and southeastern Idaho: Geol. Soc. America Bull., v. 82, p. 581–602.

Crowell, J. C., 1957, Origin of pebbly mudstones: Geol. Soc. America Bull., v. 68, p. 993–1010.

—— 1964, Climatic significance of sedimentary deposits containing dispersed megaclasts, *in* Nairn, A. E. M., ed., Problems in palaeoclimatology: New York, Interscience Publishers, Inc., p. 86–99.

Flint, R. F., 1961, Geological evidence of cold climate, *in* Nairn, A. E. M., ed., Descriptive palaeoclimatology: New York, Interscience Publishers, Inc., p. 140–155.

Flint, R. F., Sanders, J. F., and Rodgers, John, 1960, Diamictite, a substitute term for symmictite: Geol. Soc. America Bull., v. 71, p. 1809.

French, B. M., 1968, Sudbury structure, Ontario—some petrographic evidence for an origin by meteorite impact, *in* French, B. M., and Short, N. M., eds., Shock metamorphism of natural materials: Baltimore, Md., Mono Book Corp., p. 383–412.

Gabrielse, Hubert, 1967, Tectonic evolution of northern Canadian Cordillera: Canadian Jour. Earth Sci., v. 4, p. 271–298.

—— 1972, Younger Precambrian of the Canadian Cordillera: Am. Jour. Sci., v. 272, p. 521–536.

Harland, W. B., Herod, K. N., and Krinsley, D. H., 1966, The definition and identification of tills and tillites: Earth-Sci. Rev., v. 2, p. 225–256.

Jones, W. R., Peoples, J. W., and Howland, A. L., 1960, Igneous and tectonic structures of the Stillwater Complex, Montana: U.S. Geol. Survey Bull. 1071-H, p. 281–340.

Kamb, W. B., 1959, Petrofabric observations from Blue Glacier, Washington, in relation to theory and experiment: Jour. Geophys. Research, v. 64, p. 1908–1909.

Nunes, P. D., and Tilton, G. R., 1971, Uranium-lead ages of minerals from the Stillwater Igneous Complex and associated rocks, Montana: Geol. Soc. America Bull., v. 82, p. 2231–2250.

Page, N. J, and Nokleberg, W. J., 1970, Preliminary geologic map of the Stillwater Complex, Montana: U.S. Geol. Survey open-file map, scale 1:12,000.

Page, N. J, and Nokleberg, W. J., 1972, Genesis of mesozonal granitic rocks below the base of the Stillwater Complex in the Beartooth Mountains, Montana, *in* Geological Survey Research 1972: U.S. Geol. Survey Prof. Paper 800-D, p. D127–D141.

Peoples, J. W., Howland, A. L., Jones, W. R., and Flint, Delos, 1954, Geologic map, sections, and map of underground workings of the Mountain View Lake area, Stillwater County, Montana: U.S. Geol. Survey open-file report, 2 maps, 8 sections.

Pettijohn, F. J., 1963, Chemical composition of sandstones–excluding carbonate and volcanic sands–Chapter S, *in* Fleischer, Michael, ed., Data of geochemistry, 6th ed.: U.S. Geol. Survey Prof. Paper 440-S, p. S1–S21.

Stewart, J. H., 1972, Initial deposits in the Cordilleran geosyncline–Evidence of a late Precambrian (<850 m.y.) continental separation: Geol. Soc. America Bull., v. 83, p. 1345–1360.

Troxel, B. W., 1967, Sedimentary rocks of late Precambrian and Cambrian age in the southern Salt Spring Hills, southeastern Death Valley, California: California Div. Mines and Geology Spec. Rept. 92, p. 33–41.

Jour. Research U.S. Geol. Survey
Vol. 1, No. 4, July—Aug. 1973, p. 415—419

IDENTIFICATION OF A LITHIUM-BEARING SMECTITE FROM SPOR MOUNTAIN, UTAH

By HARRY C. STARKEY and WAYNE MOUNTJOY, Denver, Colo.

Abstract.—Chemical analyses, X-ray diffraction data, and cation exchange determinations are given for a lithium-bearing smectite. The X-ray data and Greene-Kelly's lithium test indicate the presence of both dioctahedral and trioctahedral phases. The exchange determinations indicate that the lithium is in the structure of the clay, and the chemical data are intermediate between those for hectorite and montmorillonite. All data indicate that the clay is a mixture of hectorite and montmorillonite.

Lithium was reported to be present, probably in montmorillonite, in the clay-size fractions of samples from a bedded rhyolite tuff at the Roadside claims in the NE¼ sec. 8, T. 13 S., R. 12 W., Spor Mountain, in western Juab County, Utah (Shawe and others, 1964). Hectorite, which is trioctahedral, is the lithium-bearing magnesium-rich end member of the smectites, whereas montmorillonite is the dioctahedral smectite that contains virtually no lithium. It appeared likely that the Spor Mountain mineral might also be trioctahedral, and an investigation was initiated to more accurately identify the clay.

Acknowledgments.—The authors express their gratitude to Daniel R. Shawe for supplying the samples used in this study. They also appreciate the various chemical determinations furnished by J. P. Cahill, I. C. Frost, (Mrs.) Johnnie Gardner, and Violet Merritt.

METHODS AND RESULTS

The samples were fractionated by disaggregating them in water, removing the sand-size fraction by wet sieving through a 230-mesh sieve, and then separating the clay and silt by centrifugation.

X-ray diffraction analyses which were made of a randomly oriented sample of each fraction showed that the disaggregation was not complete and that some of the clay minerals remained in the sand and silt fractions as aggregates. Oriented mounts of the clay fractions were air-dried and, after being given various diagnostic treatments, were also examined by X-ray diffraction.

The X-ray diffraction patterns of the randomly oriented clay-size fraction are presented in figure 1. The impurities seen in these patterns are traces of sanidine, which is present in all samples; calcite, whose presence is seen in only three patterns; and fluorite, which is present in all samples in small amounts, but which gives very strong diffraction peaks. The differences between the dioctahedral and trioctahedral minerals are indicated by the position of the 060 peak at approximately 61–62°2θ. This part of each pattern was rerun at a slower scanning speed (½°2θ/min as compared to 2°2θ/min for the complete scan). A comparison of the patterns obtained by slow scanning with patterns of hectorite and montmorillonite similarly obtained shows (fig. 2) that the more intense 060 spacings of patterns a and b are closer to the 1.50-A (62°2θ) spacing of the dioctahedral mineral montmorillonite and those of patterns e and f are closer to the 1.52-A (61°2θ) spacing of the trioctahedral mineral hectorite. The patterns for samples c and d are intermediate with slight indications of two peaks.

The value (about 1.518 A) of the 060 spacing of the hectorite sample shown in figure 2 is lower than some of the values reported in the literature. Kerr and others (1950), who reported a value of 1.527 A, and MacEwan (1961), who reported 1.53 A, were quoting, in different ways, the value of 1.527 A reported by Nagelschmidt (1938). The hectorite used in this study is A.P.I. standard H-34. Another pattern obtained from an unnumbered hectorite sample from Hector, Calif., produced a spacing of 1.515 A. Both these values agree with the 1.52 A reported by Faust, Hathaway, and Millot (1959).

The samples were treated with Greene-Kelly's lithium test. In this treatment the oriented sample is saturated with lithium chloride, washed, and then heated overnight at 300°C and X-rayed. Then it is saturated overnight with glycerol and X-rayed again. Trioctahedral minerals will expand to a spacing of about 17.7 A with the glycerol treatment, whereas dioctahedral minerals will remain collapsed with a spacing of about 9.6 A. In each of the samples, part of the clay expanded and part did not, indicating that both dioctahedral and trioctahedral phases were present. Visual estimations of the amounts of expansible, or trioctahedral, mineral give the following sequence: $b<a<c<e<d<f$.

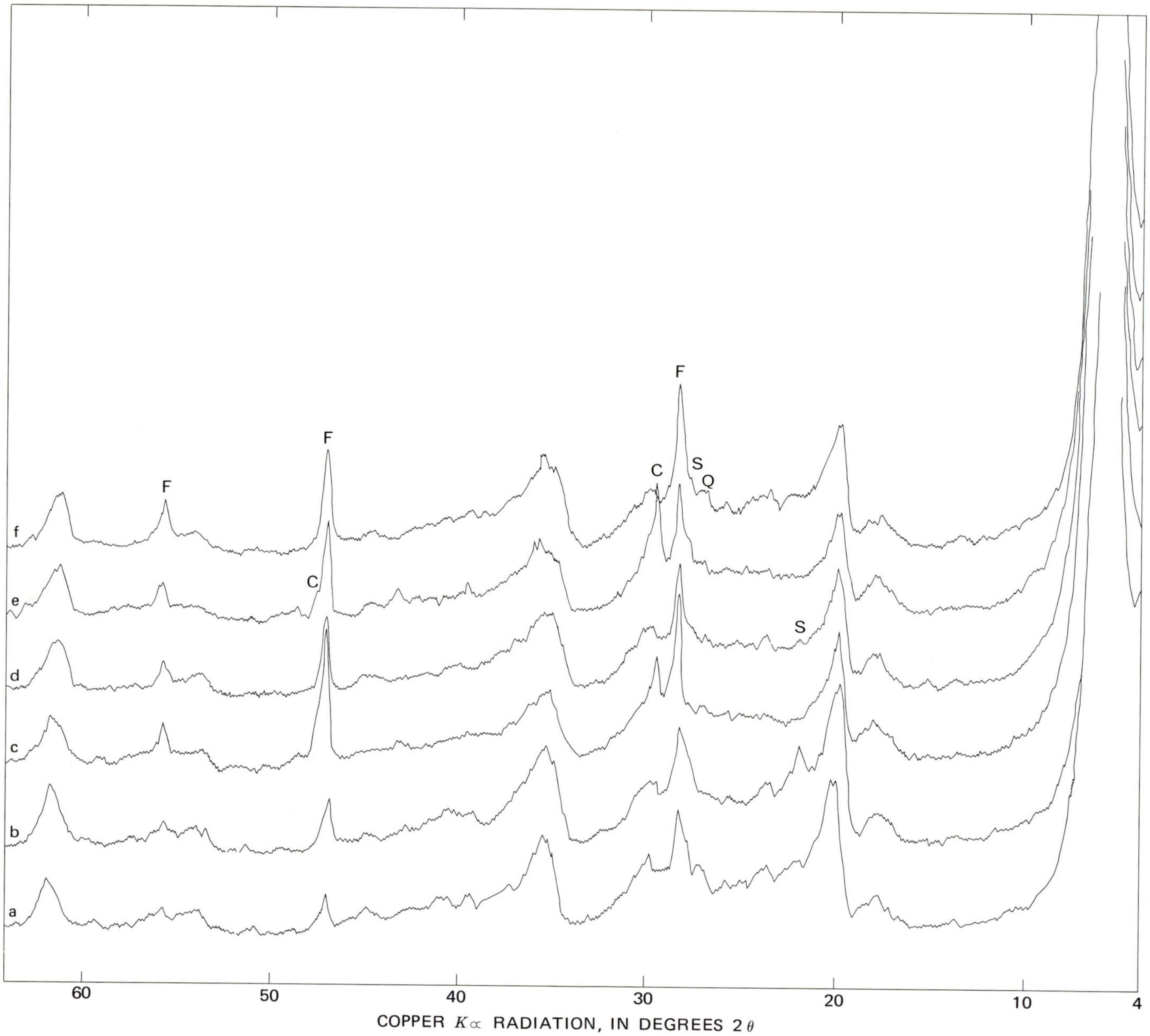

Figure 1.—X-ray diffraction patterns of randomly oriented clay-size fractions (scanning speed 2°2θ/min). Impurities: C, calcite; F, fluorite; Q, quartz; S, sanidine.

Splits of the clay fraction were chemically analyzed and the results tabulated in table 1. Adsorbed water probably accounts for the totals which are more than 100 percent because the portions for the chemical analyses and those for the water determinations were not weighed at the same time. The CO_2 determined was assumed to be in calcite and the TiO_2 in anatase or some polymorph, and these amounts together with the CaO necessary to combine with the CO_2 were subtracted from the chemical analyses. Water was also subtracted, and the analyses were recalculated to 100 percent. The values are compared to previously published analyses of hectorite and montmorillonite, also with the amounts of water subtracted (table 2). The amounts of Al_2O_3 in the samples are less than for montmorillonite but more than for hectorite. The amounts of MgO are between the two extremes, also. Lithium is not found in the standard montmorillonite; the amounts of lithium found in the samples are less than those found in the standard hectorite. These values are plotted in figure 3 to show their relationships to each other and to the standards. Fluorine is found in all the samples, but fluorine is not shown as being present in either the standard montmorillonite or the standard hectorite, although it is shown in the hectorite structural

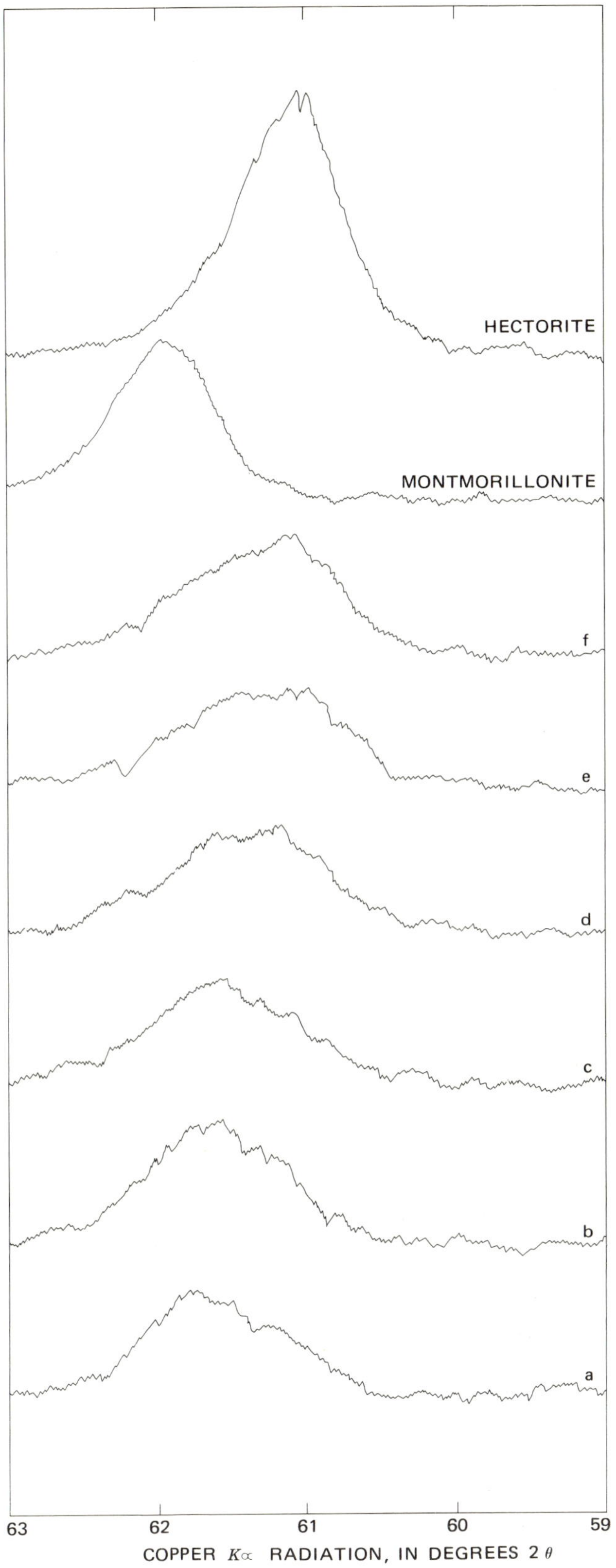

Figure 2.—X-ray diffraction pattern of the 060 region of randomly oriented clay-size fractions (scanning speed ½°2θ/min).

Table 1.—*Chemical data, in percent, for the clay-size fractions*

[SiO_2 determined colorimetrically by Wayne Mountjoy. Al_2O_3, total Fe, MgO, CaO, MnO, Be, Cs, Li, and Rb determined by atomic absorption by Wayne Mountjoy. FeO determined volumetrically by Violet Merritt. Na_2O and K_2O determined by I. L. flame photometer by Wayne Mountjoy. TiO_2 determined colorimetrically by J. P. Cahill. CO_2 determined gasometrically by I. C. Frost. F determined by specific ion electrode by (Mrs.) Johnnie Gardner.]

Sample	a	b	c	d	e	f
Field No. ..	DRS-30-63	DRS-28-63	DRS-92-63	DRS-94-63	DRS-93-63	DRS-84-63
SiO_2	56.5	57.8	53.4	55.3	53.1	52.5
Al_2O_3	10.8	11.0	10.6	8.95	8.54	7.32
Fe_2O_3	2.10	1.55	1.58	1.72	1.50	1.50
FeO	......	.17	......	.15	.14	......
MgO	9.8	9.9	12.8	14.3	13.4	15.3
CaO	2.63	2.75	6.42	4.61	7.29	5.77
MnO	.041	.019	.064	.057	.047	.019
BeO	3.77	2.28	.02	.49	.01	2.16
Na_2O	.37	.57	.21	.46	.72	.27
K_2O	.93	.80	.53	1.04	1.25	.75
Cs_2O	.01	.01	.01	.01	.01	.01
Li_2O	.42	.44	.50	.58	.57	.57
Rb_2O	.03	.03	.02	.03	.03	.02
TiO_2	.04	<.03	.04	.04	.03	<.03
F	2.38	2.52	4.02	3.84	4.04	4.06
CO_2	<.05	.32	.97	.75	2.10	.36
H_2O-	5.16	7.37	3.69	4.67	5.02	6.01
H_2O+	6.91	4.24	9.64	6.71	6.05	5.19
Subtotal .	101.94	101.80	104.51	103.71	103.85	101.84
O=F	−1.00	−1.06	−1.69	−1.62	−1.70	−1.71
Total ...	100.94	100.74	102.82	102.09	102.15	100.13

formula (Kerr and others, 1950) and is shown as 5.96 percent in the hectorite analysis given by Ross and Hendricks (1945). Some of the fluorine found in the clays under investigation is undoubtedly present as fluorite, but if we assume that the remainder of the calcium was in the fluorite, then some fluorine would still be available for the hectorite. Beryllium has been reported to be present as bertrandite crystals less than 1μ in diameter in the Spor Mountain area (Staatz, 1963). The clay fraction of sample b was split, and an X-ray pattern of the <0.5μ fraction revealed the presence of bertrandite. If it were assumed that the beryllium shown by the chemical data (table 2) was present in the form of bertrandite and if deductions were made on the basis of this assumption, only small changes would be made in the data for samples a, b, and f, and practically no change at all for samples c, d, and e.

Other splits of the clay fraction were leached with 1 *N* NH_4Cl, and the leachates were analyzed for exchangeable cations. Exchange capacities were determined by distillation of the ammonium-saturated clays. The results of the determinations of both the exchangeable cations and the exchange capacities are listed in table 3. The sum of the exchangeable cations is greater than the determined capacity because of the solubility of calcite in NH_4Cl. Determinations for aluminum,

Table 2.—*Chemical data, in percent, for the clay-size fractions compared with published hectorite and montmorillonite analyses*[1]

Sample / Field No.	a DRS-30-63	b DRS-28-63	c DRS-92-63	d DRS-94-63	e DRS-93-63	f DRS-84-63	Hectorite[2]	Montmorillonite[3]
SiO_2	63.7	65.5	61.5	62.4	62.1	59.7	63.72	65.66
Al_2O_3	12.2	12.4	12.2	10.1	9.98	8.32	.16	22.63
Fe_2O_3	2.36	1.75	1.82	1.94	1.75	1.70	.04	2.85
FeO	......	.19	......	.17	.16	......	......	.34
MgO	11.0	11.2	14.8	16.1	15.7	17.4	30.57	4.54
CaO	2.87	2.51	5.52	3.80	4.47	5.88	.19	3.04
MnO	.05	.02	.07	.07	.06	.02	......	.05
BeO	4.25	2.58	.02	.55	.01	2.46	......	......
Na_2O	.42	.64	.24	.52	.85	.30	3.57	.18
K_2O	1.05	.91	.61	1.17	1.46	.86	.27	.37
Cs_2O	.01	.01	.01	.01	.01	.01	......	......
Li_2O	.48	.48	.58	.65	.67	.64	1.45	......
Rb_2O	.03	.03	.02	.03	.03	.02	......	......
F	2.70	2.85	4.62	4.33	4.72	4.61	......	......
Subtotal	101.12	101.07	102.01	101.84	101.97	101.92		
O=F	−1.12	−1.20	−1.95	−1.83	−1.99	−1.94		
Total	100.00	99.87	100.06	100.01	99.98	99.98	99.97	99.66

[1] $CaCO_3$, TiO_2, and H_2O amounts subtracted from samples, and H_2O amounts subtracted from standard clays.
[2] A.P.I. standard 34a (Kerr and others, 1950).
[3] A.P.I. standard 23 (Kerr and others, 1950).

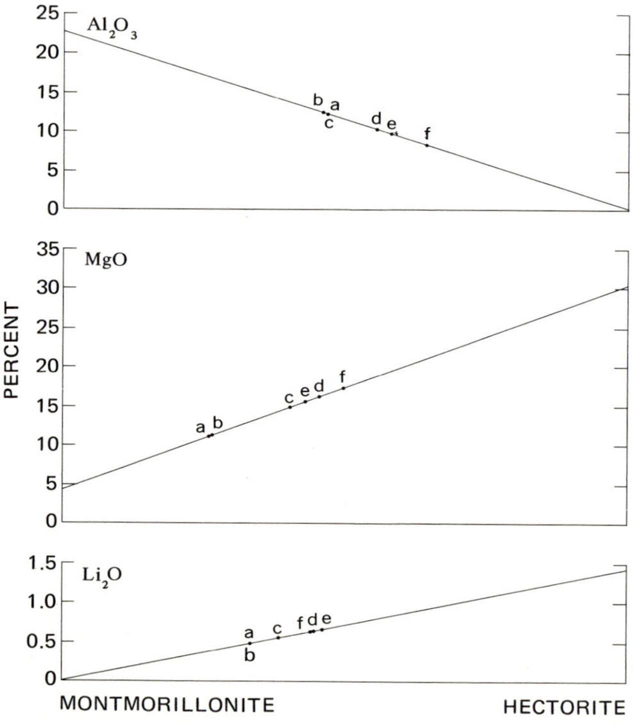

Figure 3.—Comparison of Al_2O_3, MgO, and Li_2O contents in samples a–f with those contents in hectorite and a typical montmorillonite (data from table 2).

iron, lithium, and rubidium were made on the leachates, but none of these elements was found. The values for the determined exchange capacities are within the normal ranges for hectorite and montmorillonite.

Table 3.—*Exchange determinations of the clay-size fractions*

[me/100 g clay (dried at 110°C)]

Sample	Field No.	Na	K	Ca	Mg	Sum	Determined capacity
a	DRS-30-63	3.5	1.9	41.7	38.7	85.8	78.4
b	DRS-28-63	6.9	2.0	40.8	39.4	89.1	80.8
c	DRS-92-63	3.3	1.9	85.7	40.4	131.3	84.9
d	DRS-94-63	7.7	3.4	52.6	34.5	98.2	79.6
e	DRS-93-63	17.0	4.6	99.7	33.7	155.0	78.2
f	DRS-84-63	7.5	1.5	44.6	37.5	91.1	76.8

CONCLUSIONS

Examination of the X-ray and chemical data demonstrates clearly the presence of a mixture of the two types of smectites. The X-ray patterns suggest two phases, dioctahedral and trioctahedral. Greene-Kelly's lithium test shows the two phases more clearly. The chemical data show that lithium and fluorine, which are found in hectorite but not in montmorillonite, are present but not in the amounts found in pure hectorite. The amounts of magnesium found in the samples are also intermediate between those reported for hectorite and montmorillonite. The exchange determinations indicate that the lithium is in the structure because it is not exchangeable; the exchange capacities are within the ranges expected for hectorite and montmorillonite. The samples whose more intense diffraction peaks are near 1.50 A have less fluorine, lithium, and magnesium than those whose more intense peaks are near 1.52 A. A mixture of montmorillonite and hectorite would satisfy these data.

No attempt was made to establish percentages for the clay minerals present. These clay minerals were not divided into hectorite and montmorillonite because a physical separation would have been impossible and a division based on chemical data and structural formulas would be meaningless because of the impurities present. However, estimations based on visual examinations of the X-ray diffraction patterns, the results of the Greene-Kelly treatment, and the chemical data indicate that samples a and b are high in montmorillonite content, sample f is highest in hectorite, and samples c, d, and e have intermediate amounts of the two minerals.

Other naturally occurring mixtures of hectorite and montmorillonite may exist but may be unrecognized because of the similarities of the two minerals, especially if the amount of hectorite is small. To be reasonably certain of the X-ray identification of lithium-bearing smectites, it may be necessary to employ supplementary procedures such as chemical analysis and the Greene-Kelly lithium saturation procedure in addition to the customary heating and glycolation X-ray diffraction treatments.

REFERENCES CITED

Faust, G. T., Hathaway, J. C., and Millot, Georges, 1959, A restudy of stevensite and allied minerals: Am. Mineralogist, v. 44, nos. 3–4, p. 342–370.

Kerr, P. F., and others, 1950, Analytical data on reference clay minerals: Am. Petroleum Inst. Proj. 49, Prelim. Rept. 7, 160 p.

MacEwan, D. M. C., 1961, Montmorillonite minerals, Chap. 4 *of* Brown, George, ed., The X-ray identification and crystal structures of clay minerals [2d ed.]: London, Mineralog. Soc., Clay Minerals Group, p. 143–207.

Nagelschmidt, G., 1938, On the atomic arrangement and variability of the members of the montmorillonite group: Mineralog. Mag., v. 25, no. 162, p. 140–155.

Ross, C. S., and Hendricks, S. B., 1945, Minerals of the montmorillonite group, their origin and relation to soils and clays: U.S. Geol. Survey Prof. Paper 205-B, p. 23–79 [1946].

Shawe, D. R., Mountjoy, Wayne, and Duke, Walter, 1964, Lithium associated with beryllium in rhyolitic tuff at Spor Mountain, western Juab County, Utah, *in* Geological Survey Research 1964: U.S. Geol. Survey Prof. Paper 501-C, p. C86–C87.

Staatz, M. H., 1963, Geology of the beryllium deposits in the Thomas Range, Juab County, Utah: U.S. Geol. Survey Bull. 1142-M, 36 p.

Jour. Research U.S. Geol. Survey
Vol. 1, No. 4, July—Aug. 1973, p. 421—429

STREAM-PROFILE ANALYSIS AND STREAM-GRADIENT INDEX

By JOHN T. HACK, Washington, D.C.

Abstract.—The generally regular three-dimensional geometry of drainage networks is the basis for a simple method of terrain analysis providing clues to bedrock conditions and other factors that determine topographic forms. On a reach of any stream, a gradient-index value can be obtained which allows meaningful comparisons of channel slope on streams of different sizes. The index is believed to reflect stream power or competence and is simply the product of the channel slope at a point and channel length measured along the longest stream above the point where the calculation is made. In an adjusted topography, changes in gradient-index values along a stream generally correspond to differences in bedrock or introduced load. In any landscape the gradient index of a stream is related to total relief and stream regimen. Thus, climate, tectonic events, and geomorphic history must be considered in using the gradient index. Gradient-index values can be obtained quickly by simple measurements on topographic maps, or they can be obtained by more sophisticated photogrammetric measurements that involve simple computer calculations from x, y, z coordinates.

Stream networks have regular geometric properties that can be quantitatively described. In an erosionally graded landscape (Hack, 1960, p. 89), the longitudinal profile of a stream is a property of stream geometry that can provide clues to underlying materials as well as insights into geologic processes and the geomorphic history of an area. This paper deals with a method of analyzing the longitudinal profile and develops a new unit of measurement, here called the stream-gradient index. This index relates the slope of a stream at a locality to its length at the locality and provides a basis for comparing stream reaches of different sizes.

During a study of stream profiles and streambed material in the Shenandoah Valley, Va., (Hack, 1957a, p. 87–90), it was found that a simple logarithmic graph of the stream profile provides the basis for a useful system of analysis. In this graph, the origin of the profile is at the drainage divide, which forms the source of the stream. The vertical coordinate is an arithmetic scale and represents the altitude or height above a datum. The horizontal coordinate is a logarithmic scale and represents the stream length or distance from the source. Where the stream profile is a straight line on such a plot, the profile equation is

$$H = C - k \log_e L \qquad (1)$$

where H is altitude at a point on the profile and L is stream length (horizontal distance from the drainage divide to the same point on the principal stream measured along the channel). C and k are constants. The tangent to the profile or slope, S, of the stream at a point is the derivative of equation 1,

$$\frac{dH}{dL} = kL^{-1}\text{, or } S = \frac{k}{L}. \qquad (2)$$

The slope equation can be put in the form $SL = k$.

Most natural streams do not have a logarithmic profile such as the above throughout their length, but their profiles are made up of connected series of segments of various lengths, each logarithmic in form. The value of k (equivalent to the product SL) thus differs along the stream as a whole but is constant for any particular logarithmic segment. Because the value of k defines the steepness of the logarithmic profile for such a segment, it can be considered as an index of the relative steepness of the actual profile at a point. The product SL (equivalent to the constant k in equation 1) is here called the gradient index. As will be shown, this index is useful for streams as much as several hundred miles long, regardless of the overall form of the profile.

The gradient index is a significant quantity because it is crudely related to the power of a stream to transport material of a given size and to the characteristics of the channel that resist flow. This conclusion is supported by empirical evidence. It was found, for example, that streams in the Potomac basin on the average have the following relation between particle size on the bed, channel length, and channel slope:

$$S = 25\frac{M^{0.6}}{L}, \qquad (3)$$

where S is slope, M is mean particle size on the bed (in millimeters) and L is length (in miles). Where M is constant in the equation above for a given reach of a stream, the product SL (gradient index) remains constant. An increase in particle size (M) is reflected in an increase in the product SL (see Hack, 1957a, p. 71). Several streams with nearly constant SL values over long reaches were found to have bed material that showed no systematic change in size within these reaches. The North Fork of the Shenandoah River (Hack and Young, 1959, p. 4) is an example. It has a narrow range of *SL* values and of particle sizes on the bed for a distance of about 100 miles (Hack and Young, 1959, p. 4). The Calfpasture River is another example and is discussed below. Thus, particle size clearly has a functional relation to gradient index.

The relation of the gradient index to the hydraulic geometry of stream systems is not understood. The fact that the product of slope and length has a relation to stream competence or power must be explainable in terms of the complex interrelations in the hydraulic geometry that characterize the conditions of dynamic equilibrium in streams. The theoretical aspects of channel equilibrium as related to the profile were discussed by Leopold, Wolman, and Miller (1964, p. 248–281). They stated (1964, table 7-7) that when power is equally distributed along a stream the product of slope and discharge is equal in all the reaches. Thus, if equal gradient indices are equatable with equal power, discharge must be proportional to length. Leopold, Wolman, and Miller's data show that, on the average, stream length is proportional to the 0.64 power of the drainage area. Also, bankfull discharge (which is thought to be the discharge that performs the significant work) is, on the average, proportional to the 0.75 power of the drainage area. Using these values, it is clear that bankful discharge is proportional to the 1.17 power of the channel length in the average stream. However, the data from which these figures are derived include streams that have varied flow resistance and varied power along their course and that on the average probably show a decrease in flow resistance downstream. If the data were available, one might possibly be able to show that where flow energy remains the same in a downstream direction, length and bankfull discharge would be found to be nearly directly proportional.

CALCULATION OF GRADIENT INDEX

The gradient index can be measured on topographic maps, on aerial photographs using photogrammetric methods, or by ground surveys. The parameters measured are shown in figure 1. The quantity L is the stream length measured from the

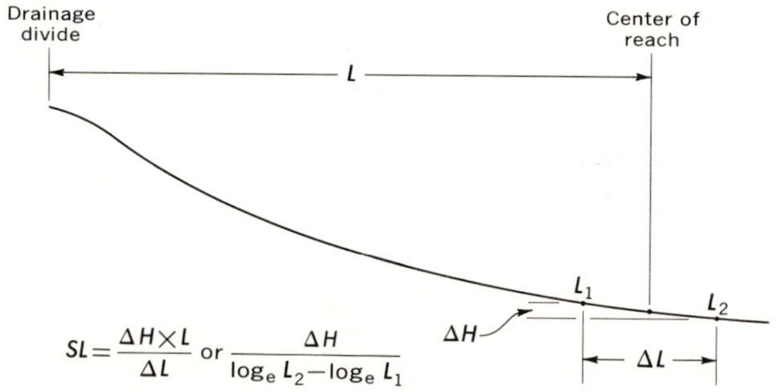

Figure 1.—Measured parameters used in calculation of gradient index. Symbols are defined in text.

drainage divide at the source of the longest stream in the drainage basin above a locality on a reach. ΔH is the difference in elevation between the ends of the reach, and ΔL is the length of the reach. The reach must be long enough so that sharp local changes in slope such as those between riffles and pools are averaged out. This distance is, of course, much longer on large streams than on small ones.

The formula for the gradient index (SL) is $SL = \dfrac{\Delta H \times L}{\Delta L}$.

Inasmuch as $L/\Delta L$ is a dimensionless ratio, the measurements of horizontal distance can be in any unit of measure. The measurements are generally made on a map with a map measure, so it is convenient to use inches. It is not necessary to make the conversion to ground scale. As the contours on United States maps are generally in feet, the quantity ΔH will be calculated in feet. The gradient index is the product of a ratio and a distance, so it is conveniently expressed as gradient-feet.

When measured in this way, the gradient index is equivalent to the product of the natural tangent to the channel slope at a locality and the distance in feet from the head of the stream to that locality. To find the value of the tangent expressed as a decimal, at any point, simply divide the index in gradient-feet by the distance in feet. The slope in feet per mile can be found by dividing the gradient index by the distance in miles. Thus, if the gradient index is 200 gradient-feet at 1 mile from the source, the slope will be 200 feet per mile; at 2 miles it will be 100 feet per mile. In the metric system, the gradient-index values would be different, as they would depend on measuring the difference in elevation at the ends of the reach in metric units rather than in feet.

Figure 2 is from an actual contour map and shows the measurements needed to find the gradient index at locality D in a reach extending from points A to B. ΔH is 40 feet, the value of the contour interval. ΔL is the distance from A to B, and L is the distance from C to D, including the bends in the stream. The distances can be measured on the map in any units desired, as long as the two measurements are in the same units.

As the validity of the gradient index depends on the general consistency of the relation between drainage area and channel length that exists in most natural stream systems, it is important that the distance L be measured along the principal (or longest) stream above the locality. The longest stream in the watershed must be followed continuously from its head to the terminating point at the locality. The operator must always proceed downstream from the head and never continue past a stream junction with a longer stream than the one being measured. A typical sequence of measurements is shown in figure 3.

Caution must be observed in calculating the *SL* value by the method above. The channel slope in the product *SL* is really a tangent to the profile at a particular point. In estimating the slope by measuring difference in height and length between the two ends of a reach, however, one is really measuring a

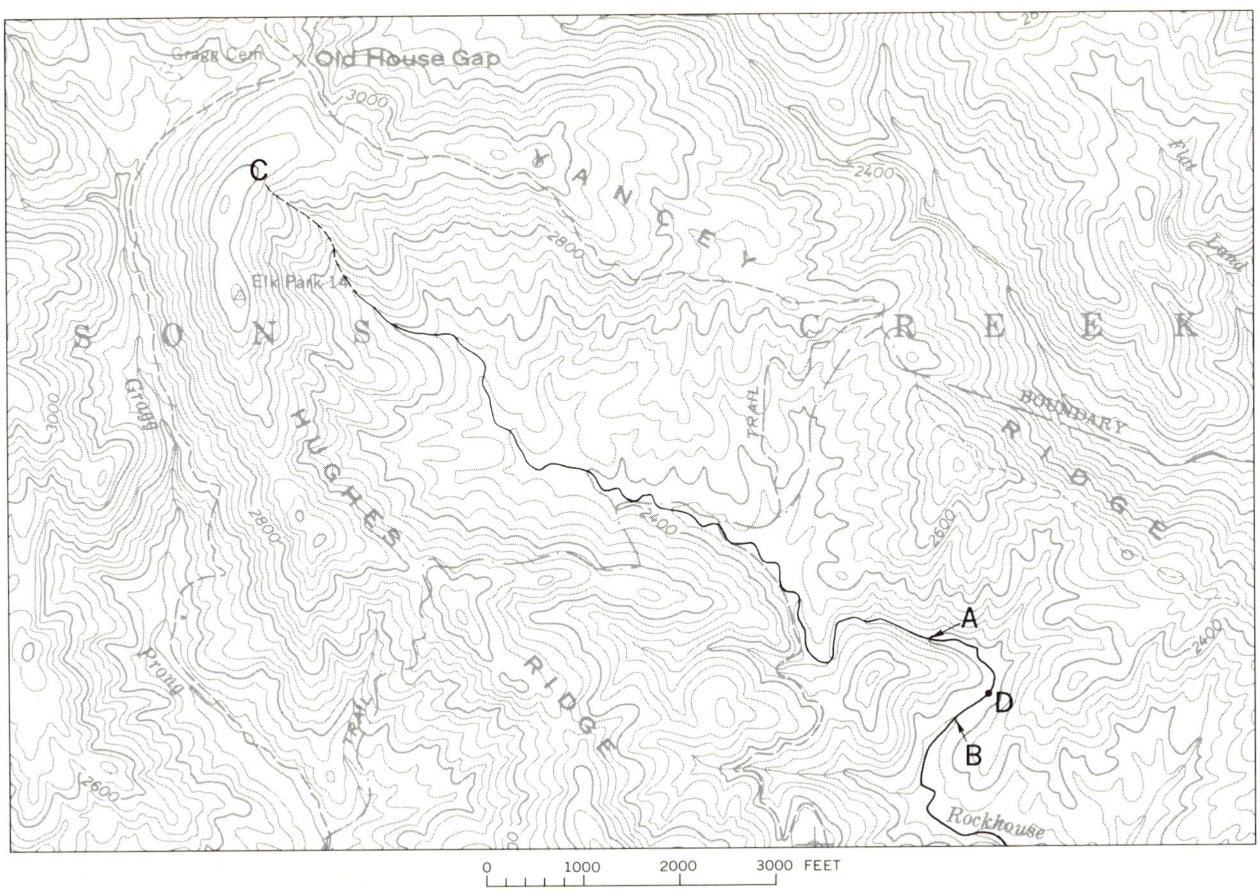

Figure 2.—Part of a topographic map used in making measurements for gradient index. From U.S. Geological Survey 7½-minute topographic map of the Grandfather Mountain quadrangle, North Carolina, 1960, 1:24,000 scale, 40-foot contour interval. See text for explanation of method.

secant of a curve. If the reach is long, this secant will not be parallel to the tangent, and the error will increase as the length of the reach increases. The error is a function of the dimensionless ratio $L/\Delta L$ and becomes larger as this ratio becomes smaller. Significant error is probably not introduced until this ratio approaches 2.0 or even 1.0. At a stream length of 100 miles, for example, the use of a secant from length 50 miles to length 150 miles would introduce an error of only about 10 percent. On the other hand, one must be careful about obtaining average SL values near the head of a stream where the curvature is high. ΔL must be kept smaller than L.

The gradient index can also be found in terms of the profile equation 1, $H = C - k \log_e L$. The gradient index is equal to the constant, k, and can be found by the formula

$$k = \frac{H_1 - H_2}{\log_e L_2 - \log_e L_1}, \qquad (4)$$

where H_1 and H_2 are map elevations at each end of the reach measured, and L_1 and L_2 are distances from the source to each end of the reach.

GRADIENT-INDEX CHANGES ALONG INDIVIDUAL STREAMS

Individual profiles can be studied graphically by simple plotting on semilogarithmic graph paper or by converting the length measurements to logarithms and plotting on arithmetic scales. In practice, this is easily done by running down the map or mosaic of maps with a map measure and recording the contour elevations and their distances from the head of the stream. The data are then plotted. On such a logarithmic graph the gradient index is proportional to the slope of the plotted profile. Its numerical value can be calculated from the tabulated data at any point. Examples of several logarithmic profiles are shown and interpreted below.

Calfpasture River.—The Calfpasture River in Virginia, a headwater tributary of the James River, is, like the North Fork of the Shenandoah River (see page 422), an example of a stream whose logarithmic profile is close to a straight line (fig. 4). The average gradient index is 260 gradient-feet but it ranges from 210 to 300. The river valley is anticlinal, floored by Devonian shale, and surrounded by mountain ridges of

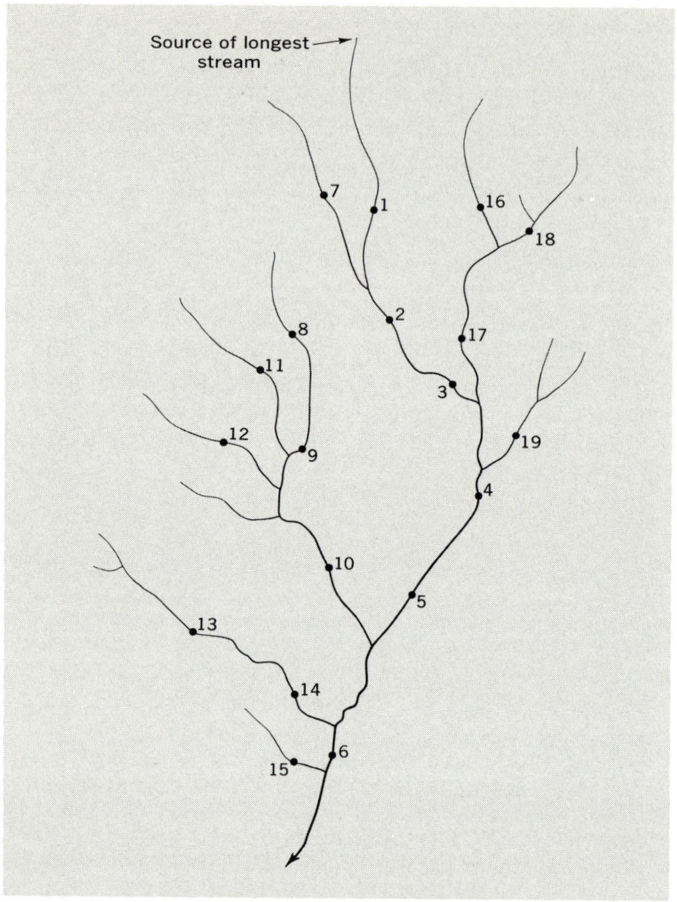

Figure 3.—A small drainage basin. Numbers represent sequence in which gradient-index values might be calculated.

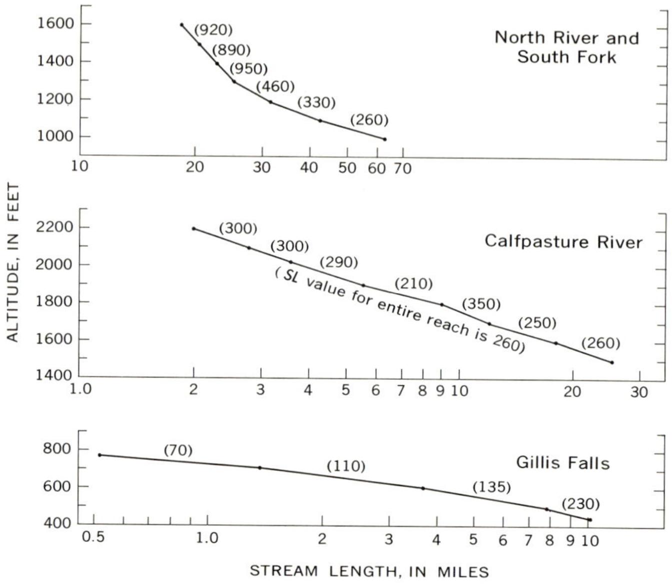

Figure 4.—Profiles of three stream reaches having (1) decreasing size of bed material downstream (North River and South Fork), (2) no systematic downstream change in size (Calfpasture River), and (3) increasing size downstream (Gillis Falls). Numbers in parentheses are *SL* values between data points. Data from topographic maps.

sandstone of Devonian and Mississippian age. Throughout the course, cobbles of sandstone are brought in by tributaries to make up the bed material, and the stream is bordered by low alluvial terraces of rounded sandstone cobbles. Shale crops out at only a few places in the stream and makes up only a very small proportion of the bed material, presumably because it breaks up into sizes too small to remain with sandstone cobbles in this part of the channel. Samples of the bed material at 10 localities along the stream range in size from 42 to 75 mm. The average size of the 10 samples is 61 mm.

The uniformity in size of the bed material suggests that the stream has uniform competence along its course because of the bedrock geology of the basin. Data on sizes of bed material are from Hack (1957a, table 8).

North River.—The North River in Virginia, the principal headwater of the South Fork, Shenandoah River, heads on Shenandoah Mountain and drains about 50 sq mi of country underlain largely by Devonian and Mississippian sandstone beds (fig. 4). It enters the limestone and shale lowland of the Shenandoah Valley about 18 miles from its source. At this point the bed material is more than 100 mm in median size. As the North River enters the Shenandoah Valley, its flood plain and terraces widen out to form a conspicuous lowland alluvial plain 2 miles wide which gradually narrows again downstream. At mile 36 the stream becomes intrenched in the limestone valley floor, and its flood plain is narrow. The size of the bed material systematically decreases from 110 mm to 42 mm (Hack, 1957a, table 8). As shown in figure 4, the profile is sharply curved on a logarithmic graph, and the values of the gradient index decrease from 1,000 to 250 as the gradient flattens. The bed material decreases in size with distance from the sandstone beds that are the source of the resistant material. Thus, the geology of the drainage basin controls the profile, as the competence and the slope are adjusted to handle the load.

Gillis Falls.—This stream, a headwater of the Patapsco River on the Maryland Piedmont, is an example of a stream with a profile of low concavity that shows an increase in the gradient index downstream (fig. 4). Size of bed material also increases downstream. This is because the watershed is underlain by soft, weathered phyllite laced by stringers and veins of resistant quartz. Though widespread in the watershed, the total volume of the quartz veins is very small in comparison with phyllite and weathered phyllite. The phyllite breaks up into small chips averaging less than 5 mm in size, whereas the quartz fragments average 80 to 100 mm. In the upstream reaches, vein quartz makes up only a small part of the bedload but forms a lag deposit on the bed and becomes more and more concentrated downstream where it constitutes the major part of the bedload. The fine-grained phyllite particles are carried out of the channel in the lower reaches. The increase in size of the bed material from 7.0 mm to 80 mm is fairly systematic. The banks of the stream are loamy clay rather than sand, and the high depth-width ratio decreases from a maximum of 0.52 at 1.7 mile to 0.05 at 11.6 miles. The high depth-width ratio probably accounts in part for the low gradient of this stream in comparison with the others just described. As shown in figure 4, the logarithmic profile graph curves downward. This does not mean that the profile is in reality convex upward but rather that the natural profile is less concave upward than the others. Note that calculated values of the product *SL* increase downstream as the competence increases.

Cranberry River.—Major differences in the materials along the course of a stream commonly cause abrupt changes in the profile, as exemplified by the Cranberry River, Ontonagon County, Mich. (fig. 5; Hack, 1965, fig. 12, and p. B22–B28). In its upper reaches this river flows through an area of till and lake deposits. At 11.5 miles it enters a buried bedrock high, and the profile abruptly changes character. The *SL* or *k* value changes from 240 to 550. At mile 16 the river again enters till, and again the profile abruptly changes.

Lower Potomac River.—The streams discussed on the preceding pages are small, and their profiles appear to be adjusted to the geology of the terrain drained by them. In contrast, the Potomac is a very large river, and its lower course has apparently been affected by changes in base level during the late geologic history of the river. A logarithmic profile of the river below the junction with the South Branch is shown in figure 6. The data for this profile are from a survey by the U.S. Engineer Office,[1] but distances are measured from the head of the South Branch, the longest headwater, in West Virginia. Because this profile is of the lower reaches of a long river, the logarithmic profile does not show much distortion as compared with a natural profile. The amount of distortion can be judged by comparing the logarithmic and true horizontal distance scales.

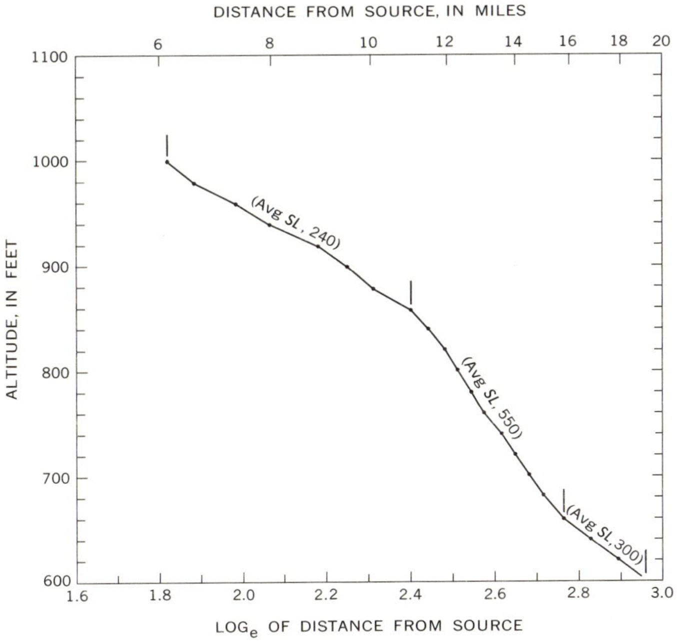

Figure 5.—Profile of the Cranberry River. Ontonagon County, Mich. The upper and lower reaches are in till; the middle reach is in sandstone.

In the upper part of the profile, above the Shenandoah River, *SL* values are comparable with the values of smaller Appalachian streams adjusted to similar rocks. Within the Valley and Ridge province below the South Branch, the river meanders through a sandstone and shale lowland. The most resistant rocks having an appreciable outcrop area along this stretch are in the Hampshire Formation, thinly interbedded shale and sandstone. Very resistant rock formations such as the Tuscarora and Pocono Sandstones also occur in the section, but they do not crop out near the channel. *SL* values average 480 gradient-feet, a figure similar to values for those streams in the Appalachian Valley that drain large areas of sandstone and shale and where most of the bed material consists of sandstone.

In the carbonate-rock area of the Appalachian Valley, the average *SL* value in the Potomac River is 429, which is higher than might be expected in carbonate rocks. However, it drops to 210 near Williamsport, Md., where the river crosses the Martinsburg Shale and to 220 in the Cambrian limestone below Shepherdstown, W. Va. An anomalously high value in the intervening reach near Dam No. 4 between Williamsport and Shepherdstown corresponds to the outcrop of the Beekmantown Dolomite, which in many places contains abundant chert.

The bed material is not readily sampled in the Potomac River because of the deep water. A random sample of part of the streambed was obtained, however, at a riffle near Shepherdstown, at the site of a onetime ford. Eighty-one fragments were measured and classified. The median size was 180 mm. The sample had the following lithologic composition: sandstone, 57 percent; limestone, 23 percent; chert, 12 percent; and not identified, 8 percent. The nearest source of sandstone is in the Valley and Ridge province, 30 to 40 miles upstream. This composition suggests that most of the bed material consists of resistant Devonian and Silurian sandstones and that they are largely responsible for the unusually steep channel slopes of the Appalachian Valley part of the stream. The average *SL* values obtained in other streams in carbonate rocks of the Shenandoah Valley are 180 in small streams and 245 in large streams. Large streams generally carry some resistant cobbles derived from headwater tributaries.

[1] Somervell, Brehon, 1929, Report to the Chief of Engineers, United States Army on investigation and survey of the Potomac River for navigation-power-flood control and irrigation: Typewritten report of U.S. Engineer Office, 167 p.

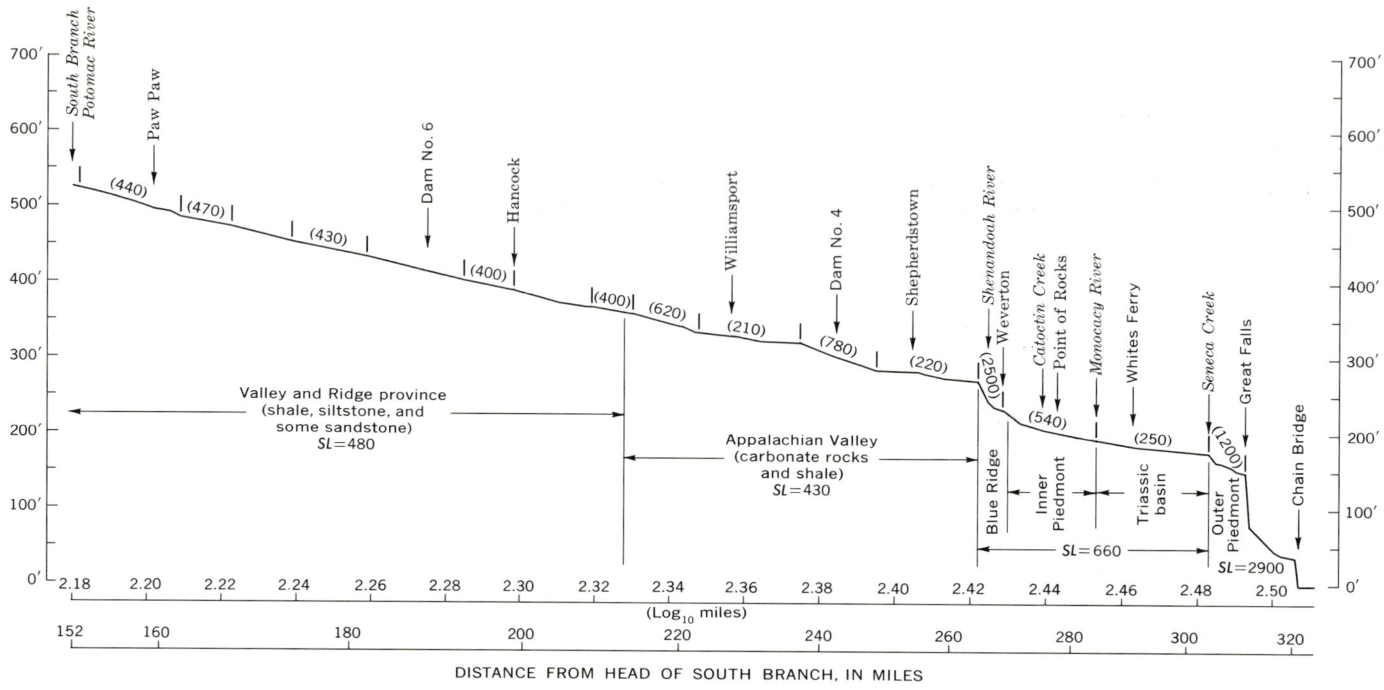

Figure 6.—Profile of the Potomac River from its junction with the South Branch to Washington, D.C. Data from Somervell, 1929 (see footnote 1). Gradient index in parentheses.

The Potomac profile steepens markedly at the water gap in the Blue Ridge. Here the river passes through the resistant quartzites and other clastic rocks of the Chilhowee Group, the metabasalt of the Catoctin Formation, and other crystalline rocks. An *SL* value of 2,500 seems high compared with *SL* values found in smaller streams in the same rocks in other places. However, this high value may simply reflect adjustment of the slope to high flow resistance encountered at the crossings of tough rock formations. In the Triassic basin between the Monocacy River and Seneca Creek, *SL* values drop again to 250, a value comparable with small streams in predominantly shale areas.

At Seneca Creek, Md., the channel slope steepens abruptly and becomes a series of rapids and falls. In this reach the average *SL* is 2,900, far higher than in the smaller streams of the adjacent Piedmont where *SL* values average less than 300. Great Falls itself corresponds to an outcrop of resistant quartz-rich gneiss (U.S. Dept. Interior, 1970, p. 11–15), so there has been some adjustment by the river to the relative resistance of the rocks. However, the anomalously high *SL* values suggest that in this reach the river is also adjusted to a lower base level than are the reaches upstream. In this connection, marine deposits of Miocene age at Ward Circle in Washington, D.C., are at 370 feet above sea level (Darton, 1950, p. 6). Marine deposits of supposed Pliocene age at Good Hope Hill in east Washington, D.C., are at 280 feet (Hack, 1955). The Pleistocene channel of the Potomac River dropped 90 feet below sea level at Alexandria, Va., approximately 12 miles downstream from Chain Bridge (Hack, 1957b, p. 823) indicating a change in base level of more than 370 feet in the last million years. Thus, the lowest part of the Potomac River gorge is probably partly adjusted to low sea level of late Wisconsin time corresponding to the −90-foot channel at Alexandria.

Two conclusions can be drawn from the profile of the Potomac River: (1) That part of the profile above the Shenandoah River is adjusted to the geology of the basin and to the profiles of other streams in the upper basin. This adjustment may extend as far as Seneca. The reaches below Seneca, however, reflect accelerated erosion related to a drop in sea level in Pliocene and post-Pliocene time. (2) The general conformity of the gradient-index values above the Shenandoah River to those of tributary streams indicates that there is probably little, if any, tendency for *SL* values to change systematically because of geometric factors related simply to the size of a stream. This conclusion is important to the usefulness of the gradient index as an analytical tool. Still larger streams, however, such as the Mississippi, may have anomalously high *SL* values. The Mississippi River is so large that the overall geometry of its basin is probably determined by factors such as the configuration of the continent and the location of mountain ranges, rather than by the evolutionary development of drainage that normally proceeds with down-wasting.

REGIONAL PLOTTING OF GRADIENT-INDEX VALUES ON MAPS

Gradient indices of streams can be studied on a regional basis by plotting regularly spaced index values on maps; contour lines can then be drawn. Several such maps have been constructed.

The procedure is to run down with a map measure all the streams in the area studied, systematically calculating *SL* values at regular intervals. It is important in doing this that stream length always be measured along the longest channel in a given basin. That is, the measurements must be ordered as shown in figure 3. The spacing of measurement points is limited by the scale and detail of the topographic maps used in the calculations as well as by the actual spacing of the streams. In the Piedmont and Appalachian regions, for example, stream channels range on the average from 0.2 to 1.0 mile apart, depending on drainage density in a region, a factor generally related to the kind of rock. Measurement localities cannot be closer to the source of a stream than about ½ mile, because close to the divide the channel is not sculptured primarily by the kinetic energy of flowing water.

Figure 7 is an example of a gradient-index map. It is based on about 400 localities measured on four 7½-minute quadrangles with 20- to 40-foot contour intervals at 1:24,000 scale. The map covers the Lenoir 15-minute quadrangle, North Carolina. It was made as part of a geomorphic study of the Blue Ridge escarpment in the Grandfather Mountain area. The problem of the Blue Ridge escarpment is not discussed here, but a few features shown on this map are pointed out as examples of interpretations that can be made.

First of all, the base of the Blue Ridge escarpment in this area corresponds closely to the trace of the Brevard zone which extends from A on the left margin of the map to A′ at the top. The Piedmont province is south and east of that zone (A–A′) and is underlain by lower Paleozoic metamorphic rock covered by saprolite. Northwest of the Brevard zone, the relief increases sharply, and rock outcrops are more numerous. In this area the rocks are gneisses of the Grandfather Mountain window.

Note the anomalously high values at B north of the Johns River. These correspond to several lenses of extremely resistant quartz-rich gneiss (Bryant and Reed, 1970, p. 66). The anomalously high *SL* values led the writer to them. The lenses were poorly exposed, generally along the bottoms of deep valleys often difficult to reach because they were covered by slash from logging operations, but they were associated with steep places in the streams.

At C, a large tributary of the Johns River almost as long as the Johns River itself, the values are anomalously high. This area corresponds to the outcrop of the Brown Mountain Granite (Bryant and Reed, 1970). The granite is a particularly massive rock with widely spaced joints. The river cuts through it in a deep picturesque gorge with many cascades.

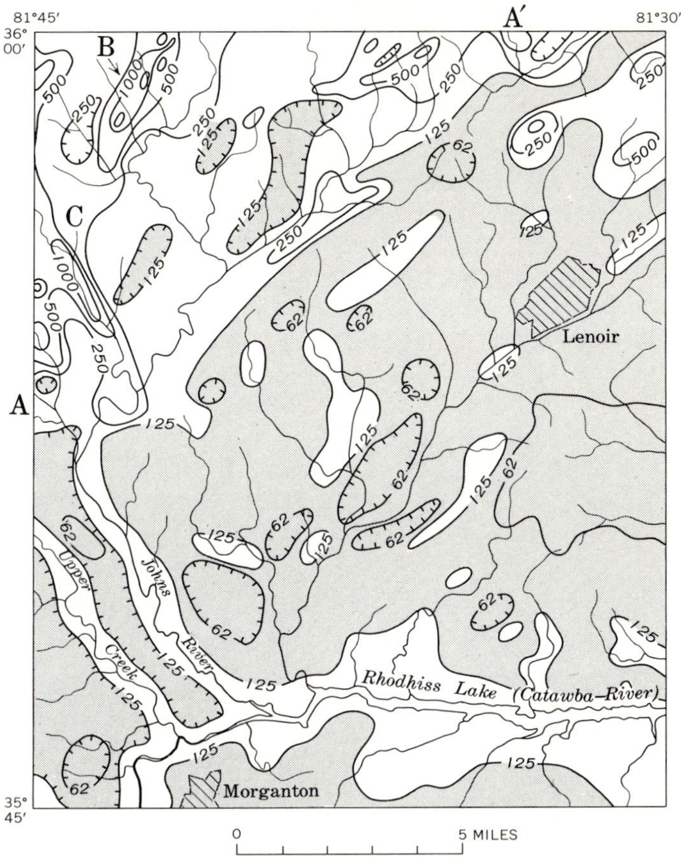

Figure 7.—Lenoir-Morganton area, North Carolina. Gradient-index values on streams are shown by contours; approximately 400 stream localities were used in making the map. Contours represent equal gradient-index values in gradient-feet; interval proportional to 2^n (62, 125, 250, 500, 1000, 2000). Areas with values less than 125 are patterned. Original data from U.S. Geological Survey Colletsville, Lenoir, Morganton North, and Drexel 7½-minute topographic quadrangles, scale 1:24,000. Letter symbols are explained in text.

SL values drop sharply in the Piedmont southeast of A–A′. An interesting feature of this region is that the large streams have higher index values than their tributaries, though the index values of the tributaries increase as they approach the large streams. The probable explanation is that the larger streams are adjusted to transport resistant material derived from resistant rocks upstream. They, therefore, require steeper slopes for a given length. The smaller streams originate in saprolite on uplands of low relief and therefore are competent to transport only fine material. The situation is analogous to that described on page 424, with reference to Gillis Falls, Md. It is a common phenomenon in the Piedmont region where the rocks are complex mineralogically. They thus have several components of varying resistance. The more resistant components, such as fragments of quartz veins or aplite dikes, concentrate downstream. As these components wear more slowly than others, the size of the bed material tends to be

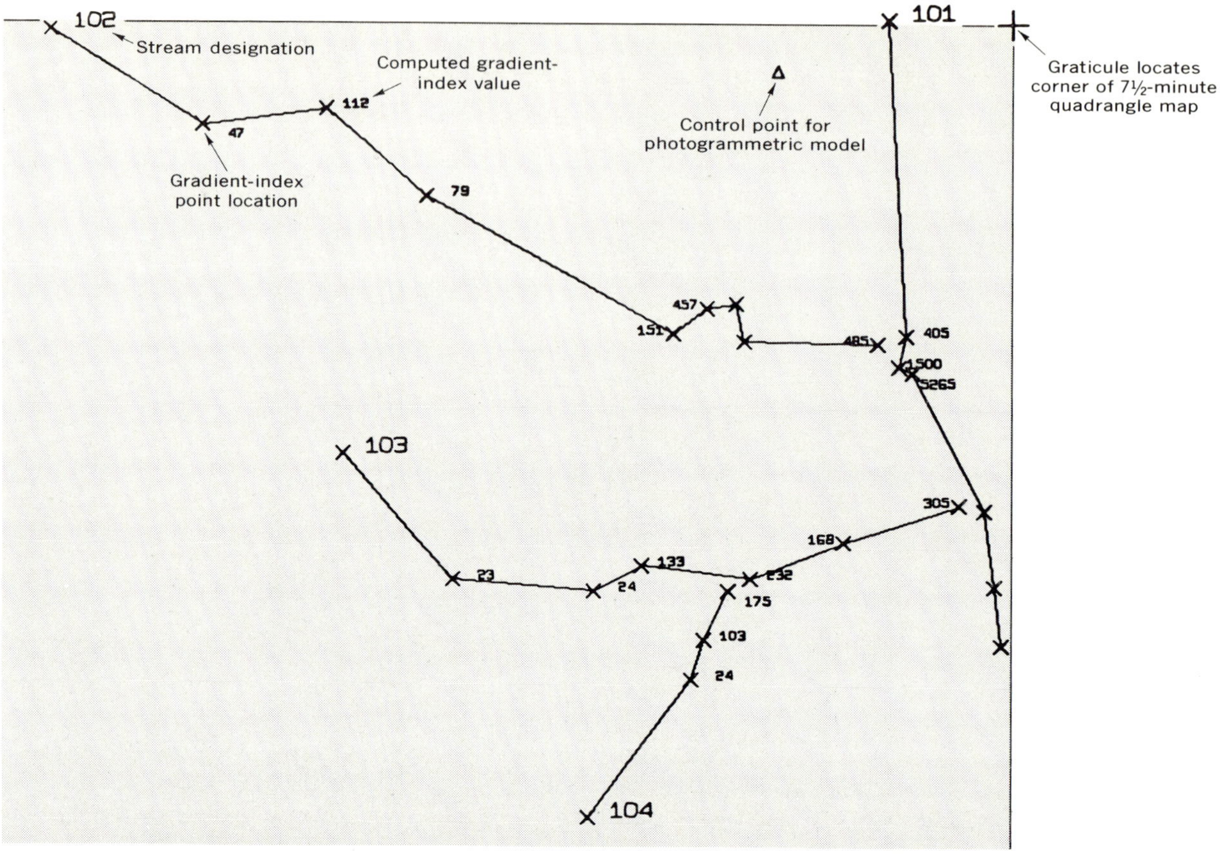

Figure 8.—Sample of a gradient-index plot of part of the Rockville quadrangle, Maryland, prepared on Cal-Comp plotter. *SL* values of some points were not computed because altitudes could not be determined accurately.

larger in the larger streams because the resistant components survive a greater distance of transport as large fragments and become relatively more abundant.

Maps similar to figure 7 can be constructed by photogrammetric measurements. By this method the spacing of points on streams is not limited by the contour interval but only by the spacing of the streams themselves and the resolution of the photogrammetric model. By use of photogrammetric equipment it is possible to plot and calculate gradient-index values automatically. A test on a model of an area in Montgomery County, Md., was made by using a Halcon stereoplotter, an optical projection instrument similar to the Kelsh plotter. The plotter was equipped with a digital readout system that provided punched cards with the x, y, and z coordinates of each measured point at model scale. A Haag-Streit coordinate plotter equipped with digital output in card form was used to measure points on the topographic map to be used as control for absolute orientation of the model. Data reduction and stream-gradient computations were made on an IBM 1130 computer. Graphic presentations of the results were plotted on a Cal-Comp plotter operated on line with the 1130 computer. Part of the graphic presentation is shown in figure 8.

GRADIENT INDEX IN DIFFERENT CLIMATIC AND GEOMORPHIC REGIONS

The examples of the gradient index cited are all in the Eastern United States, a humid region in which the density of perennial streams is high. The writer has had little experience with the index in arid regions, but it is questionable whether it would have the same meaning as it does in humid regions.

Although the index defines the slope of the channel relative to the length in arid regions, it would not necessarily correlate directly with stream power and flow resistance because the hydraulic geometry of the channel is different. For example, channel width may increase downstream in arid regions at different rates from those of humid regions because of the sparse vegetation on the banks. Presumably this is a factor influencing slope. Another factor is the relation of discharge to drainage area and length. In arid regions average discharge, as well as flood discharge, increases downstream at a regular rate only in small drainage areas a few square miles in size. Small areas are affected by individual storm cells. Although few data are available, in some larger drainage basins average discharge may actually decrease downstream.

Interpretation of the gradient index must differ to some extent in different geomorphic provinces. In the Eastern United States, most of the area is drained by converging streams with an average length proportional to the 0.64 power of the drainage area, a relation probably common to most stream-eroded landscapes in which tributaries converge downstream (Hack, 1957a, p. 63; Leopold, Wolman, and Miller, 1964, p. 144). In the Basin and Range province, however, and in other parts of the Western United States, long reaches of streams cross pediment surfaces, alluvial fans, and bahadas in which the geometric relations are different. Though the gradient index may be useful for analysis of such regions, it cannot be used in the same way as in most areas of the Eastern United States because the rates of increase in discharge downstream and the relation of the profile to stream power will not be similar.

CONCLUSION

The gradient index is useful in terrain analysis because it permits comparisons to be made of streams of different sizes. It is a sort of rule of thumb index of stream power and flow resistance. Because it is so simple to calculate from a topographic map, one of its most valuable uses may be to discover anomalously steep or gentle reaches of streams that are related to particularly resistant or soft rocks. The index may thus serve as an aid to geologic mapping, analogous to data on magnetic intensities.

Regional analysis of stream profiles can help in interpreting the geomorphology of large regions. Playfair (1802, p. 102–114) first enunciated the ideas that streams sculpture the valleys in which they flow, that their slopes are adjusted to carry away the debris in their watersheds, and that the whole river network is an adjusted system. The gradient index, when used in the general context of these ideas, can provide insights into the causes of the diversity of the landscape, including the nature of the adjustments that streams have made as well as the nature of diastrophic forces opposed to them.

REFERENCES CITED

Bryant, Bruce, and Reed, J. C., Jr., 1970, Geology of the Grandfather Mountain window and vicinity, North Carolina and Tennessee: U.S. Geol. Survey Prof. Paper 615, 190 p.

Darton, N. H., 1950, Configuration of the bedrock surface of the District of Columbia and vicinity: U.S. Geol. Survey Prof. Paper 217, 42 p. [1952]

Hack, J. T., 1955, Geology of the Brandywine area and origin of the upland of southern Maryland: U.S. Geol. Survey Prof. Paper 267-A, 43 p.

—— 1957a, Studies of longitudinal stream profiles in Virginia and Maryland: U.S. Geol. Survey Prof. Paper 294-B, p. 45–97 [1958].

—— 1957b, Submerged river system of Chesapeake Bay: Geol. Soc. America Bull., v. 68, no. 7, p. 817–830.

—— 1960, Interpretation of erosional topography in humid temperate regions: Am. Jour. Sci., v. 258-A (Bradley Volume), p. 80–97.

—— 1965, Postglacial drainage evolution and stream geometry in the Ontonagon area, Michigan: U.S. Geol. Survey Prof. Paper 504-B, p. B1–B40.

Hack, J. T., and Young, R. S., 1959, Intrenched meanders of the North Fork of the Shenandoah River, Virginia: U.S. Geol. Survey Prof. Paper 354-A, 10 p.

Leopold, L. B., Wolman, M. G., and Miller, J. P., 1964, Fluvial processes in geomorphology: San Francisco, W. H. Freeman and Co., 522 p.

Playfair, John, 1802, Illustrations of the Huttonian theory of the earth: Edinburgh, 528 p. (Reprinted by Dover Publications, Inc., New York, 1964)

U.S. Department of the Interior, 1970, The river and the rocks: Washington, D.C., U.S. Govt. Printing Office, 46 p.

Jour. Research U.S. Geol. Survey
Vol. 1, No. 4, July—Aug. 1973, p. 431—437

CURRENT SLOPE-STABILITY STUDIES IN THE SAN FRANCISCO BAY REGION

By TOR H. NILSEN and EARL E. BRABB, Menlo Park, Calif.

Study done cooperatively with Department of Housing and Urban Development and San Mateo County

Abstract.—An extensive program of slope-stability studies is presently underway in the San Francisco Bay region, California. Work to date has resulted in the publication of estimates of landslide damage, an estimated-landslide-abundance map of the region, new slope maps prepared by photomechanical processes, photointerpretive maps of landslide, colluvial, and other surficial deposits, and maps of relative slope stability. These studies indicate that landsliding is a major slope-erosion process in the region, that the damage resulting from landsliding is very great, and that additional development in the upland parts of the region should not be undertaken without careful evaluation of slope stability.

The U.S. Geological Survey is presently studying the slope-stability characteristics of the San Francisco Bay region. This work is part of a larger, more broadly based study of the region that is being done in cooperation with the U.S. Department of Housing and Urban Development. In addition, San Mateo County has provided some additional funding. The larger study, entitled "The San Francisco Bay Region Environment and Resources Planning Study," was initiated in the spring of 1970 and will last for at least 3 years. Elements of the study include new topographic mapping, geologic and geophysical studies, hydrologic studies, and regional planning studies. The overall coverage of the larger study has been outlined in the Program Design (U.S. Geological Survey and U.S. Dept. Housing and Urban Development, 1971). The purpose of the present paper is to outline the types of slope-stability studies that have been undertaken in this project and the status of the studies, and to list the publications presently available.

The San Francisco Bay region includes the nine counties that border San Francisco Bay, a total land area of about 18,000 km^2 (7,000 sq mi), with a population exceeding 5 million (fig. 1). It lies primarily within the Coast Ranges but includes part of the western Sacramento Valley. The great variety of climatic conditions, vegetation, topographic situations, and geologic conditions makes the area attractive for future growth. Population growth has historically been confined primarily to the flatlands surrounding San Francisco Bay and its adjacent waterways, the city of San Francisco, and some of the larger inland valleys. At present, however, development is spreading rapidly into adjacent hillside areas, where landsliding is becoming an increasing problem.

The geology of the region is very complex. Many different types of rocks (Schlocker, 1968, 1971) and numerous active faults (Brown, 1970; Brown and Lee, 1971) are present, and the structural and tectonic history has been complicated. Virtually all the conditions responsible for landslides are present in the San Francisco Bay region, including (1) steep, irregular slopes; (2) abundant and seasonally intense rainfall; (3) extensive human activity, including logging and the grading and cutting of slopes; (4) an abundance of rock types that are very susceptible to sliding, including extensively crushed and fractured Franciscan mélange complexes and poorly consolidated upper Tertiary to recent sediments; (5) thick unconsolidated colluvial deposits and thick weathered zones on steep slopes; (6) abundant expansible clay soils; and (7) frequent high-level seismic activity.

Several geologic studies have been conducted in the region, but they have focused primarily on mapping bedrock units, rather than on slope stability. Private engineering geology consultants have examined the slope-stability characteristics of many small parcels of land in detail, but little of this work has been published, and few regional studies have been undertaken. Some of the earlier studies that have been concerned with landslide features and slope-stability characteristics in the region, and which have provided much necessary data and insight for the current studies, include those by Kachadoorian (1956), Schlocker, Bonilla, and Radbruch (1958), Bonilla (1960a, 1960b, 1971), Radbruch (1957, 1969), Radbruch and Weiler (1963), Kojan (1968), Harding (1969), Clague (1969), Pampeyan (1970), Rogers (1971), and Waltz (1971). Within most of the region, however, information regarding the distribution of landslide deposits was very meager at the time that this slope-stability study began. New work has been directed toward the preparation of slope-stability maps at a

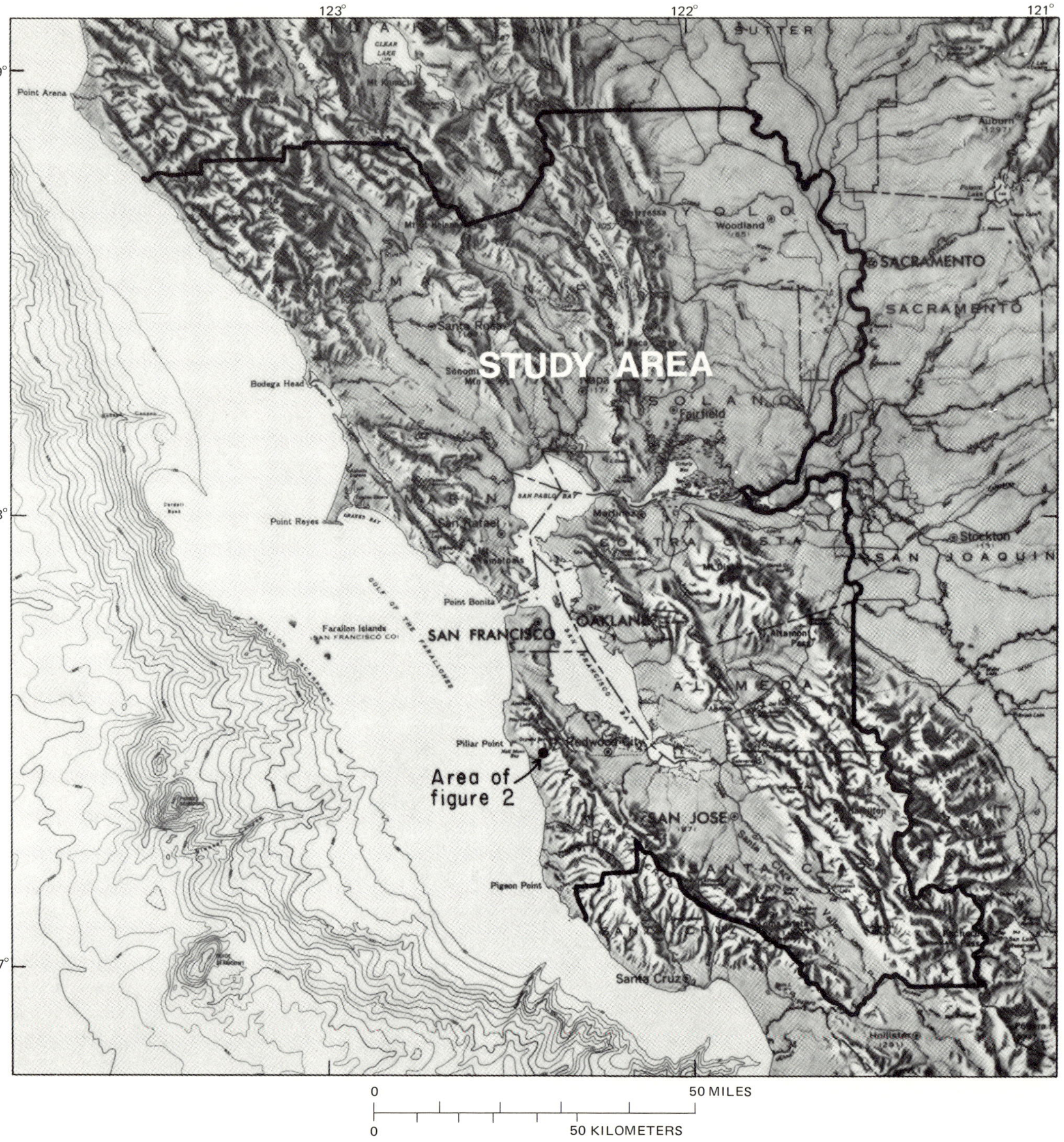

Figure 1.—Index map of the San Francisco Bay region, showing area of figure 2. Depth contour interval 100 fathoms.

regional scale (1:125,000) for the entire bay region. To attain this goal, the acquisition of much new data and much new mapping have been necessary, including the mapping of landslide deposits, bedrock geology, active faults, slopes, recent landslides, other surficial deposits, and engineering properties of bedrock and soil units.

The maps and reports from the study are being published in a three-part series: (1) Basic Data Contributions, which are based on the initial data-gathering phase of the study; (2) Technical Reports, which are derived from the basic data; and (3) Interpretive Reports, which are nontechnical and will be addressed primarily to governmental policy makers and the non-technically-oriented private sector. To date, about 40 Basic Data Contributions and a few Technical Reports have been released. Those that relate to slope-stability studies are noted separately in the list of references at the end of this paper. All of the publications and a current list of publications from the study can be obtained from the Public Inquiries Office, U.S. Geological Survey, 555 Battery Street, San Francisco, Calif. 94111.

ESTIMATED COSTS OF LANDSLIDE DAMAGE

Before the present study began, it was known that the yearly cost of landslides in the bay region was great, but no reliable figures were available. As part of the overall study of slope stability, we have attempted to estimate in several ways the costs to the community. This type of information was useful not only in pointing out the necessity of slope-stability studies prior to construction but also in informing various local governmental agencies of the costs involved in developments that did not consider geological factors.

Costs related to landsliding are generally very difficult to ascertain. Data on the costs of damage to structures, reevaluation of land or housing for tax purposes, and expenditures for road, sidewalk, sewer, and railroad repairs are available from some public agencies, but much damage goes unreported and many other costs are impossible to determine; and many public agencies do not carefully record information about landslide damage. Indeterminable costs include those for litigation, salaries of firemen and policemen, detours, and a host of others, many of them intangible.

Taylor and Brabb (1972) compiled data on landslide costs from governmental and private agencies in the San Francisco Bay region for the rainy season of 1968–69, dividing the costs into public, private, and miscellaneous categories, and enumerating costs to each county separately. They found that public and private costs totalled more than $25 million, and this figure is probably minimal.

Nilsen and Brabb (1972) investigated a group of landslides in the northeastern part of the city of San Jose that had damaged public and private facilities during a 10-year period. Their report shows the locations of landslide deposits and damaged buildings and streets and also summarizes some of the costs of the landslides to the city. During a 5-year period, San Jose spent more than $750,000 to study one of the landslides, to attempt to control its movement, and to maintain roads across it.

ESTIMATES OF LANDSLIDE ABUNDANCE

Radbruch and Wentworth (1971) made preliminary estimates of the relative abundance of landslides in the bay region by comparing types of earth materials in the region, amount of rainfall, and degree of slope. They divided the region into six categories, ranging from least abundant to most abundant landslides. Their map is an approximation, because when it was made, little information about the distribution of landslides was available. Nevertheless, it provides a reasonably good overview of the distribution of landslides in the region.

Taylor and Brabb (1972) included in their report a map (scale 1:500,000) showing all landslides that they investigated for the 1968–69 season. The map gives an impression of the distribution of structurally damaging landslides in the region, and of how many new ones might be expected from development of some hilly regions where Radbruch and Wentworth's (1971) map shows landslides to be abundant.

INVENTORY OF LANDSLIDE DEPOSITS

Maps showing the distribution of landslide deposits in the entire bay region (scale 1:62,500) are now being prepared, primarily by interpretation of aerial photographs, with minimal field checking. This technique is necessary because of the size of the area, inaccessibility of much of it, and time limitations. The inventory of landslide deposits provided by these maps will be used in conjunction with other data to prepare derivative maps showing relative slope stability.

Seven preliminary photointerpretation maps of landslide deposits have been released (Brabb and Pampeyan, 1972b; Nilsen, 1971, 1972a,b,c,d; Sims and Nilsen, 1972), and many more are being prepared. They show where landslide deposits were recognized at the time the aerial photographs were taken. Although the type of movement, date of most recent activity, and nature of the landslide materials are not indicated, the maps are nevertheless useful. Most landslide activity consists of renewed movement of older landslide deposits. The maps can therefore be used as a general guide to problem areas, and as they provide a regional picture of the past history of landslide activity, they are also useful for site investigations by consulting engineering geologists. Construction activities can alter the marginally stable character of older landslide deposits and induce renewed movement.

The photointerpretive techniques used have enabled recognition of a large number of landslide deposits in most areas and have shown that landsliding is one of the major erosional processes in the bay region. The techniques depend upon recognition of scarps, anomalous bulges and lumps, hummocky topography, ridgetop trenches and fissures, terraced slopes, abrupt slope changes, altered stream courses, discontinous drainage patterns, closed depressions, springs, and anomalous color, texture, shade, vegetation, and bedrock patterns.

SLOPE MAPS

Slope maps of selected areas within the San Francisco Bay region have been prepared by a new, experimental technique utilizing contour negatives of the Geological Survey's 1:24,000 topographic map series. The contour lines are diffused photomechanically in measured increments to produce the desired slope intervals (in percent): 0–5, 5–15, 15–30, 30–50, 50–70, and greater than 70. These six intervals are currently being used for many other studies and were selected after discussions with project geologists and city, county, and regional planners and engineers. Complete coverage of the nine

San Francisco Bay counties with slope maps at scales of 1:62,500 and 1:125,000 is planned.

Color transparencies as well as black-and-white prints have been combined several different ways to determine the best way to show slope intervals. For San Mateo County, a color transparency at a scale of 1:62,500 was superimposed on geologic and landslide maps to make a landslide-susceptibility analysis (see discussions under "Slope stability"). Inexpensive diazo prints were also prepared from positives of the color-separation negatives and were used to provide slope information for a coastline study by regional planners. Black-and-white composites as well as transparencies with dark shades of color have so far proved unsatisfactory for slope-stability studies because the contour base or other information needed for the study, such as the identification of the rock unit, cannot easily be seen.

Minor errors are introduced by the photomechanical process, especially along narrow ridge crests and valley floors, where slope categories tend to be too high. The errors can be taken into account when the contour base is examined in conjunction with the slope data.

SLOPE STABILITY

Geologic maps emphasizing engineering properties of rock units, including slope stability and shear strength, have been published for only a few parts of the bay region. Maps showing only slope stability, however, are rare. Johnson and Ellen (1968) and Johnson and Lobo-Guerrero (1968) made slope-stability maps of small areas in the town of Portola Valley. These maps were the first in the San Francisco Bay region to depict slope stability in a cartographic format that could be readily understood by urban planners. Unfortunately, neither map has been published.

A report by Blanc and Cleveland (1968) firmly established a methodology for preparing slope-stability maps in a small area of southern California. Brabb, Pampeyan, and Bonilla (1972) prepared a landslide-susceptibility map of San Mateo County based in part on the methodology of Blanc and Cleveland (1968) and in part on data provided by Bonilla (1960a,b). They (Brabb and others) avoided using the term "slope stability" because the stability of an individual slope was not analyzed. Instead, they expressed the average susceptibility of slope-material units over the region. Their map differs from others in that the landslide failure record for each rock unit in six different slope categories was systematically measured and used in the analysis. Slope and strength of the rock unit seem to be the principal factors controlling slope stability in San Mateo County—other factors, such as structural control, soil type, rainfall, climate, and vegetation, appear to be averaged through time and space so that their relative influence, at least on a regional basis, is minimal.

Brabb, Pampeyan, and Bonilla (1972) used a geologic map, landslide map, and slope map (fig. 2) to prepare the landslide-susceptibility map of San Mateo County. All three maps are at a scale of 1:62,500. Part of the geologic map, compiled by Brabb and Pampeyan (1972a), is shown on figure 2*A*. The landslide map, figure 2*B*, was prepared by Brabb and Pampeyan (1972b), largely by photointerpretation. The slope map, figure 2*C*, was prepared experimentally by the Geological Survey specifically for the slope-stability studies.

The landslide-susceptibility map, figure 2*D*, was prepared from the three aforementioned maps by the following method: the percentages of area within 35 geologic map units in San Mateo County that are covered by landslide deposits were estimated by use of a grid overlay with a grid size of 0.01 sq mi at the map scale. The geologic map units were then arbitrarily grouped in six classes, from class I with 0–1 percent area covered by landslide deposits to class VI with 54–70 percent. The class numbers express, therefore, the relative susceptibility of the geologic map units to landsliding, from I, very low, to VI, very high. The landslide deposits themselves are shown as a separate class, L. Each geologic map unit was then further evaluated to determine which slope categories were critical for the formation of landslides. If few or no landslide deposits formed on low slopes, the class number for the geologic map unit was reduced. Thus, a geologic map unit might be assigned III in comparison with the landslide susceptibility of other geologic map units, and II or I in low-slope categories where few failures occurred.

One advantage of this method is that it provides the regional planner with a way of evaluating the area between landslide deposits on the basis of the average failure record of the geologic map unit throughout a county. The method also compensates for stable formations on steep slopes and unstable formations on low slopes. The principal disadvantages are that the landslide susceptibility of flat areas adjacent to unstable slopes is underestimated, and the map does not express in absolute terms the likelihood that any given slope will fail in any given period of time. Field studies by engineering geologists are, of course, still necessary for evaluating any particular site.

The publication status of and area covered by the slope-stability and landslide maps are shown on figure 3.

CONCLUSIONS

Slope-stability studies provide basic information needed by land-use planners in the bay region. Much additional work will be required before the dynamics of downslope movements are completely understood, but the preliminary compilations (like the landslide inventory) are necessary for a broader understanding of regional slope stability. Also currently being studied are the relationships between recent landslide activity and rainfall cycles, and between landsliding and urban development, as well as the mechanics of coastal landsliding and the clay mineralogy of soils and bedrock units susceptible to sliding.

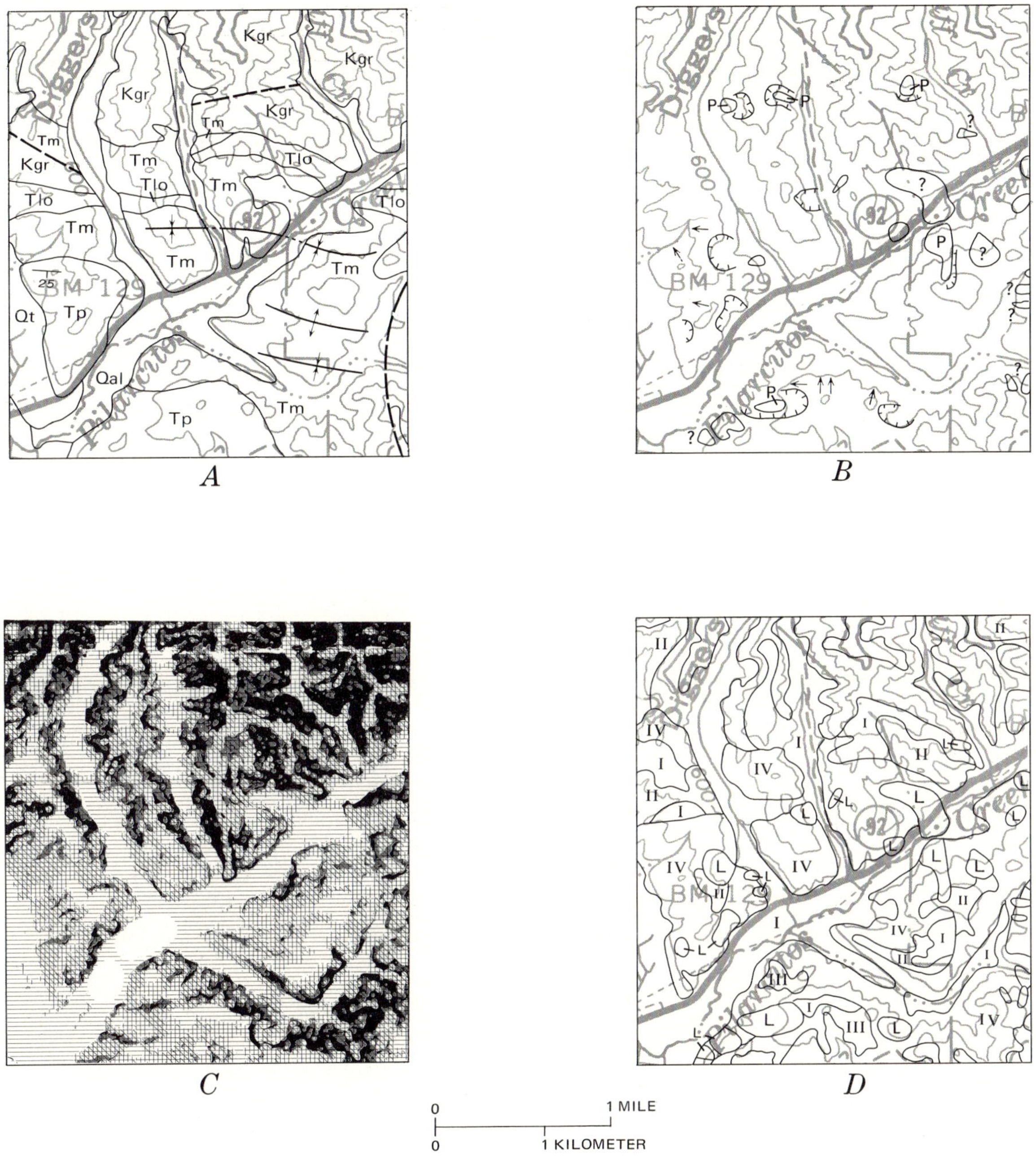

Figure 2.—Materials used for a landslide susceptibility map of San Mateo County, Calif. The area shown is near the town of Half Moon Bay about 25 km south of San Francisco (see fig. 1).

A, geologic map; includes granitic rocks of Cretaceous age (Kgr), shale and sandstone of Miocene and Pliocene age (Tp, Tm, Tlo), terrace deposits (Qt), and alluvium (Qal). Heavy dashed lines are faults; thinner lines with arrows are fold axes.

B, landslide map; the small arrows show landslide deposits 15 to 150 m in size, and the other lines show landslides larger than 150 m. The hachured lines show landslide scarps. P, probable landslide deposit; ?, questionable landslide deposit.

C, slope map; the darker the tone, the greater the slope.

D, landslide susceptibility map; the higher the roman numeral, the greater the susceptibility to landsliding. Landslide deposits (L) are shown as a separate category (the highest).

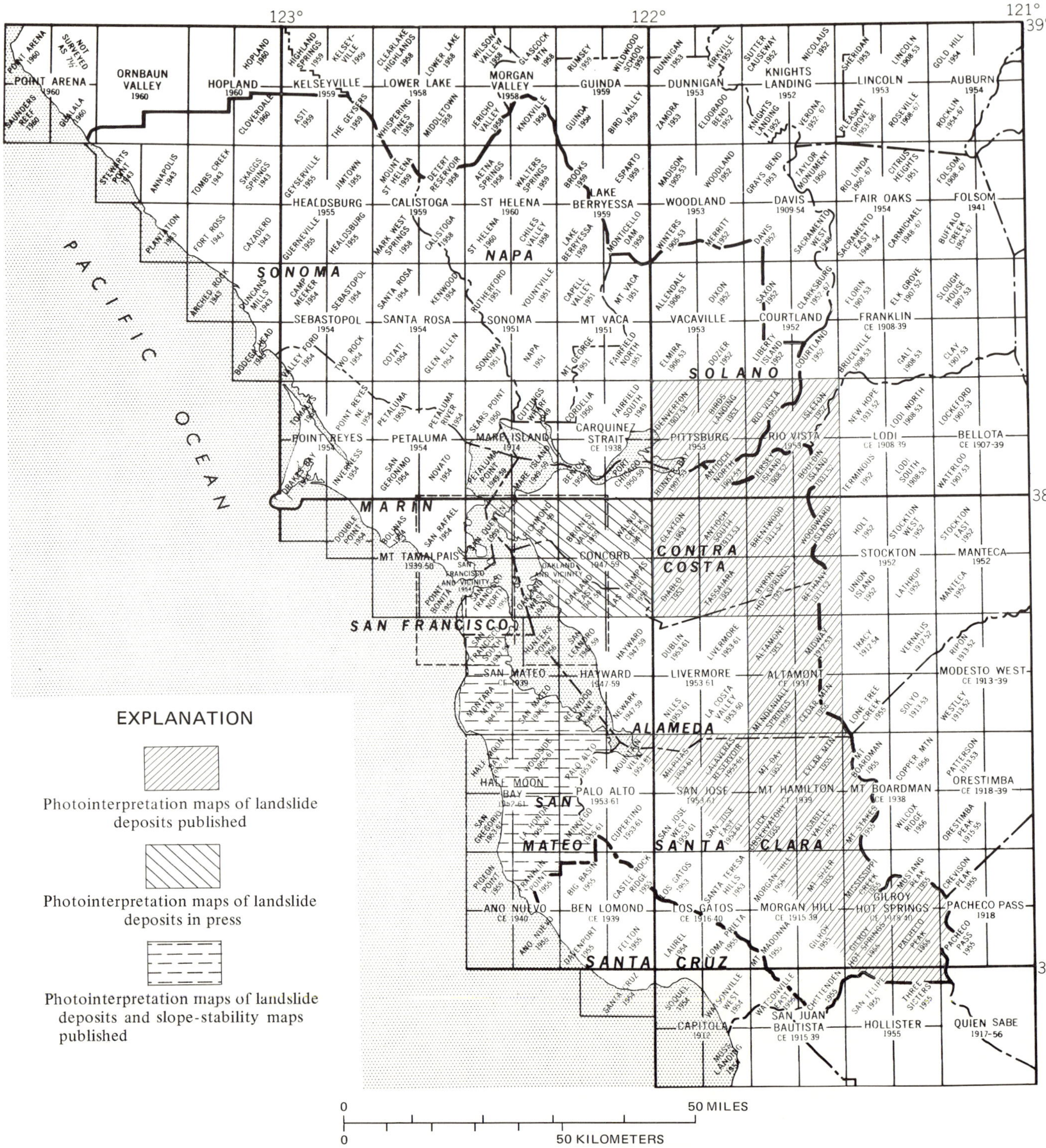

Figure 3.—Status of slope-stability studies in the San Francisco Bay region.

REFERENCES CITED

[Reports that have been released as Basic Data Contributions of the San Francisco Bay Region Environment and Resources Planning Study are noted in brackets after the formal reference citation as "BDC," with the number of the publication following]

Blanc, R. P., and Cleveland, G. B., 1968, Natural slope stability as related to geology, San Clemente area, Orange and San Diego Counties, California: California Div. Mines and Geology Spec. Rept. 98, 19 p.

Bonilla, M. G., 1960a, Landslides in the San Francisco South quadrangle, California: U.S. Geol. Survey open-file report, 44 p.

—— 1960b, A sample of California Coast Range landslides: Art. 66 *in* U.S. Geol. Survey Prof. Paper 400-B, p. B149.

—— 1971, Preliminary geologic map of the San Francisco South and part of the Hunters Point quadrangles: U.S. Geol. Survey Misc. Field Studies Map MF-311, scale 1:24,000 [BDC 29].

Brabb, E. E., and Pampeyan, E. H., compilers, 1972a, Preliminary geologic map of San Mateo County, California: U.S. Geol. Survey Misc. Field Studies Map MF-328, scale 1:62,500 [BDC 41].

—— 1972b, Preliminary map of landslides in San Mateo County, California: U.S. Geol. Survey Misc. Field Studies Map MF-344, scale 1:62,500 [BDC 42].

Brabb, E. E., Pampeyan, E. H., and Bonilla, M. G., 1972, Landslide susceptibility in San Mateo County, California: U.S. Geol. Survey Misc. Field Studies Map MF-360 [BDC 43].

Brown, R. D., Jr., 1970, Faults that are historically active or that show evidence of geologically young surface displacements, San Francisco Bay region; a progress report, October 1970: U.S. Geol. Survey Misc. Field Studies Map MF-331, scale 1:250,000 [BDC 7].

Brown, R. D., Jr., and Lee, W. H. K., 1971, Active faults and preliminary earthquake epicenters (1969–1970) in the southern part of the San Francisco Bay region: U.S. Geol. Survey Misc. Field Studies Map MF-307, scale 1:250,000 [BDC 30].

Clague, J. J., 1969, Landslides of southern Point Reyes National Seashore: California Div. Mines and Geology Mineral Inf. Service, v. 22, no. 7, p. 107–110, 116–118.

Harding, R. C., 1969, Landslides–a continuing problem for Bay area development, *in* Danehy, E. A., ed., Urban environmental geology in the San Francisco Bay region, p. 65–74: Assoc. Eng. Geologists, San Francisco Section, Spec. Pub., 162 p.

Johnson, A. M., and Ellen, S. D., 1968, Preliminary evaluation of the interaction between engineering development and natural geologic processes on the Bovet property, Town of Portola Valley, California, *with a section on* the San Andreas fault by William R. Dickinson: Report prepared for Town of Portola Valley, Calif., map scale about 1:2,400.

Johnson, A. M., and Lobo-Guerrero, A. U., 1968, Preliminary evaluation of the relative stability of ground, Marianni property, Town of Portola Valley, California, *with a section on* the San Andreas fault by W. R. Dickinson: Report prepared for Town of Portola Valley, California, 22 p.

Kachadoorian, R., 1956, Engineering geology of the Warford Mesa Subdivision, Orinda, California: U.S. Geol. Survey open-file report, 13 p.

Kojan, E., 1968, Mechanics and rates of natural soil creep: Eng. Geologists and Soil Engineers Symposium, 5th Ann., Pocatello, Idaho, April 1967, Proc., p. 233–253.

Nilsen, T. H., 1971, Preliminary photointerpretation map of landslide and other surficial deposits of the Mount Diablo area, Contra Costa and Alameda Counties, California: U.S. Geol. Survey Misc. Field Studies Map MF-310, scale 1:62,500 [BDC 31].

—— 1972a, Preliminary photointerpretation map of landslide and other surficial deposits of parts of the Altamont and Carbona 15-minute quadrangles, Alameda County, California: U.S. Geol. Survey Misc. Field Studies Map MF-321, scale 1:62,500 [BDC 34].

—— 1972b, Preliminary photointerpretation map of landslide and other surficial deposits of the Byron area, Contra Costa and Alameda Counties, California: U.S. Geol. Survey Misc. Field Studies Map MF-338, scale 1:62,500 [BDC 38].

—— 1972c, Preliminary photointerpretation map of landslide and other surficial deposits of the Mount Hamilton quadrangle and parts of the Mount Boardman and San Jose quadrangles, Alameda and Santa Clara Counties, California: U.S. Geol. Survey Misc. Field Studies Map MF-339, scale 1:62,500 [BDC 40].

—— 1972d, Preliminary photointerpretation map of landslide and other surficial deposits of parts of the Los Gatos, Morgan Hill, Gilroy Hot Springs, Pacheco Pass, Quien Sabe, and Hollister 15-minute quadrangles, Santa Clara County, California: U.S. Geol. Survey Misc. Field Studies Map MF-416, scale 1:62,500 [BDC 46].

Nilsen, T. H., and Brabb, E. E., 1972, Preliminary photointerpretation and damage maps of landslide and other surficial deposits in northeastern San Jose, California: U.S. Geol. Survey Misc. Field Studies Map MF-361, scales 1:12,000 and 1:24,000 [BDC 45].

Pampeyan, E. H., 1970, Geologic map of the Palo Alto 7½-minute quadrangle, San Mateo and Santa Clara Counties, California: U.S. Geol. Survey open-file map, scale 1:24,000 [BDC 2].

Radbruch, D. H., 1957, Areal and engineering geology of the Oakland West quadrangle, California: U.S. Geol. Survey Misc. Geol. Inv. Map I-239, scale 1:24,000.

—— 1969, Areal and engineering geology of the Oakland East quadrangle, California: U.S. Geol. Survey Geol. Quad. Map GQ-769, scale 1:24,000.

Radbruch, D. H., and Weiler, L. M., 1963, Preliminary report on landslides in a part of the Orinda Formation, Contra Costa County, California: U.S. Geol. Survey open-file report, 35 p.

Radbruch, D. H., and Wentworth, C. M., 1971, Estimated relative abundance of landslides in the San Francisco Bay region, California: U.S. Geol. Survey open-file map, scale 1:500,000 [BDC 11].

Rogers, T. H., 1971, Environmental geologic analysis of the Santa Cruz Mountain study area, Santa Clara County, California: Sacramento, California Div. Mines and Geology, 64 p.

Schlocker, Julius, 1968, The geology of the San Francisco Bay area and its significance in land use planning: Berkeley, Calif., Assoc. Bay Area Govts., Supp. Rept. IS-3, 47 p.

—— 1971, Generalized geologic map of the San Francisco Bay region, California: U.S. Geol. Survey open-file map, scale 1:500,000 [BDC 8].

Schlocker, Julius, Bonilla, M. G., and Radbruch, D. H., 1958, Geology of the San Francisco North quadrangle, California: U.S. Geol. Survey Misc. Geol. Inv. Map I-272, scale 1:24,000.

Sims, J. D., and Nilsen, T. H., 1972, Preliminary photointerpretation map of landslide and other surficial deposits of parts of the Pittsburg and Rio Vista 15-minute quadrangles, Contra Costa and Solano Counties, California: U.S. Geol. Survey Misc. Field Studies Map MF-322, scale 1:62,500 [BDC 35].

Taylor, F. A., and Brabb, E. E., 1972, Map showing distribution and cost by counties of structurally damaging landslides in the San Francisco Bay region, California, winter of 1968–69: U.S. Geol. Survey Misc. Field Studies Map MF-327, scale 1:1,000,000 [BDC 37].

U.S. Geological Survey and U.S. Department of Housing and Urban Development, 1971, Program design 1971, San Francisco Bay region environment and resources planning study, PB2-06826: Available only from U.S. Dept. Commerce Natl. Tech. Inf. Service, Springfield, Va., 123 p.

Waltz, J. P., 1971, An analysis of selected landslides in Alameda and Contra Costa Counties, California: Assoc. Eng. Geologists Bull., v. 8, no. 2, p. 153–163.

Jour. Research U.S. Geol. Survey
Vol. 1, No. 4, July—Aug. 1973, p. 439—452

DEEP-SEA FAN PALEOCURRENT PATTERNS OF THE EOCENE BUTANO SANDSTONE, SANTA CRUZ MOUNTAINS, CALIFORNIA

By TOR H. NILSEN and T. R. SIMONI, JR., Menlo Park, Calif.

Abstract.—The Butano Sandstone is an Eocene continental borderland deep-sea fan deposit located in the Santa Cruz Mountains, Calif. Paleoslope measurements from contorted strata within it yield a regional northward paleoslope for the fan. Detailed paleocurrent measurements from conglomerate clast orientations, flute casts, groove casts, current-ripple markings, small-scale cross-strata, convolute laminations, and flame structures yield a sediment-dispersal pattern characterized by northward transport of coarser grained sediments downfan along major channels and transport of finer grained sediments outward and away from channels by overspilling. The overall paleocurrent pattern is oriented radially outward from the fan apex and indicates that the growth, development, and dispersal of sediments on this ancient deep-sea fan resembled that on modern deep-sea fans.

Sedimentological studies by the writers indicate that the Butano Sandstone of the Santa Cruz Mountains was deposited as a deep-sea fan in a continental borderland setting (Nilsen, 1970, 1971). Among the attributes of the Butano that strongly suggest this depositional setting are the paleocurrent patterns derived from various sedimentary structures within it. Documentations of such patterns from ancient deep-sea fan deposits are generally lacking in geologic literature; the paleocurrent patterns and the associated sediment-dispersal model presented herein will provide an example for geologists working on other ancient fan deposits and will permit sedimentological comparisons with modern fan systems.

The Butano crops out discontinuously in the Santa Cruz Mountains over a northwest-southeast distance of about 40 miles (fig. 1). Its thickness and areal extent make it a major rock unit in the region, and it is an oil reservoir in the La Honda and Costa oil fields. The northeastern edge of its outcrop area is abruptly terminated by the Pilarcitos and San Andreas faults. Regional paleogeographic reconstructions and sedimentologic studies suggest that the missing eastern part of the ancient Butano fan is the Point of Rocks Sandstone in the Temblor Range, located approximately 190—200 miles to the southeast (Clarke and Nilsen, 1972). Because the rocks on opposite sides of the San Andreas fault have undergone considerable right-lateral offset (Dibblee, 1966a), rocks mapped by Dibblee (1966b) and Brabb (1970) as Butano(?) Sandstone in the part of the Santa Cruz Mountains east of the Pilarcitos and San Andreas faults should not be considered Butano. These rocks were originally deposited in a separate basin at least 200 miles distant from the true Butano located west of these faults (Beaulieu, 1970).

The Butano Sandstone was named by Branner, Newsom, and Arnold (1909) for massive brown and buff sandstone and minor conglomerate over 2,000 feet thick on Butano Ridge. It was later mapped and studied in greater detail in Stanford University Ph. D. theses by Touring (1959), Brabb (1960a), Cummings (1960), and Clark (1966); it was also mapped and described in several Stanford University M.S. theses and student projects during approximately the same period of time. Cummings, Touring, and Brabb (1962) have summarized the lithologic characteristics and stratigraphic relations of the Butano; Brabb (1970) and Brabb and Pampeyan (1972) have compiled recent geologic maps showing the distribution of the Butano Sandstone. The type section for its uppermost part was designated by Cummings, Touring, and Brabb (1962, p. 184) as along Little Boulder Creek in SW¼ sec. 22, SE¼ sec. 21, and N½ sec. 28, T. 8 S., R. 3 W.

The Butano ranges in age from early Eocene (Penutian) to late Eocene (Narizian) on the basis of foraminiferal studies, although most of it was deposited during the Narizian Stage of Mallory (1959). The foraminiferal studies also indicate that deposition took place in a bathyal to abyssal marine environment in a basin with unrestricted access to the ocean (Sullivan, 1962; Clark, 1966; Fairchild and others, 1969).

The Butano unconformably overlies the marine Paleocene Locatelli Formation of Brabb (1960b) and is overlain conformably by the Twobar Shale Member of Brabb (1964), a deep-sea hemipelagic shale deposit forming the lowest member of the San Lorenzo Formation. The minimum thickness of the Butano is 4,000 feet; the maximum, possibly as much as 10,000 feet. However, because it crops out as a series of isolated folded and faulted blocks, a complete section is nowhere exposed (fig. 1). Outcrops of the Butano are generally poor because of deep weathering, thick soil horizons, and extensive vegetative cover, and beds cannot generally be traced for more than 50—100 feet.

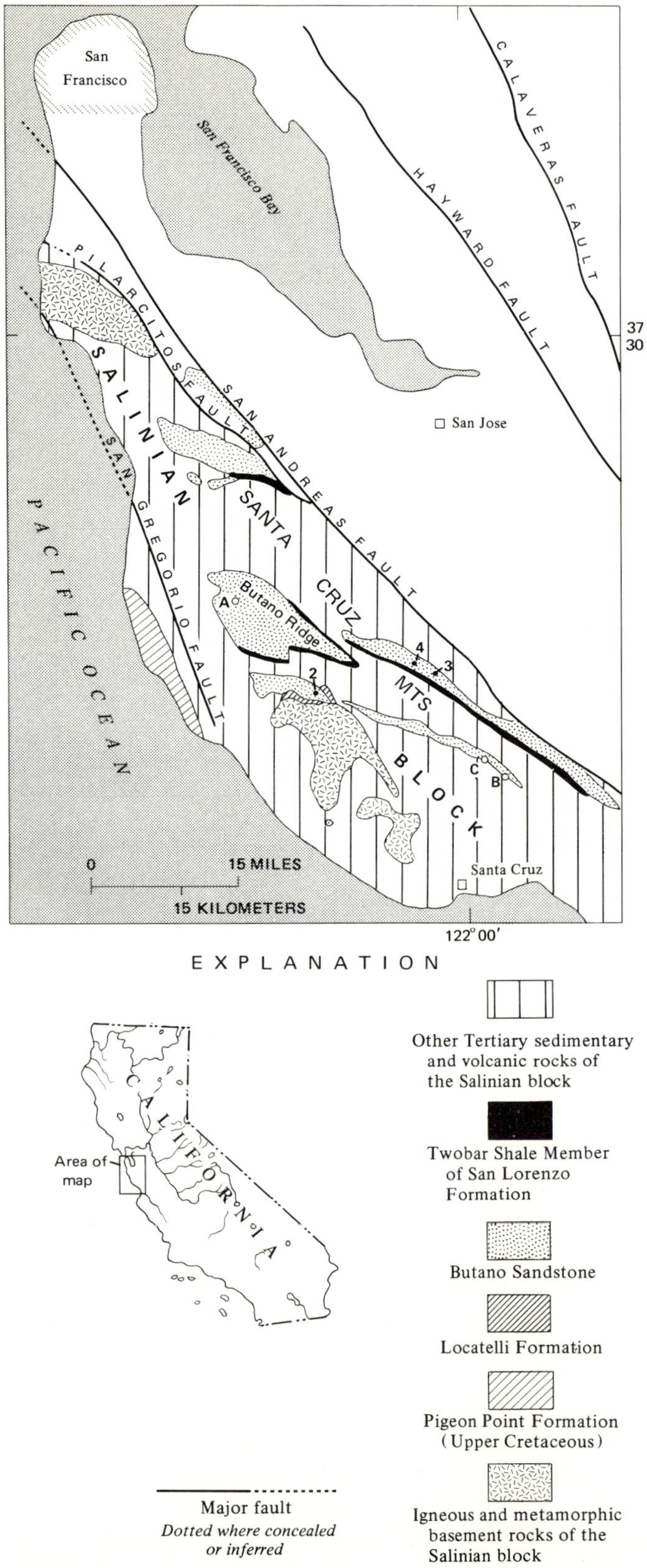

Figure 1.–Generalized geologic map of the Santa Cruz Mountains, showing the distribution of Butano Sandstone. Numbers 2, 3, and 4 are locations of figures 2, 3, and 4, respectively; A, B, and C, are locations of conglomerate fabric measurements of figure 7. Geology from Brabb (1970) and Brabb and Pampeyan (1972).

Acknowledgments.–We thank Earl E. Brabb for suggesting the study and providing much assistance during it.

SEDIMENTOLOGY

Sedimentary facies

The Butano Sandstone contains a great variety of sedimentary structures characteristic of deposition by grain-flow or other mass flow processes, turbidity currents, and downslope slumping. Sandstone, conglomerate, and shale are the major rock types. Coarser and thicker bedded deposits are most common in the southern part of the outcrop area, where thickly bedded sandstone and conglomerate that resemble fluxoturbidite and grain-flow deposits are found (Dzulynski and others, 1959; Stauffer, 1967; Stanley and Unrug, 1972).

The conglomerate, which is abundant to the south, is locally very coarse, is typically irregularly bedded, and commonly shows abrupt lateral changes in bedding thickness and coarseness (fig. 2). The sandstone typically consists of repetitively alternating deposits of thick ungraded medium- or coarse-grained Bouma *a* sandstone overlain by thin, discontinuous Bouma *e* shale (Bouma, 1962); the sandstone is commonly channeled into the underlying deposits, with considerable lateral thickening and thinning (fig. 3). These deposits are thought to represent channel deposits of the upper part (toward the south) of the Butano deep-sea fan. These channel deposits grade laterally northward into finer grained and thinner bedded channel deposits characterized by Bouma *ae* and Bouma *abe* sequences; further north, these deposits become even more thinly bedded and finer grained and are characterized by Bouma *abcde* and *bcde* sequences.

Interbedded vertically with the channel deposits and grading laterally into them are various types of interchannel deposits.

Figure 2.–Irregularly bedded, coarse-grained conglomerate from upper fan-channel deposit in the Butano Sandstone. Rock hammer (circled) located in lower center for scale. Location of photograph shown on figure 1.

In the southern part of the outcrop area, these interchannel deposits consist of repetitively alternating thin beds of fine-grained sandstone and shale, forming Bouma *cde* sequences; further north, these deposits consist of Bouma *bcde*, *cde* and *de* sequences (fig. 4). In the northernmost outcrops thick sequences of mudstone containing thinly interbedded fine-grained sandstone or siltstone with current-ripple laminations and irregular small-scale cross-laminae are conspicuous.

The various sedimentary facies show abrupt lateral changes throughout the outcrop extent of the Butano Sandstone. In fact, nearby measured sections covering the same stratigraphic intervals differ markedly, making correlation of individual beds or groups of beds virtually impossible. In vertical sequence, the facies also change abruptly, with sequences of thinly bedded, finer grained interchannel deposits irregularly alternating with sequences of thickly bedded, coarser grained channel deposits. These relations indicate continued migration of channels and changing patterns of deposition during growth of the fan.

Figure 3.—Thickly bedded, medium- to coarse-grained sandstone from upper to middle fan-channel deposit in the Butano Sandstone. Notebook in lower left is approximately 8 inches long. Location of photograph shown on figure 1.

Figure 4.—Rhythmically interbedded fine-grained sandstone and mudstone from upper to middle fan interchannel deposit in the Butano Sandstone. Location of photograph shown on figure 1.

Sedimentary structures

Sedimentary structures in the Butano are found typically within Bouma sequences, which consist of regularly interbedded cycles of coarser grained sediments that grade upward into finer grained sediments (Bouma, 1962). Sedimentary structures found include flute casts, groove casts, cross-stratification, current-ripple markings, planar bedding, convolute laminations, flame structures, dish structures, load casts, extensive bioturbation, channeling, graded bedding, shale rip-ups, diapirs, possible antidune features, amalgamated sandstone beds, mass-flow features, small-scale structures formed by the escape of gas or water, and various types of synsedimentary slumped and contorted strata. Conglomerate fabrics are variable, but some are markedly anisotropic and contain well-oriented and imbricated clasts.

Conglomerate clast size distribution

The longest dimensions of the 10 largest conglomerate clasts were measured at each conglomerate-bearing outcrop of Butano Sandstone (fig. 5). The largest clasts are concentrated into two distinct groups along the southwestern and southeastern edges of the outcrop area. These boulder accumulations probably represent deposits in major channels of the upper fan region. The maximum clast size decreases very rapidly northward from these areas, as well as between them; only scattered occurrences of very fine pebbles are found in the northern outcrops.

PALEOSLOPES AND PALEOCURRENTS

Method of study

Synsedimentary contorted strata and slumps were used to determine probable paleoslope orientations; paleocurrents were determined from conglomerate clast orientations and measurements of flute casts, groove casts, current-ripple markings, small-scale cross-strata, trough cross-strata, convolute laminations, and flame structures. A total of 565 paleocurrent indicators and 105 paleoslope indicators were measured in the field. Separate maps were prepared for each type of sedimentary structure or group of genetically related

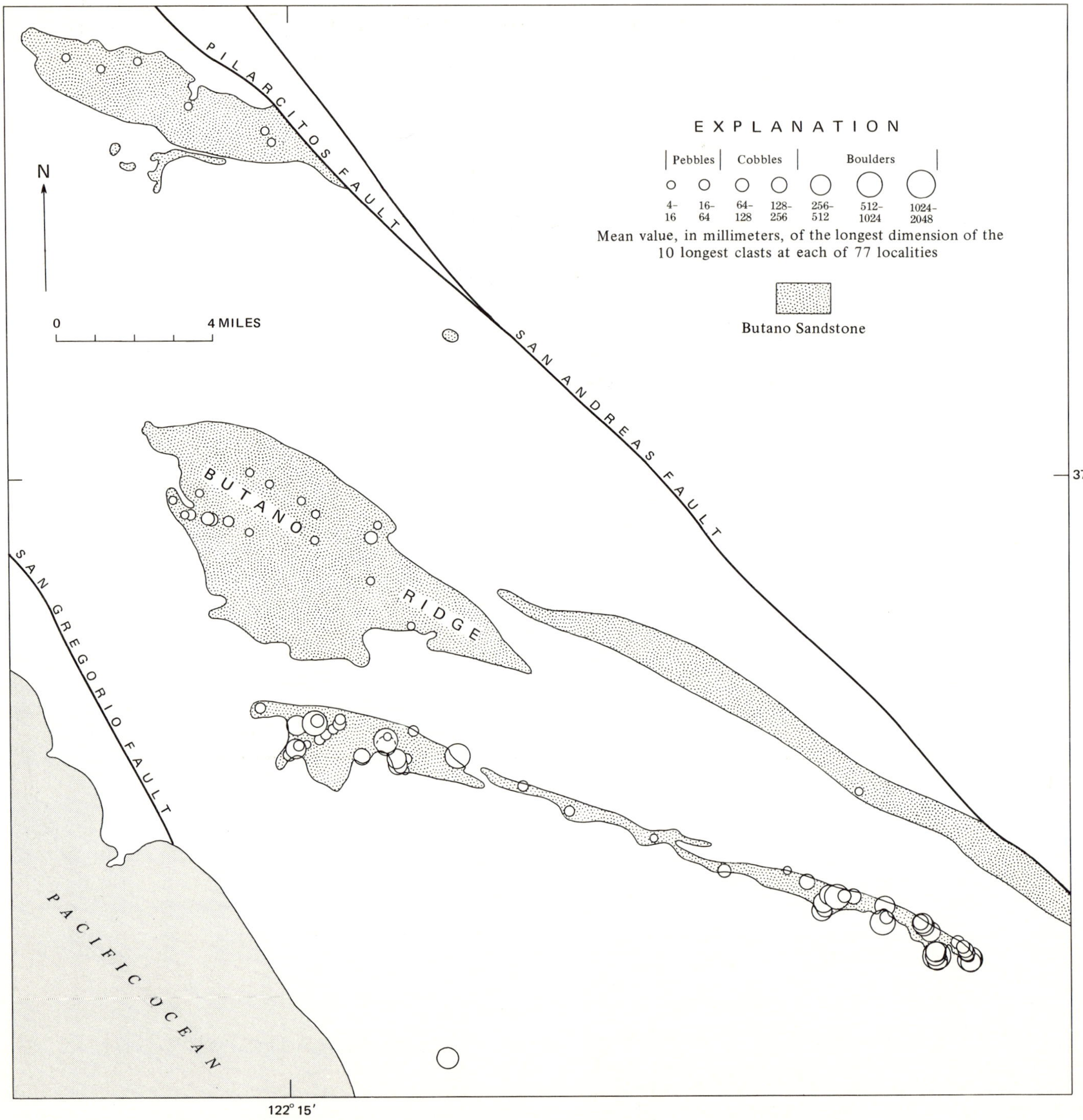

Figure 5.—Distribution of longest clasts in conglomerate beds in the Butano Sandstone.

structures so that paleocurrent and paleoslope patterns resulting from various depositional processes could be clearly differentiated.

The term paleoslope or paleocurrent "direction" is applied in this paper to derived orientations that have only one possible solution, such as from cross-strata, flute casts, and asymmetrical current-ripple markings. Paleoslope or paleocurrent "sense" is applied to derived orientations that do not have single solutions that may be in one of two directions 180° apart, such as from groove casts and symmetrical ripple markings. Some sedimentary structures that ordinarily yield paleocurrent directions were so poorly exposed or developed that only paleocurrent senses could be derived from them.

All paleoslope and paleocurrent measurements were made in the field; subsequent stereographic two-tilt restorations were made by use of computer programs developed by Parks (1970). As many as four directions from a single locality are plotted individually on the paleoslope and paleocurrent maps; where more than four direction measurements were taken at a single locality, the vector mean and standard deviation for the group of directions are plotted. The vector means have been derived according to Curray's method (1956), and standard deviations have been derived mathematically. The standard deviations have been used even where larger than about 60°, their normal useful limit for circular distributions. Paleocurrent or paleoslope directions are plotted separately from senses on all maps.

The locations of paleoslope and paleocurrent orientations are plotted without regard to their stratigraphic position within the Butano Sandstone. Thus, the patterns presented herein are composites taken from all outcrops and the entire stratigraphic range of the Butano. We have, however, separately determined that the paleoslope and paleocurrent orientations from individual measured sections have approximately as wide a spread as a similar number of orientations from a larger area. This indicates great variability in paleoslope and paleocurrent orientations over the entire surface of the fan as well as in any portion of the fan through time.

Paleoslope orientations

The Butano Sandstone contains abundant evidence for downslope subaqueous slumping and sliding. Both low-angle rotational slumps of the type described by Laird (1968) and contorted, folded strata are common. Within the proposed fan environment, downslope movements took place mainly toward the north down the probable regional paleoslope, but also more randomly into local topographic lows such as channels or interchannel areas adjacent to channel levees. The slumping and sliding probably occurred on relatively low slopes under the influence of gravity, as suggested by Dott (1963).

Paleoslope measurements were made on 105 contorted beds. In 62 places, the contorted or folded beds had a preferred orientation of asymmetry, yielding a paleoslope direction; in the remainder, the folds were either symmetrical or so complexly folded that only paleoslope senses could be determined. The mean paleoslope direction for the asymmetric contorted strata is 8°±63°, and mean paleoslope sense for the symmetric or complexly contorted strata is 32°±57° (fig. 6).

Almost all of the contorted beds range in thickness from 7 to 70 cm. Overlying and underlying beds are usually flat and undisturbed. The contorted beds most commonly consist of thinly interbedded fine-grained sandstone and mudstone of Bouma *cde* sequences; these are particularly common in interchannel and lower fan-channel deposits. As such, they are found scattered throughout much of the outcrop area. Some contorted beds may have resulted from the shearing stress applied by currents passing over flat beds, similar to the way that convolute laminations are developed (Sanders, 1960, 1965). However, most do not appear related to current movements, but to downslope sliding and slumping along bedding planes while the sediments were still unconsolidated and characterized by high pore fluid pressures.

The predominant orientation of the paleoslope directions toward the north suggests that the regional northward paleoslope of the ancient Butano fan provided the major control over the direction of movement of folded and contorted beds. Some contorted strata slumped southward, however, which suggests that variably oriented features with small-scale relief were present on the fan surface. No reliable measurements were made of the orientation of surfaces along which rotational slumping took place; most of the paleoslope data are based on measurements of contorted strata.

Paleocurrent orientations

Conglomerate fabric.—Some conglomerates in the Butano Sandstone have well-defined fabrics, with the long axes of elongate clasts oriented parallel to one another on bedding surfaces, and a strongly preferred imbrication. Unfortunately, extensive studies of clast orientations were not possible because of the high degree of induration and the lack of good exposures of conglomerate containing well-defined bedding. The conglomerate fabric orientation was, however, measured at the three localities noted on figure 1; these localities were the only suitable sites found for fabric measurements. The conglomerates at these localities undoubtedly are fan-channel deposits.

The orientations of long axes of clasts on bedding surfaces at two locations (A and B, fig. 1) are shown in figure 7; the vector means and standard deviations are 294°±51° and 324°±45° for 65 and 95 observations, respectively. The conglomerate at locality A is finer grained and has a smaller percentage of elongate clasts than the one at locality B. The conglomerates are not, however, from the same stratigraphic horizon or sedimentation unit. The poles to the maximum projection areas of 69 randomly selected flat-shaped clasts from locality C, were plotted on the lower hemisphere of an equal-area steronet projection (fig. 7); most poles plot in the north-central part of the stereonet, indicating a northward-directed imbrication that would be produced by northerly flowing currents.

These limited fabric data suggest sediment transport to the north in channels of the southeastern area (localities B and C) and to the northwest in the northwestern area (locality A); however, many more measurements are required to define the channel orientations and current directions from the conglomeratic fabric.

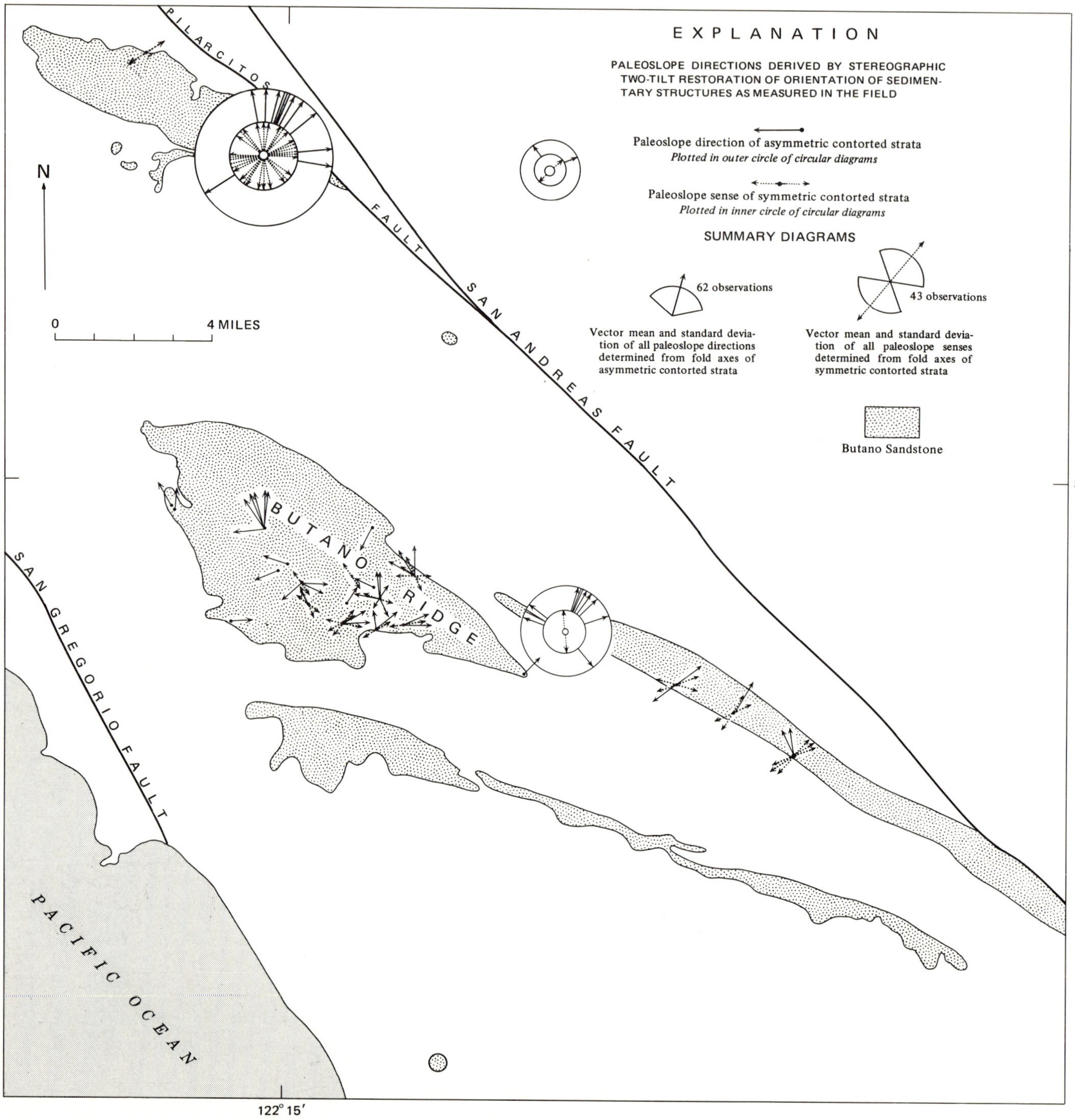

Figure 6.—Paleoslope pattern from contorted stratification in the Butano Sandstone.

Flute casts and groove casts.—Ten paleocurrent directions determined from flute casts in the Butano Sandstone yield a mean paleocurrent direction of 335°±20° (fig. 8). Nineteen additional measurements from groove casts and poorly developed flute casts with uncertain asymmetry yield northerly paleocurrent senses. Most of the flute casts and groove casts are irregularly shaped, similar to the type described by Stauffer (1967) from grain-flow deposits in the Santa Ynez Mountains, Calif. Most are sole markings at the base of thick Bouma *ae* sequences and presumably formed in main channels of the upper to lower fan area. The relatively narrow range in their orientation suggests that the main channels primarily had northerly trends.

Ripple markings.—The orientations of 44 ripple markings were measured in the Butano Sandstone. All the ripple markings visible in cross section are of the current-ripple type. On bedding surfaces, however, many are symmetrical in shape, so that only current senses could be determined from them. The mean current direction of the 25 asymmetrical current-ripple markings is 50°±62°; the mean current sense of the 19 symmetrical ripple markings is 15°±53° (fig. 9). Thus, the ripple markings show a wide range of current orientations, many at approximately right angles to the general northern paleoslope direction. The ripple markings are all small scale and are typically from Bouma *c* horizons. They are found in interchannel deposits as well as in middle and lower fan-channel and fan-fringe deposits. Thus, their variable orientations probably reflect downchannel current transport as well as overbank spilling perpendicular to the channels.

Cross-strata.—The largest number of paleocurrent measurements were from small-scale cross-strata; these are plotted in figure 10 and yield a vector mean of 8°±61°. All of the 453 inclined cross-strata are small scale, with amplitudes ranging from 2 to 10 cm; nearly all were formed by migrating current ripples and dunes. Only two trough cross-strata were noted and measured in the field; these are of larger scale than the inclined cross-strata, having amplitudes of about 20 cm. They were found at the top of thick, massive Bouma *a* deposits and may have developed when movement of entrained water from a grain-flow scoured the top of the bed after the flow had ceased (Middleton, 1969, p. GM-B-11).

The distribution of the small-scale cross-strata is similar to that of the ripple markings. However, the larger number of measurements of these structures reveals far more details of the overall paleocurrent pattern. Many paleocurrent directions are clearly at right angles to the general northern direction of transport, particularly along the eastern and western edges of the outcrop area. The northernmost outcrops yield paleocurrents that are generally directed northward. The summary rose diagram yields a radial distribution of paleocurrent directions for the postulated Butano deep-sea fan.

Convolute laminations and flame structures.—Paleocurrent measurements were made from 38 convolute laminations, three of which were so irregularly shaped that only paleocurrent senses could be determined from them (fig. 11). Four flame structures yielded scattered paleocurrent directions. The

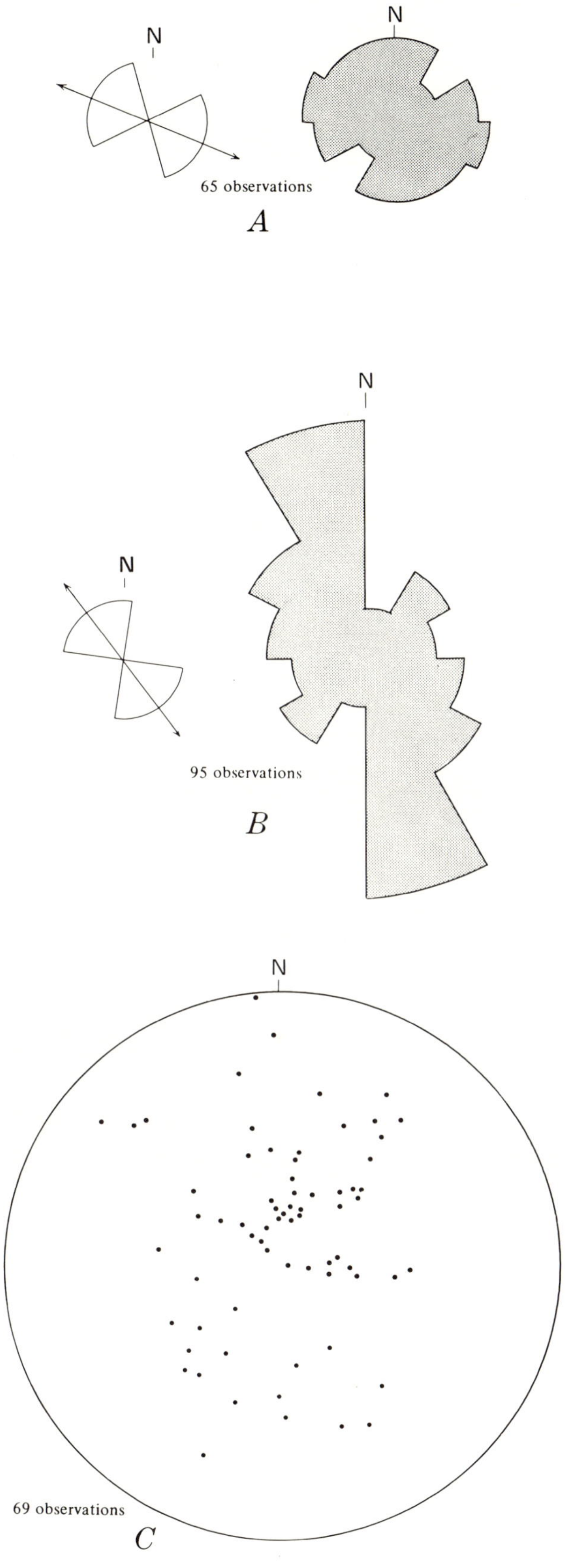

Figure 7.—Long-axis orientation of elongate clasts and imbrication of flat clasts in conglomerate of the Butano Sandstone. *A* and *B*, direction of long axes of elongate clasts on bedding surfaces; vector means and standard deviations on left, rose diagrams on right. *C*, imbrication measurements; poles to maximum projection area of flat clasts projected onto lower hemisphere of equal-area stereonet. See figure 1 for locations of measurements.

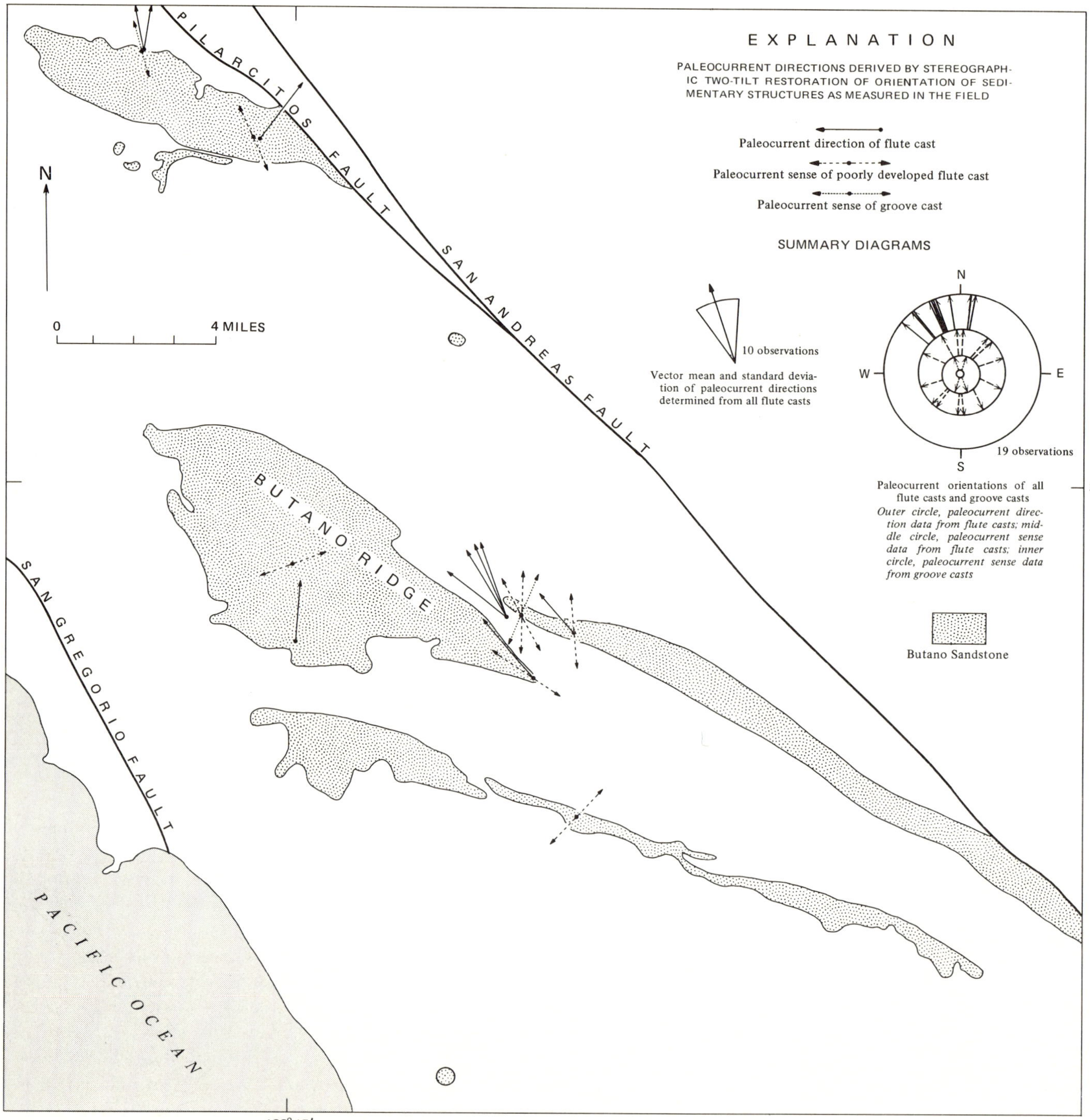

Figure 8.—Paleocurrent pattern from flute casts and groove casts in the Butano Sandstone.

convolute laminations have a wide range of paleocurrent orientations, with a vector mean of 16°±62°. These structures are characteristic of Bouma *c* deposits and are found in the same types of deposits as small-scale cross-strata and ripple markings.

Summary

The paleocurrent and paleoslope data are summarized in table 1. Flute casts and groove casts have the narrowest spread of paleocurrent orientations, probably reflecting the fact that

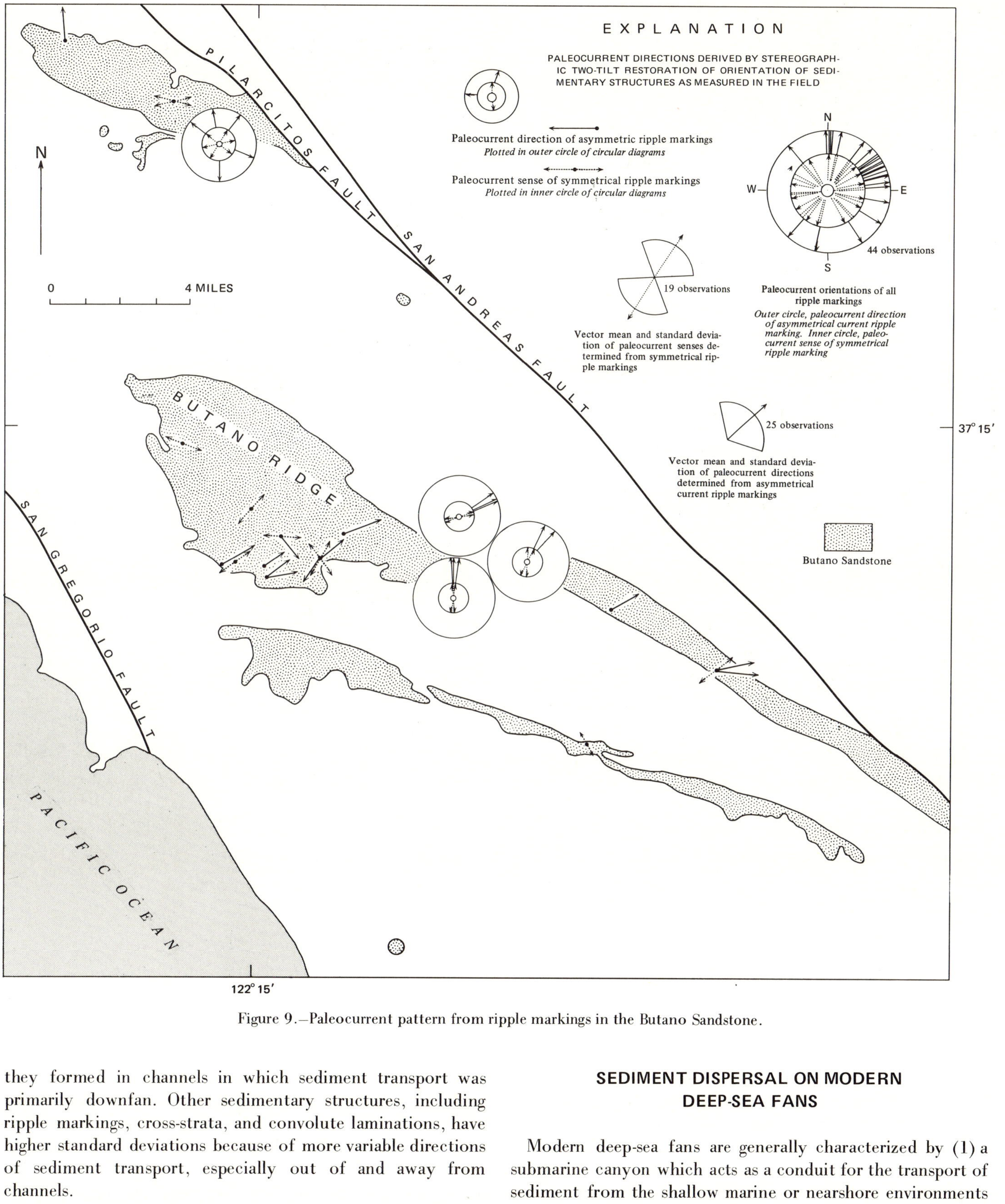

Figure 9.—Paleocurrent pattern from ripple markings in the Butano Sandstone.

they formed in channels in which sediment transport was primarily downfan. Other sedimentary structures, including ripple markings, cross-strata, and convolute laminations, have higher standard deviations because of more variable directions of sediment transport, especially out of and away from channels.

SEDIMENT DISPERSAL ON MODERN DEEP-SEA FANS

Modern deep-sea fans are generally characterized by (1) a submarine canyon which acts as a conduit for the transport of sediment from the shallow marine or nearshore environments

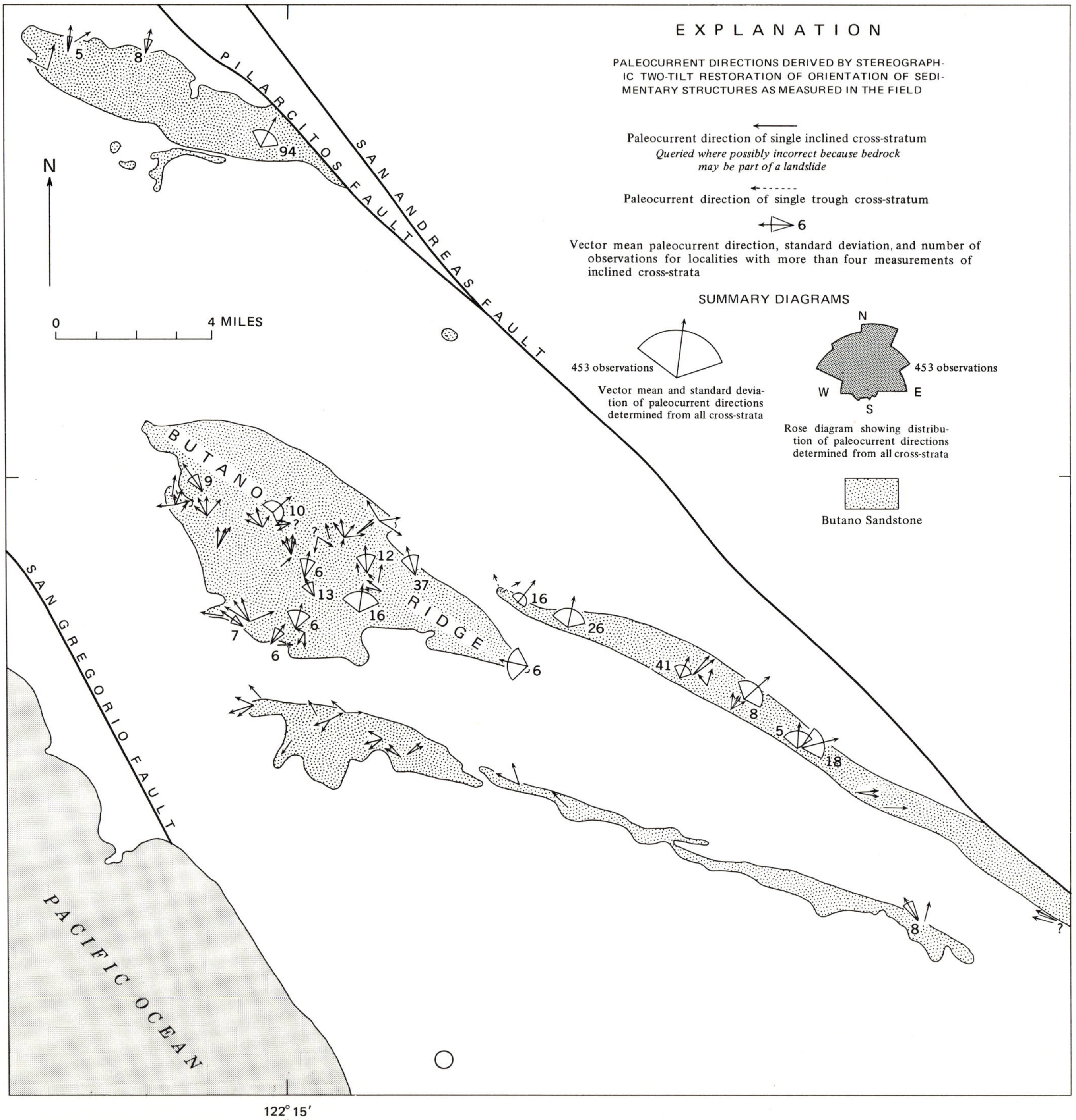

Figure 10.—Paleocurrent pattern from cross-strata in the Butano Sandstone.

to deeper water; (2) a leveed, incised upper fan valley which extends out onto the fan surface from the canyon; (3) a midfan bulge, or suprafan, formed where the leveed upper fan valley divides downfan into two or more major fan channels; (4) a distal fan area where the suprafan channels divide downfan into many smaller and shallower distributary channels; and (5) a fan-fringe area, where the sands and silts deposited on the fan grade laterally outward into hemipelagic sediments of the open ocean (Normark, 1970a; Piper, 1970; Haner, 1971; Nelson and others, 1970; Normark and Piper, 1969, 1972). Deposits are thickest and sedimentation rates highest on the suprafan area. Fan shapes are influenced by

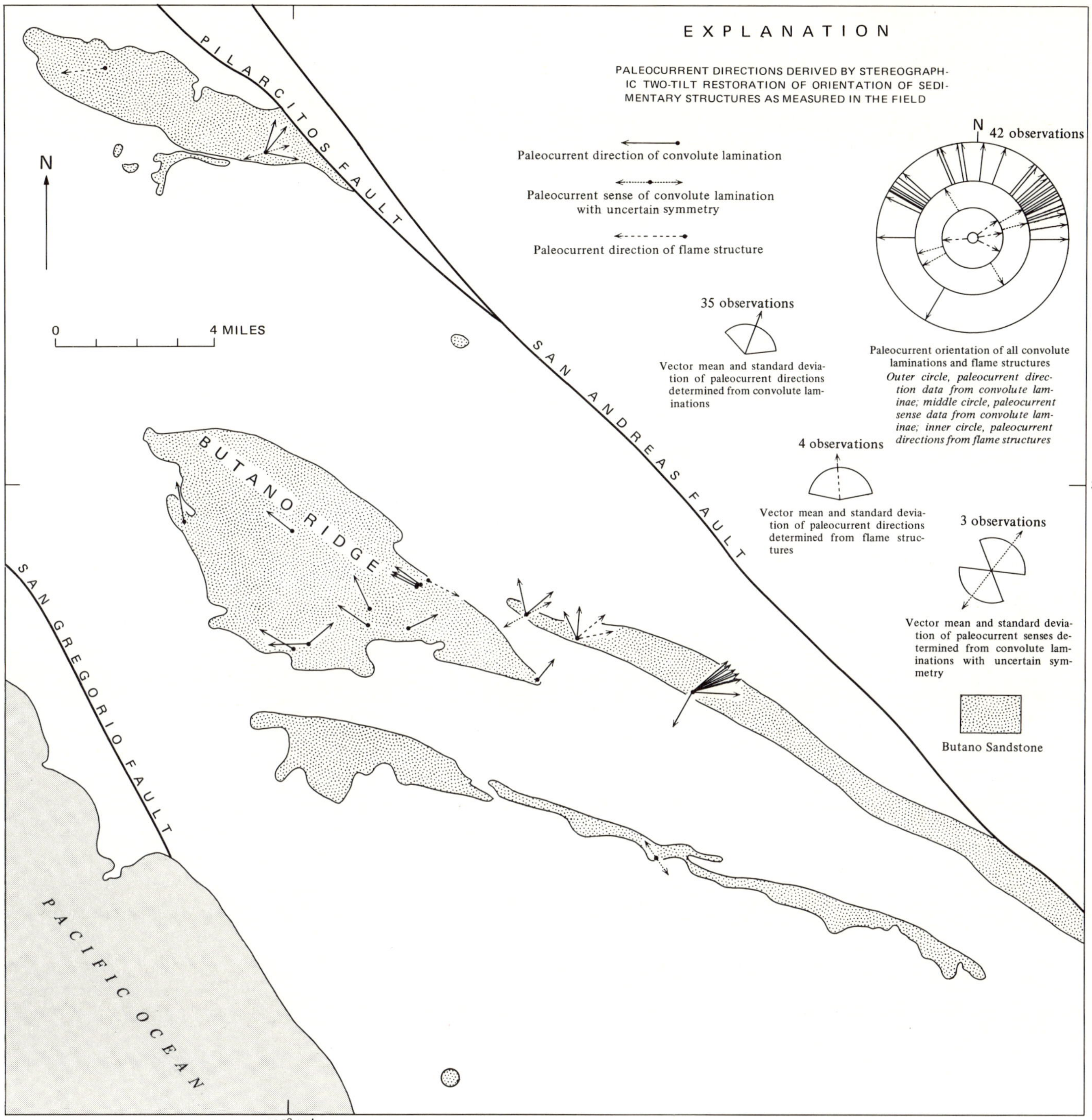

Figure 11.—Paleocurrent pattern from convolute laminations and flame structures in the Butano Sandstone.

local submarine geography, penecontemporaneous tectonism, sediment supply, and climatic factors.

The general direction of sediment transport on modern deep-sea fans is oriented radially outward from the fan apex, similar to that of alluvial fans (Bull, 1972). However, control of the depositional process by major channels yields two major components of sediment transport: (1) downfan transport along channels, and (2) overflow transport out from and commonly perpendicular to the channels. This relatively simple pattern of sediment transport is modified, however, by several other factors which may yield very complex paleocurrent patterns for ancient fan deposits.

Table 1.—*Summary of paleoslope and paleocurrent indicators*

Indicator	No. of observations	Vector mean direction or sense ± standard deviation	Type of deposit
		Paleocurrent indicators	
Conglomerate long-axis orientation.	Two localities, 65 and 95 observations.	294°±51° and 324°±45°	Channel deposits, upper fan.
Conglomerate imbrication.	One locality, 60 observations.	Northerly	Do.
Flute casts	17	335°±20°	Channel deposits
Groove casts ...	2	Northerly	Do.
Asymmetrical ripple markings.	25	50°±62°	Interchannel deposits and middle to lower fan-channel deposits.
Symmetrical ripple markings.	19	15°±53°	
Small-scale inclined cross-strata.	453	8°±61°	
Trough cross-strata.	2	Northerly	
Convolute laminations.	35	16°±62°	
Convolute laminations of uncertain asymmetry.	3	38°±60°	
Flame structures	4	343°±81°	
		Paleoslope indicators	
Asymmetrical contorted strata.	62	8°±63°	Primarily interchannel deposits and middle to lower fan-channel deposits.
Symmetrical contorted strata.	43	32°±57°	

First, complex orientations of paleocurrent directions that are measured from channel deposits will result from the meandering and braided character, particularly in midfan areas, of the fan channels. Fan channels can meander considerably, may have irregular trends, and can even be oriented perpendicular to the regional slope of the fan (Shepard, 1966; Nelson and others, 1970; Haner, 1971; Normark, 1970b). Thus, the fan channels may have orientations that are widely divergent from the general slope of the fan, and paleocurrents measured from fan-channel deposits can yield diverse paleocurrent orientations. Second, overflow deposits in the interchannel areas will have paleocurrents directed not only away from adjacent channels but also downslope from them. This additional component of flow results from the adjustment of the overflow current to the local interchannel slope orientation. Finally, contour or bottom currents are common on modern fans (Stanley and Kelling, 1969; Zimmerman, 1971). These currents commonly flow perpendicular to the general slope of the fan and rework unconsolidated surficial fan deposits. Thus, the preserved sedimentary structures and their orientations on some fan deposits may reflect these currents rather than the original depositing currents, thus yielding anomalous paleocurrent patterns.

Fan valley systems of many modern fans, particularly along the Pacific margin of North America, appear to shift toward the left through time (Menard, 1955); as the fans grow, the major deposition tends to shift periodically to the left, presumably under the influence of the Coriolis effect. The Coriolis effect deflects currents to the right in the Northern Hemisphere, so that levees on the right side of channels are generally higher than levees on the left side, because more sediment is deposited on the right. This buildup of levees on the right side may make it easier for channels to migrate leftward, thus shifting the locus of sedimentation in that direction. Consequently, the youngest or active channels are commonly located along the left side of the fan (looking downfan from the apex). As a result of this growth pattern, paleocurrent patterns from ancient fan deposits may be strongly oriented toward the left.

SEDIMENT-DISPERSAL MODEL FOR THE BUTANO SANDSTONE

The paleoslope and paleocurrent patterns of the Butano Sandstone indicate a complex system of sediment dispersal on the fan, comparable to that just outlined for modern deep-sea fans. Studies of maximum clast size, grain-size distributions, petrography, lithofacies, micropaleontology, and sedimentology of the formation indicate that deposition occurred in deep water within a tectonic basin formed on continental crust of the Salinian block (Cummings and others, 1962; Nilsen, 1971), which is an elongate fault-bounded tectonic block in the California Coast Ranges underlain by a granitic basement complex (Compton, 1966). Regional paleogeographic studies indicate that the Salinian block formed a continental borderland off the Pacific margin of California during Eocene time, perhaps similar to the present borderland off the coast of southern California (Clarke and Nilsen, 1972). Tectonic activity in this ancient borderland region created isolated uplands and intervening submarine basins in which submarine fans were deposited.

Sediments of the Butano fan were probably derived from a southern provenance area located adjacent to Monterey Bay. However, because some modern fan-channel systems diverge as much as 90° from the orientation of their adjoining submarine canyons, the location and orientation of the submarine canyon or canyons feeding the Butano fan system cannot be determined from the paleocurrent data alone. Petrographic studies of sandstone and conglomerate of the Butano Sandstone, however, indicate that granitic basement rocks and overlying sedimentary rocks of the Salinian block to the south were the major source.

Synthesis of the paleocurrent patterns from figures 7–11 permits formation of a model for sediment dispersal of the Butano Sandstone (fig. 12). Two major channels of the upper

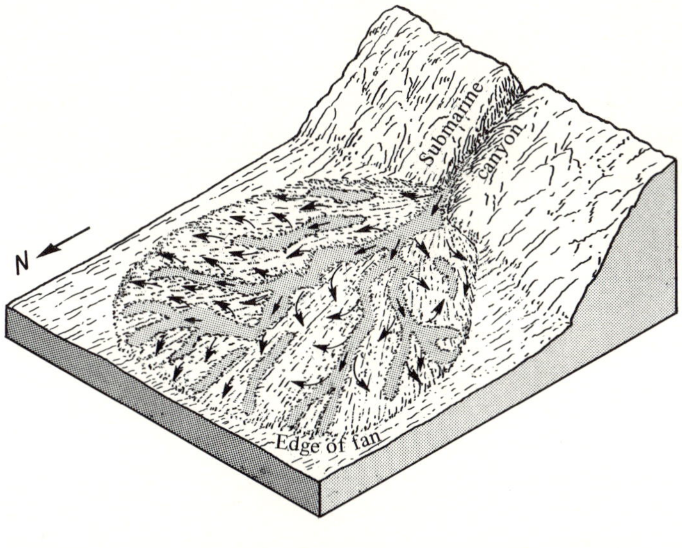

Figure 12.—Sediment-dispersal model for the Butano Sandstone, a deep-sea fan deposit. Arrows represent direction of sediment transport; shaded areas represent major channels.

fan are delineated by the distribution of maximum conglomerate clast sizes (fig. 5). These two channels may have been active at the same time, but limited fossil data indicate that deposits in the eastern channel may be older (Clark, 1966); in fact, the older channel may have been permanently replaced by the younger during growth of the fan. The sediment-dispersal model shows a clearly defined northward transport of sediments down the channels accompanied by transport outward and away from the major channels. The lower fan and fan-fringe areas contain radially oriented small distributary channels. In the lowest parts of the fan and in the fan-fringe areas, fine-grained sediments are deposited, a mixture of pelagic sediments and terrigenous detritus slowly settling out of suspension. Bottom currents may be particularly effective in redistributing these fine-grained sediments.

This type of sediment-dispersal pattern has been suggested by others for modern deep-sea fans and can now be demonstrated for an ancient deep-sea fan as well. Paleocurrent studies of ancient deep-sea fan deposits must be based on measurements of all available sedimentary structures because (1) many different subenvironments are present, (2) many different processes of deposition are active, and (3) rapid changes and growth of the fan yield complex lithofacies relations. Analysis of selected structures only does not yield sufficient data for determination of sediment-dispersal patterns.

REFERENCES CITED

Beaulieu, J. O., 1970, Cenozoic stratigraphy of the Santa Cruz Mountains, California, and inferred displacement along the San Andreas fault: Stanford, Calif., Stanford Univ. Ph. D. thesis, 202 p.

Bouma, A. H., 1962, Sedimentology of some flysch deposits, a graphic approach to facies interpretation: Amsterdam, Elsevier, 168 p.

Brabb, E. E., 1960a, Geology of the Big Basin area, Santa Cruz Mountains, California: Stanford, Calif., Stanford Univ. Ph. D. thesis, 191 p.

—— 1960b, Geology of the Big Basin area, Santa Cruz Mountains, California: Dissert. Abs., v. 21, no. 5, p. 1163.

—— 1964, Subdivision of San Lorenzo Formation (Eocene-Oligocene), west-central California: Am. Assoc. Petroleum Geologists Bull., v. 48, no. 5, p. 670–679.

—— compiler, 1970, Preliminary geologic map of the central Santa Cruz Mountains, California: U.S. Geol. Survey open-file map, scale 1:62,500.

Brabb, E. E., and Pampeyan, E. H., compilers, 1972, Preliminary geologic map of San Mateo County, California: U.S. Geol. Survey Misc. Field Studies Map MF-328, scale 1:62,500.

Branner, J. C., Newsom, J. F., and Arnold, Ralph, 1909, Description of the Santa Cruz quadrangle, California: U.S. Geol. Survey Geol. Atlas, Folio 163, 12 p.

Bull, W. B., 1972, Recognition of alluvial-fan deposits in the stratigraphic record, *in* Rigby, J. K., and Hamblin, W. K., eds., Recognition of ancient sedimentary environments: Soc. Econ. Paleontologists and Mineralogists Spec. Pub. 16, p. 63–83.

Clark, J. C., 1966, Tertiary stratigraphy of the Felton-Santa Cruz area, Santa Cruz Mountains, California: Stanford, Calif., Stanford Univ. Ph. D. thesis, 179 p.

Clarke, Samuel, and Nilsen, T. H., 1972, Postulated offsets of Eocene strata along the San Andreas fault zone, central California: Geol. Soc. America Abs. with Programs, v. 4, no. 3, p. 137–138.

Compton, R. R., 1966, Granitic and metamorphic rocks of the Salinian block, California Coast Ranges, *in* Bailey, E. H., ed., Geology of northern California: California Div. Mines and Geology Bull. 190, p. 277–288.

Cummings, J. C., 1960, Geology of the Langley Hill-Waterman Gap area, Santa Cruz Mountains, California: Stanford, Calif., Stanford Univ. Ph. D. thesis, 233 p.

Cummings, J. C., Touring, R. M., and Brabb, E. E., 1962, Geology of the northern Santa Cruz Mountains, California, *in* Bowen, O. E., ed., Geologic guide to the gas and oil fields of northern California: California Div. Mines and Geology Bull. 181, p. 179–220.

Curray, J. R., 1956, The analysis of two-dimensional orientation data: Jour. Geology, v. 64, p. 117–131.

Dibblee, T. W., Jr., 1966a, Evidence for cumulative offset on the San Andreas fault in central and northern California, *in* Bailey, E. H., ed., Geology of northern California: California Div. Mines and Geology Bull. 190, p. 375–384.

—— 1966b, Geologic map of the Palo Alto 15-minute quadrangle, California: California Div. Mines and Geology Map Sheet 8, scale 1:62,500.

Dott, R. H., Jr., 1963, Dynamics of subaqueous gravity depositional structures: Am. Assoc. Petroleum Geologists Bull. 47, p. 104–128.

Dzulynski, S., Ksiazkiewicz, M., and Kuenen, Ph. H., 1959, Turbidites in flysch of the Polish Carpathian Mountains: Geol. Soc. America Bull., v. 70, p. 1089–1118.

Fairchild, W. W., Wesendunk, P. R., and Weaver, D. W., 1969, Eocene and Oligocene Foraminifera from the Santa Cruz Mountains, California: California Univ. Pubs. Geol. Sci., v. 81, 93 p.

Haner, B. E., 1971, Morphology and sediments of Redondo Submarine Fan, southern California: Geol. Soc. America Bull., v. 82, p. 2413–2432.

Laird, M. G., 1968, Rotational slumps and slump scars in Silurian rocks, western Ireland: Sedimentology, v. 10, p. 111–120.

Mallory, V. S., 1959, Lower Tertiary biostratigraphy of the California Coast Ranges: Tulsa, Okla., Am. Assoc. Petroleum Geologists, 416 p.

Menard, H. W., 1955, Deep-sea channels, topography, and sedimentation: Am. Assoc. Petroleum Geologists Bull., v. 39, p. 236–255.

Middleton, G. M., 1969, Grain flows and other mass movements down slopes, *in* Stanley, D. J., ed., The new concepts of continental margin sedimentation: Am. Geol. Inst., Washington, D.C., p. GM-B-1 to GM-B-14.

Nelson, C. H., Carlson, P. R., Byrne, J. V., and Alpha, T. R., 1970, Physiography of the Astoria Canyon Fan System: Marine Geology, v. 8, p. 259–291.

Nilsen, T. H., 1970, Paleocurrent analysis of the flysch-like Butano Sandstone (Eocene), Santa Cruz Mountains, California: Geol. Soc. America Abs. with Programs, v. 2, no. 7, p. 636.

—— 1971, Sedimentology of the Eocene Butano Sandstone, a continental borderland submarine fan deposit, Santa Cruz Mountains, California: Geol. Soc. America Abs. with Programs, v. 3, no. 7, p. 660.

Normark, W. R., 1970a, Growth patterns of deep-sea fans: Am. Assoc. Petroleum Geologists Bull., v. 54, p. 2170–2195.

—— 1970b, Channel piracy on Monterey deep-sea fan: Deep-Sea Research, v. 17, p. 837–846.

Normark, W. R., and Piper, D. J. W., 1969, Deep-sea fan valleys, past and present: Geol. Soc. America Bull., v. 70, p. 1859–1866.

—— 1972, Sediments and growth pattern of Navy deep-sea fan, San Clemente Basin, California borderland: Jour. Geology, v. 80, p. 198–223.

Parks, J. M., 1970, Computerized trigonometric method for rotation of structurally tilted sedimentary directional features: Geol. Soc. America Bull., v. 81, p. 537–540.

Piper, D. J. W., 1970, Transportation and deposition of Holocene sediment on La Jolla deep sea fan, California: Marine Geology, v. 8, p. 211–228.

Sanders, J. E., 1960, Origin of convolute laminae: Geol. Mag., v. 97, p. 409–421.

—— 1965, Primary sedimentary structures formed by turbidity currents and related resedimentation mechanisms, *in* Middleton, G. M., ed., Primary sedimentary structures and their hydrodynamic interpretation: Soc. Econ. Paleontologists and Mineralogists Spec. Pub. 12, p. 192–219.

Shepard, F. P., 1966, Meander in valley crossing a deep-ocean fan: Science, v. 154, p. 385–386.

Stanley, D. J., and Kelling, G., 1969, Photographic investigation of sediment texture, bottom current activity, and benthonic organisms in the Wilmington submarine canyon: U.S. Coast Guard Oceanog. Rept. 22, 95 p.

Stanley, D. J., and Unrug, Rafael, 1972, Submarine channel deposits, fluxoturbidites and other indicators of slope and base-of-slope environments in modern and ancient marine basins, *in* Rigby, J. F., and Hamblin, W. K., eds., Recognition of ancient sedimentary environments: Soc. Econ. Paleontologists and Mineralogists Spec. Pub. 16, p. 287–340.

Stauffer, P. H., 1967, Grain-flow deposits and their implications, Santa Ynez Mountains, California: Jour. Sed. Petrology, v. 37, p. 487–508.

Sullivan, F. R., 1962, Foraminifera from the type section of the San Lorenzo Formation, Santa Cruz County, California: California Univ. Pubs. Geol. Sci., v. 37, no. 4, p. 233–352.

Touring, R. M., 1959, Structure and stratigraphy of the La Honda and San Gregorio quadrangles, San Mateo County, California: Stanford, Calif., Stanford Univ. Ph. D. thesis, 288 p.

Zimmerman, H. B., 1971, Bottom currents on the New England continental rise: Jour. Geophys. Res., v. 76, no. 24, p. 5865–5876.

Jour. Research U.S. Geol. Survey
Vol. 1, No. 4, July—Aug. 1973, p. 453—458

LOWER JURASSIC AMMONITE FROM THE SOUTH-CENTRAL SIERRA NEVADA, CALIFORNIA

By DAVID L. JONES and JAMES G. MOORE, Menlo Park, Calif.

Abstract.—A Lower Jurassic ammonite has been found in metasiltstone of the Boyden Cave roof pendant, south-central Sierra Nevada, Calif. Although too poorly preserved to permit positive generic and specific identification, its general shape, coiling, and ornamentation are characteristic of Early Jurassic forms. Strata associated with the fossiliferous rocks in the pendant include quartzite, andalusite hornfels, and marble. This assemblage differs strikingly from nearby volcanic rocks to the east, some of which in the Ritter Range pendant also contain Lower Jurassic fossils. The presence of nonvolcanic Lower Jurassic rocks of the Boyden Cave pendant lying west of coeval volcanic rocks of the Ritter Range pendant is anomalous and may be the result of large-scale tectonic dislocations.

Fossils indicative of age are rare in the pregranitic metamorphic remnants of the Sierra Nevada. A Lower Jurassic ammonite discovered in the south-central part of the Sierra Nevada in the summer of 1971 is therefore of regional significance. The fossil was found in a metasiltstone unit within the Boyden Cave roof pendant near the confluence of the Middle and South Forks of the Kings River (fig. 1) in the Tehipite Dome 15-minute quadrangle. Fossils of apparent Jurassic or Triassic age were found earlier in the same stratigraphic unit (Moore and Dodge, 1962), but none are as definitive as this new find.

CHARACTER AND PROBABLE AGE OF THE AMMONITE

The ammonite from the Boyden Cave roof pendant was found on a steep hillside east of Boulder Creek about 200 feet above creek level (USGS Mesozoic loc. 30196) very close to the *Pentacrinus* locality described in an earlier paper (Moore and Dodge, 1962, loc. 2). The internal mold and the external impression were found as loose blocks lying about 20 feet apart. The matrix is black siliceous metasiltstone. The proximity of the two halves indicates that they had not been transported far from their original bedrock source.

The ammonite (fig. 2) is badly deformed and eroded, and many diagnostic features, including the sutures, have been obliterated. From an individual having an original diameter of about 4 inches, it has been stretched to more than 6 inches in maximum dimension. Five whorls are clearly visible; two or three early whorls are smashed. Coiling is highly evolute. Ornamentation consists of regular, narrow, widely spaced, radial ribs that are most prominent near the umbilical shoulder and fade out high on the flanks. Most of the venter is smashed, but a suggestion of a ventral keel is discernible in the external impression.

According to R. W. Imlay (written commun., 1972), this ammonite, in ribbing and coiling, more closely resembles such Lower Jurassic (Sinemurian and Pliensbachian) genera as *Paracoroniceras* or *Metophioceras* than ammonites of either Triassic or later Jurassic age, although its poor state of preservation precludes a positive identification of even its family affinities. According to N. J. Silberling (oral commun., 1971), this ammonite is not similar to Triassic forms and is almost certainly of Early Jurassic age.

BOYDEN CAVE PENDANT

The Boyden Cave pendant (fig. 1), about 7 miles long and 3 miles wide, is composed of metamorphosed sedimentary rocks surrounded by younger granitic rocks of the Sierra Nevada batholith.

Bedding within the metasedimentary rocks is steep and locally intensely folded. The finer grained rocks have developed a cleavage, particularly in the eastern part of the pendant. Four general rock units have been recognized, from west to east: quartzitic sandstone, andalusite hornfels, marble, and metasiltstone. Directions of tops in the quartzitic sandstone are predominantly toward the west, suggesting that the sandstone is the youngest unit and that the other units are progressively older eastward, but the pendant has not been mapped in detail, and folding and faulting may have disturbed this apparent stratigraphic relation. Only the metasiltstone unit has yielded fossils, and its partial age been established.

Quartzitic sandstone unit

The westernmost and presumed youngest unit in the pendant forms a band about 9,000 feet wide composed of

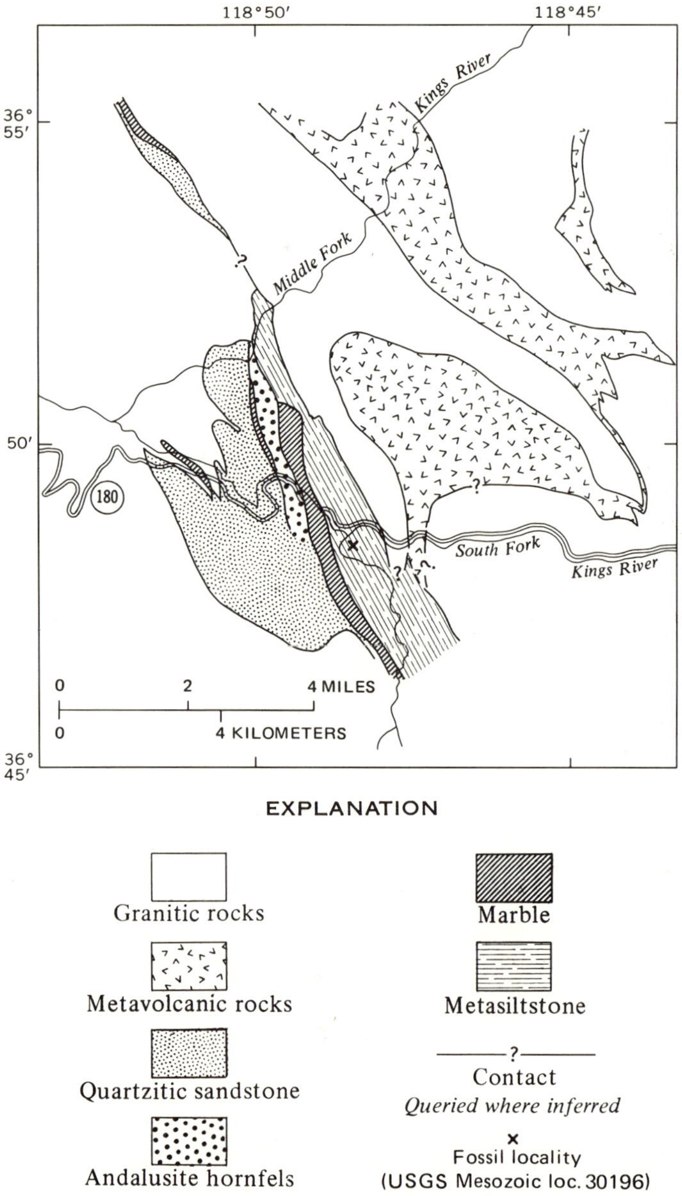

Figure 1.—Map of Boyden Cave pendant, showing lithologic units and Lower Jurassic ammonite locality.

white to gray, thick-bedded metamorphosed sandstone which is commonly crossbedded. The crossbeds average half an inch in thickness; the main beds are half a foot to several feet thick.

The rock is composed predominantly of quartz; K-feldspar is locally rather common and may make up 10–15 percent of the rock. A small amount of muscovite is present in nearly all specimens; biotite, chlorite, and epidote are rare constituents. Grains smaller than a few millimeters have recrystallized and exhibit a metamorphic texture of ragged, interlocking grains. Larger grains still preserve rounded shapes. In some places, beds are coarser grained, containing pebbles as large as 1 cm in size. Most of the pebbles are quartz; some are K-feldspar; a few are aggregates of quartz, K-feldspar, and muscovite.

Andalusite hornfels

Andalusite hornfels, formed by metamorphism of a clay-rich shaly rock, crops out in a band about 1,000 feet wide between the quartzitic sandstone and the largest marble layer. The rock weathers to a brownish color but has a faint bluish cast on fresh surfaces. It is generally mica rich and commonly schistose. In addition to quartz and spongy andalusite crystals as much as several millimeters in size, biotite and muscovite are common and magnetite is locally abundant.

Marble

The most resistant unit in the Boyden Cave pendant is a layer of massive marble about 1,000 feet thick that forms a prominent rib on both walls of the South Fork canyon. This unit is composed of calcite and dolomite containing grains as much as several millimeters in diameter. Bedding in the massive marble is weakly defined by darker layers a quarter of an inch to a foot thick. The strike of these layers wraps around the blunt northern termination of the main marble mass on the crest of the Monarch Divide. The significance of this structure is difficult to evaluate, but it does indicate that major folding and perhaps thrust faulting may have grossly modified the structure of the metasedimentary sequence.

Metasiltstone

Thin-bedded metamorphic rocks of diverse composition occur in a belt 2,000–4,000 feet wide on the east side of the Boyden Cave pendant. The ammonite described here was found near the center of this unit (fig. 1) in a siliceous metasiltstone that has been only slightly recrystallized. Associated with the ammonite are crinoid columnals and pelecypods that have been reported previously (Moore and Dodge, 1962). Thin-bedded calc-hornfels and fine-grained black carbonaceous hornfels are interbedded with the siliceous metasiltstone.

Sedimentary breccia is common in western exposures near the contact with the marble unit. In the breccia, fragments of beds of siltstone and fine-grained sandstone are included in a dark to black shaly to silty matrix; they range in size from less than 1 mm to fragments several tens of centimeters long. The breccia probably was formed by submarine slumps or turbidity flows.

In its eastern exposures, the unit consists of thin-bedded shale and siltstone interbedded with limy layers several millimeters to 20–40 cm thick.

COMPARISON WITH THE RITTER RANGE PENDANT

Lower Jurassic rocks occur about 65 miles to the north in the Ritter Range roof pendant (fig. 3), where they have been studied by Rinehart, Ross, and Huber (1959). These rocks are

A

B

Figure 2.—Lower Jurassic ammonite from Boyden Cave pendant. Natural size. USGS Mesozoic loc. 30196. USNM 185744. *A*, Rubber cast of exterior mold. *B*, Internal mold.

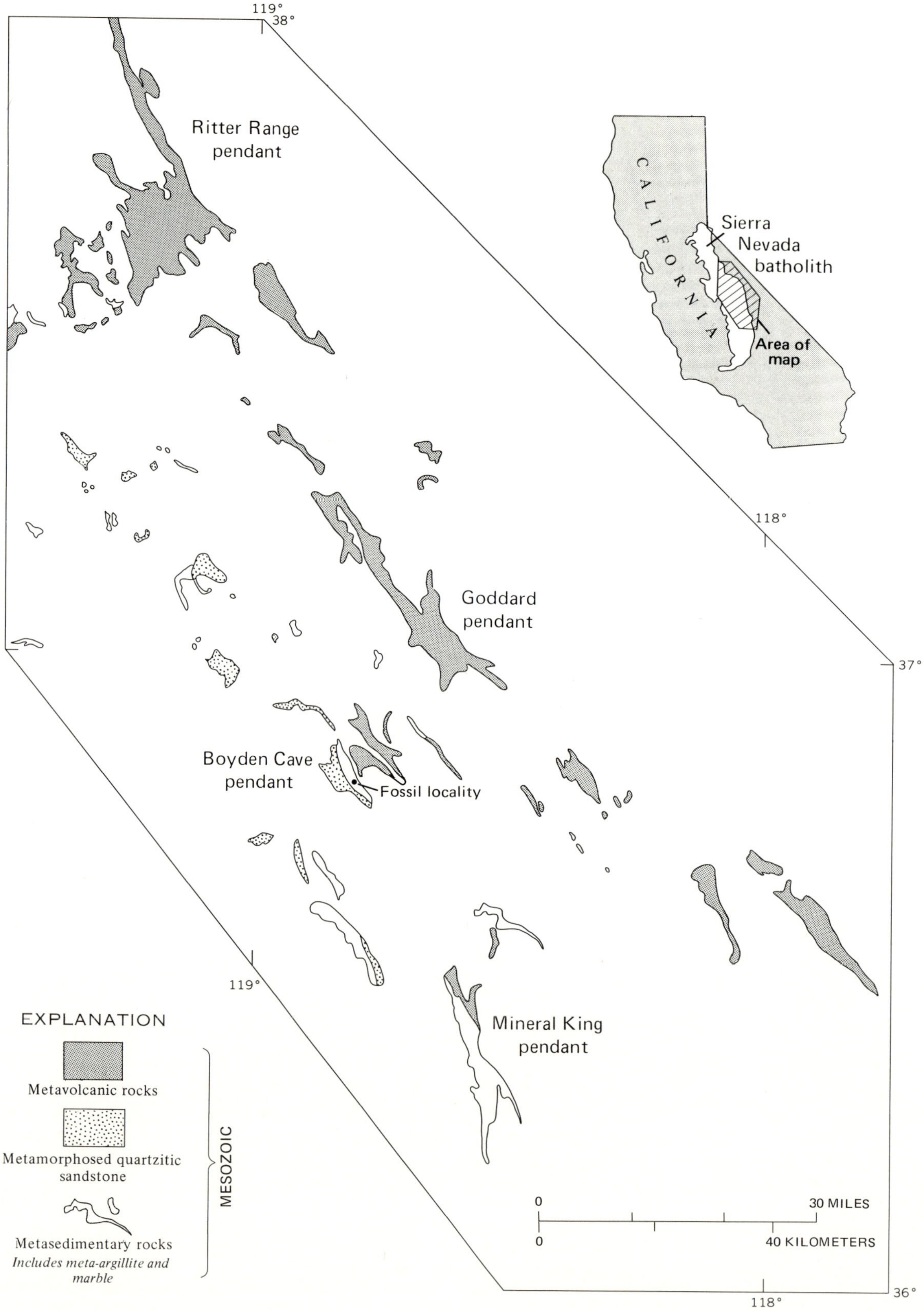

Figure 3.—Map showing location of fossil locality and general lithology of roof pendants of a part of the central Sierra Nevada batholith. Paleozoic metasedimentary roof pendants east of the Mesozoic metavolcanic rocks are not shown.

part of a volcanic sequence more than 30,000 feet thick that overlies upper Paleozoic pelitic hornfels and marble (fig. 4). They are composed chiefly of felsic metavolcanic tuffs and flows with minor interbedded calcareous and tuffaceous metasedimentary rocks. The Early Jurassic age is based mainly on fairly abundant specimens of the pelecypod *Weyla* that occur in a narrow belt of calcareous metasedimentary rock about 10,000 feet above the base of the volcanic sequence (Rinehart and others, 1959, p. 944). These fossils are poorly preserved and generally so crushed that positive specific determinations are impossible. As the genus *Weyla* is restricted mainly to strata of Sinemurian and Pliensbachian age (S. W. Muller, written commun., 1961), these specimens are grossly comparable in age to the Boyden Cave ammonite. A more definitive correlation between the two places is not possible with the poor specimens we have, but considering the great thickness of strata exposed at both places, it is reasonable to suppose at least partial age equivalency.

The columnar sections (fig. 4) show that the overall lithologic sequences of the Ritter Range pendant and the Boyden Cave pendant are totally different. Of particular significance is the absence of volcanic rocks and the presence of abundant quartz-rich sedimentary rocks in the Boyden Cave sequence.

REGIONAL SETTING

Metasedimentary rocks similar to those within the Boyden Cave pendant occur as remnants within a zone more than 70 miles long. This belt extends from the San Joaquin River

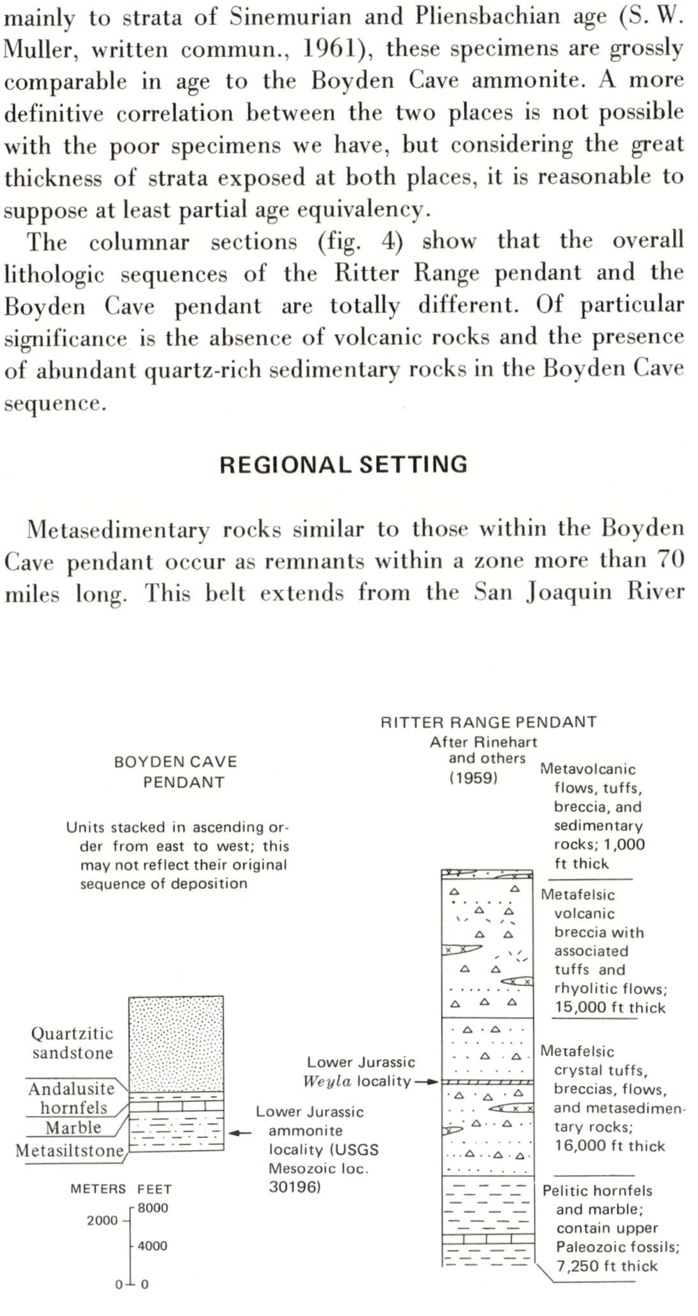

Figure 4.—Schematic columnar sections of Boyden Cave pendant and Ritter Range pendant.

drainage (Huber, 1968) on the northwest, through the Dinkey Creek area (Kistler and Bateman, 1966) and North Fork of the Kings River (Krauskopf, 1953) to the Boyden Cave pendant in the Kings River drainage, and south to the Kaweah River area (Ross, 1958). These metasedimentary remnants are characterized by relatively clean, crossbedded quartzitic sandstone interbedded with limestone and argillite and form a remarkably coherent lithologic zone (fig. 3).

The zone of pendants that includes the Boyden Cave pendant lies parallel to, and about 15 miles west of, an even more extensive zone of roof pendants composed mainly of silicic metavolcanic rocks (Bateman and others, 1963). This zone extends 130 miles from the Ritter Range pendant to a belt of similar volcanic rocks in the Inyo Mountains which overlie fossiliferous marine limestone and shale of Early and Middle Triassic age.

It has long been recognized that Lower Jurassic deposits of the Western United States comprise two distinctly different assemblages: an eastern belt characterized by quartz-rich sedimentary rocks that were deposited in shallow marine and nonmarine environments; and a western belt characterized by (1) abundant andesitic volcanic and volcaniclastic sedimentary rocks with subordinate limestone, (2) interbedded limestone and mudstone, and (3) orogenic conglomerate (Stanley and others, 1971, p. 15). The part of the western belt that is rich in volcanic material is mainly in eastern California, westernmost Nevada, northern California, and central Oregon. Stanley and his coworkers (1971, p. 12) include the volcanic rocks of the Ritter Range pendant in this volcanic belt, which they (1971, p. 17) believe represents a volcanic island arc. They postulate that a deep oceanic trench in which subduction of an oceanic plate was occurring lay on the west side of this arc.

The lack of volcanic flows and pyroclastic rocks and the quartz-rich nature of the sedimentary rocks in the Boyden Cave pendant suggest that they might have an affinity with Lower Jurassic rocks of the eastern belt, assuming that the undated lithologic units of the Boyden Cave sequence are also of Early Jurassic age. Their present position west of the westernmost known Lower Jurassic volcanic rocks is anomalous, as is the absence or sparsity of volcanic detritus despite proximity to volcanic terranes. These anomalies suggest that large-scale tectonic dislocations may have occurred and that once-distant deposits are now juxtaposed. Right-lateral faulting along northwest-trending wrench faults might be responsible for this juxtaposition, although any direct evidence for large-scale slip has been destroyed by batholithic intrusion. Alternatively, if the quartz-rich belt were originally deposited west of the volcanic belt, perhaps in an arc-trench gap, complex paleogeographic problems are introduced, as there is no obvious source terrane for these rocks in the narrow tract that intervenes between the volcanic belt and the quartzite belt. Juxtaposition by major thrusting is a possibility that should be considered along with the hypothesis for strike-slip faulting.

In summary, the presence of nonvolcanic, quartz-rich apparent Lower Jurassic sedimentary rocks close to, but west of, presumed coeval volcanic terranes suggests that the prebatholithic depositional and tectonic history of the south-central Sierra Nevada is more complex than hitherto suspected. Large-scale tectonic dislocations may be invoked to explain this anomalous relation, but data are insufficient to permit a clear understanding of this complex area.

REFERENCES CITED

Bateman, P. C., Clark, L. D., Huber, N. K., Moore, J. G., and Rinehart, C. D., 1963, The Sierra Nevada batholith—a synthesis of recent work across the central part: U.S. Geol. Survey Prof. Paper 414-D, 46 p.

Huber, N. K., 1968, Geologic map of the Shuteye Peak quadrangle, Sierra Nevada, California: U.S. Geol. Survey Geol. Quad. Map GQ-728.

Kistler, R. W., and Bateman, P. C., 1966, Stratigraphy and structure of the Dinkey Creek roof pendant in the central Sierra Nevada, California: U.S. Geol. Survey Prof. Paper 524-B, 14 p.

Krauskopf, K. B., 1953, Tungsten deposits of Madera, Fresno, and Tulare Counties, California: California Div. Mines Spec. Rept. 35, 83 p.

Moore, J. G., and Dodge, F. C., 1962, Mesozoic age of metamorphic rocks in the Kings River area, southern Sierra Nevada, California: Art. 7 *in* U.S. Geol. Survey Prof. Paper 450-B, p. B19–B21.

Rinehart, C. D., Ross, D. C., and Huber, N. K., 1959, Paleozoic and Mesozoic fossils in a thick stratigraphic section in the eastern Sierra Nevada, California: Geol. Soc. America Bull., v. 70, p. 941–946.

Ross, D. C., 1958, Igneous and metamorphic rocks of parts of Sequoia and Kings Canyon National Parks, California: California Div. Mines Spec. Rept. 53, 24 p.

Stanley, K. O., Jordan, W. M., and Dott, R. H., Jr., 1971, New hypothesis of early Jurassic paleogeography and sediment dispersal for western United States: Am. Assoc. Petroleum Geologists Bull., v. 55, no. 1, p. 10–19.

Jour. Research U.S. Geol. Survey
Vol. 1, No. 4, July—Aug. 1973, p. 459—465

THE LATE CRETACEOUS AMMONITE BACULITES UNDATUS STEPHENSON IN COLORADO AND NEW MEXICO

By W. A. COBBAN, Denver, Colo.

Abstract.—*Baculites undatus* Stephenson, originally described from the Nacatoch Sand of northeastern Texas, has been found in the Pierre Shale at 25 localities in Colorado and two in New Mexico. An early form of the species occurs in the zone of *Didymoceras cheyennense* (Meek and Hayden), and the typical form occurs in the overlying zones of *Baculites compressus* Say, *B. cuneatus* Cobban, and *B. reesidei* Elias. The species is characterized by its stout cross section, broad venter, conspicuous lateral and ventral ribs, and suture of about average complexity for the genus.

Baculites undatus Stephenson (1941, p. 405, pl. 79, figs. 5–10) is characterized by its very stout cross section, unusually broad venter, rather widely spaced conspicuous lateral ribs, and long ventral ribs. The species was originally described from the Nacatoch Sand of Navarro County in northeastern Texas. Stephenson recorded it from this formation at 10 localities in Navarro and Kaufman Counties as well as from the slightly older Neylandville Marl at one locality. The species has been recorded from Tennessee, Mississippi, Delaware, and New Jersey (Owens and others, 1970, p. 32). In recent years, specimens that seem referable to *B. undatus* have been discovered in the Pierre Shale in Colorado and New Mexico (fig. 1).

GEOGRAPHIC DISTRIBUTION IN COLORADO AND NEW MEXICO

Ammonites referable to *Baculites undatus* have been collected from the Pierre Shale at 25 localities in Colorado and two localities in New Mexico. These localities are shown on figure 1, and the descriptions of the localities are given in table 1.

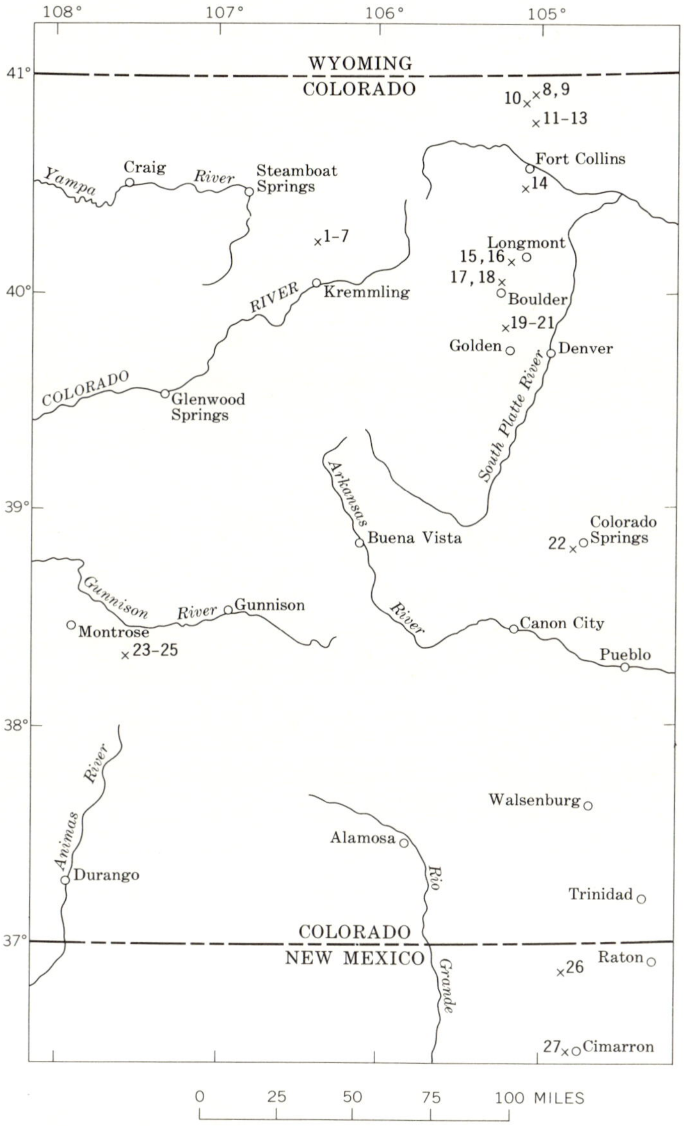

Figure 1.—Localities of *Baculites undatus* Stephenson in Colorado and New Mexico. Numbers refer to the detailed descriptions of localities in table 1.

Baculites undatus Stephenson

Figures 2–5

1941. *Baculites undatus* Stephenson, Texas Univ. Bull. 4101, p. 405, pl. 79, figs. 5–10.

Table 1.—*Localities at which fossils were collected*

Locality No. (fig. 1)	U.S. Geol. Survey Mesozoic locality No.	Collector, year of collection, description of locality, and stratigraphic assignment
1	D5991	G. A. Izett and W. A. Cobban, 1967. Center of the N½ sec. 12, T. 3 N., R. 81 W., Grand County, Colo. Pierre Shale, from limestone concretions about 380 ft above the Carter Sandstone Member.
2	D8060	G. A. Izett and W. A. Cobban, 1971. NW¼NW¼SE¼ sec. 12, T. 3 N., R. 81 W., Grand County, Colo. Pierre Shale, from limestone concretions about 380 ft above the Carter Sandstone Member.
3	D5972	G. A. Izett, 1967. E½SW¼SE¼ sec. 7, T. 3 N., R. 80 W., Grand County, Colo. Pierre Shale, from limestone concretions about 380 ft above the top of the Carter Sandstone Member.
4	D6566	G. A. Izett, 1968. SW¼NE¼NE¼ sec. 18, T. 3 N., R. 80 W., Grand County, Colo. Pierre Shale, from limestone concretions about 400 ft above the Carter Sandstone Member.
5	D1353	G. R. Scott and W. A. Cobban, 1957. NW¼SW¼ sec. 17, T. 3 N., R. 80 W., Grand County, Colo. Pierre Shale, from brown- and gray-weathering sandy limestone concretions about 420 ft above the top of the Carter Sandstone Member.
6	D1354	G. R. Scott and W. A. Cobban, 1957. W½NW¼NW¼ sec. 17, T. 3 N., R. 80 W., Grand County, Colo. Pierre Shale, from sandy limestone concretions in the interval 490–660 ft above the top of the Carter Sandstone Member.
7	D5864	G. A. Izett, 1967. SW¼SW¼NE¼ sec. 20, T. 3 N., R. 80 W., Grand County, Colo. Pierre Shale, about 400 ft above the top of the Carter Sandstone Member.
8	D370	G. R. Scott, 1955. Half a mile south of Round Butte, in the SE¼NW¼ sec. 19, T. 11 N., R. 68 W., Larimer County, Colo. Pierre Shale, Larimer Sandstone Member.
9	D372	G. R. Scott and W. A. Cobban, 1955. South of Round Butte, in the E½NW¼ sec. 19, T. 11 N., R. 68 W., Larimer County, Colo. Pierre Shale, Larimer Sandstone Member.
10	D2825	G. R. Scott, 1960. SW¼NE¼ sec. 2, T. 10 N., R. 69 W., Larimer County, Colo. Pierre Shale.
11	D2719	G. R. Scott, 1960. NW¼SE¼SW¼ sec. 12, T. 9 N., R. 69 W., Larimer County, Colo. Pierre Shale, Larimer Sandstone Member.
12	D1567	G. R. Scott and W. A. Cobban, 1971. South of Bubbles Lake, near center of the S½NW¼ sec. 7, T. 9 N., R. 68 W., Larimer County, Colo. Pierre Shale, Larimer Sandstone Member.
13	16213	R. G. Coffin, 1932. South of Bubbles Lake, in the NW¼ sec. 7, T. 9 N., R. 68 W., Larimer County, Colo. Pierre Shale, Larimer Sandstone Member.
14	D2849	G. R. Scott, 1960. NW¼NE¼NW¼ sec. 23, T. 6 N., R. 69 W., Larimer County, Colo. Pierre Shale, Rocky Ridge Sandstone Member.
15	D727	G. R. Scott, 1955. NW¼SE¼SE¼ sec. 9, T. 2 N., R. 70 W., Boulder County, Colo. Pierre Shale, from sandy limestone concretions in a sandstone unit.
16	D730	G. R. Scott, 1955. SE¼NW¼SE¼ sec. 9, T. 2 N., R. 70 W., Boulder County, Colo. Pierre Shale, from limestone concretions in a dark-gray shale unit.
17	D2740	G. R. Scott and W. A. Cobban, 1960. NW¼NW¼ sec. 3, T. 1 N., R. 70 W., Boulder County, Colo. Pierre Shale.
18	D293	G. R. Scott, 1955. Two miles north of Boulder, in the NE¼SE¼SW¼ sec. 8, T. 1 N., R. 70 W., Boulder County, Colo. Pierre Shale, from a sandy shale unit.
19	D700	G. R. Scott and W. A. Cobban, 1956. Six miles north of Golden, in the SE¼SE¼ sec. 20, T. 2 S., R. 70 W., Jefferson County, Colo. Pierre Shale, from iron-stained limestone concretions.
20	D704	G. R. Scott, R. Van Horn, and W. A. Cobban, 1956. Six miles north of Golden, in the SE¼NW¼SE¼ sec. 20, T. 2 S., R. 70 W., Jefferson County, Colo. Pierre Shale, from brown-weathering sandy concretions.
21	D705	G. R. Scott, 1956. About 6 miles north of Golden, in the SE¼NE¼ sec. 29, T. 2 S., R. 70 W., Jefferson County, Colo. Pierre Shale, from brown-weathering sandy concretions.
22	D1710	G. R. Scott, 1958. SE¼NE¼NW¼ sec. 14, T. 14 S., R. 67 W., El Paso County, Colo. Pierre Shale, from small ferruginous concretions in a bentonite-bearing gray shale unit.
23	D4311	R. G. Dickinson, 1963. Twenty-one miles southeast of Montrose in the SE¼SW¼ sec. 16, T. 47 N., R. 6 W., Montrose County, Colo. Mancos Shale, near top.
24	D4312	R. G. Dickinson, 1963. NE¼SW¼ sec. 10, T. 47 N., R. 6 W., Montrose County, Colo. Mancos Shale, near top.
25	D5435	R. G. Dickinson, 1966. SE¼NE¼ sec. 33, T. 47 N., R. 6 W., Gunnison County, Colo. Mancos Shale, about 100–200 ft below top.
26	D7484	Karen Pillmore, 1970. Casa Grande in Vermejo Park, Colfax County, N. Mex. Pierre Shale, 150–200 ft below top.
27	D4826	J. R. Gill, 1964. Two miles west of Cimarron in the NW¼NW¼NW¼ sec. 5, T. 26 N., R. 19 E., Colfax County, N. Mex. Pierre Shale, from limestone concretions 260–290 ft below top.

The holotype is a well-preserved undistorted specimen 38.5 mm in diameter at the larger end. Most of the shell material is retained; a piece missing at the larger end of the specimen reveals that the specimen is a phragmocone having a moderately simple suture. The cross section is elliptical and stout (fig. 2). At a diameter of 35.5 mm the ratio of the width to the diameter is 71 percent for the intercostal width and 85 percent for the costal width. The flanks are ornamented by strong broad arcuate nodelike ribs that have an average spacing of 1.4 for the shell diameter (diameter of shell ÷ distance between crest of ribs). Ribs of irregular height and spacing

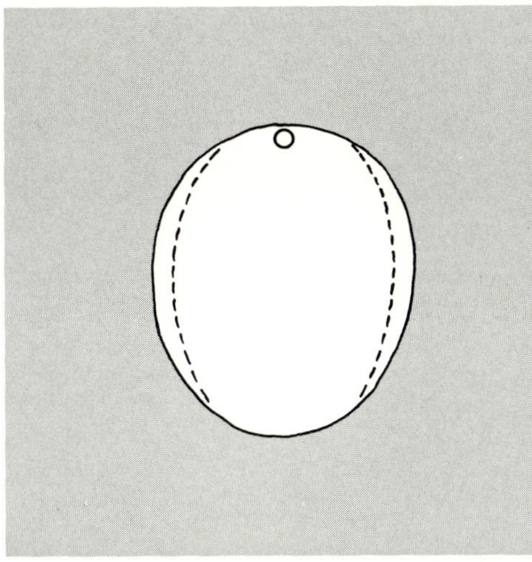

Figure 2.—Cross section, natural size, of the holotype of *Baculites undatus* Stephenson at a diameter of 36 mm. Drawn from a plaster cast. USNM 77245.

cross the very broad venter and extend well up onto the flanks. Two paratypes figured by Stephenson (1941, pl. 79, figs. 9, 10) are more strongly sculptured than the holotype. They are smaller than the holotype and have 1–2 lateral ribs per shell diameter. The paratypes and the holotype taper 5°. The holotype and one paratype (Stephenson, 1941, pl. 79, figs. 5–9) came from a locality just west of Chatfield, Tex. One of two topotypes from this locality is illustrated on figure 3, *p–r*. The other paratype came from the Nacatoch Sand near a small cemetery 1.1 miles northwest of Chatfield. A suite of 23 specimens from this locality collected by Mr. James P. Conlin, Fort Worth, Tex., presents an interesting sample of a population of *B. undatus*. These specimens range in diameter from 4 to 42 mm. Lateral ribs, which are present on all specimens (13) larger than 14 mm in diameter, may appear on some individuals as small as 7 mm. These ribs resemble those on the types and are spaced from 1 to 3 for the shell diameter with most spaced at 1.5. The specimens have angles of taper from 1° to 7°, and all have very broad venters and moderately stout to very stout subelliptical sections. A few of the specimens are illustrated on figure 3, *a–j*, and sutures of two are shown on figure 4, *c*, *d*.

According to a locality map of Stephenson (1941, loc. 762 on fig. 6), the holotype of *B. undatus* came from the upper part of the Nacatoch Sand. The specimen was associated with the type specimens of Stephenson's *Scaphites rugosus*, *S. pumilus*, and *Solenoceras multicostatum* as well as with specimens identified by Stephenson as *Solenoceras texanum* (Shumard), *Nostoceras stantoni* Hyatt, *N. helicinum* (Shumard), *Turrilites splendidus* Shumard, *Helicoceras navarroense* Shumard, and *Parapachydiscus arkansanus* Stephenson.

DESCRIPTION OF COLLECTIONS

Specimens referable to *Baculites undatus* have been found in the following zones, from oldest to youngest: *Didymoceras cheyennense* (Meek and Hayden), *Baculites compressus* Say, *B. cuneatus* Cobban, and *B. reesidei* Elias.

Zone of *Didymoceras cheyennense* (Meek and Hayden).—Eight specimens from six localities (fig. 1, locs. 17, 20, 21, 23–25) are interpreted as representing an early form of *B. undatus*. All have conspicuous lateral and ventral ribs, but none has a venter as broad as that of the typical form of the species. A septate specimen is shown on figure 5, *a*, *b*.

Zone of *Baculites compressus* Say.—Specimens that have the very broad venter and distinctive sculpture of *B. undatus* have been collected in association with *B. compressus* at three localities in Colorado (fig. 1, locs. 2, 4, 7). In addition, two specimens from two localities in New Mexico (fig. 1, locs. 26, 27) that seem certain to be *B. undatus* were not associated with other baculites, but they are probably from the zone of *B. compressus*. Distorted specimens and fragments of baculites that may be *B. undatus* were found with *B. compressus* at two other localities in Colorado (fig. 1, locs. 1, 3).

Two of the best specimens from the Kremmling, Colo., area are uncrushed internal molds that have maximum diameters of 19.5 and 25 mm (fig. 5, *h–m*). The smaller one has a taper of 4° and a stout elliptical cross section. Its nodate lateral ribs number 1–2 for the shell diameter. Ventral ribs are mostly weak and irregular in height. The specimen is a phragmocone, and its suture is shown on figure 4, *A*. The larger specimen is characterized by strong ventral ribs that extend half way up the flanks. The two specimens from New Mexico assigned to the zone of *B. compressus* are the largest individuals from this zone. One is a distorted septate fragment about 53 mm in diameter, and the other (fig. 5, *n*, *o*) is the older part of a body chamber that has a diameter of 38.7 mm at its base.

Axonoceras compressum Stephenson (1941, p. 422, pl. 89, figs. 1–5) was associated with one of the baculites from the Kremmling area (fig. 1, loc. 1) assigned to *B. undatus*. The holotype and paratypes of *A. compressum* came from the Neylandville Marl of Navarro County, Tex.

Zone of *Baculites cuneatus* Cobban.—Baculites assigned to *B. undatus* have been found in this zone at only one locality near Kremmling (fig. 1, loc. 5) in a bed of large limy sandstone concretions in the Pierre Shale about 420 feet above the top of the Carter Sandstone Member (Izett and others, 1971, p. A15). Six specimens were collected along with 150 specimens of *B. cuneatus*. The specimens of *B. undatus* are internal molds 21–37 mm in diameter. Two examples are shown on figure 5, *r–t*. A larger internal mold, about 50 mm in diameter, from this locality was collected recently by Mr. Karl Hirsh, Denver, Colo., who kindly made the specimen available for study (fig. 3, *m–o*). It has a taper of 4° and conspicuous lateral ribs that

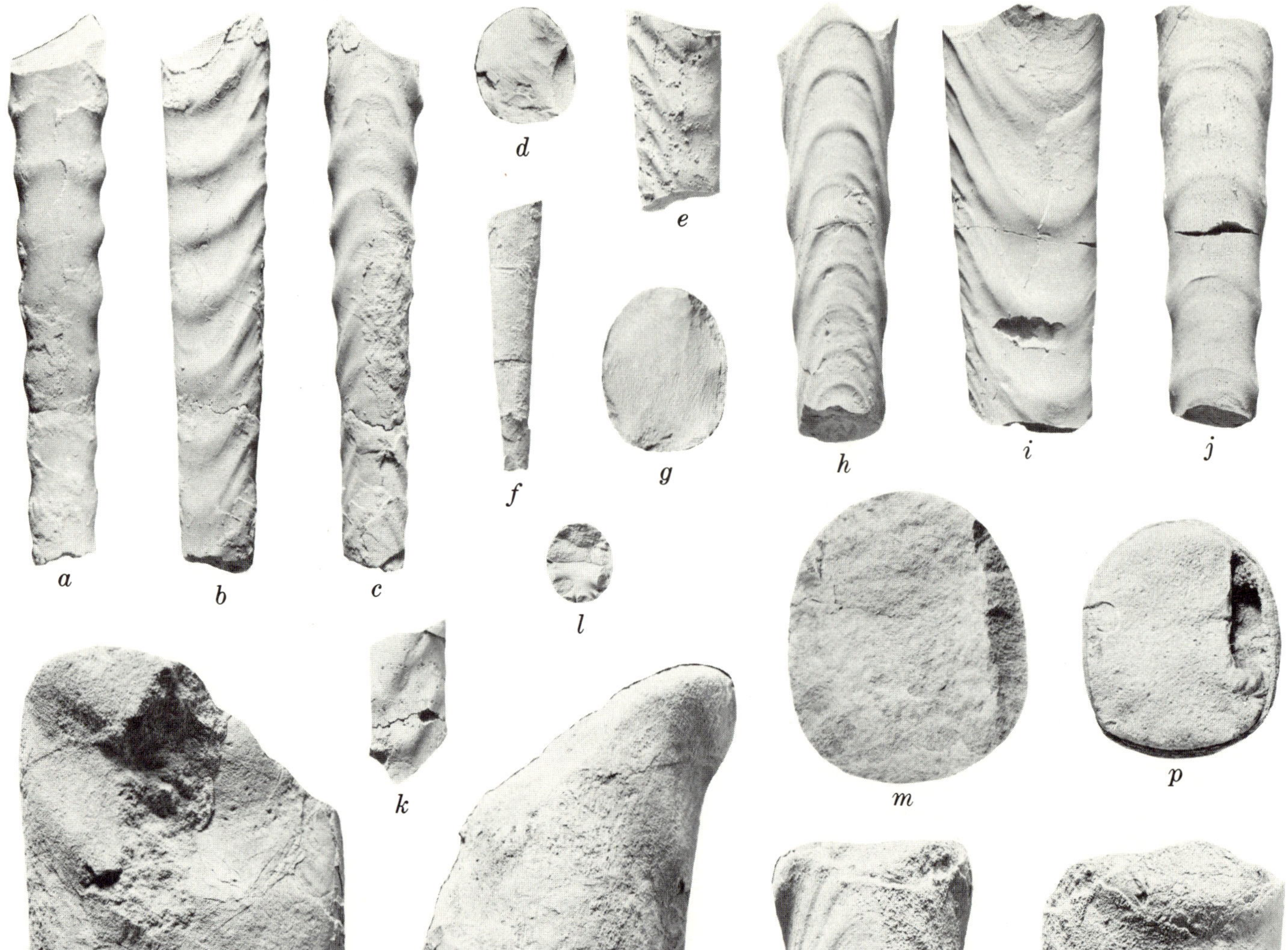

Figure 3.

Figure 3.–Specimens of *Baculites undatus* Stephenson, natural size, from Texas and Colorado.

a–d. Dorsal, lateral, ventral, and end views of hypotype USNM 182430 from the Nacatoch Sand 1.1 miles northwest of Chatfield, Navarro County, Tex.

e. Lateral view of hypotype USNM 182429 from locality of *a–d.*

f. Lateral view of hypotype USNM 182428 from locality of *a–d.*

g–j. End, ventral, lateral, and dorsal views of hypotype USNM 182431 from locality of *a–d.*

k, l. Lateral and end views of hypotype USNM 182432 from the Pierre Shale (fig. 1, loc. 2).

m–o. End, lateral, and ventral views of hypotype USNM 182437 from the Pierre Shale (fig. 1, loc. 5).

p–r. End, ventral, and lateral views of hypotype USNM 182427 from the Nacatoch Sand at USGS Mesozoic locality 762 near Chatfield, Tex.

extend to and across the venter.

The baculites from the Kremmling locality were associated with *Nostoceras dracone* Stephenson, "*Helicoceras*" *navarroense* Shumard, and *Solenoceras texanum* (Shumard). These ammonites are known from the Neylandville Marl of northeast Texas, and "*Helicoceras*" *navarroense* and *Solenoceras texanum* also occur in the overlying Nacatoch Sand (Stephenson, 1941, p. 401, 414, 418).

Zone of *Baculites reesidei* Elias.–Eight collections of fossils from this zone have baculites that seem assignable to *B. undatus* (fig. 1, locs. 6, 8–11, 13, 15, 19), and five collections contain a single specimen each that may represent this species (fig. 1, locs. 12, 14, 16, 18, 22). Most specimens are from the Fort Collins area in northern Colorado where they occur with numerous specimens of *B. reesidei* in the Larimer Sandstone Member of the Pierre Shale. The specimens of *B. undatus* are scarce in contrast to the associated *B. reesidei.* One collection (fig. 1, loc. 9) consists of 150 specimens of *B. reesidei* and a single example of *B. undatus.* The largest collection of *B. undatus* consists of six specimens 11–27 mm in diameter (fig. 1, loc. 8), and the largest individual in this collection is shown on figure 5, *e–g*, and its suture on figure 4, *B.* The largest specimen in all collections is a somewhat crushed body chamber 78 mm in diameter (fig. 1, loc. 13). A small strongly sculptured septate individual from this locality is shown on figure 5, *c, d.* This specimen has a taper of 5°. Its lateral ribs are spaced at one per shell diameter, whereas the ventral ribs are spaced at three. An unusually strongly ribbed specimen from another locality (fig. 1, loc. 10) is shown on figure 5, *p, q.* Lateral ribs, spaced one per shell diameter, extend to the venter and cross it strongly.

In the Fort Collins area, *B. undatus* is associated with several molluscan species that occur also in the Nacatoch Sand of northeastern Texas. The collection (fig. 1, loc. 8) that contains the most (six) specimens of *B. undatus* includes Stephenson's *Nuculana corbetensis, Nemodon adkinsi, Volsella uddeni, Cardium* (*Ethmocardium*) *welleri*, and *Tellina munda.* The gastropod *Capulus spangleri* Henderson and the ammonite "*Helicoceras*" *navarroense* Shumard, which have been found in the Nacatoch Sand of Texas, were associated with *B. undatus* in one of the collections (fig. 1, loc. 13).

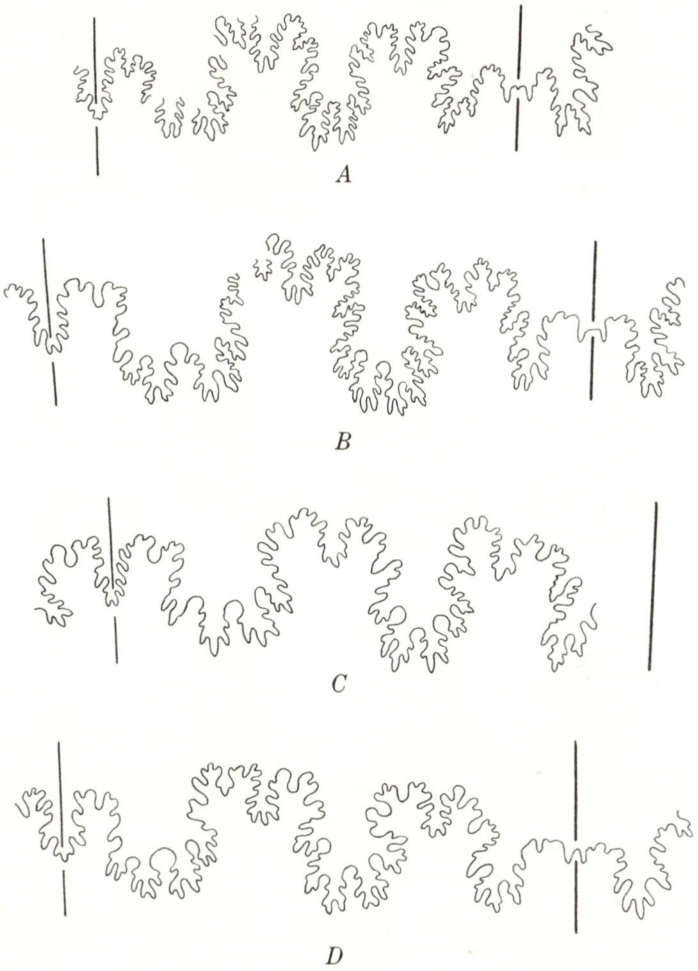

Figure 4.–Sutures of *Baculites undatus* Stephenson. *A*, Hypotype USNM 182433, × 2, at a diameter of 17 mm (fig. 5, *h–j*). *B*, Hypotype USNM 182441, × 2, at a diameter of 25.5 mm (fig. 5, *e–g*). *C*, Hypotype USNM 182430, × 4, at a diameter of 11.5 mm (fig. 3, *a–d*). *D*, Hypotype USNM 182429, × 4, at a diameter of 13 mm (fig. 3, *e*).

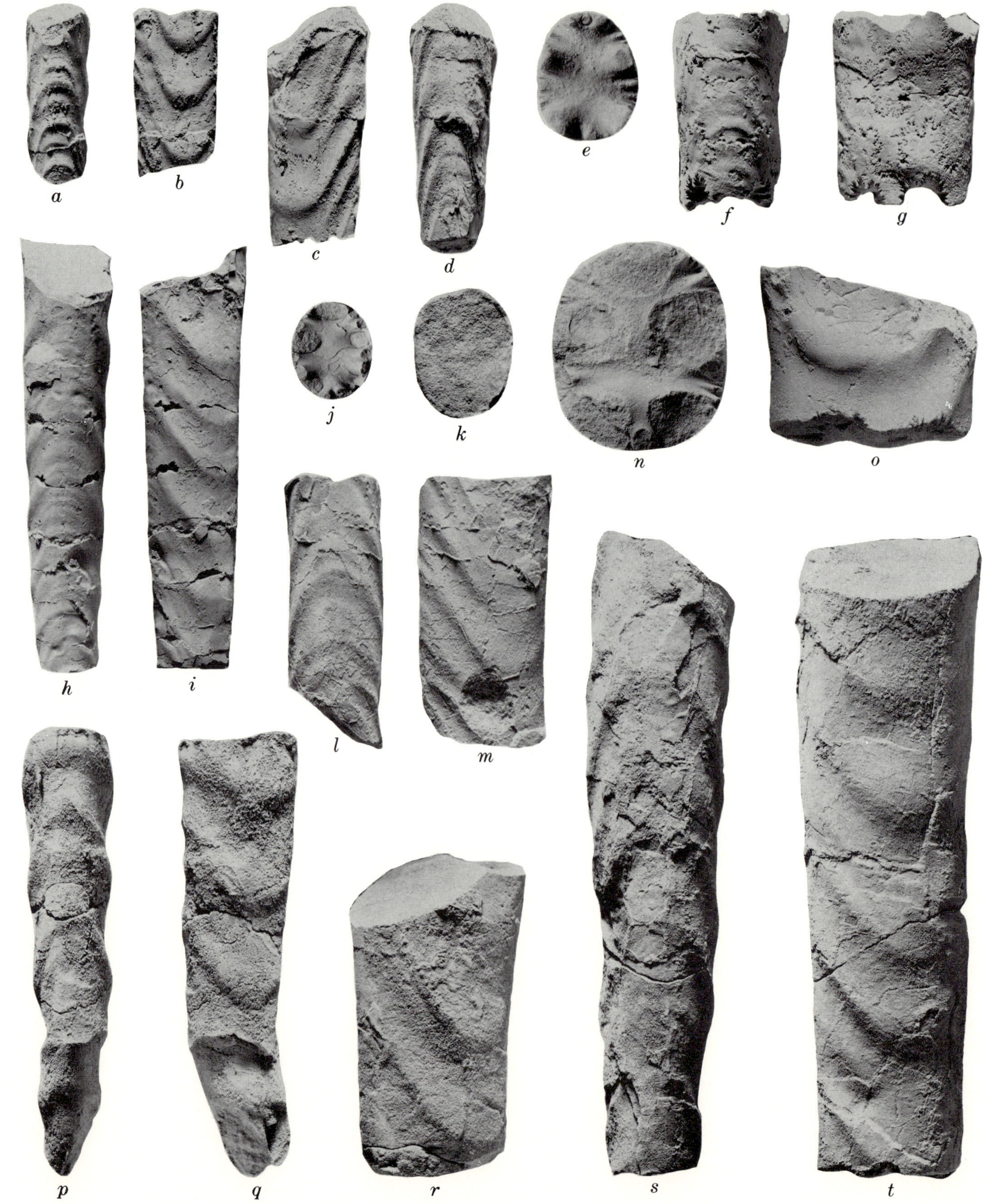

Figure 5

Figure 5.—Specimens of *Baculites undatus* Stephenson, natural size, from the Pierre Shale of Colorado and New Mexico.

a, b. Ventral and lateral views of hypotype USNM 182440 (fig. 1, loc. 21).

c, d. Lateral and ventral views of hypotype USNM 182438 (fig. 1, loc. 13).

e–g. End, ventral, and lateral views of hypotype USNM 182441 (fig. 1, loc. 8).

h–j. Ventral and lateral views and sectional view at a diameter of 18 mm of hypotype USNM 182433 (fig. 1, loc. 2).

k–m. End, ventral, and lateral views of hypotype USNM 182435 (fig. 1, loc. 5).

n, o. End and lateral views of hypotype USNM 182442 (fig. 1, loc. 26).

p, q. Ventral and lateral views of hypotype USNM 182439 (fig. 1, loc. 10).

r. Lateral view of hypotype USNM 182435 (fig. 1, loc. 5).

s, t. Ventral and lateral views of hypotype USNM 182436 (fig. 1, loc. 5).

REFERENCES CITED

Izett, G. A., Cobban, W. A., and Gill, J. R., 1971, The Pierre Shale near Kremmling, Colorado, and its correlation to the east and the west: U.S. Geol. Survey Prof. Paper. 684-A, 19 p., illus.

Owens, J. P., Minard, J. P., Sohl, N. F., and Mello, J. F., 1970, Stratigraphy of the outcropping post-Magothy Upper Cretaceous formations in southern New Jersey and northern Delmarva Peninsula, Delaware and Maryland: U.S. Geol. Survey Prof. Paper 674, 60 p., illus.

Stephenson, L. W., 1941, The larger invertebrate fossils of the Navarro group of Texas: Texas Univ. Bull. 4101, 641, p., 95 pls.

Jour. Research U.S. Geol. Survey
Vol. 1, No. 4, July—Aug. 1973, p. 467—473

POTENTIAL SHALE-OIL RESOURCES OF A STRATIGRAPHIC SEQUENCE ABOVE THE MAHOGANY ZONE, GREEN RIVER FORMATION, PICEANCE CREEK BASIN, COLORADO

By JANET K. PITMAN and JOHN R. DONNELL, Denver, Colo.

Abstract.—In the southern part of the Piceance Creek basin the upper part of the Green River Formation above the Mahogany zone contains beds of rich oil shale which may be economically recoverable by a surface-mining operation. Four units within this sequence were evaluated for thickness, distribution, oil yield, and potential shale-oil resources. In the area appraised, total estimated resources of 128.5 billion bbl of oil are contained within the sequence. It is thickest in T. 3 S., R. 96 W., where 354 feet of oil shale yields an average of 14 gal of oil per ton, with a total resource of 9.0 billion bbl. It is richest in T. 5 S., R. 96 W., where 250 feet of oil shale yields an average of 19 gal of oil per ton, with a total resource of 6.5 billion bbl. Resources are tabulated for four units of the sequence.

The decline in production of domestic crude oil and the increasing cost of imported crude oil emphasize the need for a supplementary domestic supply of oil. Extensive deposits of oil shale in the Eocene Green River Formation underlie large areas of Colorado, Utah, and Wyoming, and are potential sources of synthetic crude oil (fig. 1). The largest and richest of these deposits occur in the Piceance Creek basin, Colorado.

This report is concerned with the thickness, distribution, oil yield, and potential oil-shale resources of four units of the stratigraphic sequence above the Mahogany zone in the Piceance Creek basin, Colorado. Detailed appraisals of oil-shale resources published for the Mahogany zone and for two lower rich oil-shale zones by Donnell and Blair (1970) indicate that these three zones are of the greatest interest economically. Although the upper sequence of oil shale is not as rich as the Mahogany and lower zones, it is closer to the surface, and locally may be recoverable by surface-mining methods.

Acknowledgments.—The U.S. Bureau of Mines Oil-Shale Petroleum and Research Center at Laramie, Wyo., is the source of most of the Fischer assay data used in this report (Stanfield and others, 1954, 1957, 1960, 1967; Belser, 1951). A small amount of assay information was supplied by private companies and individuals. Computer programs for deriving average oil yield and for drawing graphs were written by George Van Trump and Margaret Roberts, of the U.S. Geological Survey.

STRATIGRAPHY

Bradley (1931) named four members of the Green River Formation in the Piceance Creek basin—Douglas Creek, Garden Gulch, Parachute Creek, and Evacuation Creek, in ascending order—and Donnell mapped and described them (Donnell, 1961; Donnell and Blair, 1970). The Douglas Creek

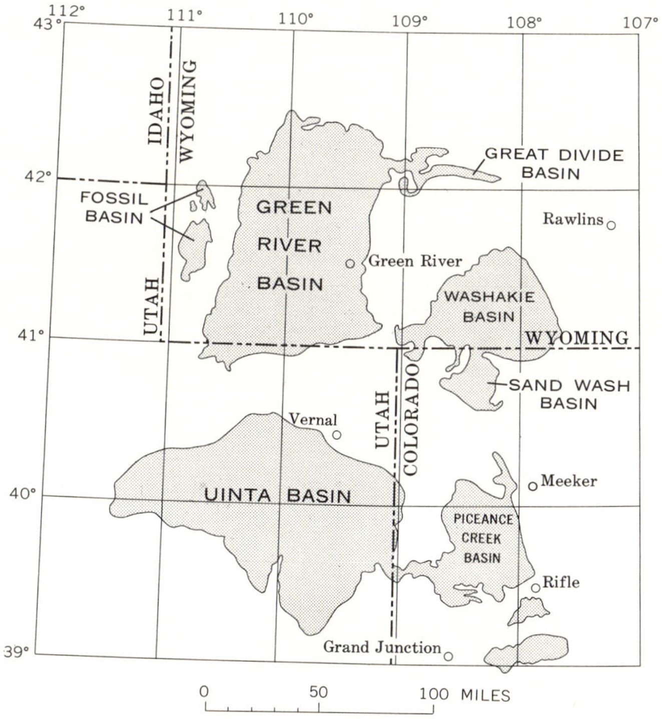

Figure 1.—Area (patterned) underlain by the Green River Formation, Colorado, Utah, and Wyoming.

consists of sandstone and minor amounts of algal and oolitic limestone; the Garden Gulch is mainly clay shale and low- to moderate-grade oil shale that grades into richer oil shale at the basin center; the Parachute Creek is almost entirely low-grade to rich oil shale that contains thin analcitized tuff beds and thin sandstone beds, finely disseminated dawsonite, pods of nahcolite, and beds of halite and nahcolite; the Evacuation Creek consists of tuffaceous siltstone and sandstone and minor amounts of low-grade oil shale and barren marlstone (Donnell and Blair, 1970).

The Parachute Creek Member has been subdivided on the basis of oil yield into zones, each of which is characterized by persistent ledges, beds, and groups of beds. Many of these have been informally named (Duncan and Denson, 1949) and are used to define the units shown on figure 2. Several groups of

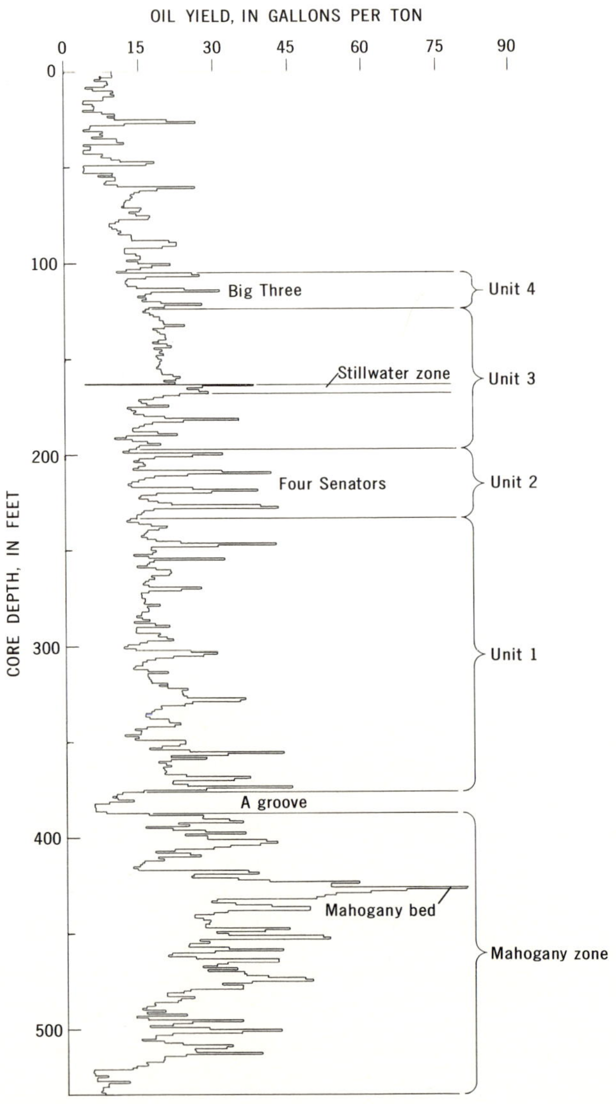

Figure 2.—Partial oil-yield graph indicating shale-oil units used in resource appraisal.

beds and oil-shale zones have been recognized in the subsurface and are traceable over a large part of the Piceance Creek basin of Colorado and the Uinta Basin of Utah (Cashion and Donnell, 1972). The most conspicuous of these is the Mahogany ledge (called Mahogany zone in the subsurface) which contains the Mahogany bed, a thin and exceedingly rich marker bed (Donnell, 1961). Another persistent marker, the A groove, is a sequence of marlstone and lean oil shale, 10–15 feet thick, that directly overlies the Mahogany zone. It is so named because it weathers to form a recess in the cliff.

About 100 feet above the top of the A groove in the southwestern part of the basin and approximately 200 feet above the A groove near the depositional center is a sequence containing four rich oil-shale beds—the Four Senators zone, which ranges in thickness from 18 to 38 feet. They yield an average of approximately 30 gal of oil per ton and are separated by tuff stringers and oil shale that yield less than 15 gal of oil per ton. Another sequence containing rich oil-shale beds, approximately 40–50 feet thick, occurs 20–30 feet above the Four Senators. The base of this sequence is marked by the Stillwater zone, a massive ledge 5–10 feet thick, which has an average oil yield of 20 gal per ton. The upper limit of the richer oil-shale sequence is marked by the Big Three. This series of three rich oil-shale beds, 1–2 feet thick, in an interval less than 25 feet, yields between 12 and 20 gal of oil per ton. In many areas as much as 200 feet of continuous oil shale has been deposited above the Big Three.

The contact between the Parachute Creek and Evacuation Creek Members is placed where the sequence of rocks changes from lean oil shale to a sequence composed predominantly of sandstone and siltstone.

PROCEDURES

Data used to construct isopach maps of oil-shale units (fig. 3) were obtained from graphs of assayed core and from electric, gamma-ray neutron, gamma-ray density, and sonic logs of other exploratory wells. Isovalue maps (figs. 4 and 5) show for each unit the variation of potential oil yield in gallons per ton and thousands of barrels per acre. Oil-yield values (gallons per ton) for each unit are based on the total thickness at each sample locality. Intervals for which no data were available were assigned the potential value of an equivalent bed in an adjacent hole. Potential resource values (yield of oil in barrels per acre) were computed from the oil yield (gallons per ton) and the thickness of the unit at each control point.

The four units were not appraised in the northern part of the basin because either the oil shale in the interval assayed yielded less than 12 gal per ton or no assay information was available.

Potential shale-oil resources for the four units are computed on a township basis and are reported in table 1.

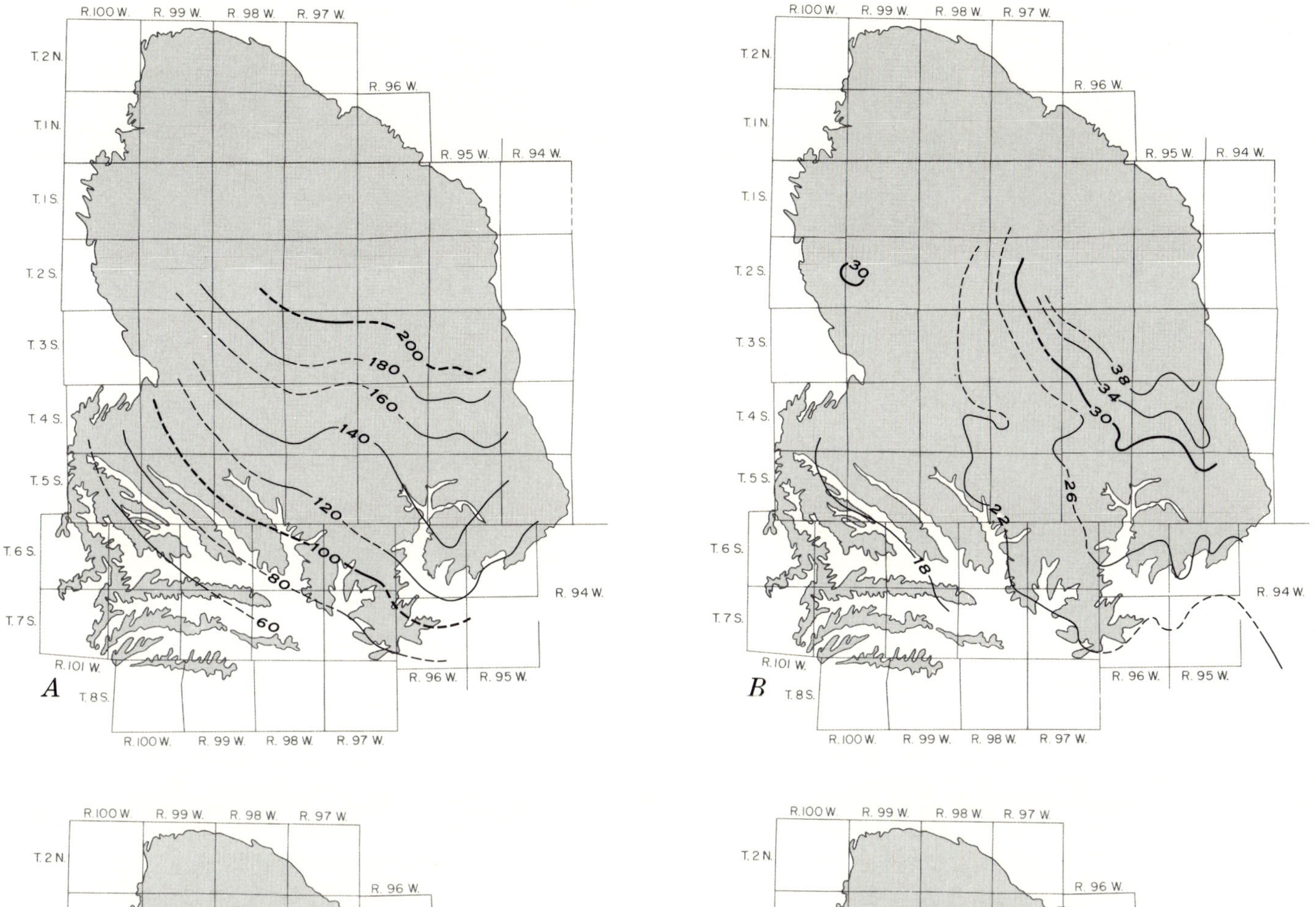

Figure 3.—Maps showing thicknesses of shale-oil units in the Piceance Creek basin. Lines are dashed where information is sparse. *A*, unit 1 (interval is 20 feet). *B*, unit 2 (4 feet). *C*, unit 3 (5 feet). *D*, unit 4 (2 feet).

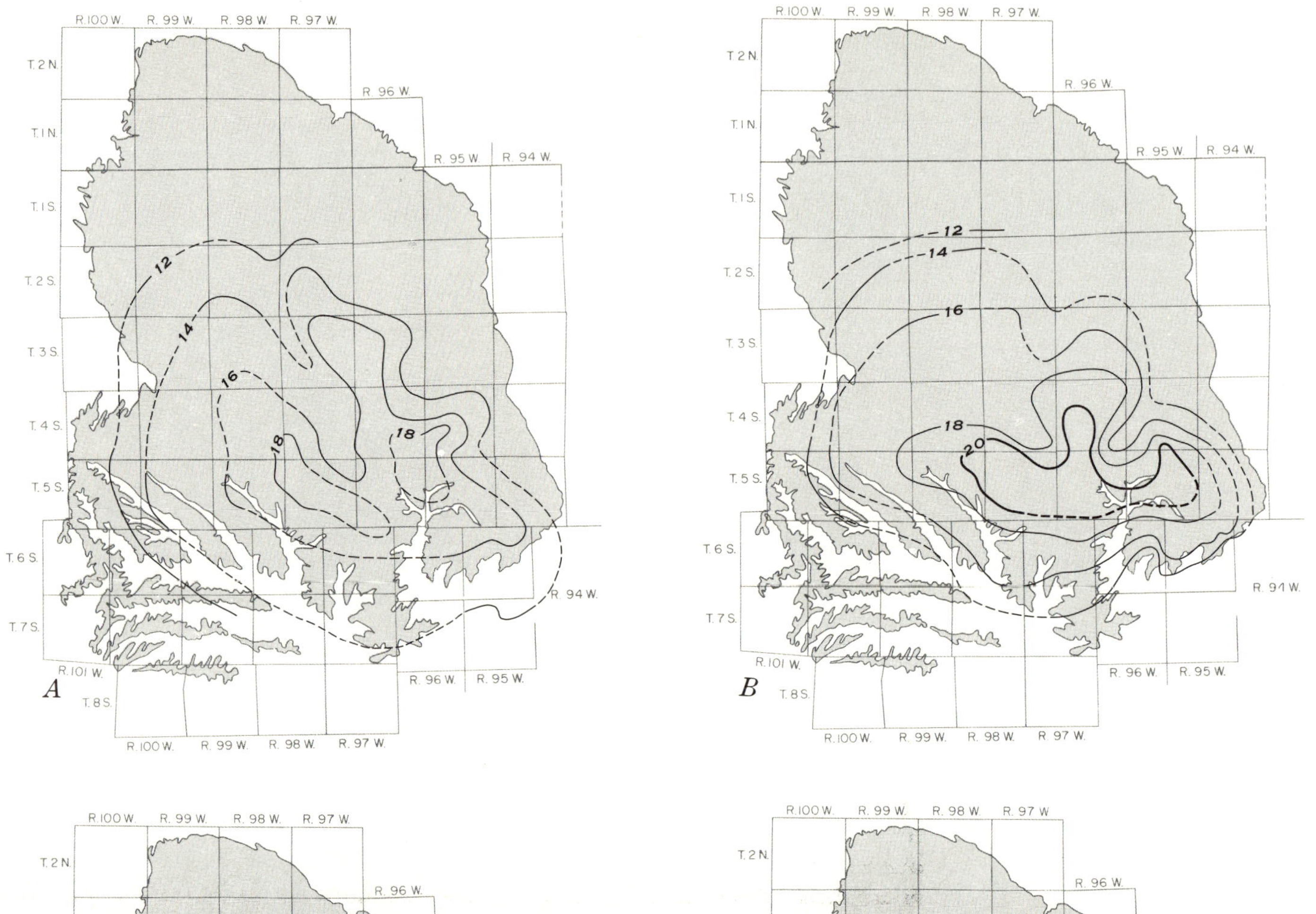

Figure 4.—Maps showing potential shale-oil yield, in gallons per ton, of *A*, unit 1, *B*, unit 2, *C*, unit 3, and *D*, unit 4, in the Piceance Creek basin. Interval is 2 gal per ton. Lines are dashed where information is sparse.

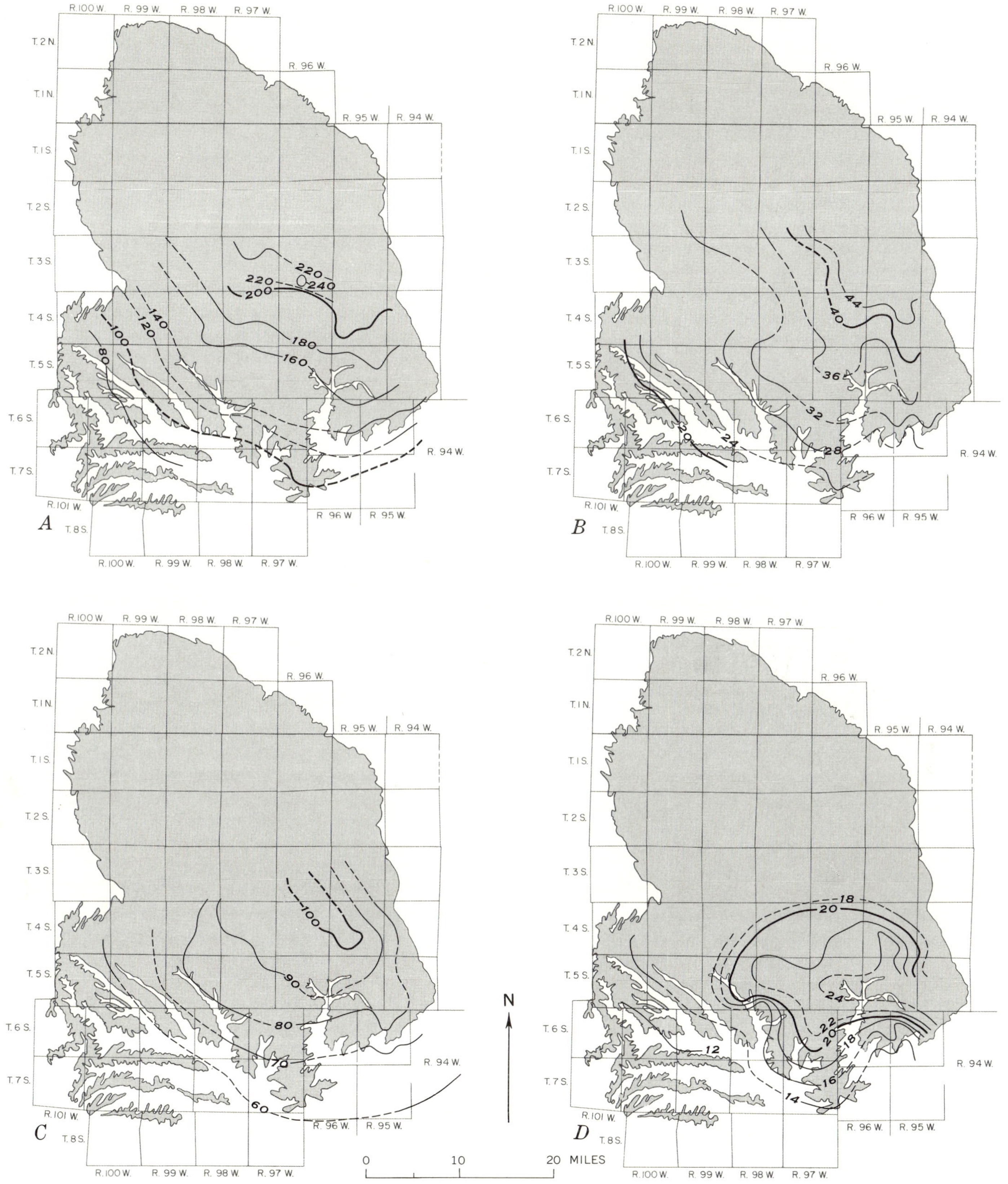

Figure 5.–Maps showing potential shale-oil yield of units in the Piceance Creek basin. Lines are dashed where information is sparse. *A*, unit 1 (interval is 20 thousand bbl per acre). *B*, unit 2 (4 thousand bbl per acre). *C*, unit 3 (10 thousand bbl per acre). *D*, unit 4 (2 thousand bbl per acre).

Table 1.—*Total resources, in billions of barrels, of the oil-shale sequence overlying the Mahogany zone*

[No allowances made for losses in mining or processing]

Location T (S.)	Location R (W.)	Unit 1	Unit 2	Unit 3	Unit 4	Total resources
2	97...	....	1.0	....	....	1.0
	98...	....	.9	....	....	.9
	99...	....	.8	....	....	.8
3	95...	....	....	1.9	....	1.9
	96...	5.4	1.1	2.5	....	9.0
	97...	5.2	.9	....	....	6.1
	98...	4.3	.7	....	....	5.0
	99...	3.6	.7	....	....	4.3
4	94...	1.7	....	.8	0.2	2.7
	95...	5.0	1.0	2.4	.5	8.9
	96...	4.4	.9	2.3	.5	8.1
	97...	4.4	.8	2.3	.5	8.0
	98...	3.7	.7	1.9	.4	6.7
	99...	2.9	.6	1.6	.4	5.5
	100...	1.2	.3	.8	.2	2.5
5	94...	3.1	....	1.5	.3	4.9
	95...	3.7	.8	1.9	.5	6.9
	96...	3.3	.8	1.9	.5	6.5
	97...	3.5	.8	2.0	.5	6.8
	98...	2.8	.6	1.6	.4	5.4
	99...	2.0	.5	1.2	.3	4.0
	100...	1.3	.3	.9	.2	2.7
6	95...	1.6	.4	.9	.2	3.1
	96...	1.7	.3	.9	.2	3.1
	97...	2.6	.6	1.5	.4	5.1
	98...	1.5	.3	.9	.2	2.9
	99...	.9	.2	.5	.1	1.7
	100...	.8	.2	....	.1	1.1
7	96...	.4	.1	....	.1	.6
	97...	.9	.2	....	.2	1.3
	98...	.4	.1	....	.1	.6
	99...	.3	.1	....	....	.4
Total.......		72.6	16.7	32.2	7.0	128.5
Area (sq mi)..		745	815	619	588	2,767

SHALE-OIL RESOURCES

The part of the Parachute Creek Member that overlies the Mahogany zone (fig. 2) is subdivided into resource units as follows:

Unit 1. Interval between the top of the A groove and the base of the Four Senators.

Unit 2. Interval containing the Four Senators.

Unit 3. Interval between the top of the Four Senators and the base of the Big Three.

Unit 4. Interval containing the Big Three.

Unit 1 varies in thickness from 60 feet near the southwest edge of the basin to more than 200 feet in the east-central part (fig. 3*A*), and ranges in average oil yield from a minimum of 12 gal per ton along the western margin of the basin to 18 gal per ton in the south-central part (fig. 4*A*). It contains approximately 80 thousand bbl of oil per acre in the southwestern part of the basin and more than 220 thousand bbl per acre in the east-central part (fig. 5*A*). For an area of approximately 745 sq mi, the interval has a total resource of 72.6 billion bbl of oil (table 1).

Unit 2 ranges in thickness from 18 feet in the southwest edge of the basin to 38 feet in the east-central part (fig. 3*B*), and yields an average of 12 gal per ton along the northwestern part of the basin to 20 gal per ton in the south-central part (fig. 4*B*). For an area of approximately 815 sq mi, unit 2 has an estimated total resource of 16.7 billion bbl of oil (table 1). The average yield per acre varies from 20 thousand bbl in the southwestern part of the basin to more than 44 thousand bbl in the east-central part (fig. 5*B*).

Unit 3 ranges in thickness from 45 feet to 85 feet (fig. 3*C*), and the oil yield varies from 12 gal per ton in the south and east-central parts of the basin to 18 gal per ton in the south-central part (fig. 4*C*). An oil yield of 60 thousand bbl per acre is estimated for the southern part of the basin, with a maximum of 100 thousand bbl per acre in the east-central part (fig. 5*C*). A total resource of 32.2 billion bbl of oil is estimated for an area of approximately 619 sq mi (table 1).

Unit 4 thickens in a northeast direction from a minimum of 10 feet in the southwestern part of the basin to more than 24 feet in the southeastern part (fig. 3*D*). The oil yield of the sequence averages 12 gal per ton along the south, west, and southeast margins of the basin and is as much as 20 gal per ton in the south-central part (fig. 4*D*). A minimum of 12 thousand bbl per acre is present in the southwestern part of the basin and a maximum of 24 thousand bbl per acre is estimated for the southeastern part (fig. 5*D*). A total resource of 7.0 billion bbl of oil is estimated for an area of approximately 588 sq mi.

In the area appraised, the four units have total estimated resources of 128.5 billion bbl of oil. The thickness and potential oil yield of the oil-shale sequence above the Mahogany zone in general increase from a minimum along the southwest basin margin to a maximum parallel to the depositional axis. Northeastward from the axis the sequence thickens and loses oil yield because of dilution by clastic material which occurs as bedded deposits or as contaminants of oil shale.

The sequence of oil shale overlying the Mahogany zone (units 1–4) is thickest in T. 3 S., R. 96 W. The total interval between the top of the A groove and the top of the Big Three is about 354 feet thick, averaging approximately 14 gal of oil per ton with a total resource of 9.0 billion bbl of oil. The sequence is richest in T. 5 S., R. 96 W., where 250 feet of oil shale yields an average of 19 gal of oil per ton, with a total resource of 6.5 billion bbl. In this area, however, the overburden above the Mahogany bed is more than 500 feet thick.

The area most favorable for a surface-mining operation is along the western margin of the basin in T. 4 S., R. 99 W. Approximately 190 feet of oil shale with an average yield of 15 gal per ton occurs within 400 feet of the surface. Some sequences as thick as 25 feet will yield an average of about 20 gal per ton.

In a surface-mining operation, perhaps low grade to moderately rich oil shales above the Mahogany zone could be saved and blended with rich oil shales from the Mahogany zone and underlying rich zones that average more than 30 gal per ton to produce a retort feed of 25 gal per ton.

REFERENCES CITED

Belser, Carl, 1951, Green River oil-shale reserves of northwestern Colorado: U.S. Bur. Mines Rept. Inv. 4769, 13 p.

Bradley, W. H., 1931, Origin and microfossils of the oil shale of the Green River formation of Colorado and Utah: U.S. Geol. Survey Prof. Paper 168, 58 p.

Cashion, W. B., and Donnell, J. R., 1972, Chart showing correlations of selected key units in the organic-rich sequence of the Green River Formation, Piceance Creek basin, Colorado, and Uinta Basin, Utah: U.S. Geol. Survey Oil and Gas Inv. Chart OC-65.

Donnell, J. R., 1961, Tertiary geology and oil-shale resources of the Piceance Creek basin between the Colorado and White Rivers, northwestern Colorado: U.S. Geol. Survey Bull. 1082-L, p. 835–891.

Donnell, J. R., and Blair, R. W., 1970, Resource appraisal of three rich oil-shale zones in the Green River Formation, Piceance Creek basin, Colorado: Colorado School Mines Quart., v. 65, no. 4, p. 73–87.

Duncan, D. C., and Denson, N. M., 1949, Geology of Naval Oil Shale Reserves 1 and 3, Garfield County, Colorado: U.S. Geol. Survey Oil and Gas Inv. Prelim. Map 94.

Stanfield, K. E., and others, 1954, Oil yields of sections of Green River oil shale in Colorado, Utah, and Wyoming, 1945–52: U.S. Bur. Mines Rept. Inv. 5081, 153 p.

——1957, Oil yields of sections of Green River oil shale in Colorado, 1952–54: U.S. Bur. Mines Rept. Inv. 5321, 132 p.

——1960, Oil yields of sections of Green River oil shale in Colorado, 1954–57: U.S. Bur. Mines Rept. Inv. 5614, 186 p.

——1967, Oil yields of sections of Green River oil shale in Colorado, 1957–63: U.S. Bur. Mines Rept. Inv. 7051, 284 p.

Jour. Research U.S. Geol. Survey
Vol. 1, No. 4, July—Aug. 1973, p. 475—482

SPECTROCHEMICAL COMPUTER ANALYSIS—INSTRUMENTATION

By A. W. HELZ, Washington, D.C.

Abstract.—A microphotometer is described for making magnetic tape recordings of spectra 480 mm long from 102- by 508-mm photographic plates. Transmission readings are recorded at a rate exceeding 1,300 per second for every 5.08 μm of length of the spectrum. A two-line cadmium fiducial line system and a developing tank for 102- by 508-mm plates also are described as equipment ancillary to a system of computer spectral analysis applied to the spectrochemical analysis of geologic materials.

The recording-computer system for a complete spectrochemical analytical procedure that was previously outlined (Helz and others, 1969) is now in routine service. Computer-prepared analytical reports show concentrations of 69 elements determined from a single 70-second microphotometric scan of a spectrum between 2,300 and 4,700 A. A search is made by the computer for about 400 spectral lines from among 92,000 optical transmission readings. All the calculations are completed automatically, including conversion of transmissions to intensities, background correction, reference to analytical curve data for concentration determination, spectral interference allowance, and choice of the "best" value on the basis of a set of line-intensity rules. Among the many changes that the procedure has undergone during the last few years are the use of 102- by 508-mm (4- by 20-inch) plates, studies of many new analytical lines, and a complete change in the line-finding logic with the attendant two-cadmium-line principle. These changes have resulted from the cooperative efforts of several of my colleagues.

Automatic trace-element analysis of geologic materials was one of the goals of this program. It was anticipated that the most refined principles of metrology would be involved because of (1) the unusually high complexity of spectra for silicate rocks and (2) the very high accuracy requirements for finding very weak lines at a predetermined wavelength (as opposed to the converse of identifying by wavelength a readily apparent line). With the objective achieved it was obvious that advantage could be taken of this system in developing many new applications.

This report describes a microphotometer designed to meet the requirements of accuracy and speed. To be effective, the microphotometer recording system had to be capable of recording a spectrum nearly 500 mm long at constant velocity from start to finish in no more than 90 seconds, making at least 1,000 transmission readings per second. Transmission readings at 5-μm intervals along the spectrum, based on known positions within the spectrum, were also required.

Acknowledgments.—C. J. Massoni not only did all the on-the-job shop work referred to in this report, but also designed a large number of mechanical refinements. Walthall (1973) devised, completed, and tested the complex computer programs in use. His work dealt with line-finding problems, line-peak definition, plate calibration, curve fitting, background treatment, element concentration calculations, report formatting, and many other details. Dorrzapf (1973) worked out details of the applied spectrochemical procedure, particularly those of the argon-oxygen shielded arc and of plate exposure and processing.

The author is particularly appreciative of help provided by A. E. Johnson and Vilmars Fimbers, of the Moore Special Tool Co., for making possible the modifications in their standard measuring machine.

RECORDING SYSTEM

The complete recording system is shown in figure 1; it includes the tape recorder, the relay rack containing most of the electronic circuits, and the microphotometer.

The recording of a single spectrum consists of first entering on the tape a 12-digit number for identification purposes. This number is determined by adjusting thumb wheel switches. Second, the memory is cleared, and third, the motor drive for the table is started. The plate containing the spectrum is moved by the motor through the scanning beam at a steady speed. A phototube constantly monitors the scanning beam, which changes in intensity as it is intercepted by the spectral lines. The photoelectric output is sampled for every 5.08 μm of travel of the spectrum plate. The reading is digitized and then stored in the memory bank. The sampling of the photoelectric output is averaged over a short but finite fraction of time between two readings in order to smooth out electronic noise fluctuations. Whenever a predetermined number of readings has accumulated in the memory bank, the entire group of readings is transferred to the tape as a single record without interruption of the constant flow of incoming

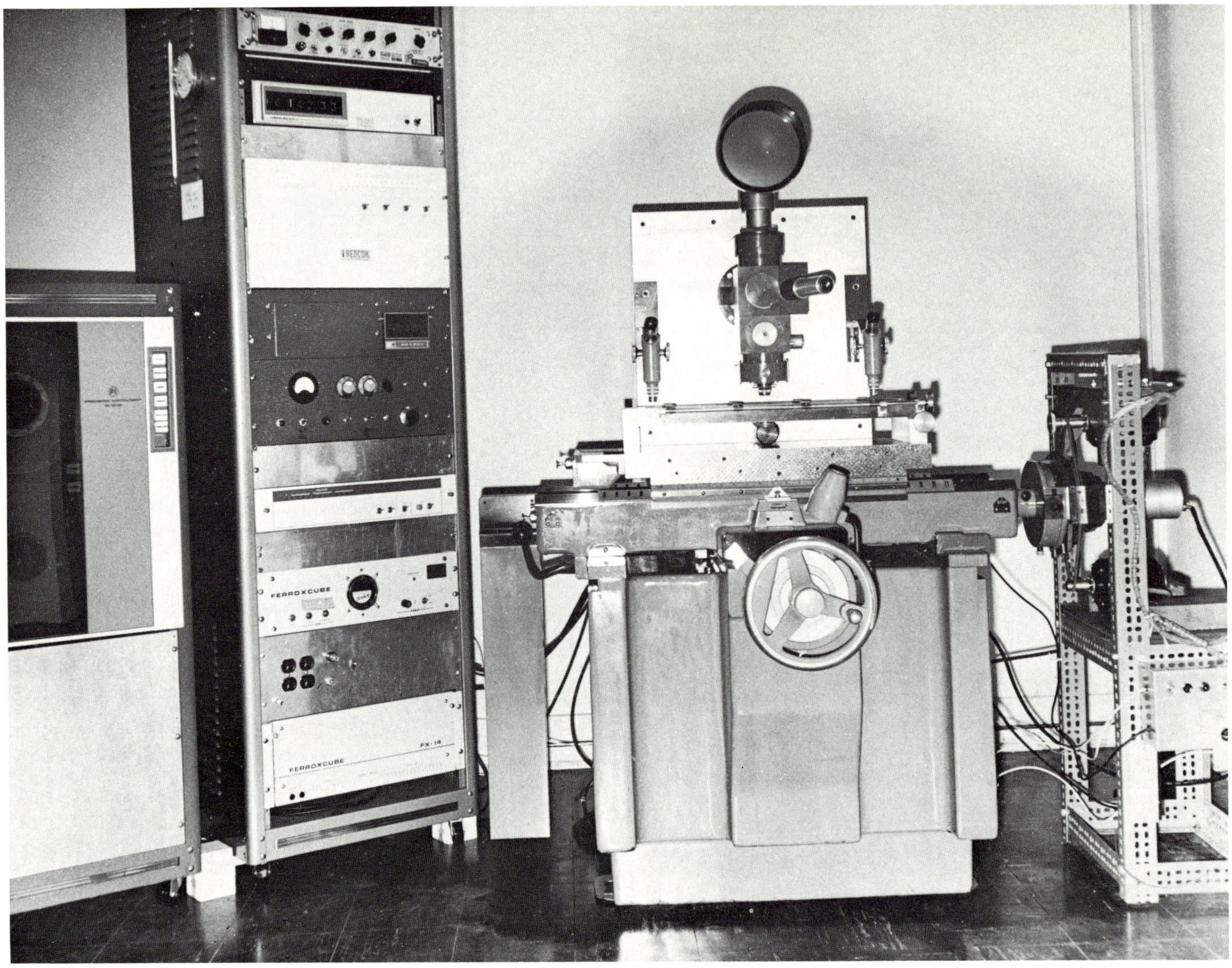

Figure 1.–Recording system. At the extreme left is the tape recorder. The tall relay rack to its right houses power supplies, counter, time devices, a-d converter, memory unit, fixed data entry, numerous control switches, and scanning lamp and phototube adjustment facilities. The microphotometer is in the center, and the power drive for the table is at the extreme right. The microphotometer is about 5½ feet tall.

readings. The tape recorder has the circuitry necessary to produce the computer-required spaces between the records. A limit switch for the table motion and a stop on the control relay rack are activated at the end of a spectrum scan.

The activated stop switch permits the one remaining incomplete record to be recorded and also produces an end-of-file mark on the tape. Thus, all the records for a single spectrum, including an identifier, are grouped into a "file." Vital to this recording process is the condition that no readings be lost. Readings made while a record is being "dumped" on tape and a gap is being formed are kept in proper order in the memory bank. The ordinal number of a reading multiplied by the reading interval determines the basic relationship between length and wavelength. The elimination of the necessity of recording explicit "length" or position data reduces the amount of recorded data by a factor of three. This saving is made possible with the use of a memory bank of sufficient storage capacity to include all the readings of one record plus the number of readings taken during the time required for the complete dumping process.

MICROPHOTOMETER

The horizontal motion of the microphotometer is provided by the Moore No. 3 Measuring Machine.[1] This machine was obtained with a simple vertical bracket in place of the standard vertical column (fig. 2). The machine was also supplied with a modification of the longitudinal traverse to provide for 483

[1] Moore Special Tool Co., Bridgeport, Conn.

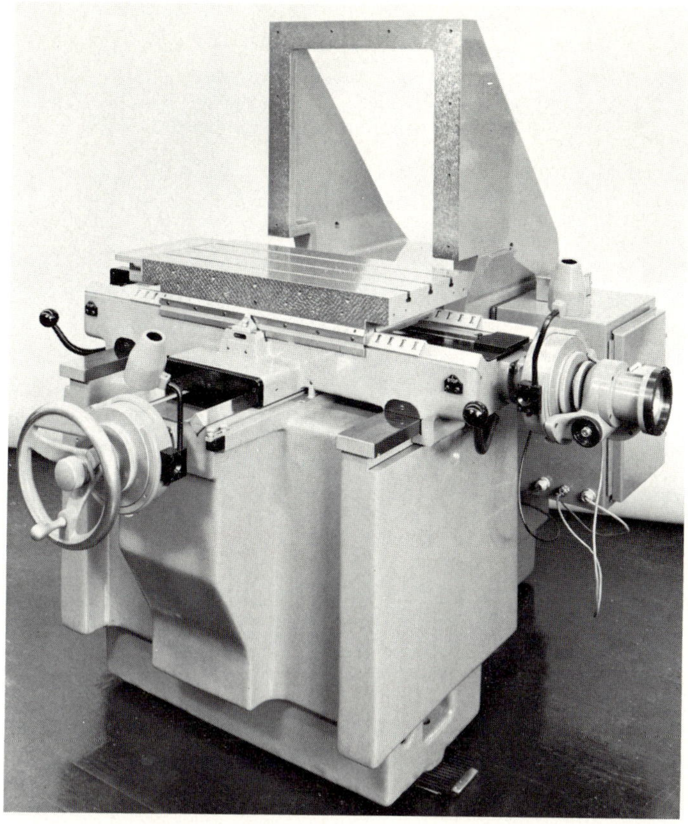

Figure 2.—Measuring machine with bracket for installing the microphotometer optics. Height is about 5 feet.

mm rather than the standard 458 mm of travel. Although this change was made at the risk of some loss of ruggedness, it was not considered serious because of the light-duty application. Concern over the comparatively high speed requirement determined our selection of roller-bearing support, on advice of the manufacturer, for the table's longitudinal motion. The heart of this machine and the fundamental length determinant of the spectral reading system is the 533-mm-long lead screw having tolerances of +0 and −0.9 μm overall and 0.4 μm in any 25-mm section (+0 and −35 millionths of an inch overall and within 15 millionths of an inch in any 1-inch section). The optical system is mounted on a 559- by 508- by 19-mm aluminum-alloy plate bolted to the vertical bracket of the measuring machine. A spectral plate holding-and-orienting device, cut from a single piece of normalized mild steel 610 by 152 by 38 mm, is mounted on the table of the measuring machine (fig. 44). This plateholder is supported at the ends, 48 mm above the table, to provide the space needed for the light path below the spectral plate. A bidirectional, incremental, rotary encoder is mounted with its axis in line with the longitudinal screw and is connected to the screw with a precision bellows coupling.

The optical system follows conventional practice for good resolution, high contrast, and low scattered or diffuse light detection. The optical system is not entirely in one plane as seemingly indicated in figure 3. For the source area and for the end with the phototube the plane of the drawing is horizontal; the remainder of the drawing is in a vertical plane.

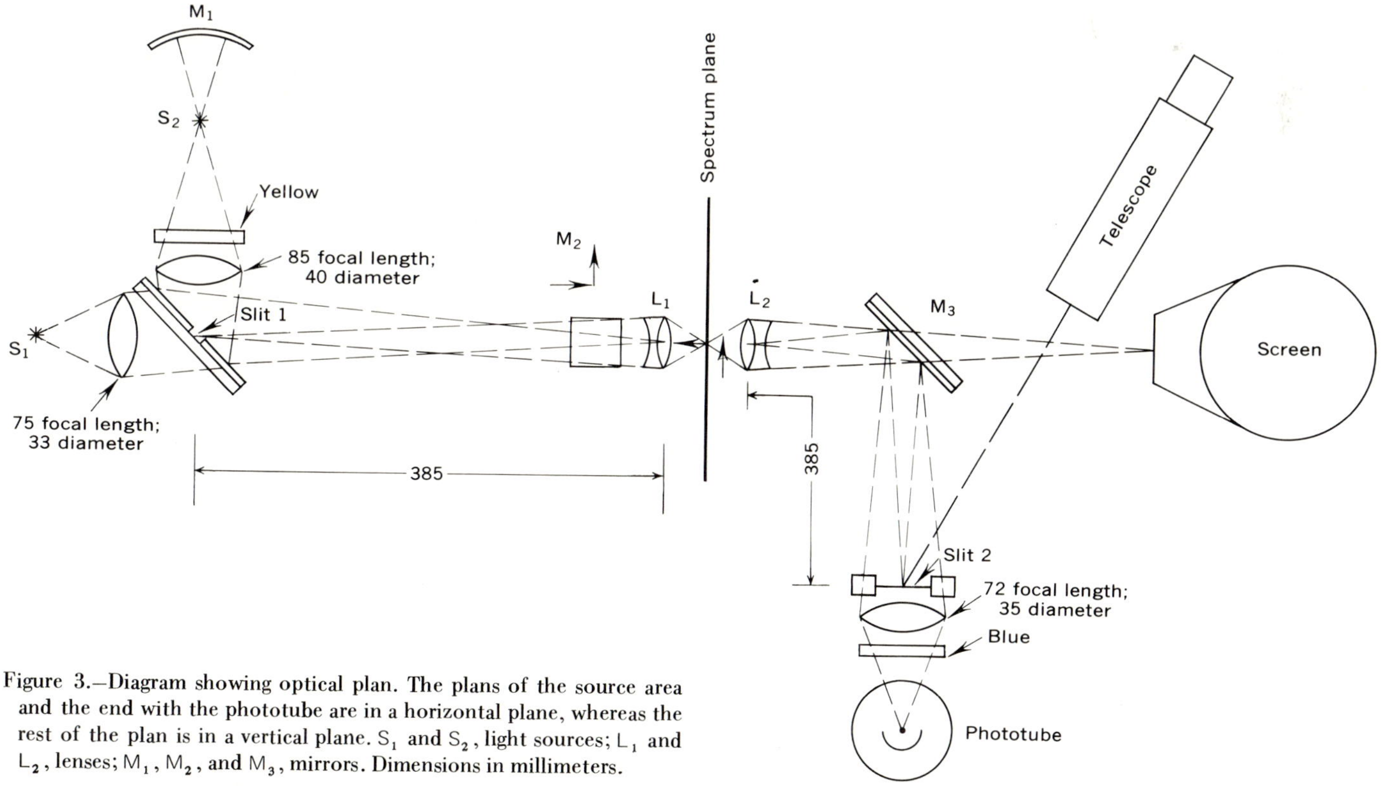

Figure 3.—Diagram showing optical plan. The plans of the source area and the end with the phototube are in a horizontal plane, whereas the rest of the plan is in a vertical plane. S_1 and S_2, light sources; L_1 and L_2, lenses; M_1, M_2, and M_3, mirrors. Dimensions in millimeters.

Two low-power light sources are used. The reading source, S_1, is d-c powered and illuminates entrance slit 1 (fig. 3). The source S_2 is a-c powered and illuminates the front mirror surface of the entrance slit. This source provides field illumination for the viewing screen. Both lamps are 6-volt, 3-amp, microscope illuminator type. The fixed entrance slit consists of a precision-ruled, 100-μm-wide window in a mirror. A 32-mm-focal-length Micro-Tessar lens, L_1, focuses an image one-tenth the slit size on the plane of the spectrum. This image for the scanning light, about 7 μm wide, was selected to be about one-quarter of the width (a sizable fraction) of a spectral line and about 1 mm in length, which is as long as practical. Precision adjustments of slit 1 for translation and rotation are provided for alinement relative to the spectral lines and slit 2. The box holding the source section of the microphotometer is shown in figure 5.

The "observer" half of the optical system starts with a 32-mm Micro-Tessar lens, L_2 in figure 3, having specifications identical with those for L_1. A blue image of the spectral area (which is illuminated through slit 1) is formed by L_2 on a second slit (slit 2) via a dichroic mirror, M_3. The yellow field illumination of the same spectral area is transmitted through the dichroic mirror to form a viewing image on the screen. Magnification of the spectrum is about 10 times at the exit slit, and 100 times at the screen. An image of slit 1 is also visible on the screen. Slit 2 has width and height adjustments and is accurately rotatable for alinement. A blue filter in front of the phototube aids in the further elimination of the light of the field illuminator source from the phototube.

The telescope indicated in figure 3 is used to set up a run but cannot be used for accurate alinement because it is positioned off axis. This was done to permit viewing past mirror M_3. Initial alinement and focal adjustments are facilitated by replacing the phototube-filter-lens combination with a low-power microscope focused on the rear of the slit. Focus, orientation, and position of the two slits and spectral lines may be accurately adjusted in this manner. Once this is accomplished and the viewing screen is adjusted, routine alinement may be made precisely on the viewing screen.

Location of the optical parts discussed above is illustrated in figure 4. The photopickup illustrated in figure 5*A* is a commercial phototube and a solid-state preamplifier. This combination has sufficient speed of response and is preferred over a multiplier phototube when the light level is adequate, because of its greater long-term stability and freedom from drift. The outboard microscopes, shown in figures 1 and 4*A*, are used to aline the spectra parallel to the table motion. The plateholder, visible in figures 4*A* and *B* with a spectral plate in position, has a rotational adjustment about a vertical axis for achieving this parallelism. The plate-supporting surface of the plateholder was machined and hand scraped to be parallel to the table, within 2.5 μm, throughout its entire motion.

A variable-speed d-c motor and a gear reduction drive were used at first for the scanning motion. However, spurious spectral lines occasionally were observed when scanning at the maximum speed, and these were traced to vibration of the vertical optical train caused by the gear drive. Although the problem was eliminated by changing the power drive, strengthening of the brackets of the optical column is recommended. The revised power drive now in use, with the worm and helical gears replaced by a 165-mm-diameter pulley, is shown in figure 6. This pulley is driven with two reversible, constant-speed, a-c motors mounted diametrically opposite the screw shaft. These motors are wired in parallel. A Buna-N O-ring, 240 mm in diameter and 7 mm in cross section, transmits the power of this dual motor arrangement with very little stress (other than that of rotation) on the precision screw and bearing.

At this writing, a motor-drive speed is used that completes scanning a spectrum in 70 seconds. Thus the rate of taking transmission readings exceeds 1,300 per second. We are hesitant to go to higher speeds because of unknown thermal effects and mechanical wear effects on the precision screw. Furthermore, we are close to the limits of speed of response of the photometric system used and also limitations of the particular recording system in use.

FIDUCIAL LINES

Computer line finding in our earlier work depended upon having Cd 2288.02 A and numerous iron lines in each spectrum. The cadmium line was obtained with an Osram-type discharge lamp and selective filtering, and the others resulted from having iron at a concentration of at least 1 percent in each sample. The latter requirement represented a nuisance value and limited the determinations of iron in the analytical scheme. As work progressed, it became apparent that the reading-number differences between given lines, even from the first to last lines in a spectrum, tended to be the same. Differences that did exist showed a definite pattern rather than random scatter, suggesting that the precision of the system, including the spacing of the microphotometer measurements, was of such a high order as to make the many-iron-fiducial-line procedure superfluous.

The differences in the length of a spectrum referred to above may be thought of as a "stretching" error. Temperature changes of either the spectrograph or the microphotometer, or both, could produce errors of this kind. However, the source of this stretching error was found to be mainly mechanical, in the spectrograph, arising from a failure of the photographic plate to slide in a fixed plane as it is racked from spectrum to spectrum. Adjustment of the plateholder reduced this problem to a tolerable level. The residual mechanical error and the plate-to-plate temperature errors are effectively diminished by the use of two cadmium fiducial lines as described below.

Cadmium fiducial lines are recorded in each spectrum with the use of a 19-mm-diameter cylindrical mask mounted as close as possible to the focal plane of the spectrograph. As diagramed in figure 7, there are three positions. When set in

Figure 4.—Front of optical support panel of microphotometer. *A*, With spectrum plate in position. *B*, Closeup view of central part of *A*. *C*, Edge of plateholder and the two Micro-Tessar lenses. *D*, Exit slit.

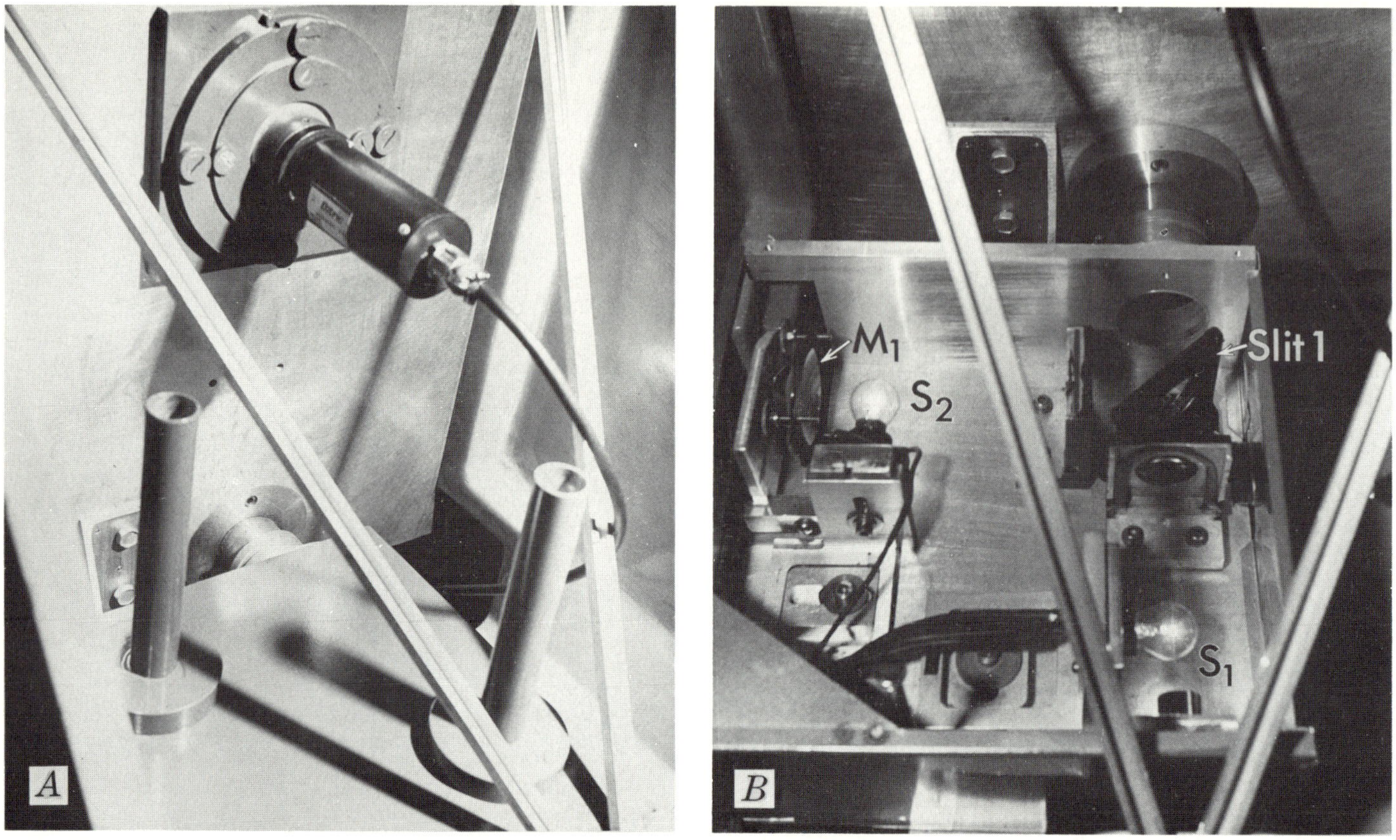

Figure 5.—Rear of optical support panel of microphotometer. *A*, The photopickup (4¼ inches long) is at the top center. The light-source section, at the bottom, is covered and has chimneys directly over the lamps for convection ventilation. *B*, A view of the box with its cover removed. The box is 10 inches square.

position 1 the entire spectral range may be exposed except for two 4-mm-wide spectral ranges, each about 20 A. Position 2 of the mask excludes from exposure all the spectrum except the same two narrow ranges. Position 3 differs from position 1 only in height of the openings. Position 1, 4 mm high, is used for iron two-step plate-calibration exposures; position 3, 2 mm high, is used for sample exposures. With this device Cd 2748.58-A and Cd 4415.70-A lines may be placed in small clear areas in each sample spectrum in exact wavelength relation to the sample lines. After the plateholder has been racked to a new position, it is exposed to cadmium radiation from an Osram-type cadmium lamp for 20 seconds through position 2 of the mask, thus exposing the photographic plate through the two small windows. A solenoid, timer-operated mirror facilitates this procedure. The mask is then rotated to position 3 for exposing a sample spectrum. Special care is taken to eliminate any disturbance of the position of the spectrum and the photographic plate between the cadmium and sample exposures.

The two cadmium lines are clearly identifiable because of the elimination of spectral background in their immediate vicinity; they are easily and uniquely located by the computer. The wide wavelength spread between the two cadmium lines assures precise data for stretching correction in the computer line-finding calculations. Using the two cadmium lines as described above has the additional advantage of maintaining precision, inasmuch as the intensities of the cadmium lines and their spectral background are under control and independent of the sample spectrum.

PHOTOGRAPHIC PLATE PROCESSING

Specially constructed plate processing, washing, and drying apparatus is required because of the 508-mm length of the spectral plates. A developing tank (fig. 8) is made of acrylic plastic sheets except for a stainless steel separator between the developer and stop-bath sections. The photographic plate is lowered into the long thin tank compartments endwise with stainless steel strips (not shown). Small volume of developing solution (450 ml), good stirring, and temperature control are basic requirements. Fixer and stop-bath solutions are circulated through heat exchangers in an external thermostatically controlled bath. The developing solution is in thermal contact with the stop bath by means of the stainless steel separator; temperature uniformity and stirring of the developer is accomplished with a gaseous burst. Nitrogen is introduced at

Figure 6.—Motor drive. The two a-c motors are mounted above and below the 165-mm pulley. The diameter of the central cylinder is about 6 inches.

Figure 7.—Diagram showing the plan of the mask mounted on the spectrograph near the focal plane. Not drawn to scale. Dimensions in millimeters are a function of the dispersion of the particular spectrograph employed. See text for explanation.

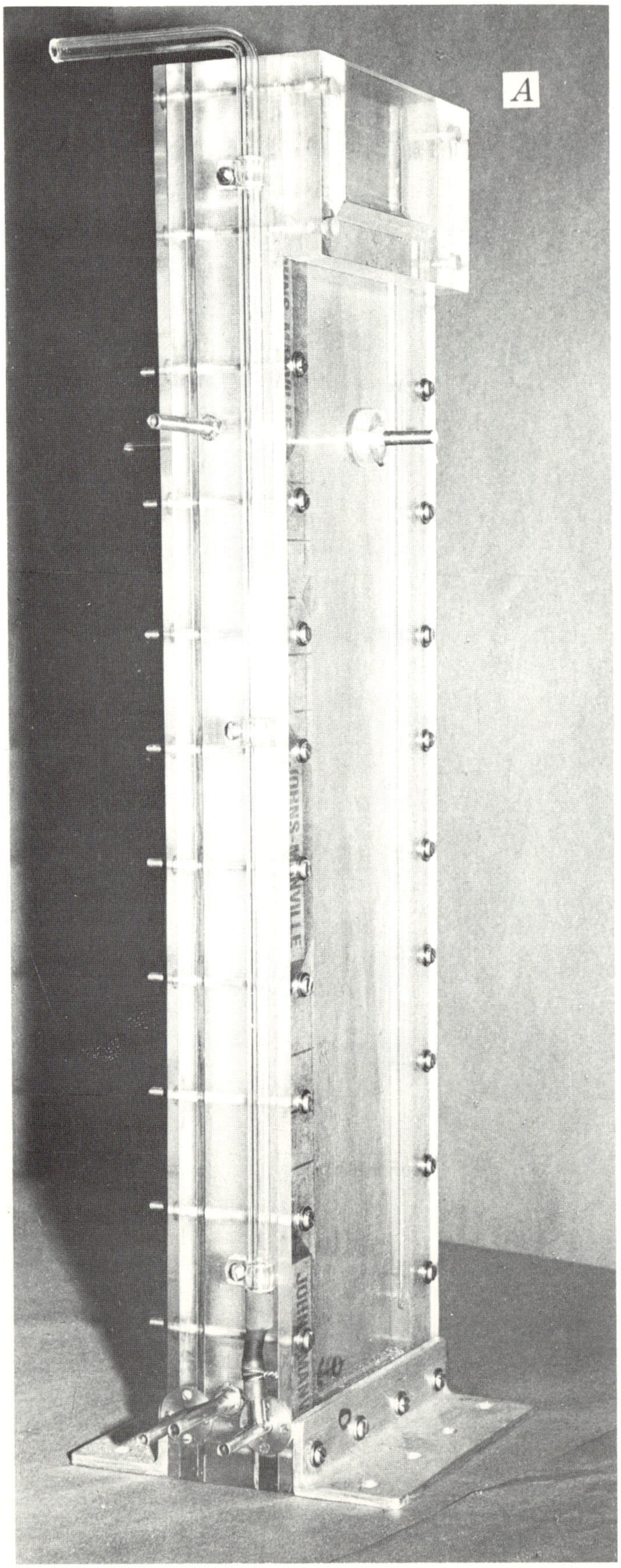

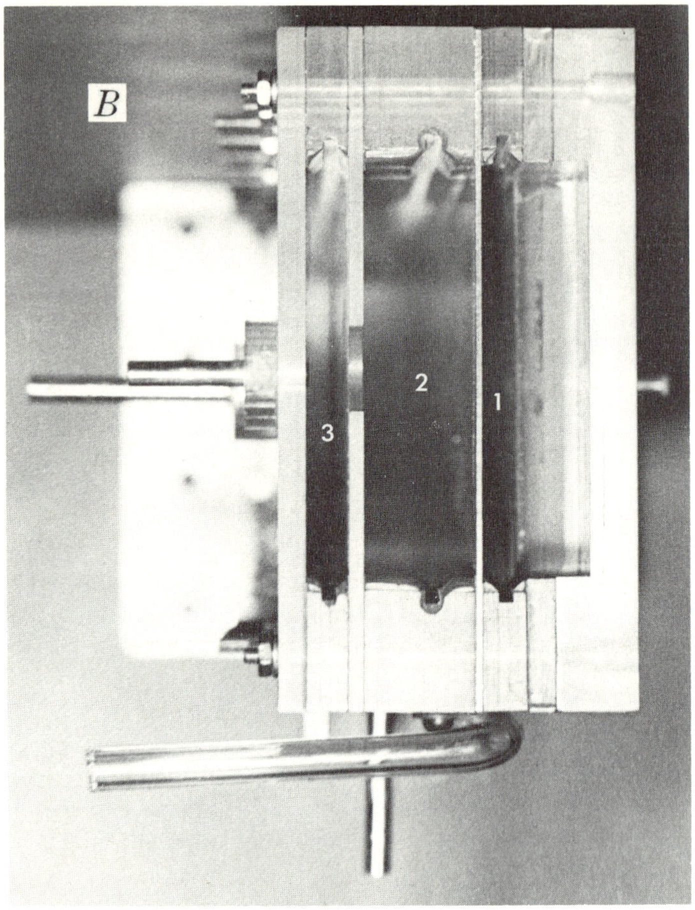

Figure 8.–Developing tank. *A*, Side view, tank is 25 inches tall. *B*, Top view. 1, Developer section; 2, stop bath; and 3, fixer. The longer dimension is 6 inches. Note in *A* and *B* that the developer section is widened near the top to prevent overflow from gaseous burst.

the top level of the tank and flows down the glass tube to the bottom where it is connected to a stainless steel "bubble" tube extending across the bottom of the tank and about 38 mm below the end of the photographic plate. Essential to proper stirring, the gas is allowed to escape to the atmosphere through an alternate vent at a constant carefully adjusted rate with enough impedance in the line to hold the liquid level in the glass tube near the bottom–just short of escaping into the developing solution. This quiet part of the cycle is timed for 8 seconds. A 2-second stirring phase obtains when a solenoid cuts off the escaping gas.

REFERENCES CITED

Dorrzapf, A. F., Jr., 1973, Spectrochemical computer analysis–argon-oxygen d-c arc method for silicate rocks: U.S. Geol. Survey Jour. Research (In press).

Helz, A. W., Walthall, F. G., and Berman, Sol, 1969, Computer analysis of photographed optical emission spectra: Appl. Spectroscopy, v. 23, no. 5, p. 508–518.

Walthall, F. G., 1973, Spectrochemical computer analysis–program description: U.S. Geol. Survey Jour. Research (In press).

Jour. Research U.S. Geol. Survey
Vol. 1, No. 4, July—Aug. 1973, p. 483—485

SOLUBILITY OF CRYOLITE AT 25°C AND 1 ATMOSPHERE PRESSURE

By C. E. ROBERSON and J. D. HEM, Menlo Park, Calif.

Abstract.—For natural cryolite from Greenland the activity product for the reaction (in water),

$$Na_3AlF_{6\ c} \rightleftharpoons 3Na^+ + Al^{3+} + 6F^- ,$$

was found to be $10^{-34.3\pm0.1}$. This is in good agreement with earlier work in which equilibrium was approached from supersaturation.

Synthetic cryolite is easily prepared at 25°C and 1 atmosphere pressure from solutions containing suitable concentrations of Na^+, Al^{3+}, and F^- (Roberson and Hem, 1968, 1969). Equilibrium was postulated after repeated analysis of the solutions showed that the ion activity products remained constant for many months. The crystalline precipitate was identified by X-ray diffraction. It is always desirable in solubility studies, however, to approach equilibrium from both supersaturation and undersaturation. This report describes the latter approach using natural cryolite from Ivigtut, Greenland, as starting material.

Acknowledgments.—We thank our colleagues of the U.S. Geological Survey: Robert Schoen for X-ray diffraction analyses, and R. A. Gulbrandsen, C. J. Lind, and J. B. Rapp for reviewing the manuscript.

EXPERIMENTAL METHOD

The cryolite was ground by mortar and pestle and was wet sieved. The fraction between 48 and 150 mesh was washed with distilled water and dried at 110°C. After further grinding, this fraction was examined by X-ray diffraction. It consisted of well-crystallized cryolite with no impurities detected by X-ray.

Two experiments were made with weighed amounts of ground cryolite and water in polyethylene bottles. For experiment 6-19-70, 1.00 g cryolite and 500 ml distilled, deionized water were used; in experiment 3-31-71, 2.00 g cryolite and 2,000 ml distilled, deionized water were used.

The solution-solid mixtures were stored at room temperature (25±1°C) and stirred occasionally during the first few days. Periodically, pH and activities for Na^+ and F^- were measured by use of electrodes. Total aluminum and sodium concentrations were determined by atomic absorption spectrophotometry. Total fluoride concentrations were measured by either a colorimetric method or by means of a specific-ion electrode method (Brown and others, 1970, p. 90, 93).

RESULTS AND DISCUSSION

Portions of the solutions from experimental runs 6-19-70 and 3-13-71 were filtered through plastic membranes with 0.1-μm pore diameter and were analyzed at various times for 17 months and 11 months, respectively. Analytical data and calculated values for pAl and K_{S0} are shown in table 1. The terms "pH," "pF," "pNa," and "pAl" represent −log $[i]$ where $[i]$ represents activities of H^+, F^-, Na^+, or Al^{3+}. The equilibrium constant K_{S0} is for zero ionic strength. The electrodes used for measuring pH and pF were calibrated with standards of known activities. Values for pNa for all but the first entry in table 1 were calculated from activity coefficients for Na^+ obtained from the Debye-Hückel equation (Klotz, 1964, p. 419) and stoichiometric concentrations of Na^+. For the first set of data (table 1), pNa was measured with a sodium-ion electrode. Our particular pNa electrode did not perform satisfactorily for the later measurements.

Because most of the dissolved aluminum is in the form of fluoride complexes rather than free aluminum ion Al^{3+}, the activity of Al^{3+} at 25°C and 1 atmosphere total pressure is calculated by means of the array of chemical equilibria and stoichiometric summarizations (Roberson and Hem, 1969, p. C3) given in equations 1 through 12. Values for $[Al^{3+}]$ can be calculated directly after substituting into equation 1 the expressions described by equations 4 through 12 and using the measured molal concentration of aluminum (C_{Al}) and measured pH and pF. In addition, one needs a measure of ionic strength for calculation of activity coefficients (γ_i). The ionic strength in these solutions is taken as approximately equal to the total sodium-ion concentration, C_{Na}. The calculations are readily performed by electronic computer.

The equilibrium constant K_{S0} for the thermodynamic solubility of cryolite is:

$$K_{S0} = [Na^+]^3 [Al^{3+}] [F^-]^6$$

Table 1.—*Analytical data, calculated activities of aluminum, and thermodynamic solubility products of cryolite*

[C_{Na} and C_{Al}, molal concentrations of Na^+ and Al^{3+}, respectively]

Age of precipitate	C_{Na} (total)	pH	pNa[a]	pF	C_{Al} (total)	pAl[b]	log K_{S0}
Experiment 6-19-70							
40 days	....	6.56	3.27	2.37	1.63×10^{-3}	13.22	-37.25
8 months	5.57×10^{-3}	5.89	2.28	2.39	1.85×10^{-3}	13.11	-34.29
14 months	5.43×10^{-3}	5.86	2.30	2.37	1.96×10^{-3}	13.16	-34.28
17 months	5.57×10^{-3}	5.55	2.28	2.38	1.78×10^{-3}	13.17	-34.29
Experiment 3-31-71							
3.5 months	5.52×10^{-3}	6.03	2.29	2.40	1.93×10^{-3}	13.06	-34.33
7.5 months	5.48×10^{-3}	5.87	2.29	2.39	1.63×10^{-3}	13.17	-34.38
11 months	5.22×10^{-3}	6.48	2.31	2.36	1.78×10^{-3}	13.24	-34.33

[a] Value for pNa for 40 days was measured by sodium selective-ion electrode. Other values for pNa were calculated from a measured concentration of Na^+ (atomic absorption) and from activity coefficients obtained from Debye-Hückel equation (Klotz, 1964, p. 419), assuming that ionic strength was approximately equal to the sodium-ion concentration.

[b] Calculated –log of free Al^{3+} activity (see text).

or

$$-\log K_{S0} = 3\text{pNa} + \text{pAl} + 6\text{pF}.$$

Values for log K_{S0} are seen to be nearly constant after 3.5 to 8 months of equilibration time (table 1). The mean value, considering all points except the first where equilibrium had not been reached, is -34.3 ± 0.1.

Equations 1—12, referred to in preceding paragraphs

$$C_{Al} = \frac{[Al^{3+}]}{\gamma_{Al^{3+}}} + \frac{[AlOH^{2+}]}{\gamma_{AlOH^{2+}}} + \frac{[Al(OH)_4^-]}{\gamma_{Al(OH)_4^-}} + \frac{[AlF^{2+}]}{\gamma_{AlF^{2+}}} + \frac{[AlF_2^+]}{\gamma_{AlF_2^+}} + \frac{[AlF_3^\circ]}{\gamma_{AlF_3^\circ}} + \frac{[AlF_4^-]}{\gamma_{AlF_4^-}} + \frac{[AlF_5^{2-}]}{\gamma_{AlF_5^{2-}}} + \frac{[AlF_6^{3-}]}{\gamma_{AlF_6^{3-}}}, \text{ and} \quad (1)$$

$$C_F = \frac{[F^-]}{\gamma_{F^-}} + \frac{[HF^\circ]}{\gamma_{HF^\circ}} + \frac{[AlF^{2+}]}{\gamma_{AlF^{2+}}} + \frac{2[AlF_2^+]}{\gamma_{AlF_2^+}} + \frac{3[AlF_3^\circ]}{\gamma_{AlF_3^\circ}} + \frac{4[AlF_4^-]}{\gamma_{AlF_4^-}} + \frac{5[AlF_5^{2-}]}{\gamma_{AlF_5^{2-}}} + \frac{6[AlF_6^{3-}]}{\gamma_{AlF_6^{3-}}}, \quad (2)$$

where

$$[HF^\circ] = [H^+][F^-]\,10^{3.17}, \quad (3)$$

$$[AlOH^{2-}] = 10^{9.23}[Al^{3+}][OH^-], \quad (4)$$

$$[Al(OH)_4^-] = 10^{33.96}[Al^{3+}][OH^-]^4, \quad (5)$$

$$[OH^-] = 10^{-14.00}[H^+]^{-1};\ [H^+] = 10^{-pH}, \quad (6)$$

$$[AlF^{2+}] = 10^{7.01}[Al^{3+}][F^-], \quad (7)$$

$$[AlF_2^+] = 10^{12.75}[Al^{3+}][F^-]^2, \quad (8)$$

$$[AlF_3^\circ] = 10^{17.02}[Al^{3+}][F^-]^3, \quad (9)$$

$$[AlF_4^-] = 10^{19.72}[Al^{3+}][F^-]^4, \quad (10)$$

$$[AlF_5^{2-}] = 10^{20.91}[Al^{3+}][F^-]^5, \text{ and} \quad (11)$$

$$[AlF_6^{3-}] = 10^{20.86}[Al^{3+}][F^-]^6. \quad (12)$$

In the present study, equilibrium was approached from undersaturation. In earlier work (Roberson and Hem, 1968, 1969), equilibrium was approached from supersaturation, including experiments where cryolite constituents Al^{3+} and F^- varied over considerable concentration ranges, and a value for log K_{S0} of -33.84 was obtained. Therefore we believed that equilibrium was closely approached in both series of experiments. The experimental uncertainty introduced by possible impurities in the solids, particle-size effects, and the magnification of analytical errors introduced by the large exponents in the solubility equilibrium equation is at least as great as the difference in the solubility products.

As a further test, the dissolution $Na_3AlF_{6\ c} = 3Na^+ + Al^{3+} + 6F^-$ was reversed by adding sodium fluoride solution to a filtered portion of the solution from experiment 3-31-71. The entry in table 1 for 11 months for experiment 3-31-71 represents the composition of the solution before adding sodium fluoride. To 250 ml of solution, separated from the cryolite by filtration through a membrane of 0.1-μm porosity, 5.21 ml of 0.50 *m* NaF was added initially and then, because no precipitate was visually observed after 5 days, 5.00 ml more of 0.50 *m* NaF was added. After 9 days from the time the first fluoride was added, a portion of the solution was filtered and a considerable amount of solid was retained on the filter. X-ray examination revealed the precipitate to be cryolite. The fact that no precipitate was observed after the first addition was probably because the crystals were very small and the index of refraction of cryolite is so near that of water.

The analytical data for the solution phase before and after adding sodium fluoride are shown below:

	Before sodium fluoride	*After sodium fluoride*
pH	6.48	6.60
pNa	2.29	1.76
pF	2.36	1.77
C_{Na}	5.22×10^{-3}	Not determined.
C_{Al}	1.78×10^{-3}	See text.
C_F	Not determined.	2.08×10^{-2}

The increased activities of Na^+ and F^-, caused by adding sodium fluoride, had decreased the aluminum concentration (C_{Al}) to such a low level that it could no longer be detected by atomic absorption (detection limit about 7.4×10^{-5} mol/l). The colorimetric method (Brown and others, 1970, p. 44) was unsuitable because of fluoride interference. However, one can calculate $[Al^{3+}]$ using measured parameters pH, pF, C_F, and ionic strength with equation 2 along with equations 3 and 7 through 12. This calculation rests on the assumptions that the difference between C_F and $\frac{[F^-]}{\gamma_{F^-}}$ is the result of complexing of fluoride with hydrogen and aluminum and that no aluminum complexes other than fluoride species are significant. For solutions having the composition and pH observed here, these are valid assumptions (Hem, 1972, p. 131). The calculation gives $[Al^{3+}] = 10^{-16.39}$. The value finally obtained for log K_{S0} for cryolite is -32.30. This is considerably larger than the value obtained in earlier precipitation experiments ($10^{-33.84}$) but such an effect is to be anticipated because of the short (9-day) aging period. A longer aging period can be expected to give a lower solubility, as the crystals increase in size.

Incidentally this experiment demonstrates the feasibility of using the fluoride electrode (together with pF, pH, C_F, and ionic strength) to determine aluminum in certain types of solutions. The accuracy of the determination is adversely affected here, however, because the amount of fluoride complexed is small compared to the total fluoride concentration. The difference between calculated K_{S0} values may be partly the result of this factor.

CONCLUSION

Data of this report are compared with earlier solubility measurements (Roberson and Hem, 1968, 1969) and show that the solubility of natural cryolite is very close to that of the synthetic product which has been aged for a few months. The activity product constant for the solubility (K_{S0}) of natural and synthetic cryolite can therefore be represented by $10^{-34.0 \pm 0.3}$

REFERENCES CITED

Brown, Eugene, Skougstad, M. W., and Fishman, M. J., 1970, Methods for collection and analysis of water samples for dissolved minerals and gases: U.S. Geol. Survey Techniques Water-Resources Inv., book 5, chap. A-1, 160 p.

Hem, J. D., 1972, Graphical methods for representing form and stability of aqueous metal ions: Chem. Geology, v. 9, p. 119–132.

Klotz, I. M., 1964, Chemical thermodynamics: New York, W. A. Benjamin, Inc., 468 p.

Roberson, C. E., and Hem, J. D., 1968, Activity product constant of cryolite at 25°C and 1 atmosphere using selective-ion electrodes to estimate sodium and fluoride activities: Geochim. et Cosmochim. Acta, v. 32, p. 1343–1351.

—— 1969, Solubility of aluminum in the presence of hydroxide, fluoride, and sulfate: U.S. Geol. Survey Water-Supply Paper 1827-C, 37 p.

Jour. Research U.S. Geol. Survey
Vol. 1, No. 4, July—Aug. 1973, p. 487—491

HYDROLOGIC CHANGES AFTER CLEAR-CUT LOGGING IN A SMALL OREGON COASTAL WATERSHED

By. D. D. HARRIS, Portland, Oreg.

Abstract.—Preliminary graphical analysis indicates that clear-cut logging of a small Oregon watershed has significantly altered certain hydrologic characteristics. After logging, moderate increases were noted in annual runoff, but no significant changes were detected in either peak or minimum flow rates. Both the annual sediment yields and the maximum monthly water temperatures increased greatly after logging; sediment yields and temperatures in the unlogged control watershed actually decreased during the postlogging period.

In 1957 a research study was begun by the Oregon Governor's Committee on Natural Resources to examine the impact of different patterns of logging on stream environment. One aspect of the study was to investigate effects of clear-cut logging on the hydrology of small streams. The U.S. Geological Survey was asked to do this particular part of the study.

To make this preliminary evaluation of logging effects, a graphical analysis was used rather than a rigorous statistical analysis of the limited postlogging data. Data will continue to be collected through the 1973 water year. The postlogging period will then coincide in length with the 7-year prelogging period. After 1973, a thorough and detailed evaluation of changes will be made with more precise study methods than those described in this report.

A small watershed, Needle Branch, in the Alsea River basin was clear cut to evaluate the effects of this logging practice on stream hydrology. Another small watershed, Flynn Creek, was used as the control watershed for comparing prelogging and postlogging hydrologic characteristics. The study watersheds are shown on the map in figure 1. The two watersheds, both of which cover less than a square mile and have the same general orientation, provide a reasonable comparison to evaluate the effects of logging.

Needle Branch has a drainage area of 0.27 sq mi (175 acres). The forest cover was 85 percent Douglas-fir and 15 percent alder and vine maple. Thirty-two acres in the headwaters had been logged in the early 1950's. The grade of sidehill slopes averages about 37 percent.

Flynn Creek has a drainage area of 0.78 sq mi (502 acres). Forest cover is about 70 percent alder and 30 percent Douglas-fir. The grade of sidehill slopes averages about 34 percent.

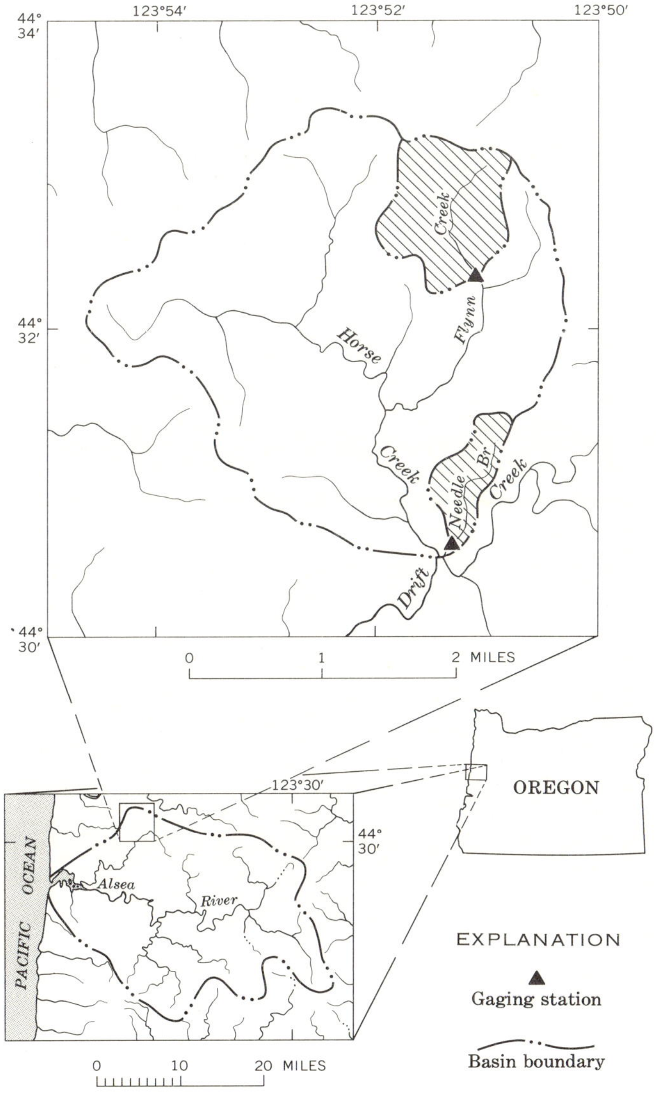

Figure 1.—Location of study watersheds (patterned) in Alsea River basin, Oregon.

DATA COLLECTED AND METHOD OF STUDY

Measurements of streamflow, sediment concentration, and water temperature near the mouths of the two study streams provided the data needed to evaluate change in their hydrologic characteristics. The records were collected at U.S. Geological Survey gaging stations, each equipped with concrete weir controls.

The study was intended to define the hydrologic characteristics of the streams for the prelogging period, 1958–65 (Harris and Williams, 1971), to compare with those for the postlogging period. The principal study method used was to relate streamflow, sediment yield, and water temperature of Needle Branch to those of Flynn Creek, the control stream. Regression lines of prelogging relations were developed for each hydrologic characteristic evaluated. Prediction limits at the 95-percent level were computed for the regressions to assess the significance of changes. The 95-percent prediction limits show the limits outside of which there is 95 percent confidence that a change has occurred. If postlogging values plot outside the prediction limits, the change resulting from logging can be considered significant.

Data for 4 years after logging, 1967–70, were compared to the prelogging relations. Because roadbuilding and logging were done throughout most of 1966, that year was not used in the evaluation.

EVALUATION OF CHANGES IN HYDROLOGIC CHARACTERISTICS

To isolate the effects of logging on streamflow, sediment yield, and water temperature, the areal distribution of precipitation must be consistent over the two watersheds. Therefore, a relation between cumulative precipitation was prepared (fig. 2) from data collected near each of the two stream-gaging stations to assure that no change in precipitation distribution occurred before or after logging. Precipitation data were available only into 1968, but the relation does indicate no change in general weather pattern after logging.

Changes in annual runoff, peak and low flows, sediment discharge, and water temperature were studied to provide a comparison of before- and after-logging characteristics. Annual runoff in inches from the two study basins for water years 1959–70 is shown in table 1. The table is divided into prelogging and postlogging periods. A comparison of annual runoff of Flynn Creek and Needle Branch during the prelogging and postlogging periods is shown in figure 3. A relation of

Table 1.—*Annual runoff, in inches, for the prelogging and postlogging periods*

Water year	Flynn Creek	Needle Branch
	Prelogging period	
1959	78.60	84.04
1960	72.18	69.55
1961	93.30	85.56
1962	66.45	61.61
1963	69.17	62.83
1964	77.21	75.28
1965	87.07	80.80
Mean	77.71	74.24
	Postlogging period	
1967	75.74	86.98
1968	68.01	85.55
1969	86.70	106.93
1970	61.77	80.51
Mean	73.06	89.99

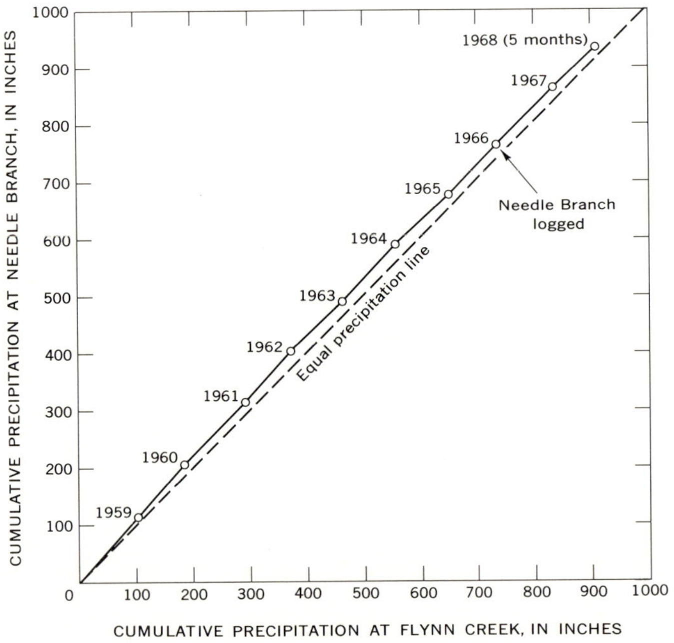

Figure 2.—Relation of cumulative annual precipitation at Needle Branch gage to that at Flynn Creek gage.

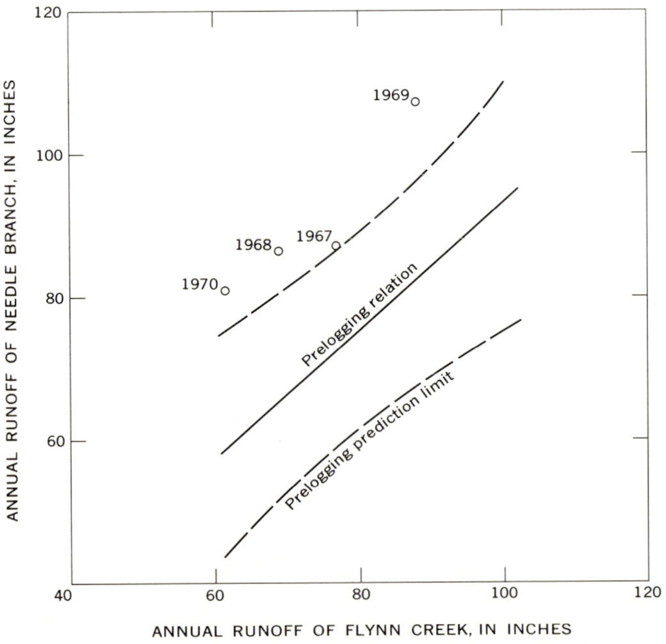

Figure 3.—Relation of annual runoff of Needle Branch to that of Flynn Creek.

cumulative runoff for the two watersheds is shown in figure 4. From table 1 and figures 3 and 4, it is evident that annual runoff in the clear-cut watershed has increased significantly since logging. The 7-year average runoff prior to logging was 3 inches less on Needle Branch than on Flynn Creek, whereas in

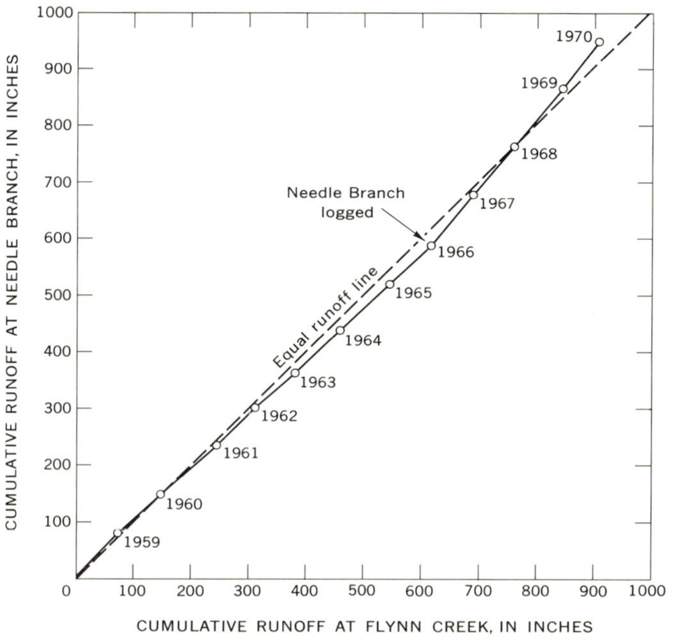

Figure 4.—Relation of cumulative annual runoff of Needle Branch to that of Flynn Creek.

the 4 years after logging Needle Branch averaged 16 inches more runoff than did Flynn Creek.

Peak flows for the prelogging and postlogging periods for the two study streams are listed in table 2. The regression of prelogging peak flows in comparison to postlogging peak flows is shown in figure 5. The peak flows show some increase after logging, but the increases may not be statistically significant.

Minimum flows for the prelogging and postlogging periods were compared by using the minimum daily flows of each September, a month with normally low flows. Minimum daily September flows on Flynn Creek and concurrent daily flows for Needle Branch are shown in table 3. No regression analysis was made for low flows because the small changes could not be detected easily by use of that method. The table does, however, indicate a small increase in low flow since logging.

Annual sediment yields for the prelogging and postlogging periods for the two study streams are listed in table 4. Figure 6 shows postlogging sediment yield compared to the prelogging regression line and the prediction limit. It is evident that sediment yields have increased significantly since logging. However, it is apparent that annual sediment yields are gradually diminishing toward prelogging conditions. The large and abrupt increase in sediment yield immediately after logging and the gradual return toward prelogging conditions

Table 2.—*Concurrent peak discharge rates on Flynn Creek and Needle Branch for all Flynn Creek peaks exceeding 50 cfs per sq mi*

Water year	Date	Flynn Creek		Needle Branch	
		(cfs)	(cfs per sq mi)	(cfs)	(cfs per sq mi)
		Prelogging period			
1959	Jan. 9 . . .	53	67.9	22	81.5
	Jan. 27 . . .	42	53.8	19	70.4
1960	Feb. 9	43	55.1	20	74.1
1961	Nov. 24 . . .	78	100.0	33	122.2
	Feb. 10 . . .	64	82.1	28	103.7
	Feb. 13 . . .	47	60.3	18	66.7
1962	Nov. 22 . . .	46	59.0	29	107.4
	Dec. 19 . . .	41	52.6	18	66.7
	Dec. 20 . . .	43	55.1	17	63.0
1963	Nov. 26 . . .	65	83.3	28	103.7
1964	Jan. 19 . . .	63	80.8	28	103.7
	Jan. 25 . . .	40	51.3	17	63.0
1965	Dec. 1 . . .	43	55.1	17	63.0
	Dec. 22 . . .	90	115.4	32	118.5
	Jan. 28 . . .	137	175.6	50	185.2
Mean		. . .	76.5	. . .	92.9
		Postlogging period			
1967	Jan. 27 . . .	70	89.7	33	122.2
1968	Feb. 19 . . .	45	57.7	25	92.6
1969	Dec. 4 . . .	45	57.7	24	88.9
	Dec. 10 . . .	43	55.1	24	88.9
	Jan. 7 . . .	41	52.6	20	74.1
1970	Jan. 18 . . .	50	64.1	25	92.6
	Jan. 23 . . .	43	55.1	22	81.5
	Jan. 27 . . .	45	57.7	19	70.4
Mean		. . .	61.2	. . .	88.9

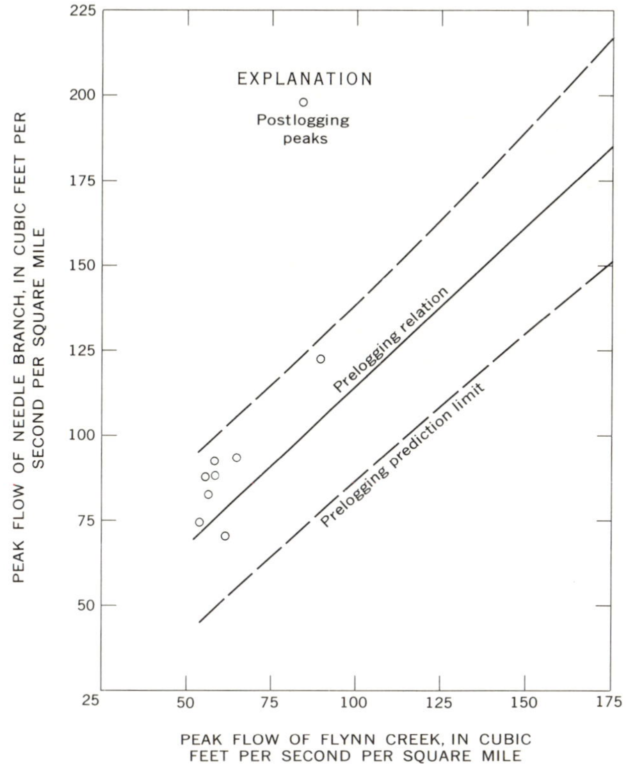

Figure 5.—Relation of peak flow of Needle Branch to that of Flynn Creek.

Table 3.—*Minimum daily September flows of Flynn Creek and concurrent flows of Needle Branch, in cubic feet per second*

Water year	Flynn Creek	Needle Branch
Prelogging period		
1959	0.36	0.11
1960	.14	.02
1961	.20	.02
1962	.20	.02
1963	.22	.06
1964	.22	.03
1965	.12	.01
Mean	[1] .21	[2] .04
Postlogging period		
1967	0.09	0.02
1968	.35	.14
1969	.18	.04
1970	.14	.02
Mean	[3] .19	[4] .06

[1] 0.27 cfs per sq mi. [2] 0.15 cfs per sq mi.
[3] 0.24 cfs per sq mi. [4] 0.22 cfs per sq mi.

Table 4.—*Annual sediment yields of the two watersheds, in tons per square mile*

Water year	Flynn Creek	Needle Branch
Prelogging period		
1959	88	59
1960	65	41
1961	338	186
1962	138	141
1963	114	117
1964	226	184
1965	1,270	430
Mean	320	165
Postlogging period		
1967	131	905
1968	66	490
1969	142	515
1970	114	232
Mean	113	536

are evident in the relation of cumulative sediment yields shown in figure 7.

Figure 8 shows maximum monthly water temperatures for the postlogging period compared to the prelogging maximum temperature regression and the prediction limits. It is evident from this illustration that water temperatures have increased greatly since logging. However, during the postlogging period, water temperatures have decreased each year toward those of the prelogging period.

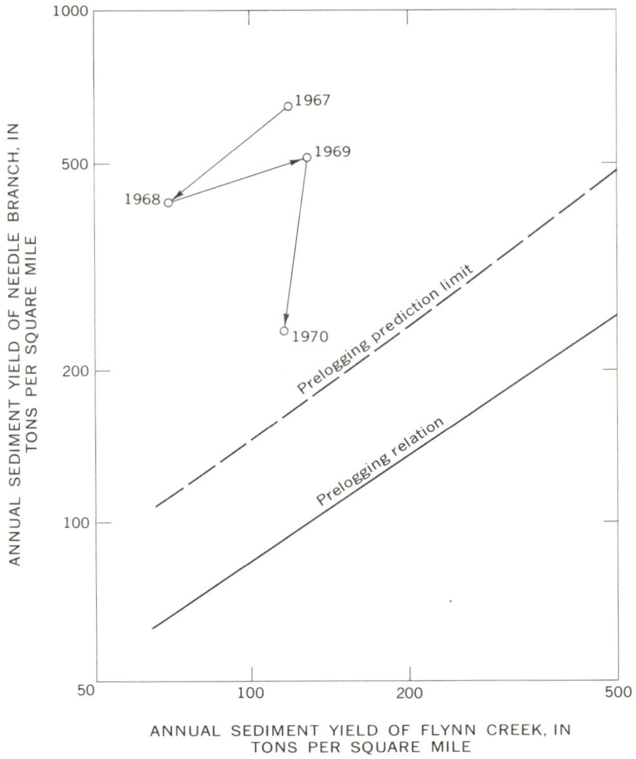

Figure 6.—Relation of annual sediment yield of Needle Branch to that of Flynn Creek.

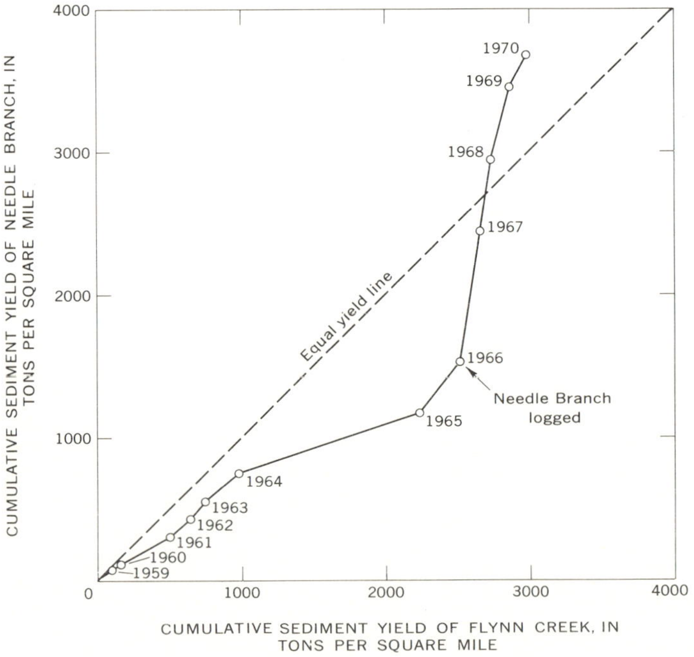

Figure 7.—Relation of cumulative annual sediment yield of Needle Branch to that of Flynn Creek.

SUMMARY

Preliminary study of the effects of clear-cut logging of a small watershed on the Oregon coast indicates that some large and some small changes have occurred in hydrologic characteristics of the stream draining the watershed. Annual runoff has increased moderately; peak flows show a small but probably not statistically significant increase, and low flows have increased only slightly, if at all. Large and significant increases appear to have occurred in sediment yields and water temperatures. During the postlogging period, however, the sediment yields and water temperatures appear to be decreasing each year toward those for the prelogging period.

REFERENCE CITED

Harris, D. D., and Williams, R. C., 1971, Streamflow, sediment-transport, and water-temperature characteristics of three small watersheds in the Alsea River basin, Oregon: U.S. Geol. Survey Circ. 642, 21 p.

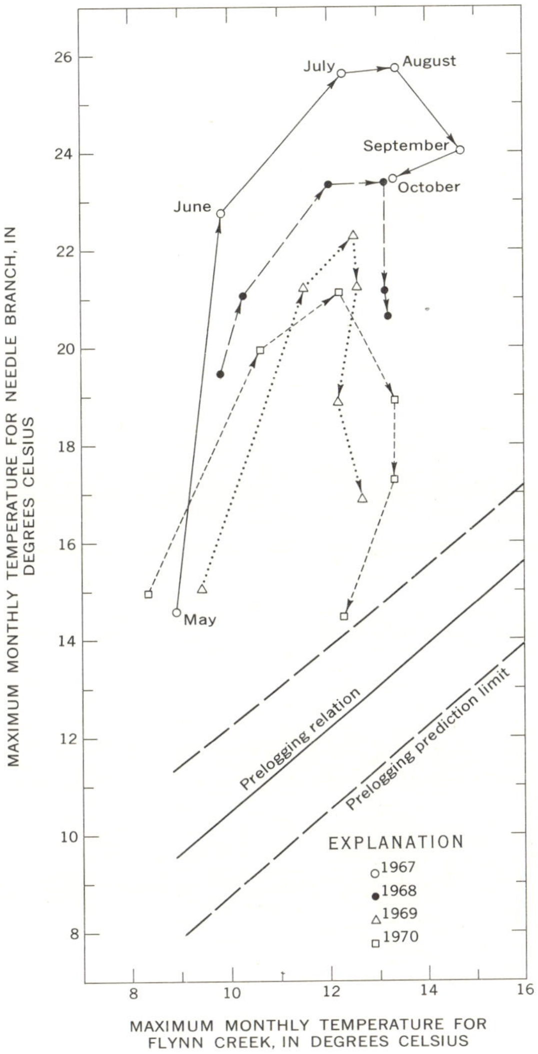

Figure 8.—Relation of maximum monthly water temperature of Needle Branch to that of Flynn Creek.

Jour. Research U.S. Geol. Survey
Vol. 1, No. 4, July—Aug. 1973, p. 493—498

APPLICATION OF THE SOURCE-AREA CONCEPT OF STORM RUNOFF TO A SMALL ARIZONA WATERSHED

By F. E. ARTEAGA[1] and S. E. RANTZ,
Davis, Calif., Menlo Park, Calif.

Abstract.—An attempt to demonstrate the source-area concept of storm runoff by analysis of the rainfall-runoff relation for the watershed of Queen Creek tributary in south-central Arizona was moderately successful. The demonstration was somewhat marred by the necessity to make several simplifying assumptions to eliminate some of the many basin variables of unknown magnitude. The percentage of watershed contributing storm runoff was related to total rainfall received—that is, antecedent and storm rainfall—on the assumption that the availability of rainfall excess from any subarea was dependent on the saturation, or near saturation, of a permeable upper layer of soil. An average unit hydrograph was used for all computed sizes of the runoff-contributing area.

During the past decade several hydrologic studies have been reported in support of the source-area concept of storm runoff. That principle, in effect, states that even during intense basinwide storms, only certain areas in a watershed—source areas—contribute storm runoff. The remaining areas are noncontributing because they can support infiltration and subsequent percolation at rates that usually exceed the rainfall intensities that are experienced. The results reported by some investigators (for example, Ragan, 1967; Dunne and Black, 1970) provide evidence that the source area is usually constant and is confined to the vicinity of the stream channel. The results reported by others (for example, Whipkey, 1965; Hewlett and Hibbert, 1967) indicate a more variable source area that increases with total storm precipitation. The source-area concept is a reasonable one. In fact, the runoff response to storm rainfall is often difficult to explain on any other basis, as will be demonstrated in the discussion that follows on storm runoff from the watershed of Queen Creek tributary at Apache Junction in south-central Arizona.

DESCRIPTION OF WATERSHED OF QUEEN CREEK TRIBUTARY

Queen Creek tributary has a drainage area of 0.50 sq mi upstream from the site at which the stream is gaged. The watershed, roughly rectangular in shape, is approximately 1.5 miles long, and altitudes range from 1,720 to 1,820 feet. The soil in the watershed is classed as a limy-sandy loam, and the vegetation is designated by the U.S. Soil Conservation Service as southern desert scrub. Runoff is ephemeral—there is no ground-water outflow (base flow)—and results primarily from summer convective storms of high intensity and short duration.

DISCUSSION OF AVAILABLE DATA

A recording rain gage is operated a quarter of a mile upstream from the water-stage recorder. During the years 1966–71, 11 storm-runoff events were recorded at the gages and were available for analysis. Rainfall and discharge for those events were tabulated at 5-minute intervals and are summarized in table 1. Inspection of the records showed that no runoff resulted unless rainfall occurred at a rate that exceeded 0.02 inch in a 5-minute interval. Consequently, the storm durations shown in column 4 of table 1 are for periods that started with a rainfall rate of 0.03 inch or more per 5 minutes and ended when the rainfall rate dropped below 0.03 inch per 5 minutes and rain did not resume soon after at a higher rate. It was therefore possible for a storm period to include a brief lull during which there were several 5-minute periods, each having less than 0.03 inch of recorded rainfall. Only two such storms occurred—those of August 12 and September 30, 1971.

The antecedent precipitation shown in column 3 of table 1 represents rainfall recorded prior to the beginning of runoff. For the major storm of September 30, 1971 (No. 11), the antecedent precipitation includes both the rainfall that occurred on September 30 prior to the onset of runoff-producing precipitation and the rainfall that occurred on the preceding day—there was no precipitation for weeks prior to September 29. As for the other three storms (8–10) for which antecedent precipitation is shown, there was no rainfall for many days immediately preceding the calendar dates of the storms.

All recorded runoff hydrographs were of simple shape,

---

[1] University of California at Davis.

Table 1.—*Summary of rainfall-runoff data*

Storm No. (1)	Date of storm (2)	Antecedent rainfall (inches) (3)	Total storm duration (minutes) (4)	Total storm rainfall (inches) (5)	Observed average basinwide runoff (inches) (6)	Average basinwide water loss (inches) (7)	Average rainfall intensity (inches per hour) (8)	Average rate of basinwide water loss (inches per hour) (9)
1	Aug. 30, 1966	0	20	1.10	0.22	0.88	3.30	2.64
2	Sept. 12, 1966	0	10	.60	.15	.45	3.60	2.70
3	July 11, 1967	0	35	.77	.08	.69	1.32	1.18
4	July 3, 1968	0	40	.70	.06	.64	1.05	.96
5	Aug. 3, 1968	0	30	.91	.15	.76	1.82	1.52
6	Sept. 16, 1969	0	20	.59	.06	.53	1.77	1.59
7	Oct. 21, 1969	0	10	.46	.07	.39	2.76	2.34
8	Sept. 5, 1970	.56	50	1.26	.33	.93	1.51	1.12
9	Sept. 5, 1970	2.30	25	.64	.17	.47	1.54	1.13
10	Aug. 12, 1971	.24	65	.86	.11	.75	.79	.69
11	Sept. 30, 1971	1.28	130	2.07	.98	1.09	.96	.50

having a single peak between rising and falling limbs, except those for the storms of August 12 and September 30, 1971 (10 and 11), which had double peaks. The two storms of September 5, 1970 (8 and 9), are considered separate events because the two bursts of runoff-producing rainfall were separated by 7¼ hours, and there was no flow in the stream for more than 5 hours during the lull in precipitation. Although we will demonstrate that runoff was apparently confined to partial areas of the watershed, the inches of runoff and water loss given in table 1 and elsewhere in this report are average basinwide values, computed as though the entire watershed—0.5 sq mi—were contributing runoff. (Water loss equals rainfall minus runoff.)

ANALYSIS OF STORM-RUNOFF CHARACTERISTICS

An attempt was first made to analyze the storm data by conventional methods using, for the sake of simplicity, only storms 1–7, none of which had antecedent rainfall. In that attempt, the computation of basinwide water loss either as an average constant loss rate for all storms (average ϕ-index), or as an average time-dependent loss rate for all storms (Horton concept), gave unsatisfactory runoff results. (A description of the ϕ-index and of the Horton theory of infiltration is given in most standard hydrology texts—for example, Linsley and others, 1958, p. 164–167, 180.)

In a step preliminary to our next attempt, we averaged the values of storm rainfall and basinwide water loss (cols. 5 and 7 of table 1) over their corresponding duration periods (col. 4). The resulting average rates are given in columns 8 and 9 and are plotted in figure 1. Inspection of figure 1, again confining our attention to storms 1–7, indicates that an open-end linear relation exists between average rate of water loss and average intensity of storm rainfall, for intensities greater than 0.77 inch per hour. That lower limit of the relation is the value at which the line of relation is intersected by a 45-degree line through the origin in figure 1—water loss cannot exceed rainfall.

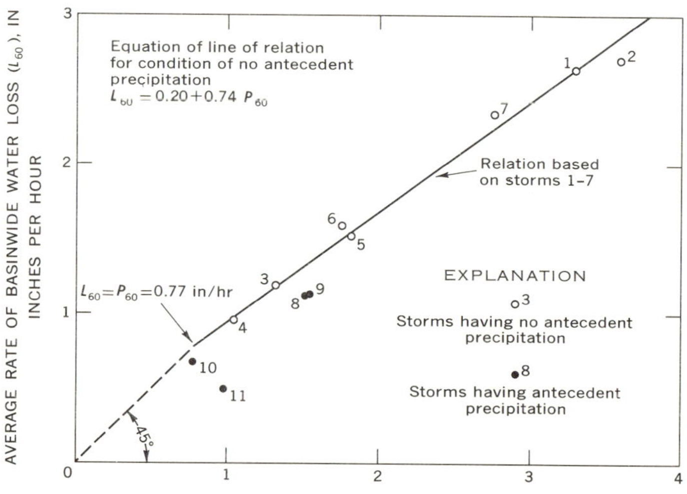

Figure 1.—Relation of average rate of basinwide water loss to average rainfall intensity for individual storms.

The direct relation (fig. 1) between average rate of water loss and average rainfall intensity is roughly consistent with the Horton infiltration theory for storms of short duration, as is the inverse relation (table 1) between average water-loss rate and storm duration. (The term "short duration" in the preceding sentence refers to durations that are too short to permit infiltration rates to reduce to their final equilibrium value.) However, as mentioned earlier, we had obtained unsatisfactory runoff results when we applied the Horton concept of a time-dependent infiltration rate to the entire watershed. It was, therefore, necessary to find some other interpretation of the line of relation in figure 1.

The equation of that relation suggests that only a part of the watershed is contributing runoff. The reasoning behind the premise of noncontributing area is as follows: The equation shown in figure 1 is

$$L_{60} = 0.20 + 0.74 P_{60} \tag{1}$$

where

L_{60} = average water-loss rate, in inches per hour, and

P_{60} = average rainfall intensity, in inches per hour. If we solve for average runoff rate in inches per hour (R_{60}), by use of the equation $R_{60} = P_{60} - L_{60}$, then

$$R_{60} = 0.26 P_{60} - 0.20, \text{ or} \quad (2)$$

$$R_{60} = 0.26 (P_{60} - 0.77). \quad (3)$$

Simplistically, we can interpret equation 3 as meaning that 74 percent of the watershed is noncontributing because its infiltration capacity exceeds the precipitation intensities experienced; the remaining 26 percent of the watershed has an infiltration capacity (ϕ-index) of 0.77 inch per hour, and all precipitation in excess of 0.77 inch per hour runs off from that partial, or source, area. If we are concerned with rainfall and runoff in 5-minute time increments, as we will be, equation 3 transforms to

$$R_5 = 0.26 (P_5 - 0.064), \quad (4)$$

where the subscript "5" refers to 5 minutes. The water loss in 5 minutes, 0.064 inch, is obtained by dividing 0.77 inch per hour (from equation 3) by 12.

Equations 3 and 4, as we have implied, are simplisms; they cannot be used in a numerical analysis of the rainfall-runoff data. Aside from the fact that some theoretical considerations with regard to infiltration are ignored in the equations, there is a practical consideration that precludes their use. We will discuss the practical shortcoming first. Points labeled 1–7 in figure 1 do not depart significantly from the line of relation for water loss in that figure. However, it is with runoff, and not water loss, that our principal concern lies. Those small departures in water loss from the relation given in equation 1 are carried through unaltered in magnitude in the relation for runoff in equation 3. Furthermore, runoff is usually small with respect to corresponding water loss, as we see from a comparison of the values in columns 6 and 7 of table 1. Consequently, although the departures from the equations represent a small percentage of water loss, they represent a large percentage of the runoff. An added complication is the fact that rainfall during many of the individual 5-minute intervals was less than the ϕ-index value of 0.064 inch in 5 minutes given in equation 4; that had the effect of further weakening the simple linear relation of storm runoff to storm rainfall.

As we have mentioned, the theoretical considerations ignored in equations 3 and 4 refer to infiltration. Infiltration capacity, and therefore rate of water loss, is not time invariant during runoff-producing storms, as the equations indicate, particularly during the first half hour of rainfall. (All but three of the storms listed had durations of 40 minutes or less.) Infiltration capacity decreases rapidly with time in the early part of a storm, and its initial value varies inversely with the initial wetness of the soil. Furthermore, during runoff-producing storms it is not necessarily the infiltration capacity (potential rate of water movement through the soil-air interface) that limits the rate of water loss throughout the storm. Commonly it is the thickness of a permeable upper layer of soil that is underlain by a less permeable layer, that becomes the limiting factor. In other words, infiltration capacity may be the limiting factor only until the permeable upper layer becomes saturated or nearly saturated, after which time it is the percolation rate through the interface of the two dissimilar soil layers that limits the rate of water loss.

We refer again to the study watershed. Figure 1 suggests that the source-area concept of storm runoff applies to the watershed of Queen Creek tributary. The consistency with which points 1–7 define the water-loss relation in figure 1 makes it unlikely that the existence of source areas can be attributed largely to the vagaries of desert rainfall with respect to areal distribution. However, uneven rainfall distribution may be a factor even in a watershed as small as our study basin. From inspecton of figure 1 we also expect the size of our source area to be variable—events having antecedent rainfall (8–11) plot below the line of relation for events having no antecedent rainfall (1–7), indicating a greater contributing area under wet antecedent conditions than under dry conditions. We undoubtedly are dealing with a heterogeneous watershed, as most watersheds are, where infiltration capacity and thickness of permeable soil horizon vary areally. Furthermore, if the source area of storm runoff varies in size and location with storm magnitude and antecedent soil moisture, for each set of conditions there will be an individual relation between rainfall excess and runoff—for example, a single unit hydrograph will not be applicable for the entire range of source-area size.

How then do we analyze storm runoff for the watershed? The only hydrologic observations available are those obtained at and near the downstream end of the watershed—the stream-gaging station provides a record of runoff from the watershed; the recording rain gage provides a record of rainfall that may or may not be completely representative of basinwide precipitation. For each storm of differing characteristics we probably have differing values of size of source area, rate of water loss, and time relation of runoff to rainfall excess. We therefore must make some simplifying assumptions that will reduce the number of variables.

The following assumptions were made for the purpose of simplifying the rainfall-runoff analysis.

1. The rainfall catch at the precipitation station is representative of rainfall over the entire watershed:

2. Infiltration capacity, at all times and at all sites, exceeds the precipitation intensity until the permeable upper soil layer reaches saturation or near saturation. The percentage of watershed contributing runoff is therefore governed by the thickness and porosity of the permeable upper soil layer. By

adopting that assumption, percentage of contributing watershed becomes a function of the total rainfall received—that is, antecedent plus storm rainfall.

3. The rate of water loss for runoff-contributing areas is equivalent to the percolation rate through the soil interface underlying the permeable upper soil layer, and that rate is a single constant value for all sites in the watershed.

4. An average unit hydrograph is applicable for all storm conditions, despite differences in size of the runoff-contributing area. As indicated earlier, the use of an average unit hydrograph is theoretically incompatible with the source-area concept of runoff, but it is used here as an expedient. The damping effect of a watershed on fluctuations in the supply of effective rainfall (rainfall excess) commonly permits the application of a linear function (unit hydrograph) to a nonlinear system (the watershed).

COMPUTATION OF VOLUME OF STORM RUNOFF

Several rates of water loss were tested, the lowest value tried being 0.02 inch per 5 minutes. A constant loss rate of 0.04 inch per 5 minutes gave best results and was selected for use. Therefore, from each 5-minute increment of storm rainfall, a water loss of 0.04 inch was subtracted. The resulting values of rainfall excess were totaled for each storm and are tabulated under the heading "Gross rainfall excess" in column 2 of table 2. Column 4 of the table shows the storm index, or rainfall associated with each runoff event, storm index being the sum of antecedent rainfall and one-half the total storm rainfall. The use of only half the total storm rainfall is explained as follows: Under our assumption that percentage of runoff-contributing area increases with the rainfall received, the contributing area during a storm will increase as the storm progresses. At the start of a runoff-producing storm the contributing area will be relatively small, its size being governed only by the quantity of antecedent rainfall (A). Near the end of the storm the contributing area will be larger, its size now being governed by the quantity of antecedent rainfall plus the total storm rainfall (S). If we assume that an index to the average size of area contributing runoff during the storm is the average of the rainfall quantities at the beginning and end of the storm, our

$$\text{storm index becomes } \frac{(A) + (A + S)}{2}, \text{ or } A + S/2.$$

To obtain the percentage of the watershed contributing runoff in each storm, the values of observed basinwide runoff (column 5 of table 2) were divided by the values of gross rainfall excess (column 2). The resulting percentages are shown in column 6. The next step was to obtain a relation between storm index and percentage of contributing area; in figure 2 a curve of relation has been fitted to values from columns 4 and 6 of table 2.

Percentages of contributing area that correspond to the tabulated values of storm index were obtained from the curve and are shown in column 7 of table 2. Multiplication of those percentages by the corresponding values of gross rainfall excess in column 2 gave the values of computed basinwide rainfall excess (basinwide storm runoff) that are shown in column 8. A graphical comparison of observed and computed volumes of runoff (column 5 versus column 8) is given in figure 3. In view of the many simplifying assumptions that were made, it is not surprising that some of the plotted points depart widely from the 45-degree line of equality in figure 3.

The widest scatter in figure 3, as in figure 2, is shown by storms 2 and 9. The wide departure of storm 2 undoubtedly

Table 2.—*Computation summary*

Storm No.	Gross rainfall excess[1] (inches)	Number of minutes of rainfall excess[2]	Storm index[3] (inches)	Observed average basinwide runoff[4] (inches)	Percentage of watershed contributing runoff: Derived from column 2[5]	Percentage of watershed contributing runoff: From curve in fig. 2	Computed basinwide rainfall excess[6] (inches)	Peak discharge (cfs): Observed	Peak discharge (cfs): Computed from unit hydrograph
(1)	(2)	(3)	(4)	(5)	(6)	(7)	(8)	(9)	(10)
1	0.94	20	0.55	0.22	23.4	23.4	0.220	126	115
2	.52	10	.30	.15	28.8	15.2	.079	88	47
3	.50	20	.38	.08	16.0	18.0	.090	42	49
4	.39	25	.35	.06	15.4	17.0	.066	40	32
5	.68	25	.46	.15	22.1	20.7	.141	70	73
6	.43	20	.30	.06	14.0	15.2	.065	26	36
7	.38	10	.23	.07	18.4	12.6	.048	38	27
8	.86	45	1.19	.33	38.4	40.5	.348	137	129
9	.44	15	2.62	.17	38.6	66.3	.292	84	162
10	.40	45	.67	.11	27.5	27.0	.108	40	39
11	1.54	60	2.32	.98	63.6	61.5	.947	278	290

[1] Sum of rainfall quantities recorded in 5-minute increments, after first excluding increments having rainfall that did not exceed 0.04 inch, and then subtracting a loss of 0.04 inch from each remaining increment of rainfall.
[2] Sum of 5-minute time increments during each of which storm rainfall exceeded 0.04 inch.
[3] Sum of antecedent rainfall (column 3 of table 1) and one-half of total storm rainfall (column 5 of table 1).
[4] From column 6 of table 1.
[5] (Column 5 ÷ column 2) × 100.
[6] Column 7 × column 2.

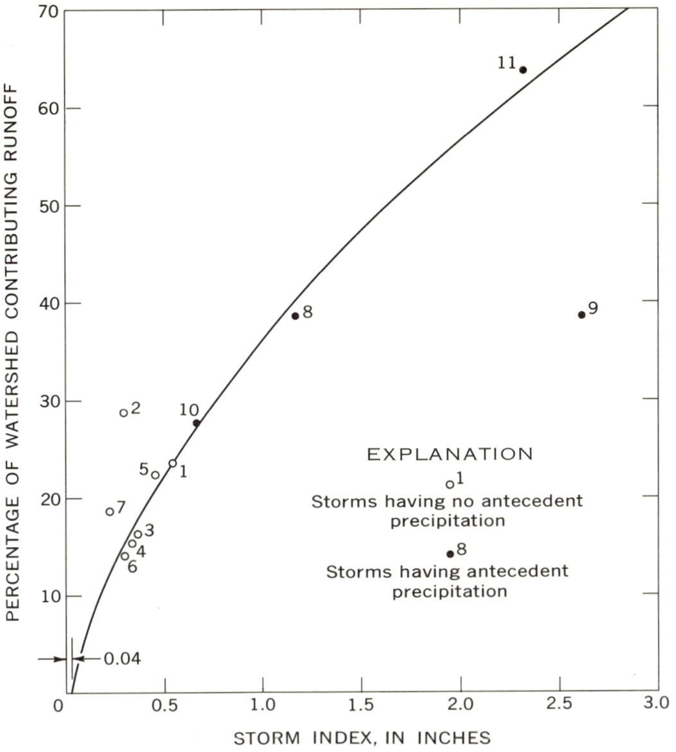

Figure 2.–Relation of percentage of watershed contributing runoff to storm index.

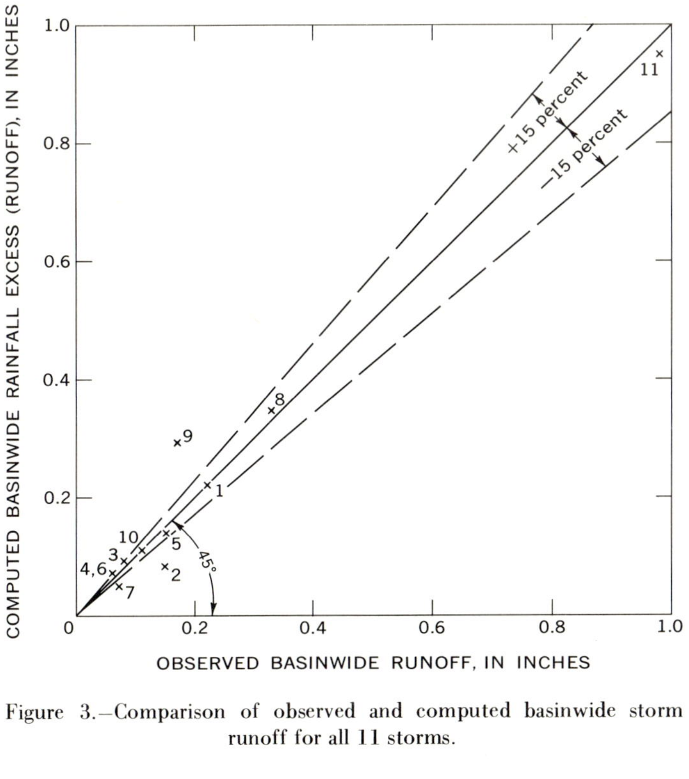

Figure 3.–Comparison of observed and computed basinwide storm runoff for all 11 storms.

results from our simplifying assumption that the infiltration capacity at all sites and at all times exceeds precipitation intensity, and that, therefore, the percentage of contributing area is independent of infiltration capacity. That assumption apparently creates no serious problems except when we have an exceedingly intense storm of such short duration that the total storm rainfall is relatively small, as, for example, in storm 2, where the total storm rainfall was 0.60 inch, but 0.55 inch occurred in the first 5 minutes. Under those circumstances we expect the rainfall intensity during the first 5 minutes to exceed the infiltration capacity over a relatively large area, all of which will tend to contribute runoff. That fact is not reflected in the graph in figure 2, where the relatively small value of total rainfall indicates a small contributing area. Consequently, the use of figure 2 causes us to underestimate the total runoff of storm 2, which in turn will cause us to later underestimate its peak discharge.

We are at a loss to explain the wide departure of storm 9 in figures 2 and 3. It is possible, of course, that the storm rainfall in the vicinity of the rain gage was much heavier than that which occurred over most of the watershed. If that were true, our use of an erroneously large value of rainfall for storm 9 would explain the discrepancy. However, one derives little satisfaction from the supposition of nonrepresentative data. The excessively large computed value of total runoff for storm 9 will cause us to later overestimate its peak discharge.

COMPUTATION OF PEAK DISCHARGE

The first step in computing peak discharge was to obtain values of basinwide rainfall excess for each 5-minute increment of storm rainfall. We previously had subtracted 0.04 inch of rainfall loss from each increment in computing what we had termed "gross rainfall excess." We now multiply each 5-minute increment of gross rainfall excess by the percentage of contributing area for the particular storm, as given in column 7 of table 2. For example, all increments of gross rainfall excess in storm 1 were multiplied by 0.234, those in storm 2 were multiplied by 0.152, and so on. It was realized that for consistency with our assumption that the percentage of contributing area increases with storm index, we should have used a variable percentage of contributing area during each storm. In other words, each 5-minute increment of rainfall actually had an antecedent rainfall that exceeded that of the preceding increment by an amount equal to the rainfall in that preceding 5-minute increment. Therefore, as the storm progressed, the contributing, or source, area should have been increased in size. However, such refinement was considered unwarranted in view of the many other simplifications that had been introduced into the analysis, and a single value for percentage of contributing area was used for each storm.

The final step in the computation of peak discharge was to apply a unit hydrograph to the 5-minute increments of basinwide rainfall excess. We had decided earlier that an average unit hydrograph would be considered applicable for all storm conditions despite differences in the size of the runoff-contributing area. The ordinates of the 5-minute unit hydrograph used are given in table 3. Figure 4 shows, as an

Table 3.—*Ordinates of 5-minute unit hydrograph*

Time (5-minute increments)	Discharge (cfs)	Time (5-minute increments)	Discharge (cfs)
0	0	9	280
1	120	10	200
2	240	11	130
3	360	12	80
4	480	13	40
5	600	14	17
6	520	15	5
7	440	16	0
8	360		

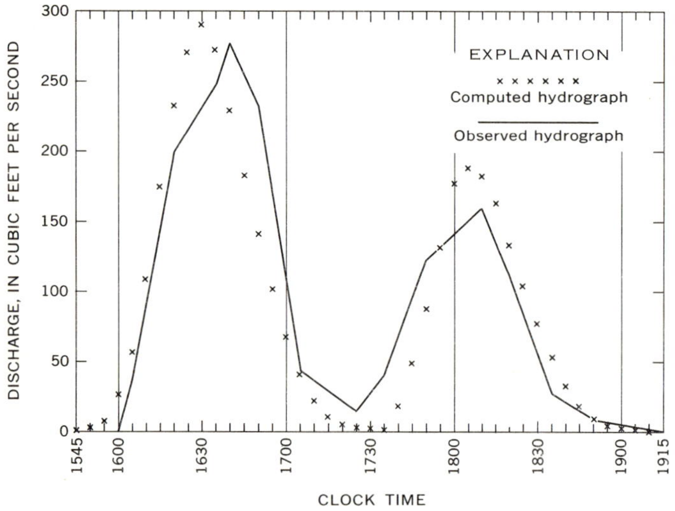

Figure 4.—Comparison of observed and computed discharge hydrographs for storm of September 30, 1971.

example, a comparison of observed and computed discharge hydrographs for the compound storm of September 30, 1971. In columns 9 and 10 of table 2, the observed and computed peak discharges for each storm are given, and figure 5 is a graphical comparison of those values.

Again, it is not surprising that some of the plotted points depart widely from the 45-degree line of equality in figure 5, in view of the many simplifying assumptions that were made, including that of uniform rainfall over the entire watershed in the amount indicated by the rain gage near the downstream end of the basin. The wide departures of computed peak discharges for storms 2 and 9 result from our failure to compute the total volume of runoff for those storms with acceptable accuracy, as explained in the preceding section of this paper.

A comparison of computed and observed time of peak discharge showed no bias in computed times. For some storms, the computed time of peak discharge was earlier than the

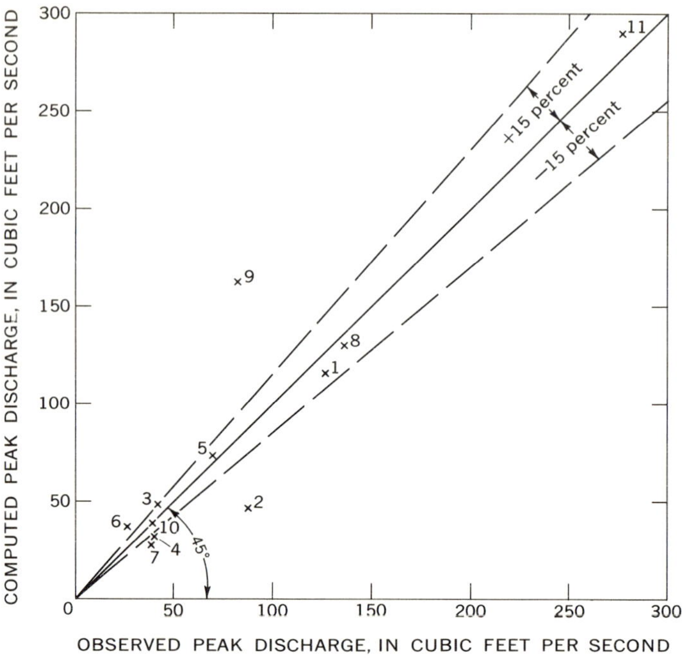

Figure 5.—Comparison of observed and computed peak discharge for all 11 storms.

observed time of peak, and for other storms the reverse was true. It was also evident from our tabulations of 5-minute increments of observed rainfall and runoff that for two storms the time synchronization of the rainfall and streamflow recording gages was poor.

SUMMARY

The relation in figure 1 of average rate of water loss to average rate of storm rainfall suggests that the concept of source areas of storm runoff is applicable to the watershed of Queen Creek tributary in south-central Arizona. The quantitative demonstration of the applicability of that concept was moderately successful, although marred by the necessity to make several simplifying assumptions to eliminate some of the many basin variables of unknown magnitude.

REFERENCES CITED

Dunne, Thomas, and Black, R. D., 1970, Partial area contributions to storm runoff in a small New England watershed: Water Resources Research, v. 6, no. 5, p. 1296–1311.

Hewlett, J. D., and Hibbert, A. R., 1967, Factors affecting the response of small watersheds to precipitation in humid areas, *in* International Symposium on Forest Hydrology: New York, Pergamon Press, p. 275–290.

Linsley, R. K., Kohler, M. A., and Paulhus, J. L. H., 1958, Hydrology for engineers: New York, McGraw-Hill Book Co., 340 p.

Ragan, R. M., 1967, An experimental investigation of partial area contributions: Internat. Assoc. Sci. Hydrology, Berne Symposium, Pub. 76, p. 241–251 [1958].

Whipkey, R. Z., 1965, Subsurface stormflow from forested slopes: Internat. Assoc. Sci. Hydrology Bull., v. 10, no. 2, p. 74–85.

Jour. Research U.S. Geol. Survey
Vol. 1, No. 4, July—Aug. 1973, p. 499

TESTS OF RHODAMINE WT DYE FOR TOXICITY TO OYSTERS AND FISH

By GARALD G. PARKER, JR., Tacoma, Wash.

Prepared in cooperation with the Lummi Indian Tribal Council

Abstract.—Because of the toxicity to oyster larvae and eggs of rhodamine B dye in concentrations greater than 1 mg/l in earlier tests, there was a concern that rhodamine WT, a similar tracer dye, would have a detrimental effect on marine life being developed under the aquaculture program of the Lummi Indian Tribe near Bellingham, Wash. Tests showed that 48-hour exposures at 24°C of 11,000 oyster eggs per liter and 6,000 12-day-old larvae per liter, in sea water with concentrations of rhodamine WT ranging from 1 μg/l to 10 mg/l, resulted in development of the eggs to normal straight-hinge larvae and no abnormalities in the larvae development. Tests made on the smolt of both silver salmon and Donaldson trout, with the fish held for 17.5 hours in a tankfull of sea water with a dye concentration of 10 mg/l at 22°C showed no mortalities or respiratory problems. With the concentration increased to 375 mg/l, and the time extended an additional 3.2 hours, still no mortalities or abnormalities were noted. The fish remained healthy in dye-free water when last checked a month after the test.

The Lummi Indian Tribe near Bellingham, Wash., is engaged in an aquaculture program that includes the propagation and sale of silver salmon, Donaldson and steelhead trout, and oysters. In cooperation with the Lummi Indian Tribal Council, the U.S. Geological Survey is conducting an evaluation of the water resources of the Lummi Indian Reservation, and part of this program required the use of rhodamine WT dye as a tracer in both the fresh- and salt-water environments.

Earlier tests using rhodamine B (Panciera, 1967) have shown that dye in concentrations greater than 1 mg/l is deleterious to oyster larvae and eggs. Marie Panciera, at the U.S. Bureau of Commercial Fisheries Biological Laboratory, Milford, Conn., found that eggs of *Crassostrea virginica* exposed to 100 mg/l dye concentrations for 48 hours did not develop and larvae that were exposed died within 2 days. In dye concentrations of 10 mg/l there was some development to the straight-hinge stage, but 27 percent of the individuals were abnormal. Development in concentrations of 1 mg/l or lower was comparable to that in control cultures.

Because of the similarity of rhodamine B to rhodamine WT, and the possibility that dye concentrations as high as 1 mg/l might reach some of the oysters and fish in the 750-acre aquaculture pond, tests were made of the effects of rhodamine WT dye on this marine life.

In cooperation with Dr. Wallace Heath, technical director of the Lummi Indian acquaculture program, and Richard L. Poole, director of oyster research, the eggs and 12-day-old larvae of the Pacific oyster *(Crassostrea gigas)* were exposed for 48 hours in water at 24°C with rhodamine WT dye concentrations that ranged from 1 μg/l to 10 mg/l. All the water used was taken from the 750-acre aquaculture pond which receives marine water directly from the Strait of Georgia. The average concentration of the eggs tested was 11,000 per liter, and the average concentration of the larvae was 6,000 per liter. The results of all the tests were comparable to those of the control cultures. All eggs tested developed to straight-hinge larvae with no abnormalities, and all the 12-day-old larvae survived with no abnormalities.

An additional test was made on smolt (4–6 inches long) of both silver salmon and Donaldson trout. Eight salmon and eight trout were held in a tank of water from the aquaculture pond with a concentration of 10 mg/l of rhodamine WT dye. The fish were held in this tank for 17.5 hours with water at 22°C. No mortalities or respiratory problems were noted, and the fish appeared similar in behavior to those in the control tank. The dye concentration in the test tank was then increased to 375 mg/l for an additional 3.2 hours. Again, no mortalities or other problems were observed. The fish tested remained healthy in dye-free water when last checked approximately 1 month after the test.

REFERENCE CITED

Panciera, Maria, 1967, The toxicity of rhodamine-B to eggs and larvae of *Crassostrea virginica*: Natl. Shellfisheries Assoc. Proc., v. 58, p. 7–8.

RECENT PUBLICATIONS OF THE U.S. GEOLOGICAL SURVEY

(Books may be ordered from the Superintendent of Documents, Government Printing Office, Washington, D.C., 20402, to whom remittances should be sent by check or money order. Give title, series No., stock No. (shown in parentheses in this list), and catalog No. [shown in brackets])

Professional Papers

313-F. Geology and phosphate deposits of the Permian rocks in central western Montana, by R. W. Swanson. 1973. p. 779–833; plates in pocket. $2.35. (2401-2201) [I 19:16:313-F]

386-D. Disposal of uranium-mill effluent by well injection in the Grants area, Valencia County, N. Mex., by S. W. West. 1972 (1973). p. D1–D28; plates in pocket. $1.55. (2401-2160) [I 19:16:386-D]

486-J. Geohydrology of the Needles area, Arizona, California, and Nevada, by D. G. Metzger and O. J. Loeltz. 1973. p. J1–J54; plates in pocket. $1.75. (2401-02212) [I 19:16:486-J]

646-C. Gravity, magnetics, and geology of the San Andreas fault area near Cholame, Calif., by W. F. Hanna, S. H. Burch, and T. W. Dibblee, Jr. 1972 (1973). p. C1–C29; plates in pocket. $3.05. (2401-2170) [I 19:16:646-C]

663-B. Structural geology of the Sun River Canyon and adjacent areas, northwestern Montana, by M. R. Mudge. 1972 (1973). p. B1–B52; plates in pocket. $4. (2401-2080) [I 19:16:663-B]

675. Landslides in the vicinity of the Fort Randall Reservoir, S. Dak., by C. F. Erskine. 1973. 64 p.; plates in pocket. $3.75. (2401-2200) [I 19:16:675]

740. Paleozoic and Precambrian rocks of Alaska and their role in its structural evolution, by Michael Churkin, Jr. 1973. 64 p. 90¢. (2401-00272) [I 19:16:740]

743-B. Stratigraphic distribution of significant Eocene palynomorphs of the Mississippi embayment, by R. H. Tschudy. 1973. p. B1–B24; 4 plates showing fossils. 75¢. (2401-00271) [I 19:16:743-B]

754-A. Glacial and postglacial geologic history of Isle Royale National Park, Mich., by N. K. Huber. 1973. p. A1–A15; plate in pocket. $1. (2401-02209) [I 19:16:754-A]

754-B. The Copper Harbor Conglomerate (middle Keweenawan) on Isle Royale, Mich., and its regional implications, by R. G. Wolff and N. K. Huber. 1973. p. B1–B15; plate in pocket. 95¢. (2401-00289) [I 19:16:754-B]

759-A. High-resolution seismic survey of an offshore area near Nome, Alaska, by A. R. Tagg and H. G. Greene. 1973. p. A1–A23. 60¢. (2401-00288) [I 19:16:759-A]

765. Geology of the oxidized uranium ore deposits of the Tordilla Hill-Deweesville area, Karnes County, Tex.; A study of a district before mining, by C. M. Bunker and J. A. MacKallor. 1973. 37 p.; plate in pocket. $1.25. (2401-00292) [I 19:16:765]

774-A. Reconnaissance geology of the northern Yukon-Koyukuk province, Alaska, by W. W. Patton, Jr. 1973. p. A1–A17. 40¢. (2401-00299) [I 19:16:774-A]

789. Geochemistry of lower Eocene sandstones in the Rocky Mountain region, by J. D. Vine and E. B. Tourtelot, *with a section on* Direct-reader spectrometric analyses, by R. G. Havens and A. T. Myers. 1973. 36 p. 75¢. (2401-00275) [I 19:16:789]

Bulletins

1258-E. A new method for the determination of three-dimensional deformation anisotropy in rock specimens, by R. A. Farrow. 1973. p. E1–E12. 25¢. (2401-00269) [I 19:3:1258-E]

1265. Ancient lavas in Shenandoah National Park near Luray, Va., by J. C. Reed, Jr. 1969. 43 p.; plate in pocket. $1.25. (Reprinted 1973).

1332-A. A preliminary report on the geology and gold deposits of the Rochford district, Black Hills, S. Dak., by R. W. Bayley. 1972 (1973). p. A1–A24; plates in pocket. $2. (2401-2173) [I 19:3:1332-A]

1346. Bedrock geology of the Cupsuptic and Arnold Pond quadrangles, west-central Maine, by D. S. Harwood. 1973. 90 p.; plates in pocket. $2.60. (2401-02205) [I 19:3:1346]

1349. General geology of the Hahns Peak and Farwell Mountain quadrangles, Routt County, Colo., by Kenneth Segerstrom and E. J. Young, *with a discussion of* Upper Triassic and pre-Morrison Jurassic rocks, by G. N. Pipiringos. 1972 (1973). 63 p.; plate in pocket. $1.25. (2401-2172) [I 19:3:1349]

1351. Geology and description of the thorium-bearing veins, Lemhi Pass quadrangle, Idaho and Montana, by M. H. Staatz. 1972 (1973). 94 p., plate in pocket. $3.75. (2401-02207) [I 19:3:1351]

1357. Placer gold deposits of Utah, by M. G. Johnson. 1973. 26 p.; plate in pocket. $1.25. (2401-00264) [I 19:3:1357]

1361. An integrated system of geologic mapping and geochemical sampling by light aircraft, by C. L. Sainsbury, K. J. Curry, and J. C. Hamilton. 1973. 28 p.; plates in pocket. 90¢. (2401-00265) [I 19:3:1361]

1369. Stratigraphy of the Washakie Formation in the Washakie Basin, Wyo., by H. W. Roehler. 1973. 40 p.; plates in pocket. 90¢. (2401-00286) [I 19:3:1369]

1371. Studies related to wilderness–primitive areas, 1972. Title page and contents for volume (published as separate chapters A–C). Free on application to the Geological Survey.

1372-D. The McHugh Complex of south-central Alaska, by S. H. B. Clark. 1973. p. D1–D10. 20¢. (2401-00273) [I 19:3:1372-D]

1372-G. The Lower Cretaceous Figuera Lava and Fajardo Formation in the stratigraphy of northeastern Puerto Rico, by R. P. Briggs. p. G1–G10. 20¢. (2401-00319) [I 19:3:1372-G]

1378. Geochemical prospecting using water from small streams in central South Carolina, by Henry Bell, III, and G. E. Siple. 1973. 26 p.; plates in pocket. $1.15. (2401-00313) [I 19:3:1378]

1379. Radiometric ages of igneous rocks from Pima, Santa Cruz, and Cochise Counties, southeastern Arizona, by R. F. Marvin, T. W. Stern, S. C. Creasey, and H. H. Mehnert. 1973. 27 p. 35¢. (2401-00283) [I 19:3:1379]

1383-A. Pine Creek volcanic assemblage at Mount St. Helens, Wash., by D. R. Crandell and D. R. Mullineaux. 1973. p. A1–A23. 40¢. (Geology of Mount St. Helens volcano, Washington.) (2401-00318) [I 19:3:1383-A]

Water-Supply Papers

1827-E. Chemical interactions of aluminum with aqueous silica at 25°C, by J. D. Hem, C. E. Roberson, C. J. Lind, and W. L. Polzer. 1973. p. E1–E57. 70¢. (2401-00229) [I 19:13:1827-E]

1998. Water resources of Hempstead, Lafayette, Little River, Miller, and Nevada Counties, Ark., by A. H. Ludwig. 1972 (1973). 41 p.; text and plates in case. $4. (2401-00215) [I 19:13:1998]

2009-C. Chemical quality of surface water in the Flaming Gorge Reservoir area, Wyoming and Utah, by R. J. Madison and K. M. Waddell. 1973. p. C1–C18; plate in pocket. 65¢. (2401-00266) [I 19:13:2009-C]

2009-D. Appraisal of ground water for irrigation in the Little Falls area, Morrison County, Minn., by J. O. Helgesen. 1973. p. D1–D40; plate in pocket. $1.25. (2401-00270) [I 19:13:2009-D]

U.S. GOVERNMENT
PRINTING OFFICE
PUBLIC DOCUMENTS DEPARTMENT
WASHINGTON, D.C. 20402
OFFICIAL BUSINESS
PENALTY FOR PRIVATE USE $300

POSTAGE AND FEES PAID
U.S. GOVERNMENT
PRINTING OFFICE
375

U.S.MAIL

JRGS HARTWOOOH R I
HARTWICK CLG LIB
ONEONTA NY 13820

JOURNAL OF RESEARCH

OF THE U.S. GEOLOGICAL SURVEY

SEPTEMBER–OCTOBER 1973
VOLUME 1, NUMBER 5

Scientific notes and summaries of investigations in geology, hydrology, and related fields

U.S. DEPARTMENT OF THE INTERIOR

UNITED STATES DEPARTMENT OF THE INTERIOR

ROGERS C. B. MORTON, Secretary

GEOLOGICAL SURVEY

V. E. McKelvey, Director

For sale by the Superintendent of Documents, U.S. Government Printing Office, Washington, D.C., 20402. Order by SD Catalog No. JRGS. Annual subscription rate, effective July 1, 1973, $15.50 (plus $3.75 for foreign mailing). Single copy $2.75. Make checks or money orders payable to the Superintendent of Documents.

Send all subscription inquiries and address changes to the Superintendent of Documents at the above address.

Purchase orders should not be sent to the U.S. Geological Survey library.

Library of Congress Card No. 72-600241

The Journal of Research consists of six issues a year (January-February, March-April, May-June, July-August, September-October, November-December) published in Washington, D.C., by the U.S. Geological Survey. It contains papers by members of the Geological Survey on geologic, hydrologic, topographic, and other scientific and technical subjects.

The Journal supersedes the short-papers chapters (B, C, and D) of the former Geological Survey Research ("Annual Review") series of professional papers. The synopsis chapter (A) of the former Geological Survey Research series will be published as a separate professional paper each year.

Correspondence and inquiries concerning the Journal (other than subscription inquiries and address changes) should be directed to the Managing Editor, Journal of Research, Publications Division, U.S. Geological Survey, Washington, D.C. 20244.

Papers for the Journal should be submitted through regular Division publication channels.

The Secretary of the Interior has determined that the publication of this periodical is necessary in the transaction of the public business required by law of this Department. Use of funds for printing this periodical has been approved by the Director of the Office of Management and Budget through February 11, 1975.

GEOGRAPHIC INDEX TO ARTICLES

[See Contents for articles concerning areas outside the United States and articles without geographic orientation]

JOURNAL OF RESEARCH

of the

U.S. Geological Survey

Vol. 1 No. 5 Sept.-Oct. 1973

CONTENTS

Abbreviations and symbols II

GEOLOGIC STUDIES

Permian paleogeography of the Arctic .... *J. T. Dutro, Jr., and R. B. Saldukas* 501

Pliocene marine fossils in the Paso Robles Formation, California .... *W. O. Addicott and J. S. Galehouse* 509

Galkhaite, (Hg,Cu,Tl,Zn) $(As,Sb)S_2$, from the Getchell mine, Humboldt County, Nev. .... *Theodore Botinelly, G. J. Neuerburg, and N. M. Conklin* 515

Disseminated pyrite in a latite porphyry at Texan Mountain, Hudspeth County, Tex. .... *T. E. Mullens* 519

Soda Creek springs—Metamorphic waters in the eastern Alaska Range .... *D. H. Richter, R. A. Lamarre, and D. E. Donaldson* 523

The Dun Mountain ultramafic belt—Permian oceanic crust and upper mantle in New Zealand .... *M. C. Blake, Jr., and C. A. Landis* 529

A calorimetric determination of the standard enthalpies of formation of huntite, $CaMg_3(CO_3)_4$, and artinite, $Mg_2(OH)_2CO_3 \cdot 3H_2O$, and their standard Gibbs free energies of formation .... *B. S. Hemingway and R. A. Robie* 535

The enthalpies of formation of nesquehonite, $MgCO_3 \cdot 3H_2O$, and hydromagnesite, $5MgO \cdot 4CO_2 \cdot 5H_2O$ .... *R. A. Robie and B. S. Hemingway* 543

Chemical analysis of rutile—A pyrocatechol violet spectrophotometric procedure for the direct microdetermination of zirconium .... *Robert Meyrowitz* 549

Spectrophotometric determination of tungsten in rocks by an isotope dilution procedure .... *E. G. Lillie and L. P. Greenland* 555

Spectrochemical computer analysis—Argon-oxygen d-c arc method for silicate rocks .... *A. F. Dorrzapf, Jr.* 559

Bathymetry of the continental margin off Liberia, West Africa .... *J. M. Robb, John Schlee, and J. C. Behrendt* 563

An accurate Invar-wire extensometer .... *W. A. Duffield and R. O. Burford* 569

Use of machine-processable field notes in a wilderness mapping project (Granite Fiords area), southeastern Alaska .... *J. G. Smith and H. C. Berg* 579

Ice ages and the thermal equilibrium of the earth .... *D. P. Adam* 587

HYDROLOGIC STUDIES

Aquifer diffusivity of the Ohio River alluvial aquifer by the flood-wave response method .... *H. F. Grubb and H. H. Zehner* 597

A study of the distribution of polychlorinated biphenyls in the aquatic environment .... *H. J. Crump-Wiesner, H. R. Feltz, and M. L. Yates* 603

Remote sensing of turbidity plumes in Lake Ontario .... *E. J. Pluhowski* 609

Method for estimating the diversion potential of streams in eastern Massachusetts and southern Rhode Island .... *G. D. Tasker* 615

Changes in floodflow characteristics of a rectified channel caused by vegetation, Jackson, Miss. .... *K. V. Wilson* 621

Recent publications of the U.S. Geological Survey .... Inside of back cover

ABBREVIATIONS AND SYMBOLS

[Singular and plural forms for abbreviations of units of measure are the same]

A . . . . angstrom units
A^3 . . . . cubic angstroms
a-c . . . . alternating current
amp . . . . amperes
atm . . . . atmospheres
bbl . . . . barrels
B.C. . . . . Before Christ
B.P. . . . . Before Present
b.y. . . . . billion years
c . . . . crystalline state
C_x . . . . molal concentration (of substance x)
cal . . . . calories
cfs . . . . cubic feet per second
Ci . . . . Curies
cm . . . . centimeters
cm^2 . . . . square centimeters
cm^3 . . . . cubic centimeters
cpm . . . . counts per minute
cu ft . . . . cubic feet
cu mi . . . . cubic miles
d-c . . . . direct current
emu . . . . electromagnetic units
eV . . . . electron volts
fpm . . . . feet per minute
ft . . . . feet
ft^3 . . . . cubic feet
g . . . . grams
gal . . . . gallons
gpd . . . . gallons per day
gpm . . . . gallons per minute
hr . . . . hours
Hz . . . . hertz (cycles per second)
in. . . . . inches
kb . . . . kilobars
kg . . . . kilograms
km . . . . kilometers
km^2 . . . . square kilometers
km^3 . . . . cubic kilometers
kV . . . . kilovolts
l . . . . liters
lb . . . . pounds
ln . . . . logarithm (natural)
m . . . . meters
m . . . . molal (concentration)
m^2 . . . . square meters
m^3 . . . . cubic meters
M . . . . molar (concentration)
me . . . . milliequivalents
MeV . . . . million electron volts
mg . . . . milligrams
mgd . . . . million gallons per day
mi^2 . . . . square miles
min . . . . minutes
ml . . . . milliliters
mm . . . . millimeters
mol . . . . moles
mr . . . . milliroentgens
mV . . . . millivolts
m.y. . . . . million years
μ . . . . microns
μm . . . . micrometers
μmho . . . . micromhos
n . . . . neutrons
N . . . . normal
ng . . . . nanograms
nm . . . . nanometers
Oe . . . . oersteds
pCi . . . . picocuries
P.d.t. . . . . Pacific daylight time
pH . . . . pH (measure of hydrogen ion activity)
ppb . . . . parts per billion
ppm . . . . parts per million
rad . . . . radiometric
rpm . . . . revolutions per minute
sec . . . . seconds
sq ft . . . . square feet
sq mi . . . . square miles
v . . . . volts
wt . . . . weight
yr . . . . years

Jour. Research U.S. Geol. Survey
Vol. 1, No. 5, Sept.-Oct. 1973, p. 501—507

PERMIAN PALEOGEOGRAPHY OF THE ARCTIC

By J. THOMAS DUTRO, JR., and R. BIRUTE SALDUKAS, Washington, D.C.

Abstract.—Three large land areas were dominant in the Arctic during the Permian: Fennoscandia, central and southern Siberia (Angara), and Canada. Smaller landmasses were in China, the Seward-Chukotskiy region, northern and eastern Siberia, and near Alaska. Coal deposits and strata bearing land plants covered a large area in central Siberia; saline basins containing red beds formed in the Zechstein, Perm, and West Texas basins as the seas withdrew, generally in the later Permian. Eugeosynclinal troughs, apparently limited to the Pacific border regions, were marked by volcanism and deposition of predominantly clastic sediments in many areas. Platform and miogeosynclinal deposits, dominated by carbonate rocks, preceded saline deposition in the basins and persisted on shallow shelves adjacent to the geosynclines. The Arctic Permian marine fauna evolved in middle Permian time because of partial isolation of the Arctic areas from the southern ocean. Endemism, latitudinal temperature controls, and the effect of ocean currents explain in large part the faunal patterns in Permian seas. Post-Permian tectonic movements account for anomalies in the present positions of some rock sequences and fossils. Northeasterly drift and counterclockwise rotation of the northern landmasses are suggested. Right-lateral shear along the southern edge of Asia is supported, followed by northward movement of peninsular India.

The Arctic seas in the Permian, particularly during the later Permian, harbored a marine invertebrate fauna that was impoverished as to variety of phyla and number of species. This Arctic Permian assemblage has been the subject of several comprehensive taxonomic papers since elements of the brachiopod fauna were first described by de Koninck (1847). Chief among these are Gobbett's (1963) description of brachiopods from Svalbard (Spitsbergen); Harker and Thorsteinsson's (1960) paper on the Permian of Grinnell Peninsula in the Canadian Arctic Islands; Dunbar's (1955) monograph of the central East Greenland brachiopods; Likharev and Einor's (1939) description of Novaya Zemlya faunas; Stepanov's (1936, 1937) papers on the Svalbard brachiopods; Zavodovskiy and others' (1970) atlas of northeastern U.S.S.R.; Stehli and Grant (1971) on Axel Heiberg Island; Grant's description of brachiopods from the Tahkandit Limestone, Alaska (in Brabb and Grant, 1971), and Waterhouse's description of brachiopods from the Yukon Territory (in Bamber and Waterhouse, 1971).

In attempting to understand the relationships of the Permian brachiopods in Arctic Alaska, Dutro (1961) proposed a correlation of Arctic Permian strata and has continued to investigate the significance of these faunas in a paleogeographic setting.

With the publication of the excellent paleotectonic maps of the Permian of the United States (McKee and others, 1967), followed by the magnificent Russian paleogeographical atlas (Nalivkin and Posner, 1969), much of the basic material for a more general synthesis of Permian paleogeography for the Northern Hemisphere became available.

We have prepared two paleogeographic maps (figs. 1, 2) on a polar projection which serve as a basis for interpretation of terrestrial and marine faunal and floral distributions at two time intervals during the Permian. The maps show the general distribution of land and sea and major lithofacies relative to present geography. They do not show the original positions of land and sea in the Permian or the relative amounts of different lithofacies or sources of clastic sediments; nor are they designed to depict drift, rotation, or other movement of continental masses (or plates), although some of these activities can be inferred (fig. 3).

Two segments of time were selected for the maps. Figure 1 depicts the Leonardian-Artinskian time and figure 2, Word-Kazanian time. Figure 1 was prepared to provide a basis for understanding the changes that occurred in the landscape during late Early Permian time. Figure 2 provides a geographic base for the biogeography shown in figure 3.

Figure 3 shows the distribution of selected elements of the biota for Word-Kazanian time. Generalized distributions of floras have been drawn from several sources but are chiefly modifications of syntheses by Andrews and Felix (1961) and by Radforth (1966). Vertebrate data were taken mostly from Olson's (1962) work.

Two major elements of the marine fauna, brachiopods and verbeekinids, are depicted on figure 3. The brachiopods were analyzed by comparing the assemblage at various localities with that of Svalbard. Twenty-five species or species groups were selected as indicators of the Arctic Permian fauna. All of them occur in Svalbard. Using a modification of the Simpson coefficient technique (Simpson, 1960), other localities were found to include varying percentages of these indicators. The results have been plotted and contoured to give an impression of the degree of relatedness to Svalbard. Distribution of later

Figure 1.–Paleogeographic map of the Northern Hemisphere during Leonardian-Artinskian time. Polar projection, scale approximately 1:67,000,000 at lat 40° N.

Figure 2.—Paleogeographic map of the Northern Hemisphere during Word-Kazanian time. Polar projection, scale approximately 1:67,000,000 at lat 40° N.

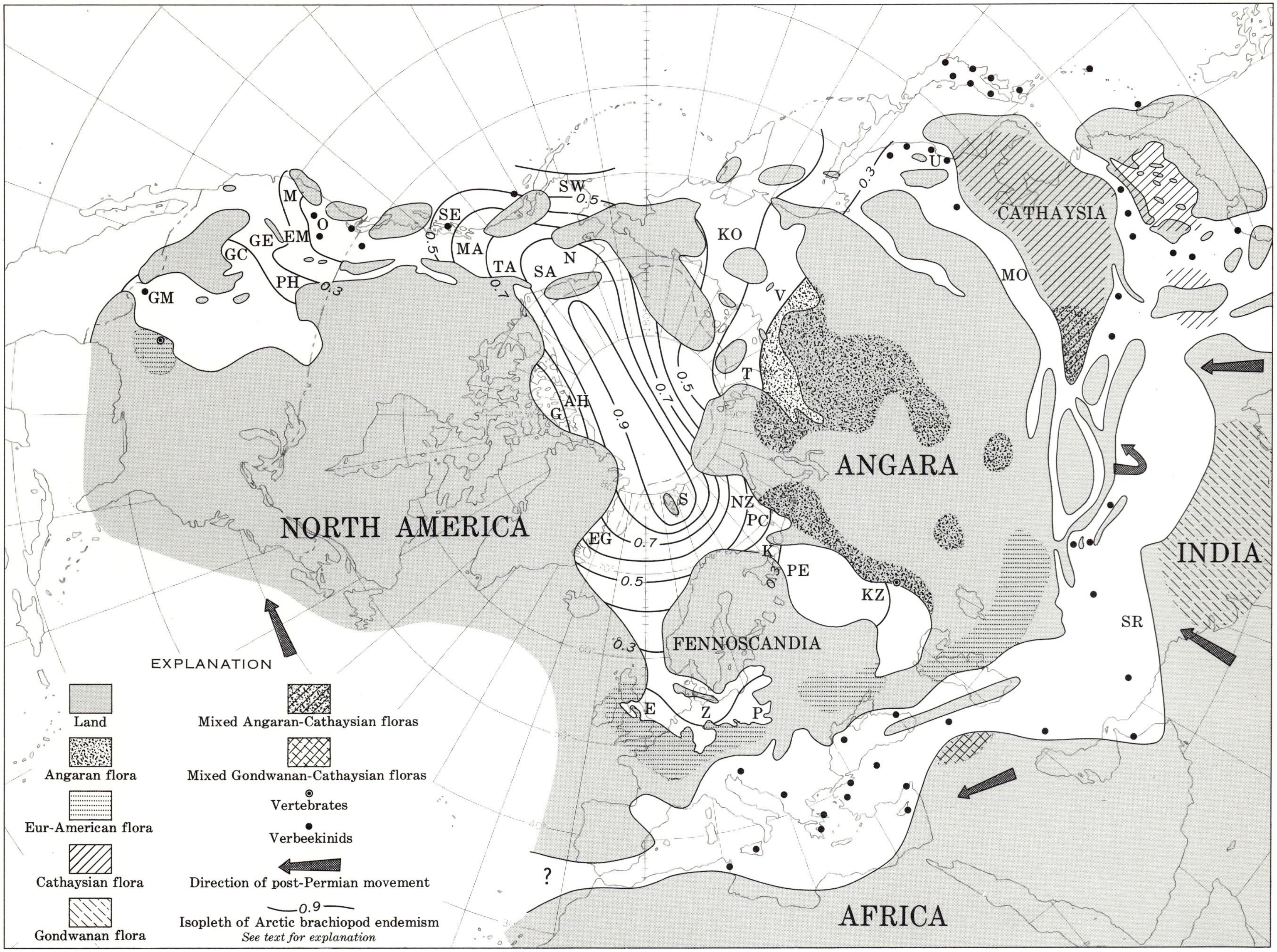

Figure 3.—Paleobiogeographic map of the Northern Hemisphere during Word-Kazanian time. Polar projection, scale approximately 1:67,000,000 at lat 40° N. AH, Axel Heiberg Island; E, England; EG, East Greenland; EM, Edna Mountain Formation; G, Grinnell Peninsula; GC, Grand Canyon region; GE, Gerster Formation; GM, Glass Mountains; K, Kanin Peninsula; KO, Kolyma basin; KZ, Kazan region; M, McCloud Limestone; MA, Mankomen Formation; MO, Mongolia; N, Nuka Formation; NZ, Novaya Zemlya; O, Oregon; P, Poland; PC, Pai-Choi Range; PE, Pechora basin; PH, Phosphoria Formation; S, Svalbard; SA, Sadlerochit Formation; SE, Southeast Alaska; SR, Salt Range; SW, Southwest Alaska; T, Taimyr Peninsula; TA, Tahkandit Limestone; U, Ussuri Valley; V, Verkhoyansk Range; Z, Zechstein basin.

Permian verbeekinid fusulinids (modified from Gobbett, 1967) shows a predominantly Tethyan pattern. Occurrences of these forms in western North America and the western Tethys area are attributed to distribution by currents from a possible center of dispersal in the east China-Japan region.

ANALYSIS OF RESULTS

Some of the major features of the Permian geography appear to be:

1. In the Carboniferous and Early Permian, North America and Laurasia were separated by a marine connection through the Russian Perm basin, which provided free exchange of marine faunas from the Tethys to the Arctic; in the latter part of the Permian, they were parts of a single large landmass.
2. The Perm basin was cut off from the Tethys by a land connection across its southern end during the late Early Permian (Kungurian).
3. Three major sites of evaporite and red bed deposition were the Perm, Zechstein, and West Texas basins.
4. Areas of coal swamp and coal deposits were the eastern United States (in the Early Permian), northern Siberia, and China.
5. A major volcanic region and, presumably, eugeosynclinal area bordered the ancient North Pacific. In the later Permian, the only connection between the world ocean and the Arctic basin was through straits between islands in the North Pacific.

THE ARCTIC PERMIAN MARINE FAUNA

The aspect of the Permian Arctic fauna that has intrigued paleontologists for a century is its domination by certain kinds of brachiopods and the virtual absence of other groups of animals. A few corals, bryozoans, and mollusks occur with the brachiopods; presence of echinoderm debris and sponge spicules indicates relative abundance of these phyla, but whole-body fossils are rare.

Among the brachiopods, a great many genera common in the tropical seas are absent; most of the assemblage can be accounted for in about 30 or 40 genera, and the characteristic forms number only about two dozen. The following species or species groups were selected for calculating the endemic ratios for the Arctic localities: *Arctitreta kempei* (Andersson), *Derbyia* cf. *D. grandis* Waagen, *Anemonaria pseudohorrida* (Wiman), *Waagenoconcha irginae* (Stuckenberg), *Kochiproductus porrectus* (Kutorga), *Thamnosia arctica* (Whitfield), *Horridonia timanica* (Toula), *Globiella* cf. *G. simensis* (Tschernyschew), *Cancrinella spitzbergiana* Gobbett, *Anidanthus aagardi* (Toula), *Kuvelousia weyprechti* (Toula), *Yakovlevia mammata* (Keyserling), *Lissochonetes spitzbergianus* (Toula), *Chonetina superba* Gobbett, *Septacamera* cf. *S. kutorgae* (Tschernyschew), *Stenocisma spitzbergiana* (Stepanov), *Rhynchopora nikitini* Tschernyschew, *Neospirifer striatoparadoxus* (Toula), *Licharewia spitzbergiana* Gobbett, *Pterospirifer alatus* (Schlotheim), *Spiriferella keilhavii* (von Buch), *Permophricadothyris asiatica* (Chao), *Martinia* sp., *Cleiothyridina royssiana* (Keyserling), *Pseudosyrinx wimani* Gobbett, and *Dielasma plica* (Kutorga).

Significant absentees from the Arctic assemblage are members of the reef-associated productoid genera, including the leptodids, richthofenids, aulostegids, and scacchinellids. Also notable is the lack of diversity in the Arctic among the spiriferoids, rhynchonelloids, and terebratuloids that one finds at most tropical and subtropical localities. Stehli (1971) has analyzed the differences between Tethyan and Boreal brachiopod facies at the family level and has concluded that the latter is completely dependent on cosmopolitan families. This reflects, in our view, an inheritance from the Carboniferous, early in the Permian when the Tethys was freely connected with the Arctic through a Uralian seaway.

At the species-group or species level, however, endemism developed in the Boreal region after the connection with the southern ocean was closed off late in the early part of the Permian. The calculated endemic ratios, showing relationships to the Svalbard fauna taken as unity, drop off regularly away from the Boreal region toward the presumed paleoequator (fig. 3). Approximately one-fifth of the taxa used in the analysis occur at most Tethyan stations, and this residue is considered to represent cosmopolitanism at the subgeneric level.

That apparent endemism and cosmpolitanism are inversely related when lower taxonomic levels are considered is not unexpected. In searching for an analog with which to compare the Boreal Permian brachiopod fauna, the molluscan distribution in restricted seas (Black Sea, Caspian Sea) comes first to mind. Runnegar and Newell (1971) have used these models to explain the Permian molluscan fauna of the Paraná basin. It seems reasonable to assume that relatively rapid evolution of marine benthonic bivalved species would take place in a relict sea in which some abnormal environmental factors were present. In the Paraná basin, Black Sea, and Caspian Sea this is probably low salinity. In the paleoarctic of the Permian, it was quite possibly related to temperature, although abnormal salinities may have been a factor in light of the formation of evaporite basins in several regions. Ustritskiy (1972) discussed the climate of the Permian and provided data that suggest that climatic gradients dispersed radially from a cold (glacial) area in north-central Siberia.

TERRESTRIAL FAUNA AND FLORA

Permian terrestrial vertebrates have been described from many places in the Northern Hemisphere, but mostly as isolated occurrences of limited faunas. One of the more comprehensive papers on these forms is Olson's (1962) analysis of north-central Texas and Uralian faunas. He concluded that vertebrates evolved separately in the two regions throughout the Early Permian. In each instance, the pattern of progression is from aquatic to upland forms. Interconnections were established by middle Permian time, however, and several migratory exchanges are postulated to account for relationships between early Late Permian genera in Texas and their Kazanian counterparts in Russia.

Paleobotanists have long considered the Permian floras as constituting four distinct provinces: (1) Eur-American, (2) Angaran, (3) Cathaysian, and (4) Gondwanan (Andrews and Felix, 1961; Radforth, 1966). Distributions of these provinces show clearly the eastward advance of the Eur-American flora into central Asia after the establishment of the land connection across the southern U.S.S.R. Two areas of floral overlap are also indicated, one in China (Angaran-Cathaysian) and one in southeast Turkey (Gondwanan-Cathaysian, see Wagner, 1962). The Gondwanan flora, as such, is found in the Northern Hemisphere only in peninsular India.

BIOGEOGRAPHIC INTERPRETATIONS

Invertebrate faunas in the Arctic inherited their basic character from the late Carboniferous faunas, mainly because a marine connection existed from the southern seas through the Perm basin. This connection was cut off in the latter part of the Early Permian, and the younger Arctic Permian assemblage reflects endemism in the northern ocean (fig. 3).

Low correlations with Svalbard are of two kinds. The presence of only a few hardy species in the Zechstein and Perm embayments undoubtedly reflects rigorous environmental conditions—high salinity—associated with the development of evaporite basins. On the other hand, a regular decrease in correlation southward along the west side of North America and the east side of Asia possibly reflects some latitudinal, perhaps temperature, factor.

Conversely, the Eur-American flora and terrestrial vertebrates evolved separately through the Early Permian but extended their ranges eastward across the land area that was formed in the southern U.S.S.R. toward the middle of the period.

Overlap of Angaran and Cathaysian floras is explained by proximity. Assumed paleowind directions would have assisted this mixing process. The seemingly anomalous flora in Turkey can be explained by large-scale tectonic activity since the Permian, as can the position of peninsular India.

TECTONIC IMPLICATIONS

The maps show rather clearly that the major land areas of the Northern Hemisphere during the middle and later Permian were part of a single large continent. The distribution of the Eur-American flora certainly implies that no Atlantic Ocean existed at that time. Land in the Southern Hemisphere seems to have been consolidated into a large but separate Gondwanan continent. A marine connection through southern Asia and the Mediterranean (pre-Tethys) best accounts for faunal relationships in the Permian oceans.

A volcanic belt paralleling the present north Pacific coast probably was the site of eugeosynclincal deposition. Rather narrow continental shelves extended southward from Alaska toward both China and the southwestern United States.

Most recent analyses of evaporite deposition conclude that major basins formed within an area extending from about lat 30° N. to 30° S., in locations far south of the present positions of the West Texas, Zechstein, and Perm basins. Consequently, significant post-Permian plate movements must have taken place.

The northern continent may have started to break up by northeastward movement accompanied by counterclockwise rotation of the three core areas—North America, Fennoscandia, and Angara (see Briden, 1968). This movement need not have been uniform, and there is reason to believe that each block moved at a different rate. After the mid-Atlantic ridge area became active, perhaps in the Jurassic, North America could have begun its westward drift, a late phase of its counterclockwise movement.

In the tropical latitudes, floral distributions suggest that great lateral motions took place. The presence of the mixed Gondwanan-Cathaysian flora in Turkey can be explained by westward shift through nearly 40° of longitude. This is about the amount of lateral shear postulated on geomagnetic grounds by Irving (1967).

A later movement of India northward from Gondwana would account for its anomalous present position both geologically and biogeographically (fig. 3). The peculiar attenuated peninsulas and islands in what is now the Himalaya region also seem to reflect this northward drift.

REFERENCES CITED

Andrews, H. N., Jr., and Felix, C. I., 1961, Studies in paleobotany: New York, John Wiley and Sons, 487 p.

Bamber, E. W., and Waterhouse, J. B., 1971, Carboniferous and Permian stratigraphy and paleontology, northern Yukon Territory, Canada: Bull. Canadian Petroleum Geology, v. 19, no. 1, p. 29–250, 27 pls., 19 figs.

Brabb, E. E., and Grant, R. E., 1971, Stratigraphy and paleontology of the revised type section for the Tahkandit Limestone (Permian) in east-central Alaska: U.S. Geol. Survey Prof. Paper 703, 26 p., 2 pls., 11 figs.

Briden, J. C., 1968, Paleoclimatic evidence of a geocentric axial dipole field, *in* Phinney, R. A., ed., The history of the earth's crust, a symposium: Princeton, N.J., Princeton Univ. Press, p. 178–194.

Dunbar, C. O., 1955, Permian brachiopod faunas of central East Greenland: Medd. Grönland, v. 110, no. 3, 169 p., 32 pls.

Dutro, J. T., Jr., 1961, Correlation of the Arctic Permian: Art. 231 *in* U.S. Geol. Survey Prof. Paper 424-C, p. C225–C228.

Gobbett, D. J., 1963, Carboniferous and Permian brachiopods of Svalbard: Norsk Polarinst. Skr., no. 127, 201 p., 25 pls.

——1967, Palaeozoogeography of the Verbeekinidae (Permian Foraminifera), *in* Adams, C. G., and Ager, D. V., eds., Aspects of Tethyan biogeography—a symposium: Systematics Assoc. Pub. 7, p. 77–91.

Harker, Peter, and Thorsteinsson, Raymond, 1960, Permian rocks and faunas of Grinnell Peninsula, Arctic Archipelago: Canada Geol. Survey Mem. 309, 146 p.

Irving, E., 1967, Paleomagnetic evidence for shear along the Tethys, *in* Adams, G. C., and Ager, D. V., eds., Aspects of Tethyan biogeography—a symposium: Systematics Assoc. Pub. 7, p. 59–76.

Koninck, L. de, 1847, Recherches sur les animaux fossiles—Pt. 1. Monographie des genres *Productus* et *Chonetes*: Liège, H. Dessain, 246 p., 20 pls.

Likharev, B. K., and Einor, O. L., 1939, [Paleontology of the Soviet Arctic, Pt. IV; Contributions to the knowledge of the upper Palaeozoic fauna of Novaya Zemlya, Brachiopoda]: Arctic Institute [U.S.S.R.] Trans., v. 127, 245 p., 28 pls. [In Russian].

McKee, E. D., Oriel, S. S., and others, 1967, Paleotectonic maps of the Permian System: U.S. Geol. Survey Misc. Geol. Inv. Map. I-450, 164 p., 20 pls., 12 figs.

Nalivkin, V. D., and Posner, V. M., eds., 1969, Devonskiy, Kamennougol'nyy i Permskiy periody [Devonian, Carboniferous, and Permian], v. 2 *of* Vinogradov, A. P., ed.-in-chief, Atlas litologo-paleogeographeskikh kart SSSR [Atlas of lithological-paleogeographical maps of the U.S.S.R.]: Moscow, Ministerstvo Geologii-Akad. Nauk SSSR, 65 pls.

Olson, E. C., 1962, Late Permian terrestrial vertebrates, U.S.A. and U.S.S.R.: Am. Philos. Soc. Trans., 1962, v. 52, pt. 2, 224 p.

Radforth, N. W., 1966, The ancient flora and continental drift, *in* Garland, G. D., ed., Continental drift: Royal Soc. Canada Spec. Pub. 9, p. 53–70.

Runnegar, Bruce, and Newell, N. D., 1971, Caspian-like relict molluscan fauna in the South American Permian: Am. Mus. Nat. History Bull., v. 146, art. 1, 66 p.

Simpson, G. G., 1960, Notes on the measurement of faunal resemblance: Am. Jour. Sci. (Bradley Volume), v. 258-A, p. 300–311.

Stehli, F. G., 1971, Tethyan and Boreal Permian faunas and their significance, *in* Dutro, J. T., Jr., ed., Paleozoic perspectives; A paleontological tribute to G. Arthur Cooper: Smithsonian Contr. Paleobiology 3, p. 337–345, 6 figs.

Stehli, F. G., and Grant, R. E., 1971, Permian brachiopods from Axel Heiberg Island, Canada, and an index of sampling efficiency: Jour. Paleontology, v. 45, no. 4, p. 502–521, pls. 61–66, 4 figs

Stepanov, D. L., 1936, [Contribution to the knowledge of the brachiopod fauna of the upper Paleozoic of Spitzbergen]: Leningrad Bubnoff State Univ. Ann., no. 9, Geol. iss., 2, p. 114–128, pls. 1–5 [In Russian].

——1937, [Permian brachiopods of Spitzbergen]: Arctic Inst. [U.S.S.R.] Trans., v. 76, p. 105–192, pls. 1–9 [In Russian].

Ustritskiy, V. I., 1972, The Permian climate (a comparison of paleobiogeographic and paleomagnetic data): Internat. Geology Rev., v. 14, no. 12, p. 1279–1286, 4 figs., table. Originally pub. as: Klimat permi (sopostavleniye paleobiogeograficheskikh i paleomagnitnykh dannykh): Akad. Nauk SSSR Izvest., Ser. Geol., 1972, no. 4, p. 3–12, 4 figs.

Wagner, R. H., 1962, On a mixed Cathaysia and Gondwana flora from SE Anatolia (Turkey): Cong. Avancement Études Stratigraphie et Géologie Carbonifère, 4th, Heerlen, 1958, Compte rendu, v. 3, p. 745–752, pls. 24–28.

Zavodovskiy, V. M. and others, 1970, [Field atlas—Permian fauna and flora of northeastern U.S.S.R.]: Magadan, Ministry Geology, RSFSR, 407 p., 101 pls. [In Russian].

Jour. Research U.S. Geol. Survey
Vol. 1, No. 5, Sept.-Oct. 1973, p. 509—514

PLIOCENE MARINE FOSSILS IN THE PASO ROBLES FORMATION, CALIFORNIA

By WARREN O. ADDICOTT and JON S. GALEHOUSE,[1]
Menlo Park, Calif., San Francisco, Calif.

Abstract.—Marine invertebrates from the Paso Robles Formation recently discovered near Atascadero, Calif., indicate that the basal part of this chiefly nonmarine deposit is of provincial early Pliocene age. Heretofore the lack of direct fossil or radiometric evidence of the age of the Paso Robles has made it a difficult unit to place in the late Cenozoic history of the Coast Ranges. The assemblage is dominated by *Ostrea vespertina* and by *Nettastomella rostrata*, a rock-boring bivalve; its mode of preservation indicates that the fossils are in place and have not been recycled from older marine formations. This occurrence suggests that during the early Pliocene a seaway connected the present southern Salinas Valley area with the northern part of the Santa Maria basin; the fossils occur about halfway between the southernmost exposures of the Pancho Rico Formation near San Miguel and fossiliferous strata east of Pismo Beach, both marine units of early Pliocene age.

The Paso Robles Formation, as originally defined by Fairbanks (1898, 1904), crops out nearly continuously over approximately 1,000 sq mi of the upper Salinas Valley in the southern part of the California Coast Ranges (fig. 1). The formation is mainly a late Cenozoic continental deposit of gravel, sand, silt, and clay. In general, the coarser sand and gravel occur as stream-channel deposits, whereas the finer sand, silt, and clay occur as flood-plain deposits. The Paso Robles has long posed a problem in interpreting the late Cenozoic geologic history of the southern part of the California Coast Ranges because of the lack of direct fossil or radiometric evidence of its age (Galehouse, 1967). Previous age determinations have been based upon such indirect criteria as long-range correlations, stratigraphic relations, and concepts of late Cenozoic diastrophic history.

This report describes the first diagnostic fossils found in the Paso Robles Formation and interprets their age and paleographic significance. It is of interest that they are of marine origin. An assemblage of oysters and other marine invertebrates was discovered in 1971 near the base of the Paso Robles Formation at a locality a few miles east of Atascadero, Calif., during a California State University stratigraphy class field trip led by Galehouse, who hereby thanks the participating students. The locality was subsequently revisited by the authors and D. L. Durham; at that time most of the material described and illustrated in this report was collected.

Acknowledgments.—We wish to acknowledge critical reviews of the manuscript by D. L. Durham, E. W. Hart, and C. A. Repenning. Hart, of the California Division of Mines, kindly made available geologic mapping and stratigraphic data

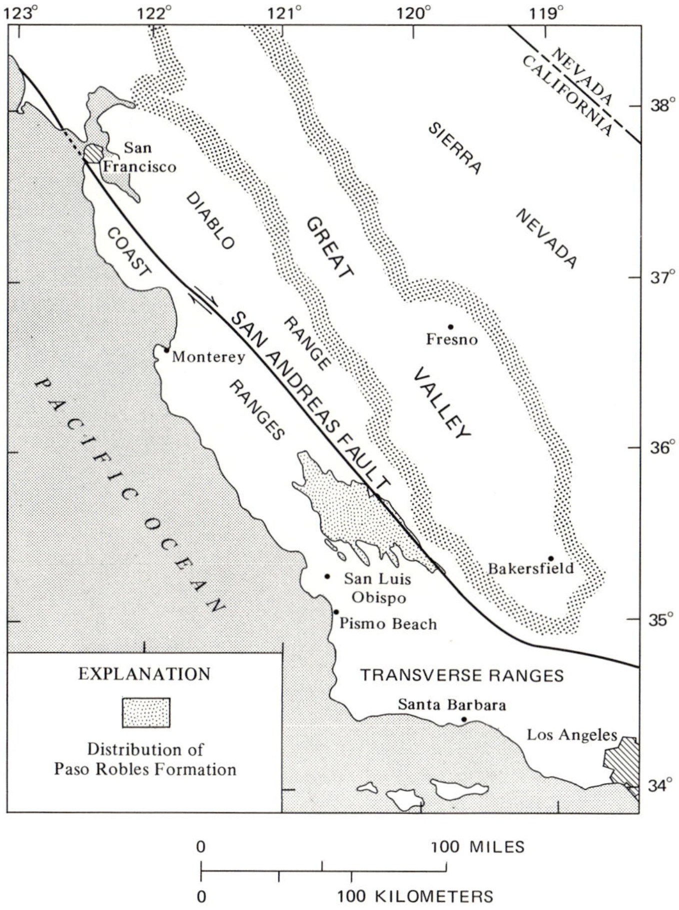

Figure 1.—Index map of central California, showing distribution of the Paso Robles Formation (from Galehouse, 1967).

[1] California State University, Department of Geology.

from his investigation of the Santa Margarita area. Fossil photography is by Kenji Sakamoto.

GEOLOGIC SETTING

The marine fossils discovered are exposed near the southern margin of an extensive area of Paso Robles terrane characteristic of the upper Salinas Valley (fig. 2). The fossil locality (USGS M4621) is in a quarry along the south side of the Atascadero-Creston road about 2 miles east of Atascadero and nearly 3,000 feet due north of the southeast corner (lat 35°30′ N.; long 120°37.5′ W.) of the Templeton, Calif., 7½-minute quadrangle (U.S. Geol. Survey topographic map). The exposure here is in the lowermost part of the Paso Robles Formation, which in this area unconformably overlies Monterey Shale (Jennings, 1958; Durham, 1973). Lithologically, the section exposed is typical of the Paso Robles Formation, consisting mainly of sand and gravel. The gravel clasts exposed in the quarry were derived from the Monterey Shale. The section exposed here differs from the Paso Robles Formation exposed elsewhere mainly in that it contains marine invertebrate fossils in place. The nonopaque heavy minerals, pebble lithology and imbrication, and foreset beds all indicate that the source area was to the south and southeast, the same as for the nonfossiliferous beds of the Paso Robles Formation in nearby outcrops. Much of the detritus probably was shed from the northern part of the La Panza Range (see Galehouse, 1967, for details).

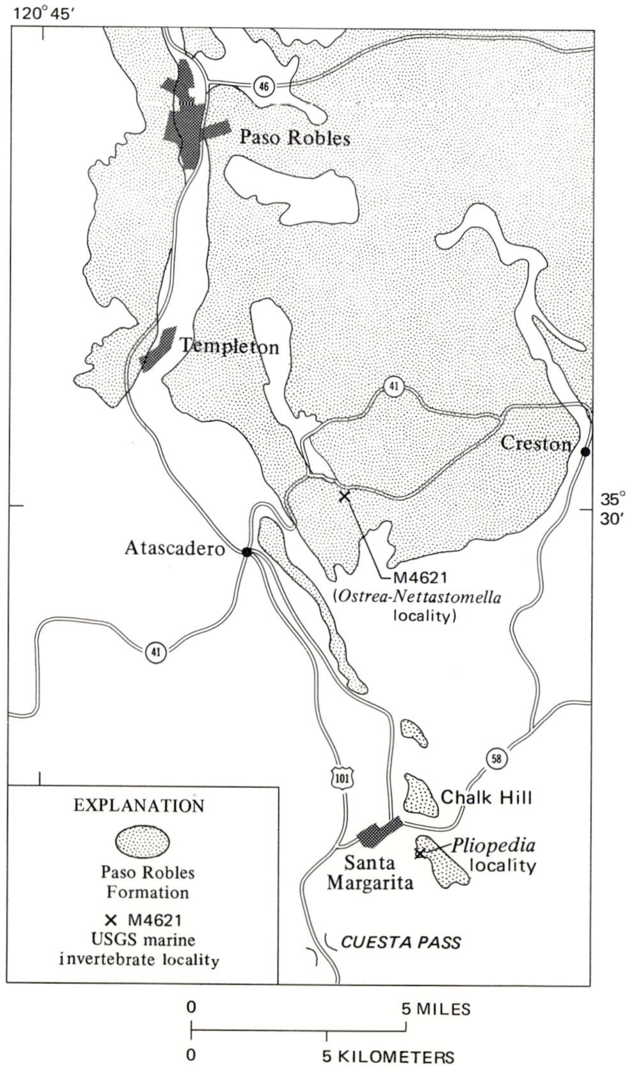

Figure 2.—Distribution of the Paso Robles Formation in the Atascadero-Santa Margarita area, central California, showing occurrences of marine fossils (after Jennings, 1958, and E. W. Hart, written commun., July 1972).

PALEONTOLOGY

Faunal assemblage

A small assemblage of epifaunal, boring, and nestling marine invertebrates, principally mollusks, has been identified from USGS Cenozoic locality M4621, and are listed here:

Marine invertebrates from the Paso Robles Formation

Pelecypods:
- *Crassostrea titan* (Conrad) (fig. 3*a*) [reworked]
- *Hinnites giganteus* (Gray) (fig. 3*i, o*)
- *Nettastomella rostrata* (Valenciennes) (fig. 3*e, j*)
- *Ostrea atwoodi* Gabb (fig. 3*p, r*)
- *Ostrea vespertina* Conrad (fig. 3*a–c, f, h, 1–n*)
- *Sphenia luticola* (Valenciennes)

Barnacle:
- *Balanus* sp. (fig. 3*g, i*)

Brachiopod:
- *Terebratalia* cf. *T. arnoldi* Hertlein and Grant (fig. 3*d, k*)

By far the most abundant species is *Ostrea vespertina* Conrad. The lower valves of this small oyster are strongly plicate and are generally ovate falcate in outline; a few of the smaller valves are more ovate. In this collection upper valves of this species are more abundant than lower valves. They vary from smooth to undulate and none are as strongly plicate as the lower valves. The upper valves closely resemble the small form of this species figured by Woodring, Stewart, and Richards (1940, pls. 8 and 10) as *O. vespertina sequens* Arnold. Indeed, in the absence of lower valves, one would probably identify the upper valves as being of *O. vespertina* forma *sequens*. Conversely, without the upper valves, the lower valves would be regarded as *O. vespertina* s.s. The oyster is here identified as *O. vespertina* in the context of variation described by Woodring (in Woodring and Bramlette, 1950) for specimens from the Santa Maria basin. Upper valves of some of the small specimens from the Santa Maria area were described as "being practically flat," the larger as being "moderately plicate to warped" (Woodring and Bramlette, 1950, p. 85). In view of this variation, it would seem that Arnold's *sequens* (1909) is best treated as a small, weakly sculptured form of *O. vespertina*.

Other calcite-shelled invertebrates, including *Ostrea atwoodi* Gabb (fig. 3*p*, *r*), are very rare in the collection from locality M4621. Aragonitic-shelled mollusks are preserved only in sand-filled borings in cobbles and small flattened boulders of relatively soft Monterey Shale (fig. 3*a*, *j*). So far as can be determined, the borings were made by the small pholadid *Nettastomella rostrata* (Valenciennes) shown in figure 3*e*, *j*. Articulated specimens of the nestling bivalve *Sphenia luticola* (Valenciennes) were found in a few of the holes.

Borings in oyster shells indicate that at least two other invertebrates were of common occurrence in this Pliocene assemblage. Some of the borings are minute holes, presumably made by a boring sponge that has honeycombed a giant oyster shell (fig. 3*q*). Other borings are circular perforations in many of the upper valves of *Ostrea vespertina* (fig. 3*h*), made by gastropods. Although no gastropods were collected from the locality, a fairly large population of carnivorous species formed an integral part of the assemblage, for nearly 50 percent of the upper valves of this oyster have one or more perforations or incomplete borings. Most of these are smoothly beveled, suggesting that they were made by a naticoid gastropod (Carter, 1968). A few are nearly vertical or have a very narrow, beveled shelf, suggesting that they were bored by a muricid or thaisid gastropod (Carter, 1968).

Depositional environment

The preservation of the *Ostrea-Nettastomella* assemblage indicates that it is generally in place and was subjected to very little postdepositional transport, whereas the lithologic constitution of the fossiliferous strata, sand and sandy gravel, is indicative of a high-energy environment. The lower valves of small oysters are preserved in their original growth positions, clinging to rounded cobbles of Monterey Shale (fig. 3*a*, *f*). Some of the larger oyster valves still have minute (2–4 mm diameter) articulated specimens of *Ostrea* attached to them. The other larger invertebrates also are generally very well preserved (fig. 3); relatively few specimens show signs of appreciable abrasion. A notable exception is an extensively bored valve of *Crassostrea titan* (fig. 3*q*) reworked from the upper Miocene Santa Margarita Formation, which is exposed about 2 miles west of the Paso Robles fossil locality (Jennings, 1958). Similar worn and broken valves of *C. titan* occur at the base of the Paso Robles Formation near Santa Margarita, about 5 miles southwest, where this formation unconformably overlies the Santa Margarita Formation (E. W. Hart, written commun., Oct. 2, 1972).

The abundance of oysters in this assemblage seems to be indicative of a brackish-water environment. Moreover, certain modern species of barnacles can tolerate brackish water (Henry, 1942), although most are found in waters of normal or nearly normal salinity. However, the co-occurrence of the small oysters and mollusks indicative of normal, or near-normal, salinity such as *Hinnites*, *Nettastomella*, and *Sphenia*, together with the brachiopod *Terebratalia*, strictly a marine genus (R. E. Grant, oral commun., July 1972), suggests that the assemblage represents a fully marine environment. The absence of aragonitic-shelled mollusks from this shallow-water assemblage, except in some of the borings made in the cobbles of Monterey Shale, is noteworthy. The inferred naticoid origin of most of the perforations in upper valves of *Ostrea vespertina*, together with the complete absence of any gastropods in the collection, suggests that aragonitic-shelled mollusks were present in the assemblage but were subsequently dissolved by ground-water action.

Age and correlation

A Pliocene age in the sense of the Pacific coast provincial megainvertebrate sequence (Weaver and others, 1944; Addicott, 1972) is indicated by *Ostrea atwoodi* Gabb and *Terebratalia* cf. *T. arnoldi* Hertlein and Grant, both of which are restricted in occurrence to strata of Pliocene age. As indicated, the one specimen of *Crassostrea titan* (Conrad) (fig. 3*q*) was reworked from older strata, the Santa Margarita Formation of late Miocene, for it is extensively abraded, whereas in-place specimens of mollusks from the Paso Robles Formation are well preserved and show very little, if any, evidence of abrasion. The other pelecypods range from the Pliocene, or possibly Miocene in the case of *Hinnites giganteus* (Gray) and *Ostrea vespertina* Conrad (Hertlein and Grant, 1972, p. 212, 218), to the Holocene. So far as we are aware, this is the first record of the minute rock borer *Nettastomella* from the Pacific coast Tertiary, although burrows doubtfully attributed to this bivalve have been reported from upper Miocene strata in the nearby Santa Maria basin (Evans, 1967). The minute nestling bivalve *Sphenia* has rarely been recorded from the Pliocene of the Pacific coast (Woodring and Bramlette, 1950; Hertlein and Grant, 1972).

The position of this assemblage within the provincial Pliocene is problematic. *Ostrea atwoodi* Gabb is known to occur in the lower and medial parts of the Pliocene sequence of the Kettleman Hills and Kreyenhagen Hills areas of the San Joaquin Valley (Nomland, 1917; Woodring and others, 1940). It is found by Durham and Addicott (1965) to be particularly characteristic of the lower Pliocene Pancho Rico Formation of the middle and lower Salinas Valley areas and has been cited by them as an early Pliocene index species in the sense of a twofold division of the epoch.

Ostrea vespertina Conrad has been reported from the late Miocene (Adegoke, 1969) and ranges throughout the provincial Pliocene; it has not, however, been recorded from the Pancho Rico Formation (Durham and Addicott, 1965). As noted, the upper valves of this abundant oyster are very weakly plicate to smooth, resembling the small variety *O. vespertina* forma *sequens* Arnold, whereas the lower valves

Figure 3.

have sharp plications (fig. 3*b*, *c*) as in *O. vespertina* Conrad s.s. The weakly sculptured form, represented by the upper valves from locality M4621, is apparently restricted in stratigraphic occurrence to the upper part of the San Joaquin Valley Pliocene sequence (Woodring and others, 1940). Woodring and Bramlette's (1950, p. 85) discussion of *O. vespertina* based upon specimens from the Santa Maria basin indicates that it is an extremely variable species. Accordingly, this seemingly unique population from the Paso Robles, which has some affinity with a late Pliocene form of *O. vespertina*, is not regarded as having chronologic significance within the provincial Pliocene. Rather, it is considered to be of pre-late Pliocene provincial age because of its occurrence with specimens of *O. atwoodi.*

In summary, the occurrence of the oyster- and *Nettastomella*-bearing sand and gravel at USGS locality M4621 in the lowermost part of the Paso Robles Formation confirms the belief that the age of this formation is at least in part early Pliocene in the sense of a twofold provincial division of the epoch. Moreover, remains of a unique marine mammal described from an isolated exposure of the Paso Robles Formation near Santa Margarita, about 8 miles south, have been assigned to the provincial Pliocene (Kellogg, 1921). They are very similar, if not congeneric, with pinniped specimens from the Pliocene Purisima Formation of the Santa Cruz area (lat 37° N.) (C. A. Repenning, oral commun., August 1972). According to Repenning, the pinniped remains from the Purisima Formation occur within, and to 30 feet above, a basal glauconite bed that has been dated at 6.7±5 m.y. (John Obradovich, written commun., 1964).

PALEOGEOGRAPHIC HISTORY

The marine invertebrate assemblage found in the Paso Robles Formation has a critical bearing on the late Cenozoic paleogeographic history of the southern Coast Ranges because it confirms earlier postulates (Durham and Addicott, 1965, p. A17–A19; Galehouse, 1967, fig. 28, p. 973) of a Pliocene marine connection between the Salinas Valley area to the north and the Santa Maria basin to the south. The faunal similarity between the Pancho Rico Formation of the middle and southern Salinas Valley area and the upper part of the Sisquoc Formation in the Santa Maria basin led Durham and Addicott (1965) to postulate an interchange of marine life between these two areas during the early Pliocene. The area of deposition was shown diagrammatically by Galehouse (1967, fig. 28) and is reprinted here, with slight modification, as figure 4. The closest Pliocene marine outcrops heretofore reported in these areas were about 40 miles apart. The fossiliferous exposure of Paso Robles Formation described herein is about halfway between the southernmost outcrop of the lower Pliocene Pancho Rico Formation southwest of San Miguel (Durham and Addicott, 1965, fig. 1) and the lower

Figure 3.—Larger marine invertebrates from the Paso Robles Formation near Atascadero, Calif. (USGS Cenozoic locality M4621). All specimens natural size unless otherwise indicated.

a. *Ostrea vespertina* Conrad. USNM 646995.
b. *Ostrea vespertina* Conrad. USNM 646996.
c. *Ostrea vespertina* Conrad. USNM 646997.
d. *Terebratalia* cf. *T. arnoldi* Hertlein and Grant. USNM 646998.
e. *Nettastomella rostrata* (Valenciennes). × 6. USNM 646999.
f. *Ostrea vespertina* Conrad. USNM 647000.
g. *Balanus* sp. USNM 647001.
h. *Ostrea vespertina* Conrad. USNM 647002.
i. *Balanus* sp. and *Hinnites giganteus* (Gray). USNM 647003.
j. *Nettastomella rostrata* (Valenciennes). × 4. USNM 647004.
k. *Terebratalia* cf. *T. arnoldi* Hertlein and Grant. USNM 647005.
l. *Ostrea vespertina* Conrad. USNM 647006.
m, n. *Ostrea vespertina* Conrad. USNM 647007.
o. *Hinnites giganteus* (Gray). USNM 647008.
p, r. *Ostrea atwoodi* Gabb. USNM 647009.
q. *Crassostrea titan* (Conrad). Reworked. USNM 647010.

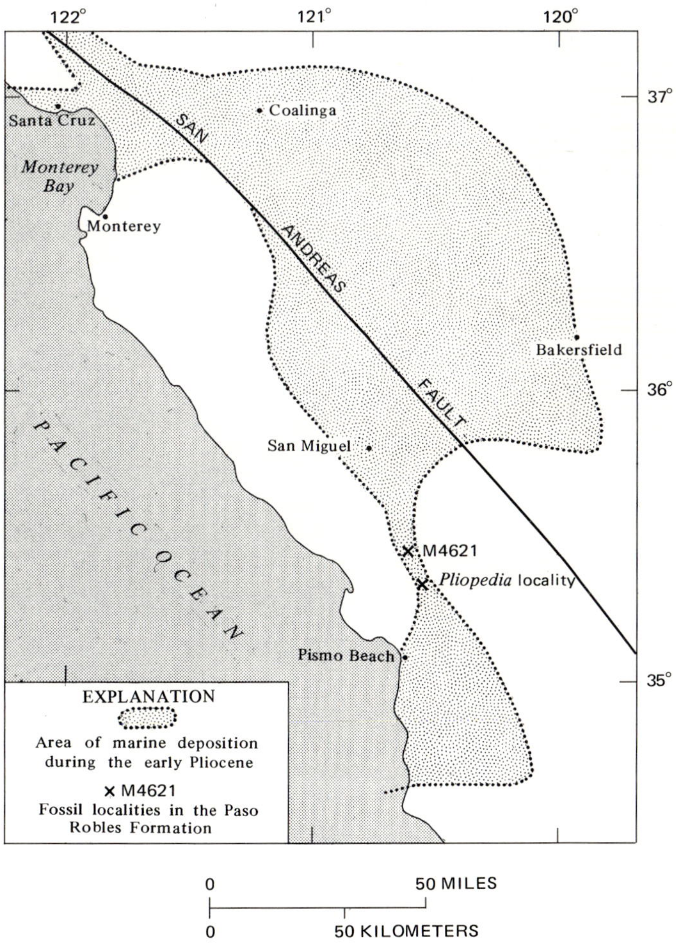

Figure 4.—Early Pliocene paleogeography of central California prior to displacement along the San Andreas fault (modified from Galehouse, 1967), showing marine fossil localities between San Miguel and Pismo Beach.

Pliocene part of the Saucelito Member of the Santa Margarita Formation of Hall (1962, fig. 5) exposed in the Huasna syncline east of Pismo Beach (fig. 4). This new fossil find is excellent substantiating evidence for the postulated marine connection between these two Pliocene basins of deposition. Further evidence of a marine environment of deposition in the southernmost exposures of the Paso Robles Formation is the occurrence of the pinniped *Pliopedia pacifica* Kellogg (1921) in exposures of the Paso Robles Formation a mile southeast of Santa Margarita (fig. 4). The type locality of this marine mammal, a unique occurrence, also is near the base of the Paso Robles Formation. Moreover, exposures of the basal Paso Robles in the vicinity of Santa Margarita are characterized by angular boulders of Monterey Shale and Vaqueros Sandstone bored by moderately large marine pholadid bivalves (E. W. Hart, written commun., Oct. 2, 1972). A specimen collected from one of these borings on Chalk Hill, about a mile northeast of Santa Margarita (fig. 2), appears to be a small *Zirfaea*. It seems clear, then, that marine Paso Robles deposition was extensive along what is now the northwestmost edge of the La Panza Range.

The exposure of oyster-bearing Paso Robles Formation east of Atascadero most likely represents the last vestige of the Pliocene marine connection between the southern Salinas Valley and the Santa Maria basin (fig. 4). The section here may also represent an intertonguing of marine and nonmarine strata marking the transition, in the upper Salinas Valley, from marine deposition that prevailed during the early Pliocene to continental deposition that has prevailed since that time.

REFERENCES CITED

Addicott, W. O., 1972, Provincial middle and late Tertiary molluscan stages, Temblor Range, California, *in* Symposium on Miocene biostratigraphy of California: Soc. Econ. Paleontologists and Mineralogists, Pacific Sec., Bakersfield, Calif., p. 1–26, pls. 1–4.

Adegoke, O. S., 1969, Stratigraphy and paleontology of the marine Neogene formations of the Coalinga region, California: California Univ. Pubs. Geol. Sci., v. 80, 241 p., 13 pls.

Arnold, Ralph, 1909, Paleontology of the Coalinga district, Fresno and Kings Counties, California: U.S. Geol. Survey Bull. 396, 173 p., 30 pls. [1910].

Carter, R. M., 1968, On the biology and palaeontology of the same predators of bivalved Mollusca: Palaeogeography, Palaeoclimatology, Palaeoecology, v. 4, no. 1, p. 29–65.

Durham, D. L., 1973, Geology of the southern Salinas Valley area, California: U.S. Geol. Survey Prof. Paper 819 (In press).

Durham, D. L., and Addicott, W. O., 1965, Pancho Rico Formation, Salinas Valley, California: U.S. Geol. Survey Prof. Paper 524-A, p. A1–A22, 5 pls.

Evans, J. W., 1967 A re-interpretation of the sand-pipes described by Adegoke: Veliger, v. 10, no. 2, p. 174–175, pl. 17.

Fairbanks, H. W., 1898, Geology of a portion of the southern Coast Ranges: Jour. Geology, v. 6, p. 551–576.

—— 1904, Description of the San Luis, Calif., quadrangle: U.S. Geol. Survey Geol. Atlas, Folio 101, 14 p.

Galehouse, J. S., 1967, Provenance and paleocurrents of the Paso Robles Formation, California: Geol. Soc. America Bull., v. 78, p. 951–978.

Hall, C. A., Jr., 1962, Evolution of the Echinoid genus *Astrodapsis:* California Univ. Pubs. Geol. Sci., v. 40, no. 2, p. 47–180.

Henry, D. P., 1942, Studies on the sessile Cirripedia of the Pacific coast of North America: Washington Univ. Pubs. Oceanography, v. 4, no. 3, p. 95–134, pls. 1–4.

Hertlein, L. G., and Grant, U. S., IV, 1972, The geology and paleontology of the marine Pliocene of San Diego, California (Paleontology: Pelecypoda): San Diego Soc. Nat. History Mem. 2, pt. 2B, p. 135–411, pls. 27–57.

Jennings, C. W., 1958, Geologic map of California, San Luis Obispo sheet, Olaf P. Jenkins edition: California Div. Mines, scale 1:250,000.

Kellogg, Remington, 1921, A new pinniped from the upper Pliocene of California: Jour. Mammalogy, v. 2, p. 212–226, illus.

Nomland, J. O., 1917, The Etchegoin Pliocene of middle California: California Univ. Pubs., Dept. Geology Bull., v. 10, no. 14, p. 191–254, pls. 6–12.

Weaver, C. E., and others, 1944, Correlation of the marine Cenozoic formations of western North America: Geol. Soc. America Bull., v. 55, no. 5, p. 569–598.

Woodring, W. P., and Bramlette, M. N., 1950, Geology and paleontology of the Santa Maria district, California: U.S. Geol. Survey Prof. Paper 222, 185 p., 23 pls. [1951].

Woodring, W. P., Stewart, R. B., and Richards, R. W., 1940, Geology of the Kettleman Hills oil field, California; stratigraphy, paleontology, and structure: U.S. Geol. Survey Prof. Paper 195, 170 p., 57 pls. [1941].

Jour. Research U.S. Geol. Survey
Vol. 1, No. 5, Sept.-Oct. 1973, p. 515–517

GALKHAITE, (Hg,Cu,Tl,Zn)(As,Sb)S_2, FROM THE GETCHELL MINE, HUMBOLDT COUNTY, NEVADA

By THEODORE BOTINELLY, GEORGE J. NEUERBURG,
and NANCY M. CONKLIN, Denver, Colo.

Abstract.—The first reported occurrence in the United States of galkhaite (Hg,Cu,Tl,Zn)(As,Sb)S_2 is at the Getchell mine, Humboldt County, Nev. The mineral occurs as brownish-black cubes associated with graphite, pyrite, and realgar. In polished section galkhaite is grayish white and isotropic with a deep-red internal reflection; reflectivity at 590 nm is 21.6 percent. Spectrographic analysis gave Hg 42 percent, Cu 5 percent, Zn 1.5 percent, Fe 0.7 percent, Tl 5 percent, As 24 percent, Sb 0.3 percent, and S (by difference) 21.3 percent. The mineral is cubic, a=10.36, and the strong lines of the X-ray powder pattern are 2.99 (100), 4.21 (90), 2.76 (80), 1.831 (70), 7.25 (60), 2.58 (40), 1.561 (40). The pattern is very similar to that of tetrahedrite except for the strong lines at 7.25, 4.21, and 2.76.

Isolation of sulfide minerals from one sample of ore from the Getchell mine, Humboldt County, Nev., by use of hydrofluoric acid (Neuerburg, 1961), yielded a small quantity of brownish-black cubes that recently proved to be the new mineral galkhaite (Gruzdev and others, 1972). This is the first reported occurrence of galkhaite in the United States and the third in the world.

The ore sample is a composite of the carbonaceous clay-shale gouge characteristic of the Getchell gold deposit (Hotz and Willden, 1964). It was collected by Ralph L. Erickson, U.S. Geological Survey, in 1961 from a part of the north pit, now removed by open-pit mining. About 125 mg of galkhaite was recovered from this one 1,200-g sample, along with graphite, pyrite, and realgar; none of the other 25 ore samples examined contained galkhaite.

The galkhaite in the Getchell ore had been provisionally identified by X-ray diffraction as tetrahedrite and found to contain thallium and mercury on X-ray fluorescence analysis by A. P. Marranzino. The diffraction pattern of galkhaite is very similar to that of tetrahedrite (table 1), except for the markedly stronger intensities of reflections from (110), (211), and (321). These discrepancies in intensity were discounted until analyses of a few milligrams of the mineral for copper, thallium, mercury, and arsenic by J. R. Watterson, A. E. Hubert, and R. L. Turner denied the possibility of tetrahedrite. A description of the Getchell mineral was submitted to Michael Fleischer in October 1971; he recognized it as identical with galkhaite, submitted by V. S. Gruzdev and colleagues to the Commission on New Minerals and Mineral Names of the International Mineralogical Association in June 1971.

Getchell galkhaite occurs as cubes and clusters of cubes less than ½ mm on edge; they are steel gray (possibly from adhering graphite) to brownish black with metallic luster, and are soft and brittle with an orange-yellow streak. In polished section the galkhaite is grayish white and isotropic, with deep-red internal reflections; the index of refraction was determined by R. E. Wilcox to be greater than 2.01. Averaged reflectivity measurements from several grains, determined by use of a Hallimond visual photometer with a SiC standard for comparison, are blue (470 nm) 25.8 percent, green (546 nm) 23.8 percent, yellow (590 nm) 21.6 percent, and red (627 nm) 21.5 percent. The X-ray diffraction pattern (table 1) is very similar to those published by Gruzdev and others (1972).

Spectrographic analysis of 10 mg of the Getchell galkhaite, diluted with sodium carbonate and quartz, yielded results (table 2) very similar to those of the type specimens. Mercury, thallium, and arsenic were determined with a pedestal-type deep electrode, National Carbon L-4-24, arced at 9 amp and 210 v for 1 minute. The other reported elements were determined by a six-step semiquantitative analysis, similar to that described by Myers, Havens, and Dunton (1961). A nondestructive X-ray fluorescence scan of the analyzed sample by J. S. Wahlberg served as a guide, and indicated that the unmeasured portion is probably all sulfur. Differences in composition with the type galkhaite (table 2) probably result from true compositional variations as well as from the different methods of analysis.

After this report was written we learned that R. C. Erd, U.S. Geological Survey, had received similar material from the Getchell mine. Gerald Czamanske made the following microprobe analysis of this material:

	Weight percent	*Moles*		*Weight percent*	*Moles*
Hg	50.2	0.2502	Cu	3.4	0.0535
As....	15.8	.2109	Zn	1.2	.0184
S......	22.6	.7048	Tl......	3.5	.0171
				96.7	

Table 1.—*X-ray powder diffraction data*

[Values in angstroms. Data on B and C from Gruzdev and others (1972)]

hkl	Galkhaite							Tetrahedrite	
	A			B		C		D	
	I	*d*(meas.)	*d*(calc.)	*I*	*d*	*I*	*d*	*I*	*d*
110	60	7.25	7.33	50	7.40	30	7.5	5	7.44
200	5	5.15	5.18	6	5.26	...	.....	10	5.21
211	90	4.21	4.23	70	4.27	50	4.2	10	4.25
220	5	3.66	3.66	5	3.72	...	.....	20	3.69
310	5	3.28	3.28	8	3.30	30	3.34	...	.....
222	100	2.99	2.99	100	3.01	100	3.01	100	3.00
321	80	2.76	2.77	80	2.78	90	2.79	10	2.78
400	40	2.58	2.59	29	2.604	50	2.61	40	2.60
411,330	10	2.44	2.44	15	2.453	30	2.47	20	2.46
420	5	2.31	2.32	4	2.327	5	2.3	10	2.33
332	20	2.21	2.21	20	2.220	30	2.22	10	2.22
422	...	.....	.....	...	.....	...	.....	10	2.12
510,431	20	2.03	2.03	20	2.040	50	2.04	30	2.04
521	20	1.892	1.891	20	1.898	40	1.90	20	1.899
440	70	1.831	1.831	50	1.841	80	1.84	80	1.838
530,433	5	1.774	1.777	6	1.786	20	1.79	10	1.781
600,442	...	.....	.....	2	1.732	20	1.73	5	1.734
611,532	20	1.681	1.681	17	1.687	40	1.69	20	1.687
620	...	.....	.....	2	1.648	5	1.66	10	1.645
541	...	.....	.....	4	1.603	5	1.61	5	1.603
622	40	1.561	1.562	29	1.569	70	1.57	60	1.570
631	...	.....	.....	6	1.534	10	1.53	5	1.535
444	10	1.495	1.495	12	1.502	30	1.501	5	1.501
710,550,543	...	.....	.....	6	1.473	10	1.474	...	.....
640	...	.....	.....	...	.....	...	.....	5	1.451
721,633,552	10	1.410	1.410	12	1.415	40	1.417	5	1.451
642	...	.....	.....	...	.....	...	.....	5	1.389
732,651	5	1.316	1.316	10	1.320	20	1.322	5	1.320
800	5	1.296	1.295	8	1.302	20	1.301	5	1.299
811,741,554	5	1.275	1.275	6	1.280	20	1.282	5	1.280
820,644	...	.....	.....	2	1.263	...	.....	...	.....
653	5	1.240	1.238	6	1.244	20	1.245	5	1.244
831,750,743	...	.....	.....	4	1.209	20	1.21	5	1.209
662	10	1.189	1.188	10	1.193	40	1.194	5	1.192
752	...	.....	.....	6	1.178	20	1.178	...	.....
840	5	1.159	1.158	8	1.164	40	1.163	...	.....
921,761,655	5	1.118	1.117	7	1.123	30	1.122	5	1.120
664	...	.....	.....	2	1.109	...	.....	...	.....
930,851,754	...	.....	.....	4	1.098	20	1.097	5	1.096
932,763	...	.....	.....	5	1.074	30	1.072	...	.....
844	5	1.058	1.057	10	1.062	50	1.064	5	1.059
770,853,941	...	.....	.....	4	1.053	30	1.051	...	.....
772,10.1.1	...	.....	.....	2	1.030	10	1.031	...	.....
943,950	...	.....	.....	3	1.011	30	1.011	...	.....
666,10.2.2	...	.....	.....	6	1.002	50	1.002	...	.....
765,952,10.3.1	...	.....	.....	4	.9924	40	.992	...	.....
961,10.3.3	...	.....	.....	2	.9580	...	.....	...	.....

A. From Getchell mine, Humboldt County, Nev. a = 10.36 A; Cu/Ni; camera diameter 114.6 mm. Intensities estimated visually.

B. From Gal-Khaya, northeastern Yakutia, U.S.S.R. a = 10.41±0.01 A; Cu$K\alpha$; camera diameter 114.6 mm.

C. From Khaidarkan, southern Kirghiz region, U.S.S.R. a = 10.41±0.02 A; Fe$K\alpha$; camera diameter 57.3 mm. Intensities converted to a scale of 100.

D. From Peruvian mine, Montezuma district, Summit County, Colo. a = 10.40 A; Cu/Ni; camera diameter 114.6 mm. Intensities estimated visually.

Table 2.—*Chemical data, in percent*

	A Getchell	B Gal-Khaya	C Khaidarkan
Hg	42	47.60	49.02
Cu	5	3.49	2.85
Zn	1.5	3.00	.60
Fe	.7	.31	.....
Tl	5	.46	2.90
As	24	23.60	19.49
Sb	.3	.59	5.51
S	(21.3)	21.00	19.31
Se	.....	.0003	.015
Sum	.....	100.05	99.695
Ag	.05	.....	.....
Cd	.07	.....	.....
Al	.1	.....	.....
Ca	.01	.....	.....
Mg	.003	.....	.....
Mn	.002	.....	.....

A. Spectrographic analysis (N. M. Conklin); sulfur by difference. $(Hg_{0.57}, Cu_{0.26}, Tl_{0.09}, Zn_{0.04}, Fe_{0.02})(Sb_{0.01}, As_{0.88})S_{2.13}$.

B. Data from Gruzdev and others (1972, p. 1196). $(Hg_{0.74}, Cu_{0.17}, Tl_{0.01}, Zn_{0.14})(Sb_{0.02}, As_{0.98})S_{2.01}$.

C. Data from Gruzdev and others (1972, p. 1196). $(Hg_{0.80}, Cu_{0.15}, Tl_{0.05}, Zn_{0.03})(Sb_{0.15}, As_{0.85})S_{1.87}$.

Additional finds of galkhaite have been reported at the Getchell mine. We have no knowledge of the exact localities within the mine, but apparently the mineral may be widespread in the Getchell deposit.

REFERENCES CITED

Gruzdev, V. S., Stepanov, V. I., Shumkova, N. G., Chernitsova, N. M., Yudin, R. N., and Bryzgalov, I. A., 1972, Galkhaite, $HgAsS_2$, a new mineral from arsenic-antimony-mercury deposits of the U.S.S.R.: Akad. Nauk SSSR Doklady, v. 205, no. 5, p. 1194–1197.

Hotz, P. W., and Willden, Ronald, 1964, Geology and mineral deposits of the Osgood Mountains quadrangle, Humboldt County, Nevada: U.S. Geol. Survey Prof. Paper 431, 128 p.

Myers, A. T., Havens, R. G., and Dunton, P. J., 1961, A spectrochemical method for the semiquantitative analysis of rocks, minerals, and ores: U.S. Geol. Survey Bull. 1084-I, p. 207–229.

Neuerberg, G. J., 1961, A method of mineral separation using hydrofluoric acid: Am. Mineralogist, v. 46, p. 1498–1501.

Jour. Research U.S. Geol. Survey
Vol. 1, No. 5, Sept.-Oct. 1973, p. 519—521

DISSEMINATED PYRITE IN A LATITE PORPHYRY AT TEXAN MOUNTAIN, HUDSPETH COUNTY, TEXAS

By THOMAS E. MULLENS, Denver, Colo.

Abstract.—A pyrite-bearing latite porphyry that contains fragments of syenite and a quartz porphyry intruded into the Cretaceous Cox Sandstone are well exposed in a roadcut at Texan Mountain, Hudspeth County, Tex. The pyrite, which occurs along tiny fractures as well as disseminated, and the multiple episodes of intrusion, coupled with copper minerals in veins in the overlying Cox Sandstone, indicate a slight potential for porphyry-type copper or molybdenum deposits at depth.

The main purpose of this report is to describe briefly the geology of a roadcut that exposes a porphyry containing disseminated pyrite as well as tiny veins of pyrite at Texan Mountain, Hudspeth County, Tex. (fig. 1). The exposed part of the porphyry is weakly mineralized and contains no minerals of economic importance, but it has several features commonly associated with porphyry copper-molybdenum deposits of the Western United States. These features, along with vein copper deposits at Texan Mountain, indicate a potential for copper or molybdenum minerals at depth. A secondary purpose of the report is to record an occurrence of a possible porphyry sulfide deposit in west Texas. McAnulty (1972, p. 12) describes disseminated copper minerals in porphyry in the Chinati Mountains northwest of Presidio, Tex. McAnulty's paper is the first to indicate the occurrence of porphyry copper deposits in west Texas, although a porphyry molybdenum deposit at Cave Peak 30 miles north of Van Horn, Tex., has been drilled extensively.

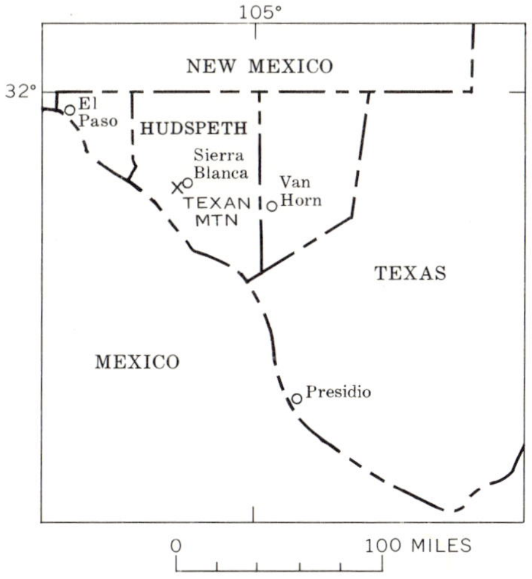

Figure 1.—Index map showing location of Texan Mountain, Hudspeth County, Tex.

The general geology of Texan Mountain is shown on plate 1 of Albritton and Smith (1965). The mountain is immediately southwest of the town of Sierra Blanca, trends northwest, is about 2 miles long, and is about 500 feet high. Sedimentary rocks exposed are assigned to the Cox Sandstone and overlying Finlay Limestone, both of Early Cretaceous age. The sedimentary rocks strike northwest and dip 20°—30° SW., and they are extensively intruded by dikes and sills of latite porphyry which are probably of early Tertiary age. Detailed descriptions of the rocks are given by Albritton and Smith (1965, p. 63—82, 88, 91—92).

Since the mapping by Albritton and Smith, some rocks along the north side of Texan Mountain have been exposed in a roadcut that trends N. 65° W. along Interstate Highway 10. The north-facing cut is about 1,100 feet long and exposes a maximum vertical section of 55 feet of rock. A section of part of the rocks exposed in the central part of the cut is shown on figure 2. The units numbered in figure 2 are described below; the order of the units is basically from west to east for units accessible at road level and from base to top for units that are well above road level. All sedimentary and metamorphosed rocks are part of the Cox Sandstone. Boundaries of units in the Cox Sandstone generally follow bedding, except for units 1, 3, and 6 which are the same stratigraphic unit but differ in composition owing to alteration.

Unit 1. Quartzite, dusky-yellow-green, dusky-green, and grayish-green, fine- to medium-grained, irregularly laminated to crossbedded. Weathers to a surface that contains many pits which average about 1 cm in diameter and 0.5 cm in depth. Slightly metamorphosed and contains sparsely disseminated epidote in clots as large as 3 cm across. As much as 20 feet exposed.

Unit 2. Quartzite and silicified siltstone. Metamorphosed but unit retains bedding structures. Various shades of

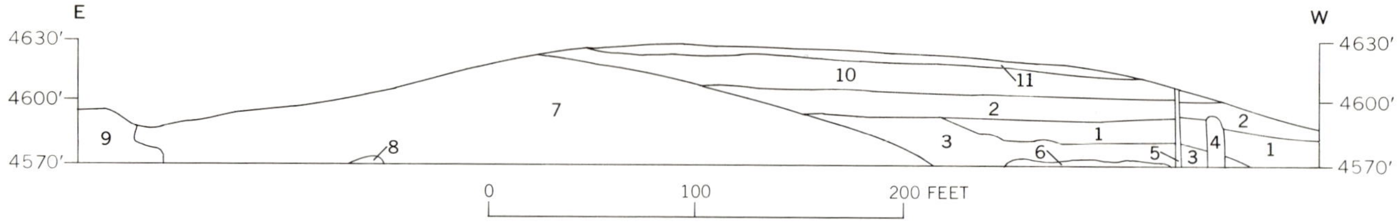

Figure 2.—Section of part of rocks exposed in north-facing cut on south side of Interstate Highway 10 at Texan Mountain, Hudspeth County, Tex. Numbered units are described in text. Altitude shown is approximate.

green and brown. Abundant epidote and sparse chlorite. Unit forms conspicuous dark-green to greenish-black band about 15 feet thick.

Unit 3. Quartzitic sandstone, very pale red to faint purple, fine- to medium-grained. Unit is only slightly metamorphosed. Irregular gradational contact with underlying (unit 6) and overlying (units 1 and 2) quartzites which are more metamorphosed.

Unit 4. Quartz porphyry dike, light-gray to white; very fine grained to aphanitic matrix and sparse anhedral 1- to 2-mm phenocrysts of quartz. Dendrites of black iron oxide common along fractures. Dike trends about N. 65° E. and is along a fault of 2 to 4 feet displacement. Intrudes into, but not through, unit 2. Mainly shows crosscutting relations, but locally seems to grade into adjacent rock.

Unit 5. Latite porphyry dike, grayish-orange; fine- to medium-grained matrix with scattered medium to coarse grains of mafic minerals. Local concentrations of anhedral phenocrysts of feldspar as large as 2 cm across. Dike trends about N. 60° E. and intrudes all exposed Cox Sandstone.

Unit 6. Quartzite, similar to unit 1 except that it does not weather to pitted surface and it contains sparse films of red iron oxide.

Unit 7. Latite porphyry, crosscutting on west side, has a sill-like extension on east side. Mainly grayish orange, but includes irregular zones of medium gray, and eastern 50 feet is mainly medium gray. Medium-grained feldspar matrix with irregular grains of mafic minerals as much as 2 mm across. About 30 percent of unit is feldspar in anhedral to euhedral phenocrysts that average about 1 cm across, but some are as much as 2.5 cm. Contains disseminated pyrite and, locally, veinlets of pyrite along fractures and concentrations of pyrite grains where no fractures are visible. Abundant red iron oxide stains derived from weathering of pyrite and mafic minerals. Unit contains scattered inclusions of dark-greenish-gray syenite as much as 60 cm long, but most are about 10 cm across, and rare angular inclusions of rhyolite, quartz, diorite, limestone, and sandstone fragments as much as 10 cm across. Gray zones seem to contain more green igneous-rock fragments, more mafic minerals and less pyrite than grayish-orange rock.

Unit 8. Large inclusion(?) of metamorphosed quartzite and siltstone of Cox Sandstone. Inclusion has green, yellow, and gray streaks, abundant red iron oxide stain, and sparse clots of epidote.

Unit 9. Metamorphosed interbedded quartzite, siltstone, and claystone, mainly shades of green; clots of epidote common, especially in claystone; and sparse chlorite. Siltstone and claystone are silicified. Very sparse blebs of green copper mineral.

Unit 10. Quartzitic sandstone, grayish-orange, seemingly unaltered. Probably typical of unaltered sandstone in Cox Sandstone.

Unit 11. Metamorphosed siltstone, claystone, and minor quartzite, grayish-green to brownish-green. Clots of epidote common in claystone.

Disseminated grains of pyrite and veinlets of pyrite along fractures are found throughout the latite porphyry (unit 7). Near road level, however, the grains and veinlets are most abundant in the western 100 feet and eastern 25 feet. The western part contains about 1.0 percent pyrite, whereas the central part of the latite porphyry contains about 0.1 percent pyrite. The pyrite weathers to tarnished and bronze surfaces that greatly resemble tarnish on chalcopyrite.

No disseminated pyrite or veinlets of pyrite were found in any natural exposures of latite porphyry on Texan Mountain. Sparsely disseminated grains of pyrite amounting to about 0.2 percent of the rock were found in a quartz latite porphyry exposed in a quarry at the northwest end of the mountain and about three-fourths of a mile west of the roadcut. The relation of the quartz latite exposed in the quarry to the latite porphyry exposed in the roadcut is not known.

Spectrographic analyses of single samples of mainly unaltered quartzite (unit 3), silicified claystone (unit 9), the quartz porphyry dike (unit 4), and the pyrite-bearing latite porphyry (unit 7) indicate that these rocks do not contain anomalous amounts of copper, lead, or zinc, or detectable molybdenum. A sample of epidote- and chlorite-bearing metamorphosed sandstone from unit 2, collected a few feet from unit 7, contained 150 ppm copper, but only 10 ppm lead and no detectable zinc or molybdenum. The copper content was less than expected, as scattered blebs of secondary copper minerals had been observed in silicified claystone.

Although no minerals of economic significance occur in the exposed part of the latite porphyry, the geologic setting indicates some potential for a porphyry copper or molybdenum deposit at depth. Several prospect pits on the northwestern third of Texan Mountain expose abundant copper minerals associated with silicified iron oxide veins that cut sandstone and limestone in the Cox Sandstone. The prospects indicate that copper was associated with the intrusive rocks. The fragments of syenite, rhyolite, and diorite in the latite porphyry and the presence of a quartz porphyry dike indicate multiple episodes of intrusion. Such multiple episodes are characteristic of the porphyry molybdenum deposits of Colorado and New Mexico (Wallace and others, 1968, p. 615–621, table 3; Ishihara, 1967) as well as many other porphyry deposits (Lowell and Guilbert, 1970, table 1). The pyrite possibly represents the pyritized outer shell of a porphyry deposit as reported by Lowell and Guilbert (1970, fig. 3).

REFERENCES CITED

Albritton, C. C., Jr., and Smith, J. F., Jr., 1965, Geology of the Sierra Blanca area, Hudspeth County, Texas: U.S. Geol. Survey Prof. Paper 479, 131 p.

Ishihara, Shunso, 1967, Molybdenum mineralization at Questa mine, New Mexico, U.S.A.: Japan Geol. Survey Rept. 218, 64 p.

Lowell, J. D., and Guilbert, J. M., 1970, Lateral and vertical alteration-mineralization zoning in porphyry ore deposits: Econ. Geology, v. 65, no. 4, p. 373–408.

McAnulty, W. N., Sr., 1972, Mineral deposits in the West Chinati stock, Chinati Mountains, Presidio County, Texas: Texas Bur. Econ. Geology Geol. Circ. 72-1, 13 p.

Wallace, S. R., Muncaster, N. K., Jonson, D. C., Mackenzie, W. B., Bookstrom, A. A., and Surface, V. E., 1968, Multiple intrusion and mineralization at Climax, Colorado, *in* Ridge, J. R., ed., Ore deposits in the United States, 1933–1967 (Graton-Sales volume): New York, Am. Inst. Mining, Metall., and Petroleum Engineers, p. 606–640.

Jour. Research U.S. Geol. Survey
Vol. 1, No. 5, Sept.-Oct. 1973, p. 523–528

SODA CREEK SPRINGS—METAMORPHIC WATERS IN THE EASTERN ALASKA RANGE

By D. H. RICHTER, R. A. LAMARRE[1],
and D. E. DONALDSON, Anchorage, Alaska

Abstract.—The Soda Creek springs are a group of small, cold mineral springs on the southern flank of the eastern Alaska Range. The spring waters contain anomalous concentrations of carbon dioxide, sodium, chlorine, sulfate, boron, and ammonia and are actively precipitating deposits of calcite and aragonite. Sparingly present in these deposits are mixed-layer illite-montmorillonite clays and zeolite minerals. Low-temperature metamorphic reactions in subjacent marine sedimentary rocks of Jurassic and Cretaceous age may have produced the fluids and silicate minerals. With only a few exceptions, cool bicarbonate-rich springs in Alaska are concentrated south of the Denali fault system in south-central Alaska, southeastern Alaska, and along the Kaltag-Tintina fault system. These areas are characterized by active or recently active tectonism, major faults and folds, and an abundance of marine sedimentary rocks.

The Soda Creek springs are a group of small, cold sodium-bicarbonate springs on the south flank of the eastern Alaska Range in southern Alaska. The unusual waters of the springs are characteristic of fluids of metamorphic origin (White, 1957b) and hence lend support to the concept of an active metamorphic-tectonic belt rimming the Pacific coast of North America (Barnes, 1970). Ecologically, the springs provide a source of essential minerals and salts to many animals of the area. Critically important is the dependence on the springs of many hundreds of Dall sheep (*Ovis dalli*), a species unique to Alaska and parts of neighboring Canada.

The springs have been named after their location on Soda Creek, a small tributary of Platinum Creek which drains into the Nabesna River. They occur at an elevation of about 3,600 feet in sec. 26, T. 9 N., R. 13 E., Copper River meridian, in the southeast corner of the Nabesna C-4 quadrangle (scale 1:63,360), and are most easily reached by a series of horse and tractor trails, approximately 11 miles long, that begin at Lost Creek on the Slana-Nabesna Road.

This note summarizes the field and laboratory data made available from several visits to the springs between 1965 and 1970 during the course of the U.S. Geological Survey's mapping program in the eastern Alaska Range and briefly discusses the geologic significance of the springs. The only known previous references to the springs are a very brief mention of their occurrence and a photograph by Moffit (1933, p. 140; 1941, pl. 6), who conducted a geologic reconnaissance of the area in 1931. Most of our data are derived from a trip during September 9–12, 1970, made especially to map the springs in detail and to sample the spring and nearby surface waters. We thank our colleagues R. M. Chapman and A. L. Clark for their unpublished chemical analyses of water from two Alaskan springs and Professor Robert C. Reynolds, of Dartmouth College, who aided in the X-ray studies of mineral deposits of the Soda Creek springs.

GEOLOGIC SETTING

Two distinct geologic terranes compose the bedrock in the vicinity of the Soda Creek springs. The older terrane, referred to as the Taku-Skolai terrane by Berg, Jones, and Richter (1972), consists of a series of low-grade regionally metamorphosed volcanic and sedimentary rocks ranging in age from Pennsylvanian to Late Triassic. The younger terrane, called the Gravina-Nutzotin belt by the same authors, consists principally of upper Mesozoic marine sedimentary rocks.

The oldest rocks in the Taku-Skolai terrane are a thick and complex series of Pennsylvanian and Permian volcanic and volcaniclastic rocks that are remnants of a late Paleozoic andesite island arc which apparently developed directly on oceanic crust (Richter and Jones, 1970). This old arc assemblage is overlain by nonvolcanogenic Permian marine argillite and minor limestone and Middle and (or) Late Triassic basalt and Late Triassic shallow-water limestone. Rocks of the younger Gravina-Nutzotin belt, unconformably overlying the Taku-Skolai terrane, consist of a thick flyschlike succession of Upper Jurassic and Lower Cretaceous argillite, graywacke, and conglomerate that were deposited in a deep, linear marine basin.

Dikes, sills, and other small irregular hypabyssal intrusions, mafic to intermediate in composition, are common throughout

[1] Present address: Bath, N.H.

the Jurassic and Cretaceous argillite in the vicinity of the springs. These rocks are probably cogenetic with upper Mesozoic granitic plutons that intrude rocks of both terranes in the general area or may be related to a younger period of intrusive activity in Tertiary time.

Bedrock exposure is relatively poor in the immediate area of the springs. Extensive glacial deposits of Wisconsin age cover much of the upland between the incised stream valleys, and most of the steep walls are mantled by colluvium. A large postglacial landslide of Triassic limestone that originated along the south valley wall of Soda Creek half a mile upstream from the springs has dammed the stream, forming a deep lake. Lake waters discharging from the base of the 1,500-foot-thick limestone dam are the present source of Soda Creek. A smaller landslide of argillite from the north valley wall, between the springs and the large landslide, occurred sometime between September 1969 and September 1970, covering several older spring deposits.

The springs are apparently located along an east-west-trending fault that juxtaposes Triassic basalt on the south with Jurassic and Cretaceous argillite on the north (fig. 1). This structure may be related to the Totschunda fault, a major active strike-slip fault (Richter and Matson, 1971) that trends across the eastern Alaska Range and passes within a mile northeast of the springs.

PHYSICAL FEATURES

The Soda Creek springs discharge from the steep vegetation-covered colluvial slope along the north bank of Soda Creek at the apexes of two conspicuous calcareous tufa cones approximately 300 feet apart (figs. 1 and 2). At least four springs have contributed to the growth of the tufa cones, but only two springs (A and C, fig. 1) have been active since our first visit to the area in 1965. The buff-colored cones are 8 to 12 feet high and as much as 60 feet wide at their bases where they have built out over the alluvial plain of Soda Creek (fig. 3). Older spring deposits overlain by slope debris exposed along the cut bank of the creek about 300 feet east of the easternmost tufa cone were covered by the 1969–70 landslide.

Water issuing from the two active springs (A and C, fig. 1) is clear, cold (5.5°C), and virtually odorless with a taste comparable to that of strong commercial soda water. Gases evolving with the water are also odorless. Discharge rates for the springs are low but on the basis of our observations appear to have been consistent for at least the past 6 years. As measured in September 1970, the principal spring (C) flows at a rate of 3 liters/min with a gas production of approximately 4 liters/min. The less active spring (A) flows 1 liter/min; gas production was not measured.

Both the active and inactive springs and their associated tufa

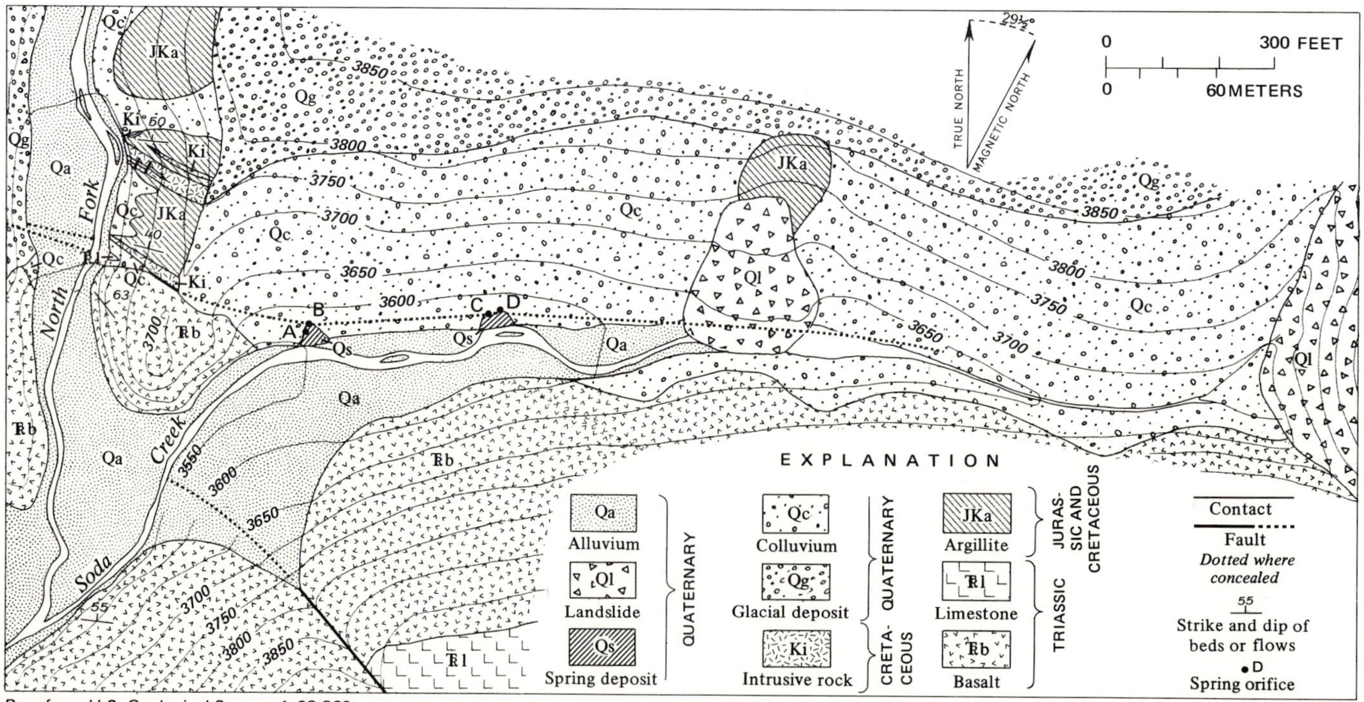

Base from U.S. Geological Survey, 1:63 360
Nabesna C-4, 1960

Geology by R. A. Lamarre
and D. H. Richter, 1970

Figure 1.—Geologic map of the Soda Creek springs area, eastern Alaska Range. The area shown is in the N½ sec. 26, T. 9 N., R. 13 E. See figure 4 for location in Alaska.

Figure 2.—General view of springs area, looking east up Soda Creek. Springs A and B are at extreme left, and springs C and D are in center partly hidden by leaning spruce tree. In middle background Soda Creek is dammed by 1969–70 landslide (L1) and in background by large limestone landslide (L2).

cones are relatively young features, probably not more than a few thousand years old. A log buried in the upper part of the tufa cone below inactive spring D has been radiocarbon dated in the laboratory of the U.S. Geological Survey (sample W-2567) at 570±250 years B.P. At the other extreme, all the cones undoubtedly have developed since the last Wisconsin glacial advance flushed the valleys of Soda and Platinum Creeks approximately 6,000 to 10,000 years ago.

CHEMISTRY OF THE SPRING WATERS

An analysis of the Soda Creek springs water (spring C) is shown in table 1. For purposes of comparison, an analysis of nearby surface water collected from Soda Creek where it discharges from the limestone dam is also shown. Water samples were filtered through 0.45μ Millipore membranes, and both a raw sample and an acidified sample (to prevent precipitation of calcium carbonate) of the filtered water were saved for analytical purposes.

The waters discharging at the springs are sodium-bicarbonate waters with high concentrations of sodium and carbon dioxide (as indicated by the high HCO_3^- and low pH), a high HCO_3^-/Cl^- ratio, and almost neutral pH. The waters are also rich in calcium, magnesium, potassium, ammonia, boron, sulfate, and chloride. The reported concentration of NH_4^+ (11 mg/l) probably represents a minimum value, as the water samples were stored several months prior to the boron and ammonia analyses. No attempt was made to analyze the copious gases evolving with the water. However, field tests showing that the gas neither supports combustion nor is combustible suggest that it is composed largely of CO_2. Furthermore, the lack of any appreciable odor is evidence against the presence of any significant amounts of H_2S.

A

B

Figure 3.—Tufa cones at springs C and D. *A*, Cones below principal spring C (left) and inactive spring D (right). View north across Soda Creek. *B*, Closeup of tufa presently being deposited on cone below spring C.

MINERALOGY OF THE SPRING DEPOSITS

The tufa cones are built of many hundreds of thin porous layers of precipitated calcium carbonate (fig. 3) containing lesser amounts of other minerals and locally abundant organic debris. Random samples of travertine collected from both the active and inactive cones range from 67 to 97 weight percent total carbonate with both calcite and aragonite present (table 2). The remainder of the travertine consists of illite-montmorillonite mixed-layer clay, epsomite, quartz, and minor amounts of gypsum, anhydrite, marcasite, analcite, natrolite, and clinoptilotite(?). Only the epsomite, which is relatively common, and the rarer gypsum may be primary precipitates.

Table 1.—*Composition, in milligrams per liter, of Soda Creek springs and meteoric water*

[Analysts: D. Donaldson and R. Barnes (B, NH_4^+), U.S. Geological Survey]

Source of water	Soda Creek springs Nabesna C-4 quadrangle (lat 62°32′ N., long 142°56′ W.)	Soda Creek (discharge from base of landslide)
pH	6.8	7.8
Temperature (°C)	5.5	7
SiO_2	12	6.5
Fe	1.8	0
Mn	.2	.02
Ca	381	48
Mg	192	11
Na	2,220	3
K	160	.5
NH_4	11	......
B	104	.1
HCO_3	7,240	171
SO_4	580	29
Cl	257	1.5
F	.7	.1
NO_3	.7	.4

Table 2.—*Mineral composition of travertine from the Soda Creek springs tufa cones*

Spring	Carbonate content, in percent (calcite and aragonite)[1]	Other minerals[2]
A (discharge rate, 1 liter/min).	81	Illite-montmorillonite, epsomite, quartz.
B (inactive)	97	Illite-montmorillonite, quartz, clinoptilolite(?), marcasite.
C, at orifice (discharge rate, 3 liters/min).	80	Illite-montmorillonite, epsomite, quartz.
C	92	Illite-montmorillonite, epsomite, anhydrite.
D (inactive)	67	Illite-montmorillonite, epsomite, gypsum, anhydrite, analcite, natrolite.

[1] Amount determined by loss in weight after acetic acid leach.
[2] Determined by X-ray diffraction of insoluble residue remaining after acetic acid leach.

Most of the other minerals are apparently carried up as particulate matter by the spring waters, although some (especially the quartz, and possibly the gypsum and anhydrite) may be of clastic windblown origin.

In the older spring deposits, covered by the 1969–70 landslide, the travertine contained small, irregular masses of marcasite associated with epsomite and antlerite, suggesting that at one time the springs were highly charged with H_2S. Also indicative of an earlier stage of higher sulfur activity are the abundant gypsum-anhydrite veins that lace the Jurassic and Cretaceous argillite peripheral to the springs.

ORIGIN

The unusual chemistry of the Soda Creek springs water and extremely large concentrations of many of its anomalous components argue against a meteoric origin for most of the water. Thermal waters of somewhat similar composition are known from a few active volcanic areas—the volcanic sodium-bicarbonate type water of White (1957a, p. 1649–1651)—but there is no geologic evidence in the eastern Alaska Range that the Soda Creek springs are related to present or recently active volcanism. White (1957a) recognized that not all sodium-bicarbonate waters are associated with areas of active volcanism and in a companion paper (White, 1957b, p. 1678–1679) suggested that many of these nonvolcanic high-bicarbonate waters may be fluids derived from the low-grade metamorphism of marine sedimentary rocks. In addition to the high bicarbonate content, White's criteria for metamorphic water included normal to low temperature, anomalous concentrations of boron and ammonia, and relatively low chloride compared with sea water.

On the basis of these criteria, the waters from the Soda Creek springs are considered to be mostly of metamorphic origin. The source from which these fluids and their unusual components have been derived is very likely the thick sequence of Jurassic and Cretaceous marine sedimentary rocks that underlie the springs area. An alternate source is the older and more deeply buried marine argillites and interbedded impure limestones of Permian age that occur at depths estimated to range from 5,000 to 8,000 feet beneath the springs. However, these Permian rocks have been regionally metamorphosed as high as the pumpellyite facies and consequently may already have lost much of their water and constituents such as boron, ammonia, and chlorine.

The mixed-layer clays and zeolite minerals found in the travertine precipitated by the springs lend additional support for a metamorphic origin of waters. Nowhere in surface exposures of either the Jurassic and Cretaceous argillites or the older Permian marine sedimentary rocks have these minerals been observed. X-ray studies of the fine-grained matrices of the Jurassic and Cretaceous argillites show the presence of quartz, both K-feldspar and Na-Ca-feldspars, calcite, chlorite, and possibly pyrophyllite. In the Permian rocks chlorite, pumpellyite, epidote, and albite have been recognized. Hence it appears that the clay and zeolites are authigenic species resulting from metamorphic reactions at depth beneath the springs. Although the temperatures and pressures in the source rocks must be relatively low, Muffler and White (1969) have shown that significant reactions involving silicate minerals occur at temperatures below 100°C.

SIGNIFICANCE OF THE SODA CREEK SPRINGS AND OTHER METAMORPHIC WATERS IN ALASKA

Recently, Barnes (1970) has reiterated and strongly supported White's suggestion of a metamorphic origin for many cool, high-bicarbonate spring waters and, on the basis of their occurrence and distribution, has proposed that marine sediments are being metamorphosed in a belt along the Pacific coast from southern California to Alaska. Because many of these springs issue from granitic, crystalline schist, and serpentinite terranes, Barnes also suggested that this was additional evidence for large-scale underthrusting of marine sediments under a tectonically active continental margin.

The presence of fluids suggestive of metamorphic origin at the Soda Creek springs extends the limits of an active metamorphic subterrane northwest into the Alaska Range. In an attempt to delineate this belt further, we have plotted in figure 4 all the relatively cool, bicarbonate-rich springs known to occur in Alaska. New analyses of three of these bicarbonate spring waters (springs 4,8; 1,2; 1,7, fig. 4) from south-central Alaska are given in table 3. On the basis of available analytical data, three types are recognized: Na-HCO_3, Ca-HCO_3, and Na-Cl-HCO_3. Water of the Na-Cl-HCO_3 type is restricted to a small part of the Copper River basin (springs 5 and 6, fig. 4) and may represent connate water modified by the addition of

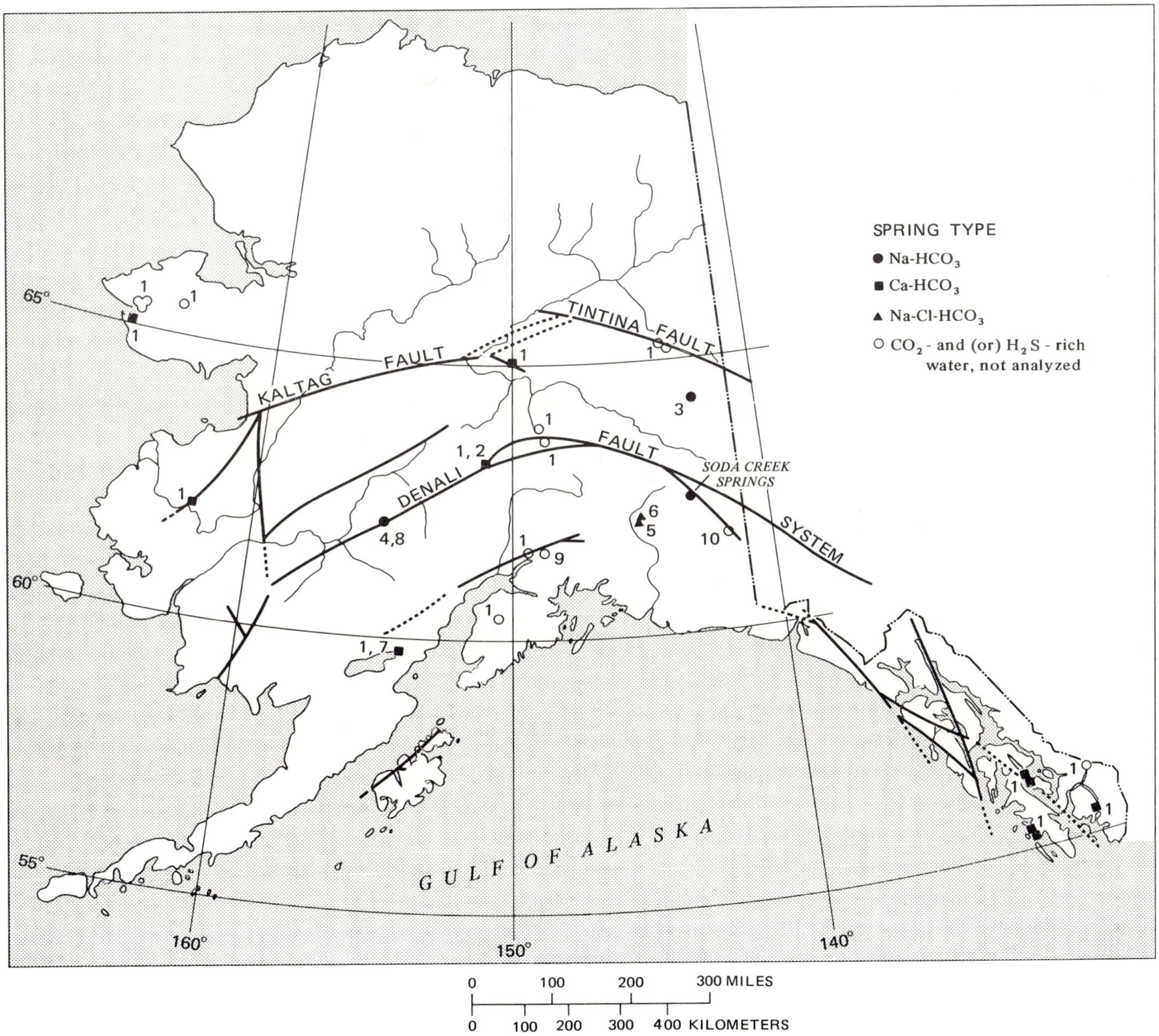

Figure 4.—Map of Alaska, showing location of known springs discharging water of possible metamorphic origin and major strike-slip faults, dashed where inferred (after Grantz, 1966). Sources of spring data: (1) Waring (1917); (2) R. M. Chapman (written commun., 1972); (3) Foster (1972); (4) A. L. Clark (written commun., 1972); (5) Grantz and others (1962); (6) Nichols and Yehle (1961); (7) U.S. Geological Survey, Water Resources Division records, Anchorage, Alaska; (8) Sainsbury and MacKevett (1965); (9) Richter (1967); and (10) D. H. Richter (unpub. data).

Table 3.–*Chemical composition, in milligrams per liter, of other bicarbonate springs in Alaska*

[Analysts: R. Barnes, 1970 (White Mountain springs); B. Walling, 1957 (Kantishna springs); C. L. Barwis, 1968 (Kakhonak springs), all U.S. Geological Survey]

Source of water	White Mountain springs (4,8)[1], McGrath A-4 quadrangle (lat 62°10′ N., long 154°53′ W.)	Kantishna springs (1,2), Mount McKinley C-2 quadrangle (lat 63°31′ N., long 150°59′ W.)	Kakhonak springs (1,7), Iliamna B-5 quadrangle (lat 59°28′ N., long 154°31′ W.)
pH	......	6.2	......
Temperature (°C)	Cool	6	4
SiO_2.....	......	36	57
Fe	......	6.8	......
Ca.......	50	405	369
Mg	43	347	106
Na	184	210	275
K	3.3	8	13
B	1.0	......	......
HCO_3....	632	1,960	2,310
SO_4	160	90	44
Cl.......	5.3	850	76
F	.....	0	.2
NO_3.....	.....	.....	.3

[1] Numbers in parentheses refer to localities in figure 4.

volcanic or metamorphic water or both (Grantz and others, 1962, p. 2000–2001).

Significantly, most of the cool bicarbonate springs of Alaska occur in southeastern Alaska, generally west of the Coast Range plutonic belt, and in south-central Alaska either along the Denali fault system or between the fault system and the continental margin. This terrane is composed chiefly of late Paleozoic and younger rocks, including widespread, thick marine sedimentary deposits. South of the Denali fault system in south-central Alaska between long 141° and 152° W., this terrane is thought to be virtually decoupled from the older terrane north of the fault (North American plate) and to be actively undergoing strong compressional deformation owing to the northward movement and impingement of the Pacific plate (Richter and Matson, 1971). In southeastern Alaska, similar deformation apparently prevailed as recently as late Tertiary time, underthrusting Mesozoic marine sedimentary rocks beneath the Coast Range plutons (Berg and others, 1972).

A few bicarbonate-rich springs occur along the Kaltag, Tintina, and related faults extending across central Alaska north of the Denali fault system. These major faults transect thick sequences of Paleozoic and Mesozoic marine sedimentary rocks and may in part represent tectonic boundaries between old crustal plates.

Only a cluster of springs on the Seward Peninsula in western Alaska and one spring in east-central Alaska (spring 3, fig. 4) do not appear to be related to young major structures and do not occur in areas underlain by marine sedimentary rocks. In both areas the terrane consists chiefly of Precambrian and old Paleozoic metamorphic rocks now part of a stable continental platform. Mesozoic and Cenozoic intrusive rocks cut the metamorphic rocks near the bicarbonate spring in east-central Alaska (Foster, 1972) and may explain the presence of the unusual water, but on the Seward Peninsula, no ready explanation for the springs is available.

In summary, we suggest that the Soda Creek springs and most of the other anomalous cool bicarbonate-rich springs in Alaska are discharging fluids characteristic of metamorphic origin. Except for the few springs on the Seward Peninsula and the one in east-central Alaska, all occur in terranes of present or recently active tectonism that include thick sections of marine sedimentary rocks, and many are located along major structures within these terranes.

REFERENCES CITED

Barnes, Ivan, 1970, Metamorphic waters from the Pacific tectonic belt of the west coast of the United States: Science, v. 168, p. 973–975.

Berg, H. C., Jones, D. L., and Richter, D. H., 1972, Gravina-Nutzotin belt–Tectonic significance of an upper Mesozoic sedimentary and volcanic sequence in southern and southeastern Alaska, *in* Geological Survey Research 1972: U.S. Geol. Survey Prof. Paper 800-D, p. D1–D24.

Foster, H. L., 1972, Preliminary geologic map of the Eagle quadrangle, Alaska: U.S. Geol. Survey Misc. Field Studies Map MF-358.

Grantz, Arthur, 1966, Strike-slip faults in Alaska: U.S. Geol. Survey open-file report, 82 p.

Grantz, Arthur, White, D. E., Whitehead, H. C., and Tagg, A. R., 1962, Saline springs, Copper River lowland, Alaska: Am. Assoc. Petroleum Geologists Bull., v. 46, p. 1990–2002.

Moffit, F. H., 1933, The Suslota Pass district, upper Copper River region, Alaska: U.S. Geol. Survey Bull. 844-C, p. 137–162.

——1941, Geology of the upper Tetling River district, Alaska: U.S. Geol. Survey Bull. 917-B, p. 115–157.

Muffler, L. J. P., and White, D. E., 1969, Active metamorphism of upper Cenozoic sediments in the Salton Sea geothermal field and the Salton trough, southeastern California: Geol. Soc. America Bull., v. 80, p. 157–182.

Nichols, D. R., and Yehle, L. A., 1961, Mud volcanoes in the Copper River basin, Alaska, *in* Rausch, G. O., ed., Geology of the Arctic: Internat. Symposium on Arctic Geology, 1st, Calgary 1960, Proc., v. 2, p. 1063–1087.

Richter, D. H., 1967, Geological and geochemical investigations in the Metal Creek area, Chugach Mountains, Alaska: Alaska Div. Mines and Minerals Geol. Rept. 25, 17 p.

Richter, D. H., and Jones, D. L., 1970, Structure and stratigraphy of the eastern Alaska Range [abs.]: Am. Assoc. Petroleum Geologists Bull., v. 54, p. 2502.

Richter, D. H., and Matson, N. A., Jr., 1971, Quaternary faulting in the eastern Alaska Range: Geol. Soc. America Bull., v. 82, p. 1529–1540.

Sainsbury, C. L., and MacKevett, E. M., Jr., 1965, Quicksilver deposits of southwestern Alaska: U.S. Geol. Survey Bull. 1187, 89 p.

Waring, G. A., 1917, Mineral springs of Alaska: U.S. Geol. Survey Water-Supply Paper 418, 114 p.

White, D. E., 1957a, Thermal waters of volcanic origin: Geol. Soc. America Bull., v. 68, p. 1637–1658.

——1957b, Magmatic, connate, and metamorphic waters: Geol. Soc. America Bull., v. 68, p. 1659–1682.

Jour. Research U.S. Geol. Survey
Vol. 1, No. 5, Sept.-Oct. 1973, p. 529—534

THE DUN MOUNTAIN ULTRAMAFIC BELT—PERMIAN OCEANIC CRUST AND UPPER MANTLE IN NEW ZEALAND

By M. C. BLAKE, JR., and C. A. LANDIS[1],
Washington, D.C., Dunedin, New Zealand

Abstract.—Geologic evidence suggests that the Dun Mountain ultramafic belt in New Zealand is the basal part of a Lower Permian ophiolite suite. By analogy with other ophiolite suites, and as a result of marine geophysical studies of the present ocean basins, the ophiolite is believed to represent oceanic crust and upper mantle upon which the Upper Permian Maitai Group was deposited. After this, much of the ultramafic belt was extensively deformed to tectonic mélange.

This paper proposes that the Dun Mountain ultramafic belt constitutes the tectonically disrupted basal part of a Lower Permian ophiolite suite which originally stratigraphically underlaid the eastern margin of the Hokonui facies of the New Zealand geosyncline.

The Dun Mountain ultramafic belt (Landis and Coombs, 1967) consists of two widely separated belts of ultramafic rock within the New Zealand geosyncline (fig. 1). One belt is on the southeast side of the Alpine fault (Red Mountain part); the other (Dun Mountain part) is on the northwest side of the fault and includes the type locality for dunite. They are considered to have been one continuous belt before a 480-km strike-slip displacement along the Alpine fault.

Acknowledgments.—The writers' research has been supported by grants from the U.S. National Science Foundation (g/18700) and New Zealand University Grants Committee (C. A. Landis) and the Fulbright Commission and Auckland University Fellowship (M. C. Blake, Jr.). The manuscript has benefitted from discussion and criticism by D. S. Coombs, E. H. Bailey, and T. P. Thayer.

HISTORICAL BACKGROUND

The origin of the Dun Mountain rocks has long been debated, and a brief review of selected interpretations is presented here. As early as 1864, the existence of an elongate belt of ultramafic rock passing through the Dun Mountain region was recognized (Hochstetter, 1864). Hochstetter was impressed by the overall conformity between the ultramafic belt and adjoining country rock (upper Paleozoic sedimentary rock and volcanic rock) and suggested that the ultramafic rock originated as a sill-like intrusion. Other early workers were equally impressed with the regular, seemingly stratigraphic, contact between the ultramafic-volcanic suite and the overlying limestones of the Maitai Group (Upper Permian), and McKay (1879) interpreted this relationship as indicating that the ultramafites and associated basaltic rocks were already on the sea floor (possibly originating as lava flows) when the Maitai limestone was deposited.

Later a post-Maitai intrusive origin for the Dun Mountain ultramafic belt came into vogue. An intrusive origin was first proposed by Park (1887, 1921) and was later developed and popularized by W. N. Benson (1926). Benson envisaged the ultramafites as intrusions, probably in a semisolid state, along major Mesozoic thrust faults. Many subsequent workers (Turner, 1930, Macpherson, 1946; Kingma, 1959) continued to favor Mesozoic intrusion along a great thrust zone.

A return to the McKay hypothesis favoring penecontemporaneity of the ultramafites with Lower Permian spilites, dolerites, and associated sediments was proposed by Grindley (1958). Grindley mapped a large segment of the Red Mountain part of the Dun Mountain belt and suggested that the ultramafites (mainly serpentinites) originated as submarine lava flows. Early Permian origin of the ultramafites was also favored by Waterhouse (1964, p. 87): "Near the close of the Lower Permian serpentine was emplaced laterally, accompanied by mild orogeny***."

Recent detailed studies of selected areas within the Dun Mountain part of the ultramafic belt by G. A. Challis, W. R. Lauder, and R. I. Walcott have led to the hypothesis of high-temperature emplacement of ultramafic magma into Lower Permian volcanic rocks. The presence of a high-temperature ultramafic intrusion in the Dun Mountain area (Lauder, 1965a,b; Challis and Lauder, 1966) is inferred from (1) structural discontinuities between peridotites (and associated serpentinites) and Maitai Group sedimentary rocks of

[1] Department of Geology, University of Otago.

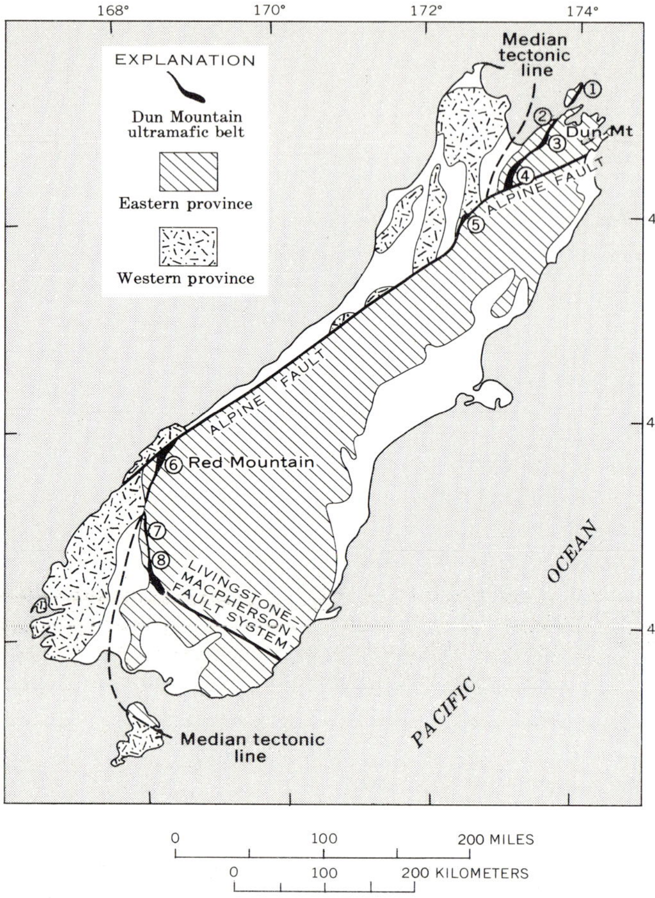

Figure 1.—Map showing location of Dun Mountain ultramafic belt, South Island, New Zealand. Localities corresponding to sections in figure 3: 1, Port Hardy, D'Urville Island; 2, Taipare, Tasman Bay; 3, Dun Mountain-Wooded Peak area; 4, Red Hills; 5, Matakitaki; 6, Red Mountain; 7, Cascade Creek; 8, Annear Creek-Upukerora Valley area. Eastern province comprises New Zealand geosyncline and contemporaneous intrusive rocks along western side of geosyncline. Hokonui belt is within eastern province west of Dun Mountain belt and southwest of Livingstone-Macpherson fault system. Western province comprises crystalline and moderate- to high-temperature-pressure metamorphosed Paleozoic rocks (Landis and Coombs, 1967). Median tectonic line is a zone of dislocation (Landis and Coombs, 1967) marking western margin of New Zealand geosyncline. Livingstone-Macpherson fault system is the boundary between two contrasting geosynclinal assemblages (Landis and Bishop, 1972). The northern extent of this fault system coincides with eastern margin of Dun Mountain ultramafic belt.

Late Permian age, (2) apparently steeply inclined concentric lithologic layering of dunite and peridotite within the Dun Mountain massif, and (3) contact metamorphism of adjoining Maitai Group country rock. Lauder (1965a, b) concluded that Dun Mountain is a volcanic pipe or magma chamber formed at the root of a Cretaceous volcano. At Red Hills, 45 km south of Dun Mountain, another large peridotite mass was described by Challis (1965a, b) and Walcott (1969). Challis regarded it as a high-temperature lopolithic intrusion. The peridotite contains near-horizontal cumulate layering that contrasts with near-vertical layering in adjoining Lower Permian spilite, a situation which seems to require deformation before emplacement of the ultramafic liquid. Evidence cited in favor of high-temperature intrusion is chiefly the unfaulted contact between cumulate ultramafite and pyroxene hornfels-facies country rock. Challis regarded the spilites and ultramafites as genetically related rocks and proposed intrusion of ultramafic liquid into deformed but comagmatic spilite. The Red Hills body was regarded as the crystallized contents of a large magma chamber at a high level within a Permian volcanic arc. Walcott (1969) also interpreted Red Hills as a high-temperature magmatic intrusion of Permian age; however, some of his observations conflict with those of Challis (see below). Both the Dun Mountain and Red Hills peridotite masses appear to be rootless; this has been interpreted (Challis and Lauder, 1966) as being due to later low-angle thrust faults.

DISCUSSION OF HYPOTHESES

We cannot fully agree with any of the origins proposed for the Dun Mountain belt, or for selected parts thereof. Some specific points of contention and our contrary interpretations are:

1. Emplacement of ultramafites along a major Mesozoic thrust fault (Benson, 1926). The intimate association and regionally concordant relation between ultramafites and the suite of Permian volcanic rocks, limestones, and volcanogenic sedimentary rocks is too widespread for us to accept a hypothesis requiring a separate and distinctive origin for each suite (see also Grindley, 1958). On the contrary, we believe that the volcanic rocks and the ultramafites are genetically related. We do acknowledge, however, a relation between Mesozoic thrust faulting and the present distribution of ultramafites brought about by localization of thrusting along a preexisting zone of weakness corresponding to both the incompetent serpentinite and an ancient plate margin (Landis and Bishop, 1972).

2. Suggested origin of ultramafic rock as submarine flow (Grindley, 1958). We agree with Grindley that gabbroic and ultramafic rocks were on, or at least near to, the Permian sea floor when spatially associated volcanic materials were emplaced. However, we can find no evidence for flows of ultramafic lava. Neither our field observations nor those of marine geologists (for example, JOIDES deep-sea drilling) provide any reason to favor extrusion of voluminous ultramafic liquid onto the sea floor.

3. Is Dun Mountain a volcanic neck? (Lauder, 1965a, b). Walcott (1969) has already discussed some of the shortcomings of this hypothesis: for example, there is no compelling evidence for intrusive contacts with Maitai rocks, whose thermal metamorphism, as described by Lauder, can be explained by low-temperature contact metasomatic effects (Coleman, 1966). In addition, no convincing evidence for a

cylindrical form of the Dun Mountain body has been presented, and the orientation of mineral layering reported by Walcott and confirmed by us conflicts with data presented by Lauder. The absence of any other evidence for Cretaceous volcanism in the Dun Mountain region (for example, mafic-ultramafic pyroclastic deposits) is noteworthy (Challis, 1965a, b).

4. Shallow roots of a Permian volcanic arc (Challis, 1965a). Challis regarded the Red Hills peridotite body as being emplaced as an ultramafic magma into a comagmatic Permian volcanic arc. Evidence to support this hypothesis includes a high-temperature unfaulted contact between the ultramafic rock and the comagmatic volcanic rocks. A fundamental problem with this hypothesis is the enormous size required for a relatively shallow magma chamber (present size of ultramafic outcrop at Red Hills is 9 by 10 km) which was emplaced beneath, but apparently never broke through, a thin (1-km) carapace of penecontemporaneous volcanic rock. In addition, significant discrepancies exist between Challis' map of the western margin of the Red Hills body and mapping by Walcott (1969), and reconnaissance studies by one of us (Landis, 1969). In particular, whereas no faults were mapped in this area by Challis, many faults in the western part of the ultramafic body were mapped by Walcott. One of these faults appears to be a major fault parallel to the ultramafite–volcanic rock contact. In addition, the presence of serpentinite adjacent to the western, supposedly high-temperature intrusive contact, and a parallel dikelike mass of serpentinite 100 m farther west, along with field data discussed elsewhere in this paper, suggest that the Red Hills mass may be part of a mélange belt. Furthermore, chemically analyzed pyroxenes from Red Hills (Challis, 1965a) have been plotted by O'Hara (1967) on his pressure-temperature grid showing estimated conditions of equilibration of some natural ultramafic assemblages. Crystallization of Red Hills pyroxenes is estimated at 1,100°C–4 kb. This corresponds to depths of 10–15 km (depending on density of overburden), a conclusion consistent with Walcott's observations of tectonite fabrics and folding in the Red Hills peridotites. Identical fabrics have been described from many other alpine ultramafic rocks (Coleman, 1971, p. 1214–1215) and attributed to high-temperature mantle deformation.

PLATE TECTONIC INTERPRETATION

Recent mapping, coupled with interpretation guided by concepts of global tectonics, has led us to propose that the Dun Mountain belt constitutes a deformed, and in part remobilized, oceanic basement of Permian age (Landis, 1969; Hatherton, 1969) on which the Permian Maitai sedimentary rocks were deposited. On the basis of analogy with the ophiolite basement which underlies the Great Valley sequence of California (Bailey and others, 1970), a similar hypothesis has been proposed by Dickinson (1971).

Our recent mapping in the Nelson-Marlborough Sounds regions supports the oceanic-crust hypothesis. Our data, along with field and petrologic observations by other workers throughout the length of the Hokonui terrane (as defined by Landis and Bishop, 1972), permit a reasonably detailed actualistic interpretation of the origin of the Dun Mountain ultramafic belt and also of the associated Permian volcanic and sedimentary rocks (Lee River and Humboldt Groups of Waterhouse, 1964).

Marine geophysical studies indicate a remarkably constant ocean-basin structure (Raitt, 1963)—a sequence progressing downward through a representative part of the sea floor is believed to comprise:

Crustal layer 1—sediments (mainly pelagic mud, chert, biogenic carbonate).	0–1.0 km
Crustal layer 2—pillow basalt and diabase.	1.6–2.0 km
Crustal layer 3—gabbro, amphibolite, metabasalt (± diorite, trondhjemite, serpentinite).	4.8 km
M—Discontinuity	
Upper mantle—harzburgite and dunite, probably underlain by lherzolite and garnet peridotite.	

The ocean-basin sequence, although generally somewhat thicker, is similar to the ophiolite suite, a partly layered rock assemblage characteristic of some orogenic belts. Typically, the ophiolite suite consists (from base to top) of dunite and peridotite (variably serpentinized) overlain by gabbro and amphibolite, pillow basalts, and capped by pelagic sediments (Moores and Vine, 1971). Several workers (Bailey and others, 1970; Davies, 1971; Coleman, 1971; Dewey and Bird, 1971; Bezzi and Piccardo, 1971) have emphasized that rock sequences and thicknesses of documented ophiolite suites are comparable to the oceanic crust–upper mantle. Stratigraphic sections from Permian geosynclinal sediments downward into the Dun Mountain rocks (figs. 2 and 3) also resemble an ocean-floor sequence (see also Coleman, 1966, figs. 5, 25, 40, and 41). The main contrasts between the Dun Mountain ophiolites and the oceanic sequences are (1) the generally sheared and incompletely developed sequences which characterize the Dun Mountain belt, and (2) the consistently thinner nature of layer 2 and layer 3 rocks of the Dun Mountain belt in comparison with oceanic crust. We believe that these discrepancies are due in part to intensive post-Permian tectonism and in part to original differences in thickness.

In most areas, we find the Dun Mountain ophiolite belt to be a tectonic mélange. Tectonic blocks of sedimentary, volcanic, gabbroic, and ultramafic rock occur as inclusions within a matrix of sheared serpentinite and argillite. Field relationships, petrography, and metasomatic alteration of these blocks were described by Coleman (1966), and our

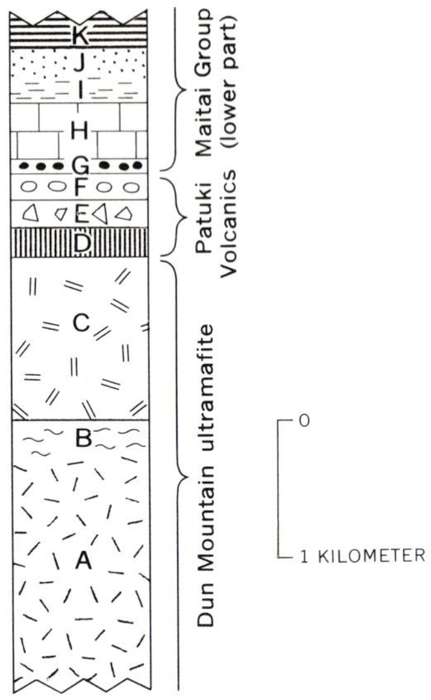

Figure 2.–Interpretive reconstruction of a representative stratigraphic section of undeformed Permian sea floor (Dun Mountain ophiolites), eastern margin of Hokonui belt.

- A, Peridotite, dunite, and less commonly lherzolite; variably serpentinized; rodingitized gabbroic to basaltic dikes.
- B, Serpentinite and argillite, generally sheared.
- C, Gabbro, dolerite, amphibolite, minor trondhjemite; extensively albitized and rodingitized; locally thermally metamorphosed.
- D, Basaltic lava, massive and layered, largely spilitized.
- E, Agglomerate plus volcanic-hypabyssal breccias.
- F, Pillow lava, extensively spilitized.
- G, Conglomerate and breccia, well to poorly bedded; predominantly volcanogenic with minor amounts of sedimentary, hypabyssal, and plutonic clasts; some interbedded black argillite and siliceous sediments.
- H, Limestone, composed mainly of bivalvian detritus; calcturbidites; interbedded volcanogenic and minor siliceous sediments.
- I, Siltstone and sandstone, fossiliferous, quartz-bearing.
- J, Sandstone, green and volcanogenic, unfossiliferous.
- K, Mudstone and fine-grained sandstone, laminated and graded, unfossiliferous.

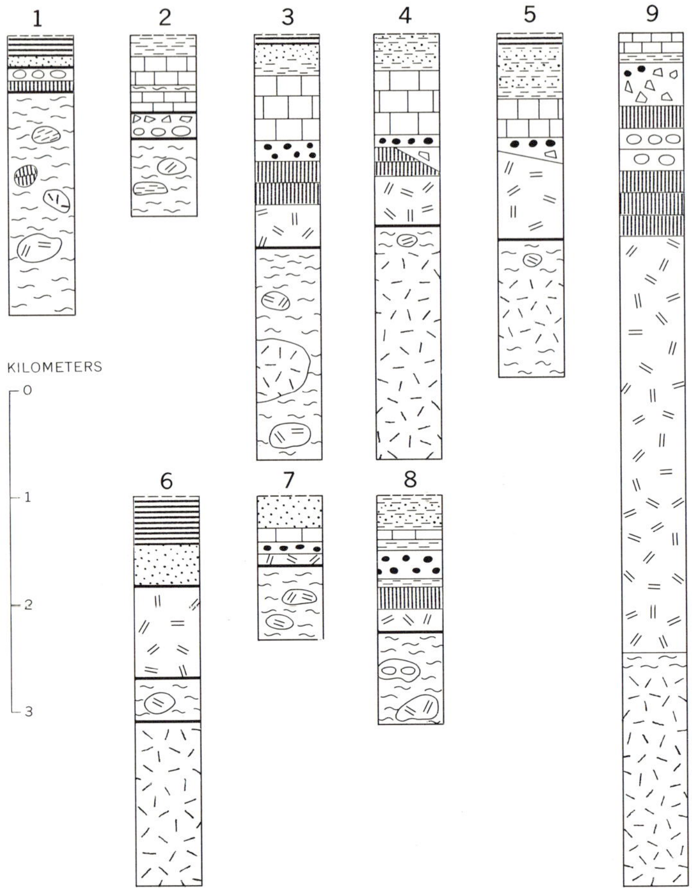

Figure 3.–Selected stratigraphic sections, somewhat diagrammatic, through Dun Mountain ultramafite and associated rocks. Data from Grindley (1958); Waterhouse (1964); Lauder (1965a, b); Walcott (1969); Coleman (1966); Landis (1969); Bell, Clarke, and Marshall (1911); Lensen (1963); Beck (1964); and unpublished work by the authors. Location of sections 1–8 shown in figure 1; section 9 is a representative sequence of oceanic crust and upper mantle. Explanation of symbols given in figure 2; heavy lines are faults. Mélange shown as rounded blocks surrounded by serpentinite; in reality, matrix includes sheared sediment as well.

studies confirm his account. Outcrop size of the blocks varies from less than 1 m to 2 by 2 km (for example, Dun Mountain massif). At Red Hills, gravity studies (Malahoff, 1965), detailed regional mapping (Walcott, 1969), and our own reconnaissance observations suggest that this ultramafic body (outcrop area, 10 by 9 km) also may be an enormous tectonic block.

Despite tectonic mixing and frequent juxtaposition of strange bedfellows (for example, peridotite and argillite), an overall ghost stratigraphy appears to persist within parts of the mélange; sedimentary and volcanic blocks tend to be more abundant near the upper (western) ophiolite contact, whereas gabbroic and ultramafic blocks are more common deeper (farther east) in the deformed ophiolite. Reduction of original thicknesses of basaltic and gabbroic layers may have occurred by attenuation during rotation of the steep-to-overturned eastern limb of the Nelson–Key Summit regional syncline formed in the Permian sedimentary rocks west of the ultramafic belt. It is also possible that the basaltic and gabbroic rocks of layers 2 and 3 were originally anomalously thin. Rapid spreading rates have been suggested as a possible cause of thin layer 2 (Moores and Vine, 1971; Dewey and Bird, 1971; Menard, 1967), and a similar origin for thin layer 3 also seems feasible.

Origin of Dun Mountain ophiolites beneath a marginal or interarc basin (Karig, 1971, 1972) should also be given consideration, especially as certain aspects of the Dun Mountain belt resemble characteristics expected for marginal-basin ophiolites (Dewey and Bird, 1971).

EVOLUTION OF DUN MOUNTAIN ULTRAMAFIC BELT

We propose that the Dun Mountain ultramafic belt originated as follows:

1. Permian sea-floor spreading, accompanied by:
   a. extrusion of submarine basalt along a ridge or marginal-basin axis;
   b. crystallization of comagmatic gabbroic rocks deeper beneath ridge and possibly of comagmatic cumulative peridotite and dunite beneath gabbro;
   c. formation of other peridotites and dunites as residue rocks by partial melting and upward expulsion of basaltic component from lherzolitic mantle. The Dun Mountain ultramafite comprises these ultramafic rocks, plus b (above), plus serpentinized derivatives;
   d. regional thermal metamorphism of basaltic and gabbroic rocks to amphibolite and greenschist facies within axial part of ridge or marginal basin;
   e. contemporaneous subduction of cooled oceanic crust plus underlying Dun Mountain oceanic mantle beneath an Early Permian volcanic arc (Brook Street terrane).
   f. deposition of Permian deep-sea sediments. Volcanic-plutonic breccias derived from layer 2 and layer 3 rocks exposed along fault scarps within ridge. Pelagic muds and calcareous and siliceous sediments (including some cherts) deposited upon layer 2 and layer 3 basement on quiet sea floor between ridge and subduction zone or within marginal basin.
2. Late Permian cessation of sea-floor spreading and subduction. Sedimentation of flyschoid sediment, predominantly of andesitic-basaltic provenance, possibly filling inactive trench (Maitai Group).
3. Folding,[2] thrusting, metamorphism, serpentinization, and internal disruption of ophiolite belt: creation of Dun Mountain mélange.
4. Division of Dun Mountain belt into Dun Mountain part and Red Mountain part by 480-km strike-slip offset along Alpine fault in Late Cretaceous-Holocene time.

Time of formation of the mélange is unclear. Possible mélange formation was initiated during Permian-Early Triassic subduction and orogenesis (compare Landis and Bishop, 1972); however, evidence for further deformation or wholesale subduction affecting the Dun Mountain belt does not appear until Late Jurassic–Early Cretaceous time, when renewed activity–Rangitata orogeny–resulted in extensive deformation, low-ratio pressure-temperature metamorphism, and mélange formation. Deformation of the ophiolite belt has continued locally and spasmodically into the Cenozoic (Fleming, 1947).

[2] Ophiolite sequences with inferred eastward-facing direction occur in certain areas (Waterhouse, 1964, p. 16, 21–23) and may indicate anticlinal folding of the Dun Mountain belt.

REFERENCES CITED

Bailey, E. H., Blake, M. C., Jr., and Jones, D. L., 1970, On-land Mesozoic oceanic crust in California Coast Ranges, *in* Geological Survey Research 1970: U.S. Geol. Survey Prof. Paper 700-C, p. C70–C81.

Beck, A. C., 1964, Geological map of New Zealand, Sheet 14, Marlborough Sounds: Wellington, New Zealand Geol. Survey, scale 1:250,000.

Bell, J. M., Clarke, E. de C., and Marshall, P., 1911, The geology of the Dun Mountain subdivision, Nelson: New Zealand Geol. Survey, new ser., Bull. 12, 71 p.

Benson, W. N., 1926, The tectonic conditions accompanying the intrusion of basic and ultrabasic igneous rocks: Natl. Acad. Sci. Mem., v. 19, no. 1, 90 p.

Bezzi, Alfredo, and Piccardo, G. B., 1971, Structural features of the Ligurian ophiolites; petrologic evidence for the "oceanic" floor of the northern Apennines geosyncline; a contribution to the problem of the alpine-type gabbro-peridotite associations: Soc. Geol. Italiana Mem., v. 10, no. 1, p. 53–63.

Challis, G. A., 1965a, The origin of New Zealand ultramafic intrusions: Jour. Petrology, v. 6, no. 2, p. 332–364.

——1965b, High-temperature contact metamorphism at the Red Hills ultramafic intrusion, Wairau Valley, New Zealand: Jour. Petrology, v. 6, no. 3, p. 395–419.

Challis, G. A., and Lauder, W. R., 1966, The genetic position of "alpine" type ultramafic rocks: Bull. Volcanol., v. 29, p. 283–304.

Coleman, R. G., 1966, New Zealand serpentinites and associated metasomatic rocks: New Zealand Geol. Survey Bull. 76, 102 p.

——1971, Plate tectonic emplacement of upper mantle peridotites along continental edges: Jour. Geophys. Research, v. 76, no. 5, p. 1212–1222.

Davies, H. L., 1971, Peridotite-gabbro-basalt complex in eastern Papua: an overthrust plate of oceanic mantle and crust: Australia Bur. Mineral Resources, Geology, and Geophysics Bull. 128, 48 p.

Dewey, J. F., and Bird, J. M., 1971, Origin and emplacement of the ophiolite suite; Appalachian ophiolites in Newfoundland: Jour. Geophys. Research, v. 76, no. 14, p. 3179–3206.

Dickinson, W. R., 1971, Clastic sedimentary sequences deposited in shelf, slope, and trough settings between magmatic arcs and associated trenches: Pacific Geology, v. 3, p. 15–30.

Fleming, C. A., 1947, Serpentinite at Wairere, Totoro survey district, King country: New Zealand Jour. Sci. and Technology, v. 29, no. 3, p. 100–115.

Grindley, G. W., 1958, The geology of the Eglinton Valley, Southland; parts of Eglinton (S131) and Mavora (S141) sheet districts: New Zealand Geol. Survey Bull. 58, 68 p.

Hatherton, Trevor, 1969, Geophysical anomalies over the eu- and miogeosynclinal systems of California and New Zealand: Geol. Soc. America Bull., v. 80, no. 2, p. 213–230.

Hochstetter, F. C. von, 1864, Geologie von Neu-Seeland. Beiträge zur Geologie der Provinzen Auckland und Nelson, *in* Reise der Osterreichischen Fregatte Novara um die Erde, in. . .1857–59. Geologischen Theil, v. 1, sec. 1: Vienna, 274 p. (English edition, translation by C. A. Fleming: Wellington, Govt. Printer).

Karig, D. E., 1971, Origin and development of marginal basins in the western Pacific: Jour. Geophys. Research, v. 76, no. 11, p. 2542–2561.

——1972, Remnant arcs: Geol. Soc. America Bull., v. 83, no. 4, p. 1057–1068.

Kingma, J. T., 1959, The tectonic history of New Zealand: New Zealand Jour. Geology and Geophysics, v. 2, no. 1, p. 1–55.

Landis, C. A., 1969, Upper Permian rocks of South Island, New Zealand–lithology, stratigraphy, structure, metamorphism and tectonics: Dunedin, New Zealand, Univ. of Otago, Ph. D. dissert., 627 p.

Landis, C. A., and Bishop, D. G., 1972, Plate tectonics and regional stratigraphic-metamorphic relations in the southern part of the New Zealand geosyncline: Geol. Soc. America Bull., v. 83, no. 8, p. 2267–2284.

Landis, C. A., and Coombs, D. S., 1967, Metamorphic belts and orogenesis in southern New Zealand: Tectonophysics, v. 4, nos. 4–6, p. 501–518.

Lauder, W. R., 1965a, The geology of Dun Mountain, Nelson, New Zealand; Pt. 1, The petrology and structure of the sedimentary and volcanic rocks of the Te Anau and Maitai Groups: New Zealand Jour. Geology and Geophysics, v. 8, no. 1, p. 3–34.

——1965b, The geology of Dun Mountain, Nelson, New Zealand; Part 2, The petrology, structure, and origin of the ultrabasic rocks: New Zealand Jour. Geology and Geophysics, v. 8, no. 3, p. 475–504.

Lensen, G. J., 1963, Geological map of New Zealand, Sheet 16, Kaikoura: Wellington, New Zealand Geol. Survey, scale 1:250,000.

Macpherson, E. O., 1946, An outline of Late Cretaceous and Tertiary diastrophism in New Zealand: New Zealand Dept. Sci. and Indus. Resources Geol. Mem. 6, 32 p.

Malahoff, Alexander, 1965, Gravimetric and geologic studies of an ultramafic mass in New Zealand: Am. Geophys. Union Trans., v. 46, p. 159–160.

McKay, Alexander, 1879, The district between the Wairau and Motueka Valleys: New Zealand Geol. Survey Rept. Geol. Explor. 1878–79, v. 12, p. 97–121.

Menard, H. W., 1967, Transitional types of crust under small ocean basins: Jour. Geophys. Research, v. 72, no. 12, p. 3061–3073.

Moores, E. M., and Vine, F. J., 1971, The Troodos Massif, Cyprus, and other ophiolites as oceanic crust; evaluation and implications: Royal Soc. London Philos. Trans., v. 268, p. 443–466.

O'Hara, M. J., 1967, Mineral parageneses in ultrabasic rocks, *in* Wyllie, P. J., ed., Ultramafic and related rocks: New York, John Wiley and Sons, p. 393–403.

Park, J., 1887, On the district between the Dart and Big Bay: New Zealand Colonial Mus. and Geol. Survey Rept. Geol. Explor. 1886–87, p. 121–137.

——1921, Geology and mineral resources of western Southland: New Zealand Geol. Survey Bull. 23, 88 p.

Raitt, R. W., 1963, The crustal rocks, *in* Hill, M. N., ed., The sea, v. 3, The earth beneath the sea: London, Interscience Publishers, p. 85–102.

Turner, F. J., 1930, The metamorphic and ultrabasic rocks of the Lower Cascade Valley, South Westland: New Zealand Inst. Trans., v. 61, p. 170–201.

Walcott, R. I., 1969, Geology of the Red Hill complex, Nelson, New Zealand: Royal Soc. New Zealand Trans., Earth Sci., v. 7, no. 5, p. 57–88.

Waterhouse, J. B., 1964, Permian stratigraphy and faunas of New Zealand: New Zealand Geol. Survey Bull. 72, 101 p.

Jour. Research U.S. Geol. Survey
Vol. 1, No. 5, Sept.-Oct. 1973, p. 535—541

A CALORIMETRIC DETERMINATION OF THE STANDARD ENTHALPIES OF FORMATION OF HUNTITE, $CaMg_3(CO_3)_4$, AND ARTINITE, $Mg_2(OH)_2CO_3 \cdot 3H_2O$, AND THEIR STANDARD GIBBS FREE ENERGIES OF FORMATION

By BRUCE S. HEMINGWAY and RICHARD A. ROBIE, Silver Spring, Md.

Abstract.—The enthalpies of formation, $\Delta H^\circ f$, of huntite, $CaMg_3(CO_3)_4$, and artinite, $Mg_2(OH)_2CO_3 \cdot 3H_2O$, have been determined by HCl solution calorimetry using a constant-volume isoperibol reaction calorimeter. For the reaction $CaO(c) + 3MgO(c) + 4CO_2(g) = CaMg_3(CO_3)_4(c)$, the enthalpy change at 298.15 K, ΔH°_{298}, is $-123{,}203 \pm 145$ cal mol^{-1}. For the reaction $2MgO(c) + 4H_2O(l) + CO_2(g) = Mg_2(OH)_2CO_3 \cdot 3H_2O(c)$, we obtained $-45{,}132 \pm 100$ cal mol^{-1}. These results combined with the standard enthalpies of formation of CaO, MgO, H_2O, and CO_2 lead to $\Delta H^\circ f_{,298}$ (huntite) = $-1{,}082{,}600 \pm 375$ cal mol^{-1} and $\Delta H^\circ f_{,298}$ (artinite) = $-698{,}043 \pm 170$ cal mol^{-1}. Using recently determined values for the standard entropies of huntite, $CaMg_3(CO_3)_4$, and artinite, $Mg_2(OH)_2CO_3 \cdot 3H_2O$, and of Mg, Ca, C, O_2, and H_2, we calculate $\Delta G^\circ f_{,298}$ (huntite) = $-1{,}004{,}707 \pm 390$ cal mol^{-1} and $\Delta G^\circ f_{,298}$ (artinite) = $-613{,}924 \pm 180$ cal mol^{-1}.

In a previous report from this laboratory (Hemingway and Robie, 1972), we presented measurements of the heat capacities of huntite and artinite between 20 and 308 K and calculated values of the entropy change, $S^\circ_{298} - S^\circ_0$, for these minerals. In this paper we present measurements of the enthalpies of formation of huntite and artinite obtained from the heat of solution of $CaMg_3(CO_3)_4$, $Mg_2(OH)_2CO_3 \cdot 3H_2O$, MgO, CaO, and H_2O in 4 *N* HCl between 24° and 37°C.

The reaction scheme used to determine the heat of formation of huntite, $CaMg_3(CO_3)_4$ was

$$CaMg_3(CO_3)_4(c) + [285HCl + 3{,}641H_2O](aq) = [CaCl_2 + 3MgCl_2 + 277HCl + 3{,}645H_2O](aq) + 4CO_2(g), \quad (1)$$

$$3MgO(c) + [285HCl + 3{,}641H_2O](aq) = [3MgCl_2 + 279HCl + 3{,}644H_2O](aq), \text{ and} \quad (2)$$

$$CaO(c) + [3MgCl_2 + 279HCl + 3{,}644H_2O](aq) = [CaCl_2 + 3MgCl_2 + 277HCl + 3{,}645H_2O](aq). \quad (3)$$

The reactions studied to obtain the enthalpy of formation of artinite, $Mg_2(OH)_2CO_3 \cdot 3H_2O$, were

$$Mg_2(OH)_2CO_3 \cdot 3H_2O(c) + [285HCl + 3{,}641H_2O](aq) = [2MgCl_2 + 281HCl + 3{,}647H_2O](aq) + CO_2(g), \quad (4)$$

$$2MgO(c) + [285HCl + 3{,}641H_2O](aq) = [2MgCl_2 + 281HCl + 3{,}643H_2O](aq), \text{ and} \quad (5)$$

$$4H_2O(l) + [2MgCl_2 + 281HCl + 3{,}643H_2O](aq) = [2MgCl_2 + 281HCl + 3{,}647H_2O](aq). \quad (6)$$

The actual reactions studied were stoichiometric for the solution of 0.0125 mol of $CaMg_3(CO_3)_4$ and of $Mg_2(OH)_2CO_3 \cdot 3H_2O$ in 950.0 g of 4.0 *N* HCl. The nominal weights of sample used were 4.413 g of $CaMg_3(CO_3)_4$, 2.549 g of $Mg_2(OH)_2CO_3 \cdot 3H_2O$, 0.701 g of CaO, 0.901 g of H_2O, and 1.008 and 1.312 g of MgO.

The gram formula weights used in the calculations are based on the 1969 values for the atomic weights (Commission on Atomic Weights, 1970). The formula weights used for $CaMg_3(CO_3)_4$ and $Mg_2(OH)_2CO_3 \cdot 3H_2O$ are 353.032 and 196.680 g mol^{-1}.[1]

MATERIALS AND APPARATUS

The MgO used for the heat of solution measurements was Johnson-Matthey Specpure reagent (JM 130). It was heated in a platinum crucible at 1,300°C for 3 hours to promote grain growth (Taylor and Wells, 1938), and stored in a desiccator over fresh Drierite prior to use. The CaO sample was obtained by heating primary standard $CaCO_3$ (Mallinckrodt, C-65) at 1,300°C in a platinum crucible for 3 hours. It was stored in a desiccator before using. The H_2O was distilled and passed through an ion-exchange column.

[1] The mole is the International System (SI) unit for that amount of substance of a system containing as many elementary entities as there are atoms in 0.012 kg of carbon-12. It is the same as the gram formula weight and is abbreviated as mol (U.S. National Bureau Standards Tech. Notes, 1972, v. 56, p. 42).

The samples of huntite and artinite used in these heat of solution studies were portions of the sample used in the low-temperature heat capacity studies of Hemingway and Robie (1972), and are described fully in that report. The hydrochloric acid was a special reagent obtained in 5-gallon lots certified by the manufacturer, Fisher Scientific Co., to be 4.00±0.01 *N*. The solution calorimeter used in our investigation and the methods of data reduction have been described by Robie and Hemingway (1972).

HEATS OF SOLUTION OF MgO, CaO, H_2O, HUNTITE, AND ARTINITE

MgO

In table 1 we have listed measurements for the heat of solution of MgO in 950.0 g of 4.0 *N*HCl for three different concentrations. These data correspond to the reactions

$$MgO(c) + [285HCl + 3{,}641H_2O](aq) = [MgCl_2 + 283HCl + 3{,}642H_2O](aq), \quad (7)$$

$$2MgO(c) + [285HCl + 3{,}641H_2O](aq) = [2MgCl_2 + 281HCl + 3{,}643H_2O](aq), \text{ and} \quad (5)$$

$$4MgO(c) + [285HCl + 3{,}641H_2O](aq) = [4MgCl_2 + 277HCl + 3{,}645H_2O](aq). \quad (8)$$

The heats of reactions 7 and 8 were measured in connection with our studies of the enthalpies of formation of nesquehonite ($MgCO_3 \cdot 3H_2O$) and hydromagnesite ($5MgO \cdot 4CO_2 \cdot 5H_2O$) which are reported in the accompanying paper (Robie and Hemingway, 1973, p. 543–547, this issue). At the time these measurements were made we had accepted the incorrect formula, ($4MgO \cdot 3CO_2 \cdot 4H_2O$), for hydromagnesite adopted by Palache, Berman, and Frondel (1951). In order to compare these measurements (at different concentrations) and to obtain the heats of the reactions

$$3MgO(c) + [285HCl + 3{,}641H_2O](aq) = [3MgCl_2 + 279HCl + 3{,}644H_2O](aq) \text{ and} \quad (2)$$

$$5MgO(c) + [285HCl + 3{,}641H_2O](aq) = [5MgCl_2 + 275HCl + 3{,}646H_2O](aq), \quad (9)$$

which we shall need to obtain the heat of formation of hydromagnesite, we shall first correct the final solutions of reactions 7, 8, 2, and 9 to the same concentrations of HCl, $MgCl_2$, and H_2O as the final solution of reaction 5. In making this correction, we have followed the method described by Taylor and Wells (1938). The concentration data for each of the reactions are listed in table 2.

The solution of 1 mol of MgO in HCl(aq) produces 1 mol of H_2O and uses up 2 mol of HCl, leading to a dilution of the acid with an attendant heat of dilution. Because the several reactions studied cause different states of dilution of the final solutions, they must be corrected for the difference in the heat of dilution of the HCl in order to properly compare the results for differing sample weights. Following Taylor and Wells (1938), we first calculate the heat of dilution associated with reactions 2, 5, 7, 8, and 9 and then take the difference between each of these results and the heat of dilution for reaction 5. The heats of dilution were calculated from the difference in the molality of HCl between the initial and final solutions for each reaction, Δm_{HCl}, the change in the relative apparent molal enthalpy, ϕL_{HCl}, in this concentration range, and the number of moles of HCl per mole of $MgCl_2$ in the final solution. For solutions of approximately 4.35 mol HCl, ϕL changes by about 220 cal for a change of one in the molality. In making the correction for the dilution of the HCl we have used the ϕL values given by Parker (1965).

It is also necessary to adjust all the data to the same final concentration of $MgCl_2$ (aq) as reaction 5. The correction is

$$(m - 0.0305) \cdot [\phi H_m - \phi H_{0.0305}] \text{ cal mol (MgO)}, \quad (10)$$

where m is the molality of $MgCl_2$ in the final solution of reaction 5, ϕH_m is the apparent molal heat content of $MgCl_2$ at molality m_f, and $\phi H_{0.0305}$ is the apparent molal heat content of 0.0305 mol $MgCl_2$, both in 4.35 mol HCl. For lack of ϕ_H data for $MgCl_2$ in 4.35 mol HCl, we have used the values of Taylor and Wells (1938) for $MgCl_2$ in 2.06 mol HCl. The numerical data used in these corrections are listed in table 3. The mean value for the heat of solution of MgO in HCl(aq) from the 10 results listed in table 1 referred to the concentration of reaction 5 is −35,898±35 cal mol^{-1} at 303.15 K. The uncertainties listed with the mean values for the heats of solution are those recommended by Rossini and Deming (1939), that is, twice the standard error or standard deviation of the mean. The uncertainty interval is equal to $2[\Sigma\delta_i^2/n(n-1)]^{1/2}$, where δ_i is the deviation of an individual observation from the mean and n is the number of observations.

After applying the corrections outlined above, the values for the enthalpy changes for reactions 7, 5, 2, and 9 are −35,847±35, −71,694±70, −107,724±105, and −179,535±175 cal, respectively.

H_2O

From table 1 the average value of the heat of solution of H_2O(l) at 303.15 K is −4.429±0.051 cal g^{-1} from which the heat of reaction 6 is −319±4 cal.

CaO

The three sets of results for the heat of solution (per gram) of CaO listed in table 1 refer respectively to the reactions

$$CaO(c) + [9MgCl_2 + 1{,}122HCl + 14{,}579H_2O](aq) = [CaCl_2 + 9MgCl_2 + 1{,}120HCl + 14{,}580H_2O](aq), \quad (11)$$

Table 1.–*Heat of solution of* MgO, H_2O, CaO, *huntite, and artinite in 950.0 g of 4.0* N HCl *at 30°C (303.15 K)*

Sample mass (g)	Temperature change corrected for heat exchange (°C)	Mean solution temperature (°C)	Heat capacities (cal deg⁻¹) Initial system	Heat capacities (cal deg⁻¹) Final system	Temperature coefficient of heat of solution (cal g^{-1} deg^{-1})	Heat of solution at 30°C (cal g^{-1})
			MgO (Fisher) (reactions 7, 5, and 8)			
0.5035	0.5168	25.41	868.30	868.33	0.064	-891.34
.5038	.5155	29.73	873.96	871.65	-4.591	-886.11
1.0078	1.0291	29.73	873.16	873.62	.462	-891.91
1.0080	1.0363	25.85	867.35	868.12	.766	-892.13
2.0161	2.0687	25.93	870.31	869.98	-.166	-892.87
2.0162	2.0474	31.89	876.58	874.70	-.929	-889.22
			MgO (Johnson-Matthey) (reaction 7)			
1.0085	1.0288	30.27	872.65	870.97	-1.664	-889.35
1.0084	1.0293	30.56	872.35	871.35	-.999	-889.98
1.0086	1.0296	30.32	871.91	871.28	-.623	-889.76
1.0087	1.0307	30.48	872.21	870.81	-1.386	-890.54
			H_2O			
			Reaction 6 (2.03 g of MgO was dissolved in the acid before measurement)			
0.9013	0.00452	27.24	870.44	870.55	0.117	-4.450
.9001	.00447	28.15	871.10	870.76	-.382	-4.378
.9026	.00463	30.25	870.37	870.60	.264	-4.458
			CaO			
			Reaction 11 (1.13 g of MgO was dissolved in the acid before measurement)			
0.1750	0.1686	29.73	872.34	871.89	-2.535	-840.22
.1758	.1683	30.60	873.77	873.78	.113	-838.61
			Reaction 12 (1.51 g of MgO was dissolved in the acid before measurement)			
.1751	0.1671	30.64	875.02	873.42	-9.143	-834.34
.1754	.1671	35.29	876.77	876.56	-1.208	-835.12
.1751	.1667	35.28	876.53	876.50	-.159	-834.05
.1754	.1686	24.38	867.89	866.53	-7.765	-833.50
.1757	.1690	24.21	867.19	869.50	13.19	-835.04
			Reaction 13 (0.806 g of MgO was dissolved in the acid before measurement)			
1.1209	1.0858	25.96	870.95	870.96	0.005	-843.64
1.1214	1.0823	26.50	869.74	872.17	2.174	-840.57
1.1213	1.0832	27.45	872.23	874.36	1.900	-843.57
1.1210	1.0831	26.87	873.43	871.54	-1.682	-842.98
			Huntite (reaction 1a)			
4.4136	0.6977	32.18	875.82	875.37	-0.103	-138.96
4.4136	.6993	31.76	874.89	874.48	-.092	-139.03
4.4138	.6980	31.76	874.79	875.26	.108	-138.81
4.4135	.6886	37.26	878.59	879.92	.302	-139.00
4.4143	.6877	37.23	878.54	879.54	.226	-138.74
4.4139	.6885	37.34	878.74	880.03	.293	-139.01
			Artinite (reaction 4a)			
2.4600	0.4803	36.32	874.18	875.24	0.430	-169.15
2.4602	.4797	36.33	874.17	875.79	.658	-168.98
2.4596	.4834	31.87	872.06	869.04	-1.230	-170.61
2.4596	.4779	30.90	874.60	874.14	-.189	-169.67
2.4598	.4755	31.00	873.33	874.61	.521	-168.68
2.4599	.4785	30.89	872.50	872.10	-.164	-169.43
2.4596	.4784	30.92	873.51	871.35	-.877	-169.45
2.4597	.4764	30.90	874.16	873.71	-.183	-169.02
2.4596	.4726	32.65	873.88	876.80	1.187	-167.50
2.4596	.4771	30.87	873.86	875.08	.495	-169.39
2.4599	.4822	36.10	875.51	875.86	.141	-170.09

Table 2.—*Concentration of* HCl*(aq) and* $MgCl_2$ *(aq) for the heat of solution of* MgO *in 4.0* N HCl

Reaction	Initial solution: Moles HCl / Moles MgO	Initial solution: Moles HCl / 1,000 g H_2O	Final solution: Moles HCl / Moles $MgCl_2$	Final solution: Moles HCl / 1,000 g H_2O	Final solution: Moles $MgCl_2$ / 1,000 g H_2O
7	285	4.345	283	4.313	0.0152
5	142.5	4.345	140.5	4.282	.0305
2	95	4.345	93	4.250	.0456
8	71.25	4.345	69.25	4.218	.0609
9	57	4.345	55	4.187	.0761

$$CaO(c) + [12MgCl_2 + 1{,}116HCl + 14{,}576H_2O](aq)$$

$$= [CaCl_2 + 12MgCl_2 + 1{,}114HCl + 14{,}577H_2O](aq), \text{ and} \quad (12)$$

$$CaO(c) + [MgCl_2 + 176HCl + 2{,}277H_2O](aq)$$

$$= [CaCl_2 + MgCl_2 + 174HCl + 2{,}278H_2O](aq). \quad (13)$$

The data for reaction 13 were taken from unpublished measurements of the present authors.

Coughlin (1956) has shown that the heat of solution of CaO in 4.0 *N* HCl is independent of the amount of CaO dissolved in 1,936 g of acid for sample weights of 0.3 to 1.6 g of CaO. We have found, however, that the heat of solution of CaO in 4.0 *N* HCl in which varying amounts of MgO had been previously dissolved depends significantly upon the amount of MgO in solution. The data listed in table 1, and the value of King, Koehler, and Adami (1962) for the heat of solution of CaO in 4.0 *N* HCl in which no MgO was present are shown in figure 1.

These results for CaO provide a concrete example of the necessity of maintaining exact stoichiometry in heat of solution measurements, a point which has been emphasized by Coughlin (1962). On the basis of these data together with the observations of Coughlin (1956) we obtain for reaction 3,

$$CaO(c) + [3MgCl_2 + 279HCl + 3{,}644H_2O](aq)$$

$$= [CaCl_2 + 3MgCl_2 + 277HCl + 3{,}645H_2O](aq),$$

$$\Delta H = -46{,}791 \pm 35 \text{ cal at } 303.15 \text{ K}.$$

Huntite and artinite

Under the actual solution conditions in the sealed calorimeter, reactions 1 and 4 should be written

$$CaMg_3(CO_3)_4(c) + [285HCl + 3{,}641H_2O](aq)$$

$$= [CaCl_2 + 3MgCl_2 + 277HCl + 3{,}645H_2O + (4-x)CO_2](aq)$$

$$+ xCO_2(g) \text{ and} \quad (1a)$$

$$Mg_2(OH)_2CO_3 \cdot 3H_2O(c) + [285HCl + 3{,}641H_2O](aq)$$

Table 3.—*Corrections to the heats of solution of* xMgO *in 4.0* N HCl *for variations in the* $MgCl_2$ *and* HCl *concentrations in the final solution*

Reaction	Δm $MgCl_2$	Correction for Δm $MgCl_2$(aq)	Change in m_{HCl} on dilution	Heat of dilution of HCl (cal)	Correction for difference in m_{HCl} in final solution (cal)	Total correction (cal)
7	−0.0153	14	0.032	−1,992	−45	−31
5	.0000	0	.063	−1,947	0	0
2	.0151	−14	.095	−1,944	3	−10
8	.0304	−27	.127	−1,935	12	−15
9	.0456	−41	.158	−1,912	35	−9

$$= [2MgCl_2 + 281HCl + 3{,}647H_2O + (1-x)CO_2](aq)$$

$$+ xCO_2(g). \quad (4a)$$

Our experimental data for reactions 1a and 4a are listed in table 1.

In order to obtain the enthalpies of reactions 1 and 4, the observed heats of reactions 1a and 4a must be corrected for the CO_2 dissolved in the acid, and the CO_2 gas must be corrected to its reference state. We shall illustrate the method of correction by using the results for huntite, $CaMg_3(CO_3)_4$. The solution of 0.0125 mol of $CaMg_3(CO_3)_4$ in HCl(aq) produces 0.050 mol of CO_2, equation 1a. In the sealed calorimeter, part of the CO_2 dissolves in the acid and part goes into the vapor space above the acid. The free internal volume of the calorimeter is 954.1 cm^3, the volume occupied by the acid is 950.0 g/1.0658 g cm^{-3} = 891.3 cm^3, and that of the vapor space (after the reaction) is 62.8 cm^3 (the density of 4.0 *N* HCl at 25°C is 1.0658 g cm^{-3}).

Henry's law states that the number of moles of a gas that dissolves in a given volume of solvent at constant temperature is proportional to the partial pressure of the gas (for example, Glasstone, 1940, p. 686). For the solution of CO_2 in HCl(aq), Henry's law holds up to approximately 5 atm; and the Henry's

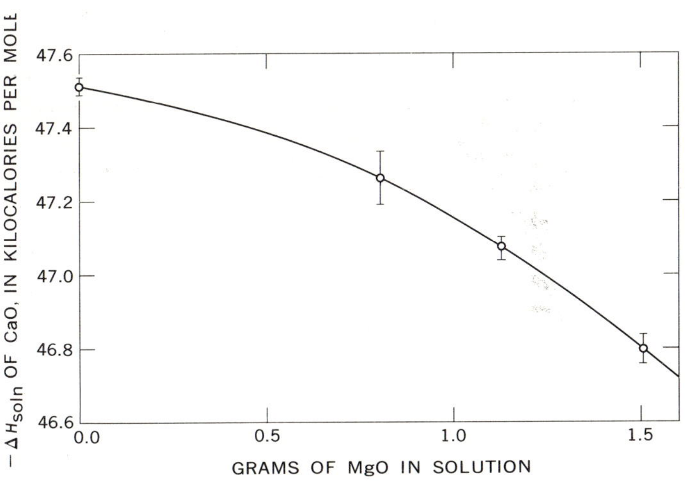

Figure 1.—Molar heat of solution of CaO in 4.0 N HCl at 30°C as a function of the amount of MgO in solution.

law constant is 0.0291±0.0001 mol l^{-1} atm^{-1} at 303.15 K, (Robb and Zimmer, 1968). We shall assume that CO_2 behaves as an ideal gas.

If we call the number of moles of CO_2 in the gas phase, n_1, and the number of moles of CO_2 dissolved in the acid, n_2, then we may write $(n_1 + n_2) = 0.05$ mol CO_2, $n_1 = p_{CO_2}$ (62.8 cm^3)/(82.056 cm^3 atm K^{-1}) (303.15 K,) and n_2 = (0.0291 mol $liter^{-1}$ atm^{-1})(0.8913 liter) p_{CO_2}. Solving simultaneously we find p_{CO_2} = 1.76 atm, n_1 = 0.0044 mol, and n_2 = 0.0456 mol.

The correction for the CO_2 dissolved in the acid is just the number of moles of dissolved CO_2 times the heat of solution of CO_2 in HCl. Robb and Zimmer (1968) give data for the solubility of CO_2 in HCl of various concentrations at 20°, 25°, and 30°C and derived a value of ΔH_{soln} of CO_2 in 0.64 mol HCl at 25°C of -4,890 cal. We have assumed that this value is also valid for 4.0 N HCl in our corrections. The correction for the dissolved CO_2 when 0.0125 mol of $CaMg_3(CO_3)_4$ dissolves in HCl is therefore (0.0456 mol) (-4,890 cal mol^{-1}) = -223.0 cal.

We must also correct for the difference in enthalpy of the CO_2 gas at 1.76 atm from that at its standard state of 1 atm. To reduce the CO_2 to its standard state we expand it reversibly and isothermally from 1.76 to 1.0 atm. For an ideal gas, the change in internal energy, dU, is 0 at constant temperature and we can write $dQ = dW$, where Q is the heat absorbed by the system and W is the work done by the expansion of the CO_2. The work done on expansion is

$$W = \int_{V_1}^{V_2} p\, dV = nRT \ln V_2/V_1 = 1.5 \text{ cal.}$$

The total CO_2 correction for the solution of 0.0125 mol of $CaMg_3(CO_3)_4$ (that is, 0.05 mol of CO_2) is thus 223.0 - 1.5 = 221.5 cal. The data in table 1 were corrected for heat exchange and reduced to the same reference temperature using the procedures discussed by Robie and Hemingway (1972). The data are also corrected for a small heat effect caused by the evaporation of H_2O into the vapor space of the sample holder when the reaction is initiated, (E. J. Prosen, written commun., May 7, 1967). This correction is usually less than 3 cal mol^{-1} of solute. The data in table 1 are given in terms of the heat of solution per gram of $CaMg_3(CO_3)_4$ or 1.0/353.032 = 0.002833 mol. The correction for 1.0 g of huntite is thus (0.002833/0.0125) · 221.5 = 50.20 cal g^{-1}. From table 1 the average value for the uncorrected heat of solution of huntite, reaction 1a, is -138.92±0.26 cal g^{-1} at 303.15 K. Adding the correction for the dissolved CO_2 gives -138.92 + 50.20 = -88.72±0.26 cal g^{-1}, and multiplying by the gram formula weight of $CaMg_3(CO_3)_4$, 353.032 g, gives -31,321±92 cal mol^{-1} as the enthalpy change for reaction 1 at 303.15 K.

From table 1 the average value for the uncorrected heat of solution of artinite is -169.27±0.37 cal g^{-1}. If we proceed in the same manner as for huntite, the correction for the dissolved CO_2 for the artinite reaction is 22.92 cal g^{-1}. The corrected heat of solution is -146.35±0.37 cal g^{-1}. The correction for the dissolved CO_2 for artinite is much smaller than for huntite because there is only one mole of CO_2 released when $Mg_2(OH)_2CO_3 \cdot 3H_2O$ dissolves in HCl. Multiplying the corrected heat of solution per gram by the formula weight gives -28,786±73 cal mol^{-1} for $\Delta H(4)$ at 303.15 K.

ENTHALPIES OF FORMATION OF HUNTITE AND ARTINITE

The enthalpy of formation of huntite from its component oxides according to the reaction

$$CaO(c) + 3MgO(c) + 4CO_2(g) = CaMg_3(CO_3)_4(c) \quad (14)$$

can be calculated from the corrected enthalpy changes for reactions 1, 2, and 3 using the relation $\Delta H(3) + \Delta H(2) - \Delta H(1) = \Delta H(14)$, from which $\Delta H(14)$ = -123,194±145 cal at 303.15 K. This value may be corrected to the reference temperature, 298.15 K, using the Kirchhoff equation,

$$d\Delta H/dT = \Delta C_p, \quad (15)$$

where ΔC_p is the difference in the molar heat capacities, at constant pressure, of the products minus the reactants. At 298.15 K the heat capacities of CO_2 (Hilsenrath and others, 1955), MgO (Barron and others, 1959), CaO (Kelley and King, 1961), and $CaMg_3(CO_3)_4$ (Hemingway and Robie, 1972) are 8.875±0.010, 8.88±0.04, 10.23±0.10, and 74.11±0.18 cal mol^{-1} K^{-1}, respectively. $\Delta C_p(14)$ is, therefore, 1.7 cal K^{-1}, and the correction to 298.15 K is -8.5 cal. The standard enthalpy change, ΔH°_{298}, for reaction 14 is, therefore, -123,203±145 cal.

In a similar fashion, the enthalpy change for the reaction

$$2MgO(c) + CO_2(g) + 4H_2O(l) = Mg_2(OH)_2CO_3 \cdot 3H_2O(c), \quad (16)$$

$-43,329 \pm 90$ cal at 303.15 K, was obtained from the corrected heats of solution for reactions 4, 5, and 6 by $\Delta H(5) + \Delta H(6) - \Delta H(4) = \Delta H(16)$. This value was corrected to 298.15 K by using the heat capacities of MgO, and CO_2 mentioned above, the value 17.995 cal $mol^{-1}K^{-1}$ for $H_2O(l)$ tabulated in the U.S. National Bureau of Standards tables, (Wagman and others, 1968), and 59.18 ± 0.18 cal $mol^{-1}K^{-1}$ for artinite measured by Hemingway and Robie (1972). The temperature coefficient for the enthalpy of reaction 16, $d\Delta H/dT$, is -39.4 ± 0.2 cal K^{-1} from which we obtain $\Delta H^\circ_{298}(16) = -43,132 \pm 100$ cal.

Combining the above values for the enthalpy changes for the formation of artinite and huntite from their constituent oxides with the enthalpies of formation from the elements of CaO, MgO, CO_2, and H_2O (Robie and Waldbaum, 1968), we obtain $-1,082,600 \pm 375$ and $-698,043 \pm 170$ cal mol^{-1} for the enthalpies of formation, $\Delta H^\circ_{f,\ 298.15}$, of $CaMg_3(CO_3)_4$ and $Mg_2(OH)_2CO_3 \cdot 3H_2O$, respectively. From this result and the entropies of $CaMg_3(CO_3)_4$ and $Mg_2(OH)_2CO_3 \cdot 3H_2O$ (Hemingway and Robie, 1972) and the entropies at 298.15 K of C (graphite), Mg, O_2, Ca, and H_2 listed in Robie and Waldbaum (1968), and by using the relation

$$\Delta G^\circ_f = \Delta H^\circ_f + T\Delta S^\circ_T, \quad (17)$$

we obtain for the Gibbs free energy of formation, $\Delta G_{f.\ 298}$, $-1,004,707 \pm 390$ and $-613,924 \pm 180$ cal mol^{-1} for huntite and artinite, respectively.

From the Gibbs free energies of formation of huntite (H) and artinite (A) and the free energies of Ca^{+2}, Mg^{+2}, CO_3^{-2}, and H_2O (Robie and Waldbaum, 1968), we can calculate the activity products, K_H and K_A, at 298.15 K for the reactions

$$CaMg_3(CO_3)_4 = Ca^{+2} + 3Mg^{+2} + 4CO_3^{-2} \text{ and} \quad (18)$$

$$Mg_2(OH)_2CO_3 \cdot 3H_2O = 2Mg^{+2} + 2OH^- + CO_3^{-2} + 3H_2O \quad (19)$$

by using the relation

$$\log K = -\Delta G^\circ_f / 2.3026\,RT. \quad (20)$$

The activity product for huntite is $K_H = (a_{Ca^{+2}})(a_{Mg^{+2}})^3 (a_{CO_3^{-2}})^4$, and $\log K_H = -30.16 \pm 0.44$. Similarly for artinite, $K_A = (a_{Mg^{+2}})^2 (a_{OH^-})^2 (a_{CO_3^{-2}})$, and $\log K_A = -18.11 \pm 0.27$.

The only previous value for the free energy of formation from the elements for huntite is that calculated by Garrels, Thompson, and Siever (1960), based on the pH of aqueous solutions in equilibrium with huntite at 1 atm CO_2 pressure. Their calculated value for ΔG°_f was $-1,007,700$ cal mol^{-1}. The free energy change on solution, reaction 17, which is, in effect, the quantity that Garrels, Thompson, and Siever (1960) measured, was 44,140 cal. This corresponds to an activity product constant for $CaMg_3(CO_3)_4$, $\log K_H = -32.4$.

Langmuir (1965, p. 737) has calculated a value for the free energy of formation of artinite based on the solubility "of an artinite-like phase with an empirical composition of $MgCO_3 \cdot Mg(OH)_2 \cdot 1.5H_2O$, in equilibrium with brucite at 20°C," measured by Kazakov, Tikhomirova, and Plotnikova (1959). Langmuir calculated 23,500 cal as the free energy for the reaction

$$Mg_2(OH)_2CO_3 \cdot 3H_2O = 2Mg^{+2} + CO_3^{-2} + 2OH^- + 3H_2O. \quad (21)$$

He combined this result with literature values for ΔG°_f of Mg^{+2}, CO_3^{-2}, OH^-, and H_2O and obtained $-612,480 \pm 1,100$ cal for the free energy of formation of artinite. Because of the uncertain nature of the material studied by Kazakov and coworkers, we believe that Langmuir's calculated ΔG°_f should be given rather little weight.

At this point it is worthwhile to emphasize that in the determination of a free energy of formation from aqueous solubility data, one measures only a small part of ΔG°_f, and then combines this value with the free energies of aqueous ions which were obtained by either calorimetric, solubility, or electrochemical cell measurements, each having its own uncertainty. Because the sum of uncertainties in the free energies of formation of the aqueous ion is often comparable to the observed free energy change for the solution reaction, one must be careful in any comparison of a free energy value obtained by calorimetric methods and one obtained from solubility data. Garrels, Thompson, and Siever (1960) have also stressed this point.

ACKNOWLEDGMENTS

We wish to thank Prof. D. L. Graf, University of Illinois, for supplying the samples of huntite and artinite used in these studies. Bruce Hemingway wishes to thank the National Science Foundation for support under NSF grants GA-1651 and GA-453 (to Prof. D. L. Graf). We are grateful to our Geological Survey colleagues, C. L. Christ and E-an Zen, for reviewing this paper and for suggesting numerous improvements in the presentation. The preparation of this report and most of the computational work was supported in part by the Office of Saline Water, U.S. Department of the Interior, under agreement No. 14-30-3040.

REFERENCES CITED

Barron, T. H. K., Berg, W. T., and Morrison, J. A., 1959, On the heat capacity of crystalline magnesium oxide: Royal Soc. [London] Proc. Ser. A, v. 250, p. 70–83.

Commission on Atomic Weights, 1970, Atomic weights for 1969: Pure and Appl. Chemistry, v. 21, p. 95–108.

Coughlin, J. P., 1956, Heats of formation of crystalline $CaO \cdot Al_2O_3$, $12CaO \cdot 7Al_2O_3$, and $3CaO \cdot Al_2O_3$: Am. Chem. Soc. Jour., v. 78, p. 5479–5482.

——1962, Solution calorimetry and silicate thermochemistry, *in* International Union of Pure and Applied Chemistry, Experimental thermochemistry, v 2 (H. A. Skinner, ed.): New York, Interscience Publishers, p. 293–320.

Garrels, R. M., Thompson, M. E., and Siever, Raymond, 1960, Stability of some carbonates at 25°C and one atmosphere total pressure: Am. Jour. Sci., v. 258, p. 402–418.

Glasstone, Samuel, 1940, Textbook of physical chemistry: New York, D. Van Nostrand, 1289 p.

Hemingway, B. S., and Robie, R. A., 1972, The heat capacities at low-temperatures and entropies at 298.15 K of huntite, $CaMg_3(CO_3)_4$, and artinite, $Mg_2(OH)_2CO_3 \cdot 3H_2O$: Am. Mineralogist, v. 57, p. 1754–1767.

Hilsenrath, J., Beckett, C. W., Benedict, W. S., Fano, L., Hodge, H. J., Masi, J. F., Nuttal, R. L., Touloukian, Y. S., and Wolley, H. W., 1955, Tables of thermal properties of gases: U.S. Natl. Bur. Standards Circ. 564, 488 p.

Kazakov, A. V., Tikhomirova, M. M., and Plotnikova, V. I., 1959, The system of carbonate equilibria: Internat. Geology Rev., v. 1, p. 1–39.

Kelley, K. K., and King, E. G., 1961, Contributions to the data on theoretical metallurgy XIV. Entropies of the elements and inorganic compounds: U.S. Bur. Mines Bull. 592, 149 p.

King, E. G., Koehler, M. F., and Adami, L. H., 1962, Heats and free energies of formation of calcium and magnesium vanadates: U.S. Bur. Mines Rept. Inv. 6049, 11 p.

Langmuir, Donald, 1965, Stability of carbonates in the system $MgO-CO_2-H_2O$: Jour. Geology, v. 73, p. 730–754.

Palache, Charles, Berman, Harry, and Frondel, Clifford, 1951, Dana's system of mineralogy [7th ed.]: New York, John Wiley and Sons, Inc., v. 2, 1124 p.

Parker, V. B., 1965, Thermal properties of aqueous uni-univalent electrolytes: Natl. Standard Reference Data Series, Natl. Bur. Standards 2, 66 p.

Robb, R. A., and Zimmer, M. F., 1968, Solubility and heat of solutions of arsenous oxide, arsenic pentoxide, and hydrochloric acid: Jour. Chem. and Eng. Data, v. 13, p. 200–203.

Robie, R. A., and Hemingway, B. S., 1972, Calorimeters for heat of solution and low-temperature heat capacity measurements: U.S. Geol. Survey Prof. Paper 755, 32 p.

——1973, The enthalpies of formation of nesquehonite, $MgCO_3 \cdot 3H_2O$, and hydromagnesite, $5MgO \cdot 4CO_2 \cdot 5H_2O$: U.S. Geol. Survey Jour. Research, v. 1, no. 5, p. 543–547.

Robie, R. A., and Waldbaum, D. R., 1968, Thermodynamic properties of minerals and related substances at 298.15°K(25.0°C) and one atmosphere (1.013 bars) pressure and at higher temperatures: U.S. Geol. Survey Bull. 1259, 265 p.

Rossini, F. D., and Deming, W. E., 1939, The assignment of uncertainties to the data of chemistry and physics, with specific recommendations for thermochemistry: Washington Acad. Sci. Jour., v. 29, p. 416–440.

Taylor, Kenneth, and Wells, L. S., 1938, Studies of heat of solution of calcium and magnesium oxides and hydroxides: U.S. Natl. Bur. Standards Jour. Research, v. 21, p. 133–149.

Wagman, D. D., Evans, W. H., Parker, V. B., Halow, I. Bailey, S. M., and Schumm, R. H., 1968, Selected values of chemical thermodynamic properties. Tables of the first thirty-four elements in the standard order of arrangement: U.S. Natl. Bur. Standards Tech. Note 270-3, 264 p.

Jour. Research U.S. Geol. Survey
Vol. 1, No. 5, Sept.-Oct. 1973, p. 543–547

THE ENTHALPIES OF FORMATION OF NESQUEHONITE, $MgCO_3 \cdot 3H_2O$, AND HYDROMAGNESITE, $5MgO \cdot 4CO_2 \cdot 5H_2O$

By RICHARD A. ROBIE and BRUCE S. HEMINGWAY, Silver Spring, Md.

Abstract.—The enthalpies of formation, $\Delta H°_f$, of nesquehonite, $MgCO_3 \cdot 3H_2O$, and hydromagnesite, $5MgO \cdot 4CO_2 \cdot 5H_2O$, have been determined by HCl solution calorimetry. For the reaction

$$MgO(c) + CO_2(g) + 3H_2O(l) = MgCO_3 \cdot 3H_2O(c),$$

the enthalpy change at 298.15 K is −29,781±40 cal mol^{-1}. For the reaction

$$5MgO(c) + 4CO_2(g) + 5H_2O(l) = 5MgO \cdot 4CO_2 \cdot 5H_2O(c),$$

the enthalpy change at 298.15 K is −120,310±120 cal. For $MgCO_3 \cdot 3H_2O$ the standard molal enthalpy and standard Gibbs free energy of formation, $\Delta H°_{f,\ 298}$ and $\Delta G°_{f,\ 298}$, are −472,576±110 and −412,040±120 cal. $\Delta H°_{f,\ 298}$ and $\Delta G°_{f,\ 298}$ for $5MgO \cdot 4CO_2 \cdot 5H_2O$ are −1,557,090±250 and −1,401,710±250 cal.

Recently Robie and Hemingway (1972b) presented heat capacity measurements for nesquehonite between 17 and 341 K and for hydromagnesite between 20 and 309 K and values for the entropy change, $S°_{298}-S°_0$, for these minerals. In this report we present measurements of the heats of solution of MgO, H_2O, $MgCO_3 \cdot 3H_2O$, and hydromagnesite ($5MgO \cdot 4CO_2 \cdot 5H_2O$) in 4.0 *N* HCl and values for their enthalpies of formation, $\Delta H°_{f,298}$, based on the enthalpy changes for the reactions

$$MgO(c) + CO_2(g) + 3H_2O(l) = MgCO_3 \cdot 3H_2O(c) \text{ and} \quad (1)$$

$$5MgO(c) + 4CO_2(g) + 5H_2O(l) = 5MgO \cdot 4CO_2 \cdot 5H_2O(c), \quad (2)$$

obtained by HCl solution calorimetry. By combining our measured entropy and enthalpy data, we have calculated values for the Gibbs free energy of formation of these minerals.

The samples of nesquehonite and hydromagnesite used in our heat of solution measurements were portions of the samples which were used by Robie and Hemingway (1972b) for low-temperature heat capacity studies. The solution calorimeter used for these studies has been described by Robie and Hemingway (1972a).

The reactions used to determine the enthalpy change for reaction 1 were

$$MgCO_3 \cdot 3H_2O(c) + [285HCl + 3{,}641H_2O](aq) = [MgCl_2 + 283HCl + 3{,}645H_2O](aq) + CO_2(g), \quad (3)$$

$$MgO(c) + [285HCl + 3{,}641H_2O](aq) = [MgCl_2 + 283HCl + 3{,}642H_2O](aq), \text{ and} \quad (4)$$

$$3H_2O(l) + [MgCl_2 + 283HCl + 3{,}642H_2O](aq) = [MgCl_2 + 283HCl + 3{,}645H_2O](aq). \quad (5)$$

Adding equations 4 and 5 and subtracting reaction 3 yields

$$MgO(c) + CO_2(g) + 3H_2O(l) = MgCO_3 \cdot 3H_2O(c) \quad (1)$$

from which $\Delta H(1) = \Delta H(4) + \Delta H(5) - \Delta H(3)$.

The following reactions were used to obtain the enthalpy change for reaction 2:

$$5MgO \cdot 4CO_2 \cdot 5H_2O(c) + [285HCl + 3{,}641H_2O(aq) = [5MgCl_2 + 275HCl + 3{,}651H_2O](aq) + 4CO_2(g), \quad (6)$$

$$5MgO(c) + [285HCl + 3{,}641H_2O](aq) = [5MgCl_2 + 275HCl + 3{,}646H_2O](aq), \text{ and} \quad (7)$$

$$5H_2O(l) + [5MgCl_2 + 275HCl + 3{,}646H_2O](aq) = [5MgCl_2 + 275HCl + 3{,}651H_2O](aq). \quad (8)$$

Adding reactions 7 and 8 and subtracting 6 yields

$$5MgO(c) + 5H_2O(l) + 4CO_2(g) = 5MgO \cdot 4CO_2 \cdot 5H_2O(c) \quad (2)$$

from which we get $\Delta H(2) = \Delta H(7) + \Delta H(8) - \Delta H(6)$.

The reactions studied were stoichiometric for the solution of 0.0125 mol of $MgCO_3 \cdot 3H_2O$ and $5MgO \cdot 4CO_2 \cdot 5H_2O$ in 950.0 g of 4.0 *N* HCl. The weight, 4.57 g, of the hydromagnesite samples used in the measurements did not correspond to 0.0125 mol of $5MgO \cdot 4CO_2 \cdot 5H_2O$ but to 0.0125 mol of $4MgO \cdot 3CO_2 \cdot 4H_2O$. This was because we originally accepted the formula for hydromagnesite listed in Dana's System of Mineralogy by Palache, Berman, and Frondel (1951), which has since been shown to be incorrect (Robie and Hemingway 1972b).

The gram formula weights used are based on the 1969 values for the atomic weights (Commission on Atomic Weights, 1970). The formula weights used for $MgCO_3 \cdot 3H_2O$ and $5MgO \cdot 4CO_2 \cdot 5H_2O$ were 138.360 and 467.638 g mol^{-1}, respectively.

In table 1 we list our measurements for the heat of solution of nesquehonite, hydromagnesite, and water in 950.0 g of 4.0 *N* HCl at 30°C. The experimental data for $MgCO_3 \cdot 3H_2O$ and hydromagnesite are for the reactions

$$MgCO_3 \cdot 3H_2O + [285HCl + 3{,}641H_2O] = [MgCl_2 + 283HCl + 3{,}645H_2O + (1-x)CO_2]\,(aq) + xCO_2(g) \text{ and} \qquad (3a)$$

$$5MgO \cdot 4CO_2 \cdot 5H_2O + [285HCl + 3{,}641H_2O] = [5MgCl_2 + 275HCl + 3{,}651H_2O + (4-x)CO_2]\,(aq) + xCO_2(g). \qquad (6a)$$

HEATS OF SOLUTION OF $MgCO_3 \cdot 3H_2O$, $5MgO \cdot 4CO_2 \cdot 5H_2O$, MgO, AND H_2O

$MgCO_3 \cdot 3H_2O$

The average value for the heat of solution of $MgCO_3 \cdot 3H_2O$ at 303.15 K (table 1) is −77.50 cal g^{-1}. The correction for the dissolved CO_2 and the reduction of the CO_2 gas to its standard state of 1 atm were made in the manner described by Hemingway and Robie (1973, p. 535–541, this issue). The correction for the dissolved CO_2 is −32.20 cal g^{-1} of nesquehonite, and that for the compression of the gas to 1 atm is 0.32 cal g^{-1}. The corrected value for the heat of reaction 3 is therefore −44.98±0.15 cal g^{-1}, or −6,223±21 cal mol^{-1} of $MgCO_3 \cdot 3H_2O$.

$5MgO \cdot 4CO_2 \cdot 5H_2O$

Three sets of values are listed in table 1 for the heat of solution of hydromagnesite. The first six measurements were made with an early design of heater. From table 1 the mean value for the heat of solution of hydromagnesite from West Pakistan is −165.01±0.19 cal g^{-1} (reaction 6a). Although we have not used the results of the heat of solution for the Coalinga, Calif., material in our final values, the data are included in table 1 to show that there is no significant difference between the two samples of well-crystallized hydromagnesite. For the dissolved CO_2 the correction is −38.12 cal g^{-1} of hydromagnesite and for the reduction of the CO_2 to 1 atm, 0.14 cal g^{-1} of hydromagnesite. The corrected value for ΔH° of reaction 6 is therefore −127.03±0.19 cal g^{-1} or −59,404±90 cal mol^{-1} at 303.15 K.

MgO

The heats of solution of MgO in 4.0 *N* HCl at the concentrations corresponding to reactions 4 and 7 were taken from the data of Hemingway and Robie (1973). At 303.15 K the values are −35,847±35 and −179,535±80 cal, respectively.

H_2O

The three sets of values for the heat of solution of H_2O in HCl (table 1) were determined with different amounts of MgO dissolved in the acid and correspond respectively to the following reactions:

$$3H_2O(l) + [2MgCl_2 + 281HCl + 3{,}643H_2O](aq) = [2MgCl_2 + 281HCl + 3{,}646H_2O](aq), \qquad (9)$$

$$3H_2O(l) + [MgCl_2 + 283HCl + 3{,}642H_2O](aq) = [MgCl_2 + 283HCl + 3{,}645H_2O](aq), \text{ and} \qquad (5)$$

$$4H_2O(l) + [4MgCl_2 + 277HCl + 3{,}645H_2O](aq) = [4MgCl_2 + 277HCl + 3{,}649H_2O](aq). \qquad (10)$$

For the heat of solution of H_2O we need reactions 5 and 8. Inasmuch as the measured heats of solution of H_2O for reactions 5, 9, and 10 differ by only 3 cal mol^{-1}, we have taken the average of the first six H_2O measurements for the heat of reaction 5. In this usage, the evaporation correction is zero. The average value is −4.298±0.004 cal g^{-1} or 3(−4.298±0.004)(18.015) = −232±1 cal for the solution of $3H_2O$. Similarly, we used the average value for the last three measurements to obtain the enthalpy change for reaction 8. The average value is −4.429±0.051 cal g^{-1}. For 5 mol of H_2O, the value is −399±2 cal.

ENTHALPIES OF FORMATION OF NESQUEHONITE AND HYDROMAGNESITE

From the data in the preceding section, the enthalpy change for the reaction

$$MgO(c) + CO_2(g) + 3H_2O(l) = MgCO_3 \cdot 3H_2O(c) \qquad (1)$$

is −29,856±40 cal at 303.15 K, and for

$$5MgO(c) + 4CO_2(g) + 5H_2O(l) = 5MgO \cdot 4CO_2 \cdot 5H_2O(c) \qquad (2)$$

is −120,530±120 cal at 303.15 K.

Table 1.—*Heat of solution of nesquehonite, hydromagnesite, and water in 4.0*N HCl *at 30°C (303.15 K)*

Sample mass (g)	Temperature change corrected for heat exchange (°C)	Mean solution temperature (°C)	Heat capacities (cal deg^{-1})		Temperature coefficient of heat of solution (cal g^{-1} deg^{-1})	Heat of solution at 30°C (cal g^{-1})
			Initial system	Final system		
Nesquehonite (reaction 3a)						
1.7203	0.1511	31.08	884.43	882.31	−1.231	−78.219
1.7203	.1506	31.03	877.64	875.86	−1.035	−77.355
1.7207	.1483	30.83	886.39	884.07	−1.351	−76.770
1.7207	.1500	31.65	881.73	879.30	−1.411	−77.687
1.7202	.1516	30.93	878.14	878.12	−.009	−77.890
1.7202	.1499	31.18	876.85	877.70	.497	−77.095
1.7205	.1510	31.25	880.53	879.03	−.875	−77.924
1.7104	.1504	31.25	877.87	875.08	−1.632	−77.762
1.7205	.1502	31.34	877.96	878.49	.307	−77.399
1.7206	.1498	31.25	878.55	879.74	.690	−77.240
1.7208	.1508	31.24	878.78	878.47	−.175	−77.686
1.7206	.1498	31.25	877.21	877.13	−.051	−77.064
1.7206	.1500	31.30	878.90	879.53	.367	−77.372
1.7204	.1596	25.06	866.16	866.96	.461	−77.629
1.7202	.1612	25.14	866.38	866.64	.149	−78.463
1.7202	.1591	25.16	864.41	867.75	1.945	−77.395
1.7206	.1578	25.16	865.49	865.89	.234	−76.666
1.7201	.1588	25.17	868.01	867.47	−.315	−77.382
Hydromagnesite, West Pakistan (reaction 6a)						
4.5690	0.8545	31.37	879.89	880.52	0.138	−165.26
4.5679	.8504	31.50	884.09	884.26	.037	−165.32
4.5686	.8482	31.48	884.26	884.99	.159	−164.95
4.5686	.8490	31.58	884.53	884.88	.078	−165.17
4.5680	.8435	31.33	884.12	885.17	.229	−163.98
4.5687	.8375	35.81	886.86	888.38	.333	−165.48
4.5687	.8395	37.13	875.53	876.95	.309	−164.39
4.5680	.8439	36.49	875.73	877.14	.307	−164.99
4.5685	.8673	25.26	868.23	870.05	.398	−165.50
4.5683	.8656	25.34	868.05	869.59	.338	−165.12
Hydromagnesite, Coalinga, Calif. (reaction 6a)						
4.5689	0.8372	35.70	880.64	883.09	0.536	−163.77
4.5681	.8307	36.44	882.66	883.79	.247	−163.55
4.5690	.8392	35.75	880.90	882.72	.398	−164.59
4.5684	.8630	25.22	867.40	869.44	.446	−164.51
4.5678	.8661	25.19	866.58	869.58	.656	−165.04
Water						
Reaction 9 (1 g of MgO was dissolved in the acid before measurement)						
0.6769	0.00324	24.64	863.88	863.83	−0.081	−4.295
.6777	.00325	24.69	863.55	862.96	−.870	−4.300
.6775	.00336	30.21	867.69	867.09	−.878	−4.292
.6766	.00334	29.40	865.74	865.87	.188	−4.299
Reaction 5 (0.5 g of MgO was dissolved in the acid before measurement)						
0.6778	0.00334	29.48	870.52	870.55	0.037	−4.305
.6780	.00334	29.65	870.15	870.17	.037	−4.296
Reaction 10 (2.0 g of MgO was dissolved in the acid before measurement)						
0.9013	0.00452	27.24	870.44	870.55	0.117	−4.450
.9001	.00447	28.15	871.10	870.76	−.382	−4.378
.9026	.00463	30.25	870.37	870.60	.264	−4.458

The correction to the reference temperature, 298.15 K, is obtained from the heat capacity data of Robie and Hemingway (1972b) for $MgO_3 \cdot 3H_2O$ and hydromagnesite. For MgO the results of Barron, Berg, and Morrison (1959) are used; the values for CO_2 and H_2O are from National Bureau of Standards tables (Wagman and others, 1968). For reaction 1, ΔC_p is −14.9 cal K^{-1} and for reaction 2, −44.0 cal K^{-1}. Thus $\Delta H^\circ_{298}(1)$ = −29,780±40 cal, and for the formation of hydromagnesite from its constituent oxides, reaction 2, $\Delta H^\circ_{298}(2)$ = −120,310±120 cal. Combining these values with the enthalpies of formation of MgO, CO_2, and H_2O tabulated by Robie and Waldbaum (1968), we obtain −472,576±110 cal and −1,557,090±250 cal for the enthalpies of formation, $\Delta H^\circ_{f,298}$, of $MgCO_3 \cdot 3H_2O$ and $5MgO \cdot 4CO_2 \cdot 5H_2O$.

GIBBS FREE ENERGIES OF FORMATION OF NESQUEHONITE AND HYDROMAGNESITE

The crystal structure of nesquehonite has recently been determined by Stephan and MacGillavry (1972). It is apparently an ordered normal hydrate. If we assume also that hydromagnesite is an ordered structure at 0 kelvin then $S^\circ_0 = 0$ for these phases and the entropy changes, $S^\circ_{298} - S^\circ_0$, for nesquehonite and hydromagnesite measured by Robie and Hemingway (1972b), 46.76±0.14 and 120.38±0.37 cal mol^{-1} K^{-1}, respectively, are the correct entropies for use in thermochemical calculations. Combining these values with the entropies of Mg, C (graphite), H_2, and O_2 given by Robie and Waldbaum (1968), we obtain $\Delta S^\circ_{298} = -203.034 \pm 0.16$ cal $mol^{-1} K^{-1}$ for the reaction

$$Mg + C\,(\text{graphite}) + 3O_2 + 3H_2 = MgCO_3 \cdot 3H_2O, \quad (11)$$

and $\Delta S^\circ_{298} = -521.161 \pm 0.40$ cal $mol^{-1} K^{-1}$ for the reaction

$$5Mg + 4C\,(\text{graphite}) + 9O_2 + 5H_2 = 5MgO \cdot 4CO_2 \cdot 5H_2O. \quad (12)$$

Substituting the enthalpy and entropy data into the relation

$$\Delta G^\circ_f = \Delta H^\circ_f - T\Delta S^\circ_T, \quad (13)$$

the standard Gibbs free energies of formation for $MgCO_3 \cdot 3H_2O$ and $5MgO \cdot 4CO_2 \cdot 5H_2O$ are −412,040±120 cal mol^{-1} and −1,401,710±260 cal mol^{-1}.

Inasmuch as the crystal structure of hydromagnesite is unknown, there exists the possibility that it might be disordered at low temperatures, that is $S^\circ_0 \neq 0$. If this were so, the entropy, S°_{298}, of hydromagnesite would be greater than 120.38 cal $mol^{-1} K^{-1}$ and $\Delta G^\circ_{f,\,298}$ for hydromagnesite would be more negative (that is, more stable) than indicated.

Our assumption that the structure of hydromagnesite is ordered, that is, does not retain any configurational entropy at 0 kelvin, is in accord with the studies of Giauque and his collaborators (for example, Brodale and Giauque, 1958), who have found that only $Na_2SO_4 \cdot 10H_2O$ (mirabilite), among the more than 10 different hydrates which they have studied at low temperatures, retained any residual entropy at 0 kelvin.

COMPARISON WITH AQUEOUS SOLUBILITY RESULTS

The solubility of $MgCO_3 \cdot 3H_2O$ has been studied by a number of investigators and the results summarized by Langmuir (1965). The several investigations are in good agreement and lead to a solubility of 0.213±0.001 mol of $MgCO_3 \cdot 3H_2O$/kg of H_2O at 25°C and 1 atm CO_2. The log of the activity product for nesquehonite (N), for the reaction

$$MgCO_3 \cdot 3H_2O = Mg^{+2} + CO_3^{-2} + 3H_2O \quad (14)$$

calculated from the solubility data and neglecting the possibility of complexing, is

$$\log K_N = (a_{Mg^{+2}})(a_{CO^{-3}})(a_{H_2O})^3 = -5.07. \quad (15)$$

Langmuir (1965) and P. B. Hostetler (oral commun., April 15, 1970) have measured the pH of aqueous solutions in equilibrium with $MgCO_3 \cdot 3H_2O$ under 1 atm of CO_2 pressure. They calculated values for $\log K_N$ from their pH data with the assumption that part of the Mg^{+2} was complexed by $MgHCO_3^+$ and (or) $MgCO_3^0$ and obtained $\log K_N = -5.59 \pm 0.10$ and -5.42 ± 0.10, respectively. The corresponding free energy changes are 7,626 and 7,394 cal for solution. Using our calorimetric value for $\Delta G^\circ_{f,\,298} = -412{,}040$ cal of $MgCO_3 \cdot 3H_2O$ and the values adopted by Robie and Waldbaum (1968) for the standard free energies of formation of Mg^{+2}, CO_3^{-2}, and H_2O, we calculate ΔG°_{298} for reaction 14 equals 6,906±250 cal, or $\log K_N = -5.06 \pm 0.18$. From the foregoing it is seen that the calorimetric data are in agreement with the solubility data only if the degree of complexing is considerably less than that calculated by Langmuir (1965).

Garrels, Thompson, and Siever (1960) and Langmuir (1965) have measured the solubility of "hydromagnesite." Garrels, Thompson, and Siever (1960) obtained a value for the Gibbs free energy of formation of hydromagnesite of −1,108,300 cal mol^{-1} based on their solubility measurements of an impure sample of material from Soda Springs, Idaho. Langmuir (1965) calculated a $\Delta G^\circ_{f,\,298}$ for hydromagnesite of −1,100,100±2,000 cal mol^{-1} from the solubility of Baker Analyzed Reagent magnesium carbonate which is presumably finely crystalline hydromagnesite. Both of these values were based upon the formula $3MgCO_3 \cdot Mg(OH)_2 \cdot 3H_2O$ which has earlier been shown to be incorrect (Robie and Hemingway, 1972b).

From the calorimetric data for hydromagnesite (HY), together with the Gibbs free energies of formation of Mg^{+2}, CO_3^{-2}, OH^-, and H_2O adopted by Robie and Waldbaum (1968), we calculate the logarithm of the activity product from the reaction

$$5MgO \cdot 4CO_2 \cdot 5H_2O = 5Mg^{+2} + 4CO_3^{-2} + 2OH^- + 4H_2O, \text{ as} \quad (16)$$

$$\log K_{HY} = (a_{Mg^{+2}})^5 (a_{CO_3^{-2}})^4 (a_{OH^-})^2 (a_{H_2O})^4$$

$$= -37.08 \pm 0.45. \quad (17)$$

ACKNOWLEDGMENTS

Bruce S. Hemingway wishes to thank the National Science Foundation for support under NSF grants GA-1651 and GA-453. The preparation of this report was supported in part by the Office of Saline Water, U.S. Department of the Interior, under agreement No. 14-30-3040.

REFERENCES CITED

Barron, T. H. K., Berg, W. T., and Morrison, J. A., 1959, On the heat capacity of crystalline magnesium oxide: Royal Soc. [London] Proc. Ser. A, v. 250, p. 70–83.

Brodale, G., and Giauque, W. F., 1958, The heat of hydration of sodium sulfate–Low temperature heat capacity and entropy of sodium sulfate decahydrate: Am. Chem. Soc. Jour., v. 80, p. 2042–2044.

Commission on Atomic Weights for 1970, Atomic weights for 1969: Pure and Appl. Chemistry, v. 21, p. 95–108.

Garrels, R. M., Thompson, M. E., and Siever, Raymond, 1960, Stability of some carbonates at 25°C and one atmosphere total pressure: Am. Jour. Sci., v. 258, p. 402–418.

Hemingway, B. S., and Robie, R. A., 1973, A calorimetric determination of the standard enthalpies of formation, of huntite, $CaMg_3(CO_3)_4$, and artinite, $Mg_2(OH)_2CO_3 \cdot 3H_2O$, and their standard Gibbs free energies of formation: U.S. Geol. Survey Jour. Research. v. 1, no. 5, p. 535–541.

Langmuir, Donald, 1965, Stability of carbonates in the system $MgO-CO_2-H_2O$: Jour. Geology v. 73, p. 730–754.

Palache, Charles, Berman, Harry, and Frondel, Clifford, 1951, Dana's system of mineralogy, [7th ed.]: New York, John Wiley and Sons, Inc. v. 2, 1124 p.

Robie, R. A., and Hemingway, B. S., 1972a, Calorimeters for heat of solution and low-temperature heat capacity measurements: U.S. Geol. Survey Prof. Paper 755, 32 p.

—— 1972b, The heat capacities at low temperatures and entropies at 298.15 K of nesquehonite, $MgCO_3 \cdot 3H_2O$ and hydromagnesite: Am. Mineralogist, v. 57, p. 1768–1781.

Robie, R. A., and Waldbaum, D. R., 1968, Thermodynamic properties of minerals and related substances at 298.15°K (25.0°C) and one atmosphere (1.013 bars) pressure and at higher temperatures: U.S. Geol. Survey Bull. 1259, 256 p.

Stephan, G. W., and MacGillavry, C. H., 1972, The crystal structure of nesquehonite, $MgCO_3 \cdot 3H_2O$: Acta Crystallographica, v. B28, p. 1031–1033.

Wagman, D. D., Evans, W. H., Parker, V. B., Halow, I., Bailey, S. M., and Schumm, R. H., 1968, Selected values of chemical thermodynamic properties. Tables of the first thirty-four elements in the standard order of arrangement: U.S. Natl. Bur. Standards Tech. Note 270-3, 264 p.

Jour. Research U.S. Geol. Survey
Vol. 1, No. 5, Sept.-Oct. 1973, p. 549—554

CHEMICAL ANALYSIS OF RUTILE—A PYROCATECHOL VIOLET SPECTROPHOTOMETRIC PROCEDURE FOR THE DIRECT MICRODETERMINATION OF ZIRCONIUM

By ROBERT MEYROWITZ,[1] Washington, D.C.

Abstract.—The ZrO_2 content of rutile is determined spectrophotometrically by a direct pyrocatechol violet procedure. The sample is decomposed by potassium pyrosulfate fusion in a transparent quartz crucible, and a sulfuric acid solution of the melt is used for the determination at a pH of 5.1. Of the elements commonly present in rutile, only titanium and niobium occur in concentrations large enough to interfere. Titanium and niobium interference is overcome by adding the titanium and niobium contents of the sample to the standard zirconium solutions used for the standard zirconium curve. The absorbance is measured at 570 nm. Beer's law is obeyed within the range of 0.05–1.50 ppm ZrO_2. In the presence of 50 ppm TiO_2, the range is 0.15–1.50 ppm ZrO_2. The tolerances of 47 elements were determined. The sensitivity is 0.0058 μg Zr/cm^2. The variables in the method were studied, and typical results are given for commercial rutile concentrates.

This is the second in a series of papers describing microprocedures and semimicroprocedures for the complete analysis of small samples of rutile, brookite, and anatase. The first paper dealt with the spectrophotometric determination of titanium, total iron, niobium, phosphorus, and vanadium (Meyrowitz, 1972). This paper describes the use of pyrocathechol violet (PCV) for the microdetermination of zirconium dioxide at concentrations of 0.1 percent or greater.

Flaschka and Farah (1956) were the first to use PCV for the determination of zirconium. The direct determination was made in the presence of disodium (ethylenedinitrilo) tetraacetate [EDTA] in acetate medium at pH 5.2. Young, French, and White (1958) used PCV in acetate medium at pH 5.1 in the presence of mercaptoacetic acid (thioglycolic acid) to eliminate the interference of moderate amounts of iron. Chernikhov, Luk'yanov, and Knyazeva (1959) used the method of Flaschka and Farah for the determination of zirconium in phosphorites. Later Chernikhov, Dobkina and Petrova (1960) found that for low zirconium concentrations the maximum absorbance was at 550 nm rather than at the 620–650 nm observed by the previous workers for high concentrations of zirconium. In addition, they used PCV for the direct determination of zirconium in titanium and its alloys. Leeb and Hecht (1963) used PCV for the determination of zirconium in titanium-free steel. After an enrichment and separation of zirconium, the absorbance of the zirconium complex was measured in the presence of mercaptoacetic acid at a pH of 5.5. Vladimirova, Yagodin, and Chekmarev (1966) proposed that PCV be used at relatively high pH (1.5–2.0 *N* sulfuric acid). However, no application was made to the analysis of materials. Staats and Brück (1967) used PCV for the determination of zirconium in steel after the extraction of most of the iron with isobutyl methyl ketone from 7 *N* HCl. Although the final determination is basically that of Flaschka and Farah (1956), the absorbance was measured at 570 nm instead of 620 nm. Luk'yanov and Knyazeva (1968) made a detailed study of the reaction of zirconium with PCV in the presence of EDTA and found that "***the colored compound formed is a three-component negatively charged complex with a Zr:EDTA:PCV ratio of 3:3:2."

In developing the method described in this paper the combined advantages of both EDTA and mercaptoacetic acid were used. The author had used mercaptoacetic acid in his PCV procedure for the direct determination of aluminum in silicate minerals (Meyrowitz, 1970).

[1] Present address: Environmental Geology Program, University of Southern California, Los Angeles, Calif. 90007.

REAGENTS AND APPARATUS

Sulfuric acid, 18 *N*.

Sulfuric acid, 1.2 *N*.

Potassium pyrosulfate, 2-percent (w/v). Transfer 10.0 g of powdered $K_2S_2O_7$ to a 15-ml transparent quartz crucible, tap to settle the contents, and place a cover on the crucible. Heat in the electric furnace from room temperature to 650°C and hold at this temperature for 30 minutes. Remove from the furnace and cool. Place crucible with contents and cover in a 150-ml beaker, add sufficient water to cover crucible, and warm to dissolve the melt. Remove and rinse crucible cover and crucible. Transfer solution to a 500-ml volumetric flask, dilute to volume with water, and mix. Store in a glass bottle.

Mercaptoacetic acid, 4-percent (v/v). Prepare fresh daily.

Disodium (ethylenedinitrilo) tetraacetate, $Na_2C_{10}H_{14}O_8N_2 \cdot 2H_2O$, 1.5-percent. Prepare 1 liter of solution. Filter the aqueous solution through a fast paper and store in a glass bottle with a plastic stopper.

Pyrocatechol violet, 0.03-percent (w/v). Prepare 500 ml, filter the aqueous solution through a slow paper, and store in glass. Discard after 5 days. The reagent available from J. T. Baker Chemical Co. is satisfactory for this procedure.

Sodium acetate, $NaC_2H_3O_2 \cdot 3H_2O$, crystal, 50-percent (w/v). Prepare 1 liter of solution. Filter through a fast paper and store in a glass bottle with a plastic stopper.

Sodium hydroxide, 0.5 *N*.

Zirconium stock solution, 100-ppm ZrO_2, 2.4 *N* H_2SO_4, 0.5-percent potassium pyrosulfate (w/v). Weigh by difference 50.00 mg of pure ZrO_2 in a 10-ml transparent quartz crucible. Add 2.5 g of $K_2S_2O_7$. Tap to settle the contents and place a cover on the crucible. Heat gently with a bunsen burner to minimize spattering. When effervescence is diminished, gradually increase the size of the flame and finally heat strongly until the melt is clear and the solution of the ZrO_2 is complete. Invert the burner and heat the crucible cover to fuse the spattered material on the underside of the crucible cover. Cool to room temperature and place crucible and cover in a 150-ml borosilicate beaker. Add 66.6 ml of 18 *N* H_2SO_4 and boil gently to dissolve the melt, stirring frequently to aid its solution. Cool. Using platinum-tipped tweezers with right-angle tips, remove the crucible cover and crucible out of the solution, rinsing each with a fine stream of water. Rinse the tweezers and the beaker. Mix frequently during these operations to prevent precipitation of the zirconium. Continuing to mix frequently, transfer the solution to a 500-ml volumetric flask and dilute to approximately 450 ml. Cool to room temperature and dilute to volume. Discard after 30 days.

Zirconium solutions containing 1.00, 2.00, 5.00, 6.00, 8.00 and 10.00 ppm ZrO_2 in 1.2 *N* H_2SO_4.

Titanium solution, 1,000-ppm TiO_2, 1.8 *N* H_2SO_4, 1.0-percent $K_2S_2O_7$ (w/v). Weigh by difference 500.0 mg of pure TiO_2 in a 15-ml transparent quartz crucible. Add 5.0 g of $K_2S_2O_7$ and follow the procedure for the preparation of the zirconium stock solution. Use 50 ml of 18 *N* H_2SO_4 instead of 66.6 ml as indicated in the procedure.

Niobium stock solution, 100-ppm Nb_2O_5, 2.4 *N* H_2SO_4, 0.4-percent $K_2S_2O_7$ (w/v). Weigh by difference 50.00 mg of pure Nb_2O_5 in a 5-ml transparent quartz crucible. Add 2.0 g of $K_2S_2O_7$. Follow the above procedure for the preparation of the zirconium stock solution. Discard after 30 days.

Niobium solutions containing 1.00, 5.00, and 10.00 ppm Nb_2O_5 in 1.2 *N* H_2SO_4.

Sodium hydroxide, 0.5 *N*. Prepare 500 ml using plastic apparatus. Store in a plastic bottle.

Cruicibles and covers, quartz, transparent, 5-, 10-, and 15-ml capacity.

Tweezers, long platinum tips with ends bent at right angles.

Furnace, electric, temperature-controlled.

Quartz plate for bottom of furnace.

Spectrophotometer, Bausch and Lomb, Spectronic 100.

Cells, absorption, 1- and 5-cm light path.

pH meter.

PROCEDURE

1. Transfer duplicate 5.00-ml aliquots from the 2.4 *N* H_2SO_4 solution of the sample (Meyrowitz, 1972, p. B157–B158) to 100-ml volumetric flasks. Rinse down the necks of the flasks with water and mix.
2. For the range 0.0–0.3 percent ZrO_2 transfer 3.00- and 5.00-ml aliquots of 1.00-ppm ZrO_2 solution, 5.00 ml of 2.00-ppm ZrO_2 solution, and 3.00 ml of 5.00-ppm ZrO_2 solution to 100-ml volumetric flasks. Rinse the necks of the flasks and mix. For the range 0.3–1.0 percent ZrO_2 transfer 5.00-ml aliquots of 5.00-, 6.00-, 8.00-, and 10.00-ppm ZrO_2 solutions to the flasks.
3. Add the amounts of titanium and niobium solutions to the standard zirconium solutions to match the sample which has been previously analyzed. Rinse the necks of the flasks and mix. Add sufficient 2.0-percent $K_2S_2O_7$ solution so that the total amount of $K_2S_2O_7$ present will be equivalent to 5.0 ml of 2.0-percent $K_2S_2O_7$.
4. Using a 10-ml Mohr pipet add, while swirling the flasks, the required amounts of 0.5 *N* NaOH to the flasks containing the standard zirconium solutions. Rinse down the necks of the flasks and mix. The number of milliliters of 0.5 *N* NaOH to be added is twice the number of milliequivalents of H_2SO_4 present in the flask less 15.6. The H_2SO_4 in the standard zirconium, titanium, and niobium solutions makes up the milliequivalent of H_2SO_4 present in the flask. Disregard the residual H_2SO_4 due to the fused $K_2S_2O_7$, as all of the flasks contain the same amount of fused $K_2S_2O_7$.
5. Add 3.0 ml of 1.2 *N* H_2SO_4 to the flasks containing the sample solutions.
6. Add 5.0 ml of mercaptoacetic acid solution. Rinse down the necks of the flasks, mix, and let stand for 10 minutes.
7. Add 5.0 ml of disodium-EDTA solution. Rinse the necks of the flasks and mix.
8. Add 10.00 ml of PCV solution with a transfer pipet. Rinse down the necks of the flasks and mix.
9. While swirling the flask, add slowly 20.0 ml of sodium acetate solution, rinse down the necks of the flasks, and mix.
10. Dilute to mark, mix, and let stand for 30 minutes.
11. Determine the absorbance at 570 nm, using water as the reference solution. Use 5-cm cells.
12. Measure the pH of all final solutions.
13. Plot a standard curve and determine the ZrO_2 content of the unknowns.

RESULTS

Absorption spectra.—Figure 1 shows the absorption spectra of the reagent blank with water as the reference solution and of the processed solutions of zirconium and titanium with the reagent blank as the reference solution. The absorbance peaks of the zirconium and titanium complexes occur at 550 nm and 545 nm, respectively. The reagent blank absorbs strongly at these wavelengths.

Effect of concentration of zirconium on the absorbance of the zirconium complex at 570 and 620 nm.—Figure 2 shows that for dilute zirconium solutions the absorbance at 570 nm is greater than at 620 nm and that the reverse is true for concentrated zirconium solutions.

Effect of pH.—The recommended procedure was followed in this study except for varying the amount of dilute H_2SO_4 present and, where necessary, adding dilute NaOH. Figure 3 shows the change in absorbance with pH for the reagent blank

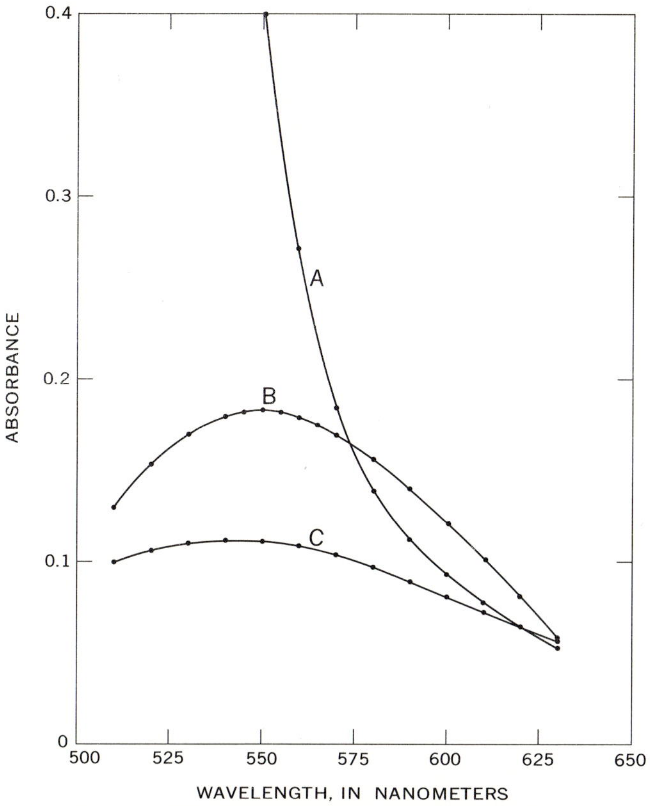

Figure 1.—Absorption spectra curves. A, reagent blank (reference solution, water); B, 0.25 ppm ZrO_2 (reference solution, reagent blank); C, 50 ppm TiO_2 (reference solution, reagent blank). Cell path, 5 cm; pH, 5.1.

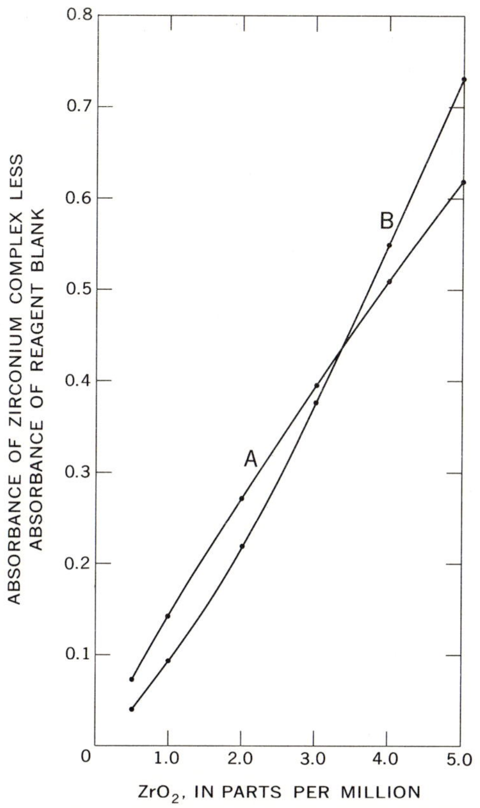

Figure 2.—Calibration curves at 570 nm (A) and 620 nm (B). Reference solution, water; cell path, 1 cm; pH, 5.2.

with water as a reference solution and for the processed zirconium and titanium solutions with the reagent blank as the reference solution. The absorbance of the reagent blank increases slowly between pH 5.0 and 5.5 and rapidly above pH 5.5. The absorbance of the processed zirconium solution increases slowly from pH 4.9 to a maximum at approximately pH 5.8 and then decreases slowly to pH 6.2. The absorbance of the processed titanium solution increases slowly between pH 4.9 and 5.2 and rapidly above pH 5.2.

Effect of development time.—The absorbance of a processed 0.25-ppm ZrO_2 solution was measured with distilled water as the reference solution. No decrease in absorbance was noted the first 30 minutes. Absorbance decreased 0.004 and 0.002 units in the next two 30-minute periods, and 0.002 units in the following hour. For a processed solution containing 0.25 ppm ZrO_2 and 50 ppm TiO_2, there was no significant change in absorbance after 2 hours.

Effect of reagent concentration.—Figure 4 shows the effect of the concentration of PCV at pH 5.1 on the absorbance of a processed 0.25-ppm solution and of a similar solution with 50 ppm TiO_2 added. For pure zirconium solutions the absorbance remains relatively constant above 50 ppm PCV. For mixtures of zirconium and titanium there is a gradual decrease at 45 to 55 ppm PCV, above which the absorbance decreases rapidly.

Adherence to Beer's law and sensitivity.—For pure zirconium solutions the system conforms to Beer's law over the range 0.05–1.50 ppm ZrO_2 with a 5-cm cell path. The sensitivity by Sandell's definition (1959, p. 83) is 0.0058 μg Zr/cm^2 at 570 nm. In the presence of 50 ppm TiO_2, the system conforms to Beer's law over the range 0.15–1.50 ppm ZrO_2 and the curve is virtually parallel to that of the pure zirconium solutions. Figures 5 and 6 show typical calibration curves for ZrO_2 with varying amounts of TiO_2 and Nb_2O_5 added.

Effect of diverse ions.—Table 1 shows the maximum concentrations ($\leqslant$5.0 ppm, except as noted) of some 46 elements, calculated as oxides, tested for effect on absorbance in the absence of zirconium, except as noted. The tolerance limit of deviation between test solution and blank was held at ±0.003 absorbance unit.

Effect of fluoride.—Table 2 shows the effect of fluoride on absorbance of zirconium solutions at different concentrations. For an aliquot of sample solution equivalent to 5.00 mg, the factor for converting parts per million of oxide and fluoride in the final solution to percentage of oxide and fluoride in the sample is 2.

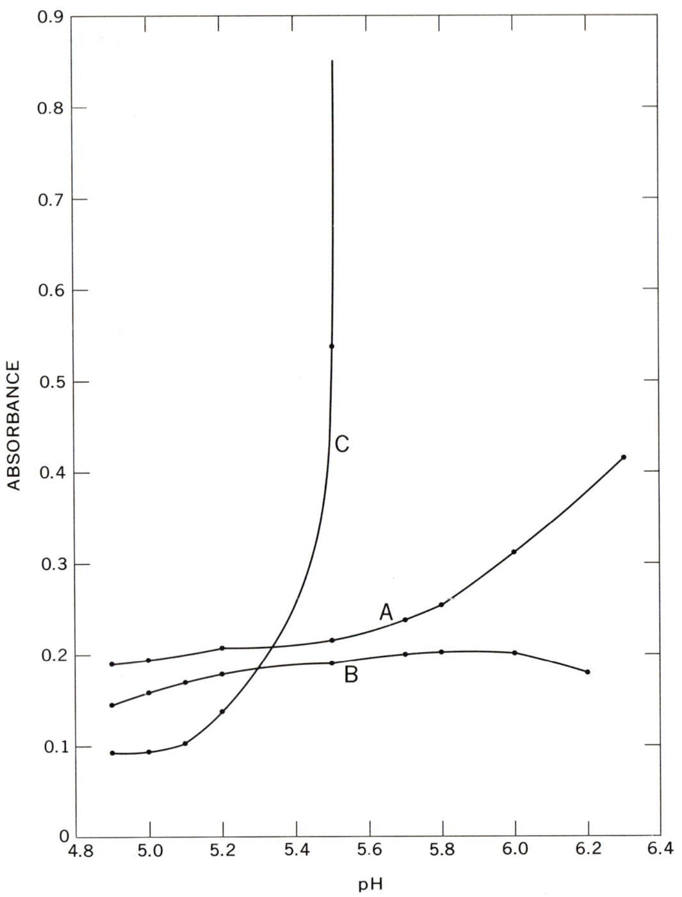

Figure 3.—Effect of pH on absorbance. A, reagent blank (reference solution, water); B, 0.25 ppm ZrO_2 (reference solution, reagent blank); C, 50 ppm TiO_2 (reference solution, reagent blank). Cell path, 5 cm; wavelength, 570 nm. B and C are absorbance of complex less absorbance of reagent blank.

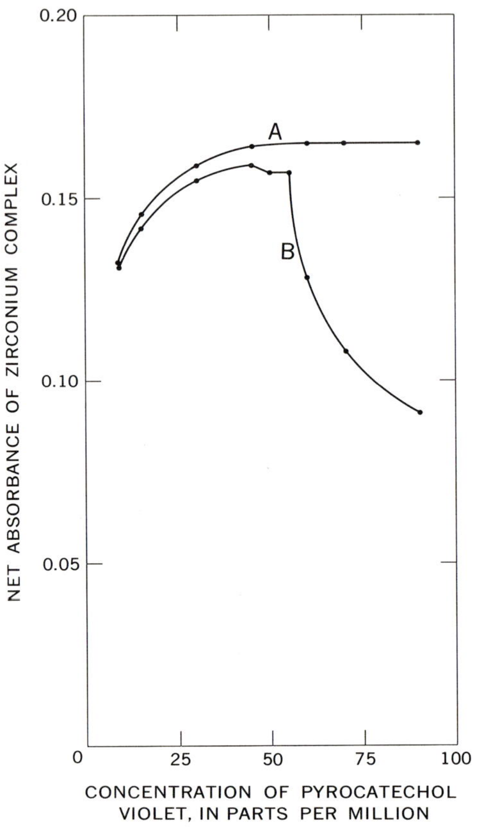

Figure 4.—Effect of concentration of pyrocatechol violet on absorbance. A, 0.25 ppm ZrO_2—absorbance of zirconium solution less absorbance of reagent blank; B, 0.25 ppm ZrO_2 and 50 ppm TiO_2—absorbance of zirconium-titanium solution less absorbance of titanium solution. Reference solution, water; wavelength, 570 nm; cell path, 5 cm; pH, 5.1.

DISCUSSION

Although the peak absorbance for the zirconium complex occurs at 550 nm, the wavelength of 570 nm was selected for the determination because of the lower absorbance of the reagent blank as shown in figure 1. The optimum range of pH for the final solution is 4.9–5.1, where the effect of small changes in concentration of reagent or TiO_2 is at a minimum and absorbance of ZrO_2 is near its maximum value (fig. 3). A pH of 5.1 was selected for the standard procedure. Samples and standards within a set should not differ by more than 0.1 pH unit. This will be obtained if the amount of acid present in the solution contains the equivalent of 15.6 me of H_2SO_4 before the mercaptoacetic reagent is added. Because the absorbancies of the final solutions change slightly with time, the solutions are read in the same order in which they are prepared.

Figure 2 is further proof of Chernikhov, Dobkina, and Petrova's (1960) assertion that for low concentrations of zirconium, the maximum absorbance of the Zr-PCV complex is not at 620 nm.

Titanium and niobium are normally the only interfering elements present in the common rutile minerals. To overcome the interference of these elements, the amounts of titanium and niobium present in the 5-ml aliquot of the sample solution are added to the standard zirconium solutions used to prepare the standard zirconium curve. The amounts of zirconium taken for the standards should bracket or be close to the unknowns. The percentage of titanium and niobium can be determined by the methods previously described (Meyrowitz, 1972, p. B158, p. B160–B162).

If the sample contains more than 1.0 percent ZrO_2, the size of the aliquot of the sample solution should be reduced so that the maximum amount of ZrO_2 is approximately 50 μg (curve B, fig. 5). Aliquots of the sample solution larger than 5.00 ml should generally not be taken. Increasing the concentration of TiO_2 above 0.5 ppm TiO_2 results in solutions of very high absorbance. At 100 ppm TiO_2 the solution becomes cloudy.

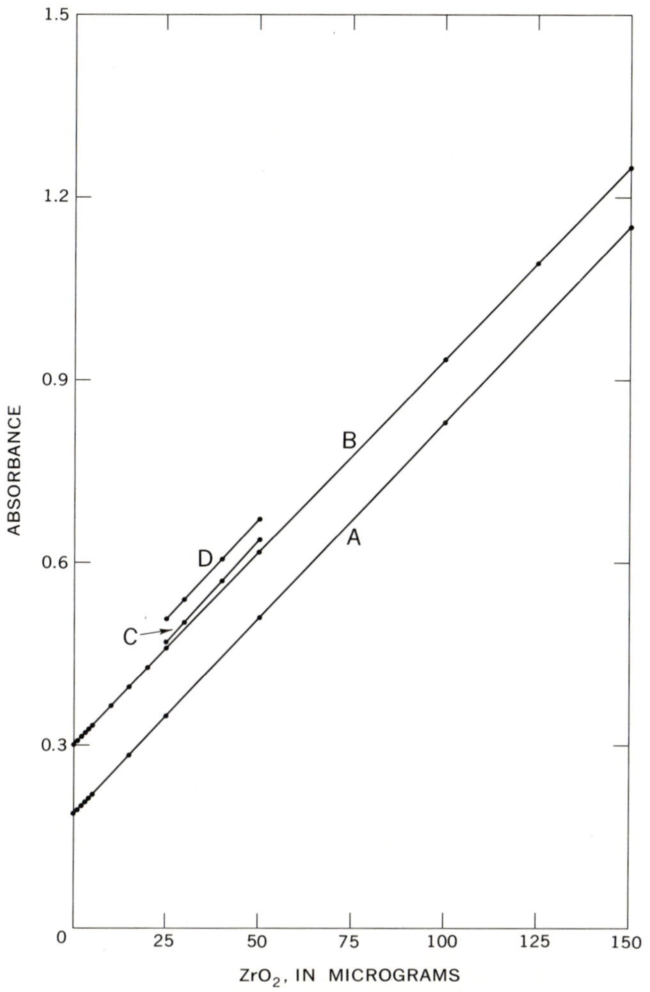

Figure 5.—Typical calibration curves. A, ZrO_2 only; B, ZrO_2 and 50 ppm TiO_2; C, ZrO_2 and 39 ppm TiO_2 and 0.14 ppm Nb_2O_5; D, ZrO_2 and 51 ppm TiO_2 and 0.19 ppm Nb_2O_5. Reference solution, water; cell path, 5 cm; wavelength, 570 nm; pH, 5.1.

If the sample contains more than 4.0 percent Nb_2O_5, use a 5.00-ml aliquot of the diluted sample solution which was prepared for the determination of TiO_2 as previously described (Meyrowitz, 1972, p. B158). In step 5 of the procedure outlined in the present paper it is necessary to add a total of 11.0 ml of 1.2 N H_2SO_4 instead of 3.0 ml as indicated in the instructions.

The concentrations of Si, Fe, Al, V, Cr, Ta, Sn, P, Mo, W, Pb, and F in most common rutiles are not sufficient to interfere with the determination of zirconium. In samples where the tolerance level is exceeded, the determination can be made by taking a smaller portion of the sample, provided that the concentration of zirconium in the final solution is not less than 0.05 ppm ZrO_2. Where it is not feasible to use a smaller portion of the sample solution, interferences can be overcome by adding the same amount of interfering element present in the analyzed solution to the standard zirconium solutions.

ANALYSIS OF COMMERCIAL RUTILE CONCENTRATES

Table 3 gives the results obtained by use of the recommended procedure for the analysis of a commercial rutile and a rutile substitute previously analyzed for TiO_2, total iron, Nb_2O_5, P_2O_5, and V_2O_5 (Meyrowitz, 1972, p. B164, table 2). Good agreement was found between the reported values for ZrO_2 and those values determined by quantitative spectrographic analysis.

REFERENCES CITED

Chernikhov, Yu. A., Dobkina, B. M., and Petrova, E. I., 1960, Determination of zirconium in titanium and its alloys by reaction with pyrocatechol violet: Zavodskaya Lab., v. 26, p. 529–531 [In Russian].

Chernikhov, Yu. A., Luk'yanov, V. F., and Knyazeva, E. M., 1959, The photometric determination of zirconium in phosphorites by means of pyrocatechol violet: Zhur. Anal. Khimii, v. 14, p. 207–210 [In Russian].

Flaschka, H., and Farah, M. Y., 1956, Eine neue, hochselektive Methode zur photometrischen Bestimmung des Zirkoniums: Zeitschr. Anal. Chemie, v. 152, p. 401–411.

(Continued on next page)

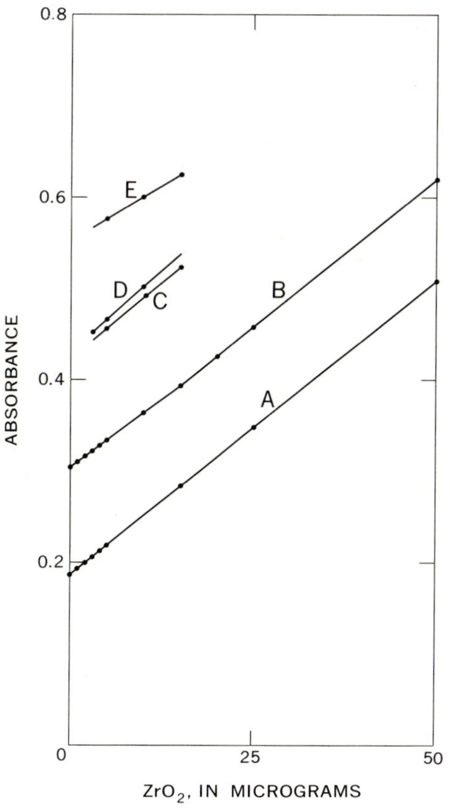

Figure 6.—Typical calibration curves. A and B are expanded lower portions of curves A and B of figure 5. C, ZrO_2 and 38 ppm TiO_2 and 0.87 ppm Nb_2O_5; D, ZrO_2 and 37 ppm TiO_2 and 0.85 ppm Nb_2O_5; E, ZrO_2 and 48 ppm TiO_2 and 1.10 ppm Nb_2O_5.

Table 1.—*Effect of diverse elements on absorbance*

[Maximum concentration of elements tested calculated as oxides, ≤5.0, except as noted. Limiting tolerance of measured absorbance of test solution versus blank, ±0.003 absorbance unit (equivalent to 0.005 ppm ZrO_2)]

Oxide	Maximum concentration (ppm)	Oxide	Maximum concentration (ppm)	Oxide	Maximum concentration (ppm)
BeO	5.0	Er_2O_3	5.0	NiO	5.0
MgO	5.0	Tm_2O_3	5.0	CuO	3.0
CaO	5.0	Yb_2O_3	5.0	ZnO	5.0
SrO	5.0	Lu_2O_3	5.0	CdO	5.0
Sc_2O_3	5.0	TiO_2	.50	B_2O_3	[1]5.0
Y_2O_3	5.0	V_2O_5	3.0	Al_2O_3	20.
La_2O_3	5.0	V_2O_4	12.	Ga_2O_3	5.0
Ce_2O_3	5.0	Nb_2O_5	.03	In_2O_3	5.0
Pr_2O_3	5.0	Ta_2O_5	.03	Tl_2O	5.0
Nd_2O_3	5.0	Cr_2O_3(as Cr^{3+})	.10	SiO_2	[1]5.0
Sm_2O_3	5.0	Cr_2O_3(as Cr^{6+})	.10	SnO_2	3.0
Eu_2O_3	5.0	MoO_3	.50	PbO	1.0
Gd_2O_3	5.0	WO_3	.20	P_2O_5	[2].50
Tb_2O_3	5.0	MnO	5.0	As_2O_5	5.0
Dy_2O_3	5.0	Fe_2O_3	13.	ThO_2	5.0
Ho_2O_3	5.0	CoO	5.0	UO_3	5.0

[1] No interference in the presence or absence of 0.25 ppm ZrO_2.
[2] No interference in the presence or absence of 1.0 ppm ZrO_2.

Table 2.—*Effect of fluoride on absorbance values of zirconium solutions*

[Results obtained by subtracting absorbance values of fluoride-containing zirconium solutions from absorbance values of pure zirconium solutions]

Zirconium concentration[1] (ppm)	Fluoride concentration (ppm)				
	0.10	0.20	0.30	0.40	0.50
0.05	0.000	0.000	−0.001	−0.001	−0.001
.25	−.001	−.001	−.002	−.002	−.004
1.00	.000	−.004	−.005	−.008	−.012

[1] Calculated as ZrO_2.

Table 3.—ZrO_2 *content of a rutile substitute and a rutile concentrate*

Weight of sample (milligrams)		ZrO_2 content (weight percent)	
Fused	Used	Procedure of this report	Quantitative spectrographic analysis[1]
U.S. Bureau of Mines rutile substitute, No. 1-250-F			
82.70	4.14	<0.1	0.03
80.31	4.02	<.1	....
103.96	5.20	<.1	....
N.S.W. Rutile Mining Co., PTY, Ltd., rutile concentrate Rm-84			
81.29	4.06	0.47	0.50
107.22	5.36	.46	....

[1] Analyzed by Janet D. Fletcher, U.S. Geological Survey.

Leeb, A. J., and Hecht, F., 1963, Beitrag zur Bestimmung von Zirkonium in Stahl: Radex-Rundschau, no. 1, p. 360–365.

Luk'yanov, V. F., and Knyazeva, E. M., 1968, The reaction of zirconium (IV) with pyrocatechol violet: Zhur. Anal. Khimii, v. 23, p. 536–540 [In Russian].

Meyrowitz, Robert, 1970, A pyrocatechol violet spectrophotometric procedure for the direct microdetermination of aluminum in silicate minerals, *in* Geological Survey Research 1970: U.S. Geol. Survey Prof. Paper 700-D, p. D225–D229.

———1972, Chemical analysis of rutile—Direct spectrophotometric determination of titanium, total iron, niobium, phosphorus, and vanadium, *in* Geological Survey Research 1972: U.S. Geol. Survey Prof. Paper 800-B, p. B157–B164.

Sandell, E. B., 1959, Colorimetric determination of traces of metals, 3d ed.: New York, Interscience Publishers, Inc., 1,032 p.

Staats, Gotthard, and Brück, Horst, 1967, Zur Bestimmung kleiner Mengen von Niob mit 4-(2-Pyridylazo)-resorcin und von Zirkonium mit Brenzcatechinviolett in Stahl: Zeitschr. Anal. Chemie, v. 230, p. 271–276.

Vladimirova, L. M., Yagodin, G. A., and Chekmarev, A. M., 1966, Photometric determination of zirconium and hafnium in sulfuric acid solutions by means of pyrocatechol violet: Zhur. Anal. Khimii, v. 22, p. 1345–1349 [In Russian].

Young, J. P., French, J. R., and White, J. C., 1958, Microdetermination of zirconium in sulfuric acid solutions with pyrocatechol violet: Anal. Chemistry, v. 30, p. 422–425.

Jour. Research U.S. Geol. Survey
Vol. 1, No. 5, Sept.-Oct. 1973, p. 555—558

SPECTROPHOTOMETRIC DETERMINATION OF TUNGSTEN IN ROCKS BY AN ISOTOPE DILUTION PROCEDURE

By E. G. LILLIE and L. PAUL GREENLAND,
Washington, D.C.

Abstract.—Samples are decomposed with hydrofluoric acid and perchloric acid in the presence of W^{181} tracer. Molybdenum is extracted from a hydrochloric acid solution with tributyl phosphate. Tungsten is separated from most other elements by extraction of the α-benzoinoximate into chloroform. Stannous chloride in concentrated hydrochloric acid is used to strip tungsten and reduce it to W^{+5}. The amount of tungsten is determined spectrophotometrically after extraction as the thiocyanate complex into amyl alcohol. The correction for chemical losses is determined by counting W^{181}.

Many procedures for the spectrophotometric determination of tungsten with thiocyanate have been published (Affsprung and Murphy, 1964; Peng and Sandell, 1963; Fogg and others, 1970a, b, 1971). Fogg, Marriott, and Burns (1970a) have made an extensive study of these procedures. In rock analyses, where concentrations of tungsten are generally low, interferences and lack of sensitivity have presented difficulties. The numerous problems associated with thiocyanate methods (Hobart and Hurley, 1962) have led to procedures using the color formed with dithiol for the determination of tungsten in rocks (Quin and Brooks, 1972; Chan and Riley, 1967). Although sensitivity is often increased in these methods, interferences, especially from molybdenum, have been noted.

The method described in this paper gives a reliable tungsten thiocyanate color owing to the prior separation of tungsten from most other sample constituents. After removal of molybdenum, iron, and some other elements by extraction with tributyl phosphate from hydrochloric acid solution, tungsten is extracted with α-benzoinoxime into chloroform and then stripped and reduced to W^{+5} with stannous chloride in concentrated hydrochloric acid. Tungsten in this virtually pure solution is reacted with thiocyanate and extracted into a small volume of amyl alcohol for the spectrophotometric determination. The selectivity of the separations of tungsten from other elements can be enhanced by accepting losses of tungsten at each separation stage; the fraction of tungsten finally recovered is determined by counting W^{181}.

Acknowledgments.—We are greatly indebted to E. Y. Campbell for assistance with the analyses. We are grateful to B. L. Ingram and D. R. Norton for very helpful reviews of an earlier version of the manuscript.

REAGENTS AND APPARATUS

Aluminum chloride solution: Dissolve 20 g of $AlCl_3 \cdot 6H_2O$ crystals in 300 ml of concentrated hydrochloric acid. Dilute to 1 liter with water.

Tributyl phosphate (TBP) solution: Mix 200 ml of tributyl phosphate with 200 ml of chloroform.

α-Benzoinoxime solution: Dissolve 4.0 g of α-benzoinoxime in 200 ml of ethanol. Prepare fresh daily.

Stannous chloride solution, concentrated: Dissolve 9.0 g of $SnCl_2 \cdot 2H_2O$ in 200 ml of concentrated hydrochloric acid. Prepare fresh daily.

Stannous chloride solution, dilute: Dilute 50 ml of concentrated stannous chloride solution to 200 ml with water. Prepare fresh daily.

Potassium thiocyanate solution: Dissolve 39 g of potassium thiocyanate in 100 ml of water. Prepare fresh weekly.

Hydrochloric acid, 6 *M*: Dilute 258 ml of concentrated hydrochloric acid to 500 ml with water.

Ethanol solution: Mix 50 ml of ethanol with 50 ml of 6 *M* hydrochloric acid.

Standard tungsten solution, 100 μg W per ml: Dissolve 0.0897 g of analytical reagent grade $Na_2WO_4 \cdot 2H_2O$ and 0.30 g of sodium hydroxide in 500 ml of water.

Tracer solution: Commercially available W^{181} was diluted with 2 percent NaOH to obtain about 10,000 counts per minute from a 0.01-ml aliquot. The specific activity was such that <0.1 μg W was added in the 0.01-ml aliquot.

Counting apparatus: A 3- by 3-in. NaI (Tl) detector coupled to a single-channel analyzer gated to pass the 59-keV tungsten X-ray was used to count W^{181}.

Extraction apparatus: Eighteen separatory funnels were placed in a rack under a fume hood. An air stream was passed through a 1-mm ID glass capillary tube inserted through the top of each funnel into the lower phase. The tubes were connected to a compressed-air source by plastic tubing. After mixing, the tubes were removed from the liquid and the layers allowed to separate. This apparatus is faster, less tedious, and just as efficient as manual or machine shaking and enables 18 samples to be analyzed per day.

ANALYTICAL METHOD

Chemical procedure

Transfer 0.5 g of sample (2—20 ppm W) into a Teflon beaker. Add 0.01 ml of the tracer solution. Prepare a counting standard for the samples at the same time by diluting 0.01 ml of tracer to 10 ml with water in a glass counting vial. To silicate samples, add 15 ml of concentrated hydrofluoric acid and 1 ml of concentrated perchloric acid and evaporate overnight on a hotplate at a surface temperature of about 120°C. To sulfide samples, add 5 ml of fuming nitric acid and evaporate to dryness on a hotplate before the addition of hydrofluoric and perchloric acids. Chemical losses from this point on may be ignored because of the final correction by counting W^{181}.

Add 15 ml of aluminum chloride solution to dissolve the salts and heat gently if necessary. Do not overheat as the acid concentration at this point is important. Transfer the solution to a 60-ml separatory funnel. Extract twice with 10 ml of TBP solution, discard the organic phases, and wash with 10 ml of chloroform.

Pipet aliquots of standard tungsten solution to cover the range of 1–10 μg into 50-ml glass beakers. Add 0.01 ml of tracer solution and 15 ml of aluminum chloride solution. Mix and transfer to 60-ml separatory funnels. Prepare a counting standard for the standard solutions at the same time by diluting 0.01 ml of tracer to 10 ml with water in a glass counting vial.

Add 5 ml of α-benzoinoxime solution to both sample and standard solutions in the separatory funnels and mix well. Extract for 2 minutes with 7 ml of chloroform. Collect the organic phase in a 20-ml glass beaker and save. Add another 5 ml of α-benzoinoxime solution to the funnels and mix. Extract for 2 minutes with another 7 ml of chloroform and add the organic phase to that from the previous extraction. Discard the aqueous phase and transfer the collected organic phases to the separatory funnel. Wash with 10 ml of dilute stannous chloride solution. Collect the organic phase in the 20-ml beaker, discard the aqueous phase, and return the organic phase to the separatory funnel. Strip with 5 ml of concentrated stannous chloride solution and discard the organic phase. Wash twice with 5 ml of chloroform.

Transfer the aqueous phase to a 15-ml glass beaker and heat for 10 minutes on a hotplate at a surface temperature of about 100°C. Cool in an ice bath and transfer to the separatory funnel. Add 0.25 ml of potassium thiocyanate solution and extract with 3.0 ml of amyl alcohol. Discard the aqueous phase. Add 1.0 ml of ethanol solution to the funnel and mix. Drain the solution into a 5-cm cell and measure the absorbance in a spectrophotometer at 405 nm against amyl alcohol.

Transfer the solution from the cell into a glass counting vial. Rinse the cell with a small quantity of ethanol and add the rinsings to the vial. Dilute the solution in the vial to 10 ml with ethanol.

Count the sample solutions, standard tungsten solutions, and the counting standards. Correct the observed counting rates for the background counting rate.

Calculations

The number of micrograms of tungsten in each standard tungsten solution extract, X, is calculated from the equation

$$X = m_1 \frac{R_1}{R_2},$$

where m_1 is the number of micrograms of tungsten initially added and R_1 and R_2 are the counting rates of the standard tungsten solution and the counting standard for the standard tungsten solution, respectively.

A calibration curve is prepared by plotting values of X against the absorbance of the standard tungsten solutions. The number of micrograms of tungsten in the final sample solution extract, m_2, is determined by reference to the calibration curve.

The number of micrograms of tungsten present in the original sample, Y, is calculated from the equation

$$Y = m_2 \frac{R_4}{R_3},$$

where R_3 and R_4 are the counting rates of the final sample solution and of the counting standard for the sample solution, respectively.

RESULTS AND DISCUSSION

The proposed procedure relies on two separations to isolate tungsten from most other elements. The α-benzoinoxime extraction has been used previously to separate tungsten and molybdenum from most other elements (Peng and Sandell, 1963; Fogg and others, 1971). A method was sought that would eliminate molybdenum interference.

The extraction of many chloride complexes, including Mo^{+6}, by oxygenated solvents has been employed widely. Mo^{99} tracer was used to study the extraction of molybdenum from hydrochloric acid solutions with tributyl phosphate into xylene. Molybdenum was extracted to an extent greater than 95 percent from hydrochloric acid solutions in the range of 2.5 to 6.0 M into xylene solutions ranging from 20 to 50 volume percent in tributyl phosphate. Chloroform eventually was selected as a diluent for the tributyl phosphate for reasons of convenience; substitution of chloroform for xylene had no effect on the extraction of molybdenum.

The extraction of most elements with tributyl phosphate increases with hydrochloric acid concentration. It was found that if the hydrochloric acid concentration was adjusted to 3.6 M, molybdenum could be removed with little loss of tungsten from the samples. As for pure standard solutions, as much as 28 percent of the tungsten present can be lost with each TBP extraction. For this reason, the TBP extractions are omitted for the standard solutions. With this separation, as much as 0.5 mg of molybdenum can be present with no apparent effect on the final color. When larger amounts are present, additional TBP extractions can be made. In addition to the removal of molybdenum, the TBP extraction removes most of the iron.

Large amounts of copper (>1.0 mg) or titanium (>1.5 mg) are partially extracted into chloroform with α-benzoinoxime. A blue-green color indicates the presence of copper. Copper interferes with the final color determination by precipitating as cuprous thiocyanate. Washing with dilute stannous chloride solution usually removes all the copper present. If the blue-green color persists, additional washings are done until the organic phase is colorless. With three washings with dilute stannous chloride solution, as much as 25 mg of copper will not interfere. The procedure accommodates as much as 1.5 mg of titanium without interference. Larger amounts interfere in the final color determination, each additional milligram of titanium being equivalent to approximately 0.5 μg of tungsten. Table 1 lists the tolerance levels of nine elements that are known to interfere with the tungsten thiocyanate color.

Table 1.—*Tolerance levels of interfering elements*

Interfering element	Maximum amount tested with no interference (mg)	Interfering element	Maximum amount tested with no interference (mg)
Fe	>50.0	V	0.05
Ti	[1]1.5	Cr	.375
Mo	[2].5	Ni	.02
Nb	.25	Mn	3.5
Cu	[3]1.0		

[1] For amounts greater than 1.5 mg Ti, each milligram is equivalent to about 0.5 μg W.
[2] Larger amounts of Mo can be tolerated by using additional TBP extractions.
[3] After three washings with dilute stannous chloride solution, as much as 25 mg Cu showed no interference.

In many methods utilizing α-benzoinoxime for the extraction of tungsten, the organic phase is collected and destroyed before the final color development. In an extensive study of the chloroform extraction of tungsten α-benzoinoximate, Peng and Sandell (1963) noted that tungsten α-benzoinoximate is unstable in strongly acidic solutions. In this method, tungsten was stripped from the chloroform solution with the same concentrated stannous chloride solution used to reduce tungsten with average tungsten losses of less than 10 percent.

The reduction of tungsten by stannous chloride has been discussed at great length in the literature (see review by Fogg and others, 1970a). In the method described in this paper, a decrease in sensitivity was noted if the concentrated stannous chloride solution of tungsten was diluted to 6 *M* hydrochloric acid before the addition of potassium thiocyanate. Dilution apparently increases the rate of oxidation of W^{+5} to W^{+6}. If the stannous chloride solution is allowed to stand for an hour or more before the addition of the potassium thiocyanate, the sensitivity is also decreased, again probably owing to oxidation of W^{+5}. The complex formed by immediate extraction with amyl alcohol was sufficiently stable for practical application, its absorbancy decreasing negligibly during a 20-minute period.

Reproducibility of the tungsten thiocyanate color is somewhat improved if the concentrated stannous chloride solution of tungsten is allowed to stand for 90 minutes before addition of the thiocyanate. Absorbances for 5 μg of tungsten, repeated over 7 days, had standard deviations of 1.7 and 5.4 percent, depending on whether samples had stood for 90 minutes before extraction or had not, respectively; corresponding molar absorptivities were 11,300 and 13,400, respectively. In either procedure, Beer's law was obeyed for the range of 1–10 μg. Apparently the W^{+5}/W^{+6} ratio decreases with time, becoming virtually stable within 90 minutes. More than 50 silicate and six sulfide samples were analyzed by two analysts; one analyst extracted immediately after reduction and the other waited 90 minutes before extraction. The values for tungsten determined by the two analysts differed by less than 10 percent for most of the samples.

The amount of tungsten lost in each separation step was found to vary from sample to sample. Table 2 shows the

Table 2.—*Average percentage loss of tungsten in the chemical separations*

Procedural step	Sample solutions	Standard tungsten solution
First TBP extraction	5.0	....
Second TBP extraction	4.8	....
Chloroform wash	.4	....
Oxime extraction	21.0	6.3
Dilute stannous chloride wash	.8	.7
Oximate stripping	7.5	17.6
First chloroform wash	.3	.4
Second chloroform wash	.4	.4
Amyl alcohol extraction	12.7	12.2
Total loss	52.9	37.6

average amount lost through the individual steps of the procedure as found by counting W^{181} in a number of samples at various separation stages. The majority of the tungsten lost in pure standard tungsten solutions occurs during the oximate stripping step. The total losses for 56 pure standard tungsten solutions ranged from 26 to 54 percent, with an average loss of 38 percent. In most of the samples, the greatest tungsten loss occurred in the oxime extraction. Total losses in 109 determinations of 38 silicate samples ranged from 32 to 64 percent, with an average loss of 49 percent. Total losses in 15 analyses of five sulfide samples ranged from 30 to 72 percent, with an average loss of 42 percent. Of 24 analyses of six other silicate samples, losses ranged from 72 to 92 percent, with an average loss of 83 percent. The reason for the large losses in the latter six samples is unknown, the only observable difference being a very low magnesium content in these samples.

Analytical precision was estimated from replicate analyses of 12 silicate and two sulfide samples containing tungsten in the 2–42 ppm range. These data (table 3) indicate a coefficient of variation of 12 percent or less for most samples. The accuracy of the method is more difficult to evaluate, but tungsten has been determined in two of the rocks studied here by a neutron activation technique. F. O. Simon (oral commun. 1972) found 1.4 and 3.8 ppm W in RGM-1 and STM-1, respectively, in good agreement with our values (table 3) of 1.8 and 4.1 ppm W, suggesting that the analytical accuracy is at least adequate.

Table 3.—*Determination of tungsten in rocks*

Sample	Description	Number of determinations	Mean quantity of tungsten (ppm)	Coefficient of variation (percent)
RGM-1	Rhyolite, USGS standard rock.	9	1.8	30
432	Sulfide	3	2.6	2.3
824	Silicate	4	2.9	7.5
822	. . . . . do.	4	3.4	9.8
STM-1	Nepheline syenite, USGS standard rock.	14	4.1	11
818	Silicate	6	4.5	18
819	. . . . . do.	4	4.9	11
823	. . . . . do.	3	5.5	5.4
811	. . . . . do.	4	6.2	9.2
810	. . . . . do.	4	9.0	12
199	. . . . . do.	4	11.0	8.3
210	. . . . . do.	4	15.3	4.4
208	. . . . . do.	4	28.9	14
430	Sulfide	4	41.7	4.0

REFERENCES CITED

Affsprung, H. E., and Murphy, J. W., 1964, The extraction and determination of tungsten with tetraphenlyarsonium chloride: Anal. Chim. Acta, v. 30, p. 501–508.

Chan, K. M., and Riley, J. P., 1967, Determination of tungsten in silicates and natural waters: Anal. Chim. Acta, v. 39, p. 103–113.

Fogg, A. G., Jarvis, T. J., Marriott, D. R. and Burns, D. T., 1971, Moderating the influence of molybdenum in the determination of tungsten, in steel, pt. 3 *of* The spectrophotometric determination of tungsten with thiocyanate: Analyst, v. 96, p. 475–479.

Fogg, A. G., Marriott, D. R., and Burns, D. T., 1970a, A review of procedures, pt. 1 *of* The spectrophotometric determination of tungsten with thiocyanate: Analyst, v. 95, p. 848–853.

—— 1970b, An experimental assessment of procedures—A recommended procedure for the determination of tungsten in steel, pt. 2 *of* The spectrophotometric determination of tungsten with thiocyanate: Analyst, v. 95, p. 854–861.

Hobart, E. W., and Hurley, E. P., 1962, Spectrophotometric determination of molybdenum and tungsten in niobium with dithiol: Anal. Chim. Acta, v. 27, p. 144–152.

Peng, P. Y., and Sandell, E. B., 1963, Simultaneous spectrophotometric determination of tungsten and molybdenum with thiocyanate after α-benzoinoxime extraction: Anal. Chim. Acta, v. 29, p. 325–334.

Quin, B. F., and Brooks, R. R., 1972, The rapid determination of tungsten in soils, stream sediments, rocks and vegetation: Anal. Chim. Acta, v. 58, p. 301–309.

Jour. Research U.S. Geol. Survey
Vol. 1, No. 5, Sept.-Oct. 1973, p. 559–562

SPECTROCHEMICAL COMPUTER ANALYSIS—ARGON-OXYGEN D-C ARC METHOD FOR SILICATE ROCKS

By A. F. DORRZAPF, JR., Washington, D.C.

Abstract.—Use of an argon-oxygen atmosphere eliminates the interference of cyanogen bands with many sensitive analytical lines. The jet-controlled atmosphere also improves the stability of the arc. These procedural changes, coupled with computerized analysis of the spectra, result in increased detectability, precision, and speed as compared to the former visual semiquantitative technique.

Complete spectrochemical analysis of geologic materials by a recording system and computer was developed by Helz, Walthall, and Berman (1969). There has been a concerted effort in the U.S. Geological Survey laboratories since then to improve and extend the capability of this method. The improved system, the procedural part of which is described in this paper, is now in routine service.

Basic changes in the recording system have been described by Helz (1973). The previous system used two 102- by 254-mm (4- by 10-inch) plates to cover the entire wavelength range. Two recordings were, therefore, required for each sample spectrum. This procedure, moreover, necessitated fiducial lines for each plate as well as massive computer storage for a complete analysis. The conversion to 102- by 508-mm (4- by 20-inch) plates allows continuous recording of a spectrum from 2300 to 4700 A, uses only two fiducial lines, simplifies computer processing, and reduces storage requirements.

Although the conversion to 508-mm plates provided continuity of recording, the cyanogen band region (3500–4216 A) was still of limited use for analyses. The intensity of these bands was reduced considerably by use of an argon-oxygen atmosphere during excitation. An additional advantage of this atmosphere is better arc control.

Acknowledgments.—The author gratefully acknowledges the guidance and assistance of Armin W. Helz and the cooperation and assistance of other colleagues, in particular Sol Berman and Frank G. Walthall.

EXPERIMENTAL METHOD

The basic guideline for this work was to keep the method simple, rapid, and as sensitive for trace and minor elements as the semiquantitative method of Myers, Havens, and Dunton (1961). To eliminate cyanogen bands, an atmosphere can be introduced around the electrodes by using some type of jet. The jet designed by Helz (1964) was preferred over the Stallwood model (Stallwood, 1954) because no glass dome is required on the Helz jet, thus eliminating cleaning of the dome between exposures. Various atmospheres have been used to eliminate cyanogen bands (Thiers, 1953; Thiers and Vallee, 1957; Shaw and others, 1958). After investigating many of these gases and combinations of argon and oxygen, we chose a mixture of 70 percent argon and 30 percent oxygen at a flow rate of 6.6 l/min.

It was necessary to increase the size of the sample used in the semiquantitative procedure from 10 mg of sample and 20 mg of graphite to 15 mg of sample and 30 mg of graphite to maintain the desired sensitivity for all elements. In addition, an increase of the initial burning time, at 5 amp, from 10 to 20 sec maintains the sensitivity for volatile elements. The details of excitation and other spectrographic conditions follow:

Electrodes: Cathode, ASTM type C-6, 2 in. long; anode, ¼-in. diam thin-walled graphite (Ultra No. 3170).
Electrode charge: 15 mg sample + 30 mg graphite (type UCP-2/200 mesh).
Spectrograph: 3.4 m Ebert design (Mark III).
Power source: 325 v open circuit d-c arc, resistance controlled.
Excitation: 15 amp d-c arc set with empty graphite electrodes.
Arc gap: 4 mm, maintained throughout burn.
Exposure: 20 sec at 5 amp followed by 130 sec at 15 amp, continuous burn.
Atmosphere: 70 percent argon + 30 percent oxygen; 6.6 l/min flow rate with top of Helz jet nozzle 2 mm below top of electrode.
Wavelength range: 2300–4700 A; first order.
Grating: 600 groove/mm; 5 A/mm reciprocal linear dispersion.
Slit: 25 μm wide and 2 mm high.
Filter: 47-percent transmission neutral-density filter.
Illumination: Arc image focused on collimator by 450-mm focal-length lens at slit.
Mask at collimator: 1.8 cm.
Emulsion: Kodak III-0 (102- by 508-mm plates).
Processing: Kodak D-19 developer, 3¼ min at 20°C; Kodak indicator stop bath, 30 sec; Kodak fixer, 8 min; wash, 20–30 min at 20°C; and dry with warm air for 20 min.

Six-step standards are prepared as described by Myers, Havens, and Dunton (1961). All standards and samples are weighed, mixed with graphite, and loaded into the electrode in

Table 1.—*Spectral lines used in spectrochemical computer analysis, listed in order of sensitivity*

Element	Wavelength (angstroms)	Concentration limits (percent)
Ag	3280.683	0.000010– 0.000681
	3382.891	.000010– .00100
Al	2660.393	0.0316 – 0.464
	2378.408	.215 – 2.15
	2669.166	2.15 –31.6
As	2860.452	0.0100 – 1.00
	2349.84	.316 – 1.00
	2370.77	.215 –10.0
	2369.67	.215 –10.0
Au	2675.95	0.000681– 0.0147
	2427.95	.00100 – .0681
	3122.781	.00215 – .100
B	2496.778	0.00100 – 0.0215
Ba	4554.042	0.000100– 0.00147
	4130.664	.00147 – .0464
	3071.591	.0100 – .215
Be	2348.610	0.000100– 0.00464
	3321.343	.000100– .0100
	3321.086	.000215– .0147
Bi	3067.716	0.000100– 0.0100
	2897.975	.00215 – .100
	3024.635	.0100 – .215
Ca	2997.314	0.0681 – 3.16
	2721.645	.464 –31.6
	3274.661	1.00 –31.6
Cd	3261.057	0.00147 – 0.0464
	3466.201	.00464 – .0681
Ce	4165.606	0.00200 – 0.136
	3201.714	.00431 – .431
Co	3453.505	0.000100– 0.00464
	3449.170	.000100– .0215
	3412.633	.000464– .0215
Cr	3593.488	0.000100– 0.00100
	4254.346	.000100– .00215
	3024.350	.000464– .0681
	2843.252	.000464– .100
	2731.908	.0100 – .681
Cs	4555.355	0.316 – 1.47
	4593.177	1.00 – 4.64
Cu	3247.540	0.000100– 0.000681
	3273.962	.000215– .00100
	2824.369	.00464 – .100
Dy	3407.80	0.000316– 0.0316
	4211.719	.000316– .0147
	3319.887	.00100 – .100
Er	3230.585	0.000215– 0.0316
	3220.730	.000681– .100
Eu	4129.737	0.000100– 0.00316
	4205.046	.000100– .00316
	2906.676	.000681– .100
	2813.95	.00100 – .100
	2727.780	.00316 – .100
Fe	3175.447	0.0506 – 5.06
	2391.474	.506 –23.5
	2385.007	1.09 –23.5
Ga	2943.637	0.000215– 0.00316
	2944.175	.00147 – .100
Gd	3549.365	0.000316– 0.0215
	3331.388	.00215 – .100
Ge	2651.178	0.000100– 0.0215
	2651.575	.00464 – .0681
	3269.494	.00464 – .0681
Hf	2916.481	0.00100 – 0.464
	3109.117	.00464 – .681
	2866.373	.00681 – .681
Hg	2536.519	0.0147 – 2.15
	3131.833	.464 – 4.64
Ho	3456.00	0.000100– 0.00681
	3398.98	.000316– .0147
In	4511.323	0.000464– 0.00681
	3039.356	.000464– .0147
Ir	3220.780	0.000681– 0.100
	2849.725	.00464 – .215
K	4044.140	0.0681 – 0.681
	4047.201	.147 – 1.00
	3446.372	1.00 –10.0
La	3245.120	0.00147 – 0.147
Li	3232.61	0.00316 – 0.215
	4273.28	.316 – 1.47
	3985.79	.464 – 4.64
Lu	2911.39	0.000316– 0.0464
Mg	2779.834	0.00215 – 0.0681
	2776.690	.00215 – .215
	2782.974	.00215 – .316
	2781.417	.00464 – .316
	3336.680	.00464 – .316
	2798.06	.00681 – .681
	3329.930	.0100 – 2.15
	2936.537	.0316 – 2.15
	2938.538	.100 – 6.81
	4571.15	1.47 –30.0
Mn	2798.271	0.000100– 0.0100
	2801.064	.000100– .0147
	2949.205	.000316– .0316
	4502.220	.00681 – .681
	3070.266	.00681 – 1.00
	3629.741	.0147 – 1.00
	2914.603	.0147 – 1.47
	2626.640	.215 – 4.64
	2713.331	.681 –10.0
	2387.02	4.64 –46.4
Mo	3864.110	0.000100– 0.00215
	3170.347	.000147– .0147
	3193.973	.000215– .0147
	2816.154	.00215 – .100
Na	3302.323	0.00464 – 0.147
	3302.988	.00681 – .316
	2853.031	.0681 – 4.64
	2852.828	.215 – 6.81
Nb	3163.402	0.000215– 0.0681
	3194.977	.000464– .100
Nd	4303.573	0.00147 – 0.0464
Ni	3492.956	0.000100– 0.00215
	3101.879	.000464– .0316
	2943.914	.00147 – .100
Os	3301.559	0.000100– 0.100
	2909.061	.00215 – .147
P	2554.93	0.0464 – 4.64
Pb	2833.069	0.000100– 0.0681
	2663.166	.00681 – .100
	2873.316	.0147 – .100
	2393.794	.0681 – 4.64
Pd	3404.580	0.000022– 0.00147
	3242.703	.000068– .00464
	3516.943	.000215– .00681
Pr	3908.431	0.000215– 0.00681
	4222.98	.00147 – .0316
	3121.571	.0316 – .100
Pt	2997.967	0.000681– 0.0464
	2659.454	.000681– .0681
	2830.295	.00215 – .100
Rb	3591.59	1.47 –10.0
	3348.72	3.16 –10.0
Re	3460.47	0.00100 – 0.0464
	3464.722	.00215 – .0681
Rh	3434.893	0.000010– 0.00147
	3692.357	.000100– .00147
	3396.85	.000147– .00464
	3502.524	0.000215– 0.00681
	3462.040	.000681– .0147
Ru	3498.942	0.000046– 0.00464
	3436.737	.000100– .0100
	2988.948	.00147 – .147
Sb	2598.062	0.00681 – 0.100
	2877.915	.00681 – .147
	3267.502	.0100 – .316
	2670.643	.100 – 2.15
	2445.515	.215 – 6.81
	2383.63	1.00 – 6.81
Sc	3911.810	0.000100– 0.00215
	4246.829	.000100– .00316
	3353.734	.000100– .00681
Si	2519.207	0.00316 – 0.100
	2987.648	.0147 – .681
	2452.136	.100 –14.7
	2577.13	2.15 –34.3
Sm	4296.750	0.000464– 0.00464
	3408.668	.00316 – .100
Sn	3175.019	0.000316– 0.0147
	3034.121	.000316– .0215
	2839.989	.00100 – .0215
	2863.327	.00681 – .0316
Sr	4077.714	0.000046– 0.000215
	4607.331	.000100– .00215
	3464.457	.00147 – .0464
	4161.796	.00464 – .147
	2931.830	.0681 – 6.81
	2569.469	1.00 –46.4
	2428.095	2.15 –46.4
Ta	3311.162	0.0147 – 1.00
	2714.674	.0316 – 1.00
Tb	3293.07	0.00147 – 0.100
	4278.51	.00464 – .100
Te	2385.76	0.0316 – 1.00
Th	4116.718	0.00215 – 0.215
	4069.210	.0100 – .316
	2837.299	.0100 – .464
	2870.413	.0147 – .681
Ti	3199.915	0.000464– 0.0464
	3186.454	.000464– .100
	2641.099	.0100 – .316
	2644.264	.0681 – .681
	2679.926	.100 – 6.81
Tl	3775.72	0.000316– 0.00681
	3519.24	.00147 – .0147
	2767.87	.00147 – .100
	3529.43	.00681 – .100
	3229.75	.100 – .681
Tm	3462.20	0.000316– 0.0100
	4094.18	.000464– .0147
U	4244.372	0.0215 – 0.464
	3270.124	.0316 – 1.00
	2865.679	.0681 – 1.00
V	3102.299	0.000147– 0.0100
	3183.406	.000147– .0215
	3134.931	.00147 – .100
W	4008.753	0.00100 – 0.0681
	2896.446	.00215 – .464
	2946.981	.00464 – .464
Y	3327.875	0.000316– 0.0215
	3195.615	.000316– .0464
Yb	3987.994	0.000068– 0.00147
	3464.370	.000681– .0100
Zn	3345.020	0.00147 – 0.0464
	3345.572	.00100 – .316
Zr	3279.265	0.000316– 0.0681

the usual manner, final tamping of the sample being accomplished with a special tamper (fig. 1).

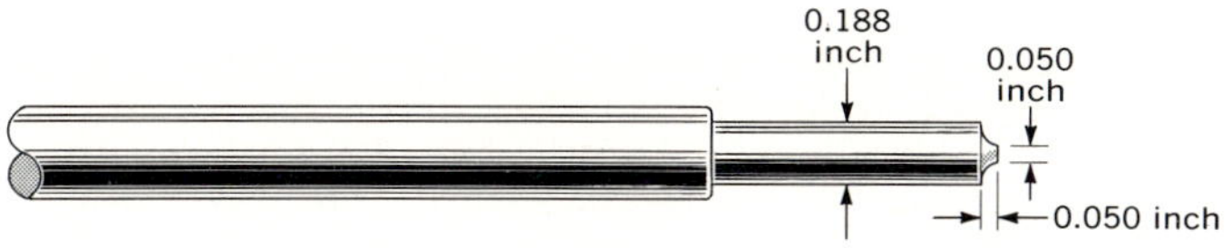

Figure 1.—Aluminum alloy tamper. This tamper provides more surface area than a flat-end tamper and facilitates the escape of gases from the sample with minimum sample loss.

Special efforts are made to assure identical conditions in the arcing of all samples and standards. The jaws in the arc stand were modified by the addition of a simple stop to permit each electrode to be grasped at the same point and cooled to the same extent during each burn.

Because the electrodes are being consumed more rapidly in the gas flow than in air, they require more frequent adjustment to maintain the arc gap. Some sample types form beads during the latter part of the arcing. The size of the bead is a function not only of the composition of the sample but of its mixing with the graphite; the better the mixing, the smaller the bead. Loss of a bead can cause low results for some of the major elements (Si, Al, Fe, and Ca). By controlling mixing and burning conditions for samples and standards, however, the results for these elements usually fall within the precision and accuracy of the method.

Each spectrum contains two cadmium reference lines superimposed with a lamp and mask assembly as described by Helz (1973), who also described the photoprocessing equipment for the 508-mm plates and the densitometer-recorder system.

Plate calibration, line finding, construction of analytical curves, and calculations are performed by the computer and will be described in detail in a subsequent paper by Walthall (1973).

RESULTS AND DISCUSSION

Detection limits and useful concentration ranges for individual lines of 68 elements determined with this technique are given in table 1. These limits and ranges are a function of the analytical lines chosen, exposure, interferences, and limitations of the recording system. A third significant figure is used solely for programing convenience. Of the 206 lines, 27 occur in the cyanogen band region and include the most sensitive lines for Ce, Cr, Eu, Gd, K, Mo, Pr, Rb, Sc, Sr, Th, Tl, W, and Yb. The detection limits for most elements are equal to or better than those obtained by the visual semiquantitative method. We are programing the computer for correcting interferences; many of the limits and ranges will be changed as a result.

A detailed study of the precision of this method, using a variety of sample types, has been made in a study of twelve U.S. Geological Survey standard rocks by F. G. Walthall, A. F. Dorrzapf Jr., and F. J. Flanagan (unpub. data). The precision is within the range of +50 to −30 percent of the amount present, as expected of a semiquantitative method, and approaches ±10–15 percent for many elements, as normally expected of a quantitative method. Data on standard diabase W-1 from this study are given in table 2.

Table 2.—*Standard deviation and coefficient of variation for standard diabase W-1*

[From F. G. Walthall, A. F. Dorrzapf, Jr., and F. J. Flanagan, unpub. data]

Element	Average concentration[1]	Standard deviation[2]	Coefficient of variation[3]
	Percent		
Si	27.7	2.3	8.30
Al	9.77	1.2	12.3
Fe	9.29	.20	2.15
Mg	6.13	.15	2.45
Ca	8.67	.45	5.19
K	.652	.096	14.7
Ti	.727	.048	6.60
Mn	.186	.006	3.23
	Parts per million		
Ba	141	9.7	6.88
Co	53.1	2.7	5.08
Cr	157	6.7	4.27
Ga	21.2	1.2	5.66
La	17.8	2.1	11.8
Nb	7.1	2.5	35.2
Ni	86.4	8.7	10.1
Pb	7.26	.73	10.1
Sr	248	15.6	6.29
Y	26.4	2.3	8.71
Yb	4.23	.24	5.67
Zn	147	4.9	3.33
Zr	142	16.3	11.5

[1] Average of six determinations; three bottles, two portions of each.
[2] Square root of the error mean square calculated in the analyses of variance.
[3] Coefficient of variation equals standard deviation times 100 divided by average concentration.

Despite marked improvements in spectrochemical methods in the last several decades, the determinations of the major constituents of a rock have been generally within the province of chemical methods. In the hope that this computer-based method might yield data for the major constituents that would be comparable to chemical determinations, duplicate portions of 20 samples have been analyzed randomly. These samples had been previously analyzed chemically.

To determine if the differences between the chemical and spectrographic data were significant, the *t* test in the form $t = \frac{\bar{d}\sqrt{n}}{s_d}$ as shown by Youden (1951, p. 28) was used. In the summary shown in table 3, the chemical data were assumed to be correct, and the differences—chemical minus spectrographic—were converted to percent of the chemical data. The average difference, $\bar{d}$, and the standard deviation of the

Table 3.—*Comparison of chemical and spectrographic data for 20 samples*

[$\bar{d}$ is the average difference in percent from chemical data, n is number of pairs, t is the t distribution with n–1 degrees of freedom. A positive difference indicates that values of chemical data are greater. NS indicates that the average difference is not significant at $t_{0.95}$]

Oxide	Range of oxide from chemical data (percent)	$\bar{d}$	n	t Calculated	t From tables
SiO_2	45.1 –76.4	+11.3	20	3.89	2.09
Al_2O_3	10.9 –22.6	+19.8	20	3.95	2.09
Fe_2O_3	1.46–16.8	+1.82	20	.812 NS	2.09
MgO	.06–13.2	+16.1	20	2.35	2.09
CaO	.34–12.7	–2.92	20	.434 NS	2.09
K_2O	.09– 6.23	+2.19	16	.460 NS	2.13
TiO_2	.09– 2.67	+24.2	20	3.83	2.09
P_2O_5	.01– .99	–16.3	10	1.89 NS	2.26
MnO	.03– .24	–11.8	20	2.79	2.09

differences, s_d, were calculated from these n differences. The tests showed that the paired differences for Fe_2O_3, CaO, K_2O, and P_2O_5 were not significant and both methods may be said to yield comparable data. Further refinements are necessary for the determination of the remaining oxides but especially for SiO_2, Al_2O_3, and TiO_2 for which the differences are significant at greater than $t_{0.99}$.

REFERENCES CITED

Helz, A. W., 1964, A gas jet for d-c arc spectoscopy: Art. 159 *in* U.S. Geol. Survey Prof. Paper 475-D, p. D176-D178.

—— 1973, Spectrochemical computer analysis–instrumentation: U.S. Geol. Survey Jour. Research, v. 1, no. 4, p. 475–482.

Helz, A. W., Walthall, F. G., and Berman, Sol, 1969, Computer analysis of photographed optical emission spectra: Appl. Spectroscopy, v. 23, no. 5, p. 508–518.

Myers, A. T., Havens, R. G., and Dunton, P. J., 1961, A spectrochemical method for the semiquantitative analysis of rocks, minerals, and ores: U.S. Geol. Survey Bull. 1084-I, p. 207–229.

Shaw, D. M., Wickremasinghe, O., and Yip, C., 1958, A simple device for the spectrochemical analysis of minerals in an inert atmosphere using the Stallwood jet: Spectrochim. Acta, v. 13, p. 197–201.

Stallwood, B. J., 1954, Air-cooled electrodes for the spectrochemical analysis of powders: Optical Soc. America Jour., v. 44, p. 171.

Thiers, R. E., 1953, The advantages of controlled atmospheres for arc spectroscopy: Appl. Spectroscopy, v. 7, p. 157–163.

Thiers, R. E., and Vallee, B. L., 1957, The effect of noble gases on the characteristics of the d-c arc, *in* Colloquim Spectroscopicum Internationale, VI, Amsterdam, 1956, Proc.: London, Pergamon Prcss, p. 179–185.

Walthall, F. G., 1973, Spectrochemical computer analysis–Program description: U.S. Geol. Survey Jour. Research, v. 1, no. 6 (In press.)

Youden, W. J., 1951, Statistical methods for chemists: New York, John Wiley and Sons, Inc., 126 p.

Jour. Research U.S. Geol. Survey
Vol. 1, No. 5, Sept.-Oct. 1973, p. 563–567

BATHYMETRY OF THE CONTINENTAL MARGIN OFF LIBERIA, WEST AFRICA

By JAMES M. ROBB, JOHN SCHLEE,
and JOHN C. BEHRENDT, Falmouth, Mass.

Abstract.—A bathymetric map based on new data allows examination of geomorphic features on the narrow continental margin off Liberia. The continental shelf in this region is relatively flat and featureless. The northwestern part of the continental slope, off Monrovia and Cape Mount, shows complex slump features and two submarine valleys. The central part of the slope is smoother, apparently as a result of progradation. The southeastern part of the slope, near Cape Palmas, is crossed oblique to the shoreline by a structural valley that has been modified by large slumps or landslides. This valley may be the termination, at the continental margin, of an oceanic fracture zone. The major slumplike features of the Liberian continental margin appear to be surface manifestations of deep faulting which has been partially masked by sedimentation.

A bathymetric contour map derived from more detailed data than were previously available has been prepared as part of geophysical studies of the continental margin of Liberia (Schlee and others, 1972; Schlee, 1972).

Reconnaissance bathymetric maps that include the continental margin off Liberia have been produced by the Association des Services Géologiques Africains (1968), Somers (1969), and Uchupi (1971). Rancurel (1965) published a map of the continental shelf of Liberia and the Ivory Coast, which included areas of sediment cover, rock outcrop, and biogenic features. Part of the eastern end of the Liberian continental margin is included in a contour map by Arens and others (1971). Part of the northwestern end is discussed by Egloff (1972). Geologic studies of the narrow continental margin of Liberia have been published by Behrendt and Wotorson (1970) and Templeton (1971).

METHODS

The survey was made aboard the RV *Unitedgeo I* in November 1971 by the U.S. Geological Survey in cooperation with the Liberian Geological Survey; it was funded by the National Science Foundation under the International Decade of Ocean Exploration (IDOE) (Schlee and others, 1972). Depths were sounded with a 3.5-kHz transducer system and corrected for sound speed variations (Matthews, 1939). A satellite system aboard the RV *Unitedgeo I* gave fixes at about 2-hour intervals accurate to about 180 m. These were supplemented by Doppler sonar and radar. Navigational accuracy was excellent. Comparison of depths at track crossings indicates positional error of less than 1 km.

Locations of sounding tracks are shown in figure 1. Data from USNS *Kane* (Lowrie and Escowitz, 1969) were included (6.5 km or greater sounding interval). In addition, a contour map and bathymetric data from R. L. McMaster (oral commun., 1972) were consulted. The curve in the edge of the continental shelf at long 8°20′ W. was taken from Rancurel (1965).

DISCUSSION

The continental margin off Liberia has been divided into three sectors characterized by different types of submarine topography (fig. 1): (1) a northwest sector, Cape Mount to Buchanan; (2) a central sector, Buchanan to east of Greenville; and (3) a southeast sector, east of Greenville to Harper.

The northwest and southeast sectors of the margin are narrow, and the slope is topographically complex. The central sector is wider and smoother. Figure 2 shows selected profiles that typify these sectors.

In the northwest sector (fig. 2, profiles 3, 6, and 12) the continental shelf is about 25 km wide. The continental slope is about 60 km wide, has an average slope of about 3°, and is characterized by many features that resemble slump and landslide scars and rubble. At least two large submarine valleys cut the slope, off the St. Paul and Farmington Rivers. The upper slope between Cape Mount and Monrovia is extremely rough; it contains many small valleys averaging about 170 m in depth and spaced at intervals of about 3 km (R. L. McMaster, oral commun., 1972). These valleys are too small to contour with the present data density or at this scale.

In contrast, off Greenville in the central sector, the surface of the slope is much smoother; the slope has smaller slump scars and no valleys. The smooth regular surface of the upper slope suggests depositional progradation. The continental shelf in the central sector is about 45 km wide; the continental slope is

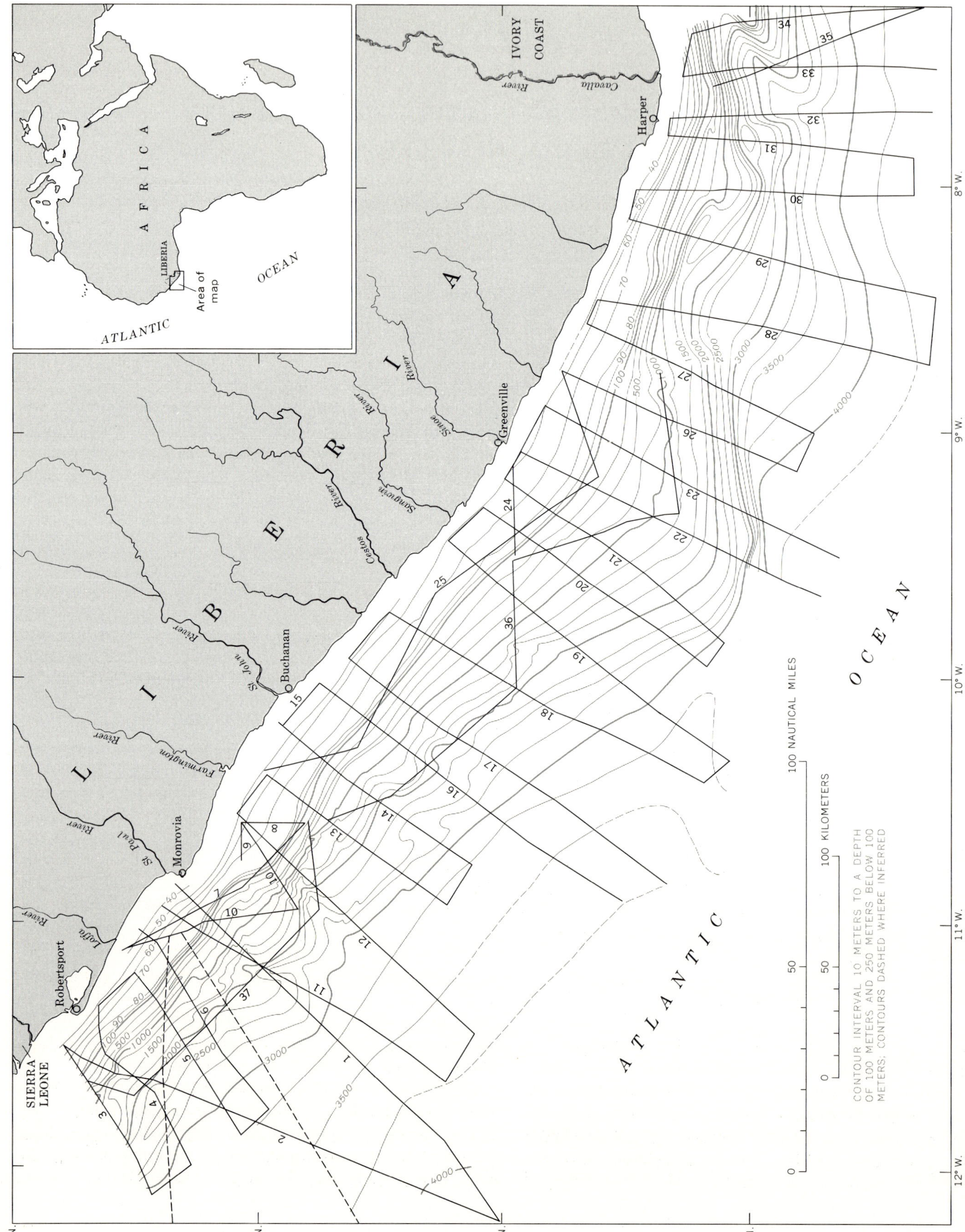

Figure 1.—Bathymetry of continental margin off Liberia. Solid sounding track lines (numbered) are those of RV *Unitedgeo I*; dashed track lines are those of USNS *Kane*.

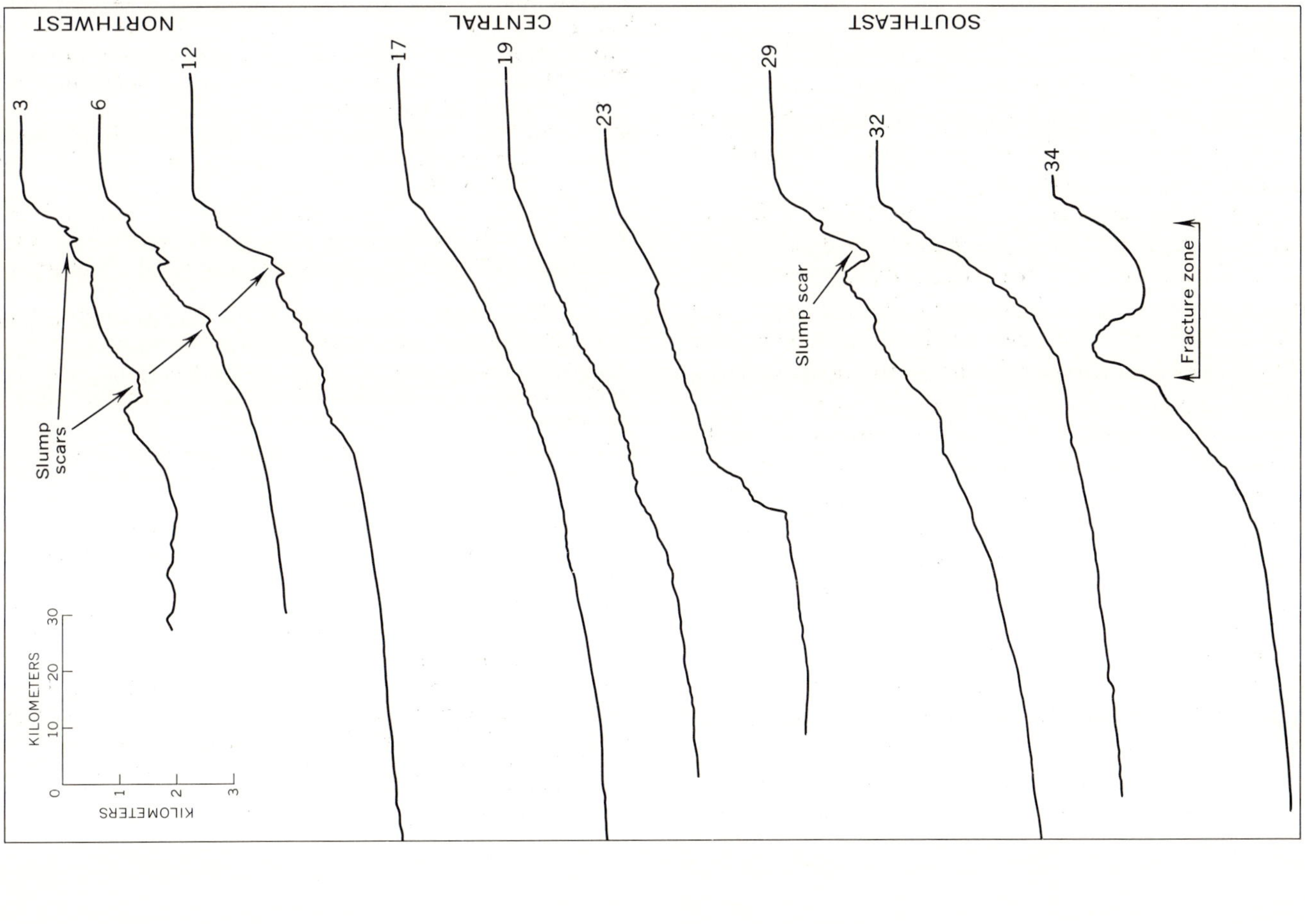

Figure 2.–Selected bathymetric profiles. For location see figure 1. Horizontal scale approximate. Vertical exaggeration about 10 times.

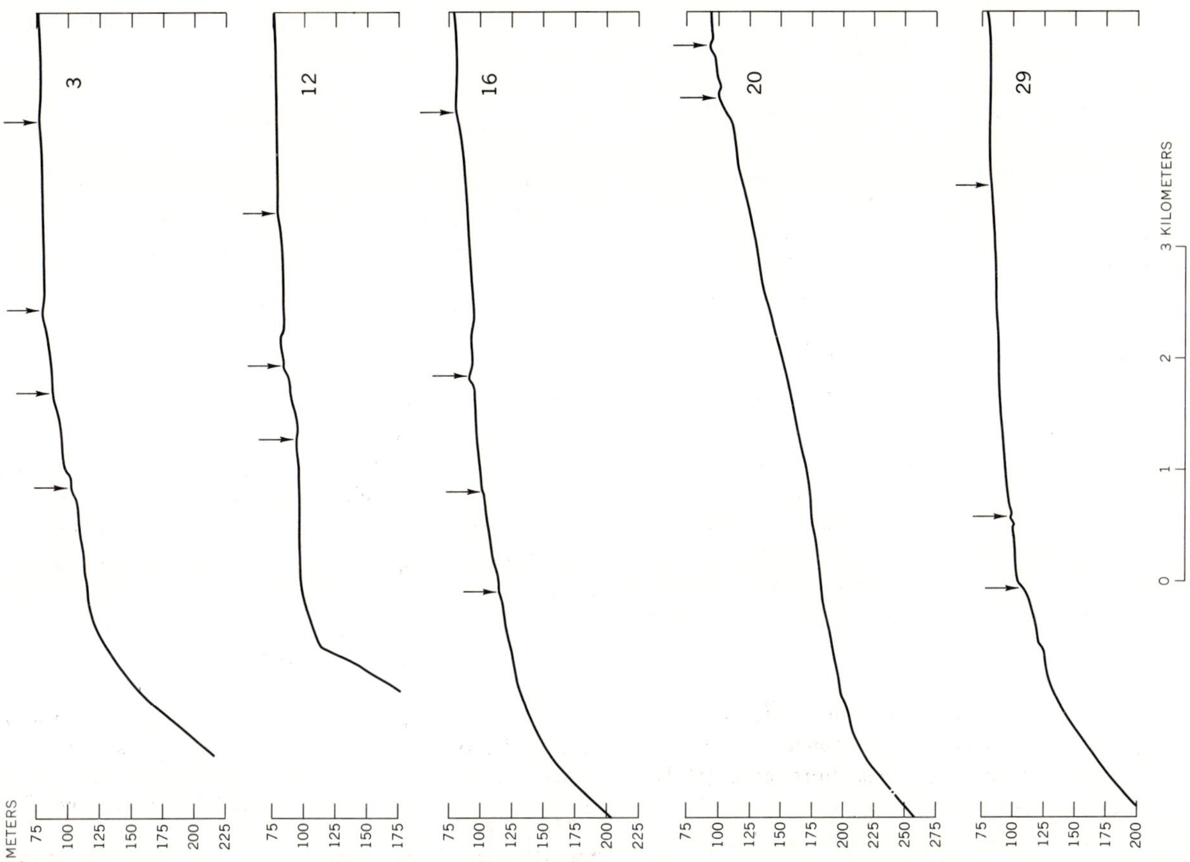

Figure 3.–Profiles of shelf edge, showing features belonging to a persistent zone of irregular topography (arrows). Tracings of 3.5-kHz records. Horizontal scale approximate. Vertical exaggeration about 10.5 times. Location of profiles shown on figure 1.

about 95 km wide and has a slope of about 1.8° (fig. 2, profiles 17, 19, and 23). A steeper (to 15°) section near the base of the slope shows a linear, easterly trend, subparallel with a valley farther east above the continental slope.

Off Harper, in the southeast sector, the continental shelf is about 20 km wide. The continental slope is about 75 km wide, has an average slope of about 3° but has slopes locally of 10° to 15° (fig. 2, profiles 29, 32, and 34). This sector is cut by a large valley trending southwest, oblique to the trend of the continental slope. We interpret this valley as the continuation, or termination at the continental margin, of the oceanic St. Paul fracture zone (Heezen and Tharp, 1965, p. 94). Seismic reflection profiles (Schlee, 1972) distinctly show a ridge in the subsurface below the southwestern wall of the valley. The valley is apparently filled by a large slump at its western end. It is probably analogous to a similar subsurface ridge-and-valley structure which Fail and others (1970), Arens and others (1971), and LePichon and Hayes (1971) described off Cape Three Points and the Ivory Coast, and which they related to the Romanche fracture zone. Uchupi (1971) showed a double ridge extending southwest from Cape Palmas into the ocean basin.

The surface of the continental shelf is generally flat and featureless along the whole coastline of Liberia, although irregularities are found in the very nearshore area (R. L. McMaster, oral commun., 1972). Small, irregular highs of 2 or 3 m relief occur on the middle and outer shelf in a few places but are more frequent southeast of long 8°20′ W. These highs are probably rock outcrops (Rancurel, 1965). A persistent zone of irregular topography occurs at depths of 80–120 m on the shelf edge (fig. 3). Such bands are common along much of the West African margin and are probably relict strandlines and coralline or algal growths formed during lower stands of sea level (McMaster and others, 1970).

The depth to the shelf break ranges from 100 to 150 m. In the northwest sector, this depth is relatively constant at about 134 m. In the central sector the break is difficult to pick, as the transition from shelf to slope is smoothly rounded. In the southeast sector, where the shelf break occurs at depths of 100–150 m, the shallower depths are at the heads of steep slopes which appear to have resulted from slumping.

By aeromagnetic methods, Behrendt and Wotorson (1970) have located several basement faults under the continental shelf. Depth to the shelf break changes from 134 to 115 m across one of these faults southeast of Monrovia (at lat 5°54′ N., long 10°46′ W.) and is consistent with their interpretation of downfaulting to the southwest. As these faults are thought to be Cretaceous in age, a surface trace may be evidence of rejuvenated faulting.

Slump features and valleys of the continental slope appear to relate closely to subsurface faulting observed in seismic reflection profiles (Schlee, 1972) and in some instances may represent fault scarps. Features of the submarine topography appear to be surface manifestations of complex subsiding blocks along the margin of the continent, although sedimentation has masked their outlines.

SUMMARY

The continental shelf off Liberia is narrow and relatively flat, marked by topographic relief only along old strandlines near the shelf break, and in a few other places where probable rock outcrops occur.

The continental slope is topographically more complex. Off the northwestern coast of Liberia it shows slumplike features and two submarine valleys. Off the central part of the country, the continental slope is smoother; its upper part may be a progradational surface. The southeastern part of the slope also shows slumplike features and contains a large structurally controlled valley which is probably an extension of the oceanic St. Paul fracture zone. The geomorphic features of the continental slope appear to be closely related to basement faulting.

REFERENCES CITED

Arens, G., Delteil, J. R., Valéry, P., Damotte, B., Montadert, L., and Patriat, P., 1971, The continental margin off the Ivory Coast and Ghana, *in* Delany, F. M., ed., The geology of the east Atlantic continental margin; 4, Africa: [Great Britain] Inst. Geol. Sci. Rept. 70/16, p. 61–78.

Association des Services Géologiques Africains, 1968, International tectonic map of Africa, sheet 4: Paris, UNESCO, scale 1:5,000,000.

Behrendt, J. C., and Wotorson, C. S., 1970, Aeromagnetic and gravity investigations of the coastal area and continental shelf of Liberia, West Africa, and their relation to continental drift: Geol. Soc. America Bull., v. 81, no. 12, p. 3563–3574.

Egloff, Julius, 1972, Morphology of ocean basin seaward of northwest Africa; Canary Islands to Monrovia, Liberia: Am. Assoc. Petroleum Geologists Bull., v. 56, no. 4, p. 694–706.

Fail, J. P., Montadert, L., Delteil, J. R., Valéry, P., Patriat, P., and Schlich, R., 1970, Prolongation des zones de fractures de l'océan Atlantique dans le Golfe de Guinée: Earth and Planetary Sci. Letters, v. 7, no. 5, p. 413–419.

Heezen, B. C., and Tharp, Marie, 1965, Tectonic fabric of the Atlantic and Indian Oceans and continental drift, *in* Blackett, P. M. S., Bullard, E., and Runcorn, S. K., eds., A symposium on continental drift: Royal Soc. London, Philos. Trans. ser. A, v. 258, no. 1088, p. 90–106.

LePichon, Xavier, and Hayes, D. E., 1971, Marginal offsets, fracture zones, and the early opening of the South Atlantic: Jour. Geophys. Research, v. 76, p. 6283–6293.

Lowrie, Allen, Jr. and Escowitz, E., eds., 1969, Kane 9, Global ocean floor analysis and research data series, v. 1: U.S. Naval Oceanog. Off.,971 p.

Matthews, D., 1939, Tables of the velocity of sound in pure water and in sea water for use in echo sounding and echo ranging: London, Admiralty Hydrog. Dept., 52 p.

McMaster, R. L., Lachance, T. P., and Ashraf, Asaf, 1970, Continental shelf geomorphic features off Portuguese Guinea, Guinea, and Sierra Leone (West Africa): Marine Geology, v. 9, no. 3, p. 203–213.

Rancurel, P., 1965, Topographie générale du plateau continental de la Cote D'Ivoire et du Liberia: Paris, Office de la Recherche Scientifique et Technique du Outre-Mer, [8 p.], 7 maps.

Schlee, John, 1972, Acoustic reflection profiles, Liberian Continental Margin: U.S. Dept. Commerce, Natl. Tech. Inf. Service, Springfield, Va., PB2-09871, 30 p.

Schlee, John, and others, 1972, USGS IDOE [Leg] 5: Geotimes, v. 17, no. 8, p. 16–17.

Somers, L. B. H., 1969, Bathymetry of the western African continental margin—Senegal to Ivory Coast: Ann Arbor, Mich., Univ. Michigan, Unpub. Ph. D. thesis (Univ. Microfilms, Ann Arbor, Mich., Thesis 70-4200 (1970)), 70 p.

Templeton, R. S. M., 1971, The geology of the continental margin between Dakar and Cape Palmas, *in* Delany, F. M., ed., The geology of the east Atlantic continental margin; 4, Africa: [Great Britain] Inst. Geol. Sci., Rept. 70/16, p. 43–60.

Uchupi, Elazar, 1971, Bathymetric atlas of the Atlantic, Caribbean, and Gulf of Mexico: Woods Hole Oceanog. Inst., Ref. No. 71-72, 11 p., 10 charts.

Jour. Research U.S. Geol. Survey
Vol. 1, No. 5, Sept.-Oct. 1973, p. 569—577

AN ACCURATE INVAR-WIRE EXTENSOMETER

By W. A. DUFFIELD and R. O. BURFORD, Menlo Park, Calif.

Abstract.—Stevens Type F water-level recorders have been modified to measure changes in the distance between two points, with amplification of up to 10 times. Such recorders are capable of measuring strains of 10^{-5} and possibly 10^{-6} over 10-m distances when corrections are made for frictional effects and temperature. In two field experiments, one on Kilauea Volcano in Hawaii, and the other on the San Andreas fault in central California, measurements by the recorders agree well with those by several different methods for the same episodes of ground deformation. Equipment for the entire system costs about $300 and requires 1 to 2 man-days for installation.

Stevens Type F water-level recorders have been used successfully for measuring crack dilation at Kilauea Volcano, Hawaii, and displacement across the San Andreas fault in central California. The instrument generally is used for lake -, stream- , or sea-level gaging, where changes in water level usually are recorded at either a one-to-one or a reduced scale through a system of gears. A simple change in the arrangement of gears, however, permits recording at amplified rather than reduced scales, so that changes of less than 1 mm can be measured very accurately. The smallest change that can be measured accurately is limited principally by friction and temperature effects, but our experience indicates that strains of 10^{-5} and possibly 10^{-6} can be measured over 10-m distances. The measurements at Kilauea Volcano have been obtained continuously since May 1971, and those across the San Andreas were made from April 15 to October 24, 1970. For both experiments, the changes indicated by the modified Stevens recorders were corroborated by independent measurements of ground motion by other means. The recorders provide a reliable, sensitive, yet inexpensive means for the continuous measurement of relative ground displacement.

Acknowledgments.—We thank James C. Savage and James H. Dieterich for helpful reviews of the manuscript.

INSTRUMENT AND INSTALLATION

The system is designed to measure the relative motion of two reference points by coupling them with a wire that is anchored at one point but is free to move a recording device at the other. Thus the recorder unit itself forms one of the reference points.

Field installations are shown in figures 1 and 2. Separation between the recorder position and the wire anchor pin is 9.6 m on Kilauea Volcano and was 12.4 m for the California system. Both systems use Invar wire 0.030 inch in diameter to link the recorder drive pulley to the anchor pin. Near the pulley, a short segment of beaded cable is spliced onto the end of the Invar wire. The beads are crimped on at uniform intervals to match recesses in the pulley, providing nonslip operation, and a 2-kg weight hangs on the free end of the beaded cable, providing constant tension on the wire.

The drive pulley of the recorder is coupled to a horizontally oriented cylinder through a system of gears that provide a mechanical amplification of cylinder rotation in the range of 8:1 to 10:1; the exact amplification depends on the arrangement of new gears. Recording charts are mounted on the cylinder, and a pen is clock driven across the chart at a constant speed of about 3 cm/day, traversing the entire chart during an 8-day period. Thus, time forms the abscissa of a completed record, and changes in the separation of the recorder and the anchor pin form the ordinate. When this separation is small compared with the width of the chart paper, the same chart can be reset and used for as many as six recording runs, each lasting up to 8 days.

The system at Kilauea is installed on a bedrock surface of dense basaltic pahoehoe. The pier for the recorder is coupled firmly to surface rocks by several 2.5-cm-square steel reinforcing bars that extend into the concrete from shallow holes in the underlying rock. The anchor reference pin is a 2.5-cm-square steel reinforcing bar that is force fit into a 30-cm-deep circular hole drilled into bedrock. Open spaces left in the hole after the square bar was emplaced were filled with concrete. Both the recorder pulley and the wire clamp on the anchor pin are positioned about 50 cm above the ground in a nearly horizontal plane. The anchor pin and recorder pier are 9.6 m apart on a line that is roughly centered on and perpendicular to a group of open surface cracks.

The system used for measurement of fault-slip displacement in California (figs. 2 and 3*A*) was installed on a thick soil. The anchor pin was a 1.5-m-long steel rod 1.4 cm in diameter, driven 1.1 m into soil and centered at the bottom of a 30-cm hole cased with a section of sewer pipe to help isolate the rod from unstable surface material. The recorder unit was bolted

A

B

Figure 1.—Extensometer field installation at Kilauea Volcano, Hawaii.

A. The recorder and wire shield. The steel bar in the right middle ground is used to monitor changes with a steel measuring tape.

B. The recorder unit. The box in front of the recording cylinder contains the clock that drives the pen.

A

B

Figure 2.—Extensometer field installation on the San Andreas fault in California.

A. General view of the installation, showing insulated instrument housing. The recorder unit is beneath the box on the left.

B. Details of recorder setup. Weights are hanging free inside a pipe in the ground. The recorder is normally covered with a metal box (shown in upper right) and protected in turn by an insulated plywood box.

to a rectangular slab of 1.3-cm waterproofed plywood (fig. 2*B*) anchored to a leveled soil surface by four steel rods driven through drill holes at the corners. The drive pulley of the recorder and the anchor pin were positioned at equal distances (6.2 m) from the center of the slip zone along a line crossing the fault trace at an angle of 20°. The top of the pulley and the wire clamp on the anchor pin were positioned about 20 cm above the surface in a nearly horizontal plane.

A major objective of the measurement experiment on the San Andreas fault was to test a rapidly deployable mechanical system on many different soil conditions. The system was designed for recording in remote areas under typical field conditions where rapid installation of several instruments

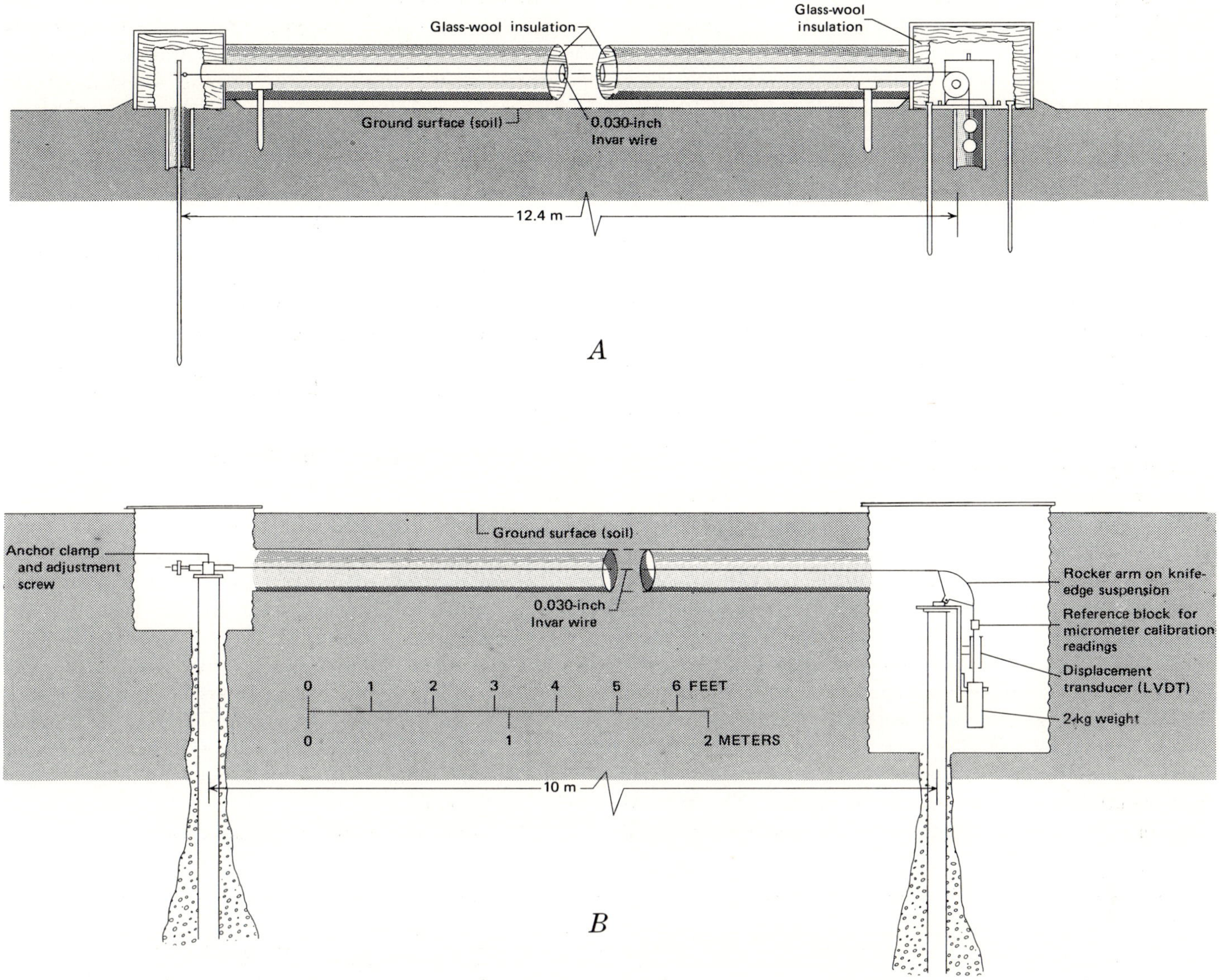

Figure 3.—Cross sections of the two instruments installed in California.
A. The 12.4-m surface installation using the water-level recorder.
B. The 10-m permanent (underground) extensometer.

followed by timely relocations might be required, such as during a period of accelerated slip or strain readjustments after an earthquake involving surface breakage along a fault. If the system were installed for long-term measurements in an area of thick soil, the results undoubtedly would be greatly improved by installing deep-set anchor and recorder piers more completely isolated from the active surface layer.

Aluminum tubing supported on brackets is used in both systems to shield the Invar wire from wind buffeting and direct sunlight. The tubing for the California system was wrapped with 3-cm glass-wool insulation which in turn was covered with aluminum foil. The recorder unit and the anchor pin were covered with sturdy plywood boxes painted with reflective white enamel and lined with glass-wool insulation. Some protection of recorder, wire, and anchor pin from animal and wind disturbance is essential, but the additional insulation probably will not be used in future installations in California. The amplitude of the diurnal thermal response was perhaps reduced by a small amount, but the principal effect of the extra insulation was a 2- to 3-hour phase lag.

In general, the distance between the recorder and the "dead" reference pin is dictated by field conditions. Longer base systems than we have used might be workable, but errors induced by temperature fluctuation and friction in the recorder are expected to increase roughly in direct proportion to wire length and should be kept to a minimum for best results.

Either mode of installation discussed here can be completed in 1 day at low cost. Total cost of materials is about $300, and labor cost will amount to 1 to 2 man-days, depending upon conditions. Weekly servicing (such as repositioning or changing the chart and resetting the pen) takes only a few minutes at the instrument site.

EVALUATION OF THE SYSTEM AND RESULTS

All records contain the effects of several sources of error, especially chart paper imperfections and instability, friction and backlash in gears and shafts of the recorder, expansion and contraction of the wire owing to air temperature changes, and wind (or animal) buffeting of the wire and weights. Most of these error sources can be controlled and their effects minimized through proper design, maintenance, and data compilation procedures.

Typically, the ruled grid on the recording paper is not precisely rectangular. Also, in mounting the paper on the recording drum, it is very difficult to orient the grid exactly parallel to the track along which the pen moves. Exposure to humid air produces additional distortions in the chart paper. Thus, a zero-change base line must be drawn by moving the pen manually along its track when the recorder is serviced at weekly intervals. All changes in drum position must be measured from the reference line rather than from the printed grid.

Friction within the shaft bearings and gears of the recorder must be carefully evaluated and considered when interpreting the records. It is possible, for example, to alter the zero-change setting slightly by a small manual rotation of the recording drum because friction and backlash in the gears keep the drum from returning exactly to its original position. This type of instrument response is thought to be the source of the small steps in the displacement record from the San Andreas fault site during contraction of the wire in the diurnal thermal cycle (fig. 4). This effect can be counteracted by manually setting the drum at the freest position during servicing at the beginning of each 7-day recording period. A small weight hung on the recording drum (fig. 5) will nearly eliminate recorder stick and gear backlash. This method has become standard practice for the San Andreas fault measurements.

The temperature-induced source of error is minimized by use of Invar rather than stainless steel or other types of wire material having relatively high coefficients of thermal expansion. Nevertheless, drift in the system due to air temperature change must be considered because the coefficient for typical Invar is about 1 ppm/°C. The trace offset on the chart due to temperature change can be closely approximated through the formula

$$D_{\Delta T} = -\Delta T \cdot K \cdot L \cdot A,$$

where

$D_{\Delta T}$ is the chart trace displacement, in millimeters, due to temperature change (positive $D_{\Delta T}$ denotes upward trace excursion on the chart from thermal contraction of the wire producing apparent extension),

ΔT is the air (or wire) temperature change in degrees centigrade (Δ_T taken as positive for temperature rise),

K is the thermal coefficient of expansion of the wire in millimeters per millimeter per degree centigrade,

L is the wire length in millimeters, and

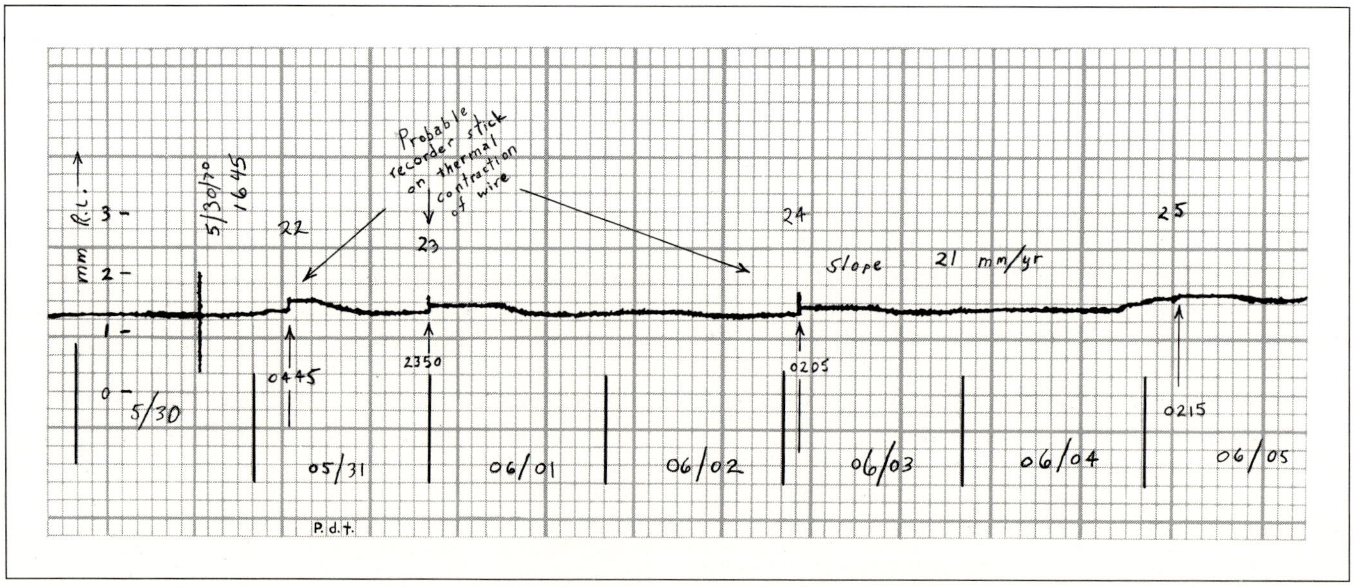

Figure 4.—Spliced records from the California site. The small steps on May 31 and June 3, 1970, were probably produced by recorder stick during thermal contraction of the Invar wire. Smoother recorder operation on June 4 shows the beginning of diurnal cooling at about 8:30 p.m. P.d.t. The spike on the left is a time mark produced by hand to mark the beginning of a recording run at 4:45 p.m. on May 30, 1970.

Figure 5.—Recorder unit with a drum weight installed to overcome recorder stick due to friction and backlash in the shafts and gears. This modification in the operation of the system was quite effective in producing smoother records. Beaded cable, with attached weight, and the system of gears that drive the drum are at left. The drum weight, W, counteracts backlash by keeping the teeth of adjacent gears in constant contact.

A is the factor of mechanical amplification for the recorder.

In a typical field situation in central California, the average daily temperature range is around 20°C, and the maximum annual change in average monthly temperature is about half that amount. Thus, the charts for a 10-m-base instrument having × 10 recorder amplification would generally show a diurnal trace excursion of 2 mm (±0.1 mm actual change in wire length equivalent to $\pm 1 \times 10^{-5}$ strain noise), superimposed on a roughly semiannual thermal drift of about 1 mm. Temperature measurements near the summit of Kilauea Volcano indicate that temperature-induced drifts of about 1.5 and 0.5 mm, respectively, can be expected for a similar system there. If short-term strain or displacement events must be resolved at levels below 1×10^{-5}, onsite continuous temperature records good to at least ±1°C should be obtained.

Ideally, the effects of friction and the thermal response of the system should be completely removed, but in practice, it is reassuring to note that the diurnal temperature cycle is faithfully recorded during most of the recording periods (fig. 6). The sinusoidal traces indicate that the gear system is free enough to record small temperature-induced changes in the length of the Invar wire, even though the presence of some friction in the system is known. Other independent lines of evidence discussed later suggest that the recording system is indeed capable of accurately measuring extremely small displacements.

The instrument has recorded some periods of slow positive strain accumulation on the flank of Kilauea Volcano and gradual right-lateral slip on the San Andreas fault (fig. 7). Strain and slip rates at the two sites are typically very low, and therefore the trace excursions on the charts are usually clearly recognizable only over a length of chart equivalent to several days, rather than hours or a single day. As a result, two slightly different data compilation procedures were worked out for Hawaii and California, both involving extrapolation of long-term trends.

The procedure devised for compiling the Kilauea records, such as those pictured in figures 6*B* and 7*B*, is to measure the separation between the zero-change reference line and the pen trace at chart positions corresponding to the initial and final midnight times for each 7-day run. The rate of change thus determined is then extrapolated to the first midnight of the next 7-day recording period, and so forth. When changes are large or sudden, such as illustrated in figure 7*B*, intermediate readings are made. No temperature corrections were applied. The arrows on the Kilauea records shown in figures 6*B* and 7*B* and the data points of figure 8 represent times when readings were made.

Data from the San Andreas slip site were compiled by projection of a zero-change reference line from the end of one chart onto the start of the next chart, usually across a time gap of 5 minutes or less. The charts were first matched two at a time and were carefully alined prior to manual projection of the zero-change reference line onto the newer record. Separations between the pen trace and the zero-change reference line were then obtained for each chart at a position corresponding to midday near the middle of each recording period. After these points were entered on a displacement–time graph, additional midday readings were obtained for periods showing conspicuous changes in displacement rates. Cumulative displacement was converted to horizontal fault-slip motion by dividing by 10 cos 20°, to correct for both mechanical amplification and the 20° angle between the instrument alinement and the trace of the fault plane. The resulting cumulative time-slip curve, shown in figure 9, is accompanied by the record from a permanent underground wire extensometer at the same site for comparison.

The permanent instrument is similar in design to the surface instrument, except that the Invar wire is 10 m long, crosses the fault at a 30° angle, and passes over a 15.2-cm-radius rocker-arm assembly pivoting on a knife-edge suspension that nearly eliminates frictional effects at the instrument pier (fig. 3*B*). Changes in pier separation are obtained by weekly micrometer measurements of the wire position relative to the instrument pier, corrected for the air temperature in the enclosure. Unfortunately, the permanent instrument broke

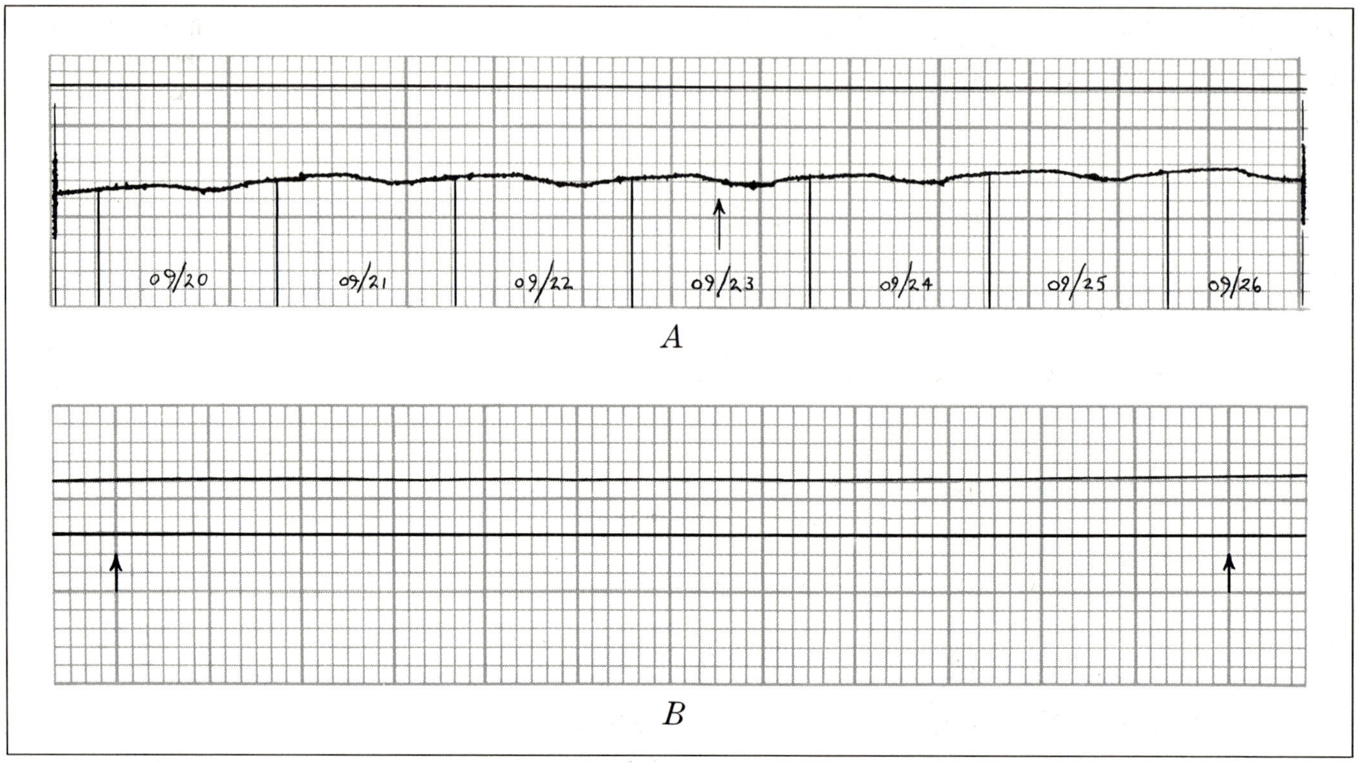

Figure 6.—Representative 7-day records showing gradual extension. The smallest division of the abscissa represents 2 hours.

A. A record from the California site obtained during the period September 19–26, 1970. A relatively quiet period during September 21–23 is preceded and followed by periods of right-lateral slip.

B. A typical record from Kilauea Volcano showing diurnal thermal response superimposed on slow, steady extension. The separation between the base line and the displacement trace was measured at the times indicated by the heavy arrows near the beginning and end of the run.

down after an unsatisfactory modification was installed on June 11, 1970. The instrument was restored to operation on June 30, and the gap in the data was closed by extrapolation. The spatial relationship between the two instruments at the site is shown in figure 10.

The close correspondence between the results for these two independent systems indicates that both responded similarly to the same phenomenon. Even though the permanent instrument was read only once a week on the average, the record obtained from those readings is herein considered to provide the standard for the comparison because the temperature and friction effects are relatively less. Differences in fine detail shown by the two traces, aside from those due to different sampling frequency, are presumably caused by different thermal environments and the lack of temperature readings and corrections for the surface system. Some minor differences are possibly due to differences in the soil behavior and response at the surface compared with that at a depth of 2 m.

CORRELATION WITH OTHER MEASUREMENTS AT KILAUEA VOLCANO

The reliability of the system at Kilauea can be further assessed by comparison with data from other types of strain and ground displacement measurements. Such comparisons provide independent tests of the meter, and three data sets are available for the volcano study area.

The instrument shown in figure 2 is located about 5 km southeast of the summit caldera of Kilauea Volcano and has been in operation since early May 1971. Part of the record is reproduced in figure 8, with principal structural and eruptive events of the volcano keyed to the record for comparison.

For the first 4 weeks of operation, the instrument measured almost no strain (fig. 8); there then began a period of positive strain, resulting in a 3.5-mm increase in the separation of the reference points. Significantly, these two periods correspond to episodes of general stagnation and tumescence of the volcano, respectively, as measured by precise leveling and trilateration (Hawaiian Volcano Observatory, unpub. data). Almost certainly the extensometer and the other surveys of ground deformation measured the same structural events. Furthermore, the period of tumescence that began in early June continued until February 1972, at which time another period of stagnation began; the extensometer and the other measurements of ground deformation again tracked one another.

On another time scale, some short-term strain events shown in figure 8 correlate with eruptive activity at Kilauea. For example, a sudden lengthening of the distance between the

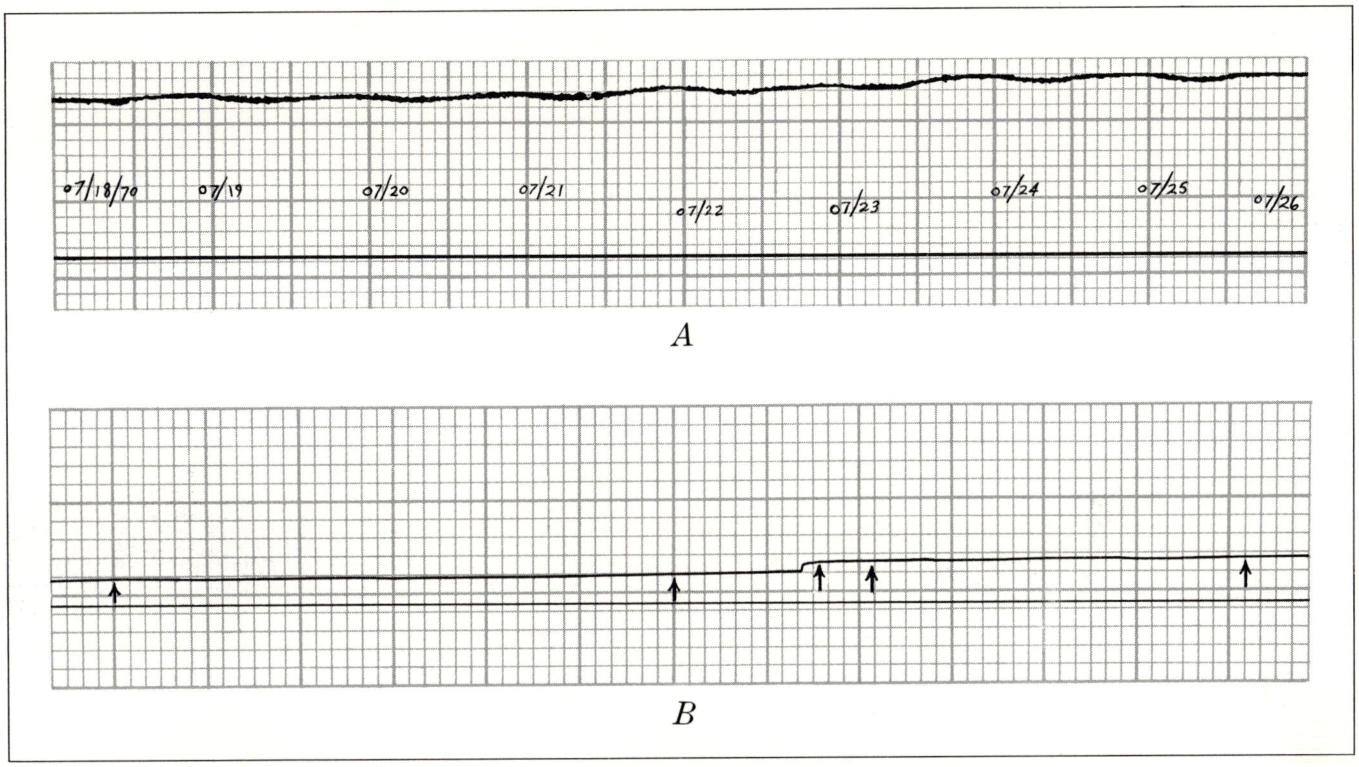

Figure 7.—Representative 7-day records showing distinct events superimposed on slow, steady extension.

A. Record from the California site for July 18–26, 1970. A period of more rapid right-lateral slip during July 21–24 ($\approx$0.1 mm/day) is preceded and followed by periods of more gradual slip ($\approx$0.02 mm/day).

B. A typical 7-day record from the Kilauea site showing an instantaneous extension step during a period of otherwise slow, steady extension. Arrows indicate times when readings were made.

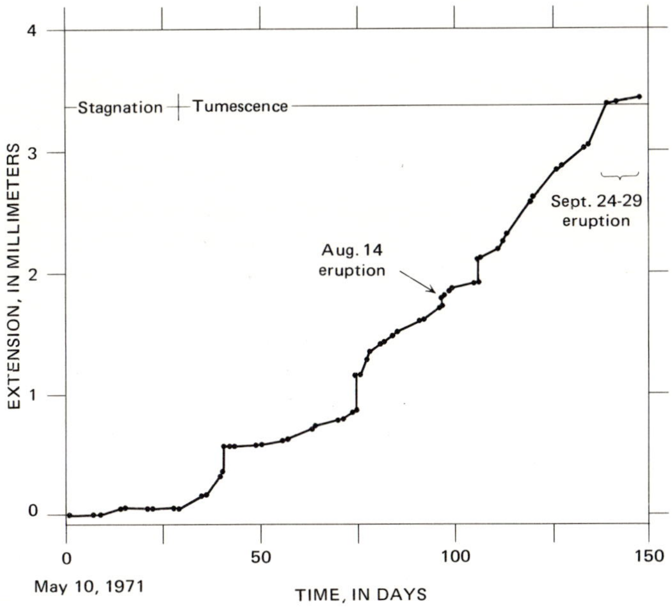

Figure 8.—Graph of 150 days of extensometer records from the Kilauea site. The small dots represent data points between which the strain rate is extrapolated. Note the correlation of strain activity with known structural and eruptive events of the volcano.

reference points correlates with a summit caldera eruption on August 14, and a marked increase in the rate of lengthening correlates with the summit caldera–southwest rift eruption of September 24–29. However, other similar events (for example, on days 41, 75, and 106 of the record) do not correlate with known eruptive activity.

These other steplike events may represent either the sudden release of frictional stress perhaps accumulated in the recorder unit over a period of time or the actual manner in which the ground deforms. Two lines of evidence favor the latter explanation. First, the events on days 41, 75, and 106 all occurred after 4- to 5-week periods of positive strain accumulation, and during these periods the recording paper and drum were repositioned weekly. Considering the method of repositioning the drum, it seems highly unlikely that frictional stress in the recorder could be an important factor except for a 7-day period between servicing of the instrument. Furthermore, the slight but definite sinusoidal shape of a typical recording (see fig. 6*B*) indicates that the recorder is free to respond to the diurnal thermal effect on the Invar wire, even though the presence of some friction in the system is known. An approximate calculation suggests that the actual amplitude of this diurnal tracing is only about half of the predicted amplitude. Nonetheless, with the recording drum set to its

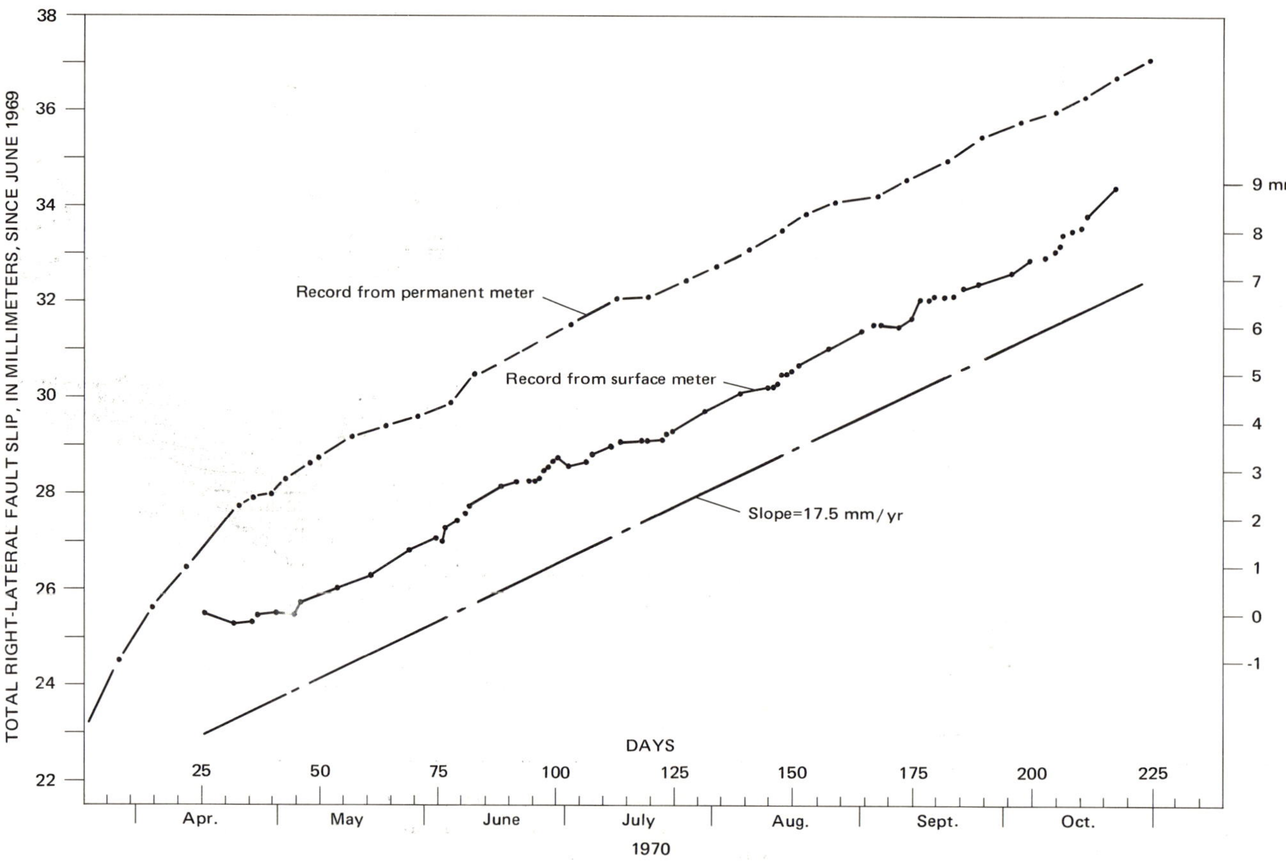

Figure 9.—Cumulative slip versus time from the permanent and surface instruments at the San Andreas fault site in California. An approximate least-squares fit to both records indicates a slope (slip rate) of 17.5 mm/yr. The negative slope and slow response of the surface meter during April are due to initial wire stretch and stabilization of the anchor pin and recorder base immediately after installation on April 14, 1970. The small dots represent temperature-corrected micrometer readings for the permanent meter and uncorrected displacement trace readings from the recorder charts of the surface meter.

freest position during weekly servicing, the large sudden positive strains on days 41, 75, and 106 seem to result from something other than the release of frictional stress in the instrument. This problem, however, needs more study.

Finally, a crude, yet very direct and independent check on the instrument response was provided by repeated measurements with a steel tape at the same location. For the period May 1971 to February 1972, the meter indicated about a 7-mm increase in the separation of reference points, while the steel tape indicated about a 5-mm increase. Considering the great difference in precision of the two methods of measurement with no temperature corrections applied, the correspondence for that time period is very good, and a claim for reliability of the wire extensometer is further supported.

SUMMARY

The modified Stevens Type F water-level recorder has been tested and has proven to be reliable in measuring creep on the San Andreas fault in California and dilation of ground cracks at Kilauea Volcano, Hawaii, where several independent checks on the system response are available; such a system could prove to be extremely useful elsewhere. The system is relatively simple, inexpensive, easily installed, and capable of measuring strains as small as 10^{-5} or even 10^{-6} if accurate temperature measurements are obtained and the appropriate corrections are applied.

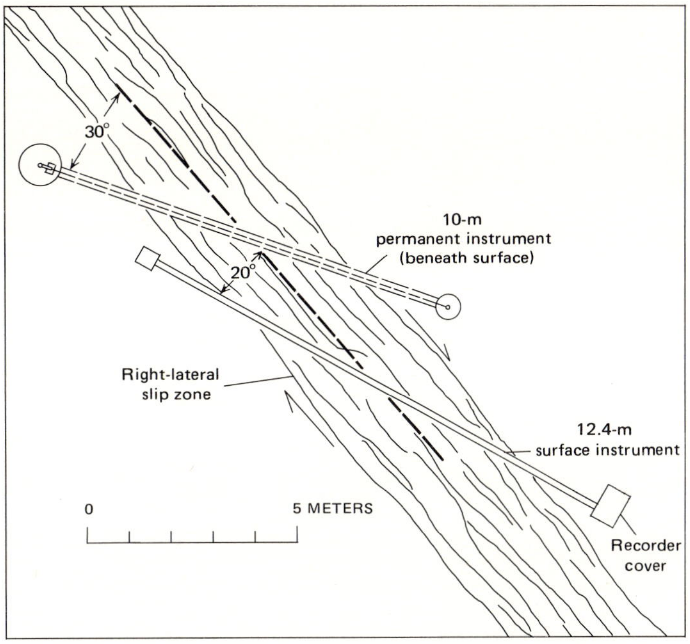

Figure 10.—Plan view of the San Andreas fault instrument site, showing the positioning of the 10-m permanently buried instrument and the 12.4-m surface instrument. The exact width of the slip zone is not known, but other observations show that it is less than 5 m.

Jour. Research U.S. Geol. Survey
Vol. 1, No. 5, Sept.-Oct. 1973, p. 579—585

USE OF MACHINE-PROCESSABLE FIELD NOTES IN A WILDERNESS MAPPING PROJECT (GRANITE FIORDS AREA), SOUTHEASTERN ALASKA

By JAMES G. SMITH and HENRY C. BERG, Menlo Park, Calif.

Abstract.—For reconnaissance geologic mapping and mineral resource evaluation of the Granite Fiords wilderness study area, we developed and used a system of machine-processable field notes. Preprinted field forms standardize notes and serve as checklists that insure collection of all available data. The use of this system cut in half the time required to record data at an outcrop. The system consists of three related but different types of preprinted field sheets, a key to abbreviations and codes, and a set of written instructions. The field sheets include a station sheet for basic outcrop data, a specimen sheet for rock samples, and a geochemical sheet for materials to be chemically analyzed. Data on the field sheets are keypunched on standard IBM cards, then arranged in subfiles and retrieved by using a card sorter. Our system is designed specifically for a region of granitic and metamorphic rocks but is easily modified for use in different geologic terranes. We offer four guidelines for developing a system of machine-processable field notes: (1) Time and money spent to develop the system must be worth its anticipated benefits. (2) The system should be as flexible as possible. (3) It is necessary to tailor the system to a particular geologic terrane or project objective. (4) The system should be as simple and self-explanatory as possible.

The authors were assigned the task of preparing a geologic map and mineral resource appraisal of the Granite Fiords wilderness study area to help determine the suitability of the area for inclusion in the National Wilderness Preservation System, as set up by the Wilderness Act of 1964. At the outset the problems appeared formidable. The study area lies in the heavy rainfall belt of coastal southeastern Alaska. Outcrops along the shore were last examined 40 to 75 years ago in rapid reconnaissance. No modern map existed. The rugged snow-covered mountains, deep fiords, and wild beauty that make the area attractive for wilderness classification greatly increase the problems of fieldwork. There are no roads or trails in the 1,000-sq-mi area of Granite Fiords. The lower mountain slopes are covered with thick stands of trees. The rugged terrane made helicopter support in mapping imperative. The most practical procedure was a kind of geologic leapfrog, wherein each geologist was set out on an outcrop and then moved by helicopter in turn. Many days of mapping passed without a geologist being able to confer with his colleagues other than in the evenings.

While planning the project, we realized that standard methods of field mapping by traversing and writing observations in a notebook would be far too slow and costly to meet project deadlines and remain within budget. If we wanted to finish on schedule, we would have to map about three to four times the area per unit of time mapped in most wilderness projects outside Alaska. Projections on the volume of data that would be acquired showed that we required fast and efficient collecting and handling. In order to speed up field mapping and standardize note taking among all project geologists, we used a system of machine-processable field notes.

At the end of the 1972 field season, we compared our note system with standard notes from past years taken in the same terrane and found that our system cut by about one-half the time required to collect the same amount of field data. During the 150 man-days in the field, we examined more than 1,000 outcrops and collected about 1,100 rocks and 2,000 geochemical samples.

This paper outlines the principles we used in developing a machine-processable note system, points out its advantages and disadvantages, and describes our system. We especially wish to call this technique to the attention of other U.S. Geological Survey geologists because we believe that its use, combined with computer-printed field-data lists, maps, and diagrams, represents a major advance over conventional methods of geologic mapping and resource appraisal. We do not suggest that other workers adopt our system exactly as it is but rather offer it as a guide in constructing their own.

Acknowledgments.—Our machine-processable field-note system is largely a modification of a system developed by J. A. Roddick and W. W. Hutchison, of the Geological Survey of Canada, for use in the geologically similar nearby areas of coastal British Columbia (Hutchison and Roddick, 1968; Roddick and Hutchison, 1972). We are especially grateful to them for helping us adapt their system to meet the special needs of the Granite Fiords project.

SUMMARY OF THE SYSTEM

Our system of machine-processable field notes is based on a set of three preprinted field sheets and standard 80-column

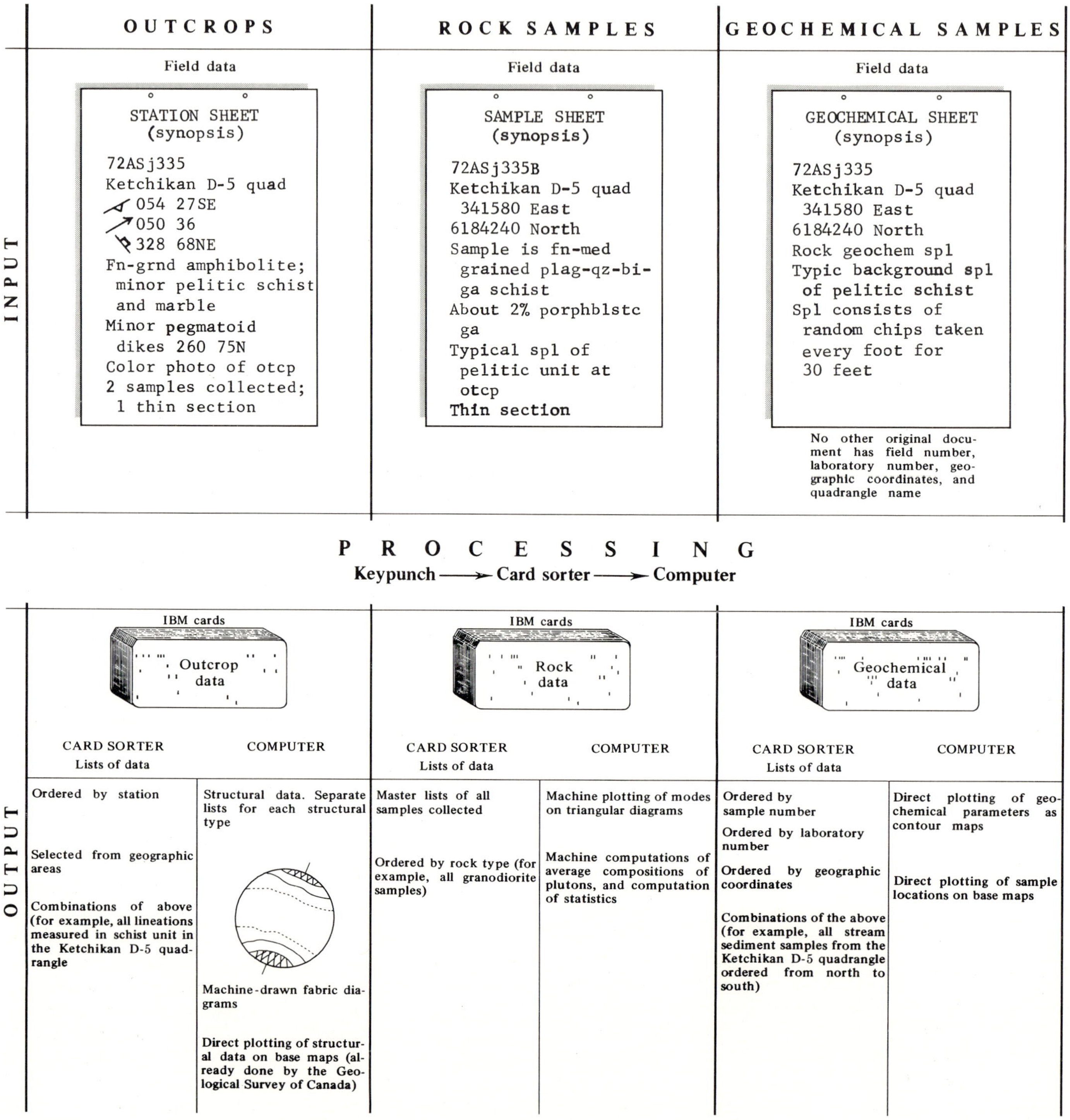

Figure 1.—Graphic synopsis of machine-processable field-note system.

IBM punch cards. A graphic synopsis, figure 1, shows input, processing steps, and different geologic problems for which we have used the output. Field data are written on the preprinted sheets (figs. 2, 3, 4), which are designed mainly for numerical data and objective observations, although a certain amount of subjective data can be recorded. Descriptions that do not fit the machine format, we write on the field sheets as ordinary notes. Separate sheets are used to describe outcrops, rock samples, and geochemical samples. Data on field sheets are keypunched on 80-column IBM cards, producing three separate master files, one for each type of sheet. Data are retrieved and subfiles for specific purposes generated using an IBM

Model 082 card sorter, a faster and cheaper method than writing data-sorting programs for a computer. We are able to sort or rearrange our cards and prepare lists of data at our convenience, without debugging or computer language problems.

PRINCIPLES

The time and money spent to develop a system of machine-processable field notes must be worth its anticipated benefits. This principle, often overlooked, is the most important. During development, systems for data collection and processing tend to become increasingly elaborate and complex with a concomitant nearly astronomical increase in effort. We tried to keep our system as simple as possible, tailoring it specifically for the metamorphic and granitic terrane known to underlie the study area rather than designing a universal note-keeping system that would work on any outcrop in the world. Without modification, our system will not work, for example, in a terrane of fossiliferous sedimentary rocks.

A second ground rule is that a system be sufficiently self-explanatory that a geologist visiting the project or a field assistant working with data can understand it with minimal explanation. Complicated formats or abstract codes lead to errors in input and to output that is difficult to understand without machine translation. For example, the most complex coding problem is to condense rock and mineral names. Generally, two characters are enough, allowing 100 codes if numbers are used or 676 codes if letters are used. An arbitrary numeric code for each rock type and mineral is easily and rapidly processed, using a relatively cheap card sorter, but difficult to remember. This leads to input errors and to printout that is unreadable without translation. Mnemonic codes for rocks and minerals are already familiar to geologists, quickly learned, and easily remembered (for example, LS = limestone, BI = biotite, and so on). Although they take slightly longer to run through the sorter and require more programing effort for computers, their advantages—reduced input errors and more readable printout—outweigh the slight speed advantage of machine-processing numeric codes.

A third requirement is flexibility: it should be possible to modify a system during a project without having to completely transform existing files. Field notes must be usable even before transfer to punch cards and without the intervention of any machine processing. Space is required for recording subjective or descriptive observations that do not fit a machine-processable format, such as outcrop sketches or relations between two fold axes.

EVALUATION

The advantages of coding geologic and geochemical field data for computer processing have been documented by several workers (Berner and others, 1972; Laurin and others, 1972; and Roddick and Hutchison, 1972). In our experience, the advantages of such a system greatly outweigh the disadvantages, many of which diminish or disappear with continued use. The drawbacks that we have encountered are summarized along with the advantages in table 1.

THE SYSTEM

The note system itself consists of the following elements:

1. Three different preprinted field sheets that may be used alone or in combination at each outcrop or geochemical sample site: a station sheet used to record basic data measured at an outcrop; a specimen sheet used to describe each rock sample; and a geochemical sheet used to describe each geochemical sample (figs. 2, 3, 4).
2. A key sheet for the data codes (table 2) (This sheet is glued inside the notebook cover.)
3. A written set of instructions on how to use the system. Complete written instructions are lengthy and tedious, however, and the system is more easily taught by example. Fortunately, the system is so quickly learned that after the first day the set of instructions can be left in camp. After a few more days, the key sheet is seldom referred to.

Station sheet

Basic geologic data about an outcrop are recorded on the station sheet (fig. 2), then keypunched on a standard 80-column IBM card for sorting, preparing lists, and so on. The station sheet is preprinted on 5- by 8-inch white looseleaf

Table 1.—*Evaluation of system of machine-processable field notes used in Granite Fiords wilderness study area, Alaska*

Advantages	Disadvantages
For most, easy to learn and use.	For some, conversion from longhand notes to data coding is a major adjustment requiring considerable concentration and effort, at least at first. Some geologists will not wish to make this adjustment.
Greatly speeds note-taking with little likelihood of omitting key observations.	Reports may not be read by individuals who are skeptical or mistrustful of computer-assisted geologic research.
Especially useful in a helicopter-supported reconnaissance mapping project carried out by numerous geologists, assistants, and short-term "guest workers."	Without modification, this system cannot be used in geologic terranes markedly different from that in Granite Fiords.
By machine sorting and listing of large volumes of geologic and geochemical field data, facilitates research and preparation of reports.	Whereas programs for computer-printed derivative geochemical maps are available to U.S. Geological Survey users, programs for such maps compiled from geologic field data are not yet widely available to Survey geologists.
Reduces time and thereby cost of preparing geologic maps, structure diagrams, and geochemical contour maps.	May create or suffer delays from keypunching backlogs.
	Rapidly produces a bulky accumulation of field data sheets.

Table 2.–*Key sheet showing codes for station, specimen, and geochemical sheets (figs. 2, 3, and 4)*

LITHOLOGY: PLUTONIC: mafic present-0 ; H-1 ; H/b-2 ; H=B-3 ; B/h-4 ; B-5 ; gabbro-1 ; diorite-2 ; qtz dior-3 ; granodior-4 ; qtz monz-5 ; granite-6 ; syenite-7 ; syenodior-8 .

MIGMATITES:
stockwork-SW
banded gn-BG
irreg b gn-IG
veined gn-VG
angular agmatite-AA
rounded agmatite-RA
elongate agmatite-EA
schlieren gn-SG
nebulite-NE

OTHER:
agglomerate-AG
alaskite-AK
amphibolite-AM
andesite-AN
aplite-AP
argillite-AR
arkose-AK
basalt-BA
breccia-BR
broken-pillow breccia-BP
calcsilicate-CS
cataclasite-CC
chert-CH
clay-CL
conglomerate-CØ
dacite-DA
dolomite-DØ
diabase-DB
dunite-DN
gneiss-GN
granulite-GA
gravel-GR
graywacke-GW
greenstone-GE
greenschist-GS
hornblendite-HB
hornfels-HF
keratophyre-KE
lamprophyre-LA
limestone-LS
marble-MB
mylonite-MY
obsidian-ØB
pegmatite-PG
phyllite-PH
phyllonite-PN
pillow breccia-PB
pillow lava-PL
quartzite-QZ
rhyolite-RH
sandstone-SS
schist-SC
semischist-SI
shale-SH
silstone-ST
skarn-SK
slate-SL
tuff-TU
unclassified:
  agmatite-UA
  gneiss-UG
  meta-UM
  plut.-UP
  sedi.-US
  volc.-UV
  migmatite-UK
volcanic breccia-VB
volcaniclastic-VC

GRAIN SIZE:

Granitic & meta:

1-glassy	
2-v. fine	<0.5 mm
3-fine	0.5–1 mm
4-medium	1–5 mm
5-coarse	5–10 mm
6-coarse	10–20 mm
7-v. coarse	20–50 mm
8-v. coarse	50–100 mm
9-giant	>10 cm

Sedimentary:

A-aphanitic	<1/16 mm
V-v. fine	1/16–1/8
F-fine	1/8–1/4
M-medium	1/4–1/2
C-coarse	1/2–1 mm
Ø-v. coarse	1–2 mm
R-granule	2–4 mm
P-f pb grav	4–8 mm
G-m pb grav	8–16 mm
B-c pb grav	16–32 mm
D-v c pb grav	32–64 mm
L-cobble	>64 mm

HETEROGENEITY:
homogeneous-H
slightly hetero-S
moder hetero-M
very hetero-V

INCLUSIONS:
Shape:
  mainly angular-A
  mainly rounded-R
  mainly elongate-E
Type:
  bedded-B
  foliated-F
  nebulous-N
  porphyroblastic-P
  granoblastic-G

SPECIMEN QUALITY:
outstanding-Ø
good-G
poor-P
heterogeneous-H
inclusion-I

STRUCTURE:

axial plane	P1 ,P2
bedding	S0
cleavage	C1 ,C2
dike	D1 ,D2
lamprophyre dk	DL
pegmatite dk	DP
fault/shear	F1 ,F2
joints	J1 ,J2
feldspath jt	JF
fold axis	A1 ,A2
lineation	L1 ,L2
mineral lin	LM
biotite lin	LB
hblnde lin	LH
silliman lin	LS
schistosity or foliation	S1 ,S2
veins	V1 ,V2

MINERALS:
actinolite-AC
albite-AB
amphibole-AM
andalusite-AD
anorthite-AN
apatite-AP
arsenopyrite-AS
augite-AU
azurite-AZ
barite-BA
beryl-BE
biotite-BI
bornite-BØ
calcite-CA
chalcedony-CD
chalcocite-CC
chalcopyrite-CP
chlorite-CL
chloritoid-CH
chromite-CM
chyrsotile-CR
clay minerals-CY
clinozoisite-CZ
cordierite-CØ
diopside-DI
epidote-EP
galena-GL
garnet-GA
glass (vol)-GS
glaucophane-GC
graphite-GR
hematite-HE
hornblende-HØ
hypersthene-HY
ilmenite-IL
kyanite-KY
limonite-LI
magnetite-MA
malachite-ML
microcline-MK
mica-MI
molybdenite-MØ
muscovite-MU
olivine-ØL
opal-ØP
orthoclase-KF
plagioclase-PC
prehnite-PN
K-spar-PF
pyrite-PY
pyroxene-PX
pyrrhotite-PR
quartz-QZ
rutile-RU
sanidine-SA
scheelite-SC
serpentine-SE
sillimanite-SI
sphalerite-SL
sphene-SP
staurolite-ST
talc-TA
tourmaline-TØ
tremolite-TR
wollastonite-WØ
zeolite-ZE
zircon-ZI

DESCRIPTIVE TERMS:
acicular-AC
allotriomorphic-AL
amygdaloidal-AM
anhedral-AN
aphanitic-AP
augen-AU
banded-BN
bedded-BD
blastophitic-BØ
blastoporphyritic-BP
boudinage-BU
cataclastic-CA
clastic-CL
crinkled-CN
cryptocrystalline-CR
decussate-DE
diktytaxitic-DI
equant-EQ
equigranular-EG
euhedral-EU
feathery-FA
felty-FE
fibrous-FB
fissile-FS
flaky-FL
foliate-FØ
glomeroporphyritic-GL
gneissose-GN
granoblastic-GB
granofelsic-GF
granular-GR
helicitic-HE
holocrystalline-HX
hornfelsic-HF
hyalopilitic-HØ
hypidiomorphic-HY
idioblastic-IB
idiomorphic-IM
inequigranular-IQ
intergranular-IG
intersertal-IS
interstitial-IT
lepidoblastic-LP
leucocratic-LC
lineated-LN
melanocratic-MC
mylonitic-MY
myrmekitic-MR
needles-NE
nematoblastic-NB
ophitic-ØP
orbicular-ØR
pegmatitic-PG
platy-PL
poikilitic-PK
porphyritic-PP
porphyroblastic-PB
protoclastic-PC
radiating-RD
schistose-SH
seriate-SE
sieve texture-SI
slaty-SL
spherulitic-SP
subhedral-SB
sugary-SU
tabular-TB
vesicular-VS
vitrophyric-VP
vitroclastic-VC
xenoblastic-XB

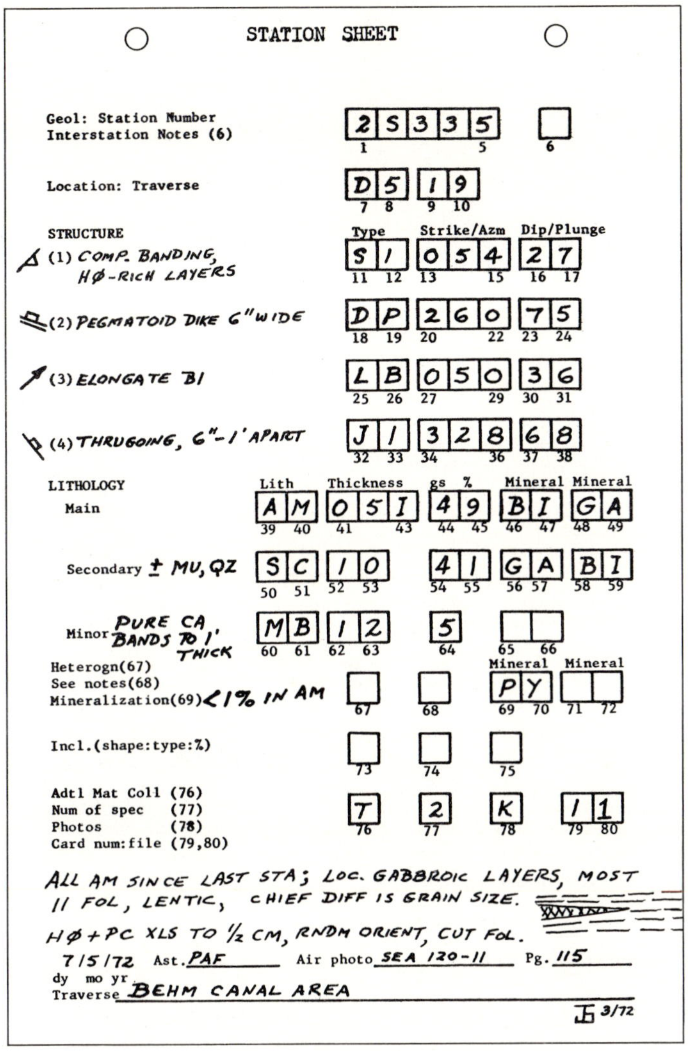
STATION SHEET

Geol: Station Number — 2 5 3 3 5 (1–5)
Interstation Notes (6) — (6)

Location: Traverse — D 5 (7 8) / 1 9 (9 10)

STRUCTURE — Type / Strike/Azm / Dip/Plunge
(1) COMP. BANDING, HØ-RICH LAYERS — S 1 (11 12) / 0 5 4 (13–15) / 2 7 (16 17)
(2) PEGMATOID DIKE 6" WIDE — D P (18 19) / 2 6 0 (20–22) / 7 5 (23 24)
(3) ELONGATE BI — L B (25 26) / 0 5 0 (27–29) / 3 6 (30 31)
(4) THRUGOING, 6"–1' APART — J 1 (32 33) / 3 2 8 (34–36) / 6 8 (37 38)

LITHOLOGY — Lith / Thickness / gs / % / Mineral / Mineral
Main — A M (39 40) / 0 5 I (41–43) / 4 9 (44 45) / B I (46 47) / G A (48 49)
Secondary ± MU, QZ — S C (50 51) / 1 0 (52 53) / 4 1 (54 55) / G A (56 57) / B I (58 59)
Minor PURE CA, BANDS TO 1' THICK — M B (60 61) / 1 2 (62 63) / 5 (64) / (65 66)

Heterogn(67) / See notes(68) / Mineralization(69) <1% IN AM — (67) / (68) / Mineral P Y (69 70) / Mineral (71 72)

Incl.(shape:type:%) — (73) / (74) / (75)

Adtl Mat Coll (76) / Num of spec (77) / Photos (78) / Card num:file (79,80) — T (76) / 2 (77) / K (78) / 1 1 (79 80)

ALL AM SINCE LAST STA; LOC. GABBROIC LAYERS, MOST // FOL, LENTIC, CHIEF DIFF IS GRAIN SIZE. HØ + PC XLS TO 1/2 CM, RNDM ORIENT, CUT FOL.

7/5/72 Ast. PAF Air photo SEA 120-11 Pg. 115
dy mo yr
Traverse BEHM CANAL AREA

JS 3/72

Figure 2.—Station sheet as filled out in the field.

paper, slightly larger than that used in a standard U.S. Geological Survey notebook. We hope to have books bound with tearout sheets as for Survey notebooks.

The format of the station sheet suits our particular mapping purposes; others could easily be devised for different areas and types of data. At first glance, the station sheet, as well as the other two sheets, presents a formidable array of boxes that most first-time users feel an almost compulsive need to fill completely. At the same time, filling all those little boxes seems to take a long time because constant reference must be made to the key sheet (table 2). As the user's confidence grows, he soon gains speed and remembers the code, for example, that foliation is coded as S1 and hornblende as HØ, without having to check the key. Then, as with handwritten notes, he becomes selective in what he records, especially with regard to what must be coded in the field and what can be deferred.

The information entered in each field of the station sheet follows (numbers are box numbers, fig. 2).

1–5: Geologist and station number. First box is for the year, second the code for the geologist. Remaining three boxes allow up to 999 separate stations.

6: The number "1" placed in this box indicates important interstation comments written on the sheet.

7–10: Location and traverse number. For Granite Fiords, the location is a mile-to-the-inch quadrangle code, because the project area includes parts of 11 different quadrangles. This gives a general location for the station, which is especially helpful for rapid helicopter reconnaissance. Structural subprovinces or mnemonic codes for geographic areas could be as easily used. Traverse number is used for further general location or keeping track of individual geologic traverses. We have not recorded this information as much as we had thought we would.

11–12, 18–19, 25–26, 32–33: Code for type of structural reading, for example, S = foliation, J = joint. Four structural readings may be recorded on one sheet. If more structural data are present than will fit on a single station sheet, additional station sheets may be used.

13–17, 20–24, 27–31, 34–38: Strike and dip of planar structures or bearing and plunge of linear features. For planar structures, the direction of dip need not be specified if the strike is always read as an azimuth with the dip to the right. For example, the foliation, S1, in figure 2, strikes N. 54° E. and dips 27° SE.; the throughgoing joint set, J1, strikes N. 32° W. and dips 68° NE. While this may seem confusing at first, one soon gets used to it. Such consistent notation facilitates computer translation of structural data to a format suitable for computer-generated fabric diagrams.

39–40, 50–51, 60–61: Rock names of main, secondary, and minor lithologies at the outcrop. A two-number code for plutonic rocks allows for both hornblende-biotite ratio and rock type. For other rock types, we use a two-letter mnemonic code, for example, AM = amphibolite, MB = marble.

41–42, 52–53, 62–63: Thickness of lithologic units; for some rocks, such as granite, these boxes would be left blank.

43: A letter code in this box designates the units of thickness used, for example, F = foot, I = inches. This system allows the range of almost three orders of magnitude from 99 to 0.1.

44, 54, 64: Grain sizes of lithologic types. See key (table 2).

45, 55: Percentage estimates, to the nearest 10 percent, of main and secondary lithologic types.

46–47, 48–49, 56–57, 58–59, 65–66: Two minerals per rock type considered significant to the geologist at the outcrop. Amphibole is not coded on figure 2 because the essential minerals of amphibolite are, by definition, hornblende and plagioclase and therefore unnecessary to code. The presence of biotite and garnet in the amphibolite, however, is considered significant.

67: Heterogeneity. Used mainly with migmatites and granitic rocks.

68: See notes. A "1" in this box indicates significant information that will not fit into the computer format, for example, field sketches or extended rock descriptions.

69–72: Mineralization. Minerals of economic interest are recorded here. Detailed information about an outcrop with significant mineralization would be coded on the geochemical sheet.

73–75: Shape, type, and abundance, to the nearest 10 percent, of inclusions in granitic rocks.

76: Additional material collected, such as thin-section samples or samples for chemical analysis. May be added later.

77: Number of samples collected at this station.

78: Photograph taken at station.

79: Records the number of station sheets used at each station.

80: File. A "1" is preprinted on each station sheet to facilitate selective machine retrieval of outcrop data.

Specimen sheet

A specimen sheet (fig. 3) is filled out for each sample collected at a station. Designed to describe the mineralogy and texture of the hand specimen rather than the entire outcrop, it is the same size as the station and geochemical sheets but is printed on blue stock. The following information is recorded on it (numbers are box numbers, fig. 3):

1–6: Geologist, station number, and sample number (= station number). The geologist and station number are the same as on the station sheet. We use a simple A, B, C system for different samples taken at the same station.

7–10: Location and traverse as on the station sheet.

11–23: Universal Transverse Mercator (UTM) grid reference. We prefer the UTM system over latitude and longitude because it is a metric decimal notation and because distances between grid lines are the same on all maps of the same scale throughout the world between lat 80° N. and 80° S. UTM grid ticks are the blue (not black) grid ticks on the margins of U.S. Geological Survey maps. Grid references are usually filled in during the evening by assistants.

24, 25: Rock name of sample.

26–29: Two textural modifiers chosen from the list of descriptive terms on the key sheet; for example, foliated = FØ, porphyroblastic = PB.

30–31: Color index. This may be a field estimate or an accurate measurement determined in the laboratory.

32: Specimen quality (for example, G, good; P, poor).

33–35: Specific gravity.

36: A "1" in this box indicates the presence of relict sedimentary features.

37–38, 45–46, 53–54, 61–62, 69–70: Names of minerals in the rock.

39–41, 47–49, 55–57, 63–65, 71–73: Percentage of each mineral present. This may be a field estimate or an accurate laboratory point count. Entry before the decimal point only indicates an estimate; an entry to the right of the decimal as well indicates a point count.

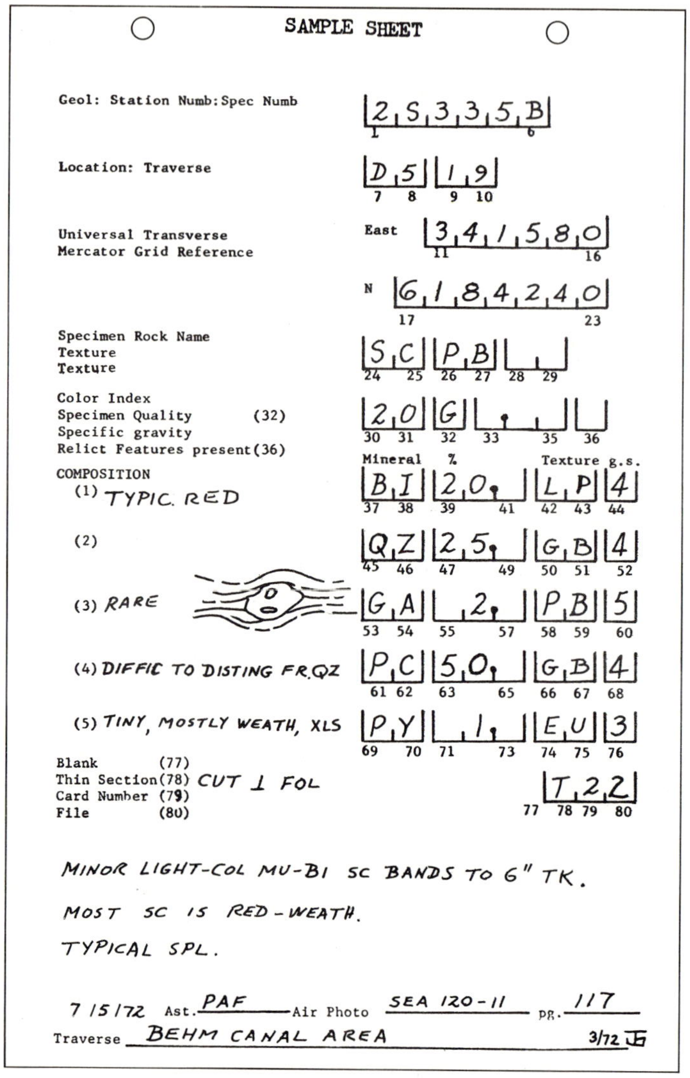

Figure 3.—Specimen (sample) sheet as filled out in the field.

42–43, 50–51, 58–59, 66–67, 74–75: Texture or habit of each mineral, taken from the list of descriptive terms on the key sheet.

44, 52, 60, 68, 76: Grain size of each mineral. A different code is used for sedimentary rocks than for igneous and metamorphic rocks.

77: Blank.

78: A "T" in this box indicates that a thin section has been prepared.

79: Records the number of specimen sheets used at each station.

80: File. A "2" is preprinted on each specimen sheet to facilitate selective machine retrieval of sample data.

Geochemical sheet

The geochemical sheet (fig. 4) is used for data on samples to be chemically analyzed by the standard 30-element semi-

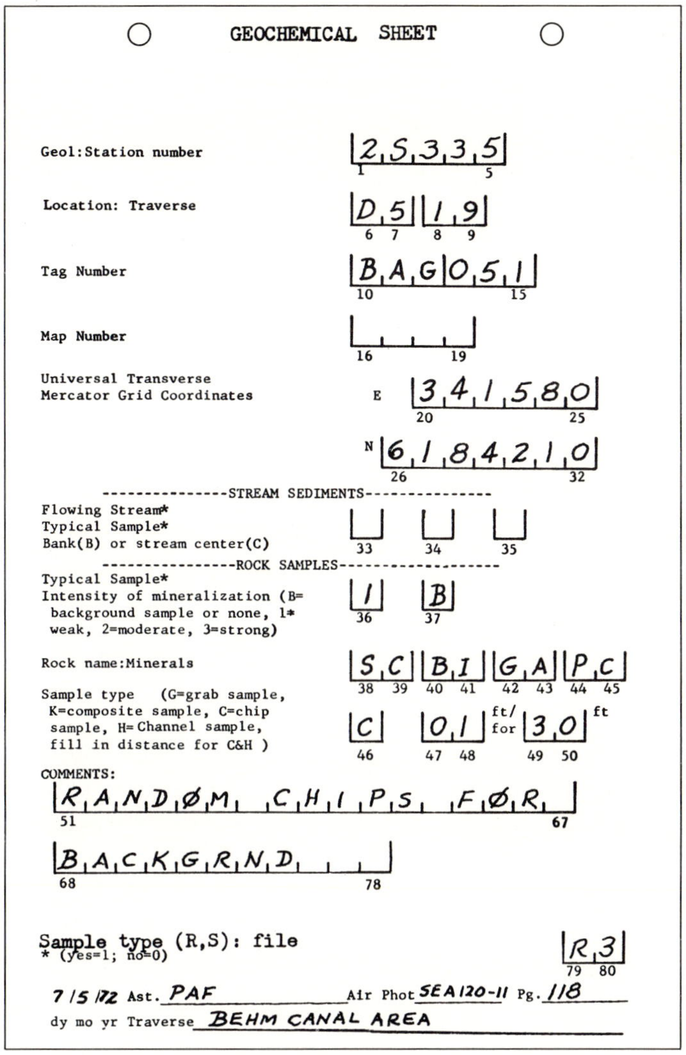
GEOCHEMICAL SHEET

Geol:Station number 2,5,3,3,5 (1–5)

Location: Traverse D,5 1,9 (6 7 8 9)

Tag Number B,A,G 0,5,1 (10–15)

Map Number (16–19)

Universal Transverse Mercator Grid Coordinates E 3,4,1,5,8,0 (20–25)

N 6,1,8,4,2,1,0 (26–32)

--------------STREAM SEDIMENTS--------------

Flowing Stream*
Typical Sample*
Bank(B) or stream center(C) (33) (34) (35)

----------------ROCK SAMPLES-------------------

Typical Sample*
Intensity of mineralization (B= background sample or none, 1= weak, 2=moderate, 3=strong) 1 (36) B (37)

Rock name:Minerals S,C B,I G,A P,C (38 39 40 41 42 43 44 45)

Sample type (G=grab sample, K=composite sample, C=chip sample, H=Channel sample, fill in distance for C&H) C (46) 0,1 (47 48) ft/for 3,0 (49 50) ft

COMMENTS:
R,A,N,D,Ø,M, C,H,I,P,S, F,Ø,R, (51–67)
B,A,C,K,G,R,N,D (68–78)

Sample type (R,S): file R,3 (79 80)
* (yes=1; no=0)

7/5/72 Ast. PAF Air Phot SEA120-11 Pg. 118
dy mo yr Traverse BEHM CANAL AREA

Figure 4.–Geochemical sheet as filled out in the field.

quantitative spectroscopic method. It is the simplest of the three to fill out, yet the most useful because it facilitates ordering and listing of geochemical results. Specific fields on this sheet, which is printed on pink stock, are explained below (numbers are box numbers, fig. 4).

1–5: Geologist and station number as on sheets 1 and 2.

6–9: Location and traverse as on sheets 1 and 2.

10–15: Used for a six-place letter and number code assigned to each sample by the U.S. Geological Survey Branch of Analytical Laboratories.

16–19: Map number (optional). A simple number arbitrarily assigned to a sample on a particular map so that cumbersome laboratory and field station numbers may later be omitted.

20–32: Universal Transverse Mercator coordinates. Same as on specimen sheet.

33–35: Filled in for stream-sediment samples only, to convey information about sample and sample site.

36–50: For specimens other than stream-sediment samples:

36: A subjective estimate by the geologist as to whether the sample is typical in amount of mineralization, and so on.

37: Intensity of mineralization indicated by a simple code.

38–45: Fields for the name of the rock and three important minerals.

46–50: Sample type and sampling interval for chip and channel samples.

51–78: Free coding space for important comments about the sample.

79: Used to indicate whether sample is stream sediment or other sample. Coding the information in this space makes for easy separation of samples.

80: File. A "3" is preprinted on each geochemical sheet to facilitate selective machine retrieval of geochemical data.

REFERENCES CITED

Berner, H., Ekström, T., Lilljequist, R., Stephansson, O., and Wikström, A., 1972, GEOMAP–A data system for geological mapping–Sec. 16, Computer-based storage, retrieval and processing of geological information: Internat. Geol. Cong., 24th, Montreal 1972, Repts., sec. 16, p. 3–11.

Hutchison, W. W., and Roddick, J. A., 1968, Recording geologic data for machine retrieval and processing: Western Miner, v. 41, p. 39–43.

Laurin, A. F., Sharma, K. N. M., Wynne-Edwards, H. R., and Franconi, A., 1972, Application of data processing techniques in the Grenville Province, Quebec, Canada: Internat. Geol. Cong., 24th, Montreal 1972, Repts., sec. 16, p. 22–35.

Roddick, J. A., and Hutchison, W. W., 1972, A computer-based system for geological field data on the Coast Mountains project, British Columbia, Canada: Internat. Geol. Cong., 24th, Montreal 1972, Repts., sec. 16, p. 36–46.

Jour. Research U.S. Geol. Survey
Vol. 1, No. 5, Sept.-Oct. 1973, p. 587—596

ICE AGES AND THE THERMAL EQUILIBRIUM OF THE EARTH

By DAVID P. ADAM, Menlo Park, Calif.

Abstract.—A model for climatic change, and particularly for the changes of the late Cenozoic, involves as its primary variables the albedo of the earth and the heat storage characteristics of the oceans. Geography exerts a strong influence. The model proposed does not require metaphysical causes or astronomical events other than known variations in the earth's orbit.

The changes that have occurred in the climate of the earth are a scientific enigma. Many qualitative and quantitative changes of past climate have been described, but their causes have remained obscure; this has resulted in a proliferation of suggested causes of climatic changes.

An ideal theory of climatic change should be able to explain the entire range of climates observable in the geologic record in terms of predictable variations in parameters known to change. The most severe test for any theory of climatic change is continental glaciation, the most extreme climatic disturbance of long duration recognized in the geologic record; a reasonable theory of glaciation should be able to explain nonglaciation as well.

The theories of climatic change are legion, and this paper will not attempt to review them. Reviews of older contributions (Charlesworth, 1957; Brooks, 1949; Schwarzbach, 1963; Shapley, 1953) and the current state of knowledge (Flint, 1971; Embleton and King, 1968; Mitchell, 1968) are available in the literature.

It has long been recognized that climatic changes represent changes in the energy budget of the earth: changes in the net amount of solar energy absorbed by the earth, in the seasonal or geographic distribution of that energy, or (now that continental drift is once again respectable) in the distribution of land and sea relative to the available energy.

The thesis developed here is that changes in the earth's energy budget can be satisfactorily explained by terrestrial causes, specifically by interactions between the thermal characteristics of the oceans and changes in albedo. The only extraterrestrial factor given any credence is the fluctuation of solar energy in the Milankovitch theory.

The main points of the model proposed here are: (1) the energy to fuel the intensified atmospheric circulation necessary to nourish Northern Hemisphere ice sheets is the heat stored in the oceans during the previous interglacial interval; (2) this energy source is tapped when perennial, high-albedo snowfields develop in the subarctic and create a strong energy gradient between themselves and the oceans, thereby initiating a glaciation; (3) a glaciation terminates when the oceans cool to the point where the energy gradient between the oceans and snowfields is no longer sufficient to nourish the ice sheets; (4) interstadial intervals arise when a surface layer of relatively fresh glacial melt water forms in the North Atlantic Ocean, isolating the warm ocean waters from the air-sea interface and decreasing the energy gradient between the oceans and the ice sheets; and (5) all of this depends to a great extent upon the present geographic configuration of the earth, as continental drift is very important in determining the climatology of the earth over long time intervals.

Nearly all the elements of the model described here have been suggested before, and there is in this sense little that is new in it. But little explicit attention has been given the thermal equilibrium of the earth as a unifying concept, and that is the primary focus of this paper.

Acknowledgments.—For comments on early versions of this manuscript, I thank T. L. Smiley, P. S. Martin, W. D. Sellers, P. E. Damon, C. Emiliani, A. Twomey, T. P. Culbert, D. M. Hopkins, and R. B. Morrison. I especially thank L. M. Gould for persistent help and encouragement. Much of this work was supported by National Science Foundation grant GB-7797 to P. S. Martin at the University of Arizona.

THE GLOBAL ENERGY BUDGET

The energy budget of the earth must be the keystone of any model of climatic change. The gross energy budget may be expressed simply as

$$G - L = S, \tag{1}$$

where G is the total energy gained from all sources, L the total energy lost to space, and S a storage term.

The incoming energy, G is derived almost entirely from the sun (Sellers, 1965); in this paper all other sources will be ignored and assumed to be constant. If the energy output of the sun is held constant, and if fluctuations of the Milankovitch type are passed over for the moment, then G is a function of the planetary albedo, α,

$$G = Q\,(1 - \alpha), \tag{2}$$

where Q is the solar energy available at the top of the atmosphere.

The outgoing energy, L, is controlled by the temperature and emissivity of the earth,

$$L = e\sigma T^4\,, \tag{3}$$

where e is the emissivity, σ the Stefan-Boltzmann constant, and T the absolute temperature. When changes in the emissivity are not large, e may be regarded as a constant, and L is then a function of T^4.

The storage term, S, is simply the difference between G and L. When energy gains exceed losses, S is positive and the earth is warming; negative values of S correspond to a cooling earth.

When the earth is at radiative equilibrium, S must equal zero. At equilibrium, the mean temperature of the earth is some value, T_{eq}, such that energy gains are just balanced by energy losses. T_{eq} is a function of α; for any value of α and geographic configuration of the earth, there is a corresponding value of T_{eq}. When $S = 0$, net energy losses from the surface of the earth must be directed outward to space, for energy losses from the surface to deeper layers represent storage.

When the climate changes, the temperature of the earth changes, and hence $S \neq 0$. Kukla (1969, 1972) and Budyko (1969) have recently emphasized the significance of the planetary albedo in producing climatic changes; the albedo is taken here as the primary controlling variable for the global energy budget. Adjustments of climate produced by albedo changes will differ in character depending upon whether S is positive or negative.

When S is positive, the earth is warming. Land surfaces warm rapidly, for their heat capacities are fairly low, and heat must be stored in a relatively thin layer near the surface. Oceanic surface temperatures also adjust fairly quickly because warming a layer of water at the surface makes that layer lighter, increasing the stability of the water column. The sea surface will warm until energy losses balance energy gains and the surface temperature reaches T_{eq}. Most of the surface energy loss will always be directed upward, but until the ocean reaches a steady state, some heat from the surface will be used to warm the deeper water. (Some evidence that this has occurred during the Holocene has been presented by Ruddiman and others, 1970.) The steady state will not occur until the oceanic depths are in equilibrium with the surface.

Adjustment of temperatures at depth will be very slow, because a water column warmed from the top is highly stable and because areas occupied by warmer surface water masses are characterized by upwelling of cooler water from beneath the thermocline to balance evaporative losses. However, surface evaporation in the middle of a gyre produces a gradual increase in salinity above the thermocline, and this tends to increase the density of the warm water and deepen the thermocline. Small positive values of S will persist until the process is complete ($T = T_{eq}$) or until T_{eq} changes.

When S is negative, the land surface cools rapidly because of the same factors that control its warming—low heat capacity and a relatively thin layer of heat storage. The surface of the ocean, however, can only change temperature relatively slowly. A parcel of water cooled at the surface becomes denser, sinks, and is replaced by a lighter parcel of warm water from beneath. In cooling, a much deeper layer of water must change to effect a given change in the surface temperature than when warming occurs. The differences between responses of the earth to warming and cooling are summarized in table 1.

Table 1.—*Selected characteristics of the response of the earth to changes in the energy budget*

	Warming ($S > 0$)	Cooling ($S < 0$)
Temperature changes:		
Land	Rapid	Rapid
Ocean surface	Rapid	Slow
Ocean at depth	Slow	Slow
Large time lags:		
Ocean surface behind land	No	Yes
Ocean at depth behind ocean surface	Yes	No

LONG-TERM CLIMATIC CHANGES

The so-called flywheel effect of the oceans can be important, even over very long time periods, as long as the earth is cooling and T_{eq} changes more rapidly than the oceans respond (table 1). The last very long period change in terrestrial climate was the general worldwide cooling in the Cenozoic, which has been amply documented (Emiliani, 1958; Schwarzbach, 1963). This cooling has been attributed to the movement of Antarctica into a polar position (Emiliani, 1958; Ewing and Donn, 1958; Donn and Ewing, 1966; Flohn, 1969; Crowell and Frakes, 1970); paleomagnetic evidence of sea-floor spreading between Australia and Antarctica suggests that since the Eocene, the two continents have separated by about 30° in a north-south direction (LePichon and Heirtzler, 1968).

A necessary condition for the development of a perennial snow cover on Antarctica was satisfied when that continent attained a polar position during the early Tertiary. It is not clear to what extent the initial early Tertiary cooling was caused by a change in the position of Antarctica and to what extent by other factors such as the emergence of the continents during the early Tertiary (Damon, 1968) and changing oceanic circulation (Hopkins, 1972; Frakes and Kemp, 1972). In any case, the high latitude and a gradually cooling climate permitted a permanent snow cover to form on Antarctica at some time during the Miocene (Denton and others, 1971; Rutford and others, 1968; Gould, 1940). This was critical for the energy budget of the earth, for it increased the planetary albedo and lowered T_{eq}.

The decrease in T_{eq} required that the earth cool ($S < 0$). The biggest obstacle to this cooling was the heat stored in the oceans. Even the bottom waters were 8°C warmer at the beginning of the Tertiary than at present (Emiliani, 1954, 1958); consequently, the entire water column had to cool by several degrees, and this involved the loss of an immense amount of heat. The oceans, because of their limited rate of heat loss, acted as a buffer to retard the cooling of the earth during the Tertiary.

With increasing knowledge of the geochronology of the Pleistocene brought about by potassium-argon dating has come a better knowledge of the timing of the several glaciations. Mountain glaciation in Antarctica (Hollin, 1969b) and around the North Pacific had begun by the Miocene, but the earliest widespread montane glaciation in temperate latitudes did not occur until about 3 m.y. ago in the Pliocene (Kent and others, 1971). Dated till deposits of this age have been recognized in Iceland (Einarsson and others, 1967), California (Curry, 1966), Argentina (Mercer, 1969a), and possibly New Zealand (Matthews and Curtis, 1966; Stipp and others, 1967). Since then, several major glacials have occurred, but as Chappell (1968) noted, a change in the periodicity of the glaciations took place around the beginning of the classical European glacial sequence, the glaciations since the Günz occurring at much closer intervals than those prior to it. Chappell attributes this change in frequency to a change in the oscillation period of the Ewing and Donn system (Ewing and Donn, 1956, 1958; Donn and Ewing, 1966); a different interpretation is made here.

With the present continents and oceans, the Antarctic ice sheet is a permanent feature of the earth and probably will remain one until the pole shifts. Wilson (1964, 1966, 1969) has proposed that the Antarctic ice may advance very rapidly on occasion because of the buildup of a layer of water at the base of the ice and a resulting significant decrease in the basal friction. This theory received strong support from the recent discovery of water at the base of a long borehole through the Antarctic ice sheet (Gow and others, 1968) and has been further discussed by Hollin (1969a, 1970) and Hughes (1970).

It seems likely that the long-period glacial cycles of the late Tertiary were produced by fluctuations in the Antarctic ice sheet, perhaps in accord with Wilson's theory. But until about 3 m.y. ago, the buffering effect of the oceans upon world climate prevented glaciations outside Antarctica except in coastal Alaska (Denton and Armstrong, 1969). Bandy (1968, p. 72), working in the Southern Hemisphere, observed that

> In addition to the classic expansions of polar planktonic foraminiferal faunas during the Quaternary, there were earlier expansions almost as great during the Middle Pliocene and the later Miocene. The first major expansion, during the later Miocene, appears to have occurred between about 10×10^6 and 11×10^6 years ago, possibly slightly more; the Middle Pliocene expansion occurred between about 5×10^6 and 7×10^6 years ago, and the Classic Pleistocene commenced about 3×10^6 years ago or perhaps slightly earlier.

I consider it likely that the early Pleistocene and earlier Tertiary mountain glaciations throughout the world were a response to worldwide cooling caused by advances of the Antarctic ice sheet. All Cenozoic glaciations prior to the Günz and Nebraskan are included.

The observed general synchroneity of Quaternary montane glaciations throughout the world with the northern continental ice sheets (and of the ice sheets with each other) can be explained by the cooling effects of the ice sheets and the oceans upon the atmosphere. This would suggest that whereas continental ice sheets as a group respond primarily to changes in precipitation and tend to control their own temperature, mountain glaciers and small icecaps may respond much more to external temperature changes, as well as to precipitation. And whereas continental ice sheets greatly affect the world climate, mountain glaciers are more passive and are controlled by the climate.

CONTINENTAL GLACIATIONS IN THE NORTHERN HEMISPHERE

Not until the Nebraskan and Günz is there strong evidence for continental glaciations in the Northern Hemisphere. I suggest that these glaciations owe their existence to a different mechanism than the earlier ones.

As the oceans cooled during the Tertiary, their warming effect upon the subarctic regions diminished. Eventually a point was reached after which the combination of a reduced warming effect of the oceans on the subarctic and major radiation minima of the earth-insolation curve (Milankovitch, 1941; Broecker, 1966; Kukla, 1972) permitted the development of perennial snowfields over large areas in the subarctic.

As in the Antarctic, the development of a perennial snowfield in the Northern Hemisphere increased the planetary albedo and lowered T_{eq}. Because of the thermal behavior of the oceans (table 1), the surface temperature of the oceans before the development of the perennial snowfields must have been either equal to or only slightly below T_{eq}. Therefore, the lowering of T_{eq} produced by the development of the perennial snowfields must have resulted in $T > T_{eq}$.

Now, when $T > T_{eq}$, the earth must cool. The landmasses, particularly in the areas of perennial snowfields, will cool rapidly, but the oceans cannot. The immediate result is a strong energy gradient between the oceans and the snowfields. To regain thermal equilibrium, heat must be transferred from the oceans to the snowfields, and the most effective mechanism for doing this is the transport of energy as latent heat. Water and energy are removed from the warm oceans and transported to the snowfields. The water precipitates as snow, and the latent heat is released and radiated to space, cooling the earth; continental ice sheets develop, and the nourishment process continues until T_{eq} changes, thermal equilibrium is reached, or the warm ocean waters are isolated from the surface.

The energy source for the intensified circulation necessary to nourish continental ice sheets is the heat stored in the oceans during the previous interglacial or nonglacial period, as originally proposed by Stokes (1955). There is no stable mode of atmospheric circulation which nourishes middle-latitude continental ice sheets, as Broecker (1966) has suggested; rather, rapid growth of ice sheets occurs during periods of major disequilibrium in the energy budget of the earth, when $T > T_{eq}$. The rate of nourishment of the ice sheets depends upon the energy gradient between the continental ice sheets and the oceans and will gradually diminish as the oceans cool.

If glaciers are nourished by the process of latent-heat transport across an energy gradient, then orographic barriers will have a strong effect upon the patterns of nourishment. Moist air cannot cross mountain ranges without losing much of its moisture and releasing its latent heat. Large mountain ranges between the continental ice sheets and warm oceans will partly isolate the icecaps from those oceans as moisture sources. This explains, in part, why the Atlantic Ocean appears to have been much more important than the Pacific in nourishing the ice sheets of the Northern Hemisphere. The Pacific is bordered by high mountain ranges around much of its northern periphery, making it difficult for large amounts of latent heat to escape from the Pacific basin, especially eastward in the direction of the prevailing atmospheric circulation.

This mechanism provides a solution to the problem of how to fuel an intensified circulation without warming the polar regions and thereby creating conditions inimical to glaciation. The heat stored in the oceans is a special energy source that can contribute substantially to the global energy budget only when the earth is rapidly cooling.

Ice sheet growth

If continental ice sheets, once started, are nourished as outlined above, then their pattern of growth may be predicted. If the rate of ablation is assumed to be some monotonic function of the rate of nourishment there must be some equilibrium area, A_{eq}, and cross-sectional convexity, C_{eq}, at which the mass budget of the ice sheet would be zero, accumulation would balance ablation, and the surface slope of the ice sheet would maintain just enough flow for these conditions to persist. The convexity of the profile may be taken to be some function of the surface slope of the ice sheet. In figure 1, a schematic representation of A_{eq}, the actual area of the ice sheet, A, and the actual convexity of its profile, C, are plotted against time for the early part of a glacial interval. A similar approach has been used by Šegota (1963).

The rate of nourishment of the ice sheet will be greatest fairly early in its history, when the energy gradient between the oceans and ice sheet is at its maximum. The rate of nourishment will then slowly decline as the oceans cool. The equilibrium area of the ice sheet, A_{eq}, will behave in a parallel fashion, as it is assumed to be a function of the rate of nourishment.

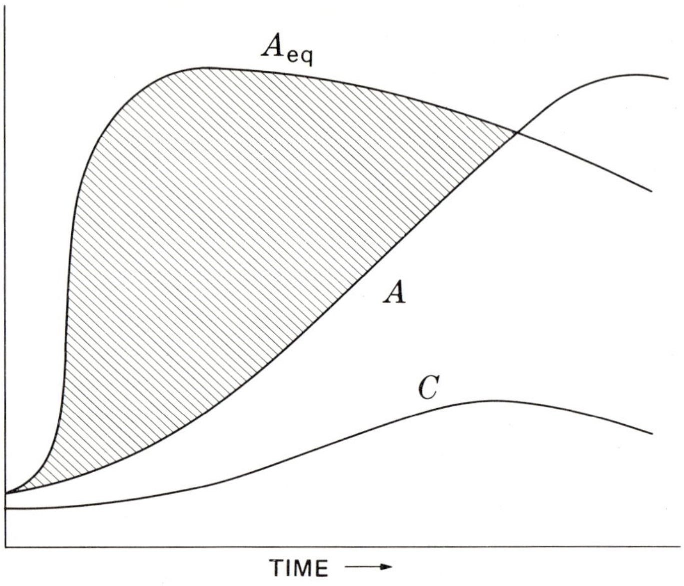

Figure 1.—Postulated relations between equilibrium area, A_{eq}; actual area of ice sheet, A; and actual convexity of the profile, C; plotted against time for the early part of a glacial interval. Scales are deliberately unspecified.

The actual size of the ice sheet, A, cannot reach A_{eq} for some time, for there is a lag in the transfer of water from the oceans onto the glacier. While $A_{eq}>A$, the ice sheet will have a positive mass budget, as indicated by the shaded area on figure 1. The response of an ice sheet to a positive mass budget is to increase the convexity of its surface, C, so as to flow more rapidly. While $A_{eq} > A$, $dC/dt > 0$, and C will attain its maximum value when $A = A_{eq}$ for the first time. But at that point, $C > C_{eq}$. As the rate of flow of the ice sheet is controlled by C, the ice sheet will continue to advance beyond A_{eq}, overextending itself. The response time for this overextension will be less than the time required for ice to pass through the glacier, for the oversteepening of the ice surface will propagate as a kinematic wave, as described by Nye (1960; 1963a, b; 1965).

The relations plotted on figure 1 suggest that, for the proposed pattern of nourishment, it is not possible for an ice sheet smaller than A_{eq} simply to grow to equilibrium size; rather, it must overshoot the mark to some degree because of the lag time between the increase in area and the corresponding adjustment of the convexity of the ice sheet to an equilibrium state. The convexity must increase as long as the mass budget is positive, and the rate of flow is a function of the convexity. Hence the profile of the ice sheet when A_{eq} is first reached must be the profile of an advancing glacier, rather than an equilibrium profile. Equilibrium can be reached only by an overextension of the ice sheet, followed by a melting back until $A = A_{eq}$ and $C = C_{eq}$. The degree of overextension will depend upon the rapidity of growth of the ice sheet.

The overextension of continental ice sheets is supported by the record of stagnation of the margins of continental ice sheets, as in Minnesota and North Dakota, where stagnant ice developed both at the end of the Wisconsin and between glacial advances (Wright and Ruhe, 1965; Florin and Wright, 1969; Clayton, 1967).

The role of melt water

The proposed overextension of ice sheets is important here because it will result in the production of large volumes of melt water within a fairly short time interval, and the way in which that melt water returns to the sea will have a critical effect upon the subsequent history of the glaciation.

Because the Pacific Ocean is largely isolated from the Northern Hemisphere continental ice sheets by mountain ranges, glaciations in the Northern Hemisphere are fueled by evaporation from the Atlantic Ocean. The effects felt there during glacial growth are a mixing and cooling of the surface layers of the ocean and an increase in salinity. Both the decrease in temperature and the increase in salinity will increase the density of the surface water and promote overturning.

When melt water is added to the oceans, the position it assumes is controlled by the relative densities of the melt water and sea water. It seems likely that the large volumes of glacial melt water, with a low density resulting from low salinity, returned to the oceans as surface water, rather than as bottom or intermediate water. I arrived at this conclusion while working on an early version of this paper (Adam, 1969). Olausson (1969; Olausson and Jonasson, 1969) independently reached the same conclusion in his "meltwater contamination theory," in attempting to reconcile the foraminiferal and O^{16}/O^{18} records for the Würm/Flandrian transition in the North Atlantic. Other workers have also discussed this problem (Weyl, 1968; Mercer, 1969b; Rasool and Hogan, 1969; Mandich, 1970).

The effects of a surface layer of melt water would be most strongly felt in the North Atlantic, for two reasons: (1) the most pronounced density changes would occur in the Atlantic, for it is the source of most of the moisture transferred to the ice sheets and hence the region of the greatest salinity and temperature changes; and (2) some 75 percent (Olausson, 1969) to 95 percent (Emiliani, 1955) of the melt water from the Northern Hemisphere continental ice sheets flowed into the North Atlantic, either directly or through the Gulf of Mexico, the Arctic Ocean, or the Mediterranean. Area figures given by Schott (1942) and von Arx (1962) indicate that the Atlantic Ocean north of the Equator, including peripheral seas, is about one-sixth the area of the total world oceans. If all the melt water entering the Atlantic spread uniformly over the surface, each 1-m rise of sea level would produce a surface layer of water from 4½ to nearly 6 m thick.

When a layer of relatively cool, fresh water overlies warmer, more saline water, the resulting lamination and stratification of the water column is very stable, as has been shown experimentally by Turner and Stommel (1964). Their experimental setup was analogous to that proposed for the ocean, except that they maintained a temperature gradient by heating their water column from beneath, whereas for a cooling ocean the gradient would be maintained by the removal of heat at the surface. They observed that the layering is very stable because the diffusivity of salt in sea water is very much lower than the conductivity of heat; because salt cannot enter the surface layer readily, the density difference can be maintained even though heat is transferred across the interface rapidly.

The behavior of a surface layer depends upon whether it is warmed primarily from the top or from the bottom. If the ocean is not cool enough that its surface temperature is near T_{eq}, then the introduction of a relatively fresh, cool layer of surface water will partially isolate the oceanic heat source from the atmosphere and reduce the rate of nourishment of the ice sheets, resulting in an interstadial period for the continental glaciers.

The proposed state of the North Atlantic during an interstadial is shown in figure 2. Heat is transferred from the warm, subsurface oceanic layers to the atmosphere only after passing through the surface water layer. Convection takes place within the surface layer and within the deeper layer, but because of the density discontinuity between the two layers, there is little or no physical transfer of water from one layer to the other. Heat moves into the surface layer by conduction; this requires that the surface layer be somewhat cooler than the deeper layer, for otherwise no heat transfer would take place. Eventually, mixing and diffusion at the base of the surface layer and evaporation at its surface will raise the salinity of the top layer to the point at which it becomes dense enough to mix with deeper water. This brings the warm water to the surface again, ending the interstadial period. The length of the interstadial depends upon the thickness of the layer of surface water formed in the Atlantic and the temperature of the deeper water.

An interstadial is thus characterized by a surface layer of water warmed primarily from beneath, as heat is transferred from the warm ocean to the continental ice sheets. The ocean still provides, in addition to current solar radiation, the extra energy necessary to maintain the ice sheets, but the size of the ice sheets is smaller than when warm ocean water is present at the air-sea interface.

The end of a glacial interval occurs when the energy gradient between the deeper water and the surface is not great enough to fuel convective overturning of the surface layer. The rate of nourishment then drops below the rate necessary to maintain continental ice sheets. They shrink, the planetary albedo drops, and T_{eq} rises. The oceanic surface layer warms from the top, producing the rapid warming of the oceans observed at the beginning of interglacial intervals (Broecker and others, 1960; Broecker and Van Donk, 1970).

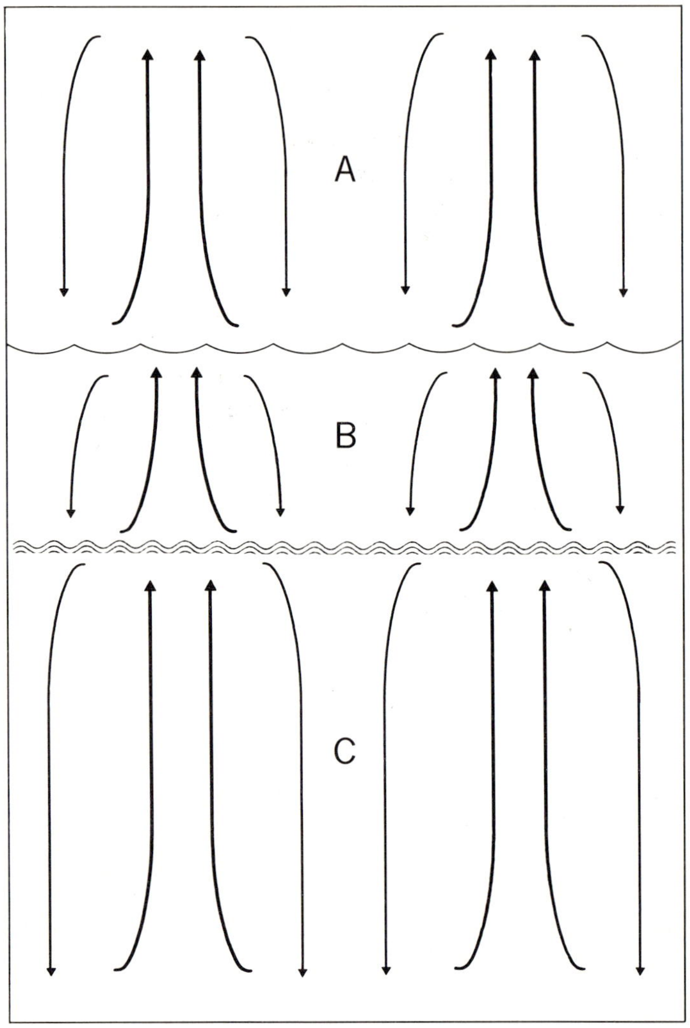

Figure 2.—Presumed cross section of the upper part of the North Atlantic Ocean during an interstadial period. A, atmosphere; B, glacial melt water, with lower salinity, temperature, and density than C; C, sea water. Heavy arrows represent warm, rising limbs of convective cells.

At the beginning of an interglacial interval, the heating of the surface layer of the ocean is restricted to a thin layer because of the initially low salinity of the surface water and the consequent high stability of the water column. Because of this high stability, the surface layer may attain a higher temperature than would be possible if mixing were to a greater depth. This condition cannot long obtain, for the salinity of the surface layer increases as salt diffuses from the bottom to concentrate within the surface layer by evaporation. When the surface layer becomes dense enough that mixing occurs with the colder water beneath it, then the surface temperature will decrease. This may explain the postglacial climatic optimum and the subsequent temperature decline.

The trigger factor

A necessary but not sufficient condition for continental glaciation is that the warming of the subarctic by the oceans must not be so great as to prevent the forming of snowfields. For this reason, the movement of Antarctica into a polar position during the Tertiary may be regarded as triggering the Pleistocene as a whole. Within the Pleistocene, the individual glaciations required some triggering mechanism, and this is the trigger factor discussed here.

The point of departure for most theories of glaciation has been the trigger factor, some combination of events that causes a glaciation to commence. This paper has developed a model for what goes on within a glaciation. If this mechanism is correct, then the trigger factor may be defined as a combination of conditions that permits a perennial snow cover to develop in the subarctic. Two theories of glaciation seem to offer plausible trigger factors: (1) the variations in incoming energy as a result of the orbital characteristics of the earth (Croll, 1875; Milankovitch, 1941; Emiliani and Geiss, 1957; Broecker, 1966; Kukla, 1969; Evans, 1971), and (2) the Ewing and Donn theory, which involves repeated freezing and thawing of the Arctic Ocean (Ewing and Donn, 1956, 1958; Donn and Ewing, 1966).

An open Arctic Ocean at first glance seems attractive as a triggering agent. It is reasonable to assume that the Arctic Ocean has not always been frozen; yet it is frozen now. The question is: Has it repeatedly frozen and thawed, and, if it has, were these changes sufficient to initiate glacial and (or) interglacial intervals?

As a logical consequence of the model proposed, the increased heat storage in the Atlantic during interglacial periods would be expected to eventually thaw the Arctic Ocean, if the interglacial lasted long enough. The open Arctic would then provide an increase in snowfall in the subarctic, permitting a perennial snow cover to develop.

While an open Arctic Ocean seems quite possible as a trigger factor, it does complicate the model, because the opening of the Arctic would decrease the planetary albedo and raise T_{eq}. This would require the development of a much larger perennial snowfield before a glaciation would commence, for the required condition is that $T_{eq} < T$. It would also seem necessary to require that the Arctic Ocean freeze over before the first interstadial, for if it did not, the interstadial decrease in size of the continental ice sheets could lower the planetary albedo to the point at which the ice sheets would disappear. Donn and Ewing (1966), in the latest version of their theory, have taken the position that the Arctic does freeze over soon after glaciation is triggered.

If an open Arctic Ocean is the trigger for continental glaciation, certain constraints are imposed upon the model that we cannot be certain are satisfied. It would be preferable to trigger continental glaciation without requiring an open Arctic.

The earth-insolation curve offers a reasonable trigger factor that does not require an open Arctic Ocean. In one recent form (Broecker, 1966), maxima and minima of summer insolation around lat 65° N. are presumed to trigger changes in the climate of the earth between glacial and nonglacial modes, which are presumed to be stable. The model presented here differs in that the glacial mode of circulation is self-limiting.

It is probable that the radiation curve can rarely switch the earth's climate to a cooling mode; once a continental ice sheet becomes established, changes in the planetary albedo produced by changes in the ice cover will be of much greater magnitude than the changes resulting from the influence of the earth-insolation curve. Once a glaciation is triggered, its subsequent course is largely independent of the earth-insolation curve.

A great attraction of the earth-insolation hypothesis is that it has a built-in time scale and is therefore subject to testing by various dating methods. Recent work by Broecker and his associates (Broecker, 1966; Broecker and Thurber, 1965; Broecker and others, 1968; Mesolella and others, 1969; Broecker and van Donk, 1970; see also Kukla, 1972; Emiliani, 1958, 1966; Evans, 1971) has provided considerable evidence in support of Milankovitch's theory. The theory proposed here, if correct, would indicate why: the summer insolation minima at lat 65° N. are able to trigger glaciations by decreasing the summer snowmelt sufficiently to permit the development of perennial snowfields.

NORTHERN VERSUS SOUTHERN HEMISPHERES

If the model proposed is valid, we are left with the esthetically unpleasing situation of two separate, and largely independent, causes for Cenozoic glaciations: (1) advances of the Antarctic ice sheet, possibly in accord with Wilson's theory, and probably most active during the initial late Cenozoic glaciations; and (2) a combination of cool oceanic surface temperatures (relative to, say, the Mesozoic) and minima of the Milankovitch radiation curve at subarctic latitudes permitting the development of perennial snowfields. In either case, the planetary albedo will rise and the earth will cool. Growth of the Antarctic ice sheet is limited by the ocean surrounding it.

An interesting asymmetry is present; a major Antarctic glacial advance would probably cause the formation of perennial snowfields and continental ice sheets in the Northern Hemisphere, but the formation of Northern Hemisphere ice sheets would either have no effect on the Antarctic ice or actually cause it to recede, because the cooling of the oceans would decrease the temperature contrast between the ice and the oceans. The Antarctic ice sheet should be largest at the end of Northern Hemisphere interglacials, assuming the rate of nourishment of the ice sheet to be greatest when the surrounding oceans are warmest. The retreats of the Antarctic ice should precede retreats elsewhere in the world by some thousands of years, unless the response time of the Antarctic ice is much longer than the response times of the Northern Hemisphere glaciers.

GREENLAND

The role of the Greenland icecap during the Pleistocene is not clearly implied by this model. However, the persistence of Greenland ice during interglacial periods can be inferred, as the ice is held in by mountains around much of its periphery and is therefore unable to overextend itself ($A > A_{eq}$) as readily as other northern continental ice sheets. The response time of the Greenland ice sheet is presumably much longer than the response time for ice sheets that flowed over fairly flat surfaces and is probably much longer than the period of the oscillations of the margins of other ice sheets. Granted that the present existence of the Greenland ice also depends strongly upon its proximity to a good moisture source, had the response time of the ice sheet been shorter and its bed flatter, it probably would have disappeared with the other Northern Hemisphere continental ice sheets at the end of the Wisconsin.

FURTHER IMPLICATIONS

The implications of this theory are of great interest, for the changes in the vertical circulation of the Atlantic Ocean and the development of layering produced by glacial melt water have not been generally considered as possibilities. It is difficult to demonstrate past changes in the vertical circulation of the oceans except under special circumstances.

One such special case is the Mediterranean Sea. Bradley (1938) proposed that the deep waters of the eastern Mediterranean should stagnate during times of high glacial runoff, because relatively fresh, cool melt water would prevent oxygenated surface water from sinking and ventilating the closed basins, as happens now (Wüst, 1961). Olausson (1961) has shown that this is indeed so in a very good discussion of the layering problem. The present stratification of the Black Sea (Caspers, 1957) and the Arctic Ocean (Donn and Ewing, 1966; Neal and others, 1969; Neshyba and others, 1971) demonstrates that very stable stratification may occur in large water bodies. It seems likely that, given a sufficient influx of melt water, similar layering could persist in the North Atlantic for time intervals on the order of a few hundred to a few thousand years.

Support for greater convective overturning of the upper portion of the Atlantic during times of glacial growth and oceanic cooling is found in the Cariaco Trench, which is now stagnant at depth but was ventilated during full-glacial time (Adam, 1971).

The surface layers formed by melt water need not have been of very low salinity. Considerable mixing with sea water must have occurred during their formation, and the only requirement is that the temperature and salinity were such that the surface layer was distinctly less dense.

If glacial melt water did contribute significantly to the surface water of the Atlantic and was restricted from mixing with the rest of the ocean by a density stratification, then, as Olausson (1969) has pointed out, some of the assumptions concerning the original oxygen-isotope composition of the surface water must be reexamined.

Another salient implication is that, with present geography and with the sun as the only energy source, the earth cannot sustain equilibrium continental glaciation except at very high latitudes, as in Antarctica, and possibly in Greenland, where the configuration of the bed gives the glacier a very long response time. Continental glaciations of the Northern Hemisphere require an additional energy source for their nourishment, for they take place largely at latitudes below the Arctic Circle, where ablational losses are large. As continental glaciations did occur, these large ablational losses must have been overbalanced by even greater rates of accumulation.

Because the available heat stored in the oceans is limited, continental glaciation in the Northern Hemisphere is a self-limiting process, and because the continental ice sheets and the oceans control the climate of the rest of the world, cold intervals are of limited duration.

Patterns of behavior that may be expected of the model presented here can be predicted and compared with known events. For example, temperature records should show rather even temperatures during interglacial intervals. The onset of glaciation should be marked by a gradual, oscillating decrease in temperature that persists until reversed by a sudden rise in temperature at the beginning of the next interglacial. Such patterns are displayed in the oxygen-isotope paleotemperature curves of many deep-sea cores, such as those given by Emiliani (1966). Of even greater interest here is the curve prepared by Šegota (1967) as a synthesis of temperature data from both oceanic and continental records. This curve, reproduced here as figure 3, clearly shows the pattern of temperature changes to be expected from this model. A similar curve has recently been prepared by Broecker and van Donk (1970).

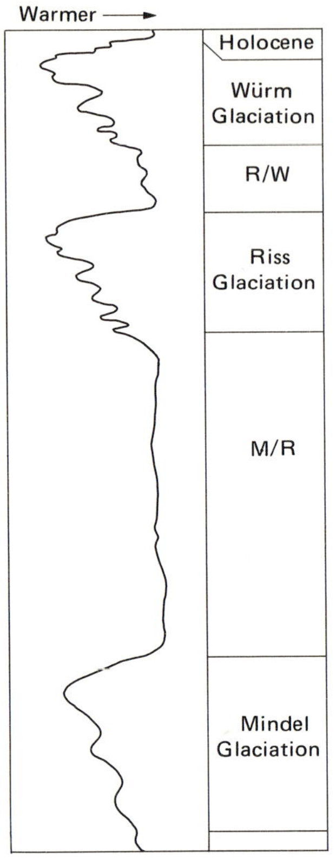

Figure 3.—Generalized paleotemperature curve for northern Europe, according to Segota (1967, fig. 3).

In addition to requiring the greatest cooling at the end of a glacial interval, the model predicts the wettest part of a glacial interval to be at the onset of the glaciation, when the rate of evaporation from the oceans is at a maximum. This pattern is expected to show up on a smaller scale during stadials. For example, Butzer (1957) has concluded from his studies of cave deposits in the Mediterranean that this pattern does obtain. The early Würm deposits in several widely separated caves are characterized by stalagmitic horizons, whereas main and late Würm deposits lack heavy stalagmitic layers but contain frost-cracked limestone fragments. Butzer interprets this sequence, which is cross-dated among several caves by artifact assemblages, to indicate a very wet, relatively warm early Würm followed by progressive cooling and drying until the beginning of the Holocene.

A similar pattern has been described in Siberia by Giterman and Golubeva (1967), who distinguish three stages of vegetational development within a "typical glacial interval." The period of glacial advance is very wet, and tundra and forest develop; the middle of the glaciation is characterized by xerophytic plants, such as *Artemisia*, *Ephedra*, and chenopods; and the period of glacial retreat is intermediate in climate between the first two phases.

It is of interest that the pluvial history in the Western United States does not seem to follow this pattern. The latest overflow of Lake Bonneville, an event which surely indicates wet conditions, occurred shortly before 12,000 years ago (Bright, 1966). Smith (1968) believes that the Searles Lake basin overflowed as late as 10,500 years ago; however, conditions of maximum wetness in the Searles Lake drainage system were marked by overflow not only of Searles Lake but also of the Panamint basin, the next basin downstream. Little is known of the times of overflow of the Panamint basin.

I attribute the difference between the Great Basin climatic record and the records from the Mediterranean and Siberia to the influence of the Pacific Ocean, the water source for rainfall and glaciation in the Far West. As the Pacific did not cool as much as the Atlantic during glacial intervals, its effectiveness as a moisture source did not decline during the later phases of glaciation. The degree of pluviosity in the Great Basin should depend upon the temperature gradient between the Pacific and the major continental ice sheets. If the temperature of the Pacific changed little, then the degree of pluviosity would depend primarily on the size of the ice sheets and the amount of radiational cooling that they produced.

The model presented would accomplish the nourishment of the ice sheets primarily from the south, a condition recognized as necessary by Donn and Ewing (1966) and by Lamb (1969; Lamb and Woodroffe, 1970). Most of the snow feeding the ice sheets would fall around the edge of the glacier, but nourishment of the interior of the ice sheet could be accomplished by the mechanism proposed by Bergeron (1965). Low-pressure cells over ice sheets produce loose, fresh snow, easily drifted toward the interior of the ice sheet; when high-pressure cells are present and winds are blowing outward from the interior, the snow surface is older, more consolidated, and resistant to wind erosion. Because snow drifts more readily toward the interior of the ice sheet than away from it, the ice sheet is able to maintain itself.

REFERENCES CITED

Adam, D. P., 1969, Ice ages and the thermal equilibrium of the earth: Arizona Univ., Tucson, Geochronology Dept. Interim Research Rept. 15, 26 p.

——1971, Palaeoclimatic significance of the stagnation of the Cariaco trench: Nature, v. 232, no. 5311, p. 469.

Bandy, O. L., 1968, Cycles in Neogene paleoceanography and eustatic changes: Palaeogeography, Palaeoclimatology, Palaeoecology, v. 5, p. 63–75.

Bergeron, Tor, 1965, The possible role of snowdrift in building up high inland icesheets, *in* M. Sears, ed., Progress in oceanography, v. 3: Oxford, Pergamon Press, p. 385–390.

Bradley, W. H., 1938, Mediterranean sediments and Pleistocene sea levels: Science, v. 88, no. 2286, p. 376–379.

Bright, R. C., 1966, Pollen and seed stratigraphy of Swan Lake, southeastern Idaho—its relation to regional vegetational history and to Lake Bonneville history: Tebiwa, v. 9, no. 2, p. 1–47.

Broecker, W. S., 1966, Absolute dating and the astronomical theory of glaciation: Science, v. 151, no. 3708, p. 299–304.

Broecker, W. S., Ewing, Maurice, and Heezen, B. C., 1960, Evidence for an abrupt change in climate close to 11,000 years ago: Am. Jour. Sci., v. 258, p. 429–448.

Broecker, W. S., and Thurber, D. L., 1965, Uranium-series dating of corals and oolites from Bahaman and Florida Key limestones: Science, v. 149, no. 3679, p. 58–60.

Broecker, W. S., Thurber, D. L., Goddard, J., Ku, T., Matthews, R. K., and Mesolella, K. J., 1968, Milankovitch hypothesis supported by precise dating of coral reefs and deep-sea sediments: Science, v. 159, no. 3812, p. 297–300.

Broecker, W. S., and van Donk, Jan, 1970, Insolation changes, ice volumes, and the O^{18} record in deep-sea cores: Rev. Geophysics and Space Physics, v. 8, no. 1, p. 169–198.

Brooks, C. E. P., 1949, Climate through the ages: London, Ernest Benn, 395 p.

Budyko, M. I., 1969, The effect of solar radiation variations on the climate of the earth: Tellus, v. 21, p. 611–619.

Butzer, K. W., 1957, Mediterranean pluvials and the general circulation of the Pleistocene: Geog. Annaler, v. 39, no. 1, p. 48–53.

Caspers, Hubert, 1957, Black Sea and Sea of Azov: Geol. Soc. America Mem. 67, v. 1, p. 801–890.

Chappell, J., 1968, Changing duration of glacial cycles from Lower to Upper Pleistocene: Nature, v. 219, p. 36–40.

Charlesworth, J. K., 1957, The Quaternary era: London, Edward Arnold Ltd., 2 v., 1,700 p.

Clayton, Lee, 1967, Stagnant-glacier features of the Missouri Coteau in North Dakota, *in* Clayton, Lee, and Freers, T. F., eds., Glacial geology of the Missouri Coteau and adjacent areas: North Dakota Geol. Survey Misc. Ser. 30, p. 25–46.

Croll, James, 1875, Climate and time in their geological relations—a theory of secular changes in the earth's climate: New York, D. Appleton and Co., 577 p.

Crowell, J. C., and Frakes, L. A., 1970, Phanerozoic glaciation and the causes of ice ages: Am. Jour. Sci., v. 268, p. 193–224.

Curry, R. R., 1966, Glaciation about 3,000,000 years ago in the Sierra Nevada: Science, v. 154, no. 3750, p. 770–771.

Damon, P. E., 1968, The relationship between terrestrial factors and climate: Meteorol. Mons., v. 8, no. 30, p. 106–111.

Denton, G. H., and Armstrong, R. L., 1969, Miocene-Pliocene glaciations in southern Alaska: Am. Jour. Sci., v. 267, p. 1121–1142.

Denton, G. H., Armstrong, R. L., and Stuiver, M., 1971, The Late Cenozoic glacial history of Antarctica, *in* Turekian, K. K., ed., The Late Cenozoic glacial ages: New Haven, Conn., Yale Univ. Press, p. 267–306.

Donn, W. L., and Ewing, Maurice, 1966, A theory of ice ages, III: Science, v. 152, no. 3730, p. 1706–1712.

Einarsson, Thorleifur, Hopkins, D. M., and Doell, R. R., 1967, A stratigraphy of Tjornes, northern Iceland, and the history of the Bering land bridge, *in* Hopkins, D. M., ed., The Bering land bridge: Stanford, Calif., Stanford Univ. Press, p. 312–325.

Embleton, Clifford, and King, C. A. M., 1968, Glacial and periglacial geomorphology: New York, St. Martin's Press, 608 p.

Emiliani, Cesare, 1954, Temperatures of Pacific bottom waters and polar superficial waters during the Tertiary: Science, v. 119, no. 3103, p. 853–855.

——1955, Pleistocene temperatures: Jour. Geology, v. 63, p. 538–578.

——1958, Ancient temperatures: Sci. American, v. 198, no. 2, p. 54–63.

——1966, Isotopic paleotemperatures: Science, v. 154, no. 3751, p. 851–857.

Emiliani, Cesare, and Geiss, J., 1957, On glaciations and their causes: Geol. Rundschau, v. 46, p. 576–601.

Evans, Percy, 1971, Towards a Pleistocene time-scale, Pt. 2 of the Phanerozoic Time-scale—A supplement: Geol. Soc. London Spec. Pub. 5, p. 123–356.

Ewing, Maurice, and Donn, W. L., 1956, A theory of ice ages [Pt. 1]: Science, v. 123, no. 3207, p. 1061–1066.

——1958, A theory of ice ages [Pt.] 2; Science, v. 127, no. 3307, p. 1159–1162.

Flint, R. F., 1971, Glacial and Quaternary geology: New York, John Wiley, 892 p.

Flohn, H., 1969, Ein geophysikalisches Eiszeit-Modell: Eiszeitalter u. Gegenwart, v. 20, p. 204–231.

Florin, Maj-Britt, and Wright, H. E., Jr., 1969, Diatom evidence for the persistence of stagnant glacial ice in Minnesota: Geol. Soc. America Bull., v. 80, p. 695–704.

Frakes, L. A., and Kemp, E. M., 1972, Influence of continental positions on Early Tertiary climates: Nature, v. 240, p. 97–100.

Giterman, R. E., and Golubeva, L. V., 1967, Vegetation of eastern Siberia during the Anthropogene period, *in* Hopkins, D. M., ed., The Bering land bridge: Stanford, Calif., Stanford Univ. Press, p. 232–244.

Gould, L. M., 1940, Glaciers of Antarctica: Am. Philos. Soc. Proc., v. 82, p. 835–877.

Gow, A. J., Ueda, H. T., and Garfield, D. E., 1968, Antarctic ice sheet—preliminary results of first core hole to bedrock: Science, v. 161, no. 3845, p. 1011–1013.

Hollin, J. T., 1969a, Ice-sheet surges and the geological record: Canadian Jour. Earth Sci., v. 6, no. 4, pt. 2, p. 903–910.

——1969b, The antarctic ice sheet and the Quaternary history of Antarctica, *in* van Zinderen Bakker, E. M., ed., Palaeoecology of Africa and Antarctica: Capetown, Balkema, p. 109–138.

——1970, Antarctic ice surges: Antarctic Jour. U.S., v. 5, no. 5, p. 155–156.

Hopkins, D. M., 1972, Changes in oceanic circulations and Late Cenozoic cold climates: Internat. Geol. Cong., 24th, Montreal 1972, Abstracts, p. 370.

Hughes, T., 1970, Convection in the antarctic ice sheet leading to a surge of the ice sheet and possibly to a new ice age: Science, v. 170, p. 630–633.

Kent, D., Opdyke, N. D., and Ewing, Maurice, 1971, Climate change in the north Pacific using ice-rafted detritus as a climatic indicator: Geol. Soc. America Bull., v. 82, p. 2741–2754.

Kukla, J., 1969, The cause of the Holocene climate change: Geologie en Mijnbouw, v. 48, no. 3, p. 307–334.

——1972, Insolation and glacials: Boreas, v. 1, no. 1, p. 63–96.

Lamb, H. H.,1969, Investigation of the climatic sequence: a meteorological-empirical approach, *in* van Zinderen Bakker, E. M., ed., Palaeoecology of Africa and Antarctica: Capetown, Balkema, p. 21–63.

Lamb, H. H., and Woodroffe, A., 1970, Atmospheric circulation during the last ice age: Quaternary Research, v. 1, no. 1, p. 29–58.

LePichon, Xavier, and Heirtzler, J. R., 1968, Magnetic anomalies in the Indian Ocean and sea-floor spreading: Jour. Geophys. Research, v. 73, p. 2101–2117.

Mandich, P. A., 1970, Comment on some ice age theories: Quartär, v. 20, p. 127–134.

Matthews, W. H., and Curtis, G. H., 1966, Date of the Pliocene-Pleistocene boundary in New Zealand: Nature, v. 212, p. 979–980.

Mercer, J. H., 1969a, Glaciation in southern Argentina more than two million years ago: Science, v. 164, p. 823–825.

——1969b, The Allerød oscillation—a European climatic anomaly?: Arctic and Alpine Research, v. 1, no. 4, p. 227–234.

Mesolella, K. J., Matthews, R. K., Broecker, W. S., and Thurber, D. L., 1969, The astronomical theory of climatic change—Barbados data: Jour. Geology, v. 77, p. 250–274.

Milankovitch, M., 1941, Kanon der Erdbestrahlung und seine Anwendung auf das Eiszeitenproblem: Kgl. Serbische Akad. Spec. Pub. 132 (Belgrade, Yugoslavia) [English translation: Canon of Insolation and the iceage problem: U.S. Dept. Commerce, Israel Program for Scientific Translations, Jerusalem, 1969, 484 p.]

Mitchell, J. M., Jr., ed., 1968, Causes of climatic change: Meteorol. Mons., v. 8, no. 30, 159 p.

Neal, V. T., Neshyba, Steve, and Denner, Warren, 1969, Thermal stratification in the Arctic Ocean: Science, v. 166, p. 373–374.

Neshyba, Steve, Neal, V. T., and Denner, Warren, 1971, Temperature and conductivity measurements under ice island T-3: Jour. Geophys. Research, v. 76, no. 33, p. 8107–8120.

Nye, J. F., 1960, The response of glaciers and ice-sheets to seasonal and climatic changes: Royal Soc. [London], Proc. Ser. A, v. 256, no. 1287, p. 559–584.

——1963a, The response of a glacier to changes in the rate of nourishment and wastage: Royal Soc. [London] Proc. Ser. A., v. 275, no. 1360, p. 87–112.

——1963b, On the theory of the advance and retreat of glaciers: Royal Astron. Soc. Geophys. Jour., v. 7, no. 4, p. 431–456.

——1965, The frequency response of glaciers: Jour. Glaciology, v. 5, no. 41, p. 567–587.

Olausson, Eric, 1961, Sediment cores from the Mediterranean Sea and the Red Sea: Swedish Deep-Sea Exped., 1947–1948, Repts., v. 8, fascicle IV, p. 337–391.

——1969, On the Würm-Flandrian boundary in deep-sea cores: Geologie en Mijnbouw, v. 48, no. 3, p. 349–361.

Olausson, Eric, and Jonasson, U. C., 1969, The Arctic Ocean during the Würm and early Flandrian: Geologiska Fören. Stockholm Förh, v. 91, p. 185–200.

Rasool, S. I., and Hogan, J. S., 1969, Ocean circulation and climatic changes: Am. Meteorol. Soc. Bull., v. 50, no. 3, p. 130–134.

Ruddiman, W. F., Tolderlund, D. S., and Bé, A. W. H., 1970, Foraminiferal evidence of a modern warming of the North Atlantic Ocean: Deep-Sea Research, v. 17, p. 141–155.

Rutford, R. H., Craddock, Campbell, and Bastien, T. W., 1968, Late Tertiary glaciation and sea-level changes in Antarctica: Palaeogeography, Palaeoclimatology, Palaeoecology, v. 5, p. 15–39.

Schott, Gerhard, 1942, Geographie des atlantischen Ozeans, 3d ed.: Hamburg, C. Boysen Verlag, 438 p.

Schwarzbach, Martin, 1963, Climates of the past; An introduction to paleoclimatology [translated and edited by R. O. Muir]: Princeton and London, Van Nostrand, 328 p.

Segota, Tomislav, 1963, Geografske Osnove Glacijacija: Radovi Geografskog Inst. Zagreb, v. 4, 119 p.

——1967, Paleotemperature changes in the upper and middle Pleistocene: Eiszeitalter u. Gegenwart, v. 18, p. 127–141.

Sellers, W. D., 1965, Physical climatology: Chicago, Univ. Chicago Press, 272 p.

Shapley, Harlow, ed., 1953, Climatic change: Cambridge, Mass., Harvard Univ. Press, 318 p.

Smith, G. I., 1968, Late-Quaternary geologic and climatic history of Searles Lake, southeastern California, *in* Morrison, R. B., and Wright, H. E., eds., Means of correlation of Quaternary successions—Internat. Assoc. Quaternary Research, 7th Cong., USA, 1965, Proc., v. 8: Salt Lake City, Utah Univ. Press, p. 292–310.

Stipp, J. J., Chappell, J. M. A., and McDougall, I., 1967, K/Ar age estimate of the Pliocene-Pleistocene boundary in New Zealand: Am. Jour. Sci., v. 265, p. 462–474.

Stokes, W. L., 1955, Another look at the ice age: Science, v. 122, no. 3174, p. 815–821.

Turner, J. S., and Stommel, Henry, 1964, A new case of convection in the presence of combined vertical salinity and temperature gradients: Natl. Acad. Sci. Proc., v. 52, p. 49–53.

von Arx, W. S., 1962, An introduction to physical oceanography: Reading, Mass., Addison-Wesley, 422 p.

Weyl, P. K., 1968, The role of the oceans in climatic change—A theory of the ice ages: Meteorol. Mons., v. 8, no. 30, p. 37–62.

Wilson, A. T., 1964, Origin of ice ages—An ice shelf theory for Pleistocene glaciation: Nature, v. 201, no. 4915, p. 147–149.

——1966, Variation in solar insolation to the south polar region as a trigger which induces instability in the antarctic ice sheet: Nature, v. 210, p. 477–478.

——1969, The climatic effects of large-scale surges of ice sheets: Canadian Jour. Earth Sci., v. 6, no. 4, p. 911–918.

Wright, H. E., Jr., and Ruhe, R. V., 1965, Glaciation of Minnesota and Iowa, *in* Wright, H. E., Jr., and Frey, D. G., eds., The Quaternary of the United States: Princeton, N.J., Princeton Univ. Press, p. 29–41.

Wüst, Georg, 1961, On the vertical circulation of the Mediterranean Sea: Jour. Geophys. Research, v. 66, no. 10, p. 3261–3271.

Jour. Research U.S. Geol. Survey
Vol. 1, No. 5, Sept.-Oct. 1973, p. 597—601

AQUIFER DIFFUSIVITY OF THE OHIO RIVER ALLUVIAL AQUIFER BY THE FLOOD-WAVE RESPONSE METHOD

By HAYES F. GRUBB and HAROLD H. ZEHNER, Louisville, Ky.

Abstract.—Aquifer diffusivity (T/S) was calculated for 10 sites in the alluvial aquifer adjacent to the Ohio River by observing the response of the aquifer to a flood wave in the river. The calculated type curves matched the observed aquifer response reasonably well at eight of the 10 sites. The diffusivities ranged from 0.4 ft^2 sec^{-1} to 10.3 ft^2 sec^{-1} and were generally in agreement with diffusivity values calculated from pump-test methods at two of the sites. Interference from pumping ½ mile upstream from one site and localized aquifer inhomogeneity at another site precluded calculation of diffusivity. Determining the shape of the ground-water recession curve may be difficult, but it can be done satisfactorily by collecting water-level data during an extended period of ground-water discharge and transposing the average recession curve to the flood period being analyzed. The flood-wave response method for estimating aquifer diffusivity provides a relatively inexpensive technique for obtaining a significant part of the data needed to predict the aquifer's response to river and pumping stresses.

Water withdrawal from the alluvial aquifer adjacent to the Ohio River in Kentucky in recent years has led to the need for predicting aquifer response to pumping and varied river-stage conditions. Aquifer characteristics such as transmissivity and storage coefficient are generally not available in the areas which have been developed in the last 15 years. To determine these aquifer characteristics by field pump-test methods in areas expected to be developed in the near future would be prohibitively expensive. Relatively inexpensive methods for estimating aquifer diffusivity (the ratio of transmissivity to the storage coefficient) from the observation of aquifer water levels have been described by Rorabaugh (1960), Bedinger and Reed (1964), and Pinder, Bredehoeft, and Cooper (1969). The purpose of this paper is to further demonstrate the applicability of the method described by Pinder and others and to illustrate some of the problems associated with its use as applied to the alluvial aquifer adjacent to the Ohio River in Kentucky.

Acknowledgments.—This work was done as part of the cooperative water resources investigations of Kentucky in cooperation with the Kentucky Geological Survey. We wish to thank M. I. Rorabaugh and John D. Bredehoeft for suggestions which were helpful in analyzing the data and George F. Pinder for providing a computer program for generating the theoretical type curves.

FLOOD-WAVE MODEL TYPE CURVES

The flood-wave response technique for determining aquifer diffusivity as described by Pinder, Bredehoeft, and Cooper (1969) consists of generating a series of type curves from a river-stage hydrograph which represents the predicted or theoretical aquifer response. Aquifer diffusivity is then obtained by selecting the curve which most closely approximates the observed ground-water hydrograph.

Theoretical type curves were prepared by use of the following equation:

$$h_p = \sum_{m=1}^{p} \sum_{n=1}^{\infty} (-1)^{n-1} \Delta H_m \left[\operatorname{erfc} 0.5U \left(\frac{\frac{2n-1}{X/L} - 1}{\sqrt{p-m}} \right) + \operatorname{erfc} 0.5U \left(\frac{\frac{2n-1}{X/L} + 1}{\sqrt{p-m}} \right) \right] \quad (1)$$

where

$$U = \frac{X}{\sqrt{(T/S)\Delta t}}$$

and

L = distance from the river to the impermeable boundary,
X = distance from the point where the aquifer response is observed to the impermeable boundary,
h_p = head at a distance $(L-X)$ from the river at time $\pm p\Delta t$,
H_m = instantaneous rise in stage at time $t = m\Delta t$ where m is an integer,
T/S = diffusivity of the aquifer, and
erfc = complementary error function.

Equation 1 relates the effects of river-stage fluctuations in a fully penetrating stream on the head in an isotropic and homogeneous aquifer of finite width. Initial head is assumed uniform in the aquifer. Impermeable materials are assumed to

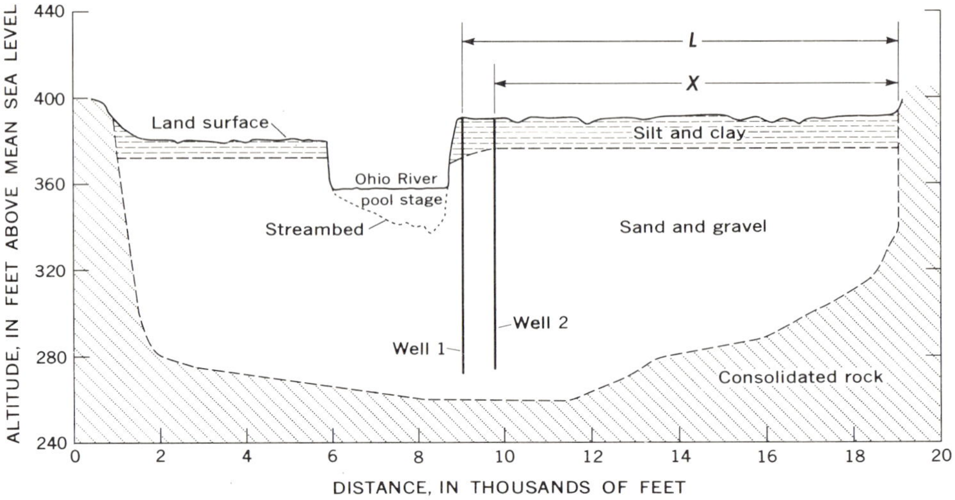

Figure 1.–Generalized cross section of the bedrock valley, showing the alluvial aquifer, the Ohio River, and the observation wells. The position of the wells relative to the river and the impermeable bedrock valley wall is indicated by L and X as defined in equation 1.

exist below the aquifer and at one side of the aquifer parallel to the stream.

Equation 1 above differs from equation 3 of Pinder, Bredehoeft, and Cooper (1969, p. 851) in that X is defined above as the distance from the point of head observation in the aquifer to the impermeable boundary (fig. 1). Pinder and others define X as the distance from the stream to the point of head observation.

METHODS

The unconsolidated aquifer adjacent to the Ohio River in Kentucky is in general glacial outwash sand and gravel containing relatively thin layers of silt and clay. Fine-grained alluvial deposits of silts and clays typically overlie the sand and gravel and are saturated in some locations. The aquifer is in a deep channel cut into consolidated sandstones, limestones, siltstones, or shales (fig. 1), depending upon location. These consolidated rocks normally have a hydraulic conductivity much lower than that of the unconsolidated sand and gravel. A more detailed description of the aquifer is given by Gallaher and Price (1966) and Walker (1957). The Ohio River is subject to a wide range of stage fluctuations owing to flooding (as much as 36 feet in 1970), which usually occurs between December and May.

The stream does not fully penetrate the aquifer at the sites selected for this study (fig. 1), and the hydraulic conductivity of the streambed is probably much smaller than that of the aquifer.

Data needed for application of the flood-wave response technique were collected at nine sites (sites 1–4 and 6–10, fig. 2) during 1970. At site 5 (fig. 2) data collected in 1946 were analyzed. At three of the sites (2, 4, and 5) aquifer characteristics had previously been determined by pump-test

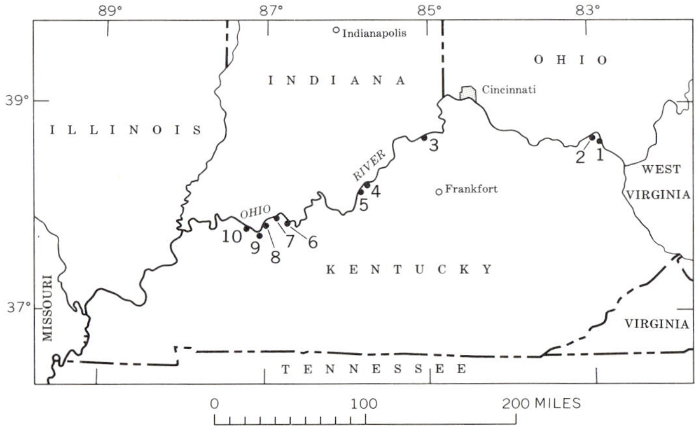

Figure 2.–Location of data-collection sites. See table 1 for names and coordinates.

methods. No data were collected at the other sites prior to this study. These other sites (1, 3, and 6–10) were selected because (1) there was a current need for information, and (2) there is a wide range in aquifer diffusivity between these sites.

At each site the following guidelines were used to locate the point of data collection: (1) a relatively straight reach of river with the valley wall parallel to the river; (2) a wide expanse of aquifer where the valley wall would approach an infinite distance from the river for the flow conditions under consideration; and (3) reasonable accessibility where the installation's interference with land use would be minimized. Sites 1 and 6 did not meet the first guideline. Site 1 is near a large river meander, and site 6 is located where the bedrock valley wall is at about a 30° angle to the river.

A 1½-inch-diameter well (well 1) was installed near the river bank at each site with the exception of site 4, where observation wells from an earlier pump test were still available. To eliminate the effects of the river's partial penetration of the aquifer and the low hydraulic conductivity of the streambed, water-level changes in this well were treated as river-stage fluctuations. Another 1½-inch-diameter well (well 2) was installed 700–1,000 feet from well 1 along a line perpendicular to the river and through well 1.

The wells were installed by lowering 1½-inch-diameter pipe inside a hollow-stem auger. A 3- to 4-foot well screen at the end of the pipe was set in the sand and gravel aquifer 5–15 feet above the bedrock surface. The wells were developed by surging air from a hose lowered to the bottom of the well until the discharging water became clear.

Water levels, from an electrical water-level-sensing device, were recorded continuously in both wells at each site for a period of several months. The period included one or more flood rises of the Ohio River.

RESULTS AND DISCUSSION

Curves calculated from water-level data at well 1 matched the observed data from well 2 at eight of the 10 sites. The best-matching type curve and the observed aquifer response at four sites are shown in figures 3 and 4. The calculated aquifer diffusivity values for all sites range from 0.40 $ft^2\ sec^{-1}$ at site 5 to 10.29 $ft^2\ sec^{-1}$ at site 4 (table 1).

Aquifer diffusivity values calculated by the flood-wave response technique compare favorably with diffusivity values computed from pump-test methods at sites 2 and 5 (table 1). The difference in diffusivity of about 750 $ft^2\ sec^{-1}$ at site 4 is attributed to at least two factors: (1) shorter duration of the stress applied to the aquifer by pumping compared with that applied by the flood, and (2) location of the water table in the

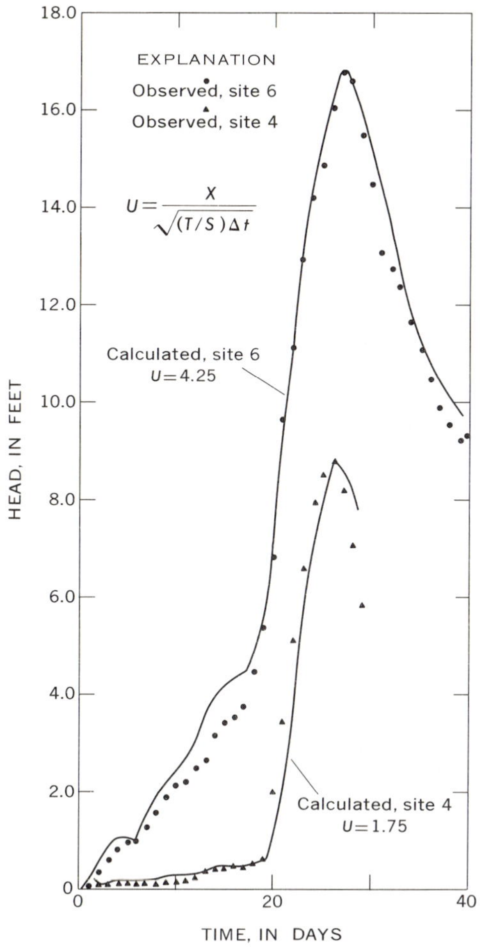

Figure 3.—Observed and calculated aquifer response for sites 4 and 6.

Table 1.—*Location, distance parameters,* U *values, and aquifer diffusivities for study sites in the Ohio River alluvial aquifer in Kentucky*

Site No.	Site name	Latitude (N.) and longitude (W.)		L (feet)	X (feet)	U	Δt (hours)	Diffusivity ($ft^2\ sec^{-1}$)	
		River well (well 1)	Observation well (well 2)					Flood-wave response method	Pump-test method
1	Bently	38°44′30″, 82°52′40″	38°44′28″, 82°52′52″	25,000	24,019	95	24	0.74	......
2	Columbia Hydrocarbons.	38°44′28″, 82°56′08″	38°44′20″, 82°56′03″	5,000	4,154	9.5	24	2.21	[1]1.82
3	Harris	38°43′35″, 85°05′25″	38°43′27″, 85°05′13″	4,350	3,350	6.0	24	3.61	......
4	Louisville Water Co.	38°16′48″, 85°42′12″	38°16′38″, 85°41′58″	3,000	1,650	1.75	24	10.29	760
5	Lees Lane	38°11′48″, 85°52′48″	38°11′45″, 85°52′41″	20,150	19,650	105	24	.40	[2].35
6	Hagman	37°55′01″, 86°45′49″	37°54′54″, 86°45′49″	4,700	3,700	4.25	24	8.77	......
7	Singleton	37°55′46″, 86°56′14″	37°55′40″, 86°56′10″	9,600	8,900	18.5	24	2.68	......
8	Givens	37°49′52″, 87°02′41″	37°49′48″, 87°02′31″	6,500	5,650	11.5	24	2.79	......
9	Owensboro Municipal Utilities.	37°47′40″, 87°03′53″	37°47′32″, 87°03′46″	9,000	7,975	([3])	...	.....	......
10	Foster	37°50′27″, 87°13′52″	37°50′19″, 87°13′59″	40,000	39,087	([4])	...	.....	......

[1]Data from Ranney, Inc., Columbus, Ohio, 1958.
[2]Rorabaugh (1946, p. 36).
[3]Wells affected by pumping.
[4]No match curve obtained.

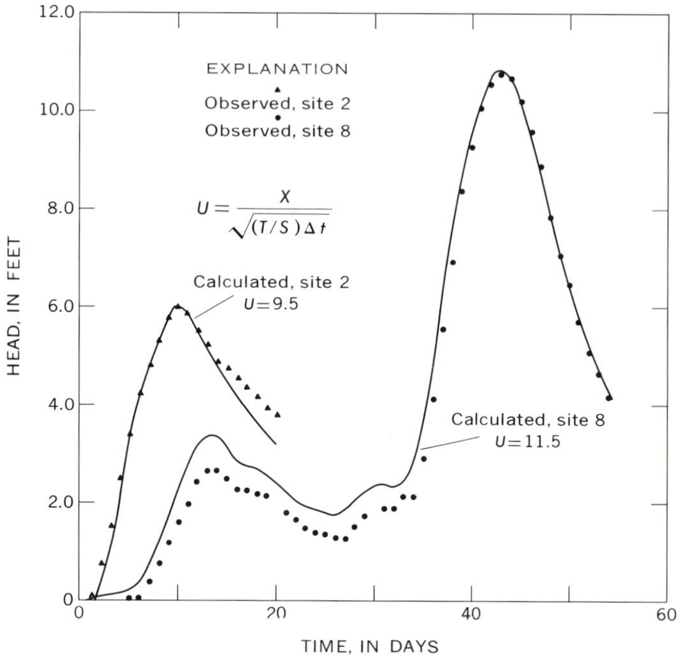

Figure 4.—Observed and calculated aquifer response for sites 2 and 8.

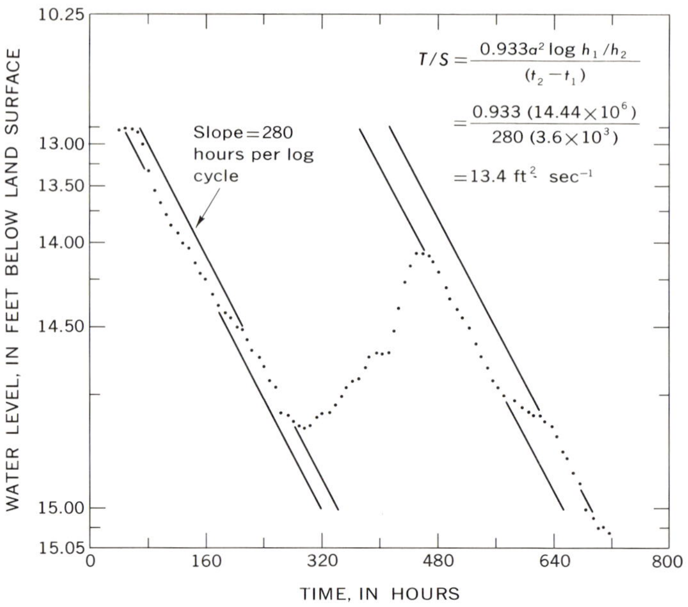

Figure 5.—Water-level hydrograph of well WC-4 (well 2) at site 4, showing the exponential shape of the recession curve.

fine-grained material overlying the aquifer at this site. Drawdown from pumping was stabilized by recharge from the river after about 0.01 day of pumping (Rorabaugh, 1956, p. 140–143). By comparison the analyzed flood period lasted for 20 days (fig. 3). A digital-model analysis for site 4 indicates that a difference in storage coefficient of about 2×10^{-2} accounts for this difference in diffusivity and probably reflects differences in flow conditions in the saturated material overlying the aquifer. Analysis of ground-water recession curves (fig. 5) as described by Rorabaugh (1960, p. 319) gives an aquifer diffusivity of 13.4 $ft^2\ sec^{-1}$, which is in close agreement with the diffusivity calculated by the flood-wave response technique.

The straight-line shape of the projected recession curve assumed by Pinder, Bredehoeft, and Cooper (1969, p. 854, fig. 3) could be a source of error. At all sites investigated in the Ohio River alluvial aquifer a straight-line projection of the recession curve resulted in a poor match of the calculated water-level hydrograph with the observed water-level hydrograph. If a reasonable match was obtained on the rising limb of the hydrograph the calculated peak and recession were generally much higher than the observed peak and recession. Rorabaugh's (1960) treatment of ground-water recession curves shows that the shape of the curve is affected by the aquifer's hydraulic characteristics, the aquifer boundaries, and time since the aquifer recharge event. These factors were such that the shape of the recession curves had not become exponential with time for the floods examined in this study. Rather than calculate theoretical recession curves for each well an average observed recession curve was transposed from a period of ground-water discharge and used as projected recession curves (fig. 6) for the flood wave analyzed.

At sites 1 and 3, data for extended periods of ground-water discharge were not available at well 2. The transposed recession curve for well 1 was used to calculate a theoretical recession curve at well 2 for these two sites.

The match of the calculated and observed hydrographs for site 8 for the first 30 days of the analyses could probably be improved by calculating a theoretical recession curve for well 2 from an average observed recession curve for well 1 (fig. 4).

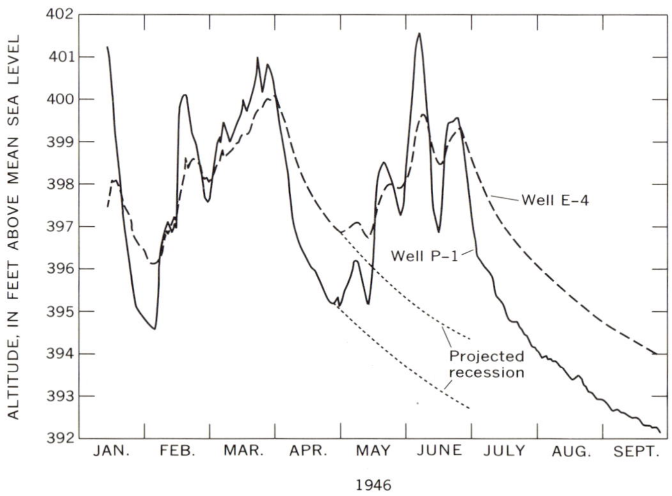

Figure 6.—Water-level hydrographs for site 5, showing projected recession curves. Well P-1 corresponds to well 1, and well E-4 to well 2.

This also applies to site 2 although this type departure of the observed data from the calculated could be the result of differential soil moisture release to the water table between well 1 and well 2 (fig. 4).

Aquifer inhomogeneities and pumping were responsible for poor matches of the calculated and the observed hydrographs at three sites: poor matches were obtained at sites 10 and 6 owing to inhomogeneities of the aquifer, and a poor match for well 2 at site 9 is attributed to the effects of pumping about ½ mile upstream.

SUMMARY

The flood-wave response technique is a relatively inexpensive method for evaluating the diffusivity of the alluvial aquifer adjacent to the Ohio River. The diffusivity values computed by this method compare favorably with those computed by pump-test methods.

Problems associated with the shape of the projected recession curves can be satisfactorily solved by collecting water-level data during extended periods of natural ground-water discharge. Effects of aquifer inhomogeneities in the vicinity of the observation wells can be reduced by using radiation logs to select the proper settings for the well screens.

Diffusivity values determined by this technique should prove useful in evaluating the overall potential of the aquifer. However, this will not eliminate the need for pump testing individual wells which can be affected by local inhomogeneities of the aquifer.

REFERENCES CITED

Bedinger, M. S., and Reed, J. E., 1964, Computing stream-induced ground-water fluctuation, *in* Geological Survey Research 1964: U.S. Geol. Survey Prof. Paper 501-B, p. B177–B180.

Gallaher, J. T., and Price, W. E., Jr., 1966, Hydrology of the alluvial deposits in the Ohio River valley in Kentucky: U.S. Geol. Survey. Water-Supply Paper 1818, 80 p.

Pinder, G. F., Bredehoeft, J. D., and Cooper, H. H., Jr., 1969, Determination of aquifer diffusivity from aquifer response to fluctuations in river stage: Water Resources Research, v. 5, no. 4, p. 850–855.

Rorabaugh, M. I., 1946, Ground-water resources of the southwestern part of the Louisville area, Kentucky: U.S. Geol. Survey open-file rept., 39 p.

——1956, Ground water in northeastern Louisville, Ky., with reference to induced infiltration: U.S. Geol. Survey Water-Supply Paper 1360-B., p. 101–169.

——1960, Use of water levels in estimating aquifer constants in a finite aquifer: Internat. Assoc. Sci. Hydrology Pub. 52, p. 314–323.

Walker, E. H., 1957, The deep channel and alluvial deposits of the Ohio Valley in Kentucky: U.S. Geol. Survey Water-Supply Paper 1411, 25 p.

Jour. Research U.S. Geol. Survey
Vol. 1, No. 5, Sept.-Oct. 1973, p. 603—607

A STUDY OF THE DISTRIBUTION OF POLYCHLORINATED BIPHENYLS IN THE AQUATIC ENVIRONMENT

By HANS J. CRUMP-WIESNER, HERMAN R. FELTZ, and MARVIN L. YATES,
Washington, D.C., Arlington, Va., Menlo Park, Calif.

Abstract.—Data gathered from monitoring activities and project studies indicate the ubiquitous occurrence and distribution of polychlorinated biphenyls in the aquatic environment. Residues have been detected in samples from 19 States, representing nearly every region of the country. Concentrations ranged from 0.1 to 4.0 μg/l in unfiltered water samples and 5.0 to 3,200 μg/kg in bottom sediments. PCB residues were also found in fish and aquatic plants. Samples were prepared by the same techniques used for general chlorinated insecticide detection, with special attention to cleanup and separation of PCB's from other compounds. Basic identification and quantification were made by dual-column electron-capture gas chromatography and confirmed by gas chromatography—mass spectrometry whenever possible. The sampling program is expected to be broadened geographically in 1973 and increased in successive years in order to more adequately define the distribution of PCB residues in the major drainage basins of the United States.

Within the past three years, polychlorinated biphenyls (PCB's) have been recognized as a major environmental contaminant. Their detection has caused widespread concern and has generated intense interest in data relating to the presence and effects of these compounds, particularly in the aquatic environment. First produced about 40 years ago, PCB compounds have become increasingly useful in such industrial applications as components in transformers and capacitors, heat exchangers, paints, inks, dyes, and dust control agents.

While much attention has been focused on the estimation of levels and potential hazards of PCB's in aquatic organisms, few data are available on the occurrence of PCB's in water and bottom sediments. The U.S. Geological Survey, through its water-quality-monitoring activities and water-resources-assessment projects, has been alert to the PCB problem since it was first reported by Widmark (1967). Although the Geological Survey has no nationwide PCB assessment program, sufficient data have accumulated from pesticide-residue programs to permit a preliminary assessment of PCB contamination of the Nation's hydrologic environment. The purpose of this paper is to present data gathered from these activities, showing the widespread occurrence of PCB's in significant concentrations in unfiltered surface water and ground water, bottom sediments, flora, and fauna.

Acknowledgment.—The authors appreciate the assistance of personnel in the U.S. Geological Survey laboratories at Austin, Tex., and Washington, D.C., in preparing data compilations.

ANALYTICAL TECHNIQUES

PCB residues were analyzed by the multiple-pesticide residue methods for water, suspended sediment, and bottom material, as described by Goerlitz and Brown (1972). The analytical procedures include not only chlorinated pesticides, but also the general class of organochlorine compounds. Special attention was given to cleanup and separation of PCB's from coextractives.

Extraction of water, sediment, and biota

One-liter unfiltered water samples were collected in precleaned glass bottles and were extracted three times with hexane. The hexane portions were combined, dried with anhydrous Na_2SO_4, and concentrated to 1 ml before cleanup and analysis by electron-capture gas chromatography (ECGC).

Fifty-gram sediment samples (dry-weight basis) were extracted with an acetone-hexane solvent. The sediment is dispersed first in acetone, and hexane is added to recover the acetone together with the desorbed material. The extract is washed with distilled water, dried over Na_2SO_4, and concentrated to 5 ml for cleanup before ECGC analysis.

The two extraction procedures used for biota are described in an analytical manual issued by the Food and Drug Administration (1971). Fish samples were extracted with petroleum ether in a blender, whereas aquatic plants were extracted with acetonitrile. The chlorinated hydrocarbon fraction was partitioned between petroleum ether and acetonitrile, dried, and concentrated to a final volume of 5 ml.

Separation

Bottom-sediment, fish, and plant extracts were cleaned up with a technique developed by Law and Goerlitz (written commun., 1971). This technique requires less time and smaller volumes of solvents for elution than other widely used methods. Liquid-solid column chromatography was employed, by use of two different types of semimicro columns in sequence, as shown in figure 1. Hexane extracts were first passed through an alumina column, and one fraction was further chromatographed on silica gel to separate PCB's from chlorinated insecticides. Successive chromatography on alumina and silica gel results in a simultaneous cleanup and separation of PCB's from the common insecticides, except aldrin, and a slight overlap of pp′ DDE. To achieve a reduction in background interference, mercury was added to remove sulfur from bottom-sediment extracts before they were applied to the silica column.

In order to insure reproducible chromatographic conditions, the activity of the adsorbents was carefully controlled. Water extracts were cleaned up on a deactivated alumina microcolumn (Law and Goerlitz, 1970). When PCB's were detected in the cleaned-up water extracts, they were also separated on a semimicro silica gel column.

Identification

Basic identification was made by dual-column ECGC (DC-200 and QF-1/OV-17) and confirmed by gas chromatography–mass spectrometry (GC–MS) when sample size and concentrations were sufficient. The amount of PCB's was

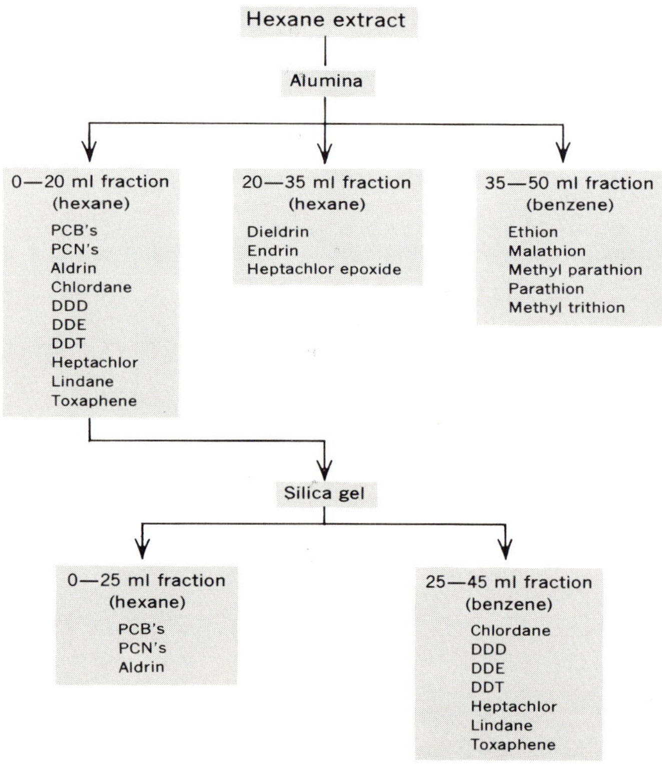

Figure 1.–Scheme for separating polychlorinated biphenyls (PCB's) and polychlorinated naphthalenes (PCN's) from pesticides.

determined by matching the unknown peaks on the chromatogram to the nearest fitting commercial formulation and measuring the areas of four corresponding peaks. Retention time and peak-area measurements were made with a digital electronic integrator. The lower detection limit for PCB residues was 0.1 μg/l in water and 5.0 μg/kg in bottom sediment. Reported levels are subject to considerable error because of the complexity of multiple peaks, some peak alteration, and the occasional presence of mixtures of PCB's in environmental samples. At best, reported values are estimates that may be as much as 50 percent in error.

DATA DESCRIPTION

Occurrences of pesticide residues in the aquatic environment have been documented over a period of years through monitoring programs of several Federal agencies. As early as 1957, studies of chlorinated hydrocarbon pesticides in major river basins were made by the Federal Water Pollution Control Administration, now a part of the Environmental Protection Agency, by use of the carbon-adsorption technique (Breidenbach and others, 1964). In 1964, interagency cooperation in pesticide-monitoring programs culminated in a proposal to begin a national monitoring program. The original program for water was described in 1967 in the first issue of the Pesticides Monitoring Journal (Green and Love, 1967). The purpose of this program, revised in 1971 (Feltz and others, 1971), is to provide continuing information on the levels of pesticide residues in the water resources of the Nation and to identify possible problem areas. Because PCB's are analyzed by the multiple-pesticide residue techniques, routine reporting of these compounds has been incorporated into current pesticide programs. At present, samples from 20 of the 161 proposed network sites are collected and analyzed by the Geological Survey. All the samples are collected from sites located west of the Mississippi River and provide continuity with a network established to evaluate the quality of water used for irrigation (Brown and Nishioka, 1967; Manigold and Schulze, 1969). Budgetary restrictions have prevented further implementation of the network.

After development of the technique to separate PCB's from pesticide residues, examination for the presence of PCB's in water and suspended- and bottom-sediment samples collected for the national monitoring program began in January 1971. Funding has been requested to increase the number of network stations to 50 in 1973, and to 100 stations in 1974, allowing a better assessment of PCB's and pesticides in major drainage basins throughout the United States. Analysis of 194 water samples and 33 bottom-sediment samples revealed no positive identifications of PCB's; however, these data are not truly representative of the entire Nation because of the limited number of sites sampled.

In 1958, the Geological Survey began operation of a bench-mark network to provide basic hydrologic data on selected stream basins throughout the United States that are expected to remain in their present natural condition or are not expected to be significantly altered by man. Locations of the 57 bench marks established in 37 States are shown in figure 2.

To insure minimum interference by man, many of the hydrologic bench marks are in national parks, wilderness areas, State parks, national forests, and areas set aside for scientific study. A detailed description of the network basins, including drainage, climate, topography, geology, vegetation, hydrology, water quality, and manmade influences, can be found in a report by Cobb and Biesecker (1971). Data gathered from 46 of these sites are presented in table 1. Despite the careful screening for pristine location of bench-mark sites, two bottom-sediment samples analyzed in the 1972 water year contained PCB residues. A value of 5.2 μg/kg was measured in the sample from South Fork Rocky Creek near Briggs, Tex., and 8.8 μg/kg in the sample from Upper Twin Creek at McGaw, Ohio.

Table 1.—*Summary of PCB residue data, national hydrologic bench-mark network, January 1971–June 1972*

Type of sample		No. of samples	Occurrences	Concentration
Water	μg/l	54	0	....
Bottom sediment	μg/kg	51	2	5.2, 8.8

The majority of the Geological Survey's water resources studies are conducted in cooperation with State water-resources and pollution-control agencies, or in response to requests from other Federal agencies. PCB data from these programs in 35 States are presented in tables 2, 3, and 4. Water samples alone, because of the low water solubility of PCB's, are not a good indicator of the widespread occurrence of the compounds, and show an incidence of slightly over 5 percent. Unfiltered water samples from 12 of the 35 States had PCB concentrations ranging from 0.1 to 4.0 μg/l. However, a significant number of suspected traces of PCB's were not reported because of several analytical limitations. Generally, resampling of areas where PCB's were first detected revealed that the compounds were still present several months later.

Bottom sediments were collected concurrently with many of the water samples reported in table 2. These samples were taken from lakes and streams that drain a variety of land-use areas generally located away from industrial centers. The data in table 3 show that the bottom-sediment samples may be used as an indicator of PCB contamination in the Nation's hydrologic environment. Significantly, of samples collected at random from 16 States, 13 contained PCB's in the range 5.0–2,400 μg/kg. Across the Nation, one of every five bottom-sediment samples examined contained PCB's.

Data available from Florida (table 4) merit special attention, because they reveal the distribution of residues in several environmental components. Only 12 of 231 unfiltered water

Figure 2.—Map showing location of hydrologic bench-mark stations. Numbers refer to list in Cobb and Biesecker (1971).

Table 2.–*Summary of PCB residue data for surface and ground water, January 1971–June 1972*

State	No. of samples	Occurrences	Concentration (μg/l)	Median concentration (μg/l)
Alaska	3	0	....	....
Arizona	8	0	....	....
Arkansas	32	0	....	....
California	161	2	0.1, 0.1	....
Colorado	32	1	.3	....
Connecticut	13	6	.1–.2	0.1
Hawaii	5	0	....	....
Iowa	24	0	....	....
Kansas	10	0	....	....
Kentucky	7	0	....	....
Louisiana	9	0	....	....
Maine	2	0	....	....
Maryland	6	1	.1	....
Massachusetts	5	1	.2	....
Michigan	2	0	....	....
Minnesota	3	2	.1, .3	....
Mississippi	8	0	....	....
Missouri	21	0	....	....
Montana	47	0	....	....
Nebraska	44	0	....	....
New Jersey	11	3	.1	.1
New Mexico	36	0	....	....
New York	325	52	.1–4.0	.3
North Dakota	40	0	....	....
Oklahoma	19	0	....	....
Oregon	13	0	....	....
Pennsylvania	2	1	.2	....
Puerto Rico	7	1	.1	....
South Dakota	18	0	....	....
Texas	660	12	.1–3.0	.4
Virginia	4	1	.1	....
Washington	25	0	....	....
West Virginia	4	0	....	....
Wisconsin	3	0	....	....
Wyoming	18	0	....	....

Table 3.–*Summary of PCB residue data for bottom sediments, January 1971–June 1972*

State	No. of samples	Occurrences	Concentration (μg/kg)	Median concentration (μg/kg)
Alaska	3	0	...	....
Arkansas	23	4	20–2,400	60
California	13	3	20–190	85
Connecticut	1	1	40	....
Hawaii	4	0	...	....
Georgia	12	10	10–1,300	300
Maryland	11	5	10–1,200	30
Mississippi	8	2	50; 170	....
New Jersey	12	10	8–250	20
Oregon	4	2	15; 140	....
Pennsylvania	16	11	10–50	20
South Carolina	11	8	30–200	50
Texas	293	23	7.9–290	80
Virginia	10	8	5–80	40
Washington	10	0	...	....
West Virginia	2	1	10	....

samples contained PCB's ranging from 0.1 to 2.1 μg/l, but over 40 percent of the associated bottom sediments analyzed during the same period were contaminatedwith PCB's ranging from 5.0 to 3,200 μg/kg. The median PCB concentrations of 20 μg/kg and 40 μg/kg found in aquatic plants and fish, respectively, follow the scheme of the biological accumulation

Table 4.–*Summary of PCB residue data from selected sampling sites in Florida, January 1971–June 1972*

Type of sample		No. of samples	Occurrences	Concentration range	Median concentration
Water	μg/l	231	12	0.1–2.1	0.2
Bottom sediment	μg/kg	118	50	5–3,200	30
Flora	μg/kg	16	5	10–50	20
Fauna	μg/kg	43	36	6–1,000	40

of the DDT family in southern Florida (Feltz and Culbertson, 1972).

DISCUSSION AND EVALUATION

Preliminary data presented in this report indicate that significant concentrations of PCB's are widespread in the water resources of the Nation. However, there are some shortcomings of data compiled from pesticide-residue programs. First, there is the problem of nonrepresentative sampling within States and some repetition of sampling in a given basin. Second, the lower limit of detection for PCB residues on the basis of a one-liter water sample is inadequate for critical evaluation. Trace amounts of less than 0.1 μg/l were detected in a significant number of samples but were excluded from the tabulation because they could not be confirmed. Third, because of the low solubility of PCB's in water, especially the higher chlorinated ones, the bulk of PCB residues in streams are associated with suspended sediment and bottom material. Therefore, PCB concentrations may be expected to vary directly with the suspended-sediment concentration in the cross section of a stream. Most surface-water samples were collected by depth integration at the center of flow, which usually does not provide a representative sample of suspended sediment. Future investigations should be made with a depth-integrating sampler using the equal-transit-rate procedure (Feltz and Culbertson, 1972). In spite of these shortcomings, evidence for the ubiquity of PCB's in the hydrologic environment is clearly established.

As others have pointed out (Goerlitz and Law, 1972), polychlorinated naphthalenes (PCN's) are compounds that have uses similar to PCB's and may possibly be present in environmental samples. They can be separated from chlorinated hydrocarbon insecticides and are eluted in the same fraction as PCB's by alumina–silica gel column chromatography. Analysis of sediment samples collected from a south Florida drainage ditch contained mixtures of PCN's ranging from 1,250 to 5,000 μg/kg, whereas the water samples overlying the sediments averaged 5.7 μg/l. Identification was confirmed by both microcoulometry and GC–MS. This may possibly be the first evidence of the occurrence of PCN's in an environmental sample and illustrates the importance of developing analytical capability for the surveillance of other organochlorine compounds that may behave like chlorinated hydrocarbon pesticides.

The entrance of PCB's into the aquatic environment is probably related primarily to low-temperature incineration of solid wastes, industrial waste disposal into waterways, and sewage outfalls. The highest levels are usually associated with industrial areas and nearby aquatic food chains. In contrast, we have noticed significant concentrations in the bottom sediments of drainage ditches, multipurpose canals, and suburban real estate lakes remote from major industrial and metropolitan areas. The presence of PCB's in real estate lakes was attributed to a variety of construction materials used in the housing industry. PCB's in surface and ground water used for public water supplies were detected through cooperative programs. The highest concentration was 4.0 μg/l in an untreated source for a city in the State of New York.

It is clear that the presence of PCB's and other organochlorine compounds in the aquatic environment merits continuing observation because of the limited evaluation that can be made from the meager data available. It is important to measure baseline levels of PCB's in streams and lakes in order to determine trends. Long-term monitoring on a systematic basis will provide the data necessary to assess the presence of PCB residues and concurrently reveal problem areas.

REFERENCES CITED

Breidenbach, A. W., and others, 1964, The identification and measurement of chlorinated hydrocarbon pesticides in surface waters: U.S. Public Health Service Pub. 1241, 70 p.

Brown, Eugene, and Nishioka, Y. A., 1967, Pesticides in selected western streams—a contribution to the National Program: Pesticides Monitoring Jour., v. 1, no. 2, p. 28–46.

Cobb, E. D., and Biesecker, J. E., 1971, The national hydrologic bench-mark network: U.S. Geol. Survey Circ. 460-D, 38 p.

Feltz, H. R., and Culbertson, J. K., 1972, Sampling procedures and problems in the determination of pesticide residues in the hydrologic environment: Pesticides Monitoring Jour., v. 6, no. 3, p. 171–178.

Feltz, H. R., Sayers, W. T., and Nicholson, H. P., 1971, National monitoring program for the assessment of pesticide residues in water: Pesticides Monitoring Jour., v. 5, no. 1, p. 54–62.

Goerlitz, D. F., and Brown, Eugene, 1972, Methods for analysis of organic substances in water: U.S. Geol. Survey Techniques Water Resources Inv. TWI 5-A3, 40 p. (Book 5, Laboratory analysis.)

Goerlitz, D. F., and Law, L. M., 1972, Chlorinated naphthalenes in pesticide analysis: Bull. Environmental Contamination and Toxicology, v. 7, p. 243–251.

Green, R. S., and Love, S. K., 1967, Network to monitor hydrologic environment covers major drainage rivers: Pesticides Monitoring Jour., v. 1, no. 1, p. 13–16.

Law, L. M., and Goerlitz, D. F., 1970, Microcolumn chromatographic cleanup for the analysis of pesticides in water: Assoc. Official Anal. Chemists Jour., v. 53, p. 1276–1286.

Manigold, D. B., and Schulze, J. A., 1969, Pesticides in selected western streams—a progress report: Pesticides Monitoring Jour., v. 3, no. 2, p. 124–135.

U.S. Food and Drug Administration, 1971, Pesticides analytical manual, v. 1: U.S. Food and Drug Adm.

Widmark, G., 1967, Pesticide residues, possible interference by chlorinated biphenyls, *in* Proceedings of the IUPAC Commission on the Development, Improvement, and Standardization of Methods of Pesticide Residue Analysis: Assoc. Official Anal. Chemists Jour., v. 50, no. 5, p. 1069.

Jour. Research U.S. Geol. Survey
Vol. 1, No. 5, Sept.-Oct. 1973, p. 609—614

REMOTE SENSING OF TURBIDITY PLUMES IN LAKE ONTARIO

By E. J. PLUHOWSKI, Arlington, Va.

Work done in cooperation with the National Aeronautics and Space Administration

Abstract.—High-altitude photography provides an effective method of monitoring the spatial extent of turbidity plumes in Lake Ontario. Large plumes generated by the Niagara, Genesee, and Oswego Rivers are identifiable on photographs obtained from about 60,000 feet above the lake on July 6, 1970, October 19, 1970, and May 29, 1971. The Niagara plume, covering as much as 43 sq mi of the lake's surface, is the largest turbidity feature. The configuration of the plumes is a function of river discharge, level of turbidity, and wind speed and direction.

To determine the utility of high-altitude photography as a means of providing synoptic hydrologic information, the National Aeronautics and Space Administration (NASA) inaugurated a series of flights beginning July 6, 1970, over parts of the Lake Ontario basin. The Lake Ontario flight pattern includes nine north-south flight lines, which form a square grid about 100 nautical miles on a side and provide coverage for the entire western part of the lake and adjacent land areas. This is approximately equal to the areal coverage provided by one image frame from the ERTS-1 satellite. Included also were two parallel flight lines over the lake's south shore, from Hamilton, Ontario, on the west to Pulaski, N.Y., on the east. The programed altitude for the RB57-F aircraft was 60,000±2,000 feet above mean sea level. Flights were made only when the cloud cover was less than 20 percent—less than 10 percent was considered optimal. The cloud-cover limitations proved to be very restrictive, especially in winter, owing to the characteristically low percentage of clear skies in the Great Lakes region. To minimize the effects of sun glitter on photograph fidelity, flights were made only at solar altitudes of 30° or greater. Glitter patterns from the sun's rays may mask water tonal discontinuities, thereby limiting the investigator's ability to identify turbidity plumes. The multispectral aerial photography provided by NASA included black and white, color, and color IR (infrared) positive transparencies.

To date, only five flight missions have been completed, owing to scheduling difficulties, aircraft and sensor malfunctions, and cloud-cover limitations. These include, in addition to the July 6, 1970, mission, flights on October 19, 1970, May 29, 1971, and June 5 and 7, 1972. Data from the June 5 and 7, 1972, missions were not received in time to be included in this paper.

Hydrologic analyses of the high-altitude photographic data are being made by the Canada Centre for Inland Waters, Ontario Water Resources Commission, McMaster University, University of Guelph, and the U.S. Geological Survey. Terrestrial research in the western Lake Ontario basin includes the use of remote-sensing techniques to identify soil-moisture conditions, drainage patterns, and areas of ground-water recharge and discharge. The effectiveness of various film and filter combinations to identify algal blooms, thermal gradients, and pollutants is being assessed on the lake and its major tributaries. The purpose of this paper is to identify the principal turbidity plumes that were found in the photographs of the south shore of Lake Ontario, and to describe lake circulation within the plumes. Specifically, the impact of wind stress on the shape, areal extent, and circulation patterns of the Niagara, Genesee, and Oswego turbidity plumes is analyzed.

NIAGARA RIVER PLUME

The Niagara River receives more than 200 mgd of industrial discharge from chemical, primary metals, and paper plants in New York State (Limnos, 1972). Much of the industrial discharge emanates from the Buffalo metropolitan area at the east end of Lake Erie near the source of the Niagara River. This heavy industrial effluent loading, when combined with the very large average flow of the river (about 200,000 cfs), produces a widespread well-defined turbidity plume in Lake Ontario on the high-altitude photographs.

Under clear skies, complete areal coverage of the Niagara River plume was obtained July 6, 1970, and October 19, 1970. A large diffuse high-pressure area over the lower Ohio River valley produced a general westerly flow of air over Lake Ontario on July 6, 1970. By way of contrast, on October 19, 1970, an easterly flow of air over the lake resulted from a high-pressure cell centered over Lake Huron. These meteorologic factors yielded nearly cloud free skies, providing an excellent opportunity to study and infer the impact of contrasting wind stresses on turbidity plumes.

The overall shape of the Niagara River plume on July 6, 1970, is shown in figure 1. The river's discharge at that time was 216,000 cfs. The plume covered an area of about 43 sq mi and was identifiable for more than 10 miles downwind from the mouth of the river. The shading on figure 1 is based on an interpretation of 9- by 9-inch color and color IR photographs at a scale of about 1:300,000. A "very bright" score was assigned to highly turbid waters, which appeared blue-white to pale blue on the photographs. A "dark" rating was given to the clear, low-turbidity water commonly found several miles offshore. This water usually appears dark blue in the color photographs and almost black in the color IR images. The intermediate patterns depict gradations of blue hues varying between the extremes of "very bright" to "dark" values. The relative brightness values shown in figures 1–5 are based on the author's visual interpretations of the photographs provided by NASA.

High turbidity values ranging from 30 to 50 JTU (Jackson Turbidity Units) were obtained in the nearshore waters west of the Niagara River on July 6, 1970. These areas appear nearly milky white in the color photographs and represent littoral drift carried by longshore currents. The configuration of several small nearshore plumes between the mouth of the Niagara River and Wilson, N.Y., suggests the presence of a large clockwise gyre. The gyre appears confined to an area between the New York shoreline and the south edge of the Niagara River plume 1 to 2 miles offshore. Westward-moving longshore currents forming the south edge of the gyre were moving in opposition to the ambient wind field. Beginning at the mouth of the Niagara River this anomalous lake circulation swept a 10-mile length of the New York State lakeshore. The direction of longshore currents was reversed about 5 miles west of Wilson, N.Y., where currents were moving downwind (eastward).

Under the influence of 5- to 8-knot easterly winds on October 19, 1970, the Niagara River plume was swept to a point within 2 miles of the entrance to the Welland Canal (fig. 2). The plume covered an area of about 35 sq mi and was visible on the photographs as far as 7.5 miles offshore. The offshore component of the easterly winds developed a wide band (3 to 4 miles) of moderately turbid water along much of the New York lakeshore. Continuous wave action striking the shore at a large angle from a normal to the beaches generated a strong littoral current, which moved sediment and drift westward toward the Niagara River jet. The narrow band of relatively clear water along the east flank of the Niagara River plume may represent upwelling caused by a concentration of westward-moving nearshore waters against the east edge of the Niagara River jet. (See area A in figure 2.) At flight time, the Niagara River jet was discharging 202,000 cfs into Lake Ontario. The oily waters of the Welland Canal were the brightest water features in the photographs. The Welland Canal plume was quickly swept westward and lost its identity abruptly in an area about 1 1/2 miles downwind.

At its mouth, the Niagara River jet is oriented toward the northwest. As the kinetic energy of the river's jet gradually dissipates in the quiescent lake water, the movement of suspended sediment, debris, and other water-borne matter becomes increasingly dependent upon wind speed and direction. On July 6, 1970 (fig. 1), the Niagara River plume, again oriented in a northwest direction at its mouth, gradually veered to a north and finally an east-northeast direction in response to a brisk 10–15 knot west-southwest wind. At its extreme boundary, the plume was visible 6 miles offshore. A region of turbulent mixing was visible in the photographs along the west edge of the plume and in a zone within the jet itself, about 1/4 mile northwest of the river's mouth. Another source of high turbidity was located at the entrance to the Welland Canal. The canal's waters are affected by oil and waste from cargo vessels and pleasure craft. Accordingly, the outflow from the canal, which averages 7,000 cfs annually (DeCooke, 1968), appeared bright in the high-altitude photographs. Once beyond the canal's entrance, the Welland Canal discharge was swept eastward by prevailing westerly winds.

GENESEE RIVER PLUME

Erodible soils and extensive agriculture within its basin combine to insure delivery of a large supply of sediment to the Genesee River. In addition to the large sediment yield of the basin, the river receives discharge from many sources, particularly from the Rochester, N.Y., metropolitan area. The resulting high levels of turbidity at the mouth of the Genesee River impart a distinctly light color to the river when viewed on aerial photographs. Accordingly, the Genesee River plume is easily delineated on most aerial photographs, owing to the normally large tonal contrast between the plume and the surrounding relatively clear waters of Lake Ontario.

A well-defined counterclockwise circulation pattern within the Genesee River plume was visible on the color and color IR photographs on October 19, 1970 (fig. 3). The plume, covering about 2 sq mi of the lake's surface, was swept westward by prevailing 6- to 8-knot east-northeasterly winds. A counterclockwise gyre, formed to the lee of the harbor breakwater, extended about 1 mile downwind from the mouth of the river (fig. 3). Turbidity ranged from 8 JTU in the Genesee River to 1 to 2 JTU in the clearer (darker) inshore waters along the base of the west breakwater. To the west of the plume, a strong northwest-trending longshore current is identifiable in the photographs. A less intense littoral current is visible east of the harbor breakwater. This westerly trending current moved around the outer end of the breakwater, mixing at that point with flow from the Genesee River.

Effluent from a submerged sewer outfall nearly 2 miles offshore is visible in the photographs (near point A on figs. 3 and 4). On October 19, 1970, effluent from the outfall was

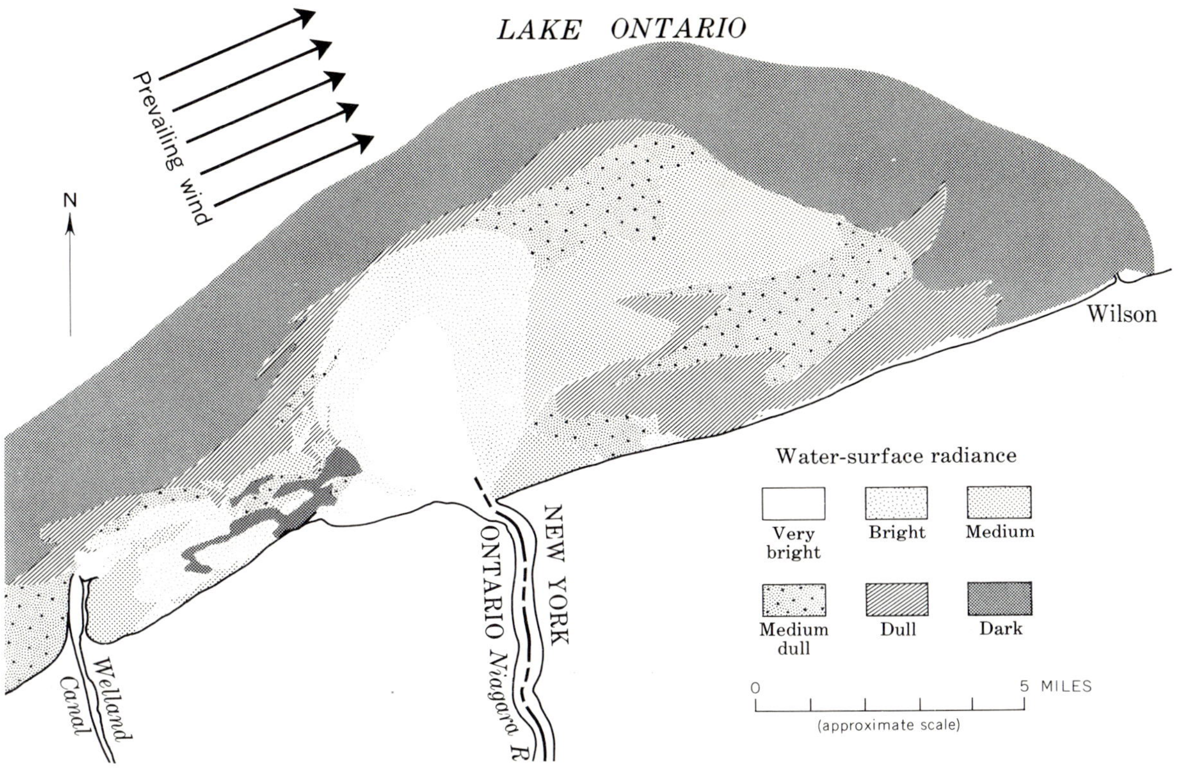

Figure 1.—Welland Canal and Niagara River plumes as interpreted from aerial photographs obtained July 6, 1970. (Photographs from NASA)

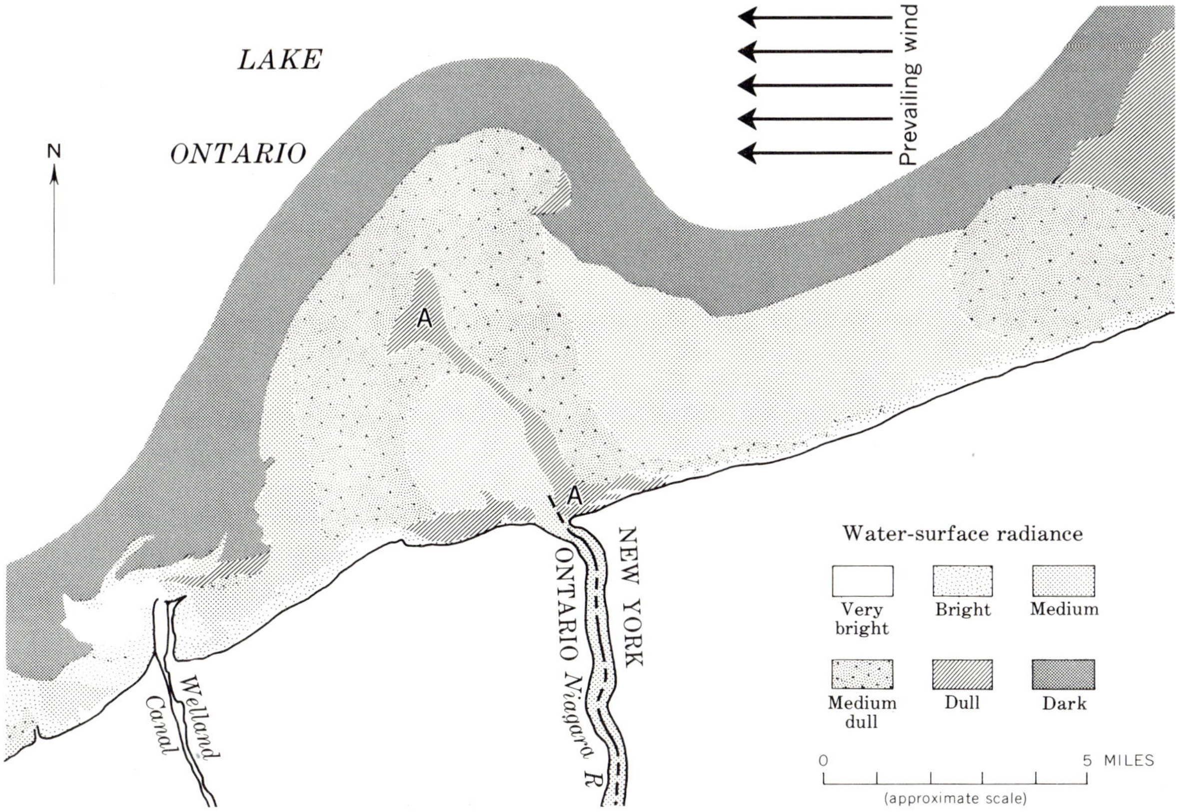

Figure 2.—Welland Canal and Niagara River plumes as interpreted from aerial photographs obtained October 19, 1970. A, area where upwelling is in progress. (Photographs from NASA)

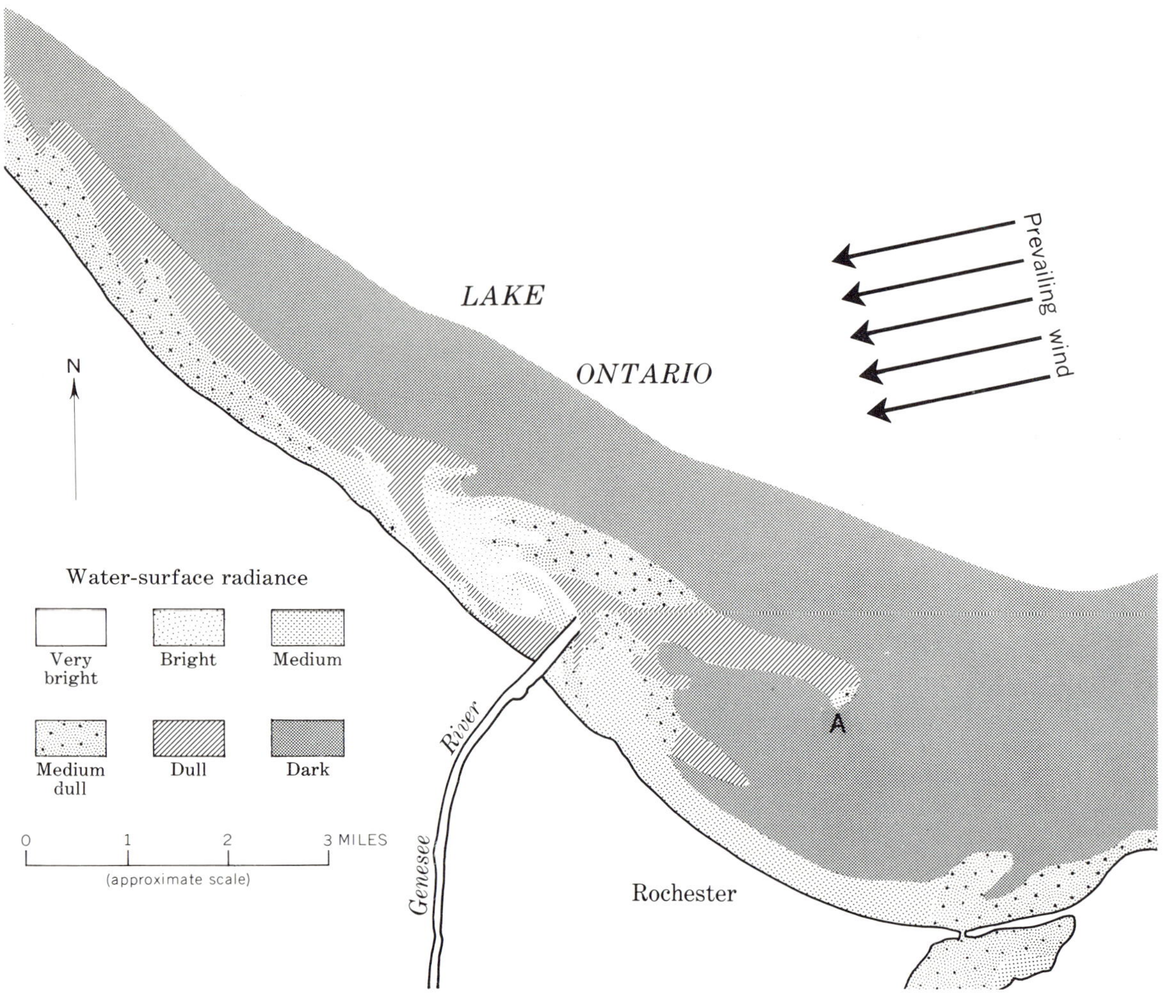

Figure 3.–Genesee River plume as interpreted from aerial photographs obtained October 19, 1970. A, approximate location of a submerged sewer outfall. (Photographs from NASA)

swept westward, eventually merging with the Genesee River plume about 1 mile northeast of the river's mouth.

The well-defined circulation patterns found on the October 19, 1970, photographs were not apparent in those obtained on May 29, 1971. Winds were calm during the forenoon of May 29, 1971, when the photographs were taken; however, earlier during the day a gentle southwesterly breeze prevailed. Because of this wind pattern, the plume drifted eastward, maintaining this direction through the forenoon (fig. 4). Discharge at the mouth of the Genesee River was 1,740 cfs on May 29, 1971, as contrasted with 2,170 cfs on October 19, 1970. Thus, on May 29, 1971, lowered river discharge and gentle winds combined to produce a sluggish circulation pattern in the turbidity plume. Some reinforcement of the Genesee River plume occurred at the submerged sewer outfall (fig. 4) when effluent from the outfall surfaced near the east edge of the plume. The Genesee River plume was extended another mile eastward and its area increased from 2.7 to 3.5 sq mi as a result of a replenished supply of suspended material from the sewer outfall.

OSWEGO RIVER PLUME

A substantial part of the sediment yield in the Oswego River basin is retained by numerous natural lakes and manmade impoundments throughout the watershed. About 6 percent of the basin's 5,100-sq-mi area represents lake surfaces (Liu and others, 1972). Extensive reaches of the Oswego River form part of the New York State Barge Canal system. Owing to these numerous manmade sediment sinks, turbidity levels at the mouth of the Oswego River are lower than might be expected. Accordingly, the Oswego River plume appears less intense on the aerial photographs than either the Genesee River or the Niagara River plumes.

The impact of a variety of wind stresses on the configuration of the Oswego River plume is shown in figure 5. Dominant

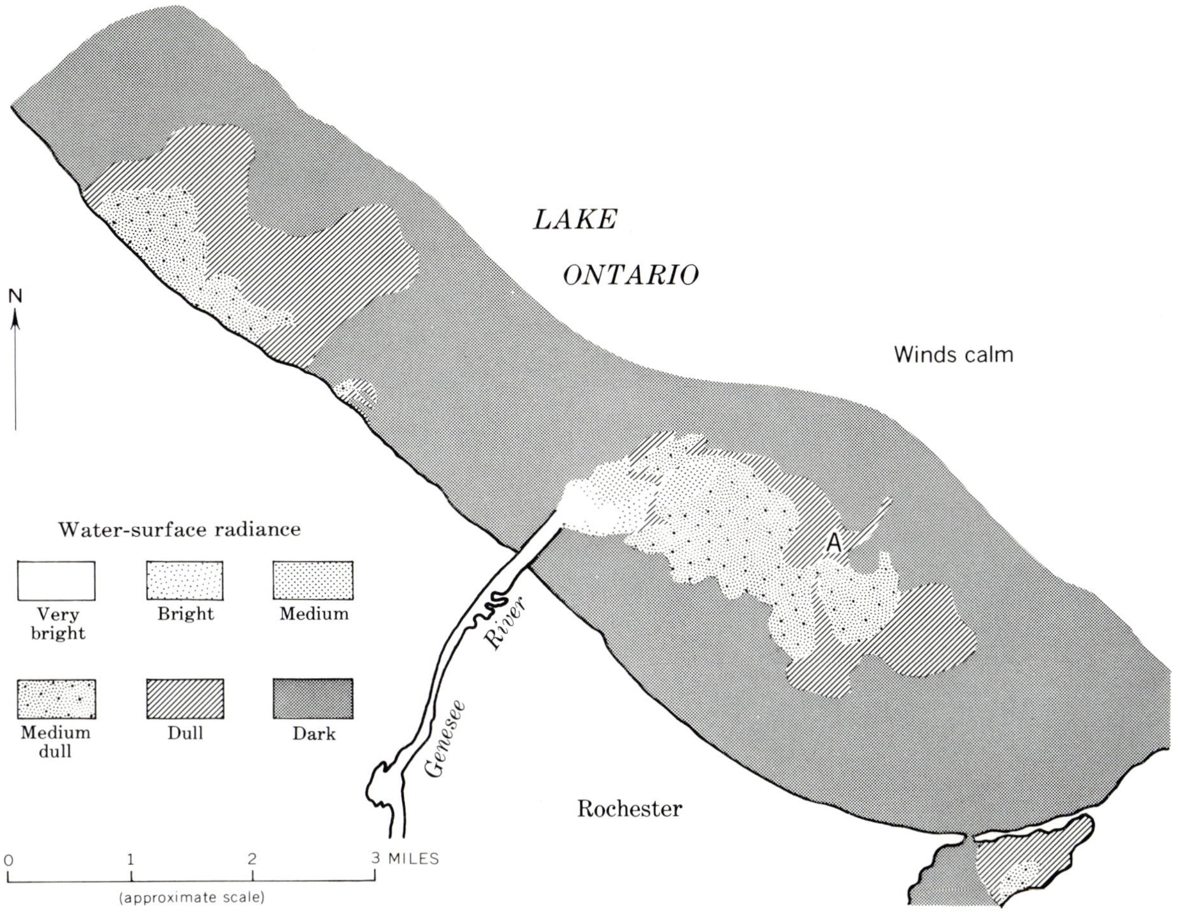

Figure 4.—Genesee River plume as interpreted from aerial photographs obtained May 29, 1971. A, approximate location of a submerged sewer outfall. (Photographs from NASA)

onshore winds on July 6, 1970, and on October 19, 1970, confined the plume to the harbor and to the lee of the harbor enclosure. The area of the plume (including the harbor) was 2.1 sq mi on July 6, 1970, and 1.2 sq mi on October 19, 1970. Under the influence of offshore winds on May 29, 1971, the areal extent of the plume expanded to about 6 sq mi. Turbidity levels ranged from 3 to 6 JTU in the river to 0.5 to 1 JTU in the clear (darker) offshore waters of Lake Ontario.

High turbidity, possibly caused by beach erosion, is evident in the high-altitude photographs on October 19, 1970, adjacent to, and to the southwest of Burt Point (fig. 5). The shoreline below Burt Point is oriented on a northeast-southwest axis, paralleling the prevailing northeast winds. A strong longshore current generated by the juxtaposition of shoreline and prevailing winds resulted in beach erosion, and the resuspension of fine-grained bottom materials. Under prevailing northwest winds on July 6, 1970, only localized areas east of Oswego, N.Y., were affected by beach erosion. No evidence of beach erosion was detected in the photographs taken May 29, 1971, when weak offshore winds prevailed.

CONCLUSIONS

High-altitude photography is an effective tool in defining turbidity plume dynamics of large and medium-sized rivers entering Lake Ontario. Plume configurations are well defined and lake circulation easily identified in the Niagara River and Genesee River plumes, but less so in the Oswego River plume. Extensive sediment trapping by lakes and canals in the Oswego River system acts to lower turbidity levels at its mouth, thereby minimizing color contrasts between the river and the receiving waters of Lake Ontario.

Strong onshore winds that subtend a large angle with a line normal to the lake's coastline will generate erosive littoral currents. The existence of such currents is readily identified in the high-altitude (60,000 feet) photographs. Coastal reaches of

Lake Ontario undergoing extensive scour by longshore currents appear blue-white to white on color photographs, contrasting sharply with the relatively clear and dark offshore waters of the lake.

REFERENCES CITED

DeCooke, B. G., 1968, The Great Lakes water levels problem: Limnos, v. 1, no. 1, p. 22–26.

Limnos, 1972, The situation lake by lake: Limnos, v. 5, no. 1, p. 19–23.

Liu, C. S., Muralidhar, D., and Tedrow, A. C., 1972, Multipurpose operation studies of a canal-lake-river system—Oswego River system, New York: Am. Water Resources Assoc., Water Resources Bull., v. 8, no. 2, p. 349.

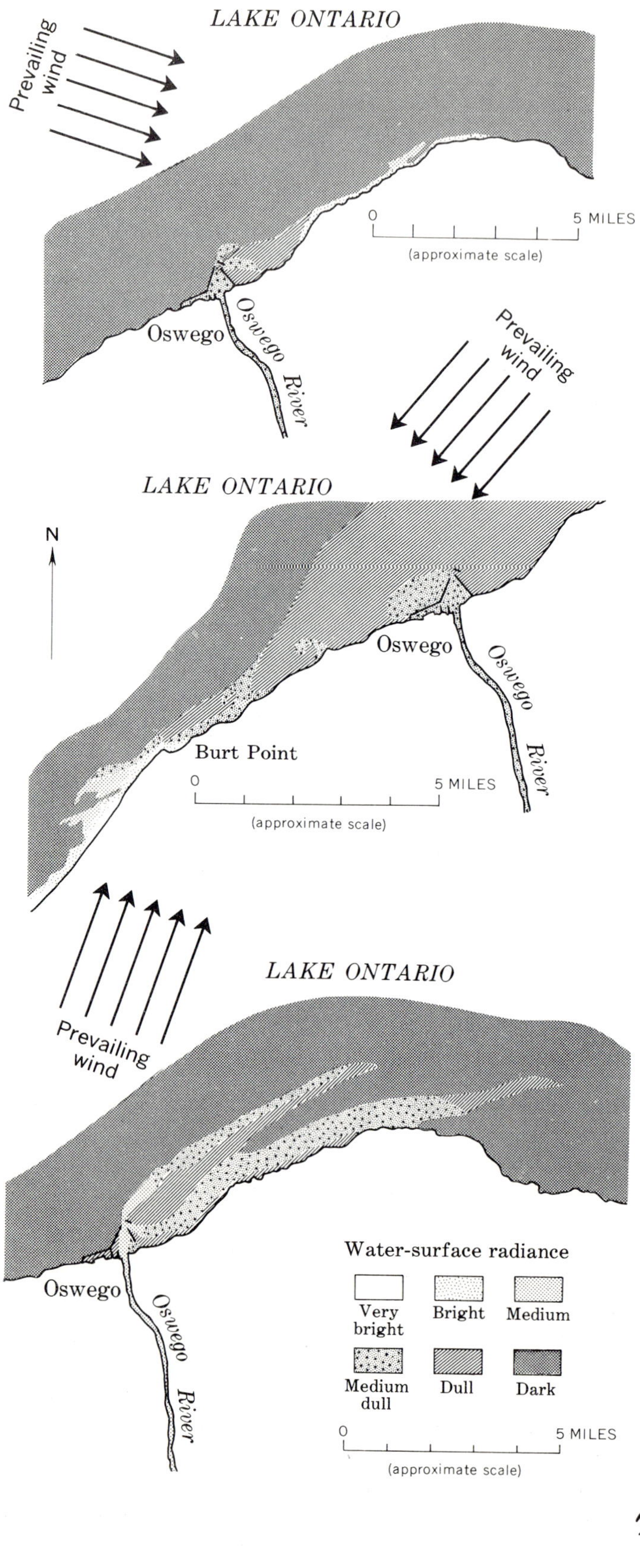

Figure 5.—Oswego River plume as interpreted from aerial photographs obtained July 6, 1970 (top), October 19, 1970 (middle), and May 29, 1971 (bottom). (Photographs from NASA)

Jour. Research U.S. Geol. Survey
Vol. 1, No. 5, Sept.-Oct. 1973, p. 615–619

METHOD FOR ESTIMATING THE DIVERSION POTENTIAL OF STREAMS IN EASTERN MASSACHUSETTS AND SOUTHERN RHODE ISLAND

By GARY D. TASKER, Boston, Mass.

Prepared in cooperation with the Massachusetts Water Resources Commission

Abstract.—A simple method is proposed for estimating the probable magnitude and frequency of streamflow that is in excess of predetermined minimum streamflows required downstream in eastern Massachusetts and southern Rhode Island. Regional curves relate these annual volumes of streamflow excess to the average annual discharge and the median 7-day annual minimum flow of the site. Use of the curves is illustrated by a hypothetical example.

Predictions of large increases in demand for water in the near future have caused planners and designers to consider additional diversions of streamflow to meet future needs. It is not unusual in eastern Massachusetts and southern Rhode Island (fig. 1) to pump water in excess of a legislated minimum flow from the stream to an off-channel storage reservoir. Therefore, proper evaluation of streamflow-diversion potential requires knowledge of the probable magnitude and frequency of streamflow in excess of a predetermined minimum streamflow.

Planners and designers desire a simple method that will give first approximations of the diversion potential of streams at sites where no continuous streamflow records are available. To help fulfill this desire, regional curves have been defined that relate annual volumes of streamflow excess to the average annual discharge and the median 7-day annual minimum flow.

DEVELOPMENT OF CURVES

Six gaging stations (table 1) were selected to represent the streams in the area. The stations were selected because each has at least 20 years of record, and the streams are not highly regulated. Diversion-probability curves for the six gaging stations are computed by the method proposed by Collings (1968). These curves assign a probability of occurrence to streamflow in excess of a specified discharge at a selected site and are computed by the following steps:

1. For each year during the period of record, the minimum streamflow required to pass downstream (F) is subtracted from the daily mean discharge, and the remaining discharge is summed to determine the annual volume of streamflow in excess of F. These computations were greatly facilitated by use of a computer program developed by A. W. Burns, U.S. Geological Survey, Boston.
2. A cumulative frequency distribution of the annual volume of streamflow in excess of F is plotted for several values of F.

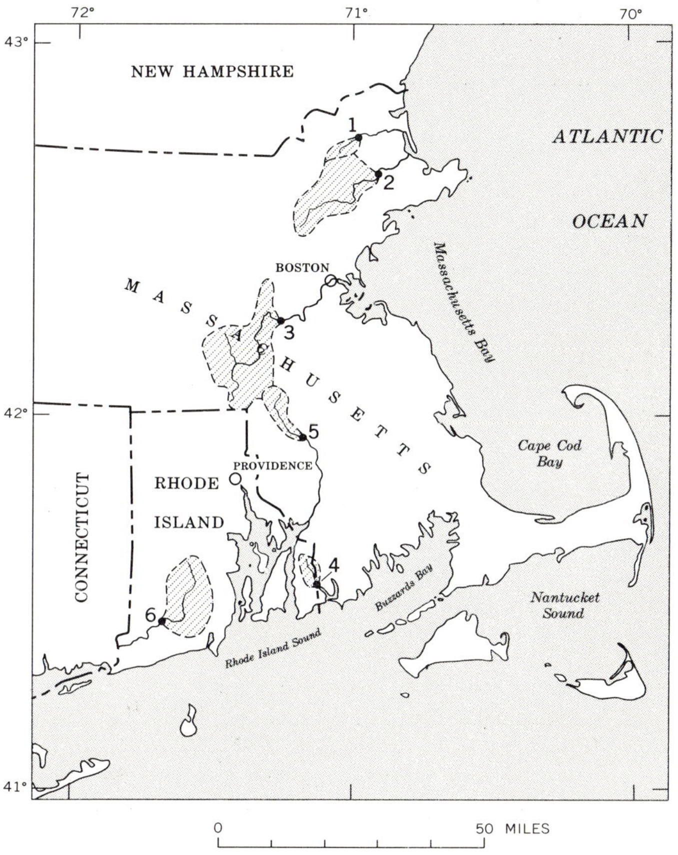

Figure 1.—Map of eastern Massachusetts and southern Rhode Island, showing the location of drainage basins (patterned) and gaging stations (table 1).

Table 1.—*Measured discharge and median 7-day annual minimum flow at gaging stations*

Station No. (fig. 1)	Station name and location	Drainage area (mi^2)	Mean annual discharge ($ft^3 sec^{-1} mi^{-2}$)	Median annual 7-day minimum flow ($ft^3 sec^{-1} mi^{-2}$)
1.	Parker River at Byfield, Mass.	21.6	1.58	0.029
2.	Ipswich River near Ipswich, Mass.	124	1.59	.048
3.	Charles River at Charles River Village, Mass.	184	1.59	.142
4.	Adamsville Brook, at Adamsville, R.I.	7.91	1.76	.020
5.	Wading River near Norton, Mass.	42.4	1.67	.113
6.	Pawcatuck River at Wood River Junction, R.I.	100	1.84	.384

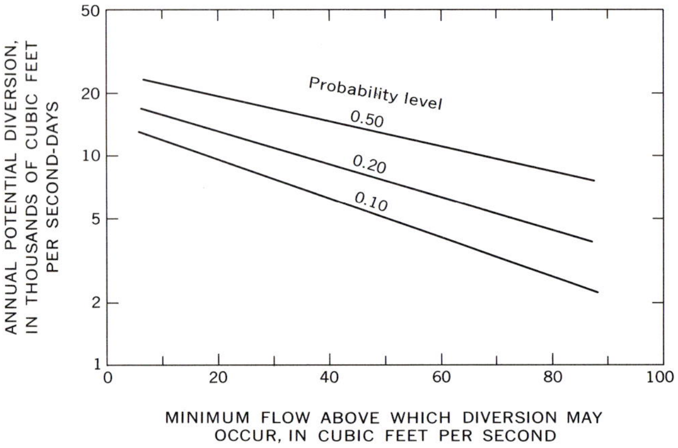

Figure 2.—Diversion-probability curves for Wading River near Norton, Mass.

3. The streamflow in excess of F for a selected frequency is determined from the cumulative frequency distribution and plotted against the several values of F. Diversion-probability curves for Wading River near Norton, Mass., are shown in figure 2 as an example.

For each of the six stations, a straight line on semilogarithmic paper provides a very good fit of the points computed by the above method. Therefore, the diversion-probability curves for these stations may be described by an equation of the form

$$V = b_0(b_1)^F \,, \quad (1)$$

where

V is the annual potential diversion, in units of volume, F is the minimum streamflow above which diversion may occur, and b_0 and b_1 are regression constants for a given stream site and probability (chance that a volume less than V will be available for diversion in any one year).

Although the constants b_0 and b_1 are estimated graphically in this study, they can be estimated by standard least-squares techniques by the following transformations:

$V = b_0(b_1)^F$,

$\log V = \log b_0 + F \log b_1$,

let $V' = \log V$, $b_0{}' = \log b_0$, and $b_1{}' = \log b_1$,

then

$$V' = b_0{}' + b_1{}'F \,, \quad (2)$$

which is the form of solution given by standard-regression computer programs for the independent variable F and dependent variable V'. Taking the inverse transforms, $b_0 = 10^{b_0{}'}$/ and $b_1 = 10^{b_1{}'}$, enables the reconstruction of equation 1 or, equivalently, in terms of the coefficients from the standard program,

$$V = 10^{(b_0{}' + b_1{}'F)} . \quad (3)$$

This fit can be solved to get the set (b_0, b_1) for every combination of stream site and probability level.

Regression constant b_0 equals the annual volume of streamflow at a selected probability level. Therefore, it is expected that areal variations in b_0 would be related to an index of areal variations in annual discharge (fig. 3). The average annual discharge was selected as an index of annual discharge because it can be estimated at ungaged sites in the area from runoff maps (Knox and Nordenson, 1955) or from regional formulas (Johnson, 1970).

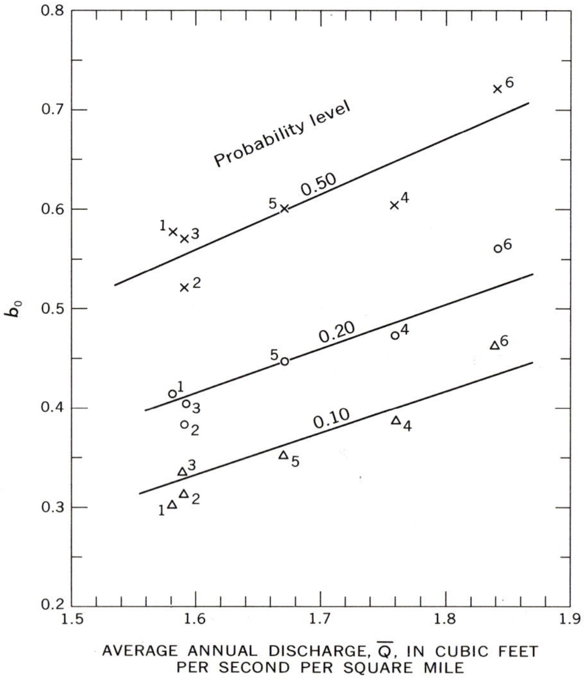

Figure 3.—Relation between b_0 and average annual discharge, Q. Data points for each probability level are gaging stations used in this report (fig. 1, table 1).

Regression constant b_1 defines the slope of the semilog curve and depends largely on how streamflow is distributed throughout the year. Consider two streams, A and B, which have equal average annual discharge but whose average within-year distribution of streamflow is represented by the flow-duration curves shown in figure 4. When $F = 0$, the

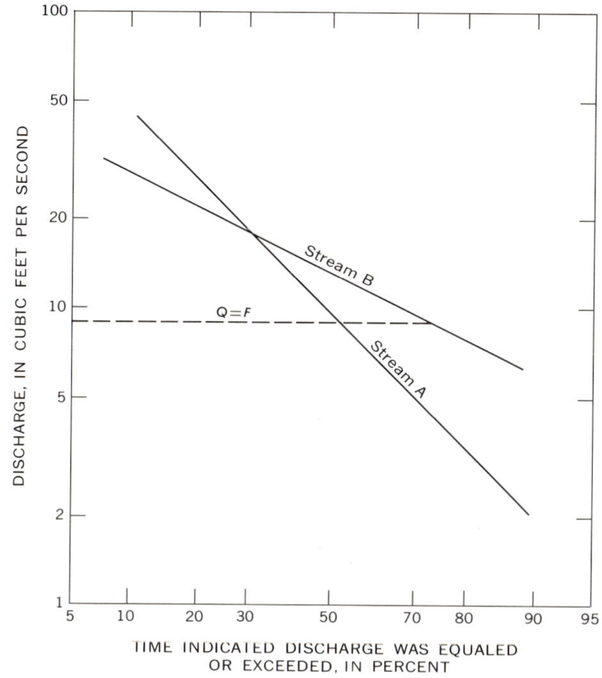

Figure 4.—Flow-duration curves.

average annual potential diversions for both streams are equal to the average annual discharge. As F increases to $F = Q$ it is apparent that the average annual potential diversion (area under the curve and above the line $Q = F$) for stream A will be greater than or equal to that of stream B for all values of F. Therefore, it would be expected that b_1 could be related to an index of the within-year distribution of streamflow (fig. 5). In eastern Massachusetts and southern Rhode Island, as in eastern and southern Connecticut (Thomas, 1966), the within-year distribution of streamflow is greatly influenced by the hydrologic properties of the unconsolidated deposits and the average flow is largely controlled by climatological factors. Because of the similarity of climatological factors and differences in hydrologic properties of the unconsolidated deposits over the area, the areal variation in average flow is small compared to the areal variation in low-flow characteristics. Therefore, a single low-flow value can be an effective index of the within-year distribution of streamflow. The median 7-day annual minimum flow was selected as an index of the within-year distribution of streamflow because it can be estimated from base-flow measurements or, in southeastern Massachusetts, from maps of ground-water availability (Tasker, 1972).

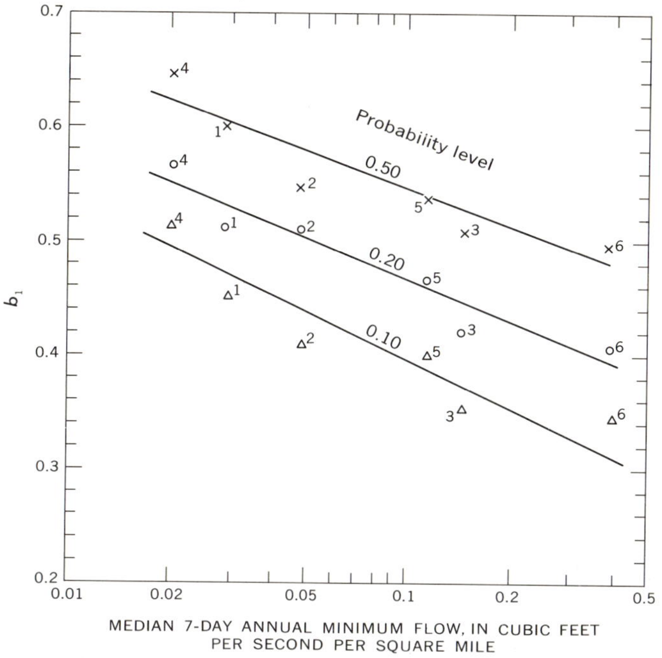

Figure 5.—Relation between b_1 and the median 7-day annual minimum flow, $Q_{m,7}$. Data points for each probability level are gaging stations (fig. 1, table 1).

In figure 3, coefficient b_0 is related to average discharge by

$$b_0 = \alpha_0 + \beta_0 \bar{Q} \tag{4}$$

for each probability level. In figure 5, coefficient b_1 is related to the medium 7-day annual minimum flow ($Q_{m,7}$)

$$b_1 = \alpha_1 + \beta_1 \log Q_{m,7} \tag{5}$$

for each probability level. These relations allow equation 1 to be expressed directly in terms of stream discharge characteristics for a particular probability level, or

$$V = (\alpha_0 + \beta_0 \bar{Q})\,(\alpha_1 + \beta_1 \log Q_{m,7})^F\ . \tag{6}$$

The parameters of this equation cannot be estimated directly by linear least squares, but can be estimated by the previously described procedure of estimating b_0 and b_1 for each basin and probability level and then relating these parameters to flow characteristics as in equations 4 and 5.

This method ignores the possible cross correlation of b_0 and b_1 (correlation coefficient equal to 0.02), as well as other factors that might further refine the relations. However, there are the physical reasons described above for the relations shown in figures 3 and 5, and the relations are statistically significant at greater than the 90-percent level. Comparisons of the potential diversion observed from streamflow records with that estimated using figures 3 and 5 and equation 1 were made for values of $F = 1.00$ and 0.25 and for probabilities of 0.50, 0.20, and 0.10 (fig. 6). The estimated potential diversion

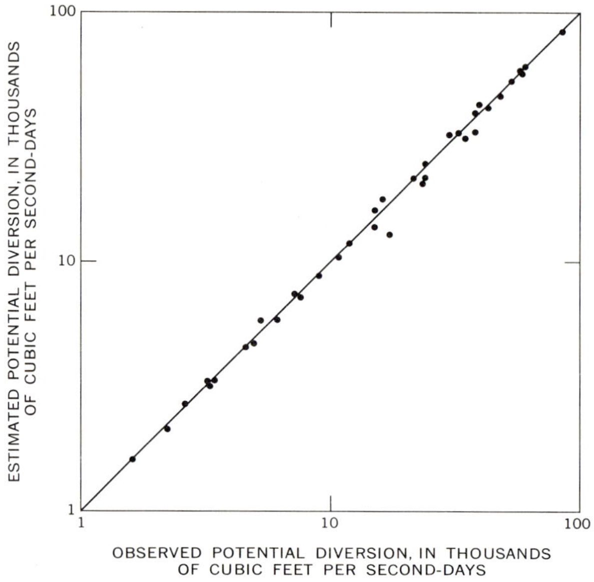

Figure 6.—Comparison of observed and estimated streamflow excess for long-term stations.

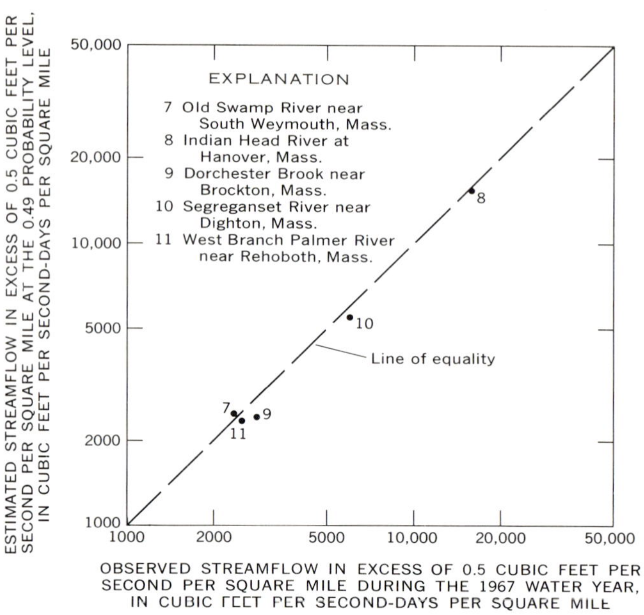

Figure 7.—Comparison of streamflow excess observed at short-term stations in 1967 and estimated streamflow excess at the 0.49 probability level.

plotted within 10 percent of the observed value in 34 of the 36 points tested and within 5 percent in 24 of the 36 points. For the six long-term stations (table 1) it is found that the volume of streamflow in excess of 0.5 $ft^3 sec^{-1} mi^{-2}$ for the 1967 water year has a probability range of 0.35 to 0.54, with an average probability of 0.49. Assuming the 1967 streamflow excess for any unregulated site in the area has a probability of occurrence of 0.49, the volume of streamflow in excess of 0.5 $ft^3 sec^{-1} mi^{-2}$ estimated by the described method at the 0.49 probability level should approximate that observed in 1967 if the method is reliable. There are five short-term unregulated gaging stations in the area for which continuous records of discharge for the 1967 water year are available. Observed values of streamflow excess for the short-term stations for the 1967 water year are plotted against the values estimated by the described method in figure 7. The close agreement between the estimated and observed values in figures 6 and 7 indicates that fairly reliable estimates of potential diversion in terms of probability can be made with little effort.

Potential diversion is usually calculated from gaging station records during a critical period, usually the 1966 water year, and extrapolated to the site of interest. However, the proposed method will allow planners and designers to assign a probability to potential diversion and compare diversion of streamflow with alternative methods of obtaining water, such as surface storage or ground-water wells.

LIMITATIONS

Applicability of empirical relations of this type to a site is dependent on similarity of the flow regimen at the site to that at the stations on which the relations are based. Consequently, the relations apply only to streams with virtually natural flow and whose drainage area, average annual discharge, and median 7-day minimum flow fall within the range of values given in table 1. In general, the relations would not apply to streams that are highly regulated, drain highly urbanized areas, or have a very large basin storage capacity.

In using figures 3 and 5 in connection with equation 1, F must be expressed in cubic feet per second per square mile and the estimate of V is given in thousands of cubic feet per second-days per square mile.

EXAMPLE

The following hypothetical example illustrates the use of the curves. A planner wants to know the median amount of diversion expected from a stream to supplement storage in a nearby reservoir. The unregulated stream has a drainage area of 10 mi^2, an average annual runoff of 1.70 $ft^3\ sec^{-1}\ mi^{-2}$, and a median 7-day annual minimum flow of 0.07 $ft^3 sec^{-1} mi^{-2}$. Requirements of downstream users will allow diversion of the flow exceeding 5 ft^3/sec. The proposed diversion system has a maximum capacity of 5 ft^3/sec.

Entering figure 3 with the average annual discharge for the basin (1.70 $ft^3 sec^{-1} mi^{-2}$), b_0 for a probability of 0.50 (median) is determined as 0.62. Entering figure 5 with the median 7-day annual minimum flow for the basin (0.07 $ft^3 sec^{-1} mi^{-2}$), b_1 for a probability of 0.50 is determined as 0.57. Substituting the values of F equal to 0.5 $ft^3 sec^{-1} mi^{-2}$, b_0 equal to 0.62, and b_1 equal to 0.57 into equation 1, the median annual volume of diversion in excess of 5 ft^3/sec is estimated as 4,680 $ft^3 sec^{-1}$ days.

At times, streamflow may exceed both the downstream requirement and the capacity of the diversion system. The median annual volume of water available from streamflow, after downstream requirements are met and beyond the capacity of the diversion system, may be determined from figures 3 and 5 and equation 1, as before, by considering *F* as the sum of the downstream requirements and the capacity of the diversion system (0.5 + 0.5). This volume is estimated as 3,530 $ft^3 sec^{-1}$ days. The difference of 1,150 $ft^3 sec^{-1}$ days between the two volumes (4,680 and 3,530 $ft^3 sec^{-1}$ days) is the estimated median annual volume of water available for diversion from the stream to the reservoir.

Similarly, figures 3 and 5 and equation 1 can be used to estimate the annual volumes that have a 20- or 10-percent chance of not being exceeded in any one year.

REFERENCES CITED

Collings, M. R., 1968, Method of volume-diversion analysis of a stream, *in* Geological Survey Research 1968: U.S. Geol. Survey Prof. Paper 600-C, p. C199–C203.

Johnson, C. G., 1970, A proposed streamflow-data program for central New England: U.S. Geol. Survey open-file rept., 49 p.

Knox, C. E., and Nordenson, T. J., 1955, Average annual runoff and precipitation in the New England–New York area: U.S. Geol. Survey Hydrol. Inv. Atlas HA-7.

Tasker, G. D., 1972, Estimating low-flow characteristics of streams in southeastern Massachusetts from maps of ground-water availability, *in* Geological Survey Research 1972: U.S. Geol. Survey Prof. Paper 800-D, p. D217–D220.

Thomas, M. P., 1966, Effect of glacial geology upon the time distribution of streamflow in eastern and southern Connecticut, *in* Geological Survey Research 1966: U.S. Geol. Survey Prof. Paper 550-B, p. B209–B212.

Jour. Research U.S. Geol. Survey
Vol. 1, No. 5, Sept.-Oct. 1973, p. 621—625

CHANGES IN FLOODFLOW CHARACTERISTICS OF A RECTIFIED CHANNEL CAUSED BY VEGETATION, JACKSON, MISSISSIPPI

By K. V. WILSON, Jackson, Miss.

Work done in cooperation with the City of Jackson

Abstract.—Extreme changes in velocity, stage, and Manning's roughness coefficient, *n*, were observed during the first year after canalization of Hanging Moss Creek at Jackson, Miss. Additional changes were observed during the following 8 years. The channel, constructed during the summer of 1963, had a 50-foot-wide bottom, 2:1 side slopes, and 12-foot depth. In March 1964, average velocities of 7.8 feet per second were measured at a 5½-foot depth in the clean channel and Manning's *n* was computed to be 0.022. In October 1964 the average velocity was 3.2 fps at a 5½-foot depth and Manning's *n* was 0.045. The channel was then lined with fairly thick vegetation consisting of small willows, weeds, and grass. In October 1970 (summer foliage existing) the average velocity was 2.0 fps at a 5½-foot depth and Manning's *n* was 0.07. Willow trees, 8 to 10 feet high, then lined the channel. In March 1971 (barren foliage), Manning's *n* was 0.05. In March 1972 (barren foliage), Manning's *n* was increased to 0.07. These observations indicate that the commonly used values of Manning's *n* for channel rectification (0.02–0.03) are low and that the carrying capacity of earthen channels may be reduced 50 percent as a result of only 1 year's growth of vegetation and 70 percent as a result of 8 year's growth. The carrying capacity during summer foliage is approximately two-thirds the carrying capacity during barren winter foliage.

This paper evaluates changes with time, velocity, Manning's *n*, and flood profiles for the rectified channel of Hanging Moss Creek at Jackson, Miss. Wilson in 1968 (p. 57–59) described changes observed during the first 3 years after construction.

During the summer of 1963, the rectification of Hanging Moss Creek was extended 11,000 feet upstream from Ridgewood Road by using the following design criteria:

1. 50-foot-wide-bottomed earthen channel with 2:1 side slopes approximately 12 feet deep.
2. Uniform grade of 0.0020 foot per foot for 2,500 feet downstream from Interstate Route 55 (formerly U.S. Highway 51) and 0.0014 foot per foot for 3,500 feet upstream from Interstate Route 55.
3. Discharge of 5,900 cfs in the vicinity of Interstate Route 55.
4. Roughness coefficient (Manning's *n*) of 0.045.

FLOODFLOW CHARACTERISTICS AT INTERSTATE ROUTE 55

Flood data collected at the Interstate Route 55 gage show an extreme variation in the new channel's characteristics during the first year after canalization and continued change during the next 8 years.

The design flow line of the new channel at the downstream side of Interstate Route 55 was at an elevation (1929 datum) of 269.91 feet above sea level, which is the culvert flow-line elevation. The design stage-discharge, stage-velocity, and stage-area relation, with an assumed Manning's *n* of 0.045, is shown on figure 1. The same relations as measured March 1964, October 1964, February 1966, October 1970, March 1971, and March 1972 are also shown on figure 1. All measurements were made at the downstream service road of Interstate Route 55, where the cross-sectional area approximates the designed channel. A comparison of these relations at different times reveals the following:

1. By March 2, 1964, scouring and filling of half a foot in the channel reduced the cross-sectional area between the elevations of 274 and 275 feet to about 10 percent less than the designed area. The third measurement of March 2, 1964, indicated an abrupt 10-percent increase in channel area and in discharge at the 275-foot stage. The average velocity at the 275-foot stage was 7.8 fps, or about double the design velocity. With this greatly increased velocity and slightly reduced area, the stage corresponding to the mean annual flood of 2,000 cfs was 274.5 feet, or 2.3 feet lower than the design stage of 276.8 feet.
2. By October 1964, moderately thick vegetation lined the new channel. The channel area, which now approximated the design area, showed no further increase in size. The average velocity at the 275-foot stage was reduced by the vegetation to only 3.2 feet per second, which is less than the design velocity at that stage. With extremely reduced velocity, the stage-discharge relation shifted about 2 feet. The stage corresponding to the mean annual flood of 2,000 cfs was increased to 276.9 feet, which was within 0.1 foot of the design stage of 276.8 feet.

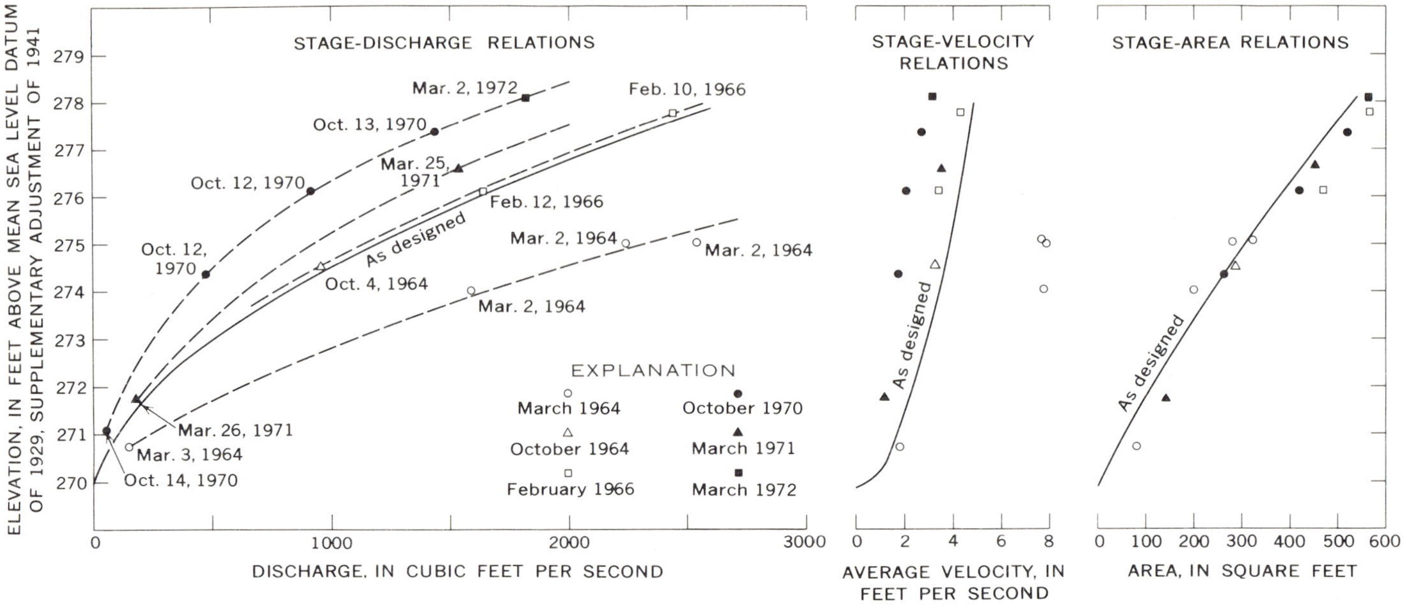

Figure 1.—Relation of stage to discharge, velocity, and area for an earthen canal constructed for Hanging Moss Creek at Jackson, Miss.

3. In February 1966 the data were similar to those for October 1964, but indicated that channel areas above the 276-foot stage were 20 percent larger than the design areas. It is probable that the consistency indicated by the 1964 and 1966 data results from summer foliage prevailing in October 1964 and winter barren foliage in February 1966.

4. By October 1970, thick vegetation lined the channel on both the bottom and banks. Channel areas were consistent with previous measurements. The average velocity at the 275-foot stage was reduced by vegetation to only 2.0 fps, which is about one-half the design velocity. With this extremely reduced velocity, the stage-discharge relation shifted an additional 1½ feet. The stage corresponding to the mean annual flood of 2,000 cfs was increased to 278.4 feet, which is 1.6 feet higher than the design stage of 276.8 feet.

5. In March 1971 velocity increased to 3.4 fps which resulted in a 40 percent increase in discharge at a 276.5-foot stage. The velocity increase was due to the barren winter foliage of the vegetation in the channel.

6. In March 1972 the data were similar to those for October 1970. Although foliage was minimal, the vegetation growth between March 1971 and March 1972 is accredited with reducing the channel's carrying capacity by 25 percent. In March 1972, the stage corresponding to the mean annual flood of 2,000 cfs was 278.4 feet, which is 1.6 feet higher than the design stage of 276.8 feet. The carrying capacity at the 278-foot elevation is 900 cfs less than the design capacity; therefore, it may be assumed that the Hanging Moss Creek channel, designed to carry a 50-year discharge of 5,900 cfs at a 12-foot depth will now carry no more than 5,000 cfs, which is less than a 25-year flood.

COMPUTATIONS OF MANNING'S n

The equation presented by Manning (1890, p. 161–207), one of the most commonly used open-channel flow formulas, is $Q = \frac{1.486}{n} AR^{2/3}S^{1/2}$, where Q is the discharge in cubic feet per second, n is the roughness coefficient, A is the cross-sectional area of the channel in square feet, R is the hydraulic radius in feet, and S is the energy gradient. All these factors are physical measurements with the exception of the roughness coefficient, which can be computed when other factors are known.

Values of Manning's n commonly used for designing earthen channels vary from 0.02 to 0.03. The calculated carrying capacity of a geometrically stable channel for any given slope is inversely related to this factor; therefore, if the n value is doubled as a result of changing channel conditions the carrying capacity is reduced 50 percent.

Manning's n was computed for reaches upstream and downstream from Interstate Route 55 for seven floods (table 1). The n values shown in the table were obtained by using known discharges, the design cross section, and slopes between bridges 1,200 feet downstream and 2,750 feet upstream.

After the flood of March 2, 1972, a four-section reach beginning 450 feet upstream from Interstate Route 55 and extending 700 feet upstream was surveyed in detail. For this short reach the Manning's n was 0.073 as compared to 0.074 for the longer reach (see table 1). A photograph showing typical roughness of March 10, 1972, (n = 0.073) is shown on figure 2.

Table 1.—*Manning's* n *values, Hanging Moss Creek at Interstate Route 55 in Jackson, Miss., 1964–72*
[Values for areas and wetted perimeters are from design cross section. Design flow line is 269.91 feet]

Date	Stage (ft)	Discharge (cfs)	Area (sq ft)	Wetted perimeter (ft)	Slope (ft/ft)		Computed *n*	
					Upstream	Downstream	Upstream	Downstream
Mar. 3, 1964	275.08	2,540	312	73.0	[1] 0.0017	[2] 0.0020	0.020	0.021
	275.01	2,240	306	72.6	[1] .0017	[2] .0020	.022	.024
Oct. 4, 1964	274.53	952	272	70.8	[1] .0017	[2] .0020	.043	.047
Feb. 10, 1966 ...	277.78	2,440	520	85.0	.00178	.00219	.045	.049
Oct. 13, 1970 ...	277.36	1,440	488	83.0	.00174	.00136	.068	.060
Mar. 25, 1971 ...	276.62	1,550	428	80.0	.00180	.00136	.053	.046
Mar. 2, 1972	278.11	1,810	550	97.6	.00214	.00140	.074	.060

[1] Estimated from profile of July 8, 1963 (slope was 0.00164).
[2] Design slope; assumed to exist during 1964.

Figure 2.—Vegetation in channel 450 feet upstream from Interstate Route 55, March 10, 1972 (n = 0.073).

During the floods of October 1964 and October 1970, summer foliage reduced the carrying capacity (increased n). In October 1970, n values were 20 to 25 percent greater than those for the following March and were approximately equal to those of March 1972. Changes in Manning's n, for the period 1964–72, in the reach upstream from Interstate Route 55 are shown on figure 3. These data indicate that n during summer foliage is one-third larger than n during barren winter conditions.

Photographs of the channel viewed upstream from Interstate Route 55 on March 25, 1971, March 29, 1971, September 9, 1971, and March 10, 1972, are shown in figure 4.

FLOOD PROFILES AND FLOW-LINE PROFILES

Floods on Hanging Moss Creek on February 10 and May 21, 1966, had peak discharges of 2,500 and 2,400 cfs, respectively, at the gage at Interstate Route 55. These peak discharges may be expected to be exceeded on the average of once in about 3 years. Profiles of these floods are compared with the design profile of the 50-year flood on figure 5.

Moderately thick vegetation consisting of willows, weeds, and grasses lined the channel. Effect of the vegetation on the flood profiles is shown by an increase in stage downstream from Ridgewood Road. The design depth for 2,500 cfs at that point is about 10 feet. The vegetation caused the depth on February 10 and May 21, 1966, to be increased to about 11 feet. This is the difference in the water surface elevation of 272 feet and the flow line of 261 feet (fig. 5).

The flood of October 13, 1970, had a peak discharge of 1,700 cfs at the gage at Interstate Route 55. This flood may be expected to be exceeded on the average of once in about 2 years. A profile of this flood is shown on figure 5.

On October 13, 1970, willows and weeds, 8 to 10 feet high, and heavy summer foliage lined the channel. Effect of this vegetation on the flood profile was to raise it to or above the profile of February 10, 1966, at which time the discharge was 2,500 cfs at Interstate Route 55. Effect of vegetation was

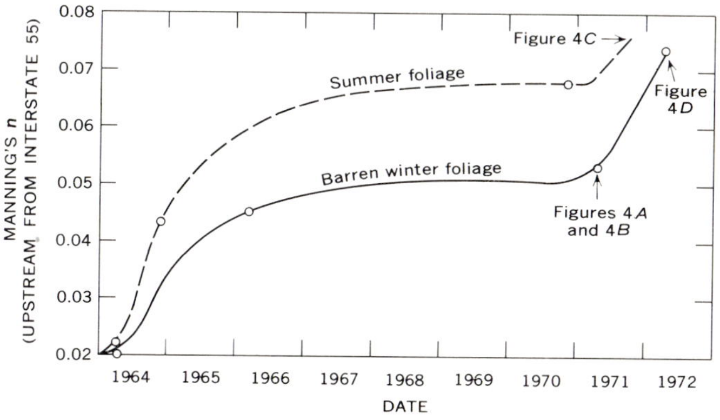

Figure 3.—Changes in Manning's n, 1964–72, and dates of photographs in figure 4.

Figure 4.—The channel viewed upstream from Interstate Route 55.

A. March 25, 1971 (near crest). Discharge, 1,600 cfs; stage at downstream service road, 276.8 feet.

B. March 29, 1971. Rod (left center) at crest of March 25.

C. September 9, 1971. Summer foliage.

D. March 10, 1972. Barren foliage; rod (upper left) at crest of March 2, 1972.

greatest at the downstream side of Ridgewood Road. The design depth for 1,700 cfs at that point is about 8½ feet. The vegetation caused the depth on October 13, 1970, to be about 13 feet. The flood stages of October 13, 1970, equaled or exceeded those of February 10, 1966, throughout the 2-mile channel reach between Sylvia Street extension and Ridgewood Road, with the exception of a short reach, just upstream from the Illinois Central Railroad, which had recently been cleared of vegetation.

The designed flow-line profile of Hanging Moss Creek between stations 10+00 and 133+00 is shown on figure 5. Cross sections were obtained upstream and downstream from all street, highway, and railroad crossings during the winter of 1968 by the U.S. Soil Conservation Service. Comparison of

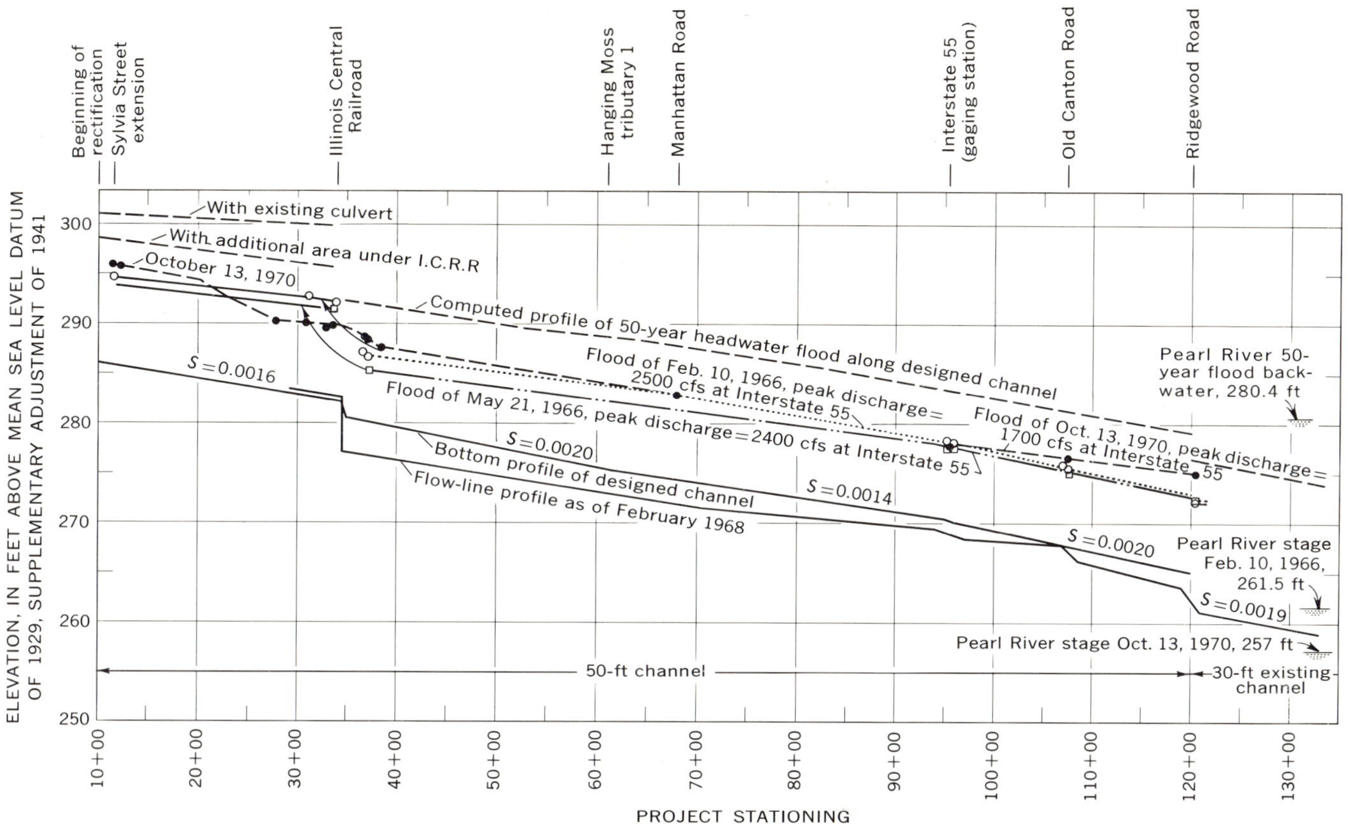

Figure 5.—Flood and flow-line profiles of Hanging Moss Creek at Jackson, Miss.

these cross sections with those of the designed channel (50-foot bottom with 2:1 side slopes approximately 12 feet deep) revealed some fairly large discrepancies. Some of these probably resulted from construction departure from the plan, but most of them are believed to have resulted from bank sloughing and degrading. A bottom profile developed from the 1968 cross sections is shown on figure 5. The 1968 profile coincides with the designed profile at the downstream side of Ridgewood Road (Sta. 120+00), at the upstream side of Old Canton Road (Sta. 107+50), and just upstream from the Illinois Central Railroad (Sta. 34+00) but shows degrading through most of the 1.6-mile reach from Ridgewood Road to the Illinois Central Railroad. Maximum degrading of more than 3 feet occurred just downstream from the railroad. A 1968 cross section 6,000 feet downstream from Ridgewood Road shows a flow line about 5 feet higher than the designed channel at that point. In summary, scour as great as 3 feet occurred between Ridgewood Road and the Illinois Central Railroad between 1963 and 1968, and fill as great as 5 feet occurred 6,000 feet below Ridgewood Road.

SUMMARY

Values of Manning's *n* commonly used for designing earthen channels vary from 0.02 to 0.03. Observations made in this study indicate that these values are low, and that the carrying capacity of earthen channels may be reduced 50 percent as a result of only 1 year's growth of vegetation and 70 percent as a result of 8 year's growth. The carrying capacity during summer foliage is only two-thirds the carrying capacity during barren winter foliage. This appraisal of the flow characteristics of a rectified channel of Hanging Moss Creek in Jackson, Miss., illustrates the desirability of using high design friction values for earthen channels and the need for establishment of an effective maintenance program to control vegetation growth.

REFERENCES CITED

Manning, Robert, 1890, On the flow of water in open channels and pipes: Inst. Civil Engineers of Ireland [Dublin] Trans., v. 20, p. 161–207.

Wilson, K. V., 1968, Flood-flow characteristics of a rectified channel, Jackson, Mississippi, *in* Geological Survey Research 1968: U.S. Geol. Survey Prof. Paper 600-D, p. D57–D59.

RECENT PUBLICATIONS OF THE U.S. GEOLOGICAL SURVEY

(Books may be ordered from the Superintendent of Documents, Government Printing Office, Washington, D.C., 20402, to whom remittances should be sent by check or money order. Give title, series No., stock No. (shown in parentheses in this list), and catalog No. [shown in brackets])

Professional Papers

306-E. Geology and paleontology of Canal Zone and adjoining parts of Panama: Description of Tertiary mollusks (additions to gastropods, scaphopods, pelecypods: Nuculidae to Malleidae), by W. P. Woodring. 1973. p. 453–539; 16 plates showing fossils. $1.75. (2401-00217) [I 19:16:306-E]

433-M. Relations among radionuclide content and physical, chemical, and mineral characteristics of Columbia River sediments, by J. L. Glenn, *with a section on* Sand and gravel mineralogy, by R. O. Van Atta. 1973. p. M1–M52. 85¢. (2401-00297) [19:16:433-M]

433-N. Radionuclides in transport in the Columbia River from Pasco to Vancouver, Wash., by W. L. Haushild, H. H. Stevens, Jr., J. L. Nelson, and G. R. Dempster, Jr. 1973. p. N1–N43. 75¢. (2401-00298) [I 19:16:433-N]

569-C. Hydrologic significance of lithofacies of the Cane River Formation or equivalents of Arkansas, Louisiana, Mississippi, and Texas, by J. N. Payne. 1972 (1973). p. C1–C17; plates in separate case. $10.90 (2401-00246) [I 19:16:569-C]

599-H. Geology of the Sierra Madera cryptoexplosion structure, Pecos County, Tex., by H. G. Wilshire, T. W. Offield, K. A. Howard, and David Cummings. 1972 (1973). p. H1–H42; plates in pocket. $2. (2401-00238) [I 19:16:599-H]

629-B. Igneous rocks in the Bingham mining district, Utah, by W. J. Moore. 1973. p. B1–B42. 85¢. (2401-00274) [I 19:16:629-B]

697. Landslides of Rio de Janeiro and the Serra das Araras escarpment, Brazil, by F. O. Jones. 1973. 42 p.; plates in pocket. $1.50. (2401-2126) [I 19:16:697]

717. Geology and ground-water characteristics of the Hanford Reservation of the U.S. Atomic Energy Commission, Wash., by R. C. Newcomb, J. R. Strand, and F. J. Frank. 1972 (1973). 78 p.; plates in pocket. $2.60. (2401-00241) [I 19:16:717]

729-A. Geology of pre-Tertiary rocks in the northern part of Yellowstone National Park, Wyo., by E. T. Ruppel, *with a section on* Tertiary laccoliths, sills, and stocks in and near the Gallatin Range, Yellowstone National Park. 1972 (1973). p. A1–A66; plates in pocket. $2.60. (2401-00242) [I 19:16:729-A]

732-B. Scour and fill in Tujunga Wash–A fanhead valley in urban southern California–1969, by K. M. Scott. 1973. p. B1–B29. 70¢. (2401-00322) [I 19:16:732-B]

734-A. Harebell Formation (Upper Cretaceous) and Pinyon Conglomerate (uppermost Cretaceous and Paleocene), northwestern Wyoming, by J. D. Love. 1973. p. A1–A54. $1. (2401-00316) [I 19:16:734-A]

736. Regional geophysical investigations in the central Colorado Plateau, by J. E. Case and H. R. Joesting. 1972 (1973). 31 p.; text and plates in case. $5.60. (2401-00222) [I 19:16:736]

757. Sedimentary framework of the western Gulf of Maine and the southeastern Massachusetts offshore area, by R. N. Oldale, Elazar Uchupi, and K. E. Prada. 1973. 10 p.; plates in pocket. $1.75. (2401-00304) [I 19:16:757]

758-A. Geology and mineral deposits of the Chulitna-Yentna mineral belt, Alaska, by C. C. Hawley and A. L. Clark. 1973. p. A1–A10; plates in pocket. $1.25. (2401-00335) [I 19:16:758-A]

764. Stratigraphy of the southern Coast Ranges near the San Andreas fault from Cholame to Maricopa, Calif., by T. W. Dibblee, Jr. 1973. 45 p. 80¢. (2401-00300) [I 19:16:764]

766. Foraminifera of the North Pacific Ocean, by P. B. Smith. 1973. 27 p.; 4 plates showing fossils. 85¢. (2401-00295) [I 19:16:766]

775. Petrography of some granitic bodies in the northern White Mountains, Calif.-Nev., by D. F. Crowder and D. C. Ross. 1973. 28 p. 70¢. (2401-00332) [I 19:16:775]

797. Petrology of the welded tuff of Devine Canyon, southeastern Oregon, by R. C. Greene. 1973. 26 p. 65¢. (2401-00331) [I 19:16:797]

801. Jurassic paleobiogeography of Alaska, by R. W. Imlay and R. L. Detterman. 1973. 34 p. 65¢. (2401-00347) [I 19:16:801]

807. Geochemical anomalies of a claypit area, Callaway County, Mo., and related metabolic imbalance in beef cattle, by R. J. Ebens, J. A. Erdman, G. L. Feder, A. A. Case, and L. A. Selby. 1973. 24 p. 65¢. (2401-00337) [I 19:16:807]

820. United States mineral resources, D. A. Brobst and W. P. Pratt, Editors. 1973. 722 p. $9.15. (2401-00307) [I 19:16:820]

838. Geologic and seismologic aspects of the Managua, Nicaragua, earthquakes of December 23, 1972, by R. D. Brown, Jr., P. L. Ward, and George Plafker. 1973. 34 p.; plate in pocket. $1.25. (2401-00340) [I 19:16:838]

Bulletins

1332-D. Lithologic characteristics of Pliocene rocks cored at Elk Hills, Kern County, Calif., by W. M. Berryman. 1973. p. D1–D56; plate in pocket. $1.20. (2401-00317) [I 19:3:1332-D]

1365. Geochemical reconnaissance of the Santa Rita Mountains, southeast of Tucson, Ariz., by Harald Drewes. 1973. 67 p.; plates in pocket. $1.25. (2101-00281) [I 19:3:1365]

1366. Bibliography of the geology and mineralogy of the rare earths and scandium to 1971, by J. W. Adams and E. R. Iberall. 1973. 195 p. $2.10. (2401-2154) [I 19:3:1366]

1367. A disseminated silver-lead-zinc sulfide occurrence at Hahns Peak, Routt County, Colo., by E. J. Young and Kenneth Segerstrom. 1973. 33 p.; plates in pocket. $1.50. (2401-00276) [I 19:3:1367]

1375. Lithologic characteristics of upper Oligocene and Miocene rocks drilled at Elk Hills, Kern County, Calif., by W. L. Adkison. 1973. 113 p.; plates in pocket. $1.50. (2401-00339) [I 19:3:1375]

1376. Some results of geochemical sampling in McCormick County, S.C., by Henry Bell III. 1973. 22 p.; plates in pocket. $1.75. (2401-00334) [No. I 19:3:1376]

1381. Geochemical characteristics of mineralized breccia pipes in the Red Mountain district, San Juan Mountains, Colo., by F. S. Fisher and W. P. Leedy. 1973. 43 p. 45¢. (2401-00320) [I 19:3:1381]

1382-A. Chemical composition of naturally occurring fluids in relation to mercury deposits in part of north-central California, by Ivan Barnes, M. E. Hinkle, J. B. Rapp, Chris Heropoulos, and W. W. Vaughn. 1973. p. A1–A19. 45¢. (2401-00296) [I 19:3:1382-A]

1382-B. Radioelement and trace-element content of the Ione Formation, central California, by H. A. Wollenberg and F. C. W. Dodge. 1973. p. B1–B17. 30¢. (2401-00328) [I 19:3:1382-B]

Water-Supply Papers

1817-D. Preparative free-flow electrophoresis as a method of fractionation of natural organic materials, by J. A. Leenheer and R. L. Malcolm. 1973. p. D1–D14. 35¢. (2401-00293) [I 19:13:1817-D]

1865. Water resources and geology of Mount Rushmore National Memorial, S. Dak., by J. E. Powell, J. J. Norton, and D. G. Adolphson. 1973. 50 p.; plate in pocket. $1.25. (2401-00323) [I 19:13:1865]

2029-B. Generalization of stream-temperature data in Washington, by M. R. Collings. 1973. p. B1–B45. 30¢. (2401-00302) [I 19:13:2029-B]

U.S. GOVERNMENT
PRINTING OFFICE
PUBLIC DOCUMENTS DEPARTMENT
WASHINGTON, D.C. 20402

OFFICIAL BUSINESS
PENALTY FOR PRIVATE USE $300

POSTAGE AND FEES PAID
U.S. GOVERNMENT
PRINTING OFFICE
375

U.S. MAIL

JRGS HARTWOOOH R 1
HARTWICK CLG LIB
ONEONTA NY 13820

JOURNAL OF RESEARCH

OF THE U.S. GEOLOGICAL SURVEY

NOVEMBER–DECEMBER 1973
VOLUME 1, NUMBER 6

Scientific notes and summaries of investigations in geology, hydrology, and related fields

U.S. DEPARTMENT OF THE INTERIOR

UNITED STATES DEPARTMENT OF THE INTERIOR

ROGERS C. B. MORTON, Secretary

GEOLOGICAL SURVEY

V. E. McKelvey, Director

For sale by the Superintendent of Documents, U.S. Government Printing Office, Washington, D.C., 20402. Order by SD Catalog No. JRGS. Annual subscription rate, effective July 1, 1973, $15.50 (plus $3.75 for foreign mailing). Single copy $2.75. Make checks or money orders payable to the Superintendent of Documents.

Send all subscription inquiries and address changes to the Superintendent of Documents at the above address.

Purchase orders should not be sent to the U.S. Geological Survey library.

Library of Congress Card No. 72-600241

The Journal of Research consists of six issues a year (January-February, March-April, May-June, July-August, September-October, November-December) published in Washington, D.C., by the U.S. Geological Survey. It contains papers by members of the Geological Survey on geologic, hydrologic, topographic, and other scientific and technical subjects.

The Journal supersedes the short-papers chapters (B, C, and D) of the former Geological Survey Research ("Annual Review") series of professional papers. The synopsis chapter (A) of the former Geological Survey Research series will be published as a separate professional paper each year.

Correspondence and inquiries concerning the Journal (other than subscription inquiries and address changes) should be directed to the Managing Editor, Journal of Research, Publications Division, U.S. Geological Survey, Washington, D.C. 20244.

Papers for the Journal should be submitted through regular Division publication channels.

The Secretary of the Interior has determined that the publication of this periodical is necessary in the transaction of the public business required by law of this Department. Use of funds for printing this periodical has been approved by the Director of the Office of Management and Budget through February 11, 1975.

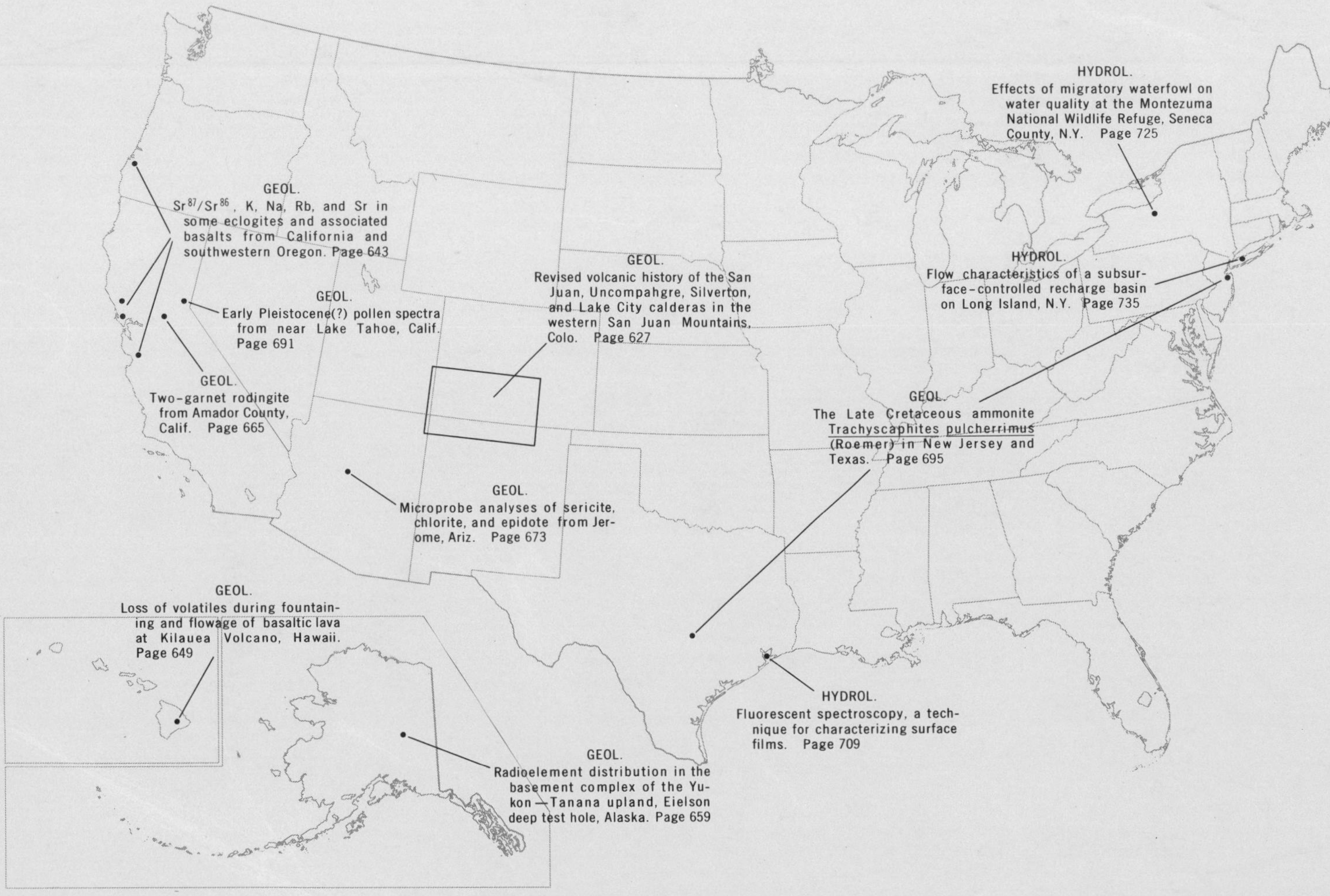

GEOGRAPHIC INDEX TO ARTICLES

[See Contents for articles concerning areas outside the United States and articles without geographic orientation]

JOURNAL OF RESEARCH
of the
U.S. Geological Survey

Vol. 1 No. 6 Nov.-Dec. 1973

CONTENTS

Abbreviations and symbols II

GEOLOGIC STUDIES

Revised volcanic history of the San Juan, Uncompahgre, Silverton, and Lake City calderas in the western San Juan Mountains, Colo. .... *P. W. Lipman, T. A. Steven, R. G. Luedke, and W. S. Burbank* 627

Sr^{87}/Sr^{86}, K, Na, Rb, and Sr in some eclogites and associated basalts from California and southwestern Oregon .... *E. D. Ghent, Z. E. Peterman, and R. G. Coleman* 643

Loss of volatiles during fountaining and flowage of basaltic lava at Kilauea Volcano, Hawaii .... *D. A. Swanson and B. P. Fabbi* 649

Radioelement distribution in the basement complex of the Yukon-Tanana upland, Eielson deep test hole, Alaska .... *C. M. Bunker, C. A. Bush, and R. B. Forbes* 659

Two-garnet rodingite from Amador County, Calif. .... *W. A. Duffield and M. H. Beeson* 665

Microprobe analyses of sericite, chlorite, and epidote from Jerome, Ariz. .... *J. T. Nash* 673

Notes on the bromine pentafluoride technique of oxygen extraction .... *Irving Friedman and J. D. Gleason* 679

Atomic absorption spectrophotometric determination of microgram levels of Co, Ni, Cu, Pb, and Zn in soil and sediment extracts containing large amounts of Mn and Fe .... *T. T. Chao and R. F. Sanzolone* 681

Archaeocycas and *Phasmatocycas*—new genera of Permian cycads .... *S. H. Mamay* 687

Early Pleistocene(?) pollen spectra from near Lake Tahoe, Calif. .... *D. P. Adam* 691

The Late Cretaceous ammonite *Trachyscaphites pulcherrimus* (Roemer) in New Jersey and Texas .... *W. A. Cobban* 695

HYDROLOGIC STUDIES

Determination of the association and dissociation of humic acid fractions by small angle X-ray scattering .... *R. L. Wershaw and D. J. Pinckney* 701

Fluorescent spectroscopy, a technique for characterizing surface films .... *M. C. Goldberg and D. H. Devonald III* 709

Problems of underground storage of wastes .... *R. L. Nace* 719

Effects of migratory waterfowl on water quality at the Montezuma National Wildlife Refuge, Seneca County, N.Y. .... *M. R. Have* 725

Flow characteristics of a subsurface-controlled recharge basin on Long Island, N.Y. .... *R. C. Prill and D. B. Aaronson* 735

ANNUAL INDEX TO VOLUME 1

Subject 745

Author 751

Recent publications of the U.S. Geological Survey .... Inside of back cover

ABBREVIATIONS AND SYMBOLS

[Singular and plural forms for abbreviations of units of measure are the same]

A	angstrom units
A^3	cubic angstroms
a-c	alternating current
amp	amperes
atm	atmosphere
bbl	barrels
B.C.	Before Christ
B.P.	Before Present
c	crystalline state
C_x	molal concentration (of substance x)
cal	calories
cfs	cubic feet per second
Ci	Curies
cm	centimeters
cm^2	square centimeters
cm^3	cubic centimeters
cpm	counts per minute
cu ft	cubic feet
cu mi	cubic miles
d-c	direct current
emu	electromagnetic units
eV	electron volts
fpm	feet per minute
ft	feet
ft^3	cubic feet
g	grams
gal	gallons
gpd	gallons per day
gpm	gallons per minute
hr	hours
Hz	hertz (cycles per second)
in.	inches
kb	kilobars
kg	kilograms
km	kilometers
km^2	square kilometers
km^3	cubic kilometers
kV	kilovolts
l	liters
lb	pounds
ln	logarithm (natural)
m	meters
m^2	square meters
m^3	cubic meters
m	molal (concentration)
M	molar (concentration)
ma	milliamperes
me	milliequivalents
MeV	million electron volts
mg	milligrams
mgd	million gallons per day
mi^2	square miles
min	minutes
ml	milliliters
mm	millimeters
mol	moles
mr	milliroentgens
mV	millivolts
m.y.	million years
μ	microns
μ^2	square microns
μcal	microcalories
μg	micrograms
μm	micrometers
μmho	micromhos
n	neutrons
N	normal
ng	nanograms
nm	nanometers
Oe	oersteds
pCi	picocuries
P.d.t.	Pacific daylight time
pH	pH (measure of hydrogen) ion activity)
ppb	parts per billion
ppm	parts per million
psi	pounds per square inch
rad	radiometric
RaeU	radium equivalent uranium
rpm	revolutions per minute
sec	seconds
sq ft	square feet
sq mi	square miles
v	volts
wt	weight
yr	years

Jour. Research U.S. Geol. Survey
Vol. 1, No. 6, Nov.-Dec. 1973, p. 627—642

REVISED VOLCANIC HISTORY OF THE SAN JUAN, UNCOMPAHGRE, SILVERTON, AND LAKE CITY CALDERAS IN THE WESTERN SAN JUAN MOUNTAINS, COLORADO

By PETER W. LIPMAN, THOMAS A. STEVEN; ROBERT G. LUEDKE;
and WILBUR S. BURBANK, Denver, Colo.;
Washington, D.C.; and Exeter, N.H.

Abstract.—The sequence of mid-Cenozoic volcanic events in the western San Juan Mountains is closely analogous to that elsewhere in the San Juan volcanic field. The Lake Fork, Picayune, and San Juan Formations were erupted from a cluster of central volcanoes from 35 to 30 m.y. ago, when dominant activity shifted to more silicic ash-flow eruptions with accompanying caldera collapses. The Uncompahgre and San Juan calderas, each about 20 km across, formed mainly from eruption of the 28-m.y.-old Sapinero Mesa Tuff. Collapse occurred concurrently with eruption, and intracaldera tuffs accumulated to a thickness of more than 700 m. Both calderas were resurgently domed together; the northeast-trending Eureka graben formed along the distended crest of that dome. The Uncompahgre caldera was then flooded by several 27- to 28-m.y.-old ash-flow sheets from easterly sources, and also by one apparently erupted from the Silverton caldera nested within the older San Juan caldera. The Lake City caldera, located within the older Uncompahgre caldera, formed about 22.5 m.y. ago in response to eruption of the Sunshine Peak Tuff.

The western San Juan Mountains are one of the major mineralized areas in the Rocky Mountain region, with about one-half billion dollars total metal production in the last 100 years (Burbank and Luedke, 1968), and the geology of this region has been studied intensively for many years. Geologic folios by Whitman Cross and his associates at the turn of the century (Cross and Purington, 1899; Cross and others, 1905, 1907) were among the first studies anywhere to determine detailed stratigraphic relations in propylitically and hydrothermally altered Tertiary volcanic rocks. These stratigraphic relations were later amplified by Larsen and Cross (1956) and subsequently modified by Luedke and Burbank (1963). Nevertheless, the stratigraphic interpretations established by the earlier workers have been generally accepted with only minor changes to the present (table 1).

Since 1930 Wilbur S. Burbank and several associates have made detailed structural studies of many of the mineralized areas; among the early noteworthy results of this work have been recognition of two ring-fault-bounded collapse features, called the Silverton and Lake City calderas (Burbank, 1933, 1938, 1941, 1947a, 1947b, 1951), and later recognition that these two structures were nested within a larger older volcanic collapse area, called the San Juan volcanic depression (Luedke and Burbank, 1963, 1968; Burbank and Luedke, 1969).

This paper reports preliminary results of recent regional studies in the San Juan Mountains (fig. 1) (Steven and others, 1973a) and detailed studies in the Lake City area by Lipman and Steven and in the Silverton area by Luedke and Burbank, which require major revisions in interpretations of the volcanic stratigraphy and related caldera-collapse structures. These revisions in turn provide plausible answers to several long-recognized stratigraphic and structural problems of the western region. In particular, the San Juan volcanic depression, rather than being a single large oval collapse structure, consists of two intersecting smaller subcircular calderas. Also, all rock units of the Silverton Volcanic Group (table 1), previously interpreted as a genetically related assemblage of lavas and tuffs that accumulated within the concurrently subsiding San Juan depression (Luedke and Burbank, 1968; Burbank and Luedke, 1969), are generally correlative with other named volcanic formations nearby in the volcanic field that were previously considered to be either older or younger than the units of the Silverton Group. Further revisions of the volcanic stratigraphy and caldera structures are likely by the time our studies are complete.

ROCK UNITS

Tertiary volcanic rocks in the western San Juan Mountains rest unconformably on pre-Tertiary nonvolcanic rocks ranging in age from Precambrian to Cretaceous. The volcanic stratigraphy is most conveniently described in terms of two suites: (1) an older suite, largely Oligocene in age, of intermediate-composition lavas and associated more silicic differentiates, including voluminous ash-flow tuffs of quartz latite and low-silica rhyolite, and (2) a younger bimodal suite of mafic and very silicic rocks of Miocene and possibly younger age. These two suites appear to have fundamental significance, both regionally in the San Juan volcanic field (Lipman and

Table 1.—*Nomenclature of Tertiary volcanic rocks in the western San Juan Mountains*

[K-Ar ages in parentheses are from Lipman, Steven, and Mehnert (1970) and from this report. Asterisk (*) indicates unit previously assigned to the Silverton Volcanic Group]

SILVERTON QUADRANGLE Cross, Howe, and Ransome (1905)	EUREKA DISTRICT Burbank and Luedke (1969)	LAKE CITY AND SILVERTON AREAS This report: ASH-FLOW SHEETS	LAKE CITY AND SILVERTON AREAS This report: LAVA FLOWS AND BRECCIAS	
Potosi volcanic series	Potosi Volcanic Group		Basalts of the Hinsdale Formation (18.0-18.4 m.y.)	Late (Miocene) bimodal volcanics
			Quartz latites of Red and Grassy Mountains (22.7 m.y.)	
	Sunshine Peak Rhyolite	Sunshine Peak Tuff (22.5 m.y.)		
			Quartz latite of Rambouillet Park	Oligocene ash-flow sequence and related lavas
		Rat Creek Tuff (> 26.5 m.y.)		
			Volcanics of Uncompahgre Peak	
		Wason Park Tuff		
		Carpenter Ridge Tuff		
			Local lavas	
		Crystal Lake Tuff		
		Fish Canyon Tuff = welded tuff of the Henson Fm.* (Burbank and Luedke, 1964) = American Flat Latite (Cross and others, 1907). (27.8 m.y.)		
			Henson* and Burns* Formations ≅Carson volcano of the Sheep Mountain Formation (Larsen and Cross, 1956)	
	Gilpin Peak[1] Tuff: GP_6	Sapinero Mesa Tuff (includes Eureka Member*)		
	Gilpin Peak[1] Tuff: GP_5	Dillon Mesa Tuff		
	Gilpin Peak[1] Tuff: GP_3	Blue Mesa Tuff		
			Local lavas and breccias	
	Gilpin Peak[1] Tuff: GP_1	Ute Ridge Tuff (28.4 m.y.)		
Silverton volcanic series: Pyroxene andesite	Silverton Volcanic Group: Henson Formation			
Burns latite	Burns Formation			
Eureka rhyolite	Eureka Tuff			
Picayune andesite	Picayune Formation			
San Juan tuff	San Juan Formation		San Juan ≅ Picayune* ≅ Lake Fork Fms. [clastic facies] (32.1 m.y.) [vent facies] [vent facies]	Early (Oligocene) intermediate-composition lavas and breccias

[1] Correlations between ash-flow sheets in the Lake City area and subunits of the Gilpin Peak Tuff mapped by Luedke and Burbank (1963) and by Burbank and Luedke (1964, 1966)

others, 1970) and widely in Cenozoic volcanic rocks of the Western United States (Christiansen and Lipman, 1972).

The Oligocene volcanic suite in the western San Juan area is discussed in terms of six progressively younger groups, as follows: (1) Early intermediate-composition lavas, breccias, and intrusives, (2) lower ash-flow sheets from sources to the southeast, (3) the Sapinero Mesa Tuff (and its Eureka Member) that formed by ash-flow eruptions from the San Juan and Uncompahgre calderas, (4) lower lavas and sediments (including the Burns and Henson Formations) that accumulated within the San Juan and Uncompahgre calderas shortly after collapse, (5) upper ash-flow sheets, mostly erupted from

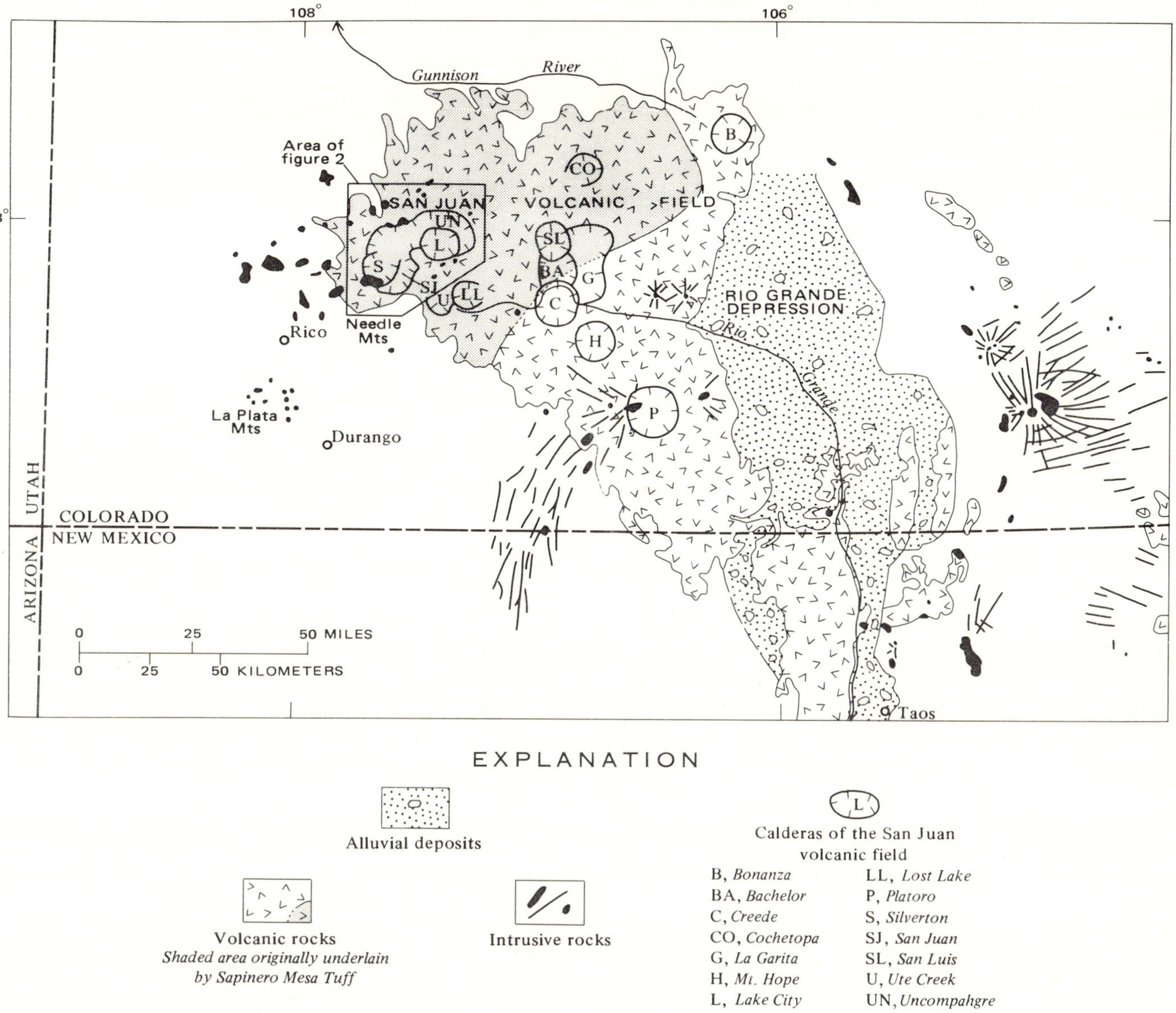

Figure 1.—Index map, showing location of the San Juan volcanic field, calderas of the San Juan Mountains, and generalized distribution of the Sapinero Mesa Tuff (and its Eureka Member) erupted from the San Juan and Uncompahgre calderas. In part modified from Cohee (1961).

sources to the east but including one—the Crystal Lake Tuff, a new name in this report—presumably erupted from the Silverton caldera, and (6) upper lavas and related intrusives that accumulated around margins of the San Juan, Uncompahgre, and Silverton calderas.

Divisions of the Miocene bimodal suite in the western San Juan area are (1) the rhyolitic Sunshine Peak Tuff erupted from the Lake City caldera, (2) silicic postcollapse lavas and intrusives of the Lake City caldera, and (3) regional mafic lavas of the Hinsdale Formation.

Pre-Tertiary Rocks

Pre-Tertiary rocks are exposed within the map area (fig. 2) south of the San Juan caldera on the north flank of the Needle Mountains, north of the San Juan caldera in the Uncompahgre River valley, and between the San Juan and Uncompahgre calderas. The last area, which consists largely of Precambrian granite, provides the main evidence that the San Juan and Uncompahgre calderas are separate structures. Precambrian gneiss of the Irving Formation and overlying Paleozoic sedimentary rocks are the major pre-Tertiary rock types in the area south of the San Juan caldera. In the Uncompahgre valley, Precambrian metasedimentary rocks of the Uncompahgre Formation are exposed below Paleozoic and Mesozoic sedimentary rocks, all of which are intruded by porphyritic granodiorite of Late Cretaceous or early Tertiary age.

Early Intermediate-Composition Lavas and Breccias

The oldest mid-Tertiary volcanic rocks in the western San Juan Mountains are lava flows, flow breccias, and mudflow breccias and conglomerates of predominantly intermediate compositions—calc-alkalic andesite, rhyodacite, and mafic quartz latite. These were erupted from numerous central volcanoes between 35 and 30 m.y. ago (Lipman and others, 1970; Luedke and Burbank, 1968). In the area considered here (fig. 2), early intermediate centers have been recognized near Larson Creek, at the head of the Cimarron River, at Matterhorn Peak, and near Carson Camp, and one or more are believed to have existed in the area north of Silverton.

Diverse formational names have been assigned to different parts of these generally equivalent early intermediate lavas and breccias. In the western San Juan region, the San Juan, Lake Fork, and Picayune Formations (table 1) represent local accumulations within a laterally intertonguing assemblage of lavas and breccias. Only two radiometric ages—32.1 m.y. for a flow breccia from the San Juan Formation (Lipman and others, 1970, table 2, no. 7) and 31.4 m.y. for a lava flow from the Lake Fork Formation (H. H. Mehnert, written commun., 1972)—are thus far available from these units, and their age range is not known.

The widespread San Juan Formation consists mainly of mudflow deposits and less voluminous associated water-laid volcaniclastic sedimentary rocks that originated as alluvial aprons around the vent-facies accumulations of the central volcanoes. Lava flows that interfinger with these volcaniclastic rocks have been mapped as part of the San Juan Formation in several areas; numerous such lava flows north of the Uncompahgre caldera were mismapped as sills in the Ouray folio (Cross and others, 1907), but these flows were later recognized and included in the San Juan Formation (Luedke and Burbank, 1963; Luedke, 1972). Flows also interfinger with the volcaniclastic rocks of the San Juan Formation northwest and southwest of the San Juan caldera (Burbank and Luedke, 1968, p. 17).

The Lake Fork Formation, as mapped by Larsen and Cross (1956, pl. 1), consists of vent-facies accumulations (lavas, flow breccias, and explosion breccias) from at least two central volcanoes, one of which is marked by the cluster of intrusions near Larson Creek about 5 km north of Lake City (fig. 2); the other, about 10 km farther northeast, was described by Larsen and Cross (1956, p. 67–68). The Lake Fork was considered by Larsen and Cross (1956, p. 64, 69) to underlie the San Juan Formation, but our recent mapping north of Lake City indicates that rocks mapped by Larsen and Cross as Lake Fork interfinger with mudflow breccias that they mapped as San Juan Formation; a similar interpretation has been inferred previously by Olson, Hedlund, and Hansen (1968, p. C8), Burbank and Luedke (1969, p. 17), and by Lipman, Steven, and Mehnert (1970, p. 2331).

The Picayune Formation consists mainly of intermediate-composition lava flows and flow breccias that previously have been considered the lowermost unit of the Silverton Volcanic Group (table 1). These rocks were believed to have accumulated mostly within the San Juan volcanic depression during early stages of its development, and to overlie the San Juan Formation unconformably (Luedke and Burbank, 1968; Burbank and Luedke, 1969).

We now interpret these lavas as downfaulted vent-facies accumulations forming the cores of early central volcanoes that were sources of the mudflow breccias in the San Juan Formation.

Apparently the areas that caved away into the San Juan and Uncompahgre calderas were near-source volcanic highlands, probably clusters of central volcanoes prior to collapse, inasmuch as lava flows interfingering with volcaniclastic rocks of the San Juan Formation increase in abundance toward the areas of the calderas (Burbank and Luedke, 1969, p. 17). Also, younger regional ash-flow sheets change from coalesced uniform sheets to local valley-filling deposits and then wedge out toward areas underlain by these vent-facies rocks. Because lavas of the Picayune Formation within the San Juan and Uncompahgre calderas occupy the same stratigraphic position—immediately below the intracaldera Eureka Member of the Sapinero Mesa Tuff—as do the other early intermediate lavas below outflow Sapinero Mesa Tuff beyond the caldera walls, they are logically considered offset parts of the same near-source accumulations.

Lower Ash-Flow Sheets

In the western San Juan area, three regionally widespread ash-flow sheets overlie the early intermediate rocks and underlie the Sapinero Mesa Tuff that resulted from the culminating eruptions of the San Juan and Uncompahgre calderas. The lower two sheets, the Ute Ridge and Blue Mesa Tuffs, were erupted from a caldera source southeast of the map area, but the overlying Dillon Mesa Tuff is uncertainly interpreted as an early eruption from the Uncompahgre caldera (table 2). Regional mapping has demonstrated that these three ash-flow sheets are correlative with units of the Gilpin Peak Tuff, as subdivided in the area west of the Silverton caldera (Burbank and Luedke, 1964, 1966).

Ute Ridge Tuff

The Ute Ridge Tuff is a new name, here applied to the lowermost widespread ash-flow sheet in the western San Juan Mountains. This unit has previously been referred to informally as the tuff of Ute Ridge (Steven and others, 1973a), and as the tuff from Storm King Mountain near the northern limit of its extent where it has been dated—somewhat discordantly—as 28.4 m.y. old (Lipman and others, 1970, table 3, no. 10). The Ute Ridge Tuff is named for excellent exposures on the lower slopes of Ute Ridge; this designated type area is about 5 km southeast of the map area (fig. 2) in the Rio Grande Pyramid 7½-minute quadrangle. The Ute Ridge Tuff is typically a densely welded red-brown phenocryst-rich quartz latite that contains 30–40 percent phenocrysts of plagioclase, sanidine, biotite, and augite. The Ute Ridge is a multiple-flow ash-flow sheet that displays well-developed compound cooling in the type area. At Ute Ridge it is as much as 200 m thick, but its thickness is rather variable owing to irregular underlying topography. It has been traced as far north as Storm King Mountain 33 km north of Ouray, southeast as far as south-flowing Weminuche Creek 36 km southeast of Silverton (Steven and others, 1973a), and it is present as small erosional remnants on high ridges west of the San Juan caldera where it has been mapped as unit 1 of the Gilpin Peak Tuff (Burbank and Luedke, 1964, 1966). The Ute Ridge appears originally to have covered an area in excess of 6,000 km^2 and had an initial volume of at least 300 km^3. The Ute Ridge Tuff probably was erupted from the Ute Creek caldera (fig. 1), now largely buried.

Blue Mesa Tuff

The Blue Mesa Tuff (Olson and others, 1968) is a relatively phenocryst-poor low-silica rhyolite that widely overlies the Ute Ridge Tuff in the western San Juan Mountains. It generally contains about 5 percent phenocrysts of sanidine and plagioclase in subequal amounts, biotite, and sparse augite; locally, near its inferred source from the Lost Lakes caldera (fig. 1), it is weakly compositionally zoned upward into a more phenocryst-rich and less-silicic tuff. The Blue Mesa, typically densely welded and pale red brown, has a black basal vitrophyre and a well-developed light-gray upper vapor-phase zone. In detail, it varies widely in welding and crystallization characteristics, especially where deposited on irregular surfaces. The Blue Mesa Tuff closely resembles several overlying phenocryst-poor rhyolites of the ash-flow sequence, especially parts of the Sapinero Mesa, Crystal Lake, and Carpenter Ridge Tuffs, and relations in some discontinuously exposed or structurally complex areas are confusing. The Blue Mesa has been mapped as unit 3 of the Gilpin Peak Tuff west of the San Juan caldera (Burbank and Luedke, 1964, 1966). In the type locality the Blue Mesa is about 75 m thick (Olson and others, 1968), but it is as much as 300 m thick on Ute Ridge and Pole Creek Mountain (Steven and others, 1973a) near its probable source at the Lost Lake caldera. The initial areal extent and volume of the Blue Mesa Tuff must have been as great or slightly greater than that of the Ute Ridge Tuff (table 2).

Dillon Mesa Tuff

The Dillon Mesa Tuff (Olson and others, 1968) is a relatively thin ash-flow sheet of red-brown phenocryst-poor rhyolite. The Dillon Mesa seems to be generally similar in phenocryst mineralogy to the underlying Blue Mesa and overlying Sapinero Mesa Tuffs, but in places it is distinguished by abundant small flakes of biotite. Although the Dillon Mesa Tuff is locally as much as 60 m thick and is densely welded in its interior, the unit is more commonly only 5–10 m thick and weakly welded throughout. It is as much as 50 m thick in the Potosi Peak-Gilpin Peak area, but it thins rapidly to the southwest (Burbank and Luedke, 1964, 1966). Southeast of the San Juan caldera this unit is as much as 20 m thick in the Pole Creek Mountain quadrangle, but it is much thinner and present only locally south of the Rio Grande or east of Pole Creek Mountain. Despite its relative thinness, the Dillon Mesa was deposited over a large area in the northwestern San Juan Mountains. The original distribution of the Dillon Mesa Tuff is incompletely known, and this tuff may have been removed by erosion over sizable areas, but it seems to have been most widespread north of the Uncompahgre caldera, where it has been traced north beyond the Gunnison River (Hansen, 1971). Several features of the Dillon Mesa, not detailed here, but including its northerly distribution, suggest that its eruption may have been related to inception of the Uncompahgre caldera. Northwest of the San Juan caldera the Dillon Mesa Tuff has been mapped as unit 5 of the Gilpin Peak Tuff. Initial volume of the Dillon Mesa is uncertain but may have been about 50–100 km^3.

Sapinero Mesa Tuff and Its Eureka Member

The most significant stratigraphic and structural reinterpretations of our recent work have resulted from recognition that the Eureka Tuff within the San Juan and Uncompahgre calderas is the intracaldera accumulation of the regionally widespread Sapinero Mesa Tuff (Olson and others, 1968). West of the San Juan caldera, the Sapinero Mesa Tuff has been mapped as unit 6 of the Gilpin Peak Tuff (Burbank and Luedke, 1964, 1966). To conform to the pattern of nomenclature that has been applied to similar stratigraphic situations elsewhere in the San Juan Mountains (Steven and others, 1973b), we propose that the formational name of the widespread outflow rocks, the Sapinero Mesa Tuff, be retained for the whole ash-flow sheet, and that the name Eureka Member of the Sapinero Mesa Tuff be applied to the same thick intracaldera assemblage of rocks previously called Eureka Rhyolite or Eureka Tuff (table 1).

The Sapinero Mesa Tuff is one of the great ash-flow sheets of the San Juan volcanic field; erosional remnants occur over an area of at least 15,000 km^2, and represent an original volume estimated in excess of 1,000 km^3. These values probably are too low, as the distribution of present erosional remnants suggests that the sheet formerly extended farther to the west (fig. 1).

The outflow Sapinero Mesa Tuff is a phenocryst-poor rhyolitic welded tuff, containing about 5 percent phenocrysts of sanidine and plagioclase in subequal amounts, biotite, and minor augite. Although compound cooling is locally evident, in most sections the Sapinero Mesa displays a simple welding-crystallization zonation—a conspicuous black vitrophyre at the base, a densely welded devitrified red-brown interior, and a light-gray upper zone of vapor-phase crystallization. Near the Uncompahgre and San Juan calderas, pumice fragments in the

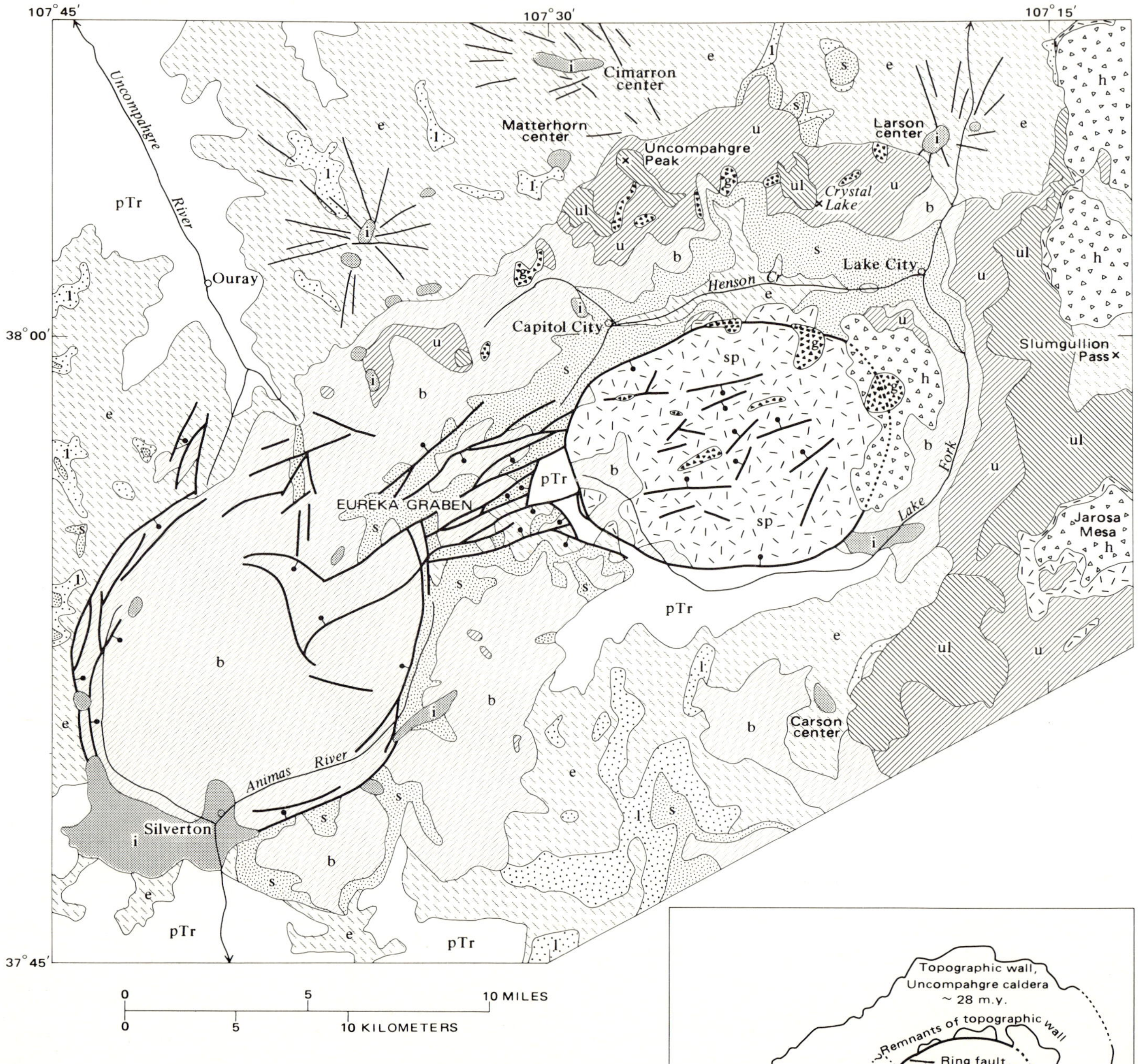

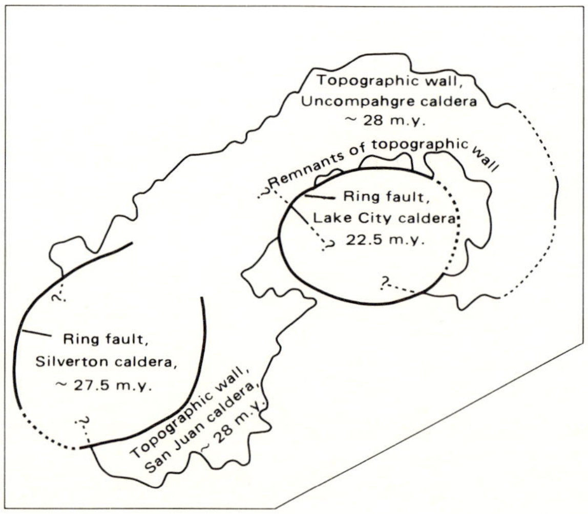

Figure 2.—Generalized geologic map of the Silverton-Lake City area. Region south of lat 38° N. modified from Steven, Lipman, Hail, Barker, and Luedke (1973a); northern area generalized from Luedke (1972) and from P. W. Lipman, D. A. Johnston, and T. A. Steven (unpub. mapping).

CORRELATION OF MAP UNITS

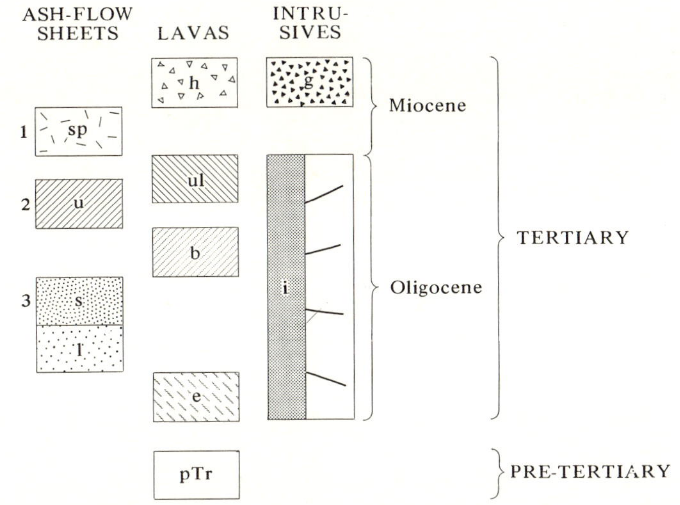

1 Time of collapse of Lake City caldera
2 Time of collapse of Silverton caldera
3 Time of collapse of San Juan and Uncompahgre calderas

DESCRIPTION OF MAP UNITS

ASH-FLOW SHEETS

- sp — Sunshine Peak Tuff (Miocene)
- u — Upper ash-flow sheets (Oligocene) – Fish Canyon, Crystal Lake, Carpenter Ridge, Wason Park, and Rat Creek Tuffs
- s — Sapinero Mesa (and Eureka Member) Tuff (Oligocene)
- l — Lower ash-flow sheets (Oligocene) – Dillon Mesa, Blue Mesa, and Ute Ridge Tuffs

LAVAS

- h — Quartz latitic lavas of Lake City caldera and basaltic lavas of the Hinsdale Formation (Miocene)
- ul — Upper lavas around margins of Uncompahgre caldera (Oligocene)
- b — Lower caldera lavas and volcaniclastic rocks (Oligocene)– Henson and Burns Formations
- e — Early intermediate-composition lavas and breccias (Oligocene)

INTRUSIVES

- g — Rhyolite and granite intrusives of Lake City caldera (Miocene)
- i — Intermediate-composition intrusives (Oligocene) – Mainly monzonite
- Dike

pTr — PRE-TERTIARY ROCKS

CONTACT

FAULT – Dotted where covered; bar and ball on downthrown side

Figure 2.

interior of the sheet are elongate and lineate, owing to extreme welding and flowage, and irregularly shaped gas cavities are as much as 0.5 m across. Lineations become obscure outward from the source and are absent near the margins of the sheet. Gas cavities diminish in size away from the source, although they remain characteristic, and near the margin of the sheet a zone of small round lithophysae is commonly well developed in the interior of the unit. Xenoliths are generally sparse, but small fragments of andesitic flow rock are somewhat more abundant near the San Juan and Uncompahgre calderas.

The intracaldera Eureka Member of the Sapinero Mesa Tuff is more variable than the outflow sheet, both in modal composition and in welding-crystallization zonation. The nature of these variations is poorly understood at present because of limited exposures, local deformation, and extensive alteration in most places. The Eureka is typically moderately to strongly propylitized greenish-gray densely welded tuff, but where least altered west of Lake City, the cooling zonation alternates from red-brown densely welded tuff to light-gray less welded tuff. No glassy tuffs have survived, but a spectacular spherulitic zone locally present near the base probably indicates former presence of a glassy zone at this horizon. Upper parts of the Eureka Member are commonly very densely welded and strikingly lineate, and in the Lake City area they closely resemble nearby outflow Sapinero Mesa Tuff. The same phenocryst phases occur in the Eureka Member as in the outflow sheet, but they are generally somewhat more abundant, typically 5–10 percent. Within and near the San Juan caldera, the phenocryst content of the Eureka Member increases upward to as much as 20–30 percent. This change may indicate that the last material erupted was somewhat more mafic, but this relation has not yet been studied in detail. The Eureka generally contains abundant lithic fragments of intermediate-composition lava and locally contains blocks of granite or quartzite that reflect the subvolcanic basement, but the amount of such detritus is locally variable. Some zones of the Eureka contain as much as 10–20 percent rock fragments, and in places included masses of landslide breccia are as much as 50 m thick. The amount of lithic material decreases markedly near the top of the Eureka Member in the Lake City area.

The thickness of the outflow Sapinero Mesa sheet averages about 50 m and is about 100 m at maximum, whereas the intracaldera Eureka Member is at least 700 m thick in places, and its base is only locally exposed. This disparity in thickness between the intracaldera and outflow tuff is interpreted to indicate subsidence of the San Juan and Uncompahgre calderas concurrently with eruption of the Sapinero Mesa. Significantly, owing in part to a difference in stratigraphic interpretation, no major outflow sheet equivalent to the Eureka was recognized previously (Luedke and Burbank, 1968, p. 194).

Thick local intracaldera accumulations characterize many calderas in the San Juan volcanic field (Steven and Ratté,

Table 2.—*Major ash-flow sheets of the western San Juan Mountains*

Tuff unit	Caldera source	Phenocryst content and composition	Estimated initial volume (km^3)	Remanent magnetic polarity[1]	K-Ar age (m.y.)[2]
Sunshine Peak	Lake City	Crystal-rich rhyolite	200–300	?	22.5
Rat Creek	San Luis	Crystal-rich quartz latite	700–800	+	>26.4
Wason Park	Creede area	Crystal-rich rhyolite	200–300	–	<26.7
Carpenter Ridge	Bachelor	Crystal-poor rhyolite	1,200–1,500	–	>26.7
Crystal Lake	Silverton	do	25–50	–	.....
Fish Canyon	La Garita	Crystal-rich quartz latite	3,000+	+	27.8
Sapinero Mesa	San Juan and Uncompahgre	Crystal-poor rhyolite	1,000+	–	.....
Dillon Mesa	Uncompahgre(?)	do	50–100	–	.....
Blue Mesa	Lost Lakes	do	400+	–	.....
Ute Ridge	Ute Creek	Crystal-rich quartz latite	300+	–	28.4

[1] +, normal magnetic polarity; –, reverse magnetic polarity; ?, undetermined.
[2] From Lipman, Steven, and Mehnert (1970) and H. H. Mehnert (written commun., 1971).

1965; Lipman and Steven, 1970; Steven and others, 1973a), and every thick intracaldera accumulation studied so far is demonstrably equivalent to a large widespread ash-flow sheet. Generally, such ash-flow sheets are not continuous across the walls of their source caldera, and equivalencies can be demonstrated only indirectly. Time relations are especially significant, as the intracaldera accumulations may differ markedly from the outflow sheets in appearance and composition owing to variations in welding, crystallization, alteration, and sorting of phenocrysts and lithic fragments.

Contemporaneity of intracaldera Eureka Member and outflow accumulations of the Sapinero Mesa Tuff can be demonstrated precisely for the Uncompahgre caldera; less direct evidence indicates the same timing for the San Juan caldera. The outflow Sapinero Mesa Tuff forms a nearly continuous sheet for about 40 km to the north of the Uncompahgre caldera, where it overlies the Blue Mesa Tuff and is overlain by Fish Canyon Tuff. At the topographic wall of the caldera, about 10 km northwest of Lake City (fig. 2), the outflow Sapinero Mesa is truncated and unconformably overlapped by the younger caldera-filling ash-flow units—the Fish Canyon, Crystal Lake, Carpenter Ridge, and Rat Creek Tuffs—that overlie the thick ponded Eureka Member within the Uncompahgre caldera. Thus, these geologic relations indicate that the outflow Sapinero Mesa can be no younger than the Uncompahgre caldera and the intracaldera Eureka no older; the caldera must have collapsed during or shortly after the emplacement of the outflow Sapinero Mesa. The Eureka cannot be older than the Sapinero Mesa, as was previously thought.

Similar unconformable relations occur on the southeast side of the San Juan caldera, at Sheep Mountain, about 13 km east of Silverton (fig. 2); there, lavas of the Burns and Henson Formations overlie Eureka within the caldera and lap out unconformably against Ute Ridge and Blue Mesa Tuffs at the caldera wall, indicating that the San Juan caldera must be younger than these tuffs. In this area the Sapinero Mesa Tuff is not present at the caldera wall, but it overlies Blue Mesa Tuff a few kilometers to the east. The San Juan caldera therefore subsided after the Blue Mesa Tuff was emplaced and before the Burns and Henson Formations accumulated, and thus within the same time interval that the Sapinero Mesa Tuff was emplaced.

Similarly, near Richmond Pass, 10 km south of Ouray on the northwest side of the San Juan caldera (Burbank and Luedke, 1964) rocks of the Henson Formation were deposited unconformably against steep slopes of the caldera wall. Here, the wall consists of an intertonguing sequence of early intermediate vent-facies lavas and volcaniclastic breccias (including rocks originally mapped as San Juan, Picayune, and Burns Formations) overlain nearly conformably by the Blue Mesa and Sapinero Mesa Tuffs (equivalent to units 3 and 6 of the Gilpin Peak Tuff). Caldera subsidence here clearly preceded the Henson eruptions but was no older than emplacement of Sapinero Mesa Tuff. A few kilometers to the northeast near Engineer Pass, 9 km southeast of Ouray, Fish Canyon Tuff confined within the San Juan caldera overlies lavas of the Burns and Henson Formations, again bracketing the time of the formation of the San Juan caldera to the interval between eruption of the Sapinero Mesa and Fish Canyon Tuffs.

All currently known geologic evidence thus indicates that both the Uncompahgre and San Juan calderas formed during the interval that the Sapinero Mesa Tuff was emplaced. This timing, as well as certain features of the distribution and lithologic variation of the Sapinero Mesa Tuff, discussed more fully in a later section, suggests to us that the eruption of this ash-flow sheet led to virtually simultaneous subsidence of the two calderas, although the Uncompahgre caldera may have begun to subside during eruption of the earlier Dillon Mesa Tuff, as mentioned previously.

Lower Caldera Lavas and Volcaniclastic Rocks

Lavas and volcanic sedimentary rocks that accumulated within and around the margins of the San Juan and Uncompahgre calderas shortly after collapse intervene between the Eureka Member of the Sapinero Mesa Tuff and the Fish Canyon Tuff. In the San Juan caldera these lavas and volcanic sedimentary rocks have been divided into the Burns and Henson Formations. The Burns Formation is a heterogeneous assemblage of rhyodacitic to quartz latitic lavas and breccias, generally containing biotite or hornblende phenocrysts, and minor tuffs and rhyolitic lavas, whereas the Henson Formation includes more abundant sedimentary rocks in association with more mafic andesites and rhyodacites, commonly characterized by pyroxene phenocrysts (Luedke and Burbank, 1963; Burbank and Luedke, 1969). These distinctions are not recognized within the Uncompahgre caldera, and probably reflect the local sequence within the San Juan caldera rather than having regional significance.

Thick intermediate-composition lavas and breccias overlying the San Juan Formation generally west of the San Juan caldera have previously been mapped as Burns Formation (Burbank and Luedke, 1964, 1966). Pending further study, these rocks are tentatively reinterpreted as parts of the early intermediate sequence because they are overlain by the Ute Ridge, Blue Mesa, and Sapinero Mesa Tuffs (units 1, 3, and 6 of the Gilpin Peak Tuff). Thin ash-flow tuffs below these lavas, previously mapped as Eureka Tuff, are now tentatively considered as local ash-flow deposits within the early intermediate sequence.

The lower lava and volcaniclastic sequence within the Uncompahgre caldera is highly variable both vertically and laterally. North of Lake City, this sequence consists mainly of fine-grained buff to gray tuffaceous sandstone and shale, representing a shallow-water deltaic or lake environment. South of Lake City the main constituents are thick lava flows, varying from sparsely porphyritic dark-gray andesite or rhyodacite to light-gray flow-laminated quartz latite or rhyolite. West of Lake City dark-gray andesitic or rhyodacitic lavas, containing conspicuous large tabular plagioclase phenocrysts, are intricately interlayered with greenish-gray andesitic sandstone.

East and southeast of the San Juan caldera and south of the Uncompahgre caldera a sequence of intermediate-composition mud-flow breccias and local interlayered lavas, described as the Carson volcano of the Sheep Mountain Formation (Larsen and Cross, 1956, p. 126–128), are bounded stratigraphically by the underlying Sapinero Mesa Tuff and overlying Fish Canyon Tuff. These predominantly volcaniclastic rocks are thus in the same stratigraphic position as the Burns and Henson Formations within the San Juan caldera and related lower lavas in the Uncompahgre caldera (table 1), and we regard the Carson rocks as a largely clastic apron, peripheral to the lower lava centers.

The lower lavas and volcaniclastic rocks vary widely in thickness within the calderas, owing to irregularities on the underlying floor and to variations in thickness around different volcanic centers. The rocks are as much as 500–600 m thick locally within both the Uncompahgre and San Juan calderas, and they wedge sharply against buried topography and adjacent caldera walls.

Upper Ash-Flow Sheets

Several ash-flow sheets, including the Fish Canyon, Carpenter Ridge, Wason Park, and Rat Creek Tuffs, flowed into the western San Juan area from caldera sources farther east. These units provide age control on the late evolution of the San Juan and Uncompahgre calderas. The Crystal Lake Tuff, which occurs locally between the Fish Canyon and Carpenter Ridge Tuffs, appears to have been erupted from the Silverton caldera nested within the San Juan caldera.

Fish Canyon Tuff

Positive identification of the Fish Canyon Tuff (Olson and others, 1968) within the Uncompahgre and San Juan calderas is one of the key pieces of evidence on which our stratigraphic reinterpretations are based, as this unit occurs widely above the Sapinero Mesa Tuff and below the Carpenter Ridge Tuff, both within and outside these calderas. The Fish Canyon is the most petrographically distinctive ash-flow sheet in the San Juan volcanic field: it is a gray phenocryst-rich quartz latite, containing 30–50 percent phenocrysts of plagioclase, sanidine, quartz, biotite, hornblende, and accessory sphene. No other major ash-flow sheet in the field contains hornblende rather than augite as the second mafic constituent after biotite. Quartz phenocrysts constitute 1–3 percent of the rock, whereas they are very rare or absent in other quartz latitic tuffs of the field. This quartz is also distinctive in that it occurs as rounded pellets, as large as 5 mm in diameter, that are riddled with wormy glass inclusions due to resorption. Finally, the abundant accessory sphene is unique.

The Fish Canyon Tuff is the most widespread (at least 15,000 km^2) and voluminous (more than 3,000 km^3) ash-flow sheet in the volcanic field. It was erupted about 27.8 m.y. ago (Steven and others, 1967; Lipman and others, 1970) from the large La Garita caldera (fig. 1). Near the Uncompahgre and San Juan calderas (fig. 2) the Fish Canyon underlies almost all the area shown as "upper ash-flow sheets." East and southeast of Lake City the Fish Canyon lies on intracaldera lavas and volcanic sandstones; northwest of Lake City it rests directly on the Eureka Member of the Sapinero Mesa Tuff; and southeast of Ouray, within the northern part of the San Juan caldera, it rests on Burns and Henson lavas. In general, the Fish Canyon Tuff within the Uncompahgre and San Juan calderas was previously mapped as American Flat Latite (Cross and others, 1907) and in part as "welded tuff of the Henson Formation" (Luedke and Burbank, 1961, 1963; Luedke, 1972).

Crystal Lake Tuff

A phenocryst-poor low-silica rhyolite ash-flow sheet lies between the Fish Canyon and overlying Carpenter Ridge Tuffs in the northern moat of the Uncompahgre caldera and also in the upper Rio Grande drainage southeast of Silverton (Steven and others, 1973a). This unit is present at Crystal Lake, about 5 km northwest of Lake City (fig. 2), and is especially well exposed on Crystal Peak just to the west; it is here named the Crystal Lake Tuff. At Crystal Peak, here designated the type area, the Crystal Lake Tuff is about 50 m thick and consists of a black basal vitrophyre, densely welded red-brown tuff in its interior, and an upper zone of vapor-phase crystallization. The lithology of the Crystal Lake Tuff closely resembles parts of other phenocryst-poor rhyolitic tuffs of the area (Blue Mesa, Sapinero Mesa, and Carpenter Ridge), and, were it not for the intervening distinctive Fish Canyon Tuff, these similar rhyolitic units could be difficult to distinguish and map consistently.

The Crystal Lake Tuff contains about 5 percent phenocrysts of sanidine and plagioclase in subequal amounts, accompanied by biotite and minor augite. Where thick and densely welded, it commonly contains highly compacted light-gray lineate pumice lenses as much as 0.5 m in length, but where the sheet is relatively thin near its margins, it is only weakly welded and contains abundant small angular fragments of intermediate-composition lava.

The Crystal Lake Tuff is thickest and most densely welded in the northern moat of the Uncompahgre caldera where it ponded to a thickness of about 200 m, but it is absent farther east in this moat, where its spread was blocked near Lake City by high parts of the resurgent dome. The Crystal Lake has been recognized outside the San Juan and Uncompahgre calderas only as a single east-trending lobe, covering an area of about 150 km^2, in the upper Rio Grande drainage. This outflow accumulation of Crystal Lake Tuff is thinner and contains fewer lithic fragments and smaller pumice lenses than that within the Uncompahgre caldera. Its distribution suggests that the Crystal Lake originated from within the San Juan caldera and flowed mainly northeast through a low divide into the Uncompahgre caldera and southeast across the San Juan caldera wall into the upper Rio Grande area. This interpretation is favored by the presence within the San Juan caldera of the structural boundary (ring fractures) of a younger caldera—the Silverton caldera—that subsided after accumulation of the Burns and Henson Formations. Maps and cross sections of the Silverton caldera (Varnes, 1963; Burbank and Luedke, 1964, 1969) indicate that this late subsidence has displacements ranging from as much as 500–700 m along the western and southern ring fractures to near zero at the northeast side. The Crystal Lake Tuff is the only sizable upper ash-flow sheet without a recognized source elsewhere in the volcanic field, and conversely the Silverton caldera is a likely source area without a related ash-flow sheet; we therefore suggest that eruption of the Crystal Lake resulted in formation of the Silverton caldera.

The Crystal Lake Tuff was erupted about 27.0–27.5 m.y. ago, as it is underlain by the 27.8-m.y.-old Fish Canyon Tuff and is overlain by the Carpenter Ridge Tuff, which in turn is overlain in the Creede area by the 26.8-m.y.-old Mammoth Mountain Tuff (table 2; Lipman and others, 1970).

The original extent of the Crystal Lake Tuff is uncertain, because it could have overflowed the San Juan caldera to the west but since have been completely removed by erosion. The original volume of the lobes in the upper Rio Grande drainage and within the Uncompahgre caldera must have been on the order of 25–50 km^3.

Carpenter Ridge Tuff

The Carpenter Ridge Tuff (Olson and others, 1968) is a voluminous ash-flow sheet of phenocryst-poor low-silica rhyolite that was erupted from the Bachelor caldera (fig. 1) in the central San Juan Mountains (Steven and others, 1973b). It crops out continuously around the eastern and northern moat areas of the Uncompahgre caldera, where it overlies the Fish Canyon and Crystal Lake Tuffs. The Carpenter Ridge is as much as 40 m thick northeast of Lake City, but even where relatively thin, it characteristically consists of a black basal vitrophyre, a densely welded red-brown central zone, and an upper light-gray vapor-phase zone. In comparison with the underlying Crystal Lake Tuff, pumice fragments in the Carpenter Ridge are smaller and less densely welded, and they lack linear structure. The phenocryst constituents and proportions are similar to those of the Crystal Lake, Blue Mesa, and Sapinero Mesa Tuffs: about 5 percent of plagioclase and sanidine in subequal amounts, biotite, and very sparse augite.

Wason Park Tuff

The Wason Park Tuff is a phenocryst-rich low-silica rhyolite erupted from the Creede area (Ratté and Steven, 1967). It occurs locally along the southeast rim of the Uncompahgre caldera and within adjacent parts of the caldera moat where it rests on the Carpenter Ridge Tuff and is overlain by rhyodacite and quartz latite of the upper lava sequence.

Rat Creek Tuff

Phenocryst-rich quartz latitic ash-flow tuff, tentatively identified as the Rat Creek Tuff (Steven and Ratté, 1965), forms a major unit within the northern and eastern moat areas of the Uncompahgre caldera. The Rat Creek Tuff was erupted from the San Luis caldera in the north-central part of the San Juan volcanic field (fig. 1). In the Uncompahgre caldera area, this tuff typically is light tan to light gray, nonwelded to partly welded, and contains 25–40 percent phenocrysts of plagioclase, biotite, and augite, and minor sanidine and quartz. As many as three petrologically indistinguishable cooling units, with an aggregate thickness of 200 m, fill a paleovalley northwest of Lake City. Southeast of Lake City, similar tuff forms a single cooling unit as much as 60 m thick interlayered within a local lava sequence (see following section). The age of the Rat Creek Tuff is greater than 26.4 m.y. and less than 26.8 m.y., as indicated by relations farther east to rocks erupted from the Creede caldera (Steven and others, 1967; Lipman and others, 1970).

Upper Lavas Around Margins of Uncompahgre Caldera

The upper caldera lavas accumulated principally within and around the margins of the Uncompahgre caldera. They are a heterogeneous assemblage of flows, breccias, and relatively minor sedimentary rocks that are interlayered at one place or another between every unit of the upper ash-flow sequence. Two of the accumulations are major: (1) at Uncompahgre Peak a succession at least 450 m thick of thick plagioclase-biotite-augite quartz latite flows, and minor interlayered sparsely porphyritic rhyodacite, occurs between the Carpenter Ridge and Rat Creek Tuffs, and (2) on the east rim of the Uncompahgre caldera a sequence as much as 250 m thick of slightly more silicic quartz latites and rhyodacites overlies the Rat Creek Tuff. In addition, andesitic sandstone 30 m in maximum thickness occurs locally between the Fish Canyon and Crystal Lake Tuffs northwest of Lake City, and several andesitic lava flows containing large tabular plagioclase phenocrysts are present in places between the Crystal Lake and Carpenter Ridge Tuffs. Southeast of Lake City, the Wason Park Tuff wedges out into a sequence of rhyodacitic flows as much as 350 m thick between the Carpenter Ridge and Rat Creek Tuffs.

Source vents have been located for only a few of these flows, but most seem to represent continued marginal eruptions related to the late evolution of the Uncompahgre caldera. One major center of this age is exposed in the Capitol City-Matterhorn Peak area, where the upper ash-flow sheets and upper lava sequence are cut by monzonitic plugs and altered by related hydrothermal activity.

Sunshine Peak Tuff

The Sunshine Peak Tuff, the youngest major ash-flow sheet of the San Juan volcanic field, is a distinctive rock characterized by 76 percent or more SiO_2 (Larsen and Cross, 1956, table 21, No. 58), abundant quartz phenocrysts, very sodic alkali feldspar phenocrysts, and a lack of plagioclase phenocrysts. The origin of the Sunshine Peak Tuff as an ash-flow deposit related to subsidence of the Lake City caldera was recognized recently (Luedke and Burbank, 1968), but the age and petrogenetic associations of this tuff unit have remained uncertain.

As originally mapped, the Sunshine Peak Tuff was shown confined to the interior of the Lake City caldera where it is 1 km or more thick; no equivalent outflow sheet was recognized outside the caldera (Larsen and Cross, 1956, pl. 1). Larsen and Cross, uncertain of the stratigraphic position of the Sunshine Peak, tentatively placed it between the Silverton and Potosi Volcanic Groups. Luedke and Burbank (1963) later included the Sunshine Peak Tuff within their redefined Potosi Group, on the basis that the Sunshine Peak was interbedded with and equivalent to Potosi rocks, as then interpreted, southeast of Lake City.

More recently, Lipman, Steven, and Mehnert (1970, p. 2344) postulated that the intracaldera Sunshine Peak might correlate with a young rhyolite welded tuff previously included in the Hinsdale Formation (Larsen and Cross, 1956, p. 193–194) which is preserved beneath capping basalt flows at Jarosa Mesa (Steven, 1967; Steven and others, 1967) and as nearby erosional remnants over a 40-km arc around the high rim south and east of the Lake City caldera. This inference, which was originally based on distribution and petrologic similarity, has been confirmed by more detailed mapping in the Lake City area and by additional K-Ar radiometric determinations. Biotite and alkali feldspar from intracaldera Sunshine Peak Tuff and a similar mineral pair from an overlying silicic intracaldera lava flow are both highly accordant, and the difference between the averaged Sunshine Peak age, 22.5 m.y., and that of the overlying lava flow, 22.7 m.y., is within analytical uncertainty (H. H. Mehnert and others, 1973). These ages are also in excellent agreement with feldspar ages from the outflow tuff at Jarosa Mesa, 22.0 and 22.9 m.y. (Steven and others, 1967).

The thick intracaldera Sunshine Peak Tuff typically shows compound cooling with numerous light-gray partly welded zones separating dark-gray more densely welded rocks. Andesitic lithic fragments are abundant, as are interlayered lenses of andesitic landslide breccia as much as 100 m thick. Lower parts of the intracaldera tuff are pervasively propylitically altered, and large areas are hydrothermally altered, especially near granite porphyry plugs. The intracaldera tuff has been resurgently domed and dips outward 10°–15° in all directions from the center of the caldera. Northeast-trending faults clearly define an apical graben at the crest of the dome (fig. 2).

In contrast to the intracaldera facies, the outflow sheet is rarely more than 50 m thick, is incipiently to only partly welded, and contains few lithic fragments. The original extent of the outflow sheet is uncertain; it now is preserved only where capped by resistant basalt flows of the Hinsdale Formation.

The original volume of the Sunshine Peak Tuff is rather uncertain because so much of the outflow sheet has been eroded. The volume of the intracaldera accumulation, calculated as 125–150 km^3, is believed reliable, but the total volume, stated as 200–300 km^3 (table 2), is only an estimate based largely on analogy with other San Juan calderas where the outflow sheets are at least as voluminous as the intracaldera accumulations.

Lavas and Intrusions of the Lake City Caldera

After subsidence, the core of the Lake City caldera was flooded by coarsely porphyritic (sanidine-plagioclase-biotite) quartz latitic lavas and intruded by granite porphyry. North of the structural boundary of the caldera, a northeast-trending chain of rhyolite porphyry plugs, dikes, and sills (fig. 2) that petrologically resemble the Sunshine Peak Tuff probably were emplaced late in the Lake City caldera cycle. The outflow Sunshine Peak Tuff on the high mesas east of the caldera is overlain by thick heterogeneous lava domes that vary from porphyritic rhyolite to sparsely porphyritic dark andesite, and by thinner flows of uniform alkalic olivine basalt. Both these rock types previously have been mapped as Hinsdale Formation (Larsen and Cross, 1956, pl. 1). A sequence of at least 15 basalt flows on the high mesas northeast of Lake City have yielded K-Ar ages (H. H. Mehnert and others, 1973) of 18.0 m.y. (top flow) and 18.4 m.y. (low flow); one of the porphyritic lava domes appears to wedge out between this basalt sequence and the underlying Sunshine Peak Tuff. We consider that in a general way these mafic rocks, together with the rhyolitic rocks of Lake City caldera, constitute a bimodal mafic-silicic association similar to that widespread elsewhere in upper Cenozoic volcanic rocks of the Western United States (Christiansen and Lipman, 1972).

Recommended Changes in Stratigraphic Nomenclature

We suggest that the terms Silverton Volcanic Group, Potosi Volcanic Group, and Gilpin Peak Tuff be abandoned as formal geologic names. The assemblage of rocks represented by each of these names includes several unrelated major volcanic units that now are believed to correlate with other named formations grouped differently elsewhere in the San Juan volcanic field (table 1).

All units of the Silverton Volcanic Group appear to correlate with older or younger formations nearby in the volcanic field. The intermediate-composition Picayune Formation is believed generally equivalent to the Lake Fork Formation and other unnamed vent-facies accumulations of lavas and breccias that intertongue with volcaniclastic rocks of the San Juan Formation. The rhyolitic Eureka Tuff is the intracaldera equivalent of outflow Sapinero Mesa Tuff and is included with the Sapinero Mesa as a member. The Burns and Henson Formations, as postcollapse accumulations of lavas, breccias, and sediments within the San Juan caldera, are in part correlative with similar lavas and breccias of the Carson center of the Sheep Mountain Formation, as used by Larsen and Cross (1956, p. 126–128). A quartz latitic welded tuff (Luedke and Burbank, 1961) interbedded within the late moat fill of the San Juan and Uncompahgre calderas, and formerly included in the redefined Henson Formation (Luedke and Burbank, 1963; Burbank and Luedke, 1969, p. 12–14), is a distal part of the Fish Canyon Tuff—the largest ash-flow sheet in the San Juan field. In the absence of a close genetic association between these varied units, the formal group classification is now superfluous, and nomenclature of the different units should be established on an individual basis.

The Potosi Volcanic Group, as redefined (Luedke and Burbank, 1963), contained only two formations—the Gilpin Peak Tuff and the Sunshine Peak (Rhyolite) Tuff. The Gilpin Peak Tuff consists largely of four ash-flow sheets that are only a part of the general Oligocene ash-flow sequence of the San Juan volcanic field. The Sunshine Peak Tuff, on the other hand, is now known to be much younger and to be petrogenetically related to the Miocene-Pliocene bimodal volcanic suite (Hinsdale Formation) long recognized to overlie the Potosi Group (Larsen and Cross, 1956, p. 193–194; Luedke and Burbank, 1968, table 1). As originally defined, the Potosi Group included all the Oligocene ash-flow sequence, as well as some early intermediate-composition rocks (Conejos Formation) of the eastern San Juan Mountains (Larsen and Cross, 1956). The Potosi Volcanic Group has thus outlived its usefulness as a meaningful assemblage of rocks, and nomenclature of the different component units is best established on the basis of regional correlations.

The major units of the Gilpin Peak Tuff correlate with at least four major ash-flow sheets that have been separately named in adjacent parts of the volcanic field (Ute Ridge, Blue Mesa, Dillon Mesa, and Sapinero Mesa Tuffs) and that were erupted from at least three separate unrelated caldera centers (Ute Creek, Lost Lake, and San Juan-Uncompahgre). Considering that each of these four sheets previously has been given formational rank elsewhere in the San Juan volcanic field, we believe that the term Gilpin Peak Tuff now lacks utility as a formal stratigraphic name.

EVOLUTION OF THE CALDERAS

The Uncompahgre and San Juan calderas developed as a closely interrelated pair and are therefore described together; the slightly younger Silverton caldera, although an integral part of this earlier history, is considered separately. The Lake City caldera formed more than 5 m.y. later, and its evolution is likewise considered separately.

Uncompahgre and San Juan Calderas

Prior to the ash-flow eruptions and related collapse of the San Juan and Uncompahgre calderas, the western San Juan region was a volcanic highland consisting of a cluster of central volcanoes surrounded by an alluvial plain of outwash debris. The near-source vent-facies rocks consist of the Picayune Formation, Lake Fork Formation, and unnamed similar lavas and breccias around local centers. The volcanoes were dissected as they grew, broad valleys were eroded in their flanks, and the intervening basins and outer flanks were mantled by volcanic detritus represented by the San Juan Formation. These rocks accumulated largely in early and middle Oligocene time, between 35 and 30 m.y. ago. Between 29 and 28 m.y. ago, the flanks of these volcanoes were partly buried by ash-flow deposits comprising the Ute Ridge and Blue Mesa Tuffs, erupted from caldera sources to the southeast. These ash-flow sheets formed discontinuous valley-filling lobes near the central volcanoes and coalesced downslope into widespread continuous sheets.

Eruption of the Dillon Mesa Tuff, that overlies the Blue Mesa Tuff, may have led to initial collapse at the Uncompahgre caldera site. The inferred 50–100 km^3 initial volume of the Dillon Mesa (table 2), though relatively small, would seemingly have been sufficient to permit subsidence of the source area (by analogy with size-volume relations of other calderas: Smith, 1960, fig. 3), and the northerly distribution of this unit makes the Uncompahgre caldera area a plausible source. This relation is inferential, however, and we know of no direct evidence supporting it.

The eruptions that deposited the Sapinero Mesa Tuff about 28 m.y. ago were more than an order of magnitude larger than those of the Dillon Mesa (table 2), and the resulting ash flows spread as much as 90 km to the northeast of the Uncompahgre caldera, as well as sizable distances in other directions (fig. 1). Both San Juan and Uncompahgre calderas are filled by 500–700 m of the intracaldera Eureka Member of the Sapinero Mesa Tuff, indicating that both calderas existed as deep depressions before the Sapinero Mesa eruptions were completed. Abundant lithic fragments and lenses of landslide breccia within the Eureka Member in both calderas indicate that their walls were oversteepened and caving during Sapinero Mesa eruptions, and the landslide material is especially abundant and coarse within the San Juan caldera.

Seemingly, therefore, both calderas were actively subsiding during eruption of the Sapinero Mesa Tuff, with the San Juan caldera being somewhat more active than the Uncompahgre caldera. Conceivably the Sapinero Mesa Tuff was erupted largely from the San Juan caldera, and the Eureka Member in the Uncompahgre caldera accumulated within an earlier basin, related to Dillon Mesa eruptions, that was undergoing slight additional subsidence. However, we favor an interpretation that the Sapinero Mesa Tuff emanated from both calderas, for three reasons. First, the Sapinero Mesa Tuff is abruptly truncated at the Uncompahgre caldera walls, indicating major subsidence during and after its eruption. Also, extension of the Sapinero Mesa ash flows so far to the northeast (fig. 1) would have been unlikely if the Uncompahgre caldera had formed a deep intervening depression. Both the Uncompahgre and San Juan calderas were resurgently domed together after the Sapinero Mesa activity ceased, indicating that the active magma chamber that supplied this tuff underlay both calderas at shallow levels. Finally, the Sapinero Mesa Tuff is among the largest ash-flow sheets in the San Juan field, and we believe that its eruption should have resulted in collapse of a larger caldera than one formed by eruption of the much smaller Dillon Mesa Tuff (table 2).

The virtually simultaneous collapse of two calderas as a result of the Sapinero Mesa eruptions, if a valid interpretation, represents an unusual geometry for caldera formation. We can only speculate that eruption of the Sapinero Mesa was from an irregularly shaped body of shallow magma, elongate to the northeast in plan, that had two separate cupolas at its roof.

The rib of Precambrian rocks separating the San Juan and Uncompahgre calderas was an unsolved problem in earlier interpretations that related eruption of the Eureka Member to the formation of a single large collapse structure, the San Juan volcanic depression (Luedke and Burbank, 1968; Burbank and Luedke, 1969, p. 17). Our recent detailed mapping has shown that these rocks constitute an unsubsided remnant of the regional Needle Mountains-Uncompahgre structural high (Kelly, 1957). The rib developed as a prominent feature only when the Sapinero Mesa eruptions caused the adjacent San Juan and Uncompahgre calderas to collapse. The early intermediate-composition lavas and breccias covered a broad surface of low relief on Precambrian and older sedimentary rocks, and the volcaniclastic beds interlayered with the lavas and breccias contain only minor detritus of Precambrian rocks. In contrast, the Eureka Member and overlying caldera-fill lavas and sediments were deposited against the Precambrian rocks on slopes of the caldera wall as steep as 60°, and Precambrian detritus is abundant both within the Eureka ash-flow tuffs and in the clastic parts of the overlying lavas and sediments. In one place, a monolithologic landslide breccia within the Eureka Member consists of Precambrian fragments as much as 10 m across, and at several localities the Eureka overlies fossil talus of Precambrian rocks at the caldera walls.

An especially interesting feature of the evolution of the San Juan and Uncompahgre calderas was their joint resurgence to form a large elliptical dome, as much as 15 km wide and at least 30 km long, with a well-developed apical graben (the Eureka graben) clearly evident in the area between the two calderas. Previously described resurgent calderas mostly have domes nested centrally within the collapsed area, such as at Valles (New Mexico), Creede (Colorado), and Timber Mountain (Nevada) calderas (Smith and Bailey, 1968), and the development of the large resurgent dome across both the San Juan and Uncompahgre calderas appeared to support the earlier concept of a large single "San Juan volcanic depression" (Luedke and Burbank, 1968; Burbank and Luedke, 1969). Complex geometric relations between caldera collapse and resurgence exist in other volcanic areas, however: two discrete resurgent domes are nested within the single large Yellowstone caldera in Wyoming (U.S. Geological Survey, 1972) and resurgence of the San Luis caldera in the San Juan field (fig. 1) was asymmetrical to the area of collapse (Steven and Lipman, unpub. data).

The geometry of the joint resurgence of the San Juan and Uncompahgre calderas is imperfectly known, because large parts of the resurgent dome have been covered by late caldera-fill rocks or have caved away as a result of the late collapses that formed the Silverton and Lake City calderas. Nevertheless, several features indicate that this resurgence produced a low-amplitude broad structure: (1) Most of the Eureka Member within these calderas is topographically lower than the outflow Sapinero Mesa Tuff, in contrast with many other well-studied resurgent calderas in which the intracaldera tuff stands higher on the resurgent dome than the general level of the outflow sheet (Smith and Bailey, 1968). (2) The Eureka Member in the Lake City area has dips only slightly steeper than overlying units of the caldera-fill sequence, mostly 20° or less, and a sizable component of this dip is due to later regional northeasterly tilting. (3) The intricate system of fractures and veins radiating from the collapsed areas, especially around the northwest and southeast sides of the San Juan caldera (Burbank and Luedke, 1969, pl. 1), indicate resurgence of an area larger than that which collapsed. The general confinement of mineralized veins in the Lake City area to the moat area of the Uncompahgre caldera suggests that the area of resurgence may have been more restricted in the northeast part of the twin caldera system.

The joint resurgent doming of the San Juan and Uncompahgre calderas began shortly after collapse, before accumulation of the lower lavas and sediments (Burns and Henson Formations), as indicated by the unconformable onlap of these caldera-fill rocks against tilted Eureka Member in the area between the two calderas (Luedke and Burbank, 1968, p. 194, fig. 9). Resurgence continued during accumulation of the thick sequence of lavas, sediments, and ash-flow tuffs within the San Juan and Uncompahgre calderas. The lavas and sediments of the Burns and Henson Formations, the initial part of this sequence, are intensely faulted along the distended crest of the dome in the Eureka graben zone. General resurgence of the two calderas together probably continued during accumulation of the middle part of the caldera-fill sequence, which consists mainly of ash-flow sheets (Fish Canyon, Carpenter Ridge, and so forth), as this ash-flow sequence dips northeast and east away from the core of the Uncompahgre caldera nearly as steeply as the underlying Eureka Tuff.

Late postcaldera lavas intertongue with and overlie the upper ash-flow sheets and probably accumulated about 27.5–26.5 m.y. ago. These rocks are preserved mainly around the north and east sides of the Uncompahgre caldera, where they overflowed the eastern caldera wall to spread at least 5–10 km farther to the east. In these areas they are as much as 300–400 m thick. The original extent of these lavas to the south and west may have been considerably greater, but they have been largely removed by erosion.

The total subsidence of the Uncompahgre and San Juan calderas is difficult to establish, because the base of the intracaldera Eureka Member is exposed only locally within the calderas, probably on relatively high parts of the caldera floor. A minimum value of 1.5–2 km is indicated by the 500–700 m thickness of the exposed Eureka, plus the 800–1,200 m thickness of overlying caldera-fill lavas, sediments, and ash-flow tuffs.

Silverton Caldera

The relatively small-volume Crystal Lake Tuff, one of the upper ash-flow sheets, apparently originated from within the San Juan caldera about 27.5–27.0 m.y. ago, and probably is related to subsidence of the Silverton caldera along ring fractures that offset the Burns and Henson Formations. This late subsidence, which in part may have reactivated earlier formed ring fractures, tilted the intracaldera rocks asymmetrically in "trapdoor" style. Maximum displacement was at the south end of the Silverton caldera, whereas little displacement appears to have taken place at the north end (fig. 2) (Burbank, 1951, p. 291). Local late resurgence has been postulated within the Silverton caldera (Luedke and Burbank, 1968; Burbank and Luedke, 1969), after the collapse probably related to eruption of the Crystal Lake Tuff, but any such late resurgence is difficult to distinguish from the earlier general doming of the two larger calderas together.

Lake City Caldera

After about a 4-m.y. period of greatly reduced volcanic activity in the western San Juan Mountains, ash-flow eruptions that produced the Sunshine Peak Tuff began about 22.5 m.y. ago in the Lake City area. Outflow Sunshine Peak Tuff must have been deposited widely in the region, although only small erosional remnants have survived. Concurrently with these eruptions, an elliptical block about 12 to 15 km across, nested within the southern part of the older Uncompahgre caldera, began to subside to form the Lake City caldera. Late eruptions of the Sunshine Peak accumulated to a thickness of as much as 1 km within the concurrently subsiding caldera, and great landslide avalanches caved off the caldera wall to spread across the caldera floor and to intertongue with the accumulating ash flows.

The ring fault along which this collapse occurred is continuously exposed for about 300° of arc around the caldera; it is nearly everywhere a single fault, typically marked by only a few feet of gouge and minor hydrothermally altered rock. It is exposed over topographic relief of as much as 600 m, and is everywhere steep, with dips varying from near vertical to about 75° inward. It is gradually being recognized that steep inward dips characterize the bounding faults of many calderas (Reynolds, 1956; Taubeneck, 1967).

Shortly after the ash-flow eruptions ceased, lava flows and domes of viscous silicic quartz latite, fed largely from vents along the ring fault, accumulated around the margins of the caldera floor. These lavas tend to overlie the Sunshine Peak Tuff conformably and dip quite steeply in places. They may largely predate resurgent doming, although the effects of doming on them are difficult to separate reliably from primary dips of the flows. An east-northeast-trending line of rhyolite intrusives was emplaced in the moat area of the older Uncompahgre caldera, north of the Lake City caldera. Compositionally these rocks closely resemble the Sunshine Peak Tuff and probably were emplaced during the same period of magmatism. Their place in the detailed sequence of events related to development of the Lake City caldera is not known, however.

Resurgence of the Lake City caldera produced a simple dome characterized by outward dips of 20°–25° on its flanks and a northeast-trending apical graben over its distended crest. The trend of this graben clearly reflects reactivation of the trends of the earlier Eureka graben system related to resurgence of the Uncompahgre and San Juan calderas. Most of the mapped faults of the Lake City resurgent structure have relatively small displacements (10–50 m) and some seem to be little more than cracks that localized weak hydrothermal alteration. The floor of the caldera is exposed on its southwest side, and the resurgence appears to have been somewhat asymmetrical, with maximum uplift in this area. Resurgence clearly resulted from upward movement of magma which crystallized as a shallow stock of granite porphyry.

Gently dipping upper contacts of the granite porphyry are exposed at bottoms of several deep erosional valleys within the Lake City caldera core, and the most intensely altered rock within the resurgent dome occurs around margins of the granite porphyry. Parts of the northern ring fault are occupied by a discontinuous stubby ring dike, which broadens and becomes coarser grained downward. Geometric relations revealed in exposures within the core indicate that the top of the granite porphyry crystallized within 1 km of the surface of the resurgent dome.

Most of the original topographic wall of the Lake City caldera has been eroded, and only a few small remnants are preserved southeast of Lake City. The present valleys of Henson Creek and the upper Lake Fork of the Gunnison River, that define a striking elliptical drainage pattern just outside the structural boundary of the Lake City caldera (fig. 2), are not directly controlled by any major fault structures. They more likely developed in the topographically low moat of the Lake City caldera and were subsequently superimposed onto older rocks outside the subsided block.

After development of the Lake City caldera, the only major late Cenozoic volcanism in the western San Juan Mountains was outpouring of thin flows of alkalic olivine basalt of the Hinsdale Formation. Only a few such erosional remnants are preserved, but these flows must formerly have been much more extensive. Locally intertongued with the flows of olivine basalt are more heterogeneous lava domes that vary in composition from basalt to rhyolite and seem to be mix lavas. Together with the rhyolites of the Lake City caldera, these basalts and mix lavas constitute a major part of the Miocene-Pliocene bimodal mafic-silicic volcanic association of the San Juan Mountains (Lipman and others, 1970). This association contrasts strikingly with the older ash-flow sheets of the San Juan field, which are Oligocene in age and belong to the older intermediate-composition volcanic association. These contrasting associations seem to have fundamental significance both in the San Juan field and widely in Cenozoic volcanic rocks of the Western United States (Christiansen and Lipman, 1972).

ECONOMIC CONSIDERATIONS

Any thorough stratigraphic and structural reinterpretation of an area affects other aspects of the geology, and in an area as intensely mineralized as the western San Juans the implications for economic geology are major. In this preliminary paper only the place and time of mineralization with respect to the caldera cycles are summarized. Burbank (1930, 1940, 1947a), Burbank and Luedke (1968), and Luedke and Burbank (1962) have demonstrated two major epochs of mineralization in the San Juan Mountains: (1) a Late Cretaceous-early Tertiary (Laramide) epoch related to intrusive centers at Ouray and, possibly, at Rico and in the La Plata Mountains, and (2) a middle to late Tertiary epoch related to the San Juan volcanic field. These major epochs still are completely valid, but the younger epoch can be subdivided into several stages, rather than just a single stage related to emplacement of postvolcanism intrusives in and around the calderas.

Elsewhere we have found that mineralization related to the different ash-flow calderas in the San Juan field occurred mostly late in the local cycle, during and spatially associated with postsubsidence magmatic activity. This activity typically emplaced lavas and intrusives along ring fractures and outward-extending radial fractures of the calderas, and was related in time and space to the mineralization. These generalizations seem valid for the individual calderas in the western San Juan Mountains, but the multiple caldera cycles resulted in several periods of mineralization.

In the Lake City area, where an exceptionally complete stratigraphic succession allows determination of detailed age relations, at least three distinct stages of mid-Tertiary mineralization can be related to different local environments of deposition. Cores of four early intermediate-composition precollapse volcanoes around the periphery of the Uncompahgre caldera are altered and mineralized, with minor ore production from one. In addition, the caldera fill in the Uncompahgre caldera is cut by monzonitic intrusives and is locally hydrothermally altered. Many associated fractures were filled by quartz-sulfide veins that have supplied most of the production from this area. The altered rocks and veins are locally truncated by the Lake City caldera wall and clearly are older than this caldera. Finally, some ring-fracture intrusives and lavas around the Lake City caldera are intensely altered, and many of the distensional fractures within the resurgent core are altered and some contain metalliferous veins.

The younger volcanic formations are absent in the highly mineralized and productive Silverton caldera area, and the relative ages of mineralization in different areas have not yet been established. The generally similar paragenesis of most of the veins has been interpreted as resulting from deposition during a single major stage of mineralization (Burbank and Luedke, 1968, 1969). However, Burbank and Luedke also noted that the veins were recurrently opened and filled with vein materials of contrasting compositions. The possibility of multistage deposition resulting in superposition of mineralization of several ages along the same fractures has never been ruled out, and remains a fascinating problem for future study.

REFERENCES CITED

Burbank, W. S., 1930, Revision of the geologic structure and stratigraphy in the Ouray district of Colorado, and its bearing on ore deposition: Colorado Sci. Soc. Proc., v. 12, no. 6, p. 151–232.

—— 1933, Vein systems of Arrastre Basin and regional geologic structure in the Silverton and Telluride quadrangles, Colorado: Colorado Sci. Soc. Proc., v. 13, no. 5, p. 135–214.

—— 1938, Silverton caldera, San Juan County, Colo. [abs.]: Washington Acad. Sci. Jour., v. 28, no. 9, p. 417–418.

—— 1940, Structural control of ore deposition in the Uncompahgre district, Ouray County, Colorado: U.S. Geol. Survey Bull. 906-E, p. 189–265.

—— 1941, Structural control of ore deposition in the Red Mountains, Sneffels, and Telluride districts of the San Juan Mountains, Colorado: Colorado Sci. Soc. Proc., v. 14, no. 5, p. 141–261.

—— 1947a, General features [of San Juan region], *in* Vanderwilt, J. W., ed., Mineral resources of Colorado: Colorado Mineral Resources Board, p. 396–408.

—— 1947b, Lake City area, Hinsdale County, *in* Vanderwilt, J. W., ed., Mineral resources of Colorado: Colorado Mineral Resources Board, p. 439–443.

—— 1951, The Sunnyside, Ross Basin, and Bonita fault systems and their associated ore deposits, San Juan County, Colorado: Colorado Sci. Soc. Proc., v. 13, no. 5, p. 285–304.

Burbank, W. S., and Luedke, R. G., 1964, Geology of the Ironton quadrangle, Colorado: U.S. Geol. Survey Geol. Quad. Map GQ-291.

—— 1966, Geologic map of the Telluride quadrangle, southwestern Colorado: U.S. Geol. Survey Geol. Quad. Map GQ-504.

—— 1968, Geology and ore deposits of the western San Juan Mountains, Colorado, *in* Ore deposits of the United States, 1933–1967 (Graton-Sales Volume), V. 1: New York, Am. Inst. Mining, Metall. and Petroleum Engineers, p. 714–733.

—— 1969, Geology and ore deposits of the Eureka and adjoining districts, San Juan Mountains, Colorado: U.S. Geol. Survey Prof. Paper 535, 73 p.

Christiansen, R. L., and Lipman, P. W., 1972, Cenozoic volcanism and plate-tectonic evolution of the Western United States, II. Late Cenozoic: Royal Soc. London Philos. Trans., v. 271, p. 249–284.

Cohee, G. V., chm., 1961, Tectonic map of the United States–exclusive of Alaska and Hawaii: U.S. Geol. Survey and Am. Assoc. Petroleum Geologists [1962].

Cross, Whitman, Howe, Ernest, and Irving, J. D., 1907, Description of the Ouray quadrangle [Colorado]: U.S. Geol. Survey Geol. Atlas, Folio 153.

Cross, Whitman, Howe, Ernest, and Ransome, F. L., 1905, Description of the Silverton quadrangle [Colorado]: U.S. Geol. Survey Geol. Atlas, Folio 120.

Cross, Whitman, and Purington, C. W., 1899, Description of the Telluride quadrangle [Colorado]: U.S. Geol. Survey Geol. Atlas, Folio 57.

Hansen, W. R., 1971, Geologic map of the Black Canyon of the Gunnison River and vicinity, western Colorado: U.S. Geol. Survey Misc. Geol. Inv. Map I-584.

Kelley, V. C., 1957, General geology and tectonics of the western San Juan Mountains, Colorado, *in* New Mexico Geol. Soc., Guidebook, 8th Field Conf., Sept. 1957: p. 154–162.

Larsen, E. S., Jr., and Cross, Whitman, 1956, Geology and petrology of the San Juan region, southwestern Colorado: U.S. Geol. Survey Prof. Paper 258, 303 p.

Lipman, P. W., and Steven, T. A., 1970, Reconnaissance geology and economic significance of the Platoro caldera, southeastern San Juan Mountains, Colorado, *in* Geological Survey Research 1970: U.S. Geol. Survey Prof. Paper 700-C, p. C19–C29.

Lipman, P. W., Steven, T. A., and Mehnert, H. H., 1970, Volcanic history of the San Juan Mountains, Colorado, as indicated by potassium-argon dating: Geol. Soc. America Bull., v. 81, p. 2329–2352.

Luedke, R. G., 1972, Geologic map of the Wetterhorn Peak quadrangle, Ouray and Hinsdale Counties, Colorado: U.S. Geol. Survey Geol. Quad. Map GQ-1011.

Luedke, R. G., and Burbank, W. S., 1961, Central vent ash-flow eruption, western San Juan Mountains, Colorado: Art. 326 *in* U.S. Geol. Survey Prof. Paper 424-D, p. D94–D96.

—— 1962, Geology of the Ouray quadrangle, southwestern Colorado: U.S. Geol. Survey Geol. Quad. Map GQ-152.

—— 1963, Tertiary volcanic stratigraphy in the western San Juan Mountains, Colorado: Art. 70 *in* U.S. Geol. Survey Prof. Paper 474-C, p. C39–C44.

—— 1968, Volcanism and cauldron development in the western San Juan Mountains, Colorado, *in* Epis, R. G., ed., Cenozoic volcanism in the southern Rocky Mountains: Colorado School Mines Quart., v. 63, no. 3, p. 175–208.

Mehnert, H. H., Lipman, P. W., and Steven, T. A., 1973, Age of the Lake City caldera and related Sunshine Peak Tuff, western San Juan Mountains, Colorado: Isochron West, no. 6, p. 31–33.

Olson, J. C., Hedlund, D. C., and Hansen, W. R., 1968, Tertiary volcanic stratigraphy in the Powderhorn-Black Canyon region, Gunnison and Montrose Counties, Colorado: U.S. Geol. Survey Bull. 1251-C, p. C1–C29.

Ratté, J. C., and Steven, T. A., 1967, Ash flows and related volcanic rocks associated with the Creede caldera, San Juan Mountains, Colorado: U.S. Geol. Survey Prof. Paper 524-H, 58 p.

Reynolds, D. L., 1956, Calderas and ring-complexes: Verh. K. Ned. Geol.-mijnb. Genoot., Geol. Ser., v. 16, p. 355-379.

Smith, R. L., 1960, Ash flows: Geol. Soc. America Bull., v. 71, p. 795–842.

Smith, R. L., and Bailey, R. A., 1968, Resurgent cauldrons, *in* Studies in volcanology—A memoir in honor of Howel Williams: Geol. Soc. America Mem. 116, p. 613–662.

Steven, T. A., 1967, Geologic map of the Bristol Head quadrangle, Mineral and Hinsdale Counties, Colorado: U.S. Geol. Survey Geol. Quad. Map GQ-631.

Steven, T. A., Lipman, P. W., Hail, W. J., Jr., Barker, Fred, and Luedke, R. G., 1973a, Geologic map of the Durango quadrangle, southwestern Colorado: U.S. Geol. Survey Misc. Geol. Inv. Map I-764. (In press.)

Steven, T. A., Lipman, P. W., and Olson, J. C., 1973b, Ash flow stratigraphy and caldera structures in the San Juan volcanic field, southwestern Colorado, *in* Cohee, G. V., and Wright, W. B., Changes in stratigraphic nomenclature by the U.S. Geological Survey, 1973: U.S. Geol. Survey Bull. 1394-A. (In press.)

Steven, T. A., Mehnert, H. H., and Obradovich, J. D., 1967, Age of volcanic activity in the San Juan Mountains, Colorado, *in* Geological Survey Research 1967: U.S. Geol. Survey Prof. Paper 575-D, p. D47-D55.

Steven, T. A., and Ratté, J. C., 1965, Geology and structural control of ore deposition of the Creede district, San Juan Mountains, Colorado: U.S. Geol. Survey Prof. Paper 487, 87 p.

Taubeneck, W. H., 1967, Notes on the Glen Coe cauldron subsidence, Argyllshire, Scotland: Geol. Soc. America Bull., v. 78, p. 1295–1316.

U.S. Geological Survey, 1972, Geologic map of Yellowstone National Park: U.S. Geol. Survey Misc. Geol. Inv. Map I-711.

Varnes, D. J., 1963, Geology and ore deposits of the South Silverton Mining Area, San Juan County, Colorado: U.S. Geol. Survey Prof. Paper 378-A, 56 p.

Jour. Research U.S. Geol. Survey
Vol. 1, No. 6, Nov.-Dec. 1973, p. 643—647

Sr^{87}/Sr^{86}, K, Na, Rb, AND Sr IN SOME ECLOGITES AND ASSOCIATED BASALTS FROM CALIFORNIA AND SOUTHWESTERN OREGON

By E. D. GHENT[1], Z. E. PETERMAN, and R. G. COLEMAN,
Menlo Park, Calif., Denver, Colo., Menlo Park, Calif.

Abstract.—Six samples of group C eclogites from California and southwestern Oregon have initial Sr^{87}/Sr^{86} ratios in the range of 0.7028 to 0.7051; Rb contents from less than 1 to 53.4 ppm; and Sr contents from 147 to 270 ppm. These data and major-element compositions suggest that the eclogites were derived from basalts older than but similar in composition to those intercalated with Mesozoic eugeosynclinal sedimentary rocks in California and western Oregon. The isotopic heterogeneity of the eclogites and associated graywackes contrasts with a uniformity of Sr^{87}/Sr^{86} in many younger calc-alkaline volcanic rocks of the circum-Pacific province. Derivation of the younger volcanic rocks from an eclogite-blueschist melange isotopically similar to those investigated here would require isotopic homogenization or integrated partial melting over sufficient volumes so as to reduce these variations in the derived melts.

Eclogites occur in a variety of geologic settings (Coleman and others, 1965) and have apparently crystallized over a range of temperature-load pressure conditions (Coleman and others, 1965; Green and Ringwood, 1967). Eclogites have been divided into three groups by Coleman and others (1965): group A, inclusions in kimberlites and alkali olivine basalts, or as layers in ultramafic rocks; group B, bands or lenses within migmatite gneiss terrains; and group C, bands or lenses within metamorphic rocks of blueschist facies. Several workers have concluded that some eclogites can form stably within the crust under low-water-pressure conditions (Green and Ringwood, 1967; Fry and Fyfe, 1969). Others have suggested that eclogites are produced in the lithosphere during subduction and are the source rocks for andesitic magmas (Ringwood and Green, 1966; Miyashiro, 1972).

Eclogites from California and Oregon occur as isolated blocks within Mesozoic eugeosynclinal rocks. They are thought to have formed from crustal rocks and to have been tectonically transported as part of a serpentinite melange (Coleman and Lanphere, 1971). Most eclogites have a bulk chemistry approximating that of basalts; however, eclogites from California and Oregon are generally richer in normative nepheline and diopside than are associated Mesozoic eugeosynclinal basaltic rocks (Ghent and Coleman, 1973). These authors have tentatively concluded that these compositions resulted from metasomatism of rocks of originally basaltic composition during the process of eclogitization.

This report is concerned with samples whose bulk chemistry, mineralogy, K-Ar ages, and field occurrences have been described elsewhere (Coleman and others, 1965; Coleman and Lanphere, 1971; Ghent and Coleman, 1973). Sr isotopes have been of value in placing constraints on and providing clues for choosing between petrogenetic models of mafic igneous rocks (see Faure and Powell, 1972). This study of Sr^{87}/Sr^{86}, and Rb and Sr contents of group C eclogites (Coleman and others, 1965) from Oregon and California was undertaken for comparison with similar data on associated Mesozoic mafic volcanic rocks, modern oceanic basalts, and andesites. Data for Mesozoic eugeosynclinal basalts and graywackes from California and Oregon have been reported by Coleman (1972) and by Sinha and Davis (1971). Few other data of this sort have been published for eclogites (Steuber and Murthy, 1966; Allsopp and others, 1969; Compston and Lovering, 1969). The analyses reported by Allsopp and others (1969) are of group A and group B eclogites, whereas the analyses by Compston and Lovering (1969) are of group A eclogites only. According to these workers, considerable amounts of Rb and radiogenic Sr are concentrated in "matrix materials" and these elements may have been introduced during the transport of the eclogites in the pipes.

Acknowledgments.—We are indebted to W. G. Ernst, University of California at Los Angeles, for giving us the analyzed powders of the metabasalts from Pacheco Pass; to W. P. Doering for the XRF Rb and Sr analyses; and to R. A. Hildreth and W. T. Henderson for the Sr isotopic measurements. Marvin Lanphere and Miles Silberman kindly reviewed the manuscript and their comments are greatly appreciated. The work was done while Ghent was at Menlo Park, Calif., on leave from the University of Calgary.

[1] University of Calgary, Calgary, Alberta, Canada.

Table 1.—*Analytical data*

[Na_2O and K_2O data for eclogites from Coleman and others (1965) and Ghent and Coleman (1973); Na_2O and K_2O data for metabasalts from Ernst and others (1970)]

Sample No.	Na_2O (wt percent)	K_2O (wt percent)	Rb (ppm)	Sr_t (ppm)	Rb/Sr	K/Rb	$(Sr^{87}/Sr^{86})_t$ [1]	$(Sr^{87}/Sr^{86})_o$ [2]	Locality and source of descriptive data
Eclogite samples									
62-RGC-58......	4.3	0.04	<1	270	0.004	>330	0.7037	0.7037	Ward Creek, Sonoma County, Calif. (Coleman and others, 1965).
100-RGC-58.....	3.1	.22	7.4	189	.039	250	.7053	.7051	Tiburon Peninsula, Marin County, Calif. (Coleman and others, 1965).
102-RGC-58.....	4.4	.20	8.4	147	.057	200	.7042	.7039	Junction School, Sonoma County, Calif. (Coleman and others, 1965).
113-RGC-58.....	3.4	.18	3.5	164	.021	430	.7037	.7035	Occidental Quarry, Sonoma County, Calif. (Coleman and others, 1965).
207-RGC-58.....	5.1	.40	18.9	139	.136	180	.7036	.7028	Valley Ford, Sonoma County, Calif. (Coleman and others, 1965).
95-69-1.........	4.29	1.20	53.4	232	.230	190	.7049	.7035	Waterman Ranch, Coos County, Oreg. (Ghent and Coleman, 1973).
Metabasalt samples									
X-72...........	2.70	0.31	6.6	105	0.063	390	0.7052	0.7048	Pacheco Pass area, California (Ernst and others, 1970).
X-81...........	3.68	.28	2.0	110	.018	1,160	.7048	.7047	Do.

[1] Measured Sr^{87}/Sr^{86} ratio. Data for Eimer and Amend standard yield an average Sr^{87}/Sr^{86} value of 0.7080.

[2] Initial Sr^{87}/Sr^{86} ratio calculated on age corrections of 150 m.y. for the eclogites and 140 m.y. for the metabasalts.

ISOTOPIC AND TRACE-ELEMENT RESULTS

Sr^{87}/Sr^{86} ratios, alkalis, and Sr contents of six eclogite samples from California and Oregon and of two basalt samples from California are presented in table 1. On a conventional isochron diagram (fig. 1), Sr^{87}/Sr^{86} values of the eclogites, except for one sample, are higher than those of ocean ridge basalts from the Juan de Fuca and Gordo Rises, and are in the range of values shown for the ophiolite suite from Cyprus, basalts from the Colebrooke Schist, and two basalts from the Franciscan Formation of the Pacheco Pass area (for mineralogy and bulk chemistry of these, see Ernst and others, 1970). Other basalts from the Franciscan Formation have significantly higher Sr^{87}/Sr^{86} values which Sinha and Davis (1971) attributed to reaction with sea water.

Rb and Sr contents of the eclogites are compared with those of basalts on figure 2. Sr in the eclogites shows less variation than in basalts from the Franciscan Formation and Colebrooke Schist and generally ranges between the values for the average ocean-ridge tholeiite and low-potassium tholeitte given by Hart

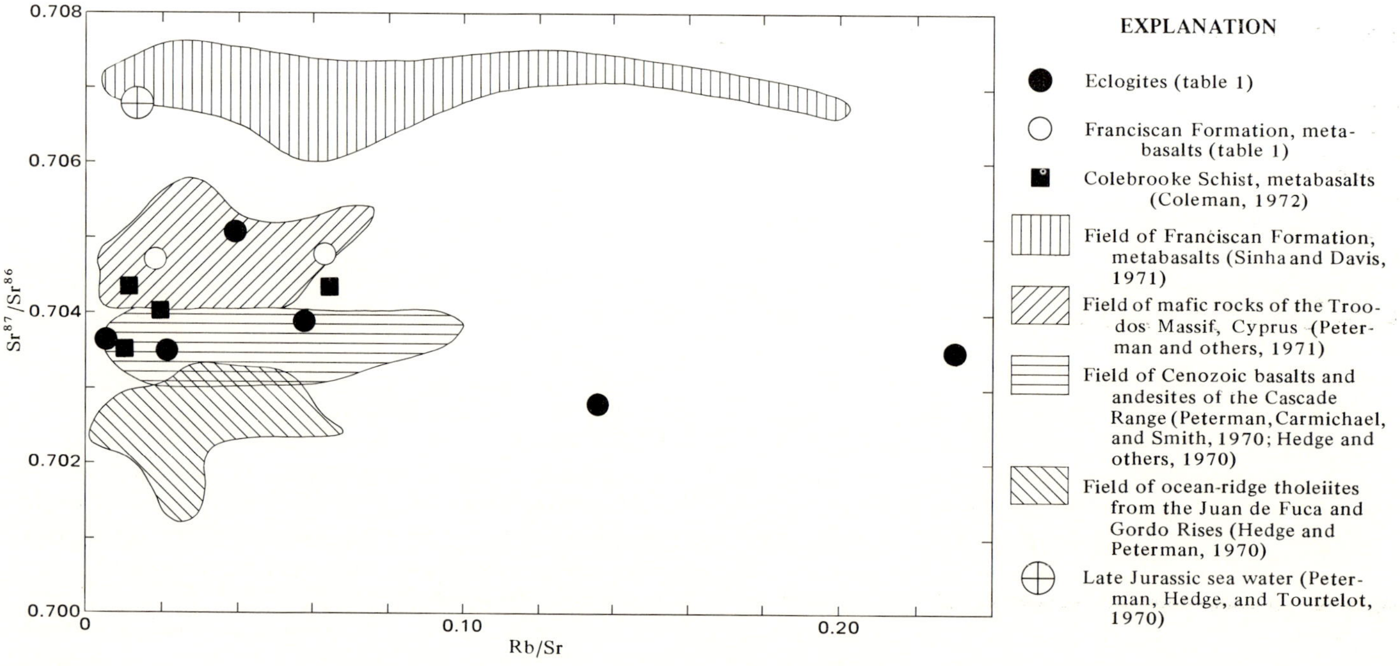

Figure 1.—Sr^{87}/Sr^{86} versus Rb/Sr diagram.

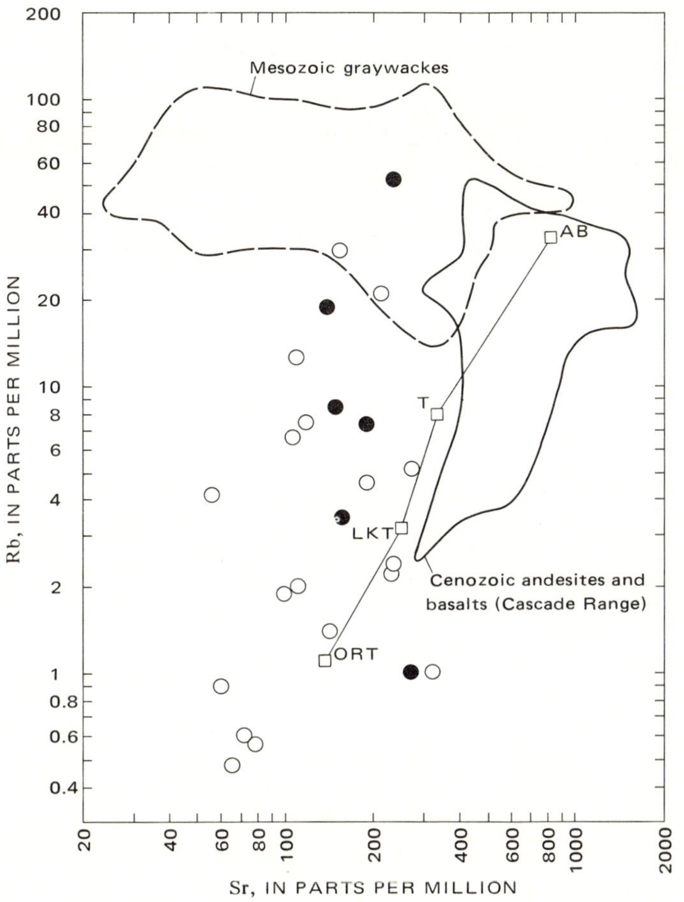

Figure 2.—Plot of Rb and Sr contents. Solid dots are eclogites (table 1); open circles are basalts from the Franciscan Formation (Sinha and Davis, 1971; table 1) and from the Colebrooke Schist (Coleman, 1972); and squares are averages of basalt types from Hart and others (1970). ORT, ocean-ridge tholeiites; LKT, low-potassium tholeiites; T, tholeiites; and AB, alkali basalts. Data defining field of Cascade andesites and basalts are from Hedge and others (1970) and Peterman, Carmichael, and Smith (1970). Data for graywackes are from Peterman and others (1967), Coleman (1972), and Peterman (unpub. data).

and others (1970). Rb shows much greater variation than Sr in the eclogites and ranges from less than 1 to 53 ppm. It should be noted that the average Rb and Sr contents for ocean-ridge tholeiites were obtained from data on the freshest material obtainable (Hart and others, 1970), and if all available data are considered, these elements show nearly as much variation as in the eclogites (see Ewart and Bryan, 1972, fig. 7).

The present Sr isotopic character, and major- and trace-element chemistry have undoubtedly been influenced by modification during eclogitization and possibly by alteration prior to this higher grade metamorphism. The initial Sr^{87}/Sr^{86} ratios calculated in table 1 should represent the isotopic composition of Sr at the time of eclogitization. As a result of a high phengite content, the Oregon eclogite has a high Rb content and high Rb/Sr ratio, yet the calculated initial Sr^{87}/Sr^{86} ratio is not anomalous with respect to the others. The lack of correlation between Sr^{87}/Sr^{86} and Rb content suggests that isotopically anomalous Sr was not introduced along with the alkalis. The possibility of alteration of the parent basalts prior to eclogitization is difficult to evaluate from these data alone. Trace-element (Hart, 1969) and isotopic (Hart, 1972) modification of submarine basalts as a result of interaction with sea water is well documented. Perhaps alteration of this type affected the parent basalts before they were subjected to eclogite metamorphism, and the Sr^{87}/Sr^{86} ratios were increased during this initial stage of alteration. The high Na contents of the eclogites may reflect an early-stage spilitization (Coleman and others, 1965; Ghent and Coleman, 1973). The migration of alkalis in pillow lavas is a well-documented phenomenon (for example, Bailey and others, 1964).

The most likely precursors of the eclogites are ocean-ridge tholeiites or eugeosynclinal basalts similar to those intercalated with the Mesozoic eugeosynclinal sediments. Coleman and others (1965) and Ghent and Coleman (1973) favor the latter source for the eclogites. Cann (1970) considers Ti to be one of the elements in basalts for which the original concentration is least affected by later alteration, and according to his data Ti ranges from 3,200 to 11,100 ppm in ocean-floor basalts, with most of the samples containing between 5,000 and 10,000 ppm. The eclogites contain between 8,400 and 19,000 ppm Ti (Coleman and others, 1965; Ghent and Coleman, 1973) and hence overlap but exceed the Ti range for ocean-floor basalts on the high side. The eugeosynclinal basalts from California and Oregon exhibit a range in Ti similar to that of the eclogites (Ernst and others, 1970; Coleman, 1972). In this respect, the eugeosynclinal rocks do not correspond to any of the volcanic series alleged by Jakeš and White (1972) to represent a continuum of igneous rock series in the island-arc domain. Younger compositional analogs of these eugeosynclinal basalts may be the tholeiites of the Eocene Siletz River Volcanics of western Oregon. These were erupted along the continental margin in evolving eugeosynclines but have chemical similarities to oceanic submarine basalts (Snavely and others, 1968).

GEOLOGIC IMPLICATIONS

A few clues provided by the present study, and much information from previous detailed investigations (Coleman and others, 1965; Coleman and Lanphere, 1971; Ghent and Coleman, 1973) lead to the following comments concerning the implications of the eclogite data:

1. Rb and Sr contents in the precursors of the eclogites were probably modified at the time of eclogitization and possibly during an earlier stage of alteration such as might result from interaction with sea water. Sr^{87}/Sr^{86} values may also have been changed during this earlier alteration. In the Late Jurassic, ocean waters contained Sr with a Sr^{87}/Sr^{86} value of 0.70675 (Peterman, Hedge, and Tourtelot, 1970) and this provides an upper limit for Sr^{87}/Sr^{86} values which could be produced by sea-water interaction on basalts (fig. 1). All

the eclogites have Sr^{87}/Sr^{86} values lower than that of Jurassic sea water; accordingly, if exchange did occur, it was variable and far from complete. Whether or not the basalt precursors underwent alteration prior to metamorphism, the initial Sr^{87}/Sr^{86} values (table 1) should be the isotopic composition of Sr at the time of eclogitization, provided that the rocks have been closed systems in Rb and Sr since that time. Tectonic transport of the eclogites in an ultramafic milieu should not have significantly modified the Rb and Sr contents because of the extremely low concentrations of these elements in the serpentinites.

2. Because of the chemical changes attendant with eclogitization, comparison of the compositions of the eclogites and unaltered basalts is difficult. Nevertheless, previous studies and the present data suggest that eugeosynclinal basalts compositionally similar to, but older than, those now exposed in the lower grade Mesozoic deposits of California and Oregon could have been the precursors of the eclogites.

3. Whatever the compositions of the parent basalts, these eclogites may represent material whose passage down a subduction zone and conversion to high-grade metamorphic rocks was somehow aborted by tectonic transport to the surface (Ernst, 1970). If this model is correct, the present data can be used to reconstruct the isotopic and chemical nature of subducted material composed of eclogite and associated rocks. From the limited data reported here, we can conclude that the eclogites are characteristically variable in Sr^{87}/Sr^{86} ratios (0.7028 to 0.7051) and Rb and Sr contents (figs. 1, 2). Associated metagraywackes show comparable variation in these parameters; Mesozoic graywackes of California and Oregon have initial Sr^{87}/Sr^{86} ratios in the range of 0.7030 to 0.7081 (Peterman and others, 1967; Coleman, 1972) and a wide range in Rb and Sr contents (fig. 2).

Without implying an actual genetic relationship, we can compare the isotopic and trace-element characteristics of the eclogite-graywacke association with those of the younger circum-Pacific calc-alkaline volcanic rocks. Obviously, if these volcanics are derived from a subducted plate, that plate is much younger than the rocks we are discussing. Most calc-alkaline volcanic rocks of the circum-Pacific province are characterized by a remarkably narrow range in Sr^{87}/Sr^{86} values of 0.7030 to 0.7040 (Hedge and Peterman, 1969). Andesites and basalts of the Cascades exemplify this limited range in Sr^{87}/Sr^{86} (fig. 1) but show much variation in Rb and Sr contents (fig. 2). To produce isotopically uniform magmas from a heterogeneous source composed of eclogite and graywacke would require either isotopic homogenization or partial melting to be integrated over sufficient volume so as to average out the isotopic variations. Isotopic homogenization among such diverse rock compositions is not supported by available data on high-grade, even granulite-facies, metamorphic rocks. Integrated partial melting of the degree necessary to reduce the isotopic variations to the required narrow range would also tend to smooth out the primary variations in Rb and Sr contents as well as in major elements. Thus it would be difficult to obtain a primary basalt melt with the compositional characteristics observed in the erupted lavas from a graywacke-eclogite mixture. In considering a similar mixed source for basalts and andesites of the Cascade Range, Hedge and others (1970) concluded that the sedimentary component would have to be minor in order to satisfy the limitation imposed by the Sr isotopic data.

At present, the degrees of freedom are many and the constraints are few. These data on eclogites merely provide some additional boundary conditions which should be considered in models postulating fusion of eclogites to produce calc-alkaline rocks.

REFERENCES CITED

Allsopp, H. L., Nicolaysen, L. O., and Hahn-Weinheimer, P., 1969, Rb/K ratios and Sr-isotopic compositions of minerals in eclogitic and peridotitic rocks: Earth and Planetary Sci. Letters, v. 5, p. 231–244.

Bailey, E. H., Irwin, W. P., and Jones, D. L., 1964, Franciscan and related rocks and their significance in the geology of western California: California Div. Mines Bull. 183, 176 p.

Cann, J. R., 1970, Rb, Sr, Y, Zr and Nb in some ocean floor basaltic rocks: Earth and Planetary Sci. Letters, v. 10, p. 7–11.

Coleman, R. G., 1972, The Colebrooke Schist of southwestern Oregon and its relation to the tectonic evolution of the region: U.S. Geol. Survey Bull. 1339, 61 p.

Coleman, R. G., and Lanphere, M. A., 1971, Distribution and age of high-grade blueschists, associated eclogites and amphibolites from Oregon and California: Geol. Soc. America Bull., v. 82, p. 2397–2412.

Coleman, R. G., Lee, D. E., Beatty, L. B., and Brannock, W. W., 1965, Eclogites and eclogites–their differences and similarities: Geol. Soc. America Bull., v. 76, p. 483–508.

Compston, W., and Lovering, J. R., 1969, The strontium isotope geochemistry of granulitic and eclogitic inclusions from the basic pipes at Delegate, eastern Australia: Geochim. et Cosmochim. Acta, v. 33, p. 691–699.

Ernst, W. G., 1970, Tectonic contact between the Franciscan melange and the Great Valley Sequence–crustal expression of a late Mesozoic Benioff zone: Jour. Geophys. Research, v. 75, p. 886–901.

Ernst, W. G., Seki, Y., Onuki, H., and Gilbert, M. C., 1970, Comparative study of low-grade metamorphism in the California Coast Ranges and the outer metamorphic belt of Japan: Geol. Soc. America Mem. 124, 270 p.

Ewart, A., and Bryan, W. B., 1972, Petrography and geochemistry of the igneous rocks from Eua, Tongan Islands: Geol. Soc. America Bull., v. 83, p. 3281–3298.

Faure, G., and Powell, J. L., 1972, Strontium isotope geochemistry: New York, Springer-Verlag, 188 p.

Fry, N., and Fyfe, W. S., 1969, Eclogites and water pressure: Contr. Mineralogy and Petrology, v. 24, p. 1–6.

Ghent, E. D., and Coleman, R. G., 1973, Eclogites from southwestern Oregon: Geol. Soc. America Bull. v. 84, p. 2471–2488.

Green, D. H., and Ringwood, A. E., 1967, An experimental investigation of the gabbro to eclogite transformation and its petrological implications: Geochim. et Cosmochim. Acta, v. 31, p. 767–833.

Hart, S. R., 1969, K, Rb, Cs contents and K/Rb, K/Cs ratios of fresh and altered submarine basalts: Earth and Planetary Sci. Letters, v. 6, p. 295–303.

——1972, Sr isotopic composition of the oceanic crust: Carnegie Inst. Washington Yearbook 71, p. 288–290.

Hart, S. R., Brooks, C., Krogh, T. W., Davis, G. L., and Nava, D., 1970, Ancient and modern volcanic rocks—a trace element model: Earth and Planetary Sci. Letters, v. 10, p. 17–28.

Hedge, C. E., Hildreth, R. A., and Henderson, W. T., 1970, Strontium isotopes in some Cenozoic lavas from Oregon and Washington: Earth and Planetary Sci. Letters, v. 8, p. 434–438.

Hedge, C. E., and Peterman, Z. E., 1969, Sr^{87}/Sr^{86} of Circum-Pacific andesites: Geol. Soc. America Abs. with Programs for 1969, pt. 7, p. 96.

——1970, The strontium isotopic composition of basalts from the Gordo and Juan de Fuca Rises, northeastern Pacific Ocean: Contr. Mineralogy and Petrology, v. 27, p. 114–120.

Jakeš, P., and White, A. J. R., 1972, Major and trace element abundances in volcanic rocks of orogenic areas: Geol. Soc. America Bull., v. 83, p. 29–40.

Miyashiro, A., 1972, Metamorphism and related magmatism in plate tectonics: Am. Jour. Sci., v. 272, p. 629–656.

Peterman, Z. E., Carmichael, I. S. E., and Smith, A. L., 1970, Sr^{87}/Sr^{86} ratios in Quaternary lavas of the Cascade Range, northern California: Geol. Soc. America Bull., v. 81, p. 311–318.

Peterman, Z. E., Coleman, R. G., and Hildreth, R. A., 1971, Sr^{87}/Sr^{86} in mafic rocks of the Troodos Massif, Cyprus, *in* Geological Survey Research 1971: U.S. Geol. Survey Prof. Paper 750-D, p. D157–D161.

Peterman, Z. E., Hedge, C. E., Coleman, R. G., and Snavely, P. D., Jr., 1967, Sr^{87}/Sr^{86} ratios in some eugeosynclinal sedimentary rocks and their bearing on the origin of granitic magma in orogenic belts: Earth and Planetary Sci. Letters, v. 2, p. 433–439.

Peterman, Z. E., Hedge, C. E., and Tourtelot, H. A., 1970, Isotopic composition of strontium in sea water throughout Phanerozoic time: Geochim. et Cosmochim. Acta, v. 34, p. 105–120.

Ringwood, A. E., and Green, D. H., 1966, An experimental investigation of the gabbro to eclogite transformation and some geophysical implications: Tectonophysics, v. 3, p. 383–427.

Sinha, A. K., and Davis, T. E., 1971, Geochemistry of Franciscan volcanic and sedimentary rocks from California: Carnegie Inst. Washington Yearbook 69, p. 394–397.

Snavely, P. D., Jr., MacLeod, N. S., and Wagner, H. C., 1968, Tholeiitic and alkalic basalts of the Eocene Siletz River Volcanics, Oregon Coast Range: Am. Jour. Sci., v. 266, p. 454–481.

Steuber, A. M., and Murthy, V. R., 1966, Strontium isotope and alkali element abundances in ultramafic rocks: Geochim. et Cosmochim. Acta, v. 30, p. 1243–1259.

Jour. Research U.S. Geol. Survey
Vol. 1, No. 6, Nov.-Dec. 1973, p. 649—658

LOSS OF VOLATILES DURING FOUNTAINING AND FLOWAGE OF BASALTIC LAVA AT KILAUEA VOLCANO, HAWAII

By DONALD A. SWANSON and BRENT P. FABBI, Menlo Park, Calif.

Abstract.—The amount of water and sulfur in pumice erupted during periods of vigorous activity during the 1969–71 Mauna Ulu eruption varied inversely with fountain height because of degassing during the fountaining. The pumice lost about 0.05 wt percent water and 0.003 wt percent sulfur during fountaining to heights of 400–540 m. Analyses suggest that the initial volatile content of Mauna Ulu lava was greater immediately preceding periods of high fountaining than during weak activity between those periods or after the last high fountains on December 30, 1969. Water and sulfur were systematically depleted during nearly isothermal flowage in lava tubes. Rapidly quenched samples of dipped melt show losses of about 0.03–0.04 wt percent water and 0.007–0.008 wt percent sulfur during flowage for several hours through a distance of 12 km. Glassy skins on cooled pahoehoe flows contain about 0.002–0.003 wt percent less sulfur than quenched melt at comparable distances from the vent, because of continued degassing under natural cooling conditions. Chlorine shows similar but less well defined trends. Pumice erupted in high fountains becomes more strongly oxidized than the parent magma, because of mixing with air while still at high temperatures.

The sudden reduction in confining pressure causes basaltic lava to degas as it erupts and flows away from the vent. Large fume clouds accompanying high lava fountains are clear evidence of degassing. Subtle but conclusive evidence of continued degassing during subsequent flowage away from the vent is provided by the observed downslope decrease in (1) the amount of fume emitted from the flowing lava, (2) the number of bubbles on the surface of the flowing lava and vesicularity of the solidified flow, and (3) the fluidity at nearly constant temperature. Swanson elaborates on this evidence of degassing during the 1969–71 Mauna Ulu eruption of Kilauea in another paper (1973). In general, the degree of degassing is important in governing the structures and textures of all solidified flows, whether subaerial (Swanson, 1973) or subaqueous (Jones, 1969; Moore, 1970a).

Chemical analysis of the volatile content of glassy, quickly chilled samples collected at various stages during an eruption is one way to measure the degree of degassing. If the quench is rapid enough, the volatile content of the resulting glass is nearly the same as that dissolved in the liquid lava at the site of collection. If not so rapid, gases are lost to a degree dependent on the rate of cooling.

We have examined the content of water, sulfur, and chlorine in many fresh, rapidly quenched samples of pumice, spatter, and flow material from the 1969–71 Mauna Ulu eruption. The rate of volatile loss is dependent in part on height of fountaining and distance of flowage, that is, on the length of time at which the sample was held at about 1 atm pressure and at magmatic temperature. The data also suggest that the lava which fountained to great heights contained more volatiles before eruption than that which erupted during weak activity or flowed out of the vent without spattering. Pumice ejected to heights of 100 m or more became more highly oxidized than the parent magma, presumably from extended contact with air at high temperatures.

Basaltic magma, if saturated, probably contains at least 0.5 wt percent water and 0.08 wt percent sulfur at confining pressures equivalent to those in Kilauea's shallow (1–3 km depth) reservoir system (Moore, 1970b; Moore and Fabbi, 1971). The distribution of these and other volatiles in the parent magma before and during the 1969–71 Mauna Ulu eruption is not known. Possibly volatiles were enriched in lower pressure (shallower depth) parts of the reservoir system owing to diffusion before eruption. Such possible enrichment cannot be evaluated in this study, however, as all analyzed samples contain only 20 percent or less of the presumed original volatile content owing to the dominance of the eruptive and flowage degassing processes. Our computed rates of volatile loss during fountaining probably are minimum rates, because we assume, for the purpose of this paper, a uniform distribution of volatiles in the magma immediately before eruption and no diffusion of volatiles into the magma from the reservoir wallrock.

Many uncertainties were involved in collecting the suite of samples examined in this paper, as is true of most collections obtained under dynamic, at times dangerous, conditions. Such uncertainties make some of the interpretations tentative. This is particularly true of samples of pumice from high fountains. One cannot possibly know the preeruption volatile history of such samples, exactly what processes take place during the time the pumice is in the fountain, and the precise trajectory of the pumice as it falls to the ground. These and other uncertainties can drastically affect the volatile content of the samples in unpredictable ways. We believe that much of the scatter in our data, especially for high fountains, is caused by such uncertainties. Furthermore, many of the changes that we examine are small and close to the analytical uncertainty. We have interpreted the results simply and find them to be reasonably consistent but emphasize the possibilities of alternative interpretations.

The fountain data, though less reliable than the flowage data, are discussed first because of the temporal sequence of the degassing processes.

Acknowledgments.—Swanson is responsible for the field observations and collection of samples; Fabbi made the sulfur and chlorine analyses. They share the interpretations. W. A. Duffield and T. L. Wright reviewed the manuscript and improved it greatly, and R. L. Christiansen and R. I. Tilling suggested stimulating alternative interpretations. We thank D. W. Peterson for help in collecting samples; E. L. Brandt, E. E. Engleman, G. O. Riddle, and V. C. Smith for the water and fluorine analyses under the direction of L. C. Peck; R. T. Okamura for the specific gravity determinations; and J. G. Moore for helpful discussion.

ANALYTICAL PROCEDURE AND EVALUATION

Sixty-two samples were analyzed for sulfur and chlorine by X-ray fluorescence using the techniques, equipment, and standards described in papers by Fabbi and Moore (1970), Moore and Fabbi (1971), and Fabbi and Espos (1972). Two pellets were analyzed for each element. The precision of the analyses is estimated to be ±0.0010 wt percent for both sulfur and chlorine. The estimated accuracy is ±0.0050 wt percent for sulfur and ±0.0020 wt percent for chlorine. Samples were analyzed for sulfur and chlorine in three batches at different times, and the results are consistent within and between batches.

Standard wet chemical analyses of 26 samples were made in the laboratories of the U.S. Geological Survey, using the methods of L. C. Peck (1964). The constituents pertinent to this study are given in table 1. Samples were submitted for analysis in four batches, for the most part in time-sequential order. Several specimens from early in the eruption were submitted in a late batch, however, and each batch contained samples of both vigorous and weak activity. Two analysts were

Table 1.—*Volatile content of completely analyzed Mauna Ulu pumice, spatter, and flow material*

[All values in weight percent. Except where noted, analyst is E. E. Engleman or V. C. Smith, U.S. Geological Survey, under the direction of L. C. Peck]

Field No.	H_2O+	H_2O-	Total H_2O	MgO	CO_2	[1]Cl	F	[1]S	Oxidation ratio[2]	Distance from Mauna Ulu (km)	Fountain height (m)	Date of activity
					Vigorous fountaining							
DAS691-3	0.04	0.03	0.07	9.14	0.01	0.0106	0.04	0.0195	9.8	....	40	May 24, 1969
693-2	.07	.00	.07	9.54	.02	.0085	.04	.017	11.0	....	100	June 13, 1969
694-5	.06	.00	.06	10.72	.02	.0088	.03	.0165	12.0	....	220	June 26, 1969
695-1	.04	.02	.06	12.18	.01	.0072	.03	.0155	10.3	....	350	July 15, 1969
697-1	.04	.01	.05	13.72	.03	.0095	.04	.0165	10.4	....	300	Aug. 6, 1969
698-1	.00	.03	.03	8.97	.02	.0087	.04	.016	12.6	....	400	Aug. 22, 1969
699-1	.00	.03	.03	9.54	.02	.0093	.04	.021	15.9	....	540	Sept. 6, 1969
6911-1	.01	.01	.02	9.00	.01	.0079	.04	.018	11.4	....	300	Oct. 20, 1969
6912-5	.01	.00	.01	14.45	.01	.0079	.03	.014	10.2	....	390	Dec. 30, 1969
					Weak fountaining							
DAS6956-5	0.02	0.00	0.02	9.08	0.02	0.0079	0.04	0.0125	9.4	....	<10	July 29, 1969
6978-9	.05	.01	.06	9.10	.02	.0082	.04	.0115	9.1	....	<10	Aug. 18–19, 1969
691112-38	.05	.01	.06	10.87	.01	.0087	.04	.0215	9.7	....	<10	Dec. 6, 1969
691112-56	.05	.00	.05	8.82	.01	.0082	.04	.011	8.8	....	<10	Dec. 29, 1969
701213-2	.03	.02	.05	8.54	.01	.0075	.04	.014	8.8	....	<10	Jan. 25, 1970
701213-35	.02	.03	.05	10.01	.02	.0066	.03	.013	8.4	....	<10	May 20–21, 1970
701213-41	.04	.01	.05	9.57	.01	.0068	.04	.018	8.4	....	<10	May 24, 1970
701213-62	.08	.01	.09	12.02	.02	.0057	.03	.0145	8.9	....	<10	July 9, 1970
701213-83	.07	.02	.09	10.92	.02	.0061	.03	.0125	8.8	....	<10	Sept. 3, 1970
701213-115	.05	.02	.07	11.54	.02	.0085	.03	.013	9.3	....	<10	Dec. 5, 1970
711213-126	.07	.01	.08	11.37	.02	.0093	.03	.013	7.6	....	<10	Feb. 13, 1971
					Lava flows[3]							
DAS711213-127	0.05	0.00	0.05	11.33	0.04	0.0065	0.03	0.012	9.0	0.4	....	Feb. 15, 1971
711213-131A	.06	.03	.09	10.69	.02	.0061	.04	.011	9.5	5.8	....	Apr. 7, 1971
711213-134	.02	.00	.02	8.14	.02	.0061	.03	.0095	10.2	10.0	....	Apr. 12, 1971
711213-134A	.03	.03	.06	11.21	.02	.0051	.03	.0095	9.7	10.0	....	Apr. 12, 1971
711213-136	.03	.03	.06	10.33	.02	.0062	.03	.0065	9.4	12.0	....	Apr. 19, 1971
711213-137	.01	.02	.03	11.96	.01	.0155	.03	.0075	8.9	12.0	....	Apr. 19, 1971

[1] X-ray fluorescence duplicate determinations of Cl and total S by B. P. Fabbi.

[2] $\frac{0.9Fe_2O_3 \times 100}{0.9Fe_2O_3 + FeO}$.

[3] Collected while liquid from flowing lava, except for sample DAS711213-137, which was collected underwater by R. L. Phillips.

also involved, and comparison of all data shows no evidence of analytical bias or drift in the results.

The estimated precision of the MgO analyses is ±0.05 wt percent or better (Wright, 1971, p. 6). Analytical precisions for the volatiles are not known. Water is notoriously difficult to determine with precision by the modified Penfield method; we believe, however, that when a set of water analyses shows distinct trends, these analyses can be reasonably interpreted as reliable. If the trends shown by the water analyses in this paper are valid and are straight-line functions, then the analytical precision for water can be estimated to be about ±0.02 wt percent.

In addition to possible analytical imprecision, the interpretation of water analyses is made difficult by the largely arbitrary division into H_2O+ and H_2O- at 110°C. Most petrologists assume that all H_2O- is contaminant and use only H_2O+ in their studies. Our samples analyzed for water were generally collected while still hot, and always before any rain fell on them. Most of them, however, were stored in a moderately humid environment for weeks to months before analysis. The true value for magmatic water in each sample is probably somewhere between the reported amounts of H_2O+ and total water.

LOSS OF VOLATILES AND OXIDATION DURING FOUNTAINING

Type of eruption

Twelve episodes of vigorous fountaining took place at Mauna Ulu, a new lava shield on Kilauea's east rift, between May 24 and December 30, 1969 (Swanson and others, 1971). Nine of these episodes featured lava fountains 100 m or more high; the maximum measured height was 540 m. Fountains of the other three episodes were 20 to 50 m high.

Beginning in July 1969, weak eruptive activity often took place between the fountaining episodes. This activity usually involved no more than a cyclic rise and fall of the lava column within the main vent, but at times the column reached the lip of the vent and spilled out on the ground surface as flows. Spattering 10 m or less in height sometimes accompanied this weak activity.

Samples

Samples of pumice from the high, vigorous fountains and spatter from the low, weak activity are the basis of the present study (table 1). These samples were, with few exceptions, collected while still warm and before rain fell. All the pumice samples were erupted during, or close to, the time of maximum fountain height. The fountain heights assigned to pumice samples in table 1 are subject to perhaps a 25-percent error because of difficulties in defining the top of a fountain and knowing the trajectory of the pumice fragments. The relative heights are considered reliable.

Most of the lava erupted in high fountains fell to the ground around the vent while still molten, gathered into a pool, and flowed away from the vent area. Only a comparatively small volume of the lava that reached the top of the fountain (itself only a small part of the total volume of erupted lava) was actually blown away as pumice fragments, most of which fell to the ground within 1 km of the vent. Such pumice fragments constitute the samples of high fountains studied in this paper. Typically, this pumice was too hot to touch when it landed but cooled within several minutes to ambient temperature.

Pumice fragments produced by the high fountains are very frothy. Some pieces are incompletely enclosed by a thin, glassy skin similar to that described and pictured by Friedman (1967). Spatter formed during weak activity is less vesicular than the pumice but still has a bulk specific gravity of less than 1. Vesicles are generally larger in the pumice than in the spatter. The larger vesicles and greater vesicularity of the pumice provide visual evidence that it degassed more completely than the spatter, and this conclusion is supported by the volatile contents.

Volatile loss

Compositions of most Kilauea lava with MgO greater than 6.8 percent, including the 1969–71 Mauna Ulu lava (Hawaiian Volcano Observatory, unpub. data), are largely controlled by the content of olivine and hence show straight-line variation when plotted on MgO variation diagrams (Powers, 1955; Wright, 1971; Wright and Fiske, 1971). Constituents not incorporated into olivine, such as volatiles, increase systematically as MgO decreases, if this relation has not been disturbed by other processes. The variation of water and sulfur with MgO, as plotted on figure 1, is not systematic, and chlorine follows a similar pattern. From this we conclude that processes other than simple olivine control have strongly influenced the volatile content.

In order to eliminate the effects of olivine control and facilitate comparison of the data, we have adjusted the analyses to an MgO value of 8 percent, using olivine control lines shown in the variation diagram, and an unpublished control line for chlorine. Each control line was drawn through the scatter of data in the diagram (fig. 1) and projects to 0 percent of the volatile constituent at Fo_{85} (about 45 percent MgO). A more precise method entails drawing a separate control line through each point and determining the appropriate adjustment for that point. As comparison of the two methods shows virtually no difference in the adjusted values, the simpler method was used. The adjusted volatile percentages (fig. 2) are all slightly higher than the unadjusted values but show similar variation trends.

One of the most critical processes affecting the volatile content is high fountaining, as indicated by the inverse relation between fountain heights of 40 m or more and content of water and, to a lesser degree, sulfur (fig. 2). Pumice erupted from low fountains during episodes of vigorous activity (filled

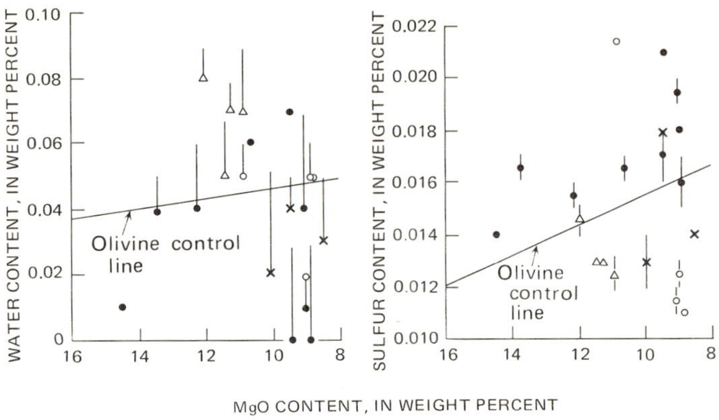

EXPLANATION

- • Vigorous fountains, May - December 1969
- ○ Weak activity, May - December 1969
- × Weak activity, January - June 1970
- △ Weak activity, July 1970 and later

Open symbols and crosses, spatter;
filled symbols, pumice

Figure 1.—Relation of water and sulfur to MgO. Symbol for water represents H_2O+, and end of line represents total water. Lines through sulfur symbols are error bars. Olivine control lines project to 0 percent water and sulfur at an olivine composition of Fo_{85}.

circles in fig. 2) contains about 0.07 wt percent total water and 0.020 percent sulfur, whereas that from high fountains contains 0.03 percent or less total water and about 0.016 percent sulfur. (Spatter erupted during weak activity, discussed below, does not follow this trend.) Except for the sample from the highest fountain (sample DAS699-1 in table 1), the inverse variation is reasonably systematic and seemingly above analytical error. We interpret this relation to indicate degassing during fountaining, high fountains allowing more time for degassing than the low ones. Chlorine may decrease from about 0.011 to 0.0085 percent with increased fountain height, but this trend is poorly defined (fig. 2).

The comparatively high content of sulfur and chlorine (checked by reanalysis) in the sample from the highest fountain cannot be adequately explained. The sample differs texturally from all others, as it is reticulite, or thread-lace scoria (Wentworth and Macdonald, 1954, p. 78), a variety of highly vesicular pumice commonly thought to form during exceptionally gassy eruptions. Accordingly, the preeruption contents of sulfur and chlorine may have been unusually high. Alternatively, the reticulite may have provided adsorption traps for sulfur and chlorine present in the fume cloud, either as gases or liquid droplets (Cadle and Frank, 1968).

The volatile content correlates with the type of eruptive activity. Most 1969 spatter samples erupted during weak activity between periods of vigorous fountaining contain less total water and sulfur and possibly less chlorine than do pumice samples from the lowest of the vigorous fountains (fig. 2). One sample[1] (DAS691112-38 in table 1) is a marked

[1] Close examination of this sample shows trace amounts of a sublimate coating many surfaces; this sublimate may be a contaminant in the analysis, explaining the high sulfur value.

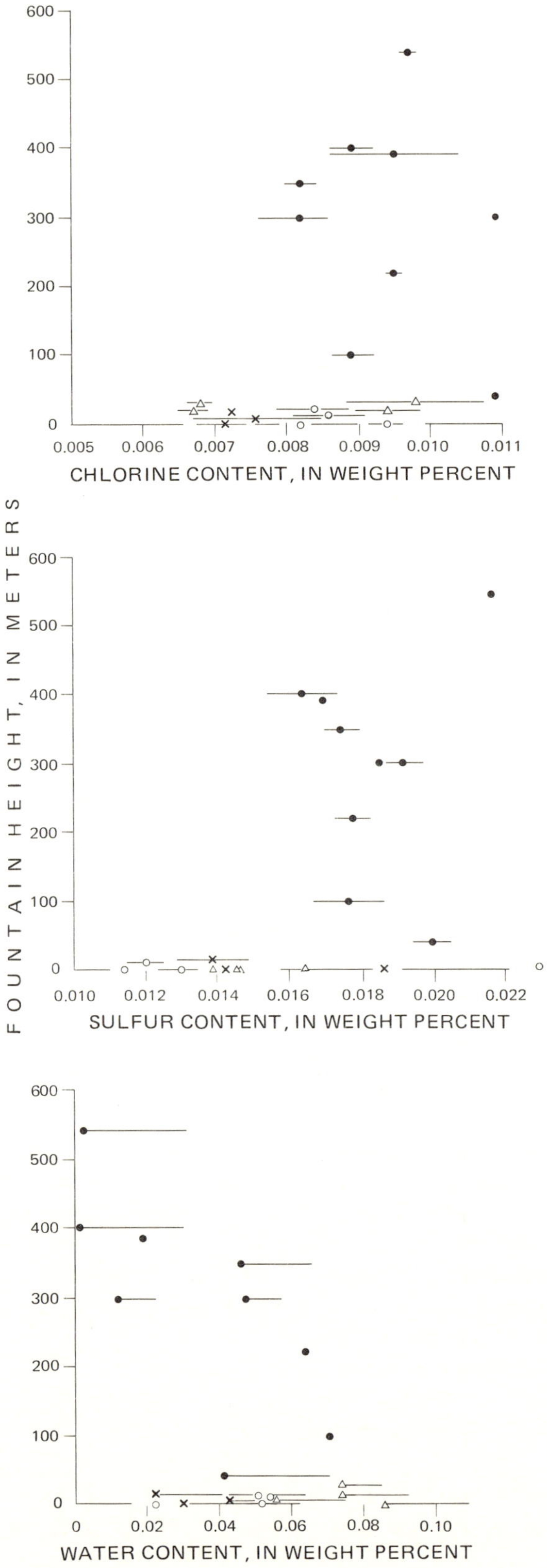

Figure 2.—Relation of water, sulfur, and chlorine to fountain height. Plotted values are adjusted for olivine control. Symbols are the same as in figure 1. Spatter samples plotted at fountain heights of less than 40 m on this and subsequent figures were actually erupted to heights of 10 m or less.

exception for it contains more sulfur than any other analyzed sample; otherwise the relation is quite clear. No other systematic chemical difference (except the degree of oxidation, as described in the next section) was noted between the pumice and spatter samples. The data suggest that the magma contained more dissolved volatiles just before high fountaining than just before weak activity, and this greater volatile content may have been instrumental in driving the fountains to greater heights. If this interpretation is correct, then the preeruption volatile content of the 1969 magma was not strictly constant, and this may account for some of the scatter in figure 2.

Available analyses (table 1) of CO_2 and fluorine show no systematic variations related to fountain height or mode of eruption. The precision of analytical techniques used for their determination probably was not sufficient to detect the small changes expected.

It could be argued that the inverse relation between fountain height and water content can be interpreted as a temporal variation in composition, for magma erupted prior to August 6 contained more water than that erupted between August 22 and December 30 (table 1). This interpretation, however, fails to explain why the three highest fountains of the eruption were produced after August 6, that is, during the time that hypothetically "dry" magma was being erupted. Also, the water content of spatter from weak activity was less before August 6 than after—a relation opposite to that of the high fountaining.

Oxidation

The degree of oxidation of Mauna Ulu pumice and spatter shows a positive correlation with fountain height. The data plotted in figure 3, adjusted for olivine control assuming an oxidation ratio, $\frac{0.9Fe_2O_3 \times 100}{0.9Fe_2O_3 + FeO}$, of 0.9 for combined olivine and spinel (T. L. Wright, written commun., 1972), indicate that pumice from vigorous fountains has an oxidation ratio of 10.4 or more, whereas all other samples except two have ratios of 10.4 or less. Some of the oxidation probably occurred during high-temperature exposure to air, so it is greater in pumice from high fountains.

The average oxidation ratio of the 11 analyses of spatter from weak activity is about 9.5 and may be a reliable value for the 1969–71 Mauna Ulu parent magma under near-surface conditions and adjusted for olivine control.

Change in water content with time

Spatter erupted during the period January through June 1970 contains about the same amount of water as spatter erupted during weak activity in 1969 (table 1; fig. 2). Spatter erupted in July 1970 and later contains more water (about 0.08 as compared with 0.05 wt percent total water). Wet chemical analyses (Hawaiian Volcano Observatory, unpub. data) indicate that several small but significant changes in major-element chemistry other than those caused by olivine control took place sequentially during the eruption, the largest in early July 1970, precisely when the water content also increased. It appears that the new batch of magma differed from that erupted earlier in water content as well as in major oxides. No change in sulfur or chlorine was detected at this time.

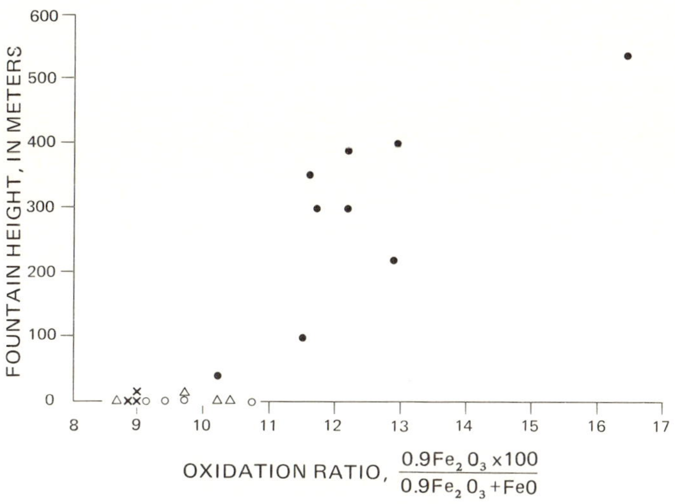

Figure 3.—Relation of oxidation ratio to fountain height. The ratios are adjusted for olivine control, assuming a ratio of 0.9 for olivine and intergrown spinel.

Comparison with the 1959 eruption

Friedman (1967) studied the water content of pumice erupted during the 1959 eruption in Kilauea Iki pit crater at Kilauea. He found an overall dependence of water content on the amount of olivine present (olivine control) but recognized deviations that he ascribed to concentration of volatiles at the top of a magma column.

Water content of Kilauea Iki pumice was plotted in relation to approximate fountain heights, which were extrapolated from data in Richter and others (1970) using the time of collection and times and heights of fountains (fig. 4). All the data have been corrected for olivine control (Murata and Richter, 1966; Wright, 1973). The water analyses are in two sets, those using the modified Penfield method (Peck, 1964) and published by Murata and Richter (1966, table 1) and those using a technique involving reaction of H_2O+ vapor with uranium metal by Friedman (1967). The two sets of analyses disagree as to absolute amount, most likely because of the difference in analytical techniques. Both sets, however, show a trend of lower water content with increased fountain height.

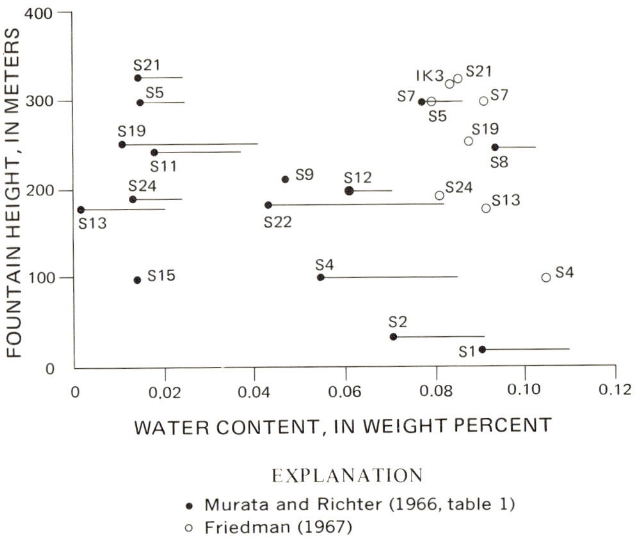

Figure 4.—Relation of water content to fountain height for pumice samples from the 1959 Kilauea eruption. Plotted values are adjusted for olivine control. Symbols for H_2O+ and total water are the same as in figure 1. Sample numbers are those given in Friedman (1967) and Murata and Richter (1966, table 1).

Friedman (1967) considered pumice of the eruption's first phase (Nov. 17–20, 1959) to contain water in amounts greater than predicted from strict olivine control, although only one analysis (S-4) deviated significantly from the olivine control line. He reasonably suggested that this concentration of water was caused by diffusion toward the top of the magma column before the eruption began. The plot of water in relation to fountain height (fig. 4) shows that S-4 was erupted from the lowest fountain of any sampled by Friedman (1967) and so had the best chance of retaining its original water content, whether or not enriched in the parent magma through diffusion. In view of the small number of samples available and the complex controls exerted by olivine content, fountain height, and possible water enrichment before eruption, we feel that no firm conclusions can be drawn concerning the cause of variation in water content of the 1959 pumice.

LOSS OF VOLATILES AND OXIDATION DURING FLOWAGE

Samples

Glassy samples were collected at regular intervals along a complex pahoehoe lava flow erupted in 1971. The flow advanced from Mauna Ulu to the ocean, 12 km to the south. It was chiefly fed through lava tubes (Peterson and Swanson, 1973), which allowed the moving lava to remain hot while permitting continuous degassing. Optical pyrometer measurements indicate that the lava cooled less than 15°C during transport in the tubes, indicating that the degassing took place under nearly isothermal conditions. Swanson gives further information on this complex lava flow in another paper (1973).

All analyzed samples listed in table 2 and plotted in figures 5–7 are of lava erupted between February and May 1971, chiefly during March and April when the flow was most active. Petrographic observations and several major-element chemical analyses suggest that the parent lava remained chemically uniform during the period of collecting.

Six samples of molten lava were obtained by dipping a metal sampling device (usually a rock hammer or a small bucket) into the flowing river free of surface crust. Each sample was quickly withdrawn and quenched in air. Lava collected in this way solidified in a few seconds but did not cool to ambient temperature for several tens of minutes unless broken into small pieces. Complete chemical analyses of five of these

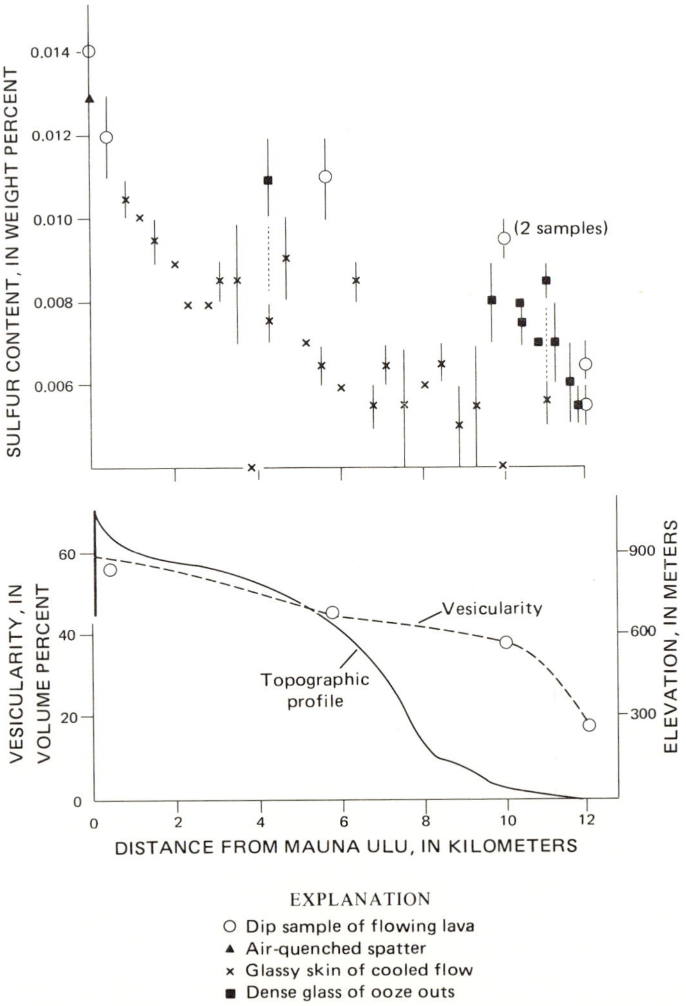

Figure 5.—Relations of sulfur content to distance of flowage, topography, and vesicularity. Lines through sulfur symbols are error bars. Dotted lines connect paired samples 10-10a and 28-28a. Heavy bar between 45- and 70-percent vesicularity indicates range of measured values for spatter. Other vesicularity values were determined on the same samples of dipped melt analyzed for sulfur and chlorine.

Table 2.—*Sulfur, chlorine, and water content of flow material from Mauna Ulu*

[X-ray fluorescence analyses of sulfur and chlorine by B. P. Fabbi. Water analyses by V. C. Smith and E. L. Brandt. All values in weight percent]

Field No.	Sulfur[1]	Chlorine[1]	H_2O+	H_2O-	Type of sample	Distance from vent (km)
DAS711213-126	0.013	0.0093	0.07	0.01	Spatter	0
711213-129	.014	.0061	....	....	Dipped from vent	0
711213-127	.012	.0065	.05	.00	Dipped from flow	.4
1	.0105	.0087	....	....	Glassy skin	.8
2	.010	.0085	....	....	do.	1.2
3	.0095	.0084	....	....	do.	1.5
4	.009	.0081	.00	.00	do.	1.9
5	.008	.0075	....	....	do.	2.3
6	.008	.0074	....	....	do.	2.8
7	.0085	.0067	....	....	do.	3.2
8	.0085	.0062	....	....	do.	3.6
9	<.004	.0060	....	....	do.	4.0
10	.0075	.0062	.03	.00	do.	4.3
10a	.011	.0064	.04	.00	Dense ooze	4.3
11	.009	.0057	....	....	Glassy skin	4.8
12	.007	.0062	....	....	do.	5.2
13	.0065	.0061	....	....	do.	5.6
DAS711213-131A	.011	.0061	.06	.03	Dipped from flow	5.8
14	.006	.0058	....	....	Glassy skin	6.0
15	.0085	.0057	....	....	do.	6.4
16	.0055	.0065	.03	.00	do.	6.8
17	.0065	.0063	....	....	do.	7.1
18	.0055	.0068	....	....	do.	7.6
19	.0060	.0065	....	....	do.	8.0
20	.0065	.0068	.00	.00	do.	8.5
21	.005	.0064	....	....	do.	8.9
22	.0055	.0064	....	....	do.	9.4
23	.008	.0061	....	....	Dense ooze	9.8
24	.004	.0055	....	....	Glassy skin	10.0
DAS711213-134	.0095	.0061	.02	.00	Dipped from flow	10.0
711213-134A	.0095	.0051	.03	.03	do.	10.0
25	.008	.0063	....	....	Dense ooze	10.4
26	.0075	.0056	....	....	do.	10.5
27	.007	.0059	....	....	do.	10.8
28	.0055	.0055	....	....	Glassy skin	11.1
28a	.0085	.0061	....	....	Dense ooze	11.1
29	.007	.0068	....	....	do.	11.3
30	.006	.0061	....	....	do.	11.7
31	.0055	.0062	....	....	do.	11.8
DAS711213-135	.0055	.0053	....	....	Dipped from flow	12.0
711213-136	.0065	.0062	.03	.03	do.	12.0
[2] 711213-137	.0075	.0155	.01	.02	Sampled under water	12.0

[1] Average of two determinations on separate pellets.
[2] Not plotted in figures 5 and 6.

samples and of numerous similar samples show no evidence of contamination from the sampler used, except for an oxidized film adjacent to the metal. Some degassing must have taken place during the period of quenching but is thought to have been minor because of the short time involved and the high viscosity of the solidifying lava.

Nine samples are of relatively dense, glassy ooze outs less than 30 cm thick. These ooze outs did not extend farther than a few meters from their point of emergence on the ground surface, usually a crack in a tumulus or the thin roof of a small lava tube. The glassiness, thinness, and small volume of the ooze outs indicate that they must have cooled very rapidly, and the comparatively small number of vesicles suggests that little degassing could have taken place during the rapid cooling.

Twenty-four samples of the chilled glassy skin on solidified and cooled flow units 1 m or more thick were analyzed. This skin, less than 2 mm thick, is so highly vesicular and flaky that winds tend to strip it from the flow in a few days. Special care was taken to avoid collecting skin next to one of the numerous small cracks along which sulfurous deposits were forming. The skin probably cooled to ambient temperatures more slowly than the melt or ooze-out samples because of heat supplied from the body of the flow.

All flow samples contain 95 percent or more glass; most carry less than 2 percent phenocrysts, all olivine. Some samples near the coastline contain small plagioclase microlites in addition to the olivine phenocrysts, reflecting slightly cooler temperatures before quenching.

For comparison, a sample of spatter and one of melt dipped from the vent at Mauna Ulu are included in table 2 and shown on figures 5–7.

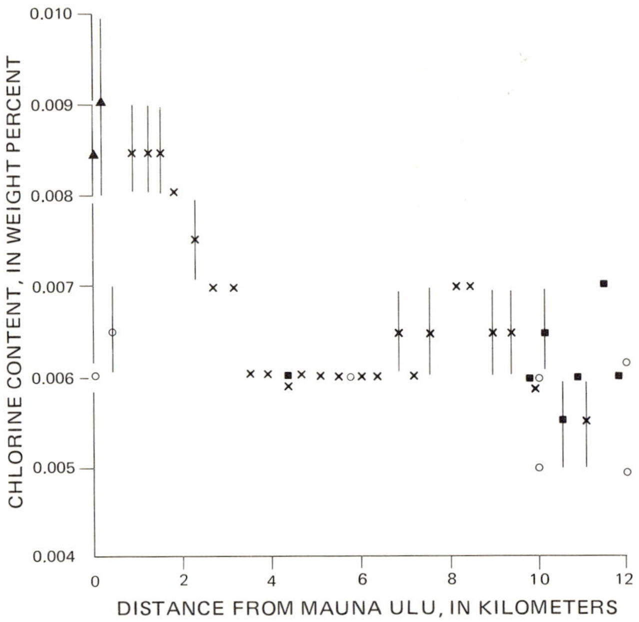

EXPLANATION

- ○ Dip sample of flowing lava
- ▲ Air-quenched spatter
- × Glassy skin of cooled flow
- ■ Dense glass of ooze outs

Figure 6.—Relation of chlorine content to distance of flowage. Lines through symbols are error bars.

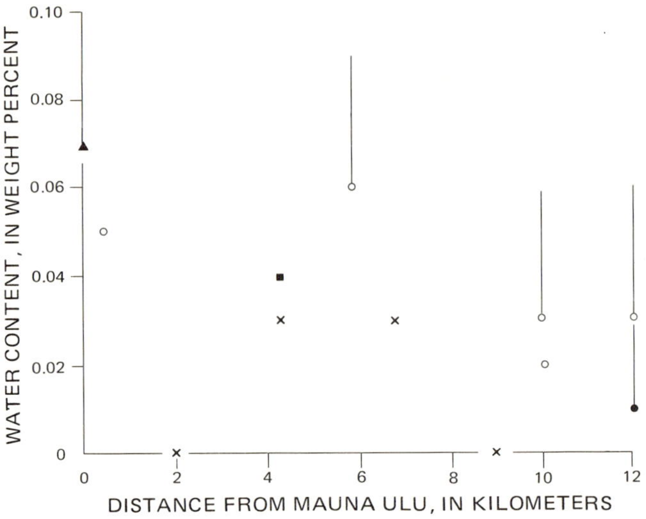

EXPLANATION

- ○ Dip sample of flowing lava
- ▲ Air-quenched spatter
- × Glassy skin of cooled flow
- ■ Dense glass of ooze outs
- ● Glassy toe collected under water

Figure 7.—Relation of water content to distance of flowage. Symbol indicates H_2O+; end of line indicates total water.

Sulfur

Sulfur is lost during flowage, as shown by the data in table 2 and figure 5. Considering only the samples of dipped melt and the air-quenched spatter—the most reliable samples—we note that about 60 percent of the sulfur originally in the lava at the vent was lost during flowage of 12 km. The average rate of loss for the first 10 km of flowage is about 0.001 percent per hour, using an average velocity of flowage of 2.5 km/hr estimated by observation through skylights in the lava tubes. The rate of loss for the last 2 km is not known, for the ground surface flattened greatly (fig. 5) and the lava spread laterally in a complex braided network of tubes where its velocity could not be adequately estimated. The flow velocity must have been considerably slower than for the preceding 10 km, however, because of the much gentler gradient, and this decreased velocity probably accounts for the abrupt loss of sulfur between 10 and 12 km. It seems likely that the rate of sulfur loss remained roughly constant throughout the duration of flowage.

Most of the dense ooze-out samples contain slightly less sulfur than predicted from the melt samples alone, suggesting a small amount of degassing during cooling.

Nearly all samples of glassy skin contain less sulfur than the melt or ooze-out samples collected at the same distance from Mauna Ulu (fig. 5), for the slower cooling of the skin allows more time for degassing. At the calculated rate of 0.001 percent per hour, this degassing must have continued for more than 2 to 4 hours after solidification of the skin, as the skin contains about 0.002 to 0.004 wt percent less sulfur than equivalent melt samples and the rate of degassing would decrease with cooling. Evidence of such prolonged degassing was always present in the field, for walking across a flow only a few hours old was made unpleasant by the SO_2 fumes being evolved.

Two paired sets of samples (10-10a and 28-28a) demonstrate clearly the relation between the sulfur content of skins and ooze outs (table 2; fig. 5). The skins contain 0.0035 and 0.003 wt percent, respectively, less sulfur than the neighboring ooze-outs.

The specific gravities of the samples dipped from melt and of four samples of spatter were determined and converted to percentage vesicularity by use of the curve in Peck, Wright, and Moore (1966, fig. 7, p. 642). A curve through the vesicularity data (fig. 5) has a shape similar to that of the sulfur-loss curve defined by the dip or ooze-out samples.

Chlorine

The amount of chlorine decreases away from the vent less markedly than sulfur (table 2; fig. 6). Melt samples suggest only a slight loss of chlorine, but skin samples show a steady decline in the first 4 km of flowage. Beyond 4 km, the chlorine content is virtually constant at about 0.006 wt percent and perhaps indicates the residual amount of chlorine that can remain trapped in the silicate framework of the melt. In this regard, none of the 141 samples of Hawaiian lavas analyzed by Iwasaki and Katsura (1964) contain less than 0.006 wt percent total chlorine.

The high chlorine content of samples between 7.5 and 9.5 km from Mauna Ulu may reflect contamination by wet sea breezes, for mist commonly hangs over this area during stormy periods involving south winds.

Other volatiles

Samples of dipped melt and air-quenched spatter suggest a loss of water of about 0.03–0.04 wt percent during flowage of 12 km (fig. 7). Samples of glassy skin show lower water contents consistent with prolonged cooling and degassing. The plotted data are not adjusted for olivine control, because MgO was not analyzed for all samples.

The one sample of lava quenched under several meters of sea water contains no more water than adjacent subaerial samples, suggesting that little if any hydration took place during high-temperature contact of lava and water. Chlorine and possibly sulfur are, however, higher than in nearby subaerial samples (table 2) despite thorough washing in distilled water, suggesting contamination by sea water.

Fluorine and CO_2 (table 1) show no consistent trends.

Oxidation ratios

The oxidation ratios (table 1) of the dipped melt samples do not increase systematically with distance traveled. This conclusion is consistent with field observations, which suggest that little if any atmospheric air entered the tubes during flowage of lava through them. In fact, there was always a very strong outward rush of hot fume at skylights in the roofs of tubes. Further, combustible material thrown into lava in the tubes burned much more slowly than on the ground surface. The tubes apparently acted as high-temperature buffers that maintained an approximately equal degree of oxidation throughout the system.

DISCUSSION

This study suggests that water, sulfur, and chlorine are lost in a systematic, measurable way from basaltic lava during vigorous fountaining and flowage. It extends the work of Moore and Fabbi (1971) to surface processes; and their seven sulfur analyses of Hawaiian pumice, spatter, and subaerially erupted lava flows (1971, table 1, p. 121) are consistent with our conclusions.

Water is lost much faster during vigorous fountaining than during flowage, when about 0.01 wt percent per hour is lost. The rate of loss during fountaining is difficult to estimate precisely, owing to the quality of the data and uncertainties as to how long the pumice fragments from different fountain heights remained airborne. Accepting the data in figure 2 and assuming that typical pumice from high fountains effectively lost water for 15 minutes longer than that from low fountains (probably longer than reasonable), we find that the rate of loss during fountaining is about 0.2 wt percent per hour, 20 times that during flowage. The actual difference is probably greater.

The rates of sulfur loss during vigorous fountaining and flowage differ greatly. The rate of loss during flowage is about 0.001 wt percent per hour, whereas that during fountaining (assuming a 15 minute longer duration of gas loss) is about 0.016 wt percent per hour, 16 times that during flowage. Again, the actual difference is probably greater.

The marked reduction in confining pressure during eruption and the subsequent breakage of rapidly formed vesicles (Muenow, 1973) must account for the rapid loss of volatiles during fountaining. During the 1969–71 Mauna Ulu eruption, magma was apparently stored at depths of 1 to 3 km (Hawaiian Volcano Observatory, unpub. data), where, if saturated, it probably contained at least 0.5 wt percent water and 0.08 wt percent sulfur (Moore, 1970b; Moore and Fabbi, 1971). Within a few minutes, as judged by the interval between the onset of seismic tremor and initial eruptive activity, this magma surged upward and reached the surface, reducing the confining pressure by about 250 to 750 bars. During this rapid rise the magma lost about 0.4 wt percent water and 0.06 wt percent sulfur, roughly 80 percent of its original water and sulfur content. With high fountaining, about 0.05 wt percent water and 0.004 wt percent sulfur were lost in addition. With flowage after fountaining or immediately upon eruption, still more volatiles were lost. These values, though necessarily approximate, demonstrate the importance of the eruptive process in determining the volatile content of the solidified lava.

The measured amounts of volatiles lost during fountaining are probably maximum values for they were obtained from pumice fragments blown far from the fountains and consequently subjected to prolonged degassing. The pumice that fell directly to the base of the fountain, where it pooled before flowing away, had less time to degas, so the volatile content of quenched glass from a near-vent flow fed by such pumice would probably be somewhat higher than our measured values.

The ratio of water lost to sulfur lost, H_2O/S, was similar during fountaining and flowage, about 12.5 for fountaining and 10 for flowage. These values are about twice the 5.7 found by Moore and Fabbi (1971) for intratelluric degassing. This difference is reasonable, as sulfur is thought to be less soluble in basaltic magma than water at confining pressures of several hundred bars (Moore and Calk, 1971) and so would be lost more rapidly than water during the early high-pressure stage of vesiculation. The ratio H_2O/S of magmatic gases lost should therefore be higher for surface degassing than for intratelluric degassing.

Sigvaldason and Elísson (1968) found that the ratio of SO_2 to water and other volatile components in volcanic gases from

Surtsey increased with advanced degassing; consequently, the S/H_2O ratio left in the residual glass should decrease. Our samples do not show this, probably because most of their degassing was at high temperatures (1,150°C or more), whereas the Surtsey gases were collected from lava in the process of cooling and thus show temperature-dependent chemical variation.

The results of this study, like those on volcanic gas at Surtsey (Sigvaldason and Elísson, 1968; Árnason and Sigurgeirsson, 1968; Björnsson, 1968), demonstrate the need for great care in selecting samples for studies of volatile contents or degree of oxidation. The effect of surface processes on both degassing and oxidation can be large and rather unexpected. For example, pumice fragments from high fountains, a common type of material used in petrologic studies, are apt to be depleted in volatiles and more highly oxidized than spatter or dipped-melt samples obtained at the vent. On the other hand, the glassy skins of tube-fed pahoehoe may preserve original oxidation ratios despite long distances of travel, whereas surface flows may become more highly oxidized after flowing only short distances from the vent (Hawaiian Volcano Observatory, unpub. data). In general, spatter at the vent would be expected to preserve original volatiles and degree of oxidation better than any other type of material.

The data for demonstrating degassing during flowage show far better internal consistency than those from the fountains. This may well reflect critical differences in the two environments. Flowage through lava tubes takes place nearly isothermally and with minimal, if any, oxidation. Fountaining, especially that higher than a few meters, involves highly oxidizing and variable thermal conditions and rapid transient effects. Aside from single samples of fountain pumice being questionable representatives of such physiochemical disequilibrium, the differences in tube versus fountain environments may cause fundamental differences in patterns of degassing, involving rates, reactions, secondary effects, and other parameters. These possibilities can best be resolved by careful sampling of high fountains, a very difficult and dangerous task.

The pattern of volatile loss, especially sulfur, with longer distance of flowage should characterize all lava flows and may be an important tool in locating source areas and inferring the direction of advance of prehistoric flows. For such a study, care should be taken to compare only those samples whose posteruption histories are similar.

REFERENCES CITED

Arnason, Bragi, and Sigurgeirsson, Thorbjörn, 1968, Deuterium content of water vapour and hydrogen in volcanic gas at Surtsey, Iceland: Geochim. et Cosmochim. Acta, v. 32, p. 807–813.

Björnsson, Sveinbjörn, 1968, Radon and water in volcanic gas at Surtsey, Iceland: Geochim. et Cosmochim. Acta, v. 32, p. 815–821.

Cadle, R. D., and Frank, E. R., 1968, Particles in the fume from the 1967 Kilauea eruption: Jour. Geophys. Research, v. 73, p. 4780–4783.

Fabbi, B. P., and Espos, L. F., 1972, X-ray fluorescence determination of chlorine in standard silicate rocks: Appl. Spectroscopy, v. 26, p. 293–295.

Fabbi, B. P., and Moore, W. J., 1970, Rapid X-ray fluorescence determination of sulfur in mineralized rocks from the Bingham mining district, Utah: Appl. Spectroscopy, v. 24, p. 426–428.

Friedman, Irving, 1967, Water and deuterium in pumice from the 1959–60 eruption of Kilauea Volcano, Hawaii, *in* Geological Survey Research 1967: U.S. Geol. Survey Prof. Paper 575-B, p. B120–B127.

Iwasaki, Bunji, and Katsura, Takashi, 1964, The chlorine content of Hawaiian lavas: Chem. Soc. Japan. Bull., v. 37, p. 1827–1833.

Jones, J. G., 1969, Pillow lavas as depth indicators: Am. Jour. Sci., v. 267, p. 181–195.

Moore, J. G., 1970a, Pillow lava in a historic lava flow from Hualalai Volcano, Hawaii: Jour. Geology, v. 78, p. 239–243.

——1970b, Water content of basalt erupted on the ocean floor: Contr. Mineralogy and Petrology, v. 28, p. 272–279.

Moore, J. G., and Calk, L., 1971, Sulfide spherules in vesicles of dredged pillow basalt: Am. Mineralogist, v. 56, p. 476–488.

Moore, J. G., and Fabbi, B. P., 1971, An estimate of the juvenile sulfur content of basalt: Contr. Mineralogy and Petrology, v. 33, p. 118–127.

Muenow, D. W., 1973, High temperature mass spectrometric gas-release studies of Hawaiian volcanic glass—Pele's Tears: Geochim. et Cosmochim. Acta, v. 37, no. 6, p. 1551–1561.

Murata, K. J., and Richter, D. H., 1966, Chemistry of the lavas of the 1959–60 eruption of Kilauea Volcano, Hawaii: U.S. Geol. Survey Prof. Paper 537-A, 26 p.

Peck, D. L., Wright, T. L., and Moore, J. G., 1966, Crystallization of tholeiitic basalt in Alae lava lake, Hawaii: Bull. Volcanol., v. 29, p. 629–656.

Peck, L. C., 1964, Systematic analysis of silicates: U.S. Geol. Survey Bull. 1170, 89 p.

Peterson, D. W., and Swanson, D. A., 1973, Observed formation of lava tubes during 1970–71 at Kilauea Volcano, Hawaii: Studies in Speleology, v. 2, pt. 6. (In press.)

Powers, H. A., 1955, Composition and origin of basaltic magma of the Hawaiian Islands: Geochim. et Cosmochim. Acta, v. 7, p. 77–107.

Richter, D. H., Eaton, J. P., Murata, K. J., Ault, W. U., and Krivoy, H. L., 1970, Chronological narrative of the 1959–60 eruption of Kilauea Volcano, Hawaii: U.S. Geol. Survey Prof. Paper 537-E, 73 p.

Sigvaldason, G. E., and Elísson, Gunnlaugur, 1968, Collection and analysis of volcanic gases at Surtsey, Iceland: Geochim. et Cosmochim. Acta, v. 32, p. 797–805.

Swanson, D. A., 1973, Pahoehoe flows from the 1969–1971 Mauna Ulu eruption, Kilauea Volcano, Hawaii: Geol. Soc. America Bull., v. 84, p. 615–626.

Swanson, D. A., Jackson, D. B., Duffield, W. A., and Peterson, D. W., 1971, Mauna Ulu eruption, Kilauea Volcano: Geotimes, v. 16, p. 12–16.

Wentworth, C. K., and Macdonald, G. A., 1954, Structures and forms of basaltic rocks in Hawaii: U.S. Geol. Survey Bull. 994, 98 p.

Wright, T. L., 1971, Chemistry of Kilauea and Mauna Loa lava in space and time: U.S. Geol. Survey Prof. Paper 735, 40 p.

——1973, Magma mixing as illustrated by the 1959 eruption, Kilauea Volcano, Hawaii: Geol. Soc. American Bull., v. 84, p. 849–858.

Wright, T. L., and Fiske, R. S., 1971, Origin of the differentiated and hybrid lavas of Kilauea Volcano, Hawaii: Jour. Petrology, v. 12, p. 1–65.

Jour. Research U.S. Geol. Survey
Vol. 1, No. 6, Nov.-Dec. 1973, p. 659—663

RADIOELEMENT DISTRIBUTION IN THE BASEMENT COMPLEX OF THE YUKON-TANANA UPLAND, EIELSON DEEP TEST HOLE, ALASKA

By C. M. BUNKER, C. A. BUSH; and R. B. FORBES,
Denver, Colo.; College, Alaska

Abstract.—Uranium, thorium, and potassium contents were determined in 94 samples of drill cuttings from a 9,774-foot-deep exploratory hole drilled entirely in crystalline schists of the basement complex of the Yukon-Tanana Upland. The data indicate two distinctively different rock types and reflect differences in the calcite content of the rock. Zones of anomalously high concentrations of the radioelements probably reflect the effects of the emplacement of the nearby Eielson pluton.

The Eielson deep test hole is about 26 miles east-southeast of Fairbanks, Alaska, and about 8 miles northeast of Eielson Air Force Base (fig. 1). The hole was drilled 9,774 feet from a collar elevation of 1,350 feet above sea level. Cores were obtained at approximately 1,000-foot intervals, and cuttings were collected at 10-foot intervals. Reported here are analyses of the radioelements uranium, thorium, and potassium in 94 samples of the cuttings from 100-foot intervals except those between 2,200 and 2,800 feet, which were unavailable.

The hole is entirely within crystalline schists of the basement complex of the Yukon-Tanana Upland, and it provides an unusual opportunity for geologic and geophysical studies of the complex. Measurements of the radioelement concentrations are a part of a series of investigations using various data obtained from the drill hole (Lachenbruch and Bunker, 1971; Forbes and F. R. Weber, unpub. data).

The principal objective of the radioelement analyses was to determine the distribution of the radioelements and that of the associated radiogenic heat through a thick vertical section of schist. The heat production and averages of the radioelement concentrations were reported by Lachenbruch and Bunker (1971). An extensive report that is being prepared by Forbes and F. R. Weber on the geology of the area and the petrology of 11 drill-core samples from the deep test hole, plus two drill-core samples from two nearby preliminary test holes, provides a basis for examining some of the possible causes for variations in the vertical distribution of the radioelements and radiogenic heat.

GEOLOGY AND PETROLOGY

R. B. Forbes and F. R. Weber, during several geologic studies in the general area of the Eielson Air Force Base, examined and analyzed the drill cores recovered from the deep test hole and supplemented these data with less critical examinations of intervening chip samples. According to results of that work, the site of the deep test hole is in a northeast-trending belt of greenschist-facies rocks, which were believed by Mertie (1937) to be of pre-middle Ordovician age. On the basis of limited K-Ar age data, the metamorphism occurred about 140 m.y. ago (Forbes and Weber, unpub. data). Characteristic rock types in the area include calc-mica schist, calc-phyllites, greenschists, phyllitic schists, slates and fine-grained quartzites which appear to be metacherts or siltstones. Where unaffected by superimposed thermal metamorphism, outcrop mineral assemblages are characteristically those of the greenschist facies. The drill-hole site is located on calc-mica schist.

Two granitic plutons, which may be parts of a continuous mass in the subsurface, are present in the greenschist-facies belt. The contact of the Eielson pluton is about 2 miles southeast of the well site; that of the Tors pluton is about 16 miles northeast. Both plutons are surrounded by contact aureoles, as much as a mile wide, which contain rocks recrystallized under temperatures equivalent to those required to produce mineral assemblages of the hornblende or pyroxene hornfels facies. In some areas contact metamorphism was accompanied by pneumatolytic alteration.

The metamorphic mineral assemblages in the section cut by the drill hole indicate that metamorphic grade increases with depth. This increase apparently represents the transition from upper-greenschist facies to lower-amphibolite facies.

The rocks in the drill hole appear to be of sedimentary parentage, with the exception of carbonate-free quartz-poor biotite amphibolites which are more likely derived from the recrystallization of basic igneous rocks. The top 3,195 feet of the section is chiefly composed of calc-mica and calc-greenschists which represent recrystallized impure (argillace-

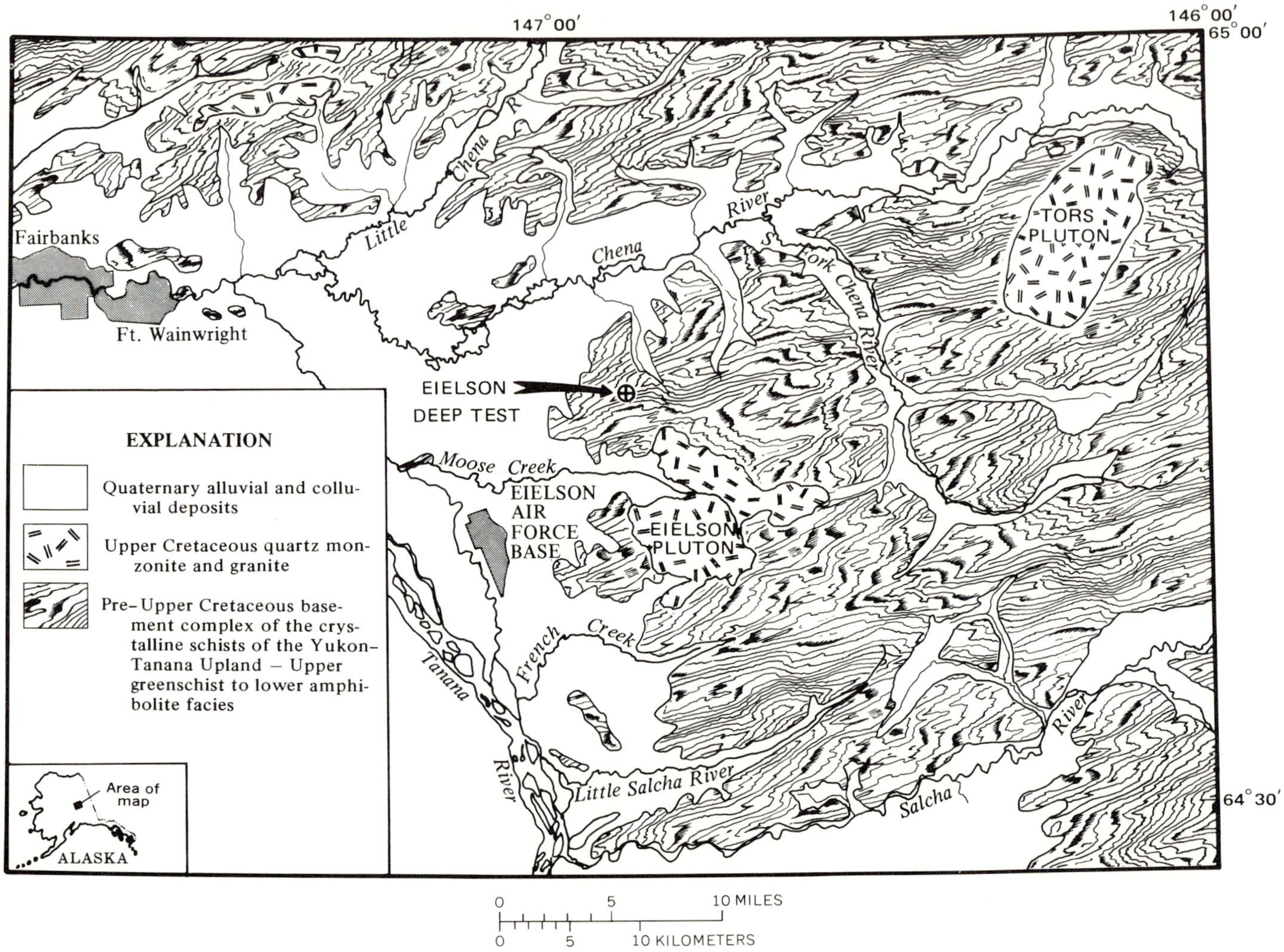

Figure 1.–Generalized geologic map of the Fairbanks district, Alaska, showing location of Eielson deep test hole.

ous) dolomitic limestones and marls. The interval from 4,065 to 9,198 feet contains both calc-magnesium and pelitic schists and sparse layers of micaceous quartzite. The deepest core (from 9,770 ft) is composed of actinolite-bearing calc-mica schists similar to those described from cores taken from the interval 3,193½ to 3,195½ feet.

ANALYTICAL METHOD

The concentrations of the radioelements in the samples were measured by gamma-ray spectrometry. The basic operational procedures and calibration techniques were described by Bunker and Bush (1966, 1967). The spectra were interpreted with the aid of a linear least-squares computer method which matches the spectrum from a sample to a library of radioelement standards and calculates the concentrations of the radioelements in the sample. The computer method is a modification of a program written by Schonfeld (1966).

Uranium concentrations are determined indirectly by measuring the radium daughters to obtain radium equivalent uranium (RaeU) values. Radium equivalent uranium is the amount of uranium, under the assumption of radioactive equilibrium, required to support the amount of daughter products that emit the radioactivity measured in a sample. Throughout the report where "U" and "uranium" are used "radium equivalent uranium" is implicit. Although thorium is also measured from daughter products, disequilibrium is improbable because of short half-lives; therefore, the concentrations are considered to be a direct measurement of parent thorium. Potassium is determined from its K^{40} constituent, which is proportional to the total potassium. The coefficients of variation for the accuracy of the data included in this report (table 1) are about 3 percent for uranium and thorium and 1 percent for potassium when compared to standards analyzed by isotope dilution and flame photometer methods.

RESULTS

The vertical distribution of the radioelement data (table 1, fig. 2) indicates two types of fairly homogeneous rock

Table 1.–*Radioelement concentrations and ratios, and calculated radiogenic heat determined from drill cuttings, Eielson deep test hole, Alaska*

Sample depth (feet)	U (ppm)	Th (ppm)	K (percent)	Heat (μcal/g-yr)	Th/U	U/K×10⁻⁴	Th/K×10⁻⁴
10–20	1.29	9.51	1.69	3.30	7.37	0.76	5.63
100–110	1.32	9.44	1.58	3.28	7.15	.84	5.97
200–210	1.67	10.83	1.67	3.84	6.49	1.00	6.49
300–310	1.79	9.68	1.77	3.72	5.41	1.01	5.47
400–410	2.18	10.93	2.14	4.36	5.01	1.02	5.11
500–510	1.52	8.89	1.57	3.31	5.85	.97	5.66
600–610	1.89	10.65	1.88	4.02	5.63	1.01	5.66
700–710	1.79	6.86	1.96	3.21	3.83	.91	3.50
800–810	2.77	8.47	1.26	4.06	3.06	2.20	6.72
900–910	1.51	10.17	1.96	3.67	6.74	.77	5.19
1,000–1,010	1.06	8.39	1.63	2.89	7.92	.65	5.15
1,310–1,320	1.98	11.61	1.83	4.26	5.86	1.08	6.34
1,400–1,410	1.62	10.97	2.00	3.92	6.77	.81	5.48
1,500–1,510	2.20	14.46	2.21	5.09	6.57	1.00	6.54
1,600–1,610	2.62	13.58	2.03	5.18	5.18	1.29	6.69
1,700–1,710	2.83	14.37	2.34	5.57	5.08	1.21	6.14
1,800–1,810	3.03	13.63	1.73	5.40	4.50	1.75	7.88
1,910–1,920	2.42	11.58	2.00	4.62	4.79	1.21	5.79
2,000–2,010	2.40	12.79	2.52	4.99	5.33	.95	5.08
2,100–2,110	3.61	15.27	2.14	6.27	4.23	1.69	7.14
2,200–2,210	2.02	12.92	1.64	4.50	6.40	1.23	7.88
2,800–2,810	2.07	11.92	2.11	4.46	5.76	.98	5.65
2,900–2,910	2.95	15.45	1.78	5.72	5.24	1.66	8.68
3,000–3,010	1.88	10.85	1.90	4.06	5.77	.99	5.71
3,100–3,110	1.53	4.82	1.29	2.43	3.15	1.19	3.74
3,200–3,210	1.51	6.09	1.30	2.67	4.03	1.16	4.68
3,300–3,310	2.78	12.15	1.99	5.00	4.37	1.40	6.11
3,400–3,410	2.77	12.80	2.01	5.12	4.62	1.38	6.37
3,500–3,510	4.22	16.59	2.62	7.11	3.93	1.61	6.33
3,600–3,610	3.10	13.74	2.19	5.60	4.43	1.42	6.27
3,710–3,720	2.70	14.40	2.01	5.39	5.33	1.34	7.16
3,800–3,810	2.94	14.12	2.40	5.62	4.80	1.22	5.88
3,900–3,910	2.63	13.02	2.20	5.12	4.95	1.20	5.92
4,000–4,010	3.17	13.61	2.57	5.73	4.29	1.23	5.30
4,100–4,110	3.98	38.08	1.62	10.96	9.57	2.46	23.51
4,200–4,210	2.69	11.39	1.43	4.63	4.23	1.88	7.97
4,300–4,310	2.83	12.65	2.04	5.15	4.47	1.39	6.20
4,400–4,410	3.08	14.20	1.87	5.59	4.61	1.65	7.59
4,500–4,510	3.60	17.10	2.48	6.72	4.75	1.45	6.90
4,600–4,610	4.83	20.37	3.55	8.56	4.22	1.36	5.74
4,700–4,710	4.24	13.88	3.02	6.69	3.27	1.40	4.60
4,800–4,810	4.81	19.71	3.14	8.30	4.10	1.53	6.28
4,900–4,910	5.73	23.71	3.77	9.94	4.14	1.52	6.29
5,000–5,010	5.37	21.95	4.19	9.44	4.09	1.28	5.24
5,100–5,110	4.54	18.79	3.73	8.08	4.14	1.22	5.04
5,200–5,210	3.43	15.93	2.82	6.45	4.64	1.22	5.65
5,300–5,310	3.84	16.76	3.06	6.98	4.36	1.25	5.48
5,400–5,410	4.16	18.51	3.34	7.64	4.45	1.25	5.54
5,500–5,510	3.82	16.97	3.66	7.17	4.44	1.04	4.64
5,510–5,520	4.30	17.87	3.45	7.64	4.16	1.25	5.18
5,520–5,530	4.81	20.03	3.62	8.49	4.16	1.33	5.53
5,530–5,540	4.14	18.16	3.10	7.49	4.39	1.34	5.86
5,600–5,610	4.32	18.49	3.06	7.68	4.28	1.41	6.04
5,700–5,710	3.84	17.14	3.00	7.04	4.46	1.28	5.71
5,800–5,810	4.73	18.76	2.97	8.01	3.97	1.59	6.32
5,900–5,910	2.91	12.92	2.50	5.38	4.44	1.16	5.17
6,000–6,010	3.11	14.31	2.72	5.87	4.60	1.14	5.26
6,100–6,110	4.39	17.45	2.93	7.49	3.97	1.50	5.96
6,200–6,210	1.89	9.65	1.72	3.77	5.11	1.10	5.61
6,300–6,310	2.85	16.24	2.16	5.91	5.70	1.32	7.52
6,400–6,410	3.04	16.97	2.26	6.22	5.58	1.35	7.51
6,500–6,510	3.46	13.05	2.93	5.93	3.77	1.18	4.45
6,600–6,610	2.57	10.65	1.86	4.51	4.14	1.38	5.73
6,700–6,710	3.52	16.25	2.75	6.56	4.62	1.28	5.91
6,800–6,810	2.80	15.77	2.75	5.94	5.63	1.02	5.73
6,900–6,910	3.00	14.41	2.59	5.77	4.80	1.16	5.56
7,000–7,010	3.09	15.09	2.32	5.90	4.88	1.33	6.50
7,100–7,110	3.47	16.44	2.93	6.61	4.74	1.18	5.61
7,200–7,210	2.89	12.70	2.20	5.24	4.39	1.31	5.77
7,300–7,310	1.62	7.19	1.10	2.92	4.44	1.47	6.54
7,400–7,410	3.39	14.61	2.45	6.06	4.31	1.38	5.96
7,500–7,510	4.30	17.10	2.33	7.19	3.98	1.85	7.34
7,600–7,610	3.79	16.52	2.41	6.72	4.36	1.57	6.85
7,700–7,710	4.29	20.37	2.99	8.01	4.75	1.43	6.81
7,800–7,810	3.68	17.75	2.92	7.02	4.82	1.26	6.08
7,900–7,910	2.35	11.88	2.10	4.66	5.06	1.12	5.66
8,000–8,010	2.84	12.90	2.54	5.34	4.54	1.12	5.08
8,100–8,110	2.73	14.44	2.62	5.59	5.29	1.04	5.51
8,200–8,210	2.68	14.89	2.21	5.53	5.56	1.21	6.74
8,300–8,310	2.85	13.86	2.57	5.55	4.86	1.11	5.39
8,400–8,410	2.76	13.03	2.24	5.23	4.72	1.23	5.82
8,500–8,510	3.15	14.13	2.48	5.80	4.49	1.27	5.70
8,600–8,610	3.30	16.73	2.78	6.51	5.07	1.19	6.03
8,700–8,710	2.71	13.48	2.33	5.30	4.97	1.16	5.79
8,800–8,810	2.95	14.69	2.55	5.78	4.98	1.16	5.76
8,900–8,910	4.49	18.38	2.75	7.70	4.09	1.63	6.68
9,000–9,010	3.90	16.17	3.40	7.00	4.15	1.15	4.76
9,100–9,110	3.98	19.00	3.20	7.57	4.77	1.24	5.94
9,200–9,210	3.66	16.88	3.08	6.88	4.61	1.19	5.48
9,300–9,310	4.26	17.87	3.03	7.50	4.19	1.41	5.90
9,400–9,410	3.51	15.66	2.78	6.44	4.46	1.26	5.63
9,500–9,510	3.23	14.99	2.39	6.00	4.64	1.35	6.28
9,600–9,610	3.71	13.94	2.12	6.07	3.76	1.75	6.58
9,700–9,710	4.89	15.95	2.54	7.45	3.26	1.93	6.28

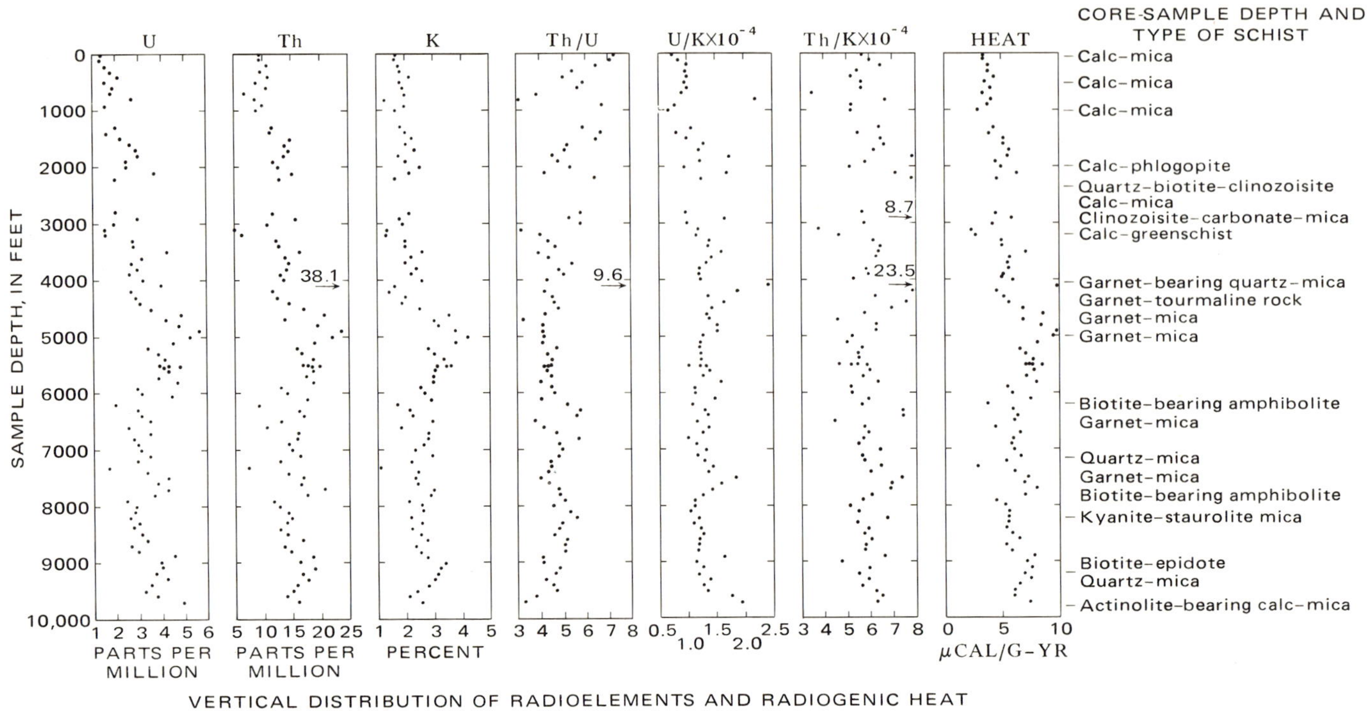

Figure 2.—Vertical distribution of radioelements and radiogenic heat, core-sample depths, and rock types.

separated at a depth of about 3,200 feet. The apparent differences observable on the vertical distribution plots are confirmed in histograms of the data (fig. 3). The data from the two rock types are also statistically different with 95-percent confidence (table 2). The averages of the radioelement concentrations may be abnormally high for both rock types because of the presence of enriched zones.

The calcic rocks, which are predominant above 3,200 feet, contain, in comparison to rocks lower in the section, significantly less uranium and slightly less thorium and potassium, and they have a lower uranium-potassium ratio. Within the calcic rocks, radioelement concentrations increase slightly at about the 1,400-foot depth, which may reflect the location of the contact between the calc-mica schist and the underlying thermally overprinted calc-phlogopite schist. Cores from depth intervals 3,193½–3,195½ and 9,766–9,770 feet are petrologically similar; however, the radioelement data do not reflect this similarity.

Zones of anomalously high concentrations of uranium, thorium, and potassium are present within the section. Parts of the entire section penetrated by the drill hole have probably been affected by thermal metamorphism and alteration associated with the emplacement of the nearby Eielson pluton, which resulted in the enrichment of radioelements to the affected parts of the section. Examples of the enriched zones are depth intervals 4,400–5,800, 7,400–7,800, and 8,900–9,500 feet. The section above 3,200 feet may also be affected by ground water moving through joint systems; the highly variable thorium-uranium ratios suggest differential mobilization of the radioelements and perhaps varying degrees of disequilibrium.

Table 2.—*Averages and standard deviations of data determined for two sections of the Eielson deep test hole*

	Averages and standard deviations[1]	
Section (depth interval, ft)	10–3,210	3,300–9,710
U (ppm)	2.06±0.62	3.52±0.52
Th (ppm)	10.93±2.74	15.96±3.97 (15.63±2.91)
K (percent)	1.84±0.31	2.64±0.58
Th/U	5.50±1.24	4.52±0.49
U/K×10⁻⁴	1.13±0.35 (1.09±0.28)	1.35±0.24 (1.33±0.20)
Th/K×10⁻⁴	5.92±1.17	5.88±0.72
Heat (μcal/g-yr)	4.18±0.98	6.47±1.40 (6.41±1.28)

[1] Values in parentheses exclude samples from depth intervals 800–810 and 4,100–4,110 ft inasmuch as values for those samples differed from the mean by more than three standard deviations.

REFERENCES CITED

Bunker, C. M., and Bush, C. A., 1966, Uranium, thorium, and radium analyses by gamma-ray spectrometry (0.184–0.352 million electron volts), *in* Geological Survey Research 1966: U.S. Geol. Survey Prof. Paper 550-B, p. B176–B181.

—— 1967, A comparison of potassium analyses by gamma-ray spectrometry and other techniques, *in* Geological Survey Research 1967: U.S. Geol. Survey Prof. Paper 575-B, p. B164–B169.

Lachenbruch, A. H., and Bunker, C. M., 1971, Vertical gradients of heat production in the continental crust—[Pt.] 2, Some estimates from bore-hole data: Jour. Geophys. Research, v. 76, no. 17, p. 3852–3860.
Mertie, J. B., Jr., 1937, The Yukon-Tanana region, Alaska: U.S. Geol. Survey Bull. 872, 276 p.
Schonfeld, Ernest, 1966, Alpha M—An improved computer program for determining radioisotopes by least-squares resolution of the gamma-ray spectra: U.S. Natl. Lab., Oak Ridge, Tenn. [Pub.] ORNL 3975, 42 p.

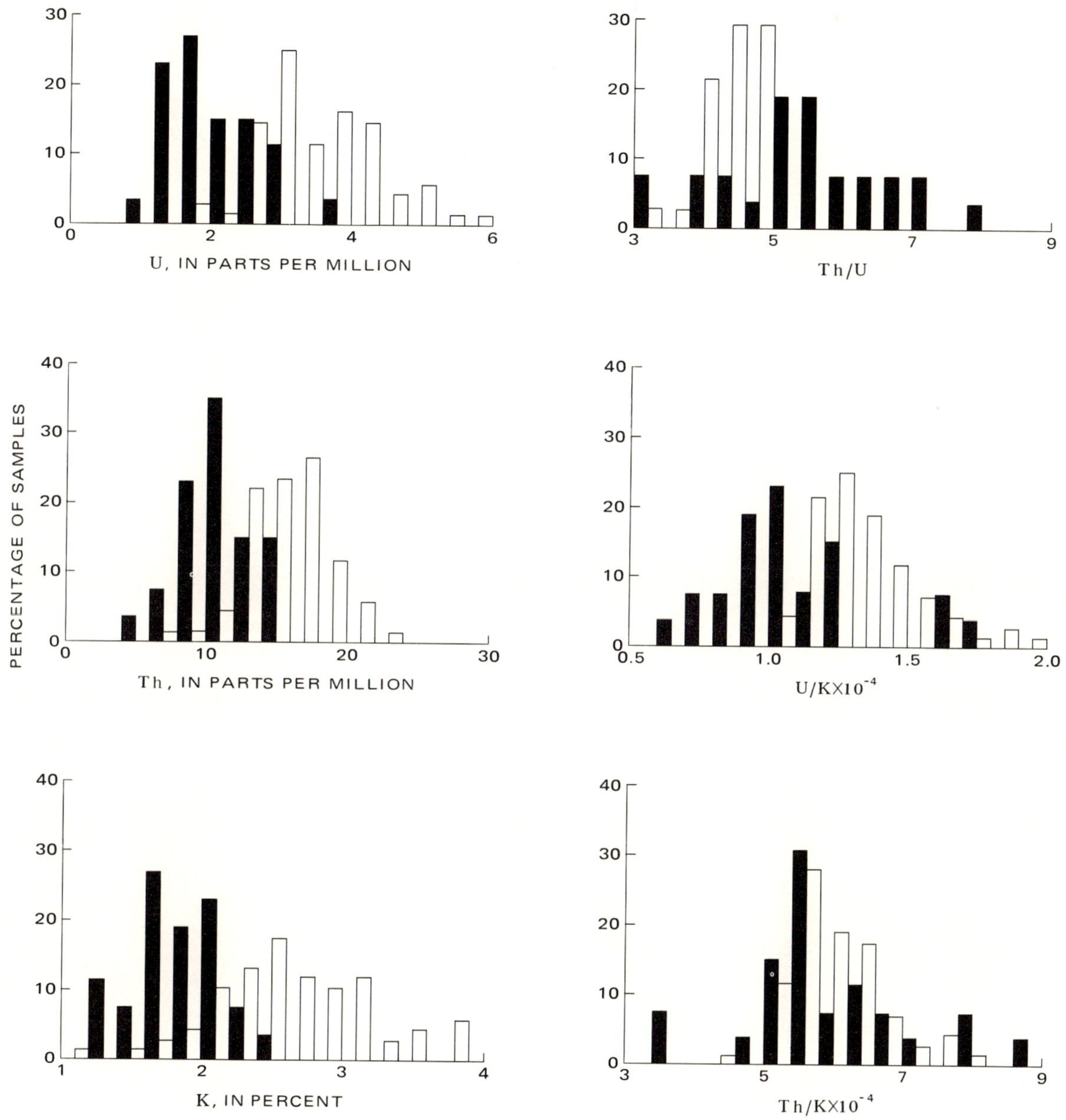

Figure 3.—Frequency distribution of radioelement data. Shaded bars are data from depth interval 10–3,210 feet (26 samples); open bars are from depth interval 3,300–9,710 feet (68 samples).

Jour. Research U.S. Geol. Survey
Vol. 1, No. 6 Nov.-Dec. 1973, p. 665—672

TWO-GARNET RODINGITE FROM AMADOR COUNTY, CALIFORNIA

By W. A. DUFFIELD and M. H. BEESON, Menlo Park, Calif.

Abstract.—Two distinct phases of garnet have been discovered in rodingite from Amador County, Calif. The two garnets are hydrogrossular and (hydro?)grossular-andradite. Only one, generally hydrogrossular, has been reported in rodingites studied by other workers. The rodingite of this study formed from a mafic dike with abundant euhedral plagioclase laths. The hydrogrossular is concentrated within the areas of these laths and is volumetrically about as abundant. The (hydro?)grossular-andradite is concentrated in the groundmass and as incursions into the plagioclase laths. The garnets apparently grew during one general episode of metasomatism, and their spatial distribution and compositions were controlled principally by the unequal distribution of iron and aluminum caused by the presence of plagioclase laths (and mafic minerals?) in the original unaltered dike.

Rodingite of the type locality in New Zealand was reported by Marshall (1911) to consist of grossular and diallage, with or without minor prehnite. Hutton (1943), in a later study, showed that the grossular contained essential water in its formula and proposed a new mineral name, hydrogrossular. Subsequently, many workers (among them, Scott, 1951; Miles, 1950; Frankel, 1959; Bilgrami and Howie, 1960) reported hydrogrossular from rodingite and closely allied rocks.

Because rodingite commonly is extremely fine grained, the separation and study of its constituent minerals are difficult, and chemical analyses of hydrogrossular from such rocks are few. Characteristically, however, rodingite is reported to contain only one garnet—hydrogrossular (see all works cited above).

We have discovered rodingite that contains two garnets, hydrogrossular and (hydro?)grossular-andradite, in roughly equal abundance. All available evidence suggests that both garnets grew simultaneously in one general period of metasomatism and that their compositions simply reflect the unequal distribution of some major elements, principally iron and aluminum, in the original unaltered rock, a mafic dike with abundant plagioclase laths. The hydrogrossular preferentially grew at the sites of the laths.

It seems likely that similar two-garnet rodingite exists elsewhere and that the presence of more than one garnet in such rocks has been overlooked in earlier studies. The garnets of this study are so similar in appearance and properties that they cannot be distinguished in thin section. They were accidentally discovered from X-ray diffractometer analysis.

Acknowledgment.—We thank R. G. Coleman and Edward G. Ghent for helpful reviews of the manuscript.

FIELD OCCURRENCE

Numerous outcrops of rodingite were discovered during a program of detailed mapping in the western foothills of the Sierra Nevada, Amador County, Calif. All lie within serpentinite masses. Most outcrops are concentrated in two relatively small areas (fig. 1), but a more thorough search within the zone of serpentinite probably would lead to more discoveries. The host serpentinite is part of a series of elongate ultramafic

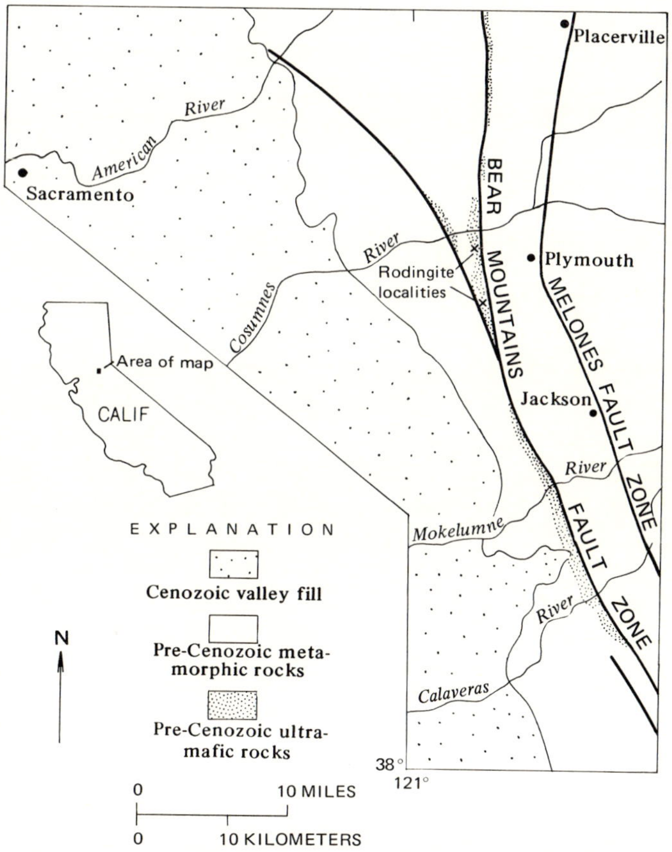

Figure 1.—Areas of ultramafic rocks (stippled) along the Bear Mountains fault zone and the two rodingite localities discussed in the text.

bodies that lie within the Bear Mountains fault zone of Clark (1960, 1964). More recent work by Duffield and Sharp (1973) indicates that the serpentinite is within a melange that possibly marks the locus of a Mesozoic subduction zone.

At both rodingite localities, the host serpentinite is pervasively sheared into pods that range in maximum diameter from several centimeters to nearly a meter. Rodingite occurs as similarly shaped bodies and as steeply dipping dikes. At the northern locality (fig. 1), a dike about 0.5 m thick is traceable along strike for several meters. The contacts of this dike are repeatedly offset several centimeters by a conjugate set of steeply dipping faults that roughly parallel shear planes in adjacent serpentinite. At the southern locality, a single dike is traceable along strike for about 35 m. The thickness there ranges from about 1 m to several centimeters; rare internal slickensided surfaces are evident, but the margins of the dike are not visibly offset. Scattered pods of rodingite, a few meters in maximum dimension, crop out at both localities; they are believed to be faulted fragments of formerly continuous dikes.

The time relations among shearing in serpentinite, emplacement of the dikes, and fault offsets on dikes are not well known, but the presence of isolated pods of rodingite and limited but clear evidence of faulting in the dikes suggest that a single period of pervasive shearing affected both rocks. Some dikes might have been preserved because they were stronger than the serpentinite within which they were enclosed.

We have studied samples of the dike at the southern locality, in the NE¼NW¼ sec. 29, T. 7 N., R. 10 E., about 60 m east of the prominent hilltop that is enclosed by the 820-foot contour on the U.S. Geological Survey topographic map of the Irish Hill 7½-minute quadrangle.

RODINGITE IN HAND SAMPLE AND IN THIN SECTION

In hand sample the rodingite is aphanitic and pale green, with a specific gravity of about 3.26 to 3.31 g/cm^3, averaging 3.30 g/cm^3. The texture of the original dike rock, although not always preserved, is often evident in thin section (figs. 2 and 3). The euhedral outlines of former plagioclase laths as much as 0.3 mm long are still clearly recognizable, and the original rock appears to have been about 50 percent plagioclase by volume. The outline of a single phenocryst of clinopyroxene(?) also has been identified (fig. 3), but judging from the several thin sections studied, such phenocrysts were rare in the original dike rock.

Original mafic dike mineralogy has been obscured by metamorphism. Scattered grains of clinopyroxene (diopside?), chlorite, and vesuvianite form about 10 percent of the rock; isotropic to weakly birefringent garnet accounts for the remaining 90 percent. The minor constituents form small grains (average about 0.1 mm in diameter) between the relict plagioclase laths. Extremely fine grained garnet replaces all plagioclase grains and a substantial amount of the groundmass.

Two distinct phases of garnet are present, although indistinguishable in thin section. Garnet is perfectly pseudomorphous

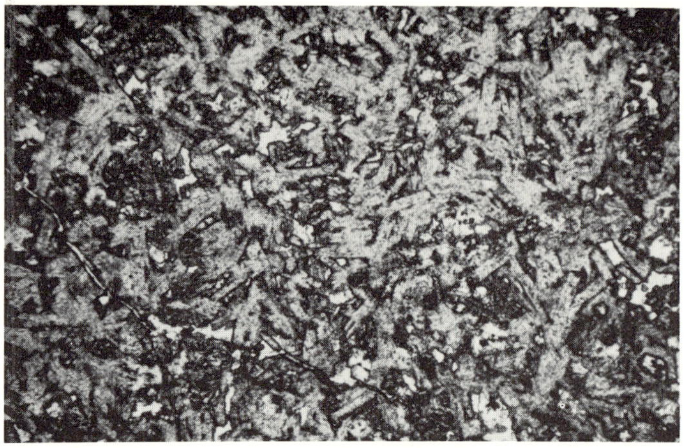

Figure 2.—Photomicrograph of rodingite showing the euhedral outlines of former plagioclase laths. Plane-polarized light.

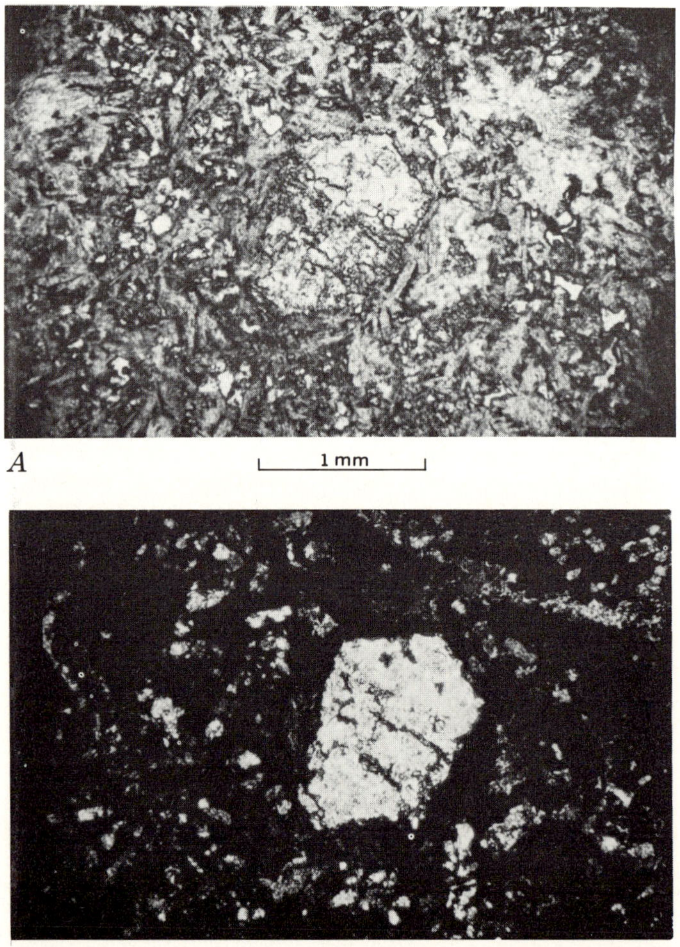

Figure 3.—Photomicrographs of rodingite showing a relict clinopyroxene(?) phenocryst. Note the euhedral outlines of former plagioclase laths. *A*, Plane-polarized light. *B*, Same view as *A*, with crossed nicols. Most of the phenocryst is replaced by chlorite.

after plagioclase laths with no evidence of its characteristic isometric crystal outline, and it forms anhedral masses in the groundmass. All garnet is turbid; the cores of relict plagioclase laths generally are relatively less turbid and tend to be slightly more birefringent than other areas of garnet, perhaps reflecting original compositional zoning in feldspar and original gross compositional contrasts between feldspar and groundmass. Microprobe analysis, discussed later, proves that one garnet phase is indeed concentrated in relict plagioclase laths and that the other is mostly in the groundmass.

METHODS OF STUDY

The presence of two distinct phases of garnet in the rodingite was discovered when X-ray diffractometer studies consistently showed closely spaced doublets for all garnet reflections (fig. 4). Attempts were then made to separate and purify mineral concentrates for further examination, but the extremely fine grain size and nearly identical properties of the two garnets partly frustrated these efforts. Chemical composition of the pure phases was estimated from comparison of chemical analyses of the mineral concentrates, and also from comparison of cell dimensions and refractive indices with determinative curves of Winchell and Winchell (1964). These results were checked by partial microprobe analysis, which also verified the suspected uneven distribution of the two garnets in the rock.

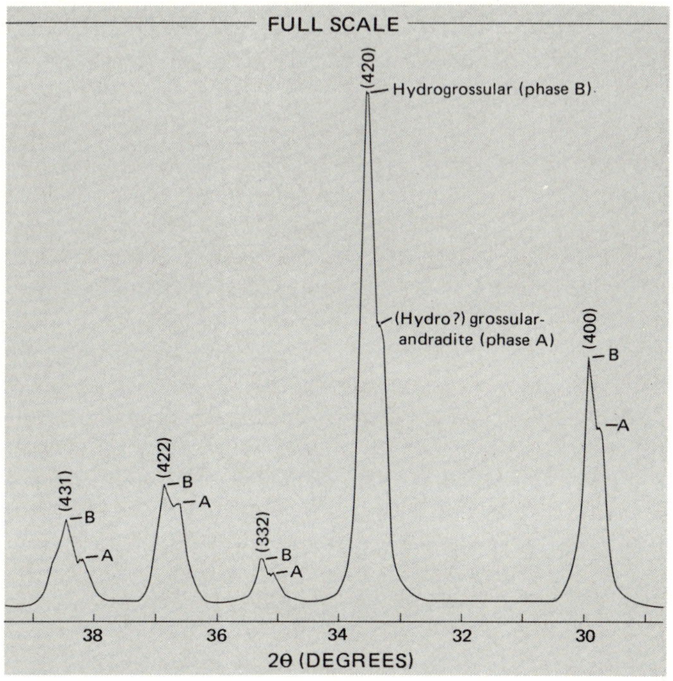

Figure 4.—Tracing of part of an X-ray diffractometer chart of garnets from the rodingite. Note that all reflections are paired and that those of phase A tend to show a slight broadening.

Mineral separation and refractive index

Standard techniques of mineral separation with heavy liquids and a Frantz magnetic separator were used to produce three mixtures (X, Y, and Z) containing different proportions of the garnets. Minerals other than garnet were easily removed from the whole-rock powder, but the two garnets were never successfully separated from one another. Best results were obtained with 320-mesh material that was elutriated to remove the finest dust.

The precise determination of refractive index was impeded by the turbid nature of the grains, but the approximate indices clearly reflect the different compositions of the two garnets and are useful in placing restraints on possible compositions for the pure phases. The refractive index of all grains is between 1.787 and 1.727. At intervals of 0.005 between these extremes, all samples studied contained some grains with indices greater than and some with indices less than all tested liquids, but this continuum was bimodal, with most indices about 1.775 and 1.740. These data suggest possible ranges in the compositions of the two phases, whereas the relatively sharp peaks characteristic of the X-ray diffraction patterns suggest the presence of two fixed compositions. The reason for this discrepancy is not known.

X-ray diffraction study

Several whole-rock powders were X-rayed to determine the size of the unit cell for each garnet. The major reflections are indexed, and unit-cell dimensions are reported in table 1.

Table 1.—*X-ray diffraction data for garnets*

[The conditions of X-ray diffraction were: Cu*K*α radiation, Ni filter, LiF internal standard. Relative intensities are in arbitrary chart units. The unit-cell edge, a_0, was determined by graphing one-half $\left(\frac{\cos^2\theta}{\sin\theta}+\frac{\cos^2\theta}{\theta}\right)$ versus a_0 for each reflection and projecting a least-squares fit to these data back to the a_0 axis (that is, $\theta = 90$)]

hkl	Phase A (hydro?)grossular-andradite)		Phase B (hydrogrossular)	
	d (A)	*I*	*d* (A)	*I*
400	3.001	63	2.983	48
420	2.683	100	2.667	100
332	2.557	13	2.543	9
422	2.451	35	2.436	24
510	2.353	17	2.338	16
521	2.190	13	2.178	13
611	1.947	17	1.934	18
444	.....	....	1.721	9
640	1.665	17	1.654	18
642	1.602	33	1.594	31
800	1.501	6	1.491	6
840	1.342	6	1.333	6
842	1.310	6	1.301	7
864	.....	....	1.107	5
1042	.....	....	1.089	3
880	.....	....	1.054	3
1222	.....	....	.967	2
a_0 .... A	12.01		B 11.92	

Splits of the three garnet concentrates, X, Y, and Z, were X-rayed to approximate the relative amounts of the two phases in each sample. Other parameters being equal, such an approximation should be possible by comparison of the heights of paired reflections on the diffractometer charts. That all reflections occur as closely spaced doublets (fig. 4) suggests that the two garnets are similar enough to make such a procedure reasonable. The results of comparing peak heights of the seven major reflections between 28° and 48° 2θ for the three mineral concentrates are given in table 2. Apparently, the most nearly pure sample (Z) is about 30 percent one garnet, hereafter called phase A, and 70 percent phase B. Concentrates X and Y consist of nearly the same proportions of the two phases.

The relative amounts of background radiation (table 2) suggest that phase A is relatively enriched in the source of such radiation. Under the conditions of the X-ray analysis used in this study (see table 2), iron is the most common constituent of silicate rocks that produces background radiation, and as shown in the next section, the mineral concentrate that contains the most phase A also contains the most iron.

Table 2.—*Peak-height analysis of garnet concentrates*

[The relative peak heights were assessed for the seven major reflections between 28° and 48° 2θ. Background radiation was compared from about 6° to 50° 2θ]

hkl	Ratio of peak heights $\left(\frac{\text{phase A}}{\text{phase B + phase A}}\right)$ of garnet concentrates		
	X	Y	Z
400	0.53	0.49	0.34
420	.40	.42	.29
332	.59	.47	.35
422	.54	.49	.33
510	.44	.51	.26
521	.51	.44	.27
611	.47	.44	.26
Average	.50	.47	.30
Standard deviation.	.060	.031	.036
Background radiation.	>Z;=Y	>Z	Least

A relative-peak-height analysis was also completed for X-rayed whole-rock samples and suggests that phase B is slightly more abundant than A, the ratio being about 6:4. This might have been surmised from the approximate modal percentage of relict plagioclase grains (see fig. 2) and the knowledge that one of the garnets appears to have preferentially replaced the feldspar laths. Thus the X-ray diffraction study suggests that an iron-poor garnet accounts for somewhat more than half of the whole rock and is preferentially concentrated in relict plagioclase laths.

Chemical analyses

Chemical analyses were run on one whole-rock sample and on the three garnet concentrates, by use of the rapid-rock-analysis methods of the U.S. Geological Survey (see table 3). The garnets are members of the grossular-andradite solid-solution series with minor amounts of other garnet molecules; one or both of the phases contains water in its formula. The analyses confirm the conclusions about relative iron contents drawn from X-ray diffraction. The sample with the lowest level of background radiation contains the least iron, and total iron varies directly with the amount of phase A in each sample (computed from relative peak heights). To a reasonable first approximation, the two garnets can be assigned to the grossular-$Ca_3Al_2O_6 \cdot 6H_2O$-andradite-$Ca_3Fe_2O_6 \cdot 6H_2O$ system.

Winchell and Winchell (1964, p. 493, fig. 388) presented graphs showing refractive index and length of unit-cell edge in relation to composition for this system. By fitting the unit-cell data and the extreme values of refractive index of this report to the graphs, the approximate limiting compositions of the two garnets can be determined: phase A—47.2 percent grossular, 41.8 andradite, 5.8 $Ca_3Al_2O_6 \cdot 6H_2O$, and 5.2 $Ca_3Fe_2O_6 \cdot 6H_2O$; phase B—86.4 percent grossular, 3.6 andradite, 9.6 $Ca_3Al_2O_6 \cdot 6H_2O$, and 0.4 $Ca_3Fe_2O_6 \cdot 6H_2O$ (all molecular percentages). These are expressed as weight percent of oxides in table 4 and are used to calculate the bulk composition of mixtures (by weight) that correspond to the three garnet concentrates, assuming the relative amounts of the two phases as determined by X-ray analysis.

It is immediately apparent that the garnet compositions calculated from refractive index and unit-cell size show more water (and correspondingly less SiO_2) than those determined by analysis and that the relative degree of hydration for the two phases is not the same as suggested by the laboratory analyses. Similarly, other constituents show some differences between the calculated analyses and the laboratory analyses, but in a gross way the agreement is fairly good. The source of the discrepancies is not known, but many undoubtedly are related to the presence in the analyzed garnets of elements other than those of the pure system assumed for the graphically derived compositions. Titanium, for instance, is known to increase the size of the unit cell when present in andradite (Deer and others, 1962). Magnesium, ferrous iron, and manganese, on the other hand, should tend to decrease the size of the unit cell. It is also possible that relations of the pure system, as depicted in graphs, are not precisely correct. In any event, the graphically derived compositions do suggest that the two minerals are indeed hydrogarnets, although the degree of hydration is not great; this conclusion is consistent with other data.

Microprobe analyses

To test further the accuracy of the indirectly derived compositions of the pure phases A and B, and to identify

Table 3.—*Chemical analyses of samples, in weight percent of oxides*

[Analyses by rapid methods (Shapiro and Brannock, 1956) supplemented by atomic absorption. Because of insufficient sample for a separate determination, H_2O+ in X and Z is assumed to be the loss of weight on ignition]

	1[a]	2[b]	50% phase A 50% phase B X	47% phase A 53% phase B Y	30% phase A 70% phase B Z
SiO_2	51.45	37.0	36.2	36.2	36.6
Al_2O_3	15.64	14.1	13.0	13.8	16.6
Fe_2O_3	3.91	7.9	11.6	9.9	7.1
FeO	7.93	1.1	.48	.64	.64
MgO	5.90	3.8	1.3	2.0	.57
CaO	9.11	32.1	34.5	34.1	36.2
Na_2O	3.13	.05	.00	.00	.02
K_2O	.98	.08	.05	.05	.03
H_2O+	.....	1.8	1.2	1.2	1.4
H_2O-	.....	.12	.....	.02	.....
TiO_2	1.48	1.0	1.4	1.4	.64
P_2O_5	.26	.20	.14	.19	.13
MnO	.21	.12	.14	.16	.13
CO_2	.....	<.05	.....	<.05	.....

[a]Analysis from Daly (1933). Represents a worldwide average for diabase, based on 90 analyses that are averaged and calculated water-free to total 100 percent.

[b]Analysis of a whole-rock sample of the rodingite of which X, Y, and Z are the three garnet concentrates; relative amounts of the two garnets as determined by the X-ray study.

Table 4.—*Chemical compositions of the garnets, in weight percent of oxides*

[Compositions for phases A and B are calculated from the molecular compositions read from the graphs of Winchell and Winchell (1964). The other three compositions are calculated by mixing phases A and B by the indicated weight percents; compare with analyses X, Y, and Z of table 3]

	Phase A	Phase B	50% phase A 50% phase B	47% phase A 53% phase B	30% phase A 70% phase B
SiO_2	34.2	36.4	35.3	35.4	35.7
Al_2O_3	11.5	22.0	16.8	16.9	18.9
Fe_2O_3	16.0	1.4	8.7	8.3	5.8
CaO	35.8	37.8	36.8	36.8	37.1
H_2O	2.5	2.4	2.5	2.5	2.5
	100.0	100.0	100.1	99.9	100.0

unambiguously any spatial segregation of the phases in the rock, several partial microprobe analyses were made on each garnet using an ARL EXM-SM electron microprobe and natural mineral standards. All data were corrected for drift, background, matrix absorption, characteristic fluorescence, and atomic number effects (Beeson, 1967; Beaman and Isasi, 1970). Quantitative analysis was difficult because of the small size of areas of uniform composition and the low visual contrast between the two garnets. Iron was monitored during all analytical runs as a convenient method of discriminating one garnet from the other; only those analyses that could be reasonably duplicated on different days and samples were retained, and these are summarized in figure 5. The range of microprobe-derived values for the pure phases shown on figure 5 probably is partly due to analytical error and partly to actual ranges in garnet compositions. For example, the data suggest, but do not prove, that the iron-rich garnet that locally occurs within relict plagioclase laths (fig. 6) may be slightly richer in iron and poorer in aluminum and titanium than that replacing glass of the groundmass. Minor broadening of some of the X-ray peaks (fig. 4) also suggests slightly different iron-rich garnets. The approximate composition of the garnet replacing glass in the groundmass (represented by G next to the composition bar in fig. 5) is invariably near the composition determined from cell-edge and index of refraction measurements.

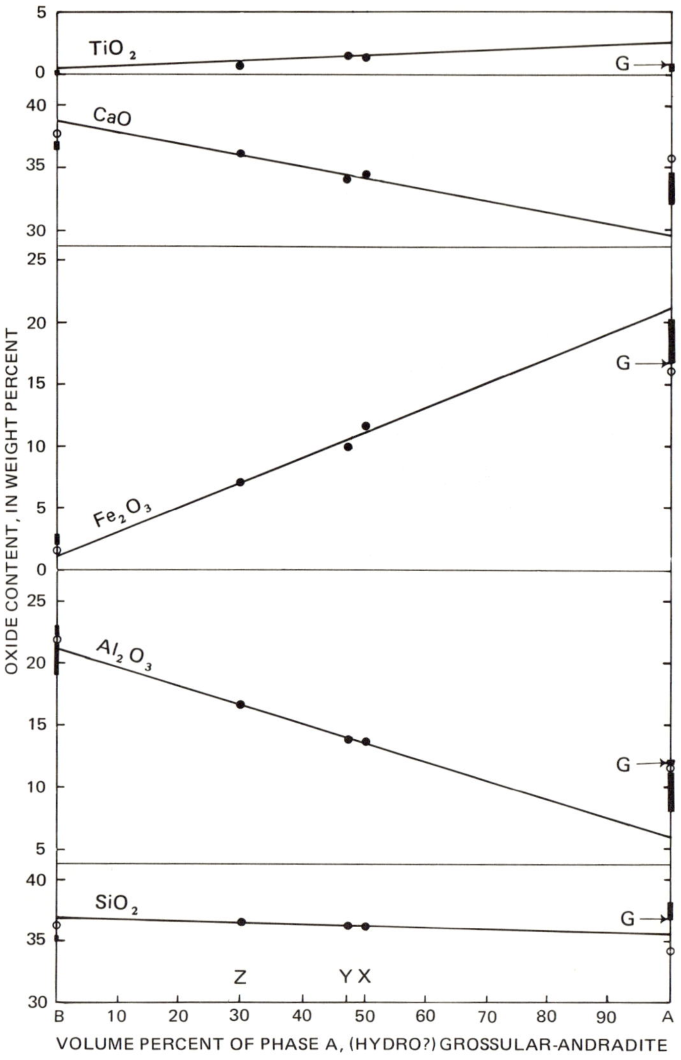

Figure 5.—A summary and comparison of the compositions of the two garnet phases as determined by: (1) fitting the length of cell edge and refractive indices to determinative curves (open circles); (2) extrapolating from the rapid-rock analyses of the three concentrates in which relative amounts of the two phases are known from peak-height studies (intersection of extrapolated lines with end-member lines); and (3) analyzing with a microprobe (range of compositions, shown by solid bars). Microprobe analyses of garnet after groundmass are indicated by G next to the bar, generally a value near that determined by cell edge and indices of refraction. The graph shows that agreement among the three methods is surprisingly good, considering that analysis of such a fine-grained material by these methods is admittedly imprecise.

Beam-scan photos (fig. 6) provide visual evidence that the iron-poor phase is indeed concentrated within relict plagioclase laths and the iron-rich phase in the groundmass; some areas of iron-rich garnet within the plagioclase laths may represent selective replacement of plagioclase cores, possibly controlled by initial zoning in the plagioclase or by fractures along cleavage directions.

SUMMARY

The approximate compositions of the two garnets have been estimated in three independent ways: (1) by fitting the unit-cell dimensions and refractive indices to determinative curves, (2) by projecting visual best-fit lines from the data points of the chemically analyzed two-garnet mineral concentrates X, Y, and Z to end-member compositions, and (3) by partial analysis with a microprobe.

Detailed comparison of the compositions determined by these three methods shows some large differences. We feel that the many difficulties of all types of analysis that we tried preclude selecting one of the three methods as best. Nonetheless, to a first approximation, all methods indicate the presence of grossular for one garnet and a member of the grossular-andradite series for the other garnet. The grossular also contains some water in its formula. The chemical data of table 3 also suggest, but do not prove, the presence of water in the other garnet. It seems likely, however, that both minerals are indeed hydrogarnets, for all evidence indicates that both formed simultaneously under the same conditions.

Structural relations in the field and textural relations in thin section indicate that the recrystallization of the original diabase dike to form rodingite occurred in a volume-for-volume manner. Otherwise, it seems unlikely that both the form of the dike and the diabasic texture would have been so perfectly preserved. It is also apparent, from a comparison of the chemical analyses of the rodingite and the average diabase of Daly (1933), that the original dike rock underwent considerable metasomatism (see table 3). As the exact composition of the unaltered rock is unknown, the details of these changes in bulk chemistry cannot be described, but silicon was clearly removed while calcium was added to the system. Total iron probably changed little, if any, but apparently much original ferrous iron was oxidized to the ferric state.

Other investigators (for example, Bilgrami and Howie, 1960; Coleman, 1967; Barnes and others, 1972) have concluded, on the basis of much more complete field and chemical data, that rodingites form from gabbroic to diabasic rocks contemporaneously with the serpentinization of enclosing or closely associated ultramafic plutons; calcium is freed from the ultramafic plutons as they are serpentinized and is then fixed primarily in hydrogrossular as the mafic rocks are altered to rodingite. This model is thought to apply to the present study; the general requirements for the serpentinization-rodingitization process are satisfied, and there are no known chemical, petrologic, structural, or other features to strain the conditions and explanations of the general model.

The presence of two garnets is unusual. Possibly, the two garnets reflect separate periods of metasomatism differing greatly in composition. This seems unlikely, however, as there is no evidence of metasomatic zoning in the dike. More likely, the dike was subjected to one general period of metasomatism, and the two garnets simply reflect the original distribution of some major elements in the unaltered rock. The relict

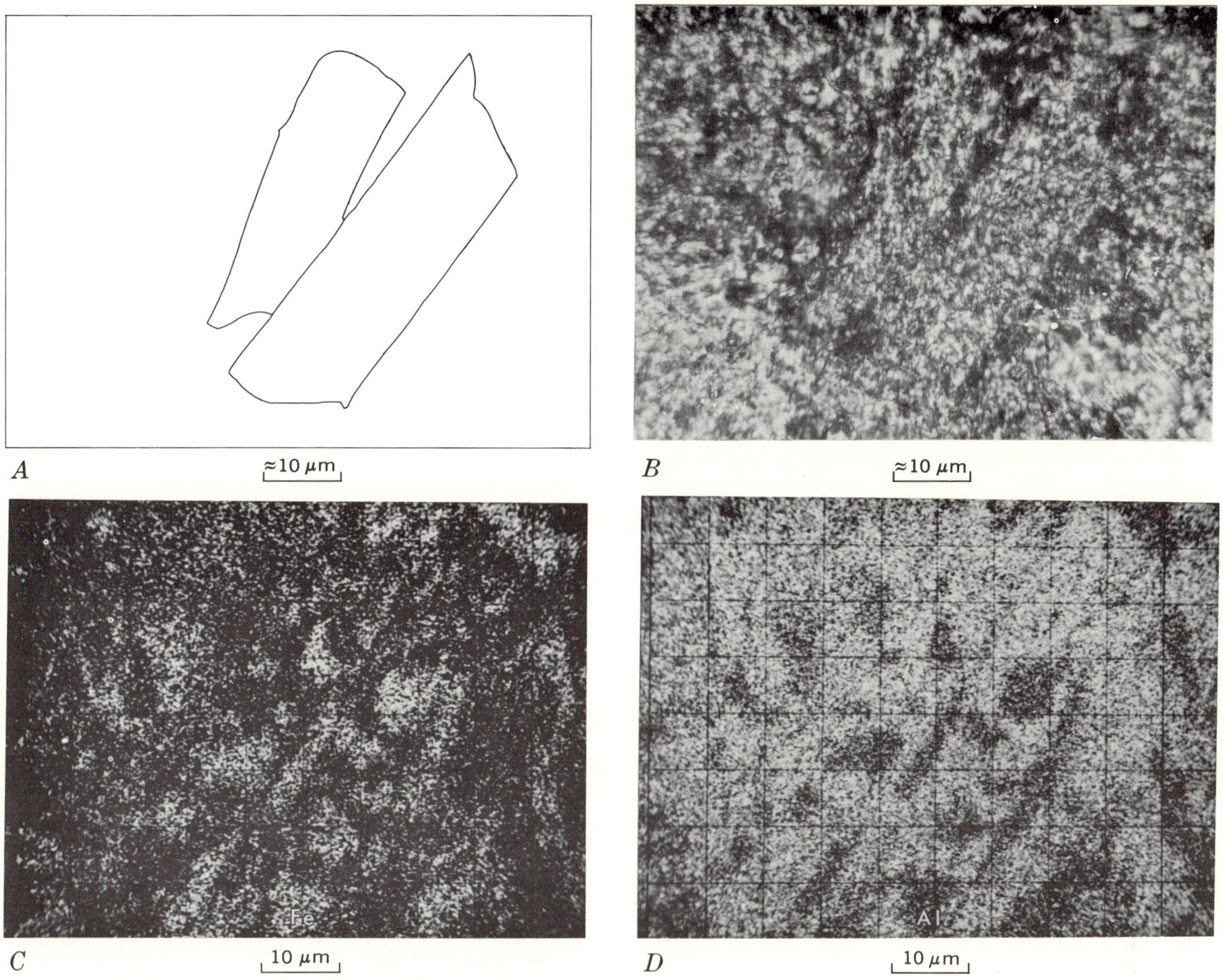

Figure 6.—Images of an area of garnet analyzed with the electron microprobe.

A. Sketch of two adjacent plagioclase laths pseudomorphed by garnet.

B. Photomicrograph of the plagioclase laths sketched in *A*. The laths contrast very little with the groundmass because both the plagioclase and the groundmass have been replaced by garnet.

C. Beam scan showing the iron distribution in approximately the area covered in *A* and *B*. Iron-rich garent occurs as patches within the plagioclase as well as in the groundmass and may reflect an initial zoning in the plagioclase. The outline of the relict plagioclase laths is therefore somewhat obscured in the beam-scan photographs.

D. Beam scan of same area shown in *C*, showing the distribution of aluminum that is antithetic to iron.

porphyritic texture described in an earlier section (see fig. 2) certainly suggests that iron in particular was unequally distributed in the original rock, and the sites where it was relatively depleted (plagioclase laths) are the prefered sites of the iron-poor hydrogarnet. We therefore suggest that the distribution of the two garnets was a direct result of the presence of plagioclase laths in the original rock and that a similar situation may be expected in other occurrences of rodingite that resulted from the metasomatism of plagioclase porphyry and perhaps many multimineralic precursor rocks.

REFERENCES CITED

Barnes, Ivan, Rapp, J. B., O'Neil, J. R., Sheppard, R. A., and Gude, A. J., III, 1972, Metamorphic assemblages and the direction of flow of metamorphic fluids in four instances of serpentinization: Contr. Mineralogy and Petrology, v. 35, p. 263–276.

Beaman, D. R., and Isasi, J. A., 1970, A critical examination of computer programs used in quantitative electron microprobe analysis: Anal. Chemistry, v. 42, no. 13, p. 1540–1568.

Beeson, M. H., 1967, A computer program for processing electron microprobe data: U.S. Geol. Survey open-file rept., 10 p., 31 p. appendix.

Bilgrami S. A., and Howie, R. A., 1960, The mineralogy and petrology of a rodingite dyke, Hindubagh, Pakistan: Am. Mineralogist, v. 45, p. 791–801.

Clark, L. D., 1960, Foothills fault system, western Sierra Nevada, California: Geol. Soc. America Bull., v. 71, p. 483–496.

—— 1964, Stratigraphy and structure of part of the western Sierra Nevada metamorphic belt, California: U.S. Geol. Survey Prof. Paper 410, 70 p. [1965]

Coleman, R. G., 1967, Low-temperature reaction zones and alpine ultramafic rocks of California, Oregon, and Washington: U.S. Geol. Survey Bull. 1247, 49 p.

Daly, R. A., 1933, Igneous rocks and the depths of the Earth: New York, McGraw-Hill Book Co., 508 p.

Deer, W. A., Howie, R. A., and Zussman, J., 1962, Rock-forming minerals: London, Longmans, Green and Co., Ltd., v. 1, 333 p.

Duffield, W. A., and Sharp, R. V., 1973, Geology of the Sierra foothills melange and adjacent areas, Amador County, California: U.S. Geol. Survey Prof. Paper 827 (In press).

Frankel, J. J., 1959, Uvarovite garnet and South African jade (hydrogrossular) from the Bushveld Complex, Transvaal: Am. Mineralogist, v. 44, p. 565–591.

Hutton, C. O., 1943, Hydrogrossular, a new mineral of the garnet-hydrogarnet series: Royal Soc. New Zealand Trans., v. 73, p. 174–180.

Marshall, Patrick, 1911, The geology of the Dun Mountain subdivision, Nelson: New Zealand Geol. Survey Bull., v. 12, p. 29–40.

Miles, K. R., 1950, Garnetized gabbros from the Eulamina district, Mount Margaret Goldfield: Western Australia Geol. Survey Bull. 103, no. 2, p. 108–130.

Scott, Beryl, 1951, A note on the occurrence of intergrowth between diopsidic augite and albite and of hydrogrossular from King Island, Tasmania: Geol. Mag., v. 58, p. 429–431.

Shapiro, Leonard, and Brannock, W. W., 1956, Rapid analysis of silicate rocks: U.S. Geol. Survey Bull. 1036-C, p. 19–56.

Winchell, A. N., and Winchell, H., 1964, Elements of optical mineralogy—Part II, Descriptions of the minerals, 4th ed.: New York, John Wiley and Sons, Inc., 551 p.

Jour. Research U.S. Geol. Survey
Vol. 1, No. 6, Nov.-Dec. 1973, p. 673—678

MICROPROBE ANALYSES OF SERICITE, CHLORITE, AND EPIDOTE FROM JEROME, ARIZONA

By J. THOMAS NASH, Menlo Park, Calif.

Abstract.—Volcanic rocks in the vicinity of the massive sulfide deposits at the United Verde mine, Jerome, Ariz., have been modified in several periods of hydrothermal alteration and greenschist metamorphism. Chlorite, $2M_1$ mica (sericite), and epidote are characteristic alteration products. Microprobe analyses for sericite, chlorite, and epidote are recalculated to structural formulas by the method employing oxygen anion equivalents. The sericite has the general composition of muscovite, but is moderately phengitic, and two samples have 6–12 percent paragonite in solid solution. Most of the chlorite is ripidolite with approximately one-third of the tetrahedral sites filled by aluminum; octahedral aluminum slightly exceeds tetrahedral. Fe:Fe+Mg+Mn ratios range from 0.34 to 0.66; low values are associated with sulfide minerals; higher values occur in a sample peripheral to the massive sulfide deposit. The epidote is a solid solution of 70 percent epidote, 30 percent clinozoisite.

The composition of fine-grained phyllosilicates developed during hydrothermal alteration is critical to the geochemistry of ore deposition, yet there is a paucity of microprobe analyses of these minerals from hydrothermal ore deposits. This paper reports the analyses of mica, chlorite, and epidote from samples taken in and near the massive sulfide deposits at Jerome, Ariz. (fig. 1).

The geology, ore deposits, wallrocks, and alteration at Jerome have been described in detail by Anderson and Creasey (1958) and by Anderson (1968). Wallrocks that contain large amounts of sericite and chlorite have recently been reinterpreted to be submarine pyroclastic tuffs and breccias constituting the Cleopatra Member of the Precambrian Deception Rhyolite (Anderson and Nash, 1972). Sericite that pervades these rocks is probably a hydrothermal alteration product of glassy or pumiceous debris (Anderson and Nash, 1972, fig. 3; fig. 2). Iron-magnesium metasomatism near the massive sulfide deposits has transformed the volcanic rocks to a chlorite-rich rock called "black schist" (Anderson and Creasey, 1958). Later metamorphism produced widespread epidote and other minerals typical of the greenschist facies.

Acknowledgments.—The author wishes to thank C. A. Anderson for introducing him to the geology of the Jerome area and for supplying several samples, and G. K. Czamanske for the microprobe standards and helpful suggestions during analysis. Czamanske and N. J Page offered helpful criticism of the manuscript.

TECHNIQUES FOR ANALYSIS AND CALCULATION

Polished thin sections of 13 selected samples were analyzed on a ARL Model EMX microprobe. Operating parameters were: 15 kilovolts accelerating potential, 0.3 microamperes sample current. LiF, ADP, and RAP crystals were used to analyze for Si, Al, Ti, Fe, Mg, Mn, Ca, K, and Na in sets of three. Beam diameter was close to 1μ. To minimize the effect of volatilization of elements under the electron beam, the beam was moved to a fresh sample area immediately before analysis. Typically, the beam was on a spot less than 15 seconds, of which about 10 seconds was used for analysis. Although X-ray intensities from a single spot, integrated for a few seconds, can yield an "analysis," the author prefers to relocate the beam and repeat counts until at least six data sets can be averaged and count statistics examined. Analyses of sericite and chlorite are for different grains in a microarea of approximately $50\mu^2$. Intensity data were corrected by computer for background, drift, atomic number, and matrix absorption (Beeson, 1967). A biotite standard was used for Si, Al, Ti, K, Fe, and Mg and an amphibole standard for Ca, Mn, and Na, as these standards have well-established uniform compositions. Because far more data were collected than can be reported here, tables of mineral analyses give the data for only one typical microarea of a sample, followed by the maximum standard deviation in any analysis of that sample.

Calculation of mineral formulas is commonly based on summation of anions ($O^{-2}+OH^{-}+F^{-}+Cl^{-}$) to a fixed number, but this technique cannot be used for microprobe analyses because water (H_2O+) and oxidation states of elements such as iron cannot be determined. Because anion analyses are unreliable, some mineralogists calculate formulas by methods that involve only oxygen to balance known cations (Foster, 1960; Borg, 1967; Robinson and others, 1971). The method used here is basically that of Foster (1960, 1962): oxide weight percentages are converted to hydrogen equivalents, then multiplied by a factor to balance the desired number of

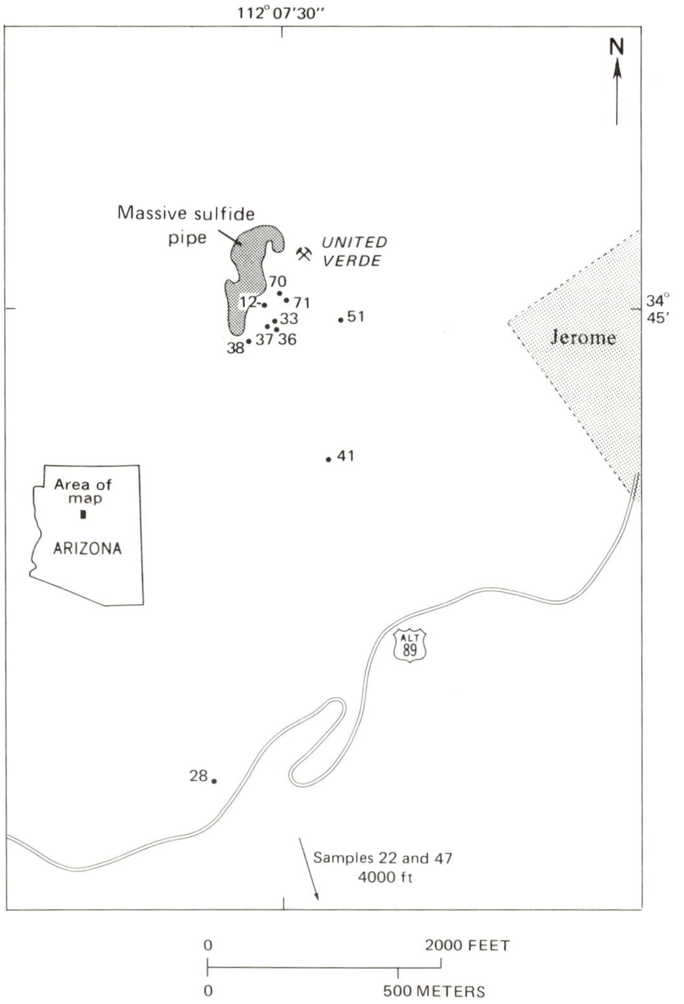

Figure 1.—Location of the United Verde mine and sample localities. Samples 70 and 71 are from the 3,300-foot underground mine level. Outline of the massive sulfide pipe from Anderson and Creasey (1958).

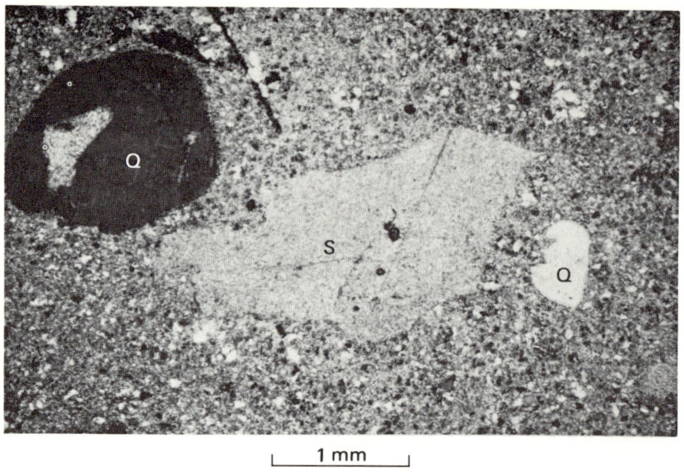

Figure 2.—Photomicrograph of crystal tuff from the Cleopatra Member of the Deception Rhyolite, showing pumice clasts replaced by sericite. S, sericite; Q, quartz. Crossed polarizers, sample 41.

negative charges in the unit cell. For sericite, summation was to 22 oxygens (44 charges), for chlorite to 28 oxygens. For epidote with one OH^- group per cell, calculations were made on the basis of a double cell and 25 oxygens rather than 12½. Computations followed the procedure of Jackson, Stevens, and Bowen (1967) as modified by T. L. Wright.

ANALYSES

Sericite

Four samples of sericite-rich Cleopatra tuff were selected for analysis. The mica in these samples is the $2M_1$ polytype as determined by X-ray diffraction. In samples 28 and 41, it occurs as very fine grained (mostly $<1\mu$) sericite pseudomorphous after fragmented pumice (fig. 2). Sample 51 is similar but has weak foliation; sample 37 is a sandier tuff in which the fine mica is disseminated throughout the matrix, a relation that probably caused the difficulty in obtaining reproducible analyses. The larger standard deviations reported in table 1 reflect grain-boundary effects and foreign grains that could not be avoided during visual positioning of the beam.

The chemistry of sericite is reckoned in terms of the general structural formula $X_2Y_4Z_8O_{20}(OH)_4$ in which X interlayer cations are large ions such as K^+ and Na^+, Y are medium-size cations such as Al^{+3}, Mg^{+2}, Fe^{+2}, and Mn^{+2} in octahedral positions, and Z are smaller cations such as Si^{+4} and Al^{+3} in tetrahedral positions. The structural calculations (table 1) show that in most analyzed microareas[1] the interlayer alkalies sum to near 1.9, which is not far below the ideal 2.0; hence, the likely H_3O^+ substitution (hydromuscovite) must be relatively small. The Y or octahedral totals are somewhat above the ideal 4.0; this probably reflects the influence of the alkali deficiency on the calculations (which forces a sum of 44 cation charges) rather than any excess of octahedral cations. These subtotals are as good as, or better than, the selected analyses of micas done by conventional wet chemical methods (Deer and others, 1962b, p. 218–220). Because offsetting errors are more apparent and water cannot be determined, the structural calculations are considered by the author to be a more sensitive test of accuracy than weight totals.

From their composition and by X-ray diffraction analysis, it is apparent that these are dioctahedral micas very similar to muscovite. In more detail, substitutions in the octahedral and interlayer positions indicate some variation in phengite and paragonite solid solution. Substitution of magnesium and iron indicates that the octahedral layer is from 10 to 56 percent phengite in the muscovite-phengite solid solution. Substitution

[1] Because the crystals analyzed are commonly smaller than the $\approx 1\mu^2$ area excited by the electron beam, we cannot refer to these as mineral grain analyses as we do for analyses of coarser material.

Table 1.—*Microprobe analyses and formulas of sericite from Jerome, Ariz.*

[Analyses by J. T. Nash. A representative analysis is given for each sample, followed by standard deviation which typically is equal to or greater than range in values in microareas of sample. Total iron expressed as FeO. Structural calculations based on 22 oxygens per unit cell.]

Sample No. and (number of analyses)	28(5)		37(3)		41(8)		51(5)	
			Chemical analysis (weight percent)					
Analysis No.	28-2	σ	37-2	σ	41-8	σ	51-2	σ
SiO_2	46.3	0.9	46.2	1.5	45.0	1.1	46.4	1.0
Al_2O_3	32.2	.6	35.6	1.0	33.4	.9	36.	.5
TiO_2	.23	.03	.10	.01	.08	.01	.01	.02
MgO	.91	.03	.76	.5	.91	.08	.63	.08
FeO	2.80	.1	.61	.4	3.08	.2	.22	.02
K_2O	10.97	.2	9.68	.6	10.47	.4	7.07	1.
Na_2O	.12	.02	.54	.1	.32	.04	1.60	.3
Total	93.5		93.5		93.3		91.9	
			Structural formula					
Si } Z	6.34	8.00	6.21	8.00	6.18	8.00	6.20	8.00
Al_{iv} } Z	1.66		1.79		1.82		1.80	
Al_{vi} } Y	3.54	4.07	3.84	4.07	3.59	4.14	3.87	4.02
Ti } Y	.02		.01		.01		.00	
Mg } Y	.19		.15		.19		.13	
Fe } Y	.32		.07		.35		.02	
K } X	1.91	1.94	1.66	1.80	1.83	1.91	1.67	1.90
Na } X	.03		.14		.08		.23	

of sodium in the mica of samples 37 and 51 suggests a range of from 12 to 25 percent for the paragonite end member.

Calcium and magnanese were determined in all analyses but are not reported in table 1. Calcium generally was at background levels, although in sample 51, which has low alkali totals and fairly high sodium content, calcium ranged from 0.03 to 0.19 weight percent and may be significant. Manganese consistently ranges from 0.00 to 0.02 weight percent and is presumed to be in the octahedral layer. Titanium ranges from 0.01 to 0.23 percent (table 1) and is presumably in octahedral sites.

Chlorite

Nine samples representing four different occurrences of chlorite were selected for analysis. Samples 22 and 47 are from Mescal Gulch, approximately 2 miles south of the United Verde mine. Chlorite in these rocks occurs as masses and clasts; no sulfides are present. This chlorite possibly formed by hydrothermal alteration during accumulation of the Cleopatra Member (Anderson and Nash, 1972, p. 857). Samples 36, 38, 70, and 71 contain chlorite-quartz-pyrite-chalcopyrite assemblages typical of the United Verde "black schist" ores. Samples 36 and 37 are from a quartz-chalcopyrite stockwork "quartz porphyry" ore (shown in fig. 2*G*, Anderson and Nash, 1972); sample 36 is from a chlorite-rich vein selvage; 37 represents adjacent sericite-rich Cleopatra with traces of incipient chlorite replacing sericite. Samples 12 and 33 are from quartz-carbonate-sulfide veins that cut "black schist" and represent vein-filling or recrystallized chlorite from the "black schist." The chlorite is typically coarse grained (fig. 3), and, except for that in sample 37, is physically well suited for microprobe analysis.

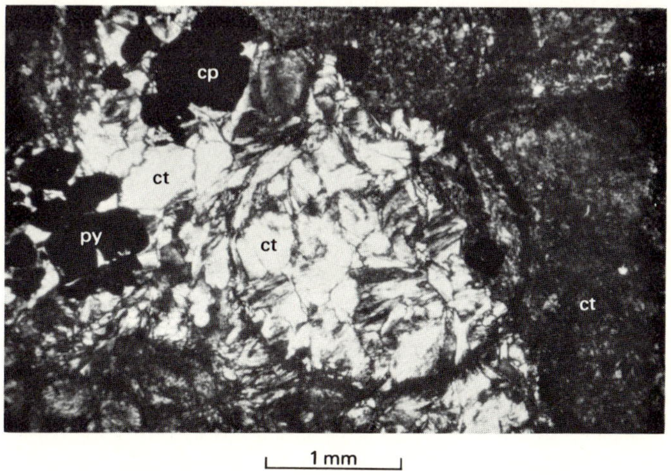

Figure 3.—Photomicrograph of chlorite-rich "black schist" ore. Dark circle is scribed to facilitate location. ct, chlorite; cp, chalcopyrite; py, pyrite. Crossed polarizers, sample 38.

Analytical determinations for most elements were quite consistent in these samples. The variation within microareas was typically similar to the variation between different areas of the same sample and is summarized in table 2. The standard deviations for sample 37 are much higher and reflect intergrown quartz and sericite that could not be entirely avoided. The variation in iron and magnesium for all the samples commonly is relatively higher than for other elements and is considered to reflect real differences within small areas of chlorite. The totals at about 84 weight percent are a few percent lower than expected if one assumes normal H_2O+ content; no reasons for this are known. Much of the deficiency could be accounted for by calculating iron as Fe_2O_3, but there are no geochemical justifications for this. The structural calculations suggest that the analyses are reasonable. Deficiencies in the octahedral position (Y = 11.87, compared with an ideal 12.00) are not large and are not necessarily a reflection of error in the analysis, as R^{+3} ions (Fe^{+3}, Al^{+3}) in octahedral positions in excess of R^{+3} in tetrahedral sites will cause this effect. Calcium, sodium, and titanium were determined but are not included in table 2 because their levels are consistently low. Calcium is consistently at background levels, sodium ranges from 0.00 to 0.04 weight percent, and titanium from 0.01 to 0.06 weight percent.

Chlorite has the general formula $Y_{12}Z_8O_{20}(OH)_{16}$, in which Y and Z cations are Fe, Mg, Mn, and Al and Si and Al, respectively. In ideal chlorites, octahedral Al should equal tetrahedral Al, but this does not obtain for most chlorites because of the presence of ferric iron or vacancies in the octahedral layer (Foster, 1962). In these chlorites octahedral Al is more abundant than tetrahedral, a relation observed by Foster (1962) in about one-third of the analyses studied by her. In such chlorites the extra charges in the octahedral layer can create vacancies in that layer as a result of substituting $2R^{+3}$ for $3R^{+2}$ (Foster, 1962, p. A8). A mechanism of this type apparently obtains in most of the Jerome chlorites because the sums of octahedral cations (Y) range from 11.69 to 11.99 relative to the ideal 12.00. The structural formulas reveal that in all the chlorites the difference between octahedral and tetrahedral Al is very close to twice the apparent deficiencies in the octahedral positions (Y). A ratio of about 3:2 would suggest substitution of Al^{+3} for Mg^{+2} and Fe^{+2}, as noted by Foster (1962). That this ratio is 2:1 rather than 3:2 suggests some other charge and position balance, such as Fe^{+3} for Fe^{+2}, and may be an artifact of calculating iron as FeO.

According to the classification of Foster (1962), most of the chlorite is ripidolite (fig. 4). By the composition-classification plot, figure 4, chlorite compositions are uniform within samples and generally similar for eight of nine samples. Sample 22, from an outlying area, contains the most iron-rich chlorite. The ranges of chlorite compositions in the other samples overlap. With the exception of sample 22 and one for which analysis of chlorite is poor, sample 37, there does not appear to be any correlation of composition with age or geologic occurrence.

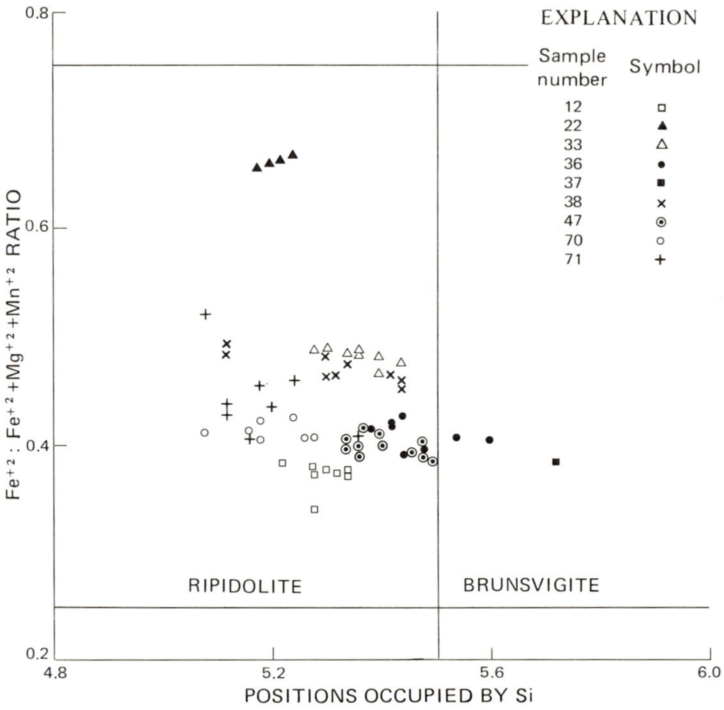

Figure 4.—Composition and classification of 64 chlorite microareas. Classification system is that of Foster (1962).

Optical properties of chlorite were employed to select areas and estimate compositions, but for some types the predictions proved erroneous. The chlorite of most microareas selected was coarse grained, length fast, nearly colorless, with very low birefringence. From these properties the chlorite was expected to have Fe:Fe+Mg ratios of <0.5 (Albee, 1962). This is confirmed by the microprobe analyses (see fig. 4). Crosscutting strands of fine-grained chlorite with anomalous blue birefringence and anticipated Fe:Fe+Mg ratios >0.5 in fact differed slightly in composition from adjacent chlorite. Chlorite in sample 47 has a peculiar circular texture resembling perlitic cracks with radial zones of different color, but these zones did not differ in composition. Green coloration in these chlorites is not simply correlated with Fe:Fe+Mg ratio; for example, chlorite in sample 47 is greener than that in samples with higher ratios.

Epidote

Epidote-group minerals are fairly common in the altered and metamorphosed volcanic rocks; they usually occur as a replacement of plagioclase in crystal tuffs. Conspicuous epidote euhedra in plagioclase were analyzed during the course of chlorite analyses.

Epidote-group minerals have the general formula $X_2Y_3Z_3(O,OH,F)_{13}$. For these analyses X = Ca+Mn, Y = Al+Fe+Ti, and Z = Si. Mg and K determinations were consistently at background levels, and Na was 0.01 percent or less. The analysis of a typical crystal is presented in table 3 along with the structural formula. Iron has been calculated as

Table 2.—*Microprobe analyses and formulas of chlorite from Jerome, Ariz.*

[Microprobe analyses by J. T. Nash. A representative analysis is given for each sample, followed by the standard deviation which is typically equal to or greater than the range in analyses for microareas of the sample. Total iron expressed as FeO. Structural calculations based on 28 oxygens per unit cell]

Sample No. and (number of analyses)	12(8)		22(4)		33(8)		36(8)		37(1)		38(9)		47(10)		70(7)		71(9)	
Chemical analysis (weight percent)																		
Analysis No.	12-8	σ	22-3	σ	33-5	σ	36-3	σ	37-1	σ	28-2	σ	47-6	σ	70-2	σ	71-1	σ
SiO_2	25.1	0.6	22.8	0.6	24.2	0.6	25.3	0.8	28.9	1.6	24.1	0.6	26.2	0.5	24.7	0.4	23.5	0.5
Al_2O_3	22.5	.4	22.1	.4	22.	.4	21.5	.6	24.8	.7	22.4	.6	22.8	.2	23.	.4	23.2	.5
MgO	17.6	.4	8.57	.2	14.1	.5	16.	.5	16.4	.3	14.2	.7	16.5	.4	16.1	.6	14.7	.4
FeO	18.8	.4	30.5	.5	23.8	.6	21.3	.6	18.4	.3	22.4	1.5	19.5	.5	21.4	.6	23.3	.6
MnO	.09	.01	.66	.03	.11	.01	.10	.01	.06	.00	.14	.02	.05	.01	.01	.00	.08	.01
Total	84.1		84.6		84.2		84.2		88.6		83.3		85.0		85.2		84.8	
Structural formula																		
Si (Z)	5.33	8.00	5.17	8.00	5.28	8.00	5.44	8.00	5.72	8.00	5.29	8.00	5.49	8.00	5.23	8.00	5.08	8.00
Al_{iv} (Z)	2.67		2.83		2.72		2.56		2.28		2.71		2.51		2.77		2.92	
Al_{vi} (Y)	2.95	11.87	3.08	11.87	2.94	11.89	2.88	11.84	3.50	11.40	3.07	11.83	3.12	11.70	2.99	11.89	3.00	11.95
Mg (Y)	5.56		2.89		4.58		5.12		4.85		4.63		5.15		5.09		4.73	
Fe (Y)	3.34		5.77		4.35		3.82		3.04		4.10		3.42		3.79		4.21	
Mn (Y)	.02		.13		.02		.02		.01		.03		.01		.02		.01	

Fe_2O_3 because that form predominates in epidote (Deer and others, 1962a, p. 197–199).

The sums in table 3 are a little low at 96 percent, as H_2O+ should be about 2 percent. However, the structural calculations show that the ratios of elements are good for the structural positions are close to ideal occupancy. SiO_2 determinations appear to be erroneously high by about 0.6 weight percent, possibly because biotite was used as the Si standard. Presumably, high SiO_2 determinations cause the structural calculations on other elements to be somewhat low. Ferric iron occupies about 0.7 positions, making these crystals approximately 70 percent epidote in the solid solution epidote-clinozoisite.

Table 3.—*Microprobe analysis and formula of epidote from Jerome, Ariz.*

[Analysis by J. T. Nash. Total iron expressed as Fe_2O_3]

Sample No. and (number of analyses)	22(4)		
Chemical analysis (weight percent)			
Analysis No.	22-2		σ
SiO_2	38.0		0.3
Al_2O_3	23.7		.8
Fe_2O_3	11.5		.4
TiO_2	.06		.01
MnO	.25		.03
CaO	22.6		.2
Total	96.1		
Structural formula			
Si	3.05	Z	3.05
Al	2.25	Y	2.95
Fe^{+3}	.70	Y	
Ti	.00	Y	
Mn	.02	X	1.98
Ca	1.96	X	

DISCUSSION

The internal consistency of the microprobe analyses and the good structural formulas resulting from them suggest that the analyses are credible. Although microprobe analysis of small isolated particles is fraught with difficulties (White, 1964; Page and others, 1968; Eugster and others, 1972), analysis of polished masses of small particles should not and apparently does not result in large errors. Structural formula calculations based on oxygen equivalents are effective for handling the microprobe analyses and put them in a readily usable form.

The moderately phengitic nature of the micas and their paragonite content presumably reflect conditions of greenschist metamorphism; the metamorphic effects are believed to be superimposed on earlier hydrothermal alteration (Anderson and Nash, 1972). The micas differ from typical phengites (Ernst, 1963) by dominance of Fe over Mg. Further, there is no evidence for very large load pressures in this environment (Anderson and Nash, 1972) as for many phengite occurrences. Mica compositions range from 2 to 21 atom percent paragonite solid solution. If these compositions are related to the muscovite-paragonite solvus (Eugster and others, 1972, fig. 9), temperatures of 200°–560°C are suggested. However, the solvus is not located with certainty (Eugster and others, 1972), and the more sodic analyses may reflect grain-boundary effects from paragonite-rich micas.

The physicochemical controls on the compositions of the chlorites and epidotes are not clear, and there are no pertinent experimental data. The chlorite analyses are in agreement with the generalization of Anderson and Creasey (1958) that chlorite near the massive sulfide deposits is more magnesian in composition than in outlying areas. Ekstrand (1963) found the opposite trend at Chibougamau, Canada, with Fe:Fe+Mg ratios of 0.75 in the sulfide zone. Although iron-magnesium metasomatism is common in massive sulfide deposits, little systematic study has been made of the mafic silicates. Presumably, chemical factors, such as fugacity of CO_2 or sulfur, or $Mg^{+2}:(H^+)^2$ are important in determining mineral stability and composition. At Jerome, chlorites formed at about 235°C and relatively high CO_2 pressures (Anderson and Nash, 1972). Sulfur fugacities cannot be determined with much certainty from the sulfide assemblage, but apparently they did not depress the activity of iron sufficiently to produce highly magnesian chlorites.

REFERENCES CITED

Albee, A. L., 1962, Relationships between the mineral association, chemical composition and physical properties of the chlorite series: Am. Mineralogist, v. 47, nos. 7–8, p. 851–870.

Anderson, C. A., 1968, Metamorphosed Precambrian silicic volcanic rocks in central Arizona, *in* Studies in volcanology—a memoir in honor of Howel Williams: Geol. Soc. America Mem. 116, p. 9–45.

Anderson, C. A., and Creasey, S. C., 1958, Geology and ore deposits of the Jerome area, Yavapai County, Arizona: U.S. Geol. Survey Prof. Paper 308, 185 p.

Anderson, C. A., and Nash, J. T., 1972, Geology of the massive sulfide deposits at Jerome, Arizona—a reinterpretation: Econ. Geology, v. 67 , no. 7, p. 845–863.

Beeson, M. H., 1967, A computer program for processing electron microprobe data: U.S. Geol. Survey open-file report, 41 p.

Borg, I. Y., 1967, On conventional calculations of amphibole formulae from chemical analyses with inaccurate $H_2O(+)$ and F determinations: Mineralog. Mag., v. 36, no. 280, p. 583–590.

Deer, W. A., Howie, R. A., and Zussman, J., 1962a, Ortho and ring silicates, v. 1, *of* Rock-forming minerals: New York, John Wiley and Sons, 333 p.

——1962b, Sheet silicates, v. 3, *of* Rock-forming minerals: New York, John Wiley and Sons, 270 p.

Eckstrand, O. R., 1963, Crystal chemistry of chlorite: Harvard Univ., Cambridge, Mass., Ph. D. thesis, 128 p.

Ernst, W. G., 1963, Significance of phengitic micas from low-grade schists: Am. Mineralogist, v. 48, nos. 11–12, p. 1357–1373.

Eugster, H. P., Albee, A. L., Bence, A. E., Thompson, J. B., and Waldbaum, D. R., 1972, The two-phase region and excess mixing properties of paragonite-muscovite crystalline solutions: Jour. Petrology, v. 13, p. 147–179.

Foster, M. D., 1960, Interpretation of the composition of trioctahedral micas: U.S. Geol. Survey Prof. Paper 354-B, p. 11–49.

——1962, Interpretation of the composition and a classification of the chlorites: U.S. Geol. Survey Prof. Paper 414-A, p. A1–A33.

Jackson, E. D., Stevens, R. E., and Bowen, R. W., 1967, A computer-based procedure for deriving mineral formulas from mineral analyses, *in* Geological Survey Research 1967: U.S. Geol. Survey Prof. Paper 575-C, p. C23–C31.

Page, N. J, Calk, L. C., and Carr, M. H., 1968, Problems of small-particle analysis with the electron microprobe, *in* Geological Survey Research 1968: U.S. Geol. Survey Prof. Paper 600-C, p. C31–C37.

Robinson, P., Ross, M., and Jaffe, H. W., 1971, Composition of the anthophyllite-gedrite series, comparisons of gedrite and hornblende, and the anthophyllite-gedrite solvus: Am. Mineralogist, v. 56, p. 1005–1041.

White, E. W., 1964, Microprobe technique for the analysis of multiphase microcrystalline powders: Am. Mineralogist, v. 49, nos. 1–2, p. 196–197.

Jour. Research U.S. Geol. Survey
Vol. 1, No. 6, Nov.-Dec. 1973, p. 679—680

NOTES ON THE BROMINE PENTAFLUORIDE TECHNIQUE OF OXYGEN EXTRACTION

By IRVING FRIEDMAN and JIM D. GLEASON,
Denver, Colo.

Abstract.—The necessity to use a dry box when loading silicate samples into reaction vessels prior to fluorination is eliminated by the use of a simple loading technique. Data presented show the reproducibility of the fluorination reaction using this technique. Sodium fluoride, when added to saline waters prior to fluorination, improves the precision of the overall technique.

In describing the use of bromine pentafluoride for the extraction of oxygen from minerals for O^{18} analysis, Clayton and Mayeda (1963) suggested that the nickel reaction vessel be opened in a dry box containing air dried by P_2O_5. This precaution was deemed necessary to prevent the uptake of water by the nickel fluoride coating in the reaction vessel and the subsequent release of oxygen from this adsorbed(?) water.

We have found that the dry box is unnecessary if the nickel reaction vessel is first filled with dry nitrogen and the mineral sample quickly introduced into the vessel through a small opening. The amount of water vapor entering the vessel is too small to be measured and too small to affect the O^{18} analysis.

The nickel reaction vessel (¾-in. OD tube) has at its open end a Swagelock fitting and Teflon front ferrules; the fitting terminates in a ¼-inch ID stainless steel tube about 2 inches long (fig. 1). This tube in turn is connected by means of another Swagelock fitting on a Teflon and stainless steel ball valve to the line leading to the reaction manifold (not shown in fig. 1).

The weighed powder sample of approximately 20 mg is placed in a special long-handled spatula (fig. 1). The line from the reaction manifold and the reaction vessel are filled with dry nitrogen at slightly more than atmospheric pressure, the valve on the line above the reaction vessel is closed, the reaction vessel is removed from the line by loosening the Swagelock fitting on the valve, and the sample on the spatula is inserted through the ¼-inch tube into the bottom of the reaction vessel. The reaction vessel is then quickly reattached to the line to the reaction manifold. The reaction vessel is exposed to the atmosphere for no longer than 1 minute, and diffusion of water vapor is minimized by the fact that a ¼-inch opening is exposed to air. The reaction vessel seldom requires cleaning—only after 20 or 30 reactions.

During the past year we repeatedly analyzed a standard quartz sample. Some analyses were made by prefluorinating the reaction tube containing the sample to remove any water contamination, and others were carried out without prefluorination. The 19 prefluorination analyses gave δO^{18} a value of +10.85 with a sigma of $0.16^{\circ}/_{oo}$. The 38 analyses without prefluorination gave an average value of +10.72 with a sigma of $0.11^{\circ}/_{oo}$. From this we conclude that contamination by

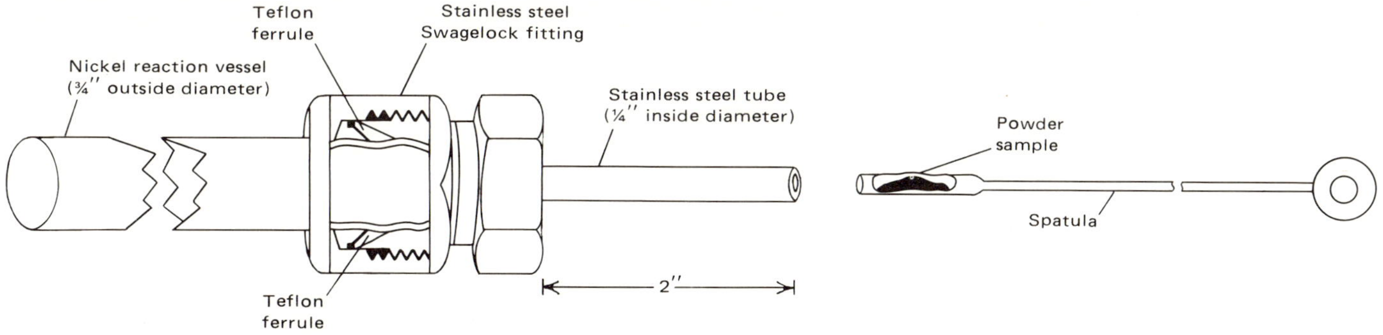

Figure 1.—Sample spatula ready for insertion of sample into reaction vessel through stainless steel tube.

water vapor is negligible during sample introduction without the use of a dry box.

In 1966 O'Neil and Epstein described the use of bromine pentafluoride for the O^{18} analysis of milligram quantities of water. We have confirmed the usefulness of this technique on water samples that are relatively "fresh." For example, replicate samples of snow water were processed and gave precisions of 0.1°/₀₀ (2 sigma). However, if we attempted to use unpurified sea-water samples, the results scattered widely, and, depending upon the technique of introduction of the water into the system, the 2 sigma values were about 2°/₀₀ to 5°/₀₀. The scatter in the data was independent of whether or not the solids that formed by evaporation of the water were heated to above 100°C.

According to Frank Manheim, U.S. Geological Survey, the discrepancy was probably related to the magnesium ions that form hydrates which are stable to temperatures above 400°C. He suggested that sodium fluoride be added to precipitate the magnesium. Accordingly, NaF (10 g/l) dried at 110°C was added to the sea water. Twelve replicate fluorinations of this treated sea water resulted in the data shown in table 1. The data points have a precision of 0.16°/₀₀ (2 sigma).

Table 1.—*Twelve replicate analyses of sea-water sample by fluorination*

[Data in per mil SMOW, Standard Mean Ocean Water]

+0.49	+0.35	+0.26	+0.33	+0.46	+0.44
+.32	+.40	+.32	+.22	+.32	+.36

Average = 0.36±0.16°/₀₀ (2 sigma).

REFERENCES CITED

Clayton, R. N., and Mayeda, T. K., 1963, The use of bromine pentafluoride in the extraction of oxygen from oxides and silicates for isotopic analysis: Geochim. et Cosmochim. Acta, v. 27, no. 1, p. 43–52.

O'Neil, J. R., and Epstein, Samuel, 1966, A method for oxygen isotope analysis of milligram quantities of water and some of its applications: Jour. Geophys. Research, v.71, no. 20, p. 4955–4961.

Jour. Research U.S. Geol. Survey
Vol. 1, No. 6, Nov.-Dec. 1973, p. 681—685

ATOMIC ABSORPTION SPECTROPHOTOMETRIC DETERMINATION OF MICROGRAM LEVELS OF Co, Ni, Cu, Pb, AND Zn IN SOIL AND SEDIMENT EXTRACTS CONTAINING LARGE AMOUNTS OF Mn AND Fe

By T. T. CHAO and R. F. SANZOLONE, Denver, Colo.

Abstract.—An atomic absorption spectrophotometric method has been developed for the determination of seven metal ions in the hydroxylamine extract of soils and sediments. Mn, Fe, and Zn are directly determined in the aqueous extract upon dilution. Co, Ni, Cu, and Pb in a separate aliquot of the extract are chelated with APDC (ammonium pyrrolidine dithiocarbamate) and extracted into MIBK (methyl isobutyl ketone) before determination. Data are presented to show the quantitative recovery of microgram levels of Co, Ni, Cu, and Pb by APDC-MIBK chelation-extraction from synthetic solutions containing as much as 2,000 μg/ml (micrograms per milliliter) Mn or 50 μg/ml Fe. Recovery of known amounts of the metal ions from sample solutions is equally satisfactory. Reproducible results are obtained by replicate analyses of two sediment samples for the seven metals.

Hydrous manganese and iron oxides are credited with being strong scavenging agents for heavy metal ions (Canney, 1966; Jenne, 1968). Information on heavy metals associated with manganese and iron oxides has been used in mineral exploration (Hawkes and Webb, 1962; Horsnail and others, 1969). Currently used extraction methods for determining metal associations do not differentiate metal ions associated with manganese oxides and those associated with iron oxides. This is mainly because the available methods dissolve both manganese and iron oxides, simultaneously, to varying and significant degrees. An extraction method has recently been developed (Chao, 1972) using a 0.1 *M* hydroxylamine hydrochloride ($NH_2OH \cdot HCl$) solution in 0.01 *M* HNO_3 (pH 2) for the preferential dissolution of manganese oxides. During dissolution of manganese oxides, the associated metal ions and minor proportions of hydrous iron oxides in the sample are brought into solution.

Atomic absorption spectrophotometry, because of its simplicity, selectivity, and sensitivity, has been chosen for the determination of metal ions in the hydroxylamine extract. Preliminary observations have shown that Mn, Fe, and Zn can be determined directly in the aqueous extract after proper dilution to compensate for the high concentrations of Mn and Fe present and for the high sensitivity for Zn. The determination of Co, Ni, Cu, and Pb in the original extract poses analytical problems. Hydroxylamine in the matrix tends to suppress absorption at the resonance lines of the metals, and metal concentrations in the extract are often too low to be analyzed directly by atomic absorption. Several investigators (Allan, 1961; Sprague and Slavin, 1964a, 1964b; Brooks and others, 1967; Burrell, 1967; Fishman and Midgett, 1968) have used APDC (ammonium pyrrolidine dithiocarbamate) -MIBK (methyl isobutyl ketone) chelation-extraction for the determination of one or more of the four metals in various samples. Not only are the metals separated from the matrix solution, but also the sensitivity of the methods is enhanced in the presence of the organic solvent. Since in none of these methods have provisions been made to deal with high concentrations of Mn and Fe relative to those of the metal ions to be determined as found in the hydroxylamine extract of soils and sediments, the major problem was to investigate whether microgram levels of Co, Ni, Cu, and Pb in solutions containing relatively large amounts of Mn and Fe could be determined by APDC-MIBK chelation-extraction and atomic absorption spectrophotometry.

This paper describes a systematic procedure for the determination of Mn, Fe, Zn, Co, Ni, Cu, and Pb in the hydroxylamine extract of soils and sediments. Mn, Fe, and Zn are determined directly in the aqueous extract after dilution. Co, Ni, Cu, and Pb, in a separate aliquot of the extract, are chelated with APDC, extracted into MIBK, and determined by atomic absorption. Data are presented to show the quantitative recovery of known amounts of Co, Ni, Cu, and Pb from solutions containing high concentrations of Mn and Fe which may occur in hydroxylamine extracts of soil and sediment samples.

Acknowledgments.—The authors wish to thank F. C. Canney and G. A. Nowlan for furnishing sediment samples used in the development of the proposed method.

EXPERIMENTAL METHOD

Apparatus

Perkin-Elmer Model 303 atomic absorption spectrophotometer equipped with a Boling burner head and single-element hollow

Table 1.—*Instrument settings for analysis of the seven metals*

[For the analysis of all metals the following settings apply: grating, ultraviolet; air pressure, 30 psi; acetylene pressure, 8 psi; aspiration rate, about 3.8 ml/min]

Element	Wave-length (A)	Slit	Scale expan-sion	Re-sponse	Lamp current (ma)	Air flow	Fuel flow
Mn	2795	3	1	1	20	7.5	6.5
Fe	2483	3	1	1	30	7.5	6.5
Zn	2139	4	5	3	15	7.5	6.5
Cu	3247	4	1	1	15	5.0	2.5
Co	2407	3	5	3	30	5.0	2.5
Ni	2320	3	5	3	25	5.0	2.5
Pb	2833	4	5	3	8	5.0	2.5

Table 2.—*Working standard solutions of metals*

Element	Standard 1	2	3	4	5
Series 1—for determinations in aqueous solution (μg/ml)					
Mn	1	2.5	5	7.5	10
Fe	1	2.5	5	7.5	10
Zn	.025	.05	.1	.2	.4
Series 2—for determinations in MIBK (μg/10 ml)					
Co	0.25	0.5	1	2	4
Ni	.25	.5	1	2	4
Cu	2.5	5	10	20	40
Pb	1.5	3	6	12	24

cathode lamps. Table 1 shows the instrument settings for the seven metals.

Sorvall SS-3 superspeed centrifuge.

Radiometer pH meter, Model 26, connected to a combination electrode.

Reagents

Extracting solution, 0.1 *M* hydroxylamine hydrochloride ($NH_2OH{\cdot}HCl$) in 0.01 *M* HNO_3 (pH = 2). Dissolve 6.95 g reagent grade $NH_2OH{\cdot}HCl$ in demineralized water, add 10 ml 1 *M* HNO_3, and dilute to approximately 900 ml in 1-liter volumetric flask. Adjust the pH of the solution with 1 *M* HNO_3 to 2 and make up to volume.

Whatman filter accelerator, one tablet cut into four.

Ammonium pyrrolidine dithiocarbamate (APDC), 1 percent (w/v). Dissolve 1 g APDC in 100 ml demineralized water. Prepare fresh daily.

Hydrochloric acid, 0.3 *M*. Mix 25 ml concentrated HCl (sp gr 1.19) with demineralized water and dilute to 1 liter.

Hydrochloric acid (1+1). Mix 100 ml concentrated HCl (sp gr 1.19) with equal volume of demineralized water.

Sodium hydroxide, 2.5 *M*. Dissolve 10 g NaOH in demineralized water and dilute to 100 ml.

Methyl isobutyl ketone (MIBK), water-saturated. Saturate 300 ml MIBK with 100 ml demineralized water by shaking vigorously in a 500-ml separatory funnel for 3 minutes. Discard the aqueous layer.

Stock standard solutions of metals. Prepare each stock standard solution from the pure metal so that the solution contains 1 mg metal per milliliter of 1-percent (v/v) concentrated HCl (sp gr 1.19) for Mn, Fe, and Zn, and 1-percent (v/v) concentrated HNO_3 (sp gr 1.42) for Co, Ni, Cu, and Pb.

Working standard solutions of metals. Prepare two series of working standard solutions from stock solutions. One series contains Mn, Fe, and Zn in 1 percent (v/v) concentrated HCl for metal determinations in aqueous solutions after dilution of the soil or sediment extracts. The second series contains Co, Ni, Cu, and Pb in 1-percent (v/v) concentrated HNO_3 for determinations of the metals after chelation with APDC and extraction into MIBK. The concentration of each metal in the two series of mixed standard solutions is presented in table 2.

Procedure

Weigh 0.10 to 0.50 g of a finely powdered soil or sediment sample (<100 mesh) along with 0.1 g Whatman filter accelerator into a 29- by 103-mm polypropylene centrifuge tube. Add 25 ml 0.1 *M* hydroxylamine in 0.01 *M* HNO_3 (pH = 2) and equilibrate the contents of the tube on a mechanical shaker for 30 minutes. Then, spin the suspension at 15,000 rpm in a Sorvall SS-3 centrifuge for 10 minutes and decant the supernatant extract into a 50-ml polyethylene bottle. The function of the ashless accelerator is to help pack the sample on the bottom of the tube during centrifugation and to prevent fine particles from dislodging upon decantation of the clear extract.

Transfer 5 ml of the extract and 1 ml HCl (1+1) into a 50-ml volumetric flask and dilute to volume. This solution is used for the determination of Mn, Fe, and Zn.

For the determination of Co, Ni, Cu, and Pb, transfer 10 ml of the extract into a 25 - by 150-mm glass culture tube. Add 10 ml demineralized water and adjust the pH of the solution with a pH meter to 2.5 to 2.7 by addition of 2.5 *M* NaOH and 0.3 *M* HCl, using a tube vibrator to aid mixing. Pipet 1 ml 1-percent APDC into the tube and adjust the pH to 2.8. Add 10 ml MIBK and shake vigorously for 1 minute. Allow the organic and aqueous phases to separate. Aspirate the upper organic layer into the flame to obtain the absorption readings for Co, Ni, Cu, and Pb. For establishing calibration curves, mix 10 ml of each of the working standard solutions (series 2 in table 2) with 10 ml of the hydroxylamine extracting solution and treat identically as for the sample extracts.

Analyze duplicate blanks with each batch of samples for correction of possible impurities present in the reagents.

RESULTS AND DISCUSSION

Calibration curves

Calibration curves for the seven metals are shown in figures 1 and 2. Linear or nearly linear relationship exists between the concentration of a given metal and its absorbance. With a 0.50-g sample taken for analysis, the range of concentrations of the seven metals that can be determined by the procedure outlined is: Mn and Fe, 500–5,000 ppm; Zn and Cu, 10–200 ppm; Co and Ni, 1–20 ppm; and Pb, 5–120 ppm. Concentrations above this range may be determined either by reducing the sample weight or by further diluting the aqueous extract with demineralized water and the organic extract with MIBK. By this technique, a wide range of concentrations of the seven

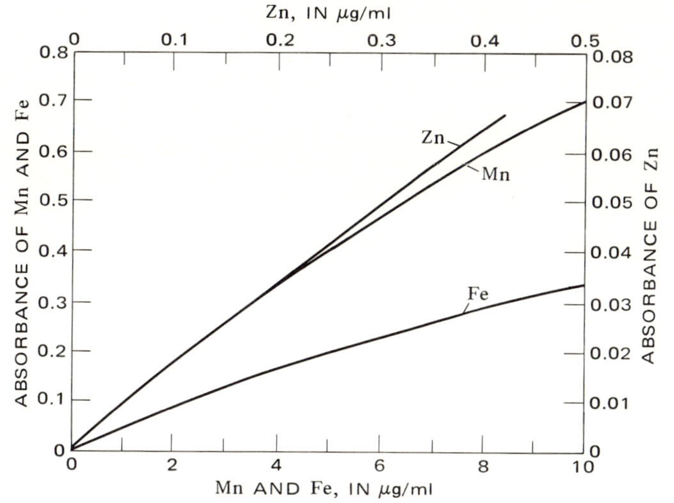

Figure 1.—Calibration curves for Mn, Fe, and Zn.

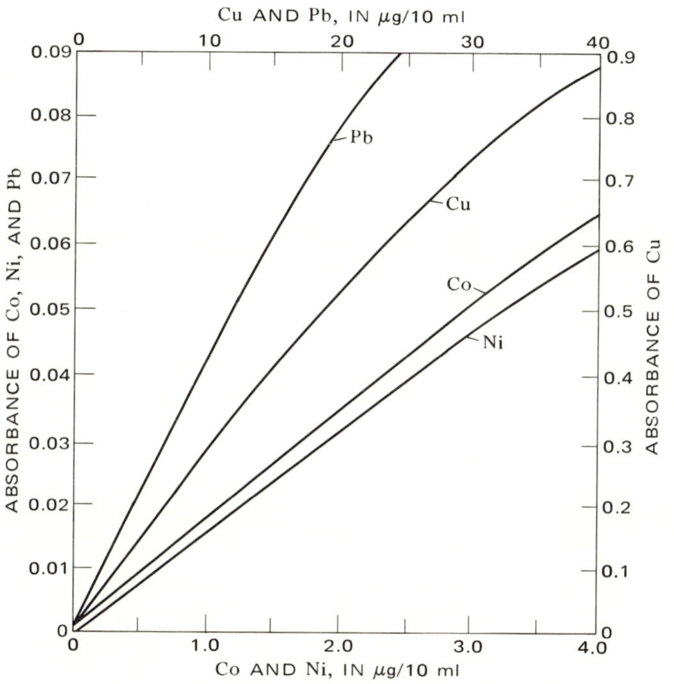

Figure 2.—Calibration curves for Co, Ni, Cu, and Pb.

metals present in background as well as mineralized samples can be covered.

The effect of Mn and Fe on Co, Ni, Cu, and Pb determinations

Analyses of more than 100 sediment samples collected from various mineralized areas show that in the hydroxylamine extract the concentration of Mn ranges from several tens to a few thousands of micrograms per milliliter and that of Fe generally ranges from 5 to 20 µg/ml, although occasionally some may range from 40 to 50 µg/ml. In order to adopt the APDC-MIBK chelate-extraction method for the determination of Co, Ni, Cu, and Pb in the hydroxylamine extract, it was essential to test whether such concentrations of Mn and Fe could interfere with the determination of microgram levels of the four metals.

Solutions were prepared containing known amounts of Co, Ni, Cu, and Pb, and of either Mn or Fe, and the same concentration of the hydroxylamine extracting solution as the sample extract. These solutions were analyzed for the metals according to the procedure just described. Recovery of the four metals in the presence of different amounts of Mn and Fe is shown in tables 3, 4, and 5. Table 3 presents data indicating no interference of 6,000 to 20,000 µg Mn (in 10 ml) with the determinations of 1 µg Co and Ni, and 5 µg Cu and Pb. Table 4

Table 3.—*Recovery of* Co, Ni, Cu, *and* Pb *from 10-ml solutions containing 0 to 20,000* µg Mn *(average of duplicates)*

Mn in 10-ml solution (µg)	Recovery (µg)			
	Co	Ni	Cu	Pb
0	1.0	1.0	5.0	5.0
6,000	1.0	1.0	5.2	5.0
10,000	1.0	1.0	5.0	5.1
16,000	1.0	1.0	5.1	5.0
20,000	1.0	1.0	5.0	5.1

Table 4.—*Recovery of* Co, Ni, Cu, *and* Pb *from 10-ml solutions containing 10,000* µg Mn *(average of four replicates)*

Element	Present (µg)	Recovered (µg)	Standard deviation (µg)	Relative standard deviation (percent)
Co	0.5	0.5	0.015	3.0
	2.0	2.1	.045	2.3
Ni	.5	.5	.027	5.4
	2.0	2.0	.046	2.3
Cu	5.0	5.2	.24	4.8
	20.0	20.2	.27	1.4
Pb	3.0	3.0	.033	1.1
	12.0	12.2	.27	2.3

shows the results of recovery of two levels of each of the four metals in the presence of a constant amount of Mn (10,000 µg in 10-ml solution) with calculated relative standard deviations for replicate analyses. Iron in amounts ranging from 50 to 500 µg in 10 ml of solution does not seem to influence the recovery of 0.5 µg Co, 1.0 µg Ni, 5.0 µg Cu, and 1.0 µg Pb as evidenced in table 5. Data on the recovery of known amounts of Co, Ni, Cu, and Pb added to hydroxylamine extracts of two sediment samples are presented in table 6.

A turbidity has been observed at the interface between the MIBK and aqueous phases with Mn concentrations greater than 10,000 µg in 10 ml solution. Presumably, this turbidity may be caused by formation of the unstable Mn-APDC complex (Mansell, 1965; Yanagisawa and others, 1968; Jenne and Ball, 1972); however, it has not interfered with the determination of any of the four metals.

Table 5.—*Recovery of* Co, Ni, Cu, *and* Pb *from 10-ml solutions containing 0 to 500 μg* Fe *(average of duplicates)*

Fe in 10-ml solution (μg)	Recovery (μg)			
	Co	Ni	Cu	Pb
0	0.5	1.0	5.0	1.0
50	.5	1.0	5.0	1.0
100	.5	1.0	4.9	...
200	.5	1.0	4.9	1.0
300	.5	1.0	5.0	...
400	.5	1.0	5.0	1.1
500	.5	1.0	5.2	.9

Table 6.—*Recovery of* Co, Ni, Cu, *and* Pb *from 10 ml of two sample solutions (hydroxylamine extracts) containing varying amounts of* Mn *and* Fe *(average of triplicates)*

Sample solution No.		Mn	Fe	Co	Ni	Cu	Pb
1	Present (μg/10 ml)	6,000	290	4.7	1.9	21.4	9.6
	Added (μg)	...	...	.7	.7	6.0	3.6
	Recovered (μg)	...	...	.7	.6	5.8	3.4
2	Present (μg/10 ml)	1,270	433	3.8	1.7	14.4	3.5
	Added (μg)	...	...	.7	.7	6.0	3.6
	Recovered (μg)	...	...	.6	.6	6.2	3.4

Two sediment samples (lab. Nos. 603305 and 613051) with distinctly different contents of hydroxylamine-extractable Mn and Fe were analyzed following the described procedure (table 7). Relative standard deviations range from 0.6 to 5.9 percent, excluding the Cu determination for sample 603305 which contains Cu at a very low concentration of 1.3 ppm.

Thus, the procedure as outlined is capable of recovering known amounts of Co, Ni, Cu, and Pb from both synthetic and sample solutions containing large amounts of Mn or Fe, and it provides reproducible results of analysis for the seven metals.

Sample size

The dissolution of manganese oxides from soil or sediment samples by acidified hydroxylamine hydrochloride is accomplished mainly through reduction; therefore, there is a limit to the amount of manganese oxides that can be brought into solution. When the reducing capacity of a fixed volume of the hydroxylamine solution is reached, no more manganese oxides will be dissolved. This statement was proved in the present investigation by experiments on the dissolution of a sample of manganese oxides containing 46.4 percent Mn and 0.4 percent Fe. There was a nearly proportional increase in Mn in the hydroxylamine extract with sample size ranging from 0.10 to 0.30 g, beyond which the dissolution of Mn leveled off to a constant value with further increments of sample size. The break of the manganese dissolution curve occurred at a manganese concentration of about 2,500 μg/ml in the extract. If 10 ml of the extract is taken for the APDC-MIBK chelation-extraction, this would mean that microgram levels of Co, Ni, Cu, and Pb can be determined in the presence of 25,000 μg Mn. The dissolution of Fe, on the other hand, decreased continuously with increasing sample size. At a sample weight of 1.00 g, no Fe was detected in the hydroxylamine extract.

Table 7.—*Eight replicate analyses of seven metals extracted from two sediment samples by 0.1* M *hydroxylamine hydrochloride in 0.01* M HNO_3 *(pH = 2)*

Sample No.	Mn	Fe	Zn	Co	Ni	Cu	Pb
603305:							
Average (ppm).	15,400	2,315	153.4	47.8	6.8	1.3	100.6
Relative standard deviation (percent).	.6	2.4	3.6	3.8	5.9	15.4	4.4
613051:							
Average (ppm).	3,733	693	122.8	38.7	8.1	19.8	55.9
Relative standard deviation (percent).	4.3	2.1	4.2	5.2	4.9	3.5	2.3

On the basis of the preceding discussion, no more than 20,000 μg Mn should be present in the 10-ml aliquot of the extract taken for analysis. This amount corresponds to 10 percent hydroxylamine-extractable Mn in the sample, assuming a sample weight of 0.50 g. Soil or sediment samples, except those containing high-manganese ferromanganese nodules or concretions, contain less than 10 percent hydroxylamine-extractable Mn. For those samples that contain more than 10 percent hydroxylamine-extractable manganese, the sample weight should be reduced accordingly.

REFERENCES CITED

Allan J. E., 1961, The determination of copper by atomic absorption spectrophotometry: Spectrochim. Acta, v. 17, p. 459–466.

Brooks, R. R., Presley, B. J., and Kaplan, I. R., 1967, APDC-MIBK extraction system for the determination of trace-elements in saline waters by atomic absorption spectrophotometry: Talanta, v. 14, p. 809–816.

Burrell, D. C., 1967, Trace elements in marine waters by atomic absorption spectrophotometry: Anal. Chim. Acta, v. 38, p. 447–455.

Canney, F. C., 1966, Hydrous manganese-iron oxide scavenging—Its effect on stream sediment survey [abs.]: Canada Geol. Survey Paper 66-54, p. 11–12.

Chao, T. T., 1972, Selective dissolution of manganese oxides from soils and sediments with acidified hydroxylamine hydrochloride: Soil Sci. Soc. America Proc., v. 36, p. 764–768.

Fishman, M. J., and Midgett, M. R., 1968, Extraction techniques for the determination of cobalt, nickel, and lead in fresh water by atomic absorption, [Chap.] 12 *in* Trace inorganics in water—A symposium: Am. Chem. Soc. Adv. Chemistry Ser. 73, p. 230–235.

Hawkes, H. E., and Webb, J. S., 1962, Geochemistry in mineral exploration: New York and Evanston, Harper and Row Publishers, 415 p.

Horsnail, R. F., Nichol, I., and Webb, J. S., 1969, Influence of variations in secondary environment on the metal content of drainage sediments: Colorado School Mines Quart., v. 64, no. 1, p. 307–322.

Jenne, E. A., 1968, Controls on Mn, Fe, Co, Ni, Cu, and Zn concentrations in soils and water—The significant role of hydrous Mn and Fe oxides, [Chap. 2] *in* Trace inorganics in waters—A symposium: Am. Chem. Soc. Adv. Chemistry Ser. 73, p. 337–339.

Jenne, E. A., and Ball, J. W., 1972, Time stability of aqueous APDC and its manganese and nickel complexes in MIBK: Atomic Absorption Newsletter, v. 11, no. 4, p. 90–91.

Mansell, R. E., 1965, Notes on the extraction of manganese with chelating agents and MIBK: Atomic Absorption Newsletter, v. 4, no. 5, p. 276–277.

Sprague, Sabina, and Slavin, Walter, 1964a, Determination of very small amounts of copper and lead in KCl by organic extraction and atomic absorption spectrophotometry: Atomic Absorption Newsletter, no. 20, p. 11–15.

——1964b, The determination of nickel in urine by atomic absorption spectrophotometry—Preliminary study: Atomic Absorption Newsletter, v. 3, no. 11, p. 160–164.

Yanagisawa, Masaaki, Suzuki, Masami, and Tukeuchi, Tsugio, 1968, Extraction of manganese dithiocarbamate complexes for atomic absorption spectrophotometry: Anal. Chim. Acta, v. 43, p. 500–502.

Jour. Research U.S. Geol. Survey
Vol. 1, No. 6, Nov.-Dec. 1973, p. 687—689

ARCHAEOCYCAS AND PHASMATOCYCAS—NEW GENERA OF PERMIAN CYCADS

By SERGIUS H. MAMAY, Washington, D.C.

Abstract.—The generic names *Archaeocycas* and *Phasmatocycas* are introduced for two previously announced but unnamed new genera of Early Permian plants; these taxa are regarded as early stages in the cycadean lineage. The names are formalized with diagnoses, illustrations, and type designations.

BACKGROUND

In a previous article (Mamay, 1969) I gave preliminary descriptions of two new genera of fossil plants on the basis of fertile organs from Lower Permian rocks of Texas and Kansas. These structures were, and are, regarded as evidence of Paleozoic origin of the cycads. Hypothetical evolutionary implications of the plants were discussed briefly, but new names were not introduced. The taxa were referred to only as "new genus A" and "new genus B." A formalized nomenclature, complete descriptions, and pertinent discussions were deferred.

The 1969 article was subsequently discussed in at least two publications by other authors. Delevoryas and Hope (1971) briefly mentioned the new fossils and some of my interpretations. Sporne (1971) also commented on the Permian fossils, duplicating some of my illustrations and pointing out the nomenclatural limbo of the material. In discussing these fossils relative to early angiosperm evolution, however, Sporne added credence to my cautiously qualified hypothesis involving derivation of a carpellike organ from new genus B, and attributed to me a claim of discovery (Sporne, 1971, p. 14: "Fig. 18. The origin of the carpel, according to Mamay * * * .") that I had neither expressed nor intended at the time of publication of the Science article. Thus, in these days of intensified search for the origins of angiospermy, the Texas fossils may become the subject of debate among theoretical plant morphologists.

In recognition of the possibly controversial future of these fossils, and in deference to inquiries as to their nomenclatural status, it seems appropriate to apply formal names at this time. This renders it possible for "new genus A" and "new genus B" to be discussed henceforth with benefit of legitimate names.

SYSTEMATIC DESCRIPTIONS

Order CYCADALES

Genus ARCHAEOCYCAS Mamay, n. gen.

New genus B. Mamay, 1969, Science, v. 164, no. 3877, p. 295–296, fig. 1.

Generic diagnosis.—Bilaterally symmetrical fertile appendage (megasporophyll) with broad midrib; several pairs of apparently sessile, closely appressed ovules borne in two lateral rows on surface of reduced basal part of lamina; ovules closely invested by lamina, each ovule with a small circular scar of attachment to lamina near midrib. Distal part of appendage expanded as flattened, sterile foliar blade.

Type species: Archaeocycas whitei Mamay, n. sp.

Figure 1*a–c*

Specific diagnosis.—Megasporophylls cuneiform, ovate, or lanceolate, 1.7 to 2.3 cm long, with greatest widths of 1.0 cm. Midribs straight, flat, faintly marked with closely set, parallel striations; midrib widths uniform or increasing distally from 1.0 to 1.3 mm at the bases, to 3.0 mm at distal termini of fertile areas; midribs flaring out conspicuously or becoming obscure in distal laminar parts of megasporophylls; sides of midribs more or less concavely scalloped through appression with ovule bases.

Proximal fertile area 1.2 to 1.6 cm long, 3.0 to 5.0 mm wide at base, nearly uniform in width or increasing distally to width of 9.0 mm. Ovules produced in opposite pairs, 4 to 6 ovules in each row. Ovules oblong, oblanceolate, rhombic or rhomboidal, tightly appressed with each other, obliquely directed forward at broad angles to the rachis. Basalmost ovules proportionately shorter, broader than distal ones; ovules 1.5 to 3 mm long (measured along lines of appression between contiguous ovules), 1.5 to 3.0 mm wide (measured along outer free margins and along lines of appression with the rachis), reaching 5 mm in greatest (diagonal) dimension. Ovules each with a small circular shallow depression or attachment scar, 0.7 to 1.0 mm in diameter, uniformly placed on the upper surfaces of ovules near the center of area of ovular appression with the midrib. Upper (adaxial) surfaces of

Figure 1.

ovules closely invested by foliar lamina; extent of lamina over lower (abaxial) ovular surfaces unknown; laminar investment of ovules showing fine closely spaced parallel striations perpendicular to midrib.

Megasporophylls abruptly modified into sterile laminar structures immediately distal to uppermost pair of ovules and contiguous with ovules; extent, venation, and margination of distal laminae obscure.

Holotype.—USGS 8877-1 (fig. 1*a*).

Occurrences.—USGS localities 8877, 8959 (Belle Plains Formation, Lower Permian, Baylor County, Tex.).

Derivation of names.—Generic name refers to the ancientness of the genus; specific name acknowledges David White's discovery of the holotype and other specimens.

Genus PHASMATOCYCAS Mamay, n. gen.

New genus A. Mamay, 1969, Science, v. 164, no. 3877, p. 295–296, fig. 1.

Generic diagnosis.—Fertile axis with two lateral rows of sessile broadly attached gymnospermous ovules; ovules simple, with blunt funnel-shaped micropyles, two distinct cuticular layers and a thick megaspore membrane; laminar tissue unknown, interseminal appendages lacking.

Type species: Phasmatocycas kansana Mamay, n. sp.

Figure 1*d–g*

Specific diagnosis.—Axial fragment 2.5 cm long, relatively stout, from 2.5 to 4.0 mm wide, rather abruptly broader at (?)basal end of specimen; surface of axis with obscure narrow longitudinal striations, lacking other characteristic markings.

Bilateral arrangement of ovules symmetrical, with no evidence of ovules between lateral rows. Ovules inserted alternately to suboppositely, extending virtually perpendicularly to axis, closely arranged so as to juxtapose against but not overlap each other. Ovules 2.8 to 4.0 mm long, 2.0 to 2.6 mm wide, ovate to oblong, broadly attached with point of attachment to axis nearly as long as greatest width of ovule; ovular apices blunt, some specimens with a shallow apical cleft or notch.

Cuticular envelopes slightly smaller than impressions of ovules, lacking ornamentation; cuticles apparently complete except for micropylar openings; apices of cuticles gradually decreasing in diameter, without marked constriction, terminating in micropylar openings from 0.2 to 0.5 mm wide; specialized chalazal features absent. Outer cuticle very thin, diaphanous, with elongate cells reaching 20 by 80 μ in dimensions, parallel to long axis of ovule. Inner cuticle apparently thicker and separate from outer; cells thick-walled, walls abruptly increasing in thickness toward the micropylar area; cells in micropylar area virtually isodiametric, averaging 10 μ in diameter. Megaspore membrane nearly filling cavity within cuticles; membrane dense, lacking ornamentation.

Small (0.25–0.33 mm in diameter) spherical sessile bodies with resinlike luster regularly alternating with ovules in each row, one such body partly imbedded in axial tissue at point between and approximately level with bases of two adjacent ovules.

Holotype.—USGS 8869-1 (figs. 1*d–g*).

Occurrence.—USGS locality 8869 (Wellington Formation, Lower Permian, Dickinson County, Kans.).

Derivation of names.—*Phasmatocycas* derives from the Greek "phasma" (apparition; phantom) and the modern generic name *Cycas; kansana* refers to geographic source of material.

REFERENCES CITED

Delevoryas, Theodore, and Hope, R. C., 1971, A new Triassic cycad and its phyletic implications: Postilla, no. 150, p. 1–21, figs. 1–12.

Mamay, S. H., 1969, Cycads: Fossil evidence of late Paleozoic origin: Science, v. 164, no. 3877, p. 295–296, fig. 1.

Sporne, K. R., 1971, The mysterious origin of flowering plants: London, Oxford Univ. Press, 16 p., 21 figs.

Figure 1.—*Archaeocycas* and *Phasmatocycas*, new genera of Permian cycads.

a–c. *Archaeocycas whitei* Mamay, n. sp. *a*, Ventral view of holotype (USGS 8877-1), × 6; *b*, lateral view of sporophyll, dark spots near midrib representing points of ovule attachment (USGS 8877-2), × 6; *c*, ventral view of sporophyll, showing circular points of ovular attachment on either side of midrib (USGS 8959-1), × 6.

d–g. *Phasmatocycas kansana* Mamay, n. sp. *d*, Macerated cuticular system of seed removed from holotype, × 30; *e*, holotype (USGS 8869-1), × 4; *f*, more enlarged part of holotype, × 6; *g*, single seed on holotype, arrows indicating resinoid globules at either side of seed base, × 21.

Jour. Research U.S. Geol. Survey
Vol. 1, No. 6, Nov.-Dec. 1973, p. 691—693

EARLY PLEISTOCENE(?) POLLEN SPECTRA FROM NEAR LAKE TAHOE, CALIFORNIA

By DAVID P. ADAM, Menlo Park, Calif.

Abstract.—Fossil pollen was recovered at Tahoe City, Calif., from beneath a 1.9-m.y.-old volcanic flow. Pollen counts of four fossil samples are compared with soil-surface pollen samples from the Sierra Nevada. The presence of *Picea* (spruce) pollen in the fossil samples suggests that summer drought conditions in the central Sierra Nevada were less severe prior to 1.9 m.y. ago than they are now.

Fossil pollen has been recovered from beneath a 1.9-m.y.-old olivine latite flow (Dalrymple, 1964; Birkeland, 1963) near the outlet of Lake Tahoe, Calif. The site (fig. 1), in a gravel quarry on the north side of the Truckee River about 0.7 km west of the Lake Tahoe dam is at an elevation of about 1,900 m in a mixed coniferous forest (*Pinus* spp., *Abies* spp., and *Libocedrus decurrens* Torr. predominate). The area now has a Mediterranean climate; summers are dry (fig. 2; see also Storer and Usinger, 1963; Russell, 1947).

The fossil pollen was recovered from a bed of clayey silt. Although the strata dip about 10°–15° SE., the fine grain size and the visible organic detritus in the pollen-bearing stratum suggest that it was laid down nearly horizontally in standing water. The fossiliferous unit, which is less than a meter thick, is conformably overlain by about 15 m of crossbedded sand, gravel, and cobbles. These sediments were probably deposited by a river flowing into the Tahoe Basin from the north, or they may have been deposited by the Truckee River in a local pond created by a lava dam.

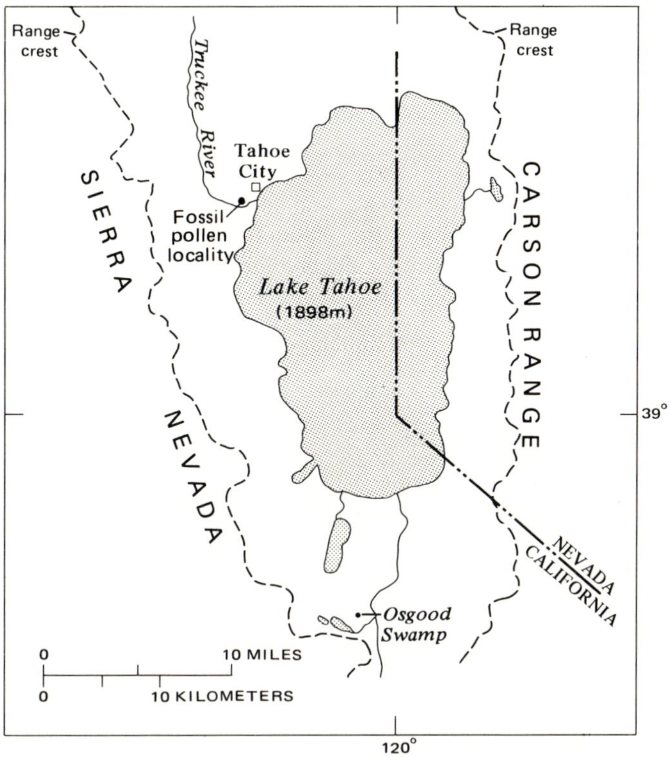

Figure 1.—Map of Lake Tahoe and vicinity, California and Nevada, showing the fossil pollen locality and Osgood Swamp. The crests of the Sierra Nevada and the Carson Range provide a rough outline of the Tahoe graben.

PROCEDURES

One soil-surface pollen sample was collected from the vicinity of the fossil samples by pooling 20 pinches of dirt from an area about 50 m square. Because of the high frequencies of *Pinus* pollen, all samples were counted using double fixed sums (Mehringer and Haynes, 1965; Adam, 1967). Two hundred grains of all pollen were counted for each sample, and this count was used to estimate the frequency of pine pollen. The second sum consisted of 100 nonpine pollen grains for all samples, except for fossil sample 2, in which 200 nonpine grains were counted. A total of some 1,686 fossil and 383 modern pollen grains was counted by this procedure. The results are presented in table 1; the frequencies for all types except pine are expressed as percentages of the second sum.

DISCUSSION

The fossil counts were compared with the soil-surface pollen sample from the site and also with transects of soil-surface pollen samples across the Sierra Nevada (Adam, 1967, figs. 3 and 4). The fossil samples most strongly resemble surface samples from about 300 m lower on the western slope of the Sierra, but with one important exception: the second sums of the fossil samples contain between 6 and 11 percent *Picea*

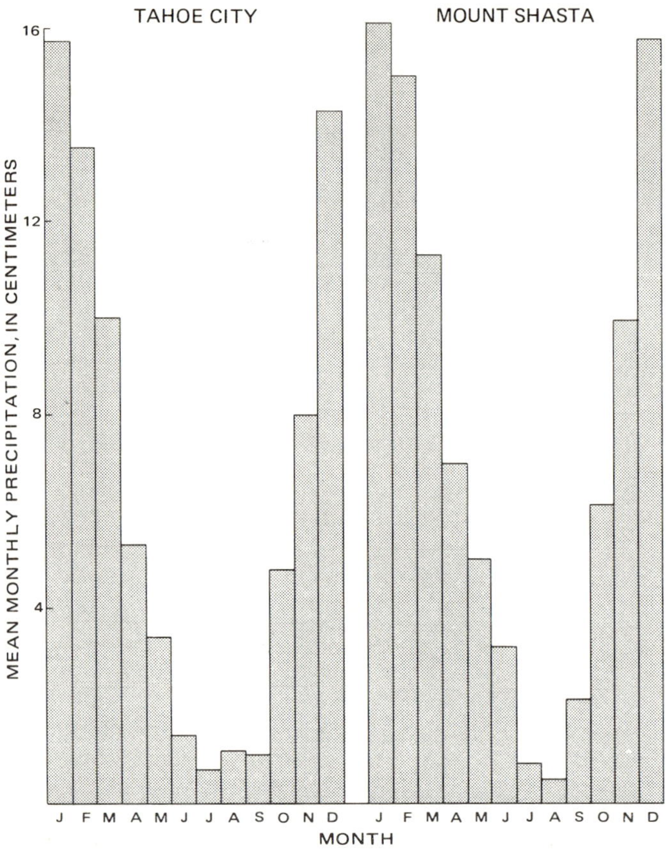

Figure 2.—Mean monthly precipitation, in centimeters, for Tahoe City and Mount Shasta, Calif. (Shasta City). Data from U.S. Weather Bureau California climatic summary.

Table 1.—*Counts of modern and fossil pollen grains from Tahoe City, Calif.*

[TCT includes Taxodiaceae, Cupressaceae, and Taxaceae; high-spine Compositae have spines >1μ; low-spine Compositae have spines <1μ; all other nomenclature follows Munz and Keck (1963)]

Pollen type	Modern pollen (percent)	Fossil pollen (percent)			
		1	2	3	4
Pinus (first count, *N*=200).	72.5	70.5	70.5	63.0	75.0
Abies	36.0	9.0	6.0	2.0	24.0
Picea	0	11.0	9.0	6.0	11.0
TCT	7.0	41.0	39.0	40.0	15.0
Tsuga	1.0	0	0	0	1.0
Pseudotsuga	0	1.0	.5	0	1.0
Arceuthobium	5.0	1.0	.5	1.0	1.0
Quercus	27.0	17.0	12.5	16.0	17.0
Fraxinus	0	0	2.5	1.0	0
Juglans	1.0	0	0	0	0
Alnus	4.0	0	0	0	0
Betula	0	0	0	1.0	0
Cornus	0	0	0	1.0	0
Cyperaceae	1.0	5.0	2.5	3.0	3.0
High-spine Compositae	4.0	1.0	1.0	0	0
Low-spine Compositae	1.0	0	1.0	1.0	1.0
Artemisia	1.0	9.0	7.0	12.0	8.0
Chenopodiaceae plus *Amaranthus*.	1.0	3.0	2.5	2.0	2.0
Sarcobatus	0	0	1.0	1.0	1.0
Ericaceae	2.0	0	0	0	0
Rhamnaceae	3.0	0	1.0	1.0	0
Gramineae	1.0	1.0	8.5	3.0	4.0
Caryophyllaceae	0	0	0	0	1.0
Polygonum, persicaria-type.	0	0	0	1.0	0
Polygonum, californicum-type.	0	0	0	0	1.0
Eriogonum	0	0	.5	1.0	0
Rosaceae	0	0	1.0	0	0
Ranunculaceae	1.0	0	0	0	0
Euphorbia	2.0	0	0	0	0
Malvaceae	0	0	0	0	1.0
Oenothera-type	0	0	0	0	1.0
Unknowns	2.0	1.0	4.0	7.0	7.0
Second sum sample (excluding pine).	100	100	200	100	100

(spruce) pollen. Spruce is not found in the Sierra Nevada today; the nearest recorded locality is on Mount Shasta, more than 250 km northwest of the fossil site (Munz and Keck, 1963; Fowells, 1965; Little, 1971). Spruce pollen is absent not only from all modern and postglacial pollen samples that I have studied from the Sierra Nevada, but also from late glacial samples from Osgood Swamp (Adam, 1967), 37.5 km south of the Tahoe City fossil site and about 100 m higher (fig. 1). However, minor amounts of *Picea* cf. *P. engelmannii* pollen occur regularly in the modern pollen rain at Searles Lake, Calif., which is located about 65 km east of the Sierra Nevada and 450 km southeast of the Tahoe City site (Leopold, 1967, and written commun., 1973). The Mount Shasta spruce population is 700 km to the northwest, but other possible sources for the Searles Lake spruce pollen are located about 450 km to the east and northeast in northern Arizona, south-central Utah, and east-central Nevada (Little, 1971).

I was unable to determine the species of spruce represented in the Tahoe City pollen. However, on the basis of modern distributions of the several North American species of *Picea* (Little, 1971), the most probable species for the spruce in the fossil samples is *P. engelmannii* Parry; the other reasonable possibility is *P. breweriana* S. Watson, which is common in Neogene floras from Nevada (Wolfe, 1969, and oral commun., 1972).

The present southern limit of the distribution of *Picea* in North America appears to be related partly to a requirement for adequate summer rainfall. Wolfe and Leopold (1967) have noted that the southern limit for spruce generally follows the 21°C July mean temperature isotherm, but they further note that the observed exceptions to this rule are a result of low precipitation. Fowells (1965, p. 299) states that for *P. engelmannii*, "Average precipitation exceeds 25 inches annually with only moderate or no seasonal deficiency."

A comparison of the mean monthly precipitation values for U.S. Weather Bureau stations at Tahoe City and Mount Shasta supports this conclusion (fig. 2). Both July and August are very dry months at both stations, but at Tahoe City the dry season includes June and September as well, whereas the Mount Shasta station receives more than 2 cm of rain in each of those months. This indicates that Engelmann spruce probably cannot tolerate more than a few months of summer drought.

Furthermore, the Sierra Nevada includes a wide range of temperature regimes, which suggests that temperature probably is not the critical factor responsible for the modern absence of spruce from the range. The absence of spruce from the Sierra Nevada is more likely the result of extended summer drought.

If this is so, then the Osgood Swamp pollen record (Adam, 1967) suggests that summer drought prevailed even during late Tioga (Wisconsinan) time and has persisted during the postglacial period. The Tahoe City samples indicate that the summer climate of the Sierra Nevada was different prior to 1.9 m.y. ago, and it is tempting to speculate that the Pacific high-pressure cell must have dominated the summer climate of northern California less than it does now.

The conditions that permitted the survival of spruce in the Sierra Nevada may have persisted over a long period. The K/Ar date provides only a minimum age for the Tahoe City deposits, although the field relations between the dated flow and the underlying sediments suggest that the samples are not very much older. However, the samples could be at least as old as the Verdi flora (about 30 km northeast), which has yielded a K/Ar date of 5.7 m.y. (Evernden and James, 1964) and which contains spruce pollen (H. E. Schorn, oral commun., 1972).

Only four of the fossil samples from Tahoe City contained pollen, and they do not provide a sufficient basis for making a detailed analysis of the paleoclimate or elevation of the site at the time of their deposition. However, the site has been destroyed by borrow operations, and thus the data cannot be duplicated. They are recorded here in the hope that they may be of use to others in a broader context.

ACKNOWLEDGMENTS

Parts of this work were done while the author held a National Science Foundation (NSF) graduate fellowship at the University of Arizona, and other support came from NSF grant GB-1959 to Paul S. Martin. V. C. LaMarche, Jr., P. J. Mehringer, Jr., J. A. Wolfe, and E. B. Leopold made suggestions which improved the manuscript.

REFERENCES CITED

Adam, D. P., 1967, Late-Pleistocene and recent palynology in the central Sierra Nevada, California, *in* Cushing, E. J., and Wright, H. E., Jr., eds., Quaternary paleoecology: New Haven, Yale Univ. Press, p. 275–301.

Birkeland, P. W., 1963, Pleistocene volcanism and deformation of the Truckee area north of Lake Tahoe, California: Geol. Soc. America Bull., v. 74, p. 1453–1464.

Dalrymple, G. B., 1964, Cenozoic chronology of the Sierra Nevada, California: California Univ. Pubs. Geol. Sci., v. 47, p. 1–41.

Evernden, J. F., and James, G. T., 1964, Potassium-argon dates and the Tertiary floras of North America: Am. Jour. Sci., v. 262, no. 8, p. 945–974.

Fowells, H. A., 1965, Silvics of forest trees of the United States: U.S. Dept. Agriculture Handbook 271, 761 p.

Leopold, E. B., 1967, Summary of palynological data from Searles Lake, *in* Pleistocene geology and palynology of Searles Valley, California–Friends of the Pleistocene, Pacific Coast Sec., Mtg., Sept. 23–24, 1967, Guidebook: p. 52–66.

Little, E. L., 1971, Atlas of the United States trees: U.S. Dept. Agriculture Misc. Pub. 1146, 8 p., 200 maps, 9 pl.

Mehringer, P. J., Jr., and Haynes, C. V., Jr., 1965, The pollen evidence for the environment of early man and extinct mammals at the Lehner mammoth site, southeastern Arizona: Am. Antiquity, v. 31, p. 17–23.

Munz, P. A., and Keck, D. D., 1963, A California flora: Berkeley, California Univ. Press, 1681 p.

Russell, R. J., 1947, Sierra climate, *in* Peattie, R., ed., The Sierra Nevada: the range of light: New York, Vanguard Press, p. 323–340.

Storer, T. I., and Usinger, R. L., 1963, Sierra Nevada natural history: Berkeley, California Univ. Press, 374 p.

Wolfe, J. A., 1969, Neogene floristic and vegetational history of the Pacific northwest: Madroño, v. 20, p. 83–110.

Wolfe, J. A., and Leopold, E. B., 1967, Neogene and Early Quaternary vegetation of northwestern North America and northeastern Asia, *in* Hopkins, D. M., ed., The Bering land bridge: Palo Alto, Stanford Univ. Press, p. 193–206.

Jour. Research U.S. Geol. Survey
Vol. 1, No. 6, Nov.-Dec. 1973, p. 695—700

THE LATE CRETACEOUS AMMONITE TRACHYSCAPHITES PULCHERRIMUS (ROEMER) IN NEW JERSEY AND TEXAS

By W. A. COBBAN, Denver, Colo.

Abstract.—*Trachyscaphites pulcherrimus*, described originally by Ferdinand Roemer in 1841 from fragments of nodose ammonites from Germany, is characterized by having five rows of tubercles on each flank of the phragmocone and three to five rows on each side of the body chamber. Weak midventral tubercles are present on some specimens. Ribbing is dense and usually irregular. The species has been recorded from upper Campanian rocks in Germany, Austria, France, Poland, and Russia. Recently a few specimens have been found at the top of the Wenonah Formation of New Jersey and in the Taylor Marl of Texas.

Trachyscaphites pulcherrimus (Roemer) has been known from the Upper Cretaceous of Europe since 1841 where it has served as a guide fossil to rocks of late Campanian age. The species is readily identified by rather dense irregular ribbing and by five rows of tubercles on the flank of the septate coil and three to five rows on each side of the body chamber. Recently several specimens were discovered near Marlboro, Monmouth County, N.J., and near Kimbro, Travis County, Tex. The New Jersey specimens, found by Messrs. John Brzostoski and Richard Heintz, River Plaza, N.J., were made available to me for study through the kind efforts of Mr. Harold Mendryk, Harrison, N.J. These specimens, internal molds of gray very fine grained soft micaceous sandstone, are from the top of the Wenonah Formation according to Mr. Mendryk (written commun., July 17, 1971). The Texas specimens are from hard limestone concretions containing much barite in the Taylor Marl on Cottonwood Creek 1 mile northwest of Kimbro, Travis County. Two of the four Texas specimens were made available for study by Dr. Keith Young, University of Texas, Austin. I greatly appreciate the loans from Mr. Brzostoski and Dr. Young and the donations from Mr. Heintz.

The photographs were made by Robert E. Burkholder, of the U.S. Geological Survey. Specimens that have USNM numbers are in the National Museum of Natural History in Washington, D.C. Plaster casts of all figured specimens are in the National Museum of Natural History and in the Cretaceous collections of the U.S. Geological Survey at the Federal Center, Denver, Colo.

According to Schlüter (1872, p. 86), Roemer (1841, p. 91) based his species on fragments of nodose scaphites. Roemer noted that the species had five rows of tubercles on each side, but his single illustration showed a lateral view of a septate coil having four rows of tubercles on a side. Schlüter accepted Roemer's description, but he assigned Roemer's illustrated specimen to the new species *Scaphites spiniger* Schlüter. Two specimens were illustrated by Schlüter as examples of *S. pulcherrimus*. The larger specimen, 90 mm in length, is preserved in the Geologisch-palaeontologisches Institut und Museum, Bonn, Germany, and a plaster cast (fig. 1*k*, *l*) is in the U.S. Geological Survey's Cretaceous collections at the Federal Center, Denver, Colo. The smaller specimen may have been lost during World War II.

TRACHYSCAPHITES PULCHERRIMUS (ROEMER)

Figures 1 and 2

1841. *Scaphites pulcherrimus* Roemer, p. 91 (not pl. 14, fig. 4).
1866. *Scaphites multinodosus* von Hauer, p. 306, pl. 1, figs. 7, 8.
1872. *Scaphites pulcherrimus* Roemer. Schlüter, p. 85, pl. 26, figs. 1–5.
1893. *Scaphites pulcherrimus* Roemer. De Grossouvre, p. 250, pl. 32, figs. 6, 9a, b [1894].
1916. *Acanthoscaphites pulcherrimus* (Roemer). Nowak, p. 63.
1925. *Scaphites (Acanthoscaphites) pulcherrimus* Roemer. Diener, p. 206.
1927. *Acanthoscaphites pulcherrimus* (Roemer). Reeside, p. 33.
1951. *Acanthoscaphites pulcherrimus* (Roemer). Mikhailov, p. 96, pl. 18, figs. 83, 84.
1959. *Acanthoscaphites pulcherrimus* (Roemer). Naidin and Shimanskii, p. 195, pl. 6, fig. 14.
1964. *Trachyscaphites pulcherrimus* (Roemer). Cobban and Scott, p. E1.
1968. *Scaphites pulcherrimus* Roemer. Arnold, p. 314, text fig. 36.

Schlüter's drawing of the larger specimen is reversed and idealized (Schlüter, 1872, pl. 26, figs. 1–3). It shows a septate coil having numerous rectiradiate ribs and five equal-spaced rows of small tubercles, and a body chamber having fewer ribs, a few conspicuous umbilical tubercles, and three outer rows of tubercles. Tubercles on opposite sides of the midline of the venter are arranged in a zigzag manner. The drawing shows the

Figure 1.

innermost of the three outer rows of tubercles on the venter extending back to and connecting with the fourth row out from the umbilicus on the septate coil. According to this arrangement, the species could be interpreted as having six rows of tubercles on a side. The plaster cast, however, reveals a rather poorly preserved specimen on which the innermost of the three outer rows of tubercles can be just as well connected to the third row out from the umbilicus on the septate coil. The cast also reveals the presence of a fourth row of very weak tubercles on the younger part of the body chamber. The specimen can be interpreted as a female by its large size, very small umbilicus, and broad body chamber having a slightly convex umbilical wall (Cobban, 1969, p. 10–11). The smaller of Schlüter's specimens is a body chamber that has a concave umbilical wall; it can be interpreted as a male. Schlüter's drawing shows seven or eight umbilical tubercles and three equal-spaced rows of tubercles on the outer third of the flank of which the innermost row is very faint.

De Grossouvre (1893, pl. 32, figs. 9a, b) illustrated a complete specimen assigned to *S. pulcherrimus* from southwestern France (Dordogne). The specimen has a slender body chamber and concave umbilical margin; I interpret this specimen as a very large male. It differs from the specimens figured by Schlüter by having all five rows of tubercles of a side persisting on the body chamber. Tubercles on opposite sides of the middle of the venter have a zigzag arrangement like that of Schlüter's larger specimen.

Frech (1915, p. 556) interpreted *S. pulcherrimus* in a different manner than did Schlüter and de Grossouvre. In the course of analyzing the scaphites of the Upper Cretaceous, Frech defined a "Gruppe des *Sc. pulcherrimus*" characterized by three to four rows of lateral tubercles as well as a midventral row.

Nowak (1916, p. 63) also included within the scope of *S. pulcherrimus* specimens that had midventral tubercles, although he did restrict it to specimens having five rows on a side. He also assigned *pulcherrimus* to his new genus *Acanthoscaphites*.

Figure 1.—*Trachyscaphites pulcherrimus* (Roemer) (*a–g, k, l*) and *T. redbirdensis* Cobban and Scott (*h–j*), natural size.

a–d. Two views each of the older two-thirds of two body chambers (males) of *T. pulcherrimus* from the Wenonah Formation near Marlboro, N.J. Private collection of John Brzostoski, River Plaza, N.J.

e–g. Three views of part of the phragmocone and part of the body chamber of another specimen, probably a female, from the Wenonah Formation. Private collection of John Brzostoski.

h–j. Three views of the phragmocone and part of the body chamber of an example of *T. redbirdensis* that has siphonal tubercles. From the Red Bird Silty Member of the Pierre Shale at USGS Mesozoic loc. D418, 1½ miles southwest of Newcastle, Wyo. Hypotype USNM 187707.

k, l. Top and side views of plaster cast of the holotype of *T. pulcherrimus*.

Mikhailov (1951, p. 96–98, pl. 18, figs. 83, 84) carefully described a nearly complete specimen 72 mm in length from siliceous marls of the Donets region in southern Russia. This specimen differed from those of Schlüter by the five rows of tubercles on the flank of the septate coil persisting onto the older half of the body chamber. Mikhailov described the rows of tubercles as umbilical, umbilicolateral, lateral, ventrolateral, and outer. He noted that only the ventrolateral and outer rows persisted to the aperture. Mikhailov also observed that ribs were thin and tended to occur in bundles separated by furrows, and that the tubercles were confined to the bundles of ribs. Such a rib and tubercle arrangement is well shown on the illustration of the septate coil of the larger specimen of Schlüter (1872, pl. 26, fig. 1). The large size, very small umbilicus, and wide body chamber of Mikhailov's specimen suggests a female. Although the specimen lacked midventral tubercles, Mikhailov assigned it to *Acanthoscaphites*. Mikhailov's terminology of umbilical, umbilicolateral, lateral, and ventrolateral for rows of tubercles will be adopted here, but ventral will be used in place of outer. For further clarity midventral tubercles will be referred to as siphonal tubercles.

The genus *Trachyscaphites* was proposed by Cobban and Scott (1964, p. E6–E7) for scaphites having three to five rows of tubercles on each flank and numerous ribs that weaken on the body chamber and tend to lack differentiation into strong primaries and secondaries as in most groups of scaphites. Cobban and Scott (1964, p. E7) noted that "*Trachyscaphites* differs from *Acanthoscaphites* by its smaller size, whorls wider than high, simpler suture, lack of midventral nodes, and straighter living chamber which has the younger part separated considerably from the chambered whorls," and that *Acanthoscaphites* "Should be restricted to a group of large tightly coiled scaphites in which midventral nodes are ordinarily present. In addition, the suture is highly incised for a scaphite, the ribs are straight, and the nodes are usually present only on the living chamber." Since the publication of Cobban and Scott's paper, a large septate coil of *T. redbirdensis*, the type species of *Trachyscaphites*, has been discovered that has a midventral row of small pointed tubercles (fig. 1*h–j*). Accordingly, the definition of *Trachyscaphites* is herein emended to include specimens with or without midventral tubercles. Inasmuch as *T. pulcherrimus* has whorls higher than wide, the degree of stoutness of whorls is removed from the definition of the genus. *Trachyscaphites* is readily distinguished from typical *Acanthoscaphites*, such as the large specimens illustrated by Nowak (1912, pl. 32), by its peculiar bundling of ribs separated by furrows, and by the three to five rows of lateral tubercles on the septate coil. *Scaphites varians* Lopuski (1911, p. 120, pl. 4, figs. 1–3, text fig. 4), usually assigned to *Acanthoscaphites* (Nowak, 1912, p. 578; Mikhailov, 1951, p. 104; Schmid, 1965), has midventral tubercles as well as three rows of lateral tubercles on the septate coil; perhaps this form should be assigned to *Trachyscaphites*.

Figure 2.

GEOGRAPHIC DISTRIBUTION AND AGE OF TRACHYSCAPHITES PULCHERRIMUS

Trachyscaphites pulcherrimus has been recorded from Germany (Roemer, 1841, p. 91; Schlüter, 1872, p. 85; Arnold, 1968, p. 314), Austria (von Hauer, 1866, p. 306), France (de Grossouvre, 1893, p. 250), Poland (Pożaryski, 1938, p. 18; Pożaryska, 1954, table 1; Błaszkiewicz, 1966, table; Cieśliński and Pożaryski, 1970, p. 212), and Russia (Mikhailov, 1951, p. 96; Naidin and Shimanskii, 1959, p. 195; Naidin, 1969, p. 181). The species seems to be confined to the upper Campanian. Pożaryska (1954, table 1) and Błaszkiewicz (1966, table) record *T. pulcherrimus* in the upper part of the upper Campanian but not at the top.

AMERICAN EXAMPLES OF TRACHYSCAPHITES PULCHERRIMUS

Parts of 10 scaphites from near the top of the Wenonah Formation near Marlboro, N.J., were available for study. All are internal molds, and most are uncrushed. Four are considered males (fig. 1*a–d*; fig. 2*a–f*), and two are considered females (fig. 2*i–k*, *n*, *o*). The others are too incomplete for assignment to either sex.

The nearest complete specimen of the females consists of most of the body chamber and part of the last septate whorl of a specimen 76.5 mm in length (fig. 2*n*, *o*). Ribs are flexuous, prorsiradiate, and tend to occur singularly or in pairs separated by poorly defined furrows. The ribbing weakens a little on the older two-thirds of the body chamber and then becomes strong again on the younger third. Tubercles on the outer septate whorl are small, pointed, nearly equal in size, and arranged in five equally spaced rows. Umbilical tubercles increase greatly in size on the body chamber where they are circular and sharp and six in number. Maximum thickness of the shell is through the umbilical tubercles at the end of the straighter part of the body chamber. The umbilicolateral tubercles, in contrast, decrease in size on the body chamber where they are very small, pointed, and more numerous than the umbilical ones. The lateral tubercles persist across the body chamber maintaining the same size as on the septate whorl. The ventrolateral and ventral tubercles are equal in number, pointed, and increase in size on the body chamber. There are no siphonal tubercles; the middle of the venter is smooth on the body chamber and ribbed on the outer septate whorl. Opposite tubercles of the ventral rows are arranged in a zigzag manner. The suture is moderately complex. This specimen closely resembles the one figured by Mikhailov.

A somewhat poorly preserved septate coil 54 mm in diameter of a large female is of interest by having siphonal tubercles on the last part (fig. 2*i–k*). These tubercles are very small, nodate, and more numerous than the ventral ones. Clearly defined siphonal tubercles are absent on the older part of the whorl where their place is taken by nodose ribs. Another specimen, probably a female, has more conspicuous nodose ribs on the middle of the venter on the younger part of the phragmocone where two occur for each tubercle in a ventral row. (fig. 1*e–g*).

Two of the four male specimens from New Jersey are represented by very well preserved complete body chambers 40 and 50 mm in height. The larger one, which has a compressed section, (fig. 2*d–f*) shows much resemblance to the smaller of Schlüter's specimens. Ribs are prorsiradiate, and umbilical tubercles, which number six, are nodate and equal in size and persist to the aperture. The rest of the ornamentation is different from that on the older half of the body chamber and that on the younger half. Ribs are rather weak and irregular in strength on the older half and strong and regular on the younger half. The older half has very small umbilicolateral and lateral tubercles and strong sharp clavate ventrolateral and ventral tubercles, whereas the younger half lacks umbilicolateral and lateral tubercles and has small nodate ventrolateral and ventral tubercles that persist to the aperture. The younger half has in addition weak nodate siphonal tubercles. On the younger half, the tubercles of each row are equal in numbers and each siphonal, ventral, and ventrolateral tubercle is alined with a rib. Tubercles on opposite sides of the midline of the venter have a zigzag arrangement. The aperture is constricted like that of other scaphites. The smaller specimen (fig. 2*a–c*) is much like the larger except that the cross section is not as compressed and the tubercles are a little stronger and sharper. The other two males (fig. 1*a–d*) consist of the older two-thirds of large stout body chambers that have unusually strong ribs. Umbilicolateral tubercles are missing, and the lateral tubercles are weak. Ventral tubercles have a zigzag arrangement.

Three of the four Texas specimens consist of body chambers with parts of the septate coils attached. The body chambers are slender and have concave umbilical walls which suggest males. The original lengths of these three specimens are estimated as 53, 65, and 68 mm. All five rows of tubercles on the side of the septate coil persist onto the body chamber of

Figure 2.–Specimens of *Trachyscaphites pulcherrimus* (Roemer) from New Jersey and Texas, natural size.

- *a–f*. Three views each of two body chambers believed to be males from the Wenonah Formation near Marlboro, N.J. Specimen *a–c*, collected by Richard Heintz, is hypotype USNM 187708; specimen *d–f* is from the private collection of John Brzostoski, River Plaza, N.J.
- *g*. Side view of part of a body chamber from the Wenonah Formation collected by Richard Heintz. Hypotype USNM 187709.
- *h*. Side view of a small laterally compressed adult (male) from the Taylor Marl 1 mile northwest of Kimbro, Tex. Univ. Texas 37972.
- *i–k*. Three views of a stout phragmocone believed to be a female from the Wenonah Formation near Marlboro, N.J. Private collection of John Brzostoski.
- *l*, *m*. Two views of an unusually large male from the same locality as *h*. Univ. Texas 33433.
- *n*, *o*. Two views of a slender female from the Wenonah Formation near Marlboro, N.J. Private collection of John Brzostoski.

the largest specimen, although the umbilicolateral and lateral tubercles are weakened there (fig. 2*l*, *m*). Siphonal tubercles are not present on this body chamber, and the tubercles of the ventral rows have a zigzag arrangement. The older part of the body chamber of the intermediate specimen has strong pointed umbilical, ventrolateral, and ventral tubercles, weaker but sharp lateral tubercles, and no umbilicolateral tubercles, whereas the younger part has all five rows of tubercles as well as very small pointed siphonal ones. The smallest specimen has compressed flanks on which are present all five rows of tubercles, although the umbilicolateral ones are barely discernible (fig. 2*h*). The midventral area on the younger part of this body chamber is not preserved. A septate coil 36 mm in diameter with a small part of the body chamber attached represents the fourth Texas specimen. It has a zigzag arrangement of the ventral tubercles and the connecting ribs. The suture is shown on figure 3.

Figure 3.—External suture, × 3, at a diameter of 32.5 mm of *Trachyscaphites pulcherrimus* (Roemer) from the Taylor Marl at USGS Mesozoic loc. 17386 on Cottonwood Creek ½ mile southwest of Manda, Travis County, Tex. Hypotype USNM 187710.

REFERENCES CITED

Arnold, Hellmut, 1968, Das Obercampan des Stemweder Berges und seine Fauna: Bremen Überseemus. Pub., v. 3, ser. A, no. 6, p. 273–342, illus.

Błaszkiewicz, Andrzej, 1966, Uwagi o stratygrafii kampanu i mastrychtu doliny środkowej Wisły [Remarks on the Campanian and Maestrichtian stratigraphy of the middle Vistula valley]: Kwart. Geol., v. 10, no. 4, p. 1060–1071. (Polish, with English summ.)

Cieśliński, Stefan, and Pożaryski.Władysław, 1970, Kreda, *in* Pożaryski, Władysław, ed., Stratygrafia Mezozoiku obrzeżenia Gór Swietokrzyskich [The stratigraphy of the Mesozoic in the margin of the Góry Świętokrzyskie]: [Poland] Inst. Geol. Prace, v. 56, p. 185–231, 5 pls.

Cobban, W. A., 1969, The Late Cretaceous ammonites *Scaphites leei* Reeside and *Scaphites hippocrepis* (DeKay) in the western interior of the United States: U.S. Geol. Survey Prof. Paper 619, 29 p., 5 pls.

Cobban, W. A., and Scott, G. R., 1964, Multinodose scaphitid cephalopods from the lower part of the Pierre Shale and equivalent rocks in the conterminous United States: U.S. Geol. Survey Prof. Paper 483-E, p. E1–E13, pls. 1–4.

Diener, Carl, 1925, Fossilium Catalogus, I, Animalia, pt. 29, Ammonoidea neocretacea: Berlin, W. Junk, 244 p.

Frech, Fritz, 1915, Die Bedeutung von *Scaphites* für die Gliederung der Oberkreide, Pt. 1 *of* Über Scaphites: Centralbl. Mineralogie Jahrg. 1915, p. 553–568.

Grossouvre, Albert de, 1893, Les ammonites de la craie supérieure, Pt. 2, Paléontologie, *of* Recherches sur la craie supérieure: Carte Géol. Détaillée France Mém., 264 p., 39 pls. [1894].

Hauer, F. R. von, 1866, Neue Cephalopoden aus den Gosaugebilden der Alpen: Kaiserlichen Akad. Wiss. Wien Sitzungsber., Math.-Naturw. Kl., v. 53, p. 300–308, 2 pls.

Lopuski, Geslaw, 1911, Przyczynki do znajomosci fauny kredowej gub Lubelskiej [Contribution to the study of the Cretaceous fauna of the Lublin Plateau] [In Polish with French summ.]: Towarzystwo Naukowe Warszawskie Sprawozdania z Posiedzen, Comptes Rendus, v. 4, p. 104–140, 4 pls.

Mikhailov, N. P., 1951, Ammonity werchnego mela yuzhnoj chasti jewropejskoj chasti SSSR i ich stratigraficheskoe znatschenie [The ammonites of the Upper Cretaceous of the southern part of the European part of the USSR and their stratigraphic significance]: Akad. Nauk SSSR Geol. Inst. Trudy, no. 129, Geol. ser. no. 50, 143 p., 19 pls.

Naidin [Najdin], D. P., 1969, Biostratigraphie und Paläogeographie der Oberen Kreide der Russischen Tafel: Geol. Jahrb., v. 87, p. 157–186, illus.

Naidin, D. P., and Shimanskii, V. N., 1959, Golovonogne Molluski *in* Moskvin, M. M., ed., Atlas verkhnemelovoi fauny severnogo Kavkaza i Kryma [Cephalopod Mollusca, *in* Atlas of the Upper Cretaceous fauna of the northern Caucasus and Crimea]: Moscow, Vses. Nauchno-Issled. Inst. Prirod. Gazov Trudy, p. 166–220.

Nowak, Jan, 1912, Die Scaphiten, Pt. 2 *of* Untersuchungen über die Cephalopoden der oberen Kreide in Polen: Acad. Sci. Cracovie Bull. Internat., 1911, ser. B, p. 547–589, pls. 32, 33.

—— 1916, Zur Bedeutung von *Scaphites* für die Gliederung der Oberkreide: K.-k. Geol. Reichsanstalt Verh., Jahrg. 1916, no. 3, p. 55–67.

Pożaryska, Krystyna, 1954, O przewodnich otwornicach z kredy górnej Polski środkowej [The Upper Cretaceous index foraminifers from central Poland]: Acta Geol. Polonica, v. 4, no. 2, p. 249–276, illus. (English summ., p. 62–72).

Pożaryski, Władysław, 1938, Stratygrafia Senonu w Przełomie Wisły między Rachowem i Puławami [Senonian stratigraphy in the breach of the Wisla River between Rachow and Pulawy in central Poland]: Poland, Inst. Géol. Bull. 6, 94 p. [German summ.]

Reeside, J. B., Jr., 1927, The scaphites, an Upper Cretaceous ammonite group: U.S. Geol. Survey Prof. Paper 150-B, p. 21–40.

Roemer, F. A., 1841, Die Versteinerungen des norddeutschen Kreidegebirges: Hannover, Germany, 145 p., 16 pls.

Schlüter, Clemens, 1871–72, 1876, Cephalopoden der oberen deutschen Kreide: Palaeontographica, 1871–72, v. 21, p. 1–120, pls. 1–35; 1876, v. 24, p. 121–264, pls. 36–55.

Schmid, Friedrich, 1965, *Acanthoscaphites tridens varians* (Lopuski 1911) aus dem Maastricht von Hemmoor (Niederelbe) in nordwest-Deutschland: Geol. Jahrb., v. 83, p. 681–692, pls. 62, 63.

Jour. Research U.S. Geol. Survey
Vol. 1, No. 6, Nov.-Dec. 1973, p. 701—707

DETERMINATION OF THE ASSOCIATION AND DISSOCIATION OF HUMIC ACID FRACTIONS BY SMALL ANGLE X-RAY SCATTERING

By R. L. WERSHAW and D. J. PINCKNEY,
Lakewood, Colo.

Abstract.—A procedure has been devised for the fractionation of humic acid samples from different environments. This procedure involves fractionation of the sample by adsorption chromatography on a Sephadex G-50 column followed by chromatography on either a G-25 or a G-100 column. The fractions of the solutions are then examined by small angle X-ray scattering. Three different types of behavior have been detected among the humic acid fractions: (1) Some fractions show very little change in aggregation at pH values above 3.5. (2) One fraction forms aggregates at pH values above and below pH 7, but at pH 7 it is completely dissociated. (3) In some fractions the degree of aggregation decreases with increasing pH. However, even at pH values as high as 11.5 some large particles are still present. These differences in association behavior are due to the interaction of different attractive and repulsive forces. In many aggregating systems only one type of attractive force is dominant; however in humic acid systems hydrogen bonding, π bonding between planar aromatic moieties, and other coulombic interactions apparently all play a role in the formation of molecular aggregates.

A number of different procedures have been used in attempts to determine the molecular weights or molecular sizes of humic acid particles in solution. Most of the classical methods of molecular weight determinations have been tried, but there is little overall agreement between the various measurements.

Scheffer and Ulrich (1960), Schnitzer and Desjardins (1962), Wershaw and Burcar (1967), and others have reviewed the literature on molecular weight determinations of humic acids. In general, they have found that measurements which are dependent upon changes in the colligative properties of thermodynamic systems yield lower molecular weights than other methods. Most of these measurements have been on unfractionated humic acids, although a few have been made on partially fractionated samples. A comparison of the results of various procedures, which might then permit us to account for the differences in apparent molecular weight from one method to another, would require a detailed knowledge of the molecular weight distribution of the particles in the solutions; unfortunately these data are not available. Some workers have attempted to measure the molecular distribution by gel-permeation chromatography. However, as we have shown (Wershaw and Pinckney, 1973), these results are at best highly questionable.

In theory it should be possible to directly measure the distribution of particle sizes in polydisperse systems by low angle X-ray scattering or ultracentrifugation. Unfortunately, in actual practice the necessary detailed information on the physical and chemical properties of all the particles in the system is generally not available (See Beeman and others, 1957; Schachman, 1959). However, the range of particle sizes can be readily evaluated, and as we shall demonstrate, this information alone can give us a valuable insight into the chemistry of the system.

Flaig and Beutelspacher (1968), Stevenson, Van Winkle, and Martin (1953), and Piret and others (1960) have studied unfractionated humic acid salt solutions by ultracentrifugation. All these authors found that the solutions were polydisperse, and they reported sedimentation average molecular weights (Z average molecular weights). Piret and others (1960) found that 90 percent by weight of the humic acid particles had molecular weights less than 3×10^5.

Wershaw and others (1967), using low angle X-ray scattering, were the first to measure some of the particle sizes in an unfractionated sodium humate solution; after this work Lindqvist (1970) found that acid hydrolysis of a chernozem sodium humate that contained a number of different size particles in solution yielded a monodisperse system in which all the particles had radii of gyration between 17 and 19 A. Others (Wershaw and others, 1967, 1970; Wershaw and Pinckney, 1971) have extended their work to measurements of particle sizes in different sodium humate fractions. They have shown that one of the sodium humate fractions isolated by gel-permeation chromatography forms molecular aggregates in solution which disaggregate at approximately pH 7; above and below this pH the molecules aggregate. In this paper we shall discuss the other types of aggregates that are found in solutions of sodium humate fractions.

All molecular weight measurement procedures when applied to polydisperse systems, such as humic acid salt solutions, yield results which are functions of the molecular weight distribution of the particles in the system. Those methods which are dependent on colligative properties will give number average molecular weights, methods such as viscosity measurements will give weight average molecular weights, and still others such as ultracentrifugation give so-called Z average molecular weights. The weight average molecular weights will be more influenced by the higher weight particles than by the lower weight particles. This effect will be even more pronounced in the Z average determinations. Comparisons of molecular determinations from one author to another and from one method to another are further complicated by the fact that the molecular weight distribution in a polyelectrolyte system in which molecular association is taking place is generally a function of the pH, the ionic strength, and the concentration of the solution (Wershaw and Pinckney, 1971).

EXPERIMENTAL PROCEDURE

The sodium humate samples were isolated from soils and natural waters. These isolates were then fractionated on Sephadex G-50[1] columns and refractionated into subfractions on Sephadex G-25 or G-100 (see Wershaw and Pinckney (1973) for a detailed description of the isolation and fractionation procedures used for the various samples). The low angle X-ray scattering measurements were made by use of the procedure outlined by Wershaw and others (1967). In our present study we were mainly interested in the smaller particles present in the various fractions, and therefore we used a 150-μm entrance slit and a 300-μm receiving slit for most of the measurements. Where measurements of the larger particles in a system were desired, an 80-μm entrance slit and a 200-μm receiving slit were used. Solutions of 0.5 percent (weight/volume) concentration of each of the fractions were prepared in various buffers (table 1). The solutions were put into a 1-mm-diameter, thin-walled quartz capillary tube for the low angle X-ray scattering measurements. The measurements of scattered intensity versus scattering angle were made on a Kratky low angle X-ray scattering goniometer. Partial monochromatization of the X-radiation was achieved by using a nickel filter and proportional detector coupled to a pulse height analyzer. The experimental data were smoothed by use of a sliding five point least-squares fit of the curve to a third degree polynomial, and the collimation effects were eliminated by a computer program developed by Lake (1967); weighting functions for our goniometer configurations were evaluated by the computer program of Buchanan and Hendricks (1967).

[1]Sephadex is a registered trademark of Pharmacia Fine Chemicals, Inc. Use of the term in this paper is for descriptive purposes only and does not constitute an endorsement of the product by the U.S. Geological Survey.

Table 1.—*Composition of buffer solutions for particle-size measurements*

[Data from Weast (1965)]

pH	0.1 M KH_2PO_4 (ml)	0.1 M $KHC_8H_4O_4$ (ml)	0.05 M Na_2PO_4 (ml)	0.1 M HCl (ml)	0.1 M NaOH (ml)
3.5	. . .	50	. . .	8.2	. . . .
5.0	. . .	50	. . .	. . .	23.9
7.0	50	. . .	. . .	. . .	29.1
8.0	50	. . .	. . .	. . .	46.1
11.0	. . .	. . .	50	. . .	4.1

DISCUSSION OF RESULTS

The scattered intensity as a function of scattering angle that is measured in a low angle X-ray scattering experiment is normally analyzed by the method of Guinier (see Guinier and Fournet, 1955). Guinier has shown that for an ensemble of randomly oriented, identical scattering particles in which there is no long range order, the scattered intensity, $I(h)$, may be represented to a close approximation by the equation

$$I(h) = I_e(h)Nn^2 e^{-h^2 R^2 /3}, \qquad (1)$$

where $I_e(h)$ is the scattered intensity that would result if a single electron were substituted for one of the scattering particles, N is the total number of particles in the ensemble, n is the number of electrons per particle, R is the radius of gyration of one of the particles, and $h = \frac{2\pi \sin 2\theta}{\lambda}$, where 2θ is the scattering angle and λ is the wavelength of the impinging X-radiation. This equation may be written as

$$\ln I(h) = \frac{-h^2R^2}{3} + \text{constant}. \qquad (2)$$

The radius of gyration of the particle, which is defined as the root mean square distance of the electrons in the particle from the center of charge, is a useful general parameter of comparative molecular or particle size.

From equation 2 it is seen that the radius of gyration may be easily calculated from the slope of a plot of ln I versus h^2; this is the so-called Guinier plot or curve. In a system in which all the scattering particles are of equal size the Guinier plot will be a straight line.

In a polydisperse system the Guinier plot, which is actually a summation of many Guinier plots, is no longer a straight line, but is concave up. If there are only a few widely different sizes of particles in the system it may be possible to discern discrete straight-line segments of the curve, and these may be used to calculate radii of gyration of the different particle sizes. In the general case, a Guinier plot of a polydisperse system of particles of uniform electron density will yield only the range of particle sizes present in the system, not the distribution of sizes (see Kratky, 1963). However, as we shall show, this information on the range of particle sizes is very useful in giving some insight into the chemical and physical properties of a polydisperse system.

In a system in which changes in the distribution of particle sizes can be brought about by altering one of the chemical or physical properties of the system, such as pH or ionic strength, then the change in distribution will be reflected in a change in the shape of the Guinier plot. If the polydispersity of the system is increased the plot will become more concave; if it is decreased the plot will flatten out and approach a straight line.

Solutions of sodium humate fractions and subfractions that we have examined by low angle X-ray scattering are polydisperse under most circumstances, and therefore the Guinier plots of these systems are commonly concave. However, pH changes alter the Guinier plots of different subfractions in three different ways. In the first group (group I) the concavity of the Guinier plots changes very little with changes in pH. In the second group (group II) the concavity decreases with increasing pH from 3.5 to 7; at pH 7 the plots are virtually straight, and then at pH values greater than 7 the concavity increases again. In the third group (group III) the concavity continually decreases with increasing pH. At pH values of about 10 some of the plots are almost straight.

There are some variations in behavior within each of the three different groups in our classification of the Guinier plots of sodium humate subfractions. These differences are most apparent in group III, and therefore we shall discuss it first. Group III may be divided into two subgroups: one in which there is a continual decrease in particle size with increasing pH; and one in which after reaching a minimum size with increasing pH, a further increase in pH causes some reaggregation. This reaggregation is evidenced by an increase in slope at low angles. The higher angle parts of the curves are virtually straight. Subfraction 3B (fig. 1) (see Wershaw and Pinckney, 1973, especially fig. 2, for identification of subfractions) is typical of the first subgroup and subfraction 4A (fig. 2) of the second subgroup; examples of the various groups will be discussed below.

In figure 1 we see that the curves for pH values greater than 3.5 are straight lines with equivalent slopes (R = 8.1 A) over practically the entire range of h values measured, and only at very low h values do the curves exhibit a slight concavity. This very low angle region was examined in more detail with an 80-μm entrance slit (fig. 3), and the following radii of gyration were measured: pH 3.5, 56.8 A; pH 5, 47.4 A; pH 7, 45.9 A; pH 8, 26.5 A; at pH 9.7 the particles were too small to give appreciable scattering with this slit system.

The Guinier curve of the Florida subfraction 4B (fig. 4) at pH 3.5 has a straight segment with a slope corresponding to a radius of gyration of 14.4 A. At smaller h values than shown in the figure the curve is concave up; this segment is due to particles with radii of gyration larger than 14.4 A. At pH 5 the radius of gyration determined from the straight segment of the curve is 8.9 A. The low angle end of the curve has much less curvature than the pH 3.5 curve. At pH 7, pH 8, and pH 9.4 the plots are virtually straight over the entire range of h values measured; however, the pH 7 curve gives a radius of gyration of 6.6 A, while at pH 8 the radius is 8.1 A and at pH 9.4 it is 8.4 A. Some of the increase in size from pH 7 to pH 9.4 may be due to changes in shape or degree of hydration of the particles in solution; however, as the volume of the 6.6-A particle is approximately half of that of the 8.4-A particle, an 8.4-A particle may simply be an aggregate of two 6.6-A particles.

In subfraction 4A (fig. 5) at pH values of about 3.5 a straight-line portion of the curve at very small angles (h^2 values from 2 to 7 $(A^{-1})^2$ has a slope corresponding to a radius of gyration of about 67 A. At even smaller angles the slope of the curve is still higher, corresponding to particles with radii of gyration larger than 67 A. At larger angles the scattered intensity of the pH 3.5 solution drops off very rapidly, the Guinier plot having a slope corresponding to a radius of gyration of about 16 to 17 A at h^2 values greater than 80×10^{-4}. The solutions of higher pH all exhibit much greater scattered intensities and lower slopes of the Guinier curves over most of the region examined. It is only at very low angles that scattered intensity from the pH 3.5 solution approaches that of the other solutions. This indicates that most of the particles in the pH 3.5 solution are greater than 67 A in radius of gyration, whereas in the higher pH solutions practically all the particles are much smaller than this. At pH 8 and pH 9.4 there appears to be some increase in the degree of aggregation. This increase may also be seen on the data measured at higher angles with the 150-μm front slit (see fig. 2).

In general all the subfractions of fraction 1 from the samples that we have studied fit into group I. In this group at pH values of 3.5 and below a marked increase in aggregation and particle size is detected; however, above pH 3.5 all the curves of a particular subfraction have virtually the same shape (see figs. 6 and 7), indicating that the distribution of particle sizes in these subfractions changes very little with increasing pH.

Several explanations could be proposed for the changes in the slope of the Guinier plots of the sodium humate subfractions that we have classified into groups II and III. These would include folding and unfolding of polymer chains, changes in the hydration of the molecules, and changes in the degree of aggregation of the molecules in solution. Although the first two possibilities may take some part in the observed flattening of the Guinier curves of the third group of subfractions, most of the change is apparently due to changes in degree of aggregation of the particles in solution. This explanation is preferred for three reasons: (1) the wide range of particle sizes that was detected, (2) the predominance of very large particles and the initiation of precipitation at low pH, and (3) the disappearance, at the higher pH values, of the very large particles which predominate at pH 3.5.

Although there is still insufficient evidence to assign mechanisms to the aggregation reactions of humic acid salts in

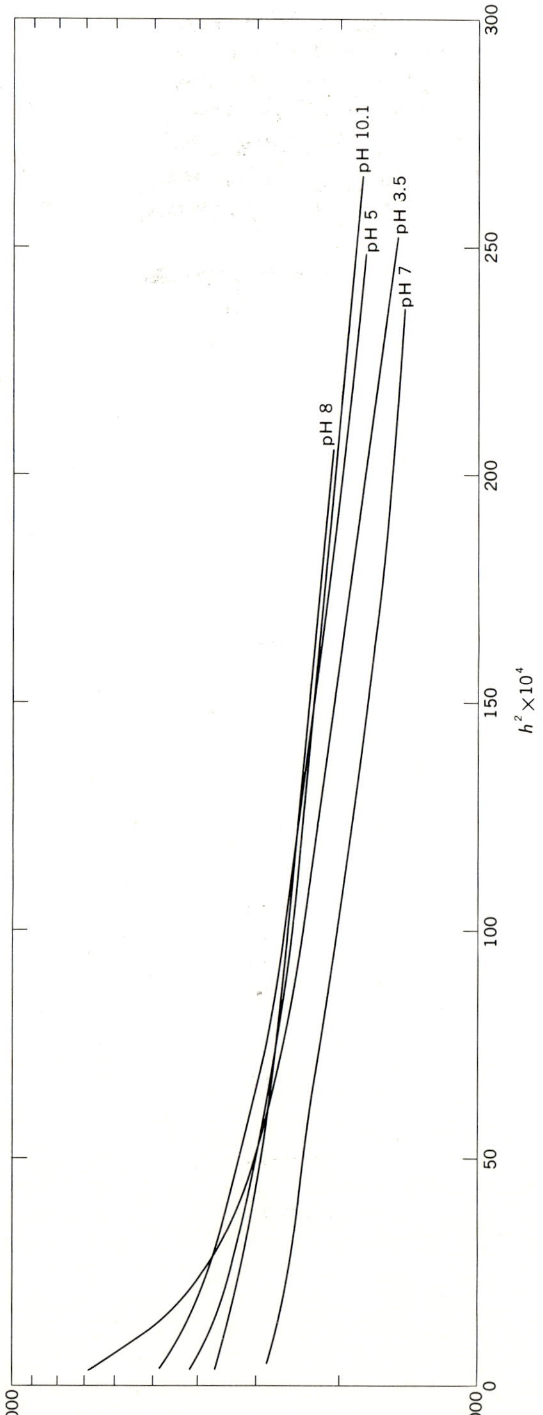

Figure 1.—Guinier plots of New Mexico subfraction 3B with 150-μm entrance slit.

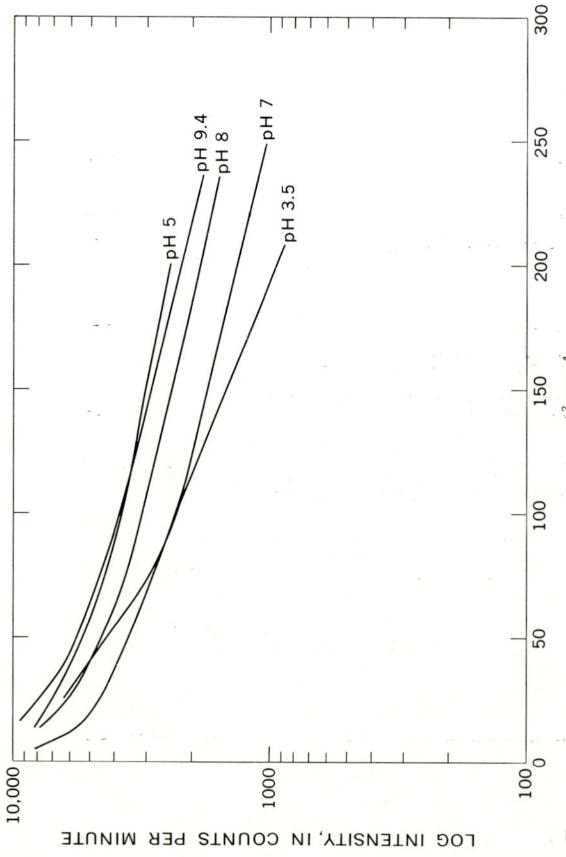

Figure 2.—Guinier plots of New Mexico subfraction 4A with 150-μm entrance slit.

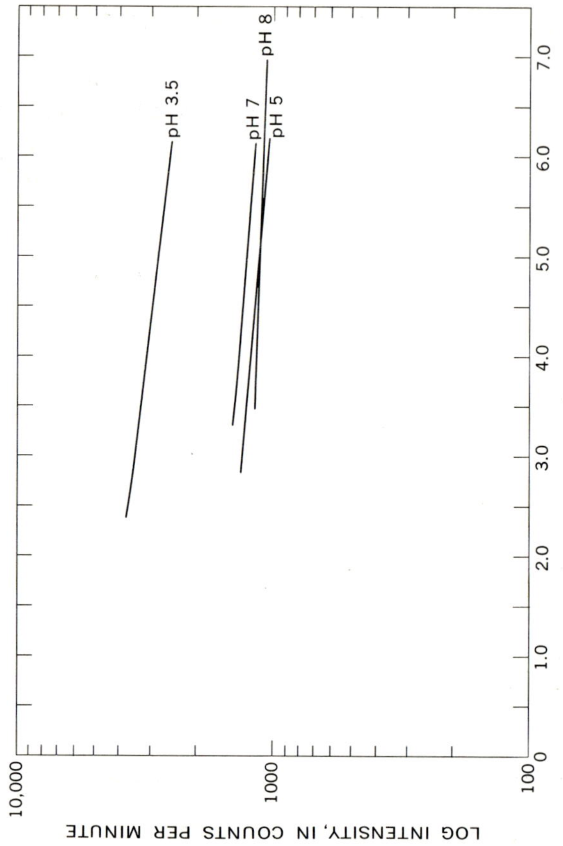

Figure 3.—Guinier plots of New Mexico subfraction 3B with 80-μm entrance slit.

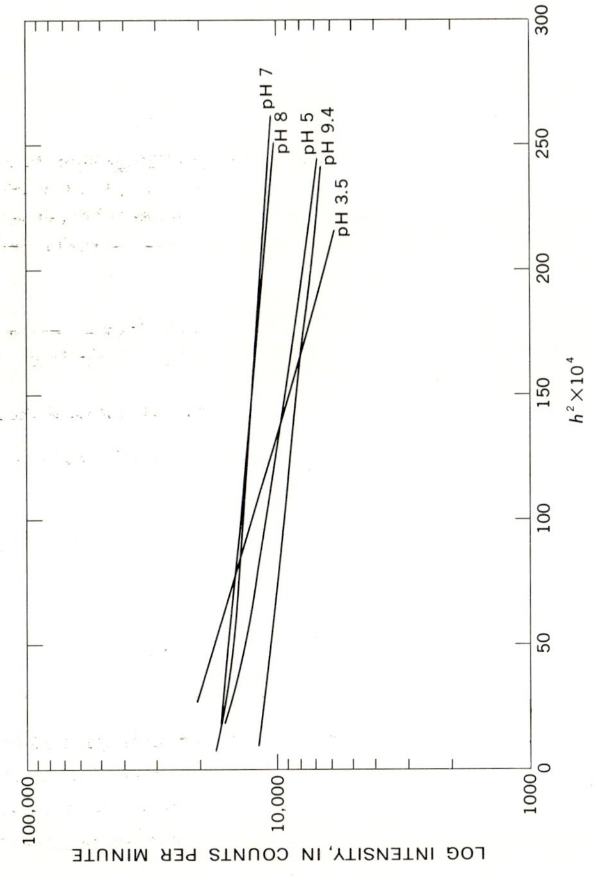

Figure 4.—Guinier plots of Florida subfraction 4B with 150-μm entrance slit.

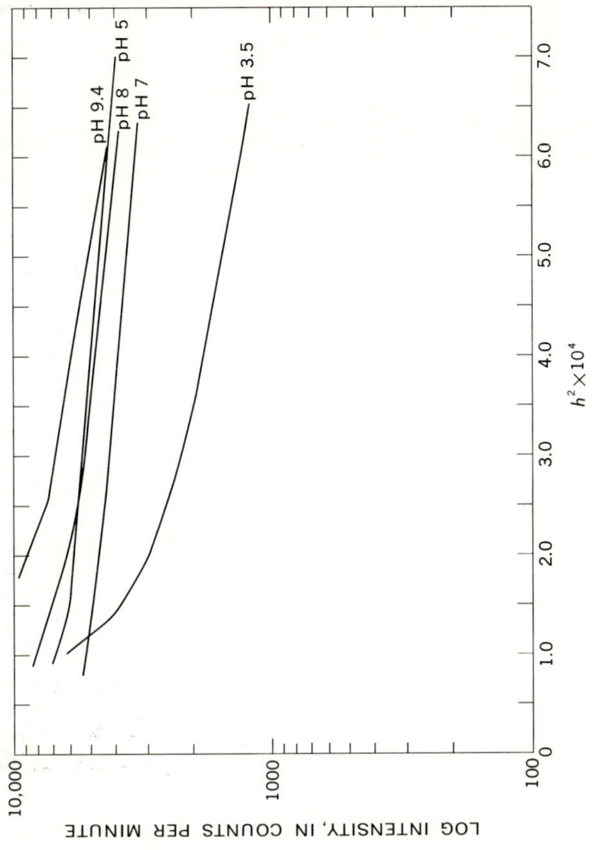

Figure 5.—Guinier plots of New Mexico subfraction 4A with 80-μm entrance slit.

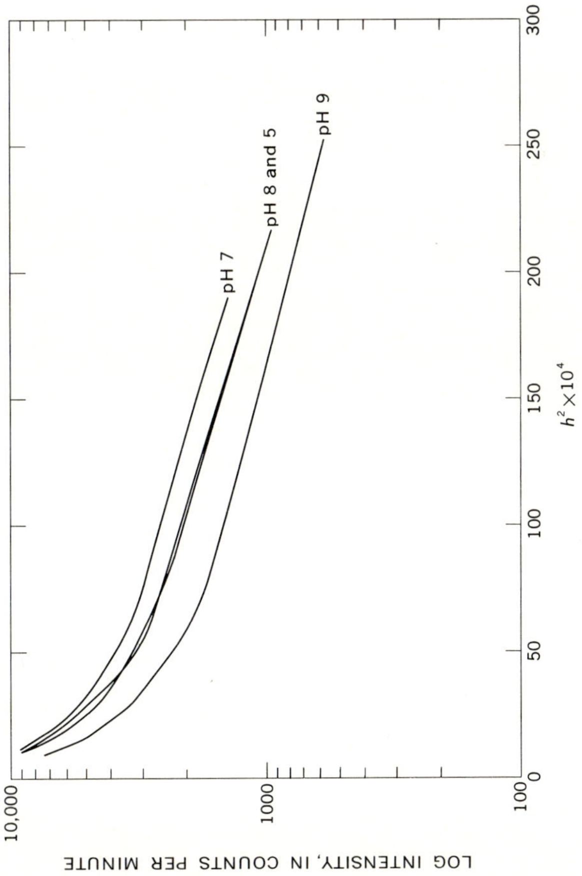

Figure 6.—Guinier plots of Florida subfraction 1A with 150-μm entrance slit.

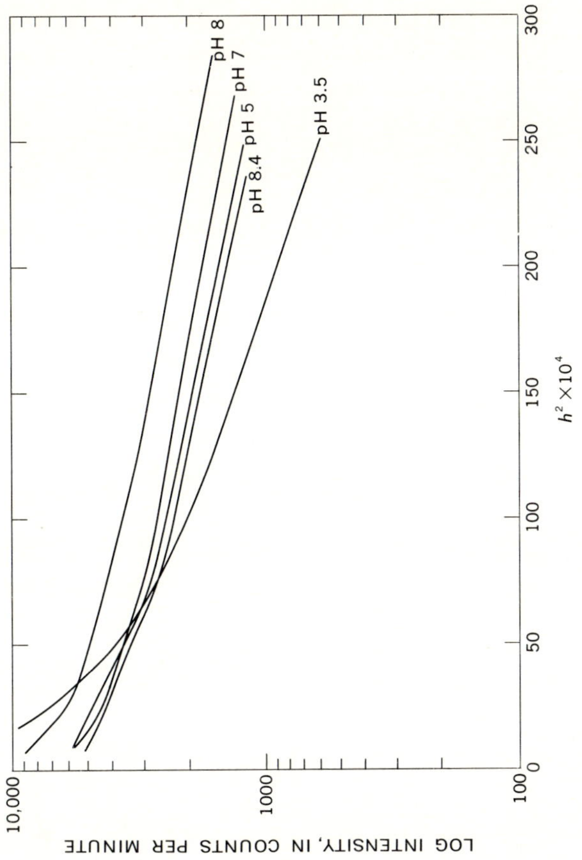

Figure 7.—Guinier plots of Florida subfraction 1B with 150-μm entrance slit.

solution, it is worthwhile to discuss several of the more likely possibilities. The mechanism or mechanisms that bring about the aggregation and disaggregation of humic acid particles will be determined by charge distribution and functional-group distribution on the exposed surfaces of the particles. A number of workers (see Wershaw and Pinckney, 1973, for references) have shown that humic acids contain abundant acid, phenol, and quinone and similar functional groups. These groups will normally participate in both intermolecular and intramolecular hydrogen bonding (Pauling, 1960).

In addition to hydrogen bonding, bonding due to coulombic attraction of charged particles will also take place in solutions of humic acid salts. In solutions, molecules of polyelectrolytes, such as the salts of humic acid, interact both with other solute molecules and with solvent molecules. These interactions are generally due to coulombic forces acting between charged sites on the molecules. Attractive forces between oppositely charged sites on the polyelectrolyte molecules or between shared counter ions and polyelectrolyte molecules will tend to cause aggregation of the polyelectrolyte molecules. This tendency to form aggregates will be opposed by the attractive forces between the polyelectrolyte molecules and the solvent molecules.

The charged sites on a polyelectrolyte molecule may arise in several different ways. Ionic compounds will dissociate in solution, producing molecules with charged sites. These charged sites may also result from charge-transfer reactions such as the transfer of an electron from a carbanion or a radical anion to another molecule (Szwarc, 1972a).

It is reasonable to assume that charge-transfer reactions between free radicals are important in the aggregation of humic acid salts in light of the high concentrations of free radicals that have been detected both in soils and humic acid preparations. Steelink and Tollin (1967) have shown that free radicals are present both in soils and in humic acid preparations. We have found very high free-radical concentrations in some of the sodium humate fractions that we have isolated, both in the solid phase and in solution. The free radicals detected in soils and humic acids may arise from the reduction of a diamagnetic molecule by a solvated electron (Kemp and Stone, 1962), enzymatic reactions, or photolysis (Commoner, 1961).

Szwarc (1970, 1972b) has reviewed the reactions of radical anions in solution with especial emphasis on electron-transfer processes. Several different types of electron-transfer reactions can lead to aggregation of the radicals. Disproportionate reactions may lead to the formation of dianions:

$$2\,B^- = B^{2-} + B.$$

The conversion of two mononegative ions into a dinegative ion and an uncharged species is facilitated by the aggregation of the dinegative ions with cations. Cations may be shared between both mononegative and polynegative anions, yielding aggregates in which the cations act as bridges between the anions. Adams, Staples, and Swzarc (1970), for example, have found evidence suggesting that in durosemiquinone systems triple ions of the type DQ, Na^+, DQ^- and DQ, $2Na^+$, DQ^- are formed. Triple ions are also formed between sodium ions and *p*-benzosemiquinone and purazine (Atherton, 1971). The formation of π-bonded charge-transfer complexes of aromatic molecules is common in solution (Effenberger and others, 1971); in some of these complexes a metal cation is sandwiched between two planar aromatic groups.

Further aggregation or polymerization can take place both in hydrogen-bonded and free-radical systems. One type of aggregation that has been intensively studied is that which takes place in the so-called living polymer systems (Szwarc, 1970). These are polymers which do not terminate, but which are able to continually add monomers to their terminal groups. Because the addition of the monomers is reversible, the living polymers may also disaggregate under suitable conditions. Thus a solution of living polymers eventually reaches a state of equilibrium.

Dipole-dipole interaction between the solvent and the polyelectrolyte molecules will cause solvent molecules to be attracted to the polyelectrolyte molecules. The cloud of solvent molecules around two polyelectrolyte molecules will interfere with their approaching each other to form a dimer. The amount of aggregation that takes place between polyelectrolyte molecules in solution will therefore be a function of the relative strengths of the solvent-solute interactions and the solute-solute interactions.

The fact that humic acid salts form molecular aggregates profoundly affects their behavior in natural water systems. One would expect them to behave like proteins and nucleic acids in living systems. Thus the enormous amount of work that has been done by those studying living systems should provide us with guidelines for study of organic polyelectrolytes in natural water systems.

SUMMARY

Fractions and subfractions of humic acid salts form molecular aggregates in solution, and the degree of aggregation is a function of both pH and concentration. Three different types of aggregation have been detected: (1) increased aggregation below pH 3.5 with little disaggregation above pH 3.5, (2) disaggregation up to pH 7 and then reaggregation above pH 7, and (3) a continual decrease in aggregation with increasing pH.

The changes in degree of aggregation of humic acid salts in solution probably reflect the interaction of several different bonding mechanisms. There are not yet enough data however, to elucidate the mechanisms of the interactions. An elucidation of the mechanisms of aggregation of humic acid salts should lead to greater understanding of the behavior of humic substances in natural water systems.

REFERENCES CITED

Adams, R. F., Staples, T. L., and Szwarc, Michael, 1970, ESR studies of electron-transfer reactions in the durosemiquinone system. Formation of the intermediate complex: Chemistry Physics Letters, v. 5, no. 8, p. 474–476.

Atherton, N. M., 1971, Recent magnetic resonance studies of ion-pairs—The complexes of O-dimesitoyl benzene and alkali metals: Internat. Cong. of Pure and Applied Chemistry, 23d, Boston, 1971, v. 4, p. 469–483.

Beeman, W. W., Kaesberg, P., Anderegg, J. W., and Webb, M. B., 1957, Size of particles and lattice defects, *in* Handbuch der Physik, v. 32: Berlin, Germany, Springer Verlag, p. 321–442.

Buchanan, M. G., and Hendricks, R. W., 1967, Program weight—A Fortran IV program for evaluation of weighting functions used in small-angle X-ray scattering: U.S. Atomic Energy Comm., Oak Ridge Natl. Lab. TM-1950, 54 p.

Commoner, Barry, 1961, Electron spin resonance studies of biochemical and biological systems: Acad. Royale Belgique Mem., Cl. Sci., v. 33, no. 3, p. 114–161.

Effenberger, Franz, Nagel, Klaus, and Agster, Wolfgang, 1971, Nucleophilic aromatic substitution—A new synthetic route to biphenyls: Angew. Chemie, internat. ed., v. 10, no. 8, p. 566–567.

Flaig, W. A. J., and Beutelspacher, H., 1968, Investigation of humic acids with the analytical ultracentrifuge, *in* Isotopes and radiation in soil organic-matter studies: Vienna, Internat. Atomic Energy Agency, p. 23–30.

Guinier, A., and Fournet, G., 1955, Small-angle scattering of X-rays: New York, John Wiley and Sons, Inc., 268 p.

Kemp, T. J., and Stone, J. J., 1962, Spectroscopic and kinetic aspects of reduction by solvated electrons: Advances in Chemical Physics, v. 4, p. 365–381.

Kratky, O., 1963, X-ray small angle scattering with substances of biological interest in diluted solutions: Prog. in Biophysics, v. 13, p. 107.

Lake, J. A., 1967, An iterative method of slit correcting small angle X-ray data: Acta Cryst., v. 23, p. 191–194.

Lindqvist, Ingvar, 1970, A small angle X-ray scattering study of sodium humate solutions: Acta Chemica Scandinavica, v. 24, p. 3068–3069.

Pauling, Linus, 1960, The nature of the chemical bond: Ithaca, N.Y., Cornell Univ. Press, 644 p.

Piret, E. L., White, R. G., Walther, H. C., Jr., and Madden, A. J., Jr., 1960, Some physico-chemical properties of peat humic acid: Royal Dublin Soc. Sci. Proc., ser. A, v. 1, p. 69–79.

Schachman, H. K., 1959, Ultracentrifugation in biochemistry: New York, Academic Press, 272 p.

Scheffer, Fritz, and Ulrich, Bernhard, 1960, Lehrbuch der Agrikulturchemie und Bodenkunde, III. Teil, Humus und Humusdungung, v. I: Stuttgart, Germany, F. Enke, 266 p.

Schnitzer, Morris, and Desjardins, J. G., 1962, Molecular and equivalent weights of the organic matter of a podzol: Soil Sci. Soc. America Proc., v. 26, p. 362–365.

Steelink, Cornelius, and Tollin, Gordon, 1967, Free radicals in soil: Soil Biochemistry, v. 1, p. 147–169.

Stevenson, F. J., Van Winkle, Q., and Martin, W. P., 1953, Physicochemical investigations of clay-adsorbed organic colloids: Soil Sci. Soc. America Proc., v. 17, p. 31–34.

Szwarc, Michael, 1970, Studies of ions and ion pairs: Science, v. 170, p. 23–31.

——1972a, Radical anions and carbanions as donors in electron-transfer processes: Accounts Chem. Research, v. 5, p. 169–176.

——1972b, Concept of ion pairs, *in* Szwarc, Michael, ed., Ions and ion pairs in organic reactions, v. 1: New York, John Wiley and Sons, Inc., 399 p.

Weast, R. C., ed., 1965, Handbook of chemistry and physics: Cleveland, The Chemical Rubber Co., 1713 p.

Wershaw, R. L., and Burcar, P. J., 1967, Physical-chemical properties of naturally occurring polyelectrolytes—I. Sodium humate: Am. Water Resources Conf., 3d, San Francisco, Calif., Nov. 8–10, 1967, Proc., p. 351–364.

Wershaw, R. L., Burcar, P. J., Sutula, C. L., and Wiginton, B. J., 1967, Sodium humate solution studied with small-angle X-ray scattering: Science, v. 157, no. 3795, p. 1429–1431.

Wershaw, R. L., Heller, S. J., and Pinckney, D. J., 1970, Measurement of the molecular size of a sodium humate fraction: Advances X-ray Analysis, v. 13, p. 609–617.

Wershaw, R. L., and Pinckney, D. J., 1971, Association and dissociation of a humic acid fraction as a function of pH, *in* Geological Survey Research 1971: U.S. Geol. Survey Prof. Paper 750-D, p. D216–D218.

——1973, The fractionation of humic acids from natural water systems: U.S. Geol. Survey Jour. Research, v. 1, no. 3, p. 361–366.

Jour. Research U.S. Geol. Survey
Vol. 1, No. 6, Nov.-Dec. 1973, p. 709—717

FLUORESCENT SPECTROSCOPY, A TECHNIQUE FOR CHARACTERIZING SURFACE FILMS

By MARVIN C. GOLDBERG and DAVID H. DEVONALD III, Lakewood, Colo.

Abstract.—A relationship is established between fluorescent spectra obtained by using a light path through the liquid solution and the fluorescent spectra obtained by a direct reading of surface reflection (remote sensing). A brief review of quantum fundamentals provides the necessary information to conclude that "see-through" and reflectance spectra are identical in wavelength response. Many floating films contain fluorescent materials; thus fluorescent spectroscopic techniques were used to obtain the fluorescent spectra of lube oil, crude oil, and lignosulfonic acid in an effort to detect, identify, and quantify these representative fluorescent materials in water solutions. For each material tested the emission maximum was established. The emission maximum was then held constant while the absorption spectrum was recorded and the absorption maximum established. The complete spectral curves are presented.

The interface between surface-water bodies and the gaseous atmosphere generally contains partially miscible floating films. These films are part of the water-quality regime; they change the evaporation kinetics and take part in the chemical hydrodynamics of dissolved and suspended material transport. The materials that comprise the films react by mechanisms such as solubilization, solution, sorption, and ion exchange. Consequently, surface films can be one of the major regulatory parameters of water quality in a hydrologic system. It is necessary to understand the mechanistic reactions of the films and to relate these data to the economics and feasability of water use and reuse (Goldberg and others, 1973; Goldberg and Weiner, 1972).

Most of the literature available concerning surface films describes the areal extent and the thickness of these films (see for example, Goolsby, 1971; Klemas, 1971; Chandler, 1971; and Measures and Bristow, 1971). Some attempts have been made to correlate surface films with undesirable ecological manifestations (Zobell, 1971; Duce and others, 1972). Yet, there remains the important aspect of correlating surface films with other water-quality variables to gain a more complete understanding of hydrologic systems.

This report establishes the background for choice of methods, techniques, and the application of specific optical phenomena that are best adapted to the study of surface films. Data are herein found that relate only to fluorescent spectroscopy using "through-the-solution" light paths. A strong case, however, is presented for the use of this method for recording fluorescent "see-through" response and correlating it with that obtained by fluorescence recorded from surface reflection.

This report also presents the fluorescent spectra of a few common materials that form surface films.

In recent years most of the surface-film data available were collected for purposes of describing oil spills. It is the common practice of investigators in this field to describe floating films by areal extent, thickness, and composition.

When referring to units of measurement for surface films it should be realized that an immiscible liquid can be described in concentration units. The criterion used to label a liquid system as an emulsion or an immiscible film is the same criterion for application of concentration units to discuss the amount of material A present in material B in two-component immiscible liquid systems. As long as an emulsion exists, concentration units can be used. Because see-through techniques are used, the Beer-Lambert relationship is presented wherein the luminosity of the solutions is discussed as the component variables—extinction coefficient, light path, and solution concentration. For this reason we discuss the standard and unknown solutions in terms of concentrations.

A remote laser fluorosensor (see Stoertz and others, 1969) can be used to trace industrial effluents and urban-runoff effluents in concentration ranges from 0.5 to 100 mg/l. The fluorescent-sensing technique will easily adapt to remote use (Weinman, NASA, written commun., 1972) with distances ranging from 20 to 2,000 feet from the sample. A boat or truck-mounted unit, and conceivably an aircraft-mounted unit could be used to rapidly scan large water areas.

FLUORESCENCE

Three components of the fluorescent effect that can be measured are: the wavelength maxima of emission, the wavelength maxima of absorption, and the fluorescent decay time. If all three are known it may be possible to identify unknown compounds. In this study only the emission and absorption were measured. The decay time can be measured with a rapidly pulsed excitation source and a synchronized fast-response detector.

Each one of the three components of the fluorescent effect characterizes the compound under observation (Parker, 1968).

Theory

From a quantum-mechanical standpoint, the solution of the Schroedinger equation yields eigenvalues that describe the energy state of an atom or molecule (Herzberg, 1945, 1950; Becker, 1969). Thus, a simplistic definition of fluorescence is given in figure 1 by plotting interatomic distance versus molecular energy eigenvalues.

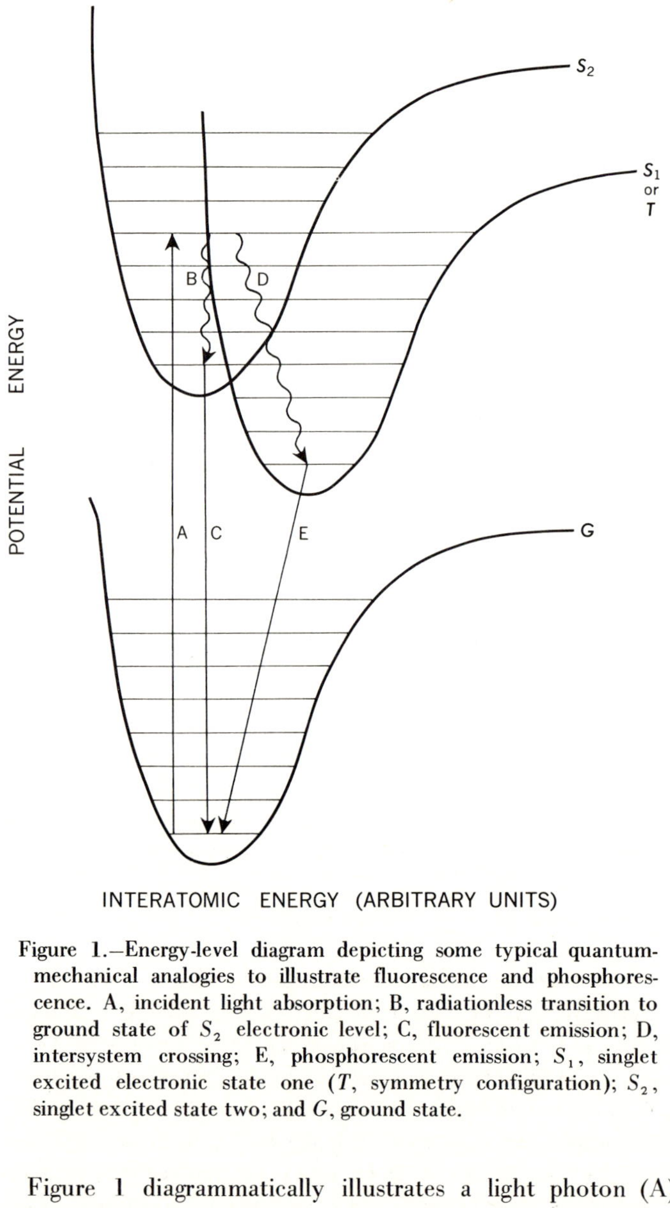

Figure 1.—Energy-level diagram depicting some typical quantum-mechanical analogies to illustrate fluorescence and phosphorescence. A, incident light absorption; B, radiationless transition to ground state of S_2 electronic level; C, fluorescent emission; D, intersystem crossing; E, phosphorescent emission; S_1, singlet excited electronic state one (T, symmetry configuration); S_2, singlet excited state two; and G, ground state.

Figure 1 diagrammatically illustrates a light photon (A) activating the ground-electronic state of an atom or molecule. The photon energizes the molecule to an excited electronic state. This excitation is instantaneous. The process of losing the excitation energy can take place in several ways. A radiationless process can occur to lower the energy level to the vibrational ground state (B) of electronic level S_2. The sequential photon emission (C) that takes place as the energy is further lowered from the ground vibrational level of electronic state S_2 to the ground state G is called fluorescence. A time delay may be evidenced between molecular energy stimulation and light emission, caused by the time it takes for a radiationless transition (B). If this time delay is lengthened by a process such as intersystem crossing (D) then the decay process is known as phosphorescence (E). The definitive difference between fluorescence and phosphorescence is the length of time between photon stimulation and photon emission. It is usually accepted as a definition that elapsed times of 10^{-9} seconds or greater categorize the phenomena as phosphorescence.

Fluorescence is a short, time-differential effect and phosphorescence a long, time-differential effect when measured from the time of the original light quantum absorption. The original absorption is usually 10^{-15} seconds duration. Fluorescence is described by the relationship

$$I = I_0 e^{-t/\tau}, \qquad (1)$$

where I = fluorescent intensity at time t,
I_0 = maximum fluorescent intensity during excitation,
t = time elapsed since removing the source of excitation, and
τ = average lifetime of the excited state.

τ is defined as the time for the fluorescent intensity to fall to $1/e$ of its initial value. It ranges in value from 10^{-10} to 10^{-5} seconds for some selected condensed ring molecules. τ can be approximated by the formula $1/\tau \approx 10^4 \cdot \epsilon$ max (Parker, 1968) where ϵ is the molecular extinction coefficient defined as

$$\log_{10} I_0/I = \epsilon c d,$$

where ϵ = the molecular extinction coefficient,
c = concentration of the water solution, and
d = optical path through the solution.

When this formula is used, the radiation lifetime can be approximated. If ϵ max is about 10^5, then the radiation lifetime is in the order of 10^{-9} seconds. To measure radiation lifetimes would necessitate a pulsed light source in the order of a nanosecond and a fast time readout. Such measurements can be obtained remotely by use of a pulsed laser such as a doubled YAG (yttrium, aluminum, garnet) and a high-speed, dual-trace oscilloscope to record the return signal. (Some comprehensive references on fluorescence are: Phillips, 1969; Guilbault, 1967; Udenfried, 1962; Berlman, 1965.)

Detection of fluorescent materials depends upon the quantum yield of fluorescence (ϕ). The ϕ is equal to (number of quanta emitted)/(number of quanta absorbed) or more appropriately:

$$I = I_0 \epsilon c d \text{ and } \phi = \frac{I}{I_0 \epsilon c d}. \quad (2)$$

Quantum efficiencies as measured by Weber and Teale (1957) are given in table 1 for selected fluorescent compounds.

Table 1.—*Quantum efficiencies (ϕ) of selected fluorescent compounds in water solution*

[Values from Weber and Teale (1957)]

Solute	Solvent	ϕ
Fluorescein	Water at pH 7	0.65
1 Amino-napthalene 3:6:8-sulfonate.	Water	.15
9 Amino-acridine	do	.98
Uranyl acetate	do	.04
Indole	do	.45
Skatole	do	.42

Measurement of oil in water

Goolsby (1971) has measured oil in environmental surface waters. Klemas (1971) reports fluorescence maxima in oils excited by ultraviolet radiation. The results of some work done by Klemas are shown in figure 2. The spectra are of diesel oil, quinine sulfate, and natural crude oil.

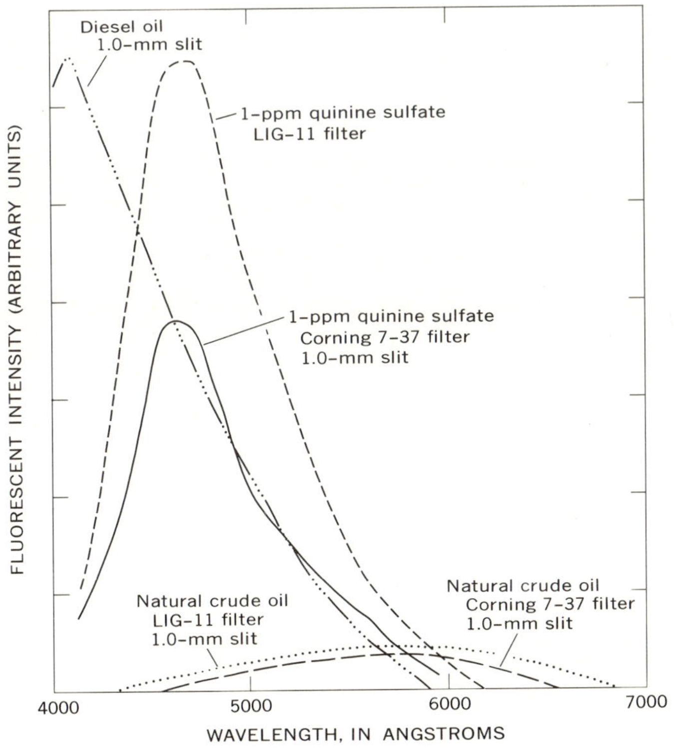

Figure 2.—Fluorescent spectra of diesel oil, quinine sulfate, and natural crude oil (after Klemas, 1971).

EQUIPMENT

All the measurements reported in the following section were made in our laboratory on an Aminco Bowman SPF spectrophotofluorometer.[1] This instrument has two single monochromators, one for the excitation source and one for scanning the fluorescent return signal (Udenfried, 1962). (See fig. 3.)

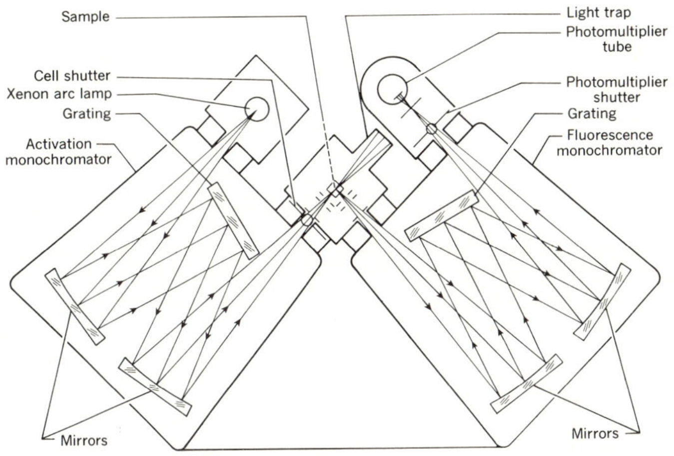

Figure 3.—Optical system of the Aminco Bowman spectrophotofluorometer.

OPTICAL SYSTEM

This double monochromator system allows a choice of excitation frequencies between 200 and 800 nanometers and a complete scan of fluorescent emission frequencies between 200 and 800 nm.

The light source is a xenon flash lamp. For purposes of broadband excitation it is sufficient. To achieve greater sensitivity a laser source should be substituted. This latter source is monochromatic. Usually there is an easily determined optimum wavelength for the fluorescent effect, as was illustrated in figure 1. In most instances a laser can be chosen that will furnish discrete light frequencies closely matching this optimum wavelength.

Measurements

A sample of crude oil donated by The Refinery Co., Denver, Colo., labeled as a crude oil from Colorado fields, was used to obtain standard fluorescent emission spectra (see fig. 4). Spectra from the above reference sample are representative of an oil film and indicate the complexity of fluorescent response from mixtures of petroleum hydrocarbons.

The fluorescent emission spectrum was scanned at several excitation frequencies in order to find the optimum excitation

[1] The use of named products in this report is for identification only and does not imply endorsement by the U.S. Geological Survey.

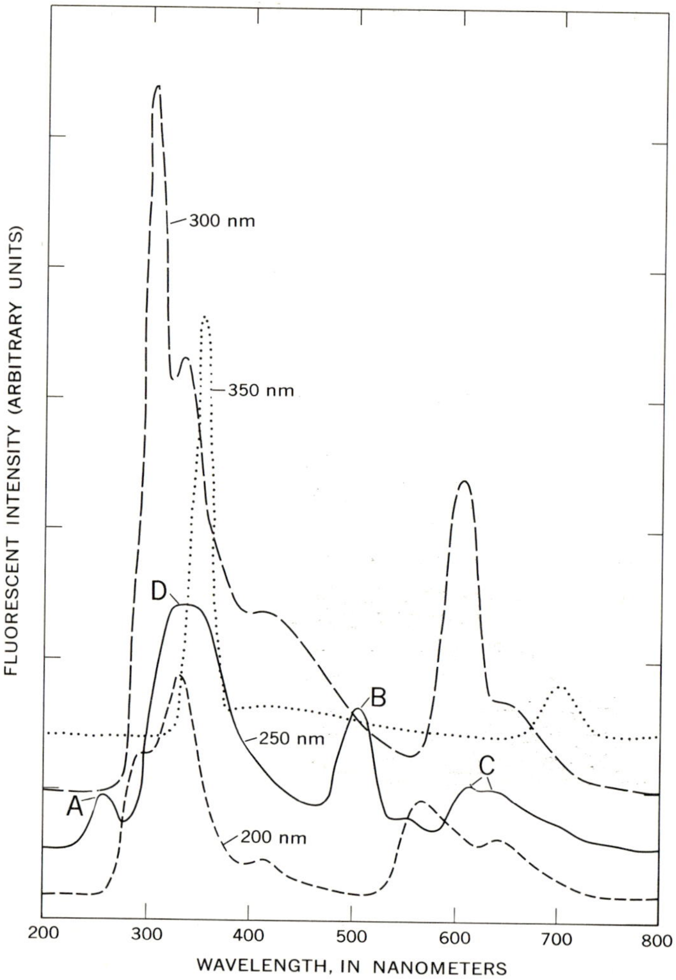

Figure 4.—Fluorescent emission of a crude-oil sample at excitation wavelengths of 200, 250, 300, and 350 nm. The peaks on the 250-nm excitation wavelength (solid line) are as follows: A, Tyndall and Rayleigh scattering; B, second order Tyndall and Rayleigh scattering; C, second order fluorescent scattering; D, fluorescent emission.

energy. Excitation frequencies evaluated were 200, 250, 300, and 350 nm. The fluorescent peak center shifts as follows:

Excitation frequency (nm)	*Fluorescent peak center (nm)*
200	330
250	340
300	340
350	...

Because the fluorescent peak center of interest responds at about 340 nm, the optimum excitation frequency must be less than 340 nm. The optimum excitation frequency was determined to be 250 nm. Most of the fluorescent emission data were recorded at this wavelength.

The solid line on figure 4 is a fluorescent spectrum of crude oil taken at excitation wavelength of 250 nm. As both fluorescence and scattering take place when the incident radiation impinges upon the sample, there will be fluorescent radiation at the same wavelength as the excitation wavelength and scattered radiation at its multiples. Note the Tyndall and Rayleigh scattering peak (A) at the fluorescent emission frequency of 250 nm and again at 500 nm. The peak (B) at 500 nm is a second order Rayleigh and Tyndall scattering, and the peak (C) from 600 to 700 nm is the second order fluorescent scatter. The peak of the oil fluorescent emission (D) occurs between 300 and 400 nm.

If the emission frequency maximum is held constant while the absorption frequency is scanned, the absorption maximum is obtained. This measurement indicates the frequencies of greatest light absorption, and is another of the three information factors that tend to pinpoint the identity from the luminous activity of the solute.

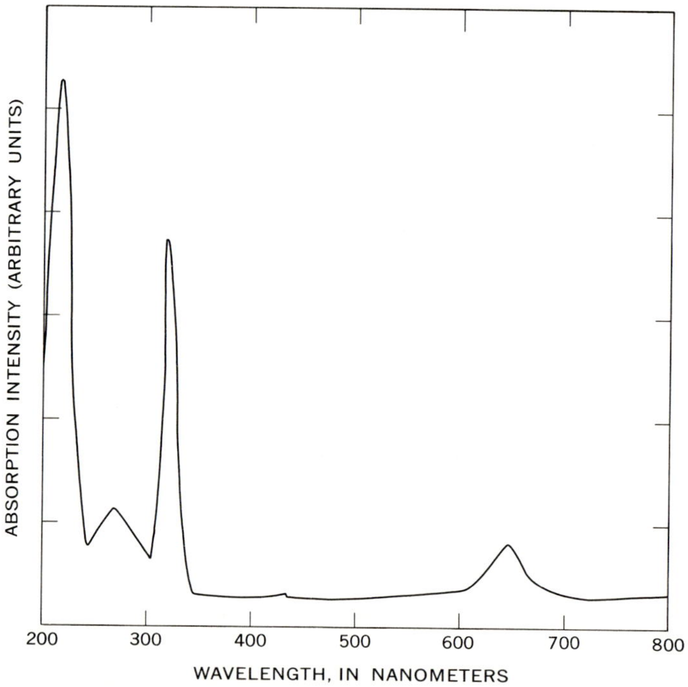

Figure 5.—Crude-oil absorption spectrum; emission wavelength set at 324 nm.

Figure 5 is an absorption spectrum of crude oil taken at emission frequency of 324 nm. The absorption maximum is 220 nm.

Another scattering effect that can appear in these samples is Raman scattering (Parker, 1959); it is a weak scattering effect that shows up at frequencies below the excitation frequency and is usually manifested as a Stokes effect. The anti-Stokes line also occurs but is hard to observe because it is three orders of magnitude less responsive than the Stokes line.[2] Unlike

[2] A Stokes line is a line that occurs below the excitation frequency. The terminology emanates from Stokes law of fluorescence; namely, scattered radiation never has a higher frequency than the excitation radiation.

Tyndall or Rayleigh scattering, the Raman scattered light is manifested by a frequency shift that is characteristic of the scattering molecule. Indeed, the frequency shift for a given molecule is independent of the frequency of the incident light.

Raman scattering from water results in a return signal that may complicate the fluorescent spectrum; thus, it must be considered in interpretation of fluorescent spectra.

Raman return signals usually are three to eight orders of magnitude below the energy of the incident light. When water is exposed to an excitation wavelength of 250 nm, the Raman shift is about 20 nm. Figure 6 is a graph of Raman shift versus excitation frequency for water. For organic compounds the Raman return signal occurs at a lesser wavelength displacement than for water. A few typical examples are listed in table 2.

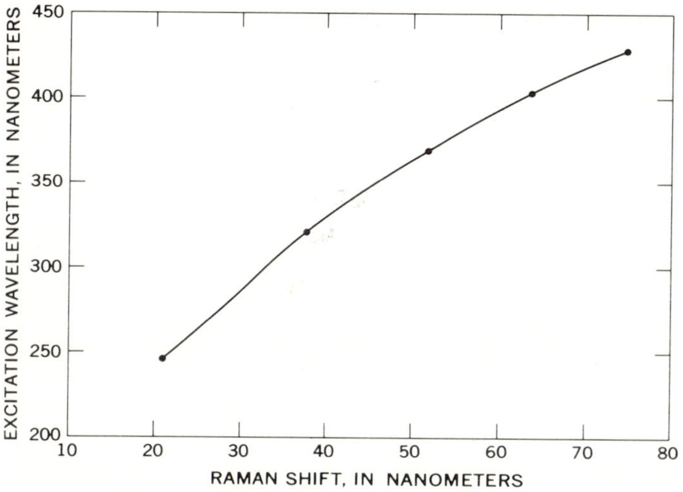

Figure 6.—Raman scatter as a function of excitation wavelength for water.

The fluorescent peaks are quantitatively related to concentration as shown by equation 2. Figure 7 is an illustration of spectra taken of three aqueous concentrations of the crude oil from Colorado fields. Integration of the area under the fluorescent peaks yields a linear calibration curve (see fig. 8). The concentration ranged over less than one order of magnitude.

A second oil sample was similarly calibrated. This sample was a government-specified, low-viscosity lube oil.[3] It should have similar characteristics to the crude oil standard. Density of the crude oil was 0.88 and density of the lube oil was 1.018.

Figure 9 is an illustration of the emission spectra of lube oil and crude oil from Colorado fields. The fluorescent response is greater for the lube oil; also, the peak is sharper and more symmetrical. A peak center occurs at 350 nm. Compounds giving similar fluorescent responses are anisole and tryptophan among others.

[3]Designated as: Lube oil I.C.E.; subzero Mil L-102958; Federal stock No. 9150-242-7603; batch, 3424; quality, S-5; density, 1.018.

Table 2.—*Most prominent Raman bands*
[Parker, 1968]

	Excitation wavelength (nm)				
	248	313	365	405	436
Water	271	350	416	469	511
Ethanol	267	344	409	459	500
Cyclohexane	267	344	408	458	499
Carbon tetrachloride	...	320	375	418	450
Chloroform	...	346	410	461	502

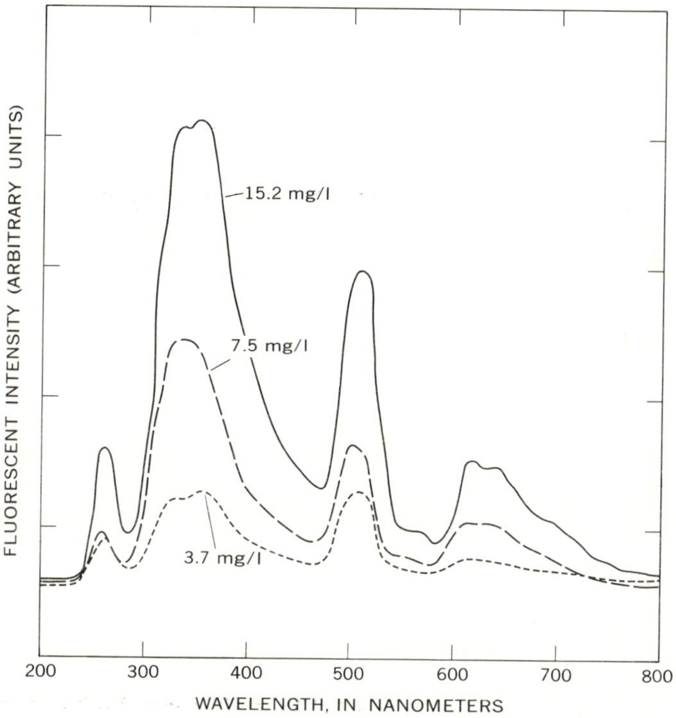

Figure 7.—Emission spectra of crude oil in concentrations of 3.7, 7.5, and 15.2 mg/l. The excitation wavelength was 250 nm.

Because these fluorescent compounds are chemically very similar, the lube oil and crude oil wavelengths of maximum fluorescent emission are also similar as illustrated in figure 9. The emission and absorption maxima are as follows:

	Emission maxima (nm)	*Absorption maxima (nm)*
Lube oil	348	228–292
Crude oil	300, 320	220

Figure 10 is a scan of the absorption of the two materials. This illustrates the broad absorption band for lube oil and the more narrow but more intense absorption band found in crude oil.

Environmental films

The Houston Ship Channel is one of many loading and pumping dock areas where one finds surface films. Samples of water were collected from the Houston Ship Channel by the

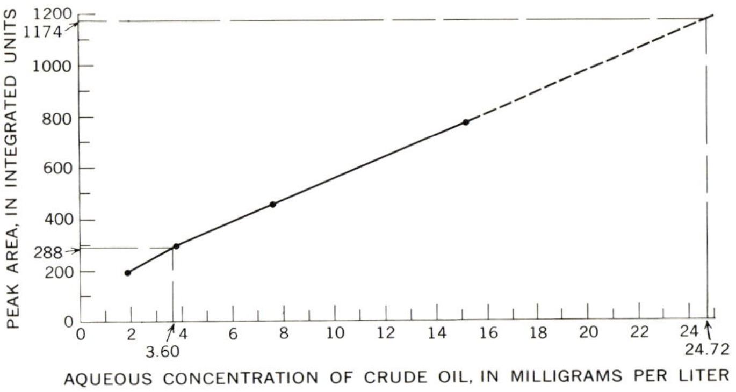

Figure 8.—Integrated peak area as a function of aqueous concentration of crude oil.

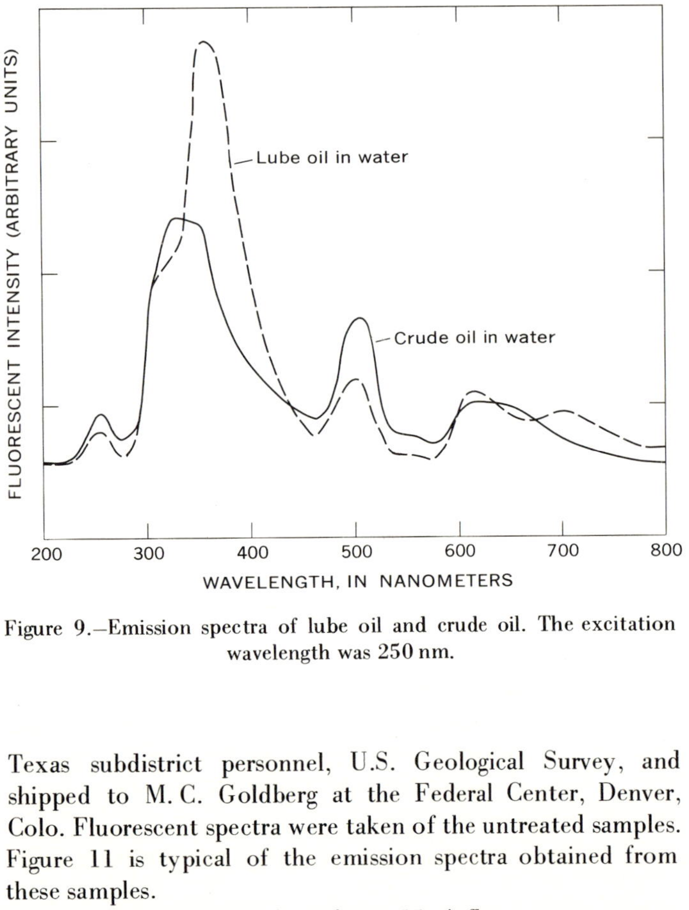

Figure 9.—Emission spectra of lube oil and crude oil. The excitation wavelength was 250 nm.

Texas subdistrict personnel, U.S. Geological Survey, and shipped to M. C. Goldberg at the Federal Center, Denver, Colo. Fluorescent spectra were taken of the untreated samples. Figure 11 is typical of the emission spectra obtained from these samples.

Two facts are evident from figure 11. A fluorescent-response peak area ranging from 325 to 400 nm exists, and a further area either of fluorescent or phosphorescent response shows up from 400 to 470 nm. Without further information, such as fluorescent decay time and (or) specific chemical identification via other methods, it is not possible to determine the chemical composition of the fluorescing compounds. It is possible to bracket the fluorescent response from certain known materials such as lube oil or crude oil samples. Within these narrow comparison limits, fluorescent emissions can be interpreted. These limits broaden as the data concerning the

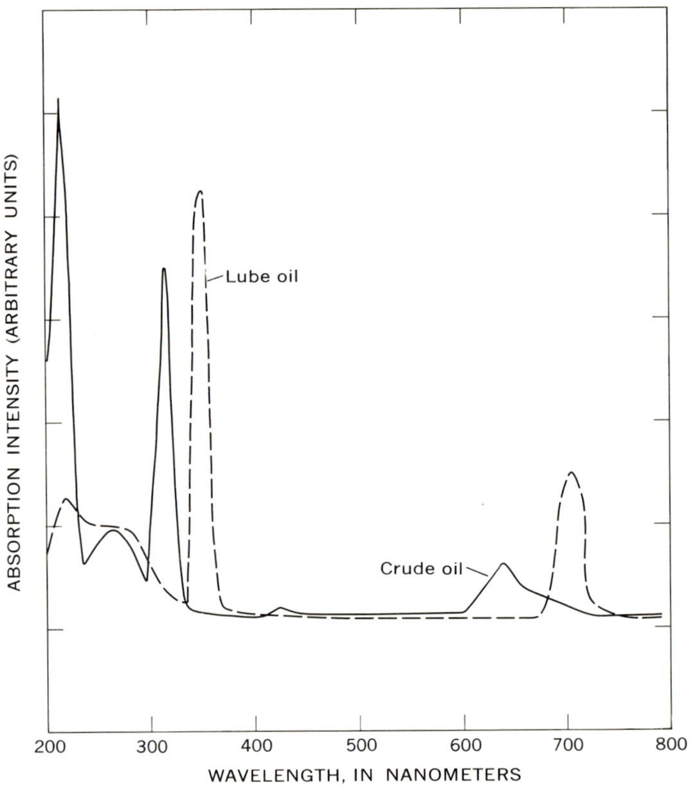

Figure 10.—Absorption maxima of crude oil and lube oil.

fluorescent compounds are increased. Many analytical procedures rely on the high sensitivity of fluorescence, but measurements are made only after a specific chemical separation insures that one is measuring the fluorescence from a pure compound.

Figure 12 illustrates the absorption spectrum of water taken from the Houston Ship Channel; emission and absorption maxima are shown in the tabulation below. As the fluorescent emission seemed to peak at 360 nm and then again at 495 nm the scan was run at 350 nm. A sharp absorption peak is present at 235 nm and a medium broad peak at 296 nm.

	Emission maxima (nm)	*Absorption maxima (nm)*
Water from Houston Ship Channel.	360(b), 400(b)	235(s), 296(b)

A comparison of the spectral fluorescent emission response from the two oil references and the Houston Ship Channel sample 3 is shown in figure 13. The fluorescent response of the Houston Ship Channel sample 3 begins at 320 nm, but the fluorescent response of both the crude and lube oils starts at 245 nm. The ship channel sample has a primary peak center at 360 nm and a secondary peak center at 400 nm. If the total peak area from the ship channel sample spectrum that lies within the crude oil reference wavelengths were considered to be oil, and the intensity of response between the Colorado

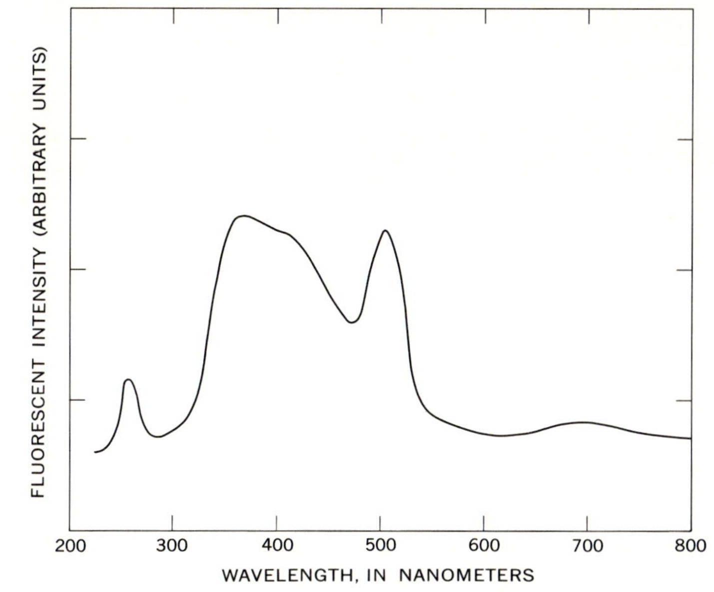

Figure 11.—Fluorescent emission spectrum of the Houston Ship Channel sample 3. The excitation wavelength was 250 nm.

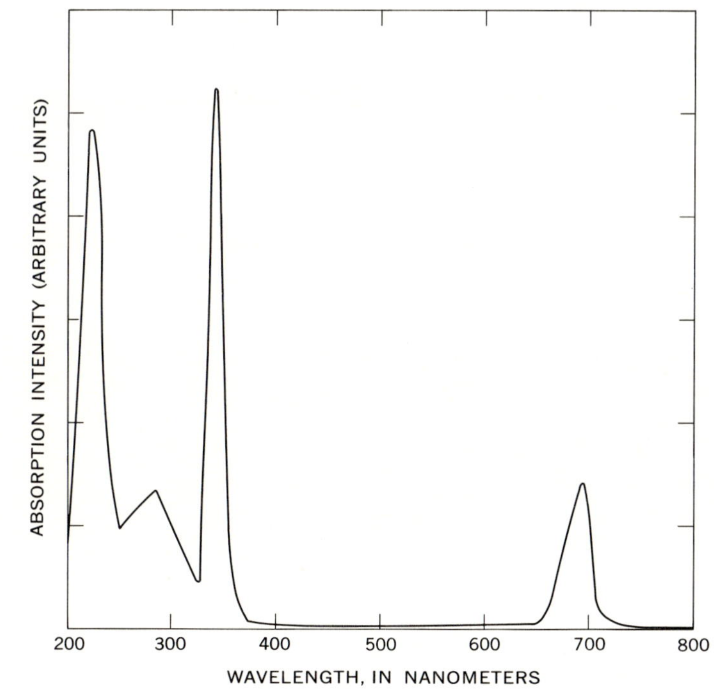

Figure 12.—The absorption spectrum of water from the Houston Ship Channel. The frequency of emission was set at 350 nm while the excitation frequency was scanned.

crude oil reference and the ship channel sample were equal, then there would be 3.6 mg/l of oil in the ship channel sample. This figure is not accurate but represents the type of data to be obtained from more refined fluorescent measurements. If the presence of oil could be confirmed by ground truth, that is, chemical laboratory analysis, then with some further

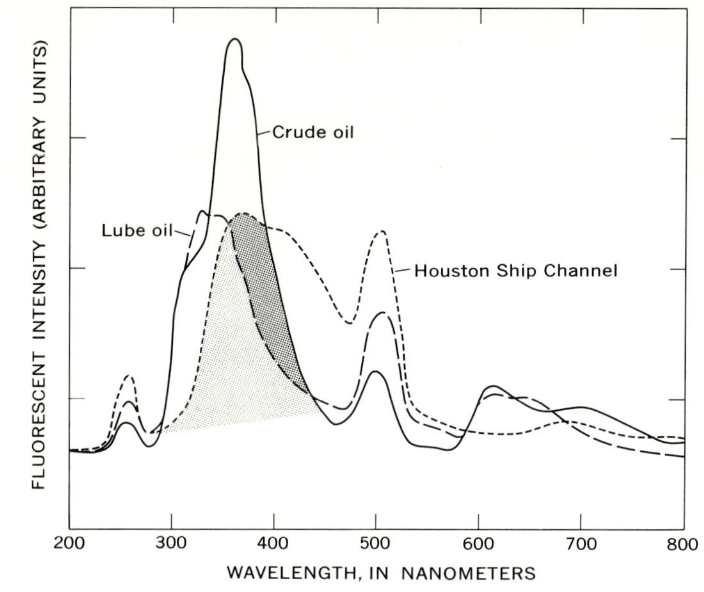

Figure 13. Fluorescent emission spectra of crude oil, lube oil, and Houston Ship Channel sample 3. The excitation wavelength was 250 nm.

chemical work such as liquid chromatography or thin-layer separations supported by infrared, ultraviolet, and mass-spectrometric identification, this type of spectral curve can be qualitatively and quantitatively complete (Guilbault, 1967; and Berlman, 1965).

Lignosulfonic acid

A characteristic material released from paper-pulp plants into holding ponds or water courses is lignosulfonic acid. This material has a natural fluorescence and seems suited as a tracer for waste discharge from paper-pulp plants.

Figure 14 is a set of concentration-dependent spectra illustrating the fluorescent response of this material. The fluorescent emission peak centers at 380 nm. Measures and Bristow (1971) report the limiting fluorescent sensitivity for calcium lignosulfonate (CA-L) at 0.5 mg/l. Thruston (1970) has shown in some streams a Ca-L background of 1–2 mg/l.

The absorption spectrum of lignosulfonic acid is given in figure 15; emission and absorption maxima are shown in the tabulation below.

	Emission maxima (nm)	*Absorption maxima (nm)*
Ligno-sulfonic acid.	380 (b)	287 (s), 245 (s), 325 (b)

It is apparent that from 220 nm to 320 nm, very strong absorption takes place. Such broadband excitation facilitates the use of broadband light sources.

DISCUSSION AND CONCLUSIONS

This study shows that the compounds chosen for investigation can be characterized by fluorescent emission and absorp-

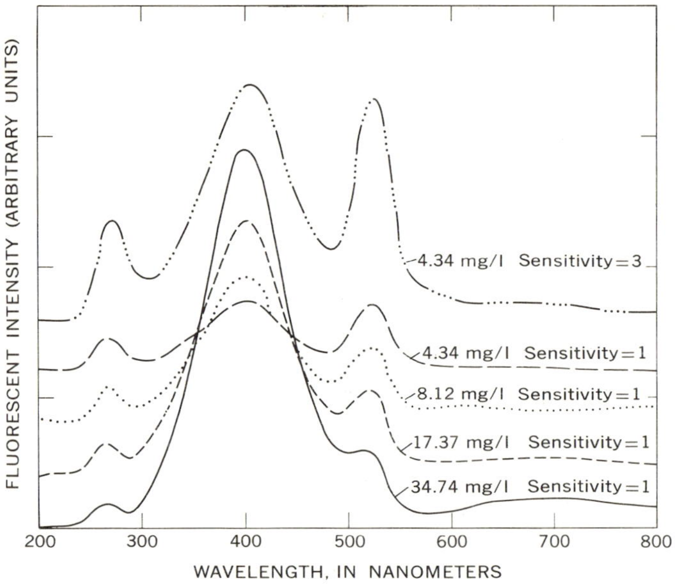

Figure 14.—Fluorescent emission spectra of lignosulfonic acid at different concentrations. The excitation wavelength was 250 nm.

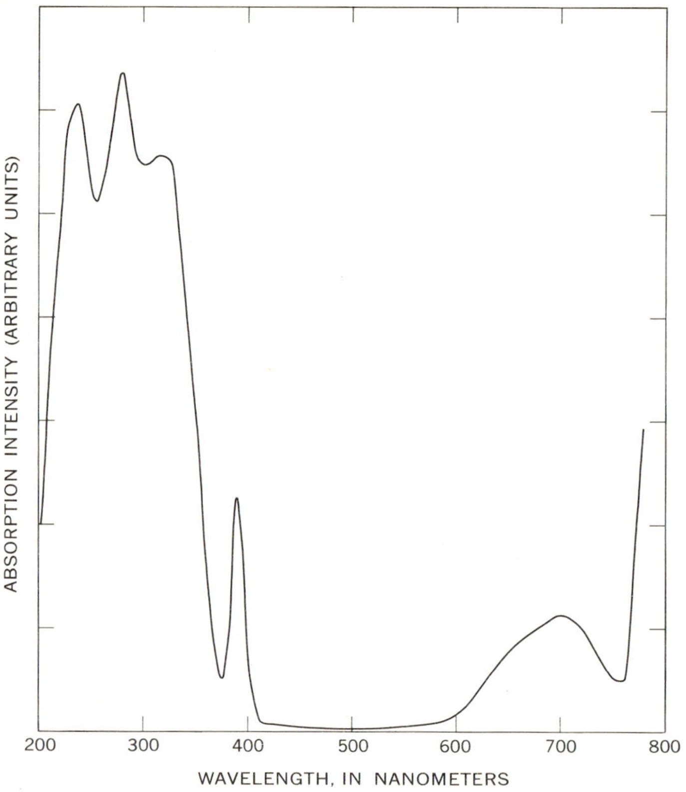

Figure 15.—Absorption spectrum of lignosulfonic acid. The emission wavelength was set at 395 nm.

tion spectroscopy. The following specific data were obtained for lube oil, crude oil, and lignosulfonic acid: The excitation frequency best suited to stimulate fluorescent emission from these materials was 250 nm. The emission maximum for lignosulfonic acid is 380 nm; absorption maxima occurred at 287, 245, and 325 nm. The crude oil emission maxima were at 300 and 320 nm; the absorption maximum occurred at 220 nm. The lube oil emission maximum differed from the crude oil maximum and was a single value occurring at 348 nm, but the absorption maximum was broader; it was displayed at 228–292 nm.

At the concentrations studied the emission curves yield a linear response to the concentration of the fluorescent material as long as the concentration did not differ by more than a factor of 10.

A sample taken from the Houston Ship Channel was analyzed. This sample exhibited a fluorescent response similar to that of the two oil standards but also exhibited additional fluorescent response from 300 to 400 nm, a longer wavelength response than from the oil samples. Very possibly this spectral curve would be unique when compared to that of other samples.

As was pointed out, the fluorescent emission is the result of a light photon returning to the ground state, but not immediately and not from the same energy level as the initial photon stimulation. The intermediate energy exchange that takes place, such as intersystem crossing, is independent of the surroundings. An emulsion or a surface film will react to light in an identical manner. Thus "through-the-solution" fluorescence is a valid method of simulating reflectance fluorescence.

Fluorescent spectroscopy is one method for characterizing materials that are known to be the main components of surface films. These films occur both on fresh water and salt water; however, with a high-powered light source and a sensitive detection system, component characterization such as that reported in this article may be applied to in situ samples regardless of location.

The information contained herein points out the usefulness of fluorescent spectroscopy as a tool to study and characterize the types of materials that comprise surface films.

REFERENCES CITED

Becker, R. S., 1969, Theory and interpretation of fluorescence and phosphorescence: New York, Wiley Interscience, 283 p.

Berlman, I. B., 1965, Handbook of fluorescence spectra of aromatic molecules: New York, Academic Press, 258 p.

Chandler, P. B., 1971, Oil pollution surveillance: Joint Conf. on Sensing of Environmental Pollutants, Palo Alto, Calif., Nov. 8–10, Paper 71-1073, 8 p.

Duce, R. A., Quinn, J. G., Olney, C. E., Piotrowicz, S. R., Ray, B. J., and Wade, T. L., 1972, Enrichment of heavy metals and organic compounds in the surface microlayer of Narragansett Bay, Rhode Island: Science, v. 176, p. 161–163.

Goldberg, M. C., DeLong, L. L., and Sinclair, Mark, 1973, Extraction and concentration of organic solutes from water: Anal. Chem., v. 45, no. 1, p. 89–92.

Goldberg, M. C., and Weiner, E. R., 1972, Applications of spectroscopy to remote determination of water quality: Nat. Oceanic and

Atmospheric Adm. and U.S. Naval Research Lab. 4th Ann. Earth Resources program rev., Manned Spacecraft Center, Houston, Tex., v. III, p. 81–11 to 81–14.

Goolsby, A. D., 1971, Water pollution detection by reflectance measurements: Joint Conf. on Sensing of Environmental Pollutants, Palo Alto, Calif., Nov. 8–10, Paper 71-1069, 6 p.

Guilbault, G. G., 1967, Fluorescence, theory, instrumentation and practice: New York, Marcel Dekker, Inc., 697 p.

Herzberg, Gerhard, 1939, Molecular spectra and molecular structure, I. Spectra of diatomic molecules: Princeton, N.J., D. Van Nostrand and Co., Inc., 1st ed., 658 p.

——1945, Molecular spectra and molecular structure, II. Infrared and Raman spectra of polyatomic molecules: Princeton, N.J., D. Van Nostrand Co., Inc., 632 p.

Klemas, Vytautas, 1971, Detecting oil on water—a comparison of known techniques: Joint Conf. on Sensing of Environmental Pollutants, Palo Alto, Calif., Nov. 8–10, Paper 71-1068, 6 p.

Measures, R. M., and Bristow, M., 1971, The development of a laser fluoresensor for remote environmental probing: Joint Conf. on Sensing of Environmental Pollutants, Palo Alto, Calif., Nov. 8–10, 7 p.

Parker, C. A., 1959, Raman spectra in spectrofluorimetry: Analyst, v. 84, p. 446.

——1968, Photoluminescence of solutions with applications to photochemistry and analytical chemistry: New York, Elsevier Publishing Co.

Phillips, R. E., 1969, Fluorometry in research and industry: Am. Lab., v. 10, p. 8–12.

Stoertz, G. E., Hemphill, W. R., and Markle, D. H., 1970, Remote analysis of fluorescence by a fraunhofer line discriminator: Marine Technology Soc., 6th Ann. Conf. and Exposition, Washington, D.C., June 29–July 1, 1970, v. 2, p. 1017–1040 [Preprints].

Thruston, A. D., Jr., 1970, A fluorometric method for the determination of liquid sulfonates in natural waters: Water Pollution Control Federation Jour., v. 42, p. 1551–1555.

Udenfried, Sidney, 1962, Fluorescence assay in biology and medicine: New York, Academic Press, 517 p.

Weber, G., and Teale, F. W. J., 1957, Determination of the absolute quantum yield of fluorescent solutions: Faraday Soc., Trans., v. 53, p. 646.

Zobell, C. E., 1971, The occurrence, effects and fate of oil polluting the sea: Internat. Air-Water Pollution, v. 7, p. 173–197.

Jour. Research U.S. Geol. Survey
Vol. 1, No. 6, Nov.-Dec. 1973, p. 719—723

PROBLEMS OF UNDERGROUND STORAGE OF WASTES

By RAYMOND L. NACE, Raleigh, N.C.

Abstract.—Problems of underground storage of waste involve geology in its broadest sense, including hydrology, geochemistry, and geophysics. Wastes may be solid, liquid, or gaseous, and they may be chemically toxic or noxious, esthetically offensive, or radioactive. Some wastes require only temporary containment, whereas others must be isolated for indefinitely long periods. The means and locale for emplacement underground depend upon many governing geological factors, including the physical, chemical, hydrological, and hydraulic properties of the host formation. These must be studied relative to the physical, chemical, and thermal properties of the waste and of potential interactions between the waste and the host formation. Thorough knowledge is essential because lack of it may lead to undesirable or disastrous environmental consequences. Escape of waste may contaminate the surface or near-surface environment; it may destroy the usefulness or accessibility of resources such as ground water, petroleum, and minerals. Effective management of underground waste requires adaptation of current technology and development of new technology.

Increasing stringency of governmental regulation of pollution by discharge of industrial, sewage, and other wastes into surface waters in the United States has caused many producers of pollutants to consider underground disposal or storage. The thesis is that underground injection of wastes would be cheaper than treatment required for discharge at the land surface. A half century of experience in oil fields, where brine (produced along with petroleum) is injected underground to avoid contamination of surface waters and fresh ground waters, has led to optimism that injection may be feasible for some industrial wastes and treated sewage. Many thousands of brine-injection wells are in use at present. In addition, thousands of injection wells are used to repressure oil-producing reservoirs.

For many years hydrogeologists have called attention to the tremendous amount of water stored in aquifers, but in the United States ground water has received little attention in regional water-resources planning. A common point of view is that ground water is available for individual, local, and small-community use, but has no significance in regional water-resources development. Ironically, the great capacity of geological formations for liquid storage now is being cited as an argument favoring their use for waste storage. At the same time, planners are awakening to the potential benefits of joint management of ground water and surface water as a single resource.

A quality of human nature is to seize upon each supposedly new alternative solution of a problem as though it were a panacea. But subsurface waste disposal is no panacea, as has been ably explained by Piper (1969). Moreover, the practice is not new. The cesspool and the septic tank, which have been used for centuries, are underground disposal devices.

Literature on underground waste injection in the United States is fairly abundant, but most of it is conjectural, some is misleading, and some is downright erroneous. A symposium on underground waste management was staged in Houston, Tex., during December 6–9, 1971. This should place the problem in perspective. Beyond that, it seems important to have an international forum, where experiences and ideas of workers from various countries may be exchanged. It would be timely for an international organization to sponsor a symposium on the topic. Meantime, one or more international organizing seminars might be useful.

Acknowledgments.—I wish to acknowledge gratefully the careful and constructive reviews of the manuscript of this article by Paul H. Jones, Francis A. Kohout, Robert Schneider, and Leonard A. Wood.

HISTORICAL NOTE

The oil industry was one of the first to generate and dispose of large volumes of waste liquid—to be specific, brine, a byproduct of petroleum production. Early in this century brine was disposed of simply by dumping it on the ground or into seepage pits. This became unacceptable because of infiltration and runoff into streams, and during the past 50 years many thousands of brine disposal systems have been installed, chiefly so-called reverse wells for underground injection of brine.[1]

Underground injection received little attention in other industries until about 20 years ago, when the atomic energy industry began a serious search for means and places to get rid of dangerous radioactive liquid wastes. The search was unsuccessful because no responsible geologist was willing to

[1] A commonly accepted definition of a water well is a hole in the ground from which water is sought or obtained. The term "reverse well" may be appropriate for a ground-water recharge hole, but it is inappropriate for a disposal structure.

say that dangerous liquid waste, injected in any given formation, would remain there for the necessary period of 600 to 1,000 years.

Underground injection of other types of wastes received little consideration by industry before about 1950. However, the number of underground waste injection systems in the conterminous United States has increased from about six in 1953, to 35 in 1963, and about 150 in 1969 (Cleary, 1969). No doubt many disposal operations exist that have not been reported or canvassed.

PREVIOUS EXPERIENCE

As previously noted, the petroleum industry has acquired a great deal of experience during the past 50 years in underground injection of waste brine solutions. The supposition is common that this wealth of experience should be applicable to the construction and operation of structures for disposal of industrial wastes. While some of the experience is applicable, the problem of industrial waste disposal is vastly different from that of brine disposal.

In some oil-field operations, water-injection holes serve to repressure the oil reservoir and thus to prolong or increase oil production. Pretreatment of injection water is common, and this practice generally raises no serious problems. The brine commonly returns to the formation from which it came; pore space having lowered pressure is available; and the brine is chemically compatible with the host formation and its contained fluids. In other operations the brine returns, not to the original host formation, but to some more shallow zone which has the capacity to accept the waste. The more shallow zone may be lithologically similar to the host zone, and no serious problem arises of chemical compatibility with the formation or its contained native liquid. Where incompatibility arises, injection may be accomplished anyway by exerting high pressures upon the relatively low volumes generally involved in any one operation.

Oil-field practices have caused countless problems, many of which have not received wide publicity. Many abandoned oil wells have not been effectively plugged, and pressure in the salaquifer has caused brine to leak out at the surface. In other abandoned wells the casing has deteriorated and brine finds its way to the land surface, into phreatic aquifers, and thence into surface streams, causing salinity problems. In extensive areas in the southern midcontinent, both underground and at the surface, waters are too saline for ordinary use. This natural condition has been aggravated by human activity, but the extent of the aggravation has not been determined.

Much oil-field experience is inapplicable to the problem of industrial wastes. Except for the uncertainty of control, the disposal of industrial wastes poses wholly different problems. These problems stem from the facts that (1) industrial plant sites have not been chosen with the feasibility in mind of underground waste disposal; (2) the properties of waste materials cover a wide range, and their physical, chemical, thermal, and radioactive properties are foreign to oil-field experience; and (3) the volumes of waste injected into a single well may be many times greater than in a brine-disposal well. The problem at hand, therefore, is new and requires the development of a wholly new technology.

CLASSIFICATION OF WASTES

Industrial and other wastes may occur in any of the three phases of matter: solid, liquid, or gaseous. Some wastes are mixtures of phases or mixtures of differing wastes in a single phase. The variety of materials in each phase is bewildering. In terms of their character the wastes may be esthetically offensive, biologically noxious or toxic, or dangerously radioactive.

These wastes may be so varied in their chemical, physical, and radiometric properties that it is not possible to classify them by simple groups. Waste effluent from a single industrial plant may contain more than 100 different chemical compounds. The liquids may include alkali, acid, chromate, nitrate, phosphate, and sulfite solutions, various organic materials such as alcohol, ketone, phenol, cyanide, and chlorinated hydrocarbon (Cleary, 1969, p. A-2). Some radioactive wastes have noxious or toxic characteristics in addition to radioactivity.

SPECIFIC PROBLEMS

Any proposed or actual waste-injection operation will entail many problems. Some of these problems will require virtually complete knowledge of the geology, hydrology, geochemistry, and seismicity of the disposal site and surrounding area. Disposal would require so much expense for site study, testing, and monitoring that, in many areas, it would be cheaper to treat the waste for surface disposal than to meet reasonable requirements for safe underground injection.

Salaquifers

In U.S. Geological Survey usage, water is classed as saline if it contains 1,000 mg/l or more of dissolved solids. Higher concentrations are used at some places for domestic and stock-water supply, and also for irrigation where less mineralized water is not available. Saline water may be used for industrial cooling also.

Traditionally, saline ground water has been considered as a nuisance, which in some places it will always be. For that reason, some advocates of underground injection of wastes have assumed that all salaquifers are potential zones for injection. The premise is that the native water is useless and that no harm will be done. This is erroneous. With advances in desalting technology, saline water becomes a resource. Kohout and others (1970) described a variety of ways in which saline water and salaquifers may be used directly and indirectly.

The total volume of saline ground water exceeds by many

times that of fresh water in the United States. This probably is true also of much of the world land area. Feth and others (1965) showed that waters containing 1,000 mg/l or more of dissolved solids underlie much of the United States. The depth to saline water is less than 150 m in somewhat more than one-third of the United States. The use of salaquifers as waste sinks, therefore, must be evaluated relative to other possible uses.

Underground storage capacity

At 15 percent porosity, a mass of 1 km^3 of rock or sediment could contain 150×10^6 m^3 of liquid. Such examples have been cited as evidence that the potential for underground injection is immense. However, all rock pores beneath the earth's unsaturated zone (zone above the water table) are saturated with fluid, either gaseous or liquid. This fluid must be displaced or compressed to provide room for injected liquid. Several ways in which additional space could be created are pressure-compression of the native fluid, hydraulic uplift of the overburden, and hydraulic fracturing.

For practical purposes, water is incompressible and little storage space could be created by compression in a salaquifer unless the contained volume of liquid is very large.

In some aquifers the weight of overburden is sustained partly by grain-to-grain contact of rock minerals and partly by hydraulic forces. Increase of hydraulic pressure in some circumstances theoretically could expand the aquifer and raise the overburden. Where the waste-injection zone is at considerable depth—on the order of thousands of meters—the required injection pressure would be very high.

Hydraulic fracturing is a technique developed in the petroleum-production industry to facilitate flow of oil from the reservoir rocks into wells. For waste disposal a modified technique may be used to accomplish the reverse process—flow of waste from an injection well into the host rock. We do not have space here to describe the technique in detail. In some geological situations it is feasible. De Laguna (1970) has described the method in detail for one set of circumstances dealing with radioactive liquid waste.

Existing stress underground can be very important to the success of waste injection. A well about 3,600 m deep, extending to the basement rock, was drilled a few miles from Denver, Colo., for the purpose of injecting noxious liquid waste in a geologic environment where it presumably could do no harm. Inasmuch as the rock is dense and very low in permeability, waste was injected at very high pressure. Within a few months after injection began, a series of mild to moderate earthquakes shook the Denver area. The possibility of a relation between the quakes and the waste injection occurred to one geologist (Evans, 1966). Study of seismic records and injection rates showed an apparent correlation. Subsequent study has confirmed this (Raleigh, 1972), although direct proof of a relation has not been established. Use of the injection well has ceased and the earthquakes have not recurred.

Chemical compatibility

Chemical compatibility of the waste liquid with the host rock and native water is an important aspect of subsurface storage. Chemical reactions may yield precipitates, clogging the openings in the host rock. The heat of reactions may also produce adverse changes in the rock. Reactions and changes in some rocks produce an increase in pore volume, further complicating the situation. Some reactions produce gases which could be noxious or inflammable. Gases are much more mobile than water, and their escape from the storage reservoir is more likely. Entrained gases in the injected fluid will drastically reduce permeability, causing higher pressures or decreased flow.

Detention time

Detention time in the waste-injection zone is an important criterion of the feasibility of injection. In the operation described by de Laguna, liquid waste is mixed with clay and cement to form a slurry. After injection the slurry solidifies in the fractures created at depths which are on the order of 100 m or more beneath the land surface. The waste will remain motionless and will not enter the surface environment until erosion exposes it thousands or millions of years in the future.

Most ground water, including that in many salaquifers, is in motion. Liquid wastes that remain liquid are potentially mobile in ground-water systems. Motion in an aquifer implies that the liquid is discharging by seepage or through springs at outcrops or by leaking into other formations. Injection of foreign fluid might accelerate motion; the waste might then migrate to locations where it is undesirable, leak into other geological formations, or appear at the land surface.

Ground-water movement in general is very slow. In highly permeable aquifers, such as clean gravel, the rates of movement may reach as much as 15 or 18 m day^{-1}. In material with only slight permeability the rate may be only a few centimeters per year. In clay, motion may be nil because molecular forces binding water to the clay may be stronger than gravitational and (or) hydraulic forces. On the other hand, osmotic forces may cause liquid to move through clay beds that separate aquifers in which the differences in salinity are large (Jones, 1969, p. 3, 63).

Presumably, some waste injection zones will be at considerable depth, where formations are virtually impermeable. Injection there can be accomplished only by hydraulic fracturing. The fluid presumably would move only so long as pressure and more liquid continued to be applied. However, some risks are involved. If fractures formed vertically rather than horizontally, liquid might migrate upward into locations where it is undesirable. Liquid might migrate upward also if it reached a permeable fault zone, or if movement occurred along a fault.

Contamination or denial of resources

The possibility that fresh ground water and surface water may be inadvertently contaminated by waste-injection operations is obvious. As is well known, few if any confined (artesian) aquifers are absolutely confined. Upward leakage through confining beds may be extremely small per unit area, but total leakage through a large area can be significant. Where the confining bed is very thick, a given molecule of liquid might require hundreds or thousands of years to pass through. On the other hand, waste liquid might react with the confining bed either to make it even less permeable or to make it more so. If the latter occurs, waste might migrate into bodies of fresh ground water or even reach the land surface.

Many useful mineral deposits remain undiscovered. Contamination of the lithosphere may deny access to such deposits. From geologic evidence it is certain that readily available mineral deposits form only a small fraction of 1 percent of the earth's crust. Projections indicate that the demand for primary minerals will increase fourfold by the year 2000. Many secondary minerals are already in short supply, and the average grade of ore mined diminishes with time.

It is therefore important to explore thoroughly each proposed injection site, if that has not been done already, in order to avoid contamination of resources or denial of access to resources.

MONITORING

The geology, hydrology, meteorology, and other aspects of the environment at an injection site must be thoroughly known and understood; in addition, it is necessary to monitor the effects of disposal operations. Advance knowledge helps prediction, and perhaps even control, of the behavior of wastes underground. It is not possible to obtain information on all important parameters of the underground environment in advance. Therefore, results of injection may not conform to predictions. Monitoring is necessary to observe actual behavior of waste in storage underground.

Monitoring may be simple under some circumstances and very complicated under others. Monitoring should always be done in the injection well. Generally, the sealed annular space between the well casing and the injection tubing is filled with an innocuous fluid that counteracts upward pressure against the seal in the lower part of the hole. Monitoring of the pressure and fluid quality in the annular space permits detection of leakage of waste from the injection tubing or through a ruptured seal. Injection pressure and the integrity of injection mechanisms must also be monitored. Case histories are on record where injection mechanisms failed, thus permitting thousands of gallons of waste liquid to discharge at the land surface where they could not be contained or recovered. Dikes around an injection well are advisable to retain wastes in the event of an accident; also storage facilities should be provided to contain wastes when injection mechanisms fail.

The nature of injected waste also must be monitored because it is commonly variable and may change drastically with changes in processes that produce the waste. Changes in the physical, chemical, and thermal properties of the waste may have a strong bearing on the feasibility of continued injection.

Monitor wells should be installed in the host formation and adjoining formations to determine the paths and rates of waste movement, reactions with the rock, and properties of residual fluids. Hydraulic phenomena must also be monitored. The hydraulic gradients in a natural aquifer may be markedly altered by the stress of waste injection.

CONCLUSIONS

Some "authorities" have hailed the idea of underground waste management as a virtual panacea for industrial waste problems. Others believe that underground injection is, at best, an interim measure that can be used only as a stopgap pending development of technology that will permit treatment of wastes so that they may be discharged safely at the land surface.

The weight of evidence seems to favor a view that, in some circumstances, waste may be disposed of safely underground. To use a simple example, treated sewage effluent discharged into a salaquifer may have better quality than the native water in the aquifer. Most wastes and problems of waste management, however, are much more complex than the example. It seems unlikely that large volumes of noxious or toxic wastes can be stored safely underground as a general practice. In many situations complete treatment and renovation of waste for surface discharge must be accomplished.

Statements about general practice, however, should not be construed to exclude consideration of underground waste storage in some areas. Data from exploration deep underground in petroleum-bearing provinces, for example, show that fluids, including saline aqueous solutions, have been held naturally in subsurface storage for millions of years. Artificially injected natural gas has been stored routinely underground in geological formations for many years with only a few reported instances of escape.

Evidently, if underground waste storage is to become predictably safe as well as technically feasible, new technology must be developed, including new kinds of appraisals of subsurface environments. Hydrologic, geochemical, and geophysical parameters must be appraised and tested; methods, devices, and procedures for testing and monitoring effects of underground emplacement must be developed. Legal and economic factors also must be considered in studies of the problem. Specific problems will require specific answers for specific instances.

REFERENCES CITED

Cleary, E. J., 1969, Public policy, legislative and legal aspects, pt. 1 *of* Perspective on the regulation of underground injection of waste-waters: Cincinnati, Ohio River Valley Water Sanitation Comm., 19 p.

de Laguna, Wallace, 1970, Radioactive waste disposal by hydraulic fracturing: Indus. Water Eng., Oct. 1970, p. 32–37.

Evans, D. M., 1966, The Denver area earthquakes and the Rocky Mountain Arsenal disposal well: Mtn. Geologist, v. 3, no. 1, p. 23–36.

Feth, J. H., and others, 1965, Preliminary map of the conterminous United States showing depth to and quality of shallowest ground water containing more than 1,000 parts per million dissolved solids: U.S. Geol. Survey Hydrol. Inv. Atlas HA-199.

Jones, P. H., 1969, Hydrology of Neogene deposits in the northern Gulf of Mexico basin: Louisiana Water Resources Research Inst. Bull. GT-2, 105 p.

Kohout, F. A., ed., 1970, Saline water, a valuable resource: Water Resources Research, v. 6, no. 5, p. 1441–1531. [Series of 16 papers reprinted as a special symposium volume]

Piper, A. M., 1969, Disposal of liquid wastes by injection underground—neither myth nor millennium: U.S. Geol. Survey Circ. 631, 15 p.

Raleigh, C. B., 1972, Earthquakes and fluid injection, *in* Cook, T. D., ed., Underground waste management and environmental implications: Am. Assoc. Petroleum Geologists Mem. 18, p. 273–279.

Jour. Research U.S. Geol. Survey
Vol. 1, No. 6, Nov.-Dec. 1973, p. 725—734

EFFECTS OF MIGRATORY WATERFOWL ON WATER QUALITY AT THE MONTEZUMA NATIONAL WILDLIFE REFUGE, SENECA COUNTY, NEW YORK

By MARK R. HAVE, Albany, N.Y.

Work done in cooperation with the Bureau of Sport Fisheries and Wildlife of the U.S. Fish and Wildlife Service

Abstract.—This study was done in response to the shellfish industry's concern that bacteria in effluent from the national wildlife refuges along the northeast coast of the United States may be adversely affecting the harvest of shellfish. A line graph shows inconsistent relationships between bird population at the Montezuma refuge and total coliform, fecal coliform, and fecal *Streptococci* counts. *Salmonella* were found in only one of 17 samples of water taken within the refuge. Counts of nonpathogenic bacteria in the two major streams flowing into the refuge, Black Brook and White Brook, were greater than they were in water flowing out of the refuge. Specific conductance of water flowing out of the refuge was less than that of water flowing into the refuge, although the effluent had higher concentrations of phosphorus and nitrogen than the influent. A settling-pond effect in the quiet water of the refuge may help explain the improvement in the quality of the water leaving the refuge. The study shows how its quality changes both chemically and biologically as water flows through the refuge. Further study is needed, however, to determine the effects that a similar effluent would have on a coastal habitat of shellfish.

The shellfish industry is concerned that effluent at national wildlife refuges along the northeast coast of the United States may be detrimental to shellfish in this area. Shellfish taken from a polluted marine environment can be contaminated with pathogenic as well as nonpathogenic bacteria. These organisms can be present in the product when it reaches the consumer; therefore, the risk of disease is present, especially in shellfish that are eaten raw or after being only briefly cooked (E. B. Pike and A. L. H. Gameson, written commun., Sept. 1969).

Moran, Van Houweling, and Ellis (1965) found *Salmonella* in feces from domestic ducks and geese, but apparently few, if any, similar studies have been done with wild ducks and geese. Therefore, the U.S. Geological Survey, in cooperation with the Bureau of Sport Fisheries and Wildlife of the U.S. Fish and Wildlife Service, monitored the quality of influent and effluent at the Montezuma National Wildlife Refuge in Seneca County, N.Y., to determine the effects of migratory waterfowl on the quality of effluent at wildlife refuges. It is beyond the scope of this study to predict the effect of effluent from a wildlife refuge on the harvest of shellfish. To be able to do this, one would need to determine the effect of wind, streamflow, and tides on the distribution of pollutants in the habitat of shellfish. The Montezuma National Wildlife Refuge study was made strictly to determine how water quality changes when water flows through a wildlife refuge.

The refuge lies 32 miles west of Syracuse, N.Y., at the north end of Cayuga Lake in Seneca County. The refuge headquarters is 4 miles northeast of Seneca Falls on New York State Route 5 and U.S. Route 20 (fig. 1). The refuge provides a typical marsh-type environment with controlled inlets and outlets.

Acknowledgment.—Much helpful data on bird population and water management were furnished by Martin S. Phillips, refuge manager at the Montezuma National Wildlife Refuge.

THE REFUGE AREA

Montezuma National Wildlife Refuge consists of 6,344 acres of cattail marshes, timbered impoundments, and cultivated fields. Originally, the refuge area was a great marsh, where, according to Jesuit missionaries, clouds of wild ducks and geese obscured the sun (U.S. Dept. Interior, 1969). An attempt to use the marshland for cultivation and the construction of the New York State Barge Canal largely drained the marshland. The refuge, established in 1938 to restore the former marshland, serves as an important resting place for birds on their migrations during spring and fall (Murphy, 1968, p. 276).

INHABITANTS

The varied habitat of the refuge provides homes for numerous birds, mammals, and fish of many species. About 270 species of birds have been observed on the refuge. Blue-winged teal, mallard ducks, and wood ducks are the most abundant nesting waterfowl. There is also a variety of herons, shore birds, terns, and songbirds. Population of waterfowl is

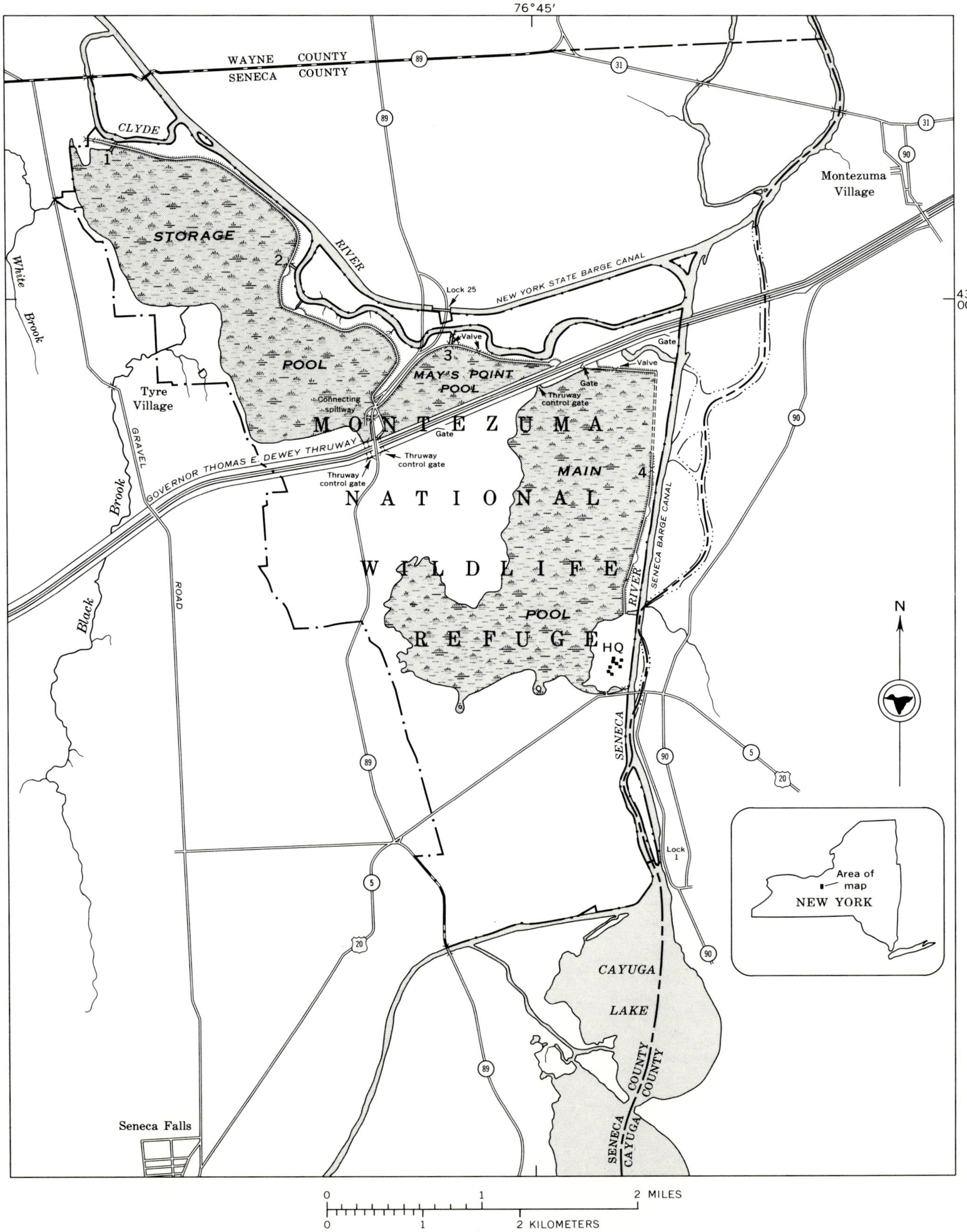
76°45′
43°
00′
WAYNE COUNTY
SENECA COUNTY
CLYDE
RIVER
STORAGE
POOL
MAY'S POINT
POOL
MAIN
POOL
MONTEZUMA
NATIONAL
WILDLIFE
REFUGE
HQ
Lock 25
Valve
Gate
Thruway control gate
Connecting spillway
NEW YORK STATE BARGE CANAL
GOVERNOR THOMAS E. DEWEY THRUWAY
SENECA BARGE CANAL
SENECA RIVER
Montezuma Village
Tyre Village
White Brook
Black Brook
GRAVEL ROAD
Lock 1
CAYUGA LAKE
SENECA COUNTY
CAYUGA COUNTY
Seneca Falls
Area of map
NEW YORK
N
0 1 2 MILES
0 1 2 KILOMETERS

Figure 1

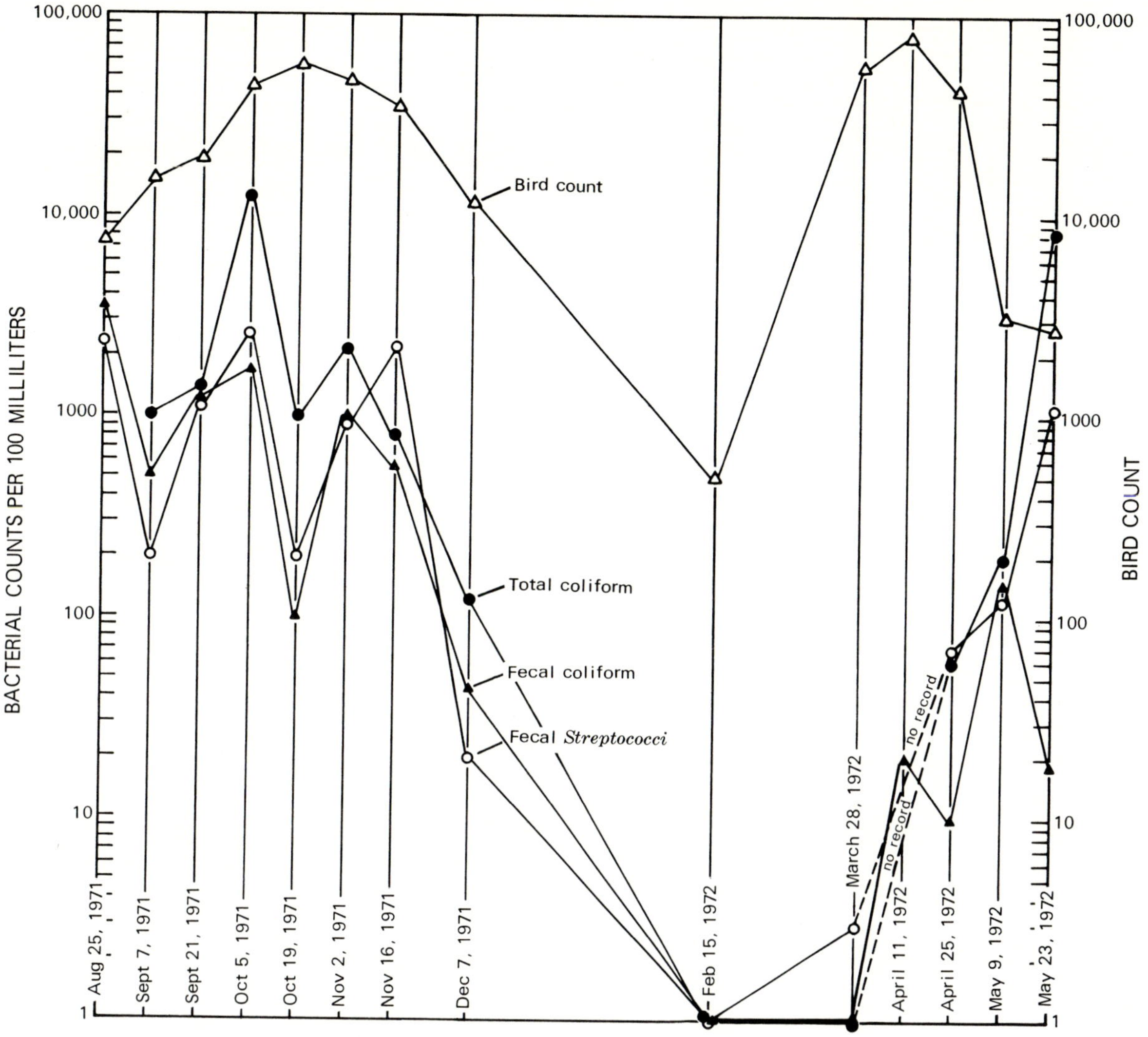

Figure 2.—Bacterial counts at Seneca spillway, Montezuma National Wildlife Refuge, near Seneca Falls, N.Y., and bird counts at the refuge. Birds are counted once a week at the refuge (not necessarily on the same day that bacteria are counted), and that count is used as the bird population for the entire week.

greatest during spring and fall migrations. (See fig. 2.) Peak counts of 70,000 geese in April and 100,000 ducks in October have been noted (U.S. Dept. Interior, 1969).

Deer and woodchucks are commonly seen on the refuge. Woodchucks are abundant and, during spring, are a nuisance along the dikes where they burrow. The marshland is an excellent habitat for muskrats. When properly managed, the activities of the muskrats help maintain marsh vegetation for use by waterfowl. The population of muskrats is controlled by trappers, who harvest between 1,000 and 8,000 annually.

Figure 1.—Montezuma National Wildlife Refuge. Dot-dash line is refuge boundary. Sampling sites within the refuge are: 1, White Brook spillway; 2, Black Brook spillway; 3, Mays Point spillway; and 4, Seneca spillway. (Modification of operating map, Montezuma National Wildlife Refuge, Seneca County, N.Y., U.S. Dept. Interior, Bureau of Sport Fisheries and Wildlife, drawing 5R-N.Y.-234-407, June 13, 1966.)

Warmwater fish are plentiful in the Clyde and the Seneca Rivers and in Cayuga Lake. Popular species include brown bullhead, northern pike, and walleye (U.S. Dept. Interior, 1969).

HYDROLOGY OF THE REFUGE

Water flowing into the refuge

The major flow into the refuge is by means of Black Brook and White Brook, which flow into the west side of Storage Pool (fig. 1). The two streams are 4.6 and 2.3 miles long and have drainage areas of 20 and 7 sq mi, respectively. They meander between long parallel ridges and through cultivated fields and pastureland. There are a few houses along each stream.

The chemical qualities of Black Brook and White Brook are similar. Both streams have a calcium bicarbonate sulfate type water. This reflects the Camillus Shale of the Salina Group in the area. The Camillus Shale belongs to the Upper Silurian Series of rocks and has an average thickness of about 525 feet. The shale contains beds of limestone, salt, and gypsum (L. J. Crain, written commun., 1969).

For this study, discharge was measured routinely only at Black Brook, the larger of the two streams. Measured discharge ranged from 0.96 cfs on October 19, 1971, to 32 cfs on April 11, 1972. On May 9, 1972, after many days of rain, flow was estimated to be 97 cfs.

Water in the refuge

The refuge has three major pools—Storage Pool, Mays Point Pool, and Main Pool. All the pools are surrounded by earthen dikes. Water in Mays Point Pool and Main Pool is obtained mainly by diverting water in Storage Pool through connecting outlets and inlets. Water levels in Storage Pool and Mays Point Pool are controlled by spillways regulating flow into the Clyde River, which is part of the New York State Barge Canal. The water level in Main Pool is controlled at its outlet, Seneca spillway, which empties into the Seneca River. The Seneca River merges with the New York State Barge Canal at the northeast corner of the refuge.

The water is a mixed type dominated by calcium, sodium, bicarbonate, sulfate, and chloride ions (U.S. Geol. Survey, unpub. data, 1971). These ions reflect swamp and lake deposits in the refuge and surrounding area. The deposits are mainly composed of silt and clay but contain peak, muck, and marl (L. J. Crain, written commun., 1969).

SAMPLING SITES AND SAMPLING FREQUENCY

Water samples for both chemical analysis and bacterial counts were collected from three primary sites—Seneca spillway, Black Brook at the gravel road, and White Brook at the gravel road (fig. 1). In general, samples were collected biweekly from August 25 through December 7, 1971, and from March 28 through May 23, 1972. Samples were also taken on February 15 and 16, 1972. Water samples for only bacterial counts were collected on April 25, 1971, at two secondary sites—Black Brook spillway and White Brook spillway—during the peak of spring runoff and the spring migration of waterfowl. Mays Point spillway was considered as a secondary sampling site, but it was not flowing at the time the other two secondary sites were sampled. Black Brook spillway was sampled again on May 9, 1972.

PARAMETERS DETERMINED

Parameters determined at the sampling sites included air and water temperatures, sampling depth, specific conductance, pH, alkalinity (reported as carbonate and bicarbonate), dissolved oxygen and percent saturation of dissolved oxygen, total coliform, fecal coliform, fecal *Streptococci*, and *Salmonella*. Discharge and gage height (stage) were determined in the field at Black Brook and at Seneca spillway. Parameters determined in the laboratory included ammonia as N (nitrogen), organic N, nitrate as N, nitrite as N, total N, phosphorus, total solids (dissolved plus undissolved) and fixed solids (residue after ignition at 600°C, Celsius, for 5 minutes), and TOC (total organic carbon).

ANALYTICAL PROCEDURES

Specific conductance, pH, alkalinity, and air and water temperatures were determined by the methods of the American Public Health Association and others (1971, p. 323, 276, 52, and 348) and Brown, Skougstad, and Fishman (1970). Dissolved-oxygen concentration was determined by a dissolved-oxygen meter. Dissolved-oxygen concentration and water temperature were used in the calculation of percent saturation of dissolved oxygen (Am. Public Health Assoc. and others, 1971, p. 480). Samples were taken near the surface, so the sampling depth was assumed to be 0.1 foot. All samples were unfiltered.

Discharge at Black Brook was measured with a current meter. Gage height was determined by measuring the distance from a reference point on the bridge to the water surface.

Discharge at Seneca spillway was calculated by the discharge equation for a contracted weir. Gage height was read from the staff gage at the spillway.

Phosphorus and total and fixed solids were collected and determined by the methods of the American Public Health Association and others (1971, p. 526 and 535) and Brown, Skougstad, and Fishman (1970).

Samples for the determination of ammonia as N, nitrate as N, and nitrite as N were collected by the method of Brown, Skougstad, and Fishman (1970, p. 17). The parameters were determined on a Technicon autoanalyzer.[1,2] The digestion and the distillation steps of the Kjeldahl method, described by Brown, Skougstad, and Fishman (1970, p. 122), were used for determining organic nitrogen. The distillate was then analyzed on the autoanalyzer. Total N was calculated by adding the concentrations of the different forms of N.

Total organic carbon was determined by the method of Goerlitz and Brown (1972, p. 4).

Total coliform, fecal coliform, and fecal *Streptococci* were determined by the membrane-filter technique described by the American Public Health Association and others (1971, p. 679, 684, and 690) and by Slack and others (1970). These parameters were determined in triplicate and were averaged for presentation in table 1.

Qualitative tests described by the American Public Health Association and others (1971, p. 698) were modified to

[1]The use of named products in this report is for identification purposes only and does not imply endorsement by the U.S. Geological Survey.

[2]Technicon Corporation, Tarrytown, N.Y., 1969, Technicon industrial method, 19-69W, 33-69W, and 35-69W.

determine whether *Salmonella* were present. At each sampling site, two 1-liter samples of water were collected and were immediately filtered through separate sterile 0.45-μm filters. One filter was placed into a vial containing a solution of tetrathionate broth, and the other was placed into a vial containing selenite broth. After the vials of broth were incubated for 24 hours at 35°C, plates of brilliant green agar, bismuth sulfite agar, and "Salmonella Shigella" agar were streaked with selenite and tetrathionate cultures. These plates were then incubated for 24 hours at 35°C. After the vials were incubated for an additional 24-hour period at 35°C, fresh plates were streaked and incubated as before. The plates were inspected for characteristic *Salmonella* colonies, and suspected colonies were restreaked onto fresh plates to purify the culture. The purified cultures were then streaked onto slants of TSA (tryptic soy agar), incubated at 35°C for 24 hours, and maintained at refrigerator temperature until final confirmation could be made.

Preparation for the confirmation tests was begun by further purifying the refrigerated cultures. This was done by streaking the slant cultures onto TSA plates and restreaking the plate cultures onto new TSA plates until pure cultures were obtained. The latest plate cultures were then streaked onto fresh TSA slants. All these transfers were incubated at 35°C.

The fresh TSA slant cultures were then streaked onto slants of urea, phenylalanine, lysine iron, and TSI (triple sugar iron) agars. Presence of *Salmonella* was indicated if the TSI test was positive and the others were negative.

The TSA slant cultures were then subjected to one more confirmation test, an agglutination test with Salmonella O antiserum poly A-1. If this test was positive, the culture was then considered to be *Salmonella*.

RESULTS AND DISCUSSION

Table 1 shows monthly counts of total coliform, fecal coliform, and fecal *Streptococci* for all the sampling sites. During the migration months of October, November, and March, 80 percent of the bacterial counts at Black Brook and White Brook were higher than those at Seneca spillway. During April, another migration month, bacterial counts at Black Brook and White Brook were higher than at any of the three spillways.

Table 1.—*Comparative bacteria counts at primary and secondary sampling sites*

[Where two dates are shown, the result is the average of the two]

Sampling site	Sampling date	Total coliform (per 100 ml)	Fecal coliform (per 100 ml)	Fecal *Streptococci* (per 100 ml)
Seneca spillway	8-25-71	([1])	3,600	2,400
	9-7, 9-21-71	1,000	900	700
	10-5, 10-19-71	7,000	940	1,400
	11-2, 11-16-71	1,400	780	1,600
	12-7-71	130	45	20
	2-15-72	<1	<1	<1
	3-28-72	<1	<1	[2] 3
	4-11, 4-25-72	160	110	140
	5-9, 5-23-72	4,400	90	670
White Brook	8-26-71	11,000	690	1,200
	9-8, 9-22-71	6,400	3,500	2,800
	10-6, 10-20-71	14,000	2,200	3,400
	11-3, 11-17-71	3,400	640	3,600
	12-8-71	2,700	650	4,800
	2-16-72	3,200	490	([3])
	3-29-72	43	20	70
	4-12, 4-26-72	1,600	89	190
	5-10, 5-24-72	2,500	1,400	1,200
Black Brook	8-26-71	45,000	24,000	13,500
	9-8, 9-21-71	61,000	5,000	76,000
	10-5, 10-19-71	5,000	230	560
	11-2, 11-16-71	2,100	270	1,900
	12-7-71	10,000	2,700	40,000
	2-15-72	1,000	290	8,700
	3-28-72	440	56	130
	4-11, 4-25-72	870	92	720
	5-9, 5-23-72	1,800	640	1,600
Black Brook spillway	4-25-72	140	10	60
	5-9-72	53	34	12
White Brook spillway	4-25-72	760	24	75

[1] Total coliform too numerous to count.
[2] Estimated.
[3] No data.

Many factors—such as sunlight, temperature, amount of organic matter, and the presence of other microorganisms—affect the concentration and the type of bacteria in water. In a literature search of the effects of various environmental factors on bacteria, Rudolfs, Falk, and Ragotzkie (1950) found much contradictory evidence. But, as a general rule, fecal coliform and fecal *Streptococci* counts reflect the degree of fecal pollution.

The generally higher counts of bacteria at White Brook and Black Brook than at Seneca spillway are probably due to wastes of farm animals and various wild animals, septic tanks, or sewage draining into the streams. In the refuge, where water is moving relatively slowly, a settling-pond effect is probably pronounced. This tends to settle bacteria, especially those that are adsorbed to particulate matter. Also, the water within the refuge may support various forms of predatory microorganisms (Salle, 1961, p. 547).

From August 25 to December 7, 1971, there was no discharge at Seneca spillway. Thus, there was very little water movement through the refuge. On December 7, 1971, the discharge at the spillway was estimated to be only 0.3 cfs. A study by Geldreich and Kenner (1969) reports that various genera of enteric bacteria in water die off at an exponential rate. This suggests that in a slowly flowing body of water there would be fewer bacteria surviving at a point downstream than at the point of entry.

During fall migration (1971), only a few birds were concentrated around the Seneca spillway area of Main Pool; therefore, high bacterial counts at the spillway were probably not the result of the corresponding bird counts. The lack of correlation between bird population and bacterial count is illustrated in figure 2.

During spring migration (1972), ducks used all pools in the refuge, but their greatest concentration (50 percent of the ducks) was at Storage Pool. Geese concentrated on Main Pool until the ice thawed on April 10; afterward, two-thirds of the geese concentrated on Storage Pool (M. S. Phillips, written commun., 1972). The lowest bacterial counts in Main Pool for the period of study occurred during the period of ice covered, when the droppings could not fall into the water and when water temperature was lowest. Because death rate for bacteria depends on temperature, the die-off rate would be greatest during the period of ice cover.

The relatively high total coliform counts on October 5 and May 23 are unexplained, but they may be due to an aftergrowth (Van Donsel and others, 1967). A nonrandom sample is another possibility for the high counts.

Qualitative tests confirmed *Salmonella* in only one of 45 samples collected from August 1971 through May 1972 at the five stations sampled. This sample, taken at Seneca spillway on September 22, 1971, was the only confirmation out of 17 samples taken from the refuge itself. One cannot assume from this single result that more *Salmonella* can be found at Seneca spillway than at any of the other sites. Geldreich (1966), in a comprehensive study of fecal coliform in the environment, pointed out that the presence of fecal coliform is indicative of the possible presence of pathogenic organisms such as *Salmonella*. It would seem to follow that the higher the fecal coliform count the higher the probability of finding pathogens. However, studies by Gallagher and Spino (1968) have shown that this assumption is questionable and that further study of the correlation is needed.

During fall migration, a fresh fecal sample taken among a flock of geese on the ground near the refuge headquarters and a water sample taken among a flock of geese that was concentrated near the middle of Main Pool were tested for *Salmonella*. None was found in either sample.

As shown in tables 2, 3, and 4, concentrations of total and fixed solids were higher in Black Brook and White Brook than they were at Seneca spillway; but the percentage of organic solids (table 5) was higher at Seneca spillway than at the other two sites. This relatively high percentage can be expected in the marsh-type water typical of the Montezuma National Wildlife Refuge.

The lower specific conductances at Seneca spillway than at White Brook or Black Brook could be the result of certain dissolved constituents, such as calcium, carbonate, and sulfate, precipitating out of solution. This precipitation could be due to the higher pH values (resulting from photosynthesis) in the refuge as compared with the values of Black Brook and White Brook. By this process, the ratio of organic solids to inorganic solids would increase. Also, the high concentrations of algae in the refuge remove various ions from the water.

Specific conductance at Seneca spillway was noticeably higher during November, December, and February than during the other months. This supports the possibility that photosynthesis plays an important role in controlling the concentration of dissolved salts in spring and summer. The specific conductance was higher at Seneca spillway than at both Black Brook and White Brook for the months of December and February.

Specific conductance and concentrations of totai and fixed solids are inversely related to the discharge in Black Brook. This is due to a dilution effect during high flows. Although discharge was not measured at White Brook, the dilution effect was observed there during corresponding sampling periods. This does not mean, though, that more total solids are being carried by Black Brook into Storage pool during periods of high concentrations of total solids than during periods of low concentrations. For example, T/d (tons per day) calculated by the formula

$$T/d = mg/l \times cfs \times 0.0027$$

for October 5, 1971, when discharge was 1.4 cfs and total-solids concentration was 1,440 mg/l, would equal 5.4. For March 28, 1972, when discharge was 29 and total-solids concentration was 388 mg/l, T/d would equal 30.

Table 2 shows that concentrations of nitrogen and phosphorus at Seneca spillway are generally higher than at Black Brook (table 3) and White Brook (table 4), particularly from August to November. Similar to bacterial counts, nutrient levels do not seem to be affected by bird population but, rather, reflect conditions in the marsh. For example, bluegreen algae, which were found at the refuge, characteristically fix atmospheric nitrogen as well as different forms of nitrogen in the water. The high concentrations of plant and animal life in the refuge corresponded to the high concentrations of phosphorus. Continuous availability of phosphorus for microbiological growth is probably accomplished by various forms of mechanical mixing of the bottom nutrients with the water. Wave action, diving birds, and carp, which stir up the bottom sediments in search of food, are the primary means of mechanical mixing in the refuge. Table 2 shows phosphorus concentrations at their lowest during the period of ice cover, when microbiological activity and mechanical mixing had least effect.

When the water temperatures decline as winter approaches, total nitrogen and total phosphorus concentrations also decline because of the decrease in microbiological activity in the refuge water. Nitrogen and phosphorus concentrations at Seneca spillway are of the same magnitude as those at Black Brook and White Brook during this period of relatively low temperatures, which extends into May.

Nitrogen and phosphorus concentrations at Black Brook increase substantially after heavy rains (table 3). For example, on September 8, 1971, discharge was 1.9 cfs, and total nitrogen and total phosphorus concentrations were 1.3 and 0.08 mg/l, respectively. On September 21, 1971, discharge was 15 cfs after a night of rain. Total nitrogen concentration was 3.7 mg/l, and total phosphorus concentration was 0.29 mg/l. The higher concentrations on September 21 probably resulted from nitrogen and phosphorus fertilizers and livestock wastes washed from the soil. Also, the larger amounts of suspended sediment stirred up from the river bottom by the faster, more turbulent flows caused by the rainfall would add more bottom nutrients to the water layer above (Greeson, 1971).

The result of photosynthesis at Seneca spillway shows up in values of pH and percent saturations of dissolved oxygen (table 2). The low percent saturations in February and March at Seneca spillway occurred while there was still much ice cover. The ice layer acted as a shield between the water and the atmospheric source of oxygen. Oxygen was utilized by respiratory processes of the biota and by oxidation of decaying materials.

FURTHER WORK NEEDED

In order to determine the effects of concentrations of parameters listed in tables 1 and 2 on water in a shellfish habitat, one would have to do a coastal water-quality study. Under the National Shellfish Sanitation Program, an industry-State-Federal cooperative program which is administered jointly by the Food and Drug Administration and State shellfish control agencies, sanitary surveys are made of each shellfish habitat before the State approves the habitat as a source of shellfish for market or for use in a controlled purification or relaying operation. The sanitary quality of each area is reappraised at least biennially (U.S. Dept. Health, Education, and Welfare, 1965, p. 10).

The purpose of the sanitary survey is to identify and evaluate factors influencing the sanitary quality of a shellfish habitat. The factors include: sources of pollution, potential or actual; volume of dilution water; effects of currents, winds, and tides in disseminating pollution throughout the growing area; bacterial quality of water and bottom sediments; die-off of polluting bacteria in the tributaries and the estuary; bottom configuration; and salinity and turbidity of the water.

A study in which data of the type obtained at the Montezuma National Wildlife Refuge is used in conjunction with a sanitary survey would be necessary to determine whether effluent from a coastal wildlife refuge adversely affects shellfish habitats.

CONCLUSIONS

The concentration of bacteria in water leaving the Montezuma National Wildlife Refuge is generally lower than that in the two largest inflowing streams (Black Brook and White Brook). This is probably due to settling of the bacteria in the quiet water of the refuge and to the die-off of bacteria between the point of entry and the sampling points. Predatory microorganisms may also influence the bacterial concentrations. *Salmonella* were detected in only one of 17 samples of water taken within the refuge.

Water leaving the refuge has lower specific conductance and generally higher dissolved-oxygen content than water flowing into the refuge. These two parameters suggest that the net effect of the refuge is to improve the quality of water that flows through it.

Table 2.—*Water-quality data for Seneca spillway at the Montezuma National Wildlife Refuge near Seneca Falls, N.Y.*

[DO, dissolved oxygen; TOC, total organic carbon]

Date / Time	8-25-71 1400	9-7-71 1500	9-21-71 1530	10-5-71 1330	10-19-71 1130	11-2-71 1100	11-16-71 1300	12-7-71 1300	2-15-72 1400	3-28-72 1345	4-11-72 1130	4-25-72 1200	5-9-72 0855	5-23-72 1130
Air temperature (°C.)	17	29	19	21	16	21	5	6	4	1	7	3.5	7	25
Water temperature (°C.)	17	24	20	20	16	17	5	0	2	3.5	5	10	9	24
Gage height (ft.)	.97	1.08	1.28	1.40	1.50	1.60	1.66	2.77	[1]2.98	2.06	1.90	1.85	1.27	1.35
Discharge (cfs.)	.0	.0	.0	.0	.0	.0	.0	[1].3	[1]1.3	1.6	11	12	[1]12	8.3
Sampling depth (ft.)	.1	.1	.1	.1	.1	.1	.1	.1	.1	.1	.1	.1	.1	.1
Specific conductance (μmhos/cm at 25°C).	545	557	594	637	602	633	667	753	838	398	350	413	507	541
pH	8.9	9.1	9.2	7.8	9.3	8.5	8.1	8.1	7.4	6.9	7.1	7.4	7.6	8.1
Carbonate (mg/l.)	8	13	16	0	16	6	0	0	0	0	0	0	0	0
Bicarbonate (mg/l.)	110	139	136	158	146	156	174	189	213	107	84	78	109	139
DO (mg/l.)	11	10	15	12	14	12	11	......	8.2	12	13	13	11	9.8
DO (percent saturation)	112	117	159	128	136	120	86	......	62	87	105	115	93	115
Ammonia as N (mg/l.)	3.4	1.5	.26	2.0	.29	1.8	1.3	.11	1.0	.5	.27	.10	.15	.02
Organic N (mg/l.)	12	5.4	4.5	5.7	4.4	6.9	5.3	1.8	1.7	1.6	2.0	2.2	1.5	2.9
Nitrate as N (mg/l.)	.2	.0	.1	.1	.0	.0	.1	.0	.2	.1	.1	.0	.1	.0
Nitrite as N (mg/l.)	.02	.01	.02	.01	.01	.01	.01	.01	.01	.01	.01	.00	.00	.01
Total N (mg/l.)	16	6.9	4.9	7.8	4.7	8.7	6.7	1.9	2.9	2.2	2.4	2.3	1.8	2.9
Phosphorus (mg/l.)	.47	.16	.27	.33	.22	.37	.31	.07	.03	.09	.13	.12	.14	.20
Total solids (mg/l.)	452	332	500	515	555	530	505	564	637	282	249	331	389	449
Fixed solids (mg/l.)	311	314	362	374	382	138	385	433	526	227	178	222	288	314
TOC (mg/l.)	13	59	51	58	33	34	34	24	20	12	21	32	35	43
Total coliform (colonies/100 ml)	....	[1]1,000	[1]1,000	13,000	1,000	2,100	800	130	<1	<1	......	60	200	8,600
Fecal coliform (colonies/100 ml)	3,600	[1]500	1,300	1,800	100	1,000	560	45	<1	<1	20	10	160	19
Fecal *Streptococci* (colonies/100 ml).	2,400	200	1,200	2,700	200	920	2,200	20	<1	[1]3	......	70	140	1,200
Remarks	Overcast; total coliform too numerous to count.	Partly cloudy.	Clear.	Partly cloudy.	Clear.	Cloudy and windy.	Overcast and windy.	Overcast; pool mostly ice covered.	Overcast and windy; pool ice covered.	Overcast and windy; pool ice covered.	Overcast.	Clear.	Overcast, windy, and rainy.	Clear.

[1] Estimated.

Table 3.—*Water-quality data for Black Brook at Tyre, N.Y.*

Date / Time	8-26-71 1030	9-8-71 1000	9-21-71 0845	10-5-71 0815	10-19-71 0800	11-2-71 0740	11-16-71 0900	12-7-71 0845	2-15-72 0900	3-28-72 0930	4-11-72 1000	4-25-72 0800	5-9-72 1530	5-23-72 0845
Air temperature (°C)	20	31	16	14	4	17	5	4	4	-1	8	2	9	17.5
Water temperature (°C)	16	25	17	15	10	12	6	1	0	1	5	7	8.5	15.5
Gage height (ft)	.18	.16	.57	.14	.14	.19	.32	2.48	[1]1.97	1.51	.94	.00	2.75	.48
Discharge (cfs)	2.1	1.9	15	1.4	.96	1.4	4.0	....	....	29	32	31	[1]97	8.9
Sampling depth (ft)	.1	.1	.1	.1	.1	.1	.1	.1	.1	.1	.1	.1	.1	.1
Specific conductance (μmhos/cm at 25°C).	1,200	1,240	816	1,420	1,680	1,610	1,360	345	643	505	570	557	318	913
pH	8.0	8.3	7.9	7.8	8.2	7.9	8.0	7.5	7.6	7.5	7.7	7.8	7.6	8.2
Carbonate (mg/l)	0	0	0	0	0	0	0	0	0	0	0	0	0	0
Bicarbonate (mg/l)	269	272	187	374	312	310	302	89	132	142	154	162	122	278
DO (mg/l)	9.7	8.5	8.0	8.4	9.8	8.5	11	....	13	14	11	12	11	10
DO (percent saturation)	98	101	82	82	87	79	90	....	86	98	88	102	94	101
Ammonia as N (mg/l)	.31	.12	.32	.15	.13	.15	.49	.37	.80	.32	.26	.12	.20	.01
Organic N (mg/l)	1.4	.88	2.6	.60	.48	.48	1.1	1.2	1.1	.88	1.1	1.1	1.2	1.1
Nitrate as N (mg/l)	.5	.3	.7	.3	.1	.0	.6	1.0	1.0	.2	.3	.2	.3	.3
Nitrite as N (mg/l)	.03	.01	.06	.01	.01	.00	.06	.03	.02	.01	.01	.01	.01	.02
Total N (mg/l)	2.2	1.3	3.7	1.1	.72	.63	2.2	2.6	2.9	1.4	1.7	1.4	1.5	1.4
Phosphorus (mg/l)	.06	.08	.29	.04	.03	.03	.06	.28	.12	.10	.07	.12	.16	.06
Total solids (mg/l)	1,220	1,090	683	1,440	1,670	1,440	1,110	370	467	388	418	468	284	790
Fixed solids (mg/l)	1,050	880	557	1,250	1,410	1,260	924	272	387	310	322	330	219	580
TOC (mg/l)	14	13	22	3	1	6	11	22	13	16	13	20	19	18
Total coliform (colonies/100 ml)	45,000	[1]1,700	[1]120,000	4,200	5,700	3,300	850	10,000	1,000	440	......	870	1,300	2,200
Fecal coliform (colonies/100 ml)	24,000	1,300	9,400	250	220	240	300	2,700	290	56	100	83	730	550
Fecal *Streptococci* (colonies/100 ml)	14,000	1,600	[1]150,000	890	240	1,000	2,800	[1]40,000	8,700	130	......	720	2,000	1,100
Remarks	Cloudy.	Partly cloudy.	Partly cloudy.	Partly cloudy.	Clear.	Intermittent rain.	Overcast and windy.	Overcast.	Overcast; ice on bottom of stream channel.	Partly cloudy and windy.	Overcast.	Clear.	Overcast and rainy.	Clear.

[1] Estimated.

Table 4.—*Water-quality data for White Brook near Tyre, N.Y.*

Date	8-26-71	9-8-71	9-22-71	10-6-71	10-20-71	11-3-71	11-17-71	12-8-71	2-16-72	3-29-72	4-12-72	4-26-72	5-10-72	5-24-72
Time	0915	1430	0800	0830	0800	0800	0745	0745	0815	0735	0930	0700	0930	0800
Air temperature . . . °C	18	31	8	13	11	10	3	4	−5	.5	9	.5	8	17
Water temperature . . . °C	16	25	12	14	11	12	5	3	0	0	5.5	4	8	15
Sampling depth . . . ft	.1	.1	.1	.1	.1	.1	.1	.1	.1	.1	.1	.1	.1	.1
Specific conductance (μmhos/cm at 25° C).	1,100	1,010	890	1,600	1,440	1,380	1,140	654	775	781	754	876	568	1,120
pH	8.2	8.5	8.1	7.9	8.1	8.0	8.0	7.7	7.6	7.8	8.1	8.0	7.9	8.1
Carbonate . . . mg/l	0	8	0	0	0	0	0	0	0	0	0	0	0	0
Bicarbonate . . . mg/l	230	282	318	310	350	400	345	221	191	239	232	265	215	320
DO . . . mg/l	8.6	8.2	9.8	7.6	6.2	8.0	11	....	14	13	12	13	11	8.4
DO (percent saturation)	87	98	91	73	56	74	88	....	93	90	92	98	96	82
Ammonia as N . . . mg/l	.16	.13	.11	.21	.24	.15	.11	.07	.20	.09	.29	.04	.05	.01
Organic N . . . mg/l	1.1	.90	.83	.55	.56	.64	.42	.61	.88	.48	.38	.49	.52	.41
Nitrate as N . . . mg/l	.2	.1	.3	.2	.1	.1	.2	1.1	1.1	.6	.5	.4	.6	.2
Nitrite as N . . . mg/l	.02	.01	.01	.01	.01	.00	.01	.01	.02	.01	.00	.00	.01	.00
Total N . . . mg/l	1.5	1.1	1.2	.97	.91	.89	.74	1.8	2.2	1.2	1.2	.93	1.2	.62
Phosphorus . . . mg/l	.10	.12	.10	.08	.11	.09	.06	.08	.07	.03	.12	.11	.07	.03
Total solids . . . mg/l	1,130	856	676	1,220	1,340	1,140	898	474	555	550	523	714	392	922
Fixed solids . . . mg/l	970	708	558	1,040	1,090	956	750	380	459	448	446	522	310	730
TOC . . . mg/l	77	13	8	4	3	3	6	9	9	5	5	18	4	7
Total coliform (colonies/100 ml)	11,000	[1]7,200	12,000	14,000	13,000	6,100	800	2,700	3,200	[1]43	......	1,600	940	4,100
Fecal coliform (colonies/100 ml)	690	[1]4,000	3,000	1,300	3,000	1,000	280	650	490	20	110	68	160	2,600
Fecal *Streptococci* (colonies/100 ml)	1,200	2,400	3,300	2,700	4,200	4,500	2,800	4,800	....	70	......	190	540	1,900
Remarks	Overcast.	Partly cloudy.	Partly cloudy.	Cloudy.	Clear windy.	Cloudy.	Overcast.	Overcast.	Partly cloudy and snowy; stream partly ice covered.	Clear.	Partly cloudy.	Clear.	Partly cloudy.	Clear.

[1] Estimated.

Table 5.—*Summary of data collected at Seneca spillway, Black Brook, and White Brook*

[TOC, total organic carbon; TC, total coliform; FC, fecal coliform; FS, fecal *Streptococci*; DO, dissolved oxygen]

Parameter	Seneca spillway				Black Brook				White Brook			
	Maximum	Minimum	Mean ($\bar{x}$)	Standard deviation (σ)	Maximum	Minimum	Mean ($\bar{x}$)	Standard deviation (σ)	Maximum	Minimum	Mean ($\bar{x}$)	Standard deviation (σ)
Discharge . . . cfs	12	0.0	3.3	0.08	97	0.96	19	1.0				
Specific conductance (μmhos/cm at 25° C).	838	350	574	.03	1,680	318	941	.83	1,600	568	1,000	22
pH	9.3	6.9	8.1	.00	8.3	7.5	7.8	.22	8.5	7.6	8.0	.00
Carbonate . . . mg/l	16	0	4	.83	0	0	0	.00	8	0	0	2.2
Bicarbonate . . . mg/l	213	78	138	1.7	374	89	222	.83	400	191	280	.55
DO . . . mg/l	15	8.2	12	.17	14	8.0	10	.14	14	6.2	10	.23
DO (percent saturation)	159	62	110	1.4	102	79	91	1.4	98	56	86	.00
Ammonia as N . . mg/l	3.4	.02	.91	.01	.80	.01	.27	.01	.29	.01	.13	.01
Organic N . . . mg/l	12	1.5	4.1	.14	2.6	.48	1.1	.05	1.1	.38	.63	.01
Nitrate plus nitrite as N (mg/l).	.2	.0	.1	.00	1.0	.0	.4	.07	1.1	.1	.4	.02
Phosphorus . . . mg/l	.47	.07	.21	.09	.29	.03	.11	.06	.12	.03	.08	.01
Total solids . . . mg/l	637	249	449	1.1	1,670	284	845	2.2	1,340	392	814	1.7
Fixed solids . . . mg/l	526	138	318	.06	1,410	219	696	.73	1,090	310	669	.28
Organic solids . . percent	74	6	29	1.4	30	12	20	1.4	27	14	18	.00
TOC . . . mg/l	59	12	34	1.9	22	1	14	.62	77	3	12	.79
TC/100 ml	13,000	<1	2,300	120	120,000	435	15,000	24,000	14,000	43	5,900	4.9
FC/100 ml	3,600	<1	650	3.9	24,000	56	2,900	110	4,000	20	1,200	160
FS/100 ml	2,400	<1	860	21	150,000	130	17,000	340	4,800	70	2,400	120

Explanation of symbols:

$$\bar{x} = \frac{\Sigma x_i}{n} \qquad \sigma = \sqrt{\frac{\Sigma x^2}{n-1}}$$

x_i = individual observation

n = total number of observations $\qquad x = x_i - \bar{x}$

REFERENCES CITED

American Public Health Association, American Water Works Association, and Water Pollution Control Federation, 1971, Standard methods for the examination of water and wastewater (13th ed.): New York, Am. Public Health Assoc. 874 p.

Brown, E. M., Skougstad, M. W., and Fishman, M. J., 1970, Methods for collection and analysis of water samples for dissolved minerals and gases: U.S. Geol. Survey Techniques Water-Resources Inv., book 5, chap. A1, 160 p.

Gallagher, T. P., and Spino, D. F., 1968, The significance of numbers of coliform bacteria as an indicator of enteric pathogens, *in* Water research: New York, Pergamon Press, v. 2, p. 169–175.

Geldreich, E. E., 1966, Sanitary significance of fecal coliforms in the environment: Federal Water Pollution Control Adm., Pub. WP-20-3, 122 p.

Geldreich, E. E., and Kenner, B. A., 1969, Concepts of fecal *Streptococci* in stream pollution: Water Pollution Control Federation Jour., v. 41, no. 8, pt. 2, p. R336–R352.

Goerlitz, D. F., and Brown, E. M., 1972, Methods for analysis of organic substances in water: U.S. Geol. Survey Techniques Water-Resources Inv., book 5, chap. A3, 40 p.

Greeson, P. E., 1971, Limnology of Oneida Lake with emphasis on factors contributing to algal blooms: U.S. Geol. Survey open-file rept., 185 p.

Moran, A. B., Van Houweling, C. D., and Ellis, E. M., 1965, The results of typing *Salmonella* from animal sources in the United States, *in* Natl. Conf. on Salmonellosis, 1964, Proc.: U.S. Public Health Service Pub. 1262. p. 33–37.

Murphy, Robert, 1968, Wild sanctuaries: New York, E. P. Dutton and Co., Inc., 288 p.

Rudolfs, W., Falk, L. L., and Ragotzkie, R. A., 1950, Literature review on the occurrence and survival of enteric, pathogenic, and relative organisms in soil, water, sewage and sludges, and on vegetation. I. Bacterial and virus diseases: Sewage and Indus. Wastes, v. 22, p. 1261–1281.

Salle, A. J., 1961, Fundamental principles of bacteriology (5th ed.): New York, McGraw-Hill, Inc., 812 p.

Slack, K. V., Biesecker, J. E., Greeson, P. E., Kolipinski, M. C., and Lipscomb, R. G., 1970, Selected procedures for biological and microbiological investigations: U.S. Geol. Survey open-file rept., 68 p.

U.S. Department of Health, Education, and Welfare, 1965, National shellfish sanitation program manual of operations. Pt. 1, Sanitation of shellfish growing areas: U.S. Dept. Health, Education, and Welfare, 32 p.

U.S. Department of the Interior, 1969, Montezuma National Wildlife Refuge: U.S. Dept. Interior, Fish and Wildlife Service, Bureau of Sport Fisheries and Wildlife Refuge Leaflet 38-R3.

Van Donsel, D. J., Geldreich, E. E., and Norman, A. C., 1967, Seasonal variations in survival of indicator bacteria in soil and their contribution to stormwater pollution: Federal Water Pollution Control Adm., 23 p.

Jour. Research U.S. Geol. Survey
Vol. 1, No. 6, Nov.-Dec. 1973, p. 735—744

FLOW CHARACTERISTICS OF A SUBSURFACE-CONTROLLED RECHARGE BASIN ON LONG ISLAND, NEW YORK

By ROBERT C. PRILL and DONALD B. AARONSON, Mineola, N.Y.

Abstract.—Ponding studies at the Woodbury recharge basin on Long Island, N.Y., show that the principal zones controlling infiltration are a surface-loam stratum and an intermediate gravelly, sandy loam stratum. The saturated hydraulic conductivities of these strata are 0.90 and 0.1 ft per day, respectively. The surface loam acts as the principal zone controlling infiltration until a perched ground-water mound develops above the intermediate gravelly, sandy loam and extends to the bottom of the surface loam; then the intermediate gravelly, sandy loam becomes the principal infiltration controlling zone. Infiltration rates at 15.6°Celsius are 1.4 ft per day when the surface loam is acting as the principal controlling zone and 0.5 ft per day when the intermediate gravelly, sandy loam is acting as the principal controlling zone. Projections of the probable infiltration rates associated with both the partial and the complete removal of the surface-loam stratum show that if recharge continues for several days total infiltration would not be greatly different whether or not the loam stratum is completely removed. The principal advantage of completely removing the surface-loam stratum is the resulting greater infiltration capacity during the early stages of ponding. This advantage is offset by potential problems associated with more intensive clogging of the subsurface controlling zone.

Recharge of ground-water reservoirs with storm runoff and highly treated domestic and industrial effluent is receiving increasing emphasis on Long Island, N.Y. Parker, Cohen, and Foxworthy (1967, p. 208) estimated that recharge of storm runoff through basins on Long Island amounted to 100 mgd in 1966. Accordingly, a major concern to Long Island water managers in selection of sites and design of recharge basins is forecasting the infiltration capacity of a basin. Among other things, such forecasting requires a quantitative description of the hydraulic properties of the materials in the unsaturated zone. Consequently, an artificial-recharge project on Long Island is presently concerned with developing such quantitative descriptions and using the data to develop and apply methods for predicting flow characteristics at basins. Study sites at which flow patterns can be evaluated quantitatively can supply valuable data for testing methods of predicting flow characteristics. More than 2,000 recharge basins are used on Long Island to collect storm runoff. Because the unsaturated zones at these basins include a wide range of lithologic conditions, the basins provide an extensive choice of sites for study. As part of the research project, seven basins on Long Island are being studied.

This report describes the flow characteristics at the Woodbury recharge basin, where infiltration rates are primarily subsurface controlled. The principal zones limiting infiltration are evaluated from test data, and the probable infiltration rates associated with alternative designs of the basin are projected to illustrate how information concerning the flow characteristics at a test site can be generalized for selecting basin design.

SITE CHARACTERISTICS

The Woodbury basin is operated by the Nassau County Department of Public Works for the collection of storm runoff. The basin is in the northeastern part of Nassau County, Long Island, N.Y., and is excavated in the Ronkonkoma terminal moraine of Pleistocene age. The basin has both a lower level and a bench level (fig. 1). However, during the 2 years in which infiltration characteristics have been studied, the level of storm runoff in the basin has never risen to the bench level.

As shown by the cross section in figure 2, the thickness of the unsaturated zone below the basin floor is about 60 feet. The principal strata in the unsaturated zone underlying the basin are a surface loam, an upper sand and gravel, an intermediate gravelly, sandy loam, and a lower sand and gravel (materials are described in this paper according to soil-survey nomenclature (Soil Survey Staff, 1951)).

FIELD MEASUREMENTS

Measurements at the Woodbury site include basin stage, temperature of the water in the basin, moisture content of materials in the unsaturated zone, water-table elevation, precipitation, and pressure head at the upper boundary of the intermediate gravelly, sandy loam stratum. Moisture content, water-table elevation, and pressure-head measurements are made at selected time intervals, generally during storms. Basin stage and temperature of the water are recorded continuously. Zero basin stage is taken as the average elevation of the lower level. Because of minor surface relief, there is a pronounced

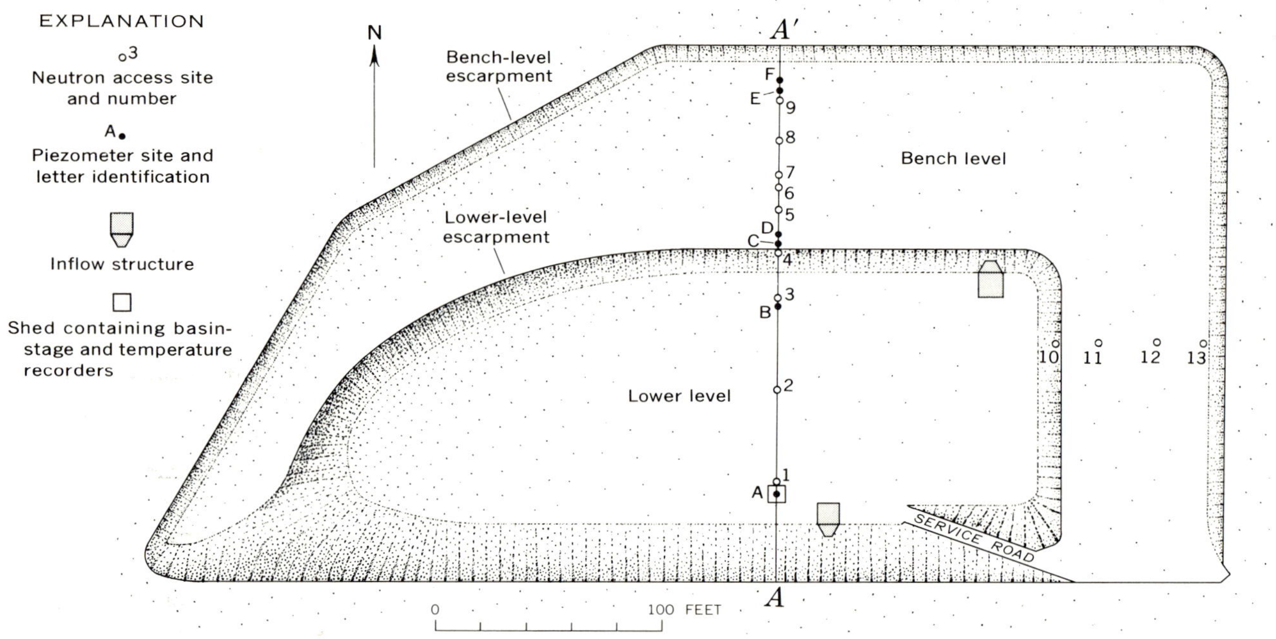

Figure 1.—Plan view of Woodbury recharge basin, showing location of instruments and structures.

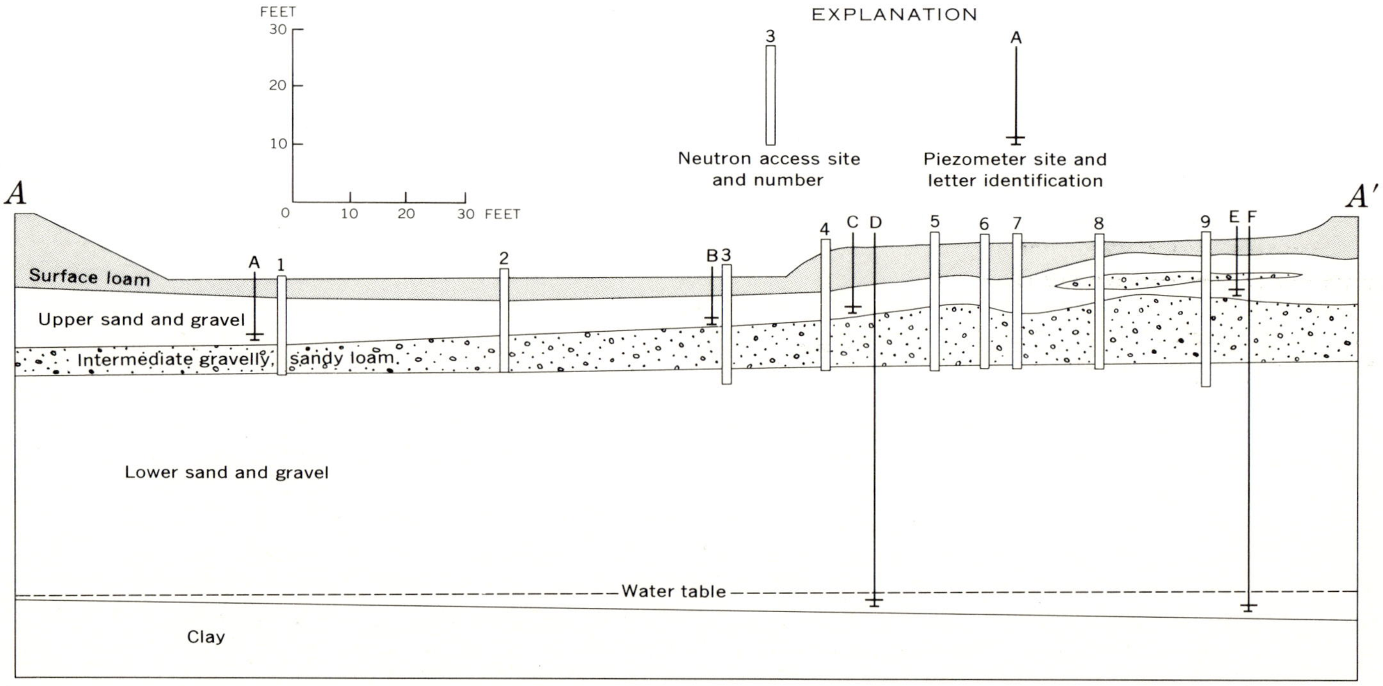

Figure 2.—Cross section of Woodbury recharge basin, showing lithology and positions of instrumentation.

increase in the flooded area as the basin stage rises from 0 to 0.15 foot.

Locations of the measuring sites are shown in figure 1. All the sites are located on a north-south traverse except for several neutron access sites used to measure moisture content by the neutron method.

The access tubing used to measure moisture content is aluminum pipe with a 2-inch outside diameter and a $^1/_{16}$-inch wall thickness. Moisture content is measured with a continuous-logging nuclear meter (Prill and Meyer, 1968) at a logging speed of 2.5 fpm.

TEST RESULTS

Three storms that occurred in September 1971, October 1971, and February 1972 were studied. Approximate inflows to the basin during the storms were 105,000 cu ft, 42,000 cu ft, and 30,000 cu ft, respectively. These inflows are equal to volumes of water having depths of 3.5 feet, 1.4 feet, and 1 foot, respectively, over an adjusted uniform basin floor having an area of 30,000 sq ft.

September 1971 storm

Water from the September storm was retained in the basin for 2.9 days. Inflow to the basin occurred intermittently and only during the first 1.6 days of ponding. Most of the data presented for this storm represent measurements after inflow ceased.

Basin stage and temperature of water in the basin after inflow ceased are shown in figure 3. The basin stage at the time inflow ceased was 0.86 foot. On the basis of basin-stage and temperature records for other storms, the volume of water that had infiltrated before this time is estimated to be 2.6 feet. The rate of decline in basin stage reflects the infiltration rate between 1.6 and 2.9 days after the start of ponding. There was a gradual decrease in the rate as the basin stage declined from 0.86 to 0.15 foot. The rate was 0.70 ft per day when the stage was at 0.75 foot and 0.65 ft per day when the stage was at 0.25 foot. As the basin stage declined below 0.15 foot, there was a gradual increase in infiltration rate. This increase was probably related to the decrease in flooded area that occurs as the basin stage drops below 0.15 foot.

Moisture logs at neutron access site 3, in the north-central part of the basin, are shown in figure 4. Because there was no inflow to the basin during the month preceding the September storm, the log showing conditions before the storm provides approximations of the soil-moisture content at various depths after complete or nearly complete field drainage. The log 1.7 days after the start of ponding shows moisture contents when the basin stage was 0.8 foot. The logs 7.5 and 10.5 days after the start of ponding show moisture contents 4.6 and 7.6 days after the end of ponding in the basin.

Pressure heads at the upper boundary of the intermediate gravelly, sandy loam stratum at piezometer B for the period from 0 to 8 days after the start of storm are shown in figure 5.

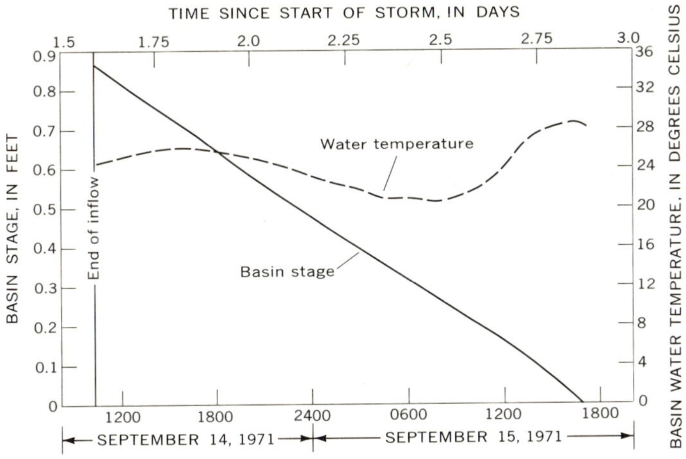

Figure 3.—Basin stage and water temperature during the September 1971 storm.

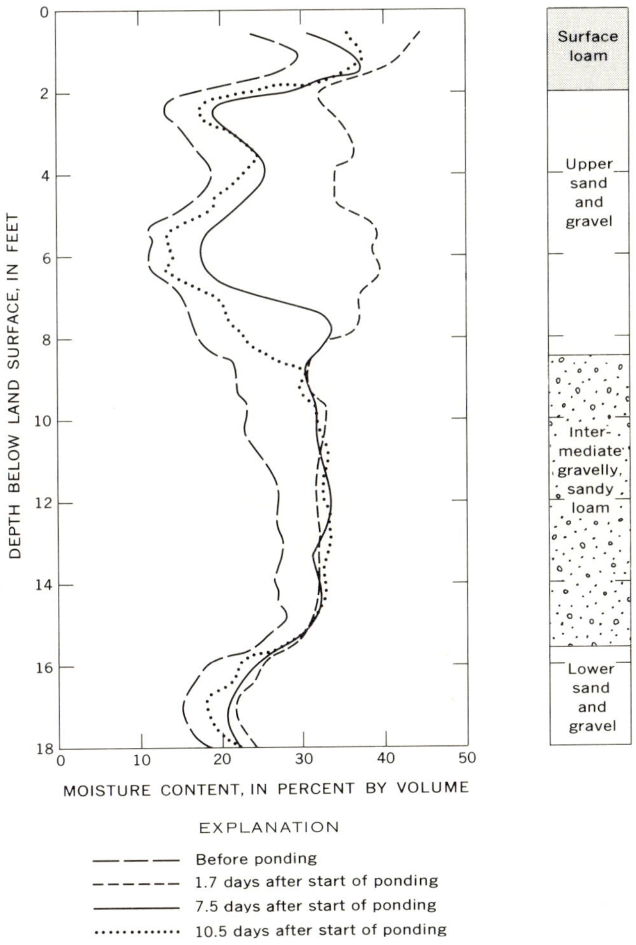

Figure 4.—Logs showing soil-moisture content at neutron access site 3 before ponding caused by September 1971 storm and after start of ponding.

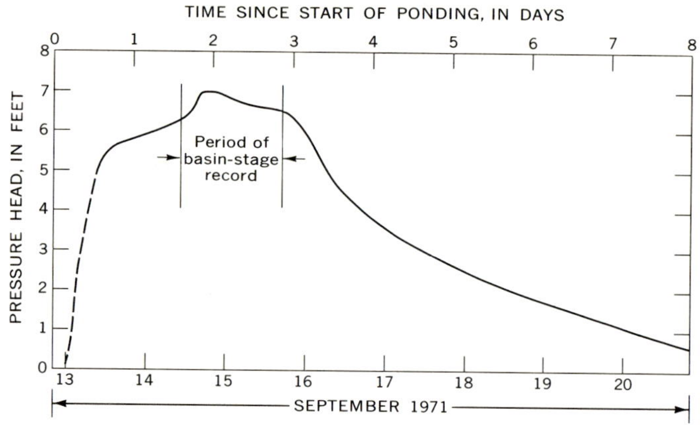

Figure 5.—Pressure head at upper boundary of intermediate gravelly, sandy loam stratum at piezometer B. Dashed where inferred.

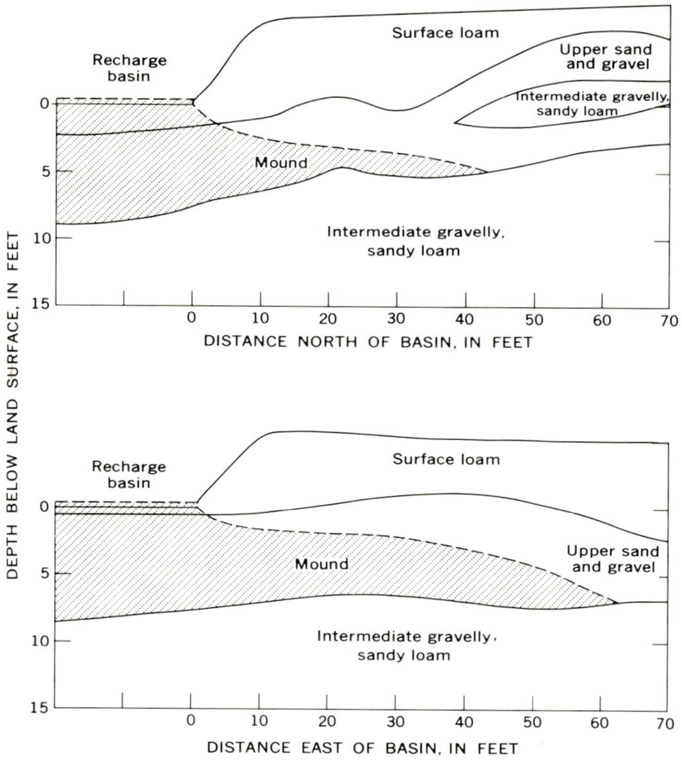

Figure 6.—Perched ground-water mound north (top) and east (bottom) of recharge basin 2.7 days after start of ponding.

Piezometer B is only 4 feet from neutron access site 3. Moisture logs at this sight (fig. 4) and head measurements in the piezometers show that the intermediate gravelly, sandy loam stratum was unsaturated before the storm. Thus, at the start of the storm, the pressure head at the upper boundary of this stratum was negative. The pressure-head data shown in figure 5 reflect a perched ground-water mound in the upper sand and gravel that develops rapidly during ponding and dissipates slowly after ponding.

Lateral spreading of the perched mound north and east of the basin 2.7 days after the start of ponding is projected in figure 6 on the basis of neutron moisture measurements. The lateral extent of the mound at this time was 60 feet east and 45 feet north of the basin. Neutron moisture measurements show that further lateral movement of the mound was insignificant.

Water-table measurements at piezometer D, 13 feet north of the basin, are shown in figure 7 for the period 1 to 10 days after the start of ponding. The first evidence of a rise in the water table at this point was noted about 1 day after the basin had drained. The water table rose 2 feet during the following week.

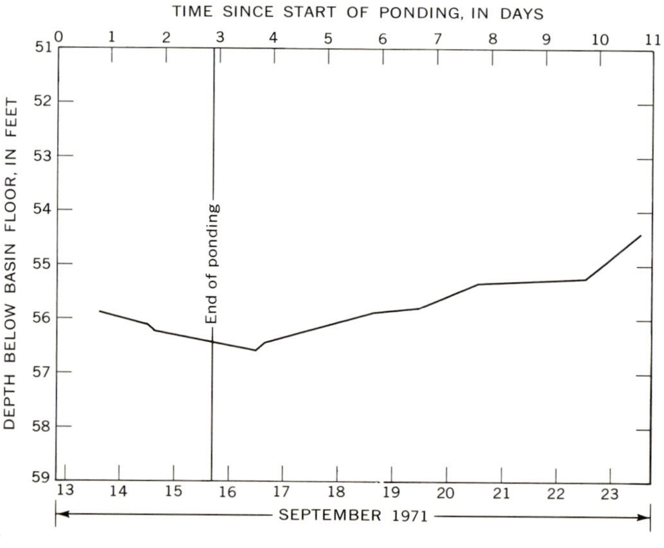

Figure 7.—Water table at piezometer D during the September 1971 storm.

October 1971 storm

Water from the October storm was retained in the basin for nearly 1 day. Total inflow into the basin was 1.4 feet. Most of the inflow (1.1 feet) was from a storm of high intensity and short duration. As shown in figure 8, inflow from this storm ended 0.3 day after the start of ponding. Total infiltration up to this time is estimated to be 0.4 foot. There was no inflow to the basin between 0.3 and 0.7 day after the start of ponding. The rate of decline in basin stage during this period shows that the infiltration rate gradually decreased with time from 1.44 ft per day when the basin stage was at 0.5 foot to 1.30 ft per day when the stage was at 0.2 foot.

A storm of low intensity occurred 0.7 day after the start of ponding. Inflow from this storm continued through much of the remaining period of record and prevented any further measurements of infiltration rate.

February 1972 storm

Water from the February storm was retained in the basin for nearly 1 day. Inflow of approximately 1 foot resulted from a

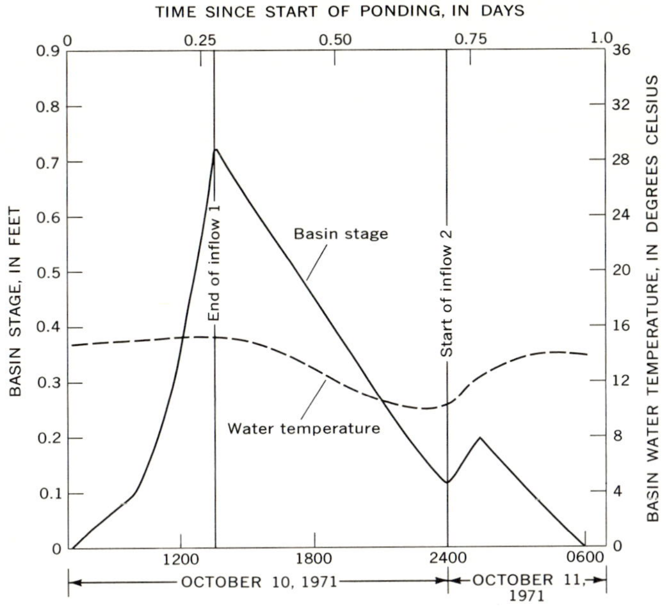

Figure 8.—Basin stage and water temperature during the October 1971 storm.

storm of high intensity and short duration. As shown in figure 9, inflow to the basin ended 0.25 day after the start of the storm. Total infiltration during the first 0.25 day of the storm is estimated to be 0.3 foot. As in the October storm, the infiltration rate decreased gradually with time. The rate was 1.02 ft per day when the stage was 0.5 foot and 0.92 ft per day when the stage was 0.2 foot. Although the storm occurred in midwinter, the materials in the unsaturated zone were not frozen because the weather before the storm was exceptionally mild.

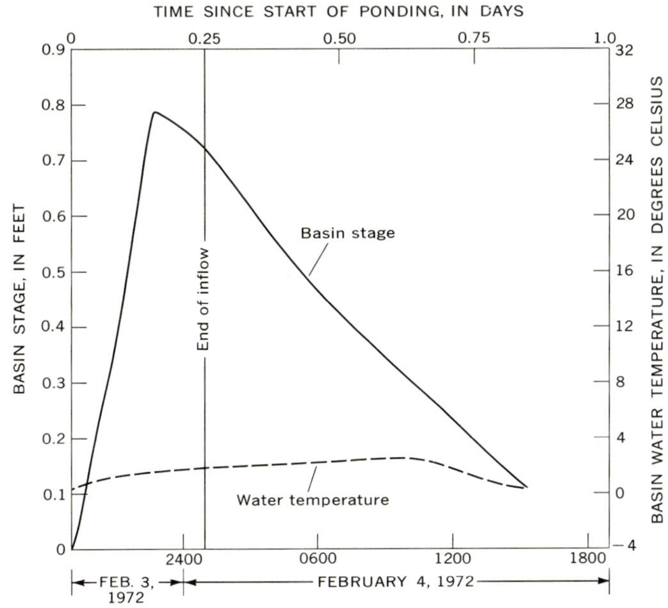

Figure 9.—Basin stage and water temperature during the February 1972 storm.

ZONES LIMITING INFILTRATION

The rate of decline in basin stage during periods when there was no inflow into the basin represents the infiltration rate. Because of differences in storm patterns, the periods for which the basin stage records could be used for determining infiltration rates were different for each of the three storms. The periods used to determine infiltration rates, as measured from the time ponding started, were from 1.6 to 2.9 days, 0.3 to 0.7 day, and 0.25 to 0.85 day for the September 1971, October 1971, and February 1972 storms, respectively. During these periods, total infiltration increased from 2.6 to 3.46 feet, 0.4 to 1.0 foot, and 0.3 to 1.0 foot, respectively.

Infiltration rates measured for the October and the February storms were markedly higher than those measured for the September storm. After adjustments were made for water temperature (Lohman and others, 1972), the average rate was 1.4 ft per day for the October and the February storms and 0.5 ft per day for the September storm. Adjusted rates are compared for the three storms in table 1 at times when the basin stage was at 0.5 foot and at 0.2 foot. As discussed later in the report, the difference in rates was largely related to changes in the hydrologic controls of the system. The higher rates for the October and the February storms, when total infiltration was less than 1 foot, reflect the intake capacity of the basin when the surface-loam stratum was acting as the principal limiting zone. The lower rates measured during the September storm, when total infiltration was between 2.60 and 3.64 feet, reflect the intake capacity of the basin when the intermediate gravelly, sandy loam stratum was acting as the principal limiting zone.

Surface-loam stratum as the principal limiting zone

During ponding, the surface-loam stratum is the principal zone limiting infiltration until the top of the perched ground-water mound that develops above the intermediate gravelly, sandy loam has extended to the bottom of the surface loam (fig. 2). Until this time, the infiltration rate will depend on the hydraulic conductivity of the surface-loam stratum and the pressure head that develops at the upper and the lower boundaries of the stratum. The pressure head that develops at the upper boundary will be positive and equivalent to the basin stage. The pressure head at the lower boundary will be negative because the hydraulic conductivity of the upper sand and gravel is many times higher than the infiltration rate. Thus, flow in the sand and gravel (above the perched mound) will be unsaturated flow and under negative pressure. Negative pressures will be small. Laboratory measurements of the relationship between unsaturated flow rates and negative pressures for the sand and gravel show that rates of 10 feet and 1 ft per day are associated with pressure heads of −0.30 and −0.57 foot of water, respectively. On the basis of these values and an assumed infiltration rate of 1.4 ft per day, the maximum pressure head that could occur at the lower

Table 1.—*Comparison of infiltration rates for basin stages of 0.2 and 0.5 foot during storms of September and October 1971 and February 1972*

Storm	Time since start of ponding (days)	Basin stage (feet)	Total infiltration (feet)	Infiltration rate (ft per day)	Water temperature (°C)	Infiltration rate adusted to 15.6°C (60°F)
September	2.6	0.2	3.3	0.63	24	0.51
	2.1	.5	3.0	.66	24	.54
October	.6	.2	.9	1.30	14	1.32
	.4	.5	.6	1.44	14	1.46
February	.7	.2	.8	.92	2	1.36
	.4	.5	.5	1.02	2	1.51

boundary of the surface-loam is about −0.5 foot. As illustrated in figure 10, the negative head at the lower boundary of the surface-loam stratum will change only slightly until the perched mound has reached the lower boundary.

The perched mound is unlikely to reach the lower boundary of the surface-loam stratum until total infiltration exceeds 1 foot, as available storage space in the upper sand and gravel is at least 1.2 feet. Thus, the infiltration rates measured during the October and the February storms should reflect the intake capacity of the basin when the surface-loam stratum is acting as the principal zone limiting infiltration.

During both the October and the February storms, the infiltration rate decreased as basin stage decreased. (See figs. 8 and 9 and table 1.) This decrease in rate was probably related to the decrease in hydraulic gradient across the loam stratum as the basin stage declined. For instance, the decrease in infiltration rate associated with a decline in basin stage from 0.5 to 0.2 foot was about 10 percent during both storms. On the basis of the probable pressure-head distribution across the loam stratum (fig. 10), a decrease of 0.3 foot in basin stage would result in a nearly 12 percent decrease in the hydraulic

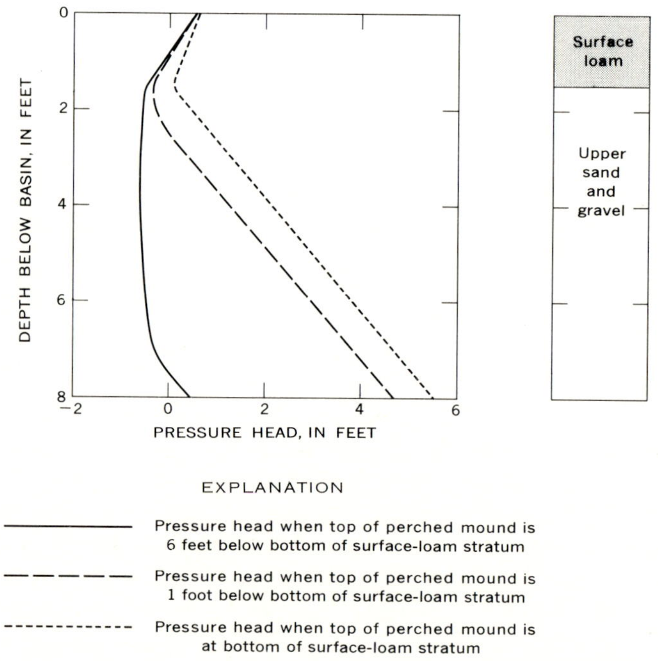

Figure 10.—Pressure head below basin when top of perched mound is in the upper sand and gravel stratum and basin stage is 0.5 foot.

gradient across the stratum. That the observed changes are similar to computed changes is evidence of the approximate correctness of the model chosen. Hence, further utilization of the model for predictive purposes seems justified.

Test data for the October and the February storms indicate that the average vertical hydraulic conductivity of the surface-loam stratum was nearly 0.8 ft per day at 15.6°C (Celsius) or 60°F. This value is based on computations using Darcy's law, which, for vertical flow, can be expressed as

$$Q = K\left(\frac{dh}{dl} + 1\right),$$

where

Q = flux,
K = vertical hydraulic conductivity,
dl = thickness of the surface-loam stratum, and
dh = change in pressure head from the lower boundary to the upper boundary of the surface-loam stratum.

Because most if not all the flow through the surface-loam stratum is probably vertical, or nearly so, the infiltration rate represents the flux through the stratum. When the basin stage during the October storm was 0.5 foot, the infiltration rate was 1.44 ft per day, and the water temperature was 14°C (table 1). Thus, Q was 1.44 feet per day, and the pressure head at the upper boundary of the surface stratum was 0.5 foot. The pressure head at the lower boundary was about −0.5 foot, as illustrated in figure 10. Thus, dh was 1.0 foot. The average thickness of the surface-loam stratum is 1.5 feet.

The computation of vertical hydraulic conductivity of the surface-loam stratum using the preceding values is as follows:

$$K = \frac{Q}{\frac{dh}{dl} + 1} = \frac{1.44 \text{ ft per day}}{\frac{1 \text{ ft}}{1.5 \text{ ft}} + 1} = 0.86 \text{ ft per day at } 14°\text{C}.$$

By correcting for viscosity, the vertical hydraulic conductivity at 15.6°C (60°F) is 0.90 ft per day.

Intermediate gravelly, sandy loam stratum as the principal limiting zone

When the perched ground-water mound rises above the lower boundary of the surface-loam stratum, the intermediate gravelly, sandy loam stratum becomes the principal zone controlling infiltration. The infiltration rate of about 0.7 ft per day observed between 1.6 and 2.9 days after the start of the September storm (fig. 3) reflects the intake capacity of the basin after the perched mound coincides with the basin stage. The nature of the pressure-head distribution below the basin during this period is shown in figure 11 for stages of 0.7 and 0.1 foot. Each of the pressure-head profiles is an extrapolation based on measured and inferred pressure heads at the lithologic boundaries. The value at the upper boundary of the surface loam is equal to basin stage. The value at the lower boundary (computed by Darcy's law) is the pressure head required to move water vertically through the surface loam at a rate of 0.7 ft per day. The pressure head at the upper boundary of the intermediate gravelly, sandy loam was determined from field measurements (fig. 5). The pressure head at the lower boundary of this stratum is negative, as flow through the lower sand and gravel is unsaturated flow.

The intermediate gravelly, sandy loam, the only stratum in which the hydraulic gradient is greater than 1 (fig. 11), is the principal zone limiting infiltration. Because the hydraulic gradient across this zone decreases by only a few percent as the basin stage decreases from 0.7 to 0.1 foot, very little change in infiltration rate would be expected when the change in basin stage is less than 1 foot. This condition explains the nearly constant infiltration rate during the September storm.

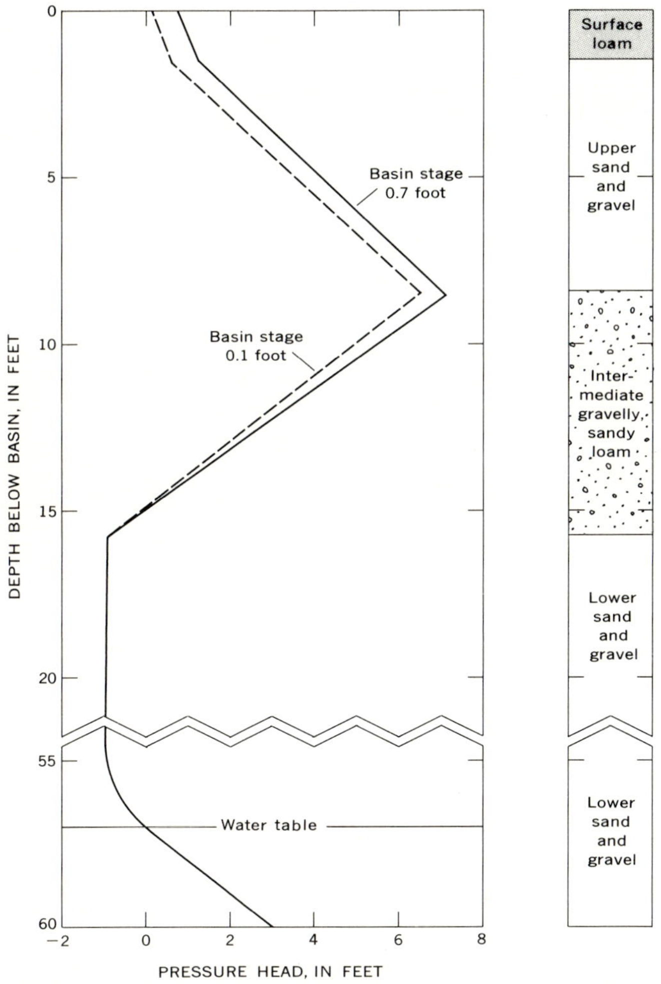

Figure 11.—Pressure head below basin when top of perched mound is coincident with basin stage.

The average hydraulic conductivity of the intermediate gravelly, sandy loam seems to be slightly less than 0.1 ft per day, on the basis of analysis of storage and pressure-head changes shown in figures 4 and 5, respectively. The data in these figures were obtained in the north-central part of the basin. After the end of infiltration, the perched ground water at this location would be almost horizontal. Thus, the flux across the gravelly, sandy loam may be approximated by multiplying the short-term specific yield of the upper sand and gravel (about 0.15, from the neutron logs shown in figure 4) by the rate of water-level decline.

At 5.8 days after the start of ponding (2.9 days after the end of infiltration), the rate of decline in pressure head at the upper boundary of the intermediate gravelly, sandy loam stratum was 0.8 ft per day. Multiplying this rate by 0.15 gives a value for the upper limit of flux (Q) through the confining zone of 0.12 ft per day. At this time, the pressure head at the upper boundary of the zone was 2.0 feet. Laboratory measurements of the relationship of hydraulic conductivity and pressure head indicate that at the above flux the pressure head at the lower boundary of the zone was about −1 foot. Thus the change in pressure head from the lower boundary to the upper boundary of the unit (dh) was 3 feet. The thickness of the unit (dl) is 8 feet. The temperature of the water was about 25°C. Assuming steady state, it follows from Darcy's law that

$$K = \frac{Q}{\frac{dh}{dl}+1} = \frac{0.12 \text{ ft per day}}{\frac{3 \text{ ft}}{8 \text{ ft}}+1} = 0.09 \text{ ft per day at } 25^{\circ}\text{C}.$$

The upper limit of hydraulic conductivity of 0.1 foot per day for the intermediate gravelly, sandy loam stratum is considerably less than that computed for the surface-loam stratum, which, when adjusted to 25°C, is 1.1 feet per day. The lower hydraulic conductivity largely reflects the greater heterogenity of the intermediate gravelly, sandy loam stratum, which produced lower porosities.

EFFECT OF MOUNDING OF THE WATER TABLE ON INFILTRATION CAPACITY

Mounding of the regional water table did not affect the infiltration capacity of the basin during the three storms. Even if the ponding were of long duration, the infiltration rate would probably be unaffected by such mounding. In order to have any noticeable affect on the infiltration capacity of the basin, the mound would have to rise to near the lower boundary of the intermediate gravelly, sandy loam stratum. The large unsaturated thickness of the lower sand and gravel stratum, about 40 feet, and the small rise in the water table during the September storm (fig. 7) would seem to rule out mounding of the regional water table as a factor controlling the infiltration rate of the basin.

COMPARISON OF ALTERNATIVE BASIN DESIGNS

Part of the potential storage capacity of recharge basins is above ground and is represented by the volume of the basin. The remainder is underground and is represented mainly by unsaturated voids in the materials underlying the basin. Because the quantity of water that can be taken into underground storage over a given period of time depends on infiltration capacity, each site, ideally, would be designed in a manner that will maximize infiltration and storage and minimize costs of construction and maintenance.

In the discussion that follows, the probable infiltration rates associated with two designs at the Woodbury site are considered to illustrate how test data of the type presented in this report might be used to evaluate different basin designs.

Alternative basin designs at the Woodbury site could involve excavating the basin into either the surface loam or the upper sand and gravel strata. Because the intermediate gravelly, sandy loam stratum is 22 to 30 feet below the land surface, excavation into this stratum is not practical.

Of two designs that might be considered, one would involve partial removal and the other complete removal of the surface-loam stratum. Cross sections of the two designs are identified in figure 12 as designs A and B. The design configuration is that of an inverted truncated pyramid. The volume of materials required to be excavated is the same for the two designs. Because a large land area is required for design A, the land-acquisition cost would be higher. However, this higher cost would be offset somewhat by the higher cost of excavating and installing inflow facilities for design B.

If water were added at a rate that would maintain a volume of about 60,000 cu ft in the basins, the water level in the basins would be as shown in figure 12. The anticipated quantity of water that would be taken into storage below the basins at 15.6°C (60°F) is shown in figure 13.

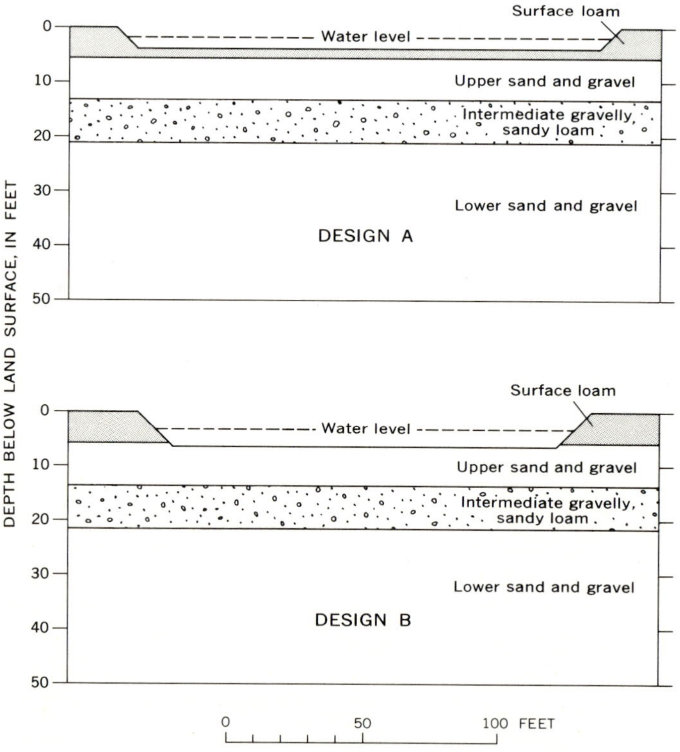

Figure 12.—Two designs for recharge basins at the Woodbury site.

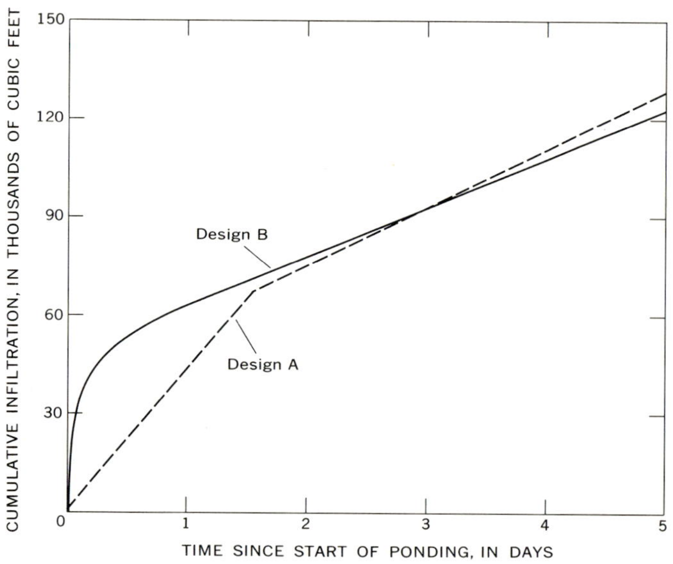

Figure 13.—Projected cumulative infiltration for two designs (fig. 12) of recharge basins at the Woodbury site.

The infiltration rate at basin B would be very high at the beginning of ponding because of the high hydraulic conductivity of the upper sand and gravel. A perched-water mound would develop rapidly above the intermediate gravelly, sandy loam stratum, and within a few hours the infiltration rate would decrease. Lateral spreading of the mound would continue for a short period. The infiltration rate would decrease at a decreasing rate during this period, after which a nearly steady-state infiltration rate would be obtained.

During the early stages of ponding, the infiltration rate at basin A would be controlled by the surface-loam stratum. The initial rate would be considerably less than at basin B but several times higher than if the rate were controlled by the intermediate gravelly, sandy loam stratum. Because a much longer time would be required for the development of the mound above the intermediate gravelly, sandy loam stratum, this stratum would not be fully effective as a controlling zone until cumulative infiltration was about 65,000 cu ft.

When the intermediate gravelly, sandy loam is fully effective as a limiting zone, the pressure head at the upper boundary of this stratum in the area immediately below the basin is similar for the two designs. Therefore, the quantity of water that would infiltrate during a given time would be directly related to the basin area. Because the basin area would be about 32,000 sq ft at basin A, as compared with 24,000 sq ft at basin B, a larger quantity would infiltrate at basin A. After about 3 days, cumulative infiltration at basin A would exceed that at basin B.

The principal advantage gained by completely removing the surface-loam stratum is that of increasing the quantity of water taken into underground storage during the early stages of ponding. After a few days of continued ponding, the quantity taken into underground storage would not be greatly different whether the stratum were completely removed or only partly removed.

The importance of the added storage capacity in the initial stages of ponding can be evaluated as illustrated in figure 14. Here the storage capacities of the two designs are compared with maximum expected runoff for 50- and 100-year intervals. Storage capacity is equal to the volume of the basin available for water storage (130,000 cu ft) plus cumulative infiltration taken from figure 13. Maximum expected runoff is equal to *IDAP*, where *I* and *D* are rain intensity and rain duration, respectively, *A* is the drainage area served by the recharge basin, and *P* is the runoff-rainfall ratio characterizing the area. Maximum expected runoffs for 50- and 100-year intervals pertain to a drainage area of 15 acres with a runoff-rainfall ratio of 0.40. Rain intensity and rain duration are obtained from precipitation-intensity data for New York City (Miller and Frederick, 1969).

As shown in figure 13, both recharge-basin designs would have sufficient storage capacity to contain the maximum expected runoff for a 50-year interval. Design B would also have sufficient storage capacity to contain the maximum expected runoff for a 100-year interval. However, the storage capacity of design A would be only marginally adequate for a 100-year interval.

The advantage of increasing underground storage during the early stages of ponding should be weighed against the likelihood that clogging of the intermediate gravelly, sandy loam stratum would be accelerated as a result of the complete stripping of the surface-loam stratum. Studies by Berend, Rebhun, and Kahana (1967) and Thomas (1968) show that when water containing particulate matter is applied over coarse-textured media the particulate matter is only partly filtered as it moves through the media. If a fine-textured stratum occurs below the coarse-textured media, a considerable amount of the particulate matter is removed near the upper boundary of the fine-textured stratum. In contrast, if water is applied over a medium or fine-textured material, much of the particulate matter is removed near the surface. The finer textured media not only acts as a more effective filter but also lowers the infiltration rate. At lower infiltration rates, more time is allowed for the settling of particulate matter from water in the reservoir.

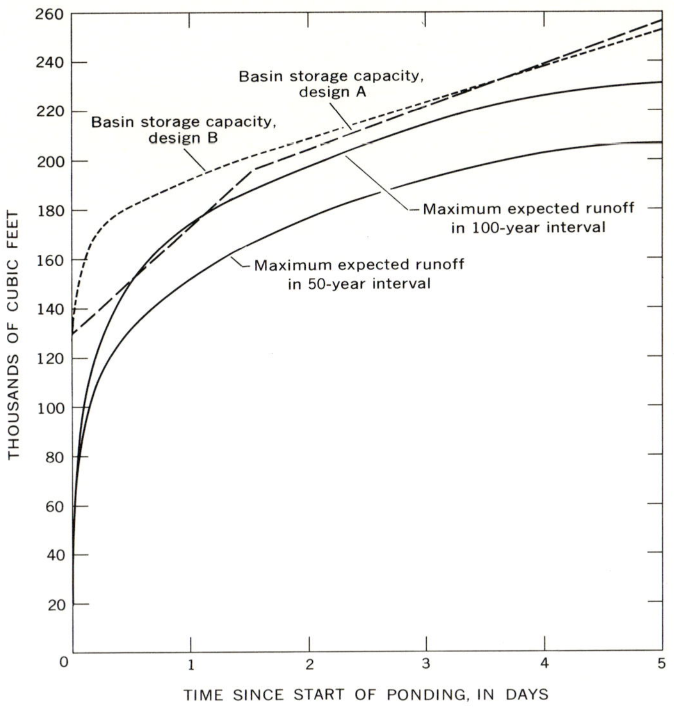

Figure 14.—Comparison between storage capacities of two recharge basin designs (fig. 12) and maximum expected runoffs for 50- and 100-year intervals.

When clogging occurs at or near the land surface, several procedures for restoring the intake capacity of the basin can be used. Among them are surface stripping, raking, and initiating vegetal growth. When clogging occurs at depth, restoring the intake capacity may not be feasible. In essence, clogging at depth may be irreversible.

SUMMARY

The principal zones limiting infiltration at the Woodbury recharge basin are a surface loam, with an average thickness of 1.5 feet, and an intermediate gravelly sandy loam, with an average thickness of 8 feet. These strata are separated by a sand and gravel stratum with a thickness of about 7 feet. The hydraulic conductivities of the limiting zones, computed from field and laboratory data, were 0.90 ft per day for the surface loam and 0.10 ft per day for the intermediate gravelly, sandy loam. The surface stratum acts as the principal zone limiting infiltration until a perched-ground-water mound develops above the intermediate gravelly, sandy loam stratum and extends to near the bottom of the surface loam. Then the intermediate gravelly, sandy loam becomes the principal limiting zone. Infiltration rates at 15.6°C were about 1.4 ft per day, when the surface loam was the principal limiting zone and 0.5 ft per day, when the intermediate gravelly, sandy loam was the principal limiting zone.

The design of a subsurface-controlled recharge basin, ideally, would provide maximum infiltration and storage at minimum costs of construction and maintenance. Design selection requires predictions of the infiltration rates that will occur if successive layers of material below the land surface are removed.

In this report, probable infiltration rates associated with two designs of the Woodbury recharge basin are projected from the interpretation of field-test data. In one design the surface-loam stratum is completely removed, and in the other the stratum is only partly removed. The projections illustrate how information concerning the flow characteristics associated with known inputs might be generalized for selecting a basin design.

Projection of infiltration rates showed that if ponding continued for several days total infiltration for the two designs would not be greatly different. The principal advantage in completely removing the surface stratum is a greater infiltration capacity during the early stages of ponding. This advantage would have to be weighed against problems that are likely to occur from clogging. Complete removal of the surface stratum is likely to result in more intensive clogging of the subsurface controlling zone. If the surface stratum is only partly removed, clogging is likely to be largely a surface phenomenon. Restoration of the infiltration capacity is much more readily achieved under this condition.

REFERENCES CITED

Berend, J. E., Rebhun, M., and Kahana, Yona, 1967, Use of storm runoff for artificial recharge: Am. Soc. Agr. Engineers Trans., v. 10, no. 5, p. 678–684.

Lohman, S. W., and others, 1972, Definitions of selected ground-water terms—revisions and conceptual refinements: U.S. Geol. Survey Water-Supply Paper 1988, 21 p.

Miller, J. F., and Frederick, R. H., 1969, The precipitation regime of Long Island, New York: U.S. Geol. Survey Prof. Paper 627-A, 21 p.

Parker, G. G., Cohen, Philip, and Foxworthy, B. L., 1967, Artificial recharge and its role in scientific water management, with emphasis on Long Island, New York, *in* Marino, M. A., ed., Symposium on ground-water hydrology, San Francisco, Calif., Nov. 6–8, 1967, Proc.: Urbana, Ill., The Am. Water Resources Assoc. Proc., ser. 4, p. 193–213.

Prill, R. C., and Meyer, W. R., 1968, Neutron moisture measurements by continuous- and point-logging procedures, *in* Geological Survey Research 1968: U.S. Geol. Survey Prof. Paper 600-B, p. B226–230.

Soil Survey Staff, 1951, Soil survey manual: U.S. Dept. Agriculture Handb. 18, 501 p.

Thomas, R. L., 1968, Coarse filter media for artificial recharge: Illinois State Water Survey, Urbana, Rept. Inv. 60, 23 p.

ANNUAL INDEX TO VOLUME 1

Journal of Research of the U.S. Geological Survey

[Issue number precedes colon; page number follows colon]

SUBJECT INDEX

A

Activity products, cryolite, in water . 4:483
fluorite, in thermal water 3:367
Aerial photography, photoimages for map bases 3:327
use in studying turbidity plumes 5:609
Aeromagnetic studies, western Montana 2:179
Africa. *See* Algeria, Liberia, Tunisia.
Age determinations, granitic rocks, Michigan 2:165
lunar samples 1:1
Mesozoic hornblendes, California 1:45
metamorphic rocks, Yucatan Channel 2:157
olivine latite flow, California .. 6:691
peat, Alaska 3:309
quartz monzonite, Montana .. 4:403
Tertiary intrusive rocks, Utah . 2:173
tuffs, volcanic breccias, and basalt, Montana 2:179
Alaska, field-note system, southeastern part 5:579
metamorphic spring waters, Alaska Range 5:523
paleontology, northern part .. 2:137
southern part 2:125
radioelement distribution, Fairbanks area 6:659
sedimentology, Admiralty Island 3:309
Algeria, 1969 flood, summary account 1:121
Ammonites, Cretaceous, Colorado and New Mexico 4:459
Cretaceous, New Jersey and Texas 6:695
Jurassic, California 4:453
Analyses. *See specific types:* Calorimetric, Cation exchange, Chemical, Microanalysis, Microprobe, Modal, Neutron activation, Radiochemical, Spectrochemical, Spectrographic, Spectrometric, Spectrophotometric, Spectroscopic, X-ray.
Analytical methods, effect of laboratory treatments on element content of gold 2:211
precautionary note on mixed solvent composition in extraction procedures ... 2:221
See also Methods and techniques.
Antimony, in orpiment, Nevada ... 1:85
Apatite, accessory, rare-earth assemblages in 3:267
from hybrid granitoid rocks, Nevada 1:89
Apollo 14, Fra Mauro breccias, geologic studies 1:1
Aquifers, change in potentiometric head, Long Island, N.Y. ... 3:345
determination of diffusivity by flood-wave response method 5:597
recharge studies, Long Island, N.Y. 3:341
specific yield studies, Arizona . 3:371
use of tracers in sand-model studies of salt encroachment 2:243
See also Ground water.
^{40}Ar-^{39}Ar age, lunar samples 1:1
Archaeocycas, new genus of Permian cycad 6:687
Arctic, paleogeography, Permian ... 5:501
Argon-oxygen d-c arc, use in spectrochemical computer analysis 5:559
Arizona, ground water, southeastern part 3:371
mineralogy, Jerome mining area 6:673
northwestern part 4:377
geomorphology Canyon de Chelly 2:193
surface water, south-central part 4:493
Arkose, California, offset along San Andreas fault 1:45
Artificial recharge, geochemistry of water 2:237
infiltration studies 6:735
use of purified sewage in 3:341
Artinite, enthalpy of formation 5:535
Astrogeology, Germany and moon, crater ejecta compared .. 1:1
Automation, photomechanical processes in cartography 2:223

B

Baculites undatus Stephenson, new occurrences, Colorado and New Mexico 4:459
Barstow Formation, California, mineralogy 4:377
Basalt, California and Oregon, isotope studies 6:643
content of potassium, uranium, and thorium 4:387
magnetization, western Montana 2:179
Basaltic lava, Kilauea Volcano, Hawaii, loss of volatiles .. 6:649
Bell Creek Gneiss, Michigan, structural geology 2:165
Bench marks, geologic, establishment by terrestrial photography 2:193
Big Sandy Formation, Arizona, mineralogy 4:377
Biostratigraphy. *See* Paleontology, Stratigraphy.
Biotite, electron microprobe analysis, for tuff-bed correlation 1:39
Birds, effects on water quality, New York 6:725

Page

Blueschist, California, metamorphism ... 1:53
Boron, in potassium feldspar of authigenic origin ... 4:377
Boyden Cave pendant, California, structural geology ... 4:453
Breccia, Fra Mauro, comparison with terrestrial ejecta ... 1:1
  magnetization, western Montana ... 2:179
Briones Sandstone, California, zeolites ... 3:255
Butano Sandstone, California, sedimentation ... 4:439

C

Calcium, ionic activity in recharge water ... 2:237
Calderas, Colorado, volcanic history 6:627
California, biostratigraphy, Paso Robles Formation ... 5:509
  geophysics, San Andreas fault . 5:569
  glacial geology, Sierra Nevada . 2:229
  isotope studies ... 6:643
  mineralogy, Sierra Nevada ... 6:665
    southern part ... 4:377
  petrology, central coast ... 3:251
    Klamath Mountains ... 1:53
    northern part ... 4:383
  pollen, Lake Tahoe area ... 6:691
  sedimentary petrology, Coast Ranges ... 3:255
  sedimentation, Santa Cruz Mountains ... 4:439
  slope-stability studies, San Francisco Bay region ... 4:431
  structural geology, Klamath Mountains ... 1:53
    Monterey Bay area ... 3:273
    Pacific coast ... 1:45
    Sierra Nevada ... 4:453
Calorimetric analysis, artinite and huntite ... 5:535
  nesquehonite and hydromagnesite ... 5:543
Cambrian, eastern United States, sedimentology ... 1:63
Canyons, submarine, Puerto Rico .. 3:293
Carbon-14 age, peat, Alaska ... 3:309
Carbonate rocks, eastern United States, dolomitization model ... 1:63
  surface runoff relations ... 3:351
Caribbean Sea. *See* Yucatan Channel.
Cartography, automated, photomechanical experiments . 2:223
Cation exchange analysis, smectite, Utah ... 4:415
Cenozoic, Colorado, revised volcanic history ... 6:627
  Colorado and New Mexico, petrology ... 4:387

Cenozoic—Continued
  model for climatic change ... 5:587
  See also Eocene, Miocene, Pleistocene, Pliocene, Tertiary.
Cesium isotopes, in water, rapid determination ... 1:113
Channels, effect of seasonal vegetation on floodflow in ... 5:621
Chemical analysis, apatite, Nevada . 1:89
  blueschist facies rocks, California ... 1:53
  Canadian River water, Texas .. 2:237
  rodingite, California ... 6:665
  smectite, Utah ... 4:415
  sulfur determination by turbidimetric method ... 1:81
Chlorite, microprobe analysis ... 6:673
Chromatography, gel-permeation, humic acid fractionation . 3:361
Climate, model for causes of changes 5:587
Closed-basin deposits, boron-bearing potassium feldspar in ... 4:377
Cobalt, determination in soil and sediment ... 6:681
Colorado, mineralogy, Gilpin County ... 3:267
  oil shale, northwestern part ... 4:467
  paleontology, Pierre Shale ... 4:459
  petrology, southern part ... 4:387
  stratigraphy, northwestern part 1:39
  volcanism, San Juan Mountains 6:627
Compeau Creek Gneiss, Michigan, structural geology ... 2:165
Computer applications, instrumentation for spectrochemical analysis ... 4:475
  machine-processable field-note system ... 5:579
  spectrochemical analysis of silicate rocks ... 5:559
Conglomerate, California, offset along San Andreas fault .. 1:45
Contamination, PCB's in aquatic environment ... 5:603
  potential effects of wastes stored underground ... 6:719
Continental margin, Liberia, bathymetry ... 5:563
Continental shelf, lower Paleozoic, carbonate sedimentology 1:63
Copper, determination in soil and sediment ... 6:681
  potential deposit, Texas ... 5:519
Corals, new species, Alaska ... 2:137
Cretaceous, Alaska, paleontology .. 2:125
  California, structural geology . 1:45
  Colorado and New Mexico, ammonites ... 4:459
  Montana, magnetic studies ... 2:179
  New Jersey and Texas, paleontology ... 6:695
Cryolite, equilibrium in water ... 4:483
Cuprobismutite, new data for ... 1:99

Cycads, new Permian genera ... 6:687

D

Diamictite, Precambrian, Montana . 4:403
Diamicton, in a landslide scarp, Alaska ... 3:309
Diffusivity, aquifer, determination by flood-wave response method ... 5:597
Dolomitization model, lower Paleozoic, eastern United States ... 1:63
Dun Mountain ultramafic belt, New Zealand, structural geology ... 5:529
Dye, rhodamine WT, effects on oysters and fish ... 4:499

E

Eclogites, California and Oregon, isotope studies ... 6:643
Economic geology, Colorado, oil shale ... 4:467
  ore-stage pyrite, in uranium deposits ... 2:151
  Texas, potential Cu and Mo deposits ... 5:519
Electron microprobe analysis. *See* Microprobe analysis.
Elkhorn Mountains volcanic field, Montana, magnetic studies 2:179
Enthalpy of formation, artinite and huntite ... 5:535
  nesquehonite and hydromagnesite ... 5:543
Eocene, California, sedimentation .. 4:439
  Colorado, oil shale ... 4:467
  Wyoming, paleontology ... 2:147
Epidote, microprobe analysis ... 6:673
Equilibria studies, cryolite in water . 4:483
  fluorite in hot springs ... 3:367
Extensometer, modified from water-level recorder ... 5:569

F

Fans, deep-sea, paleocurrent patterns 4:439
Faults, San Andreas, rocks offset by 1:45
  slip rate, measured by Invar-wire extensometer ... 5:569
Feldspar. *See* Arkose, Potassium feldspar.
Fish, effect of rhodamine WT dye on 4:499
Fission-track age, Tertiary intrusive rocks, Utah ... 2:173
Floodflow, changes caused by vegetation ... 5:621
Floods, North Africa in 1969, summary ... 1:121

Page

Flow. *See* Floodflow, Miscible-fluid flow, Streamflow.
Fluorescent spectroscopy, use in characterizing surface films 6:709
Fluoride, ionic activity in recharge water 2:237
Fluorite, equilibrium in thermal water 3:367
Fracturing, en echelon, photogeologic study 3:283
Fra Mauro breccias, Apollo 14 lunar geologic studies 1:1

G

Galkhaite, Nevada, first occurrence in United States 5:515
Garnet, two phases, California 6:665
Gastropods, Permian, new species described 1:19
Geochemistry, Colorado and New Mexico, K, Th, and U in basalt 4:387
Nevada, Belmont stock 3:289
Pacific guano island, lake water 1:105
Texas, recharge water 2:237
See also Petrology.
Geochronology. *See* Age determinations.
Geomorphology, photographic determination of geologic bench marks 2:193
use of stream-gradient indices for terrain analyses 4:421
Geophysics, California and Hawaii, ground deformation 5:569
Liberia, continental margin . . . 5:563
Montana, magnetic studies . . . 2:179
Germany, Ries crater ejecta, comparison with lunar breccias 1:1
Gibbs free energy of formation, artinite and huntite 5:535
nesquehonite and hydromagnesite 5:543
Glaciation, continental, model to explain causes 5:587
formation of joints in bedrock . 2:229
Gold, determination in phosphates by activation analysis . . . 1:79
effect of laboratory treatments on element content 2:211
spectrochemical method for determining composition 3:301
Granite, accessory apatite content, Nevada 1:89
petrography and structural relations, California 3:273
radioelement distribution, Nevada 3:289
Granite Fiords wilderness study area, Alaska, field-note system 5:579
Graptolites, Martinsburg Formation, eastern Pennsylvania 1:33

Page

Great Valley sequence, California, metamorphic facies 4:383
Green River Formation, Colorado, shale oil potential 4:467
Colorado and Utah, stratigraphy 1:39
Ground water, Alaska, Alaska Range 5:523
Arizona, Gila River flood plain 3:371
flow in karst areas 3:351
Idaho, fluorite saturation 3:367
Kentucky, Ohio River valley . . 5:597
New York, potentiometric head 3:345
recharge studies 3:341; 6:735
problems from storage of underground waste 6:719

H

Hawaii, geophysics, Kilauea Volcano 5:569
petrology, Kilauea Volcano . . . 6:649
photogeology, Kilauea Volcano 3:283
Heat, radiogenic, distribution in stock 3:289
Hectorite, in smectite, Utah 4:415
Humic acids, determination of association and dissociation by X-ray scattering 6:701
gel-permeation chromatographic fractionation . . . 3:361
Huntite, enthalpy of formation 5:535
Hydrogen, ionic activity in recharge water 2:237
Hydrologic techniques, determination of diffusivity from flood-wave response 5:597
estimation of streamflow-diversion potential 5:615
evaluation of reliability of specific-yield determination 3:371
use of sand models for miscible-fluid flow studies 2:243
See also Methods and techniques *for chemical studies of water.*
Hydromagnesite, enthalpy of formation 5:543

I

Ice sheets, continental, model to explain causes 5:587
Idaho, thermal springs, Snake River basin 3:367
Inoceramus kusiroensis, biostratigraphy, southern Alaska . 2:125
Instruments and equipment, Invar-wire extensometer 5:569
microphotometer for spectrochemical computer analysis 4:475
revolving illuminator for cartographic line-weight control 2:223

Page

Isotope dilution, use in spectrophotometric determination of tungsten 5:555
Isotope studies. *See* Cesium isotopes, Oxygen isotopes, Strontium isotopes.

J

Joints, in bedrock, formation by glaciation 2:229
Jurassic, California, structural geology 4:453

K

Kansas, new cycad genus, east-central part 6:687
Karst areas, surface runoff relation . 3:351
Kentucky, ground water, Ohio River valley 5:597
Kilauea Volcano, Hawaii, geophysics 5:569
petrology 6:649
photogeology 3:283

L

Lake City caldera, Colorado, volcanic history 6:627
Lake Ontario, remote sensing of turbidity plumes 5:609
Lakes, effects of waterfowl on water quality 6:725
geochemistry, Pacific guano island 1:105
Landslides, Alaska, Admiralty Island 3:309
California, mapping 4:431
Lava, loss of volatiles, Kilauea Volcano, Hawaii 6:649
Lead, determination in soil and sediment 6:681
Lead-alpha age, Tertiary intrusive rocks, Utah 2:173
Liberia, bathymetry of continental margin 5:563
Limestone, lower Paleozoic in eastern United States, sedimentology 1:63
Lithium, in smectite, Utah 4:415
Lithostrotion reiseri, new coral species, arctic Alaska 2:137
Lloyd aquifer, Long Island, N.Y., potentiometric surface . . 3:345
Logging, clear-cut, effects on streams 4:487
Long Island, N.Y., ground water . . . 3:341, 3:345; 6:735
Lunar analog studies, Ries crater ejecta—Apollo 14 Fra Mauro breccias 1:1

M

Magnesium, ionic activity in recharge water 2:237

Page

Magnetic studies. *See* Aeromagnetic studies.
Maine, glacial geology, Mount Desert Island 2:229
Manning's *n*, effect of seasonal vegetation on during floodflow 5:621
Mapping, geologic, machine-processable field-note system 5:579
topographic. *See* Topographic studies.
Marine geology, Liberia, continental margin 5:563
Puerto Rico, southern coast .. 3:293
Yucatan Channel, age of rocks . 2:157
Martinsburg Formation, Pennsylvania, graptolites 1:33
Massachusetts, quality of water, northeastern part 1:117
streamflow-diversion potential, eastern part 5:615
Mauna Ulu eruption, Hawaii, loss of volatiles 6:649
Mesozoic, California, structural geology 1:53
Yucatan Channel, geochronology 2:157
See also Cretaceous, Jurassic.
Metamorphic facies, indicated by vein minerals 4:383
Metamorphic rocks, geochronology, Yucatan Channel 2:157
Metamorphism, blueschist type, California 1:53
relation to spring water, Alaska 5:523
Methods and techniques, activation analysis determination of gold in phosphates 1:79
beta counting determination of radioactive cesium isotopes in water 1:113
correlation of tuff beds by electron microprobe analysis 1:39
humic acid fractionation by gel-permeation chromatography 3:361
identification of surface oil films by fluorescent spectroscopy 6:709
measurement of ground deformation with Invar-wire extensometer 5:569
microgravimetric determination of acid-insoluble impurities in minerals 2:207
prevention of water contamination in oxygen isotope analyses 6:679
spectrochemical determination of gold composition 3:301
spectrophotometric determination, Co, Ni, Cu, Pb, and Zn in soil and sediment .. 6:681

Page

Methods and techniques—Continued
spectrophotometric determination, tungsten in rocks .. 5:555
zirconium in rutile 5:549
turbidimetric determination of sulfur in rocks 1:81
use of argon-oxygen d-c arc in spectrochemical computer analysis 5:559
use of automated photomechanical devices in cartography 2:223
use of chloride content to evaluate effect of urbanization on quality of water 1:117
use of machine-processable field-note system 5:579
use of photogeology in study of en echelon fracturing ... 3:283
use of terrestrial photography for establishing geologic bench marks 2:193
X-ray analysis of humic acids .. 6:701
See also Analytical methods, Hydrologic techniques.
Michigan, structural geology, Marquette district 2:165
Microanalysis, acid-insoluble impurities in acid-soluble minerals 2:207
Microprobe analysis, biotite, Colorado and Utah 1:39
cuprobismutite, Utah 1:99
galkhaite, Nevada 5:515
orpiment, Nevada 1:85
rodingite, California 6:665
sericite, chlorite, and epidote, Arizona 6:673
Mineralogy, accessory apatites, rare-earth assemblages in 3:267
Arizona, sericite, chlorite, epidote 6:673
boron-bearing potassium feldspar in closed-basin deposits 4:377
California, central coast 3:251
rodingite in Sierra Nevada .. 6:665
determination of impurities in acid-soluble minerals 2:207
Nevada, Carlin gold deposit ... 1:85
Humboldt County 5:515
Snake Range 1:89
Utah, new data for cuprobismutite 1:99
Ohio mining district 1:99
west-central part 4:415
Miocene, California, mineralogy ... 4:377
California, sedimentary petrology 3:255
Miscible-fluid flow, use of sand models in studies 2:243
Mississippi, floodflow studies, Jackson 5:621
Mississippian, Alaska, paleontology . 2:137

Page

Modal analysis, blueschist facies rocks, California 1:53
Mollusks. *See* Ammonites, Gastropods.
Molybdenum, potential deposit, Texas 5:519
Montana, magnetic studies, western part 2:179
petrology, southwestern part . 4:403
Montmorillonite, in smectite, Utah . 4:415

N

Nesquehonite, enthalpy of formation 5:543
Neutron activation analysis, determination of gold in phosphates 1:79
Nevada, geochemistry, Belmont stock 3:289
mineralogy, Carlin gold deposit 1:85
Elko and White Pine Counties 3:267
Humboldt County 5:515
Snake Range 1:89
paleontology, Pequop Mountains 1:19
New Jersey, paleontology, Monmouth County 6:695
New Mexico, geomorphology, Santa Fe County 2:193
paleontology, northeastern part 4:459
petrology, northern part 4:387
New York, glacial geology 2:229
ground water, Long Island ... 3:341, 3:345; 6:735
quality of water, Seneca County 6:725
New Zealand, structural geology, South Island 5:529
Nickel, determination in soil and sediment 6:681

O

Ogallala Formation, Texas, geochemistry of water 2:237
Oil shale, potential oil yields, Colorado 4:467
Ophiolite, New Zealand, structural geology 5:529
Ordovician, eastern United States, sedimentology 1:63
Pennsylvania, biostratigraphy . 1:33
Oregon, isotope studies, southern part 6:643
mineralogy, eastern part 4:377
surface water, central coast ... 4:487
Orpiment, antimony in, Nevada ... 1:85
Oxygen, extraction from minerals, bromine pentafluoride technique 6:679
Oxygen isotopes, preventing water contamination during analysis 6:679
Oysters, effect of rhodamine WT dye on 4:499

Page

P

Pacific Ocean. *See* Phoenix Islands.
Paleogeography, Permian, Arctic ... 5:501
Paleontology, Alaska, northern part 2:137
Alaska, southern part 2:125
California, Pleistocene pollen . 6:691
San Luis Obispo County . 5:509
Colorado and New Mexico, ammonites 4:459
Kansas and Texas, new Permian cycad 6:687
Nevada, Pequop Mountains ... 1:19
New Jersey and Texas, ammonites 6:695
Pennsylvania, eastern part 1:33
Wyoming, Fremont County .. 2:147
Paleozoic, California, structural geology 1:53
See also Cambrian, Ordovician, Mississippian, Permian.
Parahyus vagus, second specimen from Tepee Trail Formation 2:147
Park City Group, Nevada, stratigraphy 1:19
Paso Robles Formation, California, marine fossils 5:509
PCB content, in aquatic environment, United States 5:603
Peat, exposed by landslide, Alaska .. 3:309
Pennsylvania, biostratigraphy, eastern part 1:33
Permian, Arctic, paleogeography ... 5:501
Kansas, new cycads 6:687
Nevada, paleontology 1:19
New Zealand, structural geology 5:529
Texas, new cycads 6:687
Petrography, granites, Monterey Bay, Calif., area 3:273
Petrology, Alaska, radioelements in basement 6:659
California, central coast 3:251
Klamath Mountains 1:53
northern part 4:383
Sierra Nevada 6:665
California and Oregon, Sr, K, Na, and Rb in eclogites .. 6:643
Colorado, history of calderas .. 6:627
Colorado and New Mexico, K, Th, and U in basalt 4:387
Hawaii, Kilauea Volcano 6:649
Michigan, Marquette district .. 2:165
Montana, Precambrian diamictite 4:403
Nevada, Carlin gold deposit ... 1:85
Snake Range 1:89
See also Sedimentary petrology.
Phasmatocycas, new genus of Permian cycad 6:687
Phoenix Islands, Pacific Ocean, geochemistry of water ... 1:105

Page

Phosphates, determination of gold in 1:79
Photogeology, determination of horizontal dilation direction of en echelon fracturing 3:283
Photography, satellite, mapping potential 3:315
use in establishing geologic bench marks 2:193
See also Aerial photography.
Photomechanical experiments, automated cartography 2:23
Plate tectonics, post-Permian, Northern Hemisphere 5:501
Pleistocene, California, mineralogy . 4:377
California, pollen 6:691
Pliocene, Arizona, mineralogy 4:377
California, biostratigraphy ... 5:509
Oregon, mineralogy 4:377
Plympton Formation, Nevada, stratigraphy 1:19
Pollen, Pleistocene, near Lake Tahoe, Calif. 6:691
Polychlorinated biphenyls, in aquatic environment 5:603
Porphyry copper-molybdenum deposits, potential for, Texas 5:519
Potassium, distribution in schists, Alaska 6:659
in basalts, southern Rocky Mountains 4:387
in eclogites and basalts, California and Oregon 6:643
Potassium-argon age, conglomerate clasts, California 1:45
olivine latite flow, California .. 6:691
Tertiary intrusive rocks, Utah 2:173
tuffs, volcanic breccias, and basalt, Montana 2:179
Potassium feldspar, boron-bearing, in closed-basin deposits 4:377
Potentiometric surface, Lloyd aquifer, Long Island, N.Y. 3:345
Precambrian, Michigan, structural geology 2:165
Montana, petrology 4:403
Puerto Rico, marine geology, southern coast 3:293
Pyrite as indicator of potential copper or molybdenum at depth 5:519
ore-stage, accumulation in roll-type uranium deposits ... 2:151

Q

Quality of water, effect of dye on oysters and fish 4:499
Massachusetts, northeastern part 1:117
New York, Seneca County ... 6:725
PCB content, United States ... 5:603
Phoenix Island Group, Pacific Ocean 1:105

Page

Quality of water—Continued
problems of underground waste storage 6:719
Quaternary. *See* Pleistocene.

R

Radiochemical analysis, cesium isotopes in water 1:113
See also various types of age determinations: ^{40}Ar-^{39}Ar, Carbon-14, Lead-alpha, Potassium-argon, Rubidium-strontium, Uranium-lead.
Radioelements, distribution in Belmont stock, Nevada 3:289
distribution in eclogites and basalts, California and Oregon 6:643
distribution in schist, Alaska .. 6:659
Rare earths, in accessory apatites, Nevada and Colorado ... 3:267
Recharge studies, Long Island, N.Y. 3:341; 6:735
Lubbock, Tex., area 2:237
Redox reactions, role in ore-stage pyrite accumulation in roll-type uranium deposits 2:151
Remote sensing, Lake Ontario, turbidity plumes 5:609
See also Photography, Aerial photography.
Rhodamine WT dye, effects on oysters and fish 4:499
Rhode Island, streamflow-diversion potential, southern part . 5:615
Ries crater, Germany, comparison of ejecta to Fra Mauro breccias 1:1
Rio Grande depression, Colorado and New Mexico, petrology 4:387
Rivers, estimating diversion potential 5:615
Rocky Mountains, southern region, petrology 4:387
See also Colorado, Montana, New Mexico, Wyoming.
Rodingite, two-garnet type, California 6:665
Rubidium, in eclogites and basalts, California and Oregon ... 6:643
Rubidium-strontium age, granitic rocks, Michigan 2:165
lunar samples 1:1
Runoff, effect of clear-cut logging on 4:487
effect on karst development .. 3:351
storm, source-area concept of . 4:493
Rutile, determination of zirconium in 5:549

S

Saline water, geochemistry, Pacific guano island 1:105
encroachment, sand model 2:243

Page

San Andreas fault, California, rocks offset by ... 1:45
strain measurements ... 5:569
San Francisco Bay region, California, slope-stability studies ... 4:431
San Juan caldera, Colorado, volcanic history ... 6:627
Satellites, photography, mapping potential ... 3:315
Sedimentary petrology, diagenesis of authigenic zeolites ... 3:255
Sedimentation, Alaska, diamictons in landslide ... 3:309
California, Santa Cruz Mountains ... 4:439
Sedimentology, lower Paleozoic carbonate rocks, eastern United States ... 1:63
Seismic profiling, Puerto Rico, submarine canyons ... 3:293
Septic tanks, effect on quality of water, Massachusetts ... 1:117
Sericite, microprobe analysis ... 6:673
Sewage, purified, use for recharge in New York ... 3:341
Silicate rocks, spectrochemical computer analysis ... 5:559
Silver, content in gold affected by laboratory treatments ... 2:211
Silverton caldera, Colorado, volcanic history ... 6:627
Slope-stability studies, San Francisco Bay region, California ... 4:431
Smectite, lithium-bearing, Utah ... 4:415
Sodium, in eclogites and basalts, California and Oregon ... 6:643
ionic activity in recharge water ... 2:237
Solvents, precautionary note on compositions used in extraction procedures ... 2:221
Solubility, cryolite, at 25°C and 1 atm pressure ... 4:483
Specific yield, evaluating reliability of determinations ... 3:371
Spectrochemical analysis, composition of native gold ... 3:301
computerized, argon-oxygen d-c arc method ... 5:559
microphotometer for data recording ... 4:475
Spectrographic analysis, blueschist, California ... 1:53
galkhaite, Nevada ... 5:515
orpiment, Nevada ... 1:85
Spectrometric analysis, radioelements in schist, Alaska ... 6:659
Spectrophotometric analysis, determination of Co, Ni, Cu, Pb, and Zn in soil and sediment ... 6:681
determination of tungsten ... 5:555
sulfur in rocks ... 1:81
zirconium in rutile ... 5:549
Spectroscopic analysis, fluorescent, use in characterizing surface films ... 6:709

Page

Springs, metamorphic waters, Alaska 5:523
thermal, fluorite equilibria ... 3:367
Sr^{87}/Sr^{86}, in eclogites and basalts, California and Oregon ... 6:643
Stillwater Complex, Montana, petrology ... 4:403
Stratigraphy, Alaska, diamictons in landslide ... 3:309
Colorado and Utah, Green River Formation ... 1:39
Nevada, Pequop Mountains ... 1:19
Pennsylvania, eastern part ... 1:33
Streamflow, diversion potential, method for estimating ... 5:615
effect of clear-cut logging on ... 4:487
in karst areas, characteristics ... 3:351
See also Floodflow.
Stream profiles, use in obtaining stream-gradient indices for terrain analyses ... 4:421
Strontium isotopes, in eclogites and basalts, California and Oregon ... 6:643
Structural geology, California, Klamath Mountains ... 1:53
California, Monterey Bay area ... 3:273
northern coastal area ... 1:45
Sierra Nevada ... 4:453
Michigan, Marquette district ... 2:165
New Zealand, South Island ... 5:529
post-Permian, Northern Hemisphere ... 5:501
Stuart Fork Formation, California, structural geology ... 1:53
Sulfur, determination in rocks ... 1:81
Surface water, Arizona, south-central part ... 4:493
flow in karst areas ... 3:351
Massachusetts and Rhode Island, estimating diversion potential ... 5:615
Mississippi, effect of vegetation on rectified channel ... 5:621
Oregon, central coastal area ... 4:487
PCB content, United States ... 5:603
Tunisia, 1969 flood ... 1:121
turbidity plumes in Lake Ontario ... 5:609

T

Tectonism, post-Permian, Northern Hemisphere ... 5:501
Tepee Trail Formation, Wyoming, paleontology ... 2:147
Terrain analyses, use of stream-gradient indices in ... 4:421
Tertiary, Utah, intrusive rocks ... 2:173
Yucatan Channel, geochronology ... 2:157
See also Eocene, Miocene, Pliocene.
Texas, artificial recharge, Lubbock area ... 2:237

Page

Texas—Continued
new cycad genus, north-central part ... 6:687
paleontology, Travis County ... 6:695
potential metal deposits, western part ... 5:519
Thermodynamic studies, artinite and huntite ... 5:535
cryolite in water ... 4:483
fluorite in thermal water sources ... 3:367
nesquehonite and hydromagnesite ... 5:543
Thorium, content in basalts, Rocky Mountains ... 4:387
distribution in schist, Alaska ... 6:659
Topographic studies, photoimages for map bases ... 3:327
photomechanical automated cartography ... 2:223
potential use of satellite photography ... 3:315
Toxicity studies, water, Washington 4:499
Tracers, dye, effects on oysters and fish ... 4:499
use in sand-model studies of salt encroachment in aquifers ... 2:243
Trachyscaphites pulcherrimus (Roemer), New Jersey and Texas ... 6:695
Trondhjemite, nonoccurrence in Salinian block, California ... 3:251
Tuff, correlation of beds, Colorado and Utah ... 1:39
magnetization, western Montana ... 2:179
Tungsten, spectrophotometric determination ... 5:555
Tunisia, 1969 flood, summary ... 1:121
Turbidimetric determination, sulfur in rocks ... 1:81
Turbidity plumes, remote sensing studies ... 5:609

U

Uncompahgre caldera, Colorado, volcanic history ... 6:627
Underground storage of wastes, problems ... 6:719
Uranium, content in basalts, Rocky Mountains ... 4:387
distribution in schist, Alaska ... 6:659
roll-type deposits, accumulation of ore-stage pyrite in ... 2:151
Uranium-lead age, quartz monzonite, Montana ... 4:403
Urban hydrology, effect of septic tanks on quality of water, Massachusetts ... 1:117
Utah, geochronology, Cottonwood area ... 2:173
mineralogy, Ohio mining district ... 1:99

Page

Utah—Continued
mineralogy, west-central part . . 4:415
stratigraphy, northwestern part 1:39

V

Vegetation, effect on channel floodflows 5:621
Volatiles, loss from lava, Kilauea Volcano, Hawaii 6:649
Volcanism, Colorado, mid-Cenozoic 6:627
Hawaii, recent 6:649

W

Washington, water toxicity, northern coast 4:499

Waste storage, underground, problems 6:719
Waterfowl, effects on water quality, New York 6:725
Wyoming, paleontology, Fremont County 2:147

X

X-ray analysis, association and dissociation of humic acids . 6:701
X-ray diffraction analysis, galkhaite, Nevada 5:515
rodingite, California 6:665
smectite, Utah 4:415

Y

Yucatan Channel, geochronology, metamorphic rocks 2:157

Z

Zeolites, authigenic, diagenesis 3:255
Zinc, determination in soil and sediment 6:681
Zirconium, in rutile, spectrophotometric determination . . . 5:549

AUTHOR INDEX

A

Aaronson, D. B. 6:735
Adam, D. P. 5:587; 6:691
Addicott, W. O. 5:509
Antweiler, J. C. 2:211
Armstrong, A. K. 2:137
Arteaga, F. E. 4:493

B

Bailey, E. H. 4:383
Beeson, M. H. 6:665
Behrendt, J. C. 5:563
Berg, H. C. 5:579
Berry, W. B. N. 1:33
Blake, M. C., Jr. 5:529
Botinelly, Theodore 5:515
Brabb, E. E. 3:273; 4:431
Brandt, E. L. M. 3:267
Brown, D. W. 1:105
Bunker, C. M. 3:289; 4:387; 6:659
Burbank, W. S. 6:627
Burford, R. O. 5:569
Bush, C. A. 3:289; 4:387; 6:659

C

Cahill, J. M. 2:243
Campbell, W. L. 2:211
Cannon, W. F. 2:165
Chao, E. C. T. 1:1
Chao, T. T. 6:681
Christ, C. L. 1:99
Clark, S. H. B. 2:125
Clarke, F. E. 1:121
Cobban, W. A. 4:459; 6:695
Coleman, R. G. 6:643
Conklin, N. M. 5:515
Crittenden, M. D., Jr. 2:173
Crump-Wiesner, H. J. 5:603

D

Desborough, G. A. 1:39
Devonald, D. H., III 6:709
Dillon, W. P. 2:157
Donaldson, D. E. 5:523
Donnell, J. R. 1:39; 4:467
Dorrzapf, A. F., Jr. 5:559
Doyle, F. J. 3:315
Duffield, W. A. 3:283; 5:569; 6:665
Dutro, J. T., Jr. 5:501

E

Ehlke, T. A. 3:341
Ehrlich, G. G. 3:341
Epstein, J. B. 1:33

F

Fabbi, B. P. 6:649
Feltz, H. R. 5:603
Forbes, R. B. 6:659
Fraser, G. D. 1:19
Friedman, Irving 6:679

G

Galehouse, J. S. 5:509
Garrison, L. E. 3:293
Ghent, E. D. 6:643
Gilman, C. R. 2:223
Gleason, J. D. 6:679
Goldberg, M. C. 6:709
Granger, H. C. 2:151
Greenland, L. P. 5:555
Grubb, H. F. 5:597
Gude, A. J., 3d 4:377
Gulbrandsen, R. A. 1:105

H

Hack, J. T. 4:421
Hanna, W. F. 2:179
Hanson, R. L. 3:371
Harris, D. D. 4:487
Harris, L. D. 1:63
Have, M. R. 6:725
Havens, R. G. 3:301
Helz, A. W. 4:475
Hem, J. D. 4:483
Hemingway, B. S. 5:535, 543
Heropoulos, Chris 1:85
Hotz, P. E. 1:53

J

Janzer, V. J. 1:113
Jones, D. L. 2:125; 4:383, 453

K

Kimmel, G. E. 3:345
Kistler, R. W. 2:173
Koski, R. A. 4:403

L

Lamarre, R. A. 5:523

Page

Landis, C. A. 5:529
Lanphere, M. A. 2:157
Lee, D. E. 1:89; 3:267
LeGrand, H. E. 3:351
Lewis, G. E. 2:147
Lillie, E. G. 5:555
Lipman, P. W. 4:387; 6:627
Luedke, R. G. 6:627

M

McKee, E. H. 1:45
McKenzie, M. L. 3:327
MacLeod, N. S. 2:157
Malde, H. E. 2:193
Mamay, S. H. 6:687
Mays, R. E. 1:89
Meyrowitz, Robert 2:207; 5:549
Miller, R. D. 3:309
Moore, J. G. 4:453
Morrill, G. B., III 1:117
Mosier, E. L. 2:211
Mountjoy, Wayne 4:415
Mullens, T. E. 5:519
Murata, K. J. 3:255

N

Nace, R. L. 6:719
Nakamura, Kazuaki 3:283
Nash, J. T. 6:673
Neuerburg, G. J. 5:515
Nilsen, T. H. 4:431, 439

P

Page, N. J 4:403
Palacas, J. G. 2:221
Parker, G. G., Jr. 4:499
Peterman, Z. E. 6:643
Pinckney, D. J. 3:361; 6:701
Pitman, J. K. 1:39; 4:467
Pluhowski, E. J. 5:609
Prill, R. C. 6:735

R

Radtke, A. S. 1:85, 99
Rantz, S. E. 4:493
Richter, D. H. 5:523
Robb, J. M. 5:563
Roberson, C. E. 3:367; 4:483
Roberts, A. A. 2:221
Robie, R. A. 5:535, 543
Rose, H. J., Jr. 3:267
Ross, D. C. 1:45; 3:251, 273
Rowe, J. J. 1:79

S

Sainsbury, C. L. 3:301
Saldukas, R. B. 5:501
Sanzolone, R. F. 6:681
Schlee, John 5:563
Schoen, Robert 3:367
Shapiro, Leonard 1:81
Sheppard, R. A. 4:377
Simmons, G. C. 2:165
Simoni, T. R., Jr. 4:439
Smith, J. G. 5:579
Starkey, H. C. 4:415
Stern, T. W. 2:173
Steven, T. A. 6:627
Stringfield, V. T. 3:351
Stuckless, J. S. 2:173
Sutton, A. L. 3:301
Swanson, D. A. 6:649

T

Tasker, G. D. 5:615
Taylor, C. M. 1:85, 99
Toler, L. G. 1:117
Trainer, F. W. 2:229
Trumbull, J. V. A. 3:293

V

Van Loenen, R. E. 1:89; 3:267
Vecchioli, John 3:341
Vedder, J. G. 2:157

W

Warren, C. G. 2:151
Wentworth, C. M. 1:45
Wershaw, R. L. 3:361; 6:701
Whiteley, K. R. 3:255
Wilson, K. V. 5:621
Wood, W. W. 2:237

Y

Yates, M. L. 5:603
Yochelson, E. L. 1:19

Z

Zehner, H. H. 5:597

RECENT PUBLICATIONS OF THE U.S. GEOLOGICAL SURVEY

(Books may be ordered from the Superintendent of Documents, Government Printing Office, Washington, DC 20402, to whom remittances should be sent by check or money order. Give title, series number, stock number (shown in parentheses in this list), and catalog number [shown in brackets])

Professional Papers

562-K. An experimental study of heavy-mineral segregation under alluvial-flow conditions, by L. L. Brady and H. E. Jobson. 1973. p. K1–K38. 85¢. (2401-00294) [I 19:16:562-K]

712-B. Geohydrology of the eastern part of Pahute Mesa, Nevada Test Site, Nye County, Nev., by R. K. Blankennagel and J. E. Weir, Jr. 1973. p. B1–B35; plates in pocket. $1.75. (2401-00303) [I 19:16:712-B]

716-E. Distribution, thickness, and lithology of Paleocene rocks in Pakistan, by C. R. Meissner, Jr., and Habib-ur Rahman. 1973. p. E1–E6; plates in pocket. $1.25. (2401-00341) [I 19:16:716-E]

726-D. Geophysical studies in the Yuma area, Arizona and California, by R. E. Mattick, F. H. Olmsted, and A. A. R. Zohdy. 1973. p. D1–D36; plates in pocket. $1.75. (2401-00327) [I 19:16:726-D]

748. Structural geology of the Santa Rita Mountains, southeast of Tucson, Ariz., by Harald Drewes. 1972 (1973). 35 p.; plates in pocket. $2.15. (2401-00239)[I 19:16:748]

751-B. Design and operation of the artificial-recharge plant at Bay Park, N. Y., by Ellis Koch, A. A. Giaimo, and D. J. Sulam. 1973. p. B1–B14; plate in pocket. 95¢. (2401-00321) [I 19:16:751-B]

752. Igneous rocks and related mineral deposits of the Barker quadrangle, Little Belt Mountains, Mont., by I. J. Witkind. 1973. 58 p. $1. (2401-00312) [I 19:16:752]

756. Middle Jurassic (Bajocian) ammonites from eastern Oregon, by R. W. Imlay. 1973. 100 p.; 47 plates showing fossils. $2.75. (2401-02208) [I 19:16:756]

770. Palynology of the Upper Campanian (Cretaceous) Judith River Formation, north-central Montana, by B. D. Tschudy. 1973. 42 p.; 11 plates showing fossils. $1.25. (2401-00291) [I 19:16:770]

776. Stratigraphy and geologic history of the Montana Group and equivalent rocks, Montana, Wyoming, and North and South Dakota, by J. R. Gill and W. A. Cobban. 1973. 37 p. 85¢. (2401-00342) [I 19:16:776]

791. Oligocene molluscan biostratigraphy and paleontology of the lower part of the type Temblor Formation, Calif., by W. O. Addicott. 1973. 48 p.; 9 plates showing fossils. $1.25. (2401-00284) [I 19:16:791]

798-A. Geochemistry and potassium-argon ages of plutonic rocks in the Battle Mountain mining district, Lander County, Nev., by T. G. Theodore, M. L. Silberman, and D. W. Blake. 1973. p. A1–A24. 65¢. (2401-00333) [I 19:16:798-A]

809-A. Recognition of natural brine by electrical soundings near the Salt Fork of the Brazos River, Kent and Stonewall Counties, Tex., by A. A. R. Zohdy and D. B. Jackson. 1973. p. A1–A14. 40¢. (2401-02373) [I 19:16:809-A]

820. United States mineral resources, by D. A. Brobst and W. P. Pratt, Editors. 1973. 722 p. $9.15. (2401-00307) [I 19:16:820] (Reprinted.)

841. Crystallization history of lunar feldspathic basalt 14310, by O. B. James. 1973. 29 p. 70¢. (2401-00361) [I 19:16:841]

Bulletins

1292. The geologic story of Mount Rainier, by D. R. Crandell. 1969. 43 p. 85¢. (2401-0197) [I 19:3:1292] (Reprinted 1973.)

1303. Chemical analysis of thermal water in Yellowstone National Park, Wyo., 1960–65, by J. J. Rowe, R. O. Fournier, and G. W. Morey. 1973. 31 p. 35¢. (2401-02367) [I 19:3:1303]

1372-E. Stratigraphic divisions and geologic history of the Laney Member of the Green River Formation in the Washakie Basin in southwestern Wyoming, by H. W. Roehler. 1973. p. E1–E28. 35¢. (2401-00282) [I 19:3:1372-E]

1372-H. Lower and middle Tertiary stratigraphic units of the San Emigdio and western Tehachapi Mountains, Calif., by T. H. Nilsen, T. W. Dibblee, Jr., and W. O. Addicott. 1973. p. H1–H23. 35¢. (2401-00343) [I 19:3:1372-H]

1372-J. Stratigraphic terminology of the Dakota Sandstone and Mancos Shale, west-central New Mexico, by E. R. Landis, C. H. Dane, and W. A. Cobban. 1973. p. J1–J44. 45¢. (2401-00364) [I 19:3:1372-J]

Water-Supply Papers

2018. Ground water in the Eugene-Springfield area, southern Willamette Valley, Oreg., by F. J. Frank. 1973. 65 p.; plates in pocket. $2.75. (2401-00277) [I 19:13:2018]

2028. A national study of the streamflow data-collection program, by M. A. Benson, and R. W. Carter. 1973. 44 p. 45¢. (2401-02372) [I 19:13:2028]

U.S. GOVERNMENT
PRINTING OFFICE
PUBLIC DOCUMENTS DEPARTMENT
WASHINGTON, D.C. 20402
OFFICIAL BUSINESS
PENALTY FOR PRIVATE USE $300

POSTAGE AND FEES PAID
U.S. GOVERNMENT
PRINTING OFFICE
375

U.S. MAIL

JRGS HARTWOOOH R 1
HARTWICK CLG LIB
ONEONTA NY 13820